The Law of the European Union and the European Communities

KLUWER LAW INTERNATIONAL

Kapteyn & VerLoren van Themaat

The Law of the European Union and the European Communities

with reference to changes to be made by the Lisbon Treaty

FOURTH REVISED EDITION

Edited by

**P.J.G. Kapteyn,
A.M. McDonnell,
K.J.M. Mortelmans,
C.W.A. Timmermans
and
the late L.A. Geelhoed**

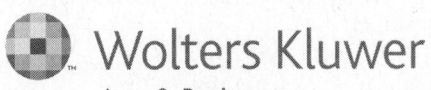
Wolters Kluwer
Law & Business

AUSTIN   BOSTON   CHICAGO   NEW YORK   THE NETHERLANDS

Published by:
Kluwer Law International
PO Box 316
2400 AH Alphen aan den Rijn
The Netherlands
Website: www.kluwerlaw.com

Sold and distributed in North, Central and South America by:
Aspen Publishers, Inc.
7201 McKinney Circle
Frederick, MD 21704
United States of America
Email: customer.care@aspenpubl.com

Sold and distributed in all other countries by
Turpin Distribution Services Ltd.
Stratton Business Park
Pegasus Drive, Biggleswade
Bedfordshire SG18 8TQ
United Kingdom
Email: kluwerlaw@turpin-distribution.com

Printed on acid-free paper.

Hardback ISBN: 978-90-411-2631-3
Paperback ISBN: 978-90-411-2816-4

The Authors and Editors

F. Amtenbrink
Professor of European Union Law, Erasmus University, Rotterdam

R. Barents
Head of Unit, Research and Documentation, European Court of Justice;
Professor of European law, University of Maastricht

The late L.A. Geelhoed
Former Advocate General, European Court of Justice

J. Inghelram
Référendaire, European Court of Justice

P.J.G. Kapteyn
Professor emeritus of European Studies, University of Amsterdam;
Former Judge, European Court of Justice

S. Kingston
Lecturer in Law, University College Dublin

P.J.Kuijper
Professor of the Law of International Organizations, University of Amsterdam

R. H. Lauwaars
Member of the Raad van State (Netherlands Council of State), The Hague

A.M. McDonnell
Europa Institute, University of Leiden;
Associate Editor Common Market Law Review

K.J.M. Mortelmans
Member of the Raad van State (Netherlands Council of State), The Hague

P.J. Slot
Professor of European law, University of Leiden

C.W.A. Timmermans
Judge, European Court of Justice

B. de Witte
Professor of European Law, European University Institute, Florence

Summary of Contents

Table of Contents

Chapter II
General Aspects of the European Union
and the European Communities
C.W.A. Timmermans

Chapter III
The Basic Principles   **115**
C.W.A. Timmermans

Chapter V
Legal Instruments, Decision-Making and EU Finances   **273**
B. de Witte, A. Geelhoed and J. Inghelram

Chapter VI
Administration of Justice 421
P.J.G. Kapteyn

Chapter VIII
The Functioning of the Internal Market: The Freedoms **575**
K.J.M. Mortelmans

Chapter XI
Horizontal and Flanking Policies   **1087**
K.J.M. Mortelmans

Foreword

Since the third English edition of this book, the editorial board of the Dutch 'parent' edition has suffered a double blow, losing two of its members. Pieter VerLoren van Themaat, who died on 4 July 2004, at the age of 88, was one of the two original authors of the first Dutch edition, which was published in the Netherlands in 1970. In the first and second English editions, he was responsible more particularly for the chapter dealing with the principles, the chapters on the internal substantive law, and the final chapter. In the third English edition the chapter on the principles and the Epilogue were still based on the texts he had drafted for the fifth Dutch edition. The second loss occurred in the course of preparing the present edition. We were confronted with the untimely death of Ad Geelhoed, member of our editorial board since the fifth Dutch edition and author of several chapters. He died on 20 April 2007 at the age of 64, six months after having finished his six year's term as Advocate General of the European Court of Justice.

This book was known in previous editions as *Introduction to the Law of the European Communities*, and it provides a comprehensive and systematic account of the law of the EC and the EU. Its extent and the depth of analysis it contains have led us to abandon the term 'Introduction' in the title of this edition. At the same time, because of the increasing importance of the so-called Second and Third Pillars, and the omnipresence of the over-arching concept of the European Union, we decided to include that entity in the title. The basis of the book nevertheless remains the same, albeit with some changes to the arrangement of material in various chapters. The chapter on administration of justice has been split into two, to allow sufficient analysis of the complex relationship between Community law and national law; the discussion of the protection of the financial interests of the Community has been added to the section dealing with the Community finances as such.

The third edition of this work was based on the fifth Dutch edition. And, following the same logic, this fourth English edition is based on the sixth Dutch edition. Nevertheless, it should be emphasized that the text has been fully updated to deal with changes taking place in the intervening years – even though the pace at which the law of the EC and the EU develops has not abated. Importantly, although this book presents the law currently in force, we have included in each chapter some indication of the major changes which will take place if and when the Treaty of Lisbon enters into force.

We are extremely grateful to Fabian Amtenbrink, Jan Inghelram and Suzanne Kingston who joined the project at extremely short notice. They carried out careful and valuable updating of the texts Ad Geelhoed had contributed to the last Dutch edition and had started to prepare for this English edition, while also substantially rewriting some parts. We decided not to replace the Epilogue, written by Ad Geelhoed in the previous Dutch edition, but instead to incorporate the latest changes in the individual chapters, where appropriate also looking ahead. We have been able to include the developments up to the beginning of 2008.

We thank all the other authors – René Barents, Pieter Jan Kuijper, Richard Lauwaars, Piet Jan Slot, Bruno de Witte – for their willingness to revise and update their chapters. We are indebted to Henk Zonneveld, librarian at the Europa Institute of Utrecht University, for providing lists of further reading for each chapter, and a section on sources of EC and EU legal materials.

It goes without saying that, wherever possible, the present edition uses the excellent translations made by Professor Laurence W. Gormley in the past when he prepared the second and third English editions. All new material has been translated or revised by Alison McDonnell.

The previous English edition appeared at a time that the Amsterdam Treaty was signed, but had not yet entered into force. The present edition also appears at a moment of change. The Lisbon Treaty is in the process of ratification, and this Foreword was written in the period of extreme uncertainty following the referendum in Ireland held on 12 June 2008, with its negative result casting a shadow of doubt as to whether – despite the political desire – that Treaty will actually enter into force. If it does, this may be the last edition in which the 'Community' has a current and not just a historical or symbolic significance.

We wish to thank Ronald van Ooik, Redmar Damsma and Lasse Burmester, University of Amsterdam, for compiling the index; Clara Besselink, Toby Besselink, Jeroen Boot, Cunzhen Huang, Brechtje Klandemans, Maaike Küthe and Joris Slot for their help in compiling the table of cases; the staff at Kluwer Law International for their professional help.

P.J.G. Kapteyn
A.M. McDonnell
K.J.M. Mortelmans
C.W.A. Timmermans

July 2008

From the Preface to the first English Edition

The work is addressed to all those who have to deal directly or indirectly with the law of the European Communities...

It is not intended for the limited group of readers looking at the same time for a full summary of the law and of the commentaries on it.... Of course, in writing the book we were in part inspired by the voluminous literature on the subject which has appeared within and without the Member States. However, as a rule we have deliberately based our argument directly on primary Community law, the several thousands of general implementing rules, the administrative practice of the Community, and the bulky jurisprudence of the Court of Justice of the European Communities. If in all cases we had also made mention of the views elaborated in the literature the scope of the book would have been considerably increased. It would however, have been a more serious draw-back that quotations from the literature, which on the whole deals with highly specialized topics in many different languages, would have diverted the reader's attention from the main purpose of the work. This purpose is to give some idea of the specific character of Community law as a new and coherent Community legal system with special emphasis on the interrelation of the various elements of Community law. Here we follow the model of the Court of Justice, which rightly places great emphasis on the special character of Community law and on the links between the different elements of this new field of law.

...

We have tried to devote as much attention to the historical, political, economic, and social background of Community law as is necessary to show that the law of the European Communities is not developing independently of that background. Community law in the form of implementing rules is, in particular, usually a compromise between diverse economic interests and political views and hence can attract a good deal of criticism. It appeared useful to us to mention explicitly a number of possible criticisms.

November 1972-June 1973   P.J.G.Kapteyn – P.VerLoren Van Themaat

Source Materials of EC and EU Law

H.G.J. Zonneveld

I   INTRODUCTION

Legislation and documents of the institutions of the European Union (EU) are made public in various ways. As well as the traditional methods of publication, this occurs increasingly via electronic media, such as databases and Internet. The EU has embraced electronic publication of documents as an important means of ensuring access to documents, particularly for individuals.[1] Access is granted to a great extent through the internet portal Europae Lex (EUR-Lex).[2] There are also various databases, more suited to professional users. In addition to these primary sources, there are a great many secondary sources(reports, press notices, literature) which give information about the functioning of the EU and European law.

II   OFFICIAL PUBLICATIONS

Although these days nearly all the documents of the EU are (also) published electronically (in databases and via Internet), the printed publications of legislation and case law are still the only official versions.

    Treaties, legislation and acts of the European Community (EC) and the EU are officially published in the printed version of the *Official Journal of the*

---

1.   See on this: V. Deckmyn, Increasing transparency in the European Union? (Maastricht: European Institute of Public Administration, 2002). Documents on the transparency policy are available at <http://ec.europa.eu/transparency/access_documents/index_en.htm>
2.   <http://eur-lex.europa.eu/>

European Union which appears every working day in all the official languages of the Union.[3]

Legislation is published in the L series of the Official Journal. Information and notices are published in the C series.

Before July 1967, the pages were numbered through the whole year (citation: O.J. 1274/61). Between 1 July 1967 and 1 January 1968, the pages were numbered per issue (citation: O.J. 1967, 100/1). After the Official Journal was split into the L series and C series in 1968, the citation style became: O.J. 1970, L 220/15 or O.J. 1970, C 220/15.

An important recent development is that not all information and notices are published in the printed versions of the Official Journal. Since 1999, legislative proposals by the Commission are only published electronically, in the C E series of the Official Journal (which can be consulted through EUR-Lex, see below). Since 1 January 2002, the minutes and the texts adopted by plenary sessions of the European Parliament are only published in the electronic version of the Official Journal, as are the common positions – together with the reasoning – concerning the legislative activity of the Council. The statements from the Economic and Social Committee and the Committee of the Regions are also only published in the electronic version of the Official Journal.

The case law of the Court of Justice of the European Communities and the Court of First Instance is officially published in the *Reports of cases before the Court of Justice and the Court of First Instance (European Court Reports)*. This consists of three parts: The decisions (judgments and orders) of the Court of Justice and the opinions of the advocates general are included in Part I (citation: [1994] ECR, I-123); the decisions of the Court of First Instance are in Part II (citation: [994] ECR, II-321). The decisions of the Court of First Instance in staff cases (from 1994) and the decisions of the Civil Service Tribunal (from 2005) are published in a separate part: *Reports of European Community Staff Cases* (or *European Court Reports – staff cases*, citation: ECR-SC).

Since 1997, the Court publishes provisional versions of decisions and opinions of the advocates general (with the aim of informing the public; these are not official) on the website of the Court of Justice: in the language of the case on the day of the decision (or in the original language on the day the Opinion is delivered), but other language versions are usually available very rapidly, especially in important cases. (see below for more electronic sources).[4]

---

3. Prior to the entry into force of the Nice Treaty, the title was: Official Journal of the European Communities.
4. <http://curia.europa.eu/jurisp/cgi-bin/form.pl?lang=en>

III GENERAL ELECTRONIC SOURCES

Up until the end of 2004, CELEX (Communitatis Europae Lex) was the official database of the ECs. Since then, EUR-Lex has taken over that task. The complete texts of the treaties, legislation, acts and case law (decisions of the courts and opinions of the advocates general (from 1995)) are available through this database, which is freely accessible via the Internet, in all the official languages of the Union (the older case law is not yet available online in all languages).

As for preparatory documents, such as Commission proposals and resolutions of the European Parliament, these texts are electronically available from roughly 1995.

Information on national implementing measures is also published, as well as parliamentary questions and answers. From roughly 1995, the full text is available.

All the Commission's 'COM documents' (White papers, green papers, proposals, reports, communications) are contained in the section 'preparatory acts'). The full text of these documents is available since 1999.

Other, commercial, databases, derived from EUR-Lex also provide access to European legislation. These include, in English: *OJ OnlinePlus* (Ellis Publications), *Justis CELEX* (Justis) and *Eurolaw* (ILI).

As well as EUR-Lex, the website of the various European institutions and bodies are an important source of documents.[5] These can be accessed through the main Europa website.[6]

A ARCHIVE WEBSITES

At various places in the world, archives have been created to preserve and give access to electronic versions of EC and EU texts. There are also a number of ongoing projects to store old, historical EC/EU documents in digital format, in order to make them available electronically. A prime example, in the Netherlands, is the Leiden website 'History of EU integration', where a great many historical documents can be found.[7] As well as EU documents, it contains news items and audio and video recordings.

Official EC/EU documents are also available through the Archive of European Integration (AEI) of the University of Pittsburgh in the United States.[8] This archive includes White papers, Green papers and Bulletin Supplements in which, in the past, important COM en SEC documents were published.

---

5. For an overview see the 'A-Z index of EU websites' compiled by the US Delegation of the European Commission at <http://www.eurunion.org/infores/euindex.htm>
6. <http://europa.eu/>
7. <http://www.eu-history.leidenuniv.nl/index.php3?m=7&c=11>
8. <http://aei.pitt.edu/>

In Luxembourg, the European NAvigator (ENA) exists.[9] A great deal of material concerning European integration is available via this website; not just official documents, but also speeches, photographs, films, cartoons, interviews, etc. Most of the material is available in the original language and in translation (English and French).

IV   OVERVIEW OF SOURCES

In the following, a brief summary is given of the most important sources for different categories of documents.

A   TREATIES

As well as being published in the C series of the Official Journal, the treaties are published in book form by the Publications Office, e.g., *Consolidated versions of the treaty on European Union and of the treaty establishing the European Community* (Luxembourg: Office for Official publications of the European Communities, 2006).

The Treaties can also be found in various other publications. The English text of the Treaties is included, inter alia, in Nigel G. Foster, *EU Treaties & Legislation: 2007–2008*, 18th edn (Oxford: Oxford University Press, 2007).

The treaties are available electronically through EUR-Lex.[10] Another useful website for electronic English language versions of the treaties is Eurotreaties.com, part of the British Management Data Foundation, was set up to bring together the basic information on the European Treaties.[11]

B   INTERNATIONAL AGREEMENTS

The EU has concluded many agreements with third countries. The texts are published in the Official Journal L series, and are also available in EUR-Lex.[12] EUR-Lex also provides links to the *Agreements Database* managed by the Council of the EU and the *Treaties Office Database* managed by the European Commission.

C   SECONDARY LAW AND OTHER ACTS

As was mentioned above, secondary law (directives and regulations) of the Community, and acts of the Institutions (also of the European Central Bank) are

---

9.   <http://www.ena.lu/mce.cfm>
10. <http://eur-lex.europa.eu/en/treaties/index.htm>
11. <http://www.eurotreaties.com/eurogeneral.html>
12. <http://eur-lex.europa.eu/en/accords/accords.htm>

published in the L series of the Official Journal. The electronic version is available in EUR-Lex, in html format, and as of 1998 also as pdf files.[13]

Twice a year, as part of the Official Journal, an overview is published of currently effective legislation: the *Directory of Community legislation in force*. An up-to-date version is available though EUR-Lex.[14]

D   PREPARATORY ACTS

There are two online databases (PreLex and OEIL) which enable one to follow the legislative process of particular acts, and access the relevant documents. PreLex[15] is managed by the Commission and gives links to the complete texts of the preparatory acts for each legislative procedure, as well as links to background information, for instance in the Bulletin of the European Union. OEIL[16] (also called *The Legislative Observatory*) is run by the European Parliament, and gives similar information for each legislative procedure, though with fewer links to the complete texts.

Legislative proposals were published, up to 1999, in the (printed) C series of the Official Journal. Since then, they are published in the electronic C E series of the Official Journal, available through EUR-Lex.[17] The proposals (including explanations) are also published as 'COM document', as are many other Commission documents. The complete texts of the COM documents (from about 1999) are available through EUR-Lex.[18] These documents are also often available via the Commission's website.[19]

The minutes of the European Parliament and answers to questions put by Member of European Parliaments (MEPs) were published up to 2001 in the C series of the Official Journal. The reports and (draft) resolutions are published separately. These documents of the European Parliament are available (since 1994) via the website of the European Parliament 'Europarl'.[20]

Common positions of the Council are published in the Official Journal (up to 2002 in the C series, thereafter in the C E series). These can also be accessed via the Public register of Council documents.[21]

---

13. <http://eur-lex.europa.eu/JOIndex.do?ihmlang=en>
14. <http://eur-lex.europa.eu/en/legis/index.htm>
15. <http://ec.europa.eu/prelex/>
16. <http://www.europarl.europa.eu/oeil/>
17. <http://eur-lex.europa.eu/en/prep/index.htm>
18. <http://eur-lex.europa.eu/COMIndex.do?ihmlang=en>
19. Via the web pages of the Commission Directorates-General and Services, at <http://ec.europa.eu/dgs_en.htm> and via the pages of the 'Activities of the European Union' at <http://europa.eu/pol/index_en.htm>
20. An overview of EP official documents can be found at: <http://www.europarl.europa.eu/guide/search/docsearch_en.htm>
21. <http://register.consilium.europa.eu/>

E   INVITATIONS TO TENDER AND PUBLIC CONTRACTS

Invitations to tender and public contracts are published in a separate supplement
'S' of the Official Journal. This information is available via internet through the
database Tenders Electronic Daily (TED).[22]

F   CASE LAW

The decisions of the Court of Justice and the Court of First Instance (and the
Opinions of the Advocates General) are published officially, as mentioned
above, in the 'European Court Reports'. The texts are also electronically available
via EUR-Lex[23] and on the website of the Court of Justice ('Curia') under 'Numerical access to the case law'.[24] More recent case law is available online in all official
languages. The provisional versions of decisions and opinions can be accessed
through the Court's website.[25]

       In the Official Journal, C Series, announcements are published about applica-
tions and actions lodged, removal of cases from the register, and judgments delivered. This information is also published in the 'Judicial proceedings' of the Court
of Justice and the Court of First Instance, together with an indication of the issues
dealt with in the judgments.[26]

       Bibliographic information concerning annotations of judgments can be found
in EUR-Lex[27] in the 'Bibliographic notice' of judgments, and via the website of the
Court of Justice.[28]

G   INFORMATION ON THE ACTIVITIES OF THE EU

The 'Bulletin of the European Union' appears monthly, with an overview of *the
activities of the EU* in that month.[29] The Bulletin is supplemented by the 'General
Report on the Activities of the European Union' which provides an overview of the
activities of the previous year.[30] In addition, there are specific reports, for instance
on competition policy[31] and agriculture.

       Every working day, the *Agence internationale d'information pour la presse*
(Brussels) produces press announcements, in French and English – known as

---

22.   <http://ted.europa.eu/>
23.   <http://eur-lex.europa.eu/RECH_jurisprudence.do?ihmlang=en>
24.   <http://curia.europa.eu/en/content/juris/juris.htm>
25.   <http://curia.europa.eu/jurisp/cgi-bin/form.pl?lang=en>
26.   <http://curia.europa.eu/en/actu/activites/index.htm>
27.   See the 'Notes relating to the decision' in the 'Bibliographic notice' of judgments.
28.   See the 'Annotation of judgments' at <http://curia.europa.eu/en/content/juris/index.htm>
29.   <http://europa.eu/bulletin/en/welcome.htm>
30.   <http://europa.eu/generalreport/en/welcome.htm>
31.   <http://ec.europa.eu/comm/competition/annual_reports/>

Agence Europe – about *the activities of the EU*. Press releases and announcements by the Institutions can be consulted via the RAPID database,[32] and indications of the latest news concerning the Institutions can be found via the 'EU Press Room'[33] and the webpage 'What's new in the EU institutions and agencies'.[34]

V JOURNALS

The most important journals concerning EU and EC law are:

Cahiers de Droit Européen (CDE)
Common Market Law Review (CML Rev.)
Il Diritto dell'Unione Europea (Dir. Un. Eur.)
Europarecht (EuR)
European Competition Law Review (ECLR)
European Journal of International Law (EJIL)
European Law Review (EL Rev.)
Europäische Zeitschrift für Wirtschaftsrecht (EuZW)
Journal des Tribunaux Droit Européen (JTDE)
Journal of Common Market Studies (JCMS)
Legal Issues of European Integration (LIEI)
Nederlands Tijdschrift voor Europees Recht (NTER)
Recht der Internationalen Wirtschaft (RIW)
Revue du droit de L'Union Européenne (RDUE) (continuation of: Revue du
    Marché Unique Européen (RMUE))
Revue du Marché Commun et de l'Union Européenne (RMC)
Revue Trimestrielle de Droit Européen (RTDE)
Rivista di Diritto Europeo (RDE)
Sociaal-Economische Wetgeving (SEW)
Yearbook of European Law (YEL)

VI SURVEYS OF LITERATURE

Various journals publish regular surveys of literature; those in *Common Market Law Review* and *Europarecht* deserve special mention.

In addition, bibliographical information can be found in ECLAS (the catalogue of the Commission library)[35] and in the surveys of literature (*Current Bibliography*) of the library of the Court of Justice.[36]

---

32. <http://europa.eu/rapid/setLanguage.do?language=en>
33. <http://europa.eu/press_room/index_en.htm>
34. <http://europa.eu/geninfo/whatsnew_inst.htm>
35. <http://ec.europa.eu/eclas/>
36. <http://curia.europa.eu/en/instit/services/bib/acqbiblio.htm>

Every year the library of the Court of Justice also publishes an overview of literature on European integration (*Legal Bibliography of European Integration*).

VII   GENERAL COMMENTARIES AND TEXTBOOKS

Barents, R. and L.J. Brinkhorst. *Grondlijnen van Europees recht*. 12de, geheel herz. dr.. (Deventer: Kluwer, 2006).

Berry, E. and S. Hargreaves. *European Union Law: Textbook*, 2nd edn (Oxford, etc.: Oxford University Press, 2007).

Chalmers, D. *European Union Law: Text and Materials*. (Cambridge: Cambridge University Press, 2006).

Cini, M. *European Union Politics*. 2nd edn (Oxford, etc.: Oxford University Press, 2007).

Craig, P.P. and G. de Búrca. *EU Law: Text, Cases, and Materials*. 4th edn (Oxford, etc.: Oxford University Press, 2008).

Cuthbert, M. *E.U. Law in a Nutshell*. 5th edn (London, etc.: Sweet & Maxwell, etc., 2006).

Davies, K. *Understanding European Union Law*. 3rd edn (Abingdon, etc.: Routledge Cavendish, 2007).

Deards, E.B.n. and S. Hargreaves. *European Union Law: Textbook*. 2nd edn (Oxford, etc.: Oxford University Press, 2007).

El-Agraa, A.M. *The European Union: Economics and Policies*. 8th edn (Cambridge: Cambridge University Press, 2007).

Fairhurst, J. *Law of the European Union*. 6th edn (Harlow, etc.: Pearson Longman, 2007).

Folsom, R.H. *European Union Law in a Nutshell*. 5th edn (St Paul, MN: Thomson/West, 2005).

Folsom, R.H. *Principles of European Union Law* (St Paul, MN: Thomson/West, 2005).

Foster, N.G. *EU Law, 2007 and 2008*. 6th edn (Oxford: Oxford University Press, 2007) (Questions & Answers).

Gautron, J.-C. *Droit européen*. 11e éd (Paris: Dalloz, 2004) (Mémentos Dalloz. Droit public – Science politique).

Geiger, R. *EUV/EGV: Vertrag über die Europäische Union und Vertrag zur Gründung der Europäischen Gemeinschaft*, 4. neubearb. und erw. Aufl.. (München: Beck, 2004).

Grabitz, E. and M. Hilf. *Das Recht der Europäischen Union*. (München: Beck, 1992) (loose-leaf).

Groeben, H. von der, J. Schwarze, et al., *Kommentar zum Vertrag über die Europäische Union und zur Gründung der Europäischen Gemeinschaft*, 6. Aufl.. (Baden-Baden: Nomos, 2004).

Hartley, T.C. *European Union Law in a Global Context: Text, Cases and Materials* (Cambridge, etc.: Cambridge University Press, 2004).

Hartley, T.C. *The foundations of European Community Law: An Introduction to the Constitutional and Administrative Law of the European Community* (New York: Oxford University Press, 2007).

Horspool, M. and M. Humphreys. *European Union Law*. 4th edn (Oxford, etc.: Oxford University Press, 2006) (Core Text Series).

Kent, P. *European Union Law*. 4th edn (London: Sweet & Maxwell, 2006) (Nutcases).

Lenaerts, K., P. Van Nuffel, et al. *Constitutional Law of the European Union*. 2nd edn (London: Thomson Sweet & Maxwell, 2005).

MacCormick, J. *Understanding the European Union: A Concise Introduction*. 3rd comprehensively rev. and upd. edn (Basingstoke, etc.: Palgrave Macmillan, 2005) (The European Union series).

Mathijsen, P.S.R.F. *A Guide to European Union Law*. 9th edn (London: Sweet & Maxwell, 2007).

Mégret, J., M. Waelbroeck, et al. *Commentaire Mégret: le droit de la CEE*, 2e éd. (Bruxelles: Éditions de l'Université de Bruxelles, 1990–2005) (15 tomes).

Moussis, N. *Access to European Union: Law, Economics, Politics*. 16th rev. edn (Rixensart: European Study Service, 2007).

Moussis, N. *Guide to European Policies*. 12th rev. edn (Rixensart: European Study Service, 2007).

Nugent, N. *The Government and Politics of the European Union*. 6th rev. and upd. edn (Basingstoke, etc.: Palgrave Macmillan, 2006) (The European Union series).

Reich, N. *Understanding EU Law: Objectives, Principles and Methods of Community Law*. 2nd edn (Antwerpen, etc.: Intersentia, 2005).

Rudden, B. and D. Wyatt. *Rudden and Wyatt's EU Treaties and Legislation*. 9th edn (Oxford, etc.: Oxford University Press, 2004).

Shaw, J., J. Hunt, et al. *Economic and Social Law of the European Union* (Basingstoke, etc.: Palgrave Macmillan, 2007).

Smit, H., P. Herzog, et al. *Smit & Herzog on the Law of the European Union* (New York: LexisNexis, 2005) (loose-leaf)

Steiner, J., L. Woods, et al. *EU Law*. 9th edn (Oxford, etc.: Oxford University Press, 2006).

Storey, T. and C. Turner. *Unlocking EU Law*. (London: Hodder Arnold, 2005).

Streinz, R. and C. Herrmann. *Europarecht*, 7. völlig neubearb. Aufl, Heidelberg: C.F. Müller Juristischer Verlag, 2005 (Schwerpunkte; 12).

Szyszczak, E.M. and A.J. Cygan. *Understanding EU Law* (London: Sweet & Maxwell, 2005).

Tridimas, T. *The General Principles of EU Law*. 2nd edn (Oxford, etc.: Oxford University Press, 2006) (Oxford EC law library).

Weatherill, S. *Cases and Materials on EU Law*. 7th edn (Oxford, etc.: Oxford University Press, 2006).

Wyatt, D., A.A. Dashwood, et al. *Wyatt and Dashwood's European Union Law*. 5th edn by Anthony Arnull, et al. (London: Sweet & Maxwell, 2006).

Table of Cases

Court of Justice of the European Communities

Judgments and orders

Table of Cases

Table of Cases

Opinions pursuant to Article 300(6) EC

Ruling delivered pursuant to the third paragraph of Article 103 of the EAEC Treaty

Court of First Instance

Civil service Tribunal

European Court of Human Rights

Table of Treaties

Protocols

A EIB Statute

B Court of Justice Statute

2 Article 119 EC

3 ESCB and ECB Statute

New Provisions (introduced by Treaty of Amsterdam)*

* This table covers wholly new provisions, or complete replacements; additions to existing provisions are included in the table of existing provisions. New Protocols are set out in the table of the Treaty of Amsterdam.

ECSC TREATY

EEA TREATY

EEC TREATY

Existing provisions

New Provisions (introduced by Treaty of Amsterdam)*

* This table covers wholly new provisions, or complete replacements; additions to existing provisions are included in the table of existing provisions. New Protocols are set out in the table of the Treaty of Amsterdam.

EU CHARTER OF FUNDAMENTAL RIGHTS

Existing provisions

New Provisions (introduced by Treaty of Amsterdam)*

* This table covers wholly new provisions, or complete replacements; additions to existing provisions are included in the table of existing provisions. New Protocols are set out in the table of the Treaty of Amsterdam.

EURATOM TREATY

CONVENTION ON CERTAIN INSTITUTIONS COMMON TO THE EUROPEAN COMMUNITIES

FIRST BUDGETARY TREATY

MERGER TREATY

TREATY ON EUROPEAN UNION

TREATY ON THE FUNCTIONING OF THE EUROPEAN UNION

Existing provisions

New Provisions (introduced by Treaty of Amsterdam)*

* This table covers wholly new provisions, or complete replacements; additions to existing provisions are included in the table of existing provisions. New Protocols are set out in the table of the Treaty of Amsterdam.

TREATY OF NICE

List of Abbreviations

AA	*Ars Aequi*
ACP	African, Caribbean and Pacific
ACT	Advance Corporation Tax
AIDS	Acquired Immunodeficiency Syndrome
AJCL	*American Journal of Comparative Law*
AJIL	*American Journal of International Law*
AÖR	*Archiv des Öffentlichen Rechts*
ASEAN	Association of Southeast Asian Nations
ASOR	Agreement on the International Carriage of Passengers by Road by means of Occasional Coach and Bus Services approved of on behalf of the European Economic Community by Council Decision 82/505/EEC of 12 July 1982
ATC	Agreement on Textiles and Clothing
BEPG	Broad Economic Policy Guidelines
BIS	Bank for International Settlements
BSE	Bovine Spongiform Encephalopathy (Mad Cow Disease)
CAP	Common Agricultural Policy
CCP	Common Commercial Policy
CDE	*Cahiers de Droit Européen*
CEBS	Committee of European Banking Supervisors
Cedefop	European Centre for the Development of Vocational Training
CEN	European Committee for Standardization
CFI	Court of First Instance
CENELEC	European Committee for Electrotechnical Standardization
CFSP	Common Foreign and Security Policy

CISA	Convention Implementing the Schengen Agreement
CMLR	*Common Market Law Reports*
CML Rev.	*Common Market Law Review*
COREPER	Committee of Permanent Representatives
COST	Coopération Scientifique et Technologique
DAS	*déclaration d'assurance*
DDR	Deutsche Demokratische Republik
Dec.	Decision
Dir.	Directive
EAEC	European Atomic Energy Community (Euratom)
EADF	European Agricultural Development Fund
EAFRD	European Agricultural Fund for Rural Development
EAGF	European Agricultural Guarantee Fund
EAGGF	European Agricultural Guidance and Guarantee Fund
EASA	European Aviation Safety Agency
EC	European Community or Treaty establishing the European Community
ECB	European Central Bank
ECE	European Commission for Europe
ECHA	European Chemicals Agency
ECHO	European Commision Humanitarian Aid
ECHR	European Convention on Human Rights
ECJ	European Court of Justice
ECLR	*European Competition Law Review*
ECMT	European Conference of Ministers of Transport
ECOFIN	Economic and Financial Affairs
ECOSOC	Economic and Social Committee (see also EESC)
ECSB	European System of Central Banks
ECSC	European Coal and Steel Community
ECtHR	European Court of Human Rights
ECU	European Currency Unit
EDC	European Defence Community
EDF	European Development Fund
EDP	Excessive Deficit Procedure
EEA	European Economic Area
EEC	European Economic Community
EEIG	European Economic Interest Grouping
EESC	Economic and Social Committee (see also ECOSOC)
EFA Rev.	*European Foreign Affairs Review*
EFF	European Fisheries Fund
EFTA	European Free Trade Association
EGTC	European Grouping of Territorial Cooperation
EHLASS	European Home and Leisure Accidents Surveillance System
EIB	European Investment Bank

EIF	European Investment Fund
EJIL	*European Journal of International Law*
ELFAA	European Low Fares Airline Association
EL Rev.	*European Law Review*
EMAS	Eco-Management and Audit Scheme
EMCF	European Monetary Cooperation Fund
EMEA	European Medicines Agency
EMI	European Monetary Institute
EMS	European Monetary System
EMU	Economic and Monetary Union
ENPI	European Neighbourhood Policy Instrument
EP	European Parliament
EPA	Economic Partnership Agreements
EPC	European Political Community
EPM	ECB Payment Mechanism
EPSO	European Personnel Selection Office
ERDF	European Regional Development Fund
ERGEG	European Regulators' Group for Electricity and Gas
ERM	European Exchange Rate Mechanism
ESA	European System of National and Regional Accounts
ESCB	European System of Central Banks
ESDP	European Security and Defence Policy
ESF	European Social Fund
ETSI	European Telecommunications Standards Institute
ETSC	European Technical and Scientific Centre
EU	European Union
EuGRZ	*Europäische Grundrechte Zeitschrift*
EUI	European University Institute
EuR	*Europarecht*
Euratom	European Atomic Energy Community
EUREKA	Pan-European network for market-oriented, industrial R&D
Eurojust	
EuZW	*Europäische Zeitschrift für Wirtschaftsrecht*
EVM	*Europa van Morgen*
FAO	Food and Agriculture Organization
FIFG	Financial Instrument for Fisheries Guidance
FII	Franked Investment Income
FPÖ	Freedom Party of Austria (*Freiheitliche Partei Österreichs*)
FR	Financial Regulation
FRONTEX	European Agency for the Management of Operational Cooperation at the External Borders of the European Union
FRY	Federal Republic of Yugoslavia
FYROM	Former Yugoslav Republic of Macedonia

GAP	General and Persistent
GATS	General Agreement on Trade in Services
GATT	General Agreement on Tariffs and Trade
GCC	Gulf Cooperation Council
GDP	Gross Domestic Product
GMO	Genetically Modified Organism
GNI	Gross National Income
GNP	Gross National Product
GSP	Generalized System of Preferences
HHI	Herfindahl-Hirschmann Index
HICPs	Harmonized Indices of Consumer Prices
HNS	Hazardous and Noxious Substances
IAEA	International Atomic Energy Agency
IAP	Integrated Action Programmes
IATA	International Air Transport Association
ICCPR	International Covenant on Civil and Political Rights
ICLQ	*International and Comparative Law Quarterly*
ICT	Information and Communication Technology
IGC	Intergovernmental Conference
IIA	Interinstitutional Agreement
ILO	International Labour Organization
IMF	International Monetary Fund
IMO	International Maritime Organization
IMP	Integrated Mediterranean Programmes
IPA	Instrument for Pre-accession Assistance
IT	Information Technology
ITER	International Thermonuclear Experimental Reactor
JCMS	*Journal of Common Market Studies*
JHA	Justice and Home Affairs
JET	Joint European Torus
JWT	*Journal of World Trade*
JZ	*Juristenzeitung*
LIEI	*Legal Issues of Economic Integration* (formerly *Legal Issues of European Integration*)
LIFE	Financial Instrument for the Environment
LJIL	*Leiden Journal of International Law*
MCA	Monetary Compensatory Amount
MEP	Member of European Parliament
MJ	*Maastricht Journal of European and Comparative Law*
NAFO	North Atlantic Fisheries Organization
NATO	North Atlantic Treaty Organization
NCB	National Central Bank
NJW	*Neue juristische Wochenschrift*
NRA	National Regulatory Authority

OCT	Overseas Countries and Territories
OECD	Organization for Economic Cooperation and Development
OEEC	Organization for European Economic Co-operation (which later became OECD)
OHIM	Office for Harmonization in the Internal Market
O.J.	*Official Journal of the European Union*
OLAF	European Anti-fraud Office (*Office de Lutte Antifraude*)
OSCE	Organization for Security and Cooperation in Europe
OTIF	Organisation Intergouvernementale pour les Transports Internationaux Ferroviaires (Organization for International Carriage by Rail)
PCA	Partnership and Cooperation Agreement
PCP	Pentachlorophenol
PDO	Protected designation of origin
PGI	Protected geographical indication
P&I Clubs	Protection & Indemnity Clubs
PIF	*protection des intérêts financiers*
PJCCM	Police and Judicial Cooperation in Criminal Matters
PNR	Passenger Name Record
PPI	Protocol on Privileges and Immunities
PSC	Political and Security Committee
PVK	Dutch Pension and Insurance Supervisory Authority
QMV	Qualified Majority Voting
REACH	Registration, Evaluation, Authorization and Restriction of Chemicals
Reg.	Regulation
REIO	Regional Economic Integration Organizations
RMT	*Rechtsgeleerd Magazijn Themis*
RTDE	*Revue Trimestrielle de Droit Européenne*
RTGS	Real-time Gross Settlement
SAA	Stabilization and Association Agreement
SARS	Severe Acute Respiratory Syndrome
SEA	Single European Act
SEW	*Sociaal-Economische Wetgeving*
SIS II	Second Generation Schengen Information System
SME	Small and Medium Enterprises
STABEX	*Système de Stabilisation des Recettes d'Exportation*
SYSMIN	System of Stabilization of Export Earnings from Mining Products
TABS-MFI	Total Assets of the Aggregated Balance Sheet of Monetary Financial Institutions
TARGET	Trans-European Automated Real-time Gross Settlement Express Transfer System
TARIC	Integrated Tariff of the European Communities

TBR	Trade Barriers Regulation
TEN	Trans European Networks
TEU	Treaty on European Union
TFEU	Treaty on the Functioning of the European Union
TRIPS	Trade-related Aspects of Intellectual Property Rights
TSG	Traditional specialty guaranteed
UCLAF	Task Force for the Coordination of the Combat against Fraud
UEFA	Union of European Football Associations
UNCED	United Nations Conference on Environment and Development
UNCTAD	United Nations Conference on Trade and Development
UNEP	United Nations Environmental Programme
UNESCO	United Nations Educational, Scientific and Cultural Organization
UNICE	Union of Industrial and Employers' Confederations of Europe
UNRWA	United Nations Relief and Works Agency
VAT	Value Added Tax
VIS	Visa Information System
WEU	Western European Union
WIPO	World Intellectual Property Organization
WTO	World Trade Organization
YEL	*Yearbook of European Law*
ZHR	*Zeitschrift für das gesamte Handels- und Wirtschaftsrecht*

Chapter I

The Genesis and Development of the European Communities and the European Union

C.W.A. Timmermans

1   THE SCHUMAN PLAN AND ITS BACKGROUND

On 9 May 1950 a press conference took place at the Quay d'Orsay to make public a proposal by the French Government which was to have far-reaching importance for European integration. The French Foreign Minister, Robert Schuman, read a sensational declaration. It contained the proposal to place the whole of Franco-German coal and steel output under a common High Authority, in an organization open to the participation of other countries of Europe.

    This proposal was sensational in two respects. In the first place it meant a turn of the tide in French policy with regard to Western Germany, a policy which had so far been directed at a continued tutelage by the Western Allies of the defeated enemy. A proposal for a Franco-German partnership in a limited but vital economic field, as the nucleus of a broader European co-operation, broke through this post-war policy. The form which was to be given to this co-operation was equally revolutionary: the grouping of coal and steel production under the direction of a common High Authority (composed of independent persons), capable of taking decisions binding on France, Germany, and any other participating countries, and which could be implemented in their territory. This proposal introduced a new

P.J.G. Kapteyn, A.M. McDonnell, K.J.M. Mortelmans and C.W.A. Timmermans (eds),
The Law of the European Union and the European Communities, pp. 1–51.
©2008 Kluwer Law International BV, The Netherlands.

element into the organizational pattern according to which the promotion of common interests by states was wont to take place in international society.

The typical feature of this latter pattern had been an intergovernmental organization, commonly based on three principles. In the first place, decisions of the organization are taken by organs composed of government representatives. Second, participating states are not legally bound by these decisions against their will; even if the basic treaty provides for binding decisions, unanimity will be required to arrive at them; decisions having no binding effect by virtue of the treaty itself will only obtain this effect in relation to states accepting them. Third, the implementation of decisions is reserved to the participating states themselves. There are, of course, exceptions to each of these three principles. But it is the abandonment of these principles as a starting point for the association of states in an international organization which justifies the *supranational*[1] label which was later to be given to the form of organization which was developed on the basis of the Schuman Declaration.

1.1   THE POWER VACUUM IN EUROPE AND THE AIM
OF EUROPEAN INTEGRATION

What was the background to this Declaration, which broke both with a main feature of post-war French foreign policy and with traditional views concerning the organization of cooperation between states?

In the spring of 1950 the world presented a grim picture, especially seen from Western Europe. The eastern part of Europe had been brought firmly within the Russian sphere of influence. The *coup d'état* of 20 February 1948 in (then) Czechoslovakia and the Berlin blockade from 24 June 1948 to 12 May 1949 had enhanced the fear of Russian expansionism. The explosion of the first Russian A-bomb in August 1949, three to four years earlier than the West had anticipated, and the strengthening of the monolithic communist block which was expected to result from the final victory of the party of Mao Zedong in China in the autumn of 1949, tended to foster even further the widely prevalent opinion in the West that the chances of a third world war had increased considerably.

The risk that Europe itself might once more be at the centre of a future conflict was recognized by many people. Indeed, armed forces of the two super-powers confronted each other there. The fuel for a conflict lay piled high: the artificial division of Germany and the militarily weak position of the garrisons of the Western Allies in West Berlin. The countries of Western Europe were busily engaged in restoring their economies with American financial aid under the Marshall Plan (1947). Politically, however, they were still at a stage of relative insignificance, while militarily they were making a first modest attempt to put up a coordinated defence of their territory against an attack from the East. Being helpless against

---

1. This term occurred in the original version of the ECSC Treaty (Art. 9), but disappeared during a later revision.

superior Russian military power and without hope of ever being able to establish any adequate defence against it, they depended on the military and financial aid of the United States under the North Atlantic Treaty, concluded on 4 April 1949. The impulse for this Treaty came on the one hand from the Brussels Treaty of 17 March 1948, on the part of the United Kingdom, France and the Benelux countries, and on the other hand from the so-called Vandenberg Resolution. This Resolution had been adopted on 11 June 1948 by the US Senate and recommended an association of the United States with 'such regional and other collective arrangements as are based on continuous and effective self-help and mutual aid'.

The international political situation which had developed after the war gave all the more impetus to a political trend which, by taking up pre-war plans and ideas, aimed at a firmly organized political and economic partnership of European nations. Europe on the basis of this partnership should muster enough strength to play its part in international politics once again, instead of being at its mercy. The vacuum which had arisen in Europe had to be filled with a new political structure which would diminish the Russian threat and reduce the dependence on the United States. Winston Churchill was the first to give full publicity to the idea of European integration after the war. On 19 September 1946, in an address at Zurich University, he submitted that it was necessary to build 'a kind of United States of Europe' for which he saw a partnership between France and Germany as the first step.

The year 1948 formed a climax for the numerous political groups which advocated a united Europe. On 7 May 1948 they jointly convened the Congress of Europe in the Hague. A great many prominent parliamentarians, scholars and statesmen not in office at the time took part. In a series of resolutions they made an appeal for the formation of a political and economic union, the calling of a European Assembly whose members were to be appointed by the national parliaments, the framing of a Charter of Human Rights, and the creation of a Court of Justice to supervise the observance of the Charter.

At the instigation of the Belgian and French Governments, these proposals were studied in the Council of the Brussels Treaty to ascertain to what extent they could be carried into effect. These discussions resulted in the Statute of the Council of Europe, signed on 5 May 1949, in which, in addition to the countries of the Brussels Treaty, Sweden, Norway, Denmark, Ireland, and Italy took part. The Statute was the result of a laboriously reached compromise, the British participants in particular having doggedly held out for an organization along purely intergovernmental lines. The British concession concerned the establishment of a Consultative Assembly in addition to the classic Committee of Ministers. This Assembly was composed of representatives of the Member States, who were to be designated in a way to be determined by each government. Although it was not expressly stated in the Statute, the intention of the framers was to pave the way for an organ in which the national parliaments might be represented, a novelty in the setup of an international organization. It was not until 1951 that the logical consequence was drawn from this intention and the Statute was amended in the sense that henceforth each parliament, at least as a general rule, was to appoint the number of delegates in the Assembly assigned to the respective country.

For the rest, the Council of Europe turned out to be a disappointment for the champions of firm European partnership. The Consultative Assembly was only able to make recommendations to the Committee of Ministers, which in turn could do little more than frame recommendations to the Member States, in practically all important cases on the basis of unanimity. Nevertheless, the Consultative Assembly, which consisted of a select group of parliamentarians, played a particularly important political role during the first few years. It was indeed from the midst of this body that the initiative came for the framing of a treaty which was eventually signed in Rome on 4 November 1950 as the European Convention for the Protection of Human Rights and Fundamental Freedoms and which entered into force on 3 September 1953. In the Assembly, the first great debates in public concerning the form and substance of future European cooperation also took place. There the different groups which had already manifested themselves at the Hague Congress became clearly apparent: the unionists, the federalists and the functionalists. The unionists desired a further development of intergovernmental cooperation between European countries. The federalists held that a European federation should be the ultimate aim. The boldest among them, the constitutionalists, wished to proceed to convene a *Constituante Européenne* which would draft and proclaim a constitution for a United States of Europe. The more prudent of the federalists, the functionalists, advocated a merger of sovereign national rights on concrete points, for instance heavy industry.

1.2   THE PROBLEM OF FRANCO-GERMAN RELATIONS
             AND THE COMMITMENT OF THE GERMAN FEDERAL
             REPUBLIC TO WESTERN EUROPE

It was this last approach which the French Government followed up when making public its plan for the establishment of a High Authority for coal and steel. Although men like Schuman and Monnet (the intellectual father of the plan) no doubt nursed conceptions of the future political structure of Europe, it was not only such conceptions which incited the French to action. The central problem was that of Franco-German relations.

The aim of French European policy was to obtain effective guarantees against a revival of a German menace to French security. Such guarantees had been sought by successive French Governments in a permanent restriction of the scope of development of German economic and political power after the collapse of the Third Reich in 1945. Especially after the final breach between the four Great Powers about the course of action to be taken with regard to Germany, this restrictive French policy appeared less and less feasible in an atmosphere of growing tension between East and West. The United States, in particular, followed by the United Kingdom, was bent on an early reconstruction of economic and political life in the Western zones of occupation of Germany. In Anglo-American circles a thriving Germany closely allied to the West was increasingly regarded as an essential condition for the recovery of Europe and as an indispensable bulwark against the dreaded Russian expansionism. With many reservations therefore, French diplomats had to acquiesce in a series of preliminary measures which led to the establishment in May 1949 of the German Federal Republic. Within, as yet, fairly narrow limits, the Occupation Statute introduced in May of that year made the Germans in the Western zones masters in their own house again.

Early in 1950, French policy reached an impasse. The negative attitude towards German economic and political recovery taxed relations with the new German state – which to an increasing degree was becoming a European political and economic reality to be reckoned with. The position of the Saar, a politically autonomous area, but economically associated with France, bade fair to become a bone of contention. The German Federal Republic, in view of the inequality involved, took a very reserved attitude towards the Ruhr Statute, which was agreed by the end of 1948 particularly at the instigation of France and which ensured allied supervision over the coal and steel industry in this district by means of an international authority. The United States and the United Kingdom showed themselves less and less willing to give an effective shape to this supervision. Finally, the French Government realized that, with the aggravation of antagonism between East and West, it would hardly be possible in the long run to resist American insistence on permitting the German Federal Republic to play its potential role in the economic, political and even military sphere among the nations of Europe to the full.

The Schuman Plan constituted a brilliant attempt to break through this impasse. The policy aim remained the same: effective guarantees against a revival of a German menace to French security. But the means for achieving this aim were changed drastically. Instead of the former negative policy, directed at a continued allied tutelage of Germany, efforts were directed towards a far-reaching partnership on a basis of parity of the two countries within a European setting. It was precisely the coal and steel sector, the traditional basis of every form of power politics, which seemed an excellent starting point for such an association. The unilateral supervision over the German coal and steel industry, embodied in the Ruhr Statute, which had not proved viable, would make way for a coal and steel regime on a broader basis, which would subject this industry in France, Germany, and other European countries which wished to participate, to supervision on an equal footing by a common High Authority. This arrangement would also place the Saar problem in a different perspective.

Thus the Schuman Plan was a political answer to a series of political problems of the first order:

> the existence of a power vacuum in Europe, viewed by many people as one of the sources of the cold war; the more effective shaping of European integration, which was widely deemed necessary; the settlement of Franco-German relations; and finally the cementing of the German Federal Republic, which was once again developing into a European power, into Western Europe on a basis of equality, but with maximum guarantees against independent German power politics, with all the dangers to Europe and world peace this could involve, also in view of the division of the former German territory into a Western and an Eastern sector.

1.3   Economic Considerations

Considerations of a more economic character were not absent, but they played a rather subsidiary part compared to the political considerations mentioned above, some of which were acute. Thanks to Marshall Aid, but also as a result of the activities of the Organization for European Economic Co-operation (the OEEC, which later became the OECD), the economic prospects for the European countries at the beginning of 1950 were not unfavourable. At the instigation of the United States and in spite of initial objections, particularly on the part of the United Kingdom, the OEEC had been established on 16 April 1948 in connection with Marshall Aid as a 'continuous organization', meaning that after termination of this aid it would still have the task of shaping economic cooperation between the participating countries of Europe. A Dutch suggestion that the OEEC be entrusted with the task of setting up a customs union on the model of the Benelux Treaty of 1944, and a French attempt to equip the organization with strong institutions had come to nothing, despite US support. These ideas had been strongly opposed in particular by the United Kingdom, but with regard to the French proposal also by Benelux, which feared excessive influence by the larger European countries.

Within the limits thus set on it, this intergovernmental organization of the traditional type had nevertheless taken the first important steps on the road towards the liberalization of trade and payments and towards a better mutual adjustment of national economic policies. However, aspirations for a far-reaching economic partnership based on abolition of tariff frontiers between the participating states, hopes widely cherished at least on the continent, could not be satisfied by the OEEC. Not only was there great difference of opinion among Member States about the nature of and the methods appropriate to a European economic partnership, but the institutional structure of the OEEC did not seem adapted to bear the load of the development and pursuance of a common policy in an economic union. Indeed, in the view of many people, this union would be the indispensable complement of the abolition of trade barriers between the countries of Europe.

Both in institutional respects and with regard to methods of European economic integration, the Schuman Plan suggested new roads. A free movement of coal and steel products might be a first step on the road towards a series of sector markets which might finally lead to full economic integration. The production and sale of coal and steel seemed a good starting point also because this sector demonstrated the striking inappropriateness of national frontiers, which cut up artificially the area where the greatest concentration of coal and iron ore in Western Europe was to be found.

2   THE ECSC TREATY OF 18 APRIL 1951

The French initiative, which was particularly sympathetically received by the United States, met with a favourable reception in several European capitals, especially Bonn. On 20 June 1950 there was a conference in Paris of the six countries (the German Federal Republic, France, Italy and the three Benelux countries) which had subscribed to the principles of the Schuman Plan. An attempt to persuade the United Kingdom to join as well had failed. The fear of being impeded in the development of its own welfare state and in the maintenance of the bonds with the Commonwealth, as well as an insufficient realization of the importance of the French proposal and the vistas it opened, caused the British Government to cling to its standpoint that only a cooperation based on coordination of national policies within the framework of an intergovernmental organization like the OEEC was acceptable.

After nine months of negotiations, the Treaty establishing the European Coal and Steel Community (ECSC) was signed in Paris on 18 April 1951. On 25 July 1952 it entered into force. According to its Article 97, it was concluded for 50 years. The basis of the common market for coal and steel thus called into being was formed by the prohibition within this market of:

(i) duties on importation or exportation or charges having equivalent effect, and quantitative restrictions;
(ii) measures and practices discriminating between producers, purchasers or consumers or interfering with the purchaser's free choice of supplier;
(iii) subsidies or aids granted by states, or special charges;
(iv) restrictive practices tending towards the sharing or exploiting of markets.[2]

In accordance with the Schuman Plan, the High Authority occupied a central place in the institutional structure of the Community. It was composed of independent persons jointly designated by the governments, had its own financial resources from a levy on coal and steel production, and was provided with powers for binding the Member States and companies coming under the Treaty regime. Thus it became a governmental authority operating in this new market, instead of or alongside the six national governments.

This breakthrough from the classic pattern of international organization, which in itself was quite revolutionary, was, however, attended by many safeguards. In the first place the powers of the High Authority were bound up strictly with the provisions of the Treaty.[3] In these provisions, the policy to be pursued in the coal and steel sector was laid down fairly precisely. As the French delegation reported after the negotiations: *'la loi ici, c'est le Traité'*. A Court of Justice was charged, in particular, with ensuring the observance of the law in the implementation of the Treaty.[4]

In the second place, the High Authority was obliged to consult governments and other interested parties frequently and cooperate closely with them. This was to

---

2. Art. 4 ECSC.
3. Art. 14 ECSC. See, generally, P. Reuter, *La Communauté Européenne du Charbon et de l'Acier* (Paris, 1953).
4. Arts. 7 and 31 et seq. ECSC.

be done either directly,[5] or in concert with the Special Council of Ministers,[6] or the Consultative Committee[7] as the case might be. The Council, which was created as a result of a Dutch initiative, was entrusted with the coordination between on the one hand the policy of the High Authority and on the other hand that of the governments responsible for the general economic policy of their countries,[8] a problem which indeed had to be provided for in a system of partial integration such as that of the ECSC system. Only in exceptional cases did the Council of Ministers itself have the power to intervene in the coal and steel market (e.g., under certain conditions in crisis situations[9]). Its task consisted chiefly in giving its opinion – unanimously or by a qualified majority vote – to the High Authority on the decisions to be taken by the latter.[10] On a number of important issues the High Authority was obliged to obtain the prior consent of the Council to its decision by means of an assent. The Council then acted as co-regulator.

Finally, the Treaty provided for a Common Assembly[11] originally composed of members of the national parliaments nominated by them, to which the High Authority was politically responsible for the implementation of the Treaty. This Assembly was given the right to dismiss the members of the High Authority collectively by the adoption of a motion of censure.[12]

The desire of the Contracting Parties not to give the High Authority too great a freedom of manoeuvre (and to this end obliging it to consult the governments and to respect democratic principles and the rule of law) only partly accounts for the heavy institutional structure of the Coal and Steel Community. Indeed, considering the strong commitment to the detailed provisions of the Treaty, the High Authority was given only modest scope for the development of a freely determined policy. The extensive institutional provisions were thus primarily justified by the political perspective, stated in the preamble to the Treaty, which was strongly influenced by the Schuman Declaration: namely the resolve 'to lay the foundations for institutions which will give direction to a destiny henceforward shared'.

Article 97 ECSC provided that the Treaty was concluded for a fixed period of fifty years. Since the Treaty was never prolonged, it lapsed definitively in 2002.[13] Coal and steel products are now in principle subject to the provisions of the EC Treaty.

---

5. Art. 46 ECSC.
6. Arts. 26–30 ECSC.
7. Arts. 18 and 19 ECSC.
8. Art. 26 ECSC.
9. Arts. 58 and 59 ECSC.
10. Art. 28 ECSC lays down special voting requirements relating to decisions and assents.
11. Arts. 20–25 ECSC.
12. Art. 24 ECSC.
13. Cf. the Protocol on the financial consequences of the expiry of the ECSC Treaty annexed to the Treaty of Nice.

3 THE FAILURE OF PLANS FOR A EUROPEAN
DEFENCE COMMUNITY AND A EUROPEAN
POLITICAL COMMUNITY

The Schuman Declaration of 9 May 1950 ushered in an era of ambitious attempts to give shape to European integration in a variety of other fields following the same model. Two of these attempts reached the stage of elaborated texts: the Treaty establishing a European Defence Community (EDC) and the draft Statute for a European Political Community (EPC).

3.1 BACKGROUND AND CONTENT OF THESE PLANS

The Treaty establishing the EDC originated in the Pleven Plan, which derived its name from the proposals of the then French Minister of Defence in October 1950. Shortly after the Schuman Declaration, the Korean conflict had broken out, a conflict which made a deep impression within Europe. To many people in the West it seemed that convincing evidence had thus been produced of the aggressive designs of Moscow-led international communism. What had happened in Korea, might be repeated in Europe. The future appeared gloomier than ever.

In August 1950 Winston Churchill (then in Opposition) launched, in the Consultative Assembly of the Council of Europe, the idea of a European army under a European Minister of Defence, although he left the British role in the dark. In September the North Atlantic Treaty Council met in New York. The US Secretary of State announced that his country was going to station more armed forces in Western Europe. His Government, however, regarded German rearmament as urgent and essential for the defence of that part of the world. The German forces would have to form part of an integrated Atlantic force which would be set up, under a common supreme command, and which was to receive political and strategic guidelines from North Atlantic Treaty Organization (NATO.)

France vigorously opposed this proposal for German rearmament. In October, Pleven submitted counter-proposals; these attempted to safeguard the objectives of French policy with regard to Germany by the methods of the Schuman Plan, and at the same time to make possible the German rearmament stubbornly urged by the US Government. A European army, composed of the smallest possible national units, would be placed under the control of a European ministry of defence, embedded in an institutional structure similar to that of the ECSC. As such, this European army would form part of the integrated Atlantic force which the North Atlantic Council had decided in September to proceed to form.

After a period of great confusion, the French proposal was ultimately adopted in principle, partly under the influence of the recently appointed Atlantic commander-in-chief, the US General Eisenhower, whose support had been enlisted for the idea. Laborious negotiations between the ECSC countries (with the United Kingdom again holding aloof) finally resulted on 27 May 1952 in the signing of the

EDC Treaty, in which an institutional structure somewhat resembling that of the ECSC was provided for.

This new Treaty met with opposition from many quarters on widely different grounds, partly of a political, partly of a more pragmatic nature. One of the major political objections, which was also raised in the circles of those wishing to promote European integration, was the fact that a European army was being created without any provision for the framing of a European defence policy and military strategy or a European foreign policy bound up therewith. Another objection concerned the weak democratic character of the EDC.

In order to meet these objections, the six foreign ministers resolved on 10 September 1952 (anticipating ratification) already to implement Article 38 of the EDC Treaty. This article had been included in the Treaty at the instigation of Italy and provided for proposals from the Parliamentary Assembly of the EDC concerning institutional reform, *inter alia*, to ensure a stronger democratic character of this Community. These proposals were to be seen in the perspective of a later federal or confederal structure, founded on the principle of division of powers and containing, in particular, a system of bicameral representation. The Common Assembly of the ECSC was supplemented by co-opted persons so as to give it a composition similar to that of the Parliamentary Assembly provided for in the EDC Treaty. The resulting '*ad hoc* Assembly' was requested by the Ministers to draft a Statute for a European Political Community: a request which went even further than the mandate contained in Article 38 of the EDC Treaty.

The invitation of the Ministers also spoke of the connection between on the one hand the establishment of such a Community and on the other hand the laying of common foundations for economic development and a fusion of essential interests of the Member States. This passage responded to a suggestion from the Dutch Foreign Minister, Beyen, who wanted to give the Latin tendency to set up institutional structures a firm startingpoint in economic reality. His ideas about this were embodied in two Dutch memoranda, of December 1952 and February 1953, in which the outlines of a European common market were sketched. This so-called Beyen Plan, which broke with the then still prevalent idea of a progressive integration of the European economy sector by sector, was later to form the basis of a successful Benelux initiative which in 1957 led to the conclusion of the EEC Treaty.[14]

The so-called '*ad hoc* Assembly' under the chairmanship of Paul-Henri Spaak, the Belgian statesman, accomplished its task energetically. In March 1953 the Statute for a European Political Community, drafted by the Assembly and adopted by a very large majority, was handed to the six Ministers. This Community would be endowed with an institutional structure resembling that of the ECSC and the EDC, although a more important role than in either of these Communities was allotted to the supranational policy-making institution and to the parliamentary element. The institutions of the EPC were to take over, on the basis of the

---

14. See, generally, R. Griffiths (ed.), *The Netherlands and the Integration of Europe 1945–1957* (Amsterdam, 1990).

respective treaties, the powers of those of the existing ECSC and the future EDC. Procedures were provided to ensure the realization of a coordinated foreign policy of the participating countries, which might in course of time become a common policy, the introduction of a Community tax to defray Community expenses, and the establishment of a common market.

A solitary opponent, the French Gaullist Michel Debré, had vainly championed a different conception in the '*ad hoc* Assembly': that of a Political Union on purely intergovernmental lines, with a Conference of Heads of Government as the top organ.

3.2   FAILURE OF THESE PLANS AND '*RELANCE EUROPÉENNE*'

The draft Statue for an EPC was not to get beyond the phase of being an object of study. The chances of ratification of the EDC Treaty by France were gradually dwindling. On 30 August 1954 the French National Assembly finally resolved to adjourn the debate on the acceptance of the EDC Treaty *sine die* – and with that, the draft Statute for an EPC also disappeared. Various factors led to this French attitude. A coalition of communists and Gaullists (whose numbers had greatly increased) had hotly opposed the EDC. The former resolutely rejected German rearmament. The latter turned against the abandonment of the instrument, *par excellence*, of national sovereignty: the French army. Moreover, in French circles there was a widespread fear of a confrontation with growing German power within an EDC without the United Kingdom.

The international situation, too, had changed. A political thaw in East-West relations appeared to set in after Stalin's death and the Korean Armistice in 1953. Besides, after the fall of Dien-Bien-Phu in August 1954, the French Government of Pierre Mendès-France had some interest in giving the Soviet Government, which was waging a vehement campaign against acceptance of the EDC, as little cause for irritation as possible, because it badly needed its support in an honourable liquidation of the French empire in Indo-China. To this should be added the French resentment of US pressure to accept the EDC Treaty. The US had far overshot the mark when, in December 1953, the US Secretary of State, Foster Dulles, had threatened an 'agonizing reappraisal of basic US policy' if the EDC should fail to be established owing to French refusal.

The efforts towards European integration had been dealt a severe blow by the decision of the French Parliament. However, thanks to an initiative of the British Foreign Secretary, Anthony Eden, the essential matter which had formed the primary concern could be settled: the admission of the German Federal Republic as a partner on terms of equality in the Atlantic alliance. The so-called Paris Agreement of 23 October 1954, which had been reached at his instigation, provided, *inter alia*, for the creation of a Western European Union, equipped with a Parliamentary Assembly and an Agency for arms control, on the basis of a modification of the Brussels Treaty of 1948, to which Italy and the German Federal Republic now also became parties. In this looser European association, the German Federal Republic, with due observance of certain restrictions, was allowed to proceed to rearmament and to make its contribution to the integrated Atlantic armed forces. The occupation regime of Western Germany, now to be admitted to NATO, was terminated, although the three Western occupying powers reserved to themselves their rights with regard to Berlin and to Germany as a whole. An agreement between France and the German Federal Republic finally provided for a settlement of outstanding disputes between the two countries. With reference to the matter of the future position of the Saar, the prospect of a plebiscite was offered, which in 1955 was to turn out in favour of confederation with the German Federal Republic.

The dismay amongst the champions of European integration about the rejection of the EDC Treaty did not, however, last long. A '*relance européenne*' was started. A Benelux memorandum of 20 May 1955 resumed the thread of the Beyen Plan: economic integration should precede political integration. The memorandum proposed the convening of a conference for the purpose of working out texts for a treaty which would give shape to far-reaching collaboration in the fields of transport infrastructure, coordination of energy policies, development of the peaceful use of atomic energy, and creation of a common market. In the two last-mentioned fields an important task was intended for a common Authority.

The reaction of the other ECSC countries was not unfavourable, although the French Government displayed an aversion to supranational institutions. The German Government also showed some reserve in this field, possibly because it was apprehensive of the *dirigiste* tendency which it felt was already embodied in the ECSC in the powers of the High Authority. The main interest shown on the French side was for cooperation in the field of atomic energy. On 1–2 June 1955 the six foreign ministers of the ECSC countries met in Messina to discuss the Benelux memorandum. It was broadly approved, although in the resolution of the Ministers the institutional provisions relating to cooperation in the field of atomic energy and the establishment of a common market were mentioned only in vague terms. It was decided to convene one or more conferences for working out treaties, and also to entrust the preliminaries for these conferences to a committee of government representatives. This was to be assisted by experts and to be presided over by a political personality who was to coordinate the activities. Paul-Henri Spaak was found willing to undertake the latter task. The United Kingdom, being a member of the Western European Union (WEU) and a power allied with the ECSC in a somewhat superficial association (meant to keep a door open) was invited to take part in the activities. This invitation was accepted, although the United Kingdom Government did not subscribe to the Messina Resolution. British participation in the work of the Intergovernmental Committee was to be only short-lived. Already in November 1955 it came to an end. The plans which had matured in the Committee could not be reconciled with the British preference for intergovernmental cooperation, preferably in the OEEC, and for a free-trade area rather than a customs union.

4   THE SPAAK REPORT AND THE CONCLUSION OF
        THE TREATIES ESTABLISHING THE EUROPEAN
        ECONOMIC COMMUNITY AND THE EUROPEAN
        ATOMIC ENERGY COMMUNITY

4.1   THE CONTENTS OF THE SPAAK REPORT

On the basis of the Messina Resolution the Intergovernmental Committee, led with great political imagination and dynamism by Paul-Henri Spaak, had set to work on 9 July 1955. In April 1956 the Spaak report was completed in its final form.[15] In the Schuman Plan, the matter of the institutions had taken priority. However, the Spaak Plan – particularly in the light of the widespread reticence about setting up supranational structures after the *débâcle* of the EDC – only dealt with this question following analysis of the substantive problems to be solved in relation to the establishment of a common market and the promotion of the peaceful use of atomic energy. The measures required for the establishment of a common market and the underlying philosophy are traced in broad outline.

'The purpose of a common market must be the creation of a large area with a common economic policy, so that a powerful unit of production is formed and continuous expansion is made possible, as well as an increased stability, an accelerated increase of the standard of living, and the development of harmonious relations between the Member States thus united'.[16]

For this, a fusion of the separate national markets was absolutely essential. The division of labour on a larger scale could put an end to the waste of economic resources. A greater certainty that the requisite sources of supply are permanently accessible makes it possible to abandon productive activities which pay no attention to costs.

This grand design is worked out further in the report around three topics. The *fusion of markets* involves the establishment of a customs union, the abolition of quantitative restrictions, free movement of services and a common agricultural policy. This fusion of markets should be accompanied by a *policy for a common market*. Indeed, in the present economic situation an expansion of markets and of competition *per se* would not yet be sufficient to ensure the more rational division of economic activities and the most favourable degree of expansion. A common competitive regime would be needed and also provisions for harmonization of laws and the development of a common transport policy. Another essential point was the coordination of national economic policies, so as to avoid difficulties with the balance of payments, if possible, and also common action for eliminating these

---

15. *Rapport des Chefs de Délégations aux Ministres des Affaires Etrangères* (Secretariat of the Intergovernmental Conference, Brussels, 21 Apr. 1956).
16. Ibid., 13 (unofficial translation).

difficulties, should they arise. *To ensure the development in this common market of European economic resources and their full use*, financial aid for investments and retraining of workers would be necessary in order to promote the transformation of enterprises, the development of economically backward regions, and professional mobility. Freedom of movement should also be given to the production factors – labour and capital.

The report further contended that the realization of this ambitious programme could only take place during a transitional period divided into stages. A multitude of tasks embracing supervision, coordination, legislation, and administration would have to be carried out, which could not possibly all be regulated in detail in the text of the treaty. Moreover, it was felt essential to ensure that flexible methods could be used in implementing the programme, because economic conditions are apt to change rapidly. A good deal therefore would have to be left to institutions, the powers of which would be clearly defined in the treaty, and to procedures, the diversity of which would match that of the problems which might arise. With regard to the institutional structure and the division of powers the report subsequently developed four principles:

(i) pending a closer unity of monetary, budgetary, and social policies of the participating countries it would be necessary to make a distinction between:

    (a) matters of general policy, which would remain the reserved domains of the governments, and

    (b) problems relating to the functioning of the common market;

(ii) the creation of an organ furnished with authority and Community responsibility would be inevitable, since:

    (a) the interest of producers and their legal certainty would demand a direct procedure (*i.e., not via* the governments) for the application and supervision of the rules concerning competition; the promptness required for enquiry and decision would not be compatible with '*la voie complexe des relations et des organisations intergouvernementales*';

    (b) the supervision of the fulfillment by the states of their obligations and the control of clauses which permit them to be temporarily relieved of these obligations under certain conditions (safeguard clauses) could hardly be subjected to '*un vote des gouvernements*': '*l'unanimité permettrait un veto ou des marchandages, la majorité pourrait traduire une coalition d'intérêts plutôt qu'une reconnaissance objective du droit*';

(iii) the general policy measures falling within the competence of the governments have so decisive an effect on the functioning of the common market that agreement between the governments should be facilitated and the coordination of these measures more effectively ensured through the use of proposals from a common institution. Certain decisions are even so indispensable for the functioning and development of the common market that, at the suggestion of this institution, acting objectively in the general interest, the rule of unanimity of the governments might be put aside, either in a strictly specified number of cases or after a given period had elapsed;

(iv) it would be necessary to provide for appeal to a judicial body and for organization of parliamentary supervision.

On the basis of these principles the report reached the conclusion that four different institutions were needed:

(a) a Council of Ministers;
(b) a European Commission;
(c) a Court of Justice; and
(d) a Parliamentary Assembly.

The functions of the two last institutions could be performed by the Court and the Common Assembly of the ECSC. The report drew a similar conclusion with regard to an organization for the peaceful development of atomic energy. Highly varied and permanent responsibilities are involved in the following:

- the promotion of research and the dissemination of scientific and technical information;
- the establishment and supervision of security norms; the encouragement of investment;
- the erection of common plants;
- the safeguarding the supplies of ores and nuclear fuel; and
- the establishment and functioning of a common market for the atomic energy industry.

Such responsibilities could rest only with a permanent institution that was capable of reacting promptly, i.e., with a Commission incorporated in an institutional structure of the same kind as that proposed for promoting the common market.

By giving priority to the practical problems involved in the objectives to be reached over the problem of the institutional structure, the Spaak Report succeeded – and this is not the least of its numerous great merits – in demonstrating in a tactical but convincing way the advantages of an institutional structure coordinated with that of the ECSC. A Commission composed of independent persons and serving the Community interest was to be the pivot around which the institutional structure would revolve. It would be able to ensure an efficient discharge of functions of supervision and administration. It would have the task of stimulating and initiating common policies and common rules, and of stimulating the coordination of national policies and national laws. Thanks to the guarantee of impartiality implied in its composition and the formulation of its task, it would even be possible to break through the rule of unanimity in the collective determination of policy measures by the governments.

4.2 THE CONCLUSION OF THE EEC AND EURATOM TREATIES

On 29 May 1956, the six foreign ministers met in Venice. At this conference they adopted the Spaak Report as basis for negotiations to frame the requisite treaties.

An intergovernmental conference, again under the leadership of Paul-Henri Spaak, was convened for this purpose on 26 June 1956. The negotiations naturally did not proceed without difficulties. Formidable problems had to be solved. Fitting the weak French economy into a common market caused great concern. On the French side all sorts of guarantees were demanded on this point. Moreover, the French Government wished its partners to share in the commercial and financial liabilities of France with regard to the overseas territories and countries associated with that country, particularly those in Africa. Nevertheless, on 25 March 1957 the Treaty establishing the European Economic Community and the Treaty establishing a European Atomic Energy Community were signed in Rome; unlike the ECSC Treaty, they were concluded for an indefinite period.[17] A smooth ratification procedure followed. The long-standing fear that the French Parliament might ultimately refuse to accept the establishment of a common market was found to be unjustified. This fear had even helped to cause questions relating to the peaceful use of atomic energy (which after the Suez crisis of 1956 in the view of many people was of even greater importance than the common market) to be settled in a separate treaty. The partners wished to prevent the fate of cooperation in this field being dependent upon that of a common market.

The successful course of the negotiations and of ratification – the treaties entered into force on 1 January 1958 – was due primarily to the indefatigable efforts of the Action Committee for the United States of Europe, a very effective European pressure group set up by Jean Monnet. Monnet, who in 1952 had been appointed the first President of the High Authority, had tendered his resignation from this office after the failure of the EDC Treaty in the French Parliament so that he might devote his full energy to the '*relance européenne*'. In the Action Committee he had managed to unite a large number of influential politicians and trade union leaders from the six countries, who had declared their willingness to make a joint effort to gain the support of their groupings for the federalist basic idea and for the specific resolutions of the Committee.

5   THE COMMUNITIES, THE UNITED KINGDOM,
              AND ENLARGEMENT TO INCLUDE OTHER
              DEMOCRATIC EUROPEAN COUNTRIES

As was to be expected, there was a reaction on the part of the other OEEC countries to the establishment of the EEC and Euratom. On a British initiative, an enquiry was started in the OEEC in the course of 1957 into the possibilities of bringing about an association in the form of a free-trade area between the OEEC countries, in which the Six would participate as one economic unit. Great differences of opinion turned out to exist on various issues about which the Six – who were apprehensive of the possibility that the integration process they had started

---

17.   Arts. 312 EC and 208 Euratom. So far no state has ceased to be a member.

might be watered down – were very much concerned. The problems which worried them included: the necessary degree of harmonization of economic and social policies, the settlement of the problem of the agricultural sector, the consequences of the lack of a common external tariff and a common external trade policy, and the institutional form for such an association. The negotiations (which started in the autumn of 1957, after the termination of the ratification procedure of the EEC Treaty) took place in the Intergovernmental Committee set up by the OEEC Council, under the leadership of the British Minister, Reginald Maudling. They came to an abrupt end in November 1958. The French Minister of Information, Jacques Soustelle, on behalf of the government of General de Gaulle, who had meanwhile come into power, informed the press (without any previous consultation with the five partners) that it was not possible to create a free-trade area without a common external tariff and without harmonization in the economic and social spheres. Thus, the door was closed to the other OEEC countries. Seven among them, *viz.* the United Kingdom, Denmark, Norway, Sweden, Austria, Switzerland and Portugal, decided in July 1959 to go their own way: on 4 January 1960, in Stockholm, the Treaty establishing a European Free Trade Association (EFTA) was concluded. Greece and Turkey associated themselves with the Community in agreements of 9 July 1961 and 12 September 1963 respectively, both based on then Article 238 EEC (now renumbered Art. 310 EC).

However, after a few years a radical change took place in the British attitude towards the Communities. On 31 July 1961 Prime Minister Harold Macmillan informed the House of Commons that in the opinion of his government 'it would be right for the United Kingdom to make a formal application, under Article 237 of the EEC Treaty for negotiations with a view to joining the Community if satisfactory arrangements could be made to meet the special needs of the United Kingdom, the Commonwealth, and EFTA'.[18] A solution of these problems, including, for the United Kingdom, those of British agriculture, would have to be found in conformity with the broad principles and purposes which inspired the concept of European unity and which were embodied in the Rome Treaty. The United Kingdom Government subsequently submitted a request to the Council of Ministers of the EEC to open negotiations with a view to a possible accession. Denmark, Norway, and Ireland followed the British example. The other EFTA countries (Austria, Sweden, Switzerland, and Portugal) on the other hand made a request for negotiations with a view to the establishment of an association or some other economic arrangement.

The negotiations with the United Kingdom started in the autumn of 1961. After 16 months of laborious and often detailed negotiations, which did result in preliminary agreement on many points, the French Government dramatically put an end to the negotiations. At his press conference of 14 January 1963, General de Gaulle plainly showed that he considered British membership of the Community premature and saw no purpose in continuing the negotiations. He alleged that the

---

18.   H.C Deb. Vol. 645, Col. 930.

United Kingdom had not appeared ready to accept a genuine common external tariff, to renounce Commonwealth preferences, to abandon the claim that its agriculture must be privileged, and to cut her ties with the EFTA countries. If the United Kingdom (and with her, inevitably the other EFTA applicant countries) were to join the Community, its character would change and its cohesion be lost. In the long run, General de Gaulle feared the Community would be swallowed up in a colossal Atlantic community, dependent on and controlled by the United States. In the General's view, the Nassau Agreements of December 1962, according to which American aid to the development of the British Skybolt Missile was stopped and the British were to receive the American Polaris Missile as a substitute, had confirmed and reinforced the dependence of the United Kingdom on the United States. With the United Kingdom, the American horse would be dragged into the European Troy. Two weeks after this press conference, on 29 January 1963, it was stated in Brussels that the existing differences of opinion with France made further negotiations impossible.

Rather more than four years after this failure, the Wilson Government considered the time ripe for the United Kingdom to apply once again. On 2 May 1967, Harold Wilson declared in the House of Commons that his Government had decided to make an application for membership of the EEC and parallel applications for membership of the ECSC and Euratom. He reported the readiness of his Government 'to accept the Treaty of Rome, subject to the necessary adjustments consequent upon the accession of a new member and provided that we receive satisfaction on the points about which we see difficulty'.[19] These points concerned in particular the operation of the Community Common Agricultural Policy: its potential effects on the cost of living, and on the structure and well-being of British agriculture; the budgetary and balance-of-payments implications of its system of financing; and certain Commonwealth problems, in particular those of New Zealand and of the sugar-producing countries, whose needs were safeguarded by the Commonwealth Sugar Agreement. Other points about which questions arose were capital movements and regional policies. However, as Wilson stated, the Government believed 'that there is nothing either in the Treaty of Rome or in the practical working of the Community which need make these problems insoluble'.[20]

The reactions of the countries of the Community to the British request for accession, followed by those of Ireland, Denmark, and Norway,[21] were again divided. From a communiqué of 19 December 1967, issued by the Council of the European Communities, it finally became evident that although no Member State had raised any fundamental objection to the enlargement of the Community, nevertheless France, unlike the European Commission and her five partners, was unwilling to start negotiations with the four countries which had sought

---

19. H.C Deb. Vol. 746, Col. 311.
20. Ibid., Col. 313.
21. Sweden, too, intimated a desire to seek a form of participation in the Community which could be reconciled with its policy of neutrality.

membership. The French Government considered it desirable that the recovery of the British economy should be completed before the request of the United Kingdom could be considered. The requests for accession presented by the four countries remained on the Council's agenda.

The resignation of General de Gaulle and the coming into office of a new French President, a confirmation of the United Kingdom's pledge to Europe by the new Heath Government and the definitive arrangement by the Community of the financing of the Common Agricultural Policy after the expiry of the transitional period finally helped to create the conditions for the re-opening of negotiations on the enlargement of the Communities. The communiqué of the meeting of the Heads of State or Government of the Six at The Hague, on 1–2 December 1969,[22] in which a conception of the future development of the Communities is set out, mentions as one of the elements of agreement the opening of negotiations with the applicant States insofar as they accept the Treaties and their political aims, the decisions taken since the entry into force of the Treaties and the choices made in the sphere of further development. After preliminary discussions within the circle of the Six, negotiations started in the summer of 1970. In the early summer of 1971 they resulted in general agreement between the Six and the United Kingdom. On 22 January 1972 the Final Act embodying the instruments of accession was signed by the six Member States, the United Kingdom, Ireland, Denmark and Norway. After the necessary ratification procedures had been completed, the United Kingdom, Ireland and Denmark acceded to the Communities on 1 January 1973.[23] Norway did not accede, the referendum on accession having gone against membership of the Communities. In the course of 1972 and 1973 free trade agreements principally relating to industrial products, were concluded with the remaining EFTA countries, Austria, Portugal, Sweden, Switzerland, Finland, Norway and Iceland.[24]

The enlargement of the Communities did not stop with the Community of nine. Greece applied to accede in 1975 and became the tenth Member State on 1 January 1981.[25] In 1977 Spain and Portugal sought membership of the Communities and after long and difficult negotiations acceded on 1 January 1986.[26] Turkey

---

22. Bull. EC 1-1970, 11 at 16 (point 13 of the communiqué). See, generally, H. von der Groeben, *The European Community: The Formative Years* (Brussels, 1985).

23. For the United Kingdom see the European Communities Act 1972 (as amended). After various renegotiations conducted by the Labour Government a referendum was held in the United Kingdom which indicated considerable majority support for Community membership (see R. Irving, 'United Kingdom Referendum' (1975–1976) EL Rev., 1).

24. For Austria see O.J. 1972, L 300/2; Portugal O.J. 1972, L 301/65 (this lapsed on Portuguese accession on 1 Jan. 1986); Sweden O.J. 1972, L 300/98; Switzerland O.J. 1972, L 300/189; Finland O.J. 1973, L 328/2; Norway O.J. 1973, L 171/2 and Iceland O.J. 1972, L 301/2. These Agreements (and particularly the Protocols thereto) were amended from time to time; the agreements with Austria, Finland, Iceland, Norway and Sweden lapsed on the entry into force of the EEA Agreement on 1 Jan. 1994.

25. O.J. 1979, L 291. See C.J. Heringa and E.F.Ch. Niehe, 'De toetreding van Griekenland tot de Europese Gemeenschappen, een overzicht van de Toetredingsinstrumenten' (1979) SEW, 599–635.

26. O.J. 1985, L 302. See M. Sohier, 'Rechtsvergelijkend overzicht van de toetredingsvoorwaarden van Spanje en Portugal' (1986) SEW, 487.

made formal application for membership on 14 April 1987,[27] as did Morocco on 8 July 1987.[28] The ongoing enlargement process is dealt with further below.

The not inconsiderable problems relating to readiness and ability to take decisions apparent in a Community of nine increased substantially in a Community of twelve. Enlargement poses particular difficulties for the maintenance and expansion of a common market and Community policy, as the divergence in the level of development and economic structure within the Community is significantly increased.[29] In these circumstances it is understandable that attempts were resumed in the 1980s (having already been undertaken in the previous decade as part of efforts towards a European Union) to reform the Community in order to prevent a watering-down of the integration process and give it, if possible, a new impetus. These efforts resulted in the Single European Act of 1986.[30]

The new dynamism in the integration process in the late 1980s, with the completion of the internal market (the so-called '1992 effect'), made the Community more attractive to those states outside it. Another contributory factor was the collapse of the Soviet hegemony in Central and Eastern Europe, first through the end of the tutelage imposed on the satellite states of Czechoslovakia, Hungary, Poland, Bulgaria and Romania, and later through the implosion of the Soviet Union itself. In the resulting turbulence, political unrest and economic insecurity, the European Community stood out as a beacon of economic prosperity and political stability.

The first territorial expansion eastward resulted from German unification on 3 October 1990. This took place without the need for a Treaty amendment, as the new German *Länder* became part of the Federal Republic of Germany, which was already a Member State.[31] Immediately prior to unification, economic and monetary union was achieved between the old German Democratic Republic and the Federal Republic, which meant that the Community Treaties could be applied

---

27. Bull. EC 4-1987, points 1.3.1 and 1.3.2. See *infra*.
28. Bull. EC 7/8-1987, point 2.2.35. This was put to one side on the ground that Morocco was not a European country (*Europa Archiv* 1987, Z 207).
29. See Bull. EC Supp. 1–3/78 as revised in COM(83)116 final. The Committee of Three Wise Men set up as a result of the European Council's discussions in Dec. 1978 in anticipation of a future enlargement to twelve Member States reported in Oct. 1979 on the adaptations to the mechanisms and procedures of the Institutions which would be necessary (Report on European Institutions presented by the Committee of Three to the European Council). See, generally, P. VerLoren van Themaat, 'Enkele kanttekeningen bij de rapporten van de drie "Wijzen" en van de Commissie-Spierenburg' (1980) SEW, 144. As to two-speed integration see, *inter alia, Gedifferentieerde Integratie in de Europese Gemeenschappen* (14th session of the Asser Instituut Colloquium Europees Recht (1984), The Hague, 1985); C.-D. Ehlermann 'How Flexible Is Community Law? An Unusual Approach to the Concept of Two Speeds' (1984) Mich.L.-Rev., 1274; E. Grabitz and B. Langeheine, 'Legal Problems Related to a Proposed "Two Tier System" of Integration within the European Community' (1981) CML Rev., 33.
30. See section 6.2, *infra*.
31. See C. Tomuschat, 'A United Germany within the European Community' (1990) CML Rev., 415; C.W.A. Timmermans, 'German Unification and Community Law' (1990) CML Rev., 437, and W. Sinninghe Damsté and W. Wedekind, 'De eenwording van Duitsland en de EG, een tussenstand' (1991) SEW, 455.

immediately in the new *Länder*.[32] The old German Democratic Republic achieved the necessary transformation of its legal system and legislation extremely quickly.

In response to the desire of the EFTA countries to strengthen their economic ties with the Community, the then President of the Commission, Jacques Delors, launched the concept of what eventually became the European Economic Area[33] on 17 January 1989. This would involve the expansion of the Community's internal market and the relevant Community legislation to embrace the EFTA countries. The negotiations which followed were difficult, as the highest possible degree of homogeneity of legislation and its adaptation in the future by the Community and the EFTA countries had to be reconciled with maintaining the independence of the Community system of decision-making and judicial protection.[34] On 2 May 1992 the EEA Agreement was signed in Oporto.[35] As a result of a referendum, Switzerland did not ratify the Agreement, which was then adapted by means of a Protocol.[36] The EEA Agreement thus entered into force on 1 January 1994, a year behind the original schedule. The EEA Agreement obliged the participating EFTA countries, to receive into their legal systems a large body of Community law and, although they would be consulted, they did not attain any power of co-decision on future amendments of that body of law by the Community. It is thus understandable that the majority of the participating EFTA countries regarded the EEA as a step on the way to actual membership of the Communities.

Accession negotiations were opened with Austria, Finland, Norway and Sweden on 1 February 1993[37] and, given the preparatory work in the EEA Agreement and the high degree of affluence of the candidate countries, came to a very speedy resolution, so that the Treaty of Accession could be signed on 24 June 1994.[38] For a second time, however, the Norwegian people decided in a referendum against accession. On 1 January 1995, Austria, Finland and Sweden acceded

---

32. As to the package of transitional measures agreed in certain fields (e.g., trade, agriculture, transport and the environment) see O.J. 1990, L 353.
33. In an address to the European Parliament, Bull. EC Supp. 1/89. For discussion of the development of the EFTA-EC relationship, see S. Norberg et al., *EEA Law* (Stockholm, 1993) 35–69. See Ch. XIII section 4.2.2. *infra.*
34. See Opinion 1/91 *EEA I,* and Opinion 1/92 *EEA II.* See also the contributions by R. Barents and W. van Gerven in J. Stuyck and A. Looijestijn-Clearie (eds), *The European Economic Area EC-EFTA* (Deventer, 1994) 57 and 33, respectively.
35. For the text of the EEA Agreement, see O.J. 1994, L 1/3. See S. Norberg et al., op. cit. *supra* note 33; T. Blanchet et al., *The Agreement on the European Economic Area (EEA)* (Oxford, 1994); J. Stuyck and A. Looijestijn-Clearie (eds), op. cit. *supra* note 34; S. Norberg, 'The Agreement on a European Economic Area' (1992) CML Rev., 1171, and J. Steenbergen, 'Het EER-Verdrag, een beknopte samenvatting' (1993) SEW, 140.
36. Concluded on 17 March 1993, Bull. EC 3-1993, point 1.3.2. The Protocol contained special provisions permitting Liechtenstein to accede, and this took place on 1 May 1995, Bull. EC 3-1995, point 1.4.49, and 4-995, point 1.4.59.
37. Bull. EC 1/2-1993, point 1.3.1.
38. See O.J. 1994, C 241/9. See also D. Booß and J. Forman, 'Enlargement: Legal and Procedural Aspects' (1995) CML Rev., 95 and M. Jorna, 'The Accession Negotiations with Austria, Sweden, Finland and Norway: A Guided Tour' (1995) EL Rev., 131.

to the European Union,[39] leaving only Norway, Liechtenstein and Iceland as partners in the EEA. The Treaty and Act of Accession and the Protocols attached
thereto were set out on the same basis as earlier accessions, namely acceptance
by the new Member States of the so-called *acquis communautaire*,[40] but with
technical adaptation of existing legislation on institutional as well as substantive
aspects. Exceptions to the *acquis* were for a limited period only.

The dismantling of the Soviet empire cleared the way for new relations with
Unlike with previous accessions, no general transitional period was necessary,
as the legal arrangements relating to the internal market were already in place in the
context of the EEA Agreement. The customs union and the Common Agricultural
Policy applied in principle as from the date of accession. The reduction in agricultural prices in the new Member States resulting from accession was compensated through a special system of regressive national support programmes. Where
environmental requirements in the new Member States were more stringent than
the Community's harmonized standards, this formed a particular problem which
resulted in the new Member States being authorized to continue to apply their
stricter standards for four years from accession, within which period Community
legislation in the field was to be reviewed. Only after this revision would the
question of the possible application of Article 95(4) EC arise.[41] As far as institutional adaptations were concerned, the United Kingdom and Spain refused to agree
to a mechanical adjustment of the provisions concerning qualified majority voting
in the Council[42] and the resulting change in the number of votes required for a
blocking minority. This problem was resolved in a somewhat unorthodox manner
in the Ioannina Declaration.[43]

The dismantling of the Soviet empire cleared the way for new relations with
the former satellite states in Central and East Europe. Sooner or later, most of them
declared their desire for full membership of the European Union. As a first stage,
the so-called Europe Agreements created the framework for close association with
these countries.[44] In June 1993, the European Council of Copenhagen agreed in
principle to accession of these countries, but set a number of general prior conditions; these conditions were, first, of a political nature, amounting to respect for the
principles of democracy and the rule of law (as confirmed later in Art. 49(1) TEU)
and, secondly, the general economic condition of a well-functioning market
economy. Applications for membership were subsequently received from Poland

---

39. As will be explained further in section 7.1 *infra*, in 1991 the Treaty of Maastricht created the
    European Union, which included and is 'founded on' the European Communities, so that from
    then on accession was to that body.
40. I.e., the total legislative achievement of the Community, including the relevant interpretations
    relating to this given by the Court of Justice. See C. Curti Gialdino, 'Some Reflections on the
    Acquis Communautaire' (1995) CML Rev., 1089–1121.
41. This provision allows Member States under certain conditions to maintain legislation which
    departs from harmonized Community rules. See Ch. VIII, section 3.3.4, *infra*.
42. Art. 205 EC.
43. Bull. EU 3-1994, point 1.3.28, O.J. 1994, C 105/1, as adapted to take account of Norway not
    acceding, O.J. 1995, C 1/1. See further, Ch. IV, section 3.3, and Ch. V, section 4.1.1 *infra*.
44. Described further in Ch. XIII section 4.2.3. *infra*.

and Hungary in 1994; from Romania, Slovakia, Estonia, Latvia, Lithuania and Bulgaria in 1995; from the Czech Republic and Slovenia in 1996. Cyprus and Malta had already applied for membership in 1990. During the European Council in Luxembourg in December 1997, it was decided to deal with all these applications in one total process, and to develop a so-called pre-accession strategy for each individual candidate state, within the framework of which considerable financial and technical assistance is given, in particular for the development of the rule of law and the strengthening of the infrastructure which this requires[45] (which can be referred to as 'good governance'). In spring 1998, the formal accession negotiations started with Cyprus, Estonia, Hungary, Poland, Slovenia and the Czech Republic; in February 2000 with Malta and the other East European countries (Bulgaria, Latvia, Lithuania, Romania and Slovakia). The European Council in Helsinki (December 1999) accepted the application for membership made earlier by Turkey, and decided to treat it in the same way as that of the other countries.[46]

The Member States agreed at an early stage that the scale of the latest expansion necessitates a reform of the institutional structure of the European Union; it was more difficult to win agreement on the substance of the reform. This was one of the most important points on the agenda for the Intergovernmental Conference convened in 1996, in conformity with Article N(2) of the Treaty on European Union (in the Maastricht version), which led to the Treaty of Amsterdam.[47] However, the parties at the negotiations did not manage to reach agreement on the required institutional changes. In 2000, a new Intergovernmental conference was convened in order to resolve the so-called 'leftovers' of Amsterdam. In December of that year, these negotiations were concluded somewhat laboriously in Nice. The national ratification procedures concerning the Treaty of Nice were only completed in October 2002, after a second Irish referendum (a first referendum in Ireland rejected the Treaty). With this, the path was cleared for the new accessions. The accession negotiations were successfully completed during the European Council of Copenhagen in December of the same year for Cyprus and Malta, the three Baltic States (Estonia, Lithuania and Latvia), Hungary, Poland, the Czech Republic, Slovakia and Slovenia. These countries acceded on 1 May 2004. Negotiations with Bulgaria and Romania were completed at the end of that same year. Both countries acceded on 1 January 2007.

With the accession of these twelve new Member States – bringing the membership of the EU to a total of twenty-seven states – the accession process has not come to an end. Formal negotiations with Turkey were opened in October 2005, but are generally expected to be lengthy; their outcome is uncertain, also because

---

45. See Reg. 622/98 on assistance to the applicant states in the framework of the pre-accession strategy, and in particular on the establishment of Accession Partnerships, O.J. 1998, L 85, and Regs. 1266 to 1268/99 on coordinating aid to the applicant countries in the framework of the pre-accession strategy, O.J. 1999, L 161.
46. In the meantime, a pre-accession strategy for Turkey has been established, Reg. 390/2001, O.J. 2001, L 58.
47. See 7.2 *infra*.

of the still unresolved problem of Cyprus. The EU and its Member States have also agreed that the Western Balkans have their future in the EU.[48] Croatia and the Former Yugoslavian republic of Macedonia have already applied for membership. Accession negotiations with Croatia were opened in 2005.

6   EUROPEAN POLITICAL COOPERATION;
                  THE EUROPEAN COUNCIL AND THE
                  SINGLE EUROPEAN ACT

6.1   EPC AND THE EUROPEAN COUNCIL

A solitary opponent, the French Gaullist Michel Debré had in vain at the beginning of 1953 championed a different idea in the '*ad hoc* Assembly' than the proposal for a supranational Political Community which it accepted.[49] He argued in favour of a Political Union on purely intergovernmental lines, with a Conference of Heads of Government as the top organ. Debré's proposal, which was viewed skeptically by his fellow-members of the Assembly, was revived in essence in 1960–1962 in General de Gaulle's proposals for the formation of a Political Union.[50]

In de Gaulle's view it was the states which were the only foundations on which Europe could be built: only the states had the necessary legitimacy to exercise authority over the peoples of Europe. Political decisions could only be taken with the agreement of those in power in those states, i.e., national governments – although according to de Gaulle's concepts of political leadership this principally meant the Heads of State or Government of all participating countries. Specialized organisms, such as the three Communities, could do useful work relating to common problems but would clearly be subordinate to unanimous political decision-making by governments. The final version of the French proposals envisaged a Political Union with the aim of approximating, coordinating and unifying policies of the Member States in the spheres of foreign policy, the economy, culture and defence, under the general leadership of a Council of Heads of State or government.

De Gaulle's plans were discussed at two Summits, one in Paris on 10–11 January 1961 and the other in Bonn on 18 July 1961; the discussion continued thereafter in the so-called Fouchet Commission, although in April 1962 this had to suspend its work without agreement having been reached. There were a number of stumbling-blocks: the intergovernmental framework, the fear of encroaching on the competence of the existing Communities, the still uncertain relations with the

---

48. See Declaration and Thessaloniki agenda for the Western Balkans of 21 Jun. 2003. Bull. EU 6-2003, point 1.6.70.
49. See the end of section 3.1 *supra*.
50. See *Le dossier de l'Union Politique* (Political Committee of the European Parliament, Jan. 1964) and H. Nijenhuis, 'De Nederlandse tactiek in de onderhandelingen over een Europese politieke unie (1960–1962): nee tegen De Gaulle!' (1986) *Internationale Spectator*, 41.

United Kingdom, and the possible weakening of relations with the United States within NATO as a result of the proposed defence cooperation. The inflexible attitude of the Netherlands, supported by Belgium, contributed substantially to the failure of the negotiations. These countries argued, in essence, that the principle of the supranational character of a political union could only be discussed if the United Kingdom participated from the outset (the negotiations on the first attempt by the United Kingdom to accede to the Communities had begun in the autumn of 1961). France was resolutely opposed to this.

Often the word 'political' in relation to de Gaulle's proposed union is thought to indicate that it concerned only external relations. This is not, however, the case; the French plans also envisaged this union laying down the powers of the governments acting by mutual agreement to take all important (i.e., political) decisions in the economic sphere. The Communities, acting under the supranational formula, would merely execute these decisions. Thus, it was always inherent in the French view that there was no place in the Communities for qualified majority decisions on important matters, nor was there any room for an independent political role for the Commission.[51]

The rigour of the French position became apparent during the constitutional crisis provoked by France in 1965 as a result of certain proposals for financing agriculture which the Commission had submitted to the Council and which were supported by the other members of the Council but were unacceptable to the French. The main reason for this crisis, however, was the possibility for the Council to decide on matters of agricultural policy with qualified majority as from 1 January 1966. The crisis took the form of a boycott by France of Council meetings (the so-called 'empty chair policy') and only came to an end with the Luxembourg Accord of January 1966. This recorded French dissent from the views of the other Member States on majority voting and was thus in reality an agreement to disagree. As a result of this Accord, the Council thenceforth avoided voting.[52]

After the failure of French plans for a Political Union and the French veto of the United Kingdom's application in January 1963, the three-monthly consultations on external policy which the foreign ministers had held since the end of 1959 were discontinued. To the great annoyance of the French Government the *other* five Member States of the Communities wanted to discuss external policy only within the framework of the WEU Council (i.e., with the United Kingdom being involved).

Only after de Gaulle's resignation, when the French position on United Kingdom accession changed, were the conditions fulfilled for a closer cooperation between the Member States in foreign policy. At the Summit at The Hague on 1–2 December 1969, at which it was decided to open negotiations with the four countries which had applied to accede to the Communities, the foreign ministers were requested to study the best method of making progress in the field of 'political

---

51. See P.J.G. Kapteyn, 'De politieke verschraling van de Europese Gemeenschappen; de EEG: een politiek verschijnsel?' (1966) *Internationale Spectator*, 51.
52. This Accord and its consequences are discussed further in Ch. V, section 4.1.1.

integration'. This task resulted in a report of a committee of Directors-General for political affairs in the six foreign ministries under the chairmanship of Davignon (from Belgium). Six-monthly meetings of the foreign ministers to discuss matters of foreign policy were proposed, to be preceded by meetings of a Political Committee of directors-general. The governments approved this report at the Luxembourg Summit on 27 October 1970 (hence it is often called the Luxembourg report); it laid the basis for European Political Cooperation (EPC). This was further expanded through the report approved at the Copenhagen Summit on 23 July 1973.[53] The report accepted by the foreign ministers in London on 13 October 1981 envisaged still further improvements in the EPC procedure.[54]

The foreign ministers of the Member States met at least four times a year. The preparation of and follow-up to the ministerial meetings was in the hands of the above-mentioned Political Committee. Discussions in EPC covered all important questions of foreign policy of concern to the Member States as a whole. The coordination of the positions of the Member States concerning the political and economic aspects of security fell within the field of EPC.[55] The European Parliament was associated with EPC, albeit often subject to restrictions because of the confidential nature of the discussions.

Cooperation in EPC was purely intergovernmental in nature. Nevertheless, coordination between Community and EPC affairs was inevitable. Economic measures affecting the Community internally, the Community's commercial policy and the way in which relations with developing countries concerning development aid were and are handled, affect the foreign policies of the Member States and are, in turn, influenced by them. Thus the Copenhagen report of 1973, with an eye to this point, envisaged the Commission being invited to give its views on subjects which could have an influence on Community activities. In practice the Commission was represented at all ministerial EPC meetings and all meetings of the Political Committee.[56]

The connection between the activities of the Communities and the work on political cooperation was expressly recognized at the Paris Summit of 9–10 December 1974, and the European Council was duly set up. It was decided that the Heads of State and Government would meet at least three times a year, accompanied by their foreign ministers, as the Council of the Communities and, at the

---

53. See *Seventh General Report on the Activities of the European Communities* (Brussels, Luxembourg, 1973) 502 et seq.
54. See Bull. EC supp. 3/81, 14 et seq.
55. Solemn Declaration on European Union agreed at the Stuttgart Summit in 1983 section 1.4.2. (Bull. EC 6-1983, 1.6.1). The reports and the Solemn Declaration were confirmed and supplemented by Title III of the Single European Act, later repealed and replaced by provisions of the Treaty of Maastricht. See, generally, S. Nuttall, *European Political Co-operation* (Oxford, 1992); G. Edwards, 'European Political Cooperation', 12 *Yearbook of European Law* (Oxford, 1992); and A. Pijpers et al. (eds), *European Political Co-operation in the 1980s* (Dordrecht, 1988).
56. B. Bot, 'Waarheen met de Europese Politieke Samenwerking'? (1977) *International Spectator*, 788.

same time, in the context of political cooperation. The foreign ministers, in order to ensure consistency in Community activities and continuity of work, were instructed to act as initiators and coordinators, meeting in the Council; at the same time they may hold political cooperation meetings. It was expressly provided that these arrangements did not affect the rules and procedures laid down in the Treaties or the provisions on political cooperation in the Luxembourg and Copenhagen reports. The Commission was to exercise its powers at all these meetings and play the part assigned to it in the various texts concerned.[57]

The setting up of the European Council institutionalized the Summit conferences which had taken place since December 1969, after de Gaulle's resignation, from time to time and with varying degrees of success.[58] At the same time, these meetings, in so far as they related to questions falling within the competence of the Communities, were at least informally incorporated into the institutional scheme of the Communities.

The formation of the European Council with, on the one hand, EPC organized on an intergovernmental basis and, on the other hand, the Council's practice since the Luxembourg Accord of not applying the qualified majority voting principle, at least in important matters, amounted to a recognition of the accuracy of some of de Gaulle's views. The thought of extending political cooperation into a more wide-ranging union was taken up again in the 1970s. At the Paris Summit in October 1972, the Heads of State and Government 'assigned themselves the key objective of converting, before the end of this decade and in absolute conformity with the signed Treaties, all the relationships between Member States into a European Union'.[59] At the Paris Summit in December 1974 the then Belgian Prime Minister, Tindemans, was asked to prepare a report on the basis of reports from the Community Institutions and his discussions with governments and circles representative of public opinion in the Community. This report on European Union, presented in December 1975,[60] was neither accepted nor rejected by the European Council. It was simply agreed that the foreign ministers and the Commission would produce an annual report to the European Council about results achieved and the feasible advances in the short term which could be made in various fields of the Union.[61]

---

57. See Bull. EC 12-1974, 7 (point 3, 4th para., of the communiqué from the Dec. 1974 Paris Summit).
58. The Hague (Dec., 1969), Paris (Oct., 1972), Copenhagen (Dec., 1973) and Paris (Dec., 1974). See, generally, Werts, *The European Council* (Amsterdam, 1992) and Glasener in Curtin and Heukels (eds), *Institutional Dynamics of European Integration* (Essays in honour of Schermers, Vol. II, Nijhoff, Dordrecht, 1994) 101.
59. Bull. EC 10-1972, 23 (point 16 of the communiqué).
60. Bull. EC Supp. 1/76. As to the reports from the Commission, the Parliament, the Court of Justice and the Economic and Social Committee, see Bull. EC Supps. 5/75 and 9/75.
61. Bull. EC 11-1976, point 2501 (93).

6.2   THE SINGLE EUROPEAN ACT (1986)

Conversion of all the relations between the Member States into a European Union was impossible in the 1970s. Only in 1981 was the thread taken up again. The German Foreign Minister Genscher and his Italian colleague Colombo put forward a draft 'European Act' which envisaged an improvement of the institutional provisions and an intensification and expansion of cooperation, also in the field of foreign policy, on the way to a European Union. Although this was not the original intention, their initiative resulted not in an amendment of the Treaties but in the Solemn Declaration on European Union adopted by the European Council at Stuttgart on 19 June 1983, which largely got bogged down in intentions about the policy to be pursued and the procedures to be applied.[62]

In the meantime there was a movement in circles in the European Parliament,[63] led by the Italian member Spinelli, which sought to achieve a fundamental reform of European cooperation. This led to the drawing up of a Draft Treaty establishing the European Union which was adopted by the European Parliament on 14 February 1984 by a large majority.[64] The Draft Treaty attracted a great deal of attention, not only in academic circles[65] but also in political circles in the Community. It was difficult for the governments not to react in some way. At the meeting in Fontainebleau on 25–26 June 1984, the European Council decided to set up an *ad hoc* Committee, composed of personal representatives of the Heads of State and Government on the lines of the Spaak Committee. This *ad hoc* Committee, under the chairmanship of Dooge, Chairman of the Irish Senate, was requested to make suggestions for improving European cooperation: in the Community field, in the field of political cooperation and in any other field. In March 1985 the Committee produced its report, albeit not a unanimous one in all parts.[66] Partly as a result of this report the European Council, at its meeting in June 1985 in Milan, and despite objections from Denmark, Greece and the United Kingdom, decided to convene a conference within the meaning of Article 236 EEC to draw up the text of a treaty on common foreign and security policy and on amendments to the EEC Treaty. This conference commenced work in September 1985 and the candidate Member States (Spain and Portugal) were invited to participate.

---

62. Bull. EC 6-1983, point 1.6.1.
63. The Assembly became formally known as the Parliament in 1987.
64. O.J. 1984, C 77/33; Bull. EC 2-1984, point 1.1.2.
65. E.g., R. Bieber et al. (eds), *An Ever Closer Union* (Brussels/Luxembourg, 1985); Capotorti et al., *The European Union Treaty* (Oxford, 1986) (also published in French as *Le Traité d'Union Européenne* (Brussels, 1985) and in German as *Der Vertrag zur Grundung der Europäischen Union* (Baden–Baden, 1986)); Lodge (ed.), *The European Community in Search of a Future* (London, 1986); J. Schwarze et al. (eds), *Eine Verfassung für Europa* (Baden-Baden, 1984); Bos (1985) SEW, 442; Capotorti (1985) CDE, 512; R. Lauwaars et al. (1985) SEW, 398; Lodge, Freestone and Davidson (1984) EL Rev., 387; Louise (1985) CDE, 530; Nickel (1984) CDE, 511; Nickel and Corbett (1984) YBEL 79; I. Pernice (1984) EuR, 126, and J. Weiler and Modrall (1985) EL Rev., 316; J.-P. Jacqué, 'The Draft Treaty Establishing the European Union' (1985) CML Rev., 19–42.
66. See Bull. EC 3-1985, point 3.5.1.

The conference had various materials before it: the report of the Dooge Committee; the report of the *ad hoc* Committee on a People's Europe (the Adonnino Committee which had also been established as a result of the Fontainebleau Summit);[67] the decisions of the Milan European Council on the realization of a single internal market by 1992,[68] and a draft revision of the treaties prepared by Luxembourg, then president-in-office of the Council. The result of the Committee's work, out of all the proposals before it, was the Single European Act which was signed on 17 February 1986 by nine Member States and on 28 February 1986 by Denmark, Italy and Greece. Both Denmark and Ireland needed to hold a referendum before ratification.[69]

The Single European Act (SEA), which came into force on 1 July 1987[70] made on the one hand a number of amendments to the existing Community Treaties. On the other hand, it contained a number of independent provisions relating to the European Council[71] and one, very detailed Article (Art. 30 SEA) which by and large confirmed the existing practice on EPC.[72] A new development was that a

---

67. Bull. EC supp. 7/85.
68. See the Commission's White Paper *Completing the Internal Market* COM (85) 310 Final, presented to the Milan European Council, 28–29 June 1985 (Bull. EC 6-1985, point 1.2.5).
69. Bull. EC Supp. 2/86. The Court of Justice has produced a collection of documents relating to the ratification process of the SEA.
70. See, e.g., J. De Ruyt, *L'Acte Unique Européen*, 2nd ed. (Brussels, 1989); A. Arnull, 'Current Survey, I. European Communities, 2. Institutional and Jurisdictional Questions. The Single European Act' (1986) EL Rev., 358; R. Bieber et al. 'Implications of the Single Act for the European Parliament' (1986) CML Rev., 767; A. Campbell, 'The Single European Act and the Implications' (1986) ICLQ, 932; D. Edward, 'The Impact of the Single Act on the Institutions' (1987) CML Rev., 19; C.D. Ehlermann, 'The Internal Market following the Single European Act' (1987) CML Rev., 361; N. Forewood and M. Clough, 'The Single European Act and Free Movement – Legal Implications of the Provisions for the Completion of the Internal Market' (1986) EL Rev., 383; D. Freestone and S. Davidson, 'Community Competence and Part III of the Single European Act' (1986) CML Rev., 793; H.J. Glaesner, 'Die Einheitliche Europäische Akte' (1986) EuR, 119; id., 'The Single European Act' (1986) YBEL, 283; C. Gulmann, 'The Single European Act: Some Remarks from a Danish Perspective' (1987) CML Rev., 31; H.G. Krenzler, 'Die Einheitliche Europäische Akte als Schritt auf dem Wege zu einer gemeinsamen europäischen Außenpolitik' (1986) EuR, 384; P. Pescatore, 'Die "Einheitliche Europäische Akte" Eine ernste Gefahr für den Gemeinsamen Markt' (1986) EuR, 153; id., 'Some Critical Remarks on the "Single European Act"' (1987) CML Rev., 9; A. Toth, 'The Legal Status of the Declarations Annexed to the Single European Act' (1986) CML Rev., 803; P. VerLoren van Themaat, 'De Europese Akte', (1986) SEW, 464, and J. De Zwaan, 'The Single European Act: Conclusion of a Unique Document' (1986) CML Rev., 747. See also the 12th. Report of the House of Lords Select Committee on the European Communities, (1985–86) *HL*, 149. As to the SEA and environmental policy, see Krämer, 'The Single European Act and Environmental Protection: Reflections on Several Provisions in Community Law' (1987) CML Rev., 659 and Vandermeersch, 'The Single European Act and the Environmental Policy of the European Economic Community' (1987) EL Rev., 407. As to the views of the Dutch government, see F. Kellermann, 'Current Survey. II Member States of the European Communities. Netherlands; The Views of the Netherlands Government on the Single European Act' (1987) EL Rev., 221.
71. Art. 2 SEA. See Capotorti in Capotorti et al. (eds), *Du droit international au droit de l'intégration* (Baden-Baden, *Liber Amicorum* Pescatore, 1987) 79 and Oppermann in ibid., 537.
72. See section 6.1 *supra*. See Frowein in Capotorti et al., ibid., 247 and Oppermann, ibid.

secretariat was set up in Brussels to assist the Presidency of EPC in preparing and implementing EPC's activities and in administrative matters. Of the amendments made to the Community Treaties, the inclusion of the internal market concept in Article 8a EEC, and the envisaged completion of the internal market by 31 December 1992 were of particular significance. To enable this completion, a new legal basis for harmonization measures was introduced in Article 100a EEC, permitting decision-making by qualified majority. New policy areas, in which the Community was already active on the basis of Article 235 EEC (now Art. 308 EC), were given a specific Treaty basis, such as environmental protection and research and technological development. The cohesion policy, designed to strengthen economic and social cohesion between the Member States of the Community, was itself strengthened. On the institutional side, the introduction of the cooperation procedure which gave the European Parliament more say in Community decision-making was particularly noteworthy, as was the attachment to the Court of Justice of a Court of First Instance, designed to deal with staff cases and to give first instance judgments on cases regularly involving complex assessment of factual issues, such as competition cases.

7   THE TREATIES OF MAASTRICHT (1992),
                 AMSTERDAM (1997) AND NICE (2001)

7.1   THE TREATY OF MAASTRICHT (1992)

After the entry into force of the Single European Act on 1 July 1987, and inspired by the progress of the market integration process, the drive towards an economic and monetary union (EMU), which had started in the early 1970s but had quickly appeared unattainable because of global monetary developments, was resumed. A completed internal market cannot continue to function without the keystone of an EMU. In a system of fixed but adaptable exchange rates, to say nothing of a system of fluctuating exchange rates, so much uncertainty remains as to the results of cross-border investments, that the economic advantages of market integration cannot be optimally utilized. Moreover, an internal market without an EMU is never a safe haven, as the risk of unilateral intervention by a Member State disturbing the market remains. These economic realities caused the Hanover European Council in June 1988 to entrust to a committee of specialists, chaired by the President of the Commission, Jacques Delors, the task of studying and proposing concrete stages towards EMU.[73] The Delors Committee Report was presented in April 1989;[74] in December 1989, the Strasbourg European Council[75] decided that the first phase of EMU could begin on 1 July 1990 with the full liberalization of capital movements. At the same time it was decided to convene

---

73. Bull. EC 6-1988, point 3.4.1.
74. Bull. EC 4-1989, points 1.1.1–1.1.9.
75. Bull. EC 12-1989, point 1.1.11.

an intergovernmental conference before the end of 1990, for the purpose of drawing up a treaty basis with a view to the final stages of EMU.

At the same time the collapse of Soviet hegemony began. The breathtaking progress of German unification and the revolutions in the neighbouring Central and East European countries created a climate of hope, but also of considerable political and economic unrest and uncertainty. The German Chancellor, Kohl, strove to anchor a united Germany firmly in a strengthened European Community, strengthened into political unity in order to support the far-reaching restructuring in the former Eastern Bloc countries and to support an effective peace and security policy in Europe. Kohl linked German cooperation on EMU (which meant that Germany would have to surrender its much-prized monetary autonomy, just like the other participants) to a real strengthening of the Community in political terms. After initial hesitation, Mitterrand, then French President, supported this idea. In a joint initiative, they presented to a special European Council in Dublin in April 1990 a proposal for the development of a common foreign and security policy.[76] In June 1990, during the regular Dublin European Council, it was agreed to convene a conference on political union to open in December 1990, alongside the intergovernmental conference on EMU.[77] The work of the two conferences was to run in parallel and to be concluded rapidly and at the same time.[78] The Dublin European Council thus confirmed the Franco-German linkage of these subjects.

Both conferences opened on 15 December 1990, following on from the Rome European Council.[79] For the conference on EMU much preparatory work had already been undertaken, including a draft treaty drawn up by the Commission.[80] With barely six months prior to its opening, the conference on political union was much less well prepared; there was merely a list of subjects which had been drawn up on the basis of contributions by the Commission[81] and some Member States.[82] On that basis, the Rome European Council requested the conference to pay particular attention to a number of issues: strengthening democratic legitimacy as well as the functioning of the Institutions; a common foreign and security policy; European citizenship (an idea of the Spanish Prime Minister Gonzales); extension of Community action and also further and deeper cooperation, in the context of the Union, in the area of justice and home affairs (for instance, immigration policy;

---

76. Bull. EC 4-1990, point I.12 (alongside their paper on political union, a paper from the Belgian Government on the subject was also considered).
77. Bull. EC 6-1990, points I.11 and Annex I (political union); I.10 (EMU).
78. This point was specifically confirmed at the Rome European Council in Dec. 1990, Bull. EC 12-1990, point I.10.
79. Bull. EC 12-1990, points 1.1.7 and 1.1.8. As to the problems of coherence between the two conferences, see the contributions by J.-V. Louis and Maganza in J. Monar et al. (eds), *The Maastricht Treaty on European Union* (Brussels, 1993) 163 and 173, respectively.
80. Bull. EC Supp. 2/91, 13–38, as to the draft treaty, see 39–62.
81. See Bull. EC Supp. 2/91, 85–179. The Commission's Opinion of 21 Oct. 1990 is set out in ibid., 75–82.
82. See, generally, J. Cloos et al., *Le Traité de Maastricht: genèse, analyse, commentaire* (Brussels, 1993) 59–83 (particularly at 75 et seq.).

organized crime; the fight against drugs, and cooperation in criminal matters), at the request of Chancellor Kohl.[83]

The negotiations proceeded pretty speedily – but at the expense of the ambitions of devotees of a Union concept, who had hoped that competence in more areas would be transferred to the Union level, and that the Community method would operate (rather than the intergovernmental method) at that level too. The United Kingdom in particular maintained its strident opposition to such a development, reflecting a certain continuity in its distrust of supranational institutions. Thus the common foreign and security policy and cooperation in justice and home affairs remained outside the Community framework, almost wholly along intergovernmental lines. An attempt by the Dutch – at the time holding the Presidency – to bring the political union and the three Communities into a unitary structure, as had been intended with EMU all along, backfired dramatically. On 30 September 1991 (Black Monday), apart from Belgium, the other Member States were not even prepared to accept the Dutch text as a basis for discussion. During the European Council at Maastricht on 9–10 December 1991 the negotiations were concluded, after certain concessions to a number of Member States, in particular to the United Kingdom in relation to social policy and EMU, and to the poorer Member States, which, led by Spain, forced a larger transfer of resources in their direction through a new cohesion fund.[84] The final text of the Treaty of Maastricht – also called the Treaty on European Union – was agreed and signed at Maastricht on 7 February 1992.[85]

The structure chosen for the Union was tripartite. The most important part, consisting of the three Communities, was strictly separated from the other two, common foreign and security policy (CFSP) and cooperation in the field of justice and home affairs (JHA), which operate in a much more intergovernmental framework. This tripartite structure – the three parts commonly being referred to as the respective 'pillars' supporting the Union as a whole – was to be regarded as an interim phase in the development of the Union. Article N(2) TEU provided for a new intergovernmental conference to be convened in 1996, *inter alia* to review this structure. The Union established by the TEU was not itself granted legal personality. It did not replace the European Communities, but brought them, as a separately organized and still autonomous part, together with the two other parts into a relationship which in legal terms was rather weakly set up. However, new Member States accede to the Union, and only thereby to the Communities. This differs from the approach of the Single European Act, which still foresaw accessions to the various Communities. The relationship between the three parts was demonstrated by the single institutional framework, the purpose of which was to ensure the consistency and continuity of the activities carried out in order to attain the Union's objectives, while respecting and building upon the *acquis communautaire*.[86]

---

83. Bull. EC 12-1990, points I.4-I.9.
84. Bull. EC 12-1991, points I.1 and I.3.
85. See J. Cloos et al., op. cit. *supra* note 82; see further the literature cited at the end of Ch. II of this book.
86. Art. C(1) TEU, Maastricht version.

The most important body in political terms was the European Council, for which the TEU lays down the tasks. The CFSP was determined by the Council, within the principles and general guidelines laid down by the European Council.[87] The Commission had a right of initiative, but not an exclusive one,[88] and the European Parliament was to be consulted by the Presidency on the main aspects and basic choices of CFSP.[89] The Court of Justice was carefully excluded from the picture.[90] As a whole, CFSP was somewhat more 'Communitarized' than was EPC, although even the institutional model of CFSP was – and is – still essentially intergovernmental, not least because decision-making is based on unanimity.

The TEU altered the name of the European Economic Community (EEC) to make it simply the European Community (EC), reflecting the long-standing reality that the Community's tasks are not solely economic in nature. The new provisions of the EC Treaty relating to EMU were set out in detail, so that this part of the Treaty in fact is a second *traité-loi*, like the ECSC Treaty, rather than a *traité-cadre*, like its other provisions. The separate preparation of the EMU and political union texts, which were integrated only in the final stages of the negotiations, was detrimental to the clarity of the final version of the Treaty. In addition to the inclusion of the principle of subsidiarity and the creation of Union citizenship, the major features of the TEU on the institutional side are the strengthening of the powers of the European Parliament – through the introduction of the co-decision procedure, the right to set up temporary Committees of Inquiry, the creation of a European Ombudsman, the formalization of the right of petition to the Parliament, the extension of the assent procedure to certain categories of international agreements, and participation in the appointment of members of the Commission – and finally the inclusion of certain new areas of activity.

The ratification of the TEU[91] met with unexpectedly severe problems in certain Member States. The negative result of the first Danish referendum was followed by fierce discussions in most Member States about the nature of the Community. In these discussions it became very apparent how weakly legitimized in the Member States Community action is, and just how much misunderstanding exists about the Community's structure and functioning. A second referendum in

---

87. Art. J.8(1) and (2) TEU, Maastricht version. See also Art. J.3(1) TEU, Maastricht version.
88. Art. J.8(3) provided that any Member State or the Commission may refer questions or make proposals to the Council within the ambit of CFSP. The Commission must be fully associated with work in the field of CFSP, Art. J.9 TEU, Maastricht version.
89. Art. J.7 TEU, Maastricht version. The Presidency must ensure that the views of the European Parliament must be taken into consideration; the Parliament must be kept regularly informed by the Presidency and the Commission of the development of CFSP, may ask questions of the Council or make recommendations to it, and holds an annual debate on progress in implementing CFSP, ibid.
90. See Art. M TEU, Maastricht version. In JHA the only involvement of the Court is if Conventions adopted by the Member States confer jurisdiction upon it, Art. K.3(2)(c), 3rd para., TEU, Maastricht version.
91. See F. Laursen and S. Vanhoonacker (eds), *The Ratification of the Maastricht Treaty: Issues, Debates and Future Implications* (Dordrecht, 1994).

Denmark produced a positive result, after the Edinburgh European Council in December 1992 had given the Danish Government support through a felicitous interpretation of certain parts of the TEU.[92] In France and the United Kingdom the ratification process proved extremely contentious, but was also ultimately successful.[93] After the German Federal Constitutional Court had ruled that German ratification would not be incompatible with the Constitution,[94] the Treaty on European Union finally came into force, nearly a year later than envisaged, on 1 November 1993.[95]

7.2   THE TREATY OF AMSTERDAM (1997)[96]

A new intergovernmental conference was already foreseen in the Treaty of Maastricht, in order to reconsider a number of (mainly) institutional problems that had not been resolved at Maastricht (structure of the Union, co-decision procedure,

---

92. Bull. EC 12-1992, 1.3. See, further, D. Howarth, 'The Compromise on Denmark and the Treaty on European Union: A Legal and Political Analysis' (1994) CML Rev., 765; D. Curtin and R. van Ooik, 'De bijzondere positie van Denemarken in de Europese Unie: een juridisch Fata Morgana'? (1993) SEW, 675 and, as to the Edinburgh European Council in general, P. VerLoren van Themaat, 'De Europese Raad van Edinburgh als goudmijn voor juristen' (1993) SEW, 423. On 6 Apr. 1998 the Danish Supreme Court dismissed an action claiming that the implementation of the EC Treaty as amended by the TEU was incompatible with Art. 20 of the Danish constitution, *Carlsen et al. v. Rasmussen*, see English translation in A. Oppenheimer (ed.) *The Relationship between European Community Law and National Law: The Cases*, Vol. II (Cambridge, 2003), 175.
93. As to England and Wales, see *R. v. Secretary of State for Foreign and Commonwealth Affairs, ex parte Rees Mogg* [1993] 3 CMLR 101 and as to Scotland, see *Monckton v. Lord Advocate* (1994) *The Times*, 12 May; see also European Communities (Amendment) Act 1993, and Szyszczak (1993) EL Rev., 248. As to France, see the discussion by Cohen (1993) EL Rev., 233.
94. *Brunner* [1994] 1 CMLR 57. See, e.g., J. Frowein, 'Das *Maastricht*-Urteil und die Grenzen der Verfassungsgerichtsbarkeit' (1994) ZaÖRV, 1; M. Herdegen, 'Maastricht and the German Constitutional Court: Constitutional Restraints for an "Ever Closer Union"' (1994) CML Rev., 235; H.-P. Ipsen, 'Zehn Glossen zum Maastricht-Urteil' (1994) EuR, 1; B. Meyring 'Intergovernmentalism and Supranationality: Two Stereotypes for a Complex Reality' (1997) EL Rev., 221; C. Tomuschat, 'Die Europäische Union unter Aufsicht des Bundesverfassungsgerichts' (1993) EuGRZ, 489; J. Wieland, 'Germany in the European Union: The Maastricht Decision of the Bundesverfassungsgericht' (1995) EJIL, 259; J. Weiler, 'Der Staat "über alles": Demos, Telos und die Maastricht-Entscheidung des Bundesverfassungsgerichts', Jean Monnet paper; J. Weiler, 'Does Europe Need a Constitution? Reflections on Demos, Telos and the German Maastricht Decision' (1995) ELJ, 219; and M. Zuleeg 'The European Constitution under Constitutional Constraints: The German Scenario' (1997) EL Rev., 19.
95. The Court of Justice has produced a series of documents on the ratification of the Treaty of Maastricht.
96. See D. O'Keeffe and P. Twomey (eds), *Legal Issues of the Amsterdam Treaty* (Oxford, 1999); Editorial: 'The Treaty of Amsterdam: Neither a Bang Nor a Whimper' (1997) CML Rev., 767–772; G. Berthu and D. Souchet, *Le Traité d'Amsterdam contre la démocratie. Texte intégral comparé et commenté*; R. Barents, *Het Verdrag van Amsterdam in Werking*, Europese Monografieën 62 (Deventer, 1999); theme issue in (1997) SEW, 343 et seq. with contributions by Barents, Donner, Posthumus Meyjes and Timmermans.

CFSP).[97] Subsequently, two important main themes were added to the agenda of this conference. First, how the Union could be brought closer to its citizens – the necessity of which had emerged so clearly in the ratification process for the Treaty of Maastricht, which had been highly problematic in a number of Member States. A second new point on the agenda was the need for reform in order to prepare the Union for the expected large number of new accessions.

The Conference started in March 1996, with at its disposal preparatory material[98] in the form of separate reports drawn up by the Parliament, the Council and the Commission, about the experiences in the application of the Treaty of Maastricht, as well as the end report of the so-called Reflection Group, presided over by Carlos Westendorp, and composed of personal representatives of the ministers of foreign affairs and the President of the European Commission, as well as two representatives of the European Parliament.

The Westendorp report comprised an inventory of the negotiation positions. The conference was concluded, as planned, in June 1997 in Amsterdam. The working method was still mainly that of classic, international diplomatic consultation, although this time with more publicity than during earlier conferences and moreover, as an interesting novelty, a certain amount of say being given to representatives of the European Parliament. Perhaps here a cautious development can be signalled which might eventually lead to a certain constitutionalization of the treaty amendment procedure, in the sense that the democratic legitimacy for these amendments would also be set at the level of the Union itself (cf. also the required assent of the European Parliament for accession of a new Member State, Art. 49 TEU).[99]

It is hard to give an overall judgment on the results of the Treaty of Amsterdam. As far as the necessary reforms with a view to enlargement are concerned, the negotiations were a failure (composition of the Commission, weighting of votes in the Council, drastic reduction of the number of cases where the Treaties provide for voting by unanimity). The solution to these problems (the so-called 'leftovers' of Amsterdam) had to be postponed for a new conference, convened in 2000. The negotiators did manage to include in the Treaty a general solution to the issue of a multi-speed Europe, that is a procedure allowing a limited number of Member States (but at least a majority of them) to use the existing institutional framework and the existing procedures to cooperate more closely in the framework of the EC and the Third pillar (i.e., police and judicial cooperation in criminal matters) of the

---

97. Cf. Art. N(3) TEU, Maastricht version.
98. See, with further references, J. Winter et al. (eds), *Reforming the Treaty on European Union* (The Hague, 1996).
99. Cf. in this context also the procedure followed for the establishment of the Charter of Fundamental Rights for the European Union, for which the drafting was put in the hands of a 'convention' composed of representatives of the national parliaments and the European Parliament, the governments of the Member States and the European Commission. A similar body was later set up in order to prepare a draft treaty for the Intergovernmental Conference convened in 2004 (see *infra* 7.3 and 8).

Union.[100] The structure of the Union was not really changed by the Treaty of Amsterdam; attempts to weld the Union and the three Communities into a single organization failed. The Union itself – the organizational construct which embraces the Communities together with the Common Foreign and Security Policy (CFSP) and police and judicial cooperation in criminal matters[101] – was structured in more detail, even though it was not explicitly accorded legal personality.[102] For instance, the CFSP was now called a policy of the Union and no longer – as in the Treaty of Maastricht – a matter for the Union together with the Member States. The concept of the Union began to acquire a constitutional significance with the explicit requirement for the Union to respect the principles of democracy and the rule of law in Article 6 TEU. The Union moreover was entrusted with the task of supervising respect for these principles, including fundamental rights, in the Member States by means of the sanction mechanism of Article 7 TEU, which enables the Union to act in situations of serious and persistent breach of these principles.

As for the development of the *acquis communautaire*, which according to Article 2, 5th indent, TEU,[103] is an objective of the Union, Amsterdam saw some positive achievements. The most significant of these was the transfer to the EC (in a new Title IV) of migration policy and judicial cooperation in civil cases, as well as private international law, which the Treaty of Maastricht had allocated to the Third Pillar. This 'Communitarization' was not perfect, however, as the decision-making procedures in this area were made more intergovernmental than the normal Community methods (requiring unanimity in the Council, and granting a joint right of initiative to the Member States) and the competence of the Court of Justice to deliver preliminary rulings was limited.[104] Denmark, Ireland and the United Kingdom decided in principle not to participate in this new area of EC policy (a so-called 'opt-out' was agreed), but with a proviso that they could later 'opt in' under certain conditions (this possibility was more restricted for Denmark). In the context of these arrangements, the Schengen regime[105] was also incorporated into the Union framework, and the various legislative provisions allocated between Title IV EC and the Third Pillar according to the respective division of competence. The Third Pillar was given a dose of the Community method insofar as the role of the European Parliament and the Commission was strengthened, and the Court of Justice was also granted a limited jurisdiction. This was, however, not the case for the CFSP, where the intergovernmental decision-making model was maintained and even strengthened, to the extent that executive tasks were entrusted to the secretariat of the Council, under the direction of a

---

100. See Ch. II, section 7.
101. This was the new wording used in the title of the Third Pillar, which had previously referred to Justice and Home Affairs.
102. See Ch. II, section 1, *infra*.
103. This objective was already contained in the Treaty of Maastricht, as Art. B, 5th indent.
104. See Arts. 67 and 68 EC.
105. The so-called Schengen arrangements (mainly concerning abolishing internal borders and increased cooperation on external controls) were originally between a number of Member States. See Ch. VIII section 4 *infra*.

secretary general, who received a new responsibility as High Representative for CFSP. The Court was still not granted any jurisdiction in this area. Finally, in institutional terms it should also be noted that the role of the European Parliament was strengthened within the system of the Community. The Parliament became a full-fledged co-legislator in the framework of the co-decision procedure, and the scope of application of that procedure was considerable extended; in other areas, the Parliament's influence was strengthened – for instance the nomination of the intended President of the Commission.

To bring the Union closer to its citizens, the principle of open government was included in the Treaty and was made subject to further regulation.[106] In this context, mention may also be made of the new coordination mechanisms concerning employment policy and the fine-tuning of the EC Treaty provisions concerning public health (Art. 152) and consumer protection (Art. 153). A far-reaching consequence for lawyers was also the re-numbering of provisions of the EU and EC treaties, in the framework of a simplification of these texts, whereby in the EC Treaty in particular a number of obsolete or superfluous provisions were removed.

7.3   THE TREATY OF NICE[107]

The Intergovernmental Conference (IGC) which had the particular task of elaborating the necessary institutional reforms to prepare the Union for the accession of ten or more new Member States, began in spring 2000 and came to an extremely laborious conclusion in December of that same year, in Nice. The results achieved for the three Amsterdam leftovers provoked mixed reactions, but at least the door was opened to a historic enlargement of the Union extending into Central and East Europe. The agreement reached on the weighing of votes in the Council met the French demand that the weight of French and German votes should remain equal. There is an additional possibility, however, of an extra condition being set for a qualified majority,[108] which is that this represents at least 62% of the total

---

106. Art. 1 TEU and 255 EC, Arts. 28 and 41 TEU.
107. V. Constantinesco, Y. Gautier and D. Simon (eds), *Le traité de Nice, premières analyses* (Strasbourg, 2001); M. Andenas and J. Usher, *The Treaty of Nice and Beyond, Enlargement and Constitutional Reform* (Oxford, 2003); R. Barents, 'Some Observations on the Treaty of Nice', (2001) MJ, 121–132; R. Barents, 'Het Verdrag van Nice: een eerste indruk' (2001) NJB, 113; M. Borchmann, 'Der *Vertrag* von Nizza', (2001) EuZW, 170–173; J.-M. Favret, 'Le traité de Nice du 26 février 2001: vers un affaiblissement irréversible de la capacité d'action de l'Union européenne'? (2001) RTDE, 271–304; J. Shaw, 'The Treaty of Nice: Legal and Constitutional Implications' (2001) EPL, 195–215; W. Wessels, 'Nice Results: The Millennium IGC in the EU's Evolution' (2001) JCMS, 197–220 (2001); T. Wiedmann, 'Der *Vertrag* von Nizza – Genesis einer Reform' (2001) EuR, 185–215; J. Wouters, 'Institutional and Constitutional Challenges for the European Union: Some Reflections in the Light of the Treaty of Nice' (2001) EL Rev., 342–356; J.W. de Zwaan, 'Het Verdrag van Nice, Een bescheiden stap in het proces van Europese integratie' (2001) SEW, 42.
108. The formulation of Art. 3 of the Protocol on the enlargement of the European Union indicates that application of this condition must be explicitly requested by a member of the Council.

population of the Union, so that account can be taken of the considerable difference between these two Member States in demographic terms. The threshold for reaching a qualified majority is raised slightly. The compromise reached in regard to the composition of the Commission is not very satisfactory, insofar as the rule that there is one Commissioner per Member State is maintained until the Commission reaches the size of twenty-seven members. If and when that situation is reached, there will be new negotiations about the ultimate size and a system of rotation. Such a large number of members involves risks for the effective operation of the Commission, and an attempt was made to compensate these risks by strengthening considerably the powers of the President of the Commission. The Commission will from now on be appointed by the Council by qualified majority, and no longer by a common decision of the governments of the Member States; the appointment will still require the approval of the European Parliament. From an institutional point of view – consider the autonomy of the Commission and the institutional balance – the appointment by the Council is unsatisfactory, but it illustrates the Member States' view of the Commission's position. As for the third Amsterdam leftover, reduction in the number of matters requiring decision-making by unanimity, the achievement at Nice was minimal. Leaving aside the common commercial policy – which from now on, barring a few exceptions, also includes trade in services and trade aspects of intellectual property law – the Member States did not manage to break through the unanimity requirement for important matters such as direct and indirect taxes, social security, and asylum and immigration legislation.

Of the other subjects dealt with in the Treaty of Nice, mention must certainly be made of the reform of the Union's judicial apparatus.[109] The Treaty lays the basis for fundamental reorganization, including the possible establishment of new judicial panels for specific areas of law (e.g., staff cases), so that the overload on the Court of Justice and Court of First Instance can be tackled (Arts. 220 and 225a EC).[110] On the whole, these developments concern the creation of legal bases, and require further decision-making by unanimity. Another achievement concerns the multi-speed regime introduced by the Treaty of Amsterdam ('enhanced cooperation'). Such a possibility is now also – to a limited extent – introduced for the CFSP. In addition, the application of this regime is made easier, as the possibility of a veto by a single Member State is removed.

Concurrently with the IGC, negotiations were taking place in another forum on a Charter of fundamental rights for the European Union. This group, called the Convention, composed of representatives of the national governments, the national parliaments, the European Parliament, the European Commission and others,

---

In the absence of such a request, a decision may be taken by qualified majority without the population criterion being met.

109. A. Johnston, 'Judicial Reform and the Treaty of Nice' (2001) CML Rev., 499–523; P.J.G. Kapteyn, 'De rechterlijke organisatie van de Europese Unie en de Intergouvernementele Conferentie 2000' (2001) NJB, 1.

110. As a first judicial panel The European Union Civil Service Tribunal was established by Council Decision of 2 Nov. 2004 (O.J. 2004, L 333/7).

succeeded in drafting, in a relatively short space of time, a text which was favourably received in many circles. The Charter of Fundamental Rights was not actually included in or attached to the Treaty of Nice. The idea of according binding legal effects to the Charter was abandoned following opposition by the United Kingdom, but also the Netherlands.[111] In the end, the Charter was 'solemnly proclaimed' by the European Parliament, the Council and the Commission.[112]

8   THE TREATY ESTABLISHING A CONSTITUTION FOR EUROPE AND THE TREATY OF LISBON

8.1   The Treaty Establishing a Constitution for Europe

Even if the Member States, in agreeing on the Treaty of Nice, considered the institutional reforms brought about by that Treaty sufficient to prepare the Union for enlargement, they adopted at the same time a Declaration on the future of the Union announcing a new round of negotiations for treaty amendments of a more constitutional nature.[113] This declaration demonstrates that the Union is in an ongoing process of reform.[114] An impetus for reform also came from the discussions triggered in 2000 by Joshka Fischer, the then German Minister for foreign affairs, on the ultimate shape of the Union, and the ensuing debate on a European Constitution.[115] It should moreover be noted that the German *Länder* had made their approval of the Treaty of Nice in the German Bundesrat conditional on the convening of a new intergovernmental conference to reach a more clear-cut division of competences between the Union and its Member States. This IGC was indeed announced at Nice for 2004.

    An essential step towards the preparation of that conference was made by the Laeken Declaration on the Future of the European Union adopted by the European Council on 15 December 2001.[116] This declaration starts by sketching the contours

---

111. Cf. the extremely critical advisory report by the Netherlands *Raad van State* of 4 Oct. 2000, Kamerstukken Tweede Kamer (Parliamentary papers Lower House) 2000–2001, No. 21501-20 A.

112. The text of the Charter was published in O.J. 2000, C 364/3.

113. Declaration No. 23 on the future of the Union.

114. B. de Witte, 'Simplification and Reorganization of the European Treaties' (2002) CML Rev., 1255–1287.

115. Cf. E.-U. Petersmann, 'Proposals for a New Constitution for the European Union: Building-Blocks for a Constitutional Theory and Constitutional Law of the EU' (1995) CML Rev., 1123–1175; I. Pernice, 'Multilevel Constitutionalism and the Treaty of Amsterdam: European Constitution-Making Revisited' (1999) CML Rev., 703–750; K. Lenaerts and M. Desomer, 'New Models of Constitution-Making in Europe: The Quest for Legitimacy' (2002) CML Rev., 1217–1253; A. Von Bogdandy and J. Bast, The European Union's Vertical Order of Competences: The Current Law and Proposals for Its Reform (2002) CML Rev., 227–268, and already much earlier G.F. Mancini, 'The Making of a Constitution for Europe' (1989) CML Rev., 595–614. See also S. Prechal, 'Een constitutionele "post-Nice" agenda?' (2001) NJB, 384.

116. Bull. EU, 12-2001, I-27.

of the agenda for the conference by listing a large number of questions grouped under four headings: a better division and definition of competence in the EU; simplification of the Union's instruments; more democracy, transparency and efficiency in the EU, including the question of the role of national parliaments; towards a constitution for European citizens. This fourth theme raises questions such as the simplification of the patchwork of existing treaties, the structure of the Union (the three pillars), the possible inclusion of the Charter of Fundamental Rights, to end up with the ultimate question, cautiously phrased, whether the simplification and reorganization of the treaties might not lead eventually to the adoption of a constitutional text in the Union.

The Laeken Declaration set out the process to be followed for the preparation of the IGC. In that respect, the Laeken Declaration breaks new ground, is really innovative and confirms the seriousness of the commitment of the Heads of States and Government to bringing the Union closer to its citizens. The preparation of the IGC was entrusted to a convention composed of 15 representatives of the Heads of State and Government of the Member States, 30 Members of national parliaments, 16 Members of the European Parliament and 2 Commission representatives; the accession candidate countries were also to be fully involved in the Convention's proceedings. The former President of France, Valéry Giscard d'Estaing was appointed as chairman of the Convention. The Convention's discussions and all its official documents should be public. The Convention did indeed work in full openness, its documents and discussion reports systematically being made available on the internet. Moreover, a Forum was set up to organize the debate with organizations representing civil society. This procedure, which in fact builds on the experience made with the convention for the elaboration of the EU Charter on fundamental rights, breaks with the traditional preparatory process of treaty amendments by secret negotiations at diplomatic level, and constitutionalizes the treaty-making process at Union level, by making it transparent and giving the process in itself a democratic legitimacy. Indeed, more than two thirds of the members of the convention were members of parliament.

The mandate given to the Convention was an open one: the final document to be produced could comprise different options, indicating the degree of support which they received, or recommendations if consensus was achieved. However, the authors of the Laeken Declaration made it quite clear that the final document would only provide the starting point for the IGC, the ultimate decisions being taken by that conference.

The Convention, which had its inaugural session in March 2002, was asked to complete its work within one year. President Giscard d'Estaing was able to submit on 18 July 2003 to the President of the European Council in Rome the final document of the Convention consisting not of a list of options but the text of a draft Treaty establishing a Constitution for Europe which the Convention had been able to adopt by consensus.[117] That draft was welcomed by the European Council

---

117. The text of this draft treaty is published in O.J. 2003, C 169/1.

as a good starting point for the IGC which began its work in October 2003. Agreement on a draft treaty establishing a Constitution for Europe was reached on 18 June 2004. The Treaty was signed in Rome on 29 October of that same year.[118] In reality, the draft treaty as adopted by the Convention was much more than a starting point for the IGC; the latter, apart from an important technical and legal revision, mainly limited its work to the most delicate institutional issues such as the system of qualified majority voting in the Council and the composition of the European Commission.[119]

The Constitution consists of four parts. Part I lays down the basic foundations, values, general objectives of the Union, its competences and institutional structure. Together with Part II, which contains the Charter of Fundamental Rights of the Union, the rules of Part I are of a more constitutional nature whereas Part III (The Policies and Functioning of the Union) mainly consolidates the existing provisions of the EU and EC Treaty – with sometimes important modifications. Part IV, finally, contains general and final provisions. Added to the Constitution are 36 Protocols and 2 Annexes which form an integral part thereof.

The Constitution does not constitute a completely new text. The impression given by its grand title: 'A Constitution for Europe' might be somewhat misleading. The Constitution is a step, in some regards an important step, in the continuous evolution of the European Communities and the European Union. Although without any doubt it brings important innovations and improvements, particularly at the institutional level[120] – most of which have been taken over by the Treaty of Lisbon (see below 8.2) – it nevertheless fully fits into that evolution and can certainly not be qualified as a revolutionary new departure. Indeed, the Constitution codifies and consolidates to a very large extent existing treaty texts, taking into account the principles developed in the case law of the Court of Justice like the basic principle of primacy of Union law over national law. That the Constitution does not dramatically change the basic characteristics of the EU is well illustrated by the emphasis put on the preservation of the Member States as basically sovereign states, and the need to preserve that quality as one of the constitutional principles of the EU (Art. I-5, para. 1).

At the beginning of 2007, the Constitutional Treaty had been ratified by 18 of the 27 Member States. However, in 2005 the Treaty had been rejected by referendum in France and The Netherlands. The negative results of these referenda to some extent repeat the experiences of the ratification process of the Maastricht

---

118. The text of the Treaty is published in O.J. 2004, C 310/1.
119. See more particularly on the work of the IGC, J.-P. Jacqué, 'De la Convention à la Conférence intergouvernementale, le projet de la Convention à l'épreuve des réalités politiques' (2005) RTDE, 227.
120. See for an analysis of the Constitution J.-C. Piris, *The Constitution for Europe: A Legal Analysis* (Cambridge, 2006); R. Barents, *Een Grondwet voor Europa, Achtergronden en commentaar* (Deventer, 2005); K. Lenaerts and P. van Nuffel, 'La Constitution pour l'Europe et l'Union comme entité politique et ordre juridique' (2005) Cahiers de droit européen, 1/2; G. Amato, H. Bribosia and B. de Witte (eds), *Genèse et destinée de la Constitution européenne/Genesis and Destiny of the European Constitution* (Brussels, 2007).

Treaty. The European Union continues to suffer from a fundamental problem of legitimacy within its Member States. The Union, its operation and its policies are met with much mistrust within some Member States. Lack of knowledge and understanding of the Union's objectives and functioning can easily be exploited to sow distrust and use the Union as a scapegoat for more general societal problems, such as caused for instance by globalization and the resulting difficulties of adaptation of national economies. What obviously also played a role both in France and The Netherlands were feelings of anxiety and uncertainty about enlargement. Another striking feature of the debate in both Member States is that objections against the Constitution did not just address its innovative parts, but also principles and rules regarding the common market which had been introduced already by the EEC Treaty of 1957. Presenting the new Treaty as a constitutional text might also have sent a wrong signal by possibly suggesting that the Constitution would entail a quantum leap and initiate a completely new phase in the process of integration. Paradoxically, Member States had chosen the constitutional language with the expectation of, by doing so, bringing the Union closer to its citizens.

8.2   THE TREATY OF LISBON

After a pause for reflection imposed by the European Council, the German presidency during the first half of 2007 prepared initiatives to sort out the crisis caused by the negative referenda on the European Constitution. The European Council of June 2007 decided to convoke a new IGC which was instructed to elaborate, within a few months, and in any event before the end of 2007, a new draft Treaty, on the basis of a detailed mandate adopted by the European Council. The mandate makes clear that this new Treaty instead of replacing the existing treaties by one single text will apply the traditional method of amending the existing treaties which will thus continue to exist. All constitutional language, including the references to the symbols of the Union (the flag, the anthem etc., contained in Art. I-8 of the Constitution) will have to be dropped. However, in substance the major institutional innovations of the Constitution, will be maintained. That explains the ambitious timetable set for this new IGC and justifies at the same time the decision not to convoke a new convention. Nevertheless, a representative of the European Commission and three Members of the European Parliament participated in this IGC.

    After the IGC had concluded its work on 19 October 2007, the new Treaty was signed at Lisbon on 13 December of that same year and baptized accordingly. The Treaty of Lisbon amends the Treaty on European Union and the EC Treaty, moreover by way of a Protocol annexed to it also the Euratom Treaty. Under the Lisbon Treaty, the European Union and the European Community will be merged into one single organization, the European Union, which replaces and succeeds the European Community. The EC Treaty is renamed Treaty on the Functioning of the European Union (TFEU). This Treaty and the TEU have the same legal value (Arts. 1 TEU (Lisbon) and TFEU).

As to the structure of both treaties and their interrelationship, it might be tempting to regard the TEU, in laying down the objectives, principles and values of the Union as well as the main features of its institutional structure, as the basic text, somewhat comparable with Part I of the Constitution. Such a comparison would, however, only partly be correct and at all events too simplistic. In fact, insofar as the innovative provisions of Part I and Part III of the Constitution have been maintained – which has largely been the case – the authors of the Treaty of Lisbon have dispersed them over both the TEU and the TFEU. In doing so, they respected fairly closely the present structure of both the EU and the EC Treaties. For instance, the detailed provisions on the common foreign and security policy have all been kept in the TEU, whereas the fundamental provisions on the delimitation of competences and the various categories of competence appear in the TFEU (Arts. 2 to 6). Likewise, some of the general provisions from Part I of the Constitution, such as those on the principle of non-discrimination on grounds of nationality, transparency, protection of personal data and the churches, are also placed in the Treaty on the Functioning of the European Union (Arts. 15 to 18 TFEU).

Like the Constitution, the Treaty of Lisbon abandons the complex and, indeed, in the long run almost unworkable distinction between the European Community and the European Union as separate but interlinked organizations and abolishes the architecture of the three pillars, This will be one of its most important innovations, the European Community and the European Union are being merged into one single, unitary structure, the European Union, with one single legal personality. However, the Euratom Treaty and with that the European Community for atomic energy will continue to exist. The former third pillar, on police and judicial cooperation in criminal matters, is almost completely made subject to the Community method, both as to the decision-making procedure and the system of judicial protection; the Common Foreign and Security Policy, however, remains governed by more intergovernmental procedures with a minimal role for the Court of Justice.

Democracy and guarantees for the respect of the rule of law within the Union's legal order will be reinforced. The position of the European Parliament in the Union's decision-making will be further strengthened as the co-decision procedure will become the 'ordinary legislative procedure'; the number of areas to which this procedure will apply is substantially increased, for instance, to include not just the former third pillar subjects, but also common agricultural and commercial policies. The Charter of Fundamental Rights, albeit not a part of the Treaties themselves, but having the same legal value, will be of a binding nature (Art. 6 TEU (Lisbon)).[121] Moreover, the TEU provides that the Union shall accede to the European Convention for the Protection of Human Rights and Fundamental Freedoms (Art. 6(2) TEU (Lisbon)).

---

121. The Charter was solemnly (re)proclaimed at a plenary session of the European Parliament by the Presidents of the Parliament, the Council and the Commission on 12 Dec. 2007 (O.J. 2007, C 303).

An important institutional modification is furthermore the introduction of the office of President of the European Council in order, *inter alia*, to improve the representation of the EU on the international level. The president, who cannot be at the same time a head of state or government, will be appointed for a term of two and a half years, renewable once (Art. 15 TEU (Lisbon)). As an institutionally fairly drastic measure to ensure coherence of the external action of the EU in the various fields of EU external competence (e.g., trade policy, development cooperation, CFSP), the function of the High Representative of the EU on foreign and security policy is merged with that of Vice-president of the European Commission responsible for external relations. The High Representative will at the same time be the permanent chairman of the Foreign Affairs Council and Vice-president of the European Commission (so-called 'double hatting') (Art. 18 TEU (Lisbon)). For the problem of qualified majority voting in the Council, one of the most contentious problems to be solved, the system of weighed voting which was basically maintained by the Treaty of Nice is replaced by a system of double majority: to obtain a qualified majority at least 55 % of the Member States, comprising at least fifteen of them and representing at least 65 % of the population of the Union must be in favour. However, a blocking minority must include at least four Member States (Art. 16 TEU (Lisbon)). Higher percentages apply when the Council does not act on a proposal from the Commission (Art. 238(2) TFEU). However, this new voting system will only enter into force as from 2014 with a further derogation period until 2017 during which Member States may require recourse to the voting rules of the Treaty of Nice (Art. 16(4) and (5) TEU (Lisbon) and Arts. 3 and 4 of the Protocol on transitional provisions).

As to the composition of the European Commission, the system of one Member per Member State will continue until 2014. The Commission to be appointed that year will be composed of a number of Members corresponding to two thirds of the number of Member States unless the European Council decides to alter this number. The Members will be chosen from among the nationals of the Member States on the basis of a system of rotation treating all Member States equally (Art. 17(5) TEU (Lisbon)).

Another important innovation is the role granted to national parliaments, not only by allowing them to be directly informed about legislative proposals of the European Commission, but also by giving them a specific responsibility for controlling respect of the principle of subsidiarity, providing as a measure of last resort also the possibility of an appeal before the Court of Justice.[122] These mechanisms are important because they could improve the legitimacy of EU action as seen at the national level by fostering national parliaments to become actively involved in the discussion of EU actions and policies.

---

122. See Protocol 1 on the role of national parliaments in the EU and Protocol 2 on the application of the principles of subsidiarity and proportionality, annexed to the treaties.

FURTHER READING

History of European Integration

Beach, D. *The Dynamics of European Integration: Why and When EU Institutions Matter.* The European Union Series. Basingstoke: Palgrave Macmillan, 2005.

Berglund, S., et al. *The Making of the European Union: Foundations, Institutions and Future Trends.* Cheltenham: Edward Elgar, 2006.

Bitsch, M.-T. *Histoire de la construction européenne de 1945 à nos jours.* Nouvelle éd. mise à jour. Bruxelles: Complexe, 2004.

Blair, A. *The European Union since 1945.* Harlow: Pearson Longman, 2005.

Booker, C. and R. North. *The Great Deception: Can the European Union Survive?* 2nd ed. London: Continuum, 2005.

Brugmans, J. *L'idée européenne, 1920–1970.* 3e éd. Brugge: De Tempel, 1970.

Chryssochoou, D.N. *Theory and Reform in the European Union.* 2nd ed. Manchester: Manchester University Press, 2003.

Courty, G. and G. Devin. *La construction européenne.* Nouv. éd. entièrement refondue et mise à jour. Collection Repères 326. Paris: La Découverte, 2005.

De Ruyt, J. *L'Acte unique européen.* 2e éd. Bruxelles: Université Bruxelles, 1989.

De Zwaan, J.W. and A.E. Kellermann. *The European Union: An Ongoing Process of Integration: Liber Amicorum Alfred E. Kellermann.* The Hague: T.M.C. Asser Press, 2004.

Devuyst, Y. *The European Union at the Crossroads: An Introduction to the EU's Institutional Evolution.* 2nd ed. European Policy, vol. 27. Brussels: P.I.E.-Peter Lang, 2003.

Dinan, D. *Europe Recast: A History of European Union.* Basingstoke: Palgrave Macmillan, 2004.

Dinan, D. *Ever Closer Union: An Introduction to European Integration.* 3rd ed. The European Union Series. Basingstoke, Hampshire: Palgrave MacMillan, 2005.

Dinan, D. *Origins and Evolution of the European Union.* The New European Union Series. Oxford: Oxford University Press, 2006.

Duff, A. *Reforming the European Union.* London: Federal Trust, 1997.

Gerbet, P. *La construction de l'Europe.* 3e éd. Paris, 1999.

Gillingham, J.R. *European Integration, 1950–2003: Superstate or New Market Economy?* Cambridge: Cambridge University Press, 2003.

Griffiths, R.T. (ed.). *The Netherlands and the Integration of Europe 1945–1957.* Amsterdam: NEHA, 1990.

Groeben, H. von der. *Aufbaujahre der Europäischen Gemeinschaft: das Ringen um den Gemeinsamen Markt und die Politische Union (1958–1966).* Baden-Baden: Nomos, 1982.

Haas, E.B. *The Uniting of Europe: Political, Social and Economic Forces 1950–1957.* 2nd ed. Stanford, CA: Stanford University Press, 1968.

Kaiser, W. and P. Starie. *Transnational European Union: Towards a Common Political Space.* Routledge Research in Transnationalism, 19. Routledge, 2005.

Koolhaas, R., et al. *History of Europe and the European Union*. Amsterdam: Archis Foundation, 2005.

Mayne, R. *The Community of Europe*. London: Victor Gollancz, 1962.

Meunier, S. and K.R. MacNamara. *Making History: European Integration and Institutional Change at Fifty*. The State of the European Union, 8. Oxford: Oxford University Press, 2007.

Middlemas, K. *Orchestrating Europe. The Informal Politics of European Union 1973–1995*. London: Fontana Press, 1995.

Milward, A.S. *Politics and Economics in the History of the European Union*. London: Routledge, 2005.

Milward, A.S. *The Reconstruction of Western Europe, 1945–51*. London: Methuen, 1984.

Milward, A.S., et al. *The Frontier of National Sovereignty*. Routledge: London, 1993.

Monnet, J. *Mémoires*. Paris: Fayard, 1976.

Moravcsik, A. (ed.). *Europe without Illusions: The Paul-Henri Spaak Lectures, 1994–1999*. Lanham: University Press of America, 2005.

Pinder, J. *The Building of the European Union* 3rd ed. Oxford: Oxford University Press, 1998.

Quermonne, J.-L. *Le système politique de l'Union européenne: Des Communautés économiques à l'Union politique*. Clefs. Politique. 4e éd. Paris: Montchrestien, 2001.

Reuter, P. *La Communauté Européenne du Charbon et de l'Acier*. Paris: Librairie Générale de Droit et de Jurisprudence, 1953.

Rogowski, R. and C. Turner. *The Shape of the New Europe*. Cambridge: Cambridge University Press, 2006.

Rücker, K. and L. Warlouzet. *Quelle(s) Europe(s)?: nouvelles approches en histoire de l'intégration européenne = Which Europe(s)?: New Approaches in European Integration History*. Euroclio. Études et documents, 36. 2me tirage. Bruxelles: PIE – P. Lang, 2007.

Snyder, F.G. *Constitutional Dimensions of European Economic Integration*. The Hague: Kluwer Law International, 1996.

Spierenburg, D. and R. Poidevin. *Histoire de la Haute Autorité de la Communauté Européenne du charbon et de l'acier: une expérience supranationale*. Bruxelles: Bruylant, 1993.

Tsoukalis, L. *What Kind of Europe?* Updated and expanded ed. Oxford: Oxford University Press, 2005.

Urwin, Derek. *The Community of Europe: A History of European Integration since 1945*. 2nd ed. London: Longman, 1997.

Van de Meerssche, P. *Europese integratie en desintegratie 1945-heden*. Antwerpen/Amsterdam: Standaard Uitgeverij, 1978.

Van de Meerssche, P. *Van Jalta tot Malta: politieke geschiedenis van Europa*. Aula-paperback. 1e druk. Utrecht: Het Spectrum, 1990.

Van Gerven, W. *The European Union: A Polity of States and Peoples*. Oxford: Hart, 2005.

Vanthoor, W.F.V. *A Chronological History of the European Union 1946–2001.* 2nd rev. and enl. ed. Cheltenham: Elgar, 2002.

Vembulu, R.P. *Understanding European Integration: History, Culture, and Politics of Identity.* Delhi: Aakar Books, 2003.

Wilkens, A. (ed.). *Le Plan Schuman dans l'Histoire; Intérêts nationaux et projet européen.* Bruxelles: Bruylant, 2004.

Wood, D.M. and B.A. Yesilada. *The Emerging European Union.* 4th ed. New York: Pearson/Longman, 2007.

Zorgbibe, C. *Histoire de l'Union Européenne.* Collection de la Fondation Robert Schuman. Paris: Albin Michel, Fondation Robert Schuman, 2005.

Economic Integration

Diebold, Jr, W. *The Schuman Plan: A Study in Economic Cooperation, 1950–1959.* New York: Praeger, 1959.

Dyson, K.H.F. and K. Featherstone. *The Road to Maastricht: Negotiating Economic and Monetary Union.* Oxford: Oxford University Press, 1999.

McDonald, F. and S. Dearden. *European Economic Integration.* 4th ed. Harlow: Financial Times/Prentice Hall, 2004.

Nello, S.S. *The European Union: Economics, Policies and History.* London: McGraw-Hill, 2005.

Pelkmans, J. *European Integration: Methods and Economic Analysis.* 3rd ed. Harlow: Prentice Hall/Financial Times, 2006.

Zervoyianni, A., et al. *European Integration.* New ed. Basingstoke: Palgrave Macmillan, 2006.

Treaty of Maastricht

Cloos, J., et al. *Le traité de Maastricht: genèse, analyse, commentaires.* Organisation internationale et relations internationals, 28. Bruxelles: Émile Bruylant, 1993.

Constantinesco, V., et al. (eds). *Traité sur l'Union Européenne.* Paris, 1995.

Corbett, R.G. *The Treaty of Maastricht: From Conception to Ratification: A Comprehensive Reference Guide.* Harlow: Longman, 1993.

Dehousse, R. (ed.). *Europa after Maastricht. An Ever Closer Union?.* Law Books in Europe. München: Beck, 1994.

Devroe, W. and J. Wouters. *De Europese Unie: het Verdrag van Maastricht en zijn uitvoering: analyse en perspectieven.* Reeks Europees Recht, 4. Leuven: Peeters, 1996.

Duff, A. and J. Pinder. *Maastricht and Beyond: Building the European Union.* London: Routledge, 1994.

Hrbek, R. (ed.). *Der Vertrag von Maastricht in der wissenschaftlichen Kontroversen: Beitr. für das Jahreskolloquium des Arbeitskreises Europäische Integration e.V., 12./14.* November 1992 in Bonn. Baden-Baden: Nomos-Verlaggesellschaft, 1993.

Ingelaere, F. *Grondlijnen van de Europese Politieke, Economische en Monetaire Unie: een verkenning van het Europese Unieverdrag.* Deurne: Story-Scientia, 1992.

Lane, R. 'New Community Competences under the Maastricht Treaty'. (1993) CML Rev., 939.

Maillet, P. (ed.) *Trois défis de Maastricht: convergence, cohésion, subsidiarité.* Paris: L'Harmattan, 1993.

Monar, J., W. Ungerer and W. Wessels (eds). *The Maastricht Treaty on European Union: Legal Complexity and Political Dynamic.* Brussels: European University Press, 1994.

O'Keeffe, D. and P.M. Twomey (eds). *Legal Issues of the Maastricht Treaty.* London: Chancery, 1994.

Schwarze, J. (ed.) *Vom Binnenmarkt zur Europäischen Union: Beiträge zur aktuellen Entwicklung des Gemeinschaftsrechts.* Schriftenreihe Europäisches Recht, Politik und Wirtschaft, Bd. 158. Baden-Baden: Nomos, 1993.

Treaty of Amsterdam

Barents, R. *Verdrag van Amsterdam in werking.* Europese Monografieën, 62. Deventer: Kluwer, 1999.

Heukels, T., et al. (eds). *The European Union after Amsterdam: A Legal Analysis.* The Hague: Kluwer, 1998.

Monar, J. and W. Wessels. *The European Union after the Treaty of Amsterdam.* London: Continuum, 2001.

O'Keeffe, D. and P.M. Twomey (eds). *Legal Issues of the Amsterdam Treaty.* Oxford: Hart, 1999.

Winter, J.A. *Reforming the Treaty on European Union: The Legal Debate.* The Hague: Kluwer Law International, 1996.

Treaty of Nice

Andenas, M.T. and J.A. Usher. *The Treaty of Nice and Beyond: Enlargement and Constitutional Reform.* Oxford: Hart, 2003.

Bond, M. and K. Feus. *The Treaty of Nice Explained.* Constitution for Europe Series, 3. London: Federal Trust for Education and Research, 2001.

Constantinesco, V., Y. Gautier and D. Simon (eds). *Le traité de Nice: premières analyses.* Strasbourg, 2001.

Melissas, D.K. and I. Pernice. *Perspectives of the Nice Treaty and the Intergovernmental Conference in 2004.* European Constitutional Law Network-Series, vol. 1. Baden-Baden: Nomos, 2002.

St. C. Bradley, K. 'Institutional Design in the Treaty of Nice'. (2001) CML Rev., 1095–1123.

The EU Charter on Fundamental Rights

Arnull, A. 'From Charter to Constitution and Beyond: Fundamental Rights in the New European Union'. (2003) *Public Law* 774–793.

Eriksen, E.O., et al. *The Chartering of Europe: The European Charter of Fundamental Rights and Its Constitutional Implications.* Baden-Baden: Nomos Verlagsgesellschaft, 2003.

Feus, K. *An EU Charter of Fundamental Rights: Text and Commentaries.* Constitution for Europe Series, 1. London: Federal Trust, 2000.

Hervey, T.K. and J. Kenner (eds). *Economic and Social Rights under the EU Charter of Fundamental Rights: A Legal Perspective.* Oxford: Hart, 2003.

Knook, A. 'The Court, the Charter and the Vertical Division of Powers in the European Union'. (2005) CML Rev., 367–398.

Peers, S. and A. Ward. *The European Union Charter of Fundamental Rights.* Oxford: Hart, 2004.

Quinn, G. and L. Flynn. *EU Charter on Fundamental Rights.* Oxford: Oxford University Press, 2001.

Schönlau, J. *Drafting the EU Charter: Rights, Legitimacy and Process.* Palgrave Studies in European Union Politics. Palgrave Macmillan, 2005.

Treaty Establishing a Constitution for Europe

Albi, A. and J. Ziller. *The European Constitution and National Constitutions: Ratification and Beyond.* European Monographs, 54. Alphen aan den Rijn: Kluwer Law International, 2007.

Amato, G., et al. *Genesis and Destiny of the European Constitution: Commentary on the Treaty Establishing a Constitution for Europe in the Light of the Travaux Préparatoires and Future Prospects = Genèse et destinée de la Constitution européenne: commentaire du Traité établissant une Constitution pour l'Europe à la lumière des travaux préparatoires et perspectives d'avenir.* Bruxelles: Bruylant, 2007.

Barnier, M., et al. *A New Constitutional Settlement for the European People.* Athens: Sakkoulas; Brussels: Bruylant, 2004.

Blankart, C.B. and D.C. Mueller. *A Constitution for the European Union.* Cambridge, MA: MIT Press, 2004.

Bogdandy, A.v. and J. Bast. *Principles of European Constitutional Law.* Modern Studies in European Law, 8. Oxford: Hart, 2006.

Brand, M. *Affirming and Refining European Constitutionalism: Towards the Establishment of the First Constitution for the European Union.* EUI Working Paper Law, no. 2004/2. San Domenico: European University Institute, 2004.

Church, C.H. and D. Phinnemore. *Understanding the European Constitution: An Introduction to the EU Constitutional Treaty.* London: Routledge, 2006.

Constantinesco, V., et al. *Le Traité établissant une Constitution pour L'Europe: analyses & commentaires.* Collections de l'Université Robert Schuman. Centre d'études internationales et européennes. Strasbourg: Presses universitaires de Strasbourg, 2005.

Cowgill, A. and A. Cowgill. *The European Constitution in Perspective: Analysis and Review of 'The Treaty Establishing a Constitution For Europe'*, including the complete text of the Treaty with all protocols and declarations as signed in Rome on 29 October 2004. Stroud: British Management Data Foundation, 2004.

Curtin, D.M., et al. *The EU Constitution: The Best Way Forward?* The Hague: T.M.C. Asser Press, 2005.

Curtin, D.M. and W. Devroe. *Mind the Gap: The Evolving EU Executive and the Constitution.* Walter van Gerven Lectures, 3. Groningen: Europa Law Publishing, 2004.

De Búrca, G. and W. Devroe. *The EU Constitution: In Search of Europe's International Identity.* Walter van Gerven Lectures, 4. Leuven: Leuven Centre for a Common Law of Europe, 2005.

De Schutter, O., et al. *Une constitution pour l'Europe: réflexions sur les transformations du droit de l'Union européenne.* Bruxelles: Larcier, 2004.

De Witte, B.E.F.M. *Ten Reflections on the Constitutional Treaty for Europe.* Florence: European University Institute, 2003.

Dehousse, R. *Une constitution pour l'Europe?* Paris: Presses de Sciences Po, 2002.

Devuyst, Y. *The European Union Transformed: Community Method and Institutional Evolution from the Schuman Plan to the Constitution for Europe.* Rev. and updated edn. European Policy, 27. Brussels: Peter Lang, 2005.

Dony, M. and E. Bribosia. *Commentaire de la Constitution de l'Union européenne.* Bruxelles: Editions de l'Université Libre de Bruxelles, 2005.

Eriksen, E.O., et al. *Developing a Constitution for Europe.* Routledge Studies on Democratizing Europe, 1. London: Routledge, 2004.

Fischer, K.H. *Der Europäische Verfassungsvertrag: Texte und Kommentar.* Baden-Baden: Nomos; Wien: Manz; Bern: Stämpfli, 2005.

FitzGerald, G. and A. O'Rourke. *Europe Re-united: A Constitutional Treaty: An Analysis.* Dublin: Institute of European Affairs, 2004.

Häberle, P. *Europäische Verfassungslehre.* 3 aktual. und erw. Aufl. Baden-Baden: Nomos, 2005.

Inglis, K. and A. Ott. *The Constitution for Europe and an Enlarging Union: Unity in Diversity?* Groningen: Europa Law Publishing, 2005.

Jacobs, A.T.J.M. *The European Constitution: How It Was Created, What It Will Change.* Nijmegen: Wolf Legal Publishers, 2005.

MacCormick, N. *Who's Afraid of a European Constitution?.* Societas: Essays in Political and Cultural Criticism, 17. Exeter: Imprint Academic, 2005.

Milton, G., et al. *The European Constitution: Its Origins, Negotiation and Meaning.* London: John Harper Publishing, 2005.

Norman, P. *The Accidental Constitution: The Making of Europe's Constitutional Treaty.* New and rev. ed. Brussels: EuroComment, 2005.

Pernice, I. and J. Zemánek. *A Constitution for Europe: The IGC, the Ratification Process and Beyond.* European Constitutional Law Network-Series, 5. Baden-Baden: Nomos, 2005.

Piris, J.-C. *The Constitution for Europe: A Legal Analysis.* Cambridge Studies in European Law and Policy. Cambridge: Cambridge University Press, 2006.

Schwarze, J. *The Birth of a European Constitutional Order: The Interaction of National and European Constitutional Law.* Schriftenreihe Europäisches Recht, Politik und Wirtschaft, Bd. 249. Baden-Baden: Nomos, 2001.

Timmermans, C.W.A. 'The Constitutionalization of the European Union'. (2002) *Yearbook of European Law*, 1–11.

Verhoeven, A. *The European Union in Search of a Democratic and Constitutional Theory.* European Monographs, 38. The Hague: Kluwer Law International, 2002.

Weiler, J.H.H. *The Constitution of Europe: 'Do the New Clothes Have an Emperor?' and Other Essays on European Integration.* Cambridge: Cambridge University Press, 1999.

Ziller, J. and M. Marquis. *The European Constitution.* The Hague: Kluwer Law International, 2005.

Chapter II

General Aspects of the European Union and the European Communities

C.W.A. Timmermans

1   THE EUROPEAN UNION

The Treaty of Maastricht formally established the European Union. According to Article 1 Treaty on the European Union (TEU), the European Union is founded on the European Communities (EC (formerly EEC)), supplemented by a Common Foreign and Security Policy (hereafter CFSP) and arrangements for Police and Judicial Cooperation in Criminal Matters (hereafter PJCCM). Pursuant to the Treaty of Amsterdam, the last-mentioned arrangements replaced what was called in the Treaty of Maastricht 'cooperation in the field of justice and home affairs'.

1.1   INTRODUCTION AND BACKGROUND

The concept of a European Union goes back further than the Intergovernmental Conference which resulted in the Treaty of Maastricht.[1] At the Paris Summit in

---

1. See for the background: E.P. Wellenstein, 'Unity, Community, Union: What's in a Name' (1992) CML Rev., 205–212; U. Everling, 'Reflections on the Structure of the European Union' (1992) CML Rev., 1053–1077 and N.M. Blokker and T. Heukels, 'The European Union: Historical Origins and Institutional Challenges', in T. Heukels, N. Blokker, M. Brus (eds), *The European Union after Amsterdam* (The Hague, 1998), 9.

P.J.G. Kapteyn, A.M. McDonnell, K.J.M. Mortelmans and C.W.A. Timmermans (eds),
The Law of the European Union and the European Communities, pp. 53–113.
©2008 Kluwer Law International BV, The Netherlands.

October 1972, the Member States confirmed their intention to transform their common relations into a European Union,[2] although nothing was stated about what this would entail, and nothing came of nothing.[3] New life was breathed into the idea with the European Parliament's Draft Treaty on European Union in 1984.[4] Prior to this, in June 1983, the European Council in Stuttgart had adopted a Solemn Declaration on European Union.[5] Subsequently, the concept of a Union was endowed with Treaty status in the Preamble to the Single European Act (SEA): there was a reference to the Stuttgart Solemn Declaration, and the resolution to implement the European Union on the basis, firstly, of the Communities operating in accordance with their own rules and, secondly, of European Cooperation among the Signatory States in the sphere of foreign policy.[6] The EC and European Political Cooperation aimed to contribute together to making concrete progress towards European unity (Art.1 SEA). In this manner the SEA gives a foretaste of the concept of a Union which was later developed in the Treaty on European Union.

1.2   A BRIEF GUIDE TO THE EUROPEAN UNION

An essential element in understanding the structure of the TEU, and thus the concept of the European Union which it establishes, is that the Treaty is the result of a hard fought-out compromise between, as always, proponents of the Community method (involving the specific role of the supranational institutions, the European Parliament, the European Commission, the Court of Justice and qualified majority voting in the Council in an increasing number of areas) and proponents of the more classic intergovernmental forms of inter-state cooperation (in which the initiative remains very much with the Member States and decisions are almost invariably taken by unanimity). The Member States were unable to accept that the supplementary policies and forms of cooperation should be brought within the Community structure, even with their own procedures and a weakening of the Community method in those areas, as the Commission and later the Dutch Presidency had originally proposed.[7] On the other hand, the institutional structure of the CFSP and PJCCM does go – certainly after the amendments in these areas brought by the Treaty of Amsterdam – further than the classic intergovernmental decision-making models. The compromise is evident.

---

2. Bull. EC 10-1972, 23.
3. See Shakespeare, *King Lear*, I.i.
4. See Bull. EC 2-1984, 1.1.2.
5. Bull. EC 6-1983, 1.6.1.
6. Preamble SEA, para. 3 (commencing 'RESOLVED to implement . . . ').
7. As to the Commission's draft structure of the Treaty, see Bull. EC Supp. 2/91, 173 et seq. The Dutch Presidency's proposal was reproduced in *Europe* Documents No. 1746/1747 of 20 Nov. 1991. See also P. VerLoren van Themaat, 'De constitutionele problematiek van een Europese Politieke Unie' (1991) SEW, 436.

1.2.1   The Structure of the Union

The Union brings together in one organization the EC (and Euratom) and the supplementary policies and forms of cooperation: CFSP and PJCCM. The Communities form a more or less closed entity within this structure, retaining their own autonomy and legally independent organization, as well as their own legal personality. Assumption into the Union has scant direct consequences for the Communities, although these have increased with the Treaty of Amsterdam (see 1.2.3 below). The Union was set up first and foremost as a home for the supplementary policies and forms of cooperation for which it creates institutional structures, bringing them and the Communities under one roof. The popular image for the architecture of the Union Treaty – a temple with three pillars – is too crude:[8] it ignores the fact that the Communities form the main load-bearing structure of the Union, and at the same time disguises the independent nature of that pillar. The formula adopted in the TEU itself (Art. 1(3) TEU), of a Union 'founded on the EC, supplemented' by the two other areas of cooperation is preferable.

1.2.2   The 'Constitution' of the Union

While the SEA in 1986 merely referred to a European Union, saying nothing about what it involved, the TEU sketches the contours for the substantive constitution, the most basic rules, of the Union. These contours have been defined further by the Treaty of Amsterdam. They are to be found in the first place in the Common Provisions in Title I and the provisions in the last two Titles VII and VIII of the Treaty. The following elements stand out in particular.

1.2.2.1   *A Union of States and of Peoples*

The task of the Union, as described in Article 1(3) TEU, is 'to organize, in a manner demonstrating consistency and solidarity, relations between the Member States and between their peoples'. This gives an excellent picture of the nature of the Union as a form of international cooperation. The Union is a union of States and also of the peoples of those States. It mixes more classic forms of intergovernmental cooperation (particularly CFSP and PJCCM) with the far more ambitious integration model pursued by the Communities. The task of the Union thus described also shows that it does not affect the identity of the Member States as such: the Union is in fact required to respect the national identities of the Member States (Art. 6(3)

---

8. Cf. P.J.G. Kapteyn, 'Inleidende beschouwingen over het Verdrag betreffende de Europese Unie' (1992) SEW, 667–673. The metaphors for the Union structure are ever more fanciful (Russian nesting dolls, gothic cathedral), see the chapter by B. de Witte, 'The Pillar Structure and the Nature of the European Union: Greek Temple or French Gothic Cathedral', in T. Heukels et al. op. cit. *supra* note 1, 51; further D. Curtin and I. Dekker, 'The EU as a "layered" International Organization: Institutional Unity in Disguise', in P. Craig and G. de Burca (eds), *The Evolution of EU Law* (Oxford, 1999), 83.

TEU). The perspective of a development in a federal direction (a *vocation fédérale*) which the Germans had insisted be included in the draft treaty text was removed at British insistence at Maastricht (gaining notoriety as the 'F-word') and replaced by the more neutral phrase 'an ever closer union' (Art. 1 TEU).

Precisely because the Union is a form of association in which the peoples are directly involved, it is important that Article 6 TEU requires the Union to respect fundamental rights. The Treaty of Amsterdam has in this context considerably strengthened the constitutional content of the Union, and thereby also the importance of the Union as a cohesive unit in two ways. First, the Union itself is now bound to the principles of liberty, democracy and the rule of law, 'principles which are common to the Member States' (Art. 6(1) TEU). In accordance with this last phrase, the TEU takes up the respect for these principles as a condition for the accession to the Union of new Member States (Art. 49 TEU). This is an important element in the so-called 'screening' process which the European Commission is carrying out with regard to the candidate countries. Secondly, a control mechanism was included in Article 7 TEU with regard to these matters, which makes it possible to impose sanctions on a Member State in case of 'a serious and persistent breach' of fundamental rights, or of the principles of liberty, democracy and the rule of law, as mentioned in Article 6 TEU. These sanctions include suspension of voting rights in the Council, and suspension of other rights and financial benefits flowing from Union membership. The Treaty of Nice adds a monitoring mechanism to this, added as a result of the experience of trying to impose sanctions on Austria by the other fourteen Member States, when Austria had a government coalition in which the extreme right FPÖ party participated.

Thus, the Union is implicitly accorded a general supervisory role with regard to the respect of human rights and the fundamental principles of the rule of law by the Member States; the task is general, since it is not restricted to the substantive scope of application of the treaties. In this way, the constitutional quality of the Union is considerably strengthened. A breach as intended under Article 7 TEU is determined by the Council at its highest level, i.e., meeting in the composition of the Heads of State or Government, and must receive the assent of the European Parliament. Such a decision cannot be reviewed by the Court of Justice, however. The Treaty of Nice has changed this by making at least the procedural aspects of application of Article 7 TEU subject to review by the Court of Justice. Sanctions concerning rights or benefits flowing from the treaties establishing the European Communities must be decided according to a procedure included in each of the treaties, with the exception of suspension of the voting rights of the Member State in question in the Council, which is decided under the TEU (Art. 7(2)) and which then applies in the framework of the Community treaties (Arts. 309 EC and 204 Euratom). The Court of Justice thus does have jurisdiction with regard to decisions on sanctions taken pursuant to the Community treaties. This nexus of procedures illustrates the complex relationship between the Union and the Communities. The drafters of the treaties have provided for separate procedures for the two Communities, in order to protect the autonomous character of the Communities, and maintain their independence. They did not succeed in this entirely, since application of these procedures is made dependent on a Union decision. We see here an example – and one could find more – of subordination of decision-making in the framework of the Community treaties to Union decision-making, and thus of the Communities to the Union (see 1.2.3 above).

The fact that the Union as such is explicitly bound to respect human rights and the principles of the rule of law means in itself a qualitative strengthening of the Union, but in addition it should not be forgotten that the guarantees offered by the Treaty on European Union itself – especially in the areas specific to the Union (CFSP and PJCCM) – are insufficient.[9] Supervision by the Court of Justice is in principle excluded in the CFSP,[10] and only guaranteed to a limited extent in PJCCM.

1.2.2.2   *Objectives of the Union*

The first four objectives set out in Article 2 TEU concern, and to a great extent correspond to, the Union's three component parts: the Communities, CFSP, and PJCCM. The details relating to Citizenship of the Union (the third objective) are set out in Articles 17 et seq. EC. The fifth objective, maintaining and building on the *acquis communautaire*, is of major significance for the relationship between the Union's component parts and their further development. The preference for the Community method as developed within the EC is evident. Thus the bringing together of the Communities with the more intergovernmental CFSP and PJCCM within the Union may not undermine the specific Community method or the so-called *acquis communautaire*, i.e., what has been achieved in the Communities. This last concept corresponds more or less to the level of integration reached in the EC framework and the corpus of legislation pertaining to it.[11] The *Union* is explicitly entrusted with the task of further developing this acquis. The Intergovernmental Conference which was called for by the Treaty of Maastricht was intended, among other things, to review the relationship between the various parts of the Union in the light of these objectives. This Intergovernmental Conference (IGC) and the Treaty of Amsterdam which was prepared there did not lead to a real change in the structure of the Union. Nevertheless, certain important steps were taken in view of the realization of these objectives: the transfer of important parts of the so-called third pillar of the Treaty of Maastricht to the EC by inserting a new Title IV in that Treaty (visas, asylum, immigration etc.), as well as a certain degree of communitarization of PJCCM by means of an extension of the role of the European Parliament and the Commission and the grant of a limited jurisdiction to the Court of Justice.

---

9. See Case C-354/04 P, *Gestoras Pro Amnistía et al. and others v. Council.*
10. Except where a field is entered for which the EC has competence, cf. Case C-170/96, *Commission v. Council* (*airport transit visas*). On this, see D. Curtin and R.H. van Ooik, 'Een Hof van Justitie van de Europese Unie?' (1999) SEW, 24. See, for an example regarding the relationship between the EC and PJCCM, Case C-176/03, *Commission v. Council* (penal sanctions in the field of environmental protection).
11. See, also on the ambiguities in the concept *acquis communautaire*, S. Weatherill, 'Safe-Guarding the acquis communautaire', in T. Heukels et al., op. cit. *supra* note 1, 153. See also C. Delcourt, 'The *acquis communautaire*: Has the Concept Had Its Day?' (1991) CML Rev., 829–870.

1.2.2.3   *Institutions of the Union*

Article 3 TEU provides that the Union is to be served by a single institutional framework. This was necessary in order to ensure the requisite consistency of the Union's activities, particularly in view of the diversity of decision-making constructs. This requirement of consistency is specified in particular as regards the Union's external activities as a whole, which are carried out on the one hand in the framework of the EC, and on the other through, in particular, the CFSP (Art. 3(2) TEU). The single institutional framework consists first of all of the European Council, which is composed of the Heads of State or Government of the Member States and the President of the Commission. The European Council provides the Union with the necessary impetus for its development and defines its general political guidelines (Art. 4 TEU). This task also embraces the EC. In practice, the European Council had already long ago developed into the most powerful, general policy-determining body for all policy areas of the Union, including the EC.[12] As for the CFSP, and to a lesser extent the PJCCM, the Treaty of Amsterdam has strengthened the role of the European Council even further by granting it formal decision-making powers.[13]

For the EC this does not hold to the same extent, even if the European Council is also mentioned here and there in the EC Treaty.[14] The true situation is different here too. In accordance with Article 4 TEU, the European Council determines the general political directions, such as for instance concerning the financing of Community policy, which are then transformed into legislation or other legally binding decisions in conformity with Community decision-making procedures. This is obviously at the cost of the autonomous position of the more supranational institutions within the Communities (cf. the right of initiative of the European Commission, the role of the European Parliament). The European Council is thus the only real organ of the Union, in that it is regulated by the Union Treaty itself. The other institutions which together with the European Council form the single institutional framework of the Union are the institutions of the Community which are placed at the disposal of the Union: the European Parliament, the Council, the Commission and the Court of Justice. However, these Community institutions are not hereby transformed into institutions of the Union. Rather, in addition to their tasks and powers as institutions of the Communities, they are given supplementary tasks for the Union's own activities (Art. 5 TEU). The importance of this observation is that even in their activities solely in the context of the Union, the Parliament, Council and the Commission must respect the institutional balance between themselves,

---

12. Cf. on this W.T. Eijsbouts, 'De raad van opperhoofden', in Bijdragen aan een Europese grondwet' (Staatsrechtconferentie, 2000), 59.
13. E.g., decisions on common strategies which are implemented by the Council with a qualified majority (Arts. 13(2) and 23(2) TEU); decisions 'on referral' in certain cases where a Member State opposes taking a decision at the normal level, for important and stated reasons of national policy (Arts. 23(2) and 40(2) TEU); in relation to enhanced cooperation (Art. 40(2) TEU) this procedure was later deleted by the Treaty of Nice.
14. Arts. 99(2), 113(3), 128(5) EC.

as laid down in the Community Treaties, save to the extent that the TEU itself expressly otherwise provides. An interpretation which lays all the emphasis on the Union character of the institutions, risks camouflaging the fact that the statute, organization and institutional position of the institutions have their basis in the Community treaties. When they act as institutions of the Union, account must be taken at the very least of this institutional acquis. Quite a different point is that, from the point of view of clarity and accessibility of the Union structure for the citizen, a stage is gradually being reached where it would be recommended that, now the Council emphatically presents itself as the Council of the European Union, the Commission and the Court of Justice should change their names accordingly.

The Council and the Commission are given the particular responsibility, in relation to the Union's tasks, for ensuring the consistency of the Union's activities as a whole; they are to work together to that end, while respecting and building upon the *acquis communautaire* (Art. 3 TEU). This means that to the extent that tension develops, particularly in relation to external policies, between the external policies of the Communities and CFSP, it is the latter which must be adapted to the former, not the other way round (otherwise this would jeopardize the *acquis communautaire*). In the exercise of their specific Union tasks, the institutions will naturally have to have regard to the principles and objectives set out in Title I TEU. Although the Court's jurisdiction for the specific Union tasks is limited (PJCCM) or virtually non-existent (CFSP), it is also part of the institutional framework of the Union. The Court moreover has jurisdiction with respect to the final provisions of the TEU. It is likely that the Court will take account of the Union dimension in the exercise of its function under the Community treaties. The normal provisions concerning judicial protection do not apply to Title I TEU, but Article 3 TEU does apply to the Court as well. Arguably, the Court takes this into account in fulfilling its task of ensuring that the law is observed (Art. 220 EC) This could be important particularly in respect of the requirement that the Union and its institutional framework respect and build upon the *acquis communautaire*.

1.2.2.4 Powers of the Union

The most far-reaching powers of the Union are those conferred on the Communities. In addition, decision-making power is conferred on the Union's Institutions for the implementation of CFSP and PJCCM. The Treaty of Amsterdam clarified that these areas really do concern powers of the Union itself, and not merely cooperation between the Member States in the framework of the Union. CFSP is a policy of the Union, and equally the PJCCM is an instrument for the realization of one of the aims of the Union, viz. the creation of an area of freedom, security and justice with a high level of safety for citizens.[15] The powers conferred on the Union in these areas generally concern the ability to take decisions which are binding on the Member States, and not the enactment of legislation which directly imposes

---

15. The PJCCM provisions are not the only instrument for realizing that aim, see also Title IV EC Treaty, esp. Art. 61. Cf. Ch. III, section 6, *infra*.

obligations on citizens. Real legislative powers such as those granted to the EC, in particular where these concern regulations, are absent for the areas of CFSP and PJCCM. For the PJCCM this is expressed in clear terms by the exclusion of the possibility of direct effect for PJCCM decisions, that is the possibility to rely on such a norm, and if necessary enforce it through a court of law, *vis-à-vis* the body for which the norm is ultimately intended. On the basis of the Treaty text alone, it is unclear whether these powers of the Union also extend to the field of international relations, and in particular whether the Union has treaty-making powers of its own in the areas of CFSP and PJCCM. There is disagreement on the interpretation of Articles 24 and 38 TEU on this point, but these provisions have in fact already been applied in that sense by the Council (see Ch. XIII).[16] That the Union itself possesses the requisite legal capacity to enable it to act in the international arena seems hard to deny; that already flows from the general aims under Article 2 TEU, second indent (to assert its identity on the international scene . . .) and has by now been amply demonstrated in the legal practice.[17]

The rather obscure wording of Article 6(4) TEU cannot confer actual powers on the Union or its Institutions. Rather this provision must be read as an instruction to the Union to furnish itself with the necessary means for an effective Union policy, using the powers and appropriate procedures otherwise conferred. This embraces in particular the necessary financial means.

1.2.2.5   Budget of the Union

Administrative expenditure of the Institutions resulting from the activities of the Union as such (CFSP and PJCCM) are charged to the budget of the Communities, as is operational expenditure (except for military or defence expenditure), unless the Council decides that it must be charged to the Member States (Arts. 28 and 41 TEU). The budget is presented these days as the budget of the European Union. That does not alter the fact that the budget is adopted according to the procedures laid down in the Community treaties.

1.2.2.6   Open Government, Subsidiarity and Respect for
            Fundamental Rights

These fundamental principles must be taken into account in the exercise of the powers of the Union (Art. 1(2); Art. 2, last paragraph; Art. 6(2) TEU). The transparency regime laid down in the framework of the EC[18] applies to all areas of

---

16. Agreement between the European Union and the Federal Republic of Yugoslavia (FRY) on the activities of the European Union Monitoring Mission in the FRY, O.J. 2001, L 125. A similar agreement has been concluded with Macedonia, O.J. 2001, L 241. For further examples see R. Gosalbo Bono, 'Some Reflections on the CFSP Legal Order' (2006) CML Rev., 337–394, at 356 footnote 50.
17. See section 5.1 *infra*.
18. Art. 255 EC on access to documents.

Union activity (cf. Arts. 28(1) and 41(1) TEU).[19] The principle of subsidiarity is further elaborated in Article 5 EC. Respect for fundamental rights already forms part of the *acquis communautaire* by virtue of the case law of the Court of Justice. Interestingly, in its Article 6, the Treaty on European Union itself makes express reference to this case law where it mentions 'general principles of Community law'. The Court is thus indirectly accepted as the authority for the further substantive development of this aspect of the Constitution of the Union at least. Finally, mention should be made of the Charter of fundamental rights (see Ch. I, section 7.3 above) which has been proclaimed as the Charter of fundamental rights of the European Union and the provisions of which are explicitly addressed also to the institutions of the Union (Art. 51 of the Charter).

1.2.2.7   Enhanced Cooperation

One of the important items on the agenda for the negotiations leading up to the Treaty of Amsterdam was the elaboration of a 'multi-speed' regime, that is to say incorporating in the Treaty itself a possibility to permit a number of Member States to make further progress in some area of integration in a more limited framework, if developments in the Community or Union as a whole are held up by one or a few Member States who do not wish to participate. The elaboration of general arrangements for this 'multi-speed' possibility – first under the title 'flexibility', which was then rebaptized 'closer cooperation', and later again 'enhanced cooperation' – was also considered necessary in the light of the expected enlargement of the Union. The basic principles and conditions for these arrangements are set out in the Union Treaty itself, in a new Title VII, and are thus part of the 'constitution' of the Union. These arrangements are then elaborated specifically for the EC (Art. 11 EC) and the PJCCM (Art. 40 TEU). At the time of the Treaty of Amsterdam, it was not considered necessary to make such arrangements for the CFSP, since in that context the possibility of 'constructive abstention' – which only applies for the CFSP – was considered to allow for sufficient flexibility; under 'constructive abstention', Member States may avoid being obliged to apply a decision (Art. 23(1) second paragraph TEU). The Treaty of Nice did, however, introduce the possibility of enhanced cooperation in CFSP, albeit more limited; we return to this in section 7 below.

1.2.2.8   Amendment of the Treaty on European Union, and
Accession to the Union

The Final Provisions of the TEU set out the procedure by which amendments may be made to the TEU itself and the other Treaties on which the Union is founded (Art. 48) and also the procedures for accession of European States to membership of the Union (Art. 49). These provisions replace the relevant provisions of the

---

19. See Ch. III, section 6.6, *infra*.

founding Treaties of the EC, which were repealed by the Treaty of Maastricht. These provisions demonstrate particularly clearly the unity of the Union structure, insofar as applicants cannot accede to the Communities alone, nor may they accede to just one of CFSP and PJCCM: they become members of the Union and by virtue thereof accede to the various parts of it. To this extent the Communities in some way lose their independent character. But, on the other hand, these provisions are a first step in breaking down the fences between the various parts of the Union. Significantly, it is the appropriate Community procedures which are applied to the Union as a whole, an approach which conforms completely to the objective of the Union to maintain in full and build on the *acquis communautaire* (Art. 2 TEU). Thus, despite the decisive role that the Member States play in CFSP and PJCCM, new members can only be admitted to these elements of the Union with the assent of the European Parliament, the influence of which on these policy areas is otherwise extremely limited.

1.2.3   Protection of the Communities

An important characteristic of the Union is the primacy of the Communities over the supplementary policies and forms of cooperation in CFSP and PJCCM. Those Member States, which advocate the Community method and fear its watering-down and infection by the more intergovernmental method of decision-making in the other Union areas, have ensured that the Communities are protected from the other elements of the Union structure. This has been achieved in three ways: first, by emphasizing the objective of the Union to maintain and build on the *acquis communautaire* (Art. 2 TEU, see also Art. 3 TEU);[20] secondly, by ensuring – as was also the case with the SEA (Art. 32 SEA) – that provisions of the TEU which do not specifically amend the Community Treaties (in particular, the provisions dealing with CFSP and PJCCM) do not affect those Treaties (Art. 47 TEU); and, finally, by envisaging the possibility of transferring to the EC certain matters which are presently reserved to PJCCM (Art. 42 TEU). This interlink or *passerelle* provision operates in one direction only. It should be noted, however, that this protection of the Community legal order against alien influences from the other areas of Union activity is by no means absolute. In some cases, the Communities are hierarchically subordinate to decision-making at Union level[21] and in some cases provisions in the TEU set the conditions for EC decision-making (e.g., Title VII on enhanced cooperation). Nevertheless, in the absence of such explicit exceptions, the Communities enjoy a certain primacy *vis-à-vis* the CFSP and PJCCM in the sense that if there is a Community competence in a certain matter, this must be

---

20. In this context, it should be recalled that on the occasion of Treaty amendments, the Member States act quite boldly with regard to this principle, e.g., at Maastricht (cf. the so-called Barber Protocol and the Protocol on Danish second homes), cf. D. Curtin, 'The Constitutional Structure of the Union: A Europe of Bits and Pieces' (1993) CML Rev., 17–69.
21. E.g., Art. 7 TEU in conjunction with Art. 309 EC, Arts. 60(1) and 301 EC, Arts. 28(2) and (3), and 41(2) and (3) TEU, Art. 44(2) TEU.

used.[22] There is no possibility simply to choose to locate, for instance, an external action in the framework of the CFSP, if a possible legal basis exists in the EC Treaty. A CFSP decision can in such a case be considered as *ultra vires* and can be contested with an action for annulment on the ground that it infringes Community competence.[23] Consequently, the protection of the Communities, in other words the division of competences between the Communities and the CFSP and PJCCM, can be guaranteed by the Court.

1.2.4 Interim Conclusion

The Union structure as this resulted from the Treaty of Maastricht could be seen as a provisional solution. Attempts made during the negotiations leading up to the Treaty of Amsterdam to arrive at a more uniform structure by means of a fusion of the Union with the EC failed miserably. So did the Constitutional Treaty, due to the negative referenda; however, the Treaty of Lisbon will achieve this fusion, if and when it enters into force. Nevertheless, the Treaty of Amsterdam did strengthen the structure of the Union by giving more body to the concept European Union and also by constitutionalizing it further. The Union as set up by the Treaty of Maastricht was a fairly loose association, but the Treaty of Amsterdam gave it the contours of a real international organization with its own institutional structure, its own competences (CFSP and PJCCM) and its own constitutional arrangements. The question of legal personality of the Union would seem to be answered by this. Taking into account the characteristics of the Union as sketched above, and more particularly the decision-making practice in CFSP, we are more and more inclined to support the opinion accepted in the academic literature that, both in its internal functioning and on the international scene the Union can already be qualified as having legal personality.[24] This is even in spite of the express intention of the drafters of the Treaty not to give explicit legal personality to the Union. Practice is here stronger than theory.

These various facts mean that for outsiders, and that includes the citizens within the Union as well as international partners, the structure of the Union is particularly lacking in transparency: a Union which, as an international organization, has its own policy responsibilities for CFSP and PJCCM, also operates through and by means of the two EC, which in turn continue to exist as separate legal persons and can themselves each be qualified as international organizations. Three international organizations seems rather a lot. The situation in relation to the position within the EC of the European Central Bank (ECB) and the European Investment Bank (EIB), which also each have legal personality and enjoy a limited

---

22. Cf. on this issue the doctoral theses by R.H. van Ooik, *De keuze der rechtsgrondslag voor besluiten van de Europese Unie* (Deventer, 1999) and R.A. Wessel, *The European Union's Foreign and Security Policy: A Legal Institutional Perspective* (The Hague, 1999).
23. Case C-170/96, *Commission v. Council* (airport transit visas), and more recently, with regard to PJCCM, Case C-176/03, *Commission v. Council* (penal sanctions).
24. See section 5.1 *infra*.

treaty-making capacity, is rather different. Their positions can easily be justified given the special nature of the relevant banking activities and, in particular as far as the ECB is concerned, that body's independent status (Art. 108 EC). Maintenance of such a structure of international organizations for the EU and EC, with one layer piled on another, seems much less rational. Whatever the outcome of the ratification process of the Lisbon Treaty, it may be expected that in practice the Union will become stronger *vis-à-vis* and at the cost of the EC. Further constitutionalization of the Union inevitably brings the risk of a certain constitutional erosion of the EC.[25]

2 DIVERSITY AND UNITY OF THE COMMUNITIES AND THE UNION, COMMUNITY LAW AND OTHER UNION LAW

2.1 DIFFERENCES IN STRUCTURE BETWEEN THE TREATIES

There are marked differences in structure between the Union Treaty where CFSP and PJCCM are concerned, on the one hand, and the Community treaties on the other, but also between the Community treaties themselves, owing to the difference in method of integration.

First, a distinction must be made between the more intergovernmentally organized CFSP and PJCCM and the more supranationally structured Communities. The CFSP covers the whole field of foreign and security policy insofar as this does not come within the scope of the competence of the Communities or the PJCCM. To give shape to this common policy, far-reaching decision-making powers have been granted to the Union, mainly concerning alignment and coordination of national foreign and security policy. The shape and exercise of these powers are predominantly organized according to classic methods of international cooperation. The emphasis is on the more intergovernmental organs: the European Council and the Council; the influence of the more supranational institutions, Parliament and Commission, is limited or very limited. The Court of Justice is completely absent. The Council and European Council combine all functions: they prepare policy, take decisions and implement them,[26] and also have the role of ensuring supervision and of settling disputes (Art. 11(2) TEU). The supporting services necessary for this are organized within the Council's own apparatus, under the authority of the Secretary-General, who is also the High representative of the CFSP. The Member States thus maintain a firm grip on the development, the

---

25. To quote the title of the farewell lecture delivered by Prof. Richard Lauwaars, when leaving his chair at the University of Amsterdam, Groningen, 1994.
26. Cf. in this context the role of presidency and secretary-general of the Council, high representative of the CFSP (Art. 18 TEU), and the policy planning and early warning unit established in the General Secretariat of the Council (Declaration 6 attached to the Treaty of Amsterdam).

implementation and the enforcement of the CFSP; the role of the other institutions which are independent of them, Parliament and Commission, is minimal.

From this point of view, the PJCCM presents a somewhat different picture. In order to create an area of freedom, security and justice, the Union also[27] has the task of promoting and giving shape to cooperation between the national police services and judicial bodies in criminal matters. The decision-making competences accorded to the Union for this purpose, aim in the first place at the operational shaping of this cooperation, in particular via Europol and Eurojust (this is the name of the European unit for judicial cooperation),[28] but in addition legislative powers are granted which make harmonization of legislation possible (for instance concerning substantive criminal law). Just as with the CFSP, the decision-making method is to a great extent intergovernmental. The real power lies with the Council and European Council, but the Commission does have a right of initiative. This right is shared with the Member States, but it may be assumed that the Commission has a better chance of success in being involved in policy-making in this area than in the CFSP, where it is also allowed to make 'proposals' (Art. 22 TEU). The role of the European Parliament is also greater here, since for most categories of decisions it has a right to be consulted. An important difference with respect to CFSP is that the Court has jurisdiction, albeit restricted. In the preparation of policy and in enforcement there are thus some elements of the Community method to be found. That is, however, not so for implementation; this belongs to the Presidency and thus lies with the Council, not the Commission, and in the future will be organized in particular via Europol and Eurojust.

As far as the Community Treaties are concerned, there were marked differences in structure and in method of integration between the European Coal and Steel Community (ECSC) Treaty[29] and the EC Treaty. The ECSC was an example of integration by sectors, which, because of the indissoluble connection between the integrated sector and those sectors of the economy of the Member States which retained their national character, was called an '*opération contre nature*' by Reuter in his commentary of 1953.[30] The explanation for this unnatural operation lay in the political motives which had led to the establishment of the ECSC. It could only be *economically* justified in the perspective of a continued economic integration, which was ultimately to embrace the whole economy of the Member States.

In contrast to the ECSC Treaty, the EC Treaty embraces practically the whole economy of the Member States and important sectors of national policy, such as social policy, environmental policy etc. Under the EC Treaty a common market, with free movement of goods, persons, services and capital, is set up together with an Economic and Monetary Union (EMU). The emphasis here is on a free operation of the market mechanism under conditions ensuring effective and undistorted

---

27. The other tasks for achieving that aim are dealt with in Title IV EC Treaty.
28. Decision 2002/187/JHA: Council Decision of 28 Feb. 2002 setting up Eurojust, O.J. 2002, L 63.
29. Which lapsed 2002, see Ch. I, section 2, *supra*.
30. P. Reuter, *La CECA*, Paris, 1953, 32. See also D. Spierenburg and R. Poidevin, *Histoire de la Haute Autorité de la CECA, Une expérience supranationale* (Brussels, 1993).

competition, or as Article 4 EC puts it, an open market economy with free competition. Outside the sectors of transport and agriculture, there is no provision for the possibility of market regulation, but that does not exclude many other forms of adjusting the market process (see Ch. III).

The EC is based on a customs union.[31] This found concrete shape in the Treaty in obligations imposed on Member States to take, according to a prescribed timetable, a series of clearly defined measures leading to the progressive elimination of mutual trade barriers and the creation of a common external tariff. Beyond this, the Treaty is principally a *traité-cadre*, or *traité de procédure*. Objectives are formulated, principles are defined, but it is left to the institutions to work out these principles and objectives in concrete measures. The most important exception to this approach is the time-table for the achievement of EMU, which is the subject of detailed Treaty provisions. Generally, though, time and adequate agreement to lay down a detailed set of rules in the EC Treaty were lacking. Moreover, it would have been unwise to do so, in some cases even inconceivable, because the measures taken would have to be appropriate to (and themselves allow adjustment to) varying circumstances.

In the EC Treaty a comprehensive policy-making and regulatory task has therefore been allotted to the institutions. Considering the vital interests which are usually at stake and the high degree of freedom in the choice of policy that was accorded – such as in the development of a common policy in the sectors of transport, agriculture and external relations – it is not surprising that this task was entrusted in the first instance to the Council, although as a rule it could act only on proposals from the Commission. It is, however, striking that the Treaty provided that even in these fields the requirement of unanimity was in the course of time to be replaced by that of a qualified majority vote as the basis for Council decisions.

To a considerable extent the system created by the EC Treaty, even when fully worked out through Council decisions, consists of rules of conduct for the national governments in the form of instructions or prohibitions. Rules of conduct for enterprises are found among the provisions for a common competition policy, while such rules have also been frequently adopted in the few sectors in which market regulation (agriculture and transport) was intended. Powers of an executive character were included in the EC Treaty only to a fairly limited degree. This is not surprising in view of the character of this Treaty as a *traité de procédure*. In so far as such powers are granted in the Treaty, they are mostly allotted to the Commission and lie generally in the sphere of the control of safeguard clauses. Since the Council may delegate powers to the Commission for carrying into effect the rules it has laid down, a further evolution of the executive activity of the Commission has been made possible. Such an activity in direct relation to the economic subjects of the Community has been explicitly provided for notably within the framework of

---

31.   There are two elements in a customs union: the abolition of internal barriers to trade and the creation of a common customs tariff *vis-à-vis* the rest of the world. In a free trade area this second element is lacking. Cf. Art. XXIV(8) GATT.

rules laid down by the Council for implementing the Treaty as regards the prohibition of discrimination in the transport sector, and as regards competition between enterprises.

The structure of Euratom recalls that of the ECSC in several respects. Here again the integration concerns one sector of the economy. A common market is set up for nuclear basic materials, products and means of production. Ample scope is given in the Treaty to the planning of scientific, technological and economic activities in so far as they are related to the development of the peaceful use of nuclear energy. A striking feature is the strong emphasis which the Treaty lays on the control of these activities with the aid of modern methods of administration, such as planning, financial incentives and the use of private law structures.

The simultaneous existence of the Union Treaty and the two Community Treaties raises the question of their interrelationship. We have already indicated in section 1.2.3. above that the Communities have to a large extent remained autonomous in relation to the Union, barring a few explicit exceptions. As for the Community Treaties themselves, Article 305 EC expressly provides that the provisions of that Treaty shall not derogate from those of the Euratom Treaty (which was concluded at the same time as the EEC Treaty). It is generally accepted that the EC Treaty, which in principle embraces all economic activities, also applies to activities in the nuclear energy sector insofar as the Euratom Treaty does not govern them[32] provided that the EC rules are not at variance with those of the Euratom Treaty. This is so even though Article 305 EC does not compel such a conclusion, since the complete exclusion of the EC system in sectors covered by the Euratom Treaty would also be compatible with the wording of that Article.

Even though the provisions of the sectoral integration Treaty take precedence as *lex specialis* over the provisions of the EC Treaty as *lex generalis*,[33] in the interpretation of the *lex specialis* the Court may call on the *lex generalis*. Thus in Ruling 1/78 the Court held that in the light of the EC Treaty the provisions of the Euratom Treaty on the nuclear common market 'appear to be nothing other than the application, in a highly specialized field, of the legal conceptions which form

---

32. Cf. *Deuxième Rapport Général sur l'Activité des Communautés Européennes, 1968* (Brussels, 1969) para. 655. See also Art. 42(1) of Reg. 1612/68, O.J. 1968, L 257/2, on the free movement of workers within the Community and the General Programmes on freedom of establishment and the freedom to provide services (O.J. 2/1962, 36). See further D. Simmonds (ed.), *Encyclopedia of European Community Law* (London, loose-leaf, 1974–94) Vol. B2, part B10, commentary on Art. 232 EEC, and E.-U. Petersmann in Von der Groeben et al. (eds), *Kommentar zum EU-/EG Vertragn* 5th ed. (Baden-Baden) Vol. 5, 545. See, in relation to the ECSC Treaty, Case 328/85, *Deutsche Babcock Handel GmbH v. Hauptzollamt Lübeck-Ost.* See in general T. Cusack, 'A Tale of Two Treaties: An Assessment of the Euratom Treaty in relation to the EC Treaty' (2003) CML Rev., 117–142.

33. Cf. Joined Cases 27–29/58, *Compagnie des hauts fourneaux et fonderies de Givors and others v. High Authority*, which showed that the High Authority, in applying special internal carriage rates in the interest of coal or steel producers (Art. 70 ECSC, 4th para.) cannot take account of the principles of an appropriate regional policy, unlike in Art. 80(2) EC (now Art. 76(2)).

the basis of the structure of the general common market'.[34] The provisions relating to the institutions common to the Communities will, in particular, be interpreted by the Court as far as possible in a uniform manner and brought into harmony with each other.[35]

2.2   COMMON FEATURES OF THE TREATIES

In spite of the marked differences, there is an obvious consistency between the Union and the Communities, since the Communities are included in the Union and therefore, together with the specific Union areas of policy, are part of one organization. This organization is characterized by one institutional framework (European Council, European Parliament, Council, Commission and Court of Justice), common objectives, and also a single budget (see above 1.2.2). Despite this consistency, it is preferable for the time being, on account of the above-mentioned differences in intensity of integration method, to continue to pay attention to the EC separately, as a predominantly autonomous legal sub-order within the larger whole made up by the Union. It is this legal order which has formed the core at the basis of the development of the integration process, and which is also the most developed legal order in terms of independence and stability. There is thus every reason to continue to speak of Community law – even after the Communities have been embraced by the Union – referring to the entirety of the legal rules concerning and enacted by the EC. The differences between the Union and the EC, between the Union legal order[36] and the EC legal order are (still?) too great to warrant replacing the term Community law with a concept 'Union law' covering all areas of the Union.

Also between the Communities themselves there are differences, as was indicated in the preceding section. Nevertheless, the general objectives have much in common,[37] and the institutional structure and the legal order called into being by or under the two Treaties display so many common features that it is justifiable to treat the Communities as a whole. The link with the Union and Union law should thereby also be kept in mind. In the discussion of the institutional and economic law of the Communities in the different chapters of the present work, the emphasis will be on the law of the EC as the most comprehensive and most important part of Community law. In view of the mutual relationship between the two Community

---

34. Ruling 1/78, at para. 15. Cf. also Case 13/60, *'Geitling' Ruhrkohlen-Verkaufsgesellschaft mbH et al. v. High Authority* in which, in the interpretation of Art. 65 ECSC, reliance was placed on Art. 81(3) EC in the light of the common inspiration behind the two provisions. In Case 6/72, *Europemballage Corporation and Continental Can Company Inc. v. Commission*, the Court refused to draw a comparison between Art. 86 EC (now 82 EC) and certain provisions of the ECSC Treaty.
35. Case 101/63, *Albert Wagner v. Jean Fohrmann et al.*; see also Case 230/81, *Luxembourg v. European Parliament*.
36. See *infra* 3.4.
37. Cf. Arts. 2 EC, 1 Euratom.

Treaties[38] it would seem appropriate to deal with the law of the Euratom as a branch of the socio-economic law of the Communities in the same way as the branches relating to agriculture and transport in the EC (see Ch. XII).

The same single institutional framework which exists now for the Union has – with the exception of the European Council – functioned for the EC almost from the beginning. Pursuant to the Convention on certain institutions common to the EC, which was concluded at the same time as the EEC and Euratom Treaties, the Parliament and the Court of Justice have functioned since the start of the EEC and Euratom as common institutions for originally three and now two Communities. The Parliament (termed the *Assemblée* in the founding Treaties), called itself the European Parliament, and this designation was adopted in the Treaties following the SEA of 1986. The Council and Commission became common institutions of the three Communities on 1 July 1967, pursuant to the Merger Treaty of 8 April 1965. Since 1 June 1977 a single Court of Auditors served all three Communities (it was listed as one of the institutions in the Treaty of Maastricht). Further, a single Economic and Social Committee (ECOSOC) functions in both the EC and Euratom. The Institutions and the Committee still enjoy all the powers they were endowed with by the founding Treaties, taking account of the conditions also provided for.[39]

The structure of Community law and the way it is implemented can also be understood as a single internal system. The *primary* law of the Communities covers the law set up by the EC and Euratom Treaties and agreements and Community decisions modifying these Treaties, such as the decisions on the Community's own resources (1970, and now 2007), the First and Second Budgetary Treaties (22 April 1970 and 22 July 1975) and the Decision and Act on direct elections to the European Parliament (20 September 1976); it embraces the SEA (28 February 1986) and the Treaties of Maastricht (7 February 1992), Amsterdam (2 October 1997) and Nice (26 February 2001). It also embraces the decisions and Treaties concerning the accession of the United Kingdom, Denmark and Ireland (1972), Greece (1979), Spain and Portugal (1985), Austria, Finland and Sweden (1994), Czech Republic, Estonia, Cyprus, Latvia, Lithuania, Hungary, Malta, Poland, Slovenia and the Slovak Republic (2003), Bulgaria and Romania (2005), as well as the Acts of Accession appended thereto in so far as they modify or supplement the earlier Treaties. The term 'Treaties' in the context of the ambit of primary Community law also covers the Annexes as well as the conventions and protocols appended to the Treaties (Arts. 311 EC, 207 Euratom). *Secondary* Community law consists of the provisions adopted by the Community Institutions on the basis of the Treaties and in order to implement them. Agreements concluded by the Communities with third countries or international organizations form a separate category of rules of Community law. This distinction between primary and secondary law can in fact also be made for Union law as such (CFSP and PJCCM).

---

38. See *supra* 2.1.
39. See now Art. 9 Treaty of Amsterdam, by which the above-mentioned Convention of 1957 and the Merger Treaty of 1965 have been repealed.

Both the primary and the secondary law of the Communities consist of two groups of rules. The first group is formed by *institutional law*. These rules relate to the field of application of the Treaties and their revision, the legal personality of the Communities, their seat, language regime and immunities. These subjects will be dealt with in the present chapter as general aspects of the Communities. In addition, institutional law embraces the rules relating to the composition of the various institutions and subsidiary bodies and the legal status of their members; the functions and powers of these institutions and bodies, and the way in which they exercise them in relation to each other, to the Member States and their organs, or to third countries, international organizations or private agents subject to Community authority. These matters will be discussed elsewhere in this book, in Chapter IV on institutional structure, Chapter V on types of legal instruments and decision-making, Chapter VI on the administration of justice, Chapter VII on application and enforcement, and partly also in Chapter XIII on external relations, where necessary attention will also be paid to the institutional aspects of the rest of Union law.

The second group of rules of Community law consists of the *substantive law* of the Communities, which will be discussed, together with the rest of substantive Union law, in the remaining chapters of this work. In the present context, discussion is confined to the treatment of some general aspects. The substantive law of the Communities can be classified according to its purposes again into two categories of rules. The first category regulates the exercise of the powers of the national policy-making and administrative organs by means of Community prohibitions and injunctions. The Member States and their organs are obliged either to abstain from certain measures or positively to take certain other measures in order to implement Community law. There can thus arise an obligation to abolish, to modify, or – if it is already in conformity with the obligation imposed – not to modify existing legislation, or to adopt new legislation. The second category of substantive law of the Communities consists of rules of conduct for private parties coming within the scope of Community law. These rules are to be found especially in the sphere of competition law.

The implementation of substantive Community law, which may ultimately lead to the application of this law in administrative acts or judicial decisions in concrete cases, may pass through many stages and has been entrusted in varying degrees to the Community Institutions and national bodies. At one end of the scale, e.g., in the sphere of competition law, the Council and/or the Commission work out primary Community law and apply it up to the stage of decisions addressed to individual enterprises, in which case national bodies have only to intervene in its enforcement (Arts. 256 EC and 164 Euratom). More often, the Member States have an important role to play in the implementation and application of Community law (common commercial policy, agricultural policy). The Commission and the Court will then chiefly have the task of exercising supervision over the way in which this role is fulfilled (Arts. 211 and 226–228 EC, 124 and 141–143 Euratom). Between the extremes of practically centralized Community administration and practically decentralized national administration there are many variations, according to the branch of Community law under consideration. The implementation will then be based on close cooperation between the Member States and the Community institutions both performing under their own responsibility their duties under Community law.[40] It is against this background that the importance of Article 10 EC should be understood; as the Court has indicated this is the expression of the more general rule imposing on the Member States and the Community institutions mutual duties of genuine cooperation and assistance.[41]

3   NATURE AND EFFECT OF COMMUNITY LAW AND
           OTHER UNION LAW

3.1   NATURE OF COMMUNITY LAW

Community law can be distinguished from traditional public international law in its content, its instruments and its sources of law.

From the formal viewpoint, Community law belongs to international law. In fact, it is partly embodied in, partly based on, treaties concluded between sovereign States. Community law, however, shows a number of properties which are foreign to traditional international law and which do not even occur in more advanced international law in this combination and intensity. *From the viewpoint of its content*, Community law is a common internal law in the Member States rather than a law between these States. Examples are the Treaty provisions on Union Citizenship and certain elements of the EMU arrangements. Further, the core of Community law is formed by the rules for the establishment and maintenance of a common market. This common market takes the place of the separate national markets and has a character analogous to that of the domestic market of one State.[42] The common market, therefore, is an internal market common to the Member States. Thus, in this market the difference between legal relations which in view of their subject-matter, persons, or place have an international or an internal character becomes blurred, as does the distinction between, on the one hand what in principle is usually the potential domain of international law and, on the other hand, the reserved domain of national law. From the viewpoint of the common market all these relations have an internal character. The law regulating these relations is *internal law common to the Member States*.[43]

---

40. Cf. Case 76/70, *Ludwig Wünsche & Co. v. Hauptzollamt Ludwigshafen/Rhein*.
41. E.g., Case 44/84, *Derrick Guy Edmund Hurd v. Kenneth Jones*; Case C-2/88 Imm., J.J. *Zwartveld* et al.
42. See Ch. III, section 3.4, *infra*. Cf. Case 270/80, *Polydor Ltd v. Harlequin Records Shops Ltd*, at para. 16: '[T]he Treaty, by establishing a common market and progressively approximating the economic policies of the Member States, seeks to unite national markets into a single market having the characteristics of a domestic market.'
43. Cf. A.G. Lagrange, in Case 8/55, *Fédération Charbonnière de Belgique v. High Authority* who spoke of the Treaty as being the charter of the Community, since the rules of law which derive from it constitute the *internal law of that Community* (italics in the original).

Further, those Community rules whose object is the establishment and functioning of the common market cannot, upon closer analysis, be reduced exclusively to mutual rights and duties of the Member States, as is often the case in traditional international law.[44] The object of these Community rules is the regulation both of the conduct of the national governments and of that of private persons (whether individuals or legal persons) with respect to and in the common market. Community law regulates *a conglomerate of mutual rights and duties between the Community and its subjects, both Member States and private persons, and between these subjects amongst themselves.*

Traditional international law is characterized, *inter alia*, by somewhat primitive instruments. Their creation, application and enforcement rest predominantly with the states, either collectively or individually. In classic intergovernmental organizations, the task of the organs is generally limited to stimulating and registering agreement between states and to furthering the observance of the points agreed upon. Their task is directed to coordination and adaptation of the legislative and administrative activities of the participating states by means of organized persuasion and political pressure. Another striking point is the modest role of international adjudication, and consequently also of the judicial element in the functioning of these organizations, although there is now some evolution in this sphere: particularly in intergovernmental organizations in the economic, financial and social fields (WTO, ILO, OECD, the IMF, the World Bank and its associated organs) a tendency towards increasing justiciability can be detected, in the form of binding executive decisions, examination and dispute resolution procedures.

Characteristic features of Community law, on the other hand, are the extensive organizational and procedural provisions that have been made and the refined legal instruments available for supplementing, working out, amending, applying and enforcing this law. They will be discussed in detail in subsequent chapters. The discussion here is confined to a short characterization, partly based on the Court's case law.

As the Court emphasizes, the Community is provided with its own institutions and has legal personality, legal capacity and right of international representation. It is vested with real powers arising from a limitation of competence or a transfer of certain powers from the states to the Community.[45] Organs have been created which are to exercise sovereign rights derived from the states.[46] These organs may carry on autonomous legislative and administrative activities within the limits set by the Treaties.

The policy-making in this Community is not exclusively in the hands of a body composed of representatives of the Member States taking decisions by a unanimous vote. A Council, which may take its decisions in many cases by a qualified majority, has to share this function with a Commission consisting of persons

---

44. Cf. Case 26/62, *NV Algemene Transporten Expeditie Onderneming Van Gend & Loos v. Nederlands Inland Revenue Administration.*
45. Case 6/64, *Flaminio Costa v. ENEL.*
46. Case 26/62, *Van Gend & Loos.*

independent of the Member States, and is increasingly dependent on cooperation in some form or another with the Parliament. Moreover, private persons who are affected as much as the Member States by the powers conferred upon the institutions, are called upon to collaborate through the European Parliament and the ECOSOC in the work of the Community.[47] The extensive powers of the Court of Justice ensure that the law is respected, as regards the functioning of the Community, in a way that is without precedent in the law of international organizations.

Finally in its sources of law, too, the picture presented by Community law is unusual in traditional international law. International law finds its sources especially in inter-state treaties and in state practice generally accepted as the law. A striking feature of Community law is the importance of the acts of the Institutions and of general legal principles as a formal source of law. Fundamental rights form an integral part of Community law and in this respect Community law offers inhabitants of the Member States a protection comparable with that afforded by their own national law.[48] The Court thus regards the Communities as being a Community based on the rule of law.[49] Being, according to its nature, largely a system of internal law which is common to the Member States, Community law moreover employs legal constructions and legal concepts which also occur in national law to a much greater extent than is the case for international law. In the definition of the content of those constructions and concepts according to Community law, therefore, national law also forms a source of inspiration.[50]

3.2   THE COMMUNITY LEGAL ORDER

It was partly on the strength of the properties described above that the Court found that the Treaties have called into being a *new, distinctive legal order*.[51] This legal order regulates the powers, rights and obligations of the Community and its subjects, and provides (an essential element of a legal order) for the procedures necessary for determining, adjudicating and where appropriate setting sanctions for infringements of the law.[52]

---

47. Ibid.
48. E.g., Case 4/73, *J.Nold, Kohlen- und Baustoffgroßhandlung v. Commission*; Case C-112/00, *Schmidberger v. Austria*; Case C-540/03, *Parliament v. Council* (directive on family reunification). See also the Charter of Fundamental Rights of the EU adopted by the European Parliament, the Council and the Commission in December 2000, O.J. 2000, C 364, and Art. 6(2) TEU. See, further, Ch. IV, section 7.5.4 *infra*.
49. Case C-2/88 Imm., *Zwartveld.*, and Opinion 1/91, *EEA Agreement I*.
50. See Ch. VI, section 1, *infra*.
51. Case 26/62, *Van Gend & Loos*. See also Case 6/64, *Costa v. ENEL*; Joined Cases 90 & 91/63, *Commission v. Luxembourg and Belgium* (which no longer mentions public international law); Case C-2/88 Imm., *Zwartveld*; Joined Cases C-6 & 9/90, *Andrea Francovich and Danila Bonifaci and others v. Italy*, and Opinion 1/91, *EEA Agreement I*.
52. Cases 90 and 91/63, *Commission v. Luxembourg and Belgium*.

The Community legal order created by the Treaty curtails the freedom of the Member States on certain points in ways other than those of traditional doctrines of international law. Thus, from the availability of the procedures necessary for determining and adjudicating infringements of the Treaty, the Court has derived a prohibition against self-help for the Member States, except for those cases in which the Treaty expressly permits it.[53] In the previous editions of this book, it was added that the traditional international doctrine of self-help may be resuscitated again if these procedures, e.g., those of Articles 226–228 EC, have produced no result, since as the Treaties stand the Community cannot take proceedings against the Member States to enforce a judgment. The Court may impose a lump sum or penalty payment at the instance of the Commission against a Member State which fails to fulfil its obligation under Article 228 EC and refuses to act upon a decision of the Court of Justice.[54] If even that should fail to produce results, we submitted on earlier occasions that the Community or the Member States could then very well take reprisals, i.e., measures which *per se* are unlawful, but which are justified as a defence against the unlawful act of another State. In view of the sanction mechanism introduced by the Treaty of Amsterdam in case of a serious or persistent breach of the principles of the rule of law by a Member State (Arts. 6 and 7 TEU), this view should be re-examined. The fact that there are good grounds for qualifying such a continued failure by a Member State to respect and act upon a judgment of the Court as such a serious and persistent breach[55] would lead us to abandon the earlier view. In view of the sanctions which are then possible pursuant to the Treaties themselves (Art. 7 TEU and 309 EC), appeal to the public international law principle of self-help and reprisals in this case seems no longer justified.

The transfer of powers from the Member States to the Community is of an irreversible nature.[56] Given that the Member States agreed to establish a Community of unlimited duration, having permanent institutions invested with real powers, stemming from a limitation of authority or transfer of powers from the states to that Community, the powers 'thus conferred could not, therefore, be withdrawn from the Community, nor could the objectives with which such powers are concerned be restored to the field of authority of the Member States alone, except by virtue of an express provision of the Treaty'.[57] Thus it cannot be argued that a Treaty provision has lapsed if the Council fails to implement it. The

---

53. Ibid.; cf. also Case C-5/94, *The Queen v. Ministry of Agriculture, Fisheries and Food, ex parte Hedley Lomas (Ireland) Ltd*; cf. the special safeguard provisions on national security (Arts. 296 and 297 EC).
54. Art. 228(2) EC. See Ch. VI, section 2.1, *infra*. See also the identically worded Art. 143(2) Euratom, 2nd and 3rd paras.
55. Cf. also the European Court of Human Rights in *Hornsby*, ECHR Reports 1997, 495.
56. Case 7/71, *Commission v. France*. See K. Mortelmans, 'Les lacunes en droit communautaire' (1981) CDE, 410, 430–431 and Usher, *European Community Law and National Law: The Irreversible Transfer?* (London, 1981).
57. Case 7/71, *Commission v. France*, para. 20.

Community does not lose its power; the Member States do not obtain the freedom to act at will in the field in question even if the Council is in default.[58]

Community solidarity is one of the fundamental principles of the Treaty and, in accordance with the obligations under Article 10 EC, lies at the very foundation of the whole Community system.[59] If a Member State unilaterally breaks, according to its own conception of national interest, the equilibrium between advantages and obligations flowing from Community membership it infringes its duty of solidarity and thus strikes at the fundamental basis of the Community legal order.[60]

3.3   EFFECT OF COMMUNITY LAW IN THE INTERNAL LEGAL SPHERE

In the view of the Court, the traditional freedom of the state to decide for itself in what way it is going to comply with treaty obligations within its national legal order, provided it does fulfil them, has also been abolished by the Community legal order. Indeed, it is assumed fairly generally that international law does not require either that international rules of law should be applied directly and as such within the national legal order, or that these rules should take priority over national law within this legal order. The method followed, for instance, in Articles 93 and 94 of the Dutch Constitution[61] is not therefore prescribed imperatively by international law.

The so-called dualist view, still prevalent particularly in Germany, Italy and the United Kingdom, that according to constitutional law, written rules of international law can be applied within the domestic legal order only after their transformation into national rules, cannot therefore be deemed to conflict with general international law. In the first two previously mentioned countries, the view is held that the transformation of the rules laid down in or under a treaty takes place in and by the act of the legislature approving the treaty or authorizing its ratification. The rules which are laid down under a treaty by international bodies created in this context[62] are generally assumed to be transformed into internal law by anticipation in the parliamentary act of approval. The transformation, in and by this national act, of rules laid down in the treaty and its implementing decisions leads to these rules obtaining the same force of law as this act itself has. In consequence, if there is a conflict between the rules transformed into national law and

---

58. Ibid. See also Case 32/79, *Commission v. United Kingdom*; Case 804/79, *Commission v. United Kingdom* and Joined Cases 47 & 48/83, *Pluimveeslachterij Midden-Nederland BV et al.* See also Ch. III, section 5.2, *infra*.
59. Joined Cases 6 & 11/69, *Commission. v. France*. See also Case 39/72, *Commission v. Italy*; Case 128/78, *Commission v. United Kingdom*. See further, Ch. III, section 5.2, *infra*.
60. Case 39/72, *Commission v. Italy*; Case 128/78, *Commission v. United Kingdom*.
61. See P. van Dijk, 'The Implementation and Application of the Law of the European Communities within the Legal Order of the Netherlands' (1968–1969) CML Rev., 283. C. Kortmann and P. Bovend'eert, *Dutch Constitutional Law* (The Hague, Kluwer, 2000).
62. Cf. the regulations mentioned in Art. 249 EC.

a later national law adopted by parliament, the latter will take priority on the basis of the adage *lex posterior derogat lege priori.*

This consequence of the transformation doctrine does not in itself conflict with general international law, although naturally the state can be fully called to account for a resultant infringement of its treaty obligations before an international forum and cannot evade its international liability by relying on its constitutional law ('a State cannot adduce as against another State its own Constitution with a view to evading obligations incumbent upon it under international law or treaties in force').[63] It should be noted that even in Member States such as France, where the transformation doctrine is not held, there was some doubt as to whether on the strength of constitutional law a national court could refuse to apply a national law of a later date in so far as it conflicts with written international law of an earlier date.[64]

The Court of Justice, however, on the basis of the Community legal order takes a quite different position from the current conception of international law, a conception which leaves the regulation of the internal effect of rules of international law to national constitutional law. The case law of the Court shows that Treaty provisions[65] (and sometimes provisions of decisions or directives addressed to Member States)[66] penetrate into the internal legal order without the aid of any national measure, to the extent that their character makes this appropriate. In other words, provisions of Community law may be directly applicable, they may produce direct effects. Provisions of Community law which leave the Community institutions and the Member States no discretionary freedom in their application or implementation will be directly effective in that the national courts can apply them, without stepping into the shoes of the legislature.[67] Such provisions, like regulations (which are by nature and function in the system of Community sources of law directly applicable),[68] must be applied by the national courts without the intervention of a legal measure designed to transpose Community law (as a whole or in respect of particular provisions) into domestic law.

The Court has made it clear that the fundamental principles and objectives of the Treaty demonstrate that 'the Community constitutes a new legal order of

---

63. Cf. the Permanent Court of International Justice, Advisory Opinion *'Treatment of Polish Nationals . . . in the Danzig Territory'* Series A/B, No. 44, (1932); cf. Vienna Convention on the Law of Treaties, United Nations, *Treaty Series*, vol. 1155, 331, Art. 27.

64. The French *Conseil d'Etat* has now ceased to maintain its earlier negative attitude, see *Nicolo* [1990] 1 CMLR 173, noted by Manin (1991) CML Rev., 499 and Kapteyn, (1991) SEW, 594. See also Decision CE No. 287110 of 8 Feb. 2007 (*Société Arcelor Atlantique et Lorraine*). The doubt which previously existed in Belgium has been extinguished since the Cour de Cassation's judgment of 29 May 1971 in *Minister of Economic Affairs v. SA Fromagerie Franco-Suisse 'Le Ski'* [1972] CMLR 330.

65. E.g., Case 26/62, *Van Gend & Loos* and (in the formulation given in the text) Case 28/67, *Firma Molkerei-Zentrale Westfalen/Lippe GmbH v. Hauptzollamt Paderborn.*

66. E.g., Case 9/70, *Franz Grad v. Finanzamt Traunstein*, Case 33/70, *SpA SACE v. Finance Minister of the Italian Republic* and Case 41/74, *Yvonne Van Duyn v. Home Office*. See further, Ch. VII, section 1, *infra.*

67. See further, Ch. VII, section 1, *infra.*

68. E.g., Case 43/71, *Politi s.a.s. v. Ministry for Finance of the Italian Republic.*

international law, for the benefit of which the States have limited their sovereign rights, albeit within limited fields, and the subjects of which comprise not only the Member States but also their nationals'.[69] Community law has effect independently of the legislation of the Member States.[70] Thus there can be no question of the transformation doctrine applying in the field of Community law; the latter applies as such in the internal legal order of the Member States.

In its approach to the Community legal order the Court of Justice has clearly rejected the most important consequence of the transformation doctrine. Community provisions which are directly effective take priority over provisions of national law even when the latter are contained in subsequent statutes or even, as is shown in *Internationale Handelsgesellschaft*, in a national constitution.[71] In its judgment in *Costa v. ENEL*,[72] the Court demonstrated that the essence of the common market stands or falls with ensuring a uniform effect of the relevant rules of Community law in every Member State. No domestic rule can be adduced before a national court against the law created by the Treaty (which springs from an original and autonomous source) lest the latter lose its Community character and the legal basis of the Community itself be impaired.[73] It may thus be concluded that the obligation to give priority in the internal legal sphere to Community law is a rule without which the rules forming the core of Community law would lose their significance or could not find any reasonable and useful application. This is an application of the 'principle of effectiveness' or '*effet utile*' in the interpretation of Community law. It is on this line of reasoning that the Court clearly based itself in a later judgment in stating that the EC Treaty had:

> established its own system of law, integrated into the legal systems of the Member States, and which must be applied by their courts. It would be contrary to the nature of such a system to allow Member States to introduce or to retain measures capable of prejudicing the practical effectiveness of the Treaty. The binding force of the Treaty and of measures taken in application of it must not differ from one state to another as a result of internal measures, lest the functioning of the Community system should be impeded and the achievement of the aims of the Treaty placed in peril.[74]

Later in its judgment in *Simmenthal*[75] the Court put it thus:

> [A]ny recognition that national legislative measures which encroach upon the field within which the Community exercises its legislative power or which are otherwise incompatible with the provisions of Community law had any legal

---

69. Case 26/62, *Van Gend & Loos*, para. 10.
70. Case 28/67, *Firma Molkerei-Zentrale Westfale/ Lippe GmbH v. Hauptzollamt Paderborn*.
71. Case 11/70, *Internationale Handelsgesellschaft mbH v. Einfuhr- und Vorratsstelle für Getreide und Futtermittel*.
72. Case 6/64, *Costa v. ENEL*.
73. Ibid.
74. Case 14/68, *Walt Wilhelm et al. v. Bundeskartellamt*, para. 6.
75. Case 106/77, *Amministrazione delle Finanze dello Stato v. Simmenthal SpA*, para. 18.

effect would amount to a corresponding denial of the effectiveness of obligations undertaken unconditionally and irrevocably by Member States pursuant to the Treaty and would thus imperil the very foundations of the Community.

The principle of primacy of Community law was to some extent confirmed in the Treaty of Amsterdam. The Protocol (No. 30) on the application of the principles of subsidiarity and proportionality, which the Treaty of Amsterdam attached to the EC Treaty, provides that the application of these principles 'shall not affect the principles developed by the Court of Justice regarding the relationship between national and Community law' (para. 2).

It falls outside the jurisdiction of the Court of Justice to decree that the national court must assign internal effect and supremacy to rules of Community law within the national sphere of law in the face of national constitutional law as this law is interpreted in the national case law. The Court can only pronounce on the effect which Community rules ought to have according to Community law within the domestic legal order. However, in its judgments, particularly in that in *Costa v. ENEL*,[76] it made an attempt to lay the foundation for a theory which might enable a national court to take a different view of the effect of Community law from that which it thinks necessary on the basis of its constitutional law in the case of ordinary rules of international law. As the Court states, the Member States have limited their sovereign rights, though in a restricted area, in favour of the new Community legal order. The final limitation of their sovereign rights results from the transfer of the rights and duties corresponding to the Treaty provisions from the national legal order into the legal order of the Community. They are 'siphoned off' from the national legal order into the Community legal order.[77]

Rules of Community law, therefore, have internal effect without reference to the national legal order, *viz.* in the area which has been created in consequence of the limitation of national sovereignty. In other words, national constitutional law with regard to the internal effect and the internal order of priority to be given to rules of international law does not apply with reference to rules of Community law, because it can apply only within the limits of sovereignty. Beyond these limits, i.e., within the Community legal order, the national court, without being hampered by constitutional restrictions, may give to the rules of Community law the effect desired by the Court of Justice. If the national court is confronted with legal measures conflicting with Community law, it must refrain from applying them, as has been indicated above, not because they are of a lower order than Community law, but because in such a case the national legislature has acted *ultra vires*.[78] In the view adopted by the Court, the Community legal order replaces a part of the

---

76. Case 6/64, *Costa v. ENEL.*
77. Ibid.
78. Cf. Lagrange, 'La primauté du droit communautaire sur le droit national', in *Droit communautaire et droit national* (Bruges, 1965) 21, 24: 'Il ne s'agit pas d'une primauté dans le sens d'une "hiérarchie" entre un droit communautaire préeminent et les droits nationaux subordonnés, mais d'une substitution du droit propre de la Communauté au droit national dans les domaines où les transferts de competence ont été opérés.'

national legal order, and it is unnecessary to use a provision of national law in order to apply Community law.[79] However, the question of whether a national judge is able to follow the Court's view is, from his point of view, in itself again a question of constitutional law (for further observations on this point see Ch. VII above).

Private parties may rely on the application of directly effective provisions of Community law in their national legal order. They can rely on such provisions in national courts, also in cases in which national legal provisions conflict with Community law.[80] This effect of Community law is not only in the interests of the legal protection of private parties. It also serves the good maintenance of Community law in general. The Court has described the result as being that the 'vigilance of individuals concerned to protect their rights amounts to an effective supervision in addition to the supervision entrusted by Articles 169 and 170 to the diligence of the Commission and of the Member States'.[81] As one author, describing the role of citizens in American federal law, has put it, citizens acting as one-man-lobbies seeking clarification and correction of the law,[82] can contribute through their vigilance to the complete and uniform application of the fundamental principles of the common market.

The extent to which they can make such a contribution depends in part on what remedies and legal procedures are available to them in order to enforce their claims and on the conditions under which they can use those procedures. Can a person who considers that another party (whether an authority or a private party) is treating him in a manner incompatible with a directly effective provision of Community law require, for instance, damages or a prohibition of that treatment, or ask for the repayment to him of sums paid but not due, or the annulment or suspension of the relevant administrative decision? Which is the competent judicial body for seeking redress, the ordinary courts or an administrative court or tribunal?

The Court of Justice has made it clear that the principle of cooperation laid down in Article 10 EC means that 'it is the national courts which are entrusted with ensuring the legal protection which citizens derive from the direct effect of the provisions of Community law';[83] it is also the national legal system which, in the absence of Community rules on this subject, designates the courts or tribunals having jurisdiction and determines the procedural conditions governing actions at law intended to ensure the protection of Community law rights.[84] The Community as a whole has no uniform provisions concerning the availability or form of

---

79. E.g., in the Netherlands, the provisions of Arts. 93, 94 and 95 of the Constitution; in the UK the European Communities Act 1972. For further observations on this point see Ch. VII, *infra*.
80. See the discussion in Ch. VII, section 1.1.4 *infra*.
81. Case 26/62, *Van Gend & Loos*, para. 16, the Articles referred to are now renumbered 226 and 227.
82. Hart in Columbia L.Rev., 1954, 489 at 493 (quoting Hurst).
83. Case 33/76, *Rewe-Zentralfinanz eG. v. Landwirtschaftskammer für das Saarland*, para. 5; see also Case 45/76, *Comet BV v. Produktschap voor Siergewassen*.
84. See also Case 13/68, *SpA Salgoil v. Italian Ministry for Foreign Trade*.

national procedures, or the legal results to which they may lead.[85] Nevertheless, the Court has always stressed that these conditions cannot be less favourable than those relating to similar actions of a domestic nature, nor may they render virtually impossible or excessively difficult the exercise of rights conferred by Community law.[86] The important case law on this subject which is still in the full thrust of development has had a certain harmonizing effect on national procedural law.[87]

3.4   OTHER LAW OF THE EUROPEAN UNION: ITS NATURE AND EFFECTS
             IN THE INTERNAL LEGAL SPHERE

How should the rest of the law of the EU, and in particular the rules concerning CFSP and PJCCM, be seen *vis-à-vis* the Community legal order and the consequences drawn by the Court of Justice concerning direct effect and the principle of primacy of Community law? Obviously, these supplementary sectors of Union activity cannot simply be counted as part of the Community legal order. That would be in conflict with the evident rejection of a unitary structure by the Member States. It is possible, however, to qualify the Union taken as a whole as one legal order, of which the Communities then comprise a part, in the form of a more or less autonomous legal sub-order. This Union legal order, though, cannot be equated with the Community legal order in terms of characteristics and quality. If one applies the criteria which led the Court to conclude that an autonomous Community legal order existed, then the differences are quite apparent.

First, it would be hard to claim that the rules of the CFSP and PJCCM form a common internal law in the Member States. To the extent that the CFSP produces 'rules', i.e., acts and decisions with legal consequences, these are mainly obligations for the Member States in shaping foreign and security policy, not rules which concern relations between national authorities and private parties, or between private parties.[88] This is different for the PJCCM. The intended cooperation between police and judicial authorities ultimately aims at criminal investigations and prosecution of individuals or firms. In addition, the Treaty on European Union provides for harmonization competences which aim at least at a minimum of common rules in the Member States. Directly applicable rules cannot be enacted however by the Union in the framework of PJCCM, since the Union does not have such rule-making competence. Moreover, for certain categories of legal acts, the possibility of direct effect is explicitly excluded.

---

85. See, e.g., Case C-312/93, *Peterbroeck, Van Campenhout & Cie SCS v. Belgium* and Joined Cases C-430 & 431/93, *Jeroen Van Schijndel et al. v. Stichting Pensioenfonds voor Fysiotherapeuten* (citing many earlier authorities).
86. See, e.g., Case 199/82, *Amministrazione delle Finanze dello Stato v. SpA San Giorgio*, Case C-432/05, *Unibet v. Justitiekanslern*.
87. See Ch. VII, *infra*.
88. Decisions relating to sanctions could be an exception in cases where they concern individuals, e.g., a prohibition on the issue of an entry visa to persons mentioned by name; cf. the CFSP decisions mentioned in note 148 *infra*.

As far as the institutional equipment of the CFSP and PJCCM is concerned, any attempt to equate the Union legal order with that of the Community in terms of characteristics also poses difficulties. These are particularly serious as far as the CFSP is concerned. It would be hard to speak of a limiting of sovereign rights by the Member States, or the exercise by the organs of the Union of 'sovereign rights derived from the States', given the all-powerful role of the Member States in the decision-making (unanimity is required) and the limited influence of the Parliament and the Commission. For the time being, the legitimacy for policy in this area will mainly need to be sought at the level of the national parliaments, and any judicial protection at the level of the national courts. That makes it difficult to consider the Union – at least, if one focuses on CFSP – as a legal order which is independent of the national legal order. Such a claim cannot be upheld in the absence of a judicial body to enforce the legal order. On the issue of institutional architecture, the PJCCM presents a more positive image, although here too the centre of gravity lies with the Member States (unanimity is the rule), and the jurisdiction of the Court of Justice is limited. This legitimacy problem in relation to PJCCM even led some Member States to make reservations regarding guarantees for the role of their own legislature in the context of approval of the Treaty of Amsterdam.[89]

Is it possible to argue that in the light of the indissoluble bond between the CFSP and PJCCM on the one hand and the Communities on the other – for the PJCCM, in particular that with Title IV of the EC Treaty – the characteristics and consequences of the legal order of the Communities should be extended to the legal order of the Union? A type of extension the Court of Justice accepted for the Brussels Convention[90] in the *Duijnstee* case?[91] This would amount to a sort of 'Baron von Münchhausen' effect – pulling oneself up by one's own bootstraps – which seems all the less defensible if one considers that the Member States deliberately chose this complex structure of the Union in order to avoid 'contamination' of the Union (intergovernmental) areas by the neighbouring Community method as much as possible, and have chosen to retain it on subsequent revision of the Treaties. If the CFSP and PJCCM had been brought into one uniform Union scheme, while retaining their existing decision-making procedures and the role of the institutions, i.e., if the Communities were incorporated into the Union, then one Union legal order would take the place of the Community legal order, and most probably the characteristics of the Community order would influence the Union order. The present Union structure is however a different one. It has apparently been the intention of the Member States thus far to avoid such an influence, and therefore they have firmly placed the Community legal order inside one securely bolted compartment within the Union.

---

89. The Netherlands Act ratifying the Treaty of Amsterdam made an explicit reservation requiring the Dutch Parliament to be systematically consulted before establishing the Dutch position in the Council for decision-making in this area, precisely because of the insufficient legitimacy of the PJCCM legal order. Cf. Act of 24 Dec. 1998, *Staatsblad* 737, Art. 3.
90. Convention of 27 Sep. 1968 on jurisdiction and the enforcement of judgments in civil and commercial matters.
91. Case 288/82, *Ferdinand M.J.J. Duijnstee v. Lodewijk Goderbauer.*

This leads us to the conclusion that the characteristics of the Community legal order cannot simply be ascribed to the Union legal order. Therefore, the consequences drawn by the Court of Justice from these characteristics cannot simply be automatically accepted for the Union either. That holds in particular for the principle of primacy. This does not in any way exclude the possibility that such a principle could be defended on other grounds, but then these should be directly related to the qualities of the Union taken on its own merits, and taking into account the elements of a process of constitutionalization mentioned above.[92] Another important aspect is how the Union develops in practice, and to what extent its legal personality – particularly in the international arena – is confirmed by the Union exercising treaty-making powers itself. The question of primacy is of practical significance at present mainly for the PJCCM, since the Court of Justice has no jurisdiction in the field of CFSP. And even for the PJCCM the question of primacy seems less urgent since the TEU explicitly excludes direct effect for most of the Union acts in this area. That would seem to imply that a Union decision cannot be relied on in proceedings before a national court, with a view to declaring national law inapplicable in case of conflict between national and Union law. Reliance on a Union decision for other purposes is hereby not excluded, for instance with regard to interpretation of national law in conformity with the Union act, which was accepted by the Court in the *Pupino* judgment,[93] or for the purpose of pleading the invalidity of a Union decision. The existence of jurisdiction of the Court of Justice to give preliminary rulings, even if on a voluntary basis for the Member States, does point in this direction.

We would not as yet choose to formulate a definitive conclusion on the primacy of what we referred to above as 'other law of the European Union' as regards national law which conflicts with it. The discussion has only recently got underway.[94] We do, though, find it difficult to defend acceptance of the principle of primacy of Union law purely on the grounds that this principle also applies for Community law and for the same reasons.

4   SCOPE AND REVISION OF THE TREATIES

4.1   TERRITORIAL SCOPE OF APPLICATION, THE ASSOCIATION SYSTEM
            OF PART IV OF THE EC TREATY, AND ACCESSION TO
            THE EUROPEAN UNION

If we consider the territorial scope of application of the Treaties, Article 299(1) EC provides that the EC Treaty applies to the Contracting Parties mentioned therein.

---

92. Cf. the grounds on which the EFTA Court accepted the existence of a legal order for the EEA (European Economic Area) in Case E-9/97, *Sveinbjörnsdóttir*; see on this Editorial Comments, 'European Economic Area and European Community: Homogeneity of legal orders'? (1999) CML Rev., 697.
93. Case C-105/03, *Criminal Proceedings against Maria Pupino*.
94. See, e.g., J. Wouters, 'National Constitutions and the European Union' (2000) LIEI, 84 and 85; S. Prechal, *Juridisch cement voor de Europese Unie* (Groningen, 2006).

Under general rules of international law it is clear that the Treaty is binding in relation to all the territory, including the non-European parts[95] falling under the sovereignty of the Parties,[96] at least in so far as the Treaty does not provide for exceptions or otherwise make special provision. Since 3 October 1990, the day of German unification, the Treaties have applied to the new *Länder* from the former Deutsche Demokratische Republik (DDR).[97] An *exception* was made for the Netherlands by a Protocol to the EC Treaty granting the possibility (which the Dutch originally made use of) of ratification of the Treaty, notwithstanding Article 299, only in respect of its European territory and for what was then Dutch New Guinea (thus excluding Surinam and the Netherlands Antilles).

Article 299(5) EC states that the Treaty applies to the Åland Islands according to special provisions.[98] According to Article 229(6) EC, the Treaty does not apply to the Faroe Islands, or the sovereign base areas of the United Kingdom in Cyprus. That paragraph of Article 299 also provides for special rules for the Channel Islands and the Isle of Man.[99] By virtue of Article 299(4) EC, the Treaty applies to the European territories for whose external relations a Member State is responsible. Monaco and San Marino do not come within this provision, but are part of the customs territory of the Community.[100] The EC Treaty does not apply to Andorra. Article 299(4) EC in fact only concerns Gibraltar, though the territory of Gibraltar is excluded from the scope of very significant parts of Community law, particularly secondary legislation relating to the common agricultural policy and the harmonization of indirect taxation.[101] Gibraltar is also excluded from the customs territory of the Community.[102]

For non-European territories over which the contracting parties exercise sovereignty special rules are laid out in Articles 299(2) and (3) EC. With regard to the French overseas departments,[103] the Azores, Madeira and the Canary Islands, the

---

95. The Euratom Treaty also applies to the non-European territories subject to the jurisdiction of the Member States (Art. 198 Euratom).

96. The territorial sea of the Member States is of course also covered by the Treaty, as being a part of their territory.

97. C. Tomuschat, 'A United Germany Within the European Community' (1990) CML Rev., 415–436; C.W.A. Timmermans, 'German Unification and Community Law' (1990) CML Rev., 437–449. As to the package of transitional measures agreed in certain fields, see O.J. 1990, L 353.

98. See Protocol No. 2 to the Act of Accession for Austria, Finland and Sweden (1994). See also WQ 1408/85 (Collins) O.J. 1986, C 48/15–16.

99. See also Protocol No. 2 to the Act of Accession 1972. Cf. Case C-293/02, *Jersey Produce Marketing Organisation Ltd v. States of Jersey, Jersey Potato Export Marketing Board.*

100. Reg. 2913/92, Art. 3(2) (O.J. 1992, L 302/1), as amended (by Reg. 82/97 (O.J. 1997, L 17/1).

101. Act of Accession (1972), Art. 28. See Romeo and Smulders (1993) YBEL, 361. See most recently Case C-349/03, *Commission v. United Kingdom.*

102. Ibid., Annex I.1.4. See, generally, WQs. 1823–1825/84 (Ford, Lomas & Megahy) O.J. 1988, C 341/1; 2109/86 (Ford) O.J. 1987, C 112/45, and 566/87 (Caamano Bernal) O.J. 1987, C 331/30.

103. Guadeloupe, French Guyana, Martinique, Réunion and (since 1976) Saint-Pierre and Miquelon (see WQ 400/76 (Lagorce) O.J. 1976, C 294/16). As to the EC system and these departments see Case 148/77, *H. Hansen jun. et al. v. Hauptzollamt de Flensburg*; Case

provisions of the Treaty apply pursuant to Article 299(2), but the Council has discretion to determine the conditions for the application of the other provisions of the Treaty to such territories. In addition, this provision mentions a number of specific economic and geographical circumstances (remoteness, insularity etc.) which handicap the development of these regions and which could justify special measures. This should be done, however, without undermining the integrity and coherence of the Community legal order. Essentially, this is an application of the substantive principle of equality (unequal treatment of unequal cases according to the degree of inequality) which compels the Community legislature to reach a delicate weighing of interests. Community law applies to Ceuta and Melilla, albeit with certain exceptions.[104]

Article 299(3) EC deals with the other non-European territories (the so-called overseas countries and territories (OCT)) and provides that only Part IV of the Treaty applies to them.[105] Part IV of the Treaty and the Council Decisions implementing it, each applicable for a period of five years[106] provide for an association arrangement for the benefit of the non-European countries and territories which have special relations with Denmark, France, the Netherlands and the United Kingdom.[107] This concerns the countries and territories listed in Annexe II of the EC Treaty, falling under the sovereignty of one of the Member States. Pursuant to Article 299(3) EC, the Treaty does not apply to OCT having special relations

---

C-163/90, *Administration des Douanes et Droits Indirects v. Legros et al.*; Joined Cases C-363/93, etc., *René Lancry SA et al. v. Direction Générale des Douanes et al.*, and Case C-212/96, *Paul Chevassus-Marche v. Conseil régional de la Réunion.* See also WQ 1839/84 (Poniatowski) O.J. 1985, C 263/1–3. Under the Lisbon Treaty, the French overseas departments will be explicitly mentioned, the reference to Saint-Pierre et Miquelon being replaced by Saint Barthélemy and Saint Martin (Art. 355(1) TFEU). According to para. 6 of the same Article, the status of these territories, with regard to the Union, as well as that of the countries and territories mentioned in para. 2 of the same Article, can be amended by a decision of the European Council.

104. See Act of Spanish and Portuguese Accession (1985), Arts. 25, 155 and Protocol No. 2.; the Act of Accession mentioned the Canary Islands explicitly, but since the Treaty of Amsterdam these are mentioned in the Treaty itself. See also, e.g., Decs. 91/315 (O.J. 1991, L 171/10) and 92/315 (O.J. 1992, L 248/74) on the Poseima programme for the Azores and Madeira. Ceuta and Melilla are not part of the customs territory of the Community (Reg. 2913/92, Art. 3(1) (O.J. 1992, L 302/1, as amended).

105. See Joined Cases C-100 & 101/89, *Peter Kaefer et al. v. French State*, and Case C-260/90, *Bernard Leplat v. Territory of French Polynesia.* See, generally, Declaration No. 25 on the representation of the interests of the OCT, adopted on the signature of the Final Act of the Intergovernmental Conferences at Maastricht on 7 Feb. 1992 (TEU Final Act). See also Case C-17/98, *Emesa Sugar (Free Zone) NV v. Aruba.*

106. See Art. 187 EC and, most recently, Council Decision of 27 Nov. 2001, O.J. 2001, L 314. See also Case C-430/92, *Netherlands v. Commission*; Joined Cases T-480 & 483/93, *Antillean Rice Mills NV et al. v. Commission*; Case C-310/95, *Road Air BV v. Inspecteur der Invoerrechten en Accijnzen*; Case C-110/97 R, *The Netherlands v. Council*; Case T-179/97 R, *Government of the Netherlands Antilles v. Council*; Case C-106/97, *Dutch Antilles Dairy Industry Inc. et al. v. Rijksdienst voor de keuringen van Vee en Vlees*; Case C-301/97, *The Netherlands v. Council*; Case T-310/97, *Netherlands Antilles v. Council.*

107. Art. 182 EC.

with the United Kingdom which are not included in Annexe II. Since 1 January 1985, the association rules also apply to Greenland, which previous to that date fell under the normal Treaty regime, as part of the Kingdom of Denmark.[108]

Association status applies to the Netherlands Antilles and to Aruba[109] (which seceded from the former on 1 January 1986) on the basis of an Agreement of 13 November 1962 between the then six Member States, amending the Treaty; this came into force on 1 October 1964.[110] A supplementary enabling act was not sufficient for this purpose (unlike in the case of Surinam[111]), as the other Member States required certain guarantees relating to the importation into the Community of petroleum products refined in the Netherlands Antilles; these arrangements were included in a Protocol attached to the Agreement.

The applicability of Part IV of the EC Treaty to 18 associated OCT in Africa and Madagascar came to an end – at least formally, for the arrangement was continued for some time – when in the years immediately succeeding the date of the conclusion of the Treaty (1958–1962) these countries gained their independence. According to Article 299 EC, the legal basis of the application of the Treaty, in this case Part IV, to these countries was the fact that, at the date of signature, they formed part of the territory over which the Contracting Parties exercised sovereignty. The moment these countries were freed from the sovereignty of the Member States this basis (strictly speaking) ceased to exist. It has never been explicitly decided whether, on the strength of the rather vague doctrine of the succession of States, they could nevertheless claim certain rights to the continuation of the treaty regime established on their behalf before their independence.

In any event, the old association Implementing Convention was replaced after 1 July 1964 by the two successive Yaoundé Conventions, each time concluded for five years. After 1 April 1976 this system was replaced by the Lomé and Cotonou Conventions.[112] Even though the Conventions do not speak of an 'association' they were concluded by the Community on the basis of Article 310 (ex 238) EC, which creates a Community competence to conclude association agreements.[113]

---

108. Treaty on Greenland, O.J. 1985, L 29/1. See F. Harhoff, 'Greenland's Withdrawal from the European Communities', (1983) CML Rev., 13 and F. Weiss, 'Greenland's Withdrawal from the European Communities', (1985), EL Rev., 173.

109. See Annexe I.A.3 of Council Decision of 27 Nov. 2001, O.J. 2001, L 314.

110. J.O. 150/64, 2414.

111. Surinam is now a party to the Lomé Convention, and its successors, since its independence on 25 Nov. 1975.

112. The fourth Lomé Convention, signed on 15 Dec. 1989, entered into force on 1 Sept. 1991, O.J. 1991, L 229/1. These Conventions embrace far more countries than those listed in Annex IV to the EC Treaty, covering the so-called ACP States. As to the predecessor regime, see K. Simmonds, 'The Third Lomé Convention' (1985) CML Rev., 389 and see, id., 'The Fourth Lomé Convention' (1991) CML Rev., 521–548. This association regime has since been thoroughly revised and replaced by the Cotonou Agreement of 23 Jun. 2000, O.J. 2000, L 317, which – barring a few exceptions – was provisionally applicable since 2 Aug. 2000, cf. O.J. 2000, L 195. See K. Arts, 'ACP-EU Relations in a New Era: The Cotonou Agreement' (2003) CML Rev., 95.

113. Preamble to the Lomé Conventions. See M. Maresceau, *Bilateral Agreements: Collected Courses of the Hague Academy of International Law* (Leiden, 2006).

It should not be deduced from the wording of Article 299 EC that the sphere of application of the EC Treaty is restricted to territory falling under the sovereignty (i.e., complete jurisdiction) of a Member State.[114] The sphere of application can stretch beyond such territory insofar as a Member State exercises sovereign rights (i.e., a functionally limited jurisdiction) under general international law, e.g., in relation to the continental shelf,[115] fishing zones[116] and exclusive economic zones. This is, naturally, provided that the matter over which this functional jurisdiction extends falls within the substantive scope of the relevant provisions of the Treaty and that they do not contain any restriction of the ambit of their application to the territory of the Member States.[117]

The SEA did not refer to the territorial scope of application of European Political Cooperation. The Treaty on European Union follows this example and remains silent on this issue for the non-Community policy areas of the Union, the CFSP and PJCCM. The obvious solution lies in analogous application of the regime under Article 299 EC, which would imply that the policies under the Second and Third Pillar do not apply to the OCT. An indication in this direction is to be found in Declaration 25 in the Final Act of the Treaty of Maastricht; the declaration makes a clear distinction between the interests of the Union as such and those of the OCT, giving in doing so at least the impression that the latter are not an integral part of the Union.[118]

4.1.1   Accession to the European Union

The territorial scope of application of the Treaties may be enlarged by accession of states to the Union, and thereby to the Communities.[119] New Member States

---

114. The customs territory of the Community is not precisely the same as the territory of the Member States, see Reg. 2913/92, Art. 3, O.J. 1992, L 302/1.

115. The Commission is of the view that the Treaty applies to the continental shelf, see its Memorandum of September 1970, SEC (70) 3095 Final, and WQ 489/73 (O'Hagan) O.J. 1974, C 49/3. The Community Customs Code, Reg. 2913/92 (O.J. 1992, L 302/1, as amended), Art. 23(2)(h) includes in the definition of goods originating in a country (thus in a Member State in the case of export from the Community) 'products taken from the seabed or subsoil beneath the seabed outside territorial waters, if that country has exclusive rights to exploit that seabed or subsoil'.

116. Since 1 Jan. 1977 the Member States have extended their fishing zones in the North-East Atlantic and the North Sea to 200 miles from their coast. See Reg. 101/76 (O.J. 1976, L 20/9) establishing a common fisheries policy; replaced by Reg. 2371/2002 (O.J. 2002, L 358/59). See also Joined Cases 3, 4 & 6/76, *Cornelis Kramer et al.* Regulations apply in principle to the same geographical area as the Treaty itself, Case 61/77, *Commission v. Ireland.*

117. See A. Koers, 'Enige ontwikkelingen ten aanzien van de externe bevoegdheden van de EEG inzake de zeevisserij' (1977) SEW, 191. On the more general question of the extraterritorial application of Community law, i.e., application to situations outside the geographical areas described here, it is difficult to make a general observation; see P.J. Slot and E. Grabandt, 'Extraterritoriality and Jurisdiction' (1986) CML Rev., 544 and Meng in Von der Groeben et al. (eds), op. cit. *supra* note 32, Vol. 5, 1207 and literature cited there.

118. Declaration on the representation of the interests of the OCT referred to in Art. 227(3) and (5)(a) and (b) of the Treaty establishing the European Community.

119. The procedure is set out in Art. 49 TEU; see Meng in Von der Groeben et al. (eds), op. cit. note 32 *supra*, Vol. 5, 1138.

accede to the Union as a whole: it is not possible for them to accede to the Communities alone or to only one or more of the supplementary policies and forms of cooperation.

An application for accession will only be entertained if it is made by a European state. This application must be addressed to the Council, which, after obtaining the opinion of the Commission, and having received the assent of the European Parliament, takes a decision on it by a unanimous vote. As may be inferred from the context of these provisions, this decision concerns the question of whether the applicant State is acceptable as a member. Before the Council can take a decision, the conditions of admission and the resultant adjustments to the Treaties forming the subject of an agreement have to be negotiated between the twenty-seven Member States and the state applying for accession. This agreement has to be ratified by all the Contracting States in accordance with their respective constitutional requirements. The conditions of admission usually cover in particular the transitional measures which have to be taken in order that the gradual integration of the new Member State in the Union in the economic and legal fields may proceed as smoothly as possible. Adjustments to the Treaties (and implementing measures) will be necessary, even if only on the composition of the institutions, voting rules and budgetary contributions. It is striking that, as regards the stage in which negotiations are conducted about the conditions of admission and the adjustment to the Treaties, there is no specific reference to the Community Institutions participating, although participation, particularly by the Commission, is not excluded. Indeed such participation is to be expected as a matter of principle (the Communities are greater than the sum of the Member States) and for the practical reason of the Commission's expertise.

In practice, a Community procedure is followed. Negotiations are conducted by the Community as such according to a uniform procedure at all levels and on all matters. The Council decides on a common position of the Community on all matters which arise in the negotiations and the Commission is invited to make the necessary proposals. Discussions in the Council are prepared by *Coreper*. The President of the Council puts forward the common position in the negotiations and defends it. If the Council so decides, particularly in relation to matters covered by existing Community policies, this task can be devolved to the Commission. Moreover, the Commission is sometimes entrusted with the discussion of a solution to specific problems with the applicant states and then reports back to the Council. Initially the Commission was disappointed about its modest role in accession negotiations, but it is clear that it can play an important part in the preparation of the Community's common position and in seeking solutions with the applicant states to specific problems. The requirement of the assent of the European Parliament was introduced by the SEA.[120]

An important innovation under the Lisbon Treaty concerns the possibility for a Member State to denounce its membership and withdraw from the Union (Art. 50 TEU (Lisbon)).

---

120. Originally introduced by Art. 8 SEA into Art. 237 EEC, now replaced by Art. 49 TEU.

As was noted above,[121] the EU, EC and Euratom Treaties were concluded for an unlimited period[122] whereas the ECSC Treaty was concluded for a period of fifty years.[123]

Just as accession is now uniformly regulated, so too amendment of the Treaties on which the Union is founded is uniformly regulated – i.e., for all the treaties on which the Union is founded – in Article 48 TEU. This accords a right of initiative not only to the Member States, but also to the Commission to propose amendments. Where appropriate, the Commission must be consulted. Further, the Council consults the European Parliament, though – unlike in the case of accession treaties – Parliament's assent is not required. In the case of institutional changes in the monetary area, the ECB is also consulted. The Council then takes a decision, by ordinary majority, to convene a conference of the representatives of the governments of the Member States, in order to lay down, by common accord, the amendments to be made to the Treaty. The amendments enter into force after being ratified by the Member States in accordance with their respective constitutional requirements.

Many international treaties contain provisions with respect to their revision. It is generally assumed that such provisions do not imply that amendment of such treaties is only permitted in conformity with the procedures laid down therein. The Contracting Parties retain the right to amend (or to terminate) the treaty in the same way as they brought it about, *viz.* by a later treaty. Does this also apply to the Community Treaties? The Dutch Government, (relying on a generally accepted rule of international law), answered this question in the affirmative during the debates in the Lower Chamber of the States General on the Act approving the Treaty of 27 October 1957, for the amendment of the ECSC Treaty.[124] The Lower Chamber did not share the standpoint of the government. It adopted a Resolution, in which it opined that revision of the Community Treaties 'could only take place in accordance with the amendment procedures laid down in these Treaties themselves'.[125] The Government declared that in practice it would abide by the opinion contained in this resolution.[126] This is a not unimportant statement, because for an amendment of the Treaties by means of a non-Community procedure the cooperation of the governments of all Member States is of course necessary. This statement on policy was also supported in the Chamber with legal arguments,[127]

---

121. In section 3.2, *supra.*
122. Arts. 51 TEU, 312 EC and 208 Euratom.
123. Art. 97 ECSC; i.e., up to and including 23 Jul. 2002.
124. Annexes to Proceedings of the Tweede Kamer (Dutch Lower House), 1957, 4763.
125. Annexes to Proceedings of the Tweede Kamer, 1957–1958, 4763. Resolution submitted by Van der Goes van Naters.
126. Proceedings of the Tweede Kamer, 1957–1958, 1088–1092.
127. Cf. M. Van der Goes van Naters, 'La Révision des traits internationaux' (1959) NTIR (special issue), 120 et seq.

arguments which, in the light of the case law of the Court referred to in section 3.1 of this chapter, above, have even gained in strength.

In fact, it appears highly questionable whether reliance on a universally recognized rule of international law, according to which, notwithstanding the prescribed revision procedures, a treaty can always be amended by a later treaty, also applies to treaties which have called into being a new legal order which limits the sovereignty of the Member States and is binding on them as well as on their nationals. Treaties, moreover, which have created an institutional structure in which an institution independent of the Member States (the Commission) takes part in the exercise of sovereign powers derived from the Member States and in which a parliamentary institution (the European Parliament) embodies the collaboration of citizens in the operation of the Communities. It is precisely the consultation of these institutions which is prescribed by the TEU in case of revision. Thus it is scarcely surprising that in the *Defrenne II* case,[128] the Court indicated that 'apart from any specific provisions, the Treaty can only be modified by means of the amendment procedure carried out in accordance with Article 236 [now repealed]'. The Court moreover considers that, even if respecting prescribed procedures, the Member States are not free to make any amendments they wish to the Treaties. Thus, in relation to the first draft European Economic Area Agreement, the Court set its face against a modification of the Treaty which threatened significant aspects of the Community legal order.[129]

For future Treaty amendments it may be expected that the formal procedure of Article 48 TEU will be preceded by a Convention to prepare such amendments, following the precedents set for the preparation of the Charter of fundamental rights and the Constitutional Treaty. When the Lisbon Treaty enters into force, the preparation by a Convention will be formalized.[130]

5   LEGAL PERSONALITY, PRIVILEGES AND IMMUNITIES, SEAT OF THE INSTITUTIONS AND LINGUISTIC REGIME OF THE UNION AND THE COMMUNITIES

5.1   LEGAL PERSONALITY

Although legal personality is not explicitly conferred on the Union, it is conferred on the Communities on which the Union is based: 'The Community shall have

---

128. Case 43/75, *Gabrielle Defrenne v. Société anonyme belge de navigation aérienne Sabena*, at para. 58. See also M. Deliège-Sequarais, 'Révision des Traités européens en dehors des procédures prévues' (1980) CDE, 539 and J.-V. Louis, 'Quelques considérations sur la révision des traités instituant le communautés' (1980) CDE, 553.

129. Opinion 1/91, *EEA Agreement I*.

130. See Art. 48 TEU (Lisbon) which also introduces simplified revision procedures in some fields.

legal personality'.[131] This reflects the intention of the Contracting Parties to confer on each of the Communities the capacity to have rights and obligations. Whether, to what extent, and in what legal sphere this is actually the case, is a question which has to be answered by reference to what the other Treaty provisions contain about the action of the Communities in legal relationships. A clear distinction must be made in this context between the legal personality in the sphere of international law and the legal personality in the sphere of national law, which concerns private law.

The private law legal personality of the Communities in the sphere of national law is established in the provision[132] that in each of the Member States they shall enjoy the most extensive legal capacity accorded to legal persons under their laws. They may, in particular, acquire or dispose of movable and immovable property and may be parties to legal proceedings. For this purpose, the Commission is to represent the EC and Euratom. Finally, it should be noted that not only the Communities themselves, but also, for example, the ECB,[133] the EIB,[134] and the Euratom Supply Agency[135] possess legal personality in the national law of the Member States. That is also true for most of the independent administrative bodies (agencies) set up by the Community.[136]

International legal personality, however, is enjoyed principally by the Communities as such, and also by the ECB[137] and the EIB.[138] The ECSC Treaty explicitly conferred on that Community, in its international relationships, the legal capacity necessary to perform its functions and to attain its objectives.[139] This formulation was reminiscent of that by which the International Court of Justice described the international legal personality of the United Nations: '[w]hereas a State possesses the totality of international rights and duties recognized by international law, the rights and duties of an entity such as the Organization must depend upon its purposes and functions...'.[140] No similar provision is to be found in the EC and Euratom Treaties. The latter only develop the general clause concerning the legal personality of the Communities insofar as

---

131. Arts. 281 EC and 184 Euratom.
132. Arts. 282 EC and 185 Euratom.
133. Art. 107(2) EC; Protocol on the Statute of the ESCB and ECB, Art. 9.
134. Art. 266 EC; Protocol on the Statute of the EIB, Art. 28.
135. Art. 54(1) Euratom.
136. See, with further references, E. Vos, 'Reforming the European Commission: What Role to Play for EU Agencies', (2000) CML Rev., 1113 and Ch. IV, section 9.4 *infra*; see also Art. 4(2) of Reg. 58/2003 laying down the statute for executive agencies, O.J. 2003, L 11/1.
137. This may be deduced from Arts. 6 and 23 of the Protocol on the Statute of the ESCB and ECB. See C. Zilioli and M. Selmayr, 'The External Relations of the Euro Area: Legal Aspects' (1999) CML Rev., 273–349 and id., 'The European Central Bank: An Independent Specialized Organization of Community Law' (2000) CML Rev., 591–643, and reaction by R. Torrent, 'Whom is the European Central Bank the Central Bank Of?' (1999) CML Rev., 1229–1241.
138. The EIB is, together with the EC and its Member States, party to the Agreement establishing the European Bank for Reconstruction and Development. See O.J. 1990, L 372.
139. Art. 6(2) ECSC.
140. *Reparation for Injuries* Case [1949] ICJ Rep. 174 at 180.

the private law legal personality in the national law of Member States is concerned. Nevertheless, it is generally assumed that the Contracting Parties meant to confer an international 'functional personality' also on the EC and Euratom.[141]

The intention to confer international 'functional' personality is substantiated by the Treaty provisions which envisage Community action in international legal relationships within the field of its functions and objectives. In the Treaties many provisions are found which relate to the power of the Communities to conclude international agreements. The EC has power to conclude tariff and commercial agreements (Art. 133(3) EC), agreements in the field of monetary policy (Art. 111 EC), cooperation agreements in the field of research, technological development and demonstration (Art. 170 EC), agreements in the environmental field (Art. 174 EC), and development cooperation agreements (Art. 181 EC). In addition, the Treaty of Nice conferred a general treaty-making power competence for economic, financial and technical cooperation measures with third countries which are not developing countries (Art. 181a EC). In the Euratom Treaty, Chapter X is devoted to 'external relations', the Community being accorded, within the limits of its powers and jurisdictions, the general power to conclude agreements or contracts with a third state or an international organization (Art. 101(1) Euratom).[142] In addition, both the EC and Euratom Treaties contain a series of provisions on the establishment and maintenance of relations with other international organizations[143] and on the conclusion of association agreements with a third state, a union of states, or an international organization (Arts. 310 EC and 206 Euratom).

Initially it was generally assumed that the Community possessed treaty-making power only in those cases in which it was expressly conferred. Since the judgment in the *ERTA* case, however, in 1971,[144] which was of immense importance for the development of the Community's external powers, it is clear that the treaty-making power of the Community arises not only from express provisions of the EC Treaty (such as Arts. 133 or 310) 'but may equally flow from other provisions of the Treaty and from measures adopted, within the framework of those provisions, by the Community institutions'.[145] The changes made to the former Article 228 EC by the TEU implicitly confirm this case law.[146]

---

141. Cf. Case 6/64, *Costa v. ENEL*, in which the Court spoke of the 'personality' and 'legal capacity' of the Community. This was confirmed in the *ERTA* judgment, Case 22/70, *Commission v. Council (ERTA)*, at para. 14, in which the Court indicated that Art. 281 EC 'means that in its external relations the Community enjoys the capacity to establish contractual links with third countries over the whole field of objectives defined in Part One of the Treaty'.

142. See also Case C-29/99, *Commission v. Council (re: Nuclear Safety Convention)*, with annotation by P. Koutrakos (2004) CML Rev., 191–208.

143. Arts. 302, 303, 304 EC and identically phrased Arts. 199, 200, 201 Euratom.

144. Case 22/70, *Commission v. Council (ERTA)*. See annotation by Brinkhorst in (1971) SEW, 479; by Waelbroeck in (1971) *Integration – Vierteljahreshefte zur Europaforschung*, 79, and Winter in (1971) CML Rev., 550.

145. Case 22/70, *Commission v. Council (ERTA)*, para. 16.

146. Cf. in particular the first three paragraphs of Art. 300 EC.

As was mentioned earlier, the Member States could not reach agreement during the negotiations leading to the Treaties of Maastricht and Amsterdam to confer international legal personality on the Union explicitly. Notwithstanding this, an objective analysis of the organization, powers, objectives and working methods of the Union, in particular since the amendments brought by the Treaty of Amsterdam, lead to the conclusion that there are sufficient elements to defend the argument that legal personality of the Union does already exist.[147] The Treaty of Nice also contributes to this, for instance in providing that the international agreements concluded under Article 24 TEU are binding on the Institutions of the Union. Moreover, there are developments in practice in the implementation of the TEU which seem to prepare the way for the acceptance of legal personality of the Union, or perhaps one should say which make it more and more difficult to deny such personality.[148] It is probably only a question of time for this acceptance to be confirmed definitively.

The *ius communicandi* of the Communities is not confined to relations with other international organizations. They also possess the right of legation, a typical attribute of international legal personality. This is a right whose existence, insofar as the passive form is concerned, is referred to only indirectly, and this only in Article 17 of the Protocol on the privileges and immunities of the EC. This Protocol provides that the Member State in whose territory the Communities have their seat shall grant the customary diplomatic immunities and privileges to the missions of third countries accredited to the Communities. About 120 missions of third

---

147. N. Blokker and T. Heukels speak of: legal personality explicitly rejected but implicitly accepted (36). 'Explicitly rejected' is in our view too strong. There was no consensus between the Member States with regard to proposals to confer legal personality. That does not imply a consensus to reject legal personality. See N. Blokker and T. Heukels, 'The European Union: Historical Origins and Institutional Challenges', in Heukels et al. op. cit. *supra* note 1, 36. Cf. also the contribution in the same publication by B. de Witte, op. cit. *supra* note 8. See further on the question of legal personality of the Union, D. Curtin and I. Dekker, op. cit. *supra* note 8, 83; A. von Bogdandy, 'The Legal Case for Unity: The European Union As a Single Organization with a Single Legal System', (1999) CML Rev., 887–910; R.A. Wessel, op. cit. *supra* note 22; id., 'The Inside Looking Out: Consistency and Delimitation in EU External Relations' (2000) CML Rev., 1135; M. Zuleeg, 'Die Organisationsstruktur der Europäischen Union: Eine Analyse der Klammerbestimmungen des Vertrags von Amsterdam' (1998) *Europarecht*, 151; P. Eeckhout, *External Relations of the EU* (Oxford, 2004), 155–160, and R. Gosalbo Bono, op. cit. *supra* note 16 at 353–357.

148. E.g., it is the Union which implements the UN Security Council's decisions on sanctions; which prohibits the issue of a travel visa to named individuals who are citizens of third countries (cf. Common Position 98/240/CFSP O.J. 1998, L 95 and Common Position 2000/696/CFSP, O.J. 2000, L 287); which presents itself as such at the annual General Assembly of the UN; which is in the process of developing its own defence policy and setting up a European intervention force in that framework, in particular for carrying out peace-keeping tasks (the so-called Petersberg tasks, Art. 17(2) TEU); which receives the missions from third countries and international organizations in Brussels, as accredited missions to the Union, but which also establishes a monitoring mission in third countries (Joint Action, 2000/811/CFSP, O.J. 2000, L 328). Cf. also the international agreements concluded between the Union and third countries mentioned in note 16 *supra*.

countries are so accredited. We mentioned earlier the current tendency for these missions to be considered accredited to the European Union, and no longer the EC.[149] The Commission maintains delegations in various countries, and these deal mainly with relations between the Community and certain third countries and organizations. There are, for example, delegations in Moscow, Washington, Ottawa, Tokyo, Caracas, Canberra, besides those to the United Nations in New York, to UNESCO and OECD in Paris, to the WTO and the ILO in Geneva and to the International Atomic Energy Agency (IAEA) in Vienna. There are also Commission delegations in a large number of African, Caribbean and Pacific (ACP) States.[150]

It may be concluded from the above that each of the Communities forms an international functional legal person and for this purpose is equipped with the requisite powers. This legal personality operates *vis-à-vis* the Member States because they have concluded the Treaties in which such personality was conferred and developed. *Vis-à-vis* third states, however, these Treaties are *res inter alios acta*. In the case of a world-wide organization (the United Nations), the International Court of Justice reached the decision that this organization possessed 'an objective international personality', not merely a legal personality with respect to its members. The argument advanced by that Court was that 'fifty States representing the vast majority of the members of the international community had the power, in conformity with international law, to bring into being an entity possessing objective international personality', i.e., a personality operating also *vis-à-vis* non-members of the United Nations.[151] This argument naturally does not apply to the Communities in this form.

It may therefore be assumed that the legal personality of the Communities *vis-à-vis* third states operates only after its existence has been recognized by these states. The recognition may be made expressly or tacitly. As has been noted above, many third states already maintain diplomatic relations with the Communities. From this as well as from the fact that many third states maintain treaty relations with the Communities it may be inferred that they have tacitly recognized their existence as a new international functional legal person. Problems in this respect caused by the former Soviet Union and its then satellite states have disappeared with the collapse of the Soviet hegemony. There has now been so universal a recognition of the legal personality of the Communities that it can safely be concluded that they have an objective international legal personality. The few states in the world which have not yet recognized the Communities will no longer be able to rely on this in international relationships to argue that for them the Communities do not exist as a legal entity.

---

149. Cf. N. Blokker and T. Heukels op. cit. *supra* note 147.
150. As to the activities of these delegations see WQ 842/85 (Rogaila) O.J. 1985, C 87/34; L. Brinkhorst, 'Permanent Missions of the EC in Third Countries: European Diplomacy in the Making' (1984) LIEI, 23, and Macleod et al., *The External Relations of the European Communities* (Oxford, 1996), 215–222.
151. *Reparation for Injuries* case [1949] ICJRep. 174 at 185.

The Lisbon Treaty explicitly grants legal personality to the European Union, the European Union and the EC being merged into one single organization, the European Union (Art. 47 TEU (Lisbon)).

5.2   PRIVILEGES AND IMMUNITIES

Ever since the entry into force of the Merger Treaty on 1 July 1967, the Communities have been subject to uniform rules on the privileges and immunities necessary for the performance of their tasks in the territories of the Member States. These rules are laid down in an annexed Protocol (Arts. 291 EC, 191 Euratom). This deals with the privileges and immunities of the Communities as such, of the members of their institutions, their officials and other servants, the representatives of the Member States taking part in the work of their institutions, and of the missions accredited to the EC. The provisions of the Protocol also apply in relation to the Union's supplementary policies and forms of cooperation to the extent that the Community institutions are entrusted with a decision-making role; to the EIB (Art. 28, Protocol on the EIB) and the ECB and its precursor, the European Monetary Institute (Art. 23, Protocol on Privileges and Immunities (hereafter: PPI), inserted by an amending protocol annexed to the TEU).[152] The members of the Court of Auditors are placed on the same footing as members of the Court of Justice (Art. 247(9) EC).

Articles 1 and 2 of the PPI lay down rules concerning the inviolability of the premises, the buildings, and the archives of the Communities. They further provide that their property and assets may not be the subject of any administrative or legislative measure of constraint without the authorization of the Court of Justice. The Court's authorization is required in order to prevent an untimely or inappropriate encroachment on the independent functioning of the Community in favour of private interests.[153] Articles 3 and 4 PPI contain rules on the exemption of the Communities from direct and indirect taxes or sales taxes and from customs duties or import or export prohibitions and restrictions. Article 6 PPI relates to freedom of communication and to travel documents (*laissez-passer*) for the members of the institutions and officials and other servants. The order of the Court in *Zwartveld* et al.[154] illustrates that the protection afforded by the Protocol is not absolute but functional in nature, and does not extend further than is necessary to avoid any interference with the functioning and independence of the Communities.

The immunity from jurisdiction normally granted to international organizations is lacking. In principle, the Communities can also be summoned to appear before national courts in the Member States without their consent, at least in so far as the Court of Justice has not been declared competent in the matter by or in

---

152. Art. 40, Protocol on the ESCB and ECB; Art. 21, Protocol on the EMI.
153. Case 4/62, *Application for Authorization to Enforce a Garnishee Order against the High Authority*.
154. Case C-2/88 Imm., *Zwartveld*.

pursuance of the Treaties (see Arts. 240 EC, 155 Euratom). In view of the extensive competence of the Court this will only very rarely occur. The Court of Justice has jurisdiction in disputes concerning the Community's non-contractual liability (Arts. 235 EC, 151 Euratom). Articles 236 EC and 152 Euratom declare that the Court also has jurisdiction in any dispute between the Communities and their servants.[155] Moreover, in many contracts of a public law or private law nature, or in general conditions applicable thereto,[156] an arbitration clause confers jurisdiction on the Court to hear disputes relating to such contracts (see Arts. 238 EC, 153 Euratom).

5.3   SEAT OF THE INSTITUTIONS

The Community Treaties contain identical provisions concerning the seat of the Community Institutions: it 'shall be determined by common accord of the governments of the Member States'. (Cf. Arts. 289 EC, 189 Euratom). After repeated decisions on provisional working places, a decision was finally adopted in 1992 at Edinburgh by common agreement of the Foreign Ministers as Representatives of the governments of the Member States.[157]

This decision largely confirmed the existing situation. Parliament has its seat in Strasbourg, where the 12 periods of monthly plenary sessions, including the budget session must be held. Periods of additional plenary sessions are held in Brussels, where the Parliament's Committees also meet. The Parliament's General Secretariat and its departments remain in Luxembourg. The Council has its seat in Brussels, but its meetings are held in Luxembourg during the months of April, June and October. The Commission also has its seat in Brussels, but certain departments are established in Luxembourg. The ECOSOC and the Committee of the Regions (which shares an organizational structure with ECOSOC) also have their seat in Brussels. The Court of Justice, the Court of Auditors, and the EIB all have their seat in Luxembourg. The institutions thus remained spread throughout Luxembourg,

---

155.   E.g., Joined Cases 43, 45 & 48/59, *Eva von Lachmüller et al. v. Commission;* Joined Cases 316/82 & 40/83, *Nelly Kohler v. Court of Auditors*; Case 38/84, *K. v. European Parliament*; Case T-497/93, *Anne Hogan v. Court of Justice.* See Staff Regs. (as amended), Art. 91.

156.   E.g., Case 220/85, *Fadex NV v. Commission* (dispute under the Commission's General Terms and Conditions governing Supply Contracts, concerning work carried out laying a floor for a TV studio); Case C-299/93, *Ernst Bauer v. Commission* (arbitration clause under a residential tenancy agreement), and Case C-42/94, *Heidemij Advies BV v. European Parliament* (arbitration clause under a contract for the extension of the Parliament's buildings in Brussels). See T. Heukels, Ch. 5 in T. Heukels and A. McDonnell (eds), *The Action for Damages in Community Law* (The Hague, 1997).

157.   O.J. 1992, C 341/1. The decision was adopted on the occasion of the Edinburgh European Council in December 1992, Bull. EC 12–92, points I.14 and I.32. See, in critical vein, P. VerLoren van Themaat, 'De Europese Raad van Edinburgh als goudmijn voor juristen' (1993) SEW, 423. The decision has now been replaced by a Protocol on the location of the seats of the institutions and of certain bodies and departments of the European Communities and of Europol, attached to the Treaty of Amsterdam.

Brussels and Strasbourg. This situation – most unsatisfactory in terms of efficiency and rational financial policy – may be explained on the basis of considerations of national prestige, but also financial and economic interests, which prevent a rational decision regarding the seat of the institutions.

In October 1993, Frankfurt was designated as the seat of the European Monetary Institute and the future ECB, and the seats of a number of other subsidiary bodies were determined.[158] By the same decision, The Hague was designated as the seat of Europol and the Europol Drugs Unit. It would have been possible to determine the seat of these bodies in the instruments establishing them, but the Member States preferred to carry out this task by intergovernmental decision-making in accordance with Article 289 EC.[159]

5.4   Linguistic Regime

Finally, a few observations are appropriate about the Communities' linguistic regime. The texts of the EC and Euratom Treaties and the Treaty on European Union are equally authentic in twenty three languages: Bulgarian, Czech, Danish, Dutch, English, Estonian, Finnish, French, German, Greek, Hungarian, Irish, Italian, Latvian, Lithuanian, Maltese, Polish, Portuguese, Romanian, Slovak, Slovenian, Spanish and Swedish.[160] Various difficulties of interpretation may well arise. It will always have to be presumed that the texts have the same meaning in all the authentic languages. If upon comparison there is found to be a difference in meaning which cannot be eliminated by application of the usual methods of interpretation, the meaning to be adopted will have to be one which reconciles the texts with each other as much as possible.[161] The 23 languages mentioned

---

158.   Decision of the Representatives of the Governments of the Member States, meeting at Head of State or Government level, 29 Oct. 1993 (O.J. 1993, C 323/1), adopted at the time of the Brussels European Council, Bull. EC 10-1993, points I.10 and I.12–I.13. See also the Protocol mentioned in the previous footnote.

159.   This was decided in Art. 2 of the Edinburgh decision (O.J. 1992, C341/1), see note 157, *supra*.

160.   Arts. 53 TEU and 314 EC as adapted by the Accession Treaty for Bulgaria and Romania 2005 (O.J. 2005, L 157/210).

161.   Cf. Art. 33, Vienna Convention on the Law of Treaties, United Nations, *Treaty Series*, vol. 1155, 331. See Case 29/69, *Erich Stauder v. City of Ulm-Sozialamt*; Case 30/77, *Régina v. Pierre Bouchereau* at para. 14: 'The different language versions of a Community text must be given a uniform interpretation and hence in the case of divergence between the versions the provision in question must be interpreted by reference to the purpose and general scheme of the rules of which it forms a part'. In circumstances in which one or more of the texts involved may have to be interpreted in a manner at variance with the natural and usual meaning of the words it is preferable, in the interests of legal certainty, to explore the possibilities of solving the points at issue without giving preference to any one of the texts involved, Case 80/76, *North Kerry Milk Products Ltd v. Minister for Agriculture and Fisheries.* See also, e.g., Case 283/81, *Srl CILFIT et al. v. Ministry of Health*; Case 9/79, *Marianne Wersdorfer, née Koschniske, v. Raad van Arbeid*; Case C-449/93, *Rockfon A/S v. Specialarbejderforbundet i Danmark, acting on behalf of Nielsen et al.*, and Case C-72/95, *Aannemingsbedrijf P.K. Kraaijeveld BV et al. v. Gedeputeerde Staten van Zuid-Holland.*

above are also official and working languages;[162] Irish, however, has a special status.[163] The *Official Journal* appears in these languages, Irish excepted. For the policy areas of the EU proper, CFSP and PJCCM, the EC language regime applies in principle.[164]

The costs of translation work (and simultaneous interpretation) are extremely high, and delays in decision-making inevitably arise because of translation problems. The use of languages in the system of the European Union has major political and cultural implications, but given the enormous costs, the question whether it is now time to apply more widely the practice of using one or more working languages becomes ever more pressing. In so far as Community acts have legal effect, however, it is important that they be available to Community citizens in their own language.[165] Similarly, it is important to safeguard the use of a person's own language in the European Parliament and, in so far as litigants are concerned, before the Court.

The use of languages in the Court is laid down in the Rules of Procedure (Arts. 29, 30 and 31).[166] The *official languages* of the Court are the twenty three languages mentioned above. Which of these is to be the language of the proceedings depends upon the plaintiff's choice, with the reservation that if the defendant is a Member State or a natural or legal person from a Member State, the language is the official language of that Member State. If there is more than one official language in this Member State, as in the case of Belgium, the plaintiff may choose whichever suits him. Upon joint request of the parties the Court may authorize the use of another official language. In special cases the Court may further authorize the total or partial use of another official language as the language of the case. If a national court makes a request for a preliminary ruling (Arts. 234 EC, 150 Euratom), the language of the proceedings shall be that of this court. Member States may use their own official language if intervening in a preliminary reference procedure. The publications of the Court of Justice appear in the official languages, Irish excepted.[167] However, in principle only the text of the Court's decision in the language of the proceedings has force of law.

---

162. See Art. 290 EC and Reg. 1. of 1958 (O.J. 17/1958 385) as amended.
163. Reg. 920/2005, O.J. 2005, L 156/3.
164. Art. 290 EC is declared applicable in these fields by Arts. 28 and 41 TEU respectively. See also Declaration No. 29, on the use of languages in the field of the CFSP, annexed to the Treaty of Maastricht.
165. Case C-361/01 P, *Kik v. OHIM*, and annotation thereof by Nic Shuihbne (2004) CML Rev., 1093–1111.
166. See Art. 64 Statute for the Court of Justice in the version established by the Treaty of Nice. The Rules of Procedure for the Court of First Instance contain similar rules in Arts. 35–37.
167. However, the Court's only working language is French, courtroom discussions being held in that language and in the absence of any interpreters.

6   CITIZENSHIP OF THE UNION

6.1   THE CONCEPT OF 'CITIZENSHIP OF THE UNION'

The new Part Two, with the title 'Citizenship of the Union', was introduced into the
EC Treaty by the Treaty of Maastricht. The title is, however, a flag which does not
cover its cargo.[168] In fact, it turns out that Union Citizenship does not exist as
something separate; it is more a question of a complementary citizenship: any
person who holds the nationality of one of the Member States is automatically
also a citizen of the Union. The Member States decide on questions of nationality.[169] Nationals of third countries, even if they are legally resident in a Member
State, do not have access to Union citizenship.[170] This complementary character
was emphasized yet again by the Treaty of Amsterdam, which added that citizenship of the Union shall not replace national citizenship. This reconfirmed, but now
in the Treaty itself, what the European Council had declared to Denmark, after
the first unsuccessful referendum in that Member State on the ratification of the
Treaty of Maastricht.[171] In fact, it seems that in some Member States, in particular
Denmark, the conferral of Union Citizenship provoked negative reactions and led
to some confusion.

With the establishment of Union Citizenship, the Member States were aiming
primarily to bring the European Union in general, and the EC in particular, closer to
the citizens, and to make clearer and more meaningful the rights citizens derive
from the integration process (cf. Art. 2(1) third indent TEU). The description
'Union citizen' is intended to express the fact that the Union does not solely
concern the Member States and their civil services, but also the citizens themselves, since they have rights directly conferred on them, as well as duties (Art.
17(2) EC). The introduction of European Citizenship was greeted with a certain
scepticism, as being mainly a rhetorical exercise with little added value compared

---

168.   As to how this political flag of the European Union came to find a home in the EC Treaty, see
       J. Cloos et al., *Le Traité de Maastricht: genèse, analyse, commentaries* (Brussels, 1993),
       162–166. Cf. moreover contributions in O'Keeffe and Twomey (eds), *Legal Issues of the
       Maastricht Treaty* (London, 1994). Cf. also W. Devroe and J. Wouters, *De Europese Unie*
       (Leuven, 1996), 144.
169.   Cf. Case C-369/90, *Mario Vicente Micheletti et al. v. Delegación del Gobierno en Cantabria.*
       On the consequences for nationals of OCT (Art. 182 et seq. EG), including the Netherlands
       Antilles and Aruba, see G.R. de Groot, 'The Relationship between the Nationality Legislation of
       the Member States of the European Union and European Citizenship', in La Torre, *European
       Citizenship* (The Hague, 1998), 115. See also Case C-200/02, *Kunqian Catherine Zhu and
       Man Lavette Chen v. Secretary of State for the Home Department.*
170.   For a critical view of this fact, see P. van Dijk, 'Free Movement of Persons: Towards European
       Citizenship' (1992) Report for *FIDE*, SEW, 277–307.
171.   As to the position of Denmark, see D. Howarth, 'The Compromise on Denmark and the Treaty
       on European Union: A Legal and Political Analysis' (1994) CML Rev., 765–805; Curtin and
       van Ooik 'De bijzondere positie van Denemarken in de Europese Unie: Een juridisch Fata
       Morgana?' (1993) SEW, 675, especially at 681–683, and for the Edinburgh conclusions, and
       decision, Bull. EC 12-1992 points I.33–I.44.

with the already existing *acquis communautaire*. Considering the evolution of the case law, the opposite appears to have happened.

6.2   THE SPECIAL RIGHTS CONFERRED BY CITIZENSHIP OF THE UNION

According to the Court of Justice, Union Citizenship is destined to be the fundamental status of nationals of the Member States.[172] Indeed, important rights result from this status.

First of all, a Union citizen may invoke the general prohibition of discrimination on grounds of nationality under Article 12 EC in enjoying the rights conferred by the Treaty (Art. 17(2) EC). This is not surprising in itself, but the Court has been creative in construing in favour of the Union citizen the condition of Article 12 according to which, in order for the prohibition to be applicable in a particular case, the matter to which a discrimination relates, must come within the scope of application of the Treaty. Whereas in the first case in which the Court ruled on this issue, *Martinez Salà*,[173] that condition was applied in the broadest possible manner, subsequent case law has followed a more sophisticated approach.[174] Indeed, as soon as the disadvantageous or discriminatory treatment of the Union's citizen is due to or related to the fact that he has exercised his right of free movement under Article 18 EC, the situation is considered to fall, *ratione materiae*, within the scope of the Treaty so as to allow him to benefit from the prohibition of Article 12 EC. In *D'Hoop*, for instance, a Belgian national was refused the so-called tideover allowance, an unemployment benefit granted under Belgian legislation to young people who have completed their studies and seeking their first employment.[175] The reason for that refusal was that Ms D'Hoop had obtained her secondary school diploma in France and not in Belgium. Consequently, it was because Ms D'Hoop had exercised her right of free movement under Article 18 EC that she could not receive the allowance. As the exercise of the right of free movement was involved, her situation was considered to come within the scope of the Treaty – which allowed her to invoke the principle of non-discrimination under Article 12 EC. This approach – and that is its advantage – makes separate analysis of whether the *sedes materiae* itself, in the case of Ms D'Hoop an allowance such as the tideover allowance, falls within the scope of the Treaty, superfluous. That there must be some transborder element is inherent in this approach. The status of Union citizen seems to be insufficient to strengthen the

---

172. Case C-184/99, *Rudy Grzelczyk v. Centre public d'aide sociale d'Ottignies-Louvain-la-Neuve* (para. 31).
173. Case C-85/96, *María Martinez Sala v. Freistaat Bayern*, see annotation by C. Tomuschat in (2000) CML Rev., 449–457 and by Schrauwen in (1999) SEW, 426–436.
174. See Case C-274/96, *Criminal proceedings against Bickel and Franz*, C-184/99, *Grzelczyck* and C-224/98, *Marie-Nathalie D'Hoop v. Office national de l'emploi*. See also Case C-209/03, *The Queen (on the application of Dany Bidar) v. London Borough of Ealing and Secretary of State for Education and Skills*.
175. Case C-224/98, *D'Hoop*.

citizen's position *vis-à-vis* his or her own country in purely internal situations in cases of so-called reverse discrimination.[176]

Secondly, and even more importantly, the right of free movement granted to the Union's citizen by Article 18(1) EC has been construed by the case law in recent years as a directly enforceable Community law right, which can thus be upheld in Member States' courts against national measures unduly restricting that right. Indeed, the Court interprets this right of free movement, in a quite similar way to the approach followed for the economic fundamental freedoms under the Treaty (see Ch. VIII above), as implying a prohibition of unjustified restrictions of this right.[177]

Admittedly, Article 18 EC grants Union citizens the right to move and reside freely within the territory of the Member States 'subject to the limitations and conditions laid down in this Treaty and by the measures adopted to give it effect'. By the time this provision came into force, a right to move and reside freely for nationals of Member States in the territory of other Member States had already been realized, albeit subject to certain conditions. First, such a right was inextricably linked with the economic rights of free movement (free movement of workers, freedom of establishment, freedom to provide services); in addition, in 1990 three Directives were adopted which conferred similar rights on a number of remaining categories of nationals who were not economically active, subject to a number of financial conditions (insurance for health costs; sufficient financial resources not to become a burden on the host state).[178] Since Article 18 EC itself also allows for such conditions, the question arises whether this provision in fact adds anything to the existing rights. The case law, already mentioned above, demonstrates that it does. Firstly, significance must be attached to the fact that the Treaty itself guarantees this right to move and reside freely as a fundamental right of Union citizens. Moreover, the EU Charter of Fundamental Rights confirms the existence of this right.[179] That the exercise of the right may be subject to limitations or conditions, as explicitly provided in Article 18(1) EC, does not detract from the existence of the right as such; this is also true for the economic freedoms. Neither does such an imposition of conditions give sufficient grounds

---

176. Cf. Joined Cases C-64 & 65/96, *Land Nordrhein-Westfalen v. Kari Uecker* and *Vera Jacquet v. Land Nordrhein-Westfalen*, on right of residence for students. Also B.J. Drijber, 'Een slotbeschouwing,' in E. Manunza and L. Senden (eds), *De EU: de interstatelijkheid voorbij?* (Nijmegen, 2006), 191.

177. See more particularly Case C-406/04, *De Cuyper v. Office national de l'emploi* and Case C-192/05, *K. Tas-Hagen, R.A. Tas v. Raadskamer WUBO van de Pensioenen Uitkeringsraad*. See also Case C-135/99, *Ursula Elsen v. Bundesversicherungsanstalt für Angestellte* which already goes a long way towards accepting this interpretation.

178. Dir. 90/364, 90/365 and 90/366, O.J. 1990, L 180. The latter Directive was replaced (after it was annulled by the Court of Justice on the ground of an incorrect legal basis in Case C-295/90, *Council v. European Parliament et al.* (Students' right of residence)) by Dir. 93/96, O.J. 1993, L 317. These three directives have been replaced by Dir. 2004/38, O.J. 2004, L 158/77; see further Ch. VIII *infra*.

179. However, for the conditions and limitations on the exercise of this right, reference is made to the EC Treaty; see Arts. 45 and 52(2) EU Charter of Fundamental Rights, O.J. 2000, C 364.

for denying direct effect to this right.[180] Since the Treaty itself so emphatically uses the term 'right' (see also Art. 2 third indent TEU), and moreover since the question whether conditions or limitations imposed by the Community legislature have been met is subject to judicial review,[181] the Court was able to acknowledge in *Baumbast* the direct effect of the right of free movement and residence according to Article 18(1) EC.[182] It seems at least defensible that the explicit acceptance of the right to move and reside freely as a Treaty right for all Union citizens should imply that any conditions and limitations imposed on the exercise of this right by the Community legislature require a special justification and must respect the principle of proportionality.[183] The *Baumbast* case points in this direction. These considerations lead us to conclude that Articles 17 and 18 EC do have an independent significance and, as the first case law on these provisions confirms, do really strengthen the rights of Union citizens as compared with the previously existing provisions of primary and secondary Community law.[184]

Pursuant to the second paragraph of Article 18 EC, the Community legislature may adopt provisions, under the co-decision procedure, to facilitate the exercise of the right to move and reside freely within the Union. Since the Treaty of Nice the requirement that the Council act unanimously is abandoned, but a price is paid for this in terms of a certain limitation in the power to adopt provisions: it is explicitly made subsidiary to other Treaty competences, so that this provision may not be used as sole basis for general arrangements concerning the right to move and reside freely for all categories of Union citizens, economically active or not.[185] A second limitation concerns the exclusion of measures concerning passports, identity cards and the like, and also social security and social protection, although this does not impinge on the existence of other legal bases in the Treaty for the regulation of these matters. The exclusion of the last two matters – social security and social protection – is interesting, since the framers of the Treaty thereby implicitly

---

180. Not even after the textual changes in Art. 18(2) brought about by the Treaty of Nice, which qualify the right to move and reside freely as an objective, but at the same time retain the term 'right'.
181. Cf. Case 41/74, *Yvonne Van Duyn v. Home Office*. In the same sense, cf. A.G. Cosmas in Case C-378/97, *Criminal proceedings against Florus Ariël Wijsenbeek*.
182. Case C-413/99, *Baumbast and R. v. Secretary of State for the Home Department*.
183. Cf. A.G. Cosmas in Case C-378/97, *Wijsenbeek*.
184. It follows from the above that there are two ways for Union citizens to enforce specific rights: first via the general prohibition on discrimination in Art. 12 EC, as in Case C-85/96, *Sala*, Case C-274/96, *Bickel and Franz* and Case C-184/99, *Grzelczyk*; and in addition, as soon as there is a connecting factor with the right to move and reside freely, on the basis of Art. 18(1) EC as a prohibition on unjustified restriction of this right. As to the relationship between these two see C. Timmermans, 'Martinez Salá and Baumbast Revisited', in M. Poiares Maduro and L. Azoulai (eds), *The Past and Future of EU Law: The Classics of EU Law Revisited on the 50th Anniversary of the Rome Treaty* (2008 forthcoming).
185. Indeed, Dir. 2004/38 on the right of citizens of the Union and their family members to move and reside freely within the territory of the Member States has as its legal basis Arts. 12, 18, 40, 44 and 52 EC (O.J. 2004, L 158/77).

acknowledge that there may be points of contact between these subjects and the right to move and reside freely.

Article 19(1) EC confers the right to vote and stand as a candidate at municipal elections[186] in the Member State where a citizen resides and of which he or she is not a national, under the same conditions as nationals of that state; Article 19(2) EC confers the right under the same conditions to vote and stand as a candidate for the European Parliament. These civil rights for non-nationals were certainly a major innovation in most of the Member States,[187] requiring an amendment of the Constitution in some cases.

Article 19(2) EC ought to be a considerable stimulus to the adoption of a uniform electoral procedure in accordance with Article 190(4) EC.[188] The fact that Article 191 EC, introduced by the Treaty of Maastricht, recognizes the importance of political parties at European level as a factor for integration within the Union may well lead to candidates who are nationals of other Member States being included in party lists or being chosen for constituencies in proportion to the number of residents who are nationals of (those) other Member States. Article 19 EC could thus contribute to strengthening the basis for legitimacy of the European Parliament as 'representatives of the peoples of the States, brought together in the Community' (Art. 189(1) EC).

Article 20 EC grants every citizen of the Union, in the territory of a third country in which the Member State of which he is a national has no representation, the right to protection by the diplomatic or consular authorities of any Member State, on the same conditions as nationals of that State. Unlike the implementing measures envisaged by Articles 18 and 19 EC, the implementing measures for this right were adopted under the intergovernmental model (i.e., by the Member States) rather than by the Community Institutions.[189] It does not appear that this is meant to replace national diplomatic and consular representation by Community representation. In order to secure this protection international negotiations (with the relevant third countries) are necessary in any event (cf. Art. 20 TEU).

Article 21 EC and Article 194 EC together made two important changes to the previously existing, and continuing, right of citizens to petition the European Parliament. Articles 21 and 195 EC introduced the possibility of recourse to an Ombudsman, appointed by the Parliament.[190] On the basis of Articles 194 and 195 EC, the rights to petition and to apply to the Ombudsman are enjoyed not only by

---

186. In many countries in the EU, these are referred to as active and passive voting rights respectively.
187. The necessary implementing measures dealing with municipal elections are contained in Dir. 94/80, O.J. 1994, L 368/38; and those dealing with elections to the European Parliament are set out in Dir. 93/109, O.J. 1993, L 329/34.
188. As noted rightly by Durand in J. Mégret et al. (eds), *Commentaire Mégret Le Droit de la CEE* Vol. 2, 2nd ed. (Brussels, 1992), 442.
189. Decision 95/553, O.J. 1995, L 314.
190. See generally A. Peters, 'The European Ombudsman and the European Constitution' (2005) CML Rev., 697–743. As to the right to petition, see, generally, E. Marias, 'The Right to Petition the European Parliament after Maastricht' (1994) EL Rev., 169.

citizens of the Union, but by any natural or legal person residing in or having its registered office in a Member State. This means that unlike the other provisions of Part Two of the EC Treaty, non-citizens of the Union benefit from these rights on equal terms with citizens of the Union. On the other hand, the rights conferred in Article 21 EC are, by the reference to Articles 194 and 195, confined in their subject-matter. In Chapter III of this book, this is discussed further in the course of examination of the functions of the European Parliament.

Pursuant to the third paragraph of Article 21 EC, citizens may write to the institutions or organs of the Community mentioned in Article 7 EC (as well as the European Ombudsman) in any of the Community languages[191] and be given an answer in that language. This formulation does not have a strong binding character. A Declaration (No. 4) attached to the Treaty of Nice is formulated more robustly, but obviously may not amend this provision.[192]

6.3   THE POSSIBILITY OF EXTENDING THE RIGHTS CONFERRED
            BY ARTICLE 18–21 EC

On the basis of the Report required to be presented every three years in accordance with Article 22, first paragraph, EC, 'and without prejudice to the other provisions of the Treaty', the Council may, under the second paragraph of Article 22, 'adopt provisions to strengthen or add to' the rights laid down in this Part Two of the EC Treaty. The Council acts unanimously on the basis of a proposal from the Commission, after consulting the European Parliament, and recommends the provisions so adopted to the Member States for adoption in accordance with their respective constitutional requirements.

The wording of Article 22 does not appear to exclude the extension of the rights in Articles 18–20 EC to persons other than citizens of the Union, in the same way as Articles 194 and 195 EC have done. On the basis of public international law considerations, it would appear difficult to envisage such an extension in respect of Article 20 EC. As far as rights on movement and residence are concerned for third country nationals who are legally resident in a Member State, the Treaty now contains a specific legal basis in its new Title IV on visa, asylum etc. (Art. 63(1)(4) EC). As regards Article 19(1) EC, on voting rights in local elections, it would appear that such an extension would founder on the rocks of general unacceptability of such an obligation, identified by Van Dijk.[193] In relation to elections to the European Parliament, such an expansion might falter on the terms of

---

191. See Art. 314 EC.
192. In any case the existing linguistic regime obliges the institutions to answer a letter in the language of the applicant (Reg. 1 EEC, O.J. 17/1958, 385, Art. 2) Cf. further in this context Art. 41(4) EU Charter on Fundamental Rights, and the Code of good administrative behaviour for staff of the European Commission in their relations with the public, of 13 Sept. 2000, O.J. 2000, L 267/63.
193. Van Dijk, FIDE report cited *supra* note 170.

Article 189 EC ('representatives of the peoples of the States'), unless that phrase is deemed to embrace legally resident third country nationals.[194]

Finally the question arises whether Article 22 EC could serve as a legal basis for the inclusion in the EC Treaty of the above-mentioned EU Charter of Fundamental Rights. The scope *ratione personae* of the Charter is, it should be noted, not restricted to citizens of the Union. The Charter is explicitly linked to Union Citizenship, first in its Preamble, and further in its Chapter V, where the most important specific rights of Union citizens are set out (Arts. 39–46 Charter). We would not exclude the possibility of using Article 22 EC for this purpose. When the Treaty of Lisbon enters into force, the Charter of Fundamental Rights will be anchored in the Treaty on European Union (Art. 6(1) TEU (Lisbon)).

7   MULTI-SPEED EUROPE, FLEXIBILITY, ENHANCED
           COOPERATION

7.1   THE CONCEPT

In connection with the succession of enlargements, as a result of which the Community of six Member States has grown into a Union with – currently – 27 Member States, the differences of opinion which existed from the beginning about the direction and ultimate goal of the European integration process have only increased. In addition, the differences in the level of economic and social development, and the resulting differences in prosperity between the Member States have also grown; the same may also be said of the opinions concerning economic, social, environmental, and other policies. This explains why over the years the call has become louder for variety in the speeds at which integration policy is formulated and implemented, for 'opt-outs', or for accepting a core group of Member States with a higher level of ambition, The terminology used is rather confusing (flexibility, Europe à la carte, variable geometry, etc.) The underlying idea, however, is clear: one or more Member States should not be able to block progress desired by the others. The standpoint adopted by the United Kingdom under John Major during the negotiations on the Treaty of Maastricht, and further the problems with the Danish ratification of that Treaty and the attitude taken by that Member State subsequently, clearly influenced the development of views on this issue.

In fact, the Community decision-making practice has had examples of multi-speed solutions for a long time already, for instance with the grant of longer implementation periods for directives to certain Member States. Such a differentiation is not difficult to reconcile with the (substantive) principle of equality, providing that it can be justified on objective grounds. An example of this is the selection criteria for Member States for entry into the third phase of monetary union, on the basis of objective criteria set by the EC Treaty itself.[195] The opt-outs

---

194. See Case C-145/04, *Spain v. United Kingdom* (on direct elections to the EP in Gibraltar).
195. Cf. Arts. 121 et seq. EC; see for another example Art. 299(2) EC.

for the United Kingdom and Denmark provided for by the EC Treaty, however, are not in conformity with the principle of equality; these countries simply do not join the euro as long as they do not wish to. More and more of such multi-speed solutions have appeared in the Treaties,[196] especially since the Treaty of Maastricht. Sometimes these turn out to be temporary, because the Member State in question gives up its exceptional position, as happened with the Protocol on Social Policy concluded at Maastricht. That Protocol enabled the other Member States to carry out a more far-reaching social policy using the EC institutions, without the United Kingdom; to that end they were also enabled to enact Community rules which applied to only eleven of the then twelve Member States. It was possible to repeal that Protocol with the Treaty of Amsterdam, but this approach served in some ways as a model for the general regime which the Treaty of Amsterdam created under the new, more neutral, name of closer cooperation.[197] This regulation in the treaties of what was formerly termed flexibility, was one of the major points on the agenda of the negotiations leading up to the Treaty of Amsterdam, as one of the necessary reforms in view of the expected new accessions. Agreement on that point was not merely a wish of those Member States wanting to go further in terms of integration. Also the more sceptical States, such as the United Kingdom, Denmark and Sweden, were interested in arranging this possibility in order to avoid the creation of groups of countries pursuing integration measures outside the framework of the Union (cf. the earlier Schengen Agreement). By including such a regime in the Treaties themselves and tying its use to strict conditions, these countries remain involved and to a certain extent able to 'keep an eye' on the way these arrangements are used.

In fact, the Treaty of Amsterdam also contains a few other specific 'multi-speed' solutions, included in four protocols annexed to the EC and EU Treaties:[198] Denmark, Ireland and the United Kingdom remain in principle outside the policy on immigration, asylum and visas provided for in the new Title IV of the EC Treaty. Nor do these three Member States, again in principle, take part in the Schengen acquis now incorporated in EC and EU (third pillar) law. Finally, the United Kingdom and Ireland may retain border controls on intra-Community movements of persons (see on this Ch. VIII).

These multi-speed solutions lead to the limited territorial application of certain parts of Community law and Union law, since they only apply to the Member States which take part. This leads to a splintering of Community law, to an extreme lack of transparency because of the technically complex nature of the regimes in

---

196. Another older example though is ex-Art. 100a(4), which was included in the EC Treaty pursuant to the SEA of 1986 (now Art. 95(4) and (5) EC).

197. The Treaty of Nice again renamed this in the English version, as 'enhanced cooperation'.

198. Protocol integrating the Schengen acquis into the framework of the European Union (1997); Protocol on the application of certain aspects of Art. 7a [now 14] of the Treaty establishing the European Community to the United Kingdom and to Ireland (1997); Protocol on the position of the United Kingdom and Ireland (1997); Protocol on the position of Denmark (1997). See on this H. Kortenberg, 'Closer Cooperation in the Treaty of Amsterdam' (1998) CML Rev., 833–854.

question, to difficult problems of demarcation and tricky questions of interpretation. That is the price which has to be paid by those who wish to go further, but also by those who wish to remain behind.

Specific multi-speed regimes will be discussed in other chapters of this book. Here, a commentary is given on the general regime for enhanced cooperation, as that was given form in the Treaty of Amsterdam, and further amended by the Treaty of Nice.

7.2   THE TREATY REGIME FOR ENHANCED COOPERATION

'Enhanced cooperation', as the method for differentiated integration institutionalized by the Treaty of Amsterdam is termed ever since the Treaty of Nice, means that a limited number of Member States (this must be a minimum of eight Member States according to Art. 43 (g) TEU) are given permission under certain conditions to implement the existing Treaties making use of the existing competences and in conformity with the existing decision-making procedures. There is thus no question of new competences. Enhanced cooperation simply means the implementation of the relevant Treaty provisions, as they are included in the Treaties, but this implementation applies only to a limited number of Member States. This method is therefore more like the 'opt-outs' for Denmark and the United Kingdom regarding the euro, than the Protocol on Social Policy which was in force for a short time, and which contained a separate regime for a social policy that was to be developed without the United Kingdom (see Ch. X above).

The Treaty regime for enhanced cooperation is set up as follows. Title VII of the Treaty on European Union sets out the basic regime, regulating the general substantive and institutional conditions. For the actual application of this regime, there are specific provisions included in the EC Treaty (Arts. 11–11a) and Titles V and VI of the TEU (Arts. 27a–27e and 40–40b), which give the requisite legal basis and – especially for Titles V and VI – some further conditions. The Treaty of Nice has grouped all the conditions of application for the EC Treaty in Title VII TEU which, as mentioned above, strengthens the impression of the character of the TEU as an overarching treaty, and therefore in a certain sense placing the EU in a hierarchical position above the EC.[199]

7.2.1   The General Regime for the Union (Title VII TEU)

Enhanced cooperation is only permitted as *ultimum remedium*, in other words, the use of the normal procedures must have turned out to be impossible. Since the Treaty of Nice, the Council is required to establish this explicitly (Art. 43a TEU). The Treaty of Nice also brought an important change by setting the required minimum number of states at eight, instead of the condition being a majority of

---

199. See section 1.2.3 *supra.*

states, as was provided under the Treaty of Amsterdam (Art. 43(g) TEU). Since this number has remained unchanged despite the last accessions[200] this could facilitate the development of a leading group of states, for instance the states participating in the euro. Measures taken in the framework of enhanced cooperation must respect the *acquis communautaire* and the Union acquis (Art. 43(c) TEU); they may not affect the 'competences, rights and obligations' of those Member States which do not take part (Art. 43(h) TEU). On the other hand, the latter may not frustrate the implementation of enhanced cooperation (Art. 44(2) TEU). A non-participant may at all times become party to enhanced cooperation, but must accept and comply with the decisions taken in that framework up until then (Art. 43b TEU).

In decision-making in the framework of enhanced cooperation, the institutions function in the same way as in the normal treaty procedures. The European Parliament and the European Commission do so in their usual composition. Only the Council is subject to special rules: all Member States may take part in the deliberations, but the decisions are adopted only by those Member States taking part. The voting rules are adapted accordingly (Art. 44(1) TEU).

The financing of expenditure linked to enhanced cooperation is borne by the participating Member States, except for the administrative costs of the institutions. However the Council may unanimously decide otherwise (Art. 44a TEU).

For the CFSP, application of a regime of enhanced cooperation was considered not necessary in the Treaty of Amsterdam, because of the introduction of a general possibility for opting out (so-called constructive abstention, Art. 23(1) TEU). The Treaty of Nice changed this situation by making enhanced cooperation also possible in the area of CFSP, albeit to a limited extent (it must relate to the implementation of a joint action or a common position, and may not relate to matters having military or defence implications (Art. 27b TEU)).

7.2.2   Enhanced Cooperation in the Framework of the EC

Some of the conditions for enhanced cooperation listed by Article 43 TEU are more particularly relevant for the EC. First, certain areas are explicitly excluded. This is the case for everything which is within the exclusive competence of the Community (Art. 43(d) TEU). In this context one should think first of the common commercial policy, the external fisheries policy and other areas of external EC policy to the extent that these competences have become exclusive.[201] In addition, it might be argued that the Treaty competences which specifically relate to the realization and maintenance of the internal market and the areas of sectoral and horizontal and flanking policies (agricultural, transport, health, environmental and consumer policies) directly linked to it, should also be considered to be exclusive in

---

200. The Lisbon Treaty will increase this minimum to nine Member States (Art. 20(2) TEU (Lisbon)).

201. The so-called *ERTA* effect, described further in Ch. XIII, section 2.3 *infra*.

this context.[202] Obviously the Treaty regime on monetary union, which is itself a specific form of enhanced cooperation, and the monetary policy carried out in that framework, fall outside the scope of application of enhanced cooperation in the sense of Article 43 TEU.

Enhanced cooperation in the remaining areas is bound to strict conditions. Of great significance is the condition that enhanced cooperation may not undermine the internal market as defined in Article 14(2) EC (Art. 43(e) TEU), and may not lead to barriers to trade or discrimination in trade between Member States, and may not distort competition between them (Art. 43(f) TEU). This last condition in particular could be applied with greater or lesser stringency given the vagueness of the criterion. For the rest, if the Treaty competences directly relating to the internal market – in particular those concerning harmonization – are not considered to be exclusive competences and therefore excluded from enhanced cooperation, then review on the basis of the conditions mentioned here might easily lead to the same result.[203] Finally, Article 43(i) provides that the specific multi-speed regime set out in the Schengen Protocol may not be affected. This does not necessarily exclude certain elements of the general regime on enhanced cooperation, which formally does not apply to the Schengen regime, nevertheless being applied – if necessary by analogy – to the extent that the provisions of the Schengen Protocol do not prevent it.

Authorization for enhanced cooperation in a specific case is granted by the Council on a proposal from the Commission and after consultation of the European Parliament (Art. 11(2) EC).[204] The Council decides by qualified majority; if a Member State so requests, the matter may also be raised in the European Council but this cannot block the procedure. For the rest, this procedure entrusts the key to enhanced cooperation to the Commission, since this institution has the exclusive right of initiative. Similarly, the Commission decides on the later participation of a Member State in already existing enhanced cooperation, and has competence to establish the special arrangements needed. It may be assumed that this competence does not go further than technical arrangements and amendments.

Article 46(c) TEU confers jurisdiction on the Court of Justice in relation to the provisions on enhanced cooperation contained in Title VII TEU 'under the conditions provided for by Articles 11 and 11a of the Treaty establishing the EC and Article 40 of this Treaty'. This rather obscure formulation should in our view be

---

202. The Court does not seem to share this view, however, at least not as far as the general harmonization competence pursuant to Art. 95 EC is concerned. In Case C-377/98, *Netherlands v. Parliament and Council* (biotechnological inventions) and Case C-491/01, *The Queen v. Secretary of State for Health, ex parte: British American Tobacco (Investments) Ltd and Imperial Tobacco Ltd* (Tobacco labelling Directive), the exercise of this competence is reviewed against the principle of subsidiarity, which indicates that the Court does not consider this to be an exclusive competence (see *infra* Ch. III, section 6.2).
203. See, however, the analysis by D. Thym, 'Supranationale Ungleichzeitigkeit im recht der Europäischen Integration' (2006) *Europarecht*, 637–655.
204. In the areas where the Parliament normally acts as co-legislator (under Art. 251 EC), Parliament must give its assent to enhanced cooperation.

understood as meaning that within the framework of the procedures in which a decision is taken on the basis of Article 11 EC or Articles 40–40b TEU, the Court has the same jurisdiction in relation to Title VII as it enjoys in accordance with the EC regime on judicial protection.[205]

The decisions and arrangements adopted in the framework of enhanced cooperation under Article 11 EC are Community law, and thus enjoy the same prerogatives of that law (primacy and possibly direct effect), and are also subject to the discipline and rules of the Community legal order. They must respect general principles of law, including fundamental rights, and also, for instance, the principle of subsidiarity. The principles developed in the case law concerning external relations must be considered to apply.[206] In this context a number of questions may arise, for instance in the area of judicial protection. Do Member States who are not participating still have a right to apply for annulment of relevant acts under Article 230 EC? May courts from countries who are not participating submit requests for preliminary rulings on rules which have been adopted in the framework of enhanced cooperation if they are confronted with them?

The general conditions of Title VII TEU seem to leave only limited opportunities for enhanced cooperation in the framework of the EC. If the condition that such cooperation does not undermine the internal market is applied strictly,[207] one might think of social policy, and certain horizontal and flanking policies insofar as they are not directly linked to the completion of the internal market (e.g., environmental policy, consumer policy, public health, culture, research and development). There has not yet been a single instance of an application of the regime for enhanced cooperation. In that context, it should be recalled that this regime was primarily developed as a safety measure for the future, in case of accession of a large number of new states.

FURTHER READING

On the Treaty of Maastricht, the Treaty of Amsterdam and the Treaty of Nice, in general, see the literature mentioned at the end of Chapter I.

Structure of the EU
Constantinesco, V. 'La structure du Traité instituant l'Union Européenne'. (1993) CDE, 251.
Curtin, D. 'The Constitutional Structure of the Union: A Europe of Bits and Pieces'. (1993) CML Rev., 17.

---

205. However, as far as enhanced cooperation in the framework of PJCCM is concerned, the Court's jurisdiction with regard to the actual measures of enhanced cooperation enacted by the Council remains limited to the more restrictive regime of Art. 35 TEU.
206. E.g., the ERTA doctrine, see Ch. XIII, sections 2.2 and 2.3 *infra*. See on this F. Tuytschaever, *Differentiation in European Union Law* (Oxford, 1999), 177.
207. Whether, for instance, this condition would allow enhanced cooperation leading to harmonization of direct taxation, seems doubtful.

Denza, E. *The Intergovernmental Pillars of the European Union.* Oxford: Oxford University Press, 2002.

Treaty Reform
De Witte, B. 'Simplification and Reorganization of the European Treaties'. (2002) CML Rev., 1255–1287.
Smith, B.P.G. *Constitution Building in the European Union: The Process of Treaty Reforms.* European Monographs, 29. The Hague: Kluwer Law International, 2002.
Winter, J.A., et al. *Reforming the Treaty on European Union: The Legal Debate.* The Hague: Kluwer Law International, 1996.

Community Legal Order and Direct Effect
Allott, P. *The Health of Nations: Society and Law beyond the State.* Cambridge: Cambridge University Press, 2002.
Bánkowski, Z. and A. Scott. *The European Union and Its Order: The Legal Theory of European Integration.* Oxford: Blackwell, 2000.
Barents, R. *The Autonomy of Community Law.* European Monographs, 45. The Hague: Kluwer Law International, 2004.
Besselink, L.F.M. *A Composite European Constitution.* Groningen: Europa Law Publishing, 2008.
Claes, M. *The National Courts' Mandate in the European Constitution.* Oxford: Hart Publishing, 2006.
Cross, E.D. 'Pre-emption of Member State Law in the EEC'. (1992) CML Rev., 447–472.
Curtin, D. 'The Province of Government: Delimiting the Direct Effect of Directives'. (1990) EL Rev., 195–223.
Curtin, D. and I. Dekker 'The European Union as a Layered International Organization: Institutional Unity in Disguise?'. In P. Craig and G. De Búrca (eds). *The Evolution of EU Law.* Oxford: Oxford University Press, 1999.
Komárek, J. 'European Constitutionalism and the European Arrest Warrant: In Search of the Limits of "Contrapunctual Principles" '. (2007) CML Rev., 9–40.
MacCormick, N. (ed.) *Constructing Legal Systems: 'European Union' in Legal Theory.* Dordrecht: Kluwer, 1997.
Pernice, I.. 'Multilevel Constitutionalism and the Treaty of Amsterdam: European Constitution-Making Revisited'. (1999) CML Rev., 703–750.
Pescatore, P. 'The Doctrine of "Direct Effect": An Infant Disease of Community Law'. (1983) CML Rev., 155.
Pliakos, A.D. 'La nature juridique de l'union européenne'. (1993) *Revue Trimestrielle de Droit Européen*, 187–224.
Prechal, S. *Directives in EC Law.* 2nd ed. Oxford: Oxford University Press, 2005.
Prechal, S. 'Remedies after "Marshall"'. (1990) CML Rev., 451–473.
Prinssen, J.M. and A.A.M. Schrauwen. *Direct Effect: Rethinking a Classic of EC Legal Doctrine.* The Hogendorp Papers, 3. Groningen: Europa Law Publishing, 2002.

Schermers, H.G. and D.F. Waelbroeck. *Judicial Protection in the European Union*. 6th ed. The Hague: Kluwer Law International, 2001.
Seidel, M.. 'Zur Verfassung der Europäischen Gemeinschaft nach Maastricht'. (1992) *Europarecht*, 125–144.

Legal Personality
De Zwaan, J.W. 'The Legal Personality of the European Communities and the European Union'. (1999) *Netherlands Yearbook of International Law*, 75–113.
Pachinger, M. *Die Völkerrechtspersönlichkeit der Europäischen Union*. Bern: Peter Lang, 2004.

Languages
Arzoz, X. (ed.). *Respecting Linguistic Diversity in the European Union*. Amsterdam: John Benjamins Publishing Company, 2008.
Assemblée nationale française. *Langues et union européenne*. Brussels: Bruylant, 2004.
Castiglione, D. and C. Longman (eds) *The Language Question in Europe and Diverse Societies: Political, Legal and Social Perspectives*. Oxford: Hart Publishing, 2007.
Creech, R. *Law and Language in the European Union: The Paradox of a Babel 'United in Diversity'*. Groningen: Europa Law Publishing, 2005.

Citizenship of the Union
Bellamy, R., et al. *Lineages of European Citizenship: Rights, Belonging, and Participation in Eleven Nation-States*. Basingstoke: Palgrave Macmillan, 2004.
Bellamy, R.P. and A. Warleigh. *Citizenship and Governance in the European Union*. London: Continuum, 2001.
Bruter, M. *Citizens of Europe?: The Emergence of a Mass European Identity*. Basingstoke: Palgrave Macmillan, 2005.
Closa, C. 'The Concept of Citizenship in the Treaty on European Union'. (1992) CML Rev., 1137.
Dell'Olio, F. *The Europeanization of Citizenship: Between the Ideology of Nationality, Immigration, and European Identity*. Aldershot: Ashgate, 2005.
Eder, K. and B. Giesen. *European Citizenship between National Legacies and Postnational Projects*. Oxford: Oxford University Press, 2001.
Einhorn, B. *Citizenship in an Enlarging Europe: From Dream to Awakening*. Basingstoke: Palgrave Macmillan, 2006.
Guild, E. *The Legal Elements of European Identity: EU Citizenship and Migration Law*. Kluwer European Law Library, 1. The Hague: Kluwer Law International, 2004.
Harmsen, R. and T.M. Wilson. *Europeanization: Institution, Identities and Citizenship*. Yearbook of European Studies = Annuaire d'études européennes, 14. Amsterdam: Rodopi, 2000.

La Torre, M. *European Citizenship: An Institutional Challenge*. European Forum, vol. 3. The Hague: Kluwer Law International, 1998.

Meehan, E. *Citizenship and the European Union*. Bonn: Zentrum für Europäische Integrationsforschung, 2000.

O'Leary, S. 'The Relationship between Community Citizenship and the Protection of Fundamental Rights in Community Law'. (1995) CML Rev., 519.

O'Leary, S. *The Evolving Concept of Community Citizenship: From the Free Movement of Persons to Union Citizenship*. European Monographs, 13. The Hague: Kluwer Law International, 1996.

O'Leary, S. 'Putting Flesh on the Bones of European Union Citizenship'. (1999) EL Rev., 68.

Pomoell, J. *European Union Citizenship in Focus: The Legal Position of the Individual in EC Law*. Erik Castrén Institute of International Law and Human Rights Research Reports 1999/04/Forum Iuris. Helsinki: Faculty of Law, 2000.

Reich, N. *Bürgerrechte in der Europäischen Union: subjektive Rechte von Union-sbürgern und Drittstaatsangehörigkeitsrecht unter besonderer Berücksichtigung der Rechtslage nach der Rechtsprechung des EuGH und dem Vertrag von Amsterdam*. Baden-Baden, Nomos, 1999.

Shaw, J. *The Transformation of Citizenship in the European Union: Electoral Rights and the Restructuring of Political Space*. Cambridge Studies in European Law and Policy. Cambridge University Press, 2007.

Vink, M.P. *Limits of European Citizenship: European Integration and Domestic Immigration Policies*. Migration, Minorities and Citizenship. Basingstoke: Palgrave Macmillan, 2005.

Weale, A. *Democratic Citizenship and the European Union*. Europe in Change. Manchester: Manchester University Press, 2005.

Differentiation, Flexibility, Closer Cooperation

De Búrca, G. and J. Scott. *Constitutional Change in the EU: From Uniformity to Flexibility?* Oxford: Hart, 2000.

De Witte, B.E.F.M., et al. *The Many Faces of Differentiation in EU Law*. Antwerpen: Intersentia, 2001.

Den Boer, M., et al. *Coping with Flexibility and Legitimacy after Amsterdam*. EIPA Publications, 98/P/02. Maastricht: European Institute of Public Administration, 1998.

Ehlermann, C.-D. 'Differentiation, Flexibility, Closer Cooperation: The New Provisions of the Amsterdam Treaty'. (1998) *European Law Journal*, 4.

Ehlermann, C.-D. Increased Differentiation or Stronger Uniformity. In J. Winter et al. (eds). *Reforming the Treaty on European Union: The Legal Debate*. The Hague: T.M.C. Asser Institute, 1995.

Grieser, V. *Flexible Integration in der Europäischen Union: neue Dynamik oder Gefährdung der Rechtseinheit?* Schriften zum europäischen Recht, Bd. 100. Berlin: Duncker & Humblot, 2003.

Kellerbauer, M. *Von Maastricht bis Nizza: Neuformen differenzierter Integration in der Europäischen Union.* Tübinger Schriften zum internationalen und europäischen Recht, Bd. 64. Berlin: Duncker & Humblot, 2003.

Kölliker, A. *Flexibility and European Unification: The Logic of Differentiated Integration.* Lanham, MD: Rowman & Littlefield, 2006.

Kortenberg, H. 'Closer Cooperation in the Treaty of Amsterdam'. (1998) CML Rev., 833.

Langner, K. *Verstärkte Zusammenarbeit in der Europäischen Union: Stärkung der Integration oder hin zu einem Europa von mehreren Geschwindigkeiten?.* Europäische Hochschulschriften. Reihe 2, Rechtswissenschaft, Bd. 4012. Frankfurt am Main: Lang, 2004.

Linke, G. *Das Instrument der verstärkten Zusammenarbeit im Vertrag von Nizza: Möglichkeiten eines Europas der differenzierten Integration.* Interdisziplinäre Europa-Studien, Bd. 3. Frankfurt am Main: Lang, 2006.

Schrauwen, A.A.M. *Flexibility in Constitutions: Forms of Closer Cooperation in Federal and Non-federal Setting.* 2nd, updated Post Nice ed. The Hogendorp Papers, 2. Amsterdam: Europa Law Publishing, 2002.

Shaw, J. 'Flexibility in a "Reorganized" and "Simplified" Treaty'. (2003) CML Rev., 279–311.

Stubb, A. *Negotiating Flexibility in the European Union: Amsterdam, Nice and Beyond.* Houndmills: Palgrave, 2002.

Tuytschaever, F. *Differentiation in European Union Law.* Oxford: Hart, 1999.

Tuytschaever, F. 'Nauwere samenwerking volgens het Verdrag van Amsterdam'. (1999) SEW, 270.

Usher, J. *Flexibility and Enhanced Cooperation in the European Union after Amsterdam: A Legal Analysis.* In T. Heukels et al. (eds). *The European Union after Amsterdam: A Legal Analysis.* The Hague: Kluwer, 1998.

Warleigh, A. *Flexible Integration: Which Model for the European Union?* Contemporary European Studies, 15. London: Sheffield Academic Press, 2002.

Further, the reader is referred to the overviews of relevant literature at the end of each of the following chapters, in which the general aspects described briefly in this chapter are dealt with in more depth (especially IV, VI and XIII).

Chapter III

The Basic Principles

C.W.A. Timmermans

1   THE STRUCTURE OF SUBSTANTIVE UNION LAW

The rules of substantive law established for the development and implementation
of Union policies can be divided into, first, the substantive law of the European
Communities, which is by far the most important source of substantive law of the
Union, and further the rules enacted in the framework of the common foreign and
security policy (hereafter: CFSP) and arrangements for police and judicial cooperation in criminal matters (hereafter: PJCCM).

   In Article 2 of Title I of the Treaty on European Union (the Common Provi-
sions), five overarching objectives for the policy areas of the Union are formulated.
The first objective paraphrases the general objectives of the European Community
Treaty (EC) mentioned in Article 2 EC, with one important difference: unlike in
Article 2 EC, the creation of an area without internal frontiers is explicitly mentioned.[1] The realization of such an area also requires action in the framework of
PJCCM, as also appears from Article 61(a) EC. The second objective, 'to assert its
identity on the international scene', will in the first place ('in particular') need to be
achieved by the CFSP, but it is also important for external policy in the other
sectors, both of the European Communities and the PJCCM. In the area of tension
between external action of the Community and that of the Member States outside

---

1. Compare this with Art. 14 EC, on the internal market.

P.J.G. Kapteyn, A.M. McDonnell, K.J.M. Mortelmans and C.W.A. Timmermans (eds),
The Law of the European Union and the European Communities, pp. 115–174.
©2008 Kluwer Law International BV, The Netherlands.

the Community framework, the Community will have to keep this Union objective in sight, as a guiding light (see Ch. XIII). The fourth objective clearly expresses the link between free movement of persons as part of the internal market and the necessary associated measures in terms of appropriate checks at external borders, and a coordinated immigration policy (Title IV EC). Of the objectives listed in Article 2 Treaty on the European Union (TEU), this one – the area of freedom, security and justice – is to the greatest extent a 'common' objective, insofar as two paths are followed for its realization: that of the EC (Title IV EC) and that of the PJCCM. Finally, the fifth objective (to maintain in full the *acquis communautaire* and build on it) is important for substantive policy and the interpretation of the legal rules enacted to that end, because it can be said to favour the EC framework as constituting the main path for Union policy. This objective can also be used to provide support for the Court's 'effectiveness' ('effet utile') methodology in the interpretation of substantive EC law (cf. Ch. VII). In that context, the question also arises to what extent the Court of Justice may take account of these Common Provisions of Title I of the TEU, even though that same Court is not granted explicit jurisdiction in relation to them by the TEU. We would not exclude the possibility of the Court taking these provisions into account as relevant considerations in interpreting the rest of Union and EC law in the framework of its jurisdiction thereto.

On account of the dominant significance of EC law as by far the most important source of substantive Union law, this will be considered in more detail in the following sections of this chapter. With the Lisbon Treaty this distinction will of course disappear, all EC law becoming Union law.

2   CONTENT AND STRUCTURE OF SUBSTANTIVE EC LAW

The substantive law of the EC sets out from the Principles contained in Part One of the EC Treaty. These are followed by Part Two, dealing with citizenship of the Union. Part Three sets out Community policies, which can be divided into eight groups of provisions: first, the provisions designed to realize the free movement of goods, persons, services, capital and payments (Titles I and III); second, the provisions on agriculture and transport (Titles II and V respectively); third, the provisions on visas, asylum, immigration etc. contained in Title IV (added by the Treaty of Amsterdam); fourth, competition, taxation and harmonization of laws now brought together in Title VI of Part Three; fifth, the important Title VII which contains the provisions relating to economic and monetary policy; sixth, the new Title VIII on employment; seventh, the provisions on the common commercial policy (CCP) in Title IX with a new Title X on Customs Cooperation. Eighth and finally, Titles XI-XXI cover ten other policy areas.

These ten other policy areas – which vary greatly in importance – cover the titles on, respectively, 'Social policy, education, vocational training and youth', 'Culture', 'Public health', 'Consumer protection', 'Trans-European networks', 'Industry', 'Economic and social cohesion', 'Research and technological development', 'Environment' and 'Development cooperation'. The Treaty of Nice added a new Title XXI on Cooperation with third countries. The provisions of the new Title IV and the Titles VII-XXI have a radically different legal nature from that of the provisions of the first three Titles and Titles V and VI of Part Three of the Treaty, as well as themselves being extremely diverse.[2]

The substantive law of the EC is built up in the Treaty as follows. Articles 2, 3 and 4 EC set out in global terms the objectives of the Treaty and the means by which they are to be achieved. This is now done in a less clear-cut manner than was the case with the original Articles 2 and 3 European Economic Community (EEC), and this will be discussed in section 2 of this chapter, below. Some of the objectives of the Community newly formulated by the Treaty of Maastricht are clearly not economic in nature. Reflecting this, the Treaty of Maastricht rebaptized the EEC as the EC, the old EEC Treaty as a consequence becoming the EC Treaty.

Each of the activities of the Community mentioned in Articles 3 and 4 EC is subsequently developed more specifically in legal provisions in Part Three of the EC Treaty, save Article 3(1)(s) on the association of the overseas countries and territories, which is worked out in its own Part Four of the Treaty. Some of these provisions contain directly effective rights (and in some cases also obligations) for nationals and firms of the Member States, directly effective obligations for the Member States and also obligations or powers to adopt implementing or further regulatory measures, in particular, but not solely, for the Community Institutions.[3] Before one gets to the detailed legal rules of Part Three, however, the Treaty lays down, also, in Part One a number of fundamental principles that are contained in Article 5 (principles of conferred powers, subsidiarity and proportionality), Article 10 (principle of loyal cooperation), Article 12 (prohibition of discrimination on grounds of nationality). In addition, Article 13 EC creates a legal basis for the adoption of measures to combat discrimination on other grounds, such as sex, race etc. The fundamental importance the Treaty attaches to the promotion of equality between men and women and the protection of the environment is underlined by the fact that these are included in the Part One as general, 'horizontal' objectives, applicable in all policy areas of the Community (these are the so-called integration provisions of Art. 3(2) EC and Art. 6 EC, respectively). Part One contains further the Articles 14–16 EC, setting out the provisions on the establishment of the internal market, and Articles 11–11a, on the regime for enhanced cooperation; the latter are discussed elsewhere in this book.[4]

The real institutional provisions, with the exception of those relating to Economic and Monetary Union (EMU), and if one discounts Articles 7–9 EC,[5] appear in Part Five of the EC Treaty, after the substantive legal principles and provisions. The place which these provisions occupy in the structure of the Treaty

2. See, further, sections 4.3 and 4.5, and, more extensively, Chs. X-XIII, *infra*.
3. Thus although the European Central Bank is not a Community institution as such (it is not mentioned in Art. 7 EC), it has important regulatory and executive powers. See, further, Chs. IV and X. Moreover, Parts One and Three of the EC Treaty also contain other obligations and powers for the Member States.
4. See Ch. II, section 7, *supra*.
5. Art. 7 lists the Community institutions. Arts. 8 and 9 establish the institutions of EMU and the European Investment Bank.

reflects the approach in the Spaak Report, whereby the nature and working methods of the institutions, and the division of powers between them have to be adapted to the effective achievement of the substantive tasks which they are to carry out, and not vice versa.[6] Thus, also, in 1956 and 1957 they were dealt with at the end of the negotiations which led to the EEC Treaty, and not at the beginning. Following this approach, it is somewhat ominous that the European Council – which is purely intergovernmental in approach – is provided for, together with a definition of its powers, in Title I of the TEU, prior to the provisions dealing with substantive matters of the Union and the Community. The European Council's political task, set out in Article 4 TEU to 'provide the Union with the necessary impetus for its development' and to 'define the general political guidelines' of the Union, also embraces the substantive legal tasks of the Communities. It must be added, however, that in accordance with Article 3 TEU, the European Council must respect and build upon the *acquis communautaire*. It cannot as such adopt any legally binding decisions in the framework of the EC; and, despite the general political guidelines which they may receive, the normal policy-making Institutions of the Communities and the European Central Bank (ECB) remain fully legally responsible for their actions, according to the relevant substantive and institutional provisions of Community law.

The placing of the European Council at the head of the TEU confirms, though, what is well known through experience, that in reality the relationship between the substantive and institutional aspects of Community law is dialectic in nature. The institutional structure and the procedures and legal instruments should of course be appropriate for an effective achievement of the various tasks to be fulfilled, but the history of the last forty years in fact demonstrates that the way in which the tasks are fulfilled depends on the institutional structure of the Communities. It has become increasingly apparent that, as a result of *inter alia* constant expansion of the Communities, external factors, and new insights, there are substantial deficiencies in that structure. The discussion of the basic principles of Community law has been maintained as one of the first chapters of this book, as it is useful for a good understanding of the institutional chapters which follow, while those chapters in turn are important for a proper understanding of the substantive law chapters which then follow. Insofar, the structure of the EC Treaty has not actually predetermined the structure of this book.

2.1   ARTICLES 2, 3 AND 4 EC AND THEIR INTER-RELATIONSHIP

2.1.1   The Objectives of the European Community

Article 2 EC maintains the first objective of the old Article 2 EEC, the promotion throughout the Community of a harmonious development of economic activities,

---

6. See Ch. I, section 4.1, *supra*.

with the addition that that development should be balanced and sustainable. The other four previous objectives have, however, been replaced by:

i)   a high level of employment and of social protection;
ii)   equality between men and women;
iii)   sustainable and non-inflationary growth;
iv)   a high degree of competitiveness and convergence of economic performance;
v)   a high level of protection and improvement of the quality of the environment;
vi)   the raising of the standard of living and quality of life; and
vii)   economic and social cohesion and solidarity among Member States.

All these modifications are of fundamental importance. The first, the fifth and the two last objectives all reflect the new tasks of the Community relating to economic and social cohesion. Article 158 EC makes it clear that this aims in particular 'at reducing disparities between the levels of development of the various regions, and the backwardness of the least-favoured regions or islands, including rural areas'.

The emphasis in the first and fourth objectives on the sustainable character of the development of economic activity, respectively growth, clearly reflects the objective of 'sustainable growth' adopted at the United Nations Conference on Environment and Development (UNCED) Conference in Rio de Janeiro in 1992;[7] this is rendered as 'sustainable economic and social development' in Article 177 EC on development cooperation. The concept of sustainable growth embraces a form and rate of growth (in the whole world, including the developing countries) which is also sustainable for future generations. This growth must therefore not lead to an exhaustion of non-renewable raw materials and natural resources (including certain energy resources). Furthermore, it must not lead to environmental damage which destroys natural resources. This environmental component of the concept of sustainable growth is confirmed by the general environmental objective of Article 2 EC.[8] The new terms of Article 2 EC emphasize that the desired economic growth must be sustainable in the long term, having regard to the availability of replacement natural resources and to what the physical and natural environment will support. The necessary reduction in the consumption of non-renewable or non-replaceable raw and natural materials and in environmental pollution does not however mean a reduction in the production of *all* goods and services. It is simply necessary to prevent both the exhaustion of non-replaceable raw and natural materials and environmental pollution. The formulation of the social dimension of Community policy in the second objective (a high level of employment and of social protection) and the seventh (the raising of the standard of living and quality of life) set out in Article 2 appears to conform to this interpretation. If 'sustainable growth' does not necessarily mean reduced growth, but simply differently directed growth of production and consumption, and probably

---

7.   31 ILM, 876 (1992).
8.   See, generally, L. Krämer, *E.C. Environmental Law*, 6th ed. (London, 2007), 8–29.

more part-time work, the objective of 'a high level of employment' is compatible with the concept of sustainable growth. The changeover to more environmentally friendly investments can indeed lead to new employment opportunities. The seventh objective, which no longer speaks of 'an accelerated raising of the standard of living' but now of 'the raising of the standard of living and quality of life' implies that material consumption (particularly of non-renewable raw and natural materials) cannot continue constantly increasing. On the other hand this sets a clear basis for the new objectives dealing with the quality of life included in Article 3(1) EC.

2.1.2   The Means of Achieving These Objectives

The objectives of the Community in Article 2 EC are reasonably clearly formulated, consistent, and adapted to the widely accepted new visions of society and its responsibilities. However, the formulation of the policy-regulatory means of achieving the stated objectives of Article 2 EC is regrettably less clear than the formulation of the old Article 2 EEC. In the latter, two regulatory means were specified: the market ('by establishing a common market') and steering mechanisms ('progressively approximating the economic policies of Member States'). In the well-known terms of Tinbergen's doctrine these correspond to negative and positive integration respectively.[9] Tinbergen defined negative integration as measures consisting of the abolition of a number of impediments to the proper operation of an integrated area; positive integration he defined as the creation of new institutions and their instruments or the modification of existing instruments. The concept of the market is maintained in Article 2 EC as the first means of achieving the Community's objectives, and is reflected in six specific parts of the new text of Article 3(1) EC[10] and in the basic principle of 'an open market economy' mentioned in Article 4 EC. But the second of the two original means has been replaced by 'establishing ... an economic and monetary union and by implementing the common policies or activities referred to in Articles 3 and 4'. Of the remaining means set out in those Articles, the establishment of the EMU is the second principal means of achieving the Community's objectives; the other means can be characterized as more specific forms of common policies or common activities.[11] These specific means are diverse in their regulatory character and extremely diverse in their practical importance.

Article 3 EC has thus at least in the first instance kept its character as a more specific development of the principal objectives specified in Article 2 EC into concrete job descriptions. These are then developed in Part Three of the EC Treaty in twenty-one Titles into provisions which may, depending on their nature and

---

9. J. Tinbergen, *International Economic Integration*, 2nd ed. (Amsterdam, 1965), 76. For application to European law see J. Pinder, 'Positive and Negative Integration: Some Problems of Economic Union in the EEC' (1968) *The World Today*, 88; J. Pelkmans, *Market Integration in the European Community* (The Hague, 1984), 4.
10. I.e., Art. 3(1)(a)–(c) and part of (d) (as far as Art. 61(a) EC is concerned) (g) and (h) EC.
11. Art. 3(1)(d) (as far as Art. 61(b)–(d) is concerned), (e), (f), and (i)–(u) EC.

content, be directly applicable.[12] In so far as the provisions are not directly applicable, they contain provisions for the development of secondary Community law in the form of regulations, directives, decisions, recommendations, opinions or other.[13] Thus substantive Community law is constructed rather as a three-stage rocket: the first stage comprises Articles 2 and 3 (supplemented by 4) EC; the second stage is Part Three of the EC Treaty (as restructured by the TEU), and the third stage is (in most cases) Community secondary legislation. Standing case law[14] makes it plain that in the interpretation of each successive stage of the rocket, due account must be taken of the preceding stages, as well as of the general principles of law, which will be considered below.

In the second place, Article 3 EC, as the reference thereto in Article 2 EC makes plain, is also designed to supplement the two principal means mentioned in Article 2, by providing a large number of specific means for realizing the principal objectives, as mentioned in Article 2.

Article 4 EC complicates still further the interpretation of Articles 2, 3 and 4 EC and their inter-relationship. It is submitted, though, that the correct interpretation of Article 4 is that it should be regarded primarily as building upon the means specified as 'establishing . . . an economic and monetary union' in Article 2 EC. Article 2 EC thus *also* refers to Article 4 EC as a means by which the Community's objectives set out in Article 2 are to be achieved. To this extent Article 4 EC is a clear supplement to the other means specified in Article 3 EC for achieving those objectives. Article 4(1) EC, which deals with the adoption of a Community economic policy, refers only in very general terms to the other means mentioned in Article 3 EC, alongside its own specific element: that the economic policy to be adopted is to be 'based on the close coordination of Member States' economic policies'. Article 4 EC, like Article 3 EC, mixes up objectives and means. It is submitted, though, that the interpretation advanced here precludes any real incompatibility between Article 4 and Articles 2 and 3, even though that may at first sight appear to be the case. The problem is that at first sight it appears that Article 4 EC seeks to achieve the objectives specified in Article 2 EC solely through means of market forces ('conducted in accordance with the principle of an open market economy with free competition'); however, in the interpretation advanced here, that is only the case for policy concerning EMU, as detailed in Title VII of Part Three of the EC Treaty. Article 4 EC leaves ample scope for other policy instruments, within the ambit of the Treaty provisions, in the policy fields

---

12. I.e., that they are binding without any intervention by either the Community Institutions, or national parliaments or administrations, see Ch. VII, section 1, *infra*.

13. I.e., the five legal instruments specified in Art. 249 EC whereby the tasks of the European Parliament and the Council together, the Council, and the Commission are to be carried out.

14. For an early example of this case law, see Case 6/72, *Europemballage Corporation and Continental Can Company Inc. v. Commission*, in which reference was made to the then Art. 3(f) EEC (now Art. 3(g) EC) in order to interpret Art. 86 EEC (now Art. 82 EC). See more recently, e.g., Case C-379/92, *Criminal proceedings against Matteo Peralta*, in which Arts. 3(f) and 7 EEC were discussed in addition to Arts. 30, 48, 52, 59, 62, 84 and 130r EEC in answering the questions referred.

mentioned in Article 3 EC which are not solely aimed at strengthening the market mechanism, such as the common agricultural policy (CAP), employment policy, social policy, and environmental policy. This raises the question to what extent the principle of an open market economy can be seen as a restatement of the first primary means of attaining the Community's objectives, the establishment of a common market, and affecting other Community policies; we discuss this further below. The complexities in the working out of Articles 2, 3 and 4 EC are certainly primarily the result of the fact that Articles 2 and 3 EC now take more express account of non-economic objectives than was the case in the old EEC Treaty.

3   THE LINK BETWEEN THE PRINCIPAL MEANS
           SPECIFIED IN ARTICLE 2 EC AND
           ARTICLES 3 AND 4 EC

3.1   THE LINK BETWEEN ARTICLES 2 AND 3 EC

It is not possible to make a clear substantive link between each of the objectives specified in Article 2 EC and certain policy areas specified in Article 3(1) EC and – with the exception of Article 3(1)(s) EC – worked out in detail in Part Three of the Treaty. All the policy areas mentioned in Article 3(1), as the opening sentence of that provision makes plain, are designed to contribute to the achievement of the Community's objectives set out in Article 2. In some cases, the link between the objectives of Article 2 and the policy areas specified in Article 3(1) is expressly underlined in the implementing provisions in Part Three. Article 159 EC, in Title XVII of Part Three, provides *inter alia* that the Member States must conduct their economic policies and coordinate them in such a way as, in addition, to attain the objectives of economic and social cohesion set out in Article 158 EC. Moreover, Article 159 further provides that the formulation and implementation of the Community's policies and actions and the implementation of the internal market must take into account the objectives set out in Article 158 and contribute to their achievement. Article 159 thereby in fact makes an explicit link between the last objective of Article 2 EC (economic and social cohesion) and all the other objectives mentioned therein. Statistics show, though, that so far the establishment of the internal market[15] has contributed more to the achievement of a harmonious and balanced development of economic activities, a high degree of convergence of economic performance, and economic and social cohesion[16] than have the measures specifically envisaged in Title XVII.[17]

---

15. I.e., liberalization of trade and investments, in accordance with Arts. 3(1)(c) and 14 EC.
16. The first, fifth and eighth objectives mentioned in Art. 2 EC.
17. Only the development of Greece was, in the past at least, an exception. For statistical details, see P. VerLoren van Themaat and N. Schrijver, 'Principles and Instruments for Implementing the Right to Development within the European Community and in the Lomé IV States', in S. Chowdhury et al. (eds), *The Right to Development in International Law* (Dordrecht, 1992), 89.

Articles 174(1) and 177(1) EC are two other examples of the inter-relationship between the objectives in Article 2 EC and most of the policy areas recited in Article 3 EC. They develop the concept of (sustainable) growth[18] as far as the aspects of sustainability and protecting the environment are concerned. Article 174(1) expressly refers to the prudent and rational utilization of natural resources as one of the objectives of the 'policy in the sphere of the environment' mentioned in Article 3(1)(l) EC. Article 177 EC refers to fostering the sustainable economic and social development of the developing countries as the first objective of the policy on development cooperation mentioned in Article 3(1)(r) EC, which is developed in the new Title XX of Part Three of the EC Treaty. Thus Titles XIX (environment) and XX (development cooperation) further elaborate certain aspects of the UNCED objective of sustainable growth.[19] As will become apparent in chapters VIII-XIII of this book, environmental policy in particular makes its influence felt on many of the policy areas mentioned in Article 3 EC. Article 178 EC requires – just as Article 159 prescribes in relation to internal economic and social cohesion within the Community – that in the policies which the Community implements which are likely to affect developing countries account be taken of the objectives referred to in Article 177 EC. On the basis that the greater includes the less, this clearly embraces each part of the policies, not merely the policies as a whole. These objectives include, in addition to sustainable economic and social development of the developing countries, the smooth and gradual integration of the latter into the world economy, just as Article 159 makes equivalent provision in relation to the internal economic and social cohesion within the Community. It is not yet apparent what consequences this will have in areas such as the CAP, industrial policy, and the CCP of the Community.

These three examples do not detract from the strong inter-relationship between the other objectives in Article 2 EC and the other policy areas mentioned in Article 3 EC.[20] Section 4 of this chapter will return to the relationships in the light of policy regulation (taking account of the diversity of means in Article 3 EC).

3.2   THE LINK BETWEEN ARTICLES 2 AND 4 EC

As has already been observed,[21] Article 4 must primarily be seen as a more specific working out of one of the *means* mentioned in Article 2 EC for the achievement of the objectives of the Community, namely the establishment of an EMU. Like Article 3 EC, Article 4 translates the objectives into more specific job descriptions. In relation to the *economic* aspect of EMU, the description in Article 4(1) is restricted to 'the adoption of an economic policy which is based on the

---

18. The 4th and 6th objectives in Art. 2 EC, discussed in section 2.2.1, *supra*.
19. See section 2.2.1, *supra*.
20. Section 2.1.2, *supra*.
21. In section 2.1.2, *supra*.

close coordination of Member States' economic policies'. From the provisions implementing Article 4(1), in particular Article 99 EC, it appears to follow that the economic policy is not primarily conceived in terms of the policy areas mentioned in Article 3 but in terms of the general socio-economic policy of the Member States. Article 99 EC only mentions 'the broad guidelines of the economic policies of the Member States'. However the disappearance of the old chapter heading 'Conjunctural Policy' for Article 103 EEC and of the possibility envisaged in the old Article 103(2) and (3) EEC for compulsory Community-level short-term economic policy measures does not mean that the broad guidelines may not cover short-term economic policy goals as well as more general structural policy objectives. This is confirmed in practice (cf. Ch. X below). Article 100 EC makes it clear that compulsory or other interventionist Community measures (such as the grant of Community financial assistance) can only be adopted exceptionally in the context of the EMU: particularly in the case of severe difficulties in the supply of certain products, but no longer in the context of a general recession. Furthermore, Article 104 EC offers the possibility of imposing in the last resort compulsory sanctions in order to avoid excessive government deficits in the Member States. However, since the coming into force of the TEU, specific stimulus measures, such as those designed to promote new or further employment opportunities[22] and specific Community measures in certain sectors or in specific policy areas outside the cases mentioned in Articles 100 and 104 EC, will have to be based on other Treaty provisions than those dealing with economic policy. Thus there appears to be a clear dividing line between the ambits of Articles 3 and 4 EC, which is consistent with the text of Article 2 EC: global economic policy falls within the scope of EMU; specific economic and social policy in particular fields falls within the ambit of the policy areas enumerated in Article 3 EC or will have to be developed with a legal basis other than those expressly provided for in Articles 3 or 4, such as Article 308 EC which has been retained from the old EEC Treaty. It cannot be deduced from the wording of Article 99(2) EC itself how far the broad economic policy guidelines may relate to specific forms of economic policy. This point is addressed further in Chapter X, below.

Article 4(2) EC provides in the first instance for the irrevocable fixing of exchange rates leading to the introduction of a single currency, the euro. Moreover, it provides for the definition and conduct of a single monetary policy and exchange-rate policy, the primary objective of both of which is to maintain price stability and, without prejudice to that objective, to support the general economic policies within the Community. This general economic policy has just as little legally binding force for the ECB as it has for the Member States. At the end of the day the ECB, according to its Statute, decides independently of

---

22. Such as those decided at the Edinburgh European Council (Bull. EC 12–1992 point I.30) and at the Brussels European Council (with the acceptance of the Commission's White Paper on Growth, competitiveness and employment (COM(93)700 Final), Bull. EC 6/93 point I.3. See further Ch. X *infra*.

any global economic guidelines established either by the European Council or by the Council.[23]

Article 4(3) EC, referring to both monetary and economic policy, provides that these activities of the Member States and the Community 'shall entail compliance with the following guiding principles: stable prices, sound public finances and monetary conditions and a sustainable balance of payments'. These principles are in fact lifted straight from the wording of the old Article 104 EEC, with the addition of 'sound public finances' and the deletion of 'a high level of employment'. The latter objective is included in Article 2 EC; employment policy belongs to the matters mentioned in Article 3 EC (cf. Art. 3(1)(i) EC). The regime developed in Title VIII to that end entails a coordination mechanism which is not legally binding; one cannot speak of a real Community employment policy.

It appears, finally, from the last phrase of Article 4(1) and (2) EC that both the coordination[24] of the Member States' economic policies, and the monetary and exchange-rate policies must be implemented in accordance with 'the principle of an open market economy with free competition'. This seems first of all to confirm that EMU will concern itself primarily with the general socio-economic policies of the Member States, including the avoidance of excessive government deficits, in addition to its monetary and exchange-rate policy functions. Secondly, the principle of an open market economy can scarcely mean anything other than a market economy characterized by a liberal commercial policy, a principle which is noticeably lacking in Articles 2 and 3 EC, although it is fortunately maintained in Article 131 EC. Thirdly, the addition of the words 'with free competition' cannot be interpreted as providing *carte blanche* for policy competition between Member States which in fact distorts competition between them (in particular through state aids, fiscal and social policies), as Articles 3(1)(g)[25] and 87–97 EC, which seek to combat such and other distortions of competition, make plain.

The concrete significance of linking the EMU to the purposes set out in Article 2 EC, which is done in the introductory words of Article 4 EC, is unclear. With the probable exception of the first objective in Article 2 (a harmonious, balanced and sustainable development of economic activities) and the non-inflationary nature of the sustainable growth referred to in the fourth objective, the objectives in Article 2 would appear to have to be achieved primarily through the means set out in Article 3 EC and developed in Part Three of the EC Treaty, although this does not exclude a supplementary, supporting or adjusting role for EMU. This is discussed further in Chapter X.

---

23. See Arts. 8 and 108 EC; ECB Statute, Art. 7. However, without prejudice to the ECB's primary objective to maintain price stability, it is to support the general economic policies in the Community, cf. Art. 105(1) EC and ECB Statute, Art. 2. See, generally, L. Gormley and J. de Haan, 'The Democratic Deficit of the European Central Bank' (1996) EL Rev., 95.
24. Generally not legally binding but not therefore necessarily ineffective.
25. To which Art. 2 EC refers (as part of Art. 3), as it does to Art. 4 EC.

4   THE MEANS FOR ACHIEVING THE OBJECTIVES
                        OF ARTICLE 2 EC

4.1   THE MEANS

On the basis of the wording of Article 2 EC, the division of the means of achieving
the objectives set out therein between Articles 3 and 4 EC and the concrete Treaty
provisions based upon them is clear. Only the means of the establishment of an
EMU is actually developed in Article 4 itself, and then worked out in the concrete
provisions of Title VII of Part Three of the EC Treaty. The two other means
specified in Article 2 EC, the establishment of a common market, and implementing the common policies or activities, which are not covered by Article 4 are dealt
with by Article 3 and the Titles of Part Three of the EC Treaty which are based
thereupon.[26] It is useful both from the viewpoint of determining the type of policy
regulation involved, and for legal practice, to distinguish which of the means listed
in Article 3 form part of the principal means of the establishment of a common
market contained in Article 2. The value of the distinction is apparent because
directly applicable Treaty obligations on the Member States and businesses
(referred to in the Treaty as 'undertakings') in Part Three of the Treaty, which
can be relied upon by private parties before their national courts,[27] occur principally in Treaty provisions dealing with the establishment of a common market
(Art. 141 EC is an exception). In relation to the policy areas mentioned in Article 4
EC, Articles 101–103 EC contain provisions (or prohibitions) which are directly
effective for the Member States themselves. In the other policy areas enumerated in
Articles 3 and 4 EC, directly effective rights and obligations for the Member States
and their subjects are often achieved by means of implementing regulations and
decisions. In other cases, completely directly effective rights and obligations for
the subjects of Member Sates can be achieved at the most by the transposition of
Community *directives* into binding national law.[28] Finally Article 3 also includes
policy areas in which legal instruments, without containing legal obligations to act
in a certain manner, merely promote a certain course of conduct. Examples include
the more or less strict recommendations and opinions, and conditional or unconditional financial incentives granted by the Community.[29] The following section
attempts to achieve a systematic division and characterization of the means set out
in Articles 3 and 4 EC to achieve the objectives specified in Article 2 EC.

---

26. I.e., all the Titles of Part Three except Title VII.
27. I.e., are directly effective. As to the distinction between direct applicability and direct effect,
    see Ch. VII, section 1, *infra*.
28. As to the conditions for direct effect of directives, and the use which may be made of that direct
    effect, see Ch. VII *infra*.
29. See J. Zijlstra, *Politique économique et problèmes de concurrence dans la CEE et les États-
    membres* (CEE études: Série concurrence No. 2) (Brussels, 1966), 39–44. For a brief summary
    of Zijlstra's planning typology, see note 60, *infra*.

4.2   THE FIRST PRINCIPAL MEANS: THE ESTABLISHMENT
             OF A COMMON MARKET

The wording of numerous provisions reveals that the concept of a common market is an essential part of countless obligations imposed by the Treaty.[30] Taking account of the case law, it is evident that the establishment of the common market embraces three aspects in particular: first, the establishment of 'an internal market characterized by the abolition, as between Member States, of obstacles to the free movement of goods, persons, services and capital'[31] secondly, 'a system ensuring that competition in the internal market is not distorted';[32] and, thirdly, a CCP.[33] The CCP marks the distinction between the concepts of a common market and a free trade area, and is necessary to guarantee *inter alia*, also in relation to imports from or exports to third countries, equal or equivalent conditions of competition for undertakings established within the common market. As the Court of Justice has made clear in myriad judgments,[34] the common market referred to in the EC Treaty is analogous in nature to the domestic market of a single state. More extensively defined, again taking the case law into account, the internal aspect of the common market in the sense of the Treaty is a market in which every participant within the Community in question is free to invest, produce, work, buy and sell, to supply or obtain services under conditions of competition which have not been artificially distorted wherever economic conditions are most favourable. The internal aspect of this definition of a common market also embraces more than the concept of an internal market set out in Article 14 EC, which merely speaks of 'an area without internal frontiers in which the free movement of goods, persons, services and capital is ensured in accordance with the provisions of this Treaty'. The element of undistorted competition[35] is absent from that definition. However, in practice, Community case law and legislation on the implementation of Article 14 by Article 95 EC demonstrate that the latter provision may indeed be used for harmonization directives which are aimed at preventing distortions to competition resulting from differences between national legal or administrative provisions of the Member States.[36] This is made possible by the text of Article 95 itself, which refers to measures approximating the laws, regulations or administrative action in Member States having as their object not merely the establishment of the internal market but also its functioning.

---

30. See Arts. 3(1)(h), 32(2), 81(1), 82, 87(1), 94, 96, 97, 119(1), 136, 296, 298 and 308 EC.
31. Art. 3(1)(a) and (c) EC, as further developed in Art. 14 EC and Titles I, III and part of IV (Art. 61(a)), as well as Arts. 94 and 95 of the Third Part of the EC Treaty.
32. Art. 3(1)(g) EC, further developed in Art. 12 and Title VI of Part Three of the EC Treaty.
33. Art. 3(1)(b) EC, further developed in Title IX of the Third Part of the EC Treaty.
34. E.g., Case 270/80, *Polydor Ltd et al. v. Harlequin Record Shops Ltd et al.* and Case 15/81, *Gaston Schul Douane Expediteur BV v. Inspecteur der Invoerrechten en Accijnzen.*
35. Competition under equal competitive conditions, as guaranteed by Arts. 12 and 81–97 EC.
36. E.g., Case C-300/89, *Commission v. Council* (Titanium Dioxide). See also C-376/98, *Germany v. Parliament and Council* (*Tobacco advertising Directive I*).

The emphasis on the fundamental instrumental significance of the common market is to be found not just in Article 2 EC, but also in Article 4 EC. Economic and monetary policies both have to be 'conducted in accordance with the principle of an open market economy with free competition'. The means of the common market is thus also a substantive principle for EMU which, unlike in Article 2 EC, is also proclaimed to be relevant for external economic and monetary policy, and embraces the whole triptych of the elements of the common market concept set out above. One small blot on the landscape is that Article 4 EC erroneously speaks of 'free competition' without also specifying undistorted competition (competition under equal conditions). However, this error has no legal consequences, as Article 4 leaves Articles 2 and 3 EC intact.[37] It is submitted that after correcting this error the Court may well take the view that the principle of an open market economy with free and undistorted competition amounts to an abbreviated restatement of the common market concept, thus embracing, as has already occurred in the case law, 'a system ensuring that competition in the internal market is not distorted' (Art. 3(1)(g) EC). The 'means' thus becomes at the same time a principle.

4.3   THE SECOND PRINCIPAL MEANS: THE ESTABLISHMENT OF AN EMU

Article 4 EC and its implementing Title VII of Part Three EC[38] are to a certain extent bridges between the means of establishing a common market and the means of policy regulation (or steering) which are examined in section 4.4, below. Thus, the chapter on economic policy[39] contains, in addition to the non-legally binding policy steering mechanism of 'broad guidelines' (Arts. 98 and 99 EC), directly effective permanent prohibitory rules (Arts. 101–103 EC).[40] These rules relate to the financial policy of the national central banks and of the Community and central governments, regional, local or other public authorities, other bodies governed by public law, and public undertakings of the Member States. They are clearly of a market economy nature, and fit into the concept of a common market explained in section 4.2, above. Articles 100 and 104 EC also provide for the possibility of compulsory temporary measures to remedy, respectively, severe supply difficulties and excessive government deficits. The steering mechanism of Community financial incentives can also be applied in exceptional cases in accordance with Articles 100 and 104(11) EC, in the form of positive or negative (sanctions) action respectively.

---

37. Other differences in emphasis in the significance of the common market concept in various of the EC Treaty Arts. mentioned in this discussion are dealt with in the relevant parts of Chs. IX-XI, *infra*.
38. Arts. 98–124 EC.
39. Arts. 98–104 EC.
40. Just as is the case with the provisions of the EC Treaty dealing with the establishment and functioning of the common market.

It may be seen from Article 4 EC that, in the final stage of EMU, the focus of monetary policy is on the irrevocable fixing of exchange rates, leading to the introduction of a single currency. Both this central task and the definition and conduct of a single monetary policy and single exchange-rate policy, with as their primary objective the maintenance of price stability, may, in accordance with Article 110 EC also involve the application of steering measures in the form of regulations, decisions, recommendations or opinions adopted by the ECB. In appropriate cases these will take account of the provisions laid down by the Council under Article 107 EC. The primary objective of the European System of Central Banks (ECSB) is the maintenance of price stability.[41] The irrevocable fixing of exchange rates contributes to this primary objective by removing the influence on prices of alterations in exchange rates within the Community. The obligations to conduct general economic policy and monetary policy in accordance with the principle of an open market economy with free competition ensure that these policies will be in conformity with the market.

EMU will thus assure greater stability of the common market economy, and will *inter alia* exclude exchange-rate risks in investment and trade within the Community, and help to prevent macro-economic disturbances of the balance within the Community. In legal terms it can even be argued that monetary union in particular is already covered by the definition of a common market set out in section 4.2, above. Within a single domestic market there are no exchange-rate barriers with the inherent transaction costs in cross-border payments and risks of market disturbances.[42] Accordingly, it is no surprise that businessmen are extremely positive about EMU: it affords more certainty in planning investment, production and sales throughout the entire territory of the common market.

4.4   POLICY REGULATION (STEERING MECHANISMS) IN ARTICLE 3 EC

Of the means specified in Article 3(1) EC, the following also have a steering character to a greater or less extent: (b) a CCP; (d) entry and movement of persons; (e) a common policy for agriculture and fisheries; (f) a common transport policy; (h) the approximation of laws; (i) the coordination of employment policies; (j) a policy in the social sphere; (k) strengthening economic and social cohesion; (l) environmental policy; (m) strengthening competitiveness of Community industry; (n) promotion of research and technological development; (o) encouragement for the establishment and development of trans-European networks; (p) contributing to the attainment of a high level of health protection; (q) a contribution to education and training of quality and to the flowering of the cultures of the Member

---

41. Arts. 4(2) and 105(1) EC; Art. 2 ECSB Statute.
42. See, generally, P. VerLoren van Themaat, 'The Relations Between the Concepts of a Common Market, a Monetary Union, an Economic Union, a Political Union and Sovereignty' (1991) CML Rev., 291 (writing before the text of this part of the TEU was agreed).

States; (r) a policy in the sphere of development cooperation; (s) the association of the overseas countries and territories; and (t) contributing to the strengthening of consumer protection. However, market economy principles are never entirely excluded in these areas and in, for example, the common transport policy they play an ever increasing part.

In certain areas ((b)–(l) and (p), (s) and (t) mentioned above) this steering character may encompass compulsory intervention by means of regulations, directives or sometimes implementing decisions; in some cases ((k) and (l)) this effect may result from the interaction with other policy areas.

In respect of the areas covered by Article 3(1)(m)–(o) EC the only available measures are financial measures or other measures which do not compel particular conduct but act as an incentive to pursue certain conduct. Article 3(1)(r) EC on development cooperation may additionally be implemented by multi-annual programmes, for which express provision is made in Article 179 EC, by coordination of Community and Member States' policies, in accordance with Article 180 EC, and by cooperation with third countries and the competent international organizations, under Article 181 EC.

The provisions implementing Article 3(1)(p) and (q) EC, dealing with the sensitive areas of education, vocational training and youth, culture, and public health,[43] seem primarily aimed at maintaining national sovereignty over non-commercial aspects of policy in those areas (the final part of each of these provisions makes this evident). Harmonization of national laws or regulations of the Member States is expressly excluded, whether completely or partly (public health).[44] Even the very weak instrument of recommendations in the field of cultural policy can only be adopted by unanimity.[45] Only incentive measures are provided for:[46] these may include financial incentives and other facilities to assist in the achievement of the non-commercial objectives set out in these provisions.

All the policy-regulation mechanisms set out in Article 3(1) are further developed in the relevant Titles of Parts Three and Four of the EC Treaty, save the matters covered by Article 3(1)(u) EC, namely measures in the spheres of energy, civil protection and tourism. These are purely programmatic in nature. According to the first Declaration attached to the Final Act of the Treaty of Maastricht, the Intergovernmental Conference which concluded the Amsterdam Treaty would examine whether new Titles for these fields should be included in the EC Treaty. The latter did not occur. In the absence of relevant amendments, other areas of Part Three of the EC Treaty, or even Article 308, if the pertinent conditions are met, may of course be applied in these policy areas.

---

43. Respectively, Arts. 149 and 150; 151; and 152 EC.
44. Arts. 149–152 EC (last paragraph in each case).
45. Arts. 151(5) EC (2nd indent).
46. Arts. 149(4); 151(5), and 152(4) EC (1st indent in each case).

4.5   THE RELATIONSHIP BETWEEN THE ESTABLISHMENT OF A COMMON MARKET, THE ESTABLISHMENT OF AN EMU, AND THE POLICY-REGULATION MECHANISMS SET OUT IN ARTICLE 3 EC

4.5.1   Policy Areas of a Predominantly Market Economy Nature

These policy areas of Article 3 EC were discussed in section 4.2, above, dealing with the establishment of a common market.

4.5.2   The Specific Policy-Regulatory Character of EMU

While, as has been submitted in section 4.3, above, Article 4 EC and Title VII of part Three of the EC Treaty on the establishment of an EMU are primarily steering measures, they are designed to operate in accordance with the market. None of the economic and monetary policy instruments developed in those provisions may affect the principle of an open market economy with free competition.

4.5.3   Policy Areas with Policy-Regulation (Steering) Mechanisms

It may well be, though, that the remaining steering mechanisms dealt with in section 4.4, above, may have a greater or less effect on the open market economy principle with free competition. The CCP and immigration policy[47] may also involve restrictions on access from third countries to the common market. As is well known, the common agricultural and fisheries policies[48] embrace obligations which are even strongly restrictive of competition and aid measures which distort competition for market participants, in order to achieve the goals set out in Article 33 EC. Nevertheless, even here, Article 32(2) EC makes it clear that the rules for the establishment of the common market apply, unless there is an express derogation from them.[49] The common transport policy[50] has in practice become much more in conformity with the market, thus more liberal, partly on account of Article 71 EC and the action by the Parliament to force liberalization in the transport sector.[51] The conditions of competition in the transport sectors in the various Member States can be extensively harmonized by means, above all, of harmonization measures in the social and fiscal spheres. There is, though, not nearly such a far-reaching market organization as in the agricultural and fisheries sectors. Unlike in the latter sectors, transport is not normally subject to malleable, repeatedly

---

47. Art. 3(1)(b) and (d) EC respectively.
48. Art. 3(1)(e) EC.
49. See also Joined Cases 80 & 81/77, *Société Les Commissionaires Réunis SARL et al. v. Receveur des Douanes*, and Case C-114/96, *Criminal proceedings against Kieffer and Thill*.
50. Art. 3(1)(f) EC.
51. Case 13/83, *European Parliament v. Council*.

changing market conditions, but to more permanent rules of market conduct which are thus more in conformity with the market, although there are temporary arrangements for the transition to a more strongly liberalized transport market.

Harmonization of laws, social policy, environmental policy, the association of overseas countries and territories, as well as health and consumer protection policy[52] may also lead to permanent binding rules of conduct, although in the latter three cases the steering measures may also be rather different in nature.

The remaining steering mechanisms in Article 3 EC[53] provide for either no or hardly any possibility of adopting binding rules affecting market behaviour; they are largely confined to the instruments of financial incentives and other facilities or incentive measures.

4.5.4   Further Comments on the Nature of the Three Means

In the implementing provisions in Part Three of the EC Treaty relating to the policy fields which have clearly non-economic objectives, namely culture, public health and consumer protection, it is made clear that account must be taken of these non-economic objectives in other areas of Community policies.[54] As mentioned earlier, similar so-called integration provisions exist for the promotion of equality between men and women (Art. 3(2) EC) and the protection of the environment (Art. 6 EC). The specific policies in some of these areas may not be achieved by harmonizing laws and regulations of the Member States.[55] To the extent that Article 3 EC also envisages more or less far-reaching steering mechanisms which are not in conformity with the market in order to achieve economic objectives, certain guarantees are always included in the implementing Treaty provisions; these ensure that competition can never be entirely prevented by these steering mechanisms, and may not be more distorted than is necessary for the achievement of the relevant goals. The question of the extent to which the principle of proportionality, laid down in Article 5 EC, is of legal importance in examining the necessity for such distortion is examined later in this chapter (see section 6.3 below). For the time being, suffice it to say that binding rules of market conduct are certainly liable to lead to more restriction of competition than state aids, as the latter virtually never completely exclude competition, even though they may considerably distort the conditions of competition for certain undertakings or groups of undertakings, and may artificially prolong the life of undertakings or industries which would not really be viable in a pure market economy. State aids will normally only obtain Community approval in particular market circumstances, on the basis of the special

---

52. Art. 3(1)(h), (j), (l), (p), (s) and (t) EC and the relevant implementing provisions in Parts Three and Four of the EC Treaty.
53. Art. 3(1)(i), (k), (m), (n), (o), (q) and (r) EC.
54. Art. 151(4) EC (culture); Art. 152(1) EC, last sentence (health); Art. 153(2) EC (consumer protection).
55. Education and vocational training (Art. 149(4) and 150(4) EC); culture (Art. 151(5) EC); public health, but here with some exceptions (Art. 152(4)(c) EC).

grounds specified in Article 87 EC, which are mostly of a temporary nature, and subject to ever more stringent conditions.

4.5.5 The Far-Reaching Economic Neutrality of the Treaty As Regards Its Economic System

Community policy regulation (steering) has gradually become more important over the years. Through the now virtually complete liberalization of free movement of goods, capital, labour and services, and of the right of establishment in other Member States for undertakings and the self-employed, it becomes ever more necessary to coordinate or even merge economic intervention by Member States. National market regulation becomes pointless if it can no longer be safeguarded against disturbances originating abroad. The EC Treaty thus had to provide for a common policy in the two sectors, agriculture and transport, which are regulated in all the Member States. Autonomous application of incidental market-regulatory measures in other sectors of trade and industry[56] is possible only subject to considerable self-restraint, lest the measures infringe the Treaty or be simply ineffective. Even the effectiveness of broader autonomous economic or monetary policy measures will decrease sharply because of the spreading of their effects throughout the common market.[57] Thus the expansionist budgetary policy of Mitterrand's regime in France during 1981–1982 led primarily to an increase in imports and with it a significant deficit in the balance of trade. Conversely, a successful counter-inflationary policy became increasingly dependent on the price of goods imported from other Member States. In the diminishing effectiveness of autonomous national economic and monetary policies and the increasing mutual dependence in an ever increasing number of policy areas lay the justification for, in turn: a common agricultural, transport and (external) commercial policy in the old EEC Treaty; the introduction of the European Monetary System in 1978; the gradual introduction of an EMU and the facilitation of a stronger Community social policy through the changes brought about by the TEU, and, a year later, at the European Council in Edinburgh in December 1992, the instigation of coordinated Community and national approaches to restoring growth and employment opportunities.[58] The increasing recognition of the importance of a coordinated environmental policy found its own justification in the cross-border nature of a large proportion

---

56. E.g., ministerial validation (and extension to all producers) of competition rules, price regulations and restrictions on expansion or contraction of capacity adopted by private regulatory bodies in the sectors. Such practices occur particularly in the Netherlands and France.

57. See J. Zijlstra, op. cit. *supra* note 29, 39–44, in which the effects of the four freedoms on, successively, wages, prices, interest rates, taxation, budgetary, structural and competition policies are discussed. While the correctness of his conclusions was then not yet generally accepted, it is nowadays. The link between the achievement of the common market and the possibility of national policy regulation is more extensively discussed in the WRR report No. 28, *De onvoltooide Europese integratie* (The Hague, 1986), 34–38, published in English as *The Unfinished European Integration* (The Hague, 1986), 34–38.

58. Bull. EC 12–1992, points I.8 and I.30.

of environmental questions. As the new text of Article 2 EC, the environment title, and the new title on development cooperation all recognize, environmental policy may also have a significant effect on internal and external economic policy.

Even after the amendments made by the Treaties of Maastricht and Amsterdam, it still follows from Articles 2, 3 and 4 EC and Part Three of the EC Treaty that the determination of the relative weight of market economy means, on the one hand, and policy regulation which may more or less conform to market principles, on the other, is left to the political decision-making process in the European Council and the Community institutions which shape Community policies, subject to review by the Court of Justice. Provided that the unity of the common market and the maintenance of sufficient effective competition are ensured, the steering measures taken by the Community Institutions for the attainment of the objectives laid down in Article 2 EC may very well be strengthened.[59] To this extent the Treaty remains largely neutral as far as the choice of economic system is concerned.

However, a number of comments should be added.

First, Article 4 EC clearly prescribes that (general) economic and monetary policy must conform to the market. Thus the general economic policy in the context of EMU will have to be confined to the lightest of Zijlstra's types of economic planning, types I and II, and possibly type III.[60] The use of financial incentives in the sense of his types IV and V will have to take place in the context of the policy areas mentioned in Article 3 EC. Monetary union may also result in binding provisions (economic planning type VI), which are necessary for its proper functioning. While the old list of more interventionist policy areas has been maintained, Article 3 has principally been expanded with policy areas in which lighter steering measures (recommendations, facilities and financial assistance measures) may be applied. The most important exceptions are the strengthening of the social dimension, environment policy and consumer protection policy. Just as in the areas in which there are common policies, so in these three areas binding measures can be adopted, as well as lighter steering measures, albeit that the binding measures, where Article 95 EC is unused in these contexts, are principally in the form of coordination directives which will be binding on citizens only after transformation into national law.

---

59. See J. Mertens de Wilmars in *Miscellanea Ganshof van der Meersch*(Brussels, 1972), 285 and P. VerLoren van Themaat, *Economic Law of the Member States of the European Communities in an Economic and Monetary Union*, EEC Studies: Competition Approximation of Legislation Series No. 20 (Brussels, 1973).

60. J. Zijlstra, op. cit. *supra* note 29, 32–33. For a summary of Zijlstra's planning types see P. VerLoren van Themaat, 'Competition and Planning in the EEC and the Member States' (1970) CML Rev., 311–314. Very briefly stated, planning type I contains only prognoses, type II quantitative assignments for macro-economic government policy, type III adds non-binding assignments for trade and industry. Type IV contains in addition unconditional and type V conditional incentives for trade and industry to act in accordance with the assignments. Planning type VI adds the instrument of coercive rules. Beyond a given degree of application this last type leads to a predominantly centrally planned economy. As to the limited importance of Zijlstra's planning typology for monetary union, see Ch. X, *infra*.

Secondly, and importantly, the degree to which steering mechanisms can be employed in practice will depend on the effectiveness of the composition, competence and working methods of the policy-making Community Institutions: the Commission, the Council and the Parliament. The Treaty of Amsterdam made a number of changes, especially in the light of the (then) forthcoming enlargement. At present, it is not certain whether these changes will be sufficient to enable the Institutions, even after further enlargement of the number of Member States, to adopt the adjustments necessary in view of the results of the open market economy to achieve the objectives specified in Article 2 EC. Such results will be the inevitable consequences of the compulsory rules and measures laid down in or under the Treaty for the establishment of a common market. The adoption of the necessary adjustments, however, depends on an effective institutional structure and on the political will of the Member States.

Thirdly, the principles of subsidiarity and proportionality laid down in Article 5 EC are of importance for the further development of the economic system of the Community. These matters are discussed in section 6, below.

In legal terms, the question of the desirable European economic system can be translated into the question of the desirable relationship between the substantive legal principles of freedom, equality and solidarity.[61] Taking a global view, the five freedoms[62] and the freedom of competition guaranteed by Articles 3(1)(g), 4 and 81 EC correspond to the principle of freedom. The various prohibitions of discrimination and other provisions of the Treaty which aim to ensure equal competitive conditions (such as the declaration of incompatibility of state aids with the common market under Art. 87 EC, and to some extent the harmonization provisions in Arts. 93–97 EC) correspond to the principle of equality. However, the growth in mutual dependence caused by the five freedoms also requires solidarity and cooperation in the solution of problems which in the past would have been solved by the Member States separately. In the past, national governments could use import and export regulations to prevent their interventions being rendered ineffective by international spillover. Since the completion of the common market, even national measures to combat the backwardness of less-favoured regions (national regional policy, which features in all the Member States) will often no

---

61. See P. VerLoren van Themaat, 'Het economisch grondslagenrecht van de Europese Gemeenschappen', in Boes et al., *Liber Amicorum Mertens de Wilmars* (Antwerp/Zwolle, 1981), 355–383 and literature cited there. As explained there (at 379), the basic economic freedoms are supported within the Community by principles of equality (e.g., Arts. 12 and 90 EC), although some substantive variants of the principle of equality (such as reducing the differences in prosperity between the various regions) can only be realized on the basis of the principle of solidarity. See also P. VerLoren van Themaat in K. Hellingman (ed.), *Europa in de steigers: van Gemeenschap tot Unie* (Deventer, 1993), 121. See also P. Allott, 'The Crisis of European Constitutionalism: Reflections on the Revolution in Europe' (1997) CML Rev., 439. In general on the so-called economic constitution of the Community, see literature mentioned at the end of this chapter.

62. I.e., free movement of goods, persons, services, capital and payments, and establishment discussed in Ch. VIII, *infra*.

longer be successful without contributions under the Community policy favouring economic and social cohesion (Community regional policy). Moreover, the policy of economic and social cohesion, in an analogous manner to national regional policy, also seeks to reduce the disparities between regions in the different Member States. Unlike the principles of freedom and equality, which are largely guaranteed in the EC Treaty itself, the principle of solidarity in fact has to be filled in by secondary legislation, even though it finds its legal basis in the Treaty itself (Cf. Arts. 2 and 158 EC).

5   THE TIMETABLE FOR THE ESTABLISHMENT OF THE
               COMMON MARKET

Save for the exceptions or derogations provided for in the Treaty, the expiry of the transitional period (which took place on 31 December 1969) constituted, in accordance with the then Article 8(7) EEC,[63] the latest date by which all the rules laid down in the Treaty had to enter into force and all the measures required for establishing the common market had to be implemented. In the course of the 1970s and the beginning of the 1980s, it became ever more apparent, though, that the hundreds of measures of secondary law necessary to complete the common market could not be adopted in time without some improvement in the decision-making process in the context of a new tight time schedule. In particular, there was a huge backlog in the liberalization of financial services and capital movements, as well as of transport, and in the numerous harmonization measures which were necessary in order to remove the barriers to trade which could, in the absence of such measures, be justified under Treaty exceptions relating to the classic four freedoms, such as Article 30 EC.

On the basis of the Commission's White Paper *Completing the Internal Market*,[64] which envisaged the adoption of some 300 measures within a tight timetable, the old EEC Treaty.was amended, in order to facilitate the completion of this most important element of the common market, by the Single European Act (SEA), which came into effect on 1 July 1987. It proved possible more or less to execute this programme by the end of the period envisaged by the Commission, namely 31 December 1992. A new Article 8a EEC (now Article 14 EC) was included in the Treaty in order to anchor the new timetable firmly. The definition of the internal market which had to be completed was set out in this article as 'an area without internal frontiers in which the free movement of goods, persons, services and capital is ensured in accordance with the provisions of this Treaty'. Article 14(1) EC provides that the measures to progressively establish the internal market were to be adopted 'over a period expiring on 31 December 1992', in accordance with the new and amended Treaty provisions and without prejudice

---

63. Later renumbered 7(7) EC, and since the Treaty of Amsterdam repealed.
64. COM(85)310 Final.

to the other provisions of the Treaty. As the measures which had to be taken were not clearly specified in advance, it would be difficult for automatic legal consequences to result if they were not adopted by that date, as had occurred in the case law on primary Treaty provisions concerning the five freedoms, on the basis of the then Article 8(7) EEC.[65] In a Declaration on Article 8a EEC, by the Intergovernmental Conference attached to the Final Act noting the adoption of the SEA, it was stated that setting the date of 31 December 1992 did not create an automatic legal effect. Case law later confirmed this.[66]

The most important gap in the completion of the internal market which still remained when the time limit of 31 December 1992 was reached, concerns the abolition of controls on persons at the internal borders. The Treaty of Amsterdam set a new term of five years for this, ending in 2003 (cf. Art. 61 under (a) EC). At the same time, protocols attached to this Treaty implicitly limited the concept of the internal market pursuant to Article 14 EC, insofar as the United Kingdom and Ireland may maintain border controls at the internal borders. However, the abolition of border controls on persons has now largely been achieved between the Member States belonging to the Schengen area (see Ch. VIII, section 4 below).

Insofar as the adoption of any adjustments was made a precondition in the Treaty for the establishment of the common market, they should have been adopted before the end of the transitional period (at the end of 1969), in accordance with the last part of old Article 8(7) EEC. This principally concerned the common agricultural, fisheries, transport, and external trade policies, as well as the programme of harmonization directives for which the new time limit of 31 December 1992 was set by the SEA. The adjustment measures relating to these common policies, which are by their very nature versatile, will, unlike the internal market, never be complete. The same is true of other areas of intervention, such as environment and social policy, which are not expressed as preconditions for the establishment of a common market. They will continually have to be adjusted to take account of changing situations and perceptions. The CAP is the clearest example of this. Of course, the Treaty provisions and secondary law relating to the establishment and proper functioning of the common market also have to be maintained and where necessary further developed even after the perceived completion of the internal market.

6   SOME FUNDAMENTAL PRINCIPLES OF THE TREATIES

This section is devoted to a number of fundamental principles which are applicable within the legal system of the EU and the EC. The fundamental nature of these principles is apparent *inter alia* from the fact that they are contained in the initial provisions of the EU Treaty or the EC Treaty (or both). The primary aim of these

---

65. E.g., Case 2/74, *Jean Reyners v. Belgian State*; Case 33/74, *Johannes Henricus Maria van Binsbergen v. Bestuur van de Bedrijfsvereniging voor de Metaalnijverheid.*
66. Case C-378/97, *Criminal proceedings against Florus Ariël Wijsenbeek.*

principles is to regulate the action of the Institutions; these are therefore principles of institutional law (principle of conferred powers, of subsidiarity, of proportionality, of loyal cooperation – to the extent this applies to relations between the Institutions – and the principle of transparency or openness). The principle of loyal cooperation (the duty to cooperate) acquires a more substantive character to the extent it is also directed at Member States. The principle of equality, in both its forms, in Articles 12 and 13 EC, directed both at Member States and at the Institutions, is also more substantive in character. This last principle is also recognized in the case law of the Court as one of the general principles of Community law.

6.1   THE PRINCIPLE OF CONFERRED POWERS

This principle, frequently called the principle of attributed powers, or sometimes simply the principle of attribution, expresses the fact that the European Union and the EC only enjoy powers which they have been granted ('conferred' or 'attributed') by the founding Treaties (and the Treaties amending these). These powers may be very extensive, also given the sometimes vague description in the relevant Treaty provisions and the interpretation of these provisions by the Court of Justice, but they are ultimately limited to what the Treaties authorize. Neither the Union nor the EC have the power to determine the scope of their own powers (so-called *Kompetenz-Kompetenz*). If they wish to extend or alter their powers, this requires a Treaty amendment according to the relevant procedure provided for in Article 48 TEU.

The principle of conferred powers is not mentioned as such in the Treaties, but it is clearly expressed, in particular in Article 5 TEU, in Article 5(1) EC (the Community 'shall act within the limits of the powers conferred upon it by this Treaty and of the objectives assigned to it therein') and in Article 7(1) EC.[67] The Court of Justice implicitly accepted this principle already in its early case law, for instance in *Van Gend en Loos*.[68] Undeniably, in its later case law, the Court of Justice has been generous and open to the functional and dynamic character of the integration process in its approach to the interpretation of conferrals of powers contained in the Treaties, in particular by accepting the existence of implicit, derived powers.[69] More recent case law, in particular the *Tobacco advertising* judgment of 6 October 2000,[70] reveals a change of direction in this context.

---

67. See moreover for the European System of Central Banks and the European Central Bank, Art. 8 EC, and for the European Investment Bank, Art. 9 EC.
68. Case 26/62, *NV Algemene Transport- en Expeditie Onderneming van Gend & Loos v. Netherlands Inland Revenue Administration*: '. . . that the Community constitutes a new legal order of international law for the benefit of which the States have limited their sovereign rights, albeit within limited fields'.
69. See Ch. IV, section 6 *infra*.
70. Case C-376/98, *Germany v. Parliament and Council* (*Tobacco advertising*). Cf. also the earlier Opinion 2/94 on the possibility of accession of the EC to the European Convention on Human

From this judgment it is evident that the political will of the Community legislature to use a particular treaty-based power for a certain objective is not sufficient, and that the Court takes its responsibility as constitutional court to supervise the limits of powers, in other words respect for the principle of conferred powers, very seriously.

More concretely, the principle of conferred powers entails that every decision aiming to have legal consequences must explicitly refer to its legal basis, i.e., the treaty provision where the power to take the decision in question may be found (or in case of exercise of a delegated competence, the provision of secondary law which provides for the delegated competence).[71] Moreover, the exercise of the power in question must in all cases be justified in the statement of reasons of the decision, in order to make the choice of legal basis amenable to legal review by the Court of Justice. In that context, the Court does not accept the subjective opinion of the Institution in question, but requires objective elements, in particular in relation to the aim and content of the decision, in order to be able to review the choice of legal basis.[72]

6.2 THE PRINCIPLE OF SUBSIDIARITY

In the core second paragraph of Article 5 EC the principle of subsidiarity is mentioned as the general canon for the practical allocation of tasks in cases in which concurrent or parallel competence of the Community and its Member States exists. This is remarkable in a number of respects. First, the subsidiarity principle originates in Catholic social doctrine, having been authoritatively laid down in the Papal Encyclicals *Quadragesimo Anno* in 1931 and *Pacem in Terris* in 1963. It is thus exclusively concerned with the relationship between the state and society, the relationship between the public authorities, citizens, families and intermediate organizations. In its origin it thus has no relevance for relationships between the different territorial administrative layers of a state, even within a federal state. Secondly, while in countries such as Italy and Portugal before the Second World War the principle was used to justify the central authority's grasp on society in a corporatist state structure, experience in Germany[73] and in the United States

---

Rights. See too Joined Cases C-317 & 318/04, *European Parliament v. Council (EC-US Agreement on Passenger Name Records PNR)*.

71. As an exception to this rule, the Court has only accepted the circumstance that the legal basis is sufficiently clearly indicated in the statement of reasons, cf. Case 45/86, *Commission v. Council (Generalized tariff preferences)*.

72. Cf. Case 45/86, *Commission v. Council* (Generalized tariff preferences) and Case C-300/89, *Commission v. Council* (Titanium Dioxide). See also more generally on the problem of legal basis Van Ooik, *De keuze der rechtsgrondslag voor besluiten van de Europese Unie* (Deventer, 1999); H. Cullen and A. Charlesworth, 'Diplomacy by Other Means: The Use of Legal Basis Litigation as a Political Strategy by the European Parliament and Member States' (1999) CML Rev., 1243–1270.

73. Where Art. 72 of the *Grundgesetz* (Basic Law) served as an important positivist example in the drafting of Art. 5 EC.

shows that it does not hinder the gradual strengthening of the powers of the central authority if this is justified by changed circumstances or perceptions.[74] Thirdly, and most importantly, in discussions about the relationship between states and international organizations, as here, the classic principle of sovereignty and its development is of far greater importance than the principle of subsidiarity, as above all the discussions in Denmark, France and the United Kingdom during the ratification procedure for the TEU made clear yet again.[75] The European Communities are still to be regarded as international organizations *sui generis*.[76] Their particular nature is expressed *inter alia* in certain analogies with federal structures. It seems dubious whether the principle of subsidiarity as such can form a useful new legal guarantee against an unjustified expansion of Community competences, and this for three reasons: first, the ideological origins of the principle of subsidiarity, which do not seem to be accepted by a majority in all the present or even likely future Member States; second, the completely different sphere of application of the principle; and, thirdly, the experiences of federal States and international organizations.[77] This said, it is now appropriate to turn to a brief legal analysis of the principle.[78]

The Treaty on European Union mentions the principle of subsidiarity explicitly in the Preamble and the Common Provisions of Title I, but refers to Article 5 EC for the description of the principle (cf. Art. 2 TEU). This means, at the very least, that the principle applies also to the European Union as such. The second paragraph of Article 5 EC is crucial in terms of the legal significance to be attached to the principle:

> In areas which do not fall within its exclusive competence, the Community shall take action, in accordance with the principle of subsidiarity, only if and

---

74. As to the first two observations, see further, P.J. Kapteyn in K. Hellingman (ed.), op. cit. note 61, supra, 41–44, and Geelhoed 'Het subsidiariteitsbeginsel: een communautair principe'? (1991) SEW, 422, who deals in particular with the German and American experiences. See also G.A. Bermann, 'Taking Subsidiarity Seriously: Federalism in the European Community and the United States' (1994) Colum.L.Rev., 331; id., 'Regulatory Federalism: European Union and United States' (Academy of International Law, The Hague), 263; *Recueil des Cours* 13, 1997.
75. S. Weatherill opined that the principle reflects concern about the scope of Community competence and its demarcation from national competence, but does little in practical terms to address that concern, cf. *Law and Integration in the European Union* (Oxford, 1995), 172.
76. A number of constitutions of the Member States, make provision for the relations with international organizations, which thereby include the EU, rather than referring to the EU specifically, e.g., Dutch Constitution (Art. 92); see C. Kortmann and L. Prakke (eds), *Constitutional Law of 15 EU Member States* (The Hague, 2004). See also P. VerLoren van Themaat, 'A neo-classical approach for the coming IGC' (1995) CML Rev., 1319.
77. Cf. also C. Durand, vol. 1 of the authoritative *Commentaire Mégret* (J.E. de Cockborne, L. Defalque, C.F. Durand, H. Prahl, G. Vandersanden, Brussels, 1992) which reaches the conclusion, after extensive analysis, that from a legal perspective the principle does not necessarily lead to different results as compared to the previous situation.
78. As to the background to and drafting of the principle of subsidiarity, see J. Cloos et al., *Le Traité: de Maastricht*, 2nd ed. (Brussels, 1994), 141–151. See further K. Lenaerts and P. van Ypersele, 'Le principe de subsidiarité et son contexte: étude de l'article 3 B du Traité CE' (1994) CDE, 3, with references to other literature and case law, and the reports for the 1994 FIDE congress in Rome. See list of further reading at the end of this chapter.

insofar as the objectives of the proposed action cannot be sufficiently achieved by the Member States and can therefore, by reason of the scale or effects of the proposed action, be better achieved by the Community.

On the basis of our introductory remarks, above, it is our opinion that the reference in this text to 'the principle of subsidiarity' does not provide any clarifications which could be useful in the process of judicial review of the other elements in this paragraph. It is clearly a political principle, which can be used both to justify and to oppose Community action In both instances, recourse must be had to the other elements in Article 5(2) EC in order to support the standpoint concerned. Before looking into that, a preliminary remark should be made. In the general discourse the principle of subsidiarity is often invoked to support arguments that the Community lacks the competence to deal with a certain matter e.g., penal law. However, this principle cannot play any role in the adjudication as such of competences. Its role is much more modest: it only governs the question of whether an existing Community competence can or should be exercised or not. Article 5(2) must be read together with Article 5(1). The principle of subsidiarity can only come into play once it has been established that a competence has been conferred on the Community at all.

Of the other elements mentioned in Article 5(2), it is primarily the concept of 'exclusive competence' which lends itself to more precise definition through case law. It is incontrovertible, on the basis of the case law, that such exclusive Community competence already exists primarily in the field of the CCP and in relation to matters of external economic relations where a transfer of competence has occurred in the internal Community sphere (see Ch. XIII, below). It is submitted that the competence conferred on the Community in relation to EMU is also by its very nature exclusive in character. In the policy areas of agriculture, fisheries and transport the case law appears to indicate that, despite the common policies provided for, Community competence is often far-reaching, but exclusiveness is not unbounded. In the fields of Community competition policy and harmonization of laws, too, it is not always clear to what extent the undeniable powers conferred on the Community have a real exclusive effect, and to what extent they merely lead to the primacy of primary and secondary Community law over national laws which are incompatible with such Community law.[79] The Court of Justice (whether immediately, or on appeal from the Court of First Instance) will gradually have to shed light on the legal significance of the term 'exclusive competence' on the basis of the general and specific objectives, and conferrals of competence in and pursuant to the EC Treaty.[80]

---

79. Community competence in the field of merger control is at least in part clearly exclusive in nature, as is explained in Ch. IX of this book; the powers in relation to Arts. 81 and 82 EC, though, are more of a guaranteed competence, which does not exclude the competence of the Member States, although Community law takes precedence over any incompatible national legal action. The Community power to control state aids, conferred by Arts. 87–89 EC is, however, exclusive in nature.

80. See for an extensive discussion of this concept on the basis of the case law, Lenaerts and van Ypersele, op. cit. *supra* note 78. It can be deduced from Case C-377/98, *Netherlands v.*

In practice it seems that Article 5(2) EC will in the meantime be important in the areas of obvious concurrent or parallel competence of the Community and the Member States. In areas in which exclusive competence (as this concept is clarified by the case law) is allocated to the Community, or, alternatively, where the Community has no competence at all, Article 5 EC is irrelevant.

The question remains, however, of the meaning of the limitation on Community competence in the remaining fields: '[T]he Community shall take action . . . only if and in so far as the objectives of the proposed action cannot be sufficiently achieved by the Member States and can therefore, by reason of the scale or effects of the proposed action, be better achieved by the Community.'

It may be recalled that the celebrated economist Jan Tinbergen developed the valuable theory of the optimal level of decision-making.[81] Under this theory, decisions with external effects (i.e., decisions affecting third parties) should be taken at a sufficiently high level that external effects outside the sphere of legal competence of the decision-making level can be neglected. Kapteyn has observed that this doctrine is remarkably compatible with a provision in the German Basic Law[82] which is comparable to Article 5 EC.[83] In accordance with Article 72(II)(2) GG, the German Federation acts in cases where the regulation of a particular matter by a piece of legislation enacted by a *Land* could harm the interest of other *Länder* or the people as a whole ('*die Gesamtheit*'). Moreover, the Tinbergen theory rightly emphasizes that the Community must be able to act in matters of a cross-border nature or with important cross-border consequences, which the Member States cannot control, either because of the principle of territoriality, or because their policy is exclusively determined by their own national interests. Thus Belgium, France or Germany have less interest in acting to combat pollution of the Meuse, the Moselle or the Rhine caused within their frontiers to the extent that, because of the location of the polluter concerned, the pollution has

---

Parliament and Council (biotechnological inventions) and Case C-491/01, *The Queen v. Secretary of State for Health, British American Tobacco (Investments) Ltd and Imperial Tobacco Ltd* (Tobacco labelling Directive) that the ECJ does not wish to accord exclusivity to the harmonization competence under Art. 95 EC, since in both cases the Court tests the exercise of this competence against the principle of subsidiarity. In relation to exclusivity of external competence see also Case C-471/98, *Commission v. Belgium*, Case C-466/98, *Commission v. United Kingdom*; C-467/98, *Commission v. Denmark;* C-468/98, *Commission v. Sweden;* C-469/98, *Commission v. Finland;* C-472/98, *Commission v. Luxemburg;* C-475/98, *Commission v. Austria;* C-476/98, *Commission v. Germany (Open skies judgments).*

81. See J. Tinbergen, *International Economic Integration*, 2nd ed. (Amsterdam, 1965), 58 and literature cited there. See also J. Tinbergen et al., *Reshaping the International Order: A Report to the Club of Rome* (New York, 1976), 86. J. Tinbergen, Naar een rechtvaardiger internationale orde, (RIO-rapport) (Amsterdam, 1977), 86.

82. The *Grundgesetz* (GG), Art. 72 deals with concurrent legislative competence. Art. 30 GG provides that: 'Except as otherwise provided or permitted by this Constitution, the exercise of governmental powers and the discharge of governmental functions is incumbent on the States [Länder].' Thus, like the Community, the Federal level in Germany operates on the basis of attributed powers.

83. P.J.G. Kapteyn, op. cit. *supra* note 74, 44.

serious consequences primarily for the Netherlands; and the Netherlands has no legal possibility of effectively acting to combat such pollution. Similar observations can be made about cross-border cartel arrangements or mergers.

In fact with the present degree of interdependence of the interests of the Member States, so many national laws and other policy measures have external effects for other Member States that a literal application of the theory of the optimal decision-making level would lead to a far-reaching centralization of powers at the Community level. Hence the importance of the words 'sufficiently' and 'better' in the text of the second paragraph of Article 5 EC: they make possible a political balancing of the interests and possibilities of the Member States individually on the one hand, and the Community as a whole on the other. The emphasis placed in that provision on not merely the effects of the proposed action but also on its scale makes it plain that the financial or economic scale of a given operation will also be decisive. The application criteria contained in Article 5 EC thus appear to leave a considerable freedom of discretion to the politically responsible Community Institutions. If in the reasoning of the positive or negative decision concerned it is stated that a Community objective is or is not involved, and moreover that Community action is or is not more effective than action by each of the Member States separately (or possibly by some of them acting together) it will be difficult to challenge successfully the result of that balancing of interests before the Court. Kapteyn has rightly observed[84] that on the basis of the words 'sufficiently' and 'better' due attention must be paid in the political balancing process to other values or interests than effectiveness in the technocratic sense, such as the interest of decision-making as close as possible to the citizens.[85] Accordingly, he rightly concluded that examination by the Court of the conclusions reached by the Community's political Institutions in the light of the second paragraph of Article 5 EC will only be of a marginal nature. The first cases to come before the Court where application of this principle has been at issue support this conclusion. The Court shows great reluctance to conduct a full review of the decision of the Community legislature as to the necessity for it to act.[86] The Court, however, does require that the view of the Community legislature on both elements of the subsidiarity test (the inadequacy of national action and the advantage of Community action) should be evident and should be explained in the statement of reasons.[87]

---

84. Kapteyn op. cit. *supra* note 74, 48.
85. 'Decisions are taken as closely as possible to the citizen', Preamble TEU.
86. Case C-84/94, *United Kingdom v. Council* (working time Directive), Case C-376/98, *Germany v. Parliament and Council* (Tobacco Advertising Directive), C-377/98, *Netherlands v. Parliament and Council* (biotechnological inventions), Case C-491/01, *The Queen v. Secretary of State for Health, British American Tobacco* (Tobacco labelling Directive) and Joined Cases C-154 & 155/04, *The Queen v. Secretary of State for Health* (Directive on Food Supplements). See also C.W.A. Timmermans, 'Is het subsidiariteitsbeginsel vatbaar voor rechterlijke contrôle'? (2007) SEW, 224–230. This article is an update of the contribution by the same author ('La justiciabilité de la subsidiarité'), to the Liber Amicorum for Judge Claus Gulmann, *Festskrift til Claus Gulmann* (Kopenhagen, 2006), 449.
87. Case C-233/94, *Germany v. Parliament and Council* (deposit-guarantee schemes) and Case C-377/98, *Netherlands v. Parliament and Council* (biotechnological inventions).

Quite apart from the possibility and intensity of judicial review in relation to the principle of subsidiarity, it should be mentioned that the Community Institutions do make a real effort to give the principle of subsidiarity real content, and to make sure that it is respected. This is apparent from, for instance, the so-called SLIM operation, a multi-annual programme aiming to simplify Community legislation.[88] In addition, in 1993 already, the European Parliament, the Council and the Commission concluded an inter-institutional agreement in order to put into practice the application of this principle in the legislative process.[89] The Treaty of Amsterdam took over the content of this Agreement more or less unchanged in a Protocol attached to the EC Treaty, so that it acquired primary law status.'[90] The predominantly political character of the principle of subsidiarity is implicitly confirmed by this Protocol, which describes the principle as 'a guide as to how [the powers conferred on the European Community by the Treaty, as interpreted by the Court of Justice] are to be exercised at the Community level', and as 'a dynamic concept'. 'It allows Community action within the limits of its powers to be expanded where circumstances so require, and conversely, to be restricted or discontinued where it is no longer justified.' The Protocol, which also concerns the principle of proportionality (discussed in the next section), requires the Commission to state, for any proposed Community legislation, the reasons justifying its compliance with the principle of subsidiarity, and in particular supporting the conclusion that a Community objective can be better achieved by the Community, providing qualitative or, wherever possible, quantitative indicators. It is worth noting that the Protocol does not require such a specific statement concerning the implementation of a subsidiarity test for the final act itself.

The Constitutional Treaty granted national parliaments particular rights with regard to the review of EU legislative proposals for respect of the subsidiarity principle. If a negative opinion were to be expressed by a minimum number of national parliaments, the proposal would have to be reconsidered but could be maintained, provided reasons are given. The Lisbon Treaty will further reinforce these rights of national parliaments, without however allowing them to veto the adoption of a proposal (Art. 12 TEU (Lisbon) and Protocol on the application of the principles of subsidiarity and proportionality).

6.3   THE PRINCIPLE OF PROPORTIONALITY

The third paragraph of Article 5 EC applies both in fields in which the Community possesses merely concurrent powers (with the Member States) and in fields in which it has exclusive powers. It thus constitutes a supplement to the principle

---

88. Council of the EU, Single Market Action Plan, CSE (97)1; Communication of the Commission: Implementing the Lisbon Programme: A Strategy for the Simplification of the Regulatory Environment (COM/2005/535).
89. Bull. EC 1993, no. 10, 125.
90. Protocol on the application of the principles of subsidiarity and proportionality.

of subsidiarity developed in the second paragraph of Article 5 EC: a supplement which has a different character and which applies to each and every action of the Community. It is expressed thus: 'Any action by the Community shall not go beyond what is necessary to achieve the objectives of this Treaty.'[91]

The principle of proportionality has been developed as a general principle of law in the case law of the Court of Justice, and continues to be developed in that case law in more and more areas.[92] As a general legal principle, it also applies to the legal order of the Union, in particular in the field of PJCCM. According to its text, the principle of proportionality contained in the third paragraph of Article 5 EC primarily relates to the *degree of intervention* in national legislation or national policy. In addition, though, in the light of Articles 2, 3, and 4 EC it also concerns the legal nature of the *means* used to achieve the general or particular objectives of the Treaty.[93] Thus not only could the principle lead to more frequent mutual recognition of legal acts of other Member States, and the establishment of minimum requirements; it could also justify the use of recommendations instead of legally binding Community measures, or of directives instead of regulations. The latter tendency, a preference for directives rather than regulations, is explicitly expressed in the Protocol on the application of the principles of subsidiarity and proportionality mentioned in the previous section (6.2). Moreover, the great emphasis which Articles 2, 3, and 4 EC place on the market economy principle should justify an interpretation of Article 5 EC in the sense that no more far-reaching interference in the market mechanism is permissible than is necessary to achieve the objectives of the EC Treaty. In addition to giving priority to measures which do not compel a particular course of action, the principle of proportionality could lead to preference for Community financial contributions supporting national policies, rather than for steering measures involving conditional financial assistance linked to a particular course of conduct, or even to preference for either of these means of assistance in the place of directives or regulations. Even in directives or regulations it would be possible to prefer less far-reaching intervention in the free-market rather than more direct intervention in matters such as prices, production and investment. It may be useful to recall in this connection that Articles 5 and 57 European Coal and Steel Community (ECSC) already expressly provided for such an order of preference in favour of the least far-reaching measures of intervention in production and the market. In the EC Treaty too, a great many examples of such an approach are evident as a result of the amendments to the old EEC Treaty introduced by the TEU.[94] Both the more free-market

---

91. K. Lenaerts and P. van Ypersele op. cit. *supra* note 78, at point 78 rightly point out that the term 'objectives of this Treaty' means the *relevant* objectives of the Treaty for the action concerned. See also their discussion of the case law on proportionality at points 78–81.

92. See for two recent analyses of the application and the development of this principle in the case law T. Tridimas, *The General Principles of EC Law*, 2nd ed. (Oxford 2006), 136 et seq., and P. van Nuffel, *De rechtsbescherming van nationale overheden in het Europees recht*, Europese Monografieën No. 64 (Deventer, 2000), 295 et seq.

93. In the same sense, C. Durand, op. cit. *supra* note 77, 429–430.

94. These matters are discussed elsewhere in this book, where substantive Community law is dealt with, e.g., Ch. XI.

developments in recent years in the field of transport policy, a field in which the text of the EC Treaty would permit a more interventionist approach, and the recent reforms in the CAP, demonstrate that a principle of less intervention is steadily gaining ground. It is thus perfectly likely that the Court of Justice in its future case law will interpret Article 5 EC as meaning that clear reasoning will usually be necessary in order to justify the necessity for more detailed legal instruments, or for stronger means of intervention in the market mechanism. Exceptions to this requirement would of course apply in the cases in which the EC Treaty itself already prescribes the use of specific means.

Finally, Article 5 EC also appears to be important for regulating the day-to-day implementation of Community policy. The principle of preference for directives rather than regulations, as already applied in the implementation of Article 95 EC,[95] means that the Community seeks to leave the implementation of the Community measures concerned to the Member States as much as possible, including the legal or administrative details of that implementation. The execution of the common customs tariff and of the CAP is also largely left to the Member States, to name but two areas in which Community law provides for detailed rules or far-reaching intervention in the operation of the market.

The most important areas of policy in which the Community Institutions themselves are charged with the day-to-day execution on the basis of the Treaty provisions are: competition law, on the basis of Articles 81–89 EC; anti-dumping policy, in the context of the CCP; and a number of safeguard provisions in primary or secondary Community law in various areas, which can only be applied at the request of Member States or interested private parties. In all these instances, it is impossible to leave the administrative execution in the fields involved to the Member States, because of the cross-border nature of the facts concerned, or their cross-border consequences, or the cross-border nature of the objectives which have to be examined (such as cross-border distortions of competition). The unsatisfactory action so far to combat fraud and evasion in the areas of the CAP and customs law make it clear that the criminal law territoriality principle, and the sometimes scant national financial loss as a result of fraud in the purely national execution of Community law, may endanger significant Community interests (including financial interests).[96] Even when the provisions to be implemented are extremely detailed, they do not always successfully prevent such risks to Community interests.

To conclude: the principle of proportionality, as set out in the third paragraph of Article 5 EC, can be seen as a general principle of law whose scope is now sufficiently clear – through numerous provisions of the EC Treaty and the case law – to be confident about the manner in which the Court of Justice will utilize it in the examination of Community action, always taking account of the margin of discretion permitted to the Community Institutions by primary or secondary Community law. In particular, as far as the non-economic objectives in the general

---

95. See the Declaration on Art. 100a EEC annexed to the Final Act of the SEA.
96. See Ch. V, section 3.3, *infra* on the protection of Communities financial interests.

interest, recognized in the Treaties or the case law, are concerned, we submit[97] that this conclusion means that the balancing cannot relate to anything other than the means by which it is sought to achieve the policy objectives thus recognized. On the basis of the analysis of Articles 2, 3, 4 and 5 EC advanced in this chapter, both the principle of subsidiarity and the principle of proportionality would seem to relate solely to the means of achieving particular objectives, not to the evaluation of the objectives themselves. In Articles 2 and 4 EC, the market economy is also a means, not an objective. Even in the examination of policy measures in the light of contradictory policy objectives set out in the Treaties, which have to be achieved simultaneously, such as in the field of agriculture, or coal and steel policy, the Court has always been very reticent in its case law, leaving the Community Institutions a wide margin of discretion.

A general conclusion could be that the preceding analysis of Article 5 seems to imply that the principle of proportionality contained therein could potentially – and certainly in legal terms – provide a more effective guarantee against too much and too detailed regulation from 'Brussels' than the principle of subsidiarity.

6.4   THE PRINCIPLE OF LOYAL COOPERATION

6.4.1   General Observations

The principle of loyal cooperation – also called Community loyalty (or solidarity) – is laid down in Article 10 EC. That Article contains two positive obligations for Member States and one negative: first, to take all appropriate measures, whether general or particular, to ensure fulfilment of the obligations arising out of the EC Treaty or resulting from action taken by the Community Institutions; secondly, to facilitate the achievement of the Community's tasks; and, thirdly, to abstain from any measures which could jeopardize the attainment of the objectives of the Treaty. The important supplementary significance of these obligations, alongside the myriad more specific obligations contained in the EC Treaty, has become more than clear from the case law. The concrete effects of these three obligations are further developed in conjunction with the obligations and objectives established in other Articles of the Treaty or in secondary legislation.[98] To this extent a parallel can be drawn with the specific obligation, phrased in similar terms, in Article 86(1) EC. Thus, for example, Article 10, or Article 86(1) for the cases falling within its scope, prohibits Member States from enacting or maintaining in force any measure which would support infringements of Article 81 EC by undertakings. Moreover, case law indicates that Article 10 links rights for individuals to

---

97.   In agreement with J. Jans, 'Evenredigheid: ja, maar waartussen'? (1992) SEW, 751–770; id., 'Proportionality Revisited' LIEI 2000/3, 239; 'Evenredigheid revisited' (2000) SEW, 270–282.
98.   See, e.g., already Case 78/70, *Deutsche Grammophon Gesellschaft mbH v. Metro-SB-Grossmarkte GmbH & Co. KG*; for an example of a resolution making specific the duty of -cooperation under Art. 5 EC, see Case 141/78, *France v. United Kingdom*.

the infringement by Member States of their obligations in other instances, such as the failure to transpose directives into national provisions on time or correctly.[99]

Due and Durand have proposed a structure for analysing the extensive case law on Article 10 EC which seems more useful than a division according to the three obligations explicitly specified in the Treaty. For the analysis of the case law which follows, we take as starting point the division made by Durand, which accords with that of Due, with some changes.[100]

6.4.2   The First Positive Obligation in Article 10 EC

6.4.2.1   The Obligation to Take All Appropriate Measures Necessary to Ensure the Effective Application of Community Law

It is unnecessary to allege an infringement of Article 10 EC in infringement proceedings under Articles 226 or 227 EC, where the primary infringement alleged relates to a specific provision of primary or secondary Community law.[101] In particular the far-reaching and complex common organizations of the agricultural markets require extensive supplementary general or particular national provisions, regulatory, budgetary, administrative and organizational, and provisions imposing sanctions and facilitating remedies, in order to ensure that the obligations arising from the EC Treaty or the Community action concerned are indeed fulfilled.[102] However, examples of such requirements stemming from Community law are far from confined to the agricultural sector, and the case law embraces examples from *inter alia* the sectors of equal treatment for men and women;[103] protection of

---

99.   Joined Cases C-6 & 9/90, *Andrea Francovich et al. v. Italian Republic* and Joined Cases C-46 & 48/93, *Brasserie du Pêcheur SA et al. v. Germany et al.*

100.   O. Due, 'Artikel 5 van het EEG-Verdrag, een bepaling met een federaal karakter'? (1992) SEW, 355; in greater detail, Durand op. cit. *supra* note 77, 26–42. See further the detailed analysis by J. Temple Lang in his general report for the XIXth FIDE Conference in Helsinki in 2000, as well as the national reports for this conference and the supplementary contribution by J. Temple Lang as a result of the discussions at the conference, 'The Duties of Cooperation of National Authorities and Courts under Article 10 EC: Two More Reflections' (2001) EL Rev., 84.

101.   O. Due, op. cit. *supra*, mentions Case C-48/89, *Commission v. Italy*, concerning the obligation to provide information. However, a failure to respond to letters from the Commission in relating to an alleged breach of Community law could be added to the substantive infringement complained of when the letter constituting formal notice is sent, and can be the subject of a specific finding of a failure by a Member State to fulfil its obligations, even if the substantive infringement alleged has not been proved, see, e.g., Case 240/86, *Commission v. Greece*. See, further, Ch. VI, section 2.1, infra.

102.   From the myriad examples, including those cited by O. Due (op. cit. *supra* note 100), C. Durand (op. cit. *supra* note 77) and by M. Zuleeg, in H. v.d. Groeben and J. Schwarze (eds), *Kommentar zum EWG-Vertrag*, (Baden-Baden, 2004), 668–678, see, e.g., Case 39/72, *Commission v. Italy*; Case 30/72, *Commission v. Italy*; Case 394/85, *Commission v. Italy*; Case C-8/88, *Germany v. Commission*; Case 68/88, *Commission v. Greece*.

103.   E.g., Case 14/83, *Sabine von Colson and Elisabeth Kamann v. Land Nordrhein-Westfalen*; Case 222/84, *Marguerite Johnson v. Chief Constable of the Royal Ulster Constabulary*; Case C-271/91, *M.Helen Marshall v. Southampton and South West Hampshire Area Health Authority.*

employees on the transfer of undertakings;[104] the free movement of goods;[105] the free movement of workers and the right of establishment;[106] transport;[107] public procurement,[108] and the environment.[109]

The obligation applies to the legislative and the executive, as well as the judicial organs of the State. An important example of the supplementary obligations for the national courts is the obligation to interpret national law in conformity with the provisions of directives, which can also be of importance in cases between private parties.[110] Moreover, the obligation covers all levels of government: central, regional or local.[111] In particular, insofar as local and regional organs enjoy autonomous powers, serious problems may arise in the practical enforcement of the respect for Community obligations. One may think of the autonomous regions in Spain or Italy, or the German *Länder*, or the Belgian autonomous regions and communities.[112] The responsibility in Community law and in public international law of a Member State also embraces responsibility for the respect of Community law by any independent policy pursued by its various territorially decentralized authorities.[113] The Member States may not, therefore, use the internal division of competences as an excuse for infringing Community law. In our opinion, then, the obligation discussed in this section entails an obligation for the Member States to take the necessary legal, administrative, or even constitutional steps to ensure that such responsibility is given effect internally.[114]

---

104. E.g., Case C-382/92, *Commission v. United Kingdom*.
105. Case C-265/95, *Commission v. France* (Spanish strawberries).
106. E.g., Case 222/86, *Union nationale des entraîneurs et cadres techniques professionnels du football (Unectef) v. Georges Heylens et al.*; Case C-340/89, *Irène Vlassopoulou v. Ministerium für Justiz, Bundes- und Europaangelegenheiten Baden-Württemberg*.
107. E.g., Case C-326/88, *Criminal Proceedings against Hansen &Soen I/S*; Case C-7/90, *Criminal proceedings against Paul Vandervenne et al.*
108. E.g., Case 31/87, *Gebroeders Beentjes BV v. The Netherlands*.
109. E.g., Case C-56/90, *Commission v. United Kingdom*.
110. See, e.g., Case 125/88, *Criminal proceedings against H. F. M. Nijman*; Case C-106/89, *Marleasing SA v. La Commercial Internacional de Alimentacion SA*; Joined Cases C-397/01 to C-403/01, *Bernhard Pfeiffer et al. v. Deutsches Rotes Kreuz, Kreisverband Waldshut eV,*. See further Ch. VII, section 1.5.3.
111. E.g., Case 103/88, *Fratelli Costanzo SpA v. Comune di Milano*; Cf. on the problem of application of Community law by local and regional authorities the inaugural lecture by B. Hessel, *Bouwen aan een stad in Europa* (Utrecht, 1999), and the literature cited therein. See also P. van Nuffel, 'What's in a Member State? Central and Decentralized Authorities before the Community Courts' (2001) CML Rev., 829–870.
112. E.g., Case C-8/88, *Germany v. Commission*.
113. E.g., Joined Cases C-46 & 48/93, *Brasserie du Pêcheur SA et al. v. Germany*.
114. E.g., Case C-8/88, *Germany v. Commission*. See, in relation to Belgium, F. van Ingelaere, 'De Europeesrechtelijke raakvlakken van de nieuwe wetgeving inzake de internationale betrekkingen van de Belgische Gemeenschappen en Gewesten' (1994) SEW, 67–82, and also J. Gerards, 'Naleving van het Europese recht door de decentrale overheden: naar een herzien stelsel van toezicht' (2000) SEW, 208–215.

6.4.2.2   *The Obligation to Ensure the Protection of Rights Stemming from Primary and Secondary Community Law*

This obligation, ensuring judicial protection for individuals in the application of Community law, should, it is submitted, be distinguished from the obligation to take all appropriate measures necessary for the attainment of the substantive objectives of the Treaty. In relation to directly effective primary or secondary Community law, this obligation is principally directed at national courts.[115] The Court has now clarified the duties of the national courts to give additional or interim relief or to impose (effective) sanctions to reinforce protection of individuals.[116] The celebrated judgments in Cases C-6 and 9/90 *Francovich*[117] and subsequent case law[118] are most important because – unlike in the *Rewe* case – they offer individuals a potentially very effective means of judicial protection in the form of damages for loss suffered through the failure to transpose Community directives on time or correctly, and through a serious infringement of Community law by any branch of government, even including the judiciary.[119] As has now been stated in a number of cases, with references to earlier case law, the obligation to ensure an adequate degree of judicial protection implies that the national legislatures must ensure the availability of proper rights of appeal (substantial and procedural rules) in relation to all relevant Community rights.[120] These obligations in the area of judicial protection will be discussed extensively and in a broader framework in Chapters VI and VII of this book.

---

115. As was already demonstrated in Case 33/76, *Rewe-Zentralfinanz eG et Rewe-Zentral AG v. Landwirtschaftskammer für das Saarland.*
116. See Case C-213/89, *The Queen. v. Secretary of State for Transport, ex parte: Factortame Ltd et al.*; Joined Cases C-6 & 9/90, *Francovich et al. v. Italy*; Joined Cases C-46 & 48/93, *Brasserie du Pêcheur*; Case C-392/93, *The Queen. v. H.M. Treasury, ex parte British Telecommunications plc*; Case C-5/94, *The Queen. v. Ministry of Agriculture, Fisheries and Food, ex parte: Hedley Lomas (Ireland) Ltd*, Case C-432/05, *Unibet (London) Ltd, Unibet (International) Ltd v. Justitiekanslern.*
117. Joined Cases C-6 & 9/90 *Francovich.*
118. Especially Joined Cases C-46 & 48/93 *Brasserie du Pêcheur.*
119. The conditions established in *Brasserie du Pêcheur* and applied in later judgments are discussed in extenso in Ch. VII, section 4, *infra*. See, in relation to the judiciary, Case C-224/01, *Köbler v. Austria.*
120. Case 61/79, *Amministrazione delle finanze dello Stato v. Denkavit Italiana*; Case 68/79, *Hans Just I/S v. Danish Ministry for Fiscal Affairs*; Case 811/79, *Amministrazione delle finanze dello Stato v. Ariete SpA*; Case 199/82, *San Giorgio*; Case 104/86, *Commission v. Italy*; Case 222/86, *Heylens*. See, further, Case C-312/93, *Peterbroeck, Van Campenhout & Cie SCS v. Belgian State*; Joined Cases C-430 & 431/93, *Jeroen van Schijndel et al. v. Stichting Pensioenfonds voor Fysiotherapeuten*; see also Case C-453/00, *Kühne and Heitz NV v. Productschap voor Pluimvee en Eieren*; Joined Cases C-392 & 422/04, *i-21 Germany GmbH (C-392/04), Arcor AG & Co. KG (C-422/04), formerly ISIS Multimedia Net GmbH & Co. KG v. Germany.*

6.4.2.3   *The Obligation to Act (Themselves) to Achieve the Objectives of the Treaty, in Particular in the Case of Inaction by the Competent Community Institution*

Good examples of the effect of this obligation can be found in the case law concerning the obligation on the Member States to take account of equivalent diplomas from other Member States when deciding on permitting nationals of another Member State to establish themselves in a professional capacity, in the absence of the Community directives envisaged in Article 47 EC.[121]

As case law from the 1980s reveals, this obligation also involves the obligation to take temporary national measures of 'positive integration',[122] where the competent Community Institution has failed to act as it should have acted, for instance, in the area of conservation measures for fish stocks, and their termination as soon as Community measures have been enacted.[123]

6.4.3   The Negative Obligation on the Member States to Abstain from Any Measure That Could Jeopardize the Attainment of the Objectives of the Treaty

It is convenient to adopt the threefold approach of Durand in order to clarify the scope of this obligation.[124]

6.4.3.1   *The Obligation to Abstain from Measures Which Could Impede the Effectiveness of Community Law*

In this connection both Durand and, more extensively, Due[125] pay particular attention to what Due calls the 'corporatist tendencies' in a number of Member States, revealed through state measures which support agreements which are restrictive of competition and incompatible with Article 81 EC, such as measures declaring the provisions of a private agreement to be generally binding, or equivalent measures. A spectacular example of this can be seen in *Ahmed Saeed Flugreisen*.[126]

---

121. As both Durand (op. cit. *supra* note 77, 32. and Due (op. cit. *supra* note 100, 358) observe. E.g., Case 71/76, *Jean Thieffry v. Conseil de l'ordre des avocats à la Cour de Paris*; Case C-340/89, *Irène Vlassopoulou v. Ministerium für Justiz, Bundes- en Europaangelegenheiten Baden-Württemberg*, and Case C-55/94, *Reinhard Gebhard v. Consiglio dell'Ordine degli Avvocati e Procuratori di Milano*. See, further, Ch. VIII, *infra*.
122. In Tinbergen's terms, see note 9, *supra*.
123. See Case 32/79, *Commission v. United Kingdom (Sea fisheries conservation measures)*; Case 325/85, *Ireland v. Commission*; Case 326/85, *Netherlands v. Commission*; Case 332/85, *Germany v. Commission*; Case 336/85, *France v. Commission*.
124. C. Durand, op. cit. *supra* note 77, 35–39.
125. C. Durand, op. cit. *supra* note 77, 35, O. Due, op. cit. *supra* note 100, 359–369.
126. Case 66/86 *Ahmed Saeed Flugreisen et al. v. Zentrale zur Bekämpfung unlauteren Wettbewerbs e.V.*

The Court found, in the context of tariff fixing in the air transport sector, that Article 10 EC (and, within its limited scope, Art. 86 EC) precluded the national authorities from encouraging the conclusion of agreements incompatible with Articles 81 or 82 EC, as the case may be, and from approving the tariffs resulting from such agreements, unless[127] those measures were indispensable for the performance of a task of general interest which the air carriers were required to carry out, provided that the nature of that task and its impact on the tariff structure were clearly established. However, such a link between Articles 10 and 81 or 82 cannot be made if there is no conduct by the undertakings involved which is itself incompatible with Articles 81 or 82. Thus, the mere fact that the authorities themselves prescribe price regulations or other measures restrictive of competition will not infringe Article 10 EC,[128] even though the measures may well come into conflict with other provisions of the Treaty, such as Article 28 EC.[129]

6.4.3.2   The Obligation to Abstain from Measures Which Could Hinder the Internal Functioning of the Community Institutions

Suffice it here to mention an example from a judgment of 1983. The Court stated that when the governments of the Member States made provisional decisions on the seats of the Community institutions they were obliged, in particular by Article 10 of the Treaty, to 'have regard to the power of the Parliament to determine its internal organization'.[130]

---

127. In the cases covered by Art. 86(2) EC.
128. See in that respect Case C-2/91, *Criminal proceedings against Wolf W. Meng*; Case C-185/91, *Bundesanstalt für den Güterfernverkehr v. Gebrüder Reiff GmbH & Co. KG.*; Case C-245/91, *Criminal proceedings against Ohra Schadeverzekeringen NV*; Case C-35/96, *Commission v. Italy*. In Case C-379/98, *PreussenElektra et al. v. Land Schleswig-Holstein*, a joint application of Arts. 10 and 87 EC was refused. At issue was a measure granting aid which could not be reviewed under Art. 87 EC, because the financial advantage pursuant to a minimum price was not financed from State funds, but by private companies. The Court rejected the Commission's application to test the measures against the Treaty rules on state aids using Art. 10 EC. See also Case C-35/99, *Arduino v. Compagnia Assicuratrice* and Joined Cases C-94 & 202/04, *Cipolla v. Rosaria Fazari, née Portolese et al.*
129. As to which, see Ch. VIII, section 3, *infra*.
130. Case 230/81, *Luxembourg v. European Parliament*, para. 37. See also Case 108/83, *Luxembourg v. European Parliament*; Joined Cases 358/85 & 51/86, *France v. European Parliament*, and Joined Cases C-213/ 88 & 39/89 *Luxembourg v. European Parliament*. The European Parliament never accepted the decision made on the allocation of seats during the Edinburgh European Council meeting in Dec. 1992, O.J. 1992, C 341/1. See R. Corbett et al., *The European Parliament*, 3rd ed. (London, 1995), 36. A Protocol on the location of the seats of the institutions was attached to the Treaty of Amsterdam See also Chapter II, section 5.3, *supra*.

6.4.3.3   *The Obligation to Abstain from any Measures Which Could Hinder the Development of the Community Integration Process*

A number of illustrations of the effect of this obligation may be given.[131] First, Member States must abstain from acting in cases where a Community measure is in preparation.[132] Another example concerns the duty on Member states to abstain from entering into agreements with third countries which affect rules which the Community has already adopted on the matter in question.[133] Moreover, in this context mention should be made of the obligation on Member States to refrain from measures which seriously endanger the realization of a result prescribed by a Directive during the implementation period for that Directive.[134] More in general, it should be born in mind that precisely because the final paragraph of Article 10 EC refers to the objectives of the Treaty, and not to concrete legal obligations, the case law on this point may well evolve further.

6.4.4   Article 10 EC As an Expression of the General Principle of Mutual Cooperation

The case law on Article 10 EC is based, as both Due and Durand observe, on the underlying *general legal principle* of mutual cooperation.[135] The case law reveals that this may be divided into four specific sets of relations: first, an obligation on national authorities and the Community institutions to cooperate with each other; secondly, a mutual assistance obligation on the Member States, thirdly, an obligation on the Community institutions to cooperate sincerely with the Member States, and fourthly an obligation of sincere cooperation between the Community institutions themselves.[136] While the mutual nature of these obligations, and the obligations on the Community institutions, are not immediately apparent from the wording of Article 10 itself (which, after all, is addressed to the Member States),

---

131. Durand, op. cit. *supra* note 77, 138.
132. Case 804/79, *Commission v. United Kingdom* (fisheries conservation), Case C-266/03, *Commission v. Luxembourg* and Case C-433/03, *Commission v. Germany*. This is certainly clear where a Commission proposal is under discussion in the context of implementing a common policy (such as agriculture, fisheries or transport. See also Dec. 3052/95 (O.J. 1995, L 321/1) on information exchange); however it is possible that outside these areas, the submission of a Commission proposal, or the mere commencement of the preparation of a proposal does not entail an obligation for the Member States (Case 174/84, *Bulk Oil (Zug) AG v. Sun International Ltd et al.*).
133. Case 22/70, *Commission v. Council* (ERTA).
134. Case C-129/96, *Inter-Environnement Wallonie ASBL v. Région wallonne*.
135. See C. Durand, op. cit. *supra* note 77, 39–42; Due op. cit. *supra* note 100, 363 et seq.
136. See Declaration 3 adopted with the Treaty of Nice, on Art. 10 EC, which states: 'The Conference recalls that the duty of sincere -cooperation which derives from Article 10 of the Treaty establishing the European Community and governs relations between the Member States and the Community institutions also governs relations between the Community institutions themselves.'

the case law of the Court becomes logical if Article 10 is itself seen as a specific expression of a more general principle.

The first of the four elements may be illustrated by the obligations on the Member States to cooperate *bona fide* with the Commission in any inquiry which the latter undertakes, and to supply the Commission with all the information requested for that purpose;[137] to consult the Commission before adopting measures which could affect a Community field,[138] and to consult the Commission in the case of difficulties in implementing Community acts (particularly in relation to state aids). Thus if, in giving effect to a decision, a Member State encounters unforeseen and unforeseeable difficulties, or perceives consequences which it feels the Commission has overlooked, it has to submit the problems to the Commission, with proposals for amendment of the decision concerned.[139] Case 94/87, *Commission v. Germany*, illustrates particularly the mutual character of the duty of cooperation between the Member States and the Community institutions, in the following terms:

> In such a case the Commission and the Member State concerned must respect the principle underlying Article [10] of the Treaty, which imposes a duty of genuine cooperation on the Member states and the Community institutions, and must work together in good faith with a view to overcoming difficulties whilst fully observing the Treaty provisions, and in particular the provisions on aid.[140]

The second type is vividly illustrated by Durand using the judgment in *Matteucci*.[141] The Court interpreted Article 7 of Regulation 1612/68[142] as meaning that the Belgian authorities were not entitled to deny an Italian national, who had been born and educated in Belgium, where her father was employed, the benefit of a scholarship to pursue studies in Germany on the ground that scholarships under a Belgo-German cultural agreement were exclusively for Belgian nationals. Article 10 EC meant that if the application of a provision of Community law was likely to be impeded by a measure adopted pursuant to a bilateral agreement, even where that agreement fell outside the field of application of the Treaty, every Member State was under a duty to facilitate the application of the provision of Community law concerned, and, to that end, to assist every other Member State which was under an obligation in Community law. Another clear recent example of this type

---

137. An example given by C. Durand op. cit. *supra* note 77, on 39. See, e.g., Case 192/84, *Commission v. Greece*.
138. C. Durand op. cit. *supra* note 77, 40. E.g., Case 186/85, *Commission v. Belgium*, and Case 141/78, *France v. United Kingdom*. See also Case C-459/03, *Commission v. Ireland* (MOX plant).
139. Case 94/87, *Commission v. Germany*.
140. Ibid., para. 9. See C. Durand op. cit. *supra* note 77, 40 and Due op. cit. *supra* note 100, 365. See also, e.g., Case C-348/93, *Commission v. Italy*, and Case C-349/93, *Commission v. Italy*.
141. Case 235/87, *Annunziata Matteucci v. Communauté française of Belgium et al.* Another example of far-reaching duties is Case C-293/03, *Gregorio My v. Office national des pensions (ONP)*.
142. O.J. 1968, L 257/2.

of mutual assistance obligation, but now in relation to social security payments to migrant workers, can be seen in *Athanasopoulos*.[143] In a wholly different field, the concepts of mutual assistance and mutual confidence have played an important role in the area of free movement of goods, so that Member States must, for example, take account of technical or chemical analyses or laboratory tests carried out in other Member States.[144] The obligation of mutual assistance among the Member States is also supported by the promotion of solidarity among Member States, which is the last of the Community's tasks specified in Article 2 EC.

The third category, the obligation on the Community institutions towards the Member States, is probably most clearly illustrated in the Order in *Zwartveld*.[145] Here, the Court obliged the Commission to give its active assistance to national legal proceedings in which the national court, hearing a case on alleged infringements of Community rules on sea fisheries, requested the production of Commission inspectors' reports and the attendance of Commission officials to give evidence, insofar as this was necessary for the preliminary investigation.[146]

Finally, pursuant to the principle of Community loyalty, it is apparent that the institutions are also under an obligation of loyal cooperation towards each other (the fourth category), which is confirmed by Declaration No. 3 adopted with the Treaty of Nice.[147]

6.4.5 A Principle of Union Loyalty

As mentioned above, the principle of loyal cooperation is also called the principle of Community loyalty. If one considers that principle as a general principle of the Community legal order, then arguably, given the close link between the Community and the Union, a similar principle should be accepted within the Union legal order. This is supported by the fact that the Union Treaty itself already contains an explicit provision – though only in relation to the CFSP – in which obligations are laid down for the Member States to cooperate loyally with one another and with the Union, whose content is similar to that of the principle of Community loyalty (Art. 11(2) TEU). Supervision of compliance with these obligations in the framework of

---

143. Case C-251/89, *Nikolaos Athanasopoulos et al. v. Bundesanstalt für Arbeit*.
144. O. Due, op. cit. *supra* note 100, 365. E.g., Case 132/80, *NV United Foods et al. v. Belgian State*; Case 272/80, *Frans-Nederlandse Maatschappij voor Biologische Producten*. See, further, Ch. VIII, *infra*.
145. Case C-2/88 Imm., *Zwartveld*.
146. O. Due, op. cit. *supra* note 100, also mentions in this context the judgment in Case C-234/89, *Stergios Delimitis v. Henninger Bräu AG*, following the same line. Here too it is stressed that, pursuant to Art. 10 EC, the Commission is under an obligation of loyal cooperation with the judicial bodies in the Member States before which cases are pending; this was in the field of the competition rules under Arts. 81 and 82 EC. See also Case C-94/00, *Roquette Frères v. Directeur général de la concurrence, de la consommation et de la répression des fraudes*.
147. Declaration on Art. 10 of the Treaty establishing the European Community, see *supra* note 136. Case C-65/93, *Parliament v. Council* (Consultation procedure); cf. also K. Mortelmans, 'The Principle of Loyalty to the Community (Article 5 EC) and the Obligations of the Community Institutions' (1998) *Maastricht Journal of European and Comparative Law*, 67–88.

the CFSP is entrusted to the Council and not the Court of Justice. The absence of such a provision for the third pillar does not imply that similar obligations do not apply in that framework. Indeed, the Court has ruled in *Pupino* that the principle of loyal cooperation also applies within the framework of PJCCM.[148]

6.5   THE PRINCIPLE OF EQUALITY

The EC Treaty contains a whole series of prohibitions of discrimination of varying import. These prohibitions can be roughly divided into three categories. The first, and as far as the EC Treaty is concerned most important category: the prohibitions on discrimination on grounds of nationality;[149] thereafter a category of broader prohibitions on discrimination, such as the prohibition of discrimination between consumers or between producers in the framework of the CAP (Art. 34(2) EC), the prohibitions on discrimination in the field of competition law (Art. 81(1)(d) EC and 82(c) EC); and thirdly the prohibition on discrimination on grounds of sex in Article 141 EC (equal pay for equal work, and equal treatment in employment and occupation, see Ch. X of this book). The new Article 13 EC on discrimination based on sex, racial or ethnic origin, religion or belief, etc., discussed below (section 6.5.2) does not strictly speaking belong in this series of prohibitions on discrimination, since it is not formulated as a prohibition, but merely provides a legal basis for further measures to be taken by the Community legislature.

    These various prohibitions on discrimination can ultimately be traced back to the same source: the general principle of equality, as that has also been explicitly recognized by the Court in its case law as an unwritten general principle of Community law.[150] Before we discuss the prohibition on discrimination on grounds of nationality contained in Article 12 EC, we present some more general remarks on the principle of equality.[151]

    The most complete description which the Court has given so far of the principle of equality concerns the above-mentioned more specific prohibition on discrimination laid down in Article 34(2) EC; the principle contained in this provision prohibiting discrimination between producers or consumers within the Community, including discrimination on grounds of nationality, means that 'comparable situations must not be treated differently and different situations must not

---

148. Case C-105/03, *Criminal proceedings against Maria Pupino*. This was confirmed in Case C-354/04 P, *Gestoras Pro Amnistía v. Council*.
149. Cf. Arts. 12; 39(2); 43; 50; 75; 90 and 294 EC.
150. Cf. Joined Cases 117/76 & 16/77, *Albert Ruckdeschel & Co. et al. v. Hauptzollamt Hamburg-St. Annen et al.*; Case 810/79, *Peter Überschär v. Bundesversicherungsanstalt für Angestellte*.
151. See the general part of the joint discussion paper by B.J. Drijber and S. Prechal, 'Gelijke behandeling van mannen en vrouwen en horizontaal perspectief' (1997) SEW, 122–167; T. Tridimas, *The General Principles of EC Law*, 2nd ed. (Oxford, 2006), 59 et seq., and C.W.A. Timmermans, 'Verboden discriminatie of (geboden) differentiatie' (1982) SEW, 426–460. See too E. Ellis, *EU Anti-Discrimination Law* (Oxford, 2005).

be treated in the same way unless such treatment is objectively justified'.[152] From this description it is apparent – and there are countless examples in the case law – that mere 'equal' treatment can in fact lead to discrimination (also called: covert, indirect or substantive discrimination); in other words, if there is a relevant difference in situations, this may require a difference in treatment, or a 'differentiating' treatment, in order to avoid infringement of the principle of equality. A classic example from the case law is *Commission v. Ireland (Sea Fisheries)*[153] which dealt with an attempt to use ostensibly objective criteria (vessel length and engine horsepower) to exclude large fishing boats from a particular stretch of Irish maritime waters. The Court was willing to see through the ostensible argument to perceive that the Irish measures indeed breached the rule of non-discrimination on grounds of nationality even though they were 'indiscriminately' applicable to Irish fishing boats and those from other Member States, when it became apparent that the larger foreign fishing vessels were for the majority caught by this rule, and the smaller Irish boats were not.

Both the essential criteria for the application of the general principle of equality – and also for the more specific prohibitions on discrimination, which are expressions of this principle – are to be found in the description quoted above. In order to determine whether an unequal, or an equal, treatment of two cases has a discriminatory character, these two cases must be compared and examined for relevant differences and similarities (test of comparability). That may appear obvious, but the execution of such a test is often more difficult than it seems, as it is not always easy to determine which aspects or elements are relevant in order to reach a judgement as to comparability or lack thereof. The second test inherent in the principle of equality is just as delicate. Determining the comparability (or lack thereof) of the relevant situations does not in itself answer the question whether there is discrimination. In principle, there is always the possibility that despite comparability of situation, unequal treatment (or, vice versa, equal treatment when situations are not comparable) can nevertheless turn out to be justified on objective grounds. The justification test immediately introduces the question of which objectives or interests at issue can be invoked, and also the question of how intensively the justification advanced in a concrete case should be reviewed, in particular in cases of judicial review. A good example of the potentially far-reaching consequences of this justification test is to be found in the case law on the prohibition of discriminatory taxation of imported goods, enshrined in Article 90 EC. In *Chemial Farmaceutici*,[154] the Court accepted the differentiated taxation of two chemically identical products as being justified on the basis of the grounds of national agricultural and energy policies adduced by the Italian Government.

---

152. Case 106/83 *Sermide v. Cassa Conguaglio Zucchero*, para. 28; Case C-309/89, *Codorniu v. Council*. Cf. also, but then for prohibition of discrimination under Art. 39 EC, Case C-411/98, *Angelo Ferlini v. Centre Hospitalier de Luxembourg*.
153. Case 61/77 *Commission v. Ireland* (Sea Fisheries).
154. Case 140/79, *Chemial Farmaceutici SpA v. DAF SpA*.

**6.5.1   The Prohibition of Discrimination on Grounds of
                 Nationality: Article 12 EC**

The most fundamental expression of the principle of equality in relation to the functioning of the common market is the prohibition of discrimination on grounds of nationality (see also Art. 21(2) EU Charter of Fundamental Rights). The fundamental nature of this prohibition is also apparent from the fact that the Treaty contains a *general* prohibition of discrimination on grounds of nationality, in Article 12, over and above the specific instances of prohibition of discrimination on grounds of nationality, in particular in the Treaty provisions intending to realize the fundamental Treaty freedoms. The case law reveals that the general prohibition in Article 12 EC only applies to the extent that no specific provisions of the Treaty with comparable effect are applicable.[155] A potential litigant seeking to invoke the prohibition of discrimination on ground of nationality will first have to ascertain whether the directly effective provisions relating to the free movement of goods, persons, services, and capital; the rules governing competition; the special non-discrimination provisions in the agricultural and transport fields[156] and in the field of taxation,[157] or Article 294 (which ensures non-discrimination with respect to participation in the capital of companies) provide a particular solution for the discrimination in question. If they do, it will be unnecessary to base the claim also on Article 12.[158]

6.5.1.1   The Scope of Application of the Treaty

If a measure is to be reviewed on the basis of the general prohibition of discrimination of Article 12 EC, then it must – according to the wording of that provision – fall 'within the scope of application of this Treaty'. In more recent case law, in particular, it may be seen that this scope of application must be interpreted broadly. For instance, measures which as such do not come within the scope of application of the specific prohibitions of restrictions on free movement of goods, services, persons and capital, but which have indirect consequences for the effective realization of these freedoms, or which can be connected to them, can come within the scope of application of the Treaty. In that context, the question which particular area of law the measure belongs to is irrelevant, as is the question whether or not the Community itself has taken action in that area, for instance by taking harmonization measures. In this way, the case law reveals that national rules in the area of criminal (procedural) law (*cautio iudicatum solvi*),[159] intellectual property law in

---

155. See, e.g., Case 411/98, *Ferlini*; Case C-179/90, *Merci convenzionali porto di Genova SpA v. Siderurgica Gabrielli SpA*; Case C-379/92, Criminal proceedings against *Peralta*, and Case C-176/96 *Lehtonen and Castors Braine v. FRBSB*.
156. Arts. 34(3), 2nd para. and 75 EC respectively.
157. Art. 90 EC.
158. See Case C-19/92, *Dieter Kraus v. Land Baden-Württemberg*.
159. Case C-29/95, *Eckehard Pastoors and Trans-Cap GmbH v. Belgium*; Case C-43/95, *Data Delecta Aktiebolag and Ronny Forsberg v. MSL Dynamics Ltd*; Case C-323/95, *David Charles*

(as yet) unharmonized areas,[160] civil rules of procedure,[161] and the law of associations,[162] have all turned out to be susceptible to review on the basis of Article 12 EC. In addition, the introduction of the status of Union citizen (Arts. 17–22 EC) appears to have direct consequences for the interpretation of the concept of the scope of application of the Treaty. If a national measure which does not come within one of the specific free movement prohibitions nevertheless affects in some way the exercise of the rights of free movement or residence of a Union citizen in another Member State, then such a measure comes within the scope of application of the Treaty, as is apparent from the *Sala* and *Bickel and Franz* cases.[163]

The earlier case law on the right of equal access – i.e., without discrimination on grounds of nationality – to higher education and universities for students from other Member States illustrates the way in which the concept of the scope of application of the Treaty is interpreted by the Court; the Court derived this right from Article 12 EC. Following studies in another Member State cannot as such be characterized as the exercise of one of the freedoms (of movement of persons, or of services).[164] The mere existence of a Treaty provision on vocational education (Art. 150 (ex 127) EC), which however on its own did not provide a legal basis for adopting binding rules on the matter, but which had led to a 'soft' form of Community policy (Council resolutions), was deemed by the Court sufficient to bring the imposition of higher fees for students from other Member States than for their own nationals, or other discriminatory conditions for following courses, within the scope of application of the prohibition of discrimination of Article 12 EC.[165] The principal elements resulting from this case law were later codified, together with rules on a right of residence for foreign students, in Directive 93/96[166] which was adopted on the basis of the second paragraph of Article 12 EC and has now been replaced by Directive 2004/38.[167]

A second example illustrating the possibilities of Article 12 EC is the *Cowan* case, dating from 1989.[168] Cowan was a British tourist who was injured as a result of a mugging in Paris. He sought compensation from the criminal injuries compensation scheme, which the French State had created. However, this was refused on the ground that he was not French, or resident in France, and did not even have a

---

    Hayes and Jeannette Karen Hayes v. Kronenberger GmbH; Case C-274/96, *Criminal proceedings against Horst Otto Bickel and Ulrich Franz*.

160. Joined Cases C-92/92 & C-326/92, *Phil Collins v. Imtrat Handelsgesellschaft mbH* and *Patricia Im- und Export and Leif Emanuel Kraul v. EMI Electrola GmbH*.
161. Case C-398/92, *Mund & Fester v. Hatrex Internationaal Transport*.
162. Case C-172/98, *Commission v. Belgium* (rules on forming associations).
163. Case C-85/96, *María Martínez Sala v. Freistaat Bayern*; Case C-274/96, *Bickel and Franz*. Cf. Ch. II, section 6.2. *supra*.
164. Unless it concerns private education for which a normal price is paid, cf. Case C-109/92, *Stephan Max Wirth v. Landeshauptstadt Hannover*.
165. Case 293/83, *Françoise Gravier v. City of Liège*.
166. O.J. 1993, L 317/59, which replaced Dir. 90/366 (O.J. 1990, L 180/30) which, as is explained in the text, *infra*, was annulled by the Court in Case C-295/90, *European Parliament v. Council*.
167. O.J. 2004, L 158/77, see further Ch. VIII *infra*.
168. Case 186/87, *Ian William Cowan v. Trésor public*.

residence permit. The Court considered this indirect discrimination on the basis of nationality to be in conflict with the Treaty, not because it constituted a restriction on Cowan's ability to receive services as a tourist, in infringement of Article 49 EC, but as an infringement of Article 12 EC, because

> when Community law guarantees a natural person the freedom to go to another Member State [in this case in the framework of the freedom to receive services] the protection of that person from harm in the Member State in question, on the same basis as that of nationals and persons residing there, is a corollary of that freedom of movement (para. 17).

The French system of compensation was thus in this case brought within the scope of application of the Treaty because of its connection with the exercise of the freedom to provide (and receive) services. The Court followed a similar approach in a more recent case, in which the requirement of the possession of Belgian nationality of at least one member of the administration of an association, or of a majority of its members, for an association to be recognized under Belgian law infringed Article 12 EC, because of the connection with the right of establishment (the forming of such an association by nationals of other Member States was thereby hindered).[169]

6.5.1.2   Covert, Indirect Discrimination

In the words of the Court in the *Sea Fisheries* case mentioned above (section 6.5 above):

> As the court has had occasion to declare in other contexts . . . the rules regarding equality of treatment enshrined in Community law forbid not only overt discrimination by reason of nationality but also all covert forms of discrimination which, by the application of other criteria of differentiation, lead in fact to the same result.[170]

Such a criterion of differentiation will often be a residence requirement in order to come within the scope *ratione personae* of a national measure.[171] In general, there is indirect or covert discrimination if a measure, even though it is equally applicable notwithstanding nationality, in its application is more disadvantageous for nationals of other Member States than for those of the state taking the measure.

6.5.1.3   Examination of Justifications

In our introductory remarks on the general principle of equality (section 6.5 above), it was remarked that review on the basis of the equality principle does not just

---

169.   Case C-172/98, *Commission v. Belgium* (rules on forming associations).
170.   Case 61/77, *Commission v. Ireland* (*Sea Fisheries*), para. 78. See generally on the concept of indirect discrimination C. Tobler, *Indirect Discrimination, A Case Study into the Development of the Legal Concept of Indirect Discrimination under EC Law* (Antwerpen/Oxford, 2005).
171.   Case C-29/95, *Pastoors*; Case C-274/96, *Bickel and Franz*.

require an examination of the comparability of the cases in question, but also of the question whether the unequal treatment of similar cases (or the equal treatment of dissimilar cases) can be justified on objective grounds. Such an examination of possible justifications occurs frequently in the case law, particularly in cases concerning possible covert or indirect discrimination.[172] A disadvantageous effect for nationals of other Member States is not sufficient to imply an infringement of Article 12 EC; the Court usually examines the justification pleaded by the Member State in question in cases of measures which do not formally discriminate according to nationality. This examination concerns not just the lawful character of the adduced public interest or government objective, but also the question whether the measure is necessary for achieving this objective and does not go further than necessary as far as the negative effects for the nationals of other Member States are concerned. In particular the more recent case law illustrates that the test of justification also includes a proportionality test.[173]

It will only rarely be the case that a formal distinction on grounds of nationality can be justified, but it is not entirely excluded. For instance, nationality is considered in the case law to be an acceptable criterion for the grant of a so-called 'expatriation allowance' for European officials pursuant to the staff regulations of officials.[174]

Also in more recent case law examples can be found of application of a nationality criterion for the limitation *ratione personae* of the scope of application of a national measure which are not as such considered to be in infringement of the prohibition in Article 12 EC, but are subject to review of the grounds adduced in justification thereof.[175] Obviously, these cases always concern 'suspicious' criteria which are subject to a 'tight fit test'.[176]

6.5.1.4   Reverse Discrimination

Article 12 EC does not forbid worse treatment of a Member State's own nationals as compared with nationals of other Member States (so-called reverse discrimination). This changes, of course, if the Member State's own nationals who are receiving worse treatment are in a cross-border situation, and therefore come within the scope of application of the Treaty. In that case they can claim the same more

---

172. Case C-398/92, *Mund & Fester v. Hatrex Internationaal Transport*; Case C-29/95, *Pastoors*; Case C-274/96, *Bickel and Franz*; Case C-411/98, *Ferlin*; Case C-209/03, *The Queen (on the application of Dany Bidar) v. London Borough of Ealing, Secretary of State for Education and Skills*.
173. Case C-29/95, *Pastoors*; Case C-323/95, *Hayes*; Case C-274/96, *Bickel and Franz*; Case C-411/98, *Ferlin*; Case C-148/02, *Carlos Garcia Avello v. Belgium*.
174. Case 37/74, *Chantal Van den Broeck v. Commission*; Case 147/79, *René Hochstrass v. ECJ*.
175. Case C-43/95, *Data Delecta Aktiebolag and Ronny Forsberg v. MSL Dynamics Ltd*.
176. L. Lusky and M. Botein 'The Law of Equality in the United States', in T. Koopmans (ed.), *Constitutional Protection of Equality* (Leyden, 1975), 31 and 37.

favourable treatment as that which holds for nationals of other Member States, as happened in *Knoors*.[177]

6.5.1.5   *The Difference between Discrimination and Distortion*

Where a difference in treatment between the nationals of different Member States is a result of differences in legislation between the Member States, one should not speak of discrimination, but of a disparity between the national legislation, which may possibly lead to a distortion of the conditions of competition; this may be overcome by means of Articles 94, 95 or 96 EC.[178] The conceptual confusion between discrimination and such distortions is regrettably still widespread.[179] The discrimination concept of the Treaty applies only to the unequal treatment of different persons by one legal subject, whereas distortions result from differences in legislation between *different* Member States. This issue is dealt with in Chapter VIII of this book.

6.5.1.6   *The Addressees of Article 12 EC*

Article 12 itself is silent as to whom it is addressed. As a fundamental legal principle it is clearly directed in any event at the Member States (including all their central, or functionally or territorially decentralized, organs or autonomous units). It also applies to the Community Institutions and other Community bodies themselves. The general system of the EC Treaty is that the obligations or prohibitions which it contains are directed only at the Member States and/or the Community Institutions, unless expressly otherwise provided, as is the case with Articles 81 and 82 EC and with a number of implementing regulations in other fields. In these cases, the provisions concerned – sometimes through Community secondary legislation – are expressly directed at undertakings, and for systematic reasons this would seem to exclude the applicability of Article 12 EC in horizontal relations. Secondly, the case law so far does not support the horizontal direct effect of Article 12 EC.[180] Against the first of these arguments, it may be objected that precisely because this provision embraces a fundamental principle, which is rightly universally held also to apply to the Community Institutions, it is in principle not obvious why it should be inapplicable to relationships between private parties.

True, horizontal effect of Article 12 EC has not been completely accepted in the case law. The *Ferlini* case of 3 October 2000, however, sets an important step in that direction, by finding that a private group of hospitals was bound by the

---

177. Case 115/78, *J. Knoors v. Secretary of State for Economic Affairs*. See further Ch. VIII of this book. See also, generally, N. Nic Shuibhne, 'Free Movement of Persons and the Wholly Internal Rule: Time to Move On'? (2002) CML Rev., 731–771.

178. See Case 14/68, *Walt Wilhelm et. al v. Bundeskartellamt*.

179. Case 155/80, *Summary proceedings against Sergius Oebel*; Joined Cases C-92/92 & C-326/92, *Phil Collins*.

180. I.e., reliance on Art. 12 EC by a private individual against another private individual.

prohibition of discrimination in Article 12 EC, although in this connection the Court referred explicitly to the fact that this group of hospitals 'exercises a certain power over individuals and is in a position to impose on them conditions which adversely affect the exercise of the fundamental freedoms guaranteed under the Treaty'.[181] This additional remark could be a sign that the Court is more reluctant to accept the horizontal effect of Article 12 EC, than for instance that of Article 39 EC, which it had already done with conviction in the *Angonese* case of 6 June 2000.[182]

From the point of view of legal certainty, Durand has rightly recommended that the applicability of Article 12 in relationships between private parties in specified fields should be defined in an implementing regulation or directive based on Article 12(2) EC.[183] It is submitted that such a measure should be based on the view, in conformity with the above-mentioned *Ferlini* judgment, that the greater the dominant position of the individual or collectively discriminating party or parties, and thus the fewer the alternatives open to the victim of the discrimination, the more likely a finding of discrimination will result. In addition, if such a measure were enacted, it could contain an obligation for the Member States to ensure that appropriate sanctions are provided for and enforced.

6.5.2 The Supplementary, Specific Non-discrimination Provision: Article 13 EC

What is immediately noticeable in this new Treaty Article, introduced by the Treaty of Amsterdam, is its limited character. Discrimination on one or more of the grounds mentioned in this provision ('sex, racial or ethnic origin, religion or belief, disability, age or sexual orientation') is not actually prohibited; Article 13 EC merely provides for a legal basis which permits the Council to enact appropriate measures to combat such forms of discrimination. Decision-making in the Council on the basis of this Article is to be by unanimity, and direct democratic legitimacy via the European Parliament is rather weak (it has only a consultative role). However, according to Article 13(2) EC, the Council may adopt measures supporting national policy to combat discrimination, with the exception of harmonization measures, by means of the co-decision procedure.

There is thus no directly effective prohibition of discrimination like that on grounds of nationality under Article 12 EC. That is remarkable, since such a prohibition does occur in the classic international fundamental rights Treaties, including the European Convention on Human Rights (Art. 14).[184] Also the

---

181. Case C-411/98, *Ferlini*, para. 50.
182. Case C-281/98, *Roman Angonese v. Cassa di Risparmio di Bolzano SpA*.
183. C. Durand, op. cit. *supra* note 77, 61 and 63.
184. It should be noted, however, that this Article only forbids such discrimination with regard to the enjoyment of the rights and freedoms set forth in that Convention. A useful overview of the relevant texts, also of national constitutional provisions in the area, is contained in the Commission Communication on certain Community measures to combat discrimination of 25 Nov. 1999, COM(1999)564 final.

European Social Charter, referred to in the preamble of the Treaty on European Union, and in Article 136 EC, contains a prohibition of such discrimination; that is also true of the EU Charter of Fundamental Rights (Art. 21). In addition, these instruments give a non-limitative list of the prohibited grounds of discrimination (i.e., using the term 'such as'), while the list in Article 13 EC can only be seen as limitative.

We would not, however, conclude from the existence of Article 13 EC that discrimination on the grounds mentioned in that provision is actually permitted in the scope of application of the Treaty as long as the Council has not taken the 'appropriate action' for the implementation of this provision. Manifest instances of discrimination on one of the grounds mentioned in Article 13 EC will usually, at least if they fall within the scope of application of the Treaty, be susceptible to condemnation as being in infringement of the general principle of equality. To that end, the above-mentioned international human rights instruments may also be relied on if necessary, as well as the common constitutional traditions of the Member States, in the light of which the Court interprets the general principles of Community law, and thus also the principle of equality (cf. Art. 6 TEU).[185]

Application of Article 13 EC is subject to two conditions. First, there should not be another Treaty provision which could serve as legal basis for the action proposed ('without prejudice to the other provisions of this Treaty'). Article 13 EC therefore has a subsidiary character. Examples of such alternative Treaty provisions are Article 137(1) EC (social exclusion, equal treatment of men and women) and Article 141 EC (discrimination on grounds of sex). As far as discrimination on grounds of race or ethnic origin and also religion are concerned, the legal bases included in the new Title IV of the EC Treaty[186] could be used. Also, Title VI of the Treaty on European Union contains an explicit reference to the prevention and combating of racism and xenophobia, in relation to Union policy provided for under PJCCM (Art. 29 TEU).

A second important condition attached to the application of Article 13 EC requires that the action proposed remains within the limits of the powers conferred by the Treaty upon the Community. This condition seems stricter that the limitation of application of the prohibition of discrimination on grounds of nationality to the 'scope of application' of the Treaty, discussed above. In fact, the Court has interpreted that concept broadly (see 6.5.1 above). It is not unlikely that by referring to the powers of the Community, the Member States wished to set narrower limits to the possible application of Article 13 EC. How should this formulation be interpreted? Obviously, it cannot mean that application of Article 13 EC requires that the Community is already competent pursuant to one of the other legal bases included in the Treaty; such an interpretation would deprive the powers granted

---

185. See recently Case C-144/04, *Werner Mangold v. Rüdiger Helm*, concerning discrimination on grounds of age and the annotation by J.H. Jans in (2007) *Legal Issues of Economic Integration*, 53–66. Cf. already Case 130/75, *Prais v. Council*.

186. On visas, asylum, immigration and other policies related to free movement of persons.

by Article 13 EC of all independent significance. In our view, this condition should be interpreted as meaning that for a measure to be based on Article 13 EC, it should concern a field which comes within the scope of application of the substantive powers of the Community. That does indeed seem more restricted that the concept 'scope of application of the Treaty', as that was interpreted in, for instance, the *Gravier* case[187] (see 6.5.1. above). On the other hand, the Community powers are described in such broad terms that, if a subject falls within the scope of application of the Treaty, then usually a Community competence can be found which can be used in that case. One may think in particular of the broadly described Community powers concerning market integration in Articles 94 and 95 EC, and the 'catch-all' competence of Article 308 EC.

The Council has established a first package of measures on the basis of Article 13 EC. In addition to a general action programme for combating discrimination for the period 2001–2006,[188] two Directives were enacted. The first Directive specifically concerns racism,[189] the second sets out a general framework for combatting discrimination concerning employment and occupation, on one of the other grounds mentioned in Article 13 EC, with the exception of sex, for which Community legislation already exists[190] (see Ch. X, below). Both Directives are organized in the same way: they give a general description of the cases of direct and indirect discrimination which fall within their scope of application; the Member States are obliged to abolish all national provisions which contain such discrimination, and also to take the necessary measures to ensure that all discriminatory provisions which are contained in individual or collective contracts or agreements, internal rules of undertakings, and rules governing the independent professions and workers' and employers' organizations, are amended or abolished. It seems to us indubitable that the first of these obligations for the Member States is directly effective. Both directives oblige the Member States, following the example of the existing Community legislation on equal treatment for men and women, to arrange for the necessary judicial and/or administrative protection for victims of discrimination, and also to lighten the burden of proof for people who consider themselves wronged in this area. As for the scope of application *ratione materiae* of the two directives, the Council has simply taken over the general restriction of Article 13 EC (within the limits of the powers conferred by the Treaty upon the Community). It should be noted that the substantive scope of application of the Directive on race discrimination, in particular, is extensively formulated. This also covers discrimination in relation to vocational training, and housing, of course on condition that the general conditions for the existence of a Community

---

187. Case 293/83, *Gravier*.
188. Council Decision of 27 Nov. 2000 establishing a Community action programme to combat discrimination (2001–2006), O.J. 2000, L 303/23.
189. Council Dir. 2000/43/EC of 29 Jun. 2000 implementing the principle of equal treatment between persons irrespective of racial or ethnic origin, O.J. 2000, L 180/22.
190. Council Dir. 2000/78/EC of 27 Nov. 2000 establishing a general framework for equal treatment in employment and occupation, O.J. 2000, L 303/16.

competence are met. As for the scope *ratione personae* of the two directives, it appears that they apply also to nationals of third countries. The possibility for third country nationals to derive rights of entrance or residence, or even access to employment or occupation, on the basis of these directives is, however, explicitly excluded.

6.6   THE PRINCIPLE OF TRANSPARENCY OR OPENNESS

In general, there is much amiss with Union citizens' knowledge of the Union, its institutions, its working methods and decision-making processes. This is an old problem, but as the integration process develops further – in depth and in breadth – this lack of knowledge undermines the legitimacy of Union action within the Member States to a greater and greater extent. The lack of familiarity, partly aggravated by the complex structure of the Union, its complicated decision-making procedures and – at least for outsiders – the impenetrability of its Institutions' functioning, forms a breeding ground for indifference; and as people are confronted with the far-reaching consequences of the Union in their daily life and in the fabric of society, this indifference rapidly translates into frustration and opposition. Such reactions may sometimes be irrational – given the lack of knowledge, that is scarcely surprising – but all in all it leads to a serious impairment of the Union's legitimacy. The ratification debates at the time of the Treaty of Maastricht, particularly after the negative result of the first Danish referendum,[191] made the extent of the problem painfully evident. This was also the period in which the policy-makers within the Union began to seek an answer to the problem by developing a policy of transparency or openness.[192] These concepts concern a diverse package of policy initiatives which quite clearly go further than the concept of open government as that was known previously in several Member States.[193] Broadly speaking, three separate areas are concerned:

  – the greatest possible openness in the legislative process within the Union, in particular as far as the role of the Council therein is concerned (given the binding nature of the Union's legislation, and – especially in the case of Community legislation – its possible direct effects for citizens and firms in the Member States, the old and hallowed practices of international, intergovernmental and, therefore, confidential negotiations were considered to be no longer acceptable);

---

191. See Ch. I, section 7.1, *supra*.
192. See on this W. Devroe and J. Wouters, *De Europese Unie* (Leuven, 1996), 316 et seq. See especially also 'The Conclusions of the European Council at Edinburgh' 1992 (Bull. EC 12/92) and the 'Interinstitutional Declaration on Democracy, Transparency and Subsidiarity' (Bull. EC 10/93).
193. E.g., in the Netherlands.

- a policy on legislation which aims to improve the accessibility of legislation, to formulate the legislation itself in as uncomplicated and clear a fashion as possible, and to make improvements in its quality;[194]
- ensuring the greatest possible access to Union documents.

This transparency policy is of fundamental importance. It aims to involve the citizens more closely in the Union's activities, and promote their participation in the process of policy formation, directly or indirectly via interest groups (the so-called 'civil society'), outside the normal channels of representative democracy. But more openness and transparency also create better conditions for holding the institutions to account as concerns the policy conducted (or not conducted), the *ex post* control, also referred to as 'accountability'. Ultimately, this transparency policy is intended to strengthen the democratic element of the Union, and thereby increase citizens' confidence in the Union's action, in other words the Union's legitimacy. The extent to which that is necessary was once again demonstrated by the referendum in Ireland in 2001, for which the turnout was less than 35%, and in which the Treaty of Nice was rejected. Deirdre Curtin spoke in 1996 of a 'spectacular alienation of the people in the various Member States'.[195] Since then not much seems to have changed,[196] as the debate preceding the referenda on the Constitutional Treaty in France and the Netherlands (in which the Constitution was rejected) has amply demonstrated.

The Treaty of Amsterdam also showed that the Member States are making serious efforts to achieve more transparency and openness in the Union. A reference was inserted in the very first provision of the Treaty on European Union, to the effect that decisions are to be taken 'as openly as possible'. Further, in the cases where the Council acts in a legislative capacity – that is defined broadly – it is to increase its openness (it must make public the results of votes and explanations of vote, as well as statements in the minutes, and must allow greater access to documents).[197] Of yet more importance is the task entrusted to the Community legislature to draw up general rules for all sectors of the Union (EC, CFSP and PJCCM) concerning the right of access to documents of the European Parliament, Council and Commission, which pursuant to Article 255 EC is enjoyed by all citizens of the Union, and also any natural or legal person residing or having its registered office in a Member State.[198] These rules have now been enacted

---

194. See on this Ch. V, section 4.1.5 *infra*.
195. D.M. Curtin, 'Betwixt and Between: Democracy and Transparency in the Governance of the European Union', in: J.A. Winter et al. (eds), *Reforming The Treaty on European Union: The Legal Debate* (The Hague, 1996), 97.
196. See the Commission White Paper on European Governance, COM(2001) 428, 8.
197. See Art. 207(3) EC, which is also declared to apply to CFSP (Art. 28 TEU) and PJCCM (Art. 41 TEU), and is further elaborated in Arts. 7, 8 and 9 and Annex II (Specific Provisions regarding public access to Council documents) of the Rules of Procedure of the Council, as established by Council Decision 2006/683/EC, Euratom, O.J. 2006, L 285/47. See also Art. 12(2) of Reg. 1049/2001 (access to documents), O.J. 2001, L 145/43 and V. Deckmyn (ed.), *Increasing Transparency in the European Union?* (Maastricht, 2002).
198. Art. 255 EC is declared applicable for the CFSP (Art. 28 TEU) and PJCCM (Art. 41 TEU).

(almost within the two year term set by the Treaty),[199] and replace the previous decisions taken by the institutions individually (for the Council and Commission, this was on the basis of a code of behaviour agreed by both).[200]

As for the consequences of the Treaty of Amsterdam for policy on legislation, first of all mention may be made of the simplification operation of the EC Treaty texts themselves, such as the deletion of superfluous provisions, and subsequent renumbering of the Treaty provisions (Arts. 6–12 of the Treaty of Amsterdam). An even more ambitious project is the operation of consolidating the treaty texts, which was put on the agenda for the negotiation of the next round of Treaty revisions, announced for 2004.[201] The Constitutional Treaty went a long way in achieving this; the Lisbon Treaty, however, since it takes the form of a series of amendments to existing Treaties, inevitably leads to a less transparent result. Finally, the Treaty of Amsterdam[202] called on the Institutions to make new initiatives in order to improve the quality of legislation. This has, in the meantime, been carried out.[203]

From the above, it is evident that the principle of transparency or openness mentioned in the title of this subsection can hardly be qualified as a general legal principle. The content of this principle is too diffuse, and the subject matters and areas in which it can be implemented are too diverse. That is different for the principle of access to documents. Now that this right of access has been anchored at the primary level of the Treaties, there are good grounds for accepting it as a fundamental right, also given the importance to be attached to decisions being taken 'as openly as possible' according to Article 1 TEU.[204] A further argument for such recognition is the fact that this right is now included, in so many words, in the EU Charter of Fundamental Rights (Art. 42). True, the Charter is not legally binding, but as an authoritative core source codifying those existing rights within the Union which can be counted as belonging to the general principles of Community law, it cannot be ignored. The qualification of the right of access to documents as a fundamental right has practical legal significance, since in that case exceptions to the right can only be accepted under strict conditions and on condition of strict judicial review thereof. A possible argument against such qualification is the fact that the relevant Treaty provision (Art. 255 EC) only recognizes

---

199. Reg. 1049/2001, O.J. 2001, L 145/43. Agencies are subject to a similar regime on access to documents, as provided for in the instrument by which they have been set up. See, e.g., Art. 23 Reg. 58/2003 laying down the statute for executive agencies, O.J. 2003, L 11/1.
200. Council Decision 93/731/EC, O.J. 1993, L 340, Commission Decision 94/90/ECSC, EC, Euratom, O.J. 1994, L 46 and Decision of the European Parliament 97/632/ECSC, EC, Euratom, O.J. 1997, L 236. The code of behaviour was published in O.J. 1993, L 340.
201. See Declaration 23 on the future of the Union, adopted with the Treaty of Nice.
202. See Declaration 39 on the quality of the drafting of Community legislation.
203. See Ch. V, section 4.1.5 *infra.*
204. See on this D.M. Curtin, 'Citizens' Fundamental Right of Access to EU Information: An Evolving Digital Passepartout'? (2000) CML Rev., 7–41; S. Prechal and M. de Leeuw, 'Transparency: A General Principle of EU Law'? in U. Bernitz, C. Gardner and J. Nergalius (eds), *General Principles of Community Law in the Process of Development* (Alphen aan den Rijn, 2008).

this right for documents of the three institutions mentioned therein, and leaves the other institutions and organs aside. On the other hand, according to a Declaration adopted together with the Treaty of Amsterdam,[205] it is apparently the intention of the framers of the Treaty to give horizontal scope of application to this right. This is confirmed by the fact that in the preamble of Regulation 1049/2001, the agencies established by the institutions are also called upon to apply the principles laid down in the Regulation.[206]

In some respects, Regulation 1049/2001 goes further than the previous regime on publication and access. There is here no space for a complete analysis of the new regime. Suffice it to mention the following major points. The scope of application covers not just documents emanating from the institutions themselves, but also documents received from third parties. The concept of a document is defined extensively, and also covers for instance information which is stored electronically. Access to documents may be effected either by consulting them on the spot or by receiving a copy, including, where available, an electronic copy, or via a register. The institutions are obliged to set up a register of documents which is available electronically.[207] There are three categories of exceptions to the right of access, which are all mandatory. The first category (public interest and privacy and the integrity of the individual) is formulated unconditionally, insofar as 'institutions shall refuse access to a document where disclosure would undermine the protection' of this interest. For the two other categories (commercial interests, court proceedings and inspections, on the one hand, and certain documents for internal use, on the other), if disclosure would undermine the protection of the interest in question, this is as such not sufficient to refuse access, but the institution must also consider whether 'there is an overriding public interest in disclosure'. This requires a balancing of interests in an individual case, which must be expressed in the reasoning of the decision refusing access. Exceptions may in principle only apply for a maximum period of 30 years. If only parts of the requested document are covered by any of the exceptions, the remaining parts of the document must be made available.[208] As regards documents received from a third party, the institution must consult the third party in order to assess whether the exceptions to access apply, unless it is clear that the document should or should not be disclosed. The third party, even if it is a Member State, cannot simply prevent disclosure, therefore. This is only different with regard to so-called

---

205. Declaration No. 41 on the provisions relating to transparency, access to documents and the fight against fraud.
206. See note 199 *supra*.
207. The Council did already have such a register, see Council Decision 2000/23/EC of 6 Dec. 1999 on the improvement of information on the Council's legislative activities and the public register of Council documents, O.J. 2000, L 9/22, now replaced by Annex II of the Council's Rules of Procedure, Decision 2006/683/EC, Euratom, O.J. 2006, L 285/47.
208. Cf. Case C-353/99 P, *Council v. Heidi Hautala*. The exception on administrative grounds which this judgment accepts (see also Case T-204/99, *Olli Mattila v. Council and Commission*), is not to be found – at least in so many words – in Art. 4(6) of Reg. 1049/2001.

sensitive documents, which are classified as 'top secret', or 'secret' in accordance with the protection of essential interests.[209]

The Court of Justice and the Court of First Instance developed important case law on the previous access regime. This remains relevant, *mutatis mutandis*, for the new regime, in particular, in our opinion, as far as the strict requirements on reasoning of a decision refusing access are concerned.[210]

FURTHER READING

Economic Constitution

Bernitz, U. and J. Nergelius. *General Principles of European Community Law: Reports from a Conference in Malmö.* European Monographs, 25. The Hague: Kluwer Law International, 2000.

Forschungsinstitut für Wirtschaftsverfassung und Wettbewerb. *Weiterentwicklung der europäischen Gemeinschaften und der Marktwirtschaft, Referate des XXV FIW-Symposions.* Köln, Berlin, Bonn, München, 1992.

Gerber, David J. 'Constitutionalizing the Economy: German Neo-liberalism, Competition Law and the "New" Europe'. (1994) *The American Journal of Comparative Law*, 25–84.

Götz, V. Verfassungsschranken interventionistischer Regulierung nach europäischem Gemeinschaftsrecht im Vergleich mit dem Grundgesetz, Vorträge, Reden und Berichte aus dem Europa Institut, Universität des Saarlandes, Nr. 166, 1989.

Groeben, Hans von der. 'Probleme einer europäischen Wirtschaftsordnung'. In *Europarecht, Energierecht, Wirtschaftsrecht, Festschrift für Bodo Börner.* Köln, Berlin, Bonn, München, 1992.

Häberle, P. 'Verfassungsrechtliche Fragen im Prozess der Europäischen Einigung'. (1992) EuGRZ, 429–236.

Hilf, M. and G. Nicolaysen. *Perspektiven für Europa: Verfassung und Binnenmarkt.* Europarecht. Beiheft, 3/2002. Baden-Baden: Nomos, 2002.

Joerges, C. 'European Economic Law, the Nation-State and the Maastricht Treaty'. In R. Dehousse (ed). *Europe after Maastricht: An Ever Closer Union?* München, 1994.

Joerges, C. *Markt ohne Staat? Die Wirtschaftsverfassung der Gemeinschaft und die Renaissance der regulatieven Politik.* EUI Working Paper Law, no. 91/15, 1991.

Mertens de Wilmars, J. 'Réflexions sur l'ordre juridicio-économique de la Communauté Européenne'. In *Interventions publiques et Droit Communautaire,* 1988.

---

209. The Council has adopted a Decision on this: cf. Council Decision 2001/264/EC of 19 Mar. 2001 adopting the Council's security regulations, O.J. 2001, L 101/1.

210. Cf. Case T-105/95, *WWF v. Commission,* Case T-174/95, *Svenska Journalistförbundet v. Council;* Case T-14/98, *Hautala.* See generally K. Lenaerts, ' "In the Union We Trust": Trust-Enhancing Principles of Community Law', (2004) CML Rev., 317–343.

Mestmäcker, E.-J. *Die Wirtschaftsverfassung in der Europäischen Union.* Vorträge und Berichte des Zentrums für Europäische Wirtschaftsrecht, Nr. 28, 1993.

Padoa-Schioppa, T. *Efficiency, Stability and Equity: A Strategy for the Evolution of the Economic System of the European Community.* Oxford, Oxford University Press, 1987.

Pescatore, P. *Les objectifs de la Communauté Européenne comme principes d'interprétation dans la jurisprudence de la Cour de Justice.* In Miscellanea W.J. Ganshof van der Meersch, II. Brussels, Bruylant, 1972.

Petersmann, E.-U. 'These zur Wirtschaftsverfassung der EG'. (1993) EuZW, 593–598.

VerLoren van Themaat, P. 'Die Aufgabenverteilung zwischen dem Gesetzgeber und dem Europäischen Gerichtshof bei der Gestaltung der Wirtschaftsverfassung der Europäischen Gemeinschaften'. In *Eine Ordnungspolitik für Europa, Festschrift für Hans von der Groeben zu seinem 80.* Geburtstag, herausgegeben von E.-J. Mestmäcker, H. Möller, H.-P. Schwarz. Baden-Baden, Nomos, 1987.

VerLoren van Themaat, P. 'Het economisch grondslagenrecht van de Europese Gemeenschappen'. In *Liber Amicorum Josse Mertens de Wilmars.* Antwerpen, Kluwer, 1982.

Waelbroeck, M. 'Le Traité CEE est-il neutre à l'égard des politiques économiques des états-membres?' In *Hacia un nuevo orden internacional y europeo (estudios en homenaje al professor Don Manuel Díez de Velasco).* Madrid, 1993.

Principles, General

Arnull, A. *The General Principles of EEC Law and the Individual.* London, Leicester University Press, 1990.

Barnard, C. *The Fundamentals of EU Law Revisited: Assessing the Impact of the Constitutional Debate.* Collected Courses of the Academy of European Law = Recueil des cours de l'Académie de droit européen. 16/2 (Oxford: Oxford University Press, 2007).

Bernitz, U. and J. Nergelius (eds). *General Principles of European Community Law.* European Monographs, 25. The Hague: Kluwer Law International, 2000.

Craig, P.P. *EU Administrative Law.* Collected Courses of the Academy of European Law, vol. 16/1. Oxford: Oxford University Press, 2006.

Folsom, R.H. *Principles of European Union Law.* St. Paul, MN: Thomson/West, 2005.

Groussot, X. *General Principles of Community Law.* The Hogendorp Papers, 6. Groningen: Europa Law Publishing, 2006.

Jans, J.H., R. de Lange, S. Prechal and R.J.G.M. Widdershoven. *Europeanisation of Public Law.* Groningen: Europa Law Publishing, 2007.

Reich, N. *Understanding EU Law: Objectives, Principles and Methods of Community Law.* 2nd amended and updated ed. with references to the Draft Constitution of 29 October 2004. Antwerpen: Intersentia, 2005.

Schwarze, J. *European Administrative Law.* 1st rev. ed. London: Sweet & Maxwell, 2006.

Tridimas, T. *The General Principles of EU Law*. 2nd ed. Oxford EC Law Library. Oxford: Oxford University Press, 2006.
Usher, J.A. *General Principles of EC Law*. London: Longman, 1998.

Subsidiarity

Begg, D., et al. *Making Sense of Subsidiarity: How Much Centralization for Europe?* London: CEPR, 1993.
Bermann, G.A. 'Taking Subsidiarity Seriously: Federalism in the European Community and the United States'. (1994) *Columbia Law Review*, 331–456.
Besselink, L.F.M., H.S.J. Albers and W.T. Eijsbouts. 'Subsidiarity in Non-federal Contexts: The Netherlands and the European Union'. (1994) SEW, 275–320.
Cananea, G.D. 'Subsidiarity in the New Draft Constitution of the European Union'. In M. Zuleeg (ed.). *Die neue Verfassung der Europäischen Union*. Baden-Baden: Nomos, 2006.
Constantinesco, V. *Subsidiarität: Zentrales Verfassungsprinzip für die Politische Union, Integration*. Institut für Europäische Politik 13, 1990, no. 4.
Duff, A. (ed.). *Subsidiarity within the European Community*. London: Federal Trust for Education and Research, 1993.
Estella de Noriega, A. *The EU Principle of Subsidiarity and Its Critique*. Oxford: Oxford University Press, 2002.
Geelhoed, L.A. 'Het subsidiariteitsbeginsel: een communautair principe?' (1991) SEW, 422–435.
Häberle, P. 'Das Prinzip der Subsidiarität aus der Sicht der vergleichenden Verfassungslehre'. (1994) *Archiv des öffentlichen Rechts*, 169–206.
Jarass, H.D. 'EG-Kompetenzen und das Prinzip der Subsidiarität nach Schaffung der Europäischen Union'. (1994) EuGrZ, 209–219.
Kapteyn, P.J.G. 'Community Law and the Principle of Subsidiarity'. (1991) *Revue des Affaires Européennes*, 35–43.
Lenaerts, K. and P. van Ypersele. 'Le principe de subsidiarité et son contexte: étude de l'article 3 B du Traité CE'. (1994) CDE, 3–85.
Toth, A.G. 'The Principle of Subsidiarity in the Maastricht Treaty'. (1992) CML Rev., 1079–1105.
Van Kersbergen, K. and B. Verbeek. 'The Politics of Subsidiarity in the European Union'. (1994) *Journal of Common Market Studies*, 215–236.

Proportionality

De Búrca, G. 'The Principle of Proportionality and Its Application in EC Law'. (1993) YEL, 105.
Ellis, E. (ed.). *The Principle of Proportionality in the Laws of Europe*. Oxford: Hart, 1999.
Emiliou, N. *The Principle of Proportionality in European Law: A Comparative Study*. European Monographs, 10. London: Kluwer, 1996.

Tridimas, T. 'The Rule of Reason and Its Relation to Proportionality and Subsidiarity'. In A. Schrauwen (ed.). *Rule of Reason: Rethinking another Classic of European Legal Doctrine*. Groningen: Europa Law Publishing, 2005.

Obligation of Loyal Cooperation

Constantinesco, V. 'L'article 5 CEE, de la bonne foi à la loyauté communautaire'. In F. Capotorti, C., et al. (eds). *Du droit international au droit de l'intégration, Liber Amicorum Pescatore*. Baden-Baden: Nomos, 1987.

Lück, M. *Die Gemeinschaftstreue als allgemeines Rechtsprinzip im Recht der Europäischen Gemeinschaft: ein Vergleich zur Bundestreue im Verfassungsrecht der Bundesrepublik Deutschland*. Baden-Baden: Nomos, 1992.

Tallberg, J. *European Governance and Supranational Institutions: Making States Comply*. Routledge Advances in European Politics, 14. London: Routledge, 2003.

Temple Lang, J. 'The Duties of Cooperation of National Authorities and Courts under Article 10 E.C.: Two More Reflections'. (2001) *European Law Review*, 84–93.

Temple Lang, J. 'The Duties of National Authorities under Community Constitutional Law'. (1998) *European Law Review*, 109–131.

Temple Lang, J. 'The Principle of Loyal Cooperation and the Role of the National Judge in Community, Union and EEA Law'. (2006) *ERA-Forum: scripta iuris europaei*, 476–501.

Equal Treatment

Dashwood, A.A. and S. O'Leary, (eds). *The Principle of Equal Treatment in EC Law*. London: Sweet & Maxwell, 1997.

Ellis, E. *EU Anti-discrimination Law*. New York, NY: Oxford University Press, 2005.

Flynn, L. 'The Implications of Article 13 EC: After Amsterdam, Will Some Forms of Discrimination Be More Equal than Others?' (1999) CML Rev., 1127.

Hervey, T.K., et al. 'Thirty Years of EU Sex Equality Law'. (2005) *Maastricht Journal of European and Comparative Law*, 305–493.

Plötscher, S. *Der Begriff der Diskriminierung im Europäischen Gemeinschaftsrecht: zugleich ein Beitrag zur einheitlichen Dogmatik der Grundfreiheiten des EG-Vertrages*. Schriften zum europäischen Recht, Bd. 90. Berlin: Duncker & Humblot, 2003.

Legal Certainty and Legitimate Expectations

Raitio, J. *The Principle of Legal Certainty in EC Law*. Law and Philosophy Library, vol. 64. Dordrecht: Kluwer Academic Publishers, 2003.

Schønberg, S.J. *Legitimate Expectations in Administrative Law*. Oxford: Oxford University Press, 2000.

Openness and Transparency

Bunyan, T. *Secrecy and Openness in the EU.* London: Kogan Page, 1999.

Curtin, D.M. 'Betwixt and Between: Democracy and Transparency in the Governance of the European Union'. In Jan A. Winter et al. (eds). *Reforming The Treaty on European Union: The Legal Debate*, The Hague: Kluwer Law International, 1996.

Curtin, D.M. 'Citizens' Fundamental Right of Access to EU Information: An Evolving Digital Passepartout?' (2000) CML Rev., 7.

Deckmyn, V. *Increasing Transparency in the European Union?* Maastricht: European Institute of Public Administration, 2002.

Deckmyn, V. and I. Thomson. *Openness and Transparency in the European Union.* Maastricht: European Institute of Public Administration, 1998.

Heitsch, C. *Die Verordnung über den Zugang zu Dokumenten der Gemeinschaftsorgane im Lichte des Transparentzprimips.* Berlin: Duncker & Humbolt, 2003.

Kranenborg, H. and W.J.M. Voermans. *Access to Information in the European Union: A Comparative Analysis of EC and Member State Legislation.* Groningen: Europa Law Publishing, 2005.

Lenaerts, K. ' "In the Union We Trust": Trust-Enhancing Principles of Community Law'. (2004) CML Rev., 317–343.

Stolk, P.J. *Transparency in Europe II: Public Access to Documents in the EU and Its Member States.* Hosted by the Netherlands during its Chairmanship of the EU Council: The Hague, 25 and 26 November 2004. The Hague: Ministry of the Interior and Kingdom Relations Constitutional Affairs and Legislation Department, 2004.

Chapter IV

Institutional Structure

R.H. Lauwaars

1   INTRODUCTION

The European Union as such has only one organ of its own: the European Council (Art. 4 TEU). For the rest, the Union makes use of the five Institutions of the European Communities: the European Parliament, the Council, the Commission, the Court of Justice and Court of Auditors (Art. 5 TEU). Together with the European Council they form the single institutional framework prescribed by Article 3 TEU, which should ensure the consistency and continuity of the Union's activities, while respecting and building upon the *acquis communautaire*. If and when the Treaty of Lisbon enters into force, the European Council as the only organ of the present Union and the five Institutions of the European Communities will be replaced by the seven Institutions of the revised Union: the European Parliament, the Council, the European Commission, the Court of Justice, the Court of Auditors as well as the European Council and the European Central Bank (Art. 13 TEU (Lisbon)).

    In view of the separate status of the European Council, this body is examined first (section 2, below). Thereafter the five Institutions of the Communities are examined in turn. The institutional structure is of decisive importance for the balance of power within the Communities, and the two most important actors are still undoubtedly the Council and the Commission, even after the changes introduced into the EC Treaty by the Treaty of Maastricht and subsequent treaties (sections 3 and 4, below). It is on the cooperation of these two Institutions

P.J.G. Kapteyn, A.M. McDonnell, K.J.M. Mortelmans and C.W.A. Timmermans (eds),
The Law of the European Union and the European Communities, pp. 175–272.
©2008 Kluwer Law International BV, The Netherlands.

that the implementation of the Treaties is largely dependent. The discussion thus focuses on their composition, tasks and powers, including the tasks which they carry out in the context of the Union.

At the outset, the European Parliament – the institution which involves the peoples of the Member States in the activities of the Community[1] – played only a modest role on the Community stage. Since 1979 the Parliament has been directly elected and its role has gradually grown in importance, a trend which was reinforced by the amendments made to the EC Treaty by the Treaty of Maastricht and later amending treaties. However, its role does not yet fully satisfy the standards which may be required of the Community and of the Union from the point of view of democracy (section 5, below).

After the examination of these three actors in the Community legislative process, attention turns to the scope of decision-making powers enjoyed by those actors (section 6, below).

The Court of Justice also has a crucial part to play in the institutional structure of the Community – though not, or much less so, of the Union – as it has to ensure the observance of the law in the implementation of the Treaty by the Institutions and the Member States (section 7, below). Its jurisdiction enables the Court to contribute to the maintenance of the balance of rights and duties, both amongst the Institutions themselves, and between them and the Member States. The Court is also in the position of being able to ensure the legal protection of private parties, which is of great importance precisely because of the limited nature of parliamentary supervision of the behaviour of the Institutions. As far as direct actions are concerned, this jurisdiction is now exercised with a few exceptions (see section 7.3.2. below) by the Court of First Instance, the establishment of which was made possible by the changes introduced by the Single European Act (SEA). Finally, attention turns to the Court of Auditors, which the Treaty on European Union also elevates to the status of a Community Institution (section 8, below); to the various independent Community bodies, including the European Central Bank (section 9, below); and the many subsidiary bodies which assist the Council and the Commission in the discharge of many of their duties (section 10, below).

2 EUROPEAN COUNCIL

2.1 ESTABLISHMENT AND COMPOSITION

As has been mentioned earlier in this book,[2] the European Council was established on the occasion of the second Paris Summit, on 9–10 December 1974. According to

---

1. Cf. case 138/79, *SA Roquette Frères v. Council*; Case 139/79, *Maizena GmbH v. Council*. See further section 5, *infra* and Arts. 189 EC and 107 Euratom. In the following sections of this chapter, the basic provisions in the Euratom Treaty concerning the institutions will be mentioned where relevant.
2. See Ch. I, section 6.1, *supra*.

the communiqué issued at the conclusion of that Summit, the Heads of State or Government announced that henceforth they would meet three times a year, accompanied by their Foreign Ministers, as a formation of the Council of the European Communities, for the work on political cooperation.[3] Although the European Council was established outside the Community framework, it has in the meantime acquired an explicit Treaty basis. According to Article 2 SEA, the European Council brings together the Heads of State or Government of the Member States and the President of the Commission; it is assisted by the Foreign Ministers and by a Member of the Commission,[4] and meets at least twice a year. Article 4(2) TEU takes over this provision more or less word-for-word, adding that the chairmanship of the European Council is held by the Head of State or Government which holds the Presidency of the Council. Initially, the European Council only included one Head of State, which was the French President (since he has uncontested primary responsibility for foreign affairs), but the Finnish President has also attended since 1995.[5]

2.1.1 Proposed Changes following the Lisbon Treaty

The European Council will have a permanent President who will be chosen by the European Council by qualified majority for a term of two and a half years, which may be renewed once. The President will be a technical chairman: his task will be to chair and stimulate the work of the European Council and to ensure the preparation and continuity of its work. He will further represent the Union on issues concerning the common foreign and security policy (Art. 15(5) and (6) TEU (Lisbon)). The European Council will consist of 29 members: the 27 Heads of State or Government of the Member States together with its President and the President of the Commission; the High Representative of the Union for Foreign Affairs and Security Policy (who was to be called the European Minister for Foreign Affairs under the Constitutional Treaty) will take part in the work of the European Council (Art. 15(2) TEU (Lisbon)).

2.2 TASKS AND POWERS

The establishment of the European Council in fact meant the institutionalization of the Summits which had been held hitherto. It was emphasized in the communiqué after the Paris Summit, however, that '[t]hese arrangements do not in any way

---

3. 8th General Report 1974, Annex, 347. Bull-EC 12-1974 7. See, generally, J. Werts, *The European Council* (Amsterdam, 1992); S. Bulmer and W. Wessels, *The European Council: Decision-Making in European Politics* (London, 1987), and the extensive literature cited therein, and Glaesner in D. Curtin and T. Heukels (eds), *Institutional Dynamics of European Integration* (*Festschrift* for Schermers, Vol. II) (Dordrecht, 1994) 101.
4. Note that the President of the European Council must invite the Economic and Finance Ministers to participate in European Council meetings when it is discussing matters relating to Economic and Monetary Union (Declaration No. 4, annexed to the Final Act of the Treaty of Maastricht).
5. M. Westlake, *The Council of the European Union* (London, 1995) 22.

affect the rules and procedures laid down in the Treaties or the provisions on political cooperation in the Luxembourg and Copenhagen Reports'.[6] There was from the outset much uncertainty as to whether the European Council was in fact a purely intergovernmental body, or whether, in certain circumstances, particularly when exercising the powers of the Council, it was in fact a special composition of the Council, and was thus acting as an Institution. Initially it appeared that the European Council adopted the position of a purely intergovernmental body. It distanced itself as much as possible from the Community decision-making process; moreover, at its meeting in London on 29–30 June 1977 it drew up a list of tasks for itself in the so-called London Declaration[7] that is significantly different from the tasks of the Council set out in Article 202 EC. That lists of tasks included:

(a) informal exchanges of view of a wide-ranging nature held in the greatest privacy and not designed to lead to formal decisions or public statements;

(b) discussions which are designed to produce decisions, settle guidelines for future action or lead to the issue of public statements expressing the agreed view of the European Council;

(c) the settlement of outstanding issues from discussions at a lower level (the European Council having a sort of appellate function to resolve stalemates in the Council.) Only in relation to this third function did the Declaration state that 'in dealing with matters of Community competence the European Council will conform to the appropriate procedures laid down in the Community Treaties and other agreements'.

However, the Stuttgart Solemn Declaration on European Union[8] struck a rather different note. There the European Council clearly stated that when it acts in matters within the scope of the European Communities, it does so in its capacity as the Council within the meaning of the Treaties.[9] While this statement is certainly not included, yet alone repeated in the TEU, it is a foundation-stone of that Treaty, albeit that the TEU reserves the name European Council for the sole body of the Union itself. This actually means that the European Council as such *cannot* exercise the powers of the Council concerning Community matters (the simple fact that the President of the Commission is a member of the European Council, but not of the Council makes the distinction plain). Accordingly, the Treaties distinguish among:

(i) The European Council as the body of the Union, consisting of the Heads of State or Government and the President of the Commission, assisted as mentioned above. This is the body whose task is now stated in Article 4(1) TEU to be to provide the Union with the necessary impetus for its development and to define the general political guidelines thereof. It also defines

---

6. Bull. EC 12-1974, 7.
7. Bull. EC 6-1977, point 2.3.1.
8. Bull. EC 6-1983, point I.6.1. See also Ch. I, section 6.2, *supra*.
9. Point 2.1.3. of the Solemn Declaration, ibid.

the principles of and general guidelines for the common foreign and security policy (CFSP), and has certain other powers in the area of CFSP.[10]

(ii) A few exceptional cases in which the European Council is mentioned *under its own name* in the EC Treaty: See Articles 11(2) (enhanced cooperation); 99(2) EC (broad guidelines for economic policy); Article 113(3) EC (ECB annual reports); and Article 128(1) and (5) EC (employment).

(iii) The Council in the composition of the Heads of State or Government, i.e., without the president of the Commission: This special composition is provided for in Articles 121 EC, dealing with the transition to the third and final stage of Economic and Monetary Union; 122 EC, dealing with discussions and decisions concerning Member States with a so-called derogation; Article 214(2) EC, dealing with the appointment of the President of the Commission.[11] This special composition of the Council is also provided for in Article 7(2) TEU, concerning the determination of the existence of a serious breach of fundamental rights by a Member State. While the Heads of State or Government prefer to function as the European Council, the Treaty does not exclude the Council meeting in this composition to deal with matters other than those set out above, such as Articles 121 and 122 EC (see Art. 203 EC, and section 3.1 below).

(iv) Decisions of the governments of the Member States at the level of Heads of State or Government. Such a decision is provided for in Article 112(2) EC which deals with the appointment of the Executive Board of the European Central Bank.[12] Such decisions can also arise outside these contexts.[13]

---

10. Arts. 13, 17 and 23(2) TEU. To the extent such impetus or guidelines concern the EC, then the Community procedures will have to be followed for their implementation (see Ch. II, section 1.2.2). In particular, such impetus may not be to the detriment of the responsibility of the (ordinary) Council in its relations with Parliament and in proceedings before the Court. The previously existing decision-making power in the area of police and judicial cooperation in criminal matters (enhanced cooperation) was removed by the Treaty of Nice; see now Art. 40a TEU.

11. According to the actual wording of Art. 214(2) EC, the competence of the European Council only concerns the nomination of the intended President, and the other competences mentioned in this provision as belonging to the Council are enjoyed by the 'ordinary' Council. The author of this chapter is however of the opinion that throughout the whole of the second paragraph of Art. 214, the term 'Council' refers to the Council meeting in the composition of the Heads of State or Government, i.e., the European Council without the President of the Commission.

12. See section 9.2, *infra*.

13. E.g., the Decision of the Heads of State or Government meeting within the European Council concerning certain problems raised by Denmark on the Treaty on European Union (Bull. EC 12-1992 point I.34; O.J. 1992, C 348/1). While the Decision on the location of the seats of the Institutions was taken during the Edinburgh European Council, it is formally merely a Decision of the Representatives of the Governments of the Member States, not a Decision of the Heads of State or Government. See ibid., point I.32 and O.J. 1992, C 341/1. See Ch. 2, section 5.3, *supra*. See further W.T. Eijsbouts, 'De Raad van opperhoofden. Over het regeringsstelsel van de Unie', in A.K. Koekkoek et al., *Bijdragen aan een Europese grondwet* (Deventer, 2000), 63–64.

Finally, the European Council of Seville of 21 and 22 June 2002, implementing the task assigned to it in Article 4(1) TEU of providing the Union with the necessary impetus for its development and defining its general political guidelines, drew up further rules concerning the preparation, the conduct and the conclusions of its meetings.[14] According to paragraph 1, the European Council meets in principle four times a year.[15] According to paragraph 3, third indent, the agenda will mention 'items for discussion with a view to adopting a decision'. Paragraph 9 provides that the political conclusions drawn from the discussion are to be brought to the attention of the (ordinary) Council, so that it can put such a 'decision' in the appropriate legally binding form, in accordance with the applicable Treaty provisions.

It cannot be denied that the relations between the European Council and the Community Institutions, particularly the Commission and the Parliament (not to mention the Court) are singularly poor. The Commission's right of initiative and the co-decision powers of the European Parliament are diminished if the European Council takes a decision of principle without the Commission having presented a proposal and the Parliament having been consulted.[16] Nevertheless, also in view of the numerous Gordian knots which the European Council has cut over the years, such as the introduction of direct elections to the European Parliament, the enlargement of the Communities, and the increase in the Communities' own resources, the overall evaluation of the European Council – at least from the point of view of effective action by the Community – must be positive.

3   THE COUNCIL OF THE EUROPEAN UNION

3.1   Name, Composition and Character

What was hitherto termed the Council of the European Communities now answers to the name of Council of the European Union[17] and consists of a representative of each of the Member States at ministerial level, authorized to commit the government of that Member State.[18] This provision, formulated as such since the Treaty on European Union, replaces Article 2(1) of the Merger Treaty, under which the Council consisted of representatives of the Member States, whereby each

---

14. See Conclusions of the Presidency, Annexe 1, Rules for organizing the proceedings of the European Council, Bull. EU 6-2002, point I-27.
15. I.e., two times in each presidency. According to Declaration No. 22 adopted with the Treaty of Nice, during each presidency, one meeting will be held in Brussels (i.e., once every six months), and once the Union has eighteen Member States (which was the case as of 1 May 2004) all the meetings will take place in Brussels.
16. See R.H. Lauwaars, 'The European Council', (1977) CML Rev., 25. A report on the outcome of each meeting, and a yearly written report on the progress achieved by the Union are presented to the European Parliament by the European Council. (Art. 4 TEU, previously point 2.1.4. of the Stuttgart Solemn Declaration).
17. See Dec. 93/591 of 8 Nov. 1993, concerning the name to be given to the Council following the entry into force of the Treaty on European Union (O.J. 1993, L 281/18).
18. Arts. 203 EC, and 116 Euratom, 1st para. in each case.

Government delegated one of its members. The present formulation makes it possible for members of regional governments to be the representatives of the Member States, providing that the minister in question is competent to commit the Member State as a whole.[19]

Despite the confusion caused by its renaming, the Council is an Institution of the Communities, just like the Commission, the European Parliament, the Court of Justice and the Court of Auditors,[20] and is put at the service of the European Union (see Arts. 3 and 5 TEU). As one of the Institutions, it is bound by the Treaties and has to fulfil the duties which they entrust to it. In law it derives its powers exclusively from the Treaties and exercises them according to the procedures laid down therein. Its decisions have the legal effect stated in the Treaties and, to the extent that they are based on the EC and Euratom Treaties, are subject to review of their legality by the Court of Justice.[21] The decisions of the Council, therefore, cannot be described as international agreements.[22]

The Council is the Institution of the Community in which the Member States are represented as such and by means of which they participate in the political and legal activities of the Communities. The members of the Council do not sit in a personal capacity, but as representatives of their Member State. Each of them acts on the instructions, and by a mandate, of his or her government. In this the Council differs from the Commission, whose members are independent.[23] In the Council, therefore, the Community interest, which the Council as an institution is as much required to protect as the Commission, will be viewed through the lens of national interests. According to the subject-matter and the political climate in the Communities the lens will be more or less tinted. A pure protection of national interests which encroaches upon essential interests of the Communities, however, conflicts with the responsibility which the Member States making up the Council bear for the protection of the interests of the Communities.[24]

In a significant sense the Council is intergovernmental: it is composed of representatives of the Member States at ministerial level. Unlike the state of affairs in most international organizations having a 'Committee of Ministers' in one form or another, in the Communities no provision has been made for meetings of the Council at the level of official deputies of the members of the Council. By expressly limiting the composition of the Council to representatives at ministerial level, the contracting parties have given evidence of their intention to include those who

---

19. R.H. Lauwaars, 'De institutionele bepalingen in het EU-Verdrag', (1992) SEW, 678–679; see also J.W. de Zwaan, *Het Comité van Permanente Vertegenwoordigers*, EM nr. 42 (Deventer, 1993), 58 and note 70 (in English as: *The Permanent Representatives Committee: Its Role in European Union Decision-Making* (Amsterdam, 1995).
20. See Arts. 7 EC and 3 Euratom.
21. The Court has at present no power to review decisions taken in the context of CFSP, and limited power to do so in the context of the third pillar (PJCCM) (Arts. 46 and 35 TEU). Questions of competence themselves may be reviewed, cf. Case C-170/96, *Commission v. Council*.
22. Cf. Case 38/69, *Commission v. Italy* (see Ch. V, section 1).
23. Arts. 213 EC and 126(2) Euratom.
24. See Joined Cases 2 & 3/60, *Niederrheinische Bergwerks-AG et al. v. High Authority* on this responsibility.

bear direct political responsibility for national policies in the decision-making process of the Communities and the Union, in order thus to make the readiness and power to take decisions as great as possible.

It must not be inferred from the obligation on governments to send someone of ministerial rank to the Council that the Council can only meet (and take decisions) in a valid way if all the governments have fulfilled this obligation. The Treaties provide for the possibility of voting by proxy.[25] This also holds for the Council when it carries out specific tasks of the Union.[26] From this it is evident that the Council can also function in the absence of one or more of its members.[27] In its Rules of Procedure, therefore, the Council has provided for the possibility that if one of its members is prevented from attending a session, he can let himself be represented.[28] However, it is clear, from the Treaty provisions concerning voting by proxy just referred to, and from the Rules of Procedure, that such a representative, since he is not a member of a government, cannot himself validly give the vote of the member of the Council; this can only be done by another member of the Council.[29]

The Council adopts its own Rules of Procedure[30] and the Presidency of the Council is held for a term of six months by one of its members in the order decided by the Council acting unanimously (Art. 203 EC).

It is left to the discretion of the governments to decide which minister they send to the Council. As a rule, the Foreign Ministers (or State Secretaries for Foreign Affairs) act as members of the Council. However, they will usually be accompanied or replaced by those of their colleagues under whose national competence particular questions come, so that in practice a 'multiple' member acts in the Council for each Member State. Usually the 'General Affairs and External Relations Council', composed of the Foreign Ministers, meets once a month; it was entrusted by the Paris Summit of December 1974 with the task of acting as initiator and coordinator, in order to ensure consistency in Community activities and continuity of work.[31]

---

25. Arts. 206 EC and 120 Euratom.
26. Arts. 28 and 41 TEU.
27. The question whether the Council can validly meet in the absence of one of its members even if this member does not send a representative and does not authorize another member to vote for him is not a purely academic question. It arose during the constitutional crisis of the EEC in the years 1965–1966, when the French government followed an 'empty chair policy' for over six months and refused to participate in the meetings of the Council. See further, in the context of the decision-making process, Ch. V, section 4.1., *infra*.
28. Art. 4, Rules of Procedure of the Council of 15 Sept. 2006, O.J. 2006, L 285/47, as amended by Council Decision of 1 Jan. 2007, O.J. 2007, L 1/9.
29. Ibid., Art. 11(3). In practice nowadays it is extremely rare for a Member State to delegate its vote, see De Zwaan, *The Permanent Representatives Committee: Its Role in European Union Decision-Making* (Amsterdam, 1995) 43.
30. Art. 207(3) EC. See generally, M. Westlake and D. Galloway, *The Council of the European Union*, 3rd. ed., (London, 2004) 28–41.
31. Bull. EC 12-1974, 7 (point 3 of the communiqué:). On the related so-called 'Marlia' procedure see WQ 730/79 (Van Miert) O.J. 1980, C 49/12.

The wide-ranging nature of the Council's activities has led to the development of specialized Council sessions – sometimes between meetings of the General Affairs Council, sometimes simultaneously – in which the Council is composed of the ministers responsible for the area under discussion. The number of these so-called sectoral or specialized Councils has become so large over the years that the General Affairs Council decided to limit them to nine in number, including Ecofin (ministers of economic and financial affairs), Agriculture, Environment, Employment and Social Policy, and competitiveness (the internal market).[32] Thus, in recent years, the Council has held around 80 sessions each year (83 in 1997, 73 in 2005)[33] and over 2,600 sessions of the Council have been held since the Merger Treaty came into force (1 July 1967).

Regular meetings are also held outside the context of the Council, particularly by the specialized ministers, such as the ministers for Finance, Justice or Education, of the Member States, in the presence of members of the Commission. As the Council stated in answer to questions asked by some members of the European Parliament,[34] these meetings are intended for 'the exchange of views and information of a general character' and may concern subjects coming under the competence of the Council. However, as soon as deliberations about decisions to be taken by the Community are necessary, these take place 'in accordance with the rules on Community competences and within the institutional framework'.

In relation to tasks which are specifically those of the Union, the ministers for Foreign Affairs or Defence constitute the Council as far as CFSP is concerned. The tasks which relate to the Third Pillar (PJCCM) are dealt with by the specialized Council for Justice and Home Affairs.

3.1.1 Proposed Changes following the Lisbon Treaty

According to Article 16(6) TEU (Lisbon) read with 236 TFEU, the Council will meet in different configurations, the list of which shall be adopted by the European Council. Two configurations are expressly mentioned: the General Affairs Council and the Foreign Affairs Council; the latter will be presided over by the High Representative (Art. 18(3) TEU (Lisbon)), that is to say the present Secretary-General of the Council who is at the same time the High Representative in the framework of the Common Foreign And Security Policy. In the future, in addition to his function as High Representative, he will be one of the Vice-Presidents of the Commission (Art. 18(4) TEU (Lisbon)).

---

32. See O.J. 2006, L 285/61 for the list of Council configurations (Annex I to the Council's Rules of Procedure).
33. Overview of the activities of the Council.
34. WQs 317/68 (Apel) J.O. 1969, C 65/5; 125/69 (Vredeling) J.O. 1969, C 94/21; 13/70 (Vredeling) J.O. 1970, C 97/2 and 284/70 (Vredeling) J.O. 1970, C 140/9. See also WQ 516/73 (O'Hagan) O.J. 1974, C 22/32. See Mortelmans, 'The extramural meetings of the Ministers of the Member States of the Community' (1974) 11 CML Rev., 62. On informal sessions see also WQs 1731/81 (Van Miert) O.J. 1982, C 129/11 and 2075 and 2076/82 (Cohen) O.J. 1983, C 118/27 and C 177/5.

The chairmanship of all other Council configurations will be held on the basis of equal rotation. Just as now, the chairmanship will be exercised for a period of six months by one of the Member States, but a new element is that the sequence of the Member States in this respect will be established by the European Council. Another new element has been laid down in Declaration No. 9: Member States will operate in teams of three chairmen for a period of 18 months; each Member State which belongs to the team will chair the sectoral Council meetings and COREPER for a period of six months, but other constructions are not to be excluded.

3.2   TASKS

According to Article 202 EC (see also Art. 115 Euratom), the Council has a coordinating task in order 'to ensure that the objectives set out in this Treaty are attained'; the task is to ensure, 'in accordance with the provisions of this Treaty', coordination of the general economic policies of the Member States;[35] in addition, it has the 'power to take decisions'. As is evident from various provisions of the Treaty, this decision-making power lies generally[36] in the field of policy-making, and amounts to what may be called, in view of the Council's freedom of decision and the importance of the subject-matter, Community legislation;[37] it also covers the substantive regulation of relations with the outside world by means of the conclusion of treaties and other agreements.[38]

The Council also has decision-making power in the fields of the supplementary policies of the Union, CFSP and PJCCM. As far as CFSP is concerned, it takes the decisions necessary for defining and implementing the common policy; these decisions may take the form of the adoption of a joint action or a common position.[39] In PJCCM, the Council may also adopt common positions; in addition it may adopt framework decisions, and may draw up conventions which it recommends to the Member States for adoption in accordance with their respective constitutional requirements.[40] Since these areas are mainly subject to intergovernmental forms of cooperation,[41] the definition of the CFSP by the Council is on the basis of the general guidelines and common strategies which are formulated by the European Council (Art. 13(1) TEU). Similarly, the PJCCM is in essence a coordination of action by the Member States in the areas mentioned in Title VI TEU (Art. 34 TEU). In the area of CFSP there is therefore a specific task for the

---

35. In Euratom, given the character of that Community as one of partial integration, the coordinating role of the Council concentrates on coordination of action by the Community on the one hand, and that of the individual Member States on the other (Art. 115, 2nd para., Euratom).
36. But see Arts. 210, 213(1)(2), 222 and 225A EC for the Council's powers concerning a number of important points on the organization of the Communities.
37. See, *inter alia*, Arts. 37(2), 40, 71(1), 83, 95, and 133 read with 300 EC.
38. Arts. 111, 300 read with 133, 170, 174(4), and 310 EC.
39. Arts. 13(3), 14 and 15 TEU.
40. Art. 34 TEU.
41. See Ch. I, section 7.2

European Council as an organ of the Union. As for the other tasks of the European Council, we refer to section 2.2 above.

3.3   VOTING REQUIREMENTS

The general rule under the Community Treaties is that the Council takes its decisions by simple majority of its members, save as otherwise provided in the Treaties themselves.[42] Mostly the Treaties prescribe unanimity or a qualified majority.[43] In the case of qualified majority voting, the votes are weighted according to the provisions of Article 205(2) EC (Art. 118(2) Euratom), as amended by Article 10(2) Act of Accession 2005. Since the entry into force of this Act on 1 January 2007 (date of accession of Bulgaria and Romania) a qualified majority is attained with 255 votes out of the 345 votes, coming from at least the majority of the Member States.[44] Under the new Article 205(4) EC, which has been added by the Protocol on Enlargement appended to the Treaty of Nice, a Member State will moreover be able to request verification that the Member States constituting the qualified majority represent at least 62% of the total population of the Union. If this condition is not met, then the decision is not adopted.[45]

If the Council is not adopting an act on a proposal from the Commission, the additional requirement is imposed that at least two-thirds of the Member States, i.e., 18 Member States, must vote in favour of the act. In practice this means that at least 12 of the smaller Member States must agree with the six large Member States on these occasions (as opposed to eight under the normal procedure). One reason for this additional requirement lies in the assumption that the interests of the smaller Member States are safer in the hands of the Commission than in a Council majority consisting mainly of the biggest Member States. In cases in which the Council adopts an act on a proposal from the Commission, unanimity is required for any deviation from that proposal.[46] If no Commission proposal is provided for, then the guarantee for the smaller Member States which is assumed to be contained in the Commission proposal is absent.

The expansion of qualified majority voting went hand-in-hand with revision of the Council's Rules of Procedure. Whereas originally provision was only made that the Council votes on the initiative of its President, since 1987 the President has also

---

42. Arts. 205(1), EC, and 118(1) Euratom
43. The number of instances in which unanimity is required has been steadily declining over the years, with each amendment of the Treaties (see Ch. 1 section 7 *supra*), but is still considerable. The most important cases where unanimity is presently required are Arts. 93; 190(4); 225(2); 269 and 308 EC.
44. Art. 205 (2) EC, as amended.
45. The size of the population of each Member State is laid down in Annex III of the Council's Rules of Procedure. The Annex will be updated by the Council as of 1 Jan. of each year. This decision will be published in the O.J. (see Art. 11, para. 5, juncto Annex III of the Rules of Procedure).
46. Arts. 250(1) EC and 119(1) Euratom.

been required to open voting proceedings on the initiative of a member of the Council or of the Commission, provided that a majority of the Council's members so decide.[47] The President draws up the provisional agenda for each meeting of the Council, and items on which a vote may be requested must be indicated as such.[48]

In the fields of CFSP and PJCCM, the Council generally decides by unanimity. Nevertheless, in CFSP, the Council acts by qualified majority when taking decisions implementing a common strategy, a joint action or a common position (Art. 23(2) TEU). In the field of PJCCM, measures implementing 'decisions' are taken by qualified majority; for procedural questions, the Council decides by simple majority (Arts. 34(2)(c) and (4) TEU). Finally it should be mentioned that in the so-called Ioannina Compromise, further rules were set in relation to the acceptance of qualified majority voting in the Council.[49]

The Declaration on the enlargement of the European Union, annexed to the Final Act of the Treaty of Nice (Declaration No. 20), includes a table showing the distribution of votes in a Union of 27 Member States. Another Declaration (No. 21) states that the threshold for qualified majority will gradually increase, so that the minimum becomes 73.4% of the votes, and the blocking minority in the enlarged Union will be 91 votes out of a total of 345.[50]

3.3.1 Proposed Changes following the Lisbon Treaty

Until 1 November 2014, the situation will remain unchanged, that is to say: majority voting will be carried out according to the rules of the Treaty of Nice, described above. As from that date the new rules will apply, according to which a qualified majority will be attained with the votes of 55% of the Member States comprising at least fifteen of them, and representing 65% of the population of the Union. However, in the period between 1 November 2014 and 31 March 2017, every Member State

---

47. See Council Decision of 20 Jul. 1987, O.J. 1987, L 219/27 (which has meanwhile been replaced). See for the current text Rules of Procedure (see *supra*), Art. 11(l).
48. Rules of Procedure (see *supra*), Art. 3. See M. Westlake and D. Galloway, *The Council of the European Union*, 3rd. ed., (London, 2004), 35–36.
49. The Ioannina compromise takes its name from an informal meeting of foreign ministers in the Greek city of Ioannina on 27 Mar. 1994. The text of the Compromise was published in *Agence Europe*, Document No. 1879 of 14 Apr. 1994. The Council Decision which is part of the compromise is also published in O.J. 1994, C 105/1; it was amended by a decision at Brussels on 1 Jan. 1995 (O.J. 1995, C 1/1). See on this also Ch. V, section 4.1.1, *infra*.
50. This figure (91) does not accord with the number of votes for a qualified majority mentioned in the Declaration on enlargement (258). After the original text of the Treaty and the Declarations was established, the Committee of Permanent Representatives (discussed immediately *infra*) fixed the number for a qualified majority at 255 (out of a total of 345 votes), which does indeed give a blocking majority of 91. At the same time, the number of votes for a qualified majority in the Union of 15 Members was set at the above-mentioned figure of 169 (originally 170). The figure of 255 votes is not included in the Declaration on enlargement. Expressed as a percentage of the total number of votes in a Union of 27 Member States (345 votes) the number of 255 votes amounts to 73.9%, which is slightly higher than the 73.4% mentioned in Declaration No. 21. See on this point J.W. de Zwaan, 'Het Verdrag van Nice' (2002) SEW, 42–52 at 43–44, and A. Arnull, Size Matters, Editorial (2001) EL Rev., 1–2.

may require that a qualified majority be set according to the previous system, that is to say according to the system established by the Treaty of Nice and which will apply until 1 November 2014 (see Art. 16(4) TEU (Lisbon) read with Art. 238 TFEU and Art. 3 Protocol on transitional provisions). Without a proposal from the Commission or from the High Representative, 72% of the Member States have to be in favour.

According to Article 16(4) TEU (Lisbon), a blocking minority must include at least four Member States; apart from that, the so-called 'Ioannina mechanism' will apply, as described in Declaration No. 7.[51]

The main rule on decision-making by the Council will be that it takes its decisions by qualified majority (Art. 16(3) TEU (Lisbon)). Under the Lisbon Treaty, qualified majority will replace unanimity in 17 cases, in particular in the field of police and judicial cooperation in criminal matters. The Lisbon Treaty further introduces about 30 new legal bases where decisions may be taken by qualified majority, *inter alia* concerning supplementary policy in the field of consular protection (see Art. 23 TFEU). Unanimity will continue to be required in fields such as defence, family law and the financial perspectives.

3.4   THE COMMITTEE OF PERMANENT REPRESENTATIVES

Although, as was mentioned in section 3.1 above, there is no provision for the Council to meet at the level of deputies,[52] a Committee of Permanent Representatives (COREPER) has been provided for as a subsidiary body of the Council.[53] The members of COREPER (as this body is known after its name in French) are ambassadors who head the Permanent Representations of each of the Member States to the Communities.[54] The task of COREPER is to prepare the Council's work and to carry out the tasks which the Council assigns to it; COREPER may adopt procedural decisions in cases provided for in the Council's Rules of Procedure.[55] COREPER is divided in two: COREPER I is made up of deputy heads of the Permanent Representations and deals with technical and legal questions; COREPER II consists of the Permanent Representatives themselves and deals with political, financial and institutional questions.[56]

---

51. See also section 3.3 and note 49 *supra*.
52. Such a procedure exists elsewhere: in the Council of Europe, decisions may be taken by Minister's Deputies, see H.G. Schermers, N.M. Blokker, *International Institutional Law*, 3rd rev. ed., The Hague/London/Boston, 1997, 393 and note 13.
53. Now governed by Arts. 207(1) EC and 121(1) Euratom. See, generally, J.W. De Zwaan, *The Permanent Representatives Committee: Its Role in European Union Decision-Making* (Amsterdam, 1995) and M. Westlake and D. Galloway, *The Council of the European Union*, 3rd ed., (London, 2004), Ch. 11.
54. Third countries have missions to the Communities, the Member States have permanent representations.
55. Arts. 207(1) EC and 121(1) Euratom. See also Rules of Procedure (see *supra*), Art. 19.
56. J.W. De Zwaan, *The Permanent Representatives Committee: Its Role in European Union Decision-Making* (Amsterdam, 1995) 140–144.

COREPER forms a permanent liaison body for the exchange of information between the national administrations and the Institutions of the Communities. Within the Member States, the individual members of COREPER participate in the formation of the national standpoints and their coordination. COREPER does not, however, have independent powers of decision, except for the procedural decisions mentioned above. Nonetheless, as the body preparing the decision-making of the Council, it plays an important role.[57]

Although COREPER was established in the framework of the EC, and has gained a prominent place in this context, it also carries out its tasks in the fields of the supplementary policies of the Union (CFSP and PJCCM). The special committees in these fields (the Political Committee for CFSP and the Coordinating Committee for PJCCM) are subordinate to COREPER. This is apparent above all from the fact that Article 207(1) EC, in which the tasks of COREPER are described, also applies to the supplementary fields. It is also apparent from Articles 25 and 36 TEU, which explicitly refer to the role of COREPER.[58]

4   EUROPEAN COMMISSION

4.1   COMPOSITION AND CHARACTER OF THE COMMISSION

The European Commission – which according to Article 7 EC is officially called simply 'a Commission' – consists of twenty-seven members 'who shall be chosen on grounds of their general competence and whose independence is beyond doubt'.[59] Members of the Commission have to be nationals of a Member State and at least one national (but no more than two) of each Member State is to be appointed. In practice this meant in the past that two nationals of each of the five large countries were appointed, whereas one national of each of the smaller countries was appointed.[60] Since 1 November 2004, when the Union comprised twenty-five Member States, the number of commissioners has been reduced to twenty-five, one from each Member State.[61] This number was increased to twenty-seven as a result of the accession of Bulgaria and Romania on 1 January 2007.

---

57. See, further, Ch. V, section 4.1.2 *infra*.
58. See J.W. de Zwaan, *The Permanent Representatives Committee: Its Role in European Union Decision-Making* (Amsterdam, 1995) 78, 79, 262–268 and 281–284. On 22 Jan. 2001, the Council set up, in the framework of the European security and defence policy, a Political and Security Committee, to deal with the tasks set out in Art. 25 TEU. The Committee is assisted by a Military Committee of the EU, set up on the same date; see O.J. 2001, L 27/1 resp. 4.
59. Art. 213(1) EC, as amended by Art. 4(1) Protocol on Enlargement and Art. 45 of the Treaty of Accession 2005. A unanimous decision of the Council is necessary in order to alter the number of members of the Commission, Art. 213(1), 2nd para., EC.
60. Art. 213(1) EC as it read until the entry of the Protocol on Enlargement on 1 Feb. 2003.
61. As a result of Art. 4(1) Protocol on Enlargement.

The governments of the Member States attempt to ensure that the composition of the Commission reflects a balanced representation of European political tendencies.[62]

Strictly speaking, the attention devoted to the division of the seats of the Commission according to nationality ought to be unnecessary, for these nationals are not representatives of the Member States. On the contrary, they have the right and the duty to perform their tasks with complete independence in the general interest of the Communities, and they are forbidden to seek or take instructions from any government or other body.[63] They are to refrain from any action incompatible with the nature of their duties.[64] The Member States have undertaken to respect this principle and not to seek to influence the members of the Commission in the performance of their tasks. During their term of office, Commissioners may not engage in any other occupation, and even after they have ceased to hold office they are required to behave with integrity and discretion as regards the acceptance of certain appointments or benefits.[65] Privileges and immunities ensure undisturbed performance of their duties.[66]

For obvious reasons, the Member States are anxious that the Commission is composed in such a way that a certain insight into and sympathy for the various national ways of thinking, the sometimes divergent national aspirations and the very real problems which beset various parts of the Community are guaranteed to a reasonable extent. A reduction in the number of commissioners appears, however,

---

62. Thus from the United Kingdom in the past a Conservative and a Labour party figure were appointed each time by common accord of the governments of the Member States. See, further, Donnelly and Ritchie in Edwards and Spence (eds), *The European Commission* 2nd ed., (London, 1997), 33–36.

63. Arts. 213(2) EC. The Commission swears an oath (or affirmation) of office before the Court of Justice, usually on the day before its first formal meeting, see, e.g., *General Report on the activities of the European Union, 1995* (Brussels, Luxembourg, 1996) point 1053. The independence question can sometimes be thorny, see the refusal of the discharge in respect of the 1992 budget, O.J. 1994, C 128/332.

64. The Commission feels that its members are free, in the exercise of their political responsibility, to conduct personal discussions with parliamentarians or members of government of their own or other countries if they wish to do so. It is convinced that during such discussions each of its members will adhere strictly to the obligations laid down in Art. 10(2) of the Merger Treaty, see WQ 10/71 (Vredeling) O.J. 1971, C 61/1. See Art. 213(2) EC.

65. This provision was relevant when the member of the Santer Commission, Bangemann, announced in Jun. 1999 that he would accept a position with the Spanish telecom firm Telefónica. The Council appealed to the Court of Justice in that case to annul Mr Bangemann's pension rights (Case C-290/99, *Council v. Bangemann*, see Council Decision of 9 Jul. 1999, O.J. 1999, L 192/55). Mr Bangemann appealed to the Court of First Instance against this Decision of the Council (Case T-208/99, *Bangemann v. Council*). Both cases have been withdrawn in the meantime, in the framework of a compromise reached between the two parties (Council Decision of 17 Dec. 1999 on the settlement of the Bangemann case, O.J. 2000, L 16/73).

66. Protocol on Privileges and Immunities of the European Communities, Arts. 20 and 12–15. The Protocol was previously annexed to the Merger Treaty, which was repealed by Art. 9 Treaty of Amsterdam; the Protocol itself is maintained by Art. 9(4) Treaty of Amsterdam.

desirable both from the point of view of internal cohesion and to ensure a more even distribution of portfolios.[67] As soon as the Union has 27 Member States, the number of commissioners is to be less than the number of Member States; the members of the Commission will then be chosen according to a system of rotation to be adopted by the Council acting unanimously.[68]

While it is the duty of the Commission to serve the general interest of the Communities as a whole, this does not mean that it has to neglect national interests in performing its duties. It will, however, have to consider all matters from the viewpoint of the Community interest. Thus, in making its contribution to the policy-making in the Council, where national interests are very much to the fore and frequently clash with each other, it will have to try to find, for these antitheses, solutions which do justice to the Community interest. It should be noted, though, that just as the Council, which is the natural representative of the various national interests, has nevertheless to protect the essential interests of the Community, the Commission for its part also has to take account of the vital interests of individual Member States. The Commission, therefore, should never help to outvote a Member State if the latter's vital interests might, in the opinion of the Commission, be prejudiced. The Commission bears this responsibility because in most cases under the EC and Euratom Treaties qualified majority decisions of the Council can only be reached with its cooperation.[69]

The process of appointing the Commission was altered by the Treaty of Nice. Since the entry into force of that Treaty, the members of the Commission are appointed by the Council in the composition of Heads of State or Government; the appointment is for a (renewable) term of five years (Art. 214(1) EC). The European Parliament plays an important role in this process. First of all, the Council nominates a person for appointment as the new president of the Commission; this nomination must be approved by the European Parliament. Then the Council, in agreement with the nominated president, draws up a list of the other candidates for membership of the Commission. Finally, the composition of the Commission as a whole is submitted for the approval of the Parliament; only following this approval may the new Commission be appointed by the Council (Art. 214(2) EC).[70] All decisions of the Council taken on the basis of this provision may be adopted by qualified majority. This is new compared with the previous

---

67. According to Art. 1 of Protocol 11 annexed to the Treaty of Amsterdam, the number of members of the Commission was to be altered to one national of each Member State. This Protocol was repealed by Art. 1 Protocol on Enlargement. See now Art. 4(2) Protocol on Enlargement.
68. Art. 4(2) Protocol on Enlargement.
69. See Ch. V, section 4.1 *infra*.
70. This right of Parliament to approve the Commission recalls the French system of investiture, i.e., a vote of confidence in the new government, a concept which had already been introduced in Community practice: see Bull. EC suppl. 1/93, speech on the occasion of the 'investiture debate on the new Commission'. This procedure resulted in a failure when in Oct. 2004 the Parliament refused to agree with the appointment of the proposed Italian commissioner Buttiglioni; the nominated President, Mr Barroso, thereupon had to withdraw his proposal for the new Commission. Only when Mr Buttiglioni had been replaced by another Italian (Mr Frattini) did Barroso succeed in obtaining Parliament's approval.

procedure, and is important since in this way it is made impossible for one Member State to prevent the appointment or reappointment of a President or Member of the Commission it does not like.[71]

While the Council, in the composition of Heads of State or Government, appoints the members of the Commission, they cannot discharge them during their five-year term of office. The Court of Justice alone, on the application of the Council or the Commission, may compulsorily retire an individual member of the Commission from office if he no longer fulfils the conditions required for the performance of his duties or if he has been guilty of serious misconduct (Art. 216 EC). The European Parliament can compel the Commission to resign as a body, by means of a motion of censure on its activities.[72]

The fact that members of the Commission are obliged to perform their duties in complete independence, in the general interest of the Communities, forbids their being prejudiced in favour of or against particular national standpoints or interests, but it does not imply that they also have to practise political neutrality and to refrain from making statements that may be regarded as interference in the domestic affairs of a Member State.[73] The Commission regards its members as being permitted to engage in national politics as long as they are not involved in specific political controversies.[74] Under certain circumstances, e.g., if the free democratic system in the Communities were in issue, there could even be an obligation on members of the Commission to comment (according to the German Secretary of State, Moersch, answering a question by a German Parliamentarian).[75]

It is a typical obligation for an *official* to refrain from interference in political questions in the performance of his duties. The Commission, however is not a body of officials which is hierarchically subordinate to the Council. It is not subject to instructions from the Council, but is a body bearing its own political responsibility. This is made clear by the provision that it must resign *en bloc* if a political body, the European Parliament, censures its policy. Moreover it is entrusted, particularly under the EC Treaty, with a task which has not only an administrative, but also a political content, as appears from the role conferred on it in the formulation of Community *policies*.

It is entirely incorrect, therefore, to equate the Commission with the secretariat of a traditional international organization, in the service of the body representing

---

71. For instance, one may recall the problems surrounding the appointment of Mr Santer as President of the Commission in Dec. 1995.
72. Arts. 201 EC and 114 Euratom. See further section 5.2.2 *infra* and Corbett et al. *The European Parliament*, 4th ed. (London, 2000).
73. See the letter of 20 Jul. 1968 from Mansholt, then Vice-President of the Commission, to Debré, then French foreign minister, which was reproduced in (1968) *Agenor* No. 8, 67–68.
74. See WQs 1175/81 (Radux) O.J. 1981, C 345/22 and 1682/85 (Vandemeulebroucke) O.J. 1986, C 55/12.
75. (1971) *Agenor* No. 21, 10. In connection with the participation of the FPÖ in the Austrian government, the Commission declared that it shared the concerns of the other 14 Member States, but for its own part strove for a workable relationship with Austria. It based itself in this on its role as guardian of the European Treaties, *Europa van Morgen* 2000/3, 25.

the member States of the organization. The Commission is one of the Institutions; it is a body with its own political responsibility, its own political task. If there is a sort of international secretariat in the Communities, it is the civil service structure of the various Community Institutions and other bodies.[76]

4.1.1 Proposed Changes following the Lisbon Treaty

The European Commission – which according to Article 13 TEU (Lisbon) will now bear this name as its official name, but which will be referred to in the Treaties as the 'Commission' – will as from 1 January 2014 no longer consist of nationals of all the Member States. According to Article 17(5) TEU (Lisbon), read with Article 244 TFEU, as from that date the Commission will consist of a number of members, including the President and the High Representative, corresponding to two-thirds of the number of Member States; the European Council may decide to alter this number. The members of the Commission will be chosen on the basis of a system of equal rotation between the Member States, whereby the following principles must be respected:

– The Member States must be treated on a strictly equal footing.
– The composition of the Commission will at all times sufficiently reflect the demographical and geographical differences between the Member States (see also Declaration No. 10).

The position of the President of the Commission will be strengthened (see Art. 17(6) (Lisbon)). According to Article 17(7) TEU (Lisbon), the European Council will propose to the European Parliament a candidate for nomination as President of the Commission 'taking into account the elections to the European Parliament and after having held the appropriate consultations' (see also Declaration No. 11).

4.2 INTERNAL ORGANIZATION

The Commission has a President and a number of Vice-Presidents, the latter appointed by the President after approval of the college of Commissioners.[77] The Commission adopts its own Rules of Procedure so as to ensure that both it and its departments operate in accordance with the provisions of the relevant Treaty.[78]

---

76. E.g., the Council's own General Secretariat (see Art. 207(2) EC). The Commission itself could be qualified as a non-plenary policy-making organ, in particular as a 'Governing Board', cf. Schermers and Blokker, *International Institutional Law* cited *supra*, 290–293, 302 and note 146. See generally on the Council secretariat M. Westlake and D. Galloway, *The Council of the European Union*, 3rd. ed. (London, 2004), Ch. 19.
77. Arts. 217(3) EC and 130 Euratom. The Vice-President(s) deputize for the President, chairing the weekly meeting of the Commission in his absence.
78. Arts. 218(2) EC and 131, 2nd para., Euratom. See Rules of Procedure of the Commission of 29 Nov. 2000, O.J. 2000, L 308/26, last amended by Decision 2006/70/EC, Euratom of 31 Jan. 2006, O.J. 2006, L 34/32.

Each member of the Commission has a personal staff – his or her *cabinet* – which assists him or her, not least by enabling him to keep abreast of matters falling within his colleagues' portfolios and thus to participate in the collegiate responsibility for the Commission's policies. The *chefs de cabinet* or their representatives meet weekly to prepare the Commission's meetings. At these preparatory meetings the points which do not need to be discussed by the Commissioners (and whose adoption will be a formality) are ascertained, and these points are known as 'A' points. Below this political level, the Commission's services are divided into at present 26 directorates-general and a number of horizontal services, such as the secretariat-general, the spokesman's service and the legal service. Each Commissioner has responsibility (sometimes shared) for one or more directorates-general, directorates or other services. As a result of the Treaty of Nice, the position of the President of the Commission has been strengthened. According to Article 217(1) and (2) EC, the members of the Commission work under the political guidance of the President; the President decides on the internal organization, and moreover on the distribution of portfolios among the members of the Commission.

The Committee of Independent Experts, which had drawn up a report in March 1999 concerning cases of 'fraud, mismanagement and nepotism', which led to the resignation of the Santer Commission, presented a follow-up report on 10 September 1999 about the operation of the Commission.[79] As a consequence of this extremely critical report, the Commission adopted a new organizational scheme. On 20 January 2000, a vice-president of the Commission (N. Kinnock) presented an 'action plan' to the European Parliament; this plan led to the adoption of a White Paper on the reform of the Commission.[80] Even before this White Paper appeared, the Commission had approved a code of conduct for its members and another code for the relations between the members of the Commission and the services.[81]

4.3 THE COMMISSION'S TASKS

4.3.1 Participation in Community Legislation

The Commission's participation in the legislative activities of the Community is particularly evident in the role it takes in the adoption of *Community legislation.*

---

79. W. van Gerven, 'Guest Editorial: Ethical and political Responsibility of EU Commissioners' (2000) CML Rev., 1–6.
80. Bull. EU 2000/3, 141.
81. In Sep. 1999. See further on the White Paper 'Reforming the Commission', COM(2000)200 final. The White paper on the reform of the Commission is not to be confused with the White Paper on Governance, COM(2001)428 final, which the Commission adopted on 25 Jul. 2001, and which concerns decentralization within the European Union and the improvement of the internal cohesion of the Community policy areas (see on this *Agence Europe* No. 8012, 23-24 Jul. 2001, 11–12, and No. 8014, 26 Jul. 2001, 17). See also V. Mehde, 'Responsibility and Accountability in the European Commission', (2003) CML Rev., 423–442; C. Möllers, 'European Governance: Meaning and Value of a Concept', (2006) CML Rev., 313–336.

In practically all cases in which decision-making power is conferred on the Council, it can act only on the basis of a proposal from the Commission. The Commission thus has the right of initiative. This is exclusive: no Commission proposal, no act by the Council.[82] The right of initiative is given even greater significance by the fact that normally the Council may amend such a Commission proposal only by unanimous vote,[83] and the fact that as long as the Council has not yet taken a decision the Commission may alter its proposal.[84]

The Commission's participation 'in the shaping of measures taken by the Council and by the European Parliament in the manner provided for in this Treaty'[85] does not always take the form of a proposal. In some cases the Commission is only empowered to adopt non-binding recommendations or opinions. Such opinions are provided for in Articles 104(5) (excessive deficits); 120(3) (protective measures in balance of payments crises); 140 (social policy) and 272(2) EC (Community budget). Recommendations forming the basis for action by the Council are provided for in Articles 99(2) and (4) (broad guidelines of economic policies of the Member States and of the Community); 104(13) (excessive deficits); 111 (exchange-rate system); 121 (fulfilment of the necessary conditions for the adoption of a single currency); 133(3) (negotiation of international agreements in the field of the common commercial policy) and 300(1) (negotiations leading to international agreements). Article 115 EC declares that the Council or a Member State may request the Commission to make a recommendation (or a proposal) for the economic and monetary matters indicated. In this last case, the Commission makes a recommendation (or a proposal) *at the request* of the Council or a Member State. This is a specific instance of the more general power conferred on the Council by Article 208 EC (cf. Art. 122 Euratom) to request the Commission to undertake any studies which the Council considers desirable for the attainment of the common objectives, and to submit to it any appropriate proposals.[86]

---

82. There are two exceptions to this exclusivity: Art. 67(1) and 107(6) EC. According to Art. 67(1), the Council takes decisions in the new Title IV, during the transitional period mentioned in the provision, on the basis of 'a proposal from the Commission or on the initiative of a Member State'; Art. 107(6) permits the Council to adopt certain provisions relating to the European Central Bank on the basis of a proposal from the Commission or a recommendation from the ECB. See also Art. 107(5) EC. The European Parliament has a quasi-right of initiative, see section 5.2.4, *infra*.

83. Art. 250(1) EC; see 119 Euratom. The exception (Art. 251(4) and (5) EC) concerns decisions of the Council adopting a joint text agreed in the Conciliation Committee with the European Parliament, which can be taken by qualified majority without the Commission having altered its proposal to reflect that joint text. See Case C-344/04, *The Queen ex parte International Air Transport Association (IATA), European Low Fares Airline Association (ELFAA) v. Department for Transport*.

84. Art. 250(2) EC, see also Art. 119 Euratom.

85. Art. 211 EC, 3rd indent; see also Art. 124 Euratom, 3rd indent.

86. As to the meaning of 'proposals' in this context, see Ch. V, section 4.1. See also Case C-27/04, *Commission v. Council*, where the Court held that, when the Council has adopted recommendations under Art. 104(7) EC, it cannot subsequently modify them without a fresh recommendation from the Commission since the latter has a right of initiative in the excessive deficit procedure.

In addition to these specific cases, the Commission has a general power to make recommendations and to adopt opinions.[87]

4.3.2 The Commission's Administrative or Executive Function

The original administrative function of the Commission is based on 'its own power of decision . . . in the manner provided for in this Treaty'.[88] Its delegated administrative function is based on 'the powers conferred on it by the Council for the implementation of the rules laid down by the latter'.[89] The administration to be performed by the Commission on the basis of these powers is wide-ranging. Thus, for example, it gives effect to the budget and to the maintenance of the Community's external relations.[90] In the EC Treaty, an original administrative function is only rarely entrusted to the Commission; in the Euratom Treaty, though, this is different. This is an obvious consequence of the difference between a framework treaty (*traité-cadre*) on the one hand and a treaty-law (*traité-loi*) or management treaty (*traité de gestion*) on the other. The administrative activities of the Commission which are directly based on the EC Treaty are mainly in the fields of the customs union, competition policy and safeguard clauses. These are in fact the main areas in which the EC Treaty exhibits the characteristics of a treaty-law or management treaty.[91] The Court has observed[92] that the Commission's own power of decision in the manner provided for in the Treaty, set out in Article 211 EC, is expressed in almost identical terms to those used in Article 202 EC to describe the same function of the Council; thus there can be no question of inferring any inherent restriction on the Commission's power of decision from the wording of Article 211 EC.

The competition regime deserves special attention. Although the *extent* of the Commission's competence is not laid down in the Treaty, but is to be defined by the Council,[93] this should not be interpreted restrictively. On the contrary, in the basic regulations dealing with the application of the competition rules,[94] the Council has given the Commission extremely broad competences, and the Commission disposes of a wide range of possible acts which it may adopt in the application of the competition rules contained in the EC Treaty although decisions under the new regulation

---

87. Arts. 211 EC, 2nd indent, and 124 Euratom, 2nd indent.
88. Arts. 211 EC and 124 Euratom, 3rd indent in each case.
89. Arts. 211 EC, and 124 Euratom, 4th indent in each case.
90. See Ch. V, section 3.2.4 and Ch. XIII, section 2.6, *infra*, respectively.
91. Note also the Commission's original administrative function in adopting conservatory measures in the event of delays in the annual decision-making process in the Council concerning agricultural prices. This is based on Arts. 10 and 211 EC.
92. Joined Cases 188-190/80, *France, Italy and United Kingdom v. Commission*.
93. Art. 83(1) and (2) first sentence and under (d) EC.
94. Such as Reg. 17/62, replaced as of 1 May 2004 by Reg. 1/2003 of 16 Dec. 2002, O.J. 2003, L 1/1.

differ in some ways from those under the old one.[95] The importance of the Commission's competence in the administration of safeguard clauses,[96] on the other hand, has declined over the years. Under these clauses, in certain circumstances specified in the Treaty, the Member States may temporarily deviate from their Treaty obligations, although this requires the authorization of the Community Institutions.[97] While, in urgent cases, the autonomous resort to protective measures is permitted exceptionally, the Institutions have the right to intervene after the measures have been taken.[98]

While the original, Treaty-based, administrative function of the Commission is confined to a small number of areas, with a narrow scope, the *delegated administrative function* assigned to it by the Council under the EC Treaty system for the implementation of the rules laid down by the Council is very wide-ranging indeed. Implementing powers for the Commission are provided for not only in those cases where the Treaty expressly lays down such a delegated administrative task,[99] but also in practically all decisions of the Council which are of any importance. If, however, these powers are considered from the viewpoint not of quantity but of quality, it must be observed that the Council usually displays an extremely narrow view of the administrative task to be entrusted to the Commission. Despite the fact that the new third indent of Article 202 EC requires the Council to confer implementing powers on the Commission,[100] the Council is still very much inclined to exercise the power it enjoys under that provision to reserve implementing measures to itself where real policy margins are implied or where decisions with important consequences are concerned. Wherever it does delegate power to adopt implementing measures, it invariably tries to ensure that the Commission's powers are subject to strict conditions, even though this clearly goes against the express desire of the Member States, as expressed on the occasion of the adoption of the SEA, that preference should be given to advisory committees (as opposed to regulatory or management committees) in the interests of speed and efficiency in the decision-making process.[101]

4.3.3   The Commission's Supervisory Function

In accordance with the proposals of the *Spaak Report*, the Commission has been directed to ensure 'that the provisions of this Treaty and of the measures taken by

---

95. Cf. Ch. IX *infra*.
96. The Commission also administers safeguard clauses in the course of its delegated administrative function in the field of the common agricultural policy; see Sack, 'The Commission's Powers under the Safeguard Clauses of the Common Organizations of Agricultural Markets', (1983) CML Rev., 757, and e.g., Reg. 1766/92 (O.J. 1992, L 181/21, most recently amended by Council Reg. 1104/2003 (O.J. 2003, L 158/1)), Art. 17 (cereals).
97. E.g., Art. 119 EC.
98. E.g., Art. 120 EC.
99. E.g., Art. 75(3) EC.
100. See section 6.4, under (a), *infra*.
101. See the Communication from the Commission to the Council, 'Conferment of Implementing Powers on the Commission', SEC(90)2589, 7 Jan. 1991. Cf. also Ch. V, section 4.1 *infra*.

the Institutions pursuant thereto are applied'.[102] This supervision extends in the first place to ensuring the observance by the Member States of their obligations under the Treaty. If the Commission considers that a Member State has failed to fulfil its obligations, it may institute proceedings which may ultimately lead to a judgment of the Court of Justice.[103] The supervisory function of the Commission also extends to ensuring the observance by private parties of their Community obligations. This appears from its powers in relation to violations of the principle of non-discrimination in transport[104] or of breach of the rules of competition by undertakings.[105] In the Council regulations in these fields,[106] control by the Commission has taken the form of a series of specific powers, particularly those by which it can oblige an undertaking to put an end to an infringement[107] and those by which it can impose fines (considered to be administrative) and/or periodic penalty payments for breaches of the rules.[108]

In order to exercise its supervisory function the Commission must of course possess the necessary information.[109] For this purpose, in addition to the data which it obtains through complaints by Member States or private parties, or through questions asked by Members of the European Parliament, it may at all times request the Member States to provide it with the requisite information. The Member States are obliged by virtue of Article 10 EC to comply with such requests.[110] Many implementing acts of the Council, particularly harmonization directives, impose a duty on Member States to provide information permitting the Commission to judge whether or not they are fulfilling their obligations.[111] An obligation to provide information to the Commission and a right of investigation by it may also arise in relation to undertakings[112] or procedures may be set up which give the Commission the requisite data[113] in some other way. Article 284 EC[114] contains a general provision according to which the Commission (within the limits and under the conditions laid down by the Council in accordance with the provisions of the Treaty) may collect any information and carry out any necessary checks. This provision has not so far led to a general regulation of the Commission's powers in this field, and initially only formed the basis for decisions of

---

102. Art. 211 EC, first indent; cf. Art. 124 Euratom, first indent.
103. Arts. 226 and 228 EC, see also Arts. 141 and 143 Euratom. See further, Ch. VI, section 2.1.
104. Art. 75(3) and (4) EC.
105. Arts. 81 and 83(2)(a) EC.
106. E.g., Reg. 11/60 (O.J. 1960, 1121) and Reg. 1/2003.
107. E.g., Reg. 1/2003, Art. 7.
108. Arts. 17 and 18 Reg. 11/60, cited *supra*, Arts. 23 and 24 Reg. 1/2003.
109. See, generally, Gil Ibanez, *The Administrative Supervision and Enforcement of EC Law: Powers, Procedures and Limits* (London, 1999).
110. See also Art. 192 Euratom.
111. E.g., Dir. 78/142 (O.J. 1978, L 44/1), Art. 6(1).
112. E.g., Reg. 11, Arts. 11 and 13, and Reg. 1/2003 Arts. 17 and 20.
113. E.g., under the old competition rules, notification of agreements in accordance with Reg. 17, Arts. 4 and 5.
114. Cf. Art. 187 Euratom, and also the extensive powers of the Commission concerning inspections for safeguard controls under Title II, Ch. VII Euratom.

the Council relating to a series of statistical enquiries to be carried out by the Commission.[115]

This last example makes it equally clear that the Commission's rights of enquiry and verification, arising under general or particular provisions of Community law, may also be essential to its policy determination function. For that function to be properly performed the necessary information must be at the Commission's disposal. Finally, it should be mentioned that with regard to information which is by nature confidential, an obligation of secrecy has been imposed on the members of the Commission as well as on members of the other Community Institutions, members of committees, and officials and other servants of the Community.[116] The obligation of secrecy is not absolute as far as the Commission is concerned. Thus, in cases before it the Commission must weigh the interest of secrecy against interests such as the proper course of investigation proceedings, the rights of the defence and the duty to state reasons for Commission decisions.[117] In addition, in accordance with Article 286 EC, since 1 January 1999, personal data processed by the institutions and bodies set up by, or on the basis of, the EC Treaty are covered by Community acts on the protection of individuals with regard to the processing and movement of such data.[118]

In pursuit of greater openness and transparency[119] the Council and the Commission issued, in 1993, a Code of Conduct concerning public access to their documents.[120] Pursuant to Article 255 EC, the Commission submitted a proposal on 26 January 2000 for Regulation concerning public access to documents held by the European Parliament, the Council and the Commission. This proposal led to

---

115. Art. 284 EC does not prevent the Commission from imposing a duty on the Member States to provide information on the basis of specific provisions: Joined Cases 188-190/80, *France et al. v. Commission;* Case C-426/93, *Germany v. Commission.*

116. Art. 287 EC and, extensively, Arts. 24–27 and 194 Euratom.

117. See Case 53/85, *AKZO Chemie BV et al. v. Commission* and Joined Cases 296 & 318/82, *Netherlands and Leeuwarder Papierwarenfabriek BV v. Commission.* See, though, Case 145/83 *Adams v. Commission:* Art. 287 enshrines a general principle. See also the Notice on internal rules of procedure for processing requests for access to the file in various competition fields, O.J. 1997, C 23/3.

118. Hijmans, 'The European Data Protection Supervisor: The Institutions of the EC Controlled by an Independent Authority' 43 CML Rev., 1313–1342. See also Reg. (EC) No 45/2001 of the European Parliament and of the Council of 18 Dec. 2000, on the protection of individuals with regard to the processing of personal data by the Community institutions and bodies and on the free movement of such data, O.J. 2001, L 8/1, and, already from an earlier date, Dir. 95/46/EC of the European Parliament and the Council of 24 Oct. 1995 on the protection of individuals with regard to the processing of personal data and on the free movement of such data, O.J. 1995, L 281/31.

119. Cf. Birmingham European Council, Conclusions of the Presidency, Annex I (Bull. EC 10-1992 point I.8). See in general, K. Lenaerts ' "In the Union We Trust": Trust-Enhancing Principles of Community Law' (2004) CML Rev., 317–343.

120. Published on 31 Dec. 1993, Dec. 93/730 (O.J. 1993, L 340/41, corr. O.J. 1994, L 23/34). See also the Commission's Communications (O.J. 1993, C 156/5 and 166/4). In Case C-58/94, *Netherlands v. Council,* the ECJ rejected the action brought by the Dutch Government against this Decision.

Regulation 1049/2001 of the European Parliament and the Council of 30 May 2001.[121] According to Article 18(1) of this Regulation, each of the Institutions mentioned must adapt its rules of procedure to the new Regulation. All three have done so in the meantime.[122]

4.3.4   Tasks in Relation to the Union

Even after the Treaty of Nice, the Commission's tasks in relation to the Union have remained fairly modest. According to Article 27 TEU, the Commission is to be 'fully associated with the work carried out in the common foreign and security policy field'. Like the Member States, the Commission has the right to refer any question relating to the common foreign and security policy to the Council, and to submit 'proposals' to the Council (Art. 22 TEU). According to Article 36 TEU, the Commission is also to be 'fully associated' in the work in the fields of Police and Judicial Cooperation in Criminal Matters; here, the Commission enjoys a right of initiative which it shares with the Member States (Art. 34(2) TEU).

5   EUROPEAN PARLIAMENT

5.1   COMPOSITION AND CHARACTER OF THE PARLIAMENT

The European Parliament, as it is now called in Article 7(1) EC (but which was originally called the Assembly),[123] consists of 'representatives of the peoples of the States brought together in the Community'.[124] Thus the members of the European Parliament are representatives of the peoples, and this body itself represents the peoples of the Community and their independence.

As representatives of the peoples, the members of the European Parliament are not bound by instructions of their governments, or of the national parliaments.[125] As representatives of the peoples they exercise their duties without instructions or obligation to consult. By the use of the words 'representatives of the peoples' the modern concept of representation, as laid down in the constitutional law of the Member States, has also been incorporated in the Treaties. The undisturbed

---

121. O.J. 2001, L 145/43.
122. See Council Decision of 29 Nov. 2001, O.J. 2001, L 319/40; Commission Decision of 5 Dec. 2001, O.J. 2001, L 345/94, and Decision of the Bureau of the European Parliament of 28 Nov. 2001, O.J. 2001, C 374/1.
123. In fact it re-baptized itself long before its name was formally changed; see the Resolutions of 20 Mar. 1958 (O.J. 1958, 6/58) and 30 Mar. 1962 (O.J. 1962, 1045). Art. 3(1) SEA brought the name 'European Parliament' into the Treaties where it changed or supplemented them.
124. Arts. 189 EC and 107 Euratom.
125. See the Act concerning the election of the representatives of the Assembly by direct universal suffrage, annexed to Dec. 76/787 (O.J. 1976, L 278/1 and 5), Art. 4(1) as last amended by Council Decision of 25 Jun. 2002, and 23 Sept. 2002 (O.J. 2002, L. 283/4).

discharge of their function is guaranteed by the arrangements in their favour contained in the Protocol on the Privileges and Immunities of the European Communities.[126]

The representatives form part of a body which represents not one people, but a plurality of peoples, although in a collective sense. By the use of the plural 'peoples', the Treaties do justice to reality, in the sense that there is not one 'European people'. By substituting for the short phrase 'Member States', commonly used throughout the Treaties, the phrase 'States brought together in the Community',[127] the Treaties emphasize the collective character of the States, not their individual character. The members of the European Parliament represent not only their own people, but also the other peoples of the Community.

The formation of European political groups which already took place in the old Common Assembly of the European Coal and Steel Community (ECSC)[128] clearly demonstrates this notion. It is the groups rather than the national parties which put their stamp on the work of the Parliament. This is evident in debates as well as in the composition of the various parliamentary bodies. The conditions for official recognition of groups are laid down in the Parliament's Rules of Procedure.[129] The creation of a group comprising independent members of the Parliament – a mixed group ('*groupe mixte*') – consisting of a number of non-attached members, was found by the Committee on Constitutional Affairs and then by the Parliament itself to be in conflict with Article 29(1) Rules of Procedure, since the members of this group maintained their political independence. The operation of that measure of the Parliament was suspended by the President of the Court of First Instance in an Order of 25 November 1999,[130] but retained by the Court of First Instance in the full proceedings.[131]

A political group must comprise members from at least one-fifth of the Member States (previously the requirement was that it should comprise members from more than one Member State). The minimum number of members required to form a political group is nineteen.

---

126. Arts. 8–10, Protocol on Privileges and Immunities. See also Act on elections mentioned *supra*, Art. 4(2)). The Court interprets the period of immunity mentioned in the Protocol on Privileges and Immunities of the European Communities (annexed to the Merger Treaty), Art. 10 in a wide sense: it is valid 'during the sessions' (and while travelling to and from the place of meeting of the Parliament). Thus in Case 149/85, *Wybot v. Faure et al.* the Court held that 'during the sessions' must be interpreted as meaning that the European Parliament is in session, even if it is not actually sitting, until the decision is taken closing its annual or extraordinary sessions. As to jurisdiction in relation to actions for non-contractual liability for acts committed on the European Parliament's premises, see Case C-201/89, *Le Pen et al. v. Puhl et al.*

127. Arts. 189 EC and 107 Euratom.

128. See P.J.G. Kapteyn, *L'Assemblée Commune de la Communauté Européenne du Charbon et de l'Acier* (Leiden, 1962) 64–103. The ECSC Treaty expired on 23 Jul. 2002.

129. Parliament's Rules of Procedure 16th ed., Jul. 2004, (O.J. 2005, L 44/1), Rule 29. According to Art. 29(1), Members may form themselves into groups according to their political affinities.

130. Order in Case T-222/99 R, *Martinez and De Gaulle v. Parliament*.

131. Joined Cases T-222/99, T-327/99 & T-329/99, *Martinez and De Gaulle v. Parliament*.

After the elections held in June 2004 and the accession of Romania and Bulgaria on 1 January 2007 there are eight groups with the following number of members and a number of non-affiliated members (at 1 August 2007):

Christian Democrats	278
Socialists	216
Liberals	104
'Green' (*Les Verts*)	44
European United Left	42
Union for Europe of the Nations	41
Independence/Democracy	23
Identity, Tradition and Sovereignty	24
Non-affiliated	13
Total	*785*

In total, the Parliament now has 785 members.[132] The Treaty of Amsterdam added a stipulation that the number of MEPs may not exceed 700.[133] The Treaty of Nice increased this to 732.[134] According to the Act of Accession 2005 (Romania and Bulgaria) this number is increased during the current session of the Parliament (until 2009) by 53 members.

Up until 1979, members of the European Parliament were appointed by and from the national parliaments in accordance with the procedure laid down by each Member State, the number of delegates per country being specified in the Treaty. This method of appointing members was envisaged as being only temporary, as was clear from the old Article 138(3) EEC[135] which required the Parliament to draw up proposals for elections by direct universal suffrage in accordance with a uniform procedure in all Member States. It also provided that the Council, acting unanimously, was to lay down the appropriate provisions which it would 'recommend to Member States for adoption in accordance with their respective constitutional requirements'.

On the basis of these provisions, the Council decided on 20 September 1976 to recommend to the Member States provisions in the form of an Act concerning the election of the representatives of the Assembly by direct universal suffrage.[136] The Act was accepted by all the Member States in accordance with their respective constitutional requirements.

The Act on direct elections does not prescribe a uniform electoral procedure for all the Member States, and national views on this point are still diverse.

---

132. Art. 11, Act of Accession (1994), as amended by Art. 5, Adaptation Decision. See further the website of the European Parliament, <www.europarl.europa.eu>. The ITS group was dissolved in Nov. 2007.
133. Old Art. 189(2) EC.
134. New Art. 189(2) EC.
135. Now, with changes, Art. 190 EC; cf. Art. 108(3) Euratom.
136. Dec. 76/787 and the Act on Direct Elections, O.J. 1976, L 278/1 and 5.

The preference for a particular electoral system, whether of proportional representation or majoritarian ('first past the post') is deeply ingrained in national traditions and political power relationships. Had it been necessary to decide on a uniform electoral procedure, the introduction of direct elections would certainly have been still further delayed. Under the Treaty provisions, the task of finding a consensus on a uniform procedure fell upon the Parliament and the Council, with the former having the right of initiative.[137] Carrying out this task has been made slightly easier by the Treaty of Amsterdam, since a new phrase has been added to Article 190(4) EC, according to which the electoral procedure may be 'in accordance with principles common to all Member States' as an alternative to being uniform. The same change was made to Article 7(2) of the Act on direct elections. Making use of this new possibility, the Parliament drew up a number of such principles in July 1998.[138]

 Until a procedure based on these principles enters into force, elections are governed in each Member State by its national provisions[139] although there are a few Community provisions which also apply.

Fixing the number of seats and dividing them according to nationality proved most problematical. In order to ensure a satisfactory representation on the basis of population of the Member States as well as ensuring a reasonable cross-section of political movements, it was felt necessary to expand the number of members and to distribute seats more proportionately than had been done prior to 1976, in relation to the old Parliament, always bearing in mind that the smallest Member State at that time, Luxembourg, had to have a certain minimum number of seats.

According to the Protocol on Enlargement,[140] as of 1 January 2004, and with effect from the 2004–2009 session, new rules for the distribution of seats apply. The drafters of the treaty approached the issue as follows: first, the number of seats for Germany was left unchanged. Then, on the basis of the link between the number of seats and the number of inhabitants per country (the principle of correspondence) the number of seats for the other 14 Member States were calculated: in total 535 seats (a reduction for some of the medium-sized countries such as the Netherlands, whose number of seats was reduced from 31 to 25). Finally, on the basis of the distribution of seats for the 15 Member States, the number of seats for the ten new Member States were calculated,[141] reaching a total for the expected

---

137. See also Art. 7(2) Act on Direct Elections.
138. O.J. 1998, C 292/66. Following this up, the Council amended the Act on Direct Elections, on 25 Jun./23 Sept. 2002 in the sense that as of 2004, elections would be on the basis of proportional representation. Council Decision 2002/772/EC, Euratom, O.J. 2002, L 283/1.
139. Act on Direct Elections, Art. 7(2): i.e., national provisions established or declared applicable for the elections.
140. Protocol attached to the Treaty on European Union and the Treaties establishing the European Communities by the Treaty of Nice.
141. Declaration on Enlargement, 1. According to the Act of Accession 2003, Art. 11, the 50 seats allotted in that list to Bulgaria and Romania – which did not accede in 2004 – were spread over the other countries, except the largest (Germany) and the 5 smallest countries; the Member States and the acceding countries further followed the distribution as laid down in the Protocol on Enlargement (total number of seats: 732).

27 Member States of 732. As has already been remarked, as from 1 January 2007, this number has been increased by 53 members as a consequence of the accession of Bulgaria and Romania on that date (reaching in total 785 members).

The Act on direct elections makes provision relating to incompatibility of functions. It is significant that a dual mandate (being a member of a national as well as the European Parliament) is expressly permitted by Article 5 of the Act.[142] However, Article 6 of the Act specifically declares certain functions to be incompatible with membership of the European Parliament, e.g., membership of the Commission, Court of Justice, Court of Auditors, the Economic and Social Committee, the Committee of the Regions, active officials or servants of any of the Community Institutions or specialized bodies attached to them.[143] Moreover, a Member of the European Parliament may not be a member of the government of a Member State. The Member States may declare, at national level, other positions to be incompatible with membership of the European Parliament.[144] The elections are held on dates fixed by the Member States within a particular period beginning on a Thursday morning and ending on the following Sunday.[145]

Members of the European Parliament are elected for five years; this was enshrined in the EC Treaty by the Treaty of Amsterdam.[146] Their credentials are verified by the Parliament; the Parliament decides whether the members elected, taking note of the results declared officially by the Member States, may be admitted according to the provisions of the Act on direct elections.[147] Evaluation of whether members elected satisfy the conditions laid down in national legislation takes place under national provisions, again, pending the entry into force of a uniform electoral procedure or one based on common principles.[148] Until that moment the filling of seats falling vacant during the Parliament's term of office occurs according to national procedures.[149]

The Act on direct elections contained no provisions relating to active and passive voting rights; the modalities remain matters for the Member States, subject now to the obligations resulting from Directive 93/109, on voting rights for EU citizens not residing in their own State;[150] this Directive implements the right conferred by Article 19 EC for every citizen of the Union – i.e., according to Article 17(1) EC, every person holding the nationality of a Member State – residing in a Member State of which he is not a national, to vote and to stand as a candidate

---

142. A dual mandate is however prohibited in various Member States.
143. Act on Direct Elections, Art. 6(1) gives the full list.
144. Ibid., Arts. 6(2) and 7(2).
145. Ibid., Art. 9.
146. Ibid., Art. 3(1), and Art. 190(3) EC.
147. Ibid., Art. 11.
148. Ibid.
149. Ibid., Art. 12. As to some of the difficulties in this regard, see Bradley and Feeney (1993) YBEL 383 at 412–413, and (1994) 14 YBEL 428–429.
150. O.J. 1993, L 329/34. See Ch. II, section 6.2, *supra.* See the Resolutions of the European Parliament O.J. 1994, C 44/159 and C 128/316.

in elections to the European Parliament in that Member State under the same conditions as nationals of that State.

Article 13 of the Act on direct elections permits the Council, acting unanimously on a proposal from the Parliament after consulting the Commission, to adopt measures to implement the Act after endeavouring to reach agreement with the Parliament in a conciliation committee consisting of the Council and representatives of the Parliament.[151] Regrettably, the first attempt to set up a Community system, based on this provision,[152] concerning the salaries and tax liability of members of the European Parliament failed through lack of unanimity. As a result, each Member State has adopted the necessary financial rules for members which it returns, as long as Parliament has not adopted any rules on the matter in the exercise of its budgetary powers. The present differences in salaries and other financial arrangements according to nationality scarcely fit in with membership of an Institution which represents the peoples of the Union assembled. Moreover, there is a real danger that financial dependence on national rules or their application could be abused in order to put pressure on members.[153]

For these reasons, but also in order to exercise more control on the members' declarations of expenses, the Parliament approved, on 3 December 1998, a draft Statute for a uniform salary for all EP members, and rules governing their expenses. The Council radically amended this draft, following which the Parliament rejected the resulting text on 5 May 1999. The legal basis was not Article 13 of the Act on direct elections, but Article 190(5) EC, a provision added by the Treaty of Amsterdam (and amended by the Treaty of Nice) which grants Parliament competence to adopt rules and set general conditions (with the approval of the Council) for the performance of the duties of its Members.[154] In 2005, the Council approved the Draft European Parliament decision on the statute for Members of the European Parliament.[155]

---

151. On the procedure, see point 5, 6 and 7 of the Joint Declaration of the European Parliament, the Council and the Commission (O.J. 1975, C 89/1). In French, this procedure is referred to as '*concertation*' rather than conciliation, which emphasizes the distinction from the 'usual' conciliation procedure within the context of Art. 251 EC; as to these procedures, see Ch. V, section 4.1 *infra*. See also Annex III to the Act on direct elections.

152. It may be doubted whether this provision can be used for this purpose: see Maas, 'Wetgevingskroniek', (1979) SEW, 686 at 696–697.

153. As an internal organization measure under Art. 199 EC, the Parliament grants members generous expenses on a lump-sum basis. In Case 208/80, *Rt. Hon. Lord Bruce of Donnington v. Eric Gordon Aspden*, the Court held that although there was no specific exemption from national taxation for members of the European Parliament, following *inter alia* Art. 10 EC, no national taxation could be levied on the lump-sum expense allowance (as this would be tantamount to exercising an administrative restriction on the free movement of members of the European Parliament), unless it could be shown under Community law that this sum was partly to be seen as pay.

154. (1998/19) EVM, 312 and (1999/8) EVM, 312.

155. Bulletin EU 7/8-2005. See the Decision of the EP of 28 Sept. 2005, adopting the Statute for Members of the European Parliament, O.J. 2005, L 262/1.

The introduction of direct elections may bring about significant changes in the institutional balance within the Community in the long term. Voters can express their views on Community policy more directly, and thus their representatives are better placed than were their indirectly elected predecessors to make the Council and the Commission aware of those views. The distribution of seats reflects the relative size of the peoples of the Member States more satisfactorily. The removal of the dependence of membership of the European Parliament on membership of national parliaments allows the members of the European Parliament to pursue their European activities on a full-time basis. These factors may contribute to a significant increase in the authority of the Parliament's pronouncements.

Such a development is by no means automatic, however, as the elections themselves have demonstrated: there has been a steady decline in average turnout since the first elections in 1979, reaching 49.8 percent in 1999 and 45.6 in 2004.[156] In addition, in a number of countries, the elections tend to be strongly influenced by national party considerations.

The way in which the Parliament carries out its tasks is also of considerable importance in establishing its authority. It will need to strengthen its internal organization and working methods, particularly through the formation of parliamentary groups and committee work; as a result, the process of political will-formation should lead to well-founded and clear pronouncements which are sufficiently convincing to mobilize public opinion in the Member States. The European Parliament will have to use to the full all the means made available in the Treaties in order to bring the influence of its political will to bear on Community policies. A European Parliament which appeals to voters by taking upon itself the tasks of steering, giving impulse to, and safeguarding the integration process can contribute significantly to changing the still heavily nationally orientated thoughts and actions of voters and political parties. Such a change would open the way for closer collaboration of national parties in the European context, or for the formation of European parties; the importance of the latter has been explicitly recognized in 191 EC, and, according to the Treaty of Nice, they will be based on regulations, including rules regarding their funding, laid down by the Council (Art. 191(2) EC).[157]

The events at the end of 1998 and the beginning of 1999, to which we will return in section 5.2.2. below, and which led to the resignation of the Santer Commission on 16 March 1999, significantly strengthened the position of the Parliament *vis-à-vis* the Commission. This led in turn to a considerable number of agreements being made between the President of the Commission and the

---

156. <www.europarl.europa.eu/elections2004/ep-election/sites/en/results1306/turnout_ep/turnout_table.html>.
157. See Reg. (EC) No. 2004/2003 of the European parliament and of the Council of 4 Nov. 2003, on the regulations governing political parties at European level and the rules regarding their funding, O.J. 2003, L 297/I. An action for annulment of this Regulation by the 'Front National' and others has been declared. inadmissible, also on appeal (Case T-17/04 and C-338/05 P, *Front National et al. v. Parliament and Council*).

Parliament when the Prodi Commission took up office on 16 September 1999, for instance over action to be taken when a member of the Commission loses the confidence of the Parliament. These agreements were later formalized in a Framework Agreement on relations between the European Parliament and the Commission, concluded on 5 July 2000.[158] Further, in September 1999, the Commission adopted the Code of Conduct for its members mentioned earlier in this chapter (see section 4.2). The present president of the Commission, Mr Barroso, has accepted the same obligations. The rejection of the candidacy of Mr Buttiglioni and the withdrawal of the entire Commission as proposed by Mr Barroso which followed upon the rejection, resulted in a further strengthening of the position of the European Parliament.

A strengthening and expansion of the Treaty-based powers of the Parliament is less essential than may be thought. It is more important to see the emergence of a clear Community power centre, that is to say a strengthened institutional structure or something more resembling a European Government, based on a transparent separation of national and Community competences and responsibilities, in which the Parliament can exercise its powers. If the Parliament develops into a political force, it will be essential for the Community power centre or government to take account of the Parliament's views and to assure itself of its support. One should recall that the development of the national systems of government into parliamentary democracies also came about principally by means of changes in the manner in which the Head of State and ministers exercised their constitutional powers, and owed far less to the actual grant of new powers to national parliaments.

5.1.1   Proposed Changes following the Lisbon Treaty

On 1 August 2007 (deadline of the original text of Ch. IV), the total number of members of the European Parliament was 785, that is to say the maximum number of members mentioned in the Treaty of Nice (732) together with the 53 members from Romania and Bulgaria. According to Article 9 of the Act of Accession 2005, during the period 2009–2014 the total number of members will be 736. The additional four members as compared with the maximum in the Treaty of Nice will be the result of an increase in the number of members from Hungary and the Czech Republic, from twenty-two to twenty-four in each case.

The Treaty of Lisbon will again change the total number of members. According to Article 14(2) TEU (Lisbon), the total number will be 751 (750 plus the

---

158. O.J. 2001, C 121/122. G. Stauner and 21 other Members of the Parliament brought an action for annulment against this agreement before the Court of First Instance (Case T-236/00, *Stauner and Others v. Parliament and Commission*). On 15 Jan. 2001, the President of the Court of First Instance dismissed the application for interim relief in this case as inadmissible. In Case T-236/00 R II, the President of the CFI again rejected an application for interim relief on 8 Oct. 2001. And on 17 Jan. 2002, the CFI (Fourth Chamber) dismissed the application for annulment as inadmissible. The Framework Agreement of 5 Jul. 2000, has been replaced by the Framework Agreement of 26 May 2005, which gave rise to the Declaration of the Council, O.J. 2005, C 161/1.

President of the European Parliament). The distribution of the seats will be based on the proposal from the European Parliament of 14 October 2007 (see Art. 2 Protocol on the Transitional Provisions and Declaration No. 5). Article 14(2) TEU (Lisbon) mentions the new parameters for the composition of the Parliament: Representation of citizens will be degressively proportional, with a minimum of six members per Member State; no Member State will have more than ninety-six seats.

5.2   POWERS AND DUTIES

According to Article 189 EC, the European Parliament exercises the powers conferred on it by the Treaties. The original limitation in Article 137 EEC to 'advisory and supervisory powers' has been removed.[159] Parliament has a general power to discuss any matter concerning the Communities, to adopt resolutions thereupon and to invite the governments of the Member States to act.[160] The European Parliament differs from the parliamentary bodies of other European organizations such as the Council of Europe, the Western European Union and Benelux – which are endowed with exclusively advisory functions – because, or at least mainly because, it has been granted powers of decision, especially its powers of co-decision concerning Community legislative measures, and its powers concerning the budget.

5.2.1   The Parliament's Role in the Decision-Making Process

The way in which the Parliament is involved in the decision-making process has developed remarkably since the coming into force of the EEC and Euratom Treaties in 1958. The decision-making process is discussed fully below,[161] but a brief explanation of the Parliament's role is appropriate here. Apart from special cases, the EC Treaty envisages four general ways in which the European parliament participates in the Council's decision-making, which are most conveniently discussed chronologically. The original, and least far-reaching involvement is the *consultation* procedure, whereby the Council consults the Parliament to ascertain its views on a Commission proposal. Such consultation was not generally required: the obligation to consult existed only where specifically laid down in the Treaty provision conferring competence on the Council to act in relation to the matter concerned. In practice, however, the Council often sought the advisory opinion of the Parliament even where this was not required by the Treaties. Moreover, the Parliament itself sometimes addresses opinions to the Council on its own initiative.[162] When consultation of the Parliament is required but has not in fact

---

159. The limitation does still exist in Art. 107 Euratom.
160. See Case 230/81, *Luxembourg v. European Parliament*. See also the Stuttgart Solemn Declaration on European Union (Bull. EC 6-1983, point I.6.1, 24 at 26).
161. See Ch. V, section 4.1, *infra*.
162. E.g., Resolution of 11 May 1979, on measures to promote the development of fish farming (O.J. 1979, C 140/117) which it accompanied by a draft proposal for a Council Regulation

taken place, the relevant measure may be annulled by Court of Justice on the ground of infringement of an essential procedural requirement.[163]

From the formula used in many of the specific provisions of the Treaties, *viz.* 'on a proposal from the Commission and after consultation of the European Parliament', it is clear that it is the Council, not the Commission, which is required to consult the Parliament; nevertheless, the additional possibility of consultation by the Commission before it submits its proposal to the Council is not excluded, since the Commission is also accountable to the Parliament for the proposals it submits. The proposal from the Commission is the subject of the consultation of the Parliament, as it constitutes, both in form and substance, the basis for the decision to be taken by the Council. The Commission may alter its proposal, as long as the Council has not acted.[164] The original text of the relevant Treaty provision[165] went on to say that the right to amend a proposal may be exercised 'in particular when the Parliament has been consulted on that proposal'. The fact that this statement has been dropped in Article 250(2) EC[166] in no way diminishes the parliamentary accountability of the Commission, but is merely a consequence of changed procedures, to be discussed below.

The consultation procedure, and thus the advisory role of the Parliament, is still significant and has been maintained in a number of policy areas which pre-date the Treaty of Maastricht.[167] It is also prescribed in various areas of Community policy introduced by the Treaties of Maastricht and Amsterdam, such as Union citizenship,[168] immigration policy etc.,[169] economic and monetary policy[170] and sectoral or supplementary policies.[171] Moreover the Parliament is also consulted on the most important aspects of CFSP and the decisions which the Council may adopt in the framework of PJCCM.[172]

With the coming into force of the SEA on 1 July 1987, a second procedure was established, the *cooperation* procedure. Unlike the consultation procedure, the

---

(O.J. 1979, C 140/120) which it invited the Commission to submit to the Council. Parliament now has the express right to request the Commission to submit appropriate proposals, see the end of this section, *infra*.

163. Case 138/79, *SA Roquette Frères v. Council* and Case 139/79, *Maizena GmbH v. Council*. See Jacobs (1981) 18 CML Rev., 219, and Lenaerts (1981) SEW 397. See also, e.g., Case 817/79, *Buyl et al. v. Commission* in relation to an examination to see if this essential requirement had been met.
164. Arts. 250(2) EC and 119(2) Euratom.
165. Old Art. 149(2) EEC, and the text of Art. 119 Euratom, 2nd para. (which is still in force)
166. And already in Art. 149(3) EEC as this read after the entry into force of the SEA.
167. For instance: Arts. 37(2) (agriculture); 71(2) (transport); 93 (tax harmonization); 94 (harmonization of laws); 225(2) (Court of First Instance); 269 (own resources) and 308 EC.
168. Arts. 19(1) and (2) (right to vote) and 22 (additional citizenship rights) EC.
169. Title IV on visas, asylum, immigration and other policies related to the free movement of persons: see Art. 67(1) and (3) EC.
170. See, e.g., Arts. 104(14) (government deficits); 107(6) (amendment Statute European System of Central Banks) and 121(2)-(4) (third phase EMU) EC.
171. Arts. 157(3) (industry); 159(3) (cohesion) and 166(4) (research and technology) EC.
172. Arts. 21(1) and 39(1) TEU.

mechanics of the cooperation procedure were set out in great detail in a new Treaty provision.[173] This procedure was designed to permit the Parliament a second reading of a proposed act. Thus in the first reading the Parliament expresses its opinion on the Commission's proposal, whereas on the second reading it expresses its opinion on the common position, adopted by the Council after examining the Commission's proposal and the Parliament's opinion given on the first reading.[174] Another difference between the consultation and the cooperation procedures is that in the latter the Parliament can reject the common position of the Council, after which the Council can only act on a second reading by unanimity.[175] Moreover, the cooperation procedure emphasizes that where amendments put forward by the Parliament[176] are taken on board by the Commission in its re-examined proposal, the Council can only deviate from them by unanimity (Art. 252(e) EC).

The Treaty of Amsterdam replaced the cooperation procedure in nearly all cases by the co-decision procedure, discussed below. The cooperation procedure only remains in the field of EMU;[177] it does not apply in relation to the Euratom Treaty.

With the changes made by the Treaty of Maastricht, a third procedure was introduced, the so-called *co-decision* procedure. The term 'co-decision procedure' is not actually used in the EC Treaty: the various substantive Treaty provisions simply say 'in accordance with the procedure referred to in Article 251' (and the cooperation procedure is now the 'procedure referred to in Article 252'). The two characteristic elements in this procedure, as amended by the Treaty of Amsterdam, are the convocation of a Conciliation Committee and the Parliament's right of co-decision. The Conciliation Committee is convened when the Council declines to adopt all or some of the amendments proposed by Parliament at the end of the first phase of the procedure, which more or less corresponds to the cooperation procedure described above (Art. 251(3) EC). The Parliament's right of co-decision concerns a joint draft text drawn up by the Conciliation Committee.[178] This text must be approved by both the Council and the Parliament; if one of the two does not approve it, then the draft text is deemed not to be adopted (Art. 251(5) EC). Nor is an act adopted if the Conciliation Committee fails to reach agreement on a joint text (Art. 251(6) EC).

The co-decision procedure applies principally in relation to acts necessary to complete the internal market in the Community, including free movement of persons, and a number of new policy areas.[179] Acts which are adopted under the

---

173. Now Art. 252 EC.
174. Art. 252(a) and (b) EC.
175. Art. 252(c) EC.
176. Parliament uses the term 'amendments', but Art. 252(c) makes it clear that these are proposed amendments
177. See, e.g., Arts. 102(2) (prohibition of privileged access); 103(2) (exclusion of liability) and 106(2) (harmonization of coinage) EC.
178. See Case C-344/04, *IATA*, on the broad powers of the conciliation committee in drawing up a text.
179. See, e.g., Arts. 40 (free movement of workers); 44(2) (establishment); 55 (freedom to provide services); 95(1) (internal market); 149(4) (vocational education); 152(4) (public health); 175(3)

co-decision procedure are signed by the Presidents of the Council and the Parliament;[180] they are referred to as being 'adopted jointly by the European Parliament and the Council'.[181] Like the cooperation procedure, the co-decision procedure does not apply in relation to the Euratom Treaty.

Finally, there are a number of cases in which the Council needs the *assent* of the European Parliament before it may act. The assent procedure had already been introduced by the SEA, and initially only concerned the accession of new Member States[182] and the conclusion of association agreements.[183] Under the assent procedure, the Parliament must explicitly give its assent to the Council acts mentioned in the relevant provisions. The Treaty of Maastricht extended the areas in which Parliament's assent is required.

The assent procedure applies at present for a number of specific matters,[184] for the establishment of a uniform European electoral procedure or of the common principles applying to European elections[185] and for certain specific types of international agreements.[186]

The procedures briefly described here are dealt with in more detail in Chapter V of this book, in section 3.1. It may already be noted that following the Lisbon Treaty, the cooperation procedure will be replaced by the consultation and the co-decision procedure respectively; in fact, the cooperation procedure is at this moment only provided for in the field of EMU. Further, the procedure of assent will be replaced by 'consent' (see e.g., Art. 7 TEU (Lisbon) and 223(1), para. 2, TFEU).

5.2.2   Political Control by the Parliament

The European Parliament is required to supervise the policy of the Commission in the two Communities. The power to dismiss the Commission *en bloc* by the adoption of a motion of censure forms the ultimate weapon under this right of supervision. Such a motion can only be carried by open vote by a two-thirds majority of the votes cast, which at the same time must represent a majority of the number of members. In view of the serious character of such a motion, a 'period of reflection' of at least three days must elapse between the motion being tabled and the vote being taken.[187]

    (environment) EC. In a decision of 22 Dec. 2004, O.J. 2004, L 396/45, the Council has extended the applicability of the co-decision procedure to some fields which are covered by Title IV of the EC Treaty viz. asylum and immigration.
180.   Art. 254(1) EC.
181.   Art. 253 EC. See also Art. 230(1) EC.
182.   See now Art. 49(1) TEU.
183.   See now, as amended, Art. 310 read with 300(3), 2nd sub-paragraph, EC.
184.   Art. 105(6) (ECB); 107(5) (ESCB) and 161(1) and (2) (Structural Funds) EC.
185.   Art. 190(4), 2nd sub-paragraph, EC.
186.   Art. 300(3) 2nd sub-paragraph, EC (*inter alia* association agreements). The Treaty of Nice adds to these: Art. 7(1) TEU (breach of fundamental rights), and 11(2) EC (enhanced cooperation in an area covered by co-decision).
187.   Arts. 201 EC and 114 Euratom.

Although a censure motion has occasionally been tabled, no such motion has ever been approved. This also holds for the censure motion on which a vote was held in the European Parliament on 14 January 1999, after the Parliament had first refused in December 1998 to approve the implementation of the budget for the financial year 1996.[188] On the other hand, the Parliament did pass another resolution on that occasion, viz. a Resolution on improving the financial management of the European Commission.[189] In that Resolution, the Parliament expressed the wish to appoint a committee of independent experts with the mandate to examine the way in which the Commission detects and deals with 'fraud, mismanagement and nepotism'. This committee was indeed appointed, and its report led – as has been mentioned above – to the resignation of the Commission on 16 March 1999. This series of events reveals once more how difficult it is for a motion of censure actually to be adopted. The reason is not so much to do with the requirements for such a motion being so cumbersome, but more that adoption of a censure motion is a leap in the dark, because until the recent coming into effect of the new appointment procedure,[190] the appointment of the new members of the Commission rested entirely with the governments collectively. As long as the Parliament did not have a say in the appointment of the new Commission, there was no guarantee that the policy of a newly appointed Commission would conform to the wishes of the Parliament.

The current procedure offers the Parliament a real opportunity to influence the composition of the Commission. After all, appointment can only take place after the Parliament has approved the nomination of the President and subsequently the nomination of the whole college of commissioners. Whether this right is sufficient to force the Council in the composition of Heads of State or Government, after a successful motion of censure, to appoint a Commission which is acceptable to Parliament, is in our opinion not entirely certain. Heads of State and Government of the Member States still enjoy more political authority in actual fact than the European Parliament. Direct elections for the Parliament have not as yet brought any real change to this situation.

Nevertheless, it should be noted that in January 1999, a motion of censure was very nearly adopted (322 votes in favour, 293 votes against and 27 abstentions).[191] Moreover, since the entry into force of the Treaty of Amsterdam, the Parliament enjoys a real co-legislative power, which means that the Commission is also dependent on the Parliament for the adoption of its proposals. The Commission will therefore be obliged to take account of the opinions of the Parliament; it can no longer assume that the mention of a vote of censure in the Treaties is an empty threat. Apart from the motion of censure, political accountability is confirmed and supported in a series of Treaty provisions, and in procedures developed by parliamentary practice which enable the European Parliament to supervise the policy and

---

188.   O.J. 1999, C 279/114.
189.   O.J. 1999, C 104/106.
190.   Art. 214 EC.
191.   (1999/1) EVM, 5.

activities of the Commission and engage it in an ongoing dialogue, of a critical nature, reviewing Community affairs. The procedure of oral and written parliamentary questions forms a particularly important means of supervision. We limit ourselves here to mentioning further the public deliberations on the mandatory general report produced annually by the Commission,[192] the statutory annual session[193] which is distributed throughout the whole year by means of a series of adjournments,[194] the participation of members of the Commission in debates,[195] the right to put questions,[196] and the system of parliamentary committees.[197] These committees (numbering 20 at present) have to prepare the decisions of the Parliament and maintain regular contact with the Commission in the periods during which the Parliament is not actually sitting.

Unlike the Commission, the Council is not formally responsible to the European Parliament. The individual members of the Council are responsible to their own national parliaments for their individual part in Community decision-making. Nevertheless, the Council and the Parliament have developed a number of formal contacts outside the legislative process which means that the Council is prepared to answer written and oral questions from members of the European Parliament[198] and to inform Parliament about its intended programme and the progress in its activities.[199] Parliament also holds an annual debate on progress in implementing CFSP and the areas covered by PJCCM and may ask questions of the Council or make recommendations to it concerning these areas.[200] Finally, the European Council sends the European Parliament a report after each of its meetings and a yearly written report on the progress achieved by the Union.[201]

5.2.3   Adopting the Budget

As a result of the First Budgetary Treaty[202] the European Parliament obtained, from 1975 onwards, the right for its President to declare the adoption of the budget, and thereby the last word on non-compulsory expenditure. As a result of the Second Budgetary Treaty[203] it also obtained from 1 June 1977, the right to reject

---

192.   As to the debate on the General Report see Art. 200 EC, and 113 Euratom.
193.   Art. 196(1) EC.
194.   See Parliament's Rules of Procedure, Rules 126, 127.
195.   Arts. 197(2) EC and 110, 2nd para. Euratom.
196.   Arts. 197(3) EC and 110, 3rd para. Euratom; see Parliament's Rules of Procedure, Rules 108–110.
197.   Rules of Procedure, Rules 174–187.
198.   Arts. 197(4) EC and 110(4) Euratom read with Rules of Procedure of the Council, Art. 26, and Parliament's Rules of Procedure, Rules 108, 110.
199.   See also 40th Overview of activities of the Council (1992), Part I 13–14.
200.   Arts. 21, 2nd para., and 39(3) TEU respectively.
201.   Art. 4, 3rd para., TEU.
202.   22 Apr. 1970, Simmonds (ed.) *Encyclopedia of European Community Law*, Vol. B (London, loose-leaf 1974–1995) para. B 8–103.
203.   22 Jul. 1975, Simmonds, ibid., para. B 8–222.

the entire draft budget 'if there are important reasons',[204] and also the right to grant the Commission discharge in respect of the implementation of the budget.[205] The Parliament's powers in this field, as set out in the relevant amended Treaty provisions[206] are discussed in more detail elsewhere.[207]

It may already be noted that following the Lisbon Treaty, the distinction between compulsory and non-compulsory expenditure will be abolished.

5.2.4 The Parliament's Other Powers

The European Parliament possesses a number of powers which are not directly connected with its supervisory, consultative or budgetary functions. Primarily these relate to its own powers of internal organization, such as adopting its Rules of Procedure,[208] and the power to adopt appropriate measures to ensure the due functioning and conduct of its proceedings.[209] In addition, the Parliament has always had two special powers:

(i) to draw up proposals for elections by direct universal suffrage in accordance with a uniform procedure in all Member States or in accordance with principles common to all Member States;[210]

(ii) to refer matters to the Court of Justice if the Council or the Commission, in infringement of the EC or Euratom Treaty, fails to act.[211]

The amendments made by the Treaty of Maastricht added to these:

(iii) the power to bring actions for annulment;[212]

(iv) the power to set up a temporary Committee of Inquiry to investigate alleged contraventions or maladministration in the implementation of Community law;[213]

(v) the power to receive petitions from any citizen of the Union, and any natural or legal person residing or having its registered office in a Member State, whether individually or in association with other citizens or

---

204. Art. 272(8) EC and 177(8) Euratom.
205. Art. 276(1) EC and 180b Euratom.
206. Arts. 272 et seq. EC and 177 et seq. Euratom.
207. Ch. V, section 3.2 *infra*.
208. Arts. 199 EC and 112 Euratom.
209. On its powers in this respect and the limits thereof see in particular: Case 230/81, *Luxembourg v. European Parliament* and Case 208/80, *Rt. Hon. Lord Bruce of Donington v. Aspden*; Case 108/83, *Luxembourg v. European Parliament*; Case 78/85, *Group of the European Right v. European Parliament*; Case 190/84, *Parti Ecologiste 'Les Verts' v. European Parliament*; Joined Cases 358/85 & 51/86, *France v. European Parliament*, and Case C-68/90, *Blot et al. v. European Parliament*.
210. Arts. 190(4) EC and 108(3) Euratom.
211. Arts. 232 EC and 148 Euratom.
212. Arts. 230, 2nd para., EC, and 146, 2nd para., Euratom. See further section 5.3 *infra*.
213. Arts. 193 EC and 107b Euratom and the Decision of the European Parliament, the Council and the Commission of 19 Apr. 1995, on the detailed provisions governing the exercise of the European Parliament's right of inquiry, O.J. 1995, L 113/2.

persons, on a matter coming within the Community's fields of activity
and which affects him, her or it directly;[214]

(vi) the power to appoint an Ombudsman empowered to receive complaints
from any citizen of the Union, and any natural or legal person residing or
having its registered office in a Member State, concerning instances of
maladministration in the activities of the Community Institutions or bodies, apart from the Court of Justice and the Court of First instance acting in
their judicial role;[215]

(vii) since the Treaty of Nice, the power to obtain the opinion of the Court of
Justice as to whether an international agreement envisaged by the EC is
compatible with the provisions of the Treaty (Art. 300(6) EC).

The Parliament has no formal right of initiative in the field of Community legislation other than that mentioned under (i) above; apart from this, the right of
initiative belongs to the Commission, although the Parliament now has what
may be called a right of quasi-initiative: it may request the Commission to submit
any appropriate proposal on matters for which it considers that a Community act is
required for the purpose of implementing the EC or Euratom Treaties.[216] By the
means of political control at its disposal (see above) the Parliament may give
additional weight to such a request.

5.2.5   Union Tasks

Like the Commission (see section 4.3.4. above), the European Parliament has only
a modest role in the second and third pillars. The first paragraph of Article 21 TEU
states that the European Parliament is to be consulted by the Presidency on the
main aspects and the basic choices of the common foreign and security policy. The
Presidency and the Commission must also keep Parliament regularly informed of
the developments in this area. As mentioned earlier, the Parliament may ask questions of the Council or make recommendations to it, and holds an annual debate on
progress in implementing the CFSP.[217]

As for Police and Judicial Cooperation in Criminal Matters, the European
Parliament must be consulted on proposals for framework decisions, decisions
and conventions in this area (Art. 39(1) TEU). The presidency and the Commission
must regularly inform the Parliament about activities in this area, and the

---

214.   This is implicit in Arts. 194 EC and 107c Euratom; cf. Art. 21, 1st para., EC.
215.   Arts. 195 EC and 107c Euratom, cf. Art. 21, 2nd para., EC. See Decision of the Parliament of
       9 Mar. 1994, 94/262 on the regulations and general conditions governing the performance of
       the Ombudsman's duties (O.J. 1994 L, 113/15), approved by the Council on 7 Feb. 1994,
       (O.J. 1994, L 54/25), and has been amended by Decision 2002/262 of the European Parliament
       of 14 Mar. 2002, O.J. 2002, L 92/13.
216.   Arts. 192 EC, 2nd para., and 107a Euratom.
217.   Art. 21, 2nd para., TEU.

Parliament enjoys the same rights concerning questions, recommendations and debate as it has in the Second Pillar.[218]

According to Article 28 TEU, the administrative expenditure relating to CFSP is charged to the budget of the European Communities; the same holds for operational expenses, except those having military or defence implications and in cases where the Council decides that they are to be borne by the Member States. The administrative expenditure relating to PJCCM is also charged to the Community budget, as are the operating expenses unless the Council decides otherwise (Art. 41 TEU). For both Pillars, the expenses which are charged to the Community budget fall under the normal Community budgetary procedure, so the European Parliament can also exert some influence on policy by this means.[219]

5.3   THE PARLIAMENT AND THE COURT OF JUSTICE

The extent to which legal remedies can be used instead of political techniques by, but also against, the Parliament is a sign of the limited development of the principles of parliamentary democracy in the Community system in comparison with the development therein of the principles of the rule of law or *Rechtsstaat*. The Parliament used its possibility to bring an action against the Council for failure to act (mentioned above) in order to obtain a judgment of the Court on whether the Council was in breach of its Treaty obligations because it had failed to adopt a common transport policy.[220] The Court was prepared to pronounce on the question, albeit not in so far-reaching a manner, and confined itself to the provisions which were to be laid down by the Council under Article 71(1)(a) and (b) EC. The Court had of course to confine itself to holding that the Council should have acted; the Court has no power to decide what provisions have to be adopted.[221] Nevertheless, the Parliament's armoury was supplemented with a weapon which, used sparingly and after reflection, forms a not insignificant means of putting pressure on the Council and its members to come to a decision. The Parliament also avails itself of the right conferred on the Community Institutions to intervene in cases pending before the Court (something which the Commission does as a matter of standard practice). Thus, for example, in the *isoglucose* cases,[222] Parliament intervened when undertakings were seeking to challenge the legality of a Council regulation

---

218. Art. 39 (2) and (3) TEU respectively.
219. Arts. 28(4) and 41(4) TEU, respectively. See Barents *Het Verdrag van Amsterdam in werking*, EM No. 62, (Deventer, 1999), 420.
220. Case 13/83, *European Parliament v. Council*. See Fennel (1985) EL Rev., 264.
221. Case 13/83, *European Parliament v. Council*. See also Case 377/87, *Parliament v. Council* (Budget procedure II). As to action by the Institution concerned after the action was brought but before judgment, see Case 377/87, *European Parliament v. Council*, but cf. Case C-41/92, *The Liberal Democrats v. European Parliament*, and see the discussion by Bradley and Feeney (1993) YBEL, 383, 392–393.
222. Case 138/79, *SA Roquette Frères v. Council*; Case 139/79, *Maizena GmbH v. Council*.

on the ground of failure properly to fulfil the requirement of consultation of the Parliament.[223]

The Parliament can be defendant as well as plaintiff; this has been clear from the start in staff cases. Later, the Parliament had to defend its decisions against challenge by other Community Institutions or other litigants. Several cases concerned decisions relating to the working places of the Parliament which were challenged by Luxembourg[224] or France.[225] The actions in the first two cases brought by Luxembourg were founded on Article 38 ECSC, which gave Member States the possibility to bring an action for annulment against a decision of the Parliament. The third Luxembourg case was after the judgment in *'Les Verts' I* in which the Court acknowledged that an action for annulment could lie under Article 230 EC against binding decisions adopted by the Parliament.[226] The *Parti écologiste 'Les Verts'* brought an action for the annulment of decisions of the Bureau of the Parliament concerning the allocation of appropriations intended for the reimbursement of expenses of political groupings which had taken part in the 1984 elections. Although Article 230 EC, in the wording then in force, only spoke of a review by the Court of the legality of acts of the Council and the Commission, the Court saw no objection to considering an appeal against acts of the Parliament. Indeed, any other interpretation would have been incompatible with the spirit of the Treaty as expressed in Article 220 EC as well as with the system whereby an appeal may lie against all decisions of the Institutions which are intended to produce legal effects.[227] In a case brought in 1986, the Council, supported by three Member States obtained a ruling that the decision of the President of the Parliament declaring the 1986 budget adopted was illegal.[228]

As for the Parliament's right itself to bring annulment proceedings, the Court's case law followed a remarkable path, initially rejecting this possibility in the *Comitology* judgment,[229] and shortly afterwards allowing it in the *Chernobyl*

---

223. See also Case 16/88, *Commission v. Council* (authorization); Case C-58/94, *Netherlands v. Council* (Rules on public access to documents), and Case T-194/94, *Carvel and Guardian Newspapers v. Council*. In Case C-201/89, *Le Pen et al. v. Puhl et al.*, the Court put questions to Parliament in the framework of a preliminary reference (See Art. 24, 2nd para., Statute Court of Justice).

224. Case 230/81, *Luxembourg v. European Parliament*; Case 108/83, *Luxembourg v. European Parliament* (see Kapteyn (1984) SEW, 427 at 436, Hartley (1984) EL Rev., 44, Hendry (1985) ELRev., 126 and Masclet (1984) RTDE, 538), and Joined Cases C-213/88 & 39/89, *Luxembourg v. European Parliament*, see Brown 'The Grand Duchy Fights Again: Comment on Joined Cases C-213/88 & C-39/89', (1993) CML Rev., 599.

225. Joined Cases 358/85 & 51/86, *France v. European Parliament* and C-345/95, *France v. European Parliament*.

226. Case 294/83, *Parti écologiste 'Les Verts' v. European Parliament* (Les Verts I).

227. Case 294/83, *'Les Verts' v. European Parliament*. In a subsequent case, Case 190/84, *Parti Ecologiste 'Les Verts' v. European Parliament* (Les Verts II), the claim was found not to be admissible, as the decisions in question did not create rights or obligations towards third parties.

228. Case 34/86, *Council v. European Parliament*, see Arnull (1986) ELRev., 43. See further, Ch. V, section 3.2, *infra*.

229. Case 302/87, *European Parliament v. Council* (Comitology). See Weiler (1989) ELRev., 334.

judgment.[230] The Court first stated that the various remedies provided for in the Treaties to protect the Parliament's prerogatives (action for failure to act, reference for a preliminary ruling etc.) and which it had found – in the *Comitology* judgment – to be sufficient for it to reject a direct right to bring proceedings for annulment, 'may prove to be ineffective or uncertain'. Observance of the institutional balance means that each of the Institutions must exercise its powers with due regard for the powers of the other Institutions, and any breach of that rule must be liable to be penalized. The Court must therefore have the possibility to ensure the protection of the prerogatives of Parliament by means of an appropriate legal remedy. The Parliament must therefore be deemed competent to bring an action for annulment against an act of the Council or the Commission 'provided that the action seeks only to safeguard its prerogatives and that it is founded only on submissions alleging their infringement' (para. 27).

The case law set out above was explicitly incorporated into Article 230 EC. Thus, actions for annulment may be brought against acts of the Parliament intended to produce legal effects *vis-à-vis* third parties.[231] And the Parliament now enjoys exactly the same right to bring actions for annulment as the Member States, the Council and the Commission; the restriction which was first included in Article 230 EC, that the action brought by the Parliament must have the purpose of protecting its prerogatives, was removed by the Treaty of Nice. Parliament is now clearly in a position to enforce respect of its rights through bringing the necessary legal proceedings, most of which will be concerned with establishing the correct legal basis of proposed legislation, in connection with the different decision-making procedures.[232] Viewed as a whole, judicial supervision forms an important supplement to the still unsatisfactory system of parliamentary supervisory and (co)legislative functions in the Community and in the Union.

5.4   PROPOSED CHANGES FOLLOWING THE LISBON TREATY: NATIONAL
            PARLIAMENTS

Besides the extension of the powers of the European Parliament, the Lisbon Treaty is intended to strengthen the role of the national parliaments of the Member States. The involvement of the national parliaments had already been recognized in Declaration No. 13 annexed to the Final Act of the Treaty of Maastricht and in a Protocol about the role of the national parliaments in the European Union attached to the Treaty of Amsterdam. But it is only in the Treaty of Lisbon that a general

---

230. Case C-70/88, *European Parliament v. Council* (Chernobyl). See Bradley (1991) ELRev., 245, annotation by G. Bebr, (1991) CML Rev., 663–680.
231. Arts. 230(1) EC and 146 Euratom, 1st para.
232. Joined Cases C-317 & 318/04, *European Parliament v. Council* and *European Parliament v. Commission* (PNR); this is one of the first uses by Parliament of its broader possibility to bring an action for annulment; here, the incorrect legal basis was taken by the Court as the reason to annul the contested measures, which will have the effect that they will be adopted on a legal basis in the third pillar, which rules out further judicial review of the substance.

provision (Art. 12 TEU (Lisbon)) is included which contains an inventory of the special rights which the national parliaments will enjoy in this respect. These rights are elaborated in the relevant Treaty Articles or Protocols. For instance, item (a) on the right to information, is elaborated in the Protocol on the role of national Parliaments in the European Union (hereafter referred to as Protocol No. 1). According to Articles 1 and 2 of this Protocol, the national parliaments have to be informed about all legislative proposals and the preparatory documents concerned. National parliaments have a period of 8 weeks to give an opinion on the compatibility of a draft legislative act with the principle of subsidiarity, in accordance with the procedure of the Protocol on the application of the principles of subsidiarity and proportionality (Art. 3); this Protocol will hereafter be referred to as 'Protocol No 2'; agendas and a report about the results of Council meetings will be sent to them directly (Art. 5).

Protocol No. 2 is mentioned in Article 12(b). Article 6 of that Protocol recalls the so-called 'early warning system' mentioned in Protocol No. 1, about the right of every national Parliament and of each chamber of a national Parliament to send a reasoned opinion to the Presidents of the European Parliament, the Council and the Commission stating that a draft legislative act does not correspond with the principle of subsidiarity. If one third of the national parliaments shares this view, the draft has to be *re-examined* (Art. 7, para. 2, Protocol No. 2). The same applies in the event that a majority of the national Parliaments has objections against a specific draft legislative act on this particular ground; but then, in case the Commission decides to maintain its original proposal, it may be overruled by a majority of 55 % of the members of the Council or a majority of the votes expressed in the European Parliament; in that case the draft legislative act has to be withdrawn (Art. 7, para. 3, Protocol No. 2). National Parliaments or a chamber of a national Parliament furthermore have a right of appeal against a legislative act on the ground of a violation of the principle of subsidiarity, be it that it has to be sent to the Court of Justice on behalf of its national Parliament or a chamber of that Parliament by the Member State concerned (Art. 8, Protocol No. 2).

According to Article 12(d) TEU (Lisbon), the national parliaments will take part in the ordinary and simplified revision procedures of the Treaties; and according to Article 12(e) TEU (Lisbon) they will be notified of applications for accession to the Union in accordance with Article 49 TEU (Lisbon).

6   SCOPE OF DECISION-MAKING POWERS

6.1   PRINCIPLE OF CONFERRED POWERS

The Council, acting alone or with the European Parliament, and the Commission have been granted powers of decision, i.e., powers to take decisions which are legally binding upon persons coming within the legal authority of the Union. This has not been done by way of a general authorization to take decisions within the scope of application of the Treaty, but by the grant of a plurality of specific powers of decision[233] which are defined as accurately as possible in the various Treaty Articles according to their nature and subject-matter. Article 5 EC sets out the general limitation that the Community must act within the limits of the powers which the Treaty confers upon it, and of the objectives assigned to it.[234] This basic principle concerning the division of competence between the Community and the Member States[235] is elaborated in the Treaties, so that each Institution may act only within the limits of the powers conferred upon it by the Treaties.[236] Each decision taken by an Institution must therefore be based directly or indirectly on one or more[237] specific provisions of the Treaties.[238]

The same principle is encountered in Article 5 TEU, according to which the Institutions exercise their powers under the conditions and for the purposes provided for by the provisions of the Treaties establishing the European Communities and also by the other provisions of the Treaty on European Union itself. It should though be noted straight away that this principle does not apply with the same degree of strictness in the second and third pillars as it does in the first pillar. As regards the decisions which may be taken in the area of CFSP, including the decisions of the European Council (general guidelines and common strategies), Article 12 TEU provides that these must be in pursuit of the objectives mentioned in Article 11 TEU. The same holds for the decisions concerning PJCCM: Article 34(2) TEU provides that these decisions must contribute to the pursuit of the objectives of the Union. Notwithstanding, subparagraphs (b) and (c) set out in more detail the aims to be pursued by framework decisions and decisions.[239]

This principle of conferred powers was an important factor in the judgment of the German Federal Constitutional Court of 12 October 1993 on the compatibility

---

233. '*Compétences d'attribution*', in English 'conferred powers' (or 'attributed powers').
234. Art. 5 EC, 1st para.
235. See Ch. III, section 6.1, *supra*.
236. Art. 7(1), 2nd sub-paragraph, EC; see also Arts. 202, 211 and 249 EC, and Arts. 3, 115, 124 and 161 Euratom. See also Art. 3(1) SEA which refers not just to the Treaties, but to Title II of the SEA itself. See Dashwood (1996) ELRev., 113.
237. Sometimes the Council bases its acts on two specific Articles of the Treaty as a compromise in the event of a dispute amongst its members as to which Article provides the correct legal basis. This can be of importance, particularly if the Articles involved provide for different voting procedures. See R. Barents, 'The internal market unlimited: Some observations on the legal basis of Community legislation', (1993) CML Rev., 85–109, H. Cullen and A. Charlesworth, 'Diplomacy by other means: The use of legal basis litigation as a political strategy by the European Parliament and Member States', (1999) CML Rev., 243-1270; R.H. van Ooik, *De keuze der rechtsgrondslag voor besluiten van de Europese Unie*, EM No. 63, (Deventer, 1999). See further, e.g., Case 68/86, *United Kingdom v. Council*; Case 131/86, *United Kingdom v. Council*; Case C-300/89, *Commission v. Council*; Case C-155/91, *Commission v. Council*; Case C-187/93, *European Parliament v. Council*.
238. See also Ch. III, section 6.1 *supra* on this. For a recent example of the relevant principle, see Case C-376/98, *Germany v. Parliament and Council* (Tobacco advertising).
239. Cf. van Ooik, op. cit. *supra* note 237 at Ch. 9.

with the German Constitution of the Maastricht Treaty on European Union.[240] That court noted that even after the changes introduced by the Treaty of Maastricht, the EC Treaty adheres to the principle of specific empowerment and the principle also applies to the TEU pursuant to its Article 5.[241] The German court then examined in detail whether this requirement was in fact respected by Article 6(4) TEU;[242] by the possibility of attributing new tasks and powers to the Union and the Community;[243] and the provisions concerning Economic and Monetary Union.[244] While the Federal Constitutional Court answered these points positively, it expressly reserved the right to examine whether legal acts taken by the Community Institutions or other bodies were within the limits of the powers conferred upon them by the Community Treaties and the TEU.[245]

6.2   FILLING IN THE *LACUNAE*: ARTICLE 308 EC

The framework of conferred powers, as just set out, reflects the desire of the contracting parties to set the clearest possible limits to the encroachment on their sovereignty. Nevertheless, the system of conferred powers means that situations may arise in which it turns out that action by the Communities is necessary in order to ensure the achievement of certain objectives, but the requisite specific powers are lacking. Thus, in the Treaties, special provision exists designed to cover such an eventuality: Article 308 EC and 203 Euratom. The Council, acting unanimously on a proposal from the Commission and after consulting the European Parliament, then takes the appropriate measures.[246]

The importance of Article 308 EC for effective Community action justifies a closer examination of its interpretation and application. Article 308 itself contains the conditions for its use. First, action by the Community must be 'necessary to attain, in the course of the operation of the common market, one of the objectives of the Community'. Thus it is clear that the *lacuna* must be in the powers granted, not in the sum of objectives of the Community. As far as objectives are concerned, these are not merely the general objectives in Article 2 EC as detailed in Article 3

---

240. *Brunner* [1994] CMLR, 57. Herdegen, Maastricht and the German Constitutional Court: Constitutional restraints for an 'ever closer union', (1994) CMLR, 235; Kokott (1996) EPL, 237; Meyring (1997) ELRev., 221; Zuleeg (1997) ELRev., 19.
241. *Prinzip der beschränkten Einzelermächtigung* (points A.I.1(b) and C.II.1(a) of that judgment): the principle of limited individual authorization.
242. Which provides that the Union shall provide itself with the means necessary to attain its objectives and carry through its policies.
243. Art. 2 TEU, 1st para., 5th indent.
244. See points C.II.2(a)–(f) of the judgment.
245. Point C.1.3 of the judgment, *in fine*.
246. Such a provision for the second and third pillar is absent, but according to some authors (e.g., van Ooik, op. cit. *supra*), the legal bases provided there also fulfil the function which Art. 308 EC fulfils in the first pillar (see 380). The author of this chapter stresses that the legal bases in the second and third pillar do not only have the function of Art. 308 EC, but also the function of the specific legal bases in the first pillar.

EC, but also the objectives mentioned in the various specific Articles of the Treaty, even if the latter can also be derived ultimately from the general objectives. The meaning of the phrase 'in the course of the operation of the common market' is not to be understood in the geographical sense, nor as restricting the operation of Article 308 EC to the strict field of the attainment of one of the two most important means by which the Community's objectives are to be achieved, namely the establishment of a common market. Rather, the application of Article 308 EC must be designed to ensure that the common market, as defined in the Treaty, may function more effectively.

The second condition which Article 308 sets out for its use is that the Treaty has not provided the necessary powers. That does not mean that no powers exist at all; it may be that powers do exist but that they do not provide for a satisfactory and effective solution, for instance where harmonization of laws by means of directives is provided for, but in actual fact uniform rules by means of regulations are needed.[247] A narrow interpretation of the ambit or reach of the powers conferred by a particular article of the Treaty, rather than a wide interpretation will obviously more easily lead to the conclusion that recourse must be had to Article 308 EC. It originally appeared that even when a wide interpretation of the powers conferred by the Treaty was justified, the Court would leave the Council a certain liberty to invoke Article 308 in the interests of legal certainty; in later cases, the Court apparently abandoned that notion.[248]

Provided that these two conditions are met, 'appropriate measures' may be taken by the Council, acting unanimously on a proposal from the Commission and after consulting the European Parliament. 'Appropriate measures' covers not merely the forms of action set out in Article 249 EC,[249] but also any other form of action which may be appropriate. On the basis of the difference in wording between Article 80(2) EC and Article 308 EC[250] it has been argued that Article 308, unlike Article 80(2), does not permit the Council to adopt acts under which it either retains the power to adopt implementing measures in a particular field itself

---

247. E.g., in the field of customs law, see Case 8/73, *Hauptzollamt Bremerhaven v. Massey-Ferguson GmbH* relating to the old Reg. 803/68 (O.J. 1968, L 148/6) on the valuation of goods for customs purposes.
248. See Case 45/86, *Commission v. Council* (generalized tariff preferences) where the Court stated, 'it follows from the very wording of Article [308] that its use as the legal basis for a measure is justified only where no other provision of the Treaty gives the Community institutions the necessary power to adopt the measure in question'. See also Case 242/87, *Commission v. Council* (Erasmus programme).
249. I.e., regulations, directives, decisions, recommendations or opinions.
250. Art. 80(2) EC provides that the 'Council may, acting by a qualified majority, decide whether, to what extent and by what procedure, appropriate provisions may be laid down for sea and air transport'. Art. 308 EC provides that if 'action by the Community should prove necessary to attain, in the course of the operation of the common market, one of the objectives of the Community and this Treaty has not provided the necessary powers, the Council shall, acting unanimously on a proposal from the Commission and after consulting the Assembly, take the appropriate measures'.

or delegates such power to the Commission under Article 211 EC.[251] This restrictive interpretation does not accord with the Council's practice in the use of Article 308.[252]

Assuming that Article 308 does not oblige the Council, when there is no specific power conferred in the Treaty, to take appropriate measures in every case, but rather allows the Council the freedom to take measures and to decide whether to entrust implementation to the Commission or in specific cases[253] to implement the measures further itself, it appears acceptable in principle that Article 308 can be the basis for creating new bodies – with legal personality – and conferring certain powers on these.[254] The usefulness of doing so is, however, heavily circumscribed by the restrictive criteria which the Court has laid down concerning the lawfulness of delegating powers of decision to bodies other than the Commission.[255]

Within the limits laid down in Article 308 EC itself, the Council can indeed use that provision in order to supplement the Treaty provisions to a certain extent and it is interesting to see how this power compares with other means of supplementing the law of the Treaties, such as the system of decisions of the representatives of the governments of the Member States meeting within the Council.[256] In the *ERTA* judgment[257] the Court did not regard the Council as being obliged to use Article 308 EC in every case where such use would be possible. This appeared to leave the door wide open for the use of decisions of the representatives of the governments of the Member States meeting within the Council as an alternative to 'appropriate measures' under Article 308 EC. Such an approach would be objectionable because it would mean that the governments could take action outside the competences and procedures of the Community.

However, the Court appears to have placed an important restriction on its remarks in the *ERTA* judgment. In *Hauptzollamt Bremerhaven v. Massey-Ferguson*[258] it stated that no objection could be raised to the application of Article 308 EC in the interests of legal certainty when it was not perhaps entirely clear that various specific Articles of the Treaty did confer the necessary powers because, in the light of the specific requirements of Article 308, 'the rules of the

---

251. Gericke, *Allgemeine Rechtssetzungsbefügnisse nach Artikel 235 EWG-Vertrag* (Hamburg, 1970) 86–87; see also Ipsen, *Europäisches Gemeinschaftsrecht* (Tübingen, 1972) 4/32 and 20/41.
252. See Gericke, ibid., 87–90.
253. Cf. Art. 202 EC, 3rd indent, 3rd sentence.
254. Thus, e.g., the Council set up the European Centre for the Development of Vocational Training (Cedefop) (by Reg. 337/75, O.J. 1975, L 39/1); the European Foundation for the Improvement of Living and Working Conditions (by Reg. 1365/75, O.J. 1975, L 139/1), and the European Agency for the Evaluation of Medicinal Products (by Reg. 2309/93, O.J. 1993, L 214/1). See further the list of agencies in section 9.4 *infra*. The question of which legal basis should be used for establishing these bodies: a specific basis, or a general basis such as Art. 308 EC, was at issue in Case C-217/04, *UK v. Parliament and Council*.
255. See section 6.4. of this Chapter, *infra*.
256. See Ch. V, section 1.7, *infra*.
257. Case 22/70, *Commission v. Council* (ERTA).
258. Case 8/73, *Hauptzollamt Bremerhaven v. Massey-Ferguson*.

Treaty on the forming of the Council's decisions or on the division of powers between the Institutions are not to be disregarded'.[259] From this it can be deduced that a decision of the representatives of the governments of the Member States meeting within the Council would not have been upheld, as the use of such a decision would have been to disregard the rules of the Treaty. Indeed, these decisions always come about without reference to the Commission's right of initiative or consultation of the European Parliament. It may be concluded that the use of such decisions is always impossible if Article 308 itself could be used. The procedures of that Article are part of 'the rules of the Treaty on the forming of the Council's decisions or on the division of powers between the Institutions' which the Court will not permit the Institutions to disregard.

Finally the question of the demarcation between Article 308 EC and Article 48 TEU on the procedure for amendment of the Treaties (including the EC Treaty) arises. That procedure in Article 48 TEU must be used whenever the conditions for the use of Article 308 EC are not fulfilled. This is particularly the case if it is necessary to confer powers for the achievement of objectives not already mentioned in the Treaty or if changes in the institutional structure of the Community are to be made. The latter would also involve a change in the institutional structure of the Union itself.[260]

The extent to which Article 308 EC has been used has shown a somewhat cyclical development. Originally the Council was rather restrained in resorting to it, and the main uses of the provision were to integrate trade in processed agricultural products into the system of the common agricultural policy and to achieve uniform regulation of customs law.[261] Post-1972 this approach changed significantly. The final communiqué of the Paris Summit in October 1972 showed a clear preference for the use of Article 308 EC (then Art. 235 EEC) as the basis of the achievement of Economic and Monetary Union and the development of complementary policies such as a common regional and social policy, a common policy for science and technology and common environmental and energy policies. A series of decisions in these sectors, based on Article 308 EC, followed in the succeeding years; at the same time more widespread use was made of Article 308 even in the traditional sectors of agriculture, the customs union, establishment and services and commercial policy.[262]

The need to fall back on Article 308 EC significantly diminished after the SEA came into force on 1 July 1987. The SEA introduced various specific powers in relation to monetary capacity, social policy, economic and social cohesion, research and technological development and the environment which have now been further developed by the changes made through the Treaty of Maastricht. Accordingly, action in matters such as environmental policy no longer normally

259. Ibid., at para. 4 (but see Case 45/86, *Commission v. Council*).
260. Cf. Arts. 3 and 5 TEU.
261. E.g., Reg. 1059/69 (O.J. 1969, L 141/1) on trade arrangements applicable to certain goods resulting from the processing of agricultural products.
262. See Lauwaars (1976) EuR 100 et seq.

has to be based on Article 308. At the same time these developments went hand-in-hand with an express limitation of the use of Article 308. Article 98 EC, introduced by the SEA (originally as Art.102a EEC), required institutional changes necessary for the establishment of Economic and Monetary Union to be undertaken by means of the procedure for amendment of the Treaties (it has since been amended).[263] A similar type of restriction is also apparent in Articles 150–152 EC in the fields of education, vocational training and youth, culture, and public health, as those provisions expressly exclude any harmonization of laws and regulations of Member States. On this basis the Edinburgh European Council concluded that the use of Article 308 EC for these purposes is also excluded.[264] Moreover the European Council declared that the principle of subsidiarity must also be respected in the application of Article 308 EC.[265]

Apart from the restrictive interpretation of Article 308 set out above, there remains the inherent objection to the use of this provision that it only provides for *consultation* of the European Parliament. Even a wide interpretation should not lead to decisions being taken on the basis of Article 308 EC which should properly be subject to full involvement of the European Parliament. As long as there is no full decision-making authority for the Parliament, or at the very least co-decision, which would lend real parliamentary democratic legitimacy to the use of Article 308,[266] fundamental decisions should, it is submitted, preferably be taken using the amendment procedure of Article 48 TEU. This latter procedure requires ratification by all the Member States in accordance with their respective constitutional requirements.

6.3   APPLICATION OF THE THEORY OF IMPLIED POWERS

It may be thought, and indeed has repeatedly been argued that the existence of Article 308 EC to cover unforeseen developments means that the theory of implied powers, which is a theory particularly well-known in the laws of federal states and international organizations, has no place in Community law. Such a view rests on scarcely convincing foundations. In the system of the European Community Treaties, which is based on an attribution of a series of specific powers to the Council and the Commission, provisions like Article 308 EC have a different scope of application from that of the theory of implied powers. As each case arises,

---

263.   The Article was amended by the Treaty of Maastricht, and this limitation was removed in view of the specific provisions introduced by that Treaty.
264.   Bull. EC 12-1992 point I.15 (final sub-point, 14, note 1). In *Brunner* [1994] CML Rev. 47, the German Constitutional Court expressly referred to this aspect of the European Council's declaration (point C.II.2.a (end)).
265.   Bull. EC 12-1992 point I.15, (13, basic principles on the implementation of Art. 5 EC). See on the subsidiarity principle Ch. III section 6.2.
266.   The Vedel Report envisaged parliamentary cooperation on, *inter alia*, the use of Art. 235 EEC as one of the first steps in the expansion of the Parliament's powers (Bull. EC 1972 Supp. 4/72) but nothing came of this.

the Treaties confer the powers required for the activities of the Communities. Article 308 grants the power to act in a case where such action is necessary to attain, in the course of operation of the common market, one of the objectives of the Communities, but this power is lacking. A new, independent power of action is created, subject to the conditions discussed in the previous section, alongside the existing ones.

On the other hand the application of the theory of implied powers in the system of the Treaties can only relate to existing powers of action. It cannot fill a gap in the totality of the specific powers conferred on the Institutions for the activities of the Communities – for this purpose a provision like Article 308 EC has been created – but it can only supplement a specific power to act, explicitly conferred on the Communities, which shows a gap. In fact, the theory is an outcome of 'a rule of interpretation generally accepted in both international and national law, according to which the rules laid down by an international treaty or a law presuppose the rules without which that treaty or law would have no meaning or could not be reasonably and usefully applied',[267] and it was adopted as such by the Court of Justice in the interpretation of the former European Coal and Steel Community Treaty. When adapted to the system for specific powers in the European Treaties, this 'principle of effectiveness' (*effet utile*) implies that such power without which an explicitly conferred specific power either would not make sense or would not permit a reasonable application, must be deemed to be included in the power that has been explicitly conferred. It is, therefore, a matter not of an independent, but a derived power, which is necessary to attain the objectives for which the main specific power is intended.

Article 308 EC and the corresponding article in the Euratom Treaty, therefore, do not in principle form an obstacle to an application of the theory of implied powers in the context of a rational interpretation of a Treaty provision. The significance of this theory for the institutional law of the Communities, however, must not be overestimated. The implied powers of decision will seldom be very wide because, first of all, they can only result from one of the specific powers which the Council and the Commission already possess and, secondly, because these specific powers have been carefully defined and delimited in the Treaties. Save in the field of external relations, the cautious case law of the Court[268] does not justify an assumption that the theory of implied powers will play a great part in the development of the powers of the Community. In the field of external relations, however, it has been clear since the *ERTA* judgment,[269] mentioned earlier, that the Community's power to conclude international agreements can arise not merely from an explicit grant of power in the Treaty[270] but also from other Treaty

---

267. Case 8/55, *Fédération Charbonnière de Belgique v. High Authority*, at 299.
268. Ibid., Case 8/55, *Fédération Charbonnière de Belgique v. High Authority*; Case 25/59, *Netherlands v. High Authority*; Joined Cases 281, 283–285 & 287/85, *Germany et al. v. Commission*, and Case C-295/90, *European Parliament v. Council* (right of residence for students).
269. Case 22/70, *Commission v. Council*.
270. As in Arts. 133 and 310 EC.

provisions and from decisions taken by the Community Institutions in connection with those provisions.[271]

6.4   DELEGATION OF POWERS

The Council, acting alone or in conjunction with the European Parliament, and the Commission may exercise their powers of decision to lay down provisions or to apply provisions laid down in the Treaties or in implementing acts. The extent to which they may delegate their powers to other Institutions, agencies or other bodies is a matter of considerable importance, as is the distinction between various types of delegation.

6.4.1   Delegation by the Council to the Commission

Delegation of powers by the Council to the Commission is expressly envisaged in the EC and Euratom Treaties.[272] The Commission exercises the powers conferred on it by the Council 'for the implementation of the rules laid down by the latter'.[273] Such delegation acquired a tighter character after the addition of a third indent to Article 202 EC by the SEA. This requires the Council to delegate to the Commission the powers of implementation. Only in exceptional circumstances may the Council reserve the right to exercise specific implementing powers itself, and the Court has ruled, in Case 16/88, *Commission v. Council*, that the Council 'must state in detail the grounds for such a decision'.[274] In the same judgment, the Court stated that the 'concept of implementation for the purposes of that article comprises both the drawing up of implementing rules and the application of rules to specific cases by means of acts of individual application' (para. 11). The rules drawn up by the Council may therefore be general in character. It is sufficient that the Council decides upon the essential elements of the matter which has to be regulated,[275] as happens for example in the regulations concerning the common organizations of the market for agricultural products 'which are intended to give

---

271. See Opinion 2/91, *ILO Convention on Safety in the Use of Chemicals at Work*; Opinion 1/94, *WTO – GATS and TRIPs*, and Opinion 2/94, *Accession to the European Convention on Human Rights*.
272. Arts. 211, 4th indent, and 202, 3rd indent EC, and Art. 124 Euratom.
273. Art. 211, 4th indent EC.
274. Case 16/88, *Commission v. Council* at para. 10. In such cases, the Council usually declares a simplified decision-making procedure to be applicable concerning the exercise of such powers acquired by 'self-authorization', as compared with those which the Treaty lays down in relation to the exercise of the basic power (e.g., no proposal by the Commission, different voting rules, or no consultation of the Parliament). In such cases, the same condition should apply as that for delegation to the Commission: the Council must lay down the essential elements of the matter according to the procedures required by the Treaty. General 'self-authorization' would, if this condition were not met, disturb the institutional balance laid down in the Treaty.
275. Case 25/70, *Einfuhr- und Vorratstelle für Getreide und Futtermittel v. Köster et Berodt & Co.*

concrete shape to the fundamental guidelines of Community policy'.[276] If the Council derives a regulatory power from the Treaty, the Council may not delegate this *in toto* to the Commission. If that were done, the implementation by the Commission would not really be an implementation of the rules laid down by the Council, but rather of those laid down by the Treaty itself!

The third indent of Article 202 EC in fact gives an express basis in the Treaty for a practice dating from the 1960s by which, in conferring implementing powers on the Commission, the Council sets out the conditions under which the Commission could exercise its powers in the provision conferring the delegation. This concerns the exercise by the Commission of the powers conferred on it in the framework of the so-called comitology procedure.[277] The second sentence of Article 202 EC, third indent permits the Council to impose certain requirements in respect of the exercise of the powers delegated to the Commission. The fourth sentence of the same indent requires the Council, acting unanimously on a proposal from the Commission and after obtaining the Opinion of the European Parliament, to lay down principles and rules to be taken into account when choosing the relevant delegation procedure.[278]

6.4.2 Delegation to Third Parties

The question of the extent of permissible delegation of powers to third parties was considered in a pair of important judgments in cases brought by an Italian company, Meroni, under the ECSC Treaty.[279] These judgments, the importance of which stretches way beyond the individual facts, show that in principle delegation is possible, even where this is not expressly provided for in the Treaties, provided that the exercise of the delegated powers is subject to the same rules as are laid down in the Treaties concerning the exercise of the powers by the delegating Institution itself, particularly as far as the obligation to state reasons for acts and subjection to judicial review are concerned.[280]

---

276. Case C-240/90, *Germany v. Commission* at para. 37. That judgment also shows that the Council may leave it up to the Commission to oblige the Member States to impose specific penalties on the basis of a delegating provision drafted in general terms.
277. See, further, Ch. V, section 4.2. *infra*.
278. See Decision of the Council No. 1999/468/EC of 28 Jun. 1999, O.J. 1999, L 184/23, laying down the procedures for the exercise of implementing powers conferred on the Commission (so-called 'Comitology Decision'), as amended by Decision of the Council No. 2006/512/EC of 17 Jul. 2006, O.J. 2006, L 200/11. A consolidated text has been published in O.J. 2006, C 255/4. See further the Declaration of the Parliament, the Council and the Commission regarding Decision No. 2006/512/EC, O.J. 2006, C 255/1 K. Lenaerts and A. Verhoeven, Towards a Legal Framework for Executive Rule-Making in the EU?: The Contribution of the New Comitology Decision, (2000), CML Rev., 645–686.
279. Case 9/56, *Meroni & Co., Industrie Metallurgiche, SpA v. High Authority*; Case 10/56, *Meroni and Co., Industrie Metallurgiche, SAS v. High Authority*.
280. Cf. the provisions of Art. 53 Euratom, 2nd para., relating to the activities of the Euratom Supply Agency.

What is not permitted, however, is the delegation of discretionary powers to institutions other than those set up by the Treaties themselves for the purpose of ensuring and controlling the exercise of those powers within the framework of their respective functions. Such a delegation would amount to a breach of a basic guarantee which the Treaties afford to the persons under the legal authority of the Communities, contained in the *balance of powers which is characteristic of the institutional structure of the Community*.[281] The only delegation which is permitted, therefore, is that of clearly defined executive powers, the use of which can be subject to strict review in the light of objective criteria which have been determined by the delegating authority.[282]

The significance of this ECSC case law for the question of delegation of powers in relation to the EC Treaty lies in the principle of the balance of powers, part of which is the Court's supervision of legality; this balance may not be disturbed. The question arises whether this case law may imply a complete prohibition of the delegation of discretionary powers in the functioning of the EC. In the ECSC system, which was characterized by strong powers conferred on the Commission by the Treaty (which were, however, narrowly defined by the Treaty), the strict test for permissible delegation was justified because if the Commission were to transfer its powers to other bodies this would be tantamount to a *carte blanche* delegation. The EC system, however, often confers very broad powers on the Council and here the emphasis of the test tends to lie on the clear and precise delimitation of the powers transferred, on the resulting restriction of free decision-making powers and not on the exclusion of all freedom.[283] Thus, in *Romano v. Institut National d'Assurance Maladie-Invalidité*[284] the Court indicated that it followed from Article 211 EC and from the judicial system created by the EC Treaty – in particular Articles 230 and 234 EC – that a body such as the Administrative Commission on Social Security for Migrant Workers could not be empowered by the Council to adopt acts having the force of law. Delegation of powers to the new independent Community bodies[285] will also have to respect the boundaries set out in this case law.[286]

6.4.3   Internal Delegation

In principle, it is not permissible for the Commission to delegate its power of decision to one of its members (so-called internal delegation), as this would

---

281. Case 10/56, *Meroni v. High Authority*. Cf. on this criterion Case 25/70, *Einfuhr- und Vorratstelle für Getreide und Futtermittel v. Köster et Berodt & Co.*
282. Case 10/56, *Meroni v. High Authority*, ibid.
283. The criterion of a clear and precise delimitation of powers was applied in Opinion 1/76 *European Laying-up Fund for Inland Waterway Vessels*, even though it did not relate in that instance to an intra-Community delegation, but to the conferral of powers on an international organization under a Treaty concluded by the Community with a third country.
284. Case 98/80 *Romano v. Institut National d'Assurance Maladie-Invalidité*.
285. See sections 9.3 and 9.4, *infra*.
286. See on the delegation of powers to new independent bodies E. Vos, 'Reforming the European Commission: What Role to Play for EU Agencies' (2000) CML Rev., 1113–1134. See further Council Reg. 58/2003 of 19 Dec. 2002, on executive agencies, O.J. 2003, L 11/1.

conflict with its collective responsibility before the European Parliament and with the requirement that the Commission take decisions by a majority of the number of its members (Art. 219(2) EC).

However, such a rigorous prohibition of delegation is impossible in view of the enormous number of Commission decisions which have to be taken, particularly in the agricultural sector. Accordingly, the Commission authorizes one or more of its individual members to take measures in the area of administration and management; this is done in the name of the Commission and taking account of the limits and conditions which it sets; the principle of collective responsibility must be fully respected.[287] The Court has been willing to accept this type of delimited internal delegation, because no power of own decision is conferred on the person mandated, and his or her power is limited to certain categories of acts in the area of administration and management and does not permit him or her to take decisions of principle in the matters concerned.[288] However, it is now clear that certain types of decision cannot be left to this procedure: in the so-called *PVC* case, the Court of First Instance (confirmed on this point on appeal by the Court of Justice) ruled that decisions finding an infringement of Article 81(1) EC and imposing substantial fines are not to be considered measures of administration and management, and may therefore not be the subject of delegation to the holder of the competition portfolio.[289] Such cases thus resemble a public law mandate rather than a real delegation of powers.

6.4.4 'Delegation' to Member States

Many Community acts provide for the adoption of implementing measures by the Member States. We shall not go further into the question whether the concept of 'delegation' is in fact applicable in these cases, let alone the consequences which could ensue.[290] It may, however, be noted that, particularly in the regulation of common organizations of the market in agricultural products and in the collection of agricultural levies, customs duties and (to some extent) Value Added Tax, as well as in the payment of agricultural refunds, national authorities often act as

---

287. Art. 13. Rules of Procedure of the Commission of 29 Nov. 2000, O.J. 2000, L 308/26. In an internal decision of 12 Jan. 2001, which has not been published in the O.J., the Commission laid down the rules for applying this provision, COM(2001)1.

288. Case 5/85, *AKZO Chemie BV et al. v. Commission*; also Case 48/69, *Imperial Chemical Industries Ltd. v. Commission*; Case 8/72, *Vereeniging van Cementhandelaren v. Commission*; Joined Cases 43 & 63/82, *Vereniging ter Bevordering van het Vlaamse Boekwezen, VBVB et al. v. Commission* and Case 8/83, *Officine fratelli Bertoli SpA v. Commission*. See also Joined Cases 46/87 & 227/88, *Hoechst AG v. Commission* and Case C-191/95, *Commission v. Germany*.

289. Case C-137/92, *Commission v. BASF AG et al.*, upholding, on this point, on appeal, the view of the Court of First Instance in Cases T-79/89 etc., *BASF AG et al. v. Commission*.

290. See Maas, 'Delegatie van bevoegdheden in de Europese Gemeenschappen' (1976) SEW, 2 and Louis, 'Delegatie van bevoegdheid in de Europese Gemeenschappen' (1978) SEW, 802–814.

administrative extensions of the Community.[291] In these circumstances the Court is not afraid to speak of power delegated to the Member States.[292] However, the Court declines to attach any consequences to such delegation, maintaining the separation of responsibility strictly.[293] The close intertwining of Community and national administrations gives rise to unsatisfactory circumstances for litigants, particularly in relation to actions for damages, as they may be uncertain whether to sue (first of all) the national authorities or the Community or, indeed, both.[294]

6.4.5   Delegation to New International Organs

The more the Community participates in international activities the more it has to face the question of how far it can accord decision-making powers to international bodies established by agreements with third countries when Community law confers these powers in the internal sphere upon the Community Institutions.[295] It is evident from Opinion 1/76 *European Laying-up Fund* that the Court regards this as lawful in so far as the powers accorded to the international body are clearly and precisely defined and limited.[296] In Opinion 1/91 *European Economic Area I* the Court confirmed that the Community is competent to conclude an international agreement providing for a system of courts whose decisions would be binding on the Contracting Parties, including the Community and its Institutions.[297] However, the Court found that the judicial arrangements in the first draft of the EEA Agreement were incompatible with Article 220 EC, and, more generally, with the very foundations of the Community, as the proposed EEA Court would have had power to determine the interpretation not merely of provisions of the EEA Agreement

---

291. See further Ch. XII section 2 *infra*.
292. Joined Cases 213–215/81, *Norddeutsches Vieh- und Fleischkontor Herbert Will et al. v. Bundesanstalt für landwirtschaftliche Marktordnung* on management of tariff quotas by the Member States. See the more general observations relating to the action of the Member States in the Community interest, in areas in which the Community alone is competent, in Case 804/79, *Commission v. United Kingdom* and Joined Cases 47 & 48/83, *Pluimveeslachterij Midden-Nederland BV et al.*
293. Cf. Joined Cases 178–180/73, *Belgium and Luxembourg v. Mertens et al.* and Case 110/76, *Pretore di Cento v. A person or persons unknown*.
294. As to this point, see Ch. VI, section 2.4 *infra*.
295. Earlier in this book, the position was defended that the European Union possesses legal personality, which implies *inter alia* that the EU can take part in international legal relations; see Ch. II, section 1.2.4 and 5.1 *supra*. Indeed, under Arts. 24 and 38 TEU, the Council can conclude agreements with third countries or other international organizations in the areas of CFSP and PJCCM respectively, which are binding on the Member States and the institutions of the Union. See on this: A. Dashwood, 'External Relations Provisions of the Amsterdam Treaty', 35 CML Rev., 1019–1045, Barents, *Het Verdrag van Amsterdam in werking*, EM nr. 62, (Deventer, 1999), 60–61, and also Ch. XII, section 2 *infra*.
296. Opinion 1/76 *European Laying-up fund for Inland Waterway Vessels*.
297. Opinion 1/91 *draft agreement for the European Economic Area*.

itself but also, because of the proposed homogeneity between EEA rules and Community rules, of the corresponding rules of Community law.[298]

6.5   POLICY FORMULATION AND IMPLEMENTATION IN THE SECOND AND
            THIRD PILLARS

As mentioned earlier, the principle of conferred powers also applies in the second and third pillars, although it is less rigid in these areas than with regard to the first (EC) pillar. Another difference is that the distribution of tasks between the Institutions is different. In the second pillar, policies are defined by the European Council (in the form of decisions on common strategies to be implemented by the Union)[299] or by the Council (joint actions and common positions).[300] The implementation of the policies thus defined is a matter for the Council or the Presidency. According to Article 18(1) TEU, the Presidency represents the Union in matters coming within the common foreign and security policy; the same organ is responsible for implementing decisions taken in this field (Art. 18(2) TEU).

The basic decisions in the area of PJCCM are taken by the Council. They can be in the form of common positions, framework decisions, decisions or conventions, and the Commission also enjoys a right of initiative in this field (Art. 34(2) TEU). The European Parliament must be consulted about the last three categories of action before the measure in question is adopted (Art. 39(1) TEU). As for representation and implementation, Article 37(2) TEU declares Articles 18 and 19 TEU to apply *mutatis mutandis*.

7   THE COURT OF JUSTICE

7.1   ONE INSTITUTION, TWO BODIES

According to Article 7(1) EC, judicial supervision in the Community is exercised by one Institution, the Court of Justice.[301] The powers and tasks of this Institution are nowadays exercised by two bodies: the original Court of Justice of the European Communities (that is: the Court which acted as an institution of the three European Communities as of 1 January 1958),[302] and the Court of First Instance subsequently attached thereto.

---

298. The changes subsequently made led the Court of Justice to find the revised draft agreement compatible with Community law. See Opinion 1/92 *EEA II.*
299. Art. 13(2) TEU.
300. Arts. 13(3), 14 and 15 TEU.
301. See also Art. 3 Euratom, 4th indent.
302. Convention on certain Institutions common to the European Communities, Arts. 3 and 4, now replaced by Art. 9 Treaty of Amsterdam.

The power to establish the Court of First Instance was created by the Single European Act. According to Article 225 EC, added by the SEA,[303] the Council, acting unanimously at the request of the Court of Justice, and after consulting the Commission and the European Parliament, was empowered to attach a Court of First Instance to the Court of Justice. This was duly done, and the Court of First Instance was established by Council Decision of 24 October 1988.[304] The judicial arrangements were radically altered by the Treaty of Nice. In order to prevent the judicial system of the European Union from becoming completely clogged up as a result of enlargement of the Union, the Treaty of Nice replaces Articles 220–225 EC (and Arts. 136–140 Euratom) with new provisions (Arts. 220–225a EC; Arts. 136–140a Euratom). These provisions provide for a number of important structural changes, either directly or by empowering the Council to take the necessary implementing decisions.[305] The basic principle for the revised judicial system is that the Court of Justice *and* the Court of First Instance, within the framework of their respective jurisdictions, must ensure observance of the law in the interpretation and application of the Treaties; the Court of First Instance is no longer a body 'attached' to the Court of Justice, but has its own autonomous position. The powers of the Court of First Instance are set out in the new Articles 225 EC (and Art. 140a Euratom). Moreover, it is stated that judicial panels may be attached to the Court of First Instance in order to exercise, in certain specific areas, the judicial competence laid down in the Treaty.[306] Accordingly, Article 10 Treaty of Nice repeals the Decision establishing the Court of First Instance mentioned above.

In the following section, we will first discuss the (original) Court of Justice, and then the Court of First Instance (hereafter CFI). It should be pointed out here already that the expression 'Court of Justice' means different things at different places in the Treaties. It may refer to the Institution as such, in which case it is the division of competence between the two bodies which determines which of the two is meant in any concrete case, or it may refer to the Court of Justice as body (as opposed to the CFI). The meaning of the expression may even change further over time, given that the division of competence between the two bodies has already changed, and may well evolve still further.[307] In the discussion below we use the expression 'Court of Justice' to refer to the Court of Justice as a body, save where expressly otherwise stated, so that the CFI is separately discussed. Finally, in

---

303.   The Article was amended by the Treaty of Maastricht. The relevant Article for Euratom is Art. 140a, also added by the SEA.
304.   Dec. 88/591, O.J. 1988, L 319/1, last amended by Council Decision of 26 Apr. 1999, O.J. 1999, L 144/52.
305.   See, e.g., Johnston, 'Judicial Reform and the Treaty of Nice' (2001) CML Rev., 499–523; P.J.G. Kapteyn, 'De rechterlijke organisatie van de Europese Unie en de Intergouvernementele Conferentie' (2001) NJB, 1–6, and J.W. de Zwaan, 'Het Verdrag van Nice. Een bescheiden stap in het proces van Europese integratie' (2001) SEW, 42–52.
306.   Arts. 220 and 225a EC; 136 and 140b Euratom.
307.   E.g., in relation to Art. 228 EC. See Lauwaars 'De institutionele bepalingen in het EU-Verdrag' (1992) SEW, 681. See further literature on the Court of Justice mentioned at the end of this chapter.

section 7.4 we will discuss the provision added by the Treaty of Nice concerning the establishment of judicial panels, and the EU Civil Service Tribunal which has been established by virtue of that article.

It may already be noted that following the Lisbon Treaty, according to Article 19(1) TEU (Lisbon), the Court of Justice of the European Union shall include the Court of Justice, the General Court and specialized courts. The problem, that with one and the same expression, the Institution as well as the judicial body was meant, will in this way be solved. The 'Court of Justice of the European Union' is the Institution, as is also indicated in Article 13 TEU (Lisbon); the 'Court of Justice' is the body which will exercise the powers which have been assigned to this particular organ.

7.2   THE COURT OF JUSTICE

7.2.1   Composition, Structure and Procedure

According to Article 221, first paragraph, EC the Court of Justice consists of one judge per Member State. As of 1 May 2004 (the date of accession of ten new Member States) it consisted of 25 judges. Because of the accession of Bulgaria and Romania on 1 January 2007 it now consists of 27 judges. It is assisted by eight advocates general.[308] It is the duty of the advocates general 'acting with complete impartiality and independence, to make, in open court, reasoned submissions on cases' which, in accordance with the Statute of the Court of Justice, require their involvement.[309] The function of the advocates general was modelled on that of the *commissaire du gouvernement* in the French *Conseil d'Etat*, though it is not in all respects comparable.[310] The task of the advocates general is of great importance, particularly as their impartial submissions on law and on the facts form an extremely valuable basis on which the Court can arrive at its judgment.[311]

---

308. Art. 222, 1st para., EC. This provision also enables the number of advocates general to be increased by the Council, acting unanimously on a request from the Court of Justice.
309. See Art. 20 Statute of the Court of Justice: in principle all cases, but not where the Court of Justice after hearing the advocate general is of the opinion that there is no new point of law at issue. The Statute of the Court of Justice is annexed to the TEU, EC Treaty and Euratom Treaty as a separate Protocol (see Arts. 245, 1st para., EC and 160, 1st para., Euratom). It replaces, from the date of entry into force of the Treaty of Nice, the two Statutes which were previously annexed to the EC and Euratom Treaties (see Art. 7 Treaty of Nice). The Statute which was annexed to the ECSC Treaty ceased to have effect on the date of expiry of the ECSC Treaty: 23 Jul. 2002.
310. Wyatt and Dashwood, *European Community Law*, 3rd ed. (London, 1993) 106, note the widely held view that in the light of its development in the Community context, the office of Advocate General must be regarded as *sui generis*. See Case C-466/00, *Arben Kaba v. Secretary of State for the Home Department* and Case C-17/98, *Emesa Sugar (Free Zone) NV v. Aruba*.
311. See Tridimas, 'The Role of the Advocate General in the Development of Community Law: Some Reflections', 34 CML Rev., 1349–1387. Until the 1990s, the Court made a practice of not referring to the Opinion, although this practice has now clearly been abandoned. The Court

The appointment of judges and advocates general has been uniformly regulated in the Treaties: they are appointed by common accord of the governments of the Member States, for a period of six years, and are chosen from 'persons whose independence is beyond doubt and who possess the qualifications required for appointment to the highest judicial offices in their respective countries or who are jurisconsults of recognized competence'.[312] Provisions relating to the taking of the oath, privileges and immunities, incompatible secondary functions, and deprivation of office are intended to ensure the independence of both judges and advocates general.[313] On the other hand the relatively short term of office which has been provided for is of doubtful wisdom, as is the fact that the appointment of judges and advocates general has been placed entirely in the hands of the governments. This forms far too small an institutional guarantee of their independence. Very great confidence indeed is thus placed both in the disinterestedness of the governments with respect to their appointment and in the moral qualities of the persons appointed, a confidence which so far has fortunately not been misplaced.

The judges appoint from among their number a President for a period of three years; this appointment is renewable.[314] According to Article 221, second paragraph, the Court sits in chambers or in a Grand Chamber; according to the third paragraph, the Court of Justice may also sit as a full Court in special cases provided for in the Statute. The Chambers consist of three or five judges; the Grand Chamber consists of 13 judges, and always includes the President of the Court and the presidents of the five-judge chambers.[315] According to Article 16, fourth paragraph of the Statute of the Court of Justice, the Court meets as a Full Court in cases of requests for the dismissal of the European Ombudsman, members of the Commission or the Court of Auditors, or in order to take certain disciplinary measures. (The only example of such a case up until now is the case brought against Edith Cresson,[316] regarding the obligations of a member of the

---

sometimes expressly adopts the reasoning of the Advocate General entirely (e.g., Case C-377/92, *Felix Koch Offenbach Couleur und Karamel GmbH v. Oberfinanzdirektion München*) or in part (e.g., Case C-36/92, *Samenwerkende Elektriciteits-Produktiebedrijven (SEP) NV v. Commission*), and quite frequently specifically adopts certain points made by the Advocate General (e.g., Case C-426/93, *Germany v. Council*, and Case C-275/94, *Roger van der Linden v. Berufsgenossenschaft der Feinmechanik und Elektrotechnik*).

312. Arts. 223 and 139 Euratom (1st para., in each case). Retiring Judges and Advocates General are eligible for reappointment, ibid. (4th para., in each case); every three years there is a partial replacement of Judges and Advocates General. The European Parliament has called for its Legal Affairs Committee to 'meet with prospective members of the Court of Justice prior to their appointment' (O.J. 1994, C 61/126). As to the meaning of the word 'jurisconsults', see K.P.E. Lasok, *The European Court of Justice, Practice and Procedure*, 2nd ed. (London, 1994) 14–15.

313. See Arts. 2-4, 6 and 8 Statute of the Court of Justice, and the Protocol on the Privileges and Immunities of the European Communities (Art. 21 with Arts. 12–15 and 18).

314. Arts. 223 EC and 139 Euratom (5th para., in each case).

315. Art. 16, Statute of the Court of Justice as amended by Decision of the Council of 26 Apr. 2004, O.J. 2004, 132/5.

316. Case C-432/04, *Commission v. Edith Cresson*.

Commission). According to paragraph 5 of the same article, the Court may decide to refer the case to the full Court where it considers that a case before it is of exceptional importance.

Since there are no Treaty provisions on the subject, the nationality of judges and advocates general has no legal relevance to their candidature for appointment. Unlike in many international jurisdictions there is no system of appointing an *ad hoc* judge from a State which is party to proceedings but has no judge of its nationality on the tribunal.[317] The Statute of the Court of Justice prevents any party seeking a change in the composition of the Court or its Chambers on the ground of the nationality of a judge or the absence of a judge of the same nationality as that party.[318] In this manner the internal Community nature of the Court's jurisdiction in the Communities is emphasized. In practice, though, the governments of the Member States do look to nationality, there usually being one national of each Member State sitting as judge. Nationality also plays a role in relation to the allocation of advocates general.

The provisions governing procedure in the Court are to be found partly in the Statute[319] and partly in the Rules of Procedure.[320] The Council may, at the Court's request and after consulting the Commission and the European Parliament, or at the Commission's request and after consulting the Court and the European Parliament, amend the provisions of the Statute by unanimous vote (with the exception of Title 1, on the status of judges and advocates general).[321] The Rules of Procedure are laid down by the Court but they require the approval of the Council, by qualified majority (before the Treaty of Nice, this had to be with unanimity).[322] Changes to Title 1 of the Statute may only be made by means of the procedure for amending the Treaties.[323]

The procedure consists of three stages:

(a) *written procedure*, starting with a request which is served on the defendant, followed by a statement of defence and a reply and a rejoinder, and finally the preliminary report of the Judge acting as *rapporteur* on whether the case requires investigation;[324]

---

317. Cf. Statute of the International Court of Justice, Art. 31.
318. Art. 18, 4th para.
319. Annexed to the EC, ECSC and Euratom Treaties, see *supra*.
320. See Rules of Procedure of the Court of Justice of the European Communities of 19 Jun. 1991, (O.J. 1991, L 176/7, as amended, latest consolidated version available on the website of the Court: <http://curia.europa.eu.>
321. Arts. 245 EC and 160 Euratom (2nd para., in each case).
322. Art. 223, 6th para., EC and Art. 160 Euratom (3rd para.). See, generally, K. Lenaerts, D. Arts, I. Maselis (ed. Robert Bray), *Procedural Law of the European Union*, 2nd ed. (London, 2006).
323. Art. 48 TEU.
324. Rules of Procedure, Arts. 37–44. See the Rules of Procedure of the Court of Justice cited *supra*. As to written procedure in references for preliminary rulings, see Statute of the Court of Justice, Art. 23 and Rules of Procedure, Art. 103–104bis.

(b) if the Court so decides, a stage of *inquiry*, in connection with which witnesses and experts may be summoned and heard;[325]

(c) *oral procedure*, ending with submissions.[326]

Parties may only address the Court through their representatives.[327] Member States and Institutions must be represented by an agent, who may be assisted by a legal adviser or by a lawyer who is authorized to practise before the court of one of the Member States or of another state which is a party to the European Economic Area Agreement; other parties must be represented by such a lawyer.[328] *Intervention* by Member States or by other Institutions, including the Parliament,[329] is permitted.[330] Any other person who establishes that he or she has an interest in the result of any case submitted to the Court may be allowed to intervene in the proceedings, but individuals are not permitted to intervene in cases between Member States *inter se*, between Member States and the Community Institutions, or between the Community Institutions themselves.[331] The submissions contained in the application for intervention must be limited to supporting the form of order sought by one of the parties.[332]

On references for a *preliminary ruling*, the parties in the main proceedings before the national court[333] may submit a statement of case or written observations, as may the Member States, the Commission and even the Council or Parliament.[334] The parties may not change the tenor of the questions referred by the national judge, or supplement them.[335] According to Article 104(3) of the Rules of Procedure, where a question referred to the Court for a preliminary ruling is identical to a question on which the Court has already ruled, where the answer to such a question may be clearly deduced from existing case law or where the answer to the question admits of no reasonable doubt, the Court may give its decision by reasoned order.[336] Under Article 104(4) there will normally be an oral part in the proceedings, except where the case is dealt with by reasoned order, or if no oral hearing has been requested by any person entitled to do so. In addition, Article 104a provides

---

325. Rules of Procedure, ibid., Arts. 45–54.
326. Ibid., Arts. 55–62. The oral procedure may be dispensed with in exceptional circumstances, ibid., Art. 44bis, if none of the parties presents a request stating why they wish to be heard.
327. Statute of the Court of Justice, Art. 32. However, where, in references for preliminary rulings, national law permits litigants to appear in person, they may do so before the Court of Justice (as the proceedings are steps in the national proceedings), see Rules of Procedure, cited *supra*, Art. 104(2).
328. Statute, Art. 19.
329. See section 5.3 *supra*.
330. Statute, Art. 40.
331. Statute, Art. 40.
332. Statute Art. 40.
333. The Court of Justice sees a reference for a preliminary ruling as being a step in the national proceedings, see Rules of Procedure, cited *supra*, Art. 104(2).
334. Statute, Art. 23.
335. See Case 44/65 *Hessische Knappschaft v. Maison Singer et Fils* [1965] ECR, 965 at 970.
336. Although, as Case C-224/01, *Gerhard Köbler v. Republic of Austria* demonstrates, the national court may nevertheless still make a mistake.

for an accelerated procedure.[337] The procedures for appeals against judgments of the Court of First Instance will be dealt with in section 7.3.1. below.

7.2.1.1   *Proposed Changes following the Lisbon Treaty*

The only amendments which have been made in respect of the composition of the Court are, first, the introduction of an advisory panel which has to be consulted about the suitability of a particular candidate for nomination as Judge or Advocate General of the Court of Justice or the General Court (Art. 255 TFEU) and, secondly, the willingness of the Member States to increase the number of Advocates General (see Declaration No. 38 regarding Article 222 [renumbered 252] of the Treaty on the Functioning of the EU in respect of the number of Advocates General at the Court of Justice). In this way Poland will obtain its 'own' Advocate General.

7.2.2   **Duties and Powers of the Court of Justice**

The Court, under Articles 220 EC and 136 Euratom, ensures the observance of the law in the interpretation and application of the Treaties and their implementing rules. To this end, a number of powers have been expressly conferred on the Court, and its powers are limited to those conferred upon it.[338] These are mainly intended to enable the Court to judge the acts and omissions of the Institutions and the Member States in accordance with Community law, and to ensure uniformity of interpretation of Community law in the application of this law by national courts. The conditions under which the Court is required to exercise these powers – the very core of its jurisdiction – and the manner in which it does so, will be discussed more fully in Chapter VI, below. This section gives a broad survey of the various powers of the Court and a number of aspects of its jurisdiction and of the functions which it performs within the Communities. This discussion deals mainly with the relevant provisions of the EC Treaty.[339]

---

337. The two latter cases in Art. 104(3) of the Rules of Procedure and the accelerated procedure were added as of 1 Jul. 2000; the aim is to meet the objections to the lengthiness of the preliminary ruling procedure. The accelerated procedure was applied in Case C-189/01, *H. Jippes et al. v. Minister for Agriculture*, a request for a preliminary ruling by the Dutch *College van Beroep voor het bedrijfsleven*. See generally Barbier de la Serre, 'Accelerated and Expedited Procedures before the EC Courts: A Review of the Practice' (2006) CML Rev., 783–815. On 1 Mar. 2008, a new so-called 'urgent procedure' was introduced which may be applied to references for a preliminary ruling relating to the areas covered by Title VI of the TEU and Title IV of Part Three of the EC Treaty, which seek to maintain and develop an area of freedom, security and justice (see Art. 104b. new of the Rules of Procedure and Art. 23a. new of the Statute of the Court of Justice, O.J. 2008, L 24/39 and 42).
338. In accordance with the concept of conferred powers in Community law. The Court is, however, prepared to take a specific power and apply it by analogy, where this seems appropriate, e.g., Case C-295/90, *European Parliament v. Council* (maintaining the effects of an annulled directive for important reasons of legal certainty, until it was replaced by a directive adopted on the correct legal basis, whereas Art. 231 EC confers this power only in relation to regulations).
339. The powers of the Court of Justice in the framework of the third pillar (PJCCM) will be discussed in section 7.5 *infra*.

The powers of the Court can be divided into three categories: settling disputes, giving binding opinions,[340] and giving preliminary rulings. An examination of the first and most extensive category of these powers shows that the jurisdiction of the Court extends to disputes about the interpretation and application of Community law between the Institutions, between Member States, and between Institutions and Member States. Originally this category also included disputes between private parties and the Institutions. Since the Council Decisions of 8 June 1993 and 7 March 1994, which altered the jurisdiction of the Court of First Instance,[341] the settlement of such disputes falls in principle within the jurisdiction of the Court of First Instance, as confirmed by the amended Article 225 EC. Since the Council Decision of 26 April 2004, certain categories of cases between Member States and Institutions are also directed in first instance to the CFI.[342] The Court of Justice is only seized of such disputes on appeal.

In the domain of settling disputes, the Court acts in the first place as the administrative court (in the continental sense) for the Communities, whose duty it is to protect the legal subjects, Member States, as well as – on appeal – private persons, against the illegal acts or omissions of the Institutions. The Court usually exercises this administrative jurisdiction[343] when it is seized of:

(1) an action for annulment of the legal acts of the Council acting jointly with the Parliament, the Council acting alone, the Commission and the European Central Bank (ECB) and acts of the European Parliament 'intended to produce legal effects vis-à-vis third parties'[344] (see also judgments on the validity of acts of the Community Institutions given in rulings on references for preliminary rulings (see also (9) below),[345] and in relation to the plea of illegality concerning regulations of the European Parliament and the Council acting jointly, the Council, the Commission and the ECB);[346]

(2) an action for a declaration that, in infringement of the Treaty, the Council or the Commission has failed to act;[347]

---

340. This happens only occasionally, although the frequency has increased recently as the Community becomes active in ever-increasing spheres of activity on the international plane.

341. Council Decision of 8 Jun. 1993, amending Council Decision 88/591/ECSC, EEC, Euratom establishing a Court of First Instance of the European Communities, O.J. 1993, L 144/21; Council Decision of 7 Mar. 1994, amending Decision 93/350/Euratom, ECSC, EEC amending Decision 88/591/ECSC, EEC, Euratom establishing a Court of First Instance of the European Communities, O.J. 1994, L 66/29.

342. See Council Decision 2004/407/EC, Euratom of 26 Apr. 2004, amending Arts. 51 and 54 of the Statute of the Court of Justice, O.J. 2004, L. 132/5, *juncto* the list of cases which have been assigned by the Court of Justice to the Court of First Instance, O.J. 2004, C 239/11. See further Arts. 51 and 54 of the Statute.

343. As to the rules on execution of judgments of the Court so far as private parties are concerned, see the final part of Ch. V, section 1.1, *in fine*, *infra*.

344. Arts. 230 EC and 146 Euratom.

345. Arts. 234 EC and 150 Euratom (1st para., point (b) in each case).

346. Arts. 241 EC and 156 Euratom.

347. Arts. 232 EC and 148 Euratom.

(3) an action against administrative penalties-an instance of unlimited jurisdiction; the Court of Justice has thus a certain penal jurisdiction;[348]

(4) a claim for damages on the basis of the non-contractual liability of the Communities;[349]

(5) an action based on an arbitration clause in a contract concluded by or on behalf of the Communities.[350]

The Court acts more like an *international court* in the following types of cases:

(6) disputes between the Commission and Member States or between Member States themselves about a Member State's failure to fulfil its obligations under one of the Treaties;[351]

(7) disputes between Member States in connection with the subject-matter of the Treaties, which are submitted to the Court under a special agreement.[352]

The Court acts as a *constitutional court* if it has to deliver an opinion[353] on whether:

(8) agreements concluded by the EC[354] or by Member States within the field of application of Euratom[355] are compatible with the respective Treaties.

In numerous opinions given under Article 300(6) EC (or its predecessor, Art. 228(1) EEC) and in a ruling under Article 103 Euratom the Court has expanded its constitutional function through making important observations on the ambit of

---

348. Arts. 229 EC and 144(b) Euratom.
349. Arts. 235 EC and 151 Euratom.
350. Arts. 238 EC and 153 Euratom. If the clause is contained in a contract governed by private law, the Court of Justice acts as a civil court. The jurisdiction applies whether the contract is governed by public or private law. See, e.g., Case 23/76, *Pellegrini v. Commission*; Case 426/85, *Commission v. Jan Zoubek*, and Case C-42/94, *Heidemij Advies BV v. European Parliament*. In actions brought by private parties this jurisdiction is now exercised by the CFI, subject to appeal to the Court of Justice.
351. Arts. 226–228 EC and 141 and 142 Euratom.
352. Arts. 239 EC, and 154 Euratom.
353. The EC Treaty uses the term 'opinion' and it seems from the context of Art. 300 EC that this has the same force as a binding judgment. The terms 'ruling' and 'adjudicating' are used in Art. 103 Euratom.
354. Art. 300(6) EC. The Court considers that an 'agreement' for these purposes is 'any undertaking entered into by entities subject to international law which has binding force, whatever its formal designation': Opinion 1/75 *OECD Understanding on a Local Cost Standard*. This concerned a binding resolution of the OECD Council: the Understanding covered export credits and guarantees. In finding that it has jurisdiction to give its opinion on a *proposed* agreement, the Court allowed itself room to opine on the division of competence between the Member States on the one hand and the Community on the other, a subject on which there was a clear difference of opinion. There need not actually be a draft agreement already prepared: it may well be that a Community Institution seeks the opinion of the Court on the general competence to accede to an existing agreement, see Opinion 2/94 *Accession by the Communities to the European Convention on Human Rights*.
355. Art. 103 Euratom, 3rd para.

the Community's external competence.[356] This point is discussed further in Chapter XIII, below.

The function of the Court as a constitutional court is not, however, exhausted by these heads of jurisdiction. In contentious proceedings, chiefly in an action for annulment or in an action aiming to establish an infringement of a Treaty provision by a Member State,[357] the Court also acts as guardian of the inviolability of the basic structural provisions of the Treaties as well as the complex balance of powers which they establish between the Institutions and between the Communities and the Member States. In particular, actions for annulment frequently provide the opportunity to examine whether the Community legislation concerned is compatible with the Treaties. This examination deals, as the Court has indicated,[358] with the constitutionality of quasi-legislative acts emanating from a public authority and which have a normative effect *erga omnes*. It is on this very ground that the right to seek the annulment of such acts has been virtually refused to private persons under the Treaties.[359] Although from the point of view of their form, the activities of the Court in the contentious proceedings mentioned here more or less resemble those of an administrative or international court, looked at from the viewpoint of their content they resemble a 'constitutional' jurisdiction.[360]

In the majority of the cases discussed above the jurisdiction of the Court is based directly on the European Treaties. This can be described as an obligatory jurisdiction, i.e., a jurisdiction which is exercised by the Court to the exclusion of national[361] or international[362] judicial bodies. In a number of cases, however, the Treaties also provide for an optional jurisdiction of the Court, i.e., a jurisdiction whose compulsory character depends on the existence of a particular unilateral or multilateral legal act other than a Treaty provision, which then forms the legal basis for jurisdiction.

A unilateral legal act as the legal basis for jurisdiction is found, for instance, in Regulation 11[363] and in both basic regulations in the competition field,[364] in which by virtue of Article 229 EC the Council conferred unlimited jurisdiction on the Court with reference to the administrative penalties laid down therein. A similar basis is also found in the Staff Regulations adopted by the Council[365] in which the settlement of disputes between the Communities and their servants is entrusted to

---

356. Most recently Opinion 2/00, *Cartagena Protocol*, and Opinion 1/03, *Lugano Convention*. See also Opinion 1/94 *WTO – GATS and TRIPs*.
357. Heads (1) and (6) *supra*.
358. Case 8/55, *Fédération Charbonnière de Belgique v. High Authority*. See also Case 18/57, *Firme J. Nold KG v. High Authority*.
359. See Ch. VI, section 3.3, *infra*.
360. See, generally, D. Curtin and D. O'Keeffe (eds), *Constitutional Adjudication in European Community Law and National Law* (Dublin, 1992).
361. Arts. 240 EC and 155 Euratom.
362. Arts. 292 EC and 193 Euratom.
363. O.J. 1960, 1121 (Art. 25). This deals with the elimination of discrimination in relation to freight prices and transport conditions.
364. See Reg. No. 1/2003, Art. 31 and Reg. No. 139/2004, Art 16. See also head (3), *supra*.
365. Reg. 259/68, O.J. 1968, L 56 (as subsequently amended), Arts. 25 and 91.

the Court by virtue of the relevant Treaty Articles.[366] Since 1 January 2007 such disputes are dealt with at first instance by the European Union Civil Service Tribunal.[367]

The Court has also been entrusted with appeals in relation to the Community Trade Mark.[368] Such appeal is against decisions of a Board of Appeal of the Office for Harmonization in the Internal Market (trade marks and designs). Article 63 of the Regulation provides for appeal by any party to the proceedings adversely affected by a decision of a Board of Appeal. The grounds of appeal and time limits are the same as those applicable for appeals against acts of the Community Institutions. Unlike those appeals, though, the Court has plenary jurisdiction insofar as it can go beyond merely annulling a decision of a Board of Appeal and can alter the decision.[369] The same applies to appeals against decisions of the Boards of Appeal of the Community Plant Variety Office.[370] Lastly, according to the new Article 229a EC, added by the Treaty of Nice, the Council may extend the jurisdiction of the Court to cover disputes relating to the application of acts concerning Community industrial property rights. This provision creates the possibility for jurisdiction in disputes between private parties, for instance between the holder of a patent and someone infringing it. This is a new power of the Court; the relevant act of the Council will have to be approved by the Member States in accordance with their respective constitutional requirements.[371]

Jurisdiction based on a multilateral legal act can be derived by the Court from an arbitration clause in contracts,[372] from a special agreement between Member States in the matter of a dispute connected with the subject-matter of the Treaties,[373] or from a convention in accordance with Article 34(2)(d) last paragraph TEU.[374] In this context, see however also the provisions on the jurisdiction of the Court of First Instance, from which it is apparent that the phrase 'Court of Justice' in all the cases mentioned above, except the last two, refer to the Court as Institution, since the

---

366. See Arts. 236 (and 288, 4th para.) EC and 152 (and 188, 3rd para.) Euratom. This jurisdiction was for a long time exercised by the Court of First Instance, subject to appeal to the Court of Justice on a point of law only.
367. See the Decision of the Council of 2 Nov. 2004, O.J. 2004, L 333/7 and the Annex to the Statute of the Court of Justice.
368. Reg. 40/94, O.J. 1994, L 11/1 (amended: O.J. 1994, L 349/83).
369. Cf. Ch. VI section 1.3.1. Appeals will in fact come before the Court of First Instance, subject to appeal on a point of law only to the Court of Justice itself.
370. See Reg. 2100/94, the Community Plant Variety Rights Regulation (O.J. 1994, L 227/1; amended by Reg. 2506/95, O.J. 1995, L 258/3) Art. 73; under Art. 73(3) the Commission and the Plant Variety Office are also entitled to appeal (which in the case of the Commission would be heard by the Court of Justice, not the CFI). Under Art. 74, in certain cases (compulsory licences and exploitation rights) appeal against decisions of the Office can be lodged directly with the Court of Justice.
371. See explanatory memorandum to the Dutch draft act of approval of the Treaty of Nice, K. II 2001–2002, 27.818 (R 1629), nr. 3, Ch. III, section 6.2.
372. See head (5) *supra*.
373. See head (7), *supra*.
374. See, e.g., convention of 26 Jul. 1995, based on Art. K.3 of the Treaty on European Union, O.J. 1995, C 316/1, and the associated Protocol on the Europol Convention (O.J. 1996, C 299/2).

powers mentioned there are also exercised by the Court of First Instance, the latter as a general rule having jurisdiction at first instance (see section 7.3.2 below).

The jurisdiction of the Court discussed so far does not cover all cases in which there may be a question of judicial application of Community law. In disputes between Member States and private persons or between private persons themselves[375] questions relating to the interpretation and application of Community law may arise before a national court. In this field, too, a specific type of jurisdiction has been conferred on the Court. It is competent:

(9) to pronounce by way of a preliminary ruling on the interpretation of the Treaty provisions and on the validity and the interpretation of acts of the Institutions of the Communities if a question on this subject is raised before a national court or tribunal.[376]

Such a court or tribunal may, or (if it functions as a jurisdiction from which there is no appeal) must request such a ruling from the Court.[377] Thanks to this jurisdiction – which in practice is the largest part of the Court's activities – the Court is able to promote the uniformity of interpretation of Community law in the legal practice of the Member States. In the discussion of references for a preliminary ruling elsewhere in this book[378] it will become apparent that as a consequence of this jurisdiction the Court can, in cooperation with national courts, make a real contribution to the judicial control of the observance of Community law by the Member States, and thus to the legal protection of individuals against acts of those Member States which infringe Community law.

Finally, it should be pointed out that an application to the Court does not have suspensory effect,[379] but that the Court may order suspension of the implementation of the contested act in an order granting interim relief; the Court can also prescribe any necessary interim measures in relation to cases brought before it.[380] This procedure is worked out in more detail in Article 39 Statute of the Court of Justice and in Articles 83–90 Rules of Procedure of the Court of Justice (see further Ch. VI).

On the jurisdiction of the Court of Justice in so-called Art. 293 conventions, similar and other international conventions, see section 7.2.3. *infra.*

375. Or in disputes between the Communities and private persons relating to contracts concluded by them or on their behalf if they do *not* entrust their settlement to the Court. The practical importance of this national jurisdiction is, though, very small (see Ch. II, section 5.2., *supra*).

376. Arts. 68 and 234 EC and 150 Euratom. As to references under Art. 234 (ex 177) EC generally, see Andenas (ed.), *Article 177 References to the European Court: Policy and Practice* (London, 1994), and literature on the Court of Justice at the end of this chapter.

377. Art. 68 EC provides for a limited preliminary rulings procedure which applies to the interpretation of Title IV EC and the validity and interpretation of acts based on the provisions of that Title.

378. See Ch. VI, section 3 *infra.*

379. An exception to this rule is made for appeals brought before the Court of Justice against decisions of the Commission, which impose sanctions for infringement of safety requirements in the field of nuclear energy (Art. 83(2) Euratom).

380. Arts. 242 and 243 EC, and 157 and 158 Euratom. The power of the Court to suspend enforcement of decisions, which impose a pecuniary obligation (Arts. 256 EC and 162 Euratom, last paragraph, in both cases), to which this procedure is also applicable, will not be further discussed here.

7.2.2.1   *Proposed Changes following the Lisbon Treaty*

The major change in this respect is that the subject-matter of the Third Pillar (Police and Judicial Cooperation in Criminal Matters) will become a part of the first one (or what is nowadays called the First Pillar, and will become the Treaty on the Functioning of the Union). Furthermore, Article 68 EC, which contains a curtailed preliminary procedure in respect of acts of the Institutions which have been adopted within the framework of Title IV of the EC Treaty (asylum, immigration and external border control) will be abolished. As a result of these two alterations the normal jurisdiction of the Court of Justice will apply, not only to the subject-matter of Title IV of the EC Treaty, but also to that of the former Third Pillar of the Union. By way of exception, however, the Protocol on the Transitional Provisions stipulates that during a period of five years, the primary and secondary law of the Third Pillar which exists at the moment of the entry into force of the Treaty on the Functioning of the Union will remain governed by the facultative preliminary procedure which is nowadays provided for in Article 35 TEU.

It should further be mentioned that according to a new paragraph of Article 267 TFEU (the ordinary preliminary procedure), preliminary questions in a case concerning a person in custody should be answered 'with the minimum of delay', which means that the Court will have to act according to the urgent procedure provided in Article 104b of the Rules of Procedure.[381]

7.2.3   Conventions under Article 293 EC; European Economic Area

Jurisdiction of the Court may also be based on a number of treaties and conventions concluded outside the Community legal order itself. This concerns primarily the treaties and conventions under Article 293 EC, that is to say the treaties and conventions concluded according to the mandate contained in that provision. For instance, since a Protocol of 3 June 1971[382] the Court has jurisdiction to give preliminary rulings concerning the interpretation of the Convention (concluded on the basis of Art. 293 EC) of 27 September 1968 on jurisdiction and the enforcement of judgments in civil and commercial matters (the Brussels Convention).[383] This Protocol was inspired by Article 234 EC, but differs in a number of respects, particularly with regard to the judicial bodies which may request a preliminary ruling from the Court of Justice. Secondly, the Court has jurisdiction to interpret so-called 'similar' conventions, that is to say treaties which are not provided for in Article 293 EC, but are concluded along the same lines, such as the

---

381. See note 337 *supra*.
382. O.J. 1975, L 204/28.
383. O.J. 1972, L 299/32, as amended several times in connection with the accession of new Member States. A codified version of the Protocol was published in O.J. 1990, C 189/25. This Convention and Protocol were replaced, except as far as Denmark is concerned, as of 1 Mar. 2002, by Reg. 44/2001 O.J. 2001, L 12/1.

European Contracts Convention (Rome Convention on the Law Applicable to Contractual Obligations of 1980).[384] In two protocols of 19 December 1988,[385] the Court of Justice is granted the same kind of jurisdiction as that in the first Protocol mentioned above. Similar powers were conferred on the Court of Justice in the Luxembourg Agreement on Community Patents (not in force).[386]

Finally, Article 111(3) of the Agreement on a European Economic Area declares the Court of Justice competent, at the request of two or more of the Contracting Parties, to rule on the interpretation of provisions of this Agreement which are identical in substance to corresponding rules of Community law.[387]

7.3   THE COURT OF FIRST INSTANCE

7.3.1   Composition, Structure and Procedure

The Court of First Instance (CFI) contains at least one judge per Member State. The number of judges is determined in the Statute of the Court of Justice. According to Article 48 of the Statute, the CFI consists of 27 judges.[388] The Judges appoint from among their number a President for a period of three years; this appointment is renewable.[389] The CFI has no permanent Advocates General: according to Article 224, first paragraph, the Statute may provide for the CFI to be assisted by advocates general. Moreover, under the Statute, a Judge may be called upon to perform the task of an Advocate General in a particular case,[390] and in such circumstances his or her function in that case is identical to that of an Advocate General of the Court of Justice.[391] The method of appointment of Judges of the CFI is also virtually identical to that of Judges and Advocates General of the Court of Justice,

---

384. O.J. 1980, L 266/1. The Commission is currently exploring possibilities of transforming this Convention into an act of Community law, cf. Editorial Comments 'On the way to a Rome I Regulation', 43 CML Rev., 913–922.
385. O.J. 1989, L 48/1 and 17, respectively.
386. O.J. 1976, L 17/1, amended by the Treaty of 15 Dec. 1989, O.J. 1989, L 40/1. This treaty never entered into force, since it failed to gain the required number of ratifications; the Commission therefore made a proposal on 1 Aug. 2000, for a Council regulation on a Community patent, COM(2000)412 FIN. In 2004, the Council definitely failed to reach agreement on a text, 9081/1/04 REV 1 (Presse 140).
387. O.J. 1994, L 1/3; this Agreement entered into force on 1 Jan. 1994.
388. Art. 224, 1st para., EC with Art. 48 Statute. We will omit mention of the corresponding provisions of the Euratom Treaty in the following.
389. Art. 224, 3rd para., EC.
390. The CFI has only sparingly made use of this possibility: see Case T-51/89, *Tetra Pak Rausing SA v. Commission*; Case T-1/89, *Rhône-Poulenc SA v. Commission*; Case T-120/89, *Stahlwerke Peine-Salzgitter AG v. Commission*, and the single Opinion given in Case T-24/90, *Automec Srl v. Commission* and Case T-28/90, *Asia Motor France SA et al. v. Commission*.
391. See section 7.2.1, *supra*.

save that the qualification for appointment is less stringent.[392] The provisions as to the oath of office, privileges and immunities and so on are also identical.[393]

According to Article 50 of the Statute, the Court of First Instance sits in Chambers of three or five Judges; in certain cases, defined in the Rules of procedure, a case may be heard in plenary session, or by a Chamber composed of a single Judge. Article 14(1) Rules of procedure of the Court of First Instance gives as reasons for hearing a case in plenary session the legal difficulty or the importance of the case or special circumstances; according to Article 14(2), cases may be heard by a single judge if they are suitable for such treatment on account of the lack of difficulty of the questions of law or fact raised, the limited importance of those cases and the absence of other special circumstances.[394] The Rules of Procedure also provide for the establishment of a Grand Chamber consisting of 13 judges.[395]

The various rules governing procedure for the CFI are to be found partly in Title III of the Statute,[396] and partly in the Rules of Procedure of the CFI. These Rules of Procedure were established by the CFI on 2 May 1991.[397] The procedure for establishing the Rules of Procedure which must now be followed, is laid down in Article 224, fifth paragraph, EC; this means the CFI must reach prior agreement with the Court of Justice, and the Rules of Procedure must be approved by the Council acting with qualified majority. (Before the Treaty of Nice this used to be unanimity).[398]

According to the preamble of the Rules of Procedure, the procedure before the CFI should be as close as possible to that of the Court of Justice itself, and is thus largely similar to that followed by the Court of Justice in direct actions for annulment or for failure to act.[399] The major innovation, compared with the procedure before the Court of Justice, is that the Court of First Instance plays a much more active role in steering the proceedings: thus it may prescribe any 'measure of organization of procedure'.[400] The aim of this measure is to ensure that cases

---

392. Judges of the CFI must possess the ability required for appointment to *high* judicial office, Arts. 223, 1st para.; and 224, 2nd para., EC (as opposed to *the highest* judicial office). The requirement further differs from that for Judges and Advocates General of the Court of Justice in that jurisconsults of recognized competence are not eligible for appointment.
393. Mentioned in section 7.2.1 *supra*. See Art. 225, 6th para., EC, according to which the Statute of the Court of Justice applies to the Court of First Instance, except where otherwise provided.
394. The Rules of Procedure of the CFI are available via the website of the Court of Justice. They were originally published in O.J. 1991, L 136/1, and have been amended many times since, most recently on 12 Oct. 2005 (O.J. 2005, L 298/1). A consolidated version is available on the website of the Court of Justice, <http://curia.europa.eu.> The reasons for delegating cases to a chamber consisting of a single judge are worked out in more detail in Art. 14 of the Rules of Procedure; the types of cases are also listed which may not be delegated to a single judge.
395. Art. 10, 1st para., Rules of Procedure; see also Art. 50, 3rd para., of the Court's Statute.
396. See Art. 53, 1st para., Statute of the Court of Justice.
397. Pursuant to Art. 11, 2nd para., of the Decision establishing the CFI, O.J. 1988, L 319/1.
398. See Statute of the Court of Justice, Art. 53, 2nd para., See also the Guidelines for lawyers and agents for the written procedure in the Court of First Instance (O.J. 1994, C 120/16).
399. Under Arts. 230 EC (annulment), or 232 EC (failure to act).
400. Rules of Procedure Art. 64.

are prepared for hearing, procedures carried out and disputes resolved under the best possible conditions.[401]

Appeal against judgments of the CFI lies to the Court of Justice. Appeal is on a point of law only.[402] Article 56 of the Statute states that

> [a]n appeal may be brought before the Court of Justice, within two months of the notification of the decision appealed against, against final decisions of the Court of First Instance and decisions of that Court disposing of the substantive issues in part only or disposing of a procedural issue concerning a plea of lack of competence or inadmissibility.[403]

Thus appeal lies against decisions on a vast number of interlocutory matters as well as final judgments. The appeal may be brought by any party which has been unsuccessful, in whole or in part, in its submissions, although interveners other than Member States or Community Institutions may bring such an appeal only if the decision of the Court of First Instance directly affects them; the Member States and Institutions may even bring an appeal in cases where they have not intervened in the case before the CFI.[404] Appeals are only possible, as was mentioned earlier, on points of law. The grounds of appeal are: lack of competence of the Court of First Instance, a breach of procedure before it which adversely affects the interests of the applicant, as well as infringement of Community law by the Court of First Instance.[405] If the appeal is well-founded, the Court of Justice quashes the decision of the Court of First Instance; it may itself give final judgment in the matter, where the state of proceedings so permits, or it may refer the case back to the Court of First Instance for judgment.[406]

7.3.2   Tasks and Powers

According to Article 225(1) EC,[407] the Court of First Instance's task is to hear and determine at first instance actions or proceedings referred to in Articles 230, 232, 235, 236 and 238 EC,[408] with the exception of those assigned to a judicial panel (to

---

401. Ibid., Art. 64(1).
402. Arts. 225(1) EC and 140a(1) Euratom. As to the further rules governing appeals, see Statute of the Court of Justice, Arts. 56–61 of the new Title IV, and Rules of Procedure of the Court of Justice, Arts. 110–123.
403. In the case of appeals against dismissal of requests to intervene, the period is two weeks, Statute of the Court of Justice, Art. 57. The period for appealing against decisions on the grant of suspensory effect, interim measures or enforcement of pecuniary obligations is also two months, Statute of the Court of Justice, Art. 54.
404. Statute Art. 56, 3rd para.
405. Statute, Art. 58. If the grounds of a judgment of the Court of First Instance reveal an infringement of Community law but the operative part is well-founded on other legal grounds, the appeal will be dismissed; Case C-32/92 P, *Andrew Macrae Moat v. Commission*.
406. Statute, Art. 61. Arts. 110–123 of the Rules of Procedure of the Court of Justice contain further rules. As to the procedure on referral back, see Rules of Procedure of the Court of First Instance Arts. 117–121.
407. And Art. 140a(1) Euratom.
408. And the corresponding provisions in the Euratom Treaty.

be discussed below) and those reserved in the Statute for the Court of Justice. According to Article 51 of the Statute of the Court of Justice, as it has stated since the entry into force of the Treaty of Nice, the Court of Justice (as a body) itself has jurisdiction in actions brought by the Member States, the Institutions and the European Central Bank. This provision has been amended by the Decision of the Council of 26 April 2004, mentioned above.[409] According to these provisions (Arts. 225, 1stpara., EC, 140A, 1stpara., Euratom and 51 of the Statute of the Court of Justice) the CFI is competent to decide upon:

(1) actions for annulment, for failure to act, or for compensation for damage, brought by legal or natural persons on the basis of the EC or Euratom Treaties;[410]

(2) actions for annulment or for failure to act which are brought by a *Member State* against a decision or a failure to take a decision of the European Parliament and/or the Council regarding the approval of State aid measures (Art. 88, 3rdpara., EC), protective measures in the field of commercial policy and the execution of earlier legislative acts (see Art. 202, third indent, EC) as well as decisions or the failure to take a decision of the Commission, with the exception of the decisions or the failure to take a decision in respect of closer cooperation (Art. 11A EC);[411]

(3) actions brought by legal or natural persons under an arbitration clause contained in a contract (whether governed by private or public law) concluded by or on behalf of the Community,[412] and

(4) appeals against judgments of the European Union Civil Service Tribunal in staff cases, i.e., disputes referred to in Articles 236 EC and 152 Euratom between the Community and its Officials or other servants which since 1 January 2007 are decided by this Tribunal.[413]

Moreover, in Articles 225(1) EC and 140a(1) Euratom, it is explicitly provided that the Statute 'may provide for the Court of First Instance to have jurisdiction for other classes of action or proceeding'. All rulings by the CFI on the basis of this paragraph are subject to appeal to the Court of Justice on points of law,[414] as dealt with in section 7.3.1 *supra*.

The rulings on appeal mentioned under (4) may exceptionally be subject to review by the Court of Justice, following a request by the first Advocate General,

---

409. O.J. 2004, L 132/5; see section 7.2.2., note 342, *supra*.
410. Under, respectively, Arts. 230 EC and 146 Euratom, 232 EC and 148 Euratom, and 235 EC and 151 Euratom.
411. See Art. 51, Statute of the Court of Justice.
412. Under Arts. 238 EC and 153 Euratom.
413. See the Decision of the Council of 2 Nov. 2004, O.J. 2004, L 333/7. See also the Decision of the President of the Court of Justice of 12 Dec. 2005, O.J. 2005, L 325/1, establishing that the Civil Service Tribunal has been regularly constituted.
414. See Arts. 225(1), 2nd para., EC, 140a(1), 2nd para., Euratom and 62 Statute of the Court of Justice.

under conditions laid down by the Statute, where there is a serious risk of the unity or consistency of Community law being affected.[415]

Finally, the CFI will have jurisdiction to give preliminary rulings in certain specific areas determined in the Statute. This possibility too was originally explicitly excluded from the powers of the CFI; but unlike in the case of direct actions brought by Member States and Community Institutions, this prohibition was explicitly maintained after the Treaties of Maastricht and Amsterdam.[416] The fact that the possibility now exists of granting jurisdiction in preliminary rulings to the CFI is an important change in terms of judicial practice. There are two safeguards provided for as well. On the one hand, the CFI may refer a case to the Court of Justice if it considers the unity or consistency of Community law is at issue; on the other hand, the Court of Justice may, following a request by the first Advocate General, subject a preliminary ruling of the CFI to review if, as is determined in Article 225(2), there is a serious risk of the unity or consistency of Community law being affected.[417]

As with applications to the Court of Justice, an application to the CFI does not have suspensory effect, but the CFI may order application of the contested act be suspended and prescribe any other necessary interim measures.[418]

The existence of one organ whose tasks and powers are carried out by two bodies raises the question of how to deal with applications addressed to the wrong Court. Article 54 Statute of the Court of Justice as amended contains the following rules for such eventualities. If an application or other procedural document addressed to the one Court is lodged by mistake with the Registrar of the other, it is immediately transmitted to the correct destination (this is merely an error of procedure). In the case of a substantive error, whereby the Court of First Instance finds that it does not have jurisdiction to hear and determine an action lodged with it, since it falls within the jurisdiction of the Court of Justice, it refers the action to the Court of Justice; in the reverse situation the Court of Justice refers the action to the Court of First Instance, which may not then decline jurisdiction.[419] Secondly, if the Court of Justice and the Court of First Instance are seized of cases concerning the same matter, the Court of First Instance may stay the proceedings until the

---

415. Arts. 225(2) and 225a, 3rd para., EC.
416. Art. 168a EC in the version following the Treaty of Maastricht: 'The Court of First Instance shall not be competent to hear and determine questions referred for a preliminary ruling under Art. 234.'
417. Art. 225(3). See also Art. 62 Statute of the Court of Justice, and Declaration No. 15 attached to the Treaty of Nice (emergency procedure). Other essential provisions of the review procedure are mentioned in the Decision of the Council of 3 Oct. 2005, O.J. 2005, L 266/60, amending the Protocol on the Statute of the Court of Justice, which is itself an elaboration of Declaration No. 13 attached to the Treaty of Nice (rect.: O.J. 2005, L 301/21).
418. Arts. 242 and 243 EC, and 157 and 158 Euratom; see further Ch. VI.
419. The CFI may of course decide to decline jurisdiction for other reasons, unrelated to the reasons which led the ECJ to refer the case to it, as happened in Case T-42/91, *Koninklijke PTT Nederland NV et al. v. Commission.*

Court of Justice has delivered judgment. The Court, too, may decide to stay the proceedings; in that case proceedings before the CFI are continued.[420]

Finally, the CFI has to declare itself to be incompetent when a Member State and an Institution dispute the same legal act; the case will then be handled by the Court of Justice. The latter provision has been added by the decision of the Council of 28 April 2004 amending the Statute and is connected with the fact that, as has already been mentioned, appeals by Member States for annulment have for the greater part been transferred to the CFI.

In the Preamble to the Decision of 24 October 1988 establishing the CFI,[421] the following reasons were given for establishing the new court. The Council considered that 'in respect of actions requiring close examination of complex facts, the establishment of a second court will improve the judicial protection of individual interests'. The Council went on to stress the need to enable the Court of Justice 'to concentrate its activities on its fundamental task of ensuring uniform interpretation of Community law'. In the background, was also the desire to relieve the Court of Justice of part of its workload. As the president of the Court of Justice stated in an open letter of 18 April 2000, in the long term, the establishment of the CFI has not been able to solve the quantitative problems sufficiently. During the period 1975–1988 – the year of establishment of the CFI – the number of new cases brought each year increased steadily from 130 to 385. In 1999, 927 new cases were brought, 543 to the Court and 384 to the CFI. This brought the number of pending cases at 1 January 2000 to 1 628 (896 at the Court of Justice and 732 at the CFI). The length of time proceedings take has reached unacceptable proportions.[422] For these reasons also, and the fact that problems were only expected to be exacerbated by the accession of twelve new Member States, it was imperative that in the Treaty of Nice the system of judicial protection in the Union would be radically changed.

7.4 JUDICIAL PANELS

According to Article 225a, first paragraph, EC and 140b, first paragraph, Euratom, the Council, acting unanimously, may create judicial panels to hear and determine at first instance certain classes of action or proceeding brought in specific areas. As mentioned earlier, appeal against decisions of these panels lies to the CFI (with the possibility of review by the Court of Justice in the third and last instance). In Declaration number 16 attached to the Treaty of Nice, the government

---

420. See the Decision of the Council of 26 Apr. 2004, amending Arts. 51 and 54 of the Statute of the Court of Justice, O.J. 2004, L 132/5. See also L. Neville Brown, 'The First Five Years of the Court of First Instance and Appeals to the Court of Justice: Assessment and Statistics' (1995) CML Rev., 743–761; K. Lenaerts, 'Het gerecht van eerste aanleg van de EG' (1990) SEW, 527–548, 539–540) and S.P. Cras, 'Zes jaar Gerecht van eerste aanleg' (1996) NJB, 477–485.
421. O.J. 1988, L 319/I.
422. G.C. Rodriguez Iglesias, 'Balancing Europe's Scales of Justice', *Financial Times*, 18 Apr. 2000; H. Rasmussen, 'Remedying the Crumbling EC Judicial System' (2000) CML Rev., 1071–1112.

representatives asked the Court of Justice and the Commission to prepare as swiftly as possible a proposal for a judicial panel with jurisdiction for disputes between the Community and its servants (so-called staff cases). In November 2004, the decision was taken to establish the EU Civil Service Tribunal.[423] This Tribunal started to function on the day of publication of the Decision of the President of the Court of Justice that the Civil Service Tribunal has been regularly constituted (12 December 2005).[424]

7.5   TASKS IN THE FRAMEWORK OF THE ACTIVITIES
            OF THE EUROPEAN UNION

As already mentioned in Chapter II, section 1.2.2., the Court is part of the institutional framework of the Union.[425] Its tasks in relation to the activities of the European Union are defined in Article 46 TEU. According to that provision, as amended by the Treaty of Nice, the provisions of the EC Treaties concerning the powers of the Court also apply to:

(a) the provisions of the Treaty on European Union[426] amending the EC Treaties;
(b) the provisions contained in the third pillar (PJCCM), under the conditions provided for by Article 35 TEU;
(c) the provisions on enhanced cooperation in Articles 43–45 TEU, under the conditions provided for by Articles 11 and 11a EC (special conditions for enhanced cooperation within the EC) and Article 40 TEU (special conditions for enhanced cooperation in the area of the third pillar);
(d) Article 6(2) TEU (respect of fundamental rights), with regard to action of the Institutions, insofar as the Court has jurisdiction under the EC Treaty and the Treaty on European Union;
(e) the purely procedural stipulations in Article 7 TEU (the determination by the Council that there is a clear risk of a serious breach of fundamental rights);
(f) Articles 46–53 TEU (the final provisions of the Treaty on European Union).

A number of remarks should be made. In the first place, it is evident from Article 46 TEU that the Court does not possess any powers in relation to the second pillar (CFSP).[427]

---

423. Council Decision of 2 Nov. 2004, establishing the European Union Civil Service Tribunal, 2004/752/EC, Euratom, O.J. 2004, L 333/7.
424. O.J. 2005, L 325/1.
425. See Art. 5 TEU.
426. Treaty of Maastricht as amended by the Treaty of Amsterdam and the Treaty of Nice.
427. However, it is apparent from Case C-170/96, *Commission v. Council*, (Airport transit visas) (to be discussed *infra*) that this lack of jurisdiction is not absolute.

In the second place, in the area of the third pillar (PJCCM) – the subject under (b) – three kinds of judicial proceedings are provided for. Article 35(1)–(5) TEU contains a *limited preliminary rulings procedure* concerning the validity and interpretation of framework decisions and decisions, the interpretation of conventions established within the framework of the third pillar, and on the validity and interpretation of implementing measures.[428] Article 35(6) TEU provides for the possibility of an action for annulment (brought by a Member State or the Commission) against framework decisions and decisions; Article 35(7) TEU concerns disputes between Member States, or between Member States and the Commission.

In the third place, the Court is given jurisdiction under (d) to review action of the Institutions against Article 6(2) TEU, which is to say the obligation contained in that provision to respect fundamental rights contained in the European Convention on Human Rights or as they result from the constitutional traditions common to the Member States. In this context, an important restriction applies, which is that this power only exists where the Court has jurisdiction under the EC Treaties and the Treaty on European Union, which means that the provision under (d) may not create a new, supplementary jurisdiction. Some authors have therefore characterized this provision as a 'cosmetic operation'.[429] Others, however, argue that there is an extension of the Court's powers, to the extent that the Court may also review acts of the Institutions in the area of the third pillar (PJCCM).[430]

In the fourth place, the provision under (e) is new, and was added by the Treaty of Nice. This addition is directly linked to the amendment of Article 7 TEU by the same Treaty, which itself was a result of the participation of the ultra-right Freedom Party, FPÖ, in the governing coalition in Austria.[431] In this matter, the Court may only verify whether the procedural conditions have been respected. At the request of the Member State in question, the Court must give a ruling within one month from the date of the determination by the Council provided for in Article 7.

---

428. This preliminary rulings procedure differs from that of Art. 234 EC insofar as it must be explicitly accepted by each Member State individually; a Member State may limit the power to put preliminary questions to the Court of Justice, to the highest judicial bodies ('court or tribunal . . . against whose decisions there is no judicial remedy under national law'; Art. 35(3) TEU). A limited preliminary rulings procedure, but which again differs from this one, is provided for under Art. 68 EC (see section 7.2.2.).

429. E.g., R. Barents, *Het Verdrag van Amsterdam in werking*, EM No. 62 (Deventer, 1999), 76 and 283.

430. E.g., the Netherlands Government, cf. Nader Rapport on the advisory opinion of the Netherlands Raad van State on the Act of approval for the Treaty of Amsterdam, K. II 1997/98, 25 922 (R1613), A, 2, and explanatory memorandum, loc. cit., No. 3, 12.

431. Cf. M. Merlingen, M. Mudde and U. Sedelmeier, 'The Right and the Righteous? European Norms, Domestic Politics and the Sanctions against Austria' (2001) JCMS, 59–77; R. Barents, 'Het Verdrag van Nice, een eerste indruk', (2001) NJB, 113–119 at. 119; J.W. de Zwaan, 'Het Verdrag van Nice. Een bescheiden stap in het proces van Europese integratie' (2001) SEW, 42–52 at. 49.

The head of jurisdiction under (f)[432] gained real significance with the so-called *Airport transit visas* case of 12 May 1998.[433] In this case, the Court derived from Article 47 TEU a power to examine whether the Council correctly chose a legal basis in the third pillar instead of a provision from the EC Treaty, and if that is not the case to annul the act of the Council. The basis for this is that according to Article 47 TEU, the Treaty on European Union may not in any way affect the EC Treaties. The Court in 2005 went on actually to annul a Council act on the basis of this reasoning in a case brought by the Commission against the Council, on the possibility of prescribing penal sanctions in environmental law.[434] It is argued that the reasoning of this case also applies to acts based on the second pillar.[435]

Apart from the provision under (b) to the extent that it concerns cases which can only be dealt with by the Court of Justice[436] (preliminary rulings, actions for annulment brought by the Commission, and settlement of disputes between Member States or between a Member State and the Commission), and that under (e), all cases mentioned in Article 46 TEU could also be brought before the CFI. The mention of the Court of Justice in the first sentence of this particle therefore refers to the Court as Institution.

8   THE COURT OF AUDITORS

Since the coming into force of the Treaty on European Union, the Court of Auditors has been the fifth institution of the Communities.[437] The provisions governing the Court of Auditors are included in a (new) fifth section of Title I (Provisions governing the Institutions) of Part Five of the EC Treaty.[438] According to Article 247(1) EC,[439] the Court of Auditors is composed of one national from each Member State, chosen 'from among persons who belong or have belonged in their respective countries to external audit bodies or who are especially qualified for this office' and their independence 'must be beyond doubt'. They are appointed for a term of six years by a qualified majority vote of the Council after consultation of the European Parliament (Art. 247(3) EC). In the general interest of the Communities, they are to be completely independent in the performance of their duties[440]

---

432. Prior to the Treaty of Nice, this was (e).
433. Case C-170/96, *Commission v. Council* (Airport transit visas).
434. Case C-176/03, *Commission v. Council*.
435. Cf. R. Barents, op. cit. 283, and D.M. Curtin and R.H. van Ooik, 'Een Hof van Justitie van de Europese Unie'? (1999) SEW, 24–38, 34.
436. Meaning: that body, and not the Institution as such.
437. Arts. 7(1) EC and 3(1) Euratom.
438. See Arts. 246–248 EC and 160a–160c Euratom. In the rest of this section, we will not mention the corresponding treaty provisions for Euratom each time.
439. As amended by the Treaty of Nice.
440. Art. 247(4) EC: 'In the performance of their duties they are prohibited from seeking or taking instructions from any government or any other body, and they must refrain from any action incompatible with their duties.'

and in this their task resembles that of the members of the Commission and the Court of Justice; indeed, their general legal position is pretty well the same.[441] The Court of Auditors examines the revenue and expenditure of the Communities.[442] It examines whether all revenue has been received and all expenditure incurred in a lawful and regular manner and whether the financial management has been sound (Art. 248(2) EC). The Treaty of Amsterdam added the obligation to report in particular on any irregularity. The control powers of the Court of Auditors were also extended by the Treaty of Amsterdam. The control is based on records and, if necessary, can be performed on the spot in the Community Institutions and on the premises of any body which manages revenue or expenditure on behalf of the Community.[443] The control also takes place in the Member States, including on the premises of any natural or legal person in receipt of payments from the budget; in the latter cases this is done in liaison with the audit bodies or competent national departments (Art. 248(3) EC). Finally, the Treaty of Amsterdam also made provision for cooperation between the Court of Auditors and the European Investment Bank (EIB). In respect of the European Investment Bank's activity in managing Community expenditure and revenue, the Court of Auditors, the Bank and the Commission should reach an agreement concerning information held by the Bank.[444]

The annual report drawn up at the close of each financial year is forwarded to the Institutions and is published, with their replies, in the Official Journal (Art. 248(4) EC). The Court of Auditors is empowered to submit observations at any time, particularly in the form of special reports, on specific questions and to deliver opinions at the request of any Community Institution.[445] The annual report of the Court of Auditors and the Institutions' replies thereto form an important part of the procedure leading to the discharge which the Parliament grants to the Commission in respect of the implementation of the budget.[446]

The Treaty of Nice added the possibility for the Court of Auditors to establish internal chambers in order to adopt certain categories of reports or opinions. This must be regulated in the Rules of Procedure, which the Court of Auditors draws up and which it adopts after approval by the Council by qualified majority.[447]

---

441. See Art. 247(5)–(9) EC.
442. Art. 248(1) EC. The Court also examines the accounts of all revenue and expenditure of all bodies set up by the Community in so far as the relevant constituent instrument does not preclude such examination, ibid.
443. Art. 248(3) EC, as it reads after the Treaty of Amsterdam.
444. Art. 248(3), 3rd para., EC.
445. Ibid.
446. Arts. 276 EC and 180b Euratom. The Court of Auditors assists the European Parliament and the Council in exercising their powers of control over the implementation of the budget, Art. 248(4) EC.
447. Art. 248(4) EC, as amended by the Treaty of Nice.

9   INDEPENDENT COMMUNITY ORGANS

9.1   THE EUROPEAN INVESTMENT BANK

The European Investment Bank (EIB) was already set up by old Article 129 EEC, which also gave it legal personality; its establishment is now confirmed by Article 9 EC.[448] Its organization, tasks and methods of working are set out in Articles 266 and 267 EC and in the Protocol on the Statute of the European Investment Bank which is annexed to the Treaty.[449] The direction and management of the Bank is entrusted to three bodies.

The Board of Governors is composed of ministers designated by the Member States, and lays down general directives for the credit policy of the EIB.[450]

The Board of Directors decides on the various operations undertaken by the Bank and ensures that it is properly run; its 28 members and 18 alternates are nominated by the Member States and the Commission according to a formula laid down in Article 11 of the EIB Statute.[451]

The Management Committee consisting of a President and eight Vice-Presidents is appointed for a period of six years by the Board of Governors, acting on a proposal from the Board of Directors and is responsible for the day-to-day running of the Bank.[452] The members of the Board of Directors and of the Management Committee are independent in the performance of their duties and are responsible only to the EIB itself. In accordance with the scheme of Article 4 of the Statute, the Member States subscribe the capital of the Bank. The latter may grant loans and guarantees to its members (the Member States) or to private or public undertakings to facilitate the financing of investment projects in all sectors of the economy of the types listed in Article 267 EC. The projects must be in the European territories of the Member States and finance is available to the extent that funds are not available from other sources on reasonable terms; the territorial restriction applies unless a derogation is authorized by unanimous vote of the Board of Governors on a proposal from the Board of Directors.[453] Various agreements concluded by the Communities with third countries or groups of third countries envisage the grant of loans by the Bank for projects in these countries.[454]

---

448. Art. 266 EC states that the EIB shall have legal personality.
449. Last revised by Act of Accession 2005, Art. 14.
450. EIB Statute, Art. 9. The measures adopted by the Board of Governors may be subject to actions for annulment, under Art. 237(b) EC, at the instance of any Member State, the Commission, or the Board of Directors.
451. As most recently amended by Protocol No. 1 of the Accession Treaty of 16 Apr. 2003, and Art. 44, Adaptation Decision. Measures adopted by the Board of Directors may be subject to annulment proceedings, under Art. 237(c) EC, at the instance of Member States or the Commission, on limited grounds.
452. EIB Statute, Art. 13.
453. Ibid., Art. 18(1).
454. See, e.g., the EC-ACP Cotonou agreement; the Association Agreement with Turkey and the agreements with other Mediterranean countries. See Ch. XIII *infra* for details of these agreements.

Finally, it should be mentioned that according to the case law of the Court of Justice, the EIB is inseparably linked to the aims of the Community, and thus falls within the Community legal order.[455]

9.2   THE EUROPEAN CENTRAL BANK, AND EUROPEAN SYSTEM OF CENTRAL BANKS

The European Central Bank (ECB) and the European System of Central Banks (ESCB) were established on 1 June 1998, although no explicit legal act was performed for their establishment: rather, it resulted from the appointment of the ECB's Executive Board, according to Articles 8 and 123(1), last paragraph, EC.[456] As of that date, the ECB had as its task the preparation of the transition to the third and final stage of the Economic and Monetary Union (EMU).[457]

As of 1 January 1999 – the date on which the third and final stage of the EMU entered into force – the ECB and ESCB have had authority to exercise their powers to the full.[458] The main objective of the ESCB is to maintain price stability. Without prejudice to this objective, the ESCB supports the general economic policies in the Community in order to contribute to the achievement of the objectives of the Community described in Article 2 EC (Art. 105(1) EC). The rules governing the ECB and the ESCB are to be found partly in the EC Treaty, and in particular Articles 105–113 EC, partly in the Protocol on the Statute of the European System of Central Banks and of the European Central Bank, attached to the EC Treaty by the Treaty of Maastricht (hereafter: ECB and ESCB Statute).

The ECB has legal personality,[459] and is governed by a Governing Council and an Executive Board (Art. 107(3) EC). The Governing Council comprises the members of the Executive Board together with the Governors of the national central banks. The Executive Board, comprising six members, one of whom is the President, is appointed by common accord of the governments of the Member States;[460] the governors of the national central banks are appointed according to the relevant national procedures.

---

455. See Case 85/86, *Commission v. Board of Governors EIB* and Case C-370/89, *SGEEM and Etroy v. EIB*.
456. Decision 98/345/EC, Decision taken by common accord of the Governments of the Member States adopting the single currency at the level of Heads of State or Government of 26 May 1998, appointing the President, the Vice-President and the other members of the Executive Board of the European Central Bank, O.J. 1998, L 154/33.
457. Art. 123(2) EC read with Art. 117(3) EC.
458. Art. 123(1), last paragraph, EC. See on this: J.-V. Louis, 'The Economic and Monetary Union: Law and Institutions' (2004) CML Rev., 575–608 and R. Smits, 'Het begin van de muntunie: besluitvorming en regelgeving' (1999) SEW, 2 et seq. at 6.
459. Art. 107(2) EC.
460. Art. 112 EC.

The ESCB is a system of 28 central banks: the 27 existing central banks of the Member States and the ECB. The ESCB does not have legal personality. Nor does it have institutions of its own, but is governed by the Governing Council and the Executive Board of the ECB.[461] In order to carry out the tasks entrusted to the ESCB, the ECB may, in the cases and under the conditions laid down in the EC Treaty and Statute of the ECB and ESCB, make regulations, take decisions, make recommendations and deliver opinions (Art. 110(1) EC). The binding acts of the ECB may be subject to actions for annulment, under Article 230 EC, and the ECB may also bring actions before the Court of Justice in order to protect its preroga- tives. The ECB also has competence to bring actions for a failure to act under Article 232 EC, and similar actions may be brought against the ECB. The appli- cability of the Protocol on Privileges and Immunities is guaranteed by Articles 40 ECB and ESCB Statute and 23 of the Protocol. (See further Ch. X of this book.)

The establishment of the ECB and ESCB brought an end to the existence of the European Monetary Institute (EMI), which had the task of preparing for the tran- sition to the third stage of economic and monetary union; the EMI also had the task of monitoring the functioning of the European Monetary System, which was the system which aimed to limit the fluctuations in exchange rates of the currencies of the Member States to certain margins, and which ceased to operate as of 1 January 1999, when the currencies of the eleven Member States which took part in EMU – as part of the euro – were irrevocably fixed.[462] This was replaced by the so-called EMS II concerning the exchange rates between the euro and the currencies of the Member States not participating in the EMU.[463]

9.3   OLAF

By Decision of 28 April 1999, the Commission established the European Anti-fraud Office (OLAF).[464] This office replaced the previously existing task force for the coordination of the combat against fraud (UCLAF)[465] and took over all the tasks of that department. Article 2 of this Decision states that the Office

---

461. Arts. 107(3) EC and 8 ECB and ESCB Statute.
462. See Council Reg. 2866/98 of 31 Dec. 1998, on the conversion rates between the euro and the currencies of the Member States adopting the euro. O.J. 1998, L 359/1. On 1 Jan. 2001, Greece became the 12th Member State to participate in the EMU; on 1 Jan. 2007, Slovenia became the 13th participating Member State.
463. See Resolution of the European Council of 16 Jun. 1997, O.J. 1997, C 236, as well as the Agreement of 1 Sept. 1998, between the European Central Bank and the national central banks of the Member States outside the euro area, laying down the operating procedures for an exchange- rate mechanism in stage three of Economic and Monetary Union, O.J. 1998, C 345/6.
464. O.J. 1999, L 136/20. 1999/352/EC, ECSC, Euratom: Commission Decision of 28 Apr. 1999, establishing the European Anti-fraud Office (OLAF) (notified under document number SEC(1999) 802). The name OLAF comes from the French title (Office de Lutte Antifraude). See also Ch. VII section 6 *infra*, and J.A.E. Vervaele, 'Naar een Europees zelfstandig bes- tuursorgaan (ZBO) voor fraude- en corruptiebestrijding in de EU'? (1999) NJB, 636–643.
465. In full: Unité de Co-ordination de la Lutte Anti-Fraude.

exercises the Commission's powers to carry out external administrative investigations for the purpose of strengthening the fight against fraud, corruption and any other illegal activity adversely affecting the Community's financial interests, and that it is responsible for carrying out internal administrative investigations.

Although the Office is part of the services of the Commission, and does not have independent legal personality, it exercises its powers in complete independence; Article 3 of the Decision says that the Director of the Office may not seek or take instructions from the Commission; the same holds for instructions from any government or any other institution or body. According to Article 4 of the Decision, a Supervisory Committee[466] is to be established responsible for the regular monitoring of the implementation by the Office of its investigative function. The members of this Committee are appointed by common accord of the European Parliament, the Council and the Commission.[467] The Committee adopted its rules of procedure on 17 November 1999.[468]

The Decision establishing OLAF was complemented by two Regulations and an interinstitutional agreement between the European Parliament, the Council and the Commission. The first Regulation (Regulation 1073/1999)[469] sets the general rules concerning the investigations to be performed by the Office (external investigations in the Member States and third countries, and internal investigations). It also includes a more detailed description of the tasks of the Supervisory Committee and the Director. The second Regulation[470] provides for similar rules in relation to Euratom. According to the interinstitutional agreement, the three Institutions agree to adopt common rules consisting of the implementing measures required to ensure the smooth operation of the investigations carried out by the Office within their institution. The other institutions, and the bodies and offices and agencies are invited to accede to this Agreement.[471]

The decision establishing the Office, the two regulations and the interinstitutional agreement all entered into force on 1 June 1999.

The implementation of the interinstitutional agreement and the invitation to other institutions, bodies, offices and agencies turned out to involve considerable problems in practice. First, 71 members of the European Parliament brought an action for annulment against the decision of the European Parliament of 18 November 1999 amending its rules of procedure in order to allow OLAF to carry out internal investigations within the Parliament.[472] This action has been

---

466. Called a 'surveillance committee' in the Decision establishing OLAF, see Art. 4.
467. See Art. 11(2) of Reg. (EC) No 1073/1999 of the European Parliament and of the Council of 25 May 1999, concerning investigations conducted by the European Anti-Fraud Office (OLAF), O.J. 1999, L 136/1. See also O.J. 1999, C 220/1.
468. O.J. 2000, L 41/12.
469. Cited *supra*.
470. Reg. 1074/1999, O.J. 1999, L 136/8.
471. O.J. 1999, L 136/15. The Agreement does not specify whether only bodies etc. of the EC and Euratom or also bodies of the EU as such (e.g., Eurojust) might accede.
472. Case T-17/00 R, *Rothley et al. v. Parliament*. See also the Order of the President of the CFI of 2 May 2000, Case T-17/00 R and the appeal (Case C-167/02 P, *Rothley et al. v. Parliament*).

declared inadmissible by the CFI, confirmed by the Court of Justice. Second, the Commission brought an action for annulment against decisions of the ECB and the EIB which were aimed at making it impossible for OLAF to carry out investigations within these bodies. Both cases have been won by the Commission.[473] OLAF is also responsible for the European Technical and Scientific Centre (ETSC) which has been charged with the analysis and classification of counterfeited euro coins (Comm. Decision No. 2005/37/EC of 29 October 2004, O.J. 2005, L 19/73).

9.4   OTHER INDEPENDENT COMMUNITY BODIES

As well as the above-mentioned bodies, the Council and Commission have established a number of other independent bodies, which we list here below (in chronological order of establishment), with their location where this has been decided:[474]

(a) European Centre for the Development of Vocational Training (Cedefop) (Council Regulation No. 337/75 O.J. 1975, L 39/1), Thessaloniki;

(b) European Foundation for the Improvement of Living and Working Conditions, Council Regulation No. 1365/75, O.J. 1975, L 139/1), Dublin;

(c) European Environment Agency (Council Regulation No. 1210/90, O.J. 1990, L 120/1),[475] Copenhagen;

(d) European Training Foundation (Council Regulation No. 1360/90), O.J. 1990, L 131/1),[476] Turin;

(e) European Monitoring Centre for Drugs and Drug Addiction (Council Regulation No. 302/93, O.J. 1993, L 36/1),[477] Lisbon;

(f) European Medicines Agency (EMEA) (Council Regulation No. 2309/93, O.J. 1993, L 214/1), London;

(g) Office for Harmonization in the Internal Market (OHIM) (Council Regulation No. 40/94, O.J. 1994, L 11/1), Alicante;

---

473. See Case C-11/00, *Commission v. ECB*, resp. Case C-15/00, *Commission v. EIB*.

474. The Euratom Supply Agency (Arts. 52–56 Euratom) and the Joint undertakings established by Council Decision under Art. 49 Euratom, which also have legal personality as a result of relevant treaty provisions, are not dealt with here. See, for the locations of certain bodies, Decision taken by common Agreement between the Representatives of the Governments of the Member States, meeting at Head of State and Government level, on the location of the seats of certain bodies and departments of the European Communities and of Europol, O.J. 1993, C 323/1.

475. Amended by Council Reg. No. 933/1999, O.J. 1999, L 117.

476. Amended by Council Regs. Nos. 2063/94, O.J. 1994, L 216, 1572/98, O.J. 1998, L 206, 2666/00, O.J. 2000, L 306, and 1648/2003, O.J. 2003, L 245/22.

477. Amended by Council Reg. No 3294/94, O.J. 1994, L 341.

(h) European Agency for Safety and Health at Work (Council Regulation No. 2062/94, O.J. 1994, L 216/1),[478] Bilbao;

(i) Community Plant Variety Office (Council Regulation No. 2100/94, O.J. 1994, L 227/1),[479] Angers;

(j) Translation Centre for the bodies of the European Union (Council Regulation No. 2965/94, O.J. 1994, L 314/1),[480] Luxembourg;

(k) European Monitoring Centre on Racism and Xenophobia (Council Regulation No. 1035/97, O.J. 1997, L 151/1), Vienna; since 1 March 2007 replaced by the European Agency for Fundamental Rights (Council Regulation No. 168/2007, O.J. 2007, L 53/1);

(l) European Agency for Reconstruction (Council Regulation No. 2454/99, O.J. 1999, L 299/1; a new Council Regulation 2666/00 was adopted on 5 December 2000 for assistance to Albania, Bosnia and Herzegovina, Croatia, the Federal Republic of Yugoslavia and the Former Yugoslav Republic of Macedonia. This new Regulation was complemented by Council Regulation 2667/00 (O.J. 2000, L 306/7), which confirmed the ongoing activities of the European Agency for Reconstruction, and by Council Regulation 2415/01 (O.J. 2001, L 327) extending the mandate to cover FYROM), Thessaloniki, with operational centres in Belgrade, Pristina, Podgorica and Skopje;

(m) European Food Safety Authority (European Parliament and Council Regulation No. 178/2002 (O.J. 2002, L 31/1);

(n) European Maritime Safety Agency (European Parliament and Council Regulation No. 1406/2002, O.J. 2002, L 201/8), presently Brussels, but will eventually be Lisbon;

(o) European Aviation Safety Agency (EASA) (European Parliament and Council Regulation No.1592/2002, O.J. 2002, L 240/1), Cologne;

(p) European Network and Information Security Agency (European Parliament and Council regulation No. 460/2004, O.J. 2004, L 77/1), presently Brussels, but will eventually be Heraklion (Greece);

(q) Eurojust (Council Decision 2002/187/JHA, O.J. 2002, L 63/1), The Hague;

(r) European Personnel Selection Office (EPSO) (O.J. 2002, L 197/53), Brussels;

(s) European Agency for the management of Operational Cooperation at the External Borders of the European Union (FRONTEX), (Council Regulation (EC) No. 2007/2004, O.J. 2004, L 349/25), Warsaw;

(t) European Chemicals Agency (ECHA), (Regulation (EC) No. 1907/2006, O.J. 2006, L 396/1), Helsinki.

---

478. Amended by Reg. (EC) No 1643/95 O.J. 1995, L 156.
479. Amended by Reg. (EC) No 2506/95, O.J. 1995, L 258.
480. Amended by Reg. (EC) No 2610/95, O.J. 1995, L 268.

10   SUBSIDIARY BODIES

10.1   THE ECONOMIC AND SOCIAL COMMITTEE OF THE EC AND EURATOM

According to Articles 7(2) EC and 3(2) Euratom, the Council and the Commission
are assisted by an Economic and Social Committee (EESC or ECOSOC).[481] All
sectors of economic and social life, including the liberal professions and the
'general interest', are represented in EESC, and since the Treaty of Nice, also
consumers. In practice, three groups of approximately equal size can be distinguished: employers in the field of industry, trade, and agriculture (with the exception of the small-scale trades), workers, and a residual group made up of
representatives of consumers' interests and experts in matters of general interest.
In total, the EESC has 344 members; the distribution between the fifteen Member
States was laid down in the EC Treaty as amended by the Treaty of Amsterdam.
The Treaty of Nice added to Article 258 EC the provision that '[t]he number of
members of the Economic and Social Committee shall not exceed 350'. The
Declaration on the enlargement of the European Union included (under (3)) the
distribution of seats for a Union of 27 Member States, with a total of 344 seats.[482]
The members of the EESC are appointed by the Council and, since the Treaty of
Nice, by qualified majority vote. They sit in a personal capacity.

    In the Treaties, the Committee is not given the status of Community Institu-
tion: it is a body which provides assistance (to the Council and the Commission).
The Council and the Commission may consult the EESC, and are required to do so
in a number of cases according to various Treaty provisions. Under the Euratom
Treaty it is invariably the Commission which is required to consult the EESC.
Under the EC Treaty, on the other hand, this obligation rests (with one exception)[483] with the Council. As regards this compulsory consultation, just as for that
of the European Parliament,[484] no distinct system has been followed in the Treaty.
It is, for instance, striking that the EC Treaty does not provide for obligatory
consultation of the EESC on decisions of the Council in the field of the rules of
competition (Arts. 81 et seq. EC). The Treaty of Maastricht gave the EESC a
Treaty-based right to issue an opinion on its own initiative in cases in which it
considers such action appropriate[485] – a right which it enjoyed as a matter of fact
since the first Paris Summit of October 1972.

    The influence of the EESC on Community policy is, however, on the whole
not as great as it might be, owing to the lack of homogeneity of the EESC itself. The

---

481. See also Arts. 257–262 EC and 165–170 Euratom; cf. also Art. 5, Convention on Certain
       Institutions common to the European Communities, now replaced by Art. 9, Treaty of Amster-
       dam. The official abbreviation is EESC, although in the past ECOSOC has been more widely
       used. Since ECOSOC is the abbreviation of the relevant UN Committee, we will here use
       EESC.
482. See now Art. 12, Act of Accession 2005.
483. Under Art. 37(2) EC.
484. As to which, see section 5.2.1, *supra*.
485. See now Arts. 262 EC and 170 Euratom.

various interest groups have the opportunity of lobbying their governments individually in a national context, and the Commission in the European context,[486] for their particular desires concerning the content of Community policy.

10.2 THE COMMITTEE OF THE REGIONS

The Council and the Commission are also assisted by the Committee of the Regions.[487] This Committee consists of representatives of regional and local bodies, and presently has 344 members (identical to the number of members of the EESC, and distributed among the Member States according to the same pattern).[488] The consultation of the Committee largely follows that applicable to the EESC,[489] with the addition that whenever the EESC is consulted, the Committee of the Regions is to be informed thereof by the Council or the Commission; where the Committee considers that specific regional interests are involved, it may issue an opinion on the matter; it may also issue own initiative opinions.[490]

The Treaty of Nice added a provision to Article 263 EC that the members of the Committee of the Regions should either hold a regional or local authority electoral mandate or be politically accountable to an elected assembly number. Here, too, as with the EESC, it is provided that the number of members shall not exceed 350. The members of this Committee are also appointed by the Council acting by qualified majority.[491]

10.3 OTHER COMMITTEES

A very important subsidiary body of the Council is the Committee of Permanent Representatives, already referred to in section 3.4. of this chapter, above.[492] In view of its influential function in the decision-making process of the Council the role of *Coreper* will be discussed more fully in section 4.1.2 of Chapter V, below.

Particularly in the EC structure there are a great many consultative committees, the institution of which is sometimes provided for in the Treaties,[493] but mainly in decisions of the Council.[494] According to their composition, two

---

486. On the conditions for interest groups to make their views known to the Commission Cf. Obradovic and Vizcaino, 'Good Governance Requirements Concerning the Participation of Interest Groups in EU Consultations', (2006) CML Rev., 1049–1085.
487. Art. 7(2) EC; see, further, Arts. 263–265 EC.
488. Art. 263 EC, as last amended by Art. 13, Act of Accession 2005.
489. See Art. 265 EC.
490. Art. 265, 3rd and 5th paras, EC.
491. Art. 263, 4th para., EC.
492. Arts. 207(1) EC and 121(1) Euratom.
493. Arts. 79, 114(2), 130, 133(3), 147 and 193 EC, see also Art. 134 Euratom.
494. See the overview in Bull. EC 1980 Supp. 2/80 and COM(84)93 final. EP activities, O.J. Supplement 1986 No.2, and the Report of the Committee on activities of the Committees

types of committees can be distinguished; those whose members are representatives of the Member States or national experts and those in which the interested parties in a given sector are represented. A tripartite composition (governments, workers and employers) is provided for *inter alia*, in the case of the Committee for the European Social Fund set up under Article 147 EC.

According to their tasks these committees can be divided into those which assist the Council, the Commission and the Member States in the preparation of a common or co-ordinated policy (policy-making committees) and those which provide the Commission with opinions in the performance of its delegated administrative duties (advisory committees).

A whole series of policy-making committees usually composed of senior officials or other highly qualified experts has been set up by the Council in the field of coordination of economic policies (in the wide sense of this term), and they have been charged in particular with the promotion of cooperation between the Member States in this field. The Treaty itself mentions the Economic and Financial Committee (Art. 114(2) EC), which took the place of the previously existing Monetary Committee as of the beginning of the third stage of EMU. In addition, on the basis of Article 202 EC, the Council appointed an Economic Policy Committee.[495]

Under the same Treaty provision, the Council has also set up an Advisory Committee on Safety, Hygiene and Health Protection at Work,[496] and a Permanent Committee for Labour Problems, which was completely restructured in 1999.[497] This committee is complimented by the Employment Committee, set up in January 2000 on the basis of Article 130 EC.[498] Finally, the Council set up, on the basis of Article 202 EC, a Social Protection Committee, whose aim is to strengthen the cooperation between the Member States in the area of social protection.[499]

There is hardly any field of administration delegated by the Council to the Commission in which the Commission is not required to consult committees, specially established for the purpose, in which the official services of the Member States working in that field are represented. The opinions issued sometimes have legal consequences, as in the case of the management committees for the organization of the markets for various agricultural products, and the regulatory

---

in 2000, O.J. 2000, C 372/2. See further on types of committee: R. Pedler and K. Bradley in D. Spence and G. Edwards (eds), *The European Commission*, 3rd ed. (London, 2006) 253 et seq. and literature cited there.

495. Dec. 74/122 (O.J. 1974, L 63/21). This Decision has since been replaced by Decision 2000/ 604/EC of 29 Sep. 2000, on the composition and the statutes of the Economic Policy Committee, O.J. 2000, L 257/28.

496. Decision 74/325/EEC, O.J. 1974, L 185/15.

497. O.J. 1999, L 72/33, by which the original decision (Dec. 70/532, O.J. 1970, L 273/25) was repealed.

498. Council Decision, 2000/98/EC, O.J. 2000, L 29/21. Council Decision 97/16/EC (O.J. 1997, L 6/32) setting up the Employment and Labour Market Committee, was thereby repealed.

499. Council Decision 2000/436/EC, setting up a Social Protection Committee, O.J. 2000, L 172/26.

committees in, *inter alia*, the field of public health and customs regulations.[500] In addition to these committees of officials there are also in many cases consultative committees, in which directly interested parties are represented, particularly, for instance, in the field of market organizations for various agricultural products,[501] agricultural structure policy,[502] social problems of agricultural workers,[503] and free movement of workers. Thus, even at the executive level, by means of these two kinds of committees national governments and interest groups generally participate in the work of the Community.

As far as the committees consisting of government representatives are concerned, the Council laid down five standard procedures for the exercise of implementing powers conferred on the Commission in its so-called 'comitology Decision' of 28 June 1999.[504]

10.4 COMMUNITY STAFF

Each of the Institutions, independent and other Community bodies (the Economic and Social Committee and the Committee of the Regions jointly) has its own staff of officials. Some 33,300 staff (including those employed at research centres) are employed on a permanent or temporary basis by the Communities (figures from end 2002).[505] The vast majority (about 24,000) are employed in the Commission's services which presently comprise 26 Directorates-General and a number of smaller services.[506] Irrespective of the Institution for which they work, all officials and other servants form part of a single Community administration in the sense that they are subject to the same set of legal rules, namely the Staff Regulations and Conditions of Employment of Servants.[507]

Under the Staff Regulations, an 'official of the Communities' means 'any person who has been appointed, as provided for in these Staff Regulations, to an established post on the staff of one of the Institutions of the Communities by an instrument issued by the Appointing Authority of that institution'.[508] The legal

---

500. See Ch. V, section 4.2, *infra*.
501. See Dec. 98/235, O.J. 1998, L 88/59.
502. Dec. 87/83, O.J. 1987, L 45/40.
503. Dec. 74/442, O.J. 1974, L 243/22, most recently amended by Dec. 87/445, O.J. 1987, L 240/24.
504. Dec. 1999/468/EC, O.J. 1999, L 184/23. as amended by Decision of the Council No. 2006/512/ EC of 17 Jul. 2006, O.J. 2006, L 200/11. See, further, section 6.4, *supra* and Ch. V, section 4.2. *infra*.
505. <http://europa.eu.int/comm/reform/2002/summary_chapter2_en.html#2_2_1> consulted 10 Nov. 2004.
506. See section 4.2, *supra*.
507. On the basis of Merger Treaty, Art. 24(1), Reg. 259/68, O.J. 1968, L 56/1, as amended on myriad occasions. Full title: Staff Regulations of Officials of the European Communities and Conditions of Employment of other servants of the European Communities, last amended by Regulation (EC, Euratom) No 723/2004 (O.J. 2004, L 124/1).
508. This also applies to persons appointed by Community bodies ('agencies') to whom the Staff Regulations apply under the Community acts establishing them. A number of bodies,

status of officials is governed entirely by public law (i.e., by the Treaties and the Staff Regulations and rules made thereunder) and is not a contractual relationship. Other members of staff (referred to as 'Other Servants') are employed on a contractual basis.[509] Most of the latter are employed as local agents performing manual labour or auxiliary services.

It is the duty of every official, just as of any national official, to be loyal to the authority which has appointed him and to the public interest of the Community for the benefit of which he is working.[510] For an international official this duty takes on a special dimension because it means that he must also show himself independent of the government of the state whose nationality he possesses and that he must not be guided by considerations of national interest. It has, therefore, been laid down that the Community official, in discharging his functions and in determining his conduct, should keep in mind solely the interests of the Communities, without seeking or accepting instructions from any government or from any authority, organization or person outside his Institution.[511]

As a rule, two criteria which are not always easy to combine are applied in recruiting officials of international organizations; they have to satisfy the most exacting demands as to ability, efficiency, and integrity, and at the same time the filling of these posts should be spread over as wide a geographical area as possible. In several organizations the latter requirement is in practice a euphemistic expression covering a system of strict national quotas for the division of the posts at every level, on the basis of criteria such as the size of population or the amount of contributions of the participating countries. Such a system, according to which vacancies fall to a given nationality, is in the interest neither of the service nor of the officials already working in the organization, because the possibilities of selection for the filling of such posts are thus seriously restricted and the chances of advancement for the officials appointed are very slim. These two criteria are also applied in the recruitment of Community officials by virtue of Article 27 of the Staff Regulations. Each Institution attempts to maintain a broad reasonable balance of nationalities across the range of posts.[512] Unlike in most international organizations, the quota system is of subsidiary importance, although it is no secret that the Member States take an active interest in senior appointments. However, the career principle is laid down in Articles 29–31 of the Staff Regulations; and these

---

including the Economic and Social Committee, are to be treated as institutions for the purposes of the Staff Regulations (Cf. Art. 1b).

509. Cf. Art.1 Staff Regulations.
510. See Case C-274/99 P, *Connolly v. Commission*, and the Order and judgment in Case T-203/95 R and Case T-203/95, *Connolly v. Commission*. See also European Parliament Debates No. 475, 192 (Commission's answer to a question by Bonde concerning Connolly, *The Rotten Heart of Europe* (London, 1995)).
511. Staff Regs., Art. 11.
512. For statistics relating to the Commission and the Council see WQs 1193/86 (Lagakos) O.J. 1986, C 337/30 and 1524/84 (Wieczorek-Zeul) O.J. 1985, C 83/31. See also WQ 585/86 (Pearce) O.J. 1986, C 299/72, and, for more recent discussion and figures, Spence and Stevens in Spence and Edwards (eds), *op. cit. supra*, 197–203.

also provide in Article 7(1) that an official is to be appointed solely in the interests of the service and irrespective of his nationality, and in Article 27 that no single post may be reserved for nationals of a particular Member State.[513]

The *privileges and immunities* of the officials and other servants are regulated in the Protocol on the Privileges and Immunities of the European Communities, annexed to the Merger Treaty.[514] The Council determines the categories of servants to which these privileges and immunities are granted.[515] According to Article 18 of the Protocol, this is in the interest of the Communities, not their own personal interest. It was also with reference to this provision that the Court decided, in the first Order in the *Zwartveld* case,[516] that the privileges and immunities have a purely 'functional character, inasmuch as they are intended to avoid any interference with the functioning and independence of the Communities', and the same applies for the officials of the Communities.[517]

The most important immunity for Community servants is the immunity from suit and legal process,[518] and the most important privilege is exemption from national taxes.[519]

The immunity from suit and legal process relates to acts performed by the officials in their official capacity, including their spoken and written words and does not, of course, apply to cases that may be brought before the Court of Justice,[520] such as those relating to their personal accountability to the Communities.[521] The phrase 'in their official capacity' should, according to the Court, be interpreted restrictively. This immunity, therefore, covers only acts which, by their nature, represent a participation of the person entitled to the immunity in the performance of the tasks of the institution to which he belongs.[522]

Community officials and other servants are exempt from national taxes on salaries, wages and emoluments paid by the Communities but are, however, liable to a tax levied by the Communities themselves which goes into the general budget.[523]

---

513. These provisions have been regularly relied on in proceedings brought before the Court of Justice and the CFI, see, e.g., Case 85/82, *Bernhard Schloh v. Council* (reservation of a particular post for a particular nationality).
514. This Protocol was maintained despite the repeal of the Merger Treaty (See Explanatory Report from the General Secretariat of the Council on the simplification of the Community Treaties, O.J. 1997, C 353/1 et seq. at 17 under III.A. See also Ch. II, section 5.2, *supra*.
515. See Protocol on Privileges and Immunities, Art. 16.
516. Case C-2/88 Imm. *J.J. Zwartveld et al.* [1990] ECR 4405.
517. Ibid., para. 19.
518. Protocol on Privileges and Immunities, Art. 12(a).
519. Ibid., Art. 13, 2nd para.
520. Ibid., Art. 12(a).
521. Art. 22. Staff Regs.
522. Case 5/68, *Sayag et al. v. Leduc et al.* In the case of criminal acts by the Institution in question, this immunity may be lifted; see Art. 18, 2nd para., Protocol on Privileges and Immunities, and the Commission Decision of 1 Mar. 1995, *Agence Europe* No. 6431, 8.
523. The tax is levied on the basis of Protocol on Privileges and Immunities, Art. 13, 1st para., by Reg. 260/68 (O.J. 1968, 56/8, as amended; last amendment O.J. 2002, L 264/15). See Case 3/83, *Abrias et al. v. Commission*.

The combination of exemption from national taxation but subjection to a Community tax prevents the effective remuneration of Community officials and other servants 'firstly and chiefly . . . from differing according to their nationality or fiscal domicile as a result of the assessment of different national taxes, and secondly . . . from being inordinately taxed as a result of double taxation'.[524]

Community officials and other servants are subject to disciplinary rules[525] and can also be held financially liable for any losses suffered by the Communities through gross negligence on their part in the exercise of their function or in connection with it.[526] The Court of Justice has unlimited jurisdiction over disputes that arise in this respect, which means in first instance the EU Civil Service Tribunal, given the division of jurisdiction between the various judicial bodies (see section 7.4 above). Indeed, pursuant to Article 91 of the Staff Regulations, any dispute concerning the legality of a decision affecting any person to whom the Staff Regulations apply[527] can be brought before the Civil Service Tribunal, without prejudice to the right of appeal to first, the Court of First Instance, and ultimately, the Court of Justice as a body. It should, finally, be mentioned that the five Institutions together with the EESC, the Committee of the Regions and the European Ombudsman in a decision of 26 January 2005[528] established a European Administrative Academy which has as its task to organize schooling activities for the officials and other servants.

FURTHER READING

1. General

Blumann, C. and L. Dubois. *Droit institutionnel de l'Union européenne*. Paris: LexisNexis Litec,. 2004.

Bolton, R. and J. Eastwood. *Guide to the EU Institutions*. London: Federal Trust for Education and Research, 2003.

Burban, J.-L. *Les institutions européennes*. 3e éd. Paris: Vuibert,. 2003.

Clapié, M. *Institutions européennes*. Champs Université. Droit 3035. Paris: Flammarion, 2003.

Craig, P.P. *EU Administrative Law*. Collected Courses of the Academy of European Law, vol. 16/1. Oxford: Oxford University Press., 2006.

Curtin, D. 'The Constitutional Structure of the Union: A Europe of Bits and Pieces'. (1993) CML Rev.

Devuyst, Y. *The European Union Transformed: Community Method and Institutional Evolution from the Schuman Plan to the Constitution for Europe.*

---

524.   Case 32/67, *Van Leeuwen v. City of Rotterdam*, at para. 3. See further on national taxation and Community officials also Case 23/68, *Johannes Gerhardus Klomp v. Inspectie der Belastingen*; Case 85/85, *Commission v. Belgium* and Case 260/86, *Commission v. Belgium*. On European Schools and national taxation see Case 44/84, *Hurd v. Jones*.
525.   Staff Regs., Arts. 86–89.
526.   *Ibid.*, Art. 22.
527.   Which includes an unsuccessful candidate: Case 130/75, *Prais v. Council*.
528.   O.J. 2005, L 37/14.

European Policy., vol. 27. Rev. and updated ed. Brussels: P.I.E.-Peter Lang., 2006.

Doutriaux, Y. and C. Lequesne. *Les institutions de l'Union européenne*. Réflexe Europe. 5e éd. mise à jour. Paris: Documentation française., 2005.

Epiney, A.,. et al. *Das institutionell Recht der Europäischen Union*. Europarecht,. vol. 1. Bern: Stämpfli, 2004.

Guéguen, D. *The New Practical Guide to the EU Labyrinth: Understanding the European Institutions Structures, Powers, Procedures through Examples, Diagrams, Summaries*. 9th ed. Brussels: European Information Service, 2006.

Hartley, T.C. *The Foundations of European Community Law: An Introduction to the Constitutional and Administrative Law of the European Community*. 6th ed. Oxford: Oxford University Press,. 2007.

Héritier, A. *Explaining Institutional Change in Europe*. Oxford: Oxford University Press,. 2007.

Hessel, B. and K.J.M. Mortelmans. 'Decentralized Government and Community Law: Conflicting Institutional Developments?' (1993) CML Rev., 905–937.

Hix, S. *The Political System of the European Union*. The European Union Series. Palgrave Macmillan, 2005.

Hosli, M.O., et al. *Institutional Challenges in the European Union*. Routledge Advances in European Politics, vol. 6. London: Routledge, 2002.

Inglis, K. 'The Union's Fifth Accession Treaty: New Means to Make Enlargement Possible'. (2004) CML Rev.

Jacqué, J.P. *Droit institutionnel de l'Union européenne*. 4me éd. Paris: Dalloz, 2006.

Lang, J.T. *The Commission and the European Parliament after Nice*. Oxford: Europaeum,. 2001.

Lasok, K. P. E. and D. Lasok. *Law and Institutions of the European Union*. 7th ed. London: Butterworths, 2001.

Leclerc, S. *Droit institutionnel de l'Union et des Communautés européennes*. Fac Universités. Série 'Mémentos'. Paris: Gualino, 2004.

Lenaerts, K. 'Some Reflections on the Separation of Powers in the European Community'. (1992) CML Rev.

Lenaerts, K., et al. *Constitutional Law of the European Union*. 2nd ed. London: Thomson Sweet & Maxwell, 2005.

Magnette, P. *Contrôler l'Europe: Pouvoirs et responsabilités dans l'Union européenne*. Études européennes/Institut d'études européennes. Bruxelles: Éd. de l'Université de Bruxelles, 2003.

Manin, P. *Droit constitutionnel de l'Union européenne*. Études internationales, no. 6. Nouv. éd. Paris: Pedone, 2004.

Manin, P. *L' Union européenne: institutions, ordre juridique, contentieux*. Etudes internationales, 6. Paris: Pedone, 2005.

Meunier, S. and K.R. MacNamara. *Making History: European Integration and Institutional Change at Fifty*. The State of the European Union, 8. Oxford: Oxford University Press, 2007.

Moreau Defarges, P. *Les Institutions européennes.* 7e éd. Compact. Science poli-
tique. Paris: Armand Colin, 2005.
Nugent, N. *The Government and Politics of the European Union.* The European
Union Series. 6th rev. and updated ed. Palgrave Macmillan, 2006.
Pertek, J. *Droit des institutions de l'Union européenne.* Thémis. Droit public.
Paris: PUF, 2004.
Peterson, J. and M. Shackleton. *The Institutions of the European Union.* The
New European Union Series. 2nd ed. Oxford: Oxford University Press, 2006.
Rideau, J. *Droit institutionnel de l'Union et des Communautés européennes.*
Manuels LGDJ. 4me éd., Paris: LGDJ, 2002.
Stevens, A. and H. Stevens. *Brussels Bureaucrats?: The Administration of the
European Union.* Basingstoke: Palgrave, 2001.
Toth, A.G. *Oxford Encyclopedia of European Community Law.* Institutional Law,
vol. I. Oxford: Clarendon Press, 1990.
Usher, J.A. *EC Institutions and Legislation.* London: Longman, 1998.
Van Raepenbusch, S. *Droit institutionnel de l'Union européenne.* Collection de la
Faculté de droit de l'Université de Liège. 4e éd. Bruxelles: Larcier, 2005.
Warleigh, A. *Understanding European Union Institutions.* London: Routledge, 2002.
Wyatt, D. and A.Dashwood. *European Union Law.* 5th ed. London: Sweet &
Maxwell, 2006.
Zarka, J.-C. *L'essentiel des institutions de l'Union européenne.* Les carrés. Droit –
Science politique. 8e éd. Paris: Gualino, 2005.

2. European Council

Bulmer, S. and W. Wessels. *The European Council.* London: Macmillan, 1987.
Eijsbouts, W.T. 'De raad van opperhoofden'. In A.K. Koekkoek et al. (eds). *Pub-
licaties van de Staatsrechtkring*, nr. 5. Deventer, 2000.
Glaesner, H.J. 'The European Council'. In D. Curtin and T. Heukels (eds). *Insti-
tutional Dynamics of European Integration, Essays in Honour of Henry G.
Schermers*, vol. II. Dordrecht/Boston/London, 1994.
Tallberg, J. 'Bargaining Power in the European Council'. Reports; 2007:1.
Stockholm: Swedish Institute for European Policy Studies (SIEPS), 2007.
Taulègne, Béatrice. *Le Conseil européen.* Paris, 1993.
Werts, J. *The European Council.* Amsterdam, 1992.

3. Council of the European Union

Dashwood, A. 'The Role of the Council of the European Union'. In D. Curtin and
T. Heukels (eds). o.c.
De Zwaan, J.W. *The Permanent Representatives Committee: Its Role in European
Union Decision-Making.* Amsterdam, 1995.
Elgström, O. *European Union Council Presidencies: A Comparative Perspective.*
Routledge Advances in European Politics, 13. London: Routledge, 2003.
Hayes-Renshaw, F. and H.S. Wallace. *The Council of Ministers.* 2nd ed. The
European Union Series. Basingstoke: Palgrave Macmillan, 2006.

Larue, T. *Agents in Brussels: Delegation and Democracy in the European Union.* Umeå: Umeå University, 2006.

Sherrington, P. *The Council of Ministers: Political Authority in the European Union.* London: Pinter, 2000.

Westlake, M., et al. *The Council of the European Union.* 3rd ed. London: Harper, 2004.

4. Commission

Bergström, C.F. *Comitology: Delegation of Powers in the European Union and the Committee System.* Oxford Studies in European Law. Oxford: Oxford University Press, 2005.

Bradley, K. St. Clair. 'Comitology and the Law: Through a Glass, Darkly'. (1992) CML Rev.

Dimitrakopoulos, D.G. *The Changing European Commission.* Manchester: Manchester University Press, 2004.

Edwards, G. and D. Spence. *The European Commission.* 2nd ed. London: Cartermill, 1997.

Endo, Ken. *The Presidency of the European Commission under Jacques Delors: The Politics of Shared Leadership.* Basingstoke/New York, 1999.

Guéguen, D. and C. Rosberg. *Comitology and other EU Committees and Expert Groups: The Hidden Power of the EU: Finally a Clear Explanation.* Brussels: Europe Information Service, 2004.

Hooghe, L. *The European Commission and the Integration of Europe: Images of Governance.* Cambridge: Cambridge University Press, 2001.

Lenaerts, K. and A. Verhoeven. 'Comitologie en scheiding der machten'. (1999) SEW, 394–413.

Nugent, N. *At the Heart of the Union: Studies of the European Commission.* 2nd ed. Houndmills, Basingstoke: Macmillan Press, 2000.

Nugent, N. *The European Commission.* Basingstoke: Palgrave, 2001.

Spence, D. and G. Edwards. *The European Commission.* 3rd ed. London: Harper, 2006.

5. European Parliament

Corbett, R. *The European Parliament's Role in Closer EU Integration.* Basingstoke: Macmillan, 1998.

Corbett, R., et al. *The European Parliament* 7th ed. London: Harper, 2007.

Heede, K. *European Ombudsman: Redress and Control at Union Level.* European Monographs, 24. The Hague: Kluwer Law International, 2000.

Hix, S., et al. *Democratic Politics in the European Parliament.* Themes in European Governance. Cambridge: Cambridge University Press, 2007.

Judge, D. and D. Earnshaw. *The European Parliament.* Basingstoke, Hampshire: Palgrave Macmillan, 2003.

Katz, R. S. and B. Wessels. *The European Parliament, the National Parliaments, and European Integration.* Oxford: Oxford University Press, 1999.

Rittberger, B. *Building Europe's Parliament: Democratic Representation beyond the Nation-State.* Oxford: Oxford University Press, 2005.
Smith, J. *Europe's Elected Parliament.* Contemporary European Studies, 5. Sheffield: Sheffield Academic Press, 1999.
Steunenberg, B. and J.J.A. Thomassen. *The European Parliament: Moving toward Democracy in the EU.* Governance in Europe. Lanham, MD: Rowman & Littlefield, 2002.

6. Competences

Christiansen, Th. and T. Larsson (eds). *The Role of Committees in the Policy Process of the European Union: Legislation, Implementation and Deliberation.* Edward Elgar Publishing, 2007.
Cullen, H. and A. Charlesworth. 'Diplomacy by Other Means: The Use of Legal Basis Litigation as a Political Strategy by the European Parliament and Member States'. (2000) CML Rev.
Franchino, F. *The Powers of the Union: Delegation in the EU.* Cambridge University Press, 2007.
Pollack, M.A. *The Engines of European Integration: Delegation, Agency, and Agenda Setting in the EU.* Oxford: Oxford University Press, 2003.
Van Ooik, R.H. *De keuze der rechtsgrondslag voor besluiten van de Europese Unie.* Europese Monografieën, 63. Deventer: Kluwer, 1999.

7. Court of Justice

Arnull, A. *The European Union and Its Court of Justice.* 2nd ed. Oxford EC Law Library.
Oxford: Oxford University Press, 2006.
Barbier de la Serre, E. 'Accelerated and Expedited Procedures before the EC Courts: A
Review of the Practice', (2006) CML Rev.
Brown, L. N., et al. (eds). *The Court of Justice of the European Communities.* 5th ed. London: Sweet & Maxwell, 2000.
Burrows, N. and R. Greaves. *The Advocate General and EC Law.* Oxford University Press, 2007.
Castillo de la Torre, F. 'Interim Measures in Community Courts: Recent Trends'. (2007) CML Rev., 273–353.
Claes, M. *The National Courts' Mandate in the European Constitution.* Oxford: Hart, 2006.
De Búrca, G. and J. H. H. Weiler. *The European Court of Justice.* Collected Courses of the Academy of European Law, vol. 10/1. Oxford: Oxford University Press, 2001.
Dehousse, R. *La Cour de justice des Communautés européennes.* 2e éd. Clefs. Politique. Paris: Montchrestien, 1997.
Johnston, A. 'Judicial Reform and the Treaty of Nice'. (2001) CML Rev., 499–523.

Kuper, R. *The Politics of the European Court of Justice.* European Dossier Series. London: Kogan Page, 1998.
Mertens de Wilmars, J. 'The Case-Law of the Court of Justice in Relation to the Review of the Legality of Economic Policy in Mixed-Economy Systems'. (1982) LIEI, 1–16.
Rasmussen, H. *On Law and Policy in the European Court of Justice: A Comparative Study in Judicial Policy-Making.* Dordrecht: Martinus Nijhoff, 1986.
Rasmussen, H. *The European Court of Justice.* Copenhagen: GadJura, 1998.
Slaughter, A.-M., A. Stone Sweet and J.H.H. Weiler. *The European Courts and National Courts: Doctrine and Jurisprudence.* Hart, 1997.

8. Court of First Instance

Kirschner, H. and K. Kluepfel. *Das Gericht erster Instanz der Europäischen Gemeinschaften: Aufbau, Zuständigkeiten, Verfahren.* 2. Aufl. Köln: Heymanns, 1998.
Millett, T. *The Court of First Instance of the European Communities.* London: Butterworths, 1990.
Vesterdorf, B. 'The Court of First Instance of the European Communities after Two Full Years in Operation'. (1992) CML Rev., 897–915.

9. European Court of Auditors

Crouy-Chanel, I. d. and C. Perron. *La Cour des comptes européenne.* Que sais-je, 3357.
Paris: PUF, 1998.
Engwirda, M.B. and A.F.W. Moonen. 'De Europese Rekenkamer: positie, bevoegdheden en toekomstperspectief'. (2000) SEW, 246–257.
Inghelsram, J. 'The European Court of Auditors: Current Legal Issues'. (2000) CML Rev., 129–146.
Skiadas, D. *The European Court of Auditors.* London: Kogan Page, 2000.

10. European Central Bank

Andenas, M. *European Economic and Monetary Union: The Institutional Framework.* International Banking and Finance Law, vol. 6. London: Kluwer, 1997.
De Haan, J., et al. *The European Central Bank: Credibility, Transparency, and Centralization.* CESifo Book Series. Cambridge, MA: MIT Press, 2005.
Howarth, D.J. and P.H. Loedel. *The European Central Bank: The New European Leviathan?* Rev. 2nd ed. Basingstoke: Palgrave Macmillan, 2005.
Marshall, M. *The Bank: The Birth of Europe's Central Bank and the Rebirth of Europe's Power.* London: Random House Business Books, 1999.
Smits, R.J.H. *The European Central Bank: Institutional Aspects.* S.l.: s.n., 1997.
Smits, R.J.H. *The European Central Bank in the European Constitutional Order.* Utrecht: Eleven International Publishing, 2003.

Waigel, C. *Die Unabhängigkeit der Europäischen Zentralbank: gemessen am Kriterium demokratischer Legitimation.* Nomos-Universitätsschriften. Recht; Bd. 305. Baden-Baden: Nomos Verlagsgesellschaft, 1999.

Zilioli, C. and M. Selmayr. 'The European Central Bank: An Independent Specialized Organization of Community Law'. (2000) CML Rev., 591–643.

Zilioli, C. and M. Selmayr. *The Law of the European Central Bank.* Oxford: Hart, 2001.

11. Committee of the Region

Hesse, J.J., et al. (eds). *Regionen in Europa = Regions in Europe = Régions en Europe.* Baden-Baden: Nomos Verlagsgesellschaft, 1995.

Theissen, R., *Der Ausschuss der Regionen (Artikel 198 a–c EG-Vertrag): Einstieg der Europäischen Union in einen kooperativen Regionalismus?* Hamburger Studien zum europäischen und internationalen Recht, Bd. 9. Berlin: Duncker und Humblot, 1996.

Warleigh, A. *The Committee of the Regions: Institutionalizing Multi-level Governance?* London: Kogan Page, 1999.

12. European Anti-Fraud Office (OLAF)

Vervaele, J.A.E. *Transnational Enforcement of the Financial Interests of the European Union: Developments in the Treaty of Amsterdam and the Corpus Juris.* Antwerpen: Intersentia Law Publishers, 1999.

White, S. *Protection of the Financial Interests of the European Communities: The Fight against Fraud and Corruption.* European Monographs, 15. The Hague: Kluwer Law International, 1998.

13. European Agencies

Chiti, E. 'The Emergence of a Community Administration: The Case of European Agencies'. (2000) CML Rev., 309–343.

Della Cananea, G. *European Regulatory Agencies.* Collectie ISUPE. Paris: Editions Rive Droite, 2005.

Geradin, D., et al. *Regulation through Agencies in the EU: A New Paradigm of European Governance.* Cheltenham: Edward Elgar, 2005.

Kreher, A. 'The EC Agencies between Community Institutions and Constituents: Autonomy, Control and Accountability: Conference Report'. San Domenico (FI): European University Institute, 1998.

Vos, E. 'Reforming the European Commission: What Role to Play for EU Agencies?' (2000) CML Rev., 1113–1134.

Chapter V

Legal Instruments, Decision-Making and EU Finances

*B. de Witte, A. Geelhoed and J. Inghelram**

1   LEGAL INSTRUMENTS

In addition to the founding treaties – European Community (EC) Treaty, Treaty on European Union (TEU), Euratom Treaty and, until recently, the European Coal and Steel Community (ECSC) Treaty – which constitute the 'primary' law of the European Union and the European Communities, there is a body of 'secondary' law, made up of the legal instruments used by the Institutions of the European Union and the European Communities. The principal legal instruments for the development and application of Community law are of course the *acts of the European Parliament and the Council acting jointly, the acts of the Council, and the acts of the Commission*. It is to these instruments that the greater part of the present section will be devoted. A second group of legal instruments which are of importance consists of *international treaties, conventions, agreements* or international legal transactions by whatever other name they may be referred to. They will be discussed in connection with the external relations of

---

*   Sections 1–3: B. de Witte. section 4: J. Inghelram, rewritten based on texts by A. Geelhoed and P.J.G. Kapteyn.

P.J.G. Kapteyn, A.M. McDonnell, K.J.M. Mortelmans and C.W.A. Timmermans (eds),
The Law of the European Union and the European Communities, pp. 273–419.
©2008 Kluwer Law International BV, The Netherlands.

the Communities in Chapter XIII, below.[1] In dealing with the acts of the European Institutions, a distinction will be made between legal instruments of the EC (with special attention being paid to regulations, directives and decisions) and the instruments of the European Union, used in the Second and Third pillars, which have different denominations and a different character. In the last subsection, attention will be paid to the acts of another organ, the European Council, and to the treaties concluded between the Member States themselves (without participation of any third countries). The latter are not, formally speaking, acts of the European Institutions, but they are closely related from a functional point of view, and that is why we treat them in this framework.

The current system of legal instruments is likely to be changed in the near future with the entry into force of the Treaty of Lisbon. The main changes that will occur on 1 January 2009, if the Treaty of Lisbon enters into force then, are summarized in section 1.8. below. The earlier sections of this chapter describe the current legal regime.

1.1   ACTS OF THE INSTITUTIONS IN GENERAL

The EC and Euratom Treaties contain a set of general provisions relating to the principal categories of acts of the Community Institutions which are in practically identical terms[2] and which specify the nature and the legal effects of such acts; they also contain rules relating to the reasoning, publication, entry into force and enforcement of these acts. No special attention will be paid to the Euratom Treaty in the following. In the ECSC Treaty (Art. 14), the instruments were given different names: that Treaty provided for general decisions, recommendations, and individual decisions. These correspond with, respectively, regulations, directives and decisions under the EC Treaty.

Article 249, first paragraph, lists the legal instruments of the EC:

> In order to carry out their task and in accordance with the provisions of this Treaty, the European Parliament acting jointly with the Council, the Council and the Commission shall make regulations and issue directives, take decisions, make recommendations or deliver opinions.

In the next paragraphs of Article 249, a brief indication of the nature of each of the instruments is given, from which it is evident first of all that regulations, directives and decisions have binding force, while recommendations and opinions have no binding force. In the rest of section 1 of this chapter, attention will be paid to the specific characteristics of the three kinds of binding instruments. Recommendations and opinions (and other acts not mentioned in Art. 249) are discussed in section 1.5 below.

---

1. Treaties concluded by the EC may provide for the establishment of bodies which are competent to take implementing decisions for these treaties (e.g., Decisions of the Joint Committee of the EEA, and decisions of the association councils established in the association agreements concluded by the EC with third countries). These decisions are often binding and are published in the *Official Journal.* They are, however, not acts of the EC; they are dealt with in Ch. XIII of this book.
2. Arts. 249–253 EC and 161–164 Euratom.

From the first paragraph of Article 249, cited above, it is apparent that the legal instruments mentioned may be enacted by three authors: the Commission, the Council, or the European Parliament and the Council acting jointly. They may only adopt these instruments in order to carry out their tasks and 'in accordance with the provisions of this Treaty'. The Institutions therefore cannot derive a general authorization to adopt such acts from this Treaty provision. Whether they may adopt an act, and in what form they can do so, will depend on the description of the powers granted to them in specific Treaty provisions (the principle of conferred powers). This principle[3] is explicitly laid down in Article 5 first paragraph EC. If the specific empowering provisions in the Treaty do not mention one or more of the three legal instruments by name, then the choice of legal instrument is determined by the nature of the measure to be taken. For example, the 'measures' mentioned in Article 95 EC embrace not merely directives but also regulations, and 'appropriate measures' in Article 308 EC embraces all legal instruments at the Council's disposal, provided that they are appropriate to the objective to be attained. The nature of the Commission's powers implies that the Commission generally adopts acts of an executive nature, and it uses mainly regulations (for generally applicable measures) or decisions (for individual measures) for that purpose, although there are also examples of implementing directives adopted by the Commission. Occasionally, the EC Treaty provides for autonomous legislative power of the Commission, explicitly empowering this Institution to issue directives.[4] The other two Institutions are more obviously endowed with a legislative role, and act mainly by means of directives and regulations; however the Council, and the Parliament and Council acting jointly, do also sometimes take decisions. Whether a legislative measure should be taken by the Council acting alone, or by the Parliament and Council acting jointly, depends on the prescribed decision-making procedure. In those policy areas where co-decision applies, the acts are adopted by the Parliament and Council jointly; in the other areas, acts are adopted by the Council.[5]

Special arrangements regarding legal instruments are contained in Article 110 EC, in which the various categories of acts of the European Central Bank (ECB) are listed: regulations, decisions, recommendations and opinions (not directives). The second paragraph of this article contains legal definitions of these acts, which are, however, identical to those contained in Article 249 EC.[6] The Statute of the ECB also gives the ECB the possibility to issue guidelines and instructions addressed to central banks. These are both binding legal instruments.[7]

---

3. See Ch. III, section 6.1 *supra*.
4. Art. 86(3) EC.
5. See section 3 of this chapter on these variations in the decision-making procedures.
6. In some language versions (e.g., Dutch), there are minimal textual differences.
7. Protocol on the Statute of the European System of Central Banks and of the ECB, Art. 12. Regarding legal instruments in the field of monetary policy, see C. Zilioli and M. Selmayr, *The Law of the European Central Bank* (Oxford, 2001), 91–112.

It should be noted from the outset that Article 249 EC gives only an incomplete picture of the legal instruments which are used in practice in the EC, even leaving aside these specific arrangements in the area of monetary policy. The text of Article 249 is still by and large the original text of the Treaty establishing the European Economic Community (EEC), but in over 50 years of practice of the Community, other instruments have been 'invented' and used which are not mentioned in Article 249 EC, most of which belong to the category 'soft law', but some of which do have binding force. These 'other' EC instruments are dealt with in section 1.5 below.[8]

The distinction between the categories of legal instruments is relevant in several respects. The legal effect varies according to the instrument and there may be a difference between rules concerning, for example, their publication and entry into force. Moreover, the distinction is relevant in those cases where the exercise of a given power is bound up with acts of a specific kind. Finally, the distinction also entails a difference in judicial protection. In general, a private person cannot appeal directly to the Court of First Instance against regulations and directives, but may do so against decisions which are addressed to him or her (or it, in the case of a legal person). However, it must be remembered that the European Court of Justice (ECJ) has ruled right from the start that, for the purpose of judicial review, what counts is not the form or name by which an Institution calls a measure, but rather its object and content; so, if a measure is effectively addressed at an individual, even though it is not called a decision, that individual will be allowed to challenge it.[9]

All regulations, directives and decisions – whether adopted by the Parliament and Council jointly, the Council or the Commission – have to *state the reasons* on which they are based and refer to any proposals or opinions which were required to be obtained in accordance with the Treaties (Art. 253 EC). This is thus a double requirement: to state reasons in general, and to refer in particular to relevant proposals etc. The requirement to refer to proposals or opinions makes it possible to check whether the decision-making procedure required by the Treaties has been followed.

---

8. For a comprehensive and systematic discussion of all the legal instruments used in EC institutional practice, pointing out the lacunae in Art. 249 EC, see A. von Bogdandy, J. Bast and F. Arndt, 'Legal Instruments in European Union Law and their Reform: A Systematic Approach on an Empirical Basis' (2004) YEL, 91–136. In a sample of EC acts existing on 1 Dec. 1999, examined by these authors, only 71% were acts belonging to the categories mentioned in Art. 249 EC, so that no less than 29% of acts belonged to a different 'un-named' category (ibid., at 124). For an overall discussion of the 'un-named acts', see S. Lefèvre, *Les actes communautaires atypiques* (Brussels, 2006).

9. See Case 20/58, *Phoenix-Rheinrohr AG Vereinigte Huetten - und Roehrenwerke v. High Authority*; Joined Cases 16 & 17/62, *Confédération nationale des producteurs des fruits et légumes et al. v. Council*; see, more generally, Joined Cases 22 & 23/60, *Raymond Elz v. High Authority*, at 188: 'it is for the Court to classify legal measures according to their nature rather than according to their form'. See also section 1.4 of this chapter.

The duty to state the reasons for the adoption of the act serves to put interested parties in a position to know the reasons for the measure involved and to allow the Court to exercise its review function.[10] If no reasons or inadequate reasons are given, this is an infringement of an essential procedural requirement – and a ground for annulment of the contested act (Art. 230 EC).

It appears from the case law of the Court of Justice and the Court of First Instance – which is very copious and detailed as regards the requirement to give reasons – that the extent of the duty to provide a statement of reasons depends on the nature of the measure in question.[11] The facts on which the measure is based have to be mentioned, as well as the arguments which were decisive for the adoption of the measure.[12] It should be possible to trace the basic elements of the train of thought of the Institution which adopted the measure in the statement of reasons.[13] The nature of the power exercised is relevant for the degree of detail with which the statement of reasons must be formulated. Since judicial control of the exercise of discretionary powers is limited,[14] it is precisely in these cases that rigorous demands will have to be made as to the care with which the statement of reasons is formulated.

The statement of reasons of a *regulation or directive* need not be as detailed as that of a decision. It may be confined to a statement about the overall situation which led to the adoption of the regulation or directive on the one hand and, on the other hand, the general weighing of interests the Community legislature has made.[15] A specific enumeration of the sometimes numerous and complicated facts which led to its adoption together with a more or less complete assessment of these facts and a specific explanation of all the details of the act are, however, not required.[16] In the case of individual *decisions*, it is necessary to mention all the

---

10. E.g., Case 250/84, *Eridania*; Case C-84/94, *United Kingdom v. Council (Working time directive)*.
11. E.g., Joined Cases 142 & 156/84, *British-American Tobacco Company Ltd et al. v. Commission*; Case C-76/01 P, *Eurocoton and others v. Council*.
12. See already Case 2/56, *Geitling selling agency for Ruhr coal et al. v. High Authority*.
13. E.g., Case 14/61, *Koninklijke Nederlandsche Hoogovens en Staalfabrieken NV v. High Authority*. See also Case 41/69, *ACF Chemiefarma NV v. Commission*, in which the Court considered (para. 78) the statement of reasons sufficient 'if it indicates clearly and coherently the considerations of fact and law on the basis of which the fine has been imposed on the parties concerned, in such a way as to acquaint both the latter and the Court with the essential factors of the Commission's reasoning'.
14. See Ch. VI, section 1.5, *infra*.
15. In the case of such legislative measures, the obligation to state reasons may seem unusual, since it is not required, in most national legal systems, for domestic legislative acts. In the EC, it serves the purpose first and foremost of protecting the policy discretion of the Member States. The ECJ has also recognized the existence of a specific duty for the Community legislature to give reasons regarding compliance with the principle of subsidiarity; Case C-377/98, *Netherlands v. Parliament and Council*.
16. Case 5/67, *W. Beus GmbH and Co. v. Hauptzollamt München*. See also Case 166/78, *Italy v. Council* and Case 167/88, *Association générale des producteurs du blé et autres céréales (AGPB) v. Office national interprofessionnel des céréales (ONIC)*.

various details which are relevant in law or as facts: thus attention is paid not merely to the text of the decision, but also to the context in which it is adopted and the corpus of legal rules governing the matter in question. Moreover, the required degree of precision of the statement of reasons for a decision will also be weighed against practical realities and the time and technical facilities available for making the decision.[17] The actual circumstances under which measures have to be adopted may sometimes be relevant in that they may lead to a reduction of the pretty rigorous demands which the Court usually makes of the reasoning of decisions. In particular, if the appellant Member State or undertaking concerned has been closely involved in the process leading to the adoption of the decision, the reasoning may be less detailed.[18] A decision which follows a well-established line of decisions may be less fully reasoned and may simply refer to the standing administrative practice of the Commission.[19] The extent of the duty to state reasons also depends on the subject matter to which the measure relates, but there is no justification for the total absence of a statement of reasons of decisions that have a negative impact on individuals, firms or states, as the case may be. This simple rule was recently reaffirmed in the high profile cases relating to the freezing of funds of suspected terrorist groups. The Court of First Instance annulled Council decisions listing such suspects because of the absence, in the preamble of the decision, of any statement of the actual reasons why *they* were listed.[20]

All regulations, the directives addressed to all Member States, as well as directives and decisions adopted by the European Parliament and Council acting jointly under the co-decision procedure, are to be published in the *Official Journal*.[21] They take effect on the date specified by them or, failing this, on the twentieth day following their publication (Art. 254 EC). Limits have been set on the freedom of the Institutions to fix the date of entry into force. Entry into force on the date of publication,[22] and *a fortiori* on an earlier date, is permitted

---

17. E.g., Case C-350/88, *Société française des Biscuits Delacre et al. v. Commission* (citing earlier case law).
18. E.g., Case 13/72, *The Netherlands v. Commission*; Case 9/83, *Eisen und Metall Aktiengesellschaft v. Commission*.
19. Case 73/74, *Groupement des fabricants de papiers peints de Belgique et al. v. Commission*; Joined Cases 142 & 156/84, *British-American Tobacco*, and Case C-350/88, *Société française des Biscuits Delacre*.
20. Case T-228/02, *Organisation des Modjahedines du peuple d'Iran v. Council*; Case T-47/03, *Sison v. Council*.
21. The Official Journal (O.J.) is currently published in twenty-three languages. The title of the Journal was not immediately altered after the entry into force of the TEU. Acts under the Second and Third Pillars, as well as acts affecting the Union as a whole, were still published in the Official Journal of the European Communities. The Treaty of Nice changed this as of 1 Feb. 2003, renaming the journal the Official Journal of the European Union (amendment of Arts. 254(1) and (2) EC by the Treaty of Nice).
22. In the absence of evidence to the contrary, a regulation is regarded as being published throughout the Community on the date appearing on the relevant issue of the Official Journal: Case 98/78, *Firma A. Racke v. Hauptzollamt Mainz*.

only if there are adequate reasons for this.[23] The Court has emphasized on several occasions that

> in general the principle of legal certainty precludes a Community measure from taking effect from a point in time before its publication, it may exceptionally be otherwise where the purpose to be achieved so demands and where the legitimate expectations of those concerned are duly respected.[24]

Clearly established case law shows moreover that substantive rules of Community law must, in order to ensure respect for the principles of legal certainty and the protection of legitimate expectations, be interpreted as applying to situations which existed before their entry into force only in so far as it clearly follows from the terms, objectives or general scheme of those rules that such an effect must be given to them.[25] The principle that penal provisions may not have retroactive effect is one of the general principles of law whose observance the Court of Justice ensures.[26]

Directives (other than those adopted by the European Parliament and the Council acting jointly under co-decision) which are not addressed to all Member States, and decisions (other than those adopted by the European Parliament and the Council acting jointly under co-decision) do not need to be published in the *Official Journal*. They must be notified to their addressees and take effect upon such notification (Art. 254 EC). Notification in accordance with the Treaty takes place on communication of the measure to the addressee and the latter being put on a position to take cognizance of it.[27] In view of the importance which directives and decisions may have for parties other than their addressees, the fact that the Community Institutions now generally publish these in the *Official Journal* even when this is not obligatory is to be welcomed. The Commission is also obliged to publish its decisions in competition cases.[28]

Finally, as far as the execution of EC decisions is concerned, it should be mentioned that decisions of the Council and the Commission which contain pecuniary obligations for private persons,[29] such as those by which the Commission imposes a fine or a penalty, have the enforceability of a court judgment. They are enforced by virtue of the rules of civil procedure in each of the Member States (Art. 256 EC). The order for their enforcement is issued by the national authority designated for this purpose by each government. Article 256 EC states that no other

---

23. Case 17/67, *Firma Max Neumann v. Hauptzollamt Hof/Saale.*
24. Case 98/78, *Firma A. Racke* at para. 20; see also Case 108/81, Case 110/81, *SA Roquette Frères v. Council.*
25. Case 21/81, *Openbaar Ministerie v. Daniël Bout et al.*
26. Case 63/83, *Regina v. Kent Kirk.* Generally, on the issue of retroactive effect see T. Heukels, *Intertemporales Gemeinschaftsrecht* (Baden-Baden, 1990); S.L. Kaleda, 'Immediate Effect of Community Law in the New Member States: Is There a Place for a Consistent Doctrine?' (2004) *European Law Journal*, 102–122; and P. Craig, *EU Administrative Law* (Oxford, 2007), 607–614.
27. Case 6/72, *Europemballage Corporation and Continental Can Company Inc. v. Commission.*
28. See Reg. 1/2003, O.J. 2003, L 1/1, Art. 30.
29. Art. 256 EC.

verification takes place except the verification of the authenticity of the document. This procedure also applies to judgments of the Court of Justice.[30]

Article 110(2) EC lays down that Articles 253, 254 and 256 apply to regulations and decisions adopted by the ECB. The ECB is not obliged to publish its decisions, recommendations and opinions pursuant to this article. Article 256 EC concerning enforcement of decisions is significant, since the Council may, under the Statute of the European System of Central Banks (ESCB) and ECB, grant (by means of a Regulation) the ECB the right to impose fines or periodic penalty payments on undertakings for failure to comply with obligations under its regulations and decisions.[31]

1.2   REGULATIONS

Regulations (in French: *règlements*) are frequently used in the Community legal system, both as legislative and administrative instruments. The three characteristic elements of a regulation are:

(a) its general application;
(b) its binding character in all respects; and
(c) its direct applicability in each Member State.[32]

The general application of a regulation concerns the impersonal, non-individualized character of the situation to which it applies, as well as legal effects it entails for the legal subjects to whom it is addressed. A measure has general application provided that 'it is applicable . . . to objectively determined situations and involves legal consequences for categories of persons viewed in a general and abstract manner'.[33] Nevertheless, it may occur that a regulation concerns private parties directly and individually, and can therefore be challenged in law before the Court of First Instance, on the basis of Article 230, fourth paragraph, EC[34] although for most regulations this will not be the case.

A regulation not only has general application, but it is also binding in every respect; thus it differs from a directive which is only binding as to the result to be achieved. Moreover, a regulation is directly applicable in all Member States.[35] The

---

30. Cf. Art. 244 EC.
31. Art. 34.3 Statute of the ESCB and ECB.
32. Art. 249, 2nd para., EC.
33. Case 6/68, *Zuckerfabrik Watenstedt GmbH v. Council* at 415 of the English edition. Cf. earlier, in a somewhat different formulation, Joined Cases 16 & 17/62, *Confédération nationale* at 478 of the English edition.
34. See, e.g., Case T-13/99, *Pfizer Animal Health SA v. Council*, paras. 84–105: a regulation prohibits the use of a certain antibiotic as an additive in feedingstuffs. This regulation is generally applicable, but it affects one undertaking directly and individually, because that is the sole producer of the antibiotic in question. See further Ch. VI, section 2.2, on judicial protection.
35. This does not mean that a regulation cannot contain rules concerning the situation in only one of the Member States or even in a part of its territory. This is implicit in the judgment in Case 30/67,

system established by a regulation must therefore 'be applied with the same binding force in all the Member States within the context of the Community legal system which they have set up and which, by virtue of the Treaty, has been integrated into their legal systems'.[36] With this rather complex formulation, the Court wishes to indicate that once a regulation has entered into force, it is part of the national legal system of each and all of the Member States, in the same way as internally enacted legislation, but that it retains its character as being EC law, which means *inter alia* that the regulation has primacy over conflicting national law.

A consequence that the Court derives from the direct applicability of regulations is that the Member States may not adopt measures applying the regulation which modify its scope or add provisions to it, unless this is provided for in the regulation itself.[37] Likewise, the Member States are not permitted to transform the contents of a regulation into national legislative provisions, since if this were so uncertainty would be created about the legal nature of the applicable provisions and the time of their entry into force. Such implementing measures would have the result of creating an obstacle to the direct effect of Community regulations and of jeopardizing their simultaneous and uniform application in the whole of the Community.[38]

In practice, however, the text of a regulation frequently provides that implementing measures must be taken either by a Community Institution (usually the Commission) or the Member States, or both.[39] Implementation by the Commission frequently takes place by means of decisions, but often also by means of (further) regulations; in the latter case, the implementing regulation must be in conformity with the basic regulation, and there is in fact a hierarchy between two legal instruments which have the same denomination: not exactly a model of transparency.... In cases of implementation by the Member States, the forms and procedures of national law apply, provided that the uniformity of application of Community law is not endangered.

Industria Molitoria Imolese SpA et al. v. Commission. Despite the limited territorial field of application such a regulation has Community-wide validity.

36. Case 17/67, *Firma Max Neumann* at 453 of the English edition.
37. Case 40/69, *Hauptzollamt Hamburg-Oberelbe v. Firma Paul G. Bollmann*; Case 74/69, *Hauptzollamt Bremen-Freihafen v. Waren-Import- Gesellschaft Krohn and Co.*
38. Case 39/72, *Commission v. Italy.* See also Case 50/76, *Amsterdam Bulb BV v. Produktschap voor Siergewassen* and Case 94/77, *Fratelli Zerbone Snc v. Amministrazione delle Finanze dello Stato* at para. 26: 'Accordingly Member States must not adopt or allow national institutions with a legislative power to adopt a measure by which the Community nature of a legal rule and the consequences which arise from it are concealed from the persons concerned.' However, in special circumstances it may be permissible for domestic laws to incorporate some elements of the Community regulations involved, 'for the sake of coherence, and in order to make them comprehensible to those to whom they apply', Case 272/83, *Commission v. Italy* at para. 27.
39. An example of a regulation requiring (quite complex) implementing measures by the Member States is Council Reg. No. 1/2003 on the implementation of the rules on competition laid down in Arts. 81 and 82 of the Treaty, O.J. 2003, L 1/1. An example of a regulation requiring implementation both by the Commission and by the Member States is Reg. 1760/2000 establishing a system for the identification and registration of bovine animals and regarding the labelling of beef and beef products, O.J. 2000, L 204/1.

In particular, national law should determine whether for the implementation of a regulation an act of the (national) legislature (i.e., a statute) is necessary, or some other legal instrument. In general, the Member States are empowered, as well as being obliged under Article 10 EC, to lay down the necessary administrative and procedural rules to enforce compliance with the Community provisions and to pre-scribe sanctions for non-compliance. In fact, the duties of the Member States when they have to implement regulations are very similar to the duties imposed on them when they implement directives, to which we will come back in greater detail in the following section (1.3). The fact that many regulations frequently require further implementing measures, either by the Member States or by the Community Institu-tions themselves, means that private individuals are not always able automatically to rely on provisions of regulations before national courts. In other words: the direct applicability of regulations does not automatically mean that all provisions of reg-ulations have direct effect.[40]

1.3   DIRECTIVES

A directive has binding force in relation to the result to be achieved for each Member State to which it is addressed but it leaves the Member States free to choose the form and methods for implementing it.[41] Along with regulations, direc-tives are the most important instruments of Community legislation. The term 'directive', and corollary terms in the various other European languages, may not suggest intrinsically that directives have binding force, but they clearly do in the European system. However, the binding force of directives is of a special kind, differing from that of regulations.

This legal instrument, for which there is no clear parallel in national or international law, raises many questions about its legal nature and the obligations it imposes on the Member States. These questions have been repeatedly brought to the attention of the Court of Justice, and have been extensively treated in legal writings.[42] For a long time, it was unclear whether the definition in Article 249 EC implied a limitation of the competence of the Community Institutions over and above that already contained in the specific Treaty article which authorized the adoption of the directive and, if so, what this limitation consisted of.

The answer to the first part of this question is, in principle, affirmative. A comparison of the legal definitions makes it clear that, for the drafters of the EC Treaty, a directive is less intrusive than a regulation or a decision. It may thus be inferred that if a specific Treaty article, such as Article 94 EC, empowers the

---

40. See, for a case in which the Court of Justice declared that a provision of a regulation lacked direct effect: Case C-403/98, *Azienda Agricola Monte Arcosu Srl v. Regione Autonoma della Sardegna.*
41. Art. 249 EC, 3rd para.
42. S. Prechal, *Directives in EC Law*, Oxford, 2nd ed., 2005, Ch. 2 to 5; also C.W.A. Timmermans, 'Community Directives Revisited' (1997) YEL, 1.

Institutions solely to adopt directives, their competence is more limited than is the case when they are empowered to adopt regulations or decisions.

But what does this limitation consist of exactly? A comparison of the legal definitions of these acts show that a directive, unlike a regulation, can impose obligations only on Member States, and not directly on individuals. It is, like a decision addressed to Member States, a means of fettering the powers of Member States by obligations and prohibitions, as is evident from its name. Furthermore, a directive differs from regulations and decisions by the fact that its binding force is limited to the result to be achieved. The distinction, however, between 'result' on the one hand and 'form and method' is not very clear: Can a directive go into details? Can it impose the introduction of uniform rules on all the Member States? The many different views on these and other questions in legal literature cannot be discussed within the scope of this section;[43] the following observations are thus restricted to a few general remarks.

In EC legal practice, the directive has developed into an important instrument for the harmonization of national legislation, whenever such harmonization seems necessary for the proper functioning of the European internal market.[44] In such cases, Community intervention is limited; not in the sense that the consequences of intervention may not be very considerable, but in the sense of a limitation of the purpose of the Community intervention: the Community may oblige the national legislature to amend national law only to the extent necessary for the functioning of the internal market. This limitation is expressed in Articles 3(1)(h) EC, in which it is laid down that Community action also includes 'the approximation of the laws of Member States to the extent required for the functioning of the common market'. It is also expressed in the concrete Treaty provisions which may serve as legal basis for harmonization directives, such as Article 93 EC ('to the extent that such harmonization is necessary') or Article 95 EC ('for the achievement of the objectives set out in Article 14', which is to say the establishment of the internal market). The limitation is also expressed, although in a slightly different way, in relation to directives concerning horizontal or sectoral policy areas (environmental protection, consumer protection, agriculture, transport, etc.): here the directive must make a concrete contribution to the achievement of the policy objectives which the EC Treaty formulates for each policy sector separately.

Thus, the 'result to be achieved', imposed by the directive, may be defined as a legal or factual situation which promotes the Community interest which the directive is to ensure. This may be, for instance, the free movement of food or cars in the common market, or a high level of consumer protection. Further, the result to be achieved by virtue of a directive will practically always necessitate amendment of national law, unless this already conforms with the directive. A directive will thus have to contain instructions as to the content of such an amendment, and to that extent a directive will impose constraints on the power of the national authorities to choose form and methods.

---

43. See, generally, S. Prechal, *Directives in EC Law*, 2nd ed. (Oxford, 2005).
44. See section 2 *infra*.

The relationship between 'result' and 'form and methods' is a flexible one, although there is a limit to the flexibility: a directive can never oblige a Member State to introduce an exhaustive set of rules entirely unconnected with the national legislation in the context of which the field concerned was regulated. If it were otherwise, the national authorities would not retain any freedom to incorporate the result to be achieved into their national legislation. However, as the Court has recognized,[45] this does not preclude a directive from containing extremely detailed substantive provisions, and thus in fact requiring the introduction of uniform rules in the law of all the Member States, depending on the specific nature of the field being regulated.

In the light of the above discussion, the conclusion may be drawn that the competence-limiting effect of the legal definition of a directive has no independent significance of its own, but is significant only in conjunction with the substantive enabling Treaty provisions which define the fields in which, and the interest on behalf of which, the Community may intervene by adopting a directive. Sometimes, the desired result can only be achieved by far-reaching rules which limit the autonomy of the Member States to a large extent, while in other cases, the text of the directive is much more 'at a distance' and leaves more freedom of manoeuvre to the Member States. What also happens more and more often is that first a 'framework directive' is adopted, which is then later filled in by means of specific directives, so that in the end the national authorities have little to regulate. The choice between these options lies in first instance with the EC Institutions which enact the directive, in which context it is obviously the role primarily of the Council to ensure that the national room for manoeuvre is not limited too much. Review of these choices may be carried out by the Court of Justice (under Art. 230 EC), at the initiative of – in particular – a Member State whose preference for a less invasive text of the directive has been overruled by a qualified majority in the Council.[46] The principles of subsidiarity and proportionality play an important role in this respect.

Directives prescribe a term within which they must be implemented by the Member States. This term varies from case to case, depending on the complexity of their content and the urgency of their application; it is often one year or less, but the term may occasionally amount to up to three years, as is the case with the general Services Directive.[47] The Commission is to be informed of the Member State's implementation, and of the text of the provisions of national law which the Member State has enacted to implement the Directive. Delays in implementation of directives are a well-known problem. If a Member State fails to implement a directive

---

45. See Case 38/77, *Enka BV v. Inspecteur der Invoerrechten en Accijnzen Arnhem*, in which the Court concluded that harmonization in the customs field could necessitate ensuring the absolute identity of provisions governing the treatment of goods imported into the Community whatever the Member State across whose frontier they are imported.
46. E.g., Case C-233/94, *Germany v. Parliament and Council.*
47. Dir. 2006/123 of the European Parliament and of the Council of 12 Dec. 2006 on services in the internal market, O.J. 2006, L 376/36 (Art. 44: transposition deadline fixed at 28 Dec. 2009).

(correctly) within the term prescribed, and to inform the Commission accordingly, the latter may bring an action for failure to fulfil treaty obligations against the Member State at fault (under Art. 226 EC). Many Member States have had to deal with this problem at some time or other, particularly in the period 1985–1995, when a particularly large number of directives were enacted in the framework of the completion of the internal market. Also, the Court of Justice has held that the Member States are not entirely free to act in the period preceding the deadline for transposition: they are not allowed to take measures, within that period, that are 'liable seriously to compromise the result prescribed' by the directive.[48]

Each Member State has the freedom to delegate powers to its domestic authorities as it considers fit and in doing so to determine the extent to which implementation will take place by means of legislation or by administrative measures (the same is true, of course, for regulations that require implementation by the Member States). This choice takes place on the basis of the relevant rules of constitutional law, which will differ from one Member State to another, so that in one Member State a directive may have to be implemented by parliament by means of a statute, while in another Member State the same directive can be implemented by the government (i.e., the administration) autonomously. The freedom of choice of 'form and methods' also includes the freedom for the legislature to choose whether to implement a directive by enacting a specific new piece of legislation, or by amending existing legislation in the area of the directive.[49] The Member States are also free to determine the role played by regional or local authorities in implementing directives; in Member States with a federal or quasi-federal structure (such as Belgium, Germany and Spain), the role may be very extensive, whereas in Member States which are more centralized (such as Netherlands and France) this role may be more limited. Often though (for instance in the field of environmental protection), even in centralized states the local authorities will have a role to play in a second phase: the general lines for the implementation of the directive are set at national level (in a statute, or government order), and the application and enforcement will be left to regional or local authorities.[50] As was said above, each Member State has the freedom to allocate powers in implementing directives (or regulations) within its domestic legal system as it considers fit, but that internal allocation of powers will not release the State from the obligation to ensure that the provisions of the directive concerned are properly implemented in national law.[51]

The form and methods of implementation of the result to be achieved must be chosen in a manner which ensures that the directive functions effectively, account being taken of its aims. A firm line of case law makes it clear that each Member

---

48. Case C-129/96, *Inter-Environnement Wallonie*, para. 45; Case C-422/05, *Commission v. Belgium*, para. 62.
49. For example, directives dealing with questions of private law are sometimes, and in some countries, transposed by means of amendments to a general Civil Code, and at other times, and in other countries, they are transposed by specific new statutes.
50. See K. Lenaerts and P. Van Nuffel, *Constitutional Law of the European Union*, 2nd ed. (London, 2005), 532–537.
51. Joined Cases 227 to 230/85, *Commission v. Belgium*.

State is obliged to implement directives in a manner which satisfies the requirement of legal certainty and thus to transpose the provisions of the directive into
national provisions having binding force,[52] which must also be enforceable *vis-à-
vis* private parties where appropriate.[53] Transposition need not necessarily require
enactment in precisely the same words in an express legal provision; thus appropriate existing measures may be sufficient, as long as the full application of the
directive is assured in a sufficiently clear and precise manner to ensure legal
certainty.[54] Mere circulars, official instructions or administrative practices,
which by their nature can always be changed as and when the authorities please
and which are not sufficiently public, are not enough to constitute proper fulfilment
of the obligation to implement directives.[55] In particular, if a directive creates
rights which may be relied on by individuals, high demands are made for the
transposition into the national legal order, so that beneficiaries may be aware of
their rights and can exercise them before their national courts if necessary.[56] The
implementation of social policy objectives pursued by a directive may be left by
the Member States in the first instance to management and labour, to be regulated,
say, by collective agreements; this possibility may even be explicitly mentioned in
the text of a directive,[57] but it will not discharge the Member States from their
obligation to ensure that all workers are afforded in full the protection required by
the directive (by, for instance declaring collective agreements to be binding in all
cases), so that the state guarantee forms a residual guarantee of effective protection
where this is not ensured by other means.[58] The same rules apply in areas of EC law

---

52. Case 239/85, *Commission v. Belgium;* Case C-340/96, *Commission v. United Kingdom of Great
    Britain and Northern Ireland.*
53. An example of a directive which obliges the national government to ensure that its provisions
    are enforceable, both in relation to the authorities and in relation to private parties, is Council
    Dir. 2000/78, establishing a general framework for equal treatment in employment and occu-
    pation, O.J. 2000, L 303/16, Art. 16 of which provides:

    Member States shall take the necessary measures to ensure that:

    (a) any laws, regulations and administrative provisions contrary to the principle of
        equal treatment are abolished;
    (b) any provisions contrary to the principle of equal treatment which are included in
        contracts or collective agreements, internal rules of undertakings or rules govern-
        ing the independent occupations and professions and workers' and employers'
        organisations are, or may be, declared null and void or are amended.

54. Case C-360/87, *Commission v. Italy*; Case C-131/88, *Commission v. Germany*; and Case C-190/
    90, *Commission v. The Netherlands.*
55. This is very often repeated in the Court's case law; see, for example, Case 102/79, *Commission v.
    Belgium*; Case 80/92, *Commission v. Belgium*; Case C-296/01, *Commission v. France*; Case
    C-132/04, *Commission v. Spain.*
56. E.g., Case C-361/88, *Commission v. Germany.*
57. E.g., Art. 18 of Dir. 2000/78 establishing a general framework for equal treatment in employ-
    ment and occupation, O.J. 2000, L 303/16.
58. Case 143/83, *Commission v. Denmark*; Case 235/84, *Commission v. Italy*; Case C-430/98,
    Commission v. Luxembourg.

other than employment law for implementation by means of covenants and self-regulation by private organizations.[59]

The direct effect of provisions of directives and their application in general by national courts is discussed in detail in Chapter VI. Here it should merely be noted that the possibility for private parties to rely, in certain cases, on a provision of a directive before a national court, does not discharge a Member State from the obligation to adopt appropriate implementing measures within the period prescribed in the directive.[60]

1.4   DECISIONS

Decisions are the means by which the Community adopts individual administrative acts, in other words, they are the means by which Community law is applied in specific cases. Given the fact that the Commission is the principal executive organ of the EU, most of these individual decisions emanate from the Commission, but there are also decisions adopted by other institutions and bodies, such as the Council or one of the EC's agencies. Decisions are binding in all respects on their addressees.[61] They can be addressed to Member States[62] or to private parties. Decisions addressed to one or all Member States are a frequently used instrument for indirect Community administration, which in some cases resembles the use of directives. As for decisions addressed to private parties, there are many types of these, just as in national administrative law. Some decisions authorize parties to do things, for instance Commission decisions authorizing a planned merger under the Merger Regulation. Other decisions may impose obligations, for example where a Member State is required to abolish or modify a particular state aid measure because it infringes the prohibition contained in Article 87 EC,[63] or a decision requiring undertakings to put an end to an infringement of the competition rules.

Private parties have the right to bring an action for annulment before the Court of First Instance (and in appeal before the Court of Justice) against a decision addressed to that party, or against a decision which, although addressed to another natural or legal person, is of direct and individual concern to the former.[64] The Court of First Instance and the Court of Justice are however also prepared to qualify an EC act which is not formally called a decision as a 'decision' in the context of an action for annulment. This possibility of 're-qualification' is explicitly offered by Article 230, fourth paragraph EC, as far as regulations are concerned: a natural or

---

59. Case C-340/96, *Commission v. United Kingdom.*
60. Case 102/79 *Commission v. Belgium,* and Case C-197/96, *Commission v. France.*
61. Art. 249 EC, 4th para.
62. In which case they are binding on all organs of the Member States concerned, including, therefore, national courts, Case 249/85, *Albako Margarinefabrik Maria von der Linde v. Bundesanstalt für landwirtschaftliche Marktordnung.*
63. Art. 88(2) EC.
64. Art. 230 EC 4th para.

legal person may bring an action against 'a decision which, although in the form of a regulation' is of direct and individual concern to the former.

A characteristic feature of a decision is considered by the Court to be the limitation of the persons to whom the decision 'is addressed'; it applies to a limited number of specified or identifiable natural or legal persons.[65] Although this does not appear to be prescribed as a formal requirement in the legal definition ('addressed' need not mean 'specified'), as a rule a decision will be recognizable by the fact that it mentions by name the persons to whom it 'is addressed'.

The case law of the Court of First Instance and the Court of Justice has frequently dealt with the problem of how to distinguish a decision from non-binding communications, opinions or recommendations, in the context of Article 230 EC. A decisive point is the Court's definition of a decision as 'a measure emanating from the competent authority, intended to produce legal effects and constituting the culmination of procedure within that authority, whereby the latter gives its final ruling in a form from which its nature can be identified'.[66] The judgments relating to whether these conditions have been met is also strongly casuistic in nature; the Court appears to be heavily influenced by the importance which a positive or negative answer may have for the legal protection of private parties.

Decisions may also, on occasion – just like regulations – require national implementing measures. Decisions addressed to Member States may contain an authorization, a prohibition, or a refusal to grant an authorization, and this then leads to the adoption, abolition, or non-adoption of national rules.

1.5   OTHER EC INSTRUMENTS

The list of legal instruments given in Articles 249 EC is not exhaustive. In addition to the three instruments possessing binding force mentioned in Article 249 EC, there is a fourth category of instruments with binding force which – for want of a better term – are often referred to, in English, as decisions '*sui generis*' or 'addressee-less decisions'.[67]

---

65. Cases 16 & 17/62, *Confédération Nationale des producteurs de fruits et légumes*, at 478 of the English edition.
66. Case 54/65, *Compagnie des Forges de Châtillon, Commentry & Neuves-Maisons v. High Authority of the ECSC* at 195 of the English edition.
67. These instruments are called in English 'decisions', and in French '*décisions*' (and published under that name in the O.J.), but in other languages there is a separate name for them. In German, for example, the 'decisions' in the sense of Art. 249 EC are called *Entscheidung*, whereas the decisions referred to in this section are called *Beschluβ*, which shows that they are truly different legal instruments. Because of the lack of a separate term, the decision-*Beschluβ* is often not perceived, and wrongly so, as a separate legal instrument in the English and French language literature.

These decisions *sui generis* play an important and often underestimated role in EC law.[68] Obviously, they cannot be used when the Treaty prescribes the use of another instrument, for instance a directive. In practice, they are used for the enactment of detailed institutional arrangements in the internal operation of the European Union, such as in laying down rules of procedure or setting up new committees or new administrative bodies. Such acts are adopted by one or more of the Institutions, depending on the subject matter.[69] The adoption of the budget also takes the form of a decision *sui generis*, as well as the acts through which the Council approves international agreements.[70] *Sui generis* decisions are also used for the adoption of multi-annual 'action programmes' in all kinds of policy areas, such as the *Socrates* programme for mobility of students and teachers.[71] Such action programmes provide for Community (co-)financing of certain projects; they do not explicitly oblige the Member States to amend their domestic legislation (in that case a directive or regulation would be more appropriate), but in practice an amendment of domestic legislation may be necessary in order to allow unimpeded application of the relevant action programme.

Other acts deserving special attention are those by which the Treaty is modified in certain aspects,[72] or rules are laid down which take the place of Treaty rules whose validity has come to an end, such as acts under Article 187 EC in respect of the application and procedure of association with overseas countries and territories. These acts regulate the subject-matter after the expiry of the

---

68. Among academic writers who have drawn attention to this legal instrument, see A. von Bogdandy, J. Bast and F. Arndt, 'Legal Instruments in European Union Law and Their Reform: A Systematic Approach on an Empirical Basis' (2004) *Yearbook of European Law*, 91, 103–106.

69. For example, Council Decision of 28 Jun. 1999, laying down the procedures for the exercise of implementing powers conferred on the Commission, O.J. 1999, L 184/23 (this is the very important 'Comitology' decision, on which see section 3.2 *infra* of this chapter); Commission Decision of 11 Nov. 2003 on establishing the European Regulators Group for Electricity and Gas, O.J. 2003, L 296/34; Commission Decision of 14 Jan. 2005 setting up the Education, Audiovisual and Culture Executive Agency, O.J. 2005, L 24/35. An example of an institutional act adopted by various institutions and bodies is the Decision of the European Parliament, the Council, the Commission, the Court of Justice, the Court of Auditors, the Economic and Social Committee and the Committee of the Regions of 20 Jul. 2000 on the organization and operation of the Office for Official Publications of the European Communities, O.J. 2000, L 183/12.

70. See, alongside numerous other examples, the Council Decision of 7 Nov. 2000 concerning the conclusion, on behalf of the Community, of the Convention for the Protection of the Rhine, O.J. 2000, L 289/30 (the text of the convention itself is published in the Official Journal as an attachment to the decision).

71. Decision No. 253/2000/EC of the European Parliament and of the Council of 24 Jan. 2000 establishing the second phase of the Community action programme in the field of education 'Socrates', O.J. 2000, L 28/1. The 'Socrates' decision was recently succeeded by Decision No. 1720/2006 of the European Parliament and of the Council of 15 Nov. 2006 establishing an action programme in the field of lifelong learning, O.J. 2006, L 327/45. Another example of a decision of this kind is: Decision No. 1718/2006 of the European Parliament and of the Council of 15 Nov. 2006 concerning the implementation of a programme of support for the European audiovisual sector (MEDIA 2007), O.J. 2006, L 327/12.

72. E.g., Art. 222 EC (Council's power, at the Court's request, to increase the number of Advocates General).

Implementing Convention annexed to the Treaty which applied during the first five years of the Community's existence.

The legal effect which acts *sui generis* have must always be determined by reference to the tenor of the provisions on which they are based. Thus, an act amending Article 222 EC will have the same binding force as the EC Treaty. The same applies to an act under Article 187 EC, which, however, cannot in itself alter the principles of Part IV of the EC Treaty, on which it must be based. The other acts are – like directives and regulations – secondary EC law, and thus subordinate to the provisions of the Treaty. They do have binding force, however, and are therefore published in the L series of the *Official Journal*, just like regulations and directives. This binding force applies, depending on the content of the act, either with regard to the Institutions or their component or subordinate bodies, or with regard to the Member States. In the latter case, an act may in fact contain provisions which could be relied on by private parties in the national courts. In this context, the general conditions for direct effect apply, which are discussed in Chapter VII of this book.

Article 249 EC mentions two types of *non-binding instruments* (recommendations and opinions), but in practice there are far more such instruments in use. *Opinions* are in fact not (definitive) acts, but preparatory acts which form one step in the procedure leading to the adoption of a definitive act. Most well known are the opinions on proposals for EC legislation given by the Economic and Social Committee, and the Committee of the Regions,[73] and above all the opinions given by the European Parliament – the last mentioned being given in the form of a particular legal instrument which the Parliament itself calls a 'Resolution'. Another type of opinion is the 'reasoned opinion' which forms a formal step in the framework of an infringement proceeding brought by the Commission against a Member State for failure to meet its Treaty obligations (Art. 226 EC). In addition to opinions, there are other sorts of preparatory acts which are not mentioned in Article 249 EC, but are mentioned elsewhere in the EC Treaty, and are also published in the C series of the *Official Journal*: proposals by the Commission for regulations or directives, common positions adopted by the Council in the framework of the co-decision procedure for legislation,[74] and (in the period between 1999 and 2004) initiatives by Member States for EC legislation in the area of free movement of persons, visas, asylum and immigration (Art. 67(1) EC). All these acts exist only in function of the definitive acts for which they form a preparatory step; they do not have an independent existence, and as such cannot be challenged in law.[75]

Recommendations are independent (definitive) acts. Although they do not have binding force for the Institution or Member States to which they are

---

73. See Ch. IV on these two bodies, at sections 10.1 and 10.2 respectively.
74. See Art. 251(2) EC, and section 3 *infra*.
75. It is possible to challenge the resultant act on grounds that a preparatory step was not taken, or was taken incorrectly. In this case there may be an 'infringement of an essential procedural requirement' in the sense of Art. 230 EC.

addressed, nevertheless in certain circumstances they may be an aid to interpretation of Community and national provisions.[76] Recommendations, when addressed to the Member States, act as a kind of surrogate directive: they often lay down very detailed standards and encourage the Member States to comply with them, but any 'implementing' national legislation is adopted on a voluntary basis.[77] The recommendations of the Council setting out the broad guidelines of economic policy[78] of the Member States, or concerning their employment policy[79] have a rather special character. These recommendations are the core of a method of governance which has become known as the 'open method of coordination'.[80] An indication of their semi-binding nature is the fact that they are published in the L series of the *Official Journal*.[81]

As well as the recommendations, there are – as we have said – many other types of *soft law*[82] to be found in the legal practice of the Community.

It is not unknown for *declarations* to be included in the minutes of meetings of the Council, relating to acts which have been adopted. Insofar as they contain declarations or reservations on the part of one or more members of the Council, they have no significance in the eyes of the Court of Justice.[83] If such declarations emanate from the Council itself, the Court declines to use them for the purpose of interpreting a provision of Community secondary legislation where no reference is made in the wording of the provision involved to the content of the declaration.[84] The Court has consistently held that the true meaning of rules of Community law can only be derived from those rules themselves, having regard to their content.[85] It is of course possible that a declaration or other statement in the minutes may be an aid, albeit not the only one, to interpretation of a provision which is unclear or equivocal.[86]

---

76. See Case C-322/88, *Salvatore Grimaldi v. Fonds des maladies professionnelles.*
77. See, for example, Recommendation of the European Parliament and of the Council of 20 Dec. 2006 on the protection of minors and human dignity and on the right of reply in relation to the competitiveness of the European audiovisual and on-line information services industry, O.J. 2006, L 378/72.
78. Art. 99(2), 3rd para., EC.
79. Art. 128(4) EC.
80. See European Council, Lisbon, 23 and 24 Mar. 2000, Conclusions of the Presidency, para. 37, Bull EU 2000-3.
81. See, e.g., Council recommendation of 19 Jun. 2000 on the broad guidelines of the economic policies of the Member States and the Community, O.J. 2000, L 210/1.
82. The term soft law is not official, and will not be encountered in the Official Journal. It is a commonly used term in the literature for indicating a variety of non-binding acts, which do have some kind of legal effect. See F. Snyder, 'Soft Law and Institutional Practice in the European Community', in S. Martin (ed.), *The Construction of Europe. Essays in Honour of Emile Noël* (Dordrecht, 1994), 197; L. Senden, *Soft Law in European Community Law* (Oxford, 2004).
83. See Case 38/69, *Commission v. Italy*. See W. Nicoll, 'Note the Hour and File the Minute' (1993) *Journal of Common Market Studies*, 559.
84. Case C-292/89, *The Queen v. Immigration Appeal Tribunal, ex parte Gustaff Desiderius.*
85. Case 237/84, *Commission v. Belgium.*
86. See Opinion of A.G. Darmon, in Case C-292/89, *The Queen v. Immigration Appeal Tribunal*. See also Case 136/78, *Ministère public v. Vincent Auer.*

Resolutions are the chosen form for acts of the European Parliament, both with regard to its contribution to the Community legislative process (opinions, amendments, rejection), and for political declarations. The Council also makes use of resolutions form time to time, for instance in order to lay down the principles of Community action in a certain area, when it does not have the competence to set binding rules, or in a period where it does not (yet) have sufficient political support for binding measures.[87] Resolutions thereby help to shape the Council's policy in a given area. Resolutions can generally only have binding force if they are intended to have legal effects and, moreover, if the power to attach such legal effects is conferred by or through the Treaties.[88] Usually it will be clear simply from the name 'resolutions' that the first of these two conditions is not fulfilled. The Court of Justice regards these resolutions as expressions of the Council's political will and nothing more: the failure to comply with such a resolution cannot in itself give rise to an infringement of Community law;[89] thus private parties cannot rely on such a resolution,[90] nor can it be invoked against them.[91] Resolutions can, though, be an aid to the interpretation of legal acts of the Institutions[92] designed to give effect to them.

Yet another category consists of the (non-binding) *notices, communications, guidelines* or *frameworks* of the Commission, in which this Institution sets out the framework for reviewing individual cases, for example in the field of competition and state aid, or describes the kind of Member State measures or behaviour which it considers to be compatible with Community law in a given area (such as the internal market freedoms).[93] Although these legal instruments do not have any intrinsic binding force with regard to private parties, and they cannot deviate from the Treaty or secondary law,[94] they can – in combination with the principle of legitimate expectations – impose a self-limitation on the Commission with regard to its individual decisional practice in the area covered by the guideline or notice.[95]

---

87. See A. von Bogdandy et al., 'Legal Instruments in European Union Law and their Reform: A Systematic Approach on an Empirical Basis' (2004) YEL, 91, 115–117.
88. E.g., the Court of Justice recognized the binding force of Annex VI of the Hague Resolution of 3 Nov. 1976 on the introduction of a fisheries zone: Case 141/78, *France v. United Kingdom*, and Case 32/79, *Commission v. United Kingdom*. Resolutions of the European Parliament may also have such legal effects, in particular when based on its power to regulate its own internal affairs, see Joined Cases C-213/88 & 39/89, *Luxembourg v. European Parliament*.
89. Joined Cases 90 & 91/63, *Commission v. Luxembourg and Belgium*.
90. Case 9/73, *Carl Schlüter v. Hauptzollamt Lörrach*.
91. Case 59/75, *Manghera*.
92. Case 43/72, *Merkur Außenhandel-GmbH & Co. v. Commission*.
93. Examples include: Commission Notice on Guidelines on the applicability of Art. 81 of the EC Treaty to horizontal cooperation agreements, O.J. 2001, C 3/2; Community Guidelines on State aid for rescuing and restructuring firms in difficulty, O.J. 1999, 288/2; Community framework for State aid in the form of public service compensation, O.J. 2005, C 297/4.
94. Case C-169/95, *Spain v. Commission*.
95. See, e.g., Joined Cases C-189/02 P, C-202/02 P, C-205/02 P to C-208/02 P & C-213/02 P *Dansk Rørindustri and others v. Commission*, in relation to the Commission's fining policy in competition cases.

Finally, there is a category of instruments which play an increasingly important role in regulating the relations between the EU Institutions in the legislative and budgetary field, namely the Interinstitutional Agreements (IIAs). As the name indicates, these are agreements concluded between two or more of the EU Institutions. They are intended to smooth the operation of the interinstitutional process by adding more detailed rules of behaviour to the often very laconic Treaty language. Among the main illustrations are the Agreements of 29 October 1993 and 6 May 1999 on budgetary discipline and the improvement of the budgetary procedure,[96] replaced by the currently applicable IIA on budgetary discipline and sound financial management of 2006;[97] the Interinstitutional Declaration of 25 October 1993 on democracy, transparency and subsidiarity and the IIA (annexed thereto) on procedures for implementing the principle of subsidiarity,[98] and the IIA on better law-making of 2003.[99] These agreements are usually published in the C series of the *Official Journal*, and do not create legal obligations for third parties. Between the Institutions themselves, the agreements may or may not have binding legal force,[100] but they certainly are considered by their signatories as authoritative guidance for their action. The practice of IIAs was confirmed by Declaration No. 3 attached to the Treaty of Nice, although here the Member States implied that such agreements can only be concluded by all three Institutions (Council, Commission and Parliament), while in practice sometimes agreements are concluded between only two of these Institutions. The legal significance of the Joint Declaration of the European Parliament, the Council and the Commission of 5 April 1977 on fundamental rights[101] was different again; it supported the case law of the Court on the subject and enabled, in cases of doubt, an interpretation of legal acts of the Institutions to be given by the Court which was in conformity with fundamental rights. The more recent Charter of Fundamental Rights of the European Union, which was launched through a 'solemn proclamation' by the presidents of the Commission, the Council and the European Parliament on 7 December 2000, could be considered as an IIA, although that term is not used in the text of the Charter or its preamble.[102]

---

96. O.J. 1993, C 331/1 and O.J. 1999, C 172/1. The 1999 Agreement replaced that of 1993.
97. O.J. 2006, C 139/1. See *infra*, section 4, on the role of these agreements in the budgetary procedure.
98. Bull. EU 10-1993 point 2.2.1 (approved by the European Parliament O.J. 1993, C 329/132)
99. O.J. 2003, C 321/1.
100. This is a controversial point. On the practice of IIAs, and their legal qualification, see J. Monar, 'Interinstitutional Agreements: The Phenomenon and its New Dynamics after Maastricht' (1994) CML Rev., 693–719; F. Snyder, 'Interinstitutional Agreements: Forms and Constitutional Limitations', in G. Winter (ed.), *Sources and Categories of European Law* (Baden-Baden, 1996), 453–466, C. Bobbert, *Interinstitutionelle Vereinbarungen im Europäischen Gemeinschaftsrecht* (Frankfurt, 2001); F. von Alemann, *Die Handlungsform der interinstitutionellen Vereinbarung* (Berlin, 2006); I. Eiselt and P. Slominski, 'Sub-constitutional Engineering: Negotiation, Content, and Legal Value of Interinstitutional Agreements in the EU' (2006) *European Law Journal*, 209–225; B. Driessen, *Interinstitutional Conventions in EU Law* (London, 2007).
101. O.J. 1977, C 103/1. See Ch. VI, section 1.4, *infra*.
102. O.J. 2000, C 364/1.

1.6   LEGAL INSTRUMENTS OF THE SECOND AND THIRD PILLARS OF THE
                        EUROPEAN UNION

When new forms of cooperation between the Member States were set up outside
the existing framework of the EC by the Treaty of Maastricht, in the fields of
common foreign and security policy (Second Pillar) and of justice and home affairs
(JHA, Third Pillar), the Member States decided to use a whole new terminology for
the legal instruments which were to be used in the framework of these new policy
areas. In this 'EU law' domain – which developed outside the tried and tested
framework of the European Communities – regulations and directives are not used,
but instead instruments which carry different names, and whose legal nature is
different. The only instrument which occurs in all three pillars is the 'decision' in
the sense of *Beschluss*.[103] As explained in the preceding section, these decisions *sui
generis* are not mentioned as such in the EC Treaty, but frequently used in practice.
In the field of foreign and security policy, something similar happens, in the sense
that a 'decision' is not included in the list of instruments set out for the Second
Pillar – though it is mentioned in other EU Treaty articles, and is used in practice. In
the Third Pillar (since the changes made by the Treaty of Amsterdam), decisions
are mentioned as 'official' legal instruments explicitly in the EU Treaty, and fulfil
a specific role.

Binding instruments of the Second and Third Pillars, and also some preparatory acts and non-binding instruments, are published in the *Official Journal*,[104] in a
separate section, entitled 'Acts adopted pursuant to Title V [or Title VI] of the
Treaty on European Union'.

Article 12 TEU lists the means by which the *Common Foreign and Security
Policy* (Second Pillar) should be given form:[105]

The Union shall pursue the objectives set out in Article 11 by:

- defining the principles of and general guidelines for the common foreign
  and security policy;
- deciding on common strategies;
- adopting joint actions;
- adopting common positions;
- strengthening systematic cooperation between Member States in the conduct of policy.

This article, unlike Article 249 EC, is not a pure list of legal instruments. It contains
a strange mixture of political working methods (the general guidelines and

---

103. See section 1.5, *supra*.
104. See Art. 17 Rules of Procedure of the Council, O.J. 2006, L 285/55.
105. See, e.g., R.A. Wessel, *The European Union's Foreign and Security Policy: A Legal Institu-
     tional Perspective* (The Hague, 1999), Ch. 5 for a thorough study of the legal nature of the acts
     under the Second Pillar, with examples from practice; see also P. Koutrakos, *EU International
     Relations Law* (Oxford, 2005), 393–404.

systematic cooperation) and formal legal instruments (common strategies, joint actions and common positions). It is the European Council which, according to Article 13(1) and (2) TEU, defines the principles and general guidelines and decides on common strategies; however, whereas the former are included in the informal 'Presidency conclusions' of the European Council, the latter are adopted as formal acts by the European Council on a proposal by the Council,[106] and published in the L series of the *Official Journal*.

The *common strategies* were introduced by the Treaty of Amsterdam, as opposed to the other two kinds of acts, which were already provided for in the Treaty of Maastricht. The Treaty of Amsterdam therefore introduced a hierarchical structure in the Second Pillar, since now in Article 13(3) TEU, it is provided that the Council implements the common strategies adopted by the European Council 'by adopting joint actions and common positions'. However, common strategies were decided by the European Council only for a few areas of foreign policy immediately after the entry into force of the Amsterdam amendments,[107] and have since fallen in disuse, so that for the most part the situation is the same as before the Treaty of Amsterdam, with policy being brought into effect solely by means of joint actions and common positions without any underlying common strategy.

Joint actions 'address specific situations where operational action by the Union is deemed to be required' (Art. 14(1) TEU). This intends a concrete 'foreign' action of the EU,[108] or measures of a financial nature,[109] although in practice the joint action instrument has also been used to set up specialized EU bodies, such as the European Defence Agency,[110] which can be called an 'operational action' only with some stretch of the imagination. *Common positions* on the other hand are not operational; Article 15 TEU states – rather vaguely – that in these common positions, the 'approach of the Union to a particular matter of a geographical or thematic nature' is defined. This 'approach' may later lead to specific operational measures: for instance, sanctions are usually adopted by means of common positions,[111] which are then actually implemented by an act of the EC (insofar as

---

106. Art. 13(3) TEU.
107. Only three common strategies have been adopted, all with a geographical focus: common strategy of 4 Jun. 1999 on Russia, O.J. 1999, L 157/1; common strategy of 11 Dec. 1999 on the Ukraine, O.J. 1999, L 331/1; common strategy of 19 Jun. 2000 on the Mediterranean, O.J. 2000, L 183/5.
108. E.g., Joint Action of 29 Jun. 1999 Council Joint Action of 29 Jul. 1999 concerning the installation of the structures of the United Nations Mission in Kosovo (UNMIK), O.J. 1999, L 201/1.
109. Council Joint Action of 16 Nov. 2000 on the holding of a meeting of Heads of State or of Government in Zagreb (Zagreb Summit), O.J. 2000, L 290/54.
110. Council Joint Action of 12 Jul. 2004 on the establishment of the European Defence Agency, O.J. 2004, L 245/17.
111. E.g., Council Common Position 98/240 of 19 Mar. 1998 on restrictive measures against the Federal Republic of Yugoslavia, O.J. 1998, L 95/1; Council Common Position 2001/931 on the application of specific measures to combat terrorism, O.J. 2001, L 344/90 (many times amended since).

economic sanctions are concerned: see Art. 301 EC) or by national measures (whether or not preceded by an EU implementing act).[112]

These three kinds of instrument are all binding on Member States. This is expressed very explicitly as far as the joint actions are concerned: according to Article 14(3) TEU, they 'commit the Member States in the positions they adopt and in the conduct of their activity'. As for common positions, it is stated that the Member States must 'ensure that their national policies conform to the common positions' (Art. 15 TEU). Given the nature of these common positions, this does not usually entail a concrete obligation to act or refrain from action, apart from the fact that the Member States (under Art. 19 TEU) are obliged to uphold the EU common positions in international organizations and at international conferences. Finally, the binding nature of the common strategies is indirectly apparent from the fact that they form the basis for binding actions or positions adopted by the Council.

Just as in EC law, one also sees in the practice of the Council the use of legal instruments not specifically listed – as such – in the EU Treaty, and in particular the *sui generis* 'decisions', which are binding acts used for the implementation of joint actions and common positions,[113] or for the institutional arrangements of the EU's external policy.[114] Binding decisions of this kind are even taken by the Council's subsidiary body in the field of Common Foreign and Security Policy (CFSP), the Political and Security Committee.[115]

In all these cases, there seems little likelihood of direct effect in the national legal order. Rights – and above all obligations – for private individuals seem to be created only after implementation of the EU acts by the national authorities. Disputes as to the possible direct effect of Second Pillar instruments may be brought before the national courts, which should decide on this themselves on the basis of their own relevant constitutional rules. The Court of Justice, it should be recalled, does not have jurisdiction for the interpretation of CFSP acts.

In order to obtain a complete picture of the instruments of the CFSP, it should also be noted that in addition to the above-mentioned binding instruments, the Council and the European Council often adopt non-binding acts. Nearly every day, the Presidency and the High Representative for the CFSP make declarations about the political situation in all corners of the world, which can be consulted on the website of the Council.[116]

As for the legal instruments of the Third Pillar, here a clear distinction is apparent between the periods before and after the entry into force of the Treaty

---

112. For a general analysis of the EU sanctions policy, see Ch. XIII, External relations.
113. See, e.g., Council Decision of 10 Nov. 2000 implementing Common Position 2000/696/CFSP concerning the maintenance of specific restrictive measures against Mr Milosevic and persons associated with him, O.J. 2000, L 287/2.
114. E.g., Council Decision of 10 May 1999 concerning the arrangements for enhanced cooperation between the European Union and the Western European Union, O.J. 1999, L 153/1.
115. See, e.g., the Political and Security Committee Decision of 25 Sep. 2007 on the appointment of the EU Force Commander for the European Union military operation in Bosnia and Herzegovina, O.J. 2007, L 288/60.
116. <www.consilium.europa.eu>.

of Amsterdam. In the Treaty of Maastricht, the area of activities of the Third Pillar was defined as 'cooperation in the fields of JHA' (heading for Title VI in its original version), and the legal instruments closely resembled those created for the Second Pillar. The instruments for cooperation in JHA were named: *joint positions, joint action* and in addition *conventions* between the Member States.[117] The two former instruments turned out not to be very practical in reality. The difference between them was not really clear, and their legal nature (above all the question of their binding force) was subject to much dispute. In the Treaty of Amsterdam, the content of the Third Pillar was narrowed (since then it covers 'police and judicial cooperation in criminal matters'). The instrument of *conventions* was retained: these are not unilateral acts of the EU, but are international treaties, and therefore are discussed separately (in section 1.7 below). Joint positions were in effect retained, but re-baptized 'common positions'. *Joint action* was abolished and replaced by two new instruments: framework decisions and decisions.

The nature of these legal instruments is today described in Article 34(2) TEU.[118] *Common positions* are comparable with the instrument with the same name in the Second Pillar: they define 'the approach of the Union to a particular matter'. The two other legal instruments created by the Treaty of Amsterdam are nearer to EC law. *Framework decisions* are clearly related to EC directives. Framework decisions have the purpose 'of approximation of the laws and regulations of the Member States' in the area of police and judicial cooperation in criminal matters. They are playing an important role as an instrument for harmonizing criminal procedure and even substantive criminal law.[119] Framework decisions are 'binding upon the Member States as to the result to be achieved but shall leave to the national authorities the choice of form and methods'. After this definition, it is explicitly stated, however, that they do not have direct effect. In this way, the Member States try to exclude the possibility that in interpreting framework decisions the Court of Justice may transpose its case law on EC directives, where – as is well known – there is a certain (limited) direct effect. However, this exclusion of direct effect does not alter the fact that framework decisions, like directives, impose a duty on Member States to take all measures that are necessary for the correct and complete implementation at the national level. Although the Commission cannot bring an infringement action before the Court of Justice for failure to implement (correctly) a framework decision, it has developed a system of monitoring and assessing Member State compliance in this area.[120] Furthermore, the Court of Justice held, in *Pupino*,[121] that the national courts have a duty to interpret

---

117. Art. K.3(2) TEU, Maastricht version.
118. See S. Peers, *EU Justice and Home Affairs Law*, 2nd ed. (Oxford, 2006), 31–37.
119. E.g., Council framework Decision of 29 May 2000 on increasing protection by criminal penalties and other sanctions against counterfeiting in connection with the introduction of the euro, O.J. 2000, L 140/1; Council Framework Decision of 13 Jun. 2002 on combating terrorism, O.J. 2002, L 164/3; Council Framework Decision of 13 Jun. 2002 on the European arrest warrant and the surrender procedures between Member States, O.J. 2002, L 190/1.
120. See M.J. Borgers, 'Implementing Framework Decisions' (2007) CML Rev., 1361–1386.
121. Case C-105/03, *Pupino*.

their national law in conformity with framework decisions, as far as they can, which may come close in practice to framework decisions having direct effect within the national legal order.

In addition to common positions and framework decisions, the Third Pillar uses *decisions*,[122] which have a residual character: they may be used 'for any other purpose consistent with the objectives of this Title'. A decision is binding on the Member States, but also lacks direct effect within the national legal orders. Finally, the Council also uses soft law instruments in the Third Pillar, in particular *resolutions*.[123]

It should once more be recalled that important parts of the policy area which prior to the Treaty of Amsterdam belonged to the Third Pillar, were transferred by that Treaty to the 'First Pillar' (the EC Treaty): asylum, immigration, visas and judicial cooperation in civil matters.[124] This means that in these areas, from the entry into force of the Treaty of Amsterdam all the EC instruments described above were used,[125] although the Third Pillar acts adopted before 1 May 1999 remained in force insofar as they were not replaced by new EC acts.

1.7   ACTS OF THE EUROPEAN COUNCIL; INTERNATIONAL TREATIES
            BETWEEN MEMBER STATES

The results of the deliberations of the European Council are published in the form of 'Conclusions of the Presidency', in the Bulletin of the European Union (and placed on the EU website), but not in the *Official Journal*. These conclusions are not formal acts of an Institution, and therefore do not have binding force. Nevertheless, in addition to a number of inconsequential but politically desirable statements, the conclusions contain important policy guidelines which are subsequently translated into binding legal instruments by the other Institutions according to the rules and procedures laid down in the EC or EU Treaty.

---

122. E.g., Council Decision of 22 Dec. 2000 establishing a European Police College (CEPOL), O.J. 2000, L 336/1; Council Decision of 28 Feb. 2002 setting up Eurojust, O.J. 2002, L 63/1.
123. E.g., Council resolution of 21 Jun. 1999 concerning a handbook for international police cooperation and measures to prevent and control violence and disturbances in connection with international football matches, O.J. 1999, C 196/1; Council resolution of 27 Nov. 2003 on combating the impact of psychoactive substances use on road accidents, O.J. 2004, C 97/1.
124. Arts. 61–69 EC. See P.J. Kuijper, 'Some Legal Problems Associated with the Communitarization of Policy on Visas, Asylum and Immigration under the Amsterdam Treaty and Incorporation of the Schengen Acquis' (2000) CML Rev., 345–366.
125. One example for each of the general EC instruments: Council Decision of 28 Sep. 2000 establishing a European Refugee Fund, O.J. 2000, L 252/12; Council Reg. (EC) No. 44/2001 of 22 Dec. 2000 on jurisdiction and the recognition and enforcement of judgments in civil and commercial matters, O.J. 2001, L 12/1; Council Dir. 2004/83 of 29 Apr. 2004 on minimum standards for the qualification and status of third country nationals or stateless persons as refugees or as persons who otherwise need international protection and the content of the protection granted, O.J. 2004, L 304/12.

In addition to the general conclusions, which are formulated by the Presidency of the European Council (after having made sure that the other Member States do not raise objections), the European Council also occasionally adopts formal decisions.[126] The Treaty of Amsterdam has bestowed concrete tasks on the European Council, which are fulfilled by means of formal decisions: the above-mentioned common strategies in the field of foreign policy (see section 1.6 above), and the (non-binding) conclusions on economic policy[127] and employment.[128] In addition, with regard to the Economic and Monetary Union (EMU), a specific role is accorded the 'Council, meeting in the composition of the Heads of State or Government'.[129] This is not the same body as the European Council (for the reason that the European Council also includes the President of the Commission), but in practice these EMU decisions are taken during a meeting of the European Council – and for these points, the President of the Commission does not take part in the deliberations. The same 'Council, meeting in the composition of the Heads of State or Government' was given a formal role by the Treaty of Amsterdam with regard to serious breaches of fundamental rights and other fundamental principles by a Member State.[130]

In addition to these binding acts which are provided by the Treaty texts, the European Council in practice adopts other decisions and acts with various names and frequently a rather uncertain legal character. The European Council often adopts *resolutions* or makes *declarations*.[131] Moreover, the European Council adopted a decision in June 1999 in Cologne, which set in motion the process leading to an EU Charter of Fundamental Rights[132] (the Charter itself was not adopted by the European Council, but by means of a 'Solemn Proclamation' of the Commission, Parliament and Council jointly).

Another, often overlooked, legal instrument of the European process of integration consists of the *treaties and conventions concluded by the Member States jointly*, which concern subjects connected with the substance of the EC Treaty or the EU Treaty.[133] These may be of great importance for the realization of the

---

126. See A. Dashwood, 'Decision-making at the Summit' (2000) *Cambridge Yearbook of European Legal Studies*, 79.
127. Art. 99(2), 2nd para., EC.
128. Art. 128(1) EC.
129. Arts. 121 and 122 EC.
130. Art. 7(2) TEU.
131. Cf., e.g., the important Resolution of 5 Dec. 1978 on the introduction of the EMS, Bull. EC 12-1987, 10 et. seq.; the Declaration on Democracy (Copenhagen European Council), Bull. EC 4-1978, 5; the EU Declaration on Globalisation, in annex to the European Council Conclusions of 14 Dec. 2007.
132. European Council Decision on the drawing up of a Charter of Fundamental Rights of the European Union. Annexe IV to the Presidency Conclusions of the Cologne European Council of 3–4 Jun. 1999, Bull. EU 6-99.
133. For a more thorough treatment of this instrument, see B. de Witte, 'Chameleonic Member States: Differentiation by Means of Partial and Parallel International Agreements', in B. de Witte, D. Hanf and E. Vos (eds), *The Many Faces of Differentiation in EU Law* (Antwerpen, 2001), 231–267.

objectives of the EU or the EC, and are concluded precisely with this in mind. Both the EC and the EU treaties explicitly provide for this possibility. In the EC Treaty, Article 293 EC refers to this instrument. This Article provides for further treaties between the Member States in the following areas: abolition of double taxation within the Community, the mutual recognition of companies or firms within the meaning of Article 48, second paragraph EC, the retention of legal personality in the event of transfer of a company's seat from one country to another, and the possibility of mergers between companies or firms governed by the laws of different countries, and the simplification of formalities governing the reciprocal recognition and enforcement of judgments of courts or tribunals and of arbitration awards. Only three treaties have come into being on this basis: the Convention of 27 February 1968 on the Mutual Recognition of Companies and Firms,[134] the Convention of 27 September 1968 on Jurisdiction and the Enforcement of Judgments in Civil and Commercial Matters (usually called the Brussels Convention)[135] and the Convention of 23 July 1990 on the Elimination of Double Taxation in connection with the adjustment of profits of associated enterprises.[136]

In addition, the EU Treaty also provides for the possibility of conventions being concluded between the Member States, in all areas covered by the Third Pillar. In the years following the entry into force of the Treaty of Maastricht, the Treaty which had introduced this provision, a large number of such conventions were concluded, but only one of these actually entered into force, which was the Europol Convention.[137] Since the entry into force of the Treaty of Amsterdam (1 May 1999), the scope of the Third Pillar has been considerably reduced, and thereby also the area in which such conventions may be concluded. The Institutions of the European Union play a specific role in the establishment of such conventions. Thus, the text of Third Pillar conventions is first established by an act of the Council, and then – the same day – signed by the representatives of the Member States (who are usually in fact the same people). The Council also often has a role to play in the implementation and application of such conventions.

Even without a link to a specific provision of the EC or EU Treaty, the Member States are free in principle to regulate certain matters which are connected to the substance of the treaties, and which are important for the achievement of their objectives, in an international agreement.[138] They can however only do this to the extent that Community law has left the regulation of these matters within their competence, and taking into account their general underlying obligation of loyal cooperation under Article 10 EC, and their specific obligations on the basis of existing primary and secondary EC or EU law (the principle of primacy). If an

---

134. Bull EC Suppl. 2/1969. This treaty has never entered into force.
135. O.J. 1972, L 299/32. Now replaced by EC Reg. 44/2001, O.J. 2001, L 12/1, except with regard to Denmark (the Regulation does not apply to Denmark, so the Convention remains in force in relation to that country).
136. O.J. 1990, L 225/10.
137. Convention on the establishment of a European Police Office, O.J. 1995, C 316/1 (entered into force 1 Oct. 1998).
138. Joined Cases C-181 & 248/91, *Parliament v. Council and Commission (Bangladesh).*

agreement concluded between the Member States were an impediment to the application of a provision of Community law, or to the proper functioning of the Institutions, then the Member States in question would be acting in breach of their obligations under Article 10 EC.[139] In that case the Commission may start proceedings for infringement of Treaty obligations against them.[140] International agreements between the Member States cannot be annulled by the Court of Justice, however, since annulment proceedings only cover actions of the Institutions (see text of Art. 230 EC). The Court has recognized its own jurisdiction to reclassify what appears to be an international agreement as an act of the Council, if the subject matter concerned falls within the exclusive competence of the Community. In such matters, after all, the Member States have forfeited their competence to conclude international agreements, and an action which they qualify as such must in fact be seen as an act of the Council, which is then subject to the applicable decision-making procedure and judicial review by the Court of Justice.[141] It may be deduced from this that the body of Member States as a whole cannot avoid judicial review by concluding international agreements in an area which belongs to the exclusive competence of the Community.

A less clearly identifiable category of legal acts is that of the 'acts of the representatives of the governments of the Member States meeting within the Council'. These 'acts of the representatives' must be clearly distinguished from acts of the Council, since they do not originate from a Community Institution, but from a diplomatic conference, although the latter has the same composition as the Council. This formal distinction between decisions of government representatives as members of an Institution (decisions of the Council) and decisions taken by these representatives as such by general agreement ('acts of the representatives') is legally significant. The rules governing the adoption of decisions of the Community Institutions, their legal effects, implementation and judicial review cannot apply to 'acts of the representatives'. The questions which may arise in this context will largely have to be answered, as far as the 'acts of the representatives' are concerned, by general international law.

Broadly speaking, two categories of cases may be distinguished, which in practice have led to the use of 'acts of the representatives'. The *first* category concerns cases in which Treaty provisions direct the governments to adopt a collective legal act for the implementation of those provisions, such as the appointment of the members of the Commission[142] and the members of the Court of Justice,[143] and determining the seat of the Institutions.[144] The *second* category

---

139. Case 44/84, *Derrick Guy Edmund Hurd v. Kenneth Jones (Her Majesty's Inspector of Taxes)*. The Court recalled, however, that this prohibition under Art. 10 EC is directed at the Member States and does not have direct effect. Private individuals may not rely on this provision in national courts.
140. Under Art. 226 EC.
141. Joined Cases C-181 & C-248/91 *Parliament v. Council and Commission*.
142. Art. 214 EC.
143. Art. 223 EC.
144. Art. 289 EC.

relates to cases in which the governments make use collectively of the discretion allowed, or allowed for the present, by the Treaties to each individual Member State to regulate a given subject-matter on its own initiative, with a view to a proper implementation of the Treaties or the realization of their objectives. An old example is the so-called acceleration decisions of 12 May 1960 and 15 May 1962.[145] On these dates, the representatives of the governments decided by general agreement to develop the customs union more rapidly than had been provided for in the EEC Treaty.[146]

The legal device of the 'acts of the representatives' was created in order to establish a simple and informal method for laying down the points agreed upon between the government representatives (usually in the margin of Council sessions) in all those cases where an act of the Council was not considered possible or opportune, and the conclusion of a formal international agreement seemed too time-consuming and laborious (in particular since such an agreement would need to be approved by the national parliaments).

Although the general term 'acts' is used – and frequently the specific acts have the title 'Decision' – there is no doubt that these are in fact international agreements,[147] although concluded in a simplified form (these are frequently referred to as 'executive agreements' in international law practice). If governments do not contemplate creating a legal obligation between the Member States, but wish to confine themselves to making each other promises concerning the policy they will follow, then they usually choose a different title, such as, for instance, 'Resolution of the representatives of the governments of the Member States meeting within the Council'.

Acts of the representatives are, however, international agreements with a strong European law element, especially where the EC Treaty directs the governments to enact collectively particular legal acts which are indissolubly linked with the functioning of the institutional system of the Communities, such as the nomination of members of the Commission and the members of the Court of Justice. The governments in such cases together carry out a task based on the Treaties and clearly defined therein, and as to which they do not have a choice as to whether or not to carry it out. The decisions taken on the basis of such a power, although not originating from an Institution within the meaning of the Treaties, form part of Community law in a broad sense, and as such are not subject to rules of national constitutional law on the conclusion of international agreements. An indication of

---

145. O.J. 1217/60 and 1284/62.
146. See old Arts. 15(2) and 24 EEC, now repealed by the Treaty of Amsterdam.
147. In some cases, perhaps doubt does arise. A well-known example is the 'Decision of the Heads of State or Government, meeting within the European Council, concerning certain problems raised by Denmark on the Treaty on European Union' (O.J. 1992, C 348/1; Bull. EC 12-1992 point I.34). This Decision dealt with the interpretation of the Treaty of Maastricht, but without modifying its text. It should probably be qualified as an agreement under international law; see D. Curtin and R. van Ooik, 'Denmark and the Edinburgh Summit: Maastricht without Tears: A Legal Analysis', in D. O'Keeffe and P. Twomey (eds), *Legal Issues of the Maastricht Treaty* (Chichester, 1994), 349–365.

the special link between these acts and the EC and EU legal order is the fact that they are taken to belong to the *acquis communautaire*. When they accede to the EU, new Member States accept that accession extends to all decisions and agreements adopted by the representatives of the Member States, meeting within the Council, and that they are in the same situation as the existing Member States in relation to 'declarations or resolutions of, or other positions taken up by, the European Council or the Council and in respect of those concerning the Community or the Union adopted by common agreement of the Member States'.[148] This provision does not, however, extend the legal scope of the measures to which it applies, and it leaves unanswered the question whether or not they have legal effects.

1.8   REFORM OF THE LEGAL INSTRUMENTS BY THE LISBON TREATY

The legal regime of EU legal instruments, as described in the previous sections of this chapter, will soon be modified if the Treaty of Lisbon enters into force. When the process of Treaty reform was started, in the framework of the Convention on the future of Europe, the question of whether and how to 'simplify' the existing system of legal instruments became prominent. A working group of the Convention was set up for this purpose, and in its final report of November 2002, that working group proposed a number of fundamental changes, in particular the abolition of the separate range of legal instruments for the Third Pillar (following logically from the proposed abolition of that pillar), a change in the denomination of the most important instruments (so that in future a legislative regulation would instead be a 'law of the EU' and a directive would be called a 'framework law of the EU'), and the introduction of a clear hierarchy between legislative and administrative (or implementing) acts.[149] These various reforms found their way into the final text of the Constitutional Treaty, but later modifications in the Lisbon Treaty meant that the new denominations 'law' and 'framework law' will not be introduced after all, and that instead the familiar instruments 'regulation' and 'directive' will be retained in their current meaning. However, other changes in the system of legal instruments have been preserved in the Lisbon Treaty, so that, if this Treaty enters into force, we will see a rather significant reform of their current regime.[150]

---

148. This formula, with small variations, was included in all Acts of Accession since 1972. The provision quoted in the text is from the Act of Accession of Bulgaria and Romania, O.J. 2005, L 157/203, Art. 3(2).

149. The European Convention, Final report of Working Group IX on Simplification, 29 Nov. 2002, CONV 42/02.

150. For commentaries on the reforms proposed in the Constitutional Treaty, see K. Lenaerts and M. Desomer, 'Towards a Hierarchy of Legal Acts in the European Union? Simplification of Legal Instruments and Procedures' (2005) *European Law Journal*, 744–765; P. Stancanelli, *Le système décisionnel de l'Union*, in G. Amato, H. Bribosia and B. de Witte (eds), *Genèse et destinée de la Constitution européenne* (Brussels, 2007), 485–543; the commentaries on Arts. I-33 to I-39, in L. Burgorgue-Larsen, A. Levade and F. Picod (eds), *Traité établissant une Constitution pour l'Europe – Commentaire article par article*, Vol. 1 (Brussels, 2007).

The most obvious change will be the disappearance of the special set of legal instruments for what is now the law of the Third Pillar. Framework decisions and conventions will no longer be available as instruments for the European Union's policy in the field of police and criminal justice cooperation. In this field, the 'mainstream' legal instruments will be used. This 'merger' of legal instruments will not be extended to what is today the Second Pillar. In the field of Common Foreign and Security Policy, regulations and directives will not be used; the main legal instrument in this field will become the *decision*, which will replace the variety of binding instruments currently in use for CFSP, namely the joint actions, common positions and decisions. This is a major terminological simplification, although it should be kept in mind that these CFSP decisions will be used for a variety of different purposes[151] corresponding to the purposes for which, today, different CFSP instruments are used. In this sense, the terminological simplification is somewhat deceptive.

There will also be a meaningful reform of the regime of 'mainstream' legal instruments, to be used except for CFSP. As was mentioned above, the Constitutional Treaty contained a radical terminological novelty by introducing the new instruments of 'laws' and 'framework laws' to replace regulations and directives having a legislative nature. This innovation was undone by the Lisbon Treaty, so that regulations and directives will continue to be, as today, the main legislative instruments of the European Union. However, the related ambition of introducing a clearer hierarchy within the system of EU acts was not abandoned. The 'amorphous' current system, in which the distinction between legislative and executive acts is not made visible by the denomination of the act (for instance, a regulation can be used both for very important legislative measures taken in co-decision and for very lowly implementing measures taken by the Commission), will be replaced by a more detailed typology of acts in which that distinction will be clearly expressed.

All the relevant rules which, in the Constitutional Treaty, were contained in the 'fundamental' Part I, were eventually incorporated by the Lisbon Treaty into the Treaty on the Functioning of the European Union (TFEU), the successor to the EC Treaty. In the new Article 288 of that Treaty, we find the same three types of binding legal instruments as are currently listed in Article 249 EC, namely *regulations*, *directives*, and *decisions*. However, each of these instruments will be available at three different tiers of law-making: for 'true' legislation, for the adoption of delegated acts and for the adoption of implementing acts, and their position in the hierarchy of law-making will be indicated in the formal denomination of the act.

The upper tier is formed by what the Treaty text calls 'legislative acts'. This term does not indicate a formal instrument, but the normative nature of some regulations, directives or decisions. This particular legislative nature will be determined by the use of a particular procedure, as is stated by the curiously worded new Article 289(3) TFEU: 'Legal acts adopted by legislative procedure shall constitute

---

151.   See Art. 25(b) TEU (Lisbon).

legislative acts.' There will not be a single legislative procedure, though. Whereas the co-decision procedure will become the normally used legislative procedure (and is in fact re-baptized as the 'ordinary legislative procedure' in Art. 289(1) TFEU), there will still be many cases in which the Treaty provides for special legislative procedures, mainly in the 'intergovernmental' matters for which the Council will be the sole author of legislation. The identification of legislative acts is not a purely formal matter. Practical legal consequences will flow from this identification: for example, the rule that the Council shall meet in public is limited to its deliberations on legislative acts;[152] the new role of national parliaments in monitoring respect for the principle of subsidiarity will refer to draft legislative acts only;[153] and the broadening of the individual right to challenge EU acts before the European Court refers to 'regulatory acts', and not therefore (presumably) legislative acts.[154]

An intermediate level of law-making, between the legislative and purely executive, will be introduced, namely the delegated acts. These will be adopted by the Commission in order to 'supplement or amend certain non-essential elements of the legislative acts' (Art. 290(1) TFEU). In contrast with implementing acts, these delegated acts will thus actually modify a legislative act, albeit only on non-essential points, provided that there is a specific delegation within the relevant legislative act, and subject to control by the institutions that have adopted that act, that is, normally speaking, by Council and Parliament.[155] In current practice, this phenomenon already exists; the Commission is frequently given the power to amend or supplement legislative acts, but this practice is considered to be covered by its general implementation powers and has no explicit Treaty basis. It remains to be seen whether the creation of a formal distinction between delegated acts and 'pure' implementing acts will add to the transparency and accountability of EU decision-making, or rather introduce additional formalism and complexity.

So, in the future, there will be nine different binding legal instruments of 'mainstream' EU law: legislative regulations, directives and decisions; delegated regulations, directives, and decisions; and implementing regulations, directives and decisions. The nature of the act will be visible from its title. Indeed, it is specified that the adjective 'delegated' shall be inserted in the title of delegated acts and that the word 'implementing' shall be inserted in the title of implementing acts.[156] Therefore, regulations, directives and decisions without an adjective in their title will be legislative acts. This will certainly add to the transparency of EU law, compared to the present situation. It is worth noting that in this new multi-tiered system, also decisions will be available at all three levels. This shows that these new-style decisions will not be identical to what are now called decisions in Article 249 EC, but are some kind of conceptual blending of the decisions in the

---

152. Art. 16(8) TEU (Lisbon).
153. New Protocol on the application of the principles of subsidiarity and proportionality.
154. New Art. 263 TFEU.
155. See the new Art. 290 TFEU for the details of this new legal regime.
156. See respectively Art. 290(3 and Art. 291(4) TFEU.

sense of Article 249 EC (which are mainly individual administrative acts, called *Entscheidung* in German) with the decisions *sui generis* (which are currently used for the adoption of certain legislative and general administrative acts, and are called in German *Beschluβ*).[157] The future decision will fulfil the rather different functions currently fulfilled by these two different types of instruments; this is expressed by the new and ambiguous definition in Article 288 TFEU: 'A decision shall be binding in its entirety. A decision which specifies those to whom it is addressed shall be binding only on them.'

The revised Treaty provisions will also refer expressly to two legal instruments which have been in frequent use for some time, namely *recommendations*[158] and *IIAs*.[159]

In conclusion, it is not altogether obvious that this new multi-layered system of legal instruments will lead to a simplification of EU law which, as was mentioned above, was a central aim of the Convention on the Future of the Union when it started discussing this matter in 2002.

2   HARMONIZATION OF NATIONAL LAW

2.1   CONCEPT AND FUNCTIONS

Article 3(1)(h) EC mentions 'the approximation of the laws of Member States to the extent required for the functioning of the common market' as one of the activities of the Community. This approximation of laws is what is generally referred to in the literature as 'harmonization'.[160]

The first and – still – most important function of such harmonization is thus, as expressed in Article 3(1)(h) EC, that of removing differences between the national legal systems which hinder the working of the *common market*, now more often called the internal market. The legislative activity of the EC in a variety of other areas mentioned in Article 3 EC (such as environmental policy, social policy, consumer protection) also consists of the 'approximation' of national laws – literally, bringing them closer together. This is harmonization in a broader sense: it is not the correct functioning of the internal market which is the main objective, but the realization of a *common policy*, in one of a number of areas indicated by the EC Treaty. In both cases, the classic instrument utilized is the directive, although harmonization sometimes also takes place by means of other legal instruments, such as regulations.

---

157. For this distinction, see section 1.5 *supra*.
158. New Art. 292 TFEU.
159. New Art. 295 TFEU.
160. In other places, such as for example in Art. 13, Art. 93, and Art. 95(4), the EC Treaty uses instead the term 'harmonization', but there is, in practice, no difference between approximation and harmonization.

For a long time, the internal market function of harmonization was foremost. In the early decades, this related to the actual *establishment* of the common market. All kinds of obstacles to free movement of goods, persons, services and capital could only be eliminated by setting common European rules. For instance, if we take the case of free movement of goods, it was apparent that customs borders and associated checks and formalities, tax borders and associated formalities resulting from the differences in legislation concerning the tax base and rate for turnover taxes and duties could only be eradicated by far-reaching harmonization. Harmonization was, and is, particularly important in all cases where obstacles to one of the freedoms resulting from differences in national legislation are justified on the grounds of interests mentioned in Articles 30, 46 or 55 EC or other general interests accepted by the Court of Justice (under the *Cassis de Dijon* case law, which currently applies to all four freedoms).[161] Such differences can only be erased by establishing one common European legislative framework, which also takes account of the interests the national legislature aims to protect. The establishment and the proper functioning of the internal or common market can be promoted by two types of legislative measures at the European level: *liberalizing* measures, which aim to abolish the 'barriers' which national law erects (negative integration), and *regulatory* measures, which replace existing national policy with policies decided at EC level (positive integration).[162] The legal framework of the EC Treaty does not contain a preference for one or the other. In fact, the Community Institutions enjoy a broad policy discretion in deciding the appropriate regulatory mix, that is, in striking a balance between market operation and public intervention, in each particular case.[163]

The Treaty provisions on *free movement of persons* and *freedom to provide services* already entail a degree of harmonization of national legislation themselves, by imposing an obligation on the Member States to bring about a real equality of access to work and professional activities (in particular in Arts. 40, 47 and 52 EC) and, hence, to eliminate from their statute books the many rules that (used to) discriminate between their own nationals and EU citizens. For *free movement of goods*, the EEC Treaty did not lay down such a specific task (except as far as customs tariffs were concerned), so that in this area, recourse had to be had to a more generally formulated competence 'for the approximation of such laws, regulations or administrative provisions of the Member States as directly affect the establishment or functioning of the common market' (Art. 94 EC). Under Article 7(7) EEC, later repealed, the harmonization required for the establishment of the

---

161. See Ch. VIII for an extensive discussion of the case law of the ECJ in this area.
162. On the concepts negative integration and positive integration see, e.g., F. Scharpf, *Governing in Europe: Effective and Democratic?* (Oxford, 1999), Ch. 2.
163. This was already recognized by the Court in Case 240/83, *Procureur de la République v. Association de défense des brûleurs d'huiles usagées (ADBHU)*. See, for general considerations on this subject, S. Weatherill, 'Supply of and Demand for Internal Market Regulation: Strategies, Preferences and Interpretation'; and B. de Witte, 'Non-market Values in Internal Market Legislation', both in N. Nic Shuibhne (ed.), *Regulating the Internal Market* (Cheltenham, 2006).

common market had to be completed before 'the expiry of the transitional period' (i.e., the end of the 1960s). As a result of the cumbersome decision-making procedures – in particular the requirement of unanimity in Article 94 EC, and the political practice following the so-called 'Luxembourg compromise',[164] this original aim proved to be an illusion. Against this background, the Commission presented its White Paper in 1985, on completing the internal market, in which it set out a detailed programme of harmonization measures which would make it possible to abolish all remaining obstacles to the internal market resulting from national legislation. In the Single European Act (SEA), concluded shortly afterwards by the Member States, this objective was written into the EEC Treaty (now Art. 14 EC). In addition, the achievement of this aim was facilitated by the introduction of Article 95 EC (originally Art. 100a EEC) which created the possibility of adopting harmonization measures with *a qualified majority* in the Council.

The significance of harmonization goes further than merely the *establishment* of the common market, which was more or less (though even now still not completely) realized by the end of 1992. After all, Article 3(1)(h) EC also mentions the *functioning* of the common market. This concerns rules which may not actually hinder access to the national markets, for goods, services or persons from other EU countries, but which do imply different *competitive conditions* from those prevailing in the country of origin. In this context, one may think of national rules concerning market behaviour of undertakings, *vis-à-vis* their competitors (intellectual property rights, competition law), *vis-à-vis* their employees (labour conditions, social protection, safety at work), *vis-à-vis* the consumers (consumer protection) and *vis-à-vis* their customers and suppliers (civil law rules for undertakings). The competitive conditions for undertakings can be further influenced by rules which are not intended to strengthen the position of certain groups, but aim to protect general interests, such as tax legislation, cultural policy and rules for environmental protection and the protection of public health. In all these cases, differences between the legislation of the various Member States can lead to a disturbance – a distortion – of competition in the internal market and may be a reason for harmonization, so as to create a *level playing field*. This, of course, creates a very wide scope for internal market—based harmonization measures and may lead to tensions in the division of powers between the EC and its Member States, a matter to which we will return in section 2.3. below.

In addition, harmonization – as was already said in the introduction to this chapter – is an instrument that is used in order to achieve other objectives of the EC, quite apart from the adequate functioning of the internal market. Examples of such other objectives are to be found throughout the EC Treaty, spread over chapters on agriculture, transport, monetary policy, social policy, environmental protection, consumer protection, immigration, non-discrimination, etc. A discussion of these policy areas, and of the main harmonization measures adopted by the Community in each of them, may be found in later chapters of this book.[165] They will not be

---

164.   See section 3.1.1, *infra*.
165.   Especially in Chs. X, XI and XII.

dealt with further here, except to the extent that they illustrate certain general issues of harmonization, such as – for instance – with regard to the concept of 'minimum harmonization'(see below, section 2.4).

2.2   THE GENERAL HARMONIZATION COMPETENCE OF
           ARTICLE 95 (AND ARTICLE 94) EC

The *general harmonization provisions* in the Treaty consist of Article 94 and Article 95 EC, the latter introduced by the SEA. The most important difference between the two from a procedural point of view, is that Article 94 EC requires the Council to adopt directives by unanimity and merely to consult the Parliament, whereas Article 95 provides for the application of the co-decision procedure (under Art. 251 EC), in which the Parliament acts as co-legislator and the Council decides by qualified majority. A second difference lies in the fact that Article 94 EC only speaks of directives, whereas Article 95 EC mentions 'measures', which can also include regulations.[166] The importance of this difference was reduced, however, by the fact that a declaration was annexed to the Final Act of the SEA stating that the Commission 'shall give precedence to the use of the instrument of a directive' when making its proposals. Although this declaration is not binding, the Commission has indeed presented the vast majority of its proposals based on Article 95 EC in the form of directives. Another difference between the two provisions is that Article 94 EC refers to 'the establishment or functioning of the *common* market', and Article 95 EC to 'the establishment and functioning of the *internal* market'. Immediately after the entry into force of the SEA, speculation was rife in the academic literature as to the possible differences between these two concepts, but the Court of Justice seems to consider that the two are synonymous.[167] Since the requirement in Article 94 that the laws and other measures 'directly affect' the common market is absent in Article 95 EC, it could even be argued that the scope of application of Article 95 EC is broader than that of Article 94 EC. If both articles could be used for a certain matter, Article 95 EC has priority (in view of the opening words of Art. 95 EC), and has for that reason evolved to become a general provision for the management of the common or internal market. Legislative practice since 1987 has confirmed this development, and also shows that Article 94 EC now has only a residual function, for instance in the area of direct taxation.

    A double price had to be paid for the agreement included in the SEA, on the part of all Member States, that for internal market legislation they would shift from decisions adopted by unanimity (under Art. 94 EC) to decisions by qualified

---

166.   In a number of cases, recommendations are also used for purposes of quasi-harmonization, see, e.g., Commission Recommendation 87/589 (O.J. 1987, L 365/72) laying down a European Code of Conduct relating to electronic payment. In such cases, compliance by the Member States is voluntary, given the soft law nature of the instrument.
167.   Case C-41/93, *France v. Commission.*

majority (under Art. 95 EC): some policy areas were explicitly excluded from the ambit of Article 95 EC, and also a safeguard clause for the Member States was included in that article. The *explicit exclusion* was made in the second paragraph of the article, and applies to fiscal matters, the free movement of persons[168] and the rights and interests of employed persons. For these three matters, Article 94 EC remains the legal basis, insofar as no specific powers are granted elsewhere in the EC Treaty.[169]

The *safeguard clause* is to be found in paragraph 4 of Article 95 EC, on the basis of which a Member State retains the possibility to maintain national provisions (deviating from the measure) even after the adoption of a harmonization measure, if this is justified on the grounds mentioned in Article 30 EC or relating to the protection of the environment or the working environment. This safeguard clause has led to many questions, both on procedural aspects and on substance; some of these were answered in the first ECJ case dealing with it, namely Case C-41/93 *France v. Commission*, in which France sought review of the Commission's decision confirming the measures Germany had notified to it, in order to maintain a prohibition on the use of the chemical substance pentachlorophenol (PCP).[170] The Court explained that as Article 95(4) permitted a derogation from a common Community measure designed to achieve one of the fundamental objectives of the Treaty, *in casu* the free movement of goods, its application is subject, in its totality, to review by the Commission and the Court.[171] Although a literal interpretation of Article 95(4) might seem to indicate otherwise, that provision is thus not a unilateral safeguard clause which the Member States can use at will for the protection of the interests specified therein.[172] The Court interpreted the procedure of Article 95(4) as meaning that 'no Member State may apply national rules derogating from the harmonized rules without obtaining confirmation from the Commission'.[173] The Commission's approval or rejection of the Member State's request is therefore an act capable of review in the sense of Article 230 EC.[174]

In a later judgment, *Kortas*, the Court of Justice added that as long as the Commission had not taken a decision – and even if a substantial amount of time

---

168. The difference between measures aimed at free movement of goods and that of persons is not always entirely clear. Dir. 91/447 (O.J. 1991, L 256/51) on the control of the acquisition and possession of weapons is a measure which in fact aims to facilitate cross border movements of persons, but which was nevertheless based on Art. 95 EC (then still Art. 100a EEC), by using the weapons themselves as the link (goods, in the sense of the EC Treaty).

169. As far as taxes are concerned, Art. 93 EC confers a specific competence in relation to harmonization of indirect taxes, so that Art. 94 EC could only be used in relation to *direct* taxes. As for free movement of persons, in the meantime extensive specific competences have been laid down elsewhere in the Treaty (Arts. 18 and 61 et seq.). On rights of workers, broad powers are conferred in Arts. 137 and 141 EC. All in all, there is thus not much left for Art. 94 to deal with.

170. Case C-41/93, *France v. Commission*.

171. Para. 24 of the judgment.

172. Para. 39.

173. Para. 28.

174. Para. 37.

had passed since notification of the national measure in question – the Member State was not permitted to apply its national rule derogating from the harmonized rule, and individuals could rely on this in an action before the national courts against application of the national rule.[175] If the Commission, as was the case in *Kortas*, failed to respond for a long period of time, an unreasonable situation resulted; the Treaty of Amsterdam settled this by introducing a time limit (of 6 months) for the Commission to respond to notifications and specifying that in the absence of a Commission decision, the national measures are deemed to be approved (Art. 95(6) EC).

The Treaty of Amsterdam also added a new paragraph 5 to Article 95, which permits Member States to adopt *new* measures derogating from a harmonized rule, to the extent these are based on 'new scientific evidence relating to the protection of the environment or the working environment on grounds of a problem specific to that Member State arising after the adoption of the harmonisation measure'. These more narrowly drawn conditions are not easy to meet. Moreover, here too the Commission must give its approval before the measures may be implemented, and it is basically for the State seeking a derogation to provide the necessary scientific evidence.[176]

Given these rather strict conditions, and given the fact that until now the Member States have rarely invoked the safeguard clauses,[177] there does not seem to be a real threat to the common market – contrary to what was feared by a number of people immediately after the entry into force of the SEA.[178] It is more likely that the possibility of invoking this clause will influence the negotiations during the legislative procedure, in the sense that attempts will be made to meet the requirements of the Member State in question to the greatest possible extent at that stage already. If, nonetheless, one of these clauses is relied on successfully, then in fact a complete Community-wide harmonization will be transformed into a territorially limited harmonization, which may at a later time recover its complete character by raising the level of protection of the directive in question to the level of the 'dissident' Member State.

In addition to these safeguard possibilities created by the EC Treaty itself, it is of course also possible that in a specific directive or regulation provision is made for temporary safeguard clauses for certain Member States,[179] or even for the

---

175. Case C-319/97, *Antoine Kortas*.
176. Joined Cases T-366/03 & T-235/04, *Land Oberösterreich and Austria v. Commission* (in this case, the region Oberösterreich sought to introduce a ban on the use of plants and seeds containing GMOs on its territory, in derogation from the relevant EC directive; the Commission's rejection of the request for derogation, because of the lack of specificity of the situation in that region, was approved by the Court).
177. See N. De Sadeleer, 'Procedures for Derogation from the Principle of Approximation of Laws under Art. 95 EC' (2003) CML Rev., 889.
178. Particularly in an article by P. Pescatore, 'Some Critical Remarks on the Single European Act' (1987) CML Rev., 9.
179. See on this G. de Búrca, 'Differentiation within the "Core"? The Case of the Internal Market', in G. de Búrca and J. Scott (eds), *Constitutional Change in the EU: From Uniformity to Flexibility?* (Oxford, 2000), 133.

possibility of derogation by all Member States, for an unlimited period, whereby the conditions for such derogation are strictly defined and subject to supervision by the Commission.[180]

2.3   SPECIFIC HARMONIZATION PROVISIONS AND THE
               LIMITS OF ARTICLE 95 EC

Although Article 95 EC is frequently used as the legal basis for harmonization measures, it is certainly not the only legal basis for such measures in the Treaty. *Within* the scope of application of Article 95 EC (i.e., the establishment and functioning of the internal market), more specific provisions take precedence. This is apparent from the words 'save where otherwise provided in this Treaty', occurring in the opening sentence of Article 95 EC. For some elements of the internal market there are indeed specific powers concerning harmonization elsewhere in the Treaty. Harmonization of national law which is necessary for the *free movement of workers* can – and should be – based on Article 40 EC, and not on Article 95 EC. Harmonization of legislation to realize the freedom to exercise a trade or profession or other economic activities has a specific legal basis in Articles 47 (*establishment*) and 55 (*services*) of the EC Treaty, and harmonization of company law has a legal basis in Article 44(2)(g) EC. A separate legal basis for the harmonization of indirect taxation (if this is necessary for the functioning of the internal market) is laid down in Article 93 EC.

Outside the scope of application of Article 95 EC, the EC Treaty contains a series of provisions concerning harmonization of laws for *specific subjects and sectors* which are not directly linked to the establishment and functioning of the internal market but have, nevertheless, a distinct economic flavour. In relation to agriculture, the case law shows that Article 37 EC confers power on the Community to harmonize legislation on veterinary, health and plant health matters, and zootechnical and botanical legislation.[181] Harmonization of legislation in the transport sector, including both its economic and social aspects, takes place on the basis of Articles 71 and 80 EC. In the field of the common commercial policy, Article 133 EC can be used to harmonize national rules relating to foreign trade. In addition to these sectoral powers – which were already included in the original text of the EEC Treaty – later Treaty amendments have granted harmonization powers in a series of other areas, of which the most important for the functioning of the market are environmental protection (Art. 175 EC), consumer protection (Art. 153 EC), labour law (Art. 137 EC) and immigration (Art. 63 EC).

Drawing a boundary between these specific harmonization powers and the general power contained in Article 95 EC is not easy. In the years following the entry into force of the SEA, Article 95 evolved, both in law and in fact, into an

---

180. An example of this is Art. 3(4) of Dir. 2000/31 on electronic commerce, O.J. 2000, L 178/1.
181. See Case 68/86, *UK v. Council*; Case 131/86, *UK v. Council*; Case 131/87, *Commission v. Council* and Case 11/88, *Commission v. Council*.

almost general power to enact rules relating to the establishment and functioning of the internal market. Indeed the wording of the provision itself reveals this tendency. Article 95(3) indicates that the power to harmonize also covers aspects of public health, environmental protection and consumer protection, and the Commission is instructed to aim, in its proposals, at a high level of protection for these public goods. Harmonization directives concerning particular policy objectives do not, therefore, always have to be based on the specific powers relating to those sectors or policies, but may also be based on Article 95 EC. In the period following the SEA, such delimitations had a practical political reason, as well, since Article 95 EC (at that time still Art. 100a EEC) and environmental policy were subject to different decision-making procedures, with different roles assigned to the main actors: Council, Commission and Parliament. In the *Titanium dioxide* case,[182] the Court of Justice interpreted Article 95 EC broadly, so that this article was to be used as the basis for harmonizing national rules on waste which is harmful to the environment. A few years later, however, in Case C-155/91, *Commission v. Council*, the Court of Justice found, on the contrary, that the harmonization of national rules on waste substances came within the specific powers relating to environmental protection, and not the general harmonization competence contained in Article 95 EC.[183] In these two judgments, the Court also formulated a general delimiting criterion which it has used ever since (even though the application of the criterion in practice is not always unambiguous): the choice of legal basis is determined by the *objective centre of gravity* or focus of the act in question, which must be determined on the basis of its aim and content. If the focus is really the establishment and functioning of the internal market (including the elimination of competitive distortions on the market), then Article 95 EC must be chosen as legal basis (or, in relevant cases, the more specific powers for free movement of persons and services); if the focus is environmental or consumer protection, or some other EC area of policy, then the relevant Treaty provision should be taken as legal basis.

Another aspect which should be mentioned concerns the so-called *negative harmonization clauses*, which the Treaty of Maastricht introduced into the EC Treaty. These are provisions which expressly state that in a certain policy area harmonization of national laws and regulations is *excluded*. This is the case for education (Art. 149(4) EC), vocational training (Art. 150(4) EC), culture (Art. 151(5) EC) and public health (Art. 152(4)(c) EC). Here too, however, a problem of delimitation arises in those cases where a harmonization measure affects the functioning of the internal market, but also regulates aspects of a 'forbidden' policy field. For instance, there is a Directive on the return of cultural objects[184] which aims to improve the functioning of the internal market for works of art (and was therefore based on Art. 95 EC – at the time still Art. 100a EEC), but which also has aims and effects in the field of cultural policy. In such cases, Article 95 (or another internal market competence) will only be available as a legal basis – and the

---

182. Case C-300/89, *Commission v. Council*.
183. Case C-155/91, *Commission v. Council* (waste management).
184. Dir. 93/7, O.J. 1993, L 74/74.

harmonization prohibition avoided – to the extent that the content of the measure is sufficiently connected to the functioning of the internal market. Otherwise, it would simply be too easy to circumvent the explicit exclusion of harmonization. This question became very prominent in the context of the legal challenge brought, in 1998, by Germany against the Directive prohibiting advertising for tobacco products, which was based on Article 95; one of the main arguments to contest the legality of this directive was that it constituted in reality a measure of health policy for which there is a prohibition of harmonization in Article 152(4) EC. However, Article 95 itself recognizes that internal market measures can also seek to protect public health, so that the real question becomes whether the measure of harmonization (in this case, a total ban on advertising) is sufficiently connected to the smooth functioning of the internal market.

The real question is, thus, how to assess whether a proposed measure is indeed a contribution to the better functioning of the internal market. In the course of the 1990s, on the basis of the practice of the EC Institutions and certain judgments of the Court of Justice, it began to seem as if Article 95 EC had grown into an all-encompassing legislative competence.[185] In addition to the myriad directives and other measures directly related to free movement of goods,[186] this provision was used for enacting Community measures on matters which could seem to be only very indirectly linked to movement of goods, or the internal market in general. Examples of this are the directives on daylight saving time[187] and the decision on the common dialling code for international telephone calls in the Community.[188] Harmonization was not limited to the approximation of national laws as such, in the sense of bringing national laws closer to on another, but also includes cases of specific action which does not involve making changes to existing laws but which facilitates the uniform application of earlier measures of harmonization.[189] Legislative practice confirms that harmonization of laws can also take place in relation to 'new' matters, which were not yet covered by legislation in the Member

---

185. See on this point R. Barents, 'The Internal Market Unlimited: Some Observations on the Legal Basis of Community Legislation' (1993) CML Rev., 85; and A. Dashwood, 'The Limits of European Community Powers' (1996) EL Rev., 113, at 120–122.
186. An overview of this multifarious legislation can be found in the Directory of EC legislation in force, updated twice a year (and now available via internet: europa.eu/eur-lex/lex/en/repert/1330.htm) in Ch. 13.30 entitled 'Internal Market: Approximation of Laws'. The following subcategories can be found, which give an impression of the areas where harmonization has taken place: motor vehicles, agricultural and forestry tractors, metrology, electrical material, foodstuffs, proprietary medicinal products, cosmetics, textiles, dangerous substances, fertilizers and the (highly diverse) subcategory 'Other sectors for approximation of laws'.
187. See Dir. 89/47, O.J. 1989, L 17/57 and all subsequent directives on this subject (most recently Dir. 2000/84, O.J. 2001, L 13/21, which made it a permanent arrangement).
188. Decision 92/264, O.J. 1992, L 137/21.
189. See already Decision 91/341 on the adoption of a programme of Community action on the subject of the vocational training of customs officials (Matthaeus programme), O.J. 1991, L 187/41; this type of 'supporting harmonization' was approved by the ECJ in Case C-217/04, *United Kingdom v. Parliament and Council*.

States, so there were no existing laws to be 'approximated'.[190] Article 95 (whether or not in combination with the specific legal basis for services or establishment) was used as an instrument of energy policy,[191] telecommunications,[192] for combating money laundering of proceeds from crime,[193] for combating trade in and use of narcotics,[194] and for the protection of privacy in relation to the processing of data.[195]

However, in the first *tobacco advertising* judgment of 2000, the Court of Justice set limits to the scope of Article 95 EC.[196] Following the challenge by Germany (already mentioned above), the Court annulled a Directive adopted by Parliament and Council which prohibited all forms of tobacco advertising. This Directive was based on the general harmonization competence of Article 95 EC, as well as the specific harmonization competence concerning freedom to provide services. The Court stated that the powers in question can only be used for two aims: on the one hand, to *improve* the functioning of the internal market (and therefore not simply to regulate that market in general terms), and on the other hand to eliminate *appreciable* distortions of competition (and therefore not distortions of competition of negligible significance). In the view of the Court some parts of the tobacco advertising directive did not meet either of these criteria: the prohibition of tobacco advertising on posters, parasols, ashtrays etc.; moreover, the prohibition of advertising spots in cinemas was not liable to contribute to an improvement in free movement of goods, or services, and was not a means of removing appreciable distortions of competition on the market for those goods or services. After the annulment of the Directive, the Council and Parliament approved a revised version which left out the elements criticized by the Court, but otherwise confirmed the ban on advertising, and this new version was upheld against a further challenge by Germany, in a judgment of 2006.[197] The net result of the 'tobacco litigation' is that the EC Institutions must now give more care to explaining (both in the Commission's explanatory memorandum and in the preamble of the final text of a directive) why the choice of the internal market legal

---

190. See Dir. 90/220 on the deliberate release into the environment of genetically modified organisms, O.J. 1990, L 61/14; Dir. 98/44 on the legal protection of biotechnological inventions, O.J. 1998, L 213/13; Dir. 98/84 on the legal protection of services based on, or consisting of, conditional access, O.J. 1998, L 320/54; Dir. 1999/93 on a Community framework for electronic signatures, O.J. 2000, L 13/12 and Dir. 2000/31 on electronic commerce, O.J. 2000, L 178/1.
191. Dir. 96/92 on common rules for the internal market in electricity, O.J. 1997, L 27/20.
192. Directives in this area have played a role in the standardization of technical regulations and in the gradual liberalization of telecom services; see *inter alia* Dir. 87/372, O.J. 1987, L 196/5; Dir. 90/544, O.J. 1990, L 310/28; Dir. 90/827, O.J. 1990, L 144/45; Dir. 97/13, O.J. 1997, L 117/15 and Dir. 98/10, O.J. 1998, L 101/24.
193. Dir. 91/308, O.J. 1991, L 166/77.
194. Dir. 92/109, O.J. 1992, L 370/76, on narcotic drugs and psychotropic substances.
195. Dir. 95/46, O.J. 1995, L 281/31.
196. Case C-376/98, *Germany v. Parliament and Council* (advertising and sponsorship of tobacco products).
197. Case C-380/03, *Germany v. Parliament and Council.*

basis is justified. However, the scope of that internal market competence remains, as before, quite extensive.

2.4   METHODS AND EXTENT OF HARMONIZATION

A classic topic in this area of EC law is that of the methods of harmonization, which usually refers to the extent to which a European harmonizing measure leaves room for supplementary national law. In the first decades of the EEC, harmonization directives went into very great detail in the field of free movement of goods, and also of free movement of persons and services, and sometimes even went so far as requiring partial or complete uniformity of national provisions. It was only after the *Cassis de Dijon* judgment that the Commission was able to take a different approach, and propose directives which went into less detail. In relation to technical standards for products – which had long been an important area for Community internal market measures – a 'new approach' was adopted as of the mid-1980s, the principal elements of which were set out in a Council Resolution of 7 May 1985[198] and worked out in the White Paper on *Completing the Internal Market*.[199] This approach was based on four elements, which were already recognizable in some of the earlier directives.[200] First, harmonization was confined to the adoption of rules protecting essential interests (such as the safety or health of the user) to which products placed on the market must conform in order to enjoy free movement throughout the Community. Secondly, the task of drawing up the technical specifications to ensure marketing of products meeting those essential requirements was entrusted to standardization bodies, taking due account of technological progress.[201] Thirdly, those technical specifications would be voluntary as opposed to mandatory (this is the key distinguishing feature of standards as opposed to technical regulations); however, national administrations are obliged to presume that products manufactured according to harmonized standards conform to the essential requirements laid down in the directives, and thus may circulate freely in the common market. This means that there is a positive incentive for a manufacturer to produce to the harmonized standards, as these products automatically enjoy a presumption of conformity. He or she remains free to manufacture to other standards if desired, but in such a case the burden of demonstrating conformity with the essential requirements of the relevant directive shifts to the manufacturer.[202]

---

198. O.J. 1985, C 136/1.
199. COM (85) 310 Final.
200. See, for a further discussion, J. Pelkmans, 'The New Approach to Technical Harmonization and Standardization' (1986–1987) *Journal of Common Market Studies*, 249.
201. These were in particular the European institutes CEN (European Committee for Standardization), CENELEC (European Committee for Electrotechnical Standardization) and ETSI (telecommunications standards).
202. See the communication of the Commission 'A global approach to certification and testing quality measures for industrial products', O.J. 1989, C 267/3.

The new approach, based on a 'model directive' has been used – in the framework of the completion of the internal market – in relation to all sorts of products, e.g., simple pressure vessels,[203] toys,[204] machines,[205] electromagnetic compatibility,[206] gas appliances,[207] personal protective equipment,[208] lifts,[209] active implantable medical devices.[210] A separate Council Decision regulates certificates and conformity assessments[211] and the CE mark of conformity which is used in this procedure, as proof of conformity with harmonized standards.[212] This form of 'private governance'[213] is still used today in the broad area of technical standard-setting. In recent years, the Commission launched a process of reform and confirmation of the standardization policy[214] which resulted, in 2006, in a new 'action plan for standardization' which was itself elaborated in close collaboration with private standard-setting bodies.[215]

Outside the area of technical standards for products, a distinction may be made in general terms between a number of methods of harmonization, the most important being *total harmonization* and *minimum harmonization*. In the academic literature, further categories are identified: *optional harmonization* and *mutual recognition* as a method of harmonization.

The simplest form is *total harmonization*, also referred to as full or complete harmonization. Total harmonization means that the Community measures deprive the Member States of the power to maintain in force rules which are at variance with the Community measures, whether stricter or less strict.[216] The free movement which is achieved in this way is total, since any appeal to Article 30 EC or other exceptions is no longer possible. There is still the possibility of appeal to the safeguard clauses in Article 95(4) and (5) EC, if the relevant conditions are met, as discussed in section 2.2 above. The concept of *total harmonization* is, however, not as simple as may appear at first sight. After all, the scope of a harmonization measure is always limited to a certain subject matter (in that sense, even total

203. Dir. 87/404, O.J. 1987, L 220/48.
204. Dir. 88/378, O.J. 1988, L 187/1.
205. Dir. 89/392, O.J. 1989, L 183/9.
206. Dir. 89/336, O.J. 1989, L 139/19.
207. Dir. 90/396, O.J. 1990, L 196/15.
208. Dir. 89/686, O.J. 1989, L 399/18.
209. Dir. 84/529, as amended by Dir. 90/486, O.J. 1990, L 270/21.
210. Dir. 90/385, O.J. 1990, L 189/17.
211. Council Decision 90/683/EEC of 13 Dec. 1990 concerning the modules for the various phases of the conformity assessment procedures which are intended to be used in the technical harmonization directives, O.J. 1990, L 380/13.
212. Dir. 93/68 and the related Council decision 93/465, O.J. 1993, L 220/1 and 23.
213. H. Schepel, *The Constitution of Private Governance* (Oxford, 2005).
214. See Commission Communication on the role of European standardisation in the framework of European policies and legislation, COM (2004) 674 of 18 Oct. 2004.
215. European Commission, *Action Plan for European Standardisation*, 15 Mar. 2007, ec. europa.eu/comm/enterprise/standards_policy/index_en.htm.
216. Except safeguard clauses contained in the directive itself. See on this Case 5/77, *Carlo Tedeschi v. Denkavit Commerciale s.r.l.* and Case 228/87, *Pretura unificata di Torino v. X.*

harmonization is only partial), and the question often arises whether a certain national rule comes within the scope of the EC measure, and therefore needs to be amended, or outside the scope of the EC measure and thus does not need changing. This problem of the *scope* of harmonization will be dealt with later in this section.

In the case of *minimum harmonization*, the Member States, as the name implies, must comply with the minimum requirements contained in the directive concerned, but are free to apply stricter or more far-reaching requirements in the area covered.[217] For certain policy areas, the Treaty expressly requires this method of harmonization to be used. This is the case for consumer protection (Art. 153(5) EC), environmental protection (Art. 176 EC), social policy (Art. 137(5) EC) and some aspects of immigration policy (Art. 63 EC).[218] In addition, minimum harmonization occurs regularly in internal market directives based on Article 95 EC. Article 95 EC does not give any indication as to which harmonization method should be used, so in these cases it will have to be identified on the basis of the text of the directive itself whether a directive involves minimum harmonization. It is quite common for a directive to contain a provision stating this explicitly (despite the fact that, by allowing stricter national standards, the internal market purpose will be less easily attained). A typical example of a minimum harmonization clause is Article 8(2) of Directive 1999/44 on the sale of consumer goods and associated guarantees, based on Article 95 EC: 'Member States may adopt or maintain in force more stringent provisions, compatible with the Treaty in the field covered by this Directive, to ensure a higher level of consumer protection'.[219] Sometimes, however, such an explicit provision is absent; in that case, the provisions of the measure taken as a whole, or the description of the concrete obligations on Member States, will have to be examined in order to see whether or not minimum harmonization is involved.[220] From the point of view of legislative technique, such an implicit approach is not satisfactory and may provoke litigation. A good example is the debate on whether Member States could impose stricter standards of product

---

217. See on this M. Dougan, 'Minimum Harmonization and the Internal Market' (2000) CML Rev., 853.
218. See furthermore Art. 152(4)(1) EC, on health standards for organs and substances of human origin, blood and blood derivatives.
219. Dir. 1999/44, O.J. 1999, L 171/12. This clause permits, e.g., Member States to set a longer time period than the period of two years laid down by the directive within which the seller may be sued for non-conformity of the good supplied. See P. Rott, 'Minimum Harmonization for the Completion of the Internal Market? The Example of Consumer Sales Law' (2003) CML Rev., 1107.
220. Among the many examples of cases in which the Court of Justice was asked whether a particular measure comprised total or minimum harmonization, see Case C-175/94, *The Queen v. Secretary of State for the Home Department, ex parte John Gallagher*; Case C-389/96, *Aher-Waggon GmbH v. Bundesrepublik Deutschland*; Joined Cases C-281 & 282/03, *Cindu Chemicals BV et al. v. College voor de toelating van bestrijdingsmiddelen*; Case C-506/04, *Graham Wilson v. Ordre des avocats du barreau de Luxembourg*.

liability than the ones mentioned in the relevant Directive of 1985; since the text of the Directive did not give a clear answer to this question, it was left to the Court to Justice to decide, rather controversially, that this Directive was one of total harmonization and that Member States were therefore not entitled to enact or maintain rules that were more protective of consumers.[221]

In any case, even in cases of minimum harmonization, more stringent national measures must also pass the test of conformity with the Treaty – as is also confirmed in the provision of Directive 1999/44 quoted above. This means that any more far-reaching national measure may not infringe the free movement of goods, persons and services guaranteed by the Treaty. More stringent national measures may only be applied to imported goods and services, or nationals of other Member States, to the extent that this does not create obstacles prohibited by the free movement provisions of the EC Treaty.[222]

As well as total harmonization and minimum harmonization, in practice there is also another method: *optional harmonization*. In that case, the directive leaves producers the choice as to whether to apply national standards or harmonized standards. Free movement is then assured for products conforming with the harmonized requirements.[223] Undertakings operating on the common market may manufacture to one – Community – set of requirements, whereas those only operating locally are not obliged to take the Community measure into account, and can continue to follow the (diverging) national requirements.

As for *mutual recognition*, this method obliges Member States to recognize the equivalence of rules and requirements imposed on products, services or persons by other Member States. If these products, services or persons meet the requirements of their country of origin, then the receiving State must accept that they do not necessarily entirely meet the requirements which apply in this country for its own products, services and persons. It is disputable whether this is actually a form of harmonization: after all, no common European standard is set, but merely an obligation for the Member States mutually to recognize each other's rules. On closer examination, however, this does turn out to be a form of harmonization; what is harmonized in this case are the national legal or administrative rules concerning market access of products and services, or concerning the professional and trade activities of individuals and undertakings. Mutual recognition thus plays

---

221. Case C-52/00, *Commission v. France* (and two other judgments on the same day); see S. Weatherill, *EU Consumer Law and Policy* (Cheltenham, 2005), 143–145.
222. So, in such cases, 'the Community legislation sets a floor, and the Treaty a ceiling, with Member States free to pursue their own policies within these boundaries'. (P. Craig and G. de Búrca, *EU Law. Text, Cases and Materials*, 4th ed. (Oxford, 2007), 626.) The question of compatibility of national measures with the free movement provisions of the EC Treaty is discussed in Ch. VIII, *infra*.
223. See extensively J. Currall, 'Some Aspects of the Relation between Articles 30–36 and Article 100 of the EEC Treaty with a Closer Look at Optional Harmonisation' (1984) YEL, 169.

a supplementary role alongside the harmonization of substantive rules in many areas. In fact, even where the substantive rules are completely harmonized, the non-recognition of administrative acts adopted in another Member State may, in practice, obstruct the importation of products or services. This difficulty will arise most clearly in cases where supervision must take place in the territory where the product is produced, whilst access to the market, or criminal prosecution, takes place in the country importing the product. Thus, if Germany were not to recognize the rules of meat inspection in French slaughterhouses, French meat could not be imported into Germany without renewed inspection, even if the rules on inspection were harmonized. Directives on harmonization, therefore, must also entail an obligation of mutual recognition of certain administrative acts.

The question of the *scope* of a directive (or other harmonization measure) is relevant for the examination of national measures in the light of the terms of the directive itself and primary Community law. If the directive *exhaustively* occupies the field, i.e., it contains all the relevant harmonized provisions on the matter concerned, there is no possibility for Member States to rely on Article 30 EC or the rule of reason justifications recognized in relation to the free movement of goods.[224] In such cases, all national measures concerning a certain matter are completely harmonized and – as a result of the pre-emptive effect of the directives – brought entirely within the scope of Community law.[225] Alongside these cases, one may distinguish cases of *non-exhaustive or partial* harmonization, where the scope of the directive in relation to a certain matter is not all-embracing; in such cases, only part of the relevant national provisions or certain aspects thereof fall within the ambit of the directive. The other aspects can therefore be regulated by the national authorities as they see fit,[226] even though account must be taken thereby of the prohibition on obstacles to intra-Community trade which flows directly from the EC Treaty.[227] This partial harmonization often marks the beginning of a process which in time will culminate in total harmonization. The Court has expressly approved the legality of such an approach.[228] As already mentioned above, the distinction between 'exhaustive' and 'partial' harmonization is not a firm one; all measures of harmonization are, by necessity, partial. In many cases, the determination of the precise scope of a directive will require a close analysis of its objectives and system,[229] which is not always easy on account of the fact that directives are frequently drafted in vague terms and use abstract formulations.

---

224. Case 148/78, *Tullio Ratti*.
225. See Case 123/76, *Commission v. Italy* and Case 815/79, *Gaetano Cremonini and Maria Luisa Vrankovich*.
226. See, e.g., case C-293/98, *Entidad de Gestión de Derechos de los Productores Audiovisuales (Egeda) v. Hostelería Asturiana SA (Hoasa)*.
227. Case C-3/99, *Cidrerie Ruwet SA v. Cidre Stassen SA, HP Bulmer Ltd*.
228. Case 37/83, *Rewe-Zentral AG v. Direktor der Landwirtschaftskammer Rheinland*.
229. See, e.g., Case 100/77, *Commission v. Italy*; Case 44/80, *Commission v. Italy* (fertilizers) and Case C-55/93, *Johannes Gerrit Cornelis van Schaik*.

3   DECISION-MAKING

3.1   LEGISLATIVE DECISION-MAKING

This subsection examines in further detail the rules and practice of legislative decision-making in the EC, and in particular the role played therein by the Commission, the Council and the European Parliament. The whole concept of 'legislation' has only recently found its way into the EC Treaty,[230] and there is no general definition as yet. EC legislation can be described as consisting of Community law acts (or 'secondary' law) which have an abstractly and generally formulated content, and which are adopted directly on the basis of an article of the Treaty.[231]

The main instruments of EC legislation, as indicated earlier in this chapter, are regulations and directives. A formal description of the concept of legislation by reference to the use of these two legal instruments would, however, not be correct. Some very detailed directives are not legislative or are intended only to implement earlier directives, regulations are used both for legislative and for general administrative measures, and decisions sometimes have a legislative nature, sometimes not. Therefore, there is so far no formal criterion for the identification of a 'legislative act' in EC law.

The special procedures leading to the adoption of the budget and the conclusion of external agreements by the Communities are not discussed here. The former are discussed in section 4 below; the procedure for the conclusion of external agreements will be dealt with in the discussion of external relations of the Union in another chapter of this book.[232]

Administrative decision-making will be dealt with in section 3.2, below. In the introduction to that section, the distinction between 'legislation' and 'administration' in EC law will also be discussed more fully. Decision-making in the intergovernmental Second and Third Pillars of the European Union will be dealt with separately in section 3.3. The reason for this separate discussion is that in the intergovernmental pillars, power is concentrated in the hands of the Council (and the European Council), and the Commission and Parliament consequently have a structurally subordinate role; moreover, in these areas it is not possible to make a clear distinction between legislation and administration.

---

230. In Art. 207(3) EC, which speaks of the cases in which the Council is 'acting in its legislative capacity'. In implementation of this article, the Council has made a (not very successful) attempt, in Art. 7 of its Rules of Procedure to indicate the cases in which it can be qualified as acting 'in its legislative capacity' (O.J. 2006, L 285/55). The concept of legislation is also employed in the Protocol on the Role of the National Parliaments in the European Union, attached to the Treaty of Amsterdam. For a scholarly analysis of the meaning of 'legislation' in the EC legal order, see A. Türk, *The Concept of Legislation in European Community Law: A Comparative Perspective* (Alphen aan den Rijn, 2006).

231. The latter characteristic distinguishes them from administrative acts, which are themselves based on a legislative act, and thus only indirectly on the EC Treaty itself.

232. See Ch. XIII.

3.1.1   The Legislative Process in General: The Role of the Institutions in the Historical Development of EC Decision-Making

No single institution can claim the title of 'the Community legislative branch' for itself. Community legislation comes about as a result of the cooperation between three Institutions: the Commission, the Council and the European Parliament. Below, we will outline the individual role of each of these three Institutions in more detail; thereafter their interaction in the framework of the various decision-making procedures will be described. An essential characteristic of the Community legislative process is in fact that it is not uniform, but that there are extremely different decision-making routes, in each of which the Institutions have a different role to play. The choice of a particular procedure for a particular subject matter depends on the legal basis which is laid down in the EC Treaty for that subject.[233] The complex division of powers between the Institutions which emerges as a result is an important element of the institutional balance created by the European Treaties.

In addition to the three most important political institutions, a number of other bodies play a general – though subordinate – role: the Economic and Social Committee, and the Committee of the Regions.[234] They are consulted on proposals for Community legislation in all cases where consultation is required under the legal basis of the proposed legislation; their advisory opinions are not binding on the other institutions. The European Council is only rarely mentioned in the EC Treaty, but according to Article 4 TEU this body has the task of laying down 'the general political guidelines' of the European Union, a role which also extends to the EC legislative process. The ECB is an important actor in the area of monetary legislation. In addition to these bodies and organs which have a formal role in the legislative process, recognized in the treaties, there are also numerous informal actors, viz. the interest groups, either purely national or organized at European level, which may exert considerable influence on the decision-making process, depending on the subject.[235]

The important function which the *Commission* usually fulfils in the decision-making process for Community legislation is based on three principles:

(1) In most cases, the Council (and Parliament) cannot take a decision without a proposal from the Commission (quasi-exclusive right of initiative).

---

233. See, on the legal basis requirement: K. Lenaerts and P. Van Nuffel, *Constitutional Law of the European Union*, 2nd ed. (London, 2005), 86–92; R.H. van Ooik, *De keuze der rechtsgrondslag voor besluiten van de Europese Unie* (Deventer, 1999), esp. Ch. 1.
234. See for more details on these bodies Ch. IV sections 10.1 and 10.2 *supra*.
235. There is extensive political science literature on their role. See, e.g., J. Greenwood, *Interest Representation in the European Union* (New York, 2003); R. Eising, 'Interest groups and the European Union', in M. Cini (ed.), *European Union Politics*, 2nd ed. (Oxford, 2007), Ch. 13.

(2) As long as the Council has not yet taken its decision, the Commission may alter its proposal.[236]

(3) The Council may only amend the Commission's proposal by unanimous vote.[237]

Unlike the second and third principles, the Commission's exclusive right of initiative is not mentioned anywhere in the EC Treaty as a general principle. However, in the vast majority of Treaty articles which serve as a legal basis for EC legislation, provision is made that a proposal must be made by the Commission. Exceptions to this rule have been made by recent Treaty revisions. The Treaty of Maastricht granted the right of initiative in the area of the EMU to the ECB to a large extent; and following the Treaty of Amsterdam, the right of initiative in the new EC areas of competence concerning immigration, visas, asylum and cooperation in civil law, was shared between the Commission and the individual Member States during a transitional phase of five years which ended in 2004. The Commission has now recovered its exclusive right of initiative also in this area.[238]

The proposal from the Commission is a fully-fledged draft measure which forms not only the formal starting-point, but also the substantive basis on which the Council takes a decision. The Commission's exclusive right of initiative in most areas also entitles it to determine whether and at what time it will submit a proposal. This of course applies only to the extent to which the specific Treaty provision which its proposal is intended to implement leaves it free to do so. If, for instance, this provision lays down a binding time-limit within which it must be implemented, the Commission is of course obliged to submit the appropriate proposals in good time. This situation was fairly common in the earlier phases of the EEC, but is now rare.

The fact that the Treaty provides for the possibility to request the Commission to submit a proposal does not detract from the Commission's right of initiative. Article 208 EC confers on the Council the right to request the Commission to undertake any studies the Council considers desirable for the attainment of the common objectives, and to submit to it any appropriate proposals. The Council does indeed frequently (by means of Resolutions or Conclusions) call on the Commission to make various legislative proposals, but it cannot actually *oblige* the Commission to make a proposal. The provisions on EMU allow not only the Council but also each individual Member State to request the Commission to make a recommendation or a proposal concerning a number of matters relating to EMU.[239] Finally, since the Treaty of Maastricht, the European Parliament may also 'request the Commission to submit any appropriate proposal on matters on

---

236. Art. 250(2) EC.
237. Art. 250(1) EC. This applies to the substance of the proposal as well as to its legal basis: the choice of the latter may affect the determination of the content of the proposed measure, Case 131/86, *United Kingdom v. Council*.
238. For the Second and Third Pillars, the Commission does not enjoy an exclusive right of initiative at all; see on this, section 3.3 *infra*.
239. Art. 115 EC.

which it considers that a Community act is required for the purpose of implementing this Treaty'.[240]

In practice, the right of initiative has often seemed to slip from the Commission's hands, particularly in the development of policies in new fields in which the Treaties contain little or no guidelines on which the Commission can develop proposals. Before making proposals in these areas, the Commission tends to sketch possible premises, objectives and instruments for such policy in communications, reports or Green Papers in order to get a better insight into the views of the other institutions. There is often also a very informal process of 'pre-negotiation'[241] even before a formal draft is tabled by the Commission. Moreover, in relation to important questions of policy, the real political initiative comes from the European Council. This body defines the main lines of policy, and the Commission is, often explicitly, given the task of submitting formal drafts of legislative acts in order to implement these policy lines. This development was strengthened by the Treaty of Maastricht. First of all, Article 4 first paragraph TEU confirms that the European Council not only provides the necessary impetus for the development of the Union, but also that it defines *the* general political guidelines thereof. These political guidelines clearly also embrace areas in which the Commission enjoys the exclusive right of initiative, as indicated above. True, these general political guidelines are not binding on the Community Institutions, since the article mentioned is without prejudice to the provisions of the EC Treaty and Euratom Treaty.[242] Thus there is no escaping the political accountability of the Commission towards the European Parliament, or the legal accountability of the Council (alone or jointly with the Parliament) and the Commission, by invoking the general political guidelines laid down by the European Council, although the latter cannot itself be brought to account. Yet in fact a practice has been established whereby the right of initiative in important policy issues is shifting to the European Council. Of course, the President and members of the Commission will be able to influence the establishment of these policy guidelines during the preparation of a European Council meeting, but such influence will depend on the capabilities and political weight of the individuals in question. In current practice, in fact, only a limited number of legislative proposals are really taken on the Commission's own political initiative. Usually, the Commission formalizes the policy options which have been chosen elsewhere – either in the text of the EC Treaty itself, or in deliberations of the European Council, or in agreements concluded with third countries.[243] Moreover, an increasing proportion of the legislative work of the Commission is devoted

---

240. Art. 192, 2nd para., EC. The European Parliament has made seventeen such requests until now (R. Corbett, F. Jacobs, and M. Shackleton, *The European Parliament*, 7th ed. (London, 2007), 239).
241. F. Hayes-Renshaw and H. Wallace, *The Council of Ministers*, 2nd ed. (Basingstoke, 2006), 201.
242. Art. 47 TEU.
243. See, e.g., the figures given by J. Peterson and E. Bomberg, *Decision-Making in the European Union* (London, 1999), 38: only 5% to 10% of the Commission proposals are, according to them, 'pure "spontaneous" Commission initiatives'.

to the elaboration of proposals for amendments to existing EC legislation, in which context the room for manoeuvre of the Commission is also limited by political agreements reached elsewhere, or by technical constraints.

The Commission may (and this is the second principle mentioned above) amend its proposal after submission. It may do so, for instance, in the light of the opinion delivered by the European Parliament. It also does so, very frequently, in order to enable the Council to reach a decision. In fact, as a rule governments will lack the requisite qualified majority or unanimity respectively to decide either to adopt the proposal or to depart from it. Negotiations (sometimes lengthy and often laborious) between the members of the Council are needed before a decision can be taken. The good offices of the Commission, as an expert and impartial agency involved in the whole procedure of decision-making in the Council, are of great importance for bringing about a compromise which does justice to the different points of view. Such a compromise must, depending on the voting requirements, be agreed by all the members of the Council or by a qualified majority. The cooperation of the Commission is indispensable, not only *de facto* but also (as regards reaching decisions by a qualified majority) *de jure* in view of the third principle set out above concerning the relationship between the Council and the Commission in the decision-making process (i.e., unanimity being required for departures from the Commission's proposals).

In practice, therefore, the position of the Commission during the decision-making process of the Council is that of an extra party in the negotiations leading to a decision of the Council: the twenty-eighth delegation in the Council's meeting room. As an extra party, it fulfils the important role of a mediator between the various national standpoints whilst also putting forward its own views, prompted by its own interpretation of the Community interest, on the decision to be taken. If qualified majority decisions are possible, this mediating function may develop into that of a decisive actor.

The provisions of the EC Treaty relating to economic and monetary policy, which were included in the EC Treaty by the Treaty of Maastricht, are something of a cuckoo in the nest of the decision-making system of the rest of the EC Treaty, as they pretty well wholly remove decision-making by the Council from the fundamental rule of acting on the basis of a proposal from the Commission, from which the Council may depart only by unanimity. The Council usually acts in this sphere on the basis of a recommendation, rather than a proposal, from the Commission.

Finally, the rule that departure from a Commission proposal is only possible on the basis of unanimity is also set aside in the framework of the second stage of the co-decision procedure between Council and Parliament, described below.[244]

The Council plays a central role in nearly all forms of EC legislation, but cannot adopt legislation entirely on its own. It is nearly always tied to a proposal from the Commission, which it may only amend under the conditions described

---

244. Art. 251 EC.

above. It must also take account of the opinions of the Parliament, to an extent which varies from case to case, depending on which decision-making procedure applies. The style of deliberations in the Council will be influenced by whether the Parliament has merely the right to give an opinion, or is not consulted at all, or whether it has the right of co-decision or the right to give its approval. The position of governments which share the opinion of the majority of the European Parliament in relation to a certain issue for which the co-decision procedure is applicable, is strengthened as compared to governments which do not share that opinion.

In the decision-making process within the Council, there is another fundamental difference linked to the question of which procedure is applicable. The EC Treaty provides that the Council takes its decisions by simple majority of the votes of the members (thus, at present, 14 out of 27), unless otherwise provided for in the Treaty.[245] In practice, this basic rule is hardly ever applicable since the Treaty 'provides otherwise' in nearly all cases: it prescribes either *unanimity*[246] or a *qualified majority*. In the latter case, the voting rules laid down in Article 205(2) EC apply, as last amended by Article 10 of the Act of Accession of Bulgaria and Romania.[247] Currently, a qualified majority is obtained with 255 out of 345 weighted votes allocated to each country according to a fixed formula. In addition, the countries voting in favour must constitute a majority of the member states (14 out of 27) and represent at least 62% of the total EU population.

With the entry into force of the SEA, the rule of unanimity was replaced in a number of cases by that of qualified majority. A further increase – both absolute and relative – in the number of areas for which the Council acted by qualified majority took place with the Treaty of Maastricht and the Treaty of Amsterdam, and also (though to a lesser extent) the Treaty of Nice.[248] In the original text of the EEC Treaty, provision was already made for the replacement of the rule of unanimity by that of a qualified majority in a number of areas after a transition period of several years. The transition led to a constitutional crisis, however, in 1965 in connection with the Commission's proposals in the field of agricultural policy – one of the areas in which qualified majority voting (hereafter QMV) would apply as of 1 January 1966. The French Government, anticipating developments, opposed an unlimited application of QMV. In its view it should not be applied if vital interests of one or more member States are at stake.

The other governments were not prepared to accept this view. This is apparent in the second part of the Luxembourg Accord of 28–29 January 1966, which provided a temporary solution to the crisis.[249] The governments were unanimously prepared to accept the idea that, whenever very important interests of one or more of

---

245. Art. 205(1) EC.
246. Art. 205(3) EC states that abstentions by Members present in person or represented do not prevent the adoption of acts which require unanimity.
247. O.J. 2005, L 157/203, at 206.
248. See on the extension of the sphere of application of QMV by the Treaty of Nice, A. Dashwood, 'The Constitution of the European Union after Nice: Law-making Procedures' (2001) EL Rev., 215.
249. Bull. EC 3–66, 8.

them were at issue, the members of the Council would try, within a reasonable time-limit, to find a solution acceptable to all of them 'while respecting their mutual interests and those of the Community, in accordance with Article 2 of the Treaty'.[250] However, they did not agree with the French standpoint 'that when very important interests are involved, the discussion must be continued until unanimous agreement is reached'.[251] Nevertheless, that point of view was followed in practice. In these circumstances, the importance of the qualified majority rule was seriously undermined. The Luxembourg compromise – often called, more accurately, an agreement to disagree – reinforced the already present tendency in the Council to avoid voting and to achieve decisions by means of a consensus, even on matters in which no important interests are at stake. Only rarely was there a vote in the Council, even on unimportant matters, save in the budgetary field.

This remained the situation until the mid-1980s. However, the fact that the SEA (1986) replaced the rule of unanimity in a number of cases by that of a qualified majority (in particular for internal market legislation) indicated that the Member States really did intend to use QMV. On 20 July 1987, the Council adopted a not insignificant change to its Rules of Procedure.[252] It was now expressly provided that the Council votes on the initiative of its President who is, furthermore, required to open voting proceedings on the invitation of a member of the Council or of the Commission, provided that a majority of the Council's members so decide.[253] Votes in the Council have not been exceptional now for a long time, even on important issues. It is now evident that the taboo on majority voting in the Council has clearly been broken, although the Luxembourg Accord was never formally revoked and from time to time a more or less implicit reference is made to them by one of the Member States.[254]

In recent years, a new conflict erupted between the Member States on the details of decision-making by QMV. The first scuffle took place during the negotiations on the accession of Austria, Finland and Sweden on the threshold for QMV. On the occasion of previous accessions, the weighting of votes required for a qualified majority had always stayed virtually the same (at about 71% of the total number of votes). The application of the formula producing the same weighting with effect from 1 January 1995 met strong resistance from the United Kingdom and Spain. They saw this as an unacceptable decrease in their possibility to block the adoption of measures by qualified majority. In a Union of Twelve, it had been possible for the United Kingdom and Spain (which had 18 votes together), aided by one of the smaller Member States having 5 votes, to block a decision, as the blocking minority was 23 votes. The British and Spanish demand to keep the

---

250. Ibid., point b(1).
251. Ibid., (2).
252. O.J. 1987 L 291/27.
253. Now Art. 11(1) Rules of Procedure, of which the current text is in O.J. 2006, L 285/47.
254. On the Luxembourg compromise and its aftermath, see J.M. Palayret, H. Wallace and P. Winand (eds), *Visions, Votes and Vetoes: The Empty Chair Crisis and the Luxembourg Compromise Forty Years on* (Brussels, 2006).

same blocking minority possibility for QMV in the EU of fifteen Member States as there had been in the EU of twelve was not met, however. The qualified majority was calculated according to the same mathematical formula (roughly 71%) as previously, coming to 62 out of 87 votes, and the blocking minority thus became 26 votes. In Ioannina, in Greece, on 29 March 1994, the Council adopted a decision on qualified majority decision-making,[255] the so-called Ioannina Compromise, whereby it was agreed that if during the decision-making process it appears that members of the Council representing a total of 23 to 25 votes were against the proposed decision, then the Council would not immediately adopt a decision by qualified majority, but would do all within its power to reach, within a reasonable time, a satisfactory solution that could be adopted by a greater qualified majority, by convincing some of the opponents.[256] In practice, however, virtually no use has been made of this compromise, although it was confirmed by the Treaty of Amsterdam.[257]

In recent years, the criteria for *weighting* of votes have been in the political limelight.[258] Since the creation of the European Communities, the weighting has never been proportional to the population, but gives relatively more weight to the smaller Member States. The perspective of accession of a number of central and eastern European states which are relatively small was a reason for the larger Member States to demand a new weighting of votes for calculating the qualified majority, in order to correct the privileged position of the smaller Member States. After the Amsterdam summit, in June 1997, failed to reach an acceptable compromise on this subject, it was put on the agenda for the 2000 Intergovernmental Conference (IGC). Indeed, in the Treaty of Nice, which was approved as the result of that IGC, a completely new arrangement was decided for the weighted votes of the various categories of Member States. This rearrangement only took effect on 1 January 2005, and not immediately on 1 February 2003, the date of entry into force of the Treaty of Nice.[259] Furthermore, in a separate Declaration attached to the Treaty of Nice, arrangements were made for the future weighted votes of the newly acceding states.[260] However, the Nice compromise on QMV was laborious and led to a complex and seemingly irrational voting regime, so that

255. O.J. 1994 C 105/1, as amended by the Council Decision of 1 Jan. 1995, O.J. 1995 C 1/1.
256. For a critical analysis, immediately after the compromise came about, see 'Editorial Comments, The Ioannina Compromise: Towards a Wider and Weaker European Union?' (1994) CML Rev., 453.
257. Declaration No. 50 attached to the Final Act of the Treaty of Amsterdam.
258. E. Best, 'The Debate over the Weighting of Votes: The Mis-Presentation of Representation?', in E. Best, M. Gray and A. Stubb (eds), *Rethinking the European Union: IGC 2000 and Beyond* (Maastricht, 2000), 105.
259. Treaty of Nice, Protocol on the enlargement of the European Union, Art. 3.
260. Treaty of Nice, Declaration No. 20 on the enlargement of the European Union, point 2. For a comprehensive view of how the question of weighting of Council votes was dealt with during the Nice Treaty negotiations, see D. Galloway, *The Treaty of Nice and Beyond* (Sheffield, 2001), Ch. 4.

the weighting of votes became a major bone of contention once again during the elaboration of the Constitutional Treaty and the Lisbon Treaty.[261]

The direct involvement[262] of the *European Parliament* in the legislative decision-making in the EC can take a variety of forms. The original form was that of simple consultation by the Council on a legislative proposal – a form which still exists; this is described in section 3.1.2, below. Over the years special procedures have been introduced in an increasing number of fields, with the aim of increasing the influence of the Parliament. In 1975, the conciliation (or *concertation*) procedure was established by mutual agreement of the Presidents of the Parliament, the Council and the Commission, which aimed, along with the increased budgetary powers granted in 1971, to give the Parliament greater influence in the adoption of Council decisions having financial implications – all within the framework of the existing consultation procedure. Then, with the coming into force of the SEA on 1 July 1987, the so-called *cooperation procedure* was introduced[263] which then applied mainly to legislation concerning the completion of the internal market. In this procedure, the Parliament can exert a not inconsiderable influence on the final act adopted by the Council, by the use of amendments. The SEA also provided for an *assent procedure*, a right of approval for the accession of new Member States[264] and the conclusion of association agreements.[265] The Treaty of Maastricht extended, as of 1 November 1993, that right to cover a number of other categories of international agreements[266] and some internal decisions. That same Treaty introduced – most importantly – the so-called *co-decision procedure*.[267] As a consequence of this procedure, the Parliament has truly evolved into a co-legislative body in the EC. In order for the Parliament to be able to fulfil this role adequately, the Parliament's rules of procedure have been amended several times, with a view to a tighter organization and speedier accomplishment of its tasks. Within the Parliament there is now a complex division of work, in the context of which the political party groups play an important role, as do the permanent parliamentary committees, meeting in Brussels, which prepare legislative resolutions for the plenary sittings of the Parliament (usually held in Strasbourg), in which the legislative resolutions are voted.[268]

---

261. See Ch. 1, section 8.2 *supra*.
262. In addition to this direct involvement, the Parliament can exert influence indirectly on the basis of its powers of control vis-à-vis the Commission. See *supra* Ch. IV, section 5.2.2.
263. Then Art. 149(2) EEC, now Art. 252 EC.
264. Then Art. 237 EEC, now Art. 49 TEU.
265. Then Art. 238 EEC, now Art. 310 EC.
266. Art. 300(3) 2nd para., EC.
267. Art. 251 EC, discussed in section 3.1.3 *infra*.
268. For a view of the internal institutional operation of the European Parliament, including the role of party groups and committees, see R. Corbett, F. Jacobs and M. Shackleton, *The European Parliament*, 7th ed. (London, 2007), Ch. 5 to 7; C. Neuhold and P. Settembri, 'The Role of European Parliament Committees in the EU Policy-making Process', in T. Christiansen and T. Larsson (eds), *The Role of Committees in the Policy-Process of the European Union* (Cheltenham, 2007), 152–181.

3.1.2   The Consultation Procedure

The consultation procedure was the normal decision-making procedure for Community legislation in the period 1958–1987. Since then, its relative importance has diminished as a result of the introduction of – first – the cooperation procedure, and then the co-decision procedure. Nevertheless, the consultation procedure remains even now of great practical significance; in particular, it applies to the vast number of Community acts concerning agricultural policy. In the discussion, a distinction will be made between various stages in the procedure (and it may already be mentioned that the first four stages also occur, with some alterations, in the co-decision procedure).

In the *first stage* the Commission's proposal is prepared by its services. As a rule national experts appointed for the purpose by the national governments at the Commission's request will participate in this stage. These experts, who are generally national officials, are consulted in their personal capacity. They are not, therefore, subject to specific instructions from their governments, neither can they commit the latter. The Commission, too, retains full freedom to act or not to act on their opinion. However, the joint working meetings enable the Commission to gauge the view of national administrations and to benefit from their expert knowledge. As mentioned earlier, many Commission proposals do not actually originate in the services of the Commission, but result from a request by the Council or the European Council, or from an international agreement concluded by the Community. Complex legislative proposals are increasingly preceded by a so-called Green Paper or some other kind of Communication, in which the Commission sets out policy options for public (online) discussion.[269] This is sometimes followed by a White Paper, in which the Commission sets out in more precise terms which policy direction it has decided to take.

In all cases, however, the *second stage* consists of the Commission's decision adopting the legislative proposal, on the basis of a detailed proposal prepared by its services; this decision is taken by a majority, pursuant to Article 219 EC, but in practice the Commission always aims to reach consensus among its members for important decisions. This Commission proposal is submitted to the Council.

In the *third stage*, consultations with the Economic and Social Committee and the Committee of the Regions take place on the Commission's proposal, if any are required by virtue of the legal basis proposed. The opinions of these bodies are not legally binding on the other Institutions, and their influence on the final act is fairly limited. At the same time, the Parliament is also consulted. Parliament's opinion is also not legally binding, but has greater political weight. The basic rule as disclosed by the Treaty provisions is that the Council consults the Parliament on the Commission's proposal, and does so on that proposal in its original form. The

---

269. To give just one example: in 1993, the Commission published a Green Paper on guarantees on consumer goods and after sales service (COM(93)509 final), which was followed by a proposal for a directive. The directive was finally adopted in 1999 (Dir. 1999/44, on certain aspects of the sale of consumer goods and associated guarantees, O.J. 1999, L 171/12).

Council does not have to wait for the Parliament's opinion before beginning its own work, described below as the fourth stage;[270] the Commission proposal is immediately subject to discussion in the working groups of the Council, while the European Parliament is still preparing its opinion. The Commission should keep the Parliament regularly informed of the progress of the proposal in the Council, otherwise the opinion would lose a good deal of its meaning. The content of the measure adopted by the Council must be clearly related in the essentials to the content of the Commission's original proposal on which the Parliament has been consulted. The duty to consult includes the requirement to re-consult whenever the text finally adopted, viewed as a whole, departs substantially from the text on which the Parliament has already been consulted, save where the amendments essentially correspond to the Parliament's wishes.[271] If the Council fails to obtain an opinion from Parliament, in principle it has no power to take a decision. However, the Council may apply for a consultation to be treated as urgent under the Rules of Procedure of the Parliament. Moreover, under Article 196 EC the Council may request the Parliament to convene an extraordinary session. This rule – that the Council must wait for the opinion of the Parliament, even though it is not bound by the content of that opinion – was formulated by the Court of Justice in its judgments in the so-called *Isoglucose* cases, in 1980.[272] The Court declared a Council act which had been adopted without the opinion of the Parliament required by the Treaty, to be invalid. The Court said at the time (when the European Parliament did not as yet have more than a consultative role in any field of Community legislative activity) that consultation

> is the means which allows the Parliament to play an actual part in the legislative process of the Community. Such power represents an essential factor in the institutional balance intended by the Treaty. Although limited, it reflects at Community level the fundamental democratic principle that the peoples should take part in the exercise of power through the intermediary of a representative assembly.[273]

In these cases, the Court left open the consequences of a *refusal* by the Parliament to give an opinion. In a later case, in 1995, where the Council had made a justified request that the Parliament bear in mind the need for the proposed measure to be adopted by a certain date, and the Parliament, notwithstanding assurances given, then decided to adjourn its plenary session without having debated the proposal, the Court regarded the Parliament as the author of its own misfortune; this was

---

270. Case C-417/93, *European Parliament v. Council.*
271. Case C-65/90, *European Parliament v. Council*; Case C-417/93, *European Parliament v. Council* and Case C-408/95, *Eurotunnel SA and Others v. SeaFrance.* Re-consultation of Parliament is not necessary if an alteration or addition leaves the essential elements of the provision as a whole unaffected, or is purely technical, i.e., comprises another method but not a substantive change, or corresponds to the wishes of the Parliament itself.
272. Case 138/79, *SA Roquette Frères v. Council of the European Communities*; Case 139/79, *Maizena GmbH v. Council.*
273. Case 138/79, *Roquette Frères*, at 3360 (para. 33).

considered a breach of the Parliament's duties of sincere cooperation with the other Institutions, and in that case (and only in that case) the Council may adopt an act in the absence of an opinion of Parliament.[274]

Understandably, the European Parliament would like to know why the Council did not follow its opinion, as often tends to be the case. If the Council were always prepared to state its reasons before the Parliament for a departure from the parliamentary opinion, this would compel it to devote some attention to these opinions. After initial resistance, the Council has become more ready to provide information about what happened to opinions from the Parliament.[275] The Council declared its readiness to exchange views on this matter during the periodic meetings with the President of the European Parliament, and agreed to explain orally, or in writing on request, the reasons for decisions deviating from opinions of the Parliament.[276]

After the consultation stage (which is what gives this legislative procedure its common name), follows the *fourth stage*, the preparation of the decision of the Council on the basis of the Commission's proposal and the opinions received. This takes place first in working groups of the Council, consisting of national officials specialized in the subject matter, which are often very influential in shaping the content of the measure.[277] These working groups normally start examining a Commission proposal as soon as it is transmitted to the European Parliament, so that there is, in reality, a partial overlap between the third and fourth stages. After the examination in a working group, the proposal moves up to the Committee of Permanent Representatives *(Coreper)*,[278] which thus fulfils its first task of 'preparing the work of the Council'.[279] The meetings of *Coreper* and the working groups are in practice always attended by officials representing the Commission. In this fourth stage, amendments to the proposal will usually be submitted by national administrations, which may or may not induce the Commission to amend its proposals. As mentioned above, the Commission is not obliged to amend its proposals, but will tend to do so if it can thus achieve consensus or a qualified majority in the Council on the main lines of its proposal. *Coreper*

---

274. Case C-65/93, *European Parliament v. Council*.
275. See now the European Parliament's Rules of Procedure (O.J. 2005, L 44/1, Rule 54). The question has diminished in importance since the introduction of the cooperation and co-decision procedures.
276. Council's note of 10 Oct. 1973, reproduced in Grabitz and Läufer, *Das Europäische Parlement* (Bonn, 1980) pp. 646–648, and the letter from the President-in-office, Bull. EC 11–1982, 53 et seq.
277. E. Fouilleux, J. de Maillard and A. Smith, 'Technical or Political? The Working Groups of the EU Council of Ministers' (2005) *Journal of European Public Policy*, 609.
278. See, on the crucial role of Coreper: J.W. de Zwaan, *The Permanent Representatives Committee: Its Role in European Union Decision-making* (Amsterdam, 1995); J. Lewis, 'National Interests: COREPER', in J. Peterson and M. Shackleton (eds), *The Institutions of the European Union*, 2nd ed. (Oxford, 2006).
279. Art. 207(1) EC. The second task is 'carrying out the tasks assigned to it by the Council'; see further, Ch. IV, section 3.4, *supra*. The chairmanship of the working groups and of *Coreper* always rotates with the rotation of the Presidency of the Council.

concludes the deliberations at this level with the decision[280] to submit the amended or unamended proposal to the Council.

The *fifth stage* takes place in the Council itself (that is, with the participation of members of the national governments), always also in the presence of members of the Commission. In cases where full agreement has been reached at the level of *Coreper* between the governments and the Commission, the draft measure is placed on the agenda of the Council as a so-called A-item, i.e., an item of the agenda on which no further discussion in the Council takes place. The Council then confines itself to adopting the draft measure without debate, unless objections are raised nonetheless during the meeting.

If no agreement has been reached at the lower levels, the matter is put on the Council's agenda as a B-item; it is then discussed by the members of the Council in order to find a common viewpoint. Such a discussion is of a negotiating nature and can well be lengthy and exhausting, certainly where unanimity is required and thus negotiations must continue until every single delegation can live with the text of the act to be adopted. The members of the Council have to make concessions on both sides, a difficult process, which on politically important issues can often be resolved only under the pressure of the circumstances: either the objective necessity to reach a decision, for example on annual agricultural price support or fishing quotas,[281] or the creation of an atmosphere of crisis by means of a time-limit in terms of an ultimatum, set by a government which can afford to do so. If the text is not approved in the end, it is sent back to the lower levels (working groups or *Coreper*), where further consensus-building work must then take place (or where the text slowly sinks into oblivion).

In the decision-making process several subjects are often combined (even subjects dealt with by different configurations of the Council), so as to meet the desire of certain Member States that concessions required from them in, say, the field of the agricultural policy, be compensated by concessions from other Member States in, say, the field of environmental policy. In the preparation of a set of measures which is balanced from the viewpoint of mutual concessions and which is acceptable to the members of the Council and to the Commission ('package deal') the knowledge of the subject and the political insight of the Commission may be of decisive importance.

In general, in the consultation procedure, the policy-making takes place mainly in close cooperation and in a constant dialogue between the Member States and the Commission. The Commission's function is to uphold the Community interest in policy-making, the members of the Council defend their national interests. Frequently the Commission, when confronted with the dilemma of taking no decision or taking a decision which is imperfect from its point of view, will give preference to the latter. This will then find expression either in the re-formulation

---

280. This is not a decision in the sense of the Treaties, as *Coreper* has no independent power of decision; see Case C-25/94, *Commission v. Council*.
281. Sometimes the Agriculture Council has been known to 'stop the clock' at midnight on the day before the deadline and continue negotiating in a marathon session.

of its original proposal or sometimes in essential amendments made subsequently. In addition to the Commission's role in adapting and revising the original text, the Presidency of the Council also plays an important role. With the support of the Council secretariat or in cooperation with the Commission, the President-in-office often tends to lay compromise proposals on the table which can break a deadlock.[282]

3.1.3   The Co-decision Procedure

Although this procedure is generally called the co-decision procedure (and equivalent names in other languages), it is not in fact officially given any name in the EC Treaty. The procedure is described in Article 251 EC. Application of the procedure is triggered by a reference in the Treaty provision serving as legal basis to the 'procedure referred to in Article 251'. This procedure was introduced by the Treaty of Maastricht in order to make the Parliament a more or less equal partner with the Council in the Community legislative process, at least in a number of policy areas. The procedure was simplified somewhat by the Treaty of Amsterdam, and certain inequalities between the Council and Parliament further levelled out; moreover, the number of policy areas to which this procedure applies was then increased. In the articles of the EC Treaty which laid down the cooperation procedure[283] after the entry into force of the SEA, the co-decision procedure now applies. The cooperation procedure has, since 1999, only applied in some parts of the EMU.

The co-decision procedure now applies in the area of free movement of workers and services, and freedom of establishment (Arts. 40, 42, 44, 46, 47 and 55 EC) and in the area of harmonization of legislation concerning the establishment and functioning of the internal market (Art. 95 EC). It also applies for the adoption of rules designed to prohibit discrimination on grounds of nationality (Art. 12 EC) and for strengthening the rights of Union citizens (Art. 18(2) EC). This procedure is also used for environmental policy (Art. 175(1) and (3) EC), development cooperation (Art. 179 EC), employment (Art. 129 EC), equal treatment of women and men in matters relating to work (Art. 141(3) EC), education (Art. 149 EC), vocational training (Art. 150 EC), culture (Art. 151 EC), public health (Art. 152 EC), consumer protection (Art. 153 EC), trans-European networks (Art. 156 EC), and research and technological development (Art. 166 EC).

The Treaty of Nice extended the application of the co-decision procedure to a number of other areas of legislative activity, so that this procedure has definitely become the 'normal' legislative procedure (though it is not the only one), and the Parliament's role as co-legislative authority is confirmed.[284]

---

282. On the role of the Presidency in this regard, see F. Hayes-Renshaw and H. Wallace, *The Council of Ministers*, 2nd ed. (Basingstoke, 2006), 149–151.
283. Described *infra* in section 3.1.4.
284. For a discussion of the cases of co-decision added by the Treaty of Nice see A. Dashwood, 'The Constitution of the European Union after Nice: Law-making Procedures' (2001) EL Rev., 215, 222–227.

The procedure is – as mentioned above – set out in Article 251 EC. The equality of the Parliament and the Council is expressed at the beginning and at the end of the procedure. Whenever the co-decision procedure applies, the Commission submits its proposal not just to the Council, but to the European Parliament and the Council.[285] Regulations, directives and decisions adopted in accordance with this procedure are signed by the President of the European Parliament and by the President of the Council[286] and are entitled 'Directive [or regulation, or other type of act] of the European Parliament and of the Council'. Actions for annulment against such acts must be addressed to the two Institutions together.[287]

The substance of the procedure contains elements of the cooperation procedure (which was, after all, introduced at an earlier date, by the SEA), but adds crucially the right of the Parliament at the end of the day to reject a text adopted against its wishes by the Council.[288]

As already mentioned, the co-decision procedure starts with the submission of the Commission proposal to the Parliament and the Council.[289] In the early stage, it is broadly similar to the consultation procedure described above. The Parliament gives its opinion on the proposal (as do the Economic and Social Committee and the Committee of the Regions, if this is required by virtue of the legal basis proposed) and then the Council establishes its viewpoint, after the preparatory work by the national civil servants meeting in Brussels in the working groups and Coreper. The Council may not simply proceed to adopting the act without more ado, as in the consultation procedure; that is only possible if it approves the Commission proposal without amendment *and* provided the European Parliament did not ask for any amendments to the Commission proposal in its opinion, or if the Parliament did ask for amendments, and these have been adopted by the Council. The Council decides in this case by qualified majority.[290] If the common position agreed by the Council departs from the Commission's proposal, then the basic rule of Article 250 EC comes into play, that this may only be done by the Council acting unanimously. Article 250 does not contain a reservation concerning Article 251(2) EC, as it does for Article 251(4) and (5) EC, which concern the later stages of the co-decision procedure.

---

285. Art. 251(2) EC.
286. Art. 254(1) EC (the President of the Council means the president-in-office of the Council in the relevant configuration).
287. E.g., Case C-376/98, *Germany v. Parliament and Council* (advertising and sponsorship of tobacco products)
288. Art. 251(5) EC. This parallels the Parliament's right to reject the draft budget, Art. 272(8) EC.
289. The following paragraphs will describe the co-decision procedure as it has applied since 1 May 1999, on the basis of the changes brought about by the Treaty of Amsterdam. This procedure was slightly different (and more complicated) in its original version laid down by the Treaty of Maastricht. For the procedure as it applied between 1993 and 1999, see the previous edition of this book, pp. 430–439.
290. In some policy areas, there are exceptions to this rule. In Art. 151(5) EC (culture), since the Treaty of Maastricht, the Council must act by unanimity at all stages of the procedure.

However, if the Council disagrees with the European Parliament, then a new stage in the co-decision procedure begins. In that case, the Council only adopts a preparatory act, which is called a *common position*.[291] This is also adopted by qualified majority (except if the Council departs from the Commission's proposal). This common position is communicated to the Parliament, which must also be informed fully by the Council of the reasons which led it to adopt the common position, and by the Commission of its own views on the common position of the Council. The Parliament then has three months[292] in which to react, and this stage is known as the second reading in the Parliament. If, within this period, the Parliament approves the common position or does not take a decision, the act in question 'shall be deemed to have been adopted in accordance with that common position' (Art. 251(2)(a) EC). That is to say, the regulation or directive (or other act) is definitively adopted without the Council considering it anew.

Within this period, though, if Parliament, by an absolute majority of its component members (which is significantly more than the majority of votes cast!), rejects the common position, then the proposed act is not adopted (Art. 251(2)(b) EC). This is an expression of the Parliament's right of veto in its most direct form. However – and this is what tends to happen more often – the Parliament can also, within the same period, and with the same majority, propose amendments to the Council's common position (Art. 251(2)(c) EC). In that case, the Council now examines the proposals in a *second reading* (Art. 251(3) EC). The Council may – within a period of three months, and by qualified majority – accept all the amendments proposed by Parliament, and in that case the act is adopted in the version proposed by the Parliament. (It should be noted, however, that if the Commission gives a negative opinion on certain amendments of the Parliament, then these amendments can only be approved by the Council acting unanimously.) The Council may also, though, stick by its earlier common position, or at least fail to reach the required majority to accept all the amendments proposed by Parliament – and this is the more likely scenario. In that case, the Conciliation Committee is convened, which consists of the twenty-seven members of the Council, or their representatives, and an equivalent number of members of the European Parliament.

The *conciliation procedure* (Art. 251(4) EC) which is thus initiated aims to reach a compromise which is acceptable to both institutions, by means of direct

---

291. This term is rather misleading. The position is not 'common' to a number of institutions, but is only held by the Council. It is also not necessarily a decision representing the common view of all the representatives of the Member States in the Council, since the common position can be adopted by qualified majority (so, against the wishes of some representatives). It also has nothing to do with a 'common position' under the Second and Third Pillars, which is one of the legal instruments which the Council can adopt in those areas, outside the scope of the EC Treaty (see section 1.6 of this chapter *supra*).

292. The periods of three months (and six weeks, see *infra*) referred to in Art. 251 EC may be extended by a maximum of one month (and two weeks, respectively) at the initiative of the European Parliament or the Council, Art. 251(7) EC.

negotiation between the Council and Parliament. The Conciliation Committee[293] has six weeks in which to do this. Within the Committee, a double majority rule applies: the draft text must be approved by a majority of the representatives of the Parliament (so, at least 14), and a qualified majority of the representatives of the Council in the Committee (with the same weighting of votes as in the decision-making in the Council itself). If such a joint text is approved, then the Parliament and the Council both have six weeks in which to adopt or reject the act in question on the basis of the agreed joint text. In the Parliament, an absolute majority of votes cast is sufficient. The Council decides with qualified majority. If the two institutions still do not accept the proposed act, despite the preparatory work of the Conciliation Committee, then it is not adopted (and the Commission must, if necessary, start all over again with a new proposal).

Despite the complexity of this procedure, it is now clear that the influence of the Parliament on legislative decision-making has increased substantially thanks to the co-decision procedure. On the other hand, this growing role of the European Parliament has led to a gradually more complex behind-the-scenes coordination between key actors of the three Institutions. This takes the form of the so-called 'trilogues', informal meetings of just a few representatives of Council, Commission and Parliament who seek to reach compromises which can then be presented and approved in the formal meetings. This phenomenon characterizes the different stages of the co-decision procedures, and not just the final phase of conciliation. It leads to more efficient decision-making (avoiding, very often, the need for a conciliation phase altogether) but there is a price to be paid in terms of transparency and accountability.[294]

3.1.4 Other Procedures

Most Community legislation these days is adopted using the co-decision procedure or the consultation procedure. A large number of different procedures are also provided for, however, in the EC Treaty, and occur in the practice of the Institutions. Some of these are generally applicable, in the sense that they are not restricted to a particular policy area, but most of them are 'made to measure' for a particular area. Even before the Treaty of Maastricht there was a proliferation of decision-making procedures, and the picture has not got any clearer since then.

The alternative procedures which are general in character are: the cooperation procedure, the assent procedure and the procedure for enhanced cooperation.

---

293. On the working methods for the Conciliation Committee, see the Interinstitutional AgreementI of 25 Oct. 1993, Bull. EC 10–1993, pp. 124–126, point 2.2.3. After the entry into force of the Treaty of Amsterdam, this was complemented by a Joint Declaration of the European Parliament, the Council and the Commission of 4 May 1999 on practical arrangements for the new co-decision procedure O.J. 1999, C 148/1, point III.
294. See M. Shackleton and T. Raunio, 'Codecision since Amsterdam: A Laboratory for Institutional Innovation and Change' (2003) *Journal of European Public Policy*, 171–187.

Article 252 EC governs the cooperation procedure, introduced by the SEA.[295] This procedure originally applied to a large number of areas of Community legislative activity. It was a precursor of the co-decision procedure, and has now (since the Treaty of Amsterdam) been replaced by the latter in all areas except four specific subjects in the field of the EMU.[296] The cooperation procedure gave the Parliament far more influence than it had under the consultation procedure.[297] Amendments to the Council's common position approved by the Parliament – which were then taken over by the Commission – could only be overruled by the Council acting unanimously. The Parliament therefore does not possess a real veto, but can influence the balance of interests within the Council in favour of its own opinions, by clever manoeuvring.[298] Despite pessimistic forecasts by many authors, who pointed out the complexity of the procedure, and were concerned about it making decision-making cumbersome, slow and even impossible, this procedure worked satisfactorily in the period 1987–1999, particularly with the implementation of the programme for realizing the internal market.[299]

The *assent procedure* is called thus because the European Parliament in this procedure does not participate in the decision-making process, but gives its assent (French: *avis conforme*) to a legal act whose content has been established by the other institutions. This procedure is utilized mainly for international agreements (on which, see Chapt. XIII). In that context it corresponds to a practice which applies at national level, whereby the national parliament approves international treaties negotiated and signed by the national governments. There are also, however, a number of instances of a European Parliament right of approval for internal legal acts: Article 7(1) and Article 7(2) TEU (action against breaches of the fundamental principles of the EU); Article 105(6) EC (extending the tasks of the ECB), Article 107(5) EC (amending the Statute of the ECB); Article 161 EC (altering the tasks of the Structural Funds); Article 190(4) EC (laying down a procedure for direct elections to the European Parliament). This assent procedure, which does not include any kind of dialogue with the Parliament prior to decision-making, and thus offers the Parliament the choice only between accepting and rejecting a final text, would seem highly unsuitable for internal legislation.

In addition, the Treaty of Amsterdam introduced a different decision-making procedure (slightly modified by the Treaty of Nice) – and as yet not utilized in practice – for legislative acts in areas in which *enhanced cooperation* takes place between a number of Member States.[300] A special procedure is laid down in order

---

295. Originally laid down in Art. 149(2) EEC.
296. See Arts. 99(5); 102(2); 103(2); and 106(2) EC.
297. For a detailed description of the cooperation procedure see the previous (English) edition of this book, pp. 427–430.
298. For a *case study* which illustrates this point of view, see C. Hubschmid and P. Moser, 'The Co-operation Procedure in the EU: Why Was the EP Influential in the Decision on Car Emission Standards?' (1997) *Journal of Common Market Studies*, 225.
299. For a general evaluation, see D. Earnshaw and D. Judge, 'The Life and Times of the European Union's Cooperation Procedure' (1997) *Journal of Common Market Studies*, 543.
300. See further on enhanced cooperation Ch. II, section 7, *supra*.

to authorize the establishment of enhanced cooperation.[301] The adoption of legislation within the context of enhanced cooperation takes place under the ordinary rules laid down in the EC Treaty for the subject matter in question,[302] with the important difference that only the representatives of those Member States participating in the enhanced cooperation take part in the adoption of decisions and voting in the Council. The threshold for QMV is lowered proportionately according to which Member States take part.[303] The Commission and the Parliament act in their normal composition.[304]

In addition to these general procedures, there are – as we already mentioned – a number of decision-making variants for *particular policy areas*. Policy relating to the *EMU* is subject to a decision-making system all of its own, some elements of which have been mentioned earlier, and which is characterized by the important role – even in legislative activities – of the ECB, and further by the fact that not all Member States participate in the decision-making (an example of enhanced cooperation which is specifically regulated in the EC Treaty). The institutional EMU law is discussed separately in Chapter X of this book. The Treaty of Maastricht provided for a completely separate legislative decision-making procedure in the area of *social policy*, as an alternative to the ordinary co-decision procedure which applies in this area: the social partners (employers' and trade union organizations) can approve an agreement, by means of consultation at European level, which is then transformed by the Council into a formal EC legal instrument, in the process of which the Council may not make any amendment to the content of the agreed act. A few directives have come into being by this procedure.[305] In the literature, however, questions have been raised as to the democratic legitimacy of this highly unusual form of legislative decision-making.[306] As for *migration and asylum law, and cooperation in civil matters*, during a period of five years after the entry into force of the Treaty of Amsterdam, there has been a transitional regime in which the initiative for legislative action was shared between the Commission and the individual Member States;[307] this was a leftover of the decision-making procedure which applied in this area before the Treaty of Amsterdam, when these subjects fell within the intergovernmental Third Pillar. A further peculiarity of this policy area – and which is not limited in time – is that Denmark, Ireland and the United Kingdom

---

301. See Art. 11(2) EC.
302. Art. 11(3) EC.
303. This is laid down in Art. 44(1) TEU. Art. 11(3) EC also refers to the provisions on enhanced cooperation in the TEU.
304. H. Bribosia, 'Différenciation et avant-gardes au sein de l'Union européenne. Bilan et perspectives du Traité d'Amsterdam' (2000) CDE, 57; J. Shaw, 'Flexibility in a "Reorganized" and "Simplified" Treaty' (2003) CML Rev., 279–311.
305. Dir. 96/34, O.J. 1996, L 145/4; Dir, 97/81, O.J 1998, L 14/9; Dir. 99/63, O.J. 1999, L 167/33; Dir. 2000/79, O.J. 2000, L 302/57. See, for an analysis of this procedure, E. Franssen, *Legal Aspects of the European Social Dialogue* (Antwerp, 2002); S. Smismans, 'The European Social Dialogue between Constitutional and Labour Law' (2007) EL Rev., 341.
306. L. Betten, 'The Democratic Deficit of Participatory Democracy in Community Social Policy' (1998) EL Rev., 20; C. Barnard, *EC Employment Law*, 3rd ed. (Oxford, 2006), 96–104.
307. Art. 67(1) EC.

only participate in the decision-making of the Council to a limited extent, pursuant to the special Protocol for these countries which was attached to the Treaty of Amsterdam.[308] In the area of *employment policy*, the Treaty of Amsterdam set up a separate decision-making procedure, which is very similar to the arrangements since the Treaty of Maastricht for the coordination of economic policy. There is continuing interaction between the Member States, the Commission, the Council and the European Council, in the context of which annual guidelines are established for the relevant national policy in mutual consultation.[309] This procedure departs sharply from the traditional legislative procedure, since the Commission does not have the formal right of initiative, but acts as a 'process manager', and also because the end product is not formal EC legislation, but decisions and acts whose legal nature is rather uncertain. This decision-making method has now been given the title 'open method of coordination' and has been extended to other policy domains in which the EC has only very limited legislative competences, and in which, therefore, the development of an EC policy requires the 'co-optation' of the relevant national authorities.[310] A departure from the usual procedures, but going in a different direction, is represented by the possibility for the Commission to adopt directives independently, without any formal participation of the other Institutions, in relation to *public undertakings*.[311] The Court of Justice confirmed, in a judgment dating from 1982,[312] that the text of the Treaty confers an independent legislative power on the Commission in this case, even though this is an unusual phenomenon within the system of the treaties. In practice, the Commission carries out a broad consultation of the parties concerned, including Member States and the European Parliament, before adopting such directives.[313]

---

308. These arrangements are extremely complex; see P.J. Kuijper, 'Some Legal Problems Associated with the Communitarization of Policy on Visas, Asylum and Immigration under the Amsterdam Treaty and Incorporation of the Schengen Acquis' (2000) CML Rev., 345–366; G. Papagianni, *Institutional and Policy Dynamics of EU Migration Law* (Leiden, 2006), Ch. 2.
309. See S. Sciarra, 'Integration through Coordination: The Employment Title in the Amsterdam Treaty' (2000) *Columbia Journal of European Law*, 209; D. Ashiagbor, 'Soft Harmonisation: the Open Method of Coordination in the European Employment Strategy' (2004) *European Public Law*, 305–332; C. Barnard, *EC Employment Law*, 3rd ed. (Oxford, 2006), Ch. 3.
310. There is a rich recent literature on the spread of the open method of coordination and on the promises and problems it contains in terms of effectiveness and accountability: P. Craig and G de Búrca, *EU Law: Text, Cases and Materials*, 4th ed. (Oxford, 2007), 150–154; E. Szyszczak, 'Experimental Governance: The Open Method of Coordination' (2006) *European Law Journal*, 486–502; K. Armstrong and C. Kilpatrick, 'Law, Governance, or New Governance? The Changing Open Method of Coordination' (2007) *Columbia Journal of European Law*, 649–677; and V. Hatzopoulos, 'Why the Open Method of Coordination is Bad for You: A Letter to the EU' (2007) *European Law Journal*, 309–342.
311. Art. 86(3) EC.
312. Joined Cases 188 & 190/80, *France, Italy and United Kingdom v. Commission*.
313. Thus, the Commission Directive on the transparency of financial relations between Member States and public undertakings, which was based on Art. 86(3) EC (Dir. 2000/52/EC of 26 Jul. 2000, O.J. 2000, L 193/75) was preceded by a draft directive which was published in the Official Journal (O.J. 1999, C 377/2).

3.1.5 Quality of EC Legislation

The quality of EC legislation is a theme which has been on the European political agenda ever since the early 1990s.[314] In a resolution adopted in 1993, the Council established a number of principles which were intended to improve the quality of drafting of EC legislation.[315] Reference was made to those principles later in Declaration No. 39 attached to the Final Act of the Treaty of Amsterdam.[316] It was stated therein that the Community Institutions should lay down guidelines in order to improve the quality of drafting of Community legislation, and also should speed up the codification of existing legislation. The guidelines – which relate mainly to technical points of drafting legislation – were established by means of an IIA in December 1998,[317] which was replaced by another, more ambitious, IIA on better law-making in 2003.[318]

Codification means the drafting and formal adoption of a text which replaces a number of existing acts in a particular area of EC legislation, without bringing about substantive changes. An IIA has been concluded with regard to this too, in which the Institutions agreed to follow a simplified procedure for such codification legislation.[319] A large number of projects have been completed,[320] but it remains a difficult process – not least because codification attempts are often interrupted by new legislative initiatives in the area to be codified. With this in mind, a new IIA was concluded in 2001 in order to facilitate the so-called 'recasting' of legislation: recasting is 'the adoption of a new legal act which incorporates in a single text both the substantive amendments which it makes to an earlier act and the unchanged provisions of that act'.[321] Unlike codification, recasting thus involves the creation of new law.[322]

For some years now, the Commission has been carrying out *impact assessments* of many of its draft legislative texts. These assessments gauge the economic,

---

314. For an overview of the development of this discussion, see R. Barents, 'The Quality of Community Legislation' (1994) *Maastricht Journal of European and Comparative Law*, 101; C.W.A. Timmermans, 'How Can One Improve the Quality of Community Legislation' (1997) CML Rev., 1229.
315. O.J. 1993, C 166/1.
316. O.J. 1997, C 340/139.
317. O.J. 1999, C 73/1.
318. O.J. 2003, C 321/1.
319. O.J. 1995, C 293/2.
320. See, e.g., Dir. 1999/42, which codifies certain directives on recognition of qualifications, O.J. 1999, L 201/77 and Dir. 1999/45, which codifies directives on the classification, packaging and labelling of dangerous preparations, O.J. 1999, L 200/1.
321. IIA of 28 Nov. 2001 on a more structured use of the recasting technique for legal acts, O.J. 2002, C 77/1, point 2.
322. An example of recasting is Dir. 2006/54 of the European Parliament and of the Council on the implementation of the principle of equal opportunities and equal treatment of men and women in matters of employment and occupation, O.J. 2006, L 204/23. For a comprehensive survey of the achievements in both codification and recasting, see European Commission, First Progress Report on the strategy for the simplification of the regulatory environment, COM (2006) 690 of 14 Nov. 2006.

social and environmental consequences of the adoption of the proposed legislation, and follow a standard methodology.[323] In 2006, for example, the Commission carried out no less than 67 such impact assessments.[324]

3.2   ADMINISTRATIVE DECISION-MAKING

The Court of Justice has ruled that in EC law, implementation 'comprises both the drawing up of implementing rules and the application of rules to specific cases by means of acts of individual application'.[325] Such implementation of EC legislation is to a large extent carried out by the Member States according to the rules and procedures of their own systems of administrative law, which cannot be dealt with in any detail within the confines of this book. It should be mentioned, however, that in this context the national authorities must take account not only of the relevant substantive rules of Community law, but also of the general principles of Community law developed by the Court of Justice aimed at the protection of individuals, as well as the general principles concerning the effect and enforcement of Community law.[326]

Frequently, however, Community legislation is implemented partly – or completely – by the Institutions of the EC themselves. In these cases too, implementation must take place in conformity with the substantive content of the legislation, and the general principles of proper Community administration. Such 'direct' implementation of legislation by the EC itself may follow three paths: autonomous administration by the Commission, implementation by the Council, or shared administration between the Council and the Commission according to the so-called 'comitology' system.

Implementation by the Council itself of a legislative decision it has adopted is an uncommon procedure – though it is explicitly provided for by Article 202 third indent EC. This provision states that the Council may reserve the right, in specific cases, to exercise directly implementing powers itself, without involving the Commission. It must give careful reasons for doing so.[327] This provision does not apply in cases where it follows from the Treaty that the Commission has the task of

---

323.   This standard method is described in an internal (but publicly available) Commission document SEC(2005)791.
324.   Report from the Commission, 'Better Lawmaking 2006', COM (2007) 286, 3.
325.   Case 16/88, *Commission v. Council*, para. 11.
326.   See J.H. Jans, R. De Lange, S. Prechal and R.J.G.M. Widdershoven, *Europeanisation of Public Law* (Groningen, 2007), Chs. 5 and 6.
327.   See Case C-257/01, *Commission v. Council* (regarding visa applications and border checks). The same piece of legislation may leave some implementing tasks to the Commission, and attribute others to the Council: for example, Reg. 2725/2000 of 11 Dec. 2000 concerning the establishment of 'Eurodac' for the comparison of fingerprints for the effective application of the Dublin Convention, O.J. 2000, L 316/1, Art. 22 reserving some implementing powers for the Council itself. This reservation of powers is justified in point 13 of the preamble of the Regulation.

drawing up rules for special situations, either explicitly (on transport, Art. 75(4) EC) or implicitly (competition, Art. 83(2)(d) EC). This *autonomous administrative task of the Commission* is characteristic in particular for the important policy sectors of competition and state aids.[328]

In most other areas, however, the Commission has a derived administrative task, assigned in a specific legislative act (usually a regulation) of the Council, or the Parliament and Council. In the exercise of these implementing tasks, the Commission is obliged in most cases to consult other bodies in its decision-making. Decision-making by the Commission is thus tied down by myriad procedures for consultation with the Council, with the individual Member States, and with committees consisting of representatives of the Member States, experts, or representatives of interested parties. A central role in this context is played by the committees of representatives of the Member States which may have an advisory or a managing role *vis-à-vis* the Commission, depending on the policy area in question. For the Council, these procedures provide a solution to the dilemma which it faced originally when enacting the relevant rules: either reserving the implementation entirely to itself, which is impractical and sometimes *de facto* impossible, or leaving the implementation entirely in the hands of the Commission, which it frequently finds to be politically undesirable. Exercise of the Commission's administrative task in close consultation with the national authorities would seem inevitable in any case, since the application of Community law 'on the ground' eventually involves the national governments and their civil services. On the other hand, this leads to an entanglement of national and Community responsibilities, which makes it very difficult for the European Parliament and the national parliament to carry out their task of scrutiny of the administration.

The name commonly used to refer to this system of institutional rules is *comitology*. The role of comitology in the implementation of EC policy in all sorts of areas (particularly in the area of agriculture and fisheries, food quality and structural funds) should not be underestimated.[329]

Involvement of committees of some type, of whatever composition, in the Commission's decision-making is one of the conditions which the Council can attach to the implementation by the Commission of the powers which the Council confers on it. The text of Article 202, third indent, EC, reflecting the modification

---

328. See Ch. IX *infra*. An example of a general administrative measure adopted autonomously by the Commission is Commission Reg. 1998/2006 of 15 Dec. 2006 on the application of Arts. 87 and 88 of the Treaty to *de minimis* aid, O.J. 2006, L 379/5.

329. See in particular: K. Lenaerts and A. Verhoeven, 'Towards a Legal Framework for Executive Rule-Making in the EU?: The Contribution of the New Comitology Decision' (2000) CML Rev., 645–686; C.F. Bergström, *Comitology: Delegation of Powers in the European Union and the Committee System* (Oxford, 2005); E. Vos, 'The Role of Comitology in European Governance', in D. Curtin and R. Wessel (eds), *Good Governance and the European Union: Reflections on Concepts, Institutions and Substance* (Antwerp, 2005), 107–124, as well as several contributions in C. Joerges and E. Vos (eds), *EU Committees: Social Regulation, Law and Politics* (Oxford, 1999), and in Th. Christiansen and T. Larsson (eds), *The Role of Committees in the Policy-Process of the European Union* (Cheltenham, 2007).

by the SEA, envisages the Council deciding in advance, acting unanimously on a proposal from the Commission and after obtaining the opinion of the European Parliament, the principles and rules for the exercise of implementing powers which it confers on the Commission in acts which it adopts. Immediately after the entry into force of the SEA, on 13 July 1987, the Council adopted Decision 87/373 on comitology[330] (hereafter: the Comitology Decision) implementing this Treaty provision and codifying the procedures which existed at that time.

The Comitology Decision provided for three procedures for participation of committees in the implementation of policy by the Commission. In the *advisory committees procedure*, the Commission must consult an advisory committee, but is not bound by the opinion of the committee – although of course in many cases the opinion of the committee will influence the Commission's further action. However, legal effects do flow from the so-called 'management committee procedure' and from the 'regulatory committee procedure'. The former procedure derives its name from the committees whose consultation was required from the start in the Commission's management of common organizations of the market under the Common Agricultural Policy. It has, however, also been applied, with certain variations, in other fields. A characteristic of the management committee procedure is the fact that the Commission is not obliged to follow the opinion of the committee consulted, but the Council itself may within a given time-limit substitute a measure for the measure taken by the Commission, if the latter is not in conformity with the opinion. If, however, the committee agrees with the Commission's draft or cannot come to an opinion, the Council cannot set aside the implementing measure of the Commission.[331] The Court upheld this system in the *Köster* case.[332]

A special variant of the management committee procedure – which differs to a considerable degree – is the regulatory committee procedure, under which the opinions to be sought relate to the Commission's exercise of its delegated regulatory powers. While in the management committee procedure, the Commission's departure from the opinion of a management committee is the condition under which the Council may intervene, in the regulatory committee procedure there is a conditional delegation of powers to the Commission. The Commission can only take the implementing measures with the consent of the committee. If no opinion or a negative one is given, the Commission must submit a proposal to the Council, which must then take a decision within a given time-limit on the basis of this proposal. If no such Council decision is forthcoming, the power of decision of the Commission becomes operative again: it adopts the proposed provisions itself.

---

330. Council Decision laying down the procedures for the exercise of implementing powers conferred on the Commission, O.J. 1987, L 197/33.
331. This was expressly confirmed by the Court in Case 35/78, *N.G.J. Schouten BV v. Hoofdproduktschap voor Akkerbouwprodukten* and in Case 95/78, *Dulciora SpA v. Amministrazione delle Finanze dello Stato.*
332. Case 25/70, *Einfuhr-und Vorratsstelle für Getreide und Futtermittel v. Köster.*

This is known in Community jargon as the *filet* procedure.[333] The Commission, like the European Parliament, had serious objections to a variant of the regulatory committee procedure which (under the first Comitology decision) gave the Council the right to veto, by a simple majority, Commission proposals, without being obliged to adopt other measures in their place (the so-called *contrefilet*, or double safety net).[334]

A particular problem arose after the introduction, by the Treaty of Maastricht, of the co-decision legislative procedure, under which acts were adopted by the Council and Parliament jointly. The delegation of powers of implementation to the Commission involved the problem that, under the comitology rules, the Council is given a right of intervention in relation to action by the Commission, but the Parliament – the co-legislative authority – was not. After long discussions, which often led to problems in relation to the adoption of acts under the co-decision procedure, parliamentary concerns were for the time being assuaged by the adoption of a *modus vivendi* between the European Parliament, the Council, and the Commission on implementing measures in relation to such acts, which provided for regular and prompt information being given to the relevant Parliamentary committee regarding the work of the comitology committees.[335] In order to reach a more definitive solution to this problem, it was agreed that the Comitology Decision would be amended. The amendments to the Comitology Decision – which were decided shortly after the Treaty of Amsterdam came into force – were of a broader nature, however.[336] The reform was aimed at increasing both the democratic legitimacy of activities of the committees (by means of a right of intervention for the European Parliament, and rules on the access to committee documents) as well as their efficiency (by means of a simplification of the existing procedures). The three existing procedures were maintained. Some substantive changes to each of the three procedures were made, and for the first time general criteria (non-binding) were laid down for the choice, by the Council, of committee procedure in a particular case.[337] A further partial reform was enacted in 2006, whereby a new comitology procedure was added to the three existing ones, namely the so-called regulatory procedure with scrutiny. This now applies to cases in which a committee considers Commission drafts for amendment of non-essential parts of EC legislation adopted under

---

333. This is the net which guarantees that a decision will be taken, as, if the Council fails to act on a matter, competence returns to the Commission.

334. The Commission thus consistently refused to propose this type of committee procedure, since it could lead to a situation in which no decision is taken, *Commission Report for the Reflection Group*, ibid.; *General Report on the activities of the European Union 1995* (Brussels, Luxembourg, 1996) point 1032.

335. O.J. 1996, C 102/1. For a clarification of the institutional context leading to this *modus vivendi*, see J.P. Jacqué, 'Implementing Powers and Comitology', in C. Joerges and E. Vos (eds), op. cit. *supra* note 329, 59.

336. Council Decision 99/468 laying down the procedures for the exercise of implementing powers conferred on the Commission, O.J. 1999, L 184/23.

337. See Lenaerts and Verhoeven, op. cit. *supra* note 329, for a detailed discussion and evaluation of the 1999 reform.

co-decision: since such Commission measures can be considered as quasi-legislative acts (they involve actual changes, albeit of a technical nature, of EC legislation), rather than mere implementation, it was thought proper to allow each of the two legislative organs, the Council and the European Parliament, to scrutinize and actually overturn an opinion of the committee involved.[338] It must also be noted that a different, and very particular, brand of comitology is used, under the name of 'the Lamfalussy process', for the adoption of quasi-legislative and administrative measures in the field of financial services.[339]

An entirely different mode of administrative decision-making occurs with the increasingly numerous *agencies*. On the one hand, the Commission has recently established some *executive agencies* that help it, essentially, to manage its spending programmes (there were five of them at the end of 2007). On the other hand, and more importantly, there is a growing number[340] of more autonomous *regulatory agencies* exercising a number of different functional roles, including information gathering, providing scientific expertise, and actual decision-making in individual cases. A clear example of a decision-making agency is the Office for the Harmonisation in the Internal Market, Trade Marks and Designs,[341] which decides on the recognition of trade marks and whose decisions can be, and are frequently, appealed before the Court of First Instance. Each of these agencies acts as a 'mini-executive', with its own decision-making procedure, and with its own mechanisms allowing for monitoring and control by the EU's main institutions.[342]

3.3   DECISION-MAKING IN THE SECOND AND THIRD PILLARS OF THE
        EUROPEAN UNION

The principles underlying the procedures for decision-making in the Second and Third Pillars differ from those in the framework of the EC Treaty. True, there is a

---

338. Council Decision 2006/512 amending Decision 1999/468, of 17 Jul. 2006, O.J. 2006, L 200/11. See 'Editorial Comment: In the Meantime . . . : Further Progress in Transparency and Democracy while the Constitution is Dormant' (2006) CML Rev., 1243, 1245–1250.

339. See D. Chalmers, C. Hadjiemmanuil, G. Monti and A. Tomkins, *European Union Law: Text and Materials* (Cambridge, 2006), 805–818.

340. At the end of 2007, the European Commission listed twenty-four Community agencies on its website, and six EU agencies under the Second and Third Pillar. Note that there is no Treaty list nor a Treaty definition of agencies, and some of the bodies listed as agencies are not actually called 'agency' but 'centre', 'authority' or 'office'. See further Ch. IV section 9.4, *supra*.

341. Reg. 40/94 of 20 Dec. 1993 on the Community trade mark, O.J. 1994, L 11/1.

342. There is a burgeoning literature on agencies. See, among others: P. Craig, *EU Administrative Law* (Oxford, 2007), Ch. 5; R. van Ooik, 'The Growing Importance of Agencies in the EU: Shifting Governance and the Institutional Balance', in D. Curtin and R. Wessel (eds), *Good Governance and the European Union: Reflections on Concepts, Institutions and Substance* (Antwerp, 2005), 125; E. Vos, 'Agencies and the European Union', in T. Zwart and L. Verhey (eds), *Agencies in European and Comparative Law* (Maastricht, 2003), 113; and various contributions, in D. Geradin, R. Muñoz and N. Petit (eds), *Regulation through Agencies in the EU. A New Paradigm of European Governance* (Cheltenham, 2005).

basic assumption that there is one general institutional framework for all EC and EU activities (Art. 3 TEU), and this principle is expressed concretely by the fact that decision-making concerning the two intergovernmental pillars takes place in the framework of Council meetings in a configuration which also deals with EC items. The General Affairs Council deals both with the CFSP and with external relations of the EC (and has moreover as task to ensure general coordination of the EU and EC policy of the Council). The JHA Council has kept its old name, even after the Treaty of Amsterdam transferred a part of its tasks from the third pillar to the First Pillar; it deals with items under both the First Pillar (including immigration and asylum) and the Third Pillar (police and judicial cooperation), in no particular order.

The powers of and the role of the Council are, though, very different under the different pillars. While under the EC Treaty the Council must usually act in close cooperation with the Commission and the European Parliament, in the Second and Third Pillars it is more or less supreme. The Parliament has only limited rights to give an opinion or receive information (Arts. 21 and 39 TEU). The Commission may make legislative proposals in the framework of the Third Pillar, but this power is shared with the individual Member States (Art. 34(2) TEU). In the framework of the Second Pillar, the entire decision-making process, from preparation to practical implementation of policy, is in the hands of the Council. In both intergovernmental pillars, the internal preparation of policy within the Council is the task of specialized committees, mentioned in the EU Treaty itself (Arts. 25 and 36 TEU); the Committee of Permanent Representatives (Coreper) has the complicated task of achieving general coordination of the Council's action in the various pillars.[343]

3.4   Changes in Decision-Making under the Treaty of Lisbon

If and when the Treaty of Lisbon enters into force, there will be some changes to the decision-making rules described above.

As far as legislative decision-making is concerned, there will be no major amendments to the procedures themselves, but the relative importance of the various procedures will change. As before, there will be no single unified procedure for making EU legislation, but the co-decision procedure (which, in its operation, will not be modified) will henceforth be called the *ordinary legislative procedure*; all the remaining procedures (including mainly the consultation and assent procedures) will be called *special legislative procedures*. This change of

---

343. See S. Duke and S. Vanhoonacker, 'Administrative Governance and CFSP', and H. Aden, 'Administrative Governance in the Fields of EU Police and Judicial Co-operation', both in H. Hofmann and A. Türk (eds) *EU Administrative Governance* (Cheltenham, 2006).

terminology is justified by the fact that co-decision will (once again) be extended to new areas of policy-making beyond those to which it currently applies, including such important areas as agriculture, external trade, 'legal' migration, and police and criminal justice cooperation. It will indeed become the main procedure through which EU legislation is adopted. This confirmation of the central role of co-decision is, however, accompanied by a number of new derogations and exceptions which detract from the transparency of the future law-making system. The current opt-outs for Denmark, Ireland and the United Kingdom in the area of migration, asylum and cooperation in civil matters will be preserved, but in addition the United Kingdom and Ireland will benefit from a new and very complex opt-out in the area of police and criminal justice (this was the price which the UK government exacted in return for allowing the application of the ordinary legislative procedure in this field).

Post-Lisbon legislative decision-making will furthermore be marked by a shift towards QMV in the Council, instead of unanimity, in a number of policy domains (which is, of course, logically connected to the extension of the co-decision procedure). QMV will happen according to an entirely new system based on a combination of the number of states and their respective population,[344] but that system will replace the current 'weighted voting' system only from 1 November 2014 onwards.

As far as non-legislative acts are concerned, the Lisbon Treaty introduces, as was mentioned in section 1.8 above, a distinction between delegated acts and implementing acts, both to be adopted by the Commission. This distinction carries with it a distinction in the political control mechanisms for these two types of acts. In the case of 'pure' implementing acts, the Commission's power will remain subject to the current comitology system, or a variation thereof. In the case of delegated acts, which will supplement or amend legislative acts, the Commission will be subject to a new and stricter control mechanism which, according to the new Article 290 TFEU, will either allow the European Parliament or the Council to revoke the delegation; or permit the entry into force of the delegated act only if Parliament or Council have not objected against it within a given period of time.

The special legislative procedure currently used under the 'third pillar' of the EU Treaty (section 3.3. above) will be abolished and replaced, as already mentioned, by the co-decision procedure accompanied by an opt-out for the UK and Ireland. On the other hand, Common Foreign and Security Policy will remain entirely subject to special procedures, with no room at all for co-decision. Important changes in this field are that, apart from the Council, the European Council will also obtain the power to adopt formal decisions, and that the High Representative of CFSP will have a general power of initiative in CFSP matters.

---

344.   As mentioned in Ch. IV, section 3.3.1 *supra*.

4   FINANCES OF THE EU

4.1   THE GENERAL BUDGET OF THE EU

**4.1.1   Historical Development prior to the Delors I Package
             Decisions of 1988**

The financial system of the Community had an eventful history, in which four
developing strands can be distinguished: the development from budgetary diversity
to unity; the development of the Community's financial autonomy; the development of financial mechanisms supporting Community policies, and the evolution
of the budgetary authority. These strands will be discussed in turn.

4.1.1.1   The Development from Budgetary Diversity to Unity[345]

Initially, the ECSC budget was divided into two budgets; one for operational
expenditure, the other for administrative expenditure. There was a similar division
for Euratom: an operating budget and the budget for research and development.
The then EEC had one single budget from the start. Since the Merger Treaty of
1965 entered into force on 1 July 1967, there was one general budget, which
included the administrative expenditure and the related revenue of the ECSC,
the revenue and expenditure of the EEC, and the revenue and expenditure of
Euratom as previously entered in its operating budget. The First Budgetary Treaty
of 22 April 1970 added to this the revenue and expenditure of the research and
investment budget of Euratom.[346]

There are, however, three exceptions[347] to the uniformity of the budget of the
Communities, which principle is nowadays enshrined in Article 268 EC: the
European Development Funds (EDFs), borrowing-and-lending operations and
guarantees of Community loans, and certain policy expenditure in the framework
of the Second and Third Pillars. These will be dealt with in section 4.2.1.1 below.

4.1.1.2   The Development of the Community's Financial Autonomy

The ECSC had financial autonomy right from the start, as a result of the power to
raise levies conferred by Article 49 ECSC. Because the administrative expenditure
of the ECSC was taken into the general budget when the Merger Treaty entered into

---

345. In Case C-284/90, *Council v. European Parliament*, at para. 26, the Court noted that the unity
      of the budget was one of two fundamental principles in budgetary matters (the other is the
      annual nature of the budget).
346. Merger Treaty, Art. 20(1) as amended by the First Budgetary Treaty, Art. 10.
347. Up to 2002, the so-called operational budget of the ECSC was outside the general budget. This
      budget was financed by special levies on coal and steel products, which were only to be used
      for specified objectives laid down in or pursuant to the ECSC Treaty. As a result, it was
      extremely difficult to integrate these in the general budget. Since the ECSC Treaty elapsed
      in 2002, this anomaly has been resolved.

force on 1 July 1967, that autonomy was partially lost. Between 1958 and 1970 the EEC and Euratom budgets were principally financed by a system of contributions from the Member States, as laid down in the old Articles 200 EEC and 172 Euratom. An extension of the Community's own resources was envisaged in the old Articles 201 EEC and 173 Euratom,[348] which should entirely or partially replace the contributions from the Member States. The first Own Resources Decision of 21 April 1970 (duly ratified by the Member States in accordance with their respective national requirements) introduced as of 1971 a system of own resources for the general budget.[349] These own resources comprised, initially:[350]

- customs duties;[351]
- agricultural levies;[352]
- a percentage of the Value Added Tax (VAT) levied by the Member States.[353]

Until the full application of the first Own Resources Decision, in 1980, the Member States paid contributions (on a degressive basis) to balance the general budget of the Community. Already in the early 1980s the budgetary ceiling, which stemmed from the revenue arising out of own resources (since the budget has to be in balance[354]) began to loom uncomfortably close. This was related to the declining revenue from customs duties as a result of the Tokyo Round of tariff reductions within the GATT, and declining revenue from the agricultural levies as a result of the increasing Community self-sufficiency for most agricultural products. The revenue from VAT turned out to show relative stagnation in relation to economic activity because of the declining share of the gross national product (GNP) accounted for by consumer expenditure in the economies of the Community's Member States. On the other hand, the expenditure of the Community continued to grow, particularly as it was unable to contain agricultural expenditure. Here too, the continual growth in Community self-sufficiency was a contributory factor.

On top of these factors, in 1981 and 1986, three relatively less prosperous Member States had acceded to the Community (Greece, Spain and Portugal), making greater calls on the existing Funds, such as the European Social Fund (ESF) and the European Regional Development Fund (ERDF), but contributing proportionally less. New policies involving intensive expenditure, and the strengthening of existing policies contributed in the 1980s to the heightened tension between the growing expenditure and the relatively stagnating revenue.

---

348. We will no longer mention the separate provisions of the Euratom Treaty in the rest of this section.
349. Council Dec. 70/243 of 21 Apr. 1970, O.J. 1970, L 94/19.
350. Other own resources included (and still include) a series of smaller items such as the proceeds of fines and penalties and the tax levied on the salaries of Community officials.
351. These were transferred to the Community in a gradual process between 1971 and 1975.
352. These have been collected by the Member States on behalf of the Community since 1971.
353. This was initially limited to a 1% ceiling calculated on a uniform basis, and was gradually applied as progress was made in harmonization of the VAT basis.
354. See Art. 268, 3rd para., EC.

In 1984, the financial possibilities accorded by the first Own Resources Decision were exhausted. Political agreement was reached at the European Council meeting in Fontainebleau in June 1984 that the VAT ceiling should be raised to 1.4%; this was given legal form with the second Own Resources Decision in May 1985,[355] and took effect from 1 January 1986.

This reform too bore scant fruit. Already in 1987, expenditure threatened (again mainly because of the agricultural guarantee expenditure) to exceed revenues. In 1979 and in 1984 attempts had been made to restrict the growth of non-compulsory expenditure, and to limit agricultural guarantee expenditure, but these attempts failed due to growing disputes between the two arms of the budgetary authority in the Community, the Parliament and the Council, and because of the fragmentation of the decision-making process in the Council, with that body – in the composition of the agricultural ministers in particular – being reluctant to accept the budgetary discipline arrangements for the agricultural sector laid down by their colleagues, the finance ministers, in the Ecofin Council.

The introduction of a system of own resources had created a troublesome apportionment problem between the Member States. Member States which import a relatively large quantity of agricultural products from outside the Community and themselves have a relatively small agricultural sector, end up contributing proportionately more to the Community and receive comparatively little benefit from the Community's agricultural spending in return. This discrepancy can become even greater if a very large proportion of the Member State's GNP is accounted for by the VAT base.

As early as 1974, just such a structural imbalance in the United Kingdom's financial relationship with the Community became a major political headache. Attempts were made on three occasions to agree some form of corrective mechanism in the forum of various European Council meetings between 1975 and 1984. The first mechanism was set out in Regulation 1172/76:[356] compensation would be provided from the Community budget to any country facing an unacceptable situation because of the unfair financial burden it was carrying, based on the partial repayment of the VAT own resources payments, provided that certain relatively stringent indicators were triggered. While the mechanism stayed in place until 1980, it was never triggered (though the United Kingdom was a net contributor during most of that period). The second attempt to appease the United Kingdom was in 1980. A Council Decision of 30 May 1980 provided for compensation in the form of specific measures to reduce regional disparities in the United Kingdom.[357] This mechanism was also not applied.

---

355. Council Dec. 85/257 of 7 May 1985, O.J. 1985, L 128/15.
356. Council Reg. (EEC) No. 1172/76 of 17 May 1976 setting up a financial mechanism, O.J. 1976, L 131/7.
357. See Council Reg. (EEC) No. 2743/80 of 27 Oct. 1980 amending Reg. (EEC) No. 1172/76 setting up a financial mechanism, O.J. 1980, L 284/1, and Council Reg. (EEC) No. 2744/80 of 27 Oct. 1980 establishing supplementary measures in favour of the United Kingdom, O.J. 1980, L 284/4.

The third attempt led to what has so far been a definitive solution to this 'British problem'. It was originally embodied in Article 3 of the second Own Resources Decision in 1985,[358] and has been repeated in the own resources decisions since. Currently,[359] three key elements are involved in this settlement:

- firstly, 66% of the difference between the United Kingdom's percentage share of VAT payments and its percentage share of allocated Community expenditure, applied to total allocated expenditure, is refunded to the United Kingdom by way of a reduction in its VAT base. A reduction to the rebate is phased in progressively by excluding a certain percentage (20% in 2009, 70% in 2010 and 100% in 2011) of enlargement-related expenditure from the calculation of the correction in favour of the United Kingdom;
- secondly, the reduction in the United Kingdom's contribution is made up by all the other Member States in accordance with their respective percentage share of VAT payments;
- thirdly, an exception applies to Austria, Germany, the Netherlands and Sweden whose financing share of the UK rebate is restricted to one fourth of their normal share.

A number of objections may be made to this complex and artificial settlement, both as matters of principle and as practical objections. What is presented as a 'solution', in fact stimulates the *juste retour* mentality of the Member States in relation to the Community, which fails to recognize the many indirect advantages of the process of European integration.[360] Moreover, on the Community's revenue side, such a compensation leads to the disappearance of the incentive to remove the causes of the undesired imbalances in the distribution of the direct benefits and burdens of the integration process on the expenditure side. The most important practical objection against such an apparently beneficial manoeuvre for the Member State concerned is that it becomes a permanent and sacrosanct arrangement, and thus encourages other Member States to try and negotiate special arrangements.

4.1.1.3   The Development of Financial Mechanisms Supporting Community Policies

As in national economic policy, since the end of the 1950s financial steering instruments have gradually assumed more importance in areas in which the Community is competent. From the outset, the ECSC and Euratom had powers anchored directly in the Treaties to administer funds. The EEC Treaty only provided for the establishment of special Funds in relation to agricultural guidance

---

358. Council Dec. 85/257 of 7 May 1985, O.J. 1985, L 128/15.
359. Art. 4 of Council Dec. 2007/436 of 7 Jun. 2007 on the system of the European Communities' own resources, O.J. 2007, L 163/17.
360. See further J. Le Cacheux, *The Poisonous Budget Rebate Debate*, Notre Europe, Studies & Research No. 41, 2005.

and guarantee policies[361] and the training and retraining of workers.[362] Since the beginning of the 1970s Community policy orientation through financial instruments has blossomed, even outside areas specifically envisaged in the then EEC Treaty.[363]

The extent of this phenomenon of expansion from the mid-1970s can be deduced from the myriad decisions, mostly on the basis of Article 308 EC, in which the changed composition of the Community was reflected, particularly in relation to regional economic policy, while in the field of scientific and technological research the scale and composition of the Community's administration of funds largely parallels the intensification of the technological race between the United States, Japan and Europe. The growing influence of the Parliament was expressed principally in the smaller programmes for specific social and regional objectives.

4.1.1.4   *The Evolution of the Budgetary Authority*

In the original EEC and Euratom Treaties, the Council was the sole budgetary authority. Until 1971 the Parliament's role in relation to the budget was purely consultative; it was the Council which adopted the budget. Unlike in normal procedures, the Council did not act on a formal proposal from the Commission as the basis for its decision-making. The Council consulted the Parliament on the draft budget which it had drawn up, after preparatory work by the Commission.

The First Budgetary Treaty of 22 April 1970[364] made various changes to the budgetary procedure and the power of decision:

– firstly, it conferred on Parliament the power to adopt the budget;
– secondly, it provided that the discharge in respect of the budget would be given by a joint decision of the Parliament and the Council;
– thirdly, it introduced a distinction between compulsory and non-compulsory expenditure,[365] although at first this distinction did not have consequences for the powers of Parliament.

---

361. Old Art. 40(4) EEC (text unchanged now Art. 34(3) EC).
362. Old Art. 123 EEC (now Art. 146 EC).
363. Important initiatives based on Art. 235 EEC (now Art. 308 EC) were: a) the establishment of the ERDP (Council Reg. (EEC) No. 724/75 of 18 Mar. 1975, O.J. 1975, L 73/1); b) the Integrated Mediterranean Programmes (Council Reg. (EEC) No. 2088/85 of 23 Jul. 1985, O.J. 1985, L 197/1). These two initiatives received a specific basis in the EC Treaty in 1986 with the articles on economic and social cohesion, now Arts. 158–162 EC. See further Ch. X, section 5, *infra*; c) the framework programmes for Community research, development and demonstration activities, adopted in the form of a Council resolution (Council Res. of 23 Jul. 1983, O.J. 1983, C 208/1), for which, also in 1986, a specific legal basis was created with what are now Arts. 163–179 EC (see further Ch. XII, section 7, *infra*).
364. O.J. 1971, L 2/1.
365. Compulsory expenditure is 'expenditure necessarily resulting from this Treaty or from acts adopted in accordance therewith', see Art. 272(4), 2nd para., EC. Non-compulsory expenditure is thus all other expenditure.

It is remarkable that in the new procedure there was no strengthening of the role of the Commission, although it had proposed to the Council that its co-responsibility should be more strongly expressed. But neither the Council nor the Parliament was willing to support such a development. This was a significant mistake, as the institution which was to play a key role in the legislative process, which in the 1970s would become ever more relevant for the Community's expenditure, was kept in a subservient, administrative function. This already made it more difficult to attune substantive and financial policy.

The Second Budgetary Treaty of 22 July 1975, which came into force on 1 June 1977,[366] made some important changes. Although these will be discussed in more detail in section 4.2 below, the most important changes are mentioned here:

- Decision-making powers on budgetary matters would henceforth be shared between the Council and the Parliament, which became the two arms of the budgetary authority, and Parliament obtained, within limits, the last word over non-compulsory expenditure (Art. 203(6) read with (9) EEC, now Art. 272(6) read with (9) EC). Alone of the Institutions, Parliament gained the power to grant the discharge in respect of the budget (under Art. 206b EEC, now Art. 276 EC).
- Budget control was to be exercised in future by the newly established Court of Auditors (Arts. 206–206a EEC, now Arts. 246–248 EC).

After the coming into force of the Second Budgetary Treaty, serious tension developed between the Parliament and the Council, at the root of which were four causes. First, the asymmetry between the powers of the Council as legislator and joint budgetary authority on the one hand, and the powers of the Parliament as joint budgetary authority on the other. Parliament sought to compensate its limitations in the sphere of policy-making and legislation by inserting a number of new budget headings and entering appropriations which could be used to commence new actions. It was able to do this by using its far-reaching power of amendment on non-compulsory expenditure, under Article 272(4) EC. The question in law was whether the power to enter a heading in the budget provided a legal basis for making a payment under that heading. That the Council did not share the Parliament's view about the budget being itself a sufficient legal basis for using appropriations, was hardly a big surprise.

The second problem was the difference in views between the Parliament and the Council on the substantive distinction between compulsory and non-compulsory expenditure; here too, the Parliament took a broad view as to the interpretation of non-compulsory expenditure, while the Council, as could have been expected, adopted a narrow interpretation.

The third cause of tension was the restriction, provided for in Article 272(9) EC, of the maximum rate of increase in non-compulsory expenditure, to be laid down by the Commission. Increases in such expenditure were in principle limited

---

366. O.J. 1977, L 359/1.

by that maximum rate, and although there was a certain degree of flexibility, the existence of the maximum rate provision was an important limitation on the Parliament's freedom of action.

Finally, the expansion in compulsory expenditure, particularly in the sphere of agricultural guarantee expenditure, in the second half of the 1970s and the first half of the 1980s, was an additional cause of friction. Given that the revenue from own resources was more or less stagnating, and given the requirement of Article 268 EC that the Community budget be in balance, this increase in agricultural expenditure was to the detriment of non-compulsory expenditure.

Thus the budgetary procedure between 1980 and 1987 was characterized by recurring friction between the Parliament and the Council, which repeatedly culminated in litigation before the Court of Justice.[367] Although the Commission attempted to mediate in these conflicts, within the limits of its rather subordinate role in the budgetary process, these efforts booked scant success. Even the Joint Declaration of the Council, Parliament and Commission of 30 June 1982,[368] which dealt with the distinction between the two types of expenditure and by which was recognized that a separate legal basis was required for the utilization of appropriations, did not lead to more harmonious collaboration. 1988 began with a fundamental impasse relating to the budget.

4.1.2 The Situation since the Delors I Package: A Multi-annual Framework for the Community Budget

The enlargement to embrace Spain and Portugal led to wider differences in the prosperity of the Member States of the Community. The less prosperous countries feared that the accelerated establishment of the internal market provided for by the SEA would make those differences in prosperity even more marked. This strengthened the demand at the political level for an extensive Community contribution for the less prosperous regions. At the same time, it appeared that controlling the compulsory agricultural expenditure was posing ever-increasing problems. The proportion of such expenditure in an already over-stretched Community budget rose to more than 70%. The differences in the views of the Council and the Parliament discussed in the preceding section meant that the annual budgetary procedure, laid down in Article 203 EEC (now Art. 272 EC), was taking longer and longer to complete; and this was further aggravated by the continually increasing gap between the resources available and the demands made upon them.

---

367. Case 34/86, *Council v. European Parliament* (in respect of the 1986 budget). The actions in respect of the 1982 budget were removed from the register on 14 Jul. 1982 and in respect of the 1988 budget the Court ruled in Case 377/87, *European Parliament v. Council*, and Case 383/87, *Commission v. Council*, that there was no need for it to proceed to give judgment. The friction did not suddenly end in 1987: see, e.g., Case C-284/90, *Commission v. European Parliament*, and Case C-41/95, *Council v. European Parliament*.

368. O.J. 1982, C 194/1. This joint declaration was replaced by the IIA of 6 May 1999 between the European parliament, the Council and the Commission on budgetary discipline and improvement of the budgetary procedure, O.J. 1999, C 172/1.

An additional factor in the size of this gap was the manifest ambitions of the Commission and the Parliament to strengthen the Community administration by means of financial instruments.

In February 1987 the Commission presented a package of comprehensive proposals for the reform of the Community's public finances, known as the Delors I package,[369] which found broad political agreement in the European Council in Brussels in February 1988.[370] The measures concerned four essential elements of Community finances. These four elements are explained, briefly, below because since 1988 they have continued to define the Community budget process and the content of the Community budget. Decision-making on the budget, as formally arranged in Article 272 EC, usually takes place within the framework formed by these four elements.

4.1.2.1   Medium-Term Perspectives

Ever since the adoption of the Delors I Package, in Brussels in February 1988,[371] the budgetary process of the Community takes place within a financial framework of a period of five to seven years. This framework is usually decided by the European Council, on the basis of a proposal by the Commission.[372] After 1988, it was determined in December 1992 by the European Council of Edinburgh,[373] in March 1999 by the Berlin European Council,[374] and in December 2005 by the Brussels European Council.[375] The four financial frameworks provide a good insight into the most important political and policy issues facing the European Union. Certain recurring problems are: the net contributions of the individual Member States, resulting from their contributions to and revenues from the Community budget; the permanent need to maintain control of the agricultural guarantee expenditures; and the tensions between the so-called Cohesion States,[376] which profit substantially from the structural funds, and the other

---

369. These were set out in two communications: *The Single European Act: A New Frontier for Europe* (COM (87) 100 Final), and *Report on the Financing of the Community Budget* (COM (87) 101 Final). These were then given concrete shape in various proposals culminating in the package of measures agreed in Jun. 1988.

370. See further L. Kolte, 'The Community Budget: New Principles for Finance, Expenditure Planning and Budget Discipline' (1988) CML Rev., 487–501.

371. Bull. EC 1/2-1988, points I.1.1–I.1.10.

372. Currently, there is no reference to the financial framework in the Treaties. This will change if the Treaty of Lisbon enters into force (see new Art. 312 TFEU).

373. Bull. EC 12-1992, points I.45–I.60.

374. Bull. EU 3-1999, points I.4–I.38. The Conclusions of the Berlin European Council are based on proposals which the Commission set out in its so-called Agenda 2000, COM (97) 2000 final.

375. Bull. EU 12-2005, point I.7.2.

376. The Cohesion States, who have a Gross National Income (GNI) of less than 90% of the Community average, were initially Spain, Portugal, Greece and Ireland. Now, the new Member States as well as Greece and Portugal have this status while Spain is eligible to the Cohesion Fund on a transitional basis; see Council Reg. (EC) No. 1083/2006 of 11 Jul. 2006 laying down general provisions on the ERDF, the ESF and the Cohesion Fund and

Member States. The financing of enlargement has also been an important issue,[377] although its final budgetary cost has ultimately been far lower than was initially assumed.[378]

Decision-making on the medium-term financial framework for the European Union is thus eminently political in character, and the European Council plays a decisive role therein. Once a decision has been taken by the European Council, this tends to be followed by the adoption of an own resources decision, an IIA between the Parliament, the Council and the Commission, and decisions or regulations on budgetary discipline. The own resources decisions fix the contributions of the Member States for a period of five to seven years. The IIAs determine the financial ceilings for the most important categories of expenditure. They form the quantitative framework within which the Community budgetary authority should operate in the relevant period. Because the financial ceilings for the most important categories of expenditure are an ideal expression of the compromises reached in the relevant European Council, the extent to which they are politically binding is high. Any description of the Community budgetary process as an institutional-legal process which ignored this political commitment would give a distorted picture of the reality of that process. The legal acts or decisions on budgetary discipline are the concluding element. They aim to prevent the Community legislature – particularly in the field of agriculture – from taking decisions which exceed the medium-term financial framework.

4.1.2.2 *Own Resources*

In the period since 1988, whenever a financial framework has been adopted, a new own resources decision has also been adopted.[379] The most important characteristics of the system of own resources decisions are:

First, in order to ensure a stable stream of revenue, from 1988 onwards the total amount of own resources was no longer linked to a single item of revenue (VAT), instead for each year overall ceilings are set for the financial resources necessary for financing the budget, expressed as a percentage of the Community's total GNP or, since the 2000 Own Resources Decision, of its total Gross National Income (GNI). This percentage is fixed in the relevant own resources decisions

---

repealing Reg. 1260/1999, O.J. L 2006, L 210/25, as amended by Council Reg. (EC) No. 1989/2006 of 21 Dec. 2006, O.J. 2006, L 411/6, and Council Reg. (EC) No. 1084/2006 of 11 Jul. 2006 establishing a Cohesion Fund and repealing Reg. 1164/94, O.J. 2006, L 210/79.

377. The 2004 enlargement gave rise to an adjustment in 2003 of the financial framework 2000–2006; see Dec. 2003/429/EC of the European Parliament and of the Council of 19 May 2003 on the adjustment of the financial perspective for enlargement, O.J. 2003, L 147/25.

378. See further A. Mayhew, 'The Financial and Budgetary Impact of Enlargement and Accession', in C. Hillion (ed.), *EU Enlargement: A Legal Approach* (Hart Publishing, Oxford-Portland Oregon, 2004), 143–167.

379. Council Dec. 88/376 of 24 Jun. 1988, O.J. 1988, L 185/24; Council Dec. 94/728 of 31 Oct. 1994, O.J. 1994, L 293/9; Council Dec. 2000/597 of 29 Sep. 2000, O.J. 2000, L 253/42, and Council Dec. 2007/436 of 7 Jun. 2007, O.J. 2007, L 163/17.

throughout the financial framework. For the current financial framework (2007–2013), the applicable maximum is 1.24%, pursuant to the 2007 Own Resources Decision.[380]

Second, since the 1988 Own Resources Decision, the VAT-based own resources have been adjusted downwards. While the maximum contribution (as a percentage) from the VAT-based own resources was fixed at 1.4% in 1985,[381] it is now fixed at 0.30% by the 2007 Own Resources Decision. Further, since 1988, the VAT base to be used for the calculation may not exceed a certain percentage (initially 55% and since the 2000 Own Resources Decision 50%) of the Member States' GNP/GNI. This capping of the VAT percentage and the VAT base tends to work degressively for the less prosperous Member States, because in those States the proportion of the VAT base in relation to GNP is relatively high.

Third, the system of traditional own resources (customs duties, agricultural levies, and the levies on sugar and isoglucose) was simplified as of 1988. Since the 2000 Own Resources Decision, 25% of these levies may be deducted as collection costs by the Member States, before the revenue is passed on to the Community.[382] The idea behind this is that the Member States then have an interest in collecting these revenues efficiently.

Fourth, and most importantly, a new 'fourth resource' was introduced by the 1988 Own Resources Decision. This fourth resource is currently[383] calculated by applying, to a base made up of the sum of the Member States' GNI,[384] a rate to be determined during the budgetary procedure in the light of the total of all other revenue. The rate is applied to the GNI of each Member State, and the resulting amount should be made available to the Community.[385] This fourth resource is intended to ensure that there is balance in the Community budget, and is, therefore, often called an 'additional resource' in budget documents. The most important side-effect of the fourth resource is to match each Member State's payments more closely to its ability to pay.

Fifth, the compensation mechanism which had been agreed for the United Kingdom in 1985 has remained in place, with certain minor adjustments since 1988. This means that the United Kingdom still benefits from a substantial correction in the form of a reduction in its VAT payments. The other Member States finance this compensation in proportion to their GNI, whereby for Germany, Sweden, Austria and the Netherlands there is a reduction of 25%.[386]

---

380. Art. 3 of Council Dec. 2007/436, see previous note.
381. Council Dec. 85/257 of 7 May 1985, O.J. 1985, L 128/15.
382. In the current 2007 Own Resources Decision, Art. 2(3).
383. Ibid., Art. 2(1)(c).
384. See, for the definition of GNI, ibid., Art. 2(7).
385. See also ibid., Art. 2(5), which provides for a gross reduction in their annual GNI contributions for Sweden and the Netherlands during the period 2007–2013.
386. Ibid., Arts. 4 and 5; see also *supra* section 4.1.1.2.

4.1.2.3   Budgetary Discipline

The three greatest threats to budgetary discipline which existed in the budgetary procedure prior to 1988 (under Art. 203 EEC) were: *first*, the tendency of the Parliament to increase the non-compulsory expenditure, in respect of which it had the most to say, as much as possible; *secondly*, the virtually autonomous continual increase in the agricultural guarantee expenditure; and, *finally*, the price (in the form of greater expenditure than was permitted) of the annual conflict between the Parliament and the Council. Therefore, inevitably, the achievement of budgetary discipline formed the central part of the Delors I package. Since then, it has been given shape in the different IIAs[387] as well as in several regulations on budgetary discipline.[388] In both these instruments, it is emphasized that the Parliament, the Council and the Commission are *jointly* responsible for the achievement of budgetary discipline, without encroaching on the powers conferred on each of them by the Treaties.

The most important elements of the current IIA will be discussed first, and then, briefly, the regulations on budgetary discipline.

4.1.2.3.1   The 2006 Interinstitutional Agreement
The core of the 2006 IIA is formed by the financial framework 2007–2013.[389] For each year, the financial framework states, per heading and subheading, the maximum amounts for which financial commitments may be undertaken (commitment appropriations) and payments made (payment appropriations). The maximum amounts are given in detail in a table attached as an Annexe to the IIA. Six separate headings of expenditure are identified:

(1) 'Sustainable growth', with subheadings 1a 'Competitiveness for Growth and Employment' (i.e., for the most part research and development expenditure; between 8.4 billion euro (in 2007) and 13 billion euro (in 2013) per year) and 1b 'Cohesion for Growth and Employment' (i.e., structural

---

387. Currently, the IIA of 17 May, 2006, O.J. 2006, C 139/1. The IIAs of 1988, 1993 and 1999 were published in O.J. 1988, L 185/33, O.J. 1993, C 331/1, and O.J. 1999, C 172/01. See further on the 1988 IIA, P. Zangl, 'The Interinstitutional Agreement on Budgetary Discipline and Improvement of the Budgetary Procedure' (1989) CML Rev., 675–685.

388. Until recently, Council Reg. (EC) No. 2040/2000 of 26 Sep. 2000 on budgetary discipline, O.J. 2000, L 244/27, meanwhile repealed by Council Reg. (EC) No. 1248/2007, O.J. 2007, L 282/3.

389. The financial framework in the 2006 IIA is a rather careful reflection of the conclusions of the Brussels European Council, apart from some limited changes and a small increase in the total amounts of commitment and payment appropriations negotiated by the European Parliament (see also A. Montagnon, 'L'accord sur le cadre financier 2007–2013' (2006) *Revue du Marché commun et de l'Union européenne*, 441). They confirm to what extent the medium-term budget planning is determined by political agreements between the Member States, in which both the net contributors and the net receivers among the Member States try to safeguard their interests as much as possible. This leaves little margin for the Community budgetary authority in the adoption of the annual budget.

funds and cohesion fund expenditure) (between 42.9 billion euro (in 2007) and 45.3 billion euro (in 2013) per year).

(2) 'Preservation and Management of Natural Resources', which refers in essence to agricultural expenditure (between 55 billion euro (in 2007) and 51.2 billion euro (in 2013) per year).

(3) 'Citizenship, freedom, security and justice', with subheadings 3a 'Freedom, Security and Justice' (between 0.6 billion euro (in 2007) and 1.4 billion euro (in 2013) per year) and 3b 'Citizenship' (0.6 billion euro per year between 2007 and 2013), which refer to expenditure for a variety of internal policies other than research and development.

(4) 'EU as a global player', which refers to expenditure for external action (between 6.2 billion euro (in 2007) and 8 billion euro (in 2013) per year).

(5) 'Administration', for the most part operational expenses of the institutions (between 6.6 billion euro (in 2007) and 7.6 billion euro (in 2013) per year).

(6) 'Compensations', which refers to certain expenditure related to the accession of Bulgaria and Romania (between 0.4 billion euro (in 2007) and 0.2 billion euro (in 2009) per year and none as of 2010).

The financial framework is adjusted annually (by the Commission), on the basis of a fixed deflator of 2% a year.[390] The budgetary discipline which the Institutions have set out in the IIA consists of four distinct elements:[391]

(i) The Institutions acknowledge that the amounts mentioned in the various headings and subheadings represent annual ceilings for expenditure from the Community budget.

(ii) The two arms of the budgetary authority (that is: Parliament and Council) accept that the maximum rates of increase for non-compulsory expenditure under Article 272(9) EC should remain within the limits of the maximum rates deriving from the financial framework.

(iii) No act adopted under the co-decision procedure by the European Parliament and the Council, or adopted by the Council, which involves exceeding the appropriations available in the budget or the allocations available in the financial framework, may be implemented until the budget has been amended, and the financial framework appropriately revised. This is one of the key conditions for the process of decision-making by consensus which is laid down in the IIA. As a result of this provision, the Community legislature is obliged to take account of the fact that the exercise of its powers in this domain can interfere with the powers of – above all – Parliament as (co-) budgetary authority.

(iv) Finally, the fact that the Community budgetary authority is tied to the available own resources is expressed. If, for any one year, the sum of total

---

390. See para. 16 IIA.
391. Paras. 12–15 IIA.

appropriations laid down in the financial framework exceeds the ceiling for own resources (1.24% of GNI), then the maximum amounts must be revised downwards. Recourse will have to be had to this provision in practice if the real economic growth in the Community stagnates.

The 2006 IIA also contains agreements between the Council and Parliament about 'earmarking' expenditure in the various categories as compulsory or non-compulsory. This division had been a recurring source of disagreement between the Parliament and the Council ever since the beginning of the 1980s, and no definition of these two concepts has been sufficient to end the disagreement.[392] The definition given in the 2006 IIA is not conclusive either.[393] The classification as compulsory or non-compulsory expenditure given in Annexe III of the IIA is based more on a – fragile – political compromise, which may be adjusted according to a conciliation procedure set out in Annexe II.[394] The classification of compulsory or non-compulsory expenditure could be disrupted if the Community legislature were to set multi-annual financial programmes – by which the budgetary authority would be bound – by legislative act. With that in mind, the consequences of such legislative acts are regulated separately.[395] These arrangements distinguish between legislative acts which are adopted under the co-decision procedure – i.e., jointly with the Parliament – and those adopted solely by the Council. Acts in the first category are in principle binding on the budgetary authority (with a margin of 5%), while those in the second category are not.

Since the 1999 IIA, the question has also been settled whether – and to what extent – a prior basic act is necessary in order to implement the appropriations listed in the budget. In the past, the Parliament had tried time and again to initiate new Community policy bypassing the Council, by using its powers as (co-) budgetary authority. This practice – which raises questions of principle concerning the

---

392. See *infra* section 4.2.3.2.
393. Para. 34 IIA defines compulsory expenditure as follows: 'The institutions consider compulsory expenditure to be expenditure necessarily resulting from the Treaties or from acts adopted in accordance therewith', which is a mere paraphrase of Art. 272(9) EC. This definition is not conclusive as far as expenditure necessarily resulting from acts adopted in accordance with the Treaties is concerned, since this would mean that the Community legislature decides what is compulsory.
394. Earlier attempts to reach compromises between the Parliament and the Council on the classification of compulsory and non-compulsory expenditure did not result in lasting agreement. The Joint Declaration of the Council, Parliament and Commission of 30 Jun. 1982 on various measures to improve the budgetary procedure, O.J. 1982, C 194/1, was followed by a number of disputes between the Parliament and the Council, which led to rulings of the Court of Justice in Case 34/86, *Council v. European Parliament*, and Case 204/86, *Greece v. Council*. In fact, in the 1980s, the quantitative ratio of compulsory to non-compulsory expenditure was still 85-15; in the 2007 budget, this ratio is about 35–65 (for commitment appropriations).
395. Paras. 37–38 IIA. Agreements were made on this subject already in the Declaration by the European Parliament, the Council and the Commission of 6 Mar. 1995 on the incorporation of financial provisions into legislative acts, O.J. 1996, C 102/4.

division of powers between the Community legislature and the Community budgetary authority,[396] and which as such has led to a number of cases before the Court of Justice[397] – was subject to detailed rules laid down in the 1999 IIA.[398] These rules are no longer included in the 2006 IIA, since they have meanwhile been incorporated in Article 49 of the Financial Regulation (FR) of 2002.[399]

Like the 1999 IIA, the 2006 IIA also contains agreements on the financing of operational expenditures for the Common Foreign and Security Policy from the general Community budget. In this context, a fine balance had to be found between on the one hand the primarily intergovernmental decision-making on the content of the CFSP and, on the other, the powers of the Community budgetary authority. The carefully drafted text reveals the extreme sensitivities involved – particularly on the part of the Parliament.[400]

The IIA has *political* significance, as the framework within which agreements are made by the Member States among themselves about how Community expenditures should be spent. This is clearly expressed at several places. The provision in the IIA that the budgetary authority is not only bound to respect the maximum amounts set out in the financial framework, but also to respect the division of those expenditures among the various categories reflects the political agreements reached between the Member States as to the distribution of expenditure.[401] An indication of how sensitive the arrangements can be is the provision that the European Parliament and the Council undertake to use to the full the maximum amounts available for the allocation of commitment appropriations provided in the financial framework for structural operations. In this way, the so-called Cohesion States have aimed to secure their share in Community expenditure.[402] The interests of the net contributor states are secured by the budgetary discipline set out in the IIA.

---

396. See further section 4.2.4. *infra*.

397. Case C-106/96, *United Kingdom v. Commission*, Joined Cases C-239 & 240/96, *United Kingdom v. Commission*, and Case C-305/96, *United Kingdom v. Commission*. After the Court had decided Case C-106/96, the United Kingdom withdrew its actions in the other cases, and they were removed from the register.

398. Paras. 36 and 37 of the 1999 IIA. Agreements on the subject had already been made in the Joint declaration of 30 Jun. 1982, O.J. 1982, C 194/1, and in a declaration to the 1993 IIA.

399. See *infra* section 4.1.4. In the new Art. 310(3) TFEU, as introduced by the Treaty of Lisbon, it is expressly mentioned that the implementation of expenditure in the budget shall require the prior adoption of a legally binding Union act providing a legal basis for its action and for the implementation of the corresponding expenditure (exceptions can be provided for in secondary legislation).

400. Para. 42 of the 2006 IIA. In 1997, a separate IIA was already concluded on this (O.J. 1997, C 286/80).

401. Para. 12 of the 2006 IIA. In the description by C. Régnier-Heldmaier, in *Commentaire J. Mégret: Le Droit de la CE et de l'Union européenne*, Vol. 11 (Éditions de l'Université de Bruxelles, Brussels, 1999), 94–98, of the negotiations which led to the 1988 and 1993 IIAs, the political significance of these agreements is clearly evident.

402. Paras. 12 of the 1999 IIA and 13 of the 2006 IIA. In the context of previous IIAs, the expenditures for the structural funds were considered to be privileged expenditures.

From the above it is apparent that the IIA has sharply diminished the policy margin of the budgetary authority under Article 272 EC. Two questions arise as a result, which the Court has had to consider on a number of occasions:

- What is the legal nature of the IIA? Is it more than simply a political agreement, and does it entail binding legal rules?[403]
- Can the Community Institutions make arrangements between themselves by which they restrict or depart from powers which are based on the Treaty?

The Court has indirectly answered the first question by reasoning that the budgetary procedure, as it is set out in the Treaty, is in fact based on an interinstitutional dialogue. That dialogue is subject to the same mutual obligations of loyal cooperation as those which govern the relations between the Member States and the Community Institutions under Article 10 EC.[404] A following step – i.e., the explicit recognition of the IIA as a legal act which binds the parties to it, and against the infringement of which they could appeal to the Court of Justice – has not so far been taken.[405] This does not detract from the fact that the existing case law implies that the IIA consists of more than a mere collection of political agreements: real legal obligations may flow from them if the rules contained are sufficiently precise.[406] As to the second question, the case law of the Court is more precise. These agreements interpret and implement the Treaty provisions on the budget, but they nevertheless cannot diminish the powers which the various Institutions derive from the Treaty.[407]

If the Treaty of Lisbon enters into force, these questions will be solved since, according to the new Article 312(2) TFEU, which mentions the multi-annual financial framework explicitly, the latter will be adopted in the form of a regulation. It will, therefore, undoubtedly have binding legal force.

4.1.2.3.2 Secondary Law on Budgetary Discipline

The agreements to respect budgetary discipline would be to no avail if the Community was unable to control agricultural guarantee expenditure, the development of which was determined by the common market organizations in agricultural products. For that reason, in 1988, a mechanism (the so-called agricultural guideline) was added to the Delors I Package, to make it possible to keep agricultural

---

403. J. Monar, 'Interinstitutional Agreements: The Phenomenon and its New Dynamics after Maastricht' (1994) CML Rev., 693–719, and H.J. Timmann, 'La procédure budgétaire pour l'exercice 1989 et la première application de l'accord interinstitutionnel' (1989) RMC, 235–242. Both authors are, cautiously, in favour of according legal consequences to the IIA.
404. Case 204/86, *Greece v. Council*, at para. 16. In Case C-41/95, *Council v. Parliament*, the legal nature of the IIA was indirectly at issue. In his Opinion in this Case, A.G. La Pergola examined the issue in more detail than the Court.
405. Contrary to C. Régnier-Heldmaier, op. cit. *supra* note 401, 35, it is our opinion that the judgment of the Court in Case C-25/94, *Commission v. Council*, does not unequivocally imply that the Court attaches legal consequences to IIAs as such which bind the parties thereto.
406. Similarly, J. Monar, op. cit. *supra* note 403, 713–719.
407. Case 204/86, *Greece v. Council*, at para. 17, and implicitly Case C-41/95, *Council v. Parliament*.

expenditure under control; this mechanism was also retained by the Edinburgh European Council in 1994.[408] After the Berlin European Council in 1999, it remained in force but with certain – important – changes which were mainly necessary in connection with changes in agricultural market policy in the course of the 1990s.[409] The mechanism was laid down in Council Reg. (EC) No 2040/2000,[410] the result of which was that the annual rate of growth of total agricultural expenditure could not exceed 74% of the annual nominal rate of growth of the Community's GNP.[411] Considering, however, that the ceilings set in the financial framework 2007–2013 preclude the need to maintain the agricultural guideline provided for in Reg. 2040/2000 and that other provisions have been rendered obsolete by new legislation on agriculture[412] and by the new FR[413] which have meanwhile been adopted, the Council has decided to repeal Reg. 2040/2000.[414]

4.1.2.4   The Reform of the Structural Funds

The third part of the Delors I package was the reform of the Structural Funds. With the accession of Greece, Spain and Portugal, the differences in regional prosperity in the Community had increased in the 1980s. The Member States on the Community's periphery and the economically less strong Member States feared that the completion of the internal market in the Community would further strengthen those differences. This was the main reason for the introduction of Articles 130a–130e EEC (now Arts. 158–162 EC) by the SEA. In February 1988, the European Council at Brussels drew the political consequences and decided to double the commitment appropriations for the structural funds in real terms by 1993, as compared with 1987, thus guaranteeing the growth of the structural funds in the medium term. At the Edinburgh European Council of December 1992, the size of the structural funds – to which the so-called Cohesion Fund had been added – was increased once more. Currently, the structural funds and the Cohesion Fund account for approximately 35% of the Community budget. The political weight of the decision-making in the European Council as to the exact size, composition and distribution of the structural funds is substantial, not merely as a mechanism for income transfers from

---

408. Respectively Council Dec. 88/377 concerning budgetary discipline, O.J. 1988, L 185/29 and Council Dec. 94/729 concerning budgetary discipline, O.J. 1994, L 293/14.
409. The biggest change in that policy was that for the most important agricultural products, a switch was made from a system of guaranteed prices to a system of producer subsidies. The former system was extremely sensitive to price and currency fluctuations on the world market, and to fluctuations in production. As a result, the expenditures on agriculture could rise or fall sharply in a short space of time. See further Ch. XII, section 1, *infra*.
410. O.J. 2000, L 244/27.
411. Ibid., Art. 3.
412. Council Reg. (EC) No. 1290/2005 of 21 Jun. 2005 on the financing of the common agricultural policy, O.J. 2005, L 209/1, as last amended by Council Reg. (EC) No. 479/2008 of 29 April 2008, O.J. 2008, L 148/1. Arts. 18–20 specifically deal with budget discipline.
413. See *infra* section 4.1.4.
414. Council Reg. (EC) No. 1248/2007 of 22 Oct. 2007, repealing Reg. (EC) No. 2040/2000 on budgetary discipline, O.J. 2007, L 282/3.

more prosperous to less prosperous regions of the Community, but also as a mechanism to compensate for – excessively – large differences in the net contributions of the Member States to the Community budget. The decision-making at the Berlin European Council in March 1999 and at the Brussels European Council in December 2005 provide a striking illustration.[415] These agreements are laid down both in the financial frameworks annexed to the IIAs, and in the basic regulations for the structural funds.[416] Although the expenditure for the structural funds, also under the most recent IIA of 2006, comes in the category of non-compulsory expenditure, over which the European Parliament has the last say, pursuant to Article 272 EC, as co-budgetary authority, that Institution in fact has little margin of appreciation with regard to these expenditures. The interested Member States tend to guard their part in the expenditures for the structural funds carefully, and they take great care that the maximum amounts laid down in the financial framework are used up. The erosion of the powers which Parliament formally derives from Article 272 EC must be balanced against the gains in terms of stability of the budgetary process since the Delors I package was accepted in 1988. In assessing this balance, it should be further noted that the co-legislative powers the European Parliament has received under Articles 161 and 162 EC in setting the objectives and organization of the structural funds and the implementing decisions relating to the ERDF have granted the possibility for greater influence on the structural policy, with its focus on expenditure. See further on this Chapter X, section 5, of this book.

4.1.3 Maastricht, Amsterdam and Nice: The Most Important Treaty Amendments

4.1.3.1 Maastricht

The Treaty of Maastricht made a number of changes to Title II of Part Five of the EC Treaty.[417] The most important amendments concern the control of the financial management of the Community. The Court of Auditors was raised to the status of a Community Institution.[418] Accordingly, the provisions relating to its composition and powers were moved from Title II of Part Five to Title I of that Part (provisions governing the Institutions).[419] This change, largely the result of British pressure, was intended to place more emphasis than hitherto on the legality, regularity and soundness in accounting terms of the Community's financial management, and thus to sharpen the responsibilities of the Parliament as well as of the

---

415. See on the latter A. Montagnon, op. cit. *supra* note 389, 441–442.
416. See further Ch. X, section 5.3. *infra*.
417. See further J. Cloos et al., *Le Traité de Maastricht*, (Bruylant, Brussels, 1994), 437–446.
418. Art. 7 EC. See further D. O'Keeffe, 'The Court of Auditors', in D. Curtin and T. Heukels (eds), *Institutional Dynamics of European Integration: Essays in Honour of Henry G. Schermers*, Vol. II (Dordrecht, 1994), 177–194.
419. To become Arts. 246, 247 and 248 EC.

Court of Auditors.[420] The greater emphasis on sound financial management and control was also reflected in a change to the rules relating to the implementation of the budget by the Commission, and a new article on the grant of the discharge by the Parliament.[421]

The changes in the actual budgetary procedure[422] were kept to a minimum, although both the Dutch delegation to the IGC which led to the Treaty of Maastricht and the Commission pressed for an amendment of these provisions to bring them more into line with the current practice since 1988. The changes involved including a provision on charging expenditure occasioned for the Community Institutions by the provisions in the TEU relating to CFSP and JHA to the Community budget.[423] The old Article 200 EEC (on the financial contributions from the Member States) was repealed.[424] Article 201 EEC (now Art. 269 EC) was completely redrafted, reflecting the existence of the Community's own resources.[425] A more important point concerns Article 270 EC, also inserted by the Treaty of Maastricht, in which the principle of budgetary discipline – introduced in the 1988 IIA – was raised to a Treaty obligation. Articles 202 and 203 EEC remained unchanged, and are now Articles 271 and 272 EC.

Attempts by various delegations to the IGC leading to the Treaty of Maastricht to include the own resources system in the Treaties themselves, in order to increase the unity of the budget further, to strengthen the role of the Parliament in the determination of the Community's own resources, to abolish the distinction between compulsory and non-compulsory expenditure, and to introduce a Community tax, came to nothing. A majority of the delegations did not want to burden a strongly institutionally orientated IGC with a financial debate, which could have arisen as a result of these proposals.

---

420. See especially Art. 248(1), 2nd para., EC, introduced by the Treaty of Maastricht, which, by imposing on the Court of Auditors the new task of providing the European Parliament and the Council with a statement of assurance as to the reliability of the accounts and the legality and regularity of the underlying transactions, also confirms the role of the Parliament.

421. Art. 205 EEC gained a new phrase 'having regard to the principles of sound financial management' (see now Art. 274 EC). The newly added Art. 206 EEC (now Art. 276 EC) sets out the grant of the discharge, which was previously summarily stated in Art. 206b EEC.

422. Arts. 268–272 EC.

423. Art. 199, 2nd para., EC (now Art. 268, 2nd para., EC). *Administrative* expenditure occasioned by the implementation of those provisions is automatically charged to the Community budget. Under the Maastricht Treaty, *operational* expenditure could be charged to the budget under the conditions set out in Arts. J.11(2) and K.8(2) TEU, respectively. Since the Amsterdam Treaty, operational expenditure is charged to the budget, except where the Council acting unanimously decides otherwise; see *infra* section 4.2.1.1.

424. The old Art. 200 EEC, which regulated the financial contributions of the Member States before the entry into force of the first Own Resources Decision, 1970, had already become redundant when the Maastricht Treaty was signed in 1992. The same was true of the old text of Art. 201 EEC.

425. See *infra* section 4.2.2.

A further important change was the introduction (by Art. 209a EEC, now Art. 280 EC) of the concept of the protection of the Community's financial interests, which is considered in section 4.3, below.

Finally, since the entry into force of the Maastricht Treaty, the Community budget is officially named the 'general budget of the European Union'.

4.1.3.2　　　　Amsterdam[426]

The Treaty of Amsterdam followed the line started in the Treaty of Maastricht. The Treaty provisions on the budget process itself (Arts. 268–272 EC) were unchanged, while the articles on the control of the financial management, and the legality and soundness of that management, were further strengthened. The same was true of the Treaty basis for Community action against fraud.

The most important amendments were the following:

- A provision was added to Article 248(1) EC requiring the statement of assurance from the Court of Auditors as to the reliability of the accounts to be published in the Official Journal. The provision concerning access to information by the Court of Auditors was sharpened and extended (Art. 248(3) EC).
- An addition to Article 274 EC places an obligation on the Member States to cooperate with the Commission, in order to ensure that the Community appropriations are used in accordance with the principles of sound financial management.
- Article 280 EC (on countering fraud) was considerably strengthened by the addition of the provision that the Community and the Member States are to take the necessary measures to counter fraud, which must act as a deterrent and afford effective protection in the Member States. Further, in this article, a legal basis was created for measures in the fields of the prevention of and fight against fraud affecting the financial interests of the Community, so as to afford effective and equivalent protection in the Member States (para. 4).

4.1.3.2.1　　　　Nice
The amendments to the financial provisions of the EC Treaty made by the Treaty of Nice were extremely limited, in line with the limited objective of that Treaty, which aimed primarily to achieve the necessary reform of the institutional provisions of the European treaties in view of the imminent enlargement. In accordance with this limited aim, Article 247 EC, laying down rules for the composition and appointment of members of the Court of Auditors, was amended. Article 248(4) EC introduces the possibility for the Court of Auditors to create internal chambers

---

426. The changes which this Treaty made to the Treaty provisions on the budget were in fact rather disappointing. A promise at the time of the 1993 IIA to review the Treaty-based distinction between compulsory and non-compulsory expenditure was not met. Nor were the Treaty provisions, in particular Art. 272 EC, adapted to the existing budget practice.

to adopt certain categories of reports or opinions[427] under the conditions laid down by its rules of procedure.[428] Article 279 EC is amended such that, as from 1 January 2007, the FRs and the rules concerning the responsibility of financial controllers, authorizing officers and accounting officers, may be adopted by qualified majority.[429]

4.1.3.2.2   Lisbon

If the Treaty of Lisbon enters into force, this will lead to several changes, many of which are to a certain extent an institutionalization at the level of the Treaty of what is now, after a long evolution, current budgetary practice. This is, for instance, the case for the financial framework, which will be mentioned explicitly in the TFEU;[430] for the changes in the provisions on the budgetary procedure;[431] and for certain aspects related to the implementation of the budget.[432] Furthermore, with the Treaty of Lisbon, the legendary distinction between compulsory and non-compulsory expenditure will disappear;[433] and, the creation of a European Public Prosecutor will become possible.[434]

4.1.4   The Financial Regulation

The most important secondary law with regard to the establishment and the implementation of the Community budget is the FR based on Article 279 EC. The FR adopted in 1977[435] applied to the management of the Community budget for many years. The evolution of Community budgetary practice, as described above, was also reflected in the changes made over the years to this Regulation. The Regulation was drastically amended in 1988, by Regulation 2049/88,[436] in order to keep the management risks attached to so-called differentiated appropriations

---

427. Until now, no such chambers have been created, although they could enhance the efficiency of the decision-making process, compared to the actual system in which reports and opinions are adopted by a majority of all 27 members.
428. A peculiarity of the amended Art. 248(4) EC is that the Council still retains the right to approve the – internal – rules of procedure of the Court of Auditors. This would seem to be in conflict with the independence of this Institution (cf. also Art. 218(2) EC, concerning the rules of procedure of the Commission, and Art. 12.3 Statute ESCB and ECB, concerning the rules of procedure of the ECB). The rules of procedure of the Court of Auditors have been published in O.J. 2005, L 18/1.
429. This provision parallels that of Art. 161, 3rd para., EC, on economic and social cohesion.
430. New Art. 312 TFEU; see *supra* section 4.1.2.3.1.
431. New Art. 314 TFEU; see *infra* section 4.2.3.1.
432. In particular, the new Art. 310(3) TFEU and, to a lesser extent, the new Art. 317 TFEU; see *infra* section 4.2.4.
433. See *infra* section 4.2.3.2.
434. New Art. 86 TFEU; see *infra* section 4.3.2.2. Other changes introduced by the Treaty of Lisbon relate to the principle of sound financial management (new Art. 310(5) TFEU; see *infra* section 4.2.1.7), own resources (new Art. 310(4) TFEU; see *infra* section 4.2.2) and the protection of financial interests (new Art. 325(4) TFEU; see *infra* section 4.3).
435. O.J. 1977, L 356/1.
436. O.J. 1988, L 185/23.

under control.[437] It was radically reformed again in 1994.[438] The changes made aimed above all at improving the presentation of lending operations and budget reserves in the budget documents. The FR of 1977, which was beginning to look like a patchwork blanket as a result of the changes made to it over time, was replaced entirely by the FR of 2002.[439] This Regulation – together with Regulation 2342/2002,[440] which contains the implementing rules for the FR (hereafter: the Implementation Regulation) – will be referred to frequently in the following discussion of the legal aspects of the Community budget.

4.2   LEGAL ASPECTS

4.2.1   Budgetary Principles

4.2.1.1   Principles of Unity and Budget Accuracy (Art. 268 EC; Arts. 4–5a of the FR of 2002)

The principle of unity of the budget was already mentioned in section 4.1.1. above. The FR makes further progress toward the realization of this principle, according to which all revenues and expenditures of the Community and all transactions which are relevant to the finances of the Community should be brought together accurately in one budget document. Nevertheless, there are still three important exceptions to the principle of unity:

4.2.1.1.1   Borrowing and Lending Operations
Article 172(4) Euratom explicitly authorizes the Community to borrow on the capital market. The EC Treaty does not contain such an explicit authorization. Since 1975, raising and granting of loans has taken place on the basis of Article 308 EC (ex Art. 235). On this basis, the mechanism for providing medium-term support

---

437. See further section 4.2.1.2. *infra*.
438. By Council Reg. (ECSC, EC, Euratom) No. 2730/94 of 31 Oct. 1994, O.J. 1994, L 293/7.
439. Council Reg. (EC, Euratom) No. 1605/2002 of 25 Jun. 2002 on the FR applicable to the general budget of the European Communities, O.J. 2002, L 248/1, as last amended by Council Reg. (EC, Euratom) No. 1525/2007 of 17 Dec. 2007, O.J. 2007, L 343/9. See further P. Craig, 'A New Framework for EU Administration: The Financial Regulation 2002', (2004) *Law and Contemporary Problems*, 107–133; V. Dussart, 'La réforme du Règlement financier communautaire: un exemple de la modernisation du droit budgétaire' (2002) *Revue française de finances publiques*, 141–163; F. Van Craeynest and I. Saarilahti, 'Le nouveau règlement financier applicable au budget general de l'Union européenne: un maillon essentiel de la réforme de la Commission' (2004) *Revue du Marché commun et de l'Union européenne*, 30–51.
440. Commission Reg. (EC, Euratom) No. 2342/2002 of 23 Dec. 2002 laying down detailed rules for the implementation of Council Reg. (EC, Euratom) No. 1605/2002 on the FR applicable to the general budget of the European Communities, O.J. 2002, L 357/1, as last amended by Commission Reg. (EC, Euratom) No. 478/2007 of 23 Apr. 2007, O.J. 2007, L 111/13.

to Member States with balance of payments difficulties,[441] and the so-called Ortoli facility[442] were set up. Of these two mechanisms, the first lost virtually all its importance with the establishment of the EMU,[443] and the second has now been abolished. They are overshadowed in importance by the external lending operations of the Community. These usually take place via the European Investment Bank (EIB), which grants loans to third countries, financed by having recourse to the capital market and utilizing its own resources. The recipient countries include a number in the Mediterranean area and some other countries, usually underdeveloped countries. The financial involvement of the Community with such transactions is reflected in the guarantees which the Community gives for these loans. After it became apparent that the issue of such guarantees sometimes involved considerable financial risks for the Community, it was decided in 1994, after the Edinburgh European Council, to establish a Guarantee Fund.[444] The aim of this Fund was to provide a buffer for the financial risks which could flow from the grant of guarantees on loans to third countries. The size of the Guarantee Fund is equivalent to about 10% of the amount granted in loans. The Fund thus fulfils a double role. First, it acts as a buffer, protecting the Community budget from financial consequences which could result from loan guarantees granted by the Community. Second, it acts as a filter preventing lending operations from becoming too ambitious, since for each loan there has to be a certain recourse to the own resources of the Community.

In 1978 already, the Commission proposed incorporating the lending activities in the budget entirely, but the Council rejected this proposal, mainly for political reasons. That would have meant the Council having to share powers with the Parliament. Nevertheless, some progress was made in shedding light on lending operations in the budget and the budget process. The guarantees for lending and borrowing operations by the Community must be entered in the budget, as must the payments to the Guarantee Fund.[445] Moreover, the claims by the Community on defaulting States are mentioned in the general overview of Community revenues. For each lending operation, the relevant Community guarantee is mentioned in the Commission section of the budget, together with an explanation giving the

---

441. Now laid down in Council Reg. (EC) No. 332/2002 of 18 Feb. 2002 establishing a facility providing medium-term financial assistance for Member States' balances of payments, O.J. 2002, L 53/1.

442. This facility was established in 1978 by Council Dec. 78/870/EEC of 16 Oct. 1978, O.J. 1978, L 298/9. It authorized the Commission to raise loans to support projects and investments contributing to greater convergence and integration of the economic policies of the Member States, and was prolonged three times, last in 1989 (by Council Dec. 87/182 of 9 Mar. 1987, O.J. 1987, L 71/34). Since 1991, no further use has been made of this facility.

443. See also Communication from the Commission to the Council: Review of the Facility Providing Medium-Term Financial Assistance to Member States under Art. 119 of the Treaty, COM (2005) 331 final.

444. Council Reg. (EC, Euratom) No. 2728/94 of 31 Oct. 1994 establishing a Guarantee Fund for external actions, O.J. 1994, L 293/1, as last amended by Council Reg. (EC, Euratom) No. 89/2007 of 30 Jan. 2007, O.J. 2007, L 22/1.

445. Art. 4(3) FR.

reference to the basic act and the volume of the operations envisaged. Finally, in a document annexed to the Commission section an overview is given of ongoing capital operations and debt management, and the capital operations and debt management for the financial year in question.[446]

The information obligations flowing from these provisions are complemented by the obligation on the Commission to report each half-year to the European Parliament and the Council on budgetary guarantees and the corresponding risks.[447]

4.2.1.1.2 The European Development Fund

The EDF is the most important instrument for financing the development agreements between the Community and a number of developing countries which, for historical reasons, have special links with certain Member States, the so-called ACP (i.e., African, Caribbean and Pacific) states.

When the EEC Treaty first entered into force in 1958, there was already an agreement attached for the development of overseas countries and territories. Ever since the Yaoundé Convention (1963), these development agreements have been concluded for five years at a time[448] with this group of countries; the group has tended to grow in the course of time. A financial protocol is attached to each of these conventions, mainly concerning the EDF. It is, therefore, slightly misleading to speak of 'the' EDF, as separate funds are created for limited periods of five years. Since 2001, the ninth EDF is in force, for the implementation of the Cotonou Convention. The various EDFs are not financed out of the Community's own resources, but out of contributions by the Member States according to a special allocation system, reflecting the historical and political connection of the various Member States with the relevant development countries. The allocation of contributions is set out in a so-called Internal Agreement between Representatives of the Governments of the Member States, meeting within the Council.[449] In the 1970s already, the Commission tried to include the EDF in the Community budget, without success. A more recent attempt, in 1995, to solve this issue, which is both politically and legally[450] controversial, was also unsuccessful.[451] The budget management rules for the EDF differ in several respects from those of the Community budget. They are to be found in the Financial regulation drawn up anew for each new EDF.[452]

---

446. Art. 46(4) FR.
447. Art. 130 FR; Art. 142(6) FR (duty to inform the Court of Auditors).
448. The second Yaondé Convention was signed in 1969; the first Lomé Convention in 1975, and from then on approximately every five years. The most recent is the Cotonou Convention, signed in 2000, O.J. 2000, L 317/3, and revised in 2005, O.J. 2005, L 209/27. See further Ch. XIII.
449. Most recently, the Internal Agreement of 2006 on the financing of Community aid under the multi-annual financial framework for the period 2008 to 2013, O.J. 2006, L 247/32.
450. On the legal problems, see the Court's decision in Joined Cases C-181 & 248/91, *Parliament v. Council and Commission (emergency aid)*.
451. Commission report on possibilities and modalities for including the EDF in the budget, Doc. SEC (94) fin.
452. The last published version is the FR of 27 Mar. 2003 applicable to the Ninth EDF, O.J. 2003, L 83/1, as amended by Council Reg. (EC) No. 309/2007 of 19 Mar. 2007, O.J. 2007, L 82/1.

4.2.1.1.3   Operational Expenditure of the Second and Third Pillars

Article 268, second paragraph, EC provides that administrative expenditure occasioned for the Institutions under the Second and Third Pillars is to be charged to the budget. This is also true for operational expenditure, except where the Council acting unanimously decides otherwise.[453]

As was mentioned above, operational expenditure for the Common Foreign and Security Policy is dealt with in an agreement between the Institutions concerned in the 2006 IIA.[454]

Although the Community financing of various 'satellite' bodies, agencies, and organizations of the Community falls within the Community budget, separate rules apply in these cases, which are worked out in detail in the FR. These bodies may be roughly divided into three groups:

(a) Bodies set up by the Communities, which exercise a Community task more or less independently, for which special expertise is needed, and which are financed more or less completely by the Communities.[455] These bodies have their own budget and their own financial regulation, which is based on a framework financial regulation adopted by the Commission.[456] The financial rules of these bodies may not depart from the framework regulation except where their specific operating needs so require and with the Commission's prior consent.[457]

(b) Executive agencies, set up by the Commission, which are entrusted with certain tasks in the management of Community programmes. They have their own operating budget[458] and the financial regulation applicable to that budget is adopted by the Commission. This regulation may deviate from the FR only if the specific operating requirements of the executive agencies so require.[459] The Commission may delegate to executive agencies as well as to bodies set up by the Communities, mentioned under a), tasks concerning the implementation of the European Communities' budget.[460]

(c) European organizations based on intergovernmental agreements which – although they are of importance for the Community – operate completely independently of the Community and its Institutions. They have their own

---

453.   Art. 28(2), (3) and (4) and Art. 41(2), (3) and (4) TEU.
454.   See *supra* section 4.1.2.3.1, and 2006 IIA, para. 42.
455.   See, for an enumeration, Ch. IV, section 9.4, *supra*. Some may also be financed by the 'consumers' of the services rendered, e.g., the Office for Harmonization in the Internal Market (OHIM) (Alicante) or the European Medicines Agency (EMEA) (London).
456.   See Commission Reg. (EC, Euratom) No. 2343/2002 of 23 Dec. 2002 on the framework FR for the bodies referred to in Art. 185 of Council Reg. (EC, Euratom) No. 1605/2002 on the FR applicable to the general budget of the European Communities, O.J. 2002, L 357/72.
457.   Art. 185 FR.
458.   Arts. 12–14 of Council Reg. (EC) No. 58/2003 of 19 Dec. laying down the statute for executive agencies to be entrusted with certain tasks in the management of Community programs, O.J. 2003, L 11/1.
459.   Art. 15 of Council Reg. (EC) No. 58/2003, previous note.
460.   Art. 54(2) FR. See also *infra* section 4.2.4.

financial regime. Nevertheless, they are relevant to the Community budget, since a not inconsiderable part of their activities is financed by the Community.[461] They are dealt with in Articles 108–113 FR, to the extent that they are financed by means of grants. These articles lay down the general principles governing the legality of the award of grants.

4.2.1.2 *The Principle of Annuality (Arts. 268 and 271 EC; Arts. 6–13 FR)*

The aim of this principle, under which budget operations must relate to a specific financial year, is to enable, at regular intervals, a full supervision of activities of the executive which have financial consequences, as well as of proper financial management (review of legality and effectiveness).[462] It is not always easy to reconcile the rule of annuality with the need to engage in multi-annual operations, which now play an increasingly important role in the budget. A solution to this problem has been found with the device of differentiated appropriations, which may be divided into commitment appropriations and payment appropriations.[463] Commitment appropriations cover, in a particular financial year, the total cost of the legal obligations entered into in respect of operations to be carried out over a period of more than one financial year. Payment appropriations cover expenditure, up to the amount entered in the budget, resulting from the commitments entered into during the financial year and/or previous financial years. In itself this is a sensible division, but it involves the risk that there is a 'time-lag' between commitments being entered into and payments being made, so that it is not always possible to determine precisely when the latter must occur. In order to maintain control over this kind of 'burden from the past', various measures were taken in 1988 in order to ensure an orderly development of commitment appropriations. These measures have been confirmed since then.[464]

In the interests of good management, it is not always possible to have these appropriations match calendar years exactly. For practical reasons, Article 271 EC, therefore, allows appropriations, other than those relating to staff expenditure, to be carried over to the next financial year. This is regulated in more detail in the FR.[465]

---

461. E.g., the European schools, and the European University Institute in Florence.
462. In Case C-284/90, *Council v. European Parliament*, at para. 26, the Court noted that the annuality of the budget was one of two fundamental principles in budgetary matters (the other is the unity of the budget).
463. Art. 7 FR.
464. These are now to be found in Art. 3(2) of the 2007 Own Resources Decision, para. 11 of the 2006 IIA and Arts. 8 and 11 FR. See Art. 5 of the Implementation Regulation for the detailed rules. See in this respect also the specific rules for structural funds in Art. 157 FR and in Art. 228 Implementation Regulation, which contains a guarantee that the earmarked funds for a Member State remain available even if that State has been obliged to repay erroneously made payments on account.
465. Art. 9 FR and Art. 6 of the Implementation Regulation.

4.2.1.3   The Principle of Equilibrium (Art. 268, Last Sentence, EC;
                 Arts. 14–15 FR)

According to this principle, budget revenue must be equal to budget expenditure in
the Community budget. In the course of implementing the budget, it may turn out
that the actual expenditures are lower or higher than were predicted. Given the
current extremely strict provisions on budgetary discipline,[466] the former will in
practice occur more frequently than the latter. If at the end of the year there is a
surplus or deficit, this may be entered in the budget for the following year as
revenue (in the case of a surplus) or as a payment appropriation (in the case of
a deficit). The discrepancy between the budget estimates and the final accounts is
presented in an amending budget.[467] With reference to the principle of equilibrium,
Article 14 FR states that the Communities may not raise loans,[468] which means that
the Communities cannot borrow in order to cover investment outlays. This obliges
EU institutions to use complex methods of financing property acquisitions which
are not always cost efficient and transparent.[469]

4.2.1.4   The Principle of Unit of Account (Art. 277 EC; Art. 16 FR)

From the very beginning, there has been a need for a common, and constant,
monetary reference value for drawing up the Community budget and for its implementation. When the ECSC first existed, and in the initial years of the EEC, use
was made of the US dollar, which provided a sufficiently stable reference value
until the end of the 1960s. After the collapse of the Bretton Woods system, which
resulted in fluctuating exchange rates, it was finally decided, in 1981, to express the
Community budget in the currency unit of the European Monetary System (EMS),
called the European Currency Unit (ECU). This solution was satisfactory to the
extent that the ECU was used as a unit of account, but it revealed shortcomings in
relation to payments, since the ECU was not universally accepted as a means of
payment.[470] The introduction of the euro as of 1999 has more or less solved this
problem; the rule in Article 277 EC now applies for the whole budget process.[471]

---

466. See *supra* section 4.1.2.3.
467. Art. 15 FR.
468. Without prejudice to the borrowing and lending operations, see *supra* section 4.2.1.1.
469. Special Report No. 2/2007 of the Court of Auditors concerning the Institutions' expenditure on
      buildings together with the Institutions' replies, O.J. 2007, C 148/1, para. 57.
470. See further X. Yataganas, in *Commentaire J. Mégret*, op. cit. *supra* note 401, 360–365.
471. Nevertheless, even now there are technical exchange rate questions between the Community's
      obligations and claims expressed in euros and the currencies of Member States who do not – as
      yet – participate in the monetary union, and of course currencies of third countries. Arts. 7–9
      Implementation Regulation lay down rules for this.

4.2.1.5   The Principle of Universality (Art. 268, First Paragraph, EC; Arts. 17–20 FR)

This principle prohibits the setting aside of certain budget revenues for certain expenditures, for instance making income from a certain source available only for a certain objective. This also implies that all income and expenditure must be entered separately, and may not be adjusted against each other.[472] This increases the transparency of the budget.[473] There are a few exceptions to the principle of universality, defined in the FR.[474]

4.2.1.6   The Principle of Specification (Art. 271, Third Paragraph, EC; Arts. 21–26 FR)

According to this principle, each appropriation must have a given purpose and be assigned to a specific objective. This principle provides a framework *ratione materiae* for the budget process. It applies at all stages – the preparation, approval, implementation and discharge – of the budget cycle. Thanks to this principle, the budgetary authority can express its policy and political priorities in the budget, and can check whether they are followed up in the subsequent stages of the budget cycle. The application of this principle means the budget must be structured according to a certain nomenclature (titles, chapters, articles, items).

In order to guarantee sufficient flexibility in the implementation of the budget, Article 274, third paragraph, EC allows for appropriations to be transferred, within certain limits laid down in the FR.[475] A distinction is made between transfers from one chapter to another, and transfers within chapters. In the former case, when considerable amounts are concerned, the budgetary authority must give its authorization.[476] In the latter, the implementing body may decide.[477]

As was already mentioned above,[478] certain categories of expenditure are very sensitive from the point of view of income distribution, such as the expenditure of the structural funds. With that in mind, the FR has separate rules for the transfer of appropriations intended for these categories of expenditure.[479]

---

472. Art. 17 FR.
473. In the past, when the Community did not yet have a general budget, the European Agricultural Guidance and Guarantee Fund (EAGGF) and the Social Fund had their own income. At present, the 'fund' is merely a certain category of expenditure, which is financed from general resources.
474. Arts. 18 and 20 FR, worked out in more detail in Arts. 11–15 Implementation Regulation.
475. See Case 204/86, *Greece v. Council*, for examples of legal problems which this may raise.
476. Arts. 22(3) and 23(2) FR, read with Art. 24 FR, and Arts. 17–20 Implementation Regulation.
477. Arts. 22(1) and (4), and 23(1) FR, and Arts. 17–20 Implementation Regulation.
478. See *supra* section 4.1.2.3.1.
479. Arts. 153, 158 and 160(2) FR.

4.2.1.7   *The Principle of Sound Financial Management*
                (Art. 274 EC; Arts. 27–28a FR)

For a long time, the notion of sound financial management referred – both in Community and national budgetary practices – to legality and so-called 'small-scale efficiency'. As long as the expenditures were formally lawful and the internal management met certain efficiency requirements, then the expenditures were considered appropriate. Gradually, the accent has shifted, with more attention being paid to large-scale efficiency and effectiveness. That is to say, the authority implementing the budget must also be able to show that expenditure is carried out effectively, in the sense that the intended policy objective has been achieved, and efficiently, in the sense that the intended policy objective could not have been achieved with less financial means or with means other than financial ones. This type of large-scale efficiency test requires quantitative efficiency and effectiveness analyses, which sometimes tend to be missing in the political decision-making on the budget. Consequently, the results of financial policy may lag far behind the intended objectives. In Articles 27 to 28a FR, the higher ambitions of modern financial management are clearly evident. The institutional context within which they must be realized in the Community is, however, not very favourable. First, the strong distributional policy preoccupations which play such an important role in the Community budget process certainly do not promote the efficient allocation of finances. At the same time, the fact that the largest part of the Community's resources is spent through or via the intermediary of the national authorities does not always promote efficient expenditure. In the reporting by the Court of Auditors in the last few years, there is, however, increasing attention for the large scale efficiency and effectiveness of financial management.[480]

In the Treaty itself, the principle of sound financial management is expressly mentioned in Article 274 EC, in the context of the implementation of the budget; it will be repeated in the new Article 310(5) TFEU, as introduced by the Treaty of Lisbon.

4.2.1.8   *The Principle of Transparency (Arts. 29–30 FR)*

Articles 29 and 30 FR reveal that the principle of transparency is understood primarily as a formal principle, according to which the budget, the amending budgets, the consolidated financial statements and the financial management reports for each institution are published in the Official Journal. The provisions of Article 30 FR, on information on the Community's borrowing-and-lending operations and the related Guarantee Fund, have the same formal meaning. Whether these provisions also guarantee the – more important – substantive

---

480. See, e.g., Special Report No. 8/2006 'Growing Success? The Effectiveness of the European Union Support for Fruit and Vegetable Producers' Operational Programmes', O.J. 2006, C 282/32, and Special Report No. 7/2006 'Rural Development Investments: Do they effectively address the problems of rural areas?', O.J. 2006, C 282/1.

transparency of the Community budget, in the sense that it is clear for interested parties what political and policy choices are expressed therein, is questionable. Neither the present decision-making on the budget, which is based on agreements laid down in the IIA, nor the incomplete realization of the principle of unity contribute to the transparency of the budgetary process as a *political* decision-making process.

4.2.2 The Community's Own Resources (Arts. 269–271 EC)

Article 269, first paragraph, EC provides that the budget shall be financed wholly from 'own resources'. The term 'own resources' has a rather ambiguous meaning,[481] since the Community's own resources are only to a very limited extent composed of income from its own 'sources' – i.e., levies based on Community legislative provisions – and the Community does not collect these itself. As a result, they tend to be seen – in the national perception – as 'our contributions' to the Community budget, with all the political implications this involves. In legal terms, these resources are indeed to be counted as own resources of the Community as soon as the corresponding claim has been determined.[482] If at the end of the year there is a surplus of own resources in relation to total expenditures, this may be entered as revenue in the budget for the following year.[483]

The payment and management of the amounts established as own resources are governed by Council Reg. (EC, Euratom) No. 1150/2000.[484] The mechanism worked out in this regulation describes the obligations of the Member States in detail:

- an obligation to establish the own resources of the Community;
- an obligation to credit them to the Commission's account within the prescribed time-limit, in twelve monthly amounts;
- an obligation to pay default interest in case of delay.

These obligations are narrowly defined, as well as being closely monitored by the Commission. Due to the rule of equilibrium, any shortfalls in revenues of own resources would indeed have to be offset either by another own resource or by an adjustment of expenditure, which could put to the test the delicate agreement arrived at by the European Council with regard to the financial framework and

---

481. See also C.-D. Ehlermann, 'The Financing of the Community: The Distinction between Financial Contributions and Own Resources' (1982) CML Rev., 571–589.
482. Case C-96/89, *Commission v. Netherlands*, at para. 37.
483. See Art. 10 FR and Art. 7 of the 2007 Own Resources Decision. See also Case C-284/90, *Council v. European Parliament*, at paras. 25–27.
484. Council Reg. (EC, Euratom) No. 1150/2000 of 22 May 2000 implementing Decision 94/728/ EC, Euratom on the system of the Communities' own resources, O.J. 2000, L 130/1, as last amended by Council Reg. (EC, Euratom) No. 2028/2004 of 16 Nov. 2004, O.J. 2004, L 352/1.

the corresponding own resources decision.[485] The Court also interprets these obligations strictly:[486]

- The default interest may be claimed, regardless of the reason for which it is paid too late into the Commission's account.[487]
- That the delay was not intentional does not provide a justification.[488]
- The fact that the Community did not suffer damage as a result of the delay is irrelevant.[489]
- Although an error committed by the customs authorities of a Member State results in the debtor not having to pay the duties in question, it does not affect that Member State's obligation to pay default interest and duties which should have been established, in the context of making available own resources.[490]

As described in section 4.1 above, the extent and composition of the Community's own resources is to a large extent determined by the dynamics of the integration process, as expressed in the Community's tasks and activities, by the differences in the ability of the various Member States to pay, and the financial consequences for the Member States of Community policies. This means that – as long as the Community does not have a tax area of its own from which the necessary financial resources can be sought – regular revision of the provisions on own resources is almost inevitable. The experiences in practice, as they have developed since the Delors I Package, are mixed. That practice offered a responsible balance between the stability in the development of the Community's revenues which is necessary for its budgetary programming in the medium term, and the equally necessary adaptation of the financial space to the changed requirements made of the Community. The disadvantage has been that the European Councils tend to decide on too rigid a financial medium-term framework for the most important categories of expenditure. This means that in situations where the Community has to take new policy initiatives, unanticipated complications in the distribution of financial aspects may arise.

In view of the negotiations on what became the 2006 IIA, the Commission proposed three options for a substantial change to the own resources system: an own resources system with:

(1) fiscal resources related to energy consumption;
(2) a fiscal VAT resource; and
(3) a fiscal resource based on corporate income.[491]

---

485. See Case C-392/02, *Commission v. Denmark*, at para. 54, and the Opinion of the AG in that case, para. 7.
486. See also Case C-378/03, *Commission v. Belgium*, at para. 48, where the Court notes that the legislation concerning the recovery of customs debts must be interpreted in the light of the aim of securing efficient and rapid availability of the Community's own resources.
487. Case C-96/89, *Commission v. Netherlands*, at para. 38.
488. Case 93/85, *Commission v. United Kingdom*, at para. 37.
489. Case C-348/97, *Commission v. Germany*, at para. 62.
490. Case C-392/02, *Commission v. Denmark*, at para. 63.
491. Financing the European Union, Commission report on the operation of the own resources system, COM (2004) 505 final.

These proposals were not accepted although the difficult negotiations on the financial framework 2007–2013 and on the UK rebate in particular demonstrated the limits of the current own resources system. In the context of the 2006 IIA, the Commission has, however, been invited to undertake a full, wide-ranging review covering all aspects of EU spending and of resources, including the UK rebate, and to report in 2008/2009.[492]

For the rest, the wording of Article 269, second paragraph, EC accords with current practice. The requirement that the decision on own resources must be adopted by unanimity and be recommended to the Member States 'for adoption in accordance with their respective constitutional requirements' forms on the one hand a barrier against a too matter-of-course expansion of own resources, but on the other hand provides the necessary medium-term flexibility.[493]

The terms of Article 270 EC logically complement Article 269 EC. In its policy development the Community must provide assurance that it remains within the financial limits imposed by the own resources decision in force. It is unlikely that this instruction applies solely to the development of new policies, as serious dangers for the prescribed financial framework may flow from the application of existing open-ended rules. Thus it is strange that only the Commission is the addressee of these provisions; the Council or a too ambitious Parliament acting under its powers to increase non-compulsory expenditure[494] may be just as threatening to the boundaries set by the own resources decision. This is addressed more appropriately in the 2006 IIA[495] as well as in the new Article 310(4) TFEU, as introduced by the Treaty of Lisbon, which imposes on the Union in general a duty not to adopt any act which is likely to have appreciable implications for the budget without providing an assurance that the expenditure arising from such an act is capable of being financed within the limit of the Union's own resources and in compliance with the multi-annual financial framework.

---

492. 3rd Declaration to the 2006 IIA. On 12 Sep. 2007, the Commission published a public consultation paper in view of the 2008/2009 budget review, SEC (2007)1188 final. See further, on alternative solutions to the current own resources system, P. Cattoir, *Tax-Based EU Own Resources: An Assessment, European Commission, Taxation Papers*, Working Paper No. 1/2004 (Luxembourg, Office for Official Publications of the European Communities, 2004); S.R.F. Plasschaert, 'Towards an Own Tax Resource for the European Union? Why? How? And When?' (2004) *European Taxation*, 470–479; W. Coussens, 'Financing the EU Budget: Time for Reform' (2004) *Studia diplomatica*, 73–92; M. Lefebre, 'Le budget européen 2007–2013: une négociation d'étape', (2006) *Revue du Marché commun et de l'Union européenne*, 445–451; J. Inghelram, 'Welke toekomst voor de financiering van de EU?' (2007) SEW, 191–200.
493. When the Treaty of Maastricht was being negotiated, the relative success of the Delors I Package led some Member States to propose including the most important elements of the 1988 Own Resources Decision in the Treaty itself. This proposal was – fortunately – not followed, because then the necessary medium-term flexibility would disappear.
494. Arts. 272(9) EC.
495. Paras. 36 and 37 of the 2006 IIA.

4.2.3   **The Budgetary Procedure (Arts. 272–273 EC)**

Article 272 EC appears at first sight to have a central function in Title II of Part Five of the Treaty. It sets out in detail the roles of the Council and the Parliament as component parts of the budgetary authority. The conflicts during the years 1975 to 1988 between the two arms of the budgetary authority primarily related to the interpretation and application of this provision. However, while Article 272 EC appears formally to govern the budgetary procedure, the substantive practice since the coming into effect of the 1988 IIA, has altered drastically. Thus Article 272 EC may be characterized as a mask, behind the very stylized appearance of which a different reality lurks. Only if the Council and the Parliament are no longer in agreement about that reality will they step out from behind the mask into the role-play of Article 272 EC, the function of which is held in reserve in the budgetary practice *extra legem* of the Community.[496] Thus it is not sufficient merely to explain the formal situation and the points of dispute between the two arms of the budgetary authority, it is necessary to bear in mind also the practice in relation to the budget, which differs from the formal scheme.

4.2.3.1   *Article 272 EC; The Divided Budgetary Authority*

As set out in Article 272 EC, the budgetary procedure has four stages.

In the *first stage* of the budgetary procedure[497] the Commission consolidates the estimates of the expenditure of each of the Institutions in a preliminary draft budget, which it puts before the Council. To this it attaches an opinion which may contain divergent estimates. After consultation with the Commission and, usually, the Parliament, the Council by qualified majority establishes the draft budget and transmits it to the Parliament. Both the draft budget and the preliminary draft will also comprise an estimate of revenue.

In the *second* stage,[498] the Parliament then has a time-limit of 45 days within which to pronounce on the draft submitted. It has the right to amend the draft budget as far as these amendments relate to non-compulsory expenditure; for compulsory expenditure, it may only propose modifications to the Council. The introduction of amendments in respect of non-compulsory expenditure is subject to a more rigorous voting procedure than normal: the Parliament can only adopt them by a majority of its *members*. For the adoption of proposed modifications, the ordinary voting procedure applies: an absolute majority of the *votes cast* is required. The draft budget as amended and with the proposed modifications is sent to the Council. If, on the other hand, the Parliament approves the draft budget as such, the budget has been finally adopted. If the draft budget is not approved

---

496. This development is not free of objections, since the IIAs, with their still unclear legal nature, cannot circumvent the powers the Institutions are granted by the Treaty; see *supra* section 4.1.2.3.1.

497. See Art. 272(1)–(3) and (4), 1st para., EC.

498. Art. 272(4) EC.

within 45 days after it was submitted to the Parliament, or if the Parliament has neither amended it nor proposed modifications within this period, the budget is considered to be finally adopted. It is the President of the Parliament who declares the budget adopted.[499]

A *third* stage commences when an amended draft budget or one in which modifications have been proposed is laid before the Council.[500] The Council, after having consulted the Commission and, where appropriate, the other Institutions concerned, may alter the amendments of the Parliament. As far as the proposed modifications are concerned, a distinction must be drawn between proposals which do not increase the total amount of expenditure of an Institution (e.g., by compensating for an increase in one budget line by a decrease in another) and those which do result in such an increase. In the first case, these proposals are deemed to be accepted unless the Council rejects them. In the second case, the reverse is true: they are deemed to be rejected unless the Council accepts them. Council decisions regarding the Parliament's amendments and those regarding its proposed modifications are taken by a qualified majority of votes. If within 15 days the Council does not alter the amendments and does not reject or (as the case may be) accepts the proposed modifications, the budget is deemed to be finally adopted. The Council informs the Parliament of this. The President of the Parliament will thereupon declare that the budget has been finally adopted.[501]

If, on the other hand, within the time-limit of 15 days the Council has altered one or more of the amendments made by the Parliament, or if the Council has rejected or altered the modifications proposed by the Parliament, the draft budget is again sent to the latter. In doing so, the Council informs the Parliament of the results of its deliberations.

A *fourth* stage thus commences.[502] The procedure then is that within 15 days of the draft budget being placed before it, the Parliament (which will have been notified of the action taken on its proposed modifications) may, acting by a majority of its members and three-fifths of the votes cast, amend or reject the alterations to its amendments made by the Council and shall adopt the budget accordingly. If within that period the Parliament has not acted the budget shall be deemed to be finally adopted. Thus, the Parliament may cancel the alterations

---

499. Art. 272(7) EC. The declaration by the President of the Parliament is open to judicial review, e.g., Case C-41/95, *Council v. European Parliament*. However, since the procedure for the approval of the budget leads only to the authorization of the commitments of expenditure, a natural or legal person cannot under any circumstances be directly concerned by the steps in the budgetary procedure. Such a person may be directly concerned only by the measures taken to implement the budget. An action for annulment filed by such a person against the adoption of the budget is, therefore, inadmissible; see Case 297/83, *Parti écologiste 'Les Verts' v. Council*, at para. 7. Moreover, remarks in the budget can neither confer individual rights nor give rise to any legitimate expectation; see Joined Cases 87/77, 130/77, 22/83, 9/84 & 10/84, *Vittorio Salerno and others v. Commission*, at para. 59.

500. Art. 272(5) EC.

501. Art. 272(7) EC.

502. Art. 272(6) EC.

made to its *amendments* by the Council. It has not been accorded the right to change the budget in accordance with its *proposals* for modification. This right is only possessed by the Council in the third stage. Whenever during this procedure a decision is, implicitly or explicitly, taken which concludes the procedure, then the President of the Parliament declares that the budget has been finally adopted.[503]

The Parliament has the last word, though. If the Parliament does not wish to accept the draft as it has emerged from the third or fourth stage, it has the right, acting by a majority of its members and two-thirds of the votes cast, 'if there are important reasons', to reject the draft budget as a whole and ask for a new draft to be submitted to it.[504]

Within the framework of this procedure, the Parliament and the Council are bound in two ways as regards the establishment of the budget, as was noted in section 4.2.1, above.

The *first restriction* derives from the combined effect of two factors: the requirement that revenue and expenditure must be balanced;[505] and financial lee-way granted by the own resources decisions drawn up under Article 270 EC.[506] Given the rigorous nature of the decision-making process for own resources decisions, and in view of the fact that since 1988 the development of own resources has been set down in multi-annual frameworks, the resulting financial room for manoeuvre for the budgetary authority is pretty much fixed.

Article 3 of the 2007 Own Resources Decision[507], based on the conclusions of the Brussels European Council, sets ceilings for both the commitment appropriations and the payment appropriations. The commitment appropriations may not exceed 1.31% of the total GNI of the Member States. The payment appropriations have an upper limit of 1.24%. This formula means that the nominal budgetary space for the Community depends partly on economic growth. The consequent uncertainties make it necessary to be cautious in establishing the budget.

The *second way* in which the Parliament and the Council are bound applies only in relation to non-compulsory expenditure, in relation to which Parliament has its own right of amendment, and the final say within the budgetary procedure. The maximum rate of increase in non-compulsory expenditure is fixed annually by the Commission on the basis of:

  – the trend, in terms of volume, of the GNP within the Community;
  – the average variation in the budgets of the Member States; and
  – the trend of the cost of living during the previous financial year.[508]

This quantitative restriction on the growth of non-compulsory expenditure is mitigated to some extent for the Parliament by the provision that in any case it may, in

---

503. Art. 272(7) EC.
504. Art. 272(8) EC.
505. Art. 268, last sentence, EC.
506. Art. 272(10) EC.
507. Council Dec. 2007/436 of 7 Jun. 2007, O.J. 2007, L 163/17.
508. Art. 272(9), 2nd para., EC.

exercising its right of amendment, increase this expenditure by up to half of the maximum rate of increase, even if the draft budget established by the Council already requires more than half of the amount available according to the maximum rate of increase prescribed by the Commission. Furthermore, it is possible, if the Parliament, the Council or the Commission consider this necessary, to exceed the prescribed maximum rate; in this case another rate can be fixed by agreement between the Council (acting by a qualified majority) and the Parliament (acting by a majority of its members and three-fifths of the votes cast).[509] Although the Court has rightly observed that no criterion has been laid down for the modification of the maximum rate of increase,[510] on the basis of the link between Articles 268, 270 and 272(9) EC it must be accepted that even if the budgetary authority were to agree a new maximum rate of increase, the requirements of a balanced budget and the currently applicable own resources decision would have to be respected.[511]

The experience with the budgetary procedure between 1977 and 1985 demonstrates that the complex budgetary procedure of Article 272 EC cannot work properly if the Council and the Parliament do not maintain good contacts and do not attempt to devise a solution for continually recurring problems with the procedure. Already in a Resolution recorded in the minutes of the Council meeting of 22 April 1970 (the date of the signature of the First Budgetary Treaty), the Council undertook to take the necessary steps to ensure close cooperation with the European Parliament on this matter. On the basis of this Resolution, numerous arrangements were established which promote mutual communication in the various phases of the budgetary procedure. The Joint Declaration of 30 June 1982,[512] which addressed this problem, was replaced by the 1999 IIA; the parts of that Declaration relating to cooperation between the two Institutions within the budgetary procedure are now to be found, with some alterations, in Part II of the 2006 IIA and, in further detail, in its Annex II. The latter provides for a conciliation procedure in which the Parliament, the Council and the Commission participate and the purpose of which is to continue discussions on the general trend of expenditure and to secure agreement between the Parliament and the Council on different issues in relation to the adoption of the budget.

The Treaty of Lisbon has written the instruments of cooperation between the two arms of the budgetary authority directly into the Treaty. Under the new Article 314 TFEU, a conciliation committee would be set up composed of the members of the Council or their representatives and an equal number of members representing the European Parliament with the Commission taking part in its proceedings. Its task would be, in case of a difference of opinion between the Parliament and the

---

509. Art. 272(9), last paragraph, EC.
510. Case 34/86, *Council v. Parliament*, at para. 34.
511. In ibid. and in Case C-41/95, *Council v. European Parliament*, at para. 26, the Court stressed the importance of an agreement, noting in the latter judgment that there has to be agreement on the total amount of expenditure to be classified as non-compulsory in order for there to be an agreement on a new rate of increase.
512. O.J. 1982, C 194/1.

Council, to reach agreement on a joint text on the basis of the positions of the two institutions. Moreover, the Treaty of Lisbon simplifies the budgetary procedure. Instead of the four above-mentioned stages, there would essentially be two stages – the first when the Council examines the draft budget and the second when the Parliament examines the position of the Council – followed, if necessary, by the conciliation committee procedure. Finally, if the Treaty of Lisbon enters into force, the distinction between compulsory and non-compulsory expenditure will disappear, which will increase the influence of the Parliament with regard to a substantial part of the expenditure.[513]

4.2.3.2   Restrictions on Parliament's Budgetary Powers

Article 272 EC constitutes an expression of the asymmetry in the division of competence in the exercise of regulatory and budgetary power between the Institutions. A budgetary procedure in which the Council has to share its powers with the Parliament, which ultimately has the last word, inevitably creates tension between the Council, as policy-maker and legislator, and the Parliament, in the exercise of its functions as budgetary authority. This tension may lead to Parliament being able to obtain certain powers of policy-determination through a wide interpretation of its budgetary powers, through opening new 'budget lines' without the requisite legal basis for their implementation. The reverse is also conceivable, if the Parliament were to be unwilling to vote resources for the implementation of Community legislation with financial implications. In order to avoid this occurring, Article 272(4) EC makes the distinction between compulsory and non-compulsory expenditure, with differing powers for the Council and the Parliament regarding these two categories of expenditure. With the benefit of hindsight, it has to be observed that this handiwork of the framers of the revisions to the Treaties, when introducing this distinction which was meant to safeguard the powers of the Council as legislator and policy-maker, has been somewhat infelicitous from the point of view of that objective. The same can be said about the maximum rate of increase provision in Article 272(9) EC. By subjecting the powers of the Parliament to such a two-part limitation, there is almost an open invitation to a permanent discussion about the demarcation between compulsory and non-compulsory expenditure, and about the leeway which the maximum rate of increase leaves for the political evaluation by the Parliament as joint budgetary authority.

The formulation of the distinction between compulsory and non-compulsory expenditure in Article 272(4) EC – by describing the former as 'expenditure necessarily resulting from this Treaty or from acts adopted in accordance therewith' – is less than wholly clear,[514] and obviously stems from the days when agricultural guarantee expenditure swallowed up the vast majority of the Community

---

513.   See also on such changes in the budgetary procedure, J. Schoo, 'Finanzen und Haushalt', in J. Schwarze (ed.), *Der Verfassungsentwurf des Europäischen Konvents*, (Nomos Verlagsgesellschaft, Baden-Baden, 2004), 127–137.
514.   See *supra* section 4.1.2.3.1.

expenditure. Because of the political weight of the Common Agricultural Policy, the authors of the Treaty apparently sought to protect that area from the consequences of giving the Parliament a joint say in the determination of the Community budget.[515]

The uncertainties about the difference between compulsory expenditure and non-compulsory expenditure also emerge from the history of the application of Article 272(9) EC.[516] It appears that the Council initially interpreted the formula in the sense that the right of amendment applied principally to administrative expenditure. In an unofficial document from the President of the Council, dated 3 February 1970,[517] such a distinction was made relating to the budget for 1970. In a Declaration[518] entered in the Council's minutes on the signing of the First Budgetary Treaty, it was stated that the Council was guided by the classification of budgetary expenditure laid down in this document, but that it recognized that 'this classification may change in the light of the operational requirements of the Communities'.[519] In the then current budgetary terms, that would mean that the right of amendment of the Parliament related to only 3.6% of the total expenditure of the Community. Moreover, since the major part of administrative expenditure is fixed, because it has a compulsory character (salaries of the existing staff of officials, rent for buildings, telephone and other expenses, etc.), this approach would mean that the Parliament's right of amendment was only of very marginal significance.

In the course of preparing the budget for 1975, Parliament agreed with the Council's view that expenditure could only be regarded as compulsory if neither the Council nor Parliament could freely fix appropriations relating to it.[520] But even this formula was unable to resolve the differences of opinion between the two Institutions, as it lacked a clear differentiating capacity.

In the Joint Declaration of 30 June 1982[521] the Institutions tried again, attaching in an annex to that Declaration a classification of then existing budget lines into

---

515. The drafters of the Treaty have at least been consistent in this respect, since the powers of the Parliament as co-legislative authority have remained extremely limited in the area of agriculture. See Art. 37(2) EC, from which it appears that Parliament has only a consultative power.
516. And the corresponding provisions in the Euratom Treaty, and in the past the ECSC Treaty.
517. The Harmel list; this was published by the Dutch government in Annexes to the proceedings of the Tweede Kamer, 1970–1971, 10915 no. 7.
518. E.P. document No. 30 Session 1970–1971.
519. This declaration related to what then became Art. 203(8) EEC relating to the maximum amount of non-compulsory expenditure (see now Art. 272(9) EC).
520. Resolution of Nov. 1974, O.J. 1974, C 155/33, para. 13.
521. O.J. 1982, C 194/1. See point I.1. of the Declaration: 'The three Institutions consider compulsory expenditure such expenditure as the budgetary authority is obliged to enter in the budget to enable the Community to meet its obligations, both internally and externally, under the Treaties and acts adopted in accordance therewith.' This Declaration was replaced by the 1999 IIA, which still contained a specific definition of compulsory expenditure (see para. 30). The definition in para. 34 of the 2006 IIA, however, merely paraphrases Art. 272(4), 2nd para. EC, which seems to imply that all attempts to theoretically define the notion of compulsory expenditure have been abandoned. In order to prevent differences of opinion – highly likely – on the interpretation and application of this definition, Annex III to the 2006 IIA includes a detailed scheme of the division into compulsory and non-compulsory expenditure.

compulsory or non-compulsory expenditure and establishing a procedure to deal with differences of opinion on new budget lines. But even this Joint Declaration could not remove the friction between the Council and the Parliament, despite the tripartite dispute resolution mechanism envisaged in Part II of that Joint Declaration.

It is not difficult to construct a satisfactory legal distinction between the two types of expenditure, by defining compulsory expenditure as being expenditure in respect of which, in the implementation of the budget under Article 274 EC, the Commission has no right to refuse to meet its obligation to pay: i.e., cases in which third parties have a legal right, on the basis of a rule of one of the Treaties or of provisions adopted thereunder – including agreements concluded by the Communities with third countries – to performance which gives rise to expenditure. In this view the simple fact that a Council measure has expressly allocated the necessary financial resources for the implementation of the measure is insufficient to render the expenditure compulsory; the decisive element is whether or not the Commission has a discretionary power.

This legal distinction, which in itself is tenable, would not, however, suffice to solve the tension between the Parliament and the Council, as the dispute is not primarily legal in nature but political. There are certain rules in the Common Agricultural Policy which do indeed leave the Commission a certain margin of evaluation as to whether there is an obligation to pay and, if there is, how much. Nevertheless, the Council has always maintained that the expenditure for such purposes is compulsory expenditure. For the provisions in the various Structural Funds regulations, the reverse is true, so that even though the appropriations are classified as non-compulsory appropriations, there are provisions which leave the Commission very little margin of discretion, if the conditions for their application are met. At the end of the day, tensions about political policy-driven differences of interpretation can only be resolved by political arrangements and dialogue between the Institutions concerned. This is the route that has been chosen, first with the Joint Declaration of 1982, then the 1988, 1993, 1999 and 2006 IIAs.[522]

The result of the 2006 IIA is that expenditure of the common agricultural policy concerning market measures and direct aids, including market measures for fisheries and fisheries agreements concluded with third parties (heading 2), certain external expenditure (e.g., aid to third countries under international agreements) and contributions provisioning the loan guarantee fund (heading 4), and most of the administrative expenditure (heading 5), are classed as compulsory expenditure. This accounted in 2007 for about 35% of total Community expenditure.[523] This

---

522. See Case 204/86, *Greece v. Council*, at para. 17: the Court observed that as far as classification of expenditure was concerned, the Community Institutions possessed a discretionary power which was limited by the separation of powers, as laid down in the EC Treaty, between the Institutions. The Court had to ensure that in the context of the dialogue the Institutions do not ignore the rules of law and do not exceed their discretionary power in a manifestly wrong or arbitrary way. Given the evident discrepancy between the budgetary practice and the treaty text, this pronouncement by the Court is of significance for other elements of the current budgetary process.

523. Taking into account the commitment appropriations in the 2007 budget.

percentage is decreasing. In 2000, more than 50% of total Community expenditure was classified as compulsory expenditure; in the 1980s, even 85%.

The distinction between compulsory and non-compulsory expenditure is less controversial at present.[524] It will even disappear if the Treaty of Lisbon enters into force. To summarize the discussion as a whole, the reasons for this evolution are: first, the increasing influence of the Parliament in Council decisions having financial implications (though influence on the Common Agricultural Policy is still limited); secondly, the arrangement, since the 1999 IIA, that the agreed financial framework applies to both categories of expenditure, to which the rider is added that a revision of the compulsory expenditure in the financial framework should not lead to a reduction in the amount available for non-compulsory expenditure;[525] thirdly, the introduction of the agricultural guideline in the decisions on budgetary discipline,[526] which forms the basis for the control of compulsory agricultural expenditure; and, fourthly, the agreement between the two arms of the budgetary authority to respect the allocations in the financial framework for, in particular, the Structural Funds and the Cohesion Fund, which are important parts of non-compulsory expenditure.[527]

The complex rules of Article 272(9) EC for the determination of the maximum rate of increase for non-compulsory expenditure lost much of their practical importance after the 1988 IIA and will disappear if the Treaty of Lisbon enters into force. The limitation which the maximum rate posed for the Parliament's right of amendment as joint budgetary authority, which was the cause of numerous conflicts between the Parliament and the Council in the 1980s, has in practice been replaced by the programmed ceilings of the financial framework, set out in the IIAs.

In this context, paragraph 15, second subparagraph, of the 2006 IIA is illustrative; it states: 'If need be, the two arms of the budgetary authority will decide [thereby complying with the voting rules laid down in Article 272(9), fifth paragraph, EC], to *lower* the ceilings set in the financial framework in order to ensure compliance with the own resources ceiling.'

This raises the question whether the Parliament may further restrict its powers under the Treaty by means of an IIA. Strictly speaking, this question must be answered in the negative, as the Community Institutions are bound by the division of powers laid down in the Treaty itself – all the more since the division of powers is closely linked to the institutional balance between the different Institutions. The contrary argument, that the Parliament by concluding an IIA is in fact exercising its

---

524. A Statement was attached to the 1993 IIA, that the provisions on the budgetary procedure, including rules on compulsory and non-compulsory expenditure, would be the subject of investigation during the 1996 IGC. The Treaty of Amsterdam, which resulted from that IGC, made a few amendments to the financial provisions in the EC Treaty, but the budgetary procedure itself, and the distinction between compulsory and non-compulsory expenditure, was not addressed.

525. Para. 21, 5th subparagraph, of the 1999 IIA and para. 23, 3rd subparagraph, of the 2006 IIA.

526. See *supra* section 4.1.2.3.2.

527. Para. 13, 2nd subpara., and para. 40 of the 2006 IIA.

powers over the medium term, is less than wholly convincing, given that Article 272(9) EC specifically envisages an *annual* determination of the maximum rate of increase, quite independently of the question whether the available own resources actually permit such a maximum increase in expenditure.[528] A solution may well be offered by the fact that each of the four IIAs concluded thus far expressly states 'This Agreement does not alter the respective budgetary powers of the various institutions, as laid down in the Treaties.'[529] This makes it possible to interpret the IIAs as political arrangements between the Institutions concerned, which expressly leave it open to the Parliament, should sufficient support exist among its members, to fall back on the formal division of powers as prescribed in the Treaties.[530] In this interpretation, Article 272(9) EC continues to fulfil a not unimportant reserve function,[531] as the possibility of using it can be a means of concentrating minds in the negotiation process between Parliament and the Commission and the Council. The pressure to concentrate minds becomes greater according to the degree to which non-compulsory expenditure forms a larger part of the total Community budget.

4.2.3.3   The Budgetary Procedure in Practice

Since the adoption of the Delors I package, the budgetary procedure in the Community can be seen as a means of financial framework programming as to the major points, in which the programming takes place every 5 to 7 years, combined with an annual fleshing out of the programme within the agreed global framework.

The medium-term financial programming is based on the political agreement achieved in the European Council on the basis of proposals from the Commission. This political consensus has a clearly intergovernmental character. It relates to the global financial room for manoeuvre of the Community, the evolution in the most important heads of expenditure, and the margin for agricultural expenditure. The political orientation from the European Council is developed in a legal framework in three forms:

- first, the own resources decisions which, in accordance with Article 270 EC, determine the Community's revenue (its financial possibilities);
- second, the decisions on budgetary discipline, with the so-called agricultural guidelines and the procedures for controlling agricultural guarantee expenditure; and

---

528. Case 204/86, *Greece v. Council*, also offers some support for this proposition.
529. Para. 3 in all IIAs.
530. Another question is whether in cases where there is still some room within the financial framework the Parliament may – in the framework of the IIA – use up that room on its own, even though it thus exceeds the maximum rate of increase, as fixed according to Art. 272(9), 1st through 3rd paras, EC. The Court answered this in the negative in Case C-41/95, *Council v. Parliament*. From this case it follows that the IIA may be binding on both arms of the budgetary authority in a political sense, but it may not circumvent the powers the Institutions are granted by the Treaty.
531. J. Monar, op. cit. *supra* note 403, 700–703.

– third, the IIAs which prescribe the margins for the Parliament and the Council for the development of expenditure by (mostly global) headings and sub-headings (although, as mentioned above, there is some uncertainty as to the legal nature of the IIA, the Community legislature tends to take the existence of an IIA, as well as the fact that the Institutions are bound to it, as fixed).

The annual budgetary procedure laid down in Article 272 EC tends to operate within the limits of these three instruments, and takes account of them. As has been explained above, these instruments are important for an accurate evaluation of the conduct of the Parliament and the Council in the exercise of their powers as the joint budgetary authority.

If at the beginning of the financial year no budget has yet been adopted, the provisions of Article 273 EC provide a technical solution.[532] In the period up to 1988, the Community was frequently forced to resort to this emergency solution.

The technical aspects of the adoption of the budget not dealt with here, are regulated in detail in Articles 31–39 FR and Articles 24–26 of the Implementation Regulation.

4.2.4 The Implementation of the Budget (Arts. 274–275 EC)

From the legal point of view, the budget has the same significance in Community law (in so far as the expenditure side is concerned) as in that of the Member States. It contains both an estimate of the various expenses and an authorization of these expenses (or of obligations to enter into these expenses) in the financial year concerned, which coincides with the calendar year.[533]

The FR[534] lays down detailed rules for the responsible bodies for the implementation of the budget, and for the procedures to be followed for the various categories of expenditure, such as the purchase of goods and services, and grants. One of the main principles of this Community accounting law is the principle of separation of functions between the authorizing officers and the accounting officers.[535] The authorizing officer, which is the institution itself and whose powers are delegated or subdelegated to staff, is responsible for implementing revenue and expenditure in accordance with the principles of sound financial management and for ensuring that the requirements of legality and regularity are complied with.[536]

---

532. These set up the system of the provisional twelfths. Not more than the equivalent of one-twelfth of the preceding financial year's budget appropriations may be spent in respect of any chapter or sub-division of the budget in any one month; see further J. Pipkorn, 'Legal Implications of the Absence of the Community Budget at the Beginning of a Financial Year' (1981), CML Rev., 141–167.
533. Arts. 271 and 272(1) EC.
534. See *supra* section 4.1.4.
535. Art. 58 FR. There is also the less important function of imprest administrator, who is competent for the collection of revenue other than own resources and for the payment of small sums (Art. 63).
536. Arts. 59–60 FR, and Arts. 45–54 Implementation Regulation.

The accounting officer is responsible for adequate accounting and the management of the financial means.[537]

The budget is the necessary legal basis for Community expenditure. The Commission, which is responsible for the implementation of the budget,[538] may not expend any monies unless the necessary appropriations are contained in the budget. Under Article 274, second paragraph, EC, the other Institutions are competent to effect their own expenditure.[539] There are different ways in which the Commission may implement the budget: either (1) on a centralized basis – which means that implementation tasks are performed either directly by its departments or indirectly, through Community or national agencies – or (2) by shared or decentralized management – implementation tasks are delegated to Member States (shared management) or to third countries (decentralized management) – or (3) by joint management with international organizations.[540]

The Commission's power under Article 274 EC to implement the budget has caused two severe differences of opinion between the Institutions concerned. The first related to the question whether and, if so, in which cases the budget forms an adequate legal basis for expenditure. Is a decision by the Council as Community legislator (or now in appropriate cases by the Parliament and the Council acting jointly) necessary in addition to provide a legal basis for such expenditure? This question was of particular currency between 1975 (when the European Parliament obtained an increased function in the adoption of the Community budget) and 1988, a period in which there were considerable policy differences between the two arms of the budgetary authority, the Parliament and the Council. In view of the asymmetry between the Parliament's powers in relation to Community legislation and its powers in relation to the budget, it was obvious that the European Parliament would attempt by means of the budgetary procedure to increase its say in Community affairs as much as possible and thus be inclined to view the budget as a sufficient legal basis for operational expenditure by the Commission. The Council, on the other hand, tended to the opposite view, viz. that the provision of an appropriation in the budget was a book-keeping exercise and that all operational expenditure by the Commission required a particular legal basis.

The current version of the Treaty offers no explicit guidance for a resolution of the legal question involved in this dispute.[541] However, two aspects are important.

---

537. Arts. 61–62 FR, and Arts. 55–65 Implementation Regulation.
538. Under Art. 274, 1st para., EC. The Treaty of Lisbon (new Art. 317 TFEU) adds that the Commission shall implement the budget *in cooperation with the Member States*. It does not, however, appear from this wording that the Commission would no longer bear the final responsibility for the implementation of the budget.
539. See the further rule in Art. 50 FR.
540. Arts. 53–57 FR, and Art. 35–43 Implementation Regulation. When implementing the budget by indirect centralised management or by decentralised management, the Commission may delegate tasks of public authority, *inter alia* to bodies set up by the Communities and to executive agencies, mentioned *supra* in section 4.2.1.1. (Art. 54 FR). See further P. Craig, 'A New Framework . . . ,' op. cit. *supra* note 439, 110–133.
541. This will change if the Treaty of Lisbon enters into force. In the new Art. 310(3) TFEU, it is expressly mentioned that the implementation of expenditure in the budget shall require the

The first is the division of competence between the Community and the Member States. The budget can never be a legal basis for expenses which go beyond the context of the provisions of the Treaties. There is no doubt, though, about the general proposition that the Community may use financial means even if the Treaties do not either expressly[542] or implicitly[543] so provide. In areas in which the Community is given power to act in a regulatory capacity on the basis of provisions of the Treaties (i.e., to influence the behaviour of legal subjects by means of non-temporary arrangements), it is also free to influence behaviour by financial means in place of, or in order to support such arrangements. This general proposition is unproblematic in cases in which the Community has a more heavy-weight regulatory competence. However, if, as in Article 140 EC, the Community competence is light, the legal basis remains uncertain. This is one of the reasons why the administration of Funds by the Community has been so strongly anchored in Article 308 EC, either alone or in conjunction with other provisions, in cases in which another adequate specific legal basis was not to be found.

The steady advance of the use of financial means by the Community administration has been one of the reasons why in sensitive areas such as education and training the Community's use of financial instruments has been so precisely delimited.[544]

The second aspect relates to the division of competence between the Institutions as such. In Case 242/87, *Commission v. Council*, the Court observed that 'under the scheme of the Treaty the conditions under which legislative and budgetary powers are exercised are not the same'.[545] Thus care is required in the exercise of these respective powers, as the one set has implications for the other. Given that in the Treaties there is no basis for the legislative powers to take precedence over the budgetary powers, or *vice versa*, the Institutions concerned must exercise their powers in such a way that they respect each other's sphere of competence as much as possible. In practice this boils down to meaning that the Parliament may not, acting as budgetary authority, formulate Community policy with normative provisions, while the Council may not, in the exercise of its legislative powers, so develop its normative provisions in financial terms that the Parliament's margin of discretion as budgetary authority completely disappears in reality. This applies irrespective of the fact that a dual legal basis (inclusion in the budget and a measure adopted by the Council on the basis of specific Treaty provisions) cannot, therefore, be required for all expenditure. In line with long-standing budgetary practice, the Court ruled in Case C-106/96, *United Kingdom v. Commission*, that implementation of Community expenditure relating to any *significant* Community action presupposes not only the entry of the relevant

---

prior adoption of a legally binding Union act providing a legal basis for its action and for the implementation of the corresponding expenditure (exceptions can be provided for in secondary legislation).

542. E.g., Art. 100 EC.
543. E.g., Art. 157 EC.
544. See Ch. X, section 6.2, *infra*.
545. Case 242/87, *Commission v. Council* (Erasmus programmes), para. 18.

appropriation in the budget of the Community, which is a matter for the budgetary authority, but in addition the prior adoption of a basic act authorizing that expenditure, which is a matter for the legislative authority. On the contrary, implementation of budgetary appropriations for Community action which does not fall within that category – namely *non-significant* Community action – does not require prior adoption of such a basic act.

This view, which will find its way into the Treaty if the Treaty of Lisbon enters into force,[546] is consistent with the nature of financial instruments as a substitute for or a supplement to the exercise of Community powers by legal instruments. Community competence for financial management is then determined and delimited by its power of regulatory management. However, such a power cannot be derived without more ado from the right to adopt the budget. The requirement of a legal basis which anchors the power to manage with financial resources will almost always involve the legislative competence of the Council.

The above leads to the conclusion that the budget is not the place for the determination of requirements relating to cases described in the abstract in which expenditure can or must take place. It also indicates how possible conflicts between the Council and the Parliament over the substance of their competence as to the budget should be resolved. In the meantime, the difference of opinion between the Council and the Parliament on this issue has lost much of its edge because of a number of developments:

- Firstly, following the judgement in Case C-106/96, *United Kingdom v. Commission*, the Parliament, the Council and the Commission reached agreement on what has to be understood under non-significant Community actions, for which expenditure can be authorized without prior adoption of a basic act. These actions include, e.g., pilot schemes of an experimental nature, preparatory actions and one-off actions.[547]
- Secondly, the same institutions recognized in the 1988, 1993, 1999 and 2006 IIAs[548] that the financial framework contained therein constituted binding expenditure ceilings for the Community.
- Thirdly, it has been agreed that, in the exercise of its legislative powers, the Council may not include binding financial references. The Council must respect the powers of the budgetary authority.[549]
- Finally, the Parliament has become more involved in legislation having financial implications, as is evidenced by, for instance, Articles 156 and 161 EC.[550]

---

546. See the new Art. 310(3) TFEU.
547. See the IIA of 13 Oct. 1998 on the legal basis and implementation of the budget, O.J. 1998, C 344/1, replaced by the 1999 IIA. The matter is now governed by Art. 49 FR.
548. See section 4.1.2.1 *supra*.
549. Para. 38 2006 IIA.
550. Para. 37 2006 IIA draws as a consequence that for legislative acts adopted under the co-decision procedure, the financial framework contained therein will constitute the prime reference for the budgetary authority.

The second controversy between the Council and the Parliament relates to whether the power of implementation of the budget conferred on the Commission under Article 274 EC is exclusive, or whether it must be shared if the implementation of the budget is inseparable from the implementation of Council decisions having financial implications. This concerns in particular Council decisions whose implementation involves committees of national experts.[551] The Commission has long maintained that the Treaties confer on it the exclusive competence in budgetary matters. In the Commission's view, where Article 202 EC left no room for co-decision by or on behalf of the Council in the implementation of the budget, and given the Commission's exclusive right to implement the budget under Article 274 EC, individual decisions on spending budgetary resources on the basis of rules laid down in a measure adopted by the Council were matters for the Commission alone, unfettered by committee procedures. This systematic interpretation is, however, untenable.[552]

It was demonstrated above that the budgetary authority may not unilaterally arrogate to itself the power of policy-making which is the province of the Community legislature. Consequently, in Community policy having financial implications the budget and the relevant policy instruments are inseparably linked. The practical complement between budgetary authority and Community legislature has a consequence for the implementation of the budget, which the Court has recognized in Case 16/88, *Commission v. Council.*[553] Thus the Court has noted that the Commission's power to implement the budget is not such as to modify the Treaty division of powers whereby general or individual measures may be adopted within certain areas; this led it to conclude that even though an individual measure might almost inevitably entail the commitment of expenditure, the measure and the commitment had to be distinguished, particularly since the power to adopt the administrative decision and the power to commit the expenditure might be entrusted, within the internal organization of each Institution, to different officials.

4.2.5   Audit, Accountability and Discharge (Arts. 248, 275–276 EC)

As has been noted in the preceding discussion, the Commission is responsible for expenditure of the Community. Just as in national budgetary and accounting law, this embraces responsibility for the legality and effectiveness of financial management. Scrutiny, based in particular on the annual activity reports and their summary, whereby the authorizing officers by delegation and the Commission

---

551. See *supra* section 3.1.
552. *Contra* R. Bieber, on Art. 274 EC, in H. von der Groeben and J. Schwarze (ed.), *Kommentar zum Vertrag über die Europäische Union und zur Gründung der Europäischen Gemeinschaft*, Vol. 4, 6th ed. (Nomos Verlagsgesellschaft, Baden-Baden, 2003), 1129–1130, and X. Yataganas, in *Commentaire J. Mégret*, op. cit. *supra* note 401, 334–336.
553. See paras. 16–17. The ruling in Case 16/88, *Commission v. Council*, was confirmed in Case C-106/96, *United Kingdom v. Commission*.

give an account of their management,[554] takes place in three phases. The first is the so-called internal audit of financial management. This is carried out by the internal auditor, in compliance with the relevant international standards.[555] Just as with national authorities and companies, this audit tends to be increasingly based on an assessment of the quality of management and control systems and procedures. The internal audit service, which should enjoy a position of functional independence within the Institution,[556] should advise its Institution on dealing with risks relating to financial management, and on the quality of the management and control systems.[557] The Institution in question sends annually to the discharge authority (the Council and the European Parliament) a report on the internal audit of the financial management.[558] Because the decision-making chain for financial management with regard to most Community expenditure and a large part of the revenues, also extends to the Member States, and the competent national authorities, as well as to third countries, the internal audit must also take place there. This complication, inherent in the implementation of the Community budget, has revealed itself to be a considerable obstacle to the realization of financial management which meets the requisite accounting standards.[559] A distinction should also be made between the review of the legality of a measure from an accounting point of view and the general legal review of a measure. The former is limited to reviewing whether the financial act by the Institution was in compliance with the relevant rules, whether the correct internal procedures have been properly followed, and whether the revenues or expenditures have been entered properly in the accounts.

The second phase consists of the so-called external audit by the Court of Auditors.[560] According to Article 248(2) EC, the Court of Auditors examines the legality and regularity of all revenue and expenditure and examines whether the financial management has been sound. The audit is based on records and, if necessary, performed on the spot in the other Institutions, on the premises of any

---

554. Art. 60(7) FR.
555. Art. 85 FR, and Art. 109 Implementation Regulation.
556. Art. 87 FR, and Arts. 113–115 Implementation Regulation. Art. 115 Implementation Regulation is remarkable in that the internal auditor is granted the power to bring an action directly before the Court of Justice against any act relating to the performance of his duties as internal auditor. This places a strong emphasis on the functional independence of the internal auditor.
557. Art. 86(1) FR.
558. Art. 86(4) FR.
559. The European Court of Auditors recommends that, in order to ensure effective and efficient internal control of EU funds, a Community internal control framework be developed containing common principles and standards, to be used as a basis for developing new or existing control systems at all levels of administration; see its Opinion No. 2/2004 on the 'single audit' model (and a proposal for a Community internal control framework), O.J. 2004, C 107/1.
560. See further C. Kok, 'The Court of Auditors of the European Communities: "The Other Court in Luxembourg"' (1989) CML Rev., 345–367; M. B. Engwirda and A. F. W. Moonen, 'De Europese Rekenkamer: Positie, bevoegdheden en toekomstperspectief' (2000) SEW, 246–257; J. Inghelram, 'The European Court of Auditors: Current Legal Issues' (2000) CML Rev., 129–146.

body which manages revenue or expenditure on behalf of the Community and in the Member States, including on the premises of any natural or legal person in receipt of payments from the budget.[561] The audit is carried out in liaison with national audit bodies (or, if these do not have the necessary powers, with the competent national departments). The expression 'in liaison with' was deliberately chosen to bring about a minimum of obligations between the national audit bodies and the Court of Auditors.[562] In practice, it means that the Court of Auditors notifies the national audit body of an audit in the Member State. The latter informs the former whether it intends to take part in the audit. The fact that it can but is not obliged to take part in the audit confirms the autonomous nature of the Court's audit rights in the Member States.[563] This liaison is not always easy, because the quality, the size and the powers of the national audit bodies are widely divergent.[564] The Court of Auditors also has a right to obtain, at its request, any document or information necessary to carry out its task[565] and a right of access to information held by the EIB in respect of the EIB's activity in managing Community expenditure and revenue.[566]

The Court of Auditors draws up an annual report after the close of each financial year, which it forwards to the other Institutions of the Community. This is published in the Official Journal, together with the reactions of the Institutions.[567] The report is based partly on specific checks of certain categories of acts of the Institutions, and partly on an assessment of the quality of management and control systems, administrative procedures and the manner in which the financial activities of the Institutions are entered in the accounts. The Court of Auditors usually concentrates on those parts of the financial management which are susceptible to carelessness and irregularities, on the basis of a prior risk analysis.

As well as the annual reports, the Court of Auditors publishes special reports, which examine certain areas of Community policy with regard to their financial regularity and effectiveness.[568] These reports too are usually published. The Court

---

561. Art. 248(3), 1st subparagraph, EC.
562. C.-D. Ehlermann, *Der Europäische Rechnungshof*, (Nomos Verlagsgesellschaft, Baden-Baden, 1976), 35.
563. Ibid.
564. R. Graf, *Die Finanzkontrolle der Europäischen Gemeinschaft*, (Nomos Verlagsgesellschaft Baden-Baden, 1999), 86–87.
565. Art. 248(3), 2nd subparagraph, EC, and Art. 142 FR.
566. Art. 248(3), 3rd subparagraph, EC. This right is governed by a tripartite agreement between the Court, the EIB and the Commission. However, it is stipulated that, in the absence of such an agreement, the Court shall nevertheless have access to information necessary for the audit of Community expenditure and revenue managed by the EIB. See further D. Skiadas, 'European Court of Auditors and European Investment Bank: An Uneasy Relationship' (1999) *European Public Law*, 215–225.
567. Art. 248(4) EC read with Art. 143(5) FR.
568. The Court of Auditors often refers to these special reports in its annual reports. The Court examines what consequences the Commission has drawn from the observations in the special reports. See, e.g., Annual Report on the financial year 2005, paras. 4.11, 5.64, 5.70, 5.76, 6.48, 7.30, 8.29, 8.47, 9.21 and 10.21, O.J. 2006, C 263/1.

of Auditors may, under certain circumstances, identify third parties in its reports but has to enable them to make observations on those points in such reports which refer to them by name, before those reports are definitively drawn up.[569]

Specifically in relation to the discharge procedure, the Court of Auditors draws up a 'statement of assurance' on the reliability of the accounts and the regularity and the legality of the underlying transactions.[570] The requirements are – for the Commission in particular – quite high, since expenditure is largely managed by national authorities, over whose activities the Commission has only partial control.[571] While the accounts of the Commission usually meet the accounting reliability requirements, the regularity and the legality of the underlying transactions, and of the payments in particular, are often more problematic.

The third phase is the actual process of discharge by the budgetary authority. The Council, acting by qualified majority, makes a recommendation to the Parliament. The Parliament then examines, as the Council already has done, the accounts and the financial statement referred to in Article 275 EC, as well as the annual report by the Court of Auditors together with the replies of the institutions, the statement of assurance, and the special reports by the Court of Auditors. The Parliament can ask the Commission to give evidence or information on the execution of expenditure or the operation of financial control systems. The Commission must take appropriate steps to act on the observations by the Council and Parliament in the decisions giving discharge, and must report on the measures taken.

On a number of occasions, the discharge procedure has led to serious conflicts between the Parliament and the Commission. In such a situation, the Parliament can postpone its decision to grant a discharge, in order to force the Commission to acquiesce in its requests.[573] Ultimately, the Parliament can refuse to grant a discharge. Such a refusal has occurred twice: in November 1984 and December 1998.

---

569. Case C-315/99 P, *Ismeri Europa v. Court of Auditors*. See further J.-F. Bernicot and J.-M. Champomier, 'L'auditeur et le juge: Cour de justice des Communautés européennes, 10 juillet 2001: Ismeri Europa Srl c/ Cour des comptes des Communautés européennes (Affaire C-315/99 P)', (2002), 'Revue française de finances publiques' 185–195; O. Mader, *Verteidigungsrechte im Europäischen Gemeinschaftsverwaltungsverfahren*, (Nomos Verlagsgesellschaft, Baden-Baden, 2006); J. Inghelram, L'arrêt Ismeri: quelles consequences pour la Cour des comptes européenne? (2001) Cahiers de droit européen, 707–728.

570. The Court of Auditors explains its 'DAS' methodology (DAS stands for *déclaration d'assurance*, the French term for statement of assurance) in detail on its web site (<www.eca.europa.eu>). See also I. Harden, F. White, and K. Donnelly, 'The Court of Auditors and Financial Control and Accountability in the European Community', (1995) *European Public Law*, 599–632; B. Friedmann, 'Défis de la certification DAS au contrôle des finances publiques communautaires', (1996) *Revue française de finances publiques*, 7–14; J. Belle, 'Institutions nationales de contrôle et Cour des comptes européenne: déclaration d'assurance annuelle et certification' (2006) *Revue française de finances publique*, 147–160.

571. This does not mean that the Commission cannot be held accountable for irregularities in the national management of Community means. The Commission indeed carries the ultimate responsibility for implementing the budget (Art. 274 EC).

572. See, e.g., Annual report for the financial year 2005, O.J. 2006, C 263/1, at 11–12.

573. X. Yataganas, in *Commentaire J. Mégret*, op. cit. *supra* note 401, 399.

Opinions differ as to the consequences of such a refusal to grant a discharge. If such a refusal is seen to imply the view that the Commission has failed to fulfil its tasks of budget management as a whole, then logically it should be followed by a motion of censure of the Commission, which – if adopted – should lead to the Commission's resignation as a body under Article 201 EC. It is also possible that the Parliament's refusal is intended to send a strong signal to the Commission, to which the latter Institution will have to respond by taking appropriate action.

In December 1998, after the publication of an extremely critical report by a Committee of Independent Experts, appointed for the purpose, on certain aspects of the Commission's internal financial management, the Commission ultimately decided collectively to tender its resignation.[574]

The scrutiny of the implementation of the budget is the conclusion of the budget cycle. For a long time, also in national constitutional practice, this was simply a formal accounting audit, which was not normally given much political significance. The last two decades have seen a change. In the first place, meticulousness and legality in the financial management of public organizations have as such become a point of political significance. This political significance also led to the sharpening of the Treaty provisions concerning the control of financial management, after serious irregularities in the management of the Community's expenditure had come to light. It has also led to a series of measures to improve financial accountability and the control of 'vulnerable' areas.[575]

In the second place, the political attention in the national sphere is shifting from the initial stages of the budgetary procedure (what are the objectives of policy with financial implications?) to the conclusion of the procedure (what results has policy implemented by financial means delivered?). The increasing importance placed on the review of efficiency and effectiveness follows on from that second question. This review is given an important place in particular in the special reports of the Court of Auditors.

Ideally, the scrutiny of the implementation of the budget should be linked to the preparation of the following budget, so that financial arrangements which prove to be susceptible to abuse are improved or replaced, and procedures for financial management are tightened, and expenditure and financial instruments which turn out to be ineffective are reconsidered. In constitutional systems where the legislative powers are exercised by the same bodies as those exercising the budgetary powers, and where the elected representatives can exercise their powers of scrutiny over an executive which bears full political responsibility for

---

574. See further 'Editorial Comments: The Report of the Committee of Independent Experts: An Ill Wind . . .' (1999) CML Rev., 269–272; P. Craig, 'The Fall and Renewal of the Commission: Accountability, Contract and Administrative Organisation' (2000) *European Law Journal*, 98–116.

575. An example are the rules in the 2002 FR on the delegation to third parties of implementing tasks by the Commission (Arts. 54–57 FR), which are clearly a response to the critique of the Committee of Independent Experts on the way in which the Commission exercised control over implementing tasks contracted out to external consultants; see on this critique, P. Craig, The Fall . . . , op. cit. previous note, 101–105.

the implementation of the budget, such a constitutional 'linking process' appears to work fairly well. In the system of the Community, that is much less so. There, the budgetary authority and the legislative authority are not identical, and the powers of scrutiny are partly exercised by an institution (the Council) which also exercises executive powers, and which, moreover, may have interests which are incompatible with the interest of a lawful and effective budget. This almost inevitably influences the manner in which the Council fulfils its role in the discharge process,[576] which is mainly limited to a check as to whether the stream of expenditure has indeed followed the pattern which the Council had envisaged when the budget was drawn up; this amounts to checking whether the basic aims of the budget in terms of distribution policy have in fact been achieved. The discharge procedure is thus for the Council primarily a source of information. The Council only gradually started to attach some political importance to the lawfulness and effectiveness of Community expenditure, and even then this was considered to be of secondary importance. Because the Council still plays a dominant role in those areas of expenditure – intensive regulation of agricultural and structural policy – which require most attention in terms of control, it cannot be expected that this institution will aim its arrows particularly accurately at these policy areas during the discharge of the budget.

4.3   THE PROTECTION OF THE FINANCIAL INTERESTS OF THE COMMUNITY: COMBATING FRAUD (ART. 280 EC)

Measures for the protection of the financial interests of the Community against fraud must be taken in the national legal order because the implementation of Community policy with financial implications is to a large extent in the hands of the Member States – as is also the collection of the Community's income. The most important items of expenditure in the Community budget are, of course, the costs of the Common Agricultural Policy (in particular the European Agricultural Guarantee Fund (EAGF) and the European Agricultural Fund for Rural Development (EAFRD)[577]) and those of the Structural funds (the ESF and the ERDF), together with the Cohesion Fund.[578] These items account for about 80% of the Community budget (which is more than 100 billion euro in commitment appropriations). They are almost entirely devoted to financing expenditure which the Member States must make in accordance with the rules of agricultural market and price policies (including interventions and restitutions) and for co-financing projects, programmes and other activities of the Member States in the framework of these funds. *Community* money is paid to beneficiaries by the *Member States* or

---

576. See R. Graf, op. cit. *supra* note 564, 123–125.
577. See Council Reg. (EC) No. 1290/2005, on the financing of the common agricultural policy, O.J. 2005, L 209/1, last amended by Council Reg. (EC) No. 479/2008 of 29 April 2008, O.J. 2008, L 148/1.
578. See Council Reg. (EC) No. 1083/2006 and Council Reg. (EC) No. 1084/2006, *supra* note 376.

used to finance works carried out or services provided under a system of shared management[579] and on the basis of a large variety of – usually complex – rules and conditions. Such a system of indirect financing increases the risk of irregularities and fraud to the detriment of the Community budget.

The risk does not only exist on the expenditure side of the budget: it also extends to the income side. In fact, the collection of the traditional own resources of the Community – customs duties and agricultural levies – also takes place in a decentralized manner. As for the third source of own resources, the VAT surcharge, it is important for the Community that when the Member States collect VAT they apply the rules correctly and take action against tax evasion. The risk of financial disadvantage that the Community runs here is lower than that related to the collection of the traditional own resources, since unlike the latter case the Member States themselves have a considerable financial interest in the proper collection of VAT.

A characteristic of irregular and fraudulent actions to the detriment of the Community budget is that they are frequently cross-border. These actions concern direct or indirect transactions for goods, services and capital, and are carried out by persons who move freely between the Member States; moreover, the existence of the market freedoms is a stimulus for internationally organized fraud. In order to investigate, prosecute, impose penalties and execute them, information must be exchanged, and cooperation between the administrative and judicial bodies of the Member States is needed. Such cooperation runs into all kinds of difficulties, however. A clear definition of the activities to be prosecuted and punished is often lacking, and the national rules concerning the nature of the sanctions to be imposed – and the related procedures – often vary considerably from one Member State to another. In addition, the already overburdened administrative and judicial bodies of the Member States have other priorities, and not just the protection of the financial interests of the Community; moreover, they are faced with conventional instruments of mutual cooperation, which frequently are rather cumbersome and inadequate in nature. In such a context, an effective fight against fraud to the detriment of the Community budget is difficult to achieve.

It was at the end of the 1980s that the outside world became aware for the first time of the huge extent of the financial damage which the Community suffers – partly as a result of laxity and carelessness on the part of national authorities – due to fraud, which is frequently internationally organized, and includes tax evasion and customs fraud. It was only then that people become sufficiently aware that this also damaged the Community's credibility; protection of the Community's financial interests gradually gained greater political priority in the Council and the Member States.[580] According to the 1994 Annual Report of the Commission on

---

579. See Art. 53b FR.
580. See Resolution of the Council and of the representatives of the Governments of the Member States, meeting within the Council of 13 Nov. 1991 concerning the protection of the financial interests of the Communities, O.J. 1991, C 328/1. See also J.A.E. Vervaele, *Fraud against the Community: The Need for European Fraud Legislation* (Kluwer, Deventer, 1992). A good

the fight against fraud, fraudulent transactions to the tune of more than one billion ECU (1.2% of the total budget) were discovered, which were to the detriment of the Community's finances.[581] The relevant Annual Report for 2006[582] reports that the total estimated financial impact of irregularities, including suspected fraud, was 1 155.32 million euro in relation to expenditure by the European Agricultural Guidance and Guarantee Fund (EAGGF)[583] – Guarantee section; 87 million euro (approx. 0.17% of total appropriations) for the EAGGF Guarantee Section; in relation to the traditional own resources, 353 million euro; in relation to the expenditure of the structural funds and cohesion fund, 703 million euro (approx. 1.83% of the structural and cohesion fund appropriations); and in relation to pre-accession funds, 12.32 million euro (approx 2.8% of the total eligible amounts).

It is scarcely surprising, then, that the Treaty of Maastricht (1992) introduced into the EC Treaty the obligation for the Community and the Member States, both individually and in cooperation, to counter fraud and any other illegal activities affecting the financial interests of the Community. This obligation is currently laid down in Article 280 EC (amended by the Treaty of Amsterdam (1997)). As to the measures to be taken, paragraphs (1) and (2) of this provision codify the principles of equivalence and effectiveness developed by the Court of Justice in this area.

Because of the frequently cross-border nature of infringements with financial implications for the Community, their prevention and investigation and the imposition of sanctions require a close cooperation, not just (horizontally) between the national bodies, but also (vertically) between these bodies and the Commission – as has been gradually recognized more and more, and is now also set out in the Treaty, in Article 280(3) EC.

Of utmost importance, finally, is the fact that since the entry into force of the Treaty of Amsterdam (1 May 1999), the fourth paragraph of Article 280 EC grants the Council the power to adopt, using the co-decision procedure and after consulting the Court of Auditors, 'the necessary measures in the fields of the prevention of and fight against fraud affecting the financial interests of the Community with a view to affording effective and equivalent protection in the Member States'. According to the last sentence of this paragraph, however, these measures will

---

overview of the development of anti-fraud policy may be found in S. White, *Protection of the Financial Interests of the European Communities: The Fight against Fraud and Corruption* (Deventer, 1998). It should be noted that there are also other Community interests – apart from financial interests – which require protection by penal law; one may think in particular of protection of the euro against counterfeiting (see Council Reg. (EC) No. 1338/2001, O.J. 2001, L 181/6).

581.   1994 Annual Report of the Commission on the protection of the Communities' financial interests and the fight against fraud (Bull. EU, 3–1995, 105, 1.6.8). Reported irregularities concerning the traditional own resources amounted in 1993 to 3.4% of income in this category.

582.   COM (2007) 390.

583.   The European Agricultural Guidance and Guarantee Fund (EAGGF) is the predecessor of the EAGF and the EAFRD.

not concern the application of national criminal law or the national administration of justice.[584]

The Commission is of the opinion that this exception does not exclude criminal law in general and as a whole from the sphere of application of Article 280(4) EC, but only the *application* of national criminal law and national administration of justice.[585] In Case C-176/03, *Commission v. Council*, the Court did not specifically address the issue of how Article 280(4) EC should be interpreted. With regard to that provision, the Court only said that it cannot be inferred from it that, in the area of environmental protection – which was at issue in that case –, any harmonization of criminal law must be ruled out even where it is necessary in order to ensure the effectiveness of Community law.[586] Moreover, the view is held by some that the essence of the Court's ruling in Case C-176/03 – the Community legislature is allowed to take measures which relate to the criminal law of the Member States if they are necessary for the full effectiveness of EC law[587] – is broad enough to apply also to other policy areas than environmental protection.[588] The ruling could thus also apply to the protection of the financial interests of the Communities, provided the application of national criminal law and national administration of justice are not affected. Article 280(4) EC does not, therefore, necessarily rule out all Community competence to adopt 'measures which relate to the criminal law of the Member States' in relation to the protection of financial interests of the Communities.[589] It should be added that this discussion will become theoretical if the Treaty of Lisbon enters into force. In the new Article 325(4) TFEU, the exception with regard to the application of national criminal law and national administration of justice has been deleted since the same Treaty makes it possible for the Council to establish a European Public Prosecutor.[590]

The Treaties of Maastricht and Amsterdam laid a solid foundation in the EC Treaty for the Community anti-fraud policy.[591] This policy, the origins of which

---

584. The same condition applies to the powers to strengthen customs cooperation which Art. 135 EC grants to the Community.
585. See the explanatory memorandum to the Proposal for a Directive of the European Parliament and of the Council on the criminal-law protection of the Community's financial interests, O.J. 2001, C 240E/125.
586. Case C-176/03, *Commission v. Council* para. 52.
587. Ibid., para. 48, confirmed in Case C-440/05, *Commission v. Council*, at para. 66.
588. See, e.g., C. Tobler, 'Annotation of Case C-176/03' (2006) CML Rev., 835–854 (at 852).
589. See also L. Kuhl and B.-R. Killmann, 'The Community Competence for a Directive on Criminal Law Protection of the Financial Interests' (2006) *Eucrim*, 100–103 (at 102); B. Hecker, *Europäisches Strafrecht*, 2nd ed. (Berlin, 2007), 162, para. 100. In its communication on the implications of the Court's judgment of 13 Sep. 2005 (Case C-176/03 *Commission v. Council*) (COM (2005) 583 final/2), the Commission confirms its opinion that Art. 280(4) EC is the correct legal basis for the Proposal for a Directive mentioned *supra* in note 585.
590. See *infra* section 4.3.2.2.
591. On this policy, see the 2006 Annual Report of the Commission on Protection of the Communities' Financial Interests – Fight against Fraud, COM (2007) 390.

are to be found in the case law of the Court of Justice,[592] had in fact already got off the ground in the years preceding the entry into force of Article 280(4) EC. Its objective was the creation and strengthening of a Community legal framework for effectively combating fraud in all areas of Community policy, and no longer only in the area of agriculture. This policy was primarily aimed at the adoption of general (horizontal) arrangements concerning two things. Not only was it opportune to lay down rules for the measures and sanctions to be imposed by the Member States in case of infringements of Community law which are detrimental to the Communities' financial interests. It was just as important to adopt rules for the checks and inspections to be carried out by the Member States and – in a supplementary capacity – the Commission, aimed at preventing such financial disadvantage, or investigating the extent of the financial disadvantage if it has already taken place. It has been correctly observed that monitoring is an essential element in enforcement.[593]

4.3.1   Administrative Sanctions

The so-called PIF Regulation (from the French name: *protection des intérêts financiers*) of the Council, dating from 1995, created the desired Community legal framework for administrative measures and sanctions, and for instituting checks.[594] The Regulation contains general arrangements for homogenous checks and administrative measures and penalties concerning irregularities with regard to Community law. It builds on the experience already gained with the sanctions applied in the area of agriculture, and on the related case law, which is discussed in Chapter VII, section 5 of this book.

Importantly, it was possible to reach agreement on a Community definition of the concept 'irregularity', which could from then on be used as a basic concept in all Community legislation. This term means:

> any infringement of a provision of Community law resulting from an act or omission by an economic operator, which has, or would have, the effect of prejudicing the general budget of the Communities or budgets managed by them, either by reducing or losing revenue accruing from own resources

---

592. Particularly through the judgments in Case 68/88, *Commission v. Greece* (see paras. 23–25); Case C-240/90, *Germany v. Commission* (see paras. 11–13), and Case C-210/91, *Commission v. Greece* (see paras. 19–20).
593. F.C.M.A. Michiels, 'Nieuwe instrumenten ter bescherming van de financiële belangen van de Europese Gemeenschappen' (1996) SEW, 362–371 (at 369).
594. Council Reg. (EC, Euratom) No. 2988/95 of 18 Dec. 1995 on the protection of the European Communities financial interests, O.J. 1995, L 312/1. See also F.C.M.A. Michiels, op. cit. previous note; P. Cullen, 'Fraud against the Community Budget: A Common Concern' (1999) *EC Tax Journal*, 61–79.

collected directly on behalf of the Communities, or by an unjustified item of expenditure (Art. 1(2), PIF Reg.).[595]

In this manner, the subject of detection and sanction is defined for all Member States. On the income side, irregularities concerning VAT do not come within the scope of the Regulation, since only the traditional own resources are 'collected directly on behalf of the Communities'. On the other hand, the definition is broad enough to include fraudulent action in the sense of the Convention on the Protection of the European Communities' financial interests,[596] to be discussed below.

The Regulation contains a number of general principles, which mainly codify the constant case law of the Court of Justice concerning the creation and imposition of administrative sanctions (Art. 2).[597] The Community legislature has, by adopting the Regulation, required that, as a general rule, all sectoral regulations comply with those principles.[598] Article 2(3) and (4) set out the division of responsibilities between the Community and the Member States. The Community legislature determines the nature and scope of the administrative measures and penalties necessary for the correct application of the rules in question; it has regard to the nature and seriousness of the irregularity, the advantage granted or received and the degree of responsibility. The procedures for applying Community checks, measures and penalties are – in accordance with 'procedural autonomy' – in principle left to the Member States, though this is 'subject to the Community law applicable'.

The Regulation makes a distinction between administrative measures and 'penalties'. Each and every irregularity should in principle lead to the withdrawal of the wrongly obtained advantage: payment or repayment of the amounts due or wrongly received, or total or partial loss of the security lodged; these measures are not seen as penalties (Art. 4).[599] Intentional irregularities or those caused by negligence may lead to the administrative penalties listed in Article 5(1). These are the same kind of sanctions encountered in relation to agricultural arrangements in Chapter VII, section 5, supplemented by a reference to:

> 'other penalties of a purely economic type, equivalent in nature and scope, provided for in the sectoral rules adopted by the Council in the light of the specific requirements of the sectors concerned and in compliance with the implementing powers conferred on the Commission by the Council' (Art. 5(1) under (g)).[600]

---

595. This definition also constitutes a reference for defining the Court of Auditors' task, introduced by the Amsterdam Treaty, to report in particular on any cases of irregularity (Art. 248(2), 1st subparagraph, EC).
596. O.J. 1995, C 316/49. Cf. 6th recital of the Regulation.
597. See on the application of Art. 2(2) concerning the retroactive application of a less severe sanction, Case C-45/06, *Campina*.
598. Case C-295/02, *Gerken*, at para. 56.
599. See, e.g., Art. 103 FR on the recovery of amounts paid when an award procedure proves to have been subject to substantial errors, irregularities or fraud attributable to the contractor.
600. G. Corstens and J. Pradel, *European Criminal Law* (The Hague-London-New York, 2002), para. 501, see the last words of (g) ('in compliance with the implementing powers conferred on the Commission by the Council'), and also the phrase 'subject to the Community law

As a general rule, 'other' irregularities may only give rise to the penalties listed here 'provided that such penalties are essential to ensure correct application of the rules' (Art. 5(2)).[601] An example of such a penalty is the exclusion from participation in procurement procedures of candidates or tenderers who have been the subject of a judgment which has the force of res judicata for fraud, corruption, involvement in a criminal organisation or any other illegal activity detrimental to the Communities' financial interests.[602]

The Regulation, moreover, lays down rules for such matters as limitation periods for proceedings (Art. 3),[603] and how to deal with a situation where financial sanctions (e.g., administrative fines) have been imposed and criminal proceedings are also commenced in relation to the same set of facts (Art. 6). It also describes the persons on whom administrative measures and sanctions may be imposed (Art. 7); these are not just the market operators – the natural or legal persons and the other entities on whom national law confers legal capacity – who have committed the irregularity, but also those who have participated in the irregularity, and those who are under a duty to take responsibility for the irregularity or to prevent it from being committed.

Finally, the Regulation contains some general (horizontal) rules, supplementing the existing sectoral rules, in the area of checks and inspections. These will be discussed further below.

4.3.2   Penal Sanctions

4.3.2.1   The Convention of 26 July 1995

In the same year as the PIF Regulation, the Council decided – in the framework of the Third Pillar – to draw up the Convention of 26 July 1995 on the protection of the European Communities' financial interests.[604] The Convention – whose

---

applicable' in Art. 2(4) (the latter is in our view less likely), as a reference to the creation or the recognition of the possibility of providing in Council regulations for the direct imposition of sanctions by the Commission, and give a number of examples.

601. This provision contains a controversial and ambiguous clause ('those penalties not equivalent to a criminal penalty that are provided for in para. 1') where in many language versions it is not clear if the relative clause is restrictive or extensive. See on this F.C.M.A. Michiels, op. cit. *supra* note 593, at 369.

602. Art. 93(1)(e) FR. A central database, which contains details of such candidates and tenderers and which receives information from authorities of the Member States and third countries, is set up and operated by the Commission, see Art. 95 FR. The FR also contains other forms of administrative sanctions, e.g., with regard to the financial actors (authorizing officers, accounting officers, and imprest administrators; see Arts. 64–68 FR).

603. See on the direct effect of Art. 3(1) and on the interruption of the limitation period, Case C-278/02, *Handlbauer*, and on the notion of continuous or repeated irregularities, Case C-279/05, *Vonk Dairy Products*.

604. O.J. 1995, C 316/49, with Explanatory Report, O.J. 1997, C 191/1. See F.C.M.A. Michiels, op. cit. *supra* note 593; P. Cullen, op. cit. *supra* note 594; G. Corstens and J. Pradel, op. cit. *supra* note 600, par. 423 et seq. For a critical view, see A. H. Klip, 'Integrated Protection of the

ratification by the Member States took a long time, just as was the case for the associated protocols[605] – aims to provide effective penal protection for these interests. Article 1 contains a definition of the concept of fraud affecting the European Communities' financial interests. The Member States undertake the obligation to take the necessary and appropriate measures to ensure that the conduct covered by the definition, as well as participation in, instigation of, or attempt at such conduct, all constitute criminal offences in their national penal law systems. They are obliged to set effective, proportionate and dissuasive criminal penalties for such conduct, making a distinction between serious and minor fraud and laying down the consequences of this distinction for the nature of the penalties (Art. 2). The Convention also contains provisions on criminal liability of heads of businesses (Art. 3), jurisdiction of the Member States (Art. 4), extradition and prosecution (Art. 5), cooperation in relation to cross-border fraud (Art. 6), and the principle of *ne bis in idem* (Art. 7).

Three supplementary protocols have been annexed to the Convention in the subsequent years. The Protocol of 27 September 1996[606] contains a definition of both passive corruption of officials (both Community and national), and active corruption (bribery), as a result of which the financial interests of the Community are or may be damaged, as well as the obligation on Member States to make these forms of corruption subject to penal sanctions. The Second Protocol of 19 June 1997[607] obliges the Member States, in the framework of the criminal offences covered by the 'PIF' instruments of the Third Pillar, to establish money laundering[608] as a criminal offence, and to take necessary measures to ensure that legal persons can be held liable as well as ensuring that the confiscation or removal of the instruments and proceeds of these offences is possible. It also contains rules on cooperation between the Commission and the Member States, and on data protection. Finally, the Protocol of 29 November 1996[609] is on the interpretation of the Convention on the protection of the European Communities' financial interests and

---

Community's Financial Interests: Shift from "State-State" Approach towards Verticalisation of the Procedure'?, in J.A.E. Vervaele (ed.), *Transnational Enforcement of the Financial Interests of the European Union* (Antwerp-Groningen-Oxford, 1999), 95–107.

605. Partly for that reason, on 23 May 2001 the Commission made a proposal for a directive, based on Art. 280(4) EC, mentioned *supra* in note 585, in which elements from the Convention and protocols are included, which according to the Commission did not concern either the application of national criminal law or national administration of justice. For a discussion of this proposal, see D.E. Comijs, *Communautair strafrecht?* (2001) NTER, 267–270. The Convention, and the protocols discussed below, entered into force on 17 Oct. 2002, with the exception of the second protocol.

606. O.J. 1996, C 313/2. See also Explanatory Report, O.J. 1998, C 11/5. See also, with a more general scope than just protection of the Communities' financial interests, the Convention on the fight against corruption involving officials of the European Communities or officials of Member States of the European Union, drawn up by the Council in 1997, O.J. 1997, C 195/1.

607. O.J. 1997, C 221/12. See also Explanatory Report, O.J. 1999, C 91/8.

608. Art. 1(e) of the Protocol refers for the definition of this concept to Art. 1, 3rd indent, of Dir. 91/308/EC, O.J. 1991, L 166/77.

609. O.J. 1997, C 151/1.

the protocols annexed thereto.[610] This jurisdictional protocol provides for voluntary acceptance by the Member States, by means of a declaration, of the jurisdiction of the Court of Justice to give preliminary rulings. The Member States can choose whether only courts of last instance may make preliminary references to the Court of Justice, or all their courts.[611]

Doubts may still arise, however, as to whether the Convention and its protocols bring effective and equivalent penal law protection of the Communities' financial interests in all Member States much nearer. They still leave important questions concerning procedures, judicial guarantees and evidence largely unregulated, in spite of the obstacles this may create for cooperation in the area of criminal law between the Member States. The diversity of criminal procedural law in the Member States is very wide regarding these matters. As to the penal sanctions to be imposed, the Member States still maintain a large degree of freedom. Moreover, the jurisdiction of the Court of Justice is limited, and dependent on the willingness of the Member States.[612]

4.3.2.2   The European Public Prosecutor

The project launched by the Commission, at the request of the Parliament, in 1995 to draw up a *Corpus Juris* offers a different perspective. The group of experts on whom this task was conferred published in 1997 the '*Corpus Juris* introducing penal provisions for the purpose of the financial interests of the European Union'[613] and in 2000 its final report, based on an extensive comparative study.[614] With a view to the protection of the Communities' financial interests, the group proposed the introduction of Community rules which do not just include eight penal provisions, but also a series of general provisions of substantive penal law and procedural rules to be taken account of in the preparation of criminal proceedings. The actual sentencing would remain in the hands of the national courts, but the investigation and prosecution would be in the hands of an independent European Office of public prosecutions, consisting of a European Public Prosecutor and, under his direction, European Public Prosecutors who are accredited in the Member States. During the preliminary investigation, a

---

610.   The jurisdictional protocol also applies to the Second Protocol, drawn up at a later date; cf. Art. 13(3) Second protocol.
611.   Cf. Art. 35 TEU (see Ch. IV, section 7.4). For the other heads of jurisdiction of the Court of Justice in relation to these matters, see Art. 8 Convention, and First Protocol, and Arts. 13–15 Second Protocol; see further G. Corstens and J. Pradel, op. cit. *supra* note 600, paras. 447, 448 and 460.
612.   See on these and other shortcomings of the PIF instruments, M. Delmas-Marty, 'The European Union and Penal Law' (1998) *European Law Journal*, 108–110 and, by the same author, 'Guest Editorial: Combatting Fraud: Necessity, Legitimacy and Feasibility of the *Corpus Juris*' (2000) CML Rev., 247–256.
613.   Under the direction of M. Delmas-Marty, Economica, Paris, 1997.
614.   M. Delmas-Marty and J.A.E. Vervaele (eds), *The Implementation of the Corpus Juris in the Member States*, Vols 1–4 (Antwerp-Groningen-Oxford, 2000–2001).

European pre-trial chamber, consisting of judges appointed by the Member States supervises strict respect for the Community rules.[615]

During the negotiation of the Nice Treaty, the Commission made a proposal to establish a European Public prosecutor,[616] which was not accepted by the European Council at Nice in December 2000.[617] The idea of a European Public Prosecutor found its way, however, into the Treaty establishing a Constitution for Europe[618] as well as into the Treaty of Lisbon. According to the new Article 86 TFEU, the Council may decide to establish a European Public Prosecutor's Office from Eurojust.[619] This decision must in principle be taken unanimously after obtaining the consent of the European Parliament, although, in the absence of unanimity, the European Council may intervene at the request of a group of at least nine Member States. The European Public Prosecutor's Office would be responsible for investigating, prosecuting and bringing to judgment, where appropriate in liaison with Europol, the perpetrators of, and accomplices in, offences against the EU's financial interests. If so decided by the Council, its powers could also include serious crime having a cross-border dimension. The Office would exercise the functions of prosecutor in the competent courts of the Member States.[620]

4.3.3 Checks and Inspections[621]

As was shown above, the PIF Regulation lays down a number of general (horizontal) rules, supplementing the existing sectoral rules in the area of checks. The Member States are obliged, in accordance with their national laws, to take the necessary measures 'to ensure the regularity and reality of transactions involving the Communities' financial interests' (Art. 8(1)). The inspection measures should be adapted to the specific character of each sector, should be proportional to the

---

615. See on the *Corpus Juris*, J.A.E. Vervaele, 'L'Union Européénne et son espace pénal europeén: Les défis du modèle Corpus Juris 2000' (2000) *Revue du droit pénal et de criminologie*, 775–779.
616. COM (2000) 608.
617. Following this refusal and building upon the *Corpus Juris* study, the Commission presented in Dec. 2001 a Green Paper on criminal-law protection of the financial interests of the Community and the establishment of a European Prosecutor, COM (2001) 715 final, as completed by COM (2003) 128 final.
618. Art. III-274.
619. See on Eurojust, Council Dec. 2002/187/JHA of 28 Feb. 2002 setting up Eurojust with a view to reinforcing the fight against serious crime, O.J. 2002, L 63/1.
620. See also L. Kuhl, 'OLAF: The Protection of the Community's Financial Interests and the Outcome of the IGC', in J.A.E. Vervaele (ed.), *European Evidence Warrant: Transnational Judicial Inquiries in the EU*, (Intersentia, Antwerp-Oxford, 2005), 167–174 (at 170–172).
621. See for more details the clear contribution by J.A.E. Vervaele, 'Community Regulation and Operational Application of Investigative Powers, the Gathering and Use of Evidence with Regard to the Infringement of EC Financial Interests', in J.A.E. Vervaele (ed.), *Transnational Enforcement of the Financial Interests of the European Union*, (Intersentia, Antwerp-Groningen-Oxford, 1999), 53–91.

objective pursued and should be so arranged that they do not cause excessive extra economic burdens or administrative costs (Art. 8(2)). Article 9 deals with the Commission's own responsibilities for the supervision of the checks carried out by the Member States (second line of supervision) and for on-the-spot checks and inspections (first line of supervision).

The first line of supervision is regulated in more detail in Regulation 2185/96,[622] which grants the Commission far-reaching powers of this nature. The Commission can carry out its own checks and inspections not just at the request of a Member State, but also for the detection of serious or transnational irregularities, or in special cases where such checks are necessary 'in order to improve the effectiveness of the protection of financial interests and so to ensure an equivalent level of protection within the Community' (Art. 2). The Commission inspections are carried out under the Commission's authority and responsibility by its officials and other servants (Art. 6). These inspectors have 'access, under the same conditions as national administrative inspectors and in compliance with national legislation, to all the information and documentation on the operations concerned which are required for the proper conduct of the on-the-spot checks and inspections' (Art. 7). As with the PIF Regulation, discussed above, on the income side this Regulation only concerns the own resources which are collected *directly* on behalf of the Communities, so not the VAT surcharge.[623]

Furthermore, in Regulation 515/97, the Council has laid down rules on the assistance which the administrative authorities of the Member States should give one another, and on their cooperation with the Commission, in order to ensure the correct application of the law on customs and agricultural matters, and the legal protection of the Communities' financial interests; this is particularly in relation to prevention and detection of infringements of this legislation, and the investigation of operations which are or appear to be contrary to those regulations.[624]

---

622. Council Reg. (Euratom, EC) No. 2185/96 of 11 Nov. 1996 concerning on-the-spot checks and inspections carried out by the Commission in order to protect the European Communities' financial interests against fraud and other irregularities, O.J. 1996, L 292/2. See L. Kuhl and H. Spitzer, 'Die Verordnung (Euratom, EG) Nr. 2185/96 des Rates über die Kontrollbefugnisse der Kommission im Bereich der Betrugsbekämpfung' (1998) EuZW, 37–44; S. Ulrich, 'Kontrollen des Europäischen Amtes für Betrugsbekämpfung (OLAF) bei Wirtschaftsbeteiligten: Befugnisse, Verfahrensrechte und Rechtsschutzmöglichkeiten bei Kontrollen vor Ort nach der VO (Euratom, EG) Nr. 2185/96' (2000) *Europäisches Wirtschafts- & Steuerrecht*, 137–147.

623. These controls are now regulated in Art. 18 of Council Reg. (EC, Euratom) No. 1150/2000 of 22 May 2000 implementing Decision 94/728/EC, Euratom on the system of the Communities' own resources, O.J. 2000, L 130/1, as last amended by Council Reg. (EC, Euratom) No. 2028/2004 of 16 Nov. 2004, O.J. 2004, L 352/1, and in Council Reg. (EC, Euratom) No. 1026/1999 of 10 May 1999 determining the powers and obligations of agents authorized by the Commission to carry out controls and inspections of the Communities' own resources, O.J. 1999, L 126/1.

624. Council Reg. (EC) No. 515/97 of 13 Mar. 1997 on mutual assistance between the administrative authorities of the Member States and cooperation between the latter and the Commission to ensure the correct application of the law on customs and agricultural matters, O.J. 1997, L 82/1, as last amended by Council Reg. (EC) No. 807/2003 of 14 Apr. 2003, O.J. 2003, L 122/36. In the area of indirect taxes (VAT), see Council Reg. (EC) No. 1798/2003 of 7 Oct. 2003 on

4.3.4 OLAF Investigations

The European Anti-Fraud Office (*Office de Lutte Anti-Fraude*, OLAF)[625] carries out 'external investigations' (in the Member States and in third countries)[626] as well as 'internal investigations' (within EU institutions, bodies, offices and agencies).[627] When carrying out investigations in the Member States, OLAF exercises the power conferred on the Commission by Council Reg. (EC) No. 2185/96.[628] OLAF is only authorized to conduct administrative investigations. It cannot, therefore, undertake all of the tasks for which police powers are required, such as searching homes or demanding access to bank accounts.[629] Its reports constitute, however, if the procedural requirements laid down in the national law of the Member State concerned have been respected, admissible evidence in administrative or judicial proceedings of the Member State in which their use proves necessary, in the same way and under the same conditions as administrative reports drawn up by national administrative inspectors.[630]

The fact that an OLAF investigation may have far-reaching consequences for individuals involved in such an investigation raises the question of judicial review of OLAF acts.[631] There appears to be little doubt that the OLAF findings can be contested either during a judicial procedure against an act of an EU institution adopted following an internal investigation[632] or during a national procedure in

---

administrative cooperation in the field of VAT and repealing Reg. (EEC) No. 218/92, O.J. 2003, L 264/1, as last amended by Council Reg. (EC) No. 1791/2006 of 20 Nov. 2006, O.J. 2006, L 363/1. On these and other forms of cooperation see, extensively, A.H. Klip and J.A.E. Vervaele (eds), *European Cooperation between Tax, Customs and Judicial Authorities*, (European Monographs Vol. 32, The Hague-London-New York, 2002), 7–48 and 249–291.

625. See also Ch. IV, section 9.3. *supra.*
626. Art. 3 of Reg. (EC) No. 1073/1999 of the European Parliament and of the Council of 25 May 1999 concerning investigations conducted by the European Anti-Fraud Office (OLAF), O.J. 1999, L 136/1.
627. Ibid., Art. 4.
628. The investigations are also governed by Arts. 5–6 of Reg. (EC) No. 1073/1999, *supra* note 626. In addition to these rules, OLAF itself has adopted and published the 'OLAF Manual' (Office for Official Publications of the European Communities, Luxembourg, 2005) which is a systematic compilation of internal instructions for its staff and can thus be seen as a series of commitments taken by OLAF in the context of its investigations; see further W. Hetzer, 'Fight against Fraud and Protection of Fundamental Rights in the European Union' (2006) *European Journal of Crime, Criminal Law and Criminal Justice*, 20–45 (at 35–40).
629. See Special Report No. 1/2005 of the Court of Auditors concerning the management of the European Anti-Fraud Office (OLAF), together with the Commission's replies, O.J. 2005, C 202/1, para. 15.
630. Reg. (EC) No. 1073/1999, *supra* note 626, Art. 9.
631. See also S. Gleβ and H.E. Zeitler, 'Fair Trial Rights and the European Community's Fight against Fraud' (2001) *European Law Journal*, 219–237; J. Wakefield, 'Good Governance and the European Anti-Fraud Office' (2006) *European Public Law*, 549–575.
632. E.g., a procedure before the EU Civil Service Tribunal against a disciplinary measure adopted on the basis of an OLAF Report.

which the findings are used following an external investigation.[633] Direct and immediate judicial protection against OLAF acts appears, however, to be less self-evident. Since OLAF is part of the Commission, a judicial procedure has to be started against the Commission and not against OLAF directly.[634] Although this does not appear to have given rise to any problems in practice, it is somewhat surprising that the Commission is legally responsible for acts adopted by OLAF although it is not allowed to give any instructions to the latter.[635]

Until now, considering that they do not bring about a distinct change in the applicant's legal position, case law has considered an action for annulment[636] to be inadmissible against several OLAF acts such as the decision to open or to re-open an administrative inquiry, the investigations themselves, and OLAF's forwarding to the administration of the report concluding the investigation[637] or to national prosecuting authorities of information on internal investigations.[638] An individual may, however, have a right to reparation under Article 288, second paragraph, EC for OLAF acts causing damage to him, provided the conditions for the application of this provision are met.[639] Direct judicial protection against OLAF acts is, therefore, not absent but appears, in practice, to be limited to the possibility to obtain an ex post compensation for damage caused. Moreover, the fact that an action for annulment against an OLAF act is considered to be inadmissible deprives the applicant of the possibility to ask for interim measures under Article 243 EC in the context of such action, and, thus, of an effective remedy in urgent matters.

---

633. In the latter case, problems of interpretation of Community law applicable to OLAF's investigation may be submitted by the competent national court to the Court of Justice for a preliminary ruling under Art. 234 EC. A question regarding the validity of an OLAF act must be submitted to the Court of Justice (see in general on this issue, e.g., Case C-461/03, *Gaston Schul Douane-expediteur*).

634. See also Opinion No. 2/99 of the Court of Auditors on the amended proposal for a Council Regulation (EC, Euratom) concerning investigations conducted by the Fraud Office, O.J. 1999, C 154/1, para. 8.

635. Art. 12(3) of Reg. (EC) No. 1073/1999, *supra* note 626. The authority of the Commission over OLAF is, however, not entirely absent since the former still has the power to adopt disciplinary sanctions against the Director of OLAF, see Art. 9(4).

636. Introduced either on the basis of Art. 236 EC (applicable to EU staff) or of 230, 4th para., EC.

637. Case T-215/02, *Gómez-Reino v. Commission*, at para. 50.

638. Case T-193/04, *Tillack v. Commission*, at para. 68. An action for annulment against a refusal by OLAF to grant access to information is admissible, see Joined Cases T-391/03 & T-70/04, *Franchet and Byk v. Commission*. The rules on access to information (Reg. (EC) No. 1049/2001 of the European Parliament and of the Council of 30 May 2001 regarding public access to European Parliament, Council and Commission documents, O.J. 2001, L 145/43) are, however, not specific to OLAF.

639. Compensation has actually been granted in Case T-309/03, *Camós Grau v. Commission*, where an OLAF investigator had been in a situation of conflict of interests, and in Case T-259/03, *Nikolaou v. Commission*, in which compensation was granted for unauthorized communication by OLAF of personal data. Compensation has also been granted in Case F-23/05, *Giraudy v. Commission*, but because of damage caused by the Commission itself in the context of an OLAF investigation.

The establishment of a European Public Prosecutor[640] would seem to offer a more favourable prospect, because then the investigations by the OLAF inspectors would most likely be led by the former, who would have clearly defined powers, and judicial supervision would be provided for the exercise of those powers.[641]

4.3.5 Sectoral Rules

Properly functioning management and control systems in the Member States are of foremost importance in order to prevent and investigate irregularities in the areas where the implementation of Community policy with financial implications for the Community budget is in the hands of the Member States, as in the case of the agricultural expenditure and the co-financing of projects, programmes and other activities of the Member States through the Structural Funds, which are financed from the Community budget. In addition, the Commission must have the possibility to carry out the so-called first and second lines of supervision, in order to check whether the Community rules are complied with within the decentralized system for managing agricultural expenditure and of implementation of the activities of the Structural funds. Therefore, sectoral rules provide for specific rules on supervision and investigations in these areas.[642]

In the area of *agricultural expenditure financed by the EAGF and the EAFRD* (which replace the European Agricultural Guidance and Guarantee Fund (EAGGF)), the obligations of the Member States have been elaborated over the years into a refined and exacting system.[643] They must adopt all legislative, regulatory and administrative provisions and take any other measures necessary to ensure effective protection of the financial interests of the Community, and particularly in order to check the genuineness and compliance of operations financed by the Agricultural Funds, to prevent and pursue irregularities and to recover sums lost as a result of irregularities or negligence.[644] Furthermore, they are obliged to inform the Commission every three months of all the irregularities which have been the subject of a primary administrative or judicial finding and must present as soon as possible follow-up reports.[645] Moreover, the Member States must introduce systems of supervision in order to guarantee that the transactions for which

---

640. See *supra* section 4.3.2.2.
641. See the new Art. 86(3) TFEU, as introduced by the Treaty of Lisbon.
642. Although most developed in the areas of agriculture and structural funds, sectoral rules also exist in other areas; see, e.g., Arts. 13–14 of Reg. (EC) No. 680/2007 of the European Parliament and of the Council of 20 Jun. 2007 laying down general rules for the granting of Community financial aid in the field of the trans-European transport and energy networks, O.J. 2007, L 162/1.
643. See S. White, op. cit. *supra* note 580, 78.
644. Art. 9 of Council Reg. (EC) No. 1290/2005, on the financing of the common agricultural policy, O.J. 2005, L 209/1, last amended by Council Reg. (EC) No. 479/2008 of 29 April 2008, O.J. 2008, L 148/1. Arts. 32–35 contain detailed rules on the way in which Member States have to deal with irregularities.
645. Commission Reg. (EC) No. 1848/2006 of 14 Dec. 2006 concerning irregularities and the recovery of sums wrongly paid in connection with the financing of the common agricultural

export subsidies are paid actually take place and are in accordance with the rules, and that agricultural intervention products are used for the prescribed purpose and/ or reach the prescribed destination.[646]

Regulation 1469/95 (sometimes called the Black List Regulation)[647] creates a system of mutual provision of information, which permits the competent authorities to identify and make known as rapidly as possible market participants who, on the grounds of experience acquired with them as regards the proper execution of their previous obligations, are considered to present 'a risk of non-reliability'[648] in connection with tendering procedures, export refunds and sales at reduced prices of intervention products, financed by the EAGF; they can then inform all the competent authorities of the Member States and the Commission. This makes it possible to take certain measures in relation to these operators, which range from reinforced checking to exclusion of the persons concerned from operations to be determined, if it is established that they have committed fraud.

Special mention should be made of the gradual introduction – in the period 1993–1995 – of an integrated management and control system for certain Community aid schemes (in the crops and livestock sectors).[649] These forms of direct income aid, which were introduced as a result of the 1992 reform of the Common Agricultural Policy, are particularly sensitive to fraud and, therefore, require special provisions for administration and control. Use is made of teledetection and electronic devises for detecting irregularities and fraud. In addition, provision is made for administrative sanctions to be imposed by the Member States. Reductions and exclusions may be imposed – having regard to the principle of

policy and the organisation of an information system in this field and repealing Council Reg. (EEC) No. 595/91, O.J. 2006, L 355/56.

646. Council Reg. (EEC) No. 386/90 of 12 Feb. 1990 on the monitoring carried out at the time of export of agricultural products receiving refunds or other amounts, O.J. 1990, L 42/6, as last amended by Council Reg. (EC) No. 14/2008 of 17 Dec. 2007, O.J. 2008, L 8/1 (see also Council Reg. (EC) No. 1234/2007, O.J. 2007, L 299/1) L 24/2, and Commission Reg. (EEC) No. 3002/92 of 16 Oct. 1992 laying down common detailed rules for verifying the use and/or destination of products from intervention, O.J. 1992, L 301/17, as amended by Commission Reg. (EC) No. 770/96 of 26 Apr. 1996, O.J. 1996, L 104/13.

647. Council Reg. (EC) No. 1469/95 of 22 Jun. 1995 on measures to be taken with regard to certain beneficiaries of operations financed by the Guarantee Section of the EAGGF, O.J. 1995, L 45/1, and the implementing Commission Reg. (EC) No. 745/96 of 24 Apr. 1996, O.J. 1996, L 102/15.

648. I.e., operators who, according to a final decision of an administrative or judicial authority, have deliberately or through serious negligence committed an irregularity in respect of relevant Community provisions and have unjustly benefited from a financial advantage or attempted to benefit therefrom; or who have been the subject, in this respect, on the basis of established facts, of a preliminary administrative or judicial report by the competent authorities of the Member State (Art. 1(2) Council Reg. (EC) No. 1469/95, cited previous note).

649. Now governed by Council Reg. (EC) No. 1782/2003 of 29 Sep. 2003 establishing common rules for direct support schemes under the common agricultural policy and establishing certain support schemes for farmers and amending Reg. (EEC) No. 2019/93, (EC) No. 1452/2001, (EC) No. 1453/2001, (EC) No. 1454/2001, (EC) 1868/94, (EC) No. 1251/1999, (EC) No. 1254/1999, (EC) No. 1673/2000, (EEC) No. 2358/71 and (EC) No. 2529/2001, O.J. 2003, L 270/1.

proportionality and the special problems linked to cases of *force majeure* as well as exceptional and natural circumstances. The reductions and exclusions should be graded according to the gravity of the irregularity committed and may go as far as the total exclusion from one or several aid schemes for a specified period.

An important concluding element in relation to the indirect Community financing of agricultural expenditure is of course the determination of the extent to which the Member States themselves should bear the financial consequences of irregular expenditure. To the extent that the consequences are borne by the Member States, and not by the Community, they will of course have a greater interest in preventing and investigating irregularities, and recovering sums wrongly paid or collecting sums due.

In relation to agricultural expenditure, the case law of the Court of Justice has played a part in enabling the Commission – in the clearance of accounts procedure – to refuse the financing of expenditure of which it has been established that this was not carried out in compliance with the relevant Community rules. The Commission may set a fixed sum or a percentage which is excluded from Community financing. Only if the irregularities or negligence cannot be attributed to the Member States, and, moreover, complete recovery of the wrongly paid sums is not possible, does the Community bear the financial consequences. As for the division of the burden of proof: it is up to the Commission to prove that the Community rules have been infringed, but the Member State must, in relevant cases, prove that the Commission has attached incorrect financial consequences to that fact.[650] Moreover, in order to prove an infringement of the rules on the common organization of the agricultural markets, the Commission is not required to demonstrate exhaustively that the checks carried out by the national authorities are inadequate, or that the data submitted by them are incorrect, but to adduce evidence of serious and reasonable doubt on its part regarding the checks or data. It is then up to the Member State to adduce the most detailed and comprehensive evidence that its inspections or figures are accurate and, if appropriate, that the Commission's statements are incorrect.[651]

This line of case law, based on Article 10 EC, in conjunction with the objectives and the system of the Common Agricultural Policy, now essentially form the basis for Article 31 of Council Regulation 1290/2005 on the financing of the common agricultural policy,[652] and the implementing provisions in the relevant Commission Regulation.[653] According to the rules which currently apply, the Commission decides the expenditure to be excluded from the Community

---

650. Cf., e.g., Case C-235/97, *France v. Commission* at para. 39. See on this development, extensively, R. Barents, 'De aansprakelijkheid van Lid-Staten in het communautaire landbouwrecht' (1997) SEW, 2–6 and the same author, *The Agricultural Law of the EC, An Inquiry into the Administrative Law of the European Community in the Field of Agriculture* (Kluwer, Deventer, 1992), 192–195.

651. Cf. e.g., Case C-329/00, *Commission v. Spain*, at para. 68.

652. See *supra* note 412.

653. Commission Reg. (EC) No. 885/2006 of 21 Jun. 2006 laying down detailed rules for the application of Council Reg. (EC) No. 1290/2005 as regards the accreditation of paying

financing, having regard in particular to the degree of non-compliance. The nature and gravity of the infringement and the financial loss suffered by the Community are also taken into account.

Before the Commission takes a decision on the expenditure to be excluded, the results of the Commission's checks and the replies of the Member State concerned are notified in writing, after which the two parties endeavour to reach agreement on the action to be taken. If no agreement is reached, the Member State may ask for a conciliation procedure to be initiated.[654] The results of this procedure are set out in a report sent to and examined by the Commission, before a decision to refuse financing is taken. The introduction of this procedure aims to reduce the number of cases, most of them with highly complex factual situations, before the Court in which Member States appeal against decisions of the Commission excluding certain sums from Community financing.

Until recently, the administration and control system in the area of *expenditure of the Structural funds* was much less detailed and less strictly regulated than that concerning expenditure on agriculture. Nor was there a procedure corresponding to the arrangements for clearing the accounts in the framework of agricultural expenditure discussed above.[655] This changed at the end of the 1990s. Detailed obligations were imposed on the Member States in relation to the arrangements for administration and control systems which aim to guarantee effective and correct implementation of the activities which are (co-)financed from the Structural funds. In addition, similar obligations of care and information apply to the Member States – taking into account the different nature of the direct financing – as in the case of agriculture expenditure.[656] Here too, a procedure has been developed which grants the Commission far-reaching powers to carry out financial corrections.

The Member States are responsible in first instance for investigating irregularities and making financial corrections – in the form of partial or complete annulment of the Community contribution to the beneficiary – which are needed as a result of a one-off or systematic irregularity.[657] If the Commission establishes that a Member State has not complied with this obligation, or that there is a serious deficiency in the management and control system of the programme, or if expenditure contained in a certified statement of expenditure is irregular and has not been

agencies and other bodies and the clearance of the accounts of the EAGF and of the EAFRD, O.J. 2006, L 171/90.

654. Art. 31(3) of Council Reg. (EC) No. 1290/2005, on the financing of the common agricultural policy, O.J. 2005, L 209/1, last amended by Council Reg. (EC) No. 479/2008 of 29 Apr. 2008, O.J. 2008, L 148/1.

655. Cf. on this X. Yataganas, in *Commentaire J. Mégret*, op. cit. *supra* note 401, par. 930–937.

656. See for the current legislation, the detailed rules on financial management in Arts. 75–102 of Council Reg. (EC) No. 1083/2006, *supra* note 376. See also Commission Reg. (EC) No. 1828/2006 of 8 Dec. 2006 setting out rules for the implementation of Council Reg. (EC) No. 1083/2006 laying down general provisions on the ERDF, the ESF and the Cohesion Fund and of Reg. (EC) No. 1080/2006 of the European Parliament and of the Council on the ERDF, O.J. 2006, L 371/1.

657. Art. 98 of Council Reg. (EC) No. 1083/2006, *supra* note 376.

corrected by the Member State, the Commission may make financial corrections by cancelling all or part of the Community contribution to an operational programme.[658]

In that case, the Commission also, after stating its reasons, requests the Member State to submit its comments and, where appropriate, carry out any corrections, within a specified period of time. If the Member State objects, there is a hearing, and thereafter a special consultation procedure, in the framework of the so-called 'partnership', between the Commission, the Member State in question, and the authorities and bodies which are designated by the Member State in accordance with national rules and practice. This procedure may eventually lead to the required financial corrections.[659] The Commission must, when deciding the amount of a correction, take account, in compliance with the principle of proportionality, of the type of irregularity or change and the extent and financial implications of the shortcomings found in the management or control systems of the Member States.

FURTHER READING

Legal Instruments
Lenaerts, K. and M. Desomer. 'Towards a Hierarchy of Legal Acts in the European Union: Simplification of Legal Instruments and Procedures'. (2005) *ELJ*, 744–765.
Louis, J.-V. In Commentaire Mégret: Le droit de la CEE, vol. 10. Deuxième Partie. Les actes des institutions. 2me éd. Bruxelles, 1993.
Prechal, A. *Directives in EC Law.* 2nd ed. Oxford: Oxford University Press, 2005.
Simon, D. *La directive européenne.* Connaissance du droit Dalloz. Droit public. Paris: Dalloz, 1997.
Simon, D. *Le système juridique communautaire.* 3e éd. mise à jour. Paris: Presses universitaires de France, 2001.
Timmermans, C. 'Community Directives Revisited'. (1998) *Yearbook of European Law*, 1–28.
Usher, J.A. *EC Institutions and Legislation.* London, 1998.
Vandamme, T.A.J.A. *The Invalid Directive: The Legal Authority of a Union Act Requiring Domestic Law Making: Europa Law.* The Hogendorp Papers, 5 2005.
Von Bogdandy, A., F. Arndt and J. Bast. 'Legal Instruments in European Union Law and Their Reform: A Systematic Approach on an Empirical Basis'. (2004) *Yearbook of European Law*, 91–136.
Winter, G. *Sources and Categories of European Union Law: A Comparative and Reform Perspective.* Schriftenreihe des Zentrums für Europäische Rechtspolitik an der Universität Bremen (ZERP), Bd. 22. Baden-Baden: Nomos Verlagsgesellschaft, 1996.

---

658. Ibid., Art. 99.
659. Ibid., Art. 100.

Zarka, J.-C. L'essentiel des institutions de l'Union européenne. 8e éd. Les carrés. Droit – Science politique. Paris: Gualino, 2005.

Harmonization

Barents, R. 'The Community and the Unity of the Common Market'. (1990) *German Yearbook of International Law*, 10.

Dougan, M. 'Minimum Harmonization and the Internal Market'. (2000) *Common Market Law Review*, 853–885.

Falkner, G., et al. *Complying with Europe: EU Harmonisation and Soft Law in the Member States*. Themes in European Governance. Cambridge: Cambridge University Press, 2005.

Kostoris Padoa-Schioppa, F. *The Principles of Mutual Recognition in the European Integration Process*. Basingstoke: Palgrave Macmillan, 2005.

Majone, G. *Regulating Europe*. London: Routledge, 1996.

Rott, P. 'Minimum Harmonization for the Completion of the Internal Market?: The Example of Consumer Sales Law'. (2003) CML Rev., 1107–1135.

Slot, P.J. 'Harmonisation'. (1996) *European Law Review*, 378–397.

Wagner, M. *Das Konzept der Mindestharmonisierung*. Schriften zum europäischen Recht, Bd. 70. Berlin: Duncker & Humblot, 2001.

Decision-Making Procedure

Alemann, F.V. *Die Handlungsform der interinstitutionellen Vereinbarung: eine Untersuchung des Interorganverhältnisses der europäischen Verfassung = Interinstitutional Agreements: A Legal Instrument of EU Constitutional Law* (English summary). Beiträge zum ausländischen öffentlichen Recht und Völkerrecht, Bd. 182. Springer, 2006.

Andersen, S.S. and K.A. Eliassen. *Making Policy in Europe*. 2nd ed. London: Sage, 2001.

Beach, D. *The Dynamics of European Integration: Why and When EU Institutions Matter*. The European Union Series. Basingstoke: Palgrave Macmillan, 2005.

Bomberg, E., J. Peterson and A. Stubb. *The European Union: How Does It Work?* 2nd ed. Oxford: Oxford University Press, 2008.

Chari, R.S. and S. Kritzinger. *Understanding EU Policy Making*. London: Pluto Press, 2006.

Christiansen, Th. and T. Larsson (eds). *The Role of Committees in the Policy-Process of the European Union*. Cheltenham: Edward Elgar, 2007.

Corbett, R., F. Jacobs and M. Shackleton. *The European Parliament*. 7th ed. London: John Harper, 2007.

Craig, P.P. and G. De Búrca. *EU Law: Text, Cases, and Materials*. 4th ed. Oxford: Oxford University Press, 2008.

Craig, P.P. and C. Harlow. *Lawmaking in the European Union*. W.G. Hart Legal Workshop Series, vol. 2. London: Kluwer, 1998.

Dashwood, A. 'European Community Legislative Procedures after Amsterdam'. (1998) Cambridge *Yearbook of European Legal Studies*, 25.

Dashwood, A. 'The Constitution of the European Union after Nice: Law-Making Procedures'. (2001) *European Law Review*, 215.

De Búrca, G. and J. Scott. *Law and New Governance in the EU and the US*. Oxford: Hart, 2006.

Denza, E. *The Intergovernmental Pillars of the European Union*. Oxford: Oxford University Press, 2002.

Devuyst, Y. *The European Union Transformed: Community Method and Institutional Evolution from the Schuman Plan to the Constitution for Europe*. Rev. and updated ed. European Policy, 27. Brussels: P.I.E.-Peter Lang, 2006.

Egeberg, M. *Multilevel Union Administration: The Transformation of Executive Politics in Europe*. Basingstoke: Palgrave Macmillan, 2006.

Franchino, F. *The Powers of the Union: Delegation in the EU*. Cambridge: Cambridge University Press, 2007.

George, S.A. and I. Bache. *Politics in the European Union*. Oxford: Oxford University Press, 2001.

Greenwood, J. *Interest Representation in the European Union*. 2nd ed. The European Union Series. Basingstoke: Palgrave Macmillan, 2007.

Hartmann, J. *Das politische System der Europäischen Union: eine Einführung*. Reihe Campus, 421: Studium. Frankfurt/Main: Campus-Verl, 2001.

Hix, S. *The Political System of the European Union*. The European Union Series. Basingstoke: Palgrave Macmillan, 2005.

Hofmann, H.C.H. and A.H. Türk. *EU Administrative Governance*. Cheltenham: Edward Elgar, 2006.

Joerges, E. and E. Vos (eds). *EU Committees: Social Regulation, Law and Politics*. Oxford, Hart Publishing 1999.

Kaltenthaler, K.C. *Policymaking in the European Central Bank: The Masters of Europe's Money*. Governance in Europe. Lanham MD: Rowman & Littlefield, 2006.

Kohler-Koch, B. and B. Rittberger. *Debating the Democratic Legitimacy of the European Union*. Lanham, MD: Rowman & Littlefield, 2007.

Moussis, N. *Guide to European Policies*. 12th rev. ed. Rixensart: European Study Service, 2007.

Niemann, A. *Explaining Decisions in the European Union*. Cambridge: Cambridge University Press, 2006.

Pedler, R.H. and G.F. Schaefer. *Shaping European Law and Policy: The Role of Committees and Comitology in the Political Process*. EIPA Publications, 96/06. Maastricht: European Institute of Public Administration, 1996.

Peterson, J. and E.E. Bomberg. *Decision-Making in the European Union*. The European Union Series. New York: St. Martin's Press, 1999.

Quermonne, J.-L. *Le système politique de l'Union européenne: Des Communautés économiques à l'Union politique*. 6e éd. recomposée et actualisée. Clefs. Politique. Paris: Montchrestien, 2005.

Richardson, J.J. *European Union: Power and Policy-Making*. 3rd ed. Routledge Research in European Public Policy. Abingdon: Routledge, 2006.

Rittberger, B. *Building Europe's Parliament: Democratic Representation beyond the Nation-State*. Oxford: Oxford University Press, 2005.

Thomson, R., et al. *The European Union Decides*. Political Economy of Institutions and Decisions. Cambridge: Cambridge University Press, 2006.

Usher, J.A. *EC Institutions and Legislation*. London: Longman, 1998.

Van Schendelen, R. *Machiavelli in Brussels: The Art of Lobbying the EU*. Amsterdam: Amsterdam University Press, 2002.

Wallace, H.S., et al. *Policy-Making in the European Union*. 5th ed. The New European Union Series. Oxford: Oxford University Press, 2005.

Wyatt and Dashwood's European Union Law. 5th ed. London: Sweet & Maxwell, 2006.

Finances

Begg, I. and N. Grimwade. *Paying for Europe*. Contemporary European Studies, 2. Sheffield: Sheffield Academic, 1998.

Bieber, R. 'On Articles 268 EC-279 EC'. In H. von der Groeben and J. Schwarze (eds). *Kommentar zum Vertrag über die Europäische Union und zur Gründung der Europäischen Gemeinschaft*. 6th ed. Baden-Baden: Nomos Verlagsgesellschaft, 2003.

Brunet, C. *La protection des intérêts financiers des Communautés européennes*. Paris: Atelier national de reproduction des thèses, 2003.

Buti, M. and M. Nava. *Towards a European Budgetary System*. EUI Working Paper RSC, no. 2003/8, Pierre Werner Chair Series. San Domenico: European University Institute, 2003.

Coget, G. 'Les ressources propres communautaires'. (1994) *Revue française de finances publiques*, 51–96.

Crespo, M.G. *Public Expenditure Control in Europe: Coordinating Audit Functions in the European Union*. Cheltenham: Edward Elgar, 2005.

European Commission. *European Union Public Finance*. Luxembourg: Office for Official Publications of the European Communities, 2002.

European Commission. *New Funds, Better Rules: Overview of New Financial Rules and Funding Opportunities 2007–2013*. Luxembourg: Office for Official Publications of the European Communities, 2007.

Freytag, M. *Der Europäische Rechnungshof. Institution, Funktion und politische Wirkung*. Baden-Baden: Nomos Verlagsgesellschaft, 2005.

Garcin, D. *La répression de la fraude au préjudice du budget communautaire*. Paris: La Documentation française, 2004.

Graf, R. *Die Finanzkontrolle der Europäischen Gemeinschaft*. Baden-Baden: Nomos Verlagsgesellschaft, 1999.

Hetzer, W. 'Fight against Fraud and Protection of Fundamental Rights in the European Union'. (2006) *European Journal of Crime, Criminal Law and Criminal Justice*, 20–45.

Kerremans, B. and H. Matthijs. *De begroting en de openbare financiën van de Europese Unie*. Antwerp/Oxford: Intersentia, 2004.

Laffan, B. *The Finances of the European Union*. Houndmills Basingstoke Hampshire: Palgrave Macmillan, 1997.

Lechantre, M. and D. Schajer. *Le budget de l'Union européenne*. Réflexe Europe. Paris: Documentation française, 2003.

Levy, R. *Managing, Monitoring and Evaluating the EU Budget: Internal and External Perspectives*. Current European Issues, 99/P/09. Maastricht: European Institute of Public Administration, 1999.

Lindner, J. *Conflict and Change in EU Budgetary Politics*. Routledge Advances in European Politics, 32. London: Routledge, 2006.

Neal, L. *The Economics of Europe and the European Union*. Cambridge: Cambridge University Press, 2007.

Petit, Y. 'La procédure de décharge sur l'exécution du budget général de l'Union européenne et ses enjeux'. In *Mélanges en hommage à Guy Isaac: 50 ans de droit communautaire*, vol. 2. Toulouse: Presses de l'Université des sciences sociales de Toulouse, 2004.

Prieß, H.-J. and H. Spitzer. 'On Art. 280 EC'. In H. von der Groeben and J. Schwarze (eds), *Kommentar zum Vertrag über die Europäische Union und zur Gründung der Europäischen Gemeinschaft*. 6th ed., vol. 4. Baden-Baden: Nomos Verlagsgesellschaft, 2003.

Régnier-Heldmaier, C., et al. *Les finances de l'Union européenne*. 2e éd. Commentaire J. Mégret: Le droit de la CE et de l'Union européenne, vol. 11. Bruxelles: Éd. de l'Université de Bruxelles, 1999.

Ruggieri, F. (ed.). *La protection des intérêts financiers de l'Union et le rôle de l'OLAF vis-à-vis de la responsabilité pénale des personnes morales et des chefs d'entreprises et admissibilité mutuelle des preuves*. Brussels: Bruylant, 2005.

Saarilahti, I. and M. Balsells Traver. 'Les innovations des procédures budgétaires communautaires'. (2006–2007) *Revue du Marché commun et de l'Union européenne*, 88–113 (Part I), 254–276 (Part II), 530–557 (Part III), 302–334 (Part IV).

Strasser, D. *The Finances of Europe*. Luxembourg: Office for Official Publications of the European Communities, 1992.

Vervaele, J.A.E. (ed.). *Transnational Enforcement of the Financial Interests of the European Union*. Antwerp/Groningen/Oxford: Intersentia, 1999.

Vervaele, J.A.E. (ed.). *European Evidence Warrant: Transnational Judicial Inquiries in the EU*. Antwerp/Oxford: Intersentia, 2005.

Weitendorf, S. *Die interne Betrugsbekämpfung in den Europäischen Gemeinschaften durch das Europäische Amt für Betrugsbekämpfung (OLAF)*. Hamburg: Lit Verlag, 2007.

Chapter VI

Administration of Justice

P.J.G. Kapteyn

1 THE LAW TO BE OBSERVED

1.1 UNWRITTEN COMMUNITY LAW

Article 220 EC provides: 'The Court of Justice and the Court of First Instance (CFI), each within its jurisdiction, shall ensure that in the interpretation and application of this Treaty the law is observed.'[1] This provision contains the very core of what has developed to become the Community legal order; moreover, this is true in two ways. First, it expresses the fact that – unlike the usual situation in inter-state legal transactions – the interpretation and application of the relevant agreement is not just a matter for the contracting parties individually and, in cases where an international organization is created, the policy organs of that organization. The lawfulness of actions of the contracting parties on the basis of the Treaties is subject to the supervision of the Court of Justice.

---

1. For the same provision regarding Euratom, see Art. 236 Euratom. The addition of the phrase 'and the Court of First Instance' to Art. 220 EC by the Treaty of Nice is superfluous, since in the original wording 'the Court of Justice' referred to the institution as such. The Treaty of Nice, which aimed to grant the Court of First Instance a more independent position, replaces the reference to the institution as such with a reference to the two bodies of which it is composed (Cf. Ch. IV, section 7.1). This reference now also covers the Staff Tribunal which is attached to the Court of First Instance. It should be noted that 'the Treaty' in this provision includes the secondary law based thereupon.

P.J.G. Kapteyn, A.M. McDonnell, K.J.M. Mortelmans and C.W.A. Timmermans (eds),
The Law of the European Union and the European Communities, pp. 421–510.
©2008 Kluwer Law International BV, The Netherlands.

Secondly, the reference to observance of the law shows that the Court's task involves more than simply the application of the Treaty provisions.[2] Interpretation and application of national laws by national courts takes place within the framework of an established legal order and legal tradition, in which these laws are embedded. The national courts may invoke the legal principles and concepts embedded in that legal order when interpreting and applying the provisions of national legislation in any dispute brought before them. Such support, taken for granted in the national system, is not at the disposal of the Court of Justice for interpreting and applying Treaty provisions. Yet it is essential, since the countless questions which arise in the context of the Court's work cannot be answered, or cannot be answered fully in legal terms, on the basis merely of the Treaty. The Court was therefore faced with the task of deriving from the Treaty texts a legal order which would provide a framework within which the law contained in the treaties could be interpreted and applied, and on the basis of which the decisions and judgments concerning that law could be accepted and regarded as law by the Member States and their organs (including their judiciaries), the other Institutions and the individual holders of Community legal rights and obligations.

The Court performed this task mainly by giving form to unwritten Community law. In its case law there are regular references to general principles of law, such as good faith, legal certainty, due diligence, the principle of equality, legitimate expectations, abuse of rights and the principle of proportionality.[3]

A passage in the judgment in *Brasserie du Pêcheur and Factortame*,[4] where the Court had to deal with the consequences of infringements of Community law by the Member States, provides a good illustration of the way in which the Court has given shape to unwritten law, and the basis on which it has done so:

> Since the Treaty contains no provision expressly and specifically governing the consequences of breaches of Community law by Member States, it is for the Court, in pursuance of the task conferred on it by Article [220 (ex 164)] of the Treaty of ensuring that in the interpretation and application of the Treaty the law is observed, to rule on such a question in accordance with generally accepted methods of interpretation, in particular by reference to the fundamental principles of the Community legal system and, where necessary, general principles common to the legal systems of the Member States.

---

2. Cf. T. Koopmans, 'The Birth of European Law at the Crossroads of Legal Traditions' (1996) AJCL, 493, 495–496.
3. See A. Arnull, *The General Principles of EEC Law and the Individual* (Leicester, 1990); H.G. Schermers and D. Waelbroeck, *Judicial Protection in the European Communities*, 6th ed. (Deventer, 2001) para. 53-238 and literature cited therein, J. Usher, *General Principles of EC Law* (London, 1998) and T. Tridimas, *The General Principles of EC Law*, 2nd ed. (Oxford, 2006). See also *Reports of the FIDE Congress*, (Paris, 1986), Vol. 1, and N. Emiliou, *The Principle of Proportionality in European Law* (London, 1996). The principle of proportionality is now made generally applicable to Community action, Art. 5 EC (final paragraph), see Ch. III, section 6.3 *supra*.
4. Joined Cases C-46/93 & C-48/93, *Brasserie du Pêcheur SA v. Bundesrepublik Deutschland* and *The Queen v. Secretary of State for Transport, ex parte: Factortame Ltd and others*, para. 27.

The possibility of relying on general principles of law in order to fill *lacunae* in Community law is not unlimited. These principles could not, for instance, be invoked to exclude parallel actions imposing sanctions for breach of national and Community competition law, at least as long as the Council had not adopted a regulation under Article 83(2)(e) EC on the matter.[5] Similarly, no limitation period for infringements of Community competition law could be deduced from these principles,[6] although the Court subsequently indicated that, in the absence of any provisions on the matter, the principle of legal certainty prevented the Commission from indefinitely delaying the exercise of its power to impose fines.[7] The Court made it clear that limitation periods must be fixed in advance in order to fulfil their function of ensuring legal certainty, and this task was a matter for the Community legislature.[8]

An illustration of the application of unwritten law can be seen in the Court's formulation of the conditions under which an administrative act conferring rights on individuals may be withdrawn. Rules on this exist in the administrative law of various Member States, but no specific rules on the matter were to be found in the ECSC Treaty, which was the context in which this came to the Court of Justice. In the case in question, the Court considered itself compelled (lest it deny justice) to solve the problem by reliance on rules recognized in the legislation, academic writing, and case law of the Member States.[9]

It has been clear that fundamental human rights are enshrined in the general principles of Community law and protected by the Court ever since the judgment in *Stauder v. City of Ulm.*[10] This point is discussed further in section 1.4 below.

It is understandable that the Court, in order to 'find' these general legal principles and rules of unwritten law, consults the national legal systems of the Member States.[11] In classic international law too 'the general principles of law recognized by civilized nations' form a source of law.[12] This source, however, flows less copiously in the international administration of justice than in that of the Communities. Indeed, in many areas, Community law shows, in its tenor as well as in its legal technique and procedures, a marked affinity with national legal systems, and above all with national administrative and economic law, and this is much more so than classic international law.

---

5. Case 14/68, *Walt Wilhelm et al. v. Bundeskartellamt.*
6. Case 41/69, *ACF Chemiefarma NV v. Commission.*
7. Case 48/69, *Imperial Chemical Industries Ltd v. Commission.*
8. Cf. Case 41/69, *ACF Chemiefarma* and Case 48/69, *Imperial Chemical Industries.* Limitation periods were laid down by Reg. 2988/74 (O.J. 1974, L 319/1).
9. Joined Cases 7/56 & 3-7/57, *Algera et al. v. Common Assembly.*
10. Case 29/69, *Stauder v. Stadt Ulm.*
11. See the Opinion of A.G. Lagrange in Case 8/55, *Fédération Charbonnière de Belgium v. High Authority.* Art. 288, 2nd para., EC (and cf. Art. 188 Euratom, 2nd para.) specifically provides for this procedure to be followed. This concerns the obligation 'to make good any damage caused' by the Community Institutions or their servants in the performance of their duties 'in accordance with the general principles common to the laws of the Member States'.
12. Statute of the International Court of Justice, Art. 38c.

The Court's finding of law, therefore, is largely an exercise in comparative law. This use of the comparative technique is not governed by an *a priori* intent to find the highest common denominator; rather is it governed by an intent to trace elements from which it is possible to build Community legal principles and rules which will offer an appropriate, fair and viable solution for the questions with which the Court is confronted. Comparative law in this sense also forms the source of inspiration for the determination of the autonomous meaning of many legal terms occurring in written Community law.[13] This comparative exercise is sometimes performed by the Advocates General in their submissions, as happened in relation to the meaning of the term 'misuse of power' – '*détournement de pouvoir*' – in the old Article 33 ECSC.[14] But as a rule it will naturally take place *in camera* during the deliberations between judges who, each of them educated and initiated in their own national legal system and way of thinking, together have to give effect to written and unwritten Community law.

Apart from the above principles, which are common to the legal systems of the Member States, there are also other principles which the Court of Justice derives from the EC Treaty itself. Thus already in *Deutsche Grammophon v. Metro-SB-Großmärkte*[15] the Court found that the second paragraph of Article 10 EC (former Art. 5) laid down 'a general duty for the Member States, the actual tenor of which depends in each individual case on the provisions of the Treaty or on the rules derived from its general scheme'. Also on the basis of Article 10 EC, the Court has derived the principle of loyal cooperation which creates obligations not merely for the Member States but also for the Community Institutions themselves,[16] and the principle of State liability in damages for loss suffered by individuals as a result of a failure by the State to fulfil its obligations under Community law.[17]

The CFI also applies unwritten law. Leaving aside the staff cases, and given the limited areas of jurisdiction which this court had in its early years, general principles of law have been particularly important in competition cases, especially

---

13. Although the meaning of such a term in Community law 'must be determined on the basis of the legal framework within which it is intended to take effect': Case 4/68, *Firma Schwarzwaldmilch GmbH v. Einfuhr und Vorratsstelle für Fette* concerning the concept of *force majeure* in Arts. 6(2)–(4) of Reg. 136/64 (J.O. 1964, 601). In Case 59/85, *State of the Netherlands v. Reed* the Court considered the term 'spouse' in Art. 10 of Reg. 1612/68 (O.J. 1968, L 257) in the light of social evolution as a provision which had effects in all Member States; thus the situation in the whole Community had to be considered, not just the situation in one Member State.

14. See the Opinion of A.G. Lagrange in Case 3/54, *ASSIDER v. High Authority*. See also A.G. Lagrange in Case 4/54, *ISA v. High Authority* and in Joined Cases 7/56 & 3-7/57, *Algera*. See further, e.g., A.G. Gand in Joined Cases 56-60/74, *Kampffmeyer v. Council and Commission* (non-contractual liability of the EC) and A.G. van Gerven in Case C-106/89, *Marleasing v. Comercial Internacional de Alimentación*(civil law sanction of nullity).

15. Case 78/70, *Deutsche Grammophon Gesellschaft mbH v. Metro-SB-Großmärkte GmbH & Co*, para. 5. See also Ch. III section 6.4 *supra*.

16. Case C-2/88, *Criminal Proceedings against Zwartveld et al.*; see also Case C-54/90, *Weddel & Co. BV v. Commission* (consideration of the Commission's proper relations with national administrations).

17. This principle was also found to be inherent in the system of the Treaty, Joined Cases C-6 & 9/90, *Francovich et al. v. Italy*. See further Ch. VII section 4.

the principles of the rights of the defence. Thus in its Order in Case T-30/89 *Hilti AG v. Commission*[18] the CFI took account of 'certain general principles of law and certain essential principles such as that of the protection of confidentiality of written communications between lawyer and client'.

1.2   PUBLIC INTERNATIONAL LAW

The Court applies Community law, finding and creating law as it goes along; but it also has the right to apply public international law.[19] As far as international law is concerned, the Community legal order is an open system. Various distinct types of case can be distinguished. The first type comprises the cases in which the Community as such is bound by norms of international law *vis-à-vis* third parties. This can result from treaties which it has concluded with third parties.[20] This may also occur on the basis of norms of international law which bind all the Member States, whenever the competence for application of these norms has actually been transferred to the Community and this transfer is recognized by third countries; this is the application of the principle of substitution.[21] Moreover, according to the Court of Justice, the Community should exercise its powers in general in conformity with public international law,[22] which includes the rules of customary international law.[23] In such cases, the legal norms which are binding on the Community as such will be directly applied by the Court of Justice in the Community legal order.[24]

---

18. T-30/89, *Hilti v. Commission*, para. 11.
19. J. Vanhamme, 'Inroepbaarheid van verdragen en volkenrechtelijke beginselen voor de Europese rechter: stand van zaken' SEW (2001), 247–256 and A. Ott, 'Thirty Years of Case-Law by the European Court of Justice on International Law: A Pragmatic Approach towards Its Integration', in V. Kronenberg (ed.), *The EU and the International Legal Order: Discord or Harmony?* (The Hague, 2001), Ch. 5.
20. Such as association agreements. On the interpretation of provisions of these see, e.g., Case 181/73, *Haegemann v. Belgian State*; Case 87/75, *Bresciani v. Amministrazione delle Finanze dello Stato* and Case 65/77, *Razantsimba*. As to free trade agreements see, e.g., Case 270/80, *Polydor Ltd et al. v. Harlequin Record Shops et al.*; Case 104/81, *Hauptzollamt Mainz v. Kupferberg & Cie.*
21. Cf. Joined Cases 21-24/72, *International Fruit Company et al. v. Produktschap voor Groenten en Fruit*. These cases concerned provisions of an international agreement (GATT) which was binding on all Member States.
22. Case C-286/90, *Anklagemindigheden v. Poulsen and Diva Navigation*.
23. Case C-162/96, *Racke v. Hauptzollamt Mainz* (*clausula rebus sic stantibus*), and Case T-115/94, *Opel Austria v. Council* (international law principle of good faith). See also P.J. Kuijper, 'From Dyestuffs to Kosovo Wine, from Avoidance to Acceptance by the European Community Courts of Customary Law as Limit to Community Action', in I. Dekker and H. Post (eds), *On the Foundation and Sources of International Law* (The Hague, 2003), 151.
24. See Joined Cases 21-24/72, *International Fruit Company*, and in the light thereof also Art. 300(7) EC. The Court concluded that the Community as such was bound by the GATT, but that the provisions of the GATT in issue were not capable of conferring rights on Community citizens which they could invoke before the courts (so-called direct effect). See to the same effect, but a slightly different reasoning, concerning the WTO agreements, Case C-149/96, *Parliament v. Council*. See also Joined Cases C-300 & 392/98, *Dior et al. v. Tuk*

The second type of case covers cases in which the Community as such is not involved, but one or more of the Member States has international obligations towards third parties which are incompatible with the obligations resulting from provisions of Community law. It is clear in any event from the first sentence of the first paragraph of Article 307 EC[25] that the provisions of the Treaty may not affect rights and obligations arising from agreements concluded before the entry into force of the EEC Treaty (or, for Member States other than the original six, before the date of their accession) between one or more Member States on the one hand and one or more third countries on the other. The principle set out in that sentence cannot, however, be applied by analogy in cases in which the Member States, after entry into force of the Treaty or after their accession to the Union, have entered into obligations with third countries whilst still being empowered to do so under Community law, and these obligations are subsequently incompatible with later Community secondary law.[26]

The third type of case covers situations in which norms of public international law have to be invoked in order to define legal relationships within the Community. The application of unwritten international law appears to be the obvious course if and insofar as the Treaties do not cover any typical problem of international law which may arise.[27] Thus in its judgment in *Van Duyn v. Home Office* the Court explained that 'it is a principle of international law, which the EEC Treaty cannot be assumed to disregard in the relations between Member States, that a State is precluded from refusing its own nationals the right of entry or residence'.[28] In the second judgment in the *Foglia v. Novello* saga[29] the Court indicated that 'in the absence of provisions of Community law in the matter, the possibility of taking

---

Consultancy BV et al. However, in its judgment in Case 87/75, *Bresciani v. Amministrazione delle Finanze dello Stato*, the Court interpreted a provision of the First Yaoundé Convention (J.O. 1964, 1430) as having direct effect from 1 Jan. 1970; likewise in relation to the old Free Trade Agreement with Portugal in Case 104/81, *Hauptzollamt Mainz v. Kupferberg & Cie.*, and in Case 192/89, *Sevince v. Staatssecretaris van Justitie*, to provisions of Decisions of the EEC-Turkey Association Council. See in more detail Ch. VII, section 1.3.

25. See also Act of Accession; Act of Greek Accession; Act of Spanish and Portuguese Accession, and Act of Austrian, Finnish and Swedish Accession (Art. 5 in each case). See, moreover, Arts. 105 and 106 Euratom.

26. Case C-476/98, *Commission v. Germany* (Open Skies Agreements), para. 69. Nor does Art. 307, 1st para., EC apply if the obligations contained in the agreement concluded before the entry into force of the EEC Treaty (or before the date of accession) are repealed by a later agreement between the same parties, see Case C-158/91, *Ministère public et al. v. Levy*, even if similar obligations are contained in the later treaty, see Case C-466/98, *Commission v. UK* (Open Skies Agreements).

27. The Court rejected an appeal based on the international law principle of self-help in Joined Cases 90 & 91/63, *Commission v. Luxembourg and Belgium* (see Ch. II, section 3.2, *supra*) and an appeal based on the international law 'local remedy' rule in a case concerning the ECSC Protocol on Privileges and Immunities of the Community in Case 6/60, *Humblet v. Belgian State*.

28. Case 41/74, *Van Duyn v. Home Office*, para. 22.

29. Case 244/80, *Foglia v. Novello*, para. 24. See Wyatt (1982) ELRev., 186 and Bebr (1982) CML Rev., 421. For the earlier judgment in this saga see Case 104/79, *Foglia v. Novello*.

proceedings before a national court against a Member State other than that in which that court is situated depends both on the laws of the latter and on the principles of international law'. In *Wood Pulp*[30] the Court noted that 'the Community's jurisdiction to apply its competition rules [to anti-competitive conduct outside the Community implemented within it] is covered by the territoriality principle as universally recognized in public international law'.

Finally, it should be noted that the Court sometimes employs international law as an auxiliary (not as an independent) source of law for the interpretation and definition of Community rules.[31] The Court tends to do so relatively sparingly, since in most cases, reliance on principles and rules of national law as an auxiliary source of law may yield a more appropriate, fair and viable result.

1.3   NATIONAL LAW

With respect to national law, the primary rule is that the Court does not apply this directly. The Court bases this primary rule on the distinctiveness of its mandate, which is limited to the interpretation and application of Community law[32] and on the principle (which it considers to be contained in the Treaties) of a strict separation between the powers of the Institutions and those of the organs of the Member States, and consequently also between those of the Court and of national judicial bodies. Accordingly, in *Stork*, the Court considered it inappropriate to pronounce on the validity of the acts of the Community Institutions under national legislation or constitutional rules.[33] The Court has equally refused to proceed on its own authority 'to annul or repeal legislative or administrative acts of a Member State'.[34] In *Stork*, the Court even held that in general it ought to abstain from pronouncements on rules of national law.[35] This is an approach to which there is a well-known exception if the Court is required, in accordance with Article 226 EC (or Art. 141 Euratom), to pronounce on whether particular internal rules of a Member State do or do not infringe obligations of that State under the Treaty.

---

30. The first judgment on jurisdiction (in 1988) in Joined Cases 89/85 etc., *Ahlström et al. v. Commission* (*Woodpulp*), para.18.
31. E.g., in relation to Art. 307 EC, Case 10/61, *Commission v. Italy* (the Commission's submission was approved by the Court) and, in relation to Art. 88 ECSC (no longer in force), Case 20/59, *Italy v. High Authority*. See also Case 14/70, *Deutsche Bakels GmbH v. Oberfinanzdirektion München*, and Joined Cases 69 & 70/76, *Dittmeyer v. Hauptzollamt Hamburg-Waltershof* (opinions of Nomenclature Committee of the Customs Cooperation Council and of the Committee on Common Customs Tariff Nomenclature, respectively, valid aids to interpretation, even though non-binding).
32. Arts. 222 EC and 136 Euratom.
33. Case 1/58, *Friedrich Stork & Cie. v. High Authority*; Joined Cases 36–38 & 40/59, *President Ruhrkohlen-Verkaufsgesellschaft et al. v. High Authority*.
34. Case 6/60, *Humblet*, 559 of the English edition.
35. Case 1/58, *Stork*, 26. The English version ('[The Court] is not normally required to rule on provisions of national law') is not as strongly worded as some other language versions, e.g., the Dutch version.

In such cases the Court does pronounce on such rules, although, if they conflict with the Treaty provisions, it cannot itself render them inoperative.[36]

There are, though, a number of exceptions to the basic rule that the Court does not apply national law as such. The Treaty provisions, or other provisions of Community law, refer, sometimes implicitly and often explicitly, to the relevant national law of a Member State.[37] When Community rules contain terms like 'representatives of Member States at ministerial level',[38] 'undertakings',[39] 'legal persons',[40] 'companies or firms constituted under civil or commercial law',[41] or 'workers'[42] the Court is faced with the question whether the reference is to the relevant national law or to a concept of Community law. If the former is the case, the question whether 'a person' or 'a thing' is covered by the term used is a question which must be judged according to the rules of the national law governing that 'person' or 'thing'. In some cases this may lead to differences in the application of rules of Community law which prejudice their objectives, or are detrimental to the persons or things concerned. In its judgments, therefore, the Court, in the absence of a reference to the national law of the Member States,[43] prefers to create Community legal concepts.[44] Finally, it should be noted that by virtue of its optional jurisdiction under an arbitration clause in a contract concluded by or on behalf of the Communities, the Court can be required to apply the law of a given state.[45]

---

36. As to the effect of the Court's judgments see Joined Cases 314–316/81 & 83/82, *Procureur de la République et al. v. Waterkeyn et al.*
37. E.g., Statute of the Court of Justice, Art. 19 refers to the relevant national law when dealing with those entitled to plead before the Court: 'a lawyer authorized to practice before a court of a Member State or of another State which is party to the Agreement on the European Economic Area' and 'University teachers being nationals of a Member State whose law accords them a right of audience'. The Court may also be confronted with questions of national law even in the absence of any express or implied reference to it in Community texts, e.g., Case 18/57, *Nold KG v. High Authority* (powers of representation and bar disciplinary measures).
38. E.g., Art. 203 EC.
39. E.g., Art. 81(1) EC.
40. E.g., Art. 230 EC.
41. E.g., Art. 48 EC, 2nd para.
42. E.g., Art. 39(1) EC.
43. Case 154/80, *Staatsecretaris van Financiën v. Coöperatieve Aardappelenbewaarplaats GA.*
44. E.g., the term 'wage-earner or assimilated worker' in Reg. No. 3 (J.O. 1958 561), Art. 19(1) in Case 75/63, *Unger v. Bedrijfsvereniging voor Detailhandel en Ambachten*; the term 'services' in Art. 50 EC in Case C-159/90, *Society for the Protection of the Unborn Child Ireland v. Grogan*; the term 'legal person' in Case 135/81, *Groupement des Agences de Voyages Asbl v. Commission*, and the term 'undertaking' in competition law in Case C-41/90, *Höfner and Elser v. Macrotron GmbH.*
45. Arts. 238 read with 288, 1st para., EC; cf. Arts. 153 read with 188, 1st para., Euratom. See Ch. IV section 7.2.2 *supra*, (under head (5) of the heads of jurisdiction). For an example of the application of Belgian law in a dispute between the Commission and a contractor see Case 318/81, *Commission v. CO.DE.MI. SpA.*

1.4   FUNDAMENTAL RIGHTS, EUROPEAN CONVENTION FOR THE
PROTECTION OF HUMAN RIGHTS AND FUNDAMENTAL FREEDOMS
(ECHR) AND THE CHARTER OF FUNDAMENTAL RIGHTS OF THE
EUROPEAN UNION

National constitutional rules concerning the protection of fundamental rights form a special category of national rules of law. In Germany, in particular, where there is an extensive system of legal protection of fundamental rights, also in the field of social and economic matters, the protection of fundamental rights in the Community's legal system received attention already in the 1950s. Thus it was German appellants who challenged various decisions of the Community Institutions before the Court of Justice, alleging that they were incompatible with national constitutionally-guaranteed rights. Initially, the Court was content to observe (not unjustifiably) that it was not competent to review decisions of the Institutions in the light of national constitutional provisions, following the primary rule mentioned in the previous section.[46]

Partly under the influence of discussions in German legal circles about the relationship between Community law and national constitutional law, and the view of many participants in those discussions that German courts were entitled to review Community decisions in the light of their own constitutional rights,[47] at the end of the 1960s the Court revised its passive stance on the matter of fundamental rights in the Community. In the celebrated judgment in Case 29/69 *Stauder v. City of Ulm*[48] the Court confirmed that fundamental human rights were part of the general principles of Community law and were protected by the Court. In doing so the Court took a view consistent with its case law on general principles of Community law which already offered guarantees affecting the sphere of human rights. This was amplified in another famous judgment, in Case 11/70 *Internationale Handelsgesellschaft mbH v. Einfuhr-und Vorratsstelle für Getreide und Futtermittel*,[49] where the Court noted that respect for fundamental human rights formed an integral part of the general principles of law protected by the Court of Justice and inspired by the constitutional traditions common to the Member States.

The fact that in ensuring protection of fundamental rights the Court must take its inspiration from the constitutional traditions common to the Member States, has as a consequence – in the Court's view – that it may not uphold measures which are incompatible with fundamental rights recognized and protected by the constitutions of those States.[50] This does not mean, however, that the Court feels compelled to ensure the same level of protection as that of the national constitution which

---

46. See Case 1/58, *Stork*; Joined Cases 36–38 & 40/59, *President Ruhrkohlen-Verkaufsgesellschaft*.
47. See Ch. VII section 2. *infra*.
48. Case 29/69, *Stauder v. Stadt Ulm*.
49. Case 11/70, *Internationale Handelsellschaft mbH v. Einfuhr-und Vorratsstelle für Getreide und Futtermittel*.
50. Case 4/73, *J. Nold, Kohlen- und Baustoffgroßhandlung v. Commission*.

guarantees the most far-reaching protection for the fundamental right in question: the constitutional traditions together form a source of inspiration for the Court when it gives shape to Community fundamental rights and the limits which may be placed on their protection.[51]

The protection of these rights is ensured within the framework of the structure and objectives of the Community.[52] In accordance with the approach in the Member States, the protection of fundamental rights is always subject to limitations laid down in accordance with the public interest. Those rights are not absolute rights,

> but must be considered in relation to their social function. Consequently, restrictions may be imposed... provided that the restrictions in fact correspond to objectives of general interest and do not constitute, in relation to the aim pursued, a disproportionate and intolerable interference, impairing the very substance of the rights guaranteed.[53]

The protection of fundamental rights is not restricted to those common to the national constitutional traditions of the Member States. It also embraces the fundamental rights guaranteed in international treaties, in particular the European Convention on Human Rights.[54] Even though it is the Member States who are parties to the Convention and not the Community, the Court observed in the second *Nold* judgment that 'international treaties for the protection of human rights on which the Member States have collaborated or of which they are signatories, can supply guidelines which should be followed within the framework of Community law'.[55] Later, in its judgment in *Rutili*[56] the Court concluded that the limitations which Regulation 1612/68[57] placed on the powers of the Member States

---

51. See on this J.H.H. Weiler, 'Fundamental Rights and Fundamental Boundaries: On the Conflict of Standards and Values in the Protection of Human Rights in the European Legal Space', in *The Constitution of Europe*, (Cambridge, 1999), 107–116. See however the objections raised by L.F.M. Besselink to such a 'common minimum standard' as exclusive Community standard, in 'Entrapped by the Maximum Standard: On Fundamental Rights, Pluralism and Subsidiarity in the European Union' (1998) CML Rev., 629–680. However, when a Member State restricts a fundamental freedom in order to safeguard fundamental rights, as justified on public policy grounds, the justification of the restriction in question does not depend on a conception shared by all Member States as regards the precise way in which a fundamental right may be protected (Case C-36/02, *Omega Spielhallen- und AutomatenaufstellungsGmbH v. Oberbürgemeisterin der Bundesstadt Bonn*, annotated by Ackermann in (2005) CML Rev., 1107). See J. Morijn, 'Balancing Fundamental Rights and Common Market Freedoms in Union Law: Schmidberger and Omega in the Light of the European Constitution' (2006) *European Law Journal*, 15–40.
52. Case 11/70, *Internationale Handelsgesellschaft*.
53. Case C-210/03 *Swedish Match AB, Swedish Match UK Ltd v. Secretary of State for Health*, para. 72; see also, *inter alia*, Case 265/87, *Hermann Schräder HS Kraftfutter GmbH & Co. KG v. Hauptzollamt Gronau*, Case C-280/93, *Germany v. Council*, Case C-293/97, *Standley and Others*, Joined Cases C-37 & 38/02, *Di Lenardo and Dilexport*, and Case C-304/01, *Spain and Finland v. Parliament and Council*).
54. Convention for the Protection of Human Rights and Fundamental Freedoms (Rome, 4 Nov. 1950).
55. Case 4/73, *Nold*.
56. Case 36/75, *Rutili v. Ministre de l'intérieur*.
57. O.J. 1968, L 257.

to control aliens were a specific manifestation of a more general principle enshrined in various provisions of the ECHR. In *Rutili* and various other judgments,[58] the Court referred to the 'principles' underlying the Convention, but in the *Hoechst* case the Court referred directly to provisions of the ECHR.[59]

Through this case law of the Court of Justice, which is followed by the CFI,[60] a reasonable protection of the fundamental rights and freedoms of citizens has been ensured in the functioning of the Community. Examples of rights which are thus protected include the right of property, freedom to exercise a profession or trade, protection of private life, and of the home, the right of access to a competent court and to a fair trial, equal treatment and – in staff cases – the right to free exercise of religious beliefs and the right of association.[61] It is important to note that these fundamental rights do not only provide protection with respect to acts of the Institutions. When a Member State implements a Community rule, or relies on a provision of the Treaty in order to justify national rules which are likely to obstruct the exercise of one of the Community freedoms, such as Article 46 EC (freedom of establishment), the Court reviews such implementation and such justifications on the basis of these fundamental rights.[62]

Since the Treaty of Maastricht, this case law is based on written law. According to Article 6(2) TEU, the European Union respects the fundamental rights resulting from the ECHR[63] and those resulting from the constitutional traditions

---

58. Case 36/75, *Rutili*; see also Case 130/75, *Prais v. Council*; Case 44/79, *Hauer v. Land Rheinland-Pfalz*; Case 63/83 *Regina. v. Kirk*; Case 222/84, *Johnston v. Chief Constable of the Royal Ulster Constabulary*. See in relation to the European Social Charter and Convention No. 111 of the ILO, Case 149/77, *Defrenne v. SABENA*, and Case C-158/91, *Ministère public et al. v. Levy*, and in relation to the International Covenant on Civil and Political Rights (ICCPR), Case 374/87, *Orkem v. Commission*, and Joined Cases C-297/88 & C-197/89, *Massam Dzodzi v. Belgian State*.

59. Joined Cases 46/87 & 227/88, *Hoechst AG v. Commission*; Case 85/87, *Dow Benelux NV v. Commission*; Joined Cases 97–99/87, *Dow Chemical Ibérica SA et al. v. Commission*. See also Case C-274/99 P, *Connolly v. Commission* (annotated by Blanquet in (2002) CML Rev., 1423). The extent to which the Court has started to take the provisions of the ECHR and the case law of the ECtHR as its standard for review is apparent from Case C-60/00, *Carpenter v. Secretary of State for the Home Department*, Case C-112/00, *Schmidberger v. Republic of Austria* and Case 117/01, *K.B. v. Service Pensions Agency, Secretary of Health*.

60. E.g., Case T-19/91, *Société d'Hygiène Dermatologique de Vichy v. Commission* (various rights of the defence).

61. See, generally, P. Alston, M. Bustelo and J. Heenan (eds), *The EU and Human Rights* (Oxford, 1999), and N.A. Neuwahl and A. Rosas, *The European Union and Human Rights* (the Hague, 1995); see also J. Coppell and A. O'Neill, 'The European Court of Justice: Taking Rights Seriously?' (1992) CML Rev., 669; J. Weiler and N. Lockhart, 'Taking Rights Seriously: The European Court and Its Fundamental Rights Jurisprudence' (1995) CML Rev., 51, 579; A. Von Bogdandy, 'The EU as a Human Rights Organization' (2000) CML Rev., 1307 and F. Jacobs, 'Human Rights in the EU: the Role of the Court of Justice' (2001) EL Rev., 331.

62. Case 5/88, *Hubert Wachauf v. Bundesamt für Ernährung und Forstwirtschaft* and Case C-2/92, *Ministry of Agriculture, Fisheries and Food, ex parte Dennis Clifford Bostock*; Case C-260/89, *Elliniki Radiophonia Tiléorassi AE(ERT) et al. v. Dimotiki Etairia Pliroforissis et al.* and Case C-368/95, *Vereinigte Familiapress Zeitungsverlags- und vertriebs GmbH v. Heinrich Bauer Verlag*.

63. The Preamble to the Treaty on European Union also refers to the 'attachment' of the contracting parties to 'fundamental social rights as defined in the European Social Charter signed at Turin

common to the Member States, 'as general principles of Community law'. This qualification does not mean that these general principles do not apply in the Second and Third Pillars. It is after all clear from this provision that the Union itself – and not just the Communities – must respect fundamental rights.[64] On the other hand, the Court's power to review acts of the institutions against these fundamental rights is limited pursuant to Article 46 under d) TEU. The Court has such power only to the extent the Court's jurisdiction extends to the review of the lawfulness of these acts on the basis of the Community treaties and the Treaty on European Union. As explained above,[65] only modest powers are granted the Court by the Treaty on European Union, and these are subject to further conditions. They do not extend to the Second Pillar (CFSP).

It would seem, therefore, that Articles 6(2) and 46 under d) TEU as such do not lead to an extension of judicial protection in the area of fundamental rights. It does not seem likely that the case law will develop to a point where limitation of standing for individual actions contained in Articles 230(4) EC is interpreted less strictly where there is a *prima facie* case that an act of one of the Institutions infringes the fundamental rights of individuals.[66]

Although the level of protection of fundamental rights which has been achieved in the Community through the case law is reasonable, that does not alter the fact that the substance of these rights is contained in unwritten law. Moreover, the protection of these rights in the application of Community law lies in last instance with the Court of Justice, and acts of the Community which are claimed to infringe such rights cannot be contested before the European Court of Human Rights (ECtHR) because the Community is not party to the ECHR.[67] The ECtHR has adopted the position that it may examine complaints against legislative provisions enacted by a Member State in implementation of a directive, even if these provisions are an almost literal transposition of the directive.[68]

---

on 18 October 1961 and in the 1989 Community Charter of the Fundamental Social Rights of Workers'. See also Art. 136 EC.

64. 'As is clear from Article 6 EU, the Union is founded on the principle of the rule of law and it respects fundamental rights as general principles of Community law. It follows that the institutions are subject to review of the conformity of their acts with the treaties and the general principles of law, just like the Member States when they implement the law of the Union' (Case C-354/04 P, *Gestoras Pro Amnistía and others* and Case C-355/04 P, *Segi and others*, para. 51). For a notable application of these general principles to the Third Pillar, see Case C-105/03, *Pupino*.

65. Ch. IV, section 7.5.

66. Case C-50/00 P (*Unión de Pequeños Agricultores v. Council*, see *infra* section 2.3.1.2.) demonstrates that the Court feels that an extension of the standing possibilities for individuals is a matter for the drafters of the treaties.

67. The European Commission of Human Rights held on 10 Jul. 1978 that a complaint by the Confédération Française Démocratique du Travail was inadmissible because legal acts of the Council could not be viewed as acts attributable to the jurisdiction of the Member States within the meaning of Art. 1 of the Convention, Yearbook ECHR 1978, 539. See also Case 66/76, *Confédération Française démocratique du Travail(CFDT) v. Council.*

68. *Cantoni v. France*, 15 Nov. 1996, Reports 1996, 1617. In its decision of 9 Feb. 1990, *M. & Co. v. Germany* (Application No. 13258/87), *Yearbook ECHR*, 1990, 46, the European Commission of

Moreover, the ECtHR has explicitly ruled that a Member State, together with all the other Member States, may be held liable for infringements of the ECHR as a result of provisions of primary Community law which, it should be recalled, escape review on grounds of lawfulness by the Court of Justice.[69]

In 2005, the ECtHR declared that state action taken in compliance with obligations flowing from that state's membership of an international organization to which it has transferred part of its sovereignty, is

> justified as long as the relevant organisation is considered to protect fundamental rights, as regards both the substantive guarantees offered and the mechanisms controlling their observance, in a manner which can be considered at least equivalent to that for which the Convention provides. Any such finding of equivalence could, however, not be final and would be susceptible to review in the light of any relevant change in fundamental rights' protection.[70,71]

Although the Court of Justice tends to take the Strasbourg case law as a standard for its own administration of justice, there is also a risk of contradictory case law concerning the protection offered by a certain fundamental right, particularly in cases where the ECtHR has not yet ruled on the issue.[72]

Human Rights deemed a complaint inadmissible. For a detailed discussion of the relevant case law from the two Courts, see S. Douglas-Scott, *A Tale of Two Courts: Luxembourg, Strasbourg and the Growing European Rights Acquis* (2006) CML Rev., 629.

69. Judgment of 18 Feb. 1999, *Matthews v. United Kingdom*, annotated by Schermers (1999) CML Rev., 673.

70. ECtHR 30 Jun. 2005, *Bosphorus v. Ireland* (Application no. 45036/98). The Court found the protection of fundamental rights by the EC to be 'equivalent' to that of the Convention system. Consequently, a presumption arose that Ireland did not depart from the requirements of the Convention when it implemented legal obligations flowing from its membership of the EC. Such a presumption could be rebutted if, in a particular case, it was considered that the protection of Convention rights was manifestly deficient. See for a critical comment, K. Kuhnert, 'Bosphorus: Double standards in European human rights protection'? (Dec. 2006) *Utrecht Law Review*.

71. Cf. the above-cited (*supra* note 68) decision of the European Commission of Human Rights *Re M. & Co. v. Germany* which declared a complaint inadmissible for that reason. For a similar reasoning in another context, the German Verfassungsgericht in *Solange II*, see Ch. VII, section 2.

72. Cf. Joined Cases 46/87 & 227/88, *Hoechst v. Commission*, Case C-374/87, *Orkem*, and a later judgment by the ECtHR in *Niemietz v. Germany*, ECHR, Series A, 251; for the position of the ECJ thereafter, see Case C-94/00, *Roquette Frères v. Directeur général de la concurrence et al.* (annotated by M. Lienemeyer and D. Waelbroeck in (2003) CML Rev., 1481) and, *inter alia*, C-308/04 P, *SGL Carbon v. Commission*, and the Opinion of A.G. Geelhoed in that case. For certain other cases in which it may be doubted whether the case law of the Court of Justice is in conformity with that of the ECtHR, see R. Lawson, 'Confusion and Conflict? Diverging Interpretations of the European Convention on Human Rights in Strasbouirg and Luxembourg', in R. Lawson and M. Blois (eds), *The Dynamics of the Protection of Human Rights in Europe: Essays in Honour of Henry G. Schermers* (Dordrecht, 1994) and M. Waelbroeck, 'Editorial: La Cour de Justice et la Convention européenne des droits de l'homme' (1996) CDE, 549–553. In its Order in Case C-17/98, *Emesa Sugar v. Aruba* (annotated by R. Lawson in (2000)

Accession of the Community to the ECHR would solve these problems: citizens would have a written text setting out the rights whose protection is guaranteed in Community law, and would be able to bring a complaint to the ECtHR in Strasbourg if they believe that a judgment of the Court of Justice has infringed these rights. The Commission already proposed that the Communities should accede to the ECHR in 1979.[73]

Accession to the Convention would require not merely the agreement of all parties to the Convention, but also the solution of a number of procedural and substantive points which would be raised by the special nature of the Communities and which would have to be resolved in an accession protocol.[74]

In 1994, in order to shed some light on the question whether Community accession would be compatible with the EC Treaty as it stands, the Council, following an initiative of the Belgian Minister of Justice Wathelet, sought the opinion of the Court of Justice under Article 300(6) EC. In Opinion 2/94, *Accession by the Communities to the European Convention on Human Rights*, the Court found that it could not rule on the compatibility of accession to the ECHR with the Treaty, since it did not have any details about the way such accession would take place.[75] The Court did examine the question whether Article 308 EC (at the time, Art. 235) could provide a legal basis for accession, and answered the question negatively.

According to the Court, accession would involve a radical change in the Community system of protection of human rights, since 'it would entail the entry of the Community into a distinct international institutional system as well as integration of all the provisions of the Convention into the Community legal order'.[76] Such a change – the institutional implications of which for both the Communities and the Member States would be far-reaching – would be of enormous constitutional significance, and would by its nature exceed the limits of the powers conferred on the Community by Article 308 EC. Accession would require an amendment of the Treaties, and so far the Member States have not amended the treaties to enable accession, not even when there was a possibility to do so in the framework of the

---

CML Rev., 83) the ECJ considered that the case law of the ECtHR concerning parties' right to reply to the opinions of advocates general in proceedings before the highest domestic courts was not applicable to its own advocates general. The ECtHR rejected the claim raised by Emesa Sugar as being a tax case which did not relate to a 'civil right or obligation' under Art. 6 ECHR.

73. See, posing the question, the Commission's *Memorandum on the Accession of the European Communities to the European Convention on Human Rights and Fundamental Freedoms* Bull. EC Supp. 2/79, part I, para. 7. The Commission repeated this in a Communication to the Council of 19 Nov. 1990, Bull. EC 10-1990, 76.

74. See the Commission's Memorandum cited *supra*, and, further H.G. Schermers, 'The Communities under the European Convention on Human Rights' (1978/1) LIEI, 1.

75. Opinion 2/94, *Accession by the Communities to the European Convention on Human Rights*. The opinion sought should concern 'an agreement envisaged', but in this case there were not even the outlines of an agreement, because all the parties to the ECHR would have to be involved in negotiating an agreement.

76. Opinion 2/94, para. 6.

Intergovernmental conferences leading to the Treaties of Amsterdam and Nice. A legal basis for accession to the ECHR is provided for by the Lisbon Treaty.[77]

The Court's Opinion met with a great deal of criticism.[78] Apparently the critics did not focus on the underlying theme of the Court's Opinion: the fundamental changes to the institutional system of the Community which accession to the ECHR would inevitable involve (e.g., review of primary Community law against the ECHR by the Court, possible changes to the preliminary reference procedure in order to enable an intervention of the ECtHR in some way and at some stage) should be arrived at in the only proper way, which is amendment to the treaties and the approval by national parliaments which that involves. It should not be arrived at by means of application by the Council of a Treaty provision which, under certain limiting conditions and after consulting the European Parliament, permits the adoption of appropriate measures to fill in gaps in the system of powers of the Treaty in order to permit the more effective functioning of the common market as it is described in the Treaty.

At the same time, the European Parliament has long been striving for the drawing-up of a catalogue of Community fundamental rights, which would also cover economic and social rights.[79] Such a catalogue of fundamental rights would then need to be approved by all the Member States as a complement to the Treaty on European Union. This effort has been partially successful. At its meeting in Cologne on 3 and 4 June 1999, the European Council decided to draft a Charter of Fundamental Rights of the European Union. A so-called 'Convention' consisting of members of the European Parliament and of the national parliaments, as well as representatives of the national governments and representatives of the European Commission, was given the task of drafting a charter, a formula which was previously unknown as far as the preparation of official acts was concerned.

Despite the fact that the decision-making procedure was frequently chaotic, the Convention managed to adopt a comprehensive draft Charter in which civil, political economic and social rights, as well as the rights attached to European Union citizenship are laid down in 54 articles. These rights are divided up on the basis of six themes: dignity, freedoms, equality, solidarity, citizens' rights, justice. According to the preamble, these rights are derived from the constitutional traditions and international obligations common to the Member States, including in particular the Treaty on European Union, the Community Treaties, the European Convention for the Protection of Human Rights and Fundamental Freedoms, the Social Charters adopted by the Community and by the Council of Europe, and the

---

77. See Art. 6(2) TEU (Lisbon). See also Protocol No. 5 relating to Art. 6(2) of the Treaty on European Union on the accession of the Union to the European Convention on the Protection of Human Rights and Fundamental Freedoms and Declaration No. 1 on Art. 6(2).

78. See, e.g., annotation by G. Gaja, (1996) CML Rev., 973–989. H.G. Schermers (1996) *NJCM-Bulletin*, 879–883) rightly states that the argument that the negative view of the Court resulted from the fact that it was loath to accept another Court superior to it is based purely on speculation.

79. See the Parliament's Resolution of 27 Apr. 1979 (O.J. 1979, C 127/68–70), the De Gucht Report (EP Docs. A3-0025/93 and A3-0025/ANN/93 and the Parliament's Resolutions of 11 Mar. 1993 (O.J. 1993, C 115/78) and 18 Jan. 1994 (O.J. 1994, C 44/32).

case law of the Court of Justice of the European Communities and of the European Court of Human Rights.

On 7 December 2000, in Nice, the Charter of Fundamental Rights of the European Union was solemnly proclaimed by the European Parliament, the Council and the Commission jointly.[80] The proclamation, however solemn, does not in itself accord the Charter any binding force in law. The legal status of the Charter, in particular the question whether it will be included in the law as contained in the treaties of the Union, was intended to be decided in the Intergovernmental Conference (IGC) of 2004, in the framework of the debate on the future of the European Union, which was launched in 2001.[81] The now defunct Constitutional Treaty, elaborated by yet another Convention and adopted by the IGC 2004,[82] referred in Article I-9 to the rights, freedoms and principles set out in the Charter which, slightly amended, would have been made legally binding as Part II of that Treaty. The Lisbon Treaty provides for a recognition of the rights, freedoms and principles set out in the Charter of Fundamental Rights, which shall have the same legal value as the Treaties (see Art. 6(1) TEU (Lisbon)).

As the Charter may be made legally binding,[83] the following comments are relevant.[84] First, the provisions of the Charter are not addressed only to the Institutions and bodies of the Union, but also to the Member States when they are implementing Union law.[85] Despite the fact that a number of the rights included in the Charter – such as the right to life, the prohibition of slavery and compulsory labour, or the freedom to found educational establishments – show no clear link with the exercise of the existing[86] Treaty competences, it is not the intention to impose a general obligation on the Member States to respect the provisions of the Charter, in addition to the obligations which already flow for them from the ECHR and other human rights treaties. The Member States are only obliged to respect the Charter to the extent they are implementing Union law.[87] National measures outside that category cannot be examined by the Court on the basis of the Charter. National measures outside that category cannot be examined by the Court on the basis of the Charter.

---

80. The text as adopted on that date was published in O.J. 2000, C 364/01.
81. See on this the Declaration on the Future of the Union, attached to the Treaty of Nice. See also in more detail Ch. I, section 8.1, *supra*).
82. O.J. 2004, C 310.
83. The Charter was (re)proclaimed in a session of the European Parliament on 12 Dec. 2007, O.J. 2007, C 303.
84. See in more detail the analysis by K. Lenaerts and E. de Smijter, 'A "Bill of Rights" for the European Union' (2001) CML Rev., 273–300. On the possible impact of the Charter on the evolution of the EU, see P. Eeckhout, 'The EU Charter of Fundamental Rights and the Federal Question' (2002) CML Rev., 945.
85. Art. 51(1) Charter.
86. The Charter does not aim to establish any new power or task for the Community or the Union, or to modify powers and tasks defined by the Treaties (Art. 51(2) Charter).
87. The limitation to 'when they are implementing Union law' seems to be more restricted than national rules 'falling within the scope of' Union (or Community) law, and insofar is not in conformity with the case law of the Court of Justice (Case C-260/89, *ERT*).

Furthermore, the rights recognized by the Charter which are based on the Community Treaties or the Treaty on European Union (such as Art. 45(1) Charter, concerning freedom of movement and residence for citizens of the European Union), are exercised under the conditions and within the limits defined by those Treaties.[88] Where the Charter contains rights which correspond to rights guaranteed by the ECHR, the content and scope of those rights is to be the same as those laid down by the ECHR, although it remains possible for a more extensive protection to be offered by Union law.[89] More in general, no provision of the Charter may be interpreted in such a way that it restricts or adversely affects human rights and fundamental freedoms as recognized by Union law and international law (including customary law) and by international agreements to which the Union, the Community or all the Member States are party, and by the Member States' constitutions.[90]

The provisions of Articles 52 and 53 Charter only partially solve the problem of the relationship between the ECHR on the one hand, as interpreted by the ECtHR, and the Charter, whose interpretation is a matter for the Court of Justice, on the other. True, it may be assumed that Article 52(3) Charter involves a duty for the Court to follow the case law of the ECtHR – in continuation of its current practice – but problems may arise in particular as a result of the fact that the descriptions of the fundamental rights derived from the ECHR differ in many ways from those of the ECHR itself.

For the time being, the Charter does not have generally binding force.[91] Probably for this reason, the Court, unlike a number of its advocates general and the CFI, was initially rather reluctant to refer in its judgments to the Charter as source of inspiration for its case law. Since 2007, however, it no longer hesitates to mention articles of the Charter as reaffirming general principles of law concerning fundamental rights.[92]

On the entry into force of the Lisbon Treaty, issues relating to fundamental rights risk becoming highly complex in view of three layers of rights co-existing at the level of Union law: the ECHR, the Charter and the fundamental rights recognized as general principles of Community (Union) law.

1.5   ROLE OF THE COURT OF JUSTICE IN THE PROCESS OF INTEGRATION

From the observations made above about the powers and functions of the Court it is clear that a vital place has been accorded to the legal element in the functioning of the Communities, something which does not tend to be the case in traditional

---

88. Art. 52(2) Charter.
89. Art. 52(3) Charter.
90. Art. 53, Charter.
91. This situation may change, if Art. 6(1) TEU (Lisbon) enters into force (see note 83 *supra*).
92. Case C-432/05, *Unibet (London) Ltd, Unibet (International) Ltd v. Justitiekanslern* and Case C-303/05, *Advocaten voor de Wereld VZW v. Leden van de Ministerraad*.

international organizations. The Court has used this opportunity in an effective manner in order to give legal support and direction to the process of integration.[93]

The most spectacular examples of this are in the case law relating to the relationship between Community law and national law,[94] the competence of the Community to conclude agreements,[95] the applicability of fundamental rights in the Community legal order,[96] and the liability of Member States for damages suffered by individuals as a result of an infringement of Community law which can be attributed to them.[97]

In a less spectacular way, though, the Court has also made an important contribution to the establishment and proper functioning of the common market. It has given concrete form to the Community rules and powers in this area and has extended and refined them by always systematically co-ordinating them and relating them to the general and the specific objectives of Community law and its component branches. With the aid of this systematic teleological interpretation,[98] Community law has been endowed with the maximal effect where this has been possible and permitted; it has been moulded into a consistent legal system which can be managed in a supple manner in order to seek solutions for the varied and ever-changing legal questions which arise in the process of integration.

There are, though, certain limits to the Court's activities; these are linked to the special nature of Community law and to the judicial function as such. Community law is predominantly social and economic law. This means that in many cases Community law must allow the Institutions sufficient discretion in the exercise of the economic management entrusted to them to take appropriate measures in the varying and varied circumstances of economic life. This discretion may concern the opportuneness of their action or the means to be chosen or both.[99] But even if action is obligatory, or if action is limited as to the means to be applied, this obligation as a rule will depend on (or the means to be applied will be determined by) an assessment of a particular set of economic facts. Such a set of facts, must

---

93. See further reading at the end of this chapter.
94. See Ch. II, section 3.3, *supra*, and Ch.VII, section 2, *infra*.
95. See Ch. XIII, section 2, *infra*.
96. See section 1.4., *supra*.
97. See Ch. VII, section 4, *infra*.
98. See P. Mathijsen, *Teleologische interpretatie der Europese verdragen* (Nijmegen, 1970); *Reports of the Judicial and Academic Conference 27–28 September 1976* (Luxembourg, 1976), and J. Mertens de Wilmars,'Réflections sur les methods d'interprétation de la Cour de justice' (1986) CDE, 5. See also L. Gormley in L. Krämer et al. (eds), *Law and Diffuse Interests in the European Legal Order* (*Festschrift* for Reich, Baden-Baden, 1997) 11, J. Bengoetxea, *The Legal Reasoning of the European Court of Justice* (Oxford, 1993) and J. Bengoetxea, N. MacCormick and L. Moral Soriano, 'Integration and Integrity in the Legal Reasoning of the European Court of Justice', in G. de Búrca and J.H.H. Weiler (eds), *The European Court of Justice* (Oxford, 2001), 43–85.
99. See Case 78/74, *Deuka, Deutsche Kraftbutter GmbH B.J. Stolp v. Einfuhr- und Vorratsstelle für Getreide und Futtermittel*. See also Case C-350/88, *Société française des Biscuits Delacre et al. v. Commission* on the Commission's margin of discretion in relation to common organizations of markets requiring continual adaptation depending on changes in the economic situation; in these circumstances there can be no legitimate expectation on the part of traders that the *status quo* will be maintained by the Community Institutions.

have been defined in Community law in an objective sense, but presuppose a certain subjective discretion in favour of the Community Institutions (or in some cases also in favour of the Member States on which the obligation has been imposed).[100] Such *unbestimmte Rechtsbegriffe* (indeterminate legal concepts) are found, for instance, in Article 134 EC.[101]

Restrictions have, of course, been imposed on judicial review of this discretion.[102] In this, the Court models its action on the national judicial control of the exercise of discretionary powers of government: judging according to principles of 'good government' and 'confining itself to an examination of the relevance of the facts and of the legal consequences' deduced from them[103] and examining whether or not the choice made in the exercise of discretion is of an arbitrary nature[104] and 'whether the evaluation of the competent authority contains a patent error or constitutes a misuse of power'.[105] In order to ensure a reasonable level of supervision, the Court generally tends to set high standards for fulfilment of the obligation to state reasons laid down in the Treaties.[106]

Whilst Community law is largely social and economic law, it is also still in the making. It is law which in many ways has to be developed by 'Community legislation' and continually adapted to changing circumstances and views. The Community legislature means, in principle, the Council, or the Council and Parliament together, but the Council has in all too many cases failed to fulfil its functions as a result of failure to take decisions, sometimes through a failure to achieve unanimity even where this was not strictly necessary. Another problem is posed by the Council's reluctance to delegate further legislative power to the Commission.

In these circumstances the Court has sometimes been obliged with the aid of the systematic teleological method of interpretation to deduce solutions from Community law for concrete problems which should have been dealt with by the Community legislature.[107] Such judicial creativity is open to objection on the ground of the lack of legal certainty,[108] and also the possible absence of

---

100. See, e.g., (in relation to Art. 90 EC 2nd para.) Case 27/67, *Firma Fink-Frucht GmbH v. Hauptzollamt München-Landsbergerstrasse.*

101. E.g., 'economic difficulties in one or more Member States', 'requisite cooperation', 'necessary protective measures', measures 'which cause the least disturbance of the functioning of the common market'.

102. In the ECSC Treaty, an attempt was made to define the restriction on the Court's control of this discretion (see Art. 33 ECSC, 1st para., 2nd sentence, no longer in force); in the other two Treaties it has been left to the Court itself to fix the limits.

103. Joined Cases 56 & 58/64, *Etablissements. Consten SARL and Grundig- Verkaufs-GmbH v. Commission.* See also Case 42/84, *Remia BV et al. v. Commission* [1985] ECR, 2545.

104. Case 5/67, *W.Beus GmbH &Co. v. Hauptzollamt München.*

105. Case 78/74, *Deuk*, para. 9: 'When examining the lawfulness of the exercise of the Commission's freedom of discretion, the courts cannot substitute their own evaluation of the matter for that of the competent authority'.

106. Art. 253 EC. See also Art. 162 Euratom. See, further, Ch. V, section 1.1, *supra.*

107. See, e.g., Case 804/79, *Commission v. United Kingdom.*

108. Perhaps with a view to this point, in its judgments in Case 22/70, *Commission v. Council* (ERTA) and Case 6/72, *Continental Can et al. v. Commission*, in which it developed a 'new'

consensus in broad societal terms for the Court's decision. In fact, this function of the Court as filling gaps in legislative provisions has lost some of its importance through the years. Following the entry into force of the Single European Act, the decision-making capacity of those Institutions whose role is to decide on policy increased. Moreover, the emphasis has been shifted increasingly to positive integration – i.e., policy integration – and in such a context the role of a judicial body such as the Court of Justice is more modest than in the framework of 'negative' integration, where it was primarily a question of deciding the details concerning extent and meaning of obligations imposed on the Member States.[109]

The role of the Court of Justice in the process of integration since the mid-1980s has sometimes led to sharp criticism retrospectively. Critics found that the Court had sought inspiration in 'guidelines which are essentially political in nature and hence, not judicially applicable', and had thus been guilty of the kind of 'judicial activism which may be an usurpation of power'.[110] This kind of criticism neglects the fact that the Court has a duty – like the other Institutions – to ensure that the tasks entrusted to the Community are carried out; but also, in the words of Lord Howe, it neglects the fact that

> the Court had no pre-existing legal system to work with. The treaty provisions it was called upon to interpret were often general in scope and silent on detail. The option of operating in a 'non-activist' manner, merely interpreting the meaning of words, was simply not open to the Court of Justice.[111]

2   DIRECT ACTIONS

In the context of a general introduction, only limited space can be given to the discussion of the conditions under which and the way in which the Court exercises its multifarious jurisdiction, as sketched in section 7.2.2 of Chapter IV, above.

---

rule, the Court concluded that on the facts the 'new' rule was inapplicable. Similarly, in exceptional circumstances the Court may limit in time the effect of its judgments, particularly, but not only, when it gives an interpretation going well beyond what was generally expected, e.g., in the application of the principle of equal pay for men and women (Art. 119 EC) in Case 43/75, *Defrenne v. SABENA*.

109. See on the difference between negative and positive integration Ch. III, section 2.1.2 *supra*. See also J. Mertens de Wilmars, 'The Case-Law of the Court of Justice in Relation to the Review of the Legality of Economic Policy in Mixed-Economy Systems' (1982) LIEI, 1–16.

110. H. Rasmussen, *On Law and Policy in the European Court of Justice: A Comparative Study in Judicial Policymaking*, (Dordrecht, 1986), 62. One of the most serious attacks on the way in which the Court fulfils its function came from the Warden of All Souls College, Oxford, (then) Sir Patrick Neill, *The European Court of Justice: A Case Study in Judicial Activism*(London, European Policy Forum, 1995). See also, very critically, T.C. Hartley, *Constitutional Problems of the European Union* (Oxford, 1999), Chs. 2 and 3, within the notes 71 and 72 references to literature by critics and defenders of the way in which the Court has interpreted the Treaty in the past.

111. G. Howe, *Euro-Justice: Yes or No?* (1997) EL Rev., 209.

The present discussion deals only with those proceedings which concern the core of the Court's jurisdiction.[112]

This section deals with the direct actions. First, those procedures which require the Court to judge whether the acts and omissions of the Member States (section 2.1) and the Institutions (section 2.2) are in conformity with Community law will be treated. Special attention will be devoted to the right of action of private parties against Community measures (section 2.3). Attention will also be paid to the possibilities for individuals to bring actions for damages before the Court on the ground of the Community's non-contractual liability (section 2.4). The activities of the Court in the field of preliminary rulings, which also belong to the core of its jurisdiction, will be discussed in the section 3 of this chapter. Finally, in section 4 interim relief at the Community courts will be discussed.

2.1   SUPERVISION OF THE ACTS OF MEMBER STATES: ACTIONS FOR INFRINGEMENT OF THE TREATY

In the proceedings which may lead to a pronouncement of the Court on the question whether a Member State has failed to fulfil one of its obligations under the Treaty, a very important function has been assigned to the Commission under Articles 226–228 EC.[113] Although the Member States themselves may also take the initiative for such a procedure,[114] in practice they have tended to leave this initiative almost entirely to the Commission, which, being an impartial body, is pre-eminently suited for this.[115]

In the first stage, the procedure initiated by the Commission has an administrative character[116] and has three aims: to give the Member State the chance to end the (possible) infringement, to give the Member State the opportunity to exercise its

---

112. The ECSC procedures are not analysed here – at least where they are not relevant for a better understanding of the EC and Euratom procedures – since the ECSC Treaty expired in 2002. See Ch. II, section 2.1 *supra*.

113. Cf. Arts. 141–143 Euratom.

114. Before such a procedure can get to Court, the complaining Member State must bring the matter before the Commission which has to deliver a reasoned opinion after each of the States involved has had the opportunity to submit observations. For the circumstances in which the power under Art. 226 is enjoyed by the Board of Directors of the European Investment Bank and the Council of the European Central Bank, see Art. 237 (a) and (d) EC.

115. Cf. Arts. 211 EC and 124 Euratom, first indent. See, for the three cases in which there was a judgment under Art. 227 EC, Case 141/78, *France v. United Kingdom*, Case C-388/95, *Belgium v. Spain* and Case C-145/04, *Spain v. UK*.

116. In certain areas, such as state aid control (Art. 88(2) EC), harmonization (Art. (95(9) EC) and security exceptions (Art. 298 EC), the Commission may bring the matter directly to the Court of Justice without going through the normal Art. 226 or 227 EC procedure (the right is also available to any interested Member State under Art. 88(2) and to any Member State under Arts. 95(9) and 298 EC; see also Arts. 38 and 92 Euratom). For the procedure under Art. 88(2) EC applicable when the Commission regards a national state aid measure as being incompatible with the common market, see Ch. IX, section 3.3 *infra*. Under Art. 237(d) EC, the Council of the European Central Bank (ECB) enjoys powers in certain areas similar to those of the

rights of defence, and to delimit the substance of the dispute with a view to possible proceedings before the Court.[117] If the Commission, in the light of the information it has received and gathered[118] is of the view that a Member State has failed to fulfil the obligations imposed on it by the Treaties themselves or the measures for their implementation, it must give this state a prior opportunity to submit its observations. This is done in a letter (*lettre de mise en demeure*) designed to set out the points at issue and to put the state in a position in which it can prepare its defence, or fulfil the obligation imposed on it by Community law.[119]

This administrative phase defines the subject matter of the dispute, which may not subsequently be extended. The fact that the Member State is given an opportunity to react to a letter sent under Article 226 is considered an essential guarantee by the Court. Non-observance of it constitutes an infringement of an essential procedural requirement.[120] The Commission, therefore, is not free to request the Court in the later (judicial) stage of the procedure to pronounce on a failure of the Member State which has not been or could not be mentioned in the administrative stage of the procedure.[121] In a great many cases, the discussions tend to lead to the Member State either convincing the Commission that it is mistaken or remedying its failure in a way that is satisfactory to the Commission.[122] The procedure has then achieved its purpose.

If the Member State refuses to put an end to the infringement and the Commission adheres to its original view, the Commission then decides on its final position. This is done by means of a (non-binding) reasoned opinion which serves to define the dispute.[123] The Commission sets out its views, giving the reasons for them[124] and invites the Member State to take the appropriate measures[125]

Commission under Art. 226 EC. The Board of Directors of the European Investment Bank (EIB) also enjoys such powers under Art. 237(a) EC.

117. Case C-362/01, *Commission v. Ireland* and Case 456/03, *Commission v. Italy*.
118. See Ch. IV, section 4.3.3. *supra*.
119. Case C-473/93, *Commission v. Luxembourg*. An opinion of the Commission relating to draft measures does not constitute a formal notice under Art. 226; moreover, draft measures may not be the object of infringement proceedings: see Order in Case C-341/97, *Commission v. Netherlands*.
120. E.g., Case C-306/91, *Commission v. Italy*.
121. Case 7/69, *Commission v. Italy*; Case 31/69, *Commission v. Italy*; see also Case 51/83, *Commission v. Italy*.
122. In 2006, in 901 out of a total of 2551 cases (i.e., 35.3%) the proceedings were terminated before a formal notice was sent, followed by 945 cases (or another 37%) before a reasoned opinion and 392 cases before referral to the Court (another 15.3%). See *XXIVth Report on Monitoring the Application of Community Law COM* (2007) 398, Annex II: Infringements Procedures: Breakdown Per Stage Reached, Legal Basis, Member State and Sector, Table 2.5.
123. Joined Cases 142 & 143/80, *Amministrazione delle Finanze dello Stato v. Essevi et al.*
124. I.e., the reasoned opinion must contain 'a coherent statement of the reasons which led the Commission to believe that the state in question has failed to fulfil an obligation under the Treaty', Case 7/61, *Commission v. Italy*.
125. These may, in appropriate cases, be specified, cf. Case 70/72, *Commission v. Germany*; however the Commission is not obliged to indicate what specific action should be taken, cf. Case C-247/89, *Commission v. Portugal*.

within a period which the Commission fixes[126] to remedy its default. A reasoned opinion has legal consequences only in relation to bringing the matter to the Court in the context of the proceedings which have been initiated.[127] By formally stating the infringement of the Treaty with which the Member State concerned is charged, the Commission's reasoned opinion concludes the pre-litigation procedure.[128] A collegiate decision of the Commission is required, but – given the limited legal consequences resulting from the decision itself – the college of Commissioners does not need to decide on the wording or put it in its final form.[129]

If the Member State does not comply with the reasoned opinion within the given period the Commission may bring the matter before the Court. The Commission enjoys discretionary power in this.[130] It is also for the Commission to decide at which moment it wishes to bring proceedings before the Court.[131] The Commission does not have to show the existence of a legal interest 'since, in the general interest of the Community, its function is to ensure that the provisions of the Treaty are applied by the Member States and to note the existence of any failure to fulfil the obligations deriving therefrom, with a view to bringing it to an end'.[132] The Commission must always ensure that its reasoned opinion and its application

---

126. The Commission will usually give two months (see, e.g., Case C-376/00, *Commission v. Italy*), although a period of one month or even less is not unknown in urgent cases.

127. Any temporary indulgence granted by the Commission in the course of Art. 226 EC proceedings (or otherwise) cannot change the obligations of the Member States under the Treaty and cannot preclude individuals from relying on rights conferred upon them by the Treaty in order to challenge any legislative or administrative measures of a Member State which may be incompatible with Community law, Joined Cases 142 & 143/80, *Amministrazione delle Finanze dello Stato v. Essevi*.

128. Case 74/82, *Commission v. Ireland*.

129. The decision to issue a reasoned opinion cannot be described as a measure of administration or management and may not be delegated; see Case C-191/95, *Commission v. Germany*. The same applies to the decision to commence proceedings before the Court under Art. 226; see Case C-191/95, *Commission v. Germany*. In this case, the principle of collegiality imposes less strict requirements than in the case of decisions to impose fines on undertakings in competition cases, see, e.g., Case C-137/92 P, *Commission v. BASF*.

130. Case C-200/88, *Commission v. Greece*; Case C-431/92, *Commission v. Germany* and Case C-236/99, *Commission v. Belgium*. According to the Lisbon Treaty, if a case is brought before the Court pursuant to Art. 226 EC on the grounds that the Member State concerned has failed to notify measures transposing a directive adopted under a legislative procedure, the Commission *may* specify, in its application to the Court, the amount of the lump sum or periodic penalty payment to be paid by the Member State concerned which it considers appropriate in the circumstances (Art. 260(3) TFEU, as amended).

131. Case 7/68, *Commission v. Italy*; Case 7/71, *Commission v. France*. The time between the infringement taking place or commencing and being brought to the Court can vary enormously: the Court has noted that the excessive duration of the pre-litigation procedure may make it more difficult for the Member State concerned to rebut the Commission's arguments, and may thus infringe the rights of the defence, see Case C-96/89, *Commission v. The Netherlands*, and more recently Case C-490/04 *Commission v. Germany*. See further, H.G. Schermers and D. Waelbroeck, op. cit. *supra* note 3, para. 1285–1288.

132. Case 167/73, *Commission v. France*.

to the Court for a finding that a Member State has failed to fulfil its obligations under a particular provision of Community law are based on the same grounds, arguments and submissions.[133]

The objective of the court proceedings is to obtain a formal pronouncement by the Court that a Member State has failed to fulfil its obligations flowing from Community law. It aims to demonstrate objectively the failure to fulfil these obligations, and from that point of view it is irrelevant whether the failure to fulfil obligations is the result of intention or negligence on the part of the Member State responsible, or of technical difficulties encountered by it.[134] Pending the proceedings before the Court, the Commission may apply to the Court under Article 243 EC, asking it to order the Member State in question to withdraw or suspend certain measures pending delivery of the judgment in the main proceedings.[135]

It is relatively seldom that infringement cases will lead to a lawsuit. The procedure is clearly intended to avoid rather than obtain a condemnation of the defaulting state. The number of actual judgments of the Court on infringement proceedings is considerably smaller than the number of cases in which the Commission deals with matters relating to the failure of Member States to fulfil obligations under the Treaty. The judgments of the Court form the tip of an iceberg: in most cases an amicable settlement is reached before the matter goes to the Court.[136]

The action which the Commission may lodge with the Court of Justice when its reasoned opinion is not complied with falls under the Court's 'unlimited' jurisdiction.[137] This means that the Court must judge the behaviour of the Member State as a whole and, in so doing, must take into account all relevant facts, such as the question of whether in the given circumstances the State has been given sufficient time to take the appropriate measures for remedying its failure.[138]

The obligations referred to in Article 226 EC may flow from primary or secondary Community law, from international law which is binding on the

---

133. E.g., Case C-52/90, *Commission v. Denmark*.
134. Case C-71/97, *Commission v. Spain*.
135. Case C-195/90 R, *Commission v. Germany*.
136. In 2006 a formal notice was sent in 998 cases (1536) and a reasoned opinion in 520 (680) cases; in the same year, 175 (189) cases were referred to the Court (the figures between brackets also include the cases against the ten Member States that acceded in 2004). See the Report mentioned in *supra* note 122, Annex II, Table 2.1. See further H.G. Schermers and D. Waelbroeck, op. cit. *supra* note 3, para. 1222, and A. Dashwood and R. White, 'Enforcement Actions under Arts. 169 and 170 EC', (1989) EL Rev. 442.
137. In cases of unlimited jurisdiction, the Court may look at all arguments, and may replace the decision by another one.
138. Whether or not the periods allowed the Member State by both the formal notice and the reasoned opinion are reasonable depends on the circumstances in the actual case; in exceptional cases, extremely short periods may be justified, especially where action must be urgently taken against an infringement, or when the Member State was entirely aware of the position of the Commission long before the proceedings were initiated. See Case 293/85, *Commission v. Belgium*.

Community,[139] but also from general principles of unwritten Community law which must be respected when a Member State acts within the scope of application of Community law.[140] A failure to fulfil such an obligation may consist of a positive action or an omission on the part of a Member State. It follows from settled case law that an administrative practice can be the subject matter of an action for failure to fulfil obligations if it is, to some degree, of a consistent and general nature.[141] Such a failure may be deduced from a series of infringements that have persisted over a protracted period. Also, as the Court held recently, in an important judgment of 26 April 2005 in the area of environmental law,[142] nothing prevents the Commission from seeking in parallel to a finding of a series of such infringements, a declaration that these were due to a general and persistent practice. Insofar as the Commission's action also seeks such a more general finding, the Court seems willing to adapt the procedural conditions under which it might be justifiable.[143] By accepting the possibility of inferring from a series of factual situations that there may be a situation of structural non-compliance by a Member State, the judgment of 26 April 2005 may have opened the way to a more effective enforcement of Community law obligations against Member States.[144,145]

The question as to whether the State has failed to fulfil its obligations[146] is of course decided by the Court in accordance with the strict standards of law. The conciliatory administrative stage of the procedure is then at an end: even if the Member State ultimately fulfils its obligation in accordance with the opinion of the Commission, the judicial procedure may be continued if the Commission decides to maintain its application.[147] According to constant case law, the question whether obligations were fulfilled or not must be determined according to the situation in the Member State at the end of the period set in the Commission's

---

139. Case C-13/00, *Commission v. Ireland*, regarding the Bern Convention.
140. Cf. Case C-260/89, *ERT*.
141. See Case C-387/99, *Commission v. Germany* and the case law cited in para. 42 of that judgment. For an example of a general and persistent practice of omitting to act, see the so-called *Spanish Strawberries* Case C-265/95, *Commission v. France*.
142. See Case C-494/01, *Commission v. Ireland*(Irish Waste).
143. See more extensively the perceptive comments on the judgment by P. Wennerås, 'A New Dawn for Commission Enforcement under Arts. 226 and 228 EC: General and Persistent (GAP) Infringements, Lump Sums and Penalty Payments' (2006) CML Rev., 31, 33–50.
144. As A.G. Geelhoed pointed out in his in Opinion in Case C-494/01 (para. 4), if the Court, in fields such as environment and public procurement where many infringements occur, can only establish *ex post facto* that the directives concerned have not been complied with in particular cases, it will not able to address basic underlying structural problems of non-compliance with the directives concerned in a Member State. It should be noted, however, that in order to demonstrate structural non-compliance, the Commission must do more than refer to a few individual cases only, see Case C-248/05, *Commission v. Ireland*.
145. See on this perspective, P. Wennerås, op. cit. *supra* note 143, 44–45.
146. See *supra* at notes 139 and 140.
147. In 2006, the Commission withdrew its application in 75 cases; See the Report mentioned in note 122 *supra*, Annex II, Table 2.5.

reasoned opinion., and the Court may not take account of changes after that date.[148] The Court regularly, and firmly, rejects requests by Member States to stay proceedings because they intend to end the failure to fulfil their obligations as soon as possible.[149]

If the action brought by the Commission is not dismissed by the Court, the latter will rule in its judgment that the Member State has failed to fulfil its obligations. In that case, the State is obliged to take the necessary measures to comply with the judgment.[150] The process of compliance must, in the interest of the immediate and uniform application of Community law, be initiated immediately and must be completed as soon as possible.[151] For the competent national authorities (a term which includes national courts as well as administrative authorities) this entails a prohibition against applying a national rule recognized as incompatible with the Treaty and, if the circumstances so require, an obligation on them to take all appropriate measures to facilitate the full application of Community law.[152] A judgment can, moreover, form the basis for liability incurred by a Member State as a result of its default, as regards other Member States, the Community or private parties.[153]

In practice, the implementation of the judgments of the Court of Justice has never been challenged by a categorical and definitive refusal to comply by the Member State concerned, although very occasionally it may have looked like it.[154] However, the number of instances in which the procedure for failure to take measures to comply with a judgment of the Court has had to be initiated is substantial, particularly as a result of the late implementation of directives by the Member States.[155] It has been repeatedly necessary for the Court to hand down a second judgment in which the failure to comply with Article 228(1) EC is

---

148. Case C-456/03, *Commission v. Italy*. For a case in which not only was the infringement ended in the course of the proceedings before the Court, but moreover that fact had been confirmed in the context of a preliminary ruling during this period, and nevertheless the Court did not take this into account, see Case C-234/91, *Commission v. Denmark*. Case 26/69, *Commission v. France*, in which the Court considered whether it should examine whether the Commission had sufficient legal interest to maintain its application, because the failure to fulfil obligations in question had already been ended at the time the application was lodged, must in retrospect be seen as a curiosity with no value of precedent.

149. See, e.g., Case C-212/98, *Commission v. Ireland* (non-transposition of a directive).

150. Arts. 228(1) EC, cf. Art. 143(1) Euratom.

151. See, e.g., Case 169/87, *Commission v. France*; Case C-387/97, *Commission v. Greece*.

152. E.g., Case 48/71, *Commission v. Italy*; Joined Cases 314–316/81 & 83/82, *Procureur de la République et al. v. Waterkeyn et al.*; Case C-101/91, *Commission v. Italy*. See Ch. III section 6.4 *supra*.

153. See, e.g., Case C-263/88, *Commission v. France*; Case 39/72, *Commission v. Italy* [1973] ECR 101. See also Case C-243/89, *Commission v. Denmark*. See Ch. VII section 4 *infra*.

154. Cf. the notorious case when France, in the late 1970s, refused the import of mutton from the UK (Case 232/78, *Commission v. France*) and Joined Cases 24 & 97/80 R, *Commission v. France*.

155. The details can be traced in the annual Reports on the application of Community law (see note 122, *supra*). E.g., on 31 Dec. 2006 the Art. 228 EC procedure had been launched in 94 cases (Table 2.3). See also T.C. Hartley, *Constitutional Problems of the European Union* (1999), Ch. 6.

established.[156] The cause of the failure by the Member States to fulfil its obligations is often to be found in the need for long drawn-out and difficult legislative procedures involved.

A remarkable achievement of the Treaty of Maastricht was that Article 228 (ex 171) EC now makes provision for the imposition by the Court of Justice of a lump sum or penalty payment on the defaulting Member State, if the latter is indeed found not to have taken the necessary measures to comply with the earlier judgment.[157] The hope is that this will act as a further incentive to compliance. If the administrative phase of the infringement procedure under Article 228(2) EC for infringement of Article 228(1) goes to the reasoned opinion, the Commission must specify the points on which the Member State has failed to comply with the Court's judgment.[158] Continued non-compliance after the deadline set out in the reasoned opinion may result in the Commission bringing the matter to the Court of Justice. Here, as with other infringement proceedings, the Commission has a discretion. If it exercises that discretion to go to the Court, the Commission is now obliged to specify, in its application to the Court, the amount of the lump sum or periodic penalty payment to be paid by the Member State concerned which it considers appropriate in the circumstances.[159] The Court's jurisdiction here too is unlimited, and, if it finds the alleged infringement proved, it decides whether the financial penalty should be imposed, and what amount will have to be paid.

The Commission has set out its intended line of behaviour in applying Article 228(2) EC in a communication of 13 December 2005.[160] In determining the amount of the lump sum or periodic penalty payment, the Commission will be guided by the main purpose of the sanctions, i.e., the need to ensure that Community law is effectively enforced. Three fundamental criteria must be taken into account: the seriousness of the infringement, the duration and the need to ensure the deterrent effect of the penalty, to end the infringement in question and prevent further infringements.

In the first proceeding in which the Commission proposed to the Court that a penalty payment should be imposed,[161] the Court considered that '[i]n the absence

---

156. Spectacular examples include Joined Cases 227–230/85, *Commission v. Belgium*; Case 169/87, *Commission v. France*.

157. See Art. 228(2) EC; cf. Art. 143 Euratom. The following discussion refers *mutatis mutandis* to the situation under the Euratom Treaty. According to the Lisbon Treaty, if a Member State has failed to notify measures transposing a directive adopted under a legislative procedure, the Court may on the Commission's initiative impose *in an Art. 226 procedure* a lump sum or penalty payment on the defaulting Member State (see *supra* note 130).

158. The procedure followed is identical to the normal Art. 226 EC proceedings described above. According to the Lisbon Treaty this procedure is simplified. A reasoned opinion will not be required anymore when the State concerned has been given the opportunity to submit its observations, see Art. 260(2) TFEU.

159. Art. 228(2) EC, 2nd para.

160. SEC(200)1658, Application of Art. 228 of the EC Treaty, replacing two earlier communications of 1996 and 1997.

161. Case C-387/97, *Commission v. Greece*. Three other cases have since been brought before the Court: Case C-278/01, *Commission v. Spain*, Case C-304/02, *Commission v. France* and Case

of provisions in the Treaty, the Commission may adopt guidelines for determining how the lump sums or penalty payments which it intends to propose to the Court are calculated, so as, in particular, to ensure equal treatment between the Member States'.[162] Such guidelines help to ensure that the Commission acts in a manner which is transparent, foreseeable and consistent with legal certainty, and aim to achieve proportionality in the amounts of the penalty payments to be proposed. Without approving these guidelines in detail, the Court was prepared to follow the Commission's approach, and to take as fundamental criteria the duration of the infringement, its degree of seriousness, and – with an eye to the deterrent effect – the ability of the Member State to pay.[163] Nevertheless, the Commission's sub-missions do not bind the Court and merely constitute a useful point of reference. 'In exercising its discretion, it is for the Court to fix the lump sum or penalty payment that is appropriate to the circumstances and proportionate both to the breach that has been found and to the ability to pay of the Member State concerned.'[164]

Until 2005 the Commission never asked for a lump sum,[165] let alone a lump sum and a periodic penalty payment simultaneously. That a more imaginative interpretation of Article 228(2) was feasible, has been shown by the judgment in the *Second French Fisheries Case*.[166] The Court not only ordered the French Republic to pay a penalty payment of EUR 57 761 250 for each period of six months from delivery of the present judgment at the end of which the previous Article 226 ruling was not yet fully complied with, but also, though this was not proposed by the Commission, imposed a lump sum penalty of EUR 20 000 000. Following the Opinion of Advocate General Geelhoed,[167] the Court found that recourse to both types of penalty EC is not precluded. Rejecting all claims to the contrary, the Court held that it was free to assess in light of the circumstances of each case the financial penalties to be imposed, regardless of the Commission's submissions. As to the different objectives of the two possible sanctions, the Court observed that the imposition of a penalty payment may serve to induce a Member

---

C-119/04, *Commission v. Italy*. Only in the last case was the sanction asked for by the Com-mission not imposed, as the Court lacked sufficient information with respect to the persistence (on the date of the examination of the facts) of the breach of obligations. See further Case C-503/04, *Commission v. Germany*, *infra* note 170.

162. Ibid., para. 84.
163. Ibid., para. 88. The Court found the Commission's suggestion that account should be taken both of the gross domestic product of the Member State concerned and of the number of its votes in the Council to be appropriate, since it enables a reasonable differentiation between the various Member States.
164. Case C-387/97, *Commission v. Greece*, paras 89 and 90 and Case C-278/01, *Commission v. Spain*, para. 41.
165. Guidelines for calculating a lump sum had till then not been provided for by the Commission.
166. Case 304/02, *Commission v. France*. It concerned the compliance by France with Community measures for fisheries conservation and the unwillingness of France to abide by a 1991 (!) ruling of the Court to the effect that France had infringed these measures.
167. The Court decided to re-open the oral procedure in order to hear the parties in the proceedings about the proposals of the Advocate General. Thereafter, the Advocate General gave a second Opinion.

State to put an end as soon as possible to a breach of obligations which, in the absence of such a measure, would tend to persist and that

> the imposition of a lump sum is based more on assessment of the effects on public and private interests of the failure of the Member State concerned to comply with its obligations, in particular where the breach has persisted for a long period since the judgment which initially established it.[168]

A less ambiguous explanation of the objective of imposing a lump sum was given by the Advocate General in his First Opinion.[169] A periodic penalty payment may be effective in finally ensuring compliance, but where a Member State succeeds in complying with the obligations it neglected before such a penalty is payable, the final result may be that no sanction at all is imposed. But having to reckon with the imposition of a lump sum if a Member State has failed to comply with a 226 EC ruling at the stage of judicial proceedings may be an incentive to put an end to the infringement before reaching that stage.[170]

The Court considers the power of the Commission to make use of the procedure to induce Member States to fulfil their obligations as an 'essential power'.[171] It has, therefore, repudiated any attempts by defaulting Member States to frustrate these procedures by means of other procedures, or to mix up the matter dealt with therein with matters that ought to have been dealt with in other procedures.[172] Thus it will be to no avail that a Member State seeks to defend itself in infringement proceedings with an argument that the directive or decision which it is alleged to have failed to implement adequately or at all is tainted by illegality. A line of cases also demonstrates that a Member State may not rely on the alleged failure by one or more other Member States in order to justify its own failure to fulfil its obligations under Community law.[173] The Court has also rejected any attempt by a Member State to justify its failure to implement provisions of Community law on the ground that the provisions have direct effect.[174] The Court is prepared to guarantee

---

168. Case 304/02, *Commission v. France*, para. 81.
169. Paras 85–88, see also his second Opinion, para. 41.
170. The new guideline of the Commission (SEC(2000)1658, para. 10.3) announcing that it will henceforth propose simultaneously a penalty per day of delay after the delivery of the judgment under Art. 228 EC, and a lump sum penalizing the continuation of the infringement between the first judgment on non-compliance and the judgment delivered under Art. 228 seems to be more in harmony with the observations of the Advocate General on the objective of the lump sum sanction than with those of the Court. See for an application of this policy Case 503/04, *Commission v. Germany*, where no periodic penalty payment was imposed as at the date of examination of the facts by the Court Germany had adopted the measures to implement the Art. 226 judgment. The Court found however that the facts of the case were such that it did not appear necessary to order payment of a lump sum.
171. Joined Cases 2 & 3/62, *Commission v. Luxembourg and Belgium*.
172. E.g., ibid.; Case 7/61, *Commission v. Italy*; Joined Cases 90 & 91/63 *Commission v. Luxembourg and Belgium*; Joined Cases 6 & 11/69, *Commission v. France*; Case 31/69, *Commission v. Italy*, Case 226/87, *Commission v. Greece*, and Case C-404/97, *Commission v. Portugal*.
173. E.g., Case 52/75, *Commission v. Italy*; Case 78/76 *Firma Steinike und Weinlig v. Germany*, and Case C-38/89 *Ministère public v. Guy Blanguernon*.
174. Case 168/85, *Commission v. Italy*.

effective use of the Commission's power to initiate proceedings against Member States involved in infringements of obligations under the Treaties.

Finally, it should be noted that the Court has expressly stated that a Member State is responsible for a failure under Article 226 EC irrespective of the question of which national agency is actually responsible for the failure, even if this agency is independent according to national constitutional law.[175] Hence, decisions of national courts may give rise to a breach of a Member State's obligations, although the use of the infringement procedure will tend to be appropriate only where there is a widely-held judicial construction which has not been disowned by the supreme court, but rather confirmed by it and which constitutes a breach of Community law that can only be brought to an end through legislation.[176]

A Member State may not rely on national provisions or practices to justify its failure to fulfil its obligations or to comply with time-limits laid down in Community acts.[177] The Member States are obliged to take the necessary steps to fulfil their Community obligations by the due date, even in circumstances of political crisis.[178] Only an appeal to absolute impossibility to fulfil its obligations properly will be accepted by the Court as defence.[179] One may question whether this extremely strict position should not be qualified somewhat if it cannot reasonably be expected of a Member State that it fulfil its obligations within the required term, as a result of circumstances which are not due to action or failure to act of that Member State.

2.2   SUPERVISION OF THE ACTS OF THE INSTITUTIONS: ACTION
                FOR ANNULMENT; ACTION AGAINST FAILURE TO ACT

The action for annulment occupies, in practice, a central place amongst the judicial remedies provided for in the Treaties.[180] At the time at which the ECSC Treaty was concluded this procedure was clearly modelled on the *recours pour excès de pouvoir* in French administrative law. In one form or another, however, it is also found in the legal systems of the other Member States in the supervision of

---

175. E.g., Case 77/69, *Commission v. Belgium*. Thus, for example, action by local authorities can be attacked by infringement proceedings against the state concerned, e.g., Case 301/84, *Commission v. United Kingdom*(O.J. 1985, C40/4, withdrawn after the local authorities had put an end to the infringement, O.J. 1985, C275/6). See also Ch. III section 6.4.2.1. *supra*.

176. In that respect, isolated or numerically insignificant judicial decisions in the context of case law taking a different direction, or a construction disowned by the national supreme court, cannot be taken into account. See Case C-129/00, *Commission v. Italy*. Infringement of Community law by judicial bodies may also be the subject of cases involving Member State liability, cf. Case C-224/01, *Köbler v. Republik Österreich*.

177. Already in Case 30/72, *Commission v. Italy*.

178. Case 79/72, *Commission v. Italy*; Case 52/75, *Commission v. Italy*, Case 10/76, *Commission v. Italy* and Case 123/76, *Commission v. Italy*.

179. Constant case law in relation to Art. 88(2) EC applications, see, e.g., C-52/84, *Commission v. Belgium*.

180. Arts. 230 EC and 146 Euratom; see Art. 35(6) TEU. See the end of this Chapter for further reading.

the legality of administrative acts; this supervision is usually done by the administrative courts.[181]

2.2.1   Action for Annulment

The acts against which an action for annulment can be brought to the Court of Justice are, in particular, regulations, directives and decisions. Furthermore, any acts of the European Parliament and the Council jointly, the Council, the Commission, and the European Central Bank may be the subject of such an action (as long as they are not recommendations or opinions), as may acts adopted by the European Parliament which are intended to have legal effects *vis-à-vis* third parties;[182] the action may also be directed against 'sui generis' acts of the Institutions[183] and of the ECB.

No action lies against mere recommendations and opinions, confirmatory measures and implementing measures in relation to decisions already taken, nor, in principle, against internal instructions,[184] or against communications and acts of an internal character. As the Court noted in its judgment in *Reynolds* ' it is settled case law that only measures the legal effects of which are binding on, and capable of affecting the interests of, the applicant by bringing about a distinct change in his legal position are acts or decisions which may be the subject of an action for annulment'.[185] The form in which such acts or decisions are cast 'is, in principle, immaterial as regards the question whether they are open to challenge under that article'.[186] It is equally clear, the Court said, that in principle an act is open to review only if it is a measure definitively laying down the position

---

181.   See generally L. Prakke and C. Kortmann (eds), *Constitutional Law of 15 EU Member States* (2004) and C. Kortmann, J. Fleuren and W. Voermans (eds), *Constitutional Law of 10 EU Member States: The 2004 Enlargement* (Deventer, 2007).

182.   The text of Art. 230 EC as amended by the Treaty of Maastricht codifies the earlier case law of the Court of Justice, see Case 294/83, *Parti écologiste 'Les Verts' v. European Parliament*. Acts relating to the Parliament's internal organization may not be subject to an action under Art. 230, see Case T-17/00, *Rothley et al. v. Parliament* (on appeal C-167/02 P). For the (limited) possibilities to bring an action for annulment against acts of the Board of Directors and Board of Governors of the EIB, see Art. 237 under (b) and (c) EC.

183.   E.g., Case 22/70, *Commission v. Council* (ERTA) in this judgment, an action by the Commission contesting a Council resolution was held admissible because the resolution had definite legal effects both on relations between the Community and the Member States and on the relationship between Institutions. See also Case 2/71, *Germany v. Commission*, Joined Cases C-213/88 & 39/89, *Luxembourg v. Parliament* and Case C-316/91, *Parliament v. Council*.

184.   C-131/03 P, *R. J. Reynolds Tobacco Holdings Inc. and others*, para. 55.

185.   Ibid., para. 54; see also Case 60/81, *International Business Machines Corporation v. Commission*, para. 9 and T-193/04, *Tillack v. Commission*, para. 67. For these purposes the Court will look to see whether such acts, although adopted, e.g., in the form of internal instructions to Community officials or codes of conduct for the Member States, aim to impose obligations which do not already flow from Community law, see, e.g., Case C-366/88, *France v. Commission*, Case C-325/91, *France v. Commission*, Case C-57/95, *France v. Commission*, Case C-180/96, *United Kingdom v. Commission*, and Case C-443/97, *Spain v. Commission*. On Council conclusions that are intended to have legal effects, see Case C-27/04, *Commission v. Council* (*stability pact*).

186.   Case 60/81, *IBM*, para. 9.

of the Commission or the Council on the conclusion of the procedure concerned and not a provisional measure intended to pave the way for the final decision.[187] In the earlier discussion of the difference between decisions and non-binding acts[188] it was observed that in drawing the line between legally assailable and non-assailable acts the Court is largely guided by the interest which the Community's subjects have in legal protection against the act at issue.

Initially, only the Member States[189] (and not their autonomous territorial entities),[190] the Council and the Commission had a general right to bring an action for annulment. The Treaty of Maastricht extended this right also to the European Parliament and to the European Central Bank for the purpose of protecting their prerogatives, and the Treaty of Amsterdam did the same for the Court of Auditors.[191] The Treaty of Nice has in the meantime granted the European Parliament a general right to bring an action for annulment. These parties and Institutions thus form a class of privileged applicants, albeit with an important limitation for the European Central Bank and the Court of Auditors. It is true that the right of action has also been granted to private parties, but only with certain restrictions which are connected to the character and the effect of the contested act. In general, their right of action is virtually confined to decisions addressed to them or, under certain conditions, other acts of an individual character. Because of the importance of the subject the details of the right of action of private parties and the problems involved are discussed separately in section 2.3. of this chapter, below.

All those who are entitled to bring an action are obliged to do so within a given period of time (two months), dating, as the case may be, either from the publication

---

187. Cf. already Case 54/65, *Compagnie des Forges de Châtillon, Commentry & Neuves-Maisons v. High Authority*. See also Case 53/85, *AKZO Chemie BV et al. v. Commission*. See also Case C-147/96, *Netherlands v. Commission*.

188. In Ch. V, section 1.4, *supra*.

189. Community law does not impose an obligation on a Member State to bring an action for annulment or for failure to act for the benefit of one of its citizens, but does not in principle preclude national law from containing such an obligation or providing for liability to be imposed on the Member State for not having acted in such a way (Case C-511/03, *Netherlands v. Ten Kate Holding Musselkanaal BV*). The Lisbon Treaty opens the possibility that Member States, in accordance with their legal order, notify *on behalf of their national Parliament or a chamber of it* actions for annulment on grounds of infringement of the principle of subsidiarity by a legislative act, see Art. 8 of the Draft Protocol No. 2 on the application of the principles of subsidiarity and proportionality. According to the same Article, the Committee of the Regions may bring such actions against legislative acts for the adoption of which the Treaty on the Functioning of the EU provides that it be consulted.

190. Cf. Order in Case C-95/97, *Région wallonne v. Commission*. See P. van Nuffel, 'What's in a Member State? Central and Decentralized Authorities before Community Courts' (2001) CML Rev., 871-901. Thus, to the extent that they have legal personality, these bodies fall under the limited right of action under Art. 230(4) EC, see, e.g., C-452/98, *Netherlands Antilles v. Council* and C-417/04 P, *Regione Siciliana*.

191. Cf. Art. 173 EC. This codifies, in respect of the European Parliament, the case law of the Court of Justice, see Case C-70/88, *European Parliament v. Council (Chernobyl)*.

of the act concerned[192] or from its notification to the applicant or, failing that, from the day on which the applicant had knowledge of that act.[193]

There are four grounds of action:

(1) lack of competence;
(2) infringement of an essential procedural requirement;
(3) infringement of the Treaty or of any rule of law relating to its application;
(4) misuse of powers.

The first ground is self-explanatory, and does not call for further discussion. Examples justifying reliance on the second ground have been mentioned before: failure to give adequate reasons or to obtain the required proposals or opinions.

The ground which has the widest scope and which in practice is the most important is undoubtedly the third, which (if the other three were not mentioned separately) might well embrace grounds one, two and four as well. The term 'any rule of law relating to the application of the Treaty' includes provisions of international agreements by which the Community itself is bound.[194] Rules of law relating to the application of the Treaty also encompass rules of unwritten law.[195]

The fourth ground, misuse of powers (*détournement de pouvoir*), refers to a concept known in the law of each of the Member States, although its content varies rather widely between the different legal systems. From the case law of the Court it appears that in its interpretation of the concept, the Court has taken the various national systems of law as sources of inspiration, but pursued its own course, finding that

> a measure is only vitiated by misuse of powers if it appears, on the basis of objective, relevant and consistent evidence to have been taken with the exclusive or main purpose of achieving an end other than that stated or evading a procedure specifically prescribed by the Treaty for dealing with the circumstances of the case.[196]

If the Court reaches the conclusion that the action for annulment is justified on one of the above-mentioned grounds, the act concerned will be declared wholly or partly void in the Court's judgment.[197] The act is then void, as of the moment it

---

192. Cf. Art. 254 EC.
193. See Art. 230 last paragraph. As to the details, see Rules of Procedure of the Court of Justice (O.J. 1991, L 176/1, most recently amended O.J. 2006, L 386/44), Arts. 80–82; Rules of Procedure of the Court of First Instance (O.J. 1991, L 136/1, corrigendum O.J. 1991, L 317/34, most recently amended O.J. 2006, L 386/45), Arts. 101–103. See also 'Practice directions' O.J. 2004, L 361/15. For a strict application of the time-limits see, e.g., Case C-406/01, *Germany v. Parliament and Council*, in which a German action was found inadmissible because it was lodged one day too late.
194. E.g., Joined Cases 21–24/72, *International Fruit Company*. Cf. section 1.2, *supra*.
195. Cf. section 1.1, *supra*.
196. Case C-110/97, *Netherlands v. Council*, para. 137 and the cases cited.
197. Arts. 231 EC and 147 Euratom.

originated and with respect to everyone (*ex tunc* and *erga omnes* effects). It is, therefore, important that express provision has been made for the competence of the Court to state, in cases of annulled regulations, which of their effects shall be considered as definitive.[198]

Such provision refers in particular to the maintenance in force of acts which have been adopted in the meantime in implementation of the annulled regulation, and the maintenance in force of the effects of a regulation in the interests of legal certainty until it is replaced. This avoids the risk that an annulment will cause unreasonable damage to the interests of the Community or others. Accordingly, in Case 59/81 *Commission v. Council*,[199] the Court ruled that in order to avoid any lack of continuity in the system of remuneration, the provisions in the annulled regulations concerning the adjustment of remuneration of Community officials should continue to have effect until such time as the Council had adopted the measures incumbent upon it in order to ensure compliance with the judgment. Although the power to maintain the effects of an annulled act is only expressly conferred in Article 231 EC in relation to regulations, the Court has applied it by analogy in relation to directives[200] and decisions;[201] it has also applied it by analogy in respect of acts of the Community Institutions in the context of preliminary references from national courts.[202] The Court will be extremely reluctant to reach a conclusion that what purports to be an act of an institution is so defective that it must be characterized as non-existent; the main reason for this reluctance being legal certainty, thus there must be 'particularly serious and manifest defects' before non-existence will be established.[203]

The Institution whose act has been declared void is required to take the necessary measures to comply with the judgment.[204] The illegality of the annulled act may, if the relevant requirements have been met, give rise to a claim for damages to be paid by the Communities to the party injured by the act. The injured party may bring an action for damages before the Court in accordance with the

---

198. Arts. 231 EC and 147 Euratom (second paragraph in each case). Qualifying the extent of the nullity is to be distinguished from partial annulment of an act. Such a partial annulment is possible if the part to be annulled may be severed from the remainder of the act. The requirement of severability is not satisfied where the partial annulment of an act would have the effect of altering its substance (Case 540/03, *Parliament v. Council*). In such a case, the Court, by annulling a particular provision of an act and maintaining the other provisions, would substitute itself for the institution whose act is in dispute, see, *inter alia*, Case C-376/98, *Germany v. Parliament and Council* and Joined Cases T-195 & 207/01, *Government of Gibraltar v. Commission*.

199. See also Case 81/72, *Commission v. Council*.

200. E.g., Case C-295/90, *Parliament v. Council*.

201. E.g., Cases 34/86, *Council v. Parliament*; C-284/90, *Council v. Parliament*, C-271/94, *Parliament v. Council* and C-22/96 *Parliament v. Council*.

202. E.g., Joined Cases C-38/90 & 151/90, *Criminal proceedings against Lomas et al.* See, further, section 3.1.4. *infra*.

203. See Case 15/85, *Consorzio Cooperative d'Abruzzo v. Commission*; for a particularly notorious example, see the *PVC saga*, Joined Cases T-79/89 *etc. BASF AG et al. v. Commission*, overturned on appeal in Case C-137/92 P, *Commission v. BASF AG et al.* (but the Court of Justice then annulled the decision).

204. Arts. 233 EC and 149 Euratom. Joined Cases C-15 & 108/91, *Josef Buckl & Söhne OHG et al. v. Commission*.

general principles of the non-contractual liability of the Community.[205] As to this, see section 2.4, below.

2.2.2 Action against Failure to Act

Apart from the action for annulment, the Treaties also provide for an action against failure to act where such failure is contrary to Community law.[206] This action is meant to induce action by the Institution which failed to act, and can be directed at the Council, the Commission, the European Parliament and the European Central Bank. The Institution in question must first be formally called upon to act. This should be done within a reasonable period of it having become clear that the Institution is not going to act.[207] If it has not acted within two months, an action may be brought before the Court.

The aim of the action is for the Court to establish an infringement of the Treaty (and the Community law based thereupon) by the relevant Institution on account of its failure to act. Such failure is involved if the Institution, after having been called upon to act, 'has not defined its position' within two months. The Member States, the Institutions, the ECB in the areas falling within its competence, and private parties (natural and legal persons) may bring such an action. The right of action of a private party, however, is subject to restrictions (see section 2.3 below).

It is noteworthy that an action against failure to act is open to all the Institutions, i.e., also to the European Parliament.[208] Probably this right was accorded to the latter to enable it to lend force to its own rights under the Treaty: the right to be consulted by the Council in the cases provided for in the Treaty, and the right to dismiss the Commission by means of a motion of censure. However, the possibility is not excluded that the Parliament might use this procedure for other purposes. Given a reasonable use of the instrument, a means has thus been given to the Parliament for compelling the Council to define its position,[209] for embarking

---

205. Art. 288 EC, 2nd para., read with Art. 235 EC; cf. Art. 188 Euratom, 2nd para., read with Art. 151 Euratom. As to remedies for unsuccessful tenderers for contracts financed by the European Development Fund see P. Kalbe, 'The Award of Contracts and the Enforcement of Claims in the Context of EC External Aid and Development Cooperation' (2001) CML Rev., 1217–1267.

206. In French an *action en carence*; Arts. 232 EC and 148 Euratom. On this action: A.G. Toth, 'The Law as it Stands on the Appeal for Failure to Act' (1975) LIEI, 65, M. Dony-Bartholmé and T. Ronse, 'Réflexions sur la spécificité du recours de carence' (2000) *Cahiers de droit européen*, 595.

207. Cf. Case 59/70, *Netherlands v. Commission*. The Court deduced this from the common purpose of Arts. 33 and 35 of the old ECSC Treaty, from which it follows that the requirements of legal certainty and of the continuity of Community action underlying the time-limits for bringing proceedings laid down in Art. 33 ECSC must also be taken into account in the exercise of the rights conferred by Art. 35 ECSC. This reasoning applies by analogy for the corresponding provisions of the EC and Euratom treaties (implicitly for Euratom in Case C-107/91, *Empresa Nacional de Urânio SA v. Commission* and explicitly for the EC in Case C-170/02 P, *Schlüsselverlag J. S. Moser GmbH*).

208. And the Court of Auditors.

209. Art. 232, 2nd para., EC.

on a dialogue with the Council, and for aiding the Commission in its efforts to induce the Council to take decisions on the basis of the proposals the Commission has submitted. Thus, this procedure was used by the Parliament in its efforts to force the Council to remedy its failure to take the necessary measures in the field of transport policy.[210]

An action against failure to act is inadmissible if the Institution has *defined its position* within two months of being requested to do so. Article 232 EC does not lay down any formal conditions on this definition of position. It is sufficient that the applicant knows where he stands, whether the Institution will act on his application or not. This can be made known by means of the adoption of an act,[211] or by means of a communication which makes the refusal to act clear, or by definite promises which can be relied on later by those who had called upon the Institution to act, insofar at least as action in the short term cannot reasonably be requested under Community law. The last possibility takes account of the fact that sometimes complex and time-consuming procedures have to be set in motion. It is also sufficient if the Institution acts in relation to the object of the request; acting in a different manner from that which the requesting party regards as desirable or necessary is also the definition of a position.[212]

Where an Institution has defined its position within the prescribed period, the Court will not look further into the question of admissibility of the request under Article 232 EC in relation to other grounds.[213] The question arises only when the Institution has failed to define its position, for example, by not replying to the request within the deadline[214] or by stating that it will not react to the request because the Article 232 EC procedure is not applicable.[215]

If the act which was the object of the action for failure to act, is in fact adopted between the action being brought and the judgment being given, the action becomes devoid of purpose. After all: the remedy in Article 232 EC is based on the premise that a declaration can be obtained from the Court that the failure to act is contrary to the Treaty, in so far as it has not been repaired by the Institution(s) concerned. The Institution(s) concerned must then, under Article 233 EC, take the necessary measures to comply with the judgment, without prejudice to any actions in respect of non-contractual liability which may result from the judgment.[216] Such

---

210. Case 13/83, *European Parliament v. Council*; see Ch. IV, section 5.3., *supra*. However, the effectiveness of this procedure should not be over-estimated, see Case C-17/90, *Pinaud Wieger Spedition GmbH v. Bundesanstalt für den Güterfernverkehr*.
211. Such a definition of a position may consist of issuing a particular procedural measure in the context of competition law, cf. Case 8/71, *Deutscher Komponistenverband v. Commission* and Case 125/78, *GEMA v. Commission*.
212. E.g., Case 8/71, *Deutscher Komponistenverband*; Joined Cases 166/86 & 220/86, *Irish Cement Ltd v. Commission*.
213. E.g., Case 48/65, *Alfons Lütticke GmbH v. Commission* and Case 42/71, *Nordgetreide GmbH & Co. KG v. Commission*.
214. E.g., Case 90/78, *Granaria BV v. Council and Commission*.
215. E.g., Case 15/70, *Chevalley v. Commission*; Case 15/71, *Mackprang v. Commission* and Case 6/70, *Gillberto Borromeo Arese et al. v. Commission*.
216. Under Art. 288, 2nd para. read with Art. 235 EC (Arts. 188, 2nd para. and 151 Euratom).

a declaration by the Court has no further point if the result has, in fact, already been achieved.[217] It is, of course, open to the requesting party to whom a definition of position has been addressed to attack it under Article 230 EC; in this case the Court will look at the admissibility of that action under the criteria of that Article.[218] Thus, the definition of the Institution's position is not automatically an act which may be the subject of an action for annulment. An action against failure to act can, for instance, fail because a position has been defined, and yet an action for annulment also fail because the definition of a position is not an act or decision which may be the subject of an action under Article 230 EC.[219]

Finally, one point should be made about the judgment of the Court. In its judgment, the Court may decide that the failure to act constitutes an infringement of the Treaty. The Institution is then obliged to take the necessary measures to comply with the judgment,[220] which is to say to take a decision or at the very least to define its position. As to the possibility of bringing an action for damages in the event of an unlawful failure to act, see section 2.4 below.

| 2.3 | SUPERVISION OF ACTS OF THE INSTITUTIONS: THE RIGHT OF ACTION BY PRIVATE PARTIES; THE PLEA OF ILLEGALITY |

2.3.1 Limited Right of Action by Private Parties (Action for Annulment)

It has already been observed above that the Member States form a class of privileged applicants in the Community judicial order. The admissibility of their action for annulment of the acts of the Institutions is subject to no conditions other than those with respect to the period within which the action must be brought and the grounds to be advanced. They do not need to prove that they have a direct interest in an action, any more than the Council or the Commission themselves. Their interest in the strict application of Treaty law and in the maintenance of the balance of power, laid down in the Treaty, between the Institutions and between the Communities and themselves is presumed.[221] An action by private parties, on the other

---

217.   See Case 377/87, *European Parliament v. Council*; Case 383/87, *Commission v. Council* and Case C-25/91, *Pesqueras Echebastar SA v. Commission* (an incorrect declaration of inadmissibility); see also Joined Cases C-15 & 108/91, *Buckl* and Joined Cases T-194/97 & 83/98, *Branco v. Commission*.
218.   Cf. Case 8/71, *Deutscher Komponistenverband* and Case 125/78, *GEMA*. See further, Case T-64/89, *Automec Srl v. Commission*. Not every letter from an Institution or from the ECB in response to a request under Art. 232, 3rd para., EC will amount to a decision for the purposes of Art. 230 EC, 2nd para. Thus a letter from the President of the European Parliament, written as a matter of courtesy, in a case in which that Institution had no power to act on the request, was not a decision, see Case C-25/92, *Miethke v. European Parliament*.
219.   Cf. e.g., Case C-282/95, *Guérin automobiles v. Commission* and Joined Cases T-194/97 & 83/98, *Branco*.
220.   Arts. 233 EC and 149 Euratom (1st para. in each case).
221.   Cf. Case 230/81, *Luxembourg v. Parliament*.

hand, is only admissible if a number of other conditions have also been fulfilled, as implied in Article 230, fourth paragraph, EC; these conditions are connected with the nature and with the effects of the contested acts.

For private parties, an action against decisions addressed to them is always open. Private parties can bring an action *de pleine juridiction* (unlimited jurisdiction) against decisions by which a fine or periodic penalty payment is imposed on them; in these actions they do not have to limit themselves to advancing the four grounds of appeal mentioned above. The Court (as an Institution, so including the CFI) has full discretion to judge the facts which led to the application of the sanction, and may substitute its decision for that of the Institution which applied the sanction; it may cancel, lower, or increase the fine or the penalty. In the EC, sanctions can be laid down in Council regulations, or in regulations adopted by the Parliament and Council jointly.[222] An action in unlimited jurisdiction against these is open only if the Council in its regulations expressly confers unlimited jurisdiction on the Court.[223]

With respect to decisions addressed to parties other than themselves, and in the case of regulations and directives, the possibility for private parties to bring an action for annulment is limited. It is to these limiting conditions that this subsection will be largely devoted.

2.3.1.1   Actions against Decisions Addressed to Other Parties

The right of appeal by private parties is subject to more far-reaching limitations in the EC and Euratom systems than was the case in the ECSC system. This is apparent from the wording, which is unmistakably intended to be more restrictive than that used in the ECSC Treaty[224] and stands in the way of the application in those newer systems of the broader interpretation which the Court had given to the ECSC provisions.[225,226]

---

222. Cf. Art. 23 of the new competition Regulation, Reg. 1/2003, O.J. 2003, L 1/1.
223. Art. 229 EC, cf. Reg. 1/2003, ibid., Art. 31.
224. In the ECSC system, undertakings had the right of action 'against decisions or recommendations concerning them which are individual in character'. (Art. 33, 2nd para. ECSC). In its case law, the Court refused to link the concepts of 'individual' on the one hand and 'concerning' on the other; it interpreted 'concerning' in the sense of interests being affected by an individual decision; thus a decision which may affect the competitive relationship between undertakings could be challenged by a competitor of the addressee.
225. By using a more restrictive wording, the contracting parties to the later treaties hoped to prevent the continuation of the 'liberal' ECSC case law of the Court in the context of the EC and Euratom.
226. Cf. Joined Cases 16 & 17/62, *Confédération nationale des producteurs de fruits et légumes et al. v. Council*: the Court admitted that the newer systems were more restrictive but felt it inappropriate for it to pronounce on their merits. For critical comments, *inter alia* H. Rasmussen, 'Why Is Article 173 Interpreted Against Private Plaintiffs?' (1980) EL Rev., 112. For a restatement of the position of the Court on this point, see the cases cited *infra* note 275.

An action is open to a private party (whether a natural or a legal person)[227] against a decision 'which, although in the form of a regulation or a decision addressed to another person, is of direct and individual concern' to the applicant.[228] Thus it is not enough that a private party is affected in his interests by a decision addressed to someone else; the decision must be 'of direct and individual concern' to the applicant.[229]

The Court had its first occasions to pronounce on the requirements for the admissibility of actions against decisions addressed to others in actions brought by private parties against Commission decisions addressed to Member States. In *Plaumann*,[230] the Commission argued that the words 'another person' – in the phrase 'a regulation or a decision addressed to another person' – could not refer to Member States 'in their capacity as sovereign authorities', and that thus individuals should not be allowed to challenge decisions of the Council or the Commission addressed to a Member State. The Court rejected that argument. It held that as Article 230 EC neither defined nor limited the scope of 'another person', the words and the natural meaning of that provision justified the broadest interpretation, particularly since 'provisions of the Treaty regarding the right of interested parties to bring an action must not be interpreted restrictively'.[231]

However, the Court evidently felt that the terms of the Treaty obliged it to take a narrow view when, in the same case, it had to define the meaning of the words 'of individual concern'. It concluded that a decision can only be of individual concern to persons other than the addressee if it affects third parties 'by reason of certain attributes which are peculiar to them or by reason of circumstances in which they are differentiated from all other persons and by virtue of these factors distinguishes them individually just as in the case of the person addressed'.[232] It appears from this formula, repeated by the Court in later judgments,[233] that private parties wishing to bring an action against decisions addressed to other persons are confronted with a formidable barrier in the fourth paragraph of Article 230 EC. The issue is not only *whether* such parties are affected by the consequences of a decision, but also *how* they are affected: this must be because of certain characteristics which are particular to them or by reason of a specific situation by reference

---

227. It should be noted that the concept of a legal person in Art. 230 EC does not necessarily coincide with that concept in the various national legal orders, cf. Case 135/81, *Groupement des Agences de Voyages, Asbl v. Commission* (referring to earlier judgments). The category of legal persons includes autonomous bodies of the Member States, see *supra* note 190.
228. Arts. 230 EC and 146 Euratom (4th para. in each case).
229. This also applies to associations which base their standing on the circumstance that the persons they represent are directly and individually concerned, see, e.g., Case C-321/95 P, *Greenpeace and Others v. Commission*.
230. Case 25/62, *Plaumann v. Commission*; for a recent application of the *Plaumann* formula by the Court of First Instance, see Case T-138/98, *ACAV and others v. Council*.
231. Case 25/62, *Plaumann* at 107 of the English version.
232. Ibid.
233. The slight variations in wording which occasionally occur are not significant, e.g., Case 26/86, *Deutz und Geldermann v. Council*; Case T-219/95 R, *Danielsson et al. v. Commission*.

to which they are individually described in a way similar to that of the addressee of the decision.[234]

A decision is also the means by which the Commission authorizes, or refuses to authorize, Member States to take certain measures by virtue of a safeguard clause. It is also by means of a decision that the Commission determines for the Member States, with binding effect, the c.i.f. prices on the basis of which they are to fix the levies and export subsidies (refunds) for particular agricultural products. Importers or exporters, for instance, may have an interest in the annulment of decisions of this type addressed to Member States. However, in the light of the formula used by the Court, the chance that an action bought by one of them will be admissible is very small. Such a party will be affected by these decisions in his or her capacity as an importer or exporter. Thus in *Plaumann* the Court classed the applicant, an importer of clementines, as a person affected 'by reason of a commercial activity which may at any time be practised by any person and is not therefore such as to distinguish the applicant in relation to the contested decision as in the case of the addressee'.[235] The capacity as an importer of a given product is not particular to him or her, but to all members of a group which can be described only in an abstract way because, at least potentially, anyone may belong to this group. Even if the number and identity of the importers affected by the consequences of such a decision could be determined, this still does not constitute a factual situation which is, as compared with all other persons, particularly relevant to them, if this results from purely fortuitous circumstances.[236]

Only in a few cases so far could the barrier of individual concern be overcome. In those cases there was no question of *fortuitous* circumstances on the basis of which certain persons, the number and identity of whom could be determined, were affected by a decision; the number and identity of these persons were determined, and could be determined at the moment at which the decision was taken and the Commission was in a position to know that its decision affected only the interests and the legal position of these persons. In these circumstances they were differentiated and distinguished individually, as compared with all other persons, in a way similar to that of the addressee of the decision.[237] Fortuitous circumstances are not at issue when the number and identity of those who will be affected by a decision can be determined, and the adoption of the decision is in any way

---

234. There is no problem in cases such as those involving a Commission decision addressed to a Member State concerning a state aid to a particular undertaking, see, e.g., Case 730/79, *Philip Morris v. Commission*, and Joined Cases 296 & 318/82, *The Netherlands et al. v. Commission*.
235. Case 25/62, *Plaumann*, at 107 of the English version.
236. Case 38/64, *Getreide-Import Gesellschaft v. Commission*. See *inter alia* Case 1/64, *Gluco-series Réunies v. Commission* and Case 97/85, *Union Deutsche Lebensmittelwerke GmbH et al. v. Commission*. Even if a party is the only importer affected by a Commission decision addressed to a Member State, that party will not be found individually concerned (unless he or she forms part of a closed class, as is explained in the text); see, in this very restrictive sense, e.g., Case 231/82, *Spijker Kwasten BV v. Commission*.
237. Joined Cases 106 & 107/63, *Alfred Toepfer et al. v. Commission*. See also Case 62/70, *Bock v. Commission*. See, further, e.g., Case 92/78, *SpA Simmenthal v. Commission*; Case 112/77,

influenced by their identity or their actual or probable conduct; there is then a causal link between the acquaintance with the specific situation in which those persons find themselves and the decision taken.[238] But even if such a causal link is missing, special circumstances may mean that the action is admissible. That may be the case, for instance, when there is a duty of care,[239] that is to say the Institution had the obligation to ascertain the effects of an intended decision for certain persons.[240]

For the action to be admissible, the decision addressed to other persons must affect a third party not only individually, but also *directly*. When does a decision addressed to Member States affect a private party directly? As a rule it is characteristic of such decisions that their consequences for private parties manifest themselves indirectly, i.e., in the national measures which have been taken or maintained under these decisions. If the national authorities have no discretion whatever in this connection, these measures may be equated to Community decisions, which accordingly may affect private parties directly.[241] But even if the national measures have a discretionary character, private parties may be affected directly by the Community decisions on which these measures are based, if the possibility that the addressee of the decision (a Member State) does not give effect to the measure 'is purely theoretical and their intention to act in conformity with it is not in doubt'.[242]

The view that the Court would not apply the test for direct and individual concern with the same strictness in considering actions brought by private parties against decisions addressed not to Member States but to *other private parties* received a certain amount of support in the judgment in *Société 'Eridania' Zuccherifici Nazionali et al. v. Commission*.[243] The formulation which the Court tends to use in examining an action by a private party against a decision addressed to a Member State is not to be found in this judgment; the Court looked at whether there were 'specific circumstances' which could enable a private party to bring an action, but did not develop the concept of 'specific circumstances' in any general definition. It did observe, though, that the 'mere fact that a measure may exercise an

---

August Töpfer & Co. GmbH v. Commission; Case 88/76, *Société pour l'exportation des sucres SA v. Commission*; Case 11/82, *Piraiki-Patraiki et al. v. Commission*, with the overview of previous case law by VerLoren van Themaat, Adv. Gen., and Case 1/84 R, *Ilford v. Commission*.

238. Cf. Waelbroeck in e.g., (1978) *Rev. Crit. de Jur. Belge.*, 105–106 and in Mégret et al. (eds), *Le Droit de la CEE*, Vol. 10, 2nd ed. (Brussels, 1993) 132.

239. See R. Barents, *Procedures en procesvoering voor het Hof van Justitie en het Gerecht van Eerste Aanleg van de EG*, 3rd ed. (Deventer, 2002), para. 297.

240. Case 11/82, *Piraiki-Patraiki*; cf. what the Court said on this case in Case C-209/94 P, *Buralux et al. v. Council*. See also Case C-152/88, *Sofrimport v. Commission* and Case C-390/95 P, *Antillean Rice Mills et al.*

241. E.g., Case C-417/04 P, *Regione Siciliana*, para. 28.

242. Case C-386/96 P, *Société Louis Dreyfus & Cie v. Commission*, at para. 44. See that judgment at paras 43-44 for a summary of the case law concerning the requirement that private parties are 'directly concerned' by decisions addressed to Member States.

243. Joined Cases 10 & 18/68, *Société 'Eridania' Zuccherifici Nazionali et al. v. Commission*.

influence on the competitive relationships existing on the market in question cannot suffice to allow any trader in any competitive relationship whatever with the addressee to be regarded as directly and individually concerned by that measure'.[244]

Particularly in the field of competition law, interested third parties had to be given ample possibilities of contesting Commission decisions (such as exemption decisions under Art. 81(3) EC) before the Court. The long-awaited judgment in a competition case came in 1977 in *Metro SB-Großmärkte*.[245] The Court declared an appeal by an interested third party (Metro) against a decision addressed by the Commission to another undertaking (SABA) to be admissible. However, it refrained from formulating any general criteria. The circumstances which differentiated the applicant from all other persons and distinguished it individually, just as in the case of the addressee, were that the contested decision was adopted in particular as a result of a complaint from Metro relating to the provisions of a selective distribution system operated by SABA, which were relied upon to justify a refusal to deal with Metro or to appoint it as a wholesaler for SABA products. The Court concluded that it was

> in the interests of a satisfactory administration of justice and of the proper application of Articles [81 (ex 85)] and [82 (ex 86)] that natural or legal persons who are entitled, pursuant to Article 3(2)(b) of Regulation No. 17, to request the Commission to find an infringement of Articles [81] and [82] should be able, if their request is not complied with either wholly or in part, to institute proceedings in order to protect their legitimate interests.[246]

The starting point remains the *Plaumann* formula; differentiating circumstances in the sense of that judgment are present, according to constant case law, if a regulation, such as Regulation 2003/1[247] in the competition field, or Regulation 2176/84[248] on anti-dumping, affords procedural guarantees to undertakings which enable them to request the Commission to find an infringement of Community rules. In such cases, undertakings must have a right of action in order to protect their legitimate interests.[249] If they have not lodged the complaint themselves then it will be relevant to examine their role in the pre-contentious proceedings, e.g., to see if they have been concerned in the development of the complaint which led to the opening of the investigation procedure, or if they have been heard, or if their observations have

---

244. Ibid., at para. 7.
245. Case 26/76, *Metro SB-Großmärkte GmbH & Co. KG v. Commission*; see also Joined Cases C-68/94 & C-30/95, *French Republic and Société commerciale des potasses et de l'azote (SCPA) and Entreprise minière et chimique (EMC) v. Commission*, and further Case T-37/92, *BEUC and NCC v. Commission*, and Case T-12/93, *CCE Vittel v. Commission*.
246. Case 26/76, *Metro*, para. 13.
247. O.J. 2003, L 1/1, and previously Reg. 17.
248. O.J. 1984, 201/1. See also Ch. XIII. Anti-dumping duties are established by regulation, see the discussion on this instrument, under 2.3.1.2. *infra*.
249. Case 26/76, *Metro*; Case 210/81, *Oswald Schmidt, trading as Demo-Studio Schmidt v. Commission*; Case 191/82, *FEDIOL v. Commission*, and Case 264/82, *Timex Corporation v. Council and Commission*.

substantially determined the conduct of the proceedings; their position on the market to which the contested legislation applies can also be taken into account.[250] A similar approach to the question of admissibility is also involved when the Commission investigates state aids, given that Article 88(2) EC gives undertakings, in general terms, the right to submit their comments to the Commission. In such cases, undertakings who have played a significant role in these proceedings must be able to show in addition that their position on the market is substantially affected by the state aid which is the subject of the decision challenged.[251]

2.3.1.2 *Actions against Regulations (and Directives)*[252]

An action by private parties against regulations *stricto sensu* is impossible. They may only institute proceedings against decisions which, 'although in the form of a regulation . . . are of direct and individual concern to them'.[253] The regulation must therefore in reality be a decision or a similar act of an individual nature, and this decision or act must be of direct and individual concern to the applicant. The purpose of this provision, according to the Court,

> is in particular to prevent the Community institutions, merely by choosing the form of a regulation, from being able to exclude an application by an individual against a decision of direct and individual concern to him and thus to make clear that the choice of form may not alter the nature of a measure.[254]

In dealing with the question of whether what purports to be a regulation is indeed one or not the Court does not take a very formalistic view. In the first place it considers that the aim and content of the purported regulation is decisive, not its form or name.[255] It is therefore necessary to examine the nature of the contested measures and in particular the legal effects which they are intended to produce or in fact produce.[256] Thus a regulation may actually be a bundle of decisions.[257]

---

250. E.g., Case 264/82, *Timex*, and Case 75/84, *Metro*.
251. Case C-106/98 P, *Comité d'Entreprise de la Société Française de Production and others*. For case law relating to associations of enterprises, Joined Cases 67,68 & 70/85, *Van der Kooy and others v. Commission* and Case C-313/90 *CIRFS v. Commission*. On these subjects more extensively J.A. Winter, 'The Rights of Complainants in State Aid Cases: Judicial Review of Commissions Decisions Adopted under Articles 88 (ex. 93) EC' (2000) CML Rev., 521.
252. The Court appears to treat directives, as acts of general application, like regulations, as far as the right of appeal by private parties is concerned; see, implicitly (and referring to earlier authorities), Case C-298/89, *Government of Gibraltar v. Council*. See also Case T-135/96, *UEAPME v. Council* and Joined Cases T-125/96 & T-152/96, *Boehringer Ingelheim Vetmedica GmbH and C.H. Boehringer Sohn v. Council*.
253. Arts. 230 EC and 146 Euratom (4th para. in each case).
254. E.g., Case 307/81, *Alusuisse v. Council and Commission.*, para. 7.
255. See Ch. V, section 1.1, *supra*.
256. Case 307/81, *Alusuisse*.
257. Joined Cases 41-44/70, *International Fruit Company et al. v. Commission*; see also Case 113/77, *NTN Toyo Bearing Company Ltd et al. v. Council*; Case 118/77, *ISO v. Council*; Case 120/77, *Koyo Seiko Co. Ltd et al. v. Council and Commission*.

Secondly, the Court recognizes the possibility that measures, even if as a whole they have the characteristics of a regulation, 'may nevertheless contain provisions addressed to specific persons in such a way as to distinguish them individually in the sense of the second paragraph of Article [230] of the Treaty'.[258]

Two questions are relevant for the admissibility of the action by a private party against a regulation (or a part thereof): (1) is it a regulation *stricto sensu* or a decision, or similar? and if the latter, (2) is this decision of direct and individual concern to the applicant? Since a decision will by definition be of direct and individual concern to a given party (a Member State or an individual), the two questions are closely linked,[259] although it is of course conceivable that a regulation must be qualified as a decision or a similar act, but that an applicant is not directly and individually affected by it, for instance because it is actually addressed to Member States.

The difference between a regulation and a decision lies exclusively in the nature of the measure itself and the legal effects which it produces and not in the procedures for its adoption.[260] The decisive factor which bestows on an act the quality of a regulation is its general import, and this implies that it 'is applicable to objectively determined situations and involves legal consequences for categories of persons viewed in a general and abstract manner'.[261] A decision, on the other hand, is characterized by the fact that the category of those to whom it is addressed is limited. It applies to a limited number of natural or legal persons that are identified or can be identified.[262] The difficulty is, however, that regulations, too, may sometimes actually apply to a limited number of identifiable persons.

According to the case law of the Court, however, the regulatory character of an act is not lost merely because it is possible to determine with a greater or lesser degree of accuracy the number or even the identity of the persons to whom it applies at any given time, provided that the measure clearly applies 'as a result

---

258. Case 30/67, *Industria Molatoria Imolese et al v. Council*, at 121 of the English edition; see also Joined Cases 16 & 17/62, *Confédération nationale des producteurs de fruits et légumes*, and Case 112/77, *August Töpfer*.

259. The Court sometimes tends to pass over the first question, see e.g., Case 40/64, *Sgarlata et al. v. Commission* and Case 123/77, *Unione Nazionale Importatori e Commercianti Motoveicoli Esteri (UNICME) et al. v. Council*; and Joined Cases C-232 & 233/91, *Odette Nikou PetridiAE et al. v. Commission*. On this question, see Lauwaars, 'The Admissibility of the Action for Annulment: The IBM Case' in D. O'Keeffe and H.G. Schermers (eds), *Essays in European Law and Integration* (Deventer, 1982), 29, 37–38. Lauwaars argues that not all acts which directly and individually concern a party must by definition be qualified as decisions. The case law mentioned at the end of this section seems to support his view. As to the rights of defence, generally, see *Due Process in the Administrative Procedure* (FIDE Congress Reports Copenhagen, 1978, Vol. 3). See also *Procedures and Sanctions in Economic Administrative Law* (FIDE Congress Reports Berlin, 1996, Vol. 3).

260. Case 307/81, *Alusuisse*.

261. Case 6/68, *Zuckerfabrik Watenstedt GmbH v. Council*, at 415 of the English edition. See also, e.g., Joined Cases 789 & 790/79, *Calpak SpA et al. v. Commission* and, further, Ch. V, section 1.2, *supra*.

262. Joined Cases 16 & 17/62, *Confédération nationale des producteurs de fruits et légumes*.

of an objective situation of fact or law which it specifies and which is in harmony with its ultimate objective'.[263] If, therefore, a provision of a regulation can be objectively justified on the basis of the regulation's imperative objective in conjunction with a specific factual context, it may retain its character as a regulation even if it applies to legal subjects whose number and identity can be determined. Likewise, provisions which restrict the application of a regulation for a particular period or by reference to a particular area or territory do not in doing so lose their normative character.[264]

As mentioned earlier,[265] directives – as acts of general application – are treated in the same way as regulations as far as the rights of private parties to challenge them are concerned. The question arises in this context whether provisions of a directive, which after all must be implemented by national rules, are capable of directly affecting private parties. This will depend on the extent to which Member States enjoy a margin of discretion in implementing the directives. Where the directive requires a more or less literal transposition of provisions it contains, which is often the case, then the condition of direct concern is met.[266]

The case law which has developed in the field of anti-dumping, in relation to attempts to challenge anti-dumping duties definitively imposed by the Council, often preceded by provisional duties imposed by the Commission, after an investigation proceeding conducted by the Commission, has abandoned a strictly literal interpretation of Article 230, fourth paragraph, EC. From this case law it is evident that for the admissibility of an action by a private party, the question whether the regulation (or a part of it) is in reality a decision, or similar act (thus an 'improper regulation'), which concerns him individually and directly, is not decisive, despite the literal wording of Article 230, fourth paragraph EC. Even a 'true' regulation can be of individual concern to an applicant,[267] a fact which was confirmed in so

---

263. Case 6/68, *Zuckerfabrik Watenstedt*, at 415 of the English edition. See also, e.g., Case 64/69, *La Compagnie Française Commerciale et Financière SA v. Commission* and Case 242/81, *Société Roquette Frères v. Council*; Joined Cases 97/86 etc., *Asteris AE et al. v. Commission*; Joined Cases C-15 & 108/91, *Buck* and Case C-167/02 P, *Willi Rothley and others v. Parliament* para. 27.

264. See Case 6/68, *Zuckerfabrik Watenstedt*, and Case 64/69, *La Compagnie Française Commerciale et Financière*. See further, e.g., Joined Cases 103–109/78, *Société des Usines de Beauport et al. v. Council*; Case 26/86, *Deutz und Geldermann v. Council*, and the Order in Case C-168/93, *Government of Gibraltar et al. v. Council*, in which a (temporary) territorial limitation of a directive was at issue.

265. See note 252 *supra*.

266. But see the judgment of the CFI in Joined Cases T-172/98 & T-175-177/98, *Salamander et al. v. Parliament and Council*. In his annotation of the case (SEW 2001, 155–159), Van Ooik points out that the CFI confuses the question of direct concern with that of the restriction on direct effect of directives. This confusion is no longer evident in, e.g., the judgment in Case T-223/01, *Japan Tobacco Inc. v. Parliament and Council*.

267. The Court tends not to pay specific attention to the question whether anti-dumping duties also meet the criterion of direct concern; see also the ball bearings cases, Case 113/77, *NTN Toyo Bearing Company Ltd et al. v. Council*; Case 118/77 *ISO v. Council*; Case 119/77, *Nippon*

many words in the *Extramet* case,[268] discussed below. In the anti-dumping case law,[269] the Court has accepted the possibility that regulations imposing anti-dumping duties may be of direct and individual concern to a particular person or group, while retaining their general normative character. Not only the party complaining of dumping practices is directly and individually concerned by the decision imposing duties, but also certain producers and exporters accused of dumping may be have standing to challenge the regulation, if they can show that they are identified in the regulation or that they were involved in the administrative proceeding leading to the adoption of the measure concerned. Also the so-called 'associated importers' (i.e., those importers whose resale price is used for the calculations which lead to the imposition of the duties, because of some kind of association between the exporter and the importer) will be able to challenge the regulation concerned.

Independent importers are normally given no standing to challenge anti-dumping regulations, as they are affected only in their general capacity as importers. Here too, an exception to the normal approach has been made by the Court, for an independent importer whose situation was unlike that of any other importer owing to the exceptional circumstances involved (in Case C-358/89 *Extramet*).[270] Outside the field of anti-dumping measures, exceptional circumstances of a similar nature have also led, on one occasion, to an action by a private party challenging a regulation being found admissible, although strictly speaking, the applicant was affected only in its capacity as a producer (Case C-309/89, *Codorniu*).[271] These two cases confirm a tendency in the case law to see the individual nature of the effects of a generally applicable rule as sufficient condition for the admissibility of an action, leaving aside the question of whether the act challenged is a true regulation. Moreover, it appears from these judgments that in exceptional cases[272] the Court is prepared to apply the test of individual concern quite flexibly

---

Seiko KK et al. v. Council and Commission; Case 120/77, *Koyo Seiko Co. Ltd et al. v. Council and Commission* and Case 121/77, *Nachi Fujikoshi Corporation et al. v. Council*.

268. Case C-358/89, *Extramet Industrie SA v. Council*, at para. 14, 'measures imposing anti-dumping duties may, without losing their character as regulations, be of individual concern in certain circumstances to certain traders'. See also the (agricultural) Case C-309/89, *Codorniu v. Council*.

269. For a recent summary of this case law, see Case C-239/99, *Nachi Europe v. Hauptzollamt Krefeld*.

270. Extramet was the largest importer of calcium metal and also the end-user of the product. Moreover, Extramet had been refused supplies from the sole Community producer which was at the same time its main competitor for the processed product.

271. Case C-309/89, *Codordiu v. Council*. This case involved a firm which as a result of a regulation would lose the right to use the term 'crémant', although it had registered the graphic mark 'Gran Crémant de Codorniu' in Spain already in 1924, and had used it ever since.

272. In Case C-358/89, *Extramet*, a strict application of the test would – given the position in which the undertaking found itself – not have made sense; in Case C-309/89, *Codordiu v. Council*, the undertaking would have lost the right to use the term 'crémant' only after five years, so that only at the end of this period, and by means of committing an illegal act in the form of using the prohibited term, would it have had the possibility of challenging the validity of the relevant provision of the regulation by means of national proceedings.

in relation to regulations. This has not led to a more general broadening of standing for private parties.[273] On the contrary, an attempt by the CFI to give an entirely new interpretation to the element of 'individual concern', in its judgment in the *Jégo Quéré* case, was firmly refused by the Court of Justice a few months later in the appeal in the *UPA* Case.[274]

> Although the condition [of being individually concerned] must be interpreted in the light of the principle of effective judicial protection by taking account of the various circumstances that may distinguish an applicant individually, such an interpretation cannot have the effect of setting aside the condition in question, expressly laid down in the Treaty, without going beyond the jurisdiction conferred by the Treaty on the Community Courts.[275]

2.3.1.3 Concluding Remarks

In the above sections, the general lines of the relevant case law have been presented, which – as some commentators have remarked[276] – have increasingly revealed a case-by-case approach on the part of the Court. The abstract formulations, such as those concerning the distinction between regulations and decisions, and individual concern, with which the Court has tried to 'translate' the restriction on the right of action for private parties contained in Article 230, fourth paragraph EC, have led to some problems in terms of application. On the one hand, they leave too much margin to lead to a clear result in all cases, and on the other hand, they offer too little basis to avoid a reference to the specific circumstances of the applicant. The development in the case law whereby in some areas – such as competition rules, state aids and anti-dumping – more concrete elements are emerging for an applicable test should thus be greeted favourably.

The case law meets two types of criticism. In the first place, it is said to lack consistency. The inevitability of a case-by-case approach, as well as the court's overload, are certainly two contributory factors. Since the establishment of the CFI, it is this court which is in first instance the source of the case law on questions of admissibility entailed by the huge quantity of actions by private parties. The

---

273. See further A. Arnull, 'Private Applicants and the Action for Annulment since Codorniu' (2001) CML Rev., 7-52 and J. Usher, 'Direct and Indirect Concern: An Effective Remedy or a Conventional Solution'? (2003) EL Rev., 102.

274. See Case T-177/01, *Jégo-Quéré v. Commission*, and on appeal Case C-263/02 P, *Jégo-Quéré v. Commission* and Case C-50/00, *Unión de Pequeños Agricultores v. Council*. A.G. Jacobs, in his Opinion in the *UPA* Case, had proposed relaxing the case law, and this was not lost on the CFI (see paras 45 and 49 of the CFI's judgment). See also the case note on *Commission v. Jégo-Quéré* by Brown and Morijn in (2004) CML Rev., 1639.

275. Case C-50/00, *Union de Pequeños Agricultores*, para. 44, repeated in Case C-167/02 P, *Willi Rothley*, para. 47.

276. E.g., R. Barents, op. cit. *supra* note 239, para. 255. For an effort two distinguish three approaches in the case law concerning challenges to regulations and decisions by individuals ('infringements of rights or breach of duties', 'degree of factual injury' and 'pure Plaumann'), see Craig and De Búrca, *EU Law*, 3rd ed. (2003) 496–500.

Court of Justice only fairly rarely has the opportunity to rule on these elements on appeal. Moreover, the CFI adopts the formal view that it is only bound to the case law of the Court of Justice in the circumstances described in Article 61, second paragraph of the Statute of the Court ('where a case is referred back to the CFI, that Court shall be bound by the decision of the Court of Justice on points of law') and according to the principle of 'res judicata'.[277] Consequently, the CFI does not hesitate to depart from the case law of the ECJ when it deems this necessary.[278]

The second type of criticism concerns matters of principle. The case law on Article 230 paragraph 4 is criticized as being unnecessarily restrictive. In this context, reference is made to the creative judicial decision-making with respect to, for instance, the active and passive right of action of the European Parliament;[279] here, the Court of Justice considered itself less bound to the letter of the Treaty provision. It should also be recalled that the Court had already bound itself at an early stage, by considering that under the EC rules on standing for private parties, stricter conditions apply than under the (old) ECSC rules, and that it was not up to the Court to pronounce on the merits of that difference.[280] It is difficult for the Court to go back on that statement.

If one views the restrictions on private parties' direct right of application for annulment in the context of the whole system of remedies at the disposal of private parties, this criticism as a matter of principle invites some comment (see the Court's comments on this in *UPA*[281]). The plea of illegality provides the opportunity to invoke the illegality of an act of the Community whenever such a Community act is applied to a private party in a particular case, by means of a decision or similar Community act.[282] Similarly, a private party may challenge the validity of a Community act before a national court at the moment the act is implemented by the authorities of a Member State and thus affects him.[283] In *Unibet*, however, the Court held that, if the only possible form of legal remedy for disputing the compatibility of a national provision with Community law would be to violate that provision in order to be able to dispute such compatibility in subsequent Court proceedings, this would be insufficient to secure effective judicial protection.[284]

---

277. Case T-162/94, *NMB et al. v. Commission*. See also Joined Cases T-177 & 377/94, *Altmann et al v. Commission*.
278. See on this A. Arnull, The *European Union and its Court of Justice*, 2nd ed. (2006) 633–637. A stark example is provided by the CFI's judgment in Case T-177/01, *Jégo Quéré v. Commission*.
279. Case C-294/83, '*Les Verts*' I and Case C-70/88, *European Parliament v. Council* (*Chernobyl*).
280. Joined Cases 16 & 17/62, *Confédération nationale des producteurs de fruits et légumes*.
281. Case C-50/00, *Unión de Pequeños Agricultores*.
282. See section 2.3.3. *infra*.
283. See section 3.1.4. *infra*. According to the principle of sincere cooperation (Art. 10 EC) national courts are required, as far as possible, to interpret and apply national procedural rules in a way that enables private parties to challenge before the courts the legality of any decision or other national measure relative to the application to them of a Community act of general application, by pleading the invalidity of such an act. The same holds true where a private party invokes a failure to take a decision which it considers to be contrary to Community law (Case C-511/03, *Ten Kate*, para. 29).
284. Case C-432/05, *Unibet*, para. 64.

Finally, private parties may sue the Community for damages which they have suffered as a result of illegal action by one of the Institutions.[285]

Nevertheless, there remain cases in which a private party cannot reasonably employ these alternative remedies.[286] The *Codorniu* case is a prime example.[287] In such situations, the case law risks infringing the right to effective judicial protection laid down *inter alia* in Article 6 ECHR, a right which, according to the same case law, must be respected by the Member States in relation to the enforcement of Community law rights.[288] Moreover, if it were possible to scrutinize a decision addressed to a Member State (or a regulation or directive) in the more balanced context of a direct action, this could avoid the need for a large number of preliminary references on its validity being brought by national courts. In addition, within the EU increasing emphasis is being put on fundamental rights and freedoms, and in that framework it would seem desirable to create more room for private individuals to challenge acts of the Institutions which *prima facie* conflict with those rights and freedoms. Finally, the time has come to link up with developments in the legal systems of the Member States concerning public interest litigation, and to grant groups which aim to protect collective material or immaterial interests, under certain conditions, a right to challenge the acts mentioned in Articles 230, first paragraph EC.[289] A more satisfactory regulation of standing for private parties in the sense described above would, however, be hard to attain without Treaty amendment, as the Court also intimated in *UPA*.[290] In that respect the Lisbon Treaty innovates by amending the provision corresponding to the present Article 230, paragraph 4, EC, so as to allow also a remedy for any natural or legal person against a regulatory act which is of direct concern to them and does not entail implementing measures (Art. 263, paragraph 4, Treaty on the Functioning of the European Union (TFEU)).

---

285. See section 2.4 *infra*.
286. K. Lenaerts, 'The Legal Protection of Private Parties under the EC Treaty: a Coherent and Complete System of Judicial Review'? in *Scritti in onore di Giuseppe Federico Mancini*, Vol. II, 591. According to the Lisbon Treaty, Member States have to 'provide remedies sufficient to ensure effective legal protection in the fields covered by Union law' (Art. 19, para. 1 TEU (Lisbon)).
287. Case C-309/89, *Codorniu v. Council*. However, the circumstances of that case regarded the impossibility of requesting in Spanish proceedings a declaration in law about the use of a graphic mark, and in that framework requesting invalidity of the relevant provision of the regulation. It would be hard to take this as a decisive criterion for admissibility before the ECJ, since the answer to the question of admissibility would then be dependent on the question whether an individual Member State offers a particular legal remedy to the applicant.
288. Case 222/84, *Johnston v. Chief Constable of the Royal Ulster Constabulary*, and Case C-185/97, *Belinda Jane Coote v. Granada Hospitality Ltd*.
289. See on this L.W. Gormley, 'Public Interest Litigation', in *Liber Amicorum in honour of Lord Slynn of Hadley* (The Hague, 2000, Vol. I), 191–201. In Case C-321/95, *Greenpeace and Others v. Commission*, an attempt was made – in vain – to use the defence of environmental interests as a ground for admissibility.
290. Case C-50/00, *Unión de Pequeños Agricultores*. The now defunct Constitutional Treaty extended the right of action by private parties by providing that they may also institute proceedings 'against a regulatory act which is of direct concern to him or her and does not

2.3.2   Limited Right of Action by Private Parties
(Action for Failure to Act)

The right of action by private parties in cases of failure to act is subject to a double restriction: the failure to act must concern an act intended to have legal effects (literally, an act other than a recommendation or opinion)[291] and addressed to that person.

How should the second of these restrictions be interpreted? Given that the Court regards Articles 230 and 232 EC as expressions of one and the same legal recourse,[292] regard may be had to the criteria relating to an action for annulment brought by a private party. Thus, it should concern an act either addressed to the applicant, or of direct and individual concern to him. After a long period of uncertainty with regard to the case law on this point, more recent case law does in fact confirm that the Court adopts this view.[293]

Under Article 232 third paragraph EC, private parties should either be potential addressees of an act which the Institutions have failed to adopt, or they should potentially be directly and individually concerned by the act in question. This means that such an action is inadmissible where it is aimed at obtaining from the Court a ruling that the Commission has failed to fulfil its Treaty obligations by not commencing infringement proceedings against a Member States under Article 226 EC. Moreover, the Commission is not under an *obligation* to start such proceedings nor, where the Commission's reasoned opinion is not complied with, is it *obliged* to bring proceedings before the Court against the Member State in question.[294]

2.3.3   The Plea of Illegality

It will be apparent from the above that a private party will hardly ever have the right to lodge a direct action for annulment of an act of the Council or the Commission which has general effect. If, however, a regulation is at issue in some other form of

---

entail implementary measures' (Art. III-365, 4th para.). See for comments the annotation of Case C-50/00, by C. Brown and J. Morijn in (2004) CML Rev., 1639,1655-1659 and A. Ward, 'The Draft EU Constitution and Judicial Review of EU Measures', in T. Tridimas and P. Nebbia (eds), *European Union Law for the Twenty-First Century*, Vol. I (Oxford, 2004) 209–221.

291.   Art. 232 para. 3. Cf. Case 15/70, *Chevalley v. Commission* and Case 6/70, *Gillberto Borromeo Arese et al. v. Commission*.

292.   Case 15/70, *Chevalley*. This does not mean, however, that Art. 232 EC can be used to evade the conditions laid down in Art. 230 EC, particularly in relation to the time-limit for bringing an action; cf. Joined Cases 10 & 18/68, *Société 'Eridania' Zuccherifici Nazionali et al. v. Commission*.

293.   Case C-107/91, *Empresa Nacional de Urânio SA v. Commission* (in relation to Art. 148 Euratom); Case C-68/95, *T. Port GmbH & Co. KG v. Bundesanstalt für Landwirtschaft und Ernährung*.

294.   Cf. Case 247/87, *Star Fruit Company SA v. Commission*. As for infringement procedures against Member States under Art. 86(3) EC, see C-141/02 P, *Commission v. T-Mobile Austria GmbH*. Private parties may complain to the Commission about infringements of Community law, see the Communication of the Commission O.J. 2002, C 244/5.

proceedings before the Court, a private party may plead the illegality of that regulation on the same grounds as those applying to an action for annulment and notwithstanding the expiration of the time limit for appeal.[295] The regulation whose legality is called into question must be applicable, directly or indirectly, to the issue with which the application is concerned.[296] Thus, for instance, private parties may raise this plea if they institute an action for annulment against a decision addressed to them which is based on a regulation or a general decision. If the plea is admitted, the Court will not apply the provisions of the regulation in that specific case, thus leading to the annulment of the decision based on those provisions.[297] The regulation itself, however, is not annulled,[298] although the Institution which issued it will, naturally, draw the appropriate conclusions and take measures to replace the illegal act.

Although Article 241 EC only lays down the application of this principle with regard to regulations, the Court regards this Article as the expression of a general principle. It covers all acts of the Institutions which, even though they are not in the form of a regulation, nevertheless produce similar legal effects. Thus the plea of illegality can be invoked against all acts which have general effect (so, probably including directives) which form the legal basis for an individual measure attacked by the applicant.[299] The Court justified this wide interpretation on the ground that it was necessary in order to protect those who were precluded by the fourth paragraph of Article 230 EC from challenging general acts.[300] But the general principle, to which Article 241 EC gives expression, does not in any way preclude a regulation from becoming definitive as against an individual in regard to whom it must be considered to be an individual decision and who could undoubtedly have sought its annulment under Article 230 EC.[301] It should be noted that the contested general act on which the individual decisions are based can be reviewed by the Court under written and unwritten Community law[302] on the same grounds as in the case of a direct action for annulment of Community acts.

---

295. Arts. 241 EC and 156 Euratom. This plea of illegality is often called 'the exception of illegality' (after the French).
296. Case 32/65, *Italy v. Council and Commission*.
297. See Case 9/56, *Meroni & Co., Industrie Metallurgiche, SpA v. High Authority (Meroni I)*.
298. See Joined Cases 31 & 33/62, *Milchwerke Heinz Wöhrmann & Sohn KG et al. v. Commission* and Joined Cases 15-33/73 etc., *Roswitha Schots, née Kortner et al. v. Council et al.*
299. The plea of illegality may, e.g., concern internal rules of an institution which, although they do not constitute the legal basis of the contested decision, determine the essential procedural requirements for adopting that decision and thus ensure legal certainty for those to whom it is addressed; Case 305/94, *LVM v. Commission*, para. 10. See also Joined Cases C-189, 202, 205-208/02 P & C-213/02 P, *Dansk Rørindustri a.o. v. Commission*, paras 209-213.
300. Case 92/78, *SpA Simmenthal v. Commission*; see also (already) van Rijn, *Exceptie van onwettigheid en prejudiciële procedure inzake geldigheid van gemeenschapshandelingen*, 1978, 172 and 261.
301. See Case C-11/00, *Commission v. European Central Bank*, para. 77.
302. Including provisions of international treaties binding on the Community, sometimes even where they do not have direct effect. See Case C-69/89, *Nakajima All Precision Co. Ltd v. Council*. See Ch. VII, section 1.2.

Any party may invoke the plea of illegality in proceedings in which an act of general application adopted by the European Parliament and the Council acting jointly, the Council, the Commission, or the ECB is at issue. The question has arisen whether the term 'proceedings' in Article 241 EC also refers to proceedings concerning a Community regulation before a national court. The Court answered this question in the negative when private parties to national proceedings made a direct application to it pursuant to Article 241, and declared their action inadmissible. The Court held that Article 241 only concerned 'a declaration of the inapplicability of a regulation . . . in proceedings brought before the Court of Justice itself under some other provision of the Treaty', and then only incidentally and with limited effect.[303] The Court did refer in this context to the possibility that the national court might request a preliminary ruling. After all, such a request for a preliminary ruling may concern 'the validity . . . of the acts of the Institutions of the Community'.[304]

As 'any party' may invoke the plea of illegality, the text of Article 241 EC does not exclude Member States and Institutions from the right to invoke the possible illegality of a general act under that article.[305] Although the Court seems to have sought the ratio of Article 241 EC particularly in the limited right of direct appeal for private parties, there is no indication that Article 241 should be interpreted otherwise. Unlike private parties, Member States and Institutions do have the right to challenge general acts, but that is not a decisive argument to deny them access to the plea of illegality. Irregularities in such an act may appear after the time limit for challenging it has passed when measures of implementation are adopted.[306] The Court has confirmed this interpretation. It is obvious, however, that Article 241 EC does not allow a Member State, when defending infringement proceedings brought by the Commission, to challenge the validity of a decision which had been addressed to it, if it had allowed the period within which it could bring an action for annulment to expire.[307]

---

303. Joined Cases 31 & 33/62, *Milchwerke Heinz Wöhrmann*, 507 of the English edition. More generally, the Court has stated that the possibility to invoke the plea of illegality does not create an independent right of action, and that the plea may only be raised indirectly in proceedings against an implementing measure. See, e.g., Joined Cases 87/77 etc., *Salerno et al. v. Commission et al.*

304. Cf. Art. 234 EC, see section 3.1.4 *infra*. See for an example Case 216/82, *Universität Hamburg v. Hauptzollamt Hamburg-Kehrwieder.*

305. The majority view in the literature is that they may. See Waelbroeck (M. and D.) and Vandersanden in Mégret et al. (eds), *Le Droit de la CEE*, Vol. 10, 2nd ed. (Brussels, 1993), 132-133 and the literature mentioned therein. Support for this view can be found in Case 32/65, *Italy v. Council and Commission* and Case C-135/93, *Spain v. Commission.*

306. Case C-11/00, *Commission v. European Central Bank*. See also A. Barav, 'The Exception of Illegality in Community Law: A Critical Analysis' (1974) CML Rev., 366, 371.

307. See, to this effect, Cases 156/77, *Commission v. Belgium*, and C-183/91, *Commission v. Greece*. These cases concerned Member States which were the addressee of decisions adopted under the first subparagraph of Art. 93(2) (now 88(2)) EC.

2.4   Actions for Damages on the Ground of the
                Community's Non-contractual Liability

At first sight, the provisions on non-contractual liability in the EC and Euratom Treaties seem to be very different from those in the ECSC Treaty. According to Article 235 EC (Art. 151 Euratom), 'The Court of Justice shall have jurisdiction in disputes relating to compensation for damage provided for in the second paragraph of Article 288.' The latter provision lays down that the Community[308] should, 'in accordance with the general principles common to the laws of the Member States, make good any damage caused by its institutions or by its servants [or the ECB and its servants] in the performance of their duties'. Article 40 ECSC, on the other hand, was clearly inspired by French administrative law. Under this provision, the Community could be sued in the Court of Justice for injury caused in carrying out the ECSC Treaty by a wrongful act or omission on the part of the Community in the performance of its functions or caused by a personal wrong by a servant of the Community in the performance of his duties.

However, it is clear that the Court's case law on liability of the EC continues the line of that relating to the ECSC liability; there is no question of a separate approach. The Court was able to pursue its general efforts towards as close an integration as possible of the law of the three Communities[309] in this field precisely because in framing the Community liability of the ECSC it pursued its own path. In doing so it implicitly (albeit not expressly) based itself on the most important principles of administrative liability in the various national legal systems, thus clearly not merely on the French system.

Looking at Article 288 EC, the question arises what is meant by general principles common to the laws of the Member States? For an answer to this question, we can refer to what was set out above (section 1.1) concerning the Court and unwritten Community law. The Court is not obliged to seek the highest common denominator in the Member States' laws on administrative liability; it should focus on tracing those elements which provide a basis for Community legal principles and rules which offer an appropriate, fair and viable solution to the problem of Community liability. The provisions of Article 288 EC should be understood 'in the sense of an orientation on the underlying principles whereby the *measure* of the responsibility of the administration is assessed in the national sphere'.[310]

In a general formulation, the Court laid down certain conditions, based on the second paragraph of Article 288 EC and the general principles to which it refers,

---

308.   The correct administration of justice requires that the Community is represented in this by the Institution or Institutions whose acts gave rise to the liability at issue. Art. 211 EEC (now Art. 282 EC) was inapplicable because it concerned legal capacity and representation only in the national legal systems. Joined Cases 63–69/72, *Werhahn Hansamuehle and others v. Council.*
309.   See Ch. II section 2.1 *supra.*
310.   Opinion A.G. Roemer in Case 25/62, *Plaumann v. Commission*, italics in the original.

which must be satisfied in order for the Community to be liable.[311] These conditions relate to:

(1) the illegality[312,313] of the conduct of which the Community Institution is accused;
(2) the existence of actual damage;
(3) a causal link between the damage claimed and the conduct alleged against the Institution.

Conduct does not just cover purely substantive acts, but also legal acts (including the failure to adopt or execute legal acts). Proceedings against the Communities in matters arising from non-contractual liability are barred after a period of five years from the event giving rise thereto.[314] That event is the occurrence of the damage.[315]

To what extent and subject to what conditions does an action for damages against the Community, as a result of or in conjunction with an action for annulment or against failure to act, offer redress to legal subjects aggrieved by unlawful action or inaction by the Community Institutions?

Certainly a suit will have a chance of success if annulment of the act (or condemnation of the inaction) on which the suit is based has already taken place. As has been shown in section 2.2.2. above,[316] Articles 233 EC and 149 Euratom refer explicitly to Articles 288 EC and 188 Euratom respectively: the obligation to take the necessary measures to comply with a judgment of the Court annulling or condemning a failure to act does not affect any obligation resulting from the Community's non-contractual liability. But even if an act has not previously been annulled (or a failure to act condemned) an action for damages on the ground of the unlawfulness of the act or failure to act may succeed.

Originally, this was not apparent. It seemed to follow from the judgment in *Plaumann*[317] that only an annulled act or a condemned failure to act could give rise

---

311. Case 4/69, *Alfons Lütticke GmbH v. Commission*.
312. Neither the wording of Art. 288, 2nd para., EC, nor the Court's case law (see Joined Cases 9 & 11/71, *Compagnie d'Approvisionnement, de transport et al. v. Commission*, Case 59/83, *Biovilac*, Case 81/86, *De Boer Buizen v. Council and Commission*, Case C-237/98 P, *Dorsch consult v. Council and Commission* and Case T-69/00, *FIAMM and FIAMM Technologies v. Council and Commission*) exclude *a priori* liability for damage resulting from lawful action of the Community, but the Court has thus far never awarded damages on this ground. According to the case law, three conditions would have to be met: the reality of the damage allegedly suffered, the causal link between it and the act on the part of the Community institutions, and the unusual and special nature of that damage. As to the meaning of the third condition, see *De Boer Buizen*, para. 17. See M.J.W. van Casteren, *Schadevergoeding bij regelmatig EG-optreden* (Deventer, 1997).
313. Case C-257/90, *Italsolar v. Commission*. Infringement of unwritten law can also lead to liability of the Community, see Case 74/74, *CNTA v. Commission*, on infringement of the principle of legitimate expectations.
314. Art. 46 Statute of the Court of Justice.
315. Cf. Case 9/56, *Meroni I* and Case 10/56, *Meroni II*.
316. At note 205 *supra*.
317. Case 25/62, *Plaumann v. Commission*. 'An administrative measure which has not been annulled cannot of itself constitute a wrongful act on the part of the administration inflicting damage upon those whom it affects'.

to a claim for damages. In later judgments the Court reconsidered this unsatisfactory position. Both in the case of an allegedly unlawful failure to act and in the case of an allegedly unlawful act the Court has expressly stated that the

> action for damages provided for by Article 178 [now 235] and the second paragraph of Article 215 [now 288] was established by the Treaty as an independent form of action with a particular purpose to fulfil within the system of actions and subject to conditions for its use, conceived with a view to its specific purpose.[318]

The independent nature of this form of action means that even though the action for damages may in certain circumstances lead to a result comparable to that achieved by an action against a failure to act, this is not a reason for its inadmissibility. The action for damages differs from an action for annulment 'in that its end is not the abolition of a particular measure but compensation for damage caused by an institution in the performance of its duties'.[319]

Although the form of action is independent, it should be borne in mind that actions for damages will be declared inadmissible if they are clearly simply designed to escape the consequences of the rejection of an action for annulment, in other words if they are in substance a disguised action for annulment or for failure to act.[320,321] However, the mere fact that some of the conditions for an action for damages coincide with those for an action for annulment is not a sufficient reason to describe the former as a misuse of the procedure.[322]

---

318. Case 4/69, *Alfons Lütticke GmbH v. Commission*, para. 6, Case 5/71, *Aktien-Zuckerfabrik Schöppenstedt v. Council* para. 3, Case C-234/02 P, *Médiateur v. Lamberts* para. 59, and Case T-193/04, *Tillack v. Commission*.

319. Case 5/71, *Schöppenstedt* para. 3. Neither may private parties be forced to seek a judgment from the Court of Justice on the validity of a measure through the Art. 234 EC mechanism in national courts before they pursue a claim for damages in the Court of Justice. Although initially Case 96/71, *R. & V. Haegeman v. Commission* indicated otherwise, in the judgment in Case 43/72, *Merkur Aussenhandels GmbH v. Commission* the Court rejected the idea of two sets of proceedings as 'not being in keeping with the proper administration of justice and the requirements of procedural efficiency'.

320. Cf. A.G. Roemer, in Case 5/71, *Schöppenstedt*, referring to earlier cases. This is, for instance, where a party tries to circumvent the inadmissibility of an application for annulment concerning the same instance of illegality and having the same financial end in view (see, in particular, Case 543/79, *Birke v. Commission and Council*, Case 799/79, *Bruckner v. Commission and Council*, and Case 175/84, *Krohn v. Commission*).

　　See also Joined Cases C-199 & 200/94, *Pesquería Vasco-Montañesa SA (Pevasa) and Compañia Internacional de Pesca y Derivados SA (Inpesca) v. Commission* and Case T-186/98, *Inpesca v. Commission*.

321. See also Case T-47/02, *Manfred and Hannelore Danzer v. Council*, in which the action for damages was dismissed as inadmissible because the applicants were seeking to obtain the same result as would be obtained if the penalties decisions taken by the Austrian authorities on the basis of national law implementing the disputed provisions of the First and Fourth Companies Directives were to be annulled. The applicants had introduced this action after the competent Austrian courts had refused to make a reference for a preliminary ruling on the validity of these provisions to the Court of Justice.

322. Joined Cases 197/80 etc., *Ludwigshafener Walzmühle Erling KG et al. v. Council and Commission*.

The judgment in *Schöppenstedt*[323] revealed that injury resulting from normative acts of the Institutions involving particular economic policy choices,[324] can also give rise to Community liability, if 'a sufficiently flagrant violation of a superior rule of law for the protection of the individual has occurred'.[325] Thus, in a legislative context a stricter criterion of liability had to be applied. Nevertheless, given that in the EC system an action challenging genuine regulations is completely excluded, this constitutes a welcome extension of judicial protection of private parties in cases of Community 'legislation', even though the chances of success in actions for damages in such cases must not be over-rated.[326]

In referring to superior rules of law it seems that the Court had in mind Treaty provisions or provisions of a superior rank than legislative acts, as well as general principles of law. In examining the lawfulness of a legislative act in the light of superior rules of law in actions for damages, the Court adopts the same approach as in actions for annulment. What is meant by a sufficiently flagrant violation has become clearer since the judgment in *Bayerische HNL Vermehrungsbetriebe*.[327] The Court had declared a Council Regulation void in three preliminary rulings.[328] When a number of undertakings sought damages from the Council and the Commission on the grounds of the annulment of the Regulation, the Court considered that the violation of a superior rule of law was insufficiently flagrant. Liability for legislative measures (normative acts) in fields in which the Community Institutions have wide discretionary powers, will not be incurred unless the Institution concerned 'has manifestly and gravely disregarded the limits on the exercise of its powers'.[329] Later case law shows that this review involves an examination of the

---

323. Case 5/71, *Schöppenstedt*.
324. The case law has always dealt with *economic* policy choices, but there is no reason to think that this is a restrictive definition of policy choices. See also A. Arnull, 'Tasting the Difference' (1987) EL Rev., 451.
325. Case 5/71, *Schöppenstedt*.
326. But for a very important example of a successful action, see Joined Cases C-104/89 & 37/90, *Mulder et al. v. Council and Commission*. This long drawn-out conflict in the milk quotas cases began in 1988 with the partial annulment of an agricultural regulation, and ended in 2000 with a judgment on the compensation for damages to be paid (the above-mentioned *Mulder* cases). This judgment provided the necessary indications for the methods for calculating damages in several hundred similar milk quota cases which were pending before the CFI. For the first judgment of the CFI following the judgment in *Mulder*, see Case T-76/94, *Jansma v. Council and Commission*. See also case note on *Mulder* by M. Ruffert in (2001) CML Rev., 781–790.
327. Joined Cases 83 & 94/76, 4, 15 and 40/77, *Bayerische HNL Vermehrungsbetriebe GmbH & Co. KG and others v. Council and Commission*, see also Case 152/88, *Sofrimport*.
328. Mentioned at para. 3.
329. Joined Cases 83/76 etc., *HNL*, para. 5. The Court based its restrictive approach on the principles prevailing in the Member States governing the liability of public authorities for damage caused to individuals by legislative measures. Although they varied considerably from one Member State to another, it was clear that public authorities only exceptionally and in special circumstances incurred liability for legislative measures which were the result of economic policy choices.

seriousness of the transgression of the limits of powers itself[330] as well as the seriousness of the consequences thereof as revealed in the number of persons affected and the scale of the injury, in the light of normal economic risks in the activities in the sectors concerned.[331]

In the meantime, however, there has been a development in the area of liability of *Member States* for infringements of Community law,[332] which could not fail to have some consequences for the case law on liability of the *Community* for such infringements. In its judgment in *Brasserie du Pêcheur and Factortame III*,[333] the Court stated the principle that

> the conditions under which the State may incur liability for damage caused to individuals by a breach of Community law cannot, in the absence of particular justification, differ from those governing the liability of the Community in like circumstances. The protection of the rights which individuals derive from Community law cannot vary depending on whether a national authority or a Community authority is responsible for the damage.[334]

The case law of the CFI, which is now the body dealing in first instance with claims for damages from individuals, did not at first draw any consequences from this, but continued to apply the tests which had been developed previously by the Court of Justice concerning the liability of the Community.

In its judgment on appeal in *Bergaderm*,[335] the Court applied, more or less *ex officio*, an improvement of the legal grounds in order to indicate that the tests concerning liability of the Community should be modified to conform with those employed by the Court in the area of liability of the Member States. It is apparent from this judgment that for liability of the Community, three conditions taken from the case law concerning liability of Member States must be fulfilled:

(1) The rule of law infringed must be intended to confer rights on individuals.
(2) The breach of the rule must be sufficiently serious.
(3) There must be a direct causal link between the infringement of the rule and the damage suffered by the applicant.[336]

As in cases of liability of Member States on the basis of Community law, the degree of discretion enjoyed by the Institution is not determined by whether the act is general or individual, a condition which always led to problems in the past.

---

330. See, e.g., Joined Cases 116 & 124/77, *G.R. Amylum NV et al. v. Council and Commission* (the defendants' behaviour was held not to verge on the arbitrary and the actions for damages were dismissed).
331. See, e.g., Case 238/78, *Ireks-Arkady GmbH v. Council et al.*
332. See Ch. VII, section 4, *infra*.
333. Joined Cases C-46 & 48/93 *Brasserie du Pêcheur* and *Factortame*.
334. Ibid., para. 42.
335. Case C-352/98 P, *Bergaderm et al. v. Commission*. See also Case C-312/00 P, *Commission v. Camar and Tico*, Case C-472/00 P, *Commission v. Fresh Marine* and Case C-282/05 P, *Holcin v. Commission*.
336. For one of the first cases in which the CFI applied the new set of conditions, see Case T-18/99, *Cordis v. Commission*.

The decisive test is not the individual nature of the act in question, but the discretion available to the institution when it was adopted.[337] A general requirement is now that the breach of the rule should be sufficiently serious, that is, a manifest and serious infringement by the Institution of the limits of its powers. If the Institution only enjoys a very limited margin of discretion – or none at all – the breach of Community law itself is already a sufficiently serious infringement. Moreover, from now on, it is no longer the *Schöppenstedt* formulation (violation of a superior rule of law for the protection of the individual)[338] which applies, but the formulation taken from the case law on Member State liability: violation of a rule of law intended to confer rights on individuals.[339]

The difference between the old test and the new test is, in fact, not so great as to have considerable impact on the evolution of the case law with respect to the non-contractual liability of the Community. Nevertheless, the application of the new tests may lead not only to a less opaque, but also to a less restrictive jurisprudence, as it implies the application of the factors laid down in the case law on state liability for determining the existence of a sufficiently serious breach.[340] Potentially these factors are more generous than the factors the Court has looked to in the past.[341]

As mentioned above, the existence of actual damage is necessary, as well as a causal link between the damage and the illegal conduct. The point of departure is complete compensation for damage suffered: not merely actual losses suffered, but also – in the absence of particular circumstances warranting a different assessment – loss of earnings.[342] The damage does not already have to have occurred: compensation for imminent damage is possible if this is foreseeable with sufficient certainty.[343] The damage may also be immaterial.[344] The requirement of causality means that the damage must be a direct consequence of the illegal conduct.[345] If the damage is partially caused by the conduct of the person suffering the damage, then responsibility may be shared.[346]

National and Community administrations often act in a complex interwoven pattern in the field of Community law. Thus in certain circumstances both can be

---

337. See C. Hilson, 'The Role of Discretion in EC Law on Non-contractual Liability' (2005) CML Rev., 677, who observes, however, that the case law on state liability now appears to be moving away from the previous emphasis on discretion.
338. Case 5/71, *Schöppenstedt*.
339. Cf. Opinion of A.G. Léger, para. 127, in Case C-224/01, *Köbler*.
340. See Joined Cases C-46 & 48/93, *Brasserie du Pêcheur SA v. Bundesrepublik Deutschland* and *The Queen v. Secretary of State for Transport, ex parte: Factortame Ltd and others*, paras 56–57. See on the significance of the judgment in Case C-352/98, *Bergaderm*, Tridimas, 'Liability for Breach of Community Law: Growing Up and Mellowing Down'? (2001) CML Rev., 301–332, 321–331.
341. See *supra*, at notes 329 and 331. See on this subject C. Hilson, op. cit. *supra* note 337.
342. Joined Cases C-104/89 & C-37/90, *Mulder*.
343. Joined Cases 56/74–60/74, *Kampffmeyer*.
344. Joined Cases 7/56 & 3/57–7/57, *Algera et al. v. Common Assembly* and e.g., C-259/96 P, *Council v. De Nil en Impens*.
345. See for examples of an insufficient causal link Joined Cases 64 & 113/76, 167/78 and 239/78, 27/79, 28/79 and 45/79, P. *Dumortier Frères SA et al. v. Council*; Case T-7/96, *Perillo v. Commission* and Case T-149/96, *Coldiretti et al. v. Council and Commission*.
346. Case C-308/87, *Alfredo Grifoni v. European Atomic Energy Community*.

held liable for the same injury; the national authorities in the national courts in the sphere of national law, the Community authorities in the Court of Justice in the Community legal order. After a long period of uncertainty about the Court's view of this, the case law can be summarized by reference to the judgment in *Krohn v. Commission*[347] as follows. If the measure involved[348] is taken by a national body in implementation of Community rules, the Court (now the CFI) will only be competent to consider an action for damages if the alleged unlawfulness on which the action is founded emanates from a Community Institution and cannot be attributed to the national body. If the national body acts under instructions of a Community Institution, then the unlawfulness is attributed to the latter. But the matter does not end there, as the admissibility of proceedings before the Community courts may in certain circumstances depend on national procedures available for the annulment of the national decision having been exhausted. It is a condition that these procedures effectively ensure the protection of interested parties through permitting redress for injury suffered. Only the existence of an effective form of action in the national courts can prevent private parties from pursuing the procedure of Articles 235 and 288 EC.[349]

In a system in which Community and national administrations are so intertwined, the division of competence for declarations for annulment or invalidity of Community legislative acts and actions for damages resulting from the application of those acts between the Court of Justice or CFI, on the one hand, and national courts, on the other, led to various objections from the point of view of judicial protection; the case law has resolved many problems, but not all of them.[350]

3   COOPERATION BETWEEN THE COURT OF JUSTICE AND NATIONAL COURTS: PRELIMINARY RULINGS

3.1   POWERS OF THE COURT AND NATIONAL COURTS, DIVISION AND COORDINATION

3.1.1   General

Under Article 234 EC[351] the Court of Justice has jurisdiction to give preliminary rulings relating in particular to the interpretation of the Treaty, acts of the Community Institutions and the validity of those acts. There would appear to be no

---

347. Case 175/84, *Krohn*, which clarifies the earlier judgments in Case 12/79, *Hans-Otto Wagner GmbH Agrarhandel KG v. Commission*; Case 133/79, *Sucrimex SA et al. v. Commission* and Case 217/81, *Compagnie Interagra SA v. Commission*.
348. The situation is completely different if it is the Community measure itself which is in issue, see Case 59/83, *Biovilac v. EEC* and Case 126/76, *Firma Gebrüder Dietz v. Commission*.
349. See in this sense also Joined Cases 197/80 etc., *Ludwigshafener Walzmühle*, Case 281/82, *Srl Unifrex v. Commission et al.* and Case 81/86, *De Boer Buizen*.
350. See Wils, 'Concurrent Liability of the Community and a Member State' (1992) EL Rev., 191, who regards joint and several liability as the only satisfactory solution.
351. See also Art. 150 Euratom. Art. 68 EC and Art. 35 TEU confer limited powers on the Court to give preliminary rulings with regard to certain subject-matters; so do some Protocols and

reason to interpret the word 'acts' restrictively. They include regulations, directives, decisions and *sui generis* measures irrespective of whether they have direct effect.[352] They also cover, at least as far as interpretation is concerned, treaties concluded by the Community with third countries or international organizations[353] or which are binding on the Community in other ways,[354] as in the case of mixed agreements to which the Community and the Member States are parties, even covering, in these mixed agreements, obligations of the Member States thereunder.[355] The Court can also interpret acts which do not produce legal effects, even if only to decide whether or not they produce legal effects.[356] It is difficult to raise questions as to the validity of these latter acts because the question of their validity arises after the question of whether or not the acts produce legal effects. Questions of interpretation can also relate to the clarification of unwritten legal principles

---

Agreements concerning judicial cooperation in civil matters, and police and judicial cooperation in criminal and customs matters.

352. See, in so many words, Case 111/75, *Impresa Costruzioni Comm. Quirino Mazzali v. Ferrovia del Renon*. A Directive of which the period for implementation is not yet over is also such an act as intended in Art. 234, see Case C-491/01, *The Queen v. Secretary of State for Health ex parte British American Tobacco (Investments) Ltd and Imperial Tobacco Ltd (Tobacco advertising II)*.

353. Constant case law since Case 181/73, *Haegemann v. Belgian State*. Implementing rules adopted by a Joint Committee on the basis of such agreements also form part of Community law and can be interpreted by the Court under Art. 234 EC, see, e.g., Case C-192/89, *Sevince v. Staatssecretaris van Justitie*; Case C- 237/91, *Kazim Kus v. Landeshauptstadt Wiesbaden* and Case C-188/91, *Deutsche Shell AG v. Hauptzollamt Hamburg-Harburg*.

354. See, *inter alia*, Joined Cases 21–24/72, *International Fruit Company* and, further, Joined Cases 267–269/81, *Amministrazione delle Finanze dello Stato v. Società Petrolifera Italiana SpA (SPI) et al.* and Joined Cases 290 & 291/81, *Compagnia Singer SpA et al. v. Amministrazione delle Finanze dello Stato v. SPI and SAMI*. In this type of judgment no act of an Institution is involved.

355. This appears to follow from Case C-18/90, *Office national de l'emploi (Onem) v. Kziber*. The Court has no jurisdiction under Art. 234 EC 'to give a ruling on the interpretation of provisions of international law which bind Member States outside the framework of Community law': Case 130/73, *Magdalena Vandeweghe et al. v. Berufsgenossenschaft für die Chemische Industrie*, para. 2, and Case 44/84, *Hurd v. Jones*. The Court does accept jurisdiction if such provisions may be applicable in situations which come within the scope of both national law and Community law (Case C-53/96, *Hermès International (a partnership limited by shares) v. FHT Marketing Choice BV*, annotated by A. von Bogdandy in (1999) CML Rev., 635, and Joined Cases C-300 & 392/98, *Dior et al. v. Tuk Consultancy BV et al.*). As to mixed agreements generally, see Ch. XIII *infra*; D. O'Keeffe and H.G. Schermers (eds), *Mixed Agreements* (Deventer, 1983); N. Neuwahl, 'Shared powers or combined incompetence? More on mixity' (1996) CML Rev., 667–687. In a number of unpublished orders mentioned in the judgment in Case C-193/98, *Pfennigmann*, the Court considered that it did not have jurisdiction to interpret provisions of an agreement which a number of member States had concluded jointly – authorized to do so by a directive – in order to implement that directive. However, it appears from this judgment that the Court was prepared to interpret a provision of the directive to which this agreement referred.

356. See Case 9/73, *Carl Schlüter v. Hauptzollamt L ö rrach* (the EMU resolution of 22 Mar. 1971) and Case 113/75, *Frecassetti v. Amministrazione delle Finanze dello Stato* (a recommendation).

inherent in Community law.[357] Even if a provision of Community law, as a result of being referred to in a national law[358] or in an agreement concluded between the parties,[359] is in substance used to determine the rules applicable in a situation not governed by Community law (being a purely domestic matter within the Member State involved), the Court will regard itself as competent to respond to questions relating to provisions of Community law posed by a national court or tribunal.

The national court is entitled, and, if a court of last instance in the case concerned, even obliged, to ask the Court for a preliminary ruling if a question of interpretation or validity is raised before it either by the parties or by the national court itself *ex officio*.[360] The national court must consider that a decision on such a question is necessary to enable it to give judgment. If these conditions are satisfied, the national court will suspend proceedings and will on its own initiative notify the Court of the decision to refer the matter.[361]

The preliminary ruling of the Court 'is binding on the national court hearing the case in which the decision is given'.[362] This does not mean that the court may not make a new preliminary reference to the Court in the same dispute. Such a new preliminary reference may be justified if the court encounters problems in interpreting or applying the judgment on the first reference, or if the national court puts a new question of law to the Court of Justice, or if it submits new facts to the Court

---

357. E.g., Case 11/70, *Internationale Handelsgesellschaft*(respect for human rights) and Case 84/78, *Ditta Angelo Tomandini Snc v. Amministrazione delle Finanze dello Stato* (protection of legitimate expectations), and Case C-331/88, *The Queen v. Ministry of Agriculture, Fisheries and Food, ex parte FEDESA and others* (principle of proportionality).

358. Joined Cases C-297/88 & C-197/89, *Dzodzi v. Belgian State*, annotated by Bravo-Ferrer-Delgrado and La Casta Muñoa in (1992) CML Rev., 152, and Case C-231/89, *Gmurzynska-Bscher v. Oberfinanzdirektion Köln*. See also Case C-28/95, *Leur-Bloem v. Inspecteur der Belastingdienst v. Ondernemingen Amsterdam 2* and Case C-130/95, *Giloy v. Hauptzollamt Frankfurt am Main-Ost*, jointly annotated by Betlem (2001) CML Rev., 157; Case C-306/99, *BIAO*. For a limit to this case law, see Case C-346/93, *Kleinwort Benson v. City of Glasgow District Council*, annotated by G. Betlem (1996) CML Rev., 33.

359. See Case C-88/91, *Federazione Italiana dei Consorzi Agrari (Federconsorzi) v. Azienda di stato per gli Interventi nel mercato Agricolo (AIMA)*.The Court refused to pronounce on the interpretation of a model agreement between national insurance bureaux provided for by Dir. 72/166, because no Community Institution was involved in the conclusion of this agreement (Case 152/83, *Demouche v. Fonds de garantie automobile*).

360. On this last point see Case 166/73, *Rheinmühlen-Düsseldorf v. Einfuhr- und Vorratsstelle für Getreide und Futtermittel (II)*. See further Joined Cases C-87–89/90, *Verholen et al. v. Sociale Verzekeringsbank*. The question whether the *ex officio* application of Community law could be restricted by national law was considered in Case C-312/93, *Peterbroeck, Van Campenhout & Cie SCS v. Belgian State*, Joined Cases C-430 & 431/93, *Van Schijndel et al. v. Stichting Pensioenfonds voor Fysiotherapeuten* and Joined Cases C-222–225/05, *J. van der Weerd a.o. v. Minister van Landbouw, Natuur en Voedselkwaliteit*. See further the discussion of these cases in Ch. VII section 3, and Prechal, 'Community Law in National Courts: The Lessons from Van Schijndel' (1998) CML Rev., 681.

361. Statute of the Court of Justice, Art. 23.

362. Case 29/68, *Milch- Fett- und Eierkontor GmbH. v. Hauptzollamt Saarbrücken*, para. 2. See also Case 52/76, *Benedetti v. Munari F.lli s.a.s.* and Case C-446/98, *Fazenda Pública v. Câmara Municipal do Porto*.

of Justice which could lead to the Court giving a different answer to a question on which it had already pronounced.[363] For courts other than those hearing the case in which the decision is given, the judgment in the preliminary ruling has 'authority of interpretation'.[364] These courts should follow the interpretation given, but of course retain the power to make a reference to the Court if they have grounds to doubt this interpretation.

Is a Member State obliged on the basis of Article 10 EC (the duty of loyal cooperation) to amend a rule of which it has become apparent in a preliminary ruling that it is not in conformity with Community law, and to amend it according to the preliminary ruling? In general, such a question will not arise, since the national court will set aside the national rule on the basis of the preliminary ruling, and the Member State will draw the appropriate consequences from this and amend the rule. The preliminary ruling may, however, concern a national rule of another Member State, other than that of the court making the reference. Such a situation occurred in the case *Belgium v. Spain*.[365] The fact that the decision in a preliminary ruling is only binding on the court which hears the case, and not on the parties to the dispute or a Member State which has intervened in the preliminary reference proceedings, or whose rule is the subject of the preliminary ruling, tends to refute a requirement in such a case to derive an obligation for a Member State on the basis of Article 10 EC to conform to a preliminary ruling. Moreover, from a formal point of view, the Court does not pronounce on the lawfulness of the national measure (that judgment is reserved to the national court), but on a question of interpretation of Community law. On the other hand, a judgment such as that given by the Court in the *Delhaize* case deals so fundamentally with the factual and legal context of the dispute, that 'interpretation' comes extremely near to 'application'.

The judgment is declaratory, and has effect *ex tunc*, even if it concerns an interpretation. The interpretation given clarifies and defines the meaning of the rule of Community law which should have been applied and understood since its coming into force. Thus the national court ought to apply the rule as so interpreted even to legal relationships which commenced before the preliminary ruling was handed down.[366] It is only in very exceptional cases[367] that the Court of Justice restricts the retroactive effect of its judgment for interested parties. This will tend to concern cases on the legal base of acts, on grounds of legal certainty, and with a

---

363. Case 14/86, *Pretore di Salo v. X*. For a more recent example, see Case C-356/98, *Arben Kaba v. Secretary of State for the Home Department* and C-466/00, same parties.
364. Cf. Joined Cases 28–30/62, *Da Costa en Schaake NV et al. v. Nederlandse Belastingadministratie.*
365. Case C-388/95, *Belgium v. Spain (Rioja)*. For the earlier preliminary ruling, see Case 47/90, *Delhaize Frères v. Promalvin and others.*
366. See Joined Cases 66, 127 & 128/79, *Amministrazione delle Finanze v. Srl Meridionale Industria Salumi et al.* Even administrative bodies may in some cases be bound to apply the rule as interpreted by the Court to legal relationships which arose or were formed before the Court gave its ruling, see Case C-453/00, *Kühne & Heitz NV*.
367. E.g., in the Case 43/75, *Defrenne v. SABENA*.

view to serious disturbances which the Court's judgment could imply for legal relations entered into in the past in good faith.[368,369]

3.1.2 Judicial Cooperation

In the words of the Court, Article 234 EC establishes

> a special field of judicial cooperation which requires the national court and the Court of Justice, both keeping within their respective jurisdiction, and with the aim of ensuring that Community law is applied in a unified manner, to make direct and complementary contributions to the working out of a decision.[370]

This definition clearly reveals the relationship between the Court of Justice and the national courts as well as the main function of Article 234 EC. The Court of Justice has not been placed hierarchically as the highest court above the national courts, but cooperates with them, each exercising its own jurisdiction. The main function of Article 234 is illuminated in the above definition: to ensure uniform application of Community law in all Member States, both as regards the interpretation of this law by the national courts and in relation to the validity or invalidity of Community acts. Moreover, as will appear in the next chapter of this book, Article 234 also fulfils an important function in the maintenance of law and in legal protection. It fosters the inclusion of Community law in the national legal orders, having direct effect and priority over national law. As the Court put it in the celebrated judgment in *Rheinmühlen-Düsseldorf*, Article 234 'is essential for the preservation of the Community character of law established by the Treaty and has the object of ensuring that in all circumstances this law is the same in all States of the Community'.[371] Any gap in the system set up could undermine the effectiveness of the provisions of both primary and secondary Community law.

---

368. Case 43/75, *Defrenne*; see *supra* section 1.5. For an early critical analysis of this case law, see M. Waelbroeck, 'May the Court of Justice Limit the Retrospective Operation of its Judgments?' (1981) YEL, 115–123. See further Case 24/86, *Blaizot et al. v. University of Liège*, and the notorious Case C-262/88, *Barber v. Guardian Royal Exchange Group;* see also the so-called *Barber* Protocol (concerning Art. 119 EC) added to the EC Treaty by the TEU, as to which see T. Hervey in D. O'Keeffe and P. Twomey (eds), *Legal Issues of the Maastricht Treaty* (Chichester, 1994), 329. For a more recent case, see, e.g., C-372/98, *The Queen v. Ministry of Agriculture, Fisheries and Food*. For a similar problem, in relation to the effect in time of declarations of invalidity, see the end of the present section, *infra*, and the literature in note 425, *infra*.

369. The financial consequences which might ensue for a Member State from a preliminary ruling are in themselves no ground for limiting the effects of a judgment of the Court (see Joined Cases C-197 & 252/94, *Bautiaa and Société française maritime v. Directeurs des services fiscaux des Landes et du* Finistère and Case C-104/98, *Buchner et al. v. Sozialversicherungsanstalt der Bauern*).

370. Case 16/65, *Firma C. Schwarze v. Einfuhr- und Vorratsstelle für Getreide und Futtermittel*, 886 of English edition.

371. Case 166/73, *Rheinmühlen II*, para. 2.

The Court has also indicated, in the famous *Costa v. ENEL* judgment, that 'Article [234] is to be applied regardless of any domestic law, whenever questions relating to the interpretation of the Treaty arise'.[372] Subsequently, the Court used these points to declare that a lower court is entitled to refer to the Court of Justice a point of law covered by a ruling of a higher court, even though the lower court may in national law be bound by the ruling of the higher court; the mere existence of such a rule in national law cannot deprive the lower court of its right to make a reference.[373] While this case concerned a German procedural rule, it is clearly of importance for other jurisdictions, particularly for the Member States with (in whole or in part) a common law tradition of binding precedents, whereby lower courts must follow rulings of higher national courts.

3.1.3 The Separate Functions of the Court of Justice and National Courts

According to a consistent line of case law, Article 234 EC is based 'on a clear separation of functions between national courts or tribunals and the Court of Justice'.[374] The jurisdiction of the Court based on Article 234 EC is confined to a decision on the interpretation of Community law and on the validity of Community acts; it does not enable the Court to investigate the facts.[375] In particular, the Court does not pronounce on the application of Community law to the facts of the case referred in the proceedings before the national court.[376] It does not, therefore, consider itself competent to examine whether, for instance, a given contractual obligation between certain parties is prohibited and consequently void in accordance with Article 81(1) and (2) EC, but confines itself to answering the questions of interpretation of that Article raised by such an obligation.[377] Nor does it have jurisdiction under Article 234 to pronounce on the question whether particular laws or administrative acts of a Member State are compatible with Community law.[378] It can, though, give the national court all the elements for the interpretation of Community law which may enable it to judge the issue of compatibility of the national

---

372. Case 6/64, *Costa v. ENEL*.
373. See Case 146/73, *Rheinmühlen-Düsseldorf v. Einfuhr- und Vorratsstelle für Getreide und Futtermittel.(III)*
374. See, e.g., Case 20/64, *Sàrl Albatros v. Société des pétroles et des Combustibles liquides (Sopéco)* and Case C-30/93, *AC-ATEL Electronics Vertriebs GmbH*.
375. Case 6/64, *Costa v. ENEL*.
376. See, *inter alia*, Joined Cases 28–30/62, *Da Costa en Schaake*. Sometimes the Court does, however, go pretty far in that direction, particularly when its interpretation is requested of terms in Community law classifying products for customs purposes, e.g., Case 40/69, *Hauptzollamt Hamburg-Oberelbe v. Firma Paul G. Bollman*. See, for a very concrete answer to a question on the interpretation of Reg. 17, Art. 4(2) Case 43/69 *Braueri A. Bilger v. Jehle et al.*, and the comments in the text *supra* (note 365) about the Case C-47/90, *Delhaize*.
377. See Case 13/61, *Kledingverkoopbedrijf de Geus en Uitdenbogerd v. Robert Bosch GmbH et al.*
378. See, *inter alia*, Case 6/64, *Costa v. ENEL* and Case 20/64, *Albatros*.

laws or acts with Community law,[379] and in order to do so it may reformulate the questions asked.[380]

The strict separation between interpretation of Community law on the one hand and application of Community law *in concreto* on the other tends of course to give rise to considerable difficulties in practice. The process of thought leading to a judicial decision cannot be readily separated into two independent parts: the interpretation of general rules and the subsequent application of the rules thus interpreted to the facts. The interpretation given by a court is also determined by the facts. A study of the various judgments given by the Court pursuant to Article 234, makes it quite obvious that the Court was inspired by the facts of the case in its interpretation of Community law and has given an interpretation for a concrete case.[381]

The Court has repeatedly emphasized that national courts must explain on what grounds they consider an answer to their questions to be necessary for judgment of the main proceedings if those grounds are not unequivocally evident from the file on the case. Moreover, in order to give an interpretation of Community law which will be of use to the national court, it is essential that the national court defines the factual and legal context in which the interpretation is requested, or at the very least explains the assumptions of fact on which the preliminary questions are posed.[382] The absence of this information may lead to the reference being found inadmissible. It should be noted that there is another reason, of a procedural nature, why it is important that the court making the preliminary reference includes this information in its reference. The Court, by means of its Registrar, informs the governments of the Member States and other interested parties of the decision making the reference, and that decision provides the basis on which they may submit observations in accordance with Article 23 of the Statute of the Court.[383]

The national court in turn will often be inclined to make its request in very concrete terms.[384] Entirely in the spirit of cooperation provided for in Article 234, the Court of Justice in this respect will exercise a minimum of formality. From the request of the national court, even if it is loosely phrased,[385] it selects those

---

379. See Case 112/75, *Directeur régional de la sécurité sociale de Nancy v. Hirardin et al.*
380. Occasionally the Court in doing so may go further that the strict framework of the questions posed. See for an early example Case 1/71, *SA Cadillon v. Firma Höss, Maschinenbau KG.* However, in Case 247/86, *Société alsacienne et lorraine de télécommunications et d'électronique (Alsatel) v. SA Novasam* the Court declined to answer a question not posed by the national court, but which the defendant and the Commission had invited it to answer.
381. On the connection between interpretation and application in the context of the Court's jurisdiction under Art. 177 EC see A. Donner, 'Les rapports entre la competénce de la Cour de justice des Communautés Européennes *et* les tribunaux internes', Chapitre III, in (1965) *Recueil des Cours, Académie de droit international*, 5–58.
382. See the information note on references from national courts for a preliminary ruling, prepared by the Court, which may be consulted on the Court's website.
383. Cf. Joined Cases 141–143/81, *Holdijk et al.* More recently Joined Cases C-320–322/90, *Telemarsicabruzzo et al. v. Circostel et al.* See also Case 244/80, *Foglia v. Novello.* An overview of the case law may be found in the order in Case C-116/00, *Laguillaume.*
384. E.g., in Case 13/61, *Kledingverkoopbedrijf de Geus en Uitdenbogerd.*
385. See, e.g., Case 251/83, *Haug-Adrion v. Frankfurter Versicherungs-AG.*

questions of interpretation or validity with respect to which it has jurisdiction. Even if questions of interpretation asked by a national court are in reality questions of the validity of Community acts, 'it is appropriate for the Court to inform the national court at once of its view without compelling the national court to comply with purely formal requirements which would uselessly prolong the procedure under Article [234] and would be contrary to its very nature'.[386]

The jurisdiction of the Court of Justice is subject solely to the existence of a request within the meaning of Article 234, without it being required to examine whether the decision of the national court has become res judicata under the provisions of the latter's domestic law.[387] Article 234 EC does not prevent a decision to make a reference from being subject to the normal appeal procedure of national law;[388] the preliminary ruling procedure will continue, however, 'as long as the request of the national court has neither been withdrawn nor become devoid of object'.[389] The Court is seized of a request within the meaning of Article 234 if the questions posed evidently relate to an interpretation of Community law or the validity of a Community measure.[390] The request must originate from the national court itself, not from the parties to the action pending before it.[391] The distribution of functions between the Court of Justice and the national court means that it is not for the former to determine whether the decision to make the reference was in accordance with the rules of national law on court organization and procedure.[392]

The strict division of powers between the Court of Justice and national courts is mandatory. It cannot be altered, nor may the exercise of those powers be impeded, in particular by agreement between private parties aiming to compel national courts to request a preliminary ruling by depriving them of their discretion under the second paragraph of Article 234.[393] The division of powers also means that the Court of Justice does not regard itself as competent to criticize the grounds

---

386. Case 16/65, *Schwarze*.
387. Case 13/61, *de Geus*.
388. Case 146/73, *Rheinmühlen III*; *contra* Opinion of A.G. Warner, in Case 166/73, *Rheinmühlen II*.
389. See Case 127/73, *Belgische Radio en Televisie et al. v. SV SABAM et al.*; in Case 106/77, *Amministrazione delle Finanze dello Stato v. Simmenthal SpA* the Court refers to this as 'its unvarying practice'. In the Chanel case in the Netherlands, the Rotterdam Rechtbank informed the Court that an appeal had been lodged against its decision to refer the case and that the effect of the appeal was to defer execution of the decision to refer. The Court suspended judgment until the appeal had been decided. The case was then removed from the register of the Court as the reference had lost its purpose after the Rechtbank notified the Court that the appeal to the Gerechtshof had been successful, see the orders of 3 Jun. 1969 and 16 Jun. 1970 in Case 31/68, *SA Chanel v. Copeha Handelsmaatschappij NV*.
390. This has been clear ever since Case 26/62, *Gend & Loos*.
391. See Statute of the Court of Justice, Art. 23 and Joined Cases 31 & 33/62, *Milchwerke Heinz Wöhrmann & Sohn KG et al. v. Commission*.
392. Case 65/81, *Reina et al. v. Landeskredietbank Baden-Württemberg* and Joined Cases C-332/92 etc., *Eurico Italia Srl et al. v. Ente Nazionale Risi*.
393. Case 93/78, *Mattheus v. Doego Fruchtimport und Tiefkühlkost eG*.

or purpose of the referring court.[394] The Court will not enquire into the relevance of the reference even if it is difficult to imagine how its answers to the questions posed could affect the resolution of the main proceedings.[395] It is for the national court to judge whether interpretation of Community law is necessary to enable it to give judgment in the action.[396] 'Questions on the interpretation of Community law referred by a national court in the factual and legislative context which that court is responsible for defining and the accuracy of which is not a matter for the Court to determine, enjoy a presumption of relevance.'[397]

That does not, however, prevent the Court investigating of its own motion the circumstances in which the national court has referred a case to it.[398] In *Foglia v. Novello*,[399] the Court was at pains to point out that it could not remain indifferent to the assessments made by national courts in the exceptional cases in which those assessments may affect the proper working of the Article 234 procedure. It had to take account not only of the interests of the parties to be proceedings but also of the interests of the Community and the Member States. In Article 234 proceedings the Court does not consider that its function is to deliver advisory opinions on general or hypothetical questions, or to answer questions in the framework of procedural constructions set up with the aim of obtaining a decision on certain issues of Community law;[400] rather its duty is to assist in the administration of justice.[401] Thus it does not have jurisdiction to reply to questions which are manifestly unconnected to a real dispute, and which therefore do not correspond to an objective requirement inherent in the resolution of a dispute.[402]

3.1.4 Questions of Validity, Specific Problems

The Court's competence to pronounce on the validity of Community acts extends not only to the formal validity, i.e., their formal existence, but also to the substantive validity, i.e., the lawfulness, of such acts. The Court put an end to the uncertainty previously surrounding this issue by examining first implicitly, and later

---

394. E.g., Case 6/64, *Costa v. ENEL.*
395. See Joined Cases 2–4/82, *SA Delhaize Frères 'Le Lion' et al. v. Belgian State* and Joined Cases 98/85 etc., *Bertini et al. v. Regione Lazio et al.*
396. E.g., Case 56/65, *Société Technique Minière v. Maschinenbau Ulm GmbH*; Case 13/68, *SpA Salgoil v. Italian Ministry for Foreign Trade*; Case 180/83, *Moser v. Land Baden-Württemberg*; Joined Cases 209–213/84, *Ministère Public v. Asjes et al.*
397. Joined Cases C-94 & 202/04, *Federico Cipolla and Others*, para. 25.
398. For an overview of the case law on the Court's criteria, see Case 112/00, *Schmidberger v. Republic of Austria*, paras 30–33.
399. Case 244/80, *Foglia v. Novello.*
400. See, e.g., Case 93/78, *Mattheus v. Doego Fruchtimport und Tiefkühlkost eG*; Case C-83/91, *Meilicke v. ADV/ORGA AG*; Joined Cases C-430 & 431/99, *Inspecteur van de Belastingdienst Douane, Rotterdam district v. Sea-Land Service Inc. et al.*
401. E.g., (citing earlier judgments) Case C-415/93, *Union Royale Belge des Sociétés de Football Association ASBL et al. v. Bosman et al.*
402. Case 244/80, *Foglia v. Novello*; Case C-286/88, *Falciola Angelo SpA v. Commune di Pavia,* and Case C-281/98, *Roman Angonese v. Cassa di Risparmio di Bolzano SpaA.* See for a case in

expressly, the lawfulness of decisions addressed to Member States.[403] The Court
has also held that its jurisdiction cannot be limited as to the grounds upon which the
validity of the measures at issue in the Article 234 proceedings may be contested;[404] thus it has jurisdiction to examine all grounds capable of invalidating
those measures, including examining their compatibility with rules of international
law.[405]

According to the Court, Article 241 EC (the plea of illegality), which is as such
not applicable in the framework of a preliminary ruling,

> expresses a general principle of law under which an applicant must, in pro-
> ceedings brought under national law against the rejection of his application, be
> able to plead the illegality of a Community measure on which the national
> decision adopted in his regard is based, and the question of the validity of that
> Community measure may thus be referred to the Court in proceedings for a
> preliminary ruling.[406]

The possibility for a party to challenge the validity of earlier acts on which a
contested decision is based by means of national proceedings exists[407] only 'if
that party was not entitled under Article 230 EC to bring a direct action challenging
those acts by which it was thus affected without having been in a position to
ask that they be declared void'.[408] If it is perfectly clear that the parties would
have had standing to challenge the act directly, but failed to do so, then they may
not later on rely on the illegality of the Community decision before the national
court.[409] Under the same reasoning, on grounds of legal certainty, a Member State
may not rely before a national court on the illegality of a Community decision

---

which the Court examined the relevance of the questions posed, Case C-343/90, *Lourenço
Dias v. Director da Alfandega do porto* and Joined Cases C-430 & 431/99, *Sea-Land Service.*

403. Joined Cases 73 & 74/63, *NV Internationale Credit- en Handelsvereniging 'Rotterdam' et al. v.
Minister van Landbouw en Visserij* (implicitly) and Case 16/65, *Schwarze*(explicitly).
404. Joined Cases 21–24/72, *International Fruit Company.*
405. For a case in which the Court examined the compatibility of a Community act with rules of
customary international law (the rebus sic stantibus clause), see Case C-162/96, *Racke v.
Hauptzollamt Mainz,* annotated by Klabbers (1999) CML Rev., 179.
406. Case C-239/99, *Nachi Europe v. Hauptzollamt Krefeld,* para. 35. In that sense, see already
Case 216/82, *Universität Hamburg v. Hauptzollamt Hamburg-Kehrwieder.*
407. Joined Cases 133–136/85, *Rau* had given a different impression.
408. Case C-239/99, *Nachi Europe,* para. 36.
409. Case C-188/92, *TWD Textilwerke Deggendorf GmbH v. Germany*; confirmed in Case C-178/
95, *Wiljo NV v. Belgian State.* TWD concerned a decision addressed to the German government requiring it to ensure that state aid received by TWD, which was found to be contrary to
Art. 93 (now 88) and 92 (now 87) be repaid. The government brought the decision to the
attention of the applicant. Cf. Case 730/79, *Philip Morris v. Commission.* The situation is
different where the private party did not have a real possibility to challenge the basic decision
in an action based on Art. 230 EC (Case 216/82, *Universität Hamburg*) or where it is unclear
whether such an action would have been admissible (Case C-241/95, *Queen v. Intervention
Board for Agricultural Produce*). See further D. Wyatt, 'The Relationship between Actions for
Annulment and References on Validity after TWD Deggendorf', in Lombay and Biondi (eds),
Remedies for Breach of EC Law (1996), Ch. 6.

addressed to it if it did not lodge an action for annulment against that decision within the time limits set by Article 230, fifth paragraph, EC.[410]

The Court has expressly held in *Firma C. Schwarze v. Einfuhr- und Vorrats- stelle für Getreide und Futtermittel*[411] that although in Article 234 EC proceedings it can decide on the validity of a measure (i.e., it can declare a measure invalid), it has no jurisdiction in such proceedings to declare a measure void. While a preliminary ruling in which the Court declares a measure of an Institution invalid is addressed only to the referring court, it is a sufficient legal basis for any other court to regard the measure as invalid. Indeed this results from the particularly imperative requirements of legal certainty in addition to those of the uniform application of Community law.[412]

Yet another problem arises in relation to questions on the validity of Com- munity acts. The lower national courts have no obligation under Article 234 to refer such questions to the Court (unless, of course, they are last instance courts in the case), and for many years it was wondered whether they could thus declare a Community measure invalid independently of a judgment of the Court of Justice. The Court explicitly ruled in *Foto-Frost v. Hauptzollamt Lübeck-Ost*[413] that national courts do not have jurisdiction to declare Community measures invalid. Divergences between national courts in different Member States as to the validity of Community acts would be liable to jeopardize the unity of the Community legal order and detract from the fundamental requirement of legal certainty. Moreover, the necessary coherence of the complete system of legal remedies established by the Treaties would be undermined. For essentially the same reasons, national courts or tribunals against whose decisions there is no judicial remedy under national law are not exempt from the obligation to seek a ruling from the Court of Justice on a question relating to the validity of the provisions of a regulation even where the Court has already declared invalid analogous provisions of another comparable regulation.[414] The Court of Justice is the only body empowered, under Article 230 EC, to annul Community acts and the coherence of the system requires that it alone should pronounce on the validity of such acts.

The Court's exclusive competence to declare a Community act invalid does not however prevent a national court,[415] in interlocutory proceedings, from

---

410. Case C-241/01, *National Farmers' Union v. Secrétariat général du gouvernement*.

411. Case 16/65, *Schwarze*.

412. Case 66/80, *International Chemical Corporation v. Amministrazione delle Finanze dello Stato*; see also Case 112/83, *Société des produits de maïs v. Administration des Douanes et droits indirects*.

413. Case 314/85, *Foto-Frost v. Hauptzollamt Lübeck-Ost*. The Court did add that the general rule might need to be qualified in certain circumstances relating to interim measures but it did not as yet elaborate on this point.

414. Case C-461/03, *Gaston Schul Douane-expediteur*. The *CILFIT* ruling concerns only questions of interpretation, and not questions relating to the validity of Community acts. See *infra* note 448.

415. As the actual status of national administrative authorities is not in general such as to guarantee that they have the same degree of independence and impartiality as national courts, they are not in a position to adopt interim measures, even in the case in which a court of a Member State takes the view that these conditions have been satisfied, see Case C-453/03, *ABNA and Others*.

suspending the enforcement of a national measure based on a Community act, such as a regulation,[416] or from granting other interim measures,[417] if it has serious doubts about the validity of the Community act involved. However, the interim measures in question may only last until Court has delivered its ruling on the validity of the Community act concerned. If the question has not yet been referred to the Court, the national court granting interim relief must make a reference itself, setting out why it believes the regulation concerned to be invalid. Moreover, the uniform application of Community law requires that identical conditions apply in all Member States with regard to the granting of suspensory relief (even though the making and examination of the application for such relief is a matter for national law). The Court has found that the conditions applying to the grant of interim relief by the Court itself in actions for annulment should also apply to the grant of interim relief by national courts. This means that the criterion of urgency has to be satisfied: it must be necessary for the suspensory measures to be adopted and take effect before the decision on the substance of the case, in order to avoid serious and irreparable damage to the party seeking such measures. Furthermore, the national court must take full account of the Community interest,[418] so that Community regulations should not be set aside too easily. Finally, in reaching its decision the national court must respect the case law of the Court of Justice and the CFI as to the validity of the Community act, as well as any interim orders in which similar interim relief has been granted at the Community level.

Sometimes there is little point in declaring an act invalid because the unlawfulness does not lie so much in what the text contains as in what it omits. In such cases, the Court contents itself with a declaration that the relevant provision is incompatible with Community law and that the competent Community Institution is obliged to adopt the necessary measures to correct the incompatibility.[419] In this sense, the Court implicitly recognizes that a declaration of invalidity in the context of Article 234 proceedings brings into operation the duty laid down in Article 233 EC to take the necessary measures to comply with the judgment; this analogous application of the terms of Article 233 (which applies on the annulment of an act or condemnation of a failure to act) is justified, as the Court later expressly

---

416. Joined Cases C-143/88 & 92/89, *Zuckerfabrik Süderdithmarschen AG et al. v. Hauptzollamt Itzehoe et al.* Referring to Case C-213/89, *The Queen. v. Secretary of State for Transport, ex parte Factortame Ltd et al.*, the Court observed that the interim legal protection which Community law ensured for individuals before national courts had to remain the same, irrespective of whether they were contesting the compatibility of national provisions with Community law or the validity of secondary Community law itself, as the dispute in both cases was in fact based on Community law.

417. Case C-465/93, *Atlanta Fruchthandelsgesellschaft and others (I) v. Bundesamt für Ernährung und Forstwirtschaft.*

418. It is up to the national court to decide, in accordance with its own rules of procedure, which is the most appropriate way of obtaining all relevant information on the Community act in question. It is not *obliged* to give the Institution which adopted the act an opportunity to express its views, see Case C-334/95, *Krüger v. Hauptzollamt Hamburg-Jonas*, paras 45–46.

419. E.g., Joined Cases 124/76 & 20/77, *SA Moulins et Huileries de Pont-à-Mousson v. Office National Interprofessionnel des Céréales.*

indicated,[420] by the necessary consistency between the preliminary ruling procedure and the procedure of an action for annulment as two mechanisms for reviewing the legality of acts of the Community Institutions.

In a series of judgments on 15 October 1980[421] the Court proceeded in preliminary rulings to apply the second paragraph of Article 231 EC (which permits the Court to uphold the effects (or some of them) of a regulation which it has annulled) in relation to a Commission regulation concerning monetary compensatory amounts for dependent products. Because a declaration of invalidity operates retroactively (*ex tunc*), on the ground of considerations of legal certainty the Court declined to allow the fact that the Regulation had been found invalid to enable the charging or payment of monetary compensatory amounts relating to periods before the date of the judgment to be challenged.[422] The operation from the date of the judgment (*ex nunc*) of the declaration of invalidity which thus resulted, and affecting everyone concerned (effect *erga omnes*), attracted much criticism;[423] the Court in other proceedings subsequently made it plain that, in the interests of a uniform application of Community law throughout the Community, any determination of a temporal limitation on the effect of a declaration of invalidity is a matter exclusively for it, and not, therefore, a matter for the national court.[424] But the criticism was clearly taken to heart, as subsequently, where the Court decided to limit the temporal effect of a declaration of invalidity, it also considered whether an

420. Case 112/83, *Société des produits de maïs*.
421. Case 4/79, *Société Co-opérative 'Providence Agricole de la Champagne' v. Office National Interprofessionnel des Céréales (ONIC)*; Case 109/79, *Sàrl Maiseries de Beauce v. ONIC* and Case 145/79, *SA Roquette Fréres v. French State Customs Administration*.
422. E.g., Case 145/79, *Roquette*. The referring courts declined to follow the judgment on this point, taking the view that only the national court had jurisdiction to determine the consequences of a declaration of invalidity, a view upheld on appeal by the Cour d'Appel, Douai (1993) Gaz. du. Pal., 292. See Servan Schreiber 'EEC Law in French Courts 1980–1984' (1986) EL Rev., 158,176–177.
423. E.g., M. Waelbroeck; 'May the Court of Justice Limit the Retrospective Operation of its Judgments?' (1981) YBEL, 115; G. Bebr, 'Preliminary Rulings of the Court of Justice, their Authority and Temporal Effect (1981) CML Rev., 475; L. Neville Brown, 'Agrimonetary Byzantinism and Prospective Overruling' (1981) CML Rev., 509; Masclet annotation of *Roquette* (1986) RTDE, 161; G. Isaac 'La modulation par la Cour de justice des effets dans le temps de ses arrets d'invalidité' (1987) CDE, 444, and E. Paulis 'Les effets des arrets d'annulation de la Cour de justice des Communautés européennes' (1987) CDE, 243. Much of the criticism is conveniently discussed by A.G. Darmon in Case C-228/92 *Roquette Frères SA v. Hauptzollamt Geldern*.
424. See the already mentioned Case 112/83, *Société des produits de maïs SA*, annotated by Bebr (1985) CML Rev., 771; the Court was giving judgment on a reference from the Tribunal d'Instance, Paris concerning the consequences of invalidity of Community measures and designed to resolve the uncertainty resulting from the national judgments in the earlier litigation. Subsequently the Cour de Cassation Cass. Comm. 10 Dec. 1985 (1986) RTDE, 195 followed the approach of the Court of Justice, unlike the Conseil d'État (1985) Rec. Lebon 233, (1985) AJDA, 615. See also on this problem the judgment of the Corte Costituzionale in Italy in *Fragd v. Amministrazione delle Finanze dello Stato* (1989) *Riv. Dir. Int.*, 103; this is also mentioned in Ch. VII *infra* at note 166.

exception to that temporal limitation was to be made in favour of certain parties which had already brought actions against the measure.[425]

3.2   NATIONAL COURTS AND TRIBUNALS: POWER AND
             OBLIGATION TO REFER

Which courts or tribunals are entitled or obliged to ask the European Court for a preliminary ruling, and under what conditions are they obliged to refer the matter? These questions relate to the interpretation of Article 234; they are, therefore, questions which may or must themselves be the subject of a request for a preliminary ruling when a national court or tribunal is confronted with them.

First of all, what is to be understood by the term 'any court or tribunal of a Member State' under Article 234 EC? It clearly covers those bodies which according to the commonly used terminology in each of these Member States belong to the judiciary in the wide sense;[426] it thus includes administrative courts. Administrative bodies which decide on administrative appeals against decisions of bodies to which they are organizationally linked will not be considered 'courts or tribunals' for the purposes of Article 234 references, even if in the national system they are regarded as exercising an appellate function, as they are not acting as third parties in relation to the authority which adopted the decision under appeal.[427]

Moreover, it is clear from the case law that it is not necessary to wait until the substantive trial of the action; a court or tribunal seized of an interlocutory point may make a reference.[428] The nature of the case before a court does not restrict the right to refer; thus Article 234 can be used in the framework of voluntary jurisdiction and in non-contentious proceedings, providing these are intended to lead to a decision of a judicial nature.[429] The corollary of a national court not being empowered to make a reference unless there is a case pending before it is that the Court of Justice has no jurisdiction to hear a reference when at the time it is made the referring court is

425. See, e.g., Case C-228/92, *Roquette Frères SA v. Hauptzollamt Geldern*. For another case of judicial transitional measures concerning the consequences of a declaration of invalidity, Case 41/84, *Pinna v. Caisse d'Allocations Familiales de la Savoie*. See also T. Koopmans, 'Retrospectivity Reconsidered', (1980) CLJ, 287.

426. It embraces even courts in associated countries and territories to which only part of the EC Treaty applies. Cf. Joined Cases 100 & 101/89, *Kaefer and Procacci v. French State*, Case C-260/90, *Leplat v. Territory of French Polynesia* (French Polynesia) and Case C-163/90, *Administration des douanes et droits indirects v. Legros and others* (La Réunion). See A. Arnull, 'The Evolution of the Court's Jurisdiction under Article 177 EEC' (1993) *EL Rev.*, 129, 132. As to the Isle of Man, see Case C-355/89, *Department of Health and Social Security v. Barr et al.* (and in particular the Opinion of A.G. Jacobs). As to Jersey, see, e.g., Case C-171/96, *Pereira Roque v. H.E. The Lieutenant Governor of Jersey*.

427. Case C-24/92, *Corbiau v. Administration des Contributions du Grand-Duché de Luxembourg*.

428. Case 107/76, *Hoffmann-La Roche v. Centrafarm Vertriebsgesellschaft Pharmazeutischer Erzeugnisse mbH*.

429. Case 199/82, *Amministrazione delle Finanze dello Stato v. SpA San Giorgio* (referring to earlier judgments); see also Case 32/74, *Friedrich Haaga GmbH*. But see Case C-111/94,

not in a position to take the ruling on the reference into account, for instance when the procedure before the referring court has terminated.[430]

Classification problems arise particularly for tribunals which lie on the border between private and public law.[431] In order to determine whether a body making a reference is a court or tribunal for the purposes of Article 234, the Court takes account of a number of factors, such as whether the body is established by law, whether it is permanent, whether its jurisdiction is compulsory, whether its procedure is *inter partes*, whether it applies rules of law and whether it is independent.[432] Recent case law demonstrates that this test is applied globally, and the Court does not apply strict criteria to the various factors individually.[433]

Arbitrators to whom parties have agreed to submit their dispute for resolution are not a court or tribunal in the sense of Article 234 EC.[434] In general, there will be an insufficiently close link between such an arbitration and the general system of judicial protection of the Member State to qualify such an arbitrator as a court or tribunal under that Article.[435] This case law is of particular interest in countries where a not insignificant proportion of the administration of justice is conducted by arbitration; such arbitration may involve the application of Community law, particularly in the competition field. The effect of refusing Article 234 EC references from arbitrators is that the Court's scope for using its influence to ensure the uniform application and maintenance of Community law for, *inter alia*, the benefit of the judicial protection of those affected by Community law is restricted.[436]

Job Centre Coop. ARL (on voluntary jurisdiction not leading to a decision of a judicial nature). For a reference by an Examining Magistrate at a Tribunal de Grande Instance, see Case 65/79, *Procureur de la République v. Chatain*. See further, e.g., Case 14/86, *Pretore di Salo v. X*(combination of the functions of public prosecutor and examining magistrate), Case C-18/93, *Corsica Ferries Italia Srl v. Corpo dei Piloti del Porto di Genova*, Case C-195/98, *Österreichischer Gewerkschaftsbund, Gewerkschaft öffentlicher Dienst v. Republik Österreich*, Case C-178/99, *Doris Salzmann* and Case *C-53/03, Syfait et al. v. GlaxoSmithKline plc et al.*

430. Case 338/85, *Fratelli Pardini SpA v. Ministero del commercio con l'estero et al.*; Case C-159/90, *Society for the Protection of the Unborn Child Ireland v. Grogan et al.*

431. See, e.g., Case 61/65,*Vaassen (née Goebbels) v. Bestuur van het Beamtenfonds voor het Mijnbedrijf*, Case 138/80, *Jules Borker* (Paris Bar Council), 246/80, Case *Broekmeulen v. Huisarts Registratie Commissie*.

432. Case C-53/03, *Syfait*, referring to earlier case law.

433. In Joined Cases C-110–147/98, *Gabalfrisa v. Agencia Estatal de Administración Tributaria (AEAT)*, the Court reached the opposite conclusion from its Advocate General with regard to the question whether the Spanish *Tribunal Económico-Administrativo Regional* was independent. See also Case C-407/98, *Abrahamsson and Anderson v. Fogelqvist*.

434. Case 102/81, *Nordsee v. Reederei Mond*.

435. Case 246/80, *Broekmeulen v. Huisarts Registratie Commissie* and Case 102/81, *Nordsee*. See W. Alexander and E. Grabandt, 'National Courts Entitled to Ask Preliminary Rulings under Article 177 of the EEC Treaty: The Case Law of the Court of Justice' (1982) CML Rev., 413–420. A court deciding on an appeal from an arbitrator's award is a 'court or tribunal' for the purposes of Art. 234 EC, even when it must give judgment 'according to what appears fair and reasonable' cf. Case C-393/92, *Gemeente Almelo et al. v. Energiebedrijf IJsselmij NV*.

436. The Court has ruled that 'where its domestic rules of procedure require a national court to grant an application for annulment of an arbitration award where such an application is founded on failure to observe national rules of public policy, it must also grant such an application where it

The next question is which courts or tribunals are not only entitled to refer questions to the Court but are also under an obligation to do so. The obligation to refer binds all courts or tribunals of a Member State 'against whose decisions there is no judicial remedy under national law'.[437]

The obligation to refer does not apply, however, if a question of Community law is raised in interlocutory proceedings and the decision to be taken does not bind the court or tribunal which later has to deal with the substance of the case. This is, however, provided that each of the parties can institute proceedings on the merits of the case (or require them to be instituted), even before the courts or tribunals of another jurisdictional system, and that during such proceedings any question of Community law provisionally decided in the summary proceedings may be re-examined and be the subject of a reference.[438]

The question has been raised whether the obligation to refer binds the highest court in the case rather than simply the highest court in the hierarchy, for instance when in a concrete case no further remedy lies because a claim is below a certain sum. This point has been the subject of divergent views (the debate between advocates of the 'concrete' theory who favour the standpoint just advanced, and the advocates of the 'abstract' theory who would restrict the obligation to the highest court in the hierarchy), but the 'concrete' theory is supported in the case law of the Court of Justice, in a paragraph of the judgment in *Costa v. ENEL* in which the Court apparently considered that the magistrate of Milan, against whose decision there was no remedy available in the concrete case, was under an obligation to refer.[439] It is now established that decisions which are open to appeal on the merits only subject to a prior declaration of admissibility are not to be considered decisions of a court against whose decisions there is no judicial remedy in the sense of Article 234 third paragraph.[440]

---

is founded on failure to comply with the prohibition laid down in Article [81(1) EC]', Case C-126/97, *EcoSwiss v. Bennetton;* annotated by A. Komninos (2000) CML Rev., 459–478. See also Case C-168/05, *Mostaza Claro* concerning the public policy character of Art. 6(1) of the Council Dir. 93/13/EEC on unfair terms in consumer contracts (O.J. 1993, L 95/29) according to which unfair terms used in a contract concluded with a consumer by a seller or supplier 'shall . . . not be binding on the consumer'. The Court held that a national court seized of an action for annulment of an arbitration award must annul that award where the agreement contains an unfair term, even though the consumer has not pleaded such invalidity in the course of the arbitration proceedings, but only in the action for annulment.

437. In some language versions of the Treaty, e.g., Dutch, there was some uncertainty as to whether this phrase meant the possibility of appeal, or the possibility of a remedy. This was clarified in Joined Cases 28–30/62, *Da Costa en Schaake.*

438. Joined Cases 35 & 36/82, *Morson and Jhanjan v. State of the Netherlands et al.* and Case 107/76, *Hoffmann-La Roche v. Centrafarm Vertriebsgesellschaft Pharmazeutischer Erzeugnisse mbH* in relation to 'einstweilige Verfügung' in German civil procedural law.

439. In Case 6/64 *Costa v. ENEL.*

440. Case C-99/00, *Kenny Roland Lyckeskog.*

Finally, the special situation should be mentioned of the highest courts of the Benelux countries, which may find themselves in a situation in which they are obliged to refer preliminary questions to the Benelux Court[441] concerning the interpretation of rules of law which are common to the Benelux countries, but which also concern questions of interpretation of Community law (e.g., a directive). When such a situation occurred, the Court of Justice ruled that the Benelux Court, being a court common to a number of Member States, is a court in the sense of Article 234 EC; the Benelux Court – like the highest national court –, whose decisions are not subject to appeal, is bound to refer the questions of Community law which are raised before it to the Court of Justice.[442]

Each of these courts is however relieved of the obligation to refer, on the basis of the authority of an interpretation provided by the Court under Article 234 EC (*'acte éclairé'*, see below), if one of these courts has already obtained a preliminary ruling from the Court of Justice on a question of Community law which is substantially the same as that now raised.

3.3   RELEVANCE, *'ACTE ÉCLAIRÉ'* AND *'ACTE CLAIR'*

Is the court of highest instance in the case always obliged to refer as soon as the condition is met that a question of Community law has been raised before it? At first sight the third paragraph of Article 234 would seem to imply this. The Court, too, in principle does not consider that there is any limitation on the obligation to refer, as soon as such a question has been raised.[443] This statement, however, can be reconciled with the theory that a second condition must be met, i.e., the one mentioned in the second paragraph of Article 234, which establishes the possibility of referring a question to the Court: the national court (also one which is obliged to refer) must consider that a decision on the point of Community law is necessary to enable it to give judgment. In fact, in order to be obliged to refer, a court or tribunal against whose decision there is no judicial remedy must first be entitled to do so in accordance with the second paragraph of Article 234.[444] If this were not so, unacceptable consequences would result. The mere fact that a question of Community law is raised, however irrelevant or absurd, would oblige the court of highest

---

441. Cf. Arts. 1, 6 and 7, Treaty Concerning the Establishment and the Statute of a Benelux Court, Treaty signed in Brussels on 31 March 1965 between the Kingdom of Belgium, the Grand Duchy of Luxembourg and the Kingdom of the Netherlands (1965) *European Yearbook*, 259–266.
442. Case C-337/95, *Parfums Christian Dior SA and Parfums Christian Dior BV v. Evora BV.*
443. Joined Cases 28-30/62, *Da Costa en Schaake.*
444. Cf. Protocol of 3 Jun. 1971 on the interpretation of the Convention of 28 Sep. 1968 on jurisdiction and the enforcement of civil and commercial judgments (concluded under Art. 220 EC, consolidated version O.J. 1998, C 27/1), Art. 3(1). The report, annexed to the Protocol, of the working group of experts made it clear that this provision was to be considered as conforming to the hitherto generally accepted interpretation of Art. 234 EC; see Case 283/81, *Srl CILFIT et al. v. Ministry of Health*, paras 9 and 10.

instance in the case to refer to the Court of Justice. This would open wide the door to chicanery.

The relevance of the question raised[445] is therefore a precondition for the right, and consequently the obligation, to refer to the Court. Article 234 leaves it to the discretion of the national court (including one which is obliged to refer) to decide whether application of Community law is necessary to enable it to give judgment in the dispute before it. It is of the greatest importance that national courts should use this discretion properly. It implies that a national court cannot be (or, as the case may be, is not) obliged to refer to the Court of Justice if it is able to settle the dispute exclusively on grounds of national law.[446]

Even if the highest court in the case considers a decision on a question raised before it necessary to enable it to settle a dispute, it is not always obliged to refer. The Court itself made an exception to this obligation. The

> authority of an interpretation under Article [234] already given by the Court may deprive this obligation of its purpose and thus empty it of its substance. Such is the case especially when the question raised is materially identical with a question which has already been the subject of a preliminary ruling in a similar case.[447]

This situation is often described as '*acte éclairé*'. The Court took the opportunity in *CILFIT* to take this further,[448] noting that the same effect (i.e., that the obligation to refer becomes devoid of purpose) 'may be produced where previous decisions of the Court have already dealt with the point of law in question, irrespective of the nature of the proceedings which led to those decisions, even though the questions at issue are not strictly identical'.[449] Thus it is clear that the previous decisions do not need to have been given in Article 234 rulings. The Court went on to stress, though, 'that in all such circumstances national courts and tribunals, including those referred to in the third paragraph of

---

445. On the marginal control exercised by the Court on the relevance of the questions posed, see the observations above concerning the functions of the Court and the national courts.

446. For instance, in a civil claim against another party who has benefited from a contractual failure of a third party, relating to a contract to which the claimant is not party, then it is not relevant whether the contract was invalid under Community law (e.g., Art. 81(2) EC) and the court is not obliged to refer. See in the Netherlands *KIM-Sieverding*, Hoge Raad [1961] NJ, 245. Cf. Case 283/81, *CILFIT* para. 10.

447. Joined Cases 28–30/62, *Da Costa en Schaake*, 31 of the English edition.

448. It is important to note that the *CILFIT* ruling only concerns questions of interpretation, and not questions relating to the validity of Community acts. National courts or tribunals against whose decisions there is no judicial remedy under national law are not exempt from the obligation to seek a ruling from the Court of Justice on a question relating to the validity of the provisions of a regulation even where the Court has already declared invalid analogous provisions of another comparable regulation. See Case C-461/03, *Gaston Schul Douane-expediteur*.

449. Case 283/81, *CILFIT*, para. 14.

Article 177, remain entirely at liberty to bring a matter before the Court of Justice if they consider it appropriate to do so'.[450] The Court always retains the possibility of reconsidering its case law.[451]

The Court in *CILFIT*[452] also added another exception to the obligation to refer, an exception which in practice was being made by the highest national courts even before the judgment in *CILFIT*. This follows French legal practice known as the '*théorie de l'acte clair*'. This theory holds that the obligation to refer does not apply if the highest court concerned is of opinion that there can be no reasonable doubt about the answers to the questions raised. Put in the words of the Court in *CILFIT*, 'the correct application of Community law may be so obvious as to leave no scope for any reasonable doubt as to the manner in which the question raised is to be resolved'.[453] But the Court has warned that it is not enough that the highest court concerned thinks that the answer is evident. Before it comes to a conclusion that there is no reasonable doubt on the point 'the national court or tribunal must be convinced that the matter is equally obvious to the courts of the other Member States and to the Court of Justice'. The national court or tribunal must assess this 'on the basis of the characteristic features of Community law and the particular

---

450. Ibid., at para. 15. E.g., the question put by the *Bundesfinanzhof* in Case 28/67, *Molkerei Zentrale Westfalen-Lippe v. Hauptzollamt Paderborn*, asking whether the Court maintained the interpretation of Art. 95 it had given in an earlier judgment. Sometimes the Court has been flooded with references on a point identical to one decided earlier; in almost exasperation it responded with a terse judgment saying that the case raised an issue identical to that in an earlier judgment, a copy of which was annexed (e.g., Joined Cases 79 & 80/84, *Procureur de la République v. Chabaud and Rémy* and Joined Cases 271–274/84 & 6–7/85, *Procureur de la République et al. v. Chiron et al.*). If a reference arrives on a point already decided, the Court's registry will draw the attention of the referring court to the earlier judgment and ask it if it wishes to maintain the reference; usually the national court then withdraws the reference, although it is, of course, perfectly entitled not to do so. That the national court may then nevertheless still fail correctly to deduce the solution under Community law to the case in hand is evident from Case C-224/01, *Köbler v. Republik Österreich*.

451. E.g., redefinition of scope of free movement of goods provisions following Joined Cases C-267 & 268/91, *Keck and Mithouard*; but see already generally, Arnull, 'Owing up to fallibility: Precedent and the Court of Justice' (1993) CML Rev., 247.

452. The role *CILFIT* played in the arbitration regarding The Iron Rhine ('IJzeren Rijn') Railway between Belgium and The Netherlands is also noteworthy. The Tribunal having to decide issues of EC law in order to enable it to render its award applied the *CILFIT* criteria by analogy (see para. 104 of the Award). In this way it tried to steer clear of Art. 292 EC which obliges Member States not to submit a dispute concerning the interpretation or application of this Treaty to any method of settlement other than those provided for therein. For the award, see the website of the Permanent Court of Arbitration, under 'Cases'.

453. Case 283/81, *CILFIT*, para. 16 et seq. See H. Rasmussen (1984) EL Rev., 242, G. Bebr (1983) CML Rev., 439 and D. Wyatt (1983) EL Rev., 179. Cf. Art. 6(4) of the Treaty concerning the establishment and the Statute of a Benelux Court (1965) *European Yearbook*, 259–266, which, however, prohibits reference to this court in such a case.

difficulties to which its interpretation gives rise'.[454] The Court then proceeded to indicate what should be borne in mind, namely:

- Community legislation is drafted in several languages, the different language versions being equally authentic. Interpretation of a provision of Community law thus involves a comparison of the different language versions.
- Even when the different language versions completely agree, Community law uses its own terminology. Moreover, legal concepts do not necessarily have the same meaning in Community law and in the law of the various Member States.[455]
- Every provision of Community law must be placed in its context and interpreted in the light of the provisions of Community law as a whole, in the light of the objectives of Community law and its state of evolution at the date on which the provision involved is to be applied.

The freedom not to refer a question to the Court of Justice will have to be used with great circumspection by the highest national court. Donner, himself then a judge of the European Court, warned:

One should be suspicious of the apparent clarity of the texts. Experience shows that the same technical term may have different meanings for lawyers coming from different countries. This is a specific danger of Community law, for the very reason that on the one hand the juridical vocabulary of the six countries is practically identical, whilst on the other hand the terms have acquired a slightly, and sometimes even profoundly, different connotation under the influence of six independent sets of case law.[456]

It must be recognized that the *acte clair* exception to the obligation to refer is necessary; it is neither in the interest of the satisfactory administration of justice nor conducive to proper cooperation between the Court of Justice and the highest judicial bodies in Member States if the latter are subjected so strongly to the control of the Court that they are automatically obliged to refer, even if there cannot be the slightest doubt on the interpretation of the text of Community law.

In this way, the main function of Article 234 – ensuring uniform application of Community law in the Member States – is reasonably safeguarded. This does not alter the fact that many if the highest national courts in the Member States, which are regularly required to apply Community law, often find the *CILFIT* case law too restrictive, and as a result are sometimes somewhat free in the use they make of it.

---

454. Case 283/81, *CILFIT*, paras 16–17.
455. E.g., the concept of 'public policy' in Arts. 30, 39 and 46 EC is just such an example: it is not a concept determined by national law alone; see, e.g., Case 36/75, *Rutili v. Ministre de l'intérieur*, and further Ch. VIII of this book.
456. *Les rapports entre la compétence de la Cour de Justice des Communautés Europiéennes et les tribunaux internes* Rec. des Cours A.D.I., 1965. II, 45 (translation by Gormley). This is even more true with 15 or 27 Member States.

In this context, the suggestion by Advocate General Jacobs to consider the CILFIT case law applicable only 'where a reference is truly appropriate to achieve the objectives of Article [234] EC, namely when there is a general question and where there is a genuine need for uniform interpretation', is an interesting one.[457] With the accession of ten new Member States, whose national courts have no experience in the application of this body of law, it seems in any case not likely that the Court will revisit its case law in order to give the highest national courts a greater responsibility of their own in deciding whether there is sufficient reason to make a reference to the Court of Justice on a question which has arisen.

3.4   SPECIAL FORMS OF PROCEDURE

Article 68 sets two restrictions to the application of Article 234 EC to Title IV of Part 3 of the EC Treaty. The first paragraph of this Article limits the category of courts and tribunals which may request preliminary rulings in relation to the interpretation of Title IV or the validity of acts based on the provisions of that Title. Only a court against whose decisions there is no judicial remedy under national law is empowered, and obliged, when such a question arises in a case before it, to put that question to the Court of Justice for a preliminary ruling if it considers that a decision on the question is necessary to enable it to give judgment.[458] Lower courts are therefore not empowered to bring preliminary references to the Court of Justice.

This restriction was imposed because the framers of the Treaty of Amsterdam did not wish to create delays to speedy national judicial proceedings in the area of migration policy, possibly at first and second instance, by time-consuming preliminary references. It is an open question whether in fact the exclusion of lower courts can prevent delays in national judicial proceedings in this area. After all, once a higher court puts a certain question to the Court, there is a substantial chance that lower courts which are confronted with the same question will suspend proceedings until the preliminary ruling of the Court of Justice in the matter. Another objection in relation to the exclusion of lower courts from the possibility to bring a preliminary reference is the danger that divergent interpretations of the provisions of Title IV and acts based thereupon, in relation to the admission of aliens, may lead to changes in flows of immigrants. In order to prevent such divergences, Article 68(3) provides for a kind of 'request for interpretation in the interest of the law'. The Council, the Commission or a Member State may request the Court of Justice to give a ruling on a question of

---

457.   Opinion in Case C-338/95, *Wiener S.I. GmbH v. Hauptzollamt Emmerich*, para. 64.
458.   Art. 68(1) EC does not alter the obligation to refer, since the formulation 'if it considers that a decision on the question is necessary to enable it to give judgment' is also a condition for the existence of the power to refer under Art. 234(2) EC, and therefore also for the existence of the obligation to refer under the third paragraph of Art. 234; cf. note 444 *supra*.

interpretation of these provisions, but such an interpretation will not apply to judgments of national courts or tribunals which have become res judicata.

The special procedures under Article 68 also apply to measures which are adopted in the field of cooperation in civil matters having cross-border implications, to the extent these are necessary for the proper functioning of the internal market (Art. 65 EC).[459] In this context,[460] Council Regulation 44/2001 of 22 December 2000 on jurisdiction and the recognition and enforcement of judgments in civil and commercial matters[461] has in the meantime been adopted. This Regulation entered into force for all Member States, with the exception of Denmark,[462] on 1 March 2002, and replaces in their mutual relationships the Brussels Convention on Jurisdiction and the Enforcement of Judgments in Civil and Commercial Matters (the Brussels Convention).[463] As of that date, the Article 68 EC procedure applies, rather than the preliminary reference procedure regulated by the 1971 Protocol on interpretation attached to the Convention. In cases on jurisdiction and enforcement of judgments that means a step backwards, as it will no longer be so that the courts of the Member States sitting in an appellate capacity may request the Court of Justice to give preliminary rulings on questions of interpretation, as was possible under the Protocol.[464]

The second restriction imposed by Article 68 EC, in its second paragraph, concerns the jurisdiction of the Court. The Court is denied jurisdiction to rule on

---

459. On this cooperation, see J. Basedow, 'The Communitarization of the Conflict of Laws under the Treaty of Amsterdam' (2000) CML Rev., 687–708.
460. On 1 March 2001 another Regulation entered into force: Council Reg. (EC) No 1347/2000 of 29 May 2000 on jurisdiction and the recognition and enforcement of judgments in matrimonial matters and in matters of parental responsibility for children of both spouses (O.J. 2000, L 160/19).
461. O.J. 2001, L 12/1.
462. According to the Protocol on the position of Denmark, attached to the Treaty of Amsterdam, that county is not bound by the provisions of Title IV EC. However, since 1 Jul. 2007, in relations with this country, Reg. 44/2001 will apply, in an amended form, in conformity with an Agreement between the European Community and the Kingdom of Denmark (O.J. 2005, L 299/62). For the jurisdiction of the Court see Art. 6 of the Agreement. The UK and Ireland, which also have an exceptional position in relation to Title IV EC, have declared on the basis of Art. 3 of the Protocol on their position attached to the Treaty of Amsterdam, that they wish to participate in the adoption and application of the Regulation. See J. Basedow, op. cit. *supra* note 459, section 4, and P.J. Kuijper, 'Some Legal Problems Associated with the Communitarization of Policy on Visas, Asylum and Immigration under the Amsterdam Treaty and Incorporation of the Schengen Acquis' (2000) CML Rev., 345 and A. McDonnell ed., 'The Evolution of the Third Pillar from Maastricht to the European Constitution: Institutional Aspects', in 'A Review of Forty Years of Community Law' (2005) 333, section 4 (Variable geometry).
463. Such protocols have also been attached to other treaties. See M.R. Mok, 'The Interpretation by the ECJ of Special Conventions Concluded Between the Member States' (1971) CML Rev., 485–494. See also note 351 *supra*.
464. See the Commission's observations in its Communication, *Adaptation of the Provisions of Title IV of the Treaty Establishing the European Community Relating to the Jurisdiction of the Court of Justice with a View to Ensuring More Effective Judicial Protection* (COM(2006)346 final), 7–8.

any measure or decision taken pursuant to Article 62(1) (abolition of controls of persons at internal borders) relating to the maintenance of law and order and the safeguarding of internal security. From the point of view of uniformity of the law and judicial protection this provision is highly regrettable.[465]

In the context of the Third Pillar (police and judicial cooperation in criminal matters), provision is made for the optional acceptance of jurisdiction of the Court of Justice to give preliminary rulings on the validity and interpretation of framework decisions and decisions, on the interpretation of conventions established under Title VI of the TEU and on the validity and interpretation of the measures implementing them.[466] The Member States can accept the Court's jurisdiction in these matters by means of a declaration. They then have the choice of whether or not to restrict the category of national courts to those against whose decisions there is no judicial remedy. These courts are not obliged to refer, but the Member States may retain the right, in their declaration, to include such an obligation in their national law.[467] As to the use made of these options, the following remarks may be made.[468] Bulgaria, Cyprus, Denmark, Estonia, Ireland, Malta, Poland, Romania, Slovakia and the United Kingdom did not make such a declaration. Of the other Member States, only Spain restricted the category of courts which could make a reference to courts of last instance. The three Benelux countries, Germany, France, Italy, Austria and Slovenia indicated that they wished to include provisions in their national law obliging courts against whose decisions there is no judicial remedy to make a reference.

Here too, the jurisdiction of the Court is restricted in an unsatisfactory manner: it may not review the validity or proportionality of operations carried out by the police or other law-enforcement services of a Member State or the exercise of the responsibilities incumbent upon Member States with regard to the maintenance of law and order and the safeguarding of internal security.[469]

---

465. In its Communication, *supra* note 464, the Commission proposes to bring the specific provisions of Art. 68 EC into line with the standard rules on judicial protection of the Treaty, in all fields covered by Title IV. Provided that the handling of preliminary rulings in particularly urgent cases could be speeded up sufficiently, the Council seems to be willing to consider this favourably, but only insofar as it concerns the removal of the restriction of Art. 68(1) EC, which prohibits national courts other than those of final instance from applying to the Court for preliminary rulings. Following discussions regarding the introduction of an 'emergency preliminary ruling procedure' which took place within the Council on the basis of two discussion papers drawn up by the Court of Justice, the Council has recently amended the Court's Statute and its Rules of Procedure to this end O.J. 2008, L 24/39–43.

466. Art. 35 TEU. The 'emergency preliminary ruling procedure' proposed by the Court (see the previous note) is meant to be also applied to the procedure under Art. 35 TEU.

467. Declaration No. 10, on Article K.7 of the Treaty on European Union, attached to the Treaty of Amsterdam.

468. Cf. list in O.J. 1999, C 120/24.

469. The first case in which the Court was called upon to give a ruling following a reference based on Art. 35 TEU was Joined Cases C-187/01 & C-385/01, *Hüseyin Gözütok and Klaus Brügge* (*ne bis in idem*). See also on the scope of the Court's jurisdiction under this Article, Case C-354/04 P, *Gestoras Pro Amnistía a.o. v. Council* and Case C-355/04 P, *Segi a.o. v. Council*.

The Treaty of Lisbon provides for the abolition of the special forms of procedure mentioned in Articles 68 EC and 35 TEU. Instead of these, the general provisions concerning the jurisdiction of the Court of Justice will be applicable. The Treaty of Lisbon imposes, however, two restrictions on the jurisdiction of the Court in the field of judicial cooperation in criminal matters and police cooperation, which at present is included in the Third Pillar, but is destined to be incorporated in the provisions on the area of freedom, security and justice of the TFEU. Firstly, Article 276 of the TFEU will forbid the Court to review the validity or proportionality of operations carried out by the police or other law-enforcement services or the exercise of the responsibilities incumbent upon Member States with regard to the maintenance of law and order and the safeguarding of internal security (cf. Art. 35(5) TEU). And secondly, Article 10 of the Protocol No. 10 on transitional provisions lays down that, as a transitional measure, Article 35 TEU will remain applicable, for a period not exceeding five years after the date of the entry in force of the Treaty of Lisbon, with respect to acts of the Union in this field which have been adopted before the entry into force of the Treaty.

4   INTERIM MEASURES BEFORE THE COMMUNITY COURTS

Appeals brought before the Court of Justice do not have suspensive effect,[470] but the Court may order the suspension of the application of a contested act if it considers that circumstances so require.[471] The Court may also order any other interim measures it considers necessary in cases brought before it.[472] It is apparent that interim measures are considered to have an accessory character, and that therefore a claim for interim relief may only be made in the framework of an action brought before the Court. The procedural rules are set out further in Article 39 Statute of the Court, in Articles 83–90 of the Rules of Procedure of the Court, and in Articles 104–110 of the Rules of Procedure of the CFI.[473]

According to Article 39 of the Statute of the Court, it is the (acting) president of the Court who, by way of summary procedure, adjudicates upon applications to

---

470. An exception to this rule is made for appeals against decisions of the Commission which impose sanctions for an infringement of safety requirements in the field of nuclear energy (Art. 83(2) Euratom). Bringing an appeal has suspensory effect, but the Court may, on application by the Commission or by any Member State concerned, order that the decision be enforced immediately.
471. Arts. 242–243 EC and 157–158 Euratom.
472. The power of the Court to suspend enforcement of decisions imposing a pecuniary obligation (Art. 256 last paragraph EC and Art. 162 Euratom), to which these procedures also apply, is not discussed here further.
473. Rules of Procedure of the Court of Justice of 19 Jun. 1991 (O.J. 1991, L 176/7, last amended 18 Dec. 2006 (O.J. 2006, L 386/44) and Rules of Procedure of the Court of First Instance of 2 May 1991 (O.J. 1991, L 36/1, last amended 18 Dec. 2006 (O.J. 2006, L 386/45).

suspend execution (or enforcement), or to prescribe other interim measures.[474] The president may, however, refer the application to (a chamber of) the Court for a decision. In practice, applications for interim measures tend to be referred in important cases, or cases which are politically sensitive, when the president prefers to allow (the chamber of) the Court to make an order.[475] In such cases, the Court postpones all other cases, and gives a decision after hearing the Advocate General.[476]

The difference between an application to suspend a measure adopted by one of the Institutions and an application for any other interim measure[477] is relevant for the question who may lodge such an application. In the first case, only parties which have brought the action against the relevant act of an Institution can also ask for that act to be suspended. In the second case, any of the parties in a case pending before the Court may request interim measures, providing this is connected to the case. Therefore, also parties which have to 'defend' themselves against an action may request 'other interim measures'.

Article 243 makes no exception according to the nature of the case.[478] A request for interim measures may be lodged not just in the framework of an action for annulment, but also in that of an action against a Member State for infringement of the Treaty.[479]

As already observed, Articles 242 and 243 EC leave no doubt that interim measures may only be granted in the framework of a case pending before the Court. The application must also be substantively connected with the main action.[480] The aim must be to reduce or prevent damage resulting from the infringement claimed in the main action. According to constant case law, interim measures may, on the basis of the provisions already mentioned,

> be adopted by the judge hearing the application for such measures if it is established that their adoption is prima facie justified in fact and in law, if

---

474. An order in such summary proceedings can be given very quickly, as is apparent from that of 5 Oct. 1969 (a Sunday!) in response to an application which had been received on 3 Oct. 1969. Case 50/69 R, *Germany v. Commission*.

475. See, e.g., the orders in Case 42/82 R, *Commission v. France*; Case C-195/90, *Commission v. Germany*; Case C-280/93 R, *Germany v. Council*; and Case C-180/96 R, *UK v. Commission*, as well as C-120/94 R, *Commission v. Greece*.

476. Art. 85 ECJ Rules of Procedure and Art. 107 CFI (without reference to the Advocate General) Rules of Procedure.

477. Art. 83(1) ECJ Rules of procedure correctly assumes that suspension is one type of interim measure.

478. See Case C-120/94 R, *Commission v. Greece* (Macedonia).

479. It has been argued that Art. 83(1) ECJ Rules of Procedure does not a priori exclude the possibility to request suspension as an interim measure before the Court in a preliminary reference case, at least insofar as the validity of an act of the Community is at issue. Since the judgment in Joined Cases C-143/88 & C-92/89, *Zuckerfabrik Süderdithmarschen*, there is less need for this. The national court is empowered, following this judgment, under certain conditions, to suspend the application of a Community measure which it considers likely to be invalid.

480. Art. 83(1) ECJ and 104(1) CFI Rules of Procedure.

they are urgent in the sense that it is necessary, in order to avoid serious and irreparable damage, that they should be laid down, and should take effect, before the decision of the Court on the substance of the action and if they are provisional in the sense that they do not prejudge the decision on the substance of the case, that is to say that they do not at this stage decide disputed points of law or of fact or neutralize in advance the consequences of the decision to be given subsequently on the substance of the action.[481]

Thus, the blueprint is laid down for the balancing of interests in any concrete case. The extent to which these conditions must be met is relative rather than absolute, because they can only be judged as a whole. For instance, the degree of urgency needed to justify interim relief will be less where, for instance, the likelihood is greater that the applicant will be proved right in the main action (the so-called *fumus boni juris*). *Vice versa*, if the importance of granting interim measures is clear, it will be sufficient that the arguments adduced by the applicant to justify his application are – according to the judge hearing the application – 'not, prima facie, entirely ungrounded'.[482] The former President of the Court, Mertens de Wilmars, has aptly referred to the balance of interests[483] and legal likelihood as the core of summary proceedings for interim relief.[484]

The interim measure is by definition temporary. If its duration is not mentioned in the Order itself, then it will lose its force as soon as the final judgment is delivered.[485] An order of the Court of Justice or of its President is not subject to appeal.[486] The enforcement of the order may be made conditional on the lodging by the applicant of security, up to a certain amount,[487] a possibility which has been made use of frequently in cases of appeals against decisions imposing financial sanctions.[488]

Making use of his right to grant the application for interim relief even before the observations of the opposite party have been submitted,[489] the

---

481. Case 20/81 R, *Arbed and others v. Commission*, para. 13.
482. See on this wording the Order of the president of the Court in Case C-149/95 P-R, *Commission v. Atlantic Container Line and others*, para. 26. According to the Commission in this case, and K. Lenaerts and D. Arts, Procedural Law of the European Union, 1999, par 13-0224, in this way 'fumus boni juris' is gradually being turned into a test of 'fumus non mali juris'. But see also F. Castillo de la Torre, 'Interim Measures in Community Courts: Recent Trends' (2007) CML Rev., 273–353.
483. A balancing of interests will always be involved. In the relevant Orders, considerations tend to be grouped under headings 'Prima facie case' (or fumus boni juris), 'urgency' and 'balance of interests'.
484. J. Mertens de Wilmars, 'Het kort geding voor het Hof van Justitie van de Europese gemeenschappen' (1986) SEW, 32–54.
485. Art. 86(3) ECJ and 107(3) CFI Rules of procedure.
486. Art. 86(1) ECJ Rules of procedure. Appeal is possible against orders of the Court of First Instance or its president.
487. Art. 86(2) ECJ and 107(2) CFI Rules of Procedure.
488. E.g., Case 392/85 R, *Finsider v. Commission*.
489. Art. 84(2) Rules of Procedure.

president sometimes orders precautionary measures in the interests of the proper administration of justice, before giving his final order on the application for interim relief, in order to prevent the proceedings for interim relief being deprived of all content and effect.[490]

Interim measures may also be laid down in relation to Member States. After first providing all parties, and the Commission, with the opportunity to seek a solution to the conflict which had arisen, when this was in vain the Court ordered Ireland to suspend operation of the two Sea Fisheries Orders (1977) with regard to fishing boats registered in one of the Member States until such time as judgment was delivered in the main proceedings, which the Commission had brought against Ireland. These Sea Fisheries Orders (1977) intended to reduce drastically fishing by foreigners in Irish fishing zones.[491]

The CFI and its President are also empowered to decide on applications for suspension or other interim measures in cases which – under Article 225(1) read with Article 51 Statute of the Court – come within the jurisdiction of that court, thus for the time being this refers mainly to direct actions brought by individuals. Further rules governing procedure may be found in Articles 104–110 Rules of Procedure of the CFI, which are the same, *mutatis mutandis*, as the relevant provisions of the Rules of Procedure of the Court of Justice. Appeal to the Court of Justice lies against an order of the CFI, one of its chambers, or its president.[492] The conditions applied by the CFI are the same as those of the Court of Justice.[493]

The importance of interim relief has grown over the years. In 1964, only 4 orders were given concerning interim measures; in 1988, this figure had increased to 20.[494] The establishment of the CFI in 1989 led to a decrease in the number of applications for interim measures before the Court of Justice, also counting those on appeal, but the number of such applications before the CFI increased steadily (to 37 in 2001 and 42 in 2000). This figure decreased significantly afterwards (to 21 in 2005 and 25 in 2006),[495] probably in relation to the newly created possibility to request an expedited procedure.[496]

---

490. See, e.g., Case 221/86 R, *Group of the European Right and National Front Party v. European Parliament*.
491. Case 61/77 R-II, *Commission v. Ireland*. See for the judgment in the main proceedings Case 61/77, *Commission v. Ireland*.
492. Art. 57, 2nd para., Statute of the Court.
493. See, e.g., Case T-23/90 R, *Peugeot v. Commission*.See further L. Cruz Vilaça, 'La procédure en référé comme instrument de protection juridictionnelle des particuliers en droit communautaire', in *Scritti in onore di Giuseppe Federico Mancini* (Milano, 1998, II), 227 et seq.
494. See the statistics included in the annexe to R. Joliet, 'Protection individuelle provisoire et droit communautaire' (1992) *Rivista di Diritto Europeo*, 253–284.
495. Court of Justice, Annual report 2006, 186, Statistics nr 13. *Miscellaneous* – Proceedings for interim measures (2000–06).
496. Art. 76a of the CFI Rules of Procedure.

FURTHER READING

General

Arnull, A. *The European Union and Its Court of Justice.* Oxford EC Law Library. 2nd ed. Oxford: Oxford University Press, 2006.

Boulouis, J., M. Darmon et al. *Contentieux communautaire.* 2e éd. Paris: Dalloz, 2001.

Brown, L. N. and T. Kennedy. *Brown & Jacobs, The Court of Justice of the European Communities.* 5th ed. London: Sweet & Maxwell, 2000.

Craig, P.P. and G. De Búrca. *EU Law: Text, Cases, and Materials.* 4th ed. Oxford: Oxford University Press, 2008.

Joliet, R. *Le droit institutionnel des Communautés européennes: le contentieux.* Liège: Faculté de Droit, d'Economie et de Science sociales de Liège, 1981.

Lasok, K.P.E. and T. Millett et al. *Judicial Control in the EU: Procedures and Principles.* Richmond: Richmond Law & Tax, 2004.

Schermers, H.G. and D.F. Waelbroeck. *Judicial Protection in the European Union.* 6th ed. The Hague: Kluwer Law International, 2001.

Stone Sweet, A. *The Judicial Construction of Europe.* Oxford: Oxford University Press, 2004.

Vandersanden, G. and A. Barav. *Contentieux communautaire.* Bruxelles: Bruylant, 1977.

Waelbroeck, M. and D. Waelbroeck. In *Commentaire Mégret, Le droit de la CEE,* vol. 10, Première Partie, La Cour de Justice. 2me éd. Bruxelles: Universite de Bruxelles, 1993.

The Law to Be Observed

Alston, P., M.R. Bustelo et al. (eds). *The EU and Human Rights.* Oxford: Oxford University Press, 1999.

Braibant, G. *La Charte des droits fondamentaux de l'Union européenne.* Points, Essais 469. Paris: Seuil, 2001.

Canor, I. *The Limits of Judicial Discretion in the European Court of Justice: Security and Foreign Affairs Issues.* Baden-Baden: Nomos, 1998.

Craig, P.P. *EU Administrative Law.* Collected Courses of the Academy of European Law, vol. 16/1. Oxford: Oxford University Press, 2006.

Eeckhout, P. 'The EU Charter of Fundamental Rights and the Federal Question'. (2002) CML Rev. 945–1009.

Gordon, R. *EC Law in Judicial Review.* Oxford: Oxford University Press, 2007.

Groussot, X. *General Principles of Community Law.* The Hogendorp Papers, 6. Groningen: Europa Law Publishing, 2006.

Peers, S. and A. Ward. *The European Union Charter of Fundamental Rights.* Oxford: Hart, 2004.

Raitio, J. *The Principle of Legal Certainty in EC Law.* Law and Philosophy Library, vol. 64. Dordrecht: Kluwer Academic Publishers, 2003.

Reich, N. *Understanding EU Law: Objectives, Principles and Methods of Community Law.* 2nd ed. Antwerpen: Intersentia, 2005.

Schwab, F. *Der Europäische Gerichtshof und der Verhältnismäßigkeitsgrundsatz; Untersuchung der Prüfungsdichte; ins besondere in der Gegenüberstellung der Kontrolle von Gemeinschaftsakten und von Maßnahmen der Mitgliedstaaten.* Europäische Hochschulschriften, Reihe 2: Rechtswissenschaft, Bd. 3424. Frankfurt am Main: Lang, 2002.

Tridimas, T. *The General Principles of EU Law.* 2nd ed. Oxford EC Law Library. Oxford: Oxford University Press, 2006.

The Law to Be Observed: Role of the Court

Alter, K. *Establishing the Supremacy of European Law: The Making of an International Rule of Law in Europe.* Oxford: Oxford University Press, 2001.

Anweiler, J. *Die Auslegungsmethoden des Gerichthofs der Europäischen Gemeinschaften.* Schriften zum internationalen und zum öffentlichen Recht, Bd. 17. Frankfurt am Main: Lang, 1997.

Bengoetxea, J. *The Legal Reasoning of the European Court of Justice.* Oxford: Clarendon Press, 1993.

De Búrca, G. and J.H.H. Weiler. *The European Court of Justice.* Collected Courses of the Academy of European Academy of Law, vol. 10/1. Oxford: Oxford University Press, 2001.

Campbell, A.I.L. and M. Voyatzi et al. *Legal Reasoning and Judicial Interpretation of European Law: Essays in Honour of Lord Mackenzie-Stuart.* Trenton London, 1996.

Dehousse, R. and W.E. Paterson. *The European Court of Justice: The Politics of Judicial Integration.* Basingstoke: Macmillan; New York, NY: St. Martin's Press, 1998.

Emmert, F. *Der Europäische Gerichtshof in Luxemburg als Garant der Rechtsgemeinschaft* Diss. University of Maastricht, 1998.

Hartley, T. 'The European Court, Judicial Objectivity and the Constitution of the European Union'. (1996) *LQRev.* 95–109 for a reaction, Arnull, A. 'The European Court and Judicial Objectivity: A Reply to Professor Hartley'. (1996) *LQRev* 411–423.

Jacobs, F. 'Human Rights in the European Union: The Role of the Court of Justice. (2001) EL Rev. 331–341.

Jetzlsperger, C. *Legitimacy through Jurisprudence?: The Impact of the European Court of Justice on the Legitimacy of the European Union.* EUI Working Paper Law, no. 2003/12. San Domenico: European University Institute, 2003.

Koopmans, T. 'The Role of Law in the Next Stage of European Integration'. (1986) ICLQ. 925–931

Kuper, R. *The Politics of the European Court of Justice.* European Dossier Series. London: Kogan Page, 1998.

Mittmann, P. *Die Rechtsfortbildung durch den Gerichtshof der Europäischen Gemeinschaften und die Rechtsstellung der Mitgliedstaaten der Europäischen Union.* Kölner Schriften zu Recht und Staat, Bd. 11. Frankfurt am Main: Lang, 2000.

Nowak, T. *How Judgments Become Law and How Law Restricts Judgments: The Influence of the European Court of Justice on the Legislative Process of the European Community.* University of Groninger, 2007.

Rasmussen, H. *On Law and Policy in the European Court of Justice.* Dordrecht, 1986; see the reviews by Cappelletti (1987) ELRev and Weiler (1987) CML Rev., but also Rasmussen (1988) ELRev.

Scheibeler, E. *Begriffsbildung durch den Europäischen Gerichtshof: autonom oder durch Verweis auf die nationalen Rechtsordnungen?* Schriften zum Europäischen Recht, Bd. 106. Berlin: Duncker & Humblot, 2004.

Sir Patrick Neill. *The European Court of Justice: A Case Study in Judicial Activism.* London: European Policy Forum, 1995; for reactions, D. Edward. *Judicial Activism: Myth or Reality?* In Campbell and Voyatzi (eds). *Legal Reasoning and Judicial Interpretation of Community Law*(1996), F. Jacobs. 'Is the Court of Justice a Constitutional Court?' In Curtin and O'Keeffe (eds). *Constitutional Adjudication in European Community and National Law* (1992) and T. Tridimas, T. 'The Court of Justice and Judicial Activism'. (1996) ELRev. 199–210.

Timmermans, C. 'The European Union's Judicial System'. In A. McDonnell (ed.). *A Review of Forty Years of Community Law: Legal Developments in the European Communities and the European Union.* The Hague: Kluwer Law International, 2005.

Remedies/Procedures

Albors-Llorens, A. *Private Parties in European Community Law: Challenging Community Measures.* Oxford: Clarendon Press, 1996.

Audretsch, H.A.H. *Supervision in European Community Law: Observance by the Member States of Their Treaty Obligations: A Treatise on International and Supra-national Supervision.* 2nd ed. Amsterdam: North-Holland, 1986.

Bölhoff, C. *Das Rechtsmittelverfahren vor dem Gerichtshof der Europäischen Gemeinschaften; Verfahren, Prüfungsumfang und Kontrolldichte.* Schriftenreihe europäisches Recht, Politik und Wirtschaft, Bd. 255. Baden-Baden: Nomos, 2001.

Brealy, M. and M. Hoskins. *Remedies in EC Law: Law and Practice in the English and EC Courts.* 2nd ed. London: Sweet & Maxwell, 1998.

Castillo De La Torre, F. 'Interim Measures in Community Courts: Recent Trends'. (2007) CML Rev. 273–353.

Van Gerven, W. 'Of Rights, Remedies and Procedures'. (2000) CML Rev. 501–536.

Gormley, L.W. 'Judicial Review in EC and EU Law: Some Architectural Malfunctions and Design Improvements?' (2002) *The Cambridge Yearbook of European Legal Studies.*

Gil Ibáñez, A.J. *The Administrative Supervision and Enforcement of EC Law: Powers, Procedures and Limits.* Oxford: Hart, 1999.

Heukels, T. and A. MacDonnell (eds). *The Action for Damages in Community Law*. The Hague: Kluwer Law International, 1997.

Kilpatrick, C. and T. Novitz et al. *The Future of Remedies in Europe*. Oxford: Hart, 2000.

Lenaerts, K. 'The Legal Protection of Private Parties under the EC Treaty: A Coherent and Complete System of Judicial Review?' In F. Mancini, *Scritti in onore di Giuseppe Federico Mancini*. Milano: A. Giuffrè, 1998, Vol.II.

Lengauer, A. *Nichtigkeitsklage vor dem EuGH: Parteistellung natürlicher und juristischer Personen* Wien: Orac, 1998.

Lewis, C. *Remedies and the Enforcement of European Community Law*. London: Sweet & Maxwell, 1996.

Micklitz, H.-W. and N. Reich. *Public Interest Litigation before European Courts*. Schriftenreihe des Vereinigten Instituts für Europäisches Wirtschafts- und Verbraucherrecht e.V., Bd. 2. Baden-Baden: Nomos, 1996.

O'Keeffe, D. (ed.). *Judicial Review in European Union Law*.: Liber Amicorum in Honour of Lord Slynn of Hadley, vol. 1. The Hague: Kluwer Law International, 2000.

Rideau, J. and F. Picod. *Code des procédures juridictionnelles de l'Union européenne*. 2e éd. Paris: Litec, 2002.

Schwartze, J. 'Judicial Review in EC Law: Some Reflections on the Origins and the Actual Legal Situation'. (2002) ICLQ 17–33.

Ward, A. *Judicial Review and the Rights of Private Parties in EU Law*. 2nd ed. New York, NY: Oxford University Press, 2007.

Wakefield, J. *Judicial Protection through the Use of Article 288(2) EC*. European Monographs, 36. The Hague: Kluwer Law International, 2002.

Wegener, B.W. *Rechte des Einzelnen: die Interessentenklage im europäischen Umweltrecht*. Schriftenreihe europäisches Recht, Politik und Wirtschaft, Bd. 203. Baden-Baden: Nomos, 1998.

Preliminary References

Andenas, M.T. *Article 177 References to the European Court: Policy and Practice*. London: Butterworths, 1994.

Anderson, D.W.K. and M. Demetriou. *References to the European Court*. 2nd ed. London: Sweet & Maxwell, 2002.

Barnard, C. and E. Sharpston. 'The Changing Face of Article 177 References'. (1997) CML Rev. 1113–1171

Donner, A. 'Les rapports entre la compétence de la Cour de justice des communautés européennes et les tribunaux internes'. (1965). *Recueil des cours - Collected Courses of The Hague Academy of International Law* vol. II, 1–58.

Pertek, J. *La pratique du renvoi préjudiciel en droit communautaire; coopération entre CJCE et juges nationaux*. Paris: Litec, 2001.

Schermers, H.G. *Article 177 EEC: Experiences and Problems*. Amsterdam: North-Holland, 1987.

Schima, B. *Das Vorabentscheidungsverfahren vor dem EuGH: Unter besonderer Berücksichtigung der Rechtslage in Österreich und Deutschland.* 2. Aufl. Wien: Manz, 2004.

Procedural Law

Barents, R. *Procedures en procesvoering voor het Hof van Justitie en het Gerecht van eerste aanleg van de EG, 3de dr.* Europese monografieën, 45. Deventer: Kluwer, 2005.

Burrows, N. and R. Greaves. *The Advocate General and EC Law.* Oxford University Press, 2007.

Hakenberg, W. and C. Stix-Hackl. *Handbuch zum Verfahren vor dem Europäischen Gerichtshof.* 2. aktualisierte Auflage. Wien: Verlag Österreich, 2000.

Koenig, C. and C. Sander. *Einführung in das EU/EG-Prozessrecht.* 2. Auflage. Tübingen: Mohr Siebeck, 2002.

Lenaerts, K. and D. Arts et al. *Procedural Law of the European Union.* 2nd ed. London: Sweet & Maxwell, 2006.

Nissen, H.-O. *Die Intervention Dritter in Verfahren vor dem Gerichtshof der Europäischen Gemeinschaften: zugleich eine rechtsvergleichende Untersuchung zu den Instituten der Drittbeteiligung vor deutschen und französischen Zivil- und Verwaltungsgerichten.* Hamburger Studien zum europäischen und internationalen Recht, Bd. 27. Berlin: Duncker & Humblot, 2001.

Plender, R. *European Courts Practice and Precedents.* London: Sweet & Maxwell, 1997.

Sinaniotis, D. *The Interim Protection of Individuals before the European and National Courts.* European Monographs, 52. Alphen aan den Rijn: Kluwer Law International, 2006.

Other

Beach, D. *Between Law and Politics: The Relationship between the European Court of Justice and EU Member States.* Copenhagen: Djøf, 2001.

Dashwood, A.A. and A. Johnston (eds). *The Future of the Judicial System of the European Union.* Oxford: Hart, 2001.

Dougan, M. *National Remedies before the Court of Justice: Issues of Harmonisation and Differentiation.* Modern Studies in European Law, vol. 4. Oxford: Hart, 2004.

Chapter VII

The Application and Enforcement of Community Law in the National Legal Systems

P.J.G. Kapteyn

Community law forms 'its own system of law, integrated into the legal systems of the Member States, and which must be applied by their courts'.[1] How does this integration of Community law in the national legal system take place? And what provisions are made for the application of Community law? The present chapter is devoted to these questions. The effect of Community law in general, and direct effect in particular, are dealt with first (section 1), then the primacy of Community law within the national legal systems (section 2). The next sections deal with access to remedies and proceedings in the national legal systems in order to guarantee the full effect of Community law and effective judicial protection (section 3), liability of Member States for damage suffered by individuals as a result of infringements of Community law which can be attributed to a Member State (section 4) and the sanctions to be established in the national legal systems for infringements of Community law (section 5).

---

1. Case 14/68, *Walt Wilhelm and others v. Bundeskartellamt*, at para. 6. See *supra* Ch. II, section 3.3. See also B. de Witte, 'Direct Effect, Supremacy, and the Nature of the Legal Order' in P. Graig and G. de Búrca (eds), *The Evolution of EU Law* (Oxford, OUP, 1999), 177.

P.J.G. Kapteyn, A.M. McDonnell, K.J.M. Mortelmans and C.W.A. Timmermans (eds),
The Law of the European Union and the European Communities, pp. 511–574.
©2008 Kluwer Law International BV, The Netherlands.

1   THE EFFECT OF COMMUNITY LAW IN THE
                    NATIONAL LEGAL SYSTEMS; DIRECT EFFECT

In its celebrated judgment in *Van Gend en Loos*[2] the Court observed that:

> the task assigned to the Court of Justice under Article [234], the object of which
> is to secure uniform interpretation of the Treaty by national courts and tribunals,
> confirms that the states have acknowledged that Community law has an author-
> ity which can be invoked by their nationals before those courts and tribunals.

For individuals to be able to rely on provisions of Community law, the provisions
concerned must be directly effective, i.e., must have direct effect (in the language
of public international law: be self-executing); in other words, they must lend
themselves by their very nature to direct application by, in this case, a court in
the national legal system. The term 'direct applicability of Community law' deals,
it has been submitted, with a different question: whether Community law has to be
transformed into domestic law;[3] a question which, as was shown in section 3.3. of
Chapter II of this book, received a negative answer from the Court.

Sometimes, the terms 'direct applicability' and 'direct effect' are used interchangeably.[4] In general, the term 'direct effect' tends to be used to describe a
situation in which a private individual can invoke or rely on a provision of Community law in national judicial proceedings.[5] A remark has to be made in this
context, however: the question whether a provision of Community law applies in
the national legal system as such, that is to say without provisions of national law
transforming it, does not correspond exactly to the question whether such provisions
can be relied on before the national courts. This is evident from the fact that even if
the view is taken that Community law is incorporated in the national legal system as
a result of the law approving the Treaty – a view which the Court has rejected[6] – that
would not automatically mean that a provision of Community law having the force
of national law could be relied upon before the national courts. This latter question
clearly depends on whether the provision lends itself to being so relied on.

As to the question when treaty provisions are apt to be directly applied by
the national courts, in the 1960s there were roughly two points of view.[7] The first,

---

2. Case 26/62, *NV Algemene Transport- en Expeditie Onderneming Van Gend en Loos v. Admin-
   istratie der Belastingen.*
3. J.A. Winter, 'Direct Applicability and Direct Effect: Two Distinct and Different Concepts in
   Community Law' (1972) CML Rev., 425–438.
4. This also holds for the Court in earlier case law. Cf. e.g., Case 50/76, *Amsterdam Bulb v.
   Produktschap voor siergewassen* and Case 31/78, *Francesco Bussone v. Ministère italien de
   l'agriculture* where the ECJ uses both direct applicability and direct effect (for Reg.).
5. All government bodies, including decentralized entities, such as municipalities, as well as courts,
   are obliged to apply directly effective provisions. Cf. Case 103/88, *Fratelli Costanzo v. Comune
   di Milano.* On this judgment, see B. de Witte, op. cit. *supra* note 1, at 192–193.
6. Cf. Case 26/62, *Van Gend en Loos.*
7. See on this the – old but still relevant – monograph by M. Waelbroeck, *Traités internationaux et
   juridictions internes dans les pays du Marché commun* (Brussels, 1969), para. 151–156, with
   further references.

which at that time was predominant, sought inspiration in an Opinion of the Permanent Court of International Justice from 1928. There it was stated:

> that, according to a well-established principle of international law an international agreement cannot, as such, create direct rights and obligations for private individuals. But it cannot be disputed that the very object of an international agreement, according to the intention of the contracting parties, may be the adoption by the parties of some definite rules creating individual rights and obligations and enforceable by the national courts.[8]

According to this view, treaty provisions can have direct effect if they create rights and obligations for individuals. It is then up to the national court to ascertain the intention of the contracting parties in this respect. Under the influence of this idea, a national court will not readily assume that a treaty provision which is expressly addressed to the contracting states can be invoked by a private party in an action pending before that court. The court will only tend to consider a treaty provision directly applicable on the basis of the intention of the contracting parties if this imposes an obligation on individuals, or grants them an individual right.

The second view concerning the direct applicability of treaty provisions is associated with the concept of 'self-executing', a concept which stems from American constitutional law practice.[9] In this view, national courts apply treaty provisions which can have effect on their own, that is to say can be applied by the courts without the intervention beforehand of legislative or administrative bodies. Whether that is so will depend on the formulation of the provision in question. This view can lead to a much broader application of treaty provisions than the first view, because the emphasis is shifted from the (subjective) issue of whether a treaty provision indicates the intention of the contracting parties to create rights and obligations for individuals, to the (objective) issue whether the treaty provision lends itself by its very nature to application by a national court, a question concerning the character of the treaty provision. Ultimately, it is only the doctrine of separation of powers which imposes a limit on the extent to which the national courts may apply directly the provisions of treaties: national courts should not usurp the role of legislature or executive.

The influence of both views can be found in the doctrine of direct effect of Community law within the national legal systems of the Member States. The question formulated by the Nederlandse Tariefcommissie in the first case in which the Court had to pronounce on the direct effect of a Treaty provision, followed the terminology of the first view – at least, that is what one can say in retrospect. The referring court in *Van Gend en Loos* asked whether Article 25 European Community (EC) (then Art. 12 European Economic Community

---

8. Permanent Court of International Justice, Jurisdiction of the Courts of Danzig, Advisory Opinion 1928, Series B, No. 15, 17–18.
9. On the relevant American doctrine and case law, see Stefan A. Riesenfeld, 'The Doctrine of Self-executing Treaties and *U.S. v. Postal*: Win at Any Price?' (1980) AJIL, 74, 892–904, and J. J. Paust, 'Self-executing Treaties' (1988) AJIL, 760–783.

(EEC)) 'has direct application within the territory of a Member State, in other words, whether nationals of such a state can, on the basis of the Article in question, lay claim to individual *rights which the courts must protect*'.[10] The answer from the Court of Justice was that the Article in question 'produces direct effects and creates individual rights which national courts must protect'.

Before examining the reasoning on the basis of which the Court came to this answer, one point should be noted: the explicit finding in *Van Gend en Loos* that the question as to whether a provision of Community law has direct effect is a question of interpretation of that provision, is of essential importance for the uniform and – as will appear – extensive application of Community law within the legal systems of the Member States. After all, that finding implies that it is not the national courts but the Court of Justice which has the final say on the question, in the framework of the preliminary reference procedure of Article 234 EC. The argument by the Dutch and Belgian governments in *Van Gend en Loos*, that the question of direct effect of the relevant Treaty provision relates not to the interpretation but to the application of the treaty in the context of the constitutional law of the Netherlands, was firmly rejected by the Court.

According to the Court in *Van Gend en Loos*, the answer to the question whether the provisions of an international treaty have direct effect depends on their spirit, their general scheme[11] and their wording. In the light of the spirit of the EC Treaty (and at the time the EEC Treaty), there is clearly a favourable predisposition towards direct effect. In *Van Gend en Loos* the Court concluded that independently of the legislation of Member States

> Community law therefore not only imposes obligations on individuals but is also intended to confer upon them rights which become part of their legal heritage. These rights arise not only where they are expressly granted by the Treaty, but also by reason of obligations which the Treaty imposes in a clearly defined way upon individuals as well as upon the Member States and upon the institutions of the Community (part II B of the judgment).

The Court derived this conclusion from the fact that 'the Community constitutes a new legal order of international law for the benefit of which the states have limited their sovereign rights, albeit in limited fields, and the subjects of which comprise not only Member States but also their nationals'.[12]

Moreover, in the case of treaty provisions, the general scheme of the Treaty and the place therein of the relevant provision are also of importance. Thus in *Van Gend en Loos* the Court pointed out that Article 12 EEC (now 25 EC) was a more

---

10. Case 26/62, *Van Gend en Loos* (our emphasis).
11. The French text uses the term 'l'economie'.
12. Cf. in relation to these arguments, the comments on the Nature of Community law, in section 3.1 of Ch. II *supra*. The 'very object' of the EC Treaty, to use the words of the Permanent Court of International Justice in its Advisory Opinion of 1928, is 'the adoption . . . of some definite rules creating individual rights and obligations and enforceable by national courts', provided one take the term 'rights' in a broad sense, i.e., as also containing the right to rely on generally binding Community norms before national courts.

specific application of Article 9 EEC (now 23 EC), which was one of the essential provisions of the customs union on which the Community was based.[13] Again, in its examination of the direct effect of the first paragraph of Article 95 (now 90 EC) in *Lütticke*[14] the Court noted that that provision 'constitutes in fiscal matters the indispensable foundation of the Common Market'.

Finally, the wording of the provision concerned is naturally of importance. As has already been observed, the fact that a Treaty provision takes the form of an obligation on the Member States is not an obstacle to its having direct effect. In myriad cases since *Van Gend en Loos* the Court has confirmed this viewpoint. Thus, for example, in *Firma Molkerei-Zentrale Westfalen-Lippe*, it repeated that directly effective 'rights arise not only where they are expressly granted by the Treaty but also by reason of obligations which the Treaty imposes in a clearly defined way upon individuals as well as upon the Member States and upon the institutions of the Community'. It added that 'it is necessary and sufficient that the very nature of the provision of the Treaty in question should make it ideally adapted to produce direct effects on the legal relationship between Member States and those subject to their jurisdiction'.[15] Under what conditions is that the case?

1.1   CONDITIONS FOR DIRECT EFFECT

Initially, the case law of the Court on the conditions for direct effect developed above all in the context of references from national courts requesting a ruling on whether private parties could rely on various provisions of the EEC Treaty, which were addressed to the Member States, in those courts against the national authorities.[16] Only at a later stage did the Court have to look at the direct effect of Community measures (regulations, directives and decisions as well as international agreements binding the Community), and then at the question to what extent provisions of Community law could be relied upon by private parties against other private parties (this is often called horizontal direct effect). The special aspects of the case law on these two issues of later date are examined in sections 1.3, 1.4 and 1.5 of this chapter, below. For the development of the case law which particularly concerned Treaty provisions imposing obligations on the Member States, the interested reader should consult the previous edition of this book. The present discussion deals with some general aspects of the doctrine of direct effect as developed in the case law of the Court of Justice through the years.

A consistent line of case law shows that a provision has direct effect if it is unconditional and sufficiently precise. It is unconditional where it is not subject, in its implementation or effects, to the taking of any measure either by the institutions

---

13. Case 26/62, *Van Gend en Loos*.
14. Case 57/65, *Lütticke v. Hauptzollamt Saarlouis* (*Lütticke II*), at 210 of the English edition.
15. Case 28/67, *Molkerei Zentrale Westfalen-Lippe v. Hauptzollamt Paderborn*, at section 1 A.
16. For an exception, see Case 13/61, *De Geus en Uitdenbogerd v. Bosch and others*, concerning what is now Art. 81(2) EC.

of the Community or by the Member States and it is sufficiently precise to be relied on by an individual and applied by the court where the obligation which it imposes is set out in unequivocal terms.[17]

Ipsen summarized the central question in examining direct effect as the presence of 'a change in the legal order applicable in the Member States brought about by Community law',[18] of an 'Alternativ-Normierung' in Community law which can be applied by the national courts. If this is not present, then the national court would be taking the place of the legislature if it were to create 'rules' itself on the basis of Community law. Thirty-five years later that pronouncement needs some adjustment, as the view on which it is based is too static. The case law has made it plain that the question of whether Community law offers 'alternative norms' – that is to say whether the national courts can apply Community law without exceeding the limits of their judicial function – may also be partly dependent on the facts of the case in which the question arises.

Still, it remains true that – whatever the facts of the case – an alternative Community law rule must be available for the court, in the sense of a sufficiently clear and unconditional norm which is not dependent on a discretionary implementing measure.[19] That alternative rule will be necessary for the court in two ways. First, in order for it to be applied instead of a national rule with which it is in conflict (or where a national rule is lacking) to the facts of the case before the court. Second, as a standard against which a national measure can be reviewed, when the court is asked either to declare a particular national measure to be in conflict with that rule, or to declare that as a result of its conflict with the Community norm that measures may not be relied on against another party, or to annul that measure or to set it aside. Even in the last category, there must be an alternative available for the national rules which seem to allow the measure in question.

However, the above does not mean that provisions which depend for their implementation on discretionary measures by the Member States can never be relied on before the national courts. The national courts can review the legality of acts on the basis of such provisions to the extent that the latter set sufficiently clear limits to the margin of discretion which the Community Institutions or the Member States are allowed where these limits are alleged to have been exceeded. This is also referred to as the objective review of legality. In the case of implementing measures by the Community itself, there has never been any doubt about this possibility. If the Council adopts regulations on state aids, on the basis of Article 89 EC, concerning the application of Articles 87 and 88, or if the Commission takes decisions on the compatibility of such state aids, then private parties can challenge the validity of such decisions or acts of the Council before the national

---

17. In that sense, see, e.g., Case 44/84, *Hurd v. Jones.* See also Case C-236/92, *Comitato di Coordinamento per la Difesa della Cava and others v. Regione Lombardia et al.* Cf. already A.G. Mayras, Opinion in Case 41/74, *Van Duyn v. Home Office.*
18. H.P. Ipsen, annotation of Case 57/65, *Lütticke II,* (1966) EuR, 356–359.
19. In this sense, I do not share the criticism of Ipsen's formulation in S. Prechal 'Does Direct Effect still Matter?' (2000) CML Rev., 1047–1069 (at 1059), based on her inaugural lecture in Tilburg.

courts under certain conditions.[20] They can invoke Article 87 EC in order to review the act of the Commission or the Council against the limits which that provision imposes on their margin of discretion.[21]

There seems no reason why this should be different where the implementation of an obligation lying not on the Community but on the Member States is dependent on discretionary measures taken by the latter. If the court is free under national law to review measures implementing national laws against those national laws, why should this possibility of review be withheld when the laws are Community rather than national in character? The case law of the Court of Justice has, in fact, developed in that direction,[22] as will appear in the discussion of actions before the national courts concerning provisions of directives (section 1.4 below). It seems therefore acceptable to define direct effect in a broad sense as 'the obligation of a court or another authority to apply the relevant provision of Community law, either as a norm which governs the case or as a standard for legal review'.[23]

The manner in which provisions of Community law have direct effect can thus be very different, depending on the procedural rules and the context of substantive legal rules involved in the concrete dispute before a national court.[24] Consequently, the requirements for direct effect of a particular provision will also vary depending on the factual and legal circumstances. Ultimately, the question will always be whether the provision relied on is sufficiently 'operational' in the context of an actual dispute so as to be applied by the court, without the court thereby exceeding the limits of its judicial function.[25]

---

20. At least, they may do so if they cannot appeal against such acts directly under Art. 230 EC, cf. Case C-188/92, *TWD Textilwerke Deggendorf GmbH v. Bundesrepublik Deutschland.*
21. Cf. Case 77/72, *Capolongo v. Azienda Agricola Maya*, at para. 6: the provisions of Art. 87(1) EC may be relied on directly before a national court 'where they have been put in concrete form by acts having general application provided for by Article [89] or by decisions in particular cases envisaged by article [88(2)]'.
22. Such cases are especially likely to arise when implementation of directives is concerned. Cf. Case 51/76, *Verbond Nederlandse ondernemingen v. Inspecteur der invoerrechten en accijnzen* (VNO) and the case law mentioned *infra* in notes 87 and 89. See also implicitly Case 88/79, *Criminal proceedings against Siegfried Grunert.*
23. S. Prechal, *Directives in European Community Law*, 2nd ed. (Oxford, 2005), at 241 and 'Direct Effect, Indirect Effect, Supremacy and the Evolving Constitution of the European Union', in Barnard (ed.), *The Fundamentals of EU Law Revisited: Assessing the Impact of the Constitutional Debate?* Collected courses of the Academy of European Law (Oxford, 2007), 35, at 37–38.
24. Cf. S. Prechal, op. cit. *supra* note 19, at 1059: 'The way in which the relevant provision will be deployed depends on the character and the subject matter of the proceedings in the national court, and also on the content and 'structure' of national rules involved'.
25. In this sense, cf. already P. Pescatore, 'The Doctrine of Direct Effect: An Infant Disease of Community Law' (1983) EL Rev., 176–177. See also para. 27 of the Opinion of A.G. Van Gerven in Case C-128/92, *Banks v. British Coal*, who referred in particular to the flexible manner in which the Court interpreted the conditions for direct effect in Case C-271/91, *Marshall v. Southampton and South West Hampshire Area Health Authority (Marshall II)*, and Joined Cases C-6 & 9/90, *Francovich and Bonifaci et al. v. Italian Republic.* See also the considerations of the judgments in Case C-63/99, *The Queen v. Secretary of State for the Home Department, ex parte Glosczuk*; Case C-235/99, *The Queen v. Secretary of State for the*

Taking into account what has been said so far, it is clear that the case law has essentially followed the view inspired by the concept of 'self-executing' provisions, and has elaborated that in its own particular way. The terminology associated with the other view, the view inspired by the Opinion of the Permanent Court of International Justice, and which equated direct effect with 'creating rights', has gradually been abandoned.[26] The only trace of this view still to be found in more recent case law is to be seen in the 'right' (apparently seen as a procedural right) to rely on a directly effective provision before a national court.[27]

The doctrine of direct effect may be explained historically as a means of involving the national courts in the enforcement and application of Community law, and therefore laying the basis for the effective application of this law in all Member States. Given the variety of rules and traditions in the Member States concerning the direct application of provisions of international agreements by national courts, the Court of Justice aimed to develop a doctrine for Community law which could be applied by the courts in all Member States in the same way, despite these divergent rules and traditions. That effort has been successful.

In the academic literature, it has been argued that there is really no reason to lay down conditions for the application of Community rules by the national courts: why should Community rules be treated differently from national rules? The situation is the same in both cases: 'a court is a court, and needs workable indications to do its job'.[28] However, it should not be forgotten that the doctrine of direct effect embraces more than a set of conditions that provisions of Community law should fulfil in order to be directly effective. The question is only raised after having established that the instrument containing these provisions can have such effect at all, according to its spirit and its general scheme. As far as the EC Treaty is concerned, this has been established ever since *Van Gend en Loos*; however, in this context abandoning the doctrine would not have much practical effect in any case, since by now it is fairly clear which articles of the EC Treaty have direct effect and which do not.

As for international agreements which are binding on the Community, be it with third countries or with other organizations, and which form an integral part of

---

Home Department, ex parte Kondova; Case C-257/99, *The Queen v. Secretary of State for the Home Department, ex parte Barkoci and Malik*, and Case C-268/99, *Jany and others v. Staats-secretaris van Justitie*, at para. 38, in which it is stated the provisions of the Association Agreement at issue are 'to be construed as establishing ... a precise and unconditional principle which is sufficiently operational to be applied by a national court'. See also Case C-141/00, *Ambulanter Pflegedienst Kügler GmbH v. Finanzamt für Körperschaften I in Berlin*.

26. See, e.g., already Case 8/81, *Becker v. Finanzamt Münster-Innenstadt*, in which the Court distinguishes between the possibility to rely on unconditional and sufficiently precise provisions and the specific case 'in so far as the provisions define rights which individuals are able to assert against the state' (para. 25).

27. See the judgments in the Case C-63/99, *Glosczuk*; Case C-235/99, *Kondova*; Case C-257/99, *Barkoci and Malik*, and Case C-268/99, *Jany*.

28. S. Prechal, op. cit. *supra* note 19, 1067. See already Pescatore, op. cit. *supra* note 25, 177, who sees direct effect as 'nothing but the ordinary state of the law'.

the Community legal order,[29] an examination of the question whether according to their spirit and general scheme (the Court also uses the terms 'object' or 'purpose and nature' of the agreement) they are apt to contain provisions having direct effect is still relevant (see section 1.3 below). Moreover, according to the case law, reliance on provisions of a directive before a national court is subject to specific limitations, which flow from the nature of that legal instrument (see section 1.4 below). External agreements and directives may thus contain provisions whose formulation in itself is sufficient to fulfil the conditions of direct effect, but which nevertheless may not be applied by the national courts.[30]

<table>
<tr><td>1.2</td><td>RELIANCE BEFORE NATIONAL COURTS ON INTERNATIONAL AGREEMENTS BINDING ON THE COMMUNITY</td></tr>
</table>

Provisions of international agreements concluded by the Community form an integral part of the Community legal order.[31] This also holds for agreements concluded by all the Member States before the entry into force of the EEC Treaty, and by which the Community is bound insofar as it has assumed the rights and obligations of the Member States on the basis of the principle of substitution (as was the case with the GATT).[32] If questions of the interpretation of international agreements binding on the Community arise before national courts, they may (or must, as appropriate) refer them to the Court of Justice under Article 234 EC. The question of the direct effect of provisions of such an agreement is one of those questions.

According to constant case law, provisions in an agreement concluded by the Community with third countries must be regarded as being directly applicable when, regard being had to its wording and the purpose and nature of the agreement itself, the provision contains a clear and precise obligation which is not subject, in its implementation or effects, to the adoption of any subsequent measure.[33]

If such a provision is directly effective, it may be relied upon before national courts to impugn the validity of Community measures. Article 234 EC does not in any way limit the Court's jurisdiction as to the grounds on which the validity of acts

---

29. Constant case law since Case 181/73, *Haegemann v. Belgian State* (*Haegeman II*).
30. Cf. B. de Witte, op. cit. *supra* note 1, at 188, who also mentions a number of other arguments.
31. Constant case law since Case 181/73, *Haegeman II*, where the Court considers such an agreement concluded by the Council as an act of one of the Institutions in the sense of Art. 234, 1st para., under (b) EC. This rather unfortunate qualification could obviously not be used by the Court in the case of agreements which are binding on the Community under the principle of substitution. For the reasoning followed in such cases, see Case 266/81, *SIOT v. Ministero delle finanze*, and Joined Cases 267–269/81, *Amministrazione delle finanze dello Stato v. SPI and SAMI*.
32. Joined Cases 21–24/72, *International Fruit Company NV and others v. Produktschap voor Groenten en Fruit* (*International Fruit Company III*); cf. Ch. VI, section 1.2, *supra*.
33. See, e.g., Case C-162/96, *Racke v. Hauptzollamt Mainz* and Joined Cases C-300/98 & C-392/98, *Parfums Christian Dior and Others*. For a slightly different wording, see Case C-344/04, *IATA and ELFAA*.

of the Institutions may be contested. The Court is bound to examine the validity of the act if that validity could be affected by incompatibility with a rule of international law.[34] Litigants before national courts are also free to allege that a national measure is incompatible with such a rule.[35]

The Court has recognized, in numerous cases, the direct effect of provisions of international agreements concluded by the Community with third countries. This was the case, for instance, with the Second Yaoundé Convention,[36] the Association Agreements with Greece,[37] and Turkey,[38] the Free Trade Agreement with Portugal,[39] and the Cooperation Agreement with Morocco.[40] The 'purpose and nature' of these agreements, to which the Association Agreements with Eastern and Central European countries can be added, was not found to stand in the way of recognition of the direct effect of provisions.[41]

In a series of preliminary references[42] concerning GATT 1947, the assessment of the spirit, general scheme and formulations of that agreement led to a very different result, however. Direct effect of provisions of GATT was excluded on the basis of the general consideration that this agreement 'is characterized by the great flexibility of its provisions, in particular those conferring the possibility of derogation, the measures to be taken when confronted with exceptional difficulties and the settlement of conflicts between the contracting parties'.[43] According to the Court, the various special characteristics showed that the rules of the GATT were not unconditional, and that an obligation to accord them the character of rules of international law which are directly applicable within the national legal systems of the contracting parties could not be based on the spirit, general scheme and terms

---

34. Joined Cases 21–24/72, *International Fruit Company III.*
35. Implicitly, Case 65/77, *Razanatsimba.*
36. Case 87/75, *Bresciani v. Amministrazione delle finanze dello Stato.*
37. Case 17/81, *Pabst and Richarz KG v. Hauptzollamt Oldenburg.*
38. Case C-192/89, *Sevince v. Staatssecretaris van Justitie*; see also Case 12/86, *Demirel v. Stadt Schwäbisch Gmünd.*
39. Case 104/81, *Hauptzollamt Mainz v. Kupferberg and Cie (Kupferberg I).*
40. Case C-18/90, *Office national de l'emploi v. Kziber.*
41. For the Europe Agreements, see, e.g., Case C-63/99, *Glosczuk.* The substantive interpretation of provisions in such agreements which are identically worded to provisions in the EC Treaty is not, however, necessarily the same, as appeared from e.g., Case 270/80, *Polydor and others v. Harlequin and others.* According to this case law,

    the extension of the interpretation of a provision in the Treaty to a comparably, similarly or even identically worded provision of an agreement concluded by the Community with a non-member country depends, inter alia, on the aim pursued by each provision in its particular context and that a comparison between the objectives and context of the agreement and those of the Treaty is of considerable importance in that regard.

    (Case C-312/91, *Metalsa*, at para. 11). See also extensively on this Opinion 1/91 (*EEA I*).
42. Joined Cases 21–24/72, *International Fruit Company III*; Case 9/73, *Schlüter v. Hauptzollamt Lörrach*; Case 266/81, *SIOT*; Joined Cases 267–269/81, *SPI and SAMI*, and Case C-280/93, *Germany v. Council (Bananas).*
43. Joined Cases 21–24/72, *International Fruit Company III*, at para. 21.

of this agreement.[44] These special characteristics also prevented the Court from taking GATT provisions into account when deciding on the legality of a regulation in the framework of an action for annulment under Article 230 EC.[45]

Similarly, the Court has not accepted the direct effect of provisions of the agreements concluded in the framework of the World Trade Organization (WTO), which on 1 January 1995 took the place of those of the GATT. Here, the Court could not simply repeat the arguments which it had used concerning the former GATT agreements. The framework within which the WTO agreements are applied differs significantly from the provisions of GATT 1947, in particular because of the strengthening of the system of safeguards and the mechanism for resolving disputes. It should be noted that in the reasoning of the Court, the central question is not whether the WTO provisions can be directly effective by their nature, but whether the consequence of the recognition of the direct effect of those provisions – i.e., giving them priority over secondary Community law – accords with the nature and general scheme of the WTO agreements.

In its judgment in Case C-149/96, *Portugal v. Council*[46] – notably a direct action and not a preliminary ruling – the Court found that, considering the possibilities of negotiated arrangements for dispute settlement, the WTO agreements 'do not determine the appropriate legal means of ensuring that they are applied in good faith in the legal order of the contracting parties' (para. 41). In relation more specifically to the application of the WTO agreements in the Community legal order – of which, after all, they form an integral part – the Court considered that, like the GATT 1947, they are based on the principle of negotiations on the basis of 'reciprocal and mutually advantageous arrangements'.[47] Since it was not disputed

---

44. Joined Cases 21–24/72, *International Fruit Company III*. For a critical view of this case law, see, e.g., E.U. Petersmann, 'Application of GATT by the Court of Justice of the European Communities' (1983) CML Rev., 397–437. See also J.H.J. Bourgeois, 'Effects of International Agreements in European Community Law: Are the Dice Cast?' (1983–1984) *Michigan Law Review*, 1250 et seq.

45. Case C-280/93, *Germany v. Council (Bananas)* and C-469/93, *Amministrazione delle finanze dello Stato v. Chiquita Italia*. The Court did find admissible an application by the Commission under Art. 226 EC for a finding that a Member State had failed to fulfil its obligations under the Treaty, on grounds of infringement of the International Dairy Arrangement concluded in the framework of the GATT, Case C-61/94, *Commission v. Germany (International Dairy Arrangement)*.

46. Case C-149/96, *Portugal v. Council (Textile products)*, see also Joined Cases C-300/98 & C-392/98, *Parfums Christian Dior*, and Case T-18/99, *Cordis v. Commission*. In Case C-53/96, *Hermès International v. FHT Marketing Choice*, the Court was able to avoid the question of the direct effect of provisions of the TRIPs agreement, concluded in the framework of the WTO; on this case law see F. Snyder, 'The Gatekeepers: The European Courts and WTO-Law' (2003) CML Rev., 313–367.

47. On that basis, they are 'distinguished, from the viewpoint of the Community, from the agreements concluded between the Community and non-member countries which introduce a certain asymmetry of obligations, or create special relations of integration with the Community, such as the agreement which the Court was required to interpret in Kupferberg'. This statement is important, because in the latter case (Case 104/81, *Kupferberg I*, at para. 4) – unlike the present one (Case C-149/96, *Portugal v. Council (Textile products)*) – the Court had considered that

that the most important trading partners (the United States and Japan) have drawn the conclusion from the subject matter and purpose of the WTO agreements that they are not to be counted among the rules applicable by their judicial organs when reviewing the legality of rules of domestic law,[48] the lack of reciprocity on this point could lead to an unbalanced application of the WTO rules.

> To accept that the role of ensuring that Community law complies with those rules devolves directly on the Community judicature would deprive the legislative or executive organs of the Community of the scope for manoeuvre enjoyed by their counterparts in the Community's trading partners (para. 46).

The Court thus came to the conclusion that 'the WTO agreements are not in principle among the rules in the light of which the Court is to review the legality of measures adopted by the Community institutions' (para. 47).[49] This is now settled case law[50] to be applied even when the Dispute Settlement Body of the WTO has stated that those measures are incompatible with those rules.[51] That does not prevent the Court from reviewing the legality of the relevant Community act in the light of the WTO rules 'where the Community intended to implement a particular obligation assumed in the context of the WTO, or where the Community measure refers expressly to the precise provisions of the WTO agreements' (para. 49) – as was already held under the GATT 1947.[52] The Court does not see this as recognizing direct effect of provisions of the GATT 1947 or of the WTO agreements, but as review in an incidental manner of the validity of a Community act in the light of the provisions of international law with which this act aims to comply, in the framework of the exception of illegality (Art. 241 EC).[53] Such a form of review shows similarities with the 'objective review of legality' mentioned above (section 1.1; see also below, section 1.4.2).[54]

'the fact that the courts of one of the parties to an international agreement concluded by the Community consider that certain of the stipulations in the agreement are of direct application whereas the courts of the other party do not recognize such direct application is not in itself such as to constitute a lack of reciprocity in the implementation of the agreement'.

48. In that sense, see also the (non-binding) declaration of the EC Council in the last recital of Decision 94/800 on the conclusion of the WTO agreements (O.J. 1994, L 336/1).

49. If the WTO agreement concerns an area in which there is already Community legislation – such as is the case for the TRIPs agreement in the field of trade marks – the Court does consider that it is competent to interpret the provisions of the agreement, see Case C-53/96, *Hermès*; Joined Cases C-300/98 & C-392/98, *Parfums Christian Dior* and Case C-89/99, *V.O.F. Schieving-Nijstad and Others v. Groeneveld*.

50. See Joined Cases C-27 & 122/00, *Omega Air and Others*, Case C-76/00 P, *Petrotub and Republica v. Council* and Case C-93/02 P, *Biret International v. Council*.

51. Cf. Case C-377/02, *Léon Van Parys NV v. BIRB*.

52. Cf. Case 70/87, *Fediol v. Commission*, and Case C-69/89, *Nakajima All Precision v. Council*.

53. Cf. paras 27 and 28 of the judgment in Case C-69/89, *Nakajima*.

54. For review on the basis of international customary law, see Case C-162/96, *Racke (clausula sic stantibus)*, annotated by J. Klabbers (1999) CML Rev., 179; see also Case T-115/94, *Opel Austria v. Council* (international legal principle of good faith), annotated by P. Fischer (1998) CML Rev., 765.

It may be assumed that the limitations Case C-149/96, *Portugal v. Council* places on review by the Community courts of Community acts in the light of provisions of the WTO agreements also hold where the national court is requested to review national or Community acts against those provisions, as appears from the *Parfums Christian Dior* cases.[55]

Finally, it should be mentioned that it is settled case law that 'Community legislation must, so far as possible, be interpreted in a manner that is consistent with international law, in particular where its provisions are intended specifically to give effect to an international agreement concluded by the Community'.[56]

1.3   RELIANCE BEFORE NATIONAL COURTS ON SECONDARY COMMUNITY LAW: DIRECTLY APPLICABLE REGULATIONS

Regulations, as the Court has said on myriad occasions, 'by reason of their nature and their function in the system of Community law ... have direct effect and are, as such, capable of creating individual rights which national courts must protect', where appropriate also 'horizontally', *vis-à-vis* other private parties.[57] The Court reached this conclusion on the basis of Article 249 EC, which provides that regulations 'shall have general application' and 'shall be directly applicable in all Member States'.

Sometimes regulations provide for implementing or further measures to be taken by the Community Institutions or by the Member States; these may involve a certain discretion for the body which adopts them.[58] Sometimes it is necessary explicitly to indicate which bodies are entrusted with implementation in the national setting. Unlike in the case of provisions of the Treaties themselves and

---

55.   Joined Cases C-300/98 & C-392/98, *Parfums Christian Dior*.
56.   Case C-284/95, *Safety Hi-Tech v. S. and T.*, at para. 22, and moreover Case C-76/00, *Petrotub and Republica v. Council*. See also Case C-61/94, *International Dairy Arrangement*, at para. 52: 'Similarly, the primacy of international agreements concluded by the Community over provisions of secondary Community legislation means that such provisions must, so far as is possible, be interpreted in a manner that is consistent with those agreements'.
57.   Cf. esp. Case 43/71, *Politi v. Ministero delle finanze*; Case 84/71, *Marimex v. Ministero delle finanze*; Case 93/71, *Leonensio v. Ministero dell' Agricoltura e Foreste*; Case 34/73, *Fratelli Variola v. Amministrazione delle finanze dello Stato*; Case 50/76, *Amsterdam Bulb* and Case 94/77, *Fratelli Zerbone Snc v. Amministrazione delle finanze dello Stato*. A regulation also creates obligations for individuals, on which they may rely before the national courts *vis-à-vis* other individuals, at least providing the latter are able to be aware of the precise extent of the obligations imposed on them by the regulation; Case C-108/01, *Consorzio del Prosciutto di Parma and Salumificio S. Rita v. Asda Stores and Hygrade Foods*.
58.   Cf. Case 230/78, *Eridania-Zuccherifici nazionali et al. v. Minstero dell' Agricoltura e Foreste et al.*: in such a case, the manner in which this competence is exercised is regulated by national (public) law; the national courts decide, however, whether the measures taken are in conformity with the content of the regulation. See on this subject, R.H. Lauwaars, 'Implementation of Regulations by National Measures' (1983) LIEI, 41 et seq. See also J.M. Bonnes, *Uitvoering van EG-verordeningen in Nederland*, (Zwolle, 1994).

in relation to decisions and directives, the national courts do not need to ask the initial question of whether a regulation satisfies the conditions for direct effect.[59]

The nature and function of a regulation mean that it has direct effect. When a national court is called to apply a provision of a regulation in a particular case, it will assess whether and, if so, to what extent, the provision can be applied without the court exceeding its judicial function. The task facing the national court is no different from that which confronts it in applying provisions of national law. These too may contain provisions which require further rules of a substantive or organizational nature,[60] or which leave a certain discretion in the hands of the administration. If a regulation does not prescribe any national implementing measures, the national court may not take account of national provisions or practices which would require such implementing measures. Otherwise 'the fundamental rule requiring the uniform application of regulations throughout the Community' would be disregarded.[61]

1.4   RELIANCE BEFORE NATIONAL COURTS ON SECONDARY COMMUNITY
             LAW: PROVISIONS OF DIRECTIVES

1.4.1   Direct Effect

Directives[62] – like decisions addressed to Member States[63] – may contain directly effective provisions. In fact, the earliest relevant case law concerned decisions addressed to Member States.[64] The reasoning followed by the Court in these

---

59. The fact that in Case 9/73, *Schlüter II*, at para. 32, the Court exceptionally went to the trouble of ascertaining that a provision of a regulation was 'itself clear and precise, and does not leave any margin of discretion to the authorities by whom it is to be applied' may probably be explained by the fact that this provision implemented an obligation of the Community under the GATT, which the Court did not consider to be directly effective in itself. In Case 87/82, *Rogers v. Arthenay*, the Court ruled that a prohibition provision was an independent and perfectly clear provision, and was therefore directly effective and did not depend on the adoption of the detailed implementing rules provided for.

60. Cf. Case C-403/98, *Azienda Agricola Monte Arcosu Srl v. Regione Autonoma della Sardegna*, annotated by V. Kronenberger (2001) CML Rev., 1545–1556.

61. Case 93/71, *Leonesio*. In this judgment, the Court decided that national budgetary rules may not frustrate the direct application of a provision of Community law, nor the exercise of pecuniary rights of individuals.

62. See on this in particular the Ch. on 'Direct Effect of Directives' (Ch. 9), in: S. Prechal, op. cit. *supra* note 23, 5.

63. Community decisions addressed to individuals determine the scope of application of a provision of Community law in concrete, individual cases. It is advisable not to use the term direct effect for such decisions, but to keep this term for the legal effect in the internal sphere of acts which are of a normative character, such as is sometimes the case for decisions addressed to the Member States.

64. Cf. Case 9/70, *Grad v. Finanzamt Traunstein*; Case 20/70, *Transports Lesage and cie. v. Hauptzollamt Freiburg* and Case 23/70, *Haselhorst v. Finanzamt Düsseldorf* (the so-called Leberpfennig cases). For a somewhat more recent example, cf. Case 249/85, *Albako v. BALM*.

cases suggested that provisions of directives taken on their own (i.e., not in combination with other directly effective provisions of Community law) might also
have such an effect. The Court confirmed this view in its judgment in *Van Duyn*.[65]

The case law on direct effect of provisions of directives, as this has evolved
since *Van Duyn*, can be summarized as follows. The basic principle is that in all
cases where a directive is correctly implemented, 'its effects extend to individuals
through the medium of the implementing measures adopted by the Member State
concerned'.[66] However, when a Member State fails to implement a directive in
national law within the time period allowed, or when the directive is not correctly
implemented, then private individuals are allowed to rely on the provisions of that
directive before the national courts as against the Member State concerned in
all cases when the content of these provisions is unconditional and sufficiently
precise.

Pronouncing on the direct effect of a provision of a directive, the Court ruled
that a provision of Community law is unconditional when the obligation it imposes
is not subject, in its implementation or effects, to the taking of any measure either
by the Institutions of the Community or by the Member States.[67] Again, according
to the Court, the provision is sufficiently precise to be relied on by an individual
and applied by the court where the obligation which it imposes is set out in
unequivocal terms.[68] Private parties can rely on provisions of directives which
meet these conditions both in relation to the state as governing authority, and the
state in its capacity as employer 'against any national provision which is
incompatible with the directive or in so far as the provisions define rights which
individuals are able to assert against the state'.[69]

The state also embraces organizations or institutions which come under its
authority or supervision, or which enjoy special powers which go beyond those
resulting from rules concerning relations between individuals. Such organizations
and institutions include, for instance, the tax authorities,[70] regional authorities,[71]
an independent police authority,[72] and a regional government body with responsibility for public health.[73] They also include – regardless of the legal form – a body
which has been made responsible, pursuant to a measure adopted by the State, for

---

65. Case 41/74, *Van Duyn*.
66. Case 8/81, *Becker v. Finanzamt Münster-Innenstadt*, at para. 19, see also Case 222/84, *Johnston v. Chief Constable of the Royal Ulster Constabulary*, at para. 51, in which the Court spoke of effects that 'reach' individuals.
67. Apart from – of course – the act implementing or transposing the directive in national law.
68. For this 'didactic' summary of the case law, see the above-mentioned Case C-236/92, *Comitato di coordinamento per la difesa della Cava*. It appears from this that the conditions in the case of provisions of directives are the same as in the case of Treaty provisions, providing the deadline for implementing the directive has elapsed.
69. Case 8/81, *Becker*, at para. 25.
70. Case 8/81, *Becker*.
71. Case 103/88, *Fratelli Costanzo*.
72. Case 222/84, *Johnston*.
73. Case 152/84, *Marshall v. Southampton and South-West Hampshire Area Health Authority* (*Marshall I*).

providing a public service under the control of the State and has for that purpose special powers beyond those which result from the normal rules applicable in relations between individuals (so-called exorbitant powers), such as a nationalized company (in the leading case this was the British Gas Corporation).[74]

Recognition of direct effect of provisions of directives is based – according to the case law – on the consideration that it would be incompatible with the binding effect which Article 249 EC ascribes to directives to exclude as a matter of principle the possibility of the obligation imposed on the Member State being relied upon by persons concerned. In particular, in cases where directives impose on Member States a duty to adopt a certain course of action, the effectiveness ('*effet utile*') of such a measure would be diminished if persons were prevented from relying upon it in proceedings before a court, and national courts were prevented from taking it into consideration as an element of Community law. The fact that Article 249 EC only speaks of direct applicability in relation to regulations may not be taken to mean *a contrario* that other categories of acts may never entail similar effects.[75] A Member State which has not adopted the implementing measures required by the directive within the prescribed period may not plead, as against individuals, its own failure to perform the obligations which the directive entails as against persons who have acted in accordance with the provisions of a directive.[76] The binding nature of a directive exists only in relation to 'each Member State to which it is addressed'.[77]

It is important to note that the recognition of direct effect to provisions of directives was far from obvious. After all, directives require by definition legislative intervention by Member States.[78] In order to be effective, provisions of directives must therefore be transposed into national law: they do not have effect directly, but only by means of their implementation in the internal legal system of the Member States. In that light, it is understandable that the Court has only wished to make an exception to this in cases where an individual relies on provisions of a directive against the Member State which has failed to implement the directive on time, or correctly, into its domestic law (so-called 'vertical' effect).

Despite this limitation, the case law of the Court on direct effect of provisions of directives has met with incomprehension and opposition in some national courts. In Germany, the *Bundesfinanzhof's* resistance to accepting the direct effect of

---

74. Case C-188/89, *Foster v. British Gas*, annotated by E. Szyszcak (1990) CML Rev., 859. See on the questions which the case law raises on this point also A.G. Van Gerven in his Opinion in this case.

75. Case 41/74, *Van Duyn*; Case 8/81, *Becker* and Case 152/84, *Marshall I.*

76. As the Court first said in Case 148/78, *Criminal Proceedings against Tullio Ratti.* In my view this should not be considered an attempt – doomed to failure – to add the Anglo-Saxon concept of 'estoppel' to the two arguments which were already developed in order to justify the acknowledgement of direct effect (binding force and effectiveness or '*effet utile*'), but rather in order to indicate the consequences which result. We refer further to the considerations of S. Prechal on this question, op. cit. *supra* note 23, 223–226.

77. Case 152/84, *Marshall I*; see further section 1.5 *infra*.

78. Cf. Art. 249(3) EC.

provisions of the Sixth Value Added Tax (VAT) Directive was finally overcome through the intervention of the *Bundesverfassungsgericht.*[79] In France the Conseil d'État had already in 1978 decided that in the absence of implementing measures incompatibility with provisions of a directive could not be relied upon directly to oppose individual decisions of the French administration, even if the directive's provisions laid down clear, precise and unconditional obligations on the Member States. From a later judgment it appears, however, that in the absence of implementing measures an individual, by raising a plea of illegality, may claim the incompatibility with regard to the directive's provisions of the administrative or statutory provisions on which the individual decision is based.[80] It is remarkable that the Conseil d'État has opened the way for private parties to attack French legislation[81] on the ground of incompatibility with the objectives of a directive, which, according to the legal definition of a directive in Article 249 EC, involves examination based on the result to be achieved by the directive.

Thus in the French administrative courts an individual is unable to obtain the annulment, on the ground of incompatibility with a directly effective provision of a directive, of an administrative decision addressed to him or her. But he or she can obtain its annulment if the national legislation on which the decision is based is incompatible with the objectives of the directive, even when the directive in question has not been transposed into national law. This so-called '*invocabilité d'exclusion*' (the objectives of the directive exclude application of the national rule) in fact makes directives more effective than they are under the case law of the Court of Justice.[82] On the other hand, the case law of the Conseil d'État is less far-reaching in that it withholds the so-called '*invocabilité de substitution*' (application of the provision of a directive in place of the national rule) from provisions of directives, even where the national court is obliged, in accordance with standing case law of the Court, to give effect to those provisions.[83]

---

79. Bundesfinanzhof 25 Apr. 1985, Europarecht (1981), 442 and Bundesverfassungsgericht, 8 Apr. 1987 (1988) CML Rev., 1; see Hilf, *Der Justizkonflikt um EG-Richtlinien: gelöst*, Europarecht 1988, 1. For the case law of the Court of Justice, see in particular Case 70/83, *Kloppenburg v. Finanzamt Leer.*

80. *Cohn-Bendit*, Conseil d'Etat 22 Dec. 1978 (1979) CML Rev., 701, annotated by P.J.G. Kapteyn; for the later judgment, see Conseil d'Etat 6 Feb. 1998, Tête et Association de sauvegarde de l'Ouest lyonnais, *Revue française de droit administratif* (1998), 407.

81. Initially only subordinate legislation, e.g., *Compagnie Alitalia* 3 Feb. 1989 (1990) CML Rev., 248, later also statutes, in the cases Rothmans International France and Philip Morris France, 28 Feb. 1992; see annotations by Dutheil de la Rochere in (1993) CML Rev., 187. The primacy of the Treaty over French primary legislation was accepted by the Conseil d'Etat in *Nicolo* (1990) CML Rev., 173; see Manin, 'The *Nicolo* case of the *Conseil d'Etat:* French Constitutional Law and the Supreme Administrative Court's Acceptance of the Primacy of Community Law over Subsequent National Statute Law' (1991) CML Rev., 499.

82. Review on the basis of the aims of the directive also seems to be broader than examining the question whether the Member State has remained within the margin of appreciation granted by the directive, the so-called objective review of legality.

83. Cf. for the distinction between these two forms of '*invocabilité*', Galmot and Bonichot, La Cour de justice des Communautés européennes et la transposition des directives en droit national,

1.4.2   Objective Review of Legality

Provisions which depend for their implementation on discretionary measures by
the Member States may in certain circumstances be relied on in the national courts
and be applied by those courts. The national court can review the legality of such an
act[84] in the light of the relevant provisions, at least to the extent that they set
sufficiently precise limits to the discretion allowed to the Member States in the
framework of implementation, and it is alleged that these limits have been
exceeded.[85] Where the discretion conferred by the provisions of the directive
has been exceeded, individuals may rely on those provisions against the national
authorities and thus obtain from the latter the setting aside of the national rules or
measures incompatible with those provisions. In such cases, it is for the authorities
of the Member State to take, according to their relevant powers, all the general or
particular measures necessary to ensure that the result sought by the directive is
achieved.[86]

In a number of cases in the 1970s[87] the Court had already ruled that the
importance of not weakening the useful effect of obligations imposed on Member
States by directives was especially relevant

> when the individual invokes a provision of a directive before a national court
> in order that the latter shall rule whether the competent national authorities, in
> exercising the choice which is left to them as to the form and the methods for
> implementing the directive, have kept within the limits as to their discretion
> set out in the directive.[88]

In its judgment in *Kraaijeveld*,[89] nearly twenty years later, the Court confirmed this
case law. In such a case, not only does Community law permit a review in the light
of provisions of a directive, but it even – as this case shows – places the court under
the obligation to carry out a review in the light of grounds derived from a binding

---

Revue française de droit administratif (1988), 1–23. See also D. Simon, *Le système juridique
communautaire*, 3e éd. mise à jour, Paris, 2001, section 343 et seq. An analysis based on this
distinction is not to be found in the Court's case law, but is used by scholars to clarify it; see, e.g.,
Prechal's three-step model of application of Community law, in C. Barnard (ed.), op. cit. note 23
supra, 41–47.

84. Not only implementing legislation, but any measure taken by national authorities, see Case
    C-127/02, *Landelijke Vereniging tot Behoud van de Waddenzee*.
85. See on this question already the observations of C.W.A. Timmermans, 'Directives: Their Effect
    within the National Legal Systems' (1979) CML Rev., 533, at 544 et seq.
86. Case 435/97, *WWF and Others v. Autonome Provinz Bozen and Others*. As to the limits to the
    direct effect of directives in 'triangular' and horizontal relations, see *infra*, 1.5
87. Case 51/76, *VNO*; Case 38/77, *Enka v. Inspecteur der invoerrechten en accijnzen* and Case
    21/78, *Delkvist v. Anklagemyndigheden*.
88. E.g., Case 51/76, *VNO*, para. 24.
89. Case C-72/95, *Kraaijeveld et al. v. Gedeputeerde Staten van Zuid-Holland*; see also Case
    C-435/97, *World Wildlife Fund*, and Case C-287/98, *State of the Grand Duchy of Luxembourg
    v. Linster*. The last case concerned review on the basis of a directive which had not been fully
    implemented on time.

rule of Community law *ex officio*, if it is under a similar obligation under national law concerning binding rules of national law.[90]

1.4.3 Interpretation in Conformity with a Directive (Duty of Consistent Interpretation)[91]

In the interpretation of national law, the national court is obliged to take greatest possible account of provisions of directives, even if they do not fulfil the conditions laid down in the case law for being directly effective. *Von Colson and Kamann v. Land Nordrhein-Westfalen*[92] shows that the obligation on Member States to achieve a particular result envisaged by a directive, as well as the obligation on them to take all general or particular measures to ensure fulfilment of that obligation (Art. 10 EC) is binding on all the authorities of Member States including, for matters within their jurisdiction, the courts. The Court ruled, in *Marleasing*,[93] that it follows that in applying national law, national courts are required to interpret national law[94] – applying interpretative methods recognised by that law – as far as possible in the light of the wording and purpose of the directive in order to achieve the result required by the third paragraph of Article 249 EC;[95] this obligation holds regardless of whether the national provisions are of earlier or later date

---

90. Case C-72/95, *Kraaijeveld*. The judgment (at para. 57) refers in that context to Joined Cases C-430 & 431/93, *Van Schijndel and Van Veen v. Stichting Pensioenfonds voor Fysiotherapeuten*. There is some lack of clarity on the question of the criteria on the basis of which it should be decided whether a rule of Community law involves binding law in the sense of 'mandatory law' (French: *règles contraignantes*); see S. Prechal, 'Community Law in National Courts: the Lessons from Van Schijndel' (1998) CML Rev., 681, at 689–700.

91. It should here be pointed out that such a duty exists not only in relation to directives, but in general to any provision of Community law. See on consistent interpretation in conformity with the EC Treaty, Case C-165/91, *Van Munster v. Rijksdienst voor Pensioenen*, and in conformity with provisions of a treaty concluded by the EC with third states, Joined Cases 300 & 392/98, *Parfums Christian Dior*.

92. Case 14/83, *Von Colson and Kamann v. Land Nordrhein-Westfalen*. See also Case C-355/96, *Silhouette International Schmied v. Hartlauer Handelsgesellschaft*.

93. Case C-106/89, *Marleasing v. Comercial Internacional de Alimentación*. For an example of an obligation to interpret *in conformity with the Treaty*, see Case C-165/91, *Van Munster*. Compare however this judgment with the later judgment in Case C-262/97, *Rijksdienst voor Pensioenen v. Engelbrecht*.

94. Not only the domestic provisions enacted in order to implement the directive in question, but national law as a whole, see Joined Cases C-397-403/01, *Bernhard Pfeiffer and Others v. Deutsches Rotes Kreuz, Kreisverband Waldshut eV*, annotated by S. Prechal (2005) CML Rev., 1445, para. 115.

95. If the application of interpretative methods recognized by national law enables, in certain circumstances, a provision of domestic law to be construed in such a way as to avoid conflict with another rule of domestic law, or the scope of that provision to be restricted to that end by applying it only insofar as it is compatible with the rule concerned, the duty of consistent interpretation even implies that a national court is bound to use those methods in order to achieve the result sought by the directive (*Pfeiffer*, para. 116).

than the directive. It exists only once the period for transposition of the directive has expired.[96]

As the Court stated in *Pfeiffer*, the duty of consistent interpretation is inherent in the system of the Treaty, 'since it permits the national court, for the matters within its jurisdiction, to ensure the full effectiveness of Community law when it determines the dispute before it'.[97] Thus, the national court would do well to examine first of all whether it can interpret the national provisions in a manner which is consistent with the relevant provision of the directive concerned, before looking at whether the latter provision can or cannot be relied upon as such against the national provisions.[98] It is clear that the duty to interpret national law in conformity with a directive is not absolute. There are inherent limits on the obligation of conforming interpretation. First, such interpretation must not lead to the imposition of obligations on individuals – although this does not exclude the possibility that interpretation in conformity with a directive may have a negative influence on the legal position of individuals. After all, provisions of directives cannot of themselves impose obligations on individuals.[99] Secondly, the Court has added an important gloss to the principle in Von Colson, namely that the duty to interpret and apply national legislation in conformity with the directive is subject to general principles of law, such as legal certainty and non-retroactivity,[100] and fundamental rights such as the right to a fair trial.[101] Thus the duty of consistent interpretation reaches for instance a limit where it has the effect of determining or aggravating the liability in criminal law of persons who act in contravention of a directive's provisions. Thirdly, the national court is under the obligation to interpret national law 'as

---

96. Case C-212/04, *Konstantinos Adeneler And Others v. ELOG*. Although a Member State cannot be reproached for not having yet adopted measures implementing a directive in national law before the period for its transposition has expired, it should be pointed out that a directive produces legal effects for the Member State to which it is addressed – and, therefore, for all the national authorities – following its publication or from the date of its notification (ibid., para. 119). It follows that during the period prescribed for transposition of a directive, the Member State must refrain from taking any measures liable seriously to compromise the attainment of the result prescribed by it (Case C-129/96, *Inter-Environnement Wallonie*, para. 45).
97. Joined Cases C-397-403/01, para. 114.
98. It is 'for the national court to the full extent of its discretion under national law, to interpret and apply domestic law in accordance with the requirements of Community law and, to the extent that such an interpretation is not possible in relation to the Treaty provisions conferring rights on individuals which are enforceable by them and which the national courts must protect, to disapply any provision of domestic law which is contrary to those provisions.' (Case C-208/05, *ITC Innovative Technology Center GmbH v. Bundesagentur für Arbeit*, para. 70).
99. The Court recalled this in Case C-106/89, *Marleasing*, referring to Case 152/84, *Marshall I*. See also Case C-168/95, *Criminal proceedings against Arcaro*.
100. The Court recalled this in Case 80/86, *Criminal proceedings against Kolpinghuis Nijmegen*, referring to Case 14/86, *Pretore di Salò v. Persons unknown*, at para. 20. See also Joined Cases C-74 & 129/95, *Criminal proceedings against X* and Case C-168/95, *Arcaro* and Case C-384/02, *Grongaard and Bang*.
101. See Case C-105/03, *Maria Pupino*, paras 58–60. See M. Fletcher, 'Extending "Indirect Effect" to the Third Pillar: the Significance of Pupino?' (2005) EL Rev., 862.

far as possible'[102] in conformity with the directive. Whether an interpretation in conformity with the directive is possible, depends on the flexibility of the provision of national law to be interpreted. Existing case law may not form any impediment, but where necessary must be amended. Any obligation to interpret national law *contra legem* is excluded however.[103]

In *Pupino*, the Court has extended the duty of consistent interpretation which exists in EC law in relation to directives, to framework decisions taken under (Third Pillar) EU law.[104] Individuals are entitled to invoke framework decisions in order to obtain a conforming interpretation of national law before the courts of the Member States. At the basis if this ruling are two main arguments: the binding character of framework decisions, formulated in terms identical to those of the third paragraph of Article 249 EC, and the existence in EU law of an unwritten obligation similar to that of loyal cooperation laid down in Article 10 EC. As direct effect of framework decisions is expressly excluded by Article 34.2(b) EU, the Court's decision highlights the conceptual difference between consistent interpretation and direct effect. Under the conditions just mentioned, individuals are entitled to invoke provisions of not only framework decisions, but also directives and other acts, directly effective or not, in order to obtain a 'conforming' interpretation of national law before the courts of the Member States.[105]

1.5   SO-CALLED HORIZONTAL, VERTICAL AND INVERSE VERTICAL
        DIRECT EFFECTS[106]

How far may private parties rely on provisions of Community law not just against the national authorities but also against other private parties? It is beyond doubt that provisions of the Treaties or of regulations[107] can impose obligations on individuals *vis-à-vis* the authorities if they are clear from their very nature and scope, as, for example, is the case for undertakings in the field of competition, or for example in the field of agriculture. However, directives which are not correctly implemented or are not implemented in time, cannot of themselves impose obligations in such a vertical manner on individuals, since a directive imposes obligations

---

102. See Joined Cases C-397-403/01, *Pfeiffer*, para. 113 and the case law cited.
103. See Case C-212/04, *Adeneler*, para. 110 and, by analogy, Case C-105/03 *Pupino*, paras 44 and 46.
104. Case C-105/03, *Maria Pupino*; see generally S. Peers, 'Salvation outside the Church: Judicial Protection in the Third Pillar after the *Pupino* and *Segi* Judgments' (2007) CML Rev., 883–929.
105. See the decision in Joined Cases 300 & 392/98, *Parfum Christian Dior*, requiring national judges to apply national rules as far as possible in the light of the wording and purpose of Art. 50 of TRIPs despite the fact that under Community law the provision lacked direct effect (para. 47).
106. See generally M. Dougan, 'When Worlds Collide! Competing Visions of the Relationship between Direct Effect and Supremacy' (2007) CML Rev., 931–963.
107. See for regulations 1.3 *supra*.

only on 'each Member State to which it is addressed'.[108] In the specific situation in which a directive is relied on against an individual by the authorities of a Member State within the context of criminal proceedings, this means that a directive cannot, of itself and independently of a national law adopted by a Member State for its implementation, have the effect of determining or aggravating the liability in criminal law of persons who act in contravention of the provisions of that directive.[109] Provisions of a directive can be invoked by individuals *vis-à-vis* the Member State which has failed to implement the directive on time, or correctly, into its domestic law: in case of such a failure, so-called *vertical direct effect* is permitted, but the Member State cannot rely on the provisions of the directive against an individual: so-called *inverse vertical direct effect* is excluded.

The issue has in practice come to a head in relation to what is known as horizontal direct effect: can private parties in their legal relationships with other private parties rely on provisions of Community law which are addressed only to the Member States? A distinction should be made in this context between Treaty provisions and provisions of directives. The implication that the Court did not exclude reliance on Treaty provisions in such circumstances was already apparent from the Court's case law on the free movement of goods under Articles 28 et seq. EC in conjunction with the second paragraph of Article 10 EC. This case law involved actions in national courts between private parties about the limits which Article 30 EC placed on the exercise of exclusive rights under national legislation relating to the protection of industrial and commercial property, as proprietors of such rights may only rely on such legislation within these limits.[110]

The Court has expressly held that the prohibition of discrimination on grounds of nationality contained in Articles 12, 39, 43 and 49 EC has horizontal direct effect. Thus the prohibition in Articles 39 and 49 EC does not merely apply to actions of public authorities but also covers other types of provisions including collective agreements or rules in the employment field and in the field of the supply of services.[111] These cases involve situations where a group or organization can exercise a certain power over private individuals, and is able to impose conditions as a result of which the exercise of fundamental freedoms guaranteed by the

---

108. Case 152/84, *Marshall I*; Case C-106/89, *Marleasing* and Case C-168/95, *Arcaro*.
109. See, *inter alia*, Cases 80/86, *Kolpinghuis Nijmegen*, and C-60/02, *X*. See also Joined Cases C-387, 391 & 403/02, *Berlusconi and Others*, paras 73–74, where the non-application of articles of the Italian penal code, due to their incompatibility with Art. 6 of the First Companies Directive, might render applicable a national provision containing a manifestly more severe criminal penalty.
110. Cf. e.g., Case 78/70, *Deutsche Grammophon v. Metro SB*. See further Ch. VIII *infra*.
111. Case 36/74, *Walrave and Koch v. Association Union Cycliste Internationale et al.* and Case C-415/93, *Union royale belge des sociétés de football association et al. v. Bosman et al.* See moreover Joined Cases C-51/96 & C-191/97, *Deliège v. Ligue francophone de judo et disciplines associées*, and Case C-176/96, *Lehtonen et al. v. Fédération royale belge des sociétés de basketball*. As a result of this case law, obstacles to intra-Community movement imposed by individuals can also be contested on the basis of these provisions, as well as the competition provisions.

Treaty may be hindered.[112] It may be concluded from the Court's judgment in *Angonese*,[113] furthermore, that in principle a private party can also rely on these non-discrimination provisions of the Treaty against another private party – one which is not a collective body.

The judgment of the Court in *Defrenne II*[114] caused more of a stir,[115] given that Article 141 (at the time Art. 119) EC is addressed explicitly to each Member State, and also that it deals with a principle rather than a clear prohibition. In that judgment, the principle of equal pay for men and women for equal work was declared applicable not only to the action of public authorities but also 'to all agreements which are intended to regulate paid labour collectively, as well as to contracts between individuals'[116] insofar as in all these cases direct and overt discrimination is involved rather than indirect and disguised discrimination. This also applies in cases of unequal pay for men and women for equal work carried out in the same establishment or service, whether private or public.[117]

In its judgment in *Defrenne II*, the Court attached to a provision which unmistakably imposed an obligation on the Member States, an obligation on private parties, namely to pay men and women equally for equal work. Giving a direct horizontal effect, i.e., creating obligations for private parties, to what was clearly a duty of the Member States under the Treaty led to the question whether horizontal direct effect could also result from provisions of *directives* which, *per se*, impose obligations on the Member States.[118]

In *Marshall v. Southampton and South-West Hampshire Area Health Authority*[119] the Court firmly stated that it cannot. According to the Court,

> it must be emphasized that according to article [249] of the [EC] treaty the binding nature of a directive, which constitutes the basis for the possibility of relying on the directive before a national court, exists only in relation to 'each member state to which it is addressed'. It follows that a directive may not of itself impose obligations on an individual and that a provision of a directive may not be relied upon as such against such a person.

---

112. Cf. Case C-411/98, *Ferlini v. Centre Hospitalier de Luxembourg.*
113. Case C-281/98, *Angonese v. Cassa di Risparmio di Bolzano*, concerning Art. 39 EC.
114. Case 43/75, *Defrenne II.*
115. See W. van Gerven, 'La contribution de l'arrêt Defrenne au développement du droit communautaire' (1977) CDE, 131 et seq.
116. Case 43/75, *Defrenne II*, at para. 39.
117. Case 43/75, *Defrenne II*. Only differences in pay which can be attributed to one source come under Art. 141(1) EC; if that is not the case, then there is no body which can be held responsible for the inequality and which could restore equal treatment (Case C-320/00, *Lawrence et al. v. Regent Office Care*).
118. It is important to recall that the provisions of a directive which the Member States are required to implement may seek to impose obligations not only on national authorities, but also on private individuals.
119. Case 152/84, *Marshall I*, para. 48. See further Case C-192/94, *El Corte Inglés*, Case C-97/96, *Daihatsu-Händler* and Case C-456/98, *Centrosteel.*

Despite the criticism which followed this negative position, the Court has maintained this stance.[120] The objections against this position have been extensively set out in the literature and the Opinions of a number of advocates general.[121]

Recognition of horizontal direct effect for provisions of directives which are not correctly implemented or not implemented on time would without doubt benefit the effectiveness of Community law, and strengthen the judicial protection of individuals. However, it should not be forgotten that this concerns an exception – and a controversial one at that – to the rule laid down in the Treaty that directives do not have direct effects in the internal legal systems of the Member States, but have effects as a result of their implementation by national authorities. This also contains the answer to the question why the type of direct effect which the Court recognized in its *Defrenne II* judgment for Treaty provisions which impose obligations on the Member States cannot be recognized for provisions of directives which impose such obligations: Treaty provisions are, unlike directives, not subject to a 'higher' rule opposing such an effect. Stretching the exception in the case of directives any further would reclassify the rule and turn it into an exception. It would also in effect 'recognize a power in the Community to enact obligations for individuals with immediate effect, whereas it has competence to do so only where it is empowered to adopt regulations'.[122]

A more concrete objection is that attracted by the extremely broad interpretation of the concept 'state in its capacity of employer', as a result of which undertakings which have been made responsible for the provision of public services are, under certain conditions, also included. Leaving aside the problem of how to determine whether an undertaking can be considered to be included in this category,[123] such an interpretation leads to a distinction that is difficult to justify, between such undertakings, which must be assimilated with branches of the state, and other undertakings which do not need to take any account of such directly effective provisions.[124] In practice, such a difference in treatment will not be likely

---

120.   Case C-91/92, *Dori v. Recreb*, at paras 22–24. See also the last three cases mentioned in the previous footnote.
121.   For a survey of the arguments pro and contra and further references, see S. Prechal Directives, op.cit. *supra* note 23, 255–258. See moreover the Opinions of A.G. Van Gerven (Case C-271/91, *Marshall II*), A.G. Jacobs (Case C-316/93, *Vaneetveld v. Le Foyer*) and extensively A.G. Lenz (Case C-91/92, *Dori*). See also F. Schockweiler, *Effets des directives non transposées en droit national à l'égard des particuliers*, in: *Hacia un nuevo orden internacional y Europeo: estudios en homenaje al profesor don Manuel Diez de Velasco*, (Madrid, 1993), 1201–1220.
122.   Case C-91/92, *Dori*, at para. 24.
123.   The formula used by the Court in Case C-188/89, *Foster et al. v. British Gas* only gives an indication, but does not contain criteria to be used elsewhere. See also in this context Joined Cases C-253-258/96, *Kampelman*.
124.   Cf. on this problem, D. Curtin, 'Directives: the Effectiveness of Judicial Protection of Individual Rights' (1990) CML Rev., 709–737, and S. Prechal, 'Remedies after Marshall' (1990) CML Rev., 451–473. See also, R. Mastroianni, 'On the Distinction between Vertical and Horizontal Direct Effect of Community Directives: What Role for the Principle of Equality?' (1999) EPL, 417, and more recently S. Prechal. Directives, op. cit. *supra* note 23, 58–61 (the concept of 'the State').

to last long, as the Member States will have every incentive to harmonize the obligations stemming from Community rules imposed on the private sector and on the public sector's economic activities as rapidly as possible. But it remains confusing to see that private parties can rely *vis-à-vis* the state not just on provisions which impose obligations on the Member State as public authority, but also on provisions imposing obligations on private parties, i.e., when the state acts as an employer.

The confusion becomes even greater as a result of the fact that permitting a private party to rely on a provision of a directive in a proceeding against the State may have disadvantageous effects for the legal position of third parties.[125] Nonetheless, 'a directive may not *of itself* impose obligations on an individual and may therefore not be relied upon as such against such a person'.[126] That leads to the hotly debated question where, in such triangular relations, the division lies between a permitted effect on the legal position of third parties, and the forbidden imposition of obligations on such third parties, between acceptable and unacceptable horizontal effects.[127] The decision in *Delena Wells* has shed more light on this question.[128] The Court there pointed out that, as directives can only create rights and not obligations for individuals, an individual 'may not rely on a directive against a Member State where it is a matter of a State obligation directly linked to the performance of another obligation falling, pursuant to that directive, on a third party'. But 'mere adverse repercussions on the rights of third parties' do not justify preventing an individual from invoking the provisions of a directive against the Member State concerned. Consequently, where, as in *Delena Wells*, the obligation on a Member State to ensure that an assessment of the environmental effects of the working of a quarry is carried out, is not directly linked to the performance of any obligation which would fall, pursuant to the directive in question, on the quarry owners, the fact that mining operations must be halted to await the results of the assessment could not be described as an inverse (vertical) direct effect of the provisions of that directive in relation to the quarry owners.[129]

The fact that unconditional and sufficiently precise provisions of directives – but which are not (or incorrectly) implemented in national law – can only have direct effects in the relations between organs of the state and private parties, does not mean that such effect may only be relied on in proceedings brought against such state organs. The judgments in *CIA Security* and *Unilever* reveal that

---

125. See, e.g., the not entirely successful attempt by the Court to deny this in Case 8/81, *Becker*, at para. 44. See also Case 103/88, *Fratelli Costanzo* and Case C-201/94, *The Queen v. The Medicines Control Agency, ex parte Smith and Nephew Pharmaceuticals* as good examples of such 'horizontal' effects. It should also be noted that certain horizontal effects can result from the case law on consistent interpretation of national law (see section 1.4.3. *supra*), as appears in particular from the judgment in Case C-106/89, *Marleasing*.
126. Case C-192/94, *El Corte Inglés v. Blázquez Rivero*, at para. 15 (our emphasis), hereby confirming once more the constant case law since the judgment in Case 152/84, *Marshall I*.
127. Cf. C.W.A. Timmermans, 'Community Directives Revisited' (1997) YEL, 1–28, at 17.
128. Case C-201/02, *Delena Wells*.
129. Ibid., paras 56–58.

sometimes such reliance is also possible in proceedings between private parties.[130] Article 9 of Directive 83/189[131] makes the entry into force of national technical regulations which should have been notified dependent on the agreement or lack of objection of the Commission; the Court has ruled that the non-applicability of such national regulations which have been adopted contrary to the Directive may be relied on in civil proceedings between private parties concerning contractual rights and obligations. The Court based its judgment on the consideration that 'Directive 83/189 does not in any way define the substantive scope of the legal rule on the basis of which the national court must decide the case before it. It creates neither rights nor obligations for individuals'.[132] It has been submitted that in this way, an indication was given about the Court's approach:[133] as long as it was merely a question of *non-application* of a national provision on grounds of its non-conformity with a rule contained in a directive (compare this with the above-mentioned '*invocabilité d'exclusion*') and not of the substitution of this provision by the rule which had been infringed (compare with the above-mentioned '*invocabilité de substitution*'), then this element can also be invoked in proceedings between private parties.[134] In this case, the directive does not of itself impose an obligation on a private party.

The decision in *Pfeiffer* proves, however, that this is not the approach of the Court,[135] though the case 'provided a textbook example of a dispute to which the distinction between substitution and exclusionary effects might have been thought to provide a solution'.[136] Referring to its case law on consistent interpretation according to which a directive cannot of itself impose obligations on an individual and cannot therefore be relied upon as such against an individual, it declared unequivocally 'that even a clear, precise and unconditional provision of a directive seeking to confer rights or impose obligations on individuals cannot of itself apply in proceedings exclusively between private parties' (para. 109). That the substitution/exclusion analysis is not accepted by the Court as a solution in horizontal relations has been confirmed by the decision in *Berlusconi*.[137]

---

130. See in particular Case C-194/94, *CIA Security International v. Signalson and Securitel* and Case C-443/98, *Unilever Italia v. Central Food*, annotated by M. Dougan (2001) CML Rev., 1503.
131. O.J. 1983, L 109.
132. See Case C-443/98, *Unilever Italia*.
133. On the various efforts to reconcile these judgments with the prohibition of horizontal direct effect for directives, see S. Prechal, Directives, op. cit. *supra* note 23, 266–268.
134. It should not be forgotten, however, that this concerns a rule which does not need to be transposed into national law in order to be applied therein, but which should be taken into account in the application of certain national measures.
135. Joined Cases C-397-403/01, *Bernard Pfeiffer and Others v. Deutsches Rotes Kreuz, Kreisverband Waldshut* annotated by S. Prechal (2005) CML Rev., 1445.
136. 'Horizontal Direct Effect – A Law of Diminishing Return?' Editorial comments (2006) *CML Rev.*, 1–8, at 5. The editorial went on to say that '[h]appily, the Court of Justice did not fall for the insidious charm of the substitution/exclusion analysis'.
137. Joined Cases C-387, 391 & 403/02, *Berlusconi and Others*, annotated by A. Biondi and R. Mastroianni (2006) CML Rev., 553 and by H. van der Wilt, (2006) *EuConst*, 309.

The question remains how to square the *CIA Security* and the *Unilever* decisions with the outcome of *Pfeiffer*. Probably, applying the *Delena Wells* criteria, the consequences of the non-applicability of such national regulations which have been adopted contrary to the directive concerned are 'mere adverse repercussions' for the other private party in the litigation.[138] It must be acknowledged, however, that academic efforts to order the case law of the Court on this point systematically tend to get wrecked time and again by new judgments which do not wholly fit in with the system designed.[139]

2   PRIMACY OF PROVISIONS OF COMMUNITY LAW; COMMUNITY LAW AND NATIONAL CONSTITUTIONAL LAW

The recognition that provisions of Community law have direct effect would not have been very significant if the question whether national courts should apply such provisions despite conflicting national law had been determined by the various ways in which each of the Member States regulates the relationship between international and national law, rather than being answered by Community law.[140] The uniform application of Community law in all Member States would in that case not have been achieved, and legal certainty would have been threatened.[141] The *Costa v. ENEL*[142] case already made it clear that the resolution of possible conflicts between Community law and the law of the Member States was not a matter of national law, but of Community law itself.

The purpose of the right to rely on directly applicable provisions of Community law 'is to ensure that provisions of Community law prevail over national provisions'.[143]

---

138. Cf. the reference in para. 57of the judgment in *Delena Wells* to the side-effects in the *CIA International Security* and *Unilever* judgments as examples of 'mere adverse repercussions on the rights of third parties'. See also S. Prechal, Directives, op. cit. *supra* note 23, 268–269.
139. See for an overview of these efforts, the critical annotation by M. Dougan of Case C-443/98, *Unilever Italia* (2001) CML Rev., 1503–1517; for a new attempt to find a theoretically convincing explanation, see Dougan, op. cit. *supra* note 106.
140. See extensively on how and why the doctrine of supremacy took hold across the EU, Karen J. Alter, *Establishing the Supremacy of European Law, the Making of an International Rule of Law* (Oxford, 2001). See also the contribution by B. de Witte, in op. cit. *supra* note 1.
141. The latter was one of the arguments employed by the A.G. in his Opinion in Case 26/62, *Van Gend en Loos*, to suggest that the Court should reject direct effect of what was then Art. 12 EEC.
142. Case 6/64, *Costa v. E.N.E.L.* The primacy of the Treaties and the law adopted by the Union on the basis of the Treaties over the law of Member States, under the conditions laid down by the settled case law of the Court, is reaffirmed by Draft Declaration No. 17 concerning primacy, attached to the Lisbon Treaty.
143. Joined Cases C-46 & 48/93, *Brasserie du pêcheur v. Bundesrepublik Deutschland and The Queen v. Secretary of State for Transport, ex parte Factortame et al. (Factortame III)*, at para. 20.

It is apparent from the judgment in *Simmenthal II*[144] that the principles of direct effect and primacy of Community law are indissolubly linked. The logical consequences of the priority of directly effective (applicable) Community law over national law were set out in that judgment by the Court in a manner which could not be misunderstood. The Court stated (para. 17) that

> in accordance with the principle of the precedence of Community law, the relationship between provisions of the Treaty and directly applicable measures of the Institutions on the one hand and the national law of the Member States on the other is such that those provisions and measures not only by their entry into force render automatically inapplicable any conflicting provisions of current national law but – in so far as they are an integral part of, and take precedence in, the legal order applicable in the territory of each of the Member States – also preclude the valid adoption of new national legislative measures to the extent to which they would be incompatible with Community provisions.

As to the consequences of such incompatible national measures, the Court appears to make here a distinction between existent ('render inapplicable') and new measures ('preclude the valid adoption'). This was, however, clearly not its intention.[145] It concludes that

> every national court must, in a case within its jurisdiction, apply Community law in its entirety and protect rights which the latter confers on individuals and must accordingly set aside any provision of national law which may conflict with it, whether prior or subsequent to the Community rule.[146]

This case law has been subsequently refined: not only national courts but all organs of the State, including administrative authorities,[147] have the duty to *disapply*[148] not only general abstract rules but also specific individual administrative decisions which contravene Community law.[149]

---

144. Case 106/77, *Amministrazione delle finanze dello Stato v. Simmenthal* (*Simmenthal II*). (Strictly speaking, this is the third *Simmenthal* judgment, but the first (Case 35/76, *Simmenthal SpA v. Ministero delle Finanze italiano*) was not as memorable as the later two).
145. Cf. Joined Cases 10-22/97, *Ministero delle Finanze v. IN.CO.GE.'90 and others*, para. 20.
146. *Simmenthal II* at para. 21. See also the dictum. Cf. R. Schütze, 'Supremacy without Pre-emption? The Very Slowly Emergent Doctrine of Community Pre-emption' (2006) CML Rev., 1023, at 1029–1030.
147. Cf. Case 103/88, *Fratelli Costanzo*. On this in practice and in national constitutional terms problematic judgment, see B. de Witte, in op. cit. *supra* note 1, 192–193.
148. 'provided always that this obligation does not restrict the power of the competent national courts to apply, from among the various procedures available under national law, those which are appropriate for protecting the individual rights conferred by Community law': Joined Cases C-10-22/97, *IN.CO.GE.'90*, para. 21.
149. See Case C-224/97, *Erich Ciola and Land Vorarlberg*, Case C-118/00, *Gervais Larsy and Inasti*, and Case C-198/01, *CIF and Autorità Garante della Concorrenza e del Mercato*, and further S. Prechal, Directives, op. cit. *supra* note 23, 67–72.

Primacy of Community law is a principle of Community law itself. It is Community law and not national law which decrees such primacy. For example, in the event of a conflict with rules of Community law, a Dutch court would disapply the relevant national provisions not on account of incompatibility with Article 94 of the Dutch Constitution but on account of their incompatibility with Community law.[150] The European Communities Act 1972 being the vehicle in the United Kingdom for the entry of Community law into the national legal system, it is not always clear whether the priority of Community law in areas where it is applicable occurs by virtue of Community law,[151] or rather by virtue of this Act.[152]

If a national court accepts the construction that it is Community law and not national law which decrees primacy, it cannot arrive at judgments like that of the French *Conseil d'État*[153] which refused on constitutional grounds to disapply a French decree (which had the force of a law) which was incompatible with an earlier EEC regulation. It is true that Article 55 of the French Constitution expressly gives priority to norms of written international law, but clearly the *Conseil d'État*, unlike the *Cour de Cassation*[154] did not consider that it had jurisdiction to consider the issue, on the basis that it would then have to consider the compatibility of the decree with the Constitution, i.e., with Article 55 itself! The question of compatibility with the Constitution is outside the jurisdiction of ordinary French courts. In the meantime, the *Conseil d'État* has revised its standpoint and has accepted the primacy of the law of international agreements, thus including Community law, even above subsequent national law.[155]

Another view which does not fit in with the Court of Justice's construction is the view which the Italian Corte Costituzionale demonstrated in the *Simmenthal* case. The Italian court took the view that it alone – and no other Italian court – was competent to decide whether a national provision was incompatible with Community law, on the ground that it had sole jurisdiction in constitutional questions. The

---

150. Cf. the Hoge Raad 2 Nov. 2004 (verplichte rusttijden), N[ederlandse] J[urisprudentie] 2005, 80.
151. Affirmative, the House of Lords, decision of 11 Oct. 1990 (Lord Bridge) in *Factortame Ltd v. Secretary of State for Transport (No.2)* (1990) CML Rev. 375, 380, and, more ambiguous, decision of 3 Mar. 1994 (Lord Keith) in *Equal Opportunities Commission v. Secretary of State for Employment* (1995) CML Rev., 641 with note by C. Harlow and E. Szyszczak.
152. See High Court, Queen's Bench Division. Divisional Court, decision of 18 Feb. 2002 (Laws LJ) in *Thoburn v. Sutherland City Council etc.* (metric martyrs case), (2003) QB 151. See on this last case M. Claes, *The National Courts' Mandate in the European Constitution* (2006), 238 and on the case law in general P. Craig, 'Britain in the European Union', in J. Jowell and D. Oliver (eds), *The Changing Constitution* (6th ed. 2007), Ch.4. On the situation in the new Member States, see A. Albi, ' "Europe" Articles in the Constitutions of Central and Eastern European Countries' (2005) CML Rev., 399.
153. *Syndicat général des fabricants de semoules de France*, 1 Mar. 1968 (1970) CML Rev., 395.
154. *Cafés Jacques Vabre*, 24 May 1975 (1975) CML Rev., 128 with note G. Bebr and (1975) CDE, 631, with note by R. Kovar.
155. In the judgment of 20 Oct. 1989, *Nicolo* (1990) CML Rev., 253, for Treaty law in general. For Community law in particular, see the judgments of 24 Sept. 1990, *Boisdet* (1991) EL Rev., 144, with note by H. Cohen and of 28 Feb. 1992, *Philip Morris* (1993) CML Rev., 187, with note by J. Dutheil de la Rochère.

conflict between national law and Community law was 'translated' into an infringement of constitutional law,[156] just as happened in the old case referred to above before the Conseil d'État in France, albeit with a difference on one point, namely that in France no court is empowered to review the constitutionality of laws once they have been promulgated, whereas in Italy the *Corte Costituzionale* is empowered to review the constitutionality of laws.

The judgment of the Court of Justice in *Simmenthal II* makes it clear that it rejects these views out of hand. Thus,

> a national court which is called upon, within the limits of its jurisdiction, to apply provisions of Community law is under a duty to give full effect to those provisions, if necessary refusing of its own motion to apply any conflicting provisions of national legislation, even if adopted subsequently, and it is not necessary for the court to request or await the prior setting aside of such provision by legislative or other constitutional means.[157]

It would be incompatible with the requirements which are the very essence of Community law, in the event of conflict between a provision of Community law and a subsequent national law 'if the solution of the conflict were to be reserved for an authority with a discretion of its own, other than the court called upon to apply Community law, even if such an impediment to the full effectiveness of Community law were only temporary'.[158] The *Corte Costituzionale* later accepted the approach of the Court of Justice on this point.[159]

The principle of the primacy of Community law also excludes review of Community law against national constitutional law. This is not only implicit from the judgment of the Court in *Simmenthal II*, it was also expressly stated in the celebrated judgment in Case 11/70 *Internationale Handelsgesellschaft*,[160] when the Court held that Community law could not,

> because of its very nature, be overridden by rules of national law, however framed, without being deprived of its character as Community law. Therefore the validity of a Community measure or its effect within a Member State cannot be affected by allegations that it runs counter to either fundamental human rights as formulated by the constitution of that state or the principles of a national constitutional structure.[161]

---

156. *In casu* the question whether infringement of Community law also meant a breach of Art. 11 of the Italian Constitution which permits restrictions of sovereignty in favour of international organizations.

157. Case 106/77, *Simmenthal II*, at para. 24.

158. Id. at para. 23.

159. *Corte Costituzionale* Judgment of 8 Jun. 1984, *Granital*, see note by G. Gaja (1984) CML Rev., 756.

160. Case 11/70, *Internationale Handelsgesellschaft v. Einfuhr- und Vorratsstelle für Getreide und Futtermittel*. See also C-473/93, *Commission v. Luxembourg* (Employment in the public service).

161. Ibid. at para. 3.

The Court was, however, willing to examine whether any analogous guarantee inherent in Community law itself had been disregarded. This made it clear that written and unwritten Community law affords guarantees comparable with those found in national constitutions and constitutional law, and that the Court of Justice itself is entrusted with the task of ensuring that such guarantees (in particular respect for fundamental rights) are protected in the Community legal order, particularly in proceedings under Article 234 EC.[162]

Problems on this point have chiefly arisen in Germany and Italy where laws (i.e., acts of parliament) may be reviewed by a constitutional court. The case law in these Member States has gradually accepted, at least as far as regulations are concerned, the theory developed by the Court of Justice of the restriction of national sovereignty *vis-à-vis* the Community legal order – which operates within the national legal sphere on its own authority and entirely independently, not transformed into national law.[163] Support for this could be found in Article 24(1) of the German Grundgesetz, which permits the transfer of sovereignty to a supranational organization, and in Article 11 of the Italian Constitution which permits the limitation of sovereign powers aimed at encouraging international organizations having the aim of assuring peace and justice between nations. It should be noted that with a view to the ratification of the Treaty of Maastricht, the entirely revised version of Article 23 of the German *Grundgesetz* now contains a number of conditions for and limitations on the transfer of sovereign powers to the European Union.[164]

In both countries, the Constitutional Courts have continually held that their Constitutions place limits on the transfer of sovereignty. The essential elements of the constitutional order, particularly fundamental rights, may not be affected by any such transfer.[165] In 1973, the *Corte Costituzionale* regarded this as rather a theoretical problem.[166] While it reserved the right to intervene if the EEC, contrary to its expectations, were to be given an unacceptable power to violate the fundamental principles of the Italian constitutional order or inalienable human rights, the *Corte Costituzionale* declined to control the constitutionality of each individual Community regulation. In Germany the *Bundesverfassungsgericht* in 1974, on the contrary, regarded itself as having jurisdiction to review regulations against the fundamental rights laid down in the German Constitution as long as (hence the popular name 'Solange judgment') the process of integration in the

---

162. See Ch. VI, section 1.4, *supra.*
163. See Ch. II, section 3.3.
164. M. Herdegen, 'Maastricht and the German Constitutional Court: Constitutional Restraints for an "Ever Closer Union" ' (1994) CML Rev., 235, at 236 with references in note 6.
165. Judgments of the Bundesverfassungsgericht of 29 May 1974: *International Handelsgesellschaft* BVerfGE 37, 271; (1974) CML Rev. 551, see Ipsen (1975) EuR 1.
166. Judgment 18/27-12-1973 *(Frontini)* (1975) CDE, 114. In a later judgment (13/21-4-1989, *Fragd*), the Constitutional Court repeated explicitly that it reserved to itself the right to review Community law against the fundamental principles of the Italian constitutional order and inalienable human rights. See moreover G. Gaja, 'New Developments in a Continuing Story: The Relationship between EEC Law and Italian Law' (1990) CML Rev., 83–95.

Community had not developed far enough so that Community law contained a codified catalogue of fundamental rights decided upon by a democratically legitimate and elected parliament which offered the same guarantees as those afforded by the German Constitution.[167]

If the judgment of the *Corte Costituzionale* was reasonably satisfactory, the same cannot be said of that of the *Bundesverfassungsgericht*. However, in a judgment of 22 October 1986[168] the *Bundesverfassungsgericht* reversed the thrust of its earlier judgment as it was convinced that the aims expressed in 1974 had been achieved. Satisfactory durable guarantees existed that the European Communities, particularly through the case law of the Court, ensured an effective protection of fundamental rights against action by the Community authorities, a protection which in essence was the same as that required as a minimum by the German Constitution, particularly because it guaranteed the essential core of fundamental rights. The Bundesverfassungsgericht based this conclusion on an exhaustive analysis of the Court's case law on the protection of fundamental rights, the Joint Declaration by the European Parliament, the Council and the Commission on Fundamental Rights, of 5 April 1977, and the Declaration of the European Council of 7 and 8 April 1978 on Democracy.[169] As long as this guarantee is present (and hence the name Solange II for this judgment) it would not hear cases seeking to challenge the constitutionality of secondary Community law. Thus, the *Bundesverfassungsgericht* has followed the approach of the *Corte Costitutionale* on this point.

It is a cause for concern, nevertheless, that the *Bundesverfassungsgericht* regards it as one of its tasks to ensure that the Community Institutions, including the Court, do not exceed the sovereign powers transferred by the German law ratifying the Treaties. Thus in *Kloppenburg*[170] it examined whether, in according vertical direct effect to certain provisions of directives, the Court of Justice had remained within the bounds of what it regarded as acceptable judicial creativity. The explicit confirmation in its judgment on the constitutionality of the Treaty of Maastricht in terms of the *Grundgesetz*, that legal acts of the Community Institutions and other bodies of the European Union which, in its opinion, were no longer covered by transfer of competences would not be binding on German territory[171] was also scarcely a great surprise.[172] In this way, the *Bundesverfassungsgericht*, as self-appointed 'highest' judge in Europe, guards the limits of Community

---

167. Decision of 29-5-1974 (*Solange I*) (1974) CML Rev. 540. See D. Soulas de Russel and U. Engels, 'L'Intégration de l'Europe à l'heure de la décision de la Cour Constitutionnelle fédérale du 29 mai 1974' (1975) *RIDC* 377.
168. Solange II (1987) EuR 51 (with note by Ipsen); (1988) CML Rev., 201 (with note by Frowein).
169. See Ch. VI, section 1.4 *supra*.
170. Decision of 8 Apr. 1987, (1988) CML Rev. 1.
171. End of Part C.I.3 of the judgment.
172. Decision of 12 Oct. 1993, see esp. part C.I.3. For the text, see *Eur.Gr.Z.* 1993, 429–448, and M. Herdegen, op. cit. *supra* note 164, at 251–262. For a critical analysis, see T. Koopmans, 'Rechter, D-mark en democratie: het Bundesverfassungsgericht en de Europese Unie, (1994) NJB, 245–251.

competence.[173] The judgment of the *Bundesverfassungsgericht* in the *Atlanta* case is encouraging, however.[174] It reveals that the judgment in the *Maastricht* case leaves the solution adopted in Solange II intact: applications for review are not admissible as long as it cannot be demonstrated on the basis of a comparison with the protection at national level that Community law, including the case law of the Court of Justice, is henceforth below the level which is necessary for the protection of fundamental rights.[175]

The view of the *Bundesverfassungsgericht* that the direct effect and supremacy of Community law can only be recognized within the boundaries of the powers conferred on the Community is in itself correct. But whether these boundaries have been respected is a matter for the Court of Justice, as it is a question of interpretation of Community law. By claiming to reserve to itself the final determination of this matter, the *Bundesverfassungsgericht* has created the possibility of conflict between the two highest courts, that in the Community and that in Germany, which could seriously threaten the uniform interpretation and application of Community law. The *Bundesverfassungsgericht* has itself declared that it has a relationship of cooperation with the Court of Justice; it is to be hoped that it will take this relationship seriously and, before reaching a definite judgment on a question, make a reference to the Court of Justice under Article 234 EC, in order for instance to raise a question of validity.[176]

National courts will always have to apply provisions of Community law to the concrete dispute before them, to the extent that this is possible without exceeding the limits of their judicial function. Moreover, in appropriate cases, national courts will have to review rules enacted by national authorities in the area of

---

173. Cf. the title of a contribution by C. Tomuschat, Die Europäische Union unter der Aufsicht des Bundesverfassungsgerichts, *Eur.Gr.Z.* 1993, 489–496. See also M. Kumm, 'Who is the Final Arbiter of Constitutionality in Europe?' (1990) CML Rev., 351. The Danish Højesteret (supreme court) takes a similar position in its judgment of 6 Apr. 1998, *Carlsen v. Rasmussen* (1999) CML Rev., 854, see K. Høegh, 'The Danish Judgment' (1999) EL Rev., 80.

174. Decision of 7 Jun. 2000, EuZW 2000, 702; annotated by F. Hoffmeister (2001) CML Rev., 791, see also K. Høegh, 'The Danish Maastricht Judgment' (1999) EL Rev., 80. Cf. Case C-466/93, *Atlanta Fruchthandelsgesellschaft et al. v. Bundesamt für Ernährung und Forstwirtschaft* (Atlanta II).

175. In its decision on the constitutionality of the Treaty of Maastricht (see note 172 *supra*), the Bundesverfassungsgericht remarked that it exercises its jurisdiction over the applicability of secondary Community law in Germany in a '*Kooperationsverhältnis*' (relationship of cooperation) with the European Court of Justice. Since the latter guarantees the protection of fundamental rights in concrete cases throughout the whole territory of the Community, the Bundesverfassungsgericht can 'sich deshalb auf eine generelle Gewährleistung der unabdingbaren Grundrechtsstandards ... beschränken ... ' [can limit itself to providing a general guarantee of the unalterable standards of fundamental rights] (Part B.2(b)).

176. For cases where a constitutional court put preliminary questions to the ECJ, see Case C-158/97, *Badeck et al. v. Hessischer Ministerpräsident* (Staatsgerichtshof des Landes Hessen), Case C-93/97, *Fédération Belge des Chambres Syndicales de Médecins ASBL v. Flemish Government et al.* (Belgian Cour d'Arbitrage) and Case C-171/01, *Wählergruppe Gemeinsam Zajedno v. Birlikte Alternative und Grüne GewerkschafterInnen* (Austrian Verfassungsgericht).

implementation of provisions of Community law against the norms contained in those provisions.[177]

In this way national courts play an important part in ensuring the judicial protection of private parties against measures taken by the Member States which are incompatible with Community law. This function was expressly confirmed by the Court of Justice in *Van Gend en Loos*.[178] Three governments had argued in their observations that only the Commission or another Member State could act against an infringement of Community law by a Member State, under Articles 226 (ex 169) and 227 (170) EC. This argument was rejected by the Court, partly because it 'would remove all direct legal protection of the individual rights of their nationals'. The Court added that there was 'the risk that recourse to the procedure under these Articles would be ineffective if it were to occur after the implementation of a national decision taken contrary to the provision of the Treaty'.

Without diminishing the essential and practical importance of the principle of primacy, it is nevertheless to be noted that a conflict between a rule of Community law and a national statutory rule of a later date will in practice usually not present itself in an acute form. As a rule, national courts will try to avoid an outright choice of one rule or the other by interpreting them in such a way that they do not conflict with each other. Indeed, national courts will not readily assume that the national legislature has acted contrary to the international obligations of the State. In this context it will hardly be relevant whether the courts concerned do or do not consider themselves obliged to give priority to the rule of Community law in accordance with national constitutional law or in accordance with Community law. The national court is in any case bound to interpret the national rules as far as possible in conformity with Community law, in order to avoid conflicts with provisions of Community law, such as directives, to which no direct effect can be attributed.[179]

It is, though, very important that national courts, especially those against whose decision there is no judicial remedy, should refer the interpretation of the rule of Community law to the Court of Justice under Article 234 EC. The intervention of the Court of Justice by means of a preliminary ruling ensures that this rule will not be interpreted in a narrow sense in order to prevent conflict with the rule of national law. If the national court wishes to avoid such a conflict, it will not be able to do so at the expense of the content or the scope of application of the Community rule, but only by means of a narrow interpretation of the national rule.

It must, therefore, be considered very important that the application of Article 234 EC should not be barred for the national court. It is not surprising that the Court opposed in such a vigorous and broad argumentation the contention

---

177. The so-called objective review of legality, see section 1.4.2 *supra*.
178. Case 26/62, *Van Gend en Loos*.
179. Cf. the interpretation of national law, in conformity with directives, discussed *supra* (section 1.4.3). See extensively T. Heukels, 'Richtlijn en Gemeenschapsrechtconforme interpretatie: nieuwe internationale dimensies', (1997) NJB, 1845–1850.

of the Italian government in *Costa v. E.N.E.L.*[180] that the request of the Milan magistrate for a preliminary ruling was 'absolutely inadmissible'. According to the Italian government, this national judge was obliged to apply the later national law, irrespective of the question whether it was contrary to the provisions of the EEC Treaty. The Milanese judge could not and should not even approach the question of how to interpret those provisions. Consequently, the Court of Justice found itself obliged to argue forcefully, on the basis of an exhaustive explanation of the supremacy of Community law, that 'Article [234] is to be applied regardless of any domestic law whenever questions relating to the interpretation of the Treaty arise'.[181]

3   ACCESS TO REMEDIES AND PROCEEDINGS IN
        NATIONAL LEGAL SYSTEMS WHICH CAN
        GUARANTEE THE FULL EFFECT OF COMMUNITY
        LAW AND EFFECTIVE JUDICIAL PROTECTION

The application of Community law takes place, at least in the decentralized structure within which the greater part of EC law is given effect, principally in the day-to-day legal activities within the Member States. The national courts thus occupy a central position in this process. It is their task to decide whether national rules and administrative acts are compatible with Community law and whether individuals have acted in accordance with the obligations incumbent on them under Community law, and also to give effect to the consequences of that decision under national law or, in some cases, under Community law itself.[182] Where necessary, they are guided in this by the Court of Justice through a preliminary ruling under Article 234 EC. The national courts may also be faced with the question whether decisions of the Community Institutions are compatible with the Community law on which they are based. It is their responsibility in particular to provide the legal protection which individuals derive from the rules of Community law and to ensure that those rules are fully effective.[183] The national judge can thus be portrayed as the judge of the common law of the Community, even if he is not always aware of this himself.

As has been explained in previous sections, the national court is obliged to interpret national law as far as possible in conformity with Community law, to apply directly effective provisions of Community law, and, in the case of conflict between the latter and national provisions, to set aside national law. However, the degree to which the national court, thus equipped, can apply Community law is in

---

180. Case 6/64, *Costa v. E.N.E.L.*
181. Ibid. at 594 of the English version.
182. See, e.g., Art. 81(2) EC (nullity) and the case law concerning liability of Member States for damage resulting from infringements of Community law attributable to them, discussed *infra* (section 4).
183. Joined Cases C-397-403/01, *Pfeiffer*, para. 111.

reality also dependent on the possibilities offered by its national legal order for this purpose. In the Community, after all,

> when provisions of the Treaty or of regulations confer power or impose obligations upon the states for the purposes of the implementation of Community law, the question of how the exercise of such powers and the fulfilment of such obligations may be entrusted by Member States to specific national bodies is solely a matter for the constitutional system of each state (the principle of institutional autonomy).[184]

Thus national law has been described as being the vehicle on which Community law must ride.[185] Whether Community law can actually be enforced depends on what legal remedies are afforded by the national legal system, and under what conditions these remedies may be used. Thus a number of questions arise. Can someone who believes that another party, whether an authority or an individual, has acted in breach of a directly effective provision of Community law seek damages for loss suffered, or an injunction restraining the conduct concerned, or the repayment of sums paid but not due, or the quashing or suspension of the relevant decision of an authority? Which appeal or limitation periods apply? And before which court must he or she then appeal, the civil courts or some kind of administrative court?

Given that the various national legal systems may display great divergence in the remedies available and in the requirements which have to be fulfilled, the complete and uniform application of Community law may actually be crowded out, despite its direct effect and primacy. The effectiveness of direct effect, as Mertens de Wilmars has put it[186] may thus be restricted. He called the resulting problems 'second generation problems', which loom up after a number of fundamental problems of the first generation (the special, independent character of the Community legal order, direct effect, and the primacy of Community law) had been solved.[187]

These second generation problems raise the question whether there are any minimum conditions for the manner in which Community law is received into national law. The Court has found that there are. This occurred first in relation specifically to the problem of sums paid but not due. Such problems arose in relation to the application of Community rules relating on the one hand to fixing

---

184. Joined Cases 51 & 54/71, *International Fruit Company et al. v. Produktschap voor Groenten en fruit* (*International Fruit Company II*), at para. 4. See in a similar sense Declaration No. 43 attached to the Treaty of Amsterdam relating to the Protocol on the application of the principles of subsidiarity and proportionality, and Declaration 19 of the Treaty of Maastricht on the Implementation of Community law.
185. The metaphor is from A.D. Keus, *report for the Vereniging voor Burgerlijk Recht en de Nederlandse Vereniging voor Europees Recht: Europees Privaatrecht, een Bonte Lappendeken* (Lelystad, 1993).
186. J. Mertens de Wilmars, 'L'efficacité des différentes techniques nationales de protection juridique contre les violations du droit communautaire par les autorités nationales et les particuliers' (1981) CDE, 379–409.
187. Ibid. See also T. Koopmans, 'Problemen van de tweede generatie', in: Josse Mertens de Wilmars, *Liber Amicorum* (Antwerpen, 1982), 119–132.

and collection of the financial charges which the Community is empowered to levy, such as customs duties and agricultural levies, and on the other hand, to the granting and payment of financial benefits such as agricultural export refunds and other subsidies which are for the account of the Community budget. It is not surprising that the case law on second generation problems initially developed in this field.[188] After all, these charges and benefits are applied and granted by the Community in indirect administration, i.e., by means of decisions of the national authorities. Disputes about the lawfulness of those decisions thus arise within the national legal orders and are decided there.

The requirement of cooperation, part of the obligation laid down in Article 10 EC, means that the national courts must provide:

> the legal protection made available as a result of the direct effect of the Community provisions both when such provisions create obligations for the subject and when they confer rights on him. It is, however, for the national legal system of each Member State to determine the courts having jurisdiction and to fix the procedures for applications to the courts intended to protect the rights which the subject obtains through the direct effect of Community law but such procedures may not be less favourable than those in similar procedures concerning internal matters and may in no case be laid down in such a way as to render impossible in practice the exercise of the rights which the national courts must protect.[189]

This passage, from the *Ferwerda* case, which expresses the earlier case law in *Rewe* and *Comet*,[190] contains three elements which apply whenever a national court is faced with a dispute involving directly effective Community provisions. The first concerns its duty to afford judicial protection. This duty is deduced from Article 10 EC, which obliges the Member States and their organs, including national courts, to ensure compliance with the obligations resulting from Community law. The second element is the procedural autonomy of the Member States' legal systems. The concept of procedure covers all substantive and organizational rules and principles applicable to actions brought to obtain such judicial protection. It only applies, of course, to the extent to which no provisions of Community law deal with the point or harmonize national provisions.[191] The third element is

---

188. See F. Hubeau, 'La répétition de l'indu en droit communautaire' (1981) RTDE, 442–470, and, more generally J. Bridge, 'Procedural Aspects of the Enforcement of European Community Law through the Legal System of the Member States' (1984) EL Rev., 28–42.

189. Case 265/78, *Ferwerda v. Produktschap voor Vee en Vlees*, at para. 10.

190. Case 33/76, *Rewe v. Landwirtschaftskammer für das Saarland*, and Case 45/76, *Comet v. Produktschap voor Siergewassen*; a more recent summary of this case law is in Case C-343/96, *Dilexport Srl v. Amministrazione delle Finanze dello Stato*. See the critical analysis by A. Biondi, 'The European Court of Justice and Certain National Procedural Limitations: Not Such a Tough Relationship' (1999) CML Rev., 1271–1287.

191. Such as in case of repayment, recovery and post-clearance recovery of import and export duties in the broad sense concerning time periods, interest on arrears, enforcement, circumstances in which remittal or recovery can be dispensed with, and appeals, titles VII and VIII of

composed of the two conditions laid down in the case law: there must be no distinction between conditions for claims brought under Community law and claims brought purely under national law (principle of equivalence, or non-discrimination), and the exercise of the rights must not be made 'virtually impossible'[192] or excessively difficult (principle of effectiveness),[193] even when such a situation would be in conformity with the non-discrimination requirement.[194]

The principle of equivalence is in fact an application of the principle of non-discrimination on grounds of nationality (Article 12 EC)[195] in the specific field of procedural conditions and procedural rules guaranteeing the Community law rights of individuals in the domestic legal systems of the Member States. It requires that the provisions at issue should be applied in an equivalent manner to claims based on infringements of Community law and claims based on infringements of national law.[196] The question what claims under national law are 'similar' to claims based on Community law can cause the national courts severe problems. The national courts, being the only courts directly acquainted with the national procedural rules, have the task of examining whether the principle of equivalence has been respected. The Court of Justice can assist them in this with information on the interpretation of Community law. For instance, it is important that the national courts examine both the subject and the main characteristics of the national claims which are alleged to be 'similar'. Moreover, when deciding the question whether a national procedural rule is less favourable than the rules concerning similar national claims, they should take into account the place of that provision in the

---

Council Reg. (EEC) No 2913/92 of 12 Oct. 1992 establishing the Community Customs Code, O.J. 1992, L 302/1 and the implementing Reg. 2454/93, O.J. 1993, L 253/1. See, e.g., also for appeal procedures in relation to public procurement, Dir. 89/665, O.J. 1989, L 95/33.

192. According to the interpretation in later case law of the requirement of effectiveness.

193. For the consequences of these principles for national law, see, e.g., Case 68/79, *Just v. Danish Ministry for Fiscal Affairs*; Case 170/84, *Bilka v. Weber von Hartz*; Case 222/84, *Johnston*, and Case 109/88, *Handels- og Kontorfunktionærernes Forbund i Danmark v. Dansk Arbejdsgiverforening, acting on behalf of Danfoss* (law on evidence), and Case 130/79, *Express Dairy Foods v. Intervention Board for Agricultural Produce* and Case 54/81, *Fromme v. BALM* (calculation of interest).

194. See also for the last, Case 199/82, *Amministrazione delle finanze dello Stato v. San Giorgio*: rules of evidence, even when applied without distinction, may not make it impossible or exceedingly difficult to be repaid duties which have been charged contrary to Community law.

195. A direct review of the discriminatory rule of national procedural law (*cautio judicatum solvi*) against Art. 12 EC was needed in Case C-43/95, *Data Delecta Aktiebolag and Ronny Forsberg v. MSL Dynamics*; Case C-323/95, *Hayes v. Kronenberger* and Case C-122/96, *Saldanha and MTS Securities Corporation v. Hiross*. These cases did not involve claims of a Community law nature being subject to such a rule, but claims based on national law brought by nationals of other Member States.

196. The requirement does not mean, of course, that a Member State is obliged to apply the most favourable national rule to claims of a Community law nature (Case C-231/96, *Edilizia Industriale Siderurgica v. Ministero delle Finanze*). It does mean that, e.g., after a ruling of the Court establishing the incompatibility pf a particular legal rule with the Treaty, a national legislature may not introduce procedural rules by which the possibilities for reclaiming taxes which have been levied under those rules contrary to Community law are specifically restricted (Case 240/87, *Deville v. Administration des impôts*).

whole proceedings before the various national bodies, including the facts of the case and any special circumstances.[197]

The principle of effectiveness, in the specific form of affording effective judicial protection (remedies) to individuals, in particular[198] where fundamental rights and freedoms conferred by Community law are at issue, has played an increasingly important role in the case law in the last decades.[199] The principle of effective judicial control reflects 'a general principle of law stemming from the constitutional traditions common to the Member States'[200] which is laid down in Articles 6 and 13 of the European Convention on Human Rights, and which has also been reaffirmed by Article 47 of the Charter of fundamental rights of the European Union,[201] and as such it is to be respected by the European Union as a fundamental right. It follows from the principle of cooperation laid down in Article 10 EC that Member States have to ensure judicial protection of an individual's rights under Community law.[202] Not only must an appeal be possible against a decision of a national authority denying a person the exercise of those rights, but the judicial control must also be effective.[203] Community law does not require a Member State to establish a procedure for judicial control of national decisions which involves a more extensive review than that carried out by the Court of Justice in similar cases.[204]

---

197. See on this problem in particular Case C-326/96, *Levez v. Jennings* and Case C-78/98, *Preston et al. v. Fletcher et al.*, and the Opinion of the A.G. in these cases. See also Steiner, 'How to Make the Action Suit the Case' (1987) EL Rev., 102–122.

198. E.M. Vermeulen, *Nederlandse rechtsbescherming in communautaire context* (Den Haag, 2001), 122–123, has rightly pointed out that in Case C-97/91, *Borelli v. Commission*, no fundamental rights from the EC Treaty were involved.

199. On this case law – referred to by them as 'third generation' – see extensively D. Curtin and K.J.M. Mortelmans, 'Application and Enforcement of Community Law by the Member States: Actors in Search of a Third Generation Script', in: D. Curtin, T. Heukels (eds), *Institutional Dynamics of European Integration, Essays in Honour of Henri G. Schermers* (Dordrecht, 1994) Vol. II, 423–438.

200. Case C-432/05, *Unibet (London) Ltd, Unibet (International) Ltd v. Justitiekanslern*, para. 37.

201. Ibid. and the case law cited therein.

202. Case C-432/05, *Unibet* para. 38.

203. See Cases 222/84, *Johnston* ('an effective judicial remedy'), 222/86, *Unectef v. Heylens*, C-13/94, *P v. S and Cornwall County Council* and C-185/97, *Coote v. Granada Hospitality*. In this sense also Case 36/75, *Rutili v. Ministre de l'intérieur*.

204. Case C-120/97, *Upjohn v. The Licensing Authority et al.*, at para. 36; where national authorities have a wide measure of discretion in implementing Community law, any national procedure for judicial review of relevant decisions of national authorities must enable the court or tribunal seized of an application for annulment of such decisions effectively to apply the relevant principles and rules of Community law when reviewing their legality. For an exception, see Joined Cases C-482/01 & C-493/01, *Georgios Orfanopoulos a.o.*: Art. 3 of Dir. 64/221/EEC on the coordination of special measures concerning the movement and residence of foreign nationals which are justified on grounds of public policy, public security or public health (O.J. 1964, 56 850) precludes a national practice not allowing circumstances arising between the administrative decision and the review by a court of the lawfulness of that decision to be taken into account.

The duty of the national courts under the said principle of cooperation to afford effective judicial protection means that they must interpret the procedural rules governing actions brought before them in such a way as to enable those rules, wherever possible, to be implemented in such a manner as to contribute to attaining this objective.[205] This may entail setting aside national legal rules in order to ensure that the protection is effective. A classic example of this in action can be seen in *Case C-213/89 R. v. Secretary of State for Transport, ex parte Factortame*,[206] which follows on directly from the judgment in the first *Simmenthal* case,[207] without leaving much intact of the 'procedural autonomy' of the United Kingdom. The Court found that a national court in interlocutory proceedings, awaiting a ruling from the Court of Justice, was obliged to set aside one or more national rules which were the sole obstacle preventing it from granting interim relief in order to ensure the full effectiveness of the judgment to be given on the existence of the rights claimed under Community law, which were alleged to be breached by national provisions. The rules involved were the presumption that national measures were compatible with Community law unless and until it they are declared incompatible, combined with the common law rule that an interim injunction does not lie against the Crown to suspend the effect of an Act of Parliament. It may well be asked whether as a result of *Factortame* the national court derives its power to suspend the operation of an Act from Community law itself, or whether it simply makes use of its power to issue interim injunctions under national law, but with a wider sphere of application than that envisaged by national law.[208]

In *Factortame* the Court did not pronounce as to the conditions under which interim relief had to be granted in the sphere of Community law. From the reference to the national rule as 'the sole obstacle' it may be deduced that the normal conditions for the grant of interim relief apply, save that this obstacle is left to one side. Such conditions were set out in *Zuckerfabrik Süderdithmarschen*.[209] This involved the question whether a national court in interlocutory proceedings could order the suspension of enforcement of a national administrative measure based on a Community regulation. According to that judgment, the national court is

---

205. Case C-432/05, *Unibet*, para. 44. See also Case C-511/03, *Staat der Nederlanden (Ministerie van Landbouw, Natuurbeheer en Visserij) v. Ten Kate Holding Musselkanaal a.o.*, para. 29 and Case C-50/00 P, *Unión de Pequeños Agricultores v. Council*, para. 42.
206. Case C-213/89, *The Queen v. Secretary of State for Transport, ex parte Factortame (Factortame I)*.
207. Case 70/77, *Simmenthal v. Amministrazione delle finanze dello Stato (Simmenthal I)*.
208. In Case 158/80, *Rewe v. Hauptzollamt Kiel*, at para. 44, the Court had explicitly stated that the Treaty 'was not intended to create new remedies in the national courts to ensure the observance of Community law other than those already laid down by national law'. In Case C-432/05, *Unibet* it added, however, that it 'would be otherwise only if it were apparent from the overall scheme of the national legal system in question that no legal remedy existed which made it possible to ensure, even indirectly, respect for an individual's rights under Community law' (para. 41).
209. Joined Cases C-143/88 & C-92/89, *Zuckerfabrik Süderdithmarschen and Zuckerfabrik Soest v. Hauptzollamt Itzehoe and Hauptzollamt Paderborn*. See also Case C-465/93, *Atlanta Fruchthandelsgesellschaft et al. v. Bundesamt für Ernährung und Forstwirtschaft (Atlanta I)*.

not, as is the case with the approach in *Factortame*, obliged to set aside national rules which would prevent it from granting relief on the basis of Community law; rather the Court of Justice found that the national court could grant interim relief only subject to the specific conditions which the Court prescribed. These conditions are analogous to those applicable when the Court itself grants interim relief.[210,211] If uniform conditions did not apply in this situation, the uniform application of Community law would be jeopardized, given the very divergent national rules involved.

Review of national procedural rules in the light of the principle of effectiveness has led to case law in a number of areas. Rules of evidence which had as a consequence that it was practically impossible or excessively difficult to have taxes, duties or dues which were levied in infringement of Community law reimbursed are contrary to Community law.[212] The burden of proof must be reversed when that is necessary to prevent employees who suffer from factual discrimination from being deprived of any effective means of enforcing the principle of equal pay.[213] It is contrary to the principle of effective judicial control for a certificate or declaration by a national authority to be treated as conclusive evidence excluding the exercise of any power of review by the courts.[214] National legislation determining an individual's standing and legal interest in bringing proceedings should not undermine the right to effective judicial protection.[215]

As to the admissibility of time-limits for bringing claims based on Community law rights, there is extensive case law. In principle, the Court considers 'that it is compatible with Community law to lay down reasonable time-limits for bringing proceedings in the interests of legal certainty, which protects both the taxpayer and the administration concerned'.[216] The judgment in *Emmott*[217] made an exception to this principle. Here the court ruled that until such time as a directive

---

210. See for these conditions, Ch. VI, section 4, *supra*.
211. The competence of the national court to admit such a suspension corresponds, according to the Court, to the competence the Court has under Art. 242 EC in the framework of applications under Art. 230 EC, cf. Joined Cases C-143/88 & C-92/89, *Zuckerfabrik Süderdithmarschen*, para. 27.
212. Case 199/82, *San Giorgio*, and Joined Cases 331, 376 & 378/85, *Les Fils de Jules Bianco and J. Girard Fils v. Directeur Général des douanes et droits indirects*. These cases concerned assumptions or rules of evidence which imposed on the tax-payer the onus of proof that wrongly levied duties which had been paid had not been passed on to third parties, or special restrictions concerning the form of evidence to be provided, such as the exclusion of all non-written evidence.
213. Case 109/88, *Danfoss*; Case C-127/92, *Enderby v. Frenchay Health Authority et al.* and Case C-400/93, *Specialarbejderforbundet i Danmark v. Dansk Industri*.
214. Case 222/84, *Johnston*. For the strict limits which the principle of effectiveness sets for the application of a hardship clause under national fiscal law, in relation to agricultural levies, see Case C-290/91, *Peter v. Hauptzollamt Regensburg*.
215. Case C-432/05, *Unibet*, para. 42 and the case law cited. See also Case C-174/02, *Streekgewest Westelijk Noord-Brabant v. Staatssecretaris van Financiën*.
216. Case C-343/96, *Dilexport*, at para. 26, with reference to earlier case law.
217. C-208/90, *Emmott v. Minister for Social Welfare and Attorney General*, annotated by E. Szyszczak (1992) CML Rev., 604.

has been properly transposed into national law, a Member State may not rely on an individual's delay in initiating proceedings against it in order to protect his or her rights to equal treatment of men and women, conferred by the directive. A period laid down by national law within which proceedings must be initiated can only start to run as of the moment at which the directive is correctly implemented. It later transpired that the scope of this case law was more limited than the considerations in the judgment led commentators to expect at the time.

Even when a Member State has not properly implemented a directive (in time), Community law does not prevent a restriction on the retroactive effect of claims to unpaid benefits or the application of a limitation period on claims to reimbursement of duties levied contrary to the directive. According to the Court, 'the particular circumstances of that case, in which the time-bar had the result of depriving the applicant of any opportunity whatever to rely on her right to equal treatment under a Community directive' were decisive in the *Emmott* case.[218] It may be assumed that the mention of 'particular circumstances' in *Emmott* should be given an independent meaning in the sense that it refers to the misleading actions of the Irish authorities, which were the cause of the non-observance of the time-limit.[219] Finally, the solution adopted in the *Emmott* case does not apply to claims to reimbursement which are not based on the direct effect of a directive.[220]

The question whether the existing obligation of the national courts to apply directly effective provisions of Community law of their own motion (*ex officio*)[221] also applies in relation to procedural rules was answered in detail in *Peterbroeck* and *Van Schijndel*.[222] In *Van Schijndel*, the Court seized the occasion to develop guidelines as to how to resolve conflicts between the principle of effectiveness on the one hand and the procedural autonomy of the Member States on the other. A balance must be sought between the interests served by the national rule that makes the application of Community law impossible or excessively difficult, and the interest of effective protection of rights which individuals derive

---

218.   According to the summary, in Case C-188/95, *Fantask and others v. Industriministeriet*, at para. 51, of the case law in Case C-338/91, *Steenhorst-Neerings v. Bestuur van de Bedrijfs-vereniging voor Detailhandel, Ambachten en Huisvrouwen*; Case C-410/92, *Johnson v. Chief Adjudication Officer (Johnson II)*; Case C-90/94, *Haahr Petroleum v. Åbenrå Havn et al.*, and Joined Cases C-114 & 115/95, *Texaco v. Middelfart Havn et al. and Olieselskabet Danmark v. Trafikministeriet et al.*

219.   See also the explicit statement by the Court in Case C-231/96, *Edilizia Industriale Siderurgica*, at para. 48, that 'it does not appear that the conduct of the Italian authorities, in conjunction with the existence of the contested time-limit, had the effect in this case, as it did in Emmott [Case C-208/90], of depriving the plaintiff company of any opportunity of enforcing its rights before the national courts.'

220.   Case C-228/96, *Aprile v. Amministrazione delle Finanze dello Stato*, see also Case C-90/94, *Haahr Petroleum* and Joined Cases C-114 & 115/95, *Texaco*.

221.   Case 166/73, *Rheinmühlen Düsseldorf v. Einfuhr- und Vorratsstelle für Getreide und Futter-mittel (Rheinmühlen II)*; Joined Cases C-87-89/90, *Verholen et al. v. Sociale Verzekeringsbank Amsterdam*.

222.   Case C-312/93, *Peterbroeck, Van Campenhout and Cie v. Belgian State*, and Joined Cases C-430 & 431/93, *Van Schijndel and Van Veen*. See S. Prechal, op. cit. *supra* note 90, 681–706.

from the direct application of Community law. The national rule in question there-fore does not automatically have to give way to the principle of effectiveness. In making that balance, the basic principles of the domestic judicial system, such as protection of the rights of the defence, the principle of legal certainty and the proper conduct of procedure, must be taken into consideration by the national court. In making the analysis, the national court must have reference to the role of the provision in question in the procedure, its progress and its special features, viewed as a whole, before the various national instances. It has been argued that the Court of Justice thus introduces a procedural 'rule of reason'.[223]

In *Van Schijndel*, the question arose whether in a case involving civil law ordinary courts must raise of their own motion points of law based on binding Community law rules, such as the competition rules of the EC Treaty. In the case concerned, it would oblige them to abandon the passive role assigned to them by going beyond the ambit of the dispute defined by the parties themselves and relying on facts and circumstances other than those on which the party with an interest in application of those provisions bases his claim. The Court ruled that it is not only if rules of national law *oblige* the national courts to raise of their own motion points of law based on binding domestic rules, but also if these national rules *enable* them to do so, that the national courts must, of their own motion,[224] raise points of law based on binding Community law rules.[225] However it added that Community law does not oblige the national court to do so insofar as the limitation of this duty

> is justified by the principle that, in a civil suit, it is for the parties to take the initiative, the court being able to act of its own motion only in exceptional cases where the public interest requires its intervention. That principle reflects conceptions prevailing in most of the Member States as to the relations between the State and the individual; it safeguards the rights of the defence; and it ensures proper conduct of proceedings by, in particular, protecting them from the delays inherent in examination of new pleas.[226]

Peterbroeck concerned a national rule of (fiscal) procedural law which prevented the court seized of an application against an administrative decision from considering whether a measure of domestic law is compatible with a provision of Community law when the latter provision has not been invoked by the litigant within a certain period after the contested decision was issued. In this case, the Court ruled that the impossibility for the court to consider of its own motion the Community law remedy 'does not appear to be reasonably justifiable by principles such as the requirement of legal certainty or the proper conduct of procedure'.[227]

---

223. Cf. S. Prechal, op. cit. *supra* note 90, 690 et seq. See more generally M. Hoskins, 'Tilting the Balance: Supremacy and National Procedural Rules' (1996) EL Rev., 365–377.
224. See also case C-72/95, *Kraaijeveld*, Case C-435/97, *World Wildlife Fund et al.*, and Case C-287/98, *Linster*.
225. See *supra* note 90 on the ambiguity with regard to the meaning of the qualification 'binding'.
226. Joined Cases C-430 & 431/93, *Van Schijndel and Van Veen*, at para. 21.
227. Case C-312/93, *Peterbroeck, Van Campenhout and Cie*, at para. 20.

Here, the fact that the national court hearing the main proceedings was the first, and only, court which could refer a preliminary question to the Court of Justice, also played a role. Indeed, the Court considered explicitly that a rule of national law preventing the procedure laid down in Article 234 EC from being followed must be set aside.[228]

In a more recent case[229] the Court has been at pains to distinguish *Peterbroeck* and other more robust rulings in which it had decided, without paying much attention to the interest served by the national provision concerned, that the principle of effectiveness precluded the application of a national provision which prevents national courts from raising of their own motion an issue as to whether the provisions of Community law have been infringed.[230]

Does the principal of effectiveness oblige an administrative body to reopen a final administrative decision, where this would enable it to remedy an infringement of Community law by the decision at issue? In *Kühne and Heitz*.[231] the Court answered this question in the affirmative, albeit under strict conditions. A later ruling confirmed that the decision in *Kühne and Heitz* must be seen as to be confined to the exceptional facts of that case. As far as national administrative bodies are concerned,[232] in accordance with the principle of legal certainty, the Community principle of effectiveness does not impose, apart from such exceptional circumstances, an obligation to reopen an administrative decision which has become final upon expiry of the reasonable time-limits for legal remedies or by exhaustion of those remedies: '[c]ompliance with that principle [legal certainty] prevents administrative acts which produce legal effects from being called into question indefinitely'.[233] Likewise, taking into account the importance, both for the Community legal order and national legal systems, of the principle of *res judicata*, the Court affirmed in *Kapferer*[234] that a national court is not required to disapply domestic rules of procedure conferring finality on a decision, even if to

---

228. Both judgments contain this consideration, referring to Case 166/73, *Rheinmühlen II.*
229. Joined Cases C-222-225/05, *J. van der Weerd and others v. Minister van Landbouw, Natuur en Voedselkwaliteit*, paras 39 and 40.
230. I.e., Cases 312/93, *Peterbroeck* (circumstances peculiar to the dispute), C-126/97, *Eco Swiss* (not dealing with the principle of effectiveness, but with that of equivalence), Joined Cases C-240-244/98 *Océano Grupo Editorial and Salvat Editores*, and Cases C-473/00 *Cofidis* and C-168/05 *Mostaza Claro* (need to ensure that consumers are given the effective protection which Council Dir. 93/13/EEC on unfair terms in consumer contracts seeks to achieve).
231. Case C-453/00, *Kühne and Heitz NV and Productschap voor Pluimvee en Eieren.*
232. See in general F. Becker, 'Application of Community Law by Member States' Public Authorities: Between Autonomy and Effectiveness' (2007) CML Rev., 1035–1056.
233. Joined Cases C-392 & 422/04, *i-21 Germany GmbH en Arcor AG and Co. KG v. Bundesrepublik Deutschland*, para. 51. See annotation by Taborowski (2007) CML Rev., 1463–1482. Where national law imposes an obligation to reopen in order to remedy an infringement of domestic law by the decision at issue, the principle of equivalence requires of course to do the same in order to remedy a Community law infringement.
234. Case C-234/04, *Rosmarie Kapferer v. Schlank and Schick GmbH.*

do so would enable it to remedy an infringement of Community law by the decision at issue.[235]

The application of Community law means that the procedural autonomy of the Member States is far from absolute, as the discussion in this section well demonstrates. The principles of equivalence and effectiveness require the national courts, informed by the case law of the Court of Justice, particularly in the context of Article 234 EC, to apply the rules and principles of national law in such a way as to ensure the full application of Community law. Of course, this is subject to the requirement that the national court must not step beyond its judicial function. The national court cannot simply create new national rules; what it can and must do is apply Community law, as interpreted by the Court of Justice, if necessary setting aside any obstacles arising from national law.

Nevertheless, the situation remains unsatisfactory from the point of view of the uniformity of judicial protection.[236] The case law of the Court of Justice sets limits and guidelines for the procedural autonomy of the Member States 'in the regrettable absence of Community provisions harmonizing procedure and time-limits',[237] but the desired uniformity can not be achieved sufficiently in this way. It is a second-best solution in the absence of a better one – which would be the harmonization of national procedural law.[238] Moreover, the current solution is bogged down by its case-driven nature, and leads to a large number of preliminary references to the Court of Justice, which in turn leads to an overburdening of the Court, without the differences in judicial protection within the Community being eliminated to a satisfactory extent. It is not just the uniformity of judicial *protection* which is threatened by the lack of harmonized rules, but also the uniform

---

235. There are situations in which the principle of *res judicata* has to be disapplied by a national court as a result of the *primacy* of Community law; see Case C-119/05, *Ministero dell'Industria, del Commercio e dell'Artigianato v. Lucchini*.
236. For a searching analysis of this situation, see D. Curtin, 'The Decentralized Enforcement of Community Rights. Judicial Snakes and Ladders', in D. Curtin and O'Keeffe (eds), *Constitutional Adjudication in European Community and National Law* (Dublin, 1992), 33–49 and W. Van Gerven, 'Of Rights, Remedies and Procedures' (2000) CML Rev., 501–536. For a strong plea for harmonization of procedural law, see C.M.G. Himsworth, 'Things Fall Apart: The Harmonization of Community Judicial Procedure Protection Revisited' (1997) EL Rev., 291–311.
237. Case 130/79, *Express Dairy Foods*, at para. 12.
238. In some sectors directives have been to this end, see, e.g., Dir. 2004/35/CE on environmental liability with regard to the prevention and remedying of environmental damage, O.J. 2004, L 143/56-75; Dir. 89/665/EEC on the coordination of the laws, regulations and administrative provisions relating to the application of review procedures to the award of public supply and public works contracts, O.J. 1989, L 395/33-35; Dir. 92/13/EEC coordinating the laws, regulations and administrative provisions relating to the application of Community rules on the procurement procedures of entities operating in the water, energy, transport and telecommunications sectors, O.J. 1992, L 76/14-20 (see also the proposal for a directive amending these two directives, SEC(2006)557), and Dir. 2003/35/EC, providing for public participation in respect of the drawing up of certain plans and programmes relating to the environment, O.J. 2003, L 156/17-25.

enforcement of Community law in general, as will appear from the discussion in the section 5 of this chapter.

4   LIABILITY OF MEMBER STATES FOR DAMAGE
                       SUFFERED BY INDIVIDUALS AS A RESULT OF
                       INFRINGEMENTS OF COMMUNITY LAW WHICH CAN
                       BE ATTRIBUTED TO A MEMBER STATE[239]

Already in older case law, the Court had noted that if damage was caused through an infringement of Community law, the state was liable to the injured party for the consequences in accordance with national law on state liability.[240] There are, however, great differences between the various national systems covering state liability.[241] The question remained, for instance, whether – and, if so, under what conditions – national law permitted liability for actions of the legislature, particularly in relation to primary legislation of a normative character.

It was thus extremely important that in its celebrated judgment in *Francovich*[242] the Court anchored the principle of state liability for damage suffered by individuals through breach of Community law attributable to the state firmly in Community law itself. Two bases were given for the principle of state liability. First, the Court found that it was inherent in the system of the EC Treaty itself, because of the requirements of the full effectiveness of Community rules, and the particular indispensability of obtaining redress where the full effectiveness of Community rules is subject to prior action on the part of the state without which individuals are unable to enforce in national courts the rights conferred on them by Community law. Secondly, the Court noted that the Member States were required, by virtue of Article 10 EC, to take all appropriate measures, whether general or particular, to ensure the implementation of Community law, and consequently to nullify the unlawful consequences of a breach of Community law.

The *conditions* under which liability will give rise to a remedy in damages depends on the nature of the breach of Community law giving rise to the loss and damage. In *Francovich* the Court considered that if a Member State fails to fulfil its obligation under Article 249(3) EC to take all the measures necessary to achieve

---

239.   See also W. van Gerven, 'Bridging the Unbridgeable: Community and National Tort Laws after Francovich and Brasserie' (1996) ICLQ, 507–544. For a discussion of the case law on this subject and the consequences for national law, see J.H. Jans, R. de Lange, S. Prechal and R.J.G.M. *Widdershoven, Europeanisation of Public Law* (2007), Ch. 8.
240.   See Case 60/75, *Russo v. AIMA*.
241.   Cf. e.g., in relation to the extent of the protection granted, Walter van Gerven et al., *Tort Law. Casebooks for the Common Law of Europe* (2000).
242.   Joined Cases C-6 & 9/90, *Francovich and Bonifaci*, annotated by G. Bebr (1992) CML Rev., 557, and confirmed in Case C-334/92, *Wagner Miret v. Fondo de garantía salarial*. See, *inter alia*, F. Schockweiler, 'La responsabilité de l'autorité nationale en cas de violation de droit communautaire' (1992) RTDE, 27, and J. Steiner, 'From Direct Effects to Francovich' (1993) ELRev., 3.

the result prescribed by a directive, a right to obtain reparation exists when three conditions are fulfilled:

1) the result prescribed by the directive should entail the grant of rights to individuals;
2) it should be possible to identify the content of those rights on the basis of the provisions of the directive; and
3) there should be a causal link between the breach of the state's obligation and the loss and damage suffered by the injured parties.

Further, the Court confirmed that reparation had to be made on the basis of national law on liability, that in the absence of Community legislation it was for the national legal order in each Member State to designate the competent courts and lay down the detailed procedural rules for legal proceedings intended to safeguard fully the rights individuals derived from Community law; and that the principles of equivalence and effectiveness, flowing from the *Rewe* and *Comet* case law (discussed in section 3 above), must be upheld.

In a series of cases in 1996[243] the Court was given the opportunity to clarify its earlier judgment and to apply the principle of state liability contained therein to other forms of breach of Community law. The judgment in *Brasserie du Pêcheur and Factortame*[244] was extremely important: this was the first occasion after *Francovich* for the Court to pronounce on the principle and conditions in a broader context. This judgment clarifies first of all that the principle does not mean that liability in damages arises only when the provisions infringed may not be directly relied on, because they are not directly effective; the principle also applies when a directly applicable provision of Community law is breached. In this case, right to reparation is a necessary corollary of the direct effect recognized for the Community provisions whose breach has caused damage.[245] The Court in *Brasserie du Pêcheur* then confirmed that the obligation for Member States to make good damage suffered by individuals as a result of infringements of Community law attributable to those states even applies to cases where it is the national legislature which is responsible for the infringement in question. Since the uniform application of Community law is a fundamental requirement of the Community legal

---

243. See Joined Cases, C-46 & 48/93, *Brasserie du Pêcheur/Factortame III*; Case C-392/93, *The Queen v. H.M. Treasury, ex parte British Telecommunications*; Case C-5/94, *The Queen v. Ministry of Agriculture, Fisheries and Food, ex parte Hedley Lomas (Ireland)* and Joined Cases C-178, 179 & 188-190/94, *Dillenkofer et al. v. Deutschland*, annotated by P. Oliver (1997) CML Rev., 635, and Joined Cases C-283, 291 & 292/94, *Denkavit Internationaal et al. v. Bundesamt für Finanzen*. On state liability for acts of the judiciary, see Case C-224/01, *Köbler v. Österreich*.
244. Joined Cases C-46 & 48/93, *Brasserie du Pêcheur/Factortame III*.
245. 'The Court has consistently held that the right of individuals to rely on the directly effective provisions of the Treaty before national courts is only a minimum guarantee and is not sufficient in itself to ensure the full and complete implementation of the Treaty' (Joined Cases C-46 & 48/93, *Brasserie du Pêcheur/Factortame III*, paras 20–22). These cases concerned Art. 30 [now 28] and Art. 52 [now 43] EC.

order, liability for decisions of constitutional authorities can not be made dependent on domestic rules as to the division of powers between them. Finally, in this judgment the Court made an important statement about the conditions establishing liability; it drew a parallel between the liability regime in relation to infringements attributable to Member States and the rules laid down in its case law on the basis of Article 288 EC concerning the non-contractual liability of the Community itself. These conditions (for liability of Member States) 'cannot, in the absence of particular justification, differ from those governing the liability of the Community in like circumstances' (para. 42). The harmonization of the two forms of liability may not be so obvious from the point of view of legal theory,[246] but from that of legal policy, the argument given by the Court in support of this seems defensible: 'The protection of the rights which individuals derive from Community law cannot vary depending on whether a national authority or a Community authority is responsible for the damage' (para. 42).

With this harmonization in mind, the Court transposed – in a different wording – the essence of the so-called *Schöppenstedt* formula,[247] concerning liability of the Community for normative acts of the Institutions which involve particular economic policy choices, to the field of liability of Member States for acts of their legislative institutions. If the breach of Community law committed by a Member State is attributable to the national legislature acting in a sphere where it has a wide discretion in making normative choices, Community law confers a right to reparation where three conditions are met:

(a) the rule of law infringed must be intended to confer rights on individuals;
(b) the breach must be sufficiently serious;
(c) and there must be a direct causal link between the breach of the obligation resting on the state and the damage sustained by the injured parties.

It should be noticed that the condition under (a) comes in the place of the so-called *Schutznormtheorie*, expressed at the time in the *Schöppenstedt* formula ('violation of a superior rule of law for the protection of the individual').[248] The Court went on to state explicitly (para. 66) that these three conditions do not mean that the state cannot incur liability for an infringement of Community law under less strict conditions on the basis of national law, as is for instance the case in the Netherlands. The decisive test for finding that a breach of Community law is sufficiently serious is whether the Member State or the Community Institution concerned manifestly and gravely disregarded the limits of its discretion. The competent

---

246. See R. Barents, 'Recente ontwikkelingen op het gebied van de rechtsbescherming in de Europese Gemeenschap', *in: Rechtsbescherming in de Europese Gemeenschap* (1997), 1–32 (op 10), who points to the difference in the position of Institutions exercising the powers conferred on them by the Treaty, and Member States who have to meet obligations of result, imposed on them by Community law.

247. See Ch. VI, section 2.4, *supra.*

248. In the meantime, the condition under a) also applies in the case of liability of the Community, see the judgment in Case C-352/98, *Bergaderm and Goupil v. Commission*, discussed in Ch. VI, section 2.4.

court must take a number of additional factors into consideration, which we will examine below.

The judgments in *Francovich* and *Brasserie du Pêcheur* concerned, respectively, the infringement of a provision (which was not directly effective) of a directive which had not been implemented in national law within the time-limit, and the infringement of directly effective provisions of the Treaty by an act of the legislature, where that infringement had already been established by the Court of Justice. How *Francovich* liability actually fitted into the theory developed in *Brasserie du Pêcheur* was still uncertain, however. The next two judgments of the Court in this area also failed to bring the necessary clarity. They concerned infringements resulting from the incorrect transposition of a directive (*British Telecommunications*)[249] and an infringement of a directly effective Treaty provision by an act of the administration, which infringement had been established in an earlier judgment of the Court (*Hedley Lomas*).[250]

The desired clarity was brought, nonetheless, by the judgment in *Dillenkofer*,[251] in which the Court expounded the state liability theory in a more general way. Here the Court put an end to the misunderstanding that the three conditions for a right to reparation mentioned in the *Brasserie du Pêcheur* judgment are different for different cases of infringements of Community law causing damage. In particular, it removed the misunderstanding that the requirement of a sufficiently serious breach is not applicable in the case of a failure to transpose a directive within the time-limit set, such as was the situation in *Francovich*. True, the Court had established that these conditions depended on the nature of the breach of Community law causing the damage, but in saying that it had merely intended to indicate that those conditions were to be applied in accordance with the particular type of situation involved (para. 24).

The condition of a sufficiently serious breach – although not mentioned as such in *Francovich* – was, according to the Court in *Dillenkofer*, inherent in the circumstances of the case. If a Member State is not faced with normative choices, and only had considerably reduced, or even no, discretion, then, as the Court had already ruled,[252] the mere infringement of Community law may be sufficient in itself to establish the existence of a sufficiently serious breach. When 'as in *Francovich*, a Member State fails, in breach of the third paragraph of Article 189 [now 249] of the Treaty, to take any of the measures necessary to achieve the

---

249. Case C-392/93, *The Queen v. H.M. Treasury, ex parte British Telecommunications.* Here the Court ruled that the infringement was not sufficiently serious, because it was based on the interpretation in good faith of a provision of a directive which could be interpreted in different ways, and the Member State had come to this interpretation on the basis of arguments which were not manifestly incorrect. See also Joined Cases C-283, 291 & 292/94, *Denkavit Internationaal et al. v. Bundesamt für Finanzen*, annotated by F. Vanistendael (1997) CML Rev., 1279.

250. Case C-5/94, *Hedley Lomas.*

251. Joined Cases C-178, 179 & 188-190/94, *Dillenkofer.* See J. Jans et al., op. cit. *supra* note 239, 330–331.

252. See Case C-5/94, *Hedley Lomas.*

result prescribed by a directive within the period it lays down, that Member State manifestly and gravely disregards the limits on its discretion' (para. 26). In this category of case, a right to reparation for damages suffered arises for individuals whenever:

> the result prescribed by the directive entails the grant of rights to them, the content of those rights is identifiable on the basis of the provisions of the directive[253] and a causal link exists between the breach of the state's obligation and the loss and damage suffered by the injured parties: no other conditions need be taken into consideration (para. 27).

This case law can be summarized as follows: there is a right to reparation for damages resulting from an infringement of Community law attributable to a Member State where three conditions are met. The first condition is that the rule of Community law which was infringed was intended to confer rights on individuals. That will tend to be the case in general if the Member State acts contrary to a directly effective provision of Community law. A special case is that of incorrect implementation of directives, or failure to implement within the time-limit set. The rule of law infringed is then the Community law rule that obliges a Member State under Article 249(3) EC to take all the measures necessary to achieve the result prescribed by a directive. In that case, a right to damages arises if the result prescribed by the relevant provision involves the conferral of rights on individuals, and the content of the rights in question can be ascertained purely on the basis of the provisions of the directive.

The case law on the application of this first condition in the case of directives is still rather meagre[254] but shows that the rights involved are those of the individuals who claim reparation for damages. Moreover, the provision of the directive at issue does not need to refer explicitly to a right of the beneficiaries to claim the result prescribed. Further, this provision may involve a certain discretion, provided it is possible to establish the minimum guarantees or rights. In this context, it is important to note that Community law only imposes an obligation to make good damage caused by the national authorities' disregard of the limits on their discretion if the condition as to the intended conferral of rights whose content can be determined is met. If, therefore, the national court, in the framework of the so-called objective review of legality,[255] comes to the conclusion that the competent national authority, in the exercise of its discretion in relation to the implementation of a directive, has exceeded the limits of that discretion, it does not automatically mean that the Member State in question is liable under Community law to make

---

253. A combination, thus, of the first two conditions in Joined Cases C-6 & 9/90, *Francovich*, and a specification in relation to directives of the first condition in *Brasserie du Pêcheur* (Joined Cases C-46 & 48/93) which states that the rule infringed must be intended to confer rights.

254. See Joined Cases C-6 & 9/90, *Francovich*; Case C-91/92, *Dori*; Joined Cases C-178, 179 & 188-190/94, *Dillenkofer*, and Case C-127/95, *Norbrook Laboratories v. Ministry of Agriculture, Fisheries and Food.*

255. Discussed in section 1.4.2. *supra.*

reparation for damage, even if the act in excess of discretion amounts to a sufficiently serious breach of Community law and has caused damage to individuals. It must also be demonstrated that the result prescribed by the directive involves the conferral of rights on individuals and that the content of these rights can be established solely on the basis of the directive's provisions.[256]

The second condition is that the breach of Community law must be sufficiently serious. In cases involving the exerc;.e of normative powers – for instance, in the implementation of directives or in setting rules for matters for which Community law leaves the national legislature a wide margin of discretion – that condition is fulfilled where the Member State manifestly and gravely exceeds the limits within which it should remain in the exercise of its powers. When the Member State in question at the moment of the infringement was not faced with normative choices, and had only considerably reduced, or even no, discretion, then the mere infringement of Community law may be sufficient to be qualified as sufficiently serious – as in the case of the failure to implement directives within the time-limit set – but this is not necessarily the case.[257] It should be borne in mind that the existence and the extent of the margin of discretion are determined by Community law and not national law.[258]

In determining whether a breach is sufficiently serious, the court must take into consideration all the factors characterizing the situation before it. These factors include the following:

- the clarity and precision of the rule infringed;
- the extent of the margin of discretion which the rule infringed allowed to national or Community bodies;
- the question whether the infringement was committed intentionally, or damage caused intentionally;
- whether an error of law was excusable or inexcusable;
- the fact that the behaviour of a Community Institution may have contributed to the infringement;
- whether or not national measures or practices which are contrary to Community law are being maintained.

Regardless of other factors, a breach of Community law is to be considered manifest and sufficiently serious if it continues despite a judgment establishing the infringement in question, or despite a preliminary ruling or constant case law of the Court in the area from which it is apparent that the relevant action is an infringement. On the other hand, the reparation of damage cannot be made

---

256. Which does not exclude an obligation to compensate damage on the basis of national law – which after all may set less restrictive conditions. For a case in which the conferral of rights on individuals by a directive was denied, see Case C-222/02, *Paul and others v. Bundesrepublik Deutschland*.
257. In that sense, see explicitly Case C-424/97, *Salomone Haim v. Kassenzahnärztliche Vereinigung Nordrhein*, at para. 41.
258. Cf. the judgment in case C-424/97, *Haim*, at para. 40.

dependent on the prior establishment by the Court of an infringement of Community law attributable to a the Member State. Nor may it depend on a condition derived from the concept of fault (in French, '*notion de faute*') going further than the sufficiently serious breach of Community law.

If one takes a closer look at these factors, they seem mainly to concern the extent to which the action causing damage can be 'blamed on' (to use a legally neutral term) the Member State; they are partly objective, and partly subjective.[259] Objective, insofar as they concern the extent to which the rule of law infringed determines the content and scope of the obligation imposed on the Member State; subjective, insofar as they refer to factors, (incriminatory or mitigating), which could have influenced the behaviour of the Member State in its failure to fulfil its obligation.

The third condition is that there is a direct causal link between the breach of the state's obligation and the damage suffered by the injured parties. Usually, the Court tends to leave the assessment of the causal link to the referring court, without giving much further guidance.[260]

When these three conditions imposed by Community law are met, the Member State must make good the damage caused, in the framework of *national* law on liability ('procedural autonomy'). This has been constant case law ever since the judgment in *Francovich*. The conditions imposed by the national legal rules concerning compensation for damage must, of course, not be less favourable than those applicable to similar national claims. Nor may they make it virtually impossible or excessively difficult to receive compensation for damage. These are the usual conditions of the *Rewe* and *Comet* case law, discussed above. At all events, the compensation must be adequate in relation to the damage suffered, so that the rights of the persons suffering the damage are effectively guaranteed.[261]

A Member State incurs liability for loss and damage caused to individuals as a result of breaches of Community law, whatever the organ of the State whose act or omission was responsible for the breach.[262] A Member State cannot plead the distribution of powers and responsibilities between the bodies within its national legal order in order to escape liability on that basis.[263] It was hardly surprising,

---

259. Cf. the judgment in Joined Cases C-46 & 48/93, *Brasserie du Pêcheur/Factortame III*, at para. 78, where in this context the Court speaks of certain objective and subjective elements which are relevant for deciding whether the infringement of Community law is sufficiently serious, and which may be linked with the notion of fault in the national legal system.
260. For an exception, where the Court itself decided that there was no causal link, see Case C-319/96, *Brinkmann Tabakfabriken v. Skatteministeriet*. In principle, it is for the national courts to review whether the conditions for state liability for infringement of Community law have been fulfilled, on the basis of the guidelines given by the Court of Justice. Sometimes, the Court conducts this review itself, when it possesses all the necessary information. See for the kind of guidelines given, e.g., Case C-278/05, *Carol Marilyn Robins and Others v. Secretary of State for Work and Pensions*.
261. Joined Cases C-94 & 95/95 *Bonifaci et al. and Berto et al. v. INPS*.
262. Case C-46/93, *Brasserie du Pêcheur*, paras 31–32.
263. Case C-302/97, *Klaus Konle v. Republik Österreich*, para. 62.

therefore, that the Court in *Köbler*[264] decided that Member States may, in principle, be liable for damage caused to individuals by infringements of Community law consisting of decisions of a national court adjudicating at last instance.

According to the Court's decision in *Köbler*, state liability arising from action of national courts is governed by the same three conditions as in the case of any other state violation of Community law: the intention to confer rights on individuals, a sufficiently serious breach, and a causal link between the breach and the damage. As to the second condition, 'regard must be had to the specific nature of the judicial function and to the legitimate requirements of legal certainty'. It follows that state liability 'can be incurred only in the exceptional case where the court has manifestly infringed the applicable law'.[265] There is an additional factor for the national court hearing a claim for reparation to take into account when assessing the seriousness of the breach, namely the non-compliance by the court in question with its obligation to make a reference for a preliminary ruling under the third paragraph of Article 234 EC.

Even though the application of the principle of state liability to judicial decisions has been accepted in one form or another by most of the Member States[266] the Court's judgment caused quite a stir and was strongly criticized by some commentators.[267] It was feared in particular that the combination of the *Köbler* liability threat and the rigid *CILFIT* criteria would henceforth induce courts of last instance to flood the Court's docket with preliminary questions, anxious, as they were imagined to be, to avoid any risk of violating their obligation under the third paragraph of Article 234 EC and of thus incurring state liability. There is however little support in the Court's case law for a finding that the failure to refer can *in itself* engage liability. It is the violation of substantive Community law by a judicial ruling which may cause damage to individuals. Disregard of the duty to refer is only one of the several factors, albeit an important one, for assessing the manifest nature of that infringement.[268]

In Member States, whether they are federal in structure or not, where decentralized (territorial) authorities with a certain degree of autonomy or other autonomous bodies under public law perform certain legislative or administrative tasks, problems may arise if the latter cause damage to individuals as a result of applying national law in conflict with Community law. The underlying idea must be the

---

264. Case C-224/01, *Gerhard Köbler v. Republik Österreich*, affirmed and reinforced in Case C-173/03, *Traghetti del Mediterraneo v. Repubblica italiana*, in which the Court ruled that, although it remains possible for national law to define the criteria relating to the nature or degree of the infringement, under no circumstances may such criteria impose requirements stricter than that of a manifest infringement of the applicable law, as set out in the *Köbler* judgment.

265. *Köbler*, para. 53.

266. Cf. *Köbler*, para. 48 and Opinion of A.G. Léger, paras 77–82.

267. See, e.g., P. Wattel, 'Köbler, Cilfit and Welhgrove: We Can't Go on Meeting Like This' (2004) CML Rev., 177; with more sense of proportion, e.g., C.D. Classen's annotation in (2004) CML Rev., 813 and J.H. Jans, 'State Liability and Infringements Attributable to National Courts: A Dutch Perspective on the Köbler Case', in: Alfred E. Kellermann, ed. *The European Union: An Ongoing Process of Integration, Liber Amicorum*, (The Hague, 2004), 165.

268. See more in detail Classen's annotation cited in the previous note.

obligation of each Member State to ensure that damage is compensated, regardless of which body committed the relevant infringement and regardless of which body should, in principle, under the law of the Member State in question, be liable to make compensation. Provided that the relevant procedures in the national legal order comply with the above-mentioned principles of equivalence and effectiveness, there is no objection under Community law to that body making good the damage suffered by individuals, either alone or together with the federal or central authorities.[269] The fulfilment by the Member State of its Community law obligations, therefore, does not necessarily require the federal or central authorities themselves to compensate damage which individuals have suffered as a result of application by decentralized bodies of national measures enacted in conflict with Community law.[270]

5   THE SANCTIONS TO BE ESTABLISHED IN THE NATIONAL LEGAL SYSTEMS FOR INFRINGEMENTS OF COMMUNITY LAW

Effective enforcement of Community law will usually require that sanctions are set under national law, of a civil, administrative, penal or disciplinary nature, for infringement of rules which the Community has enacted; appropriate proceedings must also be made available.[271] This does not only concern infringements of Community law provisions which are directly applicable in the national legal order, but also infringements of provisions of national law which have been enacted in order to implement Community law obligations, such as in the case of transposition or implementation of provisions of directives. Sanctions must be taken to cover measures which remove a benefit from or impose a disadvantage on a person on account of that person's failure to abide by certain rules. Civil law claims can also be an effective means for enforcing compliance with Community law.[272]

---

269. In any case, it is open to question whether the magic formula in the *Rewe-Comet* case law (Case 33/76, *Rewe* and Case 45/76, *Comet*) can prevent the person who suffered the damage being sent from pillar to post in this situation. See on this subject B. Hessel, *European Integration and the Supervision of Local and Regional Authorities: Experiences in the Netherlands with Requirements of European Community Law*, <http://www.utrechtlawreview.org/> Vol. 2, Issue 1 (June) 2006.
270. See on this Case C-302/97, *Konle*, and Case C-424/97, *Haim*.
271. See on this also the Council Resolution of 29 Jun. 1995 on the effective uniform application of Community law and on the penalties applicable for breaches of Community law in the internal market, O.J. 1995, C 188/1.
272. For instance, the full effect of rules concerning quality standards may require that compliance with obligations flowing from these rules can be guaranteed in civil actions between a market participant and his competitor, see Case C-253/00, *Muñoz and Superior Fruiticola v. Frumar and Redbridge Produce Marketing*. Cf. in the field of competition infringements Case C-453/99, *Courage v. Crehan* and Joined Cases C-295-298/04, *Vincenzo Manfredi v. Lloyd Adriatico Assicurazioni*. See also the Commission's Green paper *Damages actions for breach of the EC antitrust rules* COM(2005)627.

In accordance with the principles of procedural autonomy,[273] the primary responsibility for the enforcement of these provisions lies with the Member States. It is constant case law that:

> where a Community regulation does not specifically provide any penalty for an infringement or refers for that purpose to national laws, regulations and administrative provisions, Article 5 [now 10] of the EC Treaty requires the Member States to take all measures necessary to guarantee the application and effectiveness of Community law.[274]

This involves *national sanctions*. The principles of equivalence and effectiveness apply: the Member States 'must ensure in particular that infringements of Community law are penalized under conditions, both procedural and substantive, which are analogous to those applicable to infringements of national law of a similar nature and importance and which, in any event, make the penalty effective, proportionate and dissuasive'.[275] The last phrase confirms that the principle of effectiveness is predominant. The obligation contained in Article 10 EC includes, according to the Court, 'the initiation of any proceedings under administrative, fiscal or civil law for the collection or recovery of duties or levies which have been fraudulently evaded or for damages'.[276] Finally, the national authorities should proceed, with respect to infringements of Community law, with the same diligence as that which they bring to bear in implementing corresponding national laws.[277]

The obligations described by the Court apply to all bodies in the Member States in whom authoritative power is vested and therefore, within the framework of their powers, also to judicial bodies. What consequences may flow from these obligations is apparent from examples in the field of application of the directive on equal treatment of men and women in relation to access to employment, vocational training and promotion, and working conditions.[278] Article 6 of this Directive obliges the Member States to adopt in their domestic legal order the measures necessary to enable all persons who consider themselves wronged by failure to apply the principle of equal treatment 'to pursue their claims by judicial process after possible recourse to other competent authorities'.

The Court has ruled that this provision allows Member States the freedom to choose which sanctions to use. These must, however, ensure a real and effective protection of legal rights, and have a deterrent effect *vis-à-vis* the employer. If,

---

273. See section 3 *supra*.
274. Case C-177/95, *Ebony Maritime and Loten Navigation v. Prefetto della Provincia di Brindisi et al.*, at para. 35.
275. Case C-177/95, *Ebony Maritime*, at para. 35; in this sense already Case 50/76, *Amsterdam Bulb*, see also especially Case 14/83, *Von Colson*; Case 68/88, *Commission v. Greece*; Case 326/88, *Criminal proceedings against Hansen* and Case C-186/98, *Criminal proceedings against Nunes and de Matos*. See also the Council resolution in note 271 *supra*.
276. Case C-352/92, *Milchwerke Köln and Wuppertal v. Hauptzollamt Köln-Rheinau*, at para. 23, referring to the Opinion of A.G. Van Gerven.
277. Case 68/88, *Commission v. Greece*.
278. Dir. 76/207/EEC, O.J. 1976, L 39/40.

therefore, a Member State decides to use compensation as a sanction for infringement of the prohibition on discrimination, then this must at least be adequate in relation to the damage sustained.[279] Article 6 thus prohibits a national rule which sets a ceiling, a priori, for the damages to be paid in the event of discriminatory dismissal. The person who has suffered damage may rely on this Article, together with Article 5(1) of the Directive, which forbids discriminatory dismissal, as against the Member State and its organs.[280] Where a Member State chooses to employ sanctions in the field of rules on civil liability, moreover, the infringement of the prohibition of discrimination is in itself sufficient as a basis for engaging the full liability of the person who has committed the discrimination, and no regard may be had to the grounds of exemption envisaged by national law.[281]

The Community rule to be sanctioned may leave the choice of sanctions entirely open,[282] but may also contain further indications about, for instance, which persons should be subject to sanctions for which infringements,[283] or the result to be achieved with the sanctions,[284] or the procedures to be made available.[285] A Community rule may also, however, provide for specific sanction and oblige the Member States to apply these in case of infringements; we are here confronted with *Community sanctions*. The establishment of the Community sanctions obviously serves uniform and effective enforcement of Community law better than the leaving the establishment of sanctions to the Member States. Implementation of sanctions which vary between Member States as regards their nature

---

279. Case 14/83, *Von Colson*. See, e.g., also Case C-180/95, *Draehmpaehl v. Urania Immobilienservice*.
280. Case C-271/91, *Marshall II*.
281. Case C-177/88, *Dekker v. Stichting VJV-Centrum*. The question of direct (horizontal) effect was not raised by the Hoge Raad (Dutch Supreme Court) in this case. See also Case C-180/95, *Draehmpaehl*.
282. E.g., in a Reg.: 'Member States shall take appropriate legal or administrative measures in case of non-compliance with the provisions of this Regulation' or in a directive: 'The Member States shall determine the penalties applicable to breaches of the national provisions adopted pursuant to this Directive'.
283. Cf. Art. 16 Reg. 11/60 concerning the abolition of discrimination in transport rates and conditions, O.J. 1960, 52 1121.
284. Cf. Art. 31(2) Reg. 2847/93, establishing a control system applicable to the common fisheries policy, requires the Member States to take administrative action or bring criminal proceedings capable of effectively depriving those responsible of the economic benefit of the infringements, or of producing results proportionate to the seriousness of such infringements in order effectively to discourage further infringements of the same kind. Art. 31(3) then lists the kinds of administrative sanctions which may be imposed, depending on the gravity of the case.
285. See in particular Arts. 4 and 6 of Dir. 84/450 relating to the approximation of the laws, regulations and administrative provisions of the Member States concerning misleading advertising, O.J. 1984, L 250/17, and also Dir. 89/665/EEC on the coordination of the laws, regulations and administrative provisions relating to the application of review procedures to the award of public supply and public works contracts, O.J. 1989, L 395/33. On problems with the application of the latter directive in Member States where public procurement takes place by means of agreements under contract law and not administrative law, see Case C-81/98, *Alcatel Austria et al. v. Bundesministerium für Wissenschaft und Verkehr*.

and severity[286] for infringements of the same Community rules may, it must be acknowledged, disturb the proper functioning of the common market; moreover, such a situation is difficult to reconcile with the idea that citizens of the Union should receive equal treatment before the (same) law.

The inclusion of specific Community sanctions in a directive is in general harder to reconcile with the character of the directive as a legal instrument. According to Article 249 EC, after all, the choice of form and methods for achieving the result prescribed by the directive is to be left to the national authorities. It is only recently that this objection appears to carry less weight, as will be seen at the end of this section. It is thus scarcely surprising that the obligation to impose specific sanctions is encountered mainly in areas where the Community acts on the basis of its power to make regulations, and where the Community has a particular financial interest in the strict enforcement of the rules laid down. That has been, from the earliest days, the case for legislation in the field of agriculture and – to a lesser extent – fisheries,[287] and also for legislation relating to the prohibition on discriminatory transport tariffs and conditions.

In this area, the sanctions prescribed by the Community legislative Institutions and which must be applied by the Member States, have as their main aim to ensure that the Community rules concerning the levying of amounts or the receipt of premiums and subsidies are complied with by the persons who should pay the amounts or receive the subsidies. In the course of time, the Community Institutions have developed a veritable arsenal of possible *administrative sanctions.* These include: fines, non-payment of Community subsidies and premiums, recovery of subsidies and premiums, ex post recovery of Community duties and levies,

---

286. See for a good example of this the example mentioned in K.J.M. Mortelmans, 'The Application and Enforcement of Community Law by National Administrative Law', in: J.A.E. Vervaele (ed.), *Administrative Law Application and Enforcement of Community Law in the Netherlands* (Deventer, 1994), 5, at 12–13, of imposition of sanctions in Member States in the application of Reg. 2772/75 on marketing standards for eggs. See also Case C-273/90, *Meico-Fell v. Hauptzollamt Darmstadt*, at para. 12: 'It is true that the application of this criterion [punishment of specific conduct by a criminal sanction] may, owing to the substantive provisions of the criminal law of the Member States, lead to different results. However, this situation arises from the fact that in the present state of Community law the classification of a certain kind of conduct for the purposes of criminal law is not harmonized and is therefore governed by national law.'

287. For transport, see Art. 16 Reg. 11/60. In the case of customs legislation, Community sanctions are only used exceptionally: see for such an exception the fact that no repayment or remission shall be granted when the facts which led to the payment or entry in the accounts of an amount which was not legally owed are the result of deliberate action by the person concerned (Art. 236(1), last sentence, of the Customs Code, Reg. 2913/92, O.J. 1992, L 302/1). The Member States have retained powers in relation to sanctions for infringements of VAT rules – a subject matter which is regulated by means of directives – entirely for themselves. They are obliged to respect the principle of proportionality in their use of these powers, see Case 299/86, *Criminal proceedings against Drexl*, and Case C-276/91, *Commission v. France*.

possible with a surcharge, loss of deposits, temporary exclusion from the advantages of a premium or subsidy scheme (see Ch. V, section 4.3.1. above).[288]

In a case brought by Germany, the Court ruled that it is up to the legislative Institutions of the Community to decide whether the use of specific sanctions is necessary to attain the objectives of the Community Agricultural Policy – and this includes the Commission when it is exercising implementing powers delegated to it by the Council on the basis of Article 202 EC.[289] Such sanctions may be necessary, for instance, when claims for subsidies are so numerous that it is not possible to check them systematically and completely, and the uniformity of measures taken with regard to traders supplying false information needs to be guaranteed. According to the judgment in the case brought by Germany, this power implies the authorization for the Community to impose sanctions to be applied by the national authorities against traders who have committed fraud, even if the trader in question suffers, as a result of the sanction, a financial loss that is greater than the mere repayment, possibly with interest, of the wrongly received amounts. In this context, the Court rejected the argument brought by the German Government that sanctions which mean that for a certain period the trader is excluded from the right to a benefit are penal sanctions, which the Community legislature does not have the power to impose. The Court considers such sanctions to be a specific administrative instrument, which is an element of the aid scheme and intended to ensure the sound financial management of the Community's public funds.[290]

Notwithstanding the Court's ruling, these are not reparatory sanctions, intended to restore the previous, lawful situation, but are punitive sanctions aiming at the imposition of an extra disadvantage and at deterrence.[291] This distinction is important, since in the latter case – in general – the guarantees of Article 6 of the European Convention on Human Rights concerning 'criminal charges' may be applicable.[292] Critics have pointed out that, in its case law, the Court of Justice

---

288. See for the various sanctions, e.g., J.A.E. Vervaele, *Administrative Sanctioning Powers of and in the Community. Towards a System of European Sanctions?* in Vervaele (ed.), op. cit. *supra* note 286, at 179 et seq., and also R. Barents, *The Agricultural Law of the EC, An Inquiry into the Administrative Law of the European Community in the Field of Agriculture* (Kluwer, 1994), 252–253 and 277–291, and X. Yataganas, in: 'Commentaire Mégret, Le droit de la CEE', Vol. 10, *Titre V, L'exécution et le contrôle budgetaire*, 2me éd. (1999), par. 948–954.

289. Case C-240/90, *Germany v. Commission.* In view of the general nature of the reasoning followed by the Court here, this would seem to apply not only to exclusions and surcharges, but also to fines and penalty payments. For a different opinion, cf. the article by J.A.E. Vervaele, in Vervaele (ed.), op. cit. *supra* note 286, at 192. For a case where the Commission prescribes Community sanctions, see Reg. (EC) No. 2419/2001 of 11 Dec. 2001 laying down detailed rules for applying the integrated administration and control system for certain Community aid schemes, O.J. 2001, L 327/11.

290. For a clear exposition of the Court's case law see R. Barents, op. cit *supra* note 288, 277–282.

291. See particularly B.P. Vermeulen, *The Issue of Fundamental Rights in the Administrative Application and Enforcement of Community Law*, in Vervaele (ed.) op. cit. *supra* note 286, 57, at 66–70.

292. Cf. the *Oztürk* and *Bendenoun* cases, European Court of Human Rights, A.73 (1984) and A.284 (1994).

seems to deny that these sanctions are punishments in the sense of that provision, even if they do not fall under ordinary law, but under administrative law.[293] In its case law, the Court of Justice stresses the administrative nature of the sanctions, maintaining that they are not penal sanctions because they merely guarantee that an undertaking voluntarily assumed will be carried out,[294] or alternatively because the right to Community aid must be subject to the condition that the beneficiary offers all guarantees of probity and trustworthiness.[295] It would seem that this line of argument should be explained by the fear that too heavy an emphasis on the penal character of the sanctions could lead to such material and procedural requirements in relation to the imposition of the sanctions, that it would be impossible to apply them effectively.[296] Here, a tension arises between the need for effectiveness in implementing a *dirigiste* agricultural policy dating from the 1960s, on the one hand, and the requirements of the modern liberal state based on the rule of law, on the other.

In this way, the principle of effectiveness may also lead to a restriction of the application of national rules and principles intended to protect the interests of individuals. For instance, if a regulation obliges Member States to take the necessary measures in order to ensure that the Community provisions in a particular agricultural sector are complied with, it obliges them to take all legal, administrative or individual measures in their national legal systems which are necessary for the effective enforcement of Community law. If such effective enforcement requires national coercive measures to be taken within a certain time, in order to safeguard the Community interest, a Member State may not plead as an excuse that an objection raised under national law to such measures led to their suspension.[297] The national courts must also respect this requirement.

These obligations on Member States do not alter the fact, though, that the Court of Justice has found that imposition and application of sanctions to infringements of Community law, whether or not transposed into national law, may be reviewed on the basis of general legal principles, such as the requirements of legality, proportionality and non-discrimination.[298] The principle of proportionality is thus a

---

293. E.g., G. Corstens and J. Pradel, *European Criminal Law*, 2002, par. 463 and par. 464.
294. Cf. Case 117/83, *Könecke v. Balm*, at para.14, concerning deposits.
295. Case C-240/90, *Germany v. Commission*, at para. 26, concerning exclusion.
296. 'The substantive and procedural guarantees under which, at least in a system governed by the rule of law, criminal sanctions have to be imposed, would prevent in many cases an effective application of these measures', R. Barents, op. cit. note 288, 281.
297. Case C-217/88, *Commission v. Germany*. This case concerned decisions imposing on wine-growers an obligation to distill certain qualities of table wine, in implementation of Community rules.
298. E.g., Case 117/83, *Könecke* (criminal or other sanctions may only be imposed if there is a clear and unambiguous legal basis for doing so) and Case 240/78, *Atalanta Amsterdam v. Produktschap voor Vee en Vlees* (the sanctions should be with the degree of failure to implement the contractual obligations or with the seriousness of the breach of those obligations). See also Case C-29/95, *Pastoors and Trans-Cap v. Belgische Staat*, for review against the prohibition of indirect discrimination and against the principle of proportionality; Case 326/88, *Criminal proceedings against Hansen* and Case C-177/95, *Ebony Maritime* (a system of strict criminal

two-edged sword – the requirement that the sanction is proportional to the gravity of the infringement serves the interest not just of the enforcement of Community law – the sanction must be sufficiently severe to be effective and deterrent – but also of judicial protection of persons accused of infringements – the sanction may not be more severe than is necessary. The review of the severity of the sanction will, however, concern above all the necessity test. It has been remarked by a commentator that if it is necessary for the achievement of the objective of the rule in question that a sanction should be severe, and no account, or scarcely any account, should be taken of mitigating circumstances, then the Court will consider this to be justified and proportional.[299] From this point of view, too, the effectiveness of enforcement of Community law is the primary concern.

Although criminal law and criminal procedural law belong to the competence of the Member States, Community law may set limits to the exercise of this competence.[300] In addition, the principle of equivalence concerning the imposition of penalties may lead to an obligation for a Member State to set a criminal sanction on an infringement of Community law. That is without doubt. However, there are differences of opinion as to the question whether the EC Treaty provides a legal basis for the power of the Council to oblige Member States to impose not just administrative sanctions but also penal sanctions on infringements of Community law, and to harmonize some aspects of criminal procedural law of the Member States where this is considered necessary.[301]

In 2001, seeing that there were still many cases of severe non-observance of Community law on the protection of the environment which were not subject to sufficiently dissuasive and effective penalties in the Member States, the Commission deemed it necessary to establish a minimum standard on constituent elements of criminal offences in breach of this part of Community law. To this end it submitted a proposal for a *Directive of the European Parliament and of the Council on the Protection of the Environment through Criminal Law* with as legal basis Article 175(1) EC.[302] Though sharing the Commission's concerns, the Council refused to take action on the basis of the EC Treaty, but adopted a Third Pillar framework decision based on Article 34 Treaty on the European Union (TEU)

---

liability for sanctioning infringements of a regulation is not per se incompatible with Community law). See also extensively R. Barents, op. cit. note 288, 287–291.

299. A.M. de Moor-van Vugt, *Maten en gewichten, Het evenredigheidsbeginsel in Europees perspectief* (Zwolle, 1995), 111. In this context a good illustration is provided by Case C-104/94, *Cereol Italia v. Azienda agricola Castello.*

300. Case 203/80, *Criminal proceedings against Casati* and Case C-226/97 *Lemmens.* See on this subject, e.g., M. Delmas-Marty, 'The European Union and Penal Law' (1998) *European Law Journal,* 87–115.

301. See on this, e.g., Vervaele, in Vervaele (ed.), op. cit. *supra* note 286, 170–174. Most authors tend to deny any competences of the EC in the field of criminal law. In a positive sense, however, see already H.G. Sevenster, 'Criminal Law and EC Law' (1992) CML Rev., 29–70.

302. O.J. 2001, C 180/238. See for an account of earlier abortive attempts, A. Weyembergh, 'Approximation of Criminal Laws, the Constitutional Treaty and the Hague Programme' (2005) CML Rev., 1567, at 1572.

instead.[303] A majority in the Council was of the opinion that the proposal went beyond the powers conferred on the Community by the EC Treaty and that a Framework Decision, based on the said Article 34 TEU, was a correct instrument to impose on the Member States the obligation to provide for criminal sanctions.

The Commission brought an action for annulment of the framework decision before the Court, which succeeded. The framework decision was annulled on the ground that its adoption infringed Article 47 TEU,[304] as it encroached on the powers which Article 175 EC confers on the Community.[305] Accepting that 'as a general rule, neither criminal law nor the rules of criminal procedure fall within the Community's competence', the Court stated however that this finding

> does not prevent the Community legislature, when the application of effective, proportionate and dissuasive criminal penalties by the competent national authorities is an essential measure for combating serious environmental offences, from taking measures which relate to the criminal law of the Member States which it considers necessary in order to ensure that the rules which it lays down on environmental protection are fully effective.[306]

In its judgment, the Court seems to attach importance to the fact that the protection of the environment constitutes one of the essential objectives of the Community and that the provisions of the framework decision at issue left to the Member States the choice as to which criminal penalties to apply, so long as they were effective, proportionate and dissuasive. In a subsequent case, the Court clarified its position on the last point by declaring categorically that 'the determination of the type and level of the criminal penalties to be applied does not fall within the Community's sphere of competence'.[307] So, it is only with this proviso in mind that one may subscribe to the Commission's conclusion that:

> the judgment makes it clear that criminal law as such does not constitute a Community policy, since Community action in criminal matters may be based only on implicit powers associated with a specific legal basis. Hence, appropriate measures of criminal law can be adopted on a Community basis only at sectoral level and only on condition that there is a clear need to combat serious shortcomings in the implementation of the Community's objectives and to provide for criminal law measures to ensure the full effectiveness of a Community policy or the proper functioning of a freedom.[308]

---

303. Framework decision on the protection of the environment through criminal law, O.J. 2003, L 29/55.
304. The Court considers it its task under Arts. 46 and 47 TEU to ensure that acts which, according to the Council, fall under the EU Treaty do not encroach upon the powers conferred by the EC Treaty on the Community; see Case C-170/96, *Commission v. Council*.
305. Case C-176/03, *Commission v. Council*, annotated by C. Tobler (2006) CML Rev., 835.
306. Ibid., paras 47 and 48.
307. Case C-440/05, *Commission v. Council*, para. 70.
308. Communication on the implications of the Court's judgment of 13 Sep. 2005 (Case C-176/03, *Commission v. Council*) COM(2005)583, para.7.

Moreover the framework decision's penal provisions at issue in the second case, like those in the previous case, related 'to conduct which is likely to cause particularly serious environmental damage as a result, in this case, of the infringement of the Community rules on maritime safety'.[309] It remains to be seen therefore under what conditions the Community's power to provide for criminal penalties covers policy fields other than that of the protection of the environment.

Under the Treaty of Lisbon, the question whether the Council has to use its power under the EC Treaty or under Title VI of the EU Treaty to provide for criminal penalties will not be pertinent any more. According to Article 83 paragraph 2 Treaty on the Functioning of the European Union (TFEU) (which is due to replace the EC Treaty), the Union legislature may establish minimum rules with regard to the definition of criminal offences and sanctions, if the approximation of criminal laws and regulations of the Member States proves essential to ensure the effective implementation of a Union policy in an area which has been subject to harmonization measures.

The development of Community law with regard to the various measures Member States are obliged to take for the protection of the financial interests of the Community against fraud is discussed in section 4.3 of Chapter V.

FURTHER READING

Alter, K.J. *Establishing the Supremacy of European Law: The Making of an International Rule of Law in Europe.* Oxford Studies in European Law. Oxford: Oxford University Press, 2001.

Arnull, A. *The European Union and Its Court of Justice.* 2nd ed. Oxford EC Law Library. Oxford: Oxford University Press, 2006.

Barents, R. *The Agricultural Law of the EC: An Inquiry into the Administrative Law of the European Community in the Field of Agriculture.* European Monographs, 9. Deventer: Kluwer Law and Taxation Publishers, 1994.

Biondi, A. 'The European Court of Justice and Certain National Procedural Limitations: Not Such a Tough Relationship'. (1999) CML Rev., 1271–1287.

Claes, M.L.H.K. *The National Courts' Mandate in the European Constitution.* Modern Studies in European Law, 5. Oxford: Hart, 2006.

Corstens, G. and J. Pradel. *European Criminal Law* Translation from the original 1997 French version; updated text. The Hague: Kluwer Law International.

Craig, P.P. *EU Administrative Law.* Collected Courses of the Academy of European Law, vol. 16/1. Oxford: Oxford University Press, 2006.

Curtin, D.M. and R.H. van Ooik. *Revamping the European Union's Enforcement Systems with a View to Eastern Enlargement.* Working Documents/Scientific Council for Government Policy, W 110. The Hague: WRR, 2000.

De Witte, B. 'The Nature of the Legal Order'. In P. Craig and G. De Búrca (eds). *The Evolution of EU Law.* Oxford: Oxford University Press, 1999.

---

309.   Case C-440/05, *Commission v. Council*, para. 67.

Gil Ibáñez, A.J. *The Administrative Supervision and Enforcement of EC Law: Powers, Procedures and Limits.* Oxford: Hart, 1999.

Hækkerup, N. and C.R. Wagtmann. *Controls and Sanctions in the EU Law.* Copenhagen: DJØF, 2001.

Harding, C. and B. Swart (eds). *Enforcing European Community Rules.* Dartmouth: Aldershot, 1996.

Herdegen, M. 'Maastricht and the German Constitutional Court: Constitutional Restraints for an "Ever Closer Union" '. (1994) CML Rev., 235–249.

Hoskins, M. 'Tilting the Balance: Supremacy and National Procedural Rules'. (1996) EL Rev., 365–377.

Jans, J.H., et al. *Europeanisation of Public Law.* Groningen: Europa Law Publishing, 2007.

Kerchove, G.D. and A. Weyembergh (eds). *Vers un espace judiciaire pénal européen = Towards a European Judicial Criminal Area.* Bruxelles: Éditions de l'Université de Bruxelles, 2000.

Klip, A., et al. 'Special Issue on European Criminal Law'. (2005) *Maastricht Journal of European and Comparative Law*, 115–213.

Lenaerts, K. and T. Corthaut. 'Of Birds and Hedges: The Role of Primacy in Invoking Norms of EU Law'. (2006) EL Rev., 287–315.

Leonard, A. *Die Rechtsfolgen der Nichtumsetzung von EG-Richtlinien: unter besonderer Berücksichtigung der Staatshaftungs – sowie der Normerlasssklage.* Europäische Hochschulschriften. Reihe 2, Bd. 2186. Frankfurt am Main: Lang, 1997.

Louis, J.-V. In Commentaire Mégret, Le droit de la CEE, Vol. 10, Troisième Partie, Droit communautaire et droit national. 2me éd. Bruxelles: Éditions de l'Université de Bruxelles, 1993.

Nicolaides, P. *From Graphite to Diamond: The Importance of Institutional Structure in Establishing Capacity for Effective and Credible Application of EU Rules.* EIPA Publications, 2002/P/01. Maastricht: European Institute of Public Administration, 2002.

Pradel, J. and G. Corstens. *Droit pénal europeén.* Précis Dalloz. Paris: Dalloz, 2002.

Prechal, S. 'Direct Effect, Indirect Effect, Supremacy and the Evolving Constitution of the European Union'. In C. Barnard (ed.). *The Fundamentals of EU Law Revisited: Assessing the Impact of the Constitutional Debate.* Collected Courses of the Academy of European Law = Recueil des cours de l'Académie de droit européen, Vol. 16/2 35. Oxford: Oxford University Press, 2007.

Prechal, S. *Directives in EC Law.* 2nd ed. Oxford: Oxford University Press, 2005.

Prechal, S. 'Does Direct Effect Still Matter?' (2000) CML Rev., 1047–1069.

Prinssen, J.M. and A.A.M. Schrauwen. *Direct Effect: Rethinking a Classic of EC Legal Doctrine* (The Hogendorp Papers, 3). Groningen: Europa Law Publishing, 2002.

Richards, C. 'The Supremacy of Community Law before the French Constitutional Court'. (2006) EL Rev., 499–517.

Slaughter, A.-M., et al. *The European Court and National Courts: Doctrine and Jurisprudence.* Oxford: Hart, 1998.

Tallberg, J. *European Governance and Supranational Institutions: Making States Comply*. Routledge Advances in European Politics, 14. London: Routledge, 2003.

Timmermans, C. 'Community Directives Revisited'. (1998) YEL, 1–28.

Van Gerven, W. 'Bridging the Unbridgeable Community and National Tort Laws after Francovich and Brasserie'. (1996) ICLQ, 507–544.

Van Gerven, W. 'Of Rights, Remedies and Procedures'. (2000) CML Rev., 501–536.

Vervaele, J.A.E. (ed.). *Administrative Law Application and Enforcement of Community Law in the Netherlands*. Deventer: Kluwer Law and Taxation Publishers, 1994.

Vervaele, J.A.E. (ed.). *Compliance and Enforcement of European Community Law*. European Monographs, 20. The Hague: Kluwer Law International, 1999.

Chapter VIII

The Functioning of the Internal Market: The Freedoms

K.J.M. Mortelmans

1   INTRODUCTION

The establishment and functioning of the internal market are fundamentally important for the achievement of the objectives of the European Community (EC) Treaty, as is apparent from the initial provisions of the EC Treaty itself.[1] If and when the Treaty of Lisbon enters into force, Article 3 of the new version of the Treaty on European Union (TEU) will set out the aims of the European Union and mention the means by which it will pursue them. Paragraph 3 of that Article provides that the Union 'shall establish an internal market'. The Protocol on the Internal Market and Competition, annexed to the TEU and to the Treaty on the Functioning of the European Union (TFEU), includes the consideration 'that

---

1. As to the internal market, see Arts. 3(1)(c) and 14 and 15 EC; as to the common market, see Arts. 2 and 7 EC. See T. Schubert, *Der Gemeinsame Markt als Rechtsbegriff: die allgemeine Wirtschaftsfreiheit des EG-Vertrages* (Munich, 1999); P. Craig, 'The Evolution of the Single Market', in C. Barnard and J. Scott (eds), *The Law of the Single European Market. Unpacking the Premises* (Oxford, 2002), 1; L. Lohkamp, *Die rechtliche Beteutung der Marktwirtschaft im Europäischen Gemeinschaftsvertrag: zur juristischen Reichweite des marktwirtschaftlichen Verfassungsprinzips gegenüber wirtschaftspolitischen Gestaltsakten von Mitgliedstaaten und Gemeinschaft* (Berlin, 2003); C. Barnard, *The Substantive Law of the EU: The Four Freedoms*, 2nd ed. (Oxford, 2007).

P.J.G. Kapteyn, A.M. McDonnell, K.J.M. Mortelmans and C.W.A. Timmermans (eds),
The Law of the European Union and the European Communities, pp. 575–784.
©2008 Kluwer Law International BV, The Netherlands.

the internal market as set out in Article 3 of the Treaty on European Union [post-Lisbon] includes a system ensuring that competition is not distorted'. The wording of this Protocol is careless. Article 3(3) TEU (Lisbon) does not include any description of the internal market. This description is included in the current Article 2 TEU – which is what Article 3 TEU (Lisbon) intends to replace. The phrase 'an area without internal frontiers', which in Article 2 TEU constitutes a description of the internal market, is taken up in Article 3(2) TEU (Lisbon) in order to describe the area of freedom, security and justice. Such carelessness is the result of last minute work. The Protocol was added as a kind of weakening of the words 'social market economy', introduced in Article 3(3) TEU (Lisbon) and which should take the place of the current Article 3(1)(g) EC, which provides that the Community includes 'a system ensuring that competition in the internal market is not distorted'.[2]

In Chapter III, above, the establishment of the internal market was seen in the context of the substantive principles; this chapter examines the phenomenon itself, looking at both its establishment and its functioning.

In German literature – and recently, to some extent, in English-language literature[3] – a distinction is made between Community fundamental rights and Community fundamental freedoms.[4] The distinction is important in an increasing number of cases where there is a link between free movement and human rights, such as freedom of expression[5] or family life.[6]

Article 14 EC describes the internal market as 'an area without internal frontiers in which the free movement of goods, persons, services and capital is ensured in accordance with the provisions of this Treaty'.[7] The Treaty provisions and case law dealing with these freedoms are systematically discussed in the sections that follow. The emphasis is on the case law of the Court of Justice. In countless judgments, the Court has interpreted and refined its interpretation of these central provisions of the Treaty. In handing down judgments, the Court is of course

---

2. See <www.publications.parliament.uk/pa/cm200708/cmhansrd/cm080206/debtext/80206-0010.htm>. See also A. Riley, 'The EU Reform Treaty & the Competition Protocol: Undermining EC Competition Law', *CEPS Policy Brief* No. 142, Sep. 2007.
3. P. Oliver and W.-H. Roth, 'The Internal Market and the Four Freedoms' (2004) CML Rev., 407–441.
4. *Gemeinschaftsgrundrechte* and *Grundfreiheiten*: see J. Gebauer, *Die Grundfreiheiten des EG-Vertrages als Gemeinschafsgrundrechte* (Berlin, 2004); A. Brigola, *Das System der EG-Grundfreiheiten: vom Diskriminierungsverbot zum spezifischen Beschränkungsverbot* (Munich, 2004); T. Körber, *Grundfreiheiten und Privatrecht* (Tübingen, 2004).
5. See, e.g., Case C-112/00, *Eugen Schmidberger, Internationale Transporte und Planzüge v. Republik Österreich*.
6. See, e.g., Case C-60/00, *Mary Carpenter v. Secretary of State for the Home Department*.
7. The terms internal market and common market are both used in the EC Treaty, with related but distinct meanings: see Ch. III, section 4.2 *supra*. The term 'single market' is not used in the EC Treaty, but does occur in the literature. See K. Mortelmans, 'The Common Market, the Internal Market and the Single Market: What's in a Market?' (1998) CML Rev., 101–136. If and when the Lisbon Treaty enters into force, the term 'common market' will be replaced throughout the EC Treaty (then renamed the TFEU) by the term 'internal market', cf. Art. 2(2)(g) Lisbon Treaty.

primarily concerned with solving legal disputes, and not with drafting a text book;[8] nevertheless, certain clear lines in the approach of the Court can be traced.[9] Some of these lines of approach have shifted in recent years, or have become less clear[10] (see section 1.6 below). This means that a number of specific judgments by the Court do not correspond to the systematic treatment aimed at in this chapter. Partly for that reason, the footnotes in this chapter do not merely mention one or two judgments of the Court, as examples, but aim to give an extensive overview of the case law on the subject in question. This overview gives the reader the chance, on the one hand, to form an opinion of the case law of the Court together with its inconsistencies, and on the other to pick out one or more relevant cases from the veritable ocean of decisions.

The realization of the internal market does not only come about by means of case law; the Community legislature also has an important task – as is revealed by Article 14 EC. It is impossible within the confines of this work to mention all the directives and regulations which are directed at the functioning of the internal market, let alone discuss them individually. The main lines of this harmonizing process are described, however. In the other chapters of this book, dealing with the sectoral and flanking policies, the most important internal market instruments will also be discussed in some more detail. Information on harmonization techniques and the position of harmonization within general EC policy is to be found in Chapters V and III respectively.

If the Lisbon Treaty enters into force, Article 4(2) TFEU provides that the Union and the Member States have shared competence in the area of the internal market.

The area without internal frontiers is established by means of the working of a number of principles – the principle of freedom, and the principle of mutual recognition – and through harmonized or uniform rules.[11] In these introductory remarks, we deal briefly with these points

---

8. R.H. Lauwaars and C.W.A. Timmermans, *Europees Gemeenschapsrecht in kort bestek*, 6th ed. (Groningen, 2003), 198.

9. T. Kingreen, *Die Struktur der Grundfreiheiten des Europäischen Gemeinschaftsrechts* (Berlin, 1999); H.D. Jarass, 'A Unified Approach to the Fundamental Freedoms', in M. Andenas and W.-H. Roth (eds), *Services and Free Movement in EU Law* (Oxford, 2002), 141. The opinions of the Court's advocates general are very useful for gaining insight into the main lines of the case law. They set out the case law, and sometimes suggest (more or less radical) new lines of analysis, e.g., A.G. van Gerven in Case 145/88, *Torfaen Borough Council v. B & Q plc*; sometimes criticizing the Court's previous stance, see e.g., A.G. Jacobs in Case C-412/93, *Société d'Importation Edouard Leclerc-Siplec v. TF1 Publicité SA and M6 Publicité SA*. See on this K. Mortelmans, 'The Court under the Influence of Its Advocates General: An Analysis of the Case Law on the Functioning of the Internal Market,' (2005) YEL, (Oxford, 2006), 127–172.

10. For that reason, the section concerning 'the concept of freedom' from the previous edition of this book has been dropped in this edition. This distinction does not fit the current case law of the Court of Justice.

11. For the economic-policy background to these techniques, see J. Pelkmans, 'The Institutional Economics of European Integration', in M. Cappelletti, M. Seccombe and J. Weiler (eds), *Integration through Law*, Vol. 1, Book 1 (Berlin, 1986), 318; W. Molle, *The Economics of European Integration*, 14th ed. (Ashgate, 2001); J. Pelkmans, *European Integration. Methods*

1.1   THE REALIZATION OF THE INTERNAL MARKET: PROHIBITIONS
             AND EXCEPTIONS

1.1.2   The Five Freedoms

Article 3(1)(c) and Article 14 EC mention four freedoms (goods, persons, services, capital). In addition to these four, there is also – as appears from Article 56 EC – the free movement of payments, which forms a fifth freedom included in the EC Treaty in order to realize the internal market in actual fact.

During the transitional period of the common market (1958–1969), four of the freedoms (goods, persons, services and payments) were realized on the basis of the relevant procedural provisions in the Treaty and through directly effective prohibitions on the introduction of new restrictions on these freedoms, and the instruction to abolish existing restrictions (negative integration).[12] The free movement of capital was phrased in different terms in the European Economic Community (EEC) Treaty (see old Art. 67) until the amendments made by the Treaty of Maastricht brought it into line with the other freedoms. The free movement of persons resulted from on the one hand the free movement of workers (employees) and, on the other, the freedom to exercise a trade or profession. The Treaty of Maastricht introduced into the EC Treaty (Art. 17 EC) the concept of citizenship of the Union. This extension effected by the Treaty means that it is no longer only economically active persons that come within the scope of the EC Treaty, but as a rule all citizens of the Union now have the right to reside freely in the territory of another Member State, and to travel within the Community.[13] Title IV of the EC Treaty, introduced by the Treaty of Amsterdam, contains rules concerning the movement of persons from third countries.

1.1.3   The Exceptions to Free Movement

There are a number of exceptions to the Treaty provisions on the five freedoms; these can be conveniently grouped in two types.[14] The first group comprises economic safeguard clauses. The amendments made by the Treaty of Maastricht revised this group in accordance with the current state of integration. These concern provisions dealing with economic policy (Art. 100 EC), dealt with in

---

and *Economic Analysis* (Harlow, 1997); S. Weatherill, 'Pre-Emption, Harmonisation and the Distribution of Competence to Regulate the Internal Market', in C. Barnard and J. Scott (eds), *The Law of the Single European Market: Un-packing the Premises* (Oxford, 2002), 4; C. Barnard, *The Substantive Law of the EU: The Four Freedoms*, 2nd. ed. (Oxford, 2007).

12.   The Treaty articles which concerned this process, e.g., Art. 7 EC, originally Art. 8 EEC, were repealed by the Treaty of Amsterdam.

13.   Certain groups of persons not included in the concept of workers or professionals had already achieved such freedom to a degree through Community legislation; see further section 4 *infra*.

14.   A third group, which concerned the transitional period of the common market, such as Arts. 26 and 226 EEC, has now been repealed. See Case C-212/96, *Paul Chevassus-Marche v. Conseil régional de la Réunion.*

Chapter X. That chapter also examines the provision on balance of payments difficulties (Arts. 119 and 120 EC), which are temporary in nature. Article 134 EC concerning deflection of trade is dealt with in Chapter XIII on external relations. The second group comprises Articles 30, 39, 46, 55, 58, 64 and 295–297 EC.[15] The exceptions contained in these provisions, most of which lose their effect where harmonization takes place, are non-economic in nature. In addition to these two groups of general exceptions, there are a number of specific exceptions relating to undertakings with special tasks[16] or certain specific sectors.[17]

1.2   THE REALIZATION OF THE INTERNAL MARKET: POSITIVE INTEGRATION

1.2.1   Harmonization and Uniform Legislation

In a number of instances, the negative integration provisions aimed at achieving the free movement of goods[18] go hand in hand with acts adopted by the Community Institutions. The abolition of obstacles by one Member State (direct and indirect discrimination) will in many cases be insufficient to achieve an area without internal frontiers. Quality rules for goods (health requirements) and for persons (diplomas) will remain necessary in a number of instances. In many cases, these rules differ from one Member State to another – the requirement of an alcohol percentage in *Cassis de Dijon* of 15% in France and 20% in Germany is an example.[19] Such dissimilarities between the legislation of the Member States causes distortions which need to be removed.[20] The Community Institutions are granted powers to adopt harmonization measures or uniform measures, as in the case of the Community trade mark.[21] These Community rules must conform to the provisions on free movement, although in a number of cases the Court has granted the Community legislature a margin of discretion[22] (see sections 2.4.2 and 3.2.2.

---

15. See Case C-186/01, *Alexander Dory v. Bundesrepublik Deutschland*.
16. Arts. 31 and 86(2) EC.
17. Art. 38 EC in relation to agriculture, Art. 76 EC in relation to transport.
18. Note the words 'abolition … of obstacles' in Art. 3(1)(c) EC.
19. Case 120/78, *Rewe-Zentral AG v. Bundesmonopolverwaltung für Branntwein (Cassis de Dijon)*.
20. See Art. 96 EC. As to distortions of competition, see Ch. IX. As to the difference between distortion and discrimination; see also Case 14/68, *Walt Wilhelm et al. v. Bundeskartellamt*; Case C-379/92, *Criminal proceedings against Matteo Peralta*; Case C-384/93, *Alpine Investments BV v. Minister van Financiën*; and Case C-376/98, *Germany v. Parliament and Council (Tobacco advertising I)*.
21. Reg. 40/94, O.J. 1994, L 11/1.
22. Case 37/83, *Rewe-Zentral AG v. Direktor der Landwirtschaftskammer Rheinland*; Joined Cases C-427, 429 & 436/93, *Bristol-Myers Squibb, C. H. Boehringer Sohn, Boehringer Ingelheim KG and Boehringer Ingelheim A/S, and Bayer Aktiengesellschaft and Bayer Danmark A/S v. Paranova A/S*. See K.J.M. Mortelmans, 'The Relationship between the Treaty Rules and Community Measures for the Establishment and Functioning of the Internal Market: Towards a Concordance Rule' (2002), CML Rev., 1303–1346.

below). These rules contain, in a number of cases, exceptions which are substantively equivalent to those of the Treaty. Here too, these exceptions in secondary law must match the exceptions in primary law, as interpreted by the Court of Justice (see section 3.3.1 below).

Many proposals for Community measures failed to be adopted prior to the coming into force of the Single European Act (SEA) on 1 July 1987 because of the requirement of unanimity in Article 94 EC (then Art. 100 EEC). To cope with this problem, the new Article 95 EC permitted harmonization measures for the completion of the internal market to be adopted by qualified majority. By the target date of the end of 1992, most of the 300 proposals presented by the Commission as part of its internal market programme[23] had been approved by the Council.[24] As a result of this legislative operation, a number of exceptions may no longer be relied upon, or relied upon only in very limited circumstances.[25] In many cases, though, harmonization is still incomplete, so that primary Community law (free movement principle and the recognized exceptions) may still be invoked in the non-harmonized areas.[26] In a number of judgments, the Court has considered the difference between exhaustive, full and minimum harmonization.[27]

In a number of cases concerning directives, adopted by the Community legislature, on the sales and advertising of tobacco products, the Court has indicated the limits of the application of Article 95 EC. Article 95 EC does not confer on the Community legislature an exclusive competence to regulate the economic activities in the internal market. This provision is intended to improve the conditions for the establishment and functioning of the internal market. This provisions may be used as a legal basis to prevent future obstacles, but the existence of those obstacles must be likely and the measure in question must actually aim to prevent those obstacles.[28]

---

23. *Completing the Internal Market* (COM(85)310 final), also called the White Paper.
24. See Commission Recommendation of 12 Jul. 2004 on the transposition into national law of directives affecting the internal market, O.J. 2005, L 98/47.
25. Cf. Art. 95 EC. See Case 5/77, *Carlo Tedeschi v. Denkavit Commerciale*. Constant case law, see Case C-222/91, *Ministero delle Finanze and Ministero della Sanità v. Philip Morris Belgium SA and others*.
26. E.g., Case 72/83, *Campus Oil Ltd et al. v. Minister for Industry and Energy et al.*
27. See, e.g., Case C-1/96, *The Queen v. Minister of Agriculture, Fisheries and Food, ex parte Compassion in World Farming Ltd* On this, see Y. Bock, *Rechtsangleichung und Reguliering im Binnenmarkt: zum Umfang der allgemeinen Binnenmarktkompetenz* (Baden-Baden, 2005); S. Weatherill, 'Why Harmonise?' In T. Tridimas and P. Nebbia (eds), *European Union Law for the Twenty-First Century: Rethinking the New Legal Order*, Vol. 2, *Internal Market and Free Movement. Community Policies* (Oxford, 2004), 11. See further Ch. V.
28. Case C-376/98, *Germany v. Parliament and Council (Tobacco advertising I); Case C-491/01, The Queen v. Secretary of State for Health ex parte British American Tobacco (Investments) Ltd and Imperial Tobacco Ltd;* Case C-434/02, *Arnold André v. Landrat des Kreises Herford;* Case C-210/03, *Swedish Match AB, Swedish Match UK Ltd v. Secretary of State for Health;* Joined Cases C-154 & 155/04, *The Queen, on application of Alliance for Natural Health (C-154/04) and Nutri-Link Ltd v. Secretary of State for Health, and the Queen, on application of National Association of Health Stores (C-155/04) and Health Food Manufacturers Ltd v. Secretary of State for Health and National Assembly for Wales.*

1.2.2   **The Mutual Recognition Principle**

The widespread failures in the years 1970–1986 of the attempts to adopt Community measures were partially compensated by the case law of the Court of Justice on the mutual recognition of national rules, in which the celebrated judgment in *Cassis de Dijon* is something of a landmark.[29] In this case, the Court introduced a number of mandatory requirements of general interest (so-called rule-of-reason exceptions) as a counterbalance to an over-broad definition of Article 28 EC (see section 3.3.3 below).

This judgment was also the basis for the rule of mutual recognition (or mutual acceptance).[30] This rule means that Member State A must admit goods or services coming from Member State B to its territory, if those goods or services have been lawfully produced and marketed in Member State B, according to the rules applicable in Member State B.[31] Member State A may hinder the free movement of such goods only on the grounds of overriding public interest requirements, for instance in relation to consumer protection. In this way, free movement may be achieved without the need for harmonization. The application of this home state (or state of origin) principle[32] leads to competition between legal systems.[33]

In the application of the mutual recognition principle, the rules on conflict of laws from international private law play an important role. In sensitive areas, such as health protection and safety, the Community still tends to adopt harmonization

---

29. Case 120/78, *Cassis de Dijon*. A. Mattera, 'L'article 30 du traité CEE, la jurisprudence "Cassis de Dijon" et le principe de la reconnaissance mutuelle: instruments au service d'une Communauté plus respectueuse des diversités nationales' (1992), *RMC*, 13–71. The mutual recognition principle was also formulated a month before the judgment in *Cassis* in Joined Cases 110 & 111/78, *Ministère public and 'Chambre syndicale des agents artistiques et impresarii de Belgique' ASBL v. Willy van Wesemael and others*. This approach, best known from *Cassis de Dijon*, was in fact also used in Case 8/74, *Procureur du Roi v. Benoît and Gustave Dassonville*. See also R. Barents 'New Developments in Measures Having Equivalent Effect' (1981) CML Rev., 296; L. Gormley, 'Cassis de Dijon and the Communication from the Commission' (1981) EL Rev., 454.

30. V. Hatzopoulos, *Le principe communautaire d'équivalence et de reconnaissance mutuelle dans la libre prestation de services* (Brussels, 1999); N. Bernard, 'Flexibility in the European Single Market', in C. Barnard and J. Scott (eds), *The Law of the Single European Market: Unpacking the Premises* (Oxford, 2002), 101; K. Armstrong, 'Mutual Recognition', in C. Barnard and J. Scott (eds), *The Law of the Single European Market: Unpacking the Premises* (Oxford, 2002), 225.

31. For the concepts 'lawfully produced and marketed', see B. O'Connor, 'The Free Movement of Foodstuffs in EC Law' (1993), *EFLR*, 177. Cf. Case 59/82, *Schutzverband gegen Unwesen in der Wirtschaft v. Weinvertriebs*; Case C-296/00, *Prefetto Provincia di Cuneo v. Silvano Carbone*.

32. See Roth, 'Wettbewerb der Mitgliedstaaten oder Wettbewerb der Hersteller? Plädoyer für eine Neubestimmung des Art. 34 EGV' (1995) *ZHR, 78* at 85 and 91.

33. See Koopmans, 'Concurrentie tussen rechtsstelsels' (1992) SEW, 446; Reich, 'Competition between Legal Orders: A New Paradigm of EC Law?' (1992) CML Rev., 861; R. Van den Bergh, 'Towards an Institutional Legal Framework for Regulatory Competition in Europe' (2000) *Kyklos*, 435; S. Weatherill, 'Pre-emption, Harmonisation and the Distribution of Competence to Regulate the Internal Market', in C. Barnard and J. Scott (eds), *The Law of the Single European Market: Unpacking the Premises* (Oxford, 2002), 41.

measures dealing with essential requirements.[34] In these areas, there is a danger that too broad an interpretation of the mutual recognition principle would cause a reduction in national standards.[35] In its internal market programme, the Commission consciously presented the mutual recognition principle as a new strategy.[36] Depending on the subject-matter involved, the internal market is achieved through this rule of mutual recognition or through harmonized or uniform rules.[37] The Commission made an evaluation of this technique in a Communication of 15 June 1999.[38] In this document, it indicates the problems and suggests some solutions – such as a clearer policy from the Commission, better guidance of application by national authorities and increasing awareness on the part of market operators of the importance of this technique.[39] In its 'Internal Market Strategy Priorities 2003–2006', the Commission elaborated its plans further.[40] And in an interpretative communication on facilitating the access of products to the markets of other Member States[41] the Commission paid attention to the practical application of mutual recognition.

1.2.3   Notification of Information on National Rules (Securitel)

The technical rules which are adopted by the Member States can also lead to obstacles to trade. At the end of 1969 and again in early 1973, in a decision of the representatives of the Member States meeting in the framework of the Council (later elaborated as a Resolution of the Council),[42] the Member States declared themselves prepared to notify the Commission about national technical rules.

    In 1983, this duty to inform the Commission – essentially an application of the duty of loyal cooperation in Article 10 EC – was laid down in Directive 83/189.[43] This Directive has been amended frequently, was recently declared applicable to services in the information economy, and was replaced by Directive 98/34.[44]

---

34. Cf. the White Paper COM(85)310 final, para. 39.
35. This view surfaced principally in the German literature. See E. Steindorff, 'Probleme des Art. 30 EWG-Vertrag' (1984) *ZHR*, 338–355; J. Sedemund, '"Cassis de Dijon" und das neue Harmonisierungskonzept der Kommission', in J. Schwarze (Hrsg.), *Der Gemeinsame Markt Bestand und Zukunft in wirtschaftsrechtlicher Perspektive* (Baden-Baden, 1987), 37. Cf. Case C-320/93, *Lucien Ortscheit v. Eurim-Pharm Arzneimittel.*
36. COM(85) 310 final, para.61. See on this R. Bieber, R. Dehousse, J. Pinder, and J.H.H. Weiler (eds), *1992: One European Market* (Baden-Baden, 1988). See also A. Bernel, *Le principe d'équivalence ou de reconnaissance mutuelle en droit communautaire* (Zürich, 1996); D.Ch. Horng, 'The Principle of Mutual Recognition: The European Union's Practise and Development' (1999) *World Competition*, 135.
37. In respect of *Cassis de Dijon*, Community legislation now governs the matter; see Reg. 1576/89, O.J. 1989, L 160/1, most recently amended by Reg. 3378/94, O.J. 1994, L 366/1.
38. COM(99)299 final.
39. See also Resolution of the Council of 28 Oct. 1999, O.J. 1999, C 141/1.
40. COM(2003)238 final.
41. O.J. 2003, C 265/2.
42. See O.J. 1969, C 76/9 and O.J. 1973, C 9/3.
43. O.J. 1983, L 109/8.
44. O.J. 1998, L 204/37. See Case C-89/04, *Mediakabel BV v. Commissariaat voor de Media.*

The aim of the Directive is to provide the Commission with information in the area of technical standards and regulations. If the Commission considers it necessary, it may then propose a directive in order to remove the disparities in national legislation which it has found. The sanction for failure to comply with the obligation to notify the Commission – sometimes called the '*Securitel* defence'[45] – led to some commotion in a number of Member States (especially the Netherlands), but this later calmed down.[46]

1.3   GROWING PAINS AFFECTING THE INTERNAL MARKET

While 1992 was undoubtedly an important milestone in the history of the Community (see Art. 14(1) EC), the internal market was not completed by 31 December 1992, either in law or in fact.[47] The Court of Justice ruled, in the area of free movement of persons, that in the absence of the required measures of harmonization, Article 14 EC does not have direct effect.[48] Partly as a result of this, the Court took on a much less prominent role in relation to the realization of the internal market, than it did in relation to the realization of the common market.[49] In the realization of the internal market, it is the Community legislature which takes a central role. Nevertheless, in recent years there have been judgments – concerning free movement of persons and citizenship – in which the Court has taken an active role in new directions.[50] This is dealt with in section 4 below.

---

45. See Case C-194/94, *CIA Security International SA v. Signalson SA and Securitel SPRL*; Case C-226/97, *Criminal proceedings against Johannes Martinus Lemmens*; Joined Cases C-425-427/97, *Criminal proceedings against Adrianus Albers (C-425/97), Martinus van den Berkmortel (C-426/97) and Leon Nuchelmans (C-427/97)*; Case C-246/98, *Berendse-Koenen M.G. en Berendse H.D. Maatschap*; Case C-314/98, *Snellers Auto's BV v. Algemeen Directeur van de Dienst Wegverkeer*; Case C-443/98, *Unilever Italia SpA v. Central Food SpA*; Case C-55/99, *Commission v. France;* Case C-159/00, *Sapod Audic v. Eco-Emballages SA*; Case C-267/03, *Lars Erik Staffan Lindberg*.

46. See on this S. Weatherill, 'A Case Study in Judicial Activism in the 1990s: The Status before National Courts of Measures Wrongfully Un-notified to the Commission', in *Liber Amicorum in Honour of Lord Slynn of Hadley* (The Hague, 2000), 481.

47. See T. Koopmans, *De paradox van 1992* (1989) RMT, 472; E. Steindorff, *Unvollkommener Binnenmarkt* (1994) ZHR, 149; S. Weatherill, 'The Common Market: Mission Accomplished?', in V. Heiskanen and K. Kulovesi (eds), *Function and Future of European Law* (Helsinki, 1999), 33.

48. Case C-297/92, *Istituto Nazionale della Previdenza Sociale v. Corradina Baglieri*; Case C-378/97, *Criminal proceedings against Florus Ariël Wijsenbeek*.

49. See Case 2/74, *Jean Reyners v. Belgium*. In that judgment, the expiry of the transitional period for the common market was an essential element allowing the Court to recognize the direct effect of Art. 43 EC. For an explanation of the terms common market and internal market, see Ch. III.

50. Case C-224/98, *Marie-Nathalie D'Hoop v. Office national de l'emploi*; Case C-413/99, *Baumbast and R v. Secretary of State for the Home Department*; Case C-60/00, *Carpenter*; Case C-109/01, *Secretary of State for the Home Department v. Hacene Akrich* and Case C-200/02, *Kunqian Catherine Zhu and Man Lavette Chen v. Secretary of State for the Home Department*. But see Case C-1/05, *Jia v. Migrationverket*.

In 1997, the Commission presented an action plan for the Internal Market to the European Council, in which it announced that it would propose new measures. This plan was accepted by the European Council on 17 June 1997.[51] A new instrument in this context was Council Regulation 2692/98 on the functioning of the internal market in relation to the free movement of goods among the Member States.[52] This Regulation confers on the Commission a number of powers for taking action against Member States which do not take measures, or do not take sufficiently effective measures, against market operators who hinder the free movement of goods, by road blocks and similar actions.[53]

The Commission publishes a great deal of information on the degree of integration achieved (on approved and implemented directives) and also on barriers to trade erected by Member States, or not removed by them.[54] In a recommendation of 7 December 2001, the Commission proposed a network (SOLVIT) for solving internal market-related problems, which is now in operation.[55]

In its Interim report to the 2007 Spring European Council, the European Commission gave its vision for A Single Market for Citizens in the 21st Century: the single market for consumers and citizens, a single market for an integrated economy, a single market for a knowledge society and a single market for a sustainable Europe, open to the world.[56] The Presidency Conclusions of the Brussels European Council(13/14 March 2008) stated that the Single Market remains a crucial driver for enhancing living standards of European citizens and Europe's competitiveness in the globalized economy. In order to further improve the functioning of the Single Market, the following measures and actions need to be taken forward as immediate priorities:

- Ensure an effective follow-up to the Commission's Single Market Review on a yearly basis, with a focus on actions needed to boost growth and jobs by removing remaining barriers to the four freedoms of the treaty, including, where appropriate, through harmonization as well as mutual recognition.

---

51. See on this K.J.M. Mortelmans, 'The Common Market, the Internal Market and the Single Market: What's in a Market' (1998) CML Rev., 101; C. Barnard and J. Scott (eds), *The Law of the Single European Market: Unpacking the Premises* (Oxford, 2002).
52. O.J. 1998, L 337/8. See on this A. Mattera Ricigliano, *Un instrument d'intervention rapide pour sauvegarder l'unicité du Marché intérieur* (1999) *Revue du marché unique européen*, 9. See also Case C-265/95, *Commission v. French Republic*.
53. In a report published by the Commission at the beginning of 2001, the Commission said this instrument is not working well, COM(2001)160 final, *Agence Europe* 24 Mar. 2001. S. Weatherill, 'New Strategies for Managing the EC's Internal Market', in M.D.A. Freeman (ed.), *Current Legal Problems 2000* (Oxford, 2001).
54. A good source, as well as the internal market page on the website of the Commission, is the annual report on the application of Community law, e.g., 23rd Annual Report from the Commission on Monitoring the Application of Community Law (2005) COM(2006)416 final.
55. O.J. 2001, L 331/79.
56. See COM(2007)60 final, 21 Feb. 2007.

– Reinforce efforts to strengthen competition in network industries (energy, electronic communications) and to adopt the adequate regulatory frameworks. In this context, work on interconnections must be pursued and accelerated.

These policy documents reveal that the internal market is nearly completed (at least among the 15 Member States).[57] A few growing pains deserve special treatment.[58]

1.3.1 Internal Situation

The prohibitions (on obstacles to free movement) and exceptions (to free movement) concern restrictions imposed on trans-border economic activities: for instance, *Cassis de Dijon* from France that may not be marketed in Germany as *Cassis de Dijon*. If all the relevant aspects of an economic activity occur within one Member State (for instance, Dutch regulations concerning prices for bread baked and sold in the Netherlands by Dutch bakers) and there are no relevant provisions of Community secondary law, then according to the Court we are confronted with an 'internal situation', and the prohibitions of Articles 39, 43 and 49 cannot be relied upon.[59] In the discussion of the various Treaty provisions imposing prohibitions, the application of the internal situation doctrine to the various freedoms will be examined.

In *Guimont*[60] (free movement of goods) and *Reisch*[61] (free movement of capital), the Court gave an answer to the preliminary questions put to it, even though it was evident from the file that all the relevant aspects were situated within one Member State. The Court wanted to assist the national court, because it could

---

57. The Commission published early in 2003 a document, entitled 'The Internal Market: Ten Years without Frontiers'; see SEC(2002)1417. See also *Single Market News* (2003) 10th Anniversary Special, European Commission. On the possible liability of the Community for non-completion of the internal market, see Case T-113/96, *Dubois*.

58. See D. O'Keeffe and A.F. Bavasso, 'Four Freedoms, One Market and National Competence: In Search of a Dividing Line', in *Liber Amicorum in Honour of Lord Slynn of Hadley* (The Hague, 2000), 541; C. Barnard and J. Scott (eds), *The Law of the Single European Market: Unpacking the Premises* (Oxford, 2002).

59. See, e.g., Case 52/79, *Procureur du Roi v. Marc J.V.C. Debauve and others*; Case C-41/90, *Klaus Höfner and Fritz Elser v. Macrotron*; Case C-60/91, *Criminal proceedings against José António Batista Morais*; Case C-112/91, *Hans Werner v. Finanzamt Aachen-Innenstadt*; Case C-448/98, *Criminal proceedings against Jean-Pierre Guimont*. A variant is that another country is involved, but that it is a third country, e.g., Joined Cases C-64 & 65/96, *Land Nordrhein-Westfalen v. Kari Uecker and Vera Jacquet v. Land Nordrhein-Westfalen*. See Ch. Hammerl, *Inländerdiskriminierung* (Berlin, 1997); H. Tagaras, *Règles communautaires de libre circulation, discriminations à rebours et situations dites purement internes*, in *Mélanges en hommage à Michel Waelbroeck* (Brussels, 1999), 1499; P. Oliver and W.-H. Roth, 'The Internal Market and the Four Freedoms', (2004) CML Rev., 407–441, 429.

60. Case C-448/98, *Guimont*.

61. Joined Cases C-515, 519–524 & 526–540/99, *Hans Reisch et al. v. Bürgermeister der Landeshauptstadt Salzburg et al. and Anton Lassacher et al. v. Grundverkehrsbeauftragter des Landes Salzburg et al.*; Case C-300/01, *Doris Salzmann*.

not be excluded that the relevant national legislation might also be applicable to intra-Community (cross-border) situations.

Cases such as *Pistre*, *Kos* and *Lancry*,[62] concerning tariffs, are no longer based on country borders, but declare the prohibitions to apply to regional or similar barriers.[63] In *Pistre*, the Court ruled that although the national rule in fact had no link with the import of goods[64] this could not exclude the applicability of Article 28 EC: there was an obstacle to trade because the French regulations could also apply to products from other Member States.[65] In a few cases concerning Article 25 EC, the Court ruled that regional rules come within the scope of application of this prohibition.[66] The Court's judgment in *Carbonati Apuani* includes a general consideration which relates to non-tariff barriers, even though the case concerned tariff barriers.[67] In the future, the Court will be increasingly confronted with the question of the *internal* borders of the internal market.[68] This is apparent from a number of cases concerning public procurement.[69] This topic will be dealt with further in the context of the various freedoms.

1.3.2   Reverse Discrimination

In cases concerning internal situations, a person, service or product may well suffer from reverse discrimination. This means that a product, service or person from Member State A is discriminated against by that same Member State A compared with a product, service or person from Member State B, C etc. The Court has consistently found[70] that Community law is not applicable in cases where a Member State – in a field in which no common rules apply and there is no harmonization of legislation – treats national products or its own citizens less favourably than

---

62. Joined Cases C-321-324/94, *Criminal proceedings against Jacques Pistre, Michèle Barthes, Yves Milhau and Didier Oberti*; Joined Cases C-485 & 486/93, *Maria Simitzi v. Dimos Kos*; Joined Cases C-363 & 407–411/93, *René Lancry SA v. Direction Générale des Douanes, and Société Dindar Confort et al. v. Conseil Régional de la Réunion et al.*

63. M.M. Slotboom, 'L'application du Traité CE au commerce intra-étatique? Le cas de l'octroi de mer' (1996) CDE, 9.

64. This was sufficient reason for the French Government, the European Commission and the Advocate General to consider the case to concern an 'internal situation'.

65. Joined Cases C-321-324/94, *Pistre et al.* See also Case C-448/98, *Guimont*.

66. Joined Cases C-363 & 407–411/93, *Lancry et al.*; Joined Cases C-485 & 486/93, *Simitzi v. Kos*; Case C-212/96, *Chevassus*.

67. Case C-72/03, *Carbonati Apuani Srl v. Comune di Carrara*. See also Case C-441/04, *A-Punkt Schmuckhandel v. Schmidt* and Case C-293/02, *Jersey Produce Marketing Organisation v. States of Jersey et al.*

68. See the general remarks by A.G. Geelhoed in Joined Cases C- 515/99 etc., *Reisch et al.* See also Case C-293/02, *Jersey Produce Marketing Organisation Ltd v. States of Jersey et al.*

69. Case C-231/03, *Consorzio Aziende Metano (Coname) v. Comune di Cingia de' Botti* and Case C-525/03, *Commission v. Italy.*

70. See, e.g., Case 86/78, *SA des Grandes Distilleries Peureux v. Directeur des Services Fiscaux de la Haute Saone et du Territoire du Belfort*; Joined Cases 35 & 36/82, *Elestina Esselina Christina Morson v. State of the Netherlands et al., and Sweradjie Jhanjan v. State of the Netherlands*; Case 355/85, *Mr Driancourt v. Michel Cognet*; Case 308/86, *Ministère public v. R. Lambert.*

imported products or persons who make use of their rights of free movement.[71] This subject will be dealt with further in relation to the various freedoms.

1.3.3 Re-importation and Strategic Migration

A person, product or service in Member State A may benefit from the rules on free movement if activities are performed in Member State B or if the product was in circulation in Member State B. If a Belgian national exercises his or her right of free movement by, say, exercising his profession in France, and later wishes to exercise that profession in Belgium, he or she is a beneficiary of Community rights. This is not an internal situation and he or she may exercise his or her profession in Belgium under the same conditions as a Frenchman who wishes to exercise that profession in Belgium.[72] This case law has given rise to the application of re-importation constructions. In many cases a product, person or service may return to its home Member State after a stay in another Member State.

1.3.4 Abuse of Law

Sometimes, the purpose of the operation described in the previous paragraph is to escape stricter national rules on matters such as minimum prices or establishment requirements by using Articles 28, 43 or 49 EC. The Court will not permit these provisions to be relied upon if it appears from objective circumstances that the goods or services were exported simply in order to be re-imported and thereby to escape a legal requirement with which they would otherwise have had to comply.[73] In that case, a Member State is entitled to take measures designed to prevent certain of its nationals from attempting, under cover of the rights created by the Treaty, improperly to circumvent their national legislation or to prevent individuals from improperly or fraudulently taking advantage of provisions of Community law.[74] The *Centros* case, from which the preceding passage is taken, contains a reference to earlier case law, which illustrates the fact this phenomenon has been manifest in

---

71. See further D.M.W. Pickup, 'Reverse Discrimination and Freedom of Movement for Workers' (1986) CML Rev., 135–156; A. Epiney, *Umgekehrte Diskriminierungen* (Keulen, 1995); P. Oliver, 'Some Further Reflections on the Scope of Articles 28–30 (ex 30–36) EC' (1999) CML Rev., 783; N. Nic Shuibhne, 'Free Movement of Persons and the Wholly Internal Rule: Time to Move On?' 39 CML Rev., 731–771; P. Oliver and S. Enchelmaier, 'Free Movement of Goods: Recent Developments in the Case Law' (2007) CML Rev., 649–704. This point is also at issue in the relations between the EC and global organizations; see W. Weiss, 'Gibt es eine EU-Inländerdiskriminierung?: zur Kollision von Gemeinschaftsrecht mit Welthandelsrecht und Assoziationsrecht' (1999) EuR, 499.
72. Case 115/78, *J. Knoors v. Staatssecretaris van Economische Zaken.*
73. Case 229/83, *Association des Centres distributeurs Édouard Leclerc et al. v. Sàrl 'Au blé vert' et al.*; Case C-370/90, *The Queen v. Immigration Appeal Tribunal et Surinder Singh, ex parte Secretary of State for Home Department*, and Case C-23/93, *TV 10 SA v. Commissariaat voor de Media.*
74. Case C-212/97, *Centros Ltd v. Erhvervs- og Selskabsstyrelsen.*

a wide number of policy areas.[75] There is an obvious tension between legitimately profiting from the competition between national legal orders, and abuse of this. A number of judgments on transfer of a company's seat reveal how restrictively the Court applies the concept of abuse of law, and what a commotion this entails[76] (see section 6.5.1 below).

1.4   TYPES OF BARRIERS TO FREE MOVEMENT

The obstacles caused by actions of the Member States are of various types: those discussed in this chapter are tariff and non-tariff barriers and fiscal barriers.[77] The obstacles examined here are dealt with in various places in the EC Treaty. In general there is a stricter system for tariff barriers (Arts. 23–27 EC) and non-tariff barriers (Arts. 28–31 EC) than there is for fiscal barriers (Arts. 90–93 EC): the first two types of barriers *must* be removed, save where an exception may be relied upon; but fiscal systems have to be applied in a non-discriminatory manner.

These various approaches (tariff or non-tariff, import or export) work through into the case law of the Court of Justice. Let us take an example: if cattle are subject to veterinary checks and a fee is charged for the inspection, the inspection and the fee fall within the ambit of different provisions of the Treaty. Veterinary inspections in relation to export are considered under Article 29 EC; inspections on importation are assessed under Article 28 EC, and the fee in both cases is examined under Article 25 EC, or possibly Article 90 EC. An inspection fee cannot be justified on the basis of an exception which justifies the inspection itself, although if both result from Community measures (as opposed to unilateral national measures) they will both be governed in the first instance by those Community measures.[78]

The barriers are, as we indicated above, elaborated in the Treaty itself for trade in goods. For the other freedoms, the system is not explicitly elaborated.

---

75. A. Kjellgren, 'On the Borders of Abuse: The Jurisprudence of the European Court of Justice on Circumvention, Fraud and Abuses of Community Law', in M. Andenas and W.-H. Roth (eds), *Services and Free Movement in EU Law* (Oxford, 2002), 245; K. Ottersbach, *Rechtsmißbrauch bei den Grundfreiheiten des europäischen Binnenmarktes* (Baden-Baden, 2001).

76. Case C-212/97, *Centros*; Case C-208/00, *Überseering BV v. Nordic Construction Company Baumanagement (NCC)*. See also Case C-109/01, *Akrich*.

77. For a systematic analysis and a comparison between EC and GATT law, see J. Tumlir, 'GATT-Regeln und Gemeinschaftsrecht. Ein Vergleich wirtschaftlicher und rechtlicher Funktionen', in M. Hilf, F.G. Jacobs, and E.U. Petersmann (Hrsg.), *GATT und die Europäische Gemeinschaft* (Baden-Baden, 1986), 87. See also G. de Búrca, 'Unpacking the Concept of Discrimination in EC and International Trade Law', in C. Barnard and J. Scott (eds), *The Law of the Single European Market: Unpacking the Premises* (Oxford, 2002), 181; J. Scott, 'Mandatory or Imperative Requirements in the EU and the WTO', in C. Barnard and J. Scott, op. cit., note 30, 269.

78. Case 46/76, *W.J.G. Bauhuis v. The Netherlands State*.

Nevertheless, it is implicit, and is increasingly present in the case law of the Court, for instance: the link between free movement of persons and taxes (see sections 5.5 and 6.9), and fiscal measures and services (see section 7.4.1).

1.5   EXTERNAL ASPECTS OF THE INTERNAL MARKET

In the analysis of the various obstacles to free movement a distinction should be drawn between intra-Community movement and movement between a Member State and a third country.[79] The rules which apply in respect of the European Economic Area (EEA) are very similar to those applicable within the Community itself.[80] This is to some extent also true for Switzerland.[81] The Europe Agreements also contained, for some policy areas such as establishment,[82] rules which had the same content as the internal EC and the EEA rules.[83] After the accession of a number of East European countries in 2004 and 2007, similar agreements remain relevant for countries such as Russia, with whom the EC has concluded a Partnership and Cooperation Agreement.[84] The freedom of movement between the Community and other third countries is subject to different sets of rules; these depend on *inter alia* international rules (e.g., GATT/WTO).

Now that the internal market has in legal terms been achieved, and in theory controls at the internal frontiers of the Member States within the Community are no longer possible, the Community's external frontier has become of crucial importance. It is thus of major significance to indicate which persons, goods, services and capital are permitted to enter the Community's internal market and subject to what conditions. This dimension is only examined very briefly in the present chapter; more information is to be found in Chapter XIII of this book, on external relations.[85]

---

79. Cf. Art. 23 EC. M. Cremona, 'The External Dimension of the Single Market: Building (on) the Foundations', in C. Barnard and J. Scott (eds), *The Law of the Single European Market: Unpacking the Premises* (Oxford, 2002), 351.
80. See S. Norberg et al., *EEA Law: A Commentary on the EEA Agreement* (Stockholm, 1993); P. Oliver, assisted by M. Jarvis, *Free Movement of Goods in the European Community* (London, 2003), 503. See also Case C-452/01, *Margarethe Ospelt v. Schlössle Weissenberg Familienstiftung*.
81. See 'EC-Switzerland Agreements on Free Movement' (2002), O.J., L 114/6, and S. Breitenmoser, 'Sectoral Agreements between the EC and Switzerland: Contents and Context' (2003), CML Rev., 1137–1186.
82. See, e.g., Case C-268/99, *Aldona Malgorzata Jany and Others v. Staatssecretaris van Justitie*.
83. See W. Hummer, *Die räumliche Erweiterung des Binnenmarktsrechts* (2002), EuR, Beiheft 1, 75. See also Case C-30/01, *Commission v. United Kingdom*.
84. Decision 97/800, O.J. 1997, L 327/1. See Case C-265/03, *Igor Simutenkov v. Ministerio de Educación y Cultura, Real Federación Española de Fútbol*. See further Ch. XIII.
85. See also Eeckhout, *The European Internal Market and International Trade: A Legal Analysis* (Oxford, 1994).

1.6   MAIN THEMES OF THIS CHAPTER

There are a number of main themes running through this chapter, which are more or less visible at different points; it may be useful to note them here.

1.6.1   Crucial Role of the Court of Justice and the National Courts

The realization and functioning of the internal market are essentially based, in the first instance, on a number of pivotal negative integration provisions[86] and their interpretation by the Court of Justice.[87]

The majority of cases where the Court has given an interpretation of the free movement provisions are preliminary reference proceedings. The case law also gives an indication of the importance of the national courts in this area. Comparative research on judicial decisions from a number of Member States shows that the national courts in many cases, whether or not after a preliminary reference, apply the relevant Treaty provisions correctly.[88]

1.6.2   Vertical Direct Effect as a Weapon

In the course of the 1960s and 1970s, the Court indicated that the provisions prohibiting obstacles to free movement have vertical direct effect – at least as of the end of the transitional period of the common market (1 January 1970).[89] In *Wijsenbeek*,[90] the Court ruled that Article 14 EC, which concerns the entry into force of the internal market (1 January 1993), does not have the same direct effect: prior harmonization of legislation concerning visas and so on, remains necessary.[91] This line, which seemed to be clear in the 1990s has recently been abandoned in a number of cases. By means of an extensive interpretation of the concept of citizenship of the Union under Article 18 EC,[92] sometimes together with the general

---

86.   Arts. 25, 28, 39, 43, 49, 56 and 90 EC.
87.   The EFTA Court interprets the parallel provisions of the EEA Agreements. The ECJ sometimes refers to relevant case law of the EFTA Court; see Case C-192/01, *Commission v. Kingdom of Denmark*. Information on this may be found in the O.J. See P. Christiansen, 'The EFTA Court' (1997) EL Rev., 539. The CFI is only occasionally faced with such internal market provisions; see, e.g., Case T-69/89, *Radio Telefis Eireann v. Commission*; Case T-113/96, *Edouard Dubois et Fils SA v. Council and Commission*; Case T-266/97, *Vlaamse Televisie Maatschappij NV v. Commission*; Case T-313/02, *David Meca-Medina and Igor Majcen v. Commission*.
88.   M.A. Jarvis, *Application of EC Law on the Free Movement of Goods by National Courts of the Member States* (Oxford, 1998); W. Lichtenwalder, *Die Anwendung von Art. 30 EGV in der mitgliedstaatlichen Rechtsprechung* (Frankfurt am Main, 1996).
89.   E.g., Case 2/74, *Reyners*.
90.   Case C-378/97, *Wijsenbeek*.
91.   See also Case C-297/92, *Baglieri*.
92.   Cf. Case C-406/04, *De Cuyper v. Office national de l'emploi*; Case C-192/05, *K. Tas-Hagen, R.A. Tas v. Raadskamer WUBO van de Pensioen- en Uitkeringsraad* ; and more recently Case C-76/05, *Herbert Schwarz, Marga Gootjes-Schwarz v. Finanzamt Bergisch Gladbach*. See Ch. II, section 6.2 *supra*.

non-discrimination provision of Article 12 EC, and given the fact that both these provisions are directly effective, certain EU citizens who are not economically active have nevertheless been granted rights to free movement and residence, and rights linked thereto such as the right to study financing.[93] For this effect to be found, there must in general be discrimination, and not merely disparities.[94] (See further Ch. II, section 6.2. and this chapter section 4.1.1 below).

1.6.3   Horizontal Direct Effect as a Weapon?

The question whether or not the Treaty prohibitions concerning free movement have horizontal direct effect has not been absolutely decided. Cases such as *Walrave*, *Bosman*, *Deliège*, *Angonese* and *Wouters*[95] clearly indicate that this is the case with respect to free movement of workers and services where private organizations such as football associations are concerned. For the other freedoms, there is no explicit case law, and the opinions in academic literature are divided.[96] In *Sapod Audic*, the Court came to the conclusion, without any further reasoning, that Article 28 is not applicable to private agreements.[97] This point will be dealt

---

93. Cf. Case C-184/99, *Rudy Grzelczyk v. Centre public d'aide sociale d'Ottignies-Louvain-la-Neuve*, and Case C-209/03, *The Queen (on the application of Dany Bidar) v. London Borough of Ealing and Secretary of State for Education and Skills*.

94. Case C-403/03, *Egon Schempp v. Finanzamt München V*.

95. Case 36/74, *B.N.O. Walrave and L.J.N. Koch v. Association Union cycliste internationale, Koninklijke Nederlandsche Wielrenunie and Federación Española Ciclismo*; Case C-415/93, *Union royale belge des sociétés de football association ASBL v. Jean-Marc Bosman, Royal club liégeois SA v. Jean-Marc Bosman and others and Union des associations européennes de football (UEFA) v. Jean-Marc Bosman*; Joined Cases C-51/96 & C-191/97, *Christelle Deliège v. Ligue francophone de judo et disciplines associées ASBL et al. (C-51/96) and François Pacquée (C-191/97)*; Case C-281/98, *Roman Angonese v. Cassa di Risparmio di Bolzano SpA*; Case C-309/99, *J.C.J. Wouters, J.W. Savelbergh, Price Waterhouse Belastingadviseurs BV v. Algemene Raad van de Nederlandse Orde van Advocaten*. Case C-341/05, *Laval un Partneri v. Svenska Byggnasarbetareförbundet* and Case C-438/05, *The International Transport Workers' Federation and The Finnish Seamen's Union v. Viking Line and Oü Viking Line Eesti* are important in this context.

96. W.-H Roth, 'Drittwirkung der Grundfreiheiten?' in *Festschrift für U. Everling* (Baden-Baden, 1995), 1231; M. Jaensch, *Die unmittelbare Drittwirkung der Grundfreiheiten* (Baden-Baden, 1997); P. Oliver, assisted by M. Jarvis, *Free Movement of Goods in the EC* (London, 2003), 73; J. Stuyck, 'De toepassing van de bepalingen inzake het vrij verkeer uit het EG-Verdrag op niet-gouvernementele organisaties', in *Liber Amicorum R. Blanpain* (Brugge, 1998), 65; T.O. Ganten, *Die Drittwirkung der Grundfreiheiten* (Berlin, 2000); S. Van den Bogaert, 'Horizontality', in C. Barnard and J. Scott (eds), *The Law of the Single European Market: Unpacking the Premises* (Oxford, 2002), 123; J. Snell, 'Private Parties and the Free Movement of Goods and Services', in M. Andenas and W.-H. Roth (eds), *Services and Free Movement in EU Law* (Oxford, 2002), 211. M. Hintersteininger, *Binnenmarkt und Diskriminierungsverbot* (Berlin, 1999); H. Parpart, *Die unmittelbare Bindung Privater an die Personenverkehrsfreiheiten im europäischen Gemeinschaftsrecht* (Munchen, 2003); P. Oliver and W.-H. Roth, 'The Internal Market and the Four Freedoms' (2004), CML Rev., 407–441, 421.

97. Case C-159/00, *Sapod Audic*. See also Case C-325/00, *Commission v. Federal Republic of Germany*.

with further in relation to each of the freedoms (see sections 3.2.2, 5.3.1, 6.5.1, 7.4.1 and 8.3 below).

The *Spanish strawberries* case[98] brought a variant – one which is to be welcomed – from the point of view of free movement of goods. In this case, France was found to have infringed Article 10 read with Article 28, because it had not acted (sufficiently) against obstacles organized by market operators (angry farmers).[99]

1.6.4   The Combination of a Treaty Prohibition and Directive

Until the plans in the Internal Market White Paper were realized, at the end of 1992, there were many policy areas in which the Court – in the absence of Community measures – reviewed national measures purely on the basis of the EC Treaty prohibitions. Cases such as *Dassonville* and *Reyners*[100] are examples of this practice. In the 1990s, there was a clear change of direction in the Court's case law. A number of cases concern situations involving full or exhaustive harmonization. The Court, after having established this, then restricts itself to an interpretation of the relevant directive. Examples of this approach are particularly prevalent in the agricultural sector.[101] In such situations, there is no longer a possibility of relying on the exceptions in the EC Treaty itself, such as those in Article 30 EC (this is the so-called *Tedeschi* rule – see further section 3.3.1 below).

In other cases, harmonization is only partial. That is the case for a large number of minimum harmonization directives in the environmental sector and concerning consumer protection.[102] Here, the Court applies a double test. First, it looks at the content of the directive and – for national measures which go further – at the Treaty-based prohibition and the exceptions. In all cases involving the interpretation of a directive, the Court considers that the directive in question must be interpreted in the light of the Treaty provisions on free movement.[103] In a few areas where harmonization has not progressed so far – such as direct taxation – the Court was still using the same phrasing at the end of the 1990s as it had used in the 1970s. For example, the Court considered that certain measures in the area of

---

98. Case C-265/95, *Commission v. France (Spanish strawberries)*.
99. Case C-265/95, *Commission v. France (Spanish strawberries)*; Case C-112/00, *Schmidberger*. Cf. also Case C-16/94, *Édouard Dubois & Fils SA and Général Cargo Services SA v. Garonor Exploitation SA*.
100. Case 8/74, *Dassonville*; Case 2/74, *Reyners*.
101. Case C-128/94, *Hans Hönig v. Stadt Stockach*; Case C-1/96, *The Queen v. Minister of Agriculture, Fisheries and Food*.
102. Case C-315/92, *Verband Sozialer Wettbewerb eV v. Clinique Laboratoires SNC et Estée Lauder Cosmetics*; Case C-220/98, *Estée Lauder Cosmetics & Co. OHG v. Lancaster Group*; Case C-389/96, *Aher-Waggon v. Bundesrepublik Deutschland*. P. Rott, 'Minimum Harmonization for the Completion of the Internal Market? The Example of Consumer Sales Law', (2003) CML Rev., 1107; M. Dougan, 'Minimum Harmonization and the Internal Market', (2000) CML Rev., 853.
103. Case C-47/90, *Établissements Delhaize frères et Compagnie Le Lion SA v. Promalvin SA and AGE Bodegas Unidas SA*; Case C-315/92, *Clinique*. Case C-103/01, *Commission v. Federal Republic of Germany*.

taxation did not infringe Article 39 EC because no unifying or harmonizing measures had been taken so far at the level of the Community.[104]

1.6.5 The Convergence of the Freedoms and Exceptions

Under the influence of the case law of the Court there has been a growing unity in the effect of the prohibitions[105] as well as of the exceptions.[106] The judgment in *Futura*, concerning the freedom to provide services, gives a fine example.[107] In this judgment, references are made to the fundamental case law on establishment,[108] workers,[109] and goods[110] in the context of both the prohibition and the exceptions. Not just the Court of Justice, but also the Court of First Instance uses the technique of assimilation.[111] In some judgments, a convergence between the free movement rules and the competition rules can also be identified.[112]

However, important differences continue to exist, as will become apparent from an analysis of the different freedoms and, as was mentioned earlier, depending on whether or not horizontal direct effect is recognized. This is only logical, since there are in fact differences between the freedoms themselves. For instance, services – which are intangible – unlike goods cannot be stored, so there can be no time element between production and consumption. And, of course, persons have different characteristics from capital. These differences also affect the scope of

---

104. Case C-336/96, *Mr and Mrs Robert Gilly v. Directeur des services fiscaux du Bas-Rhin.*
105. P. Behrens, 'Die Konvergenz der wirtschaftlichen Freiheiten im europäischen Gemeinschafts-recht' (1992), EuR, 145; H. Jarass, 'Elemente einer Dogmatik der Grundfreiheiten Funktionen' (1995), EuR, 202, and (2000), EuR, 705; P. Oliver, 'Goods and Services: Two Freedoms Compared', in *Mélanges en hommage à Michel Waelbroeck* (Brussels, 1999), 1365; J. Snell, *Goods and Services in EC Law. A Study of the Relationship between the Freedoms* (Oxford, 2002); H.D. Jarass, 'A Unified Approach to the Fundamental Freedoms', in M. Andenas and W.-H. Roth (eds), *Services and Free Movement in EU Law* (Oxford, 2002), 141; M.P. Maduro, 'Harmony and Dissonance in Free Movement', in M. Andenas and W.-H. Roth (eds), *Services and Free Movement in EU Law* (Oxford, 2002), 41; J. Snell, 'And Then There Were Two: Products and Citizens in Community Law', in T. Tridimas and P. Nebbia (eds), *European Union Law for the Twenty-First Century: Rethinking the New Legal Order, Vol. 2, Internal Market and Free Movement: Community Policies* (Oxford, 2004), 49; P. Oliver and S. Enchelmaier, 'Free Movement of Goods: Recent Developments in the Case Law' (2007), CML Rev., 649–704, 666–671.
106. K.J.M. Mortelmans, 'Excepties bij non-tarifaire intracommunautaire belemmeringen: assim-ilatie in het nieuwe EG-Verdrag?' (1997), SEW, 182.
107. Case C-250/95, *Futura Participations SA and Singer v. Administration des contributions.* See also Case C-503/99, *Commission v. Kingdom of Belgium (Golden Shares).*
108. Case C-55/94, *Reinhard Gebhard v. Consiglio dell'Ordine degli Avvocati e Procuratori di Milano.*
109. Case C-415/93, *Bosman.*
110. Case C-120/78, *Cassis de Dijon.*
111. Case T-266/97, *VTM*; the case law on services is used in relation to a situation concerning establishment.
112. Case C-309/99, *Wouters.* See on this, K.J.M. Mortelmans, 'Towards Convergence in the Application of the Rules on Free Movement and on Competition' (2001), CML Rev., 613.

the freedoms: there is free movement of capital also for capital from third countries; but there is virtually no free movement of persons from third countries.

The starting point for the convergence of the *prohibitions* is the Court of Justice's case law on Article 28 EC, and here the judgment in *Cassis de Dijon* was a milestone.[113] In *Cassis*, the Court brought national measures (product requirements) which did not distinguish between national and imported products within the scope of the prohibition. This broad definition of the prohibition under Article 28 EC was gradually taken over in relation to the interpretation of Article 49 EC, and subsequently Articles 39 EC and 43 EC.[114] The new text concerning free movement of capital (Art. 56 EC), introduced by the Treaty of Maastricht, has brought opportunities for a further convergence of the prohibitions, and the recent case law also points in this direction.[115]

The starting point for the convergence of the *exceptions*, on the other hand, is to be found in the Treaty itself. Article 58(1)(b) EC includes a provision which is extremely similar to Articles 30, 39(3) and 46 EC. All these provisions concern public policy, public security and – with the exception of capital – public health.

Article 30 EC has also acted as a catalyst for the convergence of the rule-of-reason exceptions. The rule-of-reason exceptions formulated in *Cassis de Dijon* for the free movement of goods have also been accepted in relation to the freedom to provide services,[116] and they are gradually finding their way into other freedoms, such as the free movement of persons,[117] although this is certainly not an automatic development.[118]

1.6.6   The Court of Justice – Not Always Taking a Straight Line

The case law of the Court of Justice on the prohibitions and exceptions is constantly evolving. More and more market operators rely on Treaty prohibitions in judicial actions, so the Court must give an (indirect) answer in innumerable preliminary references to the question whether a certain national rule conflicts

---

113. Case 120/78, *Cassis de Dijon*.
114. J.C. Moitinho de Almeida, *Les entraves non discriminatoires à la libre circulation des personnes; leur compatibilité avec les articles 48 et 52 du traité CE*, in *Festskrift til Ole Due*, 1994, 241–263.
115. Case C-367/98, *Commission v. Portuguese Republic (Golden Shares)*; Case C-483/99, *Commission v. Republic of France (Golden Shares)*; Case C-503/99, *Commission v. Belgium (Golden Shares)*.
116. Compare Case C-120/78, *Cassis de Dijon* with Case C-353/89, *Commission v. Kingdom of the Netherlands (TV advertising)*.
117. E.g., Case C-379/87, *Anita Groener v. Minister for Education and the City of Dublin Vocational Educational Committee*; Case C-340/89, *Irène Vlassopoulou v. Ministerium für Justiz, Bundes- und Europaangelegenheiten Baden-Württemberg*; and Case C-19/92, *Dieter Kraus v. Land Baden-Württemberg*.
118. Case C-484/93, *Peter Svensson and Lena Gustavsson v. Ministre du Logement et de l'Urbanisme*. Here the Court did not accept the transposition of an argument about coherence of fiscal policy, taken from freedom to provide services, for freedom of capital movements.

with a directly effective Treaty prohibition – even if at first sight the rule has nothing to do with obstacles to the free movement of goods and services.[119]

The Court's answers in these cases concerning the functioning of the internal market are not always unambiguous.[120] On the one hand, the Court works in a framework of convergence, using the technique of assimilation. In this way, the case law acquires some structure. A market operator can see how a line of approach in relation to one of the freedoms may be extrapolated to apply to other freedoms, such as the extensive effect of the Treaty prohibition. On the other hand, a large (and increasing) number of judgments by the Court do not fit in these structures. This is illustrated by a few examples, which are worked out in detail below. The *Keck* case law has not (yet) been transposed to other freedoms. Since *Keck*, the Court also uses other techniques, such as hypothetical situations, in order to exclude national rules from the scope of the prohibition (see section 3.2.1). The prohibition under Article 29 EC (barriers to export of goods) has a more restricted scope than that in relation to services (*Groenveld* versus *Alpine Investments*, see sections 3.2.3 and 7.4.1 below). The condition that the rule-of-reason exceptions only hold for measures which apply indistinctly to national and non-national goods is no longer adhered to in a number of cases concerning, *inter alia*, environment and taxation. (see sections 3.3.3 and 5.3.2 below).

There are a number of reasons for this departure from a straight line of case law. First, as was already pointed out in the introduction to this chapter, the Court of Justice is primarily concerned with solving legal disputes, not writing a text-book. Secondly, the composition of the Court has changed over the years – and perhaps new judges have a new vision of the realization of the internal market. Thirdly, the Court clearly finds it difficult to rule on the obstacles it is currently confronted with on the basis of a Treaty framework which was not designed for them, or at least not sufficiently. The best example is environmental protection. This exception is not listed in Article 30, while over the years a great number of provisions on the environment have been included in the Treaty. In the absence of clear and direct footholds in the Treaty, the Court has to tie itself in knots in order to save discriminatory measures aimed at environmental protection.[121] To a certain extent, this reasoning also applies for the 'tax system' exception which was introduced in *Bachmann*, and for the exception 'a social security system's financial balance' which was introduced in *Smits and Peerbooms*.[122] Advocates general, who are sometimes caught between case-by-case approaches on the one hand and theory on the other, sometimes beg the Court to clarify things.[123] May their wish be granted!

---

119. Cf. Joined Cases C-267 & 268/91, *Criminal proceedings against Bernard Keck and Daniel Mithouard*.

120. P. Oliver, 'Could the Wording of the Court's Judgments be Improved?' (2001), EuZW, 257.

121. Case C-2/90, *Commission v. Kingdom of Belgium*; Case C-379/98, *PreussenElektra AG v. Schleswag AG*.

122. Case C-157/99, *B.S.M. Geraets-Smits v. Stichting Ziekenfonds VGZ and H.T.M. Peerbooms v. Stichting CZ Groep Zorgverzekeringen*.

123. E.g., A.G. Jacobs in Case C-379/98, *PreussenElektra*.

1.6.7   **The Role of the European Commission and**
              of National Bodies

The establishment and functioning of the internal market do not only depend on the cooperative efforts of the Court of Justice and the national courts – in particular in the interpretation of the directly effective Treaty prohibitions. The Commission also has a very important role to play; and in many cases it has done so, making use of the Article 226 EC procedure[124] and with the threat of *Francovich* liability.[125] In a number of important cases, for instance concerning food products[126] and electricity,[127] it has fulfilled its role as watchdog by bringing actions against Member States before the Court of Justice for failure to respect the Treaty prohibitions concerning the freedoms. In countless cases, the Commission has applied to the Court for a ruling that the Member States have not implemented directives in time.

Now that most of the internal market directives have been implemented, the Commission's attention is directed at the incorrect application of directives and regulations, for instance in the area of public procurement.[128]

In recent years, the task of the national legislative bodies has also come into the limelight. The liberalization of the network industries must be guided by independent national regulatory authorities (NRAs). These NRAs fulfil a role as specific competition authorities, but they also have a task in relation to the consolidation of the internal market. For instance, Article 7 of the Framework Directive on electronic communications networks provides for a consultation procedure between the European Commission and the NRAs if an NRA proposes to take a measure which would affect trade between Member States.[129]

The decentralized enforcement of competition law will mean that general competition authorities in the Member States will have to take account of the basic rules of the internal market in their own competition policy – particularly when they apply Articles 81 and 82 EC. In a number of cases, for instance in agricultural and fisheries cases,[130] and in the construction industry, there may be a combination of free movement, competition and state aids.

---

124. See Ch. VI, section 2.1. *supra.*
125. Joined Cases C-6 & 9/90, *Andrea Francovich and Danila Bonifaci and others v. Italy.* This case – and the judgment in Joined Cases C-46 & 48/93, *Brasserie du Pêcheur SA v. Bundes-republik Deutschland and The Queen v. Secretary of State for Transport, ex parte Factortame Ltd and others* – revealed that under certain conditions a Member State may be held liable for failing to comply with Treaty rules; see further Ch. VII.
126. Case 176/84, *Commission v. Hellenic Republic*; Case 178/84, *Commission v. Germany.*
127. Case C-157/94, *Commission v. Kingdom of the Netherlands*; Case C-159/94, *Commission v. France*; Case C-160/94, *Commission v. Kingdom of Spain.*
128. See, e.g., Case C-24/91, *Commission v. Kingdom of Spain*; Case C-107/92, *Commission v. Italy.*
129. Dir. 2002/21 of the European Parliament and of the Council on a common regulatory framework for electronic communications networks and services, O.J. 2002, L 108/33. Para. 38 of the preamble uses the formula from the *Dassonville* case, Case 8/74.
130. E.g., Case C-355/00, *Freskot AE v. Elliniko Dimosio* and Case C-137/00, *The Queen v. The Competition Commission et al. ex parte Milk Marque Ltd and National Farmers' Union.*

In 2003, the Commission presented a proposal to give national bodies responsibility for supervision of the internal market rules. The Commission is thus continuing on the basis of its experiences with NRAs.[131]

1.7   PLAN OF THIS CHAPTER AND ITS PLACE IN THE SCHEME
          OF THIS WORK

The various freedoms are systematically discussed in separate sections. First, the prohibition is discussed, and then the exceptions – from the point of view of the Member States also called justifications. Attention then turns to measures of positive integration in the field concerned, mentioning the most important secondary legislation, and, finally, there follows a brief indication of the external dimension.[132]

In relation to the free movement of goods, tariff and non-tariff barriers are separately examined in sections 2 and 3 below respectively. The treatment of free movement of persons starts out from the concept of 'person' in section 4, moving on to the free movement of workers in section 5, and the freedom of establishment of legal and natural persons in section 6. The freedom to provide services is examined in section 7 and the free movement of capital and payments in section 8.

This chapter elaborates on a number of substantive principles which were examined in Chapter III (freedom, equality, proportionality). The distortions of competition as a result of actions by undertakings, which the EC Treaty combats in Articles 81–86 EC, or actions by Member States in favour of certain undertakings, dealt with in Articles 87–89 EC, are discussed in Chapter IX.

There is a clear link between the present chapter and Chapters XII on sectoral policy and XIII on horizontal and flanking policies. Goods, services and persons falling under a special regime are as a rule also covered by the system of the internal market, but specific rules often apply as well. In a number of instances, the rules on free movement are also applicable in the horizontal and flanking policies. Given that those areas are non-economic policy areas, the Member States will frequently seek to invoke exceptions on grounds such as the protection of the environment, of culture, health and so on.

2   FREE MOVEMENT OF GOODS: TARIFF BARRIERS
      AND FISCAL BARRIERS

2.1   A FEW CONCEPTS

2.1.1   Tariff and Non-Tariff Barriers

The main tariff barriers to movements of goods between states are customs duties. In the original Articles 12–17 EEC – now repealed – detailed instructions were

---

131. COM(2003)238 final.
132. The external dimension is examined in more detail in Ch. XIII *infra*.

given of how these customs duties between the Member States were to be abolished. In addition, there are levies which have an equivalent effect to customs duties. This is a broad category of pecuniary charges, rather difficult to define, which have the same effect as customs duties in terms of creating an obstacle to trade. Both kinds of barriers are pecuniary charges, like indirect taxation (indirect taxes are dealt with in section 2.5).

Non-tariff barriers consist in the first place of quantitative restrictions or quotas, such as quantitative limits on imports or exports of meat or oil. The original Articles 31–33 EEC described how these restrictions were to be eliminated. As well as these barriers, there are measures which entail an equivalent effect to that of quantitative restrictions. Here, too, we are faced with a broad but difficult to describe category of obstacles; it is dealt with in section 3 below.

2.1.2   Intra-Community and Third Countries

At the internal borders, all restrictions on movements of goods must – barring certain exceptions – be eliminated. In this way, an area without internal frontiers is established (cf. Art. 14(2) EC). In sections 2 and 3, the emphasis is on the internal borders.

At the external frontiers, a uniform customs tariff and common rules are applied. This subject is dealt with further in Chapter XIII (but see also section 2.6 below).

2.1.3   Import, Export, Transit

Barriers can be imposed on different types of movements of goods. In most cases, import barriers are at issue. In this way, in many cases, a state tries to protect its own production (protectionism). States may in certain cases (such as art and antiques, or waste, or scarce or strategic products) also impose barriers on exports.

Although the right of free transit of goods within the Community is not expressly conferred in the EC Treaty,[133] the Court has always acknowledged the existence of such a principle. The Member States are prohibited from imposing transit dues or other levies in connection with transit on goods transported through their territory.[134]

2.1.4   National, Community or International Rules

In the period in which the customs union and the common market were given shape, the accent was on the elimination of national tariff and non-tariff rules which formed obstacles. These national rules retain their significance when the

---

133.   Only Art. 30 EC refers to transit.
134.   Case 266/81, *Società Italiana per l'Oleodotto Transalpino (SIOT) v. Ministero delle Finanze et al.*; Case C-16/94, *Dubois*; Case C-23/99, *Commission v. France*. See Case C-112/00, *Schmidberger* and Case C-320/03, *Commission v. Austria*.

principle of mutual recognition is applied (see section 1.1 above). This so-called negative integration is accompanied by the adoption of common (Community) rules, such as directives and regulations, which comprise positive integration. In this way, common, Community standards (product requirements or professional requirements) or common rules (for instance on the original and labelling of goods) are laid down.

In many instances, the EC and/or its Member States are party to international agreements or members of international organizations, as a consequence of the desire of the EC to contribute to the harmonious development of world trade (see Art. 131 EC). In the context of movement of goods, the WTO (successor to the GATT) is the most important organization. In Chapter XIII of this book, the relationship between the rules adopted by these international organizations, the EC rules and the national rules is discussed further.

2.1.5 The Concept of a 'Good'

Articles 23 EC et seq. use the terms 'goods' and 'products' interchangeably, and these terms are not themselves defined in the EC Treaty.[135] In Case 7/68 *Commission v. Italy*[136] the Court defined goods as 'products which can be valued in money and which are capable, as such, of forming the subject of commercial transactions'. However, in Case C-2/90, *Commission v. Belgium*[137] the Court examined whether recyclable or non-recyclable waste constituted 'goods' for the purposes of the EC Treaty. It noted that 'objects which are shipped across a frontier for the purposes of commercial transactions are subject to Article [28], whatever the nature of those transactions'.[138] The phrase 'valued in money' can provide a link with provisions on free movement of goods, but also free movement of capital.[139] Intellectual

---

135. Dir. 98/34 laying down a procedure for the provision of information in the field of technical standards and regulations, O.J. 1998, L 204/37, does contain a definition. This is not generally applicable, though. The different terms corresponding to 'good' and 'product' are also found in, e.g., the Dutch, French, Italian, Portuguese and Spanish texts, but in the German and Danish texts the same word (*Waren* and *varer*, respectively) is used.

136. Case 7/68, *Commission v. Italy* at 428 of the English edition.

137. Case 2/90, *Commission v. Belgium* at para.25. Case C-221/06, *Stadtgemeinde Frohnheiten and Gemeindebetriebe Frohnleiten GmbH v. Bundesminister für Land- und Forstwirtschaft, Umwelt und Wasserwirtschaft.*

138. Case 2/90, *Commission v. Belgium*, para. 26. See also Case C-324/93, *The Queen v. Secretary of State for Home Department, ex parte Evans Medical Ltd and Macfarlan Smith Ltd* For the concept 'waste', see also Joined Cases C-418 & 419/97, *ARCO Chemie Nederland Ltd v. Minister van Volkshuisvesting, Ruimtelijke Ordening en Milieubeheer, and Vereniging Dorpsbelang Hees et al. v. Directeur van de dienst Milieu en Water van de provincie Gelderland.*

139. Case C-97/98, *Peter Jägerskiöld v. Torolf Gustafsson*, para. 34: 'the Treaty provisions on the free movement of capital cover, in particular, operations relating to shares, bonds and other securities which, like fishing rights or fishing permits, can be valued in money and may be the subject of market transactions'.

property rights may influence trade in goods between Member States, but are themselves not 'goods'.[140]

Specific rules govern drugs,[141] counterfeit money,[142] weapons and strategic goods.[143] There are special rules for agricultural products falling within the scope of Article 32(1) EC. Save as otherwise provided in the Agriculture Title of the EC Treaty, the rules on the establishment of the common market apply to agricultural products just as to all other products.[144] An annexe to the Euratom Treaty states the products which fall within the ambit of that Treaty.[145]

There are demarcation problems with the other freedoms,[146] some of which the Court has been able to resolve. The Court has qualified electricity as falling within the concept of goods.[147] In *R. v. Thompson et al.*[148] the Court found that coins which were legal tender in a Member State were not goods; *a contrario*, coins which are no longer legal tender (e.g., after the introduction of the euro) must come under the rules on free movement of goods.[149]

There have also been demarcation problems between the concepts of 'goods' and 'services' in relation to roadworthiness tests,[150] lotteries and betting,[151]

---

140. Case C-97/98, *Jägerskiöld*.
141. Case 50/80, *Joszef Horvath v. Hauptzollamt Hamburg-Jonas*; Case 294/82, *Senta Einberger v. Hauptzollamt Freiburg*; Case 289/86, *Vereniging Happy Family Rustenburgerstraat v. Inspecteur der Omzetbelasting*; Case C-324/93, *Evans Medical*; Case C-158/98, *Staatssecretaris van Financiën v. Coffeeshop 'Siberië' v of*. For the application of this case law to alcohol, see Case C-455/98, *Tullihallitus v. Kaupo Salumets et al.*
142. Case C-343/89, *Max Witzemann v. Hauptzollamt München-Mitte*. See also Case C-275/92, *Her Majesty's Customs and Excise v. Gerhart Schindler and Jörg Schindler*.
143. See Art. 296 EC. See Case C-367/89, *Criminal proceedings against Aimé Richardt and Les Accessoires Scientifiques SNC*. See M. Trybus, 'On the Application of the EC Treaty to Armaments' (2000) EL Rev., 663.
144. Art. 32(2) EC. See Joined Cases 80 & 81/77, *Société Les Commissionnaires Réunis SARL v. Receveur des douanes; SARL Les fils de Henri Ramel v. Receveur des douanes*.
145. Similarly, an annexe listed the products falling within the scope of the ECSC Treaty (that Treaty is no longer in force). See also Case C-128/92, *H.J. Banks & Co. Ltd v. British Coal Corporation* and Case 36/83, *Mabanaft v. Hauptzollamt Emmerich*.
146. See on this, U. Everling, *Zum Begriff der Ware im Binnenmarkt der EG und sein Verhältnis zu den Dienstleistungen*, in *Festschrift für H. Hahn* (Baden-Baden, 1997), 365; P. Oliver, 'Goods and Services: Two Freedoms Compared', in *Mélanges en hommage à Michel Waelbroeck* (Brussels, 1999), 1365; J. Snell, *Goods and Services in EU Law: A Study of the Relationship between the Freedoms* (Oxford, 2002).
147. Case 6/64, *Flaminio Costa v. E.N.E.L.*; Case C-393/92, *Municipality of Almelo and others v. NV Energiebedrijf Ijsselmij*.
148. Case 7/78, *Regina v. Ernest George Thompson, Brian Albert Johnson and Colin Alex Norman Woodiwiss*.
149. See further Joined Cases C-358 & 416/93, *Criminal proceedings against Aldo Bordessa, Vicente Marí Mellado and Concepción Barbero Maestre* (coins, banknotes and bearer cheques are not goods, but means of payment).
150. Case C-55/93, *Criminal proceedings against Johannes Gerrit Cornelis van Schaik*.
151. Case C-275/92, *Schindler*, Case C-124/97, *Markku Juhani Läärä et al. v. Kihlakunnansyyttäjä (Jyväskylä) and Finland*; Case C-67/98, *Questore di Verona v. Diego Zenatti*; Case C-6/01, *Associação Nacional de Operadores de Máquinas Recreativas (Anomar) and Others v. Portugal*.

international post,[152] telephone calls,[153] television signals,[154] fishing permits[155] and in the media sector.[156] Where a national measure affects both the freedom to provide services and the free movement of goods, the Court will, in principle, examine it in relation to just one of those two fundamental freedoms if it is clear that, in the circumstances of the case, one of those freedoms is entirely secondary in relation to the other and may be attached to it.[157] Demarcation problems may also arise between the free movement of goods and the free movement of persons, particularly in the case of movement of human mortal remains or donors of organs.[158]

The nationality of the purchaser or importer of a good is irrelevant for the application of the provisions on free movement of goods.[159]

2.2   THE CUSTOMS UNION AS THE FOUNDATION OF THE COMMUNITY

Article 23 EC provides that the Community is based on a customs union covering all trade in goods and comprising the prohibition, as between Member States, of customs duties on imports and exports and all charges having equivalent effect as well as the adoption of a common customs tariff for their relations with third countries. The principle of a customs union requires that free movement of goods within that union be ensured across the whole spectrum, embracing also movement between the regions of the Community and not merely trade between the Member States.[160] A common customs tariff also necessitates on a number of points a common, and on other points a harmonized customs law. As regards customs duties of course it also entails the necessity of a common commercial policy *vis-à-vis* third countries (see further Ch. XIII of this book).

According to the definition in Article XXIV of the GATT, the concept of a customs union, subject to the permitted exceptions, also embraces the abolition of all non-tariff trade barriers in inter-state trade. The non-tariff aspects of the customs union are discussed in section 3 of this chapter, below. The Court has interpreted Articles 23–27 EC in extensive case law, and has paid particular

---

152. Joined Cases C-147 & 148/97, *Deutsche Post AG v. Gesellschaft für Zahlungssysteme mbH (GZS) (C-147/97) and Citicorp Kartenservice (C-148/97)*.
153. Case C-384/93, *Alpine Investments*.
154. Case C-390/99, *Canal Satélite Digital SL v. Administracíon General del Estado*.
155. Case C-97/98, *Jägerskiöld*.
156. Case 155/73, *Giuseppe Sacchi*; Case C-368/95, *Vereinigte Familiapress Zeitungsverlags- und vertriebs v. Heinrich Bauer Verlag*.
157. See Case C-36/02, *Omega Spielhallen- und Automatenaufstellungs v. Oberbürgermeisterin der Bundesstadt Bonn*.
158. See WQ E-3966/93 (Kostopoulos) O.J. 1994, C 340/60, on illegal trade in human organs.
159. Joined Cases 2 & 3/69, *Sociaal Fonds voor de Diamantarbeiders v. S.A. Ch. Brachfeld & Sons and Chougol Diamond Co.*
160. Joined Cases C-363 & 407–411/93, *Lancry et al.* See also Case C-293/02, *Jersey Produce Marketing Organisation*.

attention to the distinction between charges having equivalent effect to a customs duty and fiscal measures caught by Article 90 EC.

The customs union – in the narrow sense of Article 23 EC – lays the very foundations of the Community, because it forms the first important step towards achieving an optimum division of labour within the Community. By eliminating barriers to trade, the customs union tended to stimulate enlargement of the scale and growth of production of the most efficient enterprises, encouraging concentration and specialization, and at the same time the selection of the most economically favourable locations for new production plants or trade centres. Thus the customs union already made an indirect contribution to the development of the inter-state movement of persons, services and capital. At the same time it has made the economies of the Member States mutually interdependent, thereby laying a basis for the economic and monetary union (EMU).[161]

2.3   THE ORIGIN OF GOODS

Free movement of goods applies to products originating in the Community and to products originating outside it which are placed in free circulation in a Member State.[162]

Article 24 EC provides that products coming from a third country are considered as being in free circulation in a Member State 'if the import formalities have been complied with and any customs duties or charges having equivalent effect which are payable have been levied in that Member State, and if they have not benefited from a total or partial drawback of such duties or charges'.[163] The rule applies to agricultural products and to industrial products alike.[164] In Case C-296/00, *Carbone*, the Court stated that 'placing products on the market is a stage subsequent to importation. Just as a product lawfully manufactured within the Community may not be placed on the market on that ground alone, the lawful importation of a product does not imply that it will automatically be allowed onto the market'.[165] Article 23 EC makes it plain that, as far as the right to free movement within the Community is concerned, products in free circulation are definitively and wholly assimilated to products originating in a Member State, a point

---

161. K. Wöhlermann and C. de Haas, *Das Wirtschaftsrecht in der Europäischen Union am Beispiel von Inhalt und Grenzen der Warenverkehrsfreiheit* (Frankfurt am Main, 1998).
162. As to the definition of origin of goods, see the Community Customs Code, Reg. 2913/92 (O.J. 1992, L 302/1, most recently amended by Reg. 2700/2000 (O.J. 2000, L 311/17), Arts. 23–26.
163. See, generally, Case 16/65, *Firma G. Schwarze v. Einfuhr- und Vorratsstelle für Getreide und Futtermittel* at 889 of the English edition and, in relation to interpretation problems in this field, Case 34/78, *Yoshida Nederland BV v. Kamer van Koophandel en Fabrieken voor Friesland*, and Case 114/78, *Yoshida v. Industrie- und Handelskammer Kassel*. A customs union benefits goods from third countries, unlike a free trade area (where each State applies its own customs tariff to third country goods even coming from another Member State).
164. Case 69/84, *Remo Padovani and others v. Amministrazione delle finanze dello Stato*.
165. Case C-296/00, *Carbone*, at para. 31.

which means that the provisions of Article 28 EC cover both types of products without distinction.[166] This assimilation can only have full effect if the customs duties and commercial import conditions applying to the goods are the same, irrespective of the Member State in which they are placed in free circulation. The incomplete nature of the Community's common commercial policy does cause certain deflections in trade, and in certain circumstances Article 134 EC may be invoked to permit denial of Community treatment to goods originating from third countries (see further Ch. XIII).

2.4   INTRA-COMMUNITY CUSTOMS DUTIES AND CHARGES
             HAVING EQUIVALENT EFFECT

All customs duties in inter-state trade within the Community have gradually been abolished between the Member States in accordance with the obligations of the original Articles 12–17 EEC, and comparable provisions in acts of accession.

The Treaty of Amsterdam repealed those Treaty provisions, since they were no longer relevant.[167] This subject is now regulated by Article 25 EC, according to which customs duties on imports and exports, and charges having equivalent effect, are prohibited between Member States. This prohibition also applies to customs duties of a fiscal nature.

For a correct understanding of this provision, one must return to the case law of the Court on the old provisions. This was a constant line of case law, which the Court usually elaborated further when it was faced with a new set of facts. The following two sections examine the scope of the prohibition (2.4.1.) and the justifications for national measures (2.4.2.) in more detail.

2.4.1   Charges Having Equivalent Effect to Customs Duties: Definition

Such a charge is defined as 'any pecuniary charge, however small and whatever its designation and mode of application, which is imposed unilaterally on domestic or foreign goods by reason of the fact that they cross a frontier, and which is not a customs duty in the strict sense',[168] providing it is not permitted by specific

---

166. Case 41/76, *Suzanne Criel, née Donckerwolcke and Henri Schou v. Procureur de la République au tribunal de grande instance de Lille and Director General of Customs*; Case 125/88, *Criminal proceedings against H.F.M. Nijman*; Case C-296/00, *Carbone*. See P. Oliver, assisted by M. Jarvis, *Free Movement of Goods in the EC* (London, 2003), 26. For an application in EC competition law, see Case T-65/89, *BPB Industries Plc and British Gypsum Ltd v. Commission*.
167. Earlier editions of this book may be referred to for analyses of the old provisions.
168. Case 24/68, *Commission v. Italy*, para. 9; see also, e.g., Cases 2 and 3/69, *Sociaal Fonds voor de Diamantarbeiders*; Case 29/72, *S.p.A. Marimex v. Italian Finance Administration*; Case C-266/91, *Celulose Beira Industrial (CELBI) SA v. Fazenda Publica*; Case C-130/93, *Lamaire NV v. Nationale Dienst voor Afzet van Land- en Tuinbouwprodukten*; Case C-90/94, *Haahr Petroleum Ltd v. Åbenrå Havn et al.*

Treaty provisions. In this broad definition the emphasis lies on the effect the charge has as a barrier or obstacle to the free movement of goods. In *Carbonati Apuani* the Court explicitly linked the prohibition contained in Article 23 EC and Article 14 EC, the provision concerning the establishment of the internal market[169] The prohibition is also to be found in secondary legislation, and is interpreted in that context in the same way as in the EC Treaty itself.[170] The Court occasionally summarizes its case law on this point.[171]

The case law of the Court has clarified a number of aspects. It makes no difference at what point the charge is levied, whether on actual crossing of a border or subsequently.[172] The prohibition also applies when the charge is levied in relation to goods crossing a part of the Member State's territory (e.g., an island).[173] Given the fundamental nature of the customs union, even a small charge falls under the prohibition;[174] in other words, there is no *de minimis* exception. After all, the mere fact of charging anything at all, together with the administrative formalities, forms an obstacle to the free movement of goods.[175] It makes no difference whether the charge is imposed for the general benefit of the public purse, or for an autonomous fund; likewise it does not matter in what manner the pecuniary charge is levied (by the central national authorities or an independent body) or for what purpose the charge is levied.[176] It does not matter whether the charge is levied directly by the authorities, or as a result of agreements between private individuals.[177] Whether the latter still applies after the Court's judgment in *Commission v. France (Spanish strawberries)*[178] is a question which has still to be answered.[179]

The fact that the charge had a protective effect, and that the imported product – subject to the charge – competed with a national product was found to be relevant in the earliest case law, but this condition was dropped in later case law.[180]

---

169. Case C-72/03, *Carbonati Apuani*. See also Case C-293/02, *Jersey Produce Marketing Organisation.*
170. Case 34/73, *Fratelli Variola S.p.A. v. Amministrazione italiana delle Finanze*; Case 21/75, *I. Schroeder KG v. Oberstadtdirektor der Stadt Köln.*
171. Cf. Case C-234/99, *Niels Nygård v. Svineafgiftsfonden*. See also Case C-355/00, *Freskot.*
172. Case 78/76, *Steinike & Weinlig v. Federal Republic of Germany.*
173. Case C-163/90, *Administration des Douanes et Droits Indirects v. Léopold Legros and others*; Joined Cases C-485 & 486/93, *Simitzi v. Kos*; Case C-212/96, *Chevassus*; Case C-72/03, *Carbonati Apuani*, Case C-293/02, *Jersey Produce Marketing Organisation.*
174. Cases 2 and 3/69, *Sociaal Fonds voor de Diamantarbeiders.*
175. Case 34/73, *Fratelli Variola S.p.A.*
176. E.g., Case 7/68, *Commission v. Italy*; Case 29/72, *Marimex*; Case 78/76, *Steinike & Weinlig*; Case 158/82, *Commission v. Kingdom of Denmark*, and Case C-426/92, *Bundesrepublik Deutschland v. Deutsches Milch-Kontor*. Joined Cases C-441 & 442/98, *Kapniki Mikhailidis AE v. Idrima Kinonikon Asphaliseon (IKA).*
177. Case C-16/94, *Dubois.*
178. Case C-265/95, *Commission v. France (Spanish strawberries).*
179. In Case C-16/94, *Dubois*, A.G. La Pergola, came to the same conclusion as the Court – mutatis mutandis – in Case C-265/95, *Commission v. France (Spanish strawberries).*
180. Compare Joined Cases 2 & 3/62, *Commission of the European Economic Community v. Grand Duchy of Luxembourg and Kingdom of Belgium* with Cases 2 and 3/69, *Sociaal Fonds voor de Diamantarbeiders.*

Although the words 'charge . . . which is imposed unilaterally' may create the impression that charges imposed by the Community Institutions are not caught by the prohibition, the case law of the Court demonstrates that they are caught.[181] Yet the prohibition as regards acts of the Community Institutions does not have the same prohibitive character for them as for acts of the Member States (see 3.2.2. below).[182] Charges imposed by Community legal acts, such as in the past Monetary Compensatory Amounts in the agricultural sphere, were not considered by the Court to fall under the prohibition of Article 25 EC; on the contrary, as measures designed to facilitate the unity of the market by avoiding distortions which would otherwise have occurred, they were devoid of protectionist effect.[183]

2.4.2 The Grounds of Justification Related to the Prohibition

The only justifications mentioned in Title I of Part Three of the EC Treaty (i.e., the provisions on free movement of goods) are those in Article 30 EC, which may be relied upon by the Member States. However, according to the Court, these only relate to Articles 28 and 29 EC and cannot be relied upon to justify charges falling under Article 25 EC.[184] Thus – as was mentioned in section 1.4, above – a single economic operation, such as inspection and the fee charged, can fall under two different systems, so that in respect of both there will be an examination of which provisions are applicable and, if appropriate, whether a justification known to Community law exists.

In *Carbonati Apuani*, the municipality in question relied on a specific objective of the charge involved, explaining that the revenue from the tax was intended to cover the expenses borne by the Comune di Carrara as a consequence of the marble industry's activities in its territory. The tax thus responds to an interest of all operators in that industry, including those that market the goods concerned abroad. The Court replied that customs duties and charges having equivalent effect are prohibited regardless of the purpose for which they were introduced and the destination of the revenue from them.[185] The Court based its reasoning on an old judgment in which it had devoted a number of paragraphs to the characteristics and the justifications of the prohibition in Article 25 EC.[186]

---

181. E.g., Joined Cases 80 & 81/77, *Société Les Commissionnaires Réunis*.
182. Barents, 'Charges of Equivalent Effect' (1978) CML Rev., 415 at 419, and K.J.M. Mortelmans, 'The Relationship between the Treaty Rules and Community Measures for the Establishment and Functioning of the Internal Market: Towards a Concordance Rule' (2002) CML Rev., 1303–1346.
183. Case 10/73, *Rewe Zentral AG v. Hauptzollamt Kehl*; Joined Cases 80 & 81/77, *Société Les Commissionnaires Réunis*; Case 136/77, *A. Racke v. Hauptzollamt Mainz*; Case 106/81, *Julius Kind KG v. European Economic Community*; Case 337/82, *St. Nikolaus Brennerei und Likörfabrik, Gustav Kniepf-Melde v. Hauptzollamt Krefeld*.
184. Case 46/76, *Bauhuis*. In this case, protection of public health was at issue.
185. Case C-72/03, *Carbonati Apuani*.
186. Case 24/68, *Commission v. Italy*.

There are three grounds of justification according to which a charge may escape the prohibition in Article 25 EC.[187] First, that it forms part of a general system of internal taxation; this has a Treaty basis.[188] This provision cannot be qualified as an 'exception': it is a separate regime, under which the national rule may be assessed instead of Article 25 EC. The two may not apply at the same time (see section 2.5 below). The two other grounds of justification (that the charge is a recompense for a service actually rendered, or that the fees are permitted under a Community provision) can be qualified as exceptions. They are creatures of case law.

2.4.2.1   *Recompense for a Service Actually Rendered*

A recompense for a service actually rendered to the importer can fall outside the scope of the prohibition of Article 25 EC under certain conditions. There must be a specific service actually rendered by the authorities and individually conferred on the market participant.[189] The amount charged must be proportionate to the benefit received.[190] The recompense demanded may not exceed the actual cost of the service provided.[191] In *Netherlands v. Bakker*[192] the Court observed that the condition of not exceeding the actual cost of the operations in respect of which the fee was charged required there to be 'a direct link between the amount of the fee and the actual inspection in respect of which the fee is charged'. Duties paid by way of fees or dues within the meaning of Article 12(1)(e) of Directive 69/335[193] concerning indirect taxes on the raising of capital are not caught by the prohibition.[194]

The case law makes it clear that this exception is strictly interpreted by the Court;[195] it is only occasionally accepted.[196]

---

187. As stated explicitly in Case C-109/98, *CRT France International SA v. Directeur Régional des Impôts de Bourgogne.*
188. Art. 90 EC.
189. E.g., Case 24/68, *Commission v. Italy*; Case 39/82, *Andreas Matthias Donner v. Netherlands State*; Case 340/87, *Commission v. Italy*, and Case 170/88, *Ford España SA v. Estado español.*
190. Case 46/76, *Bauhuis*; Case 132/78, *SARL Denkavit Loire v. French State, administration des douanes*; Case 132/82, *Commission v. Kingdom of Belgium*; Case 158/82, *Commission v. Denmark*; and Case C-209/89, *Commission v. Italy.*
191. Case 89/76, *Commission v. Kingdom of the Netherlands.*
192. Case C-111/89, *Netherlands v. P. Bakker Hillegom BV*, para. 12. See also Case C-389/00, *Commission v. Federal Republic of Germany.*
193. O.J. 1969, L 249/25, amended by Dir. 85/303 (O.J. 1985, L 156/23) and replaced by Dir. 2008/7, O.J. 2008, L 46/11.
194. Joined Cases C-71 & 178/91, *Ponente Carni SpA and Cispadana Costruzioni SpA v. Amministrazione delle Finanze dello Stato.* See also, in relation to Art. 10(c) of Dir. 69/335, Case C-2/94, *Denkavit Internationaal BV et al. v. Kamer van Koophandel en Fabrieken voor Midden-Gelderland et al.*
195. Recently Case C-109/98, *CRT France.*
196. Case 132/82, *Commission v. Belgium*; Case 340/87, *Commission v. Italy.*

Charges levied in respect of quality controls or health inspections on crossing a frontier do not come within the scope of the term 'recompense'.[197] The Court requires that the costs occasioned by inspections prescribed in the public interest must be financed from the public purse.[198] Charging fees in return for customs services performed on private premises is also impermissible. Fees applied on an *ad valorem* basis cannot possibly be linked to the service rendered to the importer in relation to customs formalities; they are thus not acceptable.[199] If services are rendered to several undertakings at the same time, this will be unacceptable if it results in more being charged than the actual costs per undertaking.[200]

In some cases, the charge – which is frequently imposed without distinction on national and imported goods and which therefore can be qualified as an internal tax – is used to finance advertising campaigns which work either entirely or partially to the advantage of the national products. In that case, Articles 87–88 EC on state aids may come into play.[201]

2.4.2.2 Community Provisions

Where the charges are for (health) inspections carried out pursuant to Community provisions in a uniform manner, they are not considered 'charges having equivalent effect to customs duties', provided that they do not exceed the cost of carrying out the inspection.[202] This exception was formulated in Case 46/76 *Bauhuis v. Netherlands State*, concerning an inspection charge levied by the Netherlands authorities for an inspection required under a directive. The explanation given by the Court is that such inspections replace the myriad unilateral national inspections which might otherwise be justifiable under Article 30 EC;[203] they thus contribute to the free movement of goods rather than hindering it.[204]

Fees for inspections prescribed by Community legislation which are not exclusively carried out in the context of imports or exports, but also in domestic

---

197. E.g., Case 29/72, *Marimex*; Case 39/73, *Rewe-Zentralfinanz v. Direktor der Landwirtschaftskammer Westfalen Lippe*; Case 63/74, *W. Cadsky SpA v. Istituto nazionale per il Commercio Estero*; Case 87/75, *Conceria Daniele Bresciani v. Amministrazione Italiana delle Finanze*; Case 46/76, *Bauhuis*, and Joined Cases C-277, 318 & 319/91, *Ligur Carni Srl and Genova Carni Srl v. Unità Sanitaria Locale n. XV di Genova, and Ponente SpA v. Unità Sanitaria Locale n. XIX di La Spezia and v. CO.GE.SE.MA Coop a r l*.
198. Case 87/75, *Bresciani*.
199. Case 170/88, *Ford España SA*.
200. Case C-209/89, *Commission v. Italy*.
201. Case 51/74, *P.J. van der Hulst's Zonen v. Produktschap voor Siergewassen*, Case C-345/02, *Pearle BV, Hans Prijs Optiek Franchise BV, Rinck Opticiëns BV v. Hoofdbedrijfschap Ambachten* and Case C-174/02, *Streekgewest Westelijk Noord-Brabant v. Staatssecretaris van Financiën*. See further section 2.5.2. *infra* and Ch. IX *infra*.
202. The exception has been criticized by R.H. Lauwaars and C.W.A. Timmermans, *Europees Gemeenschapsrecht in kort bestek*, 6th ed. (Groningen, 2003) pages 189–190.
203. Case 46/76, *Bauhuis*; See also Case C-389/00, *Commission v. Germany*.
204. Case 18/87, *Commission v. Federal Republic of Germany*.

situations, such as technical inspection of vehicles, based on Directive 77/143 on roadworthiness tests for motor vehicles, fall within the ambit of Article 90 EC.[205]

2.5   Fiscal Barriers: National Taxation and Harmonization

A different problem is posed by the demarcation between Article 25 EC and the fiscal non-discrimination provisions of Articles 90–91 EC. The practical importance of this demarcation consists, of course, in the fact that Article 25 prohibits certain charges on imported goods, whilst Article 90 on the contrary permits the imposition of taxes on imported products, provided similar domestically produced products are subjected to the same taxes. This is why harmonization in this area is of great importance (see section 2.5.3. below). The Court of Justice has rightly observed, as early on as Case 57/65 *Alfons Lütticke GmbH v. Hauptzollamt Saarlouis*,[206] that Articles 25 and 90 EC cannot be applied at the same time to one and the same situation; a charge falls either under one heading or the other, but not both. From this point of view, Article 90 EC works at the same time both as a complement to the prohibition of customs duties and charges having equivalent effect on imports and exports, and as a justification in relation to that prohibition.[207]

Article 90 does not affect the fiscal sovereignty of the Member States as such.[208] Thus a Member State is free, providing it respects Articles 90–91 EC, to establish its system of taxation and to determine the level of fiscal tariffs until such time as harmonization of fiscal legislation has taken place.[209] Tax measures are a typical means of intervening in the economy, and are solely imposed by public authorities. These measures are therefore only attributable to the state, and cannot in any way be considered as conduct of undertakings.[210]

In the following examination of the tax provisions of the EC Treaty, a number of distinctions are made.[211] First, the various elements of the prohibition of fiscal discrimination are considered (section 2.5.1. below); secondly certain derogations from the prohibition (2.5.2 below); and, thirdly, tax harmonization is briefly examined (2.5.3. below).

---

205. O.J. 1977, L 47/47. See, e.g., Case 50/85, *Bernhard Schloh v. Auto contrôle technique SPRL.*
206. Case 57/65, *Alfons Lütticke v. Hauptzollamt Sarrelouis*; Case C-266/91, *Celulose Beira Industrial (CELBI)*; Case C-90/94, *Haahr*; Case C-234/99, *Nygård*.
207. Joined Cases 2 & 3/62, *Commission v. Luxembourg and Belgium*; Joined Cases 2 & 3/69, *Sociaal Fonds voor de Diamantarbeiders*.
208. Case 127/75, *Bobie Getränkevertrieb v. Hauptzollamt Aachen-Nord*; Case 15/81, *Gaston Schul Douane-Expediteur BV v. Inspecteur der Invoerrechten en Accijnzen, Roosendaal.*
209. On the basis of Arts. 93 or 94 EC.
210. According to A.G. Jacobs, Case C-207/01, *Altair Chimica SpA v. ENEL Distribuzione SpA*, para. 40.
211. Following Barents, 'Artikel 95 en de gemeenschappelijke markt. Preadvies voor de Vereniging voor Europees Recht' (1983) SEW, 438, and 'Nieuwe ontwikkelingen met betrekking tot het fiscale discriminatieverbod van artikel 95 EEG-Verdrag' (1991) SEW, 767.

2.5.1   The Prohibition of Fiscal Discrimination in Article 90 EC

The first paragraph of Article 90 EC prohibits the Member States from imposing, 'directly or indirectly, on the products of other Member States any internal taxation of any kind in excess of that imposed directly or indirectly on similar domestic products'. In the second paragraph of Article 90 EC, the ambit of the prohibition is extended to embrace any internal taxation of such a nature as to afford indirect protection to other products.

It is constant case law of the Court that a tax system is only compatible with Article 90 EC if it is arranged in such a way that the possibility that imported products are more heavily taxed than similar domestic products is excluded.[212] Article 90 EC itself concerns imported products; if, however, products for export are more heavily taxed than products for the domestic market and the tax concerned is part of an internal fiscal system in the sense of Article 90 EC, that provision may be applied by analogy.[213]

It is the first paragraph of Article 90 which states the main principle, starting out from a comparison of fiscal burdens on imported and national products considered to be similar. The second paragraph is directed at all forms of indirect protectionism of products which, although not similar, are indirectly or potentially in a competitive relationship with some domestic products.[214]

Article 90 EC consists of three elements, each of which are examined in turn, below: 'internal taxation'; 'products', and 'of other Member States'. On the basis of these elements two comparisons take place for the purpose of the application of the prohibition. First, a product comparison, to see whether, as the case may be, the domestic products on which the tax is levied are either similar to (Art. 90(1)) or merely competing with (Art. 90(2)) imported products. Then a fiscal comparison takes place in order to ascertain whether the tax on the imported product is, as the case may be, higher (Art. 90(1)) or protective in its effects (Art. 90(2)).[215]

By virtue of Article 91 EC, for products exported to the territory of any Member State, any repayment of internal taxation may not exceed that which has been directly or indirectly imposed on them.[216] This provision is linked to the destination country principle of taxation, according to which tax should be charged in the country in which the product is used or consumed.[217] On exportation, internal

---

212. Case C-152/89, *Commission v. Grand Duchy of Luxembourg*, Case C-68/96, *Grundig Italiana SpA v. Ministero delle Finanze*; Case C-228/98, *Kharalambos Dounias v. Ipourgos Ikonomikon (Minister for Economic Affairs)*.
213. Case 142/77, *Statens Kontrol med ædle Metaller v. Preben Larsen, and Flemming Kjerulff v. Statens Kontrol med ædle Metaller.*
214. Case 168/78, *Commission v. France.*
215. R. Barents, 'Nieuwe ontwikkelingen met betrekking tot het fiscale discriminatieverbod van artikel 95 EEG-Verdrag' (1991) SEW, 767 at 768.
216. See Case 45/64, *Commission v. Italy*; Case C-152/89, *Commission v. Luxembourg*, and Case C-153/89, *Commission v. Kingdom of Belgium.*
217. See Case C-5/05, *Staatsecretaris van Financiën v. Joustra.*

taxation borne by the products should be repaid, and on arrival in the country of destination they should be taxed there according to the applicable system.

2.5.1.1 Internal Taxation

The concept of 'internal taxation' owes its origins to Article III(2) of the GATT[218] and does not refer to domestic tax law, but is a collective term embracing all charges which are imposed on imports as well as domestic products, irrespective of their nature or purpose. The application of Article 90 EC is concerned with guaranteeing the complete neutrality of internal taxation as regards competition between imports and domestic products.[219] The tax concerned may be based on legislation, international agreements (as in the case of the Benelux countries)[220] or administrative instructions.[221]

If a fiscal charge falls to be considered as forming part of a system of internal taxation the application of the principle of non-discrimination will ensure that the principle of competitive neutrality is respected. If such a charge is discriminatory then the amount by which the charge on imports exceeds that on domestic products will still be treated as being part of the internal taxation system, albeit incompatible with Article 90 EC, and will not be treated as a charge having equivalent effect to a customs duty.[222]

The concept of a tax must be widely interpreted,[223] a conclusion which was already supported by the reference to 'internal taxation of any kind' in the first paragraph of Article 90 EC. It covers not merely taxes in the technical sense, such as consumption taxes,[224] but also parafiscal charges[225] (see further 2.5.2 below), monopoly levies,[226] inspection fees,[227] sealing and stamp duties,[228] weights and measures fees;[229] port duties[230] and environmental levies.[231]

---

218. See, generally, Case C-469/93, *Amministrazione delle Finanze dello Stato v. Chiquita Italia SpA*; M.M. Slotboom, 'Do Different Treaty Purposes Matter for Treaty Interpretation? The Elimination of Discriminatory Internal Taxes in EC and WTO Law' (2001) *Journal of International Economic Law*, 557.
219. E.g., Case 252/86, *Gabriel Bergandi v. Directeur général des impôts*; Case 323/87, *Commission v. Italy*.
220. Joined Cases C-367–377/93, *F.G. Roders BV et al. v. Inspecteur der Invoerrechten en Accijnzen*.
221. Case 17/81, *Pabst & Richarz KG v. Hauptzollamt Oldenburg*.
222. Case 7/67, *Firma Milchwerke H. Wöhrmann & Sohn KG v. Hauptzollamt Bad Reichenhall*; Case 25/67, *Firma Milch-, Fett- und Eierkontor v. Hauptzollamt Saarbrücken*.
223. Case 20/76, *Schöttle & Söhne OHG v. Finanzamt Freudenstadt*; Case C-221/06, *Stadtgemeinde Frohnheiten*.
224. E.g., Case 112/84, *Michel Humblot v. Directeur des Services Fiscaux*.
225. E.g., Case 77/72, *Carmine Capolongo v. Azienda Agricola Maya*.
226. E.g., Case 45/75, *Rewe-Zentrale des Lebensmittel-Großhandels v. Hauptzollamt Landau/Pfalz*.
227. E.g., Case 46/76, *Bauhuis*.
228. Case 77/69, *Commission v. Kingdom of Belgium*.
229. Case 142/77, *Statens Kontrol med Ódle Metaller v. Larsen*.
230. Case C-90/94, *Haahr*; Joined Cases C-114 & 115/95, *Texaco A/S v. Middelfart Havn et al., and Olieselskabet Danmark amba v. Trafikministeriet et al.* In Case C-242/95, *GT-Link A/S v. De Danske Statsbaner (DSB)*, the same facts were examined under Arts. 81 and 86 EC.
231. Case C-213/96, *Outokumpu Oy*.

2.5.1.2 Products

The term 'products' in Article 90 EC has the same meaning as that term has in Article 23 EC.[232] Thus Article 90 also applies to agricultural products[233] and to electricity.[234] Special rules which were broadly similar to Article 90 EC used to apply in respect of European Coal and Steel Community (ECSC) products, when the ECSC Treaty was in force, and based on Article 60(1) of that Treaty.[235] The fact that the origin of the product in question determines the amount of tax to be levied cannot put a tax outside the scope of Article 90 EC.[236]

Financial charges which involve a restriction of the cross-border supply of services will have to be examined in the light of Article 49 EC.[237] Moreover, Article 90 EC is inapplicable to monetary and capital transactions.[238] In certain cases, the competition provisions will come into play, in particular Article 86 EC.[239]

The production stage at which the tax is imposed is irrelevant, as can be deduced from the words 'directly or indirectly'.[240]

If the products in question are second-hand, the fact that no 'first-hand' products are produced in the relevant Member State does not mean that there is no market for second-hand products. The Court has held that other imported and resold second-hand products are to be considered similar or competing products.[241]

2.5.1.3 Of Other Member States

In this respect too, the comparison with Article 23 EC is appropriate, so that Article 90 also applies to products originating in a third country which are in free circulation in a Member State.[242] Article 90 EC does not concern products which are imported directly from third countries.[243] A charge in the framework of a general

---

232. See section 2.1, *supra*.
233. E.g., Joined Cases 36 & 71/80, *Irish Creamery Milk Suppliers Association et al. v. Government of Ireland et al., and Martin Doyle et al. v. An Taoiseach et al.*
234. Case C-213/96, *Outokumpu Oy*.
235. See Dec. 30/53. O.J. 1953, 109.
236. Case C-90/94, *Haahr*; Case C-213/96, *Outokumpu Oy*.
237. Joined Cases 62 & 63/81, *Société anonyme de droit français Seco et al. v. Établissements d'Assurance contre la Vieillesse et l'Invalidité*; Joined Cases C-430 & 431/99, *Inspecteur van de Belastingdienst Douane, Rotterdam district v. Sea-Land Service Inc. and Nedlloyd Lijnen BV*.
238. Case 267/86, *Pascal Van Eycke v. ASPA NV*.
239. Case C-242/95, *GT-Link*.
240. Case 45/64, *Commission v. Italy*; Case 28/67, *Firma Molkerei-Zentrale Westfalen/Lippe v. Hauptzollamt Paderborn*; Case 78/76, *Steinike & Weinlig*.
241. Case C-47/88, *Commission v. Kingdom of Denmark*; Case C-228/98, *Dounias*.
242. See section 2.3, *supra*, and Case 193/85, *Cooperativa Co-Frutta Srl v. Amministrazione delle Finanze dello Stato*.
243. Case C-130/92, *OTO SpA v. Ministero delle Finanze*; Joined Cases C-114 & 115/95, *Texaco*; Case C-284/96, *Didier Tabouillot v. Directeur des services fiscaux de Meurthe-et-Moselle*.

system of taxation on imports of goods coming directly from third countries is permitted, to the extent that its imposition is not incompatible with the application of the common commercial policy or with international agreements between the Community and the third countries from which the product comes.[244] National taxes which treat domestic products more severely than imports are not affected by the prohibition in Article 90 EC, i.e., reverse discrimination is permitted.[245]

2.5.1.4   Product Comparison

In the comparison of products, attention is paid to defining the relationship between the products on which the taxes to be compared are imposed. What should be done when there is no national production, as for instance in the case of cars in Denmark?[246] Article 90 intends to guarantee the complete neutrality of internal taxation as regards competition between imports and domestic products. Consequently, Article 90 may not be invoked in relation to an internal tax which, in the absence of any national production of similar or competing products, only affects imported products. The manner in which this domestic tax is levied may be examined in the framework of Article 28 EC, however.[247]

The first paragraph of Article 90 EC covers 'similar' products; once similarity is found, the tax must be equal,[248] though there are certain exceptions to this non-discrimination principle to be found in the case law (see 2.5.2. below). The Court interprets the term 'similar' in a wide sense, thus products are considered to be similar, if they 'have similar characteristics and meet the same needs from the point of view of consumers'.[249] The concept of similarity is a Community legal concept, and the first consideration is 'certain objective characteristics' of both products (or categories of products), such as their composition and method of manufacture.[250] National law, customs or consumer habits cannot be advanced in order to ascertain the similarity of products, and Community law may well provide indications as to similarity: the products may fall under the same common customs tariff classification heading, or under the same system of common organization of the market.[251]

---

244. Joined Cases C-228–234, 339 & 353/90, *Simba SpA et al. v. Ministero delle Finanze*; Case 469/93, *Chiquita Italia SpA*.
245. Case 86/78, *Peureux*.
246. Case C-383/01, *De Danske Bilimportører v. Skatteministeriet, Told- og Skattestyrelsen*.
247. Case C-47/88, *Commission v. Denmark*; Case C-383/01, *Danske Bilimportører*.
248. Cf. Case C-213/96, *Outokumpu Oy*; Case C-387/01, *Harald Weigel and Ingrid Weigel v. Finanzlandesdirektion für Vorarlberg*.
249. E.g., Case 216/81, *Cogis (Compagnia Generale Interscambi) v. Amministrazione delle Finanze dello Stato* at 2712, and Case 106/84, *Commission v. Kingdom of Denmark* at 870; Case C-265/99, *Commission v. France*; Case C-101/00, *Tulliasiamies and Antti Siilin*.
250. Case 243/84, *John Walker & Sons Ltd v. Ministeriet for Skatter og Afgifter*.
251. E.g., Case 168/78, *Commission v. France*; Case 169/78, *Commission v. Italy*; Case 170/78, *Commission v. United Kingdom*; Case 171/78, *Commission v. Kingdom of Denmark*; Case 55/79, *Commission v. Ireland*; Case 356/85, *Commission v. Kingdom of Belgium*; and Case C-230/89, *Commission v. Hellenic Republic*.

In the second paragraph of Article 90 EC, product comparison is concerned with indirect protection. The decisive element in this instance is whether the products concerned actually compete with domestic products.[252] In deciding whether there is indirect protection, identifying the relevant market is important, as was evident from cases concerning whisky and cognac, and different types of fruit.[253]

2.5.1.5   Fiscal Comparison

Fiscal comparison only involves the fiscal burdens on the products concerned. Article 90 EC provides no basis for arguments for compensating by the fiscal route an advantage or disadvantage of an economic nature.[254] The comparison takes place on the basis of the national system of internal taxation concerned, and within that framework the non-discrimination principle must be respected.[255] The comparison involves not only the rate of the tax[256] but also the basis of assessment,[257] the stage at which the tax is levied,[258] the application of any preferences and the methods of payment,[259] as well as means of enforcement.[260] In other words: a charge in the form of a domestic tax can only be considered a charge having an equivalent effect to a customs duty if the manner in which it is applied is such that the burden in fact lies only on imported products and not on national products.[261]

2.5.2   The Exceptions to the Prohibition

Practical difficulties are not a justification for discriminatory treatment of products from other Member States.[262] In certain cases, a justification may be found (i.e., an exception to the prohibition); it is interpreted strictly, however.

---

252. Case 27/67, *Firma Fink-Frucht v. Hauptzollamt München-Landsbergerstraße.*
253. Case 168/78, *Commission v. France*; Case 193/85, *Co-Frutta*; Case 356/85, *Commission v. Belgium.* However, see Case 27/76, *United Brands Company and United Brands Continentaal BV v. Commission*, where in a competition case the Court came to another conclusion for bananas. R. Barents is critical of this, op. cit. *supra* note 215, at 778.
254. Case 45/75, *Rewe-Zentrale.*
255. Case 127/75, *Bobie Getránkevertrieb*; Case C-101/00, *Tulliasiamies.*
256. Case C-90/94, *Haahr.*
257. Case 55/79, *Commission v. Ireland*; Case C-68/96, *Grundig Italiana*; Case C-213/96, *Outokumpu Oy.*
258. Case 132/78, *Denkavit Loire*, but see Joined Cases C-149 & 150/91, *Sanders Adour SNC and Guyomarc'h Orthez Nutrition Animale SA v. Directeur des Services Fiscaux des Pyrenées-Atlantiques*, and Case C-213/96, *Outokumpu Oy.*
259. Case 171/78, *Commission v. Denmark*; Case C-90/94, *Haahr*; Case C-228/96, *Aprile Srl, in liquidation, v. Amministrazione delle Finanze dello Stato*; Case C-343/96, *Dilexport Srl v. Amministrazione delle Finanze dello Stato.*
260. Case 299/86, *Criminal proceedings against Rainer Drexl.* Case C-276/91, *Commission v. France.*
261. Case 32/80, *Criminal proceedings against J.A.W.M.J. Kortmann.*
262. Case C-375/95, *Commission v. Hellenic Republic*; Case C-213/96, *Outokumpu Oy.*

2.5.2.1   Parafiscal Charges

In certain cases, the prohibition of fiscal discrimination does not operate satisfactorily: this is so for parafiscal charges which are destined to function as state aids benefiting national products or production. The policy is usually the same: a public law body levies the charge without discrimination as to the origin of the product concerned, and uses the revenue raised for its own purposes, such as promotion or research, to the benefit of national production. Article 90 EC appears not to be infringed, since the charge itself does not discriminate against imported products in any manner. The discriminatory effect, and thus the obstacle to trade, occurs later, namely when the revenue from the charge is used as selective aid. It might be thought that this would be examined in the light of Articles 87–89 EC,[263] which is the policy followed by the Commission in a number of agricultural cases.[264] However, the Court very early on adopted another approach,[265] starting out from Article 90 EC and going on via the selective state aid aspect to place such a measure firmly in the realm of Articles 25 EC, thus treating such parafiscal charges as being in reality equivalent to a customs duty: this is often called the *Capolongo* approach.[266]

The conditions for this 'back to square one' approach were developed in subsequent case law. In *Steinike*, the Court considered that a duty which has the characteristics of an internal tax, affecting both imported products and similar national, products could however constitute a charge having an effect equivalent to a customs duty if such a duty, limited to particular products, has the sole purpose of financing activities for the specific advantage of the taxed domestic products, so as to make good, wholly or in part, the fiscal charge imposed upon them.[267] These activities should be for the 'specific' advantage of the taxed domestic products. There should be identity between the national products subject to the tax and receiving the advantage, and the advantage should fully offset the burden borne

---

263. See Case C-345/02, *Pearle*. See also Joined Cases C-261 & 262/01, *Belgium v. Eugene Van Calster, Felix Cleeren (C-261/01) and v. Openbaar Slachthuis NV* and Case C-174/02, *Streekgewest Westelijk Noord-Brabant*.
264. E.g., XXIIIrd Report on Competition Policy 1993 (Brussels, Luxembourg, 1994), point 551.
265. See R. Barents, 'Artikel 95 en de gemeenschappelijke markt. Preadvies voor de Vereniging voor Europees Recht' (1983) SEW, 438 at 450.
266. Case 77/72, *Capolongo*; Case 94/74, *Industria Gomma Articoli Vari IGAV v. Ente Nazionale per la Cellulosa e per la Carta ENCC*; Case 77/76, *Fratelli Cucchi v. Avez SpA*; Case 78/76, *Steinike & Weinlig*; Case 105/76, *Interzuccheri S.p.A. v. Società Rezzano e Cavassa*; Case 222/78, *I.C.A.P. v. Walter Beneventi*; Joined Cases C-78–83/90, *Compagnie commerciale de l'Ouest et al. v. Receveur principal des douanes de La Pallice-Port*; Joined Cases C-228–234, 339 & 353/90, *Simba SpA et al. v. Ministero delle Finanze*; Case C-114/91, *Criminal proceedings against Gérard Jerôme Claeys*; Case C-266/91, *Celulose Beira Industrial (CELBI) SA*; Case C-45/94, *Cámara de Comercio, Industria y Navegación de Ceuta v. Ayuntamiento de Ceuta*; Case C-28/96, *Fazenda Pública v. Fricarnes SA*; Case C-517/04, *Koornstra v. Productschap voor Vis*. See on this *Capolongo* construction, R. Barents, 'Charges of Equivalent Effect' (1978) CML Rev., 415–434, esp. 425.
267. Case 78/76, *Steinike & Weinlig*. See also Case C-234/99, *Nygård*.

by the domestic product.[268] In *Lornoy*, the Court added that if those advantages only partly offset the burden borne by domestic products, the charge would be incompatible with Article 90, to the extent to which it discriminates against imported products.[269] It is a matter for the national court to decide on the question of whether the charge is wholly or partially offset.[270]

Later, the Court ruled that if a national charge is intended for the financing of an aid system which has been approved by the Commission under the Treaty provisions relating to state aids, this does not prevent the national arrangements from being assessed in the national courts in relation to other Treaty provisions, such as Articles 25 and 90 EC.[271]

2.5.2.2 *Fiscal Preferences and Differentiated Taxation of Products*

In the case of taxes, the purpose of the measure is less important than in the case of non-tariff barriers. The purpose of fiscal measures is to obtain revenue for the state; but on the expenditure side, such as in the grant of state aid, there may be numerous objectives of a measure, as is apparent from the *Capolongo* situation.[272] Even so, certain fiscal preferences are granted and differential taxation is levied, and these national policy objectives have to conform to the non-discrimination principle of Article 90 EC.[273] As well as national policy objectives, common policy objectives – such as environmental protection – may be concerned.[274] The Court has applied these rules in a large number of cases concerning cars,[275] and a few cases concerning alcohol,[276] oil and electricity,[277] and cigarettes.[278]

---

268. Case 77/76, *Cucchi*.
269. Case C-17/91, *Georges Lornoy en Zonen NV et al. v. Belgium*. See also Joined Cases C-78–83/90, *Compagnie commerciale de l'Ouest*; Joined Cases C-149 & 150/91, *Sanders Adour*; Joined Cases C-261 & 262/01, *Van Calster*.
270. Joined Cases C-149 & 150/91, *Sanders Adour*; Case C-72/92, *Firma Herbert Scharbatke v. Federal Republic of Germany*.
271. Case C-234/99, *Nygård*, with reference to Case 74/76, *Iannelli & Volpi SpA v. Ditta Paolo Meroni*; Case 17/81, *Pabst*; Case C-72/92, *Scharbatke*.
272. See R. Barents, 'Artikel 95 en de gemeenschappelijke markt. Preadvies voor de Vereniging voor Europees Recht' (1983) SEW, 438 at 455.
273. E.g., Case 21/79, *Commission v. Italy*.
274. Case C-213/96, *Outokumpu Oy*.
275. Case 112/84, *Humblot*; Case C-132/88, *Commission v. Hellenic Republic*; Case C-47/88, *Commission v. Denmark*; Case C-327/90, *Commission v. Hellenic Republic*; Case C-343/90, *Manuel José Lourenço Dias v. Director da Alfândega do Porto*; Case C-412/97, *ED Srl v. Italo Fenocchio*; Case C-387/01, *Weigel*. After a number of preliminary references, France was finally condemned in an infringement case; see Case C-265/99, *Commission v. France*. The Opinion of the AG refers to all the preliminary rulings. See also in the Netherlands *Hoge Raad* 6 Dec. 2002, Case 37666 (second hand cars), NJB 2003, 95.
276. In a few older Italian alcohol cases, the conditions – and in particular the prohibition on discrimination – were applied in a rather controversial manner; see Case 140/79, *Chemial Farmaceutici SpA v. DAF SpA*; Case 46/80, *SpA Vinal v. SpA Orbat*.
277. Case 21/79, *Commission v. Italy*; Case C-213/96, *Outokumpu Oy*.
278. Case C-302/00, *Commission v. France*.

As is the case with Articles 28–29 EC, the starting point of the analysis is the absence of Community rules on the matter concerned. Due to the adoption of a number of directives (see section 2.5.3. below), certain national policy measures are examined in the light of both the Treaty provisions and the EC directive.[279] Further, the preference or differentiation must be based on objective criteria, such as the engine size of motor vehicles, or the type of raw materials involved, and any advantages must serve legitimate economic or social purposes.[280] The difference may not lead to direct or indirect discrimination against the imported products concerned, or to protection of competing national products.[281] The fact that domestically produced goods are in some cases taxed more heavily than imported goods is irrelevant, since the comparison must be made with the lowest taxes on domestic products.[282]

2.5.2.3   Double Taxation

As long as there is no fiscal harmonization – or at least not complete fiscal harmonization – there is a risk of double taxation. Because the destination country principle is used generally, double taxation problems remain very much the exception. On one occasion when the Court did have to deal with such problems, it concluded that there was no infringement of Article 90 EC because the exported products and the products which were processed domestically were treated equally in fiscal terms: double taxation did indeed constitute an obstacle to trade, but it could only be removed through harmonization.[283]

There is also a danger of double taxation as long as the rules on Value Added Tax (VAT) are not completely harmonized.[284]

2.5.3   Harmonization of Taxation

For the abolition of fiscal frontiers within the Community, more is necessary than the mere application of the prohibition of fiscal discrimination contained in Article 90 EC. Article 93 EC gives the Council the power to adopt provisions for the harmonization of legislation concerning turnover taxes, excise duties and other forms of indirect taxation to the extent such harmonization is necessary to ensure the establishment and functioning of the internal market.[285] By Decision

---

279. Case C-302/00, *Commission v. France*; Case C-101/00, *Tulliasiamies*.
280. E.g., Case 148/77, *H. Hansen jun. & O.C. Balle & Co. v. Hauptzollamt Flensburg*.
281. Joined Cases 142 & 143/80, *Amministrazione delle Finance dello Stato v. Essevi SpA and Carlo Salengo*.
282. Case C-152/89, *Commission v. Luxembourg*; Case C-213/96, *Outokumpu Oy*.
283. Case 142/77, *Statens Kontrol med Ódle Metaller v. Larsen*; Case C-234/99, *Nygård*.
284. Case 15/81, *Schul I*; Case 47/84, *Staatssecretaris van Financiën v. Gaston Schul Douane-Expediteur BV (Schul II)*. See also Case 134/83, *Criminal proceedings against J. G. Abbink*.
285. The present version of Art. 93 EC differs from the original version; as to this difference, see VerLoren van Themaat (1986) SEW, 464 at 477.

2235/2002, a Community programme to improve the operation of tax systems in the internal market was adopted (as part of the Fiscalis programme 2003–2007).[286]

Various aspects of direct taxation are discussed in the context of free movement of workers (section 5.5), freedom of establishment (sections 6.5.1 and 6.9), freedom to provide services (section 7.4.1), and free movement of capital (section 8.3).

2.5.3.1   VAT and Excise Duties

The most important tax in the context of free movement of goods is undoubtedly VAT. VAT is one of the sources of income of the Community (see Ch. V). In the context of this book, we can only indicate the main lines of the EC tax rules.[287] Because the directives relating to VAT offer the Member States various choices and exceptions, the Court is confronted with many and various questions; for example, a Dutch case raised the question of VAT and cannabis.[288]

VAT is based on the principle that a general 'usage' tax is imposed on goods and services which is strictly proportional to their price, regardless of the transactions involved in the process of production and distribution prior to that stage of imposition. On every transaction, VAT is calculated by application of the respective tariff to the sales price, but the seller, when handing the VAT over to authorities, may deduct the tax he or she has paid in the process of that stage of producing the goods or services concerned. This deduction ensures that each stage of production or distribution pays a tax only on the value added at that stage.[289] VAT is imposed up to and including the retail stage, so that the last burden is borne by the consumer or ultimate user.[290]

VAT harmonization commenced during the 1960s, and the cumulative multistage turnover tax systems, which distorted competition and created barriers to trade between Member States, were abolished.[291] By 1977 the Council was able to adopt the Sixth VAT Directive, Directive 77/388,[292] which establishes a common system of VAT with a uniform basis of assessment. In order to facilitate the completion and proper functioning of the internal market, the Council was to adopt the necessary measures by the end of 1992, but disagreement about the

---

286. O.J. 2002, L 341/1. The Fiscalis Programme, which aims to ameliorate the indirect taxation systems of the internal market, was established by Decision No. 888/98, O.J. 1998, L 126/1.
287. There are a number of general text books on EC tax law, e.g., B.J.M. Terra and P.J. Wattel, *European Tax Law*, 4th ed. (Deventer, 2005).
288. Case C-158/98, *Coffeeshop Siberië*.
289. See Dir. 67/227 (O.J. English Special Edition 1967, 14), Art. 2 (as amended).
290. For a good summary of the characteristics of VAT, referring to the relevant case law, see the Opinion of AG Saggio, Case C-437/97, *Evangelischer Krankenhausverein Wien v. Abgaben-berufungskommission Wien and Wein & Co. HandelsgesmbH v. Oberösterreichische Landesregierung*, para. 17.
291. By the First and Second VAT Directives, Dirs. 67/227 and 67/228 (O.J. 1967, 71, 1301 and 1303, respectively).
292. O.J. 1977, L 145/1, most recently amended by Council Dir. 2006/69/EC (O.J. 2006, L 221/9).

nature of the appropriate system led to the adoption of an interim solution in Directive 91/680, amending Directive 77/388.[293] This Directive takes the destination country principle as the basis (VAT is in principle due in the Member State in which the goods are ultimately used). Subsequently, Directive 92/77 was adopted, on the approximation of VAT rates between the Member States.[294] The Council has adopted a number of directives (Directives 95/7, 96/42 and 96/95)[295] simplifying the VAT rules.

In relation to privatizations, a number of judgments given by the Court in infringement cases brought by the Commission against Member States, give important clarifications concerning the rules the central national authorities must abide by in order to remain exempt from VAT. The judgments concern the interpretation of Article 4(5) of Directive 77/388.[296]

Article 33 of Directive 77/388 provides that, without prejudice to other Community provisions, in particular those on excise duties, the provisions of the Directive do not prevent a Member State from maintaining or introducing a number of taxes, duties or charges which cannot be characterized as turnover taxes,[297] such as those on insurance contracts, or on betting and gambling, providing they do not lead to formalities in connection with crossing a border in the context of inter-state trade.[298] Article 33 of the Directive has also been examined in the context of other taxes.[299]

Council Directive 77/388 has been significantly amended on several occasions. For reasons of clarity and rationalization, it was 'recast' by Directive 2006/112.[300] The recast text also incorporates Directive 67/227, and the latter Directive has been repealed. Directive 2006/112 entered into force on 1 January 2007.

As far as excise duties are concerned, a general directive was adopted – Directive 92/12[301] – and a number of specific directives concerning tobacco,

---

293.   O.J. 1991, L 376/1.
294.   O.J. 1992, L 416/1.
295.   See O.J. 1995, L 102/18; O.J. 1995, L 170/34; and O.J. 1996, L 338/89.
296.   Case C-276/97, *Commission v. France*; Case C-358/97, *Commission v. Ireland*; Case C-359/97, *Commission v. United Kingdom of Great Britain and Northern Ireland*; Case C-408/97, *Commission v. Kingdom of the Netherlands*; Case C-260/98, *Commission v. Hellenic Republic*. See already Case C-202/90, *Ayuntamiento de Sevilla v. Recaudadores de Tributos de las Zonas primera y segunda.*
297.   For this concept, see Case C-200/90, *Dansk Denkavit ApS and P. Poulsen Trading ApS v. Skatteministeriet.*
298.   E.g., a Dutch special consumption tax was found not to infringe Community law; Joined Cases 93 & 94/88, *Wisselink en Co. BV et al. v. Staatssecretaris van Financiën.*
299.   Case 73/85, *Hans-Dieter and Ute Kerrutt v. Finanzamt Mönchengladbach-Mitte*; Case C-109/90, *NV Giant v. Gemeente Overijse*; Case C-318/96, *SPAR Österreichische Warenhandels AG v. Finanzlandesdirektion für Salzburg*; Case C-437/97, *Evangelischer Krankenhausverein Wien.*
300.   O.J. 2006, L 347/1.
301.   O.J. 1992, L 76/1, amended by Dir. 92/108 (O.J. 1992, L 390/124). See Case C-408/95, *Eurotunnel SA et al. v. Sea France* and Case C-434/97, *Commission v. France*; Case C-325/99, *G. van de Water v. Staatssecretaris van Financiën*; Case C-5/05, *Staatssecretaris van Financiën v. Joustra.*

alcohol and alcoholic drinks and petroleum products.[302] Regulation 2073/2004 lays down rules and procedures for administrative cooperation in the area of excise duties.[303] Regulation 218/92, concerning administrative cooperation in the field of indirect taxation (VAT) has also been significant;[304] it is replaced by Regulation 1798/2003[305] (the latter Regulation was challenged before the Court of Justice by the Commission, but the application was rejected[306]).

2.6   THE COMMON CUSTOMS TARIFF AND CHARGES HAVING
        EQUIVALENT EFFECT IN RELATION TO THIRD COUNTRIES

The levy of customs duties and charges having equivalent effect in relation to trade between the Community and third countries is part of the Community's common commercial policy, a policy which is discussed *in extenso* in Chapter XIII, below, as part of the Community's external relations. A special regime is applicable to agricultural products subject to a common organization of the market: this is described in Chapter XII, below. The discussion in this section examines the external dimension of the free movement of goods, emphasizing two aspects: the common customs tariff and the rules on charges having equivalent effect to customs duties in external trade.

2.6.1   Common Customs Tariff

In Article 131 EC, the Member States have declared their intention to follow a liberal tariff policy *vis-à-vis* third countries on a basis of reciprocity. Even before the common customs tariff entered into force, on 1 July 1968, very considerable tariff reductions were achieved in the framework of the GATT, first in the Dillon Round, but particularly later on, in the Kennedy Round (1964–1967) The common customs tariff was first introduced by Regulation 950/68,[307] but with effect from 1 January 1988 the new integrated tariff and statistical nomenclature system introduced by Regulation 2658/87[308] has replaced the old system of Regulation 950/68. This new Combined Nomenclature is based on the International Convention on the Harmonized Commodity Description and Coding System and forms the basis of the integrated tariff, with Community sub-divisions, known as the 'Taric'. The applicable duties and levies are fixed on the basis of the TARIC categories. The Commission publishes the TARIC regularly.[309]

---

302. Dirs. 92/78 (O.J. 1992, L 316/5); 92/79 to 92/94 (O.J. 1992, L 316). See also Dir. 95/59 (O.J. 1995, L 291/40). See Case C-302/00, *Commission v. France.*
303. O.J. 2004, L 359/1.
304. O.J. 1992, L 24/1.
305. O.J. 2003, L 264/1.
306. See Case C-533/03, *Commission v. Council.*
307. O.J. 1968, L 172/1.
308. O.J. 1987, L 256/1. See also the Commission's Communication, O.J. 1994, L 342/1.
309. E.g., O.J. 2000, C 115; O.J. 2002, C 104. See also O.J. 2004, C 258.

The discussion here is confined to the general system, and does not take account of particular regimes associated with certain products, e.g., agriculture or textiles; nor does it deal with preferential arrangements or association arrangements for particular countries.[310]

In May 2007, an action programme for customs in the Community was launched.[311]

2.6.2 Charges Having Equivalent Effect in relation to Third Countries

The EC Treaty contains no provisions on charges having equivalent effect to customs duties in trade with third countries. The concept is indeed referred to in Article 24(1) EC, but that provision, which deals with goods in free circulation in a Member State, contains no obligations or prohibitions as such. The Court was first confronted with charges having equivalent effect in external trade in 1973,[312] after it had already dealt with such charges in internal trade in 1969.[313] It considered that even though no mention was made in the chapter on the Customs Union of charges having equivalent effect to customs duties, that did not mean that such charges could be maintained, let alone introduced. In answering this problem, the requirements of the common customs tariff and the common commercial policy would form the starting point for its approach. Although the common customs tariff regulation did not in so many words require the repeal or equalization of such charges, it appeared from the objectives of Regulation 950/68 that it involved a prohibition on the levying by the Member States of charges other than the customs duties for which it provided, and thus of creating changes to the level of protection provided for in the common customs tariff itself. Even in the absence of protectionist characteristics, such charges could be incompatible with the common commercial policy of the Community. Accordingly, since the coming into force of the common customs tariff, the Member States are forbidden to introduce unilateral new charges or to increase the level of existing charges. As to the latter, it depends on developments in commercial policy whether they are compatible with the EC Treaty.[314]

---

310. See Ch. XIII. See also e.g., Case 17/81, *Pabst*; Case 104/81, *Hauptzollamt Mainz v. C.A. Kupferberg & Cie. KG a.A.*; Case 430/92, *Kingdom of the Netherlands v. Commission*.
311. See Decision No. 624/2007/EC of the European Parliament and of the Council of 23 May 2007 establishing an action programme for customs in the Community (Customs 2013), O.J. 2007, L 154.
312. Joined Cases 37 & 38/73, *Sociaal Fonds voor de Diamantarbeiders v. NV Indiamex et al.* See also Case 70/77, *Simmenthal SpA v. Amministrazione delle Finanze dello Stato*, and Case 30/79, *Land Berlin v. Firma Wigei, Wild-Geflügel-Eier-Import*.
313. Joined Cases 2 & 3/69, *Sociaal Fonds voor de Diamantarbeiders*; see also Case C-130/93, *Lamaire NV*.
314. Joined Cases 37 & 38/73, *Sociaal Fonds voor de Diamantarbeiders*; Case C-109/98, *CRT France*.

2.7   COMMUNITY CUSTOMS LEGISLATION

After the Common customs tariff entered into force on 1 July 1968, the Council gradually adopted directives and regulations which aimed to harmonize customs legislation, and achieve a high degree of uniformity.[315] A Community Customs Code was adopted by the Council, in Regulation 2913/92.[316] This Code entered into force on 1 January 1994, after the necessary implementing regulations had been published. As indicated in the preamble of Regulation 2913/92, this Code, based on the concept of an internal market, should contain the general rules and procedures which ensure the implementation of the tariff and other measures introduced at Community level in connection with trade in goods between the Community.

In recent years, the emphasis has been on combating fraud. The Community enacted Regulation 2988/95 on the protection of the European Communities' financial interests[317] and the Member States have concluded an agreement on the same subject.[318] See Chapter VII further on this.

3   FREE MOVEMENT OF GOODS: NON-TARIFF ASPECTS

Apart from customs duties and charges having equivalent effect, inter-state trade can also be restricted by quota systems and other quantitative restrictions or measures having equivalent effect. The EC Treaty distinguishes between restrictions on imports (Art. 28 EC) and those on exports (Art. 29 EC). The case law of the Court confirms that the prohibitions and exceptions thereto also apply to goods in transit.[319]

Certain economic law instruments, such as measures affecting or regulating prices, may be adopted by the public authorities, by the private sector, or by both acting together. If the public authorities act, this action may fall within the scope of Article 28 EC,[320] even if the body setting the price is a public body in the broader sense of the word, rather than a state authority as such.[321] If the prices are fixed by

---

315. See on this extensively D. Lasok, *The Trade and Customs Law of the EU* (The Hague, 1998).
316. O.J. 1992, L 302/1, most recently amended by Reg. 2700/2000 (O.J. 2000, L 311/17). See also Terra, *Community Customs Law* (The Hague, 1995).
317. O.J. 1995, L 312/1.
318. O.J. 1995, C 316/48. See further Ch. VII. See also on this S. White, *Protection of the Financial Interests of the EC: The Fight against Fraud and Corruption* (The Hague, 1998).
319. Case 266/81, *SIOT*; Case C-367/89, *Richardt*; Case C-112/00, *Schmidberger*; Case C-115/02, *Administration des douanes et droits indirects v. Rioglass SA and Transremar SL.*
320. E.g., Joined Cases 88–90/75, *Società SADAM et al. v. Comitato Interministeriale dei Prezzi et al.*
321. Such as *produktschappen* in The Netherlands; see, e.g., Case 82/77, *Openbaar Ministerie v. Jacobus Philippus van Tiggele.*

one or more undertakings, Articles 81 or 82 EC may be applicable.[322] There remains, though, a broad field covered by measures taken by both public and private sectors together, such as in those areas where the authorities have power to declare arrangements reached in particular branches of commerce and industry generally binding on all market participants, for instance a competition arrangement[323] or by measures whereby the action of one (public or private body) in fact makes action by the other superfluous.[324] It is in this context that the growing case law on Articles 3(1)(g), 10, 81 and 82 EC must be situated.[325]

There are several reasons why it is important whether Article 81 or Article 28 is applicable.[326] First, the exceptions to the prohibition of Article 28 are more numerous and extensive than those to Article 81(1) set out in Article 81(3);[327] secondly, Article 81 embraces measures which are confined to national territory but which create barriers to entry for imports,[328] whereas Article 28 does not embrace purely internal situations involving no real link to inter-state trade, in particular local regulation of socio-economic life.[329] Thirdly, Article 28 does not seem to have horizontal direct effect,[330] while Article 81 EC can be relied on in proceedings by a private party against a cartel. Now that Article 81(3) EC, since the entry into force of Regulation 1/2003, is directly effective, a further distinction between the application of Article 28 and Article 81 has disappeared.[331]

In section 3.1, the prohibition on quantitative restrictions is briefly mentioned; then in section 3.2 attention turns to measures having equivalent effect. In section 3.3 the exceptions to the prohibitions are considered. State monopolies of a commercial character are considered in section 3.4, before attention turns in

---

322. E.g., Joined Cases 177 & 178/82, *Criminal proceedings against Jan van de Haar and Kaveka de Meern BV.*
323. E.g., Case 123/83, *Bureau National Interprofessional du Cognac v. Guy Clair.*
324. E.g., Case 229/83, *Leclerc v. Àu blé vert.*
325. See Ch. III, section 4.5.5, *supra*, and Ch. IX, *infra* See also D. Steinberger, *Staatliche Wirtschaftsinterventionen als Verstoss gegen die Wettbewerbsregeln des EG-Vertrages* (Cologne, 1994); C.M. von Quitzow, *State Measures Distorting Free Competition in the EC* (The Hague, 2002); N. Reich 'The "November Revolution" of the European Court of Justice: Keck, Meng and Audi revisited' (1994) CML Rev., 459. See Case C-35/96, *Commission v. Italy*; Case C-309/99, *Wouters.*
326. See P. VerLoren van Themaat, 'Gaat de Luxemburgse rechtspraak over de vier vrijheden en die over het mededingingsbeleid uiteenlopen?' (1996) SEW, 398–402.
327. But see K.J.M. Mortelmans, 'Convergence in the Application of the Rules on Free Movement and on Competition' (2001) CML Rev., 613.
328. Case 8/72, *Vereeniging van Cementhandelaren v. Commission.* See also Joined Cases C-215 & 216/96, *Carlo Bagnasco et al. v. Banca Popolare di Novara soc. coop. arl. (BNP) and Cassa di Risparmio di Genova v. Imperia SpA (Carige).*
329. See section 1.3, *supra*. See also Joined Cases C-241 & 242/91 P, *Radio Telefis Eireann (RTE) and Independent Television Publications Ltd (ITP) v. Commission.*
330. See Case C-159/00, *Sapod Audic.* See also Case C-325/00, *Commission v. Germany.*
331. O.J. 2003, L 1/1.

section 3.5 to the relationship between Articles 28–30 EC and trade with third countries.

3.1 QUANTITATIVE RESTRICTIONS

Quantitative import or export restrictions include all legislative or administrative rules or administrative measures restricting the importation or exportation of one or more products according to quantitative norms or according to their value.[332] They are usually measures which distinguish between national and foreign products. Quantitative restriction only feature very rarely in the case law of the Court.[333] In many instances national measures which really belong in the category of quantitative restrictions are simply brought under the heading of measures having equivalent effect.[334]

3.2 MEASURES HAVING EQUIVALENT EFFECT

This discussion is divided into a number of subsections: in section 3.2.1 the evolution of the case law from *Dassonville* to *Keck and Mithouard* and beyond is sketched; then in the next two sections the prohibition of measures having equivalent effect is considered in relation to imports and then to exports. Finally, the relationship between Article 28 EC and other provisions of the EC Treaty is discussed (section 3.2.4.). The grounds of exception to the prohibitions are considered in the next main section, section 3.3, below.

3.2.1 Evolution of the Concept from *Dassonville* through *Keck* and *Mithouard* and Beyond

If the definition of quantitative restrictions proved easy enough, the same cannot be said of measures having equivalent effect. The latter is a catch-all concept which is not defined in the Treaty or in legislation. It is up to the courts to elaborate this vague norm, with the help of examples in practice.[335] The courts are helped in this by the Commission and by academic analyses. As was mentioned in the introduction to this chapter (section 1.6 above), the case law of the Court of Justice is not

---

332. Case 2/73, *Riseria Luigi Geddo v. Ente nazionale Risi.* See recently Case C-170/04, *Rosengren et al. v. Riksåklagaren.*
333. Case 231/78, *Commission v. United Kingdom* and Case 34/79, *Regina v. Maurice Donald Henn and John Frederick Ernest Darby.*
334. Case 40/82, *Commission v. United Kingdom*; Case 261/85, *Commission v. United Kingdom*; Case C-131/93, *Commission v. Federal Republic of Germany*; Case C-67/97, *Criminal proceedings against Ditlev Bluhme*; Case C-473/98, *Kemikalieinspektionen v. Toolex Alpha AB.*
335. See recently P. Oliver and S. Enchelmaier, 'Free Movement of Goods: Recent Developments in the Case Law', (2007) CML Rev., 649–704.

static. The line of case law sometimes becomes less clear; sometimes, the case law starts to take a different course altogether.

In 1969, the Commission made the following distinction (adopted in Directive 70/50[336]). In Article 2 of that Directive, it indicated that the concept covered measures which *make a distinction* between national products and products from other Member States, such as the requirement of controls for all imported products. In Article 3, it also included within the scope of the prohibition a well-defined category of measures which *do not distinguish* between national products and products from other Member States, viz. rules concerning the marketing of products, such as rules concerning the shape, weight or composition, but whose effects on the free movement of goods is more restrictive than the actual aim.[337]

3.2.1.1   Dassonville

In 1974, in its famous formulation in *Dassonville*, the Court chose to interpret the concept of measures having equivalent effect broadly.[338] This definition basically still holds good.[339]

In that judgment, the Court laid down the basic principle in the following terms: '[a]ll trading rules enacted by Member States which are capable of hindering, directly or indirectly, actually or potentially, intra-Community trade are to be considered as measures having an effect equivalent to quantitative restrictions'.[340] The various elements in this definition will be considered below (see section 3.2.2).

The Court added in its next paragraph that in the absence of a Community system protecting the market participant, a Member State may take *reasonable* measures to prevent unfair practices in this connection, subject to certain conditions. This contains already the core of the rule-of-reason, later referred to by the Court as the 'mandatory requirements', which appeared more clearly in *Cassis de Dijon*.

3.2.1.2   Cassis de Dijon

Although the definition given in *Dassonville* had a broad scope, it was only in the judgment in *Cassis de Dijon*[341] that it became clear that measures which do not make a distinction between national and imported products (so-called 'indistinctly applicable measures') come within the scope of application of the prohibition contained in Article 28 EC.

---

336. O.J. 1970, L 13/29.
337. P. VerLoren van Themaat (1970) SEW, 258.
338. Case 8/74, *Dassonville*.
339. It also matches the definition given by P. VerLoren van Themaat, 'Bevat artikel 30 van het EEG-Verdrag slechts een non-discriminatiebeginsel ten aanzien van invoerbeperkingen?' (1967) SEW, 632.
340. At para. 5.
341. Case 120/78, *Cassis de Dijon*.

In the same judgment, in order to compensate in some way for this broad definition, which included indistinctly applicable measures, the Court permitted national measures under certain conditions, for instance for the protection of consumers.[342] In other words, in *Cassis de Dijon*, 'mandatory requirements' were added to the existing exceptions in Article 30 EC. The Court used a so-called rule-of-reason approach in this case.

The most important condition – which in *Cassis de Dijon* was not explicitly attached to these new exceptions, but which in later case law was explicitly added to the *Cassis de Dijon* rule – was the fact that the national measure was 'indistinctly applicable'. The judgment in Case 113/80 *Commission v. Ireland*[343] a few years later removes all doubts on this point.

After *Cassis de Dijon*, the following division can be made:

- indistinctly applicable measures come under the prohibition, but may be saved by the exceptions contained in Article 30 EC and by rule-of-reason exceptions (mandatory requirements);
- distinctly applicable measures (i.e., measures which distinguish between national products and imported products) come under the prohibition, but may be saved only by the exceptions contained in Article 30 EC.

Thus, of various restrictive measures, those which are *less* restrictive (those which are indistinctly applicable) are able to rely on more possible exceptions.

3.2.1.3   Groenveld

Up until 1979, the case law of the Court of Justice did not make a distinction between import restrictions and export restrictions in relation to the application of the prohibition and the use of the exceptions.[344] In the judgment in *Groenveld*,[345] however, and later confirmed in other cases,[346] the Court restricted the prohibition of measures having equivalent effect in relation to exports to discriminatory measures and indistinctly applicable measures which are indirectly discriminatory, and which have as a result that domestic production receives a particular advantage (see further section 3.2.3).[347] The result of this restriction of

---

342. Ibid., at para. 8.
343. Case 113/80, *Commission v. Ireland*. This was also explicitly confirmed in Joined Cases C-267 & 268/91, *Keck and Mithouard*.
344. See, e.g., Case 53/76, *Procureur de la République de Besançon v. Les Sieurs Bouhelier and others*; Case 68/76, *Commission v. France*.
345. Case 15/79, *P.B. Groenveld BV v. Produktschap voor Vee en Vlees*.
346. Case 172/82, *Syndicat national des fabricants raffineurs d'huile de graissage et al. v. Groupement d'intérêt économique 'Inter-Huiles' et al.*; Case 118/86, *Openbaar Ministerie v. Nertsvoederfabriek Nederland BV*.
347. See W.-H. Roth, *Wettbewerb der Mitgliedstaaten oder Wettbewerb der Hersteller? Plädoyer für eine Neubestimmung des Art. 34 EGV* (1995) ZHR, 78–95. Cf. Case C-384/93, *Alpine Investments*. See also W.-H. Roth and P. Oliver, 'The Internal Market and the Four Freedoms' (2004) CML Rev., 407–441, 417.

the prohibition is that non-discriminatory measures which restrict or hinder exports – and this happens from time to time in environmental cases – do not come within the scope of the prohibition, and therefore do not need any further justification.[348]

3.2.1.4   Sunday Trading

In a number of cases, the question arose whether the *Dassonville/Cassis de Dijon* approach could apply unrestrictedly. In the 1980s, the Court handed down a number of judgments in which measures such as a prohibition on night transport for bread, or a prohibition of the sale of certain drinks in cafés, were found not to come within the scope of Article 28 EC.[349] As a result of these judgments, the discussion on the scope of the concept of measures having equivalent effect in relation to imports flared up again. Courts in various Member States consequently had doubts about the permissibility of Sunday trading legislation, and they put questions to the Court in this context.[350] In *Torfaen,*[351] both the Commission's agent and Advocate General Van Gerven sought to restrict the scope of the basic principle in *Dassonville*; however, the Court did not follow this approach. Indeed it did not follow that approach in any of the other Sunday trading cases dealt with in 1991 and 1992, but by and large followed its orthodox reasoning (finding the measure capable of hindering trade between Member States, and then looking at the justification advanced).[352]

3.2.1.5   Keck and Mithouard

At the end of 1993, in the judgment in Joined Cases C-267 & 268/91 *Keck and Mithouard*[353] the Court did redefine its case law in relation to Article 28 EC.

---

348. J.H. Jans, H.G. Sevenster and H.H.B. Vedder, *Europees milieurecht in Nederland*, 3rd ed. (The Hague, 2000), 332.
349. Case 155/80, *Summary proceedings against Sergius Oebel*; Case 75/81, *Joseph Henri Thomas Blesgen v. Belgium*.
350. For similar subjects, see Case C-23/89, *Quietlynn Limited and Brian James Richards v. Southend Borough Council* and Case C-350/89, *Sheptonhurst Ltd v. Newham Borough Council*; Case C-69/88, *H. Krantz v. Ontvanger der Directe Belastingen and Netherlands State*.
351. Case C-145/88, *Torfaen*.
352. Case C-312/89, *Union départementale des syndicats CGT de l'Aisne v. SIDEF Conforama, Société Arts et Meubles and Société Jima*; Case C-332/89, *Criminal proceedings against André Marchandise, Jean-Marie Chapuis and SA Trafitex*; Case C-169/91, *Council of the City of Stoke-on-Trent and Norwich City Council v. B & Q plc*. See on this, E.L. White, 'In Search of the Limits to Article 30 of the EEC Treaty' (1989) CML Rev., 235–280; K.J.M. Mortelmans, 'Article 30 of the EEC and Legislation Relating to Market Circumstances: Time to Consider a New Definition?' (1991) CML Rev., 115; J. Steiner, 'Drawing the Line: Uses and Abuses of Article 30 EEC' (1992) CML Rev., 749–774; W.P.J. Wils, 'The Search for a Rule in Article 30 EEC: Much Ado About Nothing?' (1993) EL Rev., 475–492.
353. Joined Cases C-267 & 268/91, *Keck and Mithouard*. This occurred at a time when the Court also clarified its case law on Arts. 3(1)(g), 10, 81 and 82 EC; see Reich, 'The November

This judgment was confirmed in later cases, which – to the extent they are of importance – will be discussed below.[354] After an interpretation of the judgment in *Keck and Mithouard* (hereafter: *Keck*), attention will turn to the developments in the case law following *Keck*, since the Court has not followed the *Keck* line of reasoning in all the relevant cases it has been faced with. This is not just for free movement of goods, but in particular for the other freedoms (see sections 5.3.1, 6.5.1, 7.4.1 and 8.3).

Rules on selling arrangements which make a *distinction* between national goods and imported goods come within the scope of the prohibition contained in Article 28 EC.[355] The *Keck* judgment focuses on two types of indistinctly applicable measures: product requirements and selling arrangements.

3.2.1.6   Keck: Product Requirements

The *Cassis de Dijon* case law remains fully applicable to rules concerning the requirements which must be met by products (so-called product requirements). These rules may concern designation, form, size, weight, composition, presentation, labelling, packaging, according to the non-exhaustive list given in paragraph 15 of the *Keck* judgment. This list is very similar to the list of measures given in Article 3 of Directive 70/50, mentioned above (see section 3.2.1).

3.2.1.7   Keck: Selling Arrangements

In paragraph 16 of the *Keck* judgment, the Court considered that

> contrary to what has previously been decided, the application to products from other Member States of national provisions restricting or prohibiting certain selling arrangements is not such as to hinder directly or indirectly, actually or potentially, trade between Member States within the meaning of the *Dassonville* judgment so long as those provisions apply to all relevant traders operating within the national territory and so long as they affect in the same manner, in law and in fact, the marketing of domestic products and of those from other Member States.

The term 'selling arrangements' contains two elements: 'selling' and 'arrangements'. As far as the first element is concerned, the Court also uses the term 'marketing' where necessary instead of 'selling'.[356] Thus, lease and hire are also covered, as well as sales.

Revolution of the European Court of Justice: Keck, Meng and Audi Revisited' (1994) CML Rev., 459.

354. For a general overview, see M.P. Maduro, *We The Court: The European Court of Justice and the European Economic Constitution: A Critical Reading of Article 30 of the EC Treaty* (Oxford, 1998); K. Hammer, *Handbuch zum freien Verkehr: eine Analyse der Rechtsprechung zu Art. 30 EGV vor und nach dem Urteil Keck und Mithouard* (Wenen, 1998).

355. Case C-317/92, *Commission v. Federal Republic of Germany*; Case C-320/93, *Lucien Ortscheit*.

356. Case C-320/93, *Lucien Ortscheit*.

The second element was elaborated in later case law. The following national measures come within the notion selling arrangements:[357] Sunday closing legislation,[358] shop opening hours,[359] legislation concerning restrictions on the channels available for marketing products,[360] legislation on selling at a loss,[361] advertising rules,[362] use of a trade name,[363] a rule concerning sales rounds (of a baker),[364] a general identification obligation for packaging,[365] and rules concerning the herding of animals.[366]

The case law concerning advertising rules, in particular, is ambiguous.[367] In the literature, there is criticism of the application of *Keck* to these rules.[368]

---

357. H. Matthies, 'Artikel 30 EG-Vertrag nach Keck', *Festschrift U. Everling* (Baden-Baden, 1995), 803, has examined the case law of the Court prior to *Keck*, and indicated which national rules – in his estimation – could be qualified as selling arrangements. See also the list made by AG Tesauro in his Opinion in Case C-368/95, *Familiapress*.

358. Joined Cases C-69 & 258/93, *Punto Casa SpA v. Sindaco del Comune di Capena et Comune di Capena, and Promozioni Polivalenti Venete Soc. coop. arl (PPV) v. Sindaco del Comune di Torri di Quartesolo et al.*

359. Joined Cases C-401 & 402/92, *Criminal proceedings against Tankstation 't Heukske vof and J. B. E. Boermans*; Joined Cases C-418–421,460–462, 464/93, C-9–11, 14, 15, 23, 24 and 332/94, *Semeraro Casa Uno Srl et al. v. Sindaco del Comune di Erbusco et al.*

360. Case C-391/92, *Commission v. Hellenic Republic*; Case C-387/93, *Criminal proceedings against Giorgio Domingo Banchero*; Case C-162/97, *Criminal proceedings against Gunnar Nilsson, Per Olov Hagelgren and Solweig Arrborn*; Case C-322/01, *Deutscher Apothekerverband eV v. 0800 DocMorris NV, Jacques Waterval*. But see Case C-189/95, *Criminal proceedings against Harry Franzén*.

361. Case C-63/94, *Groupement National des Négociants en Pommes de Terre de Belgique v. ITM Belgium SA and Vocarex SA*.

362. Case C-292/92, *Ruth Hünermund and others v. Landesapothekerkammer Baden-Württemberg*; Case C-412/93, *TF 1*; Joined Cases C-34–36/95, *Konsumentombudsmannen (KO) v. De Agostini (Svenska) Förlag AB (C-34/95) and TV-Shop i Sverige AB (C-35 and 36/95)*; Case C-6/98, *Arbeitsgemeinschaft Deutscher Rundfunkanstalten (ARD) v. PRO Sieben Media AG*.

363. Implicitly in Case C-255/97, *Pfeiffer Großhandel v. Löwa Warenhandel*.

364. Case C-254/98, *Schutzverband gegen unlauteren Wettbewerb v. TK-Heimdienst Sass*; Case C-20/03, *Criminal proceedings against Marcel Burmanjer, René Alexander Van Der Linden, Anthony De Jong*.

365. Case C-159/00, *Sapod Audic*; cf. Case C-416/00, *Tommaso Morellato v. Comune di Padova*.

366. According to the Pres. District Court The Hague, 5 Sep. 2001, *Groep Nederlandse veemarkten*, KG 01/979.

367. Case C-368/95, *Familiapress*, concerned an advertising rule which – according to the Court – concerned the content of the product and which therefore could not be classified as a selling arrangement. In the same sense, see Case C-470/93, *Verein gegen Unwesen in Handel und Gewerbe Köln e.V. v. Mars*. See also Case C-337/95, *Parfums Christian Dior SA and Parfums Christian Dior BV v. Evora BV*. Here, the Court included an indistinctly applicable advertising prohibition – which according to national IP rules could be imposed on a reseller – in the scope of Art. 28 EC. In Joined Cases C-34–36/95, *De Agostini*, the Court applied the *Keck* approach in the context of free movement of goods, but not to the related TV broadcasts. The Court found that Art. 49 EC applied, and the rule-of-reason exception.

368. R. Sack, 'Staatliche Werbebeschränkungen und Art. 30 und 59 EG-Vertrag' (1998) *WRP*, 103; C.W.A. Timmermans, 'Werbung und Grundfreiheiten', in J. Schwarze (ed.), *Werbung und Werbungsverbote im Lichte des europäischen Gemeinschaftsrechts* (Baden-Baden, 1999), 26;

In *Gourmet*,[369] the Court brought certain advertising rules within the scope of application of Article 28 EC. In that case, a Swedish rule concerning advertising for alcoholic drinks was concerned. The Court, sticking to the line taken in its judgment in *De Agostini*,[370] ruled that such an advertising ban did not merely prohibit a certain type of advertising, but in fact forbids the producers and importers from distributing any kind of advertising aimed at consumers, with a few, not unimportant, exceptions. Such a rule must therefore be considered as a measure which has a stronger effect on trade in products from other Member States than the trade in national products, and therefore as an obstacle to trade between Member States, which comes within the scope of application of Article 28 EC.[371] The Court applies one of the conditions from its *Keck* case law: i.e., that trade is hindered 'in fact' (see further below). In *Karner*, the advertising rules were brought under the term 'selling arrangements' because – unlike in *Gourmet* and *De Agostini*, they did not involve a total (legal or de facto) prohibition.[372] Finally, in a few cases, the *Keck* defence was rejected because the Court considered that product requirements were at issue.[373]

3.2.1.8 *Keck: Selling Arrangements; Conditions*

As is apparent from paragraph 16 of the judgment in *Keck*, quoted above, two conditions apply, which must be met cumulatively, for rules concerning certain selling arrangements to escape the application of Article 28 EC. If a certain measure comes within the category of selling arrangements, then the Court examines whether these conditions are met.[374]

The requirement that 'those provisions apply to all relevant traders' probably refers to the non-discrimination requirement on grounds of nationality.[375] In that case, one may wonder what this adds to the analysis.[376] The Court has referred to it on occasion[377] but has still failed to shed any light on the rationale or

---

R. Greaves, 'Advertising Restrictions and the Free Movement of Goods and Services' (1998) EL Rev., 305; B.J. Drijber, 'Les communications commerciales au carrefour de la dérégulation et de la réglementation' (2002) CDE, 531–610.

369. Case C-405/98, *Konsumentombudsmannen (KO) v. Gourmet International Products AB (GIP)*.
370. Joined Cases C-34–36/95, *De Agostini*.
371. Case C-405/98, *Gourmet International*; see also Case C-239/02, *Douwe Egberts v. Westrom Pharma et al.*
372. Case C-71/02, *Herbert Karner Industrie-Auktionen v. Troostwijk*.
373. Case C-315/92, *Clinique*; Case C-470/93, *Mars*; Case C-51/94, *Commission v. Federal Republic of Germany*; Case C-368/95, *Familiapress*; Case C-67/97, *Bluhme*; Case C-143/03, *Commission v. the Italy*; Case C-309/02, *Radlberger Getränkegesellschaft mbH & Co., and S. Spitz KG v. Land Baden-Württemberg*; Case C-463/01, *Commission v. Federal Republic of Germany*.
374. Joined Cases C-401 & 402/92, *'t Heukske*.
375. Joined Cases C-401 & 402/92, *'t Heukske*; Joined Cases C-69 & 258/93, *Punto Casa*.
376. See J.H. Jans (1995) SEW, 205; K.J.M. Mortelmans (1994) SEW, 124.
377. E.g., Case C-6/98, *ARD v. Pro Sieben Media*, and Case C-322/01, *Deutscher Apothekerverband v. DocMorris*.

meaning.[378] The second condition is that the measures affect the marketing of products in the same manner, 'in law and in fact'. 'In law' concerns the objective and the formulation of the legislation, while 'in fact' refers to the effects or results of the measure.[379] The effect can be demonstrated by the use of statistics.[380]

In *Heimdienst Sass*,[381] the Court examined in detail the second condition, concerning the actual marketing of the products. The Court was of the opinion that a measure which obliges travelling salesmen (in this case, market operators trading by means of sales rounds) to have a fixed establishment in the area where they trade does not affect national products and products from other Member States in the same manner, because the local operators already meet the criterion of having a permanent establishment in that region, and other market operators – thus including those from other Member States – must make extra costs.

3.2.1.9   Post-Keck

On the basis of the tendency to convergence (see section 1.6 above), one might expect the *Keck* argument to be invoked in relation to other freedoms. That has in fact occurred, but the Court has not followed this path (so far) in the context of free movement of workers,[382] freedom to provide services,[383] freedom of establishment,[384] or free movement of capital.[385]

From a number of commentaries in academic literature it was apparent that not everyone was happy with the *Keck* solution. Some had objections to the Court's approach on grounds of principle, others pointed at practical problems, particularly with regard to advertising rules and suchlike.[386] The

---

378. P. Oliver and S. Enchelmaier, 'Free Movement of Goods: Recent Developments in the Case Law' (2007) CML Rev., 649–704, at 681
379. See A.G. Van Gerven in Joined Cases C-401 & 402/92, *'t Heukske*. See for an example of inequality in law Case 152/78, *Commission v. France*, and for an example of inequality in fact Case 177/83, *Th. Kohl KG v. Ringelhan & Rennett SA and Ringelhan Einrichtungs*, and Case C-275/92, *Schindler*; Case C-405/98, *Gourmet International*.
380. Joined Cases C-34–36/95, *De Agostini*.
381. Case C-254/98, *Heimdienst Sass*. See also Case C-390/99, *Canal Satélite Digital*, and Case C-322/01, *Deutscher Apothekerverband*; Case C-20/03, *Burmanjer*.
382. Case C-415/93, *Bosman*.
383. Case C-384/93, *Alpine Investments*.
384. Joined Cases C-418–421/93, etc., *Semeraro Casa Uno*. See also Case C-309/99, *Wouters*.
385. See Case C-463/00, *Commission v. Kingdom of Spain (Golden shares)*. On the topic in general, see J.L. Da Cruz Vilaca, 'An Exercise on the Application of Keck and Mithouard in the Field of the Free Provision of Services', in *Mélanges en hommage à Michel Waelbroeck* (Brussels, 1999), 795.
386. Overviews of and commentary on post-Keck case law can be found in R. Barents, 'From Dassonville to Keck and Beyond: Old and New Trends in the Court's Case Law on Foodstuffs' (1998) EFLR, 127; L.W. Gormley, 'Two Years after Keck,' (1996) *Fordham International Law Journal*, 867; T.E. Lüder, 'Die Grenzen der Keck-Rechtsprechung' (1996) *Europäische Zeitschrift für Wirtschaftsrecht*, 615; S.O. Hödl, *Die Beurteilung von verkaufbehindernden Massnahmen im europäischen Binnenmarkt* (Baden-Baden, 1997); J. Kessler, *Das System der*

distinction between static and dynamic selling arrangements might offer a solution.[387]

There was criticism from within the Court itself, coming from Advocate General Jacobs. In his Opinion in *Leclerc-TF 1*,[388] he argued that in a number of cases – and in particular in relation to rules on advertising – it is impossible to make a clear distinction between product requirements and selling arrangements. Jacobs proposed a different criterion for the applicability of Article 28 EC: the principle that all undertakings which lawfully exercise economic activities in a Member State should have unhindered access to the whole of the Community market, except where there is a valid reason to refuse total access to a part of the market. In his view, the decisive factor is whether access to the market is significantly restricted or not. This reasoning would imply the introduction of a *de minimis* rule. The Court has not followed the proposal of Advocate General Jacobs.[389]

3.2.1.10   Access to the Market

Nevertheless, the criterion 'access to the market' of Advocate General Jacobs has had an influence on the case law; this was not in the area of free movement of goods, however, but in that of free movement of workers, the freedom of establishment and freedom to provide services (see further sections 5.3, 6.5.1 and 7.4.1 below).[390]

Warenverkehrsfreiheit im Gemeinschaftsrecht: zwischen Produktbezug und Verkaufmodali-täten (Baden-Baden, 1997); S. Weatherill, 'After Keck: Some Thoughts on How to Clarify the Clarification' (1996) CML Rev., 885; S. Weatherill, 'Recent Case Law Concerning the Free Movement of Goods: Mapping the Frontiers of Market Regulation' (1999) CML Rev., 51; P. Oliver, 'Some Further Reflections on the Scope of Arts. 28–30 (ex 30–36) EC' (1999) CML Rev., 783; W.-H. Roth, *Freier Warenverkehr nach Keck*, in *Festschrift für B. Grossfeld* (Baden-Baden, 1999), 929; H.-P. Schwintowski, *Freier Warenverkehr im europäischen Binnenmarkt: eine Fundamentalkritik an der Rechtsprechung des EuGH zu Art. 28 EG* in, *Rabels Zeitschrift für ausländisches und internationales Privatrecht* 2000, 38; G.C Rodriguez Iglesias, 'Drinks in Luxembourg: Alcoholic Beverages and the Case Law of the Court of Justice', in *Liber Amicorum in Honour of Lord Slynn of Hadley* (The Hague, 2000), 526; P. Koutrakos, 'On Groceries, Alcohol and Olive Oil: More on Free Movement of Goods after Keck' (2001) EL Rev., 391.G. Davies, 'Can Selling Arrangements Be Harmonised?' (2005) EL Rev., 370; K.J.M.Mortelmans, 'De Keck-check' (2006) NTER, 247–261.

387. Thus, K.J.M. Mortelmans, 'Article 30 of the EEC and Legislation Relating to Market Circumstances: Time to Consider a New Definition?' (1991) CML Rev., 130; in that sense, see also P. Craig and G. de Búrca, *EU Law. Text, Cases and Materials*, 3rd ed. (Oxford, 2003), 648; C. Barnard, *The Substantive Law of the EU: The Four Freedoms*, 2nd ed. (Oxford, 2007), 149; K.J.M. Mortelmans, 'De Keck-check' (2006) NTER, 259.

388. Case C-412/93, *TF 1*, see Opinion at paras. 38–42.

389. Other advocates general have also taken a critical attitude to the Keck jurisprudence, e.g., A.G. Geelhoed in Case C-239/02, *Douwe Egberts*, and A.G. Poiares Maduro in Joined Cases C-158 & 159/04, *Alfa Vita vissilopoulos v. Elliniko Dimosio et al.*

390. C. Barnard, S. Deakin, 'Market Access and Regulatory Competition', in C. Barnard and J. Scott (eds), *The Law of the Single European Market: Unpacking the Premises* (Oxford, 2002), 197.

In *Heimdienst Sass*,[391] the Court seems to make a link between its case law on selling arrangements and free movement of goods (*Keck*), on the one hand, and its case law on access to the market and the other freedoms (*Alpine Investments*), on the other.[392] A measure concerning sales rounds was first examined under the heading of selling arrangements. As mentioned above, according to the national rules, market operators had to have a fixed establishment in the region in which they made sales rounds. Local market operators obviously already met this condition. The Court ruled that this measure did not affect the sale of national products and products from other Member States in the same manner; it therefore came within the scope of the prohibition in Article 28 EC. The Court added that the measure restricted access to the market in the importing State to a greater extent for products from other Member States than for national products, even though it applied to all market operators who are active in the national territory.[393] The Court referred in this context explicitly to *Alpine Investments*, a case concerning the freedom to provide services.

3.2.1.11   Hypothetical Situations

Since handing down the judgment in *Keck*, the Court has not always opted for the *Keck* approach. In *Ligur Carni*[394] the Court did not examine the national measure in terms of product requirements and selling arrangements. It decided that the national measure fell outside the scope of application of Article 28 EC on the basis of the argument that the measure had only a hypothetical effect on imports.[395] This reasoning – which had also been followed sometimes prior to *Keck*[396] – has been repeated in a number of later (post-*Keck*) cases,[397] but has also sometimes been rejected.[398] All these cases concerned indistinctly applicable measures.

In a case concerning Article 29 EC (export restrictions), the Court has also applied the test of hypothetical effect to a measure which was distinctly applicable (i.e., it distinguished between whether goods would be supplied within the Member State concerned or exported to other Member States).[399] This test has also been applied in the area of free movement of workers, with reference to cases on free movement of goods dating from both before and after *Keck*.[400]

---

391. Case C-254/98, *Heimdienst Sass*. See also Case C-390/99, *Canal Satélite Digital*.
392. Case C-384/93, *Alpine Investments*.
393. This trend was continued in Case C-405/98, *Gourmet International*.
394. Joined Cases C-277, 318 & 319/91, *Ligur Carni Srl*.
395. P. Oliver, 'Some Further Reflections on the Scope of Arts. 28–30 (ex 30–36) EC' (1999) CML Rev., 788.
396. Case 169/91, *B & Q*.
397. E.g., Case C-379/92, *Peralta*; Case C-323/93, *Société Civile Agricole du Centre d'Insémination de la Crespelle v. Coopérative d'Elevage et d'Insémination Artificielle du Département de la Mayenne*; Case C-266/96, *Corsica Ferries France SA v. Gruppo Antichi Ormeggiatori del porto di Genova Coop. arl et al.*; Case C-44/98, *BASF AG v. Präsident des Deutschen Patentamts*.
398. Case C-67/97, *Bluhme*.
399. Case C-412/97, *ED*.
400. Case C-190/98, *Volker Graf v. Filzmoser Maschinenbau*, with reference to Case C-69/88, *Krantz* and Case C-44/98, *BASF*.

3.2.1.12 The de minimis Rule

In addition to this case law on hypothetical situations, there is some *de minimis* case law. The finding of the Court in *Van de Haar*[401] was confirmed in *Bluhme*, where the Court ruled that an extremely limited restriction still came within the scope of application of the prohibition contained in Article 28 EC.[402]

The proposal made by Advocate General Jacobs to abandon the *Keck* approach in favour of a *de minimis* approach was not adopted by the Court.[403]

In *Burmanjer*, the characteristics 'insignificant and uncertain' were added to the conditions mentioned in *Keck*.[404] In this way, a rule-oriented approach may covertly be transformed into a market-oriented approach.

3.2.1.13 Rule-Oriented or Market-Oriented Approach

This overview illustrates that there are two techniques for dealing with non-discriminatory obstacles to free movement of goods.[405] The rule-oriented approach reached its epitome in *Keck*. The market-oriented approach is most evident in the cases concerning hypothetical situations, *de minimis* etc. The *Dassonville* formula and the access to the market approach as applied to free movement of goods in *Heimdienst Sass* have elements of both approaches. As to the direction in which the Court's case law will develop further, one must always wait and see.

3.2.2 Measures Having Equivalent Effect in relation to Imports: the Prohibition (Article 28 EC)

Following on from this thematic and historical overview, from which it was clear that certain measures (selling arrangements, hypothetical situations) do not come within the scope of Article 28 EC, we will now examine the definition of the concept of measures having equivalent effect in relation to imports. The basic formulation given in *Dassonville* is still the point of departure. It is convenient to repeat that formulation: 'All trading rules enacted by Member States which are capable of hindering, directly or indirectly, actually or potentially, intra-Community trade are to be considered as measures having an effect equivalent to quantitative restrictions.'[406] This formulation is repeated in countless other

---

401. Joined Cases 177 & 178/82, *Van de Haar*; Case 269/83, *Commission v. France*; Case C-49/89, *Corsica Ferries France v. Direction générale des douanes françaises*.
402. Case C-67/97, *Bluhme*; see also C-166/03, *Commission v. France*; Case C-309/02, *Radlberger*; Case C-463/01, *Commission v. Germany*.
403. A.G. Jacobs in Case C-412/93, *TF 1*, paras. 42 et seq.
404. See Case C-20/03, *Burmanjer*, para. 31.
405. W.P.J. Wils, 'The Search for the Rule in Article 30 EEC: Much Ado About Nothing?' (1993) EL Rev., 475; W. Van Gerven, 'Constitutional Aspects of the European Court's Case-law on Arts. 30 and 36 EC as Compared with the US Dormant Commerce Clause', in *Mélanges en hommage à Michel Waelbroeck* (Brussels, 1999), 1629.
406. Case 8/74, *Dassonville* at 852.

judgments, including *Keck*. The various elements in this definition will be dealt with in the following.

3.2.2.1   *Trading Rules*

Although the phrase 'trading rules' is used in *Dassonville*, the scope of the prohibition is not restricted to trading rules as such, so the broader term 'rules'[407] or 'measures'[408] is more appropriate. As well as trading rules in the strict sense – such as rules concerning purchases or sales – all measures having a restrictive effect for production and investments are covered.[409] Obstacles affecting suppliers or consumers (such as patients) are also included.[410] The case law of the Court shows that in a number of instances even non-binding decisions or acts may be regarded as measures having equivalent effect within the meaning of Article 28 EC.[411] An intention to take a decision or measure does not, it is submitted, itself constitute a prohibited measure.[412] The term 'measure' can also cover judicial decisions,[413] decisions of professional bodies having a public regulatory function,[414] national practices as such,[415] and national practices resulting from international agreements.[416] All these examples concerned specific measures. Failure to take action on the part of a Member State can also be brought within the scope of Article 28 EC, by means of Article 10 EC.[417] Global measures such as a restrictive budgetary or credit policy do not fall under the concept of measures caught by Article 28 EC; these must now be examined in the context of the EC Treaty's provisions dealing with Economic and Monetary Union (see Ch. X).

---

407. Joined Cases 177 & 178/82, *Van de Haar*.
408. Case C-324/93, *Evans Medical*.
409. Case 190/73, *Officier van Justitie v. J.W.J. van Haaster* and Case 111/76, *Officier van Justitie v. Beert van der Hazel*.
410. Case 215/87, *Heinz Schumacher v. Hauptzollamt Frankfurt am Main-Ost*; Case C-362/88, *GB-INNO-BM v. Confédération du Commerce Luxembourgeois*; Case C-120/95, *Nicolas Decker v. Caisse de maladie des employés privés*.
411. Case 249/81, *Commission v. Ireland*; Case 21/84, *Commission v. France*.
412. See Mortelmans (1995) SEW, 65 (discussing a Dutch case).
413. See Opinion of A.G. Van Gerven in Case C-93/92, *CMC Motorradcenter v. Pelin Baskiciogullari*. Cf. Case C-108/96, *Criminal proceedings against Dennis Mac Quen et al.*; Case C-289/02, *AMOK Verlags v. A & R Gastronomie*.
414. Joined Cases 266 & 267/87, *The Queen v. Royal Pharmaceutical Society of Great Britain, ex parte Association of Pharmaceutical Importers et al.*; Case C-292/92, *Hünermund*.
415. Case C-192/01, *Commission v. Denmark*.
416. Case C-3/91, *Exportur SA v. LOR SA et al.*; Case C-324/93, *Evans Medical*; Case C-469/00, *Ravil SARL v. Bellon import SARL, Biraghi SpA*; Case C-216/01, *Budejovický Budvar, národní podnik v. Rudolf Ammersin*.
417. Case C-265/95, *Commission v. France (Spanish strawberries)*.

3.2.2.2 Member States: The Addressees of Article 28 EC

Article 28 does not mention the addressees of the prohibition. From the case law, it is evident that in first instance it is directed at Member States. It applies to measures of the public authorities at whatever level (national, regional or local).[418] Thus it embraces measures which apply only in part of a Member State, and a measure will not escape the ambit of Article 28 EC on the grounds that it also affects products coming from another part of the Member State concerned as well as products imported from other Member States.[419] Agreements concluded between various Member States may also come within the scope of Article 28 EC.[420] In *A.G.M.-COS.MET* (the case is also referred to as *Lehtinen*), the Court considered that statements which, by reason of their form and circumstances, give the persons to whom they are addressed the impression that they are official positions taken by the State, not personal opinions of the official, are attributable to the State. The decisive factor for the statements of an official to be attributed to the State is whether the persons to whom those statements are addressed can reasonably suppose, in the given context, that they are positions taken by the official with the authority of his office.[421]

Article 28 EC, being a provision of primary Community law, may also be used to contest secondary law, adopted by the Community Institutions themselves, although this has so far been without consequences for the validity of the acts in question.[422] As far as the Community Institutions themselves are concerned, the Court seems to apply the prohibition less strictly.[423] Further, there is some uncertainty as to whether the Community Institutions may rely on the exceptions to the prohibition in the same way as the Member States (see section 2.4.1. below).[424]

---

418. Case C-21/88, *Du Pont de Nemours Italiana SA v. Unità Sanitaria Locale No 2 di Carrara*; Case C-416/00, *Morellato*; Case C-255/03, *Commission v. Belgium*.
419. Joined Cases C-1 & 176/90, *Aragonesa de Publicidad Exterior SA et al. v. Departmento de Sanidad y Seguridad Social de la Generalitat de Cataluña*, and Joined Cases C-277, 318 & 319/91, *Ligur Carni Srl.* Case C-67/97, *Bluhme*; Case C-254/98, *Heimdienst Sass*.
420. Case 144/81, *Keurkoop BV v. Nancy Kean Gifts BV*; Case 286/86, *Ministère Public v. Deserbais*; Case C-3/91, *Exportur*; Case C-324/93, *Evans Medical*.
421. Case C-470/03, *A.G.M.-Cos.Met v. Suomen valtio and Lethinen*.
422. Case 15/83, *Denkavit Nederland BV v. Hoofdproduktschap voor Akkerbouwprodukten*; Case 37/83, *Rewe-Zentral*; Case C-51/93, *Meyhui NV v. Schott Zwiesel Glaswerke AG*; Case C-284/95, *Safety Hi-Tech Srl v. S. & T. Srl.*; Case C-114/96, *Criminal proceedings against Kieffer and Thill*; Case C-180/96 R, *United Kingdom v. Commission (BSE);* Joined Cases C-154 & 155/04, *Alliance for Natural Health v. Secretary of State for Health.* See on this, K.J.M. Mortelmans, 'The Relationship between the Treaty Rules and Community Measures for the Establishment and Functioning of the Internal Market: Towards a Concordance Rule' (2002) CML Rev., 1303–1346. On the relationship between an EC Directive, Arts. 28 and 30 EC and the Act of Accession (of Sweden), see Case C-434/02, *Arnold André*; Case C-210/03, *Swedish Match*.
423. Case 46/76, *Bauhuis*. Cf. A.G. Tesauro in his Opinion in Case C-41/93, *France v. Commission* (para. 6).
424. J. Currall, 'Some Aspects of the Relation between Article 30–36 and Article 100 of the EEC Treaty, with a Closer Look to Optional Harmonization' (1985) *Yearbook of European Law*,

3.2.2.3   Horizontal Direct Effect?

The Court has not clearly and incontestably established whether Articles 28–30 EC have horizontal effect.[425] The case law on industrial and commercial property points in the direction of horizontal direct effect,[426] but in *Vlaamse Reisbureaus*[427] the Court considered that Articles 28 and 29 EC only concern acts of the authorities, and not actions by undertakings. On the other hand, the Court has ruled that agreements between private parties may not derogate from the mandatory provisions of the Treaty on the free movement of goods.[428] In *Sapod Audic*[429] the Court ruled that Article 28 does not apply to private agreements.

The technique mentioned above of using Articles 10 and 28 EC together makes it possible to ensure that private operators abide by the rules on free movement of goods: the Member State is obliged to take action against market operators who try to prevent the free movement of goods within their territory.[430]

3.2.2.4   Hindering: Distinctly Applicable Measures and Indistinctly Applicable Measures

Measures which distinguish between national and imported products – whether they concern product requirements or selling arrangements – always come within the ambit of Article 28 EC.[431]

Measures which do not make such a distinction require a more refined assessment. It follows from *Keck* that non-discriminatory selling arrangements do not fall within the scope of the prohibition. Measures which are indistinctly applicable may come within the scope of the prohibition when they are discriminatory in fact. It is frequently difficult to ascertain whether the measure is of such a nature.

The conceptual difference between distinctly applicable measures and indistinctly applicable measures remains important for two reasons. First, in order to know whether Article 28 is applicable in the case of selling arrangements; second in order to know whether, for other national measures or selling arrangements, the rule-of-reason exceptions can be invoked.

191; P. Oliver, 'La législation communautaire et sa conformité avec la libre circulation des marchandises' (1979) CDE, 245.

425. See section 1.6. for literature on this point.
426. Case 16/74, *Centrafarm BV et Adriaan de Peijper v. Winthrop BV*; Case 119/75, *Terrapin (Overseas) Ltd v. Terranova Industrie CA Kapferer & Co.*
427. Case 311/85 *Asbl. Vereniging van Vlaamse Reisbureaus v. Asbl. Sociale Dienst van de plaatselijke en gewestlijke overheidsdiensten.* See also Joined Cases 177 & 178/82, *Van de Haar.*
428. Case 58/80, *Dansk Supermarked A/S v. A/S Imerco*; Case 78/70, *Deutsche Grammophon Gesellschaft mbH v. Metro-SB-Großmärkte.*
429. Case C-159/00, *Sapod Audic*; Case C-325/00, *Commission v. Germany.*
430. Case C-265/95, *Commission v. France (Spanish strawberries)*; Case C-112/00, *Schmidberger.*
431. See S. Richters, *Diskriminierung im Bereich der Warenverkehrsfreiheit* (Frankfurt am Main, 2003).

3.2.2.5 Directly or Indirectly, Actually or Potentially

The words 'directly' and 'actually' are clear. The words 'indirectly' and 'potentially', however, indicate that the prohibition has a wide scope and is not limited to actually quantifiable barriers to trade between Member States. Even after the *Keck* judgment, the Court continues to include potential obstacles to trade within the scope of Article 28 EC.[432] The term 'directly or indirectly' also occurs in the first paragraph of Article 90 EC.[433] The term 'directly' is also now used in the case law relating to Article 49 EC.[434]

The formulation in *Dassonville* is very close to the definition applied to prohibited cartel agreements under Article 81 EC: those 'which may affect trade between Member States'. Thus in *Consten and Grundig*[435] the Court noted that 'what is particularly important is whether the agreement is capable of constituting a threat, either direct or indirect, actual or potential, to freedom of trade between Member States in a manner which might harm the attainment of the objectives of a single market between States'. This is an excellent example of the interrelationship between the prohibitions on certain conduct of Member States and the prohibitions on conduct of undertakings. The EC Treaty, which seeks the removal of barriers to trade between Member States, cannot be regarded as permitting undertakings themselves to maintain or erect such barriers.[436]

3.2.2.6 Intra-Community

Article 28 EC applies not only to trade between Member States in goods originating within the Community, but also to goods originating in third countries which are in free circulation in a Member State in accordance with the conditions in Article 24 EC.[437] Article 28 does not apply to goods which come directly from third countries (see section 3.5 below).[438]

3.2.2.7 Internal Situation

Article 28 is not applicable to so-called wholly internal situations having nothing to do with intra-Community trade, as we saw in section 1.3 above. In a number of

---

432. Joined Cases C-321–324/94, *Pistre et al.*; Case C-184/96, *Commission v. France*; Case C-325/00, *Commission v. Germany*.
433. See section 2.5.1, *supra*.
434. Case C-384/93 *Alpine Investments* at paras 28 and 38.
435. Joined Cases 56 & 58/64, *Éts. Consten Sàrl and Grundig v. Commission*, at 341 of the English edition. See also Case 5/69, *Völk v. Éts. J. Vervaecke*.
436. Joined Cases 56 & 58/64, *Consten and Grundig*.
437. See Case 41/76, *Criel, née Donckerwolke et al.*; Case C-216/01, *Budvar*; see also Case 119/78, *SA des Grandes Distilleries Peureux*. See also Tegeder, 'Applying the Cassis de Dijon Doctrine to Goods Originating in Third Countries' (1994) EL Rev., 86.
438. Case 51/75, *EMI Records v. CBS United Kingdom*; Case C-296/00, *Carbone*.

fairly recent cases, the Court has interpreted this concept in more detail. The judgment in *Pistre*[439] implies that, when the national rule is discriminatory with regard to foreign products, Article 28 EC applies.[440] A rule applying without distinction to national and imported products may fall outside the scope of Article 28 EC if there are no facts linking the situation with other Member States.[441] In *Guimont*,[442] the facts of the case did not indicate any links connecting it with other Member States. Nevertheless, the Court decided that an answer to the question put by the national court would be useful, and that it was then up to the national court to decide whether Article 28 EC was relevant to the case before it.

3.2.2.8   Examples of Measures Having Equivalent Effect

Over the years the case law on Article 28 EC has given the Court extensive occasion to interpret this Article. Most of the case law has been in the form of preliminary references, under Article 234 EC. In the framework of the action programme to complete the internal market, the Commission has systematically commenced infringement proceedings against Member States where it judged this necessary; these have sometimes led to decisions of the Court on questions of general importance.[443]

Although in its case law the Court is not drawing up a textbook, but primarily resolving legal conflicts,[444] we will nevertheless impose a certain system on its work. For each subject, the most important cases will be mentioned, although we will not attempt to be exhaustive.[445] Many of the restrictions listed may be found in the summary which the Commission gave in Directive 70/50.[446]

Mentioning examples from legal practice is merely to indicate that in these cases the relationship between the national measure and the prohibition was at issue. The Court can (implicitly) decide that Article 28 EC is not applicable, or it may consider that there is a justification if it finds that Article 28 is applicable.

Selling arrangements were discussed above, in the context of the discussion of the *Keck* case law. They will not be mentioned again here, as this sort of national

---

439. Joined Cases C-321-324/94, *Pistre et al.*
440. As the Court says in Case C-448/98, *Guimont*.
441. Case 286/81, *Criminal proceedings against Oosthoek's Uitgeversmaatschappij BV*; Case 98/86, *Criminal proceedings against Arthur Mathot*; Case C-254/98, *Heimdienst Sass* and Case C-71/02 *Karner*.
442. Case C-448/98, *Guimont*; see further Case C-293/02, *Jersey Produce Marketing Organisation*.
443. Case C-157/94, *Commission v. the Netherlands*; Case C-265/95, *Commission v. France (Spanish strawberries)*.
444. R.H. Lauwaars and C.W.A. Timmermans, *Europees Gemeenschapsrecht in kort bestek*, 6th ed. (Groningen, 2003), 198.
445. This list has been drawn up on the basis of case law overviews, which appear regularly in a number of important European law journals.
446. O.J. 1970, L 13/29; see section 3.2.1. *supra*.

measure – providing it is non-discriminatory – does not come within the scope of the prohibition. Examples:

- buy-national policies:[447]
- certificates;[448]
- compulsory registration procedure;[449]
- customs formalities and delays,[450]
- difficulties in rebutting presumptions in respect of imports (evidence rules);[451]
- discrimination in public procurement;[452]
- duplicate checks, inspections or authorizations,[453]
- import licences and prior authorization requirements;[454]
- the imposition of fines or penalties;[455]
- inspections on importation;[456]
- legislation on the designation of goods;[457]

---

447. Case 249/81, *Commission v. Ireland*; Case 222/82, *Apple and Pear Development Council v. K.J. Lewis Ltd et al.*
448. Case 8/74, *Dassonville*; Case 251/78, *Firma Denkavit Futtermittel v. Minister für Ernähung, Landwirtschaft und Forsten des Landes Nordrhein-Westfalen*; Case 272/80, *Criminal proceedings against Frans-Nederlandse Maatschappij voor Biologische Producten BV*; Case 25/88, *Criminal proceedings against Esther Renée Bouchara, née Wurmser, and Norlaine*; and Case C-205/89, *Commission v. Greece*.
449. Case C-55/99, *Commission v. France*; Case C-390/99, *Canal Satélite Digital*.
450. Case 159/78, *Commission v. Italy*; Case 132/80, *United Foods NV v. Belgium*; and Case 42/82, *Commission v. France*; Case C-23/99, *Commission v. France*.
451. Joined Cases 89/74, etc., *Procureur Général at the Cour d'Appel, Bordeaux v. Arnaud et al*; Case C-192/01, *Commission v. Denmark*.
452. Case 263/85, *Commission v. Italy*; Case 45/87, *Commission v. Ireland*; Case C-21/88, *Du Pont de Nemours*; Case C-324/93, *Evans Medical*; Case C-359/93, *Commission v. Netherlands*.
453. E.g., Case 104/75, *Criminal proceedings against De Peijper*; Case 272/80, *Biologische Producten*; Case C-373/92, *Commission v. Belgium*; Case C-94/98, *The Queen v. The Licensing Authority established by the Medicines Act 1968 (represented by the Medicines Control Agency), ex parte: Rhône-Poulenc Rorer Ltd, May & Baker Ltd, SA*; Case C-390/99, *Canal Satélite Digital*; Case C-172/00, *Ferring Arzneimittel v. Eurim-Pharm Arzneimittel*; Case C-14/02, *ATRAL SA v. Belgium*; Case C-455/01, *Commission v. Italy*; Case C-112/02, *Kohlpharma v. Germany*.
454. E.g., Cases 51-54/71, *International Fruit Company NV et al. v. Produktschap voor Groenten en Fruit*; Case 41/76, *Criel, née Donckerwolke et al.*, and Case C-293/94, *Criminal proceedings against Jacqueline Brandsma*.
455. Case 41/76, *Criel, née Donckerwolke et al.*; Case 52/77, *Cayrol v. Giovanni Rivoira e Figli*; Case 179/78, *Procureur de la République v. Rivoira*; Case C-54/05, *Commission v. Finland*.
456. Case 4/75, *Rewe Zentralfinanz v. Landwirtschaftskammer (San José)*; Case 50/83, *Commission v. Italy*; Joined Cases C-277, 318 & 319/91, *Ligur Carni* and Case C-80/92, *Commission v. Belgium*.
457. Case 12/74, *Commission v. Germany*; Case 13/78, *Joh. Eggers Sohn & Co. v. Freie Hansestadt Bremen*; Case 193/80, *Commission v. Italy*; Case 16/83, *Criminal proceedings against Karl Prantl*; Case 178/84, *Commission v. Germany*; Case 182/84, *Criminal proceedings against Miro BV*; Case 286/86, *Deserbais*; Case 298/87, *Smanor*; Case C-47/90, *Delhaize* (wine of designated origin); Case C-3/91, *Exportur* (indications of provenance and designations of origin); Case C-315/92, *Clinique* (name under which cosmetics are sold); Case C-184/96,

- legislation on origin of goods;[458]
- legislation on presentation of products;[459]
- negative lists[460]
- obligation to appoint a representative in the importing Member State;[461]
- obligation to use a certain supplier;[462]
- obligation to use national products;[463]
- obligation to have a fixed establishment in country of importation;[464]
- obligation to request individual exemption;[465]
- obstacles to deliveries;[466]
- packaging requirements;[467]
- price-regulatory measures of general application;[468]
- price-regulatory measures concerning agricultural products;[469]

Commission v. France; Case C-448/98, *Guimont*; Case C-491/01, *British American Tobacco*; Case C-6/02, *Commission v. France (Salaisons d'Auvergne)*.

458. Case 41/76, *Criel, née Donckerwolke et al.*; Case 113/80, *Commission v. Ireland*; Case 207/83, *Commission v. UK*. See Reg. 2081/92 on the protection of geographical indications and designations of origin for agricultural products and foodstuffs O.J. 1992, L 208/1. Recent case law also concerns the interpretation of this and similar regulations; see Joined Cases C-321-324/94, *Pistre et al.*; Case C-87/97, *Consorzio per la tutela del formaggio Gorgonzola v. Käserei Champignon Hofmeister and Eduard Bracharz*; Joined Cases C-129 & 130/97, *Criminal proceedings against Yvon Chiciak and Fromagerie Chiciak and Jean-Pierre Fol*; Case C-312/98, *Schutzverband gegen Unwesen in der Wirtschaft v. Warsteiner Brauerei Haus Crame;* Case C-216/01, *Budvar*. In a number of cases, the validity of the Commission Decision is also examined for compatibility with free movement principles, see, e.g., Case C-469/00, *Ravil*; Case C-108/01, *Consorzio del Prosciutto di Parma, Salumificio S. Rita v. Asda Stores Ltd, Hygrade Foods Ltd.* The Court decided that the protection of these designations had priority over free movement.

459. Case 27/80, *Fietje*; Case 220/81, *Robertson*; Case 261/81, *Walter Rau Lebensmittelwerke v. De Smedt Pvb*; Case 179/85, *Commission v. Germany*; Case C-315/92, *Clinique*; Case C-293/93, *Criminal proceedings against Houtwipper*; Case 470/93, *Mars*; Case C-368/95, *Familiapress*; Case C-3/99, *Ruwet*; Case C-30/99, *Commission v. Ireland*; Case C-491/01, *British American Tobacco*.

460. Case 238/82, *Duphar BV et al. v. The Netherlands State*.

461. Case 155/82, *Commission v. Belgium*.

462. Case 72/83, *Campus Oil*; Case C-21/88, *Du Pont de Nemours*; Case C-379/98, *Preussen-Elektra*; Case C-398/98, *Commission v. Greece*.

463. Case 119/78, *SA des Grandes Distilleries Peureux*; Case 72/83, *Campus Oil*; Case C-137/91, *Commission v. Greece*; Case C-398/98, *Commission v. Greece*.

464. Joined Cases 87 & 88/85, *Société Cooperative des Laboratoires de Pharmacie Legia et al. v. Minister for Health, Luxembourg*; Case C-189/95, *Franzén*; Case C-254/98, *Heimdienst Sass*.

465. Case 82/77, *Van Tiggele*; Case 251/78, *Denkavit Futtermittel*; Case C-473/98, *Toolex*.

466. Case 155/80, *Oebel*.

467. Case 302/86, *Commission v. Denmark (bottles)*; Case C-309/02, *Radlberger*; Case C-463/01, *Commission v. Germany*.

468. E.g., Case 13/77, *NV GB-INNO-BM v. Vereniging van de Kleinhandelaars in Tabak (ATAB)*; Case 78/82, *Commission v. Italy*; Case 229/83, *Leclerc v. Àu blé vert*; Case 231/83, *Cullet et al. v. Centre Leclerc Toulouse et al.*; Case C-287/89, *Commission v. Belgium*; Joined Cases C-78-83/90, *Compagnie commerciale de l'Ouest*.

469. Case 31/74, *Galli*; Case 65/75, *Riccardo Tasca;* Joined Cases 88 & 90/75, *SADAM*; Case 154/77, *Procureur du Roi v. P. Dechmann*; Case 223/78, *Criminal proceedings against Adriano*

- price-regulatory measures concerning pharmaceutical products;[470]
- price-regulatory measures of food products;[471]
- prior authorization;[472]
- promotion of particular import channels;[473]
- promotion of particular products;[474]
- recipe laws;[475]
- requirements that imported products must conform to the requirements of the exporting country;[476]
- requirements of deposits, payments in cash;[477]
- requirements as to the use of a particular language;[478]

Grosoli; Case 5/79, *Procureur général v. Hans Buys, Han Pesch and Yves Dullieux and Denkavit France SARL*; Joined Cases 16-20/79, *Criminal proceedings against Joseph Danis and others*; Joined Cases 95 & 96/79, *Keffer and Delmelle*; Case 116/84, *Criminal proceedings against Henri Roelstraete*.

470. Case 181/82, *Roussel Laboratoria BV v. The Netherlands State*; Case 238/82, *Duphar*; Case C-249/88 *Commission v. Belgium*. See Commission Communication (O.J. 1986, C 310/7), and the transparency directive, Dir. 89/105 on the transparency of measures regulating the prices of medicinal products for human use and their inclusion in the scope of national health insurance systems (O.J. 1989, L 40/8).

471. Case 82/77, *Van Tiggele*; Joined Cases 177 & 178/82, *Van de Haar*; Joined Cases 80 & 159/85, *Nederlandse Bakkerij Stichting v. Edah BV*.

472. Case C-344/90, *Commission v. France*; Case C-192/01, *Commission v. Denmark*; Case C-24/00 *Commission v. France*; Case C-270/02 *Commission v. Italy*; Case C-95/01, *John Greenham v. Léonard Abel*; Case C-387/99, *Commission v. Germany;* Case C-150/00, *Commission v. Austria*.

473. Case 8/74, *Dassonville*; Case 104/75, *De Peijper*; Case C-359/93, *Commission v. The Netherlands*; Case C-314/98, *Snellers*.

474. Joined Cases 266 & 267/87, *Royal Pharmaceutical Society of Great Britain*, and Case C-18/88, *Régie des télégraphes et des telephones (RTT) v. GB-INNO-BM SA*; Case C-120/95, *Decker*.

475. Case 120/78, *Cassis de Dijon*; Case 788/79, *Criminal proceedings against Herbert Gilli and Paul Andres*; Case 53/80, *Officier van Justitie v. Koninklijke Kaasfabriek Eyssen BV*; Case 130/80, *Fabriek voor Hoogwaardige Voedingsprodukten Kelderman BV*; Case 94/82, *De Kikvorsch v. Groothandel Import-Export BV*; Case 174/82, *Officier van Justitie v. Sandoz BV*; Case 94/83, *Criminal proceedings against Albert Heijn BV*; Case 97/83, *Criminal proceedings against Melkunie*; Case 216/84, *Commission v. France*; Case 304/84, *Criminal proceedings against Claude Muller and others*; Case 407/85, *Drei Glocken et al. v. Unità Sanitaria Locale Centro-Sud et al.*; Case 76/86, *Commission v. Germany*; Case 52/88, *Commission v. Belgium*; Case C-67/88, *Commission v. Italy*; Case C-196/89, *Nespoli and Crippa*; Case C-269/89, *Bonfait BV*; Joined Cases C-13 & 113/91, *Criminal proceedings against Debus*; Case C-17/93, *Van der Veldt*; Case C-51/94, *Commission v. Germany*; Case C-358/95, *Morellato v. Unità Sanitaria Locale (USL) No 11, Pordenone*; Case C-12/00, *Commission v. Spain*; Case C-14/00, *Commission v. Italy*; Case C-121/00, *Criminal proceedings against Walter Hahn*; Case 416/00, *Morellato*; Case C-358/01, *Commission v. Spain*; Case C-41/02, *Commission v. Netherlands*.

476. Case 59/82, *Schutzverband gegen Unwesen in der Wirtschaft*.

477. Case 95/81, *Commission v. Italy*; Case 53/83, *Commission v. Greece;* and Case 192/84, *Commission v. Greece*.

478. Case 27/80, *Fietje*; Case C-369/89, *Piageme et al. v. BVBA Peeters*; Case C-51/93, *Meyhui*; Case C-85/94, *Piageme et al. v. Peeters*.

- stock restrictions;[479]
- quality label for domestic products;[480]
- stricter domestic limits applied to imported goods;[481]
- transport rules;[482]
- transit rules prohibiting heavy vehicles from travelling along a road section of major importance[483]
- withdrawal of licences.[484]

3.2.2.9   Burden of Proof

In infringement proceedings, the Commission is the applicant, and is the party bearing the burden of proof, in conformity with the rule *actori incumbit probatio*.[485] Preliminary proceeding form a stage in national proceedings, so the rules of evidence are determined by national procedural law.[486]

3.2.3   The Prohibition of Measures Having Equivalent Effect to Quantitative Restrictions on Exports: Article 29 EC

Although in general, a Member State will have more reasons to restrict imports than exports, there are a few situations where this is not the case: scarce goods,[487] waste,[488] strategic goods, animal-unfriendly conditions in the country of destination,[489] etc.

Article 29 EC contains a prohibition on quantitative restrictions on exports which is formulated in the same way as the prohibition in Article 28 EC relating to imports. The Court had given a broad definition of measures having equivalent effect in *Dassonville*, when dealing with measures applicable only to imports. In *Bouhelier*,[490] a few years later, the Court applied the formulation from *Dassonville* in relation to exports under Article 29 EC. In *Groenveld*, however, the Court gave a

---

479. Case 13/78, *Eggers*; Case C-323/93, *Crespelle*.
480. Case C-325/00, *Commission v. Germany*; Case C-166/03, *Commission v. France*.
481. Case C-389/96, *Aher-Waggon*.
482. Case C-350/97, *Wilfried Monsees v. Unabhängiger Verwaltungssenat für Kärnten*.
483. Case C-320/03, *Commission v. Austria*.
484. Case C-15/01, *Paranova Läkemedel AB and Others v. Läkemedelsverket*; Case C-113/01, *Paranova Oy*.
485. Case C-160/94, *Commission v. Spain* gives an example where the Commission failed to do so.
486. See on this B.J. Drijber, *Bewijsrecht in het Europees Gemeenschapsrecht: van vrij verkeer en vrij bewijs*, in S. Prechal and L. Hancher (eds), *Europees bewijsrecht: een verkenning* (Deventer, 2001), 15.
487. Case 68/76, *Commission v. France*.
488. Case C-203/96, *Chemische Afvalstoffen Dusseldorp BV v. Minister van Volkshuisvesting, Ruimtelijke Ordening en Milieubeheer*; Case C-209/98, *Entreprenørforeningens Affalds/ Miljøsektion (FFAD), acting for Sydhavnens Sten & Grus ApS v. Københavns Kommune*.
489. Case C-5/94, *The Queen v. Ministry of Agriculture, Fisheries and Food, ex parte: Hedley Lomas (Ireland)*; Case C-1/96, *The Queen v. Minister of Agriculture, Fisheries and Food*.
490. Case 53/76, *Bouhelier*.

more restrictive interpretation of the prohibition contained in Article 29 EC. The Court ruled that Article 29 concerns

> national measures which have as their specific object or effect the restriction of patterns of exports and thereby the establishment of a difference in treatment between the domestic trade of a Member State and its export trade, in such a way as to provide a particular advantage for national production or for the domestic market of the state in question at the expense of the production or of the trade of other Member States.[491]

An explanation for the difference between the prohibition in Article 28 and that in Article 29 could be that there is less chance of protectionist measures in relation to exports.[492]

This ruling – confirmed by the Court in later judgments,[493] though not always with a reference to *Groenveld*[494] – amounts to a discrimination test. Consequently, in principle, only the Treaty-based exceptions come into play, and not the rule-of-reason. This leads to problems in the sphere of environmental protection in particular (see further section 3.1.1 above)

Certain judgments of the Court give the impression that the restricted definition of the prohibition in Article 29 EC does not apply to (agricultural) products subject to a common organization of the market; in that case, the broader *Dassonville* formulation was used.[495] A possible explanation for this is the unity of the agricultural market.[496] Finally, in a fairly recent judgment the 'hypothetical situation' formula was used in relation to a distinctly applicable measure.[497]

The current confusion could be brought to an end if the Court were to declare the prohibition contained in Article 29 EC also applicable to non-discriminatory measures which hinder exports. The Court did take a step in this direction in its

---

491. Case 15/79, *Groenveld* at para. 7.
492. P. VerLoren van Themaat, 'De artikelen 30–36 van het EEG-Verdrag' (1980) *RMT*, 398.
493. Case 155/80, *Oebel*; Joined Cases 141–143/81, *Officier van Justitie v. Holdijk*; Case 286/81, *Oosthoek*; Case 29/82, *Van Luipen*; Case 172/82, *Inter-Huiles*; Case 238/82, *Duphar*; Case 240/83, *Procureur de la République v. Association de Défense des Bruleurs d'Huiles Usagées (ADBHU)*; Case 118/86, *Nertsvoederfabriek Nederland BV*; Case C-302/88, *Hennen Olie BV v. Stichting Interim Centraal Orgaan Voorraadvorming et al.*; Case C-9/89, *Spain v. Council*; Case C-332/89, *Marchandise*; Case C-3/91, *Exportur*; Case C-426/92, *Deutsches Milch-Kontor*; Case C-388/95, *Belgium v. Spain (Rioja)*; Case C-203/96, *Dusseldorp*; Case C-209/98, *Sydhavnens*; Case C-12/02, Case C-12/02, *Criminal proceedings against Marco Grilli*.
494. In Case 173/83, *Commission v. France* (waste oils) and Case C-209/98, *Sydhavnens*, the Court only used the qualification 'implicit prohibition [of exports]'.
495. Case 190/73, *Van Haaster* and Case 111/76, *Van der Hazel*; Case 94/79, *Vriend*; Case 237/82, *Jongeneel Kaas BV v. The Netherlands State*. Even after *Groenveld*, indistinctly applicable agricultural measures have been brought within the ambit of Art. 29. EC ; see Case C-47/90, *Delhaize*.
496. Cf. Case 83/78, *Pigs Marketing Board v. Raymond Redmond*; Case C-44/94, *The Queen v. Minister of Agriculture, Fisheries and Food, ex parte Fishermen's Organisations and others*.
497. Case C-412/97, *ED*. The Court refers here to the pre-*Keck* case law concerning indistinctly applicable measures.

judgment in *Alpine Investments*[498] in its interpretation of Article 49 on the freedom to provide services[499] (see section 7.4.1). There is as yet no clear case law on this issue in relation to the other freedoms, but there are certain elements which could be seen to link up with the approach taken in *Alpine Investments*, in the area of workers (section 5.3.1), establishment (section 6.5.1) and movements of capital (section 8.3).

3.2.4   Articles 28 and 29 EC and other Provisions of the EC Treaty

To the extent that import and export restrictions are also incompatible with other provisions of the treaty, such as Articles 25 and 90 EC,[500] Article 31 EC[501] or Article 87 EC,[502] the Court will apply these more specific provisions in preference to Articles 28 and 29.

In *Pfeiffer Großhandel*, the Court considered that if a national rule does not conflict with Article 43 EC, on the ground that it is justified under overriding requirements in the general interest, it could conflict with Article 28 only if, and to the extent that, it restricted the free movement of goods between Member States *other* than indirectly through the restriction of freedom of establishment.[503]

3.3   ARTICLES 28–29 EC: THE EXCEPTIONS

As was mentioned above, in section 1.1, both the drafters of the EC Treaty and the Court, which has to interpret its provisions, have attempted to find a balance between the interest in achieving the common market and the need to take into account general interests such as human health and a sustainable environment. In the Treaty itself as originally framed, the balance lay between the prohibitions contained in Articles 28 and 29 on the one hand and the exceptions contained in

---

498. Case C-384/93, *Alpine Investments*.
499. According to W.-H. Roth, 'Wettbewerb der Mitgliedstaaten oder Wettbewerb der Hersteller? Plädoyer für eine Neubestimmung des Art. 34 EGV' (1995) ZHR, 78–95. See also P. Oliver (1999) CML Rev., 802; W.-H. Roth, 'Export of Goods and Services within the Single Market: Reflections on the Scope of Arts. 29 and 49 EC', in T. Tridimas and P. Nebbia (eds), *European Union Law for the Twenty-First Century: Rethinking the New Legal Order, Vol. 2, Internal Market and Free Movement: Community Policies* (Oxford, 2004), 33.
500. E.g., Case 74/76, *Ianelli*; Case C-47/88, *Commission v. Denmark*; Case C-302/88, *Hennen Olie*; Joined Cases C-78–83/90, *Compagnie commerciale de l'Ouest*; Case 17/91, *Georges Lornoy en Zonen NV*, and Case C-266/91, *Celulose Beira Industrial (CELBI) SA*; Case C-228/98, *Dounias*; Case C-383/01, *Danske Bilimportører*; Joined Cases C-34–38/01, *Enirisorse SpA v. Ministero delle Finanze*.
501. Case C-157/94, *Commission v. Netherlands*.
502. Case 249/81, *Commission v. Ireland*; Case 18/84, *Commission v. France*; Case 103/84, *Commission v. Italy*; Case C-21/88, *Du Pont de Nemours*; and Case C-351/88, *Laboratori Bruneau v. Unità sanitaria locale RM/24 di Monterotondo*; C-379/98, *PreussenElektra*.
503. Case C-255/97, *Pfeiffer Großhandel*.

Article 30 on the other (in relation to the terminology, it was noted already above that from the point of view of the Member States these are usually referred to as *justifications*). In what can be seen as a second period of development, the Court compensated for the extension of the prohibition to indistinctly applicable measures by the development of the *Cassis de Dijon*, or rule-of-reason, exceptions, in addition to the exceptions contained in Article 30 EC. The amendments to the Treaty introduced by the SEA heralded a third period of development, so that the emphasis came to be placed less on case law developments but on the activities of the Commission and the Council which adopted measures, frequently on the basis of Article 95 EC, designed to make recourse to Articles 28–30 EC superfluous in many cases.[504] The price for such harmonization with the use of qualified majority voting was the inclusion of Article 95(4) EC, which gives the Member States the possibility to maintain certain national measures derogating from the harmonized provisions.[505]

Finally, the case law led to a new view of certain exceptions: they have in some cases become superfluous. After all, if a Member State makes a successful defence based on *Keck*, then the result is that the national measure is considered not to fall within the scope of the prohibition, and there is no need to invoke the exception. In concrete terms: it is no longer a question of a long list of exceptions in order to save legislation on shop opening hours, but higher upstream the non-applicability of the prohibition itself.

It is against this background that the exceptions to Articles 28 and 29 EC must be viewed. Those exceptions have a number of conditions in common, which are examined in section 3.3.1, below. The parting of the ways occurs in that Article 30 EC can benefit measures whether they are equally applicable or not (see section 3.3.2), whereas the case law regarding the rule-of-reason exceptions in principle only benefits indistinctly applicable measures (see section 3.3.3.). Finally, the exceptions which can be invoked in special circumstances will be examined in section 3.3.5, below.

3.3.1 The Exceptions In General

According to the Court in *Simmenthal I* and in *Tedeschi*, Article 30 EC is not designed to reserve certain matters to the exclusive jurisdiction of Member States; it merely permits national laws 'to derogate from the principle of the free movement of goods to the extent to which such derogation is and continues to be justified for the attainment of the objectives referred to in that article'.[506] This general

---

504. In pursuance of the Commission's White Paper *Completing the Internal Market* (COM(85)310 final).
505. The phases referred to here follow Mertens de Wilmars, 'Het Hof van Justitie van de Europese Gemeenschappen na de Europese Akte' (1986) SEW, 601. See further on harmonization Ch. V.
506. Case 35/76, *Simmenthal SpA v. Italian Minister of Finance* at para. 14; Case 5/77, *Tedeschi* at para. 34. See also Case 148/76, *Pubblico Ministero v. Ratti*; Case 815/79, *Criminal proceedings against Gaetano Cremonini and Maria Luisa Vrankovich*; Case C-52/92, *Commission v. Portugal*; Case C-241/01, *National Farmers' Union v. Secrétariat général du gouvernement*. See, however, Case 72/83, *Campus Oil*.

approach leads to a number of conditions which must be met for the Member States to be able to rely on these exceptions. These conditions also apply in the context of the other freedoms.

3.3.1.1   Narrow (Strict) Interpretation

This term in fact has various meanings. First, already in the 1960s the Court held that the list of exceptions contained in the first sentence of Article 30 EC was exhaustive.[507] However, the rule-of-reason exceptions do not constitute a closed class; the list of rule-of-reason exceptions in *Cassis de Dijon* is not exhaustive: the Court used the phrase 'in particular'.[508] Secondly, in Case 46/76 *Bauhuis v. The Netherlands State*[509] the Court held that Article 30 could not be understood as authorizing measures of a different nature from those referred to in Articles 28–29 EC, or where relevant Article 25 EC.[510] It is submitted that the same must be true of the rule-of-reason.[511] Finally, the application in a given case of the rule-of-reason or the first sentence of Article 30 is by no means automatic, since the national measure concerned must also be necessary and proportionate, as is explained below.

3.3.1.2   Absence of Community Measures (Tedeschi Rule)

Where Community measures provide for the harmonization of the measures necessary to ensure the protection of interests which form the objective of the Community measures in question, then recourse to Article 30 EC is no longer justified, and measures to attain these objectives must be within the framework outlined by the harmonizing measure; this was first stated by the Court in *Tedeschi*.[512] On the other hand, a national measure which implements or transposes a Community measure (for example, a Directive) cannot be considered a measure of equivalent effect to a quantitative restriction.[513]

The *Tedeschi* rule implies that Article 30 can only be invoked in the absence of Community measures occupying the field concerned. The blocking effect of the Community measures on the possibility of invoking Article 30 applies from the date by which the Community measures had to be transposed into national law,[514]

---

507. E.g., Case 7/68, *Commission v. Italy*; Case 46/76, *Bauhuis*; Case 113/80, *Commission v. Ireland*; Case 95/81, *Commission v. Italy;* and Case 229/83, *Leclerc v. Àu blé vert.*
508. Case 120/78, *Cassis de Dijon* at para. 8.
509. Case 46/76, *Bauhuis*. See also Case 32/80, *Kortmann*.
510. Case 46/76, *Bauhuis*; Case 32/80, *Kortmann*; Case C-189/01, *H. Jippes, Afdeling Groningen van de Nederlandse Vereniging tot Bescherming van Dieren, et al. v. Minister van Landbouw, Natuurbeheer en Visserij.*
511. The exceptions which concern the freedoms in general do not apply in the area of equal treatment of men and women; see Case C-186/01, *Dory*.
512. Case 5/77, *Tedeschi*.
513. Case C-123/00, *Christina Bellamy v. English Shop Wholesale*.
514. Case 35/76, *Simmenthal I*; Case C-320/93, *Lucien Ortscheit.*

or from the date on which those measures entered into force.[515] This condition also applies to rule-of-reason exceptions.[516] An international agreement to which all the Member States are parties is treated in the same way as a Community measure for these purposes.[517]

If, however, the Community measures are incomplete or are not binding, the Member Sates may invoke Article 30 or the rule-of-reason in relation to aspects not covered by the Community measures.[518] Thus in the case of minimum harmonization and other forms of incomplete harmonization the Court will look to see whether the national measures indeed remain within the space left to the Member States or whether they have strayed into the area occupied by Community legislation.[519]

3.3.1.3   Article 95(4)–(9) EC

The *Tedeschi* case law is less secure in cases where a Member State has recourse to Article 95(4)–(9) EC. This procedure, which was revised under the Treaty of Amsterdam, has so far not been used much.[520] Article 95(4) EC permits a Member State to maintain national provisions which it deems necessary on grounds of major needs referred to in Article 30, or relating to the protection of the environment or the working environment. Article 95(5) introduces a similar provision concerning national measures introduced after the relevant Community measure has been adopted. Article 95(8) provides for a special procedure in relation to public health.

In the list of protected interests in Article 95 EC, the exceptions under Article 30 EC are put on the same footing as two of the exceptions under the rule-of-reason. The fact that Article 95(3) EC mentions a rule-of-reason exception – consumer protection – which is not mentioned in Article 95(4) could imply that the list of interests mentioned in Article 95(4) is exhaustive. The case law of the Court on the strict interpretation of exceptions would point in the same direction.[521]

In the case of harmonization measures based on other Treaty provisions, such as Articles 47, 93, 94 and 308 EC, this limitation of existing case law does not exist, since these Treaty provisions do not contain arrangements similar to those of

---

515. If no transposition is required (as in the case of regulations).
516. Case C-39/90, *Denkavit Futtermittel GmbH v. Land Baden-Württemberg*.
517. Case 89/76, *Commission v. The Netherlands*.
518. Case 72/83, *Campus Oil*. See also, e.g., Case 251/78, *Denkavit Futtermittel*; Case 227/82, *Criminal proceedings against Leendert Van Bennekom*; Case 190/87, *Oberkreisdirektor des Kreises Borken v. Handelsonderneming Moormann BV*; Case 103/88, *Fratelli Costanzo SpA v. Comune di Milano*, and Case C-39/90, *Denkavit Futtermittel*.
519. E.g., Case C-11/92, *R. v. Secretary of State for Health, ex parte Gallaher Ltd et al.*; Case C-1/96, *The Queen v. Minister of Agriculture, Fisheries and Food*.
520. Case C-41/93, *France v. Commission*; Case C-112/97, *Commission v. Italy*; Case C-127/97, *Willi Burstein v. Freistaat Bayern*; Case C-319/97, *Criminal proceedings against Antoine Kortas*; Case C-512/99, *Germany v. Commission*; Case C-3/00, *Denmark v. Commission*; Joined Cases T-366/03 & T-235/04, *Land Oberösterreich v. Commission*; Case T-182/06, *The Netherlands v. Commission*. De Sadeleer, 'Procedures for Derogations from the Principle of Approximation of Laws under Article 95 EC' (2003) CML Rev., 889.
521. See beginning of this section.

Article 95 EC. In a number of cases, such as employment conditions (Art. 137) and environmental protection (Art. 176 EC), the Member States have the possibility to maintain or introduce more stringent protective measures; these must, however, be compatible with the Treaty.

3.3.1.4   Exceptions in Community Measures

Since Community measures have now been adopted in a great many sectors, it might seem that – pursuant to the *Tedeschi* rule – the possibility of invoking exceptions has become superfluous. What has happened, however, is a certain 'transfer' of exceptions: a number of directives and regulations contain exceptions mentioned in the Treaty, sometime defined in more detail,[522] sometimes merely repeated.[523] In certain cases, new exceptions are introduced, such as in a number of environmental directives: 'ecological, scientific and cultural requirements'.[524]

Many of the Court's judgments therefore deal with both Treaty-based exceptions and rule-of-reason exceptions in combination with provisions of secondary law. This phenomenon is particularly noticeable in the area of foodstuffs[525] and intellectual property (see section 3.3.2. below).

Exceptions also occur in Community measures concerning trade with third countries. The Court has explicitly indicated that the content of these must be interpreted by analogy with Article 30 EC.[526]

3.3.1.5   Interests of a Non-economic Nature

Already at an early stage the Court found that Article 30 EC protects non-economic interests;[527] thus, a Member State will not be permitted to plead economic

---

522. See, e.g., Dir. 84/450 on misleading advertising, O.J. 1984, L 250/17. See on this Case C-210/96, *Gut Springenheide and Rudolf Tusky v. Oberkreisdirektor des Kreises Steinfurt*; Case C-220/98, *Estée Lauder*.
523. Reg. 2679/98 on the functioning of the internal market in relation to the free movement of goods among the Member States, O.J. 1998, L 337/8; Dir. 2002/20, on the authorisation of electronic communications networks and services (Authorization Directive), O.J. 2002, L 108/21, para. 3 Preamble.
524. Council Dir. 79/409/EEC of 2 Apr. 1979 on the conservation of wild birds, O.J. 1979, L 103/. On this, see Case C-57/89, *Commission v. Germany*; Case C-355/90, *Commission v. Spain*; Case C-44/95, *R. v. Secretary of State for the Environment, ex parte: Royal Society for the Protection of Birds*.
525. Case C-388/95, *Belgium v. Spain (Rioja)*; Case C-101/98, *Union Deutsche Lebensmittelwerke v. Schutzverband gegen Unwesen in der Wirtschaft*; Case C-366/98, *Criminal proceedings against Yannick Geffroy*. As a result, the validity of the Commission's authorization decision may be contested via preliminary references. See, e.g., Case C-469/00, *Ravil*; Case C-108/01, *Parma ham*. See on this K.J.M. Mortelmans, 'The Relationship between the Treaty Rules and Community Measures for the Establishment and Functioning of the Internal Market: Towards a Concordance Rule' (2002) CML Rev., 1303–1346.
526. Case C-394/97, *Criminal proceedings against Sami Heinonen*.
527. E.g., Case 7/61, *Commission v. Italy*; Case 95/81, *Commission v. Italy*; Case 238/82, *Duphar*, and Case 288/83, *Commission v. Ireland*.

difficulties resulting from the removal of obstacles to intra-Community trade as a pretext for avoiding measures provided for in the Treaty.[528] This means that the Court will reject a justification based on the need to ensure the survival of a particular undertaking.[529] This restriction to interests of a non-economic nature was formulated with respect to exceptions under Article 30 EC, but it also applies in respect of the rule-of-reason justifications,[530] and has been extended to other freedoms;[531] it has also been declared applicable in relation to trade with third countries.[532] If economic difficulties arise, recourse must be had to the specific procedures contained in the EC Treaty itself, such as those in Articles 100, 119, 120 or 134 EC. In *Campus Oil*, the Court added a nuance to its case law: if a justification under Article 30 EC has been established, the fact that the national measure may promote other aims of an economic nature in addition to the objectives contained in Article 30 does not exclude the application of Article 30 EC.[533]

3.3.1.6   *Justification: Necessity and Proportionality*

The first sentence of Article 30 EC links the exceptions to the prohibition through the term 'justified' (as mentioned, the exceptions are also referred to as 'justifications'). In *Cassis de Dijon* the Court spoke of measures having to be 'necessary'.[534] It is thus manifestly evident that it is one thing for a Member State to invoke a justification, it is quite another for it to do so successfully. The criteria of the necessity and proportionality of a measure have to be satisfied.[535] These criteria are also applied in relation to justifications in the context of the other freedoms.[536]

Academic research shows the principle of proportionality as applied by the Court to be flexible in character.[537] In most judgments where Article 30 EC or the

---

528. Case 72/83, *Campus Oil*. Case 7/61, *Commission v. Italy*. See further Case 95/81, *Commission v. Italy;* Case 238/82, *Duphar*; Case 288/83, *Commission v. Ireland*; Case C-120/95, *Decker*.
529. Case C-324/93, *Evans Medical Ltd*.
530. Case C-203/96, *Dusseldorp*.
531. Case C-158/96, *Raymond Kohll v. Union des caisses de maladie*.
532. Case C-394/97, *Heinonen*; Case C-398/98, *Commission v. Greece*.
533. Case 72/83, *Campus Oil*. In Case C-157/94, *Commission v. the Netherlands*, this case law could have been clarified, but the ECJ took Arts. 31 EC and 86(2) EC as points of departure for its analysis. See also Case C-158/96, *Kohll*. Also Case C-254/98, *Heimdienst Sass*, seems to create an opening for certain measures which have other than purely economic objectives. This possibility is linked to the supply of remote and isolated districts and areas.
534. Case 120/78, *Cassis de Dijon* at para. 8. And in Case 8/74, *Dassonville*, the Court spoke of measures having to be 'reasonable'.
535. See also Ch. III, section 4. These criteria have been the subject of much discussion in academic writings Recent publications are: N. Emiliou, *The Principle of Proportionality in European Law* (The Hague, 1996); G. Hirsch, 'Das Verhältnismäßigkeitsprinzip im Gemeinschaftsrecht', in *Scritti in onore di G.F. Mancini*, vol. II (Milan, 1998), 459. E. Ellis (ed.), *The Principle of Proportionality in the Laws of Europe* (Oxford, 1999), contains analyses by e.g., W. Van Gerven, F. Jacobs and T. Tridimas.
536. A recent example is Case C-314/98, *Snellers*.
537. J.H. Jans, 'Proportionality Revisited', (2000) LIEI, 239–264.

rule-of-reason has been applied, the Court also applies the tests of necessity and/or proportionality explicitly or implicitly. The fact that the case law is frequently concerned with preliminary references under Article 234 EC has meant that in a number of cases the Court leaves the application of the test in the particular case to the national court.[538] In other cases, the Court itself gives an assessment of the justification of the measure.[539] In one case concerning infringement proceedings brought by the Commission against a Member State, the whole dispute turned on the issue of proportionality.[540]

Certain guiding principles are apparent from the case law. Van Gerven and Jans distinguish three elements,[541] though these cannot always be identified as such in each judgment, because of the case-led approach taken by the Court. Nevertheless, the three-pronged approach favoured by Van Gerven and Jans gives a good basis for analysing and understanding this subject.

First, we have the requirement of suitability. A national measure must actually be suitable for protecting the interest which has been invoked as a justification. This test concerns the causal link between the national measure and the interest to be protected. The judgment in *Cassis de Dijon* is a well-known example of this test. In that case, Germany invoked the protection of human health as a ground of justification for a higher alcohol content in German spirits than in comparable French spirits.[542] In many cases, the explicit application of the suitability test is passed over, and the necessity and proportionality tests are applied immediately. In some cases the two aspects are dealt with together.[543]

Secondly, a measure must be necessary, essential or indispensable. A measure is not 'necessary' if less far-reaching measures would be sufficient to achieve the desired result. The Court ruled, for instance, that prior authorization was indeed necessary for planning health care – this as a concrete application of the general interest protection against 'the risk of seriously undermining the financial balance of the social security system'. The Court was of the opinion that this held for hospital services but not for non-hospital services. In the latter case, prior authorization was not considered essential.[544]

Thirdly, the proportionality test in the strict sense: a balancing test. Under this test, a measure is not proportional when the obstacle to free movement of goods which it entails is out of proportion to the objective or result it aims to achieve. The

---

538. Compare Case C-145/88, *Torfaen* with Case C-312/89, *Conforama*. See on this K.J.M. Mortelmans, 'De bewijslast bij vrijverkeerzaken. De nationale rechter en de proportionaliteitstoets', in S. Prechal, L. Hancher (eds), *Europees bewijsrecht: een verkenning* (Deventer, 2001), 45.
539. Case C-189/95, *Franzén*.
540. Case C-55/99, *Commission v. France*.
541. Opinion of A.G. Van Gerven, Case C-312/89, *Conforama*; J.H. Jans, 'Proportionality Revisited' (2000) LIEI, 239–265.
542. Case C-120/78, *Cassis de Dijon*. This argument failed, since the Court found that there was already a wide variety of strengths of alcoholic drinks available on the German market.
543. Case C-385/99, *V.G. Müller-Fauré and E.E.M. van Riet v. Onderlinge Waarborgmaatschappij OZ Zorgverzekeringen*.
544. Case C-385/99, *Müller-Fauré*.

extensive case law of the Court on appropriate sanctions and penalties should be seen in this context.[545]

The principle of proportionality has been particularly frequently applied in the foodstuffs sector[546] – where the Court has on several occasions considered that appropriate labelling is sufficient to meet consumer protection requirements[547] – and in cases concerning additives, either in foods or other products. In all these cases, it is usual for the Court to refer to the state of scientific research.[548] As *Pastoors*[549] indicates, the principle of proportionality is also applied in other policy areas of the Member States and the Community (agricultural policy) and, of course, in the interpretation of the exceptions in relation to the other freedoms.[550]

A procedural twist is added to the proportionality test in many cases, insofar as the Court will insist that market participants must have access to procedural and judicial protection if a Member State decides to prohibit certain products.[551]

3.3.1.7 Burden of Proof

In infringement proceedings brought by the Commission against a Member State, that State will have to prove that its measure benefits from an exception, and that it is necessary and also applied proportionately.[552] If the Commission cannot adduce sufficient evidence to disprove this, then the application may be rejected.[553] In preliminary reference proceedings, if the Court of Justice does not make the assessment itself, it is for the national (judicial) authorities to determine whether the national measure concerned is caught by the prohibitions and, if so, whether it can stand the scrutiny under Article 30 EC or the rule-of-reason.[554] The national authorities may request information from the market participant concerned.[555] In its judgment in *Gut Springenheide*, the Court decided that the national courts may make use of information from surveys in assessing issues of consumer protection.[556]

---

545. See, e.g., Case 48/75, *Jean Noël Royer*; Case C-193/94, *Criminal proceedings against Sofia Skanavi and Konstantin Chryssanthakopoulos*; Case C-29/95, *Eckehard Pastoors and Trans-Cap v. Belgium*.
546. Case 42/82 R, *Commission v. France*.
547. Case 178/84, *Commission v. Germany*.
548. Case 174/82, *Sandoz BV*; Case 247/84, *Criminal proceedings against Léon Motte*; Case C-473/98, *Toolex*; Case C-41/02, *Commission v. Netherlands*.
549. Case C-29/95, *Pastoors*.
550. On this J.H. Jans et al., *Europeanisation of Public Law* (Groningen, 2007), 142.
551. Case C-18/88, *RTT*; Joined Cases C-46/90 & C-93/91, *Procureur du Roi v. Jean-Marie Lagauche et al.*
552. Case C-14/02, *ATRAL*.
553. Case C-157/94, *Commission v. the Netherlands*.
554. Joined Cases C-34–36/95, *De Agostini*.
555. Case 174/82, *Sandoz BV*.
556. Case C-210/96, *Gut Springenheide*. Cf. Case C-265/95, *Commission v. France (Spanish strawberries)*. This line of case law differs from earlier case law in which the ECJ explained the content of the exception itself, e.g., Case C-470/93, *Mars*. On this S. Weatherill, 'Recent Case Law Concerning the Free Movement of Goods: Mapping the Frontiers of Market Deregulation' (1999), CML Rev., 66.

The burden of proof that a measure is justified under Article 30 or the rule-of-reason lies on the Member State concerned.[557] However in the case of actions seeking to protect industrial and commercial property rights, where two undertakings are involved in a dispute, until quite recently there was no case law on the issue, nor did the specific directives and regulations lay down rules.[558] National courts came up with different solutions. In 2003, the Court handed down a detailed judgment on the matter.[559]

3.3.1.8   Conflicting General Interests

In certain special cases it is possible that the interests to be protected will conflict. For example, environmentally friendly packaging may afford the consumer less information, and questions of health protection will arise if it appears that the packaging involved is in fact less hygienic. There has not yet been any judicial pronouncement from the Court on how such conflicts in the area of free movement of goods should be resolved.[560] However, it is possible that Community law lays down some basic conditions. The Court has indicated that the protection of the health and life of humans ranks first among the interests protected by Article 30 EC.[561] The Court of First Instance adopted the same view as the Court of Justice, in *Vetmedica*,[562] though without an explicit reference; however, it added that importance should also be attached to the protection of consumer confidence.

3.3.1.9   General Interests and the EU Charter of Fundamental Rights

The increasing significance attached to the Charter of Fundamental Rights of the European Union by the Court of Justice also plays a role when it comes to the interpretation of the general interests. In *Dynamic Medien*, the Court recognized the protection of the rights of the child as a justification for obstacles to free movement of goods.[563] The Court based its reasoning on the EU Charter of

---

557. Case 251/78, *Denkavit Futtermittel*; Case 130/80, *Kelderman*.
558. On this, see A.G. Jacobs, Joined Cases C-427, 429 & 436/93, *Bristol-Myers*, Opinion, para. 100.
559. Case C-244/00, *Van Doren + Q. v. Lifestyle sports + sportswear*.
560. See on this K.J.M. Mortelmans, *Botsende algemene belangen en de werking van de interne markt* (2004) SEW, 240. In the area of free movement of persons, the Court has found that there must be a 'fair balance' between respect for family life and maintenance of public order and safety, see Case C-60/00, *Carpenter*. See also Case C-71/02, *Karner*. In Case C-61/03, *Commission v. UK*, concerning the Euratom Treaty, the interests of national security conflict with those of public health and trans-border environmental protection; see Opinion of A.G. Geelhoed at para. 59.
561. Case 104/75, *De Peijper*; Case C-320/93, *Lucien Ortscheit*; Case C-473/98, *Toolex*. See also de Opinion of A.G. Van Gerven in Case C-159/90, *The Society for the Protection of Unborn Children Ireland Ltd (SPUC) v. Stephen Grogan*, para. 37.
562. Joined Cases T-125 & 152/96, *Boehringer Ingelheim Vetmedica and C.H. Boehringer Sohn v. Council and Commission*, para. 98.
563. Case C-244/06, *Dynamic Medien Vertriebs GmbH v. Avides Media AG*.

Fundamental Rights together with the specific international instruments on which the Member States have cooperated or to which they have acceded, such as the Convention on the Rights of the Child.

In *Viking*, a similar path was taken in relation to freedom of establishment.[564]

3.3.1.10   Extra-territorial Interests

The extent to which a Member State may adopt measures hindering trade between Member States in order to protect not its own legitimate interests but those of another Member State or third country has been somewhat unclear.[565] A number of judgments throw light on this problem, albeit sometimes indirectly, but it seems that the Court avoids taking a clear stance.[566]

3.3.1.11   New Ranking of the Exceptions in the Treaty?

A number of problems have been identified in relation to the exceptions, such as: the somewhat artificial case law on indistinctly applied environmental measures and tax measures (see sections 3.3.3. and 5.3.2), the contrast in the operation of the prohibition on obstacles to exports between goods and services (see sections 3.2.3. and 7.4.1), and the importance of the so-called horizontal integration provisions (requiring certain interests to be integrated in all Community policies) for free movement provisions (see Ch. XI). These raise the question whether the provisions concerning free movement – and in particular the exceptions – are in need of revision. If these provisions were revised, the framers of the Treaty could then give a number of exceptions which are already capable of being invoked to a limited extent on a case law basis, such as environmental interests, the status of exceptions under Article 30 EC. These exceptions could then be invoked in relation to distinctly applicable measures as well.[567] The Treaty framers could then also indicate who are the addressees of the exceptions (government authorities or private parties). Moreover, attention could be paid to the convergence of the Treaty provisions and exceptions.[568]

---

564. Case C-438/05, *Viking*.

565. See on this H.G. Sevenster, *Eco-imperialisme binnen de Europese Unie: een juridisch probleem?* (Deventer, 1998); see also R. Barents, *M&R* 1998, 56, and W.-H. Roth, *Altruistische Interessenwahrnehmung im Binnenmarkt. Eine Skizze*, in *Festschrift für W. Fikentscher* (Mohr Siebeck, 1998), 723.

566. Case 172/82, *Inter-huiles*; Joined Cases 3, 4 & 6/76, *Cornelis Kramer and others*; Case 118/86, *Nertsvoederfabriek Nederland BV*; Case C-169/89, *Criminal proceedings against Gourmetterie Van den Burg*; Case C-3/91, *Exportur*; Case C-5/94, *Hedley Lomas*; Case C-1/96, *The Queen v. Minister of Agriculture, Fisheries and Food*. See for free movement of services Case C-384/93, *Alpine Investments*.

567. Cf. Case C-2/90, *Commission v. Belgium*; Case C-379/98, *PreussenElektra*.

568. See on this: K.J.M. Mortelmans, *Excepties bij non-tarifaire intracommunautaire belemmeringen: assimilatie in het nieuwe EG-Verdrag* (1997) SEW, 182; S. Weatherill, 'Recent Case Law Concerning the Free Movement of Goods: Mapping the Frontiers of Market Deregulation' (1999) CML Rev., 83; P. Oliver, 'Some Further Reflections on the Scope of Arts. 28–30

3.3.2   The Treaty-Based Exception: Article 30 EC

Article 30 EC, as an exception to the fundamental rule of the abolition of all restrictions on the free movement of goods, must be interpreted strictly.[569] This means, first of all, that the list of exceptions in Article 30 EC is exhaustive.[570] Although to some extent this standpoint is undermined by the *Cassis de Dijon* case law (see 3.3.3. below), it is still relevant where Member States introduce or maintain discriminatory measures. According to the classic case law,[571] such distinctly applicable measures may only be justified on the basis of exceptions contained in Article 30 EC. The strict interpretation of Article 30 also means that it cannot be invoked to justify measures of another type than those mentioned in Articles 28–29 EC, such as tariff barriers in the sense of Article 25 EC,[572] or state monopolies of a commercial character in the sense of Article 31 EC.[573] The Court's strict approach when reviewing attempts to rely on Article 30 is not, though, designed to remove the margin of discretion which is left to the Member States by that provision.[574]

In order for an interest or value mentioned in the first sentence of Article 30 EC to be invoked, a number of conditions must be satisfied, as was demonstrated above.[575] Thus there must be no Community legislation occupying the field; the measure must protect a non-economic interest; and it must pass the tests of necessity and proportionality. Furthermore, it must satisfy the requirement of the second sentence of Article 30 EC, namely it must not 'constitute a means of arbitrary discrimination or a disguised restriction on trade between Member States'. These conditions, like some of the heads of justification mentioned in the first sentence of Article 30, are inspired by Article XX GATT.[576] The two conditions are not systematically applied by the Court, often being dealt with together.[577]

3.3.2.1   *Arbitrary Discrimination and Disguised Restrictions on Trade*

The intention of this provision (the second sentence of Art. 30 EC) is to prevent improper use being made of the restrictions on trade which have been justified on the basis of Article 30 EC, first sentence.[578] For example, in a French case concerning a prohibition on advertising for alcoholic drinks, the Court ruled that public health was indeed at stake, but that it was a case of arbitrary

---

(ex 30–36) EC' (1999) CML Rev., 800; P. Oliver, 'Goods and Services: Two Freedoms Compared', in *Mélanges en hommage à Michel Waelbroeck* (Brussels, 2000), 1391.

569. Case 46/76, *Bauhuis*; Case 113/80, *Commission v. Ireland*.
570. Case 7/68, *Commission v. Italy*; Case 113/80, *Commission v. Ireland*.
571. See section 1.6 *supra*.
572. Case 46/76, *Bauhuis*.
573. Case C-157/94, *Commission v. the Netherlands*.
574. E.g., Case 53/80, *Eyssen*; Case 174/82, *Sandoz BV*; Case 97/83, *Melkunie*, and Case 178/84, *Commission v. Germany*.
575. Section 3.3.1.
576. See, generally, *GATT Law and Practice 1947–1994*, 6th ed. (Geneva, 1994), which discusses GATT theory and practice in this area.
577. Case 27/80, *Fietje*; Case 42/82 R, *Commission v. France*.
578. Case 34/79, *Henn and Darby*.

discrimination if products from other Member States were subject to a total ban, whereas French products were only subject to a partial ban.[579] Discrimination against parallel importers may also lead to arbitrary discrimination,[580] as can the absence of inspections of national products.[581]

The aim of the prohibition on disguised restrictions on trade between Member States is to ensure that reliance on the justifications contained in Article 30 (or the rule-of-reason) do not lead to artificial partitioning or fragmentation of markets within the common market. Such risks are particularly likely to materialize in the exercise of industrial and commercial property rights, and unsurprisingly it is in that context that much attention has been paid to the concept of a disguised restriction.[582] The first judgment in Case 40/82, *Commission v. United Kingdom*[583] demonstrates that there are other cases where this applies. The Commission has interpreted the term 'disguised restriction' in the context of Article 95(4) EC.[584]

3.3.2.2 The Interests or Values Mentioned in Article 30 EC, First Sentence

All the general interests mentioned in Article 30 have led to case law of the Court of Justice. The list below gives references (in footnotes) to the most important cases. In view of the convergence of the exceptions between the different freedoms, it is useful in examining the substance of a particular concept to analyse the case law relating to the other freedoms as well.[585] In a number of judgments, the Court gives an overall view of an exception which is mentioned at different places in the Treaty and secondary law.[586]

In many judgments, an exception is invoked, but not accepted by the Court. These cases are mentioned in the footnotes, as they also demonstrate certain characteristics of the exception, seen from the negative point of view:

- protection of industrial and commercial property (see further below);
- health and life of animals and plants;[587]

---

579. Case 152/78, *Commission v. France*. See also Case 53/76, *Bouhelier*; Case 50/85, *Schloh*.
580. Case 104/75, *De Peijper*.
581. Case 4/75, *Rewe (San José)*.
582. E.g., Case 15/74, *Centrafarm BV et al. v. Sterling Drug Inc.*; Case 102/77, *Hoffmann-La Roche & Co. AG v. Centrafarm Vertriebsgesellschaft Pharmazeutischer Erzeugnisse*; Case 144/81, *Keurkoop* and Case C-9/93, *IHT Internationale Heiztechnik et al. v. Ideal Standard et al.*
583. The 1982 judgment in this case.
584. Dec. 94/783 (O.J. 1994, L 316/43 at 47).
585. See 1.4 above.
586. For instance, some judgments concerning equal pay and internal and external security contain general arguments on the concept of 'security'; see Case C-273/97, *Angela Maria Sirdar v. The Army Board and Secretary of State for Defence*; Case C-285/98, *Tanja Kreil v. Bundesrepublik Deutschland* and Case C-186/01, *Dory*.
587. Case 4/75, *Rewe (San José)*; Case 35/76, *Simmenthal I*; Case 46/76, *Bauhuis*; Case 251/78, *Denkavit Futtermittel*; Case 132/80, *United Foods*; Joined Cases 141–143/81, *Holdijk*; Case 40/82, *Commission v. United Kingdom*; Case 73/84, *Denkavit Futtermittel GmbH v. Land Nordrhein-Westfalen*; Case C-131/93, *Commission v. Germany*; Case C-323/93, *Crespelle*; Case C-405/98, *Gourmet International*.

– health and life of humans;[588]
– national treasures possessing artistic, historic or archaeological value;[589]
– public policy;[590]
– public security;[591]
– public morality.[592]

---

588.   Case 104/75, *De Peijper*; Case 35/76, *Simmenthal I*; Case 120/78, *Cassis de Dijon*; Case 152/78,
       Commission v. France; Case 153/78, *Commission v. Germany*; Case 32/80, *Kortmann*; Case 53/
       80, *Eyssen*; Case 132/80, *United Foods*; Case 272/80, *Biologische producten*; Case 124/81,
       Commission v. United Kingdom; Case 247/81, *Commission v. Germany*; Joined Cases 2–4/82,
       SA Delhaize Frères 'Le Lion' and others v. Belgium; Case 42/82, *Commission v. France*; Case
       155/82, *Commission v. Belgium*; Case 174/82, *Sandoz BV*; Case 181/82, *Roussel*; Case 227/82,
       Van Bennekom; Case 238/82, *Duphar*; Case 50/83, *Commission v. Italy*; Case 94/83, *Albert
       Heijn*; Case 97/83, *Melkunie*; Case 176/84, *Commission v. Greece*; Case 178/84, *Commission v.
       Germany*; Case 188/84, *Commission v. France*; Case 216/84, *Commission v. France*; Case 247/
       84, *Motte*; Case 304/84, *Muller*; Case 50/85, *Schloh*; Case 54/85, *Ministère public v. Xavier
       Mirepoix*; Joined Cases 87 & 88/85, *Legia*; Case 76/86, *Commission v. Germany*; Case 118/86,
       Nertsvoederfabriek Nederland BV; Case 215/87, *Schumacher*; Case 25/88, *Wurmser*; Case 125/
       88, *Nijman*; Case C-95/89, *Commission v. Italy*; Case C-293/89, *Commission v. Greece*; Case C-
       347/89, *Freistaat Bayern v. Eurim-Pharm*; Case C-42/90, *Criminal proceedings against Jean-
       Claude Bellon*; Case C-62/90, *Commission v. Germany;* Case C-290/90, *Commission v.
       Germany*; Case C-344/90, *Commission v. France*; Case C-271/92, *Laboratoire de Prothèses
       Oculaires v. Union Nationale des Syndicats d'Opticiens de France et al.*; Case C-324/93, *Evans
       Medical*; Case C-293/94, *Brandsma*; Case C-120/95, *Decker*; Case C-358/95, *Morellato*; Case
       C-1/96, *The Queen v. Minister of Agriculture, Fisheries and Food*; Case C-180/96 R,
       United Kingdom v. Commission (BSE); Case C-180/96, *United Kingdom v. Commission (BSE
       II)*; Case C-77/97, *Österreichische Unilever v. Smithkline Beecham Markenartikel*; Case
       C-350/97, *Monsees*; Case C-209/98, *Sydhavnens*; Case C-254/98, *Heimdienst Sass*; Case C-
       473/98, *Toolex*; Case C-55/99, *Commission v. France*; Case C-121/00, *Walter Hahn*; Case
       C-172/00, *Ferring Arzneimittel*; Case C-15/01, *Paranova*; Case C-113/01, *Paranova Oy*; Case
       C-322/01, *Deutscher Apothekerverband*; Case C-112/02, *Kohlpharma*; Case C-387/99,
       Commission v. Germany; Case C-239/02, *Douwe Egberts*; Case C-150/00, *Commission v. Austria*.
589.   Case 7/68, *Commission v. Italy*. See Communication from the Commission on the Protection
       of National Treasures of November 1989, COM(89)594 final.
590.   Case 7/78, *Thomson*; Case 113/80, *Commission v. Ireland*; Case 95/81, *Commission v. Italy*;
       Case 16/83, *Prantl*; Case 72/83, *Campus Oil*; Case 177/83, *Ringelhan*; Case 231/83, *Cullet*;
       Case 288/83, *Commission v. Ireland*; Case C-124/95, *The Queen, ex parte Centro-Com Srl v.
       HM Treasury and Bank of England*; Case C-265/95, *Commission v. France (Spanish straw-
       berries)*; Case C-377/98, *Kingdom of the Netherlands v. European Parliament and Council
       (biotechnological inventions)*. See H. Schneider, *Die öffentliche Ordnung als Schranke der
       Grundfreiheiten im EG-Vertrag* (Baden-Baden, 1998); J. Fölisch, *Der gemeineuropäische
       Ordre public* (Frankfurt am Main, 1997).
591.   Case 72/83, *Campus Oil*; Case 231/83, *Cullet*; Case 174/84, *Bulk Oil (Zug) AG v. Sun
       International Limited and Sun Oil Trading Company*; Case 222/84, *Marguerite Johnston v.
       Chief Constable of the Royal Ulster Constabulary*; Case 50/85, *Schloh*; Case 406/85, *Procur-
       eur de la République v. Daniel Gofette and Alfred Gilliard*; Case 25/88, *Wurmser*; Case
       C-347/88, *Commission v. Greece*; Case C-367/89, *Richardt*; Case C-157/94, *Commission v.
       the Netherlands*; Case C-398/98, *Commission v. Greece*.
592.   Case 34/79, *Henn en Darby*; Case 121/85, *Conegate Limited v. HM Customs & Excise*; Case
       C-377/98, *Kingdom of the Netherlands v. European Parliament and Council (biotechnological
       inventions)*.

3.3.2.3   *Protection of Industrial and Commercial Property: General*

According to Article 17(2) EU Charter of Fundamental Rights, 'intellectual property shall be protected'. The scope of this provision, included in an article which is concerned with the right to property, is as yet undecided; the possible scope is connected with the legal effect of the Charter in general, which is also still rather uncertain.

Intellectual property rights may affect inter-state trade in goods, but they are not goods themselves.[593] Because the exercise of intellectual property rights does affect the free movement of goods, it comes within the scope of Articles 28 and 30 EC.

From the Court's case law, it appears that restrictions to trade resulting from intellectual property rights can also come within the scope of 'services' in the sense of the Treaty provisions on freedom to provide services.[594]

The general non-discrimination rule contained in Article 12 EC also applies to intellectual property rights.[595]

From an economic point of view, the exercise of intellectual property rights can lead to anticompetitive practices on the part of undertakings. It is therefore not surprising that this issue first arose in cases concerning Article 81 EC.[596] In this context, the Court considered that Article 30 EC and the intellectual property exception it contains, does not restrict the scope of application of Article 81 EC.[597]

Infringement proceedings are sometimes also brought before the Court in situations where cartels operate. The Court has continually recalled that the mere possession, or existence, of intellectual property rights does not lead to a dominant position in the sense of Article 82 EC.[598] Refusal to provide information about forthcoming television programmes may well constitute an abuse of a

---

593. Case C-97/98, *Jägerskiöld.*
594. Case C-97/98, *Jägerskiöld.*
595. Joined Cases C-92 & 326/92, *Phil Collins v. Imtrat Handelsgesellschaft and Patricia Im- und Export Verwaltungsgesellschaft mbH and Leif Emanuel Kraul v. EMI Electrola*; Case C-360/00, *Land Hessen v. G. Ricordi & Co. Bühnen- und Musikverlag.*
596. Joined Cases 56 & 58/64, *Consten and Grundig*; Case 24/67, *Parke, Davis and Co. v. Probel, Reese, Beintema-Interpharm and Centrafarm*; Case 40/70, *Sirena S.r.l. v. Eda S.r.l. and others*; Case 125/78, *GEMA, Gesellschaft für musikalische Aufführungs- und mechanische Vervielfältigungsrechte, v. Commission*; Case 35/83, *BAT Cigaretten-Fabriken GmbH v. Commission.*
597. Joined Cases 56 & 58/64, *Consten and Grundig.*
598. Case 24/67, *Parke-Davis*; Case 40/70, *Sirena*; Case 78/70, *Deutsche Grammophon*; Case 127/73, *Belgische Radio en Televisie v. SV SABAM and NV Fonior (BRT II)*; Case 51/75, *EMI Records*; Case 86/75, *EMI Records Limited v. CBS Grammofon A/S (EMI II)*; Case 96/75, *EMI Records Limited v. CBS Schallplatten (EMI III)*; Case 22/79, *Greenwich Film Production v. Société des auteurs, compositeurs et éditeurs de musique (SACEM) and Société des éditions Labrador*; Case 262/81, *Coditel SA, Compagnie générale pour la diffusion de la télévision, and others v. Ciné Vog Films SA and others*; Case 395/87, *Ministère public v. Jean-Louis Tournier.*

dominant position.[599] This case law is dealt with elsewhere in this book (see Ch. IX below).[600]

3.3.2.4   Protection of Industrial and Commercial Property
as a Ground of Justification

The protection of industrial and commercial property (hereafter: intellectual property rights[601]) as an exception to the prohibitions has a rather particular place in the list of protected interests in Article 30 EC. It concerns interests of certain market participants, which are protected by national legislation.[602] As indicated above, this also has consequences for the burden of proof.[603]

The tension between these rights and free movement results from the fact that national laws enable holders of, for example, patent rights to oppose by means of infringement proceedings the marketing by others of products covered by their rights. Where the national case law permitted such infringement proceedings without any further limits, this led to division of the markets.[604] Given that intellectual property infringement proceedings were primarily based on national legislation, it was obvious that national courts would make references under Article 234 EC to the Court of Justice about the extent of this head of justification. The international agreements in this area to which Member States are parties – such as the Berne Convention 1886,[605] the Paris Union Convention 1883[606] and the

---

599. Joined Cases C-241 & 242/91 P, *RTE*; Case C-418/01, *IMS Health v. NDC Health.*

600. For an extensive and recent overview of this subject, see L. Ritter, W.D. Braun and F. Rawlinson, *European Competition Law: a Practitioner's Guide*, 2nd ed. (The Hague, 2000), 555 et seq. See also R. Whish, *Competition Law*, 4th ed. (London, 2001); J. Turner, *Intellectual Property and EC Competition Law* (Richmond, 2005).

601. The term is now used as such by the ECJ; see Case C-97/98, *Jägerskiöld.*

602. On the tension between the established market participants and those from developing countries, see W. Alexander, *De betrekkelijke waarde van de intellectuele eigendom* (Zwolle, 1993).

603. See section 3.3.1. See on this Case C-244/00, *Van Doren + Q.*

604. See on this T. Koopmans, 'Mini-monopolies' (1983) RMT, 342, and L. Wichers Hoeth, 'Mini-monopolies, een reactie' (1984) RMT, 356. See also T. Koopmans, 'Intellectuele eigendom, economie en politiek' (1994) *Informatierecht/AMI*, 107–110. See for the difference between national and international trade (TRIPs), Opinion 1/94, *WTO*, para. 57 et seq.

605. Most recently revised, Paris, 24 Jul. 1971; see Case C-345/89, *Criminal proceedings against Alfred Stoeckel*; Joined Cases C-241 & 242/91 P, RTE; Joined Cases C-92 & 326/92, *Phil Collins*; Opinion 1/94, *WTO*; and Case T-56/92, *Casper Koelman v. Commission.*

606. Most recently revised, Stockholm, 14 Jul. 1967; see Case 6/81, *Industrie Diensten Groep v. J.A. Beele Handelmaatschappij*; Joined Cases 43 & 63/82, *Vereniging ter Bevordering van het Vlaamse Boekwezen, VBVB, and Vereniging ter Bevordering van de Belangen des Boekhandels, VBBB, v. Commission*; Case 182/84, *Miro*; Case 130/85, *Groothandel in, Im- en Export van Eieren en Eiprodukten Wulro BV against a decision of the Tuchtgerecht of the Stichting Scharreleieren-Controle*; Case C-235/89, *Commission v. Italy* (compulsory licences); Case C-30/90, *Commission v. United Kingdom* (Patents Act); and Opinion 1/94, *WTO*; Case C-104/01, *Libertel Groep v. Benelux-Merkenbureau.*

Trade-Related Aspects of Intellectual Property Rights (TRIPs) Agreement[607] – also play a role.

3.3.2.5 Existence, Exercise and Exhaustion of Intellectual Property Rights

The Court's approach can be summarized as follows. The actual existence of intellectual property rights is not incompatible with Articles 28–29 EC. Nevertheless, the exercise of these rights may be forbidden in a number of cases. The exception in Article 30 EC only covers the *specific object* (or specific subject matter) of patents, trade marks and similar rights. More far-reaching rights, such as the right to object to the importation of goods which have been marketed in another Member State by or with the consent of the patentee or trade mark owner, for instance by means of licences, are not saved by the terms of the first sentence of Article 30 EC. To use the terminology of the Court, the rights are said to have been exhausted as a result of the products having been marketed.[608] An analogy may be drawn here with Article 222 EC on property rights in general.[609]

3.3.2.6 Case Law on the Intellectual Property Exception

The Court has elaborated this exception in an extensive body of case law. Cases concerning misrepresentation and associated subjects are frequently treated on the basis of the rule-of-reason exceptions of consumer protection and fair business practices (see section 3.3.3. below). The various rights – patent, trade mark or plant breeder's rights, but also copyright and models and designs – have their specific characteristics. This has consequences for the case law, which is referred to here according to the various category of rights. The Court has revised its earlier case

---

607. The Marrakesh Agreement Establishing the World Trade Organization, Annex 1C: Agreement on Trade-Related Aspects of Intellectual Property Rights (TRIPs), approved by the Community for matters falling within its competence by Council Decision 94/800, O.J. 1994, L 336/1. See Case C-53/96, *Hermès International v. FHT Marketing Choice*; Case C-200/96, *Metronome Musik v. Music Point Hokamp*; Case C-89/99, *Schieving-Nijstad vof and Others v. Robert Groeneveld*; Case C-491/01, *British American Tobacco*. In Joined Cases C-300 & 392/98, *Parfums Christian Dior et al. v. Tuk Consultancy*, the Court considered that it was competent to interpret Art. 50 TRIPs agreement (Annex 1C) in general (and not merely in situations relating to trade marks). In this judgment, the ECJ also gave a careful and restrained view of the direct effect of this provision, and held that proceedings for unlawful acts were governed by national legal systems. See in this context also Case C-149/96, *Portugal v. Council* (Textiles) and Case C-431/05, *Merck Genéricos Produtos Farmacêuticos*. In Case C-377/98, *Kingdom of the Netherlands v. European Parliament and Council (biotechnological inventions)*, the ECJ considered the relationship between TRIPs and the relevant EC Directive. See also Case C-245/02, *Anheuser-Busch v. Budějovický Budvar, národní podnik* and Case C-275/06, *Productores de Música de España (Promusicae) v. Telefónica de España*.
608. Case 15/74, *Centrafarm. v. Sterling*.
609. See on the relation between Arts. 28 and 30 EC and 295 EC, Case 30/90, *Commission v. United Kingdom* (Patents Act); Case C-350/92, *Spain v. Council*; and Case C-491/01, *British American Tobacco*.

law on the so-called common origin doctrine[610] and has refined its case law in a number of areas, such as transfer of trade mark rights.[611]

Since the entry into force of a number of specific directives and regulations, the Court concentrates on the explicit EC rules. This is clearly apparent in the extensive case law on the essential function and the exhaustion of trade mark rights.[612] On the one hand, the Court considers that as a result of the Community rules, a comprehensive set of arrangements has come into existence, so that review must be on the basis of these rules and no longer on the basis of Articles 28 and 30 EC.[613] On the other hand, the Court makes use of its case law on Article 30 EC in interpreting the provisions of the directive.[614] Finally, there are a number of questions related to the application of the directive which seem – at least at first sight – as yet not to be completely regulated. In the *Silhouette* case, the Court considered that Article 7 of the Trade Mark Directive, as amended by the EEA Agreement, prohibits national rules according to which the right associated with a trade mark is exhausted for products once they are marketed by or with the consent of the owner of the mark in a country outside the EEA. In other words: Community level exhaustion, not world-wide exhaustion.[615]

At this stage, we refer (using footnotes) to the case law relating to national intellectual property law. The case law of the Court concerning Community intellectual property rules will be dealt with later in this chapter, in the context of the description of the Community legislation on intellectual property.

It is not possible in this chapter to deal with the content of this important area of case law.[616] We limit ourselves to mentioning the various rights and the most relevant cases of the Court of Justice and the Court of First Instance:

– copyright;[617]

---

610. Case C-10/89, *CNL-SUCAL v. HAG (HAG II)*. Here the Opinion of A.G. Jacobs played an important role. See also R. Joliet (1991) *GRUR Int.*, 177–184.
611. Case C-9/93, *Ideal Standard*. See G. Tritton, 'Arts. 30 to 36 and Intellectual Property: Is the Jurisprudence of the ECJ Now of an Ideal Standard?' (1994) EIPR, 422. See also W. Alexander (1995) CML Rev., 327.
612. See Arts. 3 and 7 of the trade mark Dir. 89/104, O.J. 1989, L 40/1.
613. E.g., Case C-352/95, *Phytheron International v. Jean Bourdon*.
614. E.g., Joined Cases C-427, 429 & 436/93, *Bristol-Myers*.
615. Case C-355/96, *Silhouette International Schmied v. Hartlauer Handelsgesellschaft*. This subject also led to some consternation in the Netherlands.
616. These cases are regularly annotated in *European Intellectual Property Review*; *International Review of Industrial Property and Copyright Law*; *Gewerblicher Rechtsschutz und Urheberrecht, Internationaler Teil*; *Bijblad bij de Industriële Eigendom*; *Intellectuele Eigendom & Reclamerecht*; *Ars Aequi*; *Informatierecht/AMI*.
617. Case 78/70, *Deutsche Grammophon*; Case 62/79, *Compagnie générale pour la diffusion de la télévision, Coditel, and others v. Ciné Vog Films and others*; Joined Cases 55 & 57/80, *Musik-Vertrieb membran GmbH and K-tel International v. GEMA - Gesellschaft für musikalische Aufführungs- und mechanische Vervielfältigungsrechte*; Case 58/80, *Dansk Supermarked*; Case 270/80, *Polydor and others v. Harlequin and others*; Case 262/81, *Coditel*; Joined Cases 60 & 61/84, *Cinéthèque v. Fédération nationale des cinémas français*; Case 402/85, *G. Basset v. Société des auteurs, compositeurs et éditeurs de musique (SACEM)*; Case 158/86,

- designations of origin and indications of origin;[618]
- plant-breeder's rights;[619]
- trade mark rights;[620]
- neighbouring rights;[621]
- patents;[622]
- designs and models.[623]

3.3.2.7   EC Legislation on Intellectual Property

By now, a number of instruments of positive integration in the area of intellectual property have been adopted.[624] To the extent that these are purely harmonization

---

Warner Brothers and Metronome Video v. Erik Viuff Christiansen; Case 270/86, *Cholay and Bizon's Club v. SACEM*; Case 341/87, *EMI Electrola v. Patricia Im- und Export and others*; Case 395/87, *Tournier*; Joined Cases C-241 & 242/91 P, *RTE*; Joined Cases C-92 & 326/92, *Phil Collins*. For the relation between copyright and tax, see Case 90/79, *Commission v. France*.

618. Case 8/74, *Dassonville*; Case 12/74, *Commission v. Germany*; Case 2/78, *Commission v. Belgium*; Case 207/83, *Commission v. UK*; Case 179/85, *Commission v. Germany*; Case C-47/90, *Delhaize*; Case C-3/91, *Exportur*; Case C-388/95, *Belgium v. Spain (Rioja)*; Case C-325/00, *Commission v. Germany*; Case C-469/00, *Ravil*; Case C-108/01, *Parma ham*. See on this D. Klingstein, *Schutz geographischer Angaben und Ursprungsbezeichnungen in Europa: Bewertung der VO (EWG) Nr. 2081/92 als Instrument der europäischen Qualitätspolitik in der Land- und Ernährungswirtschaft* (Göttingen, 2001).
619. Case 258/78, *L.C. Nungesser KG and Kurt Eisele v. Commission*.
620. Joined Cases 56 & 58/64, *Consten and Grundig*; Case 192/73, *Van Zuylen frères v. Hag*; Case 16/74, *Centrafarm v. Winthrop*; Case 51/75, *EMI Records*; Case 119/75, *Terrapin*; Case 102/77, *Hoffmann-la Roche*; Case 3/78, *Centrafarm BV v. American Home Products Corporation*; Case 58/80, *Dansk Supermarked*; Case 1/81, *Pfizer v. Eurim-Pharm*; Joined Cases 266 & 267/87, *Royal Pharmaceutical Society of Great Britain*; Case C-10/89, *Hag II*; Case C-238/89, *Pall Corp. v. P. J. Dahlhausen & Co.*; Case C-317/91, *Deutsche Renault AG v. AUDI AG*; Case C-9/93, *Ideal Standard*; Joined Cases C-427, 429 and 436/93, *Bristol-Myers*; Case C-349/95, *Frits Loendersloot v. George Ballantine & Son*; Case C-352/95, *Phyteron*; Case C-379/97, *Pharmacia & Upjohn v. Paranova*.
621. Joined Cases C-92 & 326/92, *Phil Collins*.
622. Case 24/67, *Parke-Davis*; Case 15/74, *Centrafarm. v. Sterling*; Case 187/80, *Merck v. Stephar and Petrus Stephanus Exler*; Case 19/84, *Pharmon v. Hoechst*; Case 434/85, *Allen & Hanburys v. Generics*; Case 35/87, *Thetford Corporation and others v. Fiamma*; Case C-235/89, *Commission v. Italy*; Case C-30/90, *Commission v. United Kingdom* (Patents Act); Case C-191/90, *Generics (UK) Ltd and Harris Pharmaceuticals Ltd v. Smith Kline & French Laboratories Ltd*; Joined Cases C-267 & 268/95, *Merck et al. v. Primecrown et al.*; Case C-316/95, *Generics v. Smith Kline & French Laboratories*; Case C-44/98, *BASF*.
623. Case 6/81, *Beele*; Case 144/81, *Keurkoop*; Case 53/87, *Consorzio italiano della componentistica di ricambio per autoveicoli and Maxicar v. Régie nationale des usines Renault*; Case 238/87, *Volvo v. Erik Veng*; Case C-23/99, *Commission v. France*.
624. See W. Cornish, *Intellectual Property* (London, 1999). J. Snell, 'European Courts and Intellectual Property: A Tale of Hercules, Zeus and Cyclops' (2004) EL Rev., 178; P. Turner-Kerr, 'Trade Mark Tangles: Recent Twists and Turns in EC Trade Mark Law' (2004) EL Rev., 345; D. T. Keeling, *Intellectual Property Rights in the EC: Vol. I, Free Movement and Competition Law* (Oxford, 2003).

measures, the Community competence is based on Articles 94 and 95 EC. In addition, the Community may create new rights on the basis of Article 307 EC.[625] Finally, Article 133(5), on the common commercial policy, contains special rules for intellectual property rights (see further Ch. XIII below).

The following instruments have been adopted or are in preparation;[626] they provide a basis for developing a substantive content at EC level for general and horizontal intellectual property matters. They are listed here in order of date of adoption:

- Council Regulation (EEC) No. 3842/86 of 1 December 1986 laying down measures to prohibit the release for free circulation of counterfeit goods, O.J. 1986, L 357/1;
- Council Directive 87/54/EEC of 16 December 1986 on the legal protection of topographies of semiconductor products, O.J. 1987, L 24/36;
- First Council Directive 89/104/EEC of 21 December 1988 to approximate the laws of the Member States relating to trade marks, O.J. 1989, L 40/1;[627]
- Agreement 89/695/EEC relating to Community patents, done at Luxembourg on 15 December 1989, O.J. 1989, L 401/1;[628]

625. See on the question of competence Opinion 1/94, *WTO*, para. 59 et seq. and 103 et seq.; Case C-350/92, *Spain v. Council*; Case C-377/98, *Netherlands v. European Parliament and Council (biotechnological inventions)*.
626. T. Cook, *EU Intellectual Property Law* (Richmond, 2005).
627. Joined Cases C-427, 429 & 436/93, *Bristol-Myers*; Joined Cases C-71–73/94, *Eurim-Pharm Arzneimittel v. Beiersdorf and others*; Case C-232/94, *MPA Pharma v. Rhône-Poulenc Pharma*; Case C-313/94, *F.lli Graffione SNC v. Ditta Fransa*; Case C-251/95, *SABEL BV v. Puma AG, Rudolf Dassler Sport*; Case C-337/95, *Dior v. Evora*; Case C-349/95, *Loendersloot*; Case C-352/95, *Phyteron*; Case C-355/96, *Silhouette*; Case C-39/97, *Canon Kabushiki Kaisha v. Metro-Goldwyn-Mayer*; Case C-63/97, *Bayerische Motoren Werke AG (BMW) and BMW Nederland BV v. Ronald Karel Deenik*; Joined Cases C-108 & 109/97, *Windsurfing Chiemsee Produktions- und Vertriebs GmbH (WSC) v. Boots- und Segelzubehör Walter Huber and Franz Attenberger*; Case C-342/97, *Lloyd Schuhfabrik Meyer v. Klijsen Handel*; Case C-375/97, *General Motors Corporation v. Yplon*; Case C-379/97, *Pharmacia & Upjohn*; Case C-173/98, *Sebago and Ancienne Maison Dubois et Fils v. GB-Unic;* Case C-425/98, *Marca Mode v. Adidas AG, Adidas Benelux*; Case C-299/99, *Koninklijke Philips Electronics NV v. Remington Consumer Products Ltd,*; Joined Cases C-414–416/99, *Zino Davidoff v. A & G Imports and Levi Strauss v. Tesco Stores*; Case C-517/99, *Merz & Krell*; Case C-2/00, *Michael Hölterhoff v. Ulrich Freiesleben*; Case C-244/00, *Van Doren + Q*; Case C-273/00, *Ralf Sieckmann*; Case C-291/00, *LTJ Diffusion v. Sadas Vertbaudet*; Case C-292/00, *Davidoff, Zino Davidoff v. Gofkid*; Case C-40/01, *Ansul v. Ajax Brandbeveiliging*; Joined Cases C-53-55/01, *Linde, Winward Industries, and Rado Uhren*; Case C-104/01, *Libertel*; Case C-206/01, *Arsenal Football Club plc v. Matthew Reed;*.Case C-418/02, *Praktiker Bau- und Heimwerkermärkte*; Case C-353/03, *Nestlé v. Mars*; Case C-405/03, *Class International v. Colgate-Palmolive*; Case C-259/04, *Elizabeth Florence Emanuel v. Continental Shelf 128*; Case C-421/04, *Matratzen Concord v. Hukla Germany*; Case C-145/05, *Levi Strauss v. Casucci*; Case C-281/05, *Moltex Holdings v. Diesel*.
628. Case C-283/01, *Shield Mark BV v. Joost Kist h.o.d.n. Memex*; Case C-408/01, *Adidas-Salomon, Adidas Benelux v. Fitnessworld Trading. Trb.* 1990, nr. 121. See in the Netherlands, Act of 15 Dec. 1994, with rules on patents, Stb. 1995, 51. See also Munich Convention of

- Council Directive 91/250/EEC of 14 May 1991 on the legal protection of computer programs, O.J. 1991, L 122/42;[629]
- Council Resolution of 14 May 1992 on increased protection for copyright and neighbouring rights (on the Berne Convention), O.J. 1992, C 138/1;
- Council Regulation (EEC) No. 1768/92 of 18 June 1992 concerning the creation of a supplementary protection certificate for medicinal products, O.J. 1992, L 182/1;[630]
- Council Regulation (EEC) No. 2081/92 of 14 July 1992 on the protection of geographical indications and designations of origin for agricultural products and foodstuffs, O.J. 1992, L 208/1;[631]
- Council Directive 92/100/EEC of 19 November 1992 on rental right and lending right and on certain rights related to copyright in the field of intellectual property, O.J. 1992, L 346/61;[632]
- Council Directive 93/83/EEC of 27 September 1993 on the coordination of certain rules concerning copyright and rights related to copyright applicable to satellite broadcasting and cable retransmission, O.J. 1993, L 248/15;[633]
- Council Directive 93/98/EEC of 29 October 1993 harmonizing the term of protection of copyright and certain related rights, O.J. 1993, L 290/9; repealed and replaced by Directive 2006/116;[634]
- Council Regulation (EC) No. 40/94 of 20 December 1993 on the Community trade mark, O.J. 1994, L 11/1;[635]
- Council Regulation (EC) No. 2100/94 of 27 July 1994 on Community plant variety rights, O.J. 1994, L 227/1;
- Council Regulation (EC) No. 3295/94 of 22 December 1994 laying down measures to prohibit the release for free circulation, export, re-export or entry for a suspensive procedure of counterfeit and pirated goods, O.J. 1994, L 341/8, as amended by Regulation 241/1999, O.J. 1999, L 27/1;[636]

---

5 Oct. 1973 on the Grant of European Patents, *Trb.* 1975, nr. 108, and 1976, nr. 101. See Case C-44/98, *BASF.*
629. Case T-198/98, *Micro Leader Business v. Commission.*
630. Case C-110/95, *Yamanouchi Pharmaceutical v. Comptroller-General of Patents, Designs and Trade Marks;* Case C-181/95, *Biogen v. Smithkline Beecham Biologicals.*
631. Joined Cases C-321–324/94, *Pistre et al.;* Case C-388/95, *Belgium v. Spain (Rioja);* Case C-87/97, *Consorzio per la tutela del formaggio Gorgonzola;* Joined Cases C-129 & 130/97, *Chiciak;* Case C-312/98, *Warsteiner Brauerei Haus Cramer;* Case C-469/00, *Ravil;* Case C-108/01, *Parma ham;* Case C-216/01, *Budvar.*
632. Case C-200/96, *Metronome Musik;* Case C-61/97, *Foreningen af danske Videogramdistributører et al. v. Laserdisken;* Case C-245/00, *Stichting ter Exploitatie van Naburige Rechten (SENA) v. Nederlandse Omroep Stichting (NOS).* Case C-192/04, *Lagardère Active Broadcast v. SPRE.*
633. Case C-293/98, *Entidad de Gestión de Derechos de los Productores Audiovisuales (Egeda) v. Hostelería Asturiana SA (Hoasa).*
634. O.J. 2006, L 372/12; Case C-60/98, *Butterfly Music Srl v. Carosello Edizioni Musicali e Discografiche Srl (CEMED);* Case C-192/04, *Lagardère.*
635. Case C-251/95, *SABEL v. Puma;* Case C-53/96, *Hermès.*
636. Case C-383/98, *The Polo/Lauren Company v. PT. Dwidua Langgeng Pratama International Freight Forwarders.*

- Directive 96/9/EC of the European Parliament and of the Council of 11 March 1996 on the legal protection of databases, O.J. 1996, L 77/20;
- Directive 98/44/EC of the European Parliament and of the Council of 6 July 1998 on the legal protection of biotechnological inventions, O.J. 1998, L 213/13;[637]
- Directive 98/71/EC of the European Parliament and of the Council of 13 October 1998 on the legal protection of designs, O.J. 1998, L 289/28;
- Council Decision 2000/278 of 16 March 2000 on the approval, on behalf of the EC, of the World Intellectual Property Organization (WIPO) Copyright Treaty and the WIPO Performances and Phonograms Treaty, O.J. 2000, L 89/6;
- Directive 2001/29/EC of the European Parliament and of the Council of 22 May 2001 on the harmonization of certain aspects of copyright and related rights in the information society, O.J. 2001, L 167/10;[638]
- Directive 2001/84/EC of the European Parliament and of the Council of 27 September 2001 on the resale right for the benefit of the author of an original work of art, O.J. 2001, L 273/32;[639]
- Council Regulation (EC) No. 6/2002 of 12 December 2001 on Community designs, O.J. 2002, L 3/1;[640]
- Directive 2004/48/EC on the enforcement of intellectual property rights, O.J. 2004, L 195/16;[641]
- Directive 2006/116/EC, on the term of protection of copyright and certain related rights O.J. 2006, L 372/12;
- Proposal for a Council Regulation on the Community patent.[642]

3.3.2.8   *The Office of Harmonization for the Internal Market*

On the basis of Regulation 40/94, undertakings may obtain a Community Trade Mark, following a single procedure, which provides uniform protection and has legal force in the whole territory of the Community. The same is true for Community Designs on the basis of Regulation 6/2002. Community Trade Marks and Community Designs are registered with the Office of Harmonization for the Internal Market (OHIM) (Trade Marks and Designs), situated in Alicante.[643]

---

637. Case C-377/98, *Netherlands v. European Parliament and Council (biotechnological inventions)*.
638. Case C-293/98, *Egeda*; Case C-479/04, *Laserdisken v. Kulturministeriet*; Case C-306/05, *SGAE v. Rafael Hoteles*; Case C-275/06, *Promusicae*.
639. See also Commission declaration in the Council minutes concerning the directive on resale rights, O.J. 2001, C 208/2.
640. See also Commission implementing Reg. 2245/2002, O.J. 2002, L 341/28.
641. See Commission Statement concerning Art. 2 of Dir. 2004/48, O.J. 2005, L 94/37. This statement concerns the scope of application of the Directive; cf. Case C-275/06, *Promusicae*.
642. COM(2000)412 final.
643. For the procedural rules, see O.J. 1996, L 28/11. On the language regime (and the position of the Dutch language), see written question E-1684/94 (Thyssen), O.J. 1995, C 30/5. See further

Appeal may be lodged against decisions of the examiners of an application for a Community Trade Mark. The case can be referred to a Board of Appeal, which is still part of the OHIM. Actions may be brought before the Court of First Instance in Luxembourg against unfavourable decisions of the Boards of Appeal.[644] Judgments of the Court of First Instance are subject to appeal at the Court of Justice on points of law only.

3.3.3   Rule-of-Reason: Case Law-Based Justifications

In the judgment in *Cassis de Dijon*,[645] the rule of mutual recognition was formulated.[646] As a counterbalance to the rule of mutual recognition, a number of so-called 'mandatory requirements' were formulated – this judgment was the first occasion on which this was done explicitly – which were added as judge-made law to the justifications under Article 30 EC.[647]

The terms rule-of-reason,[648] rule-of-reason exceptions or justifications, *Cassis de Dijon* exceptions or justifications, mandatory requirements, imperative requirements and overriding reason in the general interest all have the same scope. This is not the same as the term 'major needs', mentioned in Article 95(4) EC, which refers to the exceptions of Article 30 EC and one or more specific 'overriding interests'. Technically, from the point of view of the Treaty, the rule-of-reason exceptions are not considered as an extension of the (exhaustive) list contained in Article 30 EC. The friction between the exhaustive list of heads of justification in Article 30 EC, on the one hand, and the need for new heads of justification on the other, is resolved by the Court by means of an interpretation of Article 28 based on the principle of 'reasonableness', so that new exceptions can be seen as a continuation of Article 28. It is, after all, 'reasonable' that Member States should not create barriers to cross-border trade except where 'overriding reasons' make this necessary.[649]

Case T-107/94, *Christina Kik v. Council and Commission* (Kik I); Case C-270/95 P, *Christina Kik v. Council and Commission* (Kik II); Case T-120/99, *Christina Kik v. Office for Harmonisation in the Internal Market (Trade Marks and Designs) (OHIM)* (Kik III); Case C-361/01 P, *Christina Kik v. OHIM* (Kik IV).

644. For the first judgment, see Case T-163/98, *The Procter & Gamble Company v. OHMI (BABY-DRY)*. This judgment was annulled by the Court of Justice on appeal; see Case C-383/99 P, *The Procter & Gamble Company v. OHMI (BABY-DRY)*.

645. Case 120/78, *Cassis de Dijon*. See also Communication from the Commission concerning the consequences of the judgment given by the Court of Justice on 20 Feb. 1979 in Case 120/78 (*Cassis de Dijon*), O.J. 1980, C 256/2. See on this P.J. Slot, 'Commentaar op een opmerkelijke brief' (1981) SEW, 174–184, and C.W.A. Timmermans, 'Nogmaals: de brief van de Commissie naar aanleiding van het arrest "Cassis de Dijon"' (1981) SEW, 381–383.

646. See section 1.1. *supra*. See para. 14 of the judgment in *Cassis de Dijon*.

647. See on this M. Ahlfeld, *Zwingende Erfordernisse im Sinne des Cassis-Rechtsprechung des Europäischen Gerichtshofs zu Art. 30 EGV* (Baden-Baden, 1997); V. Hatzopoulos, '*Exigences essentielles, impératives ou impérieuses: une théorie, des théories ou pas de théorie du tout?*' (1998) RTDE, 191.

648. A. Schrauwen (ed.), *Rule of Reason: Rethinking Another Classic of EC Legal Doctrine* (Groningen, 2005).

649. See already Case 8/74, *Dassonville*.

The rule-of-reason (*Cassis de Dijon* exceptions, or whichever term one gives it) only applies if certain conditions are met: there must not be Community legislation on the matter, the measure must be non-economic, and the principles of necessity and proportionality must be met.[650] These conditions also apply to justifications under Article 30 EC. A specific condition for the rule-of-reason, however, is that the national measure must be indistinctly applicable to domestic products and products from other Member States.[651]

3.3.3.1   *Rule-of-Reason and Non-discriminatory Measures*

The exceptions under Article 30 EC are distinguished from those under the rule-of-reason in that – according to the classic case law[652] – the latter may only be invoked if the national measures are applicable without discrimination (or distinction) to both national and imported products.[653] This condition does not occur in so many words in the judgment in *Cassis de Dijon*, but was later added in a very similar case.[654] In its examination of this condition, the Court does not limit itself to a review of formal discrimination, but where relevant also examines whether there is discrimination in the factual circumstances of the case.[655]

3.3.3.2   *Rule-of-Reason and Discriminatory Measures*

It may be deduced from the so-called *Wallonian waste* case that in cases involving environmental protection, the Court is willing to accept justifications of national rules concerning waste which have a substantive discriminatory effect (i.e., where a distinction *is* made) on the basis of the rule-of-reason exception of environmental protection.[656] In its judgment in *PreussenElektra*, the Court took the same approach.[657]

Such invocation of a justification based on imperative requirements where distinctly applicable national measures are concerned, and the acceptance of such invocation by the Court, has also occurred in relation to other freedoms. These cases concerned, among other things, a justification based on the needs of the tax

---

650. See section 3.3.1. *supra.*
651. See A.G. Jacobs in Case C-379/98, *PreussenElektra*, paras. 220 to 229 and Case C-136/00, *Rolf Dieter Danner* paras. 32 to 40. Cf. Also C.W.A. Timmermans, 'Creative Homogeneity', in M. Johansson et al. (eds), *A European for All Sseasons: Liber Amicorum Sven Norberg* (Brussels, 2006), 471–484.
652. See section 1.6 *supra.*
653. See explicitly for freedom of establishment and freedom to provides services, Case C-55/94, *Gebhard*; Case C-3/95, *Reisebüro Broede v. Gerd Sandker.*
654. Case 788/79, *Gilli;* see also Case 113/80, *Commission v. Ireland*; Joined Cases C-1 & 176/90, *Aragonesa.*
655. Case 177/83, *Ringelhan.* Cf. Case C-275/92, *Schindler.*
656. Case C-2/90, *Commission v. Belgium.*
657. Case C-379/98, *PreussenElektra.*

system,[658] or a justification concerning the fairness of commercial transactions, or consumer protection.[659]

3.3.3.3 List of Justifications Based on Mandatory Requirements

In *Cassis de Dijon*, four mandatory requirements are mentioned: 'the effectiveness of fiscal supervision, the protection of public health, the fairness of commercial transactions and the defence of the consumer'. One of these, protection of public health, is really superfluous, as this general interest may already be protected on the basis of Article 30 EC.[660] In the judgment, the phrase 'in particular' is used. This phrase created the possibility to add new general interests to the original list in later case law. Some of these requirements also received a basis in the Treaty in Article 95(3) EC – viz. consumer protection, environmental protection, safety.

Since *Cassis de Dijon*, the following imperative requirements have been examined in the Court's case law:

- regulation of advertising;[661]
- promotion of culture;[662]
- protection of consumers;[663]
- protection of the environment;[664]
- protection of regional language use;[665]
- biological resources;[666]
- effectiveness of fiscal supervision;[667]

658. E.g., Case C-204/90, *Hanns-Martin Bachmann v. Belgium*.
659. Joined Cases C-34-36/95, *De Agostini*.
660. A former president of the Court of Justice later admitted that this was a drafting mistake. See J. Mertens de Wilmars, *De communautaire rechtspraak over het vrij verkeer van goederen* (1984–85) RW, No. 16, note 2. See also Joined Cases C-1 & 176/90, *Aragonesa*.
661. Case C-412/93, *TF-1*.
662. Case 229/83, *Leclerc v. Àu blé vert*; Joined Cases 60 & 61/84, *Cinéthèque*.
663. Case 27/80, *Fietje*; Case 6/81, *Beele*; Case 220/81, *Robertson*; Case 261/81, *Rau*; Case 286/81, *Oosthoek*; Case 179/85, *Commission v. Germany*; Case 25/88, *Wurmser*; Case 52/88, *Commission v. Belgium*; Case C-196/89, *Nespoli*; Case C-51/93, *Meyhui*; Case C-51/94, *Commission v. Germany*; Case C-313/94, *Graffione*; Case C-184/96, *Commission v. France*; Case C-210/96, *Gut Springenheide*; Case C-77/97, *Unilever*; Case C-383/97, *Criminal proceedings against Arnoldus van der Laan*; Case C-220/98, *Estée Lauder*; Case C-366/98, *Geffroy*; Case C-448/98, *Guimont*; Case C-3/99, *Ruwet*; Case C-358/01, *Commission v. Spain*; Case C-166/03, *Commission v. France*.
664. Joined Cases 3, 4 & 6/76, *Kramer;* Case 172/82, *Inter-huiles*; Case 240/83, *ADBHU*; Case 302/86, *Commission v. Denmark (bottles)*; Case C-2/90, *Commission v. Belgium*; Case C-159/94, *Commission v. France*; Case C-341/95, *Gianni Bettati v. Safety Hi-Tech Srl*; Case C-203/96, *Dusseldorp*; Case C-389/96, *Aher-Waggon*; Case C-67/97, *Bluhme*; Case C-314/98, *Snellers*; Case C-309/02, *Radlberger*; Case C-463/01, *Commission v. Germany*. In some cases, a link is made to Art. 174 EC: see Case C-209/98, *Sydhavnens*.
665. Case C-369/89, *Piageme v. Peeters*.
666. Joined Cases 3, 4 & 6/76, *Kramer*.
667. Case 823/79, *Criminal proceedings against Giovanni Carciati*; Case 134/83, *Abbink*.

- fairness of commercial practices;[668]
- pluriformity of the press;[669]
- product safety;[670]
- economic planning;[671]
- socio-cultural characteristics;[672]
- combating fraud;[673]
- safety for shipping;[674]
- improvement of employment conditions/ working environment;[675]
- protection of road safety;[676]
- freedom of expression;[677]
- protection of the rights of the child.[678]

3.3.4   Other Exceptions to Free Movement

Some attention was paid above, in section 3.3.1, to the specific procedure contained in Article 95(4) EC. The nature of goods (e.g., whether they are strategic goods), their origin (e.g., whether they come from third countries) and the economic situation of a Member State may be such that the normal rules of the free movement of goods must give way to an exception clause.

The Council may adopt measures to cope with severe economic difficulties or the consequences of exceptional occurrences (for instance a petroleum boycott) on the basis of Article 100 EC. If a Member State experiences a sudden crisis in its balance of payments, the EC Treaty provides that that Member State may take necessary protective measures (Art. 120(1) EC) and also provides for mutual assistance (Art. 120(2) EC), for Member States who are not members of the EMU and on a temporary basis (see further Ch. X).

Member States which have entrusted undertakings with the operation of services of general economic interest may, on the basis of Article 86(2) EC be able to

---

668.   Case 58/80, *Dansk Supermarked*; Case 6/81, *Beele*; Case 220/81, *Robertson*; Case 286/81, *Oosthoek*; Case 179/85, *Commission v. Germany*; Case 52/88, *Commission v. Belgium*; Case C-238/89, *Pall v. Dahlhausen*; Case C-77/97, *Unilever*; Case C-366/98, *Geffroy*; Case C-448/98, *Guimont*; Case C-166/03, *Commission v. France*.
669.   Case C-368/95, *Familiapress*. This exception links up with the ECHR.
670.   Case 188/84, *Commission v. France*.
671.   Case C-159/94, *Commission v. France*.
672.   Case C-145/88, *Torfaen*; Case C-169/91, *B & Q*; Joined Cases C-418-421/93 etc., *Semeraro Casa Uno.*
673.   Case C-184/96, *Commission v. France*.
674.   Case C-18/93, *Corsica Ferries v. Corpo dei piloti del porto di Genova* (*Corsica Ferries II*).
675.   Case 155/80, *Oebel*; Case C-312/89, *Conforama*; Case C-332/89, *Marchandise*.
676.   Case C-55/93, *Van Schaik*; Case C-314/98, *Snellers*.
677.   Case C-112/00, *Schmidberger*; Case C-71/02, *Karner*. This justification is linked to the ECHR.
678.   Case C-244/06, *Dynamic Medien*.

insist on an exceptional position under certain conditions for such undertakings[679] (see further Ch. IX).

There is also a certain degree of friction between market integration and regional policy (see further Ch. X).[680]

Article 296 EC contains two safeguard clauses in the interest of the security of the Member States themselves.[681] The first exempts Member States from the obligation to supply information the disclosure of which they consider contrary to the essential interest of their security. On the strength of the second clause any Member State may take such measures as it considers necessary for the protection of the essential interests of its security which are connected with the production of, or trade in, arms, munitions, and war material. On 15 April 1958 the Council, in accordance with Article 296(2) EC drew up a list of products to which the provisions of this second safeguard clause apply. This list has not been officially published. Article 296(2) EC, in the version following the Treaty of Amsterdam, grants the Council the power to amend the list (which is even explicitly mentioned in the Treaty!). A number of decisions were adopted in 1994 and 1995 in relation to dual-use goods; these were revised in 2000.[682]

Article 296(1)(b) EC explicitly provides that the measures taken by the Member States may not adversely affect the conditions of competition in the common market regarding products which are not intended for specifically military purposes. Examples of the latter could be, for instance, subsidies for national industry producing sporting-guns.[683]

Like Article 296 EC, Article 297 EC is connected with the security of the state.[684] Article 297 requires Member States to consult each other with a view to taking together the steps needed to prevent the functioning of the common market being affected by measures which a Member State may be called upon to take in the event of serious internal disturbances affecting the maintenance of law and order, in the event of war or serious international tension constituting a threat of war, or in order to carry out obligations it has accepted for the purpose of maintaining peace and international security. On the one hand, therefore, Article 297 contains a safeguard clause which in the circumstances indicated may go beyond the concept of public policy in Article 30. EC. In these circumstances, measures needed in a

---

679. Case 72/83, *Campus Oil*; Case C-157/94, *Commission v. the Netherlands*; Case C-209/98, *Sydhavnens;* Case C-17/03, *Vereniging voor Energie, Milieu en Water (VEMW) v. Directeur van de Dienst uitvoering en toezicht energie.*

680. Case C-21/88, *Du Pont de Nemours*; Case C-351/88, *Laboratori Bruneau.* See J.M. Fernández Martin and O. Stehmann, 'Product Market Integration versus Regional Cohesion in the Community' (1991) EL Rev., 216.

681. M. Trybus, 'The EC Treaty as an Instrument of European Defence Integration: Judicial Scrutiny of Defence and Security Exceptions' (2002) CML Rev., 1347.

682. O.J. 2000, L 159. See also Case C-367/89, *Richardt*; Case C-83/94, *Criminal proceedings against Leifer and others.*

683. On the equivalent Art. 27 Euratom, see Case C-61/03, *Commission v. UK.*

684. P. Koutrakos, 'Is Article 297 EC a "Reserve of Sovereignty"?' (2000) CML Rev., 1339. See also Case C-186/01, *Dory.*

situation of serious shortage in the economy can be taken, such as rationing measures, hoarding prohibitions, prohibitions of price rises, requisitioning measures, and the like. Such measures are never permitted by Article 30, on account of their economic nature, and in the event of supply difficulties due to other causes they can only to a limited extent be permitted under Article 100 EC. On the other hand, Article 297 contains an obligation for Member States to consult each other with a view to taking the steps needed to prevent interference with the functioning of the common market by such measures. It is submitted that effect must be given to this obligation as soon as one or more Member States by way of precaution establish a legal basis for measures of this kind (which has already happened) and, moreover, it is submitted that the Commission must ensure the observance of this obligation.

Article 298 EC prescribes that even within the scope of the safeguard clauses of Articles 296 and 297, conditions of competition may not be distorted by discrimination based on nationality or by subsidies. If such an effect occurs nevertheless, the Commission, together with the Member State concerned, examines how these measures can be adjusted to the rules laid down in the Treaty. There is provision for direct access to the Court (by way of derogation from the normal procedures of Arts. 226 or 227 EC) so that the Commission or another Member State may challenge any alleged misuse of Articles 296 or 297 speedily.[685] In such cases the Court's judgment is given *in camera*. This procedure under Article 298 shows some similarity to the Article 95 procedure.

The security policy of the Member States is the (joint) subject of Title V TEU in the form of the Common Foreign and Security Policy (see further Ch. XIII). Internal security (see Art. 64 EC) plays a role in Title IV of the EC Treaty, as introduced by the Treaty of Amsterdam (see section 4.3 below).

The fact that a measure results from an international agreement predating the original EEC Treaty or the accession of a Member State, and that the Member State on the basis of Article 307 maintains the measure, even though it constitutes a barrier to trade between Member States, does not remove the measure from the scope of Article 28 EC, as Article 307 EC takes effect only if the agreement places an obligation on the Member State concerned which is incompatible with the EC Treaty.[686]

3.4   STATE TRADING MONOPOLIES

Article 31(1) EC provides that the Member States should adjust their national monopolies of a commercial character, so as to ensure that no discrimination regarding the conditions under which goods are procured and marketed exists between nationals of Member States. Such a monopoly exists because the

---

685.   See Case C-120/94 R, *Commission v. Greece*.
686.   Case C-324/93, *Evans Medical*. See also Case 34/79, *Henn and Darby*; Case 121/85 *Conegate*;
       Case 286/86, *Deserbais*; Case C-158/91, *Levy*, and Joined Cases C-241 & 242/91 P, *RTE*.

government grants exclusive rights to an undertaking or a government body in relation to trade in a certain product (e.g., alcohol, tobacco, petroleum products). The term 'adjust' does not mean that all these monopolies have to be lifted.[687] This is the case, though, for exclusive rights to import,[688] and – one would assume – similarly for exclusive rights to export. Non-discriminatory taxation is compatible with Article 31(1)[689] and with Article 31(2).[690]

It can be deduced from Article 31(1) that for Article 31 to apply, there has to be an action by the state, such as a law, which (whether in combination with a production monopoly or not) grants exclusive purchase or sales rights or the possibility of control of imports or exports;[691] there must be a *de iure* or de facto monopoly.[692] Secondly, the grant must be *either* to a state service or state enterprise which is given exclusive purchase or sales powers (state monopolies),[693] *or* to an institution of the state which has the power to hinder imports or exports between Member States within the meaning of Articles 28 and 29 EC,[694] *or* to one or more private bodies (delegated monopolies to particular undertakings).[695] This last heading was included with the French mineral oil delegated monopolies of state and private undertakings in mind, but is also applied in other cases.

Article 31 EC reaches 'only activities intrinsically connected with the specific business of the monopoly'.[696] National provisions which are not closely connected with the fact that the goods in question come within a monopoly in the sense of Article 31 EC remain outside the scope of that Article.[697]

According to the standstill provision in Article 31(2) EC, Member States may not introduce any new measure which is contrary to the principles laid down in Article 31(1) EC or which restricts the scope of the articles dealing with the prohibition of customs duties and quantitative restrictions between Member States.[698]

---

687. Case 59/75, *Pubblico Ministero v. Flavia Manghera and others*; Case 91/75, *Hauptzollamt Göttingen v. Miritz*; Case 91/78, *Hansen. v. Hauptzollamt de Flensburg*.
688. Case 59/75, *Manghera*; Case 91/75, *Miritz*.
689. Case 253/83, *Kupferberg*.
690. Case 13/70, *Francesco Cinzano & Cia v. Hauptzollamt Saarbrücken*.
691. Case 30/87, *Bodson v. Pompes funèbres des régions libérées SA*; Case C-393/92, *Municipality of Almelo v. Energiebedrijf Ijsselmij*. See also Case C-189/95, *Franzén* and Case 170/04, *Rosengren*.
692. Case 10/71, *Ministère public luxembourgeois v. Madeleine Muller, Veuve J.P. Hein et al. (Port de Mertert)*.
693. Art. 31(1) EC, 1st sub-para.
694. Art. 31(1) EC, 2nd sub-para. Case 30/87, *Bodson*, concerned the powers of local authorities to establish monopolies.
695. Art. 31(1), 2nd sub-para., last sentence. See Case 161/82, *Commission v. France*.
696. Case 86/78, *Peureux*. See also Case C-438/02, *criminal proceedings against Krister Hanner*.
697. Case 120/78, *Cassis de Dijon*; Case 17/81, *Pabst*; Joined Cases C-78 to 83/90, *Compagnie commerciale de l'Ouest*; Case C-189/95, *Franzén*.
698. Case 6/64, *Costa v. E.N.E.L.*; Case 59/75, *Manghera*; Case 86/78, *Peureux*; Case 120/78, *Cassis de Dijon*; Case 90/82, *Commission v. France*.

Article 31 EC covers only goods in intra-Community movement.[699] If certain state monopolies are not covered by Article 31, they must be judged on the basis of other provisions on free movement, such as Articles 43 and 49 EC,[700] or on the basis of the competition provisions (Arts. 81, 82 and 86 EC).[701]

A number of infringement cases brought by the Commission against Member States under Article 226 EC in the area of electricity markets have shed new light on the interpretation of Article 31 EC and the relationship between this provision and the other Treaty provisions.[702] In these cases, the Commission was of the opinion that Articles 28 and 29 EC as well as Article 31 EC were infringed. The Court decided, however, that only Article 31 was infringed, with as result that the exceptions in Article 30 EC could not be invoked as justifications.[703] Article 86(2) EC (concerning the conditions under which undertakings entrusted with the operation of services of general economic interest could be protected from the competition rules) could be relied on, though.[704]

Franzén[705] concerned the Swedish retail monopoly for alcohol; here the Court of Justice made a distinction between national provisions which did fall under the monopoly and those which did not. For the former, Article 31 EC was applicable, and for the latter Article 28 EC.[706] The Swedish rules were saved because in both cases the justification on grounds of public health was accepted: Article 30 EC was invoked in relation to Article 28 EC, and this exception was read into Article 31 itself.[707]

The special provisions for the establishment of the common organizations of the market (for agricultural products) take priority, under Article 32(2) EC, in relation to the rules in Article 31 EC.[708] Service monopolies fall exclusively within the scope of Articles 49 and 86(2) EC (see section 7.5. below),[709] although they may well have an effect on monopolies relating to goods.[710] The relationship between Article 31 EC and the fiscal provisions of the Treaty (Arts. 25 and

---

699. Case 91/78, *Hansen*.
700. See Case 271/81 *Société Coopérative d'Amélioration de l'Élevage et d'Insémination Artificielle de Béarn v. Mialocq*; Cases C-46/90 and 93/9, *Lagauche*.
701. See Case 30/87, *Bodson*; Case C-393/92, *Municipality of Almelo v. Energiebedrijf Ijsselmij*.
702. Case C-157/94, *Commission v. the Netherlands*; Case C-158/94, *Commission v. Italy*; Case C-159/94, *Commission v. France*; Case C-160/94, *Commission v. Spain*.
703. Case 72/83, *Campus Oil* and Case C-347/88, *Commission v. Greece* pointed in a different direction.
704. See also Case C-438/02, *Hanner*.
705. Case C-189/95, *Franzén*.
706. In Case C-387/93, *Banchero*, the ECJ found that the national rules on retail selling of tobacco did not come under Art. 31 EC, but had to be considered selling arrangements in the sense of *Keck*.
707. Case C-189/95, *Franzén*.
708. Case 83/78, *Pigs Marketing Board*.
709. Case 155/73, *Sacchi*; Case C-393/92, *Municipality of Almelo v. Energiebedrijf Ijsselmij*; Case C-17/94, *Criminal proceedings against Denis Gervais, Jean-Louis Nougaillon, Christian Carrard and Bernard Horgue*.
710. Case 271/81, *Mialocq*.

90 EC) has been judicially considered,[711] as has that between Article 31 EC and the state aids provisions.[712]

3.5 THIRD COUNTRIES

The prohibitions in Articles 28–29 and 31 EC relate to the movement of goods between Member States.[713] Quantitative restrictions and measures having equivalent effect in trade between the Community and third countries are thus regarded as forming part of the Community's common commercial policy (see Ch. XIII). In some instances, agreements between the Community and third countries contain specific provisions,[714] but even if they are phrased identically to Articles 28–30 EC, they do not *necessarily* have the same result, as the objective of such agreements (such as the establishment of a free trade area between the Community and the country concerned) is less far-reaching than the objective of the EC Treaty itself, which *inter alia* is to establish a common market, and the activities which the Community undertakes to that end, such as harmonization of laws.[715] Nevertheless, the Court uses its case law on the content of certain justifications under Article 30 EC in situations concerning trade with third countries.[716]

4 FREE MOVEMENT OF PERSONS: MARKET PARTICIPANTS; EU CITIZENS AND THIRD-COUNTRY NATIONALS

In this section, we will first examine a number of concepts which are important for the further analysis of free movement of persons in general, and for free movement of workers and the self-employed in particular (section 4.1). Then, we will briefly outline the evolution of free movement of persons in the course of various Treaty amendments from ECSC mineworkers via citizens of the Union to third-country nationals (section 4.2). Then the rules concerning third-country nationals will be examined (section 4.3). Thereafter, the rights of market participants are discussed (section 4.4) followed by the migration rights (section 4.5). The specific intra-Community aspects of free movement of persons are not dealt with in section 4: they are discussed in section 5 (workers), section 6 (establishment) and section 7 (services).

---

711. Case 45/75, *Rewe-Zentrale*; Case 91/75, *Miritz*; Case 148/77, *H. Hansen jun.*; Case 86/78, *Peureux*; Case 17/81, *Pabst* and Joined Cases C-78-83/90, *Compagnie commerciale de l'Ouest*; Case C-383/01, *Danske Bilimportører*.
712. Case 91/78, *Hansen*.
713. E.g., Case 51/75, *EMI Records*; Case 91/78, *Hansen*; Case 190/87, *Moormann;* and Case C-191/90, *Generics v. Smith, Kline*.
714. See, e.g., Case 174/84, *Bulk Oil*.
715. E.g., Case 270/80, *Polydor*; Case 104/81, *Kupferberg*, and Case C-207/91, *Eurim-Pharm* (useful effect of the agreement).
716. Case C-394/97, *Heinonen*.

4.1   Concepts

The original EEC Treaty contained rules for market participants (employees or self-employed), in the area of movement within the territory of the Community. The Treaties of Maastricht and Amsterdam introduced provisions concerning citizenship of the European Union and provisions applying to persons coming from third countries.[717]

   In order to understand this area of law, a number of terms need to be defined.

4.1.1   Different Categories of Persons

4.1.1.1   Employees (Workers) and Self-Employed

Title III of Part Three of the EC Treaty deals with free movement of workers (Ch. 1) and the right of establishment (Ch. 2). Workers are natural persons who perform work in paid employment. Freedom of establishment applies to the self-employed and legal persons. There are clear links between the provisions for workers and those for the self-employed: for instance, the social security provisions which under Article 42 EC were designed for workers were extended to the self-employed on the basis of Article 308 EC.[718] Directives on establishment requirements and mutual recognition of diplomas for doctors were also, by the same method, declared applicable to doctors working as employed persons.[719] Directive 64/221 implementing Article 46(2) EC applies to all natural persons in the area of movement and residence within the territory of the Community.[720] It is apparent from the case law, however, that the different freedoms have individual characteristics which justify separate sets of rules and separate treatment. These rules are described in the following subsections.

*4.1.1.2   Natural Persons and Legal Persons; Nationals and
                 Companies or Firms*

The EC Treaty uses the terms 'nationals'(Arts. 43, 49 EC) and 'companies and firms'(Arts. 43, 48 EC). The EC Treaty also uses the terms 'natural persons' (Art. 47 EC) and 'legal persons' (Art. 48 EC). In some cases, it may be clearer to talk of a natural or legal person than a 'national'.

---

717.   For sociological and economic background information, see F. Weiss and F. Wooldridge, *Free Movement of Persons within the European Community* 2nd ed. (The Hague, 2007); K. Hailbronner, *Immigration and Asylum Law and Policy of the European Union* (The Hague, 2000).
718.   See Reg. 2001/83, O.J. 1983, L 230/6.
719.   Dir. 75/362, O.J. 1975, L 167/1; Dir. 75/363, O.J. 1975, L 167/14.
720.   Dir. 64/221, O.J. 1964, 850.

4.1.1.3 Persons from EC Countries and Persons from Third Countries

A distinction is made between persons (citizens, nationals, workers, the self-employed, the non-economically active) possessing the nationality of an EU (or EEA) country and persons with the nationality of a third country.[721]

The question whether a person possesses the nationality of a Member State or of another EEA State is one which is a matter for the national law of the State concerned, in conformity with international (customary) law, and taking account of Community law.[722]

This distinction between persons from EC countries and persons from third countries has consequences in the Treaty provisions. Article 14 uses the term 'internal market', within which EC nationals can in principle move freely. Article 61 EC uses the term 'external border': this is needed in order to ensure control on persons entering the territory of the EU.

The terminology used in the EC Treaty to qualify these persons is not uniform. In Article 46 EC, the Treaty uses the term 'foreign nationals'. This term, in this provision, refers to nationals of other Member States, but readers would probably first think this means nationals of third countries (since the establishment of the internal market, at least). Title IV does not use the term 'foreign nationals', but uses the term 'nationals of third countries' (Art. 62 EC) or – in specific cases, refugees and asylum seekers (Art. 63 EC).

Article 45(1) EU Charter of Fundamental Rights provides that every citizen of the Union has the right to move and reside freely within the territory of the Member States. Article 45(2) adds that freedom of movement and residence may be granted to nationals of third countries legally resident in the territory of a Member State. According to Article 52(2) of the Charter, these rights are to be exercised under the conditions and within the limits set by the EC and EU treaties.

4.1.1.4 Market Participants and the Non-economically Active

According to the case law of the Court of Justice, persons only come within the scope of Articles 39 and 43 EC if they are nationals of a Member State and exercise an economic activity.[723] Once they have the status of worker or self-employed, their family members also derive rights of entry and residence under Community law, irrespective of their own nationality.[724] Community law also provides for the

---

721. See H. Staples, *The Legal Status of Third Country Nationals Resident in the European Union* (The Hague/London, 1999); E. Sharpston, 'Different but (almost) Equal: The Development of Free Movement Rights under EU Association, Co-operation and Accession Agreements', in M. Hoskins and W. Robinson (eds.), *A True European: Essays for Judge David Edward* (Oxford, 2004), 233–245; A. Adinolfi, 'Free Movement and Access to Work of Citizens of the New Member States: The Transitional Measures' (2005) CML Rev., 469.
722. Case C-369/90, *Mario Vicente Micheletti and others v. Delegación del Gobierno en Cantabria*; Case C-192/99, *The Queen v. Secretary of State for the Home Department, ex parte Manjit Kaur.*
723. Case 36/74, *Walrave*; Joined Cases C-51/96 & C-191/97, *Deliège.*
724. Art. 10 Reg. 1612/68, O.J. 1968, L 257/2.

continuation of the right of residence after termination of the economic activity concerned.[725] During the 1980s, case law brought tourists under the beneficiaries of free movement rights, as recipients of services.[726]

A package of directives was adopted by the Council in June 1990 in order to extend the right of residence to other groups of nationals of Member States.[727] These groups were: employees and self-employed persons who have ceased their occupational activity; students; nationals of Member States who do not enjoy a right of residence under other provisions of Community law. In order to exercise these rights, these 'non-economically active' persons have to show that they have sickness insurance and that they have sufficient resources to avoid becoming a burden on the social assistance system of the host Member State during their period of residence.[728] These directives were all replaced, as of 2006, by the general Directive 2004/38 concerning rights of EU citizens in relation to movement and residence.[729] See further section 4.5.2. below.

4.1.1.5   *Citizens of the European Union*

Citizenship of the Union was established by the Treaty of Maastricht (by what is now Art. 17 EC).[730] The rights attached to citizenship include the right to move and reside freely within the territory of the Member States, and voting rights (see Art. 18 EC); the migration rights are analysed in section 4.5, below; the non-economic rights are analysed in Chapter II of this book.

From recent case law relating, in particular, to students,[731] it appears that the Court is using the provisions on citizenship as a lever to open up free movement for

---

725. Art. 39(3)(d) EC, elaborated in Reg. 1251/70, O.J. 1970, L 142/24 for workers, and in Dir. 75/34, O.J. 1975, L 14/10 for the self-employed.
726. Joined Cases 286/82 & 26/83, *Graziana Luisi and Giuseppe Carbone v. Ministero del Tesoro*; Case 186/87, *Ian William Cowan v. Trésor public*; Case C-348/96, *Criminal proceedings against Donatella Calfa*.
727. Council Dir. 90/364, 90/365, 90/366 of 13 Jul. 1990, O.J. 1990, L 180/26. Dir. 90/366 (students) was annulled: see Case C-295/90, *Parliament v. Council*. A new Directive was adopted in its place, 93/96, O.J. 1993, L 317/59. See also Case C-424/98, *Commission v. Italy*. As a result of the adoption of these Directives and the entry into force of the Treaty of Maastricht, the case law on the limited effect of free movement of persons in Case 197/86, *Steven Malcolm Brown v. The Secretary of State for Scotland*, was no longer good law. See Case C-184/99, *Grzelczyk* and Case C-413/99, *Baumbast*; Case C-456/02 *Michel Trojani v. Centre public d'aide sociale de Bruxelles (CPAS)*; Case C-209/03, *Bidar*; Case C-76/05, *Schwarz*; Case C-318/05, *Commission v. Germany;* Joined Cases C-11 & 12/06, *Morgan*.
728. See Case C-413/01, *Franca Ninni-Orasche v. Bundesminister für Wissenschaft, Verkehr und Kunst*, and Case C-408/03, *Commission v. Belgium*.
729. O.J. 2004, L 229/35; see further sections 4.2 and 4.5.2 *infra*.
730. On the temporal scope of these provisions, see Case C-224/98, *D'Hoop*.
731. See Dougan, 'Fees, Grants, Loans and Dole Cheques: Who Covers the Costs of Migrant Education within the EU?' 42 CML Rev. On the rights and duties of citizens and workers, see Joined Cases C-482 & 493/01, *Georgios Orfanopoulos et al. v. Land Baden-Württemberg and Raffaele Oliveri v. Land Baden-Württemberg*.

students, including the necessary financial arrangements.[732] This line of case law is already being extended to other citizens, and not just students.[733] Article 18(1) EC, containing the right to move and reside freely within the territory of the Member States, has been declared directly effective, notwithstanding possible limitations and conditions for the exercise of this right.

4.1.2   Internal Market and External Borders

Free movement of persons applies within the territory of the Member States of the European Union and the EEA (see Ch. II and Ch. XIII section 4.2.2). This internal market[734] is the area within which the rules on free movement apply. The Court of Justice has ruled that non-discrimination rules apply to the assessment of all legal relationships to the extent that these can be located within the territory of the Community either by the place where they are entered into or the place where they take effect.[735] As with other freedoms, though, account must be taken of so-called 'internal situations'. Nationals of a Member State who do not leave this Member State cannot rely on the rules on free movement, because then there is no Community element.[736] In *Carpenter*, the Court found a minimal connection with Community law sufficient for the application of, in this case, the freedom to provide services, in order to find that the third-country national in a family could remain in the territory of the Community.[737] It is not certain to what extent this case law will remain unchanged, although the Court in some cases still seems to tolerate reverse discrimination in the internal market with no internal borders.[738]

---

732. Case C-224/98, *D'Hoop*; Case C-184/99, *Grzelczyk*; Case C-148/02, *Carlos Garcia Avello v. État Belge*; Case C-224/02, *Heikki Antero Pusa v. Osuuspankkien Keskinäinen Vakuutusyhtiö*; Case C-209/03, *Bidar*. See in general on public benefits in other Member States, A.P. van der Mei, *Free Movement of Persons within the European Community: Cross Border Access to Public Benefits*, PhD thesis (Maastricht, 2002).
733. Case C-403/03, *Schempp*; Case C-300/04, *Eman and Sevinger*.
734. See Art. 14 EC.
735. Case 36/74, *Walrave*.
736. Case 175/78, *Saunders*; Joined Cases 35 & 36/82, *Morson and Jhanjan*; Case 180/83, *Hans Moser v. Land Baden-Württemberg*; Case C-332/90, *Volker Steen v. Deutsche Bundespost*. See recently Joined Cases C-95–98 & 180/99, *Khalil and others*.
737. Case C-60/00, *Carpenter*. This case law was further developed in Case C-109/01, *Akrich*, and Case C-200/02, *Chen;* E. Caracciolo di Torella and A. Masselot, 'Under Construction: EU Family Law' (2004) EL Rev., 32; S. Peers, 'Family Reunion and Community Law: Europe's Area of Freedom, Security and Justice' in N. Walker (ed.), *Europe's Area of Freedom, Security and Justice* (Oxford, 2004), 143–197. G. Barrett, 'Family Matters: European Community Law and Third-Country Family Members' (2003) CML Rev., 369; N. Reich and S. Harbacevica, 'Citizenship and Family on Trial: A Fairly Optimistic Overview of Recent Court Practice with regard to the Free Movement of Persons' (2003) CML Rev., 615; E. Spaventa, 'From Gebhard to Carpenter: Towards a (Non-) Economic European Constitution' (2004) CML Rev., 743–773.
738. See section 1.3 above. For an analysis of the current state of affairs in relation freedom of persons, see Opinion of A.G. Sharpston in Case C-212/06, *Government of the French Community and the Walloon Government v. Flemish Government*, pending.

The original EEC Treaty did not provide for common rules for the (free) movement of third country nationals; the Treaty of Amsterdam introduced the possibility to regulate this matter on a Community basis. In the following section, a short overview is given of the developments over the years in this area, and in particular the stages in which it has come to be regulated on a Community basis.

4.2   FREE MOVEMENT OF PERSONS: FROM ECSC MINEWORKER
            TO THIRD-COUNTRY NATIONAL

Following the analysis of the various categories of persons coming within the scope of the EC provisions, a historical overview is given of the extension of the scope *ratione personae* in the consecutive European treaties.

4.2.1   The ECSC and E(E)C Treaty (First Pillar)

Only a very few years after their nationals had been at war with each other, the Franco-German initiative which led to the ECSC Treaty in 1951 achieved free movement for workers in the coal and steel sectors between those two countries as well as with the other Member States. The EC Treaty took over the basic provisions of the ECSC Treaty for free movement of persons and developed them, so that free movement was no longer restricted to workers in specific sectors but embraced all occupations, although a distinction was drawn between the free movement of workers (Arts. 39–42 EC and the self-employed (Arts. 43–48 EC). Free movement was supposed to be achieved by the end of the transitional period for the achievement of the common market, 1 January 1970. This deadline was not met, because for many occupations the secondary provisions, such as diplomas and secondary working conditions constituted a then insurmountable obstacle.

In the course of time there has been a change of emphasis in the importance of the various freedoms. The first phase of migration largely benefited Italian workers who moved to coalfields of Northern continental Europe, but over the years the freedom to provide (and receive) services and the freedom of establishment (of both legal and natural persons) assumed greater importance. Thus Dutch skiing holidays in France or Italy might be arranged by a Dutch travel agency, which had been taken over by a company established in the United Kingdom. At the turn of the millennium, 'invisible' transactions, increasingly via e-commerce, became more important: services and capital, on a global scale.

4.2.2   Treaty of Amsterdam: An Area of Freedom, Security
            and Justice

In the Third Pillar created by the Treaty of Maastricht, a number of provisions were included in Title VI concerning 'cooperation in the field of justice and home affairs'. In legal terms, the free movement of persons was divided between the

First and Third Pillars and the Schengen Agreements,[739] in an arrangement which was far from ideal. The Treaty of Amsterdam effected a redistribution of these matters. According to Article 2, 4th indent, TEU, one of the objectives of the European Union is 'to maintain and develop the Union as an area of freedom, security and justice, in which the free movement of persons is assured in conjunction with appropriate measures with respect to external border controls, asylum, immigration and the prevention and combating of crime'.[740] Two important legal operations put this declaration of principle into effect. First, a new Title IV was added to Part Three of the EC Treaty (First Pillar). The relevant provisions – Articles 61–69 EC – are dealt with in section 4.3. below, insofar as they concern movement between the Union and third countries.

Secondly, what was left of the provisions in the Third Pillar were reformulated. Title VI TEU (the new Third Pillar) henceforth only concerns police and judicial cooperation in criminal matters, such as the establishment of Eurojust[741] and a framework programme on police and judicial cooperation in criminal matters (AGIS).[742]

The evaluation of Title IV instruments adopted enables a first assessment to be made of the free movement of third-country nationals.[743] It should be noted, that Title IV contains provisions on the maintenance of law and order and the safeguarding of internal security, also in relation to third-country nationals (see Art. 64 EC, which states that Title IV shall not affect the exercise of the responsibilities incumbent upon Member States with regard to the maintenance of law and order and the safeguarding of internal security). This provision is not subject to the jurisdiction of the Court of Justice. Under Article 68(2), the Court of Justice shall not have jurisdiction to rule on any measure or decision taken by the Council pursuant to Article 62(1) relating to the maintenance of law and order and the safeguarding of internal security. This same Title IV also contains an Article 65 EC, dealing with the harmonization of international private law, and Article 66 EC, dealing with administrative cooperation.[744]

---

739. On 14 Jun. 1985, the Benelux countries, Germany and France concluded an agreement in Schengen concerning, *inter alia*, the abolition of border controls between these Member States. The aim was to put into effect the internal market for movement of persons between the so-called Schengen countries in advance of the establishment of the internal market of the Community. On 19 Jun. 1990, the CISA was signed.

740. At the Tampere European Council, on 15–16 Oct. 1999, a political spur was given for the realization of this policy.

741. Council Decision of 28 Feb. 2002, setting up Eurojust with a view to reinforcing the fight against serious crime, O.J. 2002, L 63/1.

742. Council Decision of 22 Jul. 2002 establishing a framework programme on police and judicial cooperation in criminal matters (AGIS), O.J. 2002, L 203/5. See Ch. VII.

743. See S. Boelaert-Suominen, 'Non-EU Nationals and Council Dir. 2003/109/EC on the Status of Third-Country Nationals who Are Long-Term Residents: Five Paces Forward and Possibly Three Paces Back' (2005) CML Rev., 1011–1052.

744. See on this K. Boele and R.H. van Ooik, 'The Communitarization of Private International Law', in *International Contract Law. Articles on Various Aspects of Transnational Contract Law* (Antwerp/Oxford, Intersentia 2004), 343–383. Art. 65 EC links these measures to the proper functioning of the internal market.

4.2.3   The Incorporation of the Schengen acquis

This rearrangement and revision of provisions also had consequences for the Schengen acquis.[745] From a legal point of view, these matters are contained in four Protocols attached to the EC and EU Treaties. The institutional complications resulting from this complex arrangement are examined elsewhere in this book.[746] In Case 503/03, *Commission v. Spain*, the Court has clarified the relationship between the Schengen implementing convention and free movement of persons under the First Pillar, in particular Directive 64/221.

According to Article 1 of the Schengen Protocol, the acquis is incorporated in the Law of the Union (third pillar) and the law of the EC (mainly Title IV EC Treaty), as of the moment the Treaty of Amsterdam entered into force (1 May 1999). In this way, the intergovernmental treaty law of Schengen – and in particular of the Implementing Convention of 1990 – became in one move secondary Community law or Union law. Article 2 of the Schengen Protocol provides the legal basis of further legislation. The three other protocols concern the exceptional legal situation which certain Member States claimed during the negotiations of the Treaty of Amsterdam (the so-called opt-ins and opt-outs). In principle, the United Kingdom, Ireland and Denmark do not participate in the arrangements of Title IV EC and measures adopted in that framework. Iceland and Norway participate in the implementation of the Schengen acquis.[747] Ireland and the United Kingdom may, however, decide to participate on an ad hoc basis in legal acts[748] adopted under Title IV.[749] Denmark only has the possibility of opting in to measures which build upon the Schengen acquis.[750]

---

745. The content of the Schengen acquis is defined in Art. 1, together with the Annexe to the Protocol integrating the Schengen *acquis* into the framework of the European Union. The Schengen acquis was published in O.J. 2000, L 239. See on this P.J. Kuijper, 'Some Legal Problems Associated with the Communitarization of Policy on Visas, Asylum and Immigration under the Amsterdam Treaty and Incorporation of the Schengen acquis' (2000) CML Rev., 345. See also Council Decision 2007/471/EC, of 12 Jun. 2007 on the application of the provisions of the Schengen *acquis* relating to the SIS in the Czech Republic, the Republic of Estonia, the Republic of Latvia, the Republic of Lithuania, the Republic of Hungary, the Republic of Malta, the Republic of Poland, the Republic of Slovenia and the Slovak Republic, O.J. 2007, L 179/47, and O.J. 2008, L 53 on the application of Switzerland.
746. Ch. I, section 7.2 and Ch. II section 7, *supra.*
747. See Art. 6 Schengen Protocol.
748. Unless the act in question is building upon the Schengen *acquis*, see Case 77/05, *United Kingdom v. Council.*
749. See Art. 3 Protocol on the position of the United Kingdom and Ireland. By Council Decision of 29 May 2000, O.J. 2000, L 131/43, the United Kingdom's request to participate in all provisions of the Schengen acquis concerning the operation of the SIS, with the exception of alerts issued in the context of migration law for the purposes of refusing entry to aliens, was granted. See also Council Decision of 28 Feb. 2002 concerning Ireland's request to take part in some of the provisions of the Schengen acquis, O.J. 2002, L 64/20.
750. See the Protocol on the position of Denmark:

      Denmark shall decide within a period of 6 months after the Council has decided on a proposal or initiative to build upon the Schengen acquis, whether it will implement this decision in its

The Protocol on the application of certain aspects of Article 14 of the Treaty establishing the EC to the United Kingdom and Ireland gives these two Member States the right to maintain border controls on persons at the internal borders with other Member States (Arts. 1 and 2). The other Member States may, in turn, carry out such controls on persons coming from the United Kingdom and Ireland (Art. 3).

Pursuant to Article 35 TEU, preliminary references may be put to the Court of Justice concerning the Schengen *acquis*, under certain conditions.[751]

In June 2007, the Justice and Home Affairs Council reached agreement about a Council Decision on the stepping up of cross-border cooperation, particularly in combating terrorism and cross-border crime, incorporating in the framework of the Union important provisions of the Prüm Treaty dealing with police cooperation and information exchange on DNA-profiles, fingerprints and vehicle number-plates. These elements of the Prüm Treaty, an international police cooperation agreement signed by Belgium, Germany, Spain, France, Luxembourg, the Netherlands and Austria on 27 May 2005,[752] have now become part of the legislative framework of the European Union and will be implemented in all Member States. After this implementation, designated contact points of the law enforcement agencies in the Member States will have mutual access to each others' DNA, fingerprint and vehicle registration information systems.[753]

4.2.4 The Tampere Programme and the Hague Programme

During the European Council of Tampere, in 1999, a general programme for EU policy in the area of asylum, immigration and common checks at the external borders was adopted. This programme was gradually put into effect, against the background of the terrorist attacks in the USA of 11 September 2001. At the end of 2004, during the European Council of Brussels, with the prospect of approval of the European Constitution and with the terrorist attacks in Madrid of 11 March 2004 in mind, a new programme was adopted.[754] The objective of this so-called Hague programme is, *inter alia*, to

> improve the common capability of the Union and its Member States to guarantee fundamental rights, minimum procedural safeguards and access to justice, to provide protection in accordance with the Geneva Convention

---

national law. If it decides to do so, this decision will create an obligation under international law between Denmark and the other Member States referred to in Article 1 of the Protocol integrating the Schengen acquis into the framework of the European Union as well as Ireland or the United Kingdom if those Member States take part in the areas of cooperation in question.

751. The first references concerned the principle of *ne bis in idem;* see Joined Cases C-187 & 385/01, *Hüseyin Gözütok and Klaus Brügge*; Case C-436/04, *Criminal proceedings v. Van Esbroeck*; Case C-288/05, *Kretzinger*; Case C-367/05, *Kraaijenbrink*.
752. Council doc 10900, 7 Jul. 2005. See <www.publications.parliament.uk/pa/ld200607/ldselect/ldeucom/90/90.pdf>
753. IP/07/803, Brussels, 12 Jun. 2007.
754. O.J. 2005, C 53/1.

on Refugees and other international treaties to persons in need, to regulate migration flows and to control the external borders of the Union.

In June 2005, the Council and Commission adopted an Action Plan implementing the Hague Programme on strengthening freedom, security and justice in the European Union.[755] In 2006, there was a first evaluation.[756]

4.2.5   The Lisbon Treaty

The obstacles to ratification of the European Constitution, the uncertainty about new accessions, and the terrorist attack in London in 2005 all put the area of freedom, security and justice under intense pressure.

The Lisbon Treaty contains the following amendments to the area of freedom, security and justice. According to Article 3(2) TEU (Lisbon) the Union offers its citizens an area of freedom, security and justice without internal frontiers, in which the free movement of persons is ensured in conjunction with appropriate measures with respect to external border controls, asylum, immigration and the prevention and combating of crime. The TFEU contains a new Title on the area of freedom, security and justice, which includes Chapter I (general provisions), Chapter II (policies on border checks, asylum and immigration), Chapter III (judicial cooperation in civil matters), Chapter IV (judicial cooperation in criminal matters) and Chapter V (police cooperation). This transfer of matters from the Third Pillar to the TFEU has consequences for decision-making and judicial protection in particular. The Protocols which were attached to the Treaty of Amsterdam concerning the position of Ireland, the United Kingdom and Denmark as regards the area of freedom, security and justice remain valid.

The following text describes the law in force, before the entry into force of the Lisbon Treaty.

4.3   AN AREA OF FREEDOM, SECURITY AND JUSTICE

This section contains an analysis of Title IV of Part three of the EC Treaty, in the version after the Treaty of Amsterdam, and of the most important legislation based on that Title. We are mainly concerned here with third-country nationals. The EC market participants (i.e., the economically active) already had a number of specific rights in the area of immigration, on the basis of the provisions on free movement of workers, freedom of establishment and freedom to provide services (see 4.4. below). These rights remain intact. This is particularly important in relation to the application of restrictions. In the exercise of their economic activity, the EC market participants are subject to the restrictions of Article 39 read with 46 EC, and not the

---

755.   O.J. 2005, C 198/1.
756.   See Communication from the Commission COM(2006)331 final.

restrictions of Article 64 EC (maintenance of law and order and the safeguarding of internal security).[757]

Title IV concerns, *inter alia*, visas, asylum, immigration and other policies related to free movement of persons. In the context of the accession of new States, and international migration (and the political situation in general), and given the Hague programme, it may be expected that in the coming years a number of legislative measures will be adopted in order to realize the area of freedom, security and justice.

Title IV contains three sorts of provisions which concern third-country nationals. First, there are rules on decision-making (Arts. 67 and 68 EC) and judicial protection (Art. 68 EC). Second, the legal basis for policy (Arts. 61–65 EC). Third, a provision concerning the special position of Denmark, the United Kingdom and Ireland (Art. 69 EC).

A number of provisions of the EU Charter of Fundamental Rights deal further with this subject matter. Article 18 of the Charter concerns the right to asylum; Article 19 deals with protection in the event of removal, expulsion or extradition; Article 45(2) concerns freedom of movement and of residence.

Article 61 EC concerns a list of measures which the Council can take in view of the gradual establishment of an area of freedom, security and justice. This list is elaborated in the subsequent Treaty articles. Barring a few exceptions, the relevant measures were to be adopted by the Council within a period of five years of the entry into force of the Treaty of Amsterdam. We will here briefly indicate the outlines of policy for each topic.[758]

4.3.1 Border Controls (Article 62, under (1) EC)

All controls of persons at the internal borders had to be abolished and replaced, before 1 May 2004, by a uniform system of controls at the external borders. In view of the Protocol mentioned above, this rule does not apply to the United Kingdom and Ireland.[759] Community rules are needed for controls of persons at the external

---

757. Art. 64(2) EC provides for a procedure in emergency situations.
758. See in general I. Boccardi, *Europe and Refugees: Towards an EU Asylum Policy* (The Hague, 2002); S. Peers, 'Implementing Equality? The Directive on Long-Term Resident Third-Country Nationals (2004) EL Rev., 437; E. Guild, 'Seeking Asylum: Storm Clouds between International Commitments and EU Legislative Measures' (2004) EL Rev., 198; S. Peers, *EU Immigration and Asylum Law: Internal Market Model or Human Rights: European Union Law for the Twenty-first Century, Vol. 1* (2004), 345–360; Hailbronner, Kay, *Asylum Law in the Context of a European Migration Policy: Europe's Area of Freedom, Security and Justice* (2004), 41–88; *Collected Courses of the Academy of European Law, Vol. 13/2*; S. Peers, 'Implementing Equality? the Directive on Long-Term Resident Third Country Nationals' (2004) EL Rev., 437–460; S. Peers, 'Key Legislative Developments on Migration in the European Union' (2004) *European Journal of Migration and Law*, 67–91; F. Weiss and F. Wooldridge, *Free Movement of Persons within the European Community*, 2nd ed. (The Hague, 2007) give good overviews of existing and proposed acts.
759. Protocol on the application of certain aspects of Art. 14 of the Treaty establishing the EC to the United Kingdom and Ireland. See on this the Common Manual, as adopted by the Executive Committee established by the CISA, O.J. 2002, C 313/97.

borders. These are in the process of being prepared, in implementation of the Tampere and Hague programmes.

4.3.2   Visas[760] and Travel (Article 62, under (2) and (3) EC)

On the basis of the old Article 100c EC, which was repealed by the Treaty of Amsterdam, a number of measures had been adopted: a regulation containing a list of third countries whose nationals required a visa,[761] and a regulation on a uniform visa format.[762] A Joint Action on Airport Transit Visas was approved under the old Article K.3 TEU.[763]

Regulation 539/2001 established a list of third countries whose nationals must be in possession of a visa when crossing the external borders and of those countries whose nationals are exempt from that requirement.[764] Regulation 1091/2001 of the Council altered the Schengen Implementing Convention rules concerning free circulation for persons with a long-stay visa.[765] Regulation 1030/2002 concerns the introduction of a uniform format for residence permits for third-country nationals.[766] Regulation 415/2003 concerns the issue of visas at the border.[767] The United Kingdom has challenged the validity of two regulations: a Regulation establishing a European agency for the management of operational cooperation at the external borders[768] and a Regulation on standards for security features and biometrics in passports and travel documents.[769] The cases are pending before the European Court of Justice (ECJ).

Regulations 693/2003 and 694/2003 concern facilitated transit documents (multiple entry visa, etc.).[770] Regulation 377/2004[771] established a network of immigration liaison officers, and Decision 2004/512 set up a Visa Information System (VIS).[772] Decision 2004/573 concerns the organization of joint flights

---

760. A. Meloni, 'The Development of a Common Visa Policy under the Treaty of Amsterdam,' (2005) CML Rev., 1357–1381.
761. Reg. 574/99, O.J. 1999, L 72/2, replacing Reg. 2317/95, O.J. 1995, L 234/1, which was annulled by the ECJ, see Case C-392/95, *European Parliament v. Council of the European Union*.
762. Reg. 1683/95, O.J. 1995, L 164/1.
763. O.J. 1996, L 63/8. See on this Case C-170/96, *Commission v. Council*.
764. O.J. 2001, L 81/1.
765. O.J. 2001, L 150/4.
766. O.J. 2002, L 157/1.
767. O.J. 2003, L 64/1.
768. Council Reg. 2007/2004 of 26 Oct. 2004, establishing a European agency for the management of operational cooperation at the external borders of the Member States of the European Union, O.J. 2004, L 349/1.
769. Council Reg. 2252/2004 of 13 Dec. 2004, on standards for security features and biometrics in passports and travel documents issued by Member States, O.J 2004, L 385/1. See Case C-77/05, *United Kingdom v. Council*, and Case C-137/05, *United Kingdom v. Council*.
770. O.J. 2003, L 99/8 and L 99/15.
771. O.J. 2004, L 64/1.
772. O.J. 2004, L 213/5.

for removals from the territory of two or more Member States, of third-country nationals who are subjects of individual removal orders,[773] and Directive 2004/82 concerns obligations on carriers to provide information on passengers.[774] Regulation 1931/2006 lays down rules on local border traffic at the external land borders of the Member States and amending the provisions of the Schengen Convention.[775] Regulation 1986/2006 regards access to the Second Generation Schengen Information System (SIS II) by the services in the Member States responsible for issuing vehicle registration certificates;[776] Regulation 1987/2006 and Decision 2007/533 deal with the establishment, operation and use of the SIS II.[777]

On 12 June 2007 the Council reached a political agreement on the legislative package on the VIS: the VIS Regulation and the VIS Decision. The adoption of these instruments by the Parliament and the political agreement by Member States are necessary for the further development of the system for the exchange of visa information between Member States. The VIS Regulation will allow consulates and other competent authorities to start using the system when processing visa applications and to check visas. The VIS Decision will allow police and law enforcement authorities to consult the data under certain conditions that ensure a high level of data protection.[778]

In the Protocol on external relations of the Member States with regard to the crossing of external borders, attached to the EC Treaty by the Treaty of Amsterdam, it is laid down that the provisions on the measures on the crossing of external borders included in Article 62(2)(a) of the EC Treaty shall be without prejudice to the competence of Member States to negotiate or conclude agreements with third countries as long as they respect Community law and other relevant international agreements.

4.3.3 The Policy on Refugees and Asylum (Article 63, First Paragraph, under (1) and (2) EC)

Article 63 EC lists the measures to be adopted by the Council, which must be in accordance with the Geneva Convention on the status of refugees, and the Dublin Convention on the State responsible for examining applications for asylum lodged in one of the Member States of the ECs.[779]

By Decision of the Council of 28 September 2000, a European Refugee Fund was established.[780] Directive 2001/55 concerns minimum standards for giving

---

773. O.J. 2004, L 261/28.
774. O.J. 2004, L 261/24.
775. O.J. 2006, L 405/1.
776. O.J. 2006, L 381/1.
777. O.J. 2006, L 381/4 and O.J. 2007, L 205/63, respectively.
778. See IP/07/802.
779. See the Commission's notice on revising the Dublin Convention, SEC(2000)522. See on this I. Boccardi, *Europe and Refugees. Towards an EU Asylum Policy* (The Hague, 2002). See also Art. 18 EU Charter of Fundamental Rights.
780. Council Decision 2000/596/EC, O.J. 2000, L 252/12.

temporary protection in the event of a mass influx of displaced persons,[781] Directive 2003/9 concerns the establishment of minimum standards for the reception of asylum seekers in the Member States,[782] and Regulation 343/2003 concerns the establishment of criteria for a request for asylum.[783] A Common European Asylum System has been put in place, centred around the so-called Procedural Directive, adopted on 1 December 2005,[784] and the Directive on minimum standards for the qualification and status of third-country nationals or stateless persons as refugees or as persons who otherwise need international protection and the content of the protection granted.[785] This Directive, which had to be implemented by 2006, will result in preliminary references which need to be answered extremely rapidly.[786] In the framework of the current re-evaluation, mention should be made of the recent Green paper on the future common European asylum system.[787]

4.3.4 Immigration (Article 63, First Paragraph, under (3) and (4) EC)

Article 63, first paragraph, under (3) EC concerns conditions of entry and residence for third-country nationals.[788] In this context, Directive 2004/81 was enacted, concerning the residence permit issued to third-country nationals who are victims of trafficking in human beings[789] and Directive 2004/83 on minimum standards for the qualification and status of third-country nationals or stateless persons as refugees.[790] This Treaty provision also covers measures on illegal immigration, but the criminal law aspects of such measures come under the Third Pillar.[791] An example is Council Framework Decision 2004/757/JHA of 25 October 2004 laying down minimum provisions on the constituent elements of criminal acts and penalties in the field of illicit drug trafficking.[792]

Article 63, first paragraph, under (4) EC deals with the rights and conditions under which nationals of third countries who are legally resident in a Member State

---

781. O.J. 2001, L 212/10.
782. O.J. 2003, L 31/18.
783. O.J. 2003, L 50/1.
784. Council Dir. 2005/85 on minimum standards on procedures in Member States for granting and withdrawing refugee status, O.J. 2005, L 326/13.
785. Asylum Qualification Directive, Dir. 2004/83 of 29 Apr. 2004, O.J. 2004, L 304/12. See C. Teitgen-Colly, 'The European Union and asyLum: An Illusion of Protection' (2006) CML Rev., 1503.
786. See already Case C-465/07, *Elgafaji*.
787. COM(2007)301 final of 6 Jun. 2007. See also Report of the Commission on the evaluation of the Dublin system, COM(2007)299 final.
788. See, e.g., Council Dir. 2001/40 on the mutual recognition of decisions on the expulsion of third country nationals, O.J. 2001, L 149/34.
789. O.J. 2004, L 261/19.
790. O.J. 2004, L 304/12.
791. See Arts. 29 et seq. TEU. See Council Framework Decision 2002/946 on the strengthening of the penal framework to prevent the facilitation of unauthorized entry, transit and residence, O.J. 2002, L 328/1, and Council Dir. 2002/90/EC of 28 Nov. 2002 defining the facilitation of unauthorised entry, transit and residence, O.J. 2002, L 328/17.
792. O.J. 2004, L 335/8.

may reside in other Member States.[793] Regulation 859/2003 – based on Article 63 first paragraph, under (4) EC – extended the provisions of Regulation 1408/71 on the coordination of social security to cover nationals of third countries who are excluded from the scope of this Regulation purely as a result of their nationality.[794]

An extremely important directive is Directive 2003/86 on the right to family reunification.[795] The personal scope of this Directive extends to family members of third-country nationals, future Union citizens, and privileged third-country nationals residing lawfully in the territory of an EU Member State, and in possession of a residence permit valid for one year or longer, and who have a reasonable prospect of acquiring a permanent right of residence.

Finally, Council Directive 2003/109/EC lays down arrangements for the status of third-country nationals who are long-term residents,[796] and Council Directive 2004/114 makes arrangements for the admission of third-country nationals for the purposes of studies, pupil exchange, training and voluntary service.[797]

4.4   RIGHTS AND OBLIGATIONS OF PERSONS WHO ARE EC MARKET PARTICIPANTS (GENERAL)

EU nationals enjoy rights on the basis of the EC Treaty. These rights are elaborated per category (worker, self-employed, family member, EU national, etc.). The detailed elaboration of these rights is found mainly in secondary law.[798] In the following section (section 5), these acts of secondary law will be analysed in detail.

Free movement of market participants (workers and self-employed) – 'internal EC migration' – involves three aspects: migration, market access and ancillary rights. These aspects are dealt with in specific Treaty provisions. As far as movement from third countries is concerned, the emphasis is on the first of these, i.e., the migration rights proper.

In a series of decisions, the Court of Justice, used the general non-discrimination provision, Article 12 EC, in order to eliminate obstacles which were not related to economic motives.[799] The citizenship provisions have also been used for this.[800]

---

793. See also Art. 45(2) EU Charter of Fundamental Rights.
794. O.J. 2003, L 124/1.
795. O.J. 2003, L 251/12.
796. O.J. 2004, L 16/44. See Boelaert-Suominen, 'Non-EU Nationals and Council Dir. 2003/109/EC on the Status of Third-Country Nationals who Are Long-Term Residents: Five Paces Forward and Possibly Three Paces Back', (2005) CML Rev., 1011–1052.
797. Council Dir. 2004/114, on the conditions of admission of third-country nationals for the purposes of studies, pupil exchange, unremunerated training, or voluntary service (O.J. 2004, L 375).
798. For a very extensive overview, also of the main decisions, see F. Weiss and F. Wooldridge, *Free Movement of Persons within the European Community*, 2nd ed. (The Hague, 2007).
799. Case 186/87, *Cowan*; Case C-15/96, *Kalliope Schöning-Kougebetopoulou v. Freie und Hansestadt Hamburg*; Case C-274/96, *Criminal proceedings against Horst Otto Bickel and Ulrich Franz*; Case C-452/01, *Ospelt*.
800. Case C-224/98, *D'Hoop*; Case C-184/99, *Grzelczyk*. See also Case C-148/02, *Garcia Avello*.

4.4.1 Migration Rights

These concern the rules on the entry, admission, establishment and residence of persons. The rights of migration for EU nationals are achieved by the directly effective prohibitions of obstacles to free movement which apply for the various categories of persons concerned, and in which the principle of non-discrimination on the ground of nationality forms an essential element. These substantive rules are linked to procedural rules.[801] Thus the persons concerned must be able to appeal against adverse administrative decisions affecting them,[802] and in particular the European Convention on Human Rights must be respected.[803]

4.4.2 Rights of Access to the Market

These rights give the person concerned access to the various markets, provided that a number of conditions are fulfilled. The EU Charter of Fundamental Rights explicitly confirms the Freedom to choose an occupation and right to engage in work for every citizen of the EU (Arts. 15 and 16). Very few specific conditions are in fact laid down for workers, but for the self-employed there are qualifications requirements and establishment requirements in respect of many professions. Although these national rules apply without distinction to nationals of the host Member State and nationals of other Member States alike, in many cases they are in effect less easy to satisfy for persons moving to another Member State. Insofar as these market access conditions lead to distortions, they are overcome either by the mutual recognition principle, or by harmonization of laws, or by Community-wide uniform rules.[804]

4.4.3 Ancillary Rights

On the basis of the first two types of rights set out above an internal market for persons can be achieved. However, employees or self-employed persons who wish to migrate will only exercise their rights if a number of other guarantees are afforded, such as the portability of their social security rights, e.g., pension periods. An entrepreneur who wishes to establish an undertaking, or employ employees, or provide services, will also look to the social legislation and the fiscal climate before he chooses a location within the internal market. Both subjects, social security and taxes, will be dealt with further in this book. Social security rights will be dealt with in the framework of free movement of workers – in conformity with their place in the EC Treaty. Tax rules will be dealt with in the context of the

---

801. Case 36/75, *Roland Rutili v. Ministre de l'intérieur*; Case C-459/99, *Mouvement contre le racisme, l'antisémitisme et la xénophobie ASBL (MRAX) v. État belge*.
802. E.g., Case 222/86, *Union national des entraineurs et Cadres techniques professionnels du football (Unectef) v. Heylens et al.*
803. Case 36/75, *Rutili*. See also Art. 47 EU Charter of Fundamental Rights.
804. See section 1.2 *supra*.

discussion of each of the various freedoms (sections 5.5, 6.9, 7.4.1 and 8.4.3). Indirect taxes were dealt with in the section on free movement of goods (section 2.5 above).

4.5   MIGRATION RIGHTS (EXIT, ENTRY AND RESIDENCE)

Over the years, an enlargement has taken place in relation to both the addressees of these rights, and the content of the rights.

The Council had in the course of time enacted a number of directives concerning the right of freedom of movement and residence of 'foreign nationals',[805] and 'nationals of Member States'.[806] After the entry into force of the Treaty of Maastricht, which introduced citizenship of the European Union, and of the Treaty of Amsterdam, which established the area of freedom, security and justice, the status of citizen of the Union started to acquire a new resonance.

After years of deliberation, the Council and European Parliament approved Directive 2004/38.[807] This Directive replaced, as of 30 April 2006, the old directives concerning freedom of movement and residence of Union citizens (i.e., nationals of Member States) and their family members. Amongst other things, it codified the case law of the Court of Justice, first on free movement of workers and self-employed (market citizens) and later on non-economically active citizens. It simplifies the existing rules and updates them, for instance by taking account of social and civil developments in relation to forms of marriage and partnership. In the Hague Programme, Directive 2004/38 is used as the core of the part concerned with 'strengthening freedom'.

In the following sections, certain aspects of this directive will be referred to. The old directives will still be mentioned as well, since an explanation of the old provisions enables us to clarify the relevance of the Court's case law. We will first describe the 'old arrangements' (section 4.5.1.), and thereafter the 'new arrangements' (4.5.2.). In *Oulane*,[808] the Court already considered that there is a link between the old and new arrangements. Moreover, since a number of old provisions have been included in the new arrangements, it is still useful to give a brief analysis of the Court's case law on the old arrangements.

4.5.1   Old Arrangements

Every national of a Member State, irrespective of his or her place of residence, had the right to take up an activity as an employed person, and to pursue such activity, within the territory of another Member State under the same conditions as nationals

---

805. See Dir. 64/221, O.J. 1964, 56/850.
806. See Dir. 73/148, O.J. 1973, L 172/14.
807. O.J. 2004, L 158/77. See the corrigendum (including an incorrect reference to 'Dir. 2004/58') published at O.J. 2004, L 229/35.
808. Case C-215/03, see para.20.

of the host Member State – Article 1 Regulation 1612/68.[809] Directive 64/221 did
provide for a number of restrictions, however.

4.5.1.1   Holders of Rights

Article 1 of Directive 68/360[810] required Member States to abolish restrictions on
the movement and residence of nationals of the Member States and the members of
their families to whom Regulation 1612/68 applies. A national of a Member State
who had worked in another Member State could only derive a right of residence
under the EC Treaty on that basis if he or she was already a national of a Member
State at the time at which he or she was employed in the host Member State.
Otherwise, he was regarded as not having been employed in the host Member
State, and fell outside the scope of the Directive.[811]

    Evidently, the workers who fell within the scope of Article 39 EC were holders
of rights.[812] Further, on the basis of Regulation 1251/70,[813] a right of residence was
granted to workers after they entered employment. The right of residence was also
granted to certain family members of EC workers, on the basis of Articles 10 and
11 of Regulation 1612/68.

    Article 10 provided that the spouse[814] and their descendants under the age of
21 years or who were dependants and dependent relatives in the ascending line of the
worker and his or her spouse had the right, irrespective of their nationality, to install
themselves with a worker. In *Eind*, the Court ruled that in the event of a Community
worker returning to the Member State of which he is a national, Community law
does not require the authorities of that State to grant a right of entry and residence to a
third-country national who is a member of that worker's family because of the mere
fact that, in the host Member State where that worker was gainfully employed, that
third-country national held a valid residence permit issued on the basis of Article 10
of Regulation 1612/68. When a worker returns to the Member State of which he is a
national, after being gainfully employed in another Member State, a third-country
national who is a member of his family has a right under Article 10(1)(a) of
Regulation 1612/68, which applies by analogy, to reside in the Member State of
which the worker is a national, even where that worker does not carry on any
effective and genuine economic activities. The fact that a third-country national
who is a member of a Community worker's family did not, before residing in the
Member State where the worker was employed, have a right under national law to
reside in the Member State of which the worker is a national has no bearing on the
determination of that national's right to reside in the latter State.[815]

---

809. See also Art. 15 Charter Fundamental Rights.
810. O.J. 1968, L 257/13.
811. Case C-171/91 *Dimitrios Tsiotras v. Landeshauptstadt Stuttgart*.
812. See section 5.1. *supra*.
813. O.J. 1970, L 142/24.
814. As to unmarried partners, see Case 59/85, *Netherlands v. Ann Florence Reed*.
815. Case C-291/05, *Minister voor Vreemdelingenzaken en Integratie v. Eind*.

Article 11 provided that the worker's spouse and those of the children under the age of 21 years or dependent on the worker[816] had the right to take up any activity as an employed person throughout the territory of the host State, irrespective of their nationality.[817] The family of the worker also fell within the personal scope of the coordination arrangements relating to social security rights.[818] Both in relation to rights under Regulation 1612/68 and under the social security arrangements, family rights were derived rights, thus they depended on the worker having the status of a worker, and they ceased if the worker ceased to enjoy that status.[819] These provisions were revised in the framework of the new arrangements (see below).

In *Singh*,[820] the Court of Justice ruled that a national of a Member State who had gone to another Member State in order to work there as an employed person and returned to establish himself or herself in the State of which he or she is a national has the right, under Article 43 EC, to be accompanied by his or her spouse, even if the spouse is a third-country national, under the same conditions as those laid down in Regulation 1612/68, Directive 68/360 or Directive 73/148. In *Akrich*,[821] the Court restricted the right of residence to a spouse – a third country national – who had already been admitted to the EU in accordance with the immigration laws of an EU Member State, in the sense of being 'lawfully resident' in a Member State before moving. After the *Eind* judgment of the Court of Justice it remains to be seen whether this is still a necessary condition.[822]

4.5.1.2 Rights

Article 2 of Directive 68/360 regulated the right to leave a country. On the basis of Article 3, the Member States had to permit persons enjoying this right to leave the country on the simple production of a valid passport or identity card.[823] Without these documents, persons cannot prove their identity and the link with family members.[824] Failure to be in possession of appropriate proof of identity could only be subject to a proportionate sanction.[825] A third-country national married

---

816. Case C-10/05, *Mattern and Cokotic v. Ministre du Travail et de l'Emploi*. On the concept 'dependent' see Case 316/85, *Centre public d'aide sociale de Courcelles v. Marie-Christine Lebon*.

817. Case 267/83, *Aissatou Diatta v. Land Berlin*; Case 131/85, *Emir Gül v. Regierungspräsident Düsseldorf*; Case 249/86, *Commission v. Germany*; Case 235/87, *Matteucci*; Case C-60/00, *Carpenter*.

818. See Art. 2(1) Reg. 1408/71, O.J. 1971, L 149/2.

819. See Case 40/76 *Slavica Kermaschek v. Bundesanstalt für Arbeit*; See also Case 267/83, *Diatta*.

820. Case C-370/90, *Singh*. See Art. 23 of Dir. 2004/38.

821. Case C-109/01, *Akrich*. See also Case C-1/05, *Jia v. Migrationsverket*.

822. Case C-291/05, *Eind*.

823. Case 157/79, *Regina v. Stanislaus Pieck*; Case 321/87, *Commission v. Belgium*; Case C-68/89, *Commission v. Netherlands*; Case C-459/99, *MRAX*.

824. Case C-376/89, *Panagiotis Giagounidis v. Stadt Reutlingen*.

825. Case 48/75, *Royer*; Case 8/77, *Criminal proceedings against Concetta Sagulo, Gennaro Brenca et Addelmadjid Bakhouche*; Case C-363/89, *Danielle Roux v. Belgium*; Case C-378/97, *Wijsenbeek*; Case C-459/99, *MRAX*.

to a national of a Member State could be obliged to be in possession of a visa.[826] According to Article 4, the right of residence had to be granted to nationals and their dependent families who were able to produce specified documents.[827] The right of residence was proved by a specific residence permit, which was declaratory in nature,[828] rather than constitutive, and could not be withdrawn simply on the basis that someone was no longer in employment (Art. 7). The residence permit had to be issued free of charge or on payment of a fee which could not be higher than the dues and taxes charged for the issue of identity cards to nationals. Under Article 8 the worker could be required to report his or her presence in the territory of the host Member State.[829] Member States could not impose an unreasonably short period for the grant of a residence permit.[830]

4.5.1.3 Exceptions

The Member States could not derogate from the provisions of Directive 68/360, except on grounds of public policy, public security or public health (Art. 10). Council Directive 64/221, based on Article 46 EC, laid down the details regarding the exceptions on the basis of public policy,[831] public security or public health,[832] all of which are mentioned in Article 39(3) EC. The failure to fulfil the legal formalities concerning entry, movement and residence could in themselves not be grounds for the application of the measures in Directive 64/221.[833]

The safeguards provided by Directive 64/221 call for a broad interpretation as regards the persons to whom they apply.[834] Member States must take all steps to ensure that the safeguard of the provisions of the Directive is available to any national of another Member State who is subject to a decision ordering expulsion.[835] To exclude from the benefit of those substantive and procedural safeguards citizens of the Union who are not lawfully resident on the territory of the host Member State would deprive those safeguards of their essential effectiveness. That interpretation is borne out by the judgment in *MRAX*, in which the Court held that a national of a non-member State who is a member of the family of a Community national, but who does not fulfil the conditions necessary for lawful residence, must be able to rely on the procedural safeguards provided for by Directive 64/221.

---

826. Case C-459/99, *MRAX*.
827. Case C-376/89, *Giagounidis*; Case C-85/96, *Martínez Sala*; Case C-24/97, *Commission v. Germany*; Case C-138/02 *Collins*.
828. Case 48/75, *Royer*; Joined Cases 389 & 390/87, *Echternach and Moritz*; Case C-363/89, *Roux*; Case C-459/99, *MRAX*.
829. Case C-265/88, *Criminal proceedings against Lothar Messner*.
830. Case C-344/95, *Commission v. Belgium*.
831. See H. Schneider, *Die öffentliche Ordnung als Schranke der Grundfreiheiten im EG-Vertrag*, (Baden-Baden, 1998).
832. O.J. 1964, 850.
833. Case 48/75, *Royer*; Case C-459/99, *MRAX*.
834. See to that effect Case C-459/99, *MRAX*, para. 101.
835. See to that effect Case C-136/03, *Dörr and Ünal*, para. 49.

It must therefore be held that an interpretation to the effect that the provisions of Directive 64/221 apply only to citizens of the Union who are lawfully resident on the territory of the host Member State is not consistent with Community law.[836]

Private parties could also rely on these exceptions.[837] The Court applied these exceptions as elaborated in the context of intra-Community movement, in its case law concerning movement of workers from Turkey[838] and East Europe.[839] The concept of public policy within the meaning of Article 2 of Directive 64/221 does not correspond to that in Article 96 of the Convention Implementing the Schengen Agreement (CISA). According to the latter, an alert in the SIS for the purposes of refusing entry may be based on a threat to public policy where the person concerned has been convicted of an offence carrying a penalty involving deprivation of liberty of at least one year (Art. 96(2)(a) CISA), or if he has been subject to a measure based on a failure to comply with national regulations on the entry or residence of aliens (Art. 96(3) CISA). Unlike the rules laid down by Directive 64/221, as interpreted by the Court, such circumstances justify in themselves an alert irrespective of any specific assessment of the threat represented by the person concerned. The Court has held, however, that the rules of the Community, including the Directive, take precedence.[840]

The difference in treatment of nationals of a Member State and non-nationals[841] flows from the principle of international law that a State may not refuse entry and residence to its own nationals.[842]

Directive 64/221 did not only apply to workers, but also to nationals of the Member States who were not in employment but economically active, and to certain family members.[843] Directive 72/194 extended the scope of application to workers who remain in another Member State after their period of employment there has ceased.[844]

The public health exception was not intended to exempt employment in the sector of public health from the principle of free movement, but to create the possibility to refuse residence in another Member State to persons who may pose a danger to public health.[845]

Directive 64/221 did not define the three exceptions, but contained certain elements which enabled the Court of Justice to give an effective interpretation. The

---

836. See Case C-50/06, *Commission v. Netherlands*, paras 35–36.
837. Case C-415/93, *Bosman*; Case C-281/98, *Angonese*. For a critical view, see K.J.M. Mortelmans, *Excepties bij non-tarifaire intracommunautaire belemmeringen: assimilatie in het nieuwe EG-Verdrag?* (1997) SEW, 182–190.
838. Case C-340/97, *Nazli*.
839. Case C-268/99, *Jany*.
840. Case 503/03, *Commission v. Spain*, para. 48.
841. See section 4.1
842. See, e.g., Art. 3, 4th Protocol ECHR; Case 41/74, *Yvonne van Duyn v. Home Office*; Case C-171/96, *Roque*.
843. See section 6.5.2 *infra*.
844. O.J. 1972, L 121/32.
845. Case 131/85, *Gül*.

Court indicated – in line with its case law in the area of free movement of goods – that these Community law concepts were to be interpreted strictly where they were used to justify an exception to the principle of free movement.[846] It should be added that a particularly restrictive interpretation of the derogations from that freedom is required by virtue of a person's status as a citizen of the Union. The Court has held that that status is destined to be the fundamental status of nationals of the Member States.[847]

The content of the exceptions could not be determined unilaterally by the Member States.[848] The Court ruled that a Member State may not take measures against a national of another Member State, on the grounds of public policy, for conduct which, when attributable to the former State's own nationals, does not give rise to repressive measures or other genuine and effective measures intended to combat such conduct.[849] In this area, too, the Court has indicated that a measure which restricts one of the freedoms guaranteed by the Treaty may only be justified if it respects the principle of proportionality.[850]

As the Court already indicated explicitly in *Rutili*, Directive 64/221 contained both substantive and procedural provisions.[851] Article 2(2) of the Directive provided that the grounds of public policy, public security or public health 'shall not be invoked to service economic ends'.[852] Article 3(1) provided that measures taken on grounds of public policy[853] or public security[854] have to be justified on grounds of the individual conduct of the person concerned,[855] and Article 3(2) added that the mere existence of a criminal conviction is not enough:[856] there must be a genuine and sufficiently serious threat to the requirements of public policy.[857] The latter criterion has also been applied for convictions related to drugs.[858] In a number of judgments the Court indicated that measures limiting the right of residence to a part of the territory could only be taken by a

---

846. Case C-348/96, *Calfa*.
847. See, in particular, Case C-184/99, *Grzelczyk*, and Case C-138/02, *Collins*.
848. Case 41/74, *Van Duyn*.
849. Joined Cases 115 & 116/81, *Rezguia Adoui v. Belgium and City of Liège; Dominique Cornuaille v. Belgium*; Case C-100/01, *Ministre de l'Intérieur v. Aitor Oteiza Olazabal*.
850. Case C-100/01, *Olazabal*.
851. Case 36/75, *Rutili*; Case C-100/01, *Olazabal*.
852. Case 36/75, *Rutili*.
853. On the substance of the concept, see Case C-103/01, *Commission v. Germany*.
854. On the interpretation of the concept, see Case C-273/97, *Sirdar;* Case C-285/98, *Kreil;* and Case C-186/01, *Dory*.
855. Case 41/74, *Van Duyn;* Case 67/74, *Carmelo Angelo Bonsignore v. Oberstadtdirektor der Stadt Köln*; Case 48/75, *Royer*; Case 30/77, *Régina v. Pierre Bouchereau*; Case 98/79, *Josette Pecastaing v. Belgium*; Joined Cases 115 & 116/81, *Adoui and Cornuaille*; Case C-348/96, *Calfa*; Case C-100/01, *Olazabal*; Joined Cases C-482 & 493/01, *Orfanopoulos*.
856. Case 30/77, *Bouchereau*.
857. Case 36/75, *Rutili*; Joined Cases 115 & 116/81, *Adoui and Cornuaille*; Case C-348/96, *Calfa*; Case C-340/97, *Nazli*; Case C-268/99, *Jany*.
858. See Case C-348/96, *Calfa*, and Joined Cases C-482 & 493/01, *Orfanopoulos*.

Member State against nationals of other Member States falling under the relevant Treaty provisions in cases where such measures were also taken against nationals of that Member State, and under the same conditions as these.[859] This application of the principle of non-discrimination must also be seen in view of the unequal initial situation. The Court repeatedly ruled that in assessing the exceptions contained in Articles 39 and 46 read together with Directive 64/221, account must be taken of the fact that Member States may not expel their own nationals from their territory, and may not deny them entry.[860]

Article 3(3) of the Directive provided that expiry of the identity card or passport may not justify expulsion from the territory.[861] A Member State could not refuse a residence permit to a national of a third country who is married to a national of a Member State and who entered the territory of that State legally, and could not deport such a person merely on the ground that his or her visa had expired before the application for a residence permit.[862] Article 4 dealt with public health. The only diseases and disabilities which justified restrictions on the exercise of the right of free movement were contained in the Annex to Directive 64/221. This list was drawn up according to the state of scientific knowledge in 1964. The Commission had recommended to the Council to amend the list of diseases and disabilities, so that new contagious diseases (e.g., severe acute respiratory syndrome (SARS)) could be included. In the new arrangements on free movement of EU nationals (see below, 4.5.2) replacing Directive 64/221, the Council chose to align itself with the World Health Organization list of diseases with epidemic potential.

The procedural safeguards were contained in Articles 5–9 of Directive 64/221. The decision granting or refusing the residence permit had to be taken as quickly as possible.[863] The applicant was entitled to be informed of the decision, and of the grounds of public policy, public security, or public health on which the decision taken in his or her case was based, in a language which he or she understood.[864]

Article 8 provided that the applicant should have the same legal remedies in respect of a decision concerning entry, or refusing a residence permit, or ordering expulsion, as were available to nationals of the State concerned in respect of acts of the administration.[865] Article 9 contained some 'safety net' provisions, such as the right to be heard by a competent authority which may issue an advisory opinion, in cases where there was no right of appeal to a court of law, or where such appeal was

---

859. Case 36/75, *Rutili*; Case C-100/01, *Olazabal*.
860. Case 41/74, *Van Duijn*; Case C-348/96, *Calfa*; Case C-100/01, *Olazabal*.
861. Case 48/75, *Royer*.
862. Case C-459/99, *MRAX*.
863. Case C-357/98, *The Queen v. Secretary of State for the Home Department ex parte Nana Yaa Konadu Yiadom*.
864. Case 36/75, *Rutili*; Joined Cases 115 & 116/81, *Adoui and Cornuaille*; Case C-175/94, *The Queen v. Secretary of State for the Home Department, ex parte John Gallagher*.
865. Case 98/79, *Pecastaing*; Joined Cases C-297/88 & 197/89, *Massam Dzodzi v. Belgium*.

limited.[866] The personal scope of this provision had to be interpreted broadly[867] and should be assessed taking into account the guarantees enshrined in the European Convention on Human Rights (ECHR).[868]

4.5.2 The New Arrangements

As indicated above,[869] on 30 April 2006 the arrangements described above – dating from the 1960s and developed through case law up to the 1990s – were replaced by a new system of rights of free movement and residence for citizens of the Union and their family members, as a result of the adoption of Directive 2004/38.[870] Directive 2004/38 amends Regulation 1612/68 which concerns access to the market for workers within the Community,[871] and repeals Directives 64/221, 72/194 (public policy, public security and public health), Directives 68/360, 73/148 (movement and residence), Directive 90/364 (residence), 30/365 (residence for non-economically active) and Directive 93/96, (residence for students). Directive 2004/38 deals with three subjects: the conditions governing the exercise of the right of free movement and residence, the right of permanent residence and the limits placed on these rights. These are preceded by provisions on the personal scope of the Directive and the beneficiaries. Finally, the Directive also includes procedural guarantees.

4.5.2.1 *Personal Scope of the Directive and the Beneficiaries*

The Directive applies to Union citizens and their family members. Citizens of the Union are all persons possessing the nationality of a Member State. Family members are: spouse (or registered partner), direct descendants who are under the age of 21 or are dependants and those of the spouse or partner, the dependent direct relatives in the ascending line and those of the spouse or partner (Art. 2).

A partner in the sense of Article 2(b) of the Directive is a person with whom the citizen has contracted a registered partnership, on the basis of the legislation of a Member State, if the legislation of the host Member State treats registered partnerships as equivalent to marriage and in accordance with the conditions laid down in the relevant legislation of the host Member State (i.e., the Member State to which the citizen moves, and which triggers the exercise of his/her right of free movement and residence.) As Recital 6 of the Preamble indicates, the aim is to

---

866. See also Art. 47 EU Charter of Fundamental Rights. Joined Cases 115 & 116/81, *Adoui and Cornuaille*; Joined Cases C-65 & 111/95, *The Queen v. Secretary of State for the Home Department, ex parte Mann Singh Shingara and ex parte Abbas Radiom*; Case C-459/99, *MRAX*; Joined Cases C-482 & 493/01, *Orfanopoulos*.
867. Case 98/79, *Pecastaing*; Case C-459/99, *MRAX*.
868. Case 222/86, *Heylens*; Case C-459/99, *MRAX*.
869. See section 4.2 *supra*.
870. O.J. 2004, L 229/35.
871. Discussed further *infra*, 5.3.1. Specifically, it repeals Arts. 10 and 11 of Reg. 1612/68.

maintain the unity of the family in a broader sense. Member States are entitled to take the necessary measures in the case of marriages of convenience (Art. 35). Family members as defined in Article 2 are covered irrespective of their nationality (Art. 7(2)).

The beneficiaries are all Union citizens who move to or reside in a Member State other than that of which they are a national, and their family members (as defined in point 2 of Art. 2) who accompany or join them (Art. 3).

4.5.2.2   *The Rights of Citizens and Family Members*

Chapters II and III concern rights of exit and entry and of residence. No visa or equivalent formality may be imposed on nationals of a Member State leaving or entering another Member State. Depending on circumstances, a valid identity card or passport is sufficient (Arts. 4, 5). In relation to the right of residence, a distinction is made between short-term, long-term and permanent residence. Union citizens and their family have the right to reside on the territory of another Member State for a period of up to three months without any conditions other than the requirement to hold a valid identity card or passport. For residence of more than three months, further conditions are set: they must be workers or self-employed persons ((establishment or services); or, if they do not belong to these categories, have sufficient resources and have comprehensive sickness insurance.[872] The last two conditions are to prevent the beneficiaries from becoming an unreasonable burden on the social assistance system of the host Member State (Arts. 6, 7 and 14).

A number of provisions have been included concerning the retention of the right of residence by family members in case of death or departure of the Union citizen, or divorce (Arts. 12 and 13).

Beneficiaries must fulfil a number of administrative formalities. The most important document is a residence card, which is required for a stay of more than three months (Arts. 9–11).

The Directive introduces a right of permanent residence for citizens who have resided legally for a continuous period of five years in the host Member State. This right is also enjoyed by family members who are not nationals of a Member State and meet the five years residence requirement. Once acquired, the right of permanent residence can only be lost through absence from the host Member State for a period exceeding two consecutive years (Art. 16). Certain categories of persons, such as workers or self-employed who reach the age laid down for entitlement to an old age pension, acquire the right of permanent residence before the five year period has elapsed (Art. 17). People in this category also have to fulfil certain administrative formalities. They are issued with a Permanent residence card (Arts. 19 and 20).

---

872. For students, special conditions are set in Art. 7(1)(c).

4.5.2.3   Restrictions

The Member States may restrict the freedom of movement and residence of Union citizens and their family members on grounds of public policy, public security or public health. Article 46 provides explicitly for this possibility. Chapter VI of Directive 2004/38 indicates how these restrictions should be applied. On the one hand, the principles of the old Directive 64/221 are maintained (measures must be proportional, grounds must not be invoked to serve economic ends, restrictions must be based exclusively on the personal conduct of the individual concerned, criminal convictions may not in themselves constitute grounds for measures based on public policy of public security). On the other hand, the Directive codifies case law of the Court, particularly the requirement that the conduct of the individual concerned must represent a genuine, present and sufficiently serious threat affecting one of the fundamental interests of society[873] (Art. 27).

A new element is the principle that the Member States must take account of how long the individual concerned has resided on its territory, his/her age, state of health, family and economic situation, social and cultural integration into the host Member State and the extent of his/her links with the country of origin before taking an expulsion decision on grounds of public policy or public security (Art. 28(1)). An expulsion decision may not be taken against Union citizens, except if the decision is based on imperative grounds of public security, as defined by Member States, if they have resided in the host Member State for the previous 10 years; or in case of minors, except if the expulsion is necessary for the best interests of the child, as provided for in the United Nations Convention on the Rights of the Child of 20 November 1989 (Art. 28(3)).

The list of diseases and disabilities which was annexed to Directive 64/221 is replaced by a 'dynamic' reference to the relevant instruments of the World Health Organization. Diseases occurring after a three-month period from the date of arrival shall not constitute grounds for expulsion from the territory (Art. 29).

4.5.2.4   Procedural Guarantees

Persons concerned shall be notified in writing of any decision taken, whereby they must be able to comprehend its content and the implications for them (Art. 30). The notification must specify the court or administrative authority with which the person concerned may lodge an appeal, the time limit for the appeal. Persons concerned shall have access to judicial and, where appropriate, administrative redress procedures in the host Member State. Where application is made for an interim order to suspend enforcement of an expulsion measure, actual removal from the territory may not take place, as a general rule, until such time as the decision on the interim order has been taken (Art. 31).

---

873.   See, e.g., Case 36/75, *Rutili* and Case 30/77 *Bouchereau*.

Although the Directive does not refer to the ECHR, this Convention forms a procedural safety net and guideline, as is evident from the Court's case law.[874]

5   FREE MOVEMENT OF WORKERS

European workers are much more bound to their place of residence and their country than for instance American workers are. The free movement of workers has thus in practice been far less important than the free movement of goods and, more recently, the freedom to provide (and receive) services. It was indicated in the sections above that there could be significant migratory movements in the future, depending on the development of a common migration policy for workers from third countries. Such migration also depends on recent and future accession.

This section is limited to the rules for EU workers. The provisions contained in Articles 39–41 EC deal mainly with the legal and economic aspects of free movement: residence, establishment and market access. The social aspects are visible in Article 42 EC concerning social security matters. The employment market and working conditions policies of the Member States and the Community are governed by the terms of Articles 136–145 EC. Articles 146–148 EC on the European Social Fund and Articles 158–162 EC on the Structural Funds set out the conditions for financial stimuli for the creation of employment opportunities for certain groups or regions. These matters are discussed in Chapter X of this book.

In the light of the distinction made in section 4.1 above, the present discussion now examines first the beneficiaries of the freedom of movement for workers, in section 5.1, before turning to migration rights in section 5.2. It then proceeds to rights of market access in section 5.3, social security rights, in section 5.4, and finally personal taxation, in section 5.5.

5.1   THE CONCEPT OF A WORKER AND ARTICLES 39–42 EC

The EC Treaty itself does not define the concept of a 'worker' or the concept of employment,[875] so these concepts have had to be defined through case law. The Court of Justice has sought to give these concepts as wide an interpretation as possible, on the basis that the free movement of workers is one of the foundations of the Community, and thus the provisions conferring those freedoms must be widely interpreted. These concepts are given a Community law meaning and are not determined by reference to national legislation of the Member States.[876]

---

874. See, e.g., Case 36/75, *Rutili* and Case 222/86, *Heylens*.
875. A.C. Oliveira, 'Workers and Other Persons: A Step-by-step from Movement to Citizenship, Case Law 1995–2001' (2002) CML Rev., 77.
876. Case 75/63, *Mrs M.K.H. Hoekstra (née Unger) v. Bestuur der Bedrijfsvereniging voor Detailhandel en Ambachten*; Case 53/81, *D.M. Levin v. Staatssecretaris van Justitie*; Case 139/85, *R.H. Kempf v. Staatssecretaris van Justitie*; Case C-357/89, *V.J.M. Raulin v. Minister van Onderwijs en Wetenschappen*.

Article 10 EC (duty of loyal cooperation) requires the competent authorities in the Member States to use all the means at their disposal to achieve the aim of Article 39 EC.[877]

5.1.1 Employment

This concept must be defined in accordance with objective criteria which distinguish the employment relationship by reference to the rights and duties of the persons concerned.[878] The essential feature of an employment relationship is that for a certain period of time a person performs services for and under the direction of another person, in return for which he or she receives remuneration.[879] Activities which are non-economic in nature, such as purely amateur sport,[880] a course of study,[881] or certain appearances in national teams[882] do not fall under the concept of employment. In a number of cases, the general non-discrimination provision (Art. 12 EC) or the provisions on citizenship (Art. 18 EC) can offer the comfort of a safety net.[883] A traineeship which is used as practical preparation directly related to the actual pursuit of the occupation concerned may well be sufficient for the trainee to be regarded as a worker.[884]

The test which must be satisfied is whether effective and genuine work is being undertaken;[885] the fact that this is remunerated at less than the national minimum wage is irrelevant.[886]

---

877. Case C-165/91, *Simon J. M. van Munster v. Rijksdienst voor Pensioenen*.
878. Case 66/85, *Lawrie-Blum v. Land Baden-Württemberg*; Case C-3/87 *The Queen v. Ministry of Agriculture, Fisheries and Food, ex parte Agegate Ltd*; Case C-176/96, *Jyri Lethonen and Castors Canada Dry Namur-Braine ASBL v. Fédération royale belge des sociétés de basketball ASBL (FRBSB)*. Cf. Case C-186/01, *Dory*; Case C-413/01, *Orasche*; Case C-138/02 *Brian Francis Collins v. Secretary of State for Work and Pensions*.
879. See for an example of the application of this principle, e.g., Case 196/87 *Udo Steymann v. Staatssecretaris van Justitie*; see Case 344/87 *I. Bettray v. Staatssecretaris van Justitie*; see most recently C-43/99, *Ghislain Leclere and Alina Deaconescu v. Caisse Nationale des Prestations Familiales*. For the link between a marital relationship and the employer-employee relationship, see Case C-337/97, *C.P.M. Meeusen v. Hoofddirectie van de Informatie Beheer Groep*. For payment in kind, Case C-95/03, *Piliego*.
880. This can be deduced *a contrario* from Case 36/74, *Walrave*.
881. Case C-224/98, *D'Hoop*; Case C-184/99, *Grzelczyk*; Case 413/01, *Orasche*. See K.J.M. Mortelmans and R.H. van Ooik, *Europees recht en Nederlandse studiefinanciering* (Deventer, 2003).
882. Case 36/74, *Walrave*; Case 13/76, *Gaetano Donà v. Mario Mantero;* but see Joined Cases C-51/96 & C-191/97, *Deliège*.
883. Case C-184/99, *Grzelczyk*, which indicates that the restricted interpretation given to the scope ratione personae of the provisions in the EEC Treaty before the Treaty of Maastricht in Case 197/86, *Brown*, is no longer valid. See also Case C-403/03, *Schempp*; Case C-96/04, *Standesamt Stadt Niebüll*; Case C-406/04, *De Cuyper*; Case C-192/05, *K. Tas-Hagen*.
884. Case 66/85, *Lawrie-Blum*. See also Case C-3/90, *M. J. E. Bernini v. Minister van Onderwijs en Wetenschappen*, and Case C-413/01, *Orasche*.
885. Case 66/85, *Lawrie-Blum*; Case C-3/90, *Bernini*; Case C-278/94, *Commission v. Belgium*; Case C-224/98, *D'Hoop*; Case C-456/02, *Trojani*.
886. Case 53/81, *Levin*; Case 139/85, *Kempf*.

The question whether a person is engaged in effective and genuine work is a question of fact for the national court to decide; the irregular nature of work actually performed and the length of time may be taken into account.[887] Activities performed for the Salvation Army may be qualified as work in the sense of Article 39 EC.[888]

According to a declaration noted in the minutes of the Council meeting at which Regulation 1612/68, concerning free movement of workers, was approved, the nationals of a Member State have the right not merely to take up an offer of work, but also the right to spend up to three months in another Member State seeking work.[889] In *Antonissen*, the legal force of the declaration was diminished, and the Court ruled that in certain circumstances a period of six months to look for work was also reasonable.[890] Article 14 of Directive 2004/38[891] determines that Union citizens who have gone to another Member State to seek employment may not be expelled as long as they can provide evidence that they are continuing to seek employment and that they have a genuine chance of being engaged.

5.1.2 Nationality of Employees

According to Article 39(2) EC and Article 1 of Regulation 1612/68, free movement of workers benefits workers who are nationals of a Member State.[892] These rules apply to persons who have made use of their right of free movement.[893] They also apply to persons who possess dual nationality.[894] Nationals of a Member State who work for an international organization may rely on the free movement provisions.[895] In certain cases, nationals of a Member State who are posted to a third

---

887. Case C-357/89 *Raulin;* Case C-85/96, *María Martínez Sala v. Freistaat Bayern.*
888. Case C-456/02, *Trojani.*
889. See on this J.W.S. Pabon, *Het vrije verkeer van werknemers binnen de Europese Gemeenschap definitief tot stand gebracht* (1968) SMA, 754.
890. Case C-292/89, *The Queen v. Immigration Appeal Tribunal, ex parte Gustaff Desiderius Antonissen.* See also Case C-171/95, *Recep Tetik v. Land Berlin*; Case C-344/95, *Commission v. Belgium.*
891. O.J 2004 L 158/77.
892. Case 238/83, *Caisse d'Allocations Familiales de la Région Parisienne v. Mr and Mrs Richard Meade*; Case C-355/89, *Department of Health and Social Security v. Christopher Stewart Barr and Montrose Holdings Ltd*; Case C-171/96, *Rui Alberto Pereira Roque v. His Excellency the Lieutenant Governor of Jersey.*
893. Case 246/80, *C. Broekmeulen v. Huisarts Registratie Commissie*; Case 235/87, *Annunziata Matteucci v. Communauté française of Belgium and Commissariat général aux relations internationales of the Communauté française of Belgium.*
894. Case 292/86, *Claude Gullung v. Conseil de l'ordre des avocats du barreau de Colmar et de Saverne.*
895. Joined Cases 389 & 390/87, *G. B. C. Echternach and A. Moritz v. Minister van Onderwijs en Wetenschappen;* Case C-209/01, *Theodor Schilling, Angelika Fleck-Schilling v. Finanzamt Nürnberg-Süd.* Officials employed by the Community do come within the free movement of workers; they are not workers in the sense of the European social security rules; see Case C-411/98, *Angelo Ferlini v. Centre Hospitalier de Luxembourg.*

country may also be able to invoke Articles 39–42 EC.[896] Cross-border workers come within the scope of these provisions.[897] A national of a Member State who died before his country acceded to the Union does not come within the definition of a worker, with the result that his family members may not claim equal treatment under these provisions.[898]

Free movement of workers is regulated in Articles 28–30 of the EEA Agreement; in essence, the EC rules are declared to be applicable.[899] For workers coming from the overseas countries and territories (OCT), such as the Netherlands Antilles and Aruba, a special provision is included in Article 186 EC (cf. Art. 42 Regulation 1612/68), which does not guarantee free movement. Free movement of workers does not apply to third-country nationals.[900] Special rules have been included in a number of association agreements, concluded both with European[901] and non-European countries.[902]

In recent case law concerning prostitutes from East Europe the Court of Justice established that prostitution is an economic activity, and the persons in question could rely on the relevant provisions in the Europe Agreements, which were then in force, and concluded that the provisions on establishment in those agreements were also applicable to self-employed prostitutes. It should be noted that this concerned self-employment and not employment (see further section 6.2 below). The immigration authorities have the duty to verify that this is indeed the case.[903] This case law reveals that the distinction between employment and self-employment remains significant. There has also been case law on the Europe Agreements relating to other professions, such as university lecturers and sportsmen. In *Pokrzeptowicz-Meyer*,[904] the Court considered that Article 37(1) first indent of the Europe Agreement with Poland – corresponding to Article 39(2) EC – was directly effective. This provision was applicable as of the entry into force of the relevant Europe

896. Case 237/83 *SARL Prodest v. Caisse Primaire d'Assurance Maladie de Paris*, and Case C-214/94 *Ingrid Boukhalfa v. Bundesrepublik Deutschland*.
897. Case C-57/96, *H. Meints v. Minister van Landbouw, Natuurbeheer en Visserij*; Case C-336/96, *Gilly*; Case C-35/97, *Commission v. France*; Case C-337/97, *Meeusen*.
898. Case C-131/96, *Carlos Mora Romero v. Landesversicherungsanstalt Rheinprovinz*.
899. For EC-Switzerland relations, O.J. 2002, L 114. Breitenmoser, 'Sectoral Agreements between the EC and Switzerland: Contents and Context' (2003) CML Rev., 1137–1186.
900. Case 65/77, *Jean Razanatsimba*.
901. In particular, the so-called Europe Agreements with East European countries. See further Ch. XIII.
902. Case 65/77, *Razanatsimba*; Case C-103/94, *Zoulika Krid v. Caisse nationale d'assurance vieillesse des travailleurs salariés (CNAVTS)*; Case C-33/99, *Hassan Fahmi and M. Esmoris Cerdeiro-Pinedo Amado v. Bestuur van de Sociale Verzekeringsbank*.
903. Case C-63/99, *The Queen v. Secretary of State for the Home Department, ex parte Wieslaw Gloszczuk et Elzbieta Gloszczuk*; Case C-235/99, *The Queen v. Secretary of State for the Home Department, ex parte Eleanora Ivanova Kondova*; Case C-257/99, *The Queen v. Secretary of State for the Home Department, ex parte Julius Barkoci and Marcel Malik*; Case C-268/99, *Jany*; Case C-327/02, *Lili Georgieva Panayotova, Radostina Markova Kalcheva, Izabella Malgorzata Lis, Lubica Sopova, Izabela Leokadia Topa, Jolanta Monika Rusiecka, v. Minister voor Vreemdelingenzaken en Integratie*.
904. Case C-162/00, *Land Nordrhein-Westfalen v. Beata Pokrzeptowicz-Meyer*.

Agreement to employment contracts of limited duration which were concluded before the entry into force of the Europe Agreement for a period which ended after that entry into force. In *Kolpak*,[905] the Court considered that Article 38(1) of the Europe Agreement with Slovakia precluded the application to a professional sportsman of Slovak nationality, who is lawfully employed by a club established in a Member State, of a rule drawn up by a sports federation in that State under which clubs are authorized to field, during league or cup matches, only a limited number of players from non-member countries that are not parties to the Agreement on the EEA.

The Association agreement with Turkey grants Turkish workers within the EC extensive rights of access to the market.[906] In the case law, the concept 'worker' in the sense of the Association agreement – and in particular Decision 1/80 of the EEC-Turkey Association Council – is interpreted in the same way as the concept of worker in Article 39 EC.[907]

In *Rush Portuguesa* the Court pronounced on the rights of a certain category of workers from non-Member States.[908] The case concerned workers from Portugal who did not at the time come within the scope of Article 39 EC, as the transitional period had not yet expired. Nevertheless, they could make indirect use of the rights of freedom of movement, since the rules on provision of services were already applicable, without restriction, during the transitional period, and the Portuguese employer was therefore entitled to take his Portuguese workers to French territory to work there. This case law remains significant in the light of the recent new accessions, also with transitional arrangements for free movement of workers.[909] The whole question of Community provisions concerning posted workers proved controversial, and it was not until December 1996 that Directive 96/71 was finally adopted.[910]

---

905. Case C-438/00, *Deutscher Handballbund v. Kolpak*; see extensive annotation by J.-P. Dubey, 42 CML Rev., 499–522.
906. For an analysis of the case law on Turkish workers, see B. Cicekli, 'The Rights of Turkish Migrants in Europe under International and EU Law' (1999) *International Migration Review*, 300–353; F. Weiss and F. Wooldridge, *Free Movement of Persons within the EU*, 2nd ed. (The Hague, 2007), 207–220.
907. Case C-171/95, *Tetik*; Case C-36/96, *Faik Günaydin, Hatice Günaydin, Günes Günaydin and Seda Günaydin v. Freistaat Bayern*; Case C-98/96, *Kasim Ertanir v. Land Hessen*; Case C-340/97, *Ömer Nazli, Caglar Nazli and Melike Nazli v. Stadt Nürnberg*; Case C-188/00, *Bülent Kurz, né Yüce v. Land Baden-Württemberg* and Case C-171/01, *Wählergruppe Gemeinsam Zajedno/Birlikte Alternative und Grüne GewerkschafterInnen/UG*; Joined Cases C-317 & 369/01, *Eran Abatay and Others & Nadi Sahin v. Bundesanstalt für Arbeit*, Case C-373/02, *Sakir Öztürk v. Pensionsversicherungsanstalt der Arbeiter*.
908. Case C-113/89, *Rush Portuguesa Ld^a v. Office national d'immigration*; Case 9/88, *Mário Lopes da Veiga v. Staatssecretaris van Justitie*; Case C-43/93, *Raymond Vander Elst v. Office des Migrations Internationales*. See also Case C-445/03, *Commission v. Luxembourg*, and Case C-244/04, *Commission v. Germany*.
909. See further Ch. XIII.
910. O.J. 1997, L 18/1. See Joined Cases C-369 & 376/96, *Criminal proceedings against Jean-Claude Arblade and Arblade & Fils SARL and Bernard Leloup, Serge Leloup and Sofrage SARL*; Case C-164/99, *Portugaia Construções L^da*. Case C-490/04, *Commission v. Germany;*

5.2   MIGRATION RIGHTS (EXIT, ENTRY AND RESIDENCE)

In the previous edition of this work, these rights were discussed at this point, because they were originally developed in the context of the free movement of workers. The development of citizenship of the Union, and the position of nationals who are not economically active in that context, has led to this subject being treated more generally, in the new section 4.5 above.

5.3   RIGHTS OF ACCESS TO THE MARKET

Just as in the case of the other freedoms, the EC Treaty contains a prohibition (in this case of discrimination based on nationality) whose aim is to achieve the free movement of workers; this prohibition is discussed in section 5.3.1 below. The Treaty provides for certain exceptions on the basis of which the Member States may refuse access to their market; these exceptions are discussed in section 5.3.2, below. In both areas there has been case law on the interpretation of the relevant provisions, and the Court has taken inspiration from its case law on free movement of goods for certain aspects.[911] For this reason, where possible the same scheme and elements are used as for free movement of goods. The general warning about convergence is applicable here too (see section 1.6 above).

5.3.1   The Prohibition

5.3.1.1   Addressees

The prohibition contained in Article 39 EC does not only apply to the public authorities, but extends also to legal relationships governed by private law, such as collective bargaining agreements[912] and rules of (national) sport organizations,[913] and in some cases action by private parties.[914] The prohibition may be relied on by employers as well as employees.[915]

5.3.1.2   Internal Situation

In a number of cases the Court has indicated that workers/nationals who do not leave their own Member State, and thus do not physically carry out activities in

---

R. Giesen, 'Posting: Social Protection of Workers vs. Fundamental Freedoms?' (2003) CML Rev., 143–158; Case C-341/05, *Laval un Partneri* and Case C-438/05, *Viking*.

911.   See on this C. Barnard, 'Fitting the Remaining Pieces into the Goods and Persons Jigsaw?' (2001) EL Rev., 35.

912.   Case C-212/99, *Commission v. Italy*.

913.   Case 36/74, *Walrave*; Case C-415/93, *Bosman*; Case C-176/96, *Lethonen*; Case C-411/98, *Ferlini*.

914.   Case C-281/98, *Angonese* (see also section 1.6 *supra*).

915.   Case C-350/96, *Clean Car Autoservice v. Landeshauptmann von Wien*.

another Member State, do not fall within the ambit of the provisions, as they are in a purely internal situation.[916] An Italian who acquired French nationality and was confronted with discriminatory social security rules, was found to come within the rules on free movement of workers.[917]

5.3.1.3 Obstacles to Entry and Exit

Although the Treaty is silent on the point, obstacles to leaving the employment market of a Member State are covered by the prohibition as well as obstacles to entering the employment market of a Member State.[918]

5.3.1.4 Keck or Access to the Market

In *Bosman*,[919] the Union of European Football Associations (UEFA, which was a party in one of the national proceedings) argued that – in analogy with the *Keck* rule[920] – the rules at issue corresponded to 'selling arrangements', so that the contested acts did not fall within the scope of the prohibition. The Court rejected this argument, referring to its judgment in *Alpine Investments*,[921] concerning freedom to provide services. The Court considered that the rules in issue directly affected players' access to the employment market in other Member States and were thus capable of impeding freedom of movement for workers.[922] From this it may be inferred that in interpreting the prohibition in Article 39 EC the Court does not use a *Keck* approach, but uses the approach based on access to the market.[923]

5.3.1.5 Hypothetical Situations

In *Graf*,[924] the Court applied its case law on hypothetical situations in the area of free movement of goods,[925] with explicit references, to conclude that a national rule concerning compensation on termination of employment came outside the

---

916. E.g., Joined Cases 35 & 36/82, *Morson and Jhanjan*; Case C-332/90, *Steen*. In Case C-415/93, *Bosman*, this argument was rejected. The same thing happened in Case C-459/99, *MRAX*, where a third country national was found to have a link, since he was married to a Community national who had made use of the right of free movement.
917. Case C-55/00, *Elide Gottardo v. Istituto nazionale della previdenza sociale (INPS)*. See also Case C-212/06, *Government of the French Community and the Walloon Government v. Flemish Government*.
918. Case C-415/93, *Bosman*.
919. Case C-415/93, *Bosman*.
920. Joined Cases C-267 & 268/91, *Keck and Mithouard*.
921. Case C-384/93, *Alpine Investments*.
922. Case C-415/93, *Bosman*. See also Case C-176/96, *Lethonen*.
923. C. Barnard and S. Deakin, 'Market Access and Regulatory Competition', in C. Barnard and J. Scott (eds), *The Law of the Single European Market: Unpacking the Premises* (Oxford, 2002), 197.
924. Case C-190/98, *Graf*.
925. Case C-69/88, *Krantz*, and Case C-44/98, *BASF*.

scope of the prohibition contained in Article 39 EC. In some cases the Court has mentioned hypothetical situations in relation to its reasoning in the case at hand.[926]

5.3.1.6   Restrictive Measures: Distinctly and Indistinctly Applicable Measures

According to Article 39(2) EC, freedom of movement of workers entails the abolition of any discrimination based on nationality between workers of the Member States as regards employment, remuneration and other conditions of work and employment. This covers regional discrimination[927] as well as cases of discrimination whereby a Community national is in a less favourable position than a worker from a third country.[928]

The prohibition extends to disguised and indirect discrimination[929] such as residence requirements,[930] the registration plate of a car,[931] or a certain kind of proof of linguistic capacity,[932] as well as overt discrimination.[933] There is no discrimination if there are objective differences in the situations concerned, or objective reasons for making a distinction.[934]

Recently, in *Collins*,[935] the Court ruled that Article 39 EC, read in conjunction with Articles 12 and 17 of the Treaty, does not preclude national legislation which makes entitlement to a jobseeker's allowance conditional on a residence requirement, insofar as that requirement may be justified on the basis of objective considerations that are independent of the nationality of the persons concerned and proportionate to the legitimate aim of the national provisions. This approach (different treatment may be based on objective differences) is also used in cases where there is no specific Treaty prohibition, but the Court interprets the general

---

926. See, e.g., Case C-415/93, *Bosman*, and Case C-302/97, *Klaus Konle v. Republik Österreich*.
927. Case C-281/98, *Angonese*.
928. Case C-55/00, *Gottardo*. See also Case 235/87, *Matteucci*.
929. Case C-419/92, *Scholz v. Opera Universitaria di Cagliari and Cinzia Porcedda*; Case C-237/94, *O'Flynn v. Adjudication Officer*; Case C-15/96, *Schöning-Kougebetopoulou*; Case C-195/98, *Österreichischer Gewerkschaftsbund*; Case C-212/99, *Commission v. Italy*; Case C-224/01, *Gerhard Köbler v. Republik Österreich*.
930. Case 41/84, *Pinna v. Caisse d'allocations familiales de la Savoie*; Case 33/88, *Allué et al. v. Università degli studi di Venezia (Allué I)*; Case C-175/88, *Biehl v. Administration des contributions*; Case C-300/90, *Commission v. Belgium*; Case C-27/91, *URSSAF v. Hostellerie Le Manoir*; Case C-279/93, *Finanzamt Köln-Altstadt v. Schumacker*; Case C-18/95, *F.C. Terhoeve v. Inspecteur van de Belastingdienst Particulieren/Ondernemingen buitenland*; Case C-350/96, *Clean Car*; Case C-190/98, *Graf*; Case C-355/98, *Commission v. Belgium*.
931. Case C-232/01, *van Lent*. See also Joined Cases C-151 & 152/04, *Criminal proceedings against Nadin et al.*
932. Case C-281/98, *Angonese*.
933. Case 225/85, *Commission v. Italy*; Case C-278/94, *Commission v. Belgium*; Case C-336/94, *Dafeki v. Landesversicherungsanstalt Württemberg*; Case C-348/96, *Calfa*; Case C-258/04, *Office national de l'Emploi v. Ioannidis*.
934. Case 152/73, *Sotgiu v. Deutsche Bundespost*; Case C-237/94, *O'Flynn*.
935. Case C-138/02, *Collins*.

non-discrimination provision of Article 12 EC in order to deal with the case.[936] In certain cases involving taxation the Court took a different approach (see 5.5 below).

In a number of cases, the question arose whether indistinctly applicable measures (non-discriminatory restrictions) come within the scope of the prohibition of Article 39 EC.[937] Some of the judgments of the court from the 1980s had already pointed in this direction.[938] The *Bosman* case indicated unambiguously that certain indistinctly applicable measures came within the scope of the prohibition of Article 39.[939] This judgment fits in with the Court's case law on freedom to provide services (e.g., *Kraus*)[940] and freedom of establishment (*Gebhard*).[941]

In *Graf*,[942] the Court repeated its line of argument in *Bosman*: the Court stated that a measure which is indistinctly applicable will only be caught by Article 39 if it affects the access of workers to the employment market, which was not the case in the circumstances at issue. The Court considered that *Graf* concerned a hypothetical situation, which was not to be considered as liable to hinder freedom of movement of workers.[943]

In *Weigel*,[944] the Court considered that the Treaty offers no guarantee to a worker that transferring his activities to a Member State other than the one in which he previously resided will be neutral as regards taxation. Given the disparities in the legislation of the Member States in this area, such a transfer may be to the worker's advantage in terms of indirect taxation or not, according to circumstances. It follows that, in principle, any disadvantage, by comparison with the situation in which the worker pursued his activities prior to the transfer, is not contrary to Article 39 EC if that legislation does not place that worker at a disadvantage as compared with those who were already subject to it

5.3.1.7 Regulation 1612/68

The prohibition of discrimination on the ground of nationality is worked out in considerable detail in Regulation 1612/68.[945] The most important provisions of the regulation, which have been the subject of considerable judicial scrutiny, are those concerning employment and equality of treatment, and those concerning the

---

936. Case C-411/98, *Ferlini*. See also Case C-148/02, *Garcia Avello*. And see Ch. III of this book.
937. L. Daniele, Non-Discriminatory Restrictions to the Free Movement of Persons (1997), EL Rev., 191.
938. Case 96/85, *Commission v. France*; Case 143/87, *Stanton v. Inasti*; Joined Cases 154 & 155/87, *Inasti v. Wolf and others*; Case 33/88, *Allué I*; Case C-204/90, *Bachmann*; Case C-300/90, *Commission v. Belgium*.
939. Case C-415/93, *Bosman;* implicitly also Case C-176/96, *Lethonen*.
940. Case C-19/92, *Kraus*. See also Joined Cases C-259, 331 & 332/91, *Allué and others v. Università degli studi di Venezia and others (Allué II)*; Case C-272/92, *Spotti v. Freistaat Bayern*.
941. Case C-55/94, *Gebhard*.
942. Case C-190/98, *Graf*.
943. Case C-190/98, *Graf*. See also Case C-285/01, *Burbaud*.
944. Case C-387/01, *Weigel*.
945. O.J. 1968, L 257/2.

rights of members of a worker's family.[946] This regulation is also amended by the new Directive 2004/38, discussed above.[947] In recent case law the Court has put great emphasis on the protection of family life of nationals of the Member States.[948]

Article 3(1) concerns linguistic knowledge.[949] Article 7(1) on equal treatment has been interpreted to mean that national measures concerning absence for military service,[950] a benefit under a career-break benefit scheme,[951] special protection granted on social grounds,[952] and separation allowances[953] can all come within the scope of this provision.

The concepts of social advantages[954] and tax advantages,[955] which Article 7(2) of the regulation requires to be available on equal terms, has given rise to considerable case law. This provision applies solely to a worker and his or her family,[956] and not to persons seeking employment.[957] On many occasions the Court has been called to consider social advantages in situations where the children of migrant workers are hindered in relation to education facilities, for instance in relation to student grants.[958] Article 7(3) of the regulation specifically requires equal treatment in access to training in vocational schools and retraining centres for workers. These cases concern training with a view to the exercise of a trade or profession.[959] The case law in this area has been further developed through the

---

946. Case 94/84, *ONEM v. Deak*; Case C-337/97, *Meeusen*.
947. Section 4.5.2 *supra*.
948. Case C-459/99, *MRAX*; Case C-60/00, *Carpenter*.
949. '[C]onditions relating to linguistic knowledge required by reason of the nature of the post to be filled' are permissible: Case C-379/87, *Groener*; Case C-281/98, *Angonese*.
950. Case 15/69, *Württembergische Milchverwertung Südmilch v. Ugliola;* see, however, Case C-315/94, *de Vos v. Stadt Bielefeld*.
951. Case C-469/02, *Commission v. Belgium*.
952. Case 44/72, *Marsman v. Rosskamp*.
953. Case 152/73, *Sotgiu*.
954. Case 32/75, *Cristini v. S.N.C.F.*; Case 207/78, *Ministère public v. Even*; Case 65/81, *Reina v. Landeskreditbank Baden-Württemberg*; Case 249/83, *Hoeckx v. Openbaar Centrum voor Maatschappelijk Welzijn Kalmthout*; Case 137/84, *Ministère public v. Mutsch*; Case 59/85, *Reed*; Case 39/86, *Lair v. Universität Hannover*; Case 197/86, *Brown*; Case C-3/90, *Bernini*; Case C-326/90, *Commission v. Belgium*; Case C-310/91, *Schmid v. Belgium*; Case C-237/94, *O'Flynn*; Case C-85/96, *Martínez Sala*; Case C-185/96, *Commission v. Greece*; Case C-35/97, *Commission v. French Republic*; Case C-356/98, *Kaba I*; Case C-411/98, *Ferlini*; Case C-43/99, *Leclere*; Case C-184/99, *Grzelczyk*; Case C-466/00, *Kaba II*; Case C-299/01, *Commission v. Luxembourg*. In a number of cases, there is a close link between the social advantage and social security; see Case C-165/91, *Van Munster*; Case C-262/97, *Rijksdienst voor Pensioenen v. Engelbrecht*; Case C-386/02 *Josef Baldinger v. Pensionsversicherungsanstalt der Arbeiter*; Case C-212/05, *Hartmann v. Freistaat Bayern*; Case C-213/05, *Geveb v. Land Nordrhein-Westfalen*.
955. Case C-18/95, *Terhoeve*.
956. Case 261/83, *Castelli v. ONTPS*; Case 94/84, *Deak*; Case 157/84, *Frascogna v. Caisse des dépôts et consignations*; Case C-357/89, *Raulin*.
957. Case 316/85, *Lebon*.
958. Case 9/74, *Casagrande v. Landeshauptstadt München*; Case 39/86, *Lair*; Case 197/86, *Brown*; Case 235/87, *Matteucci*; Case C-3/90, *Bernini*; Case C-337/97, *Meeusen*; Case C-33/99, *Hassan Fahmi*; Case C-209/03, *Bidar*; Case C-258/04, *Ioannidis*.
959. Case 39/86, *Lair*; Case C-357/89, *Raulin*.

interpretation of what is now Article 150 EC, on vocational training (see Ch. XI of this book). In exceptional cases (private educational establishments), students can fall under the freedom to receive services, as they are recipients of educational services (see section 7 below).

Article 7(4) makes any clause of collective or individual agreements or any other collective regulation concerning eligibility for employment, remuneration and other conditions of work or dismissal null and void in so far as it lays down discriminatory conditions concerning workers who are nationals of other Member States.[960] Trade union and representation rights are set out in Article 8 of the regulation,[961] and equal treatment in access to housing is guaranteed by Article 9 of the Regulation.[962]

Articles 10 and 11, concerning family members of workers, were analysed above.[963] These provisions were repealed with effect from 30 April 2006, by application of Directive 2004/38.[964]

Article 12 of Regulation 1612/68 requires equal treatment in admission to the host Member State's general educational, apprenticeship and vocational training courses, if the children are residing in the territory of the host Member State.[965] This provision also embraces university education.[966]

Sometimes specific requirements are prescribed for the exercise of a particular profession in an employment situation, such as in the case of employed medical doctors. Article 6(1) of Regulation 1612/68 provides that 'the engagement and recruitment of a national of one Member State for a post in another Member State shall not depend on medical, vocational or other criteria which are discriminatory on grounds of nationality'.

Articles 47 and 55 EC, concerning establishment and services, confer competence on the Community to adopt directives concerning mutual recognition of diplomas.[967] As a result of the adoption of a number of directives, mutual recognition of diplomas has largely been achieved.[968] In some instances, the obligation to compare diplomas obtained in the Member State of origin with the requirements

---

960. Case C-15/96, *Schöning-Kougobetopoulou*.
961. Case 36/75, *Rutili*; Case C-213/90, *ASTI v. Chambre des employés privés*; Case C-465/01, *Commission v. Austria*.
962. Case 305/87, *Commission v. Greece*.
963. See section 4.5 *supra*.
964. O.J. 2004, L 229/35.
965. See, e.g., Case 76/72, *S. v. Fonds national de reclassement social des handicaps*; Case 263/86, *Belgium v. Humbel*; Case C-308/89, *Di Leo v. Land Berlin*, and Case C-7/94, *Landesamt für Ausbildungsfrdeung Land Nordrhein-Westfalen v. Gaal*; Case C-413/99, *Baumbast*.
966. Cases 389 and 390/87 *Echternach and Moritz*.
967. See also Art. 45 Reg. 1612/68, O.J. 1968, L 257/2.
968. Dir. 89/48 (O.J. 1989, L 19/16) concerning higher education diplomas awarded on completion of professional education and training of at least three years' duration; Dir. 92/51 (O.J. 1992, L 209/25) for the recognition of professional education and training; Dir. 1999/42, supplementary directive on professional activities, O.J. 1999, L 201/77. The three directives were replaced by Dir. 2005/36/EC of the European Parliament and of the Council of 7 Sep. 2005 on the recognition of professional qualifications, O.J. 2005, L 255/22.

in the host Member State is sufficient. The mutual recognition concept developed in relation to the freedom to provide services and the freedom of establishment also applies, where appropriate, to the free movement of workers.[969]

5.3.2   Exceptions to Market Access

In a number of situations a host Member State may invoke exceptions which have the effect of preventing a migrant worker who is admitted to its territory from exercising a particular activity; these concern individual cases. Employment market policy in general, as a part of social policy, falls under the system of Article 137 EC (see Ch. X of this book).

5.3.2.1   *Employment in the Public Service*

Article 39(4) EC provides that the provisions of Article 39 EC 'shall not apply to employment in the public service'. This exception – which also exists, in slightly different wording, in relation to self-employed (see Art. 45 EC) – has been narrowly interpreted by the Court of Justice, in line with its approach of interpreting fundamental freedoms broadly and exceptions narrowly.[970] Thus it cannot justify discriminatory measures against workers who have already been admitted to the public service.[971] The Member States may not extend the scope of the exception by bringing various functions within the public sector.[972] The exception only applies to a limited number of posts. According to the Court, the exception only covers posts which are typical of the specific task of the state – i.e., functions which directly or indirectly involve the exercise of public authority and which involve duties which aim to protect general interests of the state or other public bodies.[973] Thus, the Court has ruled that railway workers,[974] teachers,[975] private security staff,[976] certain medical specialists[977] and hospital directors[978] are outside the

---

969. Case 222/86, *Heylens*; Case C-234/97, *Fernández de Bobadilla v. Museo Nacional del Prado*.
970. Case C-473/93, *Commission v. Luxembourg*; Case C-173/94, *Commission v. Belgium*; Case C-290/94, *Commission v. Greece*; Case C-248/96, *Grahame and Hollanders v. Bestuur van de Nieuwe Algemene Bedrijfsvereniging*; Case C-195/98, *Österreichischer Gewerkschaftsbund*. The Commission indicated, in a communication of 18 Mar. 1988, that it would supervise the correct interpretation of this provision, O.J. 1988, C 72/2.
971. Case 152/73, *Sotgiu*; Case C-195/98, *Österreichischer Gewerkschaftsbund*; Case C-103/01, *Commission v. Germany*.
972. Case 307/84, *Commission v. France*.
973. Case 2/74, *Reyners*; Case 149/79, *Commission v. Belgium*; Case C-42/92, *Thijssen v. Controledienst voor de verzekeringen*; Case C-419/92, *Scholz*; Case C-114/97, *Commission v. Spain*.
974. Case 149/79, *Commission v. Belgium*.
975. Case 66/85, *Lawrie-Blum*; Case 33/88, *Allué I*; Case C-4/91, *Bleis v. Ministère de l'Éducation nationale*; Case C-473/93, *Commission v. Luxembourg*; Case C-90/96, *Petrie and others v. Università degli studi di Verona and Bettoni*.
976. Case C-114/97, *Commission v. Spain*.
977. Case C-15/96, *Schöning-Kougebetopoulou*.
978. Case C-285/01, *Burbaud*

scope of this exception. On the other hand, municipal architects are covered,[979] and so are management functions and state advisory functions in public research bodies for scientific and technical matters.[980]

5.3.2.2   Treaty Exceptions

The Treaty-based exceptions, contained in Article 39(3) EC, i.e., public policy, public security and public health, are mainly relied on in cases involving migration.[981] They concern primarily 'foreign nationals' (see section 4.5. above).

5.3.2.3   Rule-of-Reason Exceptions

The extensive interpretation given to the prohibition in Article 39 EC, which in certain cases also covers indistinctly applicable measures, is somewhat counter-balanced by the acceptance in the case law of exceptions based on a rule-of-reason, similar to the *Cassis de Dijon* approach in relation to free movement of goods.[982] Although, as with the other freedoms, the Court usually puts the burden of proof on the parties themselves,[983] the Court does exceptionally take the initiative in order to see whether an exception may be invoked although the parties had not mentioned this.[984]

In *Pfeiffer Großhandel*,[985] which concerned free movement of persons and freedom of establishment (as well as free movement of goods), the Court cited its earlier ruling allowing rule-of-reason exceptions in these areas under certain conditions, *Gebhard*[986] (see section 6.5.2 below). Although these justifications based on overriding requirements in the general interest should – according to previous case law – only be permitted in relation to indistinctly applicable measures, it appears from certain judgments in the area of taxation, in particular, such as *Bachmann* and *Terhoeve*,[987] that the Court in principle also considers these rule-of-reason exceptions to be applicable to distinctly applicable measures in the area of direct taxation (see further section 5.5. below). This approach is very similar to that taken in the *Wallonian waste* case[988] and the free movement of goods.[989] In *Biehl*[990] and *Bachmann*,[991] the Court introduced a fiscal exception,

---

979. Case 149/79, *Commission v. Belgium.*
980. Case 225/85, *Commission v. Italy.*
981. Case 131/85, *Gül*; Case C-114/97, *Commission v. Spain.*
982. See section 1.6 *supra.*
983. Case 251/78, *Denkavit Futtermittel.*
984. Case C-209/01, *Schilling.*
985. Case C-255/97, *PfeifferGroßhandel.*
986. Case C-55/94, *Gebhard.*
987. Case C-204/90, *Bachmann*; Case C-18/95, *Terhoeve.*
988. Case C-2/90, *Commission v. Belgium.* See also Case C-379/98, *PreussenElektra.*
989. See section 3.3.3 *supra.*
990. Case C-175/88, *Biehl.*
991. Case C-204/90, *Bachmann.* Cf. Case C-279/93, *Schumacker.*

which in the form of 'the interest of the coherence of the fiscal system' was capable in the latter case of saving the national rule at issue. In another case, *De Groot*, this defence was not successful, however.[992] In the *Terhoeve* case,[993] a number of justifications were pleaded for the national rules in question (which concerned social security premiums), which were linked to the need to simplify and coordinate the tax and social security system. The Court did not accept these arguments as grounds of justification.

In *De Groot*, the argument that the tax disadvantage was to a large extent compensated by other elements in the tax system was not accepted, in view of the fundamental nature of the free movement of persons. The Court also rejected the argument that it is legitimate for the state of residence to take into account the personal and family circumstances of a resident taxpayer only in proportion to the income derived in its territory, since it is for the state of employment to do the same with respect to the share of income taxable in its territory. The Court based itself in this on the Model Double Taxation Convention of the Organization for Economic Cooperation and Development (OECD).[994]

The Court has found that the provisions of the EC Treaty, specifically Articles 39, 43 and 49 EC, do not preclude measures aiming at a legitimate objective, such as those intended to ensure the proper management of universities, but the principle of proportionality required that they be necessary and appropriate to the objective pursued.[995] A defence based on the need for 'up-to-date' instruction was not accepted in the relevant circumstances.[996] Neither was an exception based on a provision of the Austrian Constitution relating to 'the principle of homogeneity' for employees in the public service.[997] In *Burbaud*,[998] the objective of selecting 'the best candidates in the most objective conditions possible' was accepted as an overriding reason in the general interest (though the measure at issue was not accepted, as it was found not to be necessary). In *Lent*,[999] concerning registration of vehicles, road safety was invoked as a general interest, however it could not save the national rules in question.

In *Bosman*, a number of rule-of-reason exceptions were invoked, such as the social importance of sport and training of young players. These efforts did not clear the hurdle of proportionality. The exceptions were invoked to justify both distinctly applicable and indistinctly applicable measures.[1000] In *Lethonen*, rules laid

---

992. Case C-385/00, *De Groot*. See also Case C-209/01, *Schilling*.
993. Case C-18/95, *Terhoeve*.
994. Case C-385/00, *De Groot*. See R. Neubert, *Inhalt und Grenzen der Personenverkehrsfreiheiten bei Anwendung von Doppelbesteuerungsabkommen: die Vermeidung der Doppelbesteuerung des Einkommens zwischen Diskriminierung und Nichtharmonisierung in der Europäischen Union* (Berlin, 2002).
995. Case C-106/91, *Ramrath v. Ministre de la Justice*; Joined Cases C-259, 331 & 332/91, *Allué II*; Case C-19/92, *Kraus*.
996. Case 33/88, *Allué I*; Case C-272/92, *Spotti*.
997. Case C-195/98, *Österreichischer Gewerkschaftsbund*.
998. Case C-285/01, *Burbaud*, paras. 103–104.
999. C-232/01, *Lent*.
1000. Case C-415/93, *Bosman*.

down by sports associations concerning transfer periods were at issue. The Court of Justice imposed on the national court the task of judging the proportionality of this exception, which was in principle recognized as being capable of justifying national measures.[1001]

The Court has ruled that the right to take collective action for the protection of workers is a legitimate interest which, in principle, justifies a restriction of one of the fundamental freedoms guaranteed by the Treaty.[1002]

Finally, Community secondary legislation may provide for exceptions in certain circumstances. Thus the linguistic knowledge exception to the key requirement of Article 3(1) of Regulation 1612/68 mentioned at the end of section 5.3.1, above, must be borne in mind.[1003] That exception permits 'conditions relating to linguistic knowledge required by reason of the nature of the post to be filled'. In *Groener*, the Court ruled that the requirement was justified if it was part of a policy to promote the national language, which is also the first official language, and the requirement is applied in accordance with the principles of proportionality and non-discrimination.[1004]

5.4   Social Security Systems

The European Union recognizes and respects the entitlement to social security benefits. Everyone residing and moving legally within the European Union is entitled to social security benefits and social advantages in accordance with Community law and national laws and practices (cf. Art. 34 EU Charter of Fundamental Rights).

The movement of workers may not be hindered by the loss of rights in the area of social security, such as acquired pension rights. Thus Article 42 EC provides for a competence of the Council to take measures coordinating national social security provisions for migrant workers.[1005] The main objective of these measures is to remove a crucial obstacle to the free movement of workers.[1006] The most important relevant measure is Regulation 1408/71.[1007]

The Lisbon Treaty will introduce, in Article 48 TFEU, the following emergency brake procedure: Where a member of the Council declares that a draft legislative act referred to in the first subparagraph would affect important aspects

---

1001.   Case C-176/96, *Lethonen*.
1002.   See, to that effect, Case C-438/05, *Viking*.
1003.   See also Case 137/84, *Mutsch*; Case C-274/96, *Bickel and Franz*.
1004.   Case 379/87, *Groener*. See further Case C-281/98, *Angonese*. See on this A. Wolff-Pfisterer, *Sprache als Freizügigkeitshindernis in der EU: sprachliche Anforderungen an ausländische EG-Bürger im Rahmen des Anerkennung von Befähigungsnachweisen für den Berufszugang und die Berufsausübung* (Bremen, 2002).
1005.   Case 1/67, *Ciechelsky v. Caisse regionale de sécurité sociale du Centre*.
1006.   Case C-297/92, *Baglieri*.
1007.   O.J. 1971, L 149/2.

of its social security system, including its scope, cost or financial structure, or would affect the financial balance of that system, it may request that the matter be referred to the European Council. In that case, the ordinary legislative procedure shall be suspended. After discussion, the European Council shall, within four months of this suspension, either:(a) refer the draft back to the Council, which shall terminate the suspension of the ordinary legislative procedure; or (b) take no action or request the Commission to submit a new proposal; in that case, the act originally proposed shall be deemed not to have been adopted.

5.4.1   Regulation 1408/71: Workers, Self-employed, Third-Country Nationals

On the basis of Article 42 EC, the Council introduced, in 1971, a system where by migrant workers and their family members were guaranteed, *inter alia*, that insurance periods would be cumulated and that payments would be made to persons on the territory of the Member States. This Regulation replaced the original rules, contained in Regulations 3 and 4.[1008] Regulation 1408/71 took account of practice and the case law of the Court of Justice. In 1981 the scope of Regulation 1408/71 and the implementing regulation 574/72[1009] was extended to cover the self-employed and members of their families by means of Regulation 1390/81.[1010]

Regulation 859/2003 extended the provisions of Regulation 1408/71 to include third-country nationals who were not covered by the Community provisions merely because of their nationality.[1011]

5.4.2   The Aims of Regulation 1408/71

Regulation 1408/71 does not aim to harmonize national social security systems, but coordinates their application.[1012] There was no automatic harmonization at the end of the period envisaged for the completion of the internal market.[1013] Community law, therefore, does not restrict the power of the Member States to decide on their social security systems.[1014] Nonetheless, any amendment of the national system must take account of primary Community law.[1015]

1008.   O.J. 1958, 561 and 597.
1009.   O.J. 1972, L 74/1.
1010.   O.J. 1981, L 143/1.
1011.   O.J. 2003, L 124/1.
1012.   Case 9/67, *Colditz v. Caisse d'assurance vieillesse des travailleurs salariés*; Case 41/84, *Pinna*; Case C-227/89, *Rönfeldt v. Bundesversicherungsanstalt für Angestellte*.
1013.   Case C-297/92, *Baglieri*.
1014.   Case 238/82, *Duphar*; Case C-70/95, *Sodemare and others v. Regione Lombardia*; Case C-262/97, *Engelbrecht*.
1015.   Case C-385/99, *Müller-Fauré*.

5.4.3   Content of Regulation 1408/71

Regulation 1408/71 contains the following provisions. Title I sets out the definitions of the beneficiaries of the arrangements (such as worker[1016] and self-employed persons, refugees, and stateless persons,[1017] etc.) and of the key concepts, such as residence, insurance periods, benefits and pensions, legislation, and admission to voluntary or optional continued insurance.[1018]

As far as the applicability of social security legislation is concerned, the Member States apply different (territorial) starting points: this may in cross-border movements mean that a migrant falls under the legislation of more than one Member State (positive conflict of laws) or even under the legislation of no Member State at all (negative conflict of laws). Regulation 1408/71 does not contain any provision as to its territorial scope, so the provisions of Article 299 EC apply. Title I also deals with the most important principles on which the coordination of the national systems is based, namely equality of treatment,[1019] the relationship between benefits and residence[1020] and the prevention of overlapping of benefits;[1021] it also covers certain international agreements which remain unaffected.[1022]

Title II of Regulation 1408/71 deals with the legislation applicable. Article 13 ensures that the persons to whom the Regulation applies are subject to the legislation of a single Member State only, without prejudice to their rights under the rules concerning the coordination of the social security systems, in order to avoid any plurality or purposeless overlapping of contributions and liabilities which would result from the simultaneous or alternate application of several legislative systems.[1023] This Title also covers rules for posted workers, and deals with conflicts for certain special categories of persons, such as workers employed in international transport.

The very extensive provisions of Title III set out the special provisions relating to various categories of benefits, such as sickness and maternity, invalidity, old age and survivors' pensions, accidents at work and occupational diseases; death grants, and unemployment benefits; family and child benefits; and benefits for dependent children of pensioners, and for orphans. Title IV describes the powers of the Administrative Commission on Social Security for Migrant Workers. This Commission, composed of representatives of the governments and a representative of

---

1016. Case C-85/96, *Martínez Sala*; Case C-411/98, *Ferlini*.

1017. Joined Cases C-95–98 & 180/99, *Khalil and others*.

1018. Case C-297/92, *Baglieri*.

1019. Case 41/84, *Pinna*; Case C-105/89, *Buhari Haji v. INASTI*; Case C-10/90, *Masgio v. Bundesknappschaft*; Case C-18/90, *Office national de l'emploi v. Kziber*; Case C-326/90, *Commission v. Belgium*; Case C-165/91, *Van Munster*; Case C-262/97, *Engelbrecht*.

1020. Case 300/84, *Van Roosmalen v. Bestuur van de Bedrijfsvereniging voor de Gezondheid*.

1021. Case 1/67, *Ciechelski*; Case 2/67, *De Moor v. Caisse de pension des employés privés*; Case 238/81, *Van der Bunt-Craig*; Case 296/84, *Sinatra v. FNROM*.

1022. Case C-23/92, *Grana-Novoa v. Landesversicherungsanstalt Hessen*.

1023. Case 50/75, *Caisse des pension des employés privés v. Massonet*.

the European Commission, deals with questions of interpretation,[1024] and has a
number of administrative tasks, such as translations.

For an in-depth discussion of the Regulation and the relevant case law,
reference is made to specialized literature.[1025]

Some of the judgments in this field have a general social importance, such as
the judgments on the place of residence principle for child benefits.[1026] Other
judgments have acquired a political flavour because of overt criticism by and in
certain Member States, in particular the case law concerning workers who are sick,
and certificates of illness or incapacity issued by doctors in the country of
origin.[1027] The case law on the relationship between the social security rules
and private systems is also of great importance.[1028]

5.4.4   The New Regulation

At the end of April 2004, the Council and the European Parliament adopted
Regulation 883/2004 on the coordination of social security systems.[1029] This
Regulation which takes into account the case law of the Court of Justice will
replace Regulation 1408/71 on the date that the implementing Regulation (see
Art. 91 Regulation 883/2004) comes into force – at the time of writing, no imple-
menting regulation has yet been adopted.

5.5   TAXATION AND WORKERS

The more or less complete absence of harmonization in the field of direct taxation
(see section 6.9 below), gave the Court of Justice the opportunity to condemn a
number of instances of discrimination in the area of national income taxation, in
some seminal cases.[1030]

1024. These interpretations do not bind the national and Community bodies and courts; see Case 19/
       67, *Soziale Verzekeringsbank v. Van Der Vecht.*
1025. F.J. Pennings, *Introduction to European social security law*, 4th ed. Antwerp 2003;
       M. Moore, 'Freedom of Movement and Migrant Workers' Social Security: An Overview
       of the Case Law of the Court of Justice' (2002) CML Rev., 807. See also *European Journal of
       Social Security.*
1026. Case 41/84, *Pinna.*
1027. Case C-45/90, *Paletta v. Brennet*; Case C-360/90, *Arbeiterwohlfahrt der Stadt Berlin v.
       Bötel.* See on this 'Editorial Comments: Quis Custodiet the European Court of Justice'
       (1993) CML Rev., 899–903. See further Case C-206/94, *Brennet v. Paletta.*
1028. See the discussion in the Netherlands on the introduction of a new health insurance system:
       Naar een gezond stelsel van ziektekostenverzekeringen, SER opinion 00/12 (The Hague,
       2000). See in this context Case C-158/96, *Kohll*; Case C-368/98, *Vanbraekel and others*;
       Case C-157/99, *Smits and Peerbooms*; Case C-385/99, *Muller-Fauré*; Case C-326/00, *IKA*;
       Case C-156/01, *van der Duin v. ANOZ Zorgverzekeringen*; Case C-56/01 *Inizan.*
1029. O.J. 2004, L 166/1.
1030. See K. Lenaerts and L. Bernardeau, 'L'encadrement communautaire de la fiscalité directe'
       (2007) CDE, 19; S. Kingston, 'A Light in the Darkness: Recent Developments in the ECJ's
       Direct Tax Jurisprudence' (2007) CML Rev., 1321–1359.

The Court recognizes the powers of the Member States in the field of taxation, but adds – in conformity with the case law in the area of social security, for instance[1031] – that these powers may not result in such matters being put outside the scope of application of the freedoms.[1032] For instance, an argument by Member State A based on the fact that a taxpayer has the nationality of that Member State is rejected by the Court if the individual in question has (also) worked in Member State B.[1033] Furthermore, the fact that an individual is no longer in employment at the moment of taxation does not deprive him or her of the guarantee of certain rights associated with his status as a worker.[1034]

The Court was also faced with a situation involving bilateral tax treaties to avoid double taxation.[1035] The Court stated that, in the absence of Community rules, or in this case, of Community conventions under Article 293 EC, the rules on allocation of fiscal jurisdiction contained in these bilateral treaties were not contrary to Article 39 EC. The Court added that in such situations the Member States could base themselves on international practice which has developed on the basis of the OECD model convention.[1036]

In this chapter, we will not enter into the more technical and fiscal aspects of this subject, but some remarks will be made on the general principles of European law and the case law on taxation.[1037] After all, both the interpretation of the prohibition on discrimination and the justifications adduced raise certain questions.

Article 7(2) of Regulation 1612/68 gives an explicit basis for a prohibition on discrimination. According to this provision, migrant workers enjoy the same fiscal advantages as national workers.[1038] The cases concerning taxation seldom refer to this provision – partly because the national courts do not put questions in relation to it.[1039] They are based directly on Article 39 EC.[1040] In one case (*De Groot*), the Dutch Supreme Court did put a question about Article 7(2) of Regulation 1612/68, but the Court – in view of the answer given to the first question with respect to Article 48 – did not find it necessary to answer it.[1041]

In a number of taxation cases, the argument is used – at a more fundamental level of analysis – that domestic and foreign tax subjects are not in the same

1031. Case C-18/95, *Terhoeve*.
1032. Case C-391/97, *Gschwind*; Case C-35/98, *Staatssecretaris van Financiën v. B.G.M. Verkooijen*
1033. Case C-18/95, *Terhoeve*; Case C-385/00, *De Groot*.
1034. Case C-302/98, *Sehrer*; Case C-385/00, *De Groot*.
1035. Case C-336/96, *Gilly*
1036. Case C-336/96, *Gilly*. See also Case C-307/97, *Saint-Gobain*; Case C-385/00, *De Groot*.
1037. See also R. Wernsmann 'Steuerliche Diskriminierungen und ihre Rechtfertigung durch die Kohärenz des nationalen Rechts: Zur Dogmatik der Schranken der Grundfreiheiten' (1999) EuR, 754.
1038. See section 5.3.1. *supra.*
1039. See, however, Case C-18/95, *Terhoeve* and Case C-87/99, *Zurstrassen*.
1040. Case C-175/88, *Biehl*; Case C-204/90, *Bachmann*; Case C-300/90, *Commission v. Belgium*; Case C-112/91, *Werner*; Case C-279/93, *Schumacker*; Case C-391/97, *Gschwind*; Case C-169/03, *Wallentin*.
1041. Case C-385/00, *De Groot*.

objective situation, and may therefore be treated differently. The prohibition on discrimination is then deemed not to be applicable.[1042] This is the standard route,[1043] which sometimes results in applicability,[1044] and sometimes in non-applicability of Article 39 EC.[1045] In other cases, the prohibition is first ruled to be applicable, and then, at a later stage of analysis, an objective justification is sought.[1046] In this last group, the tax-related exception 'coherence of the fiscal system' comes into play. This rule-of-reason justification, which was introduced in *Bachmann*, was later subject to more conditions in *Wielockx* and *Svensson*.[1047]

For more information on these exceptions reference is made to the rule-of-reason exceptions in relation to free movement of workers.[1048] The case law on direct taxation of individuals is closely related to that in the field of company taxation (see sections 6.5.1 and 6.5.2, below) and in the field of free movement of capital (see section 8.4 below). In *Verkooijen*, concerning free movement of capital – in relation to investments – the two 'levels of analysis' (i.e., first examining whether two situations are objectively comparable, and then whether the difference could be justified by overriding reasons in the general interest) were explicitly mentioned, with references to *Schumacker* and *Bachmann*.[1049]

6   THE RIGHT OF ESTABLISHMENT

The free movement of persons mentioned in Article 3(1)(c) EC is not restricted to those in employment.[1050] The self-employed and undertakings (companies or firms) are also offered the opportunity of exercising economic activities within the internal market. The right of establishment, provided for in Articles 43–48 EC sets out the framework within which this takes place. The freedom of establishment has much in common with the freedom to provide (and receive) services. Both involve the free exercise of a trade or profession. The framers of the EC Treaty dealt with them successively, linking them by means of an

---

1042. Case C-279/93, *Schumacker*; Case C-336/96, *Gilly*; Case C-391/97, *Gschwind*; Case C-87/99, *Zurstrassen*. Case C-520/04, *Turpeinen*.
1043. See on this R.H. Lauwaars and C.W.A. Timmermans, *Europees Gemeenschapsrecht in kort bestek*, (Groningen, 2003), 214.
1044. E.g., Case C-87/99, *Zurstrassen*.
1045. E.g., Case C-391/97, *Gschwind*.
1046. Case C-204/90, *Bachmann*; Case C-80/94, *Wielockx v. Inspecteur der directe belastingen*; Case C-107/94, *Asscher v. Staatssecretaris van Financiën*; Case C-18/95, *Terhoeve*. See on this P. Wattel, *Rechtvaardigingsgronden voor fiscale inbreuk op de EG-Verdragsvrijheden* (1997) SEW, 433. See also Case C-209/01, *Schilling*.
1047. Case C-204/90, *Bachmann*; Case C-484/93, *Svensson and Gustavsson*; Case C-80/94, *Wielockx*. See on this P.J. Wattel, op. cit. previous footnote, 427.
1048. Section 5.3.2 *supra*.
1049. Case C-35/98, *Verkooijen*.
1050. See also Arts. 15, 16 and 52 EU Charter of Fundamental Rights.

incorporation by reference of certain provisions applying to establishment (Art. 55).[1051]

Besides this linkage within the provisions on free movement of persons,[1052] the influence of the market (particularly the increase in invisible transactions) and the development of the mutual recognition principle in the case law of the Court of Justice, have over the years caused a closer relationship to develop between the provisions on the freedom to provide services and those on the free movement of goods. This has been particularly evident in the telecommunications and media sectors. As indicated above,[1053] the case law of the Court is not without ambiguity. Given the existing divergences, it is important to identify a clear definition of the concept of establishment (section 6.1), and the beneficiaries of that right (section 6.2), as well as analysing the substantive provisions (sections 6.3 and 6.4), whereby a distinction is drawn between the prohibition of discrimination and the right of establishment on the one hand, and harmonization to facilitate the exercise of the right of establishment on the other (sections 6.5 and 6.6). Harmonization of company law is examined separately in section 6.7, banking, investment and insurance and taxation are dealt with separately (sections 6.8 and 6.9).

6.1   THE CONCEPT OF ESTABLISHMENT

The concept of establishment embraces activities other than those in the course of employment, on the part of natural and legal persons.[1054] The decisive criteria in deciding whether a particular activity falls under the heading of establishment are whether an economic activity is involved, and whether the presence of the person or undertaking in the host Member State is on a permanent basis or not.

6.1.1   Economic Activity

Only economic activities fall within the scope of Article 43 EC. The Court has considered that the words 'economic activities as self-employed persons' in the Europe agreements have the same meaning and scope as the words 'activities as self-employed persons' in Article 43 EC.[1055] The Court referred in this context to its case law on freedom to provide services, which provides that the work performed must be genuine and effective and not such as to be regarded as purely

---

1051.   J.L. Hansen, 'Full Circle: Is There a Difference between the Freedom of Establishment and the Freedom to Provide Services?', in M. Andenas and W.-H. Roth (eds), *Services and Free Movement in EU Law* (Oxford, 2002), 197.

1052.   Earlier judgments, in which the legal position of the persons concerned was less clear, were based on Arts. 12, 39, 43 and 49 EC, e.g., Case 36/74, *Walrave* and Case C-370/90, *Singh*.

1053.   Section 1.6 *supra*.

1054.   Case C-79/01, *Payroll Data Services v. ADP GSI SA*; Case C-299/02, *Commission v. Netherlands*: Case C-442/02, *CaixaBank France v. Ministère de l'Économie, des Finances et de l'Industrie*.

1055.   Case C-268/99, *Jany*, para. 38.

marginal and ancillary.[1056] 'An activity by which the provider satisfies a request by the beneficiary in return for consideration without producing or transferring material goods', as the Court describes prostitution,[1057] is an economic activity in the sense of Articles 43 and 49 EC. Prostitution falls within the scope of the concept 'economic activity' regardless of the moral qualification of that work. Under certain conditions, the public policy exception may be used to justify restrictions.

Also for undertakings, the performance of economic activities is decisive, but this is more self-evident than in the case of persons (see further section 6.2).

6.1.2   Permanent Presence

This criterion is important for the distinction between establishment and services. In *Gebhard*,[1058] the Court stated that the temporary nature of the activities in question should be assessed not merely on the basis of the duration of services provided, but also taking into account the frequency, periodicity or continuity of such services. The temporary nature of the services does not exclude the possibility that the service provider creates a certain infrastructure (e.g., an office) in the host State, if that infrastructure is necessary for the provision of the service in question.

In Case 205/84, *Commission v. Germany*, the Court concluded that an undertaking of one Member State which maintains a permanent presence in another Member State falls within the scope of the provisions on establishment (rather than the provision of services), even if the presence is not in the form of a branch or agency, but merely of an office managed by the undertaking's own staff or by an independent person authorized to act on a permanent basis for the undertaking, as an agency would.[1059] Subsequently, the Court stated that the concept of establishment involved 'the actual pursuit of an economic activity through a fixed establishment in another Member State for an indefinite period'.[1060] The latter statement clearly applies to natural and legal persons alike.

6.2   THE BENEFICIARIES OF THE RIGHT OF ESTABLISHMENT

6.2.1   Natural Persons

It can be deduced from the first paragraph of Article 43 EC that all nationals of Member States enjoy the right of establishment, including those who are nationals

---

1056.   Case C-268/99, *Jany*, referring to Joined Cases C-51 & 191/97, *Deliège*.
1057.   Case C-268/99, *Jany*, para. 48. See also Joined Cases 115 & 116/81, *Adoui and Cornuaille*.
1058.   Case C-55/94, *Gebhard*; Case C-171/02, *Commission v. Portugal*.
1059.   Case 205/84, *Commission v. Germany*.
1060.   Case C-221/89, *The Queen v. Secretary of State for Transport, ex parte Factortame (Factortame II)* at para. 20. See further Case C-55/94, *Gebhard*; Case C-222/94, *Commission v. United Kingdom*; Case C-11/95, *Commission v. Belgium*; Joined Cases C-34-36/95, *De Agostini*; Case C-14/96, *Criminal proceedings against Denuit*; Case C-56/96, *VT4 v. Vlaamse Gemeenschap*.

of both a Member State and a third country.[1061] The right is not enjoyed, however, by persons who do not come from an EU (or EEA) country. In such cases, there must be an examination as to which rules apply, for instance that of an association agreement.[1062]

The EC nationals concerned may reside outside the Community.[1063] Thus, a Belgian doctor residing in the United States could establish herself as a doctor in the Netherlands. An American doctor residing in Belgium does not enjoy that right. Natural persons may have a secondary place of establishment in such forms as agencies, subsidiary undertakings or branches. The right to set up a secondary establishment remains limited to nationals of a Member State who have a primary establishment in the territory of a Member State.[1064] This requirement of establishment is also to be found in Article 49 EC on the freedom to provide services, as to which, see section 7.2, below.

Nationals of Member State A who have exercised an activity in another Member State may exercise freely their right to (re-)establish themselves in their home Member State.[1065]

6.2.2 Companies or Firms

As to companies or firms, they are treated on the same footing as natural persons for the purposes of the right of establishment (Art. 48, first paragraph EC). For this they must satisfy two conditions. The first concerns their form: the second paragraph of Article 48 EC defines 'companies or firms' as those 'constituted under civil or commercial law, including cooperative societies, and other legal persons governed by public or private law, save for those which are non-profit-making'. The decisive criterion is that they take part in economic commerce under normal commercial conditions.[1066] The *Convention on the Mutual Recognition of Companies and Legal Persons*[1067] gives a description in its Article 2 of legal persons which includes the following element: that their main or subsidiary object is to carry out economic activities, in general in return for consideration. The case law of the Court of Justice concerning rights of employees in cases of transfer of undertakings, and especially Directive 77/187[1068] can also be consulted, as well as

---

1061. Case C-369/90, *Micheletti*.
1062. For Turkey, see, e.g., Case C-37/98, *Savas*; for the Netherlands Antilles, see Case C-181/97, *Van der Kooy*.
1063. Case 107/83, *Ordre des avocats au barreau des Paris v. Klopp*; Case C-106/91, *Ramrath*.
1064. Art. 43 EC, 1st para., 2nd sentence. Thus a Greek doctor residing and practising in Lebanon may not open a subsidiary practice in Italy.
1065. Case 115/78, *Knoors*.
1066. See Case 108/96, *Mac Queen*; Case C-79/01, *Payroll Data Services*.
1067. Bull. EC Supp. 2/89. This Convention never entered into force; see Case C-208/00, *Überseering*.
1068. O.J. 1977, L 61/26. See Case C-29/91, *Redmond Stichting v. Bartol and others*; Case C-382/92, *Commission v. United Kingdom*.

the case law in the field of competition law.[1069] As the Court has indicated in both these areas, the profit-making motive is not decisive.[1070]

The second condition concerns the nationality of the entity: the first paragraph of Article 48 EC provides that they must be formed in accordance with the law of a Member State and have their registered office, central administration or principal place of business within the Community. Even a firm which does not carry out any activity in the Member State in which it has its registered office, but which has a branch in another Member State where it carries out all its commercial activities, can rely on Article 43 EC.[1071] The case law on 'pseudo-foreign firms' has led to a great deal of commotion. In these cases the difference in approach between those states which follow the real seat (siège réel) doctrine, such as Germany, and those states which take the statutory seat as linking factor, such as the Netherlands, is salient. In *Überseering*,[1072] the Court appears to have made its case law in earlier cases such as *Segers*, *Daily Mail* and *Centros*,[1073] more specific, and done so in favour of the supporters of the statutory seat.[1074]

First, the argument that such matters fall outside the scope of the freedom of establishment as long as the Convention provided for in Article 293 EC has not entered into force, is rejected. Second, the Court emphasizes the difference in legal relations in the *Daily Mail* case, on the one hand, and *Überseering* on the other. This step was necessary since – to put it very briefly – the judgment in *Daily Mail* had seemed to imply that companies could not derive any right to trans-border transfer of seat on the basis of the EC Treaty.

Companies and legal persons from third countries may not rely on Article 43 et seq. EC.[1075] The Community may conclude agreements on this matter with third countries.[1076]

6.3   THE CONTENT OF THE RIGHT OF ESTABLISHMENT

As with free movement of workers (see section 5 above), a distinction may be made between migration rights (section 6.4) and market access rights. Market access

---

1069. Case C-41/90, *Höfner*.
1070. Case C-382/92, *Commission v. United Kingdom*, with reference to Case C-41/90, *Höfner*.
1071. Case 79/85, *Segers v. Bedrijfsvereniging voor Bank- en Verzekeringswezen, Groothandel en Vrije Beroepen*; Case C-212/97, *Centros*.
1072. Case C-208/00, *Überseering*.
1073. Case 79/85, *Segers*; Case 81/87, *The Queen v. Treasury and Commissioners of Inland Revenue, ex parte Daily Mail and General Trust PLC*; Case C-212/97, *Centros*.
1074. P. Behrens and Th. Wernicke, EuZW 2002, 737 and 754; W.-H. Roth, 'From Centros to Überseering: Free Movement of Companies, Private International Law, and Community Law' (2003) ICLQ, 177–208. Wymeersch, 'The Transfer of the Company's Seat in European Company Law' (2003) CML Rev., 61–695.
1075. Cf. Opinion 1/94, *WTO*, para. 81.
1076. For a discussion of the legal situation of companies from third countries, see P. Troberg, 'Art. 58 EWG', in Von der Groeben, Thiesing and Ehlermann (eds), *Kommentar zum EU/EG-Vertrag*, 5th ed. (Baden-Baden, 1997), 1/1432.

in relation to trades and professions and for firms is subject to more regulation than in the case of workers. For that reason, a distinction is made between the prohibition of restrictions on establishment, negative integration (section 6.5) and harmonization provisions, positive integration (section 6.6).[1077] In the first case, we are dealing with national rules which restrict migration, which are prohibited except where a justification can be successfully invoked. In the second case we are dealing with professional and commercial provisions and their possible harmonization.

Separate sections are devoted to harmonization of company law, to banking, investment and insurance, and to taxation (sections 6.7, 6.8 and 6.9, respectively).

6.4   MIGRATION RIGHTS AND RESTRICTIONS

Directives 73/148 and 75/34 dealt with the abolition of restrictions on the movement and residence within the Community of nationals of Member States with regard to establishment and the provision of services.[1078] These directives involved equivalent rights to those for workers outlined in section 4.5, above, provided for by Directive 68/360. These directives only applied to natural persons and thus did not benefit legal persons.[1079]

Directive 64/221 on public policy, public security and public health, which elaborates Article 46 EC, covers migration in order to pursue an activity both as an employed and as a self-employed person. However, there is less case law in relation to establishment than in relation to workers.[1080] These Directives were replaced as of 30 April 2006 by Directive 2004/38.[1081]

6.5   PROHIBITION OF RESTRICTIONS AND THE RIGHT OF ESTABLISHMENT

As with the other freedoms, the Treaty contains a provision laying down a prohibition, in this case a prohibition on restrictions on the freedom of establishment (Art. 43 EC) and a number of exceptions (also called justifications, when invoked to 'save' national rules). In recent years, the Court has elaborated the rule-of-reason exceptions in particular.

1077.   Cf. Case 2/74, *Reyners*, para. 46–47; Case C-55/94, *Gebhard*.
1078.   O.J. 1973, L 172/14 and O.J. 1975, L 14/10. Case C-370/90, *Singh*. See on this P. Watson, 'Free Movement of Workers: A One Way Ticket' (1993) *Industrial Law Journal* 75.
1079.   Case 81/87, *Daily Mail*.
1080.   Dir. 64/221, O.J. 1964, 850. Case 79/85, *Segers*; Case C-3/88, *Commission v. Italy*; Case C-93/89, *Commission v. Ireland*; Case C-348/96, *Calfa*; Case C-268/99, *Jany*.
1081.   O.J. 2004, L 229/35; see section 4.5.2. *supra*.

6.5.1   **The Prohibition**

6.5.1.1   *Immunity of Collective Action*

In the *Viking* case, the Danish Government submitted that the right of association, the right to strike and the right to impose lock-outs fall outside the scope of the fundamental freedom laid down in Article 43 EC since, in accordance with Article 137(5) EC, as amended by the Treaty of Nice, the Community does not have competence to regulate those rights. The Court replied by stating that it was sufficient to point out that, even if, in the areas which fall outside the scope of the Community's competence, the Member States are still free, in principle, to lay down the conditions governing the existence and exercise of the rights in question, the fact remains that, when exercising that competence, the Member States must nevertheless comply with Community Consequently, the fact that Article 137 EC does not apply to the right to strike or to the right to impose lock-outs is not such as to exclude collective action such as that at issue in the main proceedings from the application of Article 43 EC.[1082]

6.5.1.2   *Addressees*

The prohibition contained in Article 43 EC applies to both central and local authorities.[1083] It may moreover be deduced from the Court's judgment in *Wouters*,[1084] that the prohibition is not only directed at government and other public authorities, but can also apply to private organizations.

6.5.1.3   *Internal Situation*

Nationals who do not leave their own country, and therefore do not exercise their professional activities in another Member State, do not come within the scope of Article 43 EC; such situations are internal situations.[1085] In internal situations, the relevant exceptions may not be invoked, either.[1086]

6.5.1.4   *Restrictions on Entering and Leaving*

Although the provisions on establishment, unlike those on non-tariff barriers to movement of goods, do not make an explicit distinction between restrictions on movement into a country and movement out of a country, it appears from the case

---

1082. Case C-438/05, *Viking*.
1083. Case C-439/99, *Commission v. Italy*.
1084. Case C-309/99, *Wouters*; Case C-438/05, *Viking*.
1085. Case 204/87, *Criminal proceedings against Bekaert*; Joined Cases C-54 & 91/88 and C-14/89, *Criminal proceedings against Nino, Prandini and others*; Case C-147/91, *Criminal proceedings against Ferrer Laderer*.
1086. Case C-108/98, *RI.SAN. v. Comune di Ischia*.

law of the Court that the prohibition also applies to movement out of a country, i.e., exit.[1087] (see also section 7.4.1).

6.5.1.5   *Keck, Hypothetical Situations and Access to the Market*

The *Keck* rule has as yet not been applied by the Court of Justice in relation to freedom of establishment. In *Semeraro Casa Uno*,[1088] a case which concerned rules on shop opening hours, the Court considered first that, in relation to the provisions on free movement of goods, the *Keck* rule was applicable. A question was also raised concerning freedom of establishment. In relation to this, the Court did not apply the *Keck* rule, but took the view that there was only a hypothetical situation.[1089] Also, in *Pfeiffer Großhandel*,[1090] where the Commission wanted to apply the *Keck* rule to establishment, the Court did not follow suit; the Court stated that the indistinctly applicable measure in question came within the scope of the prohibition, but was permissible on the grounds of a justification.

Sodemare[1091] concerned the establishment of undertakings in the social security sector; in this case the Court ruled that the prohibition was not infringed – a different verdict from that reached by the Advocate General in the case. The cautious attitude of the Court was probably linked to the specific characteristics of this sector (such as lack of profit motive, solidarity, social objectives). This line of case law fits in with the case law on the concept of an undertaking, and on insurance bodies, such as first formulated in *Poucet*,[1092] a case which the Court referred to in *Sodemare*.

In *Wouters*, the question concerning *Keck* which was explicitly posed by the Dutch Raad van State (Council of State) was not answered by the Court of Justice, in view of its answer to the other questions posed.[1093]

6.5.1.6   *Restrictive Measures: Distinctly and Indistinctly Applicable Measures*

As with the freedom to provide services, the freedom of establishment has in the first instance the character of a prohibition of discrimination on the ground that a person possesses the nationality of another Member State or of both another Member State and a third country.[1094] This covers first and foremost direct or

---

1087. Case 81/87, *Daily Mail.* See also extensively on this A.G. Lenz in Case C-381/93, *Commission v. France*, para.38; Case C-264/96, *Imperial Chemical Industries v. Colmer*; Case C-200/98, *X AB, Y AB v. Riksskatteverket*; Case C-251/98, *C. Baars v. Inspecteur der Belastingdienst Particulieren/ Ondernemingen Gorinchem.*
1088. Joined Cases C-418–421/93 etc., *Semeraro Casa Uno.*
1089. See section 3.2.1. *supra.*
1090. Case C-255/97, *Pfeiffer Großhandel.*
1091. Case C-70/95, *Sodemare.*
1092. Joined Cases C-159 & 160/91, *Poucet and Pistre v. AGF and Cancava.*
1093. Case C-309/99, *Wouters.*
1094. Case C-369/90, *Micheletti.*

manifest discrimination, such as nationality requirements.[1095] A number of recent infringement cases demonstrate that this is tough material, difficult to eradicate.[1096] In a recent case concerning national measures requiring as a condition for being able to register a ship in the Netherlands that the shareholders, directors and natural persons responsible for the day-to-day management of the Community company owning the ship have Community or EEA nationality, the Netherlands Government argued that, unlike a nationality condition linked with a Member State, a condition requiring Community or EEA nationality cannot constitute a 'restriction' for the purposes of Article 43 EC; the Court ruled however that this cannot be upheld. In the absence of a harmonized rule valid for the entire Community, a condition of Community or EEA nationality, like a condition of nationality of a specific Member State, may constitute an obstacle to freedom of establishment.[1097]

The prohibition also embraces indirect restrictions, which may relate *inter alia* to restrictions of the right to establish in two Member States;[1098] the recognition of driving licences;[1099] the manner in which a name is written;[1100] different tax rules;[1101] or a so-called golden share in privatized state companies.[1102] In *CaixaBank France*,[1103] the Court stated that a prohibition on the remuneration of sight accounts such as that laid down by the legislation at issue constitutes, for companies from Member States other than the French Republic, a serious obstacle to the pursuit of their activities via a subsidiary in the latter Member State, affecting their access to the market. That prohibition is therefore to be regarded as a restriction within the meaning of Article 43 EC. In *Meeusen*,[1104] the Court found that the provision contained in Regulation 1612/68, for workers, concerning study

---

1095. See, e.g., Case 2/74, *Reyners*; Case 90/76, *Van Ameyde v. UCI*; Case 197/84, *Steinhauser v.Ville de Biarritz*; Case 166/85, *Criminal proceedings against Bullo and Bonivento*; Case 63/86, *Commission v. Italy*; Case 147/86, *Commission v. Greece*; Case 198/86, *Conradi v. Direction de la concurrence et des prix des Hauts-de-Seine*; Case 38/87, *Commission v. Greece*; Case C-61/89, *Criminal proceedings against Bouchoucha*.

1096. Case C-101/94, *Commission v. Italy*; Case C-334/94, *Commission v. France*; Case C-62/96, *Commission v.Greece*; Case C-151/96, *Commission v. Ireland*; Case C-114/97, *Commission v. Spain*; Case C-172/98, *Commission v. Belgium*; Case C-203/98, *Commission v. Belgium*; Case C-355/98, *Commission v. Belgium*; Case C-439/99, *Commission v. Italy*.

1097. Case C-299/02, *Commission v. Netherlands*.

1098. E.g., Case 107/83 *Ordre des Avocats au Barreau de Paris v. Klopp*; Case 96/85 *Commission v. France*; Case 221/85, *Commission v. Belgium*; Case 143/87, *Stanton*; Cases 154 and 155/87 *Wolf*; Case C-106/91, *Ramrath*; Case C-55/94 *Gebhard* and Case C-53/95, *Inasti v. Kemmler*.

1099. Case 16/78, *Criminal proceedings against Michel Choquet*; Case C-193/94, *Skanavi*.

1100. Case C-168/91, *Konstantinidis v. Stadt Altensteig and Landratsamt Calw*.

1101. Case C-1/93, *Halliburton Services v. Staatssecretaris van Financiën*; Case C-250/95, *Futura*; Case C-254/97, *Baxter and others v. Premier Ministre et al.*; Case C-307/97, *Saint-Gobain*; Case C-251/98, *Baars*; Joined Cases C-397 & 410/98, *Metallgesellschaft and others v. Commissioners of Inland Revenue*; Case C-436/00, *X and Y v. Riksskatteverket*.

1102. Case C-367/98, *Commission v. Portugal (Golden Shares)*; Case C-58/99, *Commission v. Italy*; Case C-483/99, *Commission v. France (Golden Shares)*; Case C-503/99, *Commission v. Belgium (Golden Shares)*.

1103. Case C-442/02, *CaixaBank*; Case C-134/05, *Commission v. Italy*.

1104. Case C-337/97, *Meeusen*.

financing is also applicable to self-employed persons, and can therefore be read into the prohibition contained into Article 43 EC.

In *Centros*,[1105] the Court ruled that a Member State may not refuse to register a branch of a company if that company is duly registered in another Member State. Following on from this judgment, the Court decided, in *Überseering*,[1106] that the refusal of the German judicial authorities to recognize the legal personality and capacity of a company duly registered according to the laws of another Member State (in this case, the Netherlands), constitutes a restriction on the right of establishment.

At the end of 2002, the Court handed down judgments in the so-called *open skies* cases.[1107] These judgments are of utmost importance for the development of a common transport policy (see Ch. XII) and for the exercise of external competences of the Community. These judgments also contain a number of considerations which are relevant for the interpretation of restrictions on freedom of establishment in general. They concern a clause included in a bilateral treaty concluded between, in each case, one EC Member State and the United States: these clauses prejudice the undertakings or nationals of other Member States, and are therefore qualified as restrictions in the sense of Article 43 EC. The direct source of the discrimination is not the possible conduct of the United States of America but the clause on the ownership and control of airlines, concerning ownership and effective control by shareholders of the Member State in question.[1108] The Court also stated in these cases that the question whether Article 43 EC is applicable in a particular case does not depend on whether the Community has legislated in the area concerned, but on the question whether the situation under consideration is governed by Community law. Even if a matter falls within the power of the Member States, the fact remains that the latter must exercise that power consistently with Community law.[1109]

In an important case for both establishment and services, *Gebhard*,[1110] the Court ruled that the possibility for a national of a Member State to exercise his right of establishment, and the conditions under which he may exercise that right, must be determined in the light of the activities which he intends to pursue on the territory of the host Member State. National measures liable to hinder or make less attractive the exercise of fundamental freedoms guaranteed by the Treaty must fulfil four conditions: they must be applied in a non-discriminatory manner; they must be justified by imperative requirements in the general interest; they must be suitable for securing the attainment of the objective which they pursue; and they

---

1105. Case C-212/97, *Centros*. See also Case C-436/00, *X and Y*.
1106. Case C-208/00, *Überseering*. See also Case C-436/00, *X and Y* and Case C-167/01, *Kamer van Koophandel en Fabrieken voor Amsterdam v. Inspire Art Ltd.*
1107. Case C-476/98, *Commission v. Germany (Open skies)*, paras 147–156.
1108. E.g., Case C-476/98, *Commission v. Germany (Open skies)*, paras 148/156.
1109. Case C-466/98, *Commission v. United Kingdom (Open skies)*, para. 41, with reference to Case C-221/89, *Factortame II*; Case C-124/95, *Centro-Com*; Case C-264/96, *Imperial Chemical Industries*.
1110. Case C-55/94, *Gebhard*. Constant case law, see Case C-108/96, *Mac Quen*; Case C-424/97, *Haim II*; Case C-294/00, *Deutsche Paracelsus Schulen für Naturheilverfahren v. Kurt Gräbner, (Heilpraktiker)*; Case C-79/01, *Payroll Data Services*.

must not go beyond what is necessary in order to attain it.[1111] With this consideration – which is highly reminiscent of the *Cassis de Dijon* formula[1112] – the Court indicates that indistinctly applicable measures which affect the freedom of establishment may come under the prohibition;[1113] at the same time, on the basis of the last three conditions, it is clear that rule-of-reason exceptions may be relied on (see section 6.5.2, below).

This approach has been followed in a number of cases so far, such as *Futura* (concerning company taxation),[1114] and *Mac Quen* (concerning the restriction of certain optical examinations to one professional group (ophthalmologists), to the exclusion of another group (opticians)).[1115] The Court of First Instance referred to *Gebhard* in *Vlaamse Televisie Maatschapij*,[1116] but the legal question there concerned an exclusive right whereby other Belgian undertakings and undertakings from other Member States were discriminated against.

6.5.1.7   Company Law and Abuse of Law

In relation to free movement of companies, a similar widening of the prohibition can be seen.[1117] A company may also benefit from its right to freedom of establishment where it does not carry out any activities in the Member State where it is officially registered (in this case the UK) but concentrates all its activities in a branch situated in another Member State (in this case the Netherlands).[1118] In a few recent judgments, the Court did pay more attention to the possibility of abuse of law in this context.[1119] The case law was clarified further in *Überseering*.[1120]

6.5.1.8   Rules on Taxation, with or without Discrimination

The case law of the Court on freedom of establishment and taxation is still developing, but – like that on free movement of workers, services and capital – has not yet reached a stage of complete clarity (see sections 5.5, 7.4.1 and 8.3).[1121]

1111.   Case C-55/94, *Gebhard*.
1112.   Case 120/78, *Cassis de Dijon*.
1113.   K. Lackhoff, *Die Niederlassungsfreiheit des EGV - nur ein Gleichheits- oder auch een Freiheitsrecht?* (Berlin, 1999).
1114.   Case C-250/95, *Futura*.
1115.   Case C-108/96, *Mac Quen*.
1116.   Case T-266/97, *VTM*.
1117.   Case 270/83, *Commission v. France (Avoir fiscal)*; Case 79/85, *Segers*; Case C-175/88, *Biehl*; Case C-221/89, *Factortame II*; Case C-211/91, *Commission v. Belgium*; Case C-330/91, *The Queen v. Inland Revenue Commissioners, ex parte Commerzbank*; Case C-141/99, *AMID v. Belgium*. See, however, Case C-112/91, *Werner*.
1118.   Case 79/85, *Segers*; Case C-212/97, *Centros*.
1119.   Case C-367/96, *Kefalas and others v. Elliniko Dimosio and Organismos Oikonomikis Anasygkrotisis Epicheiriseon*; Case C-212/97, *Centros*.
1120.   Case C-208/00, *Überseering*. See also Case C-167/01, *Inspire Art*; Case C-171/02, *Commission v. Portugal*. See section 6.2 *supra*.
1121.   See S. Kingston, 'A Light in the Darkness: Recent Developments in the ECJ's Direct Tax Jurisprudence' (2007) CML Rev., 1321–1359.

The Court recognizes the competence of the Member States in the field of direct taxation; it adds, however, that these powers must be exercised in conformity with Community law.[1122] In a number of cases, the Court has ruled that there is indirect discrimination.[1123] In another case, the Court considered that although there was no indirect or covert discrimination, there was nonetheless a restriction on the freedom of establishment, so that the national measures in question came within the scope of the prohibition: this amounted to a measure which was 'indistinctly applicable', so that the rule-of-reason exceptions could be invoked.[1124] The Court has also had to rule in a case where provisions on establishment and provisions on capital were at issue. In this case the Court found that the Swedish rules whereby intra-group transfers were treated differently for tax purposes depending on the location of the various subsidiaries (i.e., in which Member State they were) was contrary to Article 43 EC.[1125] Given the Court's finding in relation to establishment, it did not also examine the question in the light of the rules on free movement of capital.

Recently, the Court of Justice has ruled in a number of important cases in the area of trans-border rules on companies and related fiscal arrangements. This case law has concerned, in particular, taxation of cross-border dividends and fiscal arrangements for corporate groups.[1126] In *Marks & Spencer*, the Court ruled that, as Community law now stands, Articles 43 EC and 48 EC do not preclude provisions of a Member State which generally prevent a resident parent company from deducting from its taxable profits losses incurred in another Member State by a subsidiary established in that Member State although they allow it to deduct losses incurred by a resident subsidiary. However, it is contrary to Articles 43 EC and 48 EC to prevent the resident parent company from doing so where the non-resident subsidiary has exhausted the possibilities available in its State of residence of having the losses taken into account for the accounting period concerned by the claim for relief and also for previous accounting periods and where there are no possibilities for those losses to be taken into account in its State of residence for future periods either by the subsidiary itself or by a third party, in particular where the subsidiary has been sold to that third party.[1127]

In *Test Claimants in the FII Group Litigation* ('FII' stands for 'franked investment income', which refers to a dividend received and a tax credit taken together) the Court ruled that Articles 43 EC and 56 EC must be interpreted as

---

1122. Case C-279/93, *Schumacker*; Case C-35/98, *Verkooijen*.

1123. Case C-264/96, *Imperial Chemical Industries*; Case C-307/97, *Saint-Gobain*; Case C-311/97, *Royal Bank of Scotland v. Greece*; Case C-251/98, *Baars*; Case C-141/99, *AMID*; Case C-324/00, *Lankhorst-Hohorst v. Finanzamt Steinfurt*; Case C-9/02, *Hughes de Lasteyrie du Saillant v. Ministère de l'Économie, des Finances et de l'Industrie*.

1124. Case C-250/95, *Futura*. Case C-168/01, *Bosal v. Staatssecretaris van Financiën*.

1125. Case C-200/98, *X AB and Y AB*.

1126. K. Lenaerts and L. Bernardeau, *L'encadrement communautaire de la fiscalité directe* (2007) CDE, 19; S. Kingston, 'A Light in the Darkness: Recent Developments in the ECJ's Direct Tax Jurisprudence' (2007) CML Rev., 1321–1359.

1127. Case C-446/03, *Marks & Spencer v. David Halsey (Her Majesty's Inspector of Taxes)*. See also Case C-196/04, *Cadbury Schweppes v. Commissioners of Inland Revenue* and (the later) Case C-524/04, *Test Claimants in the Thin Cap Group Litigation v. Commissioners of Inland Revenue*.

meaning that, where a Member State has a system for preventing or mitigating the imposition of a series of charges to tax or economic double taxation as regards dividends paid to residents by resident companies, it must treat dividends paid to residents by non-resident companies in the same way. The Court elaborated this basic principle further in relation to the various aspects of the national rules and the factual situation involved in the case.[1128]

In *Test Claimants in Class IV of the ACT Group Litigation* ('ACT' stands for 'advance corporation tax') the Court ruled that Articles 43 EC and 56 EC do not prevent a Member State, on a distribution of dividends by a company resident in that State, from granting companies receiving those dividends which are also resident in that State a tax credit equal to the fraction of the corporation tax paid on the distributed profits by the company making the distribution, when it does not grant such a tax credit to companies receiving such dividends which are resident in another Member State and are not subject to tax on dividends in the first State. Articles 43 EC and 56 EC do not preclude a situation in which a Member State does not extend the entitlement to a tax credit provided for in a double taxation convention concluded with another Member State for companies resident in the second State which receive dividends from a company resident in the first State to companies resident in a third Member State with which it has concluded a double taxation convention which does not provide for such an entitlement for companies resident in that third state.[1129]

In another judgment, handed down on the same day as these two *Test Claimants* cases, the Court ruled that Article 43 EC and Article 48 EC are to be interpreted as 'precluding national legislation which, in imposing a liability to tax on dividends paid to a non-resident parent company and allowing resident parent companies almost full exemption from such tax, constitutes a discriminatory restriction on freedom of establishment'.[1130]

6.5.2   Exceptions to the Prohibition of Article 43 EC

6.5.2.1   *Treaty-Based Exceptions*

The exceptions mentioned in Article 46 EC, and elaborated first in Directive 64/221 and now in Directive 2004/38, i.e., public policy, public security and public health, tend to concern migration and not market access.[1131] These exceptions also apply to free movement of services by operation of Article 55 EC.

1128.   Case C-446/04, *Test Claimants in the FII Group Litigation v. Commissioners of Inland Revenue*.

1129.   Case C-374/04, *Test Claimants in Class IV of the ACT Group Litigation v. Commissioners of Inland Revenue*, operative part of the judgment paras. 1 and 2. See also Case C-524/04, *Test Claimants in the Thin Cap Group Litigation*, Case C-231/05, *Oy* AA and Case C-347/04, *Rewe Zentralfinanz*.

1130.   Case C-170/05, *Denkavit International and Denkavit France v. Ministre de l'Économie, des Finances et de l'Industrie*, para. 41.

1131.   See sections 4.5. and 6.4 *supra*.

The protection of public health is used as a justification in relation to market access for medical professions.[1132] In the *open skies* cases, some Member States invoked the public policy exception. The Court stated that there was no direct link between the – hypothetical – danger represented by the designation of an airline by the United States and generalized discrimination against Community airlines.[1133] The limited application of Article 46 EC where market access is concerned means that Member States confronted with a situation coming within the scope of the prohibition in Article 43 EC must resort to other exceptions, for instance under the rule-of-reason.[1134] Nevertheless, the Treaty contains certain exceptions which may be used as justifications in specific situations. In these cases, the limiting conditions (non-economic aim, and proportionality) must be fulfilled.[1135]

According to Article 45 EC, the provisions concerning freedom of establishment do not apply to activities which in a particular Member State are connected, even occasionally, with the exercise of official authority. In a number of cases, the Court has given a further interpretation of Article 45, first paragraph. According to this case law, which parallels the approach to Article 39(4) EC, considered in section 5.3.2, above, these exceptions to a fundamental principle may not be invoked further than is strictly necessary to safeguard the interests which the Member States are permitted to protect.[1136] Under Article 45, second paragraph, the Council may rule that the provisions of this chapter do not apply to certain activities, but the Council has not, as yet, made use of this possibility.

Article 295 EC may also be considered to constitute an exception in the form of a genuine reservation of sovereignty. It provides that the 'Treaty shall in no way prejudice the rules in Member States governing the system of property ownership'. This provision is to be strictly interpreted: it does not, therefore, affect rules about the disposal or use of property rights.[1137]

Article 86(2) EC permits the Member States under certain conditions to make an exception to the prohibition of Article 43 EC.[1138]

1132. Case C-108/96, *Mac Quen*; Case C-385/99, *Müller-Fauré*; Case C-294/00, *Gräbner (Heilpraktiker)*.

1133. E.g., Case C-476/98, *Commission v. Germany (Open skies)*, paras 158–159.

1134. See Case C-212/97, *Centros*, para. 34: 'It should be observed, first, that the reasons put forward do not fall within the ambit of Article 56 of the Treaty.'

1135. See, e.g., Case C-436/00, *X and Y*.

1136. Case 2/74, *Reyners*, Case 147/86, *Commission v. Greece*; Case C-3/88, *Commission v. Italy*; Case C-306/89, *Commission v. Greece*; Case C-306/91, *Commission v. Italy*; Case C-42/92, *Thijssen*; Case C-114/97, *Commission v. Spain*; Case C-404/05, *Commission v. Germany*.

1137. See Case 182/83, *Robert Fearon v. Irish Land Commission*; Case C-302/97, *Konle*; Case C-367/98, *Commission v. Portugal (Golden Shares)*; Case C-483/99, *Commission v. France (Golden Shares)*; Case C-503/99, *Commission v. Belgium (Golden Shares)*; Case C-300/01, *Salzmann*. See also Case C-370/05, *Criminal proceedings against Festersen*.

1138. Case C-49/89, *Corsica Ferries I*; Case C-179/90, *Merci Convenzionali Porto di Genova v. Siderurgica Gabrielli*; Case C-18/93, *Corsica Ferries II*; Case T-266/97, *VTM*; Case C-309/99, *Wouters*.

6.5.2.2   Rule-of-Reason Exceptions

As was explained in section 6.5.1. above, *Gebhard* confirmed that indistinctly applicable measures may come within the scope of the prohibition, but also laid down the 'four conditions' approach as a result of which it was settled that rule-of-reason exceptions may also be relied on in relation to the freedom of establishment.[1139] The last two *Gebhard* conditions concern the proportionality and necessity requirements. In a number of cases, the national measures at issue failed to meet these requirements of proportionality and necessity.[1140] These exceptions are not of an economic nature – which means that industrial policy arguments can not be made.[1141] In a number of tax cases, arguments based on 'the loss of revenue' for the Member State in question were rejected, as they are based on purely economic objectives.[1142] In *Broede*,[1143] the Court explicitly applied the *Gebhard* approach to free movement of services, and in *Pfeiffer Großhandel* the same occurred for free movement of persons.[1144]

In *Futura*,[1145] the Court referred to the *Cassis de Dijon* case law when mentioning the effectiveness of fiscal supervision. In *ICI*, the justification 'the coherence of the fiscal system', which originated in the *Bachmann* judgment concerning free movement of workers,[1146] was applied by the Court, though it did not save the national rules in question.[1147]

In a number of company law cases, an exception has been formulated concerning measures to combat fraud[1148] which is closely related to the concept of public policy in Article 46 EC. In more than one case the Court has ruled that the transfer of a physical person's tax residence outside the territory of a Member State does not, in itself, imply tax avoidance. Tax evasion or tax fraud cannot be inferred generally from the fact that the tax residence of a physical person has been transferred to another Member State and cannot justify a fiscal measure which compromises the exercise of a fundamental freedom guaranteed by the Treaty.[1149]

In *Überseering*,[1150] the Court stated that it is not inconceivable that the protection of the interests of creditors, minority shareholders or employees may, in

---

1139.   See also Case C-311/97, *Royal Bank of Scotland*.
1140.   Case C-250/95, *Futura*; Case C-114/97, *Commission v. Spain*; Case C-254/97, *Baxter*.
1141.   Case C-367/98, *Commission v. Portugal (Golden Shares)*.
1142.   Case C-35/98, *Verkooijen*; Case C-436/00, *X and Y*. See also Case C-168/01, *Bosal*.
1143.   Case C-3/95, *Broede*.
1144.   Case C-255/97, *Pfeiffer Großhandel*.
1145.   Case C-250/95, *Futura*; Case 120/78, *Cassis de Dijon*. See also Case C-254/97, *Baxter* and Case C-436/00, *X and Y*; Case C-168/01, *Bosal*.
1146.   Case C-204/90, *Bachmann*.
1147.   Case C-264/96, *Imperial Chemical Industries*. See also Case C-251/98, *Baars* and Case C-436/00, *X and Y*; Case C-168/01, *Bosal*.
1148.   Case 270/83, *Commission v. France (Avoir fiscal)*; Case 79/85, *Segers*; Case C-436/00, *X and Y*. See also Case C-524/04, *Test Claimants in the Thin Cap Group Litigation*.
1149.   See, to that effect, Case C-478/98, *Commission v. Belgium*; Case C-436/00, *X and Y*, para.62, and Case C-9/02, *de Lasteyrie du Saillant*.
1150.   Case C-208/00, *Überseering*.

certain circumstances and subject to certain conditions, justify restrictions on freedom of establishment. Such objectives cannot, however, justify denying the legal capacity and, consequently, the capacity to be a party to legal proceedings of a company properly incorporated in another Member State in which it has its registered office. Such a measure is an outright negation of the freedom of establishment. The general interest of protection of shareholders was also invoked in *Payroll Data Services*, but here the requirement of necessity was not met.[1151] In *Sevic*, the Court ruled that although, due to the adoption of the Third Council Directive 78/855 harmonized rules exist in the Member States concerning internal mergers, cross-border mergers pose specific problems. In that respect, it is not possible to exclude the possibility that imperative reasons in the public interest such as protection of the interests of creditors, minority shareholders and employees[1152] and the preservation of the effectiveness of fiscal supervision and the fairness of commercial transactions,[1153] may, in certain circumstances and under certain conditions, justify a measure restricting the freedom of establishment.[1154]

In various directives dealing with banking and insurance a number of general interests are specified, such as controls for statistical purposes and appropriate measures in the case of irregularities.[1155] These exceptions relate to the same matters as various Treaty-based exceptions to the free movement of capital and payments set out in Article 58 EC.[1156]

In *CaixaBank France*,[1157] the objectives of the protection of consumers and the encouragement of medium and long-term saving were invoked as a justification. This attempt to save the national measures failed on grounds of proportionality. There have been attempts to invoke the interests of the local population in order to justify restrictions in relation to fishing,[1158] but the Court did not touch on the argument and the Advocate General took the view that if such interests were deserving of protection the residence requirement was in any event disproportionate. In certain cases concerning university titles and positions,[1159] the concept 'pressing reasons of public interest' was used, with reference to the earlier cases *Thieffry* and *Ramrath*,[1160] which recalls the *Cassis de Dijon* case law ('mandatory requirements').[1161] These cases concerned, in particular, rules on professional

---

1151. Case C-79/01, *Payroll Data Services*.
1152. Referring to Case C-208/00, *Überseering*.
1153. Referring to Case C-167/01, *Inspire Art*.
1154. Case C-411/03, *SEVIC Systems AG*.
1155. E.g., Art. 22 of Dir. 2002/12, O.J. 2000, L 121/1. See M. Tison, 'Unravelling the General Good Exception: The Case of Financial Services', in M. Andenas and W.-H. Roth (eds), *Services and Free Movement in EU Law* (Oxford, 2002), 321.
1156. Cf. Case 182/83, *Fearon*. See also Case C-370/05, *Festersen*.
1157. Case C-442/02, *CaixaBank France*, para. 13
1158. Case 3/87, *Agegate*; Case C-221/89, *Factortame II*. Cf. Case C-452/01, *Ospelt*.
1159. E.g., Case C-19/92, *Kraus*. See also Joined Cases C-259, 331 & 332/91, *Allué II*; Case C-272/92, *Spotti*; Case C-153/02, *Valentina Neri v. European School of Economics*.
1160. Case 71/76, *Jean Thieffry v. Conseil de l'ordre des avocats à la cour de Paris*; Case C-106/91, *Ramrath*.
1161. Case 120/78, *Cassis de Dijon*.

conduct and the protection of academic titles. The regulation of professional practice of lawyers was accepted as a justification in *Wouters*.[1162]

In Case C-211/91, *Commission v. Belgium* (concerning cable television), cultural policy objectives were not accepted as a ground of justification because the national measures at issue were discriminatory.[1163] In *Vlaamse Televisie Maatschapij*,[1164] the objective of plurality of the press was not accepted as a justification. In *Pfeiffer Großhandel*, an appeal to a general interest related to intellectual property rights was accepted, in this case referring to the protection of a trade name where there is a risk of confusion.[1165] This justification – which is a Treaty-based exception in the area of free movement of goods (see Art. 30 EC) – was first claimed as a rule-of-reason exception in relation to freedom to provide services[1166] and then in relation to establishment.

In the golden shares cases, the Court recognized that continuity of supply of (strategic) energy products may in principle fall within the scope of overriding requirements of the general interest,[1167] – which is an extension of the public security exception.[1168] The golden shares cases were decided on the basis of the rules on free movement of capital, but the reasoning may also be applied to freedom of establishment.

In a case concerning nationality requirements in shipping, the Court decided that this restriction cannot be justified on grounds of the exercise of effective control and jurisdiction over ships flying the Netherlands flag.[1169] In the same case, the Court considered:

> As concerns the argument that the Community itself lays down that requirement in its secondary law, it must be held that, while conditions of Community or EEA nationality might be accepted in the context of a harmonised Community scheme, they cannot be established unilaterally by Member States in their national rules (para. 24).

6.6   HARMONIZATION AND THE RIGHT OF ESTABLISHMENT:
           GENERAL

Non-discriminatory rules concerning the exercise of trade and professions may in fact hinder the establishment of nationals of other Member States more than that of

---

1162. Case C-309/99, *Wouters*. See also Case C-506/04, *Wilson v. Ordre des avocats du barreau de Luxembourg*; Case C-193/05, *Commission v. Luxembourg*.
1163. Case C-211/91, *Commission v. Belgium*. See also Case T-266/97, *VTM*.
1164. Case T-266/97, *VTM*.
1165. Case C-255/97, *Pfeiffer Großhandel*.
1166. Case 62/79, *Coditel*.
1167. Case C-367/98, *Commission v. Portugal (Golden Shares)*; Case C-483/99, *Commission v. France (Golden Shares)*; Case C-503/99, *Commission v. Belgium (Golden Shares)*; Joined Cases C-282 & 283/04, *Commission v. The Netherlands*.
1168. See Case 72/83, *Campus Oil*.
1169. Case C-299/02, *Commission v. Netherlands*, para. 21

the country's own nationals. One can think of diplomas required for the exercise of certain professions, for instance doctors, lawyers or architects.

6.6.1 Evolution

The case law in this area has evolved over time, as is well-evidenced by a number of judgments concerning the right of establishment for lawyers.[1170] The first step was the *Reyners* case,[1171] where the Court applied the non-discrimination principle. Then, in *Thieffry* and *Vlassopoulou*, possibilities for establishment were created in cases in which the person concerned did not possess the requisite 'national' qualification, but a comparable one. This was based on the General Programme on Establishment and Article 10 EC.[1172] These individual cases are in fact atypical, as the persons concerned either possessed the qualification (as in *Reyners*) or an equivalent qualification and training. Finally, specific directives concerning the legal profession were adopted and the Court moved on to the implementation and interpretation of these.[1173] An interesting case concerning Luxembourg bar dealt with setting language requirements.[1174]

6.6.2 Types of Directives

In the transitional period for the realization of the common market, there were two types of directives which were adopted in this field: directives requiring restrictions to be removed (liberalization directives), and transitional directives. The former were designed to remove existing discrimination on the ground of nationality.[1175] Transitional measures were designed to deal with those occupations for which no mutual recognition or coordination directives had yet been adopted.[1176]

1170. See also the (old) services Dir. 77/249, O.J. 1977, L 78/17. See on this Case 427/85, *Commission v. Germany;* Case C-294/89, *Commission v. France;* Case C-289/02, *AMOK.*
1171. Case 2/74, *Reyners;* see also section 6.5.1 *supra.*
1172. Case 71/76, *Thieffry;* Case C-340/89, *Vlassopoulou.* See also Case 107/83, *Klopp;* Case 292/86, *Gullung;* Case C-104/91, *Criminal proceedings against Aguirre Borrell and others;* Case C-19/92, *Kraus;* Case C-319/92, *Salomone Haim v. Kassenzahnärztliche Vereinigung Nordrhein.* See also Case C-424/97, *Haim II* and Case C-238/98, *Hugo Fernando Hocsman v. Ministre de l'Emploi et de la Solidarité;* Case C-313/01, *Christine Morgenbesser v. Consiglio dell'Ordine degli avvocati di Genova;* Case C-402/02, *Commission v. France.* See D. Kraus, 'Diplomas and the Recognition of Professional Qualifications in the Case Law of the European Court of Justice' in *A True European* (2003), 247–256.
1173. Dir. 98/5, O.J. 1998, L 77/36. See Case C-168/98, *Luxembourg v. Parliament and Council.*
1174. Case C-506/04, *Wilson v. Ordre des avocats du barreau de Luxembourg;* Case C-193/05, *Commission v. Luxembourg.*
1175. An example of this is Dir. 68/365, O.J. 1968, L 260/9, for the food manufacturing and beverage industries.
1176. An example is Dir. 64/427, O.J. 1964, 1863, activities of self-employed persons in industry and small craft industries. This directive played an important role in Case 115/78, *Knoors.* See also Case 130/88, *C.C. van de Bijl v. Staatssecretaris van Economische Zaken;* Joined Cases C-193 & 194/97, *Manuel de Castro Freitas and Raymond Escallier v. Ministre des Classes moyennes et du Tourisme.*

In order to facilitate the establishment of persons practising the free professions in the internal market, Article 47 EC provides for directives for the mutual recognition of diplomas, certificates and other evidence of formal qualifications, and the coordination of the provisions laid down by law, regulation or administrative action in Member States concerning the taking-up and pursuit of activities as self-employed persons (so-called coordination directives).

6.6.3   Mutual Recognition Directives

In the 1970s and early 1980s, much later than required by the Treaty,[1177] mutual recognition of diplomas was agreed for a wide variety of professions such as doctors,[1178] and architects.[1179] These measures concern the mutual recognition of qualifications obtained in a Member State; other specific provisions apply to the recognition of qualifications obtained in third countries.[1180]

In the Commission White Paper on the Internal Market 1985, it was noted that scant progress was being made on the basis of a profession-by-profession approach. Following the recommendations of the Adonnino Committee,[1181] the Commission urged the adoption of a general system for the recognition of higher education diplomas.[1182] This system was gradually implemented with the adoption of three general directives:

- Directive 89/48 concerning higher education diplomas awarded on completion of professional education and training of at least three years' duration.[1183]
- Directive 92/51 for the recognition of professional education and training,[1184]
- Directive 1999/42 establishing a mechanism for the recognition of qualifications in respect of the professional activities covered by the Directives on liberalization and transitional measures and supplementing the general systems for the recognition of qualifications.[1185]

1177. See Art. 47(2) EC.
1178. Dir. 93/16, O.J. 1993, L 165/1, as amended by Dir. 97/50, O.J. 1997, L 291/35. See Case C-238/98, *Hocsman*; Case C-16/99, *Ministre de la Santé v. Jeff Erpelding*; Case C-110/01, *Malika Tennah-Durez v. Conseil national de l'ordre des médecins*: Joined Cases C-10 & 11/02, *Anna Fascicolo and Others, Enzo De Benedictis and Others v. Regione Puglia* (C-10/02) *and Grazia Berardi and Others, Lucia Vaira and Others v. Azienda Unità Sanitaria Locale BA/4 and Others* (C-11/02).
1179. Dir. 85/384, O.J. 1985, L 223/15. See on this Case C-31/00, *Conseil National de l'Ordre des Architectes v. Nicolas Dreessen*.
1180. Case C-154/93, *Abdullah Tawil-Albertini v. Ministre des Affaires Sociales*.
1181. Bull. EC Supp. 7/85.
1182. White Paper on Completing the Internal Market, COM(85)310 final, para. 91.
1183. O.J. 1989, L 19/16. See Case C-164/94, *Georgios Aranitis v. Land Berlin*; Case C-232/99, *Commission v. Spain*; Case C-285/01, *Burbaud*; Case C-153/02, *Neri.*; Case C-102/02, *Ingeborg Beuttenmüller v. Land Baden-Württemberg*; Case C-330/03, *Colegio de Ingenieros de Caminos, Canales y Puertos v. Administratión del Estado*.
1184. O.J. 1992, L 209/25. See Case C-294/00, *Gräbner, (Heilpraktiker)*.
1185. O.J. 1999, L 201/77.

In 2001, the Council amended the general Directives 89/48 and 92/51 and the specific directives concerning professions in the health sector.[1186] These directives were replaced by Directive 2005/36.[1187]

6.7   HARMONIZATION OF COMPANY LAW

Article 44(2)(g) EC contains a special obligation to coordinate the safeguards which Member States require of companies or firms within the meaning of the second paragraph of Article 48 with a view to making such safeguards equivalent throughout the Community, in order to protect the interests of members and others.[1188]

Over the years, the following directives have been adopted in the field of company law. Some of these Directives have been amended. Other subjects are still under discussion.[1189]

- First Company Law Directive, Directive 68/151,[1190] deals with the publication of documents and particulars concerning companies (including the annual report and accounts) the capacity of companies and their directors and the nullity of companies.
- Second Company Law Directive, Directive 77/91,[1191] relates to the formation of public limited companies and the maintenance and alteration in their capital.
- Third Company Law Directive, Directive 78/855,[1192] covers internal mergers between joint stock companies.
- Fourth Company Law Directive, Directive 78/660,[1193] concerns annual accounts of limited liability companies.
- Draft Fifth Company Law Directive, concerned the structure of limited liability companies and the powers and obligations of their organs.[1194]
- Sixth Company Law Directive, Directive 82/891, relates to the division of public limited liability companies.[1195]

1186. See Dir. 2001/19, O.J. 2001, L 206/1.
1187. Dir. 2005/36/EC of the European Parliament and of the Council of 7 Sep. 2005 on the recognition of professional qualifications, O.J. 2005, L 255/22.
1188. E. Wymeersch, 'The Transfer of the Company's Seat in European Company Law' (2003) CML Rev., 661; V. Edwards, 'The European Company: Essential Tool or Eviscerated Dream' (2003) CML Rev., 443; P. Dryberg, 'Full Free movement of Companies in the European Community at Last?' (2003) EL Rev., 528.
1189. S. Grundman, *European Company Law* (Oxford, 2007).
1190. O.J. 1968, L 65/8; on the implementation of this directive, see Joined Cases C-387, 391 & 403/02, *Criminal proceedings against Silvio Berlusconi, Sergio Adelchi, Marcello Dell'Utri and Others.*
1191. O.J. 1977, L 26/1.
1192. O.J. 1978, L 295/36.
1193. O.J. 1978, L 222/11; see the Commission's interpretative communication, O.J. 1998, C 16/5.
1194. This proposal has been withdrawn by the Commission.
1195. O.J. 1982, L 378/47. See Case C-381/89, *Syndesmos Melon tis Eleftheras Evangelikis Ekklissias and others v. Greece and others*; Joined Cases C-19 & 20/90, *Marina Karella and*

- Seventh Company Law Directive, Directive 83/349, on consolidated accounts.[1196]
- Eighth Company Law Directive, Directive 84/253, deals with the qualifications of company auditors;[1197] it was repealed by Directive 2006/43.[1198]
- Draft ninth Directive, was intended to deal with the behaviour of groups of companies.[1199]
- Tenth Company Law Directive, Directive 2005/56 on cross-border mergers of limited liability companies.[1200]
- Eleventh Company Law Directive, Directive 89/666, deals with disclosure requirements in respects of branches set up in one Member State by companies established in another.[1201]
- Twelfth Company Law Directive, Directive 89/667,[1202] concerns single member private limited companies.
- Thirteenth Company Law Directive, Directive 2004/25, on takeover bids.[1203]

In 2002, a High Level Group of Company Experts published a report on corporate governance and the modernization of company law.[1204] Subsequently, in 2003, the European Commission established a programme of action, entitled 'Modernising Company Law and Enhancing Corporate Governance in the European Union'.[1205] In this context, the European Commission issued a recommendation on 14 December 2004 fostering an appropriate regime for the remuneration of directors of listed companies[1206] and on 15 February 2005 a recommendation on the role of non-executive or supervisory directors of listed companies and on the committees of the (supervisory) board.[1207] In this context, mention should also be made of Directive 2007/36l on the exercise of certain rights of shareholders in listed companies.[1208]

Nicolas Karellas v. Minister for Industry, Energy and Technology and Organismos Anasygkrotiseos Epicheiriseon AE; Joined Cases C-134 & 135/91, *Kerafina-Keramische-und Finanz and Vioktimatiki v. Greece and Organismos Oikonomikis Anasygkrotissis Epicheirisseon.*

1196. O.J. 1983, L 193/1.
1197. O.J. 1984, L 126/20.
1198. O.J. 2006, L 157.
1199. O.J. 1991, C 321/9; this draft prepared by the Commission is no longer under discussion. See J. Wouters, 'European Company Law: *Quo vadis?*' (2000) CML Rev., 257–307.
1200. O.J. 2005, L 310/1.
1201. O.J. 1989, L 395/36.
1202. O.J. 1989, L 395/40.
1203. O.J. 2004, L 142/12.
1204. The text of this report of the working group led by Winter may be found on the website of the Commission.
1205. COM(2003)284 final.
1206. O.J 2004, L 385/55.
1207. O.J. 2005, L 52/51.
1208. Dir. 2007/36l of 11 Jul. 2007 on the exercise of certain rights of shareholders in listed companies, O.J. 2007, L 184/17.

In July 2007 the Commission published a report setting out its views on simplifying the rules governing company law, accountancy and auditing.[1209] The first option is to address the question whether all the existing directives are still needed or whether the EU acquis in the area of company law should be reduced to those legal acts specifically dealing with cross-border problems. The second, less far-reaching option consists in focusing only on concrete, individual simplification measures in order to help EU companies. All interested parties are invited to comment on the proposals by mid-October 2007.

Not only has the Council established directives in this field based on Article 44(2)(g) EC, but it has also adopted regulations on the basis of Article 308 EC. Regulation 2137/85 introduced arrangements for European Economic Interest Grouping (EEIG).[1210]

In 2001, Regulation 2157/2001 on the European Company was finally adopted.[1211] Involvement of employees is regulated in a separate Directive (Directive 2001/86).[1212] Regulation 1606/2002 introduced rules on the application of international standards for annual accounts.[1213] This Regulation supplements the above-mentioned Directives 78/660 and 83/349. Regulation 1435/2003[1214] concerns the Statute for a European Cooperative Society; Directive 2003/72[1215] supplements the Statute for a European Cooperative Society with regard to the involvement of employees.

Finally, mention should be made of the *Convention on the Mutual Recognition of Companies and Legal Persons*, signed in Brussels on 29 February 1968, drawn up on the basis of Article 293 EC, but which has never entered into force.[1216]

6.8   HARMONIZATION OF BANKING, INVESTMENT AND INSURANCE LAW

In these sectors, a number of directives have been enacted which ensured that the free movement of financial services had a solid basis in European law at the moment the EMU began to function.[1217]

1209.   COM(2007)394 final.

1210.   O.J. 1985, L 199. See D. van Gerven and C.A.V. Aalders, *European Economic Interest Groupings*, Deventer, 1990. In 1994, the Council adopted Dir. 94/45 on the establishment of a European Works Council or a procedure in Community-scale undertakings and Community-scale groups of undertakings for the purposes of informing and consulting employees, O.J. 1994, L 254/64, amended by Dir. 97/74, O.J. 1998, L 10/22.

1211.   O.J. 2001, L 294/1. See V. Edwards, 'The European Company: Essential Tool or Eviscerated Dream?' (2003) CML Rev., 443–444.

1212.   Dir. 2001/86 supplementing the Statute for a European company with regard to the involvement of employees O.J. 2001, L 294/22.

1213.   O.J. 2002, L 243/1.

1214.   O.J 2003, L 207/1.

1215.   O.J. 2003, L 207/25.

1216.   Bull. EC Supp. 2/69. *Trb.* 1968, 113. See also Case C-208/00, *Überseering.*

1217.   N. Moloney, 'New Frontiers in EC Capital Markets Law: From Market Construction to Market Regulation' (2003) CML Rev., 809–843.

An important issue is that of the relationship between the Treaty-based freedoms and the national rules, in particular those which are in conflict with the freedoms. The Commission has published two communications giving its interpretation of exceptions based on the general good in relation to banking and insurance,[1218] but it remains to be seen in practice – on the basis of judgments of the Court of Justice – what the precise relationship is between the exercise of the freedoms in this area and clauses relating to the general good.

Using the momentum of the '1992' operation (completing the internal market – see the beginning of this chapter), and with the backing of the Court of Justice,[1219] coordinating directives were enacted in the banking, investment and insurance sectors at the end of the 1980s and beginning of the 1990s, based on the principles of mutual recognition and home state supervision. At the turn of the century, many of these directives were revised. In the following we mention the most important directives:

6.8.1   Banking

Most of the EC directives adopted in the 20th century relating to freedom of establishment and freedom to provide services for banks and credit institutions were replaced by Directive 2000/12 relating to the taking up and pursuit of the business of credit institutions.[1220] In addition, the following are important:

- Directive 94/19, on deposit-guarantee schemes;[1221]
- Directive 98/26, on settlement finality in payment and securities settlement systems;[1222]
- Directive 2000/46, on electronic money institutions;[1223]
- Directive 2001/24, on the reorganization and winding-up of credit institutions;[1224]
- Directive 2002/47, on financial collateral arrangements;[1225]
- Directive 2002/87, on the supplementary supervision of credit institutions; insurance undertakings and investment firms in a financial conglomerate;[1226]

1218. On banking services, see O.J. 1997, C 209. On insurance, see O.J. 2000, C 43. Commission Interpretative Communication: Freedom to Provide Services and the General Good in the Insurance Sector. See on this M. Tison, 'Unravelling the General Good Exception: The Case of Financial Services', in M. Andenas and W.-H. Roth (eds), *Services and Free Movement in EU Law* (Oxford, 2002), 321.

1219. Case 205/84, *Commission v. Germany*.

1220. O.J. 2000, L 126/1.

1221. O.J. 1994, L 135/5.

1222. O.J. 1998, L 166/45.

1223. O.J. 2000, L 275/39.

1224. O.J. 2001, L 125/15.

1225. O.J. 2002, L 168/43.

1226. O.J. 2003, L 35/1.

- Directive 2004/109, on the harmonization of transparency requirements in relation to issuers of certain securities;[1227]
- Directive 2005/60 on the prevention of the use of the financial system for the purpose of money laundering and terrorist financing.[1228]

6.8.2   Insurance and Pensions

The harmonization of insurance law in the EC took place in four steps:[1229] 1973/ 1979,[1230] 1988/1990,[1231] 1992[1232] and 2001–2002. In the following, we mention the most recent directives in this area:

- Directive 2001/17, on the reorganization and winding-up of insurance undertakings;[1233]
- Directive 2002/87, on the supplementary supervision of credit institutions, insurance undertakings and investment firms in a financial conglomerate;[1234]
- Directive 2002/83, concerning life assurance.[1235]
- Directive 2003/41 on the activities and supervision of institutions for occupational retirement provision.[1236]
- Directive 2005/68 on reinsurance and amending Council Directives 73/239/ EEC, 92/49/EEC as well as Directives 98/78/EC and 2002/83/EC.[1237]

6.8.3   Investment

The existing Community rules date mainly from the peak years of internal market regulation, but are gradually being revised following the so-called Lamfalussy Report.[1238]

1227.   O.J. 2004, L 390/38.
1228.   O.J. 2005, L 309/15.
1229.   See on this K. Nemeth, 'European Insurance Law: A Single Insurance Market?', EUI Working papers, Law. 2001/4.
1230.   Dir. 73/239 and Dir. 73/240, non-life insurance (direct insurance), O.J. 1973, L 228; Dir. 79/ 267, life insurance, O.J. 1979, L 63/1.
1231.   Dir. 88/357, non-life insurances, O.J. 1988, L 172/1; Dir. 90/619, life insurance, O.J. 1990, L 330/50. See Case C-191/99, *Kvaerner*.
1232.   Dir. 92/49, non-life insurance, O.J. 1992, L 228/1; Dir. 92/96, life insurance, O.J. 1992, L 360/1.
1233.   O.J. 2001, L 110/28.
1234.   O.J. 2003, L 35/1.
1235.   O.J. 2002, L 345/1. This directive replaces Dirs. 79/267, 90/619 and 92/96.
1236.   O.J. 2003, L 235/10. J. Hanlon, 'Pension Integration in the European Union' (2004) EL Rev., 74–93.
1237.   O.J. 2005, L 323/1.
1238.   Final Report of the Committee of Wise Men on the Regulation of European Securities Markets, published on 15 Feb. 2001, adopted by the European Council in Stockholm on 23 Mar. 2001.

- Directive 89/298, requirements for the prospectus to be published when transferable securities not already listed on a stock exchange are offered to the public;[1239]
- Directive 97/9, on investor-compensation schemes;[1240]
- Directive 2001/34, on the admission of securities to official stock exchange listing and on information to be published on those securities;[1241]
- Directive 2003/6, on insider dealing and market manipulation (market abuse);[1242]
- Directive 2004/39 on markets in financial instruments.[1243]

6.9   HARMONIZATION OF TAX LAW

Harmonization in the field of direct taxation – which up until now has been extremely limited – is based on Article 94 EC, as a result of the exclusion of fiscal provisions from the scope of Article 95, under paragraph 2 of that Article.[1244] Two directives have been adopted which concern fiscal arrangements for companies.[1245] In addition, a Directive was adopted early on concerning mutual assistance by the competent authorities of the Member States in the field of direct taxation.[1246]

During the European Council meeting of 19 and 20 June 2000, at Santa Maria da Feira, the report of the ECOFIN Council on a tax package was approved. This report contained the main lines for legislation, and a timetable. The intention was to reach a complete agreement by the end of 2002 at the latest. This deadline was not reached, but at the beginning of June 2003, the Council did approve two directives in this area, one on savings income and one on royalties.[1247] In 2004, the application of the Directive on savings income, together with certain specific agreements, was extended to cover Switzerland, San Marino, Liechtenstein and

1239.   O.J. 1990, L 112/24.
1240.   O.J. 1997, L 84/22.
1241.   O.J. 2001, L 184/1.
1242.   O.J. 2003, L 96/16. See also the Commission implementing Dir. 2003/124 O.J. 2003, L 339/70.
1243.   O.J. 2004, L 145/1.
1244.   See in general the Communication from the Commission, Tax Policy in the European Union: Priorities for the Years Ahead, O.J. 2001, C 284/6. See also K. Lenaerts and L. Bernardeau, 'L'encadrement communautaire de la fiscalité directe' (2007) CDE, 19.
1245.   Dir. 90/434 and Dir. 90/435 of 23 Jul. 1990, O.J. 1990, L 225. See also J. Wouters, 'The Case-Law of the ECJ on Direct Taxes: Variations Upon a Theme' (1994) *MJ*, 179–220. See Case C-43/00, *Andersen og Jensen v. Skatteministeriet*. Case C-168/01, *Bosal*; Case C-58/01, *Océ van der Grinten v. Commissioners of Inland Revenue*.
1246.   Dir. 77/799, O.J. 1977, L 336/15. See on this, Case C-204/90, *Bachmann*; Case C-420/98, *W.N. v. Staatssecretaris van Financiën*. This directive was amended by Dir. 2003/93 (O.J 2003, L 264/23). The Commission's application for the latter directive to be annulled was rejected by the ECJ, see Case C-533/03, *Commission v. Council*.
1247.   Dir. 2003/48, O.J. 2003, L 157/38 (savings); Dir. 2003/49, O.J. 2003, L 157/49 (royalties).

Monaco.[1248] The Convention on the elimination of double taxation in connection with the adjustment of profits of associated enterprises (known as the 'Arbitration Convention'), concluded on 23 July 1990,[1249] entered into force on 1 January 1995 for a period of five years. In 1999, the contracting parties adopted a Protocol amending and extending the Convention.[1250]

7 FREEDOM TO PROVIDE SERVICES

Article 3(1)(c) EC mentions the abolition of restrictions on the freedom to provide services as between Member States as one of the characteristics of the internal market.[1251] This declaration of principle is developed in Articles 49–55 EC.[1252] The provisions working this freedom out are primarily addressed to persons, and in particular to providers of services (cf. Art. 49, first paragraph, and Art. 50 EC). However, over the years this freedom has seen spectacular developments; it covers matters such as the provision of services by lawyers,[1253] but also public procurement (of works and supplies as well as of services),[1254] banking and insurance services, invisible transactions via telecommunications,[1255] cross-border provision of services in relation to lotteries[1256] and internet transactions.[1257] In some invisible transactions, particularly those relating to telecommunications, advertising and gambling, the movement of goods and the movement of services are closely related[1258] and are sometimes dealt with together.[1259]

1248. See for the relevant decisions, O.J 2004, L 385/50 and O.J. 2005, L 195/3.
1249. 90/436/EEC, O.J. 1990, L 225/10.
1250. O.J. 1999, C 202.
1251. See also Art. 15 EU Charter of Fundamental Rights.
1252. See recently, Hatzopoulos and Do, 'The Case Law of the ECJ concerning the Free Provision of Services: 2000–2005' (2006) CML Rev., 923.
1253. Recently, e.g., Joined Cases C-94 & 202/04, *Cipolla v. Fazari and Macrino v. Meloni.*
1254. See recently Case C-231/03, *Coname*, and Case C-410/04, *ANAV v. Comune di Bari.*
1255. Case C-353/89, *Commission v. Netherlands.* Joined Cases C-544 & 545/03, *Mobistar v. Commune de Fléron and Belgacom v. Commune de Schaerbeek.*
1256. Case C-275/92, *Schindler*; Case C-6/01, *Anomar*; Case C-42/02, *Diana Elisabeth Lindman.*
1257. Case C-67/98, *Zenatti*; Case C-243/01, *Piergiorgio Gambelli and others*; Joined Cases C-338, 359 & 360/04, *Criminal proceedings against Placanica and others.* Dir. 98/84 on the legal protection of services based on, or consisting of, conditional access, O.J. 1998, L 320/54; Dir. 95/46 on the protection of individuals with regard to the processing of personal data and on the free movement of such data, O.J. 1995, L 281/31; Dir. 2000/31 on certain legal aspects of information society services, in particular electronic commerce, in the Internal Market (directive on electronic commerce), O.J. 2000, L 178/1. See also Case 322/01, *Deutscher Apothekerverband.* See on this C. Perathoner, T. Schnitzer, *Internetrecht: eine europarechtliche Analyse*, Bozen, 2002. See also Case C-275/06, *Promusicae.*
1258. Cf. Case 155/73, *Sacchi*, with Joined Cases 60 & 61/84, *Cinéthèque*; cf. Case C-275/92, *Schindler*, met Case C-124/97, *Läärä*; Case C-390/99, *Canal Satélite Digital.* Case C-20/03 *Burmanjer.* See on this U. Everling, *Zum Begriff der Ware im Binnenmarkt der EG und sein Verhältnis zu den Dienstleistungen*, in *Festschrift H.J. Hahn* (Baden-Baden, 1996), 465.
1259. Joined Cases C-34–36/95, *De Agostini.* Cf. Case C-275/92, *Schindler*, with Case C-368/95, *Familiapress*; Case C-71/02, *Karner.* Case C-262/02, *Commission v. France*; Case C-429/02

The relationship between establishment and services is particularly close, and Article 55 provides that various of the provisions on establishment shall also apply in respect of the provision of services.[1260] As for the link with free movement of capital, Article 51(2) EC provides that the liberalization of banking and insurance services connected with movements of capital are to be effected in step with the liberalization of movement of capital.[1261] In *Fidium Finanz*,[1262] the Court recalled that according to settled case law, the business of a credit institution consisting of granting credit constitutes a service within the meaning of Article 49 EC.[1263] The Court mentioned Directive 2000/12/EC[1264] on the taking up and pursuit of the business of credit institutions, and stated that this seeks to regulate the activity of granting loans, *inter alia*, from the point of view of both the freedom of establishment and the freedom to provide financial services. The Court found that although Fidium Finanz was not a credit institution within the meaning of Community law, insofar as its activity did not entail the receiving of deposits or other repayable funds from the public, its activity of granting credit on a commercial basis did constitute a provision of services (see further 8.3 below).

Article 51(1) provides that the freedom to provide services in the transport field[1265] is to be governed by the provisions of the Title relating to transport.[1266] The relationship between movement of capital, payments and the provision of services has been the subject of judicial consideration,[1267] as has that between Article 49 EC and Articles 81 and 82 EC.[1268]

Bacardi France v. Télévision française 1 and Others; Case C-36/02, *Omega*; Case C-20/03, *Burmanjer*;. See on this P. Oliver, 'Goods and Services: Two Freedoms Compared', in *Mélanges en hommage à Michel Waelbroeck* (Brussels, 1999), 1368; J. Snell, *Goods and Services in EC Law* (Oxford, 2002).

1260. J.L. Hansen, 'Full Circle: Is there a Difference between the Freedom of Establishment and the Freedom to Provide Services?', in M. Andenas and W.-H. Roth (eds), *Services and Free Movement in EU Law* (Oxford, 2002), 197.

1261. Case 205/84, *Commission v. Germany*. See also Joined Cases C-358 & 416/93, *Bordessa*. See further section 8.4.2 *infra*.

1262. Case C-452/04, *Fidium Finanz v. Bundesanstalt für Finanzdienstleistungsaufsicht*.

1263. The ECJ referred to Case C-484/93, *Svensson and Gustavsson* and Case C-222/95, *Parodi*.

1264. Dir. 2000/12/EC of the European Parliament and of the Council of 20 Mar. 2000 relating to the taking up and pursuit of the business of credit institutions, O.J. 2000, L 126/1.

1265. Case 13/83, *European Parliament v. Council (transport policy)*; Case 4/88, *Lambregts Transportbedrijf PVBA v. Belgium*; Case C-49/89, *Corsica Ferries I*; Case C-17/90, *Pinaud Wieger Spedition v. Bundesanstalt für den Güterfernverkehr*; Case C-18/93, *Corsica Ferries II*; Case C-381/93, *Commission v. France*; Joined Cases C-430 & 431/99, *Sea-Land Service*; Case C-115/00, *Andreas Hoves Internationaler Transport-Service Sàrl v. Finanzamt Borken*; Case C-92/01, *Georgios Stylianakis v. Elliniko Dimosio*. See also the *Open Skies* cases, e.g., Case C-466/98, *Commission v. United Kingdom (Open Skies)*.

1266. See Opinion 1/94, *WTO*, para. 48. See further Ch. XIII of this book.

1267. Joined Cases 286/82 & 26/83, *Luisi and Carbone*; Case C-118/96, *Jessica Safir v. Skattemyndigheten i Dalarnas Län*; Case C-410/96, *Criminal proceedings against André Ambry*; Case C-302/97, *Konle*; Case C-452/01, *Ospelt*.

1268. Case 22/79, *Greenwich*; Case 7/82, *Gesellschaft zur Verwertung von Leistungsschutzrechten (GVL) v. Commission*; Joined Cases C-92 & 326/92, *Phil Collins*; Joined Cases C-147 & 148/97, *Deutsche Post*; Case C-309/99, *Wouters*; Joined Cases C-94 & 202/04, *Cipolla*.

This section first examines (in 7.1) the concept of a service, before turning to examine the beneficiaries of the freedom (7.2, below). Section 7.3 deals with migration rights, and market access rights are considered in section 7.4, below. Attention then turns to service monopolies in section 7.5 and harmonization in the field of services is examined in section 7.6. Finally, the new services Directive is examined in section 7.7.

7.1 THE CONCEPT OF A SERVICE

Article 50 EC provides that services within the meaning of the EC Treaty are those services 'normally provided for remuneration, in so far as they are not governed by the provisions relating to the free movement of goods, capital and persons'.[1269] It also provides an illustrative list of what is covered by the term services.

7.1.1 Economic Activities

The case law has gradually clarified which economic activities come within the scope of freedom to provide services. Services must be economic activities[1270] which are normally provided for remuneration.[1271] On the basis of these criteria, publicly financed education in another Member State is not regarded as falling under the freedom to provide services.[1272] Leasing is a service in the sense of Article 49 EC.[1273] Medical activities come within the scope of freedom to provide services, without a distinction between services provided within a hospital and those provided outside a hospital environment.[1274] The special nature of certain services cannot place them outside the scope of freedom to provide services.[1275] The alleged immoral character of a particular type of activity legally practised in a Member State will not play a direct role in deciding whether or not it is to be considered a service, but may lead to the application of public order exceptions.[1276]

1269. Dir. 98/34 laying down a procedure for the provision of information in the field of technical standards and regulations, O.J. 1998, L 204/37, gives a specific definition which only applies to these 'modern' services.

1270. Case 36/74, *Walrave*; Case 13/76, *Dona*; Case 15/78, *Société générale alsacienne de banque SA v. Walter Koestler*; Case 196/87, *Steymann*; Case C-275/92, *Schindler*.

1271. Case C-275/92, *Schindler*. It is evident from Case 352/85, *Bond van Adverteerders and others v. The Netherlands State*, that Art. 50 EC does not require the payment to be made by the recipient of the service. See also Joined Cases C-51/96 & C-191/97, *Deliège*; Case C-157/99, *Smits and Peerbooms*; Case C-385/99, *Müller-Fauré*; Case 355/00, *Freskot*.

1272. Case 263/86, *Humbel*; Case C-109/92, *Stephan Max Wirth v. Landeshauptstadt Hannover*; Case C-368/98, *Vanbraekel*.

1273. Case C-451/99, *Cura Anlagen v. Auto Service Leasing*.

1274. Case C-157/99, *Smits and Peerbooms*; Case C-385/99, *Müller-Fauré*.

1275. Case C-158/96, *Kohll*; Case C-157/99, *Smits and Peerbooms*.

1276. Case C-268/99, *Jany*.

7.1.2   Temporary Nature

The key demarcation between the provision of services and the right of establishment is undoubtedly to be found in the word 'temporary' in Article 50 EC.[1277]
While services are by definition provided on a temporary basis, establishment is
more permanent in nature, requiring a permanent presence in the territory of the
Member State where the economic activity is being exercised.[1278] Such permanent
presence, on a stable and continuous basis from an established professional base, or
at least presence for an indefinite period, will be identified as such even if the
presence is in the form of an office managed by an undertaking's own staff or by an
independent person permanently authorized to act.[1279]

7.2   BENEFICIARIES OF THE FREEDOM TO PROVIDE SERVICES

7.2.1   Natural Persons and Legal Persons

Whereas the nationality of the purchaser or importer in situations involving free
movement of goods is irrelevant,[1280] in relation to freedom to provide services and
establishment, the nationality (and place of residence) does have significance. The
first paragraph of Article 49 EC requires the abolition of restrictions on the freedom to provide services within the Community in respect of nationals of Member
States who are established in a Member State other than that of the person for
whom the services are intended. Thus, for the provision of services by natural
persons, establishment within the Community is required in addition to the requirement of nationality of a Member State – unlike the first establishment itself, which
merely stipulates nationality of a Member State.[1281] This combined requirement is
only made in relation to the provider of services; it does not apply to the recipient of
services. Thus third-country nationals who are established within the Community
may benefit from the freedom to provide services in their capacity as recipients of
services.[1282]

    The Council is empowered under the second paragraph of Article 49 EC to
extend the provisions on services to nationals of third countries who provide
services and who are established within the Community; the Commission

---

1277. K. Paternacki, *Zur Abgrenzung von Niederlassungsfreiheit und Dienstleistungsfreiheit bei
        Niederlassungen mit Teilfunktion* (Frankfurt/M, 2000).
1278. Case 292/86, *Gullung*; Case 196/87, *Steymann*; Case C-294/89, *Commission v. France*.
1279. See section 6.1 *supra*. Case 205/84, *Commission v. Germany*; Case C-221/89, *Factortame II*;
        Case C-55/94, *Gebhard*. Case C-215/01, *Bruno Schnitzer*; Case C-171/02, *Commission v.
        Portugal*.
1280. Joined Cases 2 & 3/69, *Sociaal Fonds voor de Diamantarbeiders*.
1281. Art. 43 EC. See section 6.2 *supra*.
1282. Case C-484/93, *Svensson and Gustavsson*. See on this P. Oliver, 'Goods and Services: Two
        Freedoms Compared', in *Mélanges en hommage à Michel Waelbroeck* (Brussels, 1999),
        1371.

presented a proposal to this effect to the Council, but the proposal was later with-drawn.[1283] In this context, the case law of the Court of Justice continues to provide the most important guidelines.[1284]

Although Articles 49 and 50 EC refer to natural persons, it appears from Articles 55 combined with 48 EC that legal persons also come within the scope of the provisions on services. They must have a link with at least one Member State in their capacity as service provider.[1285]

7.2.2 Service Transactions: Four Possibilities

The case law on the freedom to provide services has examined a great number of situations involving the cross-border provision of services, and in many cases has brought them within the scope of the provisions on freedom to provide services.[1286] The applicability of these provisions is not conditional on the prior determination of the recipient of the services.[1287] Four situations can be distinguished: the first is where the service provider moves from one Member State to another to provide the service; the second is where it is not the provider who moves but the recipient; in the third situation, neither the provider nor the recipient moves, the service being provided and received by means of telecommunication (telephone, fax, internet etc.) or mail; the fourth scenario is that both the service provider and the recipient move from their respective Member States to a third Member State so that the performance of the service takes place there.

Initially the accent clearly lay on the provider of the service moving, a situation expressly envisaged in Article 50 EC, last sentence. Indeed, early case law saw the Court too only thinking of this scenario.[1288] In such cases, Article 49 EC also applies to the employees of the service provider who accompany him for the provision of the service.[1289] The spectacular expansion to the second situation

---

1283. O.J. 1999, C 67/17. See on this J. Tiedje, *La libre prestation de services et les ressortisants de pays tiers* (1999) RMUE, 73; F. Weiss and F. Wooldridge, *Free Movement of Persons within the EU*, 2nd ed. (The Hague, 2007), 83.

1284. Case C-113/89, *Rush Portuguesa*; Case C-164/99, *Portugaia Construçoes*; Case C-43/93, *Van der Elst v. Office des migrations internationals*; Case C-445/03, *Commission v. Luxemburg*; Case C-244/04, *Commission v. Germany*. See Case C-341/05, *Laval un Partneri* and Case C-438/05, *Viking*.

1285. See General Programme for the abolition of restrictions on freedom to provide services, title I, O.J. 1962, 32.

1286. See on this A.G. Jacobs, Opinion in Case C-384/93, *Alpine Investments*. This interpretation reveals broad similarity with Art. I(2) GATS. See Opinion 1/94, *WTO*, para.43.

1287. Case C-384/93, *Alpine Investments*.

1288. Case 33/74, *Johannes Henricus Maria van Binsbergen v. Bestuur van de Bedrijfsvereniging voor de Metaalnijverheid*. Other examples are Case 16/78, *Choquet*; Case 279/80, *Criminal proceedings against Alfred John Webb*; Case 76/81, *SA Transporoute et travaux v. Minister of Public Works*.

1289. Case C-113/89, *Rush Portuguesa*; Case C-164/99, *Portugaia Construçoes*. For employees from third countries (Morocco), see Case C-43/93, *Vander Elst*.

arrived when the Court made it clear that those who were travelling to other Member States as tourists, or to receive other services, were beneficiaries of Articles 49 and 50 EC, starting with the judgment in *Luisi and Carbone*.[1290] The third situation, where the service is cross-border without provider or recipient moving is increasingly common, in particular in relation to financial services.[1291] Finally, the fourth situation is typified by the situation of tourist guides, a driver and holidaymakers on a coach trip or guided tour in another Member State, who are faced with a requirement that local guides or drivers must be used.[1292]

7.3   MIGRATION RIGHTS

The migration rights associated with the provision of services have already been examined in relation to the free movement of workers (section 4.5) and in relation to the right of establishment (6.4).[1293] Given that both the service provider and the service recipient may benefit from the freedom, regard must be had to both the demand and the supply sides of the market: thus, not just a medical doctor but also his or her patient may encounter the public health exception if he or she takes advantage of the freedom to provide or receive services.[1294]

7.4   MARKET ACCESS RULES

As with the other freedoms, the Treaty contains a prohibition in relation to services (Art. 49 EC)[1295] and a number of exceptions.

1290. Dir. 64/221, discussed in sections 4.5 and 6.4 *supra* also applied to those providing services (see Art. 1(1)). O.J. 1964, 850. Joined Cases 286/82 & 26/83, *Luisi and Carbone*. Other examples are Case 186/87, *Cowan*; Case C-159/90, *Grogan*; Case C-55/93, *Van Schaik*; Case C-274/96, *Bickel and Franz*; Case C-348/96, *Calfa*.

1291. E.g., Case C-353/89, *Commission v. Netherlands*; Case C-76/90, *Manfred Säger v. Dennemeyer*; Case C-384/93, *Alpine Investments*; Case C-60/00, *Carpenter*.

1292. Case C-154/89, *Commission v. France*; Case C-180/89, *Commission v. Italy*, and Case C-198/89, *Commission v. Greece*; Case C-398/95, *Syndesmos ton en Elladi Touristikon kai Taxidiotikon Grafeion v. Ypourgos Ergasias*.

1293. For an extensive treatment of Dir. 73/148 in the area of freedom to provide services, see Case C-60/00, *Carpenter*.

1294. Case C-157/99, *Smits and Peerbooms*; Case C-385/99, *Müller-Fauré*. Case C-372/04, *Watts v. Bedford Primary Care Trust*. See, further, the General Programme (O.J. 1962, 32), Title III. On health services, see Hatzopoulos '*Killing* National Health and Insurance Systems but *Healing* Patients? The European Market for Health Care Services after the Judgments of the ECJ in *Vanbraekel* and *Peerbooms*, (2002) CML Rev., 683–729.

1295. J. Snell and M. Andenas, 'Exploring the Outer Limits: Restrictions on the Free Movement of Goods and Services', in M. Andenas and W.-H. Roth (eds), *Services and Free Movement in EU Law* (Oxford, 2002), 69.

have any consequences for the scope of application of the prohibition contained in Article 49 EC.[1308]

In *Schindler*, although one could have considered the rule at issue to some extent to be a 'selling arrangement', the Court did not carry out a review along the lines of *Keck*.[1309] In *Alpine Investments*, the *Keck* test was considered, but the Court chose to follow a different line of reasoning – which was also followed later in relation to free movement of workers.[1310] The Court considered that, although the prohibition at issue (on so-called 'cold calling') was general and non-discriminatory, and did not have as aim or effect that the national market was at an advantage in relation to providers of services from other Member States, it was nevertheless found to affect directly access to the market in services and thus to be capable of hindering trade in services between Member States. Such a prohibition prevents the market participants in question from using a rapid and direct possibility for approaching potential clients in other Member States.[1311]

In *De Agostini*, which concerned rules on television advertising, no mention was made of the application of the *Keck* rule to services. In this same case, *Keck* was applied in relation to the examination of the compatibility of the rule in question with Article 28 EC.[1312] In two later cases, questions were put to the Court on the applicability of the *Keck* approach to services. The Court decided the cases without answering the questions.[1313]

With *Gourmet*, the Court's case law on advertising in relation to goods was brought into line with its case law on advertising services.[1314] The Court brought certain advertising rules under the prohibition of Article 28 EC, and therefore did not follow an approach along the *Keck* lines (advertising rules purely as selling arrangements). In agreement with its reasoning in *De Agostini*, the Court found that this was a measure which was capable of restricting trade.

1308. W.H. Roth, 'The European Court of Justice's Case Law on Freedom to Provide Services: is *Keck* Relevant?', in M. Andenas and W.-H. Roth (eds), *Services and Free Movement in EU Law* (Oxford, 2002), 1; J.L. da Cruz Vilaça, 'On the Application of *Keck* in the Field of Free Provision of Services', in M. Andenas and W.-H. Roth (eds), *Services and Free Movement in EU Law* (Oxford, 2002), 25; B.J. Drijber, 'Les communications commerciales au carrefour de la dérégulation et de la réglementation' (2002) CDE, 531–610. See on this Opinion of AG Léger in Case C-20/03, *Burmanjer*, para. 61.
1309. Case C-275/92, *Schindler*.
1310. Case C-415/93, *Bosman*.
1311. Case C-384/93, *Alpine Investments*. See also Case C-254/98, *Heimdienst Sass*. In this case concerning free movement of goods, the Court used the *Alpine-Investments* test.
1312. Joined Cases C-34-36/95, *De Agostini*. A comparable situation was at issue in Case C-6/98, *ARD*.
1313. Case C-309/99, *Wouters*; Joined Cases C-430 & 431/99, *Sea-Land Service*.
1314. Case C-405/98, *Gourmet International*.

7.4.1.6   *Restrictive Measure: Distinctly and Indistinctly*
                 Applicable Measures

Article 49 EC, first paragraph, EC, prohibits 'restrictions on freedom to provide services'.[1315] Restrictions which are 'inherent' in certain services, such as selection rules for sports competitions, may not be characterized as restrictions prohibited under Article 49 EC;[1316] this approach by the Court has the same effect as the *Keck* rule in relation to Article 28 EC[1317] and the *Brentjens/Wouters* approach in relation to competition rules.[1318] In all these cases, the restriction in question falls outside the application of the prohibition.

Article 49 EC implies the abolition of all discrimination against the provider or the recipient of services,[1319] even of a minor nature,[1320] on the grounds of nationality or the fact of establishment in another Member State than that in which the service is provided.[1321] This could be either equal treatment of unequal situations, or unequal treatment of equal situations.[1322] The right to equal treatment may not be made dependent on the existence of agreements based on the principle of reciprocity.[1323]

A Member State may not make the provision of services in its territory subject to compliance with all the rules applicable in the case of establishment, since otherwise the useful effect of the freedom to provide services would be negated.[1324]

The Court has found that the condition imposed by a Member State requiring private security operators to be constituted as a legal person could hamper the

---

1315. See the Commission's interpretative declaration, O.J. 1993, C 334. According to the last sentence of Art. 50 EC, the service provider may provide services in a host state under the same conditions as are imposed by that state on its own nationals. See on this Case 205/84, *Commission v. Germany.*
1316. Joined Cases C-51/96 & C-191/97, *Deliège.*
1317. Joined Cases C-267 & 268/91, *Keck and Mithouard.*
1318. Joined Cases C-115-117/97, *Brentjens' Handelsonderneming v. Stichting Bedrijfspensioenfonds voor de Handel in Bouwmaterialen*; Case C-309/99, *Wouters.*
1319. Case 168/85, *Commission v. Italy*; Case 63/86, *Commission v. Italy;* Case C-154/89, *Commission v. France*; Case C-180/89, *Commission v. Italy*; Case C-198/89, *Commission v. Greece*; Case C-260/89, *Elliniki Radiophonia Tiléorassi AE (ERT) and Panellinia Omospondia Syllogon Prossopikou v. Dimotiki Etairia Pliroforissis and Sotirios Kouvelas and Nicolaos Avdellas and others*; Case C-353/89, *Commission v. Netherlands*; Case C-58/90, *Commission v. Italy*; Case C-17/92, *Federación de Distribuidores Cinematográficos v. Spanish State*; Case C-45/93, *Commission v. Spain.*
1320. Case C-49/89, *Corsica Ferries I.*
1321. Case 33/74, *Van Binsbergen*; Case 39/75, *Robert-Gerardus Coenen and others v. Sociaal-Economische Raad*; Joined Cases 62 & 63/81, *Seco*; Case 76/81, *Transporoute*; Case 205/84, *Commission v. Germany*; Case C-224/97, *Ciola*; Case C-355/98, *Commission v. Belgium*; Case C-451/99, *Cura Anlagen.*; Case C-496/01, *Commission v. France*; Case C-189/03, *Commission v. Netherlands.*
1322. Case C-390/96, *Lease Plan Luxembourg v. Belgium.*
1323. Case 1/72, *Rita Frilli v. Belgium*; Case 186/87, *Cowan*; Case C-20/92, *Hubbard.*
1324. Case 205/84, *Commission v. Germany*; Case C-180/89, *Commission v. Italy*; Case C-20/92, *Hubbard*; Case C-393/05, *Commission v. Austria.*

activities of trans-frontier service providers established in other Member States, where they lawfully provide similar services, and constitutes a restriction within the meaning of Article 49 EC. Such a condition rules out any possibility for a trans-frontier service provider who is a natural person to provide services in that Member State. In addition, such a condition constitutes a restriction within the meaning of Article 43 EC, since it prevents Community operators who are natural persons from setting up a secondary establishment in that Member State.[1325]

As powers and rights pertaining to the exercise of state authority cannot be extended beyond national territory, their exercise does not fall within Article 49 EC.[1326] The Court came to this conclusion in a case concerning the recognition of garages in other Member States as authorized issuers of roadworthiness certificates.

Health insurance arrangements which involve requirements for prior authorization for certain medical treatment, or which give less favourable coverage for treatment received in another Member State, come within the scope of the prohibition.[1327] Article 49 EC prohibits any national rule which makes the provision of services between Member States more onerous than the provision of services within one Member State.[1328]

In the 1970s, a number of judgments were handed down which indicated that the scope of application of the prohibition in Article 49 EC went further than simply the prohibition of direct or indirect discrimination.[1329] More recent case law has confirmed these indications, stating unequivocally that – in the absence of harmonizing measures – Article 49 also concerns non-discriminatory national measures which form an obstacle to the freedom to provide services.[1330] The prohibition applies whenever the application of the national rules concerned to foreign service providers 'is not justified by overriding reasons relating to the public interest or if the requirements embodied in that legislation are already satisfied by the rules imposed on those persons in the Member State in which they are established'.[1331] Double checks are therefore viewed with great

---

1325. Case C-171/02, *Commission v. Portugal*, paras. 41 and 42.
1326. Case C-55/93, *Van Schaik*.
1327. Case C-158/96, *Kohll*; Case C-368/98, *Vanbraekel*; Case C-157/99, *Smits and Peerbooms*. See also Case C-385/99, *Müller-Fauré*; Case C-496/01, *Commission v. France*. Case C-372/04, *Watts*.
1328. Case C-381/93, *Commission v. France* and Case C-451/99, *Cura Anlagen*.
1329. Case 33/74, *Van Binsbergen*; Joined Cases 110 & 111/78, *Van Wesemael*; Case 279/80, *Webb*.
1330. Case 205/84, *Commission v. Germany*; Case C-154/89, *Commission v. France*; Case C-180/89, *Commission v. Italy*; Case C-198/89, *Commission v. Greece*; Case C-353/89, *Commission v. Netherlands*; Case C-76/90, *Säger*; Case C-384/93, *Alpine Investments*; Case C-398/95, *Syndesmos*; Case 266/96, *Corsica Ferries III*; Joined Cases C-369 & 376/96, *Arblade*; Case C-205/99, *Asociación Profesional de Empresas Navieras de Líneas Regulares (Analir) and Others v. Administración General del Estado*; Joined Cases C-430 & 431/99, *Sea-Land Service*; Case C-17/00, *De Coster*. Case C-262/02, *Commission v. France*; Case C-429/02 *Bacardi*
1331. E.g., Case C-353/89, *Commission v. The Netherlands*, para. 17.

suspicion.[1332] In its judgment in *Broede*, the Court applied the 'four conditions' approach which it had developed in *Gebhard* for establishment (see section 6.5.1), to the provision of services.[1333]

In recent years, there have been a number of judgments concerning television services: first, concerning mainly the Netherlands,[1334] but later also Belgium, the UK and France.[1335] These cases concern interpretation of the Television Directive and the minimum harmonization provisions contained therein.[1336] The Court paid particular attention to the powers of the Member States to impose restrictions, and in this context emphasized the principle of home country control.

The Court of Justice recently used Articles 43 and 49 EC – and in particular the principles of transparency and equality which they include – in order to impose the use of procurement procedures in a number of situations.[1337] In Case C-260/04, *Commission v. Italy*, the Court considered that notwithstanding the fact that public service concession contracts are, as Community law stands at present, excluded from the scope of Directive 92/50, the public authorities concluding them are, nonetheless, bound to comply with the fundamental rules of the EC Treaty, in general, and the principle of non-discrimination on the grounds of nationality, in particular. The Court then stated that the provisions of the Treaty applying to public service concessions, in particular Articles 43 and 49 EC, and the prohibition of discrimination on grounds of nationality are specific expressions of the principle of equal treatment.

> In that regard, the principles of equal treatment and non-discrimination on grounds of nationality imply, in particular, a duty of transparency which enables the concession-granting public authority to ensure that those principles are complied with. That obligation of transparency which is imposed on the public authority consists in ensuring, for the benefit of any potential tenderer, a degree of advertising sufficient to enable the service concession to be

---

1332. Case C-272/94, *Criminal proceedings against Michel Guiot and Climatec*.
1333. Case C-3/95, *Broede*; Case C-55/94, *Gebhard*.
1334. Case 352/85, *Bond van Adverteerders*; Case C-288/89, *Stichting Collectieve Antennevoorziening Gouda and others v. Commissariaat voor de Media*; Case C-353/89, *Commission v. Netherlands*; Case C-148/91, *Veronica*; Case C-23/93, *TV-10*.
1335. Case C-222/94, *Commission v. United Kingdom*; Case C-11/95, *Commission v. Belgium*; Joined Cases C-34-36/95, *De Agostini*; Case C-14/96, *Denuit*; Case C-56/96, *VT4*; Case C-17/00, *De Coster*; Case C-262/02, *Commission v. France*; Case C-429/02 *Bacardi*; Case C-89/04, *Mediakabel*; Case C-250/06, *United Pan-Europe Communications Belgium et al. v. Belgium*.
1336. Dir. 89/552, O.J. 1989, L 298/23, as amended (*inter alia* as a result of the case law of the ECJ) by Dir. 97/36, O.J. 1997, L 202/60. See on this B.J. Drijber, 'The Revised Television without Frontiers Directive: Is it Fit for the Next Century?' (1999) CML Rev., 87. The directive is adapted to take account of developments in the media: see Dir. 2007/65/EC on Audiovisual Media Services, O.J.2007, L 332. See M. Burri Nenova, 'The New Audiovisual Media Services Directive: Television *without* Frontiers, Television *without* Cultural Diversity' (2007) CML Rev., 1689–1725.
1337. Case C-231/03, *Coname* and Case C-410/04, *ANAV;* Case C-458/03, *Parking Brixen v. Gemeinde Brixen*.

opened up to competition and the impartiality of procurement procedures to be reviewed.[1338]

7.4.1.7 Fiscal Measures

Fiscal measures which may constitute an obstacle to the freedom to provide and receive services come within the scope of Article 49 EC.[1339] This fiscal case law has certain specific characteristics. The Court does not always indicate whether the measure in question is discriminatory or not. Moreover, in a number of cases, the situation has involved a Treaty-based prohibition and exceptions based on the general interest which were contained in specific directives.

In recent years in particular, an extensive case law has developed connected with the fiscal case law in relation to freedom of establishment (see section 6.5.1), free movement of workers (see section 5,5), and free movement of capital (see section 8.4.3 below).

Sometimes, more than one of the freedoms is involved.[1340] When there is thus a choice, it seems that the Court chooses to examine first that provision which leads to a finding that the Treaty has been infringed. In *Danner*, where the Court found that a voluntary pension scheme was in conflict with Article 49 EC, the questions referred concerning Articles 12, 50, 56, 58 and 87 EC were not dealt with.[1341] The Court does sometimes give a decision on more than one provision, however: in Case C-334/02, *Commission v. France*, the Court ruled that both Article 49 (services) and Article 56 EC (free movement of capital) were infringed.[1342]

7.4.2 The Exceptions to the Freedom to Provide Services

7.4.2.1 General

Restrictions which are 'inherent' in certain services – such as selection rules in competitive sporting events – fall outside the scope of the prohibition contained in

---

1338. Case C-260/04, *Commission v. Italy*, para. 24.
1339. Case 127/86, *Criminal proceedings against Ledoux*; Case C-49/89, *Corsica Ferries I*; Case C-484/93, *Svensson and Gustavsson*; Case C-222/95, *Parodi*; Case C-118/96, *Safir*; Case C-390/96, *Lease Plan*; Case C-294/97, *Eurowings Luftverkehr v. Finanzamt Dortmund-Unna*; Case C-55/98, *Skatteministeriet v. Vestergaard*; Joined Cases C-430 & 431/99, *Sea-Land Service*, Case C-451/99, *Cura Anlagen*; Case C-17/00, *De Coster*; Case C-136/00, *Danner*; Case C-234/01, *Gerritse v. Finanzamt Neukölln-Nord*; Case C-134/03, *Viacom Outdoor v. Giotto Immobilier*; Joined Cases C-544 & 545/03, *Mobistar*; Case C-451/03, *Servizi Ausiliari Dottori Commercialisti v. Calafiori;* Case C-290/04, *Scorpio Konzertproduktionen v. Finanzamt Hamburg-Eimsbüttel*.
1340. See on this the Opinion of A.G. Geelhoed in Joined Cases C-515/99 etc., *Reisch et al.*
1341. Case C-136/00, *Danner*.
1342. Case C-334/02, *Commission v. France*.

Article 49 EC; as in the *Keck* approach with Article 28, an exception does not need to be invoked to justify the measures.[1343]

The general conditions for the interpretation and application of the exceptions to Article 28 EC, discussed in section 3.3.1 above, also apply to the provisions on services. The exceptions are narrowly interpreted,[1344] and they are non-economic in nature.[1345] Despite the latter condition, the risk of seriously undermining the financial balance of the social security system may constitute an overriding reason in the general interest capable of justifying a system of prior authorizations.[1346] This is particularly so in cases of health services within a hospital.[1347] This justification was granted an explicit place in the EC Treaty by the Treaty of Nice; this is not, however, in the chapter on services, but rather in the title on social policy. Article 137(4) EC provides that the provisions adopted pursuant to this article should 'not affect the right of Member States to define the fundamental principles of their social security systems and must not significantly affect the financial equilibrium thereof'. The Court uses the term 'seriously undermining' while Article 137(4) EC speaks of 'significantly affecting'; whether these are different qualifications still needs to be clarified.[1348]

In addition, the exceptions are subject to the requirements of necessity and proportionality.[1349] The fact that in one Member State less strict rules are applied than in others does not mean that the rules in the latter are unreasonable or disproportionate.[1350]

The exceptions may only be invoked if there is no Community legislation on the matter.[1351] The Commission has issued an Interpretative Communication on the freedom to provide services and the general good in the insurance sector.[1352]

1343.   Joined Cases C-51/96 & C-191/97, *Deliège*.
1344.   Case 352/85, *Bond van Adverteerders*.
1345.   Joined Cases 62 & 63/81, *Seco*; Case 352/85, *Bond van Adverteerders*; Case C-353/89, *Commission v. Netherlands*; Case C-17/92, *Federación de Distribuidores Cinematográficos*; Case C-398/95, *Syndesmos*; Case C-158/96, *Kohll*; Case C-224/97, *Ciola*.
1346.   Case C-158/96, *Kohll*; Case C-157/99, *Smits and Peerbooms*. Case C-372/04, *Watts*.
1347.   Case C-385/99, *Müller-Fauré*.
1348.   In Case C-157/99, *Smits and Peerbooms*, handed down after the signing of the Treaty of Nice, the Court used the term 'seriously undermining', at para. 72.
1349.   Case 52/79, *Debauve*; Case 205/84, *Commission v. Germany*; Case C-154/89, *Commission v. France*; Case C-180/89, *Commission v. Italy*; Case C-198/89, *Commission v. Greece*; Case C-384/93, *Alpine Investments*; Joined Cases C-369 & C-376/96, *Arblade*; Case C-385/99, *Müller-Fauré*.
1350.   Case C-384/93, *Alpine Investments*.
1351.   Case 205/84, *Commission v. Germany*; Case C-353/89, *Commission v. Netherlands*; Case C-37/92, *Criminal proceedings against Vanacker and Lesage*.
1352.   O.J. 2000, C 43. M. Tison, 'Unravelling the General Good Exception: The Case of Financial Services', in M. Andenas and W.-H. Roth (eds), *Services and Free Movement in EU Law* (Oxford, 2002), 321.

Finally, the Court has determined that in the interpretation of a number of the exceptions the European Convention on Human Rights is of importance.[1353]

7.4.2.2 The Treaty-Based Exceptions

Articles 45[1354] and 46 EC, which were already discussed in relation to the free movement of persons and workers (section 4.5) and freedom of establishment (sections 6.4 and 6.5.2), also apply to the provision of services.

The justifications of exercise of public authority,[1355] public security,[1356] public health[1357] and the public order exception[1358] have all been invoked before the Court. In recent cases, these exceptions are also linked – where appropriate – to the ECHR.[1359] Exceptions such as public order and public security are also mentioned in secondary law in the framework of provision of services.[1360]

A Member State can only invoke justifications based on the general good if the measure in question is in conformity with fundamental rights (such as family life) whose observance the Court ensures. These conditions were explicitly considered in *Carpenter* – a case concerning the deportation of a woman who was a third country national and married to a provider of services (who himself had not made use of his right of free movement). In this case, the Court emphasized the necessity to strike a fair balance between the right to respect for family life and the maintenance of 'public order and public safety'.[1361]

Article 86(2) EC (concerning undertakings entrusted with the operation of services of general economic interest) has also been invoked on occasion.[1362] The complication of Article 95(4) and (5) EC (permitting safeguard measures by Member States despite EC harmonization) does not occur in relation to services as long as the relevant directives are based on Article 47 taken together with 55 EC, unlike some cases on free movement of goods (see section 3.3.1).

1353. Case C-260/89, *ERT*; Case C-353/89, *Commission v. Netherlands*; Case C-159/90, *Grogan*; Case C-368/95, *Familiapress*; Case C-60/00, *Carpenter*.

1354. M. Hensler and M. Kilian, *Die Ausübung hoheitlicher Gewalt im Sinne des Art. 45 EG* (2005) EuR, 192.

1355. Case C-3/88, *Commission v. Italy*; Case C-198/89, *Commission v. Greece*.

1356. Case 427/85, *Commission v. Germany*; Case C-266/96, *Corsica Ferries III*; Joined Cases C-430 & 431/99, *Sea-Land Service*. See also Case C-205/99, *Analir*, where the exception was identified in the cabotage regulation.

1357. Case C-158/96, *Kohll*; Case C-157/99, *Smits and Peerbooms*; Case C-451/99, *Cura Anlagen*; Case C-262/02, *Commission v. France*; Case C-429/02, *Bacardi*.

1358. Case 352/85, *Bond van Adverteerders*; Case C-260/89, *ERT*; Case C-348/96, *Calfa*: Case C-36/02, *Omega*.

1359. Case C-36/02, *Omega*.

1360. E.g., Dir. 2002/21, on a common regulatory framework for electronic communications networks and services (Framework Directive), O.J. 2002, L 108/33: Art. 8, security of public communications networks.

1361. Case C-60/00, *Carpenter*, para. 43.

1362. Case C-55/96, *Job Centre*; Case C-266/96, *Corsica Ferries III*; Joined Cases C-147 & 148/97, *Deutsche Post*; Case C-309/99, *Wouters*.

7.4.2.3   The Rule-of-Reason Exceptions

According to the classic doctrine, these exceptions[1363] may only be invoked to justify indistinctly applicable measures.[1364] In section 1.6 above, mention was already made of the fact that the Court does not always follow this doctrine,[1365] as appears, for example, from the case law on 'the risk of seriously undermining the financial balance [of the social security system]'.[1366]

The following general interests have been considered in case law of the Court of Justice (though not always accepted as justification for the national measure in question):[1367]

- avoiding the risk of crime;[1368]
- coherence of the fiscal system and effectiveness of fiscal supervision;[1369]
- consumer protection;[1370]
- cultural policy;[1371]
- employment conditions;[1372]
- financial balance of the social security system;[1373]
- good reputation of the financial sector;[1374]
- linguistic protection;[1375]

1363.   S. O'Leary and J.M. Fernández-Martín, 'Judicially-Created Exceptions to the Free Provision of Services', in M. Andenas and W.-H. Roth (eds), *Services and Free Movement in EU Law* (Oxford, 2002), 163.

1364.   Case C-353/89, *Commission v. Netherlands*; Case C-224/97, *Ciola*; Case C-451/99, *Cura Anlagen*; Case C-341/05, *Laval un Partneri.*

1365.   Examples may be found in the case law on taxation; see Case C-118/96, *Safir.*

1366.   Case C-157/99, *Smits and Peerbooms.*

1367.   In Case C-353/89, *Commission v. Netherlands*, the Court gave an overview of the exceptions invoked up to that date.

1368.   Case C-124/97, *Läärä.*

1369.   Case C-204/90, *Bachmann*; Case C-300/90, *Commission v. Belgium*; Case C-484/93, *Svensson and Gustavsson*; Case C-451/99, *Cura Anlagen*; Case C-422/01, *Försäkringsaktiebolaget Skandia (publ), Ola Ramstedt v. Riksskatteverket*; Case C-334/02 *Commission v. France.*

1370.   Case 220/83, *Commission v. France*; Case 252/83, *Commission v. Denmark*; Case 205/84, *Commission v. Germany*; Case C-154/89, *Commission v. France*; Case C-180/89, *Commission v. Italy*; Case C-198/89, *Commission v. Greece*; Case C-353/89, *Commission v. Netherlands*; Case C-76/90, *Säger*; Case C-275/92, *Schindler*; Case C-384/93, *Alpine Investments*; Case C-412/93, *TF-1*; Case C-222/95, *Parodi*; Case C-366/97, *Criminal proceedings against Massimo Romanelli and Paolo Romanelli*; Case C-393/05, *Commission v. Austria*; Case C-404/05, *Commission v. Germany.*

1371.   Case C-154/89, *Commission v. France*; Case C-180/89, *Commission v. Italy*; Case C-198/89, *Commission v. Greece*; Case C-353/89, *Commission v. Netherlands*; Case C-211/91, *Commission v. Belgium.*

1372.   Case C-272/94, *Guiot.*

1373.   Case C-158/96, *Kohll*; Case C-368/98, *Vanbraekel*; Case C-157/99, *Smits and Peerbooms*; Case C-385/99, *Müller-Fauré;* Case C-372/04, *Watts.*

1374.   Case C-384/93, *Alpine Investments*; Case C-42/02, *Lindman.*

1375.   Case C-211/91, *Commission v. Belgium.*

– maintenance of order in society;[1376]
– medical and hospital service of high quality, open to all;[1377]
– national, historical and artistic heritage;[1378]
– navigational safety;[1379]
– pluralism in a bilingual region;[1380]
– preventing fraud;[1381]
– professional rules protecting the recipient of services;[1382]
– proper administration of justice[1383]
– protection against advertising;[1384]
– protection of the environment;[1385]
– protection of workers and the employment market;[1386]
– protection of intellectual property rights;[1387]
– restriction of gambling, wagering and lotteries;[1388]
– right to take collective action for the protection of the workers of the host state against possible social dumping;[1389]
– road safety;[1390]
– social policy objectives;[1391]
– social policy reasons;[1392]
– technical aspects of life assurance taxation.[1393]

1376.   Case C-275/92, *Schindler*; Case C-67/98, *Zenatti*.
1377.   Case C-158/96, *Kohll*, para. 50, and Case C-157/99, *Smits and Peerbooms*, para. 73; Case C-385/99, *Müller-Fauré*, para. 73, C-496/01, *Commission v. France*.
1378.   Case 180/89, *Commission v. Italy*.
1379.   Case C-18/93, *Corsica Ferries II*.
1380.   Case C-250/06, *United Pan-Europe Communications*.
1381.   Case C-275/92, *Schindler*; Case C-67/98, *Zenatti*.
1382.   Case 33/74, *Van Binsbergen*; Joined Cases 110 & 111/78, *Van Wesemael*; Case 279/80, *Webb*; Case C-76/90, *Säger*; Case C-106/91, *Ramrath*; Case C-19/92, *Kraus*; Case C-309/99, *Wouters*.
1383.   Case C-289/02 *AMOK*.
1384.   Case C-412/93, *TF-1*.
1385.   On this point, there is no clear case law. See, however, Case C-18/93, *Corsica Ferries II* and Case C-17/00, *De Coster*. AG Lenz in his Opinion in Case C-37/92, *Vanacker*, comes to the conclusion, on the basis of his analysis of the ECJ's judgment in Case 240/83, *ADBHU*, that this exception does indeed hold for services.
1386.   Case 279/80, *Webb*; Joined Cases 62 & 63/81, *Seco*; Case C-113/89, *Rush Portuguesa*; Case C-272/94, *Guiot*; Joined Cases C-369 & C-376/96, *Arblade*.
1387.   Case 62/79, *Coditel*; Case 395/87, *Tournier*; Joined Cases C-92 & 326/92, *Phil Collins*.
1388.   Case C-124/97, *Läärä*; Case C-6/01, *Anomar*; Case C-243/01, *Gambelli*; Case C-42/02, *Lindman*; Case 15/78, *Koestler*; Case C-272/91, *Commission v. Italy*; Case C-275/92, *Schindler*.
1389.   Case C-341/05, *Laval un Partneri*.
1390.   Case C-55/93, *Van Schaik*; Case C-451/99, *Cura Anlagen*.
1391.   Case C-355/00, *Freskot*.
1392.   Case C-275/92, *Schindler*.
1393.   Case C-118/96, *Safir*.

In a number of acts of secondary law, rule-of-reason exceptions such as cultural policy[1394] and professional rules[1395] are mentioned.

7.5   SERVICE MONOPOLIES AND ARTICLE 86 EC

There is no provision relating to services which is comparable to Article 31 EC.[1396] Article 31 EC does not apply to services,[1397] but it is not excluded that a service monopoly might have an indirect effect on movement in goods.[1398] With the development of telecommunication markets, the question arose whether the principle laid down in *Manghera*[1399] for Article 31 EC – that exclusive import rights are incompatible with the EC Treaty – also applied in relation to the import of telecommunication broadcasts. In relation to a telecommunications monopoly, the Court found that although the existence of a service monopoly is not in itself incompatible with Community law, 'the manner in which such a monopoly is organized and exercised must not infringe the provisions of the Treaty on the free movement of goods and services or the rules on competition'.[1400] Service monopolies have also been considered in the areas of harbour facilities,[1401] employment placement,[1402] international postal services,[1403] waste disposal services[1404] and the legal profession.[1405] In many of these cases the Member States concerned have sought to rely on Article 86(2) EC, but to no avail.[1406] In a case on harbour facilities, the Court limited itself to the interpretation of Article 82 EC read with 86(2) EC, and did not give its judgment on service monopolies.[1407]

1394. E.g., the TV directive, Dir. 89/552, O.J. 1989, L 298/23; Dir. 2002/21, on a common regulatory framework for electronic communications networks and services (Framework Directive), O.J. 2002, L 108/33.
1395. Lawyers' services directive, Dir. 77/249, O.J. 1977, L 78/1. See Case 427/85, *Commission v. Germany*.
1396. See section 3.4 *supra*. See V. Emmerich, *Die Vereinbarkeit nationaler Dienstleistungsmonopole mit dem EWG-Vertrag*, in P. Forstmoser, *Festschrift für Max Keller zum 65. Geburtstag* (Zürich: Schulthess, 1989), 685–699; K. Hailbronner, *Öffentliche Unternehmen im Binnenmarkt - Dienstleistungsmonopole und Gemeinschaftsrecht* (1991) NJW, 593–601.
1397. Case 155/73, *Sacchi*; Case C-17/94, *Gervais*; Case C-6/01, *Anomar*.
1398. Case 271/81, *Mialocq*; Case C-17/94, *Gervais*; Case C-6/01, *Anomar*.
1399. Case 59/75, *Manghera*.
1400. Case C-260/89, *ERT*, para. 11. See also Joined Cases C-271, 281 & 289/90, *Kingdom of Spain, Kingdom of Belgium and Italian Republic v. Commission of the European Communities*; Case C-37/92, *Vanacker*.
1401. Case C-179/90, *Porto di Genova*.
1402. Case C-41/90, *Höfner*.
1403. Joined Cases C-147 & 148/97, *Deutsche Post*.
1404. Case 240/83, *ADBHU*; Case C-37/92, *Vanacker*.
1405. Case C-309/99, *Wouters*.
1406. See also Case C-438/02, *Hanner*.
1407. Case C-163/96, *Criminal proceedings against Silvano Raso and Others*.

7.6   HARMONIZATION AND FREEDOM TO PROVIDE SERVICES

In the 1970s, a number of directives were adopted concerning traditional activities in the commercial and industrial and handicrafts sectors.[1408] These directives were replaced by the third general directive on the recognition of qualifications in respect of the professional activities.[1409] Also in implementing the White Paper *Completing the Internal Market*, the Council – sometimes in cooperation with the European Parliament – adopted a number of directives in order to open up the market in services.[1410] In 2006, after protracted debate, the Services Directive was adopted (see 7.7 below).

Certain areas or sectors required special attention, such as public procurement,[1411] telecommunications[1412] and financial services. Some of the most important legislation adopted in these areas is briefly mentioned in the following.

7.6.1   Public Procurement

- Directives 89/665 and 92/13, appeal procedures;[1413]
- Directive 2004/17, utilities;[1414]
- Directive 2004/18, public works, supplies and services;[1415]
- Commission interpretative communication on concessions.[1416]

Directive 2004/18 does not include all services in its scope; concessions, for instance, come outside its field of application. In a number of cases, the Court of Justice used the principle of equality, included in Articles 43 and 49 EC – in order to impose an obligation of transparency in the use of procurement procedures.[1417]

1408. See general programme for the abolition of restrictions on freedom to provide services, O.J. 1962, 32. An example is Dir. 64/427, concerning transitional measures in respect of activities of self-employed persons in industry and small craft industries, O.J. 1964, 1863. See on this Case 130/88, *Van de Bijl.* See also Case C-58/98, *Proceedings agains Josef Corsten* and Case C-215/01, *Schnitzer.*
1409. Dir. 1999/42, O.J. 1999, L 201/77.
1410. White Paper, COM(85)310 final., paras 98–99.
1411. See S. Arrowsmith, 'An Assessment of the New Legislative Package on Public Procurement', 41 CML Rev., 1277–1325; C.H. Bovis, 'Developing Public Procurement Regulation: Jurisprudence and its Influence on Law Making', 43 CML Rev., 461–495; G. Gruber, Th. Gruber, A. Mille and M. Sachs, *Public Procurement in the EU* (Vienna, 2006).
1412. O. Castendyk, E.J. Dommering and A. Schreuer, *European Media Law,* (Alphen aan den Rijn, 2007).
1413. O.J. 1989, L 395/33 and O.J. 1992, L 76/14.
1414. O.J. 2004, L 134/1). This directive replaces Dir. 93/38, utilities, O.J. 1993, L 199/84.
1415. O.J. 2004, 134/114; this directive replaces Dir. 92/50, services, O.J. 1992, L 209/1: Dir. 93/36, supplies, O.J. 1993, L 199/1; Dir. 93/37, works, O.J. 1993, L 1991/5.
1416. O.J. 2000, C 121/2.
1417. Case C-231/03, *Coname* and Case C-410/04, *ANAV*; and recently Case C-507/03, *Commission v. Ireland.* For a different approach, see Case C-260/04, *Commission v. Italy*, para. 25. In that case, the Court of Justice applied the principle of transparency.

7.6.2   Telecommunications

- Regulation 2887/2000, on unbundled access;[1418]
- Directive 2002/19, access directive;[1419]
- Directive 2002/20, authorization directive;[1420]
- Directive 2002/21, framework directive;[1421]
- Directive 2002/22, universal services directive;[1422]
- Directive 2002/58, privacy directive;[1423]
- Directive 2002/77, telecommunications and competition.[1424]

7.6.3   Financial Services

The Community is in the process of implementing the Financial Services Action Plan.[1425] Over the years, a number of directives have been adopted (see section 6.8, above). In May 2005, the Commission published a Green paper in this area,[1426] with the intention of improving implementation of the Action Plan.

7.7   SERVICES DIRECTIVE

Directive 2006/123/EC of the European Parliament and of the Council on services in the internal market was adopted at the end of 2006, after many and heated discussions in the Member States and the European Parliament.[1427] The so-called 'country of origin principle', which had been prominent in the Commission proposal, was removed from the final text.[1428] What has remained is a directive which

1418. O.J. 2000, L 336/4.
1419. O.J. 2002, L 108/7.
1420. O.J. 2002, L 108/21.
1421. O.J. 2002, L 108/33.
1422. O.J. 2002, L 108/51.
1423. O.J. 2002, L 201/37.
1424. O.J. 2002, L 249/21.
1425. COM(1999)232. See E. Wymeersch, 'The Future of Financial Regulation and Supervision in Europe', 42 CML Rev., 987–1010.
1426. COM(2005)177.
1427. O.J. 2006, L 376/37. On the preceding debates, see 'Editorial Comments' (2006) CML Rev., 307–311. On the evolution of the proposal, see J.-V. Louis and S. Rodrigues (eds) *Les services d'intérêt général et l'Union européenne* (Brussels, 2006); O. de Schutter and S. Francq, 'La proposition de directive relative aux services dans le Marché intérieur: reconnaissance mutuelle, harmonisation et conflicts de lois dans l'Europe élargie' (2005) CDE, 603–660.
1428. B.J.Drijber, 'The Country of Origin Principle in the Proposed Directive on Services in the Internal Market' (2005) *Revue Européenne du droit de la consommation*, 14. Prior to its adoption, the directive was often referred to as the 'Bolkestein Directive', after the Commissioner in charge of the first proposal. See generally on the directive as it was adopted, C. Barnard, 'Unravelling the Services Directive' (2008) CML Rev., 323–394.

is horizontal in character, and which will certainly influence the provision of services in the coming years.

7.7.1 Background to the Directive

The removal of legal barriers to the establishment of a genuine internal market is a matter of priority for achieving the goal set by the European Council in Lisbon of 2000. Those barriers cannot be removed solely by relying on direct application of Articles 43 and 49 of the Treaty, since, on the one hand, addressing them on a case-by-case basis through infringement procedures against the Member States concerned would, especially following enlargement, be extremely complicated for national and Community institutions, and, on the other hand, the lifting of many barriers requires prior coordination of national legal schemes, including the setting up of administrative cooperation.[1429]

7.7.2 Subject Matter

Article 1 describes the subject matter: This Directive establishes general provisions facilitating the exercise of the freedom of establishment for service providers and the free movement of services, while maintaining a high quality of services. Subsequently, a number of exceptions are formulated – in terms which show signs of the underlying compromises: This Directive does not deal with the liberalization of services of general economic interest, reserved to public or private entities, nor with the privatization of public entities providing services. It does not deal with the abolition of monopolies providing services nor with aids granted by Member States which are covered by Community rules on competition and it does not affect the freedom of Member States to define, in conformity with Community law, what they consider to be services of general economic interest, how those services should be organized and financed, in compliance with the State aid rules, and what specific obligations they should be subject to. This Directive does not affect measures taken at Community level or at national level, in conformity with Community law, to protect or promote cultural or linguistic diversity or media pluralism. It does not affect Member States' rules of criminal law. However, Member States may not restrict the freedom to provide services by applying criminal law provisions which specifically regulate or affect access to or exercise of a service activity in circumvention of the rules laid down in this Directive. This Directive does not affect labour law, that is any legal or contractual provision concerning employment conditions, working conditions, including health and safety at work and the relationship between employers and workers, which Member States apply in accordance with national law which respects Community law. Equally, this Directive does not affect the social security legislation of the Member States. Lastly, this Directive does not affect the exercise of fundamental rights as recognized in the Member States and by Community law. Nor does it affect the right to

---

1429. See recitals 4-6 of the directive's Preamble.

negotiate, conclude and enforce collective agreements and to take industrial action in accordance with national law and practices which respect Community law.

7.7.3   Scope

Article 2 describes the scope: 'This Directive shall apply to services supplied by providers established in a Member State.' After this general statement, the following activities are excluded: non-economic services of general interest, financial services, electronic communications services and networks, services in the field of transport, services of temporary work agencies, healthcare services whether or not they are provided via healthcare facilities, and regardless of the ways in which they are organized and financed at national level or whether they are public or private, audiovisual services, gambling activities which involve wagering a stake with pecuniary value in games of chance, including lotteries, gambling in casinos and betting transactions, activities which are connected with the exercise of official authority as set out in Article 45 of the Treaty, social services relating to social housing, childcare and support of families and persons permanently or temporarily in need which are provided by the State, by providers mandated by the State or by charities recognized as such by the State, private security services, services provided by notaries and bailiffs, who are appointed by an official act of government. This Directive shall not apply to the field of taxation.

Article 3 deals in more detail with the relationship with other provisions of Community law, and in particular specific legislation such as Regulation1408/71 on social security and the TV Directive (see Ch. XI section 8.6 of this book). Article 3(2) states further that the directive does not concern rules of private international law, in particular rules governing the law applicable to contractual and non-contractual obligations, including those which guarantee that consumers benefit from the protection granted to them by the consumer protection rules laid down in the consumer legislation in force in their Member State.

7.7.4   Administrative Simplification

Chapter II deals with administrative simplification. Member States are to examine the procedures and formalities applicable to access to a service activity and to the exercise thereof. Where procedures and formalities examined under this paragraph are not sufficiently simple, Member States must simplify them (Art. 5). Member States must ensure that it is possible for providers to complete a number of procedures and formalities needed for access to the market through points of single contact (Art. 6).

7.7.5   Freedom of Establishment for Providers

Chapter III deals with the freedom of establishment for service providers. Member States may not make access to a service activity or the exercise thereof subject to an authorization scheme unless certain conditions are satisfied: (a) the authorization scheme does not discriminate against the provider in question; (b) the need for an authorization scheme is justified by an overriding reason relating to the public interest; (c) the objective pursued cannot be attained by means of a less restrictive measure, in particular because an a posteriori inspection would take place too late to be genuinely effective (Art. 9).

This Chapter III also contains provisions on conditions for the granting of authorization (Art. 10), the duration of authorization (Art. 11), authorization procedures (Art. 13) and prohibited requirements, such as discriminatory requirements based directly or indirectly on nationality or, in the case of companies, the location of the registered office, restrictions on the freedom of a provider to choose between a principal or a secondary establishment (Art. 14).

Article 15 provides for an extensive 'screenings operation': Member States must examine whether their legal system makes access to (or exercise of) a service activity subject to compliance with a number of listed non-discriminatory requirements, such as quantitative or territorial restrictions, an obligation on a provider to take a specific legal form, requirements relating to the shareholding of a company, and verify whether they are truly non-discriminatory, necessary and proportional. However, these conditions only apply to legislation in the field of services of general economic interest 'insofar as they do not obstruct the performance, in law or in fact, of the particular task assigned to them' (Art. 15(4)).

7.7.6 Free Movement of Services

Chapter IV deals with the freedom to provide services and related derogations. In this chapter, Article 16 contains the core provision: Member States shall respect the right of providers to provide services in a Member State other than that in which they are established. The Member State in which the service is provided shall ensure free access to and free exercise of a service activity within its territory. Member States shall not make access to or exercise of a service activity in their territory subject to compliance with any requirements which do not respect the following principles: non-discrimination, necessity and proportionality. Article 17 contains a number of derogations from the freedom to provide services, stating, *inter alia*, that Article 16 shall not apply to services of general economic interest in the postal, electricity and the gas sector, or concerning water distribution and supply services and waste water services and the treatment of waste. In these cases, the specific directives apply. Other derogations are also laid down, such as acts requiring by law the involvement of a notary, the registration of vehicles leased in another Member State or provisions regarding contractual and non-contractual obligations, including the form of contracts, determined pursuant to the rules of private international law.

7.7.7 The Transposition and Application of the Directive

The first stage of this hefty project has been completed: the Directive has been adopted. The Member States should bring into force the laws, regulations and administrative provisions necessary to comply with this directive before 28 December 2009. Only after that date will the real work begin, in the sense that the central as well as the local and regional authorities must apply the principles of the directive in practice. There is likely to be abundant case law of the Court of Justice due to the fact that a number of core provisions have not been clearly formulated.

8   FREE MOVEMENT OF PAYMENTS AND CAPITAL

On the basis of Article 73a EC, the old EEC regime[1430] was replaced as of 1 January 1994 by the new system which is set out in Articles 56–60 EC.[1431]

The delays in implementing the free movement of capital, as compared with the other freedoms, are obviously linked to the relationship between movement of capital, balance of payments and monetary policy.[1432] Articles 108 and 109 EEC, in the old regime, were intended to provide a temporary solution for balance of payments problems.

Title VII of Part 3 of the EC Treaty contains – since the entry into force of the Treaty of Amsterdam – the arrangements in legal terms implementing a model for an EMU, in which free movement of payments and free capital movements occupy an important place (see further Ch. X).

The new chapter on movement of payments and capital is structured as follows: first, there is a prohibition, contained in Article 56 EC; then, Articles 57–60 contain the various exceptions and justifications. The present section also follows that structure. The case law on free movement of capital is still developing,[1433] partly as a result of the fact that the prohibition on restrictions on free movement of capital has only been directly effective since 1994, while for the other freedoms this was the case since 1970.

1430. Basically, under the old Treaty regime there was free movement for payments, and for capital there was limited free movement.

1431. Until the entry into force of the Treaty of Maastricht, capital movements were regulated in Arts. 67–73 EEC and the directives based on Arts. 69 and 70 EEC, in particular Dir. 88/361, O.J. 1988, L 178/5. In Case C-97/98, *Jägerskold*, the Court considered that the Annexe to this directive retained its validity, even after the entry into force of Art. 56 EC et seq. The judgments concerning this directive, such as Joined Cases C-163, 165 & 250/94, *Criminal proceedings against Sanz de Lera and others,* and Case C-364/01, *The heirs of H. Barbier v. Inspecteur van de Belastingdienst Particulieren/Ondernemingen buitenland te Heerlen* thus also remain relevant for the interpretation of the new Treaty provisions. See also Case C-329/03, *Trapeza tis Ellados v. Banque Artesia* concerning First Council Directive of 11 May 1960 for the implementation of Art. 67 of the Treaty (O.J. 1960, 43, English Special Edition 1959–1962, 49).

1432. On the relation between capital movements and EMU, see Opinion A.G. Geelhoed in Case C-452/01, *Ospelt.*

1433. J.A. Usher, 'Financial Services, Taxation and Monetary Movements', in M. Andenas and W.-H. Roth (eds), *Services and Free Movement in EU Law* (Oxford, 2002), 395; S. Peers, 'Free Movement of Capital: Learning Lessons or Slipping on Spilt Milk?', in C. Barnard and J. Scott (eds), *The Law of the Single European Market: Unpacking the Premises* (Oxford, 2002), 333; L. Flynn, 'Coming of Age: The Free Movement of Capital Case Law 1993–2002' (2002) CML Rev., 773–805.

8.1   THE CONCEPTS: PAYMENTS AND MOVEMENT OF CAPITAL

The relationship between the provisions on payments and capital have been dealt with in a number of cases.[1434] This relationship conforms to the distinction made in the International Monetary Fund (IMF) Agreement.[1435]

A payment is a recompense or remuneration in the framework of a particular transaction, concerning goods or services.[1436] Capital movements concern financial operations which are essentially aimed at investment and profit-making activities for the sum in question, and not at remuneration for a good or service. Payments connected with tourism and medical services come under free movement of payments,[1437] but a mortgage which is inextricably bound with a capital movement comes under free movement of capital.[1438] Direct investment in the form of participation in an undertaking comes under free movement of capital.[1439]

Since the prohibition is set out in identical terms for the two categories (movement of capital and payments) in paragraphs 1 and 2 of Article 56 EC, the distinction is less important. It can have a role to play with regard to the application of some of the Treaty exceptions (see section 8.4. below) and in situations where capital movements or payments are linked to one of the other freedoms (see Art. 58(2) EC) or to another policy area, e.g., EMU (see Art. 59 EC).

8.2   THE BENEFICIARIES

Notwithstanding the exceptions discussed in section 8.3, below, free movement of capital and payments, both within the Community and between Member States and third countries, is not restricted in terms of categories of beneficiaries, unlike the free movement of persons and services. This means that, as with the free movement

---

1434. Case 7/78, *Thompson*; Case 203/80, *Criminal proceedings against Guerrino Casati*; Joined Cases 286/82 & 26/83, *Luisi and Carbone*; Case 157/85, *Luigi Brugnoni and Roberto Ruffinengo v. Cassa di risparmio di Genova e Imperia*; Case 308/86, *Lambert*; Case C-148/91, *Veronica*; Joined Cases C-358 & 416/93, *Bordessa*; Joined Cases C-163, 165 & 250/94, *Sanz de Lera*; Case C-222/97, *Manfred Trummer and Peter Mayer*; Case C-412/97, *ED*.

1435. 'Current' versus 'capital' transactions. See Art. XXX sub (d) IMF. See on this R. Smits, 'Freedom of Payments and Capital Movements under EMU', in *Festschrift H.J. Hahn* (Baden-Baden, 1997), 246.

1436. See Dir. 97/5, on cross-border credit transfers, O.J. 1997, L 43/25; Reg. 2560/2001, on cross-border credit transfers in Euro, O.J. 2001, L 344/13. See M. van Empel, 'Retail payments in the EU', 42 CML Rev., 1425–1444.

1437. Joined Cases 286/82 & 26/83, *Luisi and Carbone*.

1438. Case C-222/97, *Trummer*. See also Case C-464/98, *Westdeutsche Landesbank Girozentrale v. Friedrich Stefan*.

1439. Case C-367/98, *Commission v. Portugal (Golden Shares)*; Case C-483/99, *Commission v. France (Golden Shares)*; Case C-503/99, *Commission v. Belgium (Golden Shares)*; Case C-463/00, *Commission v. Spain (Golden Shares)*; Case C-98/01, *Commission v. United Kingdom (Golden Shares)*; Joined Cases C-282 & 283/04, *Commission v. The Netherlands (Golden Shares)*.

of goods, third-country nationals may also rely on Article 56 EC. This extensive liberalization is mitigated, however, by the existence of three additional exceptions (see section 8.4.1).

In *Skatteverket v. A*[1440] the Court made a number of fundamental statements on the differences between free movement of capital between Member States and that between a Member State and a third country. This judgment will be examined further below.

8.3   THE RULE: PROHIBITION OF RESTRICTIONS ON MOVEMENT

In this section, we use the same structure as for the other freedoms.

8.3.1   Addressees

Article 56 EC is directly effective.[1441] The addressees of this prohibition include both national and local authorities.[1442] In the *Euroloans* case, the Belgian Government argued that Article 56 EC was not applicable to the facts at hand, since they concerned a measure which the state had taken in its capacity as a market participant; the Court however ruled that it was a government measure, nevertheless.[1443]

It is still unclear whether private market participants come within the scope of the prohibition contained in Article 56 EC. This is certainly an important consideration in the banking sector.[1444]

8.3.2   Internal Situation

In *Reisch*, it was apparent from the file that all the elements in the main disputes were internal to one Member State, but the Court still answered the preliminary questions put to it because – as it had already stated in *Guimont* in the context of free movement of goods[1445] – it was of the opinion that an answer could be useful to the national court.[1446]

1440. Case C-101/05, *Skatteverket v. A.*
1441. This can be deduced from Joined Cases C-358 & 416/93, *Bordessa*, and Case C-35/98, *Verkooijen*.
1442. Case C-302/97, *Konle*; Joined Cases C-515/99 etc., *Reisch et al*; Case C-300/01, *Salzmann*; Case C-452/01, *Ospelt*; Joined Cases C-463 & 464/04, *Federconsumatori et al. v. Comune di Milano.*
1443. Case C-478/98, *Commission v. Belgium.*
1444. Cf. Case C-281/98, *Angonese.*
1445. Case C-448/98, *Guimont.*
1446. Joined Cases C- C-515/99 etc, *Reisch et al.* See also Case C-436/00, *X and Y*; Case C-300/01, *Salzmann.*

8.3.3   Import and Export Restrictions

Article 56 EC concerns restrictions on imports[1447] and on exports.[1448] Restrictions on intra-Community movements of capital and on movements of capital between Member States and third countries all come within the scope of the prohibition.

8.3.4   Direct Effect

Article 56(1) EC lays down a clear and unconditional prohibition for which no implementing measure is needed and which confers rights on individuals which they can rely on before the courts.[1449] In *Skatteverket v. A*,[1450] the German Government submitted that, in relations between Member States and third countries, that provision has direct effect only with regard to restrictions relating to categories of capital movement not covered by Article 57(1) EC; as regards the categories of capital movement referred to in Article 57(1), Article 57(2) confers power on the Council of the European Union to adopt liberalization measures if and to the extent that such measures make it possible to promote the operation of EMU. The German Government argued that while the Court, in *Sanz de Lera*,[1451] had acknowledged that the adoption of measures by the Council is not a prerequisite for implementing the prohibition laid down in Article 56(1) EC, it limited that interpretation to restrictions which are not covered by Article 57(1) EC. In reply, the Court stated that, as regards the movement of capital between Member States and third countries, 'Article 56(1) EC, in conjunction with Articles 57 EC and 58 EC, may be relied on before national courts and may render national rules that are inconsistent with it inapplicable, irrespective of the category of capital movement in question'.[1452]

8.3.5   Keck or Access to the Market

Konle[1453] concerned an Austrian authorization procedure for the acquisition of immovable property; here, the Court could have qualified this procedure as a 'selling arrangement' in the *Keck* sense.[1454] It did not do so – perhaps because the measure was in fact discriminatory. In the Spanish *golden shares* case,[1455] the Court rejected Spain's argument that this was a selling arrangement in the sense of

---

1447. Case C-222/97, *Trummer*.
1448. Joined Cases C-163, 165 & 250/94, *Sanz de Lera*.
1449. Joined Cases C-163, 165 & 250/94, *Sanz de Lera*, paras. 41 and 47.
1450. Case C-101/05, *Skatteverket v. A*.
1451. Joined Cases C-163, 165 & 250/94, *Sanz de Lera*.
1452. Case C-101/05, *Skatteverket v. A*, para. 27.
1453. Case C-302/97, *Konle*.
1454. See on this J. van de Gronden, 'Wetgeving ruimtelijke ordening getoetst aan de Europese regels van het vrij verkeer en de aansprakelijkheid van decentrale overheden' (1999) *NTER*, 252; J. Glöckner, 'Grundverkehrsbeschränkungen und Europarecht. Zugleich ein Beitrag zum Anwendungsbereich der Kapitalverkehrsfreiheit' (2000) EuR, 614.
1455. Case C-463/00, *Commission v. Spain*.

Keck, referring to its judgment in *Alpine Investment*[1456] and the arguments therein relating to access to the market.

8.3.6 Restrictive Measures: Distinctly and Indistinctly Applicable Measures

Save as far as the specific exceptions are concerned, which we will discuss below, Article 56 EC prohibits *all* restrictions on movement of capital and on payments within the Community and between the Member States and third countries from 1 January 1994.[1457] Thus, the obligation to use the national currency for the creation of a mortgage was found to be a restriction in the sense of Article 56 EC.[1458] As this example shows, the realization of EMU also removes a number of obstacles.[1459] Authorization systems have also been found to be within the scope of the prohibition,[1460] as well as requirements regarding the place of residence[1461] and certain tax rules concerning shares held in firms and companies which are situated (or registered) in another Member State.[1462]

8.3.7 Indistinctly Applicable Measures

Also come within the scope of the prohibition. Taking into account the wording of the prohibition ('all' restrictions: see Art. 56 EC) and the convergence between application of the Treaty provisions on the various freedoms, this is also what we would expect. Such a view is also confirmed by the decisions in *Trummer* and the *golden shares* cases.[1463]

8.3.8 Restrictions: Establishment or Capital

More and more cases concerning taxation and free movement of capital are coming before the Court. Originally, the Court avoided answering questions on Articles 56

1456. Case C-384/93, *Alpine Investment*.
1457. This may be deduced from Art. 73e EC (old). For Austria, this provision applied as of accession (1 Jan. 1995): see Case C-464/98, *Stefan*.
1458. Case C-222/97, *Trummer*. See also Case C-464/98, *Stefan*.
1459. Case C-452/01, *Ospelt*.
1460. Case C-302/97, *Konle*; Joined Cases C-515/99 etc., *Reisch et al.* See also Joined Cases C-358 & 416/93, *Bordessa* and Joined Cases C-163, 165 & 250/94, *Sanz de Lera*; Case C-300/01, *Salzmann*; Case C-452/04, *Fidium Finanz*.
1461. Case C-452/01, *Ospelt*; Case C-213/04, *Burtscher v. Stauderer*.
1462. Case C-436/00, *X and Y*; Case C-334/02, *Commission v. France*; Case C-242/03, *Ministre des Finances v. Jean-Claude Weidert and Élisabeth Paulus*; Case C-319/02, *Petri Manninen*; Case C-315/02, *Anneliese Lenz v. Finanzlandesdirektion für Tirol*; Case C-513/04, *Kerckhaert and Morres v. Belgium*; Case C-292/04, *Meilicke v. Finanzamt Bonn-Innenstadt*.
1463. Case C-222/97, *Trummer*; Case C-367/98, *Commission v. Portugal (Golden Shares)*; Case C-483/99, *Commission v. France (Golden Shares)*; Case C-503/99, *Commission v. Belgium (Golden Shares)*; Case C-463/00, *Commission v. Spain (Golden Shares)*; Case C-98/01, *Commission v. United Kingdom (Golden Shares)*.

and 58 EC,[1464] but in the judgments in *Sandoz* and *Verkooijen*, the Court interpreted these Treaty provisions in the context of, respectively, loans and investments.[1465] In the *golden shares* cases, the Commission had based its infringement action on the provisions on establishment and capital. The Court qualified the obstacles to investment as restrictions on the free movement of capital, and only dealt in a subsidiary manner with the restrictions on establishment.[1466] In Case C-436/00, *X and Y*, the situation was the reverse.[1467] In general, it may be said that Article 56 EC read with Article 58(2) EC concerns restrictions for shareholders, and Article 43 EC concerns restrictions for undertakings.[1468] In a number of test cases from the United Kingdom (with the title 'Test Claimants') concerning policy in relation to cross-border company relationships and the fiscal consequences, the Court has applied both Article 43 and Article 56 EC (see 6.5.1. above).[1469] In a few recent judgments, the Court examined double taxation conventions.[1470]

8.3.9   Restrictions: Services or Capital?

This issue was at stake in *Fidium Finanz*;[1471] the applicant company was established in Switzerland and was denied the right to grant credit to customers established in Germany on the ground that it did not have the authorization required by German law. The Court devoted a number of paragraphs to considering the questions of principle involved in the distinction between provision of services and capital movements. The distinction was particularly important because the restrictions concerning free movement of services only concern the freedom to provide services between Member States – at least as long as Article 49(2) EC on freedom to provide services in relation to third countries has not been applied by the Council – whereas restrictions on capital movements are prohibited for movements between the Member States and with third countries (and thus also Switzerland), as is laid down by Article 56(1) EC.

1464.   Case C-410/96, *Ambry*; Case C-200/98, *X AB and Y AB*.
1465.   Case C-439/97, *Sandoz v. Finanzlandesdirektion für Wien, Niederösterreich und Burgenland*; Case C-35/98, *Verkooijen*; Case C-478/98, *Commission v. Belgium*.
1466.   Case C-367/98, *Commission v. Portugal (Golden Shares)*; Case C-483/99, *Commission v. France (Golden Shares)*; Case C-503/99, *Commission v. Belgium (Golden Shares)*; Case C-463/00, *Commission v. Spain (Golden Shares*; Case C-98/01, *Commission v. United Kingdom* (Golden shares).
1467.   Case C-436/00, *X and Y*.
1468.   See on this H. Fleischer, 'Annotation of the Golden Shares Cases' (2003) CML Rev., 498.
1469.   See also Case C-157/05, *Winfried L. Holböck v. Finanzamt Salzburg-Land*; Case C-231/05, *Oy AA* and Case C-347/04, *Rewe Zentralfinanz*.
1470.   Case C-376/03, *D. v. Inspecteur van de belastingdienst*; Case C-265/04, *Bouanich v. Skatteverket*.
1471.   Case C-452/04, *Fidium Finanz*.

The Court first considered that

[c]ontrary to the chapter of the Treaty concerning the free movement of capital, the chapter regulating the freedom to provide services does not contain any provision which enables service providers in non-member countries and established outside the European Union to rely on those provisions. As the Court found in its Opinion of 15 November 1994, Opinion 1/94 [1994] ECR I-5267, paragraph 81, the objective of the latter chapter is to secure the right to provide services for nationals of Member States. Therefore, Article 49 EC et seq. cannot be relied on by a company established in a non-member country (para. 25).

The Court then ruled that the activity of granting credit on a commercial basis concerns, in principle, both the freedom to provide services and the free movement of capital. It is therefore necessary to consider whether, and if necessary to what extent, the rules in dispute affect the exercise of those two freedoms in the circumstances of the main case and whether they are capable of hindering them. The rules in dispute form part of the German legislation on the supervision of undertakings which carry out banking transactions and offer financial services. The purpose of those rules is to supervise the provision of such services and to authorize such provision only for undertakings which guarantee to conduct such transactions properly. Once the operator's access to the national market has been authorized, the preparation with a view to the loan made and the loan contract signed, that contract is carried out and the amount of the credit is actually transferred to the borrower. These rules prevent economic operators which do not have the qualities required by the German Law from having access to the German financial market. It is settled case law that all measures which prohibit, impede or render less attractive the exercise of the freedom to provide services must be regarded as restrictions of that freedom. If the requirement of authorization constitutes a restriction on the freedom to provide services, the requirement of a permanent establishment is the very negation of that freedom. For such a requirement to be accepted, it must be shown that it constitutes a condition which is indispensable for attaining the objective pursued (paras. 43–47).

The Court concluded that Article 49 EC cannot be relied on by a company, such as Fidium Finanz, which is established in a non-member country. The restrictive effects on the free movement of capital being an inevitable consequence of the restriction of services, the Court of Justice saw no need to examine the compatibility of the rules in question with the free movement of capital.

8.4   THE EXCEPTIONS TO THE PROHIBITION

The structure of the Treaty implicitly makes a distinction between exceptions which apply in general (see section 8.4.2) and those applicable to movements involving third countries (see section 8.4.1). As with the other freedoms, rule-of-reason exceptions have also been developed (see section 8.4.3).

8.4.1 Treaty-Based Exceptions Applicable to Movements Involving Third Countries

Under Article 57(1) EC, Member States are permitted to maintain certain rules which treat undertakings from third companies less favourably than undertakings from other Member States. This applies to rules concerning direct investment – including in real estate – establishment, the provision of financial services or the admission of securities to capital markets.[1472] Restrictions in the area of payments relating to transactions involving goods or services are thus excluded. The Council may, acting by a qualified majority, adopt measures on the movement of capital to or from third countries in relation to these categories, so that these restrictions may be adapted to suit new circumstances. The Council may take measures which extend these restrictions, but then unanimity is required (Art. 57(2) EC).

Where, in exceptional circumstances, movements of capital to or from third countries cause, or threaten to cause, serious difficulties for the operation of EMU, the Council may take safeguard measures for a limited period, if such measures are strictly necessary (Art. 59 EC).

Finally, in the cases envisaged in Article 301 EC, in the framework of the common external policy towards certain third countries, the Council may take measures of financial sanctions. Without prejudice to Article 297 EC, and as long as the Council has not taken measures,[1473] a Member State may take unilateral measures against a third country under certain circumstances (Art. 60 EC). See further on this Chapter XIII, section 3.3.5.[1474]

8.4.2 General Treaty-Based Exceptions

In *Skatteverket v. A.*[1475] the Court made an important pronouncement on the concept of restrictions on the movement of capital between Member States and third countries. Several Member States argued that the concept of restrictions on the movement of capital cannot be interpreted in the same manner with regard to relations between Member States and third countries as it is with regard to relations between Member States. They argued that, unlike the liberalization of the movement of capital between the Member States, which is intended to complete the internal market, the extension of the principle of free movement of capital to relations between Member States and third countries is linked to the completion of EMU. All those governments stated that, in relations with third countries, compliance with the prohibition laid down in Article 56(1) EC would lead to unilateral

---

1472. See on this extensively R. Smits, *Festschrift H.J. Hahn*, op. cit. *supra* note 1435, 254. For free movement with EEA countries, see Case C-452/01, *Ospelt*.
1473. See, e.g., Reg. 2580/2001, on specific restrictive measures directed against certain persons and entities with a view to combating terrorism, O.J. 2001, L 344/70 (post-11 Sep. 2001 measure).
1474. See on this extensively R. Smits, *Festschrift H.J. Hahn*, op. cit. note 1472, 257.
1475. Case C-101/05, *Skatteverket v. A.*

liberalization on the part of the EC without the Community securing a guarantee of equivalent liberalization on the part of the third countries concerned and, in the relations with those countries, without measures for the harmonization of national provisions, in particular on direct taxation.

The Court replied that it is clear from the case law of the Court that the extent to which the Member States are thus authorized to apply certain restrictive measures on the movement of capital cannot be determined without taking account of the fact, pointed out by several governments which submitted observations to the Court, that movement of capital to or from third countries takes place in a different legal context from that which occurs within the Community. Accordingly, because of the degree of legal integration that exists between Member States of the European Union, in particular by reason of the presence of Community legislation which seeks to ensure cooperation between national tax authorities, such as Directive 77/799, the taxation by a Member State of economic activities having cross-border aspects which take place within the Community is not always comparable to that of economic activities involving relations between Member States and third countries.[1476] According to the Court, it is possible that a Member State will be able to demonstrate that a restriction on the movement of capital to or from third countries is justified for a particular reason in circumstances where that reason would not constitute a valid justification for a restriction on capital movements between Member States.[1477] On those grounds, the argument put forward by the German and Netherlands governments – that if the concept of restrictions on movement of capital were interpreted in the same manner with regard to relations between Member States and third countries as it is with regard to relations between Member States, the Community would unilaterally open up the Community market to third countries without retaining the means of negotiation necessary to achieve such liberalization on the part of those countries – cannot be regarded as decisive.[1478]

The exceptions contained in Article 58(1) and (2) EC will be discussed below. Attention will also be paid briefly to the exceptions which apply in relation to those Member States which do not participate in EMU.

Article 58(3) EC provides that the measures referred to in paragraphs 1 and 2 may not constitute a means of arbitrary discrimination, or a disguised restriction on the free movement of capital and payments as defined in Article 56.[1479] These two conditions parallel those contained in Article 30 EC.

For the significance of the principle of proportionality in this area, reference may also be made to Article 30 EC (see section 3.3.1. above). The *golden shares* cases – in particular those against Belgium and France – give a clear indication of

---

1476. The Court referred here to Case C-446/04, *Test Claimants in the FII Group Litigation*, para.170.
1477. The Court referred here to Case C-446/04, *Test Claimants in the FII Group Litigation*, para.171.
1478. Case C-101/05, *Skatteverket v. A*, para.38.
1479. See on this Case C-319/02, *Manninen*.

the way the Court uses the principle of proportionality.[1480] In its judgment in *Sandoz*, the Court was of the opinion that the Austrian measure at issue was not appropriate for preventing fraud.[1481] In *Bordessa*, the Court applied the principles established in *Luisi and Carbone*: the requirement of prior notification is sufficient for effective supervision to be carried out; the requirement of prior authorization goes too far.[1482] In its judgment in *Association Église de scientologie*, the Court referred to its case law on the free movement of persons, and the need to be able to have access to legal redress against a restrictive measure.[1483] In line with its case law on the exceptions in the context of the other freedoms,[1484] the Court has stated that a purely economic objective may not constitute an overriding reason in the general interest capable of justifying a restriction. A Dutch provision which aimed to stimulate the national economy by encouraging private persons to invest in firms established in the Netherlands was not permitted.[1485]

8.4.2.1   Article 58(1) EC

Article 58(1)(b) EC provides for a justification on grounds of public policy or public security for all capital movements, both within the EC and with countries outside the EC. The trio with which we are familiar in relation to the other freedoms (see Arts. 39 and 46) obviously loses one of its elements – public health – in the context of capital movements. In interpreting public policy and public security,[1486] the Court refers explicitly to its case law on the free movement of persons[1487] or free movement of goods,[1488] the latter concerning the justification of security of supply of energy products (gas and petroleum) as an element of the generally formulated exceptions.

In *Albore*, the Court found that the measure in question was discriminatory. The Court considered that, although neither the order for reference nor the written observations of the Italian Government made any mention of a justification, it

---

1480. Case C-483/99, *Commission v. France (Golden shares)*; Case C-503/99, *Commission v. Belgium (Golden shares)*; Case C-463/00, *Commission v. Spain (Golden shares)*; Case C-98/01, *Commission v. United Kingdom* (Golden shares). See also Case C-478/98, *Commission v. Belgium*.
1481. Case C-439/97, *Sandoz*.
1482. Joined Cases 286/82 & 26/83, *Luisi and Carbone*; Joined Cases C-358 & 416/93, *Bordessa*.
1483. Case C-54/99, *Association Église de Scientologie de Paris and Scientology International Reserves Trust v. French Republic*, with reference to Case 222/86, *Heylens*.
1484. E.g., Case 72/83, *Campus Oil*; Case C-120/95, *Decker*; Case C-158/96, *Kohll*.
1485. Case C-35/98, *Verkooijen*. See also Case C-367/98, *Commission v. Portugal (Golden shares)*; Case C-54/99, *Église de scientologie*; Case C-315/02 *Lenz*.
1486. Joined Cases C-358 & 416/93, *Bordessa*; Joined Cases C-163, 165 & 250/94, *Sanz de Lera*; Case C-302/97, *Konle*; Case C-367/98, *Commission v. Portugal (Golden shares)*; Case C-483/99, *Commission v. France (Golden shares)*; Case C-503/99, *Commission v. Belgium (Golden shares)*.
1487. Case C-54/99, *Église de scientologie*, with reference to Case 36/75, *Rutili* and Case C-348/96, *Calfa*.
1488. Case 72/83, *Campus Oil*.

was apparent from the aim of the measure in question that it could be considered to be based on reasons of public security (Art. 58 EC) and the defence of the national territory (Art. 297 EC). The Court, which in this case did not respect its own rules on the burden of proof,[1489] eventually found the Italian measures disproportionate.[1490]

Moreover, Article 58(1)(b) EC permits a number of measures of supervision; these may concern taxation and the prudential supervision of financial institutions.[1491] Measures for administrative or statistical information may also be justified. These provisions may also be found in certain banking and insurance directives (see section 6.8 above).

Finally, Article 58(1)(a) EC permits the Member States to apply tax provisions 'which distinguish between taxpayers who are not in the same situation with regard to their place of residence or with regard to the place where their capital is invested'.[1492] A Declaration annexed to the Treaty of Maastricht limits the applicability of this exception to measures in force at the end of 1993.

8.4.2.2   Article 58(2) EC

Rather discreetly, Article 58(2) EC provides that the provisions of the chapter on payments and capital movements are without prejudice to the applicability of restrictions on the right of establishment which are compatible with the Treaty. This provision is in a manner of speaking the mirror image of Article 43(2) EC. According to the latter provision, the freedom of establishment includes the right to take up and pursue activities as self-employed persons and to set up and manage undertakings, subject to the provisions of the chapter relating to capital. There is no specific case law on the relationship between these two provisions, but recent case law on golden shares may be taken to imply that the provisions on establishment and on movement of capital – both with regard to the prohibition and the exceptions – are broadly speaking interpreted in the same manner.[1493]

8.4.2.3   Other Treaty-Based Exceptions

In the *golden shares* cases, the question arose whether Article 295 EC, concerning property ownership, could be invoked as a kind of exception in order to justify restrictions on investments in privatized undertakings. The Advocate General was of the opinion that this was possible, but the Court rejected the argument.[1494] In the Belgian *golden shares* case, the Belgian Government's plea relying on

---

1489. See section 3.3.1 *supra*.
1490. Case C-423/98, *Alfredo Albore*.
1491. Case C-478/98, *Commission v. Belgium*.
1492. Case C-439/97, *Sandoz*. See on this J.A. Usher, 'Financial Services, Taxation and Monetary Movements', in M. Andenas and W.-H. Roth (eds), *Services and Free Movement in EU Law* (Oxford, 2002), 395. See also Case C-118/96, *Safir*.
1493. Case C-463/00, *Commission v. Spain (Golden shares)*.
1494. Case C-367/98, *Commission v. Portugal (Golden shares)*; Case C-483/99, *Commission v. France (Golden shares)*; Case C-503/99, *Commission v. Belgium (Golden shares)*.

Article 86(2) was not examined by the Court, since the Belgian measure was already deemed to be justified on the grounds public policy and security.

8.4.2.4 Temporary Treaty-Based Exceptions

In the second phase (the transitional period) of the EMU, Articles 119 and 120 EC permitted the Member States participating in EMU, if they were seriously threatened with difficulties as regards their balance of payments or in the event of a sudden crisis, to impose currency restrictions under the conditions set out in those provisions.[1495] The Member States which do not participate in EMU (the 'outs', Member States with a derogation) may also use this possibility in the third phase (see Art. 120(4) read with Art. 122(6) EC).

8.4.3 Rule-of-Reason Exceptions

As a result of the broad character of the prohibition in Article 56 EC, rule-of-reason justifications may be invoked for indistinctly applicable measures, in line with the system found in relation to the other freedoms. The Court indicated this explicitly in the *golden shares* cases.[1496]

An example of a general interest justification can be found in *Veronica*, in which, under the old regime of Article 67 EEC, pluriformity of the media was at issue.[1497] In its judgment in *Trummer*, the Court grants Member States the right to take measures which are necessary to ensure the foreseeability and transparency of the mortgage system.[1498] In a few cases concerning holiday houses, the Court examined considerations of urban and country planning and tourism.[1499] In another case, the protection of small-scale agricultural holdings was examined.[1500]

A number of cases concerned situations which involved freedom to provide services and freedom of establishment alongside the fee movement of capital; in these situations, the *Bachmann* justification (cohesion or integrity of the fiscal regime) was invoked (though not successfully).[1501] In more recent case law, the justification of cohesion of the tax system was invoked in cases which only involved free movement of capital (though again unsuccessfully, either because

---

1495. See on this extensively R. Smits, *De monetaire unie na Maastricht*, in *Festschrift H.J. Hahn*, op. cit. note 1427, 250.
1496. Case C-367/98, *Commission v. Portugal (Golden shares)*; Case C-483/99, *Commission v. France (Golden shares)*; Case C-503/99, *Commission v. Belgium (Golden shares)*; Case C-112/05, *Commission v. Germany*. See also Joined Cases C-515/99 etc., *Reisch et al.* and Case C-300/01, *Salzmann*.
1497. Case C-148/91, *Veronica*.
1498. Case C-222/97, *Trummer*.
1499. Case C-302/97, *Konle*; Joined Cases C-515/99 etc., *Reisch et al.*; Case C-300/01, *Salzmann*.
1500. Case C-452/01, *Ospelt*.
1501. Case C-484/93, *Svensson and Gustavsson*; Case C-478/98, *Commission v. Belgium*.

the cohesion of the system was found not to be affected, or because the measure in question was found to be unnecessary).[1502]

In *Sanz de Lera*, the Court referred to its judgment in *Bordessa* and its interpretation of Directive 88/361 therein;[1503] Article 58(1)(b) EC was based on Article 4 of this Directive. The Court considered – in *Bordessa* – that the term '*inter alia*' used in the Directive implies that other exceptions are also permitted in addition to the objectives expressly mentioned.[1504] In *Sanz de Lera*, the Court applied this interpretation to Article 58(1)(b) EC. Using this route, the prevention of illegal activities, of money laundering, of trade in narcotics and of terrorism are all brought within the scope of the exception.[1505] The rule-of-reason exceptions can thus be read into the Treaty.

There is also a clear link between the taxation exception in Article 58(1)(a) EC and the fiscal cohesion exception in *Bachmann*.[1506] In *Verkooijen*, the Court made this link, but rejected the applicability of the exception in the case at hand.[1507]

In a case concerning Italy, the Court found that even though the need to safeguard energy supplies may, under certain conditions, justify restrictions of fundamental freedoms under the Treaty, the Italian Government had not demonstrated in what way a limitation of voting rights affecting only one specific category of public undertakings was necessary in order to attain that objective. In particular, it had not explained why it was necessary for the shares of undertakings operating in the energy sector in Italy to be held by private shareholders or by public shareholders quoted on regulated financial markets for the undertakings concerned to be able to guarantee sufficient and uninterrupted supplies of electricity and gas in the Italian market.[1508]

In an appropriate conclusion to this chapter on the freedoms, it may be mentioned that in *Verkooijen*,[1509] mentioned above, the Court gives a fine pedagogical consideration of the relationship between the freedoms and the exceptions. In answer to the argument brought by the Dutch Government concerning a possible tax advantage for taxpayers who receive dividends in the Netherlands from companies situated in other Member States, the Court stated: 'It is clear from settled case law that unfavourable tax treatment contrary to a fundamental freedom cannot be justified by the existence of other tax advantages, even supposing that such advantages exist' (para. 61). The Court referred thereby to its case law on establishment and on services,[1510] though *Verkooien* itself concerned free movement of capital.

1502.   Case C-242/03, *Weidert* and Case C-319/02, *Manninen*.
1503.   O.J. 1988, L 178/5. Joined Cases C-358 & 416/93, *Bordessa*. See also Case C-478/98, *Commission v. Belgium*.
1504.   Joined Cases C-358 & 416/93, *Bordessa*.
1505.   Joined Cases C-163, 165 & 250/94, *Sanz de Lera*.
1506.   Case C-204/90, *Bachmann*.
1507.   Case C-35/98, *Verkooijen*. See also Case C-436/00, *X and Y*.
1508.   Case C-174/04, *Commission v. Italy*.
1509.   Case C-35/98, *Verkooijen*.
1510.   Case 270/83, *Commission v. France (Avoir fiscal)*; Case C-107/94, *Asscher*; Case C-307/97, *Saint Gobain*; Case C-294/97, *Eurowings Luftverkehr*.

FURTHER READING

Internal Market, General
Barnard, C. *The Substantive Law of the EU: The Four Freedoms.* Oxford: Oxford University Press, 2007.
Barnard, C. and J. Scott. *The Law of the Single European Market: Unpacking the Premises.* Oxford: Hart, 2002.
Brigola, A. *Das System der EG-Grundfreiheiten: vom Diskriminierungsverbot zum spezifischen Beschränkungsverbot.* Europäisches Wirtschaftsrecht, Bd. 33. München: Beck, 2004.
Broberg, M.P. and N. Holst-Christensen. *Free Movement in the European Union: Cases, Commentaries and Questions.* Copenhagen: DJØF Publishing, 2004.
Davies, G.T. *EU Internal Market Law.* 2nd ed. London: Cavendish, 2003.
Davies, G.T. *Nationality Discrimination in the European Internal Market.* European Monographs, 44. The Hague: Kluwer Law International, 2003.
De Vries, S.A. *Tensions within the Internal Market: The Functioning of the Internal Market and the Development of Horizontal and Flanking Policies.* Groningen: Europa Law Publishing, 2006.
Fairhurst, J. *Law of the European Union.* 6th ed. Harlow: Pearson Longman, 2007.
Georgiadis, N.A. *Derogation Clauses: The Protection of National Interests in EC Law.*Publications of the Hellenic Institute of International and Foreign Law, 23. Bruylant: Sakkoulas, 2006.
Kostoris Padoa-Schioppa, F. *The Principles of Mutual Recognition in the European Integration Process.* Basingstoke: Palgrave Macmillan, 2005.
Mégret, J., et al. *Commentaire J. Mégret. Marché intérieur.* 3e éd. entièrement refondue et mise à jour. Bruxelles: Éd. de l'Université de Bruxelles, 2006.
Mercier, P., et al. *La libre circulation des personnes et des services.* 2e éd. ent. remaniée et augmentée. Dossiers de droit européen, no. 1. Basel: Helbing und Lichtenhahn, 2004.
Nic Shuibhne, N. *Regulating the Internal Market.* Cheltenham: Edward Elgar, 2006.
Plötscher, S. *Der Begriff der Diskriminierung im Europäischen Gemeinschaftsrecht: zugleich ein Beitrag zur einheitlichen Dogmatik der Grundfreiheiten des EG-Vertrages.* Schriften zum europäischen Recht, Bd. 90. Berlin: Duncker & Humblot, 2003.
Schrauwen, A.A.M. *Rule of Reason: Rethinking Another Classic of European Legal Doctrine.* The Hogendorp Papers, 4. Groningen: Europa Law Publishing, 2005.
Shaw, J., et al. *Economic and Social Law of the European Union.* Basingstoke: Palgrave Macmillan, 2007.
Snell, J. *Goods and Services in EC Law: A Study of the Relationship between the Freedoms.* Oxford: Oxford University Press, 2002.
Tridimas, T. and P. Nebbia. *European Union Law for the Twenty-First Century: Rethinking the New Legal Order.* Oxford: Hart, 2004.
Wallace, H., et al. *Policy-Making in the European Union.* The New European Union Series. Oxford University Press, 2005.

White, R.C.A. *Workers, Establishment, and Services in the European Union.* Oxford: Oxford University Press, 2004.

Woods, L. *Free Movement of Goods and Services within the European Community.* Aldershot: Ashgate, 2004.

Free Movement of Goods (Tariff Barriers)

Berr, C.J. and H. Trémeau. *Le droit douanier: communautaire et national.* 7e éd. Collection droit des affaires et de l'entreprise. Série: Études et recherches. Paris: Economica, 2006.

Lux, M. *Guide to Community Customs Legislation.* Pratique du droit communautaire = European Law in Practice. Brussels: Bruylant, 2002.

Lyons, T. *EC Customs La.*2nd ed. Oxford EC Law Library. Oxford: Oxford University Press, 2008.

Article 90 EC & Taxation

Dahlberg, M. *Direct Taxation in Relation to the Freedom of Establishment and the Free Movement of Capital.* EUCOTAX Series on European Taxation, vol. 9. The Hague: Kluwer Law International, 2005.

Dillmann, M. and A. Altrogge. *Europäisches Gesellschafts – und Steuerrecht: Grundlagen, Entwicklungen, Verbindungslinien.* Münchener Schriften zum Internationalen Steuerrech, H. 27. München: Beck, 2007.

Gormley, L.W. *EU Taxation Law.* Richmond Tax & Law, 2006.

Gribnau, J.L.M. Legal *Protection against Discriminatory Tax Legislation: The Struggle for Equality in European Tax Law.* London: Kluwer Law International, 2003.

Lang, M., et al. *ECJ: Recent Developments in Direct Taxation.* EUCOTAX Series on European Taxation,13. Kluwer Law International/Linde, 2006.

Pinto, C. *Tax Competition and EU Law.* The Hague: EUCOTAX Series on European Taxation, vol. 7. Kluwer Law International, 2003.

Terra, B.J.M. and J. Kajus. *A Guide to the European VAT Directives.* Amsterdam: International Bureau of Fiscal Documentation (IBFD), 2004.

Terra, B.J.M. and P.J. Wattel. *European Tax Law.* 5th ed. Alphen aan den Rijn: Kluwer Law International, 2008.

Vanistendael, F. and A. Cordewener. *EU Freedoms and Taxation: EATLP Congress, Paris 3–5 June 2004.* EATLP International Tax Series, 2. Amsterdam: IBFD Publications, 2006.

Weber, D.M. *Tax Avoidance and the EC Treaty Freedoms: A Study of the Limitations under European Law to the Prevention of Tax Avoidance.* EUCOTAX Series on European Taxation, 11. The Hague: Kluwer Law International, 2005.

Free Movement of Goods (Non-Tariff Barriers)

Jarvis, M. A. The *Application of EC Law by National Courts: The Free Movement of Goods.* Oxford: Clarendon Press, 1998.

Maduro, M. P. *We the Court: The European Court of Justice and the European Economic Situation: A Critical Reading of Article 30 of the EC Treat.* Oxford: Hart, 1998.

Millarg, I. *Die Schranken des freien Warenverkehrs in der EG: Systematik und Zusammenwirken von Cassis-Rechtsprechung und Art. 30 EG-Vertrag.* Schriftenreihe Europäisches Recht, Politik und Wirtschaft, Bd. 253. Baden-Baden: Nomos, 2001.

Oliver, P. and M.A. Jarvis. *Free Movement of Goods in the European Community: Under Articles 28 to 30 of the EC Treaty.* 4th ed. London: Sweet and Maxwell, 2003.

Richters, S. *Diskriminierung im Bereich der Warenverkehrsfreiheit.* Europäische Hochschulschriften. Reihe 2, Rechtswissenschaft, Bd. 3747. Frankfurt am Main: Lang, 2003.

Woods, L. *Free Movement of Goods and Services within the European Community.* Aldershot: Ashgate, 2004.

Free Movement of Persons and Workers

Apap, J. *Freedom of Movement of Persons: A Practitioner's Handbook.* The Hague: Kluwer, 2002.

Bigo, D. and E. Guild. *Controlling Frontiers: Free Movement into and within Europe.* Aldershot: Ashgate, 2005.

Carlier, J.-Y. and B. Coulie. *L'avenir de la libre circulation des personnes dans l'U.E.: analyse de la directive 2004/38 du 29 avril 2004 relative au droit des citoyens de circuler et de séjourner librement = The Future of Free Movement of Persons in the EU: Analysis of the Directive 2004/38 of 29 April 2004 on the Right of Citizens to Move and Reside Freely.* Collection du Centre des Droits de l'Homme de l'Université catholique de Louvain, 2. Bruxelles: Bruylant, 2006.

Cremers, J. and P. Donders. *The Free Movement of Workers in the European Union: Directive 96/71/EC on the Posting of Workers within the Framework of the Provision of Services: Its Implementation, Practical Application and Operation.* CLR Studies, 4. Bruxelles: CLR; Doetinchem: Reed Business Information, 2004.

Famira, K. *Der freie Personenverkehr in Europa: Schengen nach Amsterdam.* Schriftenreihe Europarecht, Bd. 6. Berlin: BWV Berliner Wissenschafts-Verlag; Wien : NWV Neuer Wissenschaftlicher-Verlag, 2004.

Groenendijk, C. A. and E. Guild. *In Search of Europe's Borders.* Immigration and Asylum Law and Policy in Europe, vol. 5. The Hague: Kluwer Law International, 2003.

Kutenicova, E. *Perspectives of the Free Movement of Workers in the Prospect of Enlargement of the European Union.* Rotterdam: Erasmus University, 2003.

Rogers, N. and R. Scannell. *Free Movement of Persons in the Enlarged European Union.* London: Sweet & Maxwell, 2005.

Sieveking, K. and B. Univ. *ECJ Rulings on Health Care Services and Their Effects on the Freedom of Cross-Border Patient Mobility in the EU.* ZERP-Diskussionspapier, 03/2006. [on-line]: Zentrum für Europäische Rechtspolitik, 2006.

Spaventa, E. *Free Movement of Persons in the European Union: Barriers to Movement in Their Constitutional Context.* Kluwer European Law Collection, 2. The Hague: Kluwer Law International, 2007.

Staples, H. *The Legal Status of Third Country Nationals Resident in the European Union.* European Monograph, 22. The Hague: Kluwer Law International, 1999.

Toner, H. *Partnership Rights, Free Movement, and EU Law.* Modern Studies in European Law, vol. 3. Oxford: Hart, 2004.

Van der Mei, A.P. *Free Movement of Persons within the European Community: Cross-Border Access to Public Benefits.* Oxford: Hart, 2003.

Weiss, F. and F. Wooldridge. *Free Movement of Persons within the European Community.* 2nd ed. European Monographs, 30. Alphen aan den Rijn: Kluwer Law International, 2007.

White, R.C.A. *Workers, Establishment, and Services in the European Union.* Oxford: Oxford University Press, 2004.

Right of Establishment/Company Law

Bartman, S.M. *European Company Law in Accelerated Progress.* European Company Law Series, 1. Alphen aan den Rijn: Kluwer Law International, 2006.

Costa, C.T.D. and A.d.M. Bilreiro. *The European Company Statute.* European Business Law and Practice Series, vol. 19. The Hague: Kluwer Law International, 2003.

Dumoulin, S.H.M.A. *The European Company: Corporate Governance and Cross-Border Reorganisations from a Legal and Tax Perspective.* Den Haag: Boom Juridische uitgevers, 2005.

Ferrarini, G. *Reforming Company and Takeover Law in Europe.* Oxford: Oxford University Press, 2004.

Gerster, C., et al. (eds). *European Banking and Financial Services Law.* The Hague: Kluwer Law International, 2004.

Grundmann, S. and F. Möslein. *European Company Law: Organization, Finance and Capital Markets.* Ius communitatis, 1. Antwerpen: Intersentia, 2007.

Hopt, K.J. *The European Foundation: A New Legal Approach.* Cambridge: Cambridge University Press, 2006.

Hopt, K.J. and E. Wymeersch. *European Company and Financial Law: Texts and Leading Cases.* 4th ed. Oxford: Oxford University Press, 2007.

Hulle, K.V. and H. Gesell. *European Corporate Law.* Praxis Europarecht. Nomos, 2006.

Lackhoff, K. *Die Niederlassungsfreiheit des EGV: nur ein Gleichheits – oder auch ein Freiheitsrecht?.* Münsterische Beiträge zur Rechtswissenschaft, Bd. 125. Berlin: Duncker & Humblot, 2000.

Raaijmakers, G.T.M.J. *European Regulation of Company and Securities Law.* Nijmegen: Ars Aequi, 2005.

Rickford, J. *The European Company: Developing a Community Law of Corporations: Collected Papers from the Leiden University Unilever Programme, 2002.* Antwerp: Intersentia, 2003.

Unzicker, F *Niederlassungsfreiheit der Kapitalgesellschaften in der Europäischen Union nach der Centros- und der Überseering-Entscheidung des EuGH.* Europäische Hochschulschriften. Reihe 2, Rechtswissenschaft, Bd. 3781. Frankfurt am Main: Lang, 2004.

Van Gerven, D. and P. Storm. *The European Company.* Law Practitioner Series. Cambridge: Cambridge University Press, 2006.

Warren, M. G. *European Securities Regulation* The Hague: Kluwer Law International, 2003.

Werlauff, E. *EU Company Law: Common Business Law of 28 States.* 2nd ed. Copenhagen: DJØF Publishing, 2003.

Werlauff, E. *SE: The Law of the European Company.* Copenhagen: DJØF Publishing, 2003.

Free Movement of Services

Andenas, M. and W.-H. Roth. *Services and Free Movement in EU Law.* Oxford: Oxford University Press, 2002.

Blanpain, R. *Freedom of Services in the European Union: Labour and Social Security Law: The Bolkestein Initiative.* Bulletin of Comparative Labour Relations, 58. The Hague: Kluwer Law International, 2006.

Breuss, F., et al. *Services Liberalisation in the Internal Market.* Schriftenreihe der Österreichischen Gesellschaft für Europaforschung (ECSA Austria), 6. Wien: Springer, 2008.

Freshfields Bruckhaus, D. and M. Raffan. *A Practioner's Guide to EU Financial Services Directives.* City & Financial Publishing, 2006.

Hatzopoulos, V. *Le principe communautaire d'équivalence et de reconnaissance mutuelle dans la libre prestation de services.* Bruxelles: Bruylant, 1999.

Kox, H.L.M., et al. *The Free Movement of Services within the EU.* CPB Document, no. 69. The Hague: CPB Netherlands Bureau for Economic Policy Analysis, 2004.

Rolshoven, M. *'Beschränkungen' des freien Dienstleistungsverkehrs.* Schriften zum Europäischen Recht, 86. Berlin: Duncker & Humblot, 2002.

Woods, L. *Free Movement of Goods and Services within the European Community.* Aldershot: Ashgate, 2004.

Free Movement of Capital/Payments

Booth, P. and D. Currie. *The Regulation of Financial Markets.* IEA Readings, no. 58. London: Institute of Economic Affairs, 2003.

Derleder, P. and K.-O. Knops. *Handbuch zum deutschen und europäischen Bankrecht.* Berlin: Springer, 2004.

Handoll, J. *Capital, Payments and Money Laundering in the EU*. Richmond: Richmond Law & Tax, 2006.

Hemetsberger, W., et al. *European Banking and Financial Services Law*. 2nd ed. Alphen aan den Rijn: Kluwer Law International, 2006.

Servais, D., et al. (eds). *Intégration des marchés financiers*. Commentaire J. Mégret, 3e éd., Politiques économiques et sociales, 3. Bruxelles: Éditions de l'Université, 2007.

Stünkel, K. *EG-Grundfreiheiten und Kapitalmärkte: die Auswirkungen der Grundfreiheiten auf die Integration der Sekundärmärkte*. Europäisches Wirtschaftsrecht, 42. Baden-Baden: Nomos/Beck, 2005.

Usher, J. A. *The Law of Money and Financial Services in the EC*. 2nd ed. Oxford: Oxford University Press, 2000.

Chapter IX

The Competition Policy of the EC

R. Barents

1   INTRODUCTION

The concept 'competition policy'[1] is used in this chapter in a broad sense: it
embraces the policy of the EC concerning all the matters mentioned in Articles
81–97 EC.[2] While the five freedoms relate to the *establishment* of the common
market (discussed in Ch. VIII of this book), the competition rules relate principally
to the *functioning* of the common market. The Treaty rules on competition between
undertakings (Arts. 81–86 EC, competition policy in the narrow sense), state
aids granted by the Member States (Arts. 87–89 EC), and certain aspects of harmonization of legislation (Arts. 94–97 EC), allow a considerable discretion to the
EC – unlike the provisions on the five freedoms. Competence in these areas can
primarily be used to supplement and reinforce negative integration. It is also possible, though, to use the powers contained in these provisions in a more interventionist direction. In its policy on cartels, market structure and mergers, the EC may
seek to strengthen existing competition or, in addition, it may approach cooperation between undertakings as an instrument of economic policy or coordination of
economic policy or other policies regulated in the Treaty. The powers relating
to the approval of State aids can be used to remove distortions of competition,

---

1. We will use the term 'competition' policy rather than the (US) term 'antitrust'.
2. Harmonization is dealt with in general in Ch. V of this book. In section 4 of this chapter we will
    discuss some aspects relating to competition policy.

P.J.G. Kapteyn, A.M. McDonnell, K.J.M. Mortelmans and C.W.A. Timmermans (eds),
The Law of the European Union and the European Communities, pp. 785–879.
©2008 Kluwer Law International BV, The Netherlands.

but also so as to contribute to the coordination of regional, sectoral and flanking policies. Finally, harmonization or approximation of legislation[3] can be regarded as primarily supplementing the five freedoms, i.e., removing obstacles to intra-Community trade, but also as an instrument of positive integration. Article 95 EC is a very good illustration – both in its wording and in the practice of its application – of the different gradations which the relationship between negative and positive integration can assume. The case law on the position of this provision as a legal basis, as compared with other Treaty provisions, demonstrates the practical consequences of the relationship between the two forms of integration chosen by the Community legislature.[4] In the broad sense described above, competition policy, as set out in the scheme of the Treaty and in this book, forms the bridge between the five freedoms and the binding coordination of economic policy in the framework of the economic and monetary union, as well as the Community's regional, sectoral and flanking policies.

2   THE COMPETITION RULES FOR UNDERTAKINGS

2.1   INTRODUCTION

In the field of competition rules for undertakings (Arts. 81–86 EC),[5] there is a considerable amount of legislation and quasi-legislation,[6] the Commission has an extensive practice in decision-making,[7] and there is considerable national and Community case law. The steady increase in all of these means that this area of Community law, which is of crucial importance for industry and commerce, is growing ever more complex and detailed. In addition, the mechanisms for applying Articles 81 and 82 EC have been fundamentally altered in 2003 and the following years. After the Commission presented its White Paper in 1999 on the Modernization of competition law for undertakings,[8] a new basic Regulation relating to these matters was adopted at the end of 2002, which started to apply as of 1 May 2004, replacing the old Regulation 17 – which dated from 1962.[9]

---

3. See Ch. V, section 2.
4. Case 14/68, *Walt Wilhelm and others v. Bundeskartellamt*; Case 6/72, *Europemballage Corporation and Continental Can Company Inc. v. Commission.*
5. The Lisbon Treaty will renumber the provisions 81–86 EC as Arts. 101–106 TFEU. The term 'common market' is replaced throughout the Treaty by the term 'internal market'. The reference to a system ensuring that competition is not distorted – currently in Art. 3(1)(g) EC – is not mentioned in Art. 3 TEU (Lisbon). (Art. I-3 of the Treaty establishing a Constitution for Europe did mention 'an internal market where competition is free and undistorted'.) Instead, a Protocol on the internal market and competition is annexed to the TEU (Lisbon) and the TFEU.
6. For all legislation, policy documents, and decisions see http:/europa.eu.int/comm/competition/.
7. The Commission's decisions tend to be published with considerable delay in the Official Journal.
8. O.J. 1999, C 132/1.
9. See Council Reg. (EC) No. 1/2003 of 16 Dec. 2002 on the implementation of the rules on competition laid down in Arts. 81 and 82 of the Treaty, O.J. 2003, L 1/1.

The discussion of this subject is therefore limited to a presentation and commentary of the main lines only. In this section, the principles underlying Articles 81 and 82 EC will be discussed. The *substantive competition* rules will be dealt with in sections 2.2–2.4, and the procedural and institutional competition rules will be examined in sections 2.5 and 2.6 – in this context, the changes in the mechanisms for applying the competition rules will be discussed. Merger control will be treated in section 2.7. Article 86 EC (public undertakings) will be dealt with separately (section 2.8).

2.1.1 Function of the Rules on Competition

Articles 81 and 82 EC contain directly effective prohibitions, addressed to under-takings, of the prevention, restriction or distortion of competition within the common market, subject to the conditions laid down in those provisions.[10] Both provisions are thus expressions of a system of prohibition. Constant case law of the Court shows that the function of Articles 81 and 82 EC is to guarantee the system of undistorted competition laid down in Article 3(1)(g) EC, which system in its turn serves the establishment and functioning of the common market described in Article 2 EC.[11] The function as formulated here shows clearly that the aim of these provisions is to protect the economic interests of all market participants, not just those of consumers, but also those of competitors.[12] Conduct which is not economic in character,[13] does not come within the scope of Articles 81 and 82 EC. Sport activities only fall outside the scope of the competition provisions insofar as the relevant rules are strictly necessary to ensure the proper conduct of competitive sport.[14]

In addition, this explanation of their function explains why the competition rules for undertakings have a primarily supplementary function in relation to the five freedoms. This is particularly true with respect to the free movement of goods,[15] but also holds for the other freedoms.[16] This supplementary function is expressed in

---

10. Case 127/73, *Belgische Radio en Televisie v. SV SABAM and NV Fonior* and Case 37/79, *Anne Marty SA v. Estée Lauder SA*. See for Art. 81(3), Case C-238/05, *Asnef-Equifax*.
11. Case 32/65, *Italy v. Council and Commission*; Case 6/72, *Continental Can*; Case T-22/97, *Kesko v.Commission*.
12. Case C-481/01 P (R), *NDC Health GmbH & Co. KG and NDC Health Corporation v. IMS Health Inc. and Commission*.
13. Case C-309/99, *J.C.J. Wouters, J.W. Savelbergh, Price Waterhouse Belastingadviseurs BV v. Algemene Raad van de Nederlandse Orde van Advocaten*; Case C-205/03 P, *FENIN v. Commision*.
14. Case C-519/04 P, *Meca-Medina v. Commission*.
15. Case 229/83, *Association des Centres distributeurs Édouard Leclerc and others v. SARL 'Au blé vert' and others*, para. 9; Case C-202/88, *France v. Commission (Telecom I)*, para. 4.
16. See for services Case 90/76, *S.r.l. Ufficio Henry van Ameyde v. S.r.l. Ufficio centrale italiano di assistenza assicurativa automobilisti in circolazione internazionale (UCI)* (insurance), Case 172/80, *Gerhard Züchner v. Bayerische Vereinsbank AG* (banking) and Case 45/85, *Verband der Sachversicherer e.V. v. Commission*; Joined Cases 209-213/84, *Criminal proceedings against Lucas Asjes and others, Andrew Gray and others, Jacques Maillot and others and Léo Ludwig and others* (transport); Case 311/85, *ASBL Vereniging van Vlaamse Reisbureaus v. ASBL Sociale Dienst van de Plaatselijke en Gewestelijke Overheidsdiensten* (travel) and Case C-41/90, *Klaus*

a trio of mutually related aspects. *First*, Articles 81 and 82 EC, too, are aimed at the removal of existing and the prevention of new obstacles to free movement. What is prohibited for the Member States, namely the maintenance or adoption of measures which protect national markets, cannot then be permitted for undertakings.[17] *Secondly*, distortions of competition have to be prevented within the common market once it is established. In relation to measures taken by the Member States themselves this is sought to be attained by means of Arts. 87–97 EC; in relation to actions of undertakings this is done through Arts. 81 and 82 EC.[18] Thus the Treaty expresses that the coordination of economic decisions of the market participants should primarily take place through the proper functioning of the market mechanism.[19] A properly functioning market mechanism may not be thwarted by anti-competitive agreements or by the abuse by undertakings of their dominant positions. *Thirdly*, the complementary function of Arts. 81 and 82 EC means that there is an interaction between these provisions and those relating to the *five* freedoms. The interpretation of Arts. 81 and 82 EC has a certain influence on the free movement provisions, and vice versa.[20] In particular in cases where barriers to trade result from an active, or passive, combination of government measures and action by undertakings, Community or national procedures will sometimes contain – or need to contain – provisions applying to both groups. In such situations, it is not always clear for a litigant which Treaty provisions his application should be based on, or for a national court which provisions its request for a preliminary ruling should concern. This interaction between the two groups of provisions can also play an important role in relation to action by public undertakings.[21]

This interaction demonstrates that the provisions relating to the establishment and proper functioning of the common market are more and more acquiring the character of an inter-connected unity. This explains the express recognition by the Court of the significance of Articles 28 et seq. for the system of Article 3(1)(g) EC.[22] In the context of such interconnection, of course the difference in scope of the various freedoms and the competition provisions should not be forgotten.

     Höfner and Fritz Elser v. Macrotron GmbH (employment placement); for capital movement see Case 267/86, *Pascal Van Eycke v. ASPA NV.*

17. Joined Cases 56 & 58/64, *Établissements Consten S.à.R.L. and Grundig-Verkaufs-GmbH v. Commission.* The case law offers good examples of division and control of markets by measures under private law. See e.g., Case 246/86, *SC Belasco and others v. Commission.*

18. These provisions are thus also interrelated. See on this Case C-225/91, *Matra SA v. Commission*; Case T-156/98, *RJB Mining plc. v. Commission* and Joined Cases T-197/97 & T-198/97, *Weyl Beef Products BV, Exportslachterij Chris Hogeslag BV and Groninger Vleeshandel BV v. Commission.*

19. Case C-198/01, *Industrie Fiammiferi (CIF) v. Autorità Garante della Concorrenza e del Mercato*; Case C-238/05, *Asnef-Equifax.*

20. See e.g., Case 8/74, *Procureur du Roi v. Benoît and Gustave Dassonville*; Case 15/74, *Centrafarm BV and Adriaan de Peijper v. Sterling Drug Inc*; Case 16/74, *Centrafarm BV et Adriaan de Peijper v. Winthrop BV*; Case 59/75, *Pubblico Ministero v. Flavia Manghera and others*; Case 13/77, *SA G.B.-INNO-B.M. v. Association des détaillants en tabac (ATAB)*; and Case 229/83, *Leclerc* (books).

21. See section 2.8 *infra.*

22. Case 18/88, *Régie des télégraphes et des téléphones v. GB-Inno-BM SA.*

The former category of provisions does not in principle apply to conduct of undertakings,[23] while the latter category does not, in principle, apply to legislative or administrative conduct, or other public measures (e.g., legislation on prices or on shop opening hours).[24] The case law does show that Articles 81 and 82 EC mean that the Member States may not adopt any measures which would detract from the effectiveness of these provisions, for instance by favouring,[25] requiring[26] or reinforcing[27] practices which are contrary to the competition provisions, or by depriving government action of its 'public' character by delegating responsibility for taking decisions to private parties.[28] For a good understanding of this, it should be added that if a Member State commits such an infringement, this does not detract from the applicability of the competition provisions to the undertakings in question, to the extent that these undertakings still enjoy a certain discretion with respect to their competitive action.[29] This obligation resulting from the

---

23. This may be different for Arts. 39 and 49 EC, which also have horizontal effect. For that reason, in principle it is not excluded that these articles as well as Arts. 81 and 82 may be applicable to the same set of facts. This is possible in particular in relation to rules of sporting associations. The Court has so far avoided examining the issue. See Case C-415/93, *Union royale belge des sociétés de football association ASBL v. Jean-Marc Bosman, Royal club liégeois SA v. Jean-Marc Bosman and others and Union des associations européennes de football (UEFA) v. Jean-Marc Bosman*; Joined Cases C-51/96, *Christelle Deliège v. Ligue francophone de judo (C-51/96) et disciplines associées ASBL, Ligue belge de judo ASBL, Union européenne de judo and François Pacquée (C-191/97)* and Case C-176/96, *Jyri Lehtonen and Castors Canada Dry Namur-Braine ASBL v. Fédération royale belge des sociétés de basket-ball ASBL (FRBSB)*.
24. See Case 24/67, *Parke, Davis and Co. v. Probel, Reese, Beintema-Interpharm and Centrafarm*; Case 5/79, *Procureur général v. Hans Buys, Han Pesch and Yves Dullieux and Denkavit France SARL*; Case 188/86, *Ministère public v. Régis Lefèvre*; Case 30/87, *Corinne Bodson v. SA Pompes funèbres des régions libérées*; Case C-339/89, *Alsthom Atlantique SA v. Compagnie de construction mécanique Sulzer SA Alsthom*; Case C-2/91, *Criminal proceedings against Wolf W. Meng*; Joined Cases C-104/94, *Cereol Italia Srl v. Azienda Agricola Castello Sas to C-142/94, Lingral Srl v. Comune di Chiogga*. The Commission cannot address decisions to the Member States on the basis of the competition provisions. See Case T-113/89, *Nederlandse Associatie van de Farmaceutische Industrie 'Nefarma' and Bond van Groothandelaren in het Farmaceutische Bedrijf v. Commission*.
25. Case 136/86, *Bureau national interprofessionnel du cognac v. Yves Aubert*; Case C-462/99, *Connect Austria Gesellschaft für Telekommunikation GmbH v. Telecom-Control-Kommission*; Case C-198/01, *Industrie Fiammiferi (CIF)*.
26. Case 267/86, *Van Eycke v. ASPA*.
27. Case C-2/91, *Wolf W. Meng*; Case C-185/91, *Bundesanstalt für den Güterfernverkehr v. Gebrüder Reiff GmbH & Co. KG* and Case C-245/91, *Criminal proceedings against Ohra Schadeverzekeringen NV*.
28. See Case 13/77, *INNO v. ATAB*; Case 229/83, *Leclerc* (books); Case 231/83, *Henri Cullet and Chambre syndicale des réparateurs automobiles et détaillants de produits pétroliers v. Centre Leclerc à Toulouse and Centre Leclerc à Saint-Orens-de-Gameville*; Case 311/85, *Vlaamse Reisbureaus v. Sociale Dienst van de Plaatselijke en Gewestelijke Overheidsdiensten*; Case 66/86, *Ahmed Saeed Flugreisen and Silver Line Reisebüro GmbH v. Zentrale zur Bekämpfung unlauteren Wettbewerbs e.V*; Case 267/86, *Van Eycke v. ASPA* and Case C-35/96, *Commission v. Italy* (customs agents).
29. Case T-147/89, *Société métallurgique de Normandie v. Commission* and Case T-7/92, *Asia Motor France SA, Jean-Michel Cesbron, Monin Automobiles SA, Europe Auto Service SA and SOMACO SA v. Commission*.

competition provisions, and applying to all authorities of the Member States[30] is also based on Article 10 EC.[31]

In addition, the policy on competition between undertakings has shown up the connection between the enforcement of Articles 81 and 82 EC and the co-ordination of economic policy of the Member States, in the sense that competition policy too can contribute to positive integration.[32] This follows in general terms from Article 4 EC (principle of an open market economy with free competition), and more specifically from the text of Article 81(3) EC, and already became evident at an early stage in the agricultural sector. In a situation where, as a result of greater price transparency following the introduction of the euro, competition has been intensified, competition policy plays a more significant role for the proper functioning of the economic and monetary union and the realization of the Lisbon strategy.[33] Moreover, the various horizontal integration provisions in the EC Treaty,[34] the Commission's practice – embracing decisions and communications – and the various elements of the Lisbon strategy demonstrate the existence of a link between competition law and the process of positive integration in the fields of:

- the common commercial policy;
- energy policy;
- employment policy;
- environmental policy;
- industrial policy;
- regional policy;[35]
- community research and development policy;
- cultural policy;[36]
- sport;

---

30. See Case C-198/01, *Industrie Fiammiferi (CIF)*.
31. See for the question of the applicability of Art. 81 to such action of the state authorities, Case C-2/91, *Meng*; Case C-185/91, *Reiff* and Case C-245/91, *Ohra Schadeverzekeringen*; Case C-153/93, *Bundesrepublik Deutschland v. Delta Schiffahrts-und Speditionsgesellschaft mbH*; Case C-96/94, CSC; Case T-387/94, *Asia Motor France v. Comission*; Case C-70/95, *Sodemare SA, Anni Azzurri Holding SpA and Anni Azzurri Rezzato Srl v. Regione Lombardia*. Art. 86 EC may also play a role in this delimitation. See Case C-35/96, *Commission v. Italy* (customs agents) and Case C-462/99, *Connect-Austria v. Telecom-Control-Komission*.
32. Joined Cases 6 & 7/73, *Istituto Chemioterapico Italiano S.p.A. and Commercial Solvents Corporation v. Commission*.
33. See Ch. XII.
34. Arts. 6 (environment), 16 (social and territorial cohesion), 136, 2nd para. (social policy), 151(4) (culture), 152(1) (public health), 153(2) (consumer protection), 154(2) (infrastructure), 157(1) (industrial policy) and 163(1) (research).
35. See Communication from the Commission to the Member States on the links between regional and competition policy (O.J. 1998, C 90/3).
36. Especially concerning public broadcasting, press and books. See on the problem of fixed book prices Joined Cases 43 & 63/82, *Vereniging ter Bevordering van het Vlaamse Boekwezen, VBVB, and Vereniging ter Bevordering van de Belangen des Boekhandels, VBBB, v. Commission*; Case 229/83, *Leclerc* (books) and Case C-360/92 P, *The Publishers Association v. Commission*.

- infrastructure;[37]
- public procurement;[38] and
- public health.

These parts of competition policy too reflect the mixed economic order which the Community strives to attain.

2.1.2 The System of Undistorted Competition

As has been indicated in the preceding section, it is evident from the case law that the system of undistorted competition guaranteed by Articles 81 and 82 EC forms the core of the common market. This is expressed in Article 4 EC, according to which the economic policy of the Member States and of the EC is based on the principle of an open market economy with free competition. Nevertheless, the content of the EC Treaty and the case law on the five freedoms and various economic basic rights reveal that this should not be seen as a normative *laissez-faire* system excluding any intervention at all on the part of undertakings or of the national or Community authorities.[39]

In order to guarantee this system of undistorted competition, in the first instance all practices of undertakings which create trade barriers between different national markets for certain goods or services have to be prohibited and combated. Such practices include in particular market-sharing agreements, collective exclusive dealing agreements between national producers and their distributors, agreements to adapt import prices to national price levels, collective rebate or discount agreements concerning the total turnover within one Member State, as well as import or export restrictions or bans. In this context it is sufficient to point to the parallel with the case law on Articles 28 and 29 EC.

But a prohibition of horizontal (e.g., between producers, or between distributors) and multilateral cartels is insufficient. Barriers between national markets can also result from vertical agreements, such as exclusive distribution or purchasing agreements between one producer and one distributor, particularly when they are combined with absolute territorial protection (a prohibition on sales or purchases to or from other parties within that territory) or relative territorial protection (a prohibition on active sales outside the contract territory). Market-sharing effects may also result from agreements concerning intellectual property rights. In this context, reference should be made to the case law on Arts. 28–30 EC,[40] where the Court has imposed very heavy restrictions on the possibility of dividing up the common market by the use of such rights. It is precisely in the field of industrial and commercial property rights that the link between the rules on the free movement

---

37. See the explanatory note from the Commission on the application of the competition rules on transport infrastructure projects (O.J. 1997, C 298/5).
38. See Case C-360/96, *Gemeente Arnhem and Gemeente Rheden v. BFI Holding BV.*
39. See e.g., Joined Cases C-180-184/98, *Pavlov and others v. Stichting Pensioenfonds Medische Specialisten*, and Case C-309/99, *Wouters.*
40. Considered in section 3.3.2 of Ch. VIII, *supra.*

of goods and services and those on competition between undertakings is most
evident, as appears also from the case law on Community trade mark law, in
which the Court has emphasized again and again that the interests protected by
that area of legislation – of the proprietor of the trade mark on the one hand and free
movement of goods and services on the other – must be seen in the context of
undistorted competition in a common market.[41]

The above discussion demonstrates that Arts. 81 and 82 EC do not set out to
prohibit any particular conduct of undertakings which is restrictive or distortive of
competition, but rather all forms of restriction of competition within the common
market, by means of an agreement between undertakings or a concerted practice of
undertakings, or based on the abuse of a dominant position.[42] Thus Article 81 EC not
only prohibits conduct which directly affects import or export, such as market-
sharing and restrictions or prohibitions on imports or exports, it also catches conduct
which does not aim to have such effects, but which nevertheless in practice may have
such (cross-border) effects, such as international price agreements, production and
distribution restrictions, etc. (see the examples mentioned in Article 81).[43] In relation to Article 82 EC this is expressed in the fact that action taken by a number of
undertakings may also be found to constitute abuse of a dominant position.

Thus Articles 81 and 82 EC can be regarded as an expression of the first
concept of freedom explained in Chapter VIII, above. The essential characteristic
of this principle is that, in assessing private or public conduct, attention is paid to
the *effects* of that conduct on interstate trade. This condition already occurs in the
text of Articles 81 and 82 EC, and is also apparent from the case law.[44] The well-
known *Dassonville* formula[45] is also used by the Court to determine the scope of
the competition provisions.[46] The Court stated in *Alsatel*: 'Community law applies
to any agreement, decision or concerted practice which may influence, directly or
indirectly, actually or potentially, patterns of trade between the Member States and
thereby hinder the economic interpenetration intended by the Treaty.'[47]

In the light of this concept of freedom, of which Article 81 EC is an expression,
it is understandable that in *Vereeniging van Cementhandelaren* the Court held that
even an agreement extending over the whole of the territory of a Member State by
its very nature has the effect of reinforcing the compartmentalization of markets on

---

41. See especially Case C-228/03, *The Gillette Company and Gillette Group Finland Oy v. LA-
    Laboratoires Ltd Oy*.
42. Moreover, it is apparent from the case law that no distinction is made between the terms
    'prevention', 'restriction' and 'distortion'; moreover, this triple distinction is not used in
    Arts. 82 or 87 EC.
43. Arts. 81 and 82 EC apply to every stage of the economic process, see Case 32/65, *Italy v.
    Council and Commission*.
44. Case C-250/92, *Gøttrup-Klim and others Grovvareforeninger v. Dansk Landbrugs Grovvar-
    eselskab AmbA*.
45. Case 8/74, *Dassonville*.
46. See already Joined Cases 56 & 58/64, *Consten and Grundig*.
47. Case 247/86, *Société alsacienne et lorraine de télécommunications et d'électronique (Alsatel) v.
    SA Novasam*, para. 11. See also Joined Cases C-295-298/04, *Vincenzo Manfredi et al. v. Lloyd
    Adriatico Assicurazioni SpA et al.*

a national basis, thereby holding up the economic interpenetration which the Treaty is designed to bring about and protecting domestic production.[48]

Thus, in principle, significant national cartels, national vertical price-fixing systems and – if they collectively hinder imports – even groups of national exclusive dealing agreements fall within the ambit of Article 81 EC. In relation to Article 82 EC, the same principle is expressed by the fact that an abuse of a dominant position 'in a substantial part of' the common market is prohibited.

2.1.3 The Protected Minimum of Competition

2.1.3.1 Concept

It is apparent that Articles 81 and 82 EC are not intended to bring about perfect or even maximum competition. This is evident particularly from the fact that Article 81(3) EC permits certain useful forms of cooperation even if they restrict competition, and that Article 82 does not prohibit the existence or even the 'use' of a dominant position, but only the abuse of one. However, Article 81(3)(b) EC does guarantee in its last condition that even the most useful form of cooperation between undertakings should leave a substantial degree of competition intact. In *Continental Can* the Court noted that

> the restraints on competition which the Treaty allows under certain conditions because of the need to harmonize the various objectives of the Treaty, are limited by the requirements of Articles 2 and 3. Going beyond this limit involves the risk that the weakening of competition would conflict with the aims of the common market.[49]

Thus the Court regarded Articles 81 and 82 EC as seeking to achieve the same aim, the maintenance of effective competition within the common market, and thus the two provisions had to be interpreted in a mutually coherent manner in the light of the requirements of Article 81(3)(b) EC.

In Case 26/76 *Metro SB*, the Court observed that the requirement in Articles 3(1)(g) and 81 EC that competition shall not be distorted

> implies the existence on the market of workable competition, that is to say the degree of competition necessary to ensure the observance of the basic requirements and the attainment of the objectives of the Treaty, in particular the creation of a single market achieving conditions similar to those of a domestic market.[50]

This statement makes it clear that the provisions concern competition as such, with the consequence that Article 81(1) does not only start to apply if there is an

---

48. Case 8/72, *Vereeniging van Cementhandelaren v. Commission*, para. 29.
49. Case 6/72, *Continental Can*, at para. 24.
50. Case 26/76, *Metro SB-Großmärkte GmbH & Co. KG v. Commission*, at para. 20; Case T-168/01, *GlaxoSmithKline v. Commission*, at para. 109.

interference with workable competition as defined by the Court.[51] It thus reinforces the conclusion that even in the exemption policy under Article 81(3) EC, workable competition as described must be maintained, which also appears true in respect of Article 82 EC as a result of the *Continental Can* judgment (mentioned above). The requirement of workable competition is thus a minimum requirement which must be satisfied in all cases.[52] The need to take account of this minimum requirement is also highly important for the reform of competition policy, briefly mentioned already at the beginning of section 2, above.

2.1.3.2   *Per se Prohibition or Rule of Reason?*

From the above remarks, it may be deduced that if conduct falling within the ambit of Article 81(1) EC restricts competition, and interstate trade is unfavourably affected, the prohibition contained in this provision applies. It must subsequently be examined whether the agreement in question may come within the terms of exemption from the prohibition on the basis of Article 81(3) EC. According to this view, Article 81(1) EC has the character of a per se prohibition. A quite different approach interprets Article 81(1) EC in the sense that the prohibition is only applicable if the negative aspects of the restriction of competition are more important than its positive aspects. In this approach, Article 81(1) EC is based on the so-called 'rule of reason'. However, the existence of exceptions in Article 81(3) EC, and the implication of the prohibition on cartels (maintaining workable competition), and its position in the system of the EC Treaty give good reason for arguing that the 'rule of reason' approach is not inherent in Article 81(1) EC. That is also the opinion of the Court of First Instance, which has clearly indicated that the balancing of negative and positive aspects of a restriction of competition comes by its very nature under Article 81(3) EC.[53] The position of the Court of Justice on this question is less clear though, at least to the extent that rules of deontology, or 'proper practice', are concerned. Although such rules – in particular where they involve certain prohibitions – may restrict competition and interstate trade in services, the Court of Justice has adopted the view that the prohibition contained in Article 81(1) EC does not apply to them, as long as these rules do not go further

---

51. Otherwise, 'workable competition' itself could also be further restricted on the basis of Art. 81(3) EC, and therefore lose its 'workable' character.

52. See also the description given in Case 48/69, *Imperial Chemical Industries Ltd v. Commission:*.

    The function of price competition is to keep prices down to the lowest possible level and to encourage the movement of goods between the Member States, thereby permitting the most efficient possible distribution of activities in the matter of productivity and the capacity of undertakings to adapt themselves to change. Differences in rates encourage the pursuit of one of the basic objectives of the Treaty, namely the interpenetration of national markets and, as a result, direct access by consumers to the sources of production of the whole Community. (paras. 115–116).

53. Case T-112/99, *Métropole télévision (M6), Suez-Lyonnaise des eaux, France Télécom and Télévision française 1 SA (TF1) v. Commission*; Joined Cases T-49 & 51/02, *Brasserie nationale v. Commission.*

than necessary.[54] This rather questionable judgment gives the impression that for the kind of service at issue, the Court has chosen to create a kind of separate rule-of-reason exception to the cartel prohibition, which can in principle go beyond the required minimum of competition under Article 81(3)(b).[55]

2.2   ARTICLE 81 EC

2.2.1   Article 81(1) EC

Article 81(1) contains a directly applicable prohibition of all agreements between undertakings, all decisions by associations of undertakings, and all concerted practices[56] meeting two criteria. To fall within the prohibition, they must in the first place have as their object or effect the prevention, restriction or distortion of competition within the common market. Secondly, they must tend to have an adverse effect on inter-state trade. The wording of Article 81(1) mentions some examples of agreements which – at least as a rule – meet the first criterion. The two criteria are mentioned in Article 81 in the opposite order, but the order here given is more logical, and accordingly is followed by the Commission in its decisions. It is precisely because an agreement prevents, restricts, or distorts competition in inter-state trade that it may have an adverse effect thereon.

2.2.1.1   Undertakings

In view of the objectives and nature of Articles 81 and 82 EC, the concept of an 'undertaking'[57] embraces all entities independently engaged in an economic activity,[58] consisting of a mix of material and human factors.[59] The legal status of such an entity,[60] and the way in which it is financed, is irrelevant,[61] as is the

---

54. Case C-309/99, *Wouters*.
55. As far as sports are concerned, see Case C-519/04 P, *Meca-Medina*.
56. The term 'agreements' is used hereafter as shorthand for all three forms of cooperation.
57. As to the concept of an 'association of undertakings', see especially Cases 209–215 and 218/78, *Heintz van Landewyck SARL and others v. Commission (FEDETAB)*; Case 45/85, *Verband der Sachversicherer*.
58. Case 107/82, *Allgemeine Elektrizitäts-Gesellschaft AEG-Telefunken AG v. Commission*; Joined Cases 29/83 & 30/83, *Compagnie Royale Asturienne des Mines SA and Rheinzink GmbH v. Commission* and Case T-65/89, *BPB Industries Plc and British Gypsum Ltd v. Commission*; Case T-155/04, *SELEX v. Commission*.
59. Case T-6/89, *Enichem Anic SpA v. Commission*.
60. E.g., a foundation, see Joined Cases T-213/95 & T-18/96, *Stichting Certificatie Kraanverhuurbedrijf (SCK) and Federatie van Nederlandse Kraanbedrijven (FNK) v. Commission*, or a consultative body under public law, see Case 123/83, *Bureau national interprofessionnel du cognac v. Guy Clair*.
61. Case C-41/90, *Höfner and Elser v. Macrotron*; Joined Cases C-159 & 160/91, *Christian Poucet v. Assurances Générales de France and Caisse Mutuelle Régionale du Languedoc-Roussillon* and Case C-82/01, *Aéroports de Paris v. Commission and Alpha Flight Services SAS*.

question whether or not the entity aims to make profits (e.g., pension funds).[62] The main issue is whether the entity independently provides goods or services.[63] This means, for example, that an employee[64] is not an undertaking; nor is a social security organ which does not operate along lines based on profitability criteria, but which is entirely based on the principle of solidarity.[65] A self-employed person, or member of the liberal professions or a football club may well fall within the definition of the concept.[66] However, to the extent that an agent is economically dependent on his or her principal and assumes no entrepreneurial risks other than the usual *del credere* guarantee, a commercial agent will not be regarded as an undertaking.[67] In relation to the concept of economic activity, account is taken of the question whether this is an activity of or on behalf of the public authorities, so that not every activity – even if it is 'economic' – leads to the finding that there is an undertaking.[68]

A group of companies will be regarded as one undertaking if its component parts form an economic unit, within which the parent company has the possibility in law to exercise control;[69] thus, an agreement between a parent and its subsidiaries solely concerning the internal distribution of tasks among them will fall outside

---

62. Case C-244/94, *Fédération Française des Sociétés d'Assurance, Société Paternelle-Vie, Union des Assurances de Paris-Vie and Caisse d'Assurance et de Prévoyance Mutuelle des Agriculteurs v. Ministère de l'Agriculture et de la Pêche*; Case C-67/96, *Albany International BV v. Stichting Bedrijfspensioenfonds Textielindustrie*; Joined Cases C-115-117/97, *Brentjens' Handelsonderneming BV v. Stichting Bedrijfspensioenfonds voor de Handel in Bouwmaterialen*; Case C-219/97, *Maatschappij Drijvende Bokken BV v. Stichting Pensioenfonds voor de Vervoer-en Havenbedrijven* and Joined Cases C-180-184/98, *Pavlov*.

63. Case C-35/96, *Comission v. Italy* (customs agents); Case C-475/99, *Ambulanz Glöckner v. Landkreis Südwestpfalz, Arbeiter-Samariter-Bund Landesverband Rheinland-Pfalz eV, Deutsches Rotes Kreuz Landesverband Rheinland-Pfalz eV and Vertreter des öffentlichen Interesses, Mainz*; Case C-218/00, *Cisal di Battistello Venanzio & C. Sas v. Istituto nazionale per l'assicurazione contro gli infortuni sul lavoro (INAIL)*.

64. Case C-22/98, *Criminal Proceedings against Jean Claude Becu and others*.

65. Case C-218/00, *Cisal di Battistello*; Case T-319/99, *Federación Nacional de Empresas de Instrumentación Científica, Médica, Técnica y Dental (FENIN) v. Commission*; Joined Cases C-264/01 etc., *AOK Bundesverband and others*.

66. Joined Cases C-180-184/98, *Pavlov*.

67. Joined Cases 56 and 58/64, *Consten and Grundig v. Commission*; Cases 40/73 etc., *Coöperatieve Vereniging 'Suiker Unie' UA and others v. Commission*; Case 311/85 *ASBL*; Case T-66/99, *Minoan Lines v. Commission*. See on the position of commercial agents also the Commission's Notice in O.J. 2000, C 291/1, Guidelines on vertical restraints, paras. 12–20, which concern agency agreements, and see Dir. 86/653 on independent commercial agents, O.J. 1986, L 382/17.

68. See Case C-205/03 P, *FENIN*; Case T-155/94, *SELEX*.

69. See e.g., among the extensive case law, Case 15/74, *Centrafarm BV and others v. Sterling Drug Inc.*; Case 16/74, *Centrafarm v. Winthrop*; Case 170/83, *Hydrotherm Gerátebau GmbH v. Compact del Dott. Ing. Mario Andreoli & C. sas*; Case 75/84, *Metro SB-Großmärkte GmbH & Co. KG v. Commission 'Metro III'*; Case 66/86, *Ahmed Saeed Flugreisen*; Case 30/87, *Bodson*; Case T-102/92, *Viho Europe BV v. Commission*, upheld on appeal in Case C-73/95 P, *Viho Europe BV v. Commission*; Case T-198/98, *Micro Leader Business v. Commission*.

the scope of Article 81(1) EC.[70] Infringements by the subsidiaries or branches may be attributed to the parent company.[71]

The result of the interpretation of the concept of an 'undertaking' is that certain activities of public authorities may also come within the scope of Articles 81 and 82 EC. This was already apparent from Article 86 EC on public undertakings and undertakings to which Member States grant special or exclusive rights. However, the case law does not afford complete clarity as to the dividing line between the activities which do fall under the competition provisions and those which do not. On the one hand, it could be argued on the basis of the cases concerning public employment agencies that in principle many activities of public authorities could be considered to come within the concept of an undertaking;[72] on the other hand, there is another body of case law which seems to imply that 'economic activity' cannot be interpreted so widely as to bring every public activity which could also be exercised by a private undertaking within the scope of Articles 81 and 82 EC.[73] Tasks which lie purely in the domain of public law – in this context the Court speaks of 'the exercise of public authority' or 'official powers' – do not come within the scope of Articles 81 and 82 EC,[74] although the interpretation is not without a certain case-by-case element.[75] At all events, an optimal coordination between the competition provisions on the one hand and the free movement provisions addressed to the Member States on the other, militates against a structural overlap of the scope of provisions addressed to the public authorities and those addressed to undertakings through an overly wide interpretation of the concept of an undertaking. In addressing the issue whether an entity can be considered to be an undertaking, it is recommended that account should also be had of the case law concerning 'undertaking' and 'economic activity' in the fields of VAT, state aids, and the protection of employees in cases of transfer of undertakings. On the basis of legislation and case law concerning public procurement, it may also be assumed that contracting authorities may also be considered to be an 'undertaking' in the sense of Articles 81 and 82 EC.

---

70. Case 48/69, *Imperial Chemical Industries*; Case 22/71, *Béguelin Import Co. and others v. G.L. Import Export et al.*
71. On the various problems which can occur in this context, see Case T-65/89, *British Gypsum* and Case C-297/98 P, *SCA Holding Ltd v. Commission.*
72. Case C-41/90, *Höfner and Elser v. Macrotron*; Case C-55/96, *Job Centre.*
73. Case 2/73, *Riseria Luigi Geddo v. Ente Nazionale Risi* (customs duties); Cases C-159/91 and C-160/91, *Poucet and Pistre v. Assurances Générales de France (AGF) and others*, (public health insurance); Case C-207/01, *Altair Chimica SpA v. ENEL Distribuzione SpA* (surcharges).
74. Such as air traffic control, Case C-364/92, *SAT Fluggesellschaft mbH v. Eurocontrol*, see also Case C-82/01 P, *ADP.*
75. See Case C-343/95, *Diego Calì & Figli Srl v. Servizi ecologici porto di Genova SpA (SEPG)*, on combatting pollution in harbours.

2.2.1.2   Agreements, Decisions and Concerted Practices

The concept of an agreement in the sense of Article 81(1) EC covers situations where the undertakings in question have *expressed their joint intention to conduct themselves on the market in a specific way.*[76] The essential element consists of the existence of the actual agreement of intention between at least two parties.[77] The form of that agreement is not important.[78] An agreement may be concluded in writing or orally,[79] it may be binding in character or may have the status of a 'gentlemen's agreement'.[80] It is also irrelevant what law is applicable to the agreement, or what type of agreement[81] is at issue, or whether the agreement is horizontal or vertical.[82] Equally unimportant is the fact that the agreement has ceased to exist, if the conduct in question has continued.[83]

Unilateral measures can also, in principle, be characterized as an 'agreement'; this is the case with conduct, by one party, which is apparently unilateral but which is taken in the framework of that party's contractual relations with other parties, who have therefore tacitly consented to such conduct; examples include the mention of export prohibitions on invoices,[84] or a refusal to admit a distributor to a selective distribution system, or to supply to a distributor, if the refusal is intended to consolidate the agreements between the manufacturer and its distributors.[85]

The existence of an agreement can also be deduced on the basis of participation of an undertaking in meetings at which agreements were concluded and a failure by that undertaking to explicitly distance itself from the agreement.[86]

---

76. Case 41/69, *ACF Chemiefarma v. Commission*; Case T-7/89, *SA Hercules Chemicals NV v. Commission*; Case T-41/96, *Bayer AG v. Commission*; Joined Cases T-44/02 OP etc., *Dresdner Bank and others v. Commission.*
77. Case 51/75, *EMI Records Limited v. CBS United Kingdom Limited 'EMI Records I'*; Case 86/75, *EMI Records Limited v. CBS Grammofon A/S 'EMI Records II'*; Case 96/75, *EMI Records Limited v. CBS Schallplatten GmbH 'EMI Records III'*; Case T-1/89, *Rhône-Poulenc SA v. Commission*; Case T-317/94, *Moritz J. Weig GmbH & Co. KG v. Commission.*
78. Case 243/83, *SA Binon & Cie v. SA Agence et messageries de la presse*; Case T-41/96, *Bayer.*
79. Case 28/77, *Tepea BV v. Commission*; Case T-43/92, *Dunlop Slazenger International Ltd v. Commission.*
80. Case T-141/89, *Tréfileurope Sales SARL v. Commission*; Case T-95/99, *HFB and Others v. Commission.*
81. E.g., an out-of-court settlement, see Case 65/86, *Bayer AG and Maschinenfabrik Hennecke GmbH v. Heinz Süllhöfer.*
82. I.e., between the same undertakings (sector, branch of industry) or between customers and suppliers (vertical business associates), see Joined Cases 56 & 58/64, *Consten and Grundig.*
83. Case 51/75, *'EMI Records I'*; Case 86/75, *'EMI Records II'* and Case 96/75, *'EMI Records III'*; Case 243/83, *Binon*; Case T-1/89, *Rhône-Poulenc 'PVC I'*; Case T-327/94, *SCA Holding Ltd v. Commission.*
84. See Joined Cases 32 & 36-82/78, *BMW Belgium SA and others v. Commission*; Case C-277/87, *Sandoz prodotti farmaceutici SpA v. Commission*; Case C-70/93, *Bayerische Motorenwerke AG v. ALD Auto-Leasing D GmbH.*
85. See Case 107/82, *AEG-Telefunken* and Joined Cases 25 & 26/84, *Ford-Werke AG and Ford of Europe Inc. v. Commission.*
86. Case T-35/92, *John Deere Ltd v. Commission*; Case T-29/92, *Vereniging van Samenwerkende Prijsregelende Organisaties in de Bouwnijverheid and others v. Commission 'SPO'*; Joined

The same approach is followed in the case law with regard to decisions of associations of undertakings; non-binding 'recommendations' of such bodies also fall within this category.[87] It is apparent from the case law that, if an undertaking has participated in a meeting about prices etc., the burden of proof that there were no anti-competitive intentions lies on the undertaking.[88] Truly unilateral conduct does not fall within the concept of an 'agreement'.[89] According to the case law, the concept of an 'agreement' in the sense of Article 81(1) EC does not apply to collective employment agreements, insofar as these refer to pay and other employment conditions.[90] The background to this is the special position occupied by collective employment agreements, in the framework of EC social policy.[91]

A concerted practice is a form of parallel behaviour by undertakings, which is not based on an agreement, but which aims at or leads to a restriction of competition.[92] Parallel behaviour does not automatically mean a concerted practice, as any undertaking is entitled to adapt its behaviour to its competitors' present or foreseeable behaviour. However, an undertaking must be able or willing to determine its policy autonomously, without being dependent on the behaviour of others.[93] A concerted practice does not need to be based on a previously determined strategy.[94] The concept of *concerted practices* has been defined by the Court as 'a form of co-ordination between undertakings which, without having reached the stage where an agreement properly so called has been concluded, knowingly substitutes practical cooperation between them for the risks of competition'.[95] Parallel behaviour in an oligopolistic market may amount to strong evidence of a concerted practice; the

---

Cases T-25/95 et seq., *Cimenteries CBR and Others v. Commission* (the Cement cases); Joined Cases T-44/00, *Mannesmannröhren-Werke AG v. Commission*; Joined Cases C-189/02 P etc., *Dansk Rorindustri and others v. Commission*; Case T-303/02, *Westfalen Gassen v. Commission*.

87. See Joined Cases 209-215/78, *Heintz van Landewyck SARL and others v. Commission* and Case 218/78, *Vander Elst v. Commission*; Joined Cases 96-102/82, *NV IAZ International Belgium and others v. Commission*.

88. Case C-57/02, *Acinerox v. Commission*; Joined Cases C-189/02 P, *Dansk Rorindustri*.

89. See for the problems of proof which arise in making a distinction between real and apparent unilateral conduct Case T-41/96, *Bayer AG v. Commission*; Case T-208/01, *Volkswagen AG v. Commission*; Case T-368/00, *General Motors and Opel v. Commission*.

90. Case C-67/96, *Albany International*; Joined Cases 115-117/97, *Brentjens*; Case C-219/97, *Maatschappij Drijvende Bokken*.

91. On the other hand, collective arrangements by members of the free professions do fall under the concept 'agreement'; see Joined Cases C-180-184/98, *Pavlov*.

92. Case 48/69, *Imperial Chemical Industries Ltd v. Commission*; Joined Cases 40-48/73, *'Suiker Unie' and others*.

93. Case 172/80, *Züchner*; Joined Cases 29 & 30/83, *CRAM and Rheinzink*; Case 243/83, *Binon*; Case C-238/05, *Asnef-Equifax*.

94. That is however not excluded. In that case, the distinction between an 'agreement' and a 'concerted practice' becomes fluid, see Case T-305/94, *Limburgse Vinyl Maatschappij NV, Elf Atochem SA, BASF AG, Shell International Chemical Company Ltd, DSM NV, DSM Kunststoffen BV, Wacker-Chemie GmbH, Hoechst AG, Société artésienne de vinyle, Montedison SpA, Imperial Chemical Industries plc, Hüls AG and Enichem SpA v. Commission*.

95. Case 48/69, *Imperial Chemical Industries*, para. 64; see also Joined Cases 89/85 etc., *A. Ahlström Osakeyhtiö and others v. Commission* (wood pulp); Case T-305/94, *LVM*; Joined Cases T-25/95 etc., *Cimenteries CBR and others*; Case T-303/02, *Westfalen Gassen*.

same holds for 'spontaneous' publication and exchange of information on prices etc.[96] The nature of a concerted practice will always require a careful analysis of the relevant market and the conduct of the undertakings concerned. The evidence must be such that the conduct said to be a concerted practice cannot be explained in any other way than a deliberate mutual coordination.[97]

2.2.1.3   Restriction of Competition

It is not so that every single restriction of competition on the common market is incompatible with the prohibition contained in Article 81(1) EC. In the case law, it has been assumed that the prohibition only concerns conduct by undertakings which significantly affects competition between parties and third parties.[98] This *de minimis* interpretation by the Court of the ambit of Article 81(1) EC has been further elaborated by the Commission in its regular Notices on Minor Agreements.[99]

According to constant case law, if it is apparent from the *content* of the agreement that it is apt to restrict competition between the parties and/or third parties[100] its practical effect on competition need not be examined.[101] This is for instance the case for import and export bans, whether or not in combination with absolute *territorial* protection,[102] and for price agreements.[103] An examination of the *formulation* of the individual clauses of the agreement and of its scope as a whole will be sufficient. In such cases there is also no requirement to define the relevant market which is concerned by the agreement in question.[104] In all these cases, the failure to observe the arrangements agreed is not relevant to the question of culpability.[105]

---

96. Case T-141/89, *Tréfileurope*.
97. The so-called 'indirect method of proof'. For examples, see: Case T-141/89, *Tréfileurope*, Joined Cases T-25/95 etc., *Cimenteries CBR and others*; Joined Cases 89/85 etc., *Ahlström* (wood pulp); Joined Cases T-236/01 etc., *Tokai Carbon*.
98. Case 41/69, *ACF Chemiefarma*; Case T-7/93, *Langnese Iglo GmbH v. Commission*; Case T-9/93, *Schöller Lebensmittel GmbH & Co. KG v. Commission*; Case C-214/99, *Neste Markkinointi Oy v. Yötuuli Ky and others*; Case T-25/99, *Colin Arthur Roberts and Valerie Ann Roberts v. Commission*; Joined Cases T-49-51/02, *Brasserie nationale*.
99. See section. 2.5.2 *infra*.
100. Case 32/65, *Italy v. Council & Commission*.
101. Case 56/65, *Société Technique Minière (L.T.M.) v. Maschinenbau Ulm GmbH (M.B.U.)*; Case C-277/87, *Sandoz prodotti farmaceutici*; Case T-141/89, *Tréfileurope*; Joined Cases T-39/92 & T-40/92, *Groupement des Cartes Bancaires 'CB' and Europay International SA v. Commission*; Case C-219/95 P, *Ferriere Nord SpA v. Commission*; Joined Cases T-25/95 etc., *Cimenteries and others*; Joined Cases T-44/00, *Mannesmannröhren-Werke AG v. Commission*.
102. Case 71/74, *Nederlandse Vereniging voor de fruit-en groentenimporthandel, Nederlandse Bond van grossiers in zuidvruchten en ander geimporteerd fruit 'Frubo' v. Commission and Vereniging de Fruitunie*; Case 19/77, *Miller International Schallplatten GmbH v. Commission*; Case T-66/92, *Herlitz AG v. Commission*; Case T-77/92, *Parker Pen Ltd v. Commission*.
103. Case 246/86, *Belasco*.
104. Case T-348/94, *Enso Española SA v. Commission*.
105. Case T-141/89, *Tréfileurope* and Case T-175/95, *BASF Lacke + Farben AG v. Commission*.

If the agreement does not have as its object a restriction of competition, but such a restriction will or may be the result of the agreement, then, according to constant case law, the *context* of the agreement has to be examined.[106] In the case of an exclusive dealing agreement – a kind of agreement which occurs frequently in the case law – the nature of the products or services to which the agreement relates will have to be taken into account, as well as the production or value, the position the producer and the exclusive dealer occupy in the market, and whether the rules serving to protect the exclusive dealer are very radical, effectively preventing access to the relevant market, or on the contrary allow re-exportation and parallel importation. In examining the context, account must be taken of the position of the individual agreement in the light of other agreements in the relevant market. This involves, *inter alia*, the question of whether the agreement forms part of a complex of agreements, even if there is no legal connection between those agreements. As a consequence, the fact that a great many exclusive dealing agreements with similar or complementary competition-restricting effect merely exist side by side, may mean that an individual agreement falls within Article 81(1), although the contracting parties to the individual agreements are in no way responsible for this relationship.[107]

This case law indicates that, in the framework of the 'contextual' examination, it must be established whether competition will be appreciably distorted, by means of a comparison with a situation in which that agreement does not exist.[108] This means that in making such a comparison, there is not one fixed concept of competition which is used as a criterion, but that the existing competitive situation on the relevant market will be used as a basis.[109] Depending on the market structure, this may be competition amongst many firms or amongst few, while in both cases monopolistic elements may play a role, such as in the case of products which have built up a limited monopolistic position by trade marks, special packaging, advertising etc. This makes possible, to some extent, price differentials as compared with competing products (other brands). According to the nature of the product (homogeneous or heterogeneous) and the type of agreement, a penetrating investigation of the market structure will often be necessary in order to ascertain the competition-restricting effects. From the case law it can be seen that Commission decisions are frequently annulled by the Community courts because of errors and shortcomings in the definition and analysis of the relevant markets. In this context,

---

106. Case 56/65, *'L.T.M.'*; Joined Cases 29/83 & 30/83, *'C.R.A.M.'*; Joined Cases 142/84 & 156/84, *British-American Tobacco Company Ltd and R. J. Reynolds Industries Inc. v. Commission*; Joined Cases T-213/95 & T-18/96, *SCK & FNK v. Commission*.

107. Case 23/67, *SA Brasserie de Haecht v. Consorts Wilkin-Janssen (Haecht I)*; Case C-234/89, *Stergios Delimitis v. Henninger Bräu AG*; Cases T-7/93, *Langnese-Iglo GmbH v. Commission*; Case T-9/93, *Schöller Lebensmittel*; Case C-214/99, *Neste*; Case C-551/03, *General Motors and Opel v. Commission*.

108. Case 42/84, *Remia BV and others v. Commission*; Case C-41/90, *Höfner*; Case T-34/92, *Fiatagri UK Ltd and New Holland Ford Ltd v. Commission*; Case T-35/92, *John Deere*; Case C-8/95 P, *New Holland Ford*.

109. Joined Cases T-5 & 6/00, *NVFGEG*; Case T-64/02, *Heubach v. Commission*.

it should also be noted that for a restriction of competition in the sense of Article 81(1) EC, there does not have to be an actual restriction in existence. From the description of the prohibition, given above, it follows that it is sufficient if there is a possibility for competition to be restricted (potential restriction of competition).[110] This will also depend on the market structure.[111]

Generally speaking, a restriction of competition would, on the basis of the case law, seem to be involved if two requirements are met. In the first place, the agreement will have to restrict the free market behaviour or market policy of one or more of the parties on one point or another.[112] In the second place, either an intended effect on third parties or an actual effect on the position of third parties (competitors, suppliers, or buyers) will have to be established. In the case of horizontal agreements (prices, production, distribution), an intended effect on third parties will generally follow simply from the content of the agreement, the number of parties to it, and their joint market position. As a result, a clause in a labour contract to the effect that the worker is not to establish, after termination of the contract, a competing business will not as a rule be looked upon as a restriction of competition within the sense of Article 81(1), but a multilateral price agreement will. As a rule, a more detailed examination of the market position of the parties involved, the specific characteristics of the product, and the alternatives for competitors, suppliers, or buyers will have to take place in the case of bilateral vertical agreements (exclusive dealing agreements, resale price maintenance, selective distribution, franchising, long-term selling contracts). Unlike in classic forms of cartels, which are probably what was primarily had in mind in the examples quoted in Article 81(1)(a)-(d), market domination and the resulting influence on the position of third parties does not automatically result from the restriction of competition between the parties. The effects of the agreements on the position of third parties will have to be analysed on the basis of extraneous circumstances; not all provisions of an agreement which have an effect on competition fall *per se* under the prohibition of Article 81(1) EC.[113]

Finally, it should be noted that Article 81 EC is also concerned with agreements which forbid unjustifiable or unfair competition, to the extent that such competition is not prohibited under Community or national legislation or case law.[114] This point is relevant in particular for attempts to prevent parallel importers from benefiting for example from a 'free rider' on the back of advertising

---

110. Case T-504/93, *Tiercé Ladbroke SA v. Commission*; Joined Cases T-374/94, *European Night Services Ltd (ENS), and others v. Commission*; Case C-7/95 P, *John Deere*; Joined Cases T-25/95 etc., *Cimenteries CBR and others v. Commission*; Joined Cases T-213/95 & T-18/96, *'SCK'*; Case T-168/01, *GlaxoSmthKline*; Case C-238/05, *Asnef-Equifax*.

111. For an exception to this contextual approach, see Case T-328/03, *Q2 v. Commission*.

112. Even advertising prohibitions fall under this, see Case T-144/99, *Institut des mandataires agréés v. Commission*.

113. See Case 161/84, *Pronuptia de Paris GmbH v. Pronuptia de Paris Irmgard Schillgalis*, see the different approach taken by A.G. VerLoren van Themaat therein.

114. Case 258/78, *L.C. Nungesser KG and others v. Commission*.

campaigns by official dealers in the product concerned. Here too, a parallel can be drawn with the case law on Articles 28–29 EC.[115]

2.2.1.4   The Effect on Inter-state Trade

As regards the second criterion, i.e., the possible adverse effect of the agreement (or particular clauses thereof) on trade between two or more Member States, the issue is whether the agreement in question may have an influence, direct or indirect, actual or potential, on the establishment and functioning of the common market. Here too, there is a *de minimis* rule: the effects must be appreciable or significant in order for the agreement to be caught.[116] As with the first criterion, this could be the very *object* of the agreement; in that case, no further analysis is required.[117] If an analysis is required then – according to constant case law – it must be possible to foresee with a sufficient degree of probability on the basis of a set of objective factors of law or of fact that the agreement in question may have an influence, direct or indirect, actual or potential, on trade between Member States in a manner which might harm the attainment of the objectives of a single market between states.[118] This definition from the case law makes it clear that the criterion of effect on trade between Member States is not only applicable to agreements directly concerning imports and exports.[119] Agreements whose sphere of application or effects are restricted to the territory of one Member State may create some kind of barrier to trade, and therefore have an adverse influence on the interpenetration of markets.[120] This is also true of agreements which have an indirect effect on trade between Member States by, for example, prescribing minimum prices for semi-finished products which are not traded between Member States but which form the raw materials for a final product which is traded between Member

---

115. Cf. Case 8/74, *Procureur du Roi v. Dassonville and others*; see Dir. 98/27 on unfair commercial practices, O.J. 1998, L 166/51.
116. Case 40/70, *Sirena S.r.l. v. Eda S.r.l. and others*; Case 28/77, *Tepea*; Case 30/78, *Distillers Company Limited v. Commission*.
117. Case 193/83, *Windsurfing International Inc. v. Commission*; Case T-29/92, *'SPO'*.
118. Joined Cases 56 & 58/64, *Consten and Grundig*; Case 56/65, *'L.T.M.'*; Case 5/69, *Franz Völk v. S.P.R.L. Ets J. Vervaecke*; Case 1/71, *Société anonyme Cadillon v. Firma Höss, Maschinenbau KG*; Case 99/79, *SA Lancôme and Cosparfrance Nederland BV v. Etos BV and Albert Heyn Supermart BV*; Case 126/80, *Maria Salonia v. Giorgio Poidomani and Franca Baglieri, née Giglio*; Joined Cases 89/85 etc., *Ahlström* (wood pulp); Case T-141/89, *Tréfileurope*; Case T-77/92, *Parker*; Case C-219/95 P, *Ferriere Nord*; Case C-306/96, *Javico International and Javico AG v. Yves Saint Laurent Parfums SA (YSLP)*; Joined Cases C-295-298/04, *Manfredi*; Case T-168/01, *GlaxoSmithKline*.
119. Case 43/69, *Brauerei A. Bilger Söhne GmbH v. Heinrich Jehle and Marta Jehle*; Case 8/72, *'VCH'*; Case 126/80, *Salonia*; Joined Cases 240-242/82, 261/82, 262/82, 268/82 and 269/82, *Stichting Sigarettenindustrie and others v. Commission*; Case 65/86, *Bayer v. Süllhöfer*; Case 246/86, *Belasco*.
120. Case 8/72, *'VCH'*; Case 126/80, *Salonia*; Case 161/84, *Pronuptia*; Case 65/86, *Bayer v. Süllhöfer*; Case 246/86, *Belasco*; Case T-29/92, *'SPO'*; Joined Cases T-213/95 & T-18/96, *'SCK'*; Case C-238/05, *Asnef-Equifax*.

States.[121] In certain cases, an *increase* in intra-Community trade (as a result of an agreement) may still be held to have an adverse influence in the sense of Article 81(1) EC.[122]

It has been mentioned already that the formulation in the case law of the concept of trade between Member States, in order to clarify the second main criterion, is the same as that in the classic definition of measures having equivalent effect to quantitative restrictions on imports contained in *Dassonville*.[123] This demonstrates again that Article 81(1) EC does not merely concern agreements which hinder the establishment of a market, but also agreements which hinder the functioning of that market as a market economy characterized by effective competition.

The above does not detract from the fact that the second main criterion of Article 81(1) EC functions above all as a jurisdictional criterion, drawing the dividing line between the competence of Community and national competition law.[124] This is understandable, given that an agreement which distorts competition in the common market will always have an adverse effect on trade between Member States. The proof that the first criterion is met will therefore nearly always be sufficient to assume that the second criterion is also met.

2.2.1.5   *Extra-territorial Effect*

Article 81 EC is applicable to an agreement which is *executed* within the territory of the common market, that is to say, where competition on the common market is distorted as a result of this agreement.[125] This means that the so-called 'effects doctrine' applies, even if the Court does not itself use that term; thus it makes no difference to the applicability of Article 81 EC where the parties to an agreement are situated, or where the agreement is concluded.[126] Neither is it relevant whether the agreement has been carried out by means of subsidiaries or agencies in the common market.[127] Nevertheless, the effects doctrine does not solve all problems concerning the application of Community competition law to undertakings which are not established in the EC, in particular as far as obtaining information, or

---

121.   Case 123/83, *Bureau national interprofessionnel du cognac*.
122.   Joined Cases 56 & 58/64, *Consten and Grundig*; Case T-141/89, *Tréfileurope*; Case C-238/05, *Asnef-Equifax*.
123.   Case 8/74, *Dassonville*.
124.   In this regard see Joined Cases 56 & 58/64, *Consten and Grundig*; Case 22/78, *Hugin Kassaregister AB and Hugin Cash Registers Ltd v. Commission*; Joined Cases 253/78 & 1/79 to 3/79, *Procureur de la République and others v. Bruno Giry and Guerlain SA and others*; Case 247/86, *Alsatel*; Joined Cases C-295-298/04, *Manfredi*.
125.   Joined Cases 89/85 etc., *Ahlström* (wood pulp).
126.   Case 48/69, *'ICI'*; Case 22/71, *Béguelin*; Case 28/77, *Tepea*.
127.   Case 6/72, *Continental Can*; Case 51/75, *EMI Records I*; Case 86/75, *EMI Records II* and Case 96/75, *EMI Records III*. *

imposing fines or penalty payments is concerned. This demonstrates the need to coordinate the application of Articles 81 and 82 EC by means of bilateral or multilateral agreements. With this aim, arrangements have been made by means of agreements between the EC and the USA, Canada and Japan for the exchange of information and consultation concerning the enforcement of their respective competition rules.[128] On the basis of these arrangements, for instance, inspections can be carried out on both sides of the ocean simultaneously in different offices and premises of a multinational company. In addition, the EEA Agreement and the various association and free trade agreements with other countries contain provisions which are identical to or extremely similar to Arts. 81 and 82 EC.[129]

2.2.2 Article 81(2) EC

Article 81(2) EC provides that any agreements or decisions prohibited pursuant to Article 81(1), i.e., not exempt according to Article 81(3) EC, shall be automatically void; this sanction is directly effective,[130] both retroactively and for the future.[131] This means that the prohibited agreements are unenforceable under civil law.[132] This sanction only applies to parts of the agreement which fall within the prohibition;[133] the agreement as a whole is only void if these parts cannot be severed from the other parts of the agreement.[134] This might be the case, for instance, where permissible parts of the agreement form a compensation for prohibited parts, or where the agreements are daughter contracts implementing or supplementing a void agreement. The consequences of the nullity of certain parts of an agreement for other parts of the agreement, or of the nullity of the agreement as a whole, are for national courts to decide, according to national law; such consequences may include an obligation in damages for failure to fulfil obligations or unlawful acts.[135] Damages may also be claimed by a weaker party to a contract, who was not able to avoid concluding a prohibited agreement.[136] In the framework of its policy of strengthening private enforcement of the competition provisions, the Commission published a White Paper on the subject in 2005.[137]

---

128. Resp. O.J. 1995, L 95/45; O.J. 1998, L 173/26; O.J. 1999, L 175/49 and O.J. 2003, L 183/11.
129. See also the Agreements between the EEC and Switzerland, O.J. 1972, L 300/189.
130. Case 127/73, *BRT I.*
131. Case C-453/99, *Bernard Crehan v. Courage Ltd and others*; Joined Cases C-295-298/04, *Manfredi.*
132. Case 22/71, *Béguelin.*
133. Case 56/65, *L.T.M.*
134. Joined Cases 56 & 58/64, *Consten and Grundig.*
135. Case 319/82, *Société de Vente de Ciments et Bétons de l'Est SA v. Kerpen & Kerpen GmbH und Co. KG*; Case 10/86, *VAG France SA v. Établissements Magne SA*; Joined Cases C-295-298/04, *Manfredi.*
136. Case C-453/99, *Courage.*
137. COM (2005) 672.

2.2.3   Article 81(3) EC

The prohibition of Article 81(1) EC may be declared inapplicable, either individually or generically (exemption), if two positive and two negative requirements are met. These requirements are discussed in more detail below.

In principle, Article 81(3) EC can be applied in three ways. The first manner is by means of an *exemption regulation*, usually called a block exemption, issued by the Commission on the basis of authorizing regulations enacted by the Council (on the basis of Article 83 EC). The national courts are of course bound by such regulations.[138] This manner of application, and the changes which have taken place in the last few years are discussed in section 2.2.4, below. The second manner of applying Article 81(3) EC is that of *notification* of agreements, in order to obtain individual clearance by the Commission, which was the core of the old system, which existed up until 2004. The current system is based on the principle of *direct application* of Article 81(3) EC by the national authorities and courts. These changes and the problems they entail are dealt with in section 2.5 below.

2.2.3.1   Positive Requirements

The *first* positive requirement is that the agreement must contribute to the improvement of production or distribution, to the promotion of technical or economic progress. Subjective advantages for the undertakings involved in the agreement are not sufficient; distinct objective advantages must be involved, which tend to offset the disadvantages of the restriction of competition, such as reduction of costs or improvements in quality.[139] Reduction of costs and improvement of quality are also the first factors to be considered for the fulfilment of the *second* positive requirement, *viz.* that a fair share of the benefit resulting from the objective improvements must be passed on to the consumers, for instance via lower prices or improved quality resulting from a specialization agreement, and which lead to advantages for customers which could not have been realized without the agreement.[140] The same applies to agreements relating to secondary conditions of competition, such as conditions of supply and payment, guarantees and warranties and the like.

The above observations about the concept of competition which is at the basis of the competition provisions also imply that, in applying Article 81(1) EC, account may or must be taken of national policy objectives which have been accepted at Community level. The fact that an agreement complies with national government policy is, however, not sufficient. In this respect account must be taken of the fact that the Member States have lost their powers in certain areas, either completely (such as the common commercial policy), or to the extent that their powers are subject to all kinds of rules of primary and secondary Community law.

---

138.   Case C-234/89, *Delimitis*.
139.   Joined Cases 56 & 58/64, *Consten and Grundig*; Case T-168/01, *GlaxoSmithKline*.
140.   Case C-238/05, *Asnef-Equifax*.

But even if the Member States are still free to act, the objectives concerned must be positively considered also from the Community standpoint. This may be apparent from the so-called horizontal integration provisions in the EC Treaty, and/or the existence of specific Community action programmes or other measures on the basis of horizontal regional policy, sectoral, and flanking competences of the EC. The decisional practice of the Commission contains numerous examples of the evaluation of this second requirement in the light of Community policy objectives.[141]

2.2.3.2   *Negative Requirements*

In many cases, agreements aiming at price increases and division of the market, or having such results, will already fail to obtain exemption on the basis of these two positive requirements. For the forms of cooperation which are useful, the *first* negative requirement, however, forms a difficult barrier to be overcome: this is that the agreement must not impose on the undertakings concerned any restrictions which are not indispensable to the attainment of the positive objectives (the requirement of indispensability).[142] Absolute territorial protection clauses will never get over this hurdle. The requirement of indispensability is by its nature an independent condition which stands apart from the balancing of objective advantages and restrictions of competition required by the first positive condition.

The *second* negative requirement, that the agreement must not enable the undertakings to eliminate competition in respect of a substantial part of the products in question, is a fundamental principle of the competition regime intended by the EC Treaty, as well as an additional guarantee that the three other requirements will be met. The somewhat fuller description used in Article 65(2)(c) ECSC[143] – now no longer in force – may nevertheless provide a guideline for the interpretation of this requirement, which demands a precise definition of the relevant market.[144] This shows that exclusion of competition is primarily concerned with whether the cartel in question dominates the market in relation to a substantial proportion of the suppliers or buyers. Suppliers or buyers, therefore, must have an alternative, which ensures that there is still actual competition.[145] The case law on Article 82 EC is also a source of inspiration in this respect.

---

141. See on the relationship between competition law and environmental policy Case T-289/01, *Der Grüne Punkt – Duales System Deutschland v. Commission*, and Case T-151/01, *Der Grüne Punkt – Duales System Deutschland v. Commission*.
142. Joined Cases 56 & 58/64, *Consten and Grundig*; Case T-206/99, *Métropole Télévision SA v. Commission*; and Case T-185/00, *M6 and others*.
143. See Case 13/60, *'Geitling II', Ruhrkohlen-Verkaufsgesellschaft mbH and others v. High Authority of the European Coal and Steel Community* and Case 66/63, *Netherlands v. High Authority of the European Coal and Steel Community (Ruhrkohle III)*.
144. Joined Cases 19/74 & 20/74, *Kali und Salz AG and Kali-Chemie AG v. Commission*; Joined Cases 209/78 to 215/78 & 218/78, *'Fedetab'*.
145. See especially Case C-234/89, *Delimitis*.

This requirement can be seen as an additional guarantee, because cooperation which brings economic or technical advantages compared with competitors does not require a dominant position on the market. Conversely, in the absence of such a position, the residual competition[146] will guarantee that the advantages of cooperation are passed on to purchasers.[147]

When viewed in this light, the four requirements of Article 81(3) form a logical and coherent whole, which is in keeping with the dynamic objectives of Article 2 EC. In particular, innovative agreements, changing the *status quo*, are possible; attempts to protect existing market positions on the other hand as a rule are not.

2.2.4   Application of the Cartel Prohibition in Practice

We now give a (very) brief summary of the practice in applying Articles 81(1) and (3) EC.[148]

2.2.4.1   *Prohibited Horizontal and Vertical Agreements*

Multilateral horizontal agreements *fixing prices or other selling conditions* hinder the function of price competition, which is 'to keep prices down to the lowest possible level', and endanger 'one of the basic objectives of the Treaty' which is pursued by free market pricing, 'namely the interpenetration of national markets and, as a result, direct access by consumers to the sources of production of the whole Community'.[149] This is also true of agreements as to collective resale price maintenance; credit terms;[150] tariffs and costs;[151] minimum prices;[152] fixed prices;[153] rebates, recommended prices, exchanges of information[154] and other parallel conduct which makes the pricing policy of individual undertakings so transparent that coordination can take place. The Court has pointed out that collective vertical price-fixing systems deprive resellers of all freedom to determine their sales prices, right through to the level of the consumer.[155] In practice the case law comes down to a *per se* prohibition of all horizontal price agreements.[156]

---

146. Case 43/85, *Associazione nazionale commercianti internazionali dentali e sanitari (Ancides) v. Commission.*
147. Case 75/84, *Metro SB-Großmárkte.*
148. Because of the limited space, reference will not be made to Commission decisions.
149. Case 48/69, *Imperial Chemical Industries*, para. 9.
150. E.g., Cases 209/78 etc., *SARL and others.*
151. Case 172/80, *Züchner.*
152. E.g., Case 123/83, *Bureau national interprofessionnel du cognac*; Case 136/86, *BNIC v. Aubert.*
153. Joined Cases T-213/95 & T-18/96, *SCK.*
154. Case C-176/99 P, *ARBED SA v. Commission.*
155. Joined Cases 43 & 63/82, *VBVB and others.*
156. Case T-224/00, *Archer Daniels v. Commission*; Case T-64/02, *Heubac*; Joined Cases T-5 & 6/00, *NVFGEG.*

The extensive practice in Commission decisions demonstrates moreover that price agreements virtually always go hand-in-hand with market sharing.[157] This is always prohibited, irrespective of the form it takes.[158] Export bans and obstacles to exports[159] will not escape the ambit of Article 81(1) EC, nor will obstacles to (parallel) imports.[160] The same applies in relation to market division of production or distribution.[161]

Collective exclusive dealing agreements between a considerable group of suppliers and a considerable group of professional buyers, such that a whole (national) market is inaccessible to traders from other States can also be said to be prohibited *per se*.[162]

Collective premium or rebate agreements will not benefit from exemption from the prohibition of Article 81(1) if the rebate on the total quantities purchased offered by producers to dealers only takes account of the quantities bought from the producers in a certain area or Member State.

2.2.4.2 Restrictions of Competition Permitted under Certain Conditions

The exception provided for by Article 81(3) EC with respect to the prohibition contained in the first paragraph of that Article, is mainly concerned with *vertical agreements*, i.e., agreements between two or more undertakings at different stages of production or distribution (e.g., producer, wholesaler, retailer) on the conditions concerning distribution (purchase, sale, resale). These include, *inter alia*:

- exclusive dealing agreements;[163]
- selective distribution systems (distribution by a restricted circle of traders selected on the basis of certain criteria, especially for high-quality consumer articles such as watches, perfumes, hi-fi, computers);[164] and

---

157. See especially Joined Cases T-236/01, 239/01, T-244-246/01, T-251/01 & T-252/01, *Tokai Carbon Co. Ltd, and others* (graphite electrodes).
158. See the cases mentioned earlier: Case T-141/89, *Tréfileurope*; Joined Cases T-25/95 etc., *Cimenteries CBR and others*; Joined Cases 89/85 etc., *Ahlström* (wood pulp).
159. Joined Cases 56 & 58/64, *Consten and Grundig*; Joined Cases 32/78, 36/78 to 82/78, *BMW Belgium*; Case 319/82, *SVCB v. Kerpen*.
160. Case C-279/87, *Tipp-Ex GmbH & Co. KG v. Commission*; Case T-43/92, *Dunlop*.
161. Case T-9/99, *HFB Holding für Fernwärmetechnik Beteiligungsgesellschaft mbH & Co. KG and others v. Commission*.
162. Case 8/72, *'VCH'*; Joined Cases 240/82 to 242/82, *SSI and others*; Joined Cases T-213/95 & T-18/96, *SCK*; Joined Cases T-5 & 6/00, *Nederlandse Federative Vereniging voor de Groothandel op Elektrotechnisch Gebied and Technische Unie BV v. Commission*.
163. See especially Joined Cases 56 & 58/64, *Consten and Grundig*; Case 32/65, *Italy v. Council and Commission*; Case 56/65, *'L.T.M.'*; Case 1/71, *Cadillon*; Case 22/71, *Beguelin*; Case 8/74, *Dassonville*; Case 61/80, *Coöperatieve Stremsel-en Kleurselfabriek v. Commission* and Case T-61/89, *Dansk Pelsdyravlerforening v. Commission*.
164. See especially Case 26/76, *Metro II*; Joined Cases 32 & 36-82/78, *BMW Belgium*; Case 31/80, *NV L'Oréal and SA L'Oréal v. PVBA 'De Nieuwe AMCK'*; Case 86/82, *Hasselblad (GB) Ltd v. Commission*; Case 107/82, *AEG-Telefunken*; Case 243/83, *Binon*; Joined Cases 25 & 26/84,

– franchising (exclusive supply in combination with uniformity of trade-name, trademark, furnishing, and commercial and publicity management, purchasing obligations and an obligation on the franchisee to pay the franchiser a royalty: above all used for clothing, food, restaurants, and licencing agreements (patents,[165] trade marks,[166] copyright,[167] plant bree-der's rights,[168] know-how rights, designs and models).

As a general rule, such agreements fulfil the two positive requirements for Article 81(3) EC and, at least when there is sufficient inter-brand competition, they will also meet the two negative requirements. The latter requires that such agreements are not accompanied by excessive market power on the part of the supplier or the purchaser, and that they do not contain clauses which restrict competition unnec-essarily (e.g., price agreements, obstacles to export etc.).[169]

The Commission's regulations and notices on the application of Article 81(3) EC, in general and in relation to specific agreements, are discussed in section 2.5.2, below.

2.3   ARTICLE 82 EC

2.3.1   Abuse of a Dominant Position

The most important element of Article 82 EC concerns the abuse of a dominant position on the common market or a substantial part thereof. There is a reciprocal relationship between the concept of 'abuse' and that of a 'dominant position'. On the one hand, a given practice (such as a refusal to sell or a price discrimination), which would be perfectly permissible for an undertaking having no dominant position, may constitute a prohibited abuse if it is carried out by an undertaking which enjoys a dominant position. In the latter case, the suppliers and purchasers of the dominant firm do not have alternatives, or do not have sufficient alternatives. Conversely, such conduct on the part of an undertaking may be an important indication of the very existence of a dominant position, since an undertaking which does not enjoy market power is usually not able to impose such conditions: the suppliers and purchasers will simply turn to competitors. This explains why the

---

    Ford; Case 226/84, *British Leyland Public Limited Company v. Commission*; Case C-125/05, *Vulcan Silkeborg*; Joined Cases C-376 & 377/05, *Brünsteiner*; Case C-522/03 P, *Unilever Bestfoods*.

165. Case 258/78, *Nungesser*.

166. Joined Cases 56 & 58/64, *Consten and Grundig*; Case 35/83, *BAT Cigaretten-Fabriken GmbH v. Commission*.

167. Joined Cases 55 & 57/80, *Musik-Vertrieb membran GmbH and K-tel International v. GEMA – Gesellschaft für musikalische Aufführungs- und mechanische Vervielfältigungsrechte*; Case 262/81, *Coditel SA, Compagnie générale pour la diffusion de la télévision, and others v. Ciné-Vog Films SA and others*; Case 395/87, *Ministère public v. Jean-Louis Tournier*.

168. Case 258/78, *Nungesser*.

169. See Case T-368/00, *General Motors*; Case T-67/01, *JCB Service v. Commission*.

examples in the (non-exhaustive) list contained in Article 82 EC explicitly or implicitly concern a prejudice to trading partners.

These observations shed further light on the objective of the prohibition on abuse of a dominant position. In section 2.1.2, above, it was noted that the case law reveals that Articles 81 and 82 EC pursue the same aim at different levels, namely the maintenance of effective competition within the common market.[170] Restraint of competition, which is prohibited if it results from conduct prohibited by Article 81(1) EC, cannot be lawful if such behaviour results from the conduct of a single undertaking which is able to act in that way because of its market position. An undertaking possessing a dominant position is also bound by the 'protected minimum of competition' postulated in Article 81(3)(b) EC.[171] This aim of Article 82 EC explains why the Court has ruled that a merger or takeover can also come under this prohibition. Thus, an answer was given to a heated discussion in early literature in this field as to whether Article 82 only concerned market behaviour of undertakings, or whether it also related to behaviour by an undertaking which changed the market structure. Such a distinction is not tenable, however, for at least two reasons: on the one hand, mergers and acquisitions can also be characterized as behaviour by undertakings; and on the other, because market behaviour can also lead to changes in market structure: for instance where an undertaking in a strong financial position can engage in cut-throat competition and drive smaller companies out of the market. This also reveals that abuse in the sense of Article 82 EC is an objective concept, which does not require that there should be an intention to prejudice other parties in order to be applied.[172] For that reason, the Court has ruled that abuse of a dominant position occurs 'if an undertaking in a dominant position strengthens such position in such a way that the degree of dominance reached substantially fetters competition, i.e., that only undertakings remain in the market whose behaviour depends on the dominant one'.[173] An undertaking with a dominant position has a special responsibility, as compared with an undertaking which does not occupy a dominant position, with respect to competition on the market, and must use its market power cautiously.[174] One of the consequences of this view is, for instance, that the fact that an agreement fulfils the conditions of Article 81(3) EC does not imply that the conclusion of such an agreement by an undertaking which enjoys a dominant position is excluded from the scope of the prohibition in Article 82 EC.[175]

---

170. See Case 6/72, *Continental Can.*
171. Case 6/72, *Continental Can.*
172. Case 85/76, *Hoffmann-La Roche & Co. AG v. Commission*; Case T-65/89, *British Gypsum.*
173. Case 6/72, *Continental Can*, para. 12.
174. Joined Cases T-24/93, T-25/93, T-26/93 & T-28/93, *Compagnie maritime belge transports SA and Compagnie maritime belge SA, Dafra-Lines A/S, Deutsche Afrika-Linien GmbH & Co. and Nedlloyd Lijnen BV v. Commission*; Case T-111/96, *ITT Promedia NV v. Commission*; Case T-228/97, *Irish Sugar plc v. Commission.*
175. Case T-51/89, *Tetra Pak Rausing SA v. Commission*; Case T-65/89, *British Gypsum*; Joined Cases C-395 & 396/96 P, *Compagnie maritime belge transports SA (CMBT) v. Commission* and C-396/96 P, *Dafra-Lines A/S v. Commission.*

2.3.2   One or More Undertakings

The concept of undertaking in the sense of Article 82 EC is the same as that in Article 81 EC;[176] two or more undertakings may occupy a joint dominant position. It follows from the demarcation between Articles 81 and 82 EC that the latter does not cover agreements or concerted practices of the undertakings in question, or between undertakings forming an economic entity (belonging to one concern).[177] It may be seen from the case law, that the concept of joint (or collective) dominance, which is in fact a very complicated concept, relates to situations where entities which are both legally and economically independent are closely connected on a particular market, as a result of economic factors,[178] for instance because of a technological lead compared with other market participants, or by agreements in the sense of Article 81(1) EC, whether or not these are exempt from the prohibition under paragraph 3 of Article 81. Such an oligopolistic situation may occur in a particular branch of industry (e.g., a shipping conference),[179] but also in a vertical relationship as long as the relevant undertakings are not completely integrated.[180]

2.3.3   Elements of the Prohibition of Abuse
of a Dominant Position

The Commission, the Court of First Instance, and the Court of Justice all tend to approach the application of Article 82 EC by first establishing the relevant product and geographical markets; then examining whether the undertaking(s) concerned have a dominant position in those markets, and, finally, whether there has been an abuse of that dominant position. The most important element of Article 82 EC is thus divided into four sub-parts, an approach which runs the risk of losing sight of the reciprocal relationship between abuse and a dominant position, mentioned above.[181]

---

176.   Joined Cases C-395 & 396/96 P, *CMBT*.
177.   Case 172/80, *Züchner*.
178.   Joined Cases T-68/89, T-77/89 & T-78/89, *Società Italiana Vetro SpA, Fabbrica Pisana SpA and PPG Vernante Pennitalia SpA v. Commission*; Joined Cases C-68/94 & C-30/95, *France and Société commerciale des potasses et de l'azote (SCPA) and Entreprise minière et chimique (EMC) v. Commission*; Joined Cases T-191/98, etc., *Atlantic Container Line v. Commission*; Case T-342/99, *Airtours*.
179.   Joined Cases T-24/93, T-25/93, T-26/93 & T-28/93, *CMBT*.
180.   Case T-228/97, *Irish Sugar*.
181.   The element of a negative effect on interstate trade is interpreted in the same way as for Art. 81(1) EC. See Joined Cases 6 & 7/73, *Commercial Solvents*; Case 22/79, *Greenwich Film Production v. Société des auteurs, compositeurs et éditeurs de musique (SACEM) and Société des éditions Labrador*; Case 322/81, *NV Nederlandsche Banden Industrie Michelin v. Commission*; Case T-65/89, *British Gypsum*.

2.3.3.1   Relevant Product Market

The relevant product (or service) market[182] is usually defined by an analysis of the possibility of product substitutability on both the supply and the demand sides.[183] This in effect looks at the possibilities available elsewhere to purchasers and suppliers. Demand substitutability[184] depends not only on the actual interchangeability of a product, such as bananas and other types of fruit, but also on consumer preferences.[185] Depending on the possible applications, a product may have several markets, as is the case for vitamins which may be used for bio-nutritional and industrial purposes.[186] Separate markets may exist for spare parts.[187] The existence of a separate sub-market will depend above all on a specific demand for the product or service in question.[188] The relevant product (or service) market does not imply that the competitive situation within a certain area must be entirely homogeneous.[189]

Whether supply substitutability exists will depend primarily on whether, and how easily, suppliers can easily switch their resources in order to produce and supply other products, e.g., shifting from producing aluminium cans to containers made of glass or plastic.[190]

2.3.3.2   Relevant Geographical Market

The sub-element 'relevant geographical market' is expressed in Article 82 EC by the phrase 'within the common market or in a substantial part of it'. From the case law, it is apparent that this requirement is met if the market in one Member State, or a substantial part of it, is concerned.[191] Apart from that, it appears that the relevant geographical market is mainly a function of the relevant product or service market and the area in which the abuse takes place, or in which the disadvantaged parties are located.[192] The relevant area will therefore often be characterized by a sufficiently homogeneous competitive situation.[193] This shows once more the link between the concepts of the dominant position itself, and abuse.

---

182. For more information see: Commission Notice on the definition of relevant market for the purposes of Community competition law, O.J. 1997, C 372/5.
183. Case T-83/91, *Tetra Pak*.
184. Case 322/81, *Michelin*; Case C-62/86, *AKZO Chemie BV v. Commission* (exclusionary practices); Case T-30/89, *Hilti AG v. Commission*; Case T-83/91, *Tetra Pak*; Case T-340/03, *France Télécom v. Commission*.
185. Case 27/76, *United Brands Company and United Brands Continentaal BV v. Commission*.
186. Case 85/76, *Hoffmann-La Roche & Co. AG v. Commission*.
187. Case 22/78, *Hugin Kassaregister AB and others. v. Commission* and Case 322/81, *Michelin*.
188. Case T-69/89, *Magill*; Case T-229/94, *Deutsche Bahn*.
189. Case T-139/98, *Amministrazione Autonoma dei Monopoli di Stato (AAMS) v. Commission*.
190. Case 6/72, *Continental Can*.
191. Case T-229/94, *Deutsche Bahn AG v. Commission*.
192. Joined Cases 40-48/73, 50/73, 54/73 to 56/73, 111/73, 113/73 & 114/73, *Suiker Unie*; Case 127/73, *BRT I*.
193. Case 322/81, *Michelin*; Case T-83/91, *Tetra Pak International SA v. Commission*; Case T-229/94, *Deutsche Bahn*.

2.3.3.3   Dominant Position

According to the case law, a dominant position is demonstrated by a variety of factors, none of which needs be decisive when taken separately.[194] The most important criterion is generally the market share of the undertaking in question,[195] whereby a rule of thumb is that a market share of 50% or more leads to such a dominant position.[196] Other factors, as revealed by the case law, are: the relationship between market share of the undertaking in question and that of other undertakings; the technological and economic strength of the undertaking; whether the undertaking forms part of a large concern; the existence or absence of potential competition. In the last case, factors are the size of investment required and the time needed to create production capacity.[197]

Analysis of the relevant market and the existence of a dominant position will be superfluous, or in any event less important, if the undertaking concerned enjoys a *de facto* monopoly,[198] such as a television broadcaster with regard to information on programmes to be broadcast, or a legal monopoly, such as the exclusive right to provide approvals or certificates,[199] or has a concession,[200] or that the entire market is regulated because of the existence of a monopoly.[201] In general, mere possession of industrial or intellectual property rights will not itself confer dominance, but this may be a relevant factor in determining the existence of such a dominant position.[202]

2.3.3.4   Abuse

As far as deciding that conduct of undertakings in a dominant position constitutes an abuse is concerned, in practice there is a striking parallel with the conduct which is prohibited under Article 81(1) EC. Horizontal and vertical price agreements find their parallel in Article 82 EC in the prohibition of unfair transactions.[203] When such prices are unfair is indeed a complex question, but nevertheless the Court has

---

194. Case C-250/92, *Gøttrup-Klim*; Case T-228/97, *Irish Sugar*.
195. See Case 27/76 *United Brands* and Case 85/76 *Hoffmann-La Roche*, both of which give further details.
196. Case C-62/86, *Akzo* (exclusionary practices); Case T-228/97, *Irish Sugar*; Case T-210/01, *General Electric v. Commission*.
197. Case T-210/01, *General Electric*; Case T-340/03, *France Télécom*.
198. Joined Cases C-241/91 P & C-242/91 P, *Radio Telefis Eireann (RTE) and Independent Television Publications Ltd (ITP) v. Commission*.
199. Case 26/75, *General Motors Continental NV v. Commission*, and Case 226/84, *British Leyland*; Case 311/84, *Centre belge d'études de marché-Télémarketing (CBEM) SA v. Compagnie luxembourgeoise de télédiffusion SA*.
200. Case 155/73, *Giuseppe Sacchi*; Case 30/87, *Bodson v. Pompes funèbres des régions libérées*.
201. Case T-139/98, *AAMS*.
202. Case 24/67, *Parke-Davis*; Case 40/70, *Sirena*; Case 78/70, *Deutsche Grammophon Gesellschaft mbH v. Metro-SB-Großmärkte GmbH & Co. KG*; Case 51/75, *EMI Records I*, Case T-51/89, *Tetra Pak I*.
203. Case 155/73, *Sacchi*; Case 26/75, *General Motors*; Case 247/86, *Alsatel*.

established certain general criteria.[204] The question whether a price is unfair will be closely related with the power to impose unilaterally prices on customers or suppliers.[205] There will also be abuse if, as a result of a state monopoly, an undertaking can impose dues on competitors which are not matched by services rendered.[206] The same applies to predatory pricing (in order to drive a competitor out of the market)[207] and also to price discrimination,[208] the very existence of which is usually regarded as indicative that the dominant undertaking is dividing up the common market. Rebate cartels find their parallel in the prohibition of abuse through a system of fidelity rebates and similar practices.[209] A close connection exists between collective exclusive dealing arrangements, and refusals to supply or boycott actions against unwilling purchasers or suppliers.[210] Agreements to restrict production or delivery are paralleled under Article 82 by the imposition of long-term purchasing obligations,[211] the creation of artificial scarcity,[212] refusal to supply spare parts,[213] refusal of access to 'essential facilities',[214] restrictions in granting licences and tying.[215] The refusal of access to 'essential facilities' means that a refusal by an undertaking which enjoys a dominant position to supply competitors, or potential competitors with certain goods or services, or to allow them access to certain facilities (e.g., infrastructure) may be characterized as an abuse if such supply or access is 'essential' for their conduct on the market, or for their access to the market.[216] Finally, there is also a parallel with Article 81(1) EC as far as the use of industrial or intellectual property rights by an undertaking which enjoys a dominant position is concerned.[217]

---

204. E.g., Case 27/76, *United Brands*; Case 66/86, *Ahmed Saeed Flugreisen and others v. Zentrale zur Bekämpfung unlauteren Wettbewerbs*; Case 395/87, *Ministère public v. Tournier*.
205. Case 247/86, *Alsatel v. Novasam*.
206. Case C-340/99, *TNT Traco SpA v. Poste Italiane SpA*.
207. Case 62/86, *AKZO* (exclusionary practices).
208. Case 27/76, *United Brands*; Case T-83/91, *Tetra Pak*; Case T-229/94, *Deutsche Bahn*; Case T-128/98, *Aéroports de Paris*; Case C-163/99, *Portuguese Republic v. Commission* (Portugese airports).
209. E.g., Cases 40/73 etc., *Suiker Unie*; Case 85/76, *Hoffmann-La Roche*; Case 322/81, *Michelin*; Case T-30/89, *Hilti*; Case T-219/99, *British Airways plc v. Commission*; Case T-203/01, *Michelin*.
210. E.g., Case 27/76, *United Brands*; Case 90/76, *Van Ameyde*; Case 22/78, *Hugin*.
211. Case T-65/89, *British Gypsum*.
212. Case C-41/90, *Höfner*; Case C-55/96, *Job Centre*.
213. Case T-30/89, *Hilti*.
214. See e.g., Case 311/84, *Telemarketing*; Joined Cases C-241/91 P & C-242/91 P, *RTE* (licences); Case C-7/97, *Oscar Bronner GmbH & Co. KG v. Mediaprint Zeitungs-und Zeitschriftenverlag GmbH & Co. KG, Mediaprint Zeitungsvertriebsgesellschaft mbH & Co. KG and Mediaprint Anzeigengesellschaft mbH & Co. KG* (distribution channels).
215. Case T-201/04, *Microsoft*.
216. See Case T-184/01 R, *IMS Health v. Commission* and Case C-418/01, *IMS Health*.
217. See *inter alia* Case, 53/87, *Consorzio italiano della componentistica di ricambio per auto-veicoli and Maxicar v. Régie nationale des usines*; Case 238/87, *AB Volvo v. Erik Veng (UK) Ltd*; Case 395/87, *Tournier*; Case T-69/89, *Radio Telefis Eireann v. Commission*; Case T-30/89, *Hilti*; Case T-504/93, *Ladbroke*; Case T-198/98, *Micro Leader Business v. Commission*; Case T-201/04 R II, *Microsoft v. Commission*.

2.4   SPECIAL RULES FOR AGRICULTURE

Article 36 EC empowers the Council to determine whether, and if so, to what
extent, Articles 81–86 EC shall apply to the production of or trade in agricultural
products. On the basis of that provision, in 1962 the Council adopted Regulation
26[218] which made three exceptions to the application of Article 81(1) EC in the
agricultural sector. In practice, these three exceptions – which are very unclear in
any case – only have general significance for agricultural cooperatives, the activities of which compensate for structural weaknesses in the production and trade of
agricultural produce. In many cases undertakings invoke Regulation 26 in vain, in
an attempt to escape the ambit of Article 81(1).[219]

The transport sector is no longer subject to special, divergent competition
rules.[220] In this context, reference is also made to the fact that on the basis of
the Community legislation concerning, *inter alia*, energy, public procurement,
telecommunications, media, and intellectual property, specific behaviour by
undertakings in these sectors may be prohibited, which as such would come within
the scope of Articles 81 and 82 EC.

2.5   THE GENERAL MECHANISM OF THE APPLICATION
               OF ARTICLES 81 AND 82 EC

2.5.1   The Old System and the New System

For the application of the prohibitions contained in Articles 81 and 82 EC, Article
83(1) EC provides for a competence of the Council to lay down appropriate regulations or directives, acting by a qualified majority on a proposal from the Commission and after consulting the European Parliament. With this legal basis, the
Council can authorize the Commission to lay down detailed implementing rules.
As to the manner in which the prohibitions in question are to be applied, Article
83(2) EC gives only a few indications. Only (a) of this provision is concrete:
regulations or directives referred to in paragraph 1 shall be designed in particular
to ensure compliance with the prohibitions laid down in Article 81(1) and in Article
82 by making provision for *fines and periodic penalty payments.*

For the rest, there is merely an indication of the broad areas which must be
regulated: the application of Article 81(3), the various branches of the economy,
the scope of the provisions of Articles 81 and 82, the respective functions of the

---

218. Reg. 26/62, O.J. 1962/993. (O.J. English Spec. Ed. 1959–1962, 129), codified by Reg. 1184/
      2006, O.J. 2006, L 214/7.
219. See Cases 71/74, *Nederlandse Vereniging voor Fruit en Groentenimporthandel and others v.
      Commission and others*; Case 61/80, *Coöperatieve Stremsel-en Kleurselfabriek v. Commis-
      sion*; Case 123/83, *Bureau national interprofessionnel du cognac*; Cases C-319/93 etc., *Dijk-
      stra and others v. Friesland (Frico Domo) Coperatie BA and others*; and Case C-399/93, *Oude
      Luttikhuis and others v. Verenigde Coperatieve Melkindustrie Coberco BA.*
220. See further, Ch. XII *infra* on the transport sector in general.

Commission and of the Court of Justice, the relationship between Community and national competition laws. Although Article 83 does not refer to the possibility that Articles 81 and 82 can also be applied by the Member States, it appears from the transitional rules in Article 84 that this possibility is not excluded in principle. It is laid down that the Community legislature must respect the character of the prohibitions in Articles 81 and 82 in choosing the mechanism for applying these provisions.

The old mechanism for applying the competition provisions, as this functioned on the basis of Regulation 17/62, from 1962 to 2004, was a centralized system based on authorizations. The core of this system was formed by the excusive power of the Commission to grant an exemption on the basis of Article 81(3) EC to previously notified agreements etc. which come within Article 81(1) EC, possibly for a specified period of time, and possibly under certain conditions. Agreements and so forth. which had not been notified were subject to prohibition or to fines imposed by the Commission.

In the course of time, using powers granted to it under a number of individual Council Regulations, the Commission drew up block exemption regulations, on the basis of its experiences in granting individual exemptions. These block exemptions indicated in relation to certain agreements the conditions under which Article 81(3) was not applicable, so that notification was no longer necessary. For reasons which will be discussed in section 2.4.5 below, this mechanism was radically changed as of 1 May 2004, the notification system was abolished together with the exclusive power of the Commission to grant an exemption. As of that date, the application of the prohibitions contained in Articles 81 and 82 EC has become, in its entirety, a matter of shared competences: the Commission on the one hand, and the national competition authorities (and the national courts) on the other. It has thus become a *decentralized application system*, functioning on the basis of rules concerning cooperation and division of competences, as laid down in the basic regulation, Regulation 1/2003.[221] Undertakings must therefore in principle themselves judge whether their actions fall within the prohibitions of Articles 81 and 82 EC, and thereby run the risk of having sanctions imposed on them by the Commission or the national authorities or courts.

2.5.2 Guidelines and Block Exemptions

Article 1 of Regulation 1/2003 lays down the fundamental character of Articles 81 and 82 EC: the prohibitions contained in these Articles are applicable or inapplicable *de jure*, without a prior decision on this being required. For agreements etc. which do not fall within the ambit of Article 81(1) EC, the prohibition is therefore not applicable. The same holds for agreements which do fall within the scope of Article 81(1) EC, but which fulfil the conditions mentioned in Article 81(3) EC. Article 1 confirms further that abuse of a dominant position in the sense of Article 82 EC is always

---

221. O.J. 2003, L 1/1.

prohibited. Whether Articles 81 or 82 EC apply to a particular situation is a question of proof. Article 2 lays down rules on the burden of proof. In any proceedings, national or Community, proof of an infringement of Article 81(1) or Article 82 EC must be provided by the party or the authority alleging the infringement. For the application of the exemption in Article 81(3), the burden of proof is reversed. If the Commission or a national authority (or a judicial authority) starts proceedings against an undertaking for infringement of the prohibition in Article 81(1) EC, the undertaking will have to prove that Article 81(3) applies.

We mentioned earlier that the new system for implementation of the competition rules essentially implies that undertakings and their legal counsellors must themselves assess whether the actions of the undertaking are prohibited or not. This situation creates a need for legal certainty, and the Commission meets this need to some extent by publishing its views on Articles 81 and 82 in notices, and by means of the block exemptions, somewhat modified, dating from the old system. The Commission's notices are, certainly, only binding on that institution itself, and not on national authorities; nevertheless, they form an important source of inspiration for the national authorities in their application of the Community competition rules, also in the light of the system of cooperation introduced by the basic regulation, which will be discussed below. The policy on the application of Articles 81 and 82 EC set out in the notices and the block exemptions may be summarized as follows.

We begin with the question in which cases actions of undertakings fall outside the scope of the prohibitions of Articles 81 and 82 EC. As mentioned earlier, agreements and so forth which do not appreciably affect competition (*de minimis*) fall outside the ambit of Article 81(1) EC. This requirement of an appreciable effect, developed in the case law, is described in more detail by the Commission in its regular notices on agreements of minor importance, of which the most recent was published in 2001.[222] According to these notices, agreements and so forth between small and medium enterprises are entirely excluded from the cartel prohibition.[223] Apart from this category, agreements etc. fall outside the scope of Article 81(1) EC if the joint market share of the parties involved is less than 10% (for horizontal agreements) or 15% (vertical agreements). If parallel existing networks of agreements with similar effects are concerned, then the threshold in both cases is 5%. These market share thresholds do not apply, however, to agreements with so-called 'hardcore' restrictions.

The appreciability test formulated in the case law with respect to effect on interstate trade has also been elaborated by the Commission in a notice.[224]

---

222. Commission Notice on agreements of minor importance which do not appreciably restrict competition under Art. 81(1) of the Treaty establishing the European Community (*de minimis*), O.J. 2001, C 368/7

223. These concepts are defined in recommendation 2003/351 (O.J. 2003, L 124/36). The main rule is that an SME has less than 250 employees, and a turnover or balance sheet total of no more than 50 and 43 million euros respectively.

224. O.J. 2004, C 101/81.

According to these guidelines, the general rule is that there is no question of influence on interstate trade if the joint market share of the undertakings which are parties to the agreement etc. is no greater that 5 per cent and the joint turnover no greater than 40 million euro.

As for the application of Article 81(3) EC, the Commission has published a general notice.[225] In addition, it had issued a number of block exemptions in the past, which have been adapted to the new system for implementing the Treaty prohibitions. These block exemptions, in the form of regulations, indicate that certain types of agreements etc. which meet the criteria of Article 81(3) EC, do not fall within the scope of the prohibition contained in the first paragraph of that Article. The Commission's power to issue block exemptions is derived from Council regulations based on Article 83 EC.[226] On that basis, the Commission has issued block exemptions for certain agreements in the air transport sector, categories of vertical agreements, consortia, specialization agreements, research and development, motor vehicles, insurance and technology transfer.[227] In general terms, according to these regulations, agreements come under the exemption of Article 81(3) EC if two main conditions are fulfilled. The first is that the market share of the parties involved does not exceed a certain limit. For vertical agreements this is 30%, for specialization agreements 20%, and for research and development agreements 25%. For agreements relating to technology transfer the threshold is 30% if the undertakings are not competitors, and 20% if they are competitors. The second condition is that the agreements do not contain hardcore restrictions, described in the regulations ('black list'). In practice, the block exemptions give undertakings legal certainty. As long as there are no hardcore restrictions, and the market share thresholds are not exceeded, the undertakings are in the 'safe zone'.

As mentioned already, Article 81(3) EC is applicable without a prior decision being needed; from a strictly legal point of view the block exemptions are not constitutive. An agreement therefore does not fall within the exemption of paragraph 3 *because* this is provided for in the block exemption regulations, but because that agreement as such meets the conditions of that provision. Article 81(3) EC remains, thus, the decisive criterion for the question whether the agreement is prohibited under Article 81(1) EC. For that reason, the basic regulation grants the Commission the power to withdraw the benefit of a block exemption, if it appears that the agreements described therein are not compatible with the conditions of Article 81(3) EC after all (see Art. 29 of Reg. 1/2003). The Commission has issued a number of extensive notices together with the block exemption

---

225. O.J. 2004, C 101/97.
226. For vertical agreements and intellectual property agreements: Regs. 19/65 (O.J. 1965, 533/65) and 2821/71 (O.J. 1971, L 285/46); air transport: 3976/87 (O.J. 1987, L 374/9), amended Reg. 411/2004 (O.J. 2004, L 68/1); insurance: 1534/91 (O.J. 1991, L 143/1); shipping companies: 479/92 (O.J. 1992, L 55/3).
227. Regs. 1617/93 (O.J. 1993, L 155/18), 2790/1999 (O.J. 1999, L 336/21), 823/2000 (O.J. 2000, L 100/24), 2658/2000 (O.J. 2000, L 304/3), 2659/2000 (O.J. 2000, L 304), 1400/2002 (O.J. 2002, L 203/30), 358/2003 (O.J. 2003, L 53/8), 772/2004 (O.J. 2004, L 123/11), respectively.

regulations, which contain guidelines and examples related to practice.[228] In addition, there are notices about the application of the competition rules to specific agreements, activities or sectors.[229]

Taken together, this means in practice that appreciable, hardcore restrictions are always prohibited (*per se* prohibition). This does not include all horizontal agreements, though. In the 2001 Notice on horizontal cooperation agreements, the Commission explained under which conditions – in its opinion – the cartel prohibition is not applicable to production agreements, agreements on purchasing, agreements on commercialization, agreements on standards and agreements on environmental protection.[230] When agreements are concerned which are outside the 'safe zone' mentioned above, the undertakings must themselves provide evidence that the conditions of Article 81(3) are met, in conformity with the rules on burden of proof. In that 2001 Notice, the Commission formulated a number of guidelines, emphasizing a quantified indication of the positive benefits mentioned in Article 81(3). One of the possibilities for creating more legal certainty even outside the 'safe zone' lies in the possibility, mentioned in recital 38 of the basic regulation, for the Commission to make its opinion known by means of (non-binding) communications to undertakings.[231]

**2.5.3   The Procedures for the Application of
             Articles 81 and 82 EC**

2.5.3.1   The Powers of the Commission

The powers of the Commission to apply Articles 81 and 82 EC are described in the basic regulation, and further elaborated in the implementing regulation, Regulation 773/2004.[232]

The Commission may become aware of infringements of Articles 81 and 82 EC as a result of its own investigations, or as a result of a complaint (Art. 7, Reg. 1/2003). The Commission is empowered to conduct inquiries into particular sectors or regarding particular types of agreements on its own initiative, for instance if there are indications that competition is distorted, such as price rigidity, etc. (Art. 17, Reg. 1/2003). The Commission may also initiate investigations as a result of complaints by interested parties or Member States. The implementing regulation,

---

228. On the application of Art. 81(3) EC in general (O.J. 2004, C 101/97), vertical restraints (O.J. 2000, C 291/1) and technology transfer (O.J. 2004, C 101/2).
229. Supply agreements (O.J. 1979, C 313/5), telecommunications (O.J. 1991, C 233/2 and O.J. 1998, C 265/2), transborder credit transfers (O.J. 1995, C 251/3), transport infrastructure projects (O.J. 1997, C 298/5), regional policy (O.J. 1998, C 90/3), post sector (O.J. 1998, C 39/2), cable television (O.J. 1998, C 71/4), electronic communication networks (O.J. 2002, C 165/6).
230. O.J. 2001, C 3/2.
231. See the Commission Notice on guidance letters (O.J. 2004, C 101/78). See further Case 99/79, *Lancôme* and Case 31/80, *L'Oreal*.
232. O.J. 2004, L 123/18.

mentioned above, sets out the further arrangements concerning the right of natural and legal persons to lodge a complaint, and the resulting obligations on the Commission with respect to handling complaints.[233] In addition, the Commission may request undertakings to provide information, and may – by decision – oblige undertakings to provide information, under threat of penalty payments; supply of incorrect information may lead to the imposition of fines (Art. 18, Reg. 1/2003). The Commission may interview persons who agree to be interviewed, and notes may be taken of that interview (Art. 19, Reg. 1/2003). The Commission also has extensive powers to inspect premises, land and means of transport of undertakings, it may examine the books and other records, take or obtain copies of such books and records, and may ask representatives and members of staff for explanations (Art. 20, Reg. 1/2003).[234] Under Article 21 of the basic regulation, the powers of inspection may be extended to cover the homes of directors, managers and other members of staff, if there is a reasonable suspicion that documents are kept there. The powers of inspection are exercised on grant of an authorization. If access is denied, the inspections may be ordered by decision, and be enforced by penalty payments and fines. The Commission inspectors may not use coercion or force.[235] If the undertaking opposes an investigation, the national authorities concerned are obliged to afford assistance, where appropriate the assistance of the police or of an equivalent enforcement authority, and if necessary the authorization from a judicial authority for such enforcement. Since investigations in fact amount to searches of premises, in some Member States judicial authorization is needed. Regulation 1/2003 provides that the intervention of the national judicial authority is limited to controlling the authenticity of the Commission decision, and ensuring that the measures proposed are not arbitrary nor excessive. The national courts may not examine the lawfulness of the Commission decision – only the Community courts have jurisdiction to do that.[236]

Where the Commission, acting on a complaint or on its own initiative, finds that there is an infringement of the competition rules, it starts the procedure leading to a formal decision finding an infringement. The two main principles in this procedure are the right of interested parties to be heard, and the obligation of secrecy, regulated in Articles 27 and 28 respectively of Regulation 1/2003. The practical details of the procedure are set out in the implementing regulation (mentioned above). In the framework of these infringement proceedings, the Commission issues a statement of objections, addressed to the undertakings in question. In that statement, the Commission sets a period of time within which parties may make their views known, in writing. There is a large body of case law on the content and form of the objections, the relationship between the statement of objections and the final decision of the Commission, the possibility of

---

233. And in a Notice (O.J. 2004, C 101/65).
234. Case T-65/99, *Strintzis Lines v. Commission.*
235. Joined Cases 46/87 & 227/88, *Hoechst AG v. Commission* and Case 85/87, *Dow Chemical Nederland BV v. Commission.*
236. Case C-94/00, *Roquette Frères.*

supplementary objections, and the possible reassessment of facts in the light of later developments.[237] The communication of the objections and the right to be heard are two essential elements of the infringement proceedings (see section 2.6.1 below). In its decision, the Commission may only take into account those elements which have been mentioned in the statement of objection, and on which the parties have had the opportunity to comment. The hearings are conducted by a hearing officer, who acts independently.[238] All these elements of the proceedings are set out in more detail in the implementing regulation, as is access to the file and the treatment of confidential information. Before a decision is adopted, the Commission consults the Advisory Committee on Restrictive Practices and Dominant Positions, which consists of representatives of the national competition authorities when individual cases are at issue (Art. 14 Reg. 1/2003).

Mention has been made above of the Commission's competence to issue block exemptions, its informal cartel policy, and its use of notices and communications; in addition, the basic Regulation grants the Commission the power to adopt four types of decisions. The first type concerns decisions finding an infringement and on the ending of such an infringement (Art. 7). In these decisions, the undertakings may be required to take corrective measures, either behavioural remedies (for instance, stopping certain practices) or structural remedies (for instance, selling off certain activities). The latter category may only be required if behavioural remedies would not be effective, or if behavioural remedies would turn out to be more burdensome for the undertaking concerned than the structural remedy. Secondly, the Commission may order interim measures – by decision – if there is a risk of serious and irreparable damage to competition as a result of a supposed infringement (Art. 8). Subsequently, and thirdly, the Commission has the power – by decision – to accept binding commitments from undertakings if it appears after the preliminary assessment that the undertakings are prepared to follow such a course (Art. 9).[239] This possibility is particularly important as it allows the Commission to take influential action in sectors experiencing rapid change. Finally, and fourthly, the Commission may – by decision – determine that Articles 81 or 82 EC are not applicable in a particular situation, and where Article 81 is concerned this may be either because paragraph 1 is not applicable, or the conditions of paragraph 3 are met. Such a declaratory decision may only be issued ex officio by the Commission in the general Community interest. As a result of such decisions, clarification may be provided in relation to new types of agreements or conduct.

The Commission is empowered to impose fines for infringements of primary and secondary competition law (Art. 23). Fines may not exceed 1% of the total turnover in the preceding business year when imposed for supplying incorrect

---

237. See, *inter alia*, Joined Cases T-191/98 etc., *Atlantic Container Line.*
238. The terms of reference of the hearing officers are described in Decision 2001/462 (O.J. 2001, L 162/21).
239. Case T-170/06, *Alrosa v. Commission.*

information or not supplying information within the required time-limit, or for frustrating inspections. Fines of up to 10% may be imposed for infringements of Articles 81 and 82 EC, for contravening interim measures, and for failure to comply with a commitments. Article 23 of Regulation 1/2003 also sets out rules for imposing fines on associations of undertakings and the conditions under which the members of such associations are liable. The Commission's practice shows a tendency to impose higher and higher fines on participants in horizontal agreements on pricing and market sharing and undertakings which abuse their dominant position.[240] The question remains, however, whether the imposition of fines has a sufficient deterrent effect. The Commission has drawn up guidelines for the calculation of monetary fines[241] and applies rules, also based on a notice, in order not to impose fines, or to reduce fines, if undertakings voluntarily cooperate with the Commission in order to put an end to infringements (the Leniency notice).[242] In addition, periodic penalty payments may be imposed, proportional to the average daily turnover (Art. 24).[243] Lastly, the basic regulation lays down arrangements concerning limitation periods for the imposition of penalties and for their enforcement (Arts. 25 and 26).

2.5.3.2 *The Powers of the National Authorities*

Pursuant to Article 5 of the basic regulation, the national authorities have the power, not further defined, to require that an infringement be brought to an end; to order interim measures; to accept commitments; to decide on the basis of the information in their possession that there are no grounds for action; and to impose fines, penalty payments or other sanctions. This is all to be done on the basis of national law. The inspection powers of these authorities are also subject to their national law (Art. 22). It should be understood that the national competition authorities do not act as organs of the EC, but as organs of the Member States who are jointly responsible – under Regulation 1/2003 together with Article 10 EC – for the application of Community competition law.[244] As a result of these provisions, when applying the Community competition rules, national authorities and judicial bodies are also bound to respect general legal principles and all the procedural and substantive guarantees developed in the case law of the Court concerning the protection and enforcement of Community law rights. National competition authorities are not courts or tribunals in the sense of Article 234 EC, and therefore cannot put preliminary questions to the Court of Justice on these problems.[245]

---

240. In 2006, the Commission imposed a total of 1.8 billion EUR in fines in seven cartel cases. In 2004, a fine was imposed on Microsoft of 500 million EUR for abuse of a dominant position.
241. O.J. 2006, C 210/2.
242. O.J. 2006, C 298/1.
243. Used for the first time in 2006 against Microsoft.
244. Case C-198/01, *Industrie Fiammiferi (CIF)*.
245. Case C-53/03, *Syfait et al. v. GlaxoSmithKline*.

2.5.3.3   The Co-ordination Mechanisms

Such a decentralized system for the implementation of the prohibitions contained in Articles 81 and 82 EC involves, in principle, two risks. The first risk results from the fact that the national competition authorities and national courts are also bound to apply *national* competition law. There is thus a risk that instead of Community competition law, only the (more familiar) national competition law will be applied (danger of substitution). But even if the national competition authorities and national courts do apply Community competition law, there is still the risk of divergent policy (danger of fragmentation). In order to overcome these two risks, which are a serious threat to the effectiveness of Community competition policy, the basic regulation provides for two *co-ordination mechanisms*. The danger of substitution is tackled in Article 3. To start with, the national authorities and national courts are bound whenever they apply national competition rules, also to apply Articles 81 and 82 EC. Moreover, on the basis of the primacy of Community law, it follows that anything which is prohibited by Community law may not be permitted by national law;[246] Article 3 adds that what is permitted by Community law may not be prohibited by national law. There are three exceptions to these 'anti-substitution' rules: Member States may impose more severe sanctions on unilateral action of undertakings,[247] the rules do not affect the application of national merger laws, and they do not apply to legislation which has different objectives from Articles 81 and 82 EC. This third exception refers to rules on unfair commercial practices, consumer protection etc.[248] The 'anti-substitution' rules are complicated and force the official bodies in question to choose the applicable law each time. It would probably have been simpler to apply the competence rule contained in Articles 81 and 82 EC, i.e., that Community law is only applicable where the conduct in question may have an appreciable effect on interstate trade. This criterion was, however, politically unacceptable.

In order to overcome the danger of fragmentation, the Commission and the national authorities are subject to a general obligation of mutual cooperation in applying the Community competition rules (Art. 11(1)), which may be seen as a specification of the general obligation of loyal cooperation contained in Article 10 EC.[249] This obligation is elaborated in more detail, first and foremost, in relation to an extensive exchange of information at all stages of the Community and national application proceedings and mutual support in the stages of investigation and inspection. The use of this information in general is regulated, as well as its use in evidence (Art. 12). In the second place, pursuant to Article 11(4) of the basic regulation, the national authorities are bound to inform the Commission of their

---

246. Case 14/68, *Walt Wilhelm*.
247. I.e., abuse of a dominant position. This raises the question whether abuse of a collective dominant position is also included.
248. It should be noted in this context that these rules have already been harmonized to some extent.
249. Case C-234/89, *Delimitis*; Case C-344/98, *Masterfoods Ltd v. HB Ice Cream Ltd*; Case T-340/04, *France Télécom v. Commission*.

proposed decisions. This rule is intended to bring about a dialogue between the national authorities and the Commission. Thirdly, the initiation of proceedings by the Commission relieves the competition authorities of the Member States of their competence to apply Articles 81 and 82 EC. This is also the case if the national authorities have already initiated proceedings; in that case, however, there must first be consultation before the Commission initiates proceedings, and thus deprives the national authority of its competence. In the fourth place, Article 13 of Regulation 1/2003 lays down rules for suspension or termination of proceedings if more than one national authority has initiated proceedings. The core of this institutionalized cooperation consists of the Advisory Committee on Restrictive Practices and Dominant Positions, made up of representatives of the competition authorities of the Member States which, under chairmanship of the Commission, gives advisory opinions on draft decisions of the Commission, and can hold consultations about draft decisions of national authorities and general questions of competition law (Art. 14). In this way, a network of national competition authorities has come into existence (European Competition Network); the Commission has published a notice on the functioning of this network.[250]

As far as national courts are concerned, the danger of fragmentation is prevented by the obligation laid down in Article 16 that they may not take decisions running counter to a relevant decision adopted by the Commission, and they should avoid giving decisions which would conflict with a decision contemplated by the Commission in proceedings it has initiated but not yet completed. The latter may lead to a stay of proceedings by the national court. Article 15 provides for a right of the national courts to ask the Commission for information or advice. The Commission has published a notice on this form of cooperation.[251] Article 15 also grants competition authorities and the Commission the right to submit written observations to the national courts and, with the permission of the court in question, also to submit oral observations. All of these are without prejudice to the competence or obligation of the national court to make a preliminary reference to the Court of Justice under Article 234 EC.

2.5.4   **Background and Problems of the New Mechanism for Applying Articles 81 and 82 EC**

2.5.4.1   *Policy Consideration*

It is useful to recall the background to the fundamental changes in the mechanism for applying Articles 81 and 82 EC brought about by Regulation 1/2003. It appears from the Commission's White Paper, mentioned above,[252] that the Commission's prime consideration was that this institution could no longer guarantee on its own the effective application of the competition rules in a European Union of 25 or

---

250. O.J. 2004, C 101/43.
251. O.J. 2004, C 101/54.
252. See note 8 and text, *supra*.

more Member States. On the one hand, its means are limited – both in material terms and in terms of staff – and on the other hand, competition authorities have been set up in the Member States and national competition rules have been adopted which are strongly based on those of Articles 81 and 82 EC. Secondly, the Commission is of the opinion that the system of notifications is no longer an adequate means for guaranteeing the effective application of these Treaty provisions. Given its limited means, it is not able to deal with the great number of notifications. In addition, the notification of agreements does not reveal many cases of serious infringements of the Treaty provisions, given that such practices are – by their nature – not notified. In the third place, the previous system led to uncertainty for the undertakings in question, since – as long as a decision granting exemption was not issued – the undertaking did not have any certainty as to the permissibility of the agreement concluded, and therefore could face problems in enforcing the agreement. Finally, the obligation to notify, together with the associated costs of legal advice, led to high costs, as a result of which small and medium-sized firms in particular faced a competitive disadvantage compared with large firms.

2.5.4.2   Legal Problems

The main question was and is, of course, whether Article 83 EC and the content and system of Articles 81 and 82 EC permit such a change of policy. As mentioned above, the new basic regulation, Regulation 1/2003, is based on a 'directly applicable exception system';[253] Article 81(3) EC is applicable *de jure* and any undertaking may rely on this before the national authorities and national courts. To start with, one may wonder whether the text of this provision is really so clear and unconditional that one can speak of a directly applicable provision of the Treaty. In contrast with the other provisions derogating from fundamental Treaty provisions (e.g., Arts. 30, 39(3) and (4), 46, 55 and 86(2) EC), Article 81(3) contains a discretionary power to declare the prohibition contained in the first paragraph inapplicable ('the provisions of paragraph 1 *may*, however, be declared inapplicable'). If Article 81(3) were directly applicable, a competence to declare it inapplicable would not be necessary. Let it suffice in this context to refer to the heated discussions on this question which took place prior to the introduction of Regulation 17/62. Moreover, the answer to the question whether or not a provision of Community law is directly applicable depends solely on the content and nature of that provision, and such a characteristic is not a matter which can be freely determined by the Community legislature. In addition, it is not self-evident that Article 83 EC permits the Community legislature to make a simple choice between a system of prior approval (and thus prior notification) and a system of 'legal exceptions'. This provision may also be interpreted in the sense that the Community legislature does not have such a choice, but that a system of prior approval is already implied in Article 81 itself (cf. Art. 83(2)(b) EC). Finally, the existence of

---

253.   'Exception légale' or 'Legalausnahme'.

collective exemption regulations, whose aim is merely to make these Treaty provisions concrete, mitigates against the argument that Article 81(3) EC is directly applicable. If this provision were directly applicable, secondary Community law would not be able to alter in any way its scope or application. In that case, such acts (and particularly block exemptions) would have a merely declaratory value, and national bodies would not be bound by them. These remarks raise the question whether in fact a Treaty amendment is necessary for the new mechanism for application of the competition rules. In the context of the legal problems mentioned here, it should be noted that the Court of Justice assumes, at present, that the national courts have jurisdiction to apply Article 81(3) independently.[254]

2.5.4.3 Consequences of Decentralization

Apart from these legal problems, questions may also be raised about the correctness of the premises on which the new basic regulation is based.

As far as the national competition authorities are concerned, the first question which arises is whether these bodies are capable of fulfilling the tasks which they are confronted with as a result of Community law. These bodies are not furnished in all Member States with the means – in terms of staff or material resources – to implement an effective competition policy. The Community dimension of their task requires that these bodies have the necessary clear independence in political terms, in order to give priority to the objective of effective competition over, for instance, politically popular objectives of industrial policy, social policy etc. In the second place, the question may be posed whether in fact harmonization of national rules on sanctions, procedures, powers of investigation etc. is required for decentralized application of the Treaty provisions on competition. If the policy of the various authorities in the common market is not uniform then the risk of forum-shopping arises. In the third place, the question arises whether national competition authorities will be inclined to apply their national competition rules first, with the danger that the Community rules in practice acquire a secondary character. Fourthly, and finally, the strategy of the Commission is essentially based on the establishment of a network of – from the point of view of the common market – regional authorities, which must cooperate closely on all aspects. The practical problems in forming such a network should not be underestimated. A number of legal problems may also arise in this context, for instance if an investigation necessitates trans-border inspections.

Another problem which may arise, results from the decentralization to national judicial bodies, which in many cases will be the civil courts. In many Member States, this branch of the judiciary is already seriously overloaded. Moreover, there is a danger that as a result of the complexity of the substance the national bodies will tend systematically to ask the Commission for advice, with the resulting administrative overload of that institution, or to shift the problem to

---

254. Case C-238/05, *Asnef-Equifax.*

the Court of Justice by putting preliminary questions, which could lead to a considerable delay in dealing with cases. A practical question in this context is how the Commission will supervise the obligation of the courts to inform it of pending cases. Here the question also arises whether the right of the Commission to act as amicus curiae may lead to all kinds of problems of a procedural nature. After all, such activity on the part of the Commission – which requires adequate insight in the relevant national procedural law – may lead to a substantial administrative burden. As for the Commission itself, one may wonder whether completely abandoning the system of notifications deprives this institution of an important source of information about the situation and developments on various markets. True, the Commission has the right, mentioned above, to provide clarification with regard to new forms of cooperation by means of declaratory decisions. However, this requires a high degree of alertness and continuous monitoring of new developments in the whole of the EC and outside it.

2.6　　　　　Judicial Protection in the Application of
　　　　　　the Competition Provisions

2.6.1　　　Procedural Guarantees

The procedural guarantees enjoyed by undertakings in the framework of the application of Arts. 81 and 82 EC were already laid down to some extent in Regulation 17/62. These principles have gained considerably in significance as a result of the case law of the Court of Justice and the Court of First Instance. In the new basic regulation, these developments have to a large extent been codified. The principles developed by the Community courts regarding the procedural aspects of Arts. 81 and 82 EC exert substantial influence on general Community administrative law.

The principles of proper administrative procedure[255] embrace in particular:

(i) the right of parties concerned and other interested parties to be informed of the objections raised to their conduct;
(ii) the principle of *audi alteram partem*;
(iii) the right to confidentiality of the information communicated;[256]
(iv) legal privilege;
(v) the right to remain silent (the privilege against self-incrimination);[257]

---

255. Sometimes referred to as the rights of the defence or the right of defence.
256. Case 107/82, *AEG-Telefunken*; Case 53/85, *AKZO Chemie BV and AKZO Chemie UK Ltd v. Commission* (protection of business secrets); Case T-39/90 R, *Samenwerkende Elektriciteits-produktiebedrijven NV v. Commission*; Case C-67/91, *Dirección General de Defensa de la Competencia v. Asociación Española de Banca Privada and others*; Case T-353/94, *Postbank NV v. Commission*.
257. See Joined Cases T-44/00 etc., *Mannesmannröhren-Werke AG v. Commission* and Joined Cases T-236/01 etc., *Tokai Carbon*.

    (vi) the presumption of innocence;[258]
    (vii) the *ne bis in idem* principle;[259]
    (viii) the right to have a decision taken within a reasonable period of time.[260]

These principles may not merely conflict with one another (especially the second and the third ones),[261] but also they have to be balanced against the requirements of an effective procedure for ensuring compliance with the competition rules.[262] The Court has rejected the argument that, since the Commission was at the same time investigator, prosecutor and judge there was a breach of due process, and, accordingly, a breach of Article 6(1) of the European Convention on Human Rights (right to a fair trial).[263]

    The *initiation of proceedings*, either on the Commission's own initiative, or following a complaint, which may lead to a decision of the Commission, is a purely administrative act which does not need to be notified to the undertakings concerned or otherwise announced.[264] Nor is such a step an act susceptible to judicial review.[265] The obligation on undertakings to supply information does not mean that they are obliged to provide the Commission with answers which might involve a qualification in legal terms of their conduct.[266] As for inspections by Commission officials, the case law had shown that undertakings were unable to rely on the right of respect for a person's home under Article 8(1) of the European Convention on Human Rights to resist inspections of their business premises.[267] This position is however no longer tenable since the judgment of the European Court of Human Rights in *Colas Est.*[268] According to this judgment, legal persons and business premises in principle fall within the scope of this fundamental right. The conflict which has arisen as a result of this divergent case law has been 'solved' by the Court of Justice in the sense that if the national court is required to give its assent for national assistance, it may not review the legality of the inspection decision of the Commission on the merits, but may only carry out a marginal review to ensure that the inspection is not arbitrary or disproportionate – a rule which has been taken over in the new basic regulation. The Commission is therefore obliged to inform

---

258.   Case T-38/02, *Danone v. Commission*; Joined Cases T-44/02 OP etc., *Dresdner Bank*.
259.   See on the content of this principle Joined Cases T-236/01 etc., *Tokai Carbon*.
260.   Case T-67/01, *JCB Service*; Case C-105/04 P, *Nederlandse Federatieve Vereniging voor de Groothandel op Elektrotechnisch Gebied (NFVGEG) v. Commission*.
261.   As in Case 85/76, *Hoffmann-La Roche & Co. v. Commission*.
262.   See for a summary Case C-204/00 P, *Aalborg Portland A/S and others v. Commission*, paras. 53 et seq.
263.   Joined Cases 209–215 & 218/78, *Fedetab* and Case T-348/94, *Enso-Espanola*; Joined Cases C-204/00 P, *Aalborg Portland*.
264.   Case 57/69, *Azienda Colori Nazionali – ACNA SpA v. Commission*.
265.   Case 60/81, *International Business Machines Corporation v. Commission*. Case T-64/89, *Automec Srl v. Commission*.
266.   Case 27/88, *Solvay & Cie v. Commission*; Case 374/87, *Orkem*; Case T-112/98, *Mannesmann-röhren-Werke AG, v. Commission*; Case T-59/02, *Archer Daniels v. Commission*.
267.   Joined Cases 46/87 & 227/88, *Hoechst*.
268.   ECtHR 14 April 2002.

the national court of the existence of indications which necessitate an inspection, in order to make a marginal review possible. The Commission does not have to reveal the actual content of these indications, as that could endanger the effectiveness of the inspection.[269] In the case law, so-called 'legal privilege' has also been recognized, on the basis of which the Commission may not have access to written communication between the undertaking and its lawyers (correspondence with in-house lawyers does not benefit from legal privilege).[270]

Before the Commission issues a decision finding an infringement, imposing a fine, or imposing interim measures, the undertakings concerned must be informed of the objections which the Commission is taking into account (a *statement of objections*) and given an opportunity to react to them. This may be done in writing, but may also lead to a hearing, for which the Commission takes certain procedural measures. In its final decision the Commission may only rely on matters on which those concerned have been able to make their views known.[271]

Rules have also been made for hearing *parties, complainants and third parties*. Parties must be heard. This takes place at a closed hearing with Commission officials. Such hearings are conducted by a hearing officer, who has a (more or less) independent position, in order to guarantee the objective character of the proceedings.[272] Complainants are closely involved in the proceedings; third parties may be heard. Parties also have the right of *access to the file*,[273] save insofar as documents are covered by the obligation to safeguard business secrets of (other) undertakings, and with the exception of internal Commission documents and documents of and correspondence with national authorities.[274] The Commission and its officials are subject to an *obligation of confidentiality*, and information obtained may only be used for the purpose for which it was collected.[275] There is extensive case law of the Court of First Instance on all these points.

2.6.2   Judicial Protection

All decisions of the Commission may be challenged under Article 230 EC, in first instance before the Court of First Instance, and on appeal before the Court of Justice. As a general rule, the Community courts assume the existence of a certain margin of appreciation on the part of the Commission as far as review of evidence and the conclusions to be derived therefrom for the applicability of the competition

---

269. Case C-94/00, *Roquette Frères SA v. Directeur général de la concurrence, de la consommation et de la répression des fraudes.*
270. Case 155/79, *AM & S Europe Limited v. Commission*; Case C-7/04 P-R, *Commission v. Akzo Nobel Chemicals Ltd and Akcros Chemicals Ltd*; Joined Cases T-125 & 253/03, *Akzo Nobel.*
271. Case 41/69, *ACF Chemiefarma.*
272. See Case T-250/01, *Dresdner Bank AG v. Commission.*
273. See the Notice in O.J. 1997, C 23/3.
274. See on the position of 'internal' documents: Joined Cases T-25/95 etc., *Cimenteries CBR*; Joined Cases T-44/00 etc., *Mannesmannröhren-Werke*, Joined Cases T-236/01 etc., *Tokai Carbon.*
275. Case T-198/03, *Bank Austria Creditanstalt v. Commission.*

rules are concerned, particularly if the establishment and evaluation of the facts involves what is referred to as 'a complex economic situation'.[276] It is also true that – again, in general – the Commission's margin of appreciation in relation to the application of Article 81(3) EC (under the old system) was more extensive,[277] although the difference in the review of the two paragraphs of this Article has become somewhat less pronounced over the years.[278]

There is a rich case law on the possibilities and limits of the Commission's fining policy, the communications published by the Commission in that context, the account to be taken of the duration and gravity of the infringements,[279] the principle of personal liability,[280] the determination of the relevant turnover for the calculation of the ceiling of 10%,[281] the liability of the parent company for cartel behaviour of its subsidiaries,[282] and the principle of equal treatment. The same is true for the concurrent imposition of sanctions by the Community on the one hand and the Member States and third countries on the other, and for application of the principles of *ne bis in idem*.[283]

In relation to decisions whereby the Commission imposes fines or periodic penalty payments, the Community Courts have unlimited jurisdiction within the sense of Article 229 EC: they can cancel, increase or decrease these.[284] Reductions in fines may occur if certain elements of the conduct of the undertakings are not considered to have been proved to the required standard, or if the duration of the conduct turns out to be different. The imposition of fines is not limited to deliberate infringements or recidivist cases. The Community courts also review the fines in the light of the Commission's notices on policy with regard to fines, to see if these have been correctly applied.

2.6.3   The Position of Complainants and Informants

Complaints may be brought to the Commission regarding alleged infringements of the competition rules, but complainants do not derive a right to a final decision concerning proceedings initiated following their complaint.[285] They do have a

---

276. Joined Cases 56 & 58/64, *Consten and Grundig*; Case T-168/01, *GlaxoSmithKline*.
277. Case 26/76, *Metro*; Case 42/84, *Remia*; Case T-9/93, *Schöller Lebensmittel*.
278. Case T-528/93, *Métropole*; Case T-374/94, *ENS*.
279. Joined Cases T-217 & 245/03, *FNCBV v. Commission*; Joined Cases T-109/02 etc., *Bolloré v. Commission*.
280. Case C-280/06, *Autorità Garante della Concorrenza e del Mercato v. Ente tabacchi italiani – ETI, Philip Morris*.
281. Joined Cases T-217 & 245/03, *FNCBV*; Case T-120/04, *Peroxidos Organicos v. Commission*.
282. Case T-314/01, *Avebe v. Commission*; T-330/01, *Akzo Nobel v. Commission*; T-43/02, *Jung-bunzlauer v. Commission*; T-279/02, *Degussa v. Commission*.
283. Joined Cases T-236/01 etc, *Tokai Carbon*; Case T-59/02, *Archer Daniels*; Case C-308/04 P, *SGL Carbon v. Commission*.
284. Joined Cases T-236/01 etc., *Tokai Carbon*; Case T-38/02, *Danone*.
285. Case 125/78, *GEMA, Gesellschaft für musikalische Aufführungs-und mechanische Vervielfältigungsrechte v. Commission*.

right of appeal against the rejection (total or partial) of their complaint.[286] The Court of First Instance has developed an extensive case law on the manner and extent to which the Commission must take account of arguments brought by complainants, on the setting of priorities in dealing with complaints, and the categorization of complaints.[287] A special duty of care is owed by the Commission to complainants and informers who draw its attention to infringements of Community competition law. Failure to take sufficient care can lead to substantial sums by way of damages.[288]

2.7   MERGER CONTROL

2.7.1   Background and Aim

Although the Commission's intention to take steps to control mergers dates initially from 1973, it was only at the end of 1989 that political agreement permitted a Merger Regulation to see the light of day with the adoption of Regulation 4064/89.[289] The long history of the matter demonstrates its extremely sensitive nature, on which the Member States have very divergent standpoints, against the background of their general views on questions of the power of undertakings and industrial policy in particular. Nevertheless, such preventive control is essential for the proper functioning of the common market, given that on the basis of Articles 81 and 82 EC only a partial control can be exercised over concentrations, insofar as there is an agreement,[290] or abuse of an already existing dominant position.[291] Under the regime of the first Merger Control Regulation, Community control of concentrations grew into an essential element of Community competition policy, as is evident from the fact that the number of decisions concerning merger control is far greater than the decisions on the application of Articles 81 and 82 EC. In the framework of the reform of competition policy already discussed, the new Regulation 139/2004 applied as of 1 May 2004;[292] the procedural rules are set out by the Commission in Regulation 802/2004[293] which is supplemented with a number of notices by the Commission.

---

286.   Case 26/76, *Metro II*.
287.   The so-called *Automec* case law, Cases T-64/89, *Automec I* and T-24/90, *Automec II* and many other judgments. See further the *Ufex* saga: Case T-36/92, *SFEI v. Commission*; Case C-39/93 P, *SFEI v. Commission*; Case T-77/95, *SFEI. v. Commission*; Case C-119/97 P, *Ufex v. Commission;* Case T-77/95 Rev., *Ufex v. Commission* and Case T-60/05, *Ufex et al. v. Commission*.
288.   See Case 145/83, *Stanley George Adams v. Commission* (obligation of confidentiality), concerning the circumstances of an informant who has supplied information, which partly led to the judgment *in Hoffmann-La Roche* (Case 85/76).
289.   O.J. 1989, L 195/1, amended by Reg. 1310/97, O.J. 1997, L 180/1.
290.   Joined Cases 142 and 156/84, *BAT*.
291.   Case 6/72, *Continental Can*.
292.   O.J. 2004, L 24/1. See the Commission Green Paper on the reform of Council Reg. 4064/89, COM(2001)745 final.
293.   O.J. 2004, L 133/1.

The purpose of the merger control system is to determine whether the concentration is compatible with the common market; the Commission must take account, on the one hand, of the need to maintain and develop effective competition within the common market, in view of, *inter alia*, the structure of all the markets concerned and the actual or potential competition from undertakings located within or outside the Community and, on the other hand, of a number of factors which largely, but not entirely, accord with Article 81(3) EC.[294] In the light of these factors, according to Article 2, concentrations which significantly[295] impede competition in the common market or in a substantial part of it, in particular by creating or strengthening an individual or collective dominant position,[296] should be declared incompatible with the common market. The question is obviously what is meant by 'significantly'? Recital 32 of the Regulation indicates that this must mean the effect is noticeable, and states that where the market share of the undertakings concerned does not exceed 25% this is assumed not to be the case. A further elaboration of this test is given in a notice containing guidelines on horizontal mergers.[297] Horizontal mergers take place between undertakings which either actually or potentially compete on the same market. In these guidelines, the Commission first examines the significance of market shares for the assumption of a dominant position (more than 50% always, between 40 and 50% often, and under 40% sometimes, but less than 25% never) and the application of the so-called HHI (Herfindahl-Hirschmann Index).[298] The Commission goes on to explain the possible anti-competitive effects of this type of merger: eliminating important competitive constraints and increasing the chance of coordination of conduct. The Commission also assesses the existence of compensating purchasing power, the possibility of market entry, and the significance of efficiency improvements and 'failing firm' arguments. The scope of application of the merger prohibition, as described here, differs from that of the first regulation, in which the negative effects for competition and the creation or strengthening of a dominant position were the only elements taken into account. The background to this difference was the uncertainty whether the old criterion (market dominance) also covered cases where oligopolies were created which could not be categorized as collective dominance in the sense of Article 82 EC. Even if there is no sign of a collectively dominant position, a merger may create an oligopolistic market structure, in which each undertaking is able independently to assess the behaviour

---

294. The market position of the undertakings concerned and their economic and financial power, the alternatives available to suppliers and users, their access to supplies and markets, any legal or other barriers to entry, supply and demand trends, and technical progress provided that it is to the consumers' advantage.

295. This addition differs from Art. 81(3) EC.

296. Case T-102/96, *Gencor v. Commission*; Case T-342/99, *Airtours*; Case T-464/04, *Impala v. Commission*.

297. Guidelines on the assessment of horizontal mergers under the Council Regulation on the control of concentrations between undertakings (O.J. 2004, C 31/5).

298. HHI = market share A^2 plus market share B^2.

of the other oligopolists, in other words a market structure in which coordinated behaviour is unavoidable.[299]

From the above, it is evident that the primary approach for control is based on grounds of effective competition alone. The preamble to the Regulation also makes it plain that the Commission must place its overall appraisal within the general framework of the achievement of the fundamental objectives of the EC, including economic and social cohesion. Depending on the circumstances, a trade-off between competition considerations and other objectives, in particular of an industrial policy nature, is not excluded. This results not merely from the Regulation itself, but also from the system of the Treaty, according to which the competition regime is an instrument not only of market integration, but also of policy integration. The regime of Article 3(1)(g) EC does however require the maintenance of the minimum of competition which is expressed in Article 81(3) EC, in the sense that competition may not be totally eliminated in a substantial part of the common market. The addition of the word 'significantly', pointed out above, indicates the grave danger that in the appraisal of concentrations this minimum standard will no longer be objectively applied, but that the industrial policy or other essentially political arguments (e.g., the creation of 'national champions') which are advanced may gain the upper hand.[300] The (perhaps inevitable) fierce political reactions which met the Commission after it had adopted its first decision prohibiting a merger on purely competition grounds[301] raise the question whether it possesses and will continue to possess sufficient political weight and independence to ensure in the future that merger control policy is not simply derailed into an instrument of industrial policy.[302] The same worry holds for the political dimension of global concentrations, as has been evident from the decision on the merger of American aircraft concerns.[303] This underlines the need for international coordination of merger policies.

2.7.2   Scope of Application

2.7.2.1   *Community Dimension*

Concentrations in the sense of the Regulation (Art. 3) can be generally defined as acts by which independent undertakings are merged to form a new economic entity, either horizontally or vertically, and either by means of a merger or by

---

299. See Case T-102/96, *Gencor* and recital 25 of Reg. 139/2004.
300. See also para. 29.
301. Dec. 91/619 (O.J. 1991, L 334/42) *Aerospatiale-De Havilland*, O.J. 1991, L 334/42. This criticism came primarily from French and Italian sources. During the meeting of the Commission at which this decision was adopted, the (French) chairman was absent, and the members who were of French and Italian nationality voted against.
302. The more so since at the beginning of 2005 the commissioners responsible for competition and industrial policy were ventilating quite different views.
303. Dec. *Boeing/McDonnell Douglas*, O.J. 1997, L 336/16.

means of the acquisition of control.[304] The creation of a common subsidiary (a joint venture) performing on a lasting basis all the functions of an autonomous economic entity is also a concentration. The political nature of this subject matter, which was already mentioned above, is apparent particularly in the criteria which the Regulation adopts for its scope of application. Only concentrations with a so-called 'Community dimension' fall within its scope (Art. 1). Instead of the more objective criterion of market share, two alternative turnover thresholds apply, the calculation of which is described in the regulation.[305] The first is that:

(i) the total worldwide turnover of the undertakings involved is higher than 5 billion euro; and

(ii) the individual EU turnover of each of at least two of the undertakings is higher than 250 million euro.

The second turnover threshold is:

(i) a total worldwide turnover of more than 2.5 billion euro;

(ii) a total turnover in each of three Member States of more than 100 million euro;

(iii) the individual EU turnover of each of at least two of the undertakings is higher than 250 million euro; and

(iv) a total individual EU turnover of at least two of the undertakings of more than 100 million euro.

Both the turnover thresholds are also subject to the condition that each of the undertakings concerned achieves no more than two-thirds of its aggregate Community-wide turnover within one and the same Member State. The aim of the second turnover threshold – introduced as an alternative in 1997 – was to prevent a large concern from a third country with a small EU turnover taking over small EU undertakings without coming within the scope of the Merger Regulation. Nevertheless, the thresholds chosen are high, so that many concentrations which are capable of having an effect on interstate trade and on Community competition, do not fall within the scope of the Regulation, while a consequence of the so-called two-thirds rule is that concentrations in small and large Member States can be treated differently. The turnover thresholds do not mean that the number of concentrations with a Community dimension is negligible. This number rose from 12 in 1990 to 364 in 2000, which was certainly partly due to the wave of mergers in the light of the completion of the internal market and the introduction of the euro. Since then, the number of mergers notified each year has decreased again (in 2006: 356).

2.7.2.2   Joint Ventures

A common, but not entirely adequate, distinction made in relation to joint ventures is that between concentrative and cooperative joint ventures. In the former case,

---

304. See also the Commission Notice on the notion of a concentration, O.J. 1998, C 66/2.
305. Art. 5. See also the Commission Notice on calculation of turnover, O.J. 1998, C 66/25.

there is a partial concentration. If the undertakings engaged in the joint venture leave the market on which the joint venture operates, then the agreement on which the joint venture is based may fall outside the scope of Article 81(1) EC.[306] And even if this Article is applicable, then it is still possible that as a result of the rationalization achieved, the agreement benefits from an exemption under Article 81(3) EC. In the case of cooperative joint ventures, there is a more or less far-reaching cooperation between the founding undertakings in the framework of the joint venture, so that the function of the joint venture is similar to that of a common establishment or office. Joint ventures can, however, have both cooperative and concentrative characteristics. Against this background, the Commission generally pays more attention in its evaluation to the substance of what is going on, than to the outward appearance of the form of the cooperation. Through the adoption of the rules on concentration control, this policy has entered a new phase. 'True' concentrative joint ventures, that is joint ventures which do not aim at coordination of market behaviour of the parties on a lasting basis, fall under the Merger Regulation (if they have a Community dimension); cooperative joint ventures should be assessed according to the rules of Article 81 EC. As already mentioned, this distinction is not adequate, on account of the many forms in which joint ventures may occur, with the result that the parties tended to notify a joint venture as a concentration as much as possible, because of the rapid procedures provided for by the Merger Regulation. For this reason, when the first Merger Regulation was amended in 1997, it was made clear that in assessing a joint venture under Article 81 EC the Commission must take into account, *inter alia*, the extent to which the parties remain significantly and simultaneously active on the market of the joint venture, or on (upstream or downstream) markets which are closely connected, and also the possibilities the parties have of coordinating their behaviour via the joint venture, so that competition on a significant part of the market in question could be eliminated.[307]

2.7.3   Procedure in Merger Control

2.7.3.1   *The Powers of the Commission*

The control exercised by the Commission concerns concentrations with a Community dimension. The procedure consists of two stages, for which binding time limits are provided (Art. 10). If the Commission has not taken a decision within the time limit, then the notified concentration is deemed to be compatible with the common market.[308] The first stage starts with the compulsory notification of the proposed concentration, that is to say after the conclusion of the agreement,

---

306. See the – classic but still relevant – Decision SHV-Chevron, O.J. 1975, L 38/14.
307. See on these problems of categorization the Commission Notices on full-function joint ventures, O.J. 1998, C 66/1 and O.J. 1998, C 66/3 and on ancillary restrictions, O.J. 2001, C 188/5. See on the latter, Case T-251/00, *Lagardère SCA and Canal+ SA v. Commission*.
308. See on the binding nature of these time limits Case T-251/00, *Lagardère*.

the announcement of a public takeover bid, or the acquisition of a controlling interest, but before these are implemented (Art. 4).[309] Without notification, a concentration with a Community dimension may not be implemented. The first stage lasts 25 working days, and ends with one of three types of decision (Art. 6): the concentration does not fall within the scope of the Regulation; the concentration is declared compatible with the common market, as no serious doubts have arisen in this regard, or if there are serious doubts, the parties make the necessary changes in their concentration proposals. In the last case, the time limit may be extended to 35 working days. If the concentration raises serious doubts, then the second stage commences (Art. 8). This stage lasts a maximum of 90 working days, or if commitments are offered a maximum of 105 days, and ends with a decision declaring the concentration compatible with the common market, or a conditional approval, or a decision declaring the concentration incompatible with the common market. The decisions issued by the Commission also concern so-called related restrictions necessary to a concentration.[310] The concentration may only be implemented after a decision has been adopted or after the time limit has expired. The Commission may grant a derogation from this prohibition (Art. 7). If a concentration is implemented without notification, the sanction is not nullity of the concentration. The Commission may order the concentration to be dissolved or other measures (Art. 8(4)). There is also provision for powers parallel to those of Regulation 1/2003 in relation to obtaining information (Art. 11), carrying out inspections (Art. 13), and imposing fines and periodic penalty payments. If a concentration which has been declared incompatible with the common market is implemented nonetheless, or if the conditions imposed by the Commission are not met, a fine can be imposed of up to 10% of the total turnover of the undertakings concerned (Art. 14).

The publication of Commission decisions is limited to decisions prohibiting concentrations, and decisions granting conditional approval.[311]

Informal policy also plays an important role in the field of merger control. The Regulation provides for a power of the Commission to declare a concentration compatible with the common market after the notified operation has been altered by the parties. Such alterations have the character of commitments *vis-à-vis* the Commission, which bases its decision on them. These commitments may concern the market structure (hiving off of undertakings or parts of them, sale of participations, transfer of intellectual property rights, grant of licences etc.) or market behaviour (making capacity available to traders, increase of capacity, etc.).[312] Because of the importance of informal concentration policy of this kind, decisions prohibiting a concentration, or decisions granting conditional approval represent

---

309. See on the consequences of the withdrawal of a notification Case T-310/00, *MCI Inc v. Commission*.
310. See Commission Notice on restrictions directly related and necessary to concentrations, O.J. 2005, C 56/24.
311. Often after great delay.
312. See Case T-114/02, *BaByliss SA v. Commission* and Case T-119/02, *Royal Philips Electronics NV v. Commission*.

only a very small part of the decisional practice of the Commission in this area. For 'simple' concentrations with a Community dimension the Commission has introduced a simplified procedure.[313]

Appeal against a decision of the Commission lies to the Court of First Instance,[314] and thereafter on a point of law only to the Court of Justice.[315] Article 10(5) determines that if a decision is annulled, the procedure begins anew, with a new (updated) notification.

2.7.3.2   *The Powers of the Member States*

Concentrations which do not meet the turnover thresholds of the Merger Regulation, fall within the area of competence of the Member States, even if they may have consequences for interstate trade.[316] Since many Member States have introduced their own system of concentration control, following the Community concentration control, concentrations which do not have a Community dimension will have to be notified in a number of Member States at the same time – this can lead to procedural problems as a result of differences in substantive criteria, and in the assessment of such concentrations. The paradoxical result of this situation is that concentrations which do not have a Community dimension may be subject to a much more complicated supervision than the 'one-stop-shop' system of Community supervision of concentrations. This underlines the need either to extend the scope of the Community supervision of concentrations or to harmonize national legislation on supervision of concentrations. Member States may not subject concentrations which have a Community dimension to their national law, except if the concentration in question also has consequences for certain general interests which are not covered by the Merger Regulation, such as public security and plurality of the media (Art.21). In these cases, the Commission must recognize the interests in question.[317]

Cooperation between the Commission and the Member States in the framework of the European competition network (the network of competition authorities) can take three forms. Member States may request the Commission to refer a concentration which has been notified to it to the national authorities (the so-called German clause).[318] A Member State may ask the Commission to examine a concentration

---

313. Commission Notice on a simplified procedure for treatment of certain concentrations, O.J. 2005, C 56/32.
314. Of great practical importance in this context is the fast track procedure provided for under Art. 76a of the rules of procedure of the CFI.
315. See on the questions of admissibility in relation to applications by third parties against decisions declaring a concentration to be compatible with the common market, Case T-342/00, *Petrolessence SA and Société de gestion de restauration routière SA (SG2R) v. Commission* and Case T-158/00, *Arbeitsgemeinschaft der öffentlich-rechtlichen Rundfunkanstalten der Bundesrepublik Deutschland (ARD) v. Commission.*
316. Case C-170/02 P, *Schlüsselverlag v. Commission*; Case C-42/01, *Portugal v. Commission.*
317. See Case C-42/01, *Portugal v. Commission.*
318. See Case T-119/02, *Philips* and Joined Cases T-346 & 374/02, *Cableuropa SA and others v. Commission*, Case T-87/05, *EDP v. Commission.*

which does not have a Community dimension (the so-called Dutch clause); in this case, any measures taken by the Commission only concern that Member State.[319] Finally, the Commission may itself decide to refer a concentration to a Member State to be dealt with (Art. 9), also following a request to that effect by the parties. The Commission has also published a Notice on this possibility.[320]

2.7.3.3   The Standard of Proof

Just as with cartels and dominant positions under Articles 81 and 82 EC, the Commission enjoys a certain margin of appreciation in assessing the compatibility with the common market of proposed Community concentrations. There is, however, an important difference in the two kinds of assessment, insofar as in the case of cartels and dominant positions an ex post assessment of market behaviour and changes in market structure will often be at stake, while in the assessment of the effects of a proposed concentration the emphasis lies on prospective analyses.[321] As a result, the burden of proof for the Commission is more onerous for this type of assessment, insofar as argumentation of probabilities must take place with great care, in particular concerning the definition and analysis of the relevant markets and of the foreseeable horizontal and vertical effects of a concentration.[322] In this context, according to the case law, account must be taken not only of factors which could *reinforce* a supposed effect of the concentration on existing and potential competition, but also of circumstances which could *diminish* or even annul the effect.[323]

2.8   PUBLIC UNDERTAKINGS: ARTICLE 86 EC

Article 86 EC is an extremely complicated provision, given that the rules on public undertakings and undertakings which exercise public functions form a junction between the Treaty obligations imposed on the Member States and those imposed on undertakings. During the 1980s, this provision developed into an important weapon available to the Commission – alongside the enforcement of the Community directives on public procurement – to open up the internal market in the utilities sectors such as energy supply, telecommunications and transport which

---

319. See the communication of the Commission in O.J. 2005, C 56/2. The significance of this clause has been eroded since most Member States by now have their own systems of merger control. For two cases in the Netherlands: Decisions RTL/Veronica/Endemol, O.J. 1996, L 134/32 and Blokker/Toys-R-Us, O.J. 1998, L 316/1.
320. O.J. 2005, C 56/2.
321. See Cases T-342/99, *Airtours plc v. Commission*, T-310/01, *Schneider Electric SA v. Commission* and T-5/02, *Tetra Laval BV v. Commission*, where the CFI annulled the Commission decisions prohibiting the mergers.
322. Such as the portfolio effect (large supply of products), conglomerate effect and leverage effect (extending dominant position to other markets).
323. See Case C-13/03 P, *Tetra Laval*.

had been closed off by public undertakings since time immemorial. Article 86 EC thus forms a means to set limits to the use of public and other undertakings as instruments of economic and fiscal policy and to impose these limits, in accordance with the relevant Treaty provisions, in particular those on competition.[324] To that extent, Article 86 EC also contributes to the maintenance of the system of undistorted competition prescribed by Article 3(1)(g) EC.[325]

Article 86 EC may be divided into three parts. Article 86(1) and (2) are directly effective[326] and each contains a separate substantive rule. Article 86(1) *confirms* the applicability of the Treaty provisions to actions of the Member States in relation to public undertakings. This general rule is already expressed in the other provisions of the Treaty. Article 86(2) provides for an *exception* to this rule in respect of certain undertakings. Article 86(3) contains a conferral of powers on the Commission for ensuring compliance with both of the first two limbs of Article 86. The Lisbon Treaty includes a Protocol on services of general interest, containing 'interpretative provisions' on services of general economic interest (specification of the importance of these services) and which excludes non-economic services of general interest from the scope of the treaties.

2.8.1   Article 86(1) EC

2.8.1.1   Public Undertakings and the Provisions of the Treaty

Article 86(1) EC confirms, in the first place, that the categories of undertakings mentioned therein do come within the scope of the other Treaty provisions, especially Articles 12, 81 and 82 EC. This is in fact already a result of those provisions themselves, particularly in view of the wide interpretation given by the Court to the concept of an undertaking in Articles 81 and 82 EC. In the second place, this provision confirms that the Member States must respect the other Treaty provisions in their conduct with these undertakings. This is not new either, given the line of judgments that Articles 81 and 82, in conjunction with Article 10 EC, oblige the Member States to abstain from any measures which would undermine the competition provisions of the Treaty. As well as the competition provisions – addressed to undertakings – this obligation also applies with respect to the other areas of Community law,[327] in particular for the provisions on free movement[328] and State

---

324. Case C-202/88, *France v. Commission (Telecom I)*.
325. Joined Cases C-46/90 & C-93/91, *Procureur du Roi v. Jean-Marie Lagauche and others*.
326. Case C-260/89, *Elliniki Radiophonia Tileorassi AE v. Dimotiki Etairia Pliroforissis and others (ERT)*; Case T-16/91, *Rendo NV and others v. Commission*.
327. E.g., also for provisions of directives, see Case C-188/89, *A. Foster and others v. British Gas plc*.
328. Art. 28 EC: Case 249/81, *Commission v. Ireland (Buy Irish (IER))*. Art. 29 EC: Case 302/88, *Hennen Olie BV v. Stichting Interim Centraal Orgaan Voorraadvorming Aardolieprodukten and State of the Netherlands*. Art. 31 EC: Case C-157/94, *Commission v. Netherlands* (electricity). Art. 39 EC: Case C-55/96, *Job Centre*. Art. 43 EC: Case T-266/97, *Vlaamse Televisie Maatschapij NV v. Commission*. Art. 49 EC: Case C-18/93, *Corsica Ferries Italia Srl v. Corpo dei Piloti del Porto di Genova*.

aid.[329] It is not relevant whether the State acts through its own means, using state authority, or whether it acts through undertakings whose market behaviour it has power to determine, either in law or in fact.[330] The applicability of the other Treaty provisions to measures of Member States concerning undertakings in the sense of Article 86(1) EC means that derogation from these provisions may only take place in cases provided for in those provisions, such as the exceptions specified in Articles 30[331] and 45[332] EC and in the cases where restrictions are permitted under 'the rule of reason' (overriding reason in the general interest) in respect of the freedoms.[333] An additional exception is provided for by Article 86(2) for services of general economic interest and fiscal monopolies. This also makes it plain that the interpretation of the concepts of 'public undertakings',[334] 'special[335] or exclusive rights',[336] and 'measures', must be such as to ensure that the useful effect ('*effet utile*') of these other provisions is not undermined.

2.8.1.2 Public Undertakings and the Competition Provisions

Article 86(1) EC and the case law on these provisions draw a distinction between the public undertaking on the one hand and the relevant measure of the authorities on the other. If the undertaking acts autonomously on its own account and responsibility, so that its commercial conduct can not be attributed, or not directly attributed, to the Member State, then Articles 81 and 82 EC apply to such conduct.[337] This will frequently be the case, given that the concept of an undertaking is widely interpreted in these provisions, as was mentioned above. If the market conduct of the public undertaking is not based on its own autonomous action, but can be entirely attributed to the authorities, then this conduct will not be judged on the basis of Articles 81 and 82 EC, but rather the conduct of the authorities which lies at the basis of the undertaking's conduct will be judged in the light of the other Treaty articles, through the application of Article 86(1) EC. This conduct of the authorities – that is, conferring special or exclusive rights (e.g., concessions) – can

---

329. Case 78/76, *Steinike & Weinlig v. Federal Republic of Germany*; Case 290/83, *Commission v. France* (aid to farmers financed by the operating surplus of a national agricultural credit fund); Joined Cases 67, 68 & 70/85, *Kwekerij Gebroeders van der Kooy BV and others v. Commission*; Case 57/86, *Greece v. Commission* (repayment of interest on export credits); Case T-106/95, *Fédération française des sociétés d'assurances (FFSA) and others v. Commission*.
330. See Joined Cases 188-190/80, *France, Italy and United Kingdom v. Commission* (transparency).
331. For a possibility under this heading, see Case 72/83, *Campus Oil Ltd and others v. Minister for Industry and Energy and others*.
332. Case C-260/89, *ERT*; Case C-353/89, *Commission v. Netherlands (Broadcasting Act)*.
333. Case C-202/88, *France v. Commission (Telecom I)*.
334. Joined Cases 188-190/80 *France, Italy and the United Kingdom v. Commission*; Case 118/85, *Commission v. Italy*.
335. Case C-202/88, *France v. Commission (Telecom I)*.
336. See Case 172/82, *Syndicat national des Fabricants Raffineurs d'Huile de Graissage and others v. GIE 'Inter-Huiles' and others*.
337. Case 41/83, *Italy v. Commission* (tariffs for telecommunications).

lead to the creation of national, regional[338] or local[339] monopolies for the provision (or receipt)[340] of certain goods[341] or services.[342] Since the mere existence of a dominant position (or monopoly) is not contrary to Article 82 EC, then this is also not contrary to Article 86(1) EC.[343] The situation is different if the special rights are exercised in a manner which can be qualified as a misuse of a dominant position in the sense of Article 82 EC. The distinction between the existence and the exercise of special or exclusive rights can however not be made in situations where the granting of these rights legally, or de facto, leads to a situation where the extent of competition drops below the minimum prescribed by Article 81(3) EC. This danger is particularly present in the case of conferral of exclusive rights because there, unlike in the case of a de facto monopoly, even potential competition is ruled out, since products from other Member States cannot or may not be imported (for instance, different types of telephone receivers),[344] or because the supply which is governed by the system of exclusive rights does not tally with existing demand (e.g., labour placement services).[345] In the cases mentioned earlier, the Court has explicitly referred to this danger. To the extent that conferral of exclusive rights is not covered by the exceptions in the other Treaty provisions to which Article 86(1) EC refers, such conferral results in infringement of Article 82 EC. The Court thus recognizes an approach which parallels that in Case 6/72 *Continental Can*[346] by pointing out that in this context the system of Article 3(1)(g) EC can only be maintained if the equality of competitive opportunities for the various market participants is guaranteed.[347]

---

338. Case C-323/93, *Société Civile Agricole du Centre d'Insémination de la Crespelle v. Coopérative d'Elevage et d'Insémination Artificielle du Département de la Mayenne.*
339. E.g., for funerals, see Case 30/87, *Bodson.*
340. E.g., exclusive rights to receive and process certain waste products, see Case C-203/96, *Chemische Afvalstoffen Dusseldorp BV and others v. Minister van Volkshuisvesting, Ruimtelijke Ordening en Milieubeheer.*
341. Such as generating and distributing electricity: Case C-393/92, *Municipality of Almelo and others v. NV Energiebedrijf Ijsselmij*; Case C-157/94, *Commission v. Netherlands* (electricity); C-158/94, *Commission v. Italy* (electricity). Production and distribution of gas: Case C-159/94, *Commission v. France.* Sale of tobacco products: Case C-387/93, *Criminal proceedings against Giorgio Domingo Banchero.* Bovine semen: Case C-323/93, *Crespelle.*
342. Such as transport: Case 66/86, *Ahmed Saeed Flugreisen*; Case C-18/93, *Corsica Ferries II.* Telecommunications: Case C-18/88, *RTT*; Joined Cases C-46/90 & C-93/91, *Lagauche*; Case C-69/91, *Criminal proceedings against Francine Gillon, née Decoster*; Case C-92/91, *Criminal proceedings against Annick Neny, née Taillandier.* Post: Case C-320/91, *Criminal proceedings against Paul Corbeau*; Joined Cases C-147/97 & C-148/97, *Deutsche Post AG v. Gesellschaft für Zahlungssysteme mbH GZS.* Harbour services: Case C-179/90, *Merci convenzionali porto di Genova SpA v. Siderurgica Gabrielli SpA*; Case C-242/95, *GT-Link A/S v. De Danske Statsbaner (DSB).* Employment placing: Case C-55/96, *Job Centre.* Television programmes and advertising: Case 155/73, *Sacchi*; Case C-260/89, *ERT.*
343. Case 155/73, *Sacchi*; Case C-202/88, *France v. Commission (Telecom I).*
344. See Case C-18/88, *RTT.*
345. See Case C-55/96, *Job Centre.*
346. Case 6/72, *Continental Can.*
347. Case C-260/89, *ERT*; Case C-41/90, *Höfner*; Case C-320/91, *Corbeau.*

2.8.2   Article 86(2) EC

2.8.2.1   *Services of General Economic Interest*

Article 86(2) EC concerns a separate specific category of undertakings: those entrusted with the operation of services of general economic interest or having the character of a revenue-producing monopoly. The latter variety hardly occurs any longer.[348] These undertakings too, like those mentioned in Article 86(1) EC, are subject to the rules of the Treaty. The difference is that for undertakings falling under Article 86(2), provision is made for an exception: the Treaty rules are only applicable insofar as the application of such rules does not obstruct the performance, in law or in fact, of the particular tasks assigned to them. The case law does not give a clear answer to the crucial question of what is to be understood as 'services of general economic interest'. In the relevant cases, the Court merely takes a case-by-case approach, and scarcely gives any indication why a particular activity does (management of telecommunications networks, transport services, essential postal services, public broadcasting, generation import and distribution of electricity, employment placement services) or does not (a variety of harbour services, waste disposal) deserve the label of 'service of general economic interest'.[349] From the case law mentioned, it may be deduced that that Article 86(2) is primarily concerned with tasks of the authorities which in some Member States are performed by undertakings, and the aim is to avoid the performance of these general interest tasks of the authorities being hindered by the application of the EC Treaty. This element explains further that the phrase 'services of general economic interest' must be interpreted primarily against the background of the national situation,[350] whereby the Member States are granted a certain freedom in determining whether a particular activity is included in this category.[351]

From the case law, it is clear that the concept 'undertakings entrusted with the operation of services of general economic interest' is not the same as that of 'public undertakings and undertakings to which Member States grant special or exclusive rights'. This appears first from the fact that the second paragraph speaks of 'entrusted with', which according to the Court refers to a specific task *imposed* by the authorities.[352] The mere fact that an undertaking is subject to a general or specific supervision by the authorities is not sufficient.[353] Nor can an undertaking

---

348. This concerns undertakings which enjoy exclusive rights for the production of and trade in products which are subject to special taxes, such as alcohol and tobacco. In many cases, these monopolies were already contrary to Art. 31 EC, and were therefore dismantled or adapted in the past.
349. According to the case law, a distinction should also be made between services of general economic interest and services which do not have an economic interest but are considered to belong to government prerogatives, see Case C-364/92, *SAT Fluggesellschaft*; Case C-343/95, *Cali*.
350. Case C-260/89, *ERT*.
351. Case T-32/93, *Ladbroke*.
352. Case 127/73, *BRT*; Case 7/82, *GVL*.
353. Such as the specific supervision of credit institutions and insurance, see Case 172/80, *Züchner*.

accord itself such a status.[354] Secondly, it is not so that every conferral of a special or exclusive right in the sense of Article 86(1) EC automatically means that an undertaking is entrusted with services of general economic interest in the sense of paragraph 2 of that Article.[355] This leads to the conclusion that the group of undertakings mentioned in Article 86(2) may be the same as that referred to in Article 86(1), but not necessarily so.[356] If an undertaking comes within the scope of both paragraph 1 and paragraph 2 of Article 86 EC, then the government measures in question may be justified in three circumstances: if they fall within one of the exceptions of the other Treaty provisions, on the basis of case law on restrictions in the general interest, and under Article 86(2) EC.

2.8.2.2   Conditions for Application

The most important condition for the exception under Article 86(2) to apply is that the application of the competition rules or other provisions of the EC Treaty would obstruct the performance of the particular tasks concerned. The second condition is that interstate trade must not be affected to such an extent as would be contrary to the interests of the Community. In combination, these conditions make it clear that the derogation from the competition provisions must be both necessary and proportionate. From this, it must follow that also in relation to the application of Article 86(2) EC, in principle the requirement of Article 81(3) EC must be met, that the conduct of the undertaking which restricts competition and affects trade may not wholly exclude competition for a significant part of the relevant products and services. Nevertheless, the Court does not follow this interpretation. To start with, the Court has rejected the interpretation which the Commission derived from these conditions, whereby restrictions of competition would only be allowed if the service in question could not be carried out at all, i.e., that the very existence of the undertaking concerned would be threatened.[357] The Court's judgment in *Corbeau*[358] reveals that Article 86(2) EC permits Member States

> to confer on undertakings to which they entrust the operation of services of general economic interest, exclusive rights which may hinder the application of the rules of the Treaty on competition in so far as restrictions on competition, or even the exclusion of all competition, by other economic operators are necessary to ensure the performance of the particular tasks assigned to the undertakings possessed of the exclusive rights.[359]

---

354.   Case 7/82, *Gesellschaft zur Verwertung von Leistungsschutzrechten mbH (GVL) v. Commission.*
355.   Cf. e.g., Case 10/71, *Ministère public luxembourgeois v. Madeleine Muller, Veuve J.P. Hein and others* and Case C-179/90, *Porto di Genova*, concerning harbour services. In the former case, a service of general economic interest was found to be present, in the latter this was not so.
356.   E.g., a private transport undertaking which is made responsible for transport on non-profitmaking routes and receives a subsidy in return.
357.   Case 157/94, *Commission v. Netherlands* (electricity).
358.   Case C-320/91, *Corbeau.*
359.   *Corbeau*, para. 14.

According to the same judgment, this formulation does not exclude the possibility that the access to the relevant market may be blocked entirely if that is necessary in order to enable the fulfilment of the relevant service of general economic interest under 'economically acceptable conditions' (para. 16). This last condition is understood by the Court to mean that the restriction or even exclusion of competition does not only concern the products or services which come within the special task of general economic interest, and which are frequently limited or non-profitable.[360] The restriction or exclusion of competition is also possible with regard to products or services which are themselves profitable, but where that revenue is used to compensate the less profitable or non-profitable sectors (internal cross-subsidization).[361] Article 86(2) EC may therefore also justify exclusive purchasing contracts prohibited by Article 81 EC, or import restrictions prohibited by Article 28 EC.[362] In this way, according to the Court, it may be ensured that the relevant service of general economic interest may be provided in a situation in which an economic balance is maintained. In concrete terms, this doctrine means that in the case of universal provision of services, such as post or telecommunications, whereby a proportion of the services provided will be loss-making, or have a very low profitability due to geographical factors, the access of other market participants to those parts of the activity in question which are profitable may be limited, or even excluded entirely. Well-known examples are those of the distribution of post and telephone connections in geographically isolated or sparsely populated areas (e.g., the Outer Hebrides for the UK). The significance of the exception in Article 86(2), as interpreted by the Court, is further increased by the fact that the Member State must prove that the restriction of competition is *necessary* for the provision of the relevant service of general economic interest, but that the Member State does not need to prove that there are no other less far-reaching restrictions possible.[363] It should be added that the Court hardly examines, if at all, the question of whether there is a threat to economic balance.[364]

2.8.2.3 Services of General Economic Interest and Universal Provision of Services

The wide interpretation given by the Court of the conditions for application of Article 86(2) EC raises the question of the relationship between the concept 'services of general economic interest' and that of 'universal provision of services'. Although the latter concept is far from clear, it is evident that certain elements play an important role in this, these elements including the essential character of the

---

360. Joined Cases C-147 & 148/97, *Deutsche Post AG v. Gesellschaft für Zahlungssysteme mbH GZS and Citicorp Kartenservice GmbH.*
361. Case C-340/99, *TNT Traco.*
362. Case C-393/92, *IJsselmaatschappij*; Case C-157/94, Case 157/94, *Commission v. Netherlands* (electricity).
363. Case 157/94, *Commission v. Netherlands* (electricity).
364. Joined Cases C-147 & 148/97, *Deutsche Post.*

service, the right of all persons to profit from that service, together with universal supply of the service over the whole territory, and continuity of supply. Article 16 EC, introduced by the Treaty of Amsterdam, clearly makes a connection between 'services of general economic interest' and universal provision of services, and there is a similar tendency to be discerned in the case law.[365] To this extent, the question may be raised whether Article 86(2) still has the character of an exception to the competition rules which should in principle be interpreted strictly, or that we are faced here with a more general derogation from the scope of application of the Treaty provisions.[366]

2.8.3   Article 86(3) EC

It is clear from both the text of Article 86(3) EC and the relevant case law that the power conferred on the Commission by Article 86(3) EC to address appropriate directives or decisions to Member States is intended for the purpose of applying Article 86(1) and (2).[367] Such directives or decisions are acts in the meaning of Article 249 EC.[368] Article 86(3) EC thus enables the Commission to use a directive or decision instead of following the procedure laid down in Article 226 EC (infringement proceedings).[369] Since Article 86(3) EC does not provide for an enforcement procedure of its own, the Commission will have to use the procedure of Article 226 EC if a Member State fails to comply with such a directive or decision. From the case law it also appears that with regard to the application of Article 86(3) EC, the Commission must take full account of the rights of the defence, in particular the right of the Member State and – where applicable – the undertakings concerned to be heard.[370]

As far as the substance of this power is concerned, it appears from the text of paragraph 3 that the directives and decisions may only concern the undertakings mentioned in paragraphs 1 and 2, and the acts of the authorities mentioned therein.[371] Article 86(3) EC does not, therefore, provide a legal basis for general harmonization directives as intended in Article 95 EC, nor for regulations as intended in Article 83 EC.[372] Moreover, it flows from the independent conferral of power in

---

365. See Case C-18/93, *Corsica Ferries II*, where the Court discusses universal services.
366. See for more information, the Commission Notice, Services of General Interest in Europe, O.J. 2001, C 17/4 and Green Paper on Services of General Interest, COM(2003)270 final.
367. Case C-202/88, *France v. Commission (Telecom I)*.
368. Case 226/87, *Commission v. Greece* (insurance).
369. Case C-202/88, *France v. Commission (Telecom I)*; Joined Cases C-48 & 66/90, *Netherlands and Koninklijke PTT Nederland NV and PTT Post BV v. Commission*.
370. Case 226/87, *Commission v. Greece* (insurance); Joined Cases C-48 & 66/90, *Netherlands and Koninklijke PTT Nederland NV and PTT Post BV v. Commission*; Case T-266/97, *VTM*; Case T-54/99, *max.mobil Telekommunikation Service GmbH v. Commission*. The position of complainants under the third paragraph. is, however, different from that under Arts. 81 and 82 EC, see Case C-141/02 P, *Commission v. T-Mobile Austria GmbH, formerly max-mobil Telekommunikation Service GmbH*.
371. Case C-325/91, *France v. Commission*.
372. Case C-202/88, *France v. Commission (Telecom I)*.

Article 86(3) EC that the exercise of the competence contained in that provision is not dependent on and is not influenced by the powers of the Council concerning the same matters on the basis of other provisions.[373] The Commission's power on the basis of Article 86(3) EC is discretionary.[374] Finally, the content of directives or decisions based on Article 86(3) EC is not limited to the mere establishment of infringements of paragraphs 1 and 2 of this Treaty article, but they may also include specific descriptions of certain obligations resulting from the Treaty in combination with orders that the relevant restrictions to competition be terminated.[375]

The Commission has taken a series of decisions under Article 86(3), but most important are the directives it has adopted on the basis of Article 86(3) EC: Directive 80/723 on the transparency of financial relations between Member States and public undertakings;[376] Directive 88/301 on competition in the market for telecommunications terminal equipment;[377] and Directive 2002/77 on competition in the markets for telecommunications services.[378] The last two directives elaborate a strategy for a common market in telecommunications services and equipment, which had been set out by the Commission in a Green Paper published in 1987.[379] The case law on this provision results from applications brought by various Member States against these directives.

Directive 80/723 (the transparency directive) – amended frequently – obliges Member States to have at their disposal, and if necessary to provide to the Commission, information relating to carefully defined forms in which financial means are provided to specified public undertakings. Directive 88/301 relates to special or exclusive rights of national telecom companies concerning the importation, distribution, connection, bringing into service and maintenance of terminal equipment; these activities may not be reserved to national undertakings. The Member States may prescribe that the relevant equipment must meet the essential requirements of Directive 86/361.[380] The tasks of drawing up and publishing the relevant specifications, as well as performing the necessary supervision and granting the certification of conformity thereto, must be in the hands of an independent body. As result of this directive, the national markets for such terminal equipment have been opened up, whereas previously they were completely closed, because the national telecom companies set the necessary specifications themselves,

---

373. Joined Cases 188-190/80, *France, Italy and United Kingdom v. Commission;* Joined Cases C-271/90, C-281/90 & C-289/90, *Spain, Belgium and Italy v. Commission (Telecom II);* Case C-163/99, *Portuguese Republic v. Commission* (Portugese airports).

374. Case T-32/93, *Ladbroke;* T-106/95, *FFSA.*

375. Case C-202/88, *France v. Commission (Telecom I);* Joined Cases C-271/90, C-281/90 & C-289/90, *Spain, Belgium and Italy v. Commission (Telecom II).*

376. O.J. 1980, L 195/35, amended by Dir. 2000/52, O.J. 2000, L 193/75. In Case C-325/91 *France v. Commission,* the Court annulled the Commission's Communication on the application of Arts. 92 and 93 EC and Art. 5 of Dir. 80/723 (O.J. 1991, C 273/2).

377. O.J. 1988, L 131/73, amended by Dir. 94/46 (O.J. 1994, L 286/25).

378. O.J. 2002, L 249/21, replacing the old Dir. 90/388.

379. COM(87)290 final of 30 June 1987. See further the Commission Guidelines on the application of EEC competition rules in the telecommunications sector, O.J. 1991, C 233/2.

380. O.J. 1986, L 271/21.

supervised their implementation, and marketed the equipment themselves. Framework Directive 2002/21, on a common regulatory framework for electronic communications networks and services,[381] aims to realize the internal market for telecom services; it does so by obliging Member States (i) to abolish monopolies for provision of telecom services, (ii) to introduce objective, non-discriminatory and unambiguous licencing and registration procedures, (iii) to open up monopolies for the construction and exploitation of telecommunications networks to third parties under conditions which are objective, non-discriminatory and published, and (iv) to entrust authorization and specifications to an independent body. This Directive also covers satellite communication, mobile telephony and cable television.

3   STATE AIDS (ARTICLES 87–89 EC)

3.1   FUNCTION AND SIGNIFICANCE

3.1.1   Overview

Articles 87 to 89 EC contain substantive and procedural rules concerning distortions of competition as a result of measures involving aid to undertakings from state authorities.[382] According to Article 87(1) EC, aid granted by a Member State which distorts (or threatens to distort) competition is incompatible with the common market insofar as such aid affects trade between Member States. Article 87(2) EC provides that a number of types of aid mentioned therein are *de jure* exempt from the prohibition. Article 87(3) EC – which in practice is much more important – provides for the possibility of exemption from the prohibition, and Article 88 EC provides that this exemption possibility is in the hands of the Commission. Article 88 EC provides for a supervisory mechanism, the core of which is the obligation to notify any plans to grant aid, and to refrain from granting this aid until the Commission has reached a decision as to its compatibility with the common market. Article 89 EC authorizes the Council on a proposal of the Commission to lay down implementing rules for the substantive or procedural aspects of the state aid provisions. Originally, the Commission set out its policy on state aids in a number of notices and letters addressed to the Member States. Only recently, against the background of the completion of the internal market, and the operationalization of the Economic and Monetary Union, has the Council adopted Regulation 944/98, which authorizes the Commission to enact further rules on certain categories of horizontal state aids.[383] Three Commission regulations were issued in 2001, based on Regulation 944/98, concerning aid for training, *de minimis* rules, and aid for

---

381. O.J. 2002, L 108/33, which effectively replaces Dir. 90/387.
382. The Lisbon Treaty will renumber the provisions 87–89 EC as Arts. 107–109 TFEU. The term 'common market' is replaced throughout the Treaty by the term 'internal market'.
383. O.J. 1998, L 142/1.

small and medium-sized enterprises; they were followed in 2002 by a Regulation on employment aid,[384] and in 2004 by a Regulation on aid to small and medium sized agricultural enterprises[385] The general procedural rules for the state aid provisions are set out in Regulation 659/1999,[386] further elaborated by the Commission in Regulation 794/2004.[387] In 2002, after the ECSC Treaty expired, a Council Regulation was enacted providing for separate rules for state aid to the coal industry.[388]

3.1.2 Aim

The case law reveals that Articles 87 and 88 EC form a necessary compliment to the provisions on free movement.[389] The free movement of goods and services made possible by those provisions and the optimum division of labour would be seriously undermined if Member States were to confer on their national trade and industry an artificial advantage over their competitors in other Member States through means of state aids. The provisions on state aids therefore also play a direct role in the maintenance of a regime of undistorted competition in the sense of Article 3(1)(g).[390] In addition, there is a connection between supervision of national aid measures and the coordination of national economic policy which is of increasing importance in the context of Economic and Monetary Union. If the total volume of aid which the richer Member States grant to their industries is higher than that granted by the poorer Member States, the result will be global distortions to the disadvantage of the latter. Effective control of state aids must therefore involve not merely the intensity of the aid (scope and terms), but also the (total) volume. Such control may well take place

---

384. Regs. 68/2001-70/2001, O.J. 2001, L 10/20, 30, 33; Reg. 2204/2002, O.J. 2002, L 337/3. See on the last mentioned regulation, Case C-110/03, *Belgium v. Commission*. The de minimis regulation has been replaced by Reg. 1998/06 (O.J. 2006, 385/5); the regulation on agricultural firms is supplemented by Reg. 1857/06 (O.J. 2006, L 379/9).
385. Reg. 1/2004, O.J. L 1/1.
386. O.J. 1999, L 83/1.
387. O.J. 2004, L 140/1. As a result of this, a number of Notices have become obsolete, see the Notice in O.J. 2004, C 115/1.
388. Reg. 1407/2002, O.J. 2002, L 205/1.
389. Case 173/73, *Italy v. Commission* (family allowances in the textile industry); Case 290/83, *Commission v. France*; Case 103/84, *Commission v. Italy* (subsidies for the purchase of vehicles); Case 248/84, *Federal Republic of Germany v. Commission* (compatibility of a regional aid programme); Case 310/85, *Deufil GmbH & Co. KG v. Commission*; Case C-301/87, *France v. Commission* (capital contributions, provision of loans at reduced rates of interest and reduction in social security charges); Case C-21/88, *Du Pont de Nemours Italiana SpA v. Unità sanitaria locale No. 2 di Carrara*; Case C-225/91, *Matra*; Case C-387/92, *Banco de Crédito Industrial SA, now Banco Exterior de España SA v. Ayuntamiento de Valencia*; Case C-39/94, *Syndicat français de l'Express international (SFEI) and others v. La Poste and others*; Case T-358/94, *Compagnie nationale Air France v. Commission*; Case T-14/96, *Bretagne Angleterre Irlande (BAI) v. Commission*; Case T-46/97, *SIC – Sociedade Independente de Comunicação SA v. Commission*.
390. Case 171/83 R, *Commission v. France* (interim measures); Case T-16/96, *Cityflyer Express Ltd v. Commission*.

in the context of Article 99 EC.[391] In the framework of the Lisbon strategy, the European Council in Barcelona in 2002 formulated as a main objective in relation to national state aid policy that not only should the aid be reduced as a proportion to GNP,[392] but also that the orientation of state aids should be altered so as to be geared to horizontal objectives, such as regional development, research and development, environmental policy, training, and health care.[393] In the framework of that strategy, the Commission keeps a so-called scoreboard on the extent, nature and reform of national state aid policy.[394]

3.1.3   Incompatibility or Unlawfulness

Both the content of Article 87 EC and its link with Article 88 EC make it plain that the former provision does not contain a directly effective prohibition of state aid.[395] Article 87 EC indicates the conditions under which state aid is *compatible or incompatible* with the common market. In addition to this, aid is *unlawful, and thus prohibited*, if it is granted in breach of the obligations and procedural requirements of Article 88 EC. The concepts of compatibility and lawfulness (and their counterparts incompatibility or unlawfulness) thus do not correspond entirely. Aid which is – or may be – in itself compatible with the common market (under Art. 87(2) and (3) EC) may nevertheless be unlawful, and therefore prohibited, if it is granted without due respect of the procedural obligations contained in Article 88 EC.[396]

3.2   SUBSTANTIVE ASPECTS OF ARTICLE 87 EC

3.2.1   Article 87(1) EC

3.2.1.1   The Concept of a State Aid

Given the major threat which state aids pose to the unity of the common market, it is not surprising that the Court has interpreted the concept of an aid widely.[397] The Court found, in *Denkavit Italiana*, that the concept of an aid

> refers to the decisions of Member States by which the latter, in pursuit of their own economic and social objectives, give, by unilateral and autonomous

---

391. See further Ch. X *infra*.
392. At present, about 1% of GNP.
393. In 2005 the aid mechanism that the Netherlands introduced for the reform of the system of health insurance was approved, *inter alia*, on the basis of the contribution to realization of the Lisbon process.
394. See the latest version in COM(2003)636 final.
395. Case 6/64, *Flaminio Costa v. E.N.E.L.*; Case 77/72, *Carmine Capolongo v. Azienda Agricole Maya*; Case 78/76, *Steinike*; Case C-301/87, *France v. Commission (Boussac)*; Case C-17/91, *Georges Lornoy en Zonen NV and others v. Belgian State*.
396. See Art. 1(f) read with Arts. 10–15 Reg. 659/1999.
397. Case T-613/97, *Ufex v. Commission*, para. 158.

decisions, undertakings or other persons resources or procure for them advantages intended to encourage the attainment of the economic or social objectives sought.[398]

This definition is entirely in line with modern legal views of subsidies as instruments of economic policy. This definition also makes it clear that the essential element of the concept of state aid in Article 87(1) EC is the creation of an artificial (i.e., not available under the economic conditions governing the market) advantage of whatever nature,[399] which costs the state money directly or indirectly,[400] whether by making payments or by forgoing receipts.[401] Such advantages may lower the costs of capital,[402] labour,[403] production or distribution and thereby distort existing or potential competition in the common market.[404] This holds to an even greater extent if there is already a situation of over-capacity in the relevant sector.[405] The decisive factor is the effect of the envisaged aid for the common

---

398. Case 61/79, *Amministrazione delle Finanze dello Stato v. Denkavit Italiana Srl*, at para. 31; Case T-315/02, *Deutsche Bahn v. Commission*, para. 100.

399. Case C-280/00, *Altmark Trans and Regierungspräsidium Magdeburg v. Nahverkehrsgesellschaft Altmark*; see further Ch. XII section 3.1.3 on this case. See also Case T-366/00, *Scott v. Commission* (2nd judgment).

400. Case 290/83, *Commission v. France*; Joined Cases C-72 & 73/91, *Firma Sloman Neptun Schiffahrts AG v. Seebetriebsrat Bodo Ziesemer der Sloman Neptun Schiffahrts AG*; Case C-189/91, *Petra Kirsammer-Hack v. Nurhan Sidal*; Case C-387/92, *Banco di Credito*; Case C-39/94, *SFEI*; Case T-358/94, *Air France*; Case C-342/96, *Spain v. Commission (Tubacex)*; Case C-6/97, *Italy v. Commission* (tax credit); Case T-46/97, *SIC*; Joined Cases C-52-54/97, *Epifanio Viscido, Mauro Scandella and others and Massimiliano Terragnolo and others v. Ente Poste Italiane*; Case C-75/97, *Belgium v. Commission (Maribel bis/ter scheme)*; Case C-200/97, *Ecotrade Srl v. Altiforni e Ferriere di Servola SpA (AFS)*; Joined Cases T-204 & 270/97, *Portuguese Republic v. Commission (EPAC)*; Case C-256/97, *Déménagements-Manutention Transport SA (DMT)*; Case C-295/97, *Industrie Aeronautiche e Meccaniche Rinaldo Piaggio SpA v. International Factors Italia SpA (Ifitalia), Dornier Luftfahrt GmbH and Ministero della Difesa*; Joined Cases C-15/98 & C-105/99, *Italy and Sardegna Lines – Servizi Marittimi della Sardegna SpA v. Commission*; Case C-156/98, *Federal Republic of Germany v. Commission* (aid granted to undertakings in the new German Länder – tax provision favouring investment).

401. The concept of a state aid in the sense of Art. 87(1) EC is therefore broader than the notion of a 'subsidy' in Art. 4 ECSC; see Case C-387/92, *Banco de Credito*.

402. See on investment aid especially Case T-459/93, *Siemens SA v. Commission*.

403. Case 171/83 R, *Commission v. France* (state aids – interim measures).

404. Case 173/73, *Italy v. Commission* (family allowances); Case 259/85, *France v. Commission* (state aid – textile and clothing sector); Joined Cases C-278-290/92, *Spain v. Commission* (capital contributions); Case T-214/95, *Het Vlaamse Gewest (Flemish Region) v. Commission*.

405. Case 234/84, *Belgium v. Commission* (subscription of capital of an undertaking); Case 102/87, *France v. Commission* (loan granted by the Fonds industriel de modernisation); Case C-142/87, *Belgium v. Commission* (state aid to a steel pipe and tube manufacturer); Case C-305/89, *Italy v. Commission* (capital contributions); Case C-225/91, *Matra*; Case T-214/95, *Vlaams Gewest*.

market; thus economic or social objectives, no matter how justified or worthy, will not as such suffice to permit an aid measure to escape the ambit of Article 87(1) EC.[406] Given the aim of the provisions on state aids, the argument is also not acceptable that the aid is intended to compensate for real or supposed competitive disadvantages in relation to other Member States.[407]

Case law and the Commission's practice show that the artificial advantages caught by Article 87 may take the form of direct financial payments; loan guarantees;[408] loans at lower than commercial rates of interest;[409] deferred loans; exemptions, reduction or remission of direct or indirect taxation or social security contributions;[410] export aid;[411] lower charges for goods or services delivered by the State or an undertaking under State control;[412] preference in the placing

---

406. Case 173/73, *Italy v. Commission* (family allowances); Case 310/85, *Deufil*; Case C-39/94, *SFEI*; Case T-67/94, *Ladbroke*; Case C-241/94, *France v. Commission* (concerning aid to the company Kimberly Clark Sopalin); Case T-14/96, *BAI*; Case T-46/97, *SIC*; Case C-75/97, *Belgium v. Commission*; Joined Cases T-204 & 270/97, *Portuguese Republic v. Commission* (EPAC); Case C-480/98, *Spain v. Commission*; Case T-55/99, *Confederación Española de Transporte de Mercancías (CETM) v. Commission*.
407. Joined Cases 6 & 11/69, *Commission v. France* (rate of preferential rediscount for exports); Case 173/73, *Italy v. Commission* (family allowances); Case T-214/95, *Vlaams Gewest*; Case C-6/97, *Italy v. Commission* (tax credit); Joined Cases T-298/97, T-312/97, T-313/97, T-315/97, T-600/97 to T-607/97, T-1/98, T-3/98 to T-6/98 & T-23/98, *Alzetta Mauro and others v. Commission*; Case T-55/99, *CETM*.
408. Joined Cases C-329/93, C-62/95 & C-63/95, *Federal Republic of Germany, Hanseatische Industrie-Beteiligungen GmbH and Bremer Vulkan Verbund AG v. Commission*; Case C-288/96, *Federal Republic of Germany v. Commission (JAKO Jadekost GmbH & Co. KG)*; Joined Cases T-204/97 & T-270/97, *EPAC*. See the Commission Notice on state aid in the form of guarantees, O.J. 2000, C 71/14.
409. Case 57/86, *Greece v. Commission* (repayment of interest on export credits); Case 102/87, *France v. Commission* (loan granted by the Fonds industriel de modernisation); Case T-214/95, *Het Vlaamse Gewest (Flemish Region) v. Commission*; Case C-342/96, *Spain v. Commission* (Tubacex).
410. Case 173/73, *Italy v. Commission* (family allowances); Joined Cases 62/87 & 72/87, *Exécutif régional wallon and SA Glaverbel v. Commission*; Case C-183/91, *Commission v. Greece* (tax exemption on earnings from exports); Case T-277/94, *Associazione Italiana Tecnico Economica del Cemento (AITEC) v. Commission*; Case C-342/96, *Spain v. Commission* (Tubacex); Case C-75/97 *Belgium v. Commission*; Case C-480/98, *Spain v. Commission*; Case C-278/00, *Greece v. Commission* (settlements of debts of agricultural cooperatives by public authorities); Case C-126/02, *Commission v. Belgium* (Gemo). See Commission Notice on the application of the state aid rules to measures relating to direct business taxation, O.J. 1998, C 384/3.
411. Case 57/86 *Greece v. Commission* (repayment of interest on export credits); Case C-183/91, *Commission v. Greece* (tax exemption on earnings from exports); Case C-400/92, *Federal Republic of Germany v. Commission* (concerning proposed aid by Germany to the Chinese shipping company Cosco). See Commission communication on short-term export-credit insurance (O.J. 1997, C 281/4).
412. Joined Cases 67, 68 & 70/85, *Van der Kooy*; Case 213/85, *Communities v. Netherlands* (preferential tariff for horticultural producers); Case C-56/93, *Belgium v. Commission* (preferential tariff); Case C-39/94, *SFEI*; Case T-613/97, *Ufex*.

of public contracts; distribution guarantees;[413] sales at lower prices or gifts of land;[414] aid for privatization;[415] and non-financial aid.[416]

A category of state aid measures which has led to an extensive body of case law concerns participation in equity capital by the state or by bodies controlled by the state.[417] The criterion for assessing whether such actions constitute aid is, according to the case law, the conduct of private investors. If it seems that the participation took place under conditions in which a private investor would not have made capital available – for instance, in a case where structural losses are being made, or in the absence of the perspective of making profits in the longer term[418] – then such action constitutes aid in the sense of Article 87(1) EC.[419] In a case of remission of tax obligations in the framework of a bankruptcy this situation may be different, however (the 'private creditor test').[420] The applicability of Article 87(1) EC is not avoided by situations where some companies in a group (or the holding company) become insolvent, but others continue to trade[421] or situations whereby the aid is granted to a holding company, and thereafter 'passed on'.[422] Finally, improvements in infrastructure which in fact wholly or largely benefit one undertaking or a specific group of undertakings may also be characterized as aid.[423] In the evaluation of the incompatibility of an aid with the common market, regard is had not merely to the advantage created as such but also to the context within which that advantage is created. Aid which is in principle compatible may become in fact incompatible as a whole with the common market,

---

413. Case T-14/96, *BAI*; Joined Cases T-116 & 118/01, *P&O European Ferries (Vizcaya) v. Commission*.

414. See Commission Communication on state aid elements in sales of land and buildings by public authorities, O.J. 1997, C-209/3; Joined Cases T-127 & 129/99, *Diputación Foral de Alava v. Commission and others v. Commission*; Case T-274/01, *Valmont v. Commission*; Case T-366/00, *Scott* (2nd judgment).

415. Case T-95/94, *Chambre Syndicale Nationale des Entreprises de Transport de Fonds et Valeurs and Brink's France SARL v. Commission*; Case T-157/01, *Danske Busvognmænd v. Commission*.

416. Case C-39/94, *SFEI*; Case T-613/97, *Ufex*.

417. Case 323/82, *SA Intermills v. Commission*; Case 234/84, *Belgium v. Commission* (subscription of capital of an undertaking); Case C-301/87, *France v. Commission* (capital contributions, provision of loans at reduced rates of interest and reduction in social security charges); Case C-305/89, *Italy v. Commission* (capital contributions); Joined Cases C-278-280/92, *Spain v. Commission* (capital contributions); Case C-42/93, *Spain v. Commission* (concerning aid granted by the Spanish Government to the Merco company); Joined Cases T-371 & 394/94, *British Airways plc and others v. Commission*; Case T-11/95, *BP Chemicals Ltd v. Commission*; Joined Cases T-126 & 127/96, *Breda Fucine Meridionali SpA (BFM) and Ente partecipazioni e finanziamento industria manifatturiera (EFIM) v. Commission*.

418. As well as for the existence of non-recoverable costs, see Joined Cases T-126 & 127/96, *BFM and ENIM*; Joined Cases T-228 & 223/99, WLG.

419. See further, the Communication of the Commission to the Member States of 13 Nov. 1993, O.J. 1993, C 307/3.

420. Case T-152/99, *Hijos de Andrés Molina SA (HAMSA) v. Commission*.

421. Case 323/82, *Intermills*; Case C-480/98, *Spain v. Commission*.

422. Case C-457/00, *Belgium v. Commission*.

423. Case C-225/91, *Matra v. Commission*.

because of its method of financing, for instance if it is financed by charges on both national and imported products, so that the end result is that the national products enjoy a competitive advantage.[424] Of course, an aid which is incompatible with the common market cannot be 'saved' by its method of financing.[425]

The concept of 'state' in Article 87(1) EC covers not just the central author-ities, but also (independent) sub-entities such as regions[426] or municipalities.[427] The wording of Article 87(1) EC also makes it clear that not only aid from the state but also aid financed out of the public purse is covered. This provision thus also applies to aid granted by public or private bodies (whether or not specially established for the purpose),[428] financial bodies under the control of the state,[429] public holding companies,[430] and public companies.[431] Finally, aid measures which are not actually financed through state resources but which are granted as a result of pressure from the public authorities on the body concerned are also considered state aid.[432] The Court has, however, made one exception to this case law – which actually would appear to be inconsistent with it – concerning so-called self-financed aid, where taxes charged to undertakings on the basis of a legislative provision are entirely redistributed to the same sector.[433]

Competitive advantages for a particular branch of industry which result from legal or administrative measures but are not directly quantifiable in money terms (e.g., certain employment conditions) fall outside the concept of an aid.[434] This also holds for measures of the authorities whereby a transfer of income between

---

424. Case 47/69, *France v. Commission* (system of aids to the textile industry); Case 259/85, *France v. Commission* (state aid – textile and clothing sector; Case C-17/91, *Lornoy*; Case C-204/97, *Portuguese Republic v. Commission* (aid for producers of liqueur wines and eaux-de-vie); Joined Cases C-261/01 & C-262/01, *Eugene Van Calster and others v. Belgium*; Joined Cases C-34-38/01, *Enirisorse SpA v. Ministero delle Finanze*. See on the position of state aid financed by a general tax, C-174/02, *Streekgewest Westelijk Noord-Brabant v. Staats-secretaris van Financiën*; C-175/02, *F.J. Pape v. Minister van Landbouw, Natuurbeheer en Visserijand*; and Joined Cases C-128/03 & C-129/03, *AEM SpA and others v. Autorità per l'energia elettrica e per il gas and others*.
425. Case 259/85, *France v. Commission* (state aid – textile and clothing sector); Case C-17/91, *Lornoy*.
426. Cases T-214/95, *Het Vlaamse Gewest (Flemish Region) v. Commission*; CaseT-14/96, *BAI*.
427. Joined Cases C-324/90 & C-342/90, *Federal Republic of Germany and Pleuger Worthington GmbH v. Commission*; Joined Cases C-329/93, C-62/95 & C-63/95, *Bremer Vulkan*; Case T-234/95, *DSG Dradenauer Stahlgesellschaft mbH v. Commission*.
428. Case 78/76, *Firma Steinike und Weinlig v. Germany*; Case 282/85, *Comité de développement et de promotion du textile et de l'habillement (DEFI) v. Commission*.
429. Joined Cases 296/82 & 318/82, *Netherlands and Leeuwarder Papierwarenfabriek BV v. Com-mission*; Case 57/86, *Greece v. Commission* (repayment of interest on export credits); Case T-358/94, *Air France*; and Case T-234/95, *DSG*.
430. Case C-303/88, *Italy v. Commission*; Case C-305/89, *Italy v. Commission* (capital contribu-tions).
431. Joined Cases 67/85, 68/85 & 70/85, *Van der Kooy* (gas); Case T-106/95, *FFSA* (post).
432. Case 290/83, *Commission v. France Republic*.
433. Case C-345/02, *Pearle BV, and others v. Commission*.
434. Joined Cases C-72/91 & C-73/91, *Sloman Neptun*; Case C-189/91, *Kirsammer-Hack*; Joined Cases C-52/97 to C-54/97, *Epifanio Viscido and others v. Ente Poste Italiane*.

undertakings takes place, for instance by measures intended to promote the use of 'green' electricity.[435] Aid measures granted by the EC itself similarly do not fall within the scope of Article 87(1) EC.[436]

Although the Court formulated the rule that Articles 28 and 87(1) EC may not be applied cumulatively,[437] this distinction is not always applied consistently in the case law.[438] Delimitation problems can also occur between Article 87(1) EC on the one hand and Articles 25,[439] 31,[440] 132[441] and 137 EC[442] on the other.[443] According to Article 36 EC, special rules apply to state aids in the agricultural sector.[444] In the transport sector, Article 73 EC lays down special rules.[445]

3.2.1.2 Specificity or Selectivity Criterion

Article 87(1) only applies to the concept of state aid as defined above if the advantages involved favour 'certain undertakings', which may mean one or more undertakings.[446] This specificity or selectivity criterion is needed to delimit the state aids provisions, which concern specific distortions, from the applicability of the general provisions on distortions of competition found in Articles 96 and 97 EC (for instance, a general rule on tax deductibility).[447] In accordance with the objective of the state aid provisions the Court interprets this criterion broadly.[448] Sectoral aid measures may meet this criterion,[449] but also

---

435. Case C-379/98, *PreussenElektra AG v. Schleswag AG.*
436. Joined Cases 213/81 to 215/81, *Norddeutsches Vieh-und Fleischkontor Herbert Will, Trawako, Transit-Warenhandels-Kontor GmbH & Co., and Gedelfi, Großeinkauf GmbH & Co., v. Bundesanstalt für landwirtschaftliche Marktordnung.*
437. Case 74/76, *Iannelli & Volpi SpA v. Ditta Paolo Meroni.*
438. Case 249/81, *Buy Irish (IER)*; Case 18/84, *Commission v. France* (tax advantages for newspaper publishers); Case 103/84, *Commission v. Italy* (subsidies for the purchase of vehicles); Case C-21/88, *Du Pont de Nemours*; Case C-17/91, *Lornoy.*
439. Case C-17/91, *Lornoy*; Case C-234/99, *Niels Nygård v. Svineafgiftsfonden.*
440. Case 91/78, *Hansen GmbH & Co. v. Hauptzollamt de Flensburg.*
441. Case C-142/87, *Belgium v. Commission* (state aid to a steel pipe and tube manufacturer).
442. Case C-342/96, *Spain v. Commission* (Tubacex).
443. See for a good example Case C-355/00, *Freskot AE v. Elliniko Dimosio.*
444. See Case 177/78, *Pigs and Bacon v. Commission*; Case C-311/94, *IJssel-Vliet Combinatie BV v. Minister van Economische Zaken*; Case C-173/02, *Spain v. Commission.*
445. Reg. 1370/2007, O.J. 2007, 315/1 on public passenger transport services by rail and by road (on compensation for public service obligations in transport).
446. Just as with Arts. 81 and 82 EC, also with Art. 87 EC, the notion 'undertaking' is interpreted extensively; see Case 323/82, *Intermills*; Case T-234/95, *DSG*; Joined Cases T-371 & 394/94, *British Airways.*
447. Case T-349/03, *Corsica Ferries France v. Commission*; Case C-148/04, *Unicredito v. Agenzia delle Entrate.*
448. Case C-143/99, *Adria-Wien Pipeline GmbH and others v. Finanzlandesdirektion für Kärnten*; Joined Cases T-92 & 103/00, *Territorio Histórico de Álava – Diputación Foral de Álava and others v. Commission.*
449. Case 173/73, *Italy v. Commission* (family allowances); Case 169/84, *Société CdF Chimie azote et fertilisants SA and Société chimique de la Grande Paroisse SA v. Commission*; Case C-169/95, *Spain v. Commission* (the municipality of Monreal del Campo, Piezas y Rodajes SA

regional[450] and horizontal aid.[451] The same is true of a general measure which may be applied in individual cases by discretionary powers,[452] or which may be applied only at the request of the undertaking concerned.[453]

The case law reveals that a measure which favours certain undertakings, can nevertheless have a general character – and thus fall outside the scope of Article 87(1) EC – if the specific advantage results from the 'normal application of the general system'.[454] This refers to a particular part of a general system of favourable measures, without which the general measure would lose its justification.[455] In practice, this exception has little practical significance.[456]

3.2.1.3 Inter-state Trade and Competition

For the application of these conditions, which – just as in the case of Articles 81 and 82 EC – are closely connected, an analysis of the effects of the aid is usually required.[457] Given that aid creates a competitive advantage by its very definition, this analysis does not need to be so detailed as in the case of the competition rules.[458] For the same reason, there is no requirement of a 'significant' or appreciable' effect concerning the unfavourable effects on trade or distortion of competition,[459] and it is irrelevant whether a large or a small undertaking is involved,[460] or a large or small amount of aid.[461] Nor is there a need to demonstrate

---

(PYRSA)); Case C-75/97, *Belgium v. Commission*; Case C-172/03, *Wolfgang Heiser v. Finanzamt Innsbruck*.

450. Joined Cases C-278-280/92, *Spain v. Commission* (capital contributions); Case C-88/03, *Portugal v. Commission*.

451. Also so-called indirect advantages, i.e., where the aid also benefits other undertakings as a result of the undertaking receiving the advantages, does not detract from the specificity of a state aid, see Case T-67/94, *Ladbroke*; Joined Cases T-298/97 etc., *Mauro*.

452. Case C-241/94, *Kimberly*; Case C-200/97, *Ecotrade*; Case C-256/97, *DMT*; Case T-36/99, *Lenzing AG v. Commission*.

453. Case C-156/98, *Federal Republic of Germany v. Commission* (tax concession).

454. Case 173/73, *Italy v. Commission* (family allowances),

455. See for an example of application Case C-308/01, *GIL Insurance Ltd and others v. Commissioners of Customs and Excise*.

456. Case 173/73, *Italy v. Commission* (family allowances); Case C-88/03, *Portugal* (tax exemptions).

457. See for a good example Case T-27/02, *Kronofrance SA v. Commission*.

458. Case 730/79, *Philip Morris*; Case C-142/87, *Belgium v. Commission*; Joined Cases T-447-449/93, *Associazione Italiana Tecnico Economica del Cemento (AITEC) et al. v. Commission*; Joined Cases T-298/97 etc., *Mauro*.

459. Case 730/79, *Philip Morris Holland BV v. Commission*; Case C-142/87, *Belgium v. Commission* (state aid to a steel pipe and tube manufacturer); Case T-55/99, *Confederación Española de Transporte de Mercancías (CETM) v. Commission*.

460. Joined Cases C-278/92 to C-280/92, *Spain v. Commission* (capital contributions); Case T-214/95, *Vlaams Gewest*.

461. Case C-156/98, *Federal Republic of Germany v. Commission* (tax concession); Case T-55/99, *CETM*.

an *actual* effect or distortion for these two conditions concerning trade and competition:[462] a threat of an effect or distortion is sufficient.[463] It is therefore irrelevant that the undertaking receiving the aid does not engage in intra-state trade,[464] or directs its activities mainly towards third countries.[465] This does not detract from the fact that the Commission in its decisions is obliged to explain clearly why competition threatens to be distorted and intra-Community trade affected.[466]

3.2.1.4 The Discretionary Powers of the Commission

According to constant case law, the Commission enjoys broad discretion in its assessment of the compatibility of aid according to Article 87(2) and (3) EC (see section 3.2.2. below). The question arises whether the Commission also has discretion in its assessment under Article 87(1) EC. On the basis of the text of the provision, an affirmative answer to this question is not obvious, since each of the elements mentioned in that provision is objective in nature. It flows from Article 87(2) and (3) EC, in conjunction with Article 88(2) EC, that the Commission must or may make exceptions to the prohibition on aid which is incompatible with the common market. The lack of direct effect of Article 87(1) EC does not detract from the objective character of the prohibition of incompatible aid. Quite the contrary: given the fact that the Commission enjoys excusive power to apply paragraphs 2 and 3 of Article 87 EC, it is at the very least doubtful whether the Commission also enjoys a discretionary power in the application of Article 87(1) EC. Otherwise, there would in fact be a double discretionary power on the part of the Commission: first to decide whether paragraph 1 is applicable, and second to decide whether paragraphs 2 or 3 apply, or can apply, respectively. This question has a certain practical significance, given that such a discretion could mean that the Commission could choose whether to not to take certain factors into account with regard to the applicability of paragraph 1. In that case, the step to incorporate a 'rule of reason' into Article 87(1) EC would not be far away.

The case law does not give a clear answer to the question. Although in the one hand, there have been indications on several occasions that the elements in Article 87(1) EC have an objective character,[467] on the other hand there are also

---

462. Joined Cases T-298/97 etc., *Mauro*.
463. If operating aid is involved (aid to cover running costs) then there is even the possibility of distortion of competition, Case C-86/89, *Italy v. Commission* (aid for the use of concentrated grape must); Case C-288/96, *Federal Republic of Germany v. Commission* (JAKO Jadekost GmbH & Co. KG).
464. Case C-303/88, *Italy v. Commission* (ENI-Lanerossi); Joined Cases C-278/92 to C-280/92, *Spain v. Commission* (capital contributions).
465. Case 310/85, *Deufil*; Case C-142/87, *Belgium v. Commission* (steel pipe and tube manufacturer).
466. The simple repetition of the text of the Treaty in a decision is insufficient, see Joined Cases 296/82 & 318/82, *Leeuwarder Papierfabriek* and many of the other cases mentioned elsewhere in this chapter.
467. Case T-67/94, *Ladbroke*; Case T-46/97, *SIC*; Case T-274/01, *Valmont*.

judgments which make it clear – particularly in relation to the application of the criterion of the 'market investor' – that assessments of a complex economic situation are at stake, with the conclusion inevitably that judicial review must be limited in character.[468]

3.2.2   Article 87(2) and (3) EC

3.2.2.1   *Possible Exceptions*

Two groups of exceptions apply to the incompatibility with the common market proclaimed in Article 87(1) EC. The first group is aids for the purposes specified in Article 87(2) EC; these aids are *de jure* compatible with the common market.[469] As for the list of cases in Article 87(3) EC, on the basis of which the Commission may declare aids compatible in the framework of the supervision procedure, according to constant case law this institution has a broad discretion, the exercise of which is only subject to marginal review by the Community courts.[470] The cases mentioned in Article 87(3)(a) relate to the underdeveloped areas of the Community. In relation to qualifications such as 'abnormal' or 'serious', the Court has ruled that these are defined in relation to departure from the Community average, and not the national average, so that application of this possible exception by the more prosperous Member States is limited.[471] The compatibility heading of Article 87(3)(c),[472] which deals with regional aid – which in practice is the most important heading – is interpreted in the case law, following the text of that provision, more widely, as it permits certain differences with regard to the national average to play a role.[473] In relation to this possibility of exception to the prohibition, as the wording

---

468. Case C-301/87, *France v. Commission* (capital contributions, provision of loans at reduced rates of interest and reduction in social security charges); Case C-56/93, *Belgium v. Commission* (preferential tariff); Case C-39/94, *SFEI*; Case T-67/94, *Ladbroke*; Case T-358/94, *Air France*; Case T-106/95, *FFSA*; Case T-140/95, *Ryanair Limited v. Commission*; Joined Cases T-126 & 127/96, *BFM and ENIM*; Case C-288/96, *Jadekost*; Case T-36/99, *Lenzing*; Case T-349/03, *Corsica Ferries France*.
469. See on the German clause – which is still in force – Joined Cases T-132 & 143/96, *Freistaat Sachsen, Volkswagen AG and Volkswagen Sachsen GmbH v. Commission*; Case C-156/98, *Federal Republic of Germany v. Commission* (tax concession).
470. Case 310/85, *Deufil*, and many other cases.
471. Case 248/84, *Federal Republic of Germany v. Commission* (compatibility of a regional aid programme); Joined Cases C-278/92 to C-280/92, *Spain v. Commission* (capital contributions); Case C-169/95, *Pyrsa*.
472. See over (b): Joined Cases 62/87 & 72/87, *Exécutif régional wallon and SA Glaverbel v. Commission* ('an important project of european interest'); Joined Cases T-132/96 & T-143/96, *Sachsen and Volkswagen* ('serious disturbance').
473. Joined Cases 296/82 & 318/82, *Leeuwarder Papierfabriek*; Case 259/85, *France v. Commission* (state aid – textile and clothing sector); Case C-301/87, *France v. Commission* (capital contributions, provision of loans at reduced rates of interest and reduction in social security charges); Case C-305/89, *Italy v. Commission* (capital contributions); Joined Cases C-278/92 to C-280/92, *Spain v. Commission* (capital contributions); Case C-42/93, *Merco*.

indicates,[474] an important significance is attached to the question whether the infringement of the correct functioning of the common market is compensated by the positive contribution of the aid in question to the realization of certain Community objectives (according to the principle of proportionality).[475] Finally, Article 87(3)(e) EC empowers the Council to extend the grounds on which aid may be approved as being compatible with the common market to other groups of measures, which has occurred *inter alia* in the case of shipbuilding aids, in the context of international agreements in the framework of the OECD.[476]

3.2.2.2 Commission Policy

On the basis of its discretionary powers in declaring aid compatible with the common market, the Commission has been in a position to develop a policy in relation to numerous types of aid, with respect to assessment and coordination. In general terms a distinction may be drawn between four major groups of aid measures: regional aid; sectoral aid (both in general and in relation to specific sectors); flanking policies aid (environment and research and development); and other areas. Until recently, such policy was developed mainly in Notices or Guidelines in the 'C' Series of the *Official Journal* and in letters addressed to the Member States. In the case law, the Commission's power to draw up general guidelines has been roundly acknowledged – obviously under the condition that this may not deviate from the provisions of the Treaty.[477] If these guidelines are in conformity with the Treaty provisions – or if they can be interpreted in conformity with the Treaty[478] – then they are binding on Member States in the sense that the Commission may review individual measures granting aid in the light of these guidelines.[479]

The criteria for the evaluation of *regional aid* were laid down in a Resolution of the representatives of the Member States meeting within the Council on 20 October 1971[480] on which the Commission bases its guidelines for this type of aid, as renewed periodically.[481] The general principles of this policy are as follows: in principle the

---

474. 'Aid to facilitate the development of certain economic activities or of certain economic areas, where such aid does not adversely affect trading conditions to an extent contrary to the common interest'.
475. Case 730/79, *Philip Morris*; Case T-380/94, *Association internationale des utilisateurs de fils de filaments artificiels et synthétiques et de soie naturelle (AIUFFASS) and Apparel, Knitting & Textiles Alliance (AKT) v. Commission*; Joined Cases T-371/94 & T-394/94, *British Airways*; Case T-171/02, *Regione Sardegna v. Commission*.
476. See *inter alia* Case C-400/92, *Federal Republic of Germany v. Commission* (concerning proposed aid by Germany to the Chinese shipping company Cosco); Case T-266/94, *Foreningen af Jernskibs-og Maskinbyggerier i Danmark and others v. Commission*.
477. Case C-313/90, *Comité International de la Rayonne et des Fibres Synthétiques and others v. Commission*; Case C-311/94, *IJssel-Vliet*; Case T-149/95, *Etablissements J. Richard Ducros v. Commission*; Case T-214/95, *Vlaams Gewest*.
478. Case C-139/95, *Livia Balestra v. Istituto Nazionale della Previdenza Sociale (INPS)*.
479. Case C-313/90, *CIRFS*; Case C-288/96, *Jadekost*.
480. J.O. 1971, C 111/1.
481. Guidelines on national regional aid, O.J. 1998, C 74/9.

Commission will only approve aid for initial investment, not operating aid. National state aid arrangements are coordinated under five aspects which form one whole: ceilings of aid intensity (the proportion of aid to total costs) differentiated according to the nature and gravity of the regional problems;[482] transparency; regional specificity (the aid must be targeted to a region, not to the whole Member State);[483] cumulation (for example with sectoral aid),[484] and a system of supervision. As for *sectoral aid*, coordinating criteria have been elaborated with regard to the synthetic fibres sector, and the automobile sector.[485] On the basis of the relevant Treaty provisions, a number of other regulations have been issued for the agricultural sector, fisheries, transport and shipbuilding. With regard to *flanking policies aid*, coordinating criteria have been laid down in the regulations on aid for training,[486] and aid for small and medium-sized enterprises,[487] mentioned at the beginning of section 3, and in notices concerning aid for research and development, the environment, employment, deprived urban areas and maritime transport.[488] In the fourth and last category (other measures), one may mention the guidelines on rescuing and restructuring aid,[489] government guarantees[490] and aid for the sale of land and buildings by public bodies.[491] On the basis of Article 133 EC (commercial policy), rules have been laid down, by means of decisions, concerning guidelines on export credits and project financing; these are based on OECD rules.[492] Mention should also be made of the Commission's policy concerning fiscal aid measures. This policy is based on the Code of conduct for business taxation, adopted by the Council in 1997[493] and the Commission notice on this subject drawn up on the basis of the Code of conduct.[494]

---

482. See for the applicable ceilings for the period 2007–2013, O.J. 2006, C 54/1.
483. With the exception of Luxembourg and Ireland.
484. See the 'Multisectoral Framework on Regional Aid for Large Investment Projects', O.J. 2002, C 70/8.
485. O.J. 1996, C 94/11 and O.J. 1997, C 279/1.
486. Reg. 68/2001, O.J. 2001, L 10/20; see further, the Communication from the Commission – framework on training aid (O.J. 1998, C 343/10).
487. Reg. 70/2001, O.J. 2001/1, L 10/33; see further Community guidelines on state aid for small and medium enterprises, O.J. 1996, C 213/4; see on this Case C-91/01, *Italy v. Commission* and Case T-137/02, *Pollmeier Malchow GmbH & Co. KG v. Commission*; Communication on venture capital investments in SMEs, O.J. 2006, C 194/12.
488. See the Community framework for state aid for research and development, O.J. 2006, C 323/1; the Community guidelines on state aid for environmental protection, O.J. 2001, C 37/3; the guidelines on aid to employment, O.J. 1995, C 334/4; the Guidelines on state aid for undertakings in deprived urban areas, O.J. 1997, C 146/6; Community guidelines on state aid to maritime transport, O.J. 2004, C 13/3.
489. Community guidelines on state aid for rescuing and restructuring firms in difficulty, O.J. 1999, C 288/2.
490. Commission Notice on the application of Arts. 87 and 88 of the EC Treaty to state aid in the form of guarantees, O.J. 2000, C 71/14.
491. Commission Communication on state aid elements in sales of land and buildings by public authorities, O.J. 1997, C 209/3.
492. Decisions 2001/76 and 2001/77, O.J. 2001, L 32/1, 55.
493. O.J. 1998, C 2/1.
494. O.J. 1998, C 348/2.

The Commission's policy sketched here shows that the application of Articles 87 and 88 EC lies in the transitional area between negative (liberalizing) and positive (directing) integration. Although from the viewpoint of the common market and the Economic and Monetary Union, prevention of distortion of competition must remain the point of departure, in view of the fact that aid measures are becoming a normal instrument of economic policy, this does not need to mean a per se prohibition of certain types of aid.[495] If aid measures with intrinsically laudable objectives are adopted in a large number of Member States or even in all of them, then distortions of competition should preferably be tackled through coordination of the national aid measures involved. Such coordination will then most likely require national measures to be fitted into the Community's own policy in the fields concerned, such as regional policy, agricultural policy, industrial policy relating to research and technological development, transport policy, and measures relating to infrastructure. The Community framework in these areas may, in their turn, be based on international framework arrangements, such as is the case for shipbuilding and export credits. Supervision will have to ensure that the size, modalities and duration of national aid measures do not go further than what is necessary for the realization of the objectives for which Article 87(2) and (3) make exceptions. On the other hand, differences between the various national state aid measures will only be tolerated to the extent that they can be justified from a Community point of view. A good illustration is the different ceilings for regional aid. These conditions set high standards for the efficiency of the supervisory mechanism and the political independence of the Commission which is required.[496]

3.3   ARTICLE 88 (SUPERVISION)

3.3.1   Existing and New Aid

3.3.1.1   Repressive (ex post) Supervision for Existing Aid

A clear distinction is made between existing aids and new aids in the supervision procedure.[497] According to Article 88(1) EC and Regulation 659/1999, existing aids are those which were in operation when the EC Treaty came into force in a

---

495. With the exception of operating aid, with regard to which the case law also makes an assumption of incompatibilty, see *inter alia* Case C-86/89, *Italy v. Commission* (aid for the use of concentrated grape must); Case T-459/93, *Siemens*; Joined Cases T-126/96 & T-127/96, *BFM and ENIM*; Case C-288/96, *Jadekost*.

496. A number of judgments permit one to conclude that the political character of the aid in question plays a clear role in the Commission's assessment, see e.g., Case T-67/94, *Ladbroke*; Case T-17/96, *Télévision française 1 SA (TF1) v. Commission*; Case T-95/96, *Gestevision Telecinco SA v. Commission*.

497. See especially Case C-44/93, *Namur-Les Assurances du Crédit SA v. Office National du Ducroire and the Belgian State*.

particular Member State (i.e., 1 January 1958, for the original Member States, and the date of accession for other Member States), as well as those subsequently implemented in accordance with the provisions of the Treaty, i.e., which have been notified to the Commission and which it has then approved or to which it has raised no objection.[498] According to the case law, state aids which exist at the moment a market is liberalized (e.g., in the case of transport) are also considered existing aid.[499] New aid is aid which is not part of an existing aid regime and which is not existing aid,[500] as well as any alteration to existing aid.

According to Article 88(1) EC, existing aid is only subject to a system of repressive supervision.[501] Such aid does not need to be notified, and may be implemented without prior approval by the Commission,[502] but the Commission does examine this aid in the light of the requirements of the common market, and – if necessary – will propose 'appropriate measures'. These measures are not binding,[503] but if the Commission has formulated guidelines and the Member States have accepted those guidelines, they must abide by them.[504]

3.3.1.2   *Preventive (ex ante) Supervision of New Aid*

New aid is subject to a notification system (Art. 88(3), first sentence, EC).[505] The Commission must be informed, in a proper and sufficiently detailed manner, of any plan to grant aid.[506] The obligation to notify is designed to enable the Commission to decide on the compatibility or otherwise of the measure in question with Article 87 EC.[507] Any plans to grant or alter (existing) aid[508] must be notified;[509] the Member State has no discretion in this.[510] New aid which has not been notified is unlawful (see section 3.3.2 under 3.3.2.4).

---

498. Case 120/73, *Gebrüder Lorenz GmbH v. Federal Republic of Germany et Land de Rhénanie-Palatinat*; Case C-99/98, *Republic of Austria v. Commission* (semiconductors).
499. Joined Cases T-298/97 etc., *Mauro*.
500. Except if the individual aid measure fits in an aid scheme which has already been approved, see Case T-176/01, *Ferriere Nord SpA v. Commission*.
501. Arts. 17–19 Reg. 659/1999.
502. Case C-47/91, *Italy v. Commission* (Italgrani SpA); Case C-387/92, *Banco de Credito*.
503. Case T-330/94, *Salt Union Ltd v. Commission*.
504. Case C-311/94, *IJssel-Vliet*.
505. Arts. 2–9 Reg. 659/1999.
506. Joined Cases T-126/96 & T-127/96, *BFM and ENIM*, from which it emerges that as long as the information provided is not complete, notification has not taken place.
507. Case 120/73, *Lorenz*; Case C-301/87, *France v. Commission* (capital contributions, provision of loans at reduced rates of interest and reduction in social security charges).
508. See on this notion Joined Cases 91/83 & 127/83, *Heineken Brouwerijen BV v. Inspecteur der Vennootschapsbelasting, Amsterdam and Utrecht*.
509. Also when it concerns aid granted for services of general economic interest under Art. 86(2) EC, Case C-332/98, *France v. Commission* (CELF).
510. Case 171/83 R, *Commission v. France* (interim measures); Case T-17/96, *TFI*.

3.3.2   Examination by the Commission

3.3.2.1   Preliminary Examination

After aid has been notified, the Commission is empowered, under Article 88(3), first sentence, EC 'to submit its comments'. According to the case law,[511] and its codification in Regulation 659/1999, this preliminary examination can lead to three conclusions: there is no aid; the aid is obviously compatible with the common market; the assessment of the compatibility of the aid with the common market raises doubts. In the last case, the formal investigation procedure of Article 88(2) EC must be opened. The Commission does not enjoy discretion on this point.[512] The formal investigation procedure must be opened 'without delay' in such a case, which has been interpreted by the Court in constant case law as meaning two months, corresponding with the period for appeal under Article 230 EC.[513] The preliminary examination is intended to give a first assessment of the measure in question, which according to the case law means assessing what the (real) aim of the measure is, and what the economic consequences are, so that the Commission can judge whether the effect of the aid on competition and interstate trade is such that the Community interest would be prejudiced; depending on the situation, attention may also need to be paid to possible infringement of Articles 81 or 82 EC.[514] In all three cases, the Commission finding constitutes an reviewable act, and is in the form of a decision addressed to the Member State in question.[515] In accordance with the preliminary nature of the examination, the Commission is not obliged to hear complainants or interested parties.[516] If the Commission has not made its view known at the end of the two month period, the aid may be granted,[517]

---

511. Case C-198/91, *William Cook plc v. Commission*; Case C-225/91, *Matra*; Case T-49/93, *Société Internationale de Diffusion et d'Edition (SIDE) v. Commission*; Case T-11/95, *BP Chemicals*. See for the case where the reason for doubt results from the lack of information, Art. 5 Reg. 659/1999.

512. Case T-73/98, *Société Chimique Prayon-Rupel SA v. Commission*.

513. For the first time in Case 120/73, *Lorenz*; now Art. 4(5) Reg. 659/1999.

514. Case T-49/93, *SIDE*.

515. Case C-39/94, *SFEI*; Case T-178/94, *Asociación Telefónica de Mutualistas (ATM) v. Commission*; Case T-188/95, *Waterleiding Maatschappij 'Noord-West Brabant' NV v. Commission*. In the first two cases, a decision can also be understood as an implicit refusal to start the official investigation proceedings; see Case C-367/95 P, *Commission v. Chambre syndicale nationale des entreprises de transport de fonds et valeurs (Sytraval) and Brink's France SARL*.

516. Case C-198/91, *Cook*; Case C-225/91, *Matra*; Case T-266/94, *Foreningen af Jernskibs-og Maskinbyggerier i Danmark and others v. Commission*; Case T-188/95, *Waterleiding Maatschappij 'Noord-West Brabant'*; Case C-367/95 P, *Sytraval*; Case T-158/99, *Thermenhotel Stoiser Franz Gesellschaft mbH & Co. KG v. Commission*; Case T-109/01, *Fleuren Compost BV v. Commission*.

517. Provided the Commission starts the formal investigation procedure within 15 working days, Art. 4(6) Reg. 659/1999. See Case C-99/98, *Republic of Austria v. Commission* (semiconductors).

on condition that the Commission is notified before it is implemented.[518] It then becomes existing aid.[519]

3.3.2.2   Formal Investigation Procedure

The aim of the formal investigation procedure[520] is to obtain legal certainty as to the compatibility of the aid under Article 87 EC,[521] which explains why the establishment of (in)compatibility is an exclusive power of the Commission.[522] That is also why this procedure applies even to non-notified aid. The crucial difference with the procedure for a preliminary examination is that it is contentious in character.[523] As a result, the Commission must respect the rights of the defence in all respects, in particular the right to be heard and the obligation not to rely on any information against a Member State which that Member State does not have at its disposal, and on which it has not been given an opportunity to comment.[524] From the case law it is apparent, however, that a Member State may not reproach the Commission for not having taken account of information which that State had not supplied to the Commission.[525] On the other hand, the Commission cannot justify its decision by relying on the failure of the Member State to supply certain information if the Commission has not actually ordered this information to be supplied.[526] The respect for the rights of the defence is apparent from the requirement of Article 88(2), first sentence, EC, according to which the Member States

---

518. Otherwise, the official investigation procedure may be initiated after all; see Case T-176/01, *Ferriere Nord*.
519. According to constant case law, first in Case 120/73, *Lorenz*. The Member State in question must inform the Commission first, see Art. 4(5) Reg. 659/1999 and Case C-113/00, *Spain v. Commission* (aid scheme implemented by Spain in favour of horticultural products intended for industrial processing in Extremadura).
520. Arts. 6 and 7 Reg. 659/1999.
521. Case 290/83, *Commission v. France*; Case C-198/91, *Cook*; Case T-86/96, *Arbeitsgemeinschaft Deutscher Luftfahrt-Unternehmen and Hapag Lloyd Fluggesellschaft mbH v. Commission*.
522. Case C-354/90, *Fédération Nationale du Commerce Extérieur des Produits Alimentaires and Syndicat National des Négociants et Transformateurs de Saumon v. France*; Case C-44/93, *Namur*; Case T-49/93, *SIDE*; Case C-39/94, *SFEI*; Case C-256/97, *DMT*.
523. Case C-367/95 P, *Sytraval*; Case C-78/03, *ARE v. Commission*; Case T-95/03, *AESCAM v. Commission*.
524. Case 234/84, *Belgium v. Commission* (subscription of capital of an undertaking); Case 259/85, *France v. Commission* (textile and clothing sector); Case C-301/87, *France v. Commission* (capital contributions, provision of loans at reduced rates of interest and reduction in social security charges); Case C-288/96, *Jadekost*.
525. Case C-261/89, *Italy v. Commission* (aid to aluminium undertakings); Case C-364/90, *Italy v. Commission* (special aid for certain areas of the Mezzogiorno affected by natural disasters); Case C-241/94, *France v. Commission* (concerning aid to the company Kimberly Clark Sopalin); Case C-382/99, *Netherlands v. Commission* (Dutch service stations located near the German border).
526. Case T-318/02, *Freistaat Thüringen v. Commission*.

and other interested parties[527] must be given the opportunity to make comments.[528] This takes place usually through a notice in the 'C series' of the *Official Journal*. Regulation 659/1999 sets out the obligation for the Commission to complete the formal investigation procedure within 18 months, as a general rule.[529] If that time is up, then the Commission must give a decision at the request of the Member State within two months. The formal investigation procedure is terminated with one of four decisions: there is no aid, the aid is compatible (positive decision), the aid is compatible providing certain conditions are met (conditional decision), or the aid is incompatible (negative decision).[530]

3.3.2.3 Unlawful Aid

The last sentence of Article 88(3) EC contains a so-called standstill provision: notified aid may not be put into effect as long as the Commission has not taken a preliminary or definitive decision, which means a fortiori that no aid may be granted which is not notified or which is in conflict with a negative or a conditional decision on compatibility. In all these cases, any aid granted is unlawful.[531] The standstill rule is directly effective[532] and thus forms an important tool of judicial protection for the national courts. The Regulation provides for unlawful aid in a separate procedure.[533] If unlawful aid comes to the notice of the Commission, then it must – again, without delay – investigate the matter, but it is not obliged to take a decision within 2 months, given that the Member State, by not complying with the standstill rule, has forfeited its right to speedy legal certainty.[534] Provision is made for a power of the Commission to order the Member State in question to furnish the necessary information.[535] If the Member State does not do so, then the Commission is empowered to base its investigation as to the compatibility of aid on information which it has at its disposal. While this investigation is taking place, the

---

527. In accordance with earlier case law, Art. 1(h) Reg. 659/1999 includes a person, a businessman, an assciation of undertakings whose interests are affected by the grant of aid, in particular the beneficiary of the aid, competing firms and professional associations. The right to be heard is elaborated in Art. 20 Reg. 659/1999.
528. Also the initiation of the procedure is an act subject to appeal, see Case T-98/00, *Linde AG v. Commission*; Case C-312/90, *Spain v. Commission* (aid granted by the Spanish authorities to the private group of electrical equipment producers Cenemesa, Conelec and Cademesa); Joined Cases T-195 & 207/01, *Government of Gibraltar v. Commission*.
529. See on this time limit Case T-190/00, *Regione Siciliane v. Commission*.
530. For the publication of the decisions, see Art. 26 Reg. 659/1999.
531. Art. 1(f) Reg. 659/1999.
532. Already in Case 6/64, *Costa v. ENEL* and many other cases.
533. Arts. 10–15 Reg. 659/1999, which to a great extent form a codification of the case law. See further the Commission Notices on unlawful aid, O.J. 1980, C 252/2; O.J. 1983, C 318/1; O.J. 1985, C 3/2; O.J. 1995, C 156/5.
534. Case C-39/94, *SFEI*. This can lead to problems for complainants, however, if the Commission fails to act; see Case T-95/96, *Gestevisión* and Case T-17/96, *TF1*.
535. On the consequences if the Commission fails to issue such an order, see Joined Cases C-324 & 342/90, *Federal Republic of Germany and Pleuger Worthington GmbH v. Commission*.

Commission 'may' order suspension of the aid or issue an interim order for recovery of the aid.[536] If the Member State does not comply with these orders, then the Commission may apply directly to the Court of Justice.[537] If it appears from the preliminary examination that the unlawful aid raises grave doubts as to its compatibility with the common market, then the Commission is obliged to open the formal investigation procedure. If the Commission does not follow that procedure, then it cannot issue a decision as to the (in)compatibility of the unlawful aid.[538] In the formal investigation procedure as to the compatibility of unlawful aid, the Commission is not bound to the term of 18 months.

3.3.2.4   *Recovery of Unlawful Aid*

If the Commission decides that the unlawfully granted aid is incompatible with the common market,[539] then it may order the recovery of that aid (with interest),[540] on the basis of its discretionary power derived from Article 88(2), first sentence, EC.[541] The objective of this power is to restore the status quo ante, that is to say the removal of the distortion of competition.[542] The exercise of this power thus, of necessity, complies with the proportionality principle, and a separate reasoning on that account is not needed.[543] Regulation 659/1999 does provide that recovery may not be ordered if this would be in contravention of a general principle of Community law.[544] The significance of this rule is in fact not clear, given that according to constant case law neither the Member State nor the undertakings which have profited from the incompatible aid may rely on the principle of

---

536. But not in the case of misuse of aid (Art. 16 Reg. 659/1999), i.e., aid granted in contravention of a provisional decision of approval.
537. The Regulation codifies especially Case C-301/87, *France v. Commission* (capital contributions, provision of loans at reduced rates of interest and reduction in social security charges); Case C-303/88, *Eni-Lanerossi*; Case T-49/93, *SIDE* and Case C-39/94, *SFEI*.
538. Case C-294/90, *British Aerospace Public Ltd Company and Rover Group Holdings plc v. Commission*; Case C-354/90, *FNCAEP*; Case T-17/96, *TF1*.
539. The Commission can only do this in the framework of the official investigative proceedings, see Case C-301/87, *France v. Commission* (capital contributions, provision of loans at reduced rates of interest and reduction in social security charges), Case C-294/90, *British Aerospace*; Case C-39/94, *SFEI*.
540. Art. 14 Reg. 659/1999. See further the Communication of the Commission to the Member States of 13 November 1993, O.J. 1993, C 307/3, and Case T-35/99, *Keller SpA and Keller Meccanica SpA v. Commission*.
541. Case 310/85, *Deufil*; Joined Cases C-278/92 to C-280/92, *Spain v. Commission* (capital contributions); Case C-24/95, *Land Rheinland-Pfalz v. Alcan Deutschland GmbH*.
542. See especially Case C-354/90, *FNCAEP*; Case C-350/93, *Commission v. Italy* (recovery of state aid); Case T-55/99, *CETM*.
543. Case C-142/87, *Belgium v. Commission* (state aid to a steel pipe and tube manufacturer); Case C-301/87, *France v. Commission* (capital contributions, provision of loans at reduced rates of interest and reduction in social security charges); Joined Cases T-204 & 207/97, *EPAC – Empresa para a Agroalimentação e Cereais, SA v. Commission*.
544. Further, a prescription period of 10 years applies; see Joined Cases T-366 & 369/00, *Scott SA and France v. Commission*.

protection of legitimate expectations.[545] Recovery should take place according to the procedural provisions of national law, subject to the proviso that those provisions must not be applied in such a way as to make the recovery required by Community law practically impossible.[546]

The Member State and the national courts do not enjoy any margin of discretion on this issue.[547] The recovery does not necessarily take place in the form of a transfer of money; other constructions are possible, as long as the requirement is met that the consequences of the prohibited aid are really annulled.[548] In the case law many other arguments have been rejected which attempted to justify a failure to recover prohibited aid.[549] Recently the Court has given further clarity as to the question whether and from whom the aid must be recovered if it has been 'passed on' to other undertakings, or successors in title.[550] As for recovery of unlawful aid which is later declared by the Commission to be compatible, the Court has ruled that the national courts are competent to order that the company must pay back the interest advantage which it has received in the period between the unlawful grant of the aid and the declaration of compatibility by the Commission.[551] In case of complete impossibility of recovery, constant case law dictates that the Member State must cooperate loyally with the Commission in order to find a satisfactory solution.[552]

3.3.2.5 *Derogation by the Council*

Finally, the possibility should be mentioned which is created by Article 88(2) third sentence EC for the Council to declare an aid compatible with the common market, despite the fact that it does not satisfy the normal conditions of Article 87 or a Regulation based on Article 89 EC. According to this provision, such a derogation may only be given in exceptional circumstances. The Court grants the Council

---

545. See especially Case C-24/95, *Alcan Deutschland*; Case T-55/99, *CETM* and Case C-334/99, *Federal Republic of Germany v. Commission*. But see C-182/03, *Belgium v. Commission (Forum 187)*.
546. Art. 14 Reg. 659/1999. Case C-24/95, *Alcan Deutschland*; Case C-209/00, *Commission v. Federal Republic of Germany* (WLB). The Commission is not obliged to calculate the amount which must be recovered, Case T-214/95, *Vlaams Gewest*. See on various details of calculation (taxes, rate of interest), Case T-459/93, *Siemens*.
547. Case C-24/95, *Alcan Deutschland*.
548. Case C-209/00, *WLB*.
549. Such as (without mentioning the case law) the form in which the aid was granted, the low level of aid, or the fiscal character, that there was no unjust enrichment, the high number of beneficiaries, general or special rules of company law or bankruptcy law, that bankruptcy would be unavoidable as a result of recovery, that the advantage received cannot be calculated exactly, and political tension. See *inter alia* Case C-404/00, *Commission v. Spain* and Case C-99/02, *Commission v. Italy*.
550. Joined Cases C-328/99 & C-399/00, *Italy and SIM 2 Multimedia SpA v. Commission* (Seleco); Case C-277/00, *Federal Republic of Germany v. Commission* (aid granted to System Micro-electronic Innovation GmbH); Case C-457/00, *Belgium v. Commission*.
551. Case C-199/06, *CELF*.
552. See *inter alia* Case C-75/97, *Belgium v. Commission*.

wide discretion in deciding whether this is the case.[553] This competence is used by the Council particularly in the agricultural sector, in order to approve national aid measures which are not in line with common market regulations, amounting in fact to an amendment of these regulations on the basis of Article 88(2) EC.[554]

3.3.3   Judicial Protection

3.3.3.1   Before the Community Courts

For the *Member States*, the appeal possibilities of Articles 230 and 232 EC lie open with respect to actions and failure to act of the Commission in relation to the supervisory mechanisms.[555] If a Member State has failed to contest the validity of a decision addressed to it, then the validity of that decision may not be contested later in an enforcement procedure under Article 88(2) second sentence.[556] On the other hand, the Commission may – deviating from the procedure under Article 226 EC – bring an application to the Court straight away under Article 88(2) second sentence against a Member State which fails to comply with a decision issued on the basis of this Article or on the basis of Regulation 659/1999.[557] Since all Commission decisions relating to state aids are addressed to the Member States,[558] other parties who are affected by the notified, unlawful or incompatible aid can only bring an action before the Court of First Instance against such a decision if they are directly and individually concerned, under the usual conditions of Article 230 EC.[559] These

---

553.   Case C-122/94, *Commission v. Council*.
554.   See Case C-110/02, *Commission v. Council* (aid granted by the Portuguese Government to pig farmers).
555.   A body which grants aid but which is completely under the control of the state has no standing, see Case 282/85, *DEFI*. Autonomous government bodies which grant aid have standing if they meet the requirements of direct and individual concern, see Case T-214/95, *Vlaams Gewest*; Joined Cases T-132/96 & T-146/96, *Sachsen and Volkswagen*. For the case of an autonomous government body which did not grant aid, but was an interested party, see Case T-238/97, *Comunidad Autónoma de Cantabria v. Council*; the CFI did not grant standing in that case.
556.   Case 52/84, *Commission v. Belgium* (ceramic sanitary wares); Case 94/87, *Alcan*; Case C-183/91, *Commission v. Greece* (tax exemption on earnings from exports); Case C-280/95, *Commission v. Italy* (fiscal bonus on certain taxes).
557.   See on this procedure esp. Case 213/85, *Communities v. Netherlands* (preferential tariff for horticultural producers); Case C-356/90, *Belgium v. Commission* (shipbuilding aid). An individual cannot force the Commission to make use of this procedure, see Case T-277/94, *AITEC*.
558.   The result is that a letter informing a third party of the existence of a decision is not a reviewable act, Case C-367/95 P, *Sytraval*. The decision to take 'appropriate measures' in the sense of Art. 88(1) EC, the refusal or the simple failure to take such measures are not reviewable acts either, cf. Case T-330/94, *Salt Union*.
559.   As a result, employees' associations will nearly always be excluded from the possibility of contesting a decision, see Case T-178/94, *ATM*.

conditions are met in the case of the (potential) beneficiary of the aid,[560] and that of an undertaking which is confronted with an order for recovery of aid granted.[561] The question whether a *competitor* of an undertaking which has been granted aid is individually and directly concerned by a Commission decision in this area depends, according to constant case law, in particular[562] on whether this competitor has made a complaint at an earlier stage of the proceedings, and whether the competitor has played an active part in the Commission's investigations, and also on the relevant market and that party's position in the market.[563]

The position of *parties concerned* in the sense of Article 88(2) EC may be seen as a specialized case of the requirement of direct and individual concern.[564] In this context, a distinction must be made between the preliminary examination and the formal investigation procedure. If the Commission does not initiate a formal investigation procedure – which means either that it does not consider Article 87(1) EC applicable, or that it considers the aid to be justified on the basis of Article 87(2) or (3) EC – then parties are directly and individually concerned by that decision. The background to this is that only in this way can interested parties ensure that their procedural rights under Article 88(2) EC have not been infringed, given that the preliminary examination is non-contentious in character and therefore that interested parties do not have the right to make comments.[565] In this case, the interested parties do have to lodge an application against the decision of the Commission in order to safeguard their procedural rights.[566] If a formal investigation procedure is initiated, then interested parties have had the opportunity to exercise their procedural rights, with as a result that they are not considered to be directly and individually concerned by the final decision on the mere ground that they are in

---

560. But, on the other hand, not if it is a general aid measure, within the scope of which any undertaking can come which fulfils the abstract criteria, see Joined Cases 67/85, 68/85 & 70/85, *Van der Kooy*; Case T-398/94, *Kahn Scheppvaart BV v. Commission*; Case T-188/95, *Waterleiding Maatschappij 'Noord-West Brabant'*.
561. If an undertaking has omitted to challenge the validity of an aid decision which affects it directly and individually within the time limit applicable, then it may not later challenge the order of recovery of aid granted by the Member State on the basis of a claim that the aid decision is invalid; Case C-188/92, *TWD Textilwerke Deggendorf GmbH v. Bundesrepublik Deutschland*; Joined Cases T-244/93 & T-486/93, *TWD Textilwerke Deggendorf GmbH v. Commission*; Case C-24/95, *Alcan Deutschland*.
562. But not exclusievly, see Case T-435/93, *Association of Sorbitol Producers within the EC (ASPEC), Cerestar Holding BV, Roquette Frères SA and Merck oHG v. Commission*.
563. Case 169/84, *Cofaz*; Joined Cases T-447/93 to 449/93, *AITEC*; Case T-11/95, *BP Chemicals*; Case T-149/95, *Ducros*; T-86/96, *ADLU*; Case T-88/01, *Sniace SA v. Commission*.
564. Case T-188/95, *Waterleiding Maatschappij 'Noord-West Brabant'*; Case T-69/96, *Hamburger Hafen-und Lagerhaus Aktiengesellschaft, Zentralverband der Deutschen Seehafenbetriebe eV and Unternehmensverband Hafen Hamburg eV v. Commission*.
565. Case C-313/90, *CIRFS*; Case C-198/91, *Cook*; Case C-225/91, *Matra*; Case T-49/93, *SIDE*; Case T-266/94, *Foreningen af Jernskibs-og Maskinbyggerier i Danmark and others v. Commission*; Case T-11/95, *BP Chemicals*; Case T-17/96, *TF1*.
566. Case C-78/03 P, *ARE*; Case T-95/03, *AEESCAM*.

some way affected.[567] In that case, the conditions mentioned above concerning the position of competitors apply.[568]

3.3.3.2   Before the National Courts

The national courts have jurisdiction to interpret Article 87(1) EC, for instance in order to establish whether there is a state aid, and in order to grant judicial protection. The Court of Justice has advised the national courts to cooperate as closely as possible with the Commission on this issue.[569] The national courts do not have jurisdiction, however, to decide whether a state aid may be declared compatible with the common market under Article 87(2) and (3) EC, since this is an exclusive power of the Commission.[570] Nor do the national courts have jurisdiction to judge the validity (lawfulness) of any decision of the Commission, in particular as relates to recovery of aid which has been declared incompatible.[571] Pursuant to the directly effective standstill rules of Article 88(3), last sentence, EC, interested parties can ask the Court to order the suspension or recovery of unlawful aid pending the decision of the Commission. The complainant does not need to have suffered actual damage in order to apply for this.[572] The same holds for aid which has been granted contrary to a conditional decision on compatibility.[573]

3.3.4   Aid Granted to or by Public Undertakings

In accordance with Article 86(1) EC, Articles 87 and 88 EC also apply to state aids granted to public undertakings and undertakings to which Member States grant special or exclusive rights, and, as we saw above, according to Article 86(2) EC, undertakings entrusted with the operation of services of general economic interest are subject to the Treaty rules, in particular to the rules on competition, insofar as the application of such rules does not obstruct the performance, in law or in fact, of

---

567.   Joined Cases T-447-449/93, *AITEC*; Case T-380/94, *AIUFASS and AKT*; Case T-11/95, *BP Chemicals*; Case T-149/95, *Ducros*; Case T-86/96, *ADLU*; Case T-189/97, *Comité d'entreprise de la Société française de production, Syndicat national de radiodiffusion et de télévision CGT (SNRT-CGT), et al. v. Commission*.

568.   See on the position of interest groups, Joined Cases 67/85, 68/85 & 70/85, *Van der Kooy*; Case C-313/90, *CIRFS*; Case T-442/93, *Association des Amidonneries de Céréales de la CEE, Levantina Agricola Industrial SA, Società Piemontese Amidi e Derivati SpA, Pfeifer & Langen, Ogilvie Aquitaine SA, Cargill BV and Latenstein Zetmeel BV v. Commission*; Case T-266/94 *Foreningen af Jernskibs- og Maskinbyggerier i Danmark and others v. Commission*; Case T-380/94, *AIUFASS and AKT*; Case T-86/96, *ADLU*.

569.   Case C-39/94, *SFEI*; Case C-295/97, *Piaggio*. See the Notice on cooperation between national courts and the Commission in the state aid field, O.J. 1995, C 312/8.

570.   Case C-354/90, *FNCAEP*; Case C-44/93, *Namur*; Case T-49/93, *SIDE*; Case C-256/97, *DMT*.

571.   Case C-39/94, *SFEI* and Case C-24/95, *Alcan Deutschland*.

572.   Case C-174/02, *Streekgewest Brabant* and Case C-175/02, *Pape*.

573.   Case C-354/90, *FNCAEP*; Case C-17/91, *Lornoy*; Case C-39/94, *SFEI*.

the particular tasks assigned to them. Two situations must be distinguished. In the first place, the case in which aid meets the conditions of Article 87(1) EC, but not of Article 87(2) or (3) EC. In that case, the aid may nonetheless be justified if the conditions of Article 86(2) are met.[574] This exception does not however apply to the obligation to notify, and the standstill obligation if the first obligation has not been met.[575] The second situation concerns cases where an undertaking is subject to a public service obligation under national or Community law provisions. In the case law, it is indicated that aid which is granted as compensation for the cost of the public service obligations carried out by those undertakings (e.g., a certain territorial coverage for public transport) is not considered aid in the sense of Article 87(1) EC,[576] with as a consequence that no notification has to take place. For this rule to apply, four conditions must be met.[577] First, it must be a real public service obligation clearly recognizable as such. Second, the calculation of the amount of aid as compensation for the costs must take place on the basis of previously determined objective and transparent criteria. Thirdly, the compensation may not be higher than the costs of the public service, taking into account receipts and a reasonable profit. The second and third conditions exclude the possibility that the government retroactively compensates losses, on a case-by-case basis. The fourth condition provides that if the award of the public service obligation does not take place via a public tender, the compensation must be calculated on the basis of the net costs which an average, well-run undertaking would make in carrying out the services.[578] It needs no further explanation to see that the practical application of the firth condition may be extremely complicated.[579]

The provisions on state aid also apply to the grant of aid *by* public undertakings. In that case, it must be established that the public undertaking acted under pressure from the government.[580] If the public undertaking acts as an investor, for instance by participation in equity capital, or by granting other advantages, the market investor principle is not always automatically applicable; it is possible that the public undertaking is operating on a reserved market (on the basis of special or exclusive rights), so that a comparison between that market and a market operating under conditions of private competition is not possible.[581]

---

574. Case C-387/92, *Banco de Credito*; Joined Cases T-204 & 207/97, *Portuguese Republic v. Commission* (aid for producers of liqueur wines and eaux-de-vie).

575. Case C-332/98, *France v. Commission* (CELF) and Case C-172/03, *Heiser*.

576. Case 240/83, *Procureur de la République v. Association de défense des brûleurs d'huiles usagées (ADBHU)*; Case C-53/00, *Ferring SA v. Agence centrale des organismes de sécurité sociale (ACOSS)*.

577. Case C-280/00, *Altmark*; Case C-126/01, *Ministre de l'économie, des finances et de l'industrie v. Gemo SA*; Joined Cases C-34/01 to C-38/01, *Enirisorse SpA v. Ministero delle Finanze*.

578. See Community Framework for state aid in the form of public service compensation, O.J. 2005, C 297/4.

579. See Case T-106/95, *FFSA*.

580. Case C-482/99, *France v. Commission* (Stardust).

581. Joined Cases C-83/01 etc., *Chronopost SA and others v. Union française de l'express (Ufex) and others*.

4   THE SPECIFIC PROVISIONS RELATING TO
                 DISTORTION OF COMPETITION

For a discussion of Articles 94 and 95 EC, the reader is referred to Chapter V,
section 2. As is evident from the Spaak Report[582] and the text of Articles 96 and 97
EC, these provisions in the EEC Treaty were intended as *lex specialis* in relation to
Article 94 EC, in order to be able to act more rapidly and effectively to combat
particularly flagrant distortions of competition. Nevertheless, the practical significance of these Articles has remained extremely limited. The importance of these
provisions is above all of a theoretical nature, since they throw further light on the
problem to what extent distortions of competition as a result of disparities between
national policies are still compatible with the common market.

4.1   CONTENT

Two substantive conditions must be met in order for these two provisions to be
applicable.[583] In the first place there must be *difference* between the legislative or
administrative rules of Member States. This condition makes it clear that Articles
96 and 97 EC are not intended for the elimination of discrimination. The concepts
of discrimination and difference do not overlap entirely, since in the former case
the legislation in one Member State makes a distinction between on the one hand
domestic products, services, persons and capital, and on the other hand those which
come from (or go to) another Member State. Differences result from the fact that
national legislation is not identical in two or more Member States.[584] The existence
of differences between national legislative provisions is an unavoidable consequence of the limited territorial scope of national legislation.[585]

     In the second place this difference must interfere with the conditions of com-
petition in the common market and thus cause *distortion* which should be eliminated. The wording of the provision indicates that the distortion resulting from
legislative or administrative measures must be so serious that it 'needs to be
eliminated'.[586] Distortions are usually distinguished as to whether they are global,
generic or specific. Global distortions occur at macro level, e.g., as a result of

---

582. See Ch. I *supra*.
583. These provisions are not directly effective, see Case 6/64, *Costa v. ENEL*; Case C-134/94, *Esso
      Española SA v. Comunidad Autónoma de Canarias*.
584. Case 14/68, *Walt Wilhelm*; Case 223/86, *Pesca Valentia Limited v. Ministry for Fisheries and
      Forestry, Ireland and the Attorney General*; Case C-177/94, *Criminal proceedings against
      Gianfranco Perfili*.
585. Disparities can also exist when two sets of rules are identical. If for instance a product in State
      A is subjected to the same controls as in State B, there is still a disparity as long as State A does
      not recognize the controls in State B.
586. In some language versions of the Treaty it may seem that the seriousness of the distortion is
      implied by the use of a different term from that used in general to refer to distortions of
      competition, e.g., as compared with Art. 3(1)(g) EC or Art. 81 EC.

differences in the average level of the collective tax and social security burdens, developments in labour costs, in the development of interest rates and inflation. A typical case of a global distortion is a competitive exchange rate devaluation, so that – at least in the short term – a competitive advantage is gained compared with other Member States.[587] At present, global distortions mainly concern coordination of economic policy in the framework of the multilateral supervision of the Council.

Generic distortions occur as a result of different policies in relation sectors and regions, for instance the previous low excise duty on diesel in the Netherlands, which caused sectoral distortion in favour of freight transport by road; measures favouring certain regions, and environmental taxes may also come in this category. To some extent, these distortions may be eliminated in the framework of supervision of state aids, coordination of environmental policy and policy on economic and social cohesion and trans-European networks.

On the basis of the Spaak Report, it may be assumed that Articles 96 and 97 EC were not intended for the two types of distortion mentioned so far, but only for so-called *specific distortions*. From the Spaak Report and experiences with the ECSC, it is evident that the following conditions must be met for there to be a specific distortion.[588] First, there must be a group of undertakings in a Member State which is subject to higher or lower charges than other groups of undertakings in the same Member State, for instance because of specific taxes. Secondly, in the other Member States there must not be an equal deviation for the same group of undertakings as compared with other groups of undertakings (the national intervention must have a cross-border influence on competitive relationships, thus an external effect on competition). Thirdly, the deviation in question must not be compensated by other targeted charges or benefits (the 'net effect' or balancing criterion). The use of this balancing criterion is most likely to cause problems, as it will often be extremely difficult or impossible to prove that there has been (complete) compensation. The problems with this criterion constitute one of the reasons why the significance of Articles 96 and 97 EC is so restricted in practice. In the Spaak Report a number of examples of specific distortions are given, such as specific legislation for certain sectors or branches of industry (e.g., capital-intensive, or labour-intensive),[589] differences in working hours or employment conditions, between direct and indirect taxes, price regulations, financing of the system of social security, paid vacations, rates of pay for women (!), credit facilities, etc.

If there is a specific distortion, then directives or other necessary measures may be adopted by the Council following the procedure set out in Article 96 EC in order to eliminate the distortion. Article 97 EC concerns cases where a Member State wishes to adopt a measure, as a result of which a distortion in the sense of Article 96 EC may arise.

---

587. This is why in the old Art. 107 EEC (repealed by the Treaty of Maastricht), the Member States were required to consider their rates of exchange as a matter of common concern.
588. See the answer to written question 2260/80 in O.J. 1983, C 257/1.
589. See Case 173/73, *Italy v. Commission* (family allowances).

4.2   Relationship with Other Treaty Provisions

The relationship between Articles 96 and 97 EC on the one hand and the other Treaty provisions explains why in practice the importance of the former provisions is limited. In the first place, the Court has interpreted the provisions on free movement in such a way that they do not only concern cases of discrimination, but also obstacles to free movement resulting from diverse legislation, with the result that various situations which might have justified recourse to Articles 96 and 97 EC have been brought within the scope of Articles 28, 43 and 49 EC. Secondly, Articles 87–89 EC lay down rules for an important category of distortions resulting from state aids. As a result of the broad interpretation of the concept of a state aid, the sphere of application of Articles 96 and 97 EC has been restricted even further. Moreover, Article 88(3) provides an important legal basis for coordinating national regional and sectoral policy by means of the grant of aids. Thirdly, many disparities which cause – or would have caused – distortions have been eliminated on the basis of the specific powers relating to agriculture, transport, commercial policy, social and environmental policy. Fourthly, the broad scope of Article 95 EC is also to blame for this development; the narrower interpretation of this provision in the first Tobacco advertising case does not detract from this, since the provision does still apply where significant distortions of competition are involved.[590]

Further Reading

General
Black, O. *Conceptual Foundations of Antitrust*. Cambridge: Cambridge University Press, 2005.

Competition Rules

Documentation
Barents, R. *Directory of EC Case Law on Competition*. International Competition Law Series, 28. Alphen aan den Rijn: Kluwer Law International, 2007.
Bellamy, C.W., et al. *Bellamy & Child Materials on European Community Law of Competition*. Oxford: Oxford University Press, 2008.
Jones, A. and B.E. Sufrin. *EC Competition Law: Text, Cases and Materials*. 3rd ed. Oxford: Oxford University Press, 2008.
Jones, C. and M.H.v.d. Woude. *E.C. Competition Law Handbook, 2007/2008*. London: Sweet & Maxwell, 2008.
Kokkoris, I. *Competition Cases from the European Union: The Ultimate Guide to Leading Cases of the EU and All 27 Member States*. London: Sweet & Maxwell, 2008.

---

590.   One reason is the restrictive interpretation of Arts. 96 and 97 EC by the Commission.

Korah, V. *Cases and Materials on EC Competition Law.* 3rd ed Oxford: Hart, 2006.
Struys, M., et al. *EC Merger Decisions Digest.* Kluwer Law International, 2005.
Vogelaar, F.O.W., et al. *The European Competition Rules: Landmark Cases of the European Courts and the Commission.* 2nd ed. Groningen: Europa Law Publishing, 2007.
European Commission: Competition website.
European Commission: Annual Reports on Competition Policy.

Commentaries
Amato, G. and C.-D. Ehlermann. *EC Competition Law: A Critical Assessment.* Oxford: Hart, 2007.
Bellamy, C.W., et al. *European Community Law of Competition.* 6th ed. Oxford: Oxford University Press, 2008.
Faull, J. and A. Nikpay. *The EC Law of Competition.* 2nd ed. Oxford: Oxford University Press, 2007.
Goyder, D.G. *EC Competition Law.* 4th ed. Oxford: Oxford University Press, 2003.
Korah, V. *An Introductory Guide to EC Competition Law and Practic.*9th ed Oxford: Hart, 200.
Korah, V., et al. *Competition Law of the European Community.* Matthew Bender/ LexisNexis, 2005.
Monti, G. EC *Competition Law.* Cambridge: Cambridge University Press, 2007.
Odudu, O. *The Boundaries of EC Competition Law: The Scope of Article 81.* Oxford: Oxford University Press, 2006.
Tosato, G.L., et al. *EU CompetitionLaw.* Leuven: Claeys & Casteels, 2005.
Van Bael, I. and J.-F. Bellis. *Competition Law of the European Community.* 4th ed. The Hague: Kluwer Law International, 2005.

Articles, Regular Surveys, Annotations and Overviews of Developments
In the journals: European Competition Law Review; European Competition Journal; Competition Law Journal; Europäische Zeitschrift für Wirtschaftsrecht; Wirtschaft und Wettbewerb; Fordham International Law Journal; World Competition; Common Market Law Review; European Law Review; Sociaal-Economische Wetgeving (SEW); Nederlands Tijdschrift voor Europees Recht; Markt en Mededinging.

Economic Analyses
Elhauge, E. and D. Geradin. *Global Competition Law and Economics.* Oxford: Hart, 2007.
Hildebrand, D *The Role of Economic Analysis in the EC Competition Rules.* 2nd ed. European Monographs, 17. The Hague: Kluwer Law International, 2002.
O'Donoghue, R. and A.J. Padill. *The Law and Economics of Article 82 EC.* Oxford: Hart, 2006.
Van den Bergh, R.J. and P.D.N. Camesasca. *European Competition Law and Economics: A Comparative Perspective.* 2nd ed. London: Sweet & Maxwell, 2006.

International Aspects:
Elhauge, E. and D. Geradin. *Global CompetitionLaw and Economics*. Oxford: Hart, 2007.
Schwarze, J. (Hrsg.). *Europäisches Wettbewerbsrecht im Zeichen der Globalisierung*. Schriftenreihe europäisches Recht, Politik und Wirtschaft, Bd. 268. Baden-Baden. Nomos, 2002.
Slot, P.J. and E. Grabandt. 'Extraterritoriality and Jurisdiction'. (1986) CML Rev., 545–565.

The Modernisation of EC Competition Policy
Cahill, D., et al. *The Modernisation of EU Competition Law Enforcement in the European Union*. FIDE 2004 National Reports. Cambridge: Cambridge University Press, 2004.
Deringer, A. 'Stellungnahme zum Weißbuch der Europäischen Kommission über die Modernisierung der Vorschriften zur Anwendung der Art. 85 und 86 EG-Vertrag (Art. 81 und 82 EG)'. (2000) *Europäische Zeitschrift für Wirtschaftsrecht*, 5.
Ehlermann, C.D. 'The Modernization of EC Antitrust Policy: A Legal and Cultural Revolution'. (2000) *Common Market Law Review*, 537.
Ehlermann, C.-D. and I. Atanasiu. *Modernisation of EC Antitrust Policy*. European Competition Law Annual, 2000. Oxford: Hart, 2001.
Geradin, D. *Modernisation and Enlargement: Two Major Challenges of EC Competition Law*. Antwerp: Intersentia, 2004.
Rivas, J. and M. Horspool. *Modernisation and Decentralisation of EC Competition Law*. European Business Law and Practice Series, vol. 16. The Hague: Kluwer Law International, 2000.
Rodger, B.J. 'The Commission White Paper on Modernisation of the Rules Implementing Articles 81 and 82 of the E.C. Treaty'. (1999) *European Law Review*, 653.
Stuyck, J., et al. *Modernisation of European Competition Law*. Antwerp: Intersentia, 2002.
Wesseling, R. *The Modernisation of EC Antitrust Law*. Oxford: Hart, 2000.
Wils, W. *The Modernisation of the Enforcement of Articles 81 and 82 EC: A Legal and Economic Analysis of the Commission's Proposal for a New Council Regulation Replacing Regulation No. 17*. New York: Fordham Corporate Law Institute, 2000.
Horizontal Agreements
Jephcott, M. *Horizontal Agreements and EU Competition Law*. Richmond: Richmond Law & Tax, 2005.

Vertical Agreements
Fine, F.L. *The EC Competition Law on Technology Licensing*. Sweet & Maxwell, 2006.
Goyder, J. *EU Distribution Law*. 4th ed. Oxford: Hart Publishing, 2005.

Hawk, B. 'System Failure: Vertical Restraints and EC Competition Law'. (1995) *Common Market Law Review*, 973.

Hildebrand, D. *Economic Analyses of Vertical Agreements: A Self-Assessment.* International Competition Law Series, 17. The Hague: Kluwer Law International, 2005.

Korah, V. and D. O'Sullivan. *Distribution Agreements under the EC Competition Rules.* Oxford: Hart, 2002.

Lugard, P. Vertical *Restraints under EC Competition Law.* Oxford: Hart Publishing, 2001.

Mendelsohn, M. and S. Rose. *Guide to the EC Block Exemption for Vertical Agreements.* International Competition Law Series, 4. The Hague: Kluwer Law International, 2002.

Turner, J.D.C. *Vertical Agreements and EU Competition Law.* Richmond Law & Tax, 2007.

Wijckmans, F., et al. *Vertical Agreements in EC Competition Law.* Oxford: Oxford University Press, 2006.

Merger Control

Broberg, M.P. *The European Commission's Jurisdiction to Scrutinise Mergers.* 3rd ed. European Monographs, 16. Alphen aan den Rijn: Kluwer Law International, 2006.

Camesasca, P.D. *European Merger Control: Getting the Efficiencies Right.* Antwerpen, 2000.

Cook, J. and C. Kerse. *EC Merger Control.* 4th ed. London: Sweet & Maxwell, 2005.

Drauz, G. and M. Reynolds. *EC Merger Control: A Major Reform in Progress.* Richmond: Richmond Law & Tax, 2003.

Furse, M. *The Law of Merger Control in the EC and the UK.* Oxford: Hart, 2007.

Ilzkovitz, F. and R. Meiklejohn. *European Merger Control: Do We Need an Efficiency Defence?* Cheltenham, UK: Elgar, 2006.

Kekelekis, M. *The EC Merger Control Regulation: Rights of Defence.* International Competition Law Series, vol. 21. Alphen aan den Rijn: Kluwer Law International, 2006.

Levy, N., et al. *European Merger Control Law: A Guide to the Merger Regulation.* Matthew Bender/LexisNexis, 2005.

Lindsay, A. *The EC Merger Regulation: Substantive Issues.* 2nd ed. London: Sweet & Maxwell, 2006.

Navarro Varona, E., et al. *Merger Control in the European Union: Law, Economics and Practice.* 2nd ed. Oxford: Oxford University Press, 2005.

Verloop, P. and V. Landes *Merger Control in Europe: EU, Member States and Accession States.* 4th ed. International Competition Law Series, 11. The Hague: Kluwer Law International, 2003.

Voigt, S. and A. Schmidt. *Making European Merger Policy More Predictable.* Berlin: Springer, 2005.

Joint Ventures
Lindemann, J. 'Joint Ventures and European Competition Law: A Continuing
    Challenge for the Practitioner'. In:P. Lugard et al. (eds). *On the Merits:
    Current Issues in Competition Law and Policy: Liber Amicorum Peter Plom-
    pen.* Antwerpen: Intersentia, 2005.

Essential Facilities Doctrine
Doherty, B. 'Just What Are Essential Facilities?' (2001) CML Rev., 397–436.
Glasl, D. 'Essential Facilities Doctrine in EC Antitrust Law: A Contribution to the
    Current Debate'. In R. Greaves (ed.). *Competition Law.* Aldershot, Ashgate/
    Dartmouth, 2003.
Hatzopoulos, V. 'The EC Essential Facilities Doctrine'. In G. Amato and C.-D.
    Ehlermann (eds). *EC Competition Law: A Critical Assessment.* Oxford: Hart,
    2007.
Stratakis, A. 'Comparative Analysis of the US and EU Approach and Enforcement
    of the Essential Facilities Doctrine'. (2006) *European Competition Law
    Review*, 434–442.
Temple Lang, J. 'The Principle of Essential Facilities in European Community
    Competition Law: The Position since Bronner'. (2000) *Journal of Network
    Industries*, 375–405.

Article 86 (ex 90)
Blum, F. and A. Logue. *State Monopolies under EC Law.* Chichester: Wiley, 1998.
Buendía Sierra, J.-L. *Exclusive Rights and State Monopolies under EC Law:
    Article 86 (formerly Article 90) of the EC Treaty.* Oxford: Oxford University
    Press, 1999.
Edward, D.A.O. and M. Hoskins. 'Article 90: Deregulation and EC Law. Reflec-
    tions Arising from the XVI FIDE Conference'. (1995) *Common Market Law
    Review*, 157
Geradin, D. *The Liberalization of State Monopolies in the European Union and
    Beyond.* European Monographs, 23. The Hague: Kluwer Law International,
    2000.
Heinemann, A. *Grenzen staatlicher Monopole im EG-Vertrag.* Münchener Uni-
    versitätsschriften. Reihe der Juristischen Fakultät, Bd. 116. München: Beck,
    1996.
Prosser, T. *The Limits of Competition Law: Markets and Public Services.* Oxford
    Studies in European Law. Oxford: Oxford University Press, 2005.

Services of General Interest
European Commission. *Green Paper on Services of General Interest.* COM(2003)
    270 of 21 May 2003.
Maillo, J. 'Services of General Interest and EC Competition Law'. In G. Amato and
    C.-D. Ehlermann (eds). *EC Competition Law: A Critical Assessment.* Oxford:
    Hart, 2007.

Telecommunication

Larouche, P. *Competition Law and Regulation in European Telecommunications.* Oxford : Hart, 2000.

Enforcement

Basedow, J. *Private Enforcement of EC Competition Law.* International Competition Law Series, 25. Alphen aan den Rijn: Kluwer Law International, 2007.

Ehlermann, C.-D. and I. Atanasiu. *Effective Private Enforcement of EC Antitrust Law.* European Competition Law Annual, 2001. Oxford: Hart, 2003.

Hesper, R.H.G. 'Op weg naar Europeesrechtelijke aansprakelijkheid voor schade bij schending van Europees kartelrecht'. (1999) *Rechtsgeleerd Magazijn Themis*, 143.

Ortiz Blanco, L. *European Community Competition Procedure.* 2nd ed. Oxford: Oxford University Press, 2006.

Wils, W.P.J. *Principles of European Antitrust Enforcement.* Oxford: Hart, 2005.

Zuber, Z. *Die EG-Kommission als amicus curiae.* Köln, 2001.

State Aid

Biondi, A. and P. Eeckhout. *The Law of State Aid in the European Union.* Oxford: Oxford University Press, 2004.

Dony, M., F. Renard and C. Smits. *Contrôle des aides d'Etat.* 3e éd. Brussels: Éditions de l'Université de Bruxelles, 2007.

D'Sa, R.M. *European Community Law on State Aid.* London: Sweet & Maxwell, 1998.

Hancher, L., et al. *EC State Aids.* 3rd ed. London: Sweet & Maxwell, 2006.

Jaeger, T. *Beihilfen durch Steuern und parafiskalische Abgaben.* Vienna: Neuer Wissenschaflicher Verlag, 2006.

Mégret, J., et al. *Droit communautaire de la concurrence.* 3e éd., entièrement refondue et mise à jour. 2007 (Commentaire: J. Mégret).

Nemitz, P.F. and C.W.A. Timmermans. *The Effective Application of EU State Aid Procedures: The Role of National Law and Practice.* International Competition Law Series, 29. Alphen aan den Rijn: Kluwer Law International, 2007.

Nicolaides, P., et al. *State Aid Policy in the European Community: A Guide for Practitioners.* International Competition Law Series, vol. 16. The Hague: Kluwer Law International, 2005.

Quigley, C. and A. Collins. *European State Aid Law.* 2nd ed. Oxford: Hart Publishing, 2007.

Sánchez Rydelski, M. *The EC State Aid Regime: Distortive Effects of State Aid on Competition and Trade.* London: Cameron May, 2006.

Santa Maria, A., et al. *Competition and State Aid: An Analysis of the EC Practice.* International Competition Law Series, 32. Alphen aan den Rijn: Kluwer Law International, 2007.

Chapter X

Economic, Monetary and Social Policy

F. Amtenbrink, A. Geelhoed and S. Kingston*

1   INTRODUCTION

1.1   THE LINK BETWEEN NEGATIVE AND POSITIVE INTEGRATION

As was seen in Chapter IX, above, competition policy forms a transitional area
between negative and positive integration.[1] On the one hand, it is a necessary
consequence of the liberalization of free movement of goods, persons, services
and capital by the removal of internal frontiers resulting from disparities between
national laws or from the mere existence of different national legal systems. On the
other hand, competition policy, by combating disturbances and distortions of competition, seeks to guarantee the allocative operation of the internal market. All the
aspects of competition policy involve policy choices at the Community level,
which inevitably implies *inter alia* policy integration.

Positive or policy integration is part of the task of the Community expressly
mentioned in Article 2 European Community Treaty (EC) and developed further in
Articles 3 EC and 4 EC. The link between these provisions, and the problems of
interpretation caused by their present drafting, have been discussed in Chapter III above.

---

*   Sections 1–3 F. Amtenbrink, substantially rewritten and revised based on texts by A. Geelhoed;
    Sections 4–6: S. Kingston, substantially rewritten and revised based on text by A. Geelhoed.
1.   These terms were defined in Ch. III, section 2.1.2 *supra*.

P.J.G. Kapteyn, A.M. McDonnell, K.J.M. Mortelmans and C.W.A. Timmermans (eds),
The Law of the European Union and the European Communities, pp. 881–1085.
©2008 Kluwer Law International BV, The Netherlands.

The establishment of a Monetary Union was in the long run inevitable (also from the national standpoint) because the effectiveness of purely national macro-economic and micro-economic steering measures – to the extent that they are not incompatible with the EC Treaty – is in fact lessened as liberalization (or negative integration) progresses. This has been clearly shown in various reports.[2] The completion of the internal market, at the end of 1992, including the liberalization of capital movement, has further accelerated the leakage of national ability to act in the monetary and socio-economic fields.[3] It is true that autonomously taking account of the policy of other Member States can contribute to national policy remaining effective, but the underlying tensions in the European Monetary System (EMS) in late 1992, the summer of 1993 and early 1995, showed that such 'spontaneous policy imitation' has its limits.[4] A more or less far reaching coordination of monetary and economic policies is not merely a legal obligation but an even more pressing economic necessity.[5]

In this chapter the Economic and Monetary Union (EMU) set out in Title VII of Part Three of the EC Treaty occupies centre stage. External economic policy, which encompasses *all* external elements of the internal market and the EMU, is, however, discussed in Chapter XIII.[6]

The White Paper 'Growth, Competitiveness and Employment'[7] adopted by the Commission in December 1993 confirmed again that a separation and even a sharp distinction between economic policy on the one hand and the employment and social policies set out in Titles VIII and IX of Part Three of the EC Treaty on the other, is as impossible at Community level as it is at national level. Indeed, there exist direct interactions between the legal architecture of the labour market and social security, and the growth of employment.

Employment growth, wages formation, income distribution and labour market policies are objects of economic policy as well as of social policy. The interrelations between economic policy, employment policy and social policy, which were somewhat neglected in the Treaty of Maastricht, received special attention in the Treaty of Amsterdam, with the insertion into the EC Treaty of the new Title VIII which is entirely dedicated to the coordination of national employment policies at the Community level. The Community competences in the areas of

---

2. For instance: J. Zijlstra, Politique économique et problèmes de la Concurrence dans la CEE et dans les pays membres de la CEE (CEE études, série concurrence no. 2, Brussels 1966); WRR, The Unfinished European Integration, Report no. 28 (The Hague, 1986), both discussed in Ch. III, *supra*.
3. First through the adoption of Dir. 88/361 (O.J. 1988, L 178/5), now through the terms of Arts. 56–60 EC.
4. See further, section 1.5. *infra*.
5. T. Padoa-Schioppa et al. *Stability and Equity* (Oxford, 1987). It is held there that on the one hand free circulation of products and factors and on the other hand fixed exchange rates and national monetary policies are in the long run mutually incompatible. The events of 1992 and 1993 seem to confirm this thesis.
6. With regard to the external aspects of monetary policy see further, section 3.3.5. *infra*.
7. COM(93)700, Bull. EU Supp. 6/93.

employment and social policy are discussed in sections 4 and 5 of this chapter, below.

Economic and monetary policy integration implies at the very least centralization of monetary policy at Community level, as well as discipline in the financial-economic policy of the Member States. For the less prosperous Member States, this means that they must renounce the 'easy' route to economic growth which consists of a combination of an expansive budgetary policy, an accommodating monetary policy, a relatively high level of inflation and a downward movement of exchange rates.

For the new Member States of the Community, whose gross domestic product (GDP) pro capita is still well beneath the EC average, there occurs here an awkward dilemma. On the one hand, these countries strive to become full members of the EMU as soon as possible, on the other hand they aspire to a rapid economic expansion. As will be highlighted, the strict conditions for the entry to EMU specified in Article 121(1) EC may constitute an obstacle to an expansive economic policy stance.[8] This could provide an argument in favour of conceding to these Member States an ample transitional period to prepare themselves for the special demands of EMU. A certain measure of financial equalization from the more prosperous Member States to cover the less prosperous ones for the improvement of primarily the infrastructure and the investment climate there can contribute to facilitating and shortening the trajectory to full EMU membership. The experience with Spain, Portugal, Greece and Ireland in the 1990s has taught that the contributions of the Cohesion Fund and the other structural funds provided substantial assistance in this respect.[9] Thus, the discussion of economic and social cohesion, the subject of Part Three of the EC Treaty, is also appropriate in the context of this chapter.[10]

1.2   MARKET INTEGRATION AND MONETARY POLICY INTEGRATION

With the achievement of the internal market and a common competition policy, the common market is not yet completed in the sense of a market with all the characteristics of a national market.[11] Within a national market there are no internal monetary borders, unlike the largely completed common market before the final stage of EMU. The existence of diverse national currencies causes considerable

---

8. See section 3.2.5 *infra*.
9. R. Oort, 'Economische en monetaire unie in Europa; het plan-Delors', (1990) SEW, 46–47, argues that a horizontal equalization is strictly speaking not an economic condition for the formation of an EMU. However, the experiences with the Structural Funds and the Cohesion Fund in the 1990s confirmed that capital transfers from the more prosperous to the less prosperous Member, provided that such money is well spent, could lower the barriers to the entry of EMU for the less prosperous Member States.
10. See section 6 *infra*.
11. It should be noted that in the Treaty of Lisbon the term common market is abolished. See also Ch. VIII.

transaction cost losses in intra-community traffic, which will only increase as such traffic intensifies. Moreover, the uncertainties connected to the existence of differences in parities within the common market, form an important obstacle for taking investment decisions and entering into long-term contracts. Further, they may encourage speculative money and capital movements which have no 'real' economic rationale. In addition, the liberalization of money and capital movements in the international market has made it more difficult to maintain the exchange-rate arrangements of the EMS, as the national monetary authorities may no longer impose restrictions on cross-border movements of money and capital.[12] Since the stabilizing power of EMS had diminished, the allocative effect of the common market threatened to become intrinsically fragile. As appeared in the years 1992–1995, exchange-rate movements could seriously disturb competitive relationships within that market. What remained was the temptation for national authorities to have recourse to competitive alignment of exchange rates.

The present state of monetary policy integration within the Community may be sketched as a phase in which for fifteen Member States the monetary unification is completed. Nine Member States are in a transitional phase, which sooner or later, depending on their readiness to satisfy the entry criteria, will lead to full membership in the euro area. Three Member States, the United Kingdom, Denmark and Sweden, decided for the time being not to participate in the final stage of EMU. Their present position is based on the political choice to remain for the time being as outsiders to full monetary integration.[13]

1.3   MARKET INTEGRATION AND ECONOMIC POLICY INTEGRATION

For the economic policy of the Member States, the establishment of a common market has had far-reaching consequences.[14] Various steering measures which act directly, such as national price-regulatory measures and other national interventions which affect or may affect inter-State movement of products and factors, have become unlawful, or to the extent to which they are still permitted they can be circumvented rather easily within the common market. Within a liberalized capital

---

12. See H. Hahn, 'The European Central Bank: Key to European Monetary Union or Target?' (1991) CML Rev., 783–820, in particular 788. See also A. Gamble, 'EMU and European Capital Markets: Towards a Unified Financial Market' (1991) CML Rev., 319–333; T. Padoa-Schioppa et al., op. cit., *supra* note 5; J.-V. Louis, in *Commentaire Mégret*, vol. 6, *Union économique et monétaire, cohésion économique et sociale, politique industrielle et technologie européenne*, 2ème éd. (1995) 7–8.
13. See further section 3.3.4. *infra*.
14. See e.g., WRR, The Unfinished European Integration (The Hague, 1986); A. Geelhoed, 'The Semi-Sovereign Western European State in 1995' (1990), *International Spectator*, 658–664; P. De Grauwe, 'The Autonomy of Economic Policy in a European Monetary Union' (1990), *International Spectator*, 665–668; R. Beetsma and C. Oudshoorn (eds), *Tools for Regional Stabilisation* (The Hague, 1999).

market, a relatively restrictive national monetary policy may actually have an effect contrary to that intended, if an influx of capital is thereby stimulated.

Free movement of products and production factors also results in an increased national vulnerability to external influences. In France, and a number of smaller Member States, such as The Netherlands and Belgium, this was again evident in the period from 1990 to end 1993, when the sharp oscillation in the German economy after German unification initially caused substantial disturbances in the form of higher inflation and higher interest rates than foreseen, and thereafter to stagnation with increasing unemployment and larger budget deficits. In short, the more intensive the process of market integration becomes, the more interdependent the national economies.

The arguments put forward in favour of economic policy integration so far indicate that, on the one hand, the choice for such integration is more or less made by the integration of markets. On the other hand, it is becoming ever more evident that economic policy integration also has added value as such. Market integration leads the national economies associated therein to a certain regional specialization, which is expressed in increased intra-Community trade. This economic interweaving is a positive development as long as the economic growth within the Community does not structurally lag behind that of other major economic regions in the global economy, as has been the case since the beginning of the 1990s. If the Community were to continue to have lower structural growth, this would form a handicap for the national economies which are strongly directed towards the common market, the seriousness of which should not be underestimated.[15] If large Member States, such as France, Germany and Italy, are unable to surmount existing, primarily structural, problems, this puts a damper on the Benelux economies, which are very much focused on the markets of those countries. From this perspective, the Member States have a common interest in the economic performance of the Community remaining favourable when measured by global standards.

General economic policy integration within the Community also has consequences for the Community sectoral policies discussed in Chapter XII below. This relationship became very evident for the Common Agricultural Policy in the problems concerning Monetary Compensatory Amounts (MCAs). When in the early 1970s the exchange parities within the Community fell apart, considerable consequences ensued for prices of agricultural produce expressed in national currencies. MCAs sought to compensate for such movements, although they were logically incompatible with the principle of the unity of the market.[16]

---

15. See Ch. 2 of the White Paper (COM(93)700, Bull. EU Supp. 6/93).
16. But they were accepted by the ECJ as in effect being the lesser of two evils, see Case 5/73, *Balkan Import Export v. Hauptzollamt Berlin Packhof*; Case 9/73, *Schlüter v. Hauptzollamt Lörrach*; Case 10/73, *Rewe-Zentral v. Hauptzollamt Kehl*; Case 4/79, *Providence Agricole de la Champagne*.

Taking a more general view: the more united the objectives of stability and growth are in general economic policy, the less the need to pursue sector-specific policies.

The relationship between economic policy integration and the external policy examined in Chapter XIII is to a large extent determined by the principle of an open market economy as referred to in Article 4 EC. This principle which, is reaffirmed in Article 98 EC, implies that economic policy integration within the Community must respect the preconditions of liberalized global trade to be guaranteed in the context of the WTO. As for the horizontal and flanking policies discussed in Chapter XI, below, it is primarily environment policy which is important for economic policy integration. This applies to the qualifying preconditions for economic growth which flow from environmental policy, as well as to the shaping of the instruments of that policy. Major disparities between the environment instruments of the Member States may lead to complex problems in the coordination of economic policy, as is apparent from the discussions about the introduction of eco-taxes on energy use and on other polluting activities.

1.4   MARKET INTEGRATION AND SOCIAL POLICY INTEGRATION

Although the Member States' social policies show a great divergence, both institutionally and substantively, as a result of deep-rooted social choices and policy traditions, social policy remains very closely related to general economic policy. There is a very sensitive interaction between the development of price levels in general and the development of labour costs: while employment is in the short term determined by economic growth, in the longer term it is the system of wage generation, the functioning of the labour market and the relationship between gross labour costs and labour productivity, which have the biggest impact on employment.

As relative differences in prices and costs have a much quicker and deeper effect on the competitiveness of a national economy within a completed common market, market integration calls for a much more carefully guarded link to be maintained between general economic policy and social policy than hitherto. Indeed, in a completed EMU, the development of relative labour costs might well become the central variable for national economic policy.[17]

The relationship between economic growth, employment and price stability is also playing an increasingly important role at Community level. According to the analysis in the Commission's White Paper *Growth, Competitiveness and Employment* there are convincing causal links between the disappointing development in the Community since the early 1970s and the way in which the social constitution

---

17.   Although the conclusions are diametrically opposed, this argument played a major part for A. Geelhoed, 'Why EMU has Passed the Point of in G. Amato et al. (eds) *Is European Monetary Union Dead?* (Brussels, 1994), 40–47; W. Hankel, 'Maastricht's EMU Is Too Soon', in *ibidem*, 48–60.

has been shaped at national level.[18] Because a high level of inactivity among the labour force is reflected in the level of labour costs of the still active professional population, the competitive position of the Community in the global context is put under pressure.[19]

In the global economic context, new technologies are invented, tested and applied at an ever increasing speed. Relocations of economic activities in function of relative labour costs and labour productivity are taking place on an ever increasing scale. Thus, even labour markets are becoming global markets, although some policymakers and trade unionists may still believe that even within the Community the national labour force can be protected against 'the Polish plumber'. In fact the policy response to the impact of globalization on labour markets should be more labour market flexibility, rather than job protection. In fact, rather than trying to protect jobs, policy should focus on the improvement of knowledge, as well as the competences and skills of the labour force. Modern labour market policies increasingly concentrate on the protection and reinforcement of the earning capacity of the working population in a permanently changing economic environment. Such a better tuning of supply and demand, in a qualitative sense, on the labour markets will contribute to the strengthening of economic growth in the Community. These relationships are central in the so-called Lisbon agenda.[20]

To summarize the argument: If the maintenance and strengthening of the vitality of the European economies is to be one of the central objectives of economic policy integration, also in terms of growth in employment, it is unimaginable not to involve social policy in such integration.

1.5   FORMS OF COORDINATION IN MONETARY, ECONOMIC AND SOCIAL POLICY INTEGRATION

Policy integration in the monetary, economic and social fields is considerably more difficult within the fairly light institutional construction of the Community than in more or less fully grown federal state contexts.[21] Firstly, in classic federations such as the United States and Canada the federal authorities only started to play an active role in the social and economic spheres after the federal system had already established deep roots. As general economic policy is primarily aimed at influencing macro-variables in the national economy, it was also understandable that the pursuit of active general economic policy would primarily fall within the competence of the central, in these cases, the federal authorities. A dominant role for the federal authorities could also be observed in the area of social policy, an area strongly influenced by the principle of substantive equality, which laid a relatively large claim on collective expenditure. Thus in most federations the

---

18. Ch. III of the White Paper (COM(93)700, Bull. EU Supp. 6/93).
19. The unemployment involves costs which have to be financed.
20. See Bull. EU 3-2000, 7–16.
21. WRR, op. cit., *supra* part 2, Part 3.

gradual establishment of a modern social constitution has resulted in a strengthening of the position of the federal authorities *vis-à-vis* the states.[22] This has not
occurred without friction, and in some federations, reactions are already visible
against federal authorities which are perceived as being too dominant. In this
respect it could be argued that the rejection of the Treaty establishing a Constitution for Europe in spring 2005 in the French and Dutch referenda (and that of the
Lisbon Treaty in the Irish referendum?) betrays an analogous sentiment.

In the Community, policy integration has to take place within a much lighter
and significantly less well-rooted institutional order, which is not as such uncontroversial in some Member States. Moreover, this policy integration involves
policy areas which are the subject of much constitutional discussion in all Member
States. Unlike in the federal state contexts, policy integration in the economic and
employment fields within the Community have up until now been primarily a
question of *coordination* of the Member States' policies, even in a completed
EMU. This is confirmed in so many words in Articles 4 and 99 EC. Although
Articles 2 and 3 EC are silent as to this matter, social policy also involves only
coordination and, to a much lesser extent, harmonization of the Member States'
policies, as appears from Articles 136–140 EC. This is understandable, as the most
important instruments in this field, as in the field of economic policy, are for the
time being in national hands. For monetary policy in an EMU, coordination of
national powers is insufficient. In a completed monetary union with irrevocably
fixed exchange rates, unity of monetary policy will be necessary. Thus it cannot be
determined other than at Community level.[23] Simply ascertaining that policy integration primarily implies coordination of national policies in the policy areas
discussed here says nothing as to the nature and intensity of such coordination.
Thus it is useful to develop the concept of coordination *in abstracto* somewhat
further.[24]

The concept of coordination set out in Article 4(1) EC means that primary
public competence to influence the development of their national economies
remains with the Member States. Conferring coordinating competence on the
Community means that the Member States will or must take account of coordinating intervention by the central level concerned when they exercise their primary
competences. The words 'will or must take account of' hide the fact that the degree
of compulsion of Community intervention may vary enormously, from pure prognoses to obliging the Member States to comply with the policy prescribed.

---

22. See T. Conlon, *New Federalism: Intergovernmental Reform from Nixon to Reagan* (Washing-
    ton, DC, 1988), 31–91 and M. Bullinger, 'Die Zuständigheit der Länder zur Gesetzgebung'
    (1970), *Die Öffentliche Verwaltung*, 761–773 and 785–797. The shift in competence between
    federal and state authorities lay behind this: thus the principle of subsidiarity played no role in
    this evolution, whether as a principle of policy or as a legal principle. See A. Geelhoed, Het
    subsidiariteitsbeginsel: een communautair principe? (1991) SEW, 431.
23. The Werner Committee Report (O.J. 1970, C 136/1) already came to this conclusion, which was
    moreover confirmed by the conclusions of the Delors Report (Report on the Economic and
    Monetary Union in the European Communities, Brussels, Luxembourg, 1989).
24. See already the 2nd English edition of this work edited by L.W. Gormley, 588–600.

The concept of *intervention* embraces measures which are short-term as well as those which are medium or long-term or even those which are in principle permanent in nature. The *central level concerned* qualifies the substantive scope of the relevant Community competence, which may vary from the whole field affected by general economic policy to specific functionally or sectorally defined parts of that policy.

The degree of compulsion of the broad economic policy guidelines (BEPG) mentioned in Article 99(2) EC is considerably lighter than the criteria for budgetary discipline set out in Article 104(2) EC. The broad guidelines are determined annually, whereas the criteria for budgetary discipline are more or less permanent.[25] On the other hand, the broad guidelines may encompass the entire socio-economic policy of the Member States, whereas the budgetary discipline criteria only relate to two aspects of national budgetary policy: the ratio of the planned or actual government deficit to GDP and the ratio of government debt to GDP.

In the first and second edition of this work, the coordination procedures were characterized on the basis of Zijlstra's planning typology, to which reference has been made in particular in section 4.5.5. of Chapter III of this edition, above. Indeed, there is an unmistakable analogy between influence by the public authorities ('planning') of the conduct of market participants, and the influence which a public authority which is superior in the public law hierarchy has over decision-making of lower-level authorities. Forms of such a vertical coordinating influence are to be found in all pre-federal and federal constitutional structures. They always presuppose that the coordination authority, in this case the Community, has the competence to coordinate and that the primary competence lays with the units, in this case the Member States, whose exercise of competence is to be coordinated. As in the case of 'planning' coordinating intervention may be classified according to the degree to which it has binding force, its 'intensity', so that the lightest form is making prognoses available and the heaviest form the imposition of precisely quantified obligatory tasks, compliance with which the coordinating authority may compel.[26]

Between the lightest form of prognoses and the heaviest form of precisely defined binding tasks these various other forms which can be classified. In ascending order (or binding force or intensity) these are: information; compulsory consultation procedures; recommendations; indicative tasks; conditional loans and subsidies; binding provisions. Unlike in the first and second editions, it is no longer considered appropriate to draw the analogy with Zijlstra's planning typology so far that the Community's coordinating intervention is fitted into his planning types, as the differences in principle between influencing conduct internally between authorities (coordination) and influencing conduct externally of private operators outside the sphere of authorities (planning) are too great. Thus, the completed form

---

25. These criteria have been tightened by the Stability and Growth Pact. See further, section 3.2 4. *infra.*
26. See further P. VerLoren van Themaat, *The Changing Structure of Internal Economic Law* (The Hague, 1981) 157–184.

of the heaviest type of coordination, applied over the whole breadth of the public sector, establishes an extremely centralized unit state, the component parts of which are little more than de-concentrated parts of the central authority. Before public powers were devolved to the Scottish and Welsh parliaments, the United Kingdom, which combined a strongly centralized administration with, by continental standards, an extensive and strongly liberalized market sector, demonstrated that a unitary state in the constitutional sense does not have to lead to a centrally led economy in the economic-law sense. The reverse is not the case. A centrally led economy will also in the constitutional aspect *de facto* lead to the centralization of public powers. The more an economic order leads to internal policy coordination, the more it will require centralization in the constitutional aspect. This is why at Community level there is a connection between the fairly restricted and light coordinating competence of the Community and the choice in Article 4 EC for an economic order 'conducted in accordance with the principle of an open market economy with free competition'.

For an analysis of the coordination problems in the Community, it is sensible also to draw a distinction according to the degree to which the constitutional units, whose policy is to be coordinated, are involved in the decision-making concerned. The coordinating decision-making may be the result of autonomous evaluation by the superior authority, producing a specification to which the inferior authority must conform (vertical subordinating coordination). Coordinating decision-making may also be the result of an evaluation involving consultation between the coordinating authority and the coordinee(s). The lower authorities then comply with coordinating decisions in which they themselves are involved (vertical cooperative coordination). Finally, coordinating decision-making may be the result of – voluntary – consultation between authorities at the same level. This form of coordination often displays (quasi-)contractual traits, and sometimes it results from what has been described above as spontaneous policy imitation.[27]

The first form of coordination – vertical subordinating – primarily occurs in fully grown federal systems, in which the exercise of competence at federal level and at state level is clearly delimited. It makes high demand of the legitimacy of decision-making at federal level as coordinating intervention from the federal level will not infrequently clash with the policy priorities chosen at state level. In the Community, this form of coordination is rare. An example of such a form is to be found in the so-called excessive deficit procedure of Article 104 EC. In the application of Article 104(11) EC, dealing with measures or sanctions relating to deficit reduction, the Member State concerned has no vote.[28]

The second form of coordination – vertical cooperative – is the most frequently encountered in the Community structure. This is already contained in the

---

27. See section 1.1. *supra*, and F. Scharf, 'The Joint-Decision Trap: Lessons from German Federation and European Integration' (1988), *Public Administration*, 239–278; *idem: Governing in Europe, Effective and Democratic* (Oxford, 1999). In his book, Scharf expands on the earlier article, taking into account the experiences with the coordination procedures of Arts. 99 and 104 EC.
28. See further, section 3.2.4. *infra*.

institutional shape of decision-making, which generally guarantees an intensive involvement of (representatives) of Member States, both in the preparatory phase and in the decision phase. Examples of this can be seen in the procedure for the establishment of the broad economic guidelines provided for in Article 99(2) EC, and for the annual guidelines which the Member States are to take into account in their employment policies in accordance with Article 128(2) EC.

The third form of coordination – spontaneous and (quasi-) contractual between the Member States – is not to be found in the EC Treaty in so many words. Nevertheless, it does occur on a large scale in policy practice. An example was the Dutch decision to maintain the Guilder's margin of fluctuation against the Deutschmark in the ERM at 2.25% when the margins against other currencies were set at 15% in the summer of 1993. For this 'spontaneous' horizontal coordination, arrangements were made between the German and the Dutch monetary authorities themselves.

In the recent policy practice in the coordination of economic policies under Article 99 EC, a new and interesting coordination form has been developed.[29] This form is a direct consequence of the decisions at the European Council meetings of Cardiff (June 1998) and Lisbon (March 2000). On those occasions, Member States undertook to provide at periodic intervals information on the progress they made in improving the structure of their economies. This information is to be systematically examined by the Commission. The policy practices of Member States – and the Commission's assessment of these – are subsequently published together with the global guidelines provided for in Article 99(2) EC. This procedure combines the characteristics of a light vertical coordination (information) with those of a light horizontal coordination. Member States may mutually adopt their 'best practices' – policy imitation – and exert 'peer pressure' on each other. In the description in sections 3, 4, 5 and 6, below, of economic and social policy integration in the Community particular attention will be paid to the characterization of the forms of cooperation, according to intensity, scope, permanence and type of decision-making and the particular problems which arise from them.

2   A BRIEF HISTORY OF EMU[30]

2.1   THE PROVISIONS OF THE ORIGINAL EEC TREATY

The coordination of economic and monetary policy was only summarily treated in the original European Economic Community (EEC) Treaty.[31] Among the policy

---

29. See also F. Amtenbrink and J. de Haan, 'Economic Governance in the European Union – Fiscal policy discipline versus flexibility' (2003), CML Rev, 1075–1106, who offer an alternative typology in the context of economic coordination by referring to open and closed methods of coordination.

30. See generally, D. Gros and N. Thygesen, *European Monetary Integration* (London, 1992), 3–56.

31. See the 2nd English edition of this work edited by L.W. Gormley, 598–600, 603–608 and 616–625, and literature cited there. It is remarkable that such a meagre and incomplete legal basis for economic and monetary policy integration should have led to so many thorough legal analyses.

provisions was the now repealed Article 6 EEC, which laid down in general terms an obligation on the Member States to 'coordinate their respective economic policies to the extent necessary to attain the objectives of the Treaty'. This declaration of principle was developed further in Articles 103–105 and 107–109 EEC.

The first indent of Article 145 EEC endowed the Council with responsibility to 'ensure coordination of general economic policies of the Member States'. As far as policy practice is concerned, Article 103 EEC appeared to be the most important provision. Although it was primarily meant for the coordination of short-term economic policy (conjunctural policy), it was used as the legal basis for the secondary legislation which in the 1970s was meant to build the foundations for the first steps toward an EMU. Article 103(4) EEC acquired a separate legal significance as the legal basis for Community action in case of problems in the supply of certain products, particularly during the first oil crisis in 1973. Article 104 EEC was primarily declaratory in nature: it set out the general objectives of economic policy which the Member States had to follow as members of the EEC. Article 105 EEC primarily dealt with the procedural aspects of the coordination of economic and monetary policy.

Article 107 EEC dealt with exchange-rate policy of the Member States, which was a matter of common concern. It implied that exchange-rate policy was not to be used in order to create artificial competitive advantages in the common market. The importance of these provisions decrease steadily after the final implosion in 1973 of the Bretton Woods system of fixed exchange rates. Articles 108 and 109 EEC provided for assistance and safeguard procedures respectively, for Member States faced with serious balance of payments difficulties from which – possibly – adaptation of their exchange rates could result. Since the end of the 1960s, the practical importance of these provisions too gradually diminished.[32]

The Single European Act inserted Article 102a EEC into the Treaty. The most important legal significance of that provision was that Article 102a(2) EEC expressly stated that insofar as further development in the field of economic and monetary policy (such as monetary cooperation between the Member States towards a monetary union) necessitated institutional changes, amendment of the Treaty would be required.

2.2   THE WERNER REPORT: THE FIRST ATTEMPT TO FORM AN EMU

As early as 1962, in its memorandum on the working programme of the Community during the second stage of the transitional period, the Commission had argued

---

The incompleteness of the European integration process in an economic policy sense, resulting from the fact that the rules in the then EEC Treaty demonstrated *lacunae*, clearly formed a challenge in this respect.

32. This does not diminish the great legal interest of these provisions, as they implied a considerable far-reaching limitation of national powers concerning exchange-rate policy and related policies. See in this context Joined Cases 6 & 11/69, *Commission v. France*.

that the customs union was bound to lead to an EMU if achievements so far attained were not to be jeopardized. In 1968 the Commission frankly propagated monetary unification, which in 1969 led to the so-called Barre Memorandum. After the Summit in December 1969 at The Hague had given the first impulse for this, the Council on 6 March 1970 at last decided to set up a special working group, which was to draw up a report. In this report, by reference to the various proposals, the fundamental options for a realization in stages of the EMU were to be laid down. This was the work of the so-called Werner Committee, which presented its final report on 8 October 1970.[33] Consultation of this report shows that the rationale for economic, monetary and social policy integration leading to an EMU, as summarized in sections 1.2 to 1.4 above, has essentially remained the same since that the 1970s: market integration presupposes a necessary complement to policy integration.

Based on a Commission proposal, on 22 March 1971 the corresponding resolution of the Governments of Member States was adopted.[34] According to this resolution the EMU was to take the shape of a system in which 'the principal decisions concerning economic policy will be taken at Community level, and that the powers required for this are therefore transferred from the national to the Community level. This process may result in the adoption of a single monetary unit, thus ensuring its irrevocability'. These principles were to be applied in the following fields: internal monetary and credit policy; monetary policy with regard to the rest of the world; policy with respect to the unified capital market and the movement of capital with third countries; budgetary and taxation policy in the context of policy directed at stability and growth and, finally, structural and regional policy.

Following the suggestions made in the Werner Report, the resolution foresaw the realization of EMU in subsequent stages, whereby it was expressly recognized that some of the necessary measures would require an amendment of the EEC Treaty. For the first, three-year stage the resolution itself provided for a number of measures, in particular linked to a strengthening of the coordination of short-term economic policy measures, the promotion of the free movement of capital and the coordination of the monetary and credit policies of the Member States. Moreover the Council and, where necessary, the representatives of the Member States at the end of the resolution undertook to lay down before the end of the first stage, on a proposal from the Commission, the measures which after the transition to the second stage were to lead to the full realization of an EMU, even as far as this required amendments of the Treaty.

---

33. Report to the Council and Commission on the Realisation by Stages of EMU in the Community, see note 23 *supra*. The members included, besides its president, the then Prime Minister and Minister of Finance of Luxembourg, the presidents of the Monetary Committee, the Committee of Governors of the Central Banks, the Committee for Medium-Term Economic Policy, the Committee on Short-Term Economic Policy and the Budgetary Policy Committee, as well as a representative of the Commission.
34. O.J. 1971, C 28/1. (O.J. English Spec. Ed. 2nd Series, IX, 40).

The period of euphoria about the importance of the steps that had been taken was unfortunately short-lived. In May 1971 the German Government was compelled by the growing flow of dollars to allow the exchange rate of the German mark to fluctuate freely instead of narrowing the reciprocal fluctuation margins, as had been agreed upon in March of that year. This was the forerunner of further unrest in the international monetary system which in 1973 led to the final implosion of the Bretton Woods exchange-rate system.

The first oil crisis at the end of 1973 introduced the end of the almost uninterrupted period of growth which the Community had enjoyed since 1958. Each national government attempted to limit as much as possible the damage caused by the threatening combination of inflation, stagnating economic growth and unemployment. In these efforts the absence of exchange-rate discipline was certainly not found to be a hindrance, as a lack of internal economic and monetary discipline could be as it were automatically corrected by an amendment of the now floating exchange-rate parities. These disturbances at global level form an important explanation for the fact that three years into the first stage of the envisaged EMU, the Council had made only minimal progress towards meeting the obligations which it had undertaken in its resolution of 22 March 1971.

Due to the combination of a turbulent economic and political climate at global level and a not well-considered approach to deepening economic and monetary integration, the next step by the Council in February and March 1974 was decidedly small. The most important measures were Decision 74/120[35] on the attainment of a high degree of convergence of economic policies and Directive 74/121[36] on stability, fall growth and employment in the Community. The practical significance of these instruments for the policy practice of the Member States remained limited. The convergence decisions based on the Decision 74/120 were never factors of any significance in national macro-economic decision-making. In the monetary field the Council adopted two decisions on 22 March 1971, one concerning strengthening cooperation between central banks[37] and one the creating of a procedure for the grant of medium-term financial assistance.[38]

2.3   THE EUROPEAN MONETARY SYSTEM: A USEFUL INTERLUDE

After the monetary turmoil in the second half of 1971, agreement was reached on 18 December 1971 by the Ministers of the 'Group of Ten' on new exchange rates with simultaneous widening of the fluctuation margins to 2.25% in both directions.

---

35. O.J. 1974, L 63/16, amended by Dec. 75/787 (O.J. 1975, L 330/52), supplemented by Dec. 79/
      136 (O.J. 1979, L 305/8) and repealed by Dec. 90/141 (O.J. 1990, L 78/23) on the attainment of
      progressive convergence of economic policies and performance in stage one of EMU.
36. O.J. 1974, L 63/19, also repealed by Dec. 90/141, *ibidem*.
37. Dec. 71/142, O.J. 1971, L 73/14.
38. Dec. 71/143, O.J. 1971, L 73/15, revised on several occasions and finally replaced by Reg. 1969/
      88 (O.J. 1988, L 178/1) establishing a single medium-term facility for financial assistance.

For a short while, progress towards monetary union seemed possible again. On 21 March 1972, acting on proposals from the Commission, the Council adopted a new resolution on EMU.[39] This resolution strengthened the one of 22 March 1971 on the point of coordination of the economic policies of Member States, by providing for a coordination group at top level, in which the Commission was also represented.[40] This group existed somewhat vaguely for a number of years, being quickly eclipsed by the Economic Policy Committee established by Decision 74/122,[41] which is still in existence. Furthermore, the Commission was invited to propose at the earliest possible date a binding directive for promoting stability, growth, and full employment in the Community.[42]

With regard to exchange rates, agreement was again reached on a gradual reduction of the currency fluctuations between Member States, the final aim being the abolition of any fluctuation, although fluctuations *vis-à-vis* the external world only had to respect the wider fluctuation margins permitted by the International Monetary Fund (IMF), as part of the Bretton Woods exchange-rate system. The Committee of Governors of the Central Banks (Committee of Governors)[43] had to submit before 1 July 1972 a proposal on the organization, functions and statue of a European Monetary Cooperation Fund (EMCF) which was to form a prelude to a European central banking system; although the Council was due to decide on this proposal by the end of 1972, the relevant measure, Regulation 907/73, was in fact adopted only on 3 April 1973.[44]

The EMCF was set up in order to facilitate the operation of the exchange-rate arrangements set out in the Basle Agreement and to contribute to the progressive establishment of an EMU as foreseen in the Werner Plan. In the end, the Werner Plan never got past the initial first stage. While the Member States expressed their political desire to achieve EMU, it had to be finally acknowledged that economic realities made any further development impossible.[45]

However new initiatives were taken. In March 1979 the European Monetary System (EMS) with at its centre the European Exchange Rate Mechanism (ERM I) was established.[46] All Member States, except the United Kingdom, participated in

---

39. O.J. 1972, C 38/3 (O.J. English Spec. Ed, 2nd series IX, 65).
40. This coordination group was maintained in addition to the Economic Policy Committee set up by Dec. 74/122 (O.J. 1974, L 63/21).
41. Loc. cit. (replacing earlier committees). The Committee now closely works together with the Economic and Financial Committee, established by Dec. 98/743 (O.J. 1998, L 358/109).
42. This led to Dir. 74/121 (see note 36, *supra*).
43. Established by Dec. 64/300/EEC (O.J. 1964, No. 77, 1206/64), later amended by Dec. 90/300 (O.J. 1990, L 78/25). This Committee ceased to exist at the start of the second stage of EMU on 1 Jan. 1994 (see Art. 117(1) EC in conjunction with 116(1) EC).
44. O.J. 1973, L 89/2.
45. See D. Gros and N. Thygesen, op. cit. *supra* note 30, at 20, with reference to the Majolin Report of March 1975.
46. See European Council Resolution of 5 Dec. 1978, Bull. EC 7/8–1978, on the establishment of the European Monetary System and related matters; European Council Resolution of 12/13 Mar. 1979, Bull. EC 7–1979; Agreement between the central banks of the Member States of the EEC of 13 Mar. 1979 laying down the operational procedures for the European Monetary

a differently run, partially more flexible and partially more far-reaching exchange rate and intervention system set up under the EMS-Resolution.[47] Based on a central rate, the exchange rates of the participating currencies of the Member States were kept within agreed-upon fluctuation margins. As part of the ERM, participating national central banks (NCBs) became obliged to intervene on behalf of currencies which reached the 'ceiling' or 'floor' rate. The EMCF provided borrowing facilities.[48] Despite certain legal and substantive weaknesses, the system worked relatively satisfactorily. With its grid of bilateral central rates and intervention obligations for the central banks whenever the actual exchange rates diverged more than 2.25% (for some participants 6%) from the central rate, the system clearly contributed to a relatively large degree of stability of exchange rates within the Community, certainly when compared to the fluctuating exchanger rates of the Bretton Woods system. Intervention credits in the form of very short-term facilities, short-term monetary support and the medium-term financial assistance mentioned certainly played a part. However, more important than that, the mechanism was proof of the willingness of the Member States to actively use the intervention mechanism whenever a particular currency came under pressure.

A system of stable but adjustable exchange rates as provided in the EMS cannot, however, avoid internal realignments of the central rates if inflation movements in the participating Member States diverge. In this context, the convergence in real economic policy which had occurred in the Community since 1982 undoubtedly contributed to the rather positive results of the EMS.[49]

2.4   FROM THE SINGLE EUROPEAN ACT TO THE TREATY OF MAASTRICHT
             AND EMU

The Single European Act 1986 recognized the goal of EMU in its preamble and explicitly acknowledged the existence of the EMS and the European currency unit (ECU). At the same time, this first major revision of the EC Treaty did not result in a substantial broadening of the Community competences. One positive development was that, for the first time, the aim of a close cooperation of the Member States on economic and monetary policy matters was recognized in primary Community law.[50] Moreover, with the entering into force of the SEA, after a long

---

System; Council Reg. 3180/78 of 18 Dec. 1978, O.J. 1978, L 379/1, changing the value of the unit of account used by the EMCF, as amended. Council Reg. 3181/78 of 18 Dec. 1978, O.J. 1978, L 379/2, relating to the European Monetary System. The intention had been to introduce it on 1 Jan. 1979, but its introduction was delayed largely due to French attempts to reform the system of MCAs.

47.   See also J.V. Louis, 'Het Europese Monetaire Stelsel' (1979), SEW, 441–458, and P. De Grauwe, *The EMS during 1979–1984* (Leuven, 1985).
48.   On the crisis of the ERM in 1992/93 see e.g., F. Ozkan and A. Sutherland, 'A Model of the ERM Crisis', CERP discussion paper No. 879 (1994).
49.   In the same sense, H. Hahn (1991), op. cit. *supra* note 12, at 786.
50.   Art. 102a (1) EEC.

period of little progress, the liberalization of capital movements within the Community was finally readdressed. Liberalization of capital movements has major consequences for national policy options in the monetary field, and potentially also for the working of the EMS. It was thus no coincidence that during the decision-making on the liberalization of capital movements, the desirability of a fully fledged EMU again became a live issue.[51] The basis of the negotiations on the EMU title of what became the Treaty of Maastricht was the report on EMU in the Community by the Delors Committee.[52] This committee, which had been set up in June 1988 by the European Council meeting at Hannover,[53] presented its report in April 1989, sketching out the main aspects of EMU. They are reflected in Title VII of Part Three of the EC Treaty.

In the negations leading to the present regime, four aspects played an important part:

(1) The German desire that at Community level the form, autonomy and mission of the central monetary authority should as far as possible mirror that of the Deutsche Bundesbank in the German economic legal order.

(2) The fact that in view of the geographic inequalities in economic development the fairly ambitious timetable for full monetary union might prove too short for a number of Member States.

(3) The desire to express the practical connection between the budgetary policy of the Member States and the objective of price stability, as the main objective of monetary policy at Community level, in binding obligations for the national budgetary authorities.

(4) The British and later the Danish reticence about the formation of a monetary union as such, which found expression in separate national derogations for both countries in the transition to the final stage of EMU.[54]

The political negotiations on EMU were accelerated by the collapse of the Eastern bloc, at which stage France agreed to German reunification in exchange for the latter's consent to the establishment of EMU.[55]

Both the European Council of Madrid 1989, as well as the drafters of the Treaty of Maastricht adopted the proposal set out in the Delors Report, rooted in the Werner Report, for the introduction of a European EMU in three subsequent phases or stages. In doing so, first of all it was recognized that additional steps were required to improve the convergence of the economies of the Member States, as well as the working of the internal market, before a single currency area could become a reality. Moreover, it was acknowledged that the introduction of the legal

---

51. See J. Cloos, G. Reinesch, D. Vignes, J. Weyland, *Le Traité de Maastricht* (Brussels, 1993), 39–41.

52. See note 23, *supra*.

53. *Bull.* EC 6–1988, point 3.4.1.

54. See J. Cloos et al. (1993), op. cit., *supra* note 51, 96–101. R. Corbett, *Treaty of Maastricht: From Conception to Ratification: A Comprehensive Reference Guide* (Harlow, 1993) provides also a thorough analysis of the genesis of the Treaty of Maastricht.

55. See J. Gillingham, *European Integration, 1950–2003 Superstate or New Market Economy* (Cambridge, 2004), 274–276.

institutional framework and the practical preparations for the introduction of a single currency would need time.

The first stage of EMU, which commenced on 1 July 1990, did not require the amendment of primary Community law, as it was geared towards the completion of the internal market and in particular the abolishing of all existing measures restricting capital movements and payments. Moreover, greater economic and monetary policy coordination based on the legal framework existing at the time was envisaged. Finally, the necessary preparations had to be made for the introduction of the legal framework for EMU. This was achieved by means of the Intergovernmental Conference which led to the signing and subsequent ratification of the Treaty on European Union (Treaty of Maastricht) which first and foremost introduced today's Title VII on EMU into the EC Treaty, including the provisions on the legal and economic conditions for joining the euro area and the institutional framework necessary for the conduct of a single monetary policy.[56] The Treaty of Maastricht gave legal effect to the approach chosen in the Delors Report of a full EMU in stages by effectively considering all Member States to be in stage two and thus in the antechamber to the third and final stage of EMU.[57]

Stage two of EMU commenced on 1 January 1994 as foreseen by Article 116(1) EC. Initially, the main purpose of this stage was twofold. Firstly, the necessary organs and structures, for the establishment of a single currency area had to be actually set up, including the necessary secondary Community law governing the technical aspects of the transition to stage three. Moreover, already in this stage to a large extent the strict budgetary rules and a system of coordination of the Member States' economies applied in order to ensure that the Member States would fulfil the legal and economic criteria in time for qualifying for the third and final stage of EMU within the rather strict timeframe foreseen in Article 121(3) and (4) EC.[58]

In accordance with Article 117 EC, at the start of the second stage the European Monetary Institute (EMI) was established, directed and managed by a Council, consisting of a President and the Governors of the NCBs.[59] The EMI took over the functions of the Committee of Governors and of the EMCF, both of which where dissolved at that time.[60] Its main task may be summarized as coordinating the Member State's monetary policies and, moreover, the preparatory work necessary for the establishment of the European System of Central Banks (ESCB) and the European Central Bank (ECB).[61] The latter included in particular

---

56. Signed on 7 Feb. 1992 (O.J. 1992, C 191), the Treaty entered into force on 1 Nov. 1993. Much of the groundwork was laid in a report by the Committee of Governors of the Central Banks of the Member States on a draft status and a draft Treaty on Economic and Monetary Union.
57. For more details see section 3.2.5, *infra*.
58. For details, see section 3.2.4 and 3.2.5, *infra*.
59. The EMI had legal personality. See Protocol on the Statute of the European Monetary Institute annexed to the Treaty of Maastricht (Statute EMI). The first president of the EMI was Alexandre Lamfalussy, followed by Willem Duisenberg.
60. Art. 117(2), 3rd indent EC; Art. 1(3) Statute EMI.
61. F. Amtenbrink, *The Democratic Accountability of Central Banks. A comparative study of the European Central Bank* (Oxford and Portland, Oregon, 1999), 118.

the development of the necessary instruments, procedures and strategies for stage three of EMU.[62]

The decision by the Council in the composition of the Heads of State and Government in May 1998 on the first group of Member States to fulfil the convergence criteria and the subsequent decision on the irrevocable fixing of the exchange rates of the currencies of these countries as of 1 January 1999 marked the start of stage three of EMU.[63] Already on 1 June 1998 the newly established ECB had become operational, taking over all remaining tasks from the EMI.[64] Moreover, in accordance with Article 114(2) EC the Economic and Financial Committee was set up which took over the tasks of the Monetary Committee which had been established at start of stage two in order to promote the coordination of the (economic) policies of the Member States.[65]

Evaluating the history of economic and monetary cooperation prior to the Treaty of Maastricht, it can be observed that, apart from the political will for such a move, efforts to achieve an EMU foundered on the absence of a sufficiently well-anchored basis in the EEC Treaty for monetary union which could go further than the level of mere cooperation between the Member States. Thus Regulation 907/73 establishing the EMCF[66] could not be much more than a framework for cooperation between the monetary authorities of the Member States, and the Fund as such largely remained a theoretical construction.[67] The same is true for EMS itself. Since neither Article 103 EEC nor Article 107 EEC vested powers in the Community to adopt binding measures concerning exchange rates and exchange-rate stability, the EMS-Resolution of December 1978, which required not merely consultation but also mutual agreement about the adjustment of central rates, could not be translated into a legally binding instrument.

It has been submitted above that the instruments for the coordination of general economic policy in theory afforded sufficient possibilities for the achievement of the necessary policy integration. Of particular importance appeared to be the power of the Council, set out in Article 103(2) and (3) EEC, to adopt by qualified majority the directives needed to give effect to appropriate measures unanimously agreed upon, in order to oblige Member States to comply with those measures. It has already been noted, though, that the significance in reality of short-term economic policy or macro-economic steering measures lagged far behind the legal possibilities. This was confirmed by policy practice in the 1970s and 1980s.

---

62. Generally on the tasks of the EMI, *Role and Functions of the European Monetary Institute*, Feb. 1996; U. Häde, 'Das Europäische Währungsinstitut und die Kommission' (1994), EuZW, 685–687.
63. On the decision-making leading towards the establishment of stage three of EMU and the introduction of the euro see section 3.2.5, *infra*.
64. Art. 123 EC. See also section 3.3.2, *infra*.
65. Art. 114(1) EC. With regard to the role of the Economic and Financial Committee in economic coordination see 3.2.4, *infra*.
66. Reg. 907/73 of the Council of 3 Apr. 1973 establishing a EMCF (O.J. 1973, L 89/2).
67. See D. Gros and N. Thygesen, op. cit. *supra* note 30, 21–22.

Since the beginning of the 1970s the arsenal of financial instruments at the Community's disposal has considerably enlarged, both in scope and means. The most important instruments for the coordination of general economic policy have been the so-called machinery for medium-term financial assistance[68] and financial facilities: a system of loans for assistance in the event of balance of payments difficulties.[69] It is true that policy coordination may be attached to the use of such instruments, and that they have indeed been used to a certain extent, but the importance of this instrument must not be overestimated. First, it can only be used selectively, i.e., primarily for the economically weaker Member States. As the economic policy of the stronger Member States is at the end of the day decisive for the economic development of the Community as a whole, the instrument does not appear very important at the Community level. Secondly, the scale of the single facility of the relevant macro-variables which have to be influenced is scarcely impressive. Thirdly, it appears politically not to be a simple matter to compel compliance with the conditions attached, if the Member State concerned fails to comply. Here, too, the practical results of vertical policy-coordination lag behind the theoretical legal possibilities. The cooperative slant of the decision-making on the use of the single facility, and the obstacles in reality within the Community's political and institutional context facing compulsion, where necessary, of compliance with the conditions attached to loans, leads to particular caution in linking policy instrumental conclusions to legal powers of action. In this regard, the history so far of economic and monetary policy integration presents a cautionary example. The provisions on EMU introduced by the Treaty of Maastricht into the EC Treaty must thus also be interpreted in the light of the disappointing experiences in the past.

3   ECONOMIC AND MONETARY UNION[70]

3.1   EMU as Structured by the Treaty of Maastricht

The EMU as established by the amendments to the EC Treaty resulting from the Treaty of Maastricht may be characterized as follows.

---

68. Originally set up by Dec. 71/143 (see note 38, *supra*), amended by Dec. 78/1041 (O.J. 1978, L 53/1), after the completion of EMU by Reg. 332/2002 (O.J. 2002, L 53/1).
69. Reg. 397/75 (O.J. 1975, L 46/1), replaced by Reg. 682/81 (O.J. 1981, L 73/1), amended by Reg. 131/85 (O.J. 1985, L 118/59) replaced by Reg. 1969/88 (O.J. 1988, L 178/1), establishing a single facility. After the completion of EMU this mechanism had to be replaced by an arrangement between the monetary union and the not yet participating Member States. This arrangement is provided for by Reg. 332/2002 (O.J. 2002, L 53/1).
70. The legal literature on EMU and the negotiations leading to the Treaty of Maastricht is voluminous. In the list of relevant literature annexed to this chapter a selection has been made. The economic literature is perhaps even more voluminous. Interesting contributions are to be found in K. Gretschmann (ed.), *Economic and Monetary Union, Implications for National Policy Makers* (Dordrecht, 1993) and P. De Grauwe, *The Economics of Monetary Union*, 2nd ed. (Oxford, 1994).

The *economic union* as defined by the EC Treaty embraces a fully achieved common market with free movement of products (goods and services) and factors of production (persons and capital) and free and undistorted competition. Within that framework, the main features of economic policies are coordinated and more or less stringent rules apply in respect of the budgetary policies of Member States. Within the economic union as so described, Community and national policies may be implemented, for example for the strengthening of the Community's economic structure and competitive position, and to promote a balanced regional development. Only the global economic policy coordination and the binding rules concerning the budgetary policy of the Member States are included in the EMU provisions of the EC Treaty.[71] But that certainly does not mean that the other objectives mentioned in Article 2 EC could not play a role.[72] On the contrary, Articles 4 and 98 EC expressly refer to Article 2 EC, but the Treaty provides for the achievement of those other objectives by other means than those specified in the economic policy chapter.

The *monetary union* can be described as a single currency area within, which monetary policy is centrally determined with the objective of the maintenance of price stability, in order to contribute to the achievement of the objectives set out in Article 2 EC. Monetary union must in principle satisfy three conditions:

(1) complete and irreversible convertibility of currencies;
(2) complete liberalization of capital market transactions and complete integration of banking and other money and capital markets; and
(3) abolition of fluctuation margins and coupling of exchange-rate parities.

In its final stage monetary union is governed by Articles 105–111 EC as far as substantive provisions are concerned. The institutional provisions are contained in Articles 112–115 EC. Liberalization of capital markets and movement of payments is provided for in Chapter 4 of Title Three of Part Three of the Treaty.[73] Although the description given here of a monetary union does not require the introduction of a single currency, practical arguments certainly militate in favour of such a move, which is accordingly provided for in Article 123(4) EC as the final step to full monetary union.[74]

---

71. Arts. 98–104 EC.
72. See P. VerLoren van Themaat, 'Some Preliminary Observations on the Intergovernmental Conferences: The Relations Between the Concepts of a Common Market, a Monetary Union, a Political Union and Sovereignty' (1991), CML Rev., 302–308. He rightly observes that given that an EMU also encompasses the common market, the substantive scope of the union is much wider than the coordination of macro-economic and fiscal policies alone. Therefore, the concept of economic policies in Art. 99(1) EC must be interpreted extensively, embracing both macro-economic and micro-economic or structural policies. This policy practice is reflected in the vocabulary in policy documents, such as the economic policy guidelines discussed in section 3.2.4. *infra*.
73. Arts. 56–60 EC. See Ch. VIII, section 8, *supra*.
74. Art. 123(4) EC still refers to the 'ecu' as the single currency. However, at the Madrid European Council of 15 and 16 Dec. 1995, it was decided to name the currency the 'euro'.

EMU as set out in the EC Treaty and in the relevant Protocols annexed to the EU Treaty and EC Treaty can be described as a system which combines a central monetary policy of an autonomous monetary authority at Community level with a vertical cooperative coordination of the economic policies of the Member States, a coordination which, however, has the traits for certain aspects of budgetary policy of the Member States of a vertical subordination.[75]

If the rules in Articles 102a–109 EEC were typical examples of a *traité-cadre* approach, which could be further filled in and worked out by the Community Institutions and the Member States, the present Treaty rules for EMU, in combination with the relevant Protocols, display all the facets of a *traité-loi* which in places is worked out in considerable detail. However, from this it cannot necessarily be concluded that the provisions on economic coordination stand for a stringent and enforceable system. Indeed, theoretical evidence and experience in practice in applying the Treaty system suggests that at times the opposite may be the case.

Finally it should be noted that Title VII of the EC Treaty provides for numerous legal bases allowing for the adoption of detailed rules in the form of secondary Community law.[76]

3.2   Economic Union: Articles 98–104 EC[77]

The chapter dealing with the coordination of economic policy logically falls into a number of main segments relating to general objectives and principles applicable to EMU, the rules on government financing, and the actual system of economic policy coordination in EMU. As such they include:

- The objectives and principles of economic policy coordination within the Community, which are summed up in Article 98 EC, which refers back to Articles 2 and 4 EC (see section 3.2.1.).
- The prohibitions of monetary financing, privileged access for the public sector to the financial markets, and liability for or assumption of public debt

---

75. See Art. 104 EC.
76. Including Arts. 95(5), 100(2), 102(2), 103(2), 104(14), 105(6), 106(2), 107(6) and 111 EC.
77. See: A. El-Agraa, *The European Union, Economics and Policies*, 6th ed. (London, 2001); P. De Grauwe, *The Political Economy of Monetary Union* (Cheltenham, 2001); M. Andenas, *European Economic and Monetary Union* (London, 1997); M. Baimbridge and P. Whyman (eds), *Economic and Monetary Union in Europe, Theory, Evidence and Practice* (Northampton, 2001); S. Dosenrode, *Political Aspects of the Economic Monetary Union* (Aldershot, 2002); B. Lamfalussy et al. (eds) *The Euro-Zone: A New Economic Entity?* (Brussels, 1999); J-V Louis, M. Waelbroeck et al. (1995) op. cit. *supra* note 12; R. Smits, *The European Central Bank: Institutional Aspects* (The Hague, 1997); C. Zilioli and M. Selmayr, *The Law of the European Central Bank* (Oxford, 2001); J. Stuyck (ed.), *Financial and Monetary Integration in the European Community: Legal, Institutional and Economic Aspects* (Deventer, 1993); European Central Bank, *Legal Aspects of the European System of Central Banks, Liber Amicorum Paolo Zamboni Caravelli* (Frankfurt a.M., 2005).

of other Member States by the Community and the Member States; these prohibitions are laid down in Articles 101, 102 and 103 EC, respectively in order to ensure that national authorities at all levels, bodies governed by public law and public undertakings act in conformity with the financial market conditions (see 3.2.2.).
- The special two provisions contained in Article 100 EC to deal with extraordinary circumstances (see 3.2.3.).
- The actual coordination of economic policies of the Member States, including the multilateral surveillance and excessive deficit procedure, and the possibility of judicial review (see 3.2.4.).
- The legal and economic conditions for joining the euro area and the status of Member States with a derogation (see 3.2.5.).

Each of these areas deserves separate consideration hereafter. What will become clear from this examination is that the provisions included in the EC Treaty do not establish an economic union in the sense of a unification of the national economic policies in a single European economic policy which is moreover pursued on the supranational level on behalf of the Member States.[78] Rather, a complex system of provisions is designed apparently merely to coordinate national policies based on internal market principles and budgetary policy rules and guidelines.[79]

3.2.1 The Objectives and Principles of Economic Policy Coordination (Article 98 EC)

As was already observed in Chapter III, above, in relation to Article 4 EC, the formulation of the objectives and principles for the coordination of economic policy raises some important legal questions. The express reference to the principle of an open market economy emphasizes that the necessary coordination of economic policy should be based on a well-functioning common market. Therefore, coordination of economic polices does not imply only macro-economic policies, but also micro-economic policies, directed at improving the functioning of the common market and parts thereof, as well. The qualification of the market economy as an 'open' market economy refers in particular to the relationship with the world market and thus supports the principle set out in Article 131 EC

---

78. See F. Amtenbrink, 'Integration, Coordination or Fragmentation in Economic Policy Matters ? A Comment on René Smits', in N. Lavranos and D. Obradovic (eds) *Interface between EU Law and National Law* (Groningen, 2007), 169–184. R. Smits, 'Some Reflections on Economic Policy', Legal Issues of Economic integration (2007) 5–25, 5, points out rightly that the main difference between economic and monetary policy in EMU lies in the attribution of exclusive competences to the Community in the latter area.
79. Generally on the regulatory approach of Title VII EC Treaty: F. Amtenbrink, 'Introduction to Title VII on Economic and Monetary Union', in H. Smit, P. Herzog, C. Campbell and G. Zagel, *Smit & Herzog on The Law of the European Union*, Volume 2 (New York Rev. 4-3/2007), Ch. 181-1, Ch. 181, at § 181.04.

of a liberal commercial policy. Secondly, it contains a certain instruction norm for the Member States and for the Community in the formation, attaining and implementation of their policies, that they should opt as much as possible for solutions which leave the operation of the market intact at Community level.[80] Experiences in the past have demonstrated that disparities in the composition of economic steering instruments and in their use may cause major specific or generic distortions which could unnecessarily affect the functioning of the common market. Thirdly, this reference implicitly indicates that the coordination of economic policies is *not* limited to macro-economic policy in the narrow applied sense of influencing macro-economic variables by, e.g., fiscal policy measures.[81] In the long run, the institutional structure and operation of national economies is at least as important for the economic development of the Community as a whole as the orchestration of national budgetary policies according to the different phases of the economic cycle.[82]

The phrase 'favouring an efficient allocation of resources' which is found in Article 98 EC but not in Article 4 EC can be interpreted in two ways. In one interpretation it sets out nothing more than an adjunct of free competition. In that case, the phrase would be merely repetitious. Yet, it can also be read as an independent condition for the Member States and the Commission in the conduct of their economic policies: the authorities should use their – public – resources as efficiently as possible.[83]

The real obligation to coordinate economic policies according to a cyclical procedure lies in the words: 'Member States shall conduct their economic policies . . . in the context of broad guidelines referred to in Article 99 (2).'[84]

---

80. J.-V. Louis, 'Perspectives of the EMU after Maastricht', in J. Stuyck (ed.), op. cit., *supra* note 77, 1, at 18, suggests that the commitment to the principle of an open market economy with free competition appears to have been included in Arts. 4 and 98 EC for two reasons: first in order to prevent the adoption of quantitative measures of limitation of credit allowed by financial institutions, a favourite instrument of French monetary policy in the past, and, secondly, to protect against rescue operations by the ECB as lender of last resort.

81. In the same sense: F. Van Estorff and B. Molitor, in H. Von der Groeben, J, Thiesing, C.-D. Ehlermann (eds) *Kommentar zum EU-/EG-Vertrag*, 5th ed. (Baden-Baden, 1999), 3/40.

82. Illustrative in this regard: Commission White Paper 'Growth, Competitiveness and Employment' (COM(93)700, Bull. EU Supp. 6/93).

83. Although on grammatical grounds the first interpretation appears to be more obvious, there are also arguments in favour of the second view. Strictly speaking, an efficient allocation of resources is the consequence of an effective operation of the market. Understood in that way, the addition would be superfluous. It can have particular significance only if the desired efficient allocation is extended beyond the market sector. The history of the origin of Arts. 4 and 98 EC would lend some support to this interpretation, see J. Cloos et al. (1993), op. cit., *supra* note 51 at 234.

84. The wording of Art. 98, first phrase, has ignited hot debates in the Working Group on Economic Governance of the Convention on the Future of Europe. Some members of the Working Group considered that 'in order to ensure economic growth, full employment and social cohesion, this should extend to bringing macro-economic policy within the shared competence of the Union and the Member States'. In its final report, however, to Convention Plenary, the Working Group

The last phrase of Article 98 EC, which refers to the principles set out in Article 4 EC, is far from precise. The reference concerns in particular Article 4(3) EC, which incompletely summarizes the objectives of economic policy, including stable prices, sound public finances and monetary conditions and a sustainable balance of payments.[85] It is notable that a reference to 'ensuring a high level of employment' is missing from this account, despite the fact that a high level of employment is mentioned as one of the objectives of the Union in Article 2 Treaty on the European Union (TEU) and moreover as one of the principle tasks of the Community in Article 2 EC. This objective is moreover included as a 'horizontal clause' in Article 127 EC (in Title VIII of the EC Treaty on employment).

The omission of this objective in Article 98 EC has its roots in a rather dogmatic debate on the aims of economic policy which accompanied the drafting of the EMU provisions as part of the Treaty of Maastricht. In the preparation and negotiation stages, German views about the conditions which the economic policy of Member States should satisfy with a view to monetary union were predominant. In those views the primary and central element of economic, financial and monetary policy is the maintenance of price stability. The realization of this objective is one of the preconditions for economic growth and, hence, for growth in employment. Those views implied tacitly the rejection of a counter-cyclical fiscal policy according to Keynesian prescriptions.

After the entry into force of the Treaty of Maastricht and in the run-up to the Treaty of Amsterdam, unemployment in the Community increased sharply, attaining a level of more than 10% of the total labour force, an evolution which, for evident reasons, attracted much political attention. Under those circumstances the German government was willing to see the new Title VIII, on Employment, inserted in the EC Treaty. This Title, as will be further explained in section 4, below, has as its main subject the coordination of labour market policies. However, the German and Dutch governments were not prepared to amend the existing Treaty provisions on EMU. Therefore the insertion into Article 98 EC of an explicit reference to a high level of employment, as one of the objectives of economic policy coordination, remained unattainable.

Nevertheless, given the express reference in Article 98 EC to the objectives of the Community in Article 2 EC, arguably the absence of any express mention of the employment objective in the former provision does not mean that employment

---

recommended that the current structure be kept, whereby the exclusive competence for monetary policy within the Euro-zone lies with the Community (ECSB) and economic policy with the Member States. In the final drafting stage, by the Intergovernmental Conference, of Art. I-15, any reference to a competence for the Union to coordinate the economic policies of the Member States was meticulously avoided, as appears from its present wording: 'the Member States shall coordinate their economic policies within the Union'. See: P.J. Kapteyn, 'EMU and Central Bank: Chances Missed' (2005), *European Constitutional Law Review*, 125, and D. Servais and R. Ruggeri, 'The EU Constitution: Its Impact on Economic and Monetary Union and Economic Convergence', in European Central Bank (2005), op. cit., *supra* note 77, 43, at 48–49. The Treaty of Lisbon leaves the current wording in place.

85. Similar objectives were already defined in Art. 104 of the original EEC Treaty.

could not be the subject of economic policy coordination at Community level. It could be regarded as a shortcoming in the system of the Treaty which can be overcome by interpretation. At least as important, however, is the deficiency in the policy system as such, as a result of the absence of employment as an *objective of economic policy* in EMU. In a fully established EMU, disturbances of the internal economic balance of a Member State, expressed e.g., in a relatively high level of inflation, have to be absorbed by the least mobile factor of production, that is labour.[86] Consequently, in the coordination of economic policies of the Member States, major attention has to be paid to the development of direct and indirect labour costs, to the operation of the labour market, to possible rigidities in the development of conditions of employment, and to qualitative discrepancies between labour supply and demand. This is confirmed by the economic developments in the Community since 1992, where employment questions predominate. For a long time core countries of the EMU, such as Germany, France and Italy, treated employment as a social problem to be addressed through social policy, rather than to recognize it as an objective of economic policy subject to strict economic analysis. It is this approach which has caused the high levels of structural inactivity among the working population. This by itself constitutes a serious obstacle for a balanced and sustainable economic development as stipulated by Article 2 EC.

The Employment Title of the EC Treaty includes two systematic references, respectively in Article 126(1) and in Article 128(2) EC, to the broad guidelines for the economic policies of the Member States and of the Community (BEPG) mentioned in Article 99(2) EC which have been adopted ever since the entry into force of the Treaty of Maastricht. The so-called employment guidelines must be drafted in conformity with these guidelines.[87] This furnishes further evidence as to why the absence of a mention of employment as one of the objectives of economic policy coordination in Articles 4, 98 and 99 EC may be considered as something of an anomaly.[88]

In practice, systematic attention is paid in the broad policy guidelines issued in accordance with Article 99(2) EC to the employment aspect and namely to measures that result in higher employment.[89] In recent times, employment has

---

86. A. Geelhoed (1994), op. cit., *supra* note 17, at 42. This direct relation between labour productivity, wage-inflation and the evolution of employment in a completed EMU underlines once again why the absence of employment as one of the objectives of Art. 98 EC cannot be compensated by the mention of the employment objective in Title VIII, which misses the point that the achievement of a high degree of employment is primarily to be ensured through economic policy rather than social policy.
87. See further section 4 *infra*.
88. An anomaly that is not solved by the Treaty of Lisbon.
89. See the Council's Recommendations as to the BEPG in O.J. 1994, L 7/9, O.J. 1995, L 191/24, O.J. 1996, L 179/46, O.J. 1997, L 206/12, O.J. 1998, L 200/34, O.J. 1999, L 217/34, O.J. 2000, L 210/1, O.J. 2001, L 179/1 and O.J. 2002, L 182/1, O.J. 2003, L 195/1, and O.J. 2005, L 205/28 (for the 2005–2008 period).

been given a much more prominent place in economic policy coordination. In refocusing the Lisbon Strategy on growth and employment in Europe, the European Council in 2005 has started to adopt so-called 'Integrated guidelines for jobs and growth'.[90]

It is noticeable that neither Article 98 EC nor any of the following provisions on economic policy include any reference to short-term economic policy. The fact that economic and administrative views as to the desirability and possibilities of conducting an active anti-cyclical policy have changed since the first three decades after the Second World War played a part in the removal of the old Article 102 EEC. As a matter of fact these views are strongly divergent among the Member States. Moreover, practical experiences of a demand-stimulating macro-economic policy in the 1970s, which resulted in high inflation and almost intractable budgetary deficits in combination with low economic growth ('Stagflation') on a Community-wide scale, were not such that the remaining proponents of an active anti-cyclical policy could count on much spontaneous support in the drafting of EMU provisions. However, the consequences for the practice of economic policy are not so significant. Short-term macro-economic policy is also embraced by the concept of 'economic policies'. This was confirmed when in February 2001 the ECOFIN Council addressed a recommendation to Ireland in accordance with Article 99(4) EC to pursue a more restrictive budgetary policy in view of the inflationary tensions on the Irish labour market, a clear example of Keynesian short-term macro-economic policy.[91]

3.2.2   The Rules for Deficit Financing According to Market Principles (Articles 101, 102 and 103 EC)

In most Member States, public authorities, bodies governed by public law and public undertakings have since time immemorial enjoyed a privileged position in the financing of their deficits. The most important escape from an undisciplined budgetary policy is the so-called monetary deficit financing through credit facilities afforded by the NCB. However, extensive monetary financing of government deficits poses grave risks for internal price stability, and thus for the development of interest rates on the money capital markets. For this reason, Article 101 EC prescribes a general prohibition of monetary deficit financing by the public sector

---

90. Taking the form of a recommendation on the broad guidelines for the economic policies of the Member States and the Community for the period 2005 to 2008 (O.J. 2005, L 205/28) and a decision on guidelines for the employment policies of the Member States (O.J. 2005, L 205/21). See also O.J. 2007, L 92/23 regarding the 2007 update of the broad guidelines for the economic policies of the Member States and the Community and on the implementation of the Member States' employment policies. See also section 3.2.4 *infra*.
91. Council Recommendation 2001/191/EC (O.J. 2001, L 69/22). The recommendation was thereafter published, see Council Decision 2001/192/EC (O.J. 2001, L 69/24).

in the wide sense.[92] The prohibition does not apply to publicly owned credit institutions.[93]

Complementing the prohibition of monetary financing, Article 102 EC prohibits any measure, not based on prudential considerations, establishing privileged access to financial institutions 'by Community institutions or bodies, central governments, regional, local or other public authorities, other bodies governed by public law or public undertakings'.[94] Practices such as privileging public authorities in the provision of borrowing requirements which were common in several Member States before 1994, are thus prohibited. Privileged treatment is only permissible if it results from normal business considerations based on the relatively high creditworthiness of the authority concerned as a debtor.[95]

The rules for deficit financing on strictly market conditions basis, contained in Articles 101 and 102 EC, aim to confront national budgetary authorities with the financial consequences of a budgetary policy in deficit. The financial markets will, as a rule, reflect their confidence in the authority concerned in the terms under which they are prepared to provide capital. However, the effectiveness of this corrective effect of the markets depends on the confidence that the Community or other Member States will not be liable for or assume the commitments of Member States which pursue undisciplined budgetary behaviour. Article 103 EC is designed to offer this certainty. The consequence of this 'no bail out-clause' is that weaker Member States have to offer higher interest rates on their government bonds.

---

92. See Reg. 3603/93 (O.J. 1993, L 332/1) on definitions for the application of the prohibitions referred to in Arts. 104 and 104b(1) of the Treaty. Art. 8 of this regulation adopts the definition of public undertakings used in Dir. 80/723 (O.J. 1980, L 195/35), most recently amended by Dir. 2005/81 (O.J. 2005, L 312/47) amending Dir. 80/723/EEC on the transparency of financial relations between Member States and public undertakings as well as on financial transparency within certain undertakings. See generally J. Pipkorn, 'Legal Arrangements in the Treaty of Maastricht for the Effectiveness of the Economic and Monetary Union' (1994), CML Rev., 263, at 277.
93. Art. 101(2) EC.
94. See further, Reg. 3604/93 (O.J. 1993, L 332/4) specifying definitions for the prohibition of privileged access.
95. Reg. 3604/93, ibid., Art. 2 defines prudential considerations as 'those which underlie national laws, regulations or administrative actions based on, or consistent with, EC law and designed to promote the soundness of financial institutions so as to strengthen the stability of the financial system as a whole and the protection of the customers of those institutions'. The first phrase of Art. 102 EC is not itself very clear, referring implicitly to the solvency ratio for credit institutions established by Dir. 89/647 (O.J. 1989, L 386/14), which was repealed by Dir. 2000/12 (O.J. 2000, L 126/1) relating to the taking up and pursuit of the business of credit institutions, which itself has since been recast by Dir. 2006/48 (O.J. 2006, L 177/1). These rules imply a rating of banking activities according to the degree of risk. For the more risky activities, more capital coverage is required than for less risky activities. According to these rules, loans to the central government of a Member State are regarded in the evaluation as falling within the risk-free category. That makes it simpler and cheaper for the Member States to meet their capital requirements.

No further implementation measures are required for Articles 101 and 103 EC to take effect, although the Council has made use of the possibility to adopt measures provided for in Article 103(2) EC by adopting Regulation 3603/93.[96] As regards Article 102 EC, according to Article 102(2) EC the Council had to adopt the definitions of the prohibition of privileged access to financial institutions.[97]

3.2.3 Powers to Deal with Extraordinary Circumstances (Article 100 EC)

Article 100(1) EC allows for the Council, acting by qualified majority on a proposal from the Commission to decide upon measures appropriate to an existing financial situation in a Member State, in particular if severe difficulties may arise in the supply of certain products.[98] Experience during the two oil crises in the 1970s, when the forerunner of this provision in the EEC Treaty was applied in order to adopt measures to ensure the oil supply in the Community, highlights the practical relevance of such a crisis mechanism.[99] Reflecting this particular purpose of Article 100 EC, in the Treaty of Lisbon it is foreseen that the new Article 122(1) of the Treaty on the Functioning of the EU will include an explicit reference to energy as one of the areas in which severe difficulties may arise. Moreover, the revised provision will expressly appeal to the 'spirit of solidarity between Member States'.[100]

It appears from the case law of the European Court of Justice (ECJ) that the Council may have the choice of form of the measure which it considers to be the most suitable.[101] As such, Article 100(1) EC may embrace any the legally binding measures identified in Article 249 EC.[102]

The subjection of government deficits to Community norms and the prohibition of monetary financing can make it difficult for Member States to address the

---

96. Note 92 *supra*. The Treaty of Lisbon amends Art. 103(2) EC, as the new Art. 125 of the Treaty on the Functioning of the EU (hereafter: TFEU) will state that the Council, on a proposal from the Commission and after consulting the European Parliament, may, as required, specify definitions for the application of the prohibitions referred to in today's Arts. 101–103 EC.

97. In the same sense J. Cloos, et al. (1993), 245, J. Pipkorn (1994), op. cit., *supra* note 92, 275. This provision was implemented by Reg. 3604/93 (*supra* note 94). R. Smits (1997), op. cit., *supra* note 77, draws attention to the fact that Treaty provisions, which must be implemented by secondary legislation may in combination with the latter have direct effect. There are good reasons for assuming that this is the case with Art. 102 EC. In the same sense J.-V. Louis, (1995), op. cit., *supra* note 12, 40–44. See e.g., Case 157/85, *Luigi Brugnoni and Roberto Ruffinengo v. Cassa di risparmio di Genova e Imperia*. In the Treaty of Lisbon Art. 102(2) EC is repealed.

98. This provision, originally introduced by the Treaty of Maastricht, was amended by the Treaty of Nice, thereby lowering the voting requirement in the Council from unanimity to qualified majority.

99. Art. 103(4) EEC.

100. According to Art. 1, para. 87, of the Lisbon Treaty.

101. Case 5/73, *Balkan* (para. 18). In this case, the Court ruled on Art. 103(2) EEC which referred to 'measures appropriate to the situation'.

102. See also R. Smits, 'De monetaire unie van Maastricht' (1992), SEW, 715.

consequences caused by natural disasters or exceptional occurrences beyond their control, which can trigger major economic shocks. For this reason Article 100(2) EC allows the possibility for the Council, acting by a qualified majority on a proposal from the Commission, to grant Community financial assistance subject to certain conditions. The President of the Council must inform the European Parliament of any decision taken. It becomes clear from Article 116(3) EC that such a decision can only be taken with regard to a Member State that participates in the euro area.[103]

3.2.4   Economic Coordination in EMU (Articles 99 and 104 EC, Regulations 1466/97 and 1467/97)[104]

The provisions on economic coordination relating to multilateral surveillance and the excessive deficit procedure, and the related secondary Community law, are the result of fierce legal and economic debates about the feasibility and desirability of a role for Europe in the coordination of the economic policies of the Member States.

An extensive discussion took place during the negotiations leading to the Treaty of Maastricht regarding the question whether the financial markets would be capable of correcting excessive deficits in EMU. The latter was namely argued by the United Kingdom which traditionally opposed any direct Community oversight over its internal policies. However, this view was not shared by the Member States at large, who were not willing to trust the financial markets to provide sufficient incentives for public authorities to avoid or swiftly correct public deficits. Doubts were raised about the capability of financial markets to fulfil such a function.[105] Financial markets may be able to react to an increasing country risk of an undisciplined national budgetary authority with an increase in the risk premium, resulting in a higher interest rate, but it is questionable whether an

---

103. The proposal by the Commission to introduce a mechanism to support financially Member States which need to make an extra effort to fulfil the convergence criteria for participation in the third stage of EMU was rejected at the time by a majority of Member States, who took the position that the fulfilment of these budgetary and macro-economic criteria should not be linked to financial support, without prejudice to measures to be adopted in the context of the economic and social cohesion. Despite this approach, a link nevertheless exists between EMU and the cohesion fund, which becomes clear from the Protocol on economic and social cohesion (O.J. 1992, C 191/93). According to this Protocol, the cohesion fund provides Community financial contributions to projects in the fields of environment and trans-European networks in Member States with a per capita GNP of less than 90% of the Community average which have a programme leading to the fulfilment of the conditions of economic convergence as set out in Art. 104c (now Art. 104 EC). As to the origins of this arrangement see J. Cloos et al. (1993), op. cit., *supra* note 51 151–162, and J. Pipkorn (1994), op. cit., *supra* note 92, 274.

104. The detailed description of the multilateral surveillance and excessive deficit procedure partly draws on several earlier publications: F. Amtenbrink, J. de Haan and O. Sleijpen, 'The Stability Pact- Placebo or Panacea?' (1997), *European Business Law Review*, 202–210 and 233–238; F. Amtenbrink and J. de Haan (2003), op. cit., *supra* note 29, and F. Amtenbrink and J. de Haan, 'Reforming the Stability and Growth Pact' (2006), EL Rev., 402–413.

105. R. Oort, 'Economische en Monetaire Unie, het Plan-Delors' (1990), SEW, 46–57, commenting on the Delors Report.

increase in interest rate expenditures can in the short run sway fiscal authorities to take corrective measures. What is more, the effects which an increased recourse of a Member State to the capital markets may have on the interest rates are less direct in an EMU. This may be different if the budgetary authorities of a number of Member States have to rely on the Community capital market. In such a situation, interest rates could rise to the disadvantage of Member States without excessive government deficits. Then the costs of an excessive government deficit or debt are not only born by the Member States concerned, but by all Member States. At least equally important, is the fact that such a rise in interest rates could seriously damage the investment climate to the disadvantage of the EMU as a whole. However that may be, empirical evidence gathered for the period after the introduction of EMU raises serious doubts whether financial markets actually primarily focus on public finances, directly reacting to any deterioration in the government financial position of a Member State, rather than to general economic conditions.[106]

Not only was the desirability of public intervention in the case of excessive deficits in the Member States subject to debate, but also the practicability of the legal regime introduced by the Treaty of Maastricht. In particular, Germany raised doubts about the stringency and efficiency of the rules on multilateral surveillance and excessive deficit procedure included in primary Community law, as the latter were considered too lenient and potentially dangerous for the stability of the future single currency.[107] It was in particular feared that the budgetary discipline which a number of Member States had observed in the run-up to stage three of EMU would be abandoned once the goal of participation in the euro area had been achieved, as the disciplining mechanism of Article 122(1) EC on the participation in the euro area would no longer apply. This fear was not entirely unsubstantiated, as the small economic recession which most Member States experienced from mid-1992 to mid-1994 resulted in an unexpected increase in government deficits, despite the obligation to endeavour to avoid excessive government deficits.[108] What became clear from this was that the fulfilment of the convergence criteria under normal economic conditions was no guarantee that these conditions would also still be met under less favourable economic conditions. Indeed, in the Western European social welfare states, a slowdown of economic growth results in a decrease in government incomes and an increase in government social expenditure due to rising unemployment rates. Member States which in normal economic circumstances have a government deficit below but close to the reference value stated in Article 104 EC, immediately run a considerable excessive government deficit in case of a recession. In order to prevent the latter, Member States have the option to cut

---

106. J.-P. Fitoussi, 'Fiscal Policy: Why no reaction yet by the markets?', European Parliament, Committee for Economic and Monetary affairs, Briefing paper No. 2–5 May 2005, provides evidence for the period 1/03 to 1/05 that there was no clear tendency towards an increase in the level of European interest rates despite low growth rates and high deficit paths.
107. See F. Amtenbrink and J. de Haan (2006), op. cit., *supra* note 104, 403–404.
108. Art. 116(4) EC.

government expenditure, which may however be undesirable both from an economic and social point of view.

The Stability and Growth Pact established in 1997 in the wake of the Treaty of Amsterdam was the result of an initiative by the German Minister of Finance Waigel who presented a proposal for a stability pact for Europe with the aim to reinforce Title 1 of Chapter VII of the EC Treaty.[109] The ECOFIN Council acknowledged the desirability of a reinforcement of the European fiscal policy rules, stating that government finances are crucial to preserving stable economic conditions in the Member States and in the Community.[110] What resulted from this was the adoption of two Council Regulations on the strengthening of the surveillance and coordination of budgetary positions and on speeding up and clarifying the implementation of the excessive deficit procedure.[111] The European Council Resolution attached to these Regulations represented a political rather than legally binding commitment by the Member States to implement the EC Treaty and the Council Regulations in a strict and timely manner. Together with the two Council Regulations, the European Council Resolution has become known as the Stability and Growth Pact which was agreed upon at the Amsterdam European Council of June 1997.[112]

The Stability and Growth Pact reveals the fundamental differences in opinion on the approach to economic policy (coordination) existing at the time. Firstly, the two Council Regulations fell well short of what the German government had called for.[113] Moreover, on the insistence of France, an explicit reference to economic growth had to be included, as France deplored a one-sided emphasis on stability.[114] The initial evaluation of the two Council Regulations was mixed, as serious doubts regarding both the legal and economic feasibility of economic coordination under the revised system of the Stability and Growth Pact remained.[115]

---

109. Stabilitätspakt für Europa in der dritten Stufe der WWU, press statement of the German Ministry of Finance, 10 Nov. 1995.
110. Report by the ECOFIN Council to the European Council, The Preparation for Stage Three of EMU, Annex I, Presidency Conclusions, Dublin European Council, 13 and 14 Dec. 1996.
111. The Regulations were adopted on the basis of ex Art. 103(5) EC (now Art. 99(5)) and Art. 104(c) EC (now Art. 104(14)).
112. O.J. 1997, L 209/1, last amended by Council Reg. 1055/2005 (O.J. 2005, L 174/1, amending Reg. (EC) 1466/97 on the strengthening of the surveillance of budgetary positions and the surveillance and coordination of economic policies, and O.J. 1997, L 209/6, last amended by Council Reg. 1056/2005 (O.J. 2005, L 174/5), amending Reg. (EC) No. 1467/97 on speeding up and clarifying the implementation of the excessive deficit procedure. Resolution of the European Council on the Stability and Growth Pact Amsterdam, 17 Jun. 1997 (O.J. 1997, C 236/1).
113. It had been suggested to lower the reference value for excessive government deficits under normal economic circumstances from 3% to 1%, committing Member States to balanced budgets and automatic sanctions in case of the emergence of excessive deficits. See T. Waigel, Stability Pact for Europe, Communication to the ECOFIN Council, Nov. 1995.
114. See e.g., M. Heipertz and A. Verdun, 'The Stability and Growth Pact: Theorising a Case in European Integration' (2005), JCMS, 985–1008 with further references.
115. See P. Maillet, 'Le Pacte de Stabilité de Croissance: Porteé et Limites du Compromis de Dublin?', Revue du Marché Commun et de L'Union Européenne no. 404, janvier (1997), 5–12. F. Amtenbrink, J. de Haan and Sleijpen, op. cit., supra note 104; H. Hahn, 'The Stability

As will be seen hereafter, the experience in the application of the multilateral surveillance and excessive deficit procedure since its introduction, bears out some of the initial doubts about its effectiveness, resulting in a resurgence of a broad discussion on economic coordination in EMU and calls for a revision of the multilateral surveillance and excessive deficit procedure. Based on proposals from the Commission,[116] the Council in 2005 made concrete proposals for a revision of the two Council Regulations at the centre of the Stability and Growth Pact, which were thereafter endorsed by the European Council.[117] For the Council the aim of the reform was to enhance 'the economic underpinnings of the existing framework and thus strengthen credibility and enforcement' and to make the existing framework more effective.[118] This resulted in the amendment of Council Regulation 1466/97 and Council Regulation 1467/97.[119] While the basic procedure and the institutional balance therein, provided for in Article 99 and 104 EC, has not been altered since the introduction of the latter provisions by the Treaty of Maastricht, this will change to some extent with the coming into force of the Treaty of Lisbon, as will be pointed out hereafter in relation to the relevant provisions.

Arguably the two central segments of coordination of economic policies are the actual coordination of economic policies of the Member States and of the Community in the form of the so-called multilateral surveillance procedure, basically described in Article 99 EC, and the addressing of existing government deficits and debts in the Member States above the reference value, as part of the so-called excessive deficit procedure, basically described in Article 104 EC. The provisions in the EC Treaty are further defined in several Protocols attached to the Treaties. From a practical point of view, the Protocol on the excessive deficit procedure, the Protocol on certain provisions relating to the United Kingdom of Great Britain and Northern Ireland and the Protocol on certain provisions relating to Denmark may be considered the most important.[120] These Protocols respectively define the reference values and terminology referred to in Article 104(2) EC, and determine to what extent to the rules on economic coordination in EMU apply to the United Kingdom and Denmark.

With regard to secondary Community measures, numerous regulations lay down the details for the application of the Treaty rules on economic coordination,

---

Pact for European Monetary Union: Compliance with Deficit Limit as a Constant Legal Duty' (1998), CML Rev., 77–100.
116. Communication from the Commission to Council and European Parliament, Strengthening the Co-ordination of Budgetary Policies (COM(2002)668 final); Communication from the Commission to the Council and the European Parliament, Strengthening Economic Governance and Clarifying the Implementation of the Stability and Growth Pact (COM(2004)581 final).
117. Council (ECOFIN), Improving the Implementation of the Stability and Growth Pact, Report to the European Council of 21 Mar. 2005 (No. 7423/05, UEM 97 ECOFIN 104); European Council, Presidency Conclusions, Brussels, 23 Mar. 2005 (7619/05).
118. Ibid.
119. Council Reg. (EC) 1055/2005; Council Reg. (EC) 1056/2005; both cited *supra* note 112.
120. Protocols No. 20, 25, 26 annexed to the EC Treaty by the Treaty on European Union (consolidated version, O.J. 2006, C 321 E/1).

in particular specifying definitions and introducing common accounting standards.[121] Two regulations which, due to their importance for the application of Article 99 and 104 EC, need to be highlighted are the above-mentioned Council Regulations 1466/97 and 1467/97 which, in conjunction with Article 99 EC and Article 104 EC, lay down in detail the applicable procedures.

3.2.4.1   *Multilateral Surveillance (Article 99 EC, Regulation 1466/97)*

The present Article 99 EC reproduces the major traits of policy coordination procedure set out in Decision 90/141 on the attainment of progressive convergence of economic policies and performance in the first stage of EMU.[122] Article 99(1) EC is to be read as bringing together the old Articles 6 and 103 EEC. The concept of economic policies must, as was noted above, be more widely interpreted than macro-economic policy or fiscal policy. The 'quality' and the competitive strength of the national economies and of the Community economy as a whole is only partly determined by the budgetary and monetary conditions (the so-called convergence criteria) which Article 121 EC prescribes for the transition to the third and final stage of EMU. Matters such as the quality of the labour force, the performances of the different product- and factor markets, the scope of public investment, expenditure on research and development, and so on, are of major and increasing importance for the structural strength of Western economies.[123] Thus these elements must be increasingly taken into account for the coordination of Member States' policies.

---

121. Council Reg. 3605/93 of 22 Nov. 1993, on the application of the Protocol on the excessive deficit procedure annexed to the Treaty establishing the European Community (O.J. 1993, L 332/7), last amendment Council Reg. (EC) No 2103/2005 of 12 Dec. 2005, O.J. 2005, L 337/1, amending Reg. (EC) No 3605/93 as regards the quality of statistical data in the context of the excessive deficit procedure; Council Reg. 3603/93 of 13 Dec. 1993, specifying definitions for the application of the prohibitions referred to in Arts. 104 and 104b (1) of the Treaty (O.J. 1993, L 332/1); Council Reg. 2223/96 of 25 Jun. 1996, on the European system of national and regional accounts in the Community (O.J. 1996, L 310/1), last amended Council and European Parliament Reg. 1267/2003 of 16 Jun. 2003, amending Council Reg. (EC) No 2223/96, O.J. 2003, L 180/1, with respect to the time limit for transmission of the main aggregates of national accounts, to the derogations concerning the transmission of the main aggregates of national accounts and to the transmission of employment data in hours worked; European Parliament and Council Reg. 2516/2000 of 7 Nov. 2000 modifying the common principles of the European system of national and regional accounts in the Community (ESA) 95 as concerns taxes and social contributions and amending Council Reg. 2223/96 (O.J. 2000, L 290/1); European Parliament and Council Reg. 1221/2002 of 10 Jun. 2002, on quarterly non-financial accounts for general government (O.J. 2002, L 197/1); European Parliament and Council Reg. 501/2004 of 10 Mar. 2004, on quarterly financial accounts for general government (O.J. 2004, L 81/1); Council Reg. 1222/2004 of 28 Jun. 2004, concerning the compilation and transmission of data on the quarterly government debt (O.J. 2004, L 233/1).
122. O.J. 1990, L 78/23, replacing earlier measures.
123. This is explicitly recognized in the Conclusions of the European Council of Lisbon, March 2000, See Bull. EU 3-2000, 7–18.

The multilateral surveillance of the economic policies of the Member States essentially means the monitoring of the economic developments in the Member States and the economic policy conducted by national governments, based on economic guidelines and information on planned economic policy provided by the Member States. The aims of these efforts are twofold. First and foremost: Member States are supposed to be guided towards engaging in an economic policy which will avoid the emergence of excessive government deficits as defined in Article 104(1) and (2) EC and the Protocol on the excessive deficit procedure. Moreover, economic policy coordination is geared towards sustained convergence of the economic performances of the Member States, including those not (yet) participating in the euro area.

While Article 98 EC states in broad terms that Member States must conduct their economic policies with a view to contributing to the achievement of the objectives of the Community, Article 99(1) EC obliges Member States to regard their economic policies as a matter of common concern and, furthermore to coordinate them within the Council.

In time to be taken into account by the Member States in preparing their annual budgets, in accordance with Article 99(2) EC, the Community issues multi-annual BEPG which are annually updated. The BEPG are drawn up in draft form by the Council on the basis of a recommendation from the Commission.[124] The European Council then discusses the draft. On the basis of the conclusion in that forum, the Council, acting by a qualified majority, thereafter adopts a recommendation setting out the broad guidelines.[125] The participation of the European Council and the remarkably weak position of the European Parliament, which is only informed by the Council on the recommendation setting out the BEPG, give the establishment of the BEPG an almost intergovernmental character.

Initially there was some discussion between the Member States and the Commission as to the meaning of the terms 'broad guidelines'. Some Member States – in particular Germany – defended an interpretation of the word 'broad' in the sense that the guidelines should have as their subject the economy and the economic policies within the Community as one entity. Such an approach would have inevitably resulted in a further watering down of the in any case not legally binding 'soft' coordination procedure described hereafter, as recommendations which fit a great diversity of economic situations will almost inevitably degenerate into non-committal generalizations. The majority of the Member States opted for a different interpretation. In their view, the word 'broad' should be understood as 'encompassing all the relevant subjects of economic policies'. Indeed, the wording of Article 99(2) EC does not prevent the broad guidelines from being targeted per Member State, without prejudice to the possibility of specific recommendations being made under Article 99(4) EC. In view of the diverse nature of the economic

---

124. This means the ECOFIN Council, see the Declaration in O.J. 1992, C 191/98 (Declaration No. 3 adopted on the occasion of the signature of the Final Act of the Treaty of Maastricht).

125. On the basis of Declaration No. 4, ibid., the ECOFIN ministers are invited to participate in the discussion by the European Council of matters relating to EMU.

problems in the various Member States, such an approach even seems more appropriate. Thus, more precise evaluation criteria for the purpose of multilateral surveillance could be created, contributing to the overall effectiveness of the coordination procedure as a whole.

In practice the second interpretation prevailed and the annual broad guidelines consist now of two parts. The first part is devoted to a description of the economic situation of the whole Community, the general evolution in the global and continental economies, and the preferable policy stances in view thereof. The second part is dedicated to a more or less detailed analysis of the various national economies, with rather precise recommendations as to the policy objectives to be pursued and the policy instruments that would be preferable in the specific national context. Areas covered include general economic guidelines on short-term macroeconomic policies, medium-term structural policies and long-term sustainability issues.[126] This two-tiered composition of the broad guidelines, including country-specific issues, may, at the national level, increase their interest for policymakers, employers' organizations and trade unions.

The insertion, by the Treaty of Amsterdam of the new Employment Title into the EC Treaty and the adoption of the Stability and Growth Pact at the same European Summit both contributed to the improvement of the broad guidelines' status. Indeed, the special employment guidelines provided for in the Employment Title[127] and the annual updated Convergence and Stability programmes which, as will be observed hereafter, every Member State must submit for examination by the Commission and the Council, have to be in conformity with the BEPG. By thus providing the substantive framework for the more specific coordination of national employment and budgetary policies, the interest of the broad guidelines has increased.

A further element contributing to their importance came at the European Council of Cardiff in June 1998, where the goal was defined: 'to promote the structural adaptation of Member States' economies to a more competitive environment at the global market'. This ambition resulted in the so-called 'Cardiff procedure', which amounts to comparing Member States' economies as to their weaker and stronger elements (benchmarking) at regular intervals.[128] The results of this benchmarking process provide the substantial basis for country-specific recommendations to be included into the broad guidelines. As the broad guidelines are made public, these country-specific recommendations may, potentially, attract political and public interest.

In March 2000 the European Council of Lisbon concluded ambitious and far-reaching objectives for economic growth, employment and competitiveness within the European Union.[129] These conclusions, in their turn, also led to a

---

126. Issues addressed include: e.g., budgetary positions, labour market development, investments and the development of social security systems.
127. See *infra*, section 4 of this chapter.
128. Bull. EU 6-1998, 7–21.
129. This summit also became known as the 'Dot.com summit'.

periodic check on the progress in the preparation and the implementation of the necessary policy measures, at the national level as well as the Community level. The annual reports by the Commission on the implementation of the broad guidelines also provide important information on the progress Member States are showing in the realization of the Lisbon objectives. The fact that the European Council is thus informed on a yearly basis and, sometimes, attaches special conclusions to these reports, contributes to increasing the political importance of the broad guidelines, at least at the Community level.[130]

A final factor of some significance is the relative transparency of the preparation and the implementation of the broad guidelines. All stages of the decision-making procedure are well documented and made public. In this way, interested organizations and groups are provided with a treasure of information on the quality of the different national economic policies. This comparative information (peer review) could, at least in theory, in its turn stimulate policy competition between Member States, a process leading to the adoption, adaptation and improvement of successful institutional arrangements and policy recipes (best practice). In principal, the 'soft' coordination procedure of Article 99 EC has the potential to break through the Member States' introspection for the preparation and implementation of their national economic and social policies, where benchmarking with other countries' policies in the past was the exception.

Although the broad guidelines are contained in recommendations which are in principle not legally binding, Article 99(3) and (4) EC provides for a procedure of multilateral surveillance of economic developments in each Member State and of the consistency of economic policies with the broad guidelines.[131] This assessment is primarily based on yearly updated Convergence Programmes (in the case of Member States with a derogation) and the Stability Programmes (in the case of Member States participating in the euro area) which the Member States are obliged to forward to the Council and Commission.[132] While Article 99(3) EC only states in rather broad terms that the Member States have to forward relevant information to the Commission, Articles 3 and 7 of Council Regulation 1466/97 specify in detail the contents of these programmes. Member States have to forward information on: (1) Their the medium-term budgetary objective and the adjustment path towards this objective for the general government surplus/deficit and the expected path of the general government debt ratio. (2) The main assumptions about expected economic developments and important economic variables which are relevant to the realization of the stability programme. (3) A detailed and quantitative assessment of the budgetary and other economic policy measures being taken and/or proposed to achieve the objectives of the programme. (4) An analysis

130. See e.g., Report on the Implementation of the Broad Guidelines for Economic Policy for 2001, 21 Feb. 2002 (ECOFIN/16/02-NE).
131. On the legal effect of Community instruments see Art. 249 EC.
132. According to Art. 5 of the Protocol on certain provisions relating to the United Kingdom, the latter has to 'endeavour to avoid excessive deficits'. As such, the multilateral surveillance procedure also applies to the UK.

of how changes in the main economic assumptions would affect the budgetary and debt position. (5) Reasons for a possible deviation from the required adjustment path towards the medium-term budgetary objective.[133] The medium-term character of the Stability and Growth Programmes is highlighted by the Member States' obligation to forward information which covers not only the current and preceding year, but also at least the following three years.[134]

Before its amendment in 2005, Council Regulation 1466/97 effectively imposed a single medium-term budgetary objective for all Member States of close to balance or surplus. With the 2005 reform, arguably more flexibility has been introduced into economic coordination, allowing for differences in economic situations in Member States to be taken into account in the context of economic coordination in EMU.[135] The uniform application of a medium-term objective to all Member States has been abandoned in favour of a differentiated medium-term objective for each Member State, which may diverge from the requirement of a close to balance or surplus budgetary position. For Member States participating in the euro area and those Member States participating in ERM II, the country-specific medium-term budgetary objectives must be specified within a defined range between – 1% of GDP and balance or surplus, in cyclically adjusted terms.[136] In determining the medium-term budgetary objective or the targeted adjustment path towards this objective for a given Member State, thus the relevant cyclical and structural characteristics of its economy can be taken into account in establishing the Convergence and Stability Programmes.

The multilateral surveillance of the economic policies of the Member States essentially means the monitoring of the economic developments in the Member States and the economic policy conducted by national governments based on the economic programmes submitted by the Member States. To this end, first of all, the Stability and Convergence Programmes are examined by the Council within three months of their submission, based on an assessment by the Commission and the Economic and Financial Committee.[137] This review focuses in particular on an assessment of the plausibility of the economic assumptions on which the programme is based, the appropriateness of the adjustment path towards the medium-term budgetary objective, and whether the measures being taken and/or proposed to respect that adjustment path are sufficient to achieve the

---

133. Art. 3(2) Reg. 1466/97. Convergence Programmes have to include additional information on the medium-term monetary policy objectives and the relationship between those objectives to price and exchange-rate stability (Art. 7(2) Reg. 1466/97).
134. Arts. 3(3) and 7(3) Reg. 1466/97.
135. See Council (ECOFIN), Improving the Implementation of the Stability and Growth Pact, Report to the European Council of 21 Mar. 2005, No. 7423/05, UEM 97 ECOFIN 104; European Council, Presidency Conclusions, Brussels, 23 Mar. 2005, 7619/05.
136. Art. 2a Council Reg. 1466/97, as amended. A medium-term budgetary objective can be revised in case of the implementation of a major structural reform and in any case every 4 years.
137. This period has been extended from originally two months.

medium-term objective over the economic cycle.[138] As a result of the 2005 reform of Regulation 1466/97, Articles 5(1) and 9(1) of Regulation 1466/97 now explicitly allow for the differentiation of time paths towards the medium-term objectives. At the same time a minimum annual adjustment of 0.5% of GDP has to be achieved towards the medium-term budgetary objective.[139] Moreover, the Council has to take into account whether a higher adjustment effort is made in economically good times, whereas the effort may be more limited in economically bad times. This is to ensure a more symmetrical approach to fiscal policy over the economic business cycle through enhanced budgetary discipline in economically good times, thereby avoiding pro-cyclical economic policies.

When assessing the adjustment path, the Council has to take into account the implementation of major structural reforms which have direct long-term cost-saving effects. Moreover, the Council must examine whether the contents of the Stability and Convergence Programmes facilitate the closer coordination of economic policies, and whether the economic policies of the Member State concerned are consistent with the BEPG. For the Member States with a derogation which forward Convergence Programmes, the Council also monitors whether the policies of these countries are geared to stability, ensuring that real exchange-rate misalignments and excessive nominal exchange-rate fluctuations are avoided.[140]

The legally non-binding BEPG not only serve as a point of reference for the Member States in formulating economic policy, but also for the Council. Moreover, the Convergence and Stability Programmes amount to a self-commitment by the Member States to a certain line of action.[141]

While the Commission and the Economic and Finance Committee are charged with monitoring the economic programmes and their implementation, it is the Council, acting by qualified majority on the basis of a recommendation from the Commission, which decides whether the programmes should be strengthened and whether the budgetary position in a Member State calls for an early warning and recommendations for adjustment measures in order to avoid the occurrence of an excessive deficit.[142] Article 99(4) EC foresees that such recommendations are made privately. If, in the view of the Council, the divergence of the budgetary position is persisting or even worsening, the Council must issue recommendations to the Member State concerned to take prompt corrective measures. Moreover, the Council can decide to make its recommendation public.[143]

What becomes clear from this is that the early warning mechanism does not apply automatically, but rather is based on an assessment by the Council which

---

138. Arts. 5 and 9 Council Reg. 1466/97. Updated stability programmes are in the first instance examined by the Economic and Financial Committee on the basis of assessments by the Commission (Arts. 5(3) and 9(3)).
139. Artis. 5 (1) and 9 (1) Council Reg. 1466/97. The Convergence and Stability Programmes thus have to be sufficiently ambitious.
140. Art. 10 (1) Reg. 1466/97.
141. F. Amtenbrink and J. de Haan (2003), op. cit., *supra* note 29.
142. Art. 99(4) EC and Arts. 6(2) and 10(2) Reg. 1466/97.
143. Arts. 6(3) and 10(3) Reg. 1466/97.

has to decide by qualified majority on the basis of a recommendation from the Commission.[144]

While the Council is obliged to base its own assessment on objectively definable criteria, neither Article 99 EC nor Regulation 1466/97 can effectively ensure that the BEPG and Convergence or Stability Programmes are observed by the Member States. As such, the multilateral surveillance procedure relies on the good intentions of the Member States, as Member States cannot be effectively held to account in case of non-compliance.[145] If, and to the extent that, Member States do not claim political ownership of the Community economic objectives, their implementation in the national policy areas will remain elusive, as a lack of political determination in the implementation of the broad guidelines cannot be corrected by the Community.[146] This is a consequence of the reliance on what effectively amounts to an open method of economic policy coordination and peer review.[147] The latter is particularly problematic given the fact that currently a Member State under investigation is not excluded from voting on the application of the early warning mechanism. Consequently, the impartiality of the members of the Council may vary, as it cannot be excluded that the economic situation in the Member States influences their voting behaviour. The procedure has become politicized, as was illustrated when the Council decided on several occasions not to put a Commission recommendation for the application of the early warning procedure to Germany and Portugal (February 2002) and Italy (July 2004) to the vote, despite acknowledging that these countries had departed from their respective budgetary paths.[148]

The enlargement of the EU to include new Member States most of whom at the time of accession were unable to comply with Article 104(1) EC, may further tilt the scale towards a lax application of the multilateral surveillance procedure in its present form.[149] Moreover, the failed application of the early warning procedure in 2002 and 2004 also highlights the relatively weak role of the Commission in the

---

144. There is an interesting institutional point here: the recommendations to the Member State are adopted on the basis of a recommendation from the Commission (as opposed to a proposal which is required for the recommendations to be made public). On the basis of Art. 205(2) EC, the decision to adopt the recommendation to the Member State should be taken by the heavier qualified majority (two-thirds of the Member States in favour), as the Council is not acting on a *proposal* from the Commission. The ordinary qualified majority applies in relation to a decision to make the recommendations to the Member State public.

145. As to the motives of the drafters of the Treaty of Maastricht for this soft law approach see F. Amtenbrink and J. de Haan (2003), op. cit., *supra* note 29, 1091 et seq., with further references.

146. The blatant discrepancies between the Lisbon objectives and the lack of follow-up at the national level are a case in point.

147. Generally with regard to the open and closed method of economic coordination and its shortcomings: F. Amtenbrink and J. de Haan (2003), op. cit., *supra* note 29, with further references.

148. See 2407th Council meeting (ECOFIN), Brussels, 12 Feb. 2002 (6108/02 (Presse 28)) and 2594th Council meeting (ECOFIN), Brussels, 5 Jul. 2004 (10888/04 (Presse 213)).

149. F. Amtenbrink and J. de Haan (2006), op. cit., *supra* note 104, 411, who analyse whether the reformed rules will work in an enlarged EMU.

multilateral surveillance procedure.[150] While it assesses the government financial positions in the Member States, the Commission has only its power of persuasion to move the Council to act, as its recommendation is not legally binding on the latter.[151]

The Treaty of Lisbon will not dramatically amend the present system. Its major innovation is to put the Commission at the helm of the early warning procedure by giving it the right to address a warning to the Member State concerned on its own initiative. However, the Council will remain in charge of addressing the necessary recommendations to the Member State concerned. It is foreseen that under the new arrangements the vote of the Member State concerned will not be taken into account.[152] However, this decision will continue to be based on a recommendation from the Commission, rather than a proposal from which the Council could only deviate by unanimity decision. Moreover, suggestions to introduce a separate sanction mechanism in case a Member State continuously fails to observe the BEPG have not been taken into account.[153] In addition, Member States who do not participate in the euro area (i.e., those with a derogation) will be suspended for the adoption by the Council of recommendations made to Member States within the euro area in the framework of multilateral surveillance, including on stability programmes and warnings.[154] This may in fact be counter-productive for the application of the multilateral surveillance procedure, as (some of) those Member States may have a particular interest in observing budgetary discipline in order to fulfil the convergence criteria.[155]

Finally, by not granting the European Parliament a bigger role in the establishments of the BEPG a chance has been missed to enhance the democratic legitimacy of the economic coordination and EMU as a whole.[156] However, with the increased role of the Commission in the multilateral surveillance procedure, the European Parliament will at least be able to hold the latter to account for its conduct.

---

150. The background for this limited role includes attempts in the run-up to the Treaty of Maastricht to establish EMU as a separate pillar of the EU, to which the Community institutional framework would not have applied. See J.-V. Louis, (1995), op. cit., *supra* note 12, 20–23, and J. Pipkorn (1994), op. cit., *supra* note 92, 263. The role of the European Parliament is even more limited.
151. Art. 250(1) EC.
152. Art. 121(4) TFEU. Interestingly, a qualified majority will then be defined in accordance with the amended Art. 238(3)(a) of the TFEU rather than the amended Art. 238(3)(b) which applies in case the Council acts on the recommendation of the Commission. According to Art. 238(3)(a), as from 1 Nov. 2014, if not all Council members participate in voting, a qualified majority is defined as a majority of 55% of the Council representing the participating Member States, comprising at least 65% of the population of these states. A blocking minority requires at least the minimum number of Council members representing more than 35% of the population of the participating Member States, plus one Member.
153. This was argued by A. Geelhoed in the 6th Dutch edition of this work (778).
154. Art. 139(4)(a) of the TFEU.
155. See also section 3.2.5, *infra*.
156. Generally on the role of the EP in EMU, see F. Amtenbrink, 'Integration, Coordination or Fragmentation in Economic Policy Matters? A Comment on René Smits', in N. Lavranos and D. Obradovic, op. cit., *supra* note 78, 181 et seq.

3.2.4.2   *Excessive Deficit Procedure (Article 104 EC, Regulation 1467/97)*

Rather than focusing on effective corrective measures in case of undesired budgetary developments in the Member States, and thus on preventive mechanisms, the effectiveness of the system of economic coordination depends on the procedure foreseen if an excessive government deficit actually arises, due to the weakness of the multilateral surveillance procedure as observed above.

Article 104(1) EC obliges Member States to avoid excessive government deficits, and according to Article 116(4) EC, Member States with a derogation are obliged to 'endeavour' to avoid excessive deficits.[157] The term 'excessive government deficit' is defined in Article 104(2) EC and Article 1 of the Protocol on the excessive government deficit in terms of two values, referring to the planned or actual government deficit (3% of GDP) and the government debt (60% of GDP). This exclusive focus on the government budgetary positions of the Member States, highlights the preoccupations of the drafters of the Treaty of Maastricht, especially Germany, with ensuring the stability of the future single currency.[158] Other economic policy objectives expressly mentioned in Article 2 EC, such as sustainable economic development and a high degree of employment, are mentioned neither in Articles 98 and 99 EC, nor in Article 104 EC.

The Commission monitors the development of the budgetary situation and of the stock of government debt in the Member States with a view to identifying gross errors. It examines in particular whether and to what extent Member States comply with budgetary discipline.[159] The Commission makes its assessment based on semi-annual reports which the Member States have to provide, and which must include, among other things, information concerning their planned and actual government deficits and the levels of government debt.[160]

Article 104(2) EC provides the Commission and subsequently also the Council with a certain degree of discretion in considering a government deficit above 3% of GDP as not breaching the reference value, if the deficit has declined substantially and continuously and reached a level that comes close to the reference value, or if the excess over the reference value is only exceptional and temporary. Moreover, a government debt of above 60% may be considered not to breach the reference value if the actual government debt has sufficiently diminished and is

---

157.   Those parts of the excessive deficit procedure described in Art. 104(9) and (11) EC do not apply in the case of Member States with a derogation, as well as the UK and Denmark.
158.   The inclusion of an economic paradigm in legislation geared towards economic policy decision-making is not unproblematic, as politics or new scientific insights may change the approach to economic governance over time. Moreover, immediately after the coming into existence of the Treaty of Maastricht it became clear that political aspects were given precedence over economic doctrine, as a separate chapter in the EC Treaty on employment became unavoidable. This was introduced by the Treaty of Amsterdam in 1997. For details, see section 4 *infra.*
159.   Art. 104(2) EC.
160.   Art. 4 Council Reg. 3605/93 (*supra* note 121), as amended.

approaching the reference value at a satisfactory pace.[161] What can be concluded from this is that the infringement of the quantified government deficit limits does not *de jure* signify the existence of an excessive deficit, as the reference values for establishing an excessive deficit are not absolute.[162]

The original Council Regulation 1467/97 aimed at clarifying and tightening the conditions for the application of these exceptions. To this end, in deciding on its initial recommendation, the Commission was required, in the past to consider an economic downturn only as exceptional if there had been an annual fall of real GDP of at least 2%. However, the Council was not bound by this rule, as it had discretion in deciding whether an annual fall of real GDP of less than 2% should be considered exceptional.[163] In making its overall assessment the Council had to take into account observations by the Member State concerned, thereby leaving a certain room for political bargaining. Arguably, the 2005 reform of Regulation 1467/97 has resulted in a more flexible approach to the evaluation of excessive deficits in the Member States. Commission and Council can consider an excess over the reference value resulting from a severe economic downturn as exceptional if the excess over the reference value results from a negative growth rate or an accumulated loss of output during a protracted period of very low growth relative to potential growth.[164]

What is more, in evaluating the economic situation in a given Member State the Commission must take into account numerous factors related to the development of the medium-term economic position, such as the implementation of the policies in the context of the Lisbon agenda, policies to foster research and development and to promote innovation, fiscal consolidation efforts in economically 'good times', debt sustainability, public investment, financial contributions to international solidarity, fiscal burdens related to European unification and the overall quality of public finances.[165] Moreover, the implementation of pension reforms in Member States which introduce a multi-pillar system that includes a mandatory, fully funded pillar, have to be considered by the Commission.[166]

While from an economic point of view it seems sensible to take diverging economic situations into account in determining the existence of an excessive deficit, the long list of factors to be considered risks blurring the overall assessment and offers multiple escape routes from a stringent application of the multilateral surveillance procedure.[167]

Within two weeks of the adoption by the Commission of a report to the effect that a Member State does not fulfil the requirements of Article 104(1) and (2) EC,

---

161. Art. 104(2)(a) and (b) EC.
162. Council Reg. 3605/93 (*supra*, note 121), as amended, provides for a uniform terminology to be applied also by the Member States in the context of the excessive deficit procedure.
163. Art. 2(2) and (3) Reg. 1467/97.
164. Art. 2(2) Reg. 1467/97, as amended.
165. Art. 2(3) Reg. 1467/97, as amended.
166. Art. 2(5) Reg. 1467/97, as amended.
167. M. Buti, S.C.W. Eijffinger and D. Franco, 'The Stability Pact Pains: A Forward-Looking Assessment of the Reform Debate', CEPR Discussion Paper no. 5216, 22 Sep. 2005.

the Economic and Financial Committee has to formulate an opinion on the report.[168] Thereafter, taking into account that opinion, the Commission has to address an opinion indicating the existence or the risk of an excessive deficit to the Council and moreover forward a recommendation the Council as regards the initiation of the excessive deficit procedure.[169] According to Article 3(3) Regulation 1467/97, the actual decision by the Council in accordance with Article 104(6) EC is taken as a rule within four months of the reporting of the economic data by the Member State concerned.[170] This decision is taken by qualified majority vote, whereby the Member State concerned is not excluded from the initial vote to open the excessive deficit procedure.[171] While arguably undesirable from the point of view of an effective application of the excessive deficit procedure, this may be scarcely surprising, given that Article 104(6) EC to some extent institutionalizes the influence by the Member States in the context of the Council's evaluation of the economic situation.[172]

Where a decision to start an excessive deficit procedure has been taken, the Council is required to issue general recommendations in accordance with Article 104(7) EC with a view to bringing the excessive deficit to an end.[173] While according to Article 104(7) EC these recommendations are in principle not made public, in practice Member States often agree that the recommendations should be made public immediately.[174] The Member State is given a deadline of no more than six months in order to take effective action. Moreover, the Council recommendation must establish a deadline within which the excessive government deficit has to be corrected.[175] In principle the excessive deficit must be corrected in the year following its identification.[176] As to the contents of these recommendations,

---

168. With regard to the composition and tasks of the Economic and Financial Committee which has been set up at the start of stage three of EMU: Art. 114(2) EC, Council Decision 98/743/EC of 21 Dec. 1998, on the detailed provisions concerning the composition of the Economic and Financial Committee (O.J. 1998, L 358/109) and Council Decision 1999/8/EC of 31 Dec. 1998, adopting the Statutes of the Economic and Financial Committee (O.J. 1999, L 5/71), as amended by Council Decision 2003/476/EC of 18 Jun. 2003 (O.J. 2003, L 158/58).
169. Arts. 104(3)-(6) EC and Art. 3 Reg. 1467/97.
170. Art. 3(3) of the original Reg. 1467/97 foresaw a period of 3 months. It is clear from the words 'as a rule' that this hardly amounts to a 'hard' deadline.
171. Art. 104(13) EC excludes the Member State concerned only from decisions taken in accordance with Arts. 104(7)-(11) EC.
172. According to that provision, the Council must consider any observations by the Member State concerned.
173. Despite what the wording of Arts. 104(6) and (7) and Art. 3(3) Reg. 1467/97 may suggest, the existence of an excessive deficit and the subsequent recommendations are not established in one and the same decision.
174. According to Art. 104(8) EC the publication is only foreseen after it has been established that the Member State has not taken any effective measures.
175. Art. 3(3) of the original Reg. 1467/97 foresaw a period of four months.
176. Art. 3(4) Reg. 1467/97, unless there are 'special circumstances'. An example for such an exemption can be found in the case of Hungary, where the Council allowed for a longer deadline due to the significant general government deficit upon EU accession and because of the ongoing structural shift to a modern service-oriented market economy accompanying

since the 2005 reform of Regulation 1467/97, Article 3(4) requires that the Member States concerned must be called upon to achieve a minimum annual improvement of at least 0.5% of GDP as a benchmark in the cyclically adjusted balance.[177]

The Member State's progress in correcting the excessive government deficit is monitored both by the Commission, which makes recommendations on the Member State's progress and further action to the Council, and the Council itself. Article 104(8) EC in conjunction with Article 104(13) EC implies that the Council must establish by formal vote that a Member State has not taken any effective corrective action in response to the general recommendations issued by the Council.[178] This has to take place immediately after the expiry of the deadline which the Council has set and thus no later than six months after the recommendations in accordance with Article 104(7) EC have been issued. For Member States with a derogation, the Council decision under Article 104(8) EC marks the end of the excessive deficit procedure, as the remaining steps described hereafter do not apply.[179]

For Member States participating in the euro area, the Council must – within two months of the decision under Article 104(8) EC – take a decision giving the Member State concerned notice to take, within a specified time limit, measures for the deficit reduction which the Council considers necessary in order to remedy the situation.[180] If the Member State fails to comply with the successive recommendations, a decision by the Council to apply sanctions in accordance with Article 104(11) EC must be taken, as a rule within sixteen months of the initial reporting of the economic data by the Member State concerned.[181] In principle, sanctions would take the form of a non-interest-bearing deposit to be lodged with the Commission.[182] In the case of a breach of the government deficit criterion, the initial deposit comprises a fixed component equal to 0.2% of GDP, and a variable component of 0.1% in the preceding year for each percentage point that the government deficit is above the reference value of 3%. An upper limit for a single deposit is fixed at 0.5% of GDP.[183] These sanctions can be intensified if the Member State concerned does not cooperate. Moreover, the non-interest bearing

---

the process of real convergence. See Council Recommendation of 6 Jul. 2004, to Hungary with a view to bringing an end to the situation of an excessive government deficit (11218/04) (ECOFIN 270/UEM 140).

177. For details see F. Amtenbrink and J. de Haan (2006), op. cit., *supra* note 104, 409–410.

178. This is confirmed by the wording of Art. 5(1) Reg. 1467/97.

179. See Art. 122 (3) EC. For these Member States, the incentive lies in the fulfilment of the convergence criteria laid down in Art. 121(1), 2nd indent EC. In the run-up to the decision on the Member States that would make up the initial euro area this proved to be an effective disciplining mechanism.

180. Art. 104(9) EC. Art. 5(1) Reg. 1467/97 requires the Council once more to request in its recommendation a minimum annual improvement of at least 0.5% of GDP.

181. Art. 7 Reg. 1467/96, which moreover foresees in an expedited procedure in case of a deliberately planned excessive deficit.

182. At the time of the writing of this section, this mechanism had not been applied on a single occasion.

183. Arts. 12(1) and (3) Reg. 1467/97.

deposit is converted by the Council into a fine, if two years after the decisions requiring the Member State to make a deposit, the deficit has not been corrected in the view of the Council.[184] Interestingly, Council Regulation 1467/97 does not specify the sanctions applicable in case of the non-compliance with the criterion relating to the government debt ratio, despite the fact that Article 104 (11) EC equally applies in these cases.[185]

It is apparent from Article 104(13) EC that the Council decisions in accordance with Articles 104(7)-(9), and (11) EC have to be taken on a Commission recommendation by a two-thirds majority of the votes of the Council members weighted in accordance with Article 205(2) and excluding the votes of the representative of the Member State concerned. Moreover, Member States with a derogation are excluded from voting in the context of Article 104(9) and (11) EC, as it has been observed above that they are not subject to this part of the excessive deficit procedure.[186] Article 104(13) thus lowers the hurdle for an application of the later stages of the excessive deficit procedure, as for the initial decision on the application of the excessive deficit procedure in accordance with Article 104(6) EC the double majority requirement laid down in Article 205(2) EC applies.[187] At the same time the relative weight of the votes of the Member States participating in the decision making increases, whereby the weighing of the votes is potentially more beneficial for bigger Member States participating in the euro area.[188]

Similarly to what has been observed for the multilateral surveillance procedure, the excessive deficit procedure relies on peer review. The votes of the Member State concerned are excluded once the Council decision on the existence of an excessive deficit has been taken, but it has been suggested that the participation of Member States in the voting procedure which themselves may be subject to a separate early warning or excessive deficit procedure reduces the efficiency of the excessive deficit procedure, both in deterring countries from running excessive deficits and in applying the sanctions foreseen in Article 104 EC and Regulation 1467/97.[189] The stringency of the procedure depends to a considerable extent on the political will of the Member States to observe the

---

184. Art. 12(2) and 13 Reg. 1467/97. Moreover, a new deposit has to be made.
185. Critical on this apparent lack of quantification of sanctions in the case of the government debt criterion: F. Amtenbrink and J. de Haan (2003), op. cit., *supra* note 29, 1099–1100.
186. See Arts. 122(3) and (5) EC. The same applies to the UK and Denmark. See Protocol on certain provisions relating to the United Kingdom of Great Britain and Northern Ireland and Protocol on certain provisions relating to Denmark. Nevertheless in practice the United Kingdom seems to subject itself also to Art. 104 (9) EC. At the 2753nd ECOFIN Council meeting on 10 Oct. 2006, (13600/06 (Presse 278)), the application of Art. 104(9) EC was discussed, albeit in the end rejected.
187. Acts adopted on a recommendation from the Commission require at least 255 votes in favour, cast by at least two-thirds of the Member States.
188. F. Amtenbrink and J. de Haan (2006), op. cit., *supra* note 104, at 405.
189. B. Irlenbusch, U. Leopold-Wildburger et al., 'Voting in EMU: An Experimental Study of Institutional Innovation and the Role of Communication in the Stability and Growth Pact' (2003), JCMS, 645–664.

rules, which may also depend on the particular economic situation in the Member States.[190]

The practical consequences of the system of peer review could be witnessed in 2003 in the context of the application of the excessive deficit procedure to Germany and France. In the case of both countries, the Council had established the existence of an excessive deficit.[191] Although the Commission had subsequently recommended to the Council to decide that both France and Germany had failed take effective action in response to the Council recommendations issued in accordance with Article 104(7) EC, in the case of both countries the Council failed twice to reach the two-thirds majority, first with regard to the decision establishing the failure on part of Germany and France to take sufficient action to comply with its recommendations (Art. 104(8) EC) and, thereafter with regard to the decision to issue concrete measures for deficit reduction (Art. 104(9) EC). As a result of this failure to reach the required majority in the Council, the excessive deficit procedure came to a halt, triggering a major inter-institutional conflict between the Commission and the Council.[192]

It is apparent from the experience in the application of Article 104 EC and Regulation 1467/97 that, despite its more stringent set-up as compared to the multilateral surveillance procedure, the excessive deficit procedure features the same system of peer review. The 2005 reform of Regulation 1467/97 has not changed this approach.[193] The lack of any automatism in the procedure and the absence of an independent enforcer may increase the incentives for collusion by the Council in subverting the implementation of the rules.[194] Experience so far suggests that keeping the Council firmly in charge of the procedure is likely to aggravate the problems with enforcement of the excessive deficit procedure and thus, the sustained convergence of the economic performances of the Member States. This may not only be problematic for economic policy coordination in EMU, but also for monetary policy. Given the interconnectedness of economic and monetary policy, the weakness of the current system of economic coordination, together with the diverging economic situations in the Member States and the

---

190. In this context R. Smits, 'Some Reflections on Economic Policy' (2007), *Legal Issues of European Integration*, 5, at 14 observes that the EC Treaty is 'flawed in its basic structure of EMU' as it is based 'on the misconception that enlightened self-interest will ensure coordination of economic policies'.

191. Council Decision 2003/98/EC of 21 Jan. 2003, on the existence of an excessive deficit in Germany (O.J. 2003, L 34/16) and Council Decision 2003/487/EC of 3 Jun. 2003, on the existence of an excessive deficit in France (O.J. 2003, L 165/29). See also the subsequent Council recommendations of 21 Jan. 2003 (5506/03 (Presse 15)) and of 3 Jun. 2003 (9844/03 (Presse 149)).

192. See hereafter section 3.2.4.3. on the judicial review in the multilateral surveillance and excessive deficit procedure.

193. This is also critically observed by J.-V. Louis, 'The Review of the Stability and Growth Pact' (2006), CML Rev., 85, at 105.

194. The original German proposal for a reinforcement of the excessive deficit procedure had called for an automatic application of the excessive deficit procedure. However, these ideas were resisted by a considerable number of Member States, not least because this would have essentially altered primary Community law, as Art. 104 EC does not foresee any such automatism. See F. Amtenbrink, J. de Haan and Sleijpen (1997), op. cit., *supra* note 104, at 234.

deficit situation in some Member States may arguably result in spill-over effects not just on other Member States, but also on the single monetary policy in the euro area. The ECB may feel forced to tighten or loosen its monetary policy standards, thereby also affecting those Member States whose economic situation may require a different monetary policy stance.[195]

The Treaty of Lisbon will somewhat alter the inter-institutional balance in the application of the excessive deficit procedure in favour of the Commission. Firstly, the Commission will be given the right to address its opinion on the existence of an excessive government deficit not only to the Council but also to the Member State concerned.[196] Moreover, the initial Council decision establishing the existence of an excessive deficit will be based on a Commission proposal rather than a recommendation.[197] In line with today's Article 250(1) EC, Article 293 of the Treaty on the Functioning of the EU requires the Council to act by unanimity in case it wants to amend a Commission proposal. Thus in the future, the alteration of the Commission proposal with regard to a recommendation for a Member State will require a unanimous Council decision. However, this arrangement cannot prevent the emergence of a situation similar to that observed above with regard to Germany and France, in which the required majority is not reached in the Council.[198] These majority requirements will be amended for decisions in the context of what will become Articles 126(8), (9) and (11) of the Treaty on the Functioning of the EU. The most important innovation in this regard is that the Member State under review will no longer be allowed to participate in the initial decision in accordance with today's Article 104(6) EC to open the excessive deficit procedure.[199]

However, rather like what has been observed for the multilateral surveillance procedure, the Treaty of Lisbon fails to address some of the more structural deficiencies of today's excessive deficit procedure, as the system of peer review remains firmly in place. The assessment of economic coordination in EMU as a system that is characterized by a structural imbalance between, on the one side, the relatively detailed and ambitious economic policy guidelines which the Member States have to adhere to and, on the other side, the vulnerable enforcement mechanism included in particular in Article 104 EC and Regulation 1467/97, does not have to be substantially altered against the background of the Treaty of Lisbon.

---

195. This despite the so-called 'no bail-out clause' included in Art. 103 EC. Generally with regard to spill-over effects and the role of the ECB: F. Amtenbrink and J. de Haan (2003), op. cit., *supra* note 29, 1093, with further references.
196. Art. 126(5) of the TFEU.
197. Art. 126(6) of the TFEU.
198. For more details on the complex regime introduced by the Treaty of Lisbon applicable before 1 Nov. 2014, between 1 Nov. 2014 and 31 Mar. 2017 and from 1 Apr. 2017, see Ch. V, section 3, *supra* of this work.
199. Art. 126(13) of the TFEU.

3.2.4.3 Judicial Review in the Multilateral Surveillance and Excessive Deficit Procedure

As has been observed above, the Member States are obliged to forward annually updated Stability of Convergence Programmes. Failure to forward the relevant information would constitute a breach of the reporting requirement under Article 99 EC and moreover of Article 10 EC, which obliges Member States to take all appropriate measures to ensure fulfilment of the obligations arising from the EC Treaty and from the action taken by the Community Institutions. Such an action could be initiated by the Commission or by another Member State in accordance with Article 226 or 227 EC.[200] In case of non-compliance of a Member State with a judgment by the ECJ declaring the Member State's omission in breach with Article 99 EC, sanctions could be applied to the Member State concerned as a result of the application of Article 228(2) EC. Yet, as has been observed elsewhere, such a judicial review in the context of the multilateral surveillance procedure may be little more than a theoretical course of action and moreover cannot effectively prevent the emergence of an excessive government deficit.[201]

Whether an omission by the Council to issue recommendations in accordance with Article 99(4) EC could successfully be challenged as a failure to act in accordance with Article 232 EC is questionable. The wording of Article 99(4) EC ('... the Council may ...') suggests that the Council is under no obligation to act. Article 6(2) of Regulation 1466/97 is somewhat more stringent in stating that in the event that it identifies a divergence of the budgetary position of a Member State from the medium-term budgetary objective, or the adjustment path towards it, the Council 'shall' make recommendations to the Member State concerned to take prompt corrective measures. The same applies if it is concluded thereafter that the divergence of the budgetary position is persisting or worsening.[202] The Council has a considerable degree of discretion in assessing the economic situation of Member State. The Council may thus differ from the Commission and come to the conclusion that a significant divergence does not (yet) exist. This would have to be taken into account by the ECJ if the Council's conduct was indeed challenged. Interestingly, the non-application of the early warning procedure by the Council in the case of Germany, Portugal and Italy observed above, was not challenged by the Commission.

Article 104(10) EC makes clear that the Member States' observance of the basic rule to avoid excessive government deficits cannot be subject to judicial review in the context of a Treaty infringement procedure initiated by the Commission under Article 226 EC or by another Member State under Article 227 EC.[203] Consequently, a Member State cannot be forced to comply with Article 104(1) EC by sanctions in accordance with Article 228(2) EC. It has been argued that the

---

200. Unlike Art. 104 EC, Art. 99 EC does not exclude the application of Arts. 226 and 227 EC.
201. F. Amtenbrink and J. de Haan (2003), op. cit., *supra* note 29, 1083.
202. Art. 6(3) Reg. 1466/97.
203. Excluded are Arts. 104(1)-(9) EC.

Stability and Growth Pact has resulted in an objectification of the excessive deficit procedure in a normative sense, which makes Article 104(10) EC redundant.[204] Yet, even if such an action was permissible despite the wording of Article 104 EC, its outcome would arguably be uncertain. Whether a Member State has taken effective measures comes down to an economic assessment by the Council, which once more involves a considerable degree of discretion.

On the contrary, in the context of the excessive deficit procedure, the legally binding acts of the Council or its failure to act in case of the existence of a legal obligation to that effect, can in principle be subject to judicial review in the context of an action for annulment (Art. 230 EC) or an action for failure to act (Art. 232 EC).

In fact, the scope of the obligations of the Council in the context of the excessive deficit procedure, and thus, the legal stringency of an important part of economic coordination itself, formed the subject-matter of a dispute between the Commission and the Council which finally had to be resolved by the ECJ.[205] What triggered this open inter-institutional conflict, in the form of an annulment procedure, was the above-mentioned failure of the Council in the case of Germany and France to adopt a decision according to Article 104(7) EC and, thereafter, Article 104(8) EC. Instead, applying the voting rules which relate to decisions envisaged by Article 104(9) EC, the Council basically adopted conclusions with regard to each of the two Member States concerned which moreover deviated from the Commission recommendations. These conclusions stated that the Council had decided not to act on the basis of the Commission recommendation and, moreover, that the Council agreed 'to hold the Excessive Deficit Procedure in abeyance for the time being'.[206] In the view of the Commission, the Council had effectively acted contrary to the EC Treaty by deciding not to take the two relevant decisions and, moreover, by issuing conclusions.

In its judgment the ECJ confirmed the binding character of the rules governing the excessive deficit procedure and the role assigned to the Commission therein, by rejecting the Council's course of action with regard to the issuing of conclusions. The ECJ considered that the Council had effectively broken the rules governing the excessive deficit procedure by deciding to hold the procedure in abeyance and by making this subject to the compliance by Germany and France with Council recommendations included in these conclusions. Consequently, the ECJ annulled the conclusions.

However, at the same time the ECJ acknowledged that in circumstances where the Council does not succeed in adopting a decision due to a lack of the required

---

204. Geelhoed in the 6th Dutch edition of this work (779) with reference to J.-V. Louis, (1995), op. cit., *supra* note 12, 22.
205. Case C-27/04, *Commission v. Council*. Generally on this decision: I. Maher, 'Economic Policy Coordination and the European Court: Excessive Deficits and ECOFIN Discretion' (2005), EL Rev., 831; B. Dutzler and A. Hable, The European Court of Justice and the Stability and Growth Pact: Just the Beginning?, EIoP (2005), no. 5; R. Smits, 'Het Europese Hof beslecht geschil over communautair toezicht op begrotingsdiscipline' (2004), NTER, 221.
206. See 2546th Council meeting, 25 Nov. 2003 (14492/1/03 REV 1 (en) (Presse 320)).

majority, the excessive deficit procedure is effectively held in abeyance. In this context, the ECJ did not follow the Commission's appraisal of the legal nature of such incapacity on the part of the Council. In the view of the ECJ, such a failure to reach a positive decision in the Council does not amount to a decision open to challenge under Article 230 EC.

As an *obiter dictum* the ECJ mentioned that the Commission could have recourse to Article 232 EC in a case where the Council does not adopt formal instruments recommended by the Commission pursuant to Article 104(8) and (9) EC. This raises the question what exactly the legal obligation of the Council in the context of Article 104(8) and (9) EC is, and whether this actually amounts to a legal obligation on the Council to adopt the decisions foreseen in those provisions. That would be required if the failure of the Council to take the necessary decisions were to be subject of an action for failure to act in accordance with Article 232 EC.[207] The open wording of Article 104 EC suggests that the Council is merely obliged to put the matter to the vote, whereas the somewhat more comprehensive Council Regulation 1467/97 suggests that a particular decision is to be taken.[208] What may in the end be decisive is that Article 104 EC subjects the application of the excessive deficit procedure to a political decision-making process by submitting the application of the different steps of the procedure to voting in the Council. This then includes the possibility that the required majorities may not be reached. Obliging the Council to a particular course of action would effectively disregard this legislative choice.

Overall, the judgment in Case C-27/04 confirms the major weakness of the present system of economic coordination, that is the dependence of the progress of the excessive deficit procedure on the decision of the Council. As such, the judgment can thus hardly be considered a major reinforcement of the excessive deficit procedure through the interpretative power of the ECJ.[209]

3.2.5 Legal and Economic Conditions for Joining the Euro Area and Status of Member States with a Derogation[210]

Member States not yet participating in the euro area are subject to the legal regime applying in stage two of EMU until such time as they fulfil the legal and economic conditions set out in Article 116 EC and Article 121 EC for joining the single currency and a Council decision on their inclusion in the euro area has been taken.

---

207. With regard to the requirement in the context of Art. 232 EC of an obligation to act see e.g., Case T-47/96, *Syndicat départemental de défénse de droits des agriculteurs*.
208. Of course, from a formal legal point of view, secondary Community law cannot override primary Community law.
209. This is however suggested by I. Maher, op. cit., *supra* note 204, at 841, who argues that: '... the early stages of the EDP [excessive deficit procedure: FA] are not merely a matter of politics; and that even where there is no immediate sanction other than peer pressure and the prospect of further decisions, soft law has practical and legal effects that cannot be bypassed'.
210. See generally F. Amtenbrink, 'Economic and Monetary Policy (In the Framework of EMU)', in A. Ott and K. Inglis, *Handbook on European Enlargement* (The Hague, 2002), 693–706.

Given that a considerable number of Member States of the EU have not (yet) adopted the single currency and, moreover, given the prospect of further enlargement of the EU in the coming years, the legal regime applicable in stage two of EMU retains its practical relevance to a large extent.[211]

3.2.5.1   *Legal and Economic Conditions for Joining the Euro Area: The Convergence Criteria*

The transitional phase in the run-up to the establishment of the ESCB and the ECB, as well as the adoption of a single currency, is regulated in Articles 116–124 EC and several protocols, including in particular the Protocol on the convergence criteria referred to in Article 121 EC, the Protocol on the transition to the third stage of EMU, two separate protocols on certain provisions relating to Denmark and the United Kingdom, and one on the Statute of the ESCB and ECB.[212]

Participation in the euro area and thus, in the third and final phase of EMU is not an automatic process which is linked to the accession to the EU and/or a simple political decision in the Council. In fact, with Article 121 EC the drafters the Treaty of Maastricht introduced a complex set of procedural and substantive legal and economic conditions which Member States have to fulfil in order to qualify for participation in the euro area. These conditions are generally referred to as convergence criteria. In sum, they impose far-reaching obligations on the national approach to economic and monetary policy, in particular for those Member States that actually have the ambition to join the euro area.[213]

With regard to the *legal conditions*, in stage two of EMU, Member States are required to observe the prohibition of overdraft facilities or other types of credit facilities with the ECB or with the central banks of the Member States (Art. 101 EC), as well as the prohibition on privileged access to financial institutions (Art. 102 EC).[214] According to Article 116 EC, both Article 101 and Article 102 EC apply already in stage two of EMU.[215] Article 116(5) EC moreover states that Member States 'shall, as appropriate, start the process leading to the independence of its central bank, in accordance with Article 109'. The reference to central bank independence in Article 116(5) EC is rather broad. Article 109 EC does not substantially clarify this point, as it only requires Member States to ensure that their national legislation – including the statutes of its NCB – is compatible with the EC

---

211. This excludes those provisions that only applied in the period prior the establishment of the ESCB and the ECB and the initial introduction of the euro. As of 1 Jan. 2008, 15 of the 27 Member States participate in the euro area.
212. In the order of mentioning: O.J. 1992, C 191/85, O.J. 1992, C 191/87, O.J. 1992, C 191/89, O.J. 1992, C 191/87 and O.J. 1992, C 191/79.
213. It is thus little surprising that the convergence criteria have been criticized, notably in the French and Belgian literature. See e.g., P. de Grauwe, 'The Maastricht Treaty as an Obstacle to Monetary Union', *International Economic Research Paper* no. 94 (CES, KU Leuven, 1993).
214. It results from Art. 116(2) (a) EC that they have to have adopted the necessary measures prior to entering stage two of EMU.
215. Moreover, the 'no bail-out clause' included in Art. 103(1) EC applies.

Treaty and the Statute of the ESCB. According to Article 108 EC and Article 7 ESCB Statute, neither the ECB nor a NCB when exercising the powers and carrying out the tasks and duties conferred upon them by primary Community law are allowed to seek or take instructions from Community Institutions or bodies, from any government of a Member State or from any other body. Moreover, the Community Institutions and bodies and the governments of the Member States are prompted to respect the independence of the ECB and the NCB and not to seek to influence their decision-making bodies in the performance of their tasks.[216] The actual extent of this obligation and its impact on the institutional arrangements laid down in the legal basis of a central bank can arguably only be found by using the ESCB and ECB as a yardstick. From this it becomes clear that central bank independence actually stands for a multifaceted concept, including institutional, functional, organizational and financial aspects, as well as the practice.[217]

As has been observed in the previous section, accession negotiations in the two most recent rounds of enlargement focused among other things also on EMU. This included in particular the compatibility of the statute of a country's monetary authority with the EC Treaty and the ESCB Statute. The requirement to bring national legislation in this area in line with primary Community law – and not just for the most recent accessions – has resulted in amendments of the legal basis of numerous NCBs, resulting in some instances, such as the Banque de France, in substantial alteration of the position *vis-à-vis* government.[218]

With regard to the *economic conditions*, Article 121 EC and the Protocol on the convergence criteria include the economic criteria which Member States have to fulfil in order to show that they have achieved the degree of sustainable economic convergence envisaged by the EC Treaty.

The first criterion is achievement of a *high degree of price stability*, which has to be apparent from a rate of inflation which is close to that of, at most, the three best performing Member States in terms of price stability. Article 1 of the Protocol on the convergence criteria explains that a Member State has to have a price performance that is sustainable and an average rate of inflation, observed over a period of one year before the examination, that does not exceed by more than 1.5 percentage points that of, at most, the three best performing Member States in terms of price stability.[219] The reference 'best performing Member States' has to be read as Member States both inside and outside the euro area, whereby the reference value is calculated as the simple arithmetic average of the inflation

---

216. On the independence of the ESCB and of the ECB see also hereafter section 3.3.2 *infra*.
217. Generally with regard to the evaluation of central bank independence, both *de jure* and *de facto*, cf. F. Amtenbrink, (1999) op. cit. *supra* note 61, 17 et seq.
218. With regard to the legal adjustments of the central banks of the Member States see F. Amtenbrink (1999) op. cit. *supra* note 61.
219. Inflation is measured by the harmonized indices of consumer prices (HICPs) defined in Council Reg. (EC) No 2494/95 of 23 Oct. 1995, concerning harmonized indices of consumer prices (O.J. 1995, L 257/1), as amended by Reg. (EC) No 1882/2003 of the European Parliament and the Council (O.J. 2003, L 284/1).

rates of the three best performing Member States in terms of price stability plus 1.5 percentage points.

Despite receiving less attention in the literature than the condition relating to the government financial position, the importance of this condition should not be underestimated. Indeed, the degree to which a Member State achieves convergence in the nominal price development is a good indicator for its ability to adjust its economy to the demands of a full EMU. An inflation rate that continuously deviates from the reference value despite the alignment of exchange rates decreases the economy's competitiveness, resulting in fewer employment opportunities. The ability of a Member State to achieve and maintain relative price stability is thus an indication for the ability of its economy to muster the discipline required in a full established EMU.[220]

The second criterion is *sustainability of the government financial position*, which has to be apparent from having achieved a government budgetary position without a deficit that is excessive as determined under Article 104(6)EC. According to Article 2 of the Protocol on the convergence criteria the Member State may not be the subject of an excessive deficit procedure. Accordingly, the reference values for the excessive deficit are 3% for the ratio of the planned or actual government deficit to GDP at market prices and 60% for the ratio of government debt to GDP at market prices.

The substance of this criterion is anything but undisputed among economists.[221] It has been noted that the sustainability of public finances is not only determined by the combination of government deficit and debt ratio, but moreover also by additional factors, such as the national savings balance and direct and indirect monetary financing. Moreover, there is a link between the government deficit criterion of 3% and the government debt criterion of 60%. In the case of balanced growth and excluding the possibility of monetary financing, the debt ratio will be linked to the relationship between government deficit and the growth of nominal GDP. A nominal government debt of 60% is compatible with a maximum government deficit of 3%, if the nominal GDP growth amounts to 5%. Such GDP growth can be reasonably expected under normal circumstances. Indeed, based on historical data it can be assumed that real GDP growth within the Community structurally amounts to approximately 2%. Assuming an inflation rate of 3% this amounts to a structural nominal GDP growth of approximately 5%.[222]

---

220. C. Maggiulli, 'Convergence et Union Monétaire Européenne' (1993), RMC, 620–627. Also T. van Hoek and G. Zalm, Nationaal begrotingsbeleid in Europees perspectief, in J. Alders et al., *Begrotingsbeleid en financiering Nederlandse staatsschuld, op weg naar de EMU* (Utrecht, 1992), 34–51, and S. Brittan, EMU in Perspective, in M. Andenas et al., op. cit., *supra* note 77, 101–124, in particular 109–112.

221. W. Buiter, 'De budgettaire voodoo van Maastricht' (1992) ESB, 268–272; See also T. van Hoek and G. Zalm, op. cit., *supra* note 220, and I. Harden and J. von Hagen, 'National Debt Boards: an Institutional Route to Fiscal Discipline', in M. Andenas et al., op. cit., *supra* note 77, 270–286.

222. A. Italianer, 'Begrotingsbeleid in EMU: safety first', in Alders et al., op. cit., *supra* note 220, 14–34, in particular 24 and 25; P. van den Bempt, 'The Impact of Economic and Monetary Union and Member States' Fiscal Policies', in K. Gretschmann (ed.), op. cit., *supra* note 70, 245–261.

At the time of their formulation in the Treaty of Maastricht, these government deficit criteria were rather ambitious. Most Member States nursed government deficits way above the 3% threshold, as well as having government debts considerably above the 60% limit. At the end of 1997 most Member States could manage to comply with the government deficit criterion, but where still running excessive government debts. It was this situation which resulted in the exception included in Article 104(1)(b) EC, allowing for a government debt above 60% if 'the ratio is sufficiently diminishing and approaching the reference value at a satisfactory pace' gained political and strategic importance.[223] A strict interpretation of the government debt criterion, demanding a rapid decrease of the government debt by bringing down the government deficit far below the 3% threshold before the end of 1997, was neither in line with a systematic interpretation of the law, nor desirable from an economic point of view. In fact, if the government deficit is brought below 3%, under normal economic circumstances with a real economic growth of 2–3% and an inflation rate of the same order, the conditions are created which allow for government debt ratio to gradually decrease under the 60% threshold. A similar view was taken by the Council in 1997 and 1998, when it was decided to abrogate several decisions on the existence of excessive deficits in a number of Member States.[224] This is moreover in line with the view taken by the EMI and the Commission in their respective convergence reports of March 1998.[225]

The third criterion is the observance of the *normal fluctuation margins* provided for by the exchange-rate mechanism of the EMS, for at least two years, without devaluing against the currency of any other Member State. Article 3 of the Protocol on convergence criteria adds to this that the normal fluctuation margins must be observed 'without severe tensions' and that the Member State must not have devalued its currency's bilateral central rate against any other Member State's currency 'on its own initiative'. What is arguably missing from this is the possibility that a devaluation of the currency of one or more Member States results from a revaluation of the currencies of a number of other Member States.[226]

At the time of the establishment of EMU, the inclusion of this criterion formed an insurmountable barrier for the vast majority of Member States. This was due to the turbulences in the ERM which arose in September 1992, and which led to the departure of the United Kingdom and Italy from the system and a considerable

---

223. Note for example the rather cautious way in which the EMI and the Commission handled this criterion in their convergence reports in 1998 on the eve of the decision to enter stage three of EMU. See e.g., Commission's recommendation concerning the third stage of EMU. Convergence Report 1998. Growth and employment in the stability-oriented framework of EMU, European Economy, No. 65, 1998.

224. See e.g., Council Decision 98/307/EC and 98/311/EC abrogating the decision on the existence of an excessive deficit in Belgium, as well as in Italy (O.J. 1998, L 139/9 and L 139/15). While the debt ratio was on a downward path, at the time both countries had a government debt of more than two times that of the reference value.

225. Commission, Convergence Report, Brussels, 25 Mar. 1998, 8. European Monetary Institute, Convergence Report, Frankfurt a.M., March 1998, 16 and 22.

226. See J. Cloos et al. (1993), op. cit., *supra* note 51, at 207.

adjustment in the exchange rates of the Spanish Peseta and the Portuguese Escudo within the system.[227] Given the deadlines foreseen in Article 121(4) EC this in itself should not have posed a serious problem for the Member States concerned. However, that changed following the turbulences in the summer of 1993 which resulted in a broadening of the fluctuation margins in ERM in most instances from 6 to 15%.[228] Given the vulnerability of a system of stable but adjustable exchange rates it became very questionable whether it was possible to return to the normal, i.e., previous, fluctuation margins in the ERM, in time for a positive evaluation of the corresponding convergence criterion.

In order to prevent a negative outcome, the focus turned to the objective of this criterion. Member States were supposed to discipline their conduct of monetary policy with the aim of preventing exchange-rate fluctuations caused by a destabilizing monetary policy. This was effectively the approach chosen by the Member States in the period between 1993 and 1998. Despite the broad margins foreseen in ERM, in practice the exchange rates stayed relatively close to the normal central rate. Quite remarkably, in the last year before the changeover to the single currency, no significant speculations with ERM currencies took place in the financial markets. Apparently the economic policy of the Member States enjoyed sufficient credibility in the market-place. Consequently, in the run-up to the decision on the initial group of Member States to join the euro area, a rather flexible approach was taken to the fulfilment of this convergence criterion.[229]

The *fourth and final* convergence criterion listed in Article 121(1) EC is the *durability of convergence* achieved by the Member State and of its participation in the exchange-rate mechanism of the European Monetary System as reflected in the long-term interest-rate levels.[230] According to Article 4 of the Protocol on the convergence criteria, in assessing this criterion it is observed whether a Member State over a period of one year before the examination, has had an average nominal long-term interest rate that does not exceed by more than 2% that of the three best performing Member States in terms of price stability.[231] This criterion effectively supplements the first two convergence criteria. If the economies of the Member States are convergent in terms of the level of inflation and the government budgetary situation, the free movement of capital should also result in the convergence of the long-term interest rates. The interest rate is a reflection of the level of trust

---

227. See F. Ozkan and A. Sutherland, A Model of the ERM Crisis, CEPR discussion paper no. 879, 1994, and H. Tietmayer, 'Zur politischen Fundierung des monetären Integrationsprozesses in Europa', in O. Due et al. (eds), *Festschrift für Ulrich Everling*, vol. II (Baden-Baden, 1995), 1575–1585, at 1580.
228. For the DMark and the Dutch Guilder the margins remained at +/− 2.25%.
229. Of course, the convergence criterion was formally applied, thereby allowing Sweden, which had deliberately not participated in ERM I to stay outside the euro area. On the contrary, the fact that both Finland and Italy had not yet been a full 2 years in ERM was not considered a reason to reject these Member States. See Smits (1999), op. cit., *infra* note 284, at 5.
230. In the Treaty of Lisbon, this will be amended to refer to ERM II.
231. Interest rates are measured on the basis of long-term government bonds or comparable securities, taking into account differences in national definitions.

which the financial markets have in the soundness of the economic policy of the Member States.[232]

Finally, although not formally listed as one of the convergence criteria, the last sentence of Article 121(1) EC states that the Commission in its reports on the achievement of convergence must also take account of the development of the euro, the results of the integration of markets, the situation and development of the balances of payments on current account, and the development of unit labour costs and other price indices. This provision emphasizes the link between monetary and economic policy on the one side, and market integration on the other.[233]

3.2.5.2   Decision-Making Procedure

The actual procedure for the acceptance of a Member State into the euro area is laid down in Articles 121(2)–(4) and 122(2) EC. Article 121(2)–(4) EC are partly obsolete to the extent that they govern the determination of the date on which the third and final stage of EMU starts, and the decision that a majority of Member States fulfil the conditions for joining the single currency area. As the Council initially – in December 1996 – decided that this was not the case and that it was not appropriate for the Community to enter into stage three of EMU, Article 121(4) EC thereafter automatically determined the date for the start of stage three of EMU as 1 January 1999.[234] Article 121(4) EC dropped the requirement that a majority of Member States had to fulfil the convergence criteria in order for the third stage to go ahead,[235] thereby effectively providing for a monetary integration at different speeds, as EMU would go ahead even if a majority of the Member States did not fulfil the convergence criteria. Due to the absence of any discretionary powers on the part of the Council, the examination of the convergence criteria was and still is crucial.

In the run-up to the decision on the initial group to join the euro area, Member States with the intention to join stage three of EMU from the start focused both on the improvements of their budgetary positions (namely Italy, Spain and Portugal) and, in some instances, on mustering political support for a soft approach to the application of the convergence criteria by the Commission and Council. Both the legal and political margins of discretion for the Council were, however, relatively small.[236]

---

232. T. van Hoek and G. Zalm, op. cit., *supra* note 220, 37–38, and J.-V. Louis, (1995), op. cit., *supra* note 12, at 140.
233. See also Art. 116(2) EC.
234. Council Decision 96/736/EC of 13 Dec. 1996, in accordance with Art. 109j(3) of the Treaty establishing the European Community, on entry into the third stage of EMU (O.J. 1996, L 335/24).
235. Art. 121(4) EC was introduced into the Treaty of Maastricht only at the last hour, and at the request of France. The latter wanted to ensure that the commencing of the third stage of EMU was not postponed more or less indefinitely as a result of the majority requirement included in Art. 121(3) EC. See J. Cloos et al. (2003), op. cit., *supra* note 51, 203–205.
236. In particular Germany insisted on a strict application of Art. 121 EC, not least against the background of the decision by the German Constitutional Court in the *Brunner* case (an

In line with the procedure laid down in Article 121(1), (2) and (4) EC, the Council, based on reports by the Commission and the EMI,[237] forwarded its recommendations for each Member State to the Council in the composition of the Heads of State and Government.[238] The latter confirmed for each Member State separately the qualification for stage three of EMU. This decision, which took over the considerations made in the recommendations for each Member State, confirmed that eleven of the than fifteen Member States had fulfilled 'the necessary conditions for the adoption of a single currency'.[239]

The initial decision on the move to the third and final stage of the EMU did not pass without difficulties. Despite the fact that officially all the Member States that were accepted were considered to have fulfilled the criterion of a sustainable government financial position, Belgium and Italy continued to have government debts of more than twice the allowed 60% reference value, while in principle meeting all other criteria.[240] This required recourse to the possibility provided for in Article 104(2)(b) EC to grant an exemption if the ratio of the government debt to GDP was sufficiently diminishing and approaching the reference value at a satisfactory pace.[241]

As the euro area has now been established, Article 122(2) EC applies in the case of any subsequent 'enlargements' of the euro area. At least once every two years, or at the request of a Member State with a derogation, the Commission and the ECB report to the Council in accordance with the procedure laid down in Article 121(1) EC. Unlike the initial decision on the establishment of stage three of EMU, it is the ECOFIN Council in the composition of the Member States participating in the euro area which decides by qualified majority, on a proposal from the Commission, whether a Member States fulfils the convergence criteria. The Council must consult the European Parliament and must submit an envisaged decision to discussion in the Council meeting in the composition of the Heads of State or Government. The actual decision by the Council relates to the abrogation of the derogation of a Member State from participation in stage three of EMU.[242]

English translation of the judgment has been published in CML Rev. [1994], 57–81), in particular its statements on price stability. Moreover, Art. 88 of the German Basic Law makes the transfer of monetary policy authority to the ECB subject to the observance of price stability as the primary objective.

237. See European Monetary Institute, Convergence Report (Report required by Art. 109j of the Treaty establishing the European Community), Frankfurt a.M. 1998; Commission, Convergence Report, Brussels, 1998.

238. See Council Recommendation 98/316/EC of 1 May 1998, in accordance with Art. 109j(2) of the Treaty (O.J. 1998, L 139/21); Council Decision 98/317/EC of 3 May 1998, in accordance with Art. 109j(4) of the Treaty (O.J. 1998, L 139/30). In the preamble to this decision, the special position of Denmark and the UK was recalled. With regard to Greece and Sweden, the Council determined that these countries did not fulfil all convergence criteria.

239. Art. 121(2) 2nd indent EC.

240. Albeit that Italy had not participated a full two years in ERM I.

241. In its Convergence Report 1998, op. cit., *supra* note 223, 16 and 22, the EMI urged these Member States to maintain their strict budgetary policies.

242. Council Decision 2000/427/EC of 19 Jun. 2000, in accordance with Art. 122(2) of the Treaty, on the adoption by Greece of the single currency on 1 Jan. 2001 (O.J. 2000, L 167/5); Council

According to Article 123(5) EC, the Council, acting by unanimity of the Member States of the euro area, on a proposal from the Commission and after having consulted the ECB, adopts the rate at which the euro substitutes the national currency of the Member States concerned.[243]

In the Treaty of Lisbon, it is foreseen that Article 121 EC is repealed, with only its paragraph 1 being adopted in amended form in a new Article 140(1) of the Treaty on the Functioning of the EU. Moreover, Article 122(2) EC is integrated in the new Article 140(2). According to this, the Council can only decide on the acceptance of a Member State into the euro area if it has received a recommendation of a qualified majority of the Member States in the euro area. These Member States are obliged to act within six months of the Council's receiving the Commission's proposal. The explicit mentioning of the Member States in this context arguably emphasizes the character of monetary union as a special form of enhanced cooperation.

3.2.5.3 *Status of Member States with a Derogation*[244]

Any country acceding to the EU initially finds itself in the antechamber to the euro area until such time as it fulfils the convergence criteria explained above. Under the current legal arrangements, Article 122 EC defines such Member States as 'Member States with a derogation'. This status basically entails that the legal regime introduced by Title VII of the EC does not fully apply in the case of these Member States.

It has already been observed above in the context of the excessive deficit procedure that Member States with a derogation are not subject to the prohibition of excessive government deficits as laid down in Article 104(1) EC. They are however obliged to 'endeavour to avoid excessive government deficits'.[245] Moreover, Member States with a derogation are already subject to the prohibition of overdraft facilities or other types of credit facilities with the ECB or with the central banks of the Member States (Art. 101 EC) and to the prohibition of privileged access to financial institutions (Art. 102 EC).[246]

Decision 2006/495/EC of 11 Jul. 2006, in accordance with Art. 122(2) of the Treaty, on the adoption by Slovenia of the single currency on 1 Jan. 2007 (O.J. 2006, L 195/25); Council Decision 2007/504/EC of 10 Jul. 2007, in accordance with Art. 122(2) of the Treaty, on the adoption by Malta of the single currency on 1 Jan. 2008 (O.J. 2007, L 186/32); Council Decision 2007/503/EC of 10 Jul. 2007, in accordance with Art. 122(2) of the Treaty, on the adoption by Cyprus of the single currency on 1 Jan. 2008 (O.J. 2007, L 186/29).

243. See e.g., Council Reg. 1086/2006 of 11 Jul. 2006, amending Reg. 2866/98 on the conversion rates between the euro and the currencies of the Member States adopting the euro (O.J. 2006, L 195/1) which set the conversation rate between the euro and the tolar.

244. See generally J. Cloos et al. (1993), op. cit., *supra* note 51, 224–226; R. Smits (1992), op. cit., *supra* note 102, 729–731, id. (1997), op. cit., *supra* note 77, 134–139, and J.-V. Louis, (1995), op. cit., *supra* note 12, 147–159.

245. Art. 116(4) EC.

246. According to Art. 116(2) (a) EC necessary measures have to be adopted prior to entering stage two of EMU.

It has also been observed above that Member States with a derogation are not only subject to the multilateral surveillance procedure, but also to the excessive deficit procedure, with the exception of the later parts of the procedure described in Articles 104(9) and (11) EC.[247] Since Member States with a derogation do not participate in the euro area and thus in principle remain in charge of monetary policy for their own currency area, the provisions relating to the ESCB and the ECB to a large extent do not apply.[248]

The Treaty of Lisbon aims at tidying up the current EC Treaty, which is somewhat obscure and at times repetitive as a result of the mixing of provisions which applied initially in stage two of EMU, prior to the establishment of the euro area, and provisions which apply to Member States with a derogation. To this end, as has been observed above, today's Article 122 EC will be largely repealed in favour of a new Article 140 of Treaty on the Functioning of the EU which is devoted to defining the extent of the legal obligations of Member States with a derogation in EMU.

Countries wanting to join the EU do not have to fulfil the convergence criteria for joining stage three of EMU upon accession to the EU. At the same time, not least in order to rule out any 'opting out' à la Denmark and the United Kingdom, the Copenhagen criteria which the European Council formulated in 1993 unequivocally commit any state to the aims of EMU and the eventual adoption of the single currency.[249] In the past, accession negotiations on the adoption and implementation of the *acquis communautaire* have included a separate chapter on EMU focusing, *inter alia*, on economic growth, the development of public finances, structural reforms, as well as the independent status of the NCB.[250]

The transitional provisions do not only provide the legal framework for the changeover from the second to the third stage of EMU, but moreover also regulate the relationship of the Member States participating in the single currency with those countries which for the time being conduct their own monetary policy. Based on Article 124(2) EC, Member States with a derogation have to treat their exchange-rate policy as a matter of common interest. In addition to this rather general provision, with the introduction of a single currency, the original EMS has been replaced by a new exchange-rate mechanism (hereafter ERM II), namely with the aim to provide for a stable economic environment free of exchange-rate misalignments and excessive nominal exchange-rate fluctuations in an internal market

---

247. Art. 116(3) EC.
248. See Arts. 116(3) and 122(4) EC, which exclude the application of Arts. 105(1), (2), (3) and (5), Arts. 106, 110, 111, and 112(2) (b) EC. See also Art. 43 ESCB Statute on the provisions of the ESCB Statute which do not apply to Member States with a derogation.
249. See e.g., Act concerning the conditions of accession of the Czech Republic, the Republic of Estonia, the Republic of Cyprus, the Republic of Latvia, the Republic of Lithuania, the Republic of Hungary, the Republic of Malta, the Republic of Poland, the Republic of Slovenia and the Slovak Republic and the adjustments to the Treaties on which the European Union is founded, O.J. 2003, L 236/33.
250. In the case of former Communist countries of Central and Eastern Europe, review included the progress in the transition to a market economy.

in which some but not all Member States share a single currency. Moreover, ERM II has to ensure that Member States not participating in the single currency orient their policies to stability and foster convergence with the aim of eventually ful-filling the convergence criteria. While there is no legal obligation as such to join ERM II, as has been highlighted in the previous section, participation in the ERM does form a condition for qualifying for participation in the euro area.[251]

Finally, it has to be recalled that Denmark and the United Kingdom occupy a special position outside the euro area. At the time the Treaty of Maastricht was drafted, the governments of both countries had serious reservations against the creation of a single European currency and the loss of sovereignty over monetary policy that would have been the consequence thereof.[252] The option to make the participation in the third and final stage of EMU subject to a separate decision in the Member States was rejected by a majority of Member States led by France, which wanted the whole process of the establishment of EMU to be regulated by Community law. By ratifying the Treaty of Maastricht, the Member States thus had to politically and legally commit themselves to participation in the euro area. The risk of this all-or-nothing approach was that Member States which categori-cally, or as a result of domestic political pressure, rejected the idea of a single European currency would be forced to discard the Treaty of Maastricht as a whole, thereby blocking its adoption in accordance with Article 48 TEU. To get around this problem, in the case of the United Kingdom and Denmark separate provisions were agreed upon in two protocols.[253]

The Protocol on certain provisions relating to the United Kingdom recognizes that the latter is not obliged or committed to move to the third stage of EMU without a separate decision to do so by its government and parliament, and it is under no obligation to join the euro area unless it has informed the Council that it intends to do so. Consequently, first of all, the United Kingdom remains in charge of its monetary policy. The Protocol defines in detail the extent to which the provisions of EMU apply. What results from this is that in some regards the United Kingdom can be compared to a Member State with a derogation. This is in particular the case with regard to its participation in economic coordination, as has been observed above. However, at the same time it is not fully subject to the legal requirements which Member States with a derogation have to fulfil, as for example Article 109 EC on the independence of NCBs does not apply. Despite this exemption, in practice, the United Kingdom has followed the general trend in Europe in the wake of the establishment of the ECB towards the establishment of independent central banks.[254]

The Protocol on certain provisions relating to Denmark allows the latter to decide not to participate in the third stage of EMU. As Denmark notified the

---

251. Art. 121(1) EC.
252. See e.g., J.-V. Louis, (1995) op. cit., *supra* note 12, 148.
253. Note 186 *supra*.
254. As becomes clear from a study of the Bank of England Act 1998. See generally F. Amtenbrink (1999), op. cit., *supra* note 61, at 67.

Council of such a decision, according to the Protocol Denmark has to be treated as a Member State with a derogation.[255]

Finally, Sweden constitutes a special case. Initially it was decided that it did not fulfil the convergence criteria, due to not participating in ERM.[256] By remaining outside the single currency, despite in principle fulfilling the economic conditions, and despite the absence of an exemption similar to that applicable to Denmark and the United Kingdom, the Swedish government gives effect to a referendum in 2003 in which the Swedish electorate voted against the adoption of the euro.[257]

The exclusion of those Member States with a derogation and the United Kingdom and Denmark from the euro area results de facto in an EMU with varying degrees of integration. This poses challenges to the governance of EMU not only in the context of the ESCB and the ECB, to be observed hereafter, but also in the (ECOFIN-)Council. The above-mentioned Member States are excluded from certain decisions in the context of economic coordination and monetary union.[258] Moreover, following an initiative by France, since 1997, the Ministers of Finance of the Member States participating in the euro area consult regularly on issues relating to economic and monetary policy issues related to the euro area in the so-called Euro Group.[259] Both the Commission and the ECB take part in these meetings, which are chaired by a president who is elected from among the Ministers of Finance of the Member States participating in the euro area for a period of two-and-a-half years by a majority of those Member States.[260]

While under the current legal arrangements the Euro Group has no formal decision-making power, it has been criticized for opening the door to the effective determination of economic policy outside the institutional framework of the Community, despite the fact that this has an impact on EMU which forms a central part

---

255. No. 2 of said Protocol. No. 4 implicitly provides for the possibility for Denmark to revise its decision by abrogating the exemption granted under the Protocol. In such a case the provisions of the Protocol would cease to apply (No. 5).

256. See Council Decision 98/317 of 3 May 1998, O.J. 1998, L 139/30, in accordance with Art. 109j(4) EC.

257. The turnout was 81.2%, whereby 56.2% voted against adopting the euro. Generally with regard to the legal position of Sweden: V. Miller, C. Taylor and E. Potton, The Swedish Referendum on the Euro, House of Common Library Research Paper 03/68, 15 Sep. 2003, and M. Sideek, 'Is the Purported Exclusion of Sweden from the Euroland Justified?' (2000), *European Business Law Review*, 363–372.

258. With regard to economic policy see: Arts. 104 (13) EC. With regard to monetary policy see: Arts. 11; 106(2), 111, and 112(2)(b) EC. See moreover, Art. 47 ESCB Statute, according to which the central banks of Member States with a derogation which are restricted to participating in the general Council of the ECB can only contribute to the tasks of the ESCB and the ECB.

259. Conclusions European Council of Amsterdam, 16 and 17 Jun. 1997, pt. 1.5., Bull. EU 6-1997, 10. Conclusions European Council of Luxemburg, 12 and 13 Dec. 1997, pt. 1.9 (43), Bull. EU 12-1997, 13, and Resolution of the European Council of 13 Dec. 1997, on economic policy coordination in stage 3 of EMU and on Treaty Arts. 109 and 109b of the EC Treaty (O.J. 1998, C 35/1). Usually the meetings take place prior to the meetings of the ECOFIN Council.

260. See Arts. 1 and 2 of the Protocol on the Euro Group (O.J. 2004, C 310/341).

of Community.[261] As some Member States may permanently stay outside the euro area, this may result in a split between these two groups of Member States. In fact, the Treaty of Lisbon seems explicitly to foresee a further differentiation between the Member States in the euro area and those with a derogation. A new Chapter 4 will be introduced in the future Treaty on the Functioning of the EU (which is due to replace the EC Treaty) including specific provisions for the Member States of the euro area.[262] In order to ensure the proper functioning of EMU it empowers these Member States to adopt measures specific to those Member States whose currency is the euro, with the aim of strengthening the coordination and surveillance of their budgetary discipline. Moreover, separate economic policy guidelines can be established for them, albeit that they have to be compatible with those adopted for the whole of the Union.[263] In essence this allows for the establishment of a separate multilateral surveillance regime. Moreover, the future Treaty on the Functioning of the EU explicitly recognizes the existence of the Euro Group.[264]

3.3   MONETARY UNION: ARTICLES 105–124 EC

3.3.1   General Observations

With the changeover from the second to the third stage of EMU, those Member States participating in the monetary union have given up their competences relating to monetary policy. Consequently, also the rules relating to the coordination of monetary policy applicable in stage two of EMU no longer apply. In particular, ERM II only applies to Member States which have not yet joined the euro area and thus remain in charge of their own currency. The national monetary policy of the Member States participating in the euro area is replaced by a single monetary policy, with the primary objective of securing the stability of the euro, the European single currency. In order to formulate and implement the single monetary policy in the euro area, following the decision on 3 May 1998 to move ahead with the third stage of EMU, the ESCB and the ECB were established in accordance with Article 123(1) EC.[265] The provisions governing the ESCB and the ECB

---

261. See A. Geelhoed in the 6th Dutch edition of this work (790–791 and 834–835). The emergence of this informal forum may not only be problematic from an institutional point of view, but also from a practical point of view. See: Von Hagen, op. cit., infra note 383, 66–67, who observes rightly that due to the fact that Member States in the euro area no longer have a central bank at their disposal which can support the price for government bonds, their vulnerability in the financial markets has increased. Moreover, Member States are subject to the 'no bail out clause' of Art. 101 EC.
262. Ch. 4 will include three provisions, i.e., Arts. 136–138.
263. Art. 136(1) of the TFEU.
264. Art. 137 of the TFEU.
265. The ESCB and the ECB became operational on 1 Jun. 1998, after the appointment of the president, vice-president and the other members of the Executive Board. See Dec. 98/345/EC of 26 May 1998 (O.J. 1998, L 154/33). In the period between 1 Jun. 1998 and 1 Jan. 1999, the NCBs remained in charge of the conduct of their independent monetary policies. Together

can be found in Articles 105–113 EC and in the Protocol on the Statute of the ESCB and the ECB.[266] In this context it can be argued that the dispersal of the institutional and operational rules governing the ESCB and the ECB in two separate documents has resulted in a legal basis that includes unnecessary repetitions and at times makes a difficult reading.

Together with the provisions in the EC Treaty, the Protocol enjoys the status of primary Community law. Unlike what is the case for a majority of NCBs also outside the EU, the legal basis of the ESCB and the ECB therefore has a quasi-constitutional status, as any substantial amendments of the institutional structure of the ESCB and ECB or of its primary objective requires the application of the Treaty amendment procedure laid down in Article 48 TEU. In order to allow for certain amendments of the legal basis without the need for a Treaty revision procedure, Article 107(5) EC allows for a simplified revision procedure for the more technical aspects of the legal basis of the ECB.[267]

Due to the limited space available hereafter, the legal framework of monetary union is only sketched in broad lines.[268] This overview deals with:

– the ESCB and the ECB (3.3.2.);
– the European single currency: the euro (3.3.3.);
– the relationship between the euro area and the non-participating Member States (3.3.4.);
– the external monetary policy (3.3.5.).

3.3.2   The ESCB and the ECB

Situated at the centre of monetary union, the ESCB and particularly the ECB are effectively in charge of the formulation and implementation of monetary policy in the euro area. Hereafter, the legal nature of the ESCB and ECB and the latter's internal organization (3.3.2.1.), its position in the EU's institutional framework (3.3.2.2.), and its competences and tasks (3.3.2.3.) are examined briefly.

---

with the ECB they made the necessary preparations for the changeover to the single currency. See Art. 123(1), last two sentences EC.

266. Protocol annexed to the Treaty establishing the European Community (O.J. 1992, C 191/68), as amended by the Treaty of Amsterdam (O.J. 1997, C 340/1), the Treaty of Nice (O.J. 2001, C 80/1), Council Decision 2003/223/EC (O.J. 2003, L 83/66) and the Act concerning the conditions of Accession of the Czech Republic, the Republic of Estonia, the Republic of Cyprus, the Republic of Latvia, the Republic of Lithuania, the Republic of Hungary, the Republic of Malta, the Republic of Poland, the Republic of Slovenia and the Slovak Republic and the adjustments to the Treaties on which the European Union is founded (O.J. 2003, L 236/33).

267. Including amendments of Art. 5.1, 5.2, 5.3, 17, 18, 19.1, 22, 23, 24, 26, 32.2, 32.3, 32.4, 32.6, 33.1(a) and 36 of the Statute of the ESCB. The Council can act by a qualified majority, whereby the assent of the European Parliament is required.

268. For a detailed legal analysis of the institutions and the single monetary policy see e.g., R. Smits (1997), op. cit., *supra* note 77, F. Amtenbrink (1999), op. cit., *supra* note 61, C. Zilioli and M. Selmayr (2001), op. cit., *supra* note 77. For an economic analysis see e.g., J. de Haan, S.C.W. Eijffinger and S. Waller, *The European Central Bank* (Cambridge, MA, London, 2005).

3.3.2.1   *Legal Nature of the ESCB and the ECB, and their Internal Organization*

The ESCB is a system of currently 28 central banks: the 27 central banks of the Member States (NCBs) of the EU and the ECB.[269] The legal personality of the NCBs derive from the respective national legal systems, whereas the ECB enjoys legal personality under Community law in accordance with Article 107(2) EC. The ESCB itself has no legal personality. The ECB has its seat in Frankfurt am Main, Germany.[270]

Rather than being listed in Article 7 EC as one of the institutions of the Community, the ECB enjoys a separate status, similar to the European Investment Bank, which already becomes clear from its separate mention in Article 8 EC. The reason for this status may be twofold. Firstly, unlike other Community Institutions, the ECB was set up for the purpose of a single task within the Community framework, that is the conduct of monetary policy in the single currency area. Moreover, it may be argued that the separation of the ECB from the Community Institutions is also an expression of the independent position of the ECB in the Community institutional framework which the drafters of the Treaty of Maastricht intended to ensure.[271]

While it could be argued that the separate legal personality of the different parts of the ESCB puts the latter somewhat apart from the Community, it cannot be concluded from this that the ECB enjoys a status outside the Community legal order. This cannot be concluded from the independent position of the ECB in the Community legal order either.[272] In fact the ESCB's main objective as defined in Article 105(1) EC is to pursue one of the main tasks of the Community as laid down in Articles 2 and 4 EC, i.e., to maintain price stability. Moreover, the ECB is supposed to support the general economic policies in the Community with a

---

269. Art. 106(1) EC.
270. Details are laid down in a Headquarters Agreement between the German government and the ECB (SEC/GovC/4/98/7).
271. The Treaty of Lisbon foresees listing the ECB as one of the Union Institutions in Art. 13(1) of the amended EU Treaty. However, an analysis of the TFEU makes clear that the ECB will continue to enjoy a special status. See e.g., the revised Art. 13(3) TEU which explicitly identifies the ECB apart from the other Union Institutions.
272. Differently C. Zilioli and M. Selmayr, 'The External Relations of the Euro Area: Legal Aspects' (1999), CML Rev., 273–340, and id., 'The European Central Bank: An Independent Specialized Organization of Community Law' (2000), CML Rev., 591–644, arguing that the ECB has a 'special status' outside the Community legal order. This view has been rightly rejected by R. Torrent, 'Whom is the European Central Bank the Central Bank of?: Reaction to Zilioli and Selmayr' (1999), CML Rev., 1229–1241, F. Amtenbrink and J. de Haan, 'The European Central Bank: An Independent Specialized Organization of Community Law: A Comment' (2002), CML Rev., 65–76, and B. Dutzler, 'Institutional Framework of the EMU: Is the ECB a Fourth Pillar?,' in F. Breuss, G. Fink and S. Griller (eds), *Institutional, Legal and Economic Aspects of EMU*, Series of the Research Institute of European Affairs, no. 21, Vienna 2002, 3–35. In its decision in Case C-11/00, *Commission v. ECB*, the ECJ, following the Opinion of A.G. Jacobs, rejected the ECB view that it holds a special position outside the Community legal order.

view to contributing to the achievements of the objectives of the Community.[273] The position of the ESCB and ECB within the Community legal order is also supported by the genesis and current structure of the EC Treaty provisions. With regard to the former, it is noteworthy that the EMU provisions included in the Maastricht Treaty are in principle based on former Article 102a(2) EEC, which stated that in case of further developments in the area of economic and monetary policy which would require institutional amendments, the EEC Treaty and thus, the Community legal order would need to be amended. The Delors Report on EMU took this provision into account when recommending an amendment of the EEC Treaty. Despite initial objections by some Member States, the intergovernmental conference followed this recommendation.[274] Moreover, an analysis of the current EC Treaty reveals that the relationship between the ECB and the Community Institutions are laid down in detail, whereby legally binding measures of the ECB are in principle subject to judicial review by the ECJ.[275] Hence, the general rules of Community law are in principle fully applicable in case of the ESCB and the ECB, unless explicitly stated otherwise in the EC Treaty or the Protocol.[276]

Given the fact that the ESCB comprises the ECB and the NCBs of the Member States it could be argued that the ESCB in fact constitutes a two-tier system. However, this is not to say that the power for conducting monetary policy is equally or otherwise shared by the central and decentralized levels of the system.[277] The distribution of tasks follows a different logic, as the ECB constitutes the policy-making arm of the system, whereas the NCBs of the Member States participating in the euro are mainly charged with the execution of monetary policy decisions.[278] The ESCB thus

273. On the objectives of the ECB see J.-V. Louis, (1995) op. cit., *supra* note 12, 55–57; R. Smits (1997), op. cit., *supra* note 77, 93; F. Amtenbrink and J. de Haan (2002), op. cit., *supra* note 272, 67–68.

274. J.-V. Louis, (1995), op. cit., *supra* note 12, 57.

275. R. Smits (1997), op. cit., *supra* note 77, 93; F. Amtenbrink and J. de Haan (2002), op. cit., *supra* note 272, 73–75. See also D. Janzen, *Der neue Art. 88 Satz 2 des Grundgesetzes. Verfassungsrechtliche Anforderungen an die Übertragung der Währungshoheit auf die Europäische Zentralbank*, SER vol. 26 (Berlin, 1996), 100–101.

276. Instructive in this context is Case 85/86, *Commission v. Board of Governors of the European Investment Bank* where the ECJ stated that the EIB's operational and institutional autonomy does not mean that it is totally separated from the Communities and exempted from every rule of Community law.

277. Due to this, some authors in the past have characterized the ESCB as a 'single-tier' system. See e.g., M. Potacs, 'Nationale Zentralbanken in der Wirtschafts- und Währungsunion' (1993), EuR, 23–40, at 32.

278. Based on the wording of Art. 12.1 ESCB Statute, according to which 'the ECB shall have recourse to the NCBs to carry out operations which form part of the tasks of the ESCB', the role of the NCBs in the ESCB has been described as an expression of the subsidiarity principle laid down in Art. 5 EC. See e.g., Editorial Comment, 'Executive Agencies within the EC: The European Central Bank: A Model?', (1996), CML Rev., 623–31, at 627; R. Smits (1992), op. cit., *supra* note 102, at 717, and implicitly J.-V. Louis, (1995), op. cit., *supra* note 12, 58. The execution of monetary policy by the NCBs in the ESCB can be viewed as a form of decentralized governance for which the ESCB as such remains responsible. Similar R. Smits (1997), op. cit., *supra* note 77, 112 with further references in footnotes 446 and 447. However, it is

includes features of both a centralized and a decentralized system, but the emphasis lies on the former. The functions of the NCBs are moreover not limited to those assigned by primary Community law, as they are permitted to perform other functions outside the ESCB to the extent that these do not interfere with the objectives and tasks of the ESCB.[279] NCBs can thus fulfil tasks not related to the conduct of monetary policy, such as those related to the supervision of financial institutions. With the loss of the monetary policy function in stage three of EMU, the role of NCBs in this area has been consolidated in some instances.[280]

The allocation of powers at the central level of the ESCB becomes clear from an analysis of its institutional structure, as the ESCB is governed by the decision-making bodies of the ECB, whereby the NCBs are required to act in accordance with the guidelines and instructions of the ECB.[281] The two main decision-making bodies of the ECB are the Executive Board and the Governing Council. Moreover, for the time being, the ECB has a General Council.[282]

The *Executive Board* is the managerial board of the ECB and comprises the President of the ECB, the vice-president and four additional members. They are appointed from among persons of recognized standing and professional experience in monetary and banking matters for a non-renewable period of eight years by common accord of the governments of the Member States at the level of the Heads of State or Government, on a recommendation from the Council consulting the European Parliament and the Governing Council.[283] In order to ensure continuity, the members of the first members of the Executive Board were appointed with staggered terms.[284]

The main task of the Executive Board is to implement monetary policy based on the guidelines and decisions of the Governing Council of the ECB. It is the Executive Board which issues the above-mentioned guidelines and instructions to the NCBs, so that they can fulfil their executive tasks in the ESCB. Moreover, the Executive Board is responsible for the preparation of the meetings of the Governing Board of the ECB. As *primus inter pares*, the President of the ECB

---

questionable whether this is indeed an example of the application of the subsidiarity principle, as Art. 5 EC does not apply in areas where the Community has exclusive competences, such as for monetary policy in the euro area.

279. See Art. 14.4. ESCB Statute according to which such functions must be performed on the responsibility and liability of NCBs and do not form part of the functions of the ESCB.

280. This is for example the case for De Nederlandse Bank, which in 2004 merged with the Dutch Pension and Insurance Supervisory Authority (PVK) and is in charge of prudential supervision in the Netherlands.

281. Arts. 8 and 14.3. ESCB Statute.

282. Art. 107(3) EC and Arts. 10–13 ESCB Statute.

283. Art. 11 ESCB Statute, which moreover states that only EU citizens can be members of the Executive Board.

284. As foreseen in Art. 50 ESCB Statute. Despite the fact that this provision foresaw the initial appointment of the President of the ECB for a full period of 8 years, the dispute around the person to first take this position resulted in France insisting on a political compromise allowing for a replacement of the President already after 4 years. The decision on the appointment of the first president was controversial. See R. Smits, 'Het Begin van de muntunie: besluitvorming en regelgeving' (1999), SEW, 6, and F. Amtenbrink (1999), op. cit., *supra* note 61, 255.

chairs the Executive Board and the Governing Council of the ECB and represents the ECB externally, in particular in contacts with Community Institutions such as the Council and the European Parliament.[285] Decisions of the Executive Board are in principle taken by simple majority of votes cast, whereby each member has one vote. In the event of a tie, the President of the ECB has a casting vote.[286]

The *Governing Council* is the main policy-making body of the ECB. It consists of the members of the Executive Board and the governors of the NCBs participating in the euro area. Given its mixed composition, the term of office and appointment procedures of the members of the Governing Council vary. The governors of the NCBs are appointed in accordance with the respective national provisions. While the terms of office of NCB presidents can thus in principle vary, Community law demands that national law foresees in a minimum term of five years.

The main task of the Governing Board is to take the decisions necessary to ensure the performance of the tasks entrusted to the ESCB under the EC Treaty and the ESCB Statute. The Governing Council takes the decisions relating to the definition (quantification) of the monetary policy objective and the conduct of monetary policy, namely relating to the determining of the key interest rates and the supply of reserves in the ESCB. The Governing Council moreover also establishes the guidelines which are necessary for the implementation of its decisions.[287] It can also delegate certain powers to the Executive Board.[288] According to Article 113 (1) EC, the President of the Council and a member of the Commission are entitled to participate in meetings of the Governing Council. They do not, however, have a right to vote.[289]

Although the original provisions introduced by the Treaty of Maastricht operated on the basis of a strict equality of all NCB governors, in the light of future enlargement of the euro area and the feared loss of efficiency in the main decision-making organ of the ECB, the Treaty of Nice introduced new arrangements into the ESCB Statute, allowing the Council meeting in the composition of the Heads of State or Government to amend Article 10.2. ESCB Statute on the voting in the Governing Council by unanimous vote.[290] By Decision of 21 March 2003, based

285. Art. 13 ESCB Statute.
286. Art. 11.5. ESCB Statute.
287. Based on Art. 12.3. ESCB Statute, the Governing Council has adopted Rules of Procedure which determine the internal organization of the ECB and its decision-making organs: Decision of the ECB of 19 Feb. 2004, adopting the Rules of Procedure of the ECB (ECB/2004/2) (O.J. 2004, L 80/33), Decision of the ECB of 12 Oct. 1999, concerning the Rules of Procedure of the Executive Board of the ECB (ECB/1999/7) (O.J. 1999, L 314/34), and Decision of the ECB adopting the Rules of Procedure of the General Council of the European Central Bank (ECB/2004/12) (2004/526/EC) (O.J. 2004, L 230/61).
288. Art. 12.1. ESCB Statute.
289. The president of the Council may submit a motion for deliberation to the Governing Council. Following the Lisbon Treaty, Art. 113 EC will be retained as Art. 294 of the TFEU.
290. See Art. 10.6. ESCB Statute, inserted by Art. 5 of the Treaty of Nice. This can take place either on a recommendation from the ECB and after consulting the European Parliament and the Commission, or on a recommendation from the Commission and after consulting the European

on a recommendation by the ECB,[291] the Council amended that provision. While the six members of the Executive Board retain their voting right when participating in Governing Council meetings, in principle as soon as the number of Member States – and thus NCBs – participating in the euro area exceeds 15, with the application of the new voting system the governors of the NCBs participating in the euro area will only have a voting right on a rotation basis. The NCB governors will exercise a voting right with different frequencies depending – put in a nutshell – on an indicator of the relative size of the economies of their Member States within the euro area.[292] Based on this indicator, NCB governors will be allocated to different groups. This allocation determines how often they enjoy a voting right. In any event, the maximum number of voting rights shared between all NCBs will not exceed 15.[293]

Initially, as long as the number of Member States participating in the euro area are more than 15 and less than 22, there will be two groups. The first group consists of the five NCB governors from the Member States participating in the euro area which occupy the highest positions in the country-ranking on the basis of the above-mentioned economic indicator. They will share four voting rights. The second group will include all other NCB governors. Between them, they will share the remaining 11 voting rights. Once the number of Member States participating in the euro area exceeds 22, there will be three groups: the first group will continue to consist of the five NCB governors from the participating Member States which occupy the highest positions in the country-ranking on the basis of the economic indicators, sharing four voting rights between them. The second group will be made up of half of all NCB governors, rounded up to the nearest whole number where necessary, selected from the subsequent positions of the country-ranking. They will share eight voting rights. The remaining NCB governors make up the third group, and share three voting rights.

As is currently the case, the formal voting requirement in the Governing Council will continue to be a simple majority vote of the members having a voting right, with the president having a casting vote in case of a tie.[294] A quorum exists if two-thirds of the members with a voting right participate in a decision. Within each group, the governors will have their voting rights for equal amounts of time.

Parliament and the ECB. The Council thereafter recommends the amendments to the Member States for adoption in accordance with Art. 48 TEU.

291. Council Decision 2003/223/EC (O.J. 2003, L 83/66), based on a Declaration on the new Art. 10.6 ESCB Statute annexed to the Treaty of Nice.

292. The principal component of the indicator is the Member State's GDP. The second component is the total assets of the aggregated balance sheet of monetary financial institutions (TABS-MFI) within the territory of the Member State concerned. The relative weights of the two components are 5/6 for GDP and 1/6 for TABS-MFI. But see D. Gros, 'Reforming the composition of the ECB Governing Council in view of enlargement: How not to do it!', Briefing paper for the Monetary Committee of the European Parliament, Feb. 2003, who criticizes this index, as it has arbitrary elements.

293. As of 1 Jan. 2008, 15 Member States participate in the euro area. As Denmark, Sweden and the UK continue to remain outside the euro area, the new system is in principle set to come into operation with the next enlargement of the euro area by one of the Central and Eastern European countries.

294. Art. 10.2. ESCB Statute.

Interestingly, the Council decision itself does not determine the time-span for the voting rights. Instead, the Governing Council, acting by a two-thirds majority of all its members with and without a voting right, will have to take this decision and all other necessary measures for the implementation of this new system.[295]

The new institutional structure abandons what at least *de jure* applied under the Treaty of Maastricht regime, i.e., equality of all participating central banks in the system. While the monetary policy of smaller scale economies prior to the coming into existence of the ECB was often governed by the monetary policy approach taken by the Deutsche Bundesbank, by joining EMU and the single currency, these smaller economies gained rather than lost control over monetary policy as they were put, by means of the one-man-one-vote principle, on an equal footing with the large economies. With the revision of the existing system the large economies seem to regain the upper hand.[296] Moreover, a shift in the balance of power in the Governing Council can be observed under the new arrangements. The power of the six permanently elected members of the Executive Board of the ECB, and thus of the central level, will increase relative to that of the NCB governors, the decentralized level, as the voting rights shared between the latter will not exceed 15 regardless of the number of Member States participating in the euro area.[297] Of course, from a legal point of view, given the independent position of NCB governors, the required commitment to the objectives of the ESCB and the ECB, as well as the independence of the ESCB and the ECB as a whole, little stands in the way of introducing an institutional set-up as foreseen in the ESCB Statute whereby not all central bank governors participate in voting, which should from the outset be in the common interest of the single monetary policy in the euro area. Moreover, NCB governors without a voting right are not excluded from actively participating in the deliberations in the Governing Council.

While meetings of the Governing Council are convened every two weeks, monetary policy decisions relating to the setting of key interest rates are only taken during the first meeting and thus once a month, based on a pre-determined and publicly available schedule. The second meeting is reserved for other important decisions relating, *inter alia*, to the payment systems, financial stability and important legal affairs.

The *General Council* constitutes the third decision-making body of the ECB. The General Council has taken over those functions of the former EMI which still had to be performed when the EMI was dissolved.[298] These tasks relate to the

---

295. This includes the possibility to postpone the application of the new system until such time as the number of NCB governors exceeds 18. See Art. 10.2. ESCB Statute.
296. Critical in this regard: House of Lords Select Committee on the European Union, Is the European Central Bank Working?, Session 2002–03, 42nd Report, part 3, which includes a detailed analysis of the adjusted voting system. It should be noted however that for certain decisions relating – *inter alia* – to the capital of the ECB and the transfer of foreign reserve assets from the NCBs to the ECB, the votes in the Governing Council are weighted according to the NCBs' shares in the subscribed capital of the ECB (Art. 10.3. ESCB Statute).
297. See Art. 10.2. ESCB Statute.
298. Art. 109(2) and (3) EC and Art. 44 ESCB Statute.

preparations for the changeover from the second to the third stage of EMU, and thus still need to be performed as long as there are Member States with a derogation. Consequently, in principle the General Council is a temporary body. For the time being it consists of the President and Vice-President of the ECB and *all* NCB governors, including those with a derogation, as well as the Bank of England and the Danmarks Nationalbank, the Danish central bank.[299] The specific tasks of the General Council are described in Article 47 ESCB Statute, the most important being its contribution to the preparation of Member States with a derogation for the third stage of EMU.[300] In addition, the General Council can be said to fulfil an important function in integrating Member States outside the euro area into the ESCB, with the aim of avoiding a disturbance of the single monetary policy by them.[301] In this context the General Council monitors the functioning of ERM II and serves as the forum for monetary and exchange-rate policy coordination.

3.3.2.2 The Position of the ECB in the Institutional Framework of the EU

One of the most prominent and at the same time controversial institutional aspects of EMU is the independent or autonomous position of the ECB in the Community legal order. Whether and to what extent the position of the ECB highlighted hereafter can best be described as independent or autonomous may be a definitional matter rather than involving clear-cut legal considerations. Indeed, currently neither the EC Treaty nor the ESCB Statute applies either term in defining the position of the ECB *vis-à-vis* Community and national institutions and bodies.[302] According to Black's Law Dictionary, the adjectives independent and autonomous can be understood to stand for similar concepts, as they describe respectively the state of not being 'subject to the control or influence of another' and the 'right of self government'.[303] Autonomy may be said to better describe the position of the ECB in the Community legal order which, as will explained hereafter, allows the ECB to function to a large degree without outside influence from a European or national authority. Yet, while outside influence and also control are limited, they are not completely absent in the case of the ECB.[304] Having said this, the vast literature on the ECB, as well as the ECJ, which applies the term 'independence' does so without suggesting that the ECB is entirely free of control or outside influence.[305] Moreover, the Lisbon Treaty explicitly applies the term

---

299. Art. 45.2. ESCB Statute. The other members of the Executive Board and moreover the President of the Council and a member of the Commission are allowed to participate in the meetings, albeit without voting rights.

300. Art. 47 in conjunction with Art. 44 ESCB Statute.

301. Similarly, J.-V. Louis, (1995), op. cit., 12, 151.

302. However, Art. 116(5) EC does refer to the independence of the NCBs.

303. A. Garner (ed.), *Black's Law Dictionary*, 8th edition (St. Paul, MN, 2004).

304. For this reason, A. Geelhoed in the 6th Dutch edition of this work argues in favour of using the term autonomy when referring to the position of the ECB.

305. In its decision in Case C-11/00 *Commission v. ECB*, the ECJ chooses the term 'independence' to describe the position of the ECB.

independence to the ECB, since the revised Article 282(3) of the Treaty on the Functioning of the EU will state that the ECB is independent in the exercise of its powers and in the management of its finances and that Union institutions, bodies, offices and agencies and the governments of the Member States must respect that independence.[306]

Despite its independence, the ECB does not operate in an institutional and legal vacuum. First of all, a clear link exists between the monetary policy and the economic policy of the Community.[307] Secondly, the ECB is tied into the institutional structure of the Community, as to a certain degree it is ultimately accountable for the conduct of the tasks which have been assigned to it, to the Member States as the 'Masters of the Treaty'. From a legal perspective this accountability includes the judicial review of ECB measures by the ECJ.[308] Essentially, the ECB fulfils both delegated legislative and executive functions within the Community framework, while at the same time being separated from these two branches of government which are in any event not easily separable at the European level.

Three main factors can be identified which have had a crucial impact on the position accorded the ECB in the Community legal order. Firstly, the establishment of an autonomous monetary authority was an important condition for Germany to accept the transfer of sovereignty over monetary policy. Against the background of the positive experience with the role of the Deutsche Bundesbank in the stability of the German currency, an autonomous ECB was considered a crucial prerequisite for the establishment of a stable European single currency.[309] The German position can also be explained by the extensive, albeit not always conclusive, theoretical and empirical evidence offered mainly by economists, which suggests that the conduct of an inflation-adverse monetary policy requires the removal of that policy from the political arena.[310] At the time the rules on EMU were drawn up, a majority of NCBs supported the establishment of an ECB, whose autonomous position is secured in the legal basis of the bank.[311]

---

306. For this reason unlike the Dutch edition of this work, hereafter the term independence is applied.
307. See Arts. 99, 104 and 105 EC.
308. As such the position of the ECB cannot be easily compared to that of the independent judiciary.
309. See H. Tietmeyer, The Role of the Independent Central Bank in Europe, Contribution to the 1990 IMF Seminar on Central Banking, Washington, DC, 1990.
310. See e.g., S.C.W. Eijffinger and J. de Haan, The Political Economy of Central-Bank Independence, Special Papers in Economics no. 19, International Finance Section, Department of Economics, Princeton University (Princeton, NJ, 1996), with further references. A. Alesina and G. Tabellini, Bureaucrats or Politicians?, NBER Working Paper Series no. 10241, Jan. 2004, with further references. Critical on the political economy rationale of central bank independence: W. Buiter, How Robust is the New Conventional Wisdom? The Surprising Fragility of the Theoretical Foundation of Inflation Targeting and Central Bank Independence, CEPR Discussion Paper No. 5772, Aug. 2006.
311. This preference can be clearly seen in draft ESCB Statute prepared by the Committee of Governors. See R. Smits (1997), op. cit., *supra* note 77, 159–160.

In identifying aspects of central bank autonomy, several elements can be distinguished relating to institutional, functional, organizational and financial aspects of the bank.[312] In this context moreover the issue arises whether and to what extent the ESCB as a whole and/or the ECB as the monetary policy authority is accountable for its conduct.

3.3.2.2.1 Institutional Independence

In general, institutional autonomy relates to the position of the central bank as separate in particular from the executive and legislative branch of government. An institutionally autonomous central bank does not only have its own legal personality, but more importantly can pursue its statutorily prescribed objectives free of influence from either government or parliament. This freedom of a central bank to formulate monetary policy autonomously from political institutions is sometimes referred to as political or goal independence.[313]

At present, the institutional autonomy of the ECB and the NCBs is essentially laid down in Article 107(2) EC, which establishes the legal personality of the ECB, Article 108 EC and the identical Article 7 ESCB Statute.[314] As far as the NCBs are concerned, it has been observed above that Member States are obliged to bring their NCB laws in line with the EC Treaty, as this forms one of the conditions for qualifying for participation in the third stage of EMU. In the run-up to the third stage of EMU, this resulted in substantial amendments of the central bank law of a number of Member States, whereby France may be the most prominent example of a Member State which had to depart from its previous tradition of government intervention in central bank affairs.[315]

Neither the ECB nor the NCB, nor any member of their decision-making bodies is allowed to seek or take instructions from Community Institutions or bodies, from any government of a Member State or from any other body. At the same time, Community Institutions and bodies and the governments of the Member States are prohibited from seeking to influence the members of the decision-making bodies of the ECB or of the NCBs in the conduct of their tasks.[316] The institutional independence of the ECB includes its ability to determine its internal

---

312. See e.g., J.-V. Louis, *Vers un système européen de banques centrales: projet de dispositions organiques* (Brussel, 1989), 25–28; F. Amtenbrink (1999), op. cit., *supra* note 61, 17 et seq., which differentiates between a legal and non-legal approach to the concept.

313. See e.g., S. Fischer, 'Modern Central Banking', in F. Capie et al., *The Future of Central Banking* (Cambridge, 1994), 262–308, at 292 et seq.

314. In the TFEU, the ECB's legal personality and independence is laid down in the new Art. 282(3).

315. The Bank Act 1993, specifically the provision charging the bank with formulating monetary policy, was initially declared unconstitutional by the *Conseil constitutionnel*, which argued that this effectively deprived government of its competence in accordance with the Constitution of 1958 to determine and conduct economic policies, Décision No. 93–324 DC, JORF 1993, 11014.

316. See already section 3.2.5. *supra*.

organization and to appoint its own personnel and to determine the conditions of employment of staff.[317]

3.3.2.2.2   Functional Independence

Functional independence refers to the ability of a central bank to decide on the application of its monetary policy instruments, such as the adjustment of interest rates and open market operations, free from government influence.[318] The functional independence of the ECB derives from the competences described hereafter, which provide the ECB in the performance of its tasks defined by the EC Treaty and the ESCB Statute with vast freedom in the application of its monetary policy instruments.[319] This functional autonomy is not limitless, as it can in a number of areas related to the instruments of monetary policy be more closely defined by the Council by means of secondary Community law.[320]

3.3.2.2.3   Organizational Independence

Organizational independence relates to the personal composition of the decision-making boards of a central bank and the legal arrangements concerning the appointment, the duration of office, the possibility of reappointment, and dismissal of central bank officials. This moreover also includes the incompatibility of functions outside the central bank during or subsequent to the employment with the central bank.

The members of the Executive Board of the ECB must have a recognized standing and professional experience in monetary matters. They are appointed by common accord of the Heads of State or Government of the Member States without a derogation, on a recommendation from the Council. The latter must consult both the European Parliament and the Governing Council of the ECB.[321] Under the Lisbon Treaty, the quasi-unanimity requirement, under the reference in the current EC Treaty to 'common accord', is abolished in favour of a qualified majority requirement.[322]

The term of office of the members of the Executive Board is eight years and non-renewable.[323] The relatively long term ensures that the Executive Board can

---

317. Art. 12.3. and Art. 36.1. ESCB Statute. See Decision of the ECB of 9 Jun. 1998, on the adoption of the Conditions of Employment for Staff of the ECB as last amended by Decision of 5 Jul. 2001 (ECB/2001/6) (O.J. 2001, L 201/25).
318. F. Amtenbrink (1999), op. cit., *supra* note 61, at 19. Different authors use alternative terms, such as instrument independence or political independence. With regard to the latter see D. Howarth and P. Loedel, *The European Central Bank*, 2nd ed. (New York, 2005), 128.
319. See section 3.3.2.3. *infra*.
320. See e.g., Art. 42 ESCB Statute in conjunction with Arts. 5.4, 19.1, 20 para. 2 ESCB Statute.
321. Art. 112(2) EC and Art. 11.2. ESCB Statute.
322. See Art. 283(2) TFEU, which moreover puts the European Council in charge of the appointment procedure.
323. Art. 11.2. ESCB Statute. In the run-up to the Treaty of Maastricht, the European Parliament in particular was in favour of a shorter term of office, see Resolution of the European Parliament on Economic and Monetary Union of 10 Oct. 1990 (five years). With regard to the debate on the term of office, see R. Smits (1997), op. cit., *supra* note 77, 163.

fulfil its function for a longer period of time without personal discontinuity. The exclusion of reappointment ensures that members of the Executive Board cannot consider reappointment as an incentive to bow to pressure from national governments or Community Institutions.

Members of the Executive Board of the ECB are also well-shielded from arbitrary or otherwise politically influenced dismissal, as a dismissal can only be based on the incapacity of an Executive Board member to fulfil the conditions required for the performance of his duties or on serious misconduct. Compulsory retirement requires an application by the Governing Council or the Executive Board of the ECB to the ECJ.[324] Moreover, also the dismissal of an NCB governor, which together with the Executive Board make up the Governing Council of the ECB, can only be based on the incapacity of the governor to fulfil the conditions required for the performance of his duties or on serious misconduct.[325] The decision by the national authority to dismiss a NCB governor is open to judicial review by the ECJ, which can be called upon by the NCB governor concerned or the Governing Council of the ECB.[326] The involvement of the ECJ underlines the extent to which the drafters of the Treaty of Maastricht wanted to ensure that the position of the NCB governors is not at any time the subject of political preferences of national governments.[327]

The legal requirements concerning the appointment and dismissal of NCB governors imposed upon the Member States are supposed to ensure the independence of the NCB governors and, hence, the independence of the ECB. In this context it may be somewhat inconsistent that, unlike the members of the Executive Board, Community law does not prohibit the reappointment of NCB governors.

As for the incompatibility of office with functions outside the central bank, Article 11.1. ESCB Statute states not only that Executive Board members have to perform their duties on a full-time basis, but also that they are prohibited from engaging in any occupation during their term of office, whether gainful or not, unless exemption is exceptionally granted by the Governing Council. Interestingly, neither the EC Treaty nor the ESCB Statute restrict in any way the extent to which Executive Board members can engage in professional occupation after their term

---

324. Art. 11.4. ESCB Statute. The role of the ECJ is similar to that in the context of the compulsory retirement of members of the Commission, the Court of Auditors and the European Ombudsman, see Arts. 216, 247(7) and 195(2) EC and Art. 16 para. 4 Statute of the ECJ. Interestingly, the EC Treaty does not include a similar provision for the ECB and the Statute of the ECJ does not refer to the ESCB Statute. This *lacuna*, which has been observed by A. Geelhoed in the 6th Dutch edition of this work, is not filled by the Treaty of Lisbon either.

325. Art. 14(2) ESCB Statute. See J. Usher, *The Law of Money and Financial Services in the European Community* (Oxford, 1996), 174, who refers to 'a unique example of a national office becoming subject to Community jurisdiction'.

326. Also in this context a corresponding provision in the EC Treaty determining the competent Community court and the applicable procedure is missing. Given the nature of the legal conflict involving a Member State and a Community organ, it is presently submitted that such a case should be brought before and decided by the ECJ rather than the CFI. See also R. Smits (1997), op. cit., *supra* note 77 164, note 64.

327. F. Amtenbrink (1999), op. cit., *supra* note 61, 272–273.

of office has ceased, as Article 38(1) ESCB Statute only obliges Executive Board members to professional secrecy after their duties have ceased. However, in its Code of Conduct for the members of the Governing Council, the ECB does require that members during the first year after their duties have ceased continue to avoid any conflict of interests that could arise from any new private or professional activities.[328]

3.3.2.2.4   Financial Independence

In broad terms, financial independence refers to the legal and practical arrangements related to the finances of a central bank and the extent to which the bank is subject to outside influence in this regard.[329] This includes in particular the role which government has in determining the budget of the central bank and the freedom of the latter in the management of its finances. A central bank which is subject to extensive budgetary control by government is more vulnerable to outside pressure on monetary policy.

The budget of the ECB does not form part of the general Community budget.[330] The ECB finances its operations through generated income such as from the holding of foreign reserve assets, the paid-up capital of currently ca. euro 5.7 billion[331] and seigniorage derived from the use of currency. With the exception of a certain percentage reserved for the general reserve of the ECB, net profits are distributed among the NCBs.[332]

The financial independence of the ECB embraces its exclusion from the full examination by the European Court of Auditors, which in principle is charged with the examination of the accounts of revenue and expenditure of all bodies set up by the Community.[333] In the case of the ECB, this examination is limited to the operational efficiency of the management of the ECB. It thus excludes a review of the efficiency of monetary policy operations.[334] The financial independence of the ECB does not however shield the bank from investigations by the European Anti-Fraud Office (OLAF) in accordance with Regulation 1073/1999 concerning investigations conducted by the OLAF.[335]

---

328.   O.J. 2002, C 123/9. See in particular points 4 and 6 on conflict of interests and continuance of duties respectively.
329.   F. Amtenbrink, 'Securing financial independence in the legal basis of a central bank', in S. Milton and M. Blejer, *The Capital Needs of Central Banks* (London, 2008), with further references, where three main sets of rules linked to financial independence are identified: (re-)capitalization, budget, and profit and loss distribution.
330.   See also the new Art. 314 of the TFEU which explicitly excludes the ECB from the Union's budgetary procedure.
331.   Of which circa 93% are contributed by the NCBs of the euro area and circa 7% by the other NCBs.
332.   Art. 33 ESCB Statute. The obligation for Member States to provide for the financial independence of the NCB can be deduced from the general provision of Art. 109 EC.
333.   See generally Ch. V section 3, *supra* on the Community budget.
334.   F. Amtenbrink (1999), op. cit., *supra* note 61, 330–331.
335.   In Case C-11/00, *Commission v. ECB*, the ECJ annulled decision 1999/726/EC of the European Central Bank of 7 Oct. 1999, on fraud prevention (ECB/1999/5) which had

3.3.2.2.5 Independence and Democratic Accountability

Arguably no aspect of the institutional structure of the ECB has been debated more controversially than the issue of the democratic legitimacy and accountability of the ECB in the Community legal order.[336] Yet, the debate on the position of central banks within the constitutional system is in fact much older than the Treaty of Maastricht.[337] The case for the democratic accountability of a central bank is based, on the one hand, on the legal nature of these agencies and their position within a democratic system, and on the other hand on the task with which they have been entrusted.[338] In the state context, independent central banks which are deliberately removed from the executive branch of government, fall to varying degrees outside the classic three-branch system of government, the *trias politica*, and the system of checks and balances it entails. Yet this system, and in particular the mechanisms of accountability it provides, contributes in important ways to the legitimation of the delegation of power such as found in representative democracies. From a normative point of view, the need for mechanisms of democratic accountability arguably derives from the special position which the central bank has *vis-à-vis* the democratically elected legislative and the executive. To the extent that central banks are independent, mechanisms of democratic accountability are required in order to legitimize the position of the central bank within a given constitutional system. Central banks do not operate in a constitutional vacuum. Moreover, observing the central bank from a functional point of view, its main task, i.e., monetary policy, in principle forms part economic policy. As such it should ultimately be treated like other elements of economic policy when it comes to the requirement of democratic accountability.[339]

---

established a separate, internal anti-fraud committee responsible for the monitoring of the activities of the Directorate for Internal Audit of the ECB aimed at prevention of fraud and other illegal activities detrimental to the financial interests of the ECB. The ECJ followed the noteworthy opinion of A.G. Jacobs. See also Decision of the ECB of 3 Jun. 2004, concerning the terms and conditions for OLAF investigations of the European Central Bank, in relation to the prevention of fraud, corruption and any other illegal activities detrimental to the European Communities' financial interests and amending the Conditions of Employment for Staff of the European Central Bank (ECB/2004/11) (2004/525/EC) (O.J. 2004, L 230/56). Generally with regard to the consequences of this judgment, cf. C. Zilioli and M. Selmayr, 'The Constitutional Status of the European Central Bank' (2007) CML Rev., 355, 371 et seq.

336. See e.g., R. Lastra, 'The Independence of the European System of Central Banks' (1992), *Harvard International Law Journal*, 475–519; L.W. Gormley and J. de Haan, 'The Democratic Deficit of the European Central Bank' (1996) EL Rev., 95–112; R. Smits (1997), op. cit., *supra* note 77; F. Amtenbrink (1999), op. cit., *supra* note 61, F. Amtenbrink, 'The European Central Bank: Democratically Accountable or Unrestrained?' (1999), NJB, 72–78.

337. See e.g., K. Bonin, *Zentralbanken zwischen funktioneller Unabhängigkeit und politischer Autonomie*, Dissertation (Berlin, 1978); R. Caesar, 'Die Unabhängigkeit der Notenbank im demokratischen Staat', (1980) *Zeitschrift für Politik*, 347–377.

338. F. Amtenbrink, 'The Three Pillars of Central Bank Governance: Towards a Model Central Bank Law or a Code of Good Governance?' in International Monetary Fund, *Current Developments in Monetary and Financial Law*, Volume 4 (Washington, DC, 2005), 101–132.

339. F. Amtenbrink and J. de Haan (2002), 65–66. See also T. Daintith, 'Between Domestic Democracy and Alien Rule of Law? Some Thoughts on the 'Independence' of the Bank of England', in M. Andenas et al., op. cit., *supra* note 77, 355–372.

While the act of delegation of this executive policy by an act of parliament initially legitimizes the position of the central bank in a given constitutional system, this *ex ante* mechanism of accountability cannot suffice. Indeed, in order to ensure the democratic accountability, and with it the democratic legitimacy, of independent central banks certain preconditions have to be met, such as transparency, the existence of a yardstick making it possible to judge whether the bank has properly discharged its duties and the existence of institutionalized contacts which allow for the exchange of information. Moreover, effective accountability also requires the existence of legal instruments to hold the central bank accountable. The distribution of these instruments between government and parliament provides for the democratic element in keeping the bank accountable. Examples of such instruments are the possibility to amend the legal basis of the central bank, the possibility of performance-based dismissals, the possibility of government or parliament to override central bank decisions.[340]

The choice which has been made in the Treaty of Maastricht to define the independent position, structure, competences and tasks in primary Community law, as well as the insulation of the ESCB from outside influence described above, has resulted in a central bank system whose democratic link back to the European and national government and parliaments is relatively weak. By granting the ECB a quasi-constitutional status, amendment of the legal basis of the bank is a rather ineffective and even unrealistic instrument of democratic accountability. Indeed, as past experience has shown in a EU of currently 27 Member States, achieving the required consensus for such an amendment is anything but certain. Moreover, while it will be observed hereafter that the ECB is to some extent subject to review by the European Parliament, unlike national parliaments, the latter is not in the position to alter the legal basis of the ECB. Moreover, given the extent to which the ECB and the NCBs are distanced from national government and Community Institutions, such as the Council and the Commission, neither national parliaments nor the European Parliament can hold these bodies to account for a supervisory role which they effectively do not have *vis-à-vis* the ECB and NCBs. What is more, national parliaments and government can hardly make their respective NCB governor personally responsible for a decision which has been collectively taken by the Executive Board of the ECB and the other NCB governors participating in the Governing Council.

Yet the European Parliament's difficulties in holding the ECB to account for its conduct of monetary policy is not only of an institutional nature. The evaluation of the monetary policy in the national sphere takes place first and foremost in the light of economic policy pursued by national government. The consistency of monetary policy with economic policy constitutes an important yardstick. Yet, as the Member States in principle remain in charge of economic and budgetary policy, the European Parliament misses an important yardstick for the substantive assessment of the monetary policy conducted by the ECB. What is more, given the

---

340.   For an extensive analysis of these and other elements in the context of the ESCB and the ECB see F. Amtenbrink (1999), op. cit., *supra* note 61.

diminutive role of the European Parliament in EMU, it effectively has to review the ECB's performance based on a yardstick that has been established without the input of the European Parliament.

All things considered, against the background of the Treaty-based independence of the ECB, the preconditions and instruments foreseen in primary Community law for holding the ECB accountable can only be described as underdeveloped and weak in particular when compared to some other central bank systems.[341] Mechanisms of democratic accountability are largely limited to the exchange of information in the form of dialogue with Community Institutions and reporting requirements.

As has been observed above, both the President of the Council and a member of the Commission can participate in meetings of the Governing Council without a voting right.[342] The President of the Council may submit a motion for deliberation to the Governing Council, but the Governing Council is neither obliged to take a decision on that motion for deliberation nor does the President of the Council or the member of the Commission for that matter have a formal right to override or postpone decisions taken in that forum.[343] At the same time, the President of the ECB is invited to participate in Council meetings when the Council is discussing matters relating to the objectives and tasks of the ESCB.[344] In practice, the President of the ECB or his representative participate regularly in ECOFIN Council meetings. As the drafters of the Treaty of Maastricht wanted to place the ECB at some distance from any political influence, these arrangements may seem somewhat surprising. However, as has been observed elsewhere the potential for disputes between the central bank and government may actually be the highest where such institutionalized contacts do not exist and simply take place behind closed doors, with potentially devastating effects for the credibility of the ECB

---

341. F. Amtenbrink (1999), op. cit., *supra* note 61, 359 et seq. with concrete proposals for improvements. For an early comparative indicator of central bank accountability see J. de Haan, F. Amtenbrink and S.C.W. Eijffinger, 'Accountability of Central Banks: Aspects and Quantifications' (1999), *Banca Nazionale del Lavoro Quarterly Review*, 167–193. On this point we clearly disagree with the assessment of other authors, such as e.g., R. Smits (1997), op. cit., *supra* note 77, 176–178; C. Zilioli and M. Selmayr (2001), op. cit., *supra* note 77, and by the same authors 'Recent Developments in the Law of the European Central Bank' (2005), *Yearbook of European Law*, 1–89.

342. In the Committee of Governors alternatively the president of the Council or a member of the Commission was allowed to participate. See Art. 2 of Decision 64/300/EEC (O.J. 1964, No. 77, 1206/64).

343. A similar limited right of presence existed previously in the case of the Bundesbank, see F. Amtenbrink (1999), op. cit., *supra* note 61, 222. While the existence of override mechanisms is generally considered problematic from the point of view of central bank independence, the example of the Reserve Bank of New Zealand Act 1998 and the Bank of England Act 1998 show that legal arrangements can be put in place to prevent the abuse of such a mechanism for short-term political ends. Interestingly, in line with the principle of ministerial responsibility, the previous Dutch Bank Act 1948 also foresaw in an override mechanism in favour of the Minister of Finance (Art. 26(1)). While this right has never been exercised it certainly functioned as an efficient deterrent.

344. Art. 113(2) EC.

and EMU as a whole. Conflicting monetary and general fiscal policy objectives of the central bank and government respectively call for the existence of a conflict resolution mechanism. Adequate communication channels between the government, parliament and the central bank can help to avoid misunderstandings and false expectations in particular on the part of the government but also the public at large as to what monetary policy can and cannot do.[345] At the same time, such contacts ensure that the central bank does not operate in a political or social vacuum. Public support can be an important element in shielding a central bank from unwanted political influence.[346] Parliamentary support can be equally important.

The Fed is an excellent example of a statutorily prescribed relationship between a central bank and the democratically elected parliament. Under the Humphrey-Hawkins-Procedure, Fed officials, including the president, in the past had to appear before the Senate and House of Representatives Banking Committees twice a year. In the course of time these hearings have gained great publicity and can be described as one of the cornerstones of the democratic accountability of the Fed.[347] At the same time, the value of such hearings very much depends on the quality of the reviewers and on the rhetoric abilities of the central bank officials.[348]

In the case of the ECB, according to Article 113(3) EC the President of the ECB and the other members of the Executive Board may, at the request of the European Parliament or on their own initiative, be heard by the competent committees. From the wording of this provision it cannot be concluded that the appearance before the European Parliament amounts to an obligation.[349] From the beginning, a practice has been established whereby the president of the ECB appears before the European Parliament Committee on Economic and Monetary Affairs on a quarterly basis.[350] A study of these hearings highlights the vivid interest which Member of European Parliaments (MEPs) take in the activities

---

345. F. Amtenbrink (2005), op. cit., *supra* note 338, 113 et seq.
346. J.-V. Louis, (1995), op. cit., *supra* note 12, at 75, in this context cites Goodhart: 'An independent central bank will fail and be rejected, unless it can establish broadly-based public support.'
347. F. Amtenbrink (1999), op. cit., *supra* note 61, 287.
348. As the rather famous remark by Greenspan recorded during the US Senate Banking Committee hearing of 20 Jun. 1995, goes: 'If I say something which you understand fully in this regard, I probably made a mistake.' While the legal basis of this procedure (Full Employment and Balanced Growth Act of 1978) expired in 2000, the practice continues.
349. The European Parliament had suggested the introduction of a rule according to which the president of the ECB should be heard every 6 months or whenever the European Parliament considered it feasible. See Resolution of the European Parliament on EMU of 10 Oct. 1990 (O.J. 1990, C 284/62).
350. This regular so-called monetary dialogue was established on the initiative of the European Parliament which in its rules of procedure foresees that the president of the ECB is invited to attend the meetings of said committee at least 4 times a year to make a statement and answer questions. See Rule 106 of the Rules of Procedure of the European Parliament (16th edition, Sep. 2007).

of the ESCB and ECB and in particular the latter's decisions on monetary policy. As has been observed elsewhere, MEPs focus on the issues of inflation and deflation, and the question of how the ECB can contribute to economic development with regard to growth and employment. In particular the strict preference which the ECB gives to its primary monetary objective over the secondary objective of supporting the economic policies of the Community has in the past been questioned by the elected representatives in the European Parliament.[351]

Apart from the regular appearance of the members of the Executive Board of the ECB before the relevant European Parliament standing committee, the EC Treaty and ESCB Statute also introduce reporting requirements. This includes the publication of weekly financial consolidated financial statements, quarterly reports on the activities of the ESCB and the drafting of an annual report on the activities of the ESCB and on the monetary policy of both the previous and current year addressed to the European Parliament, the Council and the Commission, and also to the European Council. The annual report is presented to the Council and to the European Parliament by the President of the ECB.[352]

The regular appearances before the European Parliament and the reporting requirements form an important element in the accountability of the ECB. Indeed, in more recent times central banks, including the ECB, have discovered transparency as an ally both in meeting demands of more openness and accountability and in communicating monetary policy.[353] However, transparency may not only refer to the degree to which a central bank provides information, but moreover to the public's understanding of the decisions taken by the monetary authorities and the reasoning behind them.[354] This includes in particular the quantification of the monetary policy objective and the strategy of the central bank in achieving the statutory objective. Indeed, communication is in the very own interest of a central bank, since it enhances the effectiveness and credibility of monetary policy, as the general public and even more so the financial markets (better) understand the banks' approach to monetary policy.[355]

Alongside numerous publications of the ECB on its approach to monetary policy, including in particular monthly reports, the ECB also holds press conferences following the first meeting of the Governing Council each month. Unlike some central banks, the ECB does not publish minutes of meetings of the

---

351. See generally with regard to these hearings F. Amtenbrink, 'On the Legitimacy and Democratic Accountability of the European Central Bank: Legal Arrangements and Practical Experience', in A. Arnull and D. Wincott, *Accountability and Legitimacy in the European Union* (Oxford, 2002), 147–163, 157 et seq.
352. Art. 113(2) EC, Art. 15 ESCB Statute.
353. Generally with regard to the transparency of the ECB see: *European Journal of Political Economy*, Vol. 23, Issue 1 (Mar., 2007), with numerous contributions on this topic.
354. R. Lastra, 'How much accountability for central banks and supervisors?' (2001) *Central Banking* 69–75; J. de Haan, F. Amtenbrink and S. Waller, 'Transparency and Credibility of the European Central Bank' (2004), JCMS, 775–794, with further references.
355. International Monetary Fund, Supporting Document to the Code of Good Practices on Transparency in Monetary and Financial Policies (Washington, DC, 2000).

Governing Board. Article 10.4 ESCB Statute, which states that the 'proceedings of the meetings shall be confidential' has been interpreted by the ECB to the effect that the proceedings of the decision-making bodies of the ECB and any committee or group established by them are confidential. The Rules of Procedure of the ECB allow the Governing Council to authorize the president of the ECB to make public (only) the outcome of their deliberations.[356] It must be acknowledged that the publication of such minutes is, at present, controversial. It can be argued that the publication of details of the deliberations at these meetings, including views expressed during the discussions and the voting behaviour of the members of the monetary policy board, could obstruct deliberations in the Governing Council and moreover subject NCB governors, in particular, to domestic political pressure.[357]

3.3.2.2.6 Independence and Judicial Review

The *ex post* democratic accountability in the form of the political control described above is complemented by *ex post* judicial control. Indeed, the independence of the ECB and its far-reaching competences and regulatory activities makes it necessary that the ECB is subject to full judicial review. To this end Article 35.1 ESCB Statute states that the acts and omissions of the ECB are open to review or interpretation by the ECJ in the cases and under the conditions laid down in the EC Treaty. Moreover, the ECB is granted standing. Article 230 EC empowers the ECJ, *inter alia*, to review the legality of legally binding acts of the ECB. Moreover, the ECB is entitled to bring an action under Article 230 paragraph 3 EC against legally binding acts adopted jointly by the European Parliament and the Council, acts of the Council, of the Commission and of the European Parliament for the purpose of protecting its prerogatives.[358] Moreover, according to Article 241 EC, in proceedings in which a regulation of the ECB is at issue, parties can plead the grounds specified in Article 230 paragraph 2 EC (grounds of lack of competence, infringement of an essential procedural requirement, infringement of the EC Treaty or of any rule of law relating to its application, misuse of powers) in order to invoke the inapplicability of that regulation.

According to Article 232 EC, the ECB can also become subject to an action for failure to act and can itself institute such an action in the areas falling within its field of competence, although if and when the EC Treaty is replaced by the Treaty on the Function of the EU, the latter condition for standing will be removed.[359] If the ECJ

---

356. Art. 23 Rules of Procedure ECB.
357. F. Amtenbrink (2002), op. cit., *supra* note 351, at 152. However, section 15(3) of the Bank of England Act 1998 highlights how the publication of such minutes can be achieved without compromising the objectives of the bank. It provides for the publication of the minutes of the established Monetary Policy Committee, while at the same time ensuring the efficiency of the decisions taken in the Committee by excluding certain market-sensitive decisions from publication for a pre-determined period of 6 weeks.
358. On the scope of these prerogatives see Ch. VI *supra* section 2.2. Decisions of the ECB to bring an action are taken by the Governing Council of the ECB (Art. 35.5. ESCB Statute).
359. Art. 265 of the TFEU moreover will extend the possibility of review of failure to act to all institutions, bodies offices or agencies of the Union.

declares an act of the ECB or a failure to act contrary to the EC Treaty, the ECB is obliged to take the necessary measures to comply with the ECJ's judgment.[360] Finally, in the context of the preliminary reference procedure provided for by Article 234(b) EC, national courts and tribunals can direct questions to the ECJ concerning the validity or interpretation of ECB acts if they consider that a decision on the question is necessary to enable them to give judgment.

According to Article 35.3 ESCB Statute, action by the ECB can become the subject of the non-contractual liability of the Community provided for in Article 288 in conjunction with Article 235 EC.[361] Whether and to what extent the NCBs are liable depends on their respective national laws; yet, it is presently submitted that this non-contractual liability of NCBs should be limited to those activities which they undertake outside the ESCB and thus outside the control of the ECB.[362]

In disputes within the ESCB between the ECB and a NCB concerning the fulfilment by the latter of its obligations under the ESCB Statute, Article 35.6 ESCB Statute introduces a procedure which has similarities to the treaty infringement procedure in Article 226 EC. In such a case the ECB (rather than the Commission) has to deliver a reasoned opinion on the matter after giving the NCB concerned the opportunity to submit its observations. If the NCB concerned does not comply with the opinion within the period laid down by the ECB, the latter may than bring the matter before the ECJ.[363]

While the acts and omissions of the ECB are thus in principle subject to judicial review, given the nature of the competences exercised by the ECB which are characterized in many areas by a considerable degree of discretion and which are based on economic assessments, an extensive jurisprudence of the ECJ on the conduct of the ECB cannot be expected.[364] This is particularly true with regard to monetary policy decisions.[365] At the same time, the institutional and substantive context of the ESCB is 'juridified' to a larger extent than has been the case in the past in many instances in NCBs. As such, the extensive jurisdiction of the ECJ relating to the ECB is certainly more than merely symbolic, as it highlights the intention of the drafters of the Treaty of Maastricht to place the ECB as much as possible within the Community legal order.[366]

---

360. Art. 233 EC.
361. Art. 288 para. 3 EC. In Art. 340 of the TFEU, para. 3 of today's Art. 288 EC is replaced: it states that the ECB, in accordance with the general principles common to the laws of the Member States, has to make good any damage caused by it or by its servants in the performance of their duties.
362. See already R. Smits (1997), op. cit., *supra* note 77, 107–108.
363. The fact that the ECB brings the action against a NCB rather than a Member State underlines the independence of the NCB as part of the ESCB. Interestingly, unlike what applies in the case of the regular infringement procedure, the ECB does not have the possibility to enforce a judgement by the ECJ in the way provided in Art. 288 para. 2 EC for Member States.
364. Similarly T. Daintith (1997), op. cit., *supra* note 77, 368–369.
365. F. Amtenbrink (1999), op. cit., *supra* note 61, 4–5, with references to attempts in the US to challenge decisions of the Fed.
366. See J.-V. Louis, (1995), op. cit., *supra* note 12, 75.

3.3.2.3   *The Competences and Tasks of the ESCB and the ECB*

The tasks and related competences of the ECB include, among other things, the definition and implementation of monetary policy, the conduct of foreign-exchange operations, payment systems oversight and advisory functions.

3.3.2.3.1   Monetary Policy[367]
The primary objective of the ECB as set out in Article 105(1) EC and Article 2 ESCB Statute is to maintain price stability. As a secondary objective, which is subordinated to that of price stability, the ECB must support the general economic policies of the Community with a view to contributing to the achievements of the objectives of the Community as laid down in Article 2 EC.[368] The inclusion of this unequivocal and single monetary policy objective in primary Community law can be attributed above all to the influence of Germany, which was only willing to surrender the monetary policy authority of the Bundesbank if a European monetary policy authority had an equally clear monetary policy objective.[369]

In conducting monetary policy, the ECB is obliged to act in accordance with the principle of an open market economy with free competition, favouring an efficient allocation of resources, and in compliance with the principles set out in Article 4 EC.[370] This link between monetary and economic policy is important as divergent development of these two policy fields would in the long run be unsustainable due to spill-over effects. On the one side, an interventionist and protectionist general economic policy would almost inevitably result in a flanking protectionist external monetary policy.[371] On the other, a monetary policy which relies on strong *dirigiste* instruments is in the long run not compatible with the principle of an open economy.[372]

With regard to the primary objective of the ECB, it is notable that neither the EC Treaty nor the ESCB Statute quantify 'price stability'. Indeed, the ECB is left to

---

367.   The legal and economic literature on the monetary policy of the ECB is extensive. See e.g., O. Issing, 'Monetary Policy Strategy in EMU', and S.C.W. Eijffinger, 'A Framework for Monetary Stability', both in J. de Beaufort Wijnholds et al., *A Framework for Monetary Stability*, Dordrecht (Boston and London, 1994), 135–148 and 309–330; A. Berg, 'Monetary Policy Strategies for the European Central Bank', in M. Andenas et al., op. cit., *supra* note 77, 125–137; J. de Haan, F. Amtenbrink and S. Waller, op. cit., *supra* note 354, with further references.
368.   This reference to the monetary policy objective will also be included in the new Art. 282(2) of the TFEU.
369.   Prior to the entry into force of the Treaty of Maastricht the German basic law (*Grundgesetz*) was amended, making the transfer of authority over monetary policy to the ESCB and ECB subject the inclusion on the European level of price stability as the primary objective. See Art. 88 sentence 2 *Grundgesetz*, as amended by law of 21 Dec. 1992 (BGBl. I, 2086).
370.   See also Art. 98 EC.
371.   The history of monetary policy in Spain and France is very instructive in this regard.
372.   Art. 18.2. ESCB Statute. See also R. Smits (1999), op. cit., *supra* note 284, 286, observes in this context that the requirement to observe the principle of open market economy has consequences for the policy instruments of the ECB. It may be concluded from this that preference must be given to indirect monetary policy instruments.

its own devices to define what this actually amounts to in numerical terms. From the point of view of democratic accountability this is not unproblematic, as the ECB itself can define the yardstick by which its performance is subsequently evaluated. It is for this reason that the EC Treaty and ESCB Statute have been criticized for granting the ECB not only instrument-independence, but also goal-independence.[373] The ECB initially announced its quantitative definition of price stability as 'a year-on-year increase in the Harmonised Index of Consumer Prices (HICP) for the euro area of below 2%.' Following concerns that, on the basis of this quantification the ECB may actually pursue a monetary policy which results in deflation, i.e., a decline in the level of prices, the ECB eventually adjusted this definition somewhat by emphasizing that it aims to maintain inflation rates below, *but close to*, 2% over the medium term.[374]

The monetary policy instruments available to the ECB are laid down in Article 105(2) EC and Articles 17–21 ESCB Statute. They include open market operations, lending facilities (standing facilities) to credit institutions (eligible counterparties), and minimum reserve requirements applied to credit institutions in the euro area.[375] As far as the indirect instruments are concerned, i.e., open market operations and lending facilities, the ECB itself establishes the general principles which have to be observed by the ECB and the NCBs in carrying out such operations.[376] On the contrary, for direct instruments, which create direct obligations for third parties, such as minimum reserve requirements, the Council has to adopt complementary legislation.[377]

The decentralized execution of monetary policy by the NCBs requires close coordination. To this end, the ECB issues the necessary instructions in the form of guidelines.[378]

Since the start of stage three of EMU and the irrevocable fixing of the exchange rates of the currencies of the Member States participating in the euro area from the time of its establishment, the conduct of monetary policy by the ECB has been monitored closely in political circles and in the market place. In the first two years of its operation, distrust of the apparently restrictive monetary policy

---

373. See e.g., F. Amtenbrink (2002), op. cit., *supra* note 351, 184 et seq.

374. See European Central Bank, *The Monetary Policy of the ECB* (Frankfurt a.M., 2004), 50–51.

375. Informative in this context: European Central Bank, *The Implementation of the Monetary Policy in the Euro Area: general documentation on the Eurosystem monetary policy instruments and procedures* (Frankfurt a.M., 2006).

376. R. Smits (1997), op. cit., *supra* note 77, 264–274.

377. See e.g., Art. 19.2. ESCB Statute which refers to Art. 42 ESCB Statute for the applicable procedure. See Reg. (EC) No. 2531/98 of 23 Nov. 1998, concerning the application of minimum reserves by the European Central Bank (O.J. 1998, L 318/1), as amended by Reg. (EC) No 134/2002 of 22 Jan. 2002 (O.J. 2002, L 24/1).

378. Guideline of the ECB of 31 Aug. 2000, on monetary policy instruments and procedures of the Eurosystem (ECB/2000/7) (O.J. 2000, L 310/1), last amended by Guideline of the ECB of 31 Aug. 2006, amending Guideline ECB/2000/7 on monetary policy instruments and procedures of the Eurosystem (ECB/2006/12) (O.J. 2006, L 352/1) and Guideline of the ECB of 20 Sep. 2007, amending Annexes I and II to Guideline ECB/2000/7 on monetary policy instruments and procedures of the Eurosystem (ECB/2007/10) (O.J. 2007, L 284/34).

prevailed in political circles, in particular in France. The rather strict approach by the ECB found its justification in the economic boom in large parts of the euro area which had resulted in inflationary pressure. This only changed after the general economic situation changed in 2001, resulting in the ECB gradually softening its monetary stand. Yet, only when the economic development in Europe showed real signs of stagnation did the ECB substantially relax its stand in the fall of 2001.

In the past, financial markets have criticized the ECB for pursuing a monetary policy strategy which is unpredictable. In this context it has been observed that the ECB does not only take action in pursuit of its primary monetary objective, that is to maintain price stability below but close to 2%, but rather takes decisions and acts in pursuit of intermediary targets, such as money growth.[379] The motive for such a focus on money growth is that while inflation may (still) be low, a growth of money that does not match the actual economic growth may in the future result in a higher price level.[380] Having said this, it has to be recognized that the ECB has taken major steps to explain its monetary policy strategy.[381]

In formulating and implementing monetary policy the ECB faces challenges deriving from its special position as a supranational monetary policy authority for a currency area where the economic developments of the Member States are not necessarily homogenous. This was certainly the case during the first two years of the ECB's existence, when the economic expansion in Member States such as Ireland, Finland and the Netherlands was not matched by the developments in the big economies, such as Germany, France and Italy. While France at the time considered the ECB's approach to monetary policy as too strict, for countries such as Ireland and the Netherlands, the very same approach was considered too lenient. This raised the question with regard to the single monetary policy in the euro area of 15 Member States by 2008, whether 'one size can fit all'.[382] The pursuit of a single monetary policy in the euro area of 15 national economies emphasizes the importance of the close economic coordination in the context of Article 99 and moreover also Article 104 EC.[383]

---

379.   See B. Friedman, 'Intermediate Targets versus Information Variables as Operating Guides for Monetary Policy', in De Beaufort Wijnholds et al. (1994), op. cit., *supra* note 367, 109–134,

380.   For an economic analysis of the relationship between inflation and money growth see e.g., G. Dwyer jr. and R. Hafer, 'Are Money Growth and Inflation Still Related?', Federal Reserve Bank of Atlanta Economic Review, Second Quarter 1999, 32–34. However M. Neumann and C. Greiber, Inflation and Core Money Growth in the Euro, Deutsche Bundesbank Discussion Paper Series 1: Studies of the Economic Research Centre No. 36/2004, 25, find evidence that this relationship 'appears to rest on relatively long-lasting cycles of monetary growth'.

381.   See e.g., the extensive documentation provided by the ECB in The Monetary Policy of the ECB, op. cit., *supra* note 374; ECB, The implementation of monetary policy (. . .), op. cit., *supra* note 375. See generally J. de Haan, S.C.W. Eijffinger and S. Waller, op. cit., *supra* note 268.

382.   See e.g., O. Issing, 'One size fits all! A single monetary policy for the euro area', Speech held at the International Research Forum, Frankfurt a.M., 20 May 2005.

383.   See J. von Hagen, 'Co-ordination of Economic Policies and Employment', in A. Lamfalussy et al., *The Euro-Zone: A New Economic Entity?* (Brussels, 1999), at 61–75.

Despite its relatively short existence, the ECB has been able to gain credibility as an inflation-adverse monetary policy authority which takes its statutorily assigned primary objective seriously, albeit that is has not necessarily been capable of sticking to its self-proclaimed definition of price stability.[384] Criticism of the ECB's approach comes, *inter alia*, from those Member States which still have difficulties in adjusting their economic policy in the light of a single currency area in which monetary policy is geared towards the single goal of price stability.[385]

3.3.2.3.2 Foreign-Exchange Operations

According to Article 105(2), second and third indent EC, the ECB conducts foreign-exchange operations consistently with Article 111 EC. The details regarding this task are laid down in Articles 23, 30 and 31 ESCB Statute.

The conduct of an internal monetary policy geared towards price stability can require exchange-rate interventions on behalf of the euro. Internal and external monetary policy are linked. On the one hand, if the value of the currency of an important trading partner of the Community suddenly increases considerably, the resulting increase in prices for imports can have a negative impact on the internal price stability. In such a situation, large amounts of the respective foreign currency may have to be sold in an attempt to lower the value of the respective currency *vis-à-vis* the euro. On the other hand, an overvalued euro may put the economies of the euro area under pressure on the global markets, with serious consequences for economic growth and employment in the EU. Such an undesirable deflationary development can, under certain conditions, be curbed through massive selling of euros.

Given the vital role of the exchange-rate policy for the European economies it may be hardly surprising that the Member States, as drafters of the Treaty of Maastricht, decided to vest the primary responsibility for the formulation of the exchange-rate policy in the Council, in fact the ECOFIN Council. However from the point of view of the independence of the ECB, this arrangement may not be ideal.[386]

Exchange-rate operations by the ECB are possible through foreign reserve assets which are provided by the NCBs. According to Article 30 ESCB Statute, NCBs have to provide the ECB with foreign reserve assets up to an amount equivalent to euro 50 000 million. The individual contributions of the NCBs have been fixed in proportion to their share in the subscribed capital of the ECB.[387] Moreover, within the margins and under the conditions set by the Council,

---

384. J. de Haan, S.C.W. Eijffinger and S. Waller, op. cit., *supra* note 268, 80, who observe that inflation in the EU has remained low despite the fact that the inflation rate has regularly exceeded the 2% reference value.

385. For a clear analysis of the ECB's approach to monetary policy see G. Corsetti and P. Presenti, Stability, Asymmetry and Discontinuity; The Launch of European Monetary Union, Brookings Papers on Economic Activity 2, 1999, 295–371. The authors rebut critics of the ECB's approach to monetary policy.

386. Art. 111 EC. This point will be further discussed in section 3.3.5. *infra*.

387. With regard to the subscription of the ECB's capital in accordance with the procedure laid down in Art. 28.1. ESCB Statute. See Council Decision (90/382/EC) of 5 Jun. 1998, on the

the ECB can demand additional foreign reserve assets.[388] While the ECB in principle has the full right to hold and manage the foreign reserves that are transferred to it and to use them for the statutorily prescribed purposes, in practice the ECB has decided to let the NCBs act as its agents in managing the foreign reserves transferred the ECB.[389] As such, NCBs are only permitted to carry out exchange-rate operations in accordance with the guidelines and instructions of the ECB.[390] While the ESCB thus in principle holds and manages the foreign reserves of the Member States, the latter are also permitted to hold and manage foreign-exchange assets (working balances) in accordance with Article 105(3) EC and once again subject to the Guidelines of the ECB.[391] Moreover, the NCBs are at liberty to perform transactions in fulfilment of their obligations towards international organizations.[392]

3.3.2.3.3   Payment Systems Oversight

As the rate of circulation of financial claims and credits in the global financial market-place has increased, so has the importance of a reliable and efficient payment system, as well as securities clearing and settlement systems. Interruptions in the payment systems can result in serious disturbances in the financial markets with undesired effects on monetary policy.[393] The role of central banks in ensuring stable payment systems has increased. In the European context this is reflected by Article 105(4), fourth indent EC and Article 3.1 ESCB Statute, according to which one of the basis tasks of the ESCB is to promote the smooth operation of payment systems.

From Article 22 ESCB Statute it becomes clear that the ECB and the NCBs are given a facilitating role, whereby the ECB is given the competence to issue regulations, to ensure efficient and sound clearing and payment systems within the Community and with third countries. The fact that the ECB has been given the competence to regulate underlines the supervisory role entrusted to the ECB in

---

statistical data to be used for the determination of the key for subscription of the capital of the European Central Bank (O.J. 1998, L 171/33) and Decision of the ECB of 15 Dec. 2006, on the NCBs' percentage shares in the key for subscription to the European Central Bank's capital (ECB/2006/21) (2007/42/EC) (O.J. 2007, L 24/1).

388. Art. 30.4. ESCB Statute.
389. See Arts. 9.2. and 12.1. ESCB Statute, according to which the ECB can manage certain of its activities through the NCBs.
390. Guideline ECB/2006/28 of 21 Dec. 2006, on the management of the foreign reserve assets of the European Central Bank by the NCBs and the legal documentation for operations involving such assets (O.J. 2007, C 17/5), last amended by Guideline of the ECB of 20 Jul. 2007 (O.J. 2007, L 196/46).
391. Guideline of the ECB of 23 Oct. 2003, for participating Member States' transactions with their foreign exchange working balances pursuant to Art. 31.3 of the Statute of the ESCB and of the ECB (ECB/2003/12) (2003/775/EC) (O.J. 2003, L 283/81).
392. Art. 31.1. ESCB Statute.
393. For more details see R. Smits (1997), op. cit., *supra* note 77, 297–306 and H. Scheller, *The European Central Bank. History, Role and Function*, 2nd ed. (Frankfurt a.M. 2006), 97 et seq.

this area.[394] Arguably the most important of the clearing and payment systems which the ESCB provide is the Trans-European Automated Real-time Gross settlement Express Transfer system, better know under its acronym TARGET, which was put in place at the start of stage three of EMU. While initially TARGET stood for a decentralized structure linking together national real-time gross settlement (RTGS) systems and the ECB Payment Mechanism (EPM), in November 2007 a revised TARGET II came into place which is based on an integrated IT infrastructure and aims at a greater harmonization of the component payments systems.[395]

The ECB also plays an important advisory role in the drafting of Community legislation relating to payment systems, such as the Directive 2007/64/EC of the European Parliament and of the Council on payment services in the internal market which foresees the establishment of a single market for payments in the EU.[396]

3.3.2.3.4 Advisory Functions

In accordance with Article 105(4) EC and Article 4 ESCB Statute, the ECB fulfils advisory functions both on the European level and the level of the Member States. These functions are threefold. The extent to which the ECB has to be consulted, observed hereafter, underlines the special position of the ECB in the Community legal order.

Firstly, in a number of places throughout the EC Treaty it is determined that the ECB has to be consulted.[397] In such instances, consulting the ECB forms an integral part of the applicable Community decision-making procedure and its participation has to be considered as an important element in the institutional balance on the Community level.[398] The participation of the ECB constitutes an 'essential procedural requirement' whose non-observance by the Community institutions can render the Community act void subject to a judgment to that effect by

---

394. Interestingly, unlike e.g., Art. 20 ESCB Statute on operational methods of monetary control, Art. 22 ESCB Statute does not require a Council decision which defines the scope of this regulatory power if the latter imposes obligations on third parties. As a result, the actual scope of the ECB's competence is unclear. An interpretation *a contrario* may be that the ECB may actually only issue regulations which do not impose such obligations on third parties.
395. Guidelines of the ECB of 26 Apr. 2007, on a TARGET2 (ECB/2007/2) (2007/600/EC) (O.J. 2007, L 237/1) and Decision of the ECB of 24 Jul. 2007, concerning the terms and conditions of TARGET2-ECB (ECB/2007/7) (2007/601/EC) (O.J. 2007, L 237/71). For more details, see ECB, *Blue Book. Payment and Securities Settlement Systems in the European Union*, Volume I (Euro Area Countries) and Volume II (Non-Euro Area Countries, 4th edition (Frankfurt a.M., Aug., 2007). The Guideline and Decision are based on the above-mentioned Art. 22 ESCB Statute. In general on payments, see M. van Empel, 'Retail Payments in the EU' (2006) CML Rev., 1425–1444.
396. O.J. 2007, L 319/1. This Directive has to be implemented by the Member States by 1 Nov. 2009.
397. See e.g., Arts. 106(2), 109(1)-(3), 112(2) (b), 123(4) and (5) EC.
398. Similar: R. Smits (1997), op. cit., *supra* note 77, 212.

the ECJ in accordance with Article 230 in conjunction with Article 231 EC.[399] Arguably the most far-reaching right in this regard is included in Article 48 TEU which describes the Treaty amendment procedure. Here, as well as the European Parliament and the Commission, the ECB has a right to be consulted in case that amendments relating to its tasks are planned.

Moreover, even if the ECB is not specifically mentioned in a legal basis, it has to be consulted on any proposed Community act in its fields of competence. The actual scope of this obligation should not be interpreted too narrowly, as it includes any measures in the field of competence of the ESCB and ECB, including among others those relating to exchange-rate policy, payment systems, prudential supervision, and more generally the regulation of the EU capital market.[400] In practice the ECB has in the past not only been consulted by the (ECOFIN) Council, but also by the Commission.[401]

Secondly, the ECB also has to be consulted by *national* authorities regarding any draft legislative provision in its fields of competence, within the limits and under the conditions set out by the Council. According to this, national authorities have to consult the ECB, in particular on currency matters, means of payment, NCBs, the collection, compilation and distribution of monetary, financial, banking, payment systems and balance of payments statistics, payment and settlement systems, and rules applicable to financial institutions insofar as they materially influence the stability of financial institutions and markets. Moreover, Member States outside the euro area must consult the ECB on any draft legislative provisions on the instruments of monetary policy.[402] The ECB itself has come up with a non-legally binding guide for national authorities.[403]

Finally, the ECB may on its own initiative submit opinions to the appropriate Community Institutions or bodies or to national authorities on matters in its fields of competence.

---

399. See e.g., Case C-65/93, *European Parliament v. Council*, with regard to the right of the European Parliament to be consulted.
400. The close relationship between the good functioning of the capital market and the efficiency of monetary policy in our opinion supports the view that the consultation of the ECB in this field is mandatory. In practice, the Council does consult the ECB on such measures. See e.g., Opinion of the ECB of 20 Feb. 2004, on the request of the Council of the European Union on a proposal for a Directive of the European Parliament and of the Council amending Council Dir. 73/239/EEC, 85/611/EEC, 91/675/EEC, 93/6/EEC and 94/19/EC and Dir. 2000/12/EC, 2002/83/EC and 2002/87/EC of the European Parliament and of the Council, in order to establish a new financial services committee organizational structure (COM(2003)659 final – 2003/0263 (COD)) (O.J. 2004, C 58/23).
401. See Opinion of the ECB of 24 Nov. 2000, at the request of the Commission of the European Communities on two draft Commission Regulations (EC) laying down detailed rules for the implementation of Council Reg. (EC) No. 2494/95 as regards minimum standards for the treatment of price reductions and as regards the timing of entering purchaser prices into the harmonized index of consumer prices (CON/00/27) (2000/C 362/11) (O.J. 2000, C 362/12).
402. Council decision (98/415/EC) of 29 Jun. 1998, on the consultation of the European Central Bank by national authorities regarding draft legislative provisions (O.J. 1998, L 189/42).
403. European Central Bank, *Guide to Consultation of the European Central Bank by National Authorities Regarding Draft Legislative Provisions* (Frankfurt a.M., 2005), Art. 2.

These formal advisory functions of the ECB have to be differentiated from the competence of the president of the ECB and the other members of the Executive Board and Governing Council of the ECB – quasi-inherent to their function – to take a position on their own authority on the budgetary and economic policy of the Community. While the ECB does not hold any formal powers in this area, given the close relationship between economic policy, for which essentially the Member States remain responsible, and monetary policy, the conduct of which is entrusted to the ECB, the latter must have the right to express its views in this regard.[404] As such the ECB takes over the tradition to be found previously in some NCB systems, where central bank officials would at times be rather outspoken about the approach to economic policy chosen by government and/or parliament.[405]

3.3.2.3.5 Prudential Supervision

According to Article 105(5) EC, the ESCB contributes to the smooth conduct of policies pursued by the competent authorities relating to the prudential supervision of credit institutions and the stability of the financial system.[406] It becomes clear from these provisions that the ECB is, in principle, not charged with prudential supervision and has no regulatory competences in this area. However, the EC Treaty provides for the possibility for the Council to confer upon the ECB specific tasks concerning policies relating to the prudential supervision of credit institutions and other financial institutions, with the exception of insurance undertakings.[407]

In the run-up to the Treaty of Maastricht, the role of the ECB in prudential supervision was the subject of much debate.[408] In most Member States, supervision of the soundness and solvency of credit institutions was entrusted to the central bank. In some Member States, this task has either been completely transferred to or is shared with a separate supervisory authority.[409] Arguments can be forwarded both in favour of and against entrusting a central bank with prudential

---

404. The regular appearances of the president of the ECB before the European Parliament and his participation in the (ECOFIN) Council meetings are two regular opportunities in this regard. Moreover, members of the Executive Board and Governing Council regularly appear in public fora. One area where ECB officials have been rather outspoken in the past is the lax application of the excessive deficit procedure.

405. Two examples for critical reflections are: J. Zijlstra, *Per Slot van Rekening* (Amsterdam, 1992), at 215–219 and 238–244, and H. Tietmeyer, 'Reflection on the German Treaty Negotiations of 1990', in S. Frowen and R. Pringle (eds), *Inside the Bundesbank* (London, 1998), 68–109.

406. See also Arts. 3.3. and 4 ESCB Statute.

407. Under Art. 105(6) EC this requires a unanimous decision in the Council on a proposal from the Commission and the consent of the European Parliament. Moreover, the ECB has to be consulted. In the TFEU, Art. 105(6) EC is amended to the effect that the Council acts by means of regulations and in accordance with a special legislative procedure which is described in the new Art. 33 EU Treaty, as foreseen in the Treaty of Lisbon.

408. Generally on the role of central banks in banking regulation: R. Lastra, *Central Banking and Banking Regulation* (London, 1996); id., *Legal Foundations of international Monetary Stability* (Oxford, 2006).

409. See D. Schoenmaker, 'Banking Supervision and Lender-of-Last-Resort in EMU', in M. Andenas et al., op. cit., *supra* note 77, 428–436.

supervision.[410] On the one hand, synergies can be achieved by combining information gained from prudential supervision and from the conduct of monetary policy, the overall responsibility of the central bank for the stability of the system as a whole and the independence position of central banks and technical expertise existing therein. Against the combining of tasks it may be argued, *inter alia*, that the latter may result in conflicts of interest between the monetary policy and supervisory tasks of the central bank, and that the position of the central bank becomes even more powerful than it already is given its role as monetary policy authority.[411]

In deciding on the role of the ECB in prudential supervision, two considerations have been most decisive. First, Community legislation on financial services (credit institutions and insurers) did not foresee any harmonization in the area of prudential supervision.[412] Second, there was a certain political resistance to the transfer of even more tasks to the new independent supranational monetary policy authority. The NCBs also indicated reservations against such a prominent role of the ECB in this area, potentially at the expense of one of their last remaining tasks after the transfer of monetary policy authority to the ECB.[413]

For the time being the role of the ECB in prudential supervision as described in the EC Treaty and ESCB Statute is limited to that of an advisor. According to Article 25.1 ESCB Statute, the ECB may offer advice to and be consulted by the Council, the Commission and the competent authorities of the Member States on the scope and implementation of Community legislation relating to the prudential supervision of credit institutions and to the stability of the financial system. It has been observed above that the general right to be consulted also includes legislative initiatives in the European or national sphere relating to financial market regulation. Given that the supervision of the financial institutions which operate in that market forms an essential element of regulation, arguably the role of the

---

410. See e.g., R. Smits (1997), op. cit., *supra* note 77, 310–327; M. Andenas and C. Hadjiemmanuil, 'Banking Supervision, The Internal Market and European Monetary Union', in M. Andenas et al., op. cit., *supra* note 77, 371–417, in particular 386–394. An instructive overview of the arguments is provided in a position paper by the European Central Bank: 'The Role of Central Banks' (Frankfurt a.M., 2001), in particular 3–7.

411. In its position paper, op. cit., *supra* note 410, at 7 et seq., the ECB argues that in the context of the institutional framework resulting from the introduction of the euro, the arguments in favour of combining these tasks outweigh those in favour of keeping them apart.

412. See Second Council Dir. 89/646/EEC of 15 Dec. 1989, on the coordination of laws, regulations and administrative provisions relating to the taking up and pursuit of the business of credit institutions and amending Dir. 77/780/EEC (O.J. 1998, L 386/1, as amended. See M. Andenas and C. Hadjiemmanuil (1997), op. cit., *supra* note 410, 381–386. Dir. 2000/12/EC of the European Parliament and of the Council of 20 Mar. 2000, relating to the taking up and pursuit of the business of credit institution which among others repealed before-mentioned Dir. and the subsequent Dir. 2006/48/EC of the European Parliament and of the Council of 14 Jun. 2006, relating to the taking up and pursuit of the business of credit institutions (O.J. 2006, L 177/1) both refer to the principle of home state supervision.

413. See J.-V. Louis, (1995), op. cit., *supra* note 12, 92 and 93, and R. Smits (1997), op. cit., *supra* note 77, 334–338.

ECB in this area is actually more powerful than the wording of Article 25.1 ESCB Statute may suggest.[414]

Past experience highlights that the concurrence of globalized financial markets and modern financial techniques and products can bear considerable risks for the stability of the financial system. The history of the financial crisis in South-East Asia in 1997, the Russian financial crisis (Rouble crisis) in 1998, as well as the global financial turmoil in 2007/2008, triggered by the US subprime mortgage crisis, highlight that large central bank interventions on short notice may become necessary in order to rescue the financial system.[415] This requires in-depth knowledge of the financial risks which credit and other financial institutions take in the course of their business. While for the time being prudential supervision remains decentralized, the ECB must be in the position to control the quality of prudential supervision and to obtain all relevant information in order to be able to act timely and adequately in case of disturbances in the increasingly integrated European financial markets.[416] Based on the so-called Lamfalussy Report of February 2001, which was subsequently adopted by the Copenhagen European Council in its Resolution of 23 March 2001 in Copenhagen, what is currently in place on the European level is a complex committee structure.[417] The Lamfalussy process is ultimately not only aimed at improvement of the regulatory approach in the Member States, but a major overhaul of the institutional design of supervision in the EU.[418] Since 1 January 2004 the Committee of European Banking Supervisors (CEBS) is in place, which comprises high level representatives from the banking supervisory authorities and the Member State's central banks.[419] The main task of the CEBS is to advise the Commission on the preparation of draft implementing measures in the field of banking activities, to contribute to the consistent implementation of Community directives and the convergence of supervisory practices throughout the Community and to enhance supervisory cooperation.

---

414. Similarly, R. Smits (1997), op. cit., *supra* note 77, 339–343 and 353. In this context Smits criticizes the fact that the Protocol on certain provisions relating to the United Kingdom and the Protocol on certain provisions relating to Denmark exclude this role of the ECB. This may be particularly problematic in the case of the UK which has the most important financial market in the EU.

415. See e.g., M. Aglietta, 'Le contrôle prudentiel dans la Communauté européenne', in J.-V. Louis and H. Bronkhorst (eds), *l'Euro et l'intégration européenne* (Bruxelles, 1999), 217–227, in particular 223–226.

416. Similar Aglietta (1999), op. cit., *supra* note 415, 223–224, and Schoenmaker (1997), op. cit., *supra* note 409, 428–442.

417. Dir. 2005/1/EC of the European Parliament and the Council of 9 Mar. 2005, amending Council Dir. 73/239/EEC, 85/611/EEC, 91/675/EEC, 92/49/EEC and 93/6/EEC and Dir. 94/19/EC, 98/78/EC, 2000/12/EC, 2001/34/EC, 2002/83/EC and 2002/87/EC in order to establish a new organisational structure for financial services committees (O.J. 2005, L 79/9).

418. See generally R. Lastra, *Legal Foundations of international Monetary Stability* (Oxford, 2006), Ch. 11; id. 'The Governance Structure for Financial Supervision and Regulation in Europe' (2003/Fall), *Columbia Journal of European Law*, 49–68.

419. Commission decision of 5 Nov. 2003, establishing the CEBS (2004/5/EC) (O.J. 2003, L 3/28).

For the time being, the current lack of European competences in the area of prudential supervision bears certain risks in case of a crisis in the financial market which spreads beyond the borders of any one country. It cannot currently be foreseen whether and to what extent the enabling clause included in Article 105(6) EC will be applied in the foreseeable future and whether this could indeed result in a single EU financial supervisory authority.[420] The Treaty of Lisbon does not change the current legal regime. Given that the financial sector has become increasingly interwoven, such European supervision would arguably also have to include insurers.[421]

3.3.2.3.6   Competences Relating to the Collection of Statistical Information

In order to be able to perform monetary policy based on adequate data, reliable statistics on the development of the relevant economic financial variables are needed. According to Article 5.1 ESCB Statute, the ECB has the right to collect the statistical information necessary to fulfil the tasks of the ESCB either from the competent national authorities or directly from economic agents. As far as possible, this task is decentralized and vested in the NCBs. Given the importance of the transparency and reliability of the submitted data, Article 5.3 ESCB Statute assigns a role to the ECB in contributing to the harmonization of the rules and practices governing the collection, compilation and distribution of statistics relating to the ECB's fields of competence. In this context it is for the Council to define the natural and legal persons subject to reporting requirements, the confidentiality regime and the appropriate provisions for enforcement.[422]

The ECB's right to collect statistics exist independent of the competence of the Community laid down in Article 285 EC to adopt measures for the production of statistics and the Commission's right to collect information provided for in Article 284 EC.[423] This does not of course exclude the possibility that, specifically, the ECB and the Commission coordinate their efforts in collecting and analysing statistical material.[424]

---

420. Generally on the need for a European regulatory agency J. Kremers, D. Schoenmaker and P. Wierts (eds), *Financial Supervision in Europe* (Cheltenham, 2003), and M. Andenas and Y. Avgerinos (eds), *Financial Markets in Europe. Towards a Single Regulator?* (The Hague, 2003).

421. This trend has e.g., resulted in the merger of De Nederlandse Bank with the Dutch Pensions and Insurance Supervisory Authority in 2004. As stated above, presently Art. 105(6) EC excludes such a transfer of authority to the ECB for insurance undertakings. Despite justified criticism in the literature, the Treaty of Lisbon does not rectify this shortcoming.

422. Art. 5.4. in conjunction with Art. 42 ESCB Statute. Council Reg. (EC) No. 2533/98 of 23 Nov. 1998, concerning the collection of statistical information by the European Central Bank (O.J. 1998, L 318/8).

423. Art. 285 EC explicitly refers to Art. 5 ESCB Statute.

424. In fact the ECB has in the past advised the Commission in this area. See Opinion of the European Central Bank of 9 Jul. 1999, at the request of the Commission of the European Communities on a draft Commission Reg. (EC) amending Commission Reg. (EC) No. 2214/96 concerning the sub-indices of the Harmonised Indices of Consumer Prices (CON/99/08) (O.J. 1999, C 285/14).

3.3.2.3.7   Legal Instruments of the ECB[425]

In the previous sections, the regulatory competences of the ECB linked to its tasks were mentioned repeatedly. The legal basis can be found in Article 110 EC and Article 34 ESCB Statute.[426]

First, the ECB can issue regulations. However, this general legislative competence is in the first instance limited in scope to a number of specific areas, including regulation in the area of monetary policy, minimum reserve requirements and clearing and payment systems.[427] Second, the EC can take decisions necessary for carrying out the tasks entrusted to the ESCB under the EC Treaty and the ESCB Statute. Finally, the ECB can make recommendations and deliver opinions. Article 110(2) EC defines the different measures with regard to their legal effects, in a similar fashion to Article 249 EC. Thus ECB regulations are generally applicable and are binding in their entirety and directly applicable in all Member States, whereas decision are binding in their entirety upon those to whom they are addressed. Recommendations and opinions have no binding force.[428]

As well as these instruments with external effect, but also internal (legal) effect within the ESCB, the ECB also has a number of instruments at its disposal which are intended to address the different components of the ESCB itself, namely guidelines (Art. 12.1. ESCB Statute) and instructions (Art. 14.3. ESCB Statute).[429] While primarily producing legal effect within the system and namely *vis-à-vis* NCBs which have to act in accordance with these guidelines and instructions, they may under certain circumstances also bind the ESCB in relation to third parties.[430] Moreover, these internal guidelines and instructions on the decentralized implementation of the monetary policy of the ECB can be of considerable importance to the different actors in the financial markets. The ECB has decided to publish all non-confidential internal legal instruments in the Official Journal of the European Union.[431]

---

425. For a more detailed analysis see e.g., R. Smits (1997), op. cit., *supra* note 77, 102–106, and C. Zilioli and M. Selmayr (2001), op. cit., *supra* note 77, 91–131.
426. The competences have to be differentiated from those special competences which Art. 42 ESCB Statute vests in the Community legislature for the subject matters identified in that provision.
427. Art. 110(1) 1st indent EC. The Council can add areas to this list.
428. Art. 110(2) EC also refers to the Arts. 253. 254 and 256 EC for procedural and formal requirements. In the Treaty of Lisbon it is foreseen that the first four subparagraphs of Art. 110(2) EC which explain the legal effect of ECB measures and include the procedural and formal requirements are deleted.
429. These guidelines should not be confused: they have nothing to do with the economic guidelines mentioned in Art. 99 EC in the context of the multilateral surveillance procedure.
430. See C. Zilioli and M. Selmayr (2001), op. cit., *supra* note 77, 108–111.
431. Decision of the European Central Bank of 10 Nov. 2000, on the publication of certain legal acts and instruments of the European Central Bank (ECB/2000/12) (2001/150/EC) (O.J. 2001, L 55/68). The guidelines are also available on the internet side of the ECB at <http://www.ecb.int>.

3.3.3   The European Single Currency: The Euro

On 1 January 1999 the rates at which the euro would substitute for the participating currencies (the conversation rates between the euro and the participating national currencies), as well as the conversion rates between participating currencies (bilateral rates) were decided in accordance with Article 123 (4) EC.[432]

According to the same provision the Council, acting by a qualified majority on a proposal from the Commission and after consulting the ECB, had to take the other measures necessary for the rapid introduction of the euro as the single currency.[433] Technically the establishment of the 'euro' as the single currency ran contrary to Article 123(4) EC which explicitly states that the ECU substitutes the national currencies and that the ECU will become a currency in its own right. This change of name, which was initiated by Germany, was decided by the Madrid European Council in December 1995.[434]

The legal framework of the European single currency is basically defined by three Regulations.[435] *Regulation 1103/97* governs the transition from the ECU, which had been used as a 'basket' currency in the context of the ERM, to the euro.[436] Article 3 arguably constitutes the central provision of Regulation 1103/97 as it regulates the legal continuity of contracts in which reference is made to the 'ecu' or a former national currency of a Member State participating in the euro area.[437]

---

432. Council Reg. 2866/98 of 31 Dec. 1998, on the conversion rates between the euro and the currencies of the Member States adopting the euro (O.J. 1998, L 359/1), Council Reg. 1478/2000 of 19 Jun. 2000, amending Reg. 2866/98 on the conversion rates between the euro and the currencies of the Member States adopting the euro (O.J. 2000, L 167/1).

433. Experience shows that the transition to the single currency also results in extensive regulatory activities in the Member States. See R. Smits (1999), op. cit., *supra* note 284, 9–11. For an overview of the legislative activities in the Netherlands see the several contributions by F. Elderson in the *Nederlandse Tijdschrift voor Europees Recht* (NTER) 2000, 175–183, NTER 2001, 55–66, and NTER 2002, 70–80.

434. *Bull.* EC EU 12-1995, 1.3. This de facto amendment of the EC Treaty by a European Council decision was problematic, as it circumvented the Treaty amendment procedure laid down in Art. 48 TEU. Moreover, the suggestion in the European Council Resolution that 'ecu' is merely a generic term which can be replaced finds no basis in primary Community law. See already R. Smits (1997), op. cit., *supra* note 77, 490–492. An action brought before the CFI in Case T-207/97, *Berthu v. Council*, against the replacement of the name 'ecu' was considered manifestly inadmissible.

435. Reg. 1103/97 on certain provisions relating to the introduction of the euro (O.J. 1997, L 162/1), as amended by Council Reg. 2595/2000 of 27 Nov. 2000, amending Reg. EC) No 1103/97 on certain provisions relating to the introduction of the euro (O.J. 2000, L 300/1); Council Reg. 974/98 of 3 May 1998, on the introduction of the euro (O.J. 1998, L 139/1), last amended by Council Reg. 1647/2006 of 7 Nov. 2006 (O.J. 2006, L 309/2); Council Reg. 2866/98 of 31 Dec. 1998, on the conversion rates between the euro and the currencies of the Member States adopting the euro (O.J. 1998, L 359/1), last amended by Council Reg. 1135/2007 of 10 Jul. 2007, (O.J. 2007, L 256/2).

436. In order to ensure legal certainty right from the start of stage three of EMU, the regulation technically had to be based on Art. 308 EC, rather than Art. 124(4) EC, which only applies at the starting date of stage three.

437. This regulation has been the subject of numerous publications: U. Wölker, 'The Continuity of Contracts in the Transition to the Third Stage of Economic and Monetary Union' (1996), CML

The actual introduction of the euro as the single currency and the replacement of the national currencies of the Member States participating in the euro area are governed by Regulation 974/98.[438] The euro adoption dates, the cash changeover date, and the phasing-out period, if applicable, for each participating Member State are set out in an Annex to that regulation. In the first place, Articles 2 and 3 of the regulation determine that with effect from the respective euro adoption, the currency of a participating Member State becomes the euro. The latter substitutes the currency of the participating Member State. In this context, the regulation also determines the transitional regime which covers the period from the adoption of the euro as single currency (in the case of the initial group of countries joining the euro area: 1 Jan. 1999) until the actual cash changeover from the national currency units to the euro.[439] Banknotes and coins denominated in a national currency unit remain legal tender within the territory of the respective Member State until six months from the respective cash changeover date. Member States are given the right to shorten this period. Moreover, Member States may, for a period of up to six months from the respective cash changeover date, lay down rules for the use of the banknotes and coins denominated in its national currency unit and take any measures necessary to facilitate their withdrawal.[440] Finally, Regulation 974/98 determines that with effect from the respective cash changeover dates, the ECB and the central banks of the participating Member States have to put into circulation banknotes denominated in euro in the participating Member States.[441]

The third regulation governing important aspects of the transition to the single currency is *Council Regulation 2866/98* which actually determines the conversion rates between the euro and the currencies of the Member States adopting the euro.[442]

According to Article 106(1) EC and Article 16 ESCB Statute, the ECB has the exclusive right to authorize the issue of banknotes within the Community. Both the ECB and the NCBs may issue such notes and in practice the ECB authorizes the NCBs to do so. Only the banknotes issued by the ECB and the NCBs have the status of legal tender within the Community. It is moreover the ECB which decides on the denominations and specifications of euro banknotes.[443]

According to Article 106(2) EC Member States in principle have the right to issue coins, albeit subject to approval by the ECB of the volume of the issue.[444]

Rev., 1996, 1107–1116; R. Dunnett, 'Some Legal Principles Applicable to the Transition to the Single Currency' (1996), CML Rev., 1996, 1133–1167; W. Rank, *Geld, geldschuld en betaling* (Deventer, 1996), 65–70.

438. Based on Art. 124(4) EC.
439. Arts. 6–9 Reg. 974/98, as amended.
440. Art. 15 Reg. 974/98, as amended.
441. Arts. 10 and 11 Reg. 974/98, as amended.
442. At the time of writing, this regulation had not yet been amended to take into account the participation of Malta in the euro area from 1 Jan. 2008.
443. Decision of the ECB of 30 Aug. 2001, on the denominations, specifications, reproduction, exchange and withdrawal of euro banknotes (ECB/2001/7) (2001/667/EC) (O.J. 2001, L 233/55).
444. See e.g., Decision of the ECB of 24 Nov. 2006, on the approval of the volume of coin issuance in 2007 (O.J. 2006, L 348/52).

Moreover, the Member States are subject to Council Regulation 975/98 which regulates the denominations and technical specifications of euro coins.[445]

3.3.4   The Relationship between the Euro Area and the Non-participating Member States

Regardless of whether Member States have not joined the euro area because they do not (yet) fulfil the convergence criteria or because they have effectively nego-tiated themselves out of the obligation to join, all of these Member States have to fulfil the convergence criteria described in Article 121(1) EC if one day they want to join the euro area.[446] Participation in an ERM is one of the convergence criteria listed in before-mentioned article. Moreover, Article 124(2) EC obliges Member States in stage two of EMU to consider their exchanger rate policy as a matter of common interest.[447] This implies the existence of an ERM after the establishment of stage three of EMU and the euro area. As the original ERM ceased to exist upon entering stage three of EMU, a ERM II in order to govern the relationship of the currencies of the Member States outside the euro area with the euro became necessary. What is more, with the establishment and completion of the monetary union the competence exchange-rate policy in the euro area became a Community competence. The NCBs of the Member States participating in the euro area have thus lost both their power over internal *and* external monetary policy. Against the background of these considerations it is remarkable that primary Community law does not foresee in an explicit competence for the Community to establish legal arrangements governing the relationship between the euro and the currencies of the Member States outside the euro area.

As Member States were reluctant to change the provisions on EMU in the run-up to stage three of EMU, a *praeter legem* solution had to be found, which came in the form of a ERM II. Based on a proposal of the EMI[448] the main lines of which were determined in a Resolution by the Amsterdam European Council in December 1996. As such, ERM II effectively combines the characteristics of an intergovernmental agreement, Community law and an agreement between central

---

445. Council Reg. 975/98 of 3 May 1998, on denominations and technical specifications of euro coins intended for circulation (O.J. 1998, L 139/6), as amended by Council Reg. 423/1999 of 22 Feb. 1999 (O.J. 1999, L 52/2).

446. From Art. 121(4) EC in conjunction with Art. 122(2) EC it is clear that Member States which fulfil the convergence criteria have to join the euro area, unless they have opted out of stage three of EMU. For this reason the convergence criteria remain relevant. See J. Usher (1999), op. cit., *supra* note 325, 14–15.

447. However, whether this amounts to an obligation for the UK and Denmark as Member States with an op-out to formally subject themselves to ERM II, as argued by A. Geelhoed in the 6th Dutch edition of this work (819) with reference to R. Smits (1997), op. cit., *supra* note 77, 466, is questionable given the open wording of Art. 122(1) EC which is similar to that found in Art. 98 EC for economic policy. Moreover, in practice the UK does not participate in ERM II.

448. European Monetary Institute, Monetary and Exchange Rate Policy Cooperation Between the Euro Area and the other EU-countries, Report of 7 Oct. 1996 to the Dublin European Council of 13 and 14 Dec. 1996, published in *Europe*, Document no. 2015/2016, 18 Dec. 1996, 9–12.

banks which also governed the original EMS.[449] This resolution has been further detailed in an agreement between the ECB and the NCBs of the Member States participating in this ERM II.[450]

Despite the condition stated in Article 121(1) EC, the Amsterdam European Council Resolution states that participation in the exchange-rate mechanism is voluntary for the Member States outside the euro area. At the time of writing this chapter, Estonia, Latvia, Lithuania and Slovakia, only four of the currently nine Member States with a derogation that have in principle committed themselves to participation in stage three of EMU (thus excluding Denmark, the United Kingdom and Sweden), actually participate in ERM II.[451] Similar to the working of ERM I, the new exchange-rate mechanism is based on central rates against the euro, whereby the standard fluctuation band is fixed at $+/-$ 15%. It is envisaged that through the implementation of stability-oriented economic and monetary policies, the central rates will remain the focus for the Member States outside the euro area participating in the mechanism. The intervention at the margins is in principle automatic and unlimited. However, unlike ERM I, the ECB and the NCBs of the Member States not participating in the euro area can suspend intervention if this threatens to conflict with their primary objective of price stability.[452]

The chosen construction has been criticized for both its formal and substantive legal deficiencies.[453] They concern first of all the choice of legal instruments for the ERM II. With the completion of the monetary union and the irrevocable fixing of the exchange rate of the currencies participating in the euro area, the regulation of the exchange-rate regime of the euro *vis-à-vis* other currencies has become a Community competence. This does not leave any room for intergovernmental solutions of the type chosen for ERM II. Even if the EC Treaty did not – and still does not – explicitly provide for the introduction of an ERM, this shortcoming should have been remedied within Community legal framework. Thus the ECO-FIN Council rather than the European Council should have acted, thereby applying

---

449. Resolution of the European Council on the establishment of an exchange-rate mechanism in the third stage of EMU Amsterdam, 16 Jun. 1997 (O.J. 1997, C 236/5). This resolution has come in place of the Resolution of the European Council establishing the European Monetary System (EMS) of 5 Dec. 1978, *Bull.* EC 6-1978, 1.5.2.

450. Agreement of 1 Sep. 1998, between the European Central Bank and the NCBs of the Member States outside the euro area laying down the operating procedures for an ERM in stage three of Economic and Monetary Union (O.J. 1998, C 345/6). This agreement has since been replaced by: Agreement of 16 Mar. 2006, between the European Central Bank and the NCBs of the Member States outside the euro area laying down the operating procedures for an ERM in stage three of Economic and Monetary Union (2006/C 73/08) (O.J. 2006, C 73/21), as amended (O.J. 2007, C 14/6).

451. This excludes Sweden. As has been pointed above, Denmark has the status of a Member State with a derogation and in that capacity participates in ERM II. The UK has opted out of participation in the third stage of EMU.

452. Agreement of 16 Mar. 2006, op. cit., *supra* note 450, Art. 3.

453. See generally J.-V. Louis, 'A Legal and Constitutional Approach for Building a Monetary Union', CML Rev., 1998, 70–72, C. Zilioli and M. Selmayr (1999), op. cit., *supra* note 272 in particular 309–313.

the Community legal instruments, namely a regulation.[454] Given the exclusive competence of the Community in this area in principle, unlike what is stated in the Resolution, any decisions in the context of the ERM II should have been subject to the Community decision-making procedure and ultimately rested with the Council.[455]

As to the substance, the statement included in the Amsterdam European Council Resolution that participation in ERM II is voluntary is problematic, given that the participation in an ERM for a period of at least two years forms one of the convergence criteria listed in Article 121(1) EC.[456] This effectively invites Member States with a derogation to escape their commitment to participate in the third stage of EMU, as non-participation in ERM II in practice allows for the (indefinite) delay of participation in the euro area.[457] Moreover, the non-binding character of ERM II contradicts if not the letter then at least the spirit of Article 124 EC, according to which in stage two of EMU Member States are supposed to treat their exchange-rate policy as a matter of common interest.[458]

Equally problematic and somewhat confusing is the statement in the Amsterdam European Council Resolution that the exchange-rate margins introduced by ERM II do not prejudice the interpretation of Article 121(1) third indent EC.[459] As the latter provision explicitly refers to the 'normal fluctuation margins provided for by the exchange-rate mechanism' the question arises what fluctuation margins if not those observed in the context of ERM II could actually be taken as a yardstick for the evaluation of this convergence criterion. Despite this legal uncertainty, in practice the Commission, and later also the Council, in past assessments have observed whether the Member State concerned has participated in ERM II for at least two years, whether the national currency has not been subject to severe tensions, and whether the bilateral central rate of that currency has not been devaluated against the euro.[460]

3.3.5   The External Monetary Policy[461]

Prior to the collapse of the Bretton Woods exchange-rate regime, arrangements in the national context were characterized by a clear separation of internal and

---

454. J. Usher (1999), op. cit., *supra* note at 16, who notes: 'It is thus an undefined act of an institution of the European Union, even though monetary policy is clearly and expressly an exclusive Community competence.' R. Smits (1999), op. cit., *supra* note 284, at 467–468 and 472–475, who suggests that Art. 308 EC could function as a legal basis.
455. See already R. Smits (1999), op. cit., *supra* note 284, at 467.
456. Point 1.6 of the Resolution.
457. This is also observed by J. Usher (1999), op. cit., *supra* note at 16.
458. In the 6th Dutch edition of this work (820) Geelhoed even argues that Art. 124(2) EC amounts to an obligation to participate in ERM II.
459. Point 2.5 of the Resolution. J. Usher (1999), op. cit., *supra* note 16, refers to 'a singular unhelpful provision'.
460. See e.g., Council Decision 2006/495/EC of 11 Jul. 2006, in accordance with Art. 122(2) of the Treaty on the adoption by Slovenia of the single currency on 1 Jan. 2007, (O.J. 2006, L 195/25).
461. See e.g., R. Smits (1999), op. cit., *supra* note 284, 367–458; J.-V. Louis, (1995), op. cit., *supra* note 12, 82–84 and 159–166, J.-V. Louis, 'Les relations internationales de l'Union

external monetary policy. The NCBs were usually charged with the conduct of the internal monetary policy, albeit not in all instances in an independent capacity. The external monetary policy remained a government domain.[462] Yet, with the floating of the exchange rates this clear separation was no longer feasible. In the European context, after the introduction of the EMS with the ERM as its centrepiece, which managed the bilateral exchange rates of the participating currencies, this applied primarily in relation to third-country currencies. In such a setting, on the one hand, the development of internal monetary policy influences the exchange rate. In particular an internal monetary policy which is directed towards price stability inevitably results in a stronger currency in the international monetary sphere.[463] On the other hand, fluctuations in international exchange rates can influence an internal monetary policy which is geared towards price stability.[464]

While a system of floating exchange rates does not require any formal decisions on the exchange rates, informal agreements on the desired developments of the exchange rates of the important international currencies may be required if these rates no longer sufficiently reflect the underlying economic ratios.[465]

The close relationship between the internal and external monetary policy also had its impact on the distribution of competences within EMU. As has been observed above, internal monetary policy in the euro area is an exclusive competence of the ECB, and thus of the Community. Also the external monetary policy must exclusively lie with the Community.[466]

économique et monétaire', EUI Working Papers, LAW no. 99/10 (Florence, 1999); C. Zilioli and M. Selmayr (1999), op. cit., *supra* note 272, 273–349; idem (2006), op. cit. 77 et seq.; W. Weiss, 'Kompetenzverteilung in der Währungspolitik und Aussenvertretung des Euro' (2002), EuR, 165–191. T. Padoa-Schioppa, 'The external representation of the euro area', introductory statement at the Sub-Committee on Monetary Affairs of the European Parliament, Brussels, 17 Mar. 1999; W. Duisenberg, The role of the ECB at the international level, speech delivered at the Annual Meeting of the Institute for International Finance, Inc. (IIF), Prague, 23 Sep. 2000.

462. According to the 1994 Annual Report of the EMI, at the time only the Austrian and Swedish central banks were in charge of exchange-rate policy.

463. This could even be witnesses in the 1980s in the context of the EMS, where the price stability oriented monetary policy of the Bundesbank forced countries with a weaker currency on several occasions to devaluate their currencies. However, a preference for price stability is not the only factor which determines the strength of a currency: the dynamics of the economy and its ability to expand are also important factors in this regard. The latter was e.g., highlighted by the exchange rate between the US Dollar and the euro between 1999 and 2002.

464. The restrictive monetary policy of the ECB in the past can – among others – be explained with the strong US Dollar which resulted in higher prices for imports (namely crude oil) from outside the EU. The risk for the monetary policy in EMU was the import of inflation from outside the EU.

465. Examples in this regard are the so-called Plaza Accord of Sep. 1985, between France, Germany, Japan, the United States and the UK to depreciate the US Dollar *vis-à-vis* the Japanese Yen and the German Mark. In Feb. 1987, agreement was reached to intervene on behalf of the US Dollar. See also R. Smits (1997), op. cit., *supra* note 77, 380 (notes 57 and 85).

466. See J.-V. Louis (1999), op. cit., *supra* note 461, 12; W. Weiss (2002), op. cit., *supra* note 461, 379.

In the past, the Member States and their NCBs have participated in international monetary institutions such as the IMF and have dominated the informal meetings on financial, monetary and economic issues, such as the G-7.[467] Moreover, most international organizations, such as the IMF, only accept States as members. What is more, in the Community context the distribution of competences is not just an issue in the vertical relationship between the national and supranational level, but also in the horizontal relationship between Community Institutions, such as the Council, the Commission and the ECB.[468] The complication derives from the fact that exchange-rate agreements can have an impact on the internal monetary policy and in particular its primary objective, i.e., price stability, while the independent ECB is actually the one that has to implement such exchange-rate agreements through exchange-rate transactions.[469]

Finally, the delineation of competences for the external policy of EMU is further complicated by the structural imbalance in the level of integration between economic and monetary policy. Whereas the latter is an exclusive Community competence for the euro area, the former remains effectively a national competence. Yet, the close relationship of economic and monetary policy requires a close coordination of the external aspects of both policy areas. This moreover calls for coordination between the Member States and the Community regarding the external economic policy of the EU. It is against this background that Article 111 EC has to be read and interpreted.[470]

Article 111(1) EC is applicable in case of the conclusion of a formal exchange-rate agreement with third countries in which the euro would participate. It provides the Council not only with the competence to conclude such an agreement on behalf of the Community, but moreover also to adopt, adjust or abandon the central rates of the euro within such an exchange-rate system. The close link between internal and external monetary policy was recognized by the drafters of Article 111(1) EC. While the competence to conclude international agreements on exchange-rate systems lies with the Council, Article 111(1) EC also emphasizes the role of the ECB: 'The Council [may], acting by a qualified majority on a recommendation from the ECB or from the Commission, and after consulting the ECB in an endeavour to reach a consensus consistent with the objective of price stability.'[471] This sentence can be interpreted in two ways. Firstly, it may be read to the effect that consultation of the ECB is only required if the Council is acting on a

---

467. The G-7 meetings are attended by the Ministers of Finance and the NCB governors of the United States, Japan, Germany, France, the UK, Italy and Canada.
468. See W. Weiss (2002), op. cit., *supra* note 461, 379.
469. This is reflected in the wording of Art. 111 EC, which describes the role of the ECB in the preparation of the decisions of the Council and emphasizes the need to act consistently with the objective of price stability.
470. With regard to the history of origins of this provision see J. Cloos et al. (1993), op. cit., *supra* note 51, 226–228. Both for R. Smits (1997), op. cit., *supra* note 77, at 375, and J.-V. Louis (1999), op. cit., *supra* note 461, at 5, there is a relationship between the complexity of Art. 111 EC and its history.
471. Our addition.

recommendation from the Commission.[472] However, Article 111(1) EC may also be interpreted as requiring the ECB always to be consulted in order to ensure that the Council acts in accordance with the primary objective of the ECB, i.e., price stability.[473] This latter, systematic rather than linguistic interpretation of Article 111 EC deserves preference in particular when taking into account the independent position granted the ECB in primary Community law for the formulation and implementation of monetary policy in the euro area. It would be incompatible with this position if the Council, while acting upon a recommendation by the ECB, could thereafter ignore that recommendation without even being required to endeavour to reach a consensus with the ECB to ensure that the planned agreement is compatible with the objective of price stability.

The question that arises in this context is what exactly the scope of the obligation of the Council with regard to the objective price stability is.[474] The phrase 'endeavour to reach a consensus' is rather vague.[475] While it can be expected that the Council makes a serious effort to reach a consensus with the ECB, it arguably cannot be concluded from Article 111(1) EC that such a consensus is *a conditio sine qua non* for the Council to act.[476] Moreover, arguably the Council is not bound by the definition of price stability which the ECB applies in conducting monetary policy. Ultimately, the decision to conclude an exchange-rate agreement is thus a political one whereby the Council can apply its own understanding of price stability. Consequently, in principle the undesirable situation could arise that the Council de facto acts contrary to the effort of the ECB to maintain price stability.[477]

The reference to *formal* agreements highlights the desire of the drafters of Article 111 EC to demarcate paragraph 1 from paragraph 2 of this provision. The former concerns formal agreements, from which stem concrete legal obligations for the contracting parties.[478] As *lex specialis*, Article 111(1) EC explicitly derogates from Article 300 EC on the conclusion of international agreements. However this provision does not introduce a new category of international agreements.[479] In the absence of (the political will for the establishment of) an international exchange-rate system, Article 111(1) EC has not yet gained any practical relevance.

---

472. See J. Cloos et al., op. cit., *supra* note 51, at 327.
473. See also R. Smits (1999), op. cit., *supra* note 284, 388.
474. For J. Cloos et al. (2003), op. cit., *supra* note 51, at 227, this amounts to a procedural provision.
475. Other language versions of this provision apply an equally vague wording.
476. F. Amtenbrink (1999), op. cit., *supra* note 61, at 205–206.
477. This mix of the internal and external monetary policy has been rightly criticized. See e.g., V. Constantinesco, R. Kovar and D. Simon, *Traité sur l'Union Européenne (signé à Maastricht le 7 février 1992): commentaire article par article* (Paris, 1995), on ex Art. 109 EC (now Art. 111 EC); Ch. Goodhard, Minutes of Evidence, in Treasury and Civil Service Committee, The Role of the Bank of England, House of Commons Paper, Session 1993–4 (London, 1993), 1–10, at 5.
478. See already R. Smits (1997), op. cit., *supra* note 77, 386–387; J.-V. Louis (1999), op. cit., *supra* note 461, at 5.
479. See Declaration on Art. 109 [now Art. 111 EC] of the Treaty establishing the European Community (O.J. 1992, C 191/99).

Article 111(2) EC applies in the absence of such an international exchange-rate system. It allows the Council to formulate general orientations for exchange-rate policy in relation to third-country currencies. Similar to Article 111(1) EC, the Council has to act either on a recommendation from the Commission and after consulting the ECB or on a recommendation from the ECB. However, rather than requiring unanimity the Council can act by qualified majority.[480] Moreover, unlike Article 111(1) EC, the second paragraph of this provision states that: 'These general orientations *shall be without prejudice* to the primary objective of the ESCB to maintain price stability.'[481] The Council in formulating such general orientations thus has to fully take into account the objective of price stability.[482]

The legal status of these 'general orientations' is somewhat unclear. It may be argued that the wording suggests the establishment of broadly defined decisions which as such are binding upon the ECB in the conduct of its exchange-rate operations.[483] If the ECB considers such a decision to contradict its statutorily prescribed primary objective of price stability, it would have to challenge the decision before the ECJ. A more accurate interpretation of Article 111(2) EC may be that the departure from the EC Treaty terminology for legally binding acts and the application of a new phrase signifies the absence of a legally binding measure which could restrict the ECB in its conduct.[484] Moreover, if the drafters of this provision had foreseen legally binding decisions, it cannot be explained why they did not included the same obligation on the part of the Council to endeavour to reach a consensus with the ECB as that in Article 111(1) EC.[485] Be it as it may, under normal circumstances the ECB can be expected to cooperate with the Council in the implementation of these 'general orientations' if and to the extent that they do not infringe the objective of price stability.

The practical relevance of Article 111(2) EC may be limited, as the Luxemburg European Council of December 1997 has made it clear that it expects the Council to apply this provision only in exceptional circumstances, such as in

---

480. In the 6th Dutch edition of this work (825, n. 319) A. Geelhoed rightly criticizes the inconsistency of this provision, which calls for the consultation of the ECB if the Council acts on a recommendation from the Commission, but lacks a similar right for the Commission if the Council acts on a recommendation from the ECB. This is an unfortunate omission given the close relationship between exchange rates and the general economic policy of the Community and the role which the Commission has in the formulation of the latter. Geelhoed argues in favour of a close link between formal competences and the substantive influence on the decision-making process in the Community institutional framework.

481. Emphasis added.

482. For M. Dean and R. Pringle, *The Central Banks* (London, 1993), at 334, the question is who will judge the compliance of the general orientations with the objective of price stability.

483. See W. Weiss (2002), op. cit., *supra* note 461, 184, and R. Stadler, *Der rechtliche Handlungs-spielraum des Europäischen Systems der Zentralbanken* (Baden-Baden, 1996), at 175–178.

484. See already R. Smits (1997), op. cit., *supra* note 77, 398–399, and J.-V. Louis (1999), op. cit., *supra* note 461, at 7.

485. See also J. Cloos et al. (2003), op. cit., *supra* note 51, at 277 with regard to the origins of this provision.

the case of clear misalignments in the exchange rate between the euro and third-country currencies.[486]

Article 111(3) EC, which like Article 111(1) EC is a *lex specialis* to Article 300 EC, is more than simply a procedural provision governing the preparation of the negotiations on agreements concerning monetary or foreign exchange regime matters. It also implicitly states that the external monetary policy is an exclusive competence of the Community. As such the wording 'concerning monetary or foreign exchange regime matters' is broader than the 'formal agreements on an exchange-rate system' to be found in Article 111(1) EC.[487] This view is confirmed by the way in which this provision is applied in practice.[488]

In analogy with Article 300(7) EC, Article 111(3) EC also somewhat superfluously confirms that international agreements concluded in accordance with Article 111 EC are binding on the Community Institutions, on the ECB and on Member States. It has been argued that it has to be concluded from the lack of a provision similar to Article 300(6) EC and the *lex specialis* character of Article 111 EC, that a review of envisaged international agreements relating to an exchange-rate regime by the ECJ on the initiative of the European Parliament, the Council, the Commission or a Member State is excluded.[489] Against this view it may be observed that Article 111 EC constitutes a *lex specialis* only to the extent that it deviates from Article 300 EC. Consequently, to the extent that this is not the case, Article 300 EC, including its paragraph 6, applies.[490] Finally, according to Article 122(3) EC, Article 111 EC does not apply to Member States with a

---

486. Resolution of the European Council of 13 Dec. 1997, on economic policy coordination in stage 3 of EMU and on Arts. 109 and 109b of the EC Treaty (O.J. 1997, C 35/1).
487. See W. Weiss (2002), op. cit., *supra* note 461, 172, and C. Zilioli and M. Selmayr (1999), op. cit., *supra* note 272, 296.
488. Against the background of several protocols and declarations annexed to the EC Treaty (see R. Smits (1997), op. cit., *supra* note 77, 380–384), the Council has taken several decisions, based on ex Art. 109(3) EC (now Art. 111(3)) in the past, in order to regulate exchange rate issues with a number of former French and Portuguese colonies, with the French oversees territories which do not form part of the EU, as well as with Monaco, San Marino and the Vatican. See: Council Decision 98/683/EC of 23 Nov. 1998, concerning exchange rate matters relating to the CFA Franc and the Comorian Franc (O.J. 1998, L 320/58); Council Decision 98/744/EC of 21 Dec. 1998, concerning exchange rate matters relating to the Cape Verde escudo (O.J. 1998, L 358/11); Council Decision 1999/95/EC of 31 Dec. 1998, concerning the monetary arrangements in the French territorial communities of Saint-Pierre-et-Miquelon and Mayotte (O.J. 1999, L 30/29); Council Decision 1999/97/EC of 31 Dec. 1998, on the position to be taken by the Community regarding an agreement concerning the monetary relations with the Republic of San Marino (O.J. 1999, L 30/33); Council Decision 1999/98/EC of 31 Dec. 1998, on the position to be taken by the Community regarding an agreement concerning the monetary relations with Vatican City (O.J. 1999, L 30/35). For a critical evaluation of these decisions and in particular the extent to which they authorize the respective Member States to independently maintain or conclude international agreements see W. Weiss (2002), op. cit., *supra* note 461, 181, and J.-V. Louis (1999), op. cit., *supra* note 461, 17–18.
489. R. Smits (1997), op. cit., *supra* note 77, 385–386.
490. J.-V. Louis (1999), op. cit., *supra* note 461, 9, and C. Zilioli and M. Selmayr (1999), op. cit., *supra* note 272, 345–346.

derogation which do not participate in the euro area.[491] Consequently these Member States also do not participate in the decision-making in the context of this provision.

International monetary relations are governed by a number of different formal international organizations, such as the IMF, and informal fora, such as G-7. Moreover, the legal character of the decision-making varies. This includes broad policy decisions, such as in the context of the IMF and G-7, as well as highly technical aspects of foreign exchange and capital mobility, such as in the context of the Bank for International Settlements (BIS). The establishment of the euro area has raised the question which issues should be addressed by the EU and who should represent it in this regard.

Article 111(4) EC vests power in the Council to decide on the position of the Community at international level as regards issues of particular relevance to EMU and on its representation. In doing so, the Council has to comply with the allocation of powers laid down in Articles 99 and 105 EC. Given its objective, it may be argued that this provision is not only addressed to the Community, but, depending on the subject-matter, also to the Member States and the ECB.[492] Article 111(4) EC foresees in two separate procedures relating, firstly, to the determining of the Community position in international fora and, secondly, relating to the representation of the Community. In both cases, decisions are taken by qualified majority on a proposal from the Commission and after consulting the ECB.

The use of Article 111(4) EC raises numerous legal, political and practical issues. This concerns in the first place the delineation of competences between the Council, acting on the basis of Article 111(4) EC, and the ECB, which according to Article 6.1 ESCB Statute decides on how the ESCB is represented in the field of international cooperation involving the tasks entrusted to the ESCB.[493] According to Article 6.2 ESCB Statute, the ECB and, subject to its approval, the NCBs can participate in international monetary institutions. Article 6.3. ESCB Statute states that these rights are without prejudice to Article 111(4) EC. Finally, Article 23 ESCB Statute allows both the ECB and the NCBs to establish relations with central banks and financial institutions in other countries and, where appropriate, with international organizations.

Based on the functions assigned to the ECB it can be argued that the ECB representing the monetary policy authority of the euro area must have the right to participate in international fora in which central banks participate directly, such as the BIS, free of instructions from the Council.[494] On the contrary, the role of the ECB is limited in the representation of EMU in international organizations of which the Member States or the Community are a member.[495]

---

491.   The application of Art. 111 EC is also excluded by the Protocol on certain provisions relating to the United Kingdom.

492.   See J.-V. Louis (1999), op. cit., *supra* note 461, 9.

493.   See generally W. Weiss (2002), op. cit., *supra* note 461, 186–189, J.-V. Louis (1999), op. cit., *supra* note 461, 13–16, and C. Zilioli and M. Selmayr (2001) op. cit. *supra* note 77, 171 et seq.

494.   See J.-V. Louis (1999), op. cit., *supra* note 461, at 14.

495.   See W. Weiss (2002), op. cit., *supra* note 461, at 186. In accordance with Art. 111(4) EC, the ECB has the right to be consulted.

Another difficulty in the application of Article 111(4) EC concerns the consequences of a decision in which it is determined that the Community solely or together with the Member States is represented in an international forum.[496] What needs to be determined in such a case is which Community Institution or organ (including the ECB) should represent the Community. This has to be decided on the basis of the distribution of competences as provided by primary Community law, in particular those relating to the Council and the ECB.[497]

A third difficulty related to representation of the Community in international arena relates to the participation in international fora in which both monetary and economic policy issues are discussed. Apart from the formal question of distribution of competences in the Community, the underlying issue is once more whether and to what extent economic and monetary policy issues can be effectively separated. While these two policy areas are closely linked and often treated as such in the international context,[498] primary Community law can be interpreted to the effect that it stands in the way of an integrative approach in the external presentation of the Community.[499]

What is at least required in EMU is a close substantive coordination between the Member States of the euro area. Yet, the closer this coordination is, the more questionable the presentation of the policy standpoints by the separate Member States becomes.[500]

The various issues mentioned above have formed the subject-matter of two European Council meetings.[501] The solutions found are rather minimalist and do not put an end to the fragmentation of the external representation of the Community in EMU matters, weakening its position in international fora.[502] This is to be

---

496. With regard to difficulties in the perception of such delegations determined by Art. 111(4) EC by other participants in international fora, see: J.-V. Louis (1999), op. cit., *supra* note 461, at 16.

497. In cases other than the conclusion of agreements it has to be assumed that external representation of the Community mirrors the internal distribution of competences. Otherwise the prerogatives which the ECB has in formulating and implementing monetary policy would be at stake. See W. Weiss (2002), op. cit., *supra* note 461, 187–188, and R. Smits (1997), op. cit., *supra* note 77, 412–413.

498. Thus e.g., in a system of floating exchange rates, the exchange rates on the international capital markets reflect differences in economic growth, inflation and generally the confidence in an economy.

499. Indeed, given the weak competences of the Community in the area of economic policy, the *ERTA* doctrine cannot easily be applied in this context.

500. This does not primarily concern the question whether the Community, the Member States or both act. What is decisive is the quality of the coordination beforehand. See J.-V. Louis (1999), op. cit., *supra* note 461, at 15.

501. Resolution of the European Council of 13 Dec. 1997, on economic policy coordination in stage 3 of EMU and on Arts. 109 and 109b of the EC Treaty (O.J. 1998, C 35/1), point 7–10. Conclusions of the Vienna European Council of 11–12 Dec. 1998, Bull. EU 12-1998, 4, section A. ii, and 25–29, Annex II, which includes the Report to the European Council on the state of preparation for Stage III of EMU, in particular the external representation of the Community.

502. See also J.-V. Louis (1999), op. cit., *supra* note 461, 23–24, with reference to the representation of the Community in the IMF.

regretted, as the EU is still not as present and influential in international organizations and fora as it should be considering that the euro has succeeded in becoming one of the most important currencies in the world, and also taking into account that the EU's GDP is roughly comparable to that of the United States of America.[503]

According to Article 111(5) EC, Member States have the right to negotiate in international bodies and conclude international agreements if and to the extent that this does not concern a Community competence or a Community agreement on EMU. Such negotiations and international agreements may fall into two categories. Firstly, there are negotiations and agreements in areas in which the Community shares its competences with the Member States, such as for example in the field of prudential supervision.[504] Secondly, Article 111(5) EC applies in cases where the Community has not (fully) replaced the Member States in international organizations, such as in the IMF.[505] In such instances the Member States are bound by the decisions which have been taken in accordance with Article 111(4) EC.[506]

Under the Treaty of Lisbon Article 111 EC will effectively be split into two separate provisions. Articles 111(1)-(3) and (5) EC are included in Article 219 which is contained in Part 5 of the Treaty on the Functioning of the EU on the external actions of the Union.[507] The amendments are mostly of a textual nature, and do not substantially alter the assessment of today's Article 111 EC offered above. Noteworthy is an amendment of the wording of today's Article 111(1) EC relating to the consultation of the ECB. From the wording of Article 219(1) it becomes clear that regardless of whether the Council acts on a recommendation of the Commission or of the ECB, the latter always has to be consulted in an endeavour to reach a consensus consistent with the objective of price stability.

Article 111(4) EC will be included in Article 138 which forms part of the Chapter 4 of the Treaty on the Functioning of the EU relating to the Euro Group, which is made up of the Member States participating in the euro area.[508] Arguably the Treaty of Lisbon aims at strengthening the coordination among of the Member States participating in the euro area. On a proposal from the Commission, the Euro Group can adopt decisions establishing common positions on matters of particular interest for EMU within the competent international financial institutions and conferences 'in order to secure the euro's place in the international monetary

---

503. J.-V. Louis (1999), op. cit., *supra* note 461, 23–24, argues that the acceptance of EMU as an entity in international economic and monetary fora depends *inter alia* on the political will of the participating Member States to enforce that acceptance. For this Member States have to accept the external consequences of the participation in the euro area first.

504. Art. 105(6) EC. This implies that the actual scope of the Member States' remaining competences has to be determined on a case-by-case basis, taking into account the case law of the ECJ on the external competences of the Community. See R. Smits (1997), op. cit., *supra* note 77, at 418.

505. See W. Weiss (2002), op. cit., *supra* note 461, 182.

506. As such Art. 111(5) EC closes a gap in the context of Art. 111(4) EC which exists for as long as the Community cannot be a full member in all international organizations.

507. Art. 219(1) – (4) TFEU.

508. Art. 138(3) TFEU. See already section 3.2.5 *supra*.

system'.[509] Moreover, the Euro Group, acting on a proposal from the Commission, can adopt appropriate measures to ensure unified representation within the international financial institutions and conferences.[510] The Euro Group has to consult the ECB.[511]

The assignments of decisions in the context of today's Article 111(4) EC to the Euro Group does not substantially change the legal situation under the EC Treaty, as it has been observed above that Article 111 EC does not apply to Member States with a derogation outside the euro area. If anything it could be argued that by referring to the 'unified representation within the international financial institutions', Article 138 of the Treaty on the Functioning of the EU is somewhat more engaging than today's Article 111(4) EC when it comes to the objective of ensuring that the EU speaks with one voice in the international arena.

4 EMPLOYMENT

4.1 FROM MAASTRICHT TO AMSTERDAM

The recession which hit large parts of the European Union from the middle of 1992 until the beginning of 1994 not only led to the postponement of the beginning of the third phase of EMU until 1 January 1999 (as the vast majority of Member States still did not fulfil the convergence criteria by the end of 1996); it also revealed the vulnerability of employment levels in Western Europe. In itself, it is wholly normal for cyclical unemployment to increase in times of economic recession. Should, however, unemployment remain at a relatively high level in a more favourable economic climate, such unemployment is structural, not cyclical. From the middle of the 1970s, it became clear that job losses in times of cyclical recession were not being recouped in boom times. The result was that, over the last three decades, unemployment in Europe at the end of every economic cycle has ended up at a higher level than at the end of the cycle beforehand. Such hysteresis, as the phenomenon is termed in economic literature, was evident in the recession at the beginning of the 1990s[512] when, within the space of two years, the increase in employment from the last half of the 1980s was swept away. The result was that average unemployment within the EC reached more than 10% of the total workforce and threatened to remain at that level.

In view of this worrying development, the European Council which met in Essen in December 1994 decided to institute what has since become known as the

---

509. Art. 138(1) TFEU.
510. Art. 138(2) TFEU.
511. No mention is made of the EP.
512. Between 1989 and 1993, unemployment in the EU increased from 12 million to 17 million, while during the same period Japan and the United States were still enjoying net increases in employment. See White Book of the European Commission, Growth, Competitiveness and Employment, EC Bull. Suppl. 6/93, 9–10.

'Essen procedure'.[513] As a result of this procedure, the European Council agreed to discuss employment issues annually on the basis of a joint report of the Ecofin and Social Policy formations of the Council of Ministers, which was to be prepared by the Economic Policy Committee and the Employment and Labour Market Committee.[514] These reports were to focus on five areas, termed the 'Essen strategy':[515] improving labour market opportunities for the workforce by investment in vocational training and education; increasing the employment intensity of growth; reducing non-wage (or indirect) labour costs to a level at which it would become economically attractive to employ low-skilled workers; improving the effectiveness of labour market policies; and, finally, improving measures to help groups that are particularly hard hit by long-term unemployment. Since the Essen European Council, attention is paid to employment growth in every meeting of this Council, sometimes on the basis of interim reports.[516] Such intensive attention paid to employment at the highest political level of the European Union, however, failed at the time to lead to immediate results. In fact, this confirmed that the issue was structural and that changes to a variety of components of Member States' socio-economic structure would be necessary to solve the problem.[517] The elaboration and implementation of the strategies necessary to achieve this at national level would take time, and the results would not become visible immediately. In addition, many of the necessary reforms encountered serious social resistance from those groups who were particularly protected by the relevant arrangements.

This context explains why, in the run-up to the Treaty of Amsterdam, most governments reacted positively to the idea of placing more emphasis on the topic of employment, which had been neglected in the Maastricht Treaty.[518] In elaborating this idea, Member States were suddenly faced with the problem that employment growth was affected by many more factors than labour market policy in the narrow

---

513. In terms of content, the Essen procedure built on the Commission's White Book cited in the previous footnote.
514. This committee is the predecessor of the Employment Committee subsequently created on the basis of Art. 130 EC. See Decision 2000/98/EC of the Council of 14 Feb. 2000, O.J. 2000, L 29/21.
515. J. Kenner, 'Employment and Macroeconomics in the EC Treaty: A Legal and Political Symbiosis' (2000), MJ, 374–397, 378.
516. EC Bull. 1994/12, para. 1.1–1.5.
517. As was pithily expressed in the White Book of the European Commission, Growth, Competitiveness and Employment, *supra* note 512, 124: 'There can certainly be no miracle cure, but there is a need for a thoroughgoing reform of the labour market, with the introduction of greater flexibility in the organization of work and the distribution of working time, reduced labour costs, a higher level of skills, and pro-active labour policies.'
518. This neglect in the text of the Treaty did not, however, mean that the problem of unemployment was neglected in the broad guidelines adopted on the basis of Art. 99(2) EC. From the first BEPG in 1993, much attention was paid to the issue of employment as an *economic* problem. No less attention was paid to the issue in subsequent publications of such guidelines.

sense. In the longer term, employment growth is determined by five economic factors:

(1) macro-economic developments, in particular the structural growth rate of the economy;
(2) the dynamics of product markets and markets in factors of production (competitiveness);
(3) in particular, the performance of the labour market;
(4) the structure of negative and positive employment incentives flowing from national tax and social security systems;
(5) the quality of the public supply of education and training, with particular emphasis on vulnerable uneducated or low-skilled groups on the labour market.

It is clear from this overview that the employment issue must, in large part, be solved using general economic policy, which falls under the EMU title of the EC Treaty.

As indicated in section 3.2.1, various Member States had major problems with the idea of re-opening this title in the run-up to the last phase of EMU.[519] As a result, the authors of the Treaty of Amsterdam finally decided to insert a separate procedure in the EC Treaty for those elements of employment policy which fell outside the scope of the coordination of general economic policy under Article 99 EC.[520]

4.2   THE LEGAL FRAMEWORK

It is immediately apparent from Article 125 EC that the substantive scope of Title VIII is limited. Although the Article talks of a 'coordinated strategy for employment', this is limited straight away by the clarification that it concerns, in particular, the promotion of 'a skilled, trained and adaptable workforce and labour markets responsive to economic change.' The substantive link to the coordination of economic policy is set down in Article 126(1) EC, which provides that Member States must conduct their employment policies in a way 'consistent with the broad guidelines of the economic policies' adopted in accordance with Article 99(2) EC. Article 126(2) EC, which is the counterpart of Article 99(1) EC, requires Member

---

519. This was especially insisted upon by Sweden and Finland. This analytically correct approach was, however, unacceptable to the United Kingdom which, under the then Conservative government, did not want to accept formal competence of any kind for the Community in employment policy. It was also unacceptable to Germany, which did not consider the re-opening of the EMU title to be open to discussion.

520. The change of government in the United Kingdom and in France in the spring of 1997, played a large part in enabling the successful resolution of negotiations on the employment title in Amsterdam. See the in many ways critical report of the Intergovernmental Conference, Brussels, Dec. 1995, 23.

States to regard promoting employment as a matter of common concern. To this end, they must coordinate their action in this respect within the Council.

Article 127 EC is remarkable for two omissions: no reference is made to the BEPG, insofar as the actions of the Community itself are concerned; and the activities of the Community which are of import for a 'high level of employment' are not detailed any further. The latter represents a shortcoming, given that employment growth in the European Union is also determined by the functioning of the internal market and by Community competition policy. The wording of Article 127 EC gives the misleading impression that the complementing Community activities will be of a financial nature.[521] This does not detract from the fact that the Community structural funds and the actions of the EIB increasingly have the explicit aim of promoting employment, in particular in small- and medium-sized enterprises.

Article 128 EC is the core provision of Title VIII. The joint annual report from the Council and the Commission to the European Council is prepared by the Ecofin and the Social Policy formations of the Council together. The guidelines for employment provided for in Article 128(2) EC are, however, largely limited to labour market policy. The economic aspects of employment are addressed in the BEPG. This complementarity is made explicit in Article 128(2) EC itself. From an institutional perspective, it is notable that the employment guidelines are drawn up by the Council on the basis of the conclusions of the European Council on a joint annual report.[522] The Council takes its decision on the basis of a Commission proposal after consulting the European Parliament, the Economic and Social Committee, and Committee of the Regions and the Employment Committee referred to in Article 130 EC.[523] The Member States' duty set out in Article 128(3) EC, to report on the principal measures taken to implement their employment policies in the light of the employment guidelines, is more far-reaching than Member States' obligations under Article 99 EC. The significance of these requirements could only become clear in due course, given that employment growth flows essentially from structural measures which will only lead to results in the longer term. Experience with the Essen procedure from 1995 to date has already demonstrated the risk

---

521. In the run-up to the Treaty of Amsterdam, a rather fundamental difference of opinion resurfaced between southern Member States, for which employment policy is mainly a question of financial incentives, and northern Member States, which argued for a more structural approach. This difference in opinion is to be seen in the text of Arts. 127(1) and 129 EC. A somewhat equivocal phrasing was ultimately agreed upon, which in our opinion wrongly disguises the fact that the most important contribution which the Community can make to employment in Europe is a properly functioning internal market and the EMU.

522. As such, the position of the European Council in the decision-making process for employment policy seems stronger than for the broad guidelines of Art. 99(2) EC. This role which seems barely compatible with the Community's institutional structure demonstrates the political importance attached to employment policy in Amsterdam. See also: J. Kenner, op. cit., *supra* note 515, 384.

523. In comparison with Art. 99(2) EC, the Commission's position (proposal rather than recommendation) and that of the Parliament (being consulted rather than merely informed) are more satisfactory.

that the annual country reports repeat themselves and provide little insight into the truly relevant developments in employment policy.[524] Article 128(4) EC is the counterpart of Article 99(4) EC. The most remarkable aspect of this provision is the role of the Employment Committee, which is composed of two representatives per Member State and two representatives from the Commission, in preparations for the examination of the implementation of Member States' employment policies in the light of the employment guidelines. This examination takes place on the basis of the annual country reports,[525] on which the Council receives the views of the Employment Committee. Should, the Council consider it appropriate in the light of its examination, it may, acting by a qualified majority on a recommendation from the Commission, make recommendations to Member States. It is on the basis of this examination that, under Article 128(5) EC, the Council and the Commission must make their joint annual report to the European Council.[526]

Article 129 EC sets out, in restrictive wording, which incentive measures may be taken by the Community to promote employment: it concerns measures primarily aimed at the labour market as such, rather than *financial* incentive measures. Further, harmonization of national measures is expressly precluded.[527] This restrictive tenor does not, however, detract from the powers of the EIB and the structural funds, for example, to use their financial instruments for economic investment in order to create new employment opportunities. Nor does it preclude the possibility that employment issues may be implicated in the policy which the

---

524. See further: J. Kenner, op. cit., *supra* note 515, 389–391.
525. Until 2005, these reports were termed National Action Plans (NAPs). From 2005, they are termed National Reform Programmes (NRPs).
526. This provision unmistakeably demonstrates that the Member States were reluctant to grant broad powers to the Commission. In contrast to Art. 99(3) EC, the Commission has no separate role in overseeing the implementation of the guidelines for employment. The task of carrying out preparatory work for the examination is given to the Employment Committee. In addition, the Commission's involvement in the Council's competence to make recommendations to Member States is restrictively termed a power of 'recommendation'. Kenner, op. cit., *supra* note 515, 390, draws the at first sight far-reaching, but not incorrect conclusion that Member States view the coordination of employment policy primarily as a dialogue between national administrations and the European Council. The consequence of this is that it will not be easy to make tough recommendations to individual Member States.
527. This somewhat overly painstaking restriction of Community competence is in itself not in conflict with the weak vertical coordination contemplated by the employment title. Nonetheless, more fundamental criticism may be made of the idea underlying the provision, i.e., that direct Community interference with national legislative competences in the employment policy field is as such undesirable. Structural rigidities caused by national legislation can have serious consequences for national employment growth and can thus damage the Community's employment objectives. As a result, a more forceful specific directive competence would not have been unsuitable. If the employment title represents the recognition that employment is an issue of Community importance, the national legislator should not be guaranteed unrestricted autonomy in the area. In the light of the Court's case law, such a legal restriction could have undesirable consequences from a policy perspective: see Joined Cases C-122 & 125/99 P, *D v. Council*. See also, E. Szyszczak 'The new social policy paradigm: A Virtuous circle' (2001) CML Rev., 1125-1170, 1138 and 1139

Community conducts towards harmonization of certain taxes.[528] Finally, Article 130 EC provides for the establishment of the advisory Employment Committee to which reference has already been made.[529]

4.3   APPLICATION IN PRACTICE

Even before the Treaty of Amsterdam came into force, a start had been made in applying the new employment title.[530] An extraordinary EU summit on employment took place on 20 and 21 November 1997 in Luxembourg. In the conclusions of this summit, the main points of the first employment guidelines were set out. These comprised 19 recommendations, grouped under four main themes:

(1) Developing entrepreneurship. This theme included recommendations to reduce administrative burdens for small and medium-sized enterprises, to reduce fiscal and administrative obstacles to setting up new enterprises, and to reduce the general fiscal and social burdens on enterprises.

(2) Improving employability. This heading included the important recommendations that every person who becomes unemployed should be offered a new position within one year, and that in the case of an unemployed young person, this time period should be just half a year. Also included were measures to improve the supply of training, work experience and the promotion of lifelong training.

(3) Encouraging adaptability. This included guidelines in order to achieve greater flexibility in the law governing employment contracts, while at the same time guaranteeing social security protection.

(4) Equal opportunities. This heading contained recommendations aimed at improving the prospects of those who are vulnerable or have fallen behind on the labour market: women, those with disabilities and the long-term unemployed.[531]

This first set of guidelines have, from year to year, been slightly modified and consolidated.[532] The principal change came with the integration of the employment guidelines and the BEPG to form the Integrated Guidelines for Growth and Jobs, 2005–2008, which took place in the context of the mid-term review of the

---

528. There is good reason for this, as in comparison with, for example, the United States, the proportion of taxation weighing on the labour factor is disproportionately high in the Community. It is primarily these 'indirect' wage costs which make basic labour in Western Europe too expensive.

529. See Council Decision 2000/98/EC of 24 Jan. 2000, establishing the Employment Committee, O.J. 2000, L 29/21.

530. The initiative for this is to be found in the resolution of 16 Jun. 1997, of the European Council on growth and employment, O.J. 1997, C 236/3.

531. This is discussed in detail in R. Blanpain, op. cit., *infra* note 664, 157–165.

532. Employment guidelines 2002, Council Decision 2002/177/EC of 18 Feb. 2002, O.J. 2002, L 60/60.

Lisbon process.[533] This has meant that, formally, the two sets of guidelines are now presented in a single document (though still passed as separate recommendations with different legal bases). In addition, Member States' annual reports on progress in implementing both sets of guidelines are now combined into a single report, termed 'National Reform Programmes'.[534] Nonetheless, there has essentially been little substantive change as regards the guidelines on employment. This is a perfectly defensible choice, as the more structural nature of the recommendations means that changing them rapidly is inadvisable. While the integrated guidelines for growth and jobs 2005–2008 set average targets of a 70% EU-wide overall employment rate, with a 60% target for women and 50% for older workers (55 to 64 years of age), no individualized quantitative targets regarding the desired employment level in Member States have been included in the Council's recommendations, though the Commission had originally proposed that such targets be included.[535] This position is understandable, given the major political and social resistance to which far-reaching reform of labour market policy, in the broad sense, can be subject.[536] In addition, as already noted above, the EU's achievements in employment ultimately depend on the structural economic growth rate. As long as uncertainties remain in this regard, all estimates of the employment rate can only amount to guesswork.[537] It is evident from the wording of Article 126 EC that employment policy remains a national competence. The employment guidelines thus represent no more than the loose indicative vertical coordination of national policy. It would seem from a comparison of Articles 99(3) and (4) EC with Articles 128(3) and (4) EC that, in principle, the employment guidelines bind the Member States to a lesser degree than the BEPG, because the recommendations which the Council may make in the case of failure to comply with the

---

533. See the Commission Communication, Integrated Guidelines for Growth and Jobs 2005–2008, COM(2005)141 final. For the employment guidelines section of the integrated guidelines, see Council Decision 2005/600 of 12 Jul. 2005, on Guidelines for the employment policies of the Member States, O.J. 2005, L 205/21; maintained by Council Decision 2006/544 of 18 Jul. 2006, on guidelines for the employment policies of the Member States, O.J. 2006, L 215/26.
534. Formerly known as 'National Action Plans' as regards the report on implementation of the employment guidelines.
535. Council Recommendation of 18 Feb. 2002, on the implementation of Member States' employment policies, O.J. 2002, L 60/70; see also the subsequent annual Council recommendations, the most recent being Council Recommendation 2007/209/EC of 27 Mar. 2007, on the 2007 update of the broad guidelines for the economic policies of the Member States and the Community and on the implementation of Member States' employment policies, O.J. 2007, L 92/23.
536. The reluctance to set targets is also now in line with the Commission's broader position on growth and employment, following its mid-term review of the Lisbon process, to move away from targets and to focus on 'actions'. See Commission Communication to the Spring European Council of 2 Feb. 2005, entitled 'Working together for growth and jobs. A new start for the Lisbon strategy', COM(2005)24 final.
537. In comparison with the United States and Japan, the level of participation of the labour force remains unusually low in the EU (at 63.8% in 2006), compared to 70% in the United States and Japan. The comparison is even more unfavourable in the case of older employees and women. See the Commission report, Policies in Support of Employment, Brussels, 2000, and the more recent Commission report, Employment in Europe 2006, Brussels, Nov. 2006.

BEPG have – pursuant to Article 99(4) EC – the indisputable aim of correcting Member State behaviour,[538] whereas this is not the case for the employment guidelines.[539] The loosely binding nature of the employment guidelines is also evident from the procedure leading to the joint annual report and from the content of this report. The methods of assessment used in these reports are informal: targeting, benchmarking, peer review, etc.[540] Nonetheless, the decision in 2005 to integrate the BEPG and the employment guidelines into a single coherent text signifies the view at Community level that success in the Lisbon process requires a two-pronged approach covering both the micro- and macro-economic aspects of the EU.

The yearly policy cycle set out in Article 128 EC concerning the employment guidelines provides a substantial amount of information for the interested observer. It also demonstrates how sensitive national policies to stimulate employment are within Member States, and the large extent to which labour market relations depend on national policy traditions and institutions. As a result, the emphases which national governments choose for their employment policies can differ substantially for political reasons.[541] This is not to say that more convergence of employment policies within the Community would be impossible. In order for this to happen, the insights which the Article 128 EC procedure can provide must play a greater role in national political and policy discourse.[542]

4.4   OUTLOOK

The indivisible inter-relation between, on the one hand, monetary and economic policy integration and, on the other hand, policy integration in the field of employment, is expressed in Articles 126(2) and 128(2) EC. It follows from the wording of these Articles that the employment guidelines must be compatible with the BEPG. It would be wrong, however, to conclude from this that, as a socio-economic goal, employment is subordinate to the economic aims set out in

---

538.   This is reinforced by the Lisbon Treaty, which expands this procedure to empower the Commission to send a preliminary 'warning letter' to a non-compliant Member State in advance of a recommendation from the Council.

539.   The European Commission's less prominent role in multilateral supervision under Art. 128(3) is, in our opinion, a factor not to be underestimated in this regard.

540.   On this, see E. Szyczczak, op. cit. *supra* note 527, 1140–1148.

541.   Thus, the unilateral institution of a 35-hour working week by the French government under Jospin in 1998 would be unacceptable, procedurally and substantively, as a measure to promote employment in the Netherlands. Likewise, the hesitations with which the Kok cabinet handled the issue of old-age pensions, at a time of impending tension on the labour market, would be difficult to understand in France.

542.   We are a long way from achieving this at present. One of the most important practical obstacles is that national parliaments are not kept sufficiently informed about the policy cycle of the employment guidelines. As a result, there is little interest subsequently in the important comparative policy information provided by this cycle. The approach seems to be somewhat more introverted in the area of employment policy to the area of general economic policy, which traditionally has had a more international focus.

Articles 4 and 98 EC.[543] As already noted in section 3.2 above, such economic aims should, in the light of Article 2 EC, be understood as intermediate aims, which help to achieve sustainable economic growth and a high level of employment. The failure to make this explicit in Articles 4 and 98 EC is simply due to the serious drafting deficiencies of the Maastricht Treaty. The situation is to some extent improved by the Lisbon Treaty, which describes the Article 3 TEU goal of establishing an internal market as based on 'balanced economic growth and price stability, a highly competitive social market economy, aiming at full employment and social progress.' However, the wording of Articles 4 and 98 EC – which, in this respect, the Lisbon Treaty leaves unchanged – has contributed to the fact that specific employment policy was traditionally dealt with in separate procedures. This has, it is true, the seeming advantage of giving the employment aims express emphasis in the EC Treaty; it also means, however, that as an aim, employment has been situated at a distance from the central economic and socio-economic debate in the Community, which takes place around the BEPG. In addition, the resulting fragmentation in decision-making on intrinsically related subjects has damaged socio-economic policy integration as a political process within the Community.[544] This is the concern which the 2005 decision to integrate the BEPG and the employment guidelines, to form the integrated guidelines for growth and jobs, was aimed at meeting. While such a move has changed little of the guidelines' substance, it has to a certain extent alleviated the problem, as it enables the BEPG and the employment guidelines to be drawn up at the same time and laid before the European Council simultaneously. The latter should preferably occur before the summer, so that national budgetary authorities can take the guidelines into account in their budget preparations. In addition, integration of the guidelines means that the broader policy convergence at which both instruments aim can better be achieved, as the difficulties of existing disparities are presented simultaneously in economic (growth) and socio-economic (employment) terms.[545] Ultimately, a further advantage of integration is that the negative consequences of disparities, which have to date seemed politically unassailable, will be sufficiently cast into the spotlight so as to encourage their discussion. An example is the minimum tax harmonization which is a

543. Both Kenner, op. cit., *supra* note 515, 375 and Szyczczak, op. cit. 1140 seem to align themselves with this misguided position, which fails to acknowledge that a completed internal market and a completed EMU by their nature can and must contribute to the achievement of ambitious targets in employment. We will return to this misunderstanding in section 6.1 below.
544. The degree to which loose vertical policy coordination becomes the subject of political and policy debate in the Member States is decisive for its success. For this reason, it is preferable to concentrate the policy coordination process in a summary of policy, which restricts itself to some general priorities combined with country-specific recommendations, rather than issuing numerous guidelines as the result of various procedures. This also makes multilateral supervision easier, which can thereby limit itself to a few essential areas. 'Qui trop embrasse, mal étreint' also holds here.
545. This also has the advantage, which is not to be underestimated, of somewhat reducing the problems of consistency Community and national level to which the existence of two types of guidelines gives rise. See also *supra*, at section 1.5.

necessary condition for the reduction of the tax burden on the labour factor. This burden forms an obstacle, which should not be underestimated, to the stimulation of, in particular, less productive workers within the EU.[546]

5   ECONOMIC AND SOCIAL COHESION[547]

5.1   ORIENTATION AND DEFINITIONS

The heading of Title XVII of the third part of the EC Treaty may be misleading. Articles 158–162 EC, inserted by the Single European Act, are not about cohesion *between* general economic policy and social policy, and are only very marginally relevant to cohesion between sectoral economic developments and the social consequences of these developments. The articles essentially concern the development of economic activity, and with that employment and welfare, in a geographically harmonious manner. This focus is made somewhat clearer by the Lisbon Treaty, which substitutes 'Economic, Social and Territorial Cohesion' as the Title heading. Given the considerable variations in the geographic distribution of welfare between and within Member States, the issue of spatially balanced economic development forms one of the central topics in the formation of the economic policy of and within the Community. It plays an important, at times dominant role in almost every Community activity, in the field of market integration as well as in that of policy integration.[548]

---

546. See: White Book of the European Commission, 'A Concerted Strategy for Modernising Social Protection' COM(99)347, 9 and 13.

547. The major political significance of Arts. 158–162 EC is not reflected in the volume of legal literature devoted to it. One of the difficulties facing a detailed account of the considerable secondary Community legislation adopted under this Title is the high turnover rate of this secondary legislation. An account of it can be little more than a snapshot, as such of mainly historical interest. This is the case for the informative account by J.V. Louis, J.C. Séché, M. Wolfcarius and Th. Margellos in Mégret part 6, 2ème éd. 1995, 167–248, which has been overtaken by subsequent legislation. The same applies to the – more concise – commentary of M. Beschel in H. von der Groeben et al. op. cit. *supra* note 81, 3/1656–1678. The dissertation of D.E. Comijs, Europese Structuurfondsen, Deventer 1998, is informative and a useful read for its analysis of the legal problems which can arise in enforcing Community structural funds policy in the national context. See further the literature at the end of this chapter. We restrict ourselves here to a concise account of the current secondary legislation and will concentrate on the most important legal and economic issues which inter-relate with spatial economic-policy within the EU.

548. This was emphasized in the European Spring Council of 2005, which, in declaring the necessity of re-launching the Lisbon Strategy to 're-focus priorities on growth and employment', stressed that 'the Union must mobilize to a greater degree all appropriate national and Community resources – *including the cohesion policy* – in the Strategy's three dimensions (economic, social and environmental) so as better to tap into their synergies in a general context of sustainable development.' (Emphasis added). On the effects of the EU's cohesion policy between 2000–2006, see the Fourth Report of the Commission on Economic and Social Cohesion, 30 May 2007, COM(2007)273 final.

The extent of geographic differences in welfare within the Community is, in the first place, determined by the integration process as a political process. Due to the accession of Ireland, Greece, Spain and Portugal, the differences in welfare within the Community have increased significantly since the beginning of the 1970s. German reunification in 1990 had similar consequences, because the welfare level of the new German Länder initially lagged far behind the Community average. The expansion of the Community to Finland, Sweden and Austria somewhat increased the proportion of more prosperous states, so the average level of welfare increased. The enlargement to include a large number of Central and Eastern European states has certainly drastically increased geographic differences in welfare.[549]

It is not, as such, possible unambiguously to determine the consequences of the integration process, as a *market integration process*, for the geographical distribution of welfare. To the extent that market integration contributes to the increase of the overall standard of living, the economically weaker parts of the Community can also profit from this. If we take the lessons of the 1990s into account, it is evident that the reallocation of economic activities, which is a necessary and desired consequence of the formation of a Community market, need not necessarily be to the disadvantage of the initially weakest economies. Thus, Spain, Portugal, Greece and Ireland have, in terms of relative growth in welfare, been able partially, and in some cases amply, to make up their initial disadvantage.[550] It is not only the formation of the Community market which leads to the phenomenon of reallocation, with its related temporary frictions; the *operation* of this market also – necessarily – has this result. This is evident in the decline and fall of former industrial and trade centres, such as Alsace-Lorraine, Merseyside and the Borinage. It is thus, in principle and substantively, wrong to consider the issue of regional variations in welfare as more or less set in stone, to be solved purely by income and capital transfer. The poorer and the richer parts of the Community remain intrinsically sensitive about geographical and

---

549. See e.g., the figures released by Eurostat in Dec. 2006, which show that, in terms of purchasing power, the average income per capita in 2005, as a percentage of the average of an EU of 25 was: 33% for Bulgaria, 89% for Cyprus, 74% for the Czech Republic, 60% for Estonia, 63% for Hungary, 48% for Latvia, 52% for Lithuania, 70% for Malta, 50% for Poland, 34% for Romania, 57% for Slovakia, 82% for Slovenia. Contrast the countries with the highest relative GDP per capita: Luxembourg (251% of the EU-25 average) and Ireland (139% of the EU-25 average). See the press release STAT/06/166 of 18 Dec. 2006.

550. In 1988, the GDP per capita for Greece, Spain, Ireland and Portugal was, respectively, 58.3%, 72.5%, 63.8%, 50.2% of the EU-15 average. In 2002 these figures were: 72.5, 83.2, 122.1, 73.7. Source: Table 1 of the Commission's interim report on economic and social cohesion of 30 Jan. 2002, COM(2002)46 final. In 2005, the GDP per capita for these countries as a percentage of the EU-25 average was: 84%, 98%, 139% and 71%. Source: Eurostat figures of 18 Dec. 2006, ibid. These figures confirm the earlier finding of W. Molle, O. Sleypen, M. Vanheukelen, 'The Impact of an Economic and Monetary Union on Member States' Fiscal Policies', in K. Gretschmann (ed.), *Economic and Monetary Union, Implications for National Policy Makers* (Dordrecht, 1993), 217–243, in particular 220–222.

sectoral reallocations which result from dynamic market activity.[551] The gravity of the frictions which a geographic shift in economic activities can cause, with all their undesirable social side effects, is determined in particular by the extent to which the Community can ensure satisfactory economic growth across the board, with an attendant high level of investment and growth in employment. This raises – once again – the issue of cohesion between *market* and *policy* integration within the Community. The achievement of the economic policy coordination aims governed by Articles 98 and 99 EC is necessary in order for economic activity within the entire Community to develop in a geographically harmonious manner. This refers not only to macro-economic policy, but also, and especially, to the Member States' policies on the so-called public supply side of their economies: the availability and the quality of physical, technological and educational infrastructure, the quality and mobility of the labour force, the quality of the operation of the market and the decision-making costs in socio-economic policy. The increasing significance attributed to these aspects probably constitutes the principal motivation for the Community's efforts to reduce geographical variations in welfare.[552] In particular, should the weaker Member States and regions lack sufficient resources to be able to offer the public services necessary for an increasingly demanding market-place, there is a risk that the dynamic variations in welfare could become permanent. This would mean that regions which, in terms of natural production conditions, are potentially attractive remain under-utilized. Such a situation is undesirable not only for the region concerned, which is confronted with an unnecessary decrease in welfare, but also for the Community as a whole, as its potential is under-exploited. Special problems of policy coordination arise at the Community level in the relationship between Community sectoral policy – in particular Community agricultural policy – and the policy to strengthen economic and social cohesion. Insofar as the marginal agricultural areas in Western Europe, to a large extent, are situated in economically weaker regions, the spatial-economic consequences of a drop in price for the most important agricultural products are very considerable. These consequences can only be absorbed temporarily by income support for the affected producers, because income transfers which lead to the preservation of enterprises which are not economically viable can, ultimately, only cause serious market disturbances. In the end, the only real solution is to improve the economic structure of the relevant agricultural areas.[553]

---

551. 'Sensitive' also implies that previously economically weaker regions can flourish rather rapidly and intensely. Southern Ireland, Catalonia and, in the Netherlands, Limburg are clear examples of this.

552. See, however, Art. 3 TEU as inserted by the Lisbon Treaty, which refers to the aim of promoting economic, social and territorial cohesion along with the arguably more value-laden aim of promoting 'solidarity between Member States.'

553. The report of the Dutch Wetenschappelijke Raad voor het Regeringsbeleid (Scientific Council for Government Policy), 'Grond voor keuzen' (Ground for Choices) (The Hague, 1992) is a very useful analysis of this pressing issue. It is once again relevant in the light of the recent enlargements of the EU, as the extension of the income support applicable within the present EU to the strongly farming-oriented acceding Member States (which, according to the

In the run-up to the completion of EMU, some expressed the concern that, within a monetary union, greater transparency of cost and price differences could lead to substantial geographic movement of economic activities, against which Member States would be powerless to defend themselves due to the loss of the exchange-rate instrument.[554] This concern is not entirely unfounded, bearing in mind the rather rigid labour markets in the EU, as geographic mobility of the labour factor is low and labour costs are little sensitive to supply and demand relations on the labour market. In such a situation, large regional variations in unemployment can, within a completed EMU, occur in the long run. Such effects will be considerably reduced if production costs reflect differences in the levels of productivity within the EMU. This presupposes three things:

(1) the disciplined development of labour conditions in the national sphere;
(2) investment in the quality of the labour factor and of the public supply-side of the market, to increase the capacity for productivity returns;
(3) more flexible labour markets which allow greater regional differentiation in labour conditions than is presently usual in large parts of Western Europe.

This issue of cohesion cannot be solved by regional economic structural policy, as experiences in the national sphere have shown.[555]

European Commission, have around 4 million farmers, added to the EU 15's farming population of around 7 million) would have led to a sharp increase in agricultural payments. As a result, direct CAP payments to farmers in the new Member States are to be phased in over 10 years, with such farmers receiving 25% of the full EU rate in 2004, rising to 30% in 2005 and 35% in 2006 (to which funds received from the EU's structural rural development fund, the European Fund for Rural Development, may be added). See in relation to this Case C-273/04, *Poland v. Council* on Art. 1(5) of Council Decision 2004/281/EC of 22 Mar. 2004, adapting the Act concerning the conditions of accession, about the extension of 'phasing in' of payments to the new Member States. The experiences with the Community agricultural policy to date demonstrates that the almost unavoidable increase in production and scaling-up of the best agricultural areas, such as Picardy and the Beauce in France and the Italian Padan plain, have already led to a certain degree of depopulation of the countryside. This phenomenon is even more pronounced in marginal agricultural areas such as Castilla in Spain, Calabria in Italy and the Massif Central in France. Direct income support can slow, but not stop, such transformation. It is expected that the phenomenon will have far-reaching socio-economic consequences for the rural areas of the new Member States of Central and Eastern Europe, whose agricultural sector still suffers from low productivity. Paradoxically, an improvement in the structure of agricultural production there will lead to a worsening of the general socio-economic structure (employment, emigration, the disappearance of socio-economic infrastructure, etc). The question is whether the consequences of this transformation can be allayed solely by regional economic structural policy. In any event, bearing in mind the experiences to date with the CAP, forms of rural development must be sought which deal more effectively with the consequences of increases in productivity and of scaling-up than the instruments used at present.

554. B. Drugman and J.-P. Laurencin, 'L'Unification monétaire, opportunité ou menace pour la cohésion au sein de l-Union européenne', (1998), RMC, 370–378.

555. This is evident from the experiences following German reunification in 1990: at that time, wholly defensibly, it was decided for political reasons to increase employment conditions in the 'new' Länder to around 60% of the then normal level in West Germany. These measures,

Experience with geographic-based socio-economic policy in the Member States and in the Community has taught us that such policy is highly vulnerable to considerations of pure political horse-trading in the distribution of funds, both on the incoming and outgoing sides of the budget. Within the Community, this has found expression in the so-called 'just return' principle, which provides that every Member State must aim at global or specific proportionality between their, on the one hand, contributions to the Community or a certain Community fund and, on the other hand, the amount spent on them by the Community.[556]

The acceptance of Delors' so-called 'First Packet' in 1988 led to a break-through on the 'just return' principle, at least in the area of regional economic policy. Since then, the vast majority of payments from the structural funds go to economically weaker regions. Globally speaking, the effectiveness of Community regional policy has improved as a result, as more resources are now being spent where they are needed the most. However, the fact that intra-Community structural payments have increased greatly (around 60 billion euro for the period 1989–1993, around 148 billion euro for the period 1993–1999, 213 billion euro for the period 2000–2006, and around 308 billion[557] for the period 2007–2013) also creates political and policy-based risks.[558]

In the first place, it appears that the capacity of the regions concerned to absorb the funds transferred can be insufficient to ensure the responsible spending of resources: resulting in 'cathedrals in the desert'.[559]

In the second place, the Member States which have relatively far weaker regions can become too dependent, in their public finances, on Community

---

inspired by social motives, failed to take into account the far greater differences in productivity between East and West. East German industry, being already highly vulnerable, had no chance of surviving competition with West German industry. Massive capital and income transfers – in the order of more than 100 billion DM per year – could not prevent, or solve, huge and stubborn unemployment in East Germany.

556. See J.V. Louis, J.C. Séché, M. Wolfcarius and Th. Margellos, op. cit., *supra* note 547, 179, 180 and 183.

557. Calculated at 2004 prices. According to the Commission, this amounts to over 347 billion euro at 2007 prices, or 35.7% of the total EU budget. See <http://ec.europa.eu/regional_policy/policy/fonds/index_en.htm>.

558. For an analysis of the effectiveness of the EU's cohesion policy in the late 1990s, see M. Beugelsdijk and S. Eijffinger, 'The Effectiveness of Structural Policy in the European Union: An Empirical Analysis for the EU-15 in 1995–2001' (2005), JCMS, 37.

559. This is the reason why, at the time of the Berlin European Council of Mar. 1999, it was agreed that contributions which the Member States would receive from the structural funds and the cohesion funds may not exceed 4% of GDP. This norm was adopted in Reg. 1260/1999 of 21 Jun. 1999, laying down general provisions on the Structural Funds, O.J. 1999, L 161/1; see Art. 7(8). It was slightly decreased and nuanced by Reg. 1083/2006 of 11 Jul. 2006, laying down general provisions on the European Regional Development Fund, the European Social Fund and the Cohesion Fund and repealing Reg. (EC) No 1260/1999, O.J. 2006, L 210/25, Annex II, para. 7, which makes the maximum amount which a given Member State may receive from the structural funds dependent on the percentage which their Gross National Income per capita from 2001–2003 represents of the EU-25 average. The relatively poorest countries (40% or less of the EU-25 average) have the highest maximum level of total contributions (3.7893%).

payments. The contribution from the structural funds to the cohesion countries (Ireland, Portugal, Spain and Greece) in the 1990s was, for example, around 3% of their GDP.[560] This dependency can have as an unintended side-effect that the Member State concerned becomes particularly vulnerable in its budgetary policy. As the size and distribution of Community payments needs to be flexible over time, in the interest of efficiency of payment, such dependency can make them vulnerable to the Community's flexibility in policy at a future date.

In the third place, the preoccupation with political horse-trading in the distribution of funds, which is almost unavoidably associated with regional economic policy, tends to stretch beyond that policy field. This occurred to a large extent in the run-up to the Treaty of Maastricht, as the Southern Member States more or less conditioned their approval of the formation of EMU on the broadening of intra-Community payments. From the perspective of the Community interest, such an approach can be counter-productive, as it leads to blockages in decision-making and to inefficient use of Community resources.

In the fourth place, political attention to inter-regional differences in welfare within the Community can lead to policy introversion, which is risky for the future of the European integration process. This can, in the long term, find expression in reservations about enlarging the European Union to economically weaker countries on the part of Member States which at present profit to a considerable degree from intra-Community structural funds. This attitude is apparent from the imbalance between intra-Community redistribution payments and resources for so-called 'external' measures, primarily directed at candidate countries.[561]

Neither the Single European Act – which introduced Articles 158–162 EC into the EC Treaty – nor the Maastricht Treaty provides a definition of the concept 'Economic and Social Cohesion'. The most we have to go on are Article 158(2) and Articles 159(1) and (2) EC. Although one might argue that a definition could be deduced from the policy which has been put in place on the basis of these Articles, the difficulty with this approach is that this policy, which since the entry into force of the Single European Act has dramatically broadened and intensified, also provides little substantive guidance. As a result, a functional definition, using definitions which are in use in national regional economic policy, offers a preferable approach: the Community's policy is aimed at optimizing the socio-economic potential of those parts of the Community which lag behind in terms of welfare and employment, and at promoting the socio-economic change which is necessary

---

560. The net contribution which a Member State receives from the Community budget can, in practice, be higher. This is so when a large contribution from the structural funds is combined with a substantial contribution from the European agricultural budget. This was the case in the 1990s for Ireland, which in 1994 received around 6% of its GDP from the Community.

561. The total amount available for candidate Member States for the period 2000–2006 amounted to around 80 billion euro, whereas the payments from the structural funds and cohesion funds alone to the 'old' 15 Member States in this period amounted to over 290 billion euro. See Annex I to the Interinstitutional Agreement between the European Parliament, the Council and the Commission of 6 May 1999 on budgetary discipline and improvement of the budgetary procedure, O.J. 1999, C 172/1.

as a result of the sectoral or spatial reallocation of economic activities. This definition demonstrates that 'Economic and Social Cohesion' should not simply achieve a pure redistribution of resources within the Community, and that it cannot take the place of the social and labour market policies of Member States and of the Community based on Articles 125–130 and 136–145 EC. Such a definition is also, in our view, sufficiently supported by the text of Article 159(1) and (2) EC.

5.2   LEGAL BASIS

Articles 158–162 EC, in their original version, are not models of clarity, because the Treaty authors were attempting not only to codify existing political regional Community policy, but also to create a Treaty basis for the expansion and the intensification of that policy. The amendments introduced by the Treaties of Maastricht, Amsterdam and Nice did not increase the transparency of the text.

Article 158 EC emphasizes regional policy in the more classical sense, that is, a policy aiming at strengthening weaker regions. This emphasis was expressly insisted upon by those Member States with relatively numerous weaker regions, which wanted to avoid the risk that, with a broader definition, Community payments might be too broadly dispersed. Compared to the original text of Article 130a EC, the current wording – that the aim of the Community's activity is to 'reduce disparities between the *levels of development*' – is a clear improvement. The former wording read simply to 'reduce . . . disparities', so this addition makes clear that the Community's activity should be, in the economic sense, instrumental and not primarily distributive. The Lisbon Treaty further clarifies the instrumental function of the policy, specifying that particular attention shall be paid to 'rural areas, areas affected by industrial transition, and regions which suffer from severe and permanent natural or demographic handicaps'.

Article 158 EC contemplates, in the first place, substantive attunement between the aims of Article 158 EC and national economic policy, which is coordinated at Community level. This implicitly raises the inter-relation between Articles 98–99 EC and Article 158 EC, which should be understood as meaning that the strengthening of macro-economic stability and growth and an increase in market dynamics can create the conditions which stimulate the development potential of weaker regions.

The system of the EC Treaty means that we must accept that the specific regional economic aims of Article 158 EC are subordinated to the general principles of economic policy in the Member States and in the Community, set out in Articles 4 and 98 EC. If one were to consider the two areas as being on the same level, or – worse – assume the opposite relationship between the two, the operation of market allocation or of trade liberalization could, in extremis, be viewed as – partly – dependent on its potential consequences for the distribution of regional welfare within the Community.[562]

---

562. Such a result would also be diametrically opposed to the case law of the Court on the four freedoms. In this case law, the Court has deliberately refused to accept economic policy

Secondly, Article 159 EC contains an obligation for the Community to take into account the aims of Article 158 EC, and to contribute to their achievement, in drawing up and implementing its policies and in realizing the internal market. It would be difficult to draw unambiguous conclusions from this two-headed obligation. The application of the principles of market unity and equality in the internal market can, in some cases, mean that marginal activities from weaker regions move to elsewhere in the Community, but practice shows that, in a favourable investment climate, the weaker regions can actually attract investment. In addition, in a completed EMU, mobility of investment can increase dramatically, a development from which even the – at present – weaker regions can profit. In each case, it is difficult to imagine how these fundamental characteristics of market integration and of monetary policy integration could be subordinated to regional economic policy aims.[563] Of course, it is nonetheless the case that, in the formulation of qualitative conditions for market integration, in competition policy and in the drawing up of sectoral policies such as agricultural and transport policy, the consequences of such policies for the geographical development of welfare and employment within the Community can be taken into account.[564]

In realizing the internal market, the balance, in composition and in sequence, of the packet of liberalizing measures was an unjustifiably neglected aspect of market integration. The priority given to the achievement of free movement of goods was, to a certain degree, at the expense of those parts of the Community with a relatively strong service sector. The delayed development of the Community transport policy harmed the economic development of the peripheral Member States, whose transport sector was relatively strong due to their location.

In competition policy, the link between the application of Articles 87–89 EC and Article 159 EC is obvious. Where Community financing in general complements national financing, this national aid must be permissible under Article 87(3) EC. Inversely, the Community's supervision of national grants of aid should prevent Member States from thwarting the Community's structural policy with their measures. The Commission can extract support for such an approach not only from Articles 87–89 EC, but also from the first and second sentences of Article 159 EC.[565]

---

arguments as a justification for restrictions on inter-state movement of goods and of factors of production; see further Ch. VIII, passim.

563. B. Drugman and J.-P. Laurencin, op. cit., *supra* note 554, 375–377, seem to be of the view that the current regional economic equilibria must not be affected by the internal market or the EMU. The cohesion policy should ensure the necessary stability.

564. It is no coincidence that, in Western Europe, highly productive agricultural areas are situated in the vicinity of large city agglomerations. Compare: Paris and the Parisian basin; London and Essex; the Ruhr valley and Dutch intensive agriculture and horticulture. In contrast, many marginal agricultural areas are situated at the periphery or in sparsely-populated areas. This modifies the inter-relation between the Community's agricultural policy and economic and social cohesion. The relation between transport networks and the development potential of peripheral areas is evident. The development of electronic networks seems, just as that of physical networks, to be an increasingly significant factor. Peripherally-situated Member States such as Finland and Ireland have unmistakeably benefited from this development.

565. See e.g., para. 16 in the preamble to Reg. 1260/1999 (though repealed by Reg. 1083/2006).

The application of the norms in the first and second sentences of Article 159 EC (which entail instructions to achieve or take account of the objectives of Article 158) seems more problematic if the Community actions required by the Treaty prove irreconcilable, or difficult to reconcile, with economic and social cohesion. The Community policy in the field of research and technological development (Articles 163–173 EC) can, for example, lead to a functionally necessary concentration of Community funds being provided in areas of the Community where high-value technological research facilities already exist, or where advanced industry is strongly represented. The distribution of these resources to economically weaker areas of the Community would make such programmes considerably less effective. Nonetheless, the interest in strengthening the competitiveness of European industry on the global market as efficiently as possible regularly comes under pressure from cohesion arguments. Further examples of the misguided invocation of cohesion arguments can be found in environmental policy, where economically weaker Member States stipulate exemptions of a temporary or substantive nature from Community requirements in the area (the drawn-out discussions on energy tax are an example), and in the Community's policy on agricultural *markets*.[566]

The Community's activities under this Title should, of course, be compatible with Community law and the other activities of the Community. Further detail is given to this coordination requirement, which is in one sense the opposite of the specific coordination principle set out in the first and second sentences of Article 159 EC, in Articles 3(1), 16 and 17 of Regulation 1083/2006.[567] In particular, Articles 16 and 17 of Regulation 1083/2006 require the objectives and implementation of the structural funds to be compatible with the Community's policies on, respectively, equality between men and women and non-discrimination and sustainable development, though the requirement is expressed less forcefully in the case of sustainable development.[568]

---

566. There is certainly a direct inter-relation between the evolution of the Community's policy on agricultural markets and the Community's policy on the structural aspect of agriculture, which is led by the Guidance section of the European Agricultural Guidance and Guarantee Fund (EAGGF). Cf. also K.J.M. Mortelmans, 'De "economische en sociale samenhang" en de "Interne Markt": enkele juridische aspecten van een LAT-relatie' (1989), SEW, 774.

567. See Art. 3(1) of Reg. 1083/2006: 'The action taken under the Funds shall incorporate, at national and regional level, the Community's priorities in favour of sustainable development by strengthening growth, competitiveness, employment and social inclusion and by protecting and improving the quality of the environment'.

568. Art. 16 provides: 'The Member States and the Commission shall ensure that equality between men and women and the integration of the gender perspective is promoted during the various stages of implementation of the Funds. The Member States and the Commission shall take appropriate steps to prevent any discrimination based on sex, racial or ethnic origin, religion or belief, disability, age or sexual orientation during the various stages of implementation of the Funds and, in particular, in the access to them. In particular, accessibility for disabled persons shall be one of the criteria to be observed in defining operations co-financed by the Funds and to be taken into account during the various stages of implementation.'; and Art. 17 provides: 'The objectives of the Funds shall be pursued in the framework of sustainable development and the Community promotion of the goal of protecting and improving the environment as set out in Art. 6 of the Treaty.'

The third sentence of Article 159 EC gives a summary of the instruments at the Community's disposal for the achievement of economic and social cohesion: the structural funds (European Agricultural Guidance and Guarantee Fund, Guidance Section; European Social Fund, European Regional Development Fund), the European Investment Bank and the other *existing* financial instruments.[569] The wording of this sentence is somewhat unfortunate, as it seems to contain an exhaustive summary of the instruments available. As Articles 158–162 EC create no general legal basis for the establishment of new funds, a specific legal basis should be sought for this in the EC Treaty, in the absence of which Article 308 EC must be used. As a result, the legal basis for the financing instrument for fisheries guidance, Regulation 1198/2006, was Articles 36 and 37 EC, and not Article 159 EC.[570]

From 1 January 2007, the European Agricultural Guidance and Guarantee Fund, Guidance Section has been replaced by the European Agricultural Fund for Rural Development (EAFRD).[571] This change took place in the context of the 2005 overhaul of the financing of the Community's Common Agricultural Policy (CAP).[572] The legal bases for the Regulation instituting the EAFRD are Articles 36, 37 and 299(2) EC.[573] Interestingly, this change was made despite the apparent limitation flowing from the wording of Articles 159 and 162 EC, which expressly refer to the EAGGF, Guidance section. This may be explained by the intention of the Community legislature to remove rural agricultural funds from the auspices of cohesion policy in its narrow sense, and to consider them from 2007 as part of the single legal framework for financing the CAP. Nonetheless, some tidying-up of the Treaty provisions on this point would serve the interest of clarity. In the period 2000–2006, the structural payments from the EAGGF, Guidance section, amounted to around 30 billion euro, that is to say around 12% of total structural payments. From 2007–2013, Community support for rural development under the EAFRD will amount to around 70 billion.[574]

---

569. Note that, though Art. 159 EC seems to define the 'structural funds' as the EAGGF, guidance section, the ESF and the ERDF, the term is often – and will in this account be – used to include the (subsequently added) Cohesion fund.

570. Reg. 1198/2006 on the European Fisheries Fund, O.J. 2006, L 223/1. This was also the case for the previous fisheries funding instrument, Reg. 2080/93, O.J. 1993, L 193/1, replaced by Reg. 1263/99, O.J. 1999, L 161/54.

571. See Council Reg. (EC) No 1698/2005 of 20 Sep. 2005, in support for rural development by the European Agricultural Fund for Rural Development (EAFRD), O.J. 2005, L 277/1.

572. This overhaul created a single legal framework for the financing of CAP spending, creating two new funds under the general EU budget, the European Agricultural Guarantee Fund (which replaced the EAGGF, Guarantee section) and the EAFRD. See Council Reg. (EC) No. 1290/2005 of 21 Jun. 2005, on the financing of the Common Agricultural Policy, O.J. 2005, L 209/1.

573. See also, Art. 34(3) EC.

574. Council Decision 2006/493 of 19 Jun. 2006, laying down the amount of Community support for rural development for the period from 1 Jan. 2007 to 31 Dec. 2013, its annual breakdown and the minimum amount to be concentrated in regions eligible under the Convergence Objective, O.J. 2006, L 195/22.

The relevant Treaty provisions for the European Social Fund (hereafter: ESF) are now Articles 146–148 EC. The ESF was, prior to the entry into force of the Single European Act, primarily an instrument of the Community social policy.[575] The Single European Act changed this. Since 1988, the activities of the ESF have been incorporated in the Community policy to strengthen economic and social cohesion. Within that framework, however, the ESF's activities are still determined by its mission as defined in Article 146 EC: its aim is 'to render the employment of workers easier and to increase their geographical and occupational mobility within the Community, and to facilitate their adaptation to industrial changes and to changes in production systems, in particular through vocational training and retraining.' It follows from this definition that the activities of the ESF fit the above-mentioned functional definition of the policy to promote economic and social cohesion. The activities of the ESF are now governed by Regulation 1081/2006.[576]

The European Regional Development Fund (ERDF) was established in 1975 on the basis of Article 308 EC.[577] After an initially rather difficult existence, dictated mainly by political horse-trading in the distribution of resources, the ERDF has benefited from new wind in its sails since the beginning of the 1980s, resulting from the introduction of the so-called Integrated Mediterranean Programmes (IMPs) and the Integrated Action Programmes (IAPs), aimed at those regions of the Communities which were faced with stronger competition due to the accession of Portugal and Spain.[578] The instrumental policy effect of these programmes, however, remained rather limited, mainly due to the modest amount of resources available.[579] With the Single European Act, the ERDF was given a place in the Treaty (Art. 160 EC), albeit in the form of the definition of its tasks rather than an explicit legal basis. The ERDF owes its present significance to the agreement reached at the European Council of February 1988 on the so-called Delors triptych.[580] This was also relevant to the amount of resources available to the structural funds and the application of these funds. The ERDF is the largest of the structural funds.

---

575. See, on the activities of the ESF in this period, D.J. Keur, 'Financiële instrumenten en coördinatie van het economisch beleid als bijdragen van de Gemeenschap aan het economisch herstel', (1982), SEW, 267–301, in particular 270–272, and J.V. Louis, J.C. Séché, M. Wolfcarius and Th. Margellos, op. cit., *supra* note 547, 177–179.

576. Reg. (EC) No. 1081/2006 of the European Parliament and of the Council of 5 Jul. 2006, on the European Social Fund and repealing Reg. (EC) No. 1784/1999, O.J. 2006, L 210/12.

577. By Reg. 724/75, O.J. 1975, L 73/1, most recently amended by Reg. (EC) No. 1080/2006 of the European Parliament and of the Council of 5 Jul. 2006, on the European Regional Development Fund and repealing Reg. (EC) No. 1783/1999, O.J. 2006, L 210/1.

578. On this, see D.J. Keur, op. cit., *supra* note 575, 272–276 and K.J.M. Mortelmans, 'Effectiviteit and billijkheid: de GMP's, de GAP's en de hervorming van de Europese structuurfondsen' (1998), SEW, 612–616.

579. See J.V. Louis, J.C. Séché, M. Wolfcarius and Th. Margellos, op. cit., *supra* note 547, 180.

580. K.J.M. Mortelmans, De 'economische en sociale samenhang' en de 'interne markt', op. cit., *supra* note 566, 768–769.

Article 158 EC places an obligation on the Commission to submit a report to the Parliament, the Council, the Economic and Social Committee and the Committee of the Regions every three years on the progress made towards achieving economic and social cohesion. 'Appropriate proposals' may accompany this report. Should specific actions prove necessary outside the funds, they may be adopted by the Council by qualified majority voting.[581] This provision, which was added at a late stage to the Treaty of Maastricht, is worthy of some comment. In the first place, requiring reports to be produced every three years is too high a frequency for the assessment of structural measures such as those concerned here. The process of decision-making, which is necessary to implement important structure-strengthening measures, in itself takes more time than that.[582] In the second place, the presentation of such a report generates, in particular, political pressure to make 'appropriate proposals'. In the third place, the specific measures flowing from the reports must fit financial projections which, for the most important categories of expense, are set out in the Inter-institutional Agreement and the requirements of budgetary discipline.[583] As there is a period of at least five years between reports on the Community's financial perspective, this constitutes a source of conflict between the Parliament and the Council, in which the 'cohesion countries' will decide their own position.

Article 160 EC gives the ERDF an implicit Treaty legal status.[584] Article 161 EC provides for three types of instrument:

(1) defining the tasks, objectives and organization of the structural funds;
(2) defining the general rules applicable to the structural funds; and
(3) ensuring coordination of the structural funds with one another and with the other existing financial instruments.

These provisions are to be enacted by the Council acting unanimously using an abridged form of co-decision procedure.[585] The Lisbon Treaty should change this, as it provides that the 'ordinary legislative procedure' (i.e., what was formerly known as the co-decision procedure) be used, with the Council acting by qualified majority.

---

581. This part of the Art. 159 EC was altered by the Treaty of Nice. Previously, 'specific actions' could only be adopted by unanimity of voting after 'consultation' of the Parliament. The co-decision provision (Art. 251 EC) presently applies.
582. Another difficulty with a time period of three years is that the presentation of the report is distorted by movements of economic cycle.
583. See further Ch. V, section 3.2. *supra.*
584. Strictly speaking, Art. 160 EC does not create a legal basis for the ERDF. The combination of the general regulation and the coordinating regulation (each based on Art. 161 EC) and the Decisions applying the ERDF (based on Art. 132 EC) now covers almost all aspects of the tasks and activities of the Fund. As a result, it is no longer necessary to rely on Art. 308 EC.
585. The Treaty of Nice added a third paragraph to Art. 161 EC, which provides that the Council should act by qualified majority from 1 Jan. 2007.

In 2006, the Council enacted the fourth generation of implementing regulations on the basis of Article 161 EC.[586] This refers to the following regulations:

- Regulation 1083/2006 laying down general provisions on the European Regional Development Fund, the European Social Fund and the Cohesion Fund;[587]
- Regulation 1080/2006 on the European Regional Development Fund;[588]
- Regulation 1081/2006 on the European Social Fund;[589]
- Regulation 1084/2006 establishing a Cohesion Fund;[590] and
- Regulation 1082/2006 on a European grouping of territorial cooperation (EGTC).[591]

One of the aims of the fourth generation reform was to simplify and clarify the role of funding instruments in the rural development and fisheries sectors.[592] To this end, the financial instrument for rural development (formerly EAGGF, Guidance division) was renamed as EAFRD and moved from the auspices of the general structural funds regulation, so that all financing instruments related to rural development policy were grouped in one single instrument financing the CAP.[593] Similarly, the Financial Instrument for Fisheries Guidance (FIFG), which had previously formally formed part of the structural funds, was renamed as the European Fisheries Fund (EFF); all financial instruments relating to the fisheries sector were grouped in a single instrument under the Common Fisheries Policy.[594]

---

586. The first general regulation with implementing regulations dates from 1993 (O.J. 2081/93, O.J. 1993, L 193/5). There is no great substantive difference between the first and the second generation of regulations. This is not the case for the third generation, which diverges significantly from both previous generations in system and in substance. The changes introduced by the fourth generation are primarily formal and structural, rather than substantive. See *infra* 5.3, and, further, J. Bachtler and C. Mendez, 'Who Governs Cohesion Policy? Deconstructing the Reforms of the Structural Funds' (2007), JCMS, 535.

587. Council Reg. (EC) No. 1083/2006 of 11 Jul. 2006, laying down general provisions on the European Regional Development Fund, the European Social Fund and the Cohesion Fund and repealing Reg. (EC) No. 1260/1999, O.J. 2006, L 210/25, as amended.

588. Reg. (EC) No. 1080/2006 of the European Parliament and of the Council of 5 Jul. 2006, on the European Regional Development Fund and repealing Reg. (EC) No. 1783/1999, O.J. 2006, L 210/1.

589. Reg. (EC) No. 1081/2006 of the European Parliament and of the Council of 5.Jul. 2006, on the European Social Fund and repealing Reg. (EC) No. 1784/1999, O.J. 2006, L 210/12.

590. Council Reg. (EC) No. 1084/2006 of 11 Jul. 2006, establishing a Cohesion Fund and repealing Reg. (EC) No. 1164/94, O.J. 2006, L 210/79.

591. Reg. (EC) No. 1082/2006 of the European Parliament and of the Council of 5 Jul. 2006, on a European grouping of territorial cooperation (EGTC), O.J. 2006, L 210/19.

592. See the Commission's Proposal for a Council Regulation laying down general provisions on the European Regional Development Fund, the European Social Fund and the Cohesion Fund, SEC(2004) 924, at para., 4 of the explanatory memorandum.

593. Council Reg. (EC) No. 1698/2005 of 20 Sep. 2005, in support for rural development by the European Agricultural Fund for Rural Development (EAFRD), O.J. 2005, L 277/1.

594. Council Reg. (EC) No. 1198/2006 of 27 Jul. 2006, on the European Fisheries Fund, O.J. 2006, L 223/1.

As noted above, in the run-up to the Treaty of Maastricht, a clear difference of opinion arose between the wealthier and less well-off Member States regarding EMU, which concerned the financial support which less well-off Member States might require in order to be able to fulfil the requirements for admission to the third phase on time.[595] Initially, Germany and the Netherlands, on grounds of principle, rejected outright requests made, particularly by Spain, to add a separate transfer mechanism. At a late stage, it was ultimately decided to complement the instruments for economic and social cohesion with a separate 'Cohesion fund'. The legal basis for this is now to be found in Article 161(2) EC. The form, tasks and methods of application of this fund, which differ from the original structural funds, were reduced into the Protocol on Economic and Social Cohesion.[596] At first, the Cohesion fund was governed by Regulation 1164/94 'establishing a Cohesion fund'.[597] This Regulation was initially applied by Regulation 1264/1999.[598] Following the 2006 'fourth generation' reform of cohesion policy, it is now governed by Regulation 1084/2006 establishing a Cohesion Fund.[599]

In contrast to the 'normal' structural funds, the payments from the Cohesion fund originally went exclusively to the then four 'cohesion countries' – Spain, Greece, Portugal and Ireland – according to an indicative method of apportionment set out in Regulation 1264/1999.[600] Under Regulation 1084/2006, Cohesion fund payments go to the twelve new Member States, as well as Spain,[601] Greece and Portugal.[602] The payments are aimed at investment in transport infrastructure and at improving the environment. In Article 155(1) EC, third indent and Article 175(5) EC, second indent, express reference is made to the Cohesion fund for trans-European networks and environmental investment.

It could be inferred from the history of the creation of the Cohesion fund, which aimed at supporting the less well-off Member States in their efforts to fulfil the EMU convergence criteria, that this financial instrument would disappear as

---

595. J. Cloos et al. (2003), *supra* note 51, 154–158.
596. O.J. 1992, C 191/93.
597. Reg. 1164/94, O.J. 1994, L 130/1. A provisional regulation based on Art. 308 EC was enacted in the form of Reg. 792/93, O.J. 1993, L 79/74, because the delay in ratification of the Treaty of Maastricht made it impossible to establish the Cohesion fund on the basis of Art. 161 EC prior to 31 Dec. 1993.
598. Reg. 1264/1999 of 21 Jun. 1999, amending Reg. 1164/94 establishing a Cohesion fund, O.J. 1999, L 161/57.
599. Council Reg. (EC) No. 1084/2006 of 11 Jul. 2006, establishing a Cohesion Fund and repealing Reg. (EC) No. 1164/94, O.J. 2006, L 210/79.
600. Since then, Ireland no longer fulfils the conditions for the financing of new projects from the Cohesion fund. This country crossed the then cut-off of 90% of the average EC GDP per capita early in the 1990s. On the performance of the four cohesion countries, see F. Barry, 'Economic Integration and Convergence Processes in the EU Cohesion Countries' (2003), JCMS, 897.
601. Spain is included as a beneficiary on a 'transitional and specific' basis only, as a Member State which would have met the threshold of 90% of EU-15 average GDP per capita, but which does not meet the threshold of 90% of EU-25 (or -27) average GDP per capita.
602. See Commission Decision 2006/596 of 4 Aug. 2006, drawing up the list of Member States eligible for funding from the Cohesion Fund for the period 2007–2013, O.J. 2006, L 243/47.

soon as all cohesion countries had been admitted to EMU. Arguments in favour of this approach could be derived from the Protocol on Economic and Social Cohesion and from Article 2(1) of the original Regulation 1164/94, which established a firm link with the achievement of EMU.[603] Against this can be put the fact that the mention of the Cohesion fund in Article 155, 161 and 175 EC seems to indicate a more permanent existence. Be that as it may, the decision at the Berlin European Council of March 1999 on the financial perspectives for the Community for 2000–2006 was that the transfer of resources from the Cohesion fund should be continued. The resources allotted to this fund up until 2006 were substantial: around 40 billion euro. Around 61 billion euro is earmarked for the fund from 2007 to 2013. The resources remain destined for investment in the environment and in trans-European networks.[604]

It is evident that this fund should play a special, if not exclusive, role as regards the newly acceded Member States: for the vast majority, their GDP per capita is far below the current Community average; they will have to make great efforts in order to fulfil the EMU criteria and generally lag far behind in their physical infrastructure and environmental quality. Whether the consequences of these evident facts will be acceptable to the 'old' Member States is, however, unclear. Experience shows that attempts to end or shift existing streams of finance can face major political obstacles.

5.3   THE IMPLEMENTATION OF ECONOMIC AND SOCIAL COHESION

With its decisions of 17 May and 21 June 1999, the Council altered the policy implementing Articles 158/162 EC, which it had applied since 1988, in two respects. First, the Community's activities in rural development were made independent from its policy on the structural funds.[605] As noted above, this approach has been

---

603. An argument for the temporary nature of the Cohesion funds can be drawn from the following passage from the Protocol on Economic and Social Cohesion: 'AGREE that the Cohesion Fund to be set up before 31 Dec. 1993, will provide Community financial contributions to projects in the fields of environment and trans European networks in Member States with a per capita GNP of less than 90% of the Community average which have a programme leading to the fulfilment of the conditions of economic convergence as set out in Art. 104c (now Art. 104 EC).' Art. 6 of Reg. 1164/94 followed this. On the link between EMU and cohesion, see F. Barry and I. Begg, 'EMU and Cohesion' (2003), JCMS, 781.
604. See further, on the application of the Cohesion fund, J.V. Louis, J.C. Séché, M. Wolfcarius and Th. Margellos, op. cit., *supra* note 547, 244–246.
605. The system of legislation implemented in 1988 comprised:
      a. A general framework Regulation which applied to all structural funds, thus including the spatial policy administered via the EAGGF, Guidance division (Reg. 2052/88, O.J. 1988, L 185/9, amended by Reg. 2081/93, O.J. 1993, L 193/5).
      b. A so-called coordinating Regulation, coordinating the activities of the various structural funds (Reg. 4253/88, O.J. 1988, L 374/1, amended by Reg. 2082/93, O.J. 1993, L 193/20);
      c. Specific Regulations for the individual funds. For the ERDF: Reg. 4254/88, O.J. 1988, L 374/15; amended by Reg. 2083/93, O.J. 1993, L 193/34. For the ESF: Reg. 4255/88,

reinforced by the 2006 wave of legislation, notably the institution of the EAFRD as the single financial instrument for rural development, to replace the EAGGF, Guidance division. In parallel with this, the aims of the Community's structural policy were reduced in 1999 to three principal aims. Second, the geographic scope of application of the spatial structural policy became more concentrated on the areas with substantial economic disadvantages. In contrast, the substantive scope of application became broader, as activities were considered for Community support which would not previously have come under typical spatial policy, such as education, vocational education and training. This has also been continued by the 2006 reforms.

The arguments for such changed were, at first sight, convincing. As indicated above (see 5.2), there is an inseparable link between market-related agricultural policy and structural agricultural policy.[606] This link is emphasized by the decision in the most recent reform to combine funding for the two areas into a single financial instrument.[607] It is also evident from the preamble to Regulation 1698/2005 on the EAFRD, recital 1 of which states that a rural development policy should 'accompany and complement' the market and income support policies of the CAP and thus contribute to achieving the CAP's objectives as laid down in the Treaty. The preamble also notes that rural development policy should 'take into account the general objectives for economic and social cohesion policy set out in the Treaty and contribute to their achievement.'[608]

In our view, another forceful argument exists for the separation, in principle, of structural agricultural or rural policy and the Community's spatial-economic policy. The Community is competent for the Community Agricultural Policy in its totality. This means that the Community itself can ensure consistency between interventions in the field of its market-related agricultural policy and its structural agricultural policy.[609] The Community's regional economic policy is, in contrast, complementary to the Member States' economic and regional economic policies. This requires a clearly different type form of preparation, planning and implementation of Community interventions. Such differences are also evident in the

---

O.J. 1988, L 374/21, amended by Reg. 2084/93, O.J. 1993, L 193/39. For the EAGGF, Guidance division: Reg. 4256/88, O.J. 1988, L 374/25, amended by Reg. 22085/93, O.J. 1993, L 193/44. In 1993, a separate structural fund for fisheries was added: Reg. 2080/93, O.J. 1993, L 193/44.

606. This relationship has already been noted by H.M.C. Gonzales, 'Het EG-landbouwstructuurbeleid: een integrerend deel van het gemeenschappelijk landbouwbeleid' (1997), SEW, 7–18.

607. The link was also emphasized in para. 9 of the preamble of Reg. 1257/1999 on the EAGGF (the precursor to EAFRD), where it is, in essence, stated that structural agricultural policy should, in principle, apply to all rural areas of the Community. The preamble expressly contemplates coordination with regional economic policy, as (then) governed by Reg. 1260/99: see, amongst others, paras 45–49 of the preamble of Reg. 1257/1999.

608. See Council Reg. (EC) No. 1698/2005 of 20 Sep. 2005, on support for rural development by the European Agricultural Fund for Rural Development (EAFRD), O.J. 2005, L 277/1.

609. These consistencies were at issue in Case C-321/99 P, *ARAP v. Commission*, in which tensions between the regulation of the sugar market and Portugal's rural development led to legal complications.

structure and application of the rural policy in Regulation 1698/2005, compared to that of Regulation 1083/2006 on the ERDF, ESF and Cohesion fund.

We will concentrate below on spatial-economic policy. For an account of rural policy, see Chapter XII, section 2.4.

5.3.1   Aims and Means

The aims, means and specific tasks of the different structural funds are described in Articles 1, 3 and 4 of Regulation 1083/2006. There are three funds which are governed by this Regulation: the ERDF, the ESF and the Cohesion fund.

The total sum available under the structural funds, around 380 billion euro, is to be distributed towards three aims: Convergence, Regional Competitiveness and Employment, and Territorial Cooperation. These objectives supersede the former Objectives 1, 2 and 3 for the 2000–2006 programming period.

The *Convergence* objective is similar to the former Objective 1. It concerns the development and structural adaptation of underdeveloped regions.[610] Around 251 billion euro, or over 81% of the total structural funds budget, has been allotted to this objective. Financing may be provided under this objective from any of the three funds governed by Regulation 1083/2006. In order to qualify for funding under this objective, the following criteria must be satisfied:

- To qualify for funding from the ERDF and ESF, the per capita GDP of the region must be below 75% of the Community average.[611] This category of region will receive around 70% of the total funds allocated to the Convergence objective.[612]
- To qualify for funding from the Cohesion Fund, the per capita Gross National Income of the Member State must be below 90% of the Community average and the Member State must be operating an economic convergence programme. Around 23% of the total allocation for the Convergence objective will be given to such Member States.[613]
- Specific ERDF funding is also available for the outermost regions (which include the Azores and the French Overseas Departments).

In contrast to first and second generation regulations, the scope of application of the Convergence objective is strictly delimited: regions in which the income per

---

610. See Art. 5 of Reg. 1083/2006.
611. The region must also be categorized at 'NUTS II' level, according to the common classification system developed by the Commission for regions, laid down in Reg. (EC) No. 1059/2003 of the European Parliament and of the Council of 26 May 2003, on the establishment of a common classification of territorial units for statistics (NUTS), O.J. 2003, L 154/1.
612. In addition, those regions where the per capita GDP would have been below 75% of the Community average in an EU of 15, but is no longer below the threshold in an EU of 27, will receive around 5% of the total Convergence allocation on a transitional basis.
613. As for the ERDF and ESF, transitional digressive financing applies to those regions who would have qualified for payments in an EU of 15.

head of population is more than 75% of the Community average are not considered for Community support under the Convergence objective.

The *Regional Competitiveness and Employment* objective aims at strengthening the competitiveness and employment levels of regions other than those which are the most disadvantaged. Regulation 1083/2006 specifies that this should be achieved, 'by anticipating economic and social changes, including those linked to the opening of trade, through the increasing and improvement of the quality of investment in human capital, innovation and the promotion of the knowledge society, entrepreneurship, the protection and improvement of the environment, and the improvement of accessibility, adaptability of workers and businesses as well as the development of inclusive job markets'.[614] It is financed by the ERDF and the ESF.[615] Around 49 billion euro, or just under 16% of total funds available, are allocated to this objective, divided equally between the ERDF and the ESF. The following regions are eligible for funding under this objective:

- regions which fell under Objective 1 during the period 2000–06, but which no longer meet the regional eligibility criteria of the Convergence objective, and which consequently benefit from transitional support (such regions will receive around 21% of the total funding for this objective);[616]
- all other regions of the Community not covered by the Convergence objective, which will receive around 79% of the total funding for this objective.

The objective of European *Territorial Cooperation* is to strengthen cross-border, trans-national and inter-regional cooperation, particularly in the fields of urban, rural and coastal development, the development of economic relations and the creation of networks of small and medium-sized enterprises.[617] It is based on the former INTERREG funding initiative, and is financed by the ERDF. Regions eligible comprise regions situated along internal land borders, certain external land borders and certain regions situated along maritime borders separated by a maximum of 150 km.[618] As is the case for the other objectives, the Commission has by decision set down the list of regions eligible under this objective.[619]

---

614. Reg. 1083/2006, Art. 3(2).
615. See Art. 6 of Reg. 1083/2006.
616. See the list drawn up by the Commission: Commission Decision 2006/597 of 4 Aug. 2006, drawing up the list of regions eligible for funding from the Structural Funds on a transitional and specific basis under the Regional competitiveness and employment objective for the period 2007–2013, O.J. 2006, L 243/49.
617. See Art. 7 of Reg. 1083/2006.
618. The region must also be classified as NUTS III level, according to the common classification system developed by the Commission for regions, laid down in Reg. (EC) No. 1059/2003 of the European Parliament and of the Council of 26 May 2003, on the establishment of a common classification of territorial units for statistics (NUTS), O.J. 2003, L 154/1.
619. Commission Decision 2006/769 of 31 Oct. 2006, drawing up the list of regions and areas eligible for funding from the European Regional Development Fund under the cross-border and trans-national strands of the European territorial cooperation objective for the period 2007 to 2013, O.J. 2006, L 312/47.

7.75 billion euro is available for this objective, amounting to just under 3% of the total cohesion funds available. Insofar as the geographic centre of gravity for payments from the ERDF and ESF duplicates the 'cohesion countries' under this objective, there is a risk that the stream of Community resources will exceed the absorption capacity of such Member States. As a result, it is provided that the total amount that every Member State can receive from the structural funds and the Cohesion fund cannot exceed a certain percentage of their GDP annually (around 3.5%, though the figure varies according to the percentage which the Member State's GNI per capita between 2001 and 2003 represents of the EU-25 average).[620] The relatively poorest countries (40% or less of the EU-25 average) have the highest maximum level of total contributions (3.7893%).

The Convergence objective is, in its tenor and form, a classic spatial-economic aim. This is not quite the case for the Regional Competitiveness and Employment objective, which includes a serious of diverging sub-aims, such as increasing and improving the quality of investment in human capital. Such a broad definition of aims seems to risk watering down the geographic rationale of the cohesion policy, as one could, in principle, find areas which satisfy such a definition almost everywhere in the Community, aside from those regions covered by the Convergence objective, which are expressly excluded from the scope of the Regional Competitiveness and Employment objective. Indeed, the Commission decision fixing Member States' allocations under this objective specifies that 14 of the 15 'old' Member States qualify for funding under the objective (with the exception of Greece, which benefits from funding under the Convergence objective).[621] In total, 16 of the 27 Member States qualify, and 9 Member States qualify on a specific and transitional basis.

The operation of the Convergence and Regional Competitiveness and Employment objectives is explicitly intended to be consistent with and complement the Community's growth and employment objectives, and the Community's other activities in these fields, including the European Employment Strategy. To that end, Regulation 1083/2006 requires the Commission and the Member States to ensure that 60% of expenditure for the Convergence objective and 75% of expenditure for the Regional Competitiveness and Employment objective for the 'old' 15 Member States is allocated to promoting competitiveness and creating jobs, and to meeting the objectives of the Integrated Guidelines for Growth and Jobs (2005 to 2008).[622] Member States which acceded to the Union after 1 May 2004 may decide to apply this provision 'at their own initiative'.[623] It can nonetheless be implied that the aims of the funds granted to the new Member States under the Convergence

---

620. Reg. 1083/2006 of 11 Jul. 2006, laying down general provisions on the European Regional Development Fund, the European Social Fund and the Cohesion Fund and repealing Reg. (EC) No. 1260/1999, O.J. 2006, L 210/25, Annex II, paras. 7.
621. Commission Decision 2006/593 of 4 Aug. 2006, fixing an indicative allocation by Member State of the commitment appropriations for the Regional competitiveness and employment objective for the period 2007–2013, O.J. 2006, L 243/32.
622. Reg. 1083/2006, Art. 9(3).
623. Ibid.

objective include contributing to the Community's employment policy. If this were not the case, then this policy would not be supported in those regions with the greatest employment problems. This would be in conflict with the tenor of the employment guidelines based on Article 128 EC.[624]

The *preoccupation with the politics of distribution*, which lies at the heart of spatial-economic policy, is expressed in Article 18(2) of Regulation 1083/2006. By this provision, the Commission proposes the indicative breakdowns, in accordance with the criteria set down in Annex II of the Regulation, of the commitment appropriations of the structural funds. These indicative breakdowns are less informal than the term 'indicative' might suggest. In particular, in the elaboration of the programmes, they are to a large extent binding, as the Commission found in a case brought by Italy under the previous generation of legislation, Case C-107/99.[625] There are numerous elements, set out in Annex II of the Regulation, which the Commission must take into account in drawing up its indicative breakdowns. The drafting of these breakdowns offers plenty of scope to arrive at a result which is consistent with the global political accord reached at the European Council in Brussels, May 2006 concerning expenditure of structural funds.[626]

It follows from the system of Regulation 1083/2006 that proposals for programmes and projects must come from the Member States. To avoid a situation where the Commission is overloaded with proposals on which it must give an opinion, Articles 25 and 26 of the Regulation provide that the Commission, after consultation of all Member States, shall issue indicative guidelines (the 'Community Strategic Guidelines on Cohesion'), which identify the Community priorities to be supported by cohesion policy and set out possible synergies with the Lisbon strategy for growth and employment. These guidelines are to be considered as pointers for the Member States which they may take into account in selecting and drawing up actions to put forward to receive a sum from the structural funds.[627] On the basis of these guidelines, each Member State must present a 'national strategic reference framework' covering the Convergence and Regional Competitiveness and Employment objectives from the period 2007 to 2013.[628]

---

624. Council Decision 2006/544 of 18 Jul. 2006, on guidelines for the employment policies of the Member States, O.J. 2006, L 215/26.
625. Case C-107/99, *Italy v. Commission*.
626. The Commission has since made the indicative breakdowns for the three objectives known: Commission Decision 2006/594 of 4 Aug. 2006, fixing an indicative allocation by Member State of the commitment appropriations for the Convergence objective for the period 2007–2013, O.J. 2006, L 243/37; Commission Decision 2006/593 of 4 Aug. 2006, fixing an indicative allocation by Member State of the commitment appropriations for the Regional competitiveness and employment objective for the period 2007–2013, O.J. 2006, L 243/32; Commission Decision 2006/609 of 4 Aug. 2006, fixing an indicative allocation by Member State of the commitment appropriations for the European territorial cooperation objective for the period 2007–2013, O.J. 2006, L 247/26.
627. See Council Decision 2006/702 of 6 Oct. 2006, on Community strategic guidelines on cohesion, O.J. 2006, L 291/11.
628. Art. 27, Reg. 1083/2006. Member States can choose to cover the European Territorial Cooperation objective as well in their national strategic reference framework.

These frameworks must be approved by the Commission. They serves as reference instruments in preparing programming of the funds covered by Regulation 1083/ 2006 and ensure that this programming is consistent with the Community Strategic Guidelines. Subsequently, Member States are to prepare an operational programme for each of the three objectives, which also cover the period 2007–2013.

Article 12(4) of Regulation 1083/2006 requires the Commission and the Member States to ensure the coordination of the actions of the various structural funds, the EIB and the Community's general financial instruments. This coordination not only concerns the question of which fund(s) should be used for a particular action, but also the composition of the intervention (subsidies *à fonds perdu*, loans and/or guarantees).

One extremely difficult issue is the compatibility of this with the existing legislative requirements which regulate the market order and hence market actors' behaviour. This issue also arises for national policy initiatives with financial means. The principle that Community intervention may not conflict with the Treaty and decisions based on the Treaty – including, amongst others, competition policy – is laid down in Article 12 of Regulation 1260/99. This principle, in our view, applies not only to individual actions supported in the framework of economic and social cohesion. It also applies to the normative decisions elaborating this policy and the application given to the policy. This is not easy to achieve in practice, as is evident from Case C-321/99 P, *ARAP v. Commission*. We will return to this requirement of compatibility below, in section 5.3.4 below.

5.3.2   General Principles

Regulation 1083/2006, provides for four main general principles for the application of the structural funds:[629]

5.3.2.1   *The Additionality Principle*

Community action with the structural funds and with other financial instruments would be largely ineffective if this tried to replace already-existent national policy with the same or comparable aims. As a result, Article 15 of Regulation 1083/2006 provides that Community action shall not replace public or equivalent structural expenditure by a Member State. The following paragraphs of this article indicate how the structural level of national expenditure must be decided upon.

There are a quite a few snags with the operation of the additionality principle in practice. As long as the level of structural expenditure in a Member State for a

---

629. Additional general principles of implementation set out in Reg. 1083/2006 are: the territorial (Member State) level of implementation (Art. 12); the principle that Community intervention should be proportionate to the amount of expenditure allocated to an operational programme (Art. 13); the principle of financial management of the funds shared between the Member States and the Commission (Art. 14); the principle of equality between men and women and non-discrimination (Art. 16), and the principle of sustainable development (Art. 17).

certain type of regional economic or labour market policy remains stable, or develops in line with current trends, it is not difficult to decide that the contribution from the structural funds is clearly complementary to national intervention. However, if a Member State reduces its national efforts shortly before the Community contribution is decided upon, this is not so easy to determine. In such a situation, the risk is great that the 'extra' Community contribution will replace the reduction in national efforts.[630] To allay that risk, Article 15 provides that the Commission will draw up a methodological paper indicating precisely how the structural national expenditure level must be decided upon and which exceptional circumstances can give rise to a justified deviation from that level. To avoid a situation that Member States might reduce their level of expenditure during the period of the six-year programme, Article 15(4) of Regulation 1083/2006 provides for a mid-term test in the course of the programme.[631]

5.3.2.2   The Complementarity Principle

This principle is set out in Article 9(1) of Regulation 1083/2006. It states that the Community's contribution is intended as a – sometimes very substantial – complement to national action. This supposes in each case that there is a national or regional or even local complement to the Community's contribution. The intention of the complementarity principle is to avoid a situation in which the Community's actions in the national sphere might become less effective. If a real and sometimes substantial contribution from the Member States is required, these States will be more critical and more selective in their proposals for programmes. Programmes where no authority in the national sphere considers themselves a 'co-owner' do not, as a result, receive the attention they deserve.

Just as with the additionality principle, there are certain snags in the operation of the complementarity principle. As long as the total volume of Community transfers for the individual Member States remains relatively limited, there will be in general few problems of co-financing.[632] At the most, national policy aims

---

630. Case C-193/02, *Netherlands v. Commission*, later withdrawn, was based on facts which created the impression that the Netherlands 'compensated' for a very substantial budgetary deficit in public labour provisions, laid down in the agreement on government of the first Kok cabinet, with contributions from the ESF. See further, for background, R. Barents, 'Nederland en de subsidies uit het Europees Sociaal Fonds' (2001), NTER, 305–310.

631. The European Court of Auditors published a critical investigation into the application of the additionality principle over the period 1989–1999 by the Commission and the Member States, which analysed the problems of application in depth. This report shows how difficult it is to apply what is, in itself, a clear principle in a national policy environment which is far from transparent. Court of Auditors, Special Report no. 6/99 on the additionality principle, O.J. 2000, C 68/1.

632. If a Member State, in its own financial planning, does not adequately take into account the co-financing obligations flowing from the complementarity principle, it can be the case that the Member State cannot make use of the Community resources reserved for it. This happened in the summer of 1996, to the then Dutch Secretary of State for Economic Affairs, Van Dok-van Weelen. The available resources for national spatial-economic policy had already been

need only be slightly altered to fulfil the requirements of complementarity. This is not the case, however, if the Community transfers for favoured Member States become relatively more substantial: if the total collective expenditure of a Member State amounts to around half of GDP, a contribution of 3.5% of GDP from the structural funds amounts to a share of 7% of the Member State's total budget. In such cases, finding the necessary national resources for co-financing may require a considerable re-organization of national collective payments. To avoid such shifts in priority for national collective payments, Community regional programmes provide for a progressive Community share of expenditure, which can be up to 85% of the total expenditure on programmes for the outermost regions or 80% for regions in Member States covered by the Cohesion Fund.

5.3.2.3   *The Programming Principle*

Initially, the Community funds mainly financed individual projects. The consistency of Community interventions between themselves, and their consistency with national interventions, did not work well. With the adoption of the Integrated Mediterranean Programmes and the Integrated Action Programmes at the beginning of the 1980s, the Commission tried for the first time to give these activities a programmatic character, in order to strengthen their consistency with each other.[633] This programmatic approach was retained in the revision of the structural funds, and is continued and further detailed, in the light of experience since 1988, in Articles 13–19 of Regulation 1260/99 and, subsequently, Article 10 and Articles 32–46 of Regulation 1083/2006.

The procedure for finalizing the programmes (which are officially termed 'operational programmes') is, to a large extent, set out in Articles 37–46 of Regulation 1083/2006. A distinction is made between finalizing operational programmes for the Convergence and Regional Competitiveness and Employment objectives (covered by Article 37) and operational programmes for the European Territorial Cooperation objective (covered by Article 38).

In the case of operational programmes for the Convergence and Regional Competitiveness and Employment objectives – the basis for which is set out by Member States in the national strategic reference framework, discussed above – Article 37 sets out a wide-ranging series of substantive requirements and criteria for the programmes, which allow the Commission to make a thorough *ex ante* and *ex post* evaluation of them. The programmes set out the Member States' strategy, priorities and specific aims, as well as the intended measures, an indicative financing plan and the provisions for the execution and control of the programmes. The Member States must submit these operational programmes to the Commission for approval. The Commission has the task of determining whether they contribute to

---

distributed to such an extent that the financial scope for co-financing was, in the most part, exhausted. This compelled substantial amendment of national policy.

633.   K.J.M. Mortelmans, Effectiviteit and billijkheid, op. cit., *supra* note 578, 612–616.

the goals and priorities of the national strategic reference framework and the Community strategic guidelines on cohesion.[634]

In the case of operational programmes for the European Territorial Cooperation objective, the procedure for their submission is contained in Regulation 1080/2006 on the ERDF, and not in the general Regulation 1083/2006.[635] However, the requirements for Member States to fulfil in drawing up these operational programmes are broadly similar. Aside from the above procedures for the so-called regular programmes, Regulation 1083/2006 also provides for separate procedures for so-called 'major' projects,[636] financial engineering instruments, and technical assistance in implementing the Regulation.

5.3.2.4 Partnership

It follows from the above that the Community's actions are decided after close discussion between the Commission and the competent national, regional or local authorities, whose details are provided by the Member State. This 'partnership' is detailed in Article 11 of Regulation 1083/2006. This provision expressly indicates that partnership respects the respective institutional, legal and financial competences of each partner completely. As a result, the Commission need not express a view on the relationship between different parts of the administration in the different Member States.

5.3.3 Management, Monitoring and Financial Control

Just as financial transfers between levels of government in the national sphere are vulnerable to abuse, improper use, and ineffective application, this can also be the case for the very substantial financial transfers which take place in the framework of economic and social cohesion.[637] In comparison with the problems which arise at national level, the difficulties at Community level are much greater, as national organization and practices in executing the programmes differ greatly, and as the Community cannot intervene directly in the national sphere.

As a result, and based on past experience, Regulation 1083/2006 provides for broad supervisory rules in order to ensure the effectiveness of the Community's financial support.[638] Member States must, for each Community finance packet,

---

634. Art. 32(4) of Reg. 1083/2006.
635. Reg. (EC) No. 1080/2006 of the European Parliament and of the Council of 5 Jul. 2006, on the European Regional Development Fund and repealing Reg. (EC) No. 1783/1999, O.J. 2006, L 210/1, Art. 12.
636. A major project is defined in Art. 39 of Reg. 1083/2006 as an operation 'comprising a series of works, activities or services intended in itself to accomplish an indivisible task of a precise economic or technical nature, which has clearly identified goals and whose total cost exceeds EUR 25 million in the case of the environment and EUR 50 million in other fields.'
637. See also Ch. V, section 3.3, *supra* on the protection of the financial interests of the Community.
638. Arts. 58–73 of Reg. 1083/2006.

designate a so-called managing authority, which is responsible for managing and implementing the relevant programme in accordance with the principles of sound financial management. This managing authority also looks after the necessary legal and other affairs for the execution of the programmes. A certifying authority and audit authority must also be set up for each operational programme. The certifying authority is tasked with certifying statements of expenditure and applications for payment before they are sent to the Commission. The function of the audit authority, which must be functionally independent of the managing authority and the certifying authority, is to verify the effective functioning of the management and control system of the operational programme. The managing authority is required to submit an annual report and a final report on the implementation of the operational programme.

In addition, Member States must designate a monitoring committee, which is has the task of ensuring the effectiveness and quality of the implementation of the operational programme. A representative of the Commission may participate in an advisory capacity in the monitoring committee.

The Member States are responsible, in the first instance, for the financial control of the finance packet. They guarantee the quality of the financial management system and the way in which the financial resources provided to them are spent. They work together with the Commission to ensure that the Community resources are spent in a manner compatible with the principle of good financial management.[639] In addition, the Commission has its own powers of control. The exercise of these competences can lead to sanctions, such as suspending interim payments, reducing advance payments or withdrawing finance provided by the funds.[640]

In the past, frequent disputes arose between the Commission and Member States, or between individuals and the Commission, concerning the execution and financial management of programmes. This has given rise to a substantial body of jurisprudence. It is notable that the Court of Justice and the Court of First Instance apply the procedural requirements for monitoring operational programmes strictly.[641]

5.3.4   Coordination

Regulation 1083/2006 contains a number of provisions to ensure the substantive coordination of Community activity in the narrow sense (contributions from the funds and other Community financial instruments) and in the broad sense (Community policy in other Community areas such as employment, environment, competition and equal treatment for men and women). These provisions may have the character of negative coordinating provisions, such as the requirement that a

---

639. Art. 70 and *infra*, Reg. 1083/2006.
640. See e.g., Arts. 91 and 92 of Reg. 1083/2006.
641. See, amongst others: Case C-291/89, *Interhotel v. Commission*; Case C-199/91, *Foyer Culturel de Sart-Tilman*; Case C-443/97, *Spain v. Commission*; Case C-158/06, *Stichting ROM-projecten v. Staatssecretaris van Economische Zaken*.

certain programme or zone may only fall under one objective at any given time,[642] or the so-called anti-cumulation provisions, which prevent a project being financed by a number of Community sources at the same time.[643] They can also have a positive tenor, such as providing that national strategic reference frameworks drawn up by Member States must expressly consider their compatibility with the Community's Integrated Guidelines for Growth and Jobs.[644] Further analysis of the numerous and sometimes unclear substantive coordination provisions of the regulations, and their legal nature, which is also at times unclear, goes beyond the scope of the present account. We will confine ourselves to the observation that, in particular, the positive coordination obligations can lead to the accumulation of aims in the programmes, which can make it even more difficult to assess and execute them.

The institutional structure of the decision-making process also aims at contributing to substantive consistency. Articles 103 and 104 of Regulation 1083/2006 provide that the Commission is assisted by two committees in executing the Regulation, a committee to coordinate the funds, and a committee set up as required by the Treaty provisions on the European Social Fund, which includes representatives of governments, trade unions and employers' organizations. This is an improvement on the previous regime under Regulation 1260/99, by which four committees assisted the Commission, which led to organizational fragmentation rather than consistency.

5.3.5   Categorization of Economic and Social Cohesion as a Policy Coordination System

Articles 158–162 EC are a typical result of incremental Treaty-making. They were inserted by the Single European Act, subsequently modified and added to by the Treaties of Maastricht, Amsterdam and Nice, where other political aims weighed more heavily than the consistency, transparency and unambiguousness of the Community measures to be taken on the basis of this Title. They gave rise to a collection of different Community funds, for which different decision-making procedures applied. The lack of attunement between Articles 161 and 162 EC is particularly notable.[645] The major substantive and political interests involved in the Community's spatial-economic policy demand a legal basis which ensures more unity and consistency of the Community's interventions and transfers.

In over 20 years since Title XVII was introduced, the policy carried out on this basis has intensified, because the resources available have increased considerably.

---

642. E.g., funding under the Regional Competitiveness and Employment objective is conditional on not being eligible for funding under the Convergence objective.

643. See e.g., Art. 34 of Reg. 1083/2006.

644. Art. 27(4), Reg. 1083/2006.

645. Art. 161 EC, first sentence, raises the possibility of grouping funds, but this option is, at last for the ERDF, the ESF, the EAGGF, Guidance division, and the Cohesion fund, purely theoretical, because the Treaty authors did not deal with this possibility in the Treaty provisions, which apply specifically to these funds. Art. 162 EC should also have been drafted in that light.

They amount at present to just under 36% of the total Community budget, that is to say, 308 billion euro. At the same time, the substantive scope of cohesion policy has increased. In addition to classic spatial-economic aims, other – in particular socio-economic – aims increasingly play a role. Experience with the regional and structural 'Fondsverwaltung'[646] in Member States has shown that decision-making in this policy area is to a large extent asymmetrical: decisions to intensify and broaden the financial transfer policy are easily taken, but decisions to reduce payments and restrict their scope face great political and social opposition. This risk increases insofar as the economically weaker Member States have a greater influence on decision-making.[647] The influence which the Community can, via the structural funds, exercise on Member State policy is unmistakeably limited by the resultant rigidities. As decision-making is so sharply focused on the interests of the politics of distribution, it becomes almost unavoidably introverted. However much the text of Regulation 1083/2006 emphasizes consistency with other Community policy areas, in the outcome of the decision-making process, the Member States pay most attention to their net balance. The spending of the Community's resources is quickly subordinated to this, a phenomenon which also damages the quality of the Community's control.

All of this reduces the potential policy effectiveness which Community transfers can have, which is not to be underestimated. This is particularly so if account is taken of the complementarity principle which requires co-financing from Member States. It can be concluded from the overview of the principles upon which the Community policy is based, and from the institutional structure of decision-making, that the policy does indeed have a *vertical coordinating effect*, but also in its organization has many *cooperative* features.[648] These features are to be seen in every stage of the decision-making process. They can be characterized by the partnership principle of Article 11 of Regulation 1083/2006. The advantages of the intensive involvement of the Member States and of their regional and local authorities in the preparation, structuring and execution of programmes is evident. The difficulties of this – the risk that national aspects will outflank the Community's control – seem insufficiently acknowledged in the literature. This can mean that policy coordination loses its effectiveness from a Community perspective.[649]

---

646. Management of funds.
647. This risk was clearly highlighted by in 1988, F.W. Scharpf, 'The Joint Decision Trap: Lessons from German Federalism and European Integration' (1988), *Public Administration*, 239–278. Experience with Title XVII has confirmed his fears. See also, F.W. Scharpf, *Regieren in Europa, Effektiv und demokratisch?* (Franfurt/New York 1999), 70–80.
648. Vertical coordination with strong cooperative features has become a very normal phenomenon in federal states. Initially, federal governments could influence states' policy unilaterally and intensively with financial transfers. Subsequently, states reacted to this by demanding greater influence on the federal 'Fondsverwaltung'. This phenomenon led in Germany to an important change in the Grundgesetz in 1989. See further, amongst others, S. Marnitz, *Die Gemeinschaft-saufgaben des Artikels 91a GG als Versuch einer verfassungsrechtlichen Institutionalisierung der bundesstaatlichen Kooperation*, (Berlin, 1974).
649. This is confirmed by two analyses by the Dutch Centraal Planbureau (Netherlands Bureau for Economic Policy Analysis): 'Funds and Games, The Economics of European Cohesion

5.4 THE EUROPEAN INVESTMENT BANK (EIB)[650]

The Treaty of Maastricht had three consequences for the EIB. The EIB is referred to in the first part of the EC Treaty, at Article 9 (though this article is deleted by the Lisbon Treaty). The provisions which had been of relevance to the bank in the EEC Treaty (Articles 129 and 130 EEC) were transferred from the part on Community policy to the (fifth) part, which governs the institutions: present Articles 266 and 267 EC. The present Article 267 EC was extended with a paragraph corresponding to the third sentence of Article 159 EC, in which the EIB is designated as one of the instruments to achieve economic and social (and, following the Lisbon Treaty, 'territorial') cohesion. Since the promotion of the development potential of the weaker areas within the Community has become one of the Community's central tasks, the political and policy interest of the role which the EIB can play in this has increased greatly. This increased attention is not only expressed in Article 159 EC and in the general and coordinating rules referred to in Article 161 EC; it is also apparent from the role attributed to the EIB, pursuant to the decisions of the Edinburgh European Council of 11 and 12 December 1992, in financing major infrastructure projects in the Member States. Although Article 154(1) EC does not expressly refer to the EIB, the potential contribution of the bank to the financing of trans-European networks for transport of goods, energy and telecommunications is highly significant.[651]

The definition of the EIB's tasks in Article 267 EC refers, on the one hand, to Article 2 EC, 'the balanced and steady development of the common market' and, on the other hand, to Articles 158–162 EC (cf. Art. 267(a), (b) and the last paragraph) and Articles 154–156 EC (cf. Art. 267(a) EC).

The means whereby the EIB performs its tasks are by making loans and giving guarantees. To do this, it relies on the capital market and on its own resources. After the latest enlargement in 2007, the EIB's subscribed capital stood at 164.8 billion euro, which is provided by the Member States (cf. Art. 4, Statute of the EIB), but of which only a – small – percentage is paid-up. The aggregate amount outstanding at any time of loans and guarantees granted by the Bank can be up to 250% of its subscribed capital, i.e., over 400 billion euro.[652] In 2006, the EIB provided 45.8 billion euro in support, with the vast majority (87%) of that amount going to the present Member States.

Policy' (The Hague, 2002), and 'Fertile Soil for Structural Funds? A Panel Data Analysis of the Conditional Effectiveness of European Cohesion Policy', CPB Discussion Paper no. 10, The Hague, 2002.

650. Compare J. Müller-Borle, in H. von der Groeben, et al., op. cit. *supra* note 81 Baden-Baden, (1997), 4/1244–1408; D.R.R. Dunnett, 'The European Investment Bank: Autonomous Instrument of Common Policy?' (1994), CML Rev., 721–763.

651. See also in this regard the conclusions of the Essen European Council of Dec. 1994, which assigned a major role to the EIB in the financing of trans-European networks.

652. Art. 18(5) of the Statute of the EIB.

The EIB is a Community organ possessing legal personality, which is autonomous within the limits indicated in the Treaty and in its Statutes.[653] This autonomy is a necessary condition in order for the bank to function as a credit institution: only in this way is it able to provide the most favourable possible conditions for borrowers on a lasting basis. This necessary financial and technical autonomy sets functional limits to the extent to which the activity of the EIB can be coordinated in the framework of Articles 155 and 159 EC using other Community instruments.[654]

Although the EIB operates according to strict banking requirements and rules, and all projects for which its co-financing is requested are evaluated in accordance with these requirements, the possibility of resorting to the EIB is, for most prospective borrowers within the economically weaker parts of the Community, attractive. As the EIB is an institution which does not aim at making profit, and as it can attract relatively cheap external resources due to its reputation (triple A rating), it can provide finance on relatively favourable terms. This attractiveness brings with it the danger of distorting competition on the capital markets and an over-reliance on the lending capacity of the EIB. As a result, Article 267 EC provides for a two-part hurdle:

(1) Financing by the EIB is always part financing (it 'facilitates' financing; see also Art. 18(2), Statute of the EIB).
(2) Recourse can only be made to the EIB if the relevant projects, by virtue of their scope and nature, cannot be entirely financed by the resources available to each of the relevant Member States. This restriction is only added by Article 267 EC for the objectives listed under (b) and (c) of that article. Pursuant to Article 18 of the Statute of the EIB, it applies equally to all of the bank's financing.

It follows from the principle that the EIB operates according to banking standards that the bank will only finance *projects*. This must be taken into account when coordinating the activity of the bank with that of the structural funds, which provide for a programmatic approach on the basis of the general Regulation 1083/2006.

Article 267 EC shows that the EIB's financing activity extends to 'all sectors of the economy'. This phrase should be interpreted broadly, as the public supply side of the market is broader than strictly 'economic' infrastructure. If it can be shown that the relevant investment is sufficiently profitable from a macro-economic perspective, then environmental investment and investment in education infrastructure can also be considered for EIB financing.[655]

---

653. The two-faceted character of the EIB as an autonomous legal person and as an organization forming part of the Community is confirmed in the consistent case law of the Court. See: Case 110/75, *Mills v. EIB*; Case 85/86, *Governing Council of the EIB*; Case C-370/89, *Société Générale d'Entreprises Electro-Mécaniques and Roland Etroy v. European Investment Bank* and, more recently, Case C-449/99 P, *European Investment Bank v. Michel Hautem*.
654. Compare Case 85/86, *Governing Council of the EIB*. See further, D.R.R. Dunnett, op. cit., *supra* note 650, 750–754.
655. J. J. Müller-Borle, op. cit., *supra* note 650 4/1273.

Up until 1994, the vast majority of the EIB's activities consisted of providing loans. This has changed. The 1992 Edinburgh European Council, already mentioned, decided to establish the European Investment Fund (EIF).[656] This fund, in which the EIB and private capital providers participate, has as its task the provision of *guarantees* on loans to smaller and medium-sized enterprises and the provision of venture capital. This fund of 3 billion euro can, with a 'leverage' of 1 to 8, generate a lending capacity of 24 billion ECU on the standard capital market.

Very substantial investment in infrastructure networks within the Community will be necessary in the coming years, in order to deal with the rapidly increasing needs of transport and communications, and in order to compensate for the fact that the new Member States lag behind considerably in this area. Their budgets – which must satisfy the tough requirements of Article 104 EC – will, temporarily, not provide enough scope for this. As a result, it is to be expected that the EIB's role in financing these investments will continue to increase.

6   SOCIAL POLICY; EQUAL TREATMENT

6.1   ORIENTATION AND HISTORY

6.1.1   Orientation

The social aspects of the EC Treaty were considerably expanded and altered by the Treaty of Amsterdam, with the addition of a separate title on employment (Title VIII, discussed above in section 4) and the restructuring and expansion of Chapter 1 of Title XI, which deals with social policy, education, vocational training and youth.[657] The role of the Community in the domain of social policy remains, however, controversial and unclear. There are three factors which explain this.

The first is the incomplete and rather unclear nature of the Treaty rules themselves, which have been amended on numerous occasions since the 1986 Single European Act, but display the typical shortcomings of an incremental Treaty-making process.[658] There was no explicit reference to the social policy of the Community in Articles 2 and 3 of the original EEC Treaty. The Treaty of

---

656. The Act establishing the EIF was signed on 5 Mar. 1993, by the Member States and came into force on 1 May 1994. The Act amends the Protocol containing the Statute of the EIB to empower the bank's Governing Council to set up the EIF. On this construction, which is very interesting – including from a legal perspective – see: D.R.R. Dunnett, op. cit., *supra* note 650, 721–763 and Müller-Borle, op. cit., *supra* note 650 4/1402–1408. The decisions relating to the EIF were published in O.J. 1994, L 173.

657. The Lisbon Treaty intends to split this title up into three separate titles: Social Policy (Title X), the European Social Fund (Title XI), and Education, Vocational Training, Youth and Sport (Title XII).

658. The difficulties with this process were already set out in L.A. Geelhoed, 'De toekomst van de Europese unie: marktintegratie en beleidsintegratie' (2001), SEW, 366–375, in particular 366–368.

Maastricht filled this lacuna by expressly including the social policy aim of 'a high level of employment and of social protection [and] the raising of the standard of living and quality of life' in the Community's Article 2 EC tasks, and by including 'a policy in the social sphere comprising a European Social Fund' in the activities set out in Article 3 EC. This provision (Art. 3(j) EC) is a good illustration of the uncertain hand of the Treaty makers in this domain: it offers no indication of the nature or scope of the Community's competence here.[659] This shortcoming has become all the more curious as a result of the considerable expansion of the Community's substantive competences in the social sphere with the Treaty of Amsterdam.[660] The Lisbon Treaty, however, cements the importance of social policy to the Union, by including within the Union's Article 3 TEU aims that of achieving a 'highly competitive social market economy, aiming at full employment and social progress', combatting 'social exclusion and discrimination' and promoting 'social justice and protection'. Furthermore, in a new departure, it adds a type of 'integration principle' in Article 9 TEU – analogous to former Article 6 EC which had been added for environmental protection requirements by the Treaty of Amsterdam – whereby, 'in defining and implementing its policies and actions, the Union shall take into account requirements linked to the promotion of a high level of employment, the guarantee of adequate social protection [and] the fight against social exclusion . . .'.

The second is the fact that the content of the concept of 'social policy' is, as such, extremely heterogeneous and susceptible to varying interpretations. As a result, no fixed point of departure exists for delimiting relevant Community and national competences, and the vertical relationship between Community and national policy (in contrast to what had been the case in general economic policy areas).[661] The codification of competences in the Treaty of the Functioning of the European Union, signed at Lisbon in 2007, fails to clarify matters, avoiding such definitional difficulties by describing 'social policy, for the aspects defined in this Treaty' as a

---

659. Nonetheless, the task as presently set out in Art. 2 EC, and further elaborated upon in Art. 136 EC, should not be considered as a non-binding declaration of intention: see Case 149/77, *Defrenne v. Sabena (Defrenne III)*, paras. 10–12.

660. The major difference with the pre-Amsterdam situation is that Art. 137(1) EC now sets out an extensive series of specific areas in which the Community has competence to legislate.

661. C. Barnard, 'Flexibility and Social Policy', in G. de Búrca and J. Scott (eds), *Constitutional Change in the EU, From Uniformity to Flexibility?* (Oxford, Hart, 2000), 196–217, 204, refers to the differing social policy traditions in, on the one hand, the United Kingdom and Ireland and, on the other hand, continental Europe, which find expression primarily in employment law and in the law of labour conditions. The Scandinavian countries adopt an intermediate position. In the Anglo-Saxon tradition, the government does not, in principle, intervene in terms of employment as agreed individually or collectively. On the continent, terms of employment are arrived at within a framework of binding legislative provisions, and the results of discussion of employment terms can as a rule be declared generally binding. In the Scandinavian countries, the social partners have somewhat more autonomy, and tend to settle detailed terms of employment. See also, C. Barnard and S. Deakin, ' "Negative" and "Positive" Harmonization of Labor Law in the European Union' (2002), *Columbia Journal of European Law*, 389.

competence shared between the Union and its Member States.[662] The complexity of the issue of division of competence further increases when one considers that the delimitation of public competences, the intermediary competences of social partners and the competence of individual employers vary widely between the various Member States and are subject to continual change. As it will be evident from the below, this complication also has consequences for the form and content of the Community's legal instruments.[663]

If one defines social policy as the totality of the public arrangements that apply particularly to the labour market and to citizens' social security, it will be clear that this definition includes most elements considered to fall under the heading in Western European welfare states.

The third factor explaining why the Community's role in social policy is controversial is the existence of large differences of opinion between Member States about the aims and design of social policy and about the delimitation of the public, intermediary, and private domains. These differences of opinion are reflected in fundamental differences of view about the role to be played by the Community in this field.[664] This is not simply a result of tension between the Anglo-Saxon and continental views of the role of government (and thus also the Community government) in relations between employees and employers.[665] Far-reaching differences of opinion concerning the proper role of government in the design of social arrangements and institutions also exist between those Member States which have traditionally aimed for a high level of public social protection.[666] This is due to the interweaving of public and private competences which, for most

---

662. Art. 4, Treaty on the Functioning of the European Union.
663. See, however, B. Bercusson, 'Episodes on the Path Towards the European Social Model', in C. Barnard, S. Deakin and G. Morris (eds), *The Future of Labour Law* (Oxford etc., 2004), 179, who is of the view that the inclusion of social and economic rights in the EU Charter of Fundamental Rights 'can be used to legitimise the actors, processes and outcomes of Social Europe', and that the Charter promises a renewal of labour law at trans-national and national levels. See also, A. Neal, 'Fundamental Social Rights in the European Union: "Floor of Rights" or "Drift to the Bottom"?', in Neal, A.C. (ed.), *The Changing Face of European Labour Law and Social Policy* (The Hague etc., 2004), 67. See further, T. Hervey and J. Kenner (eds) *Economic and Social Rights under the EU Charter of Fundamental Rights: A Legal Perspective*, (Oxford etc., 2003).
664. See R. Blanpain, 'The European Union and its Social Policy in a Global Setting', in A. Neal (ed.), *The Changing Face of European Labour Law and Social Policy* (The Hague etc., Kluwer Law International, 2004), 1, who argues that the oft-cited 'European Social Model' does not in fact exist, either at the European level or at national levels. See contra, however, Bercusson, 'The Institutional Architecture of the European Social Model' in T. Takis and P. Nebbia (eds) *European Union Law for the Twenty-First Century* (Oxford etc., 2004), 312, and the speech of Commissioner Špidla of 11 May 2006, 'The European social model: wishful thinking or reality?'
665. See R. Blanpain, op. cit., *supra* note 664, 168–172.
666. The excellent study of the CPB, Challenging Neighbours, The Hague, 1996, in which the institutional differences between the German and Dutch social-economic models are thoroughly reviewed, highlights the major differences between what would on first sight seem two rather identical versions of the 'Rhineland' model of social-economic order.

Member States, is so characteristic of this policy area. Social partners perform their own, albeit changing, role in policy-making and implementation. In this way, national social systems constitute a prime example of the expression of national ideological, cultural and social traditions.[667] The institutional equilibria set out in these systems are very vulnerable to interventions from external sources.[668] They are also vulnerable to exogenous developments on the macro- and meso-economic levels. The development and functioning of the Community market, as well as of EMU, have increased this vulnerability. This means a corresponding restriction of autonomy in national policy-making as regards national policies of employment, income, terms of labour and social security. This dual vulnerability to the actions and existence of the Community as an economic framework for integration results in a rather ambiguous relationship with European integration in the social field.

On the one hand, national supremacy is jealously, and rather egoistically, guarded; on the other hand, the Community is reproached for its unsatisfactorily handling of the social consequences of the economic integration process.[669]

In order properly to analyse the role that the Community can and must fulfil in the social field, it is necessarily to break down the largely artificial distinction made between, on the one hand, market integration and economic policy integration and, on the other hand, national social policy (including the regulation of national labour markets) and social policy integration.[670]

---

667. On this, see further H.F. Zacher, 'Wird es einen europäischen Sozialstaat geben?' (2002), EuR, 147–164.

668. C. Barnard, op. cit. *supra* note 661, 207, gives a very telling example of this in the problems with which the then British government was faced in implementing Dir. 75/129. This led to Case C-383/92, *Commission v. United Kingdom* (Collective redundancies). Many examples may also be found in the jurisprudence concerning Dir. 79/7, which show that Community norms may disturb the existing balance in national social security systems. See, amongst others, Case 71/85, *Netherlands v. Federatie Nederlandse Vakbeweging (FNV)*. See further, A. Sapir, 'Globalization and the Reform of European Social Models' (2006), JCMS, 369–390.

669. R. Blanpain, op. cit., *supra* note 664, 128–131, is very outspoken in the latter sense. He is of the view that the economic aims of the EMU, such as those highlighted in the Stability and Growth Pact, can be considered as a stage for social dumping and dualist societies. More nuanced is the conclusion of E. Szyszczak, op. cit. *supra* note 527, 1169–1170, who sees the link between economic growth, employment and social tolerance more clearly.

670. H.F. Zacher, op. cit., *supra* note 667, 151, makes an unduly sharp dichotomy between the realization of the Community market, which is a task contained in the EC Treaty with a self-contained purpose, and the tasks of a possible social Community which, insofar as already present in the EC Treaty, have (according to Zacher) an 'open' purpose. This analytically interesting approach does not sufficiently express the fact that the realization of the Community market can never be a 'neutral' operation. This project also demands choices: between a market with a higher or less high level of protection of the labour factor (or public health, or the natural environment). See also, the contrast drawn by M. Bell, *Anti-Discrimination Law and the European Union* (Oxford etc., 2002), Ch. 1, between the so-called 'market integration' and 'social citizenship' theoretical models of European social policy. On the tension between Community internal market law and Community social and labour law, see S. Giubboni, *Social Rights and Market Freedom in the European Constitution: A Labour Law Perspective* (Cambridge, 2006).

The welfare benefits flowing from the combination of market integration and economic policy integration go, to a large extent, directly to the advantage of the labour factor. A higher structural economic growth rate contributes to a structurally higher employment level and strengthens the economic basis for social security systems. At a national level, the durability of a high-quality social system in an open economy can only be ensured via a high degree of participation of the working population. Whereas the European integration process has, in terms of economic progress, made national economies more open in relation to each other and to the global market, the durability of the European economic model as a socio-economic model is only assured if that model leads to a relatively high economic growth rate and a high degree of participation. A socio-economic system that, with an economic growth rate of around 2%, leads to greater inactivity of the working population, is in the long run not sustainable on economic or social grounds.[671] Inversely, the working and design of national labour markets and national social security systems are important factors in the realization of the economic aims of the Community.[672] For this reason, intrinsically closer links exist between economic policy coordination on the basis of Articles 99 and 104 EC, employment policy coordination on the basis of Articles 125–130 EC and Community social policy on the basis of Articles 136–145 EC, than the text of the last-named provisions might suggest.[673]

The socially relevant actions of the Community extend to more than those flowing from the text of Articles 136–145 EC. Insofar as harmonization of national legislation in the social field is necessary for the realization and working of the Community market, it follows from the EC Treaty that relevant social interests

---

671. This is the theme running through the argument put forward in the analysis in the Commission White Paper entitled Growth, Competitiveness and Employment, COM(93)700 final. See also, J. Kenner, 'Employment and Macroeconomics in the EC Treaty: A Legal and Political Symbiosis?' (2000), *Maastricht Journal of European and Comparative Law*, 375.

672. See further, M. Panic, The Euro and the Welfare State, in M. Dougan and E. Spaventa (eds), *Social Welfare and EU Law* (Oxford etc., Hart, 2005), 29–36. See also, the Report of the European Commission, Industrial Relationsin Europe 2006 (available at <http://ec.europa.eu/employment_social/social_dialogue/reports_en.htm>) which concludes that high quality industrial relations make a significant contribution to economic performance, from company-level to the economy as a whole. See further, J. Driffell, 'The Centralisation of Wage Bargaining Revisited: What Have We Learnt?' (2006), JCMS, 731–756.

673. These links are almost necessarily expressed since 1994 in the BEPGs, most recently in the integrated guidelines for growth and jobs 2005–2008, which for the first time integrates the BEPGs (adopted under Art. 99(2) EC) with the employment guidelines (adopted under Art. 128(2) EC) in a single overarching document. See also, the Commission's Report, Employment in Europe 2006, available at <http://ec.europa.eu/employment_social/employment_analysis/employ_2006_en.htm>. In any event, with the Treaty of Amsterdam, a good opportunity was missed to express this connection in the Treaty's system. The spectrum of monetary policy, budgetary policy, general economic policy, employment policy and social policy would ideally be grouped in three consecutive titles. Trade policy, or rather, the external aspects of internal economic and social-economic policy, would come after this as a concluding overarching policy.

must be adequately protected.[674] This analysis is supported by the text of Article 2 EC as well as Article 136(1) EC, and the first paragraph of Article 140 EC.[675] The Lisbon Treaty further strengthens this approach, in confirming in Article 3 TEU that achieving a 'highly competitive social market economy, aiming at full employment and social progress' and combating 'social exclusion and discrimination' forms part of the Union's wider goal of achieving the internal market. In the treatment of Articles 39–42 EC above, it has already been explained that the development of free movement of workers cannot take place without the coordination of the application of national social security systems to migrating workers. In itself, Article 42 EC leaves room for the achievement of a certain convergence between national social security systems, with a view to promoting free movement of workers.[676] As the functioning of the labour markets is, within a completed EMU, also crucially important on a European scale, there should be every reason to promote this convergence in the interest of greater cross-border mobility of labour.[677] The Lisbon Treaty, which replaces unanimity of voting here with qualified majority voting – subject to an 'emergency brake' procedure[678] – is a welcome step in this direction.

The importance of the quality of the labour supply was already discussed in section 4. In Articles 149 and 150 EC, this is further expressed in the provision of a – limited – legal basis for Community actions in this area. Social aspects, and in particular employment, evidently carry considerable weight in the policy to

---

674. See also Schulte, in Von der Groeben et al. (5th ed.), op. cit., *supra* note 81, 3/920–931.

675. Art. 136, 1st para., provides, 'The Community and the Member States ... shall have as their objectives the promotion of employment, improved living and working conditions, so as to make possible their harmonization while the improvement is being maintained, proper social protection, dialogue between management and labour, the development of human resources with a view to lasting high employment and the combating of exclusion.'

676. This convergence should not be considered as static, in the sense of trying to search for a definite average or for a basic model. The design and set-up of social security is extremely sensitive to economic, social-economic and social cultural changes which take place within Western European societies. For this reason, national social security systems must regularly be updated. Convergence is therefore a very dynamic process. If Community and national legislatures stand still for – too – long, the relevant rules stand in danger of becoming incomplete and ineffective. See in this regard the Opinion of A.G. Geelhoed in Case C-413/99, *Baumbast v. Secretary of State for the Home Department*.

677. One of the current priorities of the Commission is to facilitate cross-border movement of workers by improving knowledge and coordination of social security rights for cross-border workers. To this end, in 2006, it launched a website, EUlisses (short for EU Links & Information on Social Security), which is aimed at by providing information on the social security rights of cross-border workers. See also, its proposal for a Directive on improving the portability of supplementary pension rights, SEC(2005)1293.

678. The last paragraph of Art. 42 is to be replaced by the following: 'Where a member of the Council declares that a draft legislative act referred to in the first sub-paragraph would affect important aspects of its social security system, including its scope, cost or financial structure, or would affect the financial balance of that system, it may request that the matter be referred to the European Council. In that case, the ordinary legislative procedure shall be suspended. After discussion, the European Council shall, within four months of this suspension, either: (a) refer the draft back to the Council, which shall terminate the suspension of the ordinary legislative procedure; or (b) take no action or request the Commission to submit a new proposal; in that case, the act originally proposed shall be deemed not to have been adopted.'

strengthen economic and social cohesion, which has been previously discussed. The role that the European Social Fund plays in the implementation of the Convergence and Regional Competitiveness and Employment objectives of that policy is a convincing indication of this.

Against this background, one can justifiably state that, in realizing its economic aims, the Community can also achieve social objectives.[679]

Although the Community's competences in the social field presently laid down in Articles 136–145 EC are considerably wider than those provided for in the original EEC Treaty, the possibility for the Community to intervene directly in labour markets and in the design of social security systems remains limited. The regulation of labour markets and terms of labour, and the design of social security systems and the levels of social security obligations and benefits, remain by and large matters for the Member States.[680] Aside from the differences in political opinion concerning these areas, the differences in policy traditions and culture within the Community pose, for the time being, significant obstacles to Community intervention. Further, the still very considerable differences in welfare within the Community prevent any far-reaching harmonization of labour and social security law.[681]

---

679. In the same sense, see Centre for Economic Policy Research, Making Sense of Subsidiarity, London, 1993, 101–115. The Commission re-emphasizes the role of the European Social Fund in improving the functioning of the European Employment Strategy and fostering convergence, employment and competitiveness in its Communication on the Social Agenda COM(2005)33 final. The financial support provided by the ESF has been complemented by financial support from the so-called PROGRESS programme of the Community from 2007.

680. This also follows explicitly from Art. 137(1) and (4) EC (as amended by the Treaty of Nice), which shows that, amongst other areas, the modernization of social systems and the determination of wage base remain outside the scope of Community competences to regulate.

681. Two arguments militate in favour of caution in laying down Community norms and financial, redistributive Community initiatives:

    1. In the first place, large differences in welfare and, in particular, labour productivity within the enlarged Community make the adoption of centralized norms risky as regards their scope and level. The experience of German reunification, where the – overly – rapid increase in the East German wage and benefit levels resulted in a steep increase in the unemployment rate, is an unambiguous warning in this regard.

    2. In the second place, the redistributive capacity of the Community, which has a budget of around 1.25% of Gross Community Product, is far too restricted to allow large-scale redistribution of income. See, however, the Commission's 2007 draft Communication on a new strategy of what it terms 'flexisecurity', which it defines as 'a policy strategy to enhance, at the same time and in a deliberate way, the flexibility of labour markets, work organisations and labour relations on the one hand, and security – employment security and income security – on the other' (Towards Common Principles of Flexicurity: More and better jobs through flexibility and security, available at <http://ec.europa.eu/employment_ social/news/2007/jun/flexicurity_en.pdf>). In the Commission's view, this is 'the answer to the EU's dilemma of how to maintain and improve competitiveness whilst preserving the European social model'. The Commission gets around the fact that, due to Member States' divergent labour market cultures, no 'one-size-fits-all' policy is possible, by promoting the use of 'pathways' – sets of measures that can, if introduced in conjunction with each other, improve a country's performance in terms of flexicurity – to be designed to fit each country's social security model.

Nonetheless, the scope of Member States' policy freedom is significantly influenced by the integration process.[682] As was already seen in section 3.2, the coordination of economic and budgetary policy leads to financial restrictions for national governments, which can also mean restrictions on national social policy. The rapidly increased socio-economic interdependencies within a completed EMU also materially restrict the freedom of action of national players.[683] The Community cannot allow national interventions made in the guise of employment policy or social policy, but which are discriminatory or distortive of competition, without coming into conflict with its core aims of a single market and market equality.[684] Nor can it soften the phenomenon of reallocation which is inherent in the wider dynamics of an open Community market, even in cases where the pressure of cross-border competition between markets is likely to require amending the social *acquis* in the national sphere.[685] It can, however, take action against forms of damaging policy competition in the social field using competences drawn from, amongst others, Articles 87 and 88, as well as 96 and 97 EC.[686]

6.1.2   History

The development of the Community's social policy can roughly be divided into five phases.

The first phase lasted from 1958 to 1972. In this phase, most attention was paid to the realization of free movement of persons. Regulations 3 and 4[687] and, later,

---

682.   See further, M. Dougan and E. Spaventa, 'Wish you weren't here . . . New Models of Social Solidarity in the European Union', in M. Dougan and E. Spaventa (eds), *Social Welfare and EU Law*, op. cit., *supra* note 672, 181, who refer to the notion that Member States are now 'semi-sovereign welfare states'. They argue that the idea of social solidarity is no longer merely national or local, but now has a vital Community component. In their view, this component is expressed negatively (insofar as national social choices are contrary to core Treaty provisions on economic policy) but also positively (via the emergency of a new, supranational model of solidarity based on the concept of equal treatment for Community citizens).

683.   This is also true in particular for the development of gross costs of labour. If these costs increase more quickly than labour productivity, this has unavoidable consequences for that Member State's competitive position. This also means that national governments must be cautious in raising indirect labour costs.

684.   See, *inter alia*: Case 249/81, *Commission v. Ireland*, Case 31/87, *Beentjes v. Netherlands*, Case C-21/88, *Du Pont de Nemours Italiana v. USL di Carrara*, Joined Cases C-369 & 376/96, *Criminal proceedings against Arblade*; Case C-165/98, *Criminal proceedings against Mazzoleni and ISA*, Joined Cases C-49, 50, 52–54 & 68–71/98, *Finalarte v. Urlaubs- und Lohnausgleichskasse der Bauwirtschaft et al.*

685.   Differing views are held on this: see R. Blanpain, op. cit., *supra* note 664, 435–437.

686.   The danger of such competition became acute when, due to the opposition of the UK government, the deepening of social policy integration within the Community had to be based on the Agreement on Social Policy, binding for 11 (later 14) Member States. On this, see the previous edition of this book. With the Treaty of Amsterdam, which incorporated the most important provisions of this agreement within the Treaty itself, this risk has decreased substantially.

687.   Regs. 3 and 4, O.J. 1958, 561 and 597.

the much-amended Regulation 1408/71 linking national social security systems with a view to free movement of workers, were the most important results of this period.[688]

The second phase began with the Paris summit of 1972, which sought, in addition to moving towards an EMU, a more active policy of the Community in the social field. This led to the acceptance of the Social Action Programme in January 1974. The main objectives of this programme were the attainment of full and high-quality employment, the improvement of living and working conditions and the strengthening of the participation of employees' and employers' organizations in Community policy. The first objective, as a chiefly economic policy objective, remained beyond reach in the 1970s and, to a large extent, thereafter. Some important results were achieved in particular as regards the second objective, with the adoption of three directives to protect employees' rights following collective redundancy, transfer of undertakings and employers' insolvency.[689] These

---

688. Reg. 1408/71 of 14 Jun. 1971, on the application of social security schemes to employed persons and their families moving within the Community, O.J. 1971, 2. This Regulation has been amended on many occasions, most recently by the so-called coordination regulation, Reg. 883/2004 on the coordination of social security systems, O.J. 2004, L 200/1. An official consolidated version was published in 1997: Reg. 118/97, O.J. 1997, L 28/1; the most recent (non-official) consolidated version can be found on <http://europa.eu.int/eur-lex/en/consleg/main/1971/en_1971R1408_index.html>. This regulation suffered for a long time from two serious shortcomings: it did not apply to employees from third countries and it offered no solution to link companies' social responsibilities. See in this regard C Laske, 'The Impact of the Single European Market on Social Protection for Migrant Workers' (1993), CML Rev., 515–540. One of these shortcomings – the so-called pension issue – was partly righted by Council Dir. 98/49/EC of 29 Jun. 1998, on safeguarding the supplementary pension rights of employed and self-employed persons moving within the Community, O.J. 1998, L 209/46. See further, the Commission's proposal for a Directive on improving the portability of supplementary pension rights (2005), SEC, 1293. As to the other shortcoming, in 2001, the Commission's proposal for the application of Reg. 1408/71 with a view to the rights of persons from third countries failed to get through the Council: Bull. EU 2002, no. 1/2, 38. However, steps were taken towards the solution of this problem with the adoption of Reg. 859/2003 extending the provisions of Reg. 1408/71 and Reg. 574/72 to nationals of third countries who are not already covered by those provisions solely on the ground of their nationality, O.J. 2003, L 124/1. Note, however, that this Regulation cannot be invoked in a wholly 'internal' situation. On this, see F. Pennings, 'Inclusion and Exclusion of Persons and Benefits in the New Co-ordination Regulation', in M. Dougan and E. Spaventa (eds), *Social Welfare and EU Law*, op. cit., *supra* note 672, 241.

689. Council Dir. 75/129/EEC of 17 Feb. 1975, on the approximation of the laws of the Member States relating to collective redundancies, O.J. 1975, L 48/29, amended by Dir. 92/56, O.J. 1992, L 245/3, consolidated by Dir. 98/29, O.J. 1998, L 225/16; Council Dir. 77/187//EEC of 14 Feb. 1977, on the approximation of the laws of the Member States relating to the safeguarding of employees' rights in the event of transfers of undertakings, businesses or parts of businesses, O.J. 1977, L 61/26, most recently consolidated in Dir. 2201/23, O.J. 2001, L 82/16; Council Dir. 80/987/EEC of 20 Oct. 1980 on the approximation of the laws of the Member States relating to the protection of employees in the event of the insolvency of their employer, O.J. 1980, L 283/23, amended by Dir. 87/164, O.J. 1987, L 66/11 and Dir. 2002/74, O.J. 2002, L 270/10. The last-mentioned directive gave rise to the well-known *Francovich* jurisprudence: Joined Cases C-6 & 9/90, *Andrea Francovich and Danila Bonifaci and others v. Italian Republic*.

Directives have each given rise to considerable case law. This is also the case for three Directives aimed at equal treatment of men and women on the labour market and in social security.[690] The first important Community initiatives in the field of working conditions and safety at work also date from this period.[691] The second phase came to an end with the Single European Act. It led to the addition of Articles 118a and 118b EEC. Article 118a EEC created a special legal basis for Community decisions to protect working conditions and the working environment, which up until then had primarily been based on the general harmonization article, Article 94 EC (originally Article 100 EEC). Article 118b EEC gave a first basis in the Treaty for social dialogue on a Community level.

The third phase began with the European Council of Hanover in the summer of 1988. The European Council emphasized the importance of the social aspects of the internal market, and invited the Commission to put forward a proposal in this respect. This led in the first instance to the publication of the working document, 'The Social Dimension of the Internal Market',[692] and in the second instance to a draft Social Charter.[693] The latter was broadly speaking based on the European Social Charter, to which most Member States are party.[694] Although it was diluted and shortened in many respects, it was accepted by only 11 Member States on 9 December 1989.[695] The United Kingdom refused to approve the Charter, as in its opinion the subjects dealt with therein did not come within the competences of the Community. The Charter itself did not have direct legal effect, but was of a purely declaratory character.[696] The Commission presented an action programme to implement the Charter. The proposals contained therein received little approval from the Member States, however, some of whom complained that the Commission had adopted a very extensive interpretation of Articles 100a EEC (now Article 95 EC) and 118a EEC, which provide (or, in the case of Article 118a EEC, provided) for qualified majority voting.

The self-contradictory position adopted by Member States – which in the abstract want to formulate ambitious goals for the Community in the social sphere, but which have serious reserves when the result of concretizing these goals in

---

690. Dir. 75/117, O.J. 1975, L 45/19, Dir. 76/207 O.J. 1976, L 39/40, Dir. 79/7 O.J. 1979, L 6/24. These directives and the developments to which they have given rise will be comprehensively dealt with in 6.2 *infra*.

691. Dir. 77/576/EEC of 25 Jul. 1977, on the approximation of the laws, regulations and administrative provisions of the Member States relating to the provision of safety signs at places of work, O.J. 1977, 229/12, amended by Dir. 79/640, O.J. 1979, L 183/11, was the first Directive in this area (although since replaced by Dir. 92/58 O.J. 1992, L 245/23).

692. Bull. EC 1998–9, points 1.1.1–1.1.7.

693. COM(89)248 final.

694. Turin, 18 Oct. 1961 (ETS no. 35, with relevant protocols), revised in Strasbourg, 3 May 1996 (ETS no. 163).

695. The Social Charter, as well as the action programme based on the Charter, were published in Social Europe 1990, no. 1, Luxembourg, 1990.

696. This does not prevent the Charter from being used in the interpretation of topics related to those covered therein. See e.g., Case C-322/88, *Grimaldi v. Fonds des maladies professionnelles* and Case C-106/89, *Marleasing v. Comercial Internacional de Alimentación*.

Community decisions has consequences for their national social policy – was also evident here.[697]

Be that as it may, this contradictory approach was not sufficient reason for the great majority of Member States to oppose the proposal to incorporate the aims set out in the Social Charter into the EC Treaty, or the expansion of Community powers necessary for this. Even after the watering-down of the original proposal, however, the UK remained a fierce opponent of any expansion of the Community's competences.[698] This eventually led to the Protocol on Social Policy of the Maastricht Treaty and the attached Agreement on Social Policy, agreed between the Member States of the EC with the exception of the United Kingdom. With this, the fourth phase commenced.[699] Under this dual regime, the Commission attempted, where at all possible, to find a legal basis in the Treaty for the Community's social legislation, even in the face of serious opposition from the UK.[700] The Agreement on Social Policy was only used where no other possibility existed.[701] This legislative policy meant that the gap between the legislation applicable to the '11' – and later '14' – Member States, and that applicable to the UK, remained limited. The price for this was, however, that the development of Community legislation somewhat stagnated.[702] The change of government in the United Kingdom on the eve of the conclusion of the Treaty of Amsterdam had the result that, at the last minute, the provisions of the Agreement on Social Policy could be incorporated in the text of the Treaty under Title VIII on Employment. One of the consequences of this was that the legislation which had, in the meantime, been adopted on the basis of the Agreement on Social Policy, had to be adopted once again.[703]

---

697. It is to be regretted that the proposal of the Commission in its action programme to close certain lacunae in Reg. 1408/71 was not accepted by the Council. As a result, a striking discrepancy existed *rationae personae* between the Social Charter and the aforementioned Regulation. The Charter applied to all employees active within the Community, while the Regulation only applied to Member State nationals. However, see *supra* note 688.

698. See in this regard P. Watson, 'Social Policy after Maastricht' (1993), CML Rev., 481–513, and J. Cloos et al., op. cit., *supra* note 51, 302–308.

699. The legal complications to which the Protocol and the Agreement on Social Policy gave rise are no longer an issue following the Treaty of Amsterdam. See, in this regard, the previous edition of this book.

700. Insofar as a legal basis was used which allowed qualified majority voting, such as Art. (ex) 118a EC, and the UK could be outvoted, this gave rise to severe conflicts. See Case C-84/94, *UK v. Council* (Working Time Directive), on the question whether Dir. 93/10/EEC, O.J. 1993 L 307/18, had to be based on (ex) Art. 118a EC.

701. In particular: Council Dir. 94/45/EC of 22 Sep. 1994, on the establishment of a European Works Council or a procedure in Community-scale undertakings and Community-scale groups of undertakings for the purposes of informing and consulting employees, O.J. 1994, L 254/64; Council Dir. 96/34/EC of 3 Jun. 1996, on the framework agreement on parental leave concluded by UNICE, CEEP and the ETUC, O.J. 1996, L 145/4; Council Dir. 97/80/EC of 15 Dec. 1997, on the burden of proof in cases of discrimination based on sex, O.J. 1998, L 14/6; Council Dir. 97/81/EC of 15 Dec. 1997, concerning the Framework Agreement on part-time work concluded by UNICE, CEEP and the ETUC, O.J. 1998, L 14/9.

702. C. Barnard, op. cit. *supra* note 661, 202.

703. As, under UK law, these Directives could not be transposed into UK law in a manner consistent with Art. 2(2) of the UK European Communities Act 1972, it was necessary to

The conclusion of the Treaty of Amsterdam marked the beginning of the fifth phase. This has been characterized, contrary to what may have initially been expected, not so much by a greater production of binding norms in the social field, but rather by the use of instruments that may be qualified as 'soft law'.[704] Thus, for example, one of the main instruments for implementing the EU's Social Agenda[705] is the European Employment Strategy, which aims at coordination of the employment policy priorities to which Member States should subscribe at EU level, via use of the so-called 'Open Method of Coordination'. By this method, Member States draw up national action plans setting objectives and timetables for meeting them. The Commission monitors their progress in reports drawn up each year and agreed with the Council.

6.2   SOCIAL POLICY, EDUCATION, VOCATIONAL TRAINING AND YOUTH

6.2.1   Social Provisions

The objectives of Community and national action in the social field are set out in the first paragraph of Article 136 EC. The continuity of the development of law in the social field is expressed there by referring to the European Social Charter of 1961 and to the Community Charter of the Fundamental Social Rights of Workers of 1989. The catalogue of objectives covers many subjects, developing in more detail objectives mentioned in Article 2 EC. In particular, it deals with: the promotion of employment, the improvement of living and working conditions, proper social protection, social dialogue, and the development of human resources with a view to lasting high employment and the combating of exclusion.

From the breadth of this summary it is clear that, in order to attain these goals, Community action is necessary in a far wider field than that of social policy in the narrow sense. Thus, as already emphasized above, in the first place economic growth is necessary for the promotion of employment and improved living and working conditions. In this, the procedures set out in Article 99 EC and Articles 125–130 EC play a large role. The unity and effective functioning of the Community market, as well as the Community's policy for promotion of economic and social cohesion, are important in order to develop living and working conditions. Specific Community competences may be found in Articles 149 and 150 EC, as well as in Articles 125–130 EC, for developing the Community's human resources. Exclusion can best be countered via a high level of employment, in combination with measures aimed at the weaker groups in the labour market.[706]

---

adopt them once again on the basis of Art. 94 EC. See in this regard C. Barnard op. cit. *supra* note 661, 203.

704.   E. Szyszczak, op. cit. *supra* note 527, 1137–1141.

705.   See, most recently, the Commission Communication on the Social Agenda COM(2005)33 final.

706.   This cohesion may since the end of 1997 be found in the employment guidelines. See, amongst others, Council Decision of 12 Jul. 2005, on Guidelines for Member States' employment policies 2005–2008, O.J. 2005, L 205/21.

The second paragraph of Article 136 EC, on the one hand, confirms the necessity of taking into account the differences between national policies and policy traditions in the social field and, on the other hand, emphasizes the cohesion between social and economic policy by stating the necessity of maintaining the competitiveness of the Community economy.[707] The programmatic character of Article 136 EC, in common with ex-Article 117 EEC, has certain legal implications. In its important judgment in Case 126/86, *Zaera*,[708] the Court indicated that the programmatic character of the objectives of ex-Article 117 EEC did not mean that the article had no legal consequences. These objectives were a factor in the interpretation and application of the other Treaty provisions and of secondary Community legislation in the social field. This judgment is certainly also applicable in the case of the more widely phrased Article 136 EC.

Three means for achieving the Community's aims in the social field are summarized in the third paragraph of Article 136 EC:

(i) the functioning of the common market, which will 'favour the harmonization of social systems';
(ii) the procedures provided for in the Treaty;
(iii) the approximation of provisions laid down by law, regulation or administrative action.

These three means will be discussed below in turn.

6.2.1.1   The Functioning of the Community Market

This refers primarily, though not exclusively, to the functioning of the Community labour market, which results from the free movement of workers. This Community labour market also concerns the actions of intermediary players, employees' and employers' organizations, which influence its functioning. Such influence can take place directly, for instance via the conclusion of cross-border collective labour agreements. As a rule, however, the influence is mainly indirect, via the exertion of pressure on the national and Community legislatures.[709] In each case, a certain

---

707. In the Court's case law, the complementarity of economic and social aims has been stated on many occasions, including Case 43/75, *Defrenne II*; Case 149/77, *Defrenne III*; Case 30/85, *Teuling v. Bedrijfsvereniging voor de Chemische Industrie*; Case 71/85, *FNV* and Case C-317/93, *Nolte v. Landesversicherungsanstalt Hannover*.

708. Case 126/86, *Giménez Zaera v. Instituto Nacional de la Seguridad Social and Tesorería General de la Seguridad Social*.

709. The role of the social partners remained modest for a long period. In spite of the formal realization of the free movement of workers, cross-border labour mobility remained very slight. This has increased considerably in the last decade, primarily due to workers from the 12 new Member States (though only Ireland, the UK and Sweden initially opened their markets fully upon the 2004 'big bang' accession), as well as low-qualified workers from third countries and high-qualified employees of multinational companies and in the cross-border financial services industry. None of these categories of employee is very organized at a trade union level. Although cross-border strikes did take place in the 1970s, mainly in the traditionally large-scale industries (steel, textiles, synthetic fibres), national trade union

convergence of national systems can result. Until the mid-1990s, the influence of the social partners remained rather modest, although each has long been represented in the Economic and Social Committee. This situation changed in the wake of, *inter alia*, the Agreement on Social Policy. One of the provisions of this agreement – now Article 138 EC – provided for a dialogue with the social partners, which could lead to contractual relations including agreements (cf. the present Article 139 EC). This stimulated tripartite dialogue between the social partners organized at Community level and the Commission.[710] After the conclusion of the Treaty of Amsterdam, this social dialogue had a basis in the EC Treaty itself (see Articles 138 and 139 EC); its importance was increased by the employment guidelines of Article 128 EC, which were also introduced with this Treaty. The social partners play an increasingly significant role in the preparation and implementation of the guidelines.[711] The European Council of Cologne of June 1999 further emphasized this role by instituting, in the 'European Employment Pact', a new dialogue between all players which are responsible for terms of labour and financial-economic and monetary policy.[712] The sphere of influence of the social partners thereby became far greater than the labour market and labour law in the narrow sense.[713] Their role is further emphasized by the Lisbon Treaty, through

---

movements ultimately concentrated primarily on national relations with employer organizations and governments. Even now, no real convergence as a result of free movement of workers can be said to exist in this regard. The Commission is to adopt a proposal for an optional European framework for trans-national collective bargaining: see Communication from the Commission on the Social Agenda COM(2005)33 final. See the Report of E. Ales etc. of Feb. 2006, commissioned by the Commission, Trans-national Collective Bargaining: Past, Present and Future, available at <ec.europa.eu/employment_social/labour_law/docs/transnational_agreements_ales_study_en.pdf>.

710. Such meetings had been held since 1976- the so-called Val-Duchesse dialogue (named after the chateau near Brussels where the first meeting took place). These meetings did not lead to binding commitments. Aside from the major differences in tradition and approach, the fact that the Treaty itself had no legal basis for the conclusion of binding commitments on a Community level also prevented this. The 1992 Agreement on Social Policy changed this situation, making the social dialogue less informal.

711. Compare the employment guidelines for 2005–2008 (O.J. 2005, L 205/21), which state that, in implementing the guidelines, European and national social partners should play a central role. The employment guidelines form part of the European Employment Strategy, which aims at coordination of the employment policy priorities to which Member States should subscribe at EU level, via use of the so-called 'Open Method of Coordination'.

712. Bull. EU 7-1999, 11–14, points 7.20 and Annex I of the Conclusions of the Presidency.

713. The increasingly wide direct involvement of the social partners in policy integration in the economic and social areas raises the question of the meaning of the *indirect*, purely advisory role which they play via their representation in the Economic and Social Committee. It seems unavoidable that direct social dialogue, such as it presently takes place in an increasingly wide domain, will further erode the (already rather weak) position of the Economic and Social Committee. See more generally: W. van der Voort, In Search of a Role, The Economic and Social Committee in European Decision Making, Dissertation (Utrecht, 1997). For an interesting discussion and comparison of the different institutional forms in which interest groups participate in social regulation, and in particular in EU occupational health and safety policy (e.g., the Economic and Social Committee, the Advisory Committee on Safety and Health at

the insertion of a new article by which the Union 'recognises and promotes the role of the social partners at its level, taking into account the diversity of national systems' (Art. 152 TFEU).

In addition, the completion and functioning of the Community internal market contributes overall to the objectives of Article 136 EC, through its advantageous effects on economic growth and employment and through better and lower-priced product supply. The results that countries like Spain and Ireland have achieved in welfare growth in the past decades illustrate this well.

6.2.1.2   *The Procedures Set Out in the EC Treaty*

Most relevant here are the various procedures for coordination of economic policy, employment policy and economic and social cohesion. More particularly, Articles 137–139 EC provide for special procedures for social policy. Article 137 EC is, together with Articles 138 and 139 EC, taken from the Agreement on Social Policy. The time pressure under which this transplantation was performed restricted the required drafting adjustments in this article, which took place afterwards in the Treaty of Nice. In the first paragraph of Article 137, a large number of areas are presently summarized, where the Community is to support and complement the actions of Member States. These are: a. the improvement of the working environment to protect workers' health and safety; b. working conditions; c. social security and social protection of workers; d. protection of workers where their employment contract is terminated; e. the information and consultation of workers; f. representation and collective defence of the interests of workers and employers, including co-determination, subject to paragraph 5; g. conditions of employment for third-country nationals legally residing in Community territory; h. the integration of persons excluded from the labour market, 'without prejudice to Article 150'; i. equality between men and women with regard to labour market opportunities and treatment at work; j. the combating of social exclusion; k. the modernization of social protection systems without prejudice to point (c).

The second paragraph of Article 137 provides for two methods of complementary and supporting Community action. First, the adoption of 'measures' designed to encourage cooperation between Member States through initiatives aimed at improving knowledge, developing exchanges of information and best practices, promoting innovative approaches and evaluating experiences, *excluding* any harmonization of the laws and regulations of the Member States.[714]

Work, the European Agency for Safety and Health Protection at Work, and the Social Dialogue procedure), see: S. Smismans, *Law, Legitimacy, and European Governance: Functional Participation in Social Regulation* (Oxford etc., 2004). See also M. de Vos (ed.), *A Decade Beyond Maastricht: The European Social Dialogue Revisited* (the Hague etc., Kluwer Law International, 2003) and S. Smismans, 'The European Social Dialogue between Constitutional and Labour Law' (2007), EL Rev., 341–364.

714. The Lisbon Treaty amends this so that the European Parliament and the Council propose such measures jointly, rather than the Council acting alone.

Second, the adoption of 'minimum requirement' directives, which will be gradually applied and which can have a different content per Member State. Such directives should avoid imposing administrative, financial and legal constraints in a way which would restrain the creation and development of small and medium-sized undertakings. In adopting Directives, the Council must follow the co-decision procedure of Article 251 EC, with the exception of Directives on topics falling under subparagraphs (c) (social security), (d) (protection of workers where their employment contract is terminated), (f) (representation and collective defence of workers' interests), and (g) (third-country nationals) of Article 137(1) EC, where it decides by unanimity following consultation of the European Parliament. The Council may, however, upon the proposal of the Commission and after consultation of the European Parliament, decide that the Article 251 EC procedure also applies to Article 137(1) (d), (f) and (g). For areas covered by Article 137(1) (j) and (k), Community action by means of Directive is implicitly excluded.

Article 137(3) EC raises the possibility of the Member States' entrusting the social partners with the implementation of directives adopted pursuant to Article 137(2) EC. The Lisbon Treaty amends this so as to include implementation of Directives adopted in accordance with Article 139. Member States remain, of course, responsible for correct and timely implementation.[715] Article 137(4) EC confirms, almost superfluously, that Member States remain competent as regards the fundamental principles of their social security systems to maintain or introduce more stringent protective measures compatible with the Treaty. Article 137(5) EC states that Article 137 EC does not apply to pay, the right of association, the right to strike or the right to impose lock-outs.

A number of comments should be made with regard to Article 137 EC, which now forms the central legal basis for the Community's social policy in the narrow sense. First, the article makes clear that the Community's competences are to remain subsidiary and supportive. This follows in particular from the way in which the legislative action of the Community is restrictively qualified in Article 137(2)(b) EC.[716] Second, the complementary action of the Community should primarily be found in the non-binding measures provided for by Article 137(2)(a) EC. Third, it follows expressly from the text and the system of Article 137 EC that

---

715. The question whether Directives can be implemented via collective labour agreements has been raised in cases before the Court on numerous occasions. From these cases, it can be concluded that the Court allows this, if based on national legislation which guarantees that all employees protected by the Directive in fact receive this protection, if the Directive has the desired effect in the national legal order in time, and if it is possible to contest unlawful provisions in collective labour agreements. See: Case 91/81, *Commission v. Italy* (Collective redundancy Directive), Case 165/82, *Commission v. UK* (Midwives), Case 143/83, *Commission v. Denmark* (equal treatment), Case 235/84, *Commission v. Italy* (safeguarding of employees' rights) and Case 312/86, *Commission v. France* (equal treatment).

716. '... Minimum requirements for gradual implementation, having regard to the conditions and technical rules obtaining in each of the Member States.' This temporal and substantive flexibility is viewed by C. Barnard op. cit. *supra* note 661, 205–208, as one of the characteristics of harmonization in the social field. It can also be found in older directives, such as Dir. 75/129/ EEC on collective redundancies.

the Community must, in its actions, respect as far as possible the differences in the social domain that exist within the Community. There can be no question of imposed uniformity through harmonization of legislation. This confirms already-existing legislative practice. Fourth, the long catalogue of specific sub-areas contained in Article 137(1) EC in which the Community is empowered to act will not make it easy for the Community legislature to continue in the social domain with its long practice of using the 'general' harmonization provisions of Articles 94 and 95 EC or, where these cannot be used, Article 308 EC.[717]

The fifth and final comment is that it is striking that the Community measures set out in Article 137(2)(a) EC show considerable similarity to the methods that the Community uses in the coordination of general economic policy and employment policy. This approach, using 'soft' instruments, has the advantage of enabling convergence to be promoted in the social domain as regards areas where Member States had not, up until now, accepted Community action, such as the politically very sensitive area of 'modernizing of social security systems'.[718] An additional advantage is that the comparability of convergence methods used accentuates the relationship between economic policy, employment policy and social policy, described above. As a result, the action of the Community on the basis of Article 137(2)(a) EC may become slightly – too – informal.

Article 138 EC sets out detailed regulation of contacts between the Commission and the social partners in the preparation of Community acts in the social sphere.[719] In comparison with the old Article 118b EC, this article is far more precise and compelling: the Commission is *required* to consult the social partners in two phases about all its proposals. The first consultation takes place before submission of such proposals and concerns 'the possible direction of Community action'. If the Commission is of the view that Community action is advisable, the second consultation takes place on the content of the envisaged proposal. The social partners then forward an opinion or, where appropriate, a recommendation, to the Commission. The most striking aspect of this procedure is without doubt Article 138(4) EC, which enables the social partners to, as it were, 'take over' the Commission proposal and develop it further using the Article 139 EC procedure discussed below. Article 138 EC fits in the socio-economic policy tradition based on consensus of a number of continental and Scandinavian countries. The rather imprecise text of this article gives rise to certain questions of importance for its interpretation and application.

The first question concerns the scope *ratione materiae* of Article 138 EC. As set out above, the scope of Community action that is of relevance to the social sphere is considerably wider than those areas dealt with by Articles 136–145 EC.

---

717. See also: Schulte, in Von der Groeben etc., op. cit., *supra* note 81, 3/1101.
718. See e.g., the Commission's 2007 draft Communication on 'flexisecurity', Towards Common Principles of Flexicurity: More and better jobs through flexibility and security, available at <http://ec.europa.eu/employment_social/news/2007/jun/flexicurity_en.pdf>).
719. On the role of the social partners in EU law and policy making, see C. Barnard, 'The Social Partners and the Governance Agenda' (2002), *European Law Journal*, 80.

It therefore stands to reason that the requirement to consult should include all Community initiatives with a clear social or socio-economic impact, such as measures referred to in Articles 40 and 42 EC in connection with free movement of workers or the employment guidelines referred to in Article 128 EC.[720]

The second question is whether – and if so, to what degree – the opinions or recommendations of the social partners have legal consequences, for example where these are strongly opposed or supportive of the proposed initiatives of the Commission. It seems to us that, while the positions of the social partners may be of – sometimes great – importance, this cannot detract from the fact that the Commission has sole competence to judge how it carries out its tasks under the EC Treaty.[721]

The third question concerns the legal character of the Commission's obligation to consult. Is this a general norm directing the Commission to obtain the opinion of the social partners in preparing measures in the social field, or an obligation comprising a constitutive condition for the validity of the Commission's proposals and thus for the validity of the resulting Community's decisions?[722] The wording of Articles 138(2) and (3) EC, which gives the Commission no discretion as regards its obligation to consult, would seem to support the latter interpretation. In contrast, the fact that the material scope of the article is likely to be broader than the area covered by Article 137 EC would seem to go against this interpretation. In our analysis, we would advise caution in adopting an extensive interpretation of Articles 138(2) and (3) EC. Insofar as these provisions contain an obligation to consult, this goes no further than a purely procedural condition for the legal validity of Community decisions under Articles 137 and 141(3) EC. Outside the scope of Chapter 1 of Title XI, consultation is facultative to help direct the Commission.

The fourth question is who is included under the 'social partners' heading. The Commission set out some criteria on this point in 1993, with a view to the application of Article 3 of the Agreement on Social Policy, where it defined the group of organizations with a right to be consulted.[723]

---

720. See also: C. Docksey and J.C. Séché in Von der Groeben etc., op. cit. *supra* note 81, 3/1388.
721. This also means that the Commission is not obliged to act on a request from the social partners to 'take over' a proposal and deal with it under the Art. 139 EC procedure (see Art. 138(4) EC). The reasons for this may be substantive, e.g., because the Commission doubts that the social partners will be able to find a sensible solution. They may also be political, because the Commission wishes the European Parliament to be involved as co-legislator in the relevant area.
722. C. Docksey and J.C. Séché, in Von der Groeben etc., op. cit. *supra* note 81, 3/1388.
723. Commission Communication of 14 Dec. 1993, COM(93)600 final, subsequently amended by Commission Communication of 18 Sep. 1996, COM(96)448 final. This definition has not been without controversy. It gave rise to Case T-135/96, *UEAPME v. Council*, where the organization of employers of medium and small businesses complained that they had not been involved in the agreement on parental leave, incorporated into Dir. 96/34/EC. See further, the list of consulted organizations at Annex 5 of COM(2004)557 final and S. Smismans, 'The European Social Dialogue between Constitutional and Labour Law' (2007), EL Rev., 341–364.

The wording of Article 139(1) is somewhat unhappy. The first paragraph of this article is mainly declaratory, because employee and employer organizations were already competent to enter into contractual relations in their capacity as legal persons in private law, if necessary also at the Community level. Of course, this still means that such agreements may not infringe Community or national law. Article 139(2) EC is more important. Agreements entered into at Community level can be implemented via two methods: either by the social partners themselves in the national sphere, with the possible involvement of national authorities,[724] or, in cases falling under Article 137 EC, at the collective request of the social partners by decision of the Council on the request of the Commission. The Lisbon Treaty adds the requirement that the European Parliament be 'informed'. The Council's decision is taken by qualified majority, unless the relevant agreement includes one or more provisions related to one of the areas in which unanimity is required pursuant to Article 137(2) EC. In that case, it acts unanimously.

Article 139 EC also gives rise to certain questions of interpretation. It would seem from the wording of Article 139(2) EC that the Commission and the Council are obliged to adopt the agreements put before them and take a decision in conformity with these agreements. In our view, however, the Commission remains wholly competent to examine the agreement put before it for conformity with Community law. Should it judge that the agreement is fully or partly contrary to Community law, it must refuse to make the requested proposal to the Council.[725] In turn, the Council remains competent to reject an agreement put before it by way of Commission proposal. An agreement of the social partners cannot take detract from the competences and obligations which both institutions have under the EC Treaty. Further, a different interpretation would make the distinction made in Article 139(2) EC, between areas where the Council votes with qualified majority and unanimity, superfluous.[726] A refusal by the Commission or the Council to adopt the agreement must, in our view, relate to the *entire* agreement. Should they decide only to adopt part of the agreement or to adopt it in amended form, this would usurp the freedom of negotiation that the social partners enjoy in relation to each other.[727] In contrast, the Commission and the Council can pursue the adoption of their own decision pursuant to Article 137 EC if they do not consider

---

724. See also, the Declaration on Art. 118(2) of the Treaty instituting the European Community (now Art. 137(2) EC) annexed to the Treaty of Amsterdam.
725. P. Watson, 'Social Policy after Maastricht' (1993), CML Rev., 481–513, in particular 509, seems to think otherwise. See also: C. Docksey and J.C. Séché, in Von der Groeben etc., op. cit., *supra* note 81 3/1393–1394. On the compatibility of collective agreements with the Treaty competition rules, see Case C-67/96, *Albany International BV v. Stichting Bedrijfspensioenfonds Textielindustrie*.
726. If the Council were obliged to adopt an agreement placed before it, it would make no difference in principle whether this should be done by qualified majority or unanimity.
727. This does not exclude that discussion may take place between the social partners, as parties to the agreement, the Commission and the Council, on technical questions arising with the adoption of the agreement. This occurred, for example, prior to the adoption of Dir. 96/34/EC on parental leave.

the agreement put before them to be suitable for adoption. In this analysis, a strict division remains between the public competences and responsibilities of the Community institutions and the private responsibilities of the social partners as parties to the agreement.

From Article 139(2) EC, it would seem that, for the adoption of an agreement, a Commission proposal and a Council decision on that proposal suffice. This has the unusual consequence that a simple initiative from the social partners could be enough to set aside the European Parliament's competences as a co-legislator under Article 137(2) EC.[728] It seems to us that the Treaty makers did not properly think through the relationship between Article 137 EC and the mechanism of Article 139 EC. Article 139(2) EC contains a procedure bearing a certain similarity to the possibility of declaring collective labour agreements to be generally binding, which exists in the labour law of certain Member States. The executive derives its competence to make such a declaration from express empowerment given by the normal legislature. Transposition of this legal concept into the EC Treaty would have to mean that the Community legislature as referred to in Article 137 EC had been granted the power to enable the Commission and the Council to take the decisions referred to in Article 139 EC. The present construction is institutionally and constitutionally impure. Although the European Parliament was 'involved' in the three directives[729] adopted under the comparable Article 3 of the Agreement on Social Policy,[730] the relationship between Articles 137 and 139 EC should be reviewed at the first possible opportunity. The Lisbon Treaty's amendment of Article 139, requiring that the European Parliament be 'informed' of the outcome of the Article 139(2) procedure, is clearly insufficient in this regard.

With the transposition of the core provisions of the Agreement on Social Policy into the EC Treaty, Articles 140 and 143–145 EC lost almost all of the limited relevance they had in the first place. With the Treaty of Nice, Article 144

---

728. Not only the Parliament, but also the Economic and Social Committee and the Committee for the Regions, are in this way set to one side. This consequence is even stranger if one considers that in the genesis of Art. 137 EC, long negotiations took place on the choice of legislative procedures, their scope of application and the involvement of each committee in the process. See in this regard J. Cloos et al. op. cit., *supra* note 51, 303–311 and S. Smismans, 'The European Social Dialogue between Constitutional and Labour Law' (2007), EL Rev., 341–364.

729. In the Commission Communication of 14 Dec. 1993, already referred to, 21, it promised to keep the Parliament informed about the application of Art. 139 EC. In practice, this indeed happened in the case of the three directives adopted under this provision.

730. Council Dir. 96/34/EC of 3 Jun. 1996, on the framework agreement on parental leave concluded by UNICE, CEEP and the ETUC, O.J. 1996, L 145/4, Council Dir. 97/81/EC of 15 Dec. 1997, concerning the Framework Agreement on part-time work concluded by UNICE, CEEP and the ETUC, O.J. 1998, L 14/9, Council Dir. 1999/70/EC of 18 Jun. 1999, concerning the framework agreement on fixed-term work concluded by ETUC, UNICE and CEEP O.J. 1999, L 175/43. On these Directives, see, *inter alia*, Case C-212/04, *Adeneler et al. v. Ellinikos Organismos Galaktos;* Case C-320/04, *Commission v. Luxembourg*, Case C-53/04, *Marrosu and Sardino* and Case C-180/04, *Vassalo v. Azienda Ospedaliera Ospedale San Martino di Genova e Cliniche Universitarie Convenzionate.*

EC was in any event replaced by a completely different provision. Article 140 EC is an almost word-for-word repetition of Article 118 of the original EEC Treaty. It is a general norm aimed at directing the Commission in the promotion of horizontal cooperation between Member States and in facilitating the coordination of their action in the area of social policy in the meaning of Chapter 1 of Title XI. In contrast to the present situation, the true Community competences in the chapter on social policy were, prior to the Treaty of Amsterdam, very limited.[731] A general, weak-coordinating competence for the Commission was of some import.[732] Almost all topics included under Article 140 EC fall either under Articles 125–130 EC (the employment guidelines) or under Article 137 EC, where the Commission enjoys much greater competences than Article 140 EC gives it. At present, Article 140 EC is a largely superfluous provision, of primary interest for the history and development of Community social policy.[733]

Article 143 EC contains a specific obligation for the Commission to report 'on progress in achieving the objectives of Article 136 EC, including the demographic situation in the Community'.[734] This report is forwarded every year to the European Parliament, the Council and the Economic and Social Committee. The Parliament can request that the Commission draw up reports on particular issues concerning the social situation.

The maintenance of the general Commission obligation to report in Article 145 EC, which is drawn up in similar wording to Article 143 EC, is another example of unhappy drafting by the Treaty makers in preparing the Treaty of Amsterdam. The ex-Article 144 EC, on the basis of which the Commission could be given tasks concerning the implementation of Community rules concerning, in particular, the protection of migrating workers, had remained a dead letter since 1958. This provision was, with the Treaty of Nice, replaced by a text requiring that a Social Protection Committee be established with advisory status 'to promote cooperation on social protection policies between Member States and with the Commission'. It would seem that this committee is intended to be the counterpart of the committees provided for in Articles 114 and 130 EC, on economic and financial policy, and employment policy, respectively.[735]

---

731. See the previous edition of this book.
732. However weak the competences of the Commission under this Article were, their material scope still gave rise to serious differences of opinion between the Commission and the Member States. These came to the fore in Joined Cases 281, 283–285 & 287/85, *Germany, France, Netherlands, Denmark and United Kingdom v. Commission* (migration policy). The Court held that the competences of the Commission were strictly described in the areas set out in Art. 118 EC (now 140 EC) and, as a result, that cultural aspects did not fall within these competences.
733. The Lisbon Treaty adds the provision that the European Parliament must be kept 'fully informed' of contact between the Commission and Member States under this paragraph.
734. See, in regard to the 'demographic issue', the Commission's Green Paper on demography, Confronting demographic change: a new solidarity between generations, COM(2005)94 final, and its Communication, The demographic future of Europe: From challenge to opportunity, COM(2006)571 final. A High Level group has been formed on this topic: IP/07/789.
735. This committee was established in advance of the Treaty of Nice, by Council Decision of 29 Jun. 2000, O.J. 2000, L 172/26.

This demonstrates the trend whereby, in an area of policy integration, the independent role of the Commission in preparing Community actions is restricted.[736] The question remains whether this is a desirable development from the perspective of transparency of institutional relations.[737]

6.2.1.3   *Bringing Legislative and Administrative Provisions Closer Together*

Until the entry into force of the Treaty of Amsterdam, the third of the means set out in Article 136 EC for accomplishing the aims described in this article – the approximation of provisions laid down by law, regulation or administrative action – had to be achieved primarily based on legal bases outside Chapter I on social provisions. These were: Articles 40 and 42 EC for social rights of migrating workers, Articles 94 and 95 as general harmonization provisions for the unity and functioning of the Community and internal markets respectively, and Article 308 EC as the general fall-back basis in cases where, although no specific competence exists, Community action nonetheless appears necessary. Since the entry into force of the Single European Act, ex-Article 118A (now Article 137) EC has been an important legal basis for Community legislation in the sphere of conditions of labour, safety at work and the working environment.

Although Articles 96 and 97 EC provide a special legal basis for Community action, where differences in social protection between the Member States could lead to distortion of competition, these provisions have thus far not been applied. They took on a certain relevance with the Agreement of Social Policy, which raised the possibility that the United Kingdom might engage in active policy competition with the rest of the Community in the social field. Although these provisions also remained a dead letter at this time, it cannot be excluded that their use might be necessary in a completed EMU. The resulting greater transparency of public burdens, including social burdens, makes market relations more vulnerable to policy competition via so-called social dumping than was previously the case.[738]

---

736. It follows implicitly from the new Art. 144 EC that Member States are beginning to recognize that their powers to design their social security systems – which belong to the core competences of the national welfare state – are also subject to the de facto convergence effect flowing from a completed EMU. As a result, a certain amount of vertical policy coordination is also necessary in this field. The Committee of Social Protection is a further step in this direction.
737. Another question is whether it is desirable to provide for such special committees in the Treaty itself, in particular in areas where the relationship between the Community and national competences is clearly dynamic.
738. The fear of social dumping was expressed in the past mainly by experts in social law, including P.F. van der Heyden, etc., 'Labour Law and Social Policy within the EU, The Dutch Dimension' (1994) SEW, 321–352, and more recently, R. Blanpain, op. cit., *supra* note 664, 438–439. Experience to date does not indicate that this phenomenon occurs on a large scale, although social security systems for the working population have been made more 'activating' (that is, to require more activity to obtain benefits) in most Member States. Changes in the incentive structure of social security systems should certainly not, however,

The replacement of the Agreement on Social Policy, by including Articles 136, 137, 138 and 139 EC in the EC Treaty following the Treaty of Amsterdam, was a watershed. Until then, the vast majority of Community legislation in the social field had to be based on a legal basis that was not specific to this area; the new Article 137 EC changed this. This legal basis seems, in particular following the Treaty of Nice, broad enough for minimum legislative and regulatory harmonization insofar as this is necessary for policy integration in the social domain. Indeed, in most areas covered explicitly in Article 137(1) EC, Community legislation already existed, although this was mostly based on legal bases not used solely for this field. Whether it will be possible for the Community to legislate in the most sensitive parts of this field, where unanimity is required by Article 137(2)(b) EC, is yet to be seen. Past experience shows that Community legislation in the field of social security and workers' participation in management is difficult due to major differences of opinion between the Member States. The fact that, even under the Agreement of Social Policy, no agreement could be reached on these sensitive areas, does not give rise to great expectations in this regard.[739]

It remains nonetheless interesting to observe how it was in the past possible for the Community to take decisions in the social field in the absence of a specific legal basis for this in the EC Treaty, particularly in view of the fact that the vast majority of the present Community legislation in force in the area existed prior to the entry into force of the Treaty of Amsterdam.[740] By 1 January 1998, 62 directives had been passed at Community level in the area. Six of these were in the area of labour law and terms of labour, seven in the area of equal treatment of men and women, three were related to free movement of workers, 24 concerned the protection of safety at work and working conditions.

In the case of the first category of directive, Article 94 EC (ex Art. 100 EC) was the principal legal basis used prior to the entry into force of the Single European Act. Three important directives were adopted on this legal basis: Directives 75/129 on collective redundancies,[741] 77/187 on the safeguarding of

---

be put down to social dumping. Rather, as an 'activating' social security system contributes to the robustness and competitiveness of a national economy, those in the national sphere will be thereby dissuaded from engaging in social dumping.

739. Nonetheless, the Community legislature has been active since 1998 in fields in which it had already acted, such as safety at work and the working environment, equal treatment of men and women and parental leave. See further E. Szyszczak, op. cit. *supra* note 527, 1160–1164.

740. A useful inventory of this can be found in Schulte, 'Vorbemerkung zu den Artikelen 117 bis 127 und 120', in Von der Groeben etc, op. cit. *supra* note 81, 3/1020–1027.

741. O.J. 1975, L 48/29, consolidated following amendments in Dir. 98/59/EC, O.J. 1998, L 225/16. This Directive has not given rise to substantial jurisprudence. See, amongst others, Case 284/83, *Dansk Metalarbejderforbund v. Nielsen & Søn;* Case C-449/93, *Rockfon v, Specialarbejderforbundet i Danmark, acting on behalf of Søren Nielsen and others*; Case C-188/03, *Irmtraud Junk v. Wolfgang Kühnel*; Case C-55/02, *Commission v. Portugal*; Case C-32/02, *Commission v. Italy*; Joined Cases C-187–190/05, *Agorastoudis and others v. Goodyear Hellas* and Case C-385/05, *Confédération générale du travail et al. v. Premier ministre, Ministre de l'Emploi, de la Cohésion sociale et du Logement.*

employees' rights on transfer of undertakings,[742] and 80/987 on the protection of employees in the case of employer insolvency.[743] After 1987, this legal basis was still used for Directive 91/533 on an employer's obligation to inform employees of the conditions applicable to the contract or employment relationship.[744] Post-1994, Directive 94/45 on the establishment of a European Works Council or a procedure in Community-scale undertakings and Community-scale groups of undertakings for the purposes of informing and consulting employees was based on Article 2 of the Agreement on Social Policy.[745] Directive 96/71 concerning the posting of workers in the framework of the provision of services was, in contrast, based on Articles 47(2) and 55 EC.[746] After the entry into force of the Treaty of Amsterdam, amendments of these directives, and new directives in this field, have been based on Article 137 EC.[747]

In the case of the second category of directive, Article 94 EC and – in particular – Article 308 EC (ex Art. 235 EC) were used as legal bases prior to the entry into force of the Treaty of Amsterdam. Directive 75/117 (equal pay)[748] was adopted on the basis of Article 94 EC. For the general directives, Article 308

---

742. O.J. 1977, L 61/26, subsequently amended on numerous occasions, and consolidated in Dir. 2001/23/EC, O.J. 2001, L 82/16. This Directive has given rise to a substantial amount of case law. See for a commentary: C. de Groot, 'The Council Directive of the Safeguarding of Employees' Rights in the Event of Transfers of Undertakings: An Overview of the Case Law' (1993), CML Rev., 331–349, *idem* in (1998), CML Rev., 707–726, and A. Garde, 'Recent Developments in the Law Relating to Transfers of Undertakings: An Overview of the Case Law' (2002), CML Rev., 523–550. Of the more recent case law, the following are of interest: Case C-392/92, *Schmidt v. Spar- und Leihkasse der früheren Ämter Bordesholm, Kiel und Cronshagen*; Case C-13/95, *Süzen v. Zehnacker Gebäudereinigung Krankenhausservice*; Case C-343/98, *Collino and Chiappero v. Telecom Italia*; Case C-172/99, *Oy Liikenne v. Liskojärvi and Juntunen*, and Case C-51/00, *Temco v. Samir Imzilyen et al.*

743. O.J. 1980, L 283/23. Aside from the judgment already mentioned in Joined Cases C-6 & 9/90, *Francovich and Bonifaci*, which is of a far broader significance than for this Directive alone, the following judgments are of interest: Case C-321/97, *Andersson and Wåkerås-Andersson v. Sweden*, Case C-441/99, *Riksskatteverket v. Ghareveran*; Case C-278/05, *Robins and others v. Secretary of State for Work and Pensions* and Case C-81/05, *Cordero Alonso v. Fondo de Garantía Salarial (Fogasa)*. See also, the Commission's Proposal for a codified version of this Directive, COM(2006)657 final.

744. O.J. 1991, L 288/32.

745. O.J. 1994, L 254/64, extended to the United Kingdom with Dir. 97/74, O.J. 1998, L 10/22. See, on this Directive, Case C-62/99, *Betriebsrat der bofrost* Josef H. Boquoi Deutschland West v. Bofrost**, C-440/00, *Gesamtbetriebsrat der Kühne & Nagel v. Kühne and Nagel* and Case C-349/01, *Betriebsrat der Firma ADS Anker v. ADS Anker.*

746. O.J.1997, L 18/1. This Directive was adopted in the wake of Case C-113/89, *Rush Portuguesa v. Office national d'immigration*. See also Joined Cases C-49, 50, 52–54 & 68–71/98, *Finalarte*, and the very important recent case weighing up the freedom to supply services by means of posting of workers and the (national) rights to take industrial action: Case C-341/05, *Laval un Partneri Ltd v. Svenska Byggnadsarbetareförbundet.*

747. See e.g., Dir. 2002/14 establishing a general framework for informing and consulting employees in the European Community, O.J. 2002, L 80/29. On these Directives, see W. Weiss, 'The Future of Workers' Participation in the EU,' in C. Barnard, S. Deakin and G. Morris (eds), *The Future of Labour Law*, op. cit., *supra* note 663, 251.

748. O.J. 1975, L 45/19.

EC was used, sometimes with Article 94 EC: namely, Directive 76/207 (equal treatment for men and women in access to work, etc),[749] Directive 79/7 (equal treatment for men and women in social security),[750] Directive 86/378 (equal treatment in occupational social security schemes,[751] Directive 86/613 (equal treatment of men and women engaged in a self-employed capacity).[752] The directives adopted after the entry into force of the Single European Act, Directive 92/85 (protection of pregnant employees) were based on (ex) Article 118a EC.[753] Directive 96/34 (parental leave), which followed from a framework agreement concluded by the social partners, had Article 4(2) of the Agreement on Social Policy as a legal basis.[754] Directive 97/80 (burden of proof of unequal treatment)[755] is based on Article 2(2) of the Agreement on Social Policy.

The third category of Directive, related to the free movement of workers, was based on Article 40 EC. They will not be further considered here.

The directives falling under the wide fourth category of safety at work were originally based on Articles 94 and 308 EC.[756] Following the entry into force of the Single European Act, (ex) 118a was a particularly appropriate legal basis for these.[757] Of the many directives adopted in this field through the years, the important framework Directive 89/391 on the introduction of measures to encourage improvements in the safety and health of workers at work[758] and Directive 93/104 on working time[759] should be mentioned. The former serves as a basis for further

---

749. O.J. 1976, L 39/40.
750. O.J. 1979, L 6/24.
751. O.J. 1986, L 225/40. This Directive was adopted on the basis of Arts. 94 and 308 EC.
752. O.J. 1986, L 359 /56. This Directive was adopted on the basis of Arts. 94 and 308 EC.
753. O.J. 1992, L 348/1.
754. O.J. 1996, L 145/4.
755. O.J. 1998, L 14/6. Art. 2 of the Agreement on Social Policy has now broadly become Art. 137 EC.
756. Amongst others, Dir. 77/576, O.J. 1977, L 229/12 and Dir. 79/640, O.J. 1979, L 183/11. On the development of the Community's activities in the sphere of health and safety at work, see Neal, 'Providing "Teeth" for the right to a safe and healthy working environment?' in Neal, A.C. (ed.), *The Changing Face of European Labour Law and Social Policy* (The Hague etc., 2004), 95 and the Commission Communication, Improving quality and productivity at work: Community strategy 2007–2012 on health and safety at work, COM(2007)62.
757. See e.g., Council Dir. 91/383/EEC of 25 Jun. 1991, supplementing the measures to encourage improvements in the safety and health at work of workers with a fixed-duration employment relationship or a temporary employment relationship, O.J. 1991, L 206/19 and Council Dir. 94/33/EC of 22 Jun. 1994, on the protection of young people at work, O.J. 1994, L 216/12.
758. O.J. 1989, L 183/1. See, on this, P.F. van der Heijden, 'Labour Law and Social Policy within the EU' (1994), SEW, 1994, 321–352, in particular 329–331; Case C-132/04, *Commission v. Spain*, in which the Court held that the Directive also applies in principle to the armed forces and the police; and Case C-127/05, *Commission v. UK*.
759. O.J. 1993, L 307/18, amended by Dir. 2000/34 O.J. 2000, L 195/41, consolidated and repealed by Dir. 2003/88, O.J. 2003, L 299/9. On Dir. 93/104, see the judgments of the ECJ in, *inter alia*, Case C-124/05, *Federatie Nederlandse Vakbeweging v. Netherlands;* Joined Cases C-131 & 257/04, *Robinson-Steele and others*, Case C-14/04, *Dellas and others v. Premier ministre, Ministre des Affaires sociales, du Travail et de la Solidarité*, Joined Cases C-397–403/01, *Bernhard Pfeiffer and others v. Deutsches Rotes Kreuz, Kreisverband Waldshut*, and

directives regulating a host of specific aspects of safety at work. The latter Directive is of most interest because it gave rise to a serious difference of opinion about the substantive scope of (ex) Article 118a EC, eventually leading to a Court judgment.[760]

One of the characteristics of the period from the entry into force of the Single European Act to the entry into force of the Treaty of Amsterdam was the multiplicity of conflicts about the choice of legal basis for measures in the social area. The choice between Article 94 EC, which requires unanimity of votes, Article 95 EC, which entails qualified majority voting, and the old Article 118a EEC, was particularly controversial. The inclusion of Article 137 EC, with the Treaty of Amsterdam, put an end to these differences of opinion, which had formed a serious restriction for the development of Community social legislation.[761] The scope of this article means that, as already observed, it is no longer necessary to use Article 94 EC as a more general legal basis. Whether this is also the case for Article 308 EC is yet to be seen. In any event, it is likely that the Directives on equal treatment which have up to now been partly based on Article 308 EC will, in the future, have a sufficient legal basis in Article 137 EC.[762]

This very brief overview of the most important secondary legislation in the social field does not do justice to the substantial activities which the Community has undertaken since the middle of the 1970s in the area. The Council has made numerous resolutions, recommendations and other decisions in various topics in the sphere. Investigation of this activity is interesting as it demonstrates the constants and variables of social policy on Community and national level. We shall return to this in section 6.3 below.

Within the social policy of the EU, the field of equal pay and equal treatment for men and women, has had particularly extensive and specific development, stemming from the provisions of Article 141 EC. This area will be dealt with in section 6.4 below.

6.2.2   Paid Leave

Article 142 EC states that Member States shall endeavour to maintain the existing equivalence between paid holiday schemes. As this speaks only of 'endeavour', the article has clearly no direct effect. It may be asked whether Article 142 EC still

---

Case C-342/01, *Merino Gómez v. Continental Industrias del Caucho*. See further, J. Kenner, 'Working Time, Jaeger and the Seven-Year Itch', (2004/2005) Colum. J. Eur. L. 53; and A. Bogg, 'The Right to Paid Annual Leave in the European Court of Justice: The Eclipse of Functionalism' (2006), EL Rev., 892–905.

760. Case C-84/94, *UK v. Council* (Working Time Directive).

761. Although there is still scope for argument on the question whether legislation falls within the substantive scope of Art. 137 EC: see e.g., Case C-184/02, *Spain v. Parliament and Council* (organization of the working time of road transport workers).

762. Dir. 97/80 O.J. 1998, L 14/6, amended by Dir. 98/52 O.J. 1998, L 205/66, based on Art. 2 of the Agreement on Social Policy, would likely now have been based on Art. 137 EC.

retains any purpose in view of the competences granted to the Community by Article 137(1) EC.[763]

Paid leave is now – in addition – the subject of two Directives. Directive 92/85 – the so-called 'pregnancy Directive' – has already been mentioned above.[764] This Directive, which deals primarily with the employment conditions to which women may be subjected during pregnancy and breastfeeding,[765] provides that maternity leave shall be of a minimum 14 weeks. In addition, there is a prohibition on dismissal during this period. Further, the Directive contains a guarantee of adequate payment during this maternity leave, which must be at least the level of payment that would be received in case of sick leave. Mention should also be made of Directive 96/34.[766] This Directive gives employees, whether men or women, a right to at least 3 months of parental leave for the period until their child reaches 8 years of age. Each Directive contributes to the reduction of the handicaps to which women are subject who wish to combine their activities in the workplace with parenthood. Although these measures, taken narrowly, fall outside the area of equal treatment in the workplace in the strict sense, they are highly important for the practical achievement of equality.[767] This also holds for a number of Council recommendations in the field.[768] Although these are not binding, they can indeed play a certain role in Community and national policy and legal practice.[769]

6.2.3   Education, Vocational Training and Youth

Education and training have always been areas giving rise to substantial, sometimes fundamental differences of opinion between the Community and Member States. The Member States have taken the view, even more strongly than with social policy, that education is a classic national competence and as a result falls

---

763. If leave can be viewed as an employment condition, the Community is competent to harmonize the area by Directive pursuant to Art. 137(1) EC.
764. The Court gave its view on the interpretation of this Directive in Case C-109/00, *Tele Danmark v. Handels- og Kontorfunktionærernes Forbund i Danmark*. See also, on the inclusion of pay rises in the calculation of statutory maternity pay, Case C-147/02, *Alabaster v. Woolwich*.
765. This was the reason why this Directive was based on old Art. 118 EC, which created a specific legal basis for the harmonization of legislation on working conditions. It would now be based on Art. 137 EC. See, on this Directive: E. Caracciolo di Torella (2000), EL Rev., 310–316.
766. Dir. 96/34/EC of 3 Jun. 1996, on the framework agreement on parental leave concluded by UNICE, CEEP and the ETUC, O.J. 1996, L 145/4.
767. This is still some way off. See e.g., the Commission draft Communication of 18 Jul. 2007, *Tackling the pay gap between men and women*, which states that, across the EU, women earn on average 15% less than men. On the Commission's 'gender mainstreaming' strategy to combat gender inequalities, see F. Beveridge, 'Building Against the Past: The Impact of Mainstreaming on EU Gender Law and Policy' (2007), EL Rev., 193–212.
768. See, amongst others, Council recommendation 84/635/EEC of 13 Dec. 1984 on the promotion of positive action for women, O.J. 1984, L 331/34 and Council recommendation 92/241/EEC of 31 Mar. 1992, on child care, O.J. 1992, L 123/6.
769. E.g., in Case C-476/99, *Lommers*, para. 37, the Court referred to Recommendation 92/241/EEC on child care.

outside the scope of the EC Treaty. This standpoint has proven untenable as a general approach.

In dealing with the legal framework for market integration in Chapter VIII, it has already been shown that free movement of persons and services have real consequences for national education law and policy:[770]

– children of migrating workers may take part in the educational system of the host Member State on the same footing and enjoy the same facilities as 'national' students;[771]
– insofar as education is a service, it must be offered without discrimination on the basis of nationality or origin;[772]
– students' right of residence is regulated by a separate Council Directive;[773]
– the general prohibition on discrimination on grounds of nationality applies to the national supply of education and benefits linked to this, such as study grants[774] and tax benefits;[775]
– in the framework of free movement of services, considerable harmonization of diplomas for different types of education and for a large number of professional activities has taken place.

In short, insofar as obtaining the necessary qualifications and their recognition within the Community as a whole are essential conditions to access the employ-ment market or to practise a given profession or business, those aspects of national education policy relevant to this fall within the scope of the EC Treaty.

---

770. On the potential problems that could arise for certain Member States from unrestricted free movement of students, see, A.P. van der Mei, 'EU Law and Education: Promotion of Student Mobility versus Protection of Education Systems', in M. Dougan and E. Spaventa (eds), *Social Welfare and EU Law*, op. cit., *supra* note 672. See further, Case C-147/03, *Commission v. Austria*, in which the Court held that, by failing to take the necessary measures to ensure that holders of secondary education diplomas awarded in other Member States can gain access to higher and university education organized by it under the same conditions as holders of secondary education diplomas awarded in Austria, Austria had failed to fulfil its obligations under Arts. 12 EC, 149 EC and 150 EC.

771. See, amongst others, Case 9/74, *Casagrande v. Landeshauptstadt München;* Joined cases 389 & 390/87, *G. B. C. Echternach and A. Moritz v. Minister van Onderwijs en Wetenschappen* and Case C-184/99, *Grzelczyk v. Centre public d'aide sociale d'Ottignies-Louvain-la-Neuve.*

772. See, amongst others, Case 293/83, *Gravier v. Ville de Liège.*

773. Dir. 93/96, O.J. 1993, L 317/59. On this, see *inter alia* Case C-184/99, *Grzelczyk.*

774. This can also apply for social benefits for the benefit of unemployed graduates. See Case C-278/94, *Commission v. Belgium* (young people seeking first employment) and Case C-224/98, *D'Hoop v. Office national de l'emploi.* See also Case C-209/03, *Dany Bidar v. London Borough of Ealing and Secretary of State for Education and Skills*, in which the Court held that Art. 12(1) EC precludes national legislation which grants students the right to assistance covering their maintenance costs only if they are settled in the host Member State, while precluding a national of another Member State from obtaining the status of settled person as a student even if that national is lawfully resident and has received a substantial part of his secondary education in the host Member State and has consequently established a genuine link with the society of that State.

775. Case C-76/05, *Schwarz and Gootjes Schwarz v. Finanzamt Bergisch Gladbach* and Case C-318/05, *Commission v. Germany.*

The significance of education and training goes, however, beyond market integration. The quality of the working population is increasingly one of the central areas of attention in current economic and social policy. From an economic viewpoint, the increasing intensity of knowledge of current production processes for goods and services is especially relevant. This trend is taking place over a very wide range: in agriculture, just as in logistic services or in the production of microprocessors. Economies where the supply of highly qualified labour is lower than demand will have inevitable difficulties, with little development in production, a low investment level and lower economic growth. From a social viewpoint, it is important to note that the vast majority of long-term unemployed within the Community comes from the low-educated segment of the working population. As there are clear limits to the level to which the gross salary of low-educated workers can be lowered,[776] efforts must be made to increase the level of training of this group of employees as far as possible. The speed at which new technologies and working methods are implemented in production processes is increasing. As a result, knowledge and skills become outdated quickly. A sustained capacity to remain employable on the employment market is becoming a factor affecting terms of labour – the domain of the social partners – and the form of social security benefits.

The links summarized briefly above between, on the one hand, training and knowledge and, on the other hand, economic and employment growth, can also be seen in the policy coordination on the basis of Articles 99 and 125–130 EC. Attention is paid to the issue in the BEPG as well as the employment guidelines.

The conclusions of the special European Council in Lisbon, March 2000 are, in this regard, very relevant: making the European Union an economic leader means striving for the supply of high-quality knowledge.[777] An activating and stimulating labour market policy will create the conditions which complement the protection and strengthening of the European model of the social market economy. If these ambitious goals are to be taken seriously, it will almost unavoidably mean that the direct and indirect influence of Community policy integration on national education policy will become greater.

The original EC Treaty already contained a separate article (Art. 128 EEC) in the title on social policy for vocational training which, in view of the significance of training for social policy, was an obvious complement to the general provisions of the title. Typical tensions appeared in the interpretation and application of ex-Article 128 EEC between, on the one hand, Member States' (and in Germany

---

776. In the BEPG, the reduction of so-called indirect labour costs for low-education workers is regularly emphasized. This is less simple for net labour costs, as it requires salary subsidies to be given.

777. Bull. EU 3-2000, I 14–28. See further, the Commission Communication, Delivering on the Modernisation for Universities: Education, Research and Innovation, COM(2006)208 final; the Proposal for a Regulation establishing the European Institute of Technology, COM(2006)604 final/2; the Commission Communication, A coherent set of indicators and benchmarks for monitoring progress towards the Lisbon objectives in education and training, COM(2007)61 final.

the *Länder's*) fear of far-reaching Community intervention in their treasured autonomy in the education field and, on the other hand, the evident desirability of Community initiatives in the area. In the 1980s, this tension gave rise to a bitter dispute between the Commission and certain Member States, necessitating multiple judgments of the Court.[778]

With the Treaty of Maastricht, an attempt was made to find a solution for this apparent sensitivity by creating an unambiguous legal basis for Community actions in the field of education itself (Art. 149 EC) and the field of vocational training (Art. 150 EC).[779] While these provisions were originally situated within Title XI – on social policy, education, vocational training and youth – the Lisbon Treaty changes this to create separate Titles for social policy, on the one hand, and education, vocational training, youth and sport, on the other (Titles X and XII TFEU, respectively).

Article 149 EC creates a – very restricted – legal basis for Community actions in the area of education. The Community contribution is essentially restricted to encouraging cooperation between Member States and 'where necessary' supporting and complementing their activities; in particular by emphasizing the European dimension in education, especially in language education, and by promoting cooperation between educational establishments and mobility of students and teachers (Art. 149(1) and (2) EC).[780] For this, the Council may take incentive measures under the co-decision procedure, after consultation of the Economic and Social Committee and the Committee of the Regions. The involvement of the latter committee indicates the sensitivity which exists here, in particular for the German *Länder*.

In a potentially significant move, the Lisbon Treaty expands the scope of Article 149 beyond education in the narrow sense to include the area of sport, providing that the Union shall contribute to the promotion of 'European sporting issues'. Union action in this field shall be aimed at, *inter alia*, 'developing the European dimension in sport, by promoting fairness and openness in sporting competitions.'

Article 149 EC is the legal basis for a series of incentive programmes, such as those for the exchange of students and teachers, the promotion of language

---

778. Two issues were central to this discussion: (a) What should be considered to be vocational training (the substantive scope of Art. 128 EEC)? and (b) What was the nature of the Council's competences under Art. 128 EEC? The concept of vocational training (raised by the first issue) was extensively interpreted by the Court in, amongst others, Case 293/83, *Gravier*, Case 24/86, *Blaizot v. Université de Liège* and Case C-357/89, *Raulin v. Minister van Onderwijs en Wetenschappen*. The second question was answered by the Court in Case 242/87, *Commission v. Council* (Erasmus) and Case 56/88, *UK v. Council* (Petra). These judgments are still of importance in connection with the nature of the measures that the Council can take under Art. 150(1) EC.

779. J. Cloos et al., op. cit., *supra* note 51, 317–319 and R. Lane, 'New Community Competences under the Maastricht Treaty' (1993), CML Rev., 939–979, 946–951.

780. The SOCRATES programme, which aims at promoting exchanges of students and teachers, is thus based on this Article (Decision 253/2000, O.J. 2000, L 28/1).

education and the community development of study programmes. In part, the present programmes are a development of programmes which had been based on ex-Article 128 EC.

In the area of vocational training, Article 150(1) EC provides for slightly broader Community competences. Under this article, 'The Community shall implement a vocational training policy which shall support and supplement the action of the Member States, while fully respecting the responsibility of the Member States for the content and organization of vocational training.' This rather unhappily formulated provision puts an end to previous uncertainty as to whether the Community may act on its own in this area. In addition, it follows from the text that this action does not have to be dependent on previous initiatives of the Member States. The Community may thus also take implementing decisions, as long as they do not interfere with the responsibility of the Member States for their *own* policy.[781]

It is important to note that both Articles create a Community competence to promote cooperation with third countries and with the relevant international organizations (see Art. 149(3) EC and Art. 150(3) EC).[782] The persistently delicate nature of the definition of Community competences in the area is apparent from the fourth sub-paragraph of each article. Community measures amounting to Member State harmonization of legislative and administrative provisions may not be taken in the spheres of education or vocational training on the basis of Articles 149 and 150 EC.

The policy practice of the Community on the basis of Articles 149 and 150 EC is somewhat paradoxical. On the one hand, the irrefutable social and economic importance of education and vocational training is emphasized in a host of non-binding Council and Commission decisions. These statements are supported by, from a financial point of view, relatively modest stimulation programmes. On the other hand, the Community remains very cautious in taking initiatives which could be seen by Member States as an incursion into the almost-absolute autonomy which they demand for themselves in the area. Meanwhile, higher and university educational establishments, in particular, enjoy increasing freedom of movement – which they receive in the national sphere – to market and distinguish themselves at a European level.[783] The proportion of purely privately financed higher and university education, which is increasing almost throughout the European Union, is not unrelated to this development. If this evolution continues, there is a question whether the present rather forced division of competence between the Community

781. This accords with the case mentioned above, Case 242/87, *Commission v. Council* (Erasmus) and Case 56/88, *UK v. Council* (Petra). See e.g., Decision 1720/2006 establishing an action programme in the field of lifelong learning, O.J. 2006, L 327/45.

782. These competences are regularly used. The so-called trans-European mobility programme for higher education (TEMPUS III), Council decision of 29 Apr. 1999, O.J. 1999, L 120/30, is an example. See, more recently, the ERASMUS Mundus programmes of the Commission: <http://ec.europa.eu/education/programmes/mundus/index_en.html>.

783. This development is also starting in relation to secondary school education: Case C-76/05, *Schwarz and Gootjes Schwarz* and Case C-318/05, *Commission v. Germany*.

and the Member States is sustainable in the long term. With the shift in the border between publicly and privately financed education, however, the relevance of an internal market right to education increases. The question is whether this will be recognized by the Member States.

6.3   THE FUTURE OF SOCIAL POLICY INTEGRATION

In the beginning of the 1990s, there were two radically different views about the future of social policy integration within the European Union. The first extreme position was adopted by the then-Conservative British government, which was, almost as a point of principle, of the opinion that the Community should have no competence in the social area. In its view, it was for the Member States to draw conclusions, where necessary, from the consequences of disparities between different national social systems for the competitiveness of their industry. In this view, a 'spontaneous' harmonization downwards, in the form of policy competition, was fully legitimate, as the logical consequence of market integration.[784] The other extreme position was adopted by the French and German trade union movements, which were of the view that the best guarantee of protection of the European social model lay in the harmonization of social systems along the pattern of their own national models, including minimum benefit levels.[785]

Both extremes are unsustainable, for legal-systematic reasons.

The greatest difficulty with the British view on the eve of the Treaty of Maastricht was that it completely overlooked the fact that, in a more or less completely integrated market, unrestricted policy competition in the social field could mean that the Member States' retained competences in that field would lose any real meaning. The resulting social tensions could, in the worst case scenario, cause Member States which felt 'under threat' to adopt protective measures, and this would call market integration itself into question. The interdependencies between Member States created by market integration in turn create a certain necessity for policy coordination in the social area.[786] In addition, the British view overlooked the fact that the economic policy coordination provided for in Article 99 EC

---

784. See P. Watson, 'Social Policy after Maastricht' (1993), CML Rev., 481–513, in particular 487–498. A strong ideological aversion to any intermediary involvement of the social partners in the formation and implementation of social policy also played a role in the position of the British government. In addition, it was of the view that the continental model of 'Soziale Marktwirtschaft' threatened to become unsustainable in the light of increased competition on the global level. These views were at the heart of the British government's resistance to an enlargement of Community competence in the social field in the run-up to the Treaty of Maastricht.

785. This view also seems still to be held, though in a less radical form, by certain practitioners of European social law: see amongst others R. Blanpain, op. cit., *supra* note 664, 435–440.

786. Although the original economic reasoning for Art. 141 EC in the Court's case law has been revised, the very idea that competition in social norms could result from the presence of women in the workplace within the internal market seems in itself sufficient to justify the necessity for minimal coordination at the Community level.

cannot be effective unless social policy, with its huge impact on the functioning of the labour market, is involved. Finally, the British view gave insufficient attention to the fact that the economic consequences of market integration, in the form of cross-border activities of undertakings, mean that a certain uniformity of some social provisions is desirable.[787]

The second view is, in its radicalism, not sustainable either. Aside from the considerable political and societal problems it entails, it is unrealistic in the light of the large differences in prosperity within the Community, and even more so since the latest enlargements. As the costs of the social system ultimately depend on the labour factor, every attempt to make social law and policy uniform would entail an unacceptable tax on less productive labour in less-well-off areas of the Community. The German experience after reunification shows that its pernicious socio-economic consequences, which mainly took the form of widespread and persistent unemployment, cannot be resolved by massive transfers of income.

It follows from all this that the road to more social convergence leads to more convergence in growth of employment and standard of living. The Commission recognized this in the above-mentioned White Paper on Growth, Competitiveness and Employment. This interconnection is also more than evident in the conclusions of the European Council in Lisbon, March 2000,[788] and the Commission's Social Agenda launched in the context of the mid-term review of the Lisbon strategy.[789]

The contours of the Community's social policy in the future can be sketched against this background.

First, the legislative activity of the Community will continue to focus primarily on ensuring equal access to and equal treatment on the labour market for the European working population, including the removal of barriers to the labour market for those with personal, functional or situational limitations. This will mean elaboration of the principle of equality of Articles 13 and 141 EC. The Community

---

787. It is telling that a large number of British businesses have switched 'spontaneously' to the institution of a European works council, in conformity with Dir. 94/45. See C. Barnard op. cit. *supra* note 661, 208.

788. Bull. EU 3-2000, para. 1.14–18, fundamentally relaunched in Mar. 2006 'to re-focus priorities on jobs and growth coherent with the Sustainable Development Strategy' (see the Presidency Conclusions of the Brussels European Council of 23/24 Mar. 2006 7775/06). On the relevance of this process and in particular of the 'Open Method of Coordination' to European labour law, see S. Sciarra, 'The "Making" of EU Labour Law and the "Future" of Labour Lawyers', in C. Barnard, S. Deakin and G. Morris (eds), *The Future of Labour Law*, op. cit., *supra* note 663, 201. See also, N. Bernard, 'Internal Market *v.* Open Co-ordination in EU Social Welfare Law', in M. Dougan and E. Spaventa (eds), *Social Welfare and EU Law*, op. cit., *supra* note 672, 261 and M. Daly, 'EU Social Policy after Lisbon' (2006), JCMS, 461–481.

789. Communication from the Commission on the Social Agenda, COM(2005)33 final. See also, the Report of the High Level Group on the future of social policy in an enlarged European Union (2004), commissioned by the Directorate-General for Employment and Social Affairs of the European Commission. On the outcome of the previous Social Policy Agenda (2000–2005), see the Commission Communication COM(2004)137 final, Scoreboard on Implementing the Social Policy Agenda.

has already come some way in this task, via the still-broadening scope of its secondary legislation.[790]

A second natural channel for Community legislative activities lies in ensuring the social conditions for the free movement of persons, in particular the free movement of workers. The Community has, from its first existence in the form of the ECSC, always been active in this area. Nonetheless, the very considerable legislation in this field, discussed in Chapter VIII of this book, cannot be allowed to stagnate. This legislation is extremely sensitive to cultural, societal and economic changes. If its maintenance were to fall behind – for example, because applicable only to European nationals and not to workers coming from third countries – it would no longer achieve its aim, viz. the facilitation of geographic mobility of the labour factor within the Community.[791]

Keeping this legislation up-to-date will require more activity from the Community legislature than would appear from the last decade.[792] This is all the more necessary because parts of national social security legislation for the working population are undergoing, or will shortly undergo, great change, in order to

---

790.   See *supra* section 6.2.2 and *infra* section 6.4. Aside from the directives discussed therein, mention should be made of Dir. 2000/43/EC of 29 Jun. 2000, implementing the principle of equal treatment between persons irrespective of racial or ethnic origin, O.J. 2000, L 180/22; Dir. 2000/78/EC of 27 Nov. 2000, establishing a general framework for equal treatment in employment and occupation, O.J. 2000, L 303/16; and Dir. 2004/113/EC of 13 Dec. 2004, implementing the principle of equal treatment between men and women in the access to and supply of goods and services, all of which are based on Art. 13 EC. See also, the Commission's Communication, The application of Dir. 2000/43/EC of 29 Jun. 2000, implementing the principle of equal treatment between persons irrespective of racial or ethnic origin, COM(2006)643 final. See further, M. Bell, *Anti-Discrimination Law and the European Union* (Oxford etc., 2002); E. Ellis, 'The Principle of Non-Discrimination in the Post-Nice Era', in A. Arnull and D. Wincott (eds), *Accountability and legitimacy in the European Union* (Oxford etc., Oxford University Press, 2003); D. Mabbett, 'The Development of Rights-based Social Policy in the European Union: The Example of Disability Rights' (2005), *Journal of Common Market Studies*, 97; Brennan, 'The Race Directive, Institutional Racism and Third Country Nationals', in T. Takis and P. Nebbia (eds) *European Union Law for the Twenty-First Century* (Oxford etc., 2004), 371; D. Hosking, 'Great Expectations: Protection from Discrimination because of Disability in Community Law', EL Rev., 2006, 667–689; and the Commission's Annual Reports on Equality and non-discrimination, available at <http://ec.europa.eu/employment_social/fundamental_rights/public/pubst_en.htm#stud>. On the concept of disability in Dir. 2000/78, see Case C-13/05, *Chacón Navas v. Eurest Colectividades* and, more generally, the Opinion of the Advocate General in that case. See also, Case C-144/04, *Werner Mangold v. Rüdiger Helm*, the critical views in the Opinion of A.G. Mazák in Case C-411/05, *Palacios de la Villa*; and the Editorial on Mangold (2006), CML Rev., 1.

791.   This shortcoming has already been indicated in the previous edition of this book. Attempts by the Commission to remedy Reg. 1408/71 met with no result for many years. See Bull. EU 1/2–2002, 38. This situation was to a significant extent resolved by Reg. 859/2003 extending the provisions of Reg. 1408/71 and Reg. 574/72 to nationals of third countries who are not already covered by those provisions solely on the ground of their nationality, O.J. 2003, L 124/1: see note 688 *supra* on Reg. 1408/71 generally and F. Pennings, op. cit., *supra* note 688, 241.

792.   See the Opinion of A.G. Geelhoed in Case C-413/99, *Baumbast*.

offer the greater flexibility being demanded by both the supply- and demand-side of the labour market.

A third topic of continued interest for the Community legislature is undoubtedly legislation on safety at work and working conditions. This legislation is closely connected, as the first initiatives in this field show, to the requirements of a properly functioning internal market. Aside from this, the physical protection of employees in their workplace is a classic example of an area upon which consensus can be reached at Community level. The Community labour market, which is gradually being constituted, does not tolerate the dumping of social costs of sub-standard levels of safety at work by one Member State on another Member State.[793]

The fourth topic of interest concerns the 'Betriebsverfassung', the relations between the management, employees and capital providers within an undertaking. This particularly sensitive topic delayed agreement on the statue of the European Company for more than 20 years. Even aside from this, it was a bone of contention giving rise to huge ideological differences in opinion. The adoption of Directive 94/45 on the establishment of a European Works Council, and agreement on the European Company, are milestones which are more important than what some see as the rather disappointing content of the results achieved.[794] They indicate that, within a largely completed internal market, the Community legislature should also deal with institutional relationships within undertakings.[795]

The fifth topic concerns labour relations as such. Following the activity of the Community legislature in some parts of this field in the second half of the 1970s, it only recommenced activity here in the second half of the 1990s. It is very telling that the initiative for this came primarily from the social partners, which had been brought in by the Community legislature pursuant to Article 139 EC. Further developments in this field, particularly as the fruit of social dialogue, cannot be excluded. Community legislation here will remain characterized by greater temporal flexibility and substantive differentiation than is generally the case in

---

793. See the Commission's Communication on the Social Agenda COM(2005)33 final and the Commission Communication, Improving quality and productivity at work: Community strategy 2007–2012 on health and safety at work, COM(2007)62. Note also the establishment of the European Agency for Health and Safety at Work in 1996.

794. Dir. 94/45/EC of 22 Sep. 1994, on the establishment of a European Works Council or a procedure in Community-scale undertakings and Community-scale groups of undertakings for the purposes of informing and consulting employees, O.J. 1994, L 254/64; Reg. (EC) No. 2157/2001 of 8 Oct. 2001, on the Statute for a European company (SE), O.J. 2001, L 294/1; Dir. 2001/86/EC of 8 Oct. 2001, supplementing the Statute for a European company with regard to the involvement of employees, O.J. 2001, L 294/22; and Reg. (EC) No. 1435/2003 of 22 Jul. 2003 on the Statute for a European Cooperative Society (O.J. 2003, L 207/1). See also, Case C-436/03, *Parliament v. Council* (legal basis of Reg. (EC) No. 1435/2003) and Council Dir. 2003/72 supplementing the Statute for a European Co-operative Society with regard to the involvement of employees, O.J. 2003, L 207/25.

795. E. Scyszczak, op. cit. *supra* note 327, 1161.

other areas. This reflects the considerable differences in labour relations within the Community.[796]

Community social policy is not exclusively contained in legally binding instruments. From the late 1960s onwards, the Council and the Commission have passed a host of resolutions, recommendations and declarations which, while recognizing the primarily national nature of competence in the social field, nonetheless aim at the achievement of more substantive policy convergence. The fact that the actual consequences of these activities in the national sphere have long remained disappointingly limited is also a result of the unsystematic character of the actions taken by the Council and Commission. The historiography of these activities – which cannot be dealt with here – could prove that they were often inspired by what was fashionable at the time.

Definite changes have taken place in this regard in the last decade. It is to the credit of the Delors Commission that the policy link between economic growth, employment and the functioning of the labour market (including social security) was made. We have already emphasized these links many times above in sections 3.2 and 4.2, in discussing the BEPG and the employment guidelines. The same links will, and must, give future Community action in the social field more cohesion. This will enable the social aspect of policy integration to lose the stigma of remaining one of the relatively few areas of informal cooperation.

Since the European Council of Essen in 1994, the employment issue has continuously been placed high on the agenda of European leaders. The view that this issue is very closely connected with national labour relations, the development of national conditions of work, and the institution of social security provisions for the working population, requires attention to be paid to these areas at the Community level also. If this is not done, a solution to the question of unemployment as a European problem will likely remain beyond reach. The phenomenon that we indicated in our analysis of Articles 149 and 150 EC is also apparent here: within a completed EMU, policy convergence will be necessary even in fields which the Member States consider to be at the heart of their retained competences. Recognizing this, government leaders have committed themselves to tabling the necessity of adapting national social policy at the highest political level on the agenda of European Councils while at the same time guarding against the risk that the resulting policy process might be recognized as a Community policy process.[797] The prominent position in policy-making of the Committees for Employment and Social Protection provided for in Articles 130 and 144 EC is a result.

---

796.   C. Barnard op. cit. *supra* note 661, 206–209. See e.g., the Report of the European Commission, Industrial Relations in Europe 2006 (available at <http://ec.europa.eu/employment_social/social_dialogue/reports_en.htm>), which notes that trade union membership within the EU varies between 8% and 80%. The Commission is to adopt a Green Paper on the development of labour law and industrial relations, as well as a proposal for an optional European framework for trans-national collective bargaining: see Communication from the Commission on the Social Agenda COM(2005)33 final.

797.   See also, E. Szyszczak, op. cit. *supra* note 527, 1167–1169.

It is at present too early definitively to weigh up the results of the spectacular. development in social policy integration in the past 15 years, compared with the previous situation. On the positive side of the scales, we have seen policy initiatives and political breakthroughs which, 15 years ago, seemed out of reach. This also holds for social dialogue, which has acquired much more significance than sceptics had thought possible. On the negative side, the policy process has lost transparency and the results of this process are not always recognizable or legally definable. The attention paid to social policy convergence at the highest political level does not ensure that this convergence actually takes place in national practice.[798] An increase in transparency in the decision-making processes, a clearer definition of the responsibilities and competences of the actors involved in these processes, and a sharper appraisal of the consequences of policy initiatives taken on a national level in connection with the Community, will make the necessary 'next steps' in social policy integration more effective.

6.4   EQUAL PAY AND EQUAL TREATMENT

6.4.1   Equal Pay

Article 141(1) EC (previously Art. 119 EC) requires each Member State to ensure that the principle of equal pay for male and female workers for equal work or work of equal value is applied.

The second paragraph of this article further describes what is meant by 'pay' and what equal pay 'without discrimination' means.

Article 141(3) EC directs the Community legislature to ensure the application of the principle of equality in employment and occupation described in the first paragraph. Article 141(4) leaves it open to the Member States, in ensuring equal treatment of men and women in vocational activities, to take measures of positive discrimination to make it easier for the under-represented sex to pursue such activities.

The first two paragraphs of Article 141 EC appeared in a rather different version in the original EEC Treaty. The interpretation and application of this article has gone through far-reaching developments since 1958, which seem to be still ongoing. The historical background to the inclusion of this article was the French government's fear of competitive disadvantage.[799] It was of the view that the principle of equal pay had had far greater effects in the French labour market than elsewhere in the Community. This economic approach to Article 141 EC

---

798.   For an example of a failure of Community social legislation to achieve its objectives in practice within a Member State, see C. Barnard, 'The EU Agenda for Regulating Labour Markets: Lessons from the UK in the Field of Working Time', in G. Bermann (ed.), *Law and Governance in an Enlarged Union* (Oxford etc., 2004). See further, Case C-484/04, *Commission v. UK* (Working Time).

799.   J. Currall in Von der Groeben etc., op. cit. *supra* note 81, 3/1192–1341 at 1207–1209.

is no longer used as a basis for its interpretation. As the article is primarily concerned with the labour market in the broad sense, its application has acquired a strong, though not exclusively, social flavour, since the principle of equal treatment has acquired an independent meaning in national constitutional law and international public law, quite apart from the socio-economic context in which it take effect.[800]

The content and application of the Article 141 EC principle of equality has since the 1970s been decided principally by the Court's case law. This has not only been important for the interpretation of the article itself, but also for the content and application of the secondary Community law implementing the principle of equality outside the area of pay dealt with in Article 141(1) and (2) EC. It is not possible here to give a complete overview of the jurisprudence of the Court on Article 141 EC and the Directives directly related to the article. We must restrict ourselves to looking at some of the leading cases.

In its leading judgment in *Defrenne II*, the Court held the principle laid down in Article 141(1) EC to have direct effect, including in the legal relationships between individuals (horizontal direct effect).[801]

This fundamental step immediately raised the following questions:

(a) What does equal pay for equal work or work of equal value mean?
(b) What is the framework for reference for deciding if unequal treatment has taken place?
(c) What is the content and scope of the concept of unequal treatment or discrimination?
(d) Is it possible to justify a difference in treatment?
(e) What does 'pay' mean?
(f) What is the personal scope of the Article 141 EC principle of equality?
(g) What is the substantive scope of that principle?

6.4.1.1   *Equal Pay for Equal Work or Work of Equal Value*

The principle of equality, such as at present formulated by Article 141(1) and (2) EC, lays down that the same work or work to which equal value is attributed must be remunerated in the same way, whether it is performed by a man or a woman.[802]

---

800. It appears from the Court's reluctant approach to measures with an aim of so-called positive discrimination that it too considers the principle of equal treatment on grounds of sex to be broader than a merely social principle. See, amongst others, Case C-450/93, *Kalanke v. Freie Hansestadt Bremen*, paras. 15 and 16 and Case C-476/99, *Lommers v. Minister van Landbouw, Natuurbeheer en Visserij*. See also e.g., Joined Cases C-270 & 271/97, *Deutsche Post AG v. Elisabeth Sievers and Brunhilde Schrage*, para. 57 and, for an example of the Court's considering the principle of equal treatment on grounds of age to be a general principle of Community law, Case C-144/04, *Mangold*. On this, see further the critical views in the Opinion of A.G. Mazák in Case C-411/05, *Palacios de la Villa v. Cortefiel Servicios*.
801. Case 43/75, *Defrenne v. SABENA (Defrenne II)*, para. 39.
802. See, for an illustration of the questions that can arise from the concept of equal pay, Case C-381/99, *Brunnhofer v. Bank der Osterreichischen Postparkasse*.

The application of this key rule means that, where an unjustified difference in pay is alleged, it must first be considered whether equal work or work of equal value was in fact performed. This must be done by looking at objective factors, such as the nature of the work, educational requirements, working conditions and the respective responsibilities of the men and women being compared. The mere circumstance, for example, that they are included in the same function group of a collective labour agreement is not in this respect conclusive. The Court usually gives the national judge criteria for assessing whether, on the facts, there can be said to be equal work or work of equal value, but is reluctant to make a judgment itself of the relevant facts.[803]

6.4.1.2   The Framework

The Article 141 EC norm is directed at those who can be held responsible for the application of the principle of equal pay. Differences in pay can flow from a number of 'sources'. If, for example, work performed by women is paid less in Undertaking A than identical work performed by men in Undertaking B, and each company operates wholly separately from the other, there may be two possible sources of this difference: the fact that different companies are involved, and the difference in sex. Undertaking A cannot be responsible for the fact that its level of pay for women is lower than Undertaking B's pay level for men.

As early as the *Defrenne II* case, the Court was faced with the question of how to define the set of 'sources' responsible for unequal pay. The Court held, in paragraphs still relevant today, that, among the forms of discrimination which may be identified by reference to the criteria laid down by Article 141 EC, those which have their origin in legislative provisions or in collective labour agreements must be included in particular, and that this also applies in cases where men and women receive unequal pay for equal work carried out in the same establishment or service, whether public or private.[804]

This point of departure has been retained in subsequent judgments. In some circumstances the concept of 'undertaking' has been widely applied, for example concerning pay within a company with different subsidiary companies, or within a public or semi-public service that manages a number of comparable institutions. In these cases there is still, however, one 'source' to which potential unjustified differences in pay can be attributed.

If no benchmark can be found within one undertaking or service to take as a starting point in analysing whether unequal pay exists, for example because only or primarily women carry out a given function, the case law does not permit the creation of a 'hypothetical' benchmark: 'In cases of actual discrimination falling within the scope of the direct application of Article 119 (now 141 EC), comparisons are confined to parallels which may be drawn on the basis of concrete

---

803.   See Case C-381/99, *Brunnhofer*.
804.   Case 43/75, *Defrenne II*, paras. 21 and 22.

appraisals of the work actually performed by employees of different sex within the same establishment or service.'[805]

The Court has expressed the same view in a situation where employees of different employers worked within the same overall institution.[806]

6.4.1.3   The Scope of the Concept of Discrimination

In *Defrenne II*, the Court initially chose a restricted definition of the discrimination prohibited under Article 141 EC. According to the Court, this should concern 'direct' discrimination, which can be deduced simply from differences of pay.[807] The Court quickly abandoned this restrictive interpretation, which would in practice have considerably restricted the relevance of the prohibition on discrimination, as direct discrimination rarely occurs any more in practice.[808] In *Jenkins*, the Court had to give judgment on a case where the same work was carried out within one company by two different function groups. Almost all those in the first, lower-paid, function group were women; most of those in the second function group were men. The situation was qualified as the continuation of a previously existing difference in pay via the artificial means of instituting two function groups. Such cases of disguised discrimination are *per se* considered to fall under the Article 141 EC prohibition.[809]

Indirect discrimination exists when the difference in pay is based on apparently neutral criteria which, when applied in practice, mean that a group of employees of the same sex – usually women – is disadvantaged.[810] An almost classic example from case law is differences in pay and other terms of employment between full-time and part-time workers. As in practice in society, women are usually structurally over-represented in the category of part-time workers, differences in pay between such workers and full-time workers are considered to be

---

805. Case 129/79, *Macarthys v. Smith*, para. 15, 15; see also Case C-200/91, *Coloroll Pension Trustees v. Russell and others*.
806. Case C-320/00, *Lawrence and Others v. Regent Office Care et al.* See also the Opinion of A.G. Geelhoed in Case C-256/01, *Allonby v. Accrington and Rossendale College* and the comments of S. Prechal, in 'Equality of Treatment, Non-discrimination and Social Policy: Achievements in Three Themes', in A. McDonnell (ed.), *A Review of Forty Years of Community Law: Legal Developments in the European Communities and the European Union*, (The Hague etc., 2005). C. Costello and G. Davies, 'The Case Law of the Court of Justice in the field of sex equality since 2000' (2006), CML Rev., 1567–1616.
807. Case 43/75, *Defrenne II*, paras. 20–24.
808. For recent cases involving direct discrimination, see Case C-196/02, *Nikoloudi v. Organismos Tilepikinonion Ellados* and Case C-227/04, *Maria-Luise Lindorfer v. Council of the European Union* (different actuarial values for men and women at any given age in transfer of rights to Community pension scheme). Situations where women are paid equally to men, but where men perform duties of less value, also fall under direct discrimination: see Case 157/86, *Mary Murphy and others v. An Bord Telecom Eireann*.
809. Case 96/80, *Jenkins v. Kingsgate*.
810. On the development of the concept of indirect discrimination in this area, see C. Tobler, *Indirect Discrimination* (Antwerpen, 2005).

indirect discrimination. In *Bilka*, the Court held that indirect discrimination also falls under Article 141 EC.[811] A large part of the Court's indirect discrimination judgments since then has concerned situations in which part-time workers were treated less favourably than full-time worker.[812] Other situations which can give rise to the conclusion that indirect discrimination exists include:

- Professional groups constituted unilaterally, which perform different but very similar activities for a very different fee.[813]
- Differences between female and male workers in benefits from a workers' pension fund.[814]
- Differences in pay on a piece-work basis which are not due to differences in the degree of difficulty of the work performed.[815]
- Differences in pay regulations whereby special allowances form a greater proportion of the total salary for one group than for the other. This can indicate indirect discrimination if workers of one sex are over-represented in one group of activities.[816]
- The use of the same time limit in order to qualify for an award of damages for unfair dismissal, which is structurally disadvantageous for women in comparison to men.[817]

6.4.1.4   Exceptions: Grounds of Justification

The Court has, from the first judgments in which it extended the application of Article 141 EC to cases of indirect discrimination, examined whether a measure

---

811. Case 170/84, *Bilka-Kaufhaus v. Weber von Hartz*. See also Case C-351/00, *Pirkko Niemi*.
812. From the judgments handed down up to 1 Jan. 2002, in which the concept of indirect discrimination was dealt with, 16 of the 34 cases involved part-time work. See, for more recent examples, Case C-285/02, *Elsner-Lakeberg v. Land Nordrhein-Westfalen*; Joined Cases C-4 & 5/02, *Schönheit v. Stadt Frankfurt am Main* and *Becker v. Land Hesse;* Case C-77/02, *Steinicke v. Bundesanstalt für Arbeit* and Case C-300/06, *Ursula Voβ v. Land Berlin*. This jurisprudence demonstrates that ingenious ways can be thought up to make part-time work disadvantageous in comparison to full-time work. Given that the EU has, in its employment guidelines, set itself the goal of increasing the participation rate in the labour market, a restrictive approach should be adopted with regard to national regulations and practices which make part-time work more difficult.
813. Case C-127/92, *Dr. Pamela Mary Enderby v. Frenchay Health Authority and Secretary of State for Health*.
814. Case C-132/92, *Birds Eye Wall v. Roberts*, Case C-7/93, *Bestuur van Het Algemeen Burgerlijk Pensionsfonds v. Beune*.
815. Case C-400/93, *Specialarbejderforbundet i Danmark v. Dansk Industri, formerly Industriens Arbejdsgivere, acting for Royal Copenhagen A/S*.
816. Case C-236/98, *Jämställdhetsombudsmannen v. Örebro läns landsting*.
817. Case C-167/97, *R v. Secretary of State for Employment, ex parte Seymour-Smith and Perez*. See, however, Case C-220/02, *Österreichischer Gewerkschaftsbund, Gewerkshaft der Privatangestellten v. Wirtschaftskammer Österreich* (the fact that time spent in military service is taken into account in calculating termination payment, but not time spent on parental leave, does not amount to indirect discrimination).

can be justified despite its discriminatory effect. This question was answered in the affirmative, as long as the relevant measure is necessary, appropriate and proportionate to its aim:

> It is for the national court, which has sole jurisdiction to make findings of fact, to determine whether and to what extent the grounds put forward by an employer to explain the adoption of a pay practice which applies independently of a worker's sex, but in fact affects more women than men, may be regarded as objectively justified on economic grounds. If the national court finds that the measures ... correspond to a *real need on the part of the undertaking* (emphasis added), are appropriate with a view to achieving the objectives pursued and are necessary to that end, the fact that the measures affect a far greater number of women that men is not sufficient to show that they constitute an infringement of Article 119 (now 141 EC).[818]

The Court has used this formula in considering a large variety of potential grounds of objective justification.[819]

Initially the formula was used with reference to the specific situation of the relevant employer; latterly this was expanded to categories of employer, such as small- and medium-sized undertakings.[820] Finally, the Court has also in some cases accepted that grounds of justification derived from national legislation are as such valid.[821]

The Court has, in its – rather controversial – judgments in *Danfoss* and *Cadman*, held that, while 'it is not to be excluded that recourse to the criterion of length of service may involve less advantageous treatment of women than of men',[822] an employer does not normally have to provide special justification for recourse to that criterion. Its reasoning was that, 'as a general rule', recourse to the criterion of length of service is appropriate to attain the legitimate objective of rewarding experience acquired which enables the worker to perform his duties better.[823]

---

818. Case 170/84, *Bilka*, para. 36.
819. See, amongst others, Case 237/85, *Gisela Rummler v. Dato-Druck*, Case C-171/88, *Ingrid Rinner-Kühn v. FWW Spezial-Gebäudereinigung*, Case C-189/91, *Petra Kirsammer-Hack v. Nurhan Sidal*, Case C-127/92, *Enderby*, Case C-278/93, *Edith Freers and Hannelore Speckmann v. Deutsche Bundespost*, Case C-297/93, *Rita Grau-Hupka v. Stadtgemeinde Bremen*, Case C-444/93, *Ursula Megner and Hildegard Scheffel v. Innungskrankenkasse Vorderpfalz, now Innungskrankenkasse Rheinhessen-Pfalz*, Case C-1/95, *Gerster v. Friestaat Bayern*. On the difficulty in justifying direct discrimination, see Case C-227/04, *Lindorfer* (different actuarial values for men and women in relation to pension rights are not justified by the need for sound financial management).
820. See e.g., Case C-444/93, *Megner*.
821. See, amongst others, Case C-457/93, *Lewark*.
822. Case 109/88, *Handels- og Kontorfunktionærernes Forbund i Danmark v. Dansk Arbejdsgiverforening, acting on behalf of Danfoss*, paras. 24–25; Case C-17/05, *Cadman v. Health and Safety Executive*, para. 33. See C. Costello and G. Davies, 'The Case Law of the Court of Justice in the Field of Sex Equality since 2000' (2006), CML Rev., 1567–1616.
823. *Cadman*, paras. 34–35. 'Length of service goes hand in hand with experience, and experience generally enables the worker to perform his duties better' (*Cadman*, para. 35). However,

Some critical remarks can be made regarding this development in the case law. In the first place, it must be borne in mind that, in accepting a 'ground of objective justification', this constitutes an exception to a legal rule comprising a fundamental principle of law. This should demand a high threshold to be met in order for a justification to be accepted. A 'real need' of the relevant employer should, thus interpreted, be a weighty need that is vital for the continuity of his undertaking.[824] In the second place, it is risky to expand the scope of potential justification, without more, to categories of undertakings.[825] This has the consequence that the principle of equal treatment can lose effectiveness in large sections of the economy. In the third place, one should be reluctant to accept national legislative measures as grounds of justification.[826] The protected interests should at least, here also, be weighed against the principle of equal pay as an application of the fundamental principle of equality. In this regard, it is debatable whether this weighing-up process should be left to such a considerable extent to the national judge.[827]

6.4.1.5   Pay

The Court has, since 1976, had to rule on many occasions on the content and scope of the concept 'pay' in Article 141(1) EC. From early on, in *Garland*, the Court has given a wide interpretation to this concept: 'any consideration, whether in cash or in kind, whether immediate or future, provided that the worker receives it, albeit indirectly, in respect of his employment from his employer.'[828] In a series of later judgments, the Court applied this general definition to a number of special forms of pay.[829] This case law, which is characterized by an extensive interpretation of

---

where an employee who alleges discrimination in pay can provide 'evidence capable of giving rise to serious doubts' as to whether recourse to the criterion of length of service is, in the circumstances, appropriate to attain this objective, the burden of proof shifts to the employer to prove that 'that which is true as a general rule, namely that length of service goes hand in hand with experience and that experience enables the worker to perform his duties better, is also true as regards the job in question.' (*Cadman*, para. 38). See further, G. Beck, 'The State of EU Anti-Discrimination Law and the Judgment in Cadman, or how the Legal can become the Political' (2007), EL Rev., 549–562.

824. See also J. Currall, in Von der Groeben etc., op. cit. *supra* note 81, 3/1237.
825. Such as was the case in, amongst others, Case C-278/93, *Freers and Speckmann*.
826. This also applies in our view where the relevant national legislation is based on Community legislation. See the Opinion of A.G. Geelhoed in Case C-25/02, *Katharina Rinke v. Ärztekammer Hamburg*.
827. The process primarily involves balancing the principle of equal treatment as a Community norm against the deviation from this norm considered justified by the national legislature. Such a balancing process should be carried out by the Community courts, not the national courts.
828. Case 12/81, *Garland v. British Rail*, para. 5.
829. Amongst others, compensation on termination of employment (Case C-33/89, *Maria Kowalska v. Freie und Hansestadt Hamburg*), grant of benefits for the future (Case 12/81, *Garland*), paid leave (Case C-278/93, *Freers and Speckmann*), rules on automatic classification in a higher salary grade (Case C-184/89, *Nimz v. Freie und Hansestadt Hamburg*), the availability of childcare (Case C-342/93, *Joan Gillespie and others v. Northern Health and Social Services Boards et al.*). More recently, see Case C-19/02, *Viktor Hlozek v. Roche*

the concept of pay, culminated in *Barber*.[830] In this case, the Court held that occupational pensions replacing a legislative rule (so-called 'contracted-out' regulations) should be considered to be 'pay' and that, as a result, the principle of equal pay also applied to this. This judgment was not unexpected,[831] contrary to what the rather exaggerated reactions of certain Member States would give cause to believe; it led to the so-called *Barber* Protocol to the Treaty of Maastricht,[832] by which the Member States wished to ensure that this judgment would not have retroactive effect, whether as regards pension benefits or structure. In a number of subsequent judgments, the Court interpreted its earlier decision in *Barber* in accordance with the Protocol.[833]

One of the additional critical aspects of the *Barber* judgment was that it to a large extent superseded Directive 86/378 on the implementation of the principle of equal treatment for men and women in occupational social security schemes.[834]

6.4.1.6   Personal Scope

In contrast with Article 39 EC, the applicability of Article 141 EC is not restricted to Member State nationals. It extends to all employers and employees working in the Community.[835] This accords with the character of the principle of equal pay as an instance of the fundamental principle of equality. In the first instance, it is employees who are protected via the principle of equal pay; however, it follows from the wide interpretation which the concept of 'pay' has received that family members may also rely on the principle, for example, when they have a right to an

---

  Austria Gesellschaft and Case C-220/02, *Österreichischer Gewerkschaftsbund* (benefit of taking a period of military service into account for the purpose of calculating a termination payment).

830. Case C-262/88, *Barber v. Guardian Royal Exchange Assurance Group.*

831. Case 170/84, *Bilka*, paras. 10–13, leading on from the distinction already made in Case 80/70, *Defrenne v. Belgium (Defrenne I)*, was a clear prelude to this development.

832. Protocol to Art. 119 (now Art. 141 EC) of the Treaty establishing the European Community, O.J. 1992, C 191/68.

833. On the effect of the *Barber* case, see, amongst others, Case C-109/91, *Ten Oever v. Stichting Bedrifspensionsfonds voor her Glazenwassers- en Schoonmaakbedrijf;* Case C-110/91, *Michael Moroni v. Collo*; Case C-152/91, *David Neath v. Hugh Steeper;* Case C-200/91, *Coloroll Pension Trustees*; Case C-408/92, *Smith and others v. Avdel Systems*; Case C-28/93, *V den Akker*, Case C-57/93, *Anna Adriaantje Vroege v. NCIV Instituut voor Volkshuisvesting and Stichting Pensioenfonds NCIV*, Case C-128/93, *Geertruida Catharina Fisscher v. Voorhuis Hengelo BV and Stichting Bedrijfspensioenfonds voor de Detailhandel.* The question of the consequence of the interpretation of Art. 119 (now Art. 141) EC before and after the Barber protocol was raised in a number of cases brought before the Court, including Case C-7/93, *Beune*, Case C-147/95, *Dimossia Epicheirissi Ilektrismou (DEI) v. Efthimios Evrenopoulos*, Case C-246/96, *Mary Teresa Magorrian and Irene Patricia Cunningham v. Eastern Health and Social Services Board and Department of Health and Social Services.*

834. Dir. 86/378 was subsequently amended by Dir. 96/97/EC O.J. 1997, L 46/30. See, on the consequences of the *Barber* case, D. Curtin, 'Scalping the Community Legislator: Occupational Pensions and "Barber"', (1990) CML Rev., 475–506.

835. See, on the definition of worker under Art. 141 EC, Case C-256/01, *Allonby*.

occupational pension as a surviving partner or child. *Barber* serves as an example.[836]

6.4.1.7 Substantive Scope

The Article 141 EC norm prohibits discrimination between men and women as regards pay in work relations.[837] Following on from the judgment in *P v. S*, in which the Court held that Directive 76/207 prohibits discrimination against transsexuals in dismissal,[838] it was suggested that the prohibition on discrimination set out in Article 141 EC extended to discrimination on grounds of sexual orientation. In *Grant*, the Court ruled that this is not the case.[839] That case concerned the question whether certain benefits (free travel) granted to spouses of railway workers should also be granted to a partner of the same sex. In this regard, however, it should be noted that the Treaty of Amsterdam has added the legal basis provision Article 13 EC to the EC Treaty, by which the Community 'may take appropriate action to combat discrimination based on sex, racial or ethnic origin, religion or belief, disability, age or sexual orientation'.[840]

While the Court has given a wide interpretation to the concept of 'pay', it has refused to bring elements falling under Directives 76/207 and 79/7 within this concept. In cases such as *Defrenne III*, it held that the scope of these directives and that of the principle of equal pay were mutually exclusive.[841] As regards the material scope of Directive 76/207, this has, *inter alia*, the consequence that employers' decisions on the appointment and promotion of employees should be assessed under this Directive.[842] As regards the material scope of Directive 79/7, the Court consistently assesses public social security and benefits under this Directive. In its case law, the Court closely examines whether a given benefit is an

---

836. Case C-262/88, *Barber*.
837. For this reason, the Court has found that military service restricted to men did not infringe Art. 141 EC: Case C-186/01, *Dory v. Germany*. See also, Case C-220/02, *Österreichischer Gewerkschaftsbund*, where the Court distinguishes between the nature of military service, which is performed in the 'collective interests of the nation', and that of parental leave, taken in the interests of the worker and the family: see para. 64.
838. Case C-13/94, *P v. S and Cornwall County Council*. See also, Case C-423/04, *Richards v. Secretary of State for Work and Pensions*, in which the Court held that Dir. 79/7 precludes legislation which denies a person who, in accordance with the conditions laid down by national law, has undergone male-to-female gender reassignment entitlement to a retirement pension on the ground that she has not reached the age of 65, when she would have been entitled to such a pension at the age of 60 had she been held to be a woman as a matter of national law; and Case C-117/01, *K.B. v. National Health Service Pensions Agency and Secretary of State for Health*.
839. Case C-249/96, *Grant v. South West Trains*. See K. Berthou and A. Masselot, 'Le Mariage, les Partenariats et la CJCE: Ménage à trois' (2002), CDE, 679.
840. See more generally on Art. 13 EC Ch. 3, section 6.5.2. *supra*. On the main secondary legislation adopted pursuant to this legal basis, see note 790 *supra*.
841. Case 149/77, *Defrenne III*.
842. See, amongst others, Case C-184/89, *Nimz*, Case C-1/95, *Gerster*, and Case C-313/02, *Wippel v. Peek & Cloppenburg*.

occupational or sectoral benefit – and thus 'pay' in the meaning of Article 141 EC – or, alternatively, forms part of public social security.[843]

6.4.1.8   Concluding Remarks

In principle, those alleging discrimination in pay on the ground of sex must prove this. Thus, insofar as direct or disguised discrimination is at issue, the burden of proof of such discrimination lies on the plaintiff.[844] In cases involving forms of indirect discrimination, the plaintiff may find it difficult to assemble the necessary statistical material and other relevant data. As a result, the Court has, from its first indirect discrimination judgments, placed the burden of proof in such cases on the employer.[845] Directive 97/80 now codifies the substantial case law of the Court in this area.[846]

When the Court handed down the *Defrenne II* judgment, Directive 75/117 on 'the approximation of the laws of the Member States relating to the application of the principle of equal pay for men and women' was already in force. This Directive was for a large part overtaken by the *Defrenne II* judgment, although the Court quickly adopted the somewhat broader definition of the principle of equal pay contained in Article 1 of the Directive in interpreting the old Article 119(1) EC.[847]

The obligations placed on Member States in Articles 2–6 of the Directive have led to a number of actions for breach of the obligations under the Treaty.[848]

The final issue to note is that of the consequences given by the Court to the finding of a breach of Article 141 EC. The principal rule is that those who have been discriminated against have the right to compensation for what they have been deprived of during the period of discrimination. For this, the pay level of the group

---

843. See, amongst others, Case C-7/93, *Beune*, Case C-366/99, *Joseph Griesmar v. Ministre de l'Economie, des Finances et de l'Industrie et Ministre de la Fonction publique, de la Réforme de l'Etat et de la Décentralisation*, Case C-206/00, *Henri Mouflin v. Recteur de l'académie de Reims*, and Joined Cases C-4 & 5/02, *Schönheit*.

844. Case C-381/99, *Brunnhofer*, para. 52, which refers to the previous judgment in Case C-127/92, *Enderby*, para. 13.

845. However, in cases where length of service has been taken as the differentiating criterion, the plaintiff must first provide evidence 'capable of raising serious doubts' as to whether recourse to this criterion is appropriate to achieve the legitimate objective of rewarding experience which enables the worker to perform his duties better: Case 109/88, *Danfoss*, paras. 14–16 as interpreted by Case C-17/05, *Cadman*.

846. Dir. 97/80/EC of 15 Dec. 1997 on the burden of proof in cases of discrimination based on sex, O.J. 1998, L 14/6. On this, see Case C-196/02, *Nikoloudi*. Dir. 98/52, O.J. 1998, L 205/66 expanded the scope of application of this Directive to include the United Kingdom.

847. In considering that Art. 141 EC also applies to cases of indirect discrimination, the Court had to interpret the concept of 'equal work', as contained in the version of Art. 119 EC in force prior to the Treaty of Amsterdam, as if it included the concept of 'work of equal value' contained in Art. 1 of Dir. 75/117. The evolution of this interpretation was evident in Case 96/80, *Jenkins* and Case 157/86, *Murphy*. In these cases, the Court avoided the possibility that a narrow principle of equal pay flowing from the EC Treaty would exist beside a wider principle based on secondary Community law.

848. Case 61/81, *Commission v. United Kingdom* and Case 143/83, *Commission v. Denmark*.

in relation to which they have been discriminated is taken as a benchmark.[849] Later on, however, new pay regulations may be adopted which are potentially less favourable for *all* employees, so-called 'levelling-down'.[850]

6.4.2 Equal Treatment in Employment

Directive 76/207[851] is aimed at ensuring equal treatment between men and women in three areas connected with the employment market: access to work, vocational training and promotion, and working conditions other than pay.

In terms of structure, this directive strongly resembles Directive 75/117, including the provisions relating to judicial protection of rights, protection of employees who complain of discrimination, and the information given to employees about the rights they have under these Directives.[852] The core provision of the Directive is Article 2(1), which prohibits any discrimination whatsoever on grounds of sex, either directly or indirectly by reference in particular to marital or family status.[853] In contrast to Article 141 EC, the Directive allows certain exceptions to the principle of equal treatment:

- Member States remain competent to exclude application of the Directive to certain vocational activities, for which 'by reason of the nature of the particular occupational activities concerned or of the context in which they are carried out, such a characteristic constitutes a genuine and determining occupational requirement' (Art. 2(6)).
- Deviations from the principle of equal treatment are possible in connection with the special treatment of women, in particular as concerns pregnancy and maternity (Art. 2(7)).
- Member States may take measures aimed at the promotion of equal opportunities for men and women, in particular by providing for specific advantages in order to make it easier for the under-represented sex to pursue a vocational activity or to prevent or compensate for disadvantages in professional careers (Art. 2(8)).

849. This rule was formulated as long ago as Case 43/75, *Defrenne II*, para. 15. See also, Joined Cases C-231–233/06, *National Pensions Office v. Jonkman*.
850. Case C-33/89, *Kowalska*, para. 20. The principle formulated in this case had already been developed in the Court's judgments on Dir. 79/7: see e.g., Case 71/85, *FNV*, para. 22, and Case 286/85, *Norah McDermott and Ann Cotter v. Minister for Social Welfare and Attorney-General*, para. 18.
851. Dir. 76/207/EEC of 9 Feb. 1976, on the implementation of the principle of equal treatment for men and women as regards access to employment, vocational training and promotion, and working conditions, O.J. 1976, L 39/40, amended by Dir. 2002/73, O.J. 2002, L 269/15.
852. Dir. 76/207, Arts. 6, 7 and 8.
853. The principle of equal treatment set out in Art. 2(1) has direct effect, as held in Case 152/84, *M. H. Marshall v. Southampton and South-West Hampshire Area Health Authority (Teaching)*, but does not, in contrast to Art. 141(1) EC, have horizontal direct effect. See on this, S. Prechal, 'Remedies after Marshall' (1990), CML Rev., 451–473.

The first exception speaks for itself: a position for a coloratura soprano cannot easily be filled by a man. However, the limits to this exception are reached quickly, as the Court made clear in the *Johnston* case.[854]

The Court has also been asked to give a number of judgments on the second exception, particularly in connection with the national legislation giving (pregnant) women special protection, sometimes with the consequence that access to certain professions becomes impossible for women (for example, night work for women).[855]

It is the third exception which has raised the most issues. In its controversial judgment *Kalanke*, as mentioned above, the Court held that Articles 2(1) and (4) (now, as amended, Art. 2(8)) of the Directive prohibit national regulations which, in sectors where women are underrepresented, give automatic priority to women with equal qualifications amongst candidates of different sex being considered for promotion.[856] This strict interpretation of Article 2(8) was somewhat qualified two years later in the *Marschall* judgment: although a national measure giving absolute and unconditional priority to women is not permitted, 'softer' quota regulations giving scope for individualized appreciation of the relevant circumstances did fall under the Article 2(8) exception.[857]

The judgment of the Court in *Marschall* fits with Article 141(4) EC, added by the Treaty of Amsterdam. It appears from later case law that the Court will still examine positive discrimination on the employment market critically for compliance with the fundamental principle of equal treatment.[858]

Directive 76/207 gave rise to considerable case law on the consequences of pregnancy for access to the employment market. The *Dekker* case, which is also interesting in other regards, is a classic example.[859] In that case, the Court held that Article 2(1) and Article 3(1) of the Directive prohibit a refusal to conclude an employment contract with an otherwise suitable candidate on the ground of the likely disadvantageous consequences for the employer of appointing a pregnant woman. In later judgments, the Court has frequently confirmed that dismissal of a

---

854. Case 222/84, *Marguerite Johnston v. Chief Constable of the Royal Ulster Constabulary*.
855. The main rule set out by the Court in this regard is that a general prohibition on night work for women does not fall within this exception. National legislation prohibiting night work for pregnant women is, however, permitted. Compare Case 312/86, *Commission v. France*, Case C-345/89, *Criminal proceedings against Alfred Stoeckel* and Case C-421/92, *Habermann-Beltermann*. See, however, Case C-203/03, *Commission v. Austria*, in which the Court rejected Austria's argument that this provision justified a total prohibition on the employment of women in underground work in mining, or in a high-pressure atmosphere, or in diving work. See also, Case C-284/02, *Land Brandenburg v. Ursula Sass*.
856. Case C-450/93, *Kalanke*. For the context of this judgment, the Opinion of A.G. Tesauro is instructive, which also considers the US doctrine of positive discrimination.
857. Case C-409/95, *Hellmut Marschall v. Land Nordrhein-Westfalen*.
858. See Case C-158/97, *Georg Badeck and Others, interveners: Hessische Ministerpräsident and Landesanwalt beim Staatsgerichtshof des Landes Hessen*, Case C-407/98, *Abrahamsson and Anderson v. Fogelqvist;* and Case C-319/03, *Briheche v. Ministre de l'Intérieur*.
859. Case 177/88, *Elisabeth Johanna Pacifica Dekker v. Stichting Vormingscentrum voor Jong Volwassenen*.

female employee on grounds of pregnancy is prohibited by Article 2(1) read in conjunction with Article 5(1) of the Directive.[860]

Other pregnancy-related issues, such as sickness resulting from pregnancy,[861] a legislative prohibition on night work by pregnant women,[862] unavailability for necessary tasks during the pregnancy,[863] and the consequences of pregnancy for employment based on a fixed-term contract[864] have also been the subject of rapidly expanding case law. In later jurisprudence, Directive 92/85 has played a role, in addition to Directive 76/207.[865] The definition of the substantive scope of Directive 76/207 as distinct from that of Directive 79/7 has given rise to a series of cases dealing with the legally complicated relationship between equal treatment on the employment market, equality in social security and the principle of equal pay. This complexity also follows from disparities between the relevant Community rules and between differences between occupational schemes, public social security legislation and supplementary social services in national legislation.[866] In this way, the diversity of social policies and social arrangements within the Community is reflected in the Court's jurisprudence on equal treatment.

6.4.3   Equal Treatment in Social Security

Directive 79/7[867] aims at the gradual implementation of the principle of equal treatment of men and women in social security. In comparison with Directives 75/117 and 76/207, this Directive is distinguished by its long implementation period and many exceptions.

The personal scope of the Directive is defined in Article 2. To summarize: it applies to the active working population (who have or are seeking work) and the post-active working population (who have an invalidity or old-age pension). Its substantive scope is set out in Article 3. This provision defines five categories of

---

860.   Case C-179/88, *Handels- og Kontorfunktionaerernes Forbund i Danmark v. Dansk Arbejds-giverforening (Hertz)*; Case C-32/93, *Webb v. EMO Air Cargo* and Case C-109/00, *Tele Danmark*. See A. Masselot, 'Jurisprudential Developments in Community Pregnancy and Maternity Rights' (2002), *Maastricht Journal of European & Comparative Law*, 57.
861.   See Case C-179/88, *Hertz* and Case C-191/03, *North-Western Health Board v. McKenna*.
862.   Case C-421/92, *Habermann-Beltermann v. Arbeiterwohlfahrt.*
863.   Case C-32/93, *Webb.*
864.   Case C-109/00, *Tele Danmark.*
865.   Dir. 92/85/EEC of 19 Oct. 1992, on the introduction of measures to encourage improvements in the safety and health at work of pregnant workers and workers who have recently given birth or are breastfeeding (tenth individual Directive within the meaning of Art. 16(1) of Dir. 89/391/EEC), O.J. 1992, L 348/1. See, e.g., Case C-342/01, *Merino Gómez* (coincidence of maternity leave with annual leave).
866.   See, amongst others, Case 19/81, *Burton v. British Railways Board;* Case 151/84, *Joan Roberts v. Tate & Lyle Industries Limited,* Case 152/84, *Marshall I,* Case 262/84, *Vera Mia Beets-Proper v. F. Van Lanschot Bankiers,* Case C-116/94, *Jennifer Meyers v. Adjudication Officer.*
867.   Dir. 79/7/EEC of 19 Dec. 1978, on the progressive implementation of the principle of equal treatment for men and women in matters of social security, O.J. 1979, L 6/24.

risk which fall under the scope of the Directive: sickness, invalidity, old age, accidents at work and occupational diseases and, finally, unemployment. It does not apply to payments concerning survivors' benefits or to those concerning family benefits, except in the case of family benefits granted by way of increases of benefits due in respect of the five above-mentioned risks. Article 3(3) gives a basis for further regulation of so-called occupational schemes in the future.

The core provision of the Directive is Article 4(1): 'The principle of equal treatment means that there shall be no discrimination whatsoever on ground of sex either directly or indirectly by reference in particular to marital or family status.'

Article 7(1) lists five areas which may be exempted from the scope of the Directive by Member States.[868] These optional exceptions, which substantially restrict the effect of the principle of equality laid down in Article 4(1), have proved to be a source of legal complications, because social security benefits based on *occupational* schemes fall under Article 141 EC. The principle of equality is thus fully applicable to such schemes, 'pay' within the meaning of Article 141(1) EC. As a result, the question whether a scheme is a social security scheme falling under Article 79/7 or, alternatively, falls under Article 141 EC, is legally and substantively extremely relevant. A second source of complication is the fact that benefits from public social security arrangements and those from occupational schemes often complement each other in national practice and, as is the case in the United Kingdom, can even replace each other.[869] It is thus no surprise that Directive 79/7 has led to considerable case law before the Court.

The Court was asked to rule on the direct effect of Article 4(1) of the Directive soon after the expiry of the implementation period (23 Dec. 1984). In *FNV*, the Court – unsurprisingly – confirmed that this provision had direct effect. In addition, it held that the Netherlands could not make the application of the principle of equal treatment in social security dependent on national legislation to be enacted after 23 December 1984.[870] In a similar vein, the Court held that national

---

868. Art. 7 of the Directive summarizes five exceptions: (a) the determination of pensionable age for the purposes of granting old-age and retirement pensions and the possible consequences thereof for other benefits; (b) advantages in respect of old-age pension schemes granted to persons who have brought up children; the acquisition of benefit entitlements following periods of interruption of employment due to bringing up children; (c) the granting of old-age or invalidity benefit entitlements by virtue of the derived entitlements of a wife; (d) the granting of increases of long-term invalidity, old-age, accidents at work and occupational disease benefits for a dependent wife; (e) the consequences of the exercise, before the adoption of the Directive, of a right of option not to acquire rights or incur obligations under a statutory scheme.

869. See, amongst others, Case C-154/92, *Remi van Cant v. Rijksdienst voor pensioenen*, Case C-92/94, *Secretary of State for Social Security v. Graham*, Joined Cases C-377–384/96, *August De Vriendt v. Rijksdienst voor Pensioenen, Rijksdienst voor Pensioenen v. René van Looveren et al.* See, for a useful commentary on this jurisprudence, F. Pennings, op. cit., *supra* note 688, 341.

870. Case 71/85, *FNV*. See also, Case 286/85, *McDermott and Cotter*.

implementation legislation which transposed the discriminatory aspects of previous legislation into new legislation was contrary to Article 4(1).[871]

The Court has adopted a rather strict interpretation of the personal scope of the Directive. As already observed, the Directive is aimed at social security with a connection to the employment market. From this, the Court has deduced that it does not apply to those who have never worked,[872] or those who have voluntarily stopped working, for example in order to bring up children, or those who can no longer work by reason of invalidity.[873] In addition, the Directive does not apply, in the Court's judgment, to those who care for sick or invalid family members, even where they have completed a special training for this.[874] In contrast, those who work part-time or for a short period are not excluded from the application of the Directive. This accords with the Court's view that the Directive concerns social security arrangements which are related to the employment market.[875]

The Court's reluctance to interpret the substantive scope of the Directive in an extensive manner is also to be explained against this background.[876]

In addition, the Directive expressly forbids indirect discrimination. The case law of the Court on this strongly resembles the Article 141 EC case law concerning this concept. On the one hand, the Court tends to be critical as regards national regulations which can lead to indirect discrimination.[877] On the other hand, the Community judge is rather generous in accepting grounds of objective justification for such discrimination.[878] As the Member States become better at satisfying the requirements of the Directive as regards direct discrimination in social security legislation,[879] examination of legislation for compliance as regards indirect discrimination becomes more important. This impels a more restrictive approach to

871. Case 80/87, *A. Dik, A. Menkutos-Demirci and H. G. W. Laar-Vreeman v. College van Burgemeester en Wethouders Arnhem and Winterswijk*; Case C-377/89, *Ann Cotter and Norah McDermott v. Minister for Social Welfare and Attorney General*; Joined Cases C-87–89/90, *A. Verholen and others v. Sociale Verzekeringsbank Amsterdam*.

872. Joined Cases 48, 106 & 107/88, *J. E. G. Achterberg-te Riele and others v. Sociale Verzekeringsbank*.

873. Case C-31/90, *Elsie Rita Johnson v. Chief Adjudication Officer*.

874. Case C-77/95, *Bruna-Alessandra Züchner v. Handelskrankenkasse (Ersatzkasse) Bremen*.

875. Case C-317/93, *Nolte*, Case C-444/93, *Megner*. See also, Case C-303/02, *Peter Haackert v. Pensionsversicherungsanstalt der Angestellten* (Directive applies to early old-age pension payments on account of unemployment).

876. Case C-243/90, *The Queen v. Secretary of State for Social Security, ex parte Florence Rose Smithson*, Case C-228/94, *Stanley Charles Atkins v. Wrekin District Council and Department of Transport*, Joined Cases C-245 & 312/94, *Ingrid Hoever and Iris Zachow v. Land Nordrhein-Westfalen*.

877. Case 30/85, *Teuling*, Case C-102/88, *M. L. Ruzius-Wilbrink v. Bestuur van de Bedrijfsvereniging voor Overheidsdiensten*.

878. Case C-226/91, *Jan Molenbroek v. Bestuur van de Sociale Verzekeringsbank*, Case C-343/92, *M. A. De Weerd, née Roks, and others v. Bestuur van de Bedrijfsvereniging voor de Gezondheid, Geestelijke en Maatschappelijke Belangen and others*.

879. Some problems still persist, however. See e.g., Joined Cases C-231–233/06, *Jonkman*, concerning the attempts to remedy the direct discrimination, at issue in the original *Defrenne* case, between female and male air hostesses in Belgium.

the acceptance of grounds of objective justification and a more critical appraisal of their application in the context in which they are invoked.

Further Reading

Policy Coordination

Amtenbrink, F. 'Integration, Coordination on Fragmentation in Economic Policy Matters?: A Comment on the René Smits Contribution'. In D. Obradovic and N. Lavranos (eds). *Interface between EU Law and National Law: Proceedings of the Annual Colloquium of the G.K. van Hogendorp Centre for European Constitutional Studies*. The Hogendorp Papers, 7. Groningen: Europa Law Publishing, 2007.

Arestis, P. and M. Sawyer. *Alternative Perspectives on Economic Policies in the European Union*. International Papers in Political Economy Series. Palgrave Macmillan, 2006.

Barrell, R. and J. Whitley (eds). *Macroeconomic Policy Coordination in Europe: The ERM and Monetary Union*. London: Sage, 1992.

Beetsma, R. *Monetary Policy, Fiscal Policies and Labour Markets: Macroeconomic Policymaking in the EMU*. Cambridge: Cambridge University Press, 2004.

Bratton, W.W. *International Regulatory Competition and Coordination: Perspectives on Economic Regulation in Europe and the United States*. Oxford: Clarendon Press, 1996.

Buiter, W. and Marston, R. (eds). *International Economic Policy Coordination*. New York: Cambridge University Press, 1985.

Buti, M. *Monetary and Fiscal Policies in EMU: Interactions and Coordination*. Cambridge: Cambridge University Press, 2003.

Carlberg, M. *Policy Competition and Policy Cooperation in a Monetary Union*. Berlin: Springer, 2004.

El-Agraa, A.M. *The European Union: Economics and Policies*. 8th ed. Cambridge: Cambridge University Press, 2007.

Grauwe, P.D. *The Political Economy of Monetary Union*. The International Library of Critical Writings in Economics, 134. Cheltenham: Edward Elgar, 2001.

Halberstadt, V. *Sociaal-economische beleidscoördinatie in de EU: advies over de sociaal-economische beleidscoördinatie in de EU*. Publicatie/Sociaal-Economische Raad, 00/01. Den Haag: SER, 2000.

Jordan, A. and J.A. Schout. *The Coordination of the European Union: Exploring the Capacities of Networked Governance*. Oxford: Oxford University Press, 2006.

Kassim, H. *The National Co-ordination of EU Policy: The European Level*. Oxford: Oxford University Press, 2001.

Lange, C. and Rohde, A. *Monetäre Aspekte der europäischen Integration*. Veröffentlichungen des Instituts für Empirische Wirtschaftsforschung, Bd. 35. Berlin: Duncker & Humblot, 1998.

Linsenmann, I., et al. *Economic Government of the EU: A Balance Sheet of New Modes of Policy Coordination.* Palgrave Studies in European Union Politics. Basingstoke: Palgrave Macmillan, 2007.

Maher, I. 'Economic Policy Coordination and the European Court: Excessive Deficits and ECOFIN Discretion'. (2004) EL Rev., 831–841.

Mitchell, W., et al. *Growth and Cohesion in the European Union: The Impact of Macroeconomic Policy.* Edward Elgar, 2006.

Paoda-Schioppa, T., et al. *Efficiency, Stability, and Equity: A Strategy for the Evolution of the Economic System of the European Community: A Report.* Europe in the 1990s. Oxford: Oxford University Press, 1987.

Scharpf, F.W. *Balancing Positive and Negative Integration: The Regulatory Options for Europe.* Policy Papers/the Robert Schuman Centre, 97/4. San Domenico di Fiesole (FI): European University Institute Badia Fiesolana, 1997.

Scharpf, F.W. *Governing in Europe: Effective and Democratic?* Oxford: Oxford University Press, 1999.

History of EMU

Apel, E. *European Monetary Integration: 1958–2002.* London: Routledge, 1998.

Coffey, P. *The European Monetary System: Past, Present and Future.* Dordrecht: Martinus Nijhoff Publishers, 1984.

Crowley, P.M. *Before and beyond EMU: Historical Lessons and Future Prospects.* London: Routledge, 2002.

Dyson, K.H.F. and K. Featherstone. *The Road to Maastricht: Negotiating Economic and Monetary Union.* Oxford: Oxford University Press, 1999.

Hosli, M.O. *The Euro: A Concise Introduction to European Monetary Integration.* Boulder, CO: Rienner, 2005.

Mehnert-Meland, R. *Central Bank to the European Union: European Monetary Institute, European System of Central Banks, European Central Bank: Structures, Tasks and Functions.* London: Kluwer Law International, 1995.

Pentecost, E.J. and A.v. Poeck. *European Monetary Integration: Past, Present and Future.* Cheltenham: Edward Elgar, 2001.

Sinn, H.-W. and M. Widgrén. *European Monetary Integration*, Cambridge, MA: MIT Press, 2004.

Ungerer, H. *A Concise History of European Monetary Integration: From EPU to EMU.* Westport, CN: Quorum Books, 1997.

Zestos, G. *European Monetary Integration: The Euro.* Mason, OH: South-Western, 2004.

EMU

Andenas, M.T. (ed.). *European Economic and Monetary Union: The Institutional Framework.* International Banking and Finance Law, vol. 6. London: Kluwer Law International, 1997.

Baimbridge, M. and P. Whyman (eds). *Economic and Monetary Union in Europe: Theory, Evidence, and Practice.* Northampton: E. Elgar, 2001.

Breuss, F., G, Fink. and St. Griller. (eds). *Institutional, Legal and Economic Aspects of the EMU*. Wien/New York: Springer, 2003.

Constantinesco, V., R. Kovar. and R. Simon. *Traité sur l'union Européene (signé a Maastricht le 7 fevrier 1992): commentaire article par article*. Paris: Economica, 1995.

Dosenrode, S. *Political Aspects of the Economic Monetary Union*. Aldershot: Ashgate, 2002.

Duff, A. (ed.). *Understanding the Euro*. London: Federal Trust, 1998.

Garavelli, P.Z. *Legal Aspects of the European System of Central Banks: Liber Amicorum Paolo Zamboni Garavelli*. Frankfurt am Main: European Central Bank, 2005.

Gros, D. and N. Thygesen. *European Monetary Integration*. London: Longman, 1992.

Issing, O. *Monetary Policy in the Euro Area: Strategy and Decision Making at the European Central Bank*. Cambridge: Cambridge University Press, 2001.

Jones, E. *The Politics of Economic and Monetary Union: Integration and Idiosyncrasy*. Lanham, MD: Rowman & Littlefield, 2002.

Klages, R. 'Legal Aspects of the Stability Pact in the Light of the Economic Constitution of the European Community'. (2001) *European Union Review*, 77–95.

Lamfalussy, A., et al. (eds). *The Euro-zone: A New Economic Entity?*. Collection de l'Institut d'études européennes de l'Université catholique de Louvain, 2. Bruxelles: Bruylant, 1999.

Louis, J.-V. and A.P. Komninos (eds). *The Euro. Law, Politics, Economics*. London: The British Institute of International and Comparative Law, 2003.

Louis, J.-V., et al. (eds). *Union économique et monétaire. Cohésion économique et sociale. Politique industrielle et technologique européenne*. 2e éd. Commentaire Mégret, 6. Bruxelles: Éditions de l'Université de Bruxelles, 1995.

Mehnert-Meland, R. *Central Bank to the European Union: European Monetary Institute, European System of Central Banks, European Central Bank: Structures, Tasks and Functions*. London: Kluwer Law International, 1995.

Ott. A. and K.M. Inglis. *Handbook on European Enlargement*. The Hague: T.M.C. Asser Press, 2002.

Savage, J.D. Making the EMU: *The Politics of Budgetary Surveillance and the Enforcement of Maastricht*. Oxford: Oxford University Press, 2005.

Seidel, M. *European Economic and Monetary Union: Constitutional and Legal Aspects*. Deutsch-Norwegisches Forum des Rechts, Bd. 3. Berlin: Berlin Verlag, 2001.

Sideek, M. *European Community Law on the Free Movement of Capital and the EMU*. London: Kluwer Law International, 1999.

Szász, André. *The Road to European Monetary Union*. MacMillan & St. Martin's, 1999.

Usher, J. *The Law of Money and Financial Services in the EC*. 2nd ed. Oxford: OUP, 2000.

Waigel, C. *Die Unabhängigkeit der Europäischen Zentralbank: gemessen am Kriterium demokratischer Legitimation.* Nomos-Universitätsschriften. Recht, Bd. 305. Baden-Baden: Nomos, 1999.

The European Central Bank

Amtenbrink, F. *The Democratic Accountability of Central Banks: A Comparative Study of the European Central Bank.* Oxford/Portland, OR: Hart Publishing, 1999.
De Haan, J., S.C.W. Eijffinger and S. Waller. *The European Central Bank. Credibility, Transparency and Centralization.* Cambridge, MA/London: MIT Press, 2005.
Hasse, R.H. (ed.). *The European Central Bank: Perspectives for a Further Development of the European Monetary System.* Gütersloh: Bertelsmann Foundation Publishers, 1990.
Howarth, D. and P. Loedel. *The European Central Bank.* 2nd ed. New York, 2005.
Kaltenthaler, K.C. *Policymaking in the European Central Bank: The Masters of Europe's Money.* Governance in Europe. Lanham, MD: Rowman & Littlefield, 2006.
Smits, R.J.H. *The European Central Bank: Institutional Aspects.* International Banking and Finance Law, vol. 5. The Hague: Kluwer Law International, 1997.
Zilioli, C. and M. Selmayr. *The Law of the European Central Bank.* Oxford: Hart, 2001.
Zilioli, C. and M. Selmayr. 'Recent Developments in the Law of the European Central Bank'. (2005) *Yearbook of European Law*, 1–89.

Employment Policy

Kenner, J. 'Employment and Macroeconomics in the EC Treaty: A Legal and Political Symbiosis'. (2000) *MJ*, 374–397.
Raveaud, G. 'The European Employment Strategy: Towards More and Better Jobs?' (2007) JCMS, 411.
Sciarra, S. 'The Employment Title in the Amsterdam Treaty: A Multi-language Discourse'. In D. O'Keeffe and P. Twomey (eds). *Legal Issues of the Amsterdam Treaty.* London, 1999.
Sciarra, S. 'Integration through Coordination: The Employment Title in the Amsterdam Treaty'. (2000) *Columbia Journal of European Law*, 209.

Economic and Social Cohesion

Bache, I. *Europeanization and Multilevel Governance: Cohesion Policy in the European Union and Britain.* Lanham, MD: Rowman & Littlefield, 2008.
Evans, A. *The EU Structural Funds.* Oxford: Oxford University Press, 1999.
Evans, A. *EU Regional Policy.* Oxford: Oxford University Press, 2005.
Evans, A. 'Regional Policy'. In D. Vaughan & A. Robertson (eds). *Law of the European Union.* Richmond: Richmond Publishing, 2003.

Hall, R. and A. Smith. *Competitiveness and Cohesion in EU Policies.* Oxford: Oxford University Press, 2001.

Leonardi, R. *Cohesion Policy in the European Union: The Building of Europe.* Basingstoke: Palgrave Macmillan, 2005.

Louis, J.V., J.C. Séché, M. Wolfcarius and Th. Margellos. *Commentaire Mégret*, part 6. 2ème éd, 1995.

Milio, S. and R. Leonardi. 'Title XVII: Economic and Social Cohesion'. In *Smit & Herzog on the Law of the European Union.* Newark, NJ: Matthew Bender, 2007.

Mitchell, W. and J. Muysken. *Growth and Cohesion in the European Union: The Impact of Economic Policy.* Cheltenham: Edward Elgar, 2006.

Molle, W. *European Cohesion Policy.* Regions and Cities. London: Routledge, 2007.

Shaw, J., et al. *Economic and Social Law of the European Union.* Palgrave Macmillan Law Masters Focus. Palgrave Macmillan, 2007.

Employment and Social Policy

Ashiagbor, D. *The European Employment Strategy: Labour Market Regulation and New Governance.* Oxford Monographs on Labour Law. Oxford University Press, 2005.

Barnard, C. *EC Employment Law.* 3rd ed. Oxford EC Law Library. Oxford: Oxford University Press, 2006.

Barnard, C. 'Flexibility and Social Policy'. In G. de Búrca and J. Scott (eds). *Constitutional Change in the EU: From Uniformity to Flexibility?* Oxford: Hart 2000.

Barnard, C., S. Deakin and G. Morris (eds). *The Future of Labour Law: Liber Amicorum Bob Hepple QC.* Oxford: Hart, 2004. (written from a UK perspective).

Bell, M. *Anti-discrimination Law and the European Union.* Oxford: Oxford University Press, 2002.

Blanpain, R. *European Labour Law.* 10th ed. The Hague: Kluwer Law International, 2006.

Blanpain, R., et al. *The European Social Model.* Social Europe Series, 11. Intersentia, 2006.

Brine, J. The European Social Fund and the EU: Flexibility, Growth, Stability. Contemporary European Studies, 11. London: Sheffield Academic Press, 2002.

Cornelisse, P. A., et al. *On the Convergence of Social Protection Systems in the European Union.* Department of Economics Research Memorandum, 2001.02.

Leiden: Leiden University Faculty of Law Department of Economics, 2001.

Daly, M. 'EU Social Policy after Lisbon'. (2006) JCMS, 461–481.

De Búrca, G. *EU Law and the Welfare State: In Search of Solidarity.* Collected Courses of the Academy of European Law, vol. 14/2. Oxford: Oxford University Press, 2005.

De Búrca, G., et al. *Social Rights in Europe*. Oxford: Oxford University Press, 2005.

De Schutter, O. and S. Deakin (eds). *Social Rights and Market Forces: Is the Open Coordination of Employment and Social Policies the Future of Social Europe?* Brussels: Bruylant, 2005.

Dougan, M. and E. Spaventa (eds). *Social Welfare and EU Law*. Oxford: Hart, 2005.

Ellis, E. EU *Anti-discrimination Law*. Oxford EC Law Library. New York, NY: Oxford University Press, 2005.

Fuchs, M. 'The Bottom Line of European Labour Law'. (2004) *International Journal of Comparative Labour Law and Industrial Relations*, 155, 423.

Geyer, R.R. *Exploring European Social Policy*. Cambridge: Polity Press, 2000.

Giubboni, S. and R. Inston. *Social Rights And Market Freedom in the European Constitution: A Labour Law Perspective*. Cambridge Studies in European Law and Policy. Cambridge: Cambridge University Press, 2006.

Hantrais, L. *Social Policy in the European Union*. 3rd ed. Basingstoke: Palgrave Macmillan, 2007.

Hervey, T.K. *European Social Law and Policy*. London: Longman, 1998.

Hervey, T.K. and J. Kenner (eds). *Economic and Social Rights under the EU Charter of Fundamental Rights: A Legal Perspective*. Oxford: Hart, 2003.

Hervey, T.K., et al. 'Thirty Years of EU Sex Equality Law'. (2005) *Maastricht Journal of European and Comparative Law*, 305–493.

Kenner, J. *EU Employment Law: From Rome to Amsterdam and Beyond*. Oxford: Hart, 2003.

Kvist, J. and J. Saari. *The Europeanisation of Social Protection*. London: Policy Press, 2007.

Marlier, E., et al. *The EU and Social Inclusion: Facing the Challenges*. Policy Press, 2007.

Moussis, N. *Access to Social Europe*. 5th ed. Rixensart: European Study Service, 2007.

Neal, A.C. *European Labour Law And Policy: Cases and Materials*. 2nd ed. The Hague: Kluwer Law International, 2002.

Neal, A.C. *The Changing Face of European Labour Law and Social Policy*. Studies In Employment and Social Policy, 28. The Hague: Kluwer Law International, 2004.

Nielsen, R. and E. Szyszczak. *The Social Dimension of the European Union*. 3rd ed. Business Law Series, no. 19. Copenhagen: Handelshøjskolens Forlag, 1997.

Prechal, S. 'Equality of Treatment, Non-discrimination and Social Policy: Achievements in Three Themes'. In A. McDonnell (ed.). *A Review of Forty Years of Community Law: Legal Developments in the European Communities and the European Union*. The Hague: Kluwer Law International, 2005.

Roberts, I. and B. Springer. *Social Policy in the European Union: Between Harmonization and National Autonomy*. Boulder, CO: Lynne Rienner, 2001.

Rodière, P. *Droit social de l'Union européenne.* 2e éd. Paris: Librairie générale de droit et de jurisprudence, 2002.

Sciarra, S., et al. *Employment Policy and the Regulation of Part-Time Work in the European Union: A Comparative Analysis.* Cambridge: Cambridge University Press, 2004.

Shaw, J. *Social Law and Policy in an Evolving European Union.* Oxford: Hart, 2000.

Shaw, J., et al. Economic and Social Law of the European Union. Palgrave Macmillan Law Masters Focus. Palgrave Macmillan, 2007.

Spaventa, E. and M. Dougan. *Social Welfare and EU Law.* Essays in European Law. Oxford: Hart, 2005.

Szyszczak, E. *EC Labour Law.* European Law Series. London: Longman, 2000.

Szyszczak, E. 'The New Paradigm for Social Policy: A Virtuous Circle?'. (2001) CML Rev., 1112–1170.

Teyssié, B. *Droit européen du travail.* 2e éd. Paris: Litec, 2003.

Tobler, R.C. *Indirect Discrimination: A Case Study into the Development of the Legal Concept of Indirect Discrimination under EC Law.* Social Europe Series, 10. Antwerpen: Intersentia, 2005.

Van Berkel, H.H.A. and I.H. Møller. *Active Social Policies in the EU: Inclusion through Participation?* Bristol: Policy Press, 2002.

Van Raepenbusch, S., et al. (eds). *Politique sociale; Éducation et jeunesse.* 2e éd. Commentaire Mégret, Part 7. Bruxelles: Éditions de l'Université de Bruxelles, 1998.

Vonfelt, G. *L'égalité de traitement entre hommes et femmes.* Maastricht, Institut européen d'administration publique, 2000.

Watson, P. 'Social and Employment Policy'. In D. Vaughan and A. Robertson (eds). *Law of the European Union.* Richmond: Richmond Publishing, 2003.

Welz, C. *The European Social Dialogue under Articles 138 and 139 of the EC Treaty: Actors, Processes, Outcomes.* Dissertation, Radboud University Nijmegen, 2007.

Equal Pay and Equal Treatment

Caracciolo di Torella, E. and A. Masselot. 'The Future of Sex Equality'. In T. Takis and P. Nebbia (eds). *European Union Law for the Twenty-First Century.* Oxford: Hart, 2004.

Currall J. In H. Von der Groeben, J, Thiesing and C.-D. Ehlermann (eds). *Kommentar zum EU-/EG-Vertrag.* 5th ed. Baden-Baden, 1999.

Dashwood, A.A. and S. O'Leary (eds). *The Principle of Equal Treatment in EC Law: Papers Collected by the Centre for European Legal Studies.* Cambridge/London: Sweet & Maxwell, 1997.

Hervey, T. 'Thirty Years of EU Sex Equality Law: Looking Backwards, Looking Forwards'. (2005) *Maastricht Journal of European & Comparative Law,* 307.

McCrudden, C. *Equality of Treatment between Women and Men in Social Security.* London: Butterworths, 1994.

Education, Vocational Training and Youth
Bache, I. 'The Europeanisation of Higher Education: Markets, Politics or Learning?' (2006) JCMS, 231–248.
Classen, C.D. In H. Von der Groeben, J. Thiesing and C.-D. Ehlermann (eds). *Kommentar zum EU-/EG-Vertrag*. 5th ed. Baden-Baden, 1999.
Lane, R. 'New Community Competences under the Maastricht Treaty'. (1993) CML Rev., 939–979.
Lenaerts, K. 'Education in European Community Law after "Maastricht"'. (1994) CML Rev., 7–41.

Chapter XI

Horizontal and Flanking Policies

K.J.M. Mortelmans

1   THE PLACE OF HORIZONTAL AND FLANKING
POLICIES IN THE EC TREATY

In this introductory section, we will explain what is covered by the definition of horizontal and flanking policies, and give a very brief indication of the development of these policies.

1.1   HORIZONTAL AND FLANKING POLICIES AND OTHER POLICIES

The term horizontal and flanking policies refers to a group of policies which are in some ways heterogeneous, and many of which found a basis in the EC Treaty as a result of the Treaty of Maastricht. These policies, such as environmental policy and consumer protection policy, aim to provide a corrective balance to the main thrust of action along economic policy lines – in the Community context, the internal market and competition policies. They reflect the wish to add a social, 'caring' dimension to the production of goods and services.

This approach stems from the ideology of the 1970s, and the dominant beliefs from around that time – at least in some countries – that government action can transform society. The tension between economic interests (the operation of the market) and non-economic interests is still relevant. Because of the definition of

P.J.G. Kapteyn, A.M. McDonnell, K.J.M. Mortelmans and C.W.A. Timmermans (eds),
The Law of the European Union and the European Communities, pp. 1087–1141.
©2008 Kluwer Law International BV, The Netherlands.

'non-economic interests' is a negative one, we prefer to use the collective term 'horizontal and flanking policies'.

Horizontal and flanking policies include culture, sport, education, public health, consumer policy, environmental policy and one or two others. In all cases, the link with EC law is formed by those elements of policy which involve economic activities (book prices, export of waste, medical care). In the case of horizontal and flanking policies, however, it is the other, non-economic facet which is given priority. Article 2 EC expresses this as follows in relation to environmental policy: 'the Community shall have as its task . . . to promote throughout the Community a harmonious, balanced and sustainable development of economic activities . . . a high level of protection and improvement of the quality of the environment.' The crises in relation to bovine spongiform encephalopathy (BSE) and foot-and-mouth disease are clear evidence that Community policy must take account of other aspects than merely free movement of agricultural products – such as the health of humans and animals, and even environmental protection.

Flanking and horizontal policies are to be distinguished from the policies regarding the freedoms and competition, on the one hand, and from other policy areas such as social policy or sectoral policy, on the other. Sectoral policy is discussed in Chapter XII below. The main questions in the discussion of sectoral policy relate to whether the specific (sectoral) economic provisions are applicable or the general economic provisions; in flanking and horizontal policies, the issue is that of the content of non-economic interests.

In the European Economic Area (EEA) Agreement, policy areas relating to non-economic interests are referred to as 'horizontal and flanking policies';[1] in the Court's Opinion on the Cartagena Protocol, the term 'non-commercial concerns' is used.[2] Particularly, in the period soon after the Maastricht Treaty was adopted, there was talk of 'new Community competences'[3] – but whereas this overlaps to a large extent with the matters dealt with in this chapter, this also includes some elements which in the present book are treated as social policy (structural funds) or economic policy (industrial policy, trans European networks).[4] A clear and unambiguous definition remains difficult.

1.2   THE DEVELOPMENT OF HORIZONTAL AND FLANKING POLICIES

Under Article G(A)(1) of the Treaty of Maastricht, the words 'European Economic Community' were changed into 'European Community' throughout the Treaty.

---

1. <http://secretariat.efta.int/Web/EuropeanEconomicArea/FlankingHorizontalPolicies>.
2. Opinion 2/00, *Cartagena Protocol*, at para. 35.
3. R. Lane, 'New Community Competences under the Maastricht Treaty' (1993) CML Rev., 939.
4. Some Dutch and German authors use the term 'flanking policies' (or at least its linguistic equivalent) in this broader sense; cf. R.H. Lauwaars and C.W.A. Timmermans, *Europees recht in kort bestek*, 6th ed. (Deventer, 2003), 322. See also T. Eilmansberger, 'Binnenmarktprinzipien und Flankierende Politiken', in T. Eilmansberger, *Vom Schuman-Plan zum Vertrag von Amsterdam* (Wien, 2000), 229.

This change of name, and with it a broadening of the scope of Community law,[5] was the culmination of a process which had already commenced in the 1970s. The Final communiqué of the Paris Summit in October 1972 and the Single European Act (SEA) indicated that the Community was not merely an economic one. The Community was obliged to devote more attention to the social aspects of its policies and in due course to develop into an Economic and Monetary Union, as has been explained in Chapter X of this book. Moreover, the Heads of State and Government emphasized the importance of Community action in flanking policy areas, such as research and development, and environmental policy.[6]

The communitarization of the latter policy is exemplary for the Community's approach. The first question to be addressed was whether the original European Economic Community (EEC) Treaty also sought to achieve environmental objectives.[7] Through a broad interpretation of Article 2 EEC, the two general provisions providing a basis for Community action, Articles 100 and 235 EEC, were harnessed to enable concrete action to be taken. Subsequently, with the amendments to the EEC Treaty by the SEA, specific objectives and legal bases were formulated for environmental policy. At the same time, it was indicated (in Art. 130r(4) EEC) that the principle of subsidiarity applied, and it was laid down in Article 130r(2) EEC that the relevant requirements of environmental protection formed a component part of the other tasks of Community policy.

With the Treaty of Maastricht, the same step was taken for various other flanking areas of Community policy which had been already started to develop, such as consumer protection, public health, education and culture: they were given a specific status and legal basis in the EC Treaty. Certain other flanking policies, such as civil protection and tourism were merely included in the catalogue of activities set out in Article 3 EC, finding their place in Article 3(1)(u) EC.

The Treaty of Amsterdam actually altered the content of a number of titles concerning flanking policies. This was above all the case for public health and the environment. In the first part of the EC Treaty, a provision was included concerning the integration of environmental protection in other policies of the Community.[8]

The Treaty of Nice did not bring further elaborations of horizontal and flanking policies, except an amendment to Article 175 EC, concerning the environment. In the title on commercial policy, Article 133(6) EC further specifies the shared competence of the Community and the Member States concerning the conclusion of trade agreements relating to cultural and audiovisual services, education services, and social and human health services.

In the EU Charter of Fundamental Rights, a number of provisions are devoted to subjects of the horizontal and flanking policies such as education and health.

---

5. See, generally, Lane, op. cit. *supra* note 3.
6. Bull, EC, 1972, No. 10, 15.
7. Case 91/79, *Commission v. Italy*.
8. Art. 6 EC.

On the Status of the Charter, and how this will change if and when the Treaty of Lisbon enters into force, see further Chapter 1 above.

The Treaty of Lisbon will insert two new titles in the EC Treaty (to be renamed the Treaty on the Functioning of the European Union (TFEU)): Title XXII (Art.195 TFEU) concerning tourism, and Title XXIII (Art. 196 TFEU) on civil protection. The scope of Chapter 3 of Title XI – which concerned education, vocational training and youth – will be extended to cover sport as well. According to Article 4 TFEU, the EU and the Member States will have a shared competence in the area of the environment and that of consumer protection. Article 6 TFEU provides that the Union will have competence to carry out actions to support, coordinate or supplement the actions of the Member States in the areas of, *inter alia*, public health, culture, tourism, education, vocational training, youth, sport, and civil protection.

The following sections will examine the law as it stands before the entry into force of the Treaty of Lisbon. A brief look will be taken in relation to each subject at the changes brought by the Lisbon Treaty.

2   COMMON CHARACTERISTICS OF THE HORIZONTAL AND FLANKING POLICIES

If one compares the various titles of the EC Treaty devoted to horizontal and flanking policies, it becomes clear that there is a common approach, although it is not always adhered to consistently – and that is still the case even after the amendments brought by the Treaties of Amsterdam and Nice. First of all, the *objectives* are indicated which the Community is to pursue; secondly, the *means* by which these objectives are to be pursued are specified in the form of the legal bases available for Community action, and, thirdly, the legal instruments to be used are prescribed. The various titles of the Treaty, save that dealing with consumer protection, contain a provision on the promotion of cooperation between the Member States and the Community on the one hand, and third countries on the other.[9] Attention is also paid to the cooperation between the Member States and the Community.

2.1   Harmonization or Not?

As for the scope of Community action, a distinction may be drawn between two approaches. The Community is permitted to adopt harmonization measures in the fields of the environment, consumer protection and public health – sometimes limited to certain matters.[10] This is excluded in the cases of education and culture.

---

9. See also Art. 133(6) EC.
10. This is particularly so for public health; see Case C-376/98, *Germany v. Parliament and Council*.

This restriction on the internal competences is also maintained in the external policy of the Community, as may be seen from Article 133(6) EC. The drafters of the treaties have formulated the provisions on horizontal and flanking policies in a manner which at first sight appears to limit severely the possibilities for Community action.[11] The principle of subsidiarity, the exclusion of harmonization measures, the requirement of unanimity in decision-making, and the use in some cases of non-binding instruments (recommendations) all seem have placed secure locks on the doors of the national departmental ministries. In some situations, the case law of the Court of Justice has provided a 'skeleton key' to open these doors, bringing national policy under increasing Community influence.[12]

As an alternative for (prohibited) harmonization, the Community uses the so-called open method of cooperation for certain policy rules in some flanking areas, such as education and youth.[13]

2.2   HORIZONTAL INTEGRATION PROVISIONS

As has been indicated, these are 'caring, idealistic' policy areas with economic interfaces. In Treaty terms, the horizontal integration provisions[14] function as connecting provisions; the policy which is to be 'integrated' is carried out in different ways in the different policy areas.

There are three variants. In the area of environmental protection, the principle has been raised to a higher level by the Treaty of Amsterdam, moving it from the title on environmental protection (former Art. 130s EC), to the first part of the Treaty (Art. 6 EC). In the area of culture (Art. 151(4) EC), public health (Art. 152(1) EC)[15] and consumer policy (Art. 153(2) EC)[16] the integration principle is contained in a provision of the relevant Treaty title. There is no such integrating

---

11. Y. Bock, *Rechtsangleichung und Regulierung im Binnenmarkt: zum Umfang der allgemeinen Binnenmarktkompetenz* (Baden-Baden, 2005); S. Weatherill, 'Why Harmonise?' in T. Tridimas and P. Nebbia (eds), *European Union Law for the Twenty-First Century: Rethinking the New Legal Order, vol. 2, Internal Market and Free Movement: Community Policies* (Oxford, 2004), 11.

12. Case C-120/95, *Decker v. Caisse de maladie des employés privés* (health); Case C-337/97, *C.P.M. Meeusen v. Hoofddirectie van de Informatie Beheer Groep* (education).

13. See point 37 of the conclusions of the European Council in Lisbon 23 and 24 Mar. 2000. See on this T. Bodewig, T. Voß, 'Die "offene Methode der Koordinierung" in der Europäischen Union: "Schleichende Harmonisierung" oder notwendige "Konsentierung" zur Erreichung der Ziele der EU?' (2003) EuR, 310; C. Engel, 'Integration durch Koordination und Benchmarking', in H. Hill and R. Pritschas (eds), *Europäisches Verwaltungsverfahrensrecht* (Berlin, 2004) 409; G. de Búrca, 'The Constitutional Challenge of New Governance in the European Union' (2003) EL Rev, 814.

14. See on this U. Everling, 'Zu den Querschnittsklauseln im EG-Vertrag', in *Mélanges en hommage à F. Schockweiler* (Baden-Baden, 1999), 131; D. Gasse, *Die Bedeutung der Querschnittsklauseln für die Anwendung des Gemeinschaftskartellrechts* (Frankfurt/M, 2000).

15. The Protocol on protection and welfare of animals, attached to the EC Treaty by the Treaty of Amsterdam, also contains a 'soft' integration provision; see Case C-189/01, *Jippes et al. v. Minister van Landbouw, Natuurbeheer en Visserij*.

16. Art. 129a EC did not contain an integration provision.

provision for education and vocational training. From the presence of the integration provisions, it may be deduced that the Community may adopt measures affecting health and cultural matters on the basis of other Treaty provisions, such as those concerning the internal market and competition. An example is the Television Directive, which is based on Articles 47 and 55 EC, but which contains a provision on the protection of languages and protection of children.[17]

In the Conclusions of the Presidency at the Edinburgh European Council in 1992,[18] an interpretation of Articles 126–129 EC (old versions) was advanced in the light of Article 5 EC that excludes harmonization measures. That interpretation further purports to deduce that the use of Article 308 EC for harmonization measures in pursuit of these specific objectives is excluded. It still remains to be seen whether this view is shared by the Court of Justice.[19]

Article 9 TFEU provides that 'in defining and implementing its policies and actions, the Union shall take into account requirements linked to the promotion of a high level of employment, the guarantee of adequate social protection, the fight against social exclusion, and a high level of education, training and protection of human health.'

3   ENVIRONMENTAL POLICY

In the following, we will first deal with the legal bases in the Treaty for environmental policy, in section 3.1. Then EC environmental policy itself will be briefly examined.[20] The relationship between environmental policy on the one hand and the internal market,[21] competition[22] and state aids[23] on the other, is dealt with in other chapters of this book.[24]

3.1   TREATY LEGAL BASES OF EC ENVIRONMENTAL POLICY

The SEA added a new Title VII to Part Three of the EEC Treaty, which dealt with the objectives and means of Community environmental policy. This was further

---

17. Dir. 89/552, O.J. 1989, L 298/33. See on this Case C-412/93, *Leclerc-Siplec v. TF1 and M6*. See also Art. 8 of the Framework Dir. 2002/21, on a common regulatory framework for electronic communications networks and services, O.J. 2002, L 108/33.
18. Bull, EC 12-1992, 15, note 1.
19. Cf. the view of the *Bundesverfassungsgericht* in Brunner et al. (1994) 1 CML Rev. 57, points C.II.3 (b) and (c); Case C-376/98, *Germany v. Parliament and Council* (tobacco advertising) does not clear this point up entirely either.
20. Section 3.2. In preparing this section, extensive use was made of J.H. Jans, H.G. Sevenster and H.H.B. Vedder, *Europees milieurecht in Nederland* (Den Haag, 2000), and J.H. Jans, *European Environmental Law*, 2nd revised ed. (Groningen, 2000).
21. See extensively Jans, Sevenster and Vedder, 299 et seq.
22. H.H.B. Vedder, *Competition and Environmental Protection in Europe*, PhD thesis (Amsterdam, 2003).
23. See extensively Jans, Sevenster and Vedder, 357 et seq.
24. Chs. VIII and IX *supra*.

developed, and the Treaty bases extended, by the Treaties of Maastricht, Amsterdam and Nice. Article 2 Treaty on the European Union (TEU) states that one of the objectives of the European Union is 'to promote economic and social progress . . . and to achieve balanced and sustainable development'. Article 2 EC includes the aim 'to promote throughout the Community a harmonious, balanced and sustainable development of economic activities', and speaks of 'a high level of protection and improvement of the quality of the environment'.

These objectives must be achieved by means of 'a policy in the sphere of the environment', pursuant to Article 3(1)(l) EC, which effectively achieves a codification of the legal situation which had arisen through an extensive interpretation of the old Article 2 EEC.[25]

For certain matters, such as nuclear safety and radioactive waste, the Euratom Treaty remains important. Article 1 Euratom specifies that it is the task of the Euratom Community 'to contribute to the raising of the standard of living'. By analogy with the legal situation in the EEC prior to the coming into force of the TEU, Article 1 Euratom is a proper environmental objective. Article 2 TEU is also of importance, so that in the development of its nuclear energy policy the Community must take account of the danger of environmental disasters. The absence of a specific provision in the Euratom Treaty means that in a number of instances the EC Treaty will be applicable. The decisions following the Chernobyl radiation reactor disaster, and the associated case law, illustrate this point.[26]

In the Treaties of Maastricht, Amsterdam and Nice, the environment title was elaborated on a number of points, which will be explained systematically in the following sections.

Following the Treaty of Lisbon, Article 3(3) TEU contains the following objectives: The Union shall establish an internal market. It shall work for the sustainable development of Europe based on balanced economic growth and price stability, a highly competitive social market economy, aiming at full employment and social progress, and a high level of protection and improvement of the quality of the environment. It shall promote scientific and technological advance. According to Article 3(5) TEU (Lisbon) In its relations with the wider world, the Union shall uphold and promote its values and contribute to the protection if its citizens. It shall contribute to peace, security, the sustainable development of the Earth, solidarity and mutual respect among peoples, free and fair trade, eradication of poverty and the protection of human rights, in particular the rights of the child, as well as to the strict observance and the development of international law, including respect for the principles of the United Nations Charter.

The Title on environment will be amended. Article 191 TFEU contains the explicitly formulated aim of 'promoting measures at international level to deal with regional or worldwide environmental problems, and in particular combating

---

25. Case 240/83, *Procureur de la République v. ADBHU*.
26. Case C-62/88, *Greece v. Council*; Case C-70/88, *Parliament v. Council*; Case C-146/91, *KYDEP v. Council and Commission*.

climate change'. This provision should be seen in combination with the new Title XXI, concerning energy. According to Article 194 TFEU:

> in the context of the establishment and functioning of the internal market and with regard for the need to preserve and improve the environment, the Union's policy on energy shall aim, in a spirit of solidarity between Member States, to (a) ensure the functioning of the energy market; (b) ensure security of energy supply in the Union; and (c) promote energy efficiency and energy saving and the development of new and renewable forms of energy; and (d) promote the interconnection of energy networks.

3.1.1   Objectives

According to Article 174(1) EC, the Community policy on the environment is to contribute to the following four objectives: first, preserving, protecting and improving the quality of the environment; secondly, protecting human health; thirdly, a prudent and rational utilization of natural resources, and, finally, promoting measures at international level to deal with regional or worldwide environmental problems.[27] These environmental objectives are close to or are inspired by the United Nations Environmental Conferences in Stockholm in 1972 and Rio de Janeiro in 1992. The term 'sustainable development', which played such a central role in the Rio Declaration, is not to be found in Article 174(1) EC, but can be found in Article 177 EC, which deals with development cooperation. It can also be found – since the entry into force of the Treaty of Amsterdam – in Article 6 EC, which lays down the need for environmental objectives to be integrated into other EC policies, particularly 'with a view to promoting sustainable development'. This principle also occurs in a Declaration annexed to the Final Act of the Treaty of Maastricht, on Assessment of the Environmental Impact of Community Measures. Moreover, the Title of the Community's (old) Fifth Environmental Action Programme was 'Towards Sustainability'.[28]

Article 174(3) EC sets out certain matters which the Community must take into account in preparing its policy on the environment: available scientific and technical data; environmental conditions in the various regions of the Community; the potential benefits and costs of action or lack of action, and the economic and social development of the Community as a whole and the balanced development of its regions. These matters to be taken into account are elaborated further in the EC's Sixth Environmental Action Programme.[29]

---

27. See further Case C-379/92, *Criminal Proceedings against Peralta*.
28. O.J. 1993, C 138. See also Dec. No. 2179/98 of the Parliament and Council, Towards Sustainability, O.J. 1998, L 275/1.
29. The Sixth Action Programme on the environment does not have a title focusing on a particular objective; see Dec. No. 1600/2002 of the Parliament and Council, O.J. 2002, L 242/1.

3.1.2 Principles

In implementing its environmental policy, the Community aims at *a high level of protection*. This principle was included in 1986 in Article 100a(3) EEC, concerning the Commission's harmonization proposals, but it now enjoys a more general scope and development. Article 174(2) EC adds that Community policy (not just Commission policy), while aiming at a high level of protection, must take 'into account the diversity of situations in the various regions of the Community'. This consideration is repeated in Article 174(3) fourth indent EC. Here it is added that the Community must take into account 'the economic and social development of the Community as a whole'.

The *precautionary principle*, which originated in German environmental policy, means that authorities do not have to wait for an absolutely clear, scientifically proven causal link to be established between certain activities or conduct and negative environmental effects before taking action to protect the environment. When there is a strong presumption that certain action may be environmentally damaging, action is justified 'before it is too late'.[30] The principle is not defined more fully in the Treaty but was developed in the Fifth Environmental Action programme and in a Council Resolution, annexed to the Nice European Council Conclusions, December 2000. In this Resolution, a link was made between environmental protection and Community policies concerning health and consumer protection; this was particularly in the context of the BSE (mad cow disease) crisis.

The *preventive principle* was already included in the Treaty by the amendments brought about by the SEA, and had featured earlier in the second part of the First Environmental Action Programme.[31]

The principle that environmental damage should as a priority be *rectified at source* had already been invoked before the entry into force of the TEU by the Court of Justice in Case C-2/90, *Commission v. Belgium*, with reference to the Basel Convention.[32] This principle is important for matters involving tension between free movement and environmental policy.

The principle that the *polluter pays* was already established in 1975.[33] This principle can play a role in the elaboration of Community policy in two ways. First, the Commission applies the principle in the state aids field when exercising its powers under Articles 87 and 88 EC: the Commission's practice reveals that in certain cases state aid for environmental objectives may be considered compatible

---

30. Jans, Sevenster and Vedder, op. cit. note 20, 45. See Case C-180/96, *United Kingdom v. Commission (BSE)*; Opinion 2/00, *Cartagena Protocol*; Case C-41/02, *Commission v. Netherlands*; Joined Cases C-145 & 155/04, *Spain v. United Kingdom*. See also Communication from the Commission on the precautionary principle, COM(2000)1.
31. O.J. 1973, C 112.
32. Accession to this Convention, on the control of transboundary movements of hazardous wastes and their disposal, was approved on behalf of the EC on 1 Feb. 1993, O.J. 1993, L 39.
33. Council Recommendation of 3 Mar. 1975 regarding cost allocation and action by public authorities on environmental matters, O.J. 1975, L 194/1.

with the common market.[34] Secondly, the principle can also be applied by the Community legislature when it adopts directives, particularly in determining costs in the directives on waste. In this case, Article 175(5) EC permits the Council to lay down appropriate provisions in the form of temporary derogations and/or financial support from the Cohesion Fund where the costs of a Community measure would involve disproportionate costs for the public authorities of a Member State.

With the Treaty of Amsterdam, the *integration principle* disappeared from the environment title and was granted the status of a principle in Part One (Principles) of the EC Treaty. According to Article 6 EC, the environmental protection requirements must be integrated into the definition and implementation of the Community policies and activities referred to in Article 3 EC, in particular with a view to promoting sustainable development.[35] The application of the integration principle is still in the throes of development[36] – as is evident from the case law,[37] and Commission practice.[38] In Case C-379/98, *PreussenElektra*, the integration principle was for the first time explicitly employed in the reasoning concerning the applicability of the environmental justification.[39] The EU Charter of Fundamental Rights repeats, in Article 37, that 'a high level of environmental protection and the improvement of the quality of the environment must be integrated into the policies of the Union and ensured in accordance with the principle of sustainable development.'

We will not discuss the subsidiarity principle originally included in Article 130r(4) EEC. That article, which broke new ground in the EEC Treaty, was removed from the environment title by the Treaty of Maastricht, and was replaced by the general principle of subsidiarity, now laid down in Article 5 EC.[40]

3.1.3   International Cooperation

Article 174(4), first paragraph, EC provides that the Community and the Member States shall cooperate, in their respective spheres of competence, with third countries and with the competent international organizations. Further arrangements for Community cooperation may be the subject of agreements between the Community and the third parties concerned; these are to be negotiated

---

34. See on this L. Hancher, T. Ottervanger and P.J. Slot, *E.C. State Aids*, 3rd ed. (London, 2006), Ch. 20, 493 et seq.
35. See on this N. Dhondt, *Integration of Environmental Protection into Other EC-Policies* (Groningen, 2003); M. Wasmeier, 'The Integration of Environmental Protection as a General Rule for Interpreting Community Law', CML Rev, 38/159.
36. See also Part I of Dec. No. 2179/98 of the Parliament and Council, Towards Sustainability, O.J. 1998, L 275/1.
37. Case C-62/88, *Greece v. Council*; Case C-300/89, *Commission v. Council*; Case C-17/90, *Wieger v. Bundesanstalt für den Güterfernverkehr*; Case C-379/92, *Criminal Proceedings against Peralta*; Case C-341/95, *Bettati v. Safety Hi-Tech*; Case C-513/99, *Concordia Bus Finland*.
38. E.g., Dec. of the Commission in Case CECED, O.J. 2000, L 187/47.
39. Case C-379/98, *PreussenElektra v. Schleswag*.
40. See further Ch. III *supra*.

and concluded in accordance with Article 300 EC. 'Competent international organizations' at first sight must mean UNEP (the United Nations Environment Programme), but also the Council of Europe, the International Maritime Organization (IMO), United Nations Food and Agriculture Organization (FAO), the OECD and General Agreement on Tariffs and Trade (GATT)/ World Trade Organization (WTO). Given that the Environment Title of the EC Treaty does not appear to derogate from the powers separately regulated by the Euratom Treaty, the International Atomic Energy Agency in Vienna would not appear to be covered by this provision.[41]

The second paragraph of Article 174(4) EC provides that the first paragraph is without prejudice to Member States' competence to negotiate in international bodies and to conclude international agreements. The words 'international bodies' indicate that this paragraph does not relate to purely bilateral negotiations between a Member State and a third country.

The *ERTA* declaration, adopted with the Final Act of the SEA,[42] was repeated and extended[43] in a Declaration attached to the Treaty of Maastricht. According to this Declaration, the Intergovernmental conference considered that the provision contained in Article 174(4) second paragraph EC did not affect the principles resulting from the judgment in the *ERTA* case.[44] If there had been no such declaration, it would have been possible to argue that the second paragraph of that article consciously created a different approach from the doctrine expressed in that judgment. It was clearly not the intention to do this, so that doctrine must still be applied to determine who is competent to act at international level.[45] The declaration does not however actually solve the problem of competence, as the first paragraph of Article 174(4) itself appears to indicate shared competence, whereas on the other hand, on the basis of internal Community instruments, such as those in the fisheries sector, exclusive Community competence can be argued in respect of various environmental measures.[46] In a recent Opinion, the Court ruled that for the conclusion of the Cartagena Protocol on Biosafety, the EC and the Member States enjoyed shared competences. The fact that numerous international trade agreements pursue multiple objectives and the broad interpretation of the concept of common commercial policy under the Court's case law are not such as to call into question the finding that the Protocol is an instrument falling principally within environmental policy.[47]

---

41. Cf. C-70/88, *Parliament v. Council (Chernobyl)*.
42. Declaration on Art. 130r EEC annexed to the Final Act signed on the adoption of the SEA.
43. This declaration now also applies to monetary policy and development cooperation.
44. Case 22/70, *Commission v. Council* (ERTA).
45. Opinion 2/91, *ILO Convention*.
46. See extensively, Jans, Sevenster and Vedder, op. cit. note 20, 99 et seq.
47. Opinion 2/00, *Cartagena Protocol*, para. 40.

3.1.4   **Legal Bases and Decision-Making**

3.1.4.1   *Legal Bases*

It can be deduced from Article 175 EC that Community environmental policy rests
on two general legal bases, save where there is specific provision elsewhere in the
Treaty, such as Article 37;[48] Article 71; Article 80(2); Article 93; Article 286 EC
and Article 7; Article 30; Article 31 and Article 32 Euratom. The choice between
Articles 95 and 133 EC on the one hand, and Article 175 on the other has been the
subject of important case law. The Court's judgment in Case C-300/89 *Commission v. Council* (titanium dioxide) implies that product-directed environmental
policy will have to be harmonized largely on the basis of Article 95 EC.[49] But
for waste, Article 175 EC is also available. The Court has confirmed that the
Council's use of Article 175 EC as a legal basis on its own may be justified.[50]
For the conclusion of the Cartagena Protocol on Biosafety, Article 175(1) was
found to be the correct legal basis.[51] The choice of legal basis is important because
of the differences in decision-making procedure and voting requirements, and the
conditions under which the provisions concerned may be used. These differences
were greater in the past than at present (compare Art. 95 EC with Art. 175(2) EC).[52]
Article 175 EC permits the Member States to adopt or maintain in force more
stringent preventive measures (see section 3.1.6 below). A procedure was introduced by Article 95(4) and (5) whereby even after the adoption of a harmonization
measure, national measures may be applied and even introduced, after being
approved. Article 95(4) EC (in its old version) was applied in Case C-41/93,
France v. Commission; there, the Court in fact annulled the decision of the Commission on formal grounds, but it does appear from the judgment that a national
measure may only be applied after approval by the Commission.[53] The case law
on Article 95(4) and (5) EC is still developing.[54]

3.1.4.2   *Decision-Making*

Following the Treaties of Amsterdam and Nice, the decision-making on environmental policy under Article 175 EC may be summarized as follows. First, Article

---

48. Joined Cases C-164 & 165/97, *Parliament v. Council.*
49. Case C-300/89, *Commission v. Council.*
50. Case C-155/91, *Commission v. Council*; Case C-187/93, *Parliament v. Council*; Case C-376/98,
     Germany v. Parliament and Council (tobacco advertising) is indirectly important.
51. Opinion 2/00, *Cartagena Protocol*, at para. 44.
52. Case C-36/98, *Spain v. Council.*
53. PCP Dec., O.J. 1992, L 334/8. See on this Case C-41/93, *France v. Commission*; for the new
     PCP Dec., O.J. 1994, L 316/43; N. De Sadeleer, 'Procedures for Derogations from the Principle
     of Approximation of Laws under Article 95 EC', CML Rev, 40/889.
54. See Case C-127/97, *Burstein v. Freistaat Bayern*; Case C-319/97, *Criminal Proceedings
     against Antoine Kortas*; Case C-512/99, *Germany v. Commission*; most recently, Case
     T-182/06, *The Netherlands v. Commission.*

175(1) EC lays down the co-decision procedure of Article 251 EC as the basic rule, and the Economic and Social Committee and the Committee of the Regions must be consulted.

Second, derogating from the procedure provided for in Article 175(1) EC, and without prejudice to Article 95, the Council, acting unanimously on a proposal from the Commission and after consulting the European Parliament, the Economic and Social Committee and the Committee of the Regions, decides on (a) provisions of a primarily fiscal nature; (b) measures affecting town and country planning, quantitative management of water resources or affecting, directly or indirectly, the availability of those resources, and land use, with the exception of waste management; (c) measures significantly affecting a Member State's choice between different energy sources and the general structure of its energy supply (Art. 175(2) EC). The Council may, under the conditions laid down in Article 175(1), define those matters referred to in Article 175(2) EC on which decisions are to be taken by a qualified majority. Article 175(2) EC, as reproduced here, gives the text as it results from amendment by the Treaty of Nice. In a Declaration concerning Article175 EC attached to the Final Act, the High Contracting Parties state that they are determined to see the European Union play a leading role in promoting environmental protection; full use should be made of all possibilities offered by the EC Treaty with a view to pursuing this objective, including the use of market-oriented incentives and instruments to promote sustainable development.

Third, Article 175(3) EC provides that the Council will adopt general action programmes setting out priority objectives to be attained, acting by means of the co-decision procedure. The Council will then, acting under the terms of Article 175(1) EC or Article 175(2) EC, according to the case, adopt the measures necessary for the implementation of these programmes.

3.1.5 Financing, Implementation and Enforcement

The Member States are responsible for financing and implementing Community environmental policy, without prejudice to certain measures of a Community nature (Art. 175(4) EC). Community measures include assistance from the Cohesion Fund[55] and research and development funding from programmes such as LIFE.[56]

The implementation and enforcement is left to the Member States, under supervision of the Commission in accordance with Article 211 EC. In Chapter 9 of the Fifth Environmental Action programme the Commission noted that in the past there were problems in implementation and supervision, and proposed reforms such as improvement in the preparation of measures and the quality of legislation,[57]

---

55. See Art. 175(5) EC.
56. Reg. 1655/2000, O.J. 2000, L 192/1.
57. Cf. L Krämer, 'Better Regulation for the EC Environment: On the Quality of EC Environmental Legislation' (2007) *Milieu en Recht*, 70; E. Bohne, 'Another Perspective on the Quality of EC Environmental Legislation' (2007) *Milieu en Recht*, 215.

better integration of environmental policy in other Community policies, and an increased role for the European Environment Agency.[58]

The Commission also stressed the importance of rules relating to liability for environmental damage.[59] In a Council Resolution of 7 October 1997,[60] and in the Council decision on the review of the action programme 'Towards sustainability'[61] further details are given concerning drafting, implementation and enforcement of Community environmental legislation. A Commission proposal for a directive concerning the enforcement of environmental policy by means of criminal law was changed by the Council into a Framework decision, based on Articles 29 TEU, 31(e) TEU and 34(2)(b) TEU.[62] The Commission challenged the legal basis before the Court of Justice. In its judgment, the Court stated:

> As to the content of the framework decision, Article 2 establishes a list of particularly serious environmental offences, in respect of which the Member States must impose criminal penalties. Articles 2–7 of the decision do indeed entail partial harmonisation of the criminal laws of the Member States, in particular as regards the constituent elements of various criminal offences committed to the detriment of the environment. As a general rule, neither criminal law nor the rules of criminal procedure fall within the Community's competence. However, the last-mentioned finding does not prevent the Community legislature, when the application of effective, proportionate and dissuasive criminal penalties by the competent national authorities is an essential measure for combating serious environmental offences, from taking measures which relate to the criminal law of the Member States which it considers necessary in order to ensure that the rules which it lays down on environmental protection are fully effective.[63]

The Court concluded: 'It follows from the foregoing that, on account of both their aim and their content, Articles 1–7 of the framework decision have as their main purpose the protection of the environment and they could have been properly adopted on the basis of Article 175 EC.'[64]

3.1.6   Minimum Harmonization and More Stringent National Provisions

Article 176 EC contains a so-called 'minimum harmonization' provision. According to this provision, the protective measures adopted pursuant to Article 175 do

---

58. Reg. 1210/90, O.J. 1990, L 120/1.
59. The Commission published a White Paper on this, COM(2000)66 final.
60. O.J. 1997, C 321/1.
61. O.J. 1998, L 275/1.
62. For the Commission's proposal, see COM(2001)139 final. See Framework Dec. 2003/80 of 27 Jan. 2003, O.J. 2003, L 29/55. This was based on an initiative of Denmark, with the aim of a framework decision for serious environmental crime, O.J. 2000, C 39/4.
63. Case C-176/03, *Commission v. Council*, paras 47–48.
64. Ibid., para. 51.

not prevent a Member State from maintaining or introducing more stringent protective measures. In other words, the harmonization level achieved is regarded as a minimum level, with the Member States free, according to Article 176 EC, to strive to attain a higher level of protection.[65] Measures with that objective must be compatible with the EC Treaty, and must be notified to the Commission.

Before the entry into force of the SEA, minimum harmonization provisions could be encountered in various directives.[66] Given that there is no equivalent provision to Article 176 EC in the Euratom Treaty, it is indicated in the text of measures based on that Treaty whether they are minimum provisions.[67] The possibility of taking more stringent measures is not laid down in any other Treaty provisions apart from Article 176 EC. A measure based on another Treaty article may itself provide for such a possibility.[68] In fact, Article 95 EC contains a provision which to a certain extent has the same effect as a minimum harmonization provision: the words 'maintain' and 'introduce' in paragraphs 4 and 5, respectively, of Article 95 EC indicate that both existing national measures and new measures are covered. The protection referred to in Article 176 EC ('protective measures') relates only to the protection of the environment. The provision uses the term Member State in the singular, but measures taken in common by a number of Member States (e.g., within the framework of the Benelux) may also be covered by this provision.[69] The words 'compatible with this Treaty' involve a double restriction: this relates to both primary and secondary law.[70] The sting of Article 176 EC lies in the tail of the provision. A more stringent national provision based on Article 176 EC may conflict with Articles 28–30 EC, without being able to be justified under Article 95 EC. It is also conceivable that a national provision may in some cases be incompatible with other articles of the Treaty, such as those concerning the Common Agricultural Policy, state aids or taxation.[71] The other provisions of the Treaty then take precedence over the possibility of relying on Article 176, unless the incompatibility can be removed through an environmental exception specifically relating to the provision in question, for instance in relation to Articles 28 and 87–88 EC.

3.2   EUROPEAN COMMUNITY ENVIRONMENTAL POLICY: LEGISLATION

Since the First Environmental Action Programme in 1973, environmental protection measures have regularly been adopted. While the space available does not

---

65. On the possibility of a lower level, see Jans, Sevenster and Vedder, op. cit. 179.
66. Case C-169/89, *Criminal Proceedings against Van den Burg*.
67. Case C-376/90, *Commission v. Belgium*.
68. On this see Jans, Sevenster and Vedder, op. cit., 163 et seq.
69. Cf. Art. 306 EC.
70. P. Rott, 'Minimum Harmonization for the Completion of the Internal Market? The Example of Consumer Sales Law' (2003) CML Rev., 1107; M. Dougan, 'Minimum Harmonization and the Internal Market' (2000) CML Rev., 853.
71. G. Van Calster, 'Greening the E.C.'s State Aid and Tax Regimes' (2000) ECLR, 294.

permit a detailed discussion of all of these measures, or even to mention them all, we will attempt to mention the most important ones. The original measure will be referred to, although many have been amended in the meantime, sometimes more than once. The acts listed here are 'general' in the sense that they cover more than one sector. Purely sectoral rules, for instance concerning waste products, are not included:

- Agreement of the Representatives of the Governments of the Member States meeting in Council of 5 March 1973 on information for the Commission and for the Member States with a view to possible harmonization throughout the Communities of urgent measures concerning the protection of the environment.[72]
- Council Directive 85/337/EEC on the assessment of the effects of certain public and private projects on the environment.[73]
- Council Regulation 1210/90 on the establishment of the European Environment Agency and the European Environment Information and Observation Network.[74]
- Council Directive 91/692/EEC standardizing and rationalizing reports on the implementation of certain Directives relating to the environment.[75]
- Fifth European Community programme of policy and action in relation to the environment and sustainable development.[76]
- Council Regulation 793/93 on the evaluation and control of the risks of existing substances.[77]
- Council Regulation 1836/93 on a Community eco-management and audit scheme.[78]
- Council Decision 94/69/EC concerning the conclusion of the United Nations Framework Convention on Climate Change.[79]
- Information from the Commission: Community guidelines on State aid for environmental protection.[80]
- Commission recommendation of 27 November 1996 on environmental agreements.[81]
- Council Directive 96/61/EC concerning integrated pollution prevention and control.[82]

---

72. O.J. 1973, C 9/1.
73. O.J. 1985, L 175/40.
74. O.J. 1990, L 120/1.
75. O.J. 1991, L 377/48
76. O.J. 1993, C 138/1. This programme has in the meantime been completed and replaced by the Sixth Action Programme on the environment, O.J. 2002, L 242.
77. O.J. 1993, L 84/1.
78. O.J. 1993, L 168/1.
79. O.J. 1994, L 33/11.
80. O.J. 1994, C 72/3.
81. O.J. 1996, L 333/59.
82. O.J. 1996, L 257/26.

- Commission communication environmental taxes and charges in the single market.[83]
- Council Resolution of 7 October 1997 on the drafting, implementation and enforcement of Community environmental law.[84]
- Decision No. 2179/98/EC of the European Parliament and of the Council on the review of the European Community programme of policy and action 'Towards sustainability'.[85]
- Directive 98/34/EC of the European Parliament and of the Council of 22 June 1998 laying down a procedure for the provision of information in the field of technical standards and regulations.[86]
- Regulation (EC) No. 614/2007 of the European Parliament and of the Council of 23 May 2007 concerning the Financial Instrument for the Environment (LIFE+).[87]
- Regulation (EC) No. 1980/2000 of the European Parliament and of the Council of 17 July 2000 on a revised Community eco-label award scheme.[88]
- Regulation (EC) No. 761/2001 of the European Parliament and of the Council of 19 March 2001 allowing voluntary participation by organizations in a Community eco-management and audit scheme (EMAS).[89]
- Directive 2001/42/EC of the European Parliament and of the Council of 27 June 2001 on the assessment of the effects of certain plans and programmes on the environment.[90]
- Decision No. 466/2002/EC of the European Parliament and of the Council of 1 March 2002 laying down a Community action programme promoting non-governmental organizations primarily active in the field of environmental protection.[91]
- Council Decision of 25 April 2002 concerning the approval, on behalf of the European Community, of the Kyoto Protocol to the United Nations Framework Convention on Climate Change.[92]
- Decision No. 1600/2002/EC of the European Parliament and of the Council of 22 July 2002 laying down the Sixth Community Environment Action Programme.[93]
- Council Framework Decision 2003/80/JHA of 27 January 2003 on the protection of the environment through criminal law.[94]

---

83. O.J. 1997, C 224/6.
84. O.J. 1997, C 321/1.
85. O.J. 1998, L 275/1.
86. O.J. 1998, L 204/37.
87. O.J. 2007, L 149/1.
88. O.J. 2000, L 237/1.
89. O.J. 2001, L 114/1.
90. O.J. 2001, L 197/30.
91. O.J. 2002, L 75/1.
92. O.J. 2002, L 130/1.
93. O.J. 2002, L 242/1. See also the Commission's proposal for the Sixth Action Programme, 'Environment 2010: Our future, Our Choice', COM(2001)31 final.
94. O.J. 2003, L 29/55. This Framework Decision was annulled by the Court of Justice in Case C-176/03, *Commission v. Council*, mentioned above.

- Directive 2003/4/EC of the European Parliament and of the Council of 28 January 2003 on public access to environmental information.[95]
- Directive 2004/35/CE of the European Parliament and of the Council of 21 April 2004 on environmental liability with regard to the prevention and remedying of environmental damage.[96]
- Council Decision 2005/370/EC, on the conclusion of the Convention on access to information, public participation in the decision-making process and access to justice in environmental matters (Århus Convention).[97]
- Regulation (EC) No. 1907/2006 concerning the Registration, Evaluation, Authorisation and Restriction of Chemicals (REACH).[98]

4   CONSUMER PROTECTION

In the following, we will first deal with the Treaty provisions on consumer policy, in section 4.1. The EC's consumer protection policy will then be briefly described in section 4.2.[99] As a preliminary point, it useful to consider who are the market participants included in the notion of consumer as a matter of EC law. The EC Treaty is silent as to the meaning of the notion 'consumer', even though the term 'consumers' features in Articles 33(1)(e), 34(2), 81(3), 82 under (b), 87(2)(a) EC as well as in the provisions on consumer protection as such.[100]

In Community secondary legislation, a consumer is defined as a natural person who, in transactions covered by the relevant act, is acting for purposes which can be regarded as outside his trade or profession.[101] Traders do not fall under this definition.[102] In the Court's case law on the rule of reason applied in relation to Article 28 EC (the so-called 'mandatory requirements' later called 'overriding reasons in the general interest') the concept of a consumer has a similar meaning.

---

95. O.J. 2003, L 41/26.
96. O.J. 2004, L 143/56.
97. O.J. 2005, L 124/1.
98. O.J. 2006, L 396/1.
99. G. Howells and T. Wilhelmsson, 'EC Consumer Law: Has it Come of Age?' (2003) EL Rev., 370.
100. The various language versions sometimes have different terms in these provisions, e.g., the French text has *consommateurs* in Arts. 33(1)(e), 34(2), and 82 under (b) EC and *utilisateurs* in Art. 81(3) EC.
101. See e.g., Council Dir. 85/577/EEC to protect the consumer in respect of contracts negotiated away from business premises, O.J. 1985, L 372/31, Art. 2: '"Consumer" means a natural person who, in transactions covered by this Directive, is acting for purposes which can be regarded as outside his trade or profession.'
102. Case C-361/89, *Criminal Proceedings against Di Pinto*. For the meaning of this concept in the context of the Brussels Convention, see Case 150/77, *Bertrand v. Ott*, and Case C-89/91, *Shearson Lehman Hutton v. TVB*. See K.J.M. Mortelmans and J.S. Watson, 'The Notion of Consumer in Community Law: A Lottery?' in J. Lonbay (ed.) *Enhancing the Legal Position of the European Consumer* (London, 1996), 36–57. See also Joined Cases C-541/99 & C-542/99, *Cape v. Idealservice Srl*.

Here, the term 'average consumer' or something similar is often used.[103] The protection of non-end users is covered in the case law by the term 'fairness of commercial transactions', 'fair trading' or suchlike.[104] Moreover, the interests of consumers as market participants are in the first instance protected by Community law on the free movement of goods, services and capital,[105] and the rules on competition.[106]

4.1   TREATY BASES FOR CONSUMER POLICY

In the original EEC Treaty there was no specific basis for consumer protection policy. Paragraph 3 of Article 100a EEC – an article which was added to the Treaty by the SEA – provided that in its proposals for harmonization relating to the establishment and functioning of the internal market concerning, *inter alia*, consumer protection, the Commission was to take as a base a high level of protection. Nevertheless, consumer protection is not included in the list of exceptions set out in Article 95(4) EC, as it is now numbered. These days, more attention is paid in the EC Treaty to the interests of consumers. Article 3(1)(t) EC prescribes that Community action will include 'a contribution to the strengthening of consumer protection'; 'contribution' implies a less far-reaching activity than 'policy', which is prescribed for environmental protection.

The Title on consumer protection, introduced by the Treaty of Maastricht, was amended by the Treaty of Amsterdam, though not fundamentally so.[107] The EU Charter of Fundamental Rights repeats in Article 38 that Union policies shall ensure a high level of consumer protection.

Article 153(3) EC provides that the Community contributes in two ways to the achievement of a high level of consumer protection, required by Article 153(1) EC. The first means is through measures adopted pursuant to Article 95 EC in the context of the completion of the internal market. Article 95(3) EC obliges the Commission to ensure a high level of consumer protection, but according to Article 153 EC such an obligation also rests on the Community itself.

A second means for promoting the interests of consumers is through the adoption, by the co-decision procedure under Article 251 EC, of specific action supporting, supplementing and monitoring the policy pursued by Member States; the objectives of such action are to protect the health, safety and economic interests of consumers, and to promote their right to information and education and their right to organize themselves in order to safeguard their interests.[108] On the one

---

103. See Case C-51/93, *Meyhui v. Schott Zwiesel Glaswerke*; Case C-210/96, *Gut Springenheide and Tusky v. Oberkreisdirektor des Kreises Steinfurt*; Case C-104/01, *Libertel v. Benelux-Merkenbureau*.
104. See Ch. VIII, s. 3.3.3 *supra*.
105. See Ch. VIII *supra*.
106. See Ch. IX *supra*. K. Cseres, *Competition Law and Consumer Protection* (The Hague, 2005).
107. J.H.V. Stuyck, 'European Consumer Law After the Treaty of Amsterdam: Consumer Policy in or Beyond the Internal Market' (2000) CML Rev., 367.
108. This list is more extensive than that contained in old Art. 129A EC.

hand, Article 153 EC mentions interests such as health and safety, which are also dealt with elsewhere in the Treaty – see Articles 95, 137 and 152 EC. On the other hand, it contains some specific consumer rights, such as consumers' right to information and representation. The right to judicial protection is absent from this article;[109] however, Title IV of Part 3 of the EC Treaty, on policies related to free movement of persons, does give some footholds to overcome this lacuna.[110]

Unlike in the Title on culture (see section 6 below), the use of the term 'measures' in Article 153(3) without any clause excluding harmonization measures, demonstrates that harmonization measures are possible. A general framework for Community activities in favour of consumers has been established by the Council and Parliament, in a decision adopted on 25 January 1999.[111]

Article 153(5) EC lays down that Member States may maintain or introduce more stringent protective measures.[112]

4.2   EC CONSUMER POLICY

Community policy is implemented on the basis of action plans, which then lead to the adoption of concrete measures.

4.2.1   Programme of Action

In a Resolution of 2 December 2002, the Council asked the Commission, among other things, to emphasize the integration of consumer policy in other sectors of Community policy and to emphasize consumer interests in services of general interest. The Commission was also asked to devote attention to the enforcement of consumer law.[113]

On 8 December 2003, the Council and Parliament established a general framework for financing Community actions in support of consumer policy for the years 2004–2007.[114] On 6 April 2005, the Commission adopted a Health and Consumer protection Strategy and a proposal for a European Parliament and Council Decision creating the Community Programme for Health and Consumer protection

---

109. Cf. the Resolution of the Council on consumer redress, O.J. 1987, C 176/2. See also the Commission Recommendation on the principles applicable to the bodies responsible for out-of-court settlement of consumer disputes, O.J. 1998, L 115/31; the Council Resolution of 25 May 2000 on a Community-wide network of national bodies for the extra-judicial settlement of consumer disputes, O.J. 2000, C 155/1; and Commission Recommendation of 4 Apr. 2001 on the principles for out-of-court bodies involved in the consensual resolution of consumer disputes, O.J. 2001, L 109/56.
110. See Council Dir. 2003/8 to improve access to justice in cross-border disputes, O.J. 2003, L 26/41.
111. Dec. No. 283/1999/EC O.J. 1999, L 34/1.
112. The significance of this is discussed in section 3.1.6. above in relation to environmental protection.
113. O.J. 2003, C 11/2.
114. Dec. 20/2004, O.J. 2004, L 5/1.

2007–2013. The strategy and programme proposal bring together and extend the current EU Public Health Programme and the current programme in support of EU consumer policy.[115]

In 2006, the Commission published its programme for consumer policy for the period 2007–2013.[116] The aim of the programme is avowedly to complement, support and monitor the policies of the Member States and to contribute to protecting the health, safety and economic and legal interests of consumers, as well as to promoting their rights to information, to education and to organise themselves in order to safeguard their interests. The aim will be pursued through the following objectives (a) to ensure a high level of consumer protection, notably through improved evidence, better consultation and better representation of consumers' interests; and (b) to ensure the effective application of consumer protection rules, in particular through enforcement cooperation, information, education and redress.[117] Early in 2007, the Commission published a Green paper on the review of the Consumer Acquis.[118] In a resolution of 31 May 2007 on the Consumer Policy Strategy of the EU (2007–2013) the Council called upon the Commission to implement this strategy.[119]

4.2.2   Current Policy

Current EC consumer policy is based on three sorts of measures:

> First, there are national measures concerning products and services which have consumer policy elements; the EC law conditions for these were discussed in Chapter VIII. Secondly, there are directives, adopted on the basis of various Treaty provisions, which deal with specific issues of concern to consumers. The following directives and related case law may be mentioned:
>
> – misleading advertising (Directive 84/450);[120]
> – product liability (Directive 85/374);[121]

---

115. COM(2005)115 final.
116. O.J. 2006, L 404/39. See also the Commission's Green Paper on European consumer protection, COM(2001)531 final.
117. Dec. 1926/2006 O.J. 2006, L 404/39.
118. O.J. 2007, C 61/1.
119. O.J. 2007, C 166.
120. O.J. 1984, L 250. Cf. Case C-373/90, *Criminal Proceedings against X*; Case C-112/99, *Toshiba Europe v. Katun Germany*; Case C-44/01, *Pippig Augenoptik v. Hartlauer Handelsgesellschaft*; Case C-356/04, *Lidl Belgium v. Franz Colruyt*; Case C-381/05, *De Landsheer v. Comité Interprofessionnel du Vin de Champagne and Veuve Cliquot Ponsardin*.
121. O.J. 1985, L 210. Cf. Case C-339/89, *Alsthom v. Sulzer*; Case C-293/91, *Commission v. France*; Case C-300/95, *Commission v. United Kingdom*; Case C-203/99, *Veedfeld v. Århus Amtskommune*; Case C-183/00, *Gonzáles Sánchez v. Medicina Asturiana*; Case C-402/03, *Skov v. Bilka*; Case C-127/04, *Declan O'Byrne v. Sanofi Pasteur MSD*; Case C-177/04, *Commission v. French Republic*. See further the Green Paper on Liability for Defective Products, COM(1999)396 final. See, finally, Council Resolution of 19 Dec. 2002 on amendment of the liability for defective products directive, O.J. 2003, C 26/2.

- doorstep selling (Directive 85/577);[122]
- consumer credit (Directive 87/102);[123]
- package tours (Directive 90/314);[124]
- unfair terms in consumer contracts (Directive 93/13);[125]
- timesharing (Directive 94/47);[126]
- cross-border credit transfers (Directive 97/5);[127]
- distance selling (Directive 97/7);[128]
- comparative advertising (Directive 97/55);[129]
- unfair business-to-consumer commercial practices (Directive 2005/29);[130]
- misleading and comparative advertising (codification);[131]
- consumer credit agreements;[132]
- injunctions for the protection of consumers' interests (Directive 98/27);[133]
- sale of consumer goods and associated guarantees (Directive 1999/44);[134]
- food labelling (Directive 2000/13);[135]
- presentation and sale of tobacco products (Directive 2001/37);[136]
- electronic commerce (Directive 2000/31);[137]

122. O.J. 1985, L 372. Cf. Case 382/87, *Buet et al. v. Ministère public*; Case C-361/89, *Criminal Proceedings against Di Pinto*; Case C-91/92, *Faccini Dori v. Recreb*; Case C-45/96, *Bayerische Hypotheken- und Wechselbank v. Dietzinger*; Case C-423/97, *Travel Vac v. Manuel José Antelm Sanchis*; Case C-481/99, *Heininger v. Bayerische Hypo- und Vereinsbank*; Case C-20/03, *Criminal Proceedings against Burmanjer et al.* Case C-350/03, *Schulte v. Deutsche Bausparkasse Badenia*; Case C-229/04, *Crailsheimer Volksbank v. Conrads et al.* This directive does not apply to the unsolicited offer of services; see Case C-384/93, *Alpine Investments v. Minister van Financiën*.
123. O.J. 1987, L 42. Cf. Case C-192/94, *El Corte Inglés v. Blázquez Rivero*; Case C-208/98, *Berliner Kindl Brauerei v. Siepert*.
124. O.J. 1990, L 158. Cf. Joined Cases C-178, 179 & 188–190/94, *Dillenkofer et al. v. Bundesrepublik Deutschland*; Case C-364/96, *Verein für Konsumenteninformation v. Österreichische Kreditversicherungs*; Case C-140/97, *Rechberger et al. v. Österreich*; Case C-237/97, *AFS Intercultural Programs Finland*; Case C-168/00, *Leitner v. TUI Deutschland*.
125. O.J. 1993, L 95/29.
126. O.J. 1994, L 280/83.
127. O.J. 1997, L 43/25.
128. O.J. 1997, L 144/19.
129. O.J. 1997, L 290/18. Cf. Case C-126/91, *Schutzverband gegen Unwesen i.d. Wirtschaft v. Rocher*. See also the case law relating to Art. 28 EC in Ch. VIII *supra*.
130. O.J. 2005, L 149, see J. Stuyck, E. Terryn and T. van Dyck, 'Confidence through Fairness? The New Directive on Unfair Business-to-Consumer Commercial Practices in the Internal Market' (2006) CML Rev., 107–152.
131. Dir. 2006/114/EC of the European Parliament and of the Council of 12 Dec.2006 concerning misleading and comparative advertising (codified version), O.J. 2006, L 376/21.
132. Draft directive on consumer credit agreements formally adopted by the Competitiveness Council on 21 May 2007.
133. O.J. 1998, L 166/51.
134. O.J. 1999, L 171/12.
135. O.J. 2000, L 109/29. This directive replaces Dir. 79/112, O.J. 1979, L 33/1.
136. O.J. 2001, L 194/26.
137. O.J. 2000, L 178/1. Cf. Case C-322/01, *Deutscher Apothekerverband v. DocMorris*. See A. Lopez-Tarruella, 'A European Community Regulatory Framework for Electronic

- product safety (Directive 2001/95);[138]
- distance marketing of financial services (Directive 2002/65);[139]
- unfair commercial practices (Directive 2005/29).[140]

These directives also provide the link for the application of Regulation 2006/2004 on cooperation between national authorities responsible for the enforcement of consumer protection laws.[141]

Thirdly, there are measures for which Article 153 EC provides an explicit legal basis. The following measures have been adopted on the basis of this provision:

- Decision No. 3092/94 introducing a Community system of information on home and leisure accidents (European Home and Leisure Accidents Surveillance System (EHLASS)).[142]
- Directive 98/6 on consumer protection in the indication of the prices of products offered to consumers.[143]
- Decision No. 276/1999 adopting a multiannual Community action plan on promoting safer use of the Internet by combating illegal and harmful content on global networks.[144]

5 PUBLIC HEALTH

Article 3(1)(p) EC declares that the Community is to make 'a contribution to the attainment of a high level of health protection'. The Treaty of Maastricht added to the EC Treaty a Title on public health (containing one article: now Art. 152 EC). This provision was further elaborated by the Treaty of Amsterdam – partly as a result of a number of affairs, such as the BSE crisis[145] and scandals concerning AIDS contamination. Firstly, a number of – albeit limited – harmonization powers were granted to the Community. Secondly, certain matters which had previously been dealt with in the provisions on agriculture were brought under the Title on public health.[146]

Commerce', CML Rev., 38/1337: M.Y. Schaub, *European Legal Aspects of E-commerce* (Groningen, 2004).
138. O.J. 2002, L 11/4. On the previous directive (92/59, O.J. 1992, L 228/25), see Case C-359/92, *Germany v. Council*.
139. O.J. 2002, L 271/16.
140. O.J. 2005, L 149/22.
141. O.J. 2004, L 364/1.
142. O.J. 1994, L 331/1.
143. O.J. 1998, L 80/27.
144. O.J. 1999, L 33/1.
145. See in this context Case C-180/96, *United Kingdom v. Commission*.
146. See also Council Conclusions of 26 Nov. 1998 on the future framework for Community action in the field of public health, O.J. 1998, C 390/1.

In a resolution of the Council annexed to the conclusions of the European Council in Nice, December 2000, attention was paid to the precautionary principle, partly as a result of the BSE crisis. This principle plays a role in the health policy of the Community, as well as in its environmental policy.

Finally, Article 35 of the EU Charter of Fundamental Rights provides that everyone has the right of access to preventive health care and the right to benefit from medical treatment under the conditions established by national laws and practices. This provision also states that a high level of human health protection shall be ensured in the definition and implementation of all Union policies and activities.

The inclusion of the Title on public health in the EC Treaty necessitates a delimitation of the scope of this Title in relation to other Treaty provisions dealing with the subject.

The Treaty of Lisbon will bring some alteration to the Title on public health. Article 168(5) TFEU provides that the European Parliament and the Council may also adopt incentive measures, under the ordinary legislative procedure, which are designed:

> to protect and improve human health and in particular to combat the major cross-border health scourges, measures concerning monitoring, early warning of and combating serious cross-border threats to health, and measures which have as their direct objective the protection of public health regarding tobacco and the abuse of alcohol, excluding any harmonisation of the laws and regulations of the Member States.

Article 168(7) TFEU provides that Union action shall respect the responsibilities of the Member States for the definition of their health policy and for the organization and delivery of health services and medical care. The responsibilities of the Member States shall include the management of health services and medical care and the allocation of the resources assigned to them.

5.1   HEALTH AND OTHER EC POLICY

Articles 30, 39 and 46(1) EC indicate that the Member States may refuse entry to certain products or persons for reasons justified by grounds of (public) health.[147] Article 46(2) EC grants the Council power to issue directives aiming to coordinate

---

147. Case 238/82, *Duphar et al. v. the Netherlands*; Joined Cases C-159 & 160/91, *Poucet and Pistre v. AGF and Cancava*; Case C-120/95, *Decker v. Caisse de maladie des employés privés*; Case C-108/96, *Criminal Proceedings against Mac Quen et al.*; Case C-158/96, *Kohll v. Union des caisses de maladie*; Case C-368/98, *Vanbraekel et al. v. Alliance nationale des mutualités chrétiennes*; Case C-411/98, *Ferlini v. Centre Hospitalier de Luxembourg*; Case C-157/99, *Smits v. Ziekenfonds VGZ and Peerbooms v. CZ Groep Zorgverzekeringen*; Case C-385/99, *Müller-Fauré v. Onderlinge Waarborgmaatschappij*; Case C-372/04, *Watts v. Bedford Primary Care Trust*; C. Newdick, 'Citizenship, Free Movement and Health Care: Cementing Individual Rights by Corroding Social Solidarity' (2006) CML Rev, 1645–1668; see in general Ch.VIII *supra*.

the provisions providing for special treatment for foreign nationals on grounds of public health. For example, the annexe to Directive 64/221 contained a list of diseases which could form an obstacle to free movement for the person in question.[148] This Directive was repealed by Directive 2004/38/EC of the European Parliament and of the Council of 29 April 2004 on the right of citizens of the Union and their family members to move and reside freely within the territory of the Member States.[149] The Council has chosen to align itself with the World Health Organization list of diseases with epidemic potential.

Article 47 EC gives the Council competence to issue directives relating to medical professions.[150] Health insurance aspects are dealt with in Regulation 1408/71 on social security.[151] Article 133 EC on commercial policy permits certain measures to be taken in relation to movement between the EU and third countries[152] – it refers specifically to agreements relating to trade in human health services. Article 137 EC concerns health and safety of workers: numerous directives have been adopted in this area, which are discussed further in Chapter X of this book.[153] The Environment Title and Consumer Protection Title, discussed in sections 3 and 4, above, also aim to play a role in relation to health and safety issues.[154] On 6 April 2005 the Commission adopted a Health and Consumer protection Strategy and a proposal for a European Parliament and Council Decision creating the Community Programme for Health and Consumer protection 2007–2013. The strategy and programme proposal bring together and extend the current EU Public Health Programme and the current programme in support of EU consumer policy.[155]

One chapter of the Euratom Treaty is devoted to protection of health.[156]

Article 29 TEU, in Title VI on Police and Judicial Cooperation in Criminal Matters also relates to health, in particular concerning the fight against drug addiction.

As a result of privatization of health insurance,[157] Articles 81 and 82 EC are starting to play a more important role,[158] although in practice it will be mainly

---

148. O.J. 1964, 850.
149. O.J. 2004, L 158/77. See Ch. VIII, s. 4.5.2 *supra*.
150. Dir. 93/16 on medical doctors, O.J. 1993, L 165/1, and Dir. 85/584 on pharmacies, O.J. 1985, 372/42. Both these directives have been replaced by Dir. 2005/36/EC of the European Parliament and of the Council of 7 Sep. 2005 on the recognition of professional qualifications, O.J. 2005, L 255/22.
151. See Ch. VIII.
152. For example, Council Reg. 953/2003 to avoid trade diversion into the European Union of certain key medicines, O.J. 2003, L 135/5.
153. E.g., Dir. 91/383, O.J. 1991, L 206/19.
154. Cf. Arts. 174(1) EC and 153(1) EC respectively.
155. COM(2005)115.
156. Cf. Arts. 30–39 Euratom.
157. See on this M. McKee, E. Mossialos and R. Baeten (eds), *The Impact of EU Law on Health Care Systems* (Brussels, 2002); E. Mossialos and M. McKee, *EU Law and the Social Character of Health Care* (Brussels, 2002).
158. Joined Cases C-159 & 160/91, *Poucet and Pistre*; Case C-245/91, *Criminal Proceedings against Ohra Schadeverzekeringen*; Case T-319/99, *Fenin v. Commission*; Case C-205/03 P,

national competition law which applies. Free movement and privatization on the one hand and waiting lists on the other, encourage more and more patients to seek medical treatment in a different EU Member State from the State where they reside. The health insurers tolerate, and in some cases encourage, this mobility, although they were extremely hesitant at first.

The Council has considered the desirability of a European system for evaluation and supervision of medicinal products[159] and has devoted attention to patient mobility.[160]

Numerous directives have been adopted concerning health aspects of goods and agricultural products on the basis of Articles 33, 43, 47, 55, 94, 95 and 133 EC. This subject illustrates the hiatus in the Communities in this area. On the one hand, Articles 47, 55 and 95 EC – which concern the internal market – do not give the Community a general competence to adopt directives which primarily affect health (as opposed to the free movement of goods and services). On the other hand, the Title on health does not contain a harmonization provision.

On the basis of Article 95 EC – the general harmonization provision concerning the internal market-directives and regulations may be adopted which in some way relate to health. This can be deduced from Article 95(3) EC, which obliges the institutions to take as a base a high level of protection when adopting measures concerning, *inter alia*, health. Further, Article 95(8) EC provides that when a Member State raises a specific problem on public health in a field which has been the subject of prior harmonization measures, the Commission shall immediately examine whether to propose appropriate measures to the Council.

A number of measures adopted by the Community Institutions on the basis of Article 95 EC have been the subject of decisions by the Court of Justice concerning their validity (in particular in relation to the correct legal basis). The *general* Directive 98/43 concerning advertising and sponsoring of tobacco products, which was based on Articles 47, 55 and 95 EC, was annulled by the Court of Justice on the grounds that its legal basis was insufficient.[161] The Council and the European Parliament subsequently enacted Directive 2003/03,[162] which concerns *specific* advertising measures. Germany brought an application for annulment of the new directive, giving the Court the occasion to examine whether the new directive could be adopted on the basis of Article 95 EC. According to the German Government, this new more limited directive on tobacco products still concerned Community health policy, and could therefore not be based on Article 95 EC. Germany lost the case, however[163]

     Commission v. Fenin. See D. Pieters and S. Van den Bogaert, *The Consequences of European Competition Law for National Health Policies* (Antwerpen, 1997).

159. Council conclusions of 29 Jun. 2000 on Medicinal Products and Public Health, O.J. 2000, C 218/10.

160. Conclusions of the Council and of the Representatives of the Member States meeting in the Council of 19 Jul. 2002 on patient mobility and health care developments in the European Union, O.J. 2002, C 183/1.

161. O.J. 1998, L 213/9. Case C-376/98, *Germany v. Parliament and Council.*

162. O.J. 2003, L 152.

163. Case C-380/03, *Germany v. Parliament and Council.*

In another case concerning tobacco products, *BAT and Imperial Tobacco*,[164] the Court examined the validity of Directive 2001/37, which concerns the manufacture, presentation and sale of tobacco products;[165] it came to the conclusion – in the light of the preliminary questions raised – that the directive was not invalid. The 'snus' cases[166] follow on from *BAT and Imperial Tobacco*; the Court ruled that a prohibition on the marketing of 'snus' (a tobacco product for oral use) was in accordance with the Treaty, because the Community legislature made protection of human health a decisive factor in its choices.[167]

5.2   'HEALTH' IN THE TITLE ON PUBLIC HEALTH

It is unclear whether the term 'health' in Article 3(1)(p) EC has a broader meaning than the term 'public health' used in Title XIII of Part Three of the EC Treaty. In any event, just as with culture and education, which are examined in the next two sections below, a distinction may be drawn between individual measures and the global policy of a Member State. In the first case there are clear links to free movement issues and to competition policy;[168] in the second case the link is weaker and any questions concern the system as such. The first category of measures may be connected to the Public Health Title by the integration provision, Article 152(1) EC.

The Title on Public Health follows the general structure set out in section 2 above. The first sentence of Article 152(1) EC contains an integration provision: 'A high level of human health protection shall be ensured in the definition and implementation of all Community policies and activities.'[169] This provision has more binding force, and is more generally formulated than its predecessor, the last sentence of former Article 129(1) EC. The Community contributes towards the achievement of this high level of protection by encouraging cooperation between the Member States, and, if necessary, lending support to their action. Article 152(1) EC then goes on to indicate that Community action should be directed towards

---

164. Case C-491/01, *The Queen v. Secretary of State for Health, ex parte: British American Tobacco and Imperial Tobacco*.
165. O.J. 2001, L 194/26.
166. Case C-210/03, *The Queen, on the application of: Swedish match v. Secretary of State for Health*; Case C-434/02, *Arnold André v. Landrat des Kreises Herford*.
167. See also Joined Cases C-154 & 155/04, *Spain v. United Kingdom*.
168. Case 238/82, *Duphar et al. v. the Netherlands*; Joined Cases C-159 & 160/91, *Poucet and Pistre*; Case C-120/95, *Decker v. Caisse de maladie des employés privés*; Case C-108/96, *Criminal Proceedings against Mac Quen et al.*; Case C-158/96, *Kohll v. Union des caisses de maladie*; Case C-368/98, *Vanbraekel et al. v. Alliance nationale des mutualités chrétiennes*; Case C-411/98, *Ferlini v. Centre Hospitalier de Luxembourg*; Case C-157/99, *Smits v. Ziekenfonds VGZ and Peerbooms v. CZ Groep Zorgverzekeringen*; Case C-385/99, *Müller-Fauré v. Onderlinge Waarborgmaatschappij*; Joined Cases C-264, 306, 354 & 355/01, *AOK Bundesverband et al. v. Ichthyol-Gesellschaft Cordes, Hermani & Co. et al.*; V. Hatzopoulos, 'Killing National Health and Insurance Systems but Healing Patients' (2003) CML Rev, 683.
169. See most recently Council Resolution of 18 Nov. 1999, O.J. 2000, C 86/3.

improving public health, preventing human illness and diseases, and obviating sources of danger to human health. This action covers the fight against the major health scourges, by promoting research into their causes, their transmission and their prevention, as well as health information and education. The last sentence of Article 152(1) EC states that the Community shall complement the Member States' action in reducing drugs-related health damage, including information and prevention.[170] This is aimed at the position of (potential) drug addicts. It is Article 29 TEU which enables the Union to take measures to combat illegal trade in drugs.[171]

According to Article 152(3) EC, the Community and the Member States promote cooperation with third countries and the competent international organizations in the sphere of public health. In this context one may think of the World Health Organization[172] and the Council of Europe. Article 133(6) EC provides that commercial agreements relating to human health services fall within the shared competence of the Community and its Member States. Article 152(4) EC lays down the competences of the Council to take measures on the basis of this provision. In the old (Treaty of Maastricht) version, the Council was only competent to take incentive measures. In the new version, the Council may – under the co-decision procedure – adopt other measures: these may include harmonization directives, which are possible in relation to two subjects.[173] First: measures setting high standards of quality and safety of organs and substances of human origin, blood and blood derivatives;[174] such measures should involve minimum harmonization. Secondly, in derogation from Article 37 EC (on agriculture): measures in the veterinary and phytosanitary fields which have as their direct objective the protection of public health. This last competence illustrates the tension between agricultural policy and health policy. The BSE crisis[175] and the foot-and-mouth

170. See Council Conclusions of 24 Jul. 1997, O.J. 1997, C 241/7.
171. Proposal for a Council framework decision laying down minimum provisions on the constituent elements of criminal acts and penalties in the field of illicit drug trafficking, O.J. 2001, C 270 E/21/144.
172. See memorandum concerning the framework and arrangements for cooperation between the World Health Organization and the Commission of the European Communities, O.J. 2001, C 1/9. Council Dec. of 2 Jun. 2004 concerning the conclusion of the WHO Framework Convention on Tobacco Control (O.J. 2004, L 213/8).
173. Joined Cases C-453/03, C-11, 12 & 194/04, *ABNA et al. v. Secretary of State for Health, Food and Standards Agency*. See also Case C-376/98, *Germany v. Parliament and Council*, where the Court states that 'harmonising measures in that field [public health policy] are expressly prohibited by Art. 129(4) first indent, of the EC Treaty (now, after amendment, Article 152(4), 1st para. EC)' (para. 35).
174. See Council Recommendation of 29 Jun. 1998 on the suitability of blood and plasma donors and the screening of donated blood in the European Community, O.J. 1998, L 203/14. See also Dir. 2002/98, setting standards of quality and safety for the collection, testing, processing, storage and distribution of human blood and blood components, O.J. 2003, L 33/30 and Dir. 2004/23 on setting standards of quality and safety for the donation, procurement, testing, processing, preservation, storage and distribution of human tissues and cells, O.J. 2004, L 102/48.
175. Case C-180/96, *United Kingdom v. Commission*.

crisis[176] have forced the Community to take drastic measures, which have consequences for agricultural policy in general. After some difficulties, the European Food Safety Authority was finally established in 2002. At the same time, and in the same Regulation, procedures were established for food safety matters.[177]

Regulation 726/2004 laying down Community procedures for the authorization and supervision of medicinal products for human and veterinary use also established a European Medicines Agency.[178] Regulation 851/2004 established a European Centre for disease prevention and control.[179]

In 1999, the Council and the European Parliament approved a number of decisions adopting programmes of action on injury prevention[180] and on rare diseases.[181] The Council has also paid consideration to alcohol-related harm,[182] Creutzfeldt-Jakob disease[183] and antimicrobial agents.[184]

Finally, by Decision No. 1786/2002/EC, the European Parliament and the Council adopted a programme of Community action in the field of public health (2003–2008).[185] This was followed by Decision No. 1350/2007/EC of the European Parliament and of the Council of 23 October 2007 establishing a second programme of Community action in the field of health (2008–13)[186]

6   CULTURAL POLICY

For many years, national cultural bodies or those pleading on their behalf, claimed that their cultural policy was not – and should not be – affected by EEC law, and later EC law. Judgments by the Court of Justice on related policy areas, such as sport[187] media,[188] and on cultural activities or output themselves,[189] have all helped to remove any doubt on this point.

---

176. Case C-189/01, *Jippes et al. v. Minister van Landbouw, Natuurbeheer en Visserij*.
177. Reg. 178/2002 of the European Parliament and of the Council, laying down the general principles and requirements of food law, establishing the European Food Safety Authority and laying down procedures in matters of food safety, O.J. 2002, L 31/1. See also COM(2000)716 final, Proposal for a regulation in matters of food, and the Green Paper on integrated product policy presented by the Commission COM(2001)68 final.
178. O.J. 2004, L 136/1.
179. O.J. 2004, L 142/1.
180. O.J. 1999, L 46/1.
181. O.J. 1999, L 155/1.
182. O.J. 2001, C 175/1.
183. O.J. 2001, C 175/2.
184. O.J. 2002, L 34/13.
185. O.J. 2002, L 271/1.
186. O.J. 2007, L 301/3.
187. Case 36/74, *Walrave and Koch v. Association Union Cycliste Internationale* .
188. Case 352/85, *Bond van Adverteerders v. the Netherlands*; Case C-353/89, *Commission v. Netherlands*.
189. Case 197/84, *Steinhauser v. Ville de Biarritz*; Case 379/87, *Groener v. Minister for Education and City of Dublin Vocational Education Committee*; Case C-154/89, *Commission v. France*; Case C-180/89, *Commission v. Italy*; Case C-198/89, *Commission v. Greece*; Case C-388/01, *Commission v. Italy*.

Now that it is clear that a great many cultural activities come within the scope of the Treaty's prohibitions, by virtue of the fact that they are economic activities,[190] exceptions on grounds of cultural policy are receiving more attention.[191] In the area of state aids, such an exception received a basis in the Treaty following the Treaty of Maastricht (Art. 87(3)(d) EC).[192] The decision-making practice of the Commission – in particular concerning prices of books – reveals that an exception on these grounds can also play a role in relation to Article 81 EC; the book trade provides plenty of illustrations of the tensions between cultural interests, competition and free movement rules.[193]

In a Resolution of 17 December 1999, the Council urges free movement of persons working in the cultural sector.[194] In Directive 2001/84, rules were laid down for resale rights for the benefit of the author of an original work of art.[195]

With the entry into force of the Treaty of Maastricht, a title on culture was included in the EC Treaty (former Art. 128 EC). The Treaty of Amsterdam amended this article (which is now Art.151 EC) in relation to its integration provision, adding the aim 'to respect and to promote the diversity of its cultures.'[196]

Article 151 EC deals with cultural policy in general, and does not concern the relationship between cultural activities and free movement.[197] This Article follows the scheme of the other new titles, and is redolent of the subsidiarity principle. It elaborates Article 3(1)(q) EC, which provides that the Community contributes 'to the flowering of the cultures of the Member States'. This phrase is repeated in Article 151(1) EC and in that provision is filled out in a more balanced manner: 'The Community shall contribute to the flowering of the cultures of the Member

---

190. On the relationship between culture and VAT, see Case C-144/00, *Criminal Proceedings against Hoffmann.*

191. See, e.g., A. Biondi, 'The Merchant, the Thief and the Citizen: The Circulation of Works of Art Within the EU' (1997) CML Rev, 1173.

192. C. Koenig and J. Kühling, *Mitgliedstaatliche Kulturförderung und gemeinschaftliche Beihilfekontrolle durch die EG-Kommission* (2000) EuZW, 195.

193. See Council Dec. of 22 Sep. 1997 on cross-border fixed book prices in European linguistic areas, O.J. 1997, C 305/2, and Council Resolution of 8 Feb.1999 on fixed book prices in homogeneous cross-border linguistic areas, O.J. 1999, C 42/3, and Council Resolution of 12 Feb. 2001 on the application of national fixed book-price systems, O.J. 2001, C 73/5. A. Obert, *Die Preisbindung im Buchhandel in Deutschland und im Vereinigten Königreich in der Sicht des Europäischen Rechts* (München, 2000). The 'Sammelrevers' Case, O.J. 2000, C 162/25, shows that the integration of cultural objectives and competition rules is not an easy matter, see M. Engelmann, *Die Zukunft der Buchpreisbindung im europäischen Binnenmarkt: dargestellt anhand des Systems der deutsch-österreichischen Buchpreisbindung* (Berlijn, 2002).

194. O.J. 2000, C 8/3. See also Council Conclusions of 17 Dec. 1999 on cultural industries and employment in Europe, O.J. 2000, C 8/10, and Council Resolution of 26 May 2003 on the horizontal aspects of culture, O.J. 2003, C 136/1.

195. O.J. 2001, L 273/32. See also declaration in the Council minutes concerning the Directive on resale rights, O.J. 2001, C 208/2.

196. For an example, see Art. 8 Dir. 2002/21 on a common regulatory framework for electronic communications networks and services (Framework Dir.), O.J. 2002, L 108/33.

197. R.C. Smith, 'Article 151 EC and European Identity', in R.C. Smith (ed.), *Culture and European Union Law* (Oxford, 2004), 277.

States, while respecting their national and regional diversity and at the same time bringing the common cultural heritage to the fore.'[198]

Community action in this field has a supplementary character, and is aimed at the improvement of the knowledge and dissemination of the culture and history of the European peoples; conservation and safeguarding of cultural heritage of European significance; non-commercial cultural exchanges, and artistic and literary creation, including the audiovisual sector. The relevant programmes of action indicate how this incentive policy is to be worked out year-by-year. For some programmes – such as the programme to promote linguistic diversity of the Community in the information society – there was uncertainty as to the legal basis: cultural policy or industrial policy.[199] The Council adopted new work plans on European cooperation in the field of culture, by resolutions of 25 June 2002 and 19 December 2002.[200] On 26 May 2003, the Council adopted a Resolution on the horizontal aspects of culture: increasing synergies with other sectors and Community actions, and exchanging good practices in relation to the social and economic dimensions of culture.[201]

The integration provision for cultural aspects is contained in Article 151(4) EC.[202]

Article 151(3) EC contains an obligation for the Community and the Member States to foster cooperation with third countries and the competent international organizations, such as the Council of Europe and United Nations Educational, Scientific and Cultural Organization (UNESCO).[203] The *ERTA* Declaration attached to the Treaty of Maastricht[204] does not apply to the culture Title. Article 133(6) EC provides that agreements relating to trade in cultural and audiovisual services fall within the shared competence of the Community and its Member States. As for trade in cultural goods, reference is made to Council Regulation 3911/92 on the export of cultural goods.[205]

---

198. See Case C-479/04, *Laserdisken v. Kulturministeriet.*
199. O.J. 1996, L 306/40. See Case C-42/97, *Parliament v. Council.*
200. O.J. 2002, C 162/5 and O.J. 2003, C 13/5.
201. O.J. 2003, C 136/1.
202. See on this G. Ress and J. Ukrow, *Auswirkungen von Art. 128 Abs, 4 EGV auf die wettbewerbsrechtliche Beurteilung von Buchpreisbindungen* (1999) *Zeitschrift für europarechtliche Studien*, 1-74. See also Council Resolution of 20 Jan. 1997 on the integration of cultural aspects into Community actions, O.J. 1997, C 36/4, and written question No. E-0773/98 (Larive), O.J. 1999, C 13/8.
203. J. A. McMahon, 'Preserving and Promoting Differences? The External Dimension of Cultural Cooperation', in R.C. Smith (ed.), *Culture and European Union Law* (Oxford, 2004), 277.
204. Declaration on Arts. 109, 130r and 130y of the Treaty establishing the European Community, by which the Member States declared that certain provisions did not affect the principles resulting from Court's judgment in the ERTA case.
205. O.J. 1992, L 395/1, as amended. See also Dir. 93/7, O.J. 1993, L 74/74 (return of cultural artefacts). See S. Gimbrère and T. Pronk, 'The Protection of Cultural Property: From UNESCO to the European Community with Special Reference to the Case of the Netherlands', *Netherlands Yearbook of International Law*, vol. XXII-I (1992), 223–273; A. Peya, *Die Ausfuhr von Kulturgütern im nationalen und Gemeinschaftsrecht* (Frankfurt am Main, 2002);

Article 151(5) EC makes it plain that the Community must restrict itself to incentive measures, and may not proceed to harmonization measures.[206] In this line, mention may be made of the Decision of 25 May 1999 establishing a Community action for the European Capital of Culture event for the years 2005–2019[207] and the Decision of 14 February 2000 establishing the Culture 2000 programme;[208] this programme is the successor to the Kaleidoscope Programme,[209] the Ariane Programme[210] and the Raphael programme.[211]

Finally, we should mention Decision 792/2004 establishing a Community action programme to promote bodies active at European level in the field of culture,[212] and the Council Resolution of 16 November 2007 on a European Agenda for Culture.[213]

It may be noted that Article 3 TEU (Lisbon) provides that the Union 'shall respect its rich cultural and linguistic diversity, and shall ensure that Europe's cultural heritage is safeguarded and enhanced.'

7   EDUCATION

7.1   Education and Free Movement

Although the system of education and educational policy as such are not included in the subjects which the Treaty has put within the competence of the Community Institutions,[214] educational activities are increasingly being affected by the free movement rules.

A steady stream of case law on students[215] and teachers[216] demonstrates that these groups can be categorized in a number of cases as recipients or providers of

---

A. Biondi, 'The Gardener and Other Stories: The Peregrinations of Cultural Artefacts within the European Union', in R.C. Smith (ed.), *Culture and European Union Law* (Oxford, 2004), 153.

206.   See Communication of the Commission of 25 Oct. 1994, COM(94)356 final. Even before 1992, aid was often granted to cultural activities, such as translations. This occurred on the basis of ad hoc measures or via the European Social Fund and the European Regional Fund.

207.   Dec. 1419/1999/EC of the European Parliament and of the Council, O.J. 1999, L 166/1.

208.   Dec. 508/2000/EC of the European Parliament and of the Council, O.J. 2000, L 63/1. As of 2007, Dec. No. 1855/2006/EC of the European Parliament and of the Council of 12 Dec. 2006, establishing the Culture Programme (O.J. 2006, L 372/1), applies.

209.   Dec. 719/96, O.J. 1996, L 99/20.

210.   To promote knowledge and distribution of European literary works, Dec. 2085/97, O.J. 1997, L 291/26.

211.   For the preservation of cultural heritage, Dec. 2228/97, O.J. 1997, L 305/31.

212.   Dec. 792/2004/EC of the European Parliament and of the Council of 21 Apr. 2004, O.J. 2004, L 138/40.

213.   O.J. 2007, C 287/1.

214.   Case 293/83, *Gravier v. Ville de Liège*.

215.   M. Dougan, 'Fees, Grants, Loans and Dole Cheques: Who Covers the Costs of Migrant Education within the EU?' (2005) 42 CML Rev., 943–986.

216.   Case C-224/01, *Köbler v. Österreich*.

services, or as employees.[217] The Court's interpretation of Articles 39 and 49 EC – and associated measures such as Regulation 1612/68[218] – has had an impact on the education competences of the Member States in areas, such as student grants, in which they felt that they were 'Community-proof' – even if they were sometimes pulling the wool over their own eyes.[219] The case law of the Court is far-reaching. If a measure, such as a bilateral agreement in the field of education and culture, does not come within the scope of the EC Treaty, but obstructs free movement because it results in discrimination, then the Member States are obliged under Article 10 EC to adopt measures to facilitate free movement.[220]

Furthermore, Community law – and especially the provisions on citizenship (Arts 17–18 EC) – prohibits a Member State from refusing to grant a tideover allowance to one of its nationals, a student seeking her first employment, on the sole ground that that student completed her secondary education in another Member State.[221] The general anti-discrimination provision, Article 12 EC, taken together with Articles 149 and 150 EC may provide a basis for condemning the education policy of a Member State.[222] The EC law status of students and teachers is further developed in secondary law, such as Directive 89/48 on the general system of mutual recognition of diplomas for higher education of at least three years' duration and Directive 92/51 on the second general system for mutual recognition of courses of shorter duration;[223] these two directives have been

---

217. See Ch. VIII, ss 4.1, 5.3.1 and 6.6, *supra*. See also Recommendation of the European Parliament and of the Council of 10 Jul. 2001 on mobility within the Community for students, persons undergoing training, volunteers, teachers and trainers, O.J. 2001, L 215/30.
218. O.J. 1968, L 257/2.
219. In Joined Cases 389 & 390/87, *Echternach et al. v. Minister van Onderwijs en Wetenschappen*, the government of the Netherlands defended positions which had already been rejected by the Court even before this case. See also Case C-357/89, *Raulin v. Minister van Onderwijs en Wetenschappen*. The situation has not changed much over the years: see Case C-337/97, *Meeusen v. Hoofddirectie van de Informatie Beheer Groep*.
220. Case 235/87, *Matteucci v. Communauté française de Belgique*.
221. Case C-224/98, *D'Hoop v. Office national de l'emploi*. See also case C-184/99, *Grzelczyk v. Centre public d'aide sociale d'Ottignies-Louvain-la-Neuve*; Case C-76/05, *Schwarz and Gootjes Schwarz v. Finanzamt Bergisch Gladbach*; Case C-318/05, *Commission v. Germany*.
222. In Case C-147/03, *Commission v. Austria*, the Court declared that 'by failing to take the necessary measures to ensure that holders of secondary education diplomas awarded in other Member States can gain access to higher and university education organised by it under the same conditions as holders of secondary education diplomas awarded in Austria, the Republic of Austria has failed to fulfil its obligations under Arts. 12 EC, 149 EC and 150 EC'(operative part of the judgment).
223. Dir. 89/48, O.J. 1989, L 19/16; Dir. 92/51, O.J. 1992, L 209/25. The application of these directives, and Dir. 93/96, see next footnote, led to problems in various Member States. See e.g., Case C-285/01, *Burbaud v. Ministère de l'Emploi et de la Solidarité*; Case C-153/02, *Neri v. European School of Economics*; Case C-209/03, *The Queen, on the application of: Bidar v. London Borough of Ealing and Secretary of State for Education and Skills*. Case C-330/03, *Colegio de Ingenieros de Caminos, Canales y Puertos v. Administratión del Estado*; Case C-149/05, *Harold Price v. Conseil des ventes volontaires de meubles aux enchères publique*. See D. Kraus, 'Diplomas and the Recognition of Professional Qualifications in the Case Law

replaced by Directive 2005/36/EC.[224] An important piece of secondary law, Directive 93/96 on the right of residence for students, was replaced as of 30 April 2006 by Directive 2004/38.[225]

Pursuant to Article 133(6) EC, commercial agreements relating to educational services fall within the shared competence of the Community and its Member States.[226]

7.2   EDUCATION SYSTEMS

The chapter on education in the EC Treaty[227] does not deal with individual free movement questions in the education sector, but with the broad thrust of education policy.[228] It elaborates the reference in Article 3(1)(q) EC to the aim of a Community contribution to education and training of quality.

Unlike cultural policy – a policy which is even mentioned in the same phrase in Article 3(1)(q) EC – Article 149 EC does not contain an integration provision. This is noteworthy, since the relationship between education and free movement has been elaborated far more clearly than is the case for culture, both in secondary law and case law.

Article 13 of the EU Charter of Fundamental Rights acknowledges academic freedom. Article 14 of this Charter provides that everyone has the right to education and to have access to vocational and continuing training. This right includes the possibility of receiving compulsory education free of charge. The freedom to found educational establishments with due respect for democratic principles, and the right of parents to ensure the education and teaching of their children in conformity with their religious, philosophical and pedagogical convictions is to be respected, in accordance with the national laws governing the exercise of such freedom and right. This last provision in the Charter corresponds to the wording of the EC Treaty, but it goes further in the area of education provided free of charge. The same is true for the provision on academic freedom.

Through unambiguous drafting in the Treaty, the Member States have ensured that their responsibility for the content of teaching, the organization of education systems, and cultural and linguistic diversity is 'fully' respected (Art. 149(1) EC).

---

of the European Court of Justice', in M. Hoskins and W. Robinson (eds), *A True European* (London, 2003), 247–256.

224. Dir. 2005/36/EC of the European Parliament and of the Council of 7 Sep. 2005 on the recognition of professional qualifications, O.J. 2005, L 255/22.

225. Dir. 93/96, O.J. 1993, L 317 (the earlier directive); see O.J. 2004, L 229/35 for the new directive. See further Ch. VIII, sections 4.2 and 4.5.2, *supra*.

226. See the decisions on cooperation in education with Canada and the United States, O.J. 2001, L 71.

227. Chapter 3 of Title XI, on Education, Vocational Training and Youth. Art. 149 EC concerns education, and Art. 150 concerns vocational training.

228. A. Fürst, *Die bildungspolitischen Kompetenzen der europäischen Gemeinschaft* (Frankfurt/M, 1999).

The Community contributes to the development of quality education by encouraging cooperation between Member States, and by supporting and supplementing their action.

7.3   INCENTIVE MEASURES

The activities of the Community aimed at developing the European dimension in education are somewhat more concrete: encouraging mobility of students and teachers, promoting cooperation between educational establishments, and encouraging the development of distance education. For these purposes the Council is empowered, on the basis of Article 149(4) EC, to adopt incentive measures, though it is prohibited from adopting harmonization measures. The old programmes on mobility of students (Erasmus),[229] the cooperation between universities and industry (Comett),[230] the promotion of the knowledge of foreign languages (Lingua)[231] and the Tempus Programme on trans-European mobility for university studies[232] are examples of this approach. Previously, such activities were based on Articles 128 EEC or 235 EEC.

By now, these programmes have been replaced by the Socrates II programme,[233] the Leonardo da Vinci programme[234] and the Tempus III programme,[235] with the necessary transitional arrangements. An Erasmus Mundus programme[236] and an e-learning programme have also recently started to operate.[237]

The Robert Schumann programme was established in order to improve awareness of Community law within the legal professions.[238] There is also a programme for legal practitioners in the area of civil law (Grotius-civil).[239] Of great importance is the Fifth Framework Programme for activities in the area of research, technological development and demonstration activities.[240] In the Council's conclusions of 17 December 1999, a Resolution is devoted to the development of

---

229. Council Decs. 87/327, O.J. 1987, L 16625 and 89/663, O.J. 1989, L 395/23. See Case 242/87, *Commission v. Council.*
230. Dec. 89/27, O.J. 1989, L 13/28. See Joined Cases C-51, 90 & 94/89, *United Kingdom et al. v. Council.*
231. Dec. 89/489, O.J. 1989, L 239/24.
232. Dec. 93/246, O.J. 1993, L 112/34.
233. For Socrates I, see Dec. 819/95, O.J. 1995, L 87/10; for Socrates II, Dec. 253/2000, O.J. 2000, L 28/1. See the Agreements with the United States and Canada, Decs. 2001/196 and 2001/197, O.J. 2001, L 71.
234. See Dec. 1999/382, O.J. 1999, L 146/33.
235. O.J. 1999, L 120/30 and O.J. 2002, L 195/34 (third phase).
236. Dec. 2317/2003, O.J. 2003, L 345/1.
237. Dec. 2318/2003, O.J. 2003, L 335/23
238. Dec. 1496/98, O.J. 1998, L 196/24.
239. Reg. 290/2001, O.J. 2001, L 43/1 extending the programme, which was previously based on Joint Action 96/636, O.J. 1996, L 287/3. This was thus previously a Third Pillar act; the change is based on Arts. 61(c) and 67(1) EC. See also Grotius II – criminal, O.J. 2001, L 186.
240. O.J. 1999, L 26/1. For the implementing rules, O.J. 1999, L 26/46.

new working procedures for European cooperation in the field of education and training.[241] An important recent initiative is the establishment in 2004 of a Community action programme to promote bodies active at European level and to support specific activities in the field of education and training.[242]

On 13 December 2004, Council Directive 2004/114 on the conditions of admission of third-country nationals for the purposes of studies, pupil exchange, unremunerated training or voluntary service was adopted.[243]

7.4   INFORMATION SOCIETY AND BOLOGNA PROCESS

During the Lisbon European Council of 23 and 24 March 2000, important initiatives were taken concerning education and training, aimed at living and working in the so-called information society or knowledge-based society. The European education and training systems need to be adapted to the needs of the information society, and the need for more high-quality employment. This new approach is based on three pillars: the development of local learning centres, the promotion of information technology skills, and more transparency in the area of qualifications. In this context, the Council reached an agreement in May 2003 on European benchmarks,[244] and a single Community framework for the transparency of qualifications and competences (Europass) has been set up by Decision 2241/2004.[245]

The Nice European Council, of December 2000, approved a Resolution of the Council concerning the mobility of students and teachers. This Community policy creates a framework for the initiatives of a number of Ministers of education – the so-called Sorbonne Declaration.[246] The introduction of a Bachelors/Masters model for higher education in Member States which did not previously use such a model fits in with this. The recommendations on quality assurance in higher education and quality evaluation in school education also complement this line of development.[247] In addition, many Member States are reconsidering their system of student grants to take account of developments in student mobility.

---

241. O.J. 2000, C 8/6.
242. Dec. No. 791/2004/EC of the European Parliament and of the Council of 21 Apr. 2004 O.J. 2004, L 138/31.
243. O.J. 2004, L 375/12.
244. Council Conclusions of 5 May 2003 on reference levels of European average performance in education and training (Benchmarks), O.J. 2003, C 134/3.
245. Dec. No. 2241/2004/EC of the European Parliament and of the Council of 15 Dec. 2004 on single Community framework for the transparency of qualifications and competences (Europass), O.J. 2004, L 390/6.
246. In 1998, on the occasion of the 800th anniversary of the Sorbonne, a number of ministers of education signed a declaration, the aim of which was to achieve greater mobility of students by harmonizing the architecture of the European higher education system, agreeing on mutual recognition based on the Anglo-Saxon undergraduate-graduate structure. This was followed up by the Bologna Declaration, see note 247 *infra*.
247. O.J. 1998, L 270/56 and O.J. 2001, L 60/51.

These European initiatives, either developed within EC fora or in the margins thereof (Sorbonne Declaration and Bologna process),[248] have led to a detailed work programme of the Council, adopted in 2002, on the follow-up of the objectives of Education and training systems in Europe.[249] That these subjects continue to receive close attention is revealed in the conclusions of the Council of 21 February 2005 on Education and Training in the framework of the mid-term review of the Lisbon Strategy[250] and the Council Conclusions of 24 May 2005 on new indicators in education and training.[251] The Council Resolution of 15 November 2007 moreover, recognizes education and training as a key driver of the Lisbon Strategy.[252]

Finally, mention should be made of Regulation (EC) No. 1906/2006 of the European Parliament and of the Council of 18 December 2006 laying down the rules for the participation of undertakings, research centres and universities in actions under the Seventh Framework Programme and for the dissemination of research results (2007–2013),[253] and the Recommendation of the European Parliament and of the Council of 15 February 2006 on further European cooperation in quality assurance in higher education.[254] In November 2007, the Council and of the Representatives of the Governments of the Member States, meeting within the Council, adopted conclusions on improving the quality of teacher education.[255]

7.4.1   Vocational Training and Research

The provisions concerning vocational training, which are also included in the Education Chapter of the Treaty, are discussed in Chapter X of this book, above.[256] Given that research and technology policy is closely related to industrial policy, it is discussed in Chapter XII, below.

8   OTHER HORIZONTAL AND FLANKING POLICIES

Since the changes brought by the Treaty of Maastricht, the horizontal and flanking activities now embrace a great many aspects of the activities of the national

---

248. In 1999, the ministers of education of twenty-nine countries met to discuss the future development of higher education in Europe. The post-summit declaration – the Bologna Declaration – expressed the goal of developing a European Higher Education Area by 2010. The ensuing process is known as the Bologna process.
249. O.J. 2002, C 142/1.
250. O.J. 2005, C 85/1.
251. O.J. 2005, C 141/7.
252. O.J. 2007, C 300/1.
253. O.J. 2006, L 391/1.
254. O.J. 2006, L 64/60.
255. O.J. 2007, C 300/6.
256. See e.g., Council Resolution of 19 Dec. 2002 on the promotion of enhanced European cooperation in vocational education and training, O.J. 2003, C 13/2.

authorities, even though some matters are dealt with only marginally. The Treaties of Amsterdam and Nice have not changed this situation as such. Some of these policy areas deserve brief mention.

8.1   Tourism

The Court has interpreted the freedom to provide services as also embracing the freedom to receive services, and as a result many tourists have been able to make use of the freedom to receive services as well as the free movement of persons.[257] Article 3(1)(u) EC permits the Community to take measures in the field of tourism, and the first Declaration annexed to the Final Act on the occasion of the signature of the Maastricht Treaty required a report to be submitted by the Commission by 1996 which would form the basis for consideration of introducing, *inter alia*, a Title on tourism into the EC Treaty.[258] In that Declaration the Commission stated that Community action in, *inter alia*, the sphere of tourism would be pursued on the basis of the present provisions of the EC Treaty. The Treaties of Amsterdam and Nice did not pay specific attention to tourism.[259]

A number of incentive measures in relation to tourism have been approved, and attention is paid to the relationship between tourism and the environment.[260] Other measures of some importance in this area are the directives on package tours, on timesharing and statistical information on tourism.[261] In 2002, the Council passed a resolution on the future of European tourism.[262]

Following the Treaty of Lisbon, Article 195 TFEU provides that 'The Union shall complement the action of the Member States in the tourism sector, in particular by promoting the competitiveness of Union undertakings in that sector.' In this context, action by the Union shall aim (a) to encourage the creation of a favourable environment for the development of undertakings in this sector and (b) to promote cooperation between the Member States, particularly by the exchange of good practice. The European Parliament and the Council, acting in accordance with the ordinary legislative procedure, shall establish specific measures to complement actions within the Member States to achieve the objectives

---

257. Joined Cases 286/82 & 26/83, *Luisi and Carbone v. Ministero dello Tesoro*; Case 186/87, *Cowan v. Trésor public*; Joined Cases C-163, 165 & 250/94, *Criminal proceedings against Sanz de Lera et al.*; Case C-348/96, *Criminal proceedings against Donatella Calfa*. See E. Tichadou, *Der Schutz des Touristen in der Rechtsprechung des Europäischen Gerichtshofs* (2002) *Zeitschrift für europarechtliche Studien*, 299–319.
258. In the Luxembourg draft for the EU Treaty, separate titles were included for tourism and civil protection, see *Europe Documents* No. 1722/1723, 5 Jul. 1991.
259. The Commission found it unnecessary to make proposals in 1996. See *Agence Europe* 3 Apr. 1996, No. 6701, 9.
260. The Commission issued a report on this in Nov. 2000; see *Agence Europe* 30 Nov. 2000, No. 7852, 12.
261. Dir. 90/314, O.J. 1990, L 158/59, resp. Dir. 94/47, O.J. 1994, L 280/83; Dir. 95/57, O.J. 1995, L 291/32.
262. O.J. 2002, C 135/1.

referred to in this article, excluding any harmonization of the laws and regulations of the Member States.

8.2 CIVIL PROTECTION

Tourism and civil protection are mentioned in one and the same breath in the EC Treaty, in Article 3(1)(u) EC, and in the declaration attached to the Maastricht Treaty.[263] In relation to civil protection, one may mention a number of measures concerning public radio paging,[264] personal protective equipment[265] and wireless telecommunications.[266] In addition, the Community has signed the Convention on the Transboundary Impact of Industrial Accidents.[267] This type of Community action is closely linked to environmental policy (for instance, the directive adopted after the Seveso disaster).[268] The Community Action programme on civil protection[269] and a number of resolutions and decisions on the capacity, training and assistance interventions in the field of civil protection should also be mentioned.[270] Since the terrorist attacks of 11 September 2001, this subject is receiving more attention in the EC: Council Decision 2001/792, adopted already on 23 October 2001, established a Community mechanism to facilitate cooperation in civil protection assistance interventions[271] In the Council's Conclusions of 27 November 2003 on strengthening Community cooperation in the field of civil protection assistance, the Commission was encouraged to make further efforts. The Council Conclusions of 27 November 2003 on strengthening Community cooperation in the field of civil protection assistance set out the Community framework,[272] and by Council Resolution of 22 December 2003, further strengthening of Community cooperation in the field of civil protection research was declared to be desirable.[273] Finally, Council Decision 2007/162 established a Civil Protection Financial Instrument.[274]

---

263. Declaration No. 1 on civil protection, energy and tourism, adopted with the Final Act of the Maastricht Treaty.
264. Recommendation 90/543, O.J. 1990, L 310/23, and Council Dir. 90/544/EEC of 9 Oct. 1990 on the frequency bands designated for the coordinated introduction of pan-European land-based public radio paging in the Community, O.J. 1990, L 310/28. See Case C-14/02, *ATRAL v. État belge.*
265. Dir. 89/686, O.J. 1989, L 399/18. See Case C-103/01, *Commission v. Germany.*
266. Dir. 91/287 and recommendation 91/288, O.J. 1991, L 144.
267. Twenty-sixth General Report EC 1992, No. 611.
268. Council Dir. 82/501/EEC of 24 Jun. 1982 on the major-accident hazards of certain industrial activities, O.J. 1982, L 230. See Case C-190/90, *Commission v. Netherlands.*
269. Council Dec. of 9 Dec. 1999, O.J. 1999, L 327/53.
270. O.J. 2001, C 82/1; O.J. 2001, L 297/7; O.J. 2002, C 43/1.
271. Council Dec. 2001/792 EC, Euratom of 23 Oct., O.J. 2001, L 297/7.
272. O.J. 2003, C 317/1.
273. O.J. 2004, C 8/2.
274. Council Decision 2007/162 of 5 Mar. 2007 establishing a Civil Protection Financial Instrument O.J. 2007, L 71/9.

If and when the Treaty of Lisbon enters into force, Article 196 TFEU provides that the Union 'shall encourage cooperation between Member States in order to improve the effectiveness of systems for preventing and protecting against natural or man-made disasters.' The Union's action will have three aims:

(a) To support and complement Member States' action at national, regional and local level in risk prevention, in preparing their civil-protection personnel and in responding to natural or man-made disasters within the Union.

(b) To promote swift, effective operational cooperation within the Union between national civil-protection services.

(c) To promote consistency in international civil-protection work.

The measures necessary to help achieve these objectives are to be established by the European Parliament and Council, acting in accordance with the ordinary legislative procedure. Any harmonization of the laws and regulations of the Member States is excluded.

8.3   SPORT

The importance of sport for the development of European integration has been acknowledged in recent years. There is frequent traffic in this context, both of sportsmen and women and of fans. Recent case law of the Court, building on earlier case law, has stimulated the Community to develop a policy on sport. The case law concerned free movement of sportsmen and women[275] and competition rules.[276]

---

275. Case 36/74, *Walrave and Koch v. Association Union Cycliste Internationale et al.*; Case 13/76, *Dona v. Mantero*; Case 222/86, *Unectef v. Heylens*; Case T-46/92, *Scottish Football v. Commission*; Case C-415/93, *Union royale belge des sociétés de football association et al. v. Bosman et al.*; Joined Cases C-51/96 & C-191/97, *Deliège v. Ligue francophone de judo et disciplines associées*; Case C-176/96, *Lehtonen and Castors Braine v. Fédération royale belge des sociétés de basket-ball*; Case C-438/00, *Deutscher Handballbund v. Kolpak*; Case T-313/02, *Meca-Medina and Majcen v. Commission*; Case C- 265/03, *Simutenkov v. Ministerio de Educación y Cultura and Real Federación Española de Fútbol*. Case C-519/04 P, *Meca-Medina and Majcen v. Commission*. See also Case C-264/98, *Tibor Balog v. Royal Charleroi Sporting Club* (O.J. 1998, C 278). The last mentioned case was withdrawn – under pressure from the football federations – on the day the Opinion of the Advocate General was due to be delivered, see *Agence Europe* 30 Mar. 2001, No. 7935 and O.J. 2001, 173/32). The Advocate General published the main arguments of the Opinion (which was as such never delivered) in A. Egger and C. Stix-Hackl, 'Sports and Competition Law: A Never-ending Story?' (2002), ECLR, 81. See S. Weatherill, '"Fair Play Please!"', Recent Developments in the Application of EC Law to Sport' (2003) CML Rev., 51-93; J.-F., Pons, 'La politique européenne de concurrence et le sport' (2002) RDUE, 241–259.

276. Screensport/European Broadcasting Union, O.J. 1991, L 63/32; 1990 World Cup football, O.J. 1992, L 326/31; Eurosport/Sky, O.J. 1993, C 76/8; BSkyB, O.J. 1993, C 94/6; Audiovisual-Sport; O.J. 1997, C 120/5; Formula 1, O.J. 1997, C 36/7; DFB, O.J. 1999, C 6/10; 1998 World Cup football, O.J. 2000, L 5/55; Eurovision, O.J. 2000, L 151/33; Fifa, *Agence Europe* 19 Jun. 2000

There is also a clear overlap with the rules on the media[277] and free movement of persons (for the 'supporters');[278] in these cases it is the passive enjoyment of sport which is concerned.

In a declaration on sport attached to the Treaty of Amsterdam, the importance of sport and its social role were highlighted. The Vienna European Council of December 1998 asked the Commission to report on this subject. The Report was presented at the Helsinki European Council, at the end of 1999.[279] In this Report, the Commission aimed to put sport on the agenda of the Member States, also with a view to Treaty amendments. Although the Community can act in cases of discrimination, distortions of competition, and abuses of dominant positions, and can adopt incentive measures, it has no direct competences in the field of sport. The Helsinki report does not only deal with top sport: the social and educational roles of sport are also considered. The report also discusses the need for measures to combat doping practices.[280]

The Nice European Council, December 2000, resulted in an extensive declaration on the social function of sport, which must be taken into account in the implementation of Community policy. The Treaty of Nice did not, however, lead to the inclusion of a special title on sport in the EC Treaty: despite intensive lobbying, the groups which wanted a special status for sport did not see their wishes granted.[281] The Commission, in applying competition law, and the courts, in applying the free movement provisions, will have to use the framework of Treaty law, supplemented with various declarations and resolutions, and dicta of the Court of Justice.[282] In its recent competition policy, the Commission recognizes the considerable social importance of sport, and takes this into account.[283] On 11 July 2007, the Commission adopted a White Paper on Sport;[284] this was the first

---

and *Agence Europe* 10 and 11 Jun. 2002. See also Joined Cases T-528, 542, 543 & 546/93, *Métropole television et al.*

277. D. Brinckman and E. Vollebregt, 'The Marketing of Sport and its Relation to EC Competition Law' (1998) ECLR, 281; H. Flaming, 'Exclusive Rights to Broadcast Sporting Events in Europe' (1999) ECLR, 143. See the commitment decision adopted by the Commission on 19 Jan.ry 2005, based on Reg. 1/2003, concerning the German Football League, IP/05/62.

278. Recommendation of the Commission of 22 Apr. 1996 on guidelines for preventing and restraining disorder connected with football matches, O.J. 1996, C 131/1; Council Dec. of 25 Apr. 2002 concerning security in connection with football matches with an international dimension, O.J. 2002, L 121/1.

279. Report from the Commission to the European Council with a view to safeguarding current sports structures and maintaining the social function of sport within the Community framework, COM(1999)644 final. On this see S. Weatherill, 'The Helsinki Report on Sport' (2000) ELRev, 282.

280. See COM(1999)643 final Community support plan to combat doping in sport.

281. See the Report in K. van Miert, *Mijn Europese Jaren* (Tielt, 2000), 157.

282. E.g., on the inherent restrictions (selections), see Joined Cases C-51/96 & C-191/97, *Deliège v. Ligue francophone de judo et disciplines associées*.

283. Commission Communication pursuant to Art. 19(3) Reg. 17, UEFA, O.J. 1999, C 363/2. See also Case T-193/02, *Piau v. Commission* (the appeal against the CFI judgment, Case C-171/05, *Piau v. Commission*, was rejected).

284. COM(2007)391 final.

comprehensive initiative on sport by the Commission, adopted in full respect of the principle of subsidiarity, the autonomy of sport organizations and the current EU competences in this area. The White Paper develops the concept of the specificity of sport, provides legal clarity for stakeholders and makes concrete proposals, forming an Action Plan named after Pierre de Coubertin which will guide the Commission in its sport-related activities during the coming years.

Following the Treaty of Lisbon, Article 165(2), last indent, TFEU provides that developing the European dimension in sport, by promoting fairness and open-ness in sporting competitions and cooperation between bodies responsible for sports, and by protecting the physical and moral integrity of sportsmen and sports-women, especially the youngest sportsmen and sportswomen.

8.4   YOUTH AND THE ELDERLY

In Articles 24 and 25 EU Charter of Fundamental Rights, a number of rights enjoyed by children and by the elderly are recognized.

Policy relating to children and young people has been given a place in the EC Treaty in the chapter on education, vocational training and youth. Unlike these other two policy areas, 'youth' is not mentioned in the list of Community activities in Article 3 EC. In a Resolution of the Council of 27 June 2002, the first steps were taken towards a common policy.[285]

According to Article 149(2) EC, Community action is aimed, *inter alia*, at encouraging the development of youth exchanges and of exchanges of socio-educational instructors. Article 150(2) EC provides for certain measures concerning vocational training for young people. In November 2006, an action programme in the field of lifelong learning was established.[286] In 2004, the Council and European Parliament adopted an action programme to promote bodies active at European level in the field of youth, following on from the establishment in 2000 of the 'Youth' Community action programme.[287] The 'Youth in action' programme for the period 2007–2013, with a number of mainly social objectives, was established by Decision 1719/2006.[288]

An action programme to prevent and combat violence against children, young people and women (the Daphne III programme) has also been adopted.[289]

---

285. O.J. 2002, C 168/2. See also Council Conclusions of 6 May 2003 regarding the future of youth activities in the context of the new generation of programmes, O.J. 2003, C 115/1.
286. Dec. No. 1720/2006/EC of the European Parliament and of the Council of 15 Nov. 2006, O.J. 2006, L 327/45.
287. Dec. No. 790/2004, O.J. 2004, L 138/24. Dec. 1031/2000, O.J. 2000, L 117/1. See also O.J. 2000, C 374/5.
288. Dec. No. 1719/2006/EC of the European Parliament and of the Council of 15 Nov. 2006 establishing the Youth in Action programme for the period 2007–2013, O.J. 2006, L 327/30.
289. Decision No. 779/2007/EC of the European Parliament and of the Council of 20 Jun. 2007 establishing for the period 2007–2013 a specific programme to prevent and combat violence against children, young people and women and to protect victims and groups at risk (Daphne III

Other significant measures include Conclusions of the Council on child sex tourism,[290] Council Decision of 29 May 2000 to combat child pornography on the Internet,[291] a Council framework Decision on combating the sexual exploitation of children and child pornography[292] a resolution on sporting activities in the European Community youth programmes[293] and a Council recommendation on the drinking of alcohol by young people, in particular children and adolescents.[294]

Finally, mention may be made of two Council Resolutions on participation by and information for young people, in 2003 and 2005,[295] the Resolution of the Council and the Representatives of the Governments of the Member States of 24 May 2005 meeting within the Council on the evaluation of activities conducted in the framework of European cooperation in the youth field,[296] and the Conclusions by the Council of 21 February 2005 on Youth in the framework of the mid-term review of the Lisbon Strategy.[297]

In a recent judgment, the Court of Justice recognized the protection of the rights of the child as a general interest, which may justify a restriction on the free movement of goods.[298]

If the Lisbon Treaty enters into force, According to Article 3(3) TEU (Lisbon), the Union 'shall combat social exclusion and discrimination, and shall promote social justice and protection, equality between women and men, solidarity between generations and protection of the rights of the child.' Paragraph 5 of that article states that, in its relations with the wider world, the Union shall uphold and promote its values and contribute to the protection if its citizens. It goes on to lay down that the Union shall contribute to the protection of human rights, in particular the rights of the child, as well as to the strict observance and the development of international law, including respect for the principles of the United Nations Charter.

8.5   SPATIAL PLANNING

Planning policy is not yet actively pursued at Community level.[299] Various activities in this policy area are fragmented and could well be brought together to

---

programme) as part of the General Programme 'Fundamental Rights and Justice', O.J. 2007, L 173/19.
290. O.J. 1999, C 379. See also Council Dec. of 28 Jun. 2001 establishing a second phase of the programme of incentives, exchanges, training and cooperation for persons responsible for combating trade in human beings and the sexual exploitation of children (Stop II), O.J. 2001, L 186/7.
291. O.J. 2000, L 138/1. See also de Council Conclusions of 17 Dec. 1999, O.J. 2000, C 8/8.
292. Council Framework Dec. 2004/68/JHA of 22 Dec. 2003, O.J. 2004, L 13/44.
293. O.J. 2000, C 8/5. See also Dec. 291/2003 establishing the European Year of Education through Sport 2004, O.J. 2003, L 43/1.
294. O.J. 2001, L 161/38.
295. Resolutions of 25 Nov. 2003 and 24 May 2005, O.J. 2003, C 295/6 and O.J. 2005, C 141/3.
296. O.J. 2005, C 141/1.
297. O.J. 2005, C 85/5.
298. Case C-244/06, *Dynamic Medien Vertriebs v. Avides Media.*
299. See H.D. Jarass, 'Europäisierung des Planungsrechts' (2000) *Deutsches Verwaltungsblatt*, 945.

promote coherence and transparency. Town and country planning is explicitly mentioned in the Title on environmental policy (Art. 175(2) EC),[300] but is also relevant in the Titles on Economic and Social Cohesion (regional policy), Transport, Trans-European Networks, and Industry. Directive 2007/2/EC of the European Parliament and of the Council of 14 March 2007 establishes an Infrastructure for Spatial Information in the European Community (Inspire).[301]

Given Article 295 EC (by which the national systems of property ownership are unaffected by the Treaty) and the subsidiarity principle, the Community will never be able to take such far-reaching measures as are possible for national authorities, whether central, regional or local. Thus the Community cannot enforce compulsory purchase of land or property, but national property rules may be examined under the Treaty[302] or under Community policies – such as the market organization in wine and wine products – and in the light of the First Protocol to the European Convention on Human Rights.[303]

Article 17 of the EU Charter of Fundamental Rights provides that:

> everyone has the right to own, use, dispose of and bequeath his or her lawfully acquired possessions. No. one may be deprived of his or her possessions, except in the public interest and in the cases and under the conditions provided for by law, subject to fair compensation being paid in good time for their loss. The use of property may be regulated by law in so far as is necessary for the general interest.

8.6   MEDIA

Media policies pursued at national level are in many cases at odds with the freedoms guaranteed by Community law, particularly with the freedom to provide services.[304] Many Member States have found that the application of the principle of proportionality, in particular, means that obligations to purchase from particular sources, discriminatory advertising provisions, establishment requirements and other restrictions will not withstand Community scrutiny.[305] Articles 81, 82 and 86 EC and the merger rules are also regularly applied to cases in the media sector.[306] The same applies for Article 87 EC in relation to state aid to broadcasting

---

300. On this see J.H. Jans, H.G. Sevenster and H.H.B. Vedder, *Europees milieurecht in Nederland* (Den Haag, 2000), 54.
301. O.J. 2007, L 108/1.
302. Case 182/83, *Fearon v. Irish Land Commission*; Case C-302/97, *Konle v. Republik Österreich*; Case C-452/01, *Ospelt v. Schlössle Weissenberg*; Case C-370/05, *Criminal Proceedings against Festersen*.
303. Case 44/79, *Hauer v. Land Rheinland-Pfalz*.
304. V. Schmitz, *Die kommerzielle Kommunikation im Binnenmarkt im Lichte der neueren Rechtsprechung zur Warenverkehrsfreiheit* (Baden-Baden, 2000).
305. See further Ch. VIII, *supra*.
306. D. Geradin, 'Access to Content by New Media Platforms: A Review of the Competition Law Problems' (2005) EL Rev, 68.

companies.[307] A Protocol on the system of public broadcasting in the Member States was adopted with the Treaty of Amsterdam. In many cases, subjects at the intersection of sport and media are concerned (see section 8.3 above).

In 1984, the Commission published a Green Paper on 'Television without frontiers'.[308] As a follow-up, the TV Directive (89/552) was adopted.[309] Partly in reaction to the Court's case law, this Directive was amended by Directive 97/36.[310] It may be deduced from the case law of the Court of Justice and the Court of First Instance that a 'true' public broadcasting company can rely on general interest exceptions (culture, media pluralism, regional diversity) to retain rights to broadcast.[311] In 2007, the TV Directive was adapted to take account of the developments in the area of the media.[312]

By Decision of 15 November 2006 a programme of support for the European audiovisual sector (MEDIA 2007) was adopted.[313]

Article 133(6) EC provides that commercial agreements relating to trade in cultural and audiovisual services fall within the shared competence of the Community and its Member States.

FURTHER READING

Horizontal and Flanking Policies, General

Bergkamp, L. *European Community Law for the New Economy.* Antwerp: Intersentia. 2003.

de Vries, S. A. *Tensions within the Internal Market: The Functioning of the Internal Market and the Development of Horizontal and Flanking Policies.* Groningen: Europa Law Publishing. 2006.

Gronden, J. W. van de and K. J. M. Mortelmans. *Mededinging en niet-economische belangen.* Deventer: Kluwer. 2001 (Mededingingsmonografieën; dl. 3).

---

307. A. Bartosch, 'Öffentlichrechtliche Rundfunkfinanzierung und EG-Beihilfenrecht. Eine Zwischenbilanz' (1999) EuZW, 176; P. Kreijger, *De financiering van de publieke omroep in Europa: nieuw beleid van de Europese Commissie* (2003) *Mediaforum*, 82. See further H. Zeinstra, *Mediaforum* (2003), 163.
308. COM(84)300 final.
309. Dir. 89/552, O.J. 1989, L 298/33. Case C-412/93, *Leclerc-Siplec v. TF1 and M6*; Case C-245/01, *RTL Television v. Niedersächsische Landesmedienanstalt für privaten Rundfunk*. Case C-89/04, *Mediakabel v. Commissariaat voor de Media*; Case T-33/01, *Infront v. Commission*.
310. O.J. 1997, L 202/60. On this see B.J. Drijber, 'The Revised Television Without Frontiers Directive: Is It Fit for the Next Century?' (1999) CML Rev., 87. See further Council Conclusions of 19 Dec. on the 'Television without Frontiers' Directive, O.J. 2003, C 13/1. See also the interpretative declaration by the Commission of 28 Apr. 2004, O.J. 2004, C 102/2.
311. See most recently Case T-266/97, *Vlaamse Televisie Maatschappij v. Commission*.
312. Dir. 2007/65/EC on Audiovisual Media Services, O.J. 2007, L 332.
313. Decision No. 1718/2006/EC of the European Parliament and of the Council of 15 Nov. 2006 concerning the implementation of a programme of support for the European audiovisual sector (MEDIA 2007), O.J. 2006, L 327/12.

Lane, R. 'New Community Competences under the Maastricht Treaty'. (1993) CML Rev.: 939–979.

Moussis, N. S. *Access to European Union: Law, Economics, Policies.* 16th Rev. ed. Rixensart: European Study Service. 2007.

Moussis. N. *Guide to European Policies.* 12th Rev. ed. Rixensart: European Study Service, 2007.

Shaw. J., et al., *Economic and Social Law of the European Union.* Basingstoke: Palgrave Macmillan. 2007.

Environment

Bailey, I. *New Environmental Policy Instruments in the European Union : Politics, Economics, and the Implementation of the Packaging Waste Directive.* Aldershot: Ashgate. 2003.

Baker, S., 'European Union Biodiversity Policy'. San Domenico: European University Institute. 2002 (EUI working papers RSC; 2002/44).

Betlem, G. and E. Brans. *Environmental Liability in the EU: The 2004 Directive Compared with US and Member State Law.* London: Cameron. 2006.

Chave, P. A. *The EU Water Framework Directive: An Introduction.* London: IWA Publishing, 2001.

Comte, F. and L. Krämer. *Environmental Crime in Europe: Rules of Sanctions.* Groningen: Europa Law Publishing. 2004 (The Avosetta Series; 5).

Davies, P. G. G. *European Union Environmental Law: An Introduction to Key Selected Issues.* Aldershot: Ashgate, 2004.

de Sadeleer, N. *Implementing the Precautionary Principle: Approaches from the Nordic Countries, EU and USA.* London: Earthscan. 2007.

Demmke, C.and M. Unfried (eds). *European Environmental Policy: The Administrative Challenge for the Member States.* Maastricht: European Institute of Public Administration. 2001 (Capacity building for integration; Current European issues; EIPA; 2001/P/04).

Dhondt, N. M. L. *Integration of Environmental Protection into other EC Policies : Legal Theory and Practice.* Groningen: Europa Law Publishing, 2003 (The Avosetta series; 2)

Douma, W. T. *European Environmental Case Law.* The Hague: T.M.C. Asser Press. 2002.

Douma, W. T. *The Precautionary Principle: Its Application in International European and Dutch Law.* S.l.: s.n. 2003.

Faure, M. G. and G. Heine. *Criminal Enforcement of Environmental Law in the European Union.* The Hague: Kluwer Law International, 2005. (Comparative Environmental Law & Policy Series; 8).

Frenz, W. *Außenkompetenzen der Europäischen Gemeinschaften und der Mitgliedstaaten im Umweltbereich : Reichweite und Wahrnehmung.* Berlin: Duncker & Humblot. 2001. (Schriften zum europäischen Recht; Bd. 77).

Glachant, M. *Implementing European Environmental Policy: The Impacts of Directives in the Member States.* Cheltenham: Edward Elgar.2001.

Hedemann-Robinson, M. *Enforcement of European Union Environmental Law: Legal Issues and Challenges.* London: Routledge-Cavendish. 2007.

Jans, J.H. and H.H.B. Vedder. *European Environmental Law*, 3rd ed. Groningen: Europa Law Publishing, 2008.

Jordan, A. *Environmental Policy in the European Union: Actors, Institutions and Processes.* 2nd fully rev. ed. London: Earthscan. 2005.

Kemp, R. Treatment of an EU Directive: Compliance with the Urban Waste Water Treatment Directive in Germany, Spain, England and Wales, and the Netherlands. S.l.: s.n. Drukker: Norderstedt : Books on Demand GmbH, 2002.

Knill, C. and J. D. Liefferink. *Environmental Politics in the European Union: Policy-making, Implementation and Patterns of Multi-level Governance.* Manchester: Manchester University Press. 2007.

Krämer, L. *Casebook on EU Environmental Law.* Oxford: Hart. 2002.

Krämer, L. *EC Environmental Law.* 6th rev. and updated ed. London: Sweet & Maxwell. 2007.

Krämer, L. *European Environmental Law.* Aldershot: Ashgate/Dartmouth. 2003 (The International Library of Environmental Law and Policy).

Lee, M. *EU Environmental Law: Challenges, Change and Decision-making.* Oxford: Hart. 2005 (Modern Studies in European Law; 6).

Lenschow, A. *Environmental Policy Integration: Greening Sectoral Policies in Europe.* London: Earthscan. 2002.

Loula, E. *Conflicting Integration: The Environmental Law of the European Union.* Antwerp. 2004.

MacCormick, J. *Environmental Policy in the European Union*, Basingstoke: Palgrave, 2001.

Macrory, R. *Reflections on 30 Years of EU environmental Law: A High Level of Protection?: Proceedings of the Avosetta Group of European Environmental Lawyers.* Groningen: Europa Law Publishing. 2006. (The Avosetta series; 7).

Macrory, R., et al. *Principles of European Environmental Law: Proceedings of the Avosetta Group of European Environmental Lawyers.* Groningen: Europa Law Publishing. 2004. (The Avosetta series; 4).

Maxwell, J. W. and R. Reuveny. *Trade and Environment: Theory and Policy in the Context of EU Enlargement and Economic Transition.* Cheltenham: Edward Elgar. 2005. (Fondazione Eni Enrico Mattei (FEEM). Series on Economics, Energy and Environment).

Onida, M.and L. Krämer. *Europe and the Environment: Legal Essays in Honour of Ludwig Krämer.* Groningen: Europa Law Publishing. 2004.

Peeters, M. G. W. M. and K. R. Deketelaere. *EU Climate Change Policy: The Challenge of New Regulatory Initiatives.* Cheltenham: Edward Elgar. 2006 (New Horizons in Environmental Law).

Rengeling, H.-W. *Handbuch zum europäischen und deutschen Umweltrecht : Eine systematische Darstellung des europäischen Umweltrechts mit seinen Auswirkungen auf das deutsche Recht und mit rechtspolitischen Perspektiven*, 2. Auflage, Köln: Heymanns, 2003.

Rijswick, H. F. M. W. v. and T. Barton. *The Water Framework Directive: Implementation into German and Dutch Law.* Utrecht: University of Utrecht Centrum voor Omgevingsrecht en Beleid/NILOS; Trier: University of Trier. 2003.

Romi, R. *L'Europe et la Protection Juridique de l'Environnement.* 3e éd. Paris: Victoires-Editions. 2004 (Collection Environnement / Victoires-Éditions).

Scheuer, S. *EU Environmental Policy Handbook: A Critical Analysis of EU Environmental Legislation: Making it Accessible to Environmentalists and Decision Makers.* Brussels: European Environmental Bureau (EEB). 2005.

Somsen, H. 'Discretion in European Community Environmental Law: An Analysis of ECJ Case Law'. CML Rev. 40/1413.

Somsen, H. *Protecting the European Environment: Enforcing European Community Environmental Law in the Age of Subsidiarity.* Hull: University of Hull. 1999.

Therivel, R. *Strategic Environmental Assessment in Action.* London: Earthscan. 2004.

Weale, A. *Environmental Governance in Europe: An Ever Closer Ecological Union?.* Oxford: Oxford U.P. 2002.

Wennerås, P. E. *EC Environmental Law in National and Community Courts.* S.l.: s.n. 2006.

Ziegler, A. R. *Trade and Environment Law in the EC.* Oxford, 1996.

Zito, A. R. *Creating Environmental Policy in the European Union.* 2nd pr., Basingstoke: Palgrave. 2001.

Consumers

Bourrinet, J. and F.G. Snyder. *La Sécurité Alimentaire dans l'Union Européenne.* Bruxelles: Bruylant. 2003 (Travaux du CERIC 1).

Collins, H. *The Forthcoming EC Directive on Unfair Commercial Practices.* The Hague: Kluwer Law International. 2004 (Private Law in European Context Series; 5).

Coteanu, C. *Cyber Consumer Law and Unfair Trading Practices.* Ashgate 2005 (Markets and the Law).

Cseres, K.J. *Competition Law and Consumer Protection.* The Hague: Kluwer Law International. 2005 (European Monographs; 49).

Henning-Bodewig, F. *Unfair Competition Law: European Union and Member States.* Kluwer Law International. 2006 (International Competition Law Series; 18).

Hodges, C. *European Regulation of Consumer Product Safety.* Oxford: Oxford University Press. 2005.

Holland, D. and H. Pope. *EU Food Law and Policy.* The Hague: Kluwer Law International. 2004.

Howells G.G. and Weatherill St. *Consumer Protection Law.* 2nd ed. Ashgate: Aldershot/ 2005.

Howells, G.G., et al. *European Fair Trading Law: The Unfair Commercial Practices Directive.* Aldershot: Ashgate. 2006 (Markets and the Law).

Kilbey, I. 'Consumer Protection Evaded via the Internet' (2005) EL Rev.: 123.

MacMaoláin, C. *EU Food Law: Protecting Consumers and Health in a Common Market.* Oxford: Hart. 2007 (Modern Studies in European Law; 13).

Mahiou, A. and H.v. Hamel, *La Sécurité Alimentaire = Food Security and Food Safety.* Leiden: Nijhoff. 2006 (Les Livres de Droit de l'Ácadémie).

Nebbia, P. *Unfair Contract Terms in European Law: A Study in Comparative and EC Law*, Oxford: Hart. 2007 (Modern Studies in European Law; Vol. 15).

Nebbia, P. and T. Askham. *EU Consumer Law.* Richmond: Richmond Law & Tax. 2004.

O'Rourke, R. *European Food Law.* 3rd ed. London: Sweet & Maxwell. 2005.

Pasa, B., et al. *The Harmonization of Civil and Commercial Law in Europe.* Budapest: Central European University Press. 2005 (A Guide to European Private Law; 2).

Pitt, G. *Butterworth's Commercial and Consumer Law Handbook.* 4th ed. London: Butterworth/LexisNexis. 2003.

Radeideh, M. *Fair Trading in EC Law : Information and Consumer Choice in the Internal Market* Groningen: Europa Law Publishing. 2005.

Reich, N. and H.W. Micklitz. *Europäisches Verbraucherrecht.* 4. aktualisierte Aufl. Baden-Baden: Nomos. 2003.

Rickett, C. E. F. and T. G. W. Telfer. *International Perspectives on Consumers' Access to Justice.* Cambridge: Cambridge University Press. 2003.

Rösler, H. *Europäisches Konsumentenvertragsrecht : Grundkonzeption, Prinzipien und Fortentwicklung.* München: Beck. 2004 (Europäisches Wirtschaftsrecht; Bd. 32).

Rott, P. 'Minimum Harmonization for the Completion of the Internal Market? The Example of Consumer Sales Law'. (2003) CML Rev.:1107–1135.

Schieble, C. *Produktsicherheitsgesetz und europäisches Gemeinschaftsrecht.* Baden-Baden: Nomos. 2003. (Schriftenreihe Europäisches Verbraucherrecht; 13).

Sheridan, B. and R. Coleman. *EU Biotechnology Law & Practice.* London: Sweet and Maxwell, 2007.

Twigg-Flesner, C. *Consumer Product Guarantees.* Aldershot: Ashgate. 2003.

van der Meulen, B.M.J. and M. van der Velde, *Food Safety Law in the European Union: An introduction.* Wageningen: Wageningen Academic Publishers. 2004 (European Institute for Food Law Series; 1).

Vos, E. and F. Wendler. *Food Safety Regulation in Europe: A Comparative Institutional Analysis.* Antwerpen: Intersentia. 2006 (Ius Commune Europaeum; 62).

de Vrey, R.W. *Towards a European Unfair Competition Law: A Clash between Legal Families: A Comparative Study of English, German and Dutch Law in Light of Existing European and International Legal Instruments.* Leiden: Nijhoff. 2006. (Intellectual Property Law Library; 1).

Weatherill, S., *EU Consumer Law and Policy.* New and Expanded ed. Cheltenham: Edward Elgar. 2005 (Elgar European Law).

Weatherill, S. and U. Bernitz. *The Regulation of Unfair Commercial Practices under EC Directive 2005/29: New Rules and New Techniques.* Oxford: Hart Publishing. 2007 (Studies of the Oxford Institute of European and Comparative Law; 4).

Wetzig, W. *Einfluss der EG und der WTO auf das Lebens'mittelrecht : Bindung an internationale und ausländische Standards.* Frankfurt am Main: Lang. 2000 (Europäische Hochschulschriften. Reihe 2; Bd. 2832).

Whittaker, S. *Liability for Product: English Law, French Law, and European Harmonisation.* Oxford: Oxford University Press. 2005.

Health Policy and Health Care

Abraham, J. and G. Lewis. *Regulating Medicines in Europe: Competition, Expertise and Public Health.* London: Routledge. 2000.

Belcher, P.J. *The Role of the European Union in Health Care: Overview.* Zoetermeer: Council for Health and Social Service, 1999.

Cabral, P. 'The Internal Market and the Right to Cross-border Medical Care'. (2004) EL Rev.: 673.

Exter, A.P. and J. Sándor. *Frontiers of European Health Law: Yearbook 2002.* Rotterdam: Erasmus University Press. 2003.

Hervey, T.K. and J.V. McHale. *Health Law and the European Union.* Cambridge: Cambridge University Press. 2004 (Law in Context).

Holland, D. and H. Pope. *EU Food Law and Policy.* The Hague: Kluwer Law International. 2004.

Horton, L.R. *European Union Pharmaceutical and Medical Device Regulation: Regulatory Affairs Professionals Society.* 2005.

Lisman, J.and J.R.A. Schoonderbeek. *An Introduction to EU Pharmaceutical Law.* 1st ed. London: Brookwood Booklets. 2005.

MacKee, M., et al. The Impact of EU Law on Health Care Systems. 2002. Bruxelles: Lang. 2002 (Work and Society; Vol. 39).

MacKee, M., et al. *Health Policy and European Union Enlargement.* Maidenhead: Open University Press. 2004.

Mossialos, E. *EU Law and the Social Character of Health Care*, Frankfurt am Main: Peter Lang. 2002.

Nickless, J.A. *The Consequences of European Competition Law for Social Health Care Providers.* Antwerpen: Maklu. 1998 (Reeks Gezondheidszorgverzekering en Europa 26–27).

O'Rourke, R. *European Food Law.* 3rd ed. London: Sweet & Maxwell. 2005.

Randall, E. *The European Union and Health Policy.* Basingstoke: Palgrave. 2001.

Schneider, H.-P and T. Stein. *The European Ban on Tobacco Advertising: Studies Concerning its Compatibility with European Law.* Baden-Baden: Nomos-Verlagsgesellschaft, 1999.

Schweitzer, M., et al. *EG-Binnenmarkt und Gesundheitsschutz : am Beispiel der neuen Tabakrichtlinie der Europäischen Gemeinschaft.* Heidelberg: Verlag Recht und Wirtschaft. 2002.

Sheridan, B. *EU Biotechnology Law & Practice: Regulating Genetically Modified & Novel Food Products.* Bembridge: Palladian Law. 2001.

Sieveking, K. and B. Univ. 'ECJ Rulings on Health Care Services and Their Effects on the Freedom of Cross-Border Patient Mobility in the EU'. [on-line]:

Zentrum für Europäische Rechtspolitik. 2006 (ZERP-Diskussionspapier; 03/2006).

Somsen, H. *The Regulatory Challenge of Biotechnology: Human Genetics, Food and Patents.* Cheltenham: Edward Elgar. 2007.

Steffen, M. *Health Governance in Europe: Issues, Challenges, and Theories.* Routledge, 2005 (Routledge/ECPR Studies in European Political Science; 40).

Theofilatou, M. *The Emerging Health Agenda: The Health Policy of the European Community.* S.l.: s.n., 2000.

Vos, E. *Institutional Frameworks of Community Health and Safety Regulation: Committees, Agencies and Private Bodies.* Oxford: Hart. 1999.

Walters, D. *Regulating Health and Safety Management in the European Union: A Study of the Dynamics of Change.* Bruxelles: P.I.E.-Peter Lang,. 2002 (Work & Society; no. 35).

Culture

Ahrens, R. *Europäische Sprachenpolitik = European Language Policy.* Heidelberg: Winter. 2003 (Anglistische Forschungen; Bd. 329).

Benn, M.N.J. *The Cultural Dimension in EC Law.* London: Kluwer Law International. 1997.

Creech, R.L. *Law and Language in the European Union : The Paradox of a Babel 'United in Diversity'.* Groningen: Europa Law Publishing. 2005.

de Groof, J., et al. *Cultural and Educational Rights in the Enlarged Europe.* Wolf Legal Publishers, 2005.

Everling, U. *Buchpreisbindung im deutschen Sprachraum und Europäisches Gemeinschaftsrecht = Book Price Fixing in the German Language Area and European Community Law = Fixation des Prix du Livre dans l'Espace Germanophone et le Droit Communautaire Européen.* Baden-Baden: Nomos. 1997.

Flood, P.and D. Kevin. *Media and Cultural Policy in the Enlarged European Union.* Mahwah, NJ: Lawrence Erlbaum Associates. 2004 (Trends in communication; Vol. 12 Issue 4).

Jund, S., et al. 'Culture et marché.' ERA – Forum 2005:128.

Loman, J.M.E. et. al. *Culture and Community Law: Before and after Maastricht.* Deventer: Kluwer Law and Taxation. 1992.

MacMahon, J.A. *Education and Culture in European Community Law.* London: The Athlone Press. 1995.

Maurer, C.H.M. *Die Ausfuhr von Kulturgütern in der Europäischen Union.* Frankfurt am Main: Haag and Herchen. 1997.

Meinhof, U.H. and A. Triandafyllidou. *Transcultural Europe: Cultural Policy in a Changing Europe.* Palgrave: Macmillan, 2006.

Obert, A. *Die Preisbindung im Buchhandel in Deutschland und im Vereinigten: Königreich in der Sicht des europäischen Rechts.* München: Beck. 2000.(Urheberrechtliche Abhandlungen des Max-Planck-Instituts für; Ausländisches und Internationales Patent-, Urheber- und; Wettbewerbsrecht, München; H. 33).

Peya, A. *Die Ausfuhr von Kulturgütern im nationalen und Gemeinschaftsrecht.* Frankfurt am Main: Lang, 2002 (Europäische Hochschulschriften. Reihe 2; Bd. 3543).

Sarikakis, K. *Media and Cultural Policy in the European Union.* Amsterdam: Rodopi. 2007 (European Studies; 24).

Schmahl, S., *Die Kulturkompetenz der Europäischen Gemeinschaft*, Baden-Baden: Nomos, 1996 (Nomos Universitätsschriften. Recht; Bd. 223).

Shore, C.N. *Building Europe: The Cultural Politics of European Integration.* London: Routledge, 2000

Smith, R.C. *Culture and European Union Law*, Oxford: Oxford University Press. 2004.

Wemmer, B. *Die neuen Kulturklauseln des EG-Vertrages: eine Analyse der Art. 128 EGV und Art. 92 Abs. 3 lit. d) EGV.* Frankfurt am Main: Lang. 1996 (Europäische Hochschulschriften. Reihe 2, Rechtswissenschaft; Bd. 1874).

De Witte, B. *Language Law of the European Union: Protecting or Eroding Linguistic Diversity* in R.C. Smith. *Cultural and Educational Rights in the Enlarged Europe.* Wolf Legal Publishers. 2005: Culture and European Union Law: Oxford, 2004: 205.

Education

Bergan, S. *Recognition Issues in the Bologna Process.* Strassbourg: Council of Europe. 2003.

Fürst, A. *Die Bildungspolitischen Kompetenzen der Europäischen Gemeinschaft : Umfang und Entwicklungsmöglichkeiten.* Frankfurt: Lang. 1999 (Schriften zum internationalen und zum öffentlichen Recht; 32).

Gori, G. *Towards an EU Right to Education.* The Hague: Kluwer Law International. 2001 (European monographs; 28).

de Groof, J. and G. Lauwers. *Cultural and Educational Rights in the Enlarged Europe*: Wolf Legal Publishers, 2005.

Hackl, E. *Towards a European Area of Higher Education: Change and Convergence in European Higher Education.* San Domenico: European University Institute. 2001. (EUI working paper RSC; no. 2001/9).

Lenaerts, K. 'Education in European Community Law after 'Maastricht'. (1994) CML Rev.: 7–42.

Lonbay J. 'Reflections on Education and Culture in EC Law' in R.C. Smith. *Culture and European Union Law.* Oxford, 2004: 243.

Margellos, T.M., et al. *Politique Sociale, Education et Jeunesse.* 2e éd. ent. refondue et mise à jour. Bruxelles: Éd. de l'Université de Bruxelles. 1998 (Commentaire J. Mégret : Le droit de la CE et de l'Union européenne; 7).

Phillips, D. *European Union Education and Training Policy.* Colchester: Routledge. 2006 (Comparative education; vol. 42, no. 1 (special issue 31) February 2006).

Phillips, D. and H. Ertl, *Implementing European Union Education and Training Policy: A Comparative Study of Issues in Four Member States.* Dordrecht: Kluwer Academic Publishers, 2003.

Rauhvargers, A., et al. *Recognition in the Bologna Process: Policy Development and the Road to Good Practice.* Strasbourg: Council of Europe Publishing. 2006 (Council of Europe Higher Education Series; no. 4).

Reinalda, B. and E. Kulesza. *The Bologna Process: Harmonizing Europe's Higher Education.* 2nd rev. Opladen: Barbara Budrich Publishers. 2006.

Schleicher, K. and P.J. Weber, *Zeitgeschichte europäischer Bildung.* 1970–2000. Münster: Waxmann, 2002 (Umwelt, Bildung, Forschung; Bd. 8).

Tomusk, V. *Creating the European Area of Higher Education: Voices from the Periphery: Springer.* 2006. (Higher Education Dynamics; 12).

Tourism

McDonald, M., et al. *European Community Tourism Law and Practice.* Dublin, 2003.

Tichadou, E. 'Der Schutz des Touristen in der Rechtsprechung des Europäischen Gerichtshofs'. (2002) *ZEuS*: 299–319.

Tonner, K. 'Consumer Protection and the European Union's Tourism Policy'. (1998) CLJ: 32–46.

Wouters, J. 'La Libre Circulation des Touristes dans la Jurisprudence de la Cour de Justice'. (1994) *CE. JTDE*:102–104.

Civil Protection

European Commission, Communication from the Commission to the European Parliament, the Council, the European Economic and Social Committee and the Committee of the Regions : Improving the Community Civil Protection Mechanism, COM(2005) 137.

Sport

Blanpain, R. *The Legal Status of Sportsmen and Sportswomen under International, European and Belgian National and Regional Law.* The Hague: Kluwer Law International. 2003 (Studies in Employment and Social Policy; 22).

Bogusz, B., et al. *The Regulation of Sport in the European Union.* Cheltenham: Elgar, 2007.

Caiger, A. and S. Gardiner. *Professional Sport in the European Union: Regulation and Re-regulation.* The Hague: T.M.C. Asser Press. 2000.

Parrish, R. and S. Miettinen. *The Sporting Exception in European Union Law.* The Hague: T.M.C. Asser Press, 2008. (Asser International Sports Law Series).

Pons, J.-Fr. *Sport and European Competition Law.* Fordham Conference. 1999.

Siekmann, R.C.R. and J. Soek. *The European Union and Sport: Legal and Policy Documents.* The Hague: T.M.C. Asser Press. 2005.

van den Bogaert, S. *Practical Regulation of the Mobility of Sportsmen in the EU Post 'Bosman'.* The Hague: Kluwer Law International. 2005. (European Monographs; 48).

Weatherill, S. 'European Football Law', in *Collected Courses of the 7th Session of the Academy of European Law.* Den Haag. 1999. 339–382.

Weatherill, S. 'Sport as Culture in EC Law'. in R.C. Smith. *Culture and European Union Law.* Oxford, 2004: 113.

Weatherill, S. 'The Helsinki Report on Sport'. (2000) EL Rev.: 282–292.

Weatherill, S. *European Sports Law: Collected Papers.* The Hague: T.M.C. Asser Press. 2007. (Asser International Sports Law Series).

De Waele, J.-M. and A. Husting. *Sport et Union Européenne.* Bruxelles: Éditions de l'Université de Bruxelles. 2001.

Spatial Planning

Adams, N. and J. Alden. *Regional Development and Spatial Planning in an Enlarged European Union.* Aldershot: Ashgate. 2006.

Altrock, U., et al. *Spatial Planning and Urban Development in the New EU Member States: From Adjustment to Reinvention.* Aldershot: Ashgate Publishing. 2006 (Urban and Regional Planning and Development Series).

Balchin, P. and L. Sýkora. *Regional Policy and Planning in Europe.* London: Routledge. 1999.

Doria, L., et al. *Rethinking European Spatial Policy as a Hologram: Actions, Institutions, Discourses.* Ashgate Publishing. 2006 (Urban and Regional Planning and Development Series).

Faludi, A. K. F. and B. Waterhout. *The Making of the European Spatial Development Perspective: No. Masterplan.* London: Routledge. 2002 (The RTPI Library Series; 2).

Faludi, A. *European Spatial Planning.* Cambridge, MA: Lincoln Institute of Land Policy. 2002.

Jönsson, C., et al. *Organizing European Space.* London: Sage. 2000.

Tewdwr-Jones, M. and R. H. Williams. *The European Dimension of British Planning.* London: Spon Press. 2001.

Media

Castendyk, O., Dommering, E.J. and Scheuer, A., *European Media Law*, Kluwer Law International. 2007.

Daufeldt, D. *Duale Rundfunkordnung im digitalen und europäischen Medienzeitalter*, S.l.: s.n., 2002.

Flood, P. and D. Kevin. *Media and Cultural Policy in the Enlarged European Union.* Mahwah, NJ: Lawrence Erlbaum Associates. 2004 (Trends in Communication; Vol. 12 issue 4).

Harcourt, A. *The European Union and the Regulation of Media Markets.* Manchester: Manchester University Press. 2005 (European Policy Research Unit Series).

Holmes J. 'European Community Law and the Cultural Aspects of Television'. In R.C. Smith. *Culture and European Union Law.* Oxford. 2004:169.

Holoubek, M., et al. *Regulating Content: European Regulatory Framework for the Media and Related Creative Sectors.* Alphen van den Rijn: Kluwer Law International. 2007 (European Monographs; 53).

Institut für Europäisches Medienrecht. *Die Zukunft der Fernsehrichtlinie = The Future of the 'Television without Frontiers' Directive.* Baden-Baden: Nomos. 2005. (Schriftenreihe des Instituts für Europäisches Medienrecht (EMR); Bd. 29).

Levy, D. A. L. *Europe's Digital Revolution: Broadcasting Regulation, the EU and the Nation State.* London: Routledge. 1999 (Routledge Research in European Public Policy; 5).

Nihoul, P. and P. Rodford. *EU Electronic Communications Law: Competition and Regulation in the European Telecommunications Market.* Oxford: Oxford University Press. 2004.

Nikoltchev, S. *Audiovisual Media Services without Frontiers: Implementing the Rules.* Strasbourg: European Audiovisual Observatory. 2006 (IRIS special).

Nitsche, I. *Broadcasting in the European Union: The Role of Public Interest in Competition Analysis.* The Hague: T.M.C. Asser Press. 2001.

Roider, C. *Perspektiven einer europäischen Rundfunkordnung : eine Untersuchung der gemeinschaftsrechtlichen Direktiven unter besonderer Berücksichtigung des Pluralismusgebots.* Berlin: Duncker & Humblot. 2001 (Schriften zum Europäischen Recht; Bd. 81).

Sarikakis, K. *Media and Cultural Policy in the European Union.* Amsterdam: Rodopi. 2007 (European studies; 24).

Sarikakis, K. *Powers in Media Policy: The Challenge of the European Parliament.* Oxford: Lang, 2004.

Smith, R.C. 'Rethinking European Union Competence in the Field of Media Ownership: the Internal Market, Fundamental Rights and European Citizenship'. (2004) EL Rev., 652.

Chapter XII

Sectoral Policies

R. Barents and P.J. Slot*

1   GENERAL COMMENTS

1.1   BACKGROUND

A sectoral policy consists of measures which relate to one specific sector of socio-
economic life; as a result, the relevant market (or markets) for goods or services is
subject to a separate legal regime which deviates, to a greater or lesser extent, from
the general rules of economic law. Under the Community treaties, this is the case
for agriculture, transport and nuclear energy, and this used to be the case for coal
and steel, until the expiry of the European Coal and Steel Community (ECSC)
Treaty in 2002. Since the Treaty of Maastricht, there also exists a Community
competence in relation to industrial policy, which in principle could be exercised
using a sectoral approach; but its practical significance is limited. The European
Community (EC) has developed a specific policy for telecommunications on the
basis of the various harmonization powers. Research and technological development policy as well as policy on trans-European networks are actually not sectoral
policies but functional policies, but they are also discussed in this chapter because
they are directly related to sectoral policy in the strict sense, particularly as concerns industry, transport and telecommunications.

---

*   Section 1: R. Barents and P.J. Slot; section 2: R. Barents; remaining sections: P.J. Slot.

P.J.G. Kapteyn, A.M. McDonnell, K.J.M. Mortelmans and C.W.A. Timmermans (eds),
The Law of the European Union and the European Communities, pp. 1143–1271.
©2008 Kluwer Law International BV, The Netherlands.

The EC Treaty lacks a specific set of rules for the energy sector.[1] The background to this is that at the time the original European Economic Community (EEC) Treaty entered into force, nuclear (or atomic) energy was seen as the most important source of energy for the future, while at the same time account had to be taken of the need to make the (then) EEC less dependent on imported oil – an element which became particularly salient as a result of the interruption of supplies of this energy source due to the Suez crisis in 1956. The importance attached to nuclear energy is evident from the fact that separate arrangements were made for this matter, outside the EEC, in the Euratom Treaty, which established the European Atomic Energy Community (EAEC, or Euratom). In reality, the picture turned out quite differently. The 'promised land' of atomic energy was never fully reached. As a result, the substantial dependence of the EC on imported oil has remained – which explains why a Community system of reserves was built up after the 1974 oil crisis. It was only in the perspective of the completion of the internal market that the EC started to be more active in opening up the natural gas and electricity sectors, which tended to be controlled by state enterprises. The liberalization of these sectors is now on the Union's agenda.[2]

The reason behind the existence of the two most important sectoral policies provided for in the EC Treaty – agriculture and transport – is that these two sectors were subject to specific and often far-reaching intervention measures in the Member States, dating back to the period after the First World War for most countries. Bringing about a common market in these two sectors would mean that the national regulatory measures could no longer be maintained. As a result, it was necessary to provide for special Community measures, as is evident from Articles 3(1)(e) EC and 32(4) EC on agriculture, and 3(1)(f) EC and 51(1) EC on transport.

1.2   LEGAL CHARACTERISTICS

Any sectoral policy obviously has its own characteristics, flowing from the nature of the product or service involved. Nevertheless, a number of common legal elements may be mentioned, linked to the fact that a sectoral policy concerns a specific set of arrangements which deviates from the general regulatory framework; these determine to a large extent the form and further development of such policies.

In the first place, sectoral policies, even more than other areas of economic life, reveal a great interdependence between positive and negative integration: the

---

1. The anodyne reference to 'measures in the sphere of energy' in Art. 3(1)u EC cannot be viewed as forming a set of rules. The Lisbon Treaty will include energy in the areas of shared competences, under Art. 4(2)(i) Treaty on the Functioning of the European Union (TFEU). That Treaty will also contain a specific Art. 194, on energy. The Euratom Treaty will however remain in force.
2. Art. 194 TFEU, following the Lisbon Treaty, identifies as objectives the functioning of the energy market, security of supply, energy efficiency and saving, as well as interconnection of energy networks.

one is simply not possible without the other. For the agricultural sector, this meant a Community policy consisting of a large number of market regulations for the most important agricultural products. These regulations were – barring a few exceptions – put into place already before the end of the transitional period (1970), so that free movement of agricultural products was already achieved in the second half of the 1960s. In the transport sector, a quite different picture was evident: because the implementation of a common transport policy only took shape at the end of the 1980s, there could be no question of freedom to provide services in this sector up until then. At the same time, the far-reaching form of integration required by a sectoral policy means that it is also susceptible to developments of a general economic nature in areas where integration has not progressed that far. This is particularly evident in the developments in the agricultural sector as a result of the lapse of the fixed exchange rate system but without the establishment of the economic and monetary union. In the period 1968–1993, as a result of that situation, the common market for agricultural products was in actual fact split up by a system of monetary compensatory amounts levied or granted per Member State, so as to be able to carry out a price policy which was based on a common unit of account.

In the second place, this interrelationship is expressed by the fact that specific rules in the framework of the sectoral policy have an impact on almost all elements covered by general rules in the EC Treaty; this is for instance the case for competition law in the agricultural sector, for which a separate regulation was adopted deviating from the general regime of Articles 81 and 82 EC. In the transport sector, specific provisions on the social aspects of transport, provisions on access to the market, and technical rules were necessary to accompany liberalization. In the agricultural sector, there is a different regime for state aids, and the free movement of agricultural products requires a far-reaching harmonization of all rules relating to health of humans, animals and plants.

In the third place, the regulation of these sectors is strongly influenced by considerations of an income policy nature. The interventions in these sectors result from specific problems of supply and demand, in particular the existence of a large number of small-scale and marginal firms. The political necessity to guarantee the continued existence of these firms requires measures which tend to 'correct' the results of the working of the market mechanism to a far-reaching extent. All kinds of subsidies and other protective measures therefore continually · involve the danger that they contribute to a tendency which often already exists in any case, i.e., the formation of surpluses. For the agricultural sector, characterized by overproduction, this situation is patently obvious. The fisheries sector is plagued by a large surplus capacity, as a result of, among other things, diminishing fish stocks and excess fishing capacity. Similar situations may be found in the steel industry and inland waterway transport. The need to protect the national transport sectors against external competition was one of the most important reasons why a common policy in this sector could only be realized at a much later stage.

In the fourth place, the interrelationship between positive and negative integration is revealed by the fact that it was in the agriculture and transport sectors that the question of the extent of the Community's external powers first arose.[3]

As a fifth characteristic, it may be mentioned that each sector has its own particular type of administrative law. In the framework of the completion of the internal market and the global trend towards liberalization of trade, the common transport policy has been constructed along rather liberal lines since the end of the 1980s. The same influence has been felt in the area of agricultural policy, which has also been pushed in a more market-oriented direction since that period, as a result of which the rigid market regulations focused on price intervention have been replaced by arrangements for direct income support to agricultural producers.

The reduction in the degree of intervention in these sectors has increased the possibilities of paying more attention to environmental aspects, so that the general environmental policy of the EC has been made more coherent and, in turn, can take its place at global level. In more general terms, policy in these sectors reveals an increasing degree of integration in the overall policy of the EC. This is particularly evident from the place of sectoral policies in the framework of initiatives aimed at reducing the great regional differences – in the agricultural sector, by means of rural policy, which is itself part of the general spectrum of regional policy instruments, and in the transport sector *inter alia* by means of the trans-European networks. Both these developments lead to an increase in EC involvement in questions of urban and rural planning. This does not make the implementation of sectoral policies at the Community level any easier: the objectives of those policies are not always identical with the objectives of horizontal and flanking policies, and there has to be a continual balancing of the two. This last aspect is revealed, amongst other things, by the case law on the extent and nature of the discretionary powers of the Community legislature in these areas.

2   AGRICULTURE AND FISHERIES

2.1   THE NATURE OF THE AGRICULTURAL PROBLEMS

Public authorities have since time immemorial been concerned about agriculture. Already in the nineteenth century there had developed the specialty presently known as agricultural law. It was principally concerned with the legal status of the farmer's land (title, mortgages and succession, etc.). At the beginning of the twentieth century, and particularly in the period between the two world wars, agricultural markets were subject to intensive government intervention. To an important extent, this market regulation was due to a number of specific

---

3.   Case 22/70, *Commission v. Council (ERTA)*; Joined Cases 3, 4 & 6/76, *Kramer et al.*

characteristics of the agricultural sector compared with other sectors of the economy. Some of the structural causes of the permanent problems, which are relevant to an understanding of European agricultural policy, will be briefly mentioned here.[4]

Neither the demand for nor the supply of agricultural products is very susceptible to rises or falls in prices (this is known as low price elasticity of supply and demand). In the short-term, the volume of production depends – particularly for plant products – mainly on climatological factors. In addition, there is a weak price elasticity (and for a number of products also a weak income elasticity) of demand, i.e., changes in price or income have little effect on demand. For generations already, the agricultural sector has been confronted by massive surpluses or sometimes massive shortages, resulting in unstable markets and price relationships. Many agricultural products are substitutable, both in terms of demand and supply, so that unstable situations for one product exercise a direct effect on the situation of other products. A surplus of milk, for example, may lead to the wholesale slaughter of milk cows, and an increase in the supply of beef, which can interfere with the market for pork.

In the long term these problems stem from the structure of supply and demand. On the demand side problems may arise through a low or stagnating population growth, so that the improvements in mechanization, intensive farming and productivity cannot be fully absorbed: structural surpluses then result. In many countries, principally the southern Member States, agricultural structures are relatively underdeveloped, primarily due to natural factors such as hill and mountain farming, climate, and inadequate infrastructure, and the level of organization of production and trade in agricultural products is relatively low. These structural weaknesses often go hand in hand with social inequalities and retarded economic development. Such factors also play a role in the agricultural sectors in the new Member States in Central and Eastern Europe, who also have to face the problems linked to the transition from collective forms of organization to market economies. Another important element in the problem is the relative immobility of production. In some countries, agricultural land is scarce and more profitable production requires an active policy of land reallocation, infrastructural improvements and so on. It is still the case that most agricultural holdings are in the hands of marginal or almost marginal family enterprises, which, while economically of limited significance, have a social and electoral influence which should not be underestimated. Moreover, farmers are vitally important for management of the environment and natural surroundings.

This brief overview makes it clear that any form of intervention in the agricultural markets must deal not merely with short-term problems (market and price policies), it must also embrace the longer term (agricultural structures). Intervention in the context of market and price policies almost always aims to increase prices or producer incomes. Two types of short-term intervention should be

---

4. For more extensive discussion see M. Tracy, *Agriculture in Europe. Challenges and Response, 1880–1980*, 2nd ed. (London, 1982).

distinguished: the first involves supplements to the income of the producers, in the form of subsidies – whether product-related or not. In this situation, there is free price formation for agricultural products, and farmers sell their products at market prices, but receive 'deficiency payments' so as to assure them a certain income. This was long the system followed in the United Kingdom, but even before its accession to the Communities the United Kingdom government started to adapt this system to the Community system. The second type – which was the standard practice in most European countries apart from the United Kingdom and Ireland – involves a system of price interventions, whereby surplus production which would depress prices is taken out of the national market through government financed purchases. This of course requires effective prevention of the undermining of this equilibrium by much cheaper imports from third countries; variable import levies have thus been imposed to bring third-country imports up to the Community price level, and export subsidies have been paid to compensate farmers for the lower prices on the world market. In some cases this policy was accompanied by centralization of imports and exports of agricultural products. Price-stabilizing measures may also take the form of production quotas, which may be used in order to avoid disastrous price competition and the resulting demise of many marginal producers. The choice for one method or the other depends on myriad political, economic and financial considerations, and has been a subject of constant debate particularly in the economic literature.[5] Agricultural structural policy has not only to offer a long-term perspective for short-term interventions and their effects on the structure of supply and demand, it must also contribute to a harmonious development of the agricultural sector in public policy as a whole. Such policy is often related to competition policy (for instance in relation to cooperatives), and production and marketing structures, and is closely linked to regional and environmental policy.

2.2   THE AGRICULTURAL TITLE IN THE EC TREATY

2.2.1   The Common Agricultural Policy

It follows from old Article 7 EEC and the present Article 14 EC that the agricultural sector also forms part of the common market. This was by no means obvious, as is apparent from the fact that the first sentence of Article 32(1) explicitly states that the common market extends to agriculture and trade in agricultural products.[6] Given that for years all Member States had been regulating agricultural markets

---

5. *Ibidem.*
6. Case 83/78, *Pigs Marketing Board v. Raymond Redmond* and Case 177/78, *Pigs and Bacon Commission v. Mc Carren and Company Ltd.* If and when the Treaty of Lisbon enters into force, Art. 38 TFEU states 'The internal market shall extend to agriculture, fisheries and trade in agricultural products', since the term 'common market' is everywhere replaced by 'internal market'. For the rest, the Treaty if Lisbon does not entail substantial changes for material law in the agricultural sector.

to a greater or lesser extent in the framework of various types of market regulation, the application of the free movement of goods provisions after the transitional period would have irrevocably led to the undermining of these national market organizations which were primarily based on price interventions coupled with import and export regulation. The common market in the agricultural sector could therefore only be established by specific measures involving the communitarization of the national regulatory policies, a principle which is already set out in Article 3(1)(e) EC and developed in Articles 32–38 EC. What precisely these measures should be – which comprise 'a' or 'the' common policy – is not specified in the Treaty itself. These provisions only sketch a framework consisting of a number of objectives,[7] some global indication of instruments,[8] and a broad grant of powers.[9] Articles 3(1)(e) and 32(2) and (4) EC do express the factually and legally indissoluble link between the CAP and the common market for agricultural products.[10] The one is unimaginable without the other, as is confirmed by Article 37(3)(b) EC, which provides that the Community policy in this sector has the objective of creating a situation which is comparable to that of a national market.[11] The CAP thus embodies the most far-reaching form of integration provided for in the EC Treaty, namely a total fusion of positive and negative integration.[12] It is particularly on that point that the CAP has great economic and also legal significance for the whole integration process. The CAP not only serves to establish the common market, it is of essential importance for the whole of Community policy, in particular relating to the strengthening of economic and social cohesion, environmental policy, commercial policy, public health, consumer protection and development cooperation. The Court has recognized in very clear terms this connection between the CAP and negative and positive integration aspects.[13]

2.2.2 Objectives

The connection between market integration and policy integration explained above is apparent from the objectives of the CAP set out in Article 33(1) EC and the

---

7. Art. 33 EC.
8. Arts. 34–36 EC.
9. Art. 37 EC.
10. Case 250/84, *Eridania v. Cassa conguaglio zucchero*; Case C-27/90, *SITPA v. ONIFLHOR*; Joined Cases C-133, 300 & 362/93, *Crispoltoni and others v. Fattoria Autonoma Tabacchi et al.*
11. Case 31/74, *Galli* and Case 68/86, *United Kingdom v. Council*.
12. In relation to the common organizations of the markets this principle means that after the end of the transitional period the free movement of goods provisions have become an integral part of these organizations, see Joined Cases 3, 4 & 6/76, *Kramer*; Case 83/78, *Pigs Marketing Board*; Case 251/78, *Denkavit Futtermittel* and Case 29/82, *Van Luipen*. This 'integral part' principle is confusingly sometimes referred to as the 'open market' principle, see in particular Case 190/73, *Officier van Justitie v. Van Haaster*, and Case 111/76, *Officier van Justitie v. Van den Hazel*; Case 94/79, *Vriend*, and Case C-44/94, *The Queen v. Minister of Agriculture, Fisheries and Food, ex parte Fishermen's Organisations et al.*
13. Joined Cases 80 & 81/77, *Commissionnaires réunis and Ramel v. Receveur des douanes*; Case 4/79, *Providence Agricole*.

general guidelines expressed in Article 33(2) EC. By their very nature these objectives, both as to the short term and the long term, and constituting an integral whole, can only be achieved in a completely communitarized agricultural market. The Court has drawn the important conclusion from this that the concept of a CAP, which is not clearly defined anywhere in the Agriculture Title, has an objective and indivisible character. Thus all measures which relate to the realization of free movement of agricultural products contribute by their nature to these objectives, and as such constitute a matter falling within the competence of the Community under Article 37 EC. This is particularly true for the harmonization of national legislation relating to veterinary, health and phytosanitary matters, zootechnical and plant improvement questions, and the complex mass of legislation involving the production, composition, presentation of and trade in straight and compound animal feedingstuffs.[14]

As has been indicated above, these objectives cover all aspects of agricultural policy. The objectives specified in Article 33(1)(a) and (b) relate primarily to structural policy; those in Article 33(1)(c), (d) and (e) mainly concern market and price policy. The achievement of these objectives, which in some ways are even in conflict with one another, requires, according to long-established case law, that the Community legislature should possess a wide margin of discretion so that account may be taken of, as appropriate, the political, economic and budgetary situation, and priorities established.[15] This choice of priorities means that in order to ensure the maintenance of the common market, it may even be split up, in principle on a temporary basis, by Community measures, if complete free movement is no longer possible for compelling reasons (e.g., crisis management in the framework of combatting cattle diseases). Against this background, the Community was entitled to apply the monetary compensatory amounts which were necessary when the system of fixed exchange rates became untenable at the beginning of the 1970s.[16] Another consequence of the competence to set priorities is that, within certain limits, Community legislation may take account in the field of agricultural policy of certain 'horizontal' interests, such as the protection of animal welfare, public health and other aspects.[17]

The precise relationship between short-term and long-term policies is not clearly expressed in the objectives. On the one hand it can be deduced from the

---

14. Cf. Case 68/86, *United Kingdom v. Council*; Case 131/86, *United Kingdom v. Council*; Case C-131/87, *Commission v. Council*; Case C-11/88, *Commission v. Council*; Case C-180/96, *United Kingdom v. Commission*.

15. E.g., Case 5/67, *Beus v. Hauptzollamt München*; Joined Cases 63–69/72, *Wilhelm Werhahn Hansamühle et al. v. Council*; Joined Cases 197–200, 243, 245 & 247/80, *Ludwigshafener Walzmühle v. Council and Commission*; Case 59/83, *Biovilac v. EEC*; Case C-311/90, *Hierl v. Hauptzollamt Regensburg*; Case C-353/92, *Greece v. Council*; Case C-280/93, *Germany v. Council*.

16. E.g., Case 5/73, *Balkan Import Export v. Hauptzollamt Berlin Packhof*; Joined Cases 80 & 81/77, *Commissionnaires réunis and Ramel v. Receveur des douanes*.

17. Joined Cases 141–143/81, *Holdijk*; Case C-146/91, *KYDEP v. Council and Commission*; Case C-336/00, *Huber*; Case C-189/01, *Jippes*.

introductory word 'thus' in Article 33(1)(b) EC that increasing the individual earnings of persons engaged in agriculture should principally be achieved by structural measures.[18] On the other hand, the improvement of individual earnings can also be seen in a normative context, in the sense that there is an obligation to realize such an increase, which implies a more or less permanent short-term intervention policy. The relationship between the two components of agricultural policy is a matter for the Council's discretionary power.[19] This background explains why the Court has never accepted that Article 33 EC could be a source of individual rights relating to income (with, as a consequence, a certain intervention policy) or economic freedom (with, as a consequence, the absence or limitation of such an intervention policy).[20] Thus Article 33 forms an obligation for the Community and the Member States to take various steps, but it does not confer direct rights on operators in the agricultural sector.[21] In any event, both limbs of Article 33 EC make it plain that the CAP, in legal terms as in other terms, cannot only consist of a market and price policy. The factual accuracy of this legal statement has been confirmed in more than 40 years of the existence of the CAP. While an improvement in producer incomes remains a matter of purely short-term policy, the inevitable consequence is that the price level to be achieved on the market through intervention is fixed at the level of the marginal undertaking, with the result that a major incentive is created for industrialized agricultural producers to increase production. The disregard of the structural component of agricultural policy has contributed to the fact that about 80% of agricultural production is accounted for by approximately 20% of agricultural firms, whereas there has only been very limited change in agricultural structures through the years.

2.2.3 Scope

As has been noted above, the EC Treaty is silent as to what is meant by 'a' or 'the' Common Agricultural Policy (CAP). Article 32(2) and (3) EC do give a description of what are agricultural products, referring to the list of products contained in Annex I to the EC Treaty.[22] The text of both these parts of Article 32 EC – together with the case law – makes it clear that whether or not a product is on that

---

18. Joined Cases 36 & 71/80, *Irish Creamery Milk Suppliers Association et al. v. Government of Ireland et al.*; Case 297/82, *De Samvirkende Danske Landboforeninger v. Ministry of Fiscal Affairs.*
19. E.g., Case 114/76, *Bela-Mühle Josef Bergmann v. Grows-Farm*. The Court annulled the contested regulation finding that there was a discriminatory distribution of the burden of costs between the various agricultural sectors, and that the obligation involved was not necessary to attain the objective in view.
20. E.g., Case 139/79, *Maizena v. Council*; Case 106/81, *Kind v. EEC*; Case 281/84, *Zuckerfabrik Bedburg v. Council and Commission*; Case C-280/93, *Germany v. Council*.
21. Case 114/76, *Bela-Mühle*; Case 138/78, *Stölting v. Hauptzollamt Frankfurt-Jonas*; Case 237/82, *Jongeneel Kaas.*
22. Case 61/80, *Coöperatieve Stremsel- en Kleurselfabriek v. Commission*; Case 123/83, *BNIC v. Clair*; Case T-61/89, *Dansk Pelsdyravlerforening v. Commission.*

list is decisive.[23] This limitative list did not, though, prevent products being brought within the scope of application of the Title on Agriculture which are not specified therein, but which are economically or functionally of essential importance to the products which are mentioned therein.[24] A practical consequence of this demarcation of the Title on Agriculture by means of a list of agricultural products is that the EC Treaty does not make clear what should be understood by the concepts of agricultural holding or producers of agricultural products; this can lead to problems in relation to measures which are not linked to products but to groups of people.[25]

According to the text of Article 32 EC and the list of fish, crustaceans and molluscs in Annex I, the provisions of the Title on Agriculture also apply to saltwater and freshwater fisheries.[26] In 1977, the EC – following the example of many third countries – extended its fishing waters to 200 sea miles from the coast. This extension necessitated the development of a policy for the conservation of the biological resources of the sea, and for the division of the scarce fishing rights in the thus extended Community seas between the Member States and third countries. The power to pursue such a policy and the power associated therewith to enter into international agreements has been recognized by the Court of Justice.[27]

2.2.4   Means

Article 32(2) and (4) EC make it plain that the means to achieve the objectives and guidelines set out in Article 33 EC concern both the free movement of agricultural products (the common market) and a policy specifically relating to the agricultural sector (the common policy). The significance and connection of these two instruments has been clarified in the case law of the Court in two respects. First, since the end of the transitional period the Member States may not maintain in force any measures which conflict with the free movement of goods provisions.[28] This means in practical terms that national market organizations have become well nigh impossible, a principle which applies also if the Community has not taken or been able to take common measures in a particular sector.[29] In relation to the

---

23. Case 61/80, *Coöperatieve Stremsel- en Kleurselfabriek*; Case 77/83, *CILFIT*; Case C-295/88, *Corman v. Belgian State and Grand Duchy of Luxembourg*.
24. Originally Art. 308 EC was used, later always Art. 37 EC.
25. As to this problem, see Case 85/77, *Société Azienda Avicola Sant'Anna v. Istituto Nazionale della Previdenza Sociale (INPS) and Servizio Contributi Agricoli Unificati (SCAU)*; Case 139/77, *Denkavit v. Finanzamt Warendorf*; Case 312/85, *Villa Banfi v. Regione Toscana*, Case C-162/91, *Tenuta in Bosco v. Ministero delle finanze dello Stato*; Case C-403/98, *Monte Arcosu*.
26. It should be noted that, if the Treaty of Lisbon enters into force, Art. 38(1) TFEU explicitly indicates that the CAP also concerns the fisheries sector.
27. Joined Cases 3, 4 & 6/76, *Kramer*.
28. Case 48/74, *Charmasson v. Ministre de l'économie and des finances*; Case 118/78, *Meijer v. Department of Trade et al.*; Case 232/78, *Commission v. France*; Joined Cases 194 & 241/85, *Commission v. Greece*; Case 119/86, *Spain v. Council et al.*
29. See Case 232/78, *Commission v. France*. In non-regulated sectors Art. 38 EC, which envisages the possibility of countervailing measures, retains some significance; this provision has only been applied in the alcoholic drinks sector, see Case 337/82, *St. Nikolaus Brennerei und*

Member States, the common market takes precedence over national market organizations, although the exceptions of Article 30 EC remain applicable as long as the
measures based thereupon have not been superseded by harmonization of laws.[30]
In relation to the Community itself, however, the situation is different, and is
actually to be regarded as the mirror-image of the prohibition of unilateral intervention measures by the Member States. Although the Community is also bound by
the free movement of goods provisions,[31] it is entitled, should the Community
interest so require, to adopt measures on the basis of Article 37 EC, which in
principle could involve a temporary division of the common market. Apart from
the monetary compensation measures, mentioned above, the case law has accepted
the de facto division on national lines by production quotas (e.g., sugar) or dual
market organizations established per Member State.[32] An example of this latter
approach can be seen in the old sheepmeat market organization, which, as a result
of political problems, was based on a system of premiums 'per ewe' for the United
Kingdom, and in the other Member States on a system of price intervention. This
meant that mutton and lamb exported from the United Kingdom to the other
Member States was subject to an export levy equal to the ewe premium received
(the clawback system). In these and other cases the Court regarded such measures
as permissible, as long as they were based on Community action which aimed to
maintain the common market as much as possible, or to complete it at a later
stage.[33] Moreover, the initial failure on the part of the Council to take conservation
measures led to important case law concerning the powers of the Commission
and the Member States in a situation of 'legal vacuum' resulting from political
disagreement.[34]

2.2.5 Regulation of the Market

Article 34(1) EC makes it clear that the core of the CAP is the common regulation
of agricultural markets, and that this may take three forms: either common rules on
competition, or compulsory coordination of the various national market organizations, or a European market organization. From this summary it is apparent that the

---

 Likörfabrik v. Hauptzollamt Krefeld; Case 114/83, *Société d'initiatives et de coopération
 agricoles v. Commission*; Case 181/85, *France v. Commission*.

30. E.g., See Case 251/78, *Denkavit Futtermittel*; Case 40/82, *Commission v. United Kingdom*;
 Case 261/85, *Commission v. United Kingdom*; Case 118/86, *Openbaar Ministerie v. Nertsvoe-
 derfabriek Nederland*; Case 29/87, *Dansk Denkavit v. Landbrugsministeriet*; Case C-5/94, *The
 Queen v. Ministry of Agriculture, Fisheries and Food, ex parte Hedley Lomas*.
31. Joined Cases 80 & 81/77, *Commissionnaires réunis and Ramel*; Case 179/78, *Procureur de la
 République v. Michelangelo Rivoira et al.*; Case 15/83, *Denkavit Nederland*; Case 199/84,
 Procuratore della Republica v. Migliorini and Fischl. See K.J.M. Mortelmans, 'The Relationship between the Treaty Rules and Community Measures for the Establishment and Functioning
 of the Internal Market: Towards a Concordance Rule', (2002) CML Rev., 1303–1346.
32. E.g., Case 138/79, *Roquette v. Council*; Case 139/79, *Maizena*.
33. Case 106/81, *Kind*; Case 61/86, *United Kingdom v. Commission*; Case 162/86, *Livestock Sales
 Transport v. Intervention Board for Agricultural Produce*.
34. Case 804/79, *Commission v. United Kingdom*.

concept of a European market organization means nothing other than that the Community legislature should prescribe which of these models of regulation should be chosen in order to achieve the objectives specified in Article 33 EC.[35] The legal difference between the agricultural sector and other sectors of the economy is such that the choice of model for the coordination of supply and demand in the former requires an express decision by the Community.[36] As has been noted, the model to be chosen may range from the relatively liberal model of competition rules (dealing with cooperatives, quality rules for agricultural products, and external protection through the Common Customs Tariff) to a more interventionist model in the form of a real sectoral or other type of market regulation for the Community market as a whole.[37]

From the non-exhaustive summary[38] of measures in the first and third sentences of Article 34(2) EC, it appears that the framers of the Treaty had a preference for price intervention policy, based on certain guarantees for the producer and on protection from external forces, which is also indicated by the reference to guarantee funds in Article 34(3) EC. The decisive criterion for the measures to be applied is their necessity in the light of Article 33 EC.[39] This is also apparent from the wording of Articles 35 and 36 EC, concerning, respectively, a number of issues linked to the structure of agriculture and competition. The powers conferred on the Community have always been broadly interpreted,[40] so that many types of measures not enumerated in Article 34(2) have been accepted which tend to restrict economic freedom much more than the types of measures which are enumerated therein; examples of such measures are production restrictions,[41] production prohibitions,[42] purchase and delivery obligations,[43] various types of import and production levies (such as the well-known co-responsibility levies and the

---

35. See Cases 6/71, *Rheinmühlen Düsseldorf v. Einfuhr- und Vorratsstelle für Getreide und Futtermittel*; Case 153/73, *Holz & Willemsen v. Council and Commission*; Case 8/78, *Milac v. Hauptzollamt Freiburg*.
36. Case 51/74, *Van der Hulst v. Produktschap voor Siergewassen.*
37. The terms 'a common organization of agricultural markets' and a 'European market organization' used in Art. 34(1) are in fact two distinct concepts, as is also clear from the German version of the EC Treaty (*eine gemeinsame Organization der Agrarmärkte* and *eine Europäische Marktordnung*). Thus the former covers all three models specified in that provision, whereas the latter is a Community-wide common organization, see Cases 90 & 91/63, *Commission v. Luxembourg and Belgium*; Case 48/74, *Charmasson*; Joined Cases 194 & 241/85, *Commission v. Greece*. The English and French versions of Art. 34(1) EC make this somewhat less clear, and are sometimes invoked to support the argument that 'a common organization' has to be 'a European market organization'.
38. Case C-240/90, *Germany v. Commission.*
39. Ibid. and Case 34/70, *Syndicat national du commerce extérieur des céréales et al. v. O.N.I.C.*
40. Case 57/72, *Westzucker v. Einfuhr- und Vorratsstelle für Zucker.*
41. Case 230/78, *Eridania*; Case 139/79, *Maizena*; Case 84/87, *Erpelding v. Secrétaire d'État à l'Agriculture and à la Viticulture.*
42. In order to reduce surpluses, Case C-331/88, *The Queen v. Ministry of Agriculture, Fisheries and Food, ex parte FEDESA et al.*
43. Case 114/76, *Bela-Mühle Josef Bergmann.*

super levies)[44] and various types of deposit obligations.[45] It should be observed that so far the Court has not condemned any category of intervention measures to be as such incompatible with the provisions of the EC Treaty or with general principles of law.[46]

The market-regulatory action by the Community may have the objective of conserving certain natural resources, as is the case with catch quotas for sea fishing.[47] The term 'all measures' in Article 34(2) EC does not merely refer to the substantive provisions of the CAP, but also to their implementation (control and enforcement).[48] An important element in the regulation of markets is formed further by the extensive and highly detailed harmonization of veterinary, health, phytosanitary and technical aspects of agriculture, plant and animal improvement, and the fight against animal and plant disease which is associated with these. There is extensive case law on all these aspects.[49] The importance of this element for the unity of the market, and the interrelationship of agricultural policy and the requirements of public health and consumer protection has been revealed in recent years in particular by the problems relating to BSE (mad cow disease), foot-and-mouth disease, avian 'flu (bird 'flu), and various other animal illnesses.[50]

The regulation of the various markets is limited by the two standards of legality set out in the second sentence of Article 34(2) EC: proportionality and non-discrimination. The proportionality principle[51] restricts intervention in the market mechanism to what is necessary in the light of the objectives of the CAP, though it should be mentioned that the evaluation of the necessity of

---

44. The basic criterion for levies is to be found in Case 17/67, *Neumann v. Hauptzollamt Hof/Saale*. See also Case 108/81, *Amylum v. Council*; Case 179/84, *Bozzetti v. Invernizzi*; Case 265/87, *Schräder v. Hauptzollamt Gronau*; Case C-8/89, *Zardi v. Consorzio agrario provinciale di Ferrara*.
45. Case 11/70, *Internationale Handelsgesellschaft v. Einfuhr- und Vorratsstelle für Getreide und Futtermittel*.
46. Case 203/86, *Spain v. Council*; Case 84/87, *Erpelding*.
47. Joined Cases 3, 4 & 6/76, *Kramer et al.*
48. As to sanctions, see Case C-240/90, *Germany v. Commission*.
49. See especially Case 70/77, *Simmenthal v. Amministrazione delle finanze dello Stato*; Case 137/77, *Stadt Frankfurt v. Neumann*; Case 30/79, *Land Berlin v. Wigei*; Joined Cases 2–4/82, *Delhaize*; Case 1/83, *IFG v. Freistaat Bayern*; Case 37/83, *Rewe-Zentrale*; Case 214/88, *Amministrazione delle finanze dello Stato v. Politi*; Case C-143/91, *Criminal proceedings against Van der Tas*; Case C-52/92, *Commission v. Portugal*; Case C-432/92, *The Queen v. Minister of Agriculture, Fisheries and Food, ex parte Anastasiou*; Case C-315/93, *Flip and Verdegem v. Belgian State*; Case C-86/94, *De Venhorst v. Staatssecretaris van Landbouw, Natuurbeheer en Visserij*; Case C-27/95, *Woodspring District Council v. Bakers of Nailsea*; Case C-105/95, *Daut v. Oberkreisdirektor des Kreises Gütersloh*; Case C-183/95, *Affish v. Rijksdienst voor de keuring van Vee en Vlees*; Case C-100/96, *British Agrochemicals Association*; Case C-106/97, *DADI and Douane-Agenten*.
50. Case C-157/96, *The Queen v. Ministry of Agriculture, Fisheries and Food and Commissioners of Customs & Excise, ex parte National Farmers' Union et al.*; Case C-180/96, *United Kingdom v. Commission*; Case C-365/99, *Portugal v. Commission*; Case C-428/99, *Van den Bor*; Case C-241/01, *National Farmers' Union*.
51. As to which, see, generally, Ch. III of this book and literature mentioned therein.

measures is a matter for the Council's margin of discretion pursuant to Article 37 EC.[52] The non-discrimination principle refers, although the wording appears to suggest otherwise, to equal treatment among producers, or among consumers, including the processing industry (but not as between producers and consumers).[53] Both criteria have evolved in the Court's case law as concrete expressions of the general legal principles of proportionality and equality.[54] The Member States are also bound by these principles when they implement the CAP.[55]

2.2.6   Competition

Article 36 EC is closely linked to Article 34 EC; the latter provision governs the extent to which the Community may affect competition in the common market through its regulatory action in order to achieve the objectives of Article 33 EC. In the case law it has been expressly recognized that the CAP takes priority over the system of undistorted competition prescribed by Article 3(1)(g) EC,[56] and that such competition is only one of the interests which the Community may take into account in the framework of its discretionary powers.[57] Article 36 EC governs the interference with competition in the common market for agricultural products by undertakings (primarily cooperatives) and by the Member States (through state aids). Depending on which of the three models is chosen for the CAP,[58] such private or national measures restricting competition may play a useful role, subject of course to this taking place on the basis of a Community law framework. Thus Article 36 EC permits the establishment of a distinct competition regime for the agricultural sector.[59]

In the absence of a Council decision on the matter, the application of the competition rules of the Treaty (Arts. 81–89 EC) is suspended.[60] Once taken, the Council decision may involve applying those rules, or not, in whole or in part, conditionally or unconditionally, to all or to certain sectors and activities. In Regulation 26/62[61] the Council used this power to permit, as far as the competition rules for undertakings are concerned, three, somewhat unclear, exceptions to the prohibitions contained in Article 81(1) EC; the principal practical

---

52. E.g., Case 5/73, *Balkan Import Export*; Case C-280/93, *Germany v. Council*; Case C-150/94, *United Kingdom v. Council*; Case C-17/98, *Emesa Sugar*; Case C-306/93, *SMW Winzersekt v. Land Rheinland-Pfalz*.
53. Case 5/73, *Balkan Import Export*; Case C-306/93, *SMW Winzersekt*.
54. Case 153/73, *Holz & Willemsen*; Joined Cases 117/76 & 16/77, *Ruckdeschel et al. v. Hauptzollamt Hamburg-St. Annen*.
55. Case 111/76, *Van den Hazel*; Joined Cases 201 & 202/85, *Klensch v. Secrétaire d'État*.
56. Joined Cases 41–44/70, *International Fruit Company et al. v. Commission*; Case 139/79, *Maizena*.
57. Case 68/86, *United Kingdom v. Council*; C-280/93 R, *Germany v. Council*.
58. Art. 34(1) EC.
59. Case C-280/93 R, *Germany v. Council*; Case C-456/00, *France v. Commission*.
60. Case 73/79, *Commission v. Italy*; Case 337/82, *St. Nikolaus Brennerei und Likörfabrik*.
61. O.J. 1962, p. 993; codified by Reg. 1184/2006, O.J. 2006, L 214/7.

importance of these is for agricultural cooperatives.[62] As far as the rules on state aids are concerned, Regulation 26 only provides for the application of Article 88(1) and the first sentence of Article 88(3) EC. The non-applicability of Articles 87–89 EC is in fact of scant practical importance, given that in various schemes of common organization of the market those provisions are specifically declared applicable.[63] For this reason, the market organizations are also based on Article 36 EC as well as on Article 37 EC. The practical effect of the measures on the applicability of Articles 87–89 EC is that those provisions are inapplicable only in relation to sectors not covered by a common organization of the market.[64] If these articles do apply, their application may not be used to justify a derogation from the rules of the CAP.[65] The only exception to this is in the case of the clause on exceptional circumstances in Article 88(2) third sentence EC. On the basis of this clause, the Council may, in exceptional circumstances, decide that national aid shall be considered to be compatible with the common market, in derogation from the provisions of Article 87 or from the regulations provided for in Article 89, with the result that, in fact, the functioning of a common market organization may be interfered with, at least temporarily. This lack of Community coordination is of particular significance in the organization of the market in wine, which suffers structurally from surpluses.[66]

Article 36 EC applies only to the coordination of national aid measures, which are subject to Articles 87–89 EC.[67] National aid measures can also undergo far-reaching coordination on the basis of Article 37 EC, for example by obliging or permitting the Member States to apply certain types of aid measures. Thus both on the basis of Article 36 and on the basis of Article 37, the Community has wide powers to coordinate national aid measures, a power which is of great importance, primarily for structural policy.

---

62. See Case 71/74, *Fruit- en Groentenimporthandel and Frubo v. Commission*; Case 61/80, *Coöperatieve Stremsel- en Kleurselfabriek*; Case T-61/89, *Dansk Pelsdyravlerforening*; Joined Cases T-70 & 71/92, *Florimex and VGB v. Commission*; Case C-250/92, *Gøttrup-Klim and others Grovvareforeninger v. Dansk Landbrugs Grovvareselskab*; Case C-319/93, *Dijkstra et al. v. Friesland (Frico Domo) Coöperatie et al.*; Case C-399/93, *Oude Luttikhuis et al. v. Verenigde Coöperatieve Melkindustrie Coberco*. Of these, the last two are the most important, see Ackermann (1997) 34 CML Rev., 695 and P.J. Slot (1997) SEW, 204.
63. But even these clauses contain exceptions, e.g., in the case of sugar and milk, see Case 105/76, *Interzuccheri S.p.A. v. Società Rezzano e Cavassa*; Case 73/79, *Commission v. Italy*.
64. In that case, Art. 38 EC is applicable see note 29 *supra*.
65. Case C-456/00, *France v. Commission*.
66. Case C-122/94, *Commission v. Council*; Case C-309/95, *Commission v. Council*; Case 110/02, *Commission v. Council*.
67. Art. 36 EC clearly does not apply to Community aid measures, as they do not fall within the ambit of Arts. 87–89 EC, see Joined Cases 213–215/81, *Norddeutsches Vieh- und Fleischkantor Herbert Will et al. v. Bundesanstalt für landwirtschaftliche Marktordnung*.

2.2.7   Allocation of Powers

The real legal basis for the CAP is to be found in the very widely drafted
Article 37(2) EC. This provision also covers the conclusion of international agreements, a power which the Community has used extensively in relation to agreements with third countries concerning reciprocal access to fishing grounds.[68]

A constant line of case law demonstrates that Article 37 EC confers wide
discretionary powers on the basis of which the Community legislature may take
all measures which it regards as appropriate and necessary for the priorities
established in the light of the objectives set out in Article 33 EC.[69] The consultation procedure provided for in Article 37 EC is at present a notable exception
to the more generally prescribed co-decision procedure. Under the Treaty of
Lisbon, the ordinary legislative procedure (the new term for the co-decision
procedure) will also apply in the field of agriculture. Although Article 37 provides for qualified majority voting, it is in this sector that the Luxembourg
Accords of 1966[70] are still of great importance. The Council still tends to take
the most important decisions on the basis of unanimity, as is illustrated by the
annual marathon sessions for fixing the common prices and other aspects of market
and price policy. The use of the (de facto) 'right of veto' has even meant that on a
number of occasions the Council has been unable to reach decisions, so that it has
been impossible to fix prices for the forthcoming agricultural year. In part on the
basis of the case law on the failure by the Council to fulfil its obligations in the
fisheries sector,[71] the Commission has developed the practice of adopting
the necessary measures itself, on the basis of Articles 10 and 212 EC,[72] in the
absence of a Council decision.

As to the allocation of powers in the agricultural sector between the Community and the Member States, it appears from Article 34(2)(b) EC that the CAP does
not *a priori* mean that the Member States are no longer competent to take measures
in this sector.[73] The mere existence of common organizations of the market
concerned will not make the Member States incompetent. But the model of
organization chosen by the Community may well mean that the Member States
are unable to adopt any unilateral measures at all, or will be able to adopt only
very few such measures.[74] Thus, constant case law indicates that the common

---

68. See Joined Cases 3, 4 & 6/76 *Kramer et al.*
69. E.g., Joined Cases 83 & 94/76, 4, 15 & 40/77, *HNL v. Council and Commission*; Case 138/78,
     Stölting; Case 197/80, *Ludwigshafener Walzmühle*; Joined Cases C-267–285/88, *Wuidart
     et al. v. Laiterie coopérative eupenoise et al.*; Case C-306/93, *SMW Winzersekt*; Case
     C-122/94, *Commission v. Council.*
70. See Ch. V, section 4.1.1 *supra.*
71. Case 804/79, *Commission v. United Kingdom.*
72. Joined Cases 47 & 48/83, *Pluimveeslachterij Midden-Nederland.*
73. Joined Cases 141–143/81 *Holdijk*; Case 237/82, *Jongeneel Kaas.*
74. See e.g., Case 68/76, *Commission v. France*; Case 16/83, *Prantl*; Case 55/83, *Italy v.
     Commission*; Case 148/85, *Direction générale des impôts v. Forest*; Case 216/86, *Antonini v.
     Prefetto di Milano* [1987] ECR 2919.

organizations of the market mean that at the production and wholesale stages the Member States have scarcely any room for manoeuvre left in relation to the volume of production and prices, whereas the possibility to apply national aid measures concerning incomes, production or trading is expressly or implicitly excluded by the market organization schemes.[75] It is constant case law that where there is a regulation on the common organization of the market in a given sector, the Member States are under an obligation to refrain from taking any measures which might undermine it.[76]

2.2.8 Implementation and Application

Constant case law makes it plain that the Council is bound to prescribe the general rules of the measures concerned according to the procedure laid down in Article 37(2) EC.[77] In cases where the Council reserves to itself the right to adopt implementing measures, they can be adopted according to a simplified procedure, without consultation of the European Parliament.[78] More detailed implementation is left to the Commission, which may or may not have to act through a committee procedure (so-called 'comitology').[79] On the basis of their general obligation to implement Community law, under Article 10 EC, the Member States are obliged to adopt all necessary measures to guarantee the application and effectiveness of Community law in general and of the acts concerned in particular.[80] This means for instance that they must specify which bodies are charged with implementation and application. Initially it was usual for the regulation to use only general terms when obliging the Member States to take such measures. Gradually the Community legislation has come to contain more specific obligations concerning national implementation, particularly in relation to controls (especially financial irregularities and fraud), procedures, organizational matters and penalties.[81] The system of

---

75. E.g., Case 218/85, *Cerafel v. Le Campion*, which summarizes the rules on Member State competence.
76. Case C-1/96, *The Queen v. Minister of Agriculture, Fisheries and Food, ex parte Compassion in World Farming*; Case C-507/99, *Denkavit*.
77. Case 25/70, *Einfuhr- und Vorratsstelle für Getreide und Futtermittel v. Köster*; Case 121/83, *Zuckerfabrik Franken v. Hauptzollamt Würzburg*; Case 46/86, *Romkes v. Officier van Justitie*; Case C-357/88, *Hopermann v. BALM*; Case C-240/90, *Germany v. Commission*; Case C-156/93, *Parliament v. Commission*.
78. See Art. 202 EC, 3rd indent, 3rd sentence.
79. Joined Cases 194–206/83, *Asteris v. Commission*; Case 278/84, *Germany v. Commission*; Case 22/88, *Vreugdenhil et al. v. Minister van Landbouw en Visserij*; Joined Cases C-9, 23 & 150/95, *Belgium and Germany v. Commission*; Case C-228/99, *Silos*; Case C-317/99, *Kloosterboer Rotterdam*. As to comitology in general, see Ch. V, section 4.2, *supra*.
80. See Case 68/88, *Commission v. Greece*.
81. See in particular Reg. 3508/92, O.J. 1992, L 355/1, establishing an integrated administration and control system for certain Community aid schemes, see Case C-354/95, *Queen v. Minister for Agriculture, Fisheries and Food, ex parte: National Farmers' Union et al.*; Case C-369/98, *Fischer*; Case C-131/00, *Nilsson*; Case C-304/00, *Strawson and Gagg & Sons*; Case C-417/00, *Agrargenossenschaft Pretzsch*. See further Ch. VII section 6 *supra*.

lump sums and penalty payments under Article 228 EC can play an important role in this area.[82]

2.3   MARKET AND PRICE POLICY

The term 'market and price policy' usually covers the body of rules by means of which the Community Institutions try to bring supply and demand of agricultural products into balance in the short term (usually not longer than 1 year), in such a way as to ensure that producers are guaranteed a reasonable income, in conformity with the aims of Article 33 EC.

In the period from 1964 to approximately the beginning of the 1990s, this policy was implemented mainly in the form of product-related measures in the framework of sectoral common organizations of the market. These organizations brought about the free movement of agricultural products, whose prices on the internal market were influenced by a panoply of subsidies and levies, in order to reach a price level which was determined in the political arena. The determination of these common prices took place annually in the Council, usually during marathon sessions in the course of which the Member States negotiated with one another in order to guarantee their own specific agricultural interests.

These common organizations of the market also entailed an isolation of the internal market from the world market, by means of a system of import levies and export subsidies, in order to counteract the distortionary effects of the world prices – which tended to be lower than the Community prices. This rigid system, characterized by more or less unlimited guarantees for producers, originated in the 1960s, when the European agricultural sector was characterized by a low level of development, and the EC was not self-sufficient for most food products. As a result of all these measures, a favourable climate for the increase of production was created.

In combination with the rapid mechanization of the agricultural sector, major progress in seed improvement techniques and better feed for animals, larger and larger surpluses soon started to come into being. At the same time, the steadily increasing production was accompanied by a weak population growth, a food level which was already high, the tendency to more awareness and selectivity in food habits, and better yield in the preparation of food products. The result was that ever-increasing budget expenditure was necessary to take products off the market through intervention buying, disposal, or subsidized disposal, and exportation with the help of export refunds. This in turn led to ever more complex agricultural regulations with hundreds of detailed subsidy rules for nearly every aspect of the economic process from production to consumption.

As a result, agricultural policy became more and more self-contradictory: on the one hand because of the various instruments aimed at increasing production

---

82. Case C-304/02, *Commission v. France.*

and on the other with countless instruments in order to neutralize the negative effects flowing from that increase. After 1984, the threat of the actual insolvency of the Community as a result of the explosion of agricultural expenditure (about 70% of the budget) led in 1988 to the whole of agricultural expenditure being subjected to a binding medium term plan. Gradually, the various guarantees to producers were limited in the framework of a policy which aimed to bring prices on the internal market nearer to those on the world market. These developments led to the introduction of various general and specific systems of direct income support, in order to compensate for the reduction or abolition of the price guarantees. The increasingly stringent obligations at the international level – in the framework of the GATT and thereafter the WTO – as well as the demands of developing countries for increased access to the Community market, also played an important role in the process of reforming the common organizations of the market. At present, market and price policy is increasingly influenced by, amongst other things, considerations of climate and environmental policy, energy saving, and a gradually emerging scarcity of agricultural products on the world market as a result of the greater demand from China and other developing countries in the course of industrialization.

In brief, market and price policy embraces the following regulations. The more than 20 common organizations of the market, which formed the legal framework for market intervention in the various agricultural sectors in the period 1968–2007, were to a large extent abolished in 2007 and replaced by one horizontal regulation[83] which puts into place, in the course of 2008, one common organization of the market for 21 agricultural products[84] and three special measures.[85] Just as with the old sectoral common organizations of the market, this basic regulation is further elaborated by Council regulations (under a simplified procedure) and Commission regulations (sometimes under the committee procedures, mentioned above). The difference is, however, that as a result of the horizontal approach, the legislative load is considerably lightened, since in principle each market intervention instrument is no longer dealt with separately for each product, but is set out in one horizontal implementing regulation. The application of the basic regulation, and of the implementing regulations based on it, is the responsibility of national authorities which must be established or indicated by the Member States for this purpose, in conformity with their obligations under Article 10 EC. The horizontal regulation contains the main rules for the various instruments (intervention purchases, aid for private storage, various aid measures), by means of which the Community tries to achieve a particular price level in the internal market for the most important food products, tries to control production using systems of

83. Council Reg. 1234/2007, O.J. 2007, L 299/1.
84. Cereals, rice, sugar, dried fodder, seeds, hops, olive oil, flax and hemp, vegetables and fruits, processed vegetables and fruits, bananas, wine, flowers and live plants, raw tobacco, bovine meat, milk and dairy products, pigmeat, sheepmeat and goatmeat, eggs, poultry and 'other products'.
85. For ethylalcohol, bees and silkworms.

production restrictions (sugar, milk), aims to improve quality (by trade and production standards); it also contains rules for the involvement of producers' organizations.

Protection in relation to the world market is ensured by means of the common customs tariff, with in some cases the possibility of import levies and export subsidies, combined with various multilateral and bilateral rules for trade and for managing the import quotas agreed in that context.

In addition to the horizontal common organization of the market, there are measures for direct income support payments. Unlike the product-related measures – in which context the products and sectors have to be treated equally in order to prevent distortions of competition in the internal market – these 'person-related' measures offer greater opportunities for regional diversification, and thus also more freedom for the Member States in implementing them. The income support payments may also be made dependent on particular conditions for compulsory or voluntary setting-aside of land, non-intensive production, taking into account of certain environmental protection requirements and measures to support various other interests.[86]

Over the years, a large body of case law of the Court of Justice has emerged on the administrative law aspects of these market organization instruments, in particular on the scope of application and the conditions for the various levies and subsidies, the powers of the national authorities in relation to their implementation, the liability of the producer and the undertaking for the failure to meet these conditions, the various possibilities for sanctions provided for in the Community legislation, and the compatibility of all these mechanisms with general principles of law and fundamental rights. It is not possible to go in detail into all these points within the confines of this book; the reader is referred to the further reading indicated at the end of this chapter.

2.4   RURAL DEVELOPMENT POLICY

Rural development policy is at present the usual term for referring to that part of the CAP which concerns the totality of measures intended for structural improvements. This policy aspect only began to acquire real importance after 1988, in the framework of the limitation of guarantee expenditures and the increase in expenditure in the context of the Structural Funds in order to improve social and economic cohesion. It is clear that an improvement in the structure of the agricultural sector can make an important contribution to increased cohesion in the EC, given the enormous differences in income per capita, per unit of labour, added value per person employed in the agricultural sector, size of holding and productivity – in which context it should also be noted that more than 40% of Community agriculture is situated in mountain and hill regions. The general aim of

---

86. Council Reg. 1782/2003, O.J. 2003, L 270/1 (direct support payments).

structural policy in agriculture is to organize Community agricultural production in the perspective of sustainable agriculture, aimed at providing one, coherent framework of rules for economic, social and environmental aspects of agriculture. In the framework of the general policy aimed at strengthening economic and social cohesion by means of the structural funds and other financial instruments, the rural development policy should particularly contribute to strengthening the competitiveness of the agricultural sector (research and development, information and communication technology (ICT), biofuels), environmental and natural improvement (maintenance of landscape features, environment-friendly production and animal-friendly production, biological agriculture) and the integration of diverse other elements in agricultural policy (infrastructure, tourism, ICT, micro-undertakings, culture, etc.).[87] For this purpose, a framework regulation was adopted in 1999, in which all the existing structural measures are brought together in one coherent structure.[88] This framework presently encompasses the following areas of action: improvement of the structure of individual agricultural firms (lowering production costs, conversion of production, improving quality, improving the natural environment, and diversification) by granting investment aid; setting-up aid for young farmers, support for vocational training, support for early retirement from farming; compensatory support for less-favoured areas and areas with environmental restrictions, such as mountain areas (maintaining the countryside), sustainable farming methods, good farming practice, organic agriculture, environmental measures (introduction of environmental planning, aid for extensification); aid for improving processing and marketing of agricultural products; aid for forestry and aid for promoting the adaptation and development of rural areas (land improvement, reparcelling, water resources management, encouragement for tourist and craft activities, renovation and development of villages, etc.). The Member States should draw up plans, which are to be approved by the Commission, after which their implementation under the conditions set may be financed by the EC for 50% or more from the European Agricultural Development Fund (EADF).[89]

For the fisheries sector, a separate structural policy exists. In the coming years, structural improvement in this sector will centre on reducing fishing capacity, which is presently far too great.

The interrelationship between agricultural policy and quality-improvement policy is expressed both in the general rules for the protection of names of agricultural products and foodstuffs, and a great many existing specific arrangements. The aim of these rules is to promote the diversity of agricultural products, to protect product names against misuse and imitation, and to help consumers by giving them information concerning the specific character of the products. For this purpose,

---

87. Council Decision 2006/144, O.J. 2006, L 55/1: strategic directives for rural development.
88. Council Reg. (EC) No. 1257/1999 on support for rural development from the European Agricultural Guidance and Guarantee Fund (EAGGF) and amending and repealing certain Regulations, O.J. 1999, L 160/80.
89. Council Reg. 1698/2005, L 277/1. See further Ch. X section 5 *supra*.

three systems were devised: a *protected designation of origin* (PDO) can be granted to products for which the production, processing and preparation take place within a given geographical area; a *protected geographical indication* (PGI) can be granted to products where the geographical link occurs in at least one of the stages of production, processing or preparation; and a *Traditional Speciality Guaranteed* (TSG) does not refer to the origin, but highlights the traditional character, either in the composition or means of production.[90]

2.5   FINANCING

Expenditure for market and price policy is financed from the European Agricultural Guarantee Fund (EAGF), which forms part of the Community budget and is thus financed from the Community's own resources – of which import levies on agricultural products and other production levies form part. The basic regulation on the financing of the CAP governs the organization of expenditure and the annual clearance of accounts.[91] Expenditure is carried out by *paying agencies* designated by the Member States; these are charged with the approval of payment requests for the numerous subsidies, the bookkeeping and the organization of administrative and physical checks. In this process, these bodies must apply Community legislation. Financing takes place by means of advances made available to the Member States by the Commission. At the end of each financial year, the Member States forward to the Commission their annual statement of expenditure together with an attestation regarding the completeness, accuracy and veracity of the accounts transmitted, and on the basis of this, the Commission clears the accounts – or refuses to do so. This procedure for clearing the accounts regularly leads to disputes between the Commission and the Member States regarding whether the legislation in question has been applied correctly. If this is not the case, the expenditure is not – or not completely – reimbursed, so that the Member State is responsible for wrongly paid amounts. The basic regulation provides for a dispute settlement procedure; the final decision may be appealed to the Court of Justice. This has led to a large amount of case law over the years, in which the Court has defined further the consequences of the strict liability of the Member States for payments made in breach of Community legislation.[92] The procedure for clearance of accounts is a matter which exclusively concerns the Member States and the Commission; individuals have no possibility to challenge decisions relating to this

---

90. Reg. 2081/92 (geographical indications and designations of origin) and Reg. 2082/92 (certificates of specific character for agricultural products and foodstuffs), see especially Joined Cases C-321–324/94, *Criminal proceedings against Pistre et al.*; Case C-289/96, *Denmark v. Commission*; Case C-87/97, *Consorzio per la tutela del formaggio Gorgonzola*; Joined Cases C-129 & 130/97, *Criminal proceedings against Chiciak and Fol*; Case C-312/98, *Haus Cramer*; Case C-269/99, *Carl Kühne et al.*; Case C-108/01, *Consorzio del Prosciutto di Parma and Salumificio S. Rita*.

91. Reg. 1258/1999, O.J. 1999, L 101/22, which replaces the old basic Reg. 729/70, O.J. 1970, L 94/1.

92. See Case C-247/98, *Greece v. Commission* and Case C-373/99, *Greece v. Commission*.

procedure before the Community courts, even if they are indirectly affected by such decisions.[93] Since 1988, guarantee expenditure has been tied to an annual ceiling fixed for the medium-term (six years) in the framework of general budgetary discipline. In the framework of budgetary discipline, at the end of the planning period 2006–2013, the expenditures for direct market intervention in the agricultural sector will have gone down to about 43% of the total.

2.6   THE GENERAL IMPORTANCE OF AGRICULTURAL POLICY
             FOR INTEGRATION

2.6.1   Historical Significance

In many ways, Community agricultural law is of great importance for Community law as a whole. This position can be explained historically. Up until about 1990, agricultural policy was the only truly common policy of the EC, and it would be no exaggeration to state that up to then, this policy formed the backbone of the integration process, amongst other things because of the implications of the CAP for the common market as a whole, the socio-economic position of the agricultural sector in general, and its regional policy aspects in particular, its significance for external and commercial policy, the relationship between agriculture and the environment, and the consequences of the CAP for the Community budget.

Already in the early years of the Community, the CAP played a crucial role in achieving agreement between France and the Federal Republic of Germany as to the course of the integration process which had been set in motion. For instance, competition policy, participation of the Community in international trade negotiations, and the harmonization of turnover taxes were successively made conditions for the further development of the agricultural policy. The crucial position of agriculture was further demonstrated during the crisis concerning the future financing of the Community in 1966, with the French 'empty chair' policy which was finally resolved by the Luxembourg Accords, and again during the struggle which lasted for nearly a decade over the division of budgetary burdens among the Member States, especially concerning the British share in the financing of the CAP. The agreement at the conclusion of the 1988 Brussels European Council on setting ceilings for agricultural expenditure made it possible to consider further development of the regional policy of the EC in the framework of the structural funds. The scarcely concealed threat by the French in the final months of 1993 to invoke the Luxembourg Accords in relation to the agreement reached between the Commission and the United States about agricultural exports in the framework of the GATT Uruguay Round again illustrated the key role played by the CAP in the corpus of intra-Community relations. The same comment could be made of the problems concerning the financing of agricultural expenditure after the 2004

---

93.   Joined Cases 89 & 91/86, *Étoile commerciale and CNTA v. Commission*; Case T-244/00, *Coillte Teoranta v. Commission*.

accession of ten new Member States, which formed one of the great obstacles in the successful conclusion of accession negotiations.

2.6.2 The Significance for Community Law in General

Against this background, the significance of Community agricultural law for Community law in general may be summarized as follows. *To start with*, agricultural law is still today, both qualitatively and quantitatively the most important component part of Community law. About a quarter of Community legislation and about one-sixth of the court's case law deals with the agricultural sector. Although at first sight agricultural law may be regarded as a special part of general Community law, the influential relationship is in fact to a great extent the reverse, in view of the major influence which legislation and case law in the agricultural sector have exercised on the other component parts of Community law.

From the constitutional viewpoint, agricultural law has set the standard for the development of general doctrines, such as the supremacy of Community law, especially regulations and their consequences for individuals and the Member States. Moreover, important doctrines such as the scope of judicial control of discretionary decision-making by the Community legislature, the non-contractual liability of the Community for unlawful legislative acts, and the general and particular implications of the implementation obligation incumbent on the Member States, have been largely developed in agricultural case law. The same applies for the division of powers between the Community Institutions themselves, as is demonstrated by the case law on the disputes between the Commission, the Parliament and the Council on the use of Article 37 EC as a legal basis, and on the possibility and limits of the Council's reserving to itself the right to adopt implementing legislation as opposed to delegating it to the Commission (comitology).[94] Of major importance also is the case law on the delimitation of powers between the Community on the one hand and the Member States on the other.

In substantive law terms, agricultural law is of importance because of the development and application of general principles of law, such as legal certainty (protection of acquired rights and of legitimate expectations),[95] equality and proportionality,[96] and not least the potential, though in practice limited, importance of various fundamental rights for the policy freedom of the Community legislature.[97] Further, Community agricultural law has seen the development of specific substantive legal instruments, such as the integrated application of subsidies and levies in order to steer the behaviour of its economic subjects, and the development of its own specific enforcement instruments, especially the technique of guarantee

---

94. See Ch. V of this book.
95. E.g., Case 74/74, *CNTA v. Commission.*
96. Joined Cases 117/76 & 16/77, *Ruckdeschel et al. v. Hauptzollamt Hamburg-St. Annen*; Joined Cases 124/76 & 20/77, *Moulins Pont-à-Mousson v. ONIC.*
97. Case 44/79, *Hauer v. Land Rheinland-Pfalz.*

deposits and the associated problems of the possibilities of and limits to administrative sanctions.

It may thus be stated that Community agricultural law occupies a unique position in the wider corpus of Community law, which is firmly linked to the fact that the CAP reflects the most far-reaching form of integration provided for in the EC Treaty. At the same time, agricultural law also illustrates the problems which arise if negative and positive integration are not sufficiently coherent. In the absence of an Economic and Monetary Union, the exchange rate fluctuations as of the early 1970s could only be compensated by the extremely complicated system of MCAs (monetary compensation amounts), so that in reality the common market for agricultural products had already become to a large extent a legal fiction – a situation which could only be ended after 1993. The differentiated integration as a result of the fact that not all Member States belong to the euro-zone requires a system of agromonetary measures, which is highly complex, even if it is on a limited scale; this all goes to show yet again that the various aspects of the integration process are interconnected. The extensive case law on these matters is still of great importance for the significance of general principles of law as a means of control on the exercise of discretionary powers. Further, agricultural law also shows the consequences of the lack of a link between on the one hand the far-reaching substantive law integration and on the other hand an institutional framework which in effect is based on intergovernmental decision-making. The unanimity policy of the Council and the consequent loss of authority for the Commission has led to the Council – in the heydays of price intervention policy – in fact operating as an intergovernmental price cartel, which assured the continued existence of even the most inefficient undertakings. This meant that the claim on limited financial resources was an important factor in the tardiness in paying attention to the structural component of agricultural policy, which could contribute to the Community's economic and social cohesion.

2.6.3 Equality (Non-discrimination) and Differentiation

Community agricultural law contributes, albeit negatively, to the operationalization of the principle of subsidiarity. It may be recalled that a policy of price intervention leads by its very nature to a far-reaching centralization of legislation at the highest level. Given that in the framework of such a policy the competitive position of agricultural products is altered, particularly by the application of levies and subsidies, every actual or potential divergent application or interpretation of the rules concerned involves the possibility of distortions, which in turn may affect the proper functioning of the common organizations of the market and thus free movement.[98] The principle of uniform application and interpretation which has

---

98. Case 30/67, *Industria Molatoria Imolese et al. v. Council*; Case 40/69, *Hauptzollamt Hamburg Oberelbe v. Bollmann*; Case 34/70, *Syndicat national du commerce extérieur des céréales et al.*; Case 39/70, *Norddeutsches Vieh- und Fleischkontor v. Hauptzollamt Hamburg St*; Case 49/71, *Hagen OHG*; Case 39/72, *Commission v. Italy*; Joined Cases 67–85/75, *Lesieur v. Commission*;

long been recognized in the case law, means that the role of the Member States is largely limited to the strict application of these rules in individual cases.[99] In addition to a large and continuing legislative production which does not benefit the accessibility and internal consistency of Community rules, this character trait of the common organizations of the market means that no account can be taken of regional differences in production and trade structures. Thus, as has already been noted, differences in, for example, common prices, import levies and various subsidies may give rise to distortions of competition. This also demonstrates the inadequacy of price intervention as the only or most important instrument of the CAP, given that this policy, based on the formal principle of equality, does not do sufficient justice to the agricultural structure of the Community, characterized as it is by great diversity – which is indeed acknowledged in Article 33(2) EC. Seen in this light, the re-orientation from price intervention to direct income support is of major importance, given that the unity of the common market in the long term cannot be maintained by price intervention alone – an aspect which also plays a major role in the light of the latest enlargements of the Union. The CAP thus demonstrates that the centralization of legislation is a result of the chosen model of market intervention, which was in the 1960s supported virtually unanimously by all the parties involved. A policy of direct income support and structural policy instruments, based on regional differentiation, involves far greater possibilities for the Member States to apply framework Community legislation, within certain limits, and supplement it having regard to their own specific circumstances.

2.7   SOME CHARACTERISTICS OF COMMUNITY AGRICULTURAL
             ADMINISTRATIVE LAW

2.7.1   Instrumental Character

There are far too many interesting but also extremely complex aspects of Community administrative law in the agricultural sector to discuss them in detail here. But this administrative law is largely instrumental in character, and is concerned with steering the behaviour of economic subjects (producers, traders, processing industries, etc.) in such a way as to contribute to what the case law usually refers to

---

Case 50/76, *Amsterdam Bulb v. Produktschap voor siergewassen*; Case 265/78, *Ferwerda*; Case 4/79, *Providence agricole de la Champagne*; Case 64/81, *Corman v. Hauptzollamt Gronau*; Case 55/87, *Moksel v. BALM*.

99. See Case 74/69, *Hauptzollamt Bremen Freihafen v. Krohn*; Case 39/70, *Norddeutsches Vieh- und Fleischkontor*; Case 93/71, *Leonensio v. Minstero dell' Agricoltura e Foreste*; Case 18/72, *Granaria v. Produktschap voor Veevoeder*; Case 26/72, *Vereenigde Oliefabrieken v. Produktschap voor Margarine, Vetten en Olien*; Case 2/73, *Geddo v. Ente Nazionale Risi*; Case 119/73, *Getreide- und Futtermittel Handelsgesellschaft v. Einfuhr- und Vorratsstelle für Getreide und Futtermittel*; Case 153/73, *Holz & Willemsen*; Case 23/75, *Rey Soda v. Cassa Conguaglio Zucchero*; Case 118/76, *Balkan Import Export v. Hauptzollamt Berlin Packhof*.

as the proper functioning of the common organization of the market concerned – which in turn contributes to the achievement of the objectives specified in Article 33 EC.[100] For the most part this steering of conduct takes place by raising or lowering the costs of or revenue from certain economic transactions (investments, production, processing, supply, import and export, etc.). Thus, through the imposition of an import levy the costs of an import transaction are raised, and through the grant of a production subsidy the costs of production are lowered. The buying-in of agricultural produce by intervention agencies involves the grant of a subsidy, by means of a purchase at a price which could not be achieved on the market. It is not relevant whether this steering of conduct takes place in the framework of price and market policy or in the framework of rural development policy, nor whether the financing of the measures takes place on the basis of Community law or on the basis of national measures in a Community framework.

This approach demonstrates, *first*, that the choice of the beneficiary or the person burdened largely rests on considerations of effectiveness. In order to combat overproduction, co-responsibility levies, or other measures, may for example be placed on producers, as occurred in the dairy and cereals sectors. In order to stimulate the processing of agricultural products, a consumption aid may, for instance, be granted to the processing industry, or a production subsidy to the producer. Direct income support ultimately aims to guarantee the continuity of agricultural production, possibly under certain conditions, for instance conformity with particular environmental requirements. These examples show that the attribution of rights and obligations under the system of subsidies and levies is heavily dependent on the objectives chosen, such as restraint of production or guaranteeing a certain price level. Although these rights and obligations are meant to act ultimately to the advantage or disadvantage of the producer, it is perfectly possible that those rights and obligations are imposed in other phases of the process between production and consumption.[101]

Secondly, this administrative law illustrates a far-reaching integration of the levies and subsidies instruments, so that it is possible to speak of just one category of administrative acts, the application of financial amounts. Depending on the objectives, structure of the market, budgetary considerations and the like, these amounts may be applied in the form of a subsidy or in the form of a levy, for instance a subsidy for taking products off the market, or a levy in order to limit production. The extensive case law on various subsidy and levy mechanisms demonstrates that the fixing of these amounts in concrete cases and the status of acquired rights is based on a number of common principles. In all this, it is irrelevant whether the economic subject is granted a benefit or bears a burden;[102] what

---

100. E.g., Case 21/85, *Maas v. Bundesanstalt für landwirtschaftliche Marktordnung.*
101. Joined Cases C-143/88 & 92/89, *Zuckerfabrik Süderdithmarschen and Zuckerfabrik Soest v. Hauptzollamt Itzehoe and Hauptzollamt Paderborn.*
102. Case 65/69, *Compagnie d'approvisionnement, de transport and de crédit v. Commission;* Case 73/69, *Oehlmann & Co. v. Hauptzollamt Münster;* Case 16/70, *Necomout v. Hoofdproduktschap voor Akkerbouwprodukten et al.;* Joined Cases 9 & 11/71, *Compagnie d'approvisionnement, de*

is relevant is that by the application of such a financial amount, his or her conduct is steered in a direction which the Community legislature regards as necessary for the proper functioning of the mechanisms concerned.

2.7.2   Strict Liability

The concluding remark in the previous paragraph explains, *thirdly*, why the application of this combined levy and subsidy law is characterized by its predominantly objective character, and therefore the associated 'standardized' character of these amounts.[103] What is decisive for the existence of the rights or obligations is simply whether the conditions in the legislation concerned have been fulfilled, not whether the party concerned desired to bring about this legal (and financial) result or not.[104] The failure to fulfil the many and often extremely detailed conditions which are attached to many subsidies, means that the right to certain amounts is foregone, or that the party concerned is liable to repay the amounts involved, that a deposit lodged as a security is declared forfeit, or that the party is excluded, wholly or partially, from the grant of subsidies in the future, irrespective of whether the market participant was personally responsible for the failure to fulfil the conditions, or was guilty or negligent, or acted in good faith, and so on.[105] The case law shows that through this system, the party concerned is confronted with a far-reaching strict liability, from which he or she can only escape on grounds of *force majeure*.[106] The Community's levy and subsidy policy demonstrates that

---

        transport and de crédit et al. v. Commission; Case 13/72, *Netherlands v. Commission*; Case 74/74, *CNTA*; Joined Cases 67–85/75, *Lesieur*; Case 64/87, *Versele-Laga v. Robegra*; Case 195/87, *Cehave v. Hoofdproduktschap voor Akkerbouwprodukten*.

103.   Case 16/65, *Schwarze v. Einfuhr- und Vorratsstelle für Getreide und Futtermittel*; Case 31/70, *Deutsche Getreide- und Futtermittel Handelsgesellschaft v. Hauptzollamt Hamburg Altona*; Case 38/70, *Deutsche Tradax v. Einfuhr- und Vorratsstelle für Getreide und Futtermittel*; Case 58/86, *Coopérative agricole d'approvisionnement des Avirons v. Receveur des douanes*.

104.   See Case C-110/99, *Emsland-Stärke*.

105.   E.g., Case 122/78, *Buitoni*; Case 240/78, *Atalanta*; Case 147/81, *Merkur v. Hauptzollamt Hamburg-Ericus*; Case 272/81, *RU-MI v. FORMA*; Case 117/83, *Könecke v. BALM*; Case 124/83, *Direktaratet for Markedsordningerne v. Corman*; Case 20/84, *De Jong v. VIB*; Case 299/84, *Neumann v. BALM*; Case 288/85, *Hauptzollamt Hamburg-Jonas v. Plange Kraftfutterwerke*; Case 298/86, *Commission v. Belgium*; Case C-118/89, *Lingenfelser*; Case C-285/91, *Merck*; Case C-8/92, *General Milk Products v. Hauptzollamt Hamburg-Jonas*; Joined Cases C-433 & 434/92, *BALM v. Frick and Murr*; Case C-12/94, *Uelzena Milchwerke v. Antpöhler*; Case C-63/00, *Schilling and Nehring*.

106.   See e.g., Case 4/68, *Schwarzwaldmilch v. Einfuhr- und Vorratsstelle für Fette*; Case 68/77, *IFG v. Commission*; Case 6/78, *Union française de céréales v. Hauptzollamt Hamburg-Jonas*; Case 71/82, *BALM v. Brüggen*; Case 284/82, *Busseni v. Commission*; Case 266/84, *Denkavit France v. FORMA*; Case 109/86, *Theodorakis*; Case 71/87, *Greece v. Inter-Kom*; Case 113/88, *Leukhardt v. Hauptzollamt Reutlingen*; Case C-155/89, *Belgian State v. Philipp Brothers*; Case C-85/90, *Dowling v. Ireland et al.*; Case C-312/91, *Metalsa*; Case C-124/92, *An Bord Bainne and Inter-Agra*; Case C-136/93, *Transáfrica v. Administración del Estado español*; Case C-210/00, *Käserei Champignon Hofmeister*; Case C-208/01, *Parras Medina*.

individual freedom can be limited to a great extent through both levies and sub-sidies, by the simple lack of any possibility of alternatives. In many cases the undertaking can do nothing other than submit to these levies or subsidies, with the conditions attached to them, simply in order to exercise its economic activities.

2.7.3 Marginal Judicial Review

Fourthly, this instrumental position of the individual under Community agricul-tural law also has consequences for judicial protection. The case law demonstrates, in global terms, that the principle of legal certainty primarily boils down to a prohibition of retroactive legislation, although this is not without exceptions, and that the principle of the protection of legitimate expectations is very restric-tively interpreted in order not to restrict the freedom of action of the Community legislature to adapt existing legislation to economic reality at any time.[107] The principle of non-discrimination is also strongly dependent on the freedom which is left to the legislature to decide, in the context of its objectives and policy, what may or may not be regarded as like or equal.[108] Furthermore, the case law shows that the practical significance of the principle of proportionality depends on the fundamental rights enjoyed by the individual concerned. The significance of these fundamental rights is pretty small, given that constant case law holds that they do not restrict the freedom of the Community legislature even to pre-scribe far-reaching limits to the exercise of the right to property, the freedom to pursue a trade or profession, and the freedom of contract.[109] If the individual cannot lay claim to a right, but only to an interest, the failure to take account of that individual interest will only infringe the principle of proportionality if it can be shown that the measure involved is therefore to be regarded as not being appropriate or necessary in the light of the objectives of Article 33 EC, which – given the extensive freedom of the legislature – will only rarely be the case.[110]

---

107. Case 126/76, *Dietz v. Commission*; Case 26/77, *Balkan v. Hauptzollamt Berlin Packhof*; Joined Cases 44–51/77, *Union Malt*; Case 78/77, *Lührs v. Hauptzollamt Hamburg-Jonas*; Case 125/77, *Koninklijke Scholten-Honig et al. v. Hoofdproduktschaap voor Akkerbouwprodukten*; Case 146/77, *British Beef Company Limited v. Intervention Board for Agricultural Produce*; Case 84/78, *Ditta Angelo Tomadini Snc v. Amministrazione delle finanze dello Stato*; Case 98/78, *Racke v. Hauptzollamt Mainz*; Case 230/78, *Eridania*; Case 84/81, *Staple Dairy Products*; Case 224/82, *Meiko*; Case 59/83, *Biovilac*; Case C-402/98, *ATB et al.*
108. Case 43/72, *Merkur Aussenhandels v. Commission*; Case 8/78, *Milac*; Case 166/78, *Italy v. Council*; Case 139/79, *Maizena*; Joined Cases 292 & 293/81, *Lion*; Case 8/82, *Wagner v. BALM*; Case 15/83, *Denkavit Nederland*; Case 59/83, *Biovilac*; Case 106/83, *Sermide*; Case 179/84, *Bozzetti*; Joined Cases 424 & 425/85, *Frico v. Voedselvoorzienings In- en Verkoopbureau*; Case 84/87, *Erpelding*; Joined Cases C-181, 182 & 218/88, *Deschamps et al. v. Ofival*; Case C-15/95, *EARL de Kerlast*; Case C-372/96, *Pontillo*; Case C-56/99, *Gascogne Limousin viandes*; Case C-117/99, *Unilet and Le Bars*.
109. See e.g., Case 44/79, *Hauer*; Case C-22/94 *The Irish Farmers Association*.
110. Case 114/76, *Bela-Mühle Josef Bergmann*; Case 120/86, *Mulder*; Case 300/86, *Van Landschoot v. Mera*; Case 170/86, *Von Deetzen v. Hauptzollamt Hamburg-Jonas*.

In general, the case law on these general legal principles confirms that the judicial control on the exercise of discretionary powers leans strongly in the direction of a prohibition of arbitrariness.[111]

3   TRANSPORT POLICY

3.1   INTRODUCTION

The EC Treaty deals with transport in a separate Title. For a number of reasons the framers of the EC Treaty felt it necessary to establish a common policy for the transport sector, and this is given expression in Article 3(1)(f) EC.[112] The special status of transport in the Treaty is in part due to the fact that the transport sector was highly regulated in all the original Member States. Moreover, it was seen as crucial for the establishment of a common market.

3.1.1   The Special Character of Transport

The idiosyncrasies of the transport sector have been described extensively elsewhere.[113] We confine ourselves here to mentioning a few of the most relevant points. First, the great dependence on infrastructure and the associated problem of cost allocation. This allocation does not take place in the same way *in each* Member State individually, particularly as far as road and rail transport are concerned. Moreover, it does not take place in the same way *within* the various Member States. This was one of the issues which came to the fore in the discussion about the allocation of costs in road transport. The lack of agreement in the Community about the allocation of these costs blocked progress in the development of the common transport policy for years. This was primarily the result of divergent views in Germany, which followed a policy of fixing tariffs for road transport in such a way that rail transport faced no real competition.[114] German seaport policy was also conducted for a long time with the assistance of low railway tariffs.[115] On the other hand, the national railways were subsidized to a great extent

---

111. See already e.g., Case 138/79, *Roquette.*
112. The 'Spaak report' mentioned services in Ch. III, Services, and proposed that free provision of transport services should also be realized by the end of the transitional period at the latest. See further J. Erdmenger, in Nomos von der Groeben/Schwarze, *Vertrag über die Europäische Union und Vertrag zur Gründung der Europäischen Gemeinschaft,* 6th ed. Baden-Baden, 2003, 1899.
113. For an extensive background discussion, see the 2nd edition of this work (ed. Gormley) (Deventer, 1989) 705–711. See also R. Greaves, *Transport Law of the European Communities* (Athlone, 1991), 2. See also Erdmenger in von der Groeben/Schwarze op. cit. *supra,* note 112, 1897–1992.
114. See Case C-185/91, *Bundesanstalt für den Güterfernverkehr v. Reiff.*
115. This is confirmed by the decision of the Commission concerning the German railways, O.J. 1994, L 104/34. The appeal brought against this decision was rejected by the Court of First Instance in Case T-229/94, *Deutsche Bahn v. Commission.*

in virtually all the Member States.[116] In inland waterway transport the allocation problem was far less significant; the problems in this sector were primarily caused by a relatively small sector, and the small family firms. This sector suffers predominantly from structural overcapacity.

Another feature which hindered the development of a common transport policy was the existence of strongly divergent national intervention systems.

Further, it should be recalled that it is impossible to stock-pile transport services: transport capacity, therefore, has to be adapted to peak demands, which leads to overcapacity during the other periods. When combined with high fixed charges, among which wages must now be included, this may lead to disastrous price competition. Particularly in depressed areas, such as Southern Italy, but also elsewhere, there is overcapacity especially with regard to return freights. Since the transport charges as a rule are already defrayed on the outward journey, transport during the return journey will yield profit even if the price is extremely low.

Finally, attention should be drawn to the international character of sea and air transport in particular.

3.1.2 The Development of a Common Transport Policy

In the light of all the specificities of the transport sector, the development of a common transport policy was a long time in the making. Despite the obstacles caused by the various elements – some of which were mentioned above – a common transport policy has now finally been more or less realized. These developments were set in motion by the celebrated action brought by the European Parliament against the Council for failure to establish a common policy in the field of transport,[117] by the changes introduced by the Single European Act (SEA),[118] by a couple of major judgments on Article 234 EC references (*Asjes* and *Ahmed Saeed*),[119] and by the Commission's programme for completing the Internal Market.[120] The following elements have also been crucial in making a coherent policy possible: the adoption of the Third Aviation Package and the *'open skies'* judgments in the air transport sector;[121] the adoption of rules on cabotage in

---

116. See Scharf in L. Hancher, T.R. Ottervanger, and P.J. Slot, *E.C. State Aids*, 3rd ed. (London, 2006), Ch. 16-015, 382.
117. Case 13/83, *Parliament v. Council (common transport policy)*.
118. The SEA altered the voting requirements of Art. 80 EC, to permit decision-making by qualified majority.
119. Joined Cases 209–213/84, *Ministère public v. Asjes*; Case 66/86, *Ahmed Saeed Flugreisen et al. v. Zentrale zur Bekämpfung unlauteren Wettbewerbs*.
120. See White Paper Completing the Internal Market, COM(85)310 final, Luxembourg, 1985.
121. This package consisted principally of Regs. 2407/92 (O.J. 1992, L 240/1) on licencing of air carriers; 2408/92 (O.J. 1992, L 240/8, as amended) on access for Community air carriers to intra-Community air routes; 2409/92 (O.J. 1992, L 240/15) on fares and rates for air services; 2410/92 (O.J. 1992, L 240/18) and 2411/92 (O.J. 1992, L 240/19) which amended the competition rules in the air sector; and 95/93 (O.J. 1993, L 14/1) on common rules for slot allocation at Community airports. The *open skies* judgments are: Case C-466/98 *Commission v. United Kingdom*; Case C-467/98, *Commission v. Denmark*; Case C-468/98, *Commission v. Sweden*;

road transport[122] and maritime transport;[123] and the adoption of Directive 93/89, allowing costs of road infrastructure to be charged to users.[124] As will become evident from the discussion of the developments in the various transport sectors, this policy is now often driven by other considerations, such as safe skies and combatting terrorism, as well as enhanced environmental awareness. In addition, the role of the EU in the world has changed dramatically since the original six Member States set out to develop a common transport policy, and the EU's transport policy increasingly reflects this trend.[125]

As will appear from the sector-by-sector description of the transport regime, there is a clear model based on a market economy orientation. In this model, the price and capacity rules from the national regulatory systems have disappeared. Interference in prices is now possible only in a very few precisely defined exceptional situations. The qualitative conditions for access to the profession are regulated for each sector. Such professional qualifications have only an indirect effect on market access. Furthermore, there are specific rules for each sector, such as the driving and rest hours provisions for road transport.[126]

The market economy model has come about for a number of reasons. First, it turned out to be impossible to achieve an internal market using one all-embracing philosophy on intervention in prices and capacity. This was primarily because the national systems were based on specific policy objectives reflecting national political considerations. Moreover, in the course of the 1980s, the intervention system was abandoned in a number of Member States.[127] This was particularly true for road transport. In the field of air transport, the market model was chosen as a result of external influences: deregulation in the United States which created strongly competitive airline companies, and competition from the Far East. Moreover, the deregulation doctrine gradually made its influence felt in the Community as well.[128] In addition, the progressive development of the internal market certainly played a role. The liberalization in the rail transport sector was provided for in

---

Case C-469/98, *Commission v. Finland*; Case C-471/98, *Commission v. Belgium*; Case C-472/98, *Commission v. Luxembourg*; Case C-475/98, *Commission v. Austria*; Case C-476/98, *Commission v. Germany*, annotated by P.J. Slot and J. Dutheil de la Rochère, in 40 CML Rev., 2003, 697–713.

122. Reg. 3118/93, O.J. 1993, L 279/1.
123. Reg. 3577/92, O.J. 1992, L 364/7.
124. Dir. 93/89, O.J. 1993, L 279/32; this directive was later annulled on procedural grounds by the Court of Justice, and replaced by Dir. 1999/62/EC on the charging of heavy goods vehicles for the use of certain infrastructures, O.J. 1999, L 187/42.
125. See e.g., Case C-344/04, *IATA and ELFAA*, which concerns the question whether Reg. 261/2004 on compensation for denied boarding is compatible with Arts. 19, 22 and 29 of the Montreal Convention.
126. Reg. 3820/85 (O.J. 1985, L 370/1) Dir. 2006/22/EC provides for minimum conditions for the implementation O.J. 2006, L 102/35. See also, as to tachographs, Reg. 3821/85 (O.J. 1985, L 370/8, most recently amended by Reg. 561/2006 on the harmonization of certain social legislation relating to road transport (O.J. 2006, L 102/1)).
127. As to the changes in the Dutch approach, see Slot, 'Sturing en vervoer' (1992) SEW, 514.
128. For instance, the United Kingdom and The Netherlands pursued a very clear *open skies* policy.

Directive 91/440[129] which concerned the separation of functions in the Community's railways and access to the rail network. Here too, external developments, particularly in the United States, played a role.

The market economy model is supplemented on a number of points. In road transport, a crisis mechanism is provided for in emergency cases.[130] Elements of environmental protection are becoming more and more evident.[131] Furthermore, there are specific rules for the establishment of public service obligations. As mentioned above, measures aimed at combating terrorism as well as measures to promote safe skies and seas have recently taken a prominent role.

These developments have not always been positively viewed. Particularly those who have argued that harmonization of conditions of competition should always be achieved before liberalization takes place claim that such harmonization is still insufficient.[132] For instance: as a result of great differences in road taxes between the United Kingdom and the Netherlands, it is attractive for British transport companies to register their lorries in the Netherlands. In France, the provision of transport services using a Dutch number plate and a Community authorization issued by the British authorities[133] led to prosecution under criminal law. As a result, the British firm requested a Community authorization in the Netherlands. The Dutch authorities refused, on the ground that the Dutch legislation contained a requirement that the requesting firm must be established in the Netherlands, and must permanently and factually direct its road haulage activities from this place of establishment. This requirement would seem to be in conflict with Article 43 EC,[134] and would also seem to be incompatible with the provisions of Regulation 3118/93 and Directive 93/89.[135]

With the entry into force of Regulation 1/2003 and Regulation 411/2004, the application of Articles 81 EC and 82 EC (the competition rules) in the maritime and air transport sectors has finally been aligned with the general competition rules; in the maritime sector this was accompanied by the repeal, in 2006, of Regulation

---

129. O.J. 1991, L 305/22.
130. Reg. 3916/90 (O.J. 1990, L 375/10) for international carriage of goods by road; see also Reg. 3118/93, O.J. 1993, L 279/1, Art. 7, for cabotage.
131. See e.g., M. Humphreys, 'The Polluter Pays Principle in Transport Policy' (2001), EL Rev., 451–467.
132. See V. Schmitt, 'Die Harmonisierung der Wettbewerbsbedingungen in der EG-Binnenverkehrspolitik' (1993) EuZW, 305 et seq.
133. The Community authorization is regulated in Arts. 3 and 5 Reg. 881/92, O.J. 1992, L 95/1.
134. See Case C-212/97, *Centros*; Case C-208/00, *Überseering*. See also the Dutch College van Beroep voor het Bedrijfsleven (CBB) Nos. 93/2197/094/301 and 93/2197/094/302, Lübbert *v.* NIWO, UCB 1997 nr.6, in which it was held that the applicant should be given the possibility of fulfilling the requirement of permanent and actual management by other means than being established in the Netherlands.
135. Reg. 3118/93, O.J. 1993, L 279/1, the cabotage regulation. Dir. 93/89, O.J. 1993, L 279/32, taxation road transport. See on this the important judgment in Case C-115/00, *Hoves Internationaler Transport-Service*, where the Court ruled that in the case of cabotage transport, the host Member State may not levy road vehicle taxes on vehicles registered in another Member State.

4056/86.[136] Since the liberalization of these sectors, the competition rules have also been applied on a number of occasions. These developments will be discussed in sections 3.11 and 3.12 below.

3.1.3   Services of General Economic Interest

The notion of public services, or services of general economic interest, has become a key concept in Community law and politics.[137] It is a notion that is particularly important in all sectors that have been the target of liberalization: transport, energy, telecommunications, postal services; it is also relevant in other sectors such as broadcasting. The Treaty of Amsterdam in 1997 added a new Article 16 EC, according to which 'the Community and the Member States, each within their respective powers and within the scope of application of this Treaty, shall take care that such services operate on the basis of principles and conditions which enable them to fulfil their missions'.[138] Article 36 of the EU Charter of Fundamental Rights recognizes and respects services of general economic interest. The European Council of 20–21 June 2007 adopted a Protocol on services of general interest which is now part of the Lisbon Treaty.[139]

---

136.   See Reg. 1/2003, O.J. 2003, L 1/1, and Reg. 411/2004, O.J. 2004, L 68/1. Reg. 4056/86, O.J. 1986, L 378/4, was repealed by Council Reg. (EC) No. 1419/2006 of 25 Sep. 2006, O.J. 2006, L 269/1.

137.   Its political importance was highlighted during the French campaign for the referendum on the Constitutional Treaty in the spring of 2005. One of the arguments of the 'No' camp was that the Community was gradually undermining the public services. Note also that the concepts of public service obligations and services of general economic interest are of significance in the field of EC free movement law as well as under the competition rules: see e.g., the discussion of the free movement of goods in the *Energy cases* (note 550, *infra*) and of the free movement of capital in the various *Golden shares* cases (note 153, *infra*). Recent articles include T. Prosser, 'Competition Law and Public Services: From Single Market to Citizenship rights?' (2005) EPL, 543 and G. Napolitano, 'Towards a European Legal Order for Services of General Economic Interest,' (2005) EPL, 565.

138.   See M. Ross, 'Article 16 EC and Services of General Interest: From Derogation to Obligation', (2000) EL Rev., 22.

139.   Protocol No. 9 on Services of General Interest:

The High Contracting Parties, Wishing to emphasise the importance of services of general interest Have agreed upon the following interpretative provisions, which shall be annexed to the Treaty on European Union and to the Treaty on the Functioning of the European Union:
    Article 1
    The shared values of the Union in respect of services of general economic interest within the meaning of Article 16 EC Treaty include in particular:

    – the essential role and the wide discretion of national, regional and local authorities in providing, commissioning and organizing services of general economic interest as closely as possible to the needs of the users;
    – the diversity between various services of general economic interest and the differences in the needs and preferences of users that may result from different geographical, social or cultural situations;
    – a high level of quality, safety and affordability, equal treatment and the promotion of universal access and of user rights;

The terminology is not always entirely clear: the Commission uses the term 'services of general interest' to include both services of general interest and services of general economic interest.[140] The Protocol also refers to both terms. It would be helpful to make a clear distinction between the two concepts and use the term services of general economic interest only for market activities i.e., activities performed by undertakings, and services of general interest for non-market activities i.e., performed by entities that are not undertakings.[141]

There has been a lively discussion on the proper function of public services and the extent to which such services are exempt from the competition rules and the state aid rules; the latter question is largely dealt with by reference to Article 86(2) EC.[142] A new element has been added by the Court's judgment in the *Altmark* case,[143] which provided important guidelines for the compatibility of financial compensation for such services with the state aid rules. It is worth quoting this important judgment extensively. The Court ruled that: 'public subsidies intended to enable the operation of urban, suburban or regional scheduled transport services are not caught by that provision [Art. 87(1) EC] where such subsidies are to be regarded as compensation for the services provided by the recipient undertakings in order to discharge public service obligations. For the purpose of applying that criterion, it is for the national court to ascertain that the following conditions are satisfied:

- first, the recipient undertaking is actually required to discharge public service obligations and those obligations have been clearly defined;
- second, the parameters on the basis of which the compensation is calculated have been established beforehand in an objective and transparent manner;
- third, the compensation does not exceed what is necessary to cover all or part of the costs incurred in discharging the public service obligations, taking into account the relevant receipts and a reasonable profit for discharging those obligations;
- fourth, where the undertaking which is to discharge public service obligations is not chosen in a public procurement procedure, the level of

---

Article 2
The provisions of the Treaties do not affect in any way the competence of Member States to provide, commission and organise non-economic services of general interest.

140. See the Communication from the Commission on this subject (COM(2000)580 final, of 20 Sep. 2000), as well as its 'Non-Paper' on 'Services of General Economic Interest and State Aid' (COMP-2002-01759) of 12 Nov. 2002. On 12 May 2003, the Commission published a Green Paper on services of general economic interest (COM(2003)270 final). In this publication, the Commission examines a variety of public service obligations and the Community instruments in force in the field of services of general interest. The Commission issued a White Paper on the same topic in 2004 (COM(2004)374 final).
141. That would make it clear that services of general interest do not come within the scope of the Treaty provisions. It would also make Art. 2 of the Protocol redundant.
142. Art. 86(2) EC deals specifically with undertakings entrusted with the operation of services in the general interest. See further Ch. IX *supra*.
143. Case C-280/00, *Altmark Trans and Regierungspräsidium Magdeburg*.

compensation needed has been determined on the basis of an analysis of the costs which a typical undertaking, well run and adequately provided with means of transport so as to be able to meet the necessary public service requirements, would have incurred in discharging those obligations, taking into account the relevant receipts and a reasonable profit for discharging the obligations.'[144]

The *Altmark* judgment has led to further questions about the interpretation of the four conditions that it laid down, as well as about the relationship between those conditions and Article 86(2) EC. The Commission adopted Decision 2005/842 based on Article 86(3) EC to deal with cases where the *Altmark* conditions are not met.[145] This Decision exempts Member States from the notification duty where compensation for a public service obligation is less than 30 million euro per annum and is granted to undertakings with an annual turnover of less than 100 million euro. According to Article 1 of the Decision, such compensation is to be regarded as compatible with the common market. The Decision also excludes compensation granted to hospitals and for social housing. In addition, the Commission has adopted a Community Framework for state aid given in the form of public service compensation.[146] The Framework addresses situations that do not fall within the scope of application of the above-mentioned Decision and specific projects that Member States have decided to notify.[147] The Commission enacted a directive amending the Financial Transparency Directive,[148] and published further relevant documents in November 2007.[149] The Commission's view on the appropriate scope of the *Altmark* judgment is also explained in several state aid decisions.[150] It can implicitly be gleaned from these cases, as well as from the Commission's decisions based on Article 86(3) EC, that the Commission considers that in those instances where the *Altmark* conditions are *not* fulfilled, an exemption from the

---

144. Ibid., para. 95.
145. Commission Decision 2005/842/EC on the application of Art. 86(2) EC to state aid in the form of public service compensation granted to certain undertakings entrusted with the operation of services of general economic interest, O.J. 2005, L 312/67. Art. 2 also exempts public service compensation to maritime and air transport links to islands which do not exceed 300,000 passengers, as well as compensation for airports with less than 1,000,000 passengers and ports with less than 300,000 passengers.
146. Community Framework for state aid in the form of public service compensation, O.J. 2005, C 297/4.
147. Para. 21 of the preamble of the decision.
148. Commission Dir. 2005/81/EC of 28 Nov. 2005, amending Dir. 80/723/EEC on the transparency of financial relations between Member States and public undertakings as well as on financial transparency within certain undertakings, O.J. 2005, L 312/47.
149. Services of general interest, including social services of general interest: A new European commitment, COM(2007)725 final; accompanying document SEC(2007)1516.
150. See e.g., para. 6.4 of the Commission Dec. of 15 Oct. 2003 on the measures implemented by Italy for RAI SpA, O.J. 2004, L 119/1; Commission Dec. of 20 Oct. 2004, concerning the aid scheme by Spain for the airline Intermediacíon Area, O.J. 2005, L 110/52; Commission Dec. 2004/838/EC of 10 Dec. 2003 on State aid implemented by France for France 2 and France 3, O.J. 2004, L 361/21.

effects of Article 87(1) EC (which prohibits most state aid) may be possible on the basis of Article 86(2) EC, provided that the compensation is commensurate with the extra cost of providing the public service. Regulation 1370/2007 provides for the follow-up of the *Altmark* case law in the inland transport sector.[151]

The foregoing discussion presupposes that the relevant public service obligations have been established in accordance with the requirements of Community law. This question was the subject of *Analir* and *Coname*. In the *Analir* judgment,[152] although the Court of Justice granted the Member States a fairly wide discretion in establishing public service obligations, it also imposed clear conditions upon the exercise of that discretion: 'They must be based on objective, non-discriminatory criteria which are known in advance to the undertakings concerned, in such a way as to circumscribe the exercise of the national authorities' discretion.'[153] Although *Analir* involved an interpretation of specific provisions in the regulation on cabotage in maritime transport,[154] the conditions formulated in *Analir* can be taken to be of more general significance across the whole transport sector and, indeed, for other sectors in which such public service obligations arise.[155]

In the *Coname* judgment, the European Court of Justice (ECJ) provided further guidance in this matter for cases where no compensation is involved.[156] The direct award of a concession must, on the basis of Articles 43 and 49 EC, comply with transparency requirements such as to enable an undertaking from another Member State to have access to appropriate information so that it would be in a position to apply for the concession. The Court stressed that the transparency requirements do not necessarily imply an obligation to hold a tender.[157] It should be observed that the fourth condition of the *Altmark* judgment requires transparency and suggests a preference for a tender procedure when the authorities provide for compensation for the services. The case law is not entirely conclusive on this requirement. The *Coname* and the *Altmark* judgments do not require a tender, but another recent judgment (*Brixen*) seems to impose such a

---

151. O.J. 2007, L 315/1; the regulation is discussed *infra* in section 3.6.
152. Case C-205/99, *Analir*. See the annotation by Slot in (2003) CML Rev., 159–168. The so-called 'golden shares' cases – Case C-367/98, *Commission v. Portugal*; Case C-483/99, *Commission v. France*; C-503/99 *Commission v. Belgium* – provide, particularly in the last of these cases, a further clarification of the demands that must be met by any such approval process.
153. Case C-205/99, *Analir*, at para. 38.
154. Reg. 3577/92 on maritime cabotage, O.J. 1992, L 364/7.
155. According to the Commission, the frequent use of public service obligations by the Member States has led to the maintenance of a wide variety of procedures and conditions in these areas. On this basis, the Commission has proposed a new regulation to harmonize the creation of such public service obligations (O.J. 2002, C 151E/146). This new regulation would replace Reg. 1191/69/EC, O.J. 1969, L 156/1. The updated proposal COM(2005)319 does not apply to inland waterway transport, therefore Regs. 1169/69 and 1107/70 will continue to apply for this sector.
156. Case C-231/03, *Coname*.
157. The concession in the *Coname* case was rather small and this may have led the ECJ not to require a tender.

requirement.[158] Both Commission Decision 2005/842, based on Article 86(3), and the Framework mentioned above are silent on this question. The Commission decisions in individual cases suggest a strong preference for tendering, even to the extent that the presence of a tender establishes a rebuttable presumption that the transparency conditions are satisfied.[159]

3.1.4   The Concept of Transport

The EC Treaty contains no definition of the concept of transport as such,[160] although it does indicate the scope of application of the transport Title. It can be deduced from Article 80 EC that in any event road, rail and inland waterway transport fall within the ambit of transport, referred to in Community jargon as inland transport. This term is used hereafter to describe these three sectors collectively. Maritime and air transport also now fall under the transport sectors regulated on the basis of the EC Treaty, although Article 80 EC itself initially left that open. Article 80 EC is silent about transport by pipeline, although this is in common parlance also referred to as transport. This is an area which gives rise to particular questions which are primarily addressed within the Community in the context of a common energy policy.[161]

3.2   THE RELATIONSHIP BETWEEN THE GENERAL PRINCIPLES OF THE
         EC TREATY AND THE SPECIAL PROVISIONS OF THE TRANSPORT TITLE

The relationship between the general principles and the special provisions has given rise to much discussion, but by now most questions have been answered in the case law of the Court of Justice. The transport Title contains no provisions which regulate this relationship. This contrasts with the agriculture Title, where Articles 32(2) and 36 EC determine the relationship with the common market and competition respectively. Article 51(1) EC does provide that the free movement of services in the field of transport is to be governed by the provisions in the title

---

158. Case C-458/03, *Parking Brixen*. *Brixen* provides a useful clarification of the question when the award of public service concessions can be regarded as a transaction to which the public procurement rules of the Community apply and when this is not the case. In this context it should be noted that *Coname* was a judgment of the Grand Chamber of the ECJ, and *Brixen* was a judgment of a chamber of 5 judges.
159. And, by analogous reasoning, that the absence of a tender creates a rebuttable presumption that the transparency requirements have *not* been satisfied.
160. Whereas a definition of agricultural products, at least, is given; see Art. 32 EC.
161. See e.g., Dec. 1229/2003/EC of the European Parliament and of the Council of 26 Jun. 2003 laying down a series of guidelines for trans-European energy networks and repealing Decision No. 1254/96/EC, O.J. 2003, L 176/11–28. See generally, section 5.3. *infra*. See specifically on pipelines, M.M. Roggenkamp, Het juridisch kader van pijpleidingen in de olie- en gasindustrie, PhD thesis Leiden, 1999, 33 et seq.

relating to transport. Article 70 EC provides that the objectives of the Treaty in the field of transport are to be pursued by Member States within the framework of a common transport policy.

In the transport policy case,[162] the Court ruled that on the basis of Article 71(1)(a) and (b) EC the Council is *obliged* to bring about the free movement of services in the transport sector, and that the scope of those obligations is clearly laid down in the Treaty. For the rest, the general rules of the Treaty are applicable to transport, as various judgments have made clear – the application of the competition rules being confirmed in *Asjes* and *Ahmed Saeed Flugreisen*.[163] Although, therefore, the free movement of services had to be achieved, it was for the Council to take the measures it felt necessary to accompany the required liberalization measures.[164] The crisis mechanism for road transport, for example, is just such an accompanying measure; such measures may be based on Article 71 EC.[165] The Court's ruling in that same transport policy case also made it clear that Articles 49 and 50 EC are not directly applicable in the transport sector: specific measures were needed.[166] The question whether Article 71(1)(a) and (b) is directly effective was side-stepped by the Court in *Pinaud Wieger*.[167]

The non-discrimination principle in Article 12 EC can not provide a legal basis for the realization of the freedom to provide services in this area. While it is true that as a general rule of the Treaty,[168] Article 12 applies to transport,[169] questions relating to the freedom to provide services in the transport sector fall under Articles 70, 71 and 80(2) EC, by virtue of Article 51(1) EC – as the Court has confirmed in *Corsica Ferries II*.[170]

The wording of Article 80 EC has given rise to additional questions about the applicable Treaty regime for maritime and air transport,[171] but it is now clear from the case law that the general rules of the Treaty apply to these sectors

---

162. Case 13/83, *Parliament v. Council* at para. 64.
163. See Case 167/73, *Commission v. France*; Case 156/77, *Commission v. Belgium*; Joined Cases 209–213/84, *Asjes*; Case 66/86, *Ahmed Saeed Flugreisen*.
164. Case 13/83, *Parliament v. Council*.
165. See Reg. 3916/90 on measures to be taken in the event of a crisis in the market in the carriage of goods by road, O.J. 1990, L 375/10.
166. Case 13/83, *Parliament v. Council*.
167. Case C-17/90, *Pinaud Wieger v. Bundesanstalt für den Güterfernverkehr*. In that case, A.G. Darmon was (like A.G. Jacobs in Case 4/88, *Lambregts Transportbedrijf v. Belgium*) of the opinion that the obligation to achieve the free movement of services was directly effective. The virtual completion of the common transport policy for inland transport reduces the importance of this discussion, as direct effect is really important for those areas where no secondary Community legislation has been adopted. For air transport to third countries, free movement of services must still be brought about on the basis of Art. 80(2), as will be shown below; the wording of this provision excludes the possibility of direct effect.
168. Case 167/73, *Commission v. France*.
169. Cf. Opinion of A.G. van Gerven, in Case C-18/93, *Corsica Ferries v. Corpo dei piloti del porto di Genova*.
170. Case C-18/93, *Corsica Ferries Italia v. Corpo dei piloti del porto di Genova*.
171. See further J. Erdmenger op. cit. *supra* note 112, 1966–1992.

as well.[172] The Court of Justice ruled (in *Corsica Ferries I*) that on the basis of Article 80(2) EC the freedom to provide services in the areas covered by that provision needed to be implemented by the Council.[173] For these sectors too, the use of Article 12 EC as a legal basis for the application of the freedom to provide services is excluded.[174] As will be explained below, the Council finally managed to reach agreement on the freedom to provide services in the field of maritime transport both within the Community and between the Community and third countries in 1986,[175] and in the field of air transport within the Community in 1992.[176]

3.3   EXTERNAL RELATIONS IN THE TRANSPORT FIELD: GENERAL
              OBSERVATIONS

As already mentioned in the introduction to this section, relations with third countries in the transport field are extremely important. It is no mere coincidence, therefore, that two fundamental decisions of the Court of Justice – the judgment in the *ERTA* case[177] and Opinion 1/76 on the *European Laying-up Agreement for Inland Waterway Vessels*[178] – have international transport as their subject matter. These pronouncements of the Court indicate that the Community has competence to conclude international agreements in order to implement existing Community transport policy, and to put new policy into effect. In Opinion 1/94 on the WTO, the Court ruled that international agreements in transport matters are not covered by

---

172. Case 167/73, *Commission v. France*; Joined Cases 209–213/84, *Asjes*, and Case 66/86, *Ahmed Saeed Flugreisen.*
173. Case C-49/89, *Corsica Ferries France v. Direction générale des douanes*. In Case C-381/93, *Commission v. France*, the Court declared the rules which were the subject of Case C-49/89, *Corsica Ferries France* to be incompatible with Art. 1 of Reg. 4055/86 (O.J. 1986, L 378/1). The cases concerned a charge levied on embarkation and disembarkation of passengers travelling to or from ports in other Member States whenever ships used harbour facilities (on the mainland or on an island), whereas in the case of transport between two French ports the charge was levied only on embarkation (on the mainland or on an island). The charge was moreover levied at a higher level for passengers travelling from and to another Member State than for passengers whose journeys were only internal.
174. Case C-18/93, *Corsica Ferries Italia*. The principle of Art. 12 EC can be applied in relation to other measures, such as environmental, safety and social measures.
175. Reg. 4055/86 applying the principle of freedom to provide services to maritime transport between Member States and between Member States and third countries, O.J. 1986, L 378/1, amended by Reg. 3573/90, O.J. 1990, L 353/16.
176. Reg. 2408/92 on access for Community air carriers to intra-Community air routes, O.J. 1992, L 240/8.
177. Case 22/70, *Commission v. Council (ERTA)*. See ch. XIII on the *ERTA* case.
178. Cf. Opinion 1/76, *European Laying-up Agreement*. These principles have been reiterated in the ECJ's judgments in Case C-266/03, *Commission v. Luxembourg*; Case C-433/03, *Commission v. Germany*.

Article 133 EC.[179] In that Opinion, the ECJ also found that when internal competence can be effectively exercised only at the same time as external competence, the latter will be exclusive.[180] These decisions and opinions of the Court are discussed further in Chapter XIII. In this chapter, a brief summary will be given of existing external relations in the field of transport.

In relation to road transport, the European Conference of Ministers of Transport (ECMT)[181] and the Economic Commission for Europe (ECE)[182] are the most important bodies. Virtually all the Member States participate, and the Community has observer status, in both fora. The ECE has undertaken much work in the field of technical provisions, and the ECMT plays an important role in the promotion of relations with third countries. In inland waterway transport matters, the Central Commission for Navigation on the Rhine, in which the Community also has observer status, has long been an important forum.[183] This Commission is responsible for implementing and promoting free navigation on the Rhine, as laid down in the Convention of Mannheim.[184] The Intergovernmental Organization for International Carriage by Rail (OTIF) was set up on 1 May 1985;[185] the EC is a member of OTIF.

The maritime transport division of the United Nations Conference on Trade and Development (UNCTAD) has drafted a number of conventions, the most important of which is that laying down a code of conduct for Liner Conferences.[186] The Community has observer status in UNCTAD. In recent years, UNCTAD has lost much of its influence. In the field of safety and the protection of the marine environment, the International Maritime Organization (IMO, based in London) is the relevant body, and is also a part of the UN. In IMO, the European Commission has observer status.[187] Given the world-wide nature of the IMO, EC legislation in this area nearly always takes the rules laid down by this body as basis for more far-reaching rules; nevertheless, with the continuing growth of EC policy, there is increasing tension. The Organization for Economic Cooperation and Development (OECD, based in Paris) played an important role in the preparation of the decision-making by the Western countries (the so-called B Group) in the UNCTAD

---

179. Opinion 1/94, WTO, para. 48; such competence falls under Arts. 71 and 80 EC. The Treaty of Nice did not alter this.
180. Opinion 1/94, WTO, para. 89.
181. ECMT is administratively part of the OECD.
182. Which is a regional commission of the United Nations Economic and Social Council.
183. France, Germany, Belgium, the Netherlands and Switzerland are members. The special problems concerning Switzerland were dealt with in Opinion 1/76, *European Laying-up Agreement*. See further M. Decker, Juridische aspecten van de codificatie en harmonisering van de Europese internationale rivierenregimes, PhD thesis, Antwerpen, 2003.
184. See below, section 3.10.
185. As a consequence of the Convention of 9 May 1980 (COTIF). Its predecessor was the Central Office for International Carriage by Rail which was set up in 1893.
186. UNCTAD Convention on a Code of Conduct for Liner Conferences ((1974) 13 ILM 917).
187. F. Hoffmeister and P.J. Kuijper, 'The Status of the EU at the UN: Institutional Ambiguities and Political Realities', in J. Wouters, F. Hoffmeister and T. Ruys, *EU-UN: An Ever Growing Partnership* (eds.) (The Hague, 2006).

framework, as well as in the adoption of its own policies, as demonstrated by the Code of Liberalization of Current Invisible Operations.[188] The Community has observer status in the OECD, likewise, but the Commission plays an active role in the OECD's work.[189]

For the air transport field, the International Civil Aviation Organization is the world-wide forum responsible for economic and technical cooperation in civil aviation, and the EC has recently achieved an upgraded participant status therein;[190] at European level the relevant organizations are the European Civil Aviation Conference – which aims to improve the coordination, better utilization and development of European air traffic – and Eurocontrol, in relation to air safety. On 8 October 2002, the Member States and the EC signed a Protocol on the Accession of the EC to the revised Eurocontrol Convention. With all these organizations, a certain tension arises as a result of the increasingly extensive activities of the EC.

Concrete relations with third countries concerning maritime, air and road transport are usually set out in bilateral conventions, which means that there is an extensive set of rules, particularly in the aviation sector. Any incompatibility between these conventions and the EC Treaty must be eliminated, in accordance with the second paragraph of Article 307 EC.[191] In the aviation sector, such problems were at issue in the so-called '*open skies*' cases.[192] Such bilateral agreements are increasingly being replaced by agreements between the EC itself and third countries. Special mention should be made in this context of the agreements between the EC and Switzerland in the area of rail and road transport and aviation.[193]

---

188. OECD, Paris, 1992.
189. <www.OECD.org/about/0,3347,en_33873108_33873325_1_1_1_1_1,00.html>
190. F. Hoffmeister and P.J. Kuijper, 'The Status of the EU at the UN', op. cit. *supra*, note 187.
191. In Joined Cases C-62 & 84/98, *Commission v. Portugal*, the ECJ ruled that Portugal had not fulfilled its obligations under Art. 3 of Reg. 4055/86 (O.J. 1986, L 378/1). The shipping agreements with Angola and Yugoslavia breached the principle of non-discrimination. Portugal was therefore under an obligation to denounce the agreements. The Court did not need to interpret Art. 307, because both agreements contained a clause enabling denunciation. Agreements without discriminatory cargo-sharing clauses may be prolonged on the basis of an authorization by the Council. See Council Decision 2001/855/EC authorizing the automatic renewal or continuation in force of provisions governing matters covered by the common commercial policy contained in the friendship, trade and navigation treaties and trade agreements concluded between Member States and third countries, O.J. 2001, L 320/13. The annexe to the Decision contains a long list of such agreements.
192. See further section 3.12 *infra*. Case C-466/98 *Commission v. United Kingdom*; Case C-467/98, *Commission v. Denmark*; Case C-468/98, *Commission v. Sweden*; Case C-469/98, *Commission v. Finland*; Case C-471/98, *Commission v. Belgium*; Case C-472/98, *Commission v. Luxembourg*; Case C-475/98, *Commission v. Austria*; Case C-476/98, *Commission v. Germany*.
193. O.J. 2002, L 114. The agreements can be found at <www.europa.admin.ch/e/index.htm>. See on this S. Breitenmoser, 'Sectoral Agreements between the EC and Switzerland: Contents and Control', CML Rev., 2003. See also R. Bieber, F. Maiani and M.Delaloye, *Droit européen des transports* (Helbing & Lichtenhahn, Bruylant, L.G.D.J., Brussels 2006), Ch. XIII, 357–381.

3.4   COMPETITION IN THE TRANSPORT SECTOR: GENERAL OBSERVATIONS

Up until 1 May 2004, the whole transport sector was subject to special competition rules, diverging from those which were applicable in other sectors. Since this date, the general rules of Regulation 1/2003 also apply to the transport sector.[194] Air transport between Member States and third countries is not excluded from the Regulation's scope any longer.[195] The rules for these sectors and block exemptions are dealt with in sections 3.11 and 3.12 below.

3.5   THE TREATY PROVISIONS ON TRANSPORT

3.5.1   Article 70 EC

Article 70 EC confirms the rule laid down in Article 51(1) EC that the freedom to provide services in the field of transport is to be achieved in the context of the common transport policy. It also places that policy in the perspective of the general objectives of the EC Treaty. The Treaty itself gives no further indication of the objectives of a common transport policy, unlike Article 33 for the CAP. In the absence of indications in the Treaty a considerable discussion ensued in the literature.[196] The Commission has produced various papers and communications elaborating the common transport policy.[197] The concept was extensively discussed in the transport policy case,[198] in which the common transport policy was described as 'a coherent set of rules'.[199] The importance of a correct definition of the concept was somewhat diminished by the Court's conclusion that it was for the Council to determine the objectives and means of that policy. As a result of that judgment, the Council proceeded to draw up programmes for the achievement of a common policy in the various branches of transport.[200] In the discussion about a common transport policy, a major debate continued for a long time between the proponents

---

194. Reg. 1/2003, on the implementation of the rules on competition laid down in Arts. 81 and 82 of the Treaty, O.J. 2003, L 1/1. Art. 43 of this regulation repeals Reg. 141/62 which provided for an exemption of the transport sector from the scope of Reg. 17/62. Reg. 1419/2006 (O.J. 2006, L 269/1) repealed Reg. 4056/86 (which set special rules for applying Arts. 81 and 82 in the maritime transport sector) with the exception of Art. 1(3)(b) and(c), Arts. 3 to 7, Art. 8(2) and Art. 26 which continue to apply for conferences satisfying the requirements of Reg. 4056/86 for a transitional period of two years. Art. 2 of Reg. 1419/2006 provides that Art. 32 of Reg. 1/2003 shall be deleted, which means that international tramp vessel services and maritime cabotage are henceforward subject to the general competition rules of Arts. 81, 82, 86 and Reg. 1/2003.
195. Reg. 411/2004, O.J. 2004, L 68, amending Regs. 3975/87 and 3976/87, as well as Reg. 1/2003.
196. See the suggested further reading at the end of this chapter.
197. Of which the most important recently is the White Paper, 'European Transport Policy for 2010: Time to Decide', COM(2001)370 final, 12 Sep. 2001.
198. Case 13/83, *Parliament v. Council.*
199. At para. 46.
200. Resolution of 12 Sep. 1985, O.J. 1985, C 262/69.

of liberalization and the supporters of harmonization. Now that the common transport policy has largely been achieved, the importance of that discussion has receded.

3.5.2 Article 71 EC

Article 71 EC is the core of the transport policy. It first indicates the procedural framework for the establishment of the policy. Then, Article 71(1)(a) and (b) prescribe that in any event common rules must be established for international transport to or from the territory of a Member State or passing across the territory of one or more Member States, and that rules must be established for the conditions under which non-resident carriers may operate transport services within a Member State (cabotage transport). The Court has ruled[201] that the Council may adopt the measures it deems necessary to guide the required liberalization. Such measures may be based on Article 71(1)(d) EC, as well as on the words 'taking into account the distinctive features of transport' in the first sentence of Article 71(1) EC. The Council has a wide margin of discretion on this point.[202] In particular the Council may decide what degree of market intervention is necessary. On the basis of Article 71 EC, the Council established a system to cope with any possible crisis in road transport.[203] The Commission collects data necessary to monitor the market and to detect a possible crisis.[204] If a Member State considers that there is a crisis, it may request the Commission to investigate; if the Commission considers that there is a crisis, it may adopt measures to restrict the supply capacity; such measures may last for up to six months and may be renewed once for up to six months more.[205] Article 71(1)(c) EC was added by the Treaty of Maastricht, conferring express competence on the Community to adopt measures to improve transport safety.[206]

3.5.3 Article 72 EC

Article 72 EC obliges the Member States not to introduce provisions which make the conditions of transport for transporters from other Member States less favourable.[207] In Case C-195/90, *Commission v. Germany*, the Court gave a broad

---

201. In the *transport policy* case: Case 13/83, *Parliament v. Council*.
202. The Court confirmed this in Case C-17/90, *Pinaud Wieger*.
203. Reg. 3916/90, O.J. 1990, L 375/10.
204. Ibid., Art. 3.
205. Ibid., Art. 4.
206. Dir. 2002/15, O.J. 2002, L 80/35, on the organization of the working time of persons performing mobile road transport activities, was adopted also with the aim of improving road safety. As will be shown in sections 3.11 and 3.12 *infra*, this power has been used extensively in the area of sea and air transport. Specific competence in transport safety permits a wide range of Community action in this area. See e.g., the 'Commission Communication on a European Road Safety Action Programme', COM(2003)311 Final, 2 Jun. 2003.
207. In Case C-320/03 R, *Commission v. Austria*, the President of the ECJ ordered Austria to suspend the sectoral ban on driving, designed to reduce emissions. In Case C-320/03, *Commission v. Austria*, the Full Court ruled that the Austrian ban was contrary to Arts. 28 and 29 EC.

interpretation of this obligation, so that measures designed to terminate hitherto more favourable conditions for transporters from other Member States, and place them on an equal footing with national undertakings also fell foul of Article 72 EC. That provision ceases to have effect when the measures specified in Article 71(1) EC are adopted. In view of the drafting, it can be accepted that Article 72 EC is directly effective.[208] This standstill clause may still be relevant for new accessions, even after the achievement of a common transport policy.

3.5.4 Article 73 EC

Article 73 EC provides that aid measures which meet the needs of coordination of transport, or which represent reimbursement 'for the discharge of certain obligations inherent in the concept of a public service' are compatible with the Treaty; these principles are further elaborated in Regulations 1191/69 and 1107/70.[209] Article 73 is generally regarded as supplementing the exceptions to the prohibition on state aids listed in Article 87(2) and (3) EC. Articles 87 and 88 EC are otherwise applicable to the transport sector.[210] Article 73 EC may also be seen as an exception to Article 86(2) EC.[211] Moreover, the provisions in the fields of public service and competition, discussed above, are important for the interpretation of this provision.

3.5.5 Article 74 EC

Article 74 EC provides that measures taken within the framework of the Treaty in respect of transport rates and conditions must take account of the economic circumstances of carriers. This appears to confirm the rationale for a common transport policy discussed in section 3.1 above, and is a clear obligation which the Council has to take into account in the adoption of measures under Article 71 EC.[212]

---

208. As appears from Joined Cases C-184 & 221/91, *Oorburg and Van Messem v. Wasser- und Schiffahrtsdirektion Nordwest.*
209. O.J. 1969, L 156/1 on action by Member States concerning the obligations inherent in the concept of a public service in transport by rail, road and inland waterway, as last amended by Reg. (EEC) No. 1893/91 (O.J. 1991, L 169/1). Reg. (EEC) No. 1107/70 of 4 Jun. 1970 on the granting of aids for transport by rail, road and inland waterway, O.J. 1970, L 130/1. The Commission adopted (20 Jul. 2005) a proposal for a regulation on public passenger transport services by rail and by road Brussels, COM(2005)319 final, 2000/0212 (COD) which repeals the two previous regulations; on 25 Jul. 2007, the Commission adopted a position on the amendments proposed by the EP, COM(2007)460 final. The Commission has also taken a decision on the application of Art. 86(2) EC to state aid in the form of public services compensation granted to certain undertakings entrusted with the operation of services of general economic interest, O.J. 2005, L 312/67. See section 3.1.3 above and section 3.6 on state aids.
210. See Case 156/77, *Commission v. Belgium.*
211. Cf. Case C-387/92, *Banco Exterior de España v. Ayuntamiento de Valencia.*
212. Cf. also the judgment in Case C-17/90, *Pinaud Wieger.*

3.5.6   Article 75 EC

Article 75 EC required the abolition at the latest before the end of the second stage of the transitional period of discriminatory carriage rates and conditions; it is a *lex specialis* in relation to Article 12 EC. It may be assumed that Article 75 is directly effective. The obligation is worked out in more detail in Regulations 11/60[213] and 3626/84.[214]

3.5.7   Article 76 EC

Article 76 EC contains a prohibition on Member States imposing, in respect of transport operations carried out within the Community, rates and conditions involving any element of support or protection in the interest of one or more particular undertakings or industries. Here it should be mentioned that, to the extent that such support or protection constitutes aid in the sense of Article 87 EC – which, in view of the wide definition of state aid which the Court applies, is very likely – Articles 87 and 88 EC will apply in addition to Article 73 EC, as will the case law and legislation on services of general economic interest.

3.5.8   Article 77 EC

Article 77 EC prohibits the carriers from imposing charges or dues in respect of the crossing of frontiers (in addition to the transport rates) which are in excess of a reasonable level after taking the costs actually incurred thereby into account. The Member States are obliged to endeavour to reduce those costs. This provision shows certain similarities with the prohibition of charges having equivalent effect to customs duties. If it can be shown in a particular case that the charges are disproportionate to the costs, it is submitted that shippers will be able to rely on Article 77 EC against carriers.

3.5.9   Articles 78 and 79 EC

Article 78 EC has largely lost its significance after German unification, just like Article 87(2)(c) EC, as a result of the Commission's restrictive interpretation of the latter provision.[215]

Article 79 EC establishes an Advisory committee for Transport, which is attached to the Commission.

---

213. Reg. 11/60, O.J. 1960, 121.
214. Reg. 3626/84, O.J. 1984, L 335/4.
215. The Commission's interpretation was endorsed by the Court in Case C-156/98, *Germany v. Commission.* See Hancher, Ottervanger, Slot, op. cit. *supra* note 116 para. 4-008-4010 at 107; See also Heidenhain, *Handbuch des Europäischen Beiheilferechts* (München, 2003), 188 et seq.

3.5.10 Article 80 EC

The drafting of Article 80(2) EC was revised by the SEA;[216] moreover a reference to Article 80 was included in Article 14(1) EC. The drafting of Article 80(2) EC is decidedly infelicitous, as the first sentence still refers to the Council deciding 'by what procedure' appropriate provisions for sea and air transport are to be laid down, whereas the second sentence prescribes that of Article 71(1) and (3) EC. It is also regrettable that the word 'whether' in that same sentence was not removed: keeping the present drafting still gives rise to doubt about the obligation to establish a common policy for maritime and air transport. The change in the decision-making process to permit qualified majority voting is, though, a clear improvement.

3.6 Inland Transport: General Observations[217]

Before looking at the secondary law in each of the transport branches individually, it is appropriate to give an overview of measures which apply in more than one branch.

3.6.1 Framework Programmes

The EC Treaty suggests that transport policy should be more or less a coherent whole.[218] On various occasions, the Council has adopted resolutions or decisions in which working programmes were set out. The last of these taken in the form of a decision was as long ago as 14 December 1967;[219] subsequently, such policy intentions were laid down as resolutions. An important example is a Council resolution of 12 September 1985,[220] which can be seen as the Council's response to the judgment in the transport policy case, mentioned above.[221] Furthermore, the Commission has adopted a number of Communications in which it has proposed programmes for its future activities.[222] The Schaus Memorandum of 10 April 1961

---

216. Art. 16(5) and (6) SEA. This amendment was a reaction to the judgment of the ECJ in Case 13/83, *Parliament v. Council (common transport policy)*.
217. As was mentioned in section 3.1, the term 'inland transport' covers road, rail, and inland waterway transport.
218. Cf. the discussion in Case 13/83, *Parliament v. Council*.
219. Dec. 67/790, O.J. 1967, 322/4. A first step in the development of a common transport policy was the adoption of the decision establishing a procedure for prior examination and consultation of Member States' proposed transport measures (Council Decision, O.J. 1962, 720, amended by Dec. 73/402, O.J. 1973, L 347/48).
220. O.J. 1985, C 262/99. Here, the Council took on the obligation of bringing about a common transport policy before 1 Jan. 1993. As is evident from the text, this resolution has been more or less completely achieved.
221. Case 13/83, *Parliament v. Council*.
222. See e.g., COM(83)85 final (O.J. 1983, C 154/1), and more recently, 'Common Transport Policy Action Programme 1995–2000', COM(95)302 final of 12 Jul. 1995; 'Connecting

formed the original basis for the Commission's activities, and gave the initial orientation for the development of a common transport policy.[223] As for the more recent developments, in 1998 the Commission published a communication on the common transport policy, entitled 'Sustainable mobility: Perspectives for the future'.[224] This was followed in 2001 by a white paper.[225] One of the concrete results of this white paper was the adoption of the so-called Marco Polo Programme, on freight transport.[226] Another element of the Community policy is the Alpine Convention in the field of transport and its Protocol.[227] In 1998, the Commission made a new attempt to grasp the nettle of charges for the use of transport infrastructures.[228]

3.6.2   **Public Services**[229]

Public service obligations are closely related to services of general economic interest, which were discussed above in section 3.1. For inland transport, some additional comments may be made. In Regulation 1191/69, the Council made provision for the removal of differences between the Member States' legislation concerning the treatment of public service obligations in the transport sector.[230] This regulation has been superseded by Regulation 1370/2007 discussed below.[231] In that sector in particular such differences are capable of significantly distorting competition. In order to attain the desired aim, common principles for the removal or treatment of public service obligations were established. As for the rail sector,

---

the Union's Transport Infrastructure to its Neighbours: Towards a Co-operative Pan-European Transport Network Policy', COM(97)172 final of 23 Apr. 1997, and most recently the White Paper of 2001, mentioned below.

223. Bull. EC 4-1961 5, see Tromm, *Juridische aspecten van het communautaire vervoersbeleid*, Tilburg, 1990, 125 et seq.
224. COM(98)716 final of 1 Dec. 1998.
225. White Paper, 'European Transport Policy for 2010: Time to Decide', 12 Sep. 2001, COM(2001)370 final.
226. Reg. (EC) No. 1692/2006 on the granting of Community financial assistance to improve the environmental performance of the freight transport system (Marco Polo Programme II) O.J. 2006, L 328/1. The Marco Polo Programme features three types of action: firstly, modal shift actions, which should focus on shifting as much cargo as possible under current market conditions from road to short sea shipping, rail and inland waterways; secondly, catalyst actions, which should change the way non-road freight transport is conducted in the Community; and thirdly, common learning actions, which should enhance knowledge in the freight logistics sector and foster advanced methods and procedures of cooperation in the freight market.
227. O.J. 2007, L 323/13.
228. White paper COM(98)466 final of 22 Jul. 1998.
229. See also section 3.1.3 *supra*.
230. Reg. 1191/69, O.J. 1969, L 156/1. In Case C-412/96, *Kainuun Liikenne Oy*, the Court ruled that Member States have a margin of discretion in deciding on a request to end a public service obligation.
231. O.J. 2007, L 315/1.

common rules and methods for the financial compensations arising from the normalization of railway accounts were laid down in Regulation 1192/69.[232]

3.6.3 State Aids[233]

As was noted above, Articles 87–88 EC apply in the transport sector in the normal way, albeit supplemented by Article 73 EC.[234] In Decision 65/271[235] the Council adopted a programme for the harmonization of national provisions on competition affecting the inland transport sectors, further elaborated in subsequent regulations.[236] Regulation 1370/2007 lays down the conditions under which competent authorities may compensate for the costs incurred when imposing or contracting public services obligations.[237] Article 3 of that regulation indicates when aid measures are permissible.

Regulation 1108/70 lays down rules for an accounting system for expenditure on infrastructure in respect of transport by rail, road and inland waterways.[238]

These regulations should be seen as a complement to the regulations mentioned above dealing with public service obligations and financial compensation. Until the *XVth Report on Competition Policy*[239] no mention was made of aids in the transport sector, but since then many annual reports have noted the large-scale support granted to national railways. Problems relating to inland waterway transport are also frequently encountered, and they have been countered with a Community aid regime.[240] In other inland transport sectors only incidental problems are reported. In 2002, the Council adopted three decisions on the basis of which aid in

---

232. Reg. 1192/69, O.J. 1969, L 156/8.
233. An extensive overview of state aid rules in the transport sector may be found in L. Hancher, T. Ottervanger and P.J. Slot, op. cit. Ch. 16, although that discussion does not deal with Reg. 1370/2007.
234. It should also be noted that according to the Commission Regional Aid Guidelines 2007 special rules apply for the transport sector.
235. O.J. 1965, 1500.
236. Reg. 1191/69, O.J. 1969, L 156/1 and Reg. 1192/69, O.J. 1969, L 156/8.
237. O.J. 2007, L 315/1. An example of application of the previous Reg. 1191/69 may be found in the Commission decision on aid for NS Cargo for a shuttle link between Rotterdam and Prague, O.J. 2001, L 38/43.
238. Reg. 1108/70, O.J. 1970, L 130/4. This regulation is further elaborated in Reg. 2598/70, O.J. 1970, L 278/1 and Reg. 281/71, O.J. 1971, L 33/11. It should also be mentioned that pursuant to its Art. 4, Dir. 80/723, O.J. 1980, L 195/35, amended by Dir. 2000/52, O.J. 2000, L 193/75, on the transparency of financial relations between Member States and public undertakings, does not apply in the transport sector.
239. For 1985 (Brussels and Luxembourg, 1986).
240. Reg. 1101/89 O.J. 1989, L 166/125. In the Joined Cases C-248 & 249/95, *SAM Schiffahrt and Stapf v. Germany*, the Court confirmed the validity of the regulation. In Case T-155/97, *Natural van Dam and Danser Container Line v. Commission*, the Court of First Instance confirmed the Commission's wide powers for granting exceptions, though in this case an exception was not granted. Case T-63/98, *Transpo Maastricht and Ooms v. Commission* similarly concerns the refusal of a request for an exemption. The regime was extended for a period of four years by Reg. 718/99, O.J. L 90/1.

the form of a reduction in or exemption from duties on diesel fuel was permitted.[241] In the maritime and air transport sectors there have been considerable aid operations, and the Commission has drawn up specific guidelines for aid in these sectors.[242] These are discussed in sections 3.11 and 3.12, below.

3.6.4   Competition

A separate system governed competition in inland transport up until the entry in force of Regulation 1/2003, 1 May 2004, in accordance with Regulation 1017/68.[243] At present, only Articles 3 and 4 of that Regulation are still in force.[244] Article 3 provides for an exemption for technical agreements; Article 4 provides for an exemption for groups of small and medium-sized undertakings. Article 3 agreements are unconditionally placed outside the scope of the prohibition of Article 81(1) EC; Article 4 provides for conditional exemption of agreements from Article 81(1). The retention of these two articles has the effect that the case law under Regulation 1017/68 relating to the substantive issues retains its relevance under the new competition regime. Because maritime transport is no longer subject to a special competition regime, as it was under Regulation 4056/86, the delimitation between inland transport and maritime transport is no longer an issue.[245]

3.7   ROAD TRANSPORT

3.7.1   Economic Regulation

As was briefly indicated in section 3.1.2 above, a common transport policy has been more or less established for professional freight transport by road.[246] Given

---

241. Decision 361/2002 (Netherlands), 362/2002 (Italy) and 363/2002 (France), O.J. 2002, L 131/12 et seq. The decisions were taken on the basis of Art. 88(2), 3rd para., EC. A Commission decision in which a Spanish aid measure for commercial vehicles was found to infringe Art. 87(1) EC, was annulled in Case C-409/00, *Spain v. Commission.*
242. O.J. 1994, C 350/5, air transport and O.J. 1997, C 205/5, sea transport.
243. Reg. 1017/68, O.J. 1968, L 175/1. This follows from the new Reg. 1/2003, see section 3.4 *supra.*
244. Art. 36 of Reg. 1/2003.
245. The previous delimitation problems were highlighted in Case C-264/95 P, *Commission v. Union internationale des chemins de fer.* The Court here confirmed the interpretation of the CFI that the sale of train tickets falls within the scope of Reg. 1017/68. See further the Commission decisions Transatlantic, O.J. 1994, L 376/1; Far Eastern Freight, O.J. 1994, L 378/17, TACA; O.J. 1999, L 95/1, on the delimitation of the respective scope of Reg. 1017/68 and Reg. 4056/86. See further on this section 3.11 *infra.* Although similar questions could arise in relation to the delimitation of Reg. 1017/68 and Reg. 3975/87 (air transport), these have not so far arisen.
246. Transport on own account has been liberalized ever since 1962. Dir. 2006/94 consolidates the 1962 rules and subsequent amendments, O.J. 2006, L 374/5.

that road freight transport forms a very large part of the professional freight transport sector, the economic importance of this system is very great indeed. Regulation 881/92[247] establishes a system of Community licences, based on qualitative criteria.[248] Directive 84/647 is also relevant, as it sets rules for the use of vehicles hired without drivers for the carriage of goods by road.[249]

Once a road haulage operator has a Community authorization, he or she may freely undertake international transport throughout the Community, as Regulation 881/92 has lifted all the earlier restrictions. Transport to third countries remains dependent on the agreements which have been concluded with those countries. In 1992, important transit agreements were concluded with Austria[250] and Switzerland;[251] the agreements with Austria were transformed into ordinary Community legislation after Austrian accession.[252] As was mentioned in section 3.3 above, new agreements have been concluded with Switzerland, as a result of which Switzerland is de facto part of the EC transport market.[253]

The holder of a Community authorization may carry out cabotage transport throughout the Community.[254] The liberalization of cabotage transport was made possible after a solution was found to the very divergent fees for the use of

---

247. O.J. 1992, L 95/1.
248. The Community authorizations are issued by the competent authorities in the Member State of establishment, ibid., Art. 5 of the Regulation. The qualitative criteria for access to the occupation of road haulage operator are set out in Dir. 96/26, O.J. 1996, L 124/1, amended by Dir. 98/76, O.J. 1998, L 277/35. In Case C-274/01, *Commission v. Belgium*, Belgium was found to be in breach of its Treaty obligations by failing to implement this Directive within the time limit.
249. O.J. 1984, L 335/72. The directive is amended by Dir. 90/398, O.J.1990, L 202/46. The directive was the subject of a preliminary ruling in Joined Cases C-228 & 289/01, *Bourrasse and Perchicot*.
250. Dec. 92/577, O.J. 1992, L 373/4. This agreement contains an original Ecopoints system (distribution of rights of transit for heavy goods vehicles), see Reg. 3637/92, O.J. 1992, L 373/1.
251. See Dec. 92/578, O.J., 1992, L 373/26. On the basis of Art. 4 of the new agreement between the EC and Switzerland (see note 193 *supra*), the first agreement remained in force until 2004.
252. Reg. No. 2327/2003 of the European Parliament and of the Council of 22 Dec. 2003, establishing a transitional points system applicable to heavy goods vehicles travelling through Austria for 2004, within the framework of a sustainable transport policy, O.J. 2003, L 345/30. According Art. 3(3) of the regulation these rules remain in force until the 2006 if no fresh legislation is adopted. After 2006, no transitional points system shall be applied. Council Reg. 863/2004 adapted this regulation to the accession of the ten new countries, O.J. 2004, L 161/44. A good overview of this problem may be found in the Opinion of A.G. Jacobs of 11 Jul. 2002, in Case C-112/00, *Schmidberger*.
253. See note 193 *supra*. O.J. 2002, L 114. Recent measures include: Decision No. 1/2004 of the Community/Switzerland Inland Transport Committee of 22 Jun. 2004, concerning the charging system applicable to vehicles in Switzerland for the period from 1 Jan. 2005, until the opening of the Lötschberg base tunnel or 1 Jan. 2008 at the latest 2005/249/EC; and Decision No. 2/2004 of the Community/Switzerland Inland Transport Committee of 22 Jun. 2004, amending Annex 1 to the agreement between the EC and the Swiss Confederation on the carriage of goods and passengers by rail and road.
254. Reg. 3118/93, O.J. 1993, L 279/1. Art. 1(2) empowers other carriers who are designated by national legislation to undertake such transport. Cabotage, it will be recalled, means a transport operation performed between two places in one country by a non-resident carrier.

infrastructure in the various Member States. Article 6 of Directive 1999/62 sets minimum rates for motor vehicle taxes.[255] These taxes are levied by the Member State of establishment, and not the Member State where the cabotage transport is carried out.[256] Under Article 7, Member States remain competent to introduce tolls or other road user charges, although they may not discriminate on the ground of carrier nationality or consignment origin or destination, nor may they give rise to any undue hindrance.[257] The directive also contains certain rules to ensure uniform application.

If there are serious disturbances in relation to cabotage, safeguard measures may be invoked.[258] For cabotage transport, the rates and contractual conditions of the host state apply.[259] In a real internal market of course such a provision should not apply any more.[260] Some countries, such as the Netherlands, the United Kingdom and Germany, no longer apply rate provisions; such provisions for domestic transport are still found in Italy, Spain and Greece.

For international transport there are no common rules for rates and contractual conditions: Regulation 4058/89[261] prescribes that the rates for international carriage are to be freely fixed between the parties to the haulage contract,[262] and the Member States have to establish a system whereby the rates charged are communicated to the national authorities, pending the introduction of a definitive system of market observation.[263]

Regulation 2679/98 aims to prevent serious disruption of the free movement of goods caused by any situation which physically or otherwise prevents, delays or diverts the import of these goods into, their export from or transport across a Member State; it is in a category of its own.[264]

---

255. The original directive, Dir. 93/89 (O.J. 1993, L 279/32) was later annulled on procedural grounds by the Court of Justice; it was replaced by Dir. 1999/62/EC on the charging of heavy goods vehicles for the use of certain infrastructures, O.J. 1999, L 187/42.

256. Case C-115/00, *Hoves Internationaler Transport-Service*.

257. In Case C-157/02, *Rieser Internationale Transporte*, the Court ruled that Austrian hauliers, like the hauliers of the other Member States, may rely on Arts. 7(b) of Dir. 93/89 and 7(4) of Dir. 1999/62 in order to claim that because of the (excessive) rate for the full itinerary on the Austrian Brenner motorway they suffer discrimination in comparison with road users using parts only of the itinerary on that motorway.

258. Reg. 3916/90, O.J. 1990, L 375/10 for international transport and Art. 7 Reg. 3118/93, O.J. 1993, L 279/1 for cabotage transport.

259. Reg. 3118/93, Art. 6. Cf. Case C-17/90, *Pinaud Wieger*.

260. Cf. Case C-113/89, *Rush Portuguesa v. Office national d'immigration*, and the posted workers Dir. 96/71 O.J. 1997, L 18/1. In a real internal market, the rates of the land of establishment would apply, as in the case of the free movement of goods, or – if these are lower – the rates in the Member State of destination or origin of the transport.

261. O.J. 1989, L 390/1.

262. Reg. 4058/89, Art. 2.

263. Ibid., Art. 3. Strangely, the preamble to Reg. 3916/90 (on the crisis mechanism; see *supra*) makes no mention of this system. Reg. 1172/98, O.J. 1998, L 163/1 obliges the Member States to collect statistical data, so that the Commission can carry out its tasks in relation to carriage of goods by road.

264. O.J. 1998, L 337/8. See on this C. Gimeno Verdego, 'La Réponse Communautaire aux blocages des réseaux de transport; application et perspectives d'avenir du règlement No. 2679/98 en vue de la protection du Marché Intérieur', (2002) CDE, 45–93.

3.7.2 Requirements with regard to Safety and the Environment

A number of measures concerning road transport are rather more general in scope, and have the effect – at least as a secondary consequence – of bringing the competitive conditions between the Member States closer together. The first of these to be mentioned here is the introduction of a Community driving licence.[265] The Community has also taken action on the harmonization of the technical control of motor vehicles and their trailers.[266] The original directive introduced the obligation of mutual recognition of roadworthiness tests according to Community rules. It was amended a number of times, and the rules were eventually consolidated in Directive 96/96.[267] Directive 2000/30 provides for rules on the technical roadside inspection of the roadworthiness of commercial vehicles.[268] As a result of these measures, lorries are assured of free movement. The formalities for the cross-frontier transport of goods have been adapted to the development of the internal market within the Community.[269]

A particular milestone in the achievement of the common transport policy – one which was of great economic importance – was the adoption of Directive 85/3 on weights, dimensions and certain other technical characteristics,[270] later replaced

---

265. See now Dir. 91/439, O.J. 1991, L 237/1, amended by Dir. 96/47, O.J. 1996, L 235/1 and Dir. 97/26, O.J. 1997, L 150/41 and Dir. 2006/126, O.J 2006, L 403/18. As is apparent from the ruling in Case C-230/97, *Criminal proceedings against Awoyemi*, third country nationals may also benefit from the system of the directive. A driving licence obtained in one Member State is also valid in other Member States. In Case C-246/00, *Commission v. Netherlands*, the Court found that the Netherlands had failed to comply with its obligations under Arts. 1(2) and 6(1)(c) of, and point 4 of Annex III to, Council Dir. 91/439/EEC of 29 Jul. 1991 on driving licences, as amended by Council Dir. 96/47/EC of 23 Jul. 1996.

266. Dir. 77/143, O.J. 1977, L 47/47; later repealed and replaced by Dir. 96/96, O.J. 1996, L 46/1, corr. O.J. 1998, L 93/22.

267. Ibid.

268. O.J. 2000, L 203/10. In Case C-375/03, *Commission v. Luxembourg*, Luxembourg was found to have failed its obligations to implement the directive. Other relevant measures include: Dir. 94/12/EC relating to measures to be taken against air pollution by emissions from motor vehicles and amending Dir. 70/220/EEC, O.J. 1994, L 100/19; Dir. 98/70/EC of the European Parliament and of the Council of 13 Oct. 1998 relating to the quality of petrol and diesel fuels and amending Dir. 93/12/EEC O.J. 1998, L 350/58; Dir. 98/69 relating to measures to be taken against air pollution by emissions from motor vehicles and amending Dir. 70/220/EEC, O.J. 1998, L 350/1; Dir. 1999/96/EC on the approximation of the laws of the Member States relating to measures to be taken against the emission of gaseous and particulate pollutants from compression ignition engines for use in vehicles, and the emission of gaseous pollutants from positive ignition engines fuelled with natural gas or liquefied petroleum gas for use in vehicles and amending Council Dir. 88/77/EEC, O.J. 1999, L 44/1.

269. Dir. 91/342, O.J. 1991, L 187/47, amending Dir. 83/643, O.J. 1983, L 359/8. See further Reg. 719/91, O.J. 1991, L 78/6 and Reg. 1593/91, O.J. 1991, L 148/11 on the use in the Community of TIR carnets and ATA carnets as transit documents. The abolition of systematic frontier controls on the movement of goods between Member States has meant the repeal of earlier legislation.

270. O.J. 1985, L 2/14 (amended on numerous occasions).

by Directive 96/53.[271] The long-running debate on the subject matter covered by these measures well demonstrates the competing interests of transporters who are anxious to transport goods as efficiently and cheaply as possible, freight vehicle manufacturers seeking to gain market dominance through their own standards, safety considerations, and, last but not least, environmental interests.

Directive 94/55 lays down rules for the transport of dangerous goods by road.[272]

The community directives on the protection of ambient air quality play a vital role for the road transport sector.[273] In a remarkable judgment, the ECJ ruled that Austria was entitled to implement more stringent environmental standards ahead of the deadline set by the relevant directive.[274] An important measure for the protection of the environment is found in Protocol No. 9 of the Accession Treaty for Austria[275] on the system of ecopoints for lorries in transit through Austria.[276]

Over the past decades, road transport has grown much faster than the other inland transport modes. This raises environmental concerns, since road transport causes more pollution than the other modes of transport. Shifting the balance between the modes of transport is therefore at the heart of the sustainable development strategy. Regulation 1692/2006, establishing the Marco Polo II programme, implements this strategy.[277]

The Council has also taken steps to ensure the duty-free admission of fuel contained in commercial vehicle fuel tanks,[278] as differences in the duty-free

---

271. O.J. 1996, L 235/59, corr. O.J. 1998, L 19/83.
272. O.J. 1994, L 319/7. This directive was amended by Dir. 95/50, O.J. 1995, L 249/35 and supplemented by Dir. 2001/26, O.J. 2001, L 168/23 with rules for uniform procedures for the control of transport of dangerous substances.
273. Dir. 96/62, on ambient air quality assessment and management,. O.J. 1996, L 296/55; and Dir. 1999/30 relating to limit values for sulphur dioxide, nitrogen dioxide and oxides of nitrogen, particular matter and lead in ambient air, O.J. 1999, L 163/41 amended by Commission decision 2001/744, O.J. 2001, L 278/35.
274. Case C-320/03, *Commission v. Austria.* Nevertheless the ECJ ruled against the Austrian ban on driving because it failed the proportionality test. Earlier the President of the ECJ ordered Austria to suspend the ban, Case C-320/03 R, *Commission v. Austria.* See case note on Case C-320/03, *Commission v. Republic of Austria* by A. Schrauwen, (2006) CML Rev., 1447–1456 and further references therein.
275. O.J. 1994, C 241/21 and 1995, L 1.
276. Commission Reg. 3298/94, O.J. 1994, L 341/20, laid down detailed arrangements for the implementation of this system. In Case C-445/00, *Austria v. Council*, Austria successfully challenged Council Reg. 2012/2000 amending the ecopoints system. In Case C-356/01, *Austria v. Commission*, Austria unsuccessfully challenged the Commission's decision not to propose legislation reducing the number of ecopoints for the year 2002. Reg. 2327/2003 (O.J. 2003, L 345/30) established a regime for 2004. After 2006, no transitional points system is applicable. The regulation was challenged by Austria in Case C-161/04, *Austria v. Parliament and Council*, but Austria later withdrew its application. The A.G. had proposed that the application should be rejected.
277. O.J. 2006, L 328/1, on the granting of Community financial assistance to improve the environmental performance of the freight transport system (Marco Polo II Programme). See section 3.6 *supra.*
278. Dir. 68/297, O.J. 1968, L 175/15 and Dir. 85/347, O.J. 1985, L 183/22.

exemptions lead to clear distortions of competition, especially where there are major differences in the level of diesel excise duty. Finally, provisions concerning the use of vehicles hired without drivers for the carriage of goods by road, are contained in the above-mentioned Directive 84/647.[279]

The interest of ensuring that adequate arrangements exist in relation to insurance was taken care of in Directive 72/166.[280]

3.7.3 Regulation of Social Aspects

One of the most important reasons why the transport sector has been subject to special rules in all the Member States and thus also at Community level is the social aspect. Many small firms operate in this sector and many measures were adopted with a view to protecting them against cut-throat competition. In this way, questions concerning the social aspects of transport have always been considered important. In order to promote the dialogue between the social partners the Commission has established sectoral committees.[281]

The harmonization of certain provisions of social policy has also played an important role. It was in this field that the celebrated litigation in Case 22/70 *Commission v. Council* took place, relating to the ERTA Agreement which governs international road transport involving through third countries.[282] Regulation 3820/85 contains the provisions relating to manning, driving times, and rest periods, as well as a prohibition of certain types of incentive payments.[283] The other aspects of working time in relation to road transport are regulated in Directive 2002/15.[284]

An important piece of legislation in this respect was the regulation on the introduction of the tachograph (euphemistically called 'recording equipment' in

---

279. O.J. 1984, L 335/72, amended by Dir. 90/398, O.J. 1990, L 202/46.

280. Dir. 72/166, O.J. 1972, L 103/1. The directive has been amended by Dir. 72/430, O.J. 1972, L 291/162 and Dir. 84/5, O.J. 1984, L 8/17. The most important obligation is that the Member States cease to require presentation of a Green card at their borders; furthermore they are obliged to take all possible steps to ensure that vehicles registered in their countries have at least third-party insurance.

281. Commission Decision 98/500/EC on the establishment of Sectoral Dialogue Committees promoting the Dialogue between the social partners at European level O.J. 1998, L 225/27.

282. The European Agreement concerning the Work of Crews of Vehicles engaged in International Road Transport (Geneva, 1 Jul. 1970 to 31 Mar. 1971, TS 103 (1978); Cmnd 7401), ERTA, also frequently known by its acronym in French, AETR. The Community rules apply to transport within the Community. For transport outside the Community, the Council established, by Reg. 2829/77, O.J. 1977, L 334/1, the application of the ERTA agreement. Art. 3 of this Regulation provides that the agreements concluded with third countries on the basis of Art. 2(2) ERTA are to be concluded by the Community. In addition, the TIR agreement of 14 Nov. 1975 should be mentioned, Reg. 3237/76, O.J. 1976, L 368/1, approved by Reg. 2112/78, O.J. 1978, L 252/1.

283. O.J. 1985, L 325/1. See on the interpretation of Art. 8 of the Regulation, on rest periods, Case C-439/01, *Cipra and Kvasnicka.* Dir. 2006/22/EC lays down minimum conditions for the implementation, O.J. 2006, L 102/35.

284. O.J. 2002, L 80/35.

the legislation, but in plain English labelled as the 'spy in the cab').[285] Article 3 required vehicles intended to transport goods or persons by road, and registered in a Member State, to be fitted with recording equipment complying with the terms of the regulation. This equipment registers, amongst other things, compliance with rules on driving time and rest periods. Differences in national practice with respect to control of compliance with this regulation can lead to considerable distortion of competition. This and other regulations concerning social aspects have led to a great deal of case law, mainly following preliminary references.[286]

3.8   CARRIAGE OF PASSENGERS BY ROAD

The common regime for carriage of passengers by road is based on controlling access to the occupation of passenger transport operator, through requirements as to good repute, appropriate financial standing and professional competence.[287] These requirements are further elaborated by the Member States.

On the other hand, international coach and bus transport is governed by Regulation 684/92.[288] By virtue of Article 3 of that regulation, any passenger transport operator authorized in his or her Member State of establishment who satisfies the requirements as to access to the profession and road safety requirements, may provide bus and coach services within the Community. Regular services and so-called 'special regular services' (previously called shuttle services) are subject to authorization by the Member States. Own-account services are possible on the basis of a control document or certificate issued by the competent authorities of the Member State in which the vehicle is registered.[289] The holder of a Community authorization may also carry out cabotage services.[290]

---

285. Reg. 1463/70, O.J. 1970, L 164/1. Consolidated version Reg. 3821/85, O.J. 1985, L 370/8, most recently amended by Reg. 561/2006 on the harmonization of certain social legislation relating to road transport (O.J. 2006, L 102/1).

286. See e.g., Case C-394/92, *Criminal proceedings against Michielsen and Geybels Transport Service*; Case C-235/94, *Criminal proceedings against Bird*; Case C-29/95, *Pastoors and Trans-Cap v. Belgium*. In the last mentioned case, a Belgian rule whereby a 50% higher fine was demanded from nationals of other Member States than for Belgian nationals for infringements of Reg. 3820/85 and Reg. 3821/85, was found to be in breach of Art. 12 EC; Case C-335/94, *Mrozek and Jäger*.

287. Dir. 96/26 (O.J. 1996, L 124/1) which replaces earlier legislation. Cf. Art. 2. The Directive has been amended a number of times (as can be gleaned from the consolidated version in Eurlex). The access of non-resident carriers to the market in national road passenger transport services within a Member State is regulated in Reg. 12/98, O.J. 1998, L 4/10.

288. O.J. 1992, L 74/1 amended by Reg. 11/98 (O.J. 1998, L 4/1), replacing earlier legislation.

289. All services other than regular services may be provided without the need for any form of authorization, see the amendments made by Reg. 11/98, ibid.

290. Reg. 12/98, O.J. 1998, L 4/10. Under Art. 3, cabotage includes occasional services, special regular services covered by a contract and regular services in the course of a regular international service.

Finally, it should be mentioned that the Agreement on the International Carriage of Passengers by Road by means of Occasional Coach and Bus Services (ASOR) was concluded, for transport to, via, or from third countries.[291]

3.9 RAIL TRANSPORT

The main objective of the policy in this sector has always been to promote the healthy financial position of the railways and to guarantee reasonable conditions of competition *vis-à-vis* transport by road and inland waterways. The fact that railways have been and for the most part still are public undertakings has been an important factor in this. The Member States have taken on an important part of the infrastructure costs, which makes the competitive relationship with other forms of transport very difficult, and it is unsurprising that there is still no satisfactory solution within the Community to the problem of the allocation of rail infrastructure costs. In addition, a solution needs to be found to the problem of transport on unprofitable lines, which is important for regional policy considerations. Various measures of Community secondary law therefore are directed at obtaining transparency in regard to the financial relations of the railways, and the relations between the railways and the Member States.

Directive 91/440 was a first step in the liberalization of rail transport. The directive requires a clear separation to be made between the management and accounts concerning the various functions of the railways: on the one hand the provision of transport services, and on the other hand the management of railway infrastructure.[292] Under Article 10, access and transit rights must be ensured for third parties. This directive was amended by Directive 2001/12.[293] The most important change concerned the broadening of access rights for freight transport. In addition, the requirements on separation ('unbundling') and granting access to the network were tightened up. Directive 95/18 establishes a procedure for granting a Community railway licence, and lays down the relevant conditions.[294] Rules for the allocation of railway infrastructure capacity, and the levying of charges for the use of railway infrastructure are laid down in Directive 2001/14.[295] These

---

291. Council Decision of 12 Jul. 1982, concluding the Agreement, O.J. 1982, L 230/38; implementing rules were laid down in Reg. 56/83, O.J. 1983, L 10/1.
292. O.J. 1991, L 237/25. Under Art. 12, this directive is without prejudice to Dir. 90/531 on public procurement in the so-called excluded sectors. One of the first measures in this area was decision 75/327, O.J. 1975, L 152/3. The directive has been amended by Dir. 2007/58, O.J. 2007, L 315/44.
293. O.J. 2001, L 75/1.
294. O.J. 1995, L 143/70. The licence is not valid for transport through the channel tunnel. Dir. 95/18 was amended by Dir. 2001/13 (O.J. 2001, L 75/26) which harmonized the conditions for the grant of an authorization, so that access to transport throughout the whole Community is achieved. Safety requirements were also tightened up.
295. O.J. 2001, L 75/29. There have been several infringement proceedings for failure to implement the respective directives: Case C-482/03, *Commission v. Ireland* (Dir. 2001/14), Case C-477/03, *Commission v. Germany* (Dir. 2001/12, 13 and 14), Case C-483/03, *Commission v. United Kingdom*

requirements have since been amended by Directive 2004/49,[296] which lays down more detailed rules for safety certification. Directives 2001/12 and 2001/14 provide the legal basis for the creation of a Regulatory Body, and for such a body's powers.[297] This body has now been established[298] and is entrusted with the task of promoting safety standards and competitiveness. The Community has adopted rules for the certification of train drivers.[299] Furthermore Regulation 1371/2007 lays down rules on rail passengers' rights and obligations.[300]

Regulation 1017/68, applying rules of competition to transport by rail, road and inland waterway, has occasionally been applied in the rail sector.[301]

Moreover, mention should be made of two important directives which aim to stimulate the interoperability of trans-European high-speed railway systems.[302]

Common rules for the normalization of the accounts of railway undertakings have long been in force.[303] Regulation 2830/77 set out measures which were needed in order to make the accounting systems and annual accounts of railway undertakings comparable.[304] The Member States have also long been obliged to abolish all 'obligations to carry' and all tariff obligations.[305] Further rules were also laid down concerning state aids.[306] The considerable increase in the transport of dangerous goods by rail led to the adoption of Directive 96/49, concerning harmonization legislation for the transport of dangerous goods.[307]

(Dir. 2001/12,13 and 14), Case C-550/03, *Commission v. Greece* (Dir. 2001/12, 13 and 14), and Case C-481/03, *Commission v. Luxembourg* (Dirs. 2001/12 and 13).

296.   O.J. 2004, L 164/44.
297.   In respectively Art. 10(7) of Dir. 2001/12 and Art. 30 and 31 of Dir. 2001/14.
298.   Reg. (EC) No. 881/2004 establishing a European railway agency O.J. 2004, L 164/1.
299.   Dir. 2007/59 O.J. 2007, L 315/51.
300.   O.J. 2007, L 315/14.
301.   Joined Cases T-374, 375, 384 & 388/94, *European Night Services et al. v. Commission*; Case T-14/93, *Union internationale des chemins de fer v. Commission* and Case C-264/95 P, *Commission v. Union internationale des chemins de fer*; Case T-229/94, *Deutsche Bahn v. Commission* and Case C-436/97 P, *Deutsche Bahn v. Commission*; Joined Cases T-79 & 80/95, *SNCF and British Railways v. Commission*. See also the case of Channel Tunnel Rail Link, O.J. 1999, C 6/7, where the Commission gave a so-called comfort letter for the development of the Channel tunnel link.
302.   Dir. 96/48, O.J. 1996, L 235/6 and Dir. 2001/16, O.J. 2001, L 110/1. In Case C-441/00, *Commission v. United Kingdom*; Case C-460/00, *Commission v. Greece*, the United Kingdom and Greece, respectively, were found to have failed to fulfil their obligations by not implementing Dir. 96/48.
303.   Reg. 1192/69, O.J. 1969, L 156/8.
304.   Reg. 2830/77, O.J. 1977, L 334/13. Further rules are found in Reg. 2183/78, O.J. 1978, L 258/1; Dir. 80/1177, O.J. 1980, L 350/23, on statistical registration; Decision 82/529, O.J. 1982, L 234/5, price formation.
305.   Reg. 1191/69, O.J. 1969, L 156/1, Art. 2.
306.   Reg. 1107/70, O.J. 1970, L 130/1, last amended by Reg. 3578/92, O.J. 1992, L 364/11. These regulations were discussed in section 3.6 *supra*.
307.   O.J. 1996, L 235/25, amended by Commission Dir. 96/87, O.J. 1996, L 335/45. Another important measure in this context is Dir. 2000/18, O.J. 2000, L 118/41, on minimum examination requirements for safety advisers for the transport of dangerous goods by road, rail or inland waterway.

3.10   Inland Waterway Transport

The basic rules on access to the market in the international transport of goods and passengers by inland waterway are laid down in Regulation 1356/96.[308] This regulation implements the principle of freedom to provide services in this sector.

Inland waterway transport in the Community occupies a special position insofar as one of the most important inland waterway routes in the Community, the Rhine and its tributaries, is governed by the Mannheim Convention. This Convention guarantees free navigation of the Rhine not simply for the riparian States, but also for other countries; as a result of the opening of the Rhine-Main-Danube canal, giving East European inland waterway fleets access to the Rhine waterway network, the traditional free navigation was confined to vessels having a real connection with one of the contracting parties to the Convention. This was laid down in a Protocol to the Revised Mannheim Convention. On the basis of the protocol, rules of application were established; the application of these rules in the Community is ensured by Regulation 2919/85.[309] Obviously, this protocol has lost its importance as a result of the accession of the remainder of the Danube Member States.

Regulation 3921/91 grants cabotage rights to Community carriers.[310]

In this area, too, there are rules relating to access to the occupation of carrier of goods by waterway in national and international transport, and on mutual recognition of diplomas, certificates and other titles relating to this occupation.[311] As for the other branches of transport, the conditions of access to the profession have been harmonized. Article 3 of the relevant directive sets professional competence as the condition for access to the occupation. The requirements for this are set out in annexes. If a comparison is made with the directives for other transport sectors, it is remarkable that here the requirements concerning reliability and creditworthiness are lacking. Article 7 of the directive states that diplomas and certificates issued in accordance with the directives are to be mutually recognized. Directive 96/50 sets the conditions for granting national national boatmasters' certificates for the carriage of goods and passengers by inland waterway in the Community.[312]

---

308. Council Reg. (EC) No. 1356/96 of 8 Jul. 1996 on common rules applicable to the transport of goods or passengers by inland waterway between Member States with a view to establishing freedom to provide such transport services. O.J. 1996, L 175/7.

309. O.J. 1985, L 280/4. A good overview may be found in M. Decker, *Juridische aspecten van de codificatie en harmonisering van de Europese internationale rivierenregimes*, PhD thesis, Antwerpen, 2003.

310. O.J. 1991, L 373/1. In its judgments in Case C-266/03, *Commission v. Luxembourg* and Case C-433/03, *Commission v. Germany*, the ECJ ruled that this regulation does not govern transport by carriers established in non-Member States.

311. Dir. 87/540, O.J. 1987, L 322/20.

312. O.J. 1996, L 235/31. In Case C-468/00, *Commission v. France*, France was found to have failed to fulfil its obligations by implementing this directive too late.

In recent years, inland waterway transport has been characterized above all by structural overcapacity. As a reaction to this, the Community has laid down rules for the restructuring of the sector.[313]

Of the Community measures in this field, the following should also be mentioned: Directive 76/135, which regulated reciprocal recognition of navigability licences;[314] Directive 2006/87, which lays down technical requirements for inland waterway vessels;[315] Regulation 1365/2006 on statistics of goods transport by inland waterways;[316] and Directive 2005/44, which provides rules for the deployment of ICTs on inland waterways, in order to increase the safety and efficiency of transport by inland waterway.[317]

3.11   Maritime Transport

3.11.1   Economic Regulation

Until recently, the core of maritime transport policy[318] consisted of Regulation 954/79[319] implementing the UNCTAD Convention on a Code of Conduct for Liner Conferences[320] and the package of measures adopted in December 1986: the last comprising Regulation 4055/86 on the application of the principle of the

---

313.   Reg. 1101/89, O.J. 1989, L 116/25. The measures consisted of a reduction of overcapacity by means of a scrapping programme coordinated at Community level, and associated measures to ensure that the existing overcapacity did not become even greater, or new elements add to overcapacity. To implement this, Art. 8 contained the so-called old-for-new rule: new tonnage could only be put into use if the equivalent old tonnage was scrapped without receiving a scrapping premium. In Case T-155/97, *Natural van Dam*, an application for annulment was brought against a refusal of the Commission to grant an exemption under Art. 3(8)(c) Reg. 1101/89. In 1997, the Commission produced a report on the effect of the scheme, COM(97)555 final of 3 Nov. 1997. The Commission was of the opinion that the scheme had worked satisfactorily. Nevertheless, it believed that the scheme needed to be prolonged, although at a lower intensity. Reg. 718/99 (O.J. 1999, L 90/1) prolonged the scheme for 4 years. Commission Reg. 336/2002, O.J. 2002, L 53/11 amended Reg. 805/1999 (O.J. 1999, L 102/64) containing implementing rules.

314.   O.J. 1976, L 21/10. On the basis of Art. 3 of the directive, navigability licences issued by other Member States in accordance with the directive are valid in all Member States, provided the licence was issued or last extended not more than five years previously and has not expired. On the basis of Art. 3(4), additional requirements may be set if dangerous goods are being transported; these requirements should be based on the Agreement on transport of dangerous goods on the Rhine (ADNR).

315.   Dir. 2006/87 laying down technical requirements for inland waterway vessels and repealing Council Directive 82/714/EEC, O.J. 2006, L 389 /1.

316.   O.J. 2006, L 264/1. Implementing rules are laid down in Reg. 425/2007, O.J. 2007, L 103/26.

317.   O.J. 2005, L 255/152. More detailed rules are provided in Regs. 414, 415 and 416/2007, O.J. 2007, L 105/1 et seq.

318.   L. Ortiz Blanco, *Shipping Conferences under EC Antitrust Law, Criticism of a Legal Paradox* (London, 2007).

319.   O.J. 1979, L 121/1. It may be concluded from Case 355/87, *Commission v. Council* that Art. 1 of this regulation does not involve an obligation to be a party to the UNCTAD agreement.

320.   Conferences are cartels of shipping lines on a particular route.

freedom to provide services,[321] Regulation 4056/86 on the application of the competition rules to this field,[322] Regulation 4057/86 on unfair pricing practices in the maritime sector,[323] and Regulation 4058/86 on free access to cargoes.[324] Cabotage transport has also been liberalized.[325] Member States do, however, retain the possibility to impose public service obligations for cabotage transport.[326]

After a thorough review of the industry by the Commission, Regulation 4056/86 was repealed in 2006.[327] The Council concluded that shipping conferences no longer fulfil the conditions of Article 81(3) EC. The Council further observed that the mechanisms of Regulation 1/2003 are also appropriate for the entire maritime sector and therefore abolished the exemption for cabotage and tramp vessels.[328] A year later regulation 954/79 was repealed as well;[329] it was noted that the repeal of Regulation 4056/86 made it impossible for the Member States to fulfil their obligations under the Convention on a Code of Conduct for Liner Conferences and thus made the repeal of the implementing regulation 954/79 inevitable. Therefore Regulation 4057/86 is presently the only regulation specifically applicable to liner services.[330] The regime is characterized by free access to the market, as well as the protection of this free market.[331]

---

321. O.J. 1986, L 378/1, corr. in O.J. 1988, L 117/33.
322. O.J. 1986, L 378/4, corr. in O.J. 1988, L 117/34.
323. O.J. 1986, L 378/14, corr. in O.J. 1988, L 117/35.
324. O.J. 1986 L 378/21, corr. in O.J. 1988, L 117/36.
325. Reg. 3577/92, O.J. 1992, L 364/7. Art. 6 lays down a number of transitional periods. The last of these (for Greece) expired on 1 Nov. 2002. In Decision 93/125, O.J. 1993, L 49/88, Spain was asked to repeal the unilateral safeguard measures it had taken based on Reg. 3577/92. In Case C-160/99, *Commission v. France*, France was found to have failed to fulfil its obligations by failing to adapt its national legislation to Reg. 3577/92. In the 4th report on the implementation of the cabotage Regulation, COM(2002)203 final of 24 Apr. 2002, the Commission concluded that participation of foreign vessels in national cabotage had remained limited. The difference in manning costs is an important reason for this. In Case C-400/99, *Italy v. Commission*, para. 65, the ECJ ruled that: 'any aid in excess of what is necessary to cover the public service obligations provided for in the contracts at issue cannot come within the scope of Article 4(3) of Regulation No. 3577/92.' In Case T-17/02, *Olsen v. Commission* the CFI found Reg. 3577/92 not applicable to the facts. In Case C-288/02, *Commission v. Greece*, Greece was found to have infringed Arts. 1, 3 and 6 of the regulation. In Case C-323/03, *Commission v. Spain*, Spain was found to have infringed Arts. 1,4 and 9 of Reg. 3577/92 by reserving access to the Ria de Vigo sea lanes to a single operator for a period of 20 years.
326. See on this Case C-205/99, *Analir*. See further section 3.1 *supra*.
327. Recital 3 of the preamble of Reg. 1419/2006, repealing Reg. 4056/86, O.J. 2006, L 269/1. The history of the regulation of competition in the liner transport sector has been extensively analysed by L. Ortiz Blanco, *Shipping Conferences under EC Antitrust Law: Criticism of a Legal Paradox* (Hart Publishing, 2007).
328. Art. 3 of Reg. 1419/2006 abolishes Art. 32 of Reg. 1/2003 which excluded these services from the scope of Reg. 1/2003
329. Reg. 1490/2007, O.J. 2007, L 332/1. The regulation will enter into force on 18 Oct. 2008, the same date as Reg. 1419/2006.
330. Tramp shipping services do not come under Reg. 954/79 and Reg. 4057/86. This has always been a free market world-wide; such services do fall under Reg. 4055/86.
331. Decision 167/2006/EC of the European Parliament and of the Council of 18 Jan. 2006 concerning the activities of certain third countries in the field of cargo shipping, O.J. 2006,

In Regulation 479/92[332] the Council empowered the Commission to grant a block exemption for liner consortia. After the abolition of Regulation 4056/86, the block exemption Regulation 823/2000 adopted pursuant to Regulation 479/92 is the only remaining special feature of the application of the competition rules in the maritime sector.[333]

Regulation 4056/86 was applied frequently and even though the regulation has now been repealed the Commission decisions continue to provide useful guidance.[334] Commission policy in this context was to set limits to the broad exemptions granted by the regulation, and to harmonize this area as much as possible with the application of the competition rules in other sectors. Thus, price agreements for intermodal transport were only accepted for the maritime transport leg and not for the onward inland transport.[335] In addition, the Commission decision on

---

L 33/18, is intended to provide for the necessary measures to adopt countermeasures in respect of the cargo shipping activities of certain third countries.

332. O.J. 1992, L 55/3.

333. Reg. 823/2000, O.J. 2000, L 100/24, amended by Reg. 611/2005, O.J. 2005, L 101,10. This block exemption applies to consortia participating in conferences and outside them both According to recital 7 and Art. 4 of the Regulation, the non-utilization of vessel capacity within a consortium is not an essential feature of consortia. According to Art. 3(2)(b) temporary capacity adjustments are exempted. The Commission has indicated that it will also have a critical look at this block exemption.

334. See the Decisions on Secrétama, O.J. 1990, L 35/23, on providing incorrect information; French-West African shipowners, O.J. 1992, L 134/1, and CEWAL, O.J. 1993, L 34/20, on prohibited reservation of loads and exclusion of competitors. The application against this decision was rejected by the CFI, Joined Cases T-24–26 & 28/93, *Compagnie maritime belge transports et al. v. Commission.* On appeal, Joined Cases C-395 & 396/96 P, *Compagnie maritime belge transports et al. v. Commission*, the ECJ confirmed the decision of the CFI. In para. 48 of this judgment, the Court stated that, by its very nature and in the light of its objectives, a liner conference can be characterized as a collective entity which presents itself as such on the market. On a particular market, a liner conference can therefore be considered to hold a collective dominant position. The judgment gives a number of important clarifications of the concepts of liner conferences and collective dominant positions, and abuses thereof in the form of selective price cuts and loyalty rebates. See also the follow-up decision by the Commission COMP/D2/32448 and 32450. On the basis of Art. 12 of the regulation, exemptions are frequently applied for, see e.g., P&O Stena Line, O.J. 2001, C 76/2. See for an overview the annual reports on competition policy.

335. This is evident particularly in the decisions Trans Atlantic Agreement, O.J. 1994, L 376/1; Far Eastern Freight Conference, O.J. 1994, L 378/17 and TACA, O.J. 1999, L 95/1. See annotation of the TACA decision by P.J. Slot in NTER (1999), p. 260 et seq. Appeals were brought against these decisions, which were eventually (after seven years) rejected: Case T-395/94, *Atlantic Container Line et al. v. Commission* and Case T-86/95, *Compagnie générale maritime et al. v. Commission.* These judgments give an excellent and detailed overview of both the issues raised and the procedural course of events. Joined Cases T-191 & 212–214/98, *Atlantic Container Line et al. v. Commission* [2003] ECR II-3275 annulled the Commission decision insofar as it imposed a fine. The Commission, in Nov. 2002, gave an individual exemption for the revised Trans-Atlantic Conference Agreement, IP/02/1677. This decision seems to provide a model for other conference agreements. For the Far Eastern Freight Conference, the Commission found an infringement in 2000, in the form of price-fixing, O.J. 2000, L 268/34. In Case T-213/00, *CMA CGM et al. v. Commission*, this decision was annulled.

Protection & Indemnity Clubs (P & I Clubs) is important in this context.[336] Although that decision was based on Regulation 17 rather than Regulation 4056/86, it is nevertheless an important decision for maritime transport. In the decision, the parties sought a negative clearance and individual exemption for mutual insurances for damage and liability.

Articles 87 and 88 EC have been applied on myriad occasions in the shipping sector since 1985.[337] Community guidelines on state aid to maritime transport were adopted in 1997 and revised in 2004.[338] These guidelines lay down a more flexible approach than in other sectoral regimes. Because of the great difference in competitiveness between ships registered in the Community and those outside – which frequently sail under a low-cost flag – operating aid is permitted by way of exception; this must be exceptional, temporary and degressive.

Regulation 4055/86 on the freedom to provide services aims to apply this principle to maritime transport between the Member States themselves, and between them and third countries.[339] The regulation provided for the gradual abolition of unilateral national restrictions. The regulation also governs the conditions under which Member States may conclude cargo-sharing arrangements with third countries.[340] Article 3 of the regulation provides that the Member States are to abolish rules on cargo-sharing arrangements contained in existing bilateral agreements. The Commission has brought infringement proceedings a number of times in order to make Member States comply with this obligation.[341] Also, a number of proceedings have been brought in which differences in harbour dues and charges for vessel traffic services were challenged.[342]

Regulation 4057/86 on unfair pricing practices in the maritime sector amounts to the establishment of anti-dumping rules in liner transport.[343]

---

336. Decision 1999/329/EC, O.J. 1999, L 125/12. P & I clubs provide a kind of mutual insurance.
337. Scharf in: L. Hancher, T.R. Ottervanger, P.J. Slot, op. cit., Ch. 16, paras 16-033–16-044 394–401.
338. O.J. 1997, C 205/5. An interesting application of the guidelines may be found in the Commission decision on state aid granted by Spain to Ferries Golfo de Vizcaya, O.J. 2001, L 89/28. The decision was taken after an earlier decision was annulled by the CFI, Case T-14/96, *BAI v. Commission*. The 2004 guidelines were published in O.J. 2004, C 13/3. They follow the same basic approach. The guidelines have been adopted by the EFTA Surveillance Authority, O.J. 2007, L 240/9.
339. It is apparent from Art. 1(1) Reg. 4055/86 that the application is restricted to the free provision of services between the Member States themselves, and between the Member States and third countries. Cabotage transport was excluded; this was liberalized by Reg. 3577/92.
340. In Case 355/87, *Commission v. Council*, the Commission challenged Council Decision 87/475, O.J. 1987, L 272/37, which authorized Italy to conclude a bilateral marine transport agreement with Algeria.
341. Joined Cases C-176 & 177/97, *Commission v. Belgium and Luxembourg*; Joined Cases C-62 & 84/98, *Commission v. Portugal* (agreement with Angola and former Yugoslavia); Case C-295/00, *Commission v. Italy*.
342. Joined Cases C-430 & 431/99, *Sea-Land Service and Nedlloyd Lijnen*; Case C-435/00, *Geha Naftiliaki et al.*
343. Reg. 15/89, O.J. 1989, L 4/1 imposed a compensatory duty on the South-Korean merchant marine company Hyundai. See Seong Deog Yi and Chong Ju Choi, 'The Community's Unfair Pricing Practice in the Maritime Transport Sector' (1991) EL Rev., 279–294.

Regulation 4058/86 on free access to cargoes is intended to coordinate the individual reactions of the various Member States to restrictions imposed on their vessels in maritime transport to third countries where such restrictions result from government measures. The Commission has presented a proposal for an agreement to be concluded in this area with the People's Republic of China.[344]

The Commission is regularly obliged to urge the Member States to comply with the general Treaty rules in the implementation of maritime policy. This mainly involves the infringement of the principle of freedom of establishment in national legislation on registration of vessels.[345]

3.11.2   Safety and Environmental Issues

Recent years have seen a sharp increase in measures on safety and environmental issues. In assessing this development, it should be realized that after the Second World War this field was regulated by the IMO, and that in the Member States' traditional shipping policy this world-wide regulatory system was strongly supported. A shift away from this world-wide approach began to take place as a result of public opinion, which was no longer satisfied with the EC's hesitancy in the areas of safety and environmental pollution. The frequent and well-publicized large-scale shipping disasters – disasters in both human and environmental terms – have played a very important role.[346]

EC policy in general in this area is characterized by deference to the basic principles drawn up by the IMO, although there is a certain tension between the two organizations. The cautious start to this policy consisted of two directives,

---

344. The text of the draft agreement may be found in O.J. 2002, C 181/16 E/08 176. Bulletin 12/2002 point 1.4.83. The agreement was ratified in spring 2008.

345. Case C-334/94, *Commission v. France* (nationality requirements for owner and crew; this case concerned failure to comply with the judgment in Case 167/73, *Commission v. France*); see also Case C-62/96, *Commission v. Greece* and Case C-151/96, *Commission v. Ireland*. See further Case C-290/94, *Commission v. Greece*, concerning the requirement that vessels used for public transport in Greece should have Greek crews. Case C-90/94, *Haahr Petroleum v. Åbenrå Havn et al.*; Joined Cases C-114 & 115/95, *Texaco v. Middelfart Havn et al. and Olieselskabet Danmark v. Trafikministeriet et al.*, and Case C-242/95, *GT-Link v. De Danske Statsbaner*, concern duties on goods imported from other Member States. Case C-297/00, *Commission v. Luxembourg* concerns the failure to implement Dir. 98/35 on minimum level of training of seafarers. In Case C-266/96, *Corsica Ferries France v. Gruppo Antichi Ormeggiatori del porto di Genova et al.*, the Court ruled that Arts. 28, 10, 81, 82 and 86 EC and the provisions of Reg. 4055/86 do not preclude legislation which requires shipping companies established in another Member State, when their vessels make port stops in the first Member State, to have recourse to the services which local mooring groups supply for a charge. In Case C-405/01, *Colegio de Oficiales de la Marina Mercante Española*, the ECJ ruled that Spain had failed to observe the obligation of Art. 39 EC by reserving the posts of master and chief mate to its nationals. In Case C-299/02, *Commission v. Netherlands*, the ECJ found that the Netherlands, by adopting legislation concerning the nationality of the shareholders of companies owning seagoing ships which they wish to register in the Netherlands and other related requirements, failed to fulfil its obligations under Arts. 43 and 48 EC.

346. This is summarized in the Commission report for the Biarritz European Council, on the Community's strategy for safety at sea, COM(2000)603 final of 29 Sep. 2000. The shipwreck of the Prestige in 2002 led to further legislative action.

concerning the pilotage of vessels by deep-sea pilots in the North Sea and the English Channel, and minimum requirements for certain tankers entering or leaving Community ports, respectively.[347]

Since 1995, the linchpin of Community policy has been the important Directive 95/21 on port state control.[348] This directive obliges the Member States to inspect vessels calling at their ports in order to enforce compliance with the safety, environmental and social (living and working conditions) requirements contained in various IMO conventions – and implicitly also the relevant EC directives mentioned below. The principle of port state control is an important deviation from the usual principle of international public law under which treaties are only binding on the parties to them.[349] The 'no more favourable treatment' principle which is set out in various IMO – and International Labour Organization (ILO) – conventions concerning maritime transport, means that ships registered in a state which is not party to the convention may also be inspected, in order to ensure compliance with the rules laid down in the conventions. For maritime transport, where large numbers of vessels are registered in states with low-cost flags, these states usually not being party to the conventions mentioned here, the principle is of great importance. Article 7b of the directive provides that authorities of the Member States shall ban sub-standard ships. The Commission shall publish a list of such ships.[350] In 2001, Directive 95/21 was supplemented by changes which were agreed in the framework of the IMO, and was further tightened.[351] The following measures are in force in this area:[352]

– Directive 94/58 on minimum training requirements for seafarers.[353]
– Regulation 3051/95 on safety procedures for ro/ro passenger vessels.[354]

---

347. Dir. 79/115, O.J. 1979, L 33/32 and Dir. 79/116, O.J. 1979, L 33/33.
348. O.J. 1995, L 157/1. The directive was amended and adapted to the developments in the IMO by Commission Dir. 98/42, O.J. 1998, L 184/40. An important amendment was made by Dir. 2001/16, O.J. 2002, L 19/17. The directive is based on the Memorandum of Understanding on Port State Control. With this Memorandum, the EU Member States have joined a number of other Western European States in order to exercise so-called Port State Control. On the basis of this principle, vessels are inspected for safety and environmental requirements in the ports of participating countries. In Case C-315/98, *Commission v. Italy*, Italy was found to have failed to fulfil its obligations for not having implemented this directive. Several other Member States have been found to have failed to implement the directive: Case C-439/02, *Commission v. France*; Case C-225/04, *Commission v. Finland.*
349. See on this G.C. Kasoulides, *Port State Control and Jurisdiction: Evolution of the Port State Regime*, Dordrecht, 1993; Z. Oya Özçayir, *Port State Control*, LLP, London, 2001.
350. O.J. 2007, C 222/2 provides a list of ships that were refused access to Community ports between 1 Oct. 2006 and 31 Aug. 2007, pursuant to Art. 7b of Council Dir. 95/21/EC on the port state control of ships.
351. Dir. 2001/106, O.J. 2002, L 19/17.
352. It should be emphasized that since the more recent disasters involving the 'Erika' and the 'Prestige' new legislation may be expected. For instance, the Commission has proposed that the Member States become parties to the Bunkers Convention, which lays down rules on liability for damage resulting from oil from ships' bunkers, O.J. 2002, C 51E/371.
353. O.J. 1994, L 319/28 amended by Dir. 98/35, O.J. 1998, L 172/1.
354. O.J. 1995, L 320/14 amended by Reg. 179/98, O.J. 1998, L 19/35.

- Directive 94/57, on common rules and standards for ship inspection and survey organizations.[355]
- Directive 96/98 on marine equipment.[356]
- Directive 98/18 on safety rules and standards for passenger ships.[357]
- Directive 98/41 on registration of persons sailing on board passenger ships operating to or from ports of the Member States of the Community.[358]
- Directive 1999/95 concerning the enforcement of provisions in respect of seafarers' hours of work on board ship.[359]
- Directive 2001/25 on the mutual recognition of seafarers' certificates issued by the Member States.[360]
- Directive 2001/96 establishing harmonized requirements and procedures for the safe loading and unloading of bulk carriers.[361]
- Directive 2002/6 on reporting formalities for ships arriving in and/or departing from ports of the Member States of the Community.[362]
- Directive 2002/59, establishing a Community vessel traffic monitoring and information system.[363]
- Regulation 417/2002 on the accelerated phasing-in of double hull or equivalent design requirements for single hull oil tankers.[364]
- Decision 2002/971, authorizing the Member States, in the interest of the Community, to ratify or accede to the International Convention on Liability and Compensation for Damage in Connection with the Carriage of Hazardous and Noxious Substances by Sea, 1996 (the HNS Convention).[365]

---

355. O.J. 1994, L 319/20, amended by Dir. 97/58 of the Commission, O.J. 1997, L 274/8. The directive was radically amended by Dir. 2001/105, O.J. 2002, L 19/9. In Case C-368/97, *Commission v. Belgium* and Case C-431/97, *Commission v. Ireland*, these Member States were found to have failed to fulfil their obligations for not implementing the directive. In Decision 98/295/EC the Commission recognized the 'Hellenic Register of Shipping', in accordance with Art. 4(3) Dir. 94/57/EC for a period of 3 years. By Decision 2005/623 O.J. 2005, L 219/43 recognition has been extended for another 3 years. By Decision 2006/660, O.J. 2006, L 272/17 the Polish register of shipping was recognized for a period of 3 years.
356. O.J. 1997, L 46/25.
357. O.J. 1998, L 144/1. In Case C-140/01, *Commission v. Belgium*, Belgium was found to have failed to fulfil its obligations to implement the directive correctly. This directive was amended by Dir. 2002/25, O.J. 2002, L 98/1 so as to comply with the new international instruments, the amendments to the IMO International Convention for the Safety of Life at Sea (SOLAS).
358. O.J. 1998, L 188/35.
359. O.J. 1999, L 167/33. In Case C-410/03, *Commission v. Italy*, Italy was found to have failed to fulfil its obligations to implement the directive.
360. O.J. 2001, L 136, 17 amended by Dir. 2005/45, O.J. 2005, L 255/160.
361. O.J. 2002, L 13/9.
362. O.J. 2002, L 67/31.
363. O.J. 2002, L 208/10. This directive replaces Dir. 93/75.
364. O.J. 2002, L 64/1. This regulation replaces Reg. 2978/94.
365. O.J. 2002, L 337/55.

    – Directive 2005/35 on ship-source pollution and on the introduction of
penalties for infringements.[366]

A new package of seven legislative proposals was adopted by the Commission in
autumn 2005. These proposals seek to enhance the standards of the port state
control regime, as well as other related safety issues. The Community safety policy
may look impressive if measured in terms of legislation, but it has two fundamental
flaws: one is that enforcement will always lag behind legislation, and this is particularly true in the field of international shipping where it is difficult for one
jurisdiction to impose its enforcement policy. The second, and probably more
important, flaw is the fact that it has so far been impossible to pierce the corporate
veil when it comes to punishing the real culprits. As a result, *mala fide* shipowners
can hide behind corporate structures set up in countries hosting flags of
convenience. The UNCTAD convention on registration of ships, which was
designed to tackle this problem, has remained a dead letter.[367] The Community
has attempted to remedy this by its Port State control policy and in particular the
Directive 95/21 discussed above.

    The fight against terrorism in the Community increasingly leaves its mark in
the maritime sector with the adoption of rules intended to enhance ship and port
facility security.[368] Directive 2005/65 introduces Community measures to enhance
port security in the face of threats of security incidents.[369] In addition, the Community has concluded an important agreement with the USA on container security.[370]

3.12   AIR TRANSPORT

It is certainly in the air transport sector that the changes as a result of liberalization
have been the most conspicuous. The spectacular growth in air travel has also
increased the need to regulate the airspace. This is reflected in the 'Single

---

366. O.J. 2005, L 255/11. A framework Decision No. 2005/667/JHA, O.J. 2005, L 255/164, supplemented the directive with a view to strengthening maritime safety by approximating the
legislation of the Member States providing for criminal penalties. In a judgment of the grand
chamber of the ECJ, Case C-440/05, *Commission and Parliament v. Council*, the Court held
that Arts. 2, 3 and 5 of the framework decision, providing for enforcement rules, could have
been validly adopted on the basis of Art. 80(2) EC and consequently the Framework decision
was annulled. By contrast the Court held that the provisions determining the type and level of
criminal penalties could not be adopted on the basis of Art. 80(2) EC, since this does not fall
within the sphere of competence of the Community. The validity of Dir. 2005/35 was unsuccessfully challenged in Case C-308/06, *Intertanko*. The ECJ held, in its judgment of 3 June
2008, that the Directive could not be assessed in the light of Marpol 73/78 or UNCLOS.
367. United Nations Convention on Conditions for Registration of Ships, Geneva, 7 Feb. 1986, not
in force, ILM Vol. 26, No. 5 p. 1229 et seq Sep. 1987.
368. Reg. (EC) No. 725/2004 O.J. 2004, L 129/6.
369. Dir. 2005/65/EC, O.J. 2005, L 310/28.
370. Agreement between the EC and the United States of America on intensifying and broadening
the agreement on customs cooperation and mutual assistance in customs matters to include
cooperation on container security and related matters, O.J. 2004, L 304/34.

European Sky' project, designed to promote efficiency and safety in the use of the airspace and air traffic control. The fight against terrorism also impacts clearly on the rules in this sector.

3.12.1   The Main Lines of the Regulatory System

Since 1 April 1997, there has been a single Community market for air transport by virtue of Regulation 2408/92.[371] Any Community airline company which possesses a Community authorization (issued by a Member State) is free to fly both national and international routes within the Community.[372] The application of this principle in practice has not been without problems.[373] Member States are entitled to impose public service obligations.[374] They are also entitled to distribute air traffic between various airports which are part of one airport system; the way in which the Italian authorities exercised this power led to considerable conflict at the time the new Malpensa airport near Milan came into use.[375]

Within the internal air transport market, the capacity and price restrictions which had long existed are now defunct. Under Regulation 2409/92, the airlines established within the Community have the freedom to set their rates as they wish, but it is still possible for safeguard measures to be adopted if cut-throat competition emerges.[376] In addition, the competition rules for the conduct of intra-Community air transport have been elaborated. The regime for the single European sky was extended by means of separate bilateral agreements to include Switzerland.[377] Norway and Iceland are included on the basis of the European Economic Area.

---

371. O.J. 1992, L 240/8. In Case C-70/99, *Commission v. Portugal* and Case C-447/99, *Commission v. Italy*, both countries were found to have failed to fulfil their obligations, because they set higher rates for intra-Community flights than internal flights, in breach of Art. 3(1) of the Regulation.
372. Reg. 2407/92, O.J. 1992, L 240/1.
373. Cf. Commission decision, O.J. 1994, L 127/32; the French airline Air Inter contested this decision, but the application was rejected by the CFI in Case T-260/94, *Air Inter v. Commission*; see further Case C-174/94 R, *France v. Commission*. Further, the ECJ ruled, in Case C-92/01, *Stylianakis*, that Art. 3(1) of the Regulation prohibits charging a higher airport tax for flights to other Member States than for internal flights.
374. Art. 4 of Reg. 2408/92. See in this context also Case C-205/99, *Analir*, and the discussion of public service obligations in 3.1 *supra*. In Case C-181/00, *Flightline*, the Court ruled that if a Member State imposes a public service obligation on the basis of Art. 4, this does not mean that that Member State must waive its right under Art. 3(2) to restrict competition in cabotage services in its territory.
375. The issue was decided in Case C-361/98, *Italy v. Commission*, in which the Court fully supported the Commission's policy. In the challenged decision, the Commission had declared the preferential treatment of Alitalia to be in breach of Art. 8(3) Reg. 2408/92, since it infringed the non-discrimination principle.
376. O.J. 1992, L 240/15. In Jul. 2006 the Commission proposed modernizing and simplifying Regs. 2407/92, 2408/92 and 2409/92, COM(2006)396 final.
377. O.J. 2002, L 114; see further note 193, *supra*. This highly interesting agreement declares the EC competition regime applicable for transport between the EC and Switzerland. Further implementing rules are regularly enacted by the Community/Switzerland air transport committee, e.g., Decision 1/2005 and Decisions 1–4/2006.

3.12.2   **Air Transport between the Community and Third Countries: The 'Open Skies' Cases**

Air transport between the Community and third countries is still subject to the negotiation of bilateral agreements between the Community and third countries – which is the usual mode in air transport. It should be noted, however, that the rules governing the internal aviation market and the general Treaty rules also have consequences for relations with third countries. This was made crystal clear in the extremely important '*open skies*' judgments of the Court of Justice.[378] In these cases, the Commission started infringement procedures against a number of Member States on the grounds that by concluding bilateral aviation agreements with the United States – so-called *Open Skies* Agreements – they had infringed their obligations under Community law. The Commission based its case primarily on the existence of an exclusive external competence of the Community in the sense of Opinion 1/76. The Court rejected this argument. The Commission's second argument was based on the *ERTA* principle;[379] here the Court followed the Commission in the sense that it accepted that Regulation 2409/92[380] laid down rules on rates and fares which preclude the Member States from making agreements on this matter with third countries.[381] The same was true for the subject matter of Regulation 2299/89[382] and Regulation 95/93,[383] concerning respectively computerized reservation systems and common rules for the allocation of slots at Community airports. Finally, the Court accepted the Commission's argument that the clause on the ownership and control of airlines in the bilateral agreements was contrary to the principle of freedom of establishment laid down in Article 43 EC.

This ruling of the Court has clearly spurred on the development of an external policy with regard to the so-called 'hard' rights, such as landing rights. The Court's statement that a clause on ownership and control is incompatible with Article 43 EC means, above all, that there is no point for the Member States in concluding this kind of agreement: they will have to allow other EC airlines to share the rights negotiated and obtained on the basis of any bilateral agreement.[384] In the meantime, the Community has adopted a regulation laying down rules for Member

---

378. Case C-466/98 *Commission v. United Kingdom*; Case C-467/98, *Commission v. Denmark*; Case C-468/98, *Commission v. Sweden*; Case C-469/98, *Commission v. Finland*; Case C-471/ 98, *Commission v. Belgium*; Case C-472/98, *Commission v. Luxembourg*; Case C-475/98, *Commission v. Austria*; Case C-476/98, *Commission v. Germany*. In a later case, Case C-523/04, *Commission v. Netherlands*, the Court held that by concluding a bilateral agreement with the USA the Netherlands failed to fulfil its obligations under the EC Treaty notably Arts. 10 and 43, as well as Reg. 2409/92, 2299/89 as amended by Reg. 3089/93.
379. Case 22/70, *Commission v. Council* (ERTA); see generally Ch. XIII.
380. On fares and rates for air services, O.J. 1992, L 240/15.
381. According to the Court, Case C-476/98, *Commission v. Germany* at para. 126, this competence is an exclusive Community competence.
382. O.J. 1989, L 220/1.
383. O.J. 1993, L 14/1.
384. See e.g., C. Panayi, 'Exploring the Open Skies: EC-Incompatible Treaties between Member States and Third Countries' (2006) *Yearbook of European Law*, 315–362.

States negotiating agreements with third countries.[385] More importantly, the Community now negotiates agreements with third countries itself.[386] For this purpose, the Council has given the Commission a mandate to negotiate with the USA. Following the publication of the Commission's communication on 'Developing the agenda for the Community's external aviation policy',[387] the Council adopted conclusions on developing that agenda.[388] The conclusions provide a good summary of the present aims and the state of the external aviation policy. This is based on a three-pronged approach: first, negotiations between the EC and the USA as well as other bilateral agreements at a Community level; second, efforts to establish a wider European Common Aviation Area and a suitable arrangement with Russia; third, bilateral agreements between Member States and third countries with respect to the principles of Regulation 847/2004. As a result a number of important agreements have now been concluded,[389] the most important one being the agreement with the USA.[390] Another important agreement has been with Russia on Siberian over-flights.[391]

As a corollary of the new direction of external policy, the scope of the competition rules has been extended to transport between the Community and third countries.[392]

3.12.3 Other Obstacles for the Internal Market in Air Transport Services

The most pressing problem is one of air traffic management, requiring a solution to problems of take-off and landing slots.[393] The basic Regulation 95/93[394] does give

---

385. Reg. 847/2004, of the European Parliament and the Council on the negotiation and implementation of air service agreements between Member States and third countries, O.J. 2004, L 157/7.
386. See e.g., the agreement concluded with Chile, O.J. 2006, L 300/45.
387. COM(2005)79 final.
388. O.J. 2005, C 173/1.
389. E.g., with Chile, Pakistan, Mongolia, Armenia and Kyrgistan, see the General Report on the activities of the European Union, 2006 and the Bulletin of the EU; and with New Zealand: O.J. 2007, L 256/27.
390. O.J. 2007, L 134/4. The agreement has yet to be ratified. See J. Balfour, 'EC External Aviation Relations: The Community's Increasing Role, and the New EC/US Agreement' (2008) CML Rev., 443–463.
391. See the website <http://ec.europa.eu/transport/air_portal/international/index_en.htm>.
392. Reg. 411/2004, O.J. 2004, L 68/1.
393. Various airports in the EC are seriously congested, e.g., London Heathrow, Amsterdam Schiphol. Because the slots are allocated on the basis of previous services, it is difficult for newcomers on the market to acquire attractive take-off and landing times. This limits the competitive possibilities for new entrants, which they should have on the basis of the new legislation. The availability of these slots is thus probably one of the most important elements for the further development of EC aviation policy. See V. de Boe, 'Allocation of Slots to Airlines: What Role for Competition Law?', (December 2005) *Journal for Network Industries*, 293–332.
394. O.J. 1993, L 14/1. Further, Dir. 2002/30 (O.J. 2002, L 85/40) sets out rules and procedures for the introduction of noise-related operating restrictions at Community airports. These rules have obviously had an effect on the capacity of these airports.

common rules for the allocation of slots at congested airports and further procedural rules, but does not really get to grips with the problem of allocation of scarce capacity. The regulation was amended in 2004 as a first step in a comprehensive revision process.[395] The issue of the ownership of slots – and thus whether slots can be sold or traded – was not addressed. The Commission has frequently had to deal with the issue in the framework of merger control, and in deciding on individual exemptions. In those situations, the Commission has often required parties to give up slots, in order to guarantee competition.[396]

To an increasing extent, measures will have to be taken to tackle the fragmented organization of air traffic control within Europe, if intra-European traffic is not to suffer even greater delays. Here too, questions of competence are highly relevant. The Community does not have clear and adequate powers in this area.[397] Like maritime transport, the transfer of competences to the Community in this field is a sensitive issue within the Member States. Supervision of air traffic has for years been subject to world-wide rules drawn up by the International Civil Aviation Organization; in the European context, Eurocontrol is the specialized agency. In 2004 the EC adopted four regulations establishing the framework for the so-called 'single European sky'.[398] This institutional framework consolidates the position of Eurocontrol; as a consequence the EC has become a member of Eurocontrol; a memorandum of Cooperation between the two has been agreed upon.[399] These arrangements will promote a more efficient and safe use of the European air

---

395. Reg. 793/2004, O.J. 2004, L 138/50.
396. Commission decision on the route London (Heathrow)-Brussels 92/552, O.J. 1992, L 353/32; Commission decision Lufthansa/SAS 96/180, O.J. 1996, L 54/28–42; Commission notice concerning the alliance between British Airways and American Airlines, O.J. 1998, C 239/ 10; Commission decision COMP/37.730, O.J. 2002, L 242/25. The Report on Competition Policy 2004 gives an extensive summary of the KLM/Air France merger (COMP/M 3280 and the Air France/Alitalia alliance (COMP/38.248) p. 84–88. See also the Lufthansa/Swiss (COMP/M 3770) decision.
397. See on this C. Probst, in: P.D. Dagtoglou, G. Jarolim and T. Soames, *European Air Law Association*, Vol. 13 (The Hague, 1999), 147 et seq. The Commission has also been unable to win sufficient political support, and has therefore not yet submitted any proposal on this. See also written question P-0312/01 (Atkins), O.J. 2001, C 235E/76.
398. Reg. 549/2004, O.J. 2004, L 96/1. Reg. 550/2004, O.J. 2004, L 96/10 on the provision of air navigation services in the single European sky; Reg. 551/2004, O.J. 2004, L 96/20, on the organization and use of the airspace in the European sky; Reg. 552/2004, O.J. 2004, L 96/ 26, on the interoperability of the European Air Traffic Management network. Regs. 1032 and 1033/2006 O.J. 2006, L 186/27 et seq, provide for detailed rules of the latter. See B. van Houtte, 'The Single European Sky: EU Reform of Air Traffic Management' (2004), CML Rev., 1595. Reg. 219/2007 O.J. 2007, L 64/1, establishes a joint Undertaking to develop the new generation European air traffic manage (SESAR); see on the proposal for the regulation: House of Commons European Scrutiny Committee, Sixteenth Report of Session 2005–2006.
399. O.J. 2004, L 304/210.

space.[400] Further improvements may lie ahead if military air traffic management can be integrated.[401]

Directive 96/67 deals with the important matter of ground handling services at Community airports.[402] Moreover, in this area the Commission has issued a considerable number of individual decisions, which all aim to abolish existing dominant positions.[403] The commercially important field of computerized reservation systems seems now to be satisfactorily regulated – also given that the general competition law instruments (Arts. 82 and 86 EC) can be applied in full to this field.

Intra-Community air freight transport has also been liberalized.[404]

3.12.4   The Most Important Regulations

Regulation 2407/92 on licencing of air carriers, sets out in its Article 5 economic and financial requirements for obtaining a licence.[405] The most controversial point in this context is the definition of effective ownership and control. The intention of this requirement is obviously to exclude companies from third countries, contrary to Article 48 EC.[406] It is remarkable that there is no reciprocity clause.[407] The problem of effective ownership and control is still more complex for aviation, because in the bilateral aviation treaties, landing rights are linked to this criterion. It has also acquired a new dimension as a result of the *open skies* cases, discussed above. The Council conclusions on developing the agenda for the Community's external aviation policy, also mentioned above, reveal that ownership relations are an element therein.[408]

---

400. As is obvious to every air traveller, congestion in the European air space causes very considerable delays. Further measures have been enacted: Dir. 2006/23 lays down rules for a Community Air Traffic Controller Licence, O.J. 2006, L 114/22.

401. Commission Reg. 2150/2005 laying down common rules for the flexible use of airspace, O.J. 2005, L 342/20 sets out rules to ensure better cooperation between civil and military entities responsible for air traffic management.

402. O.J. 1996, L 272/36. In Case C-386/03, *Commission v. Germany*, the ECJ ruled that the German legislation was not in conformity with the provisions of this directive. See on this subject section 3.13 on seaports and airports *infra*.

403. See further section 3.13 *infra*.

404. Art. 3 Reg. 2408/92, O.J. 1992, L 240/8. See also R.J. Fennes, International Air Cargo Transport Services: Economic Regulation and Policy, PhD thesis, Leiden, 1997.

405. Art. 9 Reg. 2407/92 provides that the granting and validity at any time of an operating licence shall be dependent upon the possession of a valid air operator's certificate specifying the activities covered by the operating licence and complying with the criteria to be established in a prospective regulation. These have been established in Reg. 3922/91, O. J. 1991, L 377/1. The rules have been amended by Regs. 1899/2006 and 1900/2006, O.J. 2006, L 377/1 and 176.

406. See on this problem P.J. Slot, 'Harmonised Licensing Requirements', in: P.D. Dagtoglou (ed.), *European Air Law Conference Papers* 5 (Deventer, 1993), 21 et seq.

407. Reg. 954/79 on the ratification of the UN Convention on a Code of Conduct for Liner Conferences does contain such a reciprocity clause, in Art. 4, to give one example.

408. O.J. 2005, C 173/1, point 12 refers to investment possibilities. The negotiations with the US also relate to the restriction of ownership clause in the US legislation restricting ownership of non-US citizens to 24.9%, which is far below the 49% in Reg. 2407/92.

3.12.5 The Competition Rules in the Air Transport Sector

For the air transport sector, too, the new Regulation 1/2003 brought considerable changes as of 1 May 2004, and the special rules for air transport which had been in existence until then were to a large extent abandoned. Henceforth the air transport sector is subject to the rules in Regulation 1/2003. The block exemption for technical agreements in Article 2 of Regulation 3975/87 is all that remains in force. Regulation 3976/87, providing the basis for enacting rules for block exemptions, remains in force more or less in its entirety. On the basis of the latter, the Commission adopted Regulation 1459/2006 on agreements and concerted practices concerning consultations on passenger tariffs on scheduled air services and slot allocation.[409] Another important change is the extension of the scope of the competition rules to third countries.[410]

Ever since competition rules were adopted for this sector, the Commission has applied them actively.[411] This is particularly so for the policy towards the very prevalent alliances in this sector,[412] and for mergers.[413]

---

409. O.J. 2006, L 272/3. This regulation expired 31 Oct. 2007.
410. Reg. 411/2004, O.J. 2004, L 68/1. The agreement between the EC and its Member States and Switzerland, O.J. 2002, L 114/1 extends the application of the competition and the state aid rules to Switzerland. It also provides for a division of competences between the Commission and the Swiss competition authorities. See S. Breitenmoser, 'Sectoral Agreements between the EC and Switzerland: Contents and Context.' 40 CML Rev., 2003, 1137–1186.
411. Regs. 3975/87 and 3976/87 were enacted in 1987. See e.g., the decisions concerning *Sabena*, O.J. 1988, L 317/47, relating to including competitors' flights in the computerized system; IATA, relating to passenger organization and freight, O.J. 1991, L 258/18 et seq.; *Air Lingus*, O.J. 1992, L 96/34, relating to abuse of dominant position and a refusal of interlining; *SAS/Maersk*, O.J. 2001, L 265/15, which was a case of classic division of the market. The application contesting this decision, Case T-241/01, *Scandinavian Airlines System v. Commission*, was dismissed. Various informal actions can be noted in recent annual reports. In addition, it is important to note that the merger control regulation has been applied on many occasions to mergers of Air France with Air Inter and Sabena, BA and BCAL, BA and American Airlines, KLM-Transavia, KLM/Air France and Lufthansa/Swiss and Lufthansa/Eurowings.
412. See XXVIIth Report on Competition policy, 1997, points 90–92; XXVIIIth Report on Competition policy, 1998, points 101–104; XXIXth Report on Competition policy, 1999, points 88–94. See e.g., the interesting report of the alliance between British Midland/Lufthansa/SAS, O.J. 2001, C 83/6, in which an overview is given of the proposed agreements which were considered necessary in order to prevent too much concentration on the route London-Frankfurt.
413. Both the KLM/Air France COMP/M (3280) and Lufthansa/Swiss, COMP/M (3770), merger decisions provide a good illustration of the competition issues in this sector including the Commission's approach of the difficult issue of definition of the relevant markets. See also Lufthansa/Eurowings COMP/M (3940). The case of the proposed merger between KLM and Martinair, COMP/M 1608, the Commission imposed a fine for providing incomplete and misleading information, O.J. 2005, L 50/10. See also Angela Cheng-Jui Lu, *International Airline Alliances*, 2003, Kluwer Law International.

3.12.6   State Aids

The Commission also carries out an active policy with regard to Articles 87 and 88 EC. In the *Sabena* and *Aer Lingus* decisions, the Commission showed that national state aid measures would be investigated carefully, and where aid is approved this may be under strict conditions.[414] The large extent of state ownership[415] of national airline companies in most Member States, makes this policy area a hornets' nest. The approval of the extensive packages of aid for Air France,[416] TAP, Iberia and Olympic[417] have been subject to severe criticism. The recovery of unlawfully granted aid in the *Olympic* case caused a lot of upheaval as a result of the unco-operative attitude of the Greek government.[418] The Commission has drawn up guidelines for aid in the aviation sector, on the basis of the experience it has acquired.[419] In 2005 the Commission adopted additional guidelines on financing of airports and start-up aid to airlines departing from regional airports.[420]

3.12.7   Other Rules

The impact of the terrorist attacks of 11 September 2001 was even greater on the aviation sector than in other areas, and this is to be seen in subsequent Community legislation. Thus, Regulation 2320/2002 establishing common rules in the field

---

414.   O.J. 1991, L 300/48, Sabena; O.J. 1994, L 54/30, Aer Lingus. See also the answer to written question 809/93 (V.d. Waal), on aid to Air France, O.J. 1993, C 350/8. In this case, the Commission was of the opinion that the loan (of 1.25 billion francs) to Air France, on the basis of the so-called market investor principle, was acceptable. Aid operations for Air France (20 billion francs), TAP Portugal and Olympic Airways were also approved, subject to certain conditions, O.J. 1994, L 254/73 and L 258/26, L 279/29 and L 273/22 respectively. See further Scharf in: L. Hancher, T.R. Ottervanger, P.J. Slot, op. cit. Ch. 16, 16-045 – 16-56, 401–411.
415.   The only national carrier in the EC without government participation is British Airways.
416.   The application contesting this decision, Case T-358/94, *Air France v. Commission*, was rejected by the CFI. The application by British Airways (Joined Cases T-371 & 394/94, *British Airways et al. and British Midland Airways v. Commission*) was partly accepted by the CFI. The application against the decision of the Commission approving the second tranche of the aid package for Aer Lingus, was rejected in Case T-140/95, *Ryanair v. Commission*, although the CFI subjected the Commission's conduct to a critical examination.
417.   The aid to Olympic Airways was approved subject to a great number of conditions. From the written question E-4112/00, O.J. 2001, C 235 E/71, it appears that the Commission is not confident that these conditions are being met.
418.   NN 4/2003 to be found at the website of DG COMP: <http://ec.europa.eu/comm/competition/index_en.html>
419.   O.J. 1994, C 350.
420.   O.J. 2005, C 312/1 the guidelines were adopted in the aftermath of the Commission decision concerning advantages granted by the Walloon Region and Brussels South Charleroi Airport to the airline Ryanair in connection with its establishment at Charleroi (notified in Number C (2004) 516) O.J. 2004, L 137/1. Para. 41 of the guidelines notes that compensation to category D airports (less that 1 million passengers per year) is exempted according to Art. 2(d) of the Commission decision of 13 Jul. 2005, O.J. 2005, L 312/67; see also section 3.1.3. *supra*. Scharf in: L. Hancher, T.R. Ottervanger, P.J. Slot, op. cit. Ch. 16, 16-057 – 16-67, 411–419.

of civil aviation security was adopted.[421] Air transport to the USA, in particular, is subject to increased safety measures. As a result, the Community concluded an agreement with the USA on the transfer of passenger data.[422]

Directive 2000/79 sets out rules for an agreement on the organization of working time of mobile workers in civil aviation.[423]

Environmental protection is gaining an ever more prominent position in Community legislation in this area. Directive 2002/30 should be mentioned, concerning the establishment of rules and procedures with regard to the introduction of noise-related operating restrictions at Community airports.[424] Here mention should also be made of the increasing importance of Community rules on the limitation of the use of old, noisy aircraft;[425] on its adoption, this legislation originally led to considerable conflicts with the USA.

As for safety: in 2004, a directive was adopted for a harmonized approach to the effective enforcement of international safety standards by the Member States. According to the rules of this directive, aircraft landing in the Member States should undergo an inspection if there is any suspicion that they do not comply with international safety standards.[426] In December 2005 the Community stepped up its safety policy and adopted a regulation which lays down the procedure for establishing a blacklist for unsafe airlines.[427] Directive 94/56 lays down basic principles for the inspection of accidents and incidents in civil aviation.[428]

---

421. O.J. 2002, L 355/1. Reg. 894/2002, O.J. 2002, L 142/3 (corrigendum O.J. 2004, L 204/28), which aims to prevent airlines from losing their slots as a result of the fact that they have to limit their activities temporarily because of sharply reduced demand, was already mentioned above.

422. Council Decision 2004/496 on the conclusion of an agreement between the EC and the United States of America on the processing and transfer of PNR data by Air Carriers to the United States Department of Homeland Security, Bureau of Customs and Border Protection, O.J. 2004, L 183/83. The decision was challenged by the Parliament in Joined Cases C-317 & 318/04, *Parliament v. Council and Commission, inter alia* on the grounds of an incorrect legal basis; the ECJ found that indeed the legal basis was wrong and annulled the agreement, while maintaining its effects; the Council has concluded a new agreement on a different legal basis, O.J. 2007, L 204/18. Case C-318/04 concerned Commission Decision 2004/535 on the level of protection of the data concerned.

423. O.J. 2000, L 302/57. The agreement is based on Art. 139(2) EC, and was the result of consultations between employers' and employees' organizations.

424. O.J. 2002, L 85/40.

425. Dir. 2006/93, O.J. 2006, L 374/1. The previous directive was drafted with the aim, inter alia, of ending the conflict between the EU and the USA.

426. Dir. 2004/36 of the EP and of the Council on the safety of third-country aircraft using Community airports. O.J. 2004, L 143/76.

427. Reg. 2111/2005 of the European Parliament and the Council on the establishment of a Community list of air carriers subject to an operating ban within the Community and on informing air transport passengers of the identity of the operating air carrier, and repealing Art. 9 of Dir. 2004/36. The adoption of the regulation followed unilateral action by certain Member States. The list is regularly updated, most recently by Reg. 787/2007, O.J. 2007, L 175/10.

428. O.J. 1994, L 319/14. In Case C-138/99, *Commission v. Luxembourg* and Case C-494/99, *Commission v. Greece,* Luxembourg and Greece were found to have failed to fulfil their obligations for failure to implement this directive.

As part of a policy to increase protection to passengers, Regulation 261/2004 on compensation for denied boarding was adopted.[429] The new regulation increases the airlines' responsibilities considerably, which led the International Air Transport Association (IATA) and the European association of low cost airlines to challenge the legality of the regulation on a number of grounds.[430] According to the associations, the regulation was incompatible with Articles 19 and 22(1) of the Montreal Convention. The ECJ did not find a conflict between the rules of the regulation and those of the Montreal convention. Nevertheless this is yet another example of Community rules being extended to areas previously only covered by international agreements.[431]

It is also worth mentioning that the EC is party to the Montreal Convention, it takes part in its negotiations and adopts its rules to the extent that these come within the scope of the Community powers.[432]

The Community also participates in the work of the Chicago convention, amongst other things in designing rules for the protection of the environment. In order to implement the rules of the Chicago convention, the Community has established a European Aviation Safety Agency. This agency has the task of certifying the safety of aeronautical products and to verify that they meet essential airworthiness and environmental protection requirements relating to civil aviation.[433]

3.13   SEAPORTS AND AIRPORTS

Ports are usually natural monopolies – this holds both for sea transport (seaports) and air transport (airports). The monopoly position tends to be strengthened by

---

429. Reg. 261/2004 of the European Parliament and of the Council establishing common rules on compensation and assistance to passengers in the event of denied boarding and of cancellation or long delay of flights, and repealing Reg. (EEC) No. 295/91, O.J. 2004, L 46, 1.
430. See Case C-344/04, *IATA and ELFAA*; the Court rejected all the arguments of the parties, and upheld the Regulation. See case note by K. St. C. Bradley, (2006), CML Rev., 1101–1124 and correspondence J. Balfour, (2007), CML Rev., 555–560.
431. The ECJ stated in paras. 44 and 45:

'It is clear from Articles 19, 22 and 29 of the Montreal Convention that they merely govern the conditions under which, after a flight has been delayed, the passengers concerned may bring actions for damages by way of redress on an individual basis, that is to say for compensation, from the carriers liable for damage resulting from that delay. It does not follow from these provisions, or from any other provision of the Montreal Convention, that the authors of the Convention intended to shield those carriers from any other form of intervention, in particular action which could be envisaged by the public authorities to redress, in a standardised and immediate manner, the damage that is constituted by the inconvenience that delay in the carriage of passengers by air causes, without the passengers having to suffer the inconvenience inherent in the bringing of actions for damages before the courts.'

432. See e.g., Council Decision 2001/539/EC, O.J. 2001, L 194/38.
433. Reg. 1592/2002, O.J. 2002, L 240/1. The Reg. has been amended by Reg. 334/2007, O.J. 2007, L 88/39.

the fact that it is increasingly difficult to construct new ports, for reasons of environmental protection and of spatial planning. Strictly speaking, ports fall outside the scope of application of the transport title of the Treaty. Nevertheless, port activities are intimately connected with transport. As a result of the completion of the internal market and the considerable growth in transport, there is an increasingly urgent need to address the position of ports within the Community. With this background in mind, in 1997 the Commission issued a Green Paper on Sea Ports and Maritime Infrastructure.[434] The key elements in the Green Paper are: the role of ports in the trans-European Transport Network, EU enlargement and connections to neighbouring third countries, the role of ports as transfer points in the intermodal transport chain, the development of short sea shipping, maritime safety[435] and protection of the environment. In addition, attention is paid to financing and charging for ports and maritime infrastructure. This last subject crops up regularly in the context of application of the state aid rules. A draft directive concerning market access to port services[436] was rejected by the European Parliament.[437]

Over the last ten years, an important body of case law has built up on the compatibility of exclusive rights in ports with provisions of the Treaty.[438] The exclusive rights of certain dock-workers in the Port of Genoa were found to be in breach of Article 86(1) EC.[439] In various judgments, lines have been drawn, with gradually increasing clarity, between activities which can be categorized as a typical exercise of state authority – and which therefore fall outside the scope of the prohibitions of the competition rules,[440] entrepreneurial activities in the form of exclusive rights which can be justified under Article 86(2) EC,[441] and entrepreneurial activities which do not deserve any kind of special treatment.[442] Port services are recognized as Services of General Economic Interest.[443] The

---

434. COM(97)678 final of 10 Dec. 1997.

435. This is an issue also touching port state control, see *supra* section 3.11.

436. O.J. 2002, C 299E/1. The draft directive only applies to seaports.

437. The Commission withdrew its proposal (COM(2004)654), O.J. 2006, C 64/3.

438. These development are summarized in P.J. Slot and A. Skudder, 'The Legal Regime of Ports and Airports under Community Law', *Liber Amicorum Lord Slynn*, 2000, 361. An overview of the application of Arts. 81, 82 and 86 EC in the area of airports and airport services may be found in the contributions by T. Soames, H. Bammer, H. Dillmann, H. Bittlinger, in: P.D. Dagtoglou, G. Jarolim, T. Soames, *European Air Law Association*, Volume 13 (The Hague, 1999), 85–146.

439. Case C-179/90, *Merci Convenzionali Porto di Genova v. Siderurgica Gabrielli*. An important aspect of this case is that the ECJ considers the port of Genoa to be a substantial part of the common market. The judgment in this case immediately set the tone for application of the competition rules to seaports and airports.

440. Case C-343/95, *Calì & Figli v. Servizi Ecologici Porto di Genova*, concerning environmental inspections carried out by a private undertaking Cf. also Case C-22/98, *Becu et al.*, dock workers as a group do not constitute an undertaking.

441. Case C-266/96, *Corsica Ferries France*, mooring services and the prices charged for such services.

442. Case C-35/96, *Commission v. Italy*, on the activity of customs agents.

443. See section 3.1.3 *supra*.

relevant decision of the Commission exempts compensation for smaller ports and airports from the prohibition of Article 86 EC.[444] State aid to larger airports is covered by the Commission's guidelines on the financing of airports.[445]

National legislation concerning these activities is also assessed on the basis of principles developed in the case law on Articles 3(1)(g) and 81 and 82 EC, i.e., preventing distortions of competition.[446] In various decisions on airports and seaports, the Commission has followed similar lines;[447] this also holds for decisions concerning merger control.[448] As mentioned above, a Community directive applies for ground handling services in the air transport sector.[449] The Commission has also applied the state aid rules in relation to seaports.[450] Sometimes, ports still apply rules which involve differences in treatment that are incompatible with the general Treaty rules; for instance, a surcharge on normal duties applying to goods coming from other Member States is obviously not permitted under

---

444. Decision 2005/842 on the application of Art. 86(2) EC to aid in the form of public service compensation granted to certain undertakings entrusted with the operation of services of general economic interest, O.J. 2005, L 312/67; Art. 2(1)(d) thereof exempts airports with less than 1 million passengers and ports with less than 300,000 passengers. Presumably bigger ports and airports can still benefit from the same principle in view of the Commission's framework for state aid in the form of public service compensation, O.J. 2005, C 297/4 and/or the judgment in C-280/00, *Altmark*. There are Commission Guidelines on state aid to airports, see Scharf in: L. Hancher, T.R. Ottervanger, P.J. Slot, op. cit., Ch. 16, 16-057 – 16–67, 411–419.

445. O.J. 2005, C 312/1.

446. Cf. Ch. IX *supra*. This is especially so when excusive or special rights are involved.

447. Decision 98/513 of 11 Jun. 1998, O.J. 1998, L 230/10. The application against this decision was rejected by both the CFI, in Case T-128/98, *Aéroports de Paris v. Commission*, and the ECJ, in Case C-82/01 P, *Aéroports de Paris v. Commission*. Decision of 28 Jun. 1995, O.J. 1995, L 216/8, Zaventem, discriminatory rate; Decision of 14 Jan. 1998, Frankfurt airport, O.J. 1998, L 72/30, ramp ground-handling services (catering and refuelling) are not inseparably connected with the actual air transport; decision of 10 Feb. 1999, O.J. 1999, L 69/31, landing rights at airports; Decision of 10 Feb. 1999, O.J. 1999, L 69/24, Ilmailulaitos/Luftfartsverket; Decision Rødby-Puttgarden, O.J. 1994, L 55/52; B & I Line plc/ Sealink Harbours Ltd, Decision of 11 Jun. 1992, CMLR [1992] 5, 255; Sea Containers/Stena Sealink, O.J. 1994, L 15/8.

448. See the decision Hutchison Whampoa, M.1412; in this case, the Commission initiated the second phase, but the parties withdrew their merger plans because they considered the conditions imposed by the Commission unacceptable. <http://ec.europa.eu/comm/competition/ mergers/cases/index/m28.html#m_1412. O.J. 1999, C 74/5>

449. See section 3.12 *supra*.

450. See the decision on tugboats in the port of Rotterdam, O.J. 2002, L 314/97. The decision was appealed by the Dutch government: see Case C-368/01 and Case C-314/02 (transferred to CFI as Joined Cases T-218 & 228/04) *Netherlands v. Commission*. The decision was also appealed by the tugboat companies: Case T-326/02, *Kotug International*, Case T-327/02, *Muller Marine*; Case T-328/02, *Smit Harbour Towage*; Case T-329/02, *URS Nederland* and Case T-330/02, *Wagenborg*. All these cases were later withdrawn and removed from the register, allowing for negotiations. See also the Communication from the Commission, Community guidelines on financing of airports and start-up aid to airlines departing from regional airports, O.J. 2005, C 312/1.

Article 90 EC.[451] The Commission has also proposed a directive on airport charges.[452]

3.14 INFRASTRUCTURE AND COMBINED TRANSPORT

As was emphasized in section 3.1, above, transport is strongly dependent on an adequate infrastructure, and it is thus not surprising that the Community has adopted a number of measures specially concerning this aspect.[453] In 1998, the Commission issued a White Paper examining the policy options for pricing in relation to transport infrastructure.[454] In 2004, the Community adopted a directive on minimum safety requirements for tunnels in the Trans-European Road Network.[455]

Directive 92/106 provides for liberalization of combined transport.[456] The importance of stimulating intermodal freight transport was emphasized yet again in 2000, in a Council resolution.[457]

4 THE EUROPEAN ATOMIC ENERGY COMMUNITY: EURATOM[458]

4.1 INTRODUCTION

The position of atomic (or nuclear) energy has changed drastically since the entry into force of the Euratom Treaty in 1958. On the one hand, a mature nuclear industry has emerged which covers the entire fuel cycle with all its potential.[459] On the other hand, the future of nuclear energy is determined by its social and

---

451. Joined Cases C-114 & 115/95, *Texaco*; Joined Cases C-430 & 431/99, *Sea-Land Service and Nedlloyd Lijnen*; Case C-435/00, *Geha Naftiliaki et al.*
452. COM(2006)820 final.
453. See item 7.10 of Community legislation in force, Transport infrastructure.
454. COM(1998)466
455. Dir. 2004/54, O.J. 2004, L 167/39.
456. O.J. 1992, L 368/38. In Case C-444/99, *Commission v. Italy*, Italy was found to have failed to fulfil its obligations by failing to implement this directive.
457. 14 Feb. 2000, O.J. 2000, C 56/1.
458. See for more extensive information on the situation with regard to Euratom law, the literature mentioned at the end of this chapter. The Euratom Supply Agency gives a useful overview of the activities within Euratom in its Annual Report.
459. According to the Commission in its Communication on the nuclear industries in the European Union (an illustrative nuclear programme according to Art. 40 of the Euratom Treaty), COM(96)339 final, 25 Sep. 1996, 28. The definitive text of the programme is in COM(97)401 final, 25 Jun. 1997. This communication puts the development of nuclear energy in the context of the white paper 'An Energy Policy for the European Union', COM(95)682, of 13 Dec. 1995. The communication gives a good overview of the current policy objectives for EU nuclear energy policy.

political acceptance. In a number of Member States, it began to seem as though the development of atomic energy was no longer a feasible option. The continued use of existing atomic energy plants in certain Member States, such as Germany,[460] Italy, Sweden and the Netherlands, no longer seemed politically acceptable.[461] Germany, Italy and Sweden took political decisions to dismantle the existing power plants. Yet the recent steep increase in the oil price and the enormous growth in the demand for energy in China, India and other burgeoning economies have very rapidly changed this perspective. Several governments which were sceptical about nuclear energy have now again embraced it as an energy source. In this new context, the most important aim of the Euratom Treaty, the development of a strong common nuclear energy industry,[462] may become relevant again. The Euratom Treaty has not played a major role in the energy policy of the Community, largely as a result of the actual situation on energy markets. At the time the Euratom Treaty was drafted, it could not have been predicted that it would not be nuclear energy, but oil and natural gas which would replace coal as the primary sources of energy. This has, of course, been reflected in the development of Euratom policy, and explains the somewhat limited activities for the relevant policy areas. The go-it-alone French nuclear policy also played a role in these developments.

As a result of the existence of a fully fledged atomic energy industry in certain Member States, such as France, some competitive openings have opened for the European industry on the world market, which is not (yet) stagnating as a result of political considerations. Promoting the chances of the European industry on the world market has become a new objective of the Euratom.

A third objective, that of promoting nuclear safety, has gradually become extremely important. Three things particularly influence this: the fact that public opinion turned against nuclear energy, the large-scale disasters involving nuclear power plants, and the collapse of the communist system. The last-mentioned development led to an increased risk of a proliferation of nuclear material and an increasing lack of maintenance and repairs to dangerous nuclear plants in the former communist countries.[463] The subject of nuclear safety was also an important element in accession negotiations.[464]

---

460. See D.H. Scheunig, 'Europarechtliche Aspekte einer Beendigung der Kernenergienutzung in der Bundesrepublik Deutschland,' EuR 2000, 1–23.
461. This is clearly different in France, and to some extent Belgium. It also holds for the newly acceded States such as Lithuania, Slovakia and the Czech Republic.
462. According to preamble and Art. 1 Euratom Treaty.
463. In its answer to written question E-1182/00 (Muscardini), O.J. 2001, C 103 E/6, the Commission gives a good overview of the Community activities in this area.
464. In the chapter on energy, the Commission website on accession mentions nuclear safety as a very important objective. The decommissioning of the Ignalina reactor in Lithuania was one of the results of these negotiations, see note 502, *infra*.

The institutional structure set out in the Euratom Treaty is, certainly in comparison with the EC Treaty, limited.[465] There is no intervention by Parliament in the legislative process. A working party of the European Parliament believes that Parliament should play a role in the decision-making process.[466] This subject may be expected to attract further attention now that accession of new Member States with operational nuclear power plants has put the subject of nuclear safety firmly on the agenda again.

4.2   THE MOST IMPORTANT CHARACTERISTICS OF THE EURATOM TREATY

4.2.1   Aims

As appears at once from Articles 1 and 2 Euratom, the character of Euratom is quite different from that of the EC, and also from that of the ECSC (now no longer in force). The focus of its task is the development of research and the dissemination of technical knowledge (Arts. 2(a) and 4–29 Euratom). Article 2 refers further to:

- The establishment of uniform safety standards.[467]
- The facilitation of investments.
- The ensuring of regular and equitable supplies of ores and nuclear fuels.
- The guaranteeing by appropriate measures of control that nuclear materials are not diverted for purposes other than those for which they are intended.
- The exercise of property rights in respect of special fissile materials.
- The establishment of a common market for specialized materials and equipment.
- Free movement of capital for nuclear investment, and freedom of employment for specialists within the Community.
- And finally the establishment with other countries and with international organizations of any contacts likely to promote progress in the peaceful uses of nuclear energy. The Atomic Energy Community has no powers in relation to the use of ores and nuclear fuels for military purposes.

---

465. The Lisbon Treaty intends to change this and align the institutional and financial provisions of the Euratom Treaty with those of the EU Treaty and the Treaty on the Functioning of the EU; see Protocol No. 12 Amending the Treaty Establishing the EAEC.

466. See the report 'The European Parliament and the Euratom Treaty: Past, present and future', *Agence Europe* No. 8280, 2002.

467. The wording of Art. 2 Euratom corresponds badly in this respect with the further working-out of the Treaty itself. The safety standards for the protection of the health of workers and the general population are worked out in Chapter III under the title Health and Safety. The term 'safeguards' is correctly used in Chapter VII for control against the misuse of nuclear energy for military purposes.

4.2.2   Scope

In its judgment in Case C-61/03, *Commission v. United Kingdom*, the Court of Justice ruled that the Treaty is not applicable to uses of nuclear energy for military purposes.[468]

4.2.3   Powers

As appears from the definition of its tasks in Article 2, Euratom, unlike the EC, has certain powers for the independent development and dissemination of research and knowledge. In the period of the development of atomic energy, the establishment of a common market,[469] achieved within one year, was and remains of less importance than this task of independent management. It is principally the research agreements and the patent ownership of Euratom which have attracted the attention of the legal community. Further original features which have received attention from lawyers and, particularly since the Chernobyl disaster, of others, are the tasks of ensuring safety control, the common ownership of fissile materials, the common enterprises, and the regulation of civil liability for nuclear risks.

**4.2.4   A Brief Outline of the Principal Original Points
                of the Euratom Treaty**

As is well known, in the last twenty years nuclear energy policy has become the subject of increasing controversy on the grounds of fears about environmental pollution, danger to population, the risk of proliferation of nuclear weapons and the uncertainty of supplies of raw fissile materials. The wording of the Treaty appears to have had an eye to all these dangers and on each of these points the Euratom Treaty already contains a number of guarantees and provides for powers to develop those guarantees. It should be noted, moreover, that so far the objections referred to above principally relate to the process of nuclear *fission*; they do not apply to the same degree or in the same way to the process of nuclear *fusion* which is now being developed. The wording of Article 1 Euratom – which speaks of the Community's task being 'to contribute to raising of the standard of living in the Member States and to the development of relations with other countries by creating the conditions necessary for the speedy establishment and growth of nuclear industries' – would not be so easily ratified in all Member States now as it was in 1957.

     As far as positive law is concerned the fears expressed above have not as yet had any clearly visible effect on this area of Community law. It seems certain that these fears would not be allayed simply by terminating the Euratom Treaty or making it in practice a dead letter. Both of these solutions would merely mean that the development of nuclear energy would thenceforth continue without control or coordination at Community level. The risks would if anything increase rather

---

468. Case C-61/03, *Commission v. UK*. This view was reiterated in Case C-65/04, *Commission v. UK*.
469. Arts. 92–100 Euratom.

than decrease. For critics as well as for proponents of nuclear energy, the best perspective would appear to lie in managing at the Community level and in broader international cooperation (particularly in the framework of the International Atomic Energy Agency in Vienna) the movement of emphasis, differentiated between the Member States, from existing nuclear energy technology to other energy sources and energy-saving measures. After the Chernobyl disaster, various measures were taken relating to the maximum permitted levels of radioactive contamination.[470] Moreover, measures were taken for rapid exchange of information in case of risks of radioactive contamination,[471] cooperation in civil protection,[472] information for the public,[473] international cooperation,[474] as well as assistance in case of nuclear accidents.[475]

4.3 RESEARCH

The struggle to draw the boundary between a joint research programme and national research programmes should be viewed against the background of Articles 4–7, 10, and 215 Euratom. It is already apparent from Article 4 Euratom that the joint research programme, the implementation of which is entrusted to the Commission, has a supplementary character, and that the Commission's main task is promoting nuclear energy research by the Member States. Article 172 Euratom empowers the Commission to issue loans for the financing of research or investment; the ceiling for such loans was later raised to 4 billion euro.[476]

---

470. Reg. 3954/87 laying down maximum permitted levels of radioactive contamination of foodstuffs and of feedingstuffs following a nuclear accident or any other case of radiological emergency, O.J. 1987, L 317/11. See also: Reg. 944/89, O.J. 1989, L 101/17, on less important foodstuffs; Reg. 2219/89, O.J. 1989, L 211/4, on the conditions for the export of foodstuffs and of feedingstuffs after a nuclear accident or in other cases of radiological emergency; Reg. 770/90, O.J. 1990, L 83/78 on maximum permitted levels of radioactive contamination of feedingstuffs following a nuclear accident or any other case of radiological emergency; Reg. 737/90, O.J. 1990, L 82/1, on the conditions governing imports of agricultural products originating in third countries following the accident at Chernobyl. The last of these was amended by Reg. 616/2000, O.J. 2000, L 75/1. The preamble of this amending regulation states that radioactive contamination of certain agricultural products originating in the third countries most affected by the accident still exceeds the maximum permitted levels of radioactivity.
471. Decision 87/600, O.J. 1987, L 371/76. The Community is also party to the IAE Convention on Early Notification of a Nuclear Accident O.J. 2005, L 314/22; see Commission decision of 25 Nov. 2005, O.J. 2005, L 314/21.
472. Resolution of 25 Jun. 1987, O.J. 1987, C 176/1.
473. Dir. 89/618, O.J. 1989, L 357/31.
474. Programme of the Commission of 4 Feb. 1992, O.J. 1992, C 142/5.
475. The Community is party to the IAEA Convention (26 Sep. 1986) on assistance in the case of a nuclear accident or radiological emergency, O.J. 2005, L 314/28, see Commission decision of 25 Nov. 2005: O.J. 2005, L 314/27.
476. Council Decision 82/170, O.J. 1982, L 78/21; Dec. 77/271 (O.J. 1977, L 88/11, most recently amended by Dec. 90/212 (O.J. 1990, L 112/26).

Articles 5 and 6 provide for a fairly weak form of coordination of national research programmes. In this context, research contracts and expert assistance can constitute financial incentives; subsidies are not allowed. For the first five years the joint research programme was laid down during the negotiations on the Treaty (Art. 215 and Annex V Euratom) and subsequently it had to be laid down for a period not exceeding five years by the Council, acting by unanimity on a proposal from the Commission, which must consult on the subject a Scientific and Technical Committee set up for this purpose (Art. 7 Euratom).

The most recent programme runs to 2012.[477] Since 1972, two four-year programmes were adopted which also dealt with non-nuclear matters such as information technology. After the Paris Summit in 1972, there was a trend to adopt multiannual research programmes outside the Euratom area; initially these were based on the old Article 235 EEC.[478] Title XVIII of Part Three of the EC Treaty offers an independent legal basis for such Community multiannual programmes in addition to that provided by the Euratom Treaty. Indeed, the idea in drafting that Title was to make a link with the relevant articles of the Euratom Treaty.[479]

In view of the French and later Dutch opposition to an extensive joint programme, it is interesting to mention that Article 6 Euratom permits the Commission to place facilities, equipment, or expert assistance of the Community at the disposal of Member States, persons, or undertakings, either for payment or free of charge. Examples of the facilities referred to in Article 6 are the Joint Research Centre, set up under Article 8 Euratom, and its establishments at Ispra, Geel, Karlsruhe, and Petten.[480] In 1978, after a long period of difficult negotiation concerning its place of establishment the 'Joint European Torus' (JET) Joint Undertaking was set up to conduct research into thermonuclear fusion at Culham in Oxfordshire (United Kingdom).[481] The research programme for the Joint Research Centre for 2002–2006 was established by Council Decision 2002/838.[482] Article 10 Euratom provides for the possibility of entrusting Member

---

477. Decision 2002/668, O.J. 2002, L 232/34 and 2002/837, Euratom, O.J. 2002, L 294/74. Decision 2006/970 Concerning the Seventh Framework Programme of the EAEC (Euratom) for nuclear research and training activities (2007 to 2011) O.J. 2006, L 400/60. Rectification O.J. 2007, L 54/21. See also Reg. No 1908/2006 of 19 Dec. 2006 laying down the rules for the participation of undertakings, research centres and universities in action under the Seventh Framework Programme of the EAEC and for the dissemination of research results, O.J. 2006, L 400/1. Further implementing decisions have been enacted by the Council, see 2006/976/Euratom, O.J. 2006, L 400/405 and 2006/977/Euratom, O.J. 2006, L 400/435. Rectifications see O.J. 2007, L 54/4, L 54/139 and L 54/149.
478. See Sixth General report 1972, 254.
479. As was pointed out in the explanatory memorandum to the proposal for approval of the SEA by the Dutch Parliament (Kamerstukken 1985–86, 10626, no. 3, 7).
480. By Decision 96/282, O.J. 1996, L 107/12, the Commission reorganized this Joint Research Centre.
481. O.J. 1978, L 151/10.
482. O.J. 2002, L 294/86. Council Decision 2004/185 adopted a supplementary research programme, O.J. 2004, L 57, 25. The seventh framework 2007–2013 has been adopted by Decision 2006/970 Concerning the Seventh Framework Programme of the EAEC (Euratom) for nuclear research and training activities (2007 to 2011) O.J. 2006, L 400/60.

States, persons, or undertakings, third countries, international organizations or nationals of third countries with the implementation of certain parts of the Community's research programme. This possibility has often been made use of by means of the conclusion of research or association contracts.[483]

Since 1985 Euratom participates in International Thermonuclear Experimental Reactor (ITER) – an international consortium for the development of nuclear fusion.[484]

As a curiosity it should finally be mentioned that Article 9 Euratom lays down, amongst other things, the obligation to set up an institution at university level. The particulars of its operation were to be settled by the Council, acting by a qualified majority on a proposal from the Commission. Unfortunately no time-limit was set for the implementation of this duty to set up a 'European University' – which need by no means be confined to the science of nuclear energy. The European University Institute (EUI) which was founded from scratch in 1973 can be regarded as a substitute for this Community university institution. The EUI is not in fact based on Article 9 Euratom but on a separate convention[485] and is now having increasing success in the fields of historical, economic, legal and political science research, but does not work in the field of the natural or applied sciences.

4.4   DISSEMINATION OF KNOWLEDGE

The Community may acquire patents – both by means of its own research programme and by purchase. Article 12 Euratom imposes on the Commission the obligation to grant to Member States, persons and undertakings, at their request, non-exclusive licences under these patents, provided that the applicants are in a position effectively to exploit the inventions to which they relate. The same applies *mutatis mutandis* to applications for sub-licences of licences held by the Community. The Commission may indeed attach conditions to such licences and sub-licences, in order to contribute to the achievement of the tasks of the Community referred to in Articles 1 and 2 Euratom.

Articles 14, 15 and 16 Euratom provide for other means for the Community to obtain and disseminate (under carefully developed guarantees as to exclusive dissemination among interested parties within the Community) confidential information in the field of atomic energy. Articles 5 and 16 contain important obligations to report to the Commission on national research programmes (also of private business) and national patent applications.

---

483. See on this P.S.R.F. Mathijsen in: *Miscellanea Ganshof van der Meersch* (Brussels, 1972), 1098 et seq.
484. Decision 2007/198/Euratom: Council Decision of 27 Mar. 2007, establishing the European Joint Undertaking for ITER and the Development of Fusion Energy and conferring advantages upon it, O.J. 2007, L 90/58. On 24 Oct. 2007, the ITER Organization for fusion research and development was formally established.
485. O.J. 1976, C 29/1.

Articles 17–23 contain an original, but complicated procedure for the grant of compulsory licences of a non-exclusive character to the Community or to the joint undertakings to be discussed below, or under certain conditions also to others. In practice, however, these articles have not yet turned out to be of any importance.

Article 24 formed the basis of the important Security Regulation in the matter of secrecy.[486] Articles 24–28 themselves contain rules on secrecy for the protection of defence interests which are also of interest to industry.

4.5   HEALTH PROTECTION

With a view to the protection of the health of the general public and of workers, Articles 30–39 Euratom provide for the establishment of basic standards within the Community and compulsory compliance with these basic standards, and additional measures by Member States. Article 37 Euratom requires Member States to provide the Commission with data about the disposal of nuclear waste. This article was highlighted in the Court's judgment in *Saarland v. Minister for Industry, Post, Telecommunications and Tourism.*[487] The basic rules are set out in Directive 89/618, 96/29, Directive 97/43 and Directive 2003/122.[488] The Chernobyl disaster led to stricter rules for the protection of health and cooperation in such matters.[489]

---

486. Reg. 3, O.J. 1958, 406.
487. In Case 187/87, *Land de Sarre v. Ministre de l'Industrie*, the Court held that Art. 37 Euratom must be interpreted as meaning that Member States are required to provide the Commission with general data relating to any plans for the disposal of radioactive waste *before* authorization of the disposal is granted. After the plans have been made known to the Commission, they are assessed by the Commission which then publishes its opinion on them, see e.g., the Opinion on the Covra waste processing and storage facility at Sloe, O.J. 1992, L 121/44. See further the Opinion of the Commission on the basic nuclear facility Pierrelatte, O.J. 1995, L 114/28 and the Opinion of the Commission on the Windscale advanced gas-cooled reactor, O.J. 1996, L 48/13.
488. Dir. 89/618/Euratom on informing the general public about health protection measures to be applied and steps to be taken in the event of a radiological emergency, O.J. 1989, L 357/31; Dir. 96/29/Euratom laying down basic safety standards for the protection of the health of workers and the general public against the dangers arising from ionizing radiation, O.J. 1996, L 159/1; Dir. 97/43/Euratom on health protection of individuals against the dangers of ionizing radiation in relation to medical exposure, O.J. 1997, L 180/22 and Dir. 2003/122/ Euratom on the control of high-activity sealed radioactive sources and orphan sources, O.J. 2003, L 346/57. See on the earlier directives in this area Case C-246/88, *Commission v. Italy.* In Case C-483/01, *Commission v. France*, the ECJ held that France had not properly implemented the provisions of Dir. 96/29; in Case C-218/02, *Commission v. United Kingdom*, and in Case C-155/06, *Commission v. United Kingdom*, the UK was held to be in breach of its obligation to implement Dir. 96/29; in Case C-484/01, *Commission v. France*, France was condemned for not properly implementing Dir. 97/43; in Case C-177/03, *Commission v. France*, the ECJ held that France had failed to implement Arts. 2, 3, 6 and 7 of Dir. 89/618.
489. Reg. 3954/87, O.J. 1987, L 371/11; Council Reg. 1493/93 on shipments of radioactive substances between the Member States and Decision 93/552, on the standard document for such shipments, O.J. 1993, L 148/1 and L 268/83, are also important. Dir. 92/3, O.J. 1992, L 35/24, lays down rules radioactive waste. As of 25 Dec. 2008, the directive will be replaced by Dir. 2006/117, O.J. 2006, L 337/21.

The Commission regularly issues opinions on Member States' plans for the disposal of nuclear waste.[490] The ECJ has rejected the Commission's view that Article 37 Euratom requires Member States to provide it with information on the disposal of radioactive waste from military installations.[491] However, the Court did underline the vital importance of the objective of protecting the health of the public against the dangers related to the use of nuclear energy, including for military purposes. It suggested that the pursuit of that objective may be effected by appropriate measures on the basis of the relevant provisions of the EC Treaty.

4.6   SAFETY CONTROL

The rules of Articles 77–85 Euratom concerning safety control, which are important in connection with the Treaty on the Non-Proliferation of Nuclear Weapons (the Non-Proliferation Treaty),[492] should be distinguished from the provisions for health protection. The supervisory task with which the Commission is entrusted in this context serves to ensure that ores, source materials, and special fissile materials are not diverted from their intended uses as stated by the users, and to ensure the observance of the provisions of any agreements on the subject between the Community and third States or an international organization.[493] In this context, the important co-operation agreement with the United States[494] and the agreement with the International Atomic Energy Agency (IAEA)[495] are of particular importance. In implementation of the provisions of the Non-Proliferation Treaty, a separate agreement was concluded between the Member States without atomic weapons (at the time: Belgium, Denmark, Germany, Ireland, Italy, Luxembourg, the Netherlands) and the IAEA.[496] The important IAEA Convention on Nuclear Safety was adopted and ratified on behalf of the Community.[497] The Commission has put forward a proposal for a Council directive laying down the basic obligations and general principles on the safety of nuclear installations.[498] The

---

490. See e.g., Commission opinion on Pierrelatte, O.J. 2005, C 195/02; opinion on Centre de l'Aube, O.J. 2005, C 195/03; opinion on Medical University Hannover, O.J. 2005, C 225/02; further reports to be found on the website of DG TREN.
491. Case C-61/03, *Commission v. United Kingdom.* It was certainly no coincidence that in the proceedings the UK government was supported by the French government. This view was confirmed in Case C-65/04, *Commission v. United Kingdom.*
492. London, Moscow and Washington, 1 Jul. 1968 (7 ILM 809, 729 UNTS 161).
493. Commission Reg. 302/2005, O.J. 2005, L 54/1 lays down the relevant rules.
494. The old agreement dating from 1960 expired at the end of 1995 and the new agreement applies from 12 Apr. 1996, see Dec. 96/314, O.J. 1996, L 120/1.
495. O.J. 1975, L 329/28.
496. Agreement 78/164/Euratom, O.J. 1978, L 51/1.
497. O.J. 1999, L 318/20. In Case C-29/99, *Commission v. Council*, the Commission challenged the Council's decision because it was of the opinion that a considerable number of Convention provisions fall within Community competence. The ECJ found for the Commission on several accounts.
498. COM(2003)32 final of 30 Jan. 2003. The amended proposal, COM(2004) 526 final is still with the Council and the EP.

Community has also acceded to the amended Convention on the Physical Protection of Nuclear Material and Nuclear Facilities.[499]

In order to ensure the observance of these provisions, Article 83 Euratom provides for purely administrative sanctions – the most far-reaching of these are the temporary placing of the undertaking under the administration of a person or board, and the complete or partial withdrawal of source materials or special fissionable materials.[500] With regard to France and the United Kingdom it is of interest that under Article 84 Euratom the control may not extend to materials used for defence purposes. The implementing provisions on safeguards were extensively revised in 2005 [501] In relation to non-military materials and equipment the United Kingdom, Euratom and the IAEA concluded a separate cooperation agreement in 1976, and France, Euratom and the IAEA concluded such an agreement in 1978.

The accession of new Member States has given rise to special programmes assisting them with the decommissioning of nuclear power plants.[502]

4.7   INVESTMENTS

The Commission must periodically publish programmes indicating, in particular, the production targets for nuclear energy and the various types of investment required to attain them (Art. 40 Euratom). Article 41 Euratom imposes an obligation on persons and undertakings to communicate certain types of investment projects to the Commission.[503] The Commission's powers of coordination on the subject under Article 43 Euratom are not very far-reaching and in fact only imply giving an opinion. What is far more important is that the Community may, by virtue of Articles 6, 47, 171, 172 and 174 Euratom, directly participate in investments. The first programme for this purpose provided in particular for a considerable amount of participation in the construction of reactors for electric power stations. Since 1977 the Commission has been empowered to issue

---

499. O.J. 2007, L 190/12.
500. See Case C-308/90, *Advanced Nuclear Fuels v. Commission.* By Decisions 90/413 (O.J. 1990, L 209/270) and 90/465 (O.J. 1990, L 241/14) the company concerned was placed under administration on the basis of Art. 83(1) Euratom. In an unpublished decision the Court granted the immediate enforcement of these decisions, later rejecting the substantive appeal.
501. Reg. 302/2005 O.J. 2005, L 54/1. See on the original safeguards regulation: J. Hilbert, 'Un renouveau de l'activité réglementaire dans le domaine nucléaire? Le nouveau système de contrôle de sécurité', (1977) RTDE, 282–291.
502. Reg. (EC) No. 1990/2006 on the implementation of Protocol 4 on the Ignalina nuclear power plant in Lithuania to the Act of Accession of the Czech Republic, Estonia, Cyprus, Latvia, Lithuania, Hungary, Malta, Poland, Slovenia and Slovakia Ignalina Programme, O.J. 2006, L 411/10. Reg. (Euratom) No. 549/2007 on the implementation of Protocol No. 9 on Unit 1 and Unit 2 of the Bohunice V1 nuclear power plant in Slovakia to the Act concerning the conditions of accession to the European Union of the Czech Republic, Estonia, Cyprus, Latvia, Lithuania, Hungary, Malta, Poland, Slovenia and Slovakia, O.J. 2007, L 131/1
503. See Reg. 4/58, O.J. 1958, 417 and Reg. 1/58, O.J. 1958, 511.

Euratom loans for the purpose of contributing to the financing of nuclear power stations.[504]

4.8   JOINT UNDERTAKINGS

Undertakings of fundamental importance for the development of the nuclear indus-try in the Community can be established under Article 45 Euratom as Joint Under-takings pursuant to Articles 46–51 Euratom. The Treaty does not require these 'joint ventures' to involve undertakings from more than one Member State, and in practice only one really international enterprise (in this case a joint Belgian and French one) was established under this regime before 1978.[505] The Commission has rightly observed that the JET Joint Undertaking is the first real joint under-taking within the meaning of the Euratom Treaty.[506] However, although the Court in 1987 found that the Community character of JET did not embrace the conditions of employment there for personnel of British nationality,[507] in 1996 the Court of First Instance actually decided the contrary.[508] The legal position of joint under-takings is hybrid. Legal personality is conferred by the Council decision which establishes a joint undertaking and this decision also lays down its Statutes (articles of association). The latter may diverge from national law which is otherwise applicable. Furthermore, Article 49 Euratom provides that not only shall joint undertakings have legal personality; they shall also enjoy the most extensive legal capacity accorded to legal persons under the respective national laws of each of the Member States. From the possibility of the Community's participation in financing laid down in Article 47, a power to take part in the management has also been derived. Finally, the advantages mentioned in Annex III to the Treaty may be granted to a Joint Undertaking. The most important of these advantages are the very far-reaching tax exemptions that may be granted.

---

504.   O.J. 1977, L 88/9, amended in 1979, O.J. 1980, L 12/28, and in 1982, O.J., 1982, L 78/21.
505.   That was the Société d'énergie nucléaire franco-belge des Ardennes (SENA). The Statutes (articles of association) of this undertaking were amended, and the amendment approved by the Commission in 1987, cf. O.J. 1987, L 148/1. Further approval was given to RWE-Bayerwerk, O.J. 1988, L 160/49, amended by decision 96/243, O.J. 1996, L 80/62 and JET, O.J. 1993, L 222/4.
506.   *Twelfth General Report* (Brussels, Luxembourg, 1979) point 397.
507.   See Case 271/83, *Ainsworth v. Commission and Council*, and contrary to the opinions of A.G. VerLoren van Themaat and A.G. Mischo.
508.   Joined Cases T-177 & 377/94, *Altmann et al. v. Commission*. This was possible because of changes in the nature of the JET from a short-term project into a more permanent project. The short-term nature had been crucial to the ECJ's earlier judgment. The CFI could depart from the earlier judgment of the ECJ as the identity of the litigants and their arguments were different. The CFI judgment was not appealed. The new judgment is of importance not merely in relation to staff cases as such, but also in relation to the JET structure and its history.

4.9   SUPPLY OF ORES, SOURCE MATERIALS AND SPECIAL FISSILE
               MATERIALS

Articles 52–76 Euratom concern supplies of materials used in the nuclear sector: ores, source materials and special fissile materials. At one stage, there was actually disagreement as to whether these articles were still in force.[509] The question was answered in the affirmative by the Court of Justice in its important judgment in *Commission v. France.*[510] Various proposals for modification of these provisions have been made, but so far to no avail.

The chief principles on which these articles are based are those of equal access to resources and of a common supply policy.[511] In connection with the first principle, all practices designed to grant certain users a privileged position are prohibited.

For the realization of the second principle, an Agency was set up – the Euratom Supply Agency – which possesses, amongst other things, the exclusive right of concluding contracts relating to the supply of ores, source materials, or special fissile materials coming from inside or from outside the Community, and a right of option on these materials produced in the territory of the Community.[512] In Case 7/71, *Commission v. France,* mentioned above, the Court confirmed that no import contracts may be concluded with other Member States or third countries outside the framework of the supply agency. An exception has been made in Regulation 17/66 to the Agency's monopoly in respect of imports from third countries for small quantities (in conformity with Art. 74), but this exception does not apply to special fissile materials.[513] In the *Industrias Nucleares do Brasil* judgment, the ECJ held that the obligation of Article 75 to notify imports and exports to the Agency also extends to uranium enrichment.[514] A 'supervised exception' applies if the Agency is unable, within a reasonable period, to fulfil an order for supplies or is able to fulfil it only at an excessive price (Art. 66 Euratom). In practice, the liberalization of the supply policy for materials (other than special fissile materials) went even further. Under a regulation dating back to 1960, transactions relating to these materials can be concluded directly between producers and consumers: such

---

509.   Art. 76 states that 'seven years after the entry into force of this Treaty, the Council may confirm these provisions' and, in the event they are not confirmed, 'new provisions . . . shall be adopted.' The procedure of confirmation and revision came to a deadlock in the Council.
510.   Case 7/71, *Commission v. France.* The case mainly concerned Arts. 52, 55, 64 and 75 Euratom.
511.   Art. 52 Euratom. See, generally, Allen, *The Euratom Treaty,* Ch. VI: 'New Hope or False Dawn?' (1983) CML Rev., 473.
512.   Arts. 57 and 58 Euratom. The statutes are in O.J. 1958, 539.
513.   Reg. 17/66, O.J. 1966, 4057.
514.   Joined Cases C-123 & 124/04, *Industrias Nucleares do Brasil and Siemens v. UBS AG and Texas Utilities Electric Corporation.* A grand chamber of the ECJ interpreted Art. 75(c) to mean that this provision also applies when similar but not identical nuclear material are shipped back. Furthermore the Court interpreted the concept of third-country undertaking referred to in Art. 196(b).

contracts are to be communicated to the Agency, which has a right of veto.[515] With regard to imports and exports of special fissile materials, the intervention of the Agency is necessary, partly in view of the existing international cooperation agreements. For intra-Community transactions, on the other hand, the necessity of active intervention of the Agency would appear doubtful. The statutes of the Agency have been amended by Council Decision 73/45/Euratom[516] and also on the accession of new Member States.[517] The basic regulation of 1960 was amended in 1975, to match changing circumstances.[518] In two sets of proceedings, the Court of First Instance and the Court of Justice have confirmed the broad discretionary powers of the Agency in relation to purchase and supply of fissile materials, as laid down in Articles 57–63 Euratom.[519]

Under Article 53 Euratom, the Commission is given a supervisory role *vis-à-vis* the Agency. The Court has held that where a Member State has requested the Commission to give a decision under the second paragraph of that article, the Commission is indeed under an obligation to do so.[520]

4.10   THE REGULATION OF THE RIGHT OF OWNERSHIP OF SPECIAL
            FISSILE MATERIALS

A legal curiosity which has attracted a good deal of attention in the literature is the provision in Article 86 Euratom, according to which all the special fissile materials defined in Article 197 are the property of the Community. Exceptions exist only for materials processed for foreign owners[521] and for materials held on lease from the United States under the cooperation agreement.[522] According to Article 87, the Member States, persons, or undertakings only have the – most extensive – right of use and consumption of special fissile materials properly in their possession, subject to their obligations resulting from the provisions of the Treaty. The property right of the Community arises at the moment of production or import of the

---

515. EAEC Supply Agency: Rules of the Supply Agency of the EAEC determining the manner in which demand is to be balanced against the supply of ores, source materials and special fissile materials, O.J. 1960, 777, prolonged to 31 Dec. 1969, O.J. 1964, 240.
516. O.J. 1973, L 83/20.
517. See the relevant accession treaties.
518. O.J. 1975, L 193/37.
519. Joined Cases T-458 & 523/93, *ENU v. Commission*, and the appeal Case C-357/95 P, *ENU v. Commission*; Joined Cases T-149 & 181/94, *Kernkraftwerke Lippe-Ems v. Commission*, and the appeal Case C-161/97 P, *Kernkraftwerke Lippe-Ems v. Commission* at para. 97.
520. Case C-107/91, *ENU v. Commission*. ENU had asked the Agency, under Art. 57 Euratom, to dispose of 350 tons of uranium. Neither the Agency nor the Commission took a decision on this request. As a result of the Court's ruling in this case, the Commission did take a decision. That decision was contested in Joined Cases T-458 & 523/93, *ENU*, and on appeal in Case C-357/95 P, *ENU*, but the application was rejected in both instances.
521. Art. 75 Euratom.
522. A new agreement has been concluded with the United States; the decision approving the agreement is in O.J. 1996, L 120/1; see further General Report EU 1996, point 368, 158.

special fissile materials. If they have been produced or imported for the account of a Member State, a person, or an undertaking, the price is refunded by the Community. In this context Articles 88–89 Euratom provide for a special account. Fluctuations of value are to be borne by the person in possession of the material, so the Community itself cannot grow any poorer or richer from this property right.

4.11   THE COMMON MARKET IN THE FIELD OF NUCLEAR ENERGY

On the basis of Article 305(2) EC it must be assumed that the provisions of the EC Treaty are applicable to the extent that the Euratom Treaty does not diverge from them. This is important, for instance, with regard to the right of establishment, capital movement, the competition rules, approximation of laws, the power laid down in Article 308 EC to make arrangements for unforeseen problems, the common commercial policy, and (last but not least) a common or coordinated general energy policy. The latter will have to be brought about on the basis of the EC Treaty, since the Euratom Treaty – except with regard to the supply of source materials – gives no powers in this respect. As will be seen in the next section, the powers conferred by the EC Treaty in this respect are also limited, although not totally non-existent. The basic rule is that the core activities of the EAEC fall under the specific rules of the Euratom Treaty, and other activities fall under the EC Treaty. The applicability of Articles 81 and 82 EC in the atomic energy sector has been confirmed by the Commission on many occasions.[523] The same is true for the rules on merger control. On the other hand, the supply contracts concluded by the Agency and the activities under Chapter 6 (on supplies, see section 4.10 above) do not come within the scope of Articles 81 and 82 EC.

As for the establishment of a common market for the source materials and other goods and products playing a part in the use of nuclear energy and enumerated in Euratom lists A1 and A2 of Annex IV to the Treaty, Article 93 Euratom provides for an abolition of customs duties, charges with equivalent effect, and quantitative restrictions in imports and exports in internal trade.[524] For these source materials and auxiliary materials, machines, equipment, vehicles, packaging materials, and tools mentioned in lists A1 and A2, which by their nature are specially intended for the field of nuclear energy, the common customs tariff was also established at an earlier date.[525]

Article 96 Euratom provides for free movement of workers for specialized employment in the nuclear field.[526] With regard to the social security of the workers concerned, general EC law applies, as mentioned earlier in this section.

---

523. See especially the decision United Reprocessors, O.J. 1976, L 51/7, see further also the decision Scottish Nuclear, O.J. 1991, L 178/31. See the answer of the Commission to parliamentary question 169/71 (Vredeling), O.J. 1972, C 5/1. See T.F. Cusack, 'A Tale of Two Treaties: An Assessment of the Euratom Treaty in Relation to the EC Treaty', CML Rev., 2003, 117.
524. This article was amended by the Treaty of Amsterdam. The original article provided for abolition before 1 Jan. 1959.
525. By agreements on 22 Dec. 1958 (J.O. 406/59 and 410/59).
526. Implemented by a directive of 5 Mar. 1962, O.J. 1962, 1650.

Article 97 Euratom contains a directly applicable prohibition on the application of restrictions based on nationality to natural or legal persons, whether public or private, coming within the jurisdiction of a Member State and desiring to participate in the construction within the Community of nuclear facilities of a scientific or an industrial character.

Article 98 Euratom provides for an obligation on the part of Member States to take all necessary measures to facilitate the conclusion of insurance contracts covering atomic risks. The directives required in this article were, however, considered unnecessary in view of the Paris Convention on third-party liability in the nuclear field concluded on 29 July 1960 within the framework of the Organization for European Economic Cooperation (OEEC)[527] and supplemented on 31 January 1963 on the initiative of the Community.[528] The Commission has indeed addressed recommendations to the Member States on the implementation of these treaties and has drawn up, in cooperation with producers and insurers, a skeleton policy for the insurance of third-party liability in the permanent nuclear facilities of Member States. However, partly with a view to Article 85 EC, the Commission was opposed to giving a binding character to this skeleton policy. The parties are free to agree on different conditions. This whole problem of third-party liability for atomic risks has received much attention in the legal literature.[529]

Articles 99 and 100 Euratom on the liberalization of capital and payments have lost their significance since the coming into force of Article 56 EC, which is directly effective.[530]

4.12   EXTERNAL RELATIONS UNDER THE EURATOM TREATY

Numerous agreements and conventions have been concluded by the Community, on the basis of Articles 101 and 102 Euratom, with third countries (including the United States of America, Argentina, Australia, Brazil, Canada, Russia,[531] Japan,[532] and, with reference to the JET project, Sweden and Switzerland) as well as with the OECD (the 'Dragon Agreement') and with the International Atomic Energy Agency.[533] The seventh Framework programme has been extended to Switzerland.[534]

---

527. Vol. 55 *American Journal of International Law* (1961), 1082.
528. ILM vol. 2 1963, 685 et seq. Various additional Protocols were concluded in 1982.
529. See on this N.L.J.T. Horbach, 'Liability versus Responsibility under International Law', PhD thesis, Leiden, 1996, et seq.
530. See, further, Ch.VIII, section 8, *supra*.
531. Council decision 2003/462, O.J. 2003, L 155, 35.
532. O.J. 2007, L 246/32.The agreement is published O.J. 2007, L 246/34.
533. See T.F. Cusack, 'External Relations of the European Atomic Energy Community in the Fields of Supply and Safeguards: Background and Developments in 1982 and 1983' (1983) *Yearbook of European Law*, 347–369. On 8 Mar. 2001, the Council approved a cooperation agreement between Euratom and the United States in the field of fusion energy research and development, O.J. 2001, L 148/78.
534. O.J. 2007, L 189/24 et seq.

Article 103 Euratom provides for supervision and the possibility of intervention by the Commission in the matter of the conclusion of agreements or conventions between Member States and third countries, to the extent that they concern the field of application of the Euratom Treaty. This provision has become of great political importance in connection with the Non-Proliferation Treaty.[535] Articles 104–106 Euratom lay down general rules on the relation between old and new agreements or conventions with third countries, international organizations or nationals of third countries, on the one hand, and the Euratom Treaty on the other. These articles are also of significance for private agreements with the external world.[536] In 2002, the Court of Justice handed down an important ruling concerning the accession of Euratom to the Convention on Nuclear Safety of the IAEA.[537] The Court found that, on the basis of Community law, the Council is obliged to give a full declaration of the competences of the Member States and of the Euratom in a decision on accession to a convention.[538] In 2005 the Council adopted a decision approving the accession of Euratom to the Joint Convention on the Safety of Spent Fuel Management and on the safety of Radioactive Waste Management.[539]

4.13   NON-CONTRACTUAL LIABILITY

Article 188 EA provides for non-contractual liability of Euratom in similar wording to that of Article 288 EC. In the *Autosalone Ispra* judgment the Court of First Instance (CFI) rejected an action for such damages.[540]

5   ENERGY POLICY

5.1   GENERAL INTRODUCTION

Like agriculture and transport, energy is usually considered to be a sensitive sector of the economy.[541] Nevertheless, the EC Treaty does not provide for special

---

535. See also section 4.6 *supra* on the relationship between the powers of the Community and those of the Member States in the area of external relations. In the field of nuclear energy, see the important Ruling 1/78, delivered pursuant to the third paragraph of Art. 103 of the EAEC Treaty, on Draft Convention of the International Atomic Energy Agency on the Physical Protection of Nuclear Materials, Facilities and Transports. The Convention has now entered into force, see note 499 *supra*.
536. These articles were amended by the Treaty of Amsterdam in order to clarify when agreements with third countries have effect for acceding states.
537. Case C-29/99, *Commission v. Council*. In 2004, the Council adopted a joint action 2004/495/ CFSP on support for IAEA activities under its Nuclear Security Programme
538. Case C-29/99, *Commission v. Council*. In this case, the Court ruled that the decision challenged did not fulfil that obligation, and annulled the relevant declaration made by the EAEC according to the provisions of Art. 30(4)(iii) of the Nuclear Safety Convention. See the annotation by P. Koutrakos in (2004) CML Rev., 191–208.
539. Decision 2005/84/Euratom O.J. 2005, L 30/10.
540. Case T-250/02, *Autosalone Ispra Snc v. European Atomic Energy Community*.
541. The Spaak Report already earmarked energy as a sector requiring urgent action.

powers, although Article 3(1)(u) EC now specifically envisages 'measures' in this area.[542] The Declaration on civil protection, energy and tourism, adopted with the Treaty of Maastricht,[543] does envisage the possibility of a separate Title on energy being included in the Treaty.[544] Moreover, energy is mentioned as one of the sectors for which trans-European networks should be developed.[545]

In a Declaration on Article 231 EC (as it now is) attached to the Final Act on the occasion of signature of the SEA, the then Intergovernmental Conference confirmed that the Community's activities in the sphere of the environment may not interfere with national policies regarding the exploitation of energy resources, a declaration which the national governments regarded as confirming their sovereignty over mineral resources. This still influences the willingness of the Member States to agree on a common energy policy.[546] It is interesting to draw the parallel with the development of the common transport policy, outlined in section 3.1 above. In the energy market – with the exception of nuclear energy – the general provisions of the EC Treaty apply, so for that part of the energy market there is in principle no other regulatory regime than the liberal market regime of the Treaty itself. It would be possible to introduce a specific regime in any new energy Title, but that would require unity of approach among the Member States as to the type of regime required. As long as this is lacking, the sole option for the Community appears to be the formation of a liberalized energy market. Thus, in fact, the same choice has been made as for transport policy. As will be seen in the discussion of the directives on the internal market in electricity and natural gas,[547] this picture needs some fine tuning. The regime introduced by these directives contains a number of clearly sector-specific characteristics. Both directives leave considerable room for national energy policy, in particular because public service obligations can be imposed. The interest in these public service obligations is constantly growing.[548] This characteristic is amplified by the fact that case law

---

542. While it is unclear what sort of measures are meant, it may be assumed on the basis of the general principles of the Treaty that they may not derogate from the fundamental rules, save where specifically permitted. A comparison with Art. 71(1)(d) EC may be made. Cf. section 3.2 *supra*. As was mentioned in notes 2 and 3 *supra*, the Lisbon Treaty intends to insert a separate Title on energy in the EC Treaty (renamed the Treaty on the Functioning of the European Union). It would also abolish the present Art. 3(1)(u) EC, but lists energy as an area of shared competence.

543. Annexed to the Final Act on the occasion of the signature of the Treaty of Maastricht.

544. The Commission stated in the same declaration that it would pursue its action on the basis of the present provisions.

545. See section 6.4, *infra*.

546. This became clear in the discussion on the Commission's proposal on upstream licencing, which has now become Dir. 94/22 (O.J. 1994, L 164/3). Norway was particularly opposed to the proposal. A similar standpoint was evident in the negotiations on the European Energy Charter, discussed in section 5.3, *infra*. The new Art. 194, to be inserted by the Lisbon Treaty in the TFEU, reflects a similar view.

547. Dir. 96/92 concerning common rules for the internal market in electricity, O.J. 1997, L 27/20 (also referred to as the electricity directive); and Dir. 98/30, concerning common rules for the internal market in natural gas, O.J. 1998, L 204/1 (also referred to as the natural gas directive). Both these directives have now been replaced, see *infra*.

548. See also section 3.1 *supra*.

of the Court of Justice on Articles 86 EC leaves broad discretion for the establishment of the content of these public service obligations.[549]

The importance of public service obligations has also been demonstrated by the inclusion of a new article on this in the EC Treaty, Article 16 EC, inserted by the Treaty of Amsterdam. This provision obliges the Community and the Member States to ensure that services of general economic interest operate on the basis of principles and conditions which enable them to fulfil their missions.[550]

Now that the public service obligations have been given their proper role in the context of the energy policy, attention has shifted to the principle of security of supply. As a result, the national regulators have been endowed with market monitoring powers to address security of supply issues.

Three factors of further importance for the development of energy policy are (a) that these sectors are partly covered by the Euratom Treaty, (b) that up until July 2002 they were covered by the ECSC Treaty as far as coal was concerned, and (c) that the EC Treaty deals with the other energy sectors.[551] As the ECSC Treaty expired on 23 July 2002, it is not discussed further at this point in the present edition. Interested readers may consult the previous edition for more information.[552]

5.2   Energy Policy Prior to 1996: A Brief Overview

5.2.1   Introduction

In making an assessment of the Community energy policy, as with any other sectoral policy, one needs to ask to what extent specific measures are necessary alongside the application of the general Treaty provisions on free movement and competition. In that context, it is also important to know whether these general

---

549. Energy cases: Case C-157/94, *Commission v. Netherlands*; Case C-158/94, *Commission v. Italy*; Case C-159/94, *Commission v. France*; Case C-160/94, *Commission v. Spain.* See on this annotation by Slot in (1998) CML Rev., 1183 et seq. See further Joined Cases C-147 & 148/97, *Deutsche Post*; Case C-209/98, *Sydhavnens Sten & Grus.* See also the judgment in Case C-205/99, *Analir et al.*, discussed in section 3.1 *supra. Analir* may be taken as a guideline for Member States in relation to the imposition of public service obligations. Further useful indications may be found in the so-called 'golden shares' cases: Case C-367/98, *Commission v. Portugal*; Case C-483/99, *Commission v. France*; Case C-503/99, *Commission v. Belgium.* The last of these in particular gives further clarification of the requirements which an approval procedure must meet.

550. See section 3.1.3 *supra.*

551. The scope of application of the various Treaties is discussed in Ch. II, section 2, *supra.*

552. See, however, Ch. I of this book for the relevant historical information; Chs. V and VI also refer to the ECSC Treaty where relevant for background information. The research fund for coal and steel are regulated in the Decision of the Representatives of the Governments of the Member States, meeting within the Council 2002/234, O.J. 2002, L 79/42. A good overview of the market intervention system of the ECSC Treaty is given by E. Steindorff, Markt und hoheitliche Verantwortung in der EG (2000) ZHR, 223–273. See also J. Grunwald, 'Das Ende der Epoche – das Erbe der EGKS', (2003) EuZW, 193.

Treaty articles are actually applied in practice, and if so whether this takes place with the same intensity as in other sectors. In general it can be said that application in the energy sector as a whole has been more difficult than in other sectors. The reasons for this are set out below.

The application of Articles 28 and 31 EC took some time to get off the ground. It was some years before the Commission tackled the national monopolies in the oil and petroleum sector in the various Member States.[553] It was only in the early 1990s that the Commission raised questions about import and export monopolies in the electricity and natural gas sectors – and, moreover, these were mainly permitted by the Court on the basis of Article 86(2) EC.[554] The application of Articles 81 and 82 EC was also rare in the energy sector.[555] On the other hand, the rules on mergers (under Regulation 4064/89 and now Regulation 139/2004) – which applied to all sectors – were applied frequently.[556] As is apparent from section 5.4 below, the state aid rules have regularly been at issue in this sector. This brief sketch of the application of the general Treaty rules only applies to the oil, natural gas and electricity sectors; the other energy sectors were subject to the rules of the ECSC and Euratom treaties. As will appear below, the incomplete application of thee general Treaty rules has left its mark on the development of sectoral measures.

5.2.2   From the Beginning and up to 1988

At the start of the European integration process, with the establishment of the ECSC, King Coal played a dominant role in the provision of energy. The availability of cheap oil, and, from 1961, natural gas, meant that the importance of the coal sector declined rapidly. The reduction in coal production did not go smoothly: social considerations and the desire that the Community should not become wholly dependent on imports of oil and coal led to massive aid programmes in the Member States. But EEC policy was initially very liberally oriented, influenced by cheap oil. After the oil crisis in 1973 particular attention was paid to reducing external dependency. Directives based on the old Article 103(4) EEC established a crisis mechanism.[557]

---

553. See T.C. Daintith, L. Hancher, *Energy Strategy in Europe*, Berlijn, 1986 and Case C-347/88, *Commission v. Greece.*

554. See energy cases etc. *supra* note 549.

555. See J. Faull, A. Nickpay, *The EC Law of Competition*, 2nd ed. (OUP, Oxford, 2007), Ch. 10; P.D. Cameron, *Competition in Energy Markets* (OUP, Oxford, 2007), Part III; C.W. Jones (ed.), *EU Energy Law*, Vol. II, 'EU Competition Law & Energy Markets' (Leuven, 2005); P.J. Slot, 'Energy and Competition', (1994) CML Rev., 511–547.

556. See the commentaries cited in the previous footnote. An interesting merger control decision is BP Amoco/Arco, parties had undertaken significant commitments relating to divestiture of pipelines, O.J. 2001, L 18/1. An overview of the most important developments up until 2000 may be found in M. Albers, 'Energy Liberalisation and EC Competition Law', (2001) *Fordham Corporate Law Institute*, 393 et seq.

557. Dir. 73/238 (O.J. 1973, L 228/1), was preceded by Dir. 68/414 O.J. 1968, L 308, on minimum stocks of crude oil and/or petroleum products. See for further measures the literature mentioned at the end of this chapter.

The second oil crisis led to an extension of these measures[558] and also to various measures concerned with energy saving.[559]

In 1981 the Commission developed a new policy strategy.[560] In the relevant communication, the Commission said, in so many words, that as a result of the very divergent situations in the Member States[561] while Community objectives were required, neither a common (centralized) policy nor uniformity in the diversification of energy sources pursued was necessary. A common policy would be necessary only in areas in which the Community itself possessed specific or even exclusive powers. Policy in the 1980s was characterized by information obligations, numerous recommendations, annual reports on national energy policy, and financial incentives.

5.2.3   Towards an Internal Energy Market

5.2.3.1   Introduction

As of 1988, the objective of achieving an internal market was emphasized, especially after the publication of the Commission's working document *The Internal Energy Market.*[562] This meant in practice creating normal, healthy conditions of

---

558. The crisis measures implement the International Energy Agency's rules (Dir. 73/238, O.J. 1973, L 228/1). They are supplemented by an agreement between the major oil companies which was the subject of exemption under Art. 81(3) EC (Dec. 83/671 (O.J. 1983, L 376/30) *International Energy Agency*, renewed by Dec. 94/153 (O.J. 1994, L 68/35)). The obligation on oil companies to maintain emergency stocks has in some countries been restrictively applied in a manner incompatible with the internal market, thus the companies have been obliged to keep stocks on national territory, without being allowed to count stocks elsewhere, see CEPS, *Relaunching the Debate on Energy Policy* (Brussels, 1993) 16. The judgment in Case 72/83, *Campus Oil*, shows that the system is not regarded as affording complete guarantees of security of supply. The same may be concluded from the Belgian Golden Shares Case C-503/99, *Commission v. Belgium*. In Case C-347/88, *Commission v. Greece*, the Court did not take such a lenient view of the Greek rules. In Case C-398/98, *Commission v. Greece*, this country was found to have failed to fulfil its obligations under Art. 28 EC by establishing and maintaining a system for stocks of petroleum products which obliged undertakings to obtain supplies of petroleum products from refineries established in Greece. In O.J. 2002, C 331E/ 249, 3 proposed guidelines for amendments to the system are published.
559. See further: E.D. Cross, B. Delvaux, L. Hancher, P.J. Slot, G. van Calster and W. Vanderberge 'EC Energy Law', in *Energy Law in Europe* 2nd ed. (Oxford, 2007).
560. See T.C. Daintith and L. Hancher, *Energy Strategy in Europe* (Berlin, 1986).
561. One of the most important objectives of the study by Daintith and Hancher (ibid.) is to make clear that these differences do not only concern the strongly divergent weight of the different energy sources and the structure of the market but also the objectives, principles and instruments of the legal regulation of energy supplies (ibid. 33–128). Particularly the different ways in which the states participate in production do not lend themselves, on the basis of Art. 295 EC, to a transfer of powers to the Community. For a long time, the competition rules of the EC Treaty were not applied to oligopolistic market structures or even monopolistic market structures in sectors of the market. See Slot, 'Energy and Competition' (1994) CML Rev., 511.
562. COM(88)238 Final; this document can be seen as a sectoral elaboration of the White paper on completing the internal market COM(85)310 final.

competition in the markets for the separate sources of energy: coal, gas, oil, and electricity. It also meant healthy competition between the different forms of energy. In that working document, the Commission did not make it clear whether it was concerned with competition *within* the individual energy markets or *between* them. It is submitted, though, that there should be no contradiction between intra-fuel and inter-fuel competition. The Commission's working document gave an overview of the many obstacles to the internal market in energy which existed at that time. Extensive aid measures, particularly in the coal sector, constituted major obstacles, the stream of which the Commission attempted to bring under control.[563] Decisions approving aid in Spain, Portugal and Germany show that the Commission was willing to approve large-scale aid.[564]

5.2.3.2 Characteristics of the Energy Sector That Influenced the Development of a Community Energy Policy

The security of supplies has always played an important role. It is useful for analytical purposes to distinguish between security of supplies as a geopolitical concept and as an operational concept. In the former concept, this manifested itself heavily in the development of energy policy after the oil crises. In this context, the emphasis is on measures to reduce dependency on external energy sources, particularly oil, but also, increasingly, gas. The second concept is often invoked to justify exclusive rights to produce, transport and distribute energy. In the latter two of these activities, the concept is particularly invoked in the network-based forms of energy: gas and electricity. In some instances, the one concept follows the other.

The case law on the exceptions under Articles 28, 31 and 86(2) EC and Commission policy in the application of Articles 81, 82 and 86(2) EC lead to the conclusion that a great many problems were involved in reaching a satisfactory definition of the possibility of exceptions on the basis of security of supplies. For many years the not uncontroversial judgment in *Campus Oil* set the tone: the Member States had the feeling that the exception was far-reaching for two main reasons. On the one hand, the Court accepted that in the case of interests of security of supply, the possibility of justification under Article 30 EC was not excluded by the mere fact that other, economic, objectives could be achieved by one and the same measure; at the same time, the Court's view of the proportionality of the measures concerned meant that the prices fixed by the government were found acceptable.[565]

---

563. Decision 2064/86, ECSC, O.J. 1986, L 177/1.
564. See e.g., Decisions 93/135, 93/145 and 93/151, ECSC, O.J. 1993, L 55/64, L 57/26 and L 59/33, respectively. The aid in the BRD amounted to roughly 5 billion DM per year. See further L. Hancher, T.R. Ottervanger, and P.J. Slot, *E.C. State Aids*, 3rd ed. (London, 2006), Ch. 13, for an overview of state aid to the energy sector.
565. Case 72/83, *Campus Oil*.

In the meantime, in *Almelo v. IJsselmaatschappij*,[566] and the electricity cases,[567] the Court has recognized that restrictions of competition for energy utilities are permitted on the basis of Article 86(2) EC: account must be taken of the economic conditions under which the undertaking operates, in particular the costs it has to bear and the rules, particularly as to environmental policy, to which it is subject. For the application of Article 86(2) EC it is not necessary that the undertaking in question cannot fulfil a special task incumbent on it in any other manner; it is sufficient that this task cannot be fulfilled under economically acceptable conditions.

5.2.3.3   *Further Reasons for Slow Development*

Any analysis of the slow development of the Community energy policy should bear in mind that, due to a number of factors, this policy is only susceptible to control to a limited extent. First, the price of crude oil. The significance of this factor for the whole energy sector is enormous,[568] as the policy of all other energy providers (gas, coal, nuclear energy, hydro-electric power and alternative energy sources such as wind farms) is ultimately determined by the price of oil. Because the world's largest oil and gas reserves are located outside the Community, the Community's influence on the price of oil is pretty well in inverse proportion to the importance of that price. Thus Community policy has aimed at facilitating a reduction in the risk of price movements.

After the Chernobyl disaster, the possibility of turning to nuclear energy was for a long time pretty well blocked in many Member States, save France[569] and some of the new Member States. The recent steep increase in the price of oil seems to have altered this.[570] The possibility of using coal produced in the Community for energy production is strongly hindered by the fact that its production price is about twice the world market price. Moreover, environmental requirements pose ever-increasing restrictions on coal, even though new technology has made major reductions in emissions possible.[571] The development of combined heat and power stations has led to a major increase in energy efficiency.[572] As these power stations run on gas, this caused an increase in the use of gas.

---

566.   Case C-393/92, *Gemeente Almelo et al. v. Energiebedrijf IJsselmij*. This judgment builds on the decision in Case C-320/91, *Criminal proceedings against Corbeau*, see Hancher (1994) CML Rev., 105 and (1995) CML Rev., 305.
567.   Case C-157/94, *Commission v. Netherlands*; Case C-158/94, *Commission v. Italy*; Case C-159/94, *Commission v. France*; Case C-160/94, *Commission v. Spain*.
568.   This can be witnessed in the sudden change in the appreciation of nuclear energy that has taken place over the last two years, see section 4.1 *supra*.
569.   Which in the 1990s produced some 77% of its electricity requirements from nuclear energy (Power in Europe, 22 Oct. 1993, No. 160).
570.   See section 4.1 *supra*.
571.   Dir. 84/360 on the combating of air pollution from industrial plants, O.J. 1984, L 188/20, requires Member States to use the best technology for steam and gas turbine units of power stations. In Case C-364/03, *Commission v. Greece*, Greece was censored for not having defined policies for the best available technology for steam engine units.
572.   S. Wiersema, 'Industrial Combined Heat and Power: Comparison between Netherlands and Denmark', *Utilities Law Review* 1991, 170 et seq.

Finally, the network-bound nature of gas and electricity should not be forgotten. This element has frequently led to the existence of exclusive rights to transport and distribution;[573] this contrasts with the right to *produce* electricity, which does not need to be exclusive. As has been noted above, the existence of these exclusive rights has rendered the application of the competition rules very difficult.

The production of gas and oil, which are activities linked to concessions, also gives rise to problems in relation to procurement. For that reason, Directive 2004/17, on procurement procedures of entities operating in the water, energy, transport and postal services sectors, also included the production, transport and distribution of energy within its scope.[574] Directive 94/22 ensures that the conditions for granting and using authorizations for the prospection, exploration and production of hydrocarbons are brought into line with Community law.[575]

The geopolitical aspect of security of supplies has also led to major attention being focused on external policy. This has translated into an active policy in relation to the major oil-producing countries in the framework of the Gulf Cooperation Council as well as several bilateral agreements. The European Energy Charter Treaty and the Basic Agreement were supposed to address this issue in particular by improving energy relations with Russia.[576] Russia has not ratified the Treaty, so it has not played an important role in securing energy supplies.[577] The Treaty also dealt with energy issues, such as transit, for the Eastern European countries, but since most of them have now become Member States of the EU,

---

573. Cf. P.J. Slot and A.M. Skudder, 'Common Features of Community Law Regulation in the Network-bound Sectors' (2001) CML Rev., 87–129.

574. O.J. 2004, L 134/1. Under Art. 30, it is possible to obtain an exemption from the requirements of the directive for the prospection and production of oil and gas, providing that, inter alia, the grant of authorizations takes place in a non-discriminatory manner. The general criteria for the grant of such exemptions can be found in Decision 93/327, O.J. 1993, L 129/25. Further rules are laid down in Commission Decision 2005/15/EC of 7 Jan. 2005 on the detailed rules for the application of the procedure provided for in Art. 30 of Dir. 2004/17/EC of the European Parliament and of the Council coordinating the procurement procedures of entities operating in the water, energy, transport and postal services sectors, O.J. 2005, L 7/7–17. See Van Calster, Cross, Delvaux, Hancher, Slot and Vandenberge, in Roggenkamp et al., *EU Energy Law*, 2nd ed. (OUP, 2007), Ch. 6 (G)(6).

575. O.J. 1994, L 164/3, corr. O.J. 1996, L 79/30. See also Van Calster et al. op. cit., *supra* note 574, Ch. 6(H).

576. The Energy Charter Treaty and accompanying declarations are in O.J. 1994, C 344/3. See T. Walde (ed.), *The Energy Charter Treaty* (The Hague, 1996), and the contribution by C. Bamberger, T. Waelde and J. Lineham on the Charter in: M.M. Roggenkamp, A. Ronne and C. Redgwell (eds), *Energy Law in Europe* (Oxford, 2001). The current developments in the area of the Energy Charter Treaty may be found at: <www.encharter.org>. In December 1998, the 'Rules Concerning the Conduct of Conciliation of Transit Disputes' were approved. This is an important instrument which may considerably stimulate through transport of energy. On this subject, a report is included each year in the General report of activities of the EU, see e.g., 1998, point 399, 143, where it is mentioned that the Treaty entered into force, and that 13 Member States were already parties.

577. Another important producer of oil and gas, Norway, has not ratified the Treaty either. Nevertheless, the Treaty is still relevant for issues such as transit.

such matters are now subject to Community law. In 1996, the Commission issued a communication setting out a strategy for energy cooperation with Asia.[578]

5.3   POLICY SINCE 1996

5.3.1   Introduction

The adoption of the directives on the internal market for electricity and natural gas[579] finally gave concrete shape to the Community energy policy. Around the same time, the Commission published a white paper on energy policy.[580] This white paper fits in with the policy set out in the directives, and at the same time supplements it. It is based on the integration of energy markets. In addition, it proposes a balanced approach to competition and environmental concerns. The latter are largely embodied in the directive on the promotion of renewable energy sources[581] and the directive on cogeneration.[582] The external dimension is also explicitly highlighted, on account of the Community's great dependence on external energy sources. Finally, the white paper states that reliable supply must be guaranteed.

   In 1997, the Community issued a communication in which it gave an overall view of energy policy and actions.[583] The electricity and natural gas directives were amended in 2003 with the aim of stepping up the liberalization effort.[584] At the same time, a regulation facilitating access to the network for cross-border exchanges in electricity was adopted.[585] Two years later, a regulation on access

---

578.   COM(96)308 final, 18 Jul. 1966. The communication concludes that the Community can contribute significantly to meeting the energy and environmental challenges; that a considerable contribution can be made by European businesses, which is vital for hundreds of thousand of jobs in Europe where the markets are almost saturated.

579.   Dir. 96/92 concerning common rules for the internal market in electricity, O.J. 1997, L 27/20 and Dir. 98/30, concerning common rules for the internal market in natural gas, O.J. 1998, L 204/1. See for a comparative overview, P.J. Slot and A.M. Skudder, 'Common Features of Community Law Regulation in the Network-Bound Sectors' (2001) CML Rev., 87–129.

580.   'An Energy Policy for the European Union', COM(95)682 final, 13 Dec. 1995.

581.   Dir. 2001/77 on the promotion of electricity produced from renewable energy sources in the internal electricity market, O.J. 2001, L 283/33.

582.   Dir. 2004/8 on the promotion of cogeneration based on a useful heat demand in the internal market, O.J. 2004, L 52/50.

583.   COM(97)167 final, 23 Apr. 1997. The most important conclusions of the communication are that policy should be more transparent. In addition, it should be intensified, and made more efficient. This is all proposed in the context of the existing instruments; new instruments are not proposed.

584.   Dir. 2003/54 concerning common rules for the internal market in electricity, repealing Dir. 96/92, O.J. 2003, L 176/37. Dir. 2003/55 concerning common rules for the internal market in natural gas, repealing Dir. 98/30, O.J. 2003, L 176/57.

585.   Reg. 1228/2003 of the European Parliament and of the Council of 26 Jun. 2003 on conditions for access to the network for cross-border exchanges in electricity, O.J. 2003, L 176/1. Commission decision 2006/770/EC has amended the annex, O.J. 2006, L 312/59. In Case

to the natural gas transmission network was enacted,[586] providing for tariffs for access to networks (Art. 3) and other specific rules for access.

The Community has made a, timid, effort to address the security of supply for electricity, with Directive 2005/89.[587] Article 3(1) thereof requires Member States to ensure a high level of security of electricity supply by taking the necessary measures to facilitate a stable investment climate and by defining the roles and responsibilities of competent authorities. In 2006, the Commission published a Green Paper, entitled 'A European Strategy for Sustainable, Competitive and Secure Energy.'[588] The paper identifies six priority areas: competitiveness and the internal market, diversification of the energy mix, solidarity, sustainable development, innovation and technology and external policy. The latter has assumed particular importance as a result of the steep increase in the oil price in 2005 and early 2006, as well as the fragile energy relations with Russia.[589] In 2007, the sector enquiry into the European gas and electricity was published which concluded that there are several areas where competition is not functioning properly.[590] In September 2007 the Commission adopted proposals for a third package of legislative proposals.[591]

5.3.2 The Directives on the Internal Market for Electricity and Natural Gas[592]

The directives follow a comparable system, although there are also important differences. The following paragraphs will only discuss the main lines of the

---

C-414/04, *European Parliament and Commission v. Council*, the Court annulled Reg. 1223/2004 amending Reg. 1228/2003 thereby extending the date of application of certain provisions to Slovenia.

586. Reg. 1775/2005 of the European Parliament and of the Council of 28 Sep. 2005 on access to natural gas transmission networks, O.J. 2005, L 289/1.

587. Dir. 2005/89/EC of the European Parliament and of the Council of 18 Jan. 2006 concerning measures to safeguard security of electricity supply and infrastructure investment, O.J. 2006, L 33/22.

588. COM(2006)105 final of 8 Mar. 2006. The objectives therein were reiterated by the European Council of 8–9 Mar. 2007, cf. paras. 27 and 28 of Presidency Conclusions.

589. These relations set the context of an ongoing dialogue for the preparation of bilateral treaty.

590. DG Competition report on energy sector inquiry, 10 Jan. 2007, SEC(2006)1724.

591. COM(2007)529 final; COM(2007)530 final; COM(2007)531 and COM(2007)532 final, of 19 Sep. 2007. The proposals seek to amend Dir. 2004/54 on the internal market for electricity, Dir. 2004/55 on the internal market for natural gas, Reg. 1228/2003 on cross-border exchanges in electricity and Reg. 1775/2005 on access to natural gas transmission networks, and propose establishing an Agency for cooperation among energy regulators.

592. Dir. 2003/54 concerning common rules for the internal market in electricity, O.J. 2003, L 176/37. Dir. 2003/55 concerning common rules for the internal market in natural gas, O.J. 2003, L 176/57. Although the first directives were only enacted in 1996 they have already been replaced by a second generation of directives. Paragraph 2 of the preamble of the 2003 directives summarizes the shortcomings and the possibilities for improving the functioning of the market. An extensive commentary on the directives is given in C.W. Jones, *EU Energy Law*, Vol. I, 'The Internal Energy Market' (Claeys & Casteels, Leuven, 2004). For a shorter

regime in the two sectors. It should be borne in mind that the directives in both sectors aim to break up a far-reaching system of exclusive and special rights for the production, transport and distribution of electricity and natural gas. Member States must observe the principle of non-discrimination.[593] The 'market-proof' nature of the existing system was further strengthened by the fact that the production, transport and distribution functions were – and still are – frequently in the hands of vertically integrated undertakings. The basic principle of the directives is that access must be granted to the electricity grid and the gas network, respectively.[594] According to Article 20 of the directive on the internal electricity market, Member States must ensure third party access to the transmission and distribution system, based on published tariffs applicable to all eligible customers (regulated access). Article 18 of the directive on the internal market for natural gas provides for regulated access to the transmission and distribution system. For access to storage, Article 19 of the gas directive leaves Member States the choice between negotiated access and regulated access, and Article 20 obliges Member States to ensure that undertakings and eligible parties obtain access to upstream pipeline networks, but leaves them the choice of the instruments.

Another important principle is the so-called 'unbundling' obligation.[595] Integrated electricity and gas undertakings may abuse the fact that they combine a number of activities. They may be tempted to indulge in cross-subsidization: they may, for instance, give reductions to larger customers – who might otherwise go to competitors – using the substantial income they receive on the market for small-scale customers – who do not (as yet) have any alternative. Therefore, the directives lay down that the distribution and transmission systems are operated through separate entities where vertically integrated undertakings exist. The rules for

---

comment see P.D. Cameron: 'The Internal Market in Energy: Harnessing the New Regulatory Regime' (2005) EL Rev., 631 et seq. In Case C-259/01, *Commission v. France*, France was found to have failed to implement Dir. 98/30 within the time limits. For a long time, Italy and Spain applied legislation which limited the participation of energy companies from other Member States in the absence of reciprocity. This legislation was aimed at the French EDF, because France refused to liberalize the energy markets according to the rules in the directives. See *Agence Europe* No. 8319, 2002. Proposals have since been presented for adapting the directives and laying down rules for access to the network for cross-border exchanges in electricity, O.J. 2001, C 240E/11/60 and E/12/72 respectively. In Case C-413/04, *Parliament and Commission v. Council* the Court annulled Dir. 2004/85which extended the implementation period of Dir. 2003/54 for Estonia

593. Art. 3(1) of Dir. 2003/54 and of Dir. 2003/55. In Joined Cases C-128 & 129/03, *AEM SpA v. Autorita per l'energia elettrica e per il gas*, the Court interpreted this rule. It held that an increased charge for a transitional period for access could be acceptable.

594. In the case of electricity, this involves high-voltage, medium voltage and low voltage distribution systems. In the case of natural gas, this involves both local and regional pipeline networks. In Case C-439/06, the court ruled that Art. 20(1) of the electricity directive does not allow an exemption for certain operators, cf Case C-439/06, *Citiworks v. Flughafen Leipzig/Halle*.

595. A comparable principle of transparency is laid down in Dir. 80/723, O.J. 1980, L 195/35, amended by Dir. 2000/52, O.J. 2000, L 193/75, on the transparency of financial relations between Member States and public undertakings. The directive has been amended by Dir. 2005/81, O.J. 2005, L 312/47 to take into account Case C-280/00, *Altmark*.

unbundling are found in the Articles 10 (for transmission operators), 15 (for distribution system operators) and 19 (for the unbundling of the accounts) of the electricity market directive.[596]

Another important principle is that – in theory at least – it should be possible for any firm that so wishes to start generating electricity; alternatively, if a system exists whereby a licence is required for the production of electricity, these should be issued on a non-discriminatory basis. The electricity market directive provides in Article 6 for a non-discriminatory authorization procedure or, in Article 7, a tendering procedure.[597] For the production of natural gas, Art 3 et seq. of Directive 94/22 (on prospection, exploration and production of hydrocarbons) state that non-discriminatory conditions must apply to the issue of authorizations for exploring and producing natural gas.[598]

Both the electricity market directive and the natural gas market directive provide for rules concerning transmission: on the one hand, a secure, reliable and efficient system must be operated and maintained, and on the other hand there must be no discrimination (Article 12 natural gas directive). Both directives oblige the Member States gradually to open up the market for competition, and both require that from 1 July 2007 all customers must be 'eligible', i.e., able to choose their supplier.[599]

The two directives require Member States to establish national regulatory authorities providing for effective regulation. The Commission has set up a European Regulators Group for Electricity and Gas (ERGEG) which constitutes an advisory mechanism for encouraging cooperation and coordination of national regulatory authorities. This European Regulators Group (a semi-official body) assumes an increasingly important role in the management of the internal market for electricity and gas. The directives allow the Member States to impose public service obligations to ensure a high level of consumer protection, security (including security of supply), and environmental protection.[600] Such measures have to conform to the case law of the ECJ on Article 86 EC and have to be notified to the Commission.

The directives also contain a number of important exceptions. Access to the electricity grid or the gas network may be refused if there is insufficient capacity.[601] It is possible to refuse access to the gas network if a natural gas undertaking would encounter, serious economic and financial difficulties because of long-term commitments.[602] In the electricity directive, Article 26 provides a

---

596. The corresponding articles in the gas directive are 9, 13 and 17. According to recital 8 of the preamble of the electricity directive, and recital 10 of the gas directive, the respective entities must be separated legally (the distribution system operators have until Jul. 2007 to do so), ownership unbundling is not mentioned in the directives.

597. Art. 4 of the gas directive requires Member States to grant non-discriminatory authorizations to build and operate natural gas facilities.

598. O.J. 1994, L 164/3.

599. Art. 21 of the electricity directive and Art. 23 of gas directive.

600. Art. 3 of both directives.

601. Art. 20(2) of the electricity directive and Art. 21 of the gas directive.

602. Art. 27.

more or less comparable derogation possibility.[603] Article 22 of the natural gas directive allows for an exemption from the access provisions for new infrastructure projects where that is necessary in view of the level of risk of the investment.[604] Both directives contain safeguard clauses allowing Member States temporarily to take measures to deal with sudden crises.[605] Article 11(4) of the electricity directive grants Member States the power to take measures to stimulate energy from indigenous primary energy fuel sources.[606] It may be remarked that the liberalization intended by the directives is frustrated to the extent that some Member States such as France, Spain and Italy still maintain price controls for certain consumers.

The implementation of the directives is being carried out fairly smoothly, although it can not be predicted yet whether all Member States will manage to implement correctly and on time.[607] There are also regular frictions between countries which favour a restrictive interpretation of the obligations contained in the directives, and Member States which pursue a more far-reaching liberalization. These differences in the extent of liberalization can still lead to new distortions of competition. The Commission follows developments closely, not least because it is obliged – on the basis of the directives – to examine the imposition of public service obligations for conformity with the general rules of the Treaty, in particular Article 86(2) EC.[608] This is why the Commission made a proposal to establish a European regulatory agency which, according to the Commission should ensure uniform application of the rules.[609]

---

603. This provision was invoked by the Netherlands, and other Member States, in order to solve the problem of the 'millstones': these were contracts which were concluded under the previous regime (the Dutch 1989 Electricity Act) or expensive generating stations which have been built in the past. In a series of decisions, the Commission has for the most part rejected such requests. O.J. 1999, L 319/1 et seq. See further *infra* section 5.4.

604. All applications for such exemptions have so far been granted by the Commission. See T. Van der Vijver, 'Exemptions to Third Party Access for New Infrastructures in the European Community Gas Sector' (2008), ECLR, 229–237.

605. Art. 24 of the electricity directive and Art. 26 of the gas directive.

606. In his Opinion in Case C-379/98, *PreussenElektra* at para. 208 A.G. Jacobs rejects the possibility that this provision (at the time, Art. 8(4) of the old electricity Dir. 96/92) might be used to justify an extra duty on alternative energy. He held the same view in relation to Arts. 3(2) and 11(3) of the old directive (96/92), see paras. 211 et seq.

607. Art. 30(2) of Dir. 2003/54 (electricity) allows Member States until 1 Jul. 2007 to implement the unbundling of the distribution system operators. Art. 33(2) of Dir. 2003/55 (gas) contains a similar provision.

608. In 2001, the Commission published a communication on completing the internal energy market (COM(2001)125 final), giving an overview of the state of affairs concerning progress in implementing the directives, and proposing amendments to the existing legislation. For the electricity sector, an informal body of regulators, network operators and other stakeholders has been established, the Florence Regulatory Forum, named after the city where it meets every year. For the gas sector, a similar forum has been established, meeting in Madrid. The reports of the annual meetings give a good overview of the most important problems in the sector. They are available on the website of DG Energy, <ec.europa.eu/energy/electricity/florence/index_en.htm>.

609. COM(2007)530 final 19 Sep. 2007.

5.3.3 Other Measures to Support Liberalization

In addition to the implementation of the internal market directives, the Commission continues to make active use of its competition arsenal[610] as well as the other general provisions of the Treaty.[611] The liberalization of the internal market has been supported by an active competition policy of the Commission.[612] Thus the Commission has reached agreement with Algeria's Sonatrach and Gazprom of Russia whereby territorial restrictions from all existing natural gas export contracts were deleted.[613] The liberalization has in turn led to fresh co-operative activities, some in the form of joint ventures and mergers. After the entry into force of Regulation 1/2003, which had the effect of abolishing the Commission's power to grant individual exemptions,[614] the Commission has to rely mainly on its powers in the field of approval of mergers. The power to impose conditions when accepting remedies has been employed with considerable effectiveness.[615] On the other hand, Article 1 of the merger control regulation 139/2004 excludes the Commission's jurisdiction when there is a Community dimension, but two-thirds turnover is achieved in one Member State. This means that the Commission has no powers to vet major national mergers.[616]

---

610. See on this M. Albers, 'Energy Liberalisation and EC Competition Law', (2001) *Fordham Corporate Law Institute* 393. See further e.g., the action of the Commission in relation to natural gas coming from Nigeria, whereby territorial sales restrictions were removed, *Agence Europe* 12 Dec. 2002, IP 02/1869. The active application of competition policy in this field is also apparent from recent annual reports on competition policy.
611. See Case C-173/05, *Commission v. Italy*, where the Italian environmental tax on methane gas was found to be incompatible with Arts. 23, 25 and 133 EC. Within the EEA similar principles are applied, see Case E-2/06, *EFTA Surveillance Authority v. Norway*, where the EFTA court found that the obligation to surrender all installations of a hydropower installation to the Norwegian state after the expiry of the concession period was an infringement of Art. 31 (the equivalent of the freedom of establishment) and Art. 40 (the equivalent of the freedom of capital movement) of the EEA agreement.
612. Report on Competition Policy 2004, paras. 293–299, Report on Competition Policy 2003, paras 86–100. See C.W. Jones (ed.), *EU Energy Law*, vol II, op. cit. for an extensive treatment of this topic. See also Van Calster et al. in M. Roggenkamp et al., *Energy Law in Europe*, 2nd ed. (OUP, 2007), op. cit., *supra* note 574, Ch. 6, D(5).
613. Sonatrach: press release IP/07/1074 (11 Jul. 2007); Gazprom: press releases IP/03/1345 (6 Oct. 2003) and IP/05/195 (17 Feb. 2005).
614. Except for the, limited, power of Art. 10 of the Regulation.
615. Jones op. cit. paras. 4.121- 4.146 provides ample references; see E. Morgan de Rivery and V. Guérand, 'Case COMP/M.3410 Total/Gaz de France Merger Control as a Tool to Greater Liberalisation in the Gas Sector' (2005) ECLR, 624 for a concrete illustration of this policy. See also Case T- 87/05, *EDP v. Commission*, where the CFI rejected Energias de Portugal's challenge of the Commission's refusal to accept commitments.
616. Thus the Commission had to conclude that it lacked jurisdiction in the case of the hostile take-over bid by Gas Natural for Endesa. Case COMP/M 3986. Endesa's appeal against this decision was dismissed by the CFI: Case T-417/05, *Endesa SA v.Commission*,(that judgment was appealed to the ECJ, Case C-122/06, *Endesa SA v. Commission*, but the appeal was later withdrawn).

Following the Commission's 1988 working document, legislation was already adopted in the area of transparency of gas and electricity prices; the transparency directive took a first, cautious step in the direction of providing information on market relations for industrial users of gas and electricity.[617] In addition to the internal market directives, regulations have been adopted on access to cross-border exchanges for electricity and natural gas.[618] Both regulations lay down basic principles with regard to tarification and capacity allocation. They also provide for the adoption of guidelines for further relevant principles and methodologies. The regulations require non-discriminatory and transparent charges for network use. The available capacities of these lines should be set at the maximum levels consistent with the safety standards of secure network operation. Cross-border exchanges are also promoted by the Community policy on trans-European energy networks.[619]

The liberalization of the energy sector has not been an unequivocal success. Competition is still limited, and this led the Commission to launch a sectoral inquiry.[620] The preliminary findings identify three main issues: first, market concentration, since most gas and electricity markets remain highly concentrated; second, vertical foreclosure, since incumbents often retain a firm control on entry third, a lack of market integration.[621]

5.3.5   External Energy Policy

The Community has adopted important measures for energy saving and the environment. For these topics the reader is referred to specialized literature.[622] Since 1996, external policy has developed further and – as a consequence of the EU's energy dependency[623] – more rapidly. A number of elements may be noted in addition to what was discussed in section 5.2.3.3. above. The Council has adopted a Regulation containing a programme to promote international cooperation in the energy sector.[624] The EU has established an Energy Community, enhancing the

---

617. Dir. 90/377, O.J. 1990, L 185/16.
618. Reg. 1228/2003, O.J. 2003, L 176/1 as amended by Reg. 1223/2004 O.J. 2004, L 233/3 (which was annulled by the ECJ in Case C-414/04, *European Parliament and Commission v. Council*) and Reg. 1775/2005, O.J. 2005, L 289/1. Commission decision 2006/770/EC has amended the annex, O.J. 2006, L 312/59.
619. Decision No. 1229/2003, O.J. 2003, L 176/11.
620. Multi-sector inquiry, Report of 16.02.06 DG COMP.
621. See the website DG Comp. <www.europa.eu.int/comm/competition/index_en.html>.
622. E.g., Van Calster et al. in M. Roggenkamp et al., *Energy Law in Europe*, 2nd ed. (Oxford, 2007), op. cit., *supra* note 574, Chs. G.2 and 4.
623. This dependency on external energy sources is summarized in the green paper: 'A European Strategy for Sustainable, Competitive and Secure Energy' COM(2006)105 final.
624. O.J. 1997, L 104/1. Council Reg. (EC) No. 701/97 of 14 Apr. 1997 amending a programme to promote international cooperation in the energy sector: Synergy programme. As was mentioned in section 4.2, the external dimension is taking an increasingly prominent place in Commission policy documents.

security supply of Greece and strengthening relations with the Western Balkans.[625] The recent rise in oil prices and the interruptions in the gas supply from Russia in early 2006 further underscored the need to develop an international framework for stable energy supplies.[626] The EU participates in the OECD work in the field of energy. Energy is an important topic in the EU – Gulf Co-operation Council.[627] In other cases it is part of bilateral treaties.[628]

For an overview of the extensive secondary legislation in the various parts of the energy sector, reference is made to the suggested further reading at the end of this chapter. Energy policy includes, among other things, promotion of energy conservation and alternative energy sources, such as wind energy and biomass energy.[629] In *PreussenElektra* the Court of Justice recognized promotion of alternative energy sources explicitly as a justification for national measures infringing the general prohibition of Article 28 EC, even if they are discriminatory.[630]

5.4   STATE AIDS

Articles 87 and 88 EC have been frequently applied in the energy sector.[631] Even before liberalization, they already provided the basis for significant application of the state aid rules in the sector.[632] For instance, the judgment in *Van der Kooy*[633] had important implications for the Dutch government's policy regarding energy tariffs, as the Court of Justice found that the fixing of the contested tariff could be

---

625. Council decision of 29 May 2006, O.J. 2006, L 198/15. The Treaty is published in the same issue of the O.J. 18 et seq.
626. The EU-Russia summit in early 2006 as well as the summit in autumn 2007, was largely devoted to this topic.
627. See <http://ec.europa.eu/external_relations/gulf_cooperation/intro/index.htm>. See also the CE-GOLFE 3501/06 communiqué of 15 May 2006, available through that website.
628. See e.g., the Euro-Mediterranean Agreement with Algeria, O.J. 2005, L 265/2.
629. In this area, too, the Commission has issued a number of communications: Green Paper for a Community Strategy, Energy for the future: renewable sources of energy COM(96)576 final, 20 Nov. 1996; on the energy dimension of climate change, COM(97)196 final, 14 May 1997; 'A Community Strategy to Promote Combined Heat and Power (CHP) and to Dismantle Barriers to Its Development', COM(97)514 final, 15 Oct. 1997; 'White Paper for a Community Strategy and Action Plan on Energy for the Future: Renewable Sources of Energy', COM(97)599; and the 'Proposal for a Directive on the Promotion of Electricity from Renewable Energy Sources in the Internal Electricity Market' COM(2000)279 final. See the green paper, 'A European Strategy for Sustainable, Competitive and Secure Energy' COM(2006)105 final.
630. Case C-379/98, *PreussenElektra*.
631. C.W. Jones, (ed.) *EU Energy Law*, vol. II 'EU Competition Law and Energy Markets', Part V, by L. Hancher provides an extensive treatment of the subject. For a typical case involving a state enterprise see the Commission decision on state aid granted by France to EDF, O.J. 2005, L 49/9.
632. See on this further L. Hancher, T.R. Ottervanger, P.J. Slot, op. cit. *supra*, Ch. 19; and P.J. Slot, 'Competition and Energy', (1994) CML Rev., 511 et seq.
633. Joined Cases 67, 68 & 70/85, *Van der Kooy v. Commission*.

imputed to the Dutch government. Furthermore, in both that judgment and in *Cofaz*[634] the Court carried out a detailed examination of the tariffs of the Dutch Gasunie. As a result of these judgments and the Commission's decision after *Cofaz*[635] the following conclusions may be drawn: differences in the level of energy tariffs are justified, first, to the extent that they result from actual reductions in costs; second, to the extent that they form part of a general system applicable to the industry as a whole; third, to the extent that there is a commercial reason for them;[636] and, fourth, to the extent that they serve an objective recognized by Community law, are necessary for that purpose, and are reasonably proportionate to that objective.[637] As the energy sector is one where many public sector undertakings are active, this case law has led to Community control of tariffs. In *PreussenElektra*, the Court of Justice limited the application of the state aid rules by ruling that extra payments for energy from alternative (renewable) sources which must be borne by producers and consumers in accordance with statutory provisions are not state aid.[638]

The adoption of the directive on the internal electricity market has given rise to a discussion about compensation for stranded costs. According to Article 24 of Directive 96/92 Member States can ask the Commission for a derogation from certain provisions of the directive. The Commission has adopted a communication indicating to what extent compensation may be given for stranded costs.[639] The ECJ has interpreted the exemption of Article 24 strictly. It also denied Member States that have not availed themselves of the procedure of Article 24 of the directive the possibility of recourse to Article 86(2) EC. It ruled that: 'priority access to a portion of the capacity for the cross-border transmission of electricity conferred on an operator by reason of commitments assumed before the Directive

---

634.   Case 169/84, *Cofaz v. Commission.*
635.   See O.J. 1992, C 344/4. This contains a useful summary of the Commission's views on when a state undertaking's conduct is objectively justified. The Commission applies the so-called market investor principle. See also, for a comparable approach, the decision on tariffs for gas used as a raw material by industry, O.J. 1994, C 35/6.
636.   See on this especially Case C-56/93, *Belgium v. Commission*, in which Belgium challenged, in vain, the Commission decision mentioned in the previous note.
637.   Cf. Joined Cases 67, 68 & 70/85, *Van der Kooy.* The objective recognized by Community law was environmental protection, and both the Commission and the Court were of opinion that the reduction in the gas tariffs went beyond what was necessary to ensure that the greenhouse growers would not switch from gas to coal. A recent investigation of preferential electricity rates concerned the rates charged to various firms in the paper industry by EDF. The Commission concluded that some rates were covered by the de minimis rule, that certain others were justified in a situation characterized by overcapacity, and EDF still covered the variable costs, as well as 57% of the fixed costs, O.J. 2001, L 95/18.
638.   Case C-379/98, *PreussenElektra.* An essential element is the Court's finding that the contribution was born by private undertakings and not utilities in which the national authorities had decisive influence. See also the annotation by Goossens and Emmerechts, (2001) CML Rev., 991 et seq.
639.   Report on Competition Policy 2001, §§ 346–353 see L. Hancher in: C.W. Jones (ed.), *EU Energy Law*, vol. II 'EU Competition Law and Energy Markets', Part V.

entered into force, but without compliance with the procedure set out in Article 24 of the Directive, is contrary to Articles 7(5) and 16 of the Directive.'[640]

6   INDUSTRIAL POLICY, RESEARCH AND
           TECHNOLOGICAL DEVELOPMENT, AND
           TRANS-EUROPEAN NETWORKS

6.1   INTRODUCTION

The titles on Industrial policy and trans-European networks were added to the EC Treaty by the Treaty of Maastricht; they are Titles XVI and XV, respectively, of Part Three of the Treaty. Title XVIII on Research and Technological development had already been added by the SEA, but was extended by the Treaty of Maastricht. The extension concerned in particular the scope of this Title: in addition to the objective of strengthening the research and technological foundations of Community industry and promoting the Community's international competitive position, research activities are now provided for in relation to activities falling under other chapters of the Treaty. This expansion is the logical complement of the Treaty developments in these areas and the widening of the objectives of the Community. The Lisbon Treaty provides that in the areas of research, technological development and space, the Union shall have competence to carry out activities, in particular to define and implement programmes; however, the exercise of that competence shall not result in Member States being prevented from exercising theirs.[641]

The provisions on trans-European networks, added by the Treaty of Maastricht, should be regarded in the first place as a supplement to the achievement of the internal market for transport, telecommunications and energy.[642] They also intend to create a framework for measures to open up regional and local communities, particularly in the outermost and insular regions of the Community, and to promote economic and social cohesion. The provisions on trans-European networks thus have a wider functional ambit than sectoral policy as such.

Policy on Research and Technological development received an important boost from the European Council of Lisbon, 23 and 24 March 2000, which was specially convened for this policy area.[643] The European Council aimed to launch a

---

640. Case C-17/03, *VEMW* at para. 71. The grand chamber of the Court followed a strict harmonization approach basing its judgment on the fact that Art. 24 of the directive provides for total harmonization. Thus the ECJ bypassed the preliminary question by the national court asking whether such a measure can be exempted under Art. 86(2) EC.

641. Cf. Art. 4 TFEU. The Lisbon Treaty also provides for some minor changes in the text of the current Art. 163 EC. These changes, as well as the changes made to the current Art. 3 EC, do not seem to change much in the Community powers in this area.

642. Particularly in view of the internal market achieved for electricity and now agreed for gas, referred to in section 5.3 *supra*.

643. See <http://europa.eu.int/comm/off/index_en.htm>.

strategy to promote employment, economic reform and social cohesion, as part of a so-called 'knowledge society' or knowledge-based society. The Council conclusions provide for the preparation of the transition to a knowledge-based economy and society by better policies for the information society and R&D, as well as by stepping up the process of structural reform for competitiveness and innovation and by completing the internal market. The creation of a European area for research and innovation was formulated as one of the objectives.

The Lisbon strategy is a comprehensive interdependent series of reforms. The gist of the strategy consists of reforms by the Member States acting in concert so as to be more effective. It is mainly based on the open method of coordination, supported by Community action. An important element of the strategy is the promotion of the knowledge society focusing on R&D. So far the impact of the strategy has been limited due to a lack of commitment from both the Member States and the EU.[644]

In 2005 the Commission published two Communications on growth and employment proposing a fresh start for the Lisbon strategy.[645] The second Communication notes that:

the Community contributes to the overall economic and employment policy agenda by
    completing the internal market and by implementing common policies and activities that
        support and complement national policies. It will in particular concentrate on a number of
            key actions with high value-added [sic]:

– the support of knowledge and innovation in Europe,
– the reform of the state aid policy,
– the improvement and simplification of the regulatory framework in which business operates,
– the completion of the Internal Market for services,
– the completion of an ambitious agreement in the Doha round,
– the removal of obstacles to physical, labour and academic mobility,
– the development of a common approach to economic migration,
– the support of efforts to deal with the social consequences of economic restructuring.

---

644. See 'Facing the Challenge. The Lisbon Strategy for Growth and Employment'. Report from the high level group chaired by Wim Kok, Nov. 2004. available at <http://europa.eu.int/commission/Lisbon_strategy/index_en.html>.

645. Communication to the Spring European Council: 'Working Together for Growth and Jobs: A New Start for the Lisbon Strategy', COM (2005)24 of 2 Feb. 2005 and Communication from the Commission to the Council and the European Parliament: 'Common Actions for Growth and Employment: The Community Lisbon Programme' COM(2005)330 final of 20 Jul. 2005. The latter Communication builds on the first.

At the same, the Commission published further communications on industrial policy which will be discussed below.[646]

Although the industry Title (Title XVI) was only added by the Treaty of Maastricht, the problems with which it deals were certainly not new even then. Industrial policy has been the subject of discussion pretty well since the beginning of the EEC. The Commission published an extensive memorandum on this subject already in 1970.[647]

Of the policies discussed here, research and technological development can be seen as a horizontal and flanking policy, and for that reason the observations made in sections 1 and 2 of Chapter XI, above, are also relevant here. Given that research and technological development is so closely linked to industrial policy, however, it is discussed here.

Nevertheless, unlike the Treaty's provisions on horizontal and flanking policies, there is no common approach in the subjects examined here. Both trans-European networks and industrial policy are somewhat extraneous to the system of the Treaty; this is particularly true of industrial policy. The provisions of the Industry Title are scarcely couched in terms of obligations and contain hardly any concrete instruments. The Titles on research and development and trans-European networks do clearly confer competence on the Community, and are thus important in the light of the first paragraph of Article 5 EC.[648]

Section 1 of Chapter XI, above, examined the place of horizontal and flanking policies in the EC Treaty. It should also be noted that research and technological development has found a place as an objective in Article 3(1)(n) EC, and that industrial policy and trans-European networks are mentioned in Article 3(1)(m) and (o) EC, respectively.

6.2   INDUSTRIAL POLICY

6.2.1   Treaty Foundations

The text of Article 157 EC clearly bears the traces of a compromise between the age-old difference of views about the need for an industrial policy and the form it should take. The conflict was principally between the more *dirigiste* approach based on southern European thinking, and the liberal non-interventionist

---

646. Communication from the Commission: 'Fostering Structural Change: An Industrial Policy for an Enlarged Europe', COM (2004)274 final 20 Apr. 2004; Communication from the Commission: 'Implementing the Community Lisbon Programme: A Policy Framework to Strengthen EU Manufacturing: Towards a More Integrated Approach for Industrial Policy'. COM(2005)474 final, 5 Oct. 2005.

647. Often called the Colonna memorandum: La Politique industrielle de la Communauté (Brussels, 1970).

648. The wording of the new Art. 4(3) TFEU resulting from the Lisbon Treaty – 'the exercise of that competence shall not result in Member States being prevented from exercising theirs' – seems to restrict the impact of the Community power in this area.

approach.[649] The original draft was much more *dirigiste* in nature, but resistance from the northern, more market-oriented Member States led to the present text.

A number of points stand out on reading Article 157 EC. Article 157(1) formulates guidelines for promoting greater competitiveness, with the following aims:

- speeding up the adjustment of industry to structural changes;
- encouraging an environment favourable to initiative, and to the development of undertakings throughout the Community, particularly small and medium-sized undertakings;
- encouraging an environment favourable to cooperation between undertakings; and
- fostering better exploitation of the industrial potential of policies of innovation, research and technological development.

It is very important that all this takes place in accordance with a system of open and competitive markets. This point is emphasized by the last paragraph of Article 157(3), which states that this title may not provide a basis for the introduction of measures which could lead to a distortion of competition. This would appear to be a clear confirmation of the free-market philosophy of the more liberally-minded Member States.

For the interventionist-minded Member States, Article 157 EC merely offers an instrument for consultation and coordination. Article 157(3) EC provides that the Community shall contribute to the achievement of the objectives set out in Article 157(1) through the policies and activities it pursues under other provisions of the Treaty. This appears on the one hand to confirm the approach that industrial policy can be pursued without the need for common steering measures, other than policy coordination. This corresponds to the theory and practice of the old Article 103 EEC, which was used for measures in case of actual or threatened shortages, and offered the possibility of adopting market-regulatory measures.[650] The first measures implementing the White Paper *Growth, Competitiveness and Employment*[651] showed that coordination may also be based on Article 99 EC. On the other hand, Article 157 EC also offers the possibility of using other instruments of the Treaty in a manner which does not always reflect a liberal trading policy. Use of the anti-dumping regulation is a clear example.[652] Remarkable cases can also be seen in the sphere of competition law.[653] The importance of the practical application of Article 87 EC in this context is discussed below.

---

649. See, generally, the literature mentioned at the end of this chapter.
650. See the 2nd ed. of this work (1989) 605–608.
651. COM(93)700, Bull. EU Supp. 6/93.
652. See Case C-358/89, *Extramet Industrie v. Council*. Péchiney succeeded in persuading the Community to take action against imports of raw materials by Extramet, a competitor of Péchiney, even though Extramet had been forced to import raw materials because of Péchiney's refusal to supply it (they competed in respect of a product of the raw material).
653. Case T-28/90, *Asia Motor France et al. v. Commission* and Case T-7/92, *Asia Motor France et al.*

Article 157 EC does afford Community competence on one point: on the basis of Article 157(3) EC, the Council may, acting unanimously, adopt specific measures supporting the action taken by the Member States.[654]

6.2.2 The European Investment Bank

Much of the activity of the European Investment Bank (EIB) is directed at the innovative and knowledge-based European economy.[655]

6.2.3 The Various Means Used

As the respective communications of the Commission[656] show, industrial policy in the Community is primarily pursued through techniques of negative integration, by removing technical, administrative, fiscal and other barriers to trade. But in addition to this approach, the positive integration method has become increasingly important. For the problem of technical barriers to trade, this has led to the promotion of standardization of norms.[657] The Bangemann Memorandum on the competitiveness and prospects of the Community automobile industry is an interesting example of Community industrial policy.[658] The basic approach in that memorandum is that by increasing the competitive strength of European industry, its future will be safeguarded. The Community's task is thus to create a supporting framework in the form of a free market based on competition. This supporting framework would be achieved through horizontal structural policy instruments, which would in particular take the form of improved education and training of workers, as envisaged in Article 146 EC, and research and technological development. In addition external measures were envisaged, such as the extension of the voluntary export restraint agreement with Japan.[659]

---

654. The Treaty of Nice has amended the procedure. Measures will now be adopted in accordance with the co-decision procedure (Art. 251).

655. EUR 10.7 billion. Through its 'Innovation 2010 Initiative' ('i2i'), the EIB supports the EU's Lisbon Strategy for an information and knowledge-based economy. The EIB's target is to mobilize EUR 50 billion by the end of the decade, to increase the EU's innovative capacity and enhance its longer-term competitiveness. Since the start of 'i2i' in 2000, the EIB has advanced loans for innovative investment worth EUR 34.8 billion, of which EUR 10.7 billion in 2005 alone. See <www.eib.org/news/press/press.asp?press=3074>.

656. Communication from the Commission: 'Fostering Structural Change: An Industrial Policy for an Enlarged Europe', COM(2004)274 final, 20 Apr. 2004; Communication from the Commission: 'Implementing the Community Lisbon Programme: A Policy Framework to Strengthen EU Manufacturing: Towards a More Integrated Approach for Industrial Policy', COM(2005)474 final, 5 Oct. 2005.

657. See on this the Commission communication on the broader use of standardization in Community policy, COM(95)412 final, 30 Oct. 1995.

658. COM(94)49 final, 23 Feb. 1994.

659. A similar approach may be found in the Commission's dealings with the steel industry, *Agence Europe* No. 1881 (supplement), 28 Apr. 1994.

The only more or less concrete 'positive' measure of industrial policy was a communication issued in 1996 by the Commission about 'benchmarking' the competitiveness of European industry.[660] The aim of this was to provide undertakings and national authorities with an instrument for measuring their competitiveness, in order to be able to improve it.

A more recent Commission Communication proposes cross-sectoral policy initiatives such as the Intellectual Property Rights and Counterfeiting Initiative, a new legislative Simplification Programme as well as sector-specific initiatives.[661] Annex 2 of this Communication lists 27 sectors for which specific actions are foreseen. As the Communication shows, the Commission continues to make efforts to promote international industrial cooperation.[662]

6.2.4   The Role of Competition Policy

Competition policy also plays an important part in industrial policy, and the policy in relation to joint ventures can be seen as a horizontal instrument for industrial policy purposes.[663] Positive developments can be reported in the context of merger control: the Commission has so far based its examination of almost all mergers notified to it on pure competition criteria;[664] it has resisted the temptation to allow industrial policy arguments to prevail. The Commission's competition policy reveals several examples of situations where industrial policy considerations are taken into account. Before the entry into force of Regulation 1/2003, this was mostly in the context of exemptions under Article 81(3) EC, often when considering whether a fair share of the benefit goes to consumers.[665] In this context, it is also important that cooperative joint ventures may be assessed under the merger control regulation. Commission policy on state aids leaves the Member States a relatively large margin for the promotion of national industry; this is clearly illustrated in the automobile branch, for instance.[666]

---

660. COM(96)463 final, 9 Oct. 1996.
661. COM(2005)474.
662. Id. p. 9.
663. Cf. A.M. van den Bossche, Gemeenschappelijke ondernemingen in het Europees mededingingsrecht, Gent, 1994. See also F.W. Vogelaar, Van Joint Ventures, mededinging en de nieuwe eeuw, *Markt en Mededinging* 2001, 129 et seq.
664. K. Stockmann, 'Balanced Harmonisation and State Sovereignty, Antitrust – Merger Control – A German Perspective', (1994) *Connecticut Journal of International Law*, 565–606. In the decision Mannesmann/Vallourec/Ilva, O.J. 1994, L 102/15, the potential competition from East European suppliers is explicitly taken into account for approving the merger. See also J.T. Halverson, 'EC Merger Control: Competition Policy or Industrial Policy', (1992) LIEI, 49–66.
665. See e.g., the decision Ford-VW, O.J. 1993, L 20/14.
666. Cf. C.R.A. Swaak, European Community Law and the Automobile Industry, Den Haag, 1999, in particular Ch. 8, 277–342; see further L. Hancher, T.R. Ottervanger and P.J. Slot, *E.C. State Aids*, 2nd ed. (London, 1999), Ch. 12. See e.g., in particular the Commission decision Renault, O.J. 1988, L 220/30.

6.2.5 Other Factors[667]

Community industrial policy does not include the defence sector – which is one major reason why the overall industrial development in Europe trails behind the USA.[668]

Research and technological development policy is also an important instrument in an active industrial policy, and, as will be evident from the following section, the Community possesses wider powers in this sphere. The same is true of trans-European networks, albeit to a lesser degree.

6.3 RESEARCH AND TECHNOLOGICAL DEVELOPMENT[669]

6.3.1 Introduction

Title XVIII of the EC Treaty contains the provisions relating to Community research and technological development.[670] The need for Community activities in the field of research and technological development arises in part from the greatly increased importance of such activities for the economic development and competitiveness of industry. Important product markets such as telematics, chips and pharmaceuticals are characterized by the shorter and shorter life-cycles of their products. Thus the time within which new generations of chips can be profitably produced has been reduced to a very few years.[671] There has also been an enormous increase in the scale of investment for new products, so that billions of euros go into the development of, for instance, a new model range of cars or aircraft designs. It was thus inevitable that because of this trend there should be an increasing number of joint ventures among the major players.[672] Barriers to market entry such as high promotion costs, have also greatly increased.

But these developments do not in themselves lead to the conclusion that Community action is necessary. Rather, such a conclusion follows from the evidence that research and technological development policy fragmented along national lines result in fewer patents and less technological innovation, as compared with the United States and Japan for instance. The technological harvest is less in Europe than in those countries, not least due to a lack of expenditure on

---

667. For a detailed examination of the various areas, see R. Hellman, Industrie, in: von der Groeben op. cit. *supra* note 112 Schwarze, 1196–1245.
668. See M. Trybus and N.D.White (eds), *European Security Law* (Oxford, 2006).
669. An extensive overview is given by Juliane Hilf in: von der Groeben Schwarze, op. cit. *supra* note 112, 1261–1378.
670. The Lisbon Treaty makes some amendments to Art. 163 EC.
671. See *inter alia* De Jong, *Dynamic Market Theory* (Leiden, 1989), 85.
672. E.g., *Volvo Car and Mitshubishi*, the take-over of Fokker by DASA, the merger of Boeing with McDonnell-Douglas, cf. e.g., the Commission decision on Boeing-McDonnell-Douglas, O.J. 1997, L 336/16.

research and technological development.[673] The promotion of R&D is one of the key areas of the Lisbon strategy.[674]

The latest summary of the Community programme is outlined in the 2005 Commission Communication. It seeks to provide a better regulatory environment for R&D in the Union by mobilizing funding, intensifying cooperation between the public and private sector R&D, and improving research and innovation policies in the Member States. Regular Council meetings address the competitiveness of the European Union.[675]

6.3.2   The Legal Framework

The legally relevant horizontal character of this Community policy is generally indicated in Article 163 EC. The 'vertical' objective of strengthening the scientific and technological bases of Community industry and encouraging it to become more competitive at international level is mentioned first. Article 163(2) goes on to demonstrate that it is not enough to 'encourage undertakings, including small and medium-sized undertakings, research centres and universities in their research and technological development activities': cooperation is also necessary.[676] It is also necessary to open up matters such as procurement practices, and to encourage the development of common standards (since divergent national standards have the effect of protecting 'national champions' which would otherwise be insufficiently competitive in the end), and the abolition of legal and fiscal barriers to cooperation. Legal barriers include divergent public law technical regulations, the legal monopolies accorded in the field of telecommunications, and, despite the various Patent Conventions, divergent national patent protection.

As was indicated in section 6.1 above, the provisions of Title XVIII were amended by the Treaty of Maastricht, and further by the Treaty of Amsterdam. They appear to lay a heavier accent on the Community's activities than was hitherto the case, as is expressed in Article 163(3) EC. Compared with the provisions introduced by the SEA, it is primarily the procedural provisions which have been adapted. At the moment, the procedure of Article 251 EC is to be followed (the co-decision procedure) without the requirement of the Council acting by

---

673. See M. André, *Research and Technological Development Policy*, 3rd ed., (Luxembourg, 1988). Expenditure on research and technological development in the United States is not only significantly higher, the fragmentation there is much less. See Hellmann, op. cit., *supra* note 669.

674. Commission Communication, More Research and Innovation: Investing for Growth and Employment: A Common Approach COM(2005)488 final. See also the Council Resolution of 15 Nov. 2007 on education and training as a key driver of the Lisbon Strategy, O.J. 2007, C 300/1.

675. In 2007, four meetings were held, discussing *inter alia* joint technology initiatives.

676. See the block exemptions for research and development agreements, also mentioned in Ch. IX of this book, Reg. 2659/2000 (O.J. 2000, L 304/3), and technology transfer agreements, Reg. 772/2004 (O.J. 2004, L 123/11).

unanimity, as was previously the case. The new rules are designed to facilitate a more coherent and a more global approach, and they should facilitate a better institutional balance in decision-making.[677] The European Parliament has obtained a greater say: under Article 172 EC, the co-decision procedure of Article 251 EC is followed for the adoption of the multiannual framework programme and for supplementary programmes; under Article 166(4) EC the specific programmes are adopted after consulting the European Parliament. In actual practice, the co-decision procedure has led to long-running blockades between the Council and the Parliament, and it may be wondered whether it is suitable for programmatic decision-making.

6.3.3 Community Action in the Area of Research

Article 164 EC makes it plain that the Community's actual research and development activities are solely complementary to those of the Member States. This does not exclude very expensive research in certain areas being promoted exclusively at Community level, whether or not in cooperation with third countries or international organizations. Indeed this happens for projects such as the JET project in Culham, mentioned above, and express provision for such research, technological development and demonstration is made in Article 164(b) EC. Article 171 EC empowers the Community to set up joint undertakings for Community research and technological development: the Galileo satellite company is a good example.[678] Nevertheless, the large Member States in particular still seem to persist in the illusion that in the most important areas, research and technological development of sufficient scale and quality can be undertaken exclusively or largely at national level. This misconception is evident not merely from practice concerning standards and procurement in highly technologically developed sectors, but also from their attempts to reduce the Community research budget to below the minimum which Community-level industrial organizations such as Union of Industrial and Employers' Confederations of Europe (UNICE) regard as necessary. Thus the link between technological development and the achievement of the internal market as a large domestic market for technologically advanced industries, an achievement which is essential for the very viability of undertakings in those large Member States themselves, risks being forgotten.

6.3.4 Supplementary Nature of Community Policy

Typical of the fact that Community policy is seen as supplementing national policy is the fact that in Article 165 EC the coordination of national policy by the Member

---

677. See J. Cloos, G. Reinesch, D. Vignes and J. Weyland, *Le Traité de Maastricht* (Brussels, 1993), 293 et seq. and P. Twomey and D. O'Keeffe (eds), *Legal Issues of the Amsterdam Treaty* (Oxford, 1999).
678. Reg. 876/2002, O.J. 2002, L 138/1, amended by Reg. 1943/2006, O.J. 2006, L 367/21. Galileo is a world-wide system of satellites providing Global Positioning System (GPS) data.

States is clearly given pride of place in the implementation of this Title. Cooperation and specialization may be promoted, and Article 165(2) EC permits the Commission to take the initiative in this regard also. The Commission's supervision of state aids may also make a contribution. Without the Community's own activities and financial support, the coordination of national policies will probably have insufficient effect, if experience in other areas is any guide. In general, the Commission adopts a positive stance towards aid measures for research and technological development.[679] Article 163 EC has been used on occasion as an extra justification for national aid measures.[680] Aids which are clearly designed to foster research and technological developments, such as fundamental research, will be accepted, but aids for normal modernization and improvement of production facilities will not be considered to be compatible with the common market.

6.3.5   Framework Programmes

The way Community activities are to function is set out in Articles 166–172 EC. According to Article 166(1) EC, the multiannual framework programme adopted by the Council establishes the scientific and technological objectives to be achieved and fixes the relevant priorities, indicates the broad lines of the activities to be undertaken, and fixes the maximum overall amount and detailed rules for Community financial participation in the framework programme, as well as the respective shares in each of the activities provided for. In 2002, the Sixth framework programme was adopted.[681] The total budget for the Sixth framework programme (2002–2006) was set at 16.3 billion euro. This framework programme matches the decisions taken at the European Council of Lisbon, in 2000. The budget for the seventh framework programme for the period 2007–2013 is 50.5 billion euro.[682] These funds are intended to have a leverage effect on national research spending. The target for the latter is 3% of gross domestic product (GDP).

Article 166(2) EC provides for the possibility of adaptations to be made after the establishment of a programme.

The multiannual framework programme adopted by the Council under the co-decision procedure is then implemented by specific programmes which are developed within each activity, which also make the necessary financial provisions (Art. 166(3) EC).

The Council determines under Article 167 EC the rules for the participation of undertakings, research centres and universities, and for the dissemination of research results. In this context, one may think of the conditions for the grant

---

679. See Community framework for state aid for research and development, O.J. 1996, C 45/5. See further L. Hancher, T.R. Ottervanger, P.J. Slot, op. cit., Ch. 21.
680. See O.J. 1994, C 244/2.
681. Decision No. 1513/2002 EC, O.J. 2002, L 232/1. The specific programmes are found in O.J. 2002, L 294/1.
682. Council Decision No. 1982/2006/EC of 18 Dec. 2006, concerning the Seventh Framework Programme of the European Community for research, technological development and demonstration activities (2007–2013) O.J. 2006, L 412/1.

of patents and patent licences.[683] As a result of Articles 168 and 169 EC, provision may be made in the framework programme for the adoption of supplementary programmes, in which only some Member States participate and finance, subject to possible Community participation. Pursuant to Article 170 EC, the Community may make provision for cooperation in research with third countries or international organizations, according to the rules laid down in Article 300 EC.

On the basis of Article 171 EC read with Article 172(1) EC, the Council may, acting by qualified majority and after consulting the European Parliament and the Economic and Social Committee, set up joint undertakings or other structures necessary for the efficient execution of Community research and technological development programmes. As far as joint undertakings are concerned, Articles 45–51 Euratom, would seem to be significant, by analogy, although these provisions are not explicitly declared to be applicable. Again, JET in Culham is the obvious example (concerning joint nuclear fusion research). It also appears that more generally an effort has been made in this Title to ensure coherence with similar provisions of the Euratom Treaty.[684]

Prior to competence in this field being based on a separate Title in the Treaty, recourse was primarily had to Article 308 EC.[685]

6.3.6 Other Developments

The EC Treaty no longer explicitly refers to the link between research and technological development, the establishment of the internal market, and competition policy in particular,[686] but it is still important to emphasize that link. As has been explained above, competition law provides for block exemptions which also implement Community policy on research and technological development. The Commission's policy in applying Arts. 81 and 82 EC is heavily influenced by the promotion of research and technological development, and the same is true of the case law of the Court of Justice and the Court of First Instance.[687]

A number of important acts have been adopted on the basis of the Title on Research and Development.[688] Article 173 EC requires the Commission to

---

683. Cf. Arts. 12–23 Euratom.
684. This appears from the explanatory note of the Dutch government accompanying the proposal for ratification of the SEA.
685. See on this the publication by the T.M.C. Asser Instituut, *Technical Development and Cooperation in Europe, Legal Aspects* (1987). See further M. André, op. cit. *supra* note 673.
686. In the text introduced by the SEA, this was Art. 130F(3) EEC. The changes to Art. 163 EC introduced by the Lisbon Treaty emphasize the creation of a common area for research.
687. See for a summary e.g., L. Ritter and W.D. Braun, *European Competition Law* (Deventer, 2004), 787–868 and C.W. Bellamy and G.D. Child, *Common Market Law of Competition* (London, 2002), Ch. 8.
688. The most important programmes are described in the *General Report of the Activities of the EU* (2001), 123 et seq.

produce an annual report on research and technological development activities. These reports contain a useful summary of the policy carried out.[689]

6.4   TRANS-EUROPEAN NETWORKS

6.4.1   Introduction

The idea of developing trans-European networks was born in the late 1980s and early 1990s.[690] The Commission saw the stimulation of trans-European networks as an important component in the completion of the internal market. Later on, interests of economic and social cohesion were also linked to such networks. Portugal was a good example of a Member State with a major interest in good transit links,[691] and the same undoubtedly applies for Greece, Austria, Finland, Sweden and the new Member States.

6.4.2   Legal Framework

The basic concept is set out in Article 154(1) EC: the Community contributes to the achievement of the objectives concerned, which means that, as in the case of research and development policy, its action is complementary. On the one hand, the aim is to achieve the objectives of the internal market (set out in Art. 14 EC) and economic and social cohesion (set out in Article 158 EC), and on the other to enable citizens of the Union, economic operators and regional and local communities to derive full benefit from the setting-up of an area without internal frontiers. The trans-European networks should be established in the areas of transport, telecommunications and energy infrastructures. Article 154(2) EC emphasizes that within the framework of a system of open and competitive markets, Community action is aimed at promoting both the interconnection and interoperability of these networks and also access to them.[692]

All this was brought together in the 1993 White Paper *Growth, Competitiveness and Employment*:[693] Trans-European networks should create better, safer and cheaper transport, telecommunications and energy; they should make planning for

---

689. Report 2003, COM(2005)233 final; Report 2004, COM(2005)517 final; Report 2005, COM(2006)685 final; Report 2006, COM(2007)519 final.
690. See J. Erdmenger in: von der Groeben and Schwarze, *Vertrag über die Europäische Union und Vertrag zur Gündung der Europäische Gemeinschaft, Kommentar EU-/EG-Vertrag*, (Nomos, Baden-Baden, 2003), 1171–1195: J.A. Vinois, Les réseaux transeuropéens: une nouvelle dimension donnée au Marché unique (1993) *Revue du Marché Unique Euroéen*, 99–125.
691. J. Cloos, G. Reinesch, D. Vignes and J. Weyland, op. cit., *supra* note 677, 299.
692. This last addition shows that the rules in the directives for an internal market in electricity and natural gas aiming to ensure access to the network and pipelines for third parties also fit into this general framework. Cf. the remarks in section 5.3 *supra* concerning these directives.
693. Commission, 'Growth, Competitiveness and Employment: The Challenges and Ways Forward into the 21st Century' COM(93)700 final, Bull. EC, Suppl. 6/93, 15.

the whole European territory possible and also promote relations with Eastern Europe.[694] These objectives should be achieved by removing legal obstacles, stimulating private investors for projects of European interest, and a selection of projects from among those already agreed (such as transport infrastructure projects) or to be approved (such as energy structure projects).

6.4.3 The Instruments

Article 155 EC mentions as instruments the establishment of guidelines covering the objectives, priorities and broad lines of policy in this area. Further, the Community is to implement any measures that may prove necessary to ensure the interoperability of the networks, particularly as regards standardization. The Community may support projects of common interest supported by Member States; a contribution may be made through the Cohesion Fund and the structural funds. The largest financial contributions are provided by the EIB:[695] the promotion of trans-European Networks is actually one of the objectives of the EIB.[696]

The guidelines are adopted under the first paragraph of Article 156 EC by the Council in accordance with the co-decision procedure of Article 251 EC and after consulting the Economic and Social Committee and the Committee of the Regions. For Guidelines and projects of common interest which relate to the territory of a Member State, the approval of the Member State concerned is required. Article 155(2) EC obliges the Member States to coordinate among themselves the policies which they pursue at national level which may have a significant impact on the development of trans-European networks; the Commission may take initiatives, in close cooperation with the Member State concerned, to promote such coordination.

Finally, Article 155(3) EC permits the Community to cooperate with third countries to promote projects of common interest and ensure the interoperability of networks. This is particularly important for the Central and East European countries.[697]

Guidelines have now been adopted in a number of areas.[698] These guidelines all have the same structure: first, the general objectives are set out. Then, the priorities of Community policy are laid down. The guidelines provide for a greater

---

694. The parallel with the objectives of the European Energy Charter Treaty is clear, see note 580, *supra.*
695. See table 11 of the General Report of the Activities of the Community 2003 192.
696. See D.R.R. Dunnett, 'The European Investment Bank: Autonomous Instruments of Common Policy' (1994), CML Rev., 721 et seq. Since 1993, the EIB has approved nearly 100 billion in loans. The aim for the period 2004–2010 is to reach 50 billion. <http://europa.int/scadplus>.
697. See on this the General Report of the Activities of the Community 1998, point 390, 137.
698. Decision 1692/96/EC, O.J. 1996, L 228/1, Community guidelines for the development of the trans-European transport network. Decision 1254/96/EC, O.J. 1996, L 161/147, guidelines for trans-European energy networks. Decision 1336/97/EC, O.J. 1997, L 183/12, guidelines for trans-European telecommunications networks (this decision is further elaborated in decision of the Commission 97/548, O.J. 1997, L 225/25); and decision 2717/95/EC, O.J. 1995, L 282/16, guidelines for the development of the EURO-ISDN (Integrated Services Digital Network) as a trans- European network.

interoperability, partly as a result of focused activity by the European standardization organizations, such as CEN and CENELEC.[699] In the area of rail transport, two directives have been adopted aiming to promote the interoperability of
trans-European high speed rail links.[700]

The overall scheme for the development of trans-European networks has still
not really taken shape. This is exacerbated by the fact that the guidelines in the
area of interoperability leave a great deal in the hands of the Member States – in
accordance with the principle of subsidiarity. The coordination of European and
national decision-making procedures therefore remains crucial. Ideally, the most
important connecting axes should be decided at European level, after balancing
the interests of the Member States which may be conflicting and even
contradictory; these main axes should then be taken as the points of departure
for national planning. This obviously requires a far-reaching national contribution in the European decision-making process. For instance: once the cross-
frontier part of the Betuwe Line[701] has been agreed in Brussels after negotiations
involving Germany and the Netherlands, the Dutch should no longer seek to
impose unilateral changes to the plan. At the later stage of working out the
trans-European networks in detail by the various Member States, the procedure
for authorizations and consents needs to be streamlined as far as possible.[702]
Article 155 EC would appear to afford possibilities for such a policy to be drafted
and adopted. However, as mentioned above, only very limited use of this
provision has been made so far.

It may be expected that the directives for the internal market in electricity and
gas, discussed in section 5 above, and the problems which have arisen in relation to
trans-border transport in the implementation of these directives will give a further
stimulus in the area of policy on trans-European networks.

Council Regulation 2236/95 sets general rules for the grant of financial assistance.[703] Such assistance may only be given for projects of common interest; these
must also be in conformity with the general objectives of the Community – for
instance with regard to environmental policy. Regulation 680/2007 establishes a
programme determining the general rules for the granting of Community financial
aid in the field of TEN-Transport and TEN-Energy.[704]

---

699. European Committee for Standardization and European Committee for Electrotechnical Standardization.
700. Dir. 96/48/EC, O.J. 1996, L 235/6 and Dir. 2001/16, O.J. 2001, L 110/1.
701. The proposed new goods traffic link from Rotterdam to the German industrial heartland and
net.
702. Cf. M.M. Roggenkamp, 'Obstacles to the Establishment of Transnational Energy Networks:
A Matter of National Legislation' (1992), *Utilities Law Review*, 127–132. A complete stream-
lining – as has occurred for intra-Community air transport licences, as regulated by Reg. 2407/92,
O.J. 1992, L 240/1 – is not feasible, inter alia because of the close link between trans-European
networks and questions of national environmental planning.
703. O.J. 1995, L 228/1. The regulation has been amended several times, lastly by Reg. 1159/2005,
O.J. 2005, L 191/16
704. O.J. 2007, L 162/1.

Advances made in the area of trans-European networks are discussed in an annual report drawn up by the Commission.[705]

FURTHER READING

Agriculture

Ackrill, R. *The Common Agricultural Policy. Sheffield*: Sheffield Academic Press. 2000 (Contemporary European Studies; 9).

Barents, R. *The Agricultural Law of the EC: An Inquiry into the Administrative Law of the European Community in the Field of Agriculture*. Deventer: Kluwer Law and Taxation Publishers. 1994 (European Monographs; 9).

Cardwell, M.N. The European Model of Agriculture. Oxford: Oxford University Press. 2004 (Oxford Studies in European Law).

Garzon, I. *Reforming the Common Agricultural Policy: History of a Paradigm Change*. Basingstoke: Palgrave Macmillan. 2006 (Palgrave Studies in European Union Politics).

Greer, A. *Agricultural Policy in Europe*. Manchester: Manchester University Press. 2005.

Holland, D. and H. Pope. *EU Food Law and Policy*. The Hague: Kluwer Law International, 2004.

Ingersent, K.A., et al. *The Reform of the Common Agriculture Policy*. Basingstoke, MacMillan. 1998.

McMahon, J.A. *EU Agricultural Law*. Oxford: Oxford University Press. 2007.

Magnusson, A. *The EU Common Agriculture Policy and a Changing World Trade Order*. Sindelfingen: Libertas. 2006 (Libertas Paper; 63).

Senior Nello, S. *Food and Agriculture in an Enlarged EU*. San Domenico: European University Institute. 2002 (EUI Working Papers RSC; 2002/58).

Usher, J.A. *EC Agricultural Law*. 2nd ed. Oxford: Oxford University Press. 2001.

Transport

Bartlik, M. *The Impact of EU Law on the Regulation of International Air Transportation*. Aldershot: Ashgate. 2007.

Cheng-Jui Lu, A.. *International Airline Alliances*. Kluwer Law International. 2003.

Dagtoglou, P.D. 'European Air Law and Policy: Recent Developments'. Sixteenth Annual Conference. Brussels, 5 November 2004. Athens: Sakkoulas; Brussels: Bruylant 2005 (EALA Papers; Vol. 20).

---

705. See e.g., Annual Report for 1999, COM(2000)591 final, 22 Sep. 2000. See further the critical Special Report. No. 9/2000 by the Court of Auditors concerning Trans-European-Networks (TEN) – Telecommunications, accompanied by the Commission's replies, O.J. 2000, C 166/1; it is reported here that the Commission made Structural Fund payments for telecommunications despite ongoing infringement procedures against the Member State concerned, for failing to transpose market-liberalization directives in the telecoms sector.

Erdmenger, J. in: von der Groeben/ Schwarze, Vertrag über die Europäische Union und Vertrag zur Gündung der Europäische Gemeinschaft, Kommentar, EU-/ EG-Vertrag, Nomos, Baden-Baden, 2003.

Farantouris, N.E. *European Integration and Maritime Transport.* Athens: Sakkoulas. 2003.

Faull, J. and A. Nikpay. *The EC Law of Competition.* 2nd ed. Oxford: Oxford University Press. 2007: Ch. 14.

Goh, J. *European Air Transport Law and Competition.* Chichester: Wiley. 1997.

Gómez-Ibáñez, J.A. *Competition in the Railway Industry: An International Comparative Analysis.* Edward Elgar. 2006 (Transport Economics, Management and Policy Series).

Greaves, R. *EC Transport Law.* Harlow: Longman. 2000.

Hooydonk, E.V. and E. Bruyninckx. *European Seaports Law: The Regime of Ports and Port Services under European Law and the Ports Package: Antwerp Maritime Law Seminars.* Antwerpen: Apeldoorn: Maklu. 2003.

Stevens, H. *Transport Policy in the European Union.* Basingstoke: Palgrave Macmillan. 2004.

Ortiz Blanco, L. and B.V. Houtte. *EC Competition Law in the Transport Sector.* Oxford: Clarendon Press. 1996.

Travis, R. *Air Transport Liberalisation in the European Community 1987–1992: A Case of Integration.* Uppsala: Universitetet. 2001 (Skrifter utgivna av Statsvetenskapliga föreningen i Uppsala; 145).

Euratom

Cusack, T.F. 'A Tale of Two Treaties: An Assessment of the Euratom Treaty in Relation to the EC Treaty'. (2003) CML Rev., 117–142.

Dumoulin, M. and P. Guillen. *L'E'nergie Nucléaire en Europe: Des Origines à Euratom: Actes des Journées d'Etudes de Louvain-la-Neuve des 18 et 19 Novembre 1991.* Bern: Lang, 1994.

Grünwald, J. 'Neuere Entwicklungen des Euratom-Rechts'. (1998) *Zeitschrift fur Europarechtliche Studien*, 275–310.

Grünwald J. and M.C.L. Brüssel. 'Neuere Entwicklungen des Euratom-Rechts'. (1990) EuZW, 209–214.

Lindroos, A. 'The Role of Euratom in the Non-Proliferation Regime'. (1997) *Finnish Yearbook of International Law*, 307–335.

Nocera, F. *The Legal Regime of Nuclear Energy: A Comprehensive Guide to International and European Union Law.* Antwerpen: Intersentia. 2006.

O'Driscoll, M. *The European Parliament and the Euratom Treaty: Past, Present and Future.* Luxembourg: European Parliament. 2002 (Energy and Research Series. Working Paper; ENER 114 EN).

Pirotte, O. and P. Girard. *Trente Ans d'Expérience Euratom: La Naissance d'une Europe nucléaire.* Brussel. 1988.

Trüe, C. Legislative Competences of Euratom and the European Community in the Energy Sector: The 'Nuclear package' of the Commission. (2003) EL Rev., 664–685.

Energy
Cabau, E. and C. Jones. *EU Energy Law*, Vol. II: *EU Competition Law and Energy Markets* 2nd ed. Leuven: Claeys & Casteels. 2007.

Cameron, P.D. *Competition in Energy Markets: Law and Regulation in the European Union.* 2nd ed. Oxford: Oxford University Press. 2007.

Cameron, P.D. *Legal Aspects of EU Energy Regulation: Implementing the New Directives on Electricity and Gas Across Europe.* Oxford: Oxford University Press. 2005.

Cross, E.D., L. Hancher and P. J. Slot. 'EC Energy Law'. In Roggenkamp, M. M., A. Rønne et al. *Energy Law in Europe: National, EU and International Law and Institutions.* Oxford: Oxford University Press. 2001.

Delbeke, J. *EU Energy Law.* Leuven: Claeys & Casteels. 2006.

Eising, R. *Liberalisierung und Europäisierung: die regulative Reform der Elektrizitätsversorgung in Großbritannien, der Europäischen Gemeinschaft und der Bundesrepublik Deutschland.* Opladen: Leske und Budrich. 2000 (Gesellschaftspolitik und Staatstätigkeit; Bd. 20).

Faross, P. 'Energiepolitik' in: *von der Groeben/Schwarze Vertrag über die Europäische Union und Vertrag zur Gündung der Europäische Gemeinschaft.* 6 ed. Kommentar, EU-/EG-Vertrag, Baden-Baden. 2003.

Faull, J. and A. Nikpay. *The EC Law of Competition.* 2nd ed., Oxford: Oxford University Press. 2007. Ch. 12.

Geradin, D. *The Liberalization of Electricity and Natural Gas in the European Union.* The Hague: Kluwer Law International. 2001 (European Monographs; 27).

Hammer, U., et al. *European Energy Law Report 3*: Intersentia. 2006 (Energy & Law; 4).

Jarass, H. *Europäisches Energierecht: Bestand-Fortentwicklung-Umweltschutz.* Berlijn. 1996.

Jones, C. and W. Webster. *EU Energy Law*, Vol. 1: *The Internal Energy Market.* 2nd ed. Leuven: Claeys & Casteels. 2006.

Pfrang, E. *Towards Liberalisation of the European Electricity Markets: The Directive Concerning Common Rules for an Internal Market in Electricity in the Frame of the Competition and Internal Market Rules of the EC Treaty.* Frankfurt am Main: Lang. 1999 (Schriften zum Staats- und Völkerrecht; Bd. 80).

Roggenkamp, M.M. Energy *Law in Europe: National, EU and International Regulation.* 2nd ed. Oxford: Oxford University Press. 2007.

Roggenkamp, M.M. and F. Boisseleau. *The Regulation of Power Exchanges in Europe.* Antwerpen: Intersentia. 2005 (Energy & Law; 2).

Roggenkamp, M.M. and U. Hammer. *European Energy Law Report.* 4: Intersentia. 2007 (Energy & Law; 5).

Schaub, A. *Europäische Energiebinnenmarktpolitik und Umweltpolitik.* Baden-Baden. Nomos 1996 (Frankfurter Schriften zum Umweltrecht; Bd. 14).

Seeger, B.J. *Die Durchleitung elektrischer Energie nach neuem Recht.* Baden-Baden; Nomos, 2002 (Veröffentlichungen des Instituts für Energierecht an der Universität zu Köln; Bd. 103).

Vandersanden, G., et al. *Culture: Santé; Consommateurs; Reseaux transeuropéens; Recherche et développement technologique: Environnement; Énergie, 2me éd., Bruxelles.* Éditions de l'Université de Bruxelles. 1996 (Commentaire Mégret; part 8).

Werring, L. and P. Bertoldi. *EU Energy Law.* Vol. III: *EU Environmental Law: Energy Efficiency and Renewable Energy Sources.* Leuven: Claeys and Casteels. 2006.

Trans-European Networks

Geradin, D. *Remedies in Network Industries: EC Competition Law vs. Sector-specific Regulation.* Antwerp: Intersentia. 2004.

Johnson, D. and C. Turner. *Strategy and Policy for Trans-European Networks.* Basingstoke: Palgrave Macmillan. 2007.

Industrial Policy, Research and Technology Policy

Bianchi, P. *Industrial Policies and Economic Integration: Learning from European Experiences.* London: Routledge. 1998.

Borrás, S. *The Innovation Policy of the European Union: From Government to Governance.* Cheltenham: Elgar, 2003.

Cloos, J., G. Reinesch, D. Vignes and J. Weyland. *Le Traité de Maastricht.* Brussel. 1993: r288 e.v.

Cowling, K. *Industrial Policy in Europe: Theoretical Perspectives and Practical Proposals.* London: Routledge, 1999.

Darmer, M., et al. *Industry and the European Union: Analysing Policies for Business.* Cheltenham: Elgar. 2000.

Devine, P.J. and Y.S. Katsoulacos. *Competitiveness, Subsidiarity and Industrial Policy.* London: Routledge. 1996.

Edler, J. and S. Kuhlmann. *Changing Governance of Research and Technology Policy: The European Research Area.* Cheltenham: Elgar. 2003.

Erdmenger, J. In von der Groeben. Schwarze, J. Vertrag über die Europäische Union und Vertrag zur Gündung der Europäische Gemeinschaft, Kommentar, EU-/EG-Vertrag, Nomos, Baden-Baden. 2003, 1171–1195.

Hilf, J., In von der Groeben. Schwarze, J. Vertrag über die Europäische Union und Vertrag zur Gündung der Europäische Gemeinschaft, Kommentar, EU-/EG-Vertrag, Nomos, Baden-Baden. 2003, 1261–1378.

Hellmann, R. In von der Groeben. Schwarze, J. Vertrag über die Europäische Union und Vertrag zur Gündung der Europäische Gemeinschaft, Kommentar, EU-/EG-Vertrag, Nomos, Baden-Baden. 2003, 1196–1245.

Johnson, D. and C. Turner. *European Business.* 2nd ed. London: Routledge. 2006.

Johnson, P. *Industries in Europe: Competition, Trends and Policy Issues.* Cheltenham: Edward Elgar. 2003.

Kassim, H. and A. Menon. *The European Union and National Industrial Policy.* London: Routledge. 1996.

Lawton, T.C. *European Industrial Policy and Competitiveness: Concepts and Instruments.* Basingstoke: Macmillan; New York: St. Martin's Press. 1999.

Mundschenk, S. *Competitiveness and Growth in Europe: Lessons and Policy Implications for the Lisbon Strategy.* Cheltenham: Edward Elgar. 2006.

Papon, P. *L'Europe de la Science et de la Technologie.* Grenoble: Presses Universitaires de Grenoble. 2001 (Transeurope).

Peterson, J. and M. Sharp. *Technology Policy in the European Union.* Basingstoke: Hampshire; Macmillan. 1998.

Sauter, W. *Competition Law and Industrial Policy in the EU.* Oxford: Clarendon Press. 1997.

Stajano, A. *Research, Quality, Competitiveness: European Union Technology Policy for the Information Society.* New York, NY: Springer. 2006.

Vandersanden, G., et al. *Culture; Santé; Consommateurs; Reseaux Transeuropéens; Recherche et Développement Technologique; Environnement; Énergie.* 2me éd. Bruxelles, Éditions de l'Université de Bruxelles. 1996 (Commentaire Megret; partl 8).

Waelbroeck, M. and J.-V. Louis, Union E'conomique et Monétaire Cohésion E'conomique et Sociale Politique Industrielle et Technologique Européenne, 2me éd. Bruxelles, Éditions l'Université de Bruxelles 1995 (Commentaire Megret; part 6).

Chapter XIII

External Relations

P.J. Kuijper

1   INTRODUCTION

It is only logical that a common market such as that created by the three Community Treaties manifests itself externally, towards third countries, as one unit. First and foremost, the establishment of a customs union involves the creation of a common customs tariff. Then, 'other trade regulations'[1] *vis-à-vis* third countries must also be made uniform. The internal market and its achievements need a certain protection in their external elements, and this protection should in principle be based on uniform measures. There are also exogenous factors which contribute to the need to pursue a common external policy. The establishment of a common market of now 27 European States naturally has a major effect on the world economy, which involves for the European Union a heavy responsibility for the functioning of the international economic system. It is evident from Article 131 EC, which prescribes that the Community should contribute to a harmonious development of world trade and to a reduction in barriers to trade, that the founding fathers of the Community were conscious of this responsibility from the very

---

1.   These terms come from Art. XXIV GATT, which maintains an exception for customs unions and free trade areas, on which the Communities rely in order not to be obliged to grant the advantages of the Community system to third countries in accordance with the most-favoured nation principle which underlies GATT/WTO system.

P.J.G. Kapteyn, A.M. McDonnell, K.J.M. Mortelmans and C.W.A. Timmermans (eds),
The Law of the European Union and the European Communities, pp. 1273–1365.
©2008 Kluwer Law International BV, The Netherlands.

beginning. Article 56 EC, introduced by the Treaty of Maastricht, and Article 11 Treaty on European Union (TEU) also confirm that external openness, also with regard to monetary union and the Common Foreign and Security Policy (CFSP), remains a fundamental characteristic of the European Union.

Since the very beginning, European integration has also had political objectives, which are expressed along with other objectives in the first paragraph of the Preamble to the EC Treaty. Economic integration also gave rise to expectations in third countries concerning a common political stance by the Member States. As regards external matters, the possibility of a common political action was initially created in the context of European Political Cooperation.[2] This loose intergovernmental cooperation framework found a more solid form in the so-called Second Pillar of the TEU, the provisions concerning CFSP. These provisions are largely intergovernmental in nature, so that in external relations the Union has two sets of instruments at its disposal: the Community instruments provided for in the EC and Euratom Treaties; and the intergovernmental instruments set out in Title V of the Treaty on European Union.

When looking at the European Union's external relations, it is useful to bear in mind that the question whether the Union itself has international legal personality was initially a controversial one, and that the treaty-making powers of the Union, separate from the Member States, have only slowly asserted themselves through practice, and were finally clarified by the Nice Treaty. As far as the two Communities are concerned, there is no shadow of a doubt on this point; both are equipped with international legal personality and the competence to conclude treaties.

With regard to foreign (economic) policy, one can make a distinction between unilateral (autonomous) measures directed at third countries, and agreements with third countries. Not all CFSP instruments fit in this scheme though; some of them have more of the character of internal acts, preparing or setting policy. According to Article 13(1) TEU, the CFSP is based on general guidelines defined by the European Council. In addition, Article 13(2) TEU states that the European Council takes decisions on common strategies to be implemented by the Union in areas where the Member States have important interests in common: these are clearly instruments which have a predominantly internal character. Article 13(3) TEU lays down the Council's possibilities to decide that a certain matter should be the subject of a joint action or a common position, which it does on the basis of the guidelines and strategies defined by the European Council. These are clearly autonomous instruments of the CFSP. In addition, Article 24 TEU provides for the possibility of agreements with third countries or international organizations in implementation of the CFSP.

Unilateral (autonomous) measures of the Community are usually adopted in the form of regulations – for instance in the area of commercial policy or assistance for third countries, such as the European Neighbourhood Policy Instrument

---

2.   See Ch. I, section 6 *supra*.

(ENPI). Agreements with third countries form the other instrument for implementing the external policy of the EC. Initially, specific mention of these was to be found only in the areas of commercial policy[3] and associations.[4] The Single European Act (SEA) in 1986 and the Treaty of Maastricht in 1992 led to express mention of competence to conclude agreements in the field of monetary policy,[5] research and technology,[6] environment,[7] and development cooperation.[8] The old provision on common action in international organizations[9] was deleted from the EC Treaty by the Maastricht Treaty, and has been – only partly – replaced by Article 19(1) TEU. The Maastricht Treaty has also introduced a whole Title devoted to development cooperation, which, like commercial policy, can take the form of both autonomous measures and agreements with third countries and international organizations.[10] The Treaty of Nice has added an article on economic, financial and technical cooperation measures with third countries (not developing countries).[11] The amendments made by the Maastricht Treaty, now to be found in Article 300 EC, also set out in greater detail than was the case in the old European Economic Community (EEC) Treaty the different arrangements for concluding such agreements. Finally, ever since the beginning – i.e. 1958 – account has been taken of the general desirability of maintaining all appropriate relations or, as the case may be, developing cooperation with other international organizations.[12] Using these instruments, the Community has given form and substance to its relations with the outside world on an extensive scale and sometimes in a very intensive way.

The new articles in the EC Treaty brought in by the SEA and the Treaty of Maastricht, mean that the development of a simple commercial policy, primarily embracing free movement of goods, into a much more extensive external economic policy, through the doctrine of implied powers accepted by the Court of Justice and the use of Article 308 EC, has as it were been codified. This creates clarity, but also removes a certain dynamism from the development of the law.

In this chapter, attention will first be paid to the Union's external competence, in general, and that of the EC in particular. Legal aspects of external relations involving Euratom will be discussed only incidentally in the treatment of the external competence of the EC.[13] A distinction will be made between the competences deriving from the Treaty on European Union – both CFSP and police and

---

3. Art. 133 EC.
4. Art. 310 EC.
5. Art. 111 EC.
6. Art. 170 EC.
7. Art. 174(4) EC.
8. Art. 181 EC.
9. Art. 116 EEC.
10. Arts. 177 et seq. EC.
11. Art. 181a EC.
12. Arts. 302 et seq. EC.
13. Section 4 of Ch. XII *supra* deals with Euratom in general, and section 4.12 with external relations under the Euratom Treaty.

judicial cooperation – and the real Community competence in the external sphere, but they will be treated together to the extent this is possible, since increasingly one sees an interpenetration of the two. In discussing Community competence, a distinction is drawn between express and implied external competence, and between exclusive Community competence and competence shared between the Community and its Member States.[14] In relation to the latter, the discussion then turns to mixed agreements and to Community membership of international organizations.[15] The treatment of all these issues will include consideration of the question how far they also apply in relation to the Treaty on European Union. Finally, the manner in which the external powers of the Community are exercised is examined, particularly as regards the power to conclude agreements. The exercise of CFSP powers, and the substance of these powers, will also be dealt with briefly, in section 2.6.

Section 3 of this chapter then examines in some detail the Community's common commercial policy, turning first to the concept of commercial policy and to the exclusive nature of that policy.[16] In section 3.2 the principles of the Community's commercial policy are examined in the framework of the GATT/WTO and in conjunction with the completion of the internal market and the developments in Central and Eastern Europe. The next section gives a brief description of the most important commercial policy instruments at the Community's disposal for the pursuit of autonomous commercial policy, and of practice concerning trade and cooperation agreements concluded by the Community and the Member States.[17]

Finally, in section 4, the system of Community agreements is examined. These agreements can be viewed as forming a series of concentric circles, in which the European Economic Area (EEA) is the innermost and various cooperation agreements with countries in Asia and Latin America form the outermost circle.[18] In this context, the so-called development associations and the relatively new Treaty provisions on development are also examined. Moreover, in section 4.4, the Community agreements are also examined from a sectoral viewpoint and briefly related to autonomous external policy in the various sectors concerned.

2   EXTERNAL COMPETENCE OF THE EUROPEAN UNION

2.1   EXTERNAL COMPETENCES UNDER THE SECOND AND THIRD PILLARS

The European Union has been equipped with an express treaty-making competence, both in the area of CFSP (Title V) and police and judicial cooperation

---

14. See sections 2.2 and 2.3 *infra*, respectively.
15. See sections 2.4 and 2.5 *infra*, respectively.
16. Section 3.1 *infra*.
17. Section 3.3 *infra*.
18. Section 4.1 *infra*.

(Title VI) – the so-called Second and Third Pillars. According to Article 24 TEU, this power to conclude agreements concerns agreements which it is necessary to conclude with one or more states or international organizations 'in implementation of this title'. Since, according to Articles 24(4) and 38 TEU, the provisions of this article also apply to matters falling under Title VI, there can be no doubt that the agreements in question may concern both these areas of the European Union.

The question whether this is a true treaty-making competence of the Union – or whether these are agreements concluded by the Council on behalf of the Member States – has been largely put to rest by the Treaty of Nice, which determines that agreements concluded under Article 24 shall be binding on the Institutions of the Union (a provision borrowed in part from paragraph 7 of Article 300 EC), which indicates that the agreement in question is concluded on behalf of the Union.[19] On the other hand, the Member States at Nice were still incapable of agreeing to grant international personality to the Union. However, in line with the, now abandoned, Constitutional Treaty, the Treaty of Lisbon foresees that the European Union and the EC will be united in one European Union with a single legal personality.

As far as practice is concerned, the European Union has signed and concluded a fast growing number of international agreements with third states, primarily relating to military and police missions in the Balkans and in Africa, mostly Status of Forces Agreements with the host states of these operations and agreements on the participation of third states in such operations.[20] Furthermore there are a few Union agreements in the field of the third Pillar (Title VI of the Treaty on European Union), interestingly enough primarily with the United States. These agreements relate to extradition and mutual assistance and to the transfer of what is termed the Passenger Name Records (PNR) and are primarily related to what is termed the war on terror.[21]

The most reasonable conclusion at the present stage of the development of Union law would seem to be that the Union disposes of a functional international personality largely determined by the scope of its treaty-making practice and at

---

19. It is interesting to note that the other element of Art. 300(7) EC Treaty is missing from Art. 24 TEU, namely, the fact that the Union agreements also bind the Member States. This is not bothersome in the domain of CFSP, but all the more so in the field of the Third Pillar (Title VI), where the citizens of the Member States are implicated.
20. A quick count of CFSP-based international agreements on the website of the Council Secretariat shows that the Council has concluded some 73 agreements based on Art. 24 TEU, of which 11 are Status of Forces Agreements (SOFAs) or comparable treaties or Protocols thereto. There are 53 agreements with third states about their participation in various police and military operations, and 9 relate to the security of information that is exchanged between the EU and a third state.
21. There are 6 agreements based on Arts. 24 and 38 TEU (Third Pillar agreements). The Agreements on Extradition and Mutual Assistance with the USA were signed and declared to be provisionally applied by Council Decision 2003/516, O.J. 2003, L 181/25; they have not yet entered into force. The Agreement on the processing and transfer of PNR data by air carriers to the US Department of Homeland Security was signed and declared to be provisionally applied on 23 and 26 July 2007, O.J. 2007, L 204/18; this agreement has also not yet entered into force.

the very least recognized by the states that have concluded agreements with the Union.[22]

2.2   EXPRESS AND IMPLIED EXTERNAL COMPETENCE OF THE EC

Unlike the European Coal and Steel Community (ECSC) and EC Treaties, but like the EU Treaty (cf. Art. 24 TEU), the Euratom Treaty, in Article 101, expressly provides that the Community may enter into obligations by concluding agreements or contracts with a third state, an international organization or a national of a third state 'within the limits of its powers and jurisdiction'. In the Court's interpretation this phrase means within the limits of its external as well as internal powers.[23] This appears to anchor the parallel between internal and external competence (*in foro interno, in foro externo*) firmly in Community law for Euratom matters. The EC Treaty confines itself to conferring specific powers in the external field.[24] As a result of the Court's case law, particularly the judgments in Case 22/70, *Commission v. Council (ERTA)*[25] and Cases 3, 4 and 6/76 *Kramer et al.* and the findings in Opinion 1/75 on the *OECD Understanding on a Local Cost Standard* and Opinion 1/76 on a *European Laying-up Fund for Inland Waterway Vessels*, a similar situation started to prevail at a fairly early stage to that provided for in the Euratom Treaty.[26]

The Court bases the *capacity* of the Community to enter into binding agreements with other subjects of international law throughout the whole range of objectives set out in Part One of the Treaty on Article 281 EC, which confers legal personality on the Community.[27] Whether the Community has the *competence* to enter into agreements in a particular case depends on the question whether

---

22. Cf. *Reparation for Injuries Suffered in the Service of the United Nations*, 1949 ICJ Reports, 174 et seq. It is interesting to note that such a derivation of implied powers in the external field from practice is only possible in the inter-governmental Second Pillar. In the First Pillar the ECJ has always rejected the idea that practice could lead to the acquisition of powers by the Institutions: only the Treaty counts for the Court; see Case C-327/91, *France v. Commission*. For the contrary view of the ICJ in respect of the UN system, see *Legal Consequences for States of the Continued Presence of South-Africa in Namibia*, 1971 ICJ Reports, 12 et seq., at para. 22, where the practice of abstention of the permanent members has legally modified the meaning of Art. 27(3) UN Charter.
23. According to P. van Dijk in his annotation of Ruling 1/78, *Draft Convention of the International Atomic Energy Agency on the Physical Protection of Nuclear Materials, Facilities and Transports*, (1979) SEW, 191.
24. Arts. 111; 133; 149(3); 150(3); 151(3); 170; 174(4); 181; 300–304 and 310 EC.
25. In French: AETR.
26. Cf. Ruling 1/78, *Draft Convention of the International Atomic Energy Agency* at para. 36, where the Court spoke of 'the necessity for harmony between international action by the Community and the distribution of jurisdiction and powers within the Community which the Court of Justice had occasion to emphasise in its case law originating with the judgment of 31 Mar. 1971 [i.e., Case 22/70, *Commission v. Council (ERTA)*] on the European agreement on road transport'.
27. Case 22/70, *Commission v. Council (ERTA)*; Joined Cases 3, 4 & 6/76, *Kramer*. See Ch. II, section 4.1.

a Treaty provision expressly, as in the cases of the provisions referred to above,[28] or implicitly provides the power to do so. Such an implied power may also result from the actions of the Community Institutions in the context of the provisions concerned. It follows that such a power cannot be derived from the mere existence of an internal power linked to a general provision such as that contained in Article 101 Euratom, but must be derived using the *effet utile* principle (the principle of effectiveness) from the interpretation of specific provisions relating to the Community's internal powers – or where appropriate the Community's implementation of these provisions. There must always be an examination of whether the powers expressly conferred to adopt measures internal to the Community necessarily include in any particular case the power to enter into international commitments (the so-called *ERTA* doctrine):[29]

> The Court has concluded *inter alia* that whenever Community law has created for the institutions of the Community powers within its internal system for the purpose of attaining a specific objective, the Community has authority to enter into the international commitments necessary for the attainment of that objective even in the absence of an express provision in that connexion.[30]

Thus it appears justified to speak of *derived* or *implied* external powers in the sense of the theory of implied powers discussed in section 6.3 of Chapter IV of this book.

Such derived powers appear to have been avoided in the parts of the EC Treaty introduced by the SEA and the Maastricht Treaty, by expressly including the power to conclude agreements in the relevant provisions.[31] On the other hand, Declaration No. 10 attached to the Final Act on the occasion of signature of the Maastricht Treaty states that the *ERTA* doctrine is unaffected by these provisions.

The discussion above, like the case law cited, has spoken of entering into international *commitments*. The external competence of the Community is, as this phrase expressly makes clear, not confined to the conclusion of agreements. It also covers the power, with deference to the Treaty,[32] to set up international organizations[33] or to accede to them[34] and to cooperate in the elaboration of decisions of international bodies and in that context to enter into international commitments.[35]

---

28. Note 24 *supra.*
29. Case 22/70, *Commission v. Council (ERTA)*; Joined Cases 3, 4 & 6/76, *Kramer*. This doctrine also includes the question of the exclusivity of these powers; see section 2.3 *infra.*
30. Opinion 1/76, *Draft Agreement Establishing a European Laying-Up Fund for Inland Waterway Vessels*, para. 3.
31. Cf. Arts. 111; 170; 174(4); 181 EC.
32. For the difficulties which may arise see Opinion 1/76, *Laying-up fund.*
33. Opinion 1/76, *Laying-Up Fund.*
34. Joined Cases 3, 4 & 6/76, *Kramer.*
35. Joined Cases 3, 4 & 6/76, *Kramer.* Cf. also Case 61/77, *Commission v. Ireland* and Opinion 1/75, *Local Cost Standard*, in relation to the interpretation of the concept of an 'agreement' in Art. 300(1) EC.

2.3   WHEN IS EXTERNAL COMPETENCE OF THE EU OR THE
                   EC EXCLUSIVE?

The mere existence of an expressly conferred or derived external competence need
not mean that this competence is also *exclusive*, i.e., that only the Community has
the right to exercise this competence in relation to the outside world, to the exclusion of the Member States. The question of exclusivity depends on whether the
Treaty or its application involves a transfer of powers to the Community. Thus the
exclusive character of the external competence of the Community which is
expressly conferred by the Treaty in the field of the common commercial policy
has been confirmed by the Court: after the end of the transitional period, the
Member States have transferred their competence in this field to the Community.
This is discussed further in section 3.1.2 below.

A derived external competence will have an exclusive character in certain
circumstances, as developed in the Court's case law. First, in certain exceptional
cases a derived external competence may be *ipso facto* exclusive, where it is
necessary for the attainment of an objective of the Treaty that the external competence is exercised by the Community alone, to the exclusion of the Member
States.[36] This was the case, for instance, when the capacity of transport on the
Rhine needed to be regulated: an agreement with Switzerland was absolutely
necessary for this. The Court made it clear initially that cases where an exclusive
power can be implicitly derived in such a direct manner will remain extremely
limited, i.e., to those cases when there is an almost physical necessity,[37] and later
took an even more restrictive view, requiring that the internal competence and the
'necessary' external competence be exercised simultaneously.[38]

Secondly, Treaty provisions may confer an exclusive character on internal
competence with effect from a particular time, and thereby also involve the exclusivity of the external powers derived from these.[39] In practice, this category is very
similar to the first: the Act of Accession (1972), concerning the UK, Ireland and
Denmark, provided for an exclusive competence of the Community in the area of
fish conservation measures at the latest from the sixth year after accession. It was
clear for the Court that this also necessitated agreements with third countries in
this field.

The third possibility is that the *exercise* of internal competence may lead to the
exclusivity of the derived external competence linked to it. This is the case if and in
so far as the internal measures taken as a result of the exercise of the internal
competence could be affected or their scope altered by a Member State concluding

---

36. Opinion 1/76, *Laying-Up Fund.*
37. Opinion 1/94, *WTO-GATS and TRIPS.*
38. Opinion 1/03, *Lugano Convention.* In this way, this approach to the exclusivity of external
     powers becomes indistinguishable from the *ERTA* approach discussed below, since an exercise
     of internal powers is now necessary for the exercise of the corresponding external powers, the
     latter no longer being completely independent from the former.
39. Joined Cases 3, 4 & 6/76, *Kramer.*

an agreement with a third country concerning the same subject matter either on its own or together with other Member States.[40] In such a case, this would endanger the attainment of the objectives of the Community rules, and prevent the Community as such from protecting the Community interest.[41] After first having made an attempt to systematize its case law since *ERTA* in a set of judgments handed down in November 2002,[42] the Court produced a new restatement of its case law in its *Lugano Convention* Opinion of 2006.[43] With some additions and explanations this restatement is followed here.

The crucial question is the following: in what circumstances can Community rules be affected or their scope altered by international obligations undertaken by Member States? According to the Court's case law, this is the case where the international obligations fall within the scope of Community rules (regardless of whether these are rules resulting from a common policy mentioned in the Treaty, such as agriculture or transport, or other common rules)[44] or, at least, within an area which is already covered to a large extent by Community rules, especially in the case of progressive harmonization on the road to the internal market.[45] In such cases, the Member States can no longer enter into international commitments outside the framework of the Community, not even in the absence of conflict or identity between these commitments and the internal Community rules.[46] Such parallel international action by the Member States could interfere with the unhindered exercise of the internal Community competence.

In its *Lugano Convention* Opinion, the Court consolidates three situations that it also previously considered decisive for exclusive external competence (clauses granting negotiating powers with third states to the Community, normally the Commission; clauses concerning the treatment of third state nationals; and situations of complete harmonization of a sector)[47] into one. It refers back to *ERTA* itself, where it said that the conclusion of an agreement by the Member States that is incompatible with the unity of the common market and the uniformity of Community law is not allowed.[48] On the other hand, harmonization at the level of

---

40. Case 22/70, *Commission v. Council (ERTA)*.
41. Case C-471/98, *Commission v. Belgium (Open Skies)*.
42. Case C-471/98, *Commission v. Belgium (Open Skies)*. The other open skies judgments handed down on the same day were: Case C-466/98, *Commission v. United Kingdom*; C-467/98, *Commission v. Denmark*; C-468/98, *Commission v. Sweden*; C-469/98, *Commission v. Finland*; C-472/98, *Commission v. Luxembourg*; C-475/98, *Commission v. Austria*; C-476/98, *Commission v. Germany*.
43. Opinion 1/03, *Lugano Convention*.
44. See Case 22/70, *Commission v. Council (ERTA)* and Opinion 2/91, *Convention N° 170 of the International Labour Organization*.
45. Opinion 1/03, *Lugano Convention*, recalling Opinion 2/91, *ILO Convention*.
46. Opinion 2/91, *ILO Convention* and Opinion 1/03, *Lugano Convention*.
47. Opinion 1/94, *WTO - GATS and TRIPS*. The latter two are now characterized as situations where the nature of the existing Community rules is such that any agreement in that area would necessarily affect the relevant Community rules within the meaning of the *ERTA* judgment.
48. Opinion 1/03, *Lugano Convention*, referring to point 31 of Case 22/70, *Commission v. Council (ERTA)*.

minimum standards (minimum harmonization) leads to the conclusion that the Member States wished to reserve the competence to negotiate with third countries, at least partially: they may legitimately apply stricter rules in conformity with Community law, and may undertake international commitments in relation to those stricter rules without altering the scope of the Community rules.[49] Such minimum harmonization occurs in the field of social policy (Art. 137(2) EC), consumer protection (Art. 153 EC), and environmental protection (Art. 176 EC); in these areas, this possibility is provided for in the EC Treaty, but in practice it also occurs in harmonization of legislation in the area of technical standards (Art. 95 EC). In all these areas it will generally not be easy to arrive at an exclusive external competence of the Community; at best, the Council could agree voluntarily to apply the potential competence of the Community in such fields – which Member States will normally not allow. This situation seems anomalous in domains where Community legislation is often very intense (e.g., in the area of the environment), but where the Community is doomed to remain an international nobody as a consequence of this approach.

Finally, the Court has clearly stated that no exclusive external Community competence is established as a consequence of distortions in the internal market (in particular, in relation to the freedom to provide services and freedom of establishment) which result from commitments undertaken by Member States with third countries.[50] There is a connection here with the narrow interpretation which the Court has so far given to the Community commercial policy and its exclusive character.[51]

On the other hand, it is not self-evident that where Member States are given the task of implementing provisions of an international agreement, such an agreement also comes within the competence of the Member States as such, so that it would have to be concluded by, at the very least, a mixed agreement. Where an agreement comes within the exclusive external competence of the Community, the fact that the Member States must take implementing measures or amend their national legislation does not alter this fact; it is the Community which remains competent to negotiate at international level.[52]

As yet, it has not been clarified whether or not the Treaty-making powers contained in Article 24 TEU are exclusive, and it is doubtful whether there ever will be clarity about this since – as explained above – the doctrine of exclusivity of external competences of the EC is above all judge-made law. The Court of Justice has no jurisdiction in the area of CFSP, and only limited jurisdiction in the area of police and judicial cooperation. The intergovernmental character of the cooperation within the Union – as has thus far mainly been the case – would argue against exclusive competence of the Union. Given the strict loyalty requirements which Article 11(2) TEU imposes on the Member States in the area of CFSP, Member

---

49.   Opinion 2/91, *ILO Convention*, accepted by Opinion 1/03, *Lugano Convention*.
50.   Cf. Case C-471/98, *Commission v. Belgium*, para. 70.
51.   See *infra*, sections 3.1.1 and 3.1.2.
52.   Opinion 2/91, *ILO Convention*.

States are not permitted to conclude agreements which would be at odds with existing CFSP instruments. The Court has decided that such an obligation of loyal cooperation also exists in the domain of the third pillar.[53]

2.4　MIXED AGREEMENTS

As long as, and in so far as, no internal transfer of powers has occurred and no use has been made of derived external competence, each of the Member States remains competent to enter into international commitments in the areas concerned, subject in any event to respecting the obligations flowing from Community law. In doing so the Member States might hinder the Community's use at a later stage of the internal competence and the external competence derived therefrom. It is true that the Community itself is not bound by such arrangements or legally obliged to respect them but it may well be in fact forced to take account of them in the exercise of its powers. Only an application by analogy of the second paragraph of Article 307 EC, (which is not applicable to obligations entered into by Member States after the coming into force of the EEC Treaty)[54] could perhaps offer a solution.

If, however, the Treaty obliges the Community to fulfil an obligation to regulate a matter by a particular date, the Member States may not enter into any commitments which hinder the Community in the execution of its task. The Court bases this obligation on the provisions of Article 10 EC.[55] It would appear justified to regard such an obligation as being present also when there is no such set date but the Community is preparing to exercise its powers as, for example, in cases where the Council has set itself a date, or has asked the Commission to make proposals, or cases where the Commission has itself taken steps to prepare the decision-making process in the Council.

The Court has also drawn a strict distinction between the external competence of the Community on the one hand and that of the Member States on the other in relation to mixed agreements. These are permitted only if the agreements also cover subjects in relation to which the Community has no express or implied external powers.[56]

The Community often cannot avoid giving some explanation about the division of competence between the Community and its Member States.[57] Given that it

---

53. Case C-105/03, *Pupino*, paras 41–42.
54. Or in the case of Member States acceding subsequently, after accession to the EU (or, at the time, the EEC), see e.g., Act of Accession (1972), Art. 5.
55. Joined Cases 3, 4 & 6/76, *Kramer*.
56. Cf. Opinion 1/76, *Laying-Up Fund*.
57. Originally, in Ruling 1/78 *Draft Convention of the IAEA*, it was of the view that the exact nature of the division of powers between Community and Member States was 'a domestic question in which third parties have no need to intervene'. However, in most recent cases it treats declarations of competence as normal and as an instrument to interpretation; see e.g., Case C-459/03, *Commission v. Ireland (MOX Plant)*, paras 104, 116.

is inherent in the *ERTA* doctrine that this division is not fixed for all time, but may evolve, considerable problems may result. Annex IX to the United Nations Convention on the Law of the Sea[58] illustrates the complicated arrangements which may in certain circumstances arise from the participation of the Community and the Member States in multilateral agreements. The Annex sets out the conditions under which international organizations such as the EC may become parties to the Convention.[59] In spite of all these practical difficulties, and other ones, more and more mixed agreements are being concluded, even though on a broader interpretation of the Community's relevant external competence (e.g., Arts. 133 and 310 EC) this would be unnecessary. Thus, despite the broad interpretation of Article 310 EC by the Court,[60] almost all Association Agreements are concluded in the form of mixed agreements. Certain provisions of the Treaty of Nice may even lead to mixed trade agreements if the agreements relate to trade in cultural and audiovisual services, educational services, and social and human health services, provided that they lead to harmonization in these sectors that is otherwise prohibited.[61]

Sometimes such recourse to mixed agreements is unavoidable, particularly if it is desired to embrace aspects relating to CFSP together with matters falling within Community competence in one and the same agreement. This was already the case in the Europe Agreements with the countries of Central and Eastern Europe, in the time of European Political Cooperation. This trend continues in the partnership agreements with the countries of the former Soviet Union (the so-called Commonwealth of Independent States (CIS) countries), and the countries of the Mediterranean. Because treaty-making power of the Union is still subject to some differences of opinion,[62] agreements in which Community and CFSP matters are included at the same time are frequently in the form of traditional mixed agreements and not agreements of the Union and the Community together.

As for the possibility of mixed agreements involving the Community on the one hand and the Union and the Member States on the other in the framework of Article 24 TEU, let it suffice to say that that article authorizes the Union to conclude all necessary agreements 'in implementation of Titles V and VI', which clearly demonstrates that the Council cannot go beyond these two titles in concluding agreements according to the (intergovernmental) procedure of Article 24 TEU. In addition Article 47 TEU protects the Community method against inroads by the Union.

---

58. Montego Bay, Jamaica, 10 Dec. 1982.
59. See the critical comment by K.R. Simmonds, 'The Community's Declaration upon Signature of the UN Convention on the Law of the Sea' (1986) CML Rev., 521–544.
60. See Case 12/86, *Meryem Demirel v. Stadt Schwäbisch Gmünd.*
61. See section 3.1.1. *infra.* The interpretation of the relevant paragraphs of Art. 133 is controversial; see Case C-13/07, *Commission v. Council, Vietnam,* pending.
62. See section 2.1 *supra.*

2.5   MEMBERSHIP OF INTERNATIONAL ORGANIZATIONS

It is obvious that if the Community has the power to conclude international agreements, it may also accede to international organizations which are concerned with subjects which fall within the competence of the Community.[63] International organizations are, after all, usually established by international agreements, most of which also contain specific provisions on membership, accession and voting. Even if accession is an obvious step from the perspective of the Community and its powers, these and other similar provisions of the treaties establishing the organizations concerned often pose problems for Community accession. For instance, most international organizations accept only states as members, relegating international organizations including the Community (and the Union; now that the Union also enjoys at least the beginnings of treaty-making power, these considerations also apply to the Union) to the status of observers. This is particularly so in the case of the United Nations and its specialized organizations, in which the Community has long had observer status.[64] In those international organizations that do provide for the possibility of other international organizations acceding, and which are active in the areas of exclusive Community competence, there is no obstacle to Community accession. The international fisheries organizations are celebrated examples of such bodies.[65] The Community usually possesses one vote in such circumstances.

Most international organizations need to adapt their statutes if the Community is to be able to participate as a full member. This is often a far from simple matter: even with an international organization such as the UN Food and Agriculture Organization (FAO), which works in fields – agriculture and fisheries – which fall to an overwhelming degree within Community competence, and even the Community's exclusive competence, it required an enormous effort to obtain acceptance of the Community as a member. In order for this to take place, Article II of the FAO Constitution had to be amended. To this end, in 1991 a number of specific provisions concerning regional economic integration organizations (REIOs) were approved. A REIO may only accede to the FAO if the majority of its member states is a member of the FAO, and if those member states have transferred competence in the areas of activity of the FAO to the REIO concerned, which on that basis may adopt decisions binding those member states. Although these provisions are cast in general terms, it is clear that they primarily envisage the Community, and that as yet no other international organization satisfies those criteria. On the one hand, accession of the Community to the FAO is an important

---

63. See generally F. Hoffmeister, 'Outsider or Frontrunner? Recent Developments under International and European Law on the Status of the European Union in International Organizations and Treaty Bodies' (2007) CML Rev., 41–68.
64. See J. Wouters, F. Hoffmeister and T. Ruys (eds), *The UN and the EU: an Ever Stronger Partnership*; for observer status, see R.G. Sybesma-Knol, *The Status of Observers in the United Nations* (Leiden, 1981), Ch. VI-I.
65. Cf. Convention on Future Multilateral Cooperation in the North-West Atlantic Fisheries (NAFO), O.J. 1978, L 378/2; the Community is member of 3 other fisheries organizations.

step forwards, on the other hand the conditions are very onerous.[66] In particular, the exercise by the Community of the right to speak and vote in the various FAO organs gives rise to great difficulties in practice.[67] In order to deal with these, the Council and the Commission have agreed on arrangements governing the division of tasks between the Commission and the Member States. Even though the arrangements agreed on were informal in character, the Court found that they expressed the obligation of cooperation between the Community and the Member States in the framework of mixed agreements, and as such were binding: when the Council decided to give the Member States the right to vote in the framework of the FAO on the adoption of a fisheries agreement, this decision was annulled by the Court.[68] Following the FAO example, so-called REIO clauses have been included in many other multilateral treaties and the statutes of international organizations.[69]

2.6   EXERCISE OF EXTERNAL COMPETENCES

2.6.1   Treaty-making Power

According to the text of Article 24 TEU, the agreements covered by this provision, that is to say agreements of the Second and Third Pillar, are concluded by the Council on a recommendation from the Presidency. The Presidency conducts the negotiations, assisted by the Commission where appropriate, after it has been authorized to do so by the Council. Since the amendments made by the Treaty of Nice, the Council acts unanimously when the agreement covers an issue for which unanimity is required for the adoption of internal decisions, and by qualified majority where this is provided for in relation to the internal decisions.[70] It is clear that the more limited role of the Commission and the greater role of the Presidency, especially in the CFSP area, are also expressed in these provisions

---

66. The Community was unable to prevent the FAO involving itself to a considerable extent in the division of powers between a REIO and its Member States. On application for FAO membership, a REIO must submit a declaration as to the division of competence, and the FAO has to be informed of any change therein. The REIO and its Member States exercise their votes alternatively: thus if the REIO votes, the Member States may not, and vice versa. If the REIO votes, it enjoys the number of votes equal to the number of its Member States who are members of the FAO.

67. Cf. R. Frid, 'The European Economic Community, a Member of a Specialized Agency of the United Nations' (1993) EJIL, 239–255. In the World Trade Organization (WTO) the Community has the number of votes of its Member States, but there are not such detailed rules as in the FAO agreement; see Art. IX:1 WTO Agreement.

68. Case C-25/94, *Commission v. Council.*

69. See e.g., recently the Codex Alimentarius, a number of commodity agreements, such as the International Coffee and Cocoa agreements, as well as the Hague Conference for Private International Law. A great many multilateral environmental agreements also contain REIO clauses, such as the Biodiversity Convention and the associated Biosafety Protocol.

70. Arts. 23(2) and 34(3) TEU.

and in their application. It is mostly in the Third Pillar and in matters closely related to Community law that the role of the Commission in the negotiation of agreements to be concluded by the Union is important because of its undeniable expertise in these matters. As has been pointed out earlier, the agreements are now explicitly said to bind the Institutions of the Union – but not (yet) the Member States, as is the case in Article 300(7) EC. This omission is connected to paragraph 5 of Article 24, which gives Member States the opportunity to declare that they must follow their internal constitutional procedures before they can be bound by a projected agreement. This provision, which is notoriously difficult to apply, emphasizes again the intergovernmental nature of the cooperation between the Member States in the Second and Third Pillars.[71] In the future, after the pillar structure is abolished by the Treaty of Lisbon, there will only be agreements of the Union and they will be negotiated primarily by the High Representative or by the Commission, depending on whether the subject matter of the projected agreement falls primarily under the CFSP or under 'Community' external relations.[72]

The old Article 228 EEC regulated the procedure for concluding international agreements by the Community in a rather fragmentary manner, not always free from obscurity. Article 300 EC was however significantly reshaped by the treaties of Maastricht, Amsterdam and Nice, so as to comprise a number of provisions which systematically bring together all the procedures for negotiating and concluding agreements. Before negotiations are formally opened, the Commission makes recommendations to the Council, which then authorizes the Commission to open the necessary negotiations. Frequently the Commission will already have conducted informal exploratory discussions. The Commission then conducts the formal negotiations, in consultation with a special committee appointed by the Council. In the area of commercial policy there is a special committee established pursuant to Article 133 EC. The Commission follows any instructions ('directives') it receives from the Council; these are not always given, however, and they are not as such binding: the Commission may thus stray from its negotiating mandate, if it believes the course of the negotiations make that inevitable, but will need the cooperation of the Council if the negotiations are to result in the conclusion of an agreement.

The signing, provisional application (where appropriate) and conclusion of an agreement is decided on by the Council. This power of the Council is exercised 'subject to the powers vested in the Commission in this field' (Art. 300(2) EC). It is not entirely clear what these words mean. In the past, the Commission had developed a practice whereby it concluded, independently, so-called administrative agreements with ministries or governments of third countries, and thus applied,

---

71. The phrase 'the other members of the Council may agree that the agreement shall nevertheless apply provisionally', in particular, raises numerous questions. Do 'the other members' decide this for themselves or for the Union as a whole? If the former, what is the use of provisional agreement 'à géométrie variable' for the Union's treaty partners? If the latter, by which procedure do they so decide, and what if 'the other members' happen to be in the minority?
72. See Art. 218 TFEU inserted by the Treaty of Lisbon.

albeit on a modest scale, the criteria of Article 101 Euratom by analogy.[73] The Court has however held that this analogous application of Article 101 Euratom is unjustified, and its judgment on the agreement concluded by the Commission and the United States in the area of cooperation in the field of competition law enforcement, leaves little if any room for this practice.[74]

For the authorization to open negotiations, the issue of directives, as well as the signing, provisional application and the final conclusion of the agreement, the Council acts, in principle, by qualified majority. Unanimity for all these decisions is required when the agreement covers a field for which unanimity is required for the adoption of internal rules, and for the association agreements based on Article 310 EC.[75]

The provisions of Article 300(3) EC, dealing with the powers of the European Parliament are hardly beacons of clarity, and practice has also failed so far to provide the necessary elucidation. In principle, the Parliament has to have been consulted (and thus to have delivered its opinion) on all agreements before they are concluded by the Council. Parliamentary approval, as exists in most of the Member States, is thus not required, and for commercial policy agreements even the opinion of Parliament does not have to be obtained. Certain specific types of agreement do need the assent of Parliament before they may be concluded. These are: first of all, the association agreements based on Article 310 EC, or 'other agreements establishing a specific institutional framework by organizing cooperation procedures'. This requirement applies, secondly, to agreements which have important budgetary implications for the Community; and, thirdly, to agreements entailing amendment of an act adopted under the co-decision procedure of Article 251 EC.

These provisions should be seen in the light of the Court's case law on the democratic legitimacy of legal acts of the Community.[76] A broad interpretation is therefore justified, and in particular the category of 'other agreements establishing a specific institutional framework' should be interpreted as covering virtually all international organizations; also the 'important budgetary implications' for the Community budget should not be interpreted too narrowly.[77] Such an approach also has consequences for the interpretation of the Parliament's competences concerning the conclusion of commercial agreements; if democratic legitimacy is placed in the foreground, it must be accepted that certain commercial agreements

---

73. Under Art. 101 Euratom, in certain cases – where the subject matter of an international agreement falls within the competence of the Commission and can be effected within the limits of the relevant budget – the Commission may negotiate and conclude agreements entirely on its own.
74. See Case C-327/91, *France v. Commission*. In a later case, also brought by France against the Commission (Case C-233/02), the Court approved a non-binding arrangement concluded by the Commission with the relevant US authorities on the Trans-Atlantic Regulatory Dialogue.
75. Art. 300(2) 1st para. EC.
76. Case C-300/89, *Commission v. Council (titanium dioxide)*.
77. In Case C-189/97, *Parliament v. Council*, the Court ruled that a sum representing 1% of the whole of the payment appropriations allocated for external operations of the Community does not have important implications for the Community budget. The Court rejected a comparison with the overall Community budget as a basis for 'important implications'.

also need the assent of the European Parliament, as they fall within one of the three categories of agreements requiring assent, specified in the second paragraph of Article 300(3) EC, even though under the first paragraph of Article 300(3) EC commercial agreements as such do not even need to be submitted for the opinion of Parliament.[78]

Of course the time factor may well be important in relation to seeking the opinion or the assent of the Parliament. If the former is sought, the Council may, according to the urgency of the matter, prescribe a time-limit for the delivery of Parliament's opinion, and in the absence of the opinion within that period the Council may conclude the agreement. If Parliament's assent is required, the Council and the Parliament may, in an urgent situation, agree upon a time-limit for the assent.[79]

The opinion or assent of Parliament is not required if the Council decides to suspend an agreement; the EC Treaty considers this as the other side of provisional application and the same decision-making rules apply.[80] This is also the case if the Council has to establish a position to be adopted on behalf of the Community in a body set up by an agreement, when that body is called upon to adopt decisions having legal effects. Prior to the Treaty of Nice, this was only the case in relation to bodies set up by *association* agreements.[81] Both these situations require a certain speed of action, which does not leave the possibility for an opinion or assent of Parliament; Parliament should be immediately informed of any provisional application, suspension or Community position established.

A practical addition, introduced by an amendment made by the Treaty of Maastricht, is the possibility for the Council to authorize the Commission to approve modifications to agreements (usually of subsidiary importance) on behalf of the Community, where the agreement being modified provides for modifications to be adopted by a simplified procedure or by a body set up by the agreement.[82] The

---

78. This will also depend on whether a broad or narrow interpretation of the term 'commercial policy' is used. Since the Court in Opinion 1/94, *WTO*, chose a narrow interpretation, it was difficult to imagine that trade agreements could ever entail amendments to Community acts adopted under the co-decision procedure (e.g., in the area of free movement of persons and services, and harmonization of legislation), so there could scarcely be a conflict between the beginning of the 1st subpara. and the 2nd subpara. of Art. 300(3) EC. The more extensive interpretation of commercial policy in the Treaty of Nice does not fundamentally alter this, since only the 'old' trade agreements are excluded from consultation of Parliament.
79. Art. 300(3), last subpara. EC.
80. Art. 300(2) 2nd subpara. EC.
81. The extension of this provision from decisions of Association Councils (normally largely controlled by the Community) to decisions of organs of international organizations generally, has not taken sufficient account of the reality of the practice of decision-making in international organizations, where negotiations on texts continue until the last minute and the projected text of a decision is not known sufficiently beforehand to allow the Commission to make a proposal for a position to be taken by the EC and for the Council to adopt it.
82. Art. 300(4) EC. One should here think above all of lists of products, etc., which are attached to agreements and which form an integral part thereof, but which may be amended by means of a simplified procedure. See e.g., the lists of endangered species attached to the CITES Agreement (to which the Community is still not a party).

Council may attach specific conditions to such authorization. It is unclear whether this addition should be read in conjunction with the opening words of Article 300(2) EC, 'the powers vested in the Commission in this field', so that in fact it leads to a restriction of the treaty-making powers left to the Commission by those opening words.

It is evident that where the Council envisages concluding an international agreement which involves amendments to the EC Treaty or TEU, it will have to follow the treaty amendment procedure prescribed by Article 48 TEU;[83] this has not yet ever come to pass. If there is doubt about the compatibility of a proposed international agreement with the EC Treaty, the European Parliament, the Council, the Commission or a Member State may obtain the opinion of the Court of Justice. When in the past the Court has given a negative opinion, it is the agreement which has been adapted, not the EC Treaty.[84]

Finally, Article 300(7) EC contains the guarantee – also useful for third countries – that not just the Community and its Institutions, but also the Member States are bound by agreements concluded by the Community. This means, according to the Court, that in complying with an agreement concluded by the Community, a Member State also fulfils an obligation *vis-à-vis* the Community.[85] If necessary the Commission or a Member State could react to a breach by one of the Member States of an agreement concluded by the Community by bringing infringement proceedings under, as appropriate, Articles 226 and 227 EC.[86] The liability of the Community for infringements by Member States of Community agreements is, however, recognized by third countries: the Community is recognized as being subject to WTO panels if one of the Member States allegedly does not meet its obligations under the WTO.[87]

Derogations from the procedure of Article 300 EC are provided for in the context of the provisions on Economic and Monetary Union.[88] In the case of conclusion of an agreement on an exchange-rate system for the euro in relation to non-Community currencies, the Council takes a decision, acting unanimously on a recommendation from the European Central Bank (ECB) or from the Commission and after consulting the ECB. The authorization to negotiate and the directives for negotiation are also dealt with differently from Article 300 EC; there are not even clear rules as to who should conduct the negotiations. Where agreements concerning monetary or foreign-exchange regime matters need to be negotiated, the Council decides the arrangements for the negotiation and for the conclusion of

---

83. Art. 300(5) EC.
84. E.g., Opinion 1/92, *European Economic Area II*.
85. See Case 104/81, *Hauptzollamt Mainz v. Kupferberg*.
86. See Case C-61/94, *Commission v. Germany*, and other cases cited in C. Kaddous, *Le droit des relations extérieures dans la jurisprudence de la Cour de Justice des Communautés européennes* (1998), 34–40. The Commission may even bring infringement procedures against Member States for not having observed mixed agreements relating to matters that are not covered by Community legislation; see Case C-239/03, *Etang de Berre*.
87. Cf. the Panel and Appellate Body report in Case DS 62, 67 and 68, *EC-Computer Equipment*.
88. See on this also *supra* Ch. X, especially section 3.3.5.

such agreements on a recommendation from the Commission and after consulting the ECB. Although the Commission is to be fully associated with the negotiations, it is not necessarily the negotiating body. According to Article 111(3) EC, the arrangements must ensure that the Community expresses a single position. This provision could be of importance for the establishment of the position of the EC within the International Monetary Fund (IMF), but has not yet been applied in this context.

2.6.2 Autonomous External Action by the Community

The Community does not only exercise its external powers in a contractual manner through the conclusion of agreements; it can also act autonomously in external matters. This can be seen most clearly in the exercise of autonomous commercial policy competence, which is dealt with in sections 3.3.1–3.3.5 below. The Community also acts autonomously in external matters in a variety of other areas of international relations: it performs unilateral public international law acts, reacts to such acts of states and other international legal persons, and issues letters of protest and the like.

The oldest and most well-known example of this type of action is that of investigations, followed by decisions, in the competition field against undertakings established outside the Community; these involve the unilateral exercise of Community legal authority over those undertakings.[89] On the other hand, the Community has protested strongly at what it regarded as excessive exercise of jurisdictional powers by the United States, especially in the field of export controls.[90] Moreover, it is unavoidable that the Community from time to time becomes entangled in questions of recognition of other states and regimes.[91] The Community must also from time to time adopt standpoints on the international law of treaties. The Community even participated in the conference on the law of treaties between states and international organizations and between international

---

89. Wood pulp decision, O.J. 1985, L 85/1; Joined Cases 89/85, 104/85, 114/85, 116/85, 117/85 & 125/85 to 129/85, *A. Ahlström Osakeyhtiö and others v. Commission (wood pulp)*. See also the decision in Gencor, O.J. 1997, L 11/30 and Case T-102/96, *Gencor v. Commission*.

90. ILM 1982, 891–904, on the so-called pipeline protest. Later similar protests were made against the Helms/Burton Act, Bull. EC 10/1996, point 1.4.81.

91. For instance, the Commission, on behalf of the Community, has refused recognition of North-Cyprus, see Bull. EC 11–1983. The consequences of this non-recognition were, according to the Court of Justice, radical: the impossibility of accepting certificates of origin and phytosanitary certificates from non-recognized authorities, see Case C-432/92, *The Queen v. Minister of Agriculture, Fisheries and Food, ex parte S. P. Anastasiou (Pissouri) Ltd and others (EEC-Cyprus Association Agreement)*. Later, in the framework of European Political Cooperation (EPC), the Community and the Member States developed criteria for the recognition of states which had been part of the former USSR; see Bull. EC 12-1991, point 1.4.5. Since there seemed to be less immediate necessity afterwards and there was less agreement on the criteria to be applied to the countries of ex-Yugoslavia, no efforts have been made subsequently in the CFSP framework to develop criteria for the recognition of third States.

organizations[92] although in treaty law questions the Commission prefers to rely on the (1969) Vienna Convention on the Law of Treaties than on the Convention resulting from that conference.[93] As a result of German unification and the great tumult in Eastern Europe and the former Soviet Union, the Community has also had to determine its position in relation to questions of state succession on a number of occasions.[94] The Commission is also very active representing the Community in relation to the work of the International Law Commission on the international responsibility of international organizations.[95]

The exercise of these autonomous external powers, through which the Community and its Institutions also contribute to international legal practice and thus to the formation or confirmation of international customary law, in practice occurs according to procedures which are to a large extent the same as those applicable to the exercise of the power to conclude agreements. Given that the emphasis in this type of instance is placed on policy questions, it is primarily the Commission which acts externally, albeit normally in consultation with the special Committee for commercial policy, or other appropriate bodies or committees under the Council. It is to be expected that the European Parliament, which now possesses increased responsibilities in the field of external affairs, will in the future also wish to be involved in consultations on the exercise of autonomous external competence. This is clearly different for matters which are firmly embedded in the CFSP. Examples are the Protocol on Biological and Toxin Weapons, the Treaty on the Non-Proliferation of Nuclear Weapons and policy on Antipersonnel landmines; in these cases, it is purely a question of coordination of national positions by means of a common position under Article 15 TEU and not of developing Community policy in CFSP.

2.7   THE CFSP: INSTRUMENTS AND RELATION TO COMMUNITY LAW

Earlier in this chapter, in section 1, it was already pointed out that the CFSP has four different instruments: general guidelines and common strategies of the European Council;[96] joint actions[97] and common positions,[98] both of which are

---

92. See P. Manin, 'The European Communities and the Vienna Convention on the Law of Treaties between States and International Organizations or between International Organizations' (1987) CML Rev., 457–481.

93. Cf. P.J. Kuyper, 'The Court and Tribunal of the EC and the Vienna Convention on the Law of Treaties 1969' (1998) LIEI, 1–24.

94. Cf. P.J. Kuyper, 'The Community and State Succession in Respect of Treaties', in D. Curtin, T. Heukels (eds), *The Institutional Dynamics of European Integration, Essays in Honour of H.G. Schermers* (Dordrecht, 1994), 619–640.

95. See E. Paasivirta and P.J. Kuijper, 'Does One Size Fit All?: the European Community and the Responsibility of International Organizations' (2005) NYIL, 169–226.

96. Art. 12, first and second indent; Art. 13(1) and (2) TEU.

97. Art. 12, third indent; Art. 14(1) TEU.

98. Art. 12, fourth indent; Art. 15 TEU.

established by the Council in principle by consensus.[99] The Council has also created an additional category of so-called decisions, which is not explicitly mentioned in the Treaty.[100] Up to now, the European Council has not adopted official guidelines in accordance with Article 13(1) TEU, but this has not prevented the Council from referring in acts adopted under Article 14 TEU to similar conclusions of the European Council from before the entry into force of the Treaty of Maastricht.[101] Instead of adopting guidelines, the European Council continues to work with declarations – just as it did before Maastricht. In some cases, such as the policy for the Mediterranean area, such declarations are used as building blocks for a common strategy.[102] Perhaps it must be accepted that such declarations contain *de facto* guidelines.[103]

Two other common strategies have been elaborated thus far by the European Council apart from that for the Mediterranean region: one for Russia and one for Ukraine. They have played a certain role and served as basis for Joint Actions, especially in respect of the Mediterranean Policy. They have, however, largely lost their relevance in the light of the changed circumstances both in the Mediterranean and in Eastern Europe.

The distinction between the two other instruments of the CFSP is not always equally clear in practice. Although the description of the two instruments in Articles 14 and 15 TEU clearly shows that joint actions are more operational in character, and common positions more declaratory, they are frequently swapped around and there is a lack of consistency in practice. For instance, it is noticeable that common positions are used as a first step in the implementation of sanctions of the UN Security Council, on the basis of Article 301 EC, while joint actions are used to effect restrictions on the export of dual-use goods. According to the Treaty of Lisbon, the European Council will still give general guidelines, but not adopt common strategies. The other two categories of CFSP acts will disappear and be replaced by a single category: 'decisions'. These decisions can bear on 'actions', on 'positions', and on 'arrangements for implementation'.[104]

---

99. Art. 23(1) TEU. Since Amsterdam, there is a rule of constructive abstention included in the article, i.e., an abstention shall not prevent the adoption of a decision. Moreover an abstention may be accompanied by a declaration to the effect that the Member State accepts that the decision in question binds the Union (constructive abstention). These provisions seem to have been borrowed from Arts. 5 and 6 of the OECD Treaty.

100. Art. 13(3) TEU speaks of decisions 'necessary for defining and implementing' the CFSP, but this seems rather to be a general reference to joint actions and common positions.

101. In various decisions, reference was made to the guidelines of the European Council of 29 Oct. 1993. See Decision 93/603/CFSP, O.J. 1993, L 286/1, and Decision 94/276/CFSP, O.J. 1994, L 119/1.

102. See Common Strategy 2000/458/CFSP on the Mediterranean region, which builds on the Barcelona (1995) and Berlin (1999) declarations.

103. This is unsatisfactory, since in this way it can only be decided ex post whether certain parts of declarations of the European Council were in fact guidelines as intended in Art. 13(1) TEU.

104. Art. 24 TEU (Lisbon). This will also solve the problem signalled in note 100 *supra* with respect to 'decisions' under the old TEU. See further Ch. V *supra* on the new categories of legal acts in the Lisbon Treaty.

The extent to which implementation of CFSP in practice relies on Community instruments and action by the European Commission has been commented.[105] It has been shown above already that various Community instruments – both contractual and autonomous in nature – are required for the implementation of the Common Strategy for the Mediterranean area. The same is obviously true for the Common Strategies for Russia and the Ukraine: these are to a large degree dependent on the partnership and cooperation agreements (PCAs) with these countries, and the autonomous financial instruments such as ENPI and the instrument for assistance to industrialized and high income countries.[106] Nevertheless, joint actions and common positions are also to a significant extent dependent on implementation by Community instruments; this is particularly evident in the case of the sanctions and measures for dual-use goods, already mentioned above.[107] In crisis situations, the Community financing instrument that enables the Commission to give various forms of emergency aid in order to re-establish stability may play an important role.[108]

The Court of Justice has ruled on the issue of the relationship between the two pillars, in a judgment which is also of more general significance for the relation between CFSP and the EC. The Member States may not take refuge in CFSP measures in order to withdraw certain matters from Community competence. This is not permitted when the Community is involved, under its own competence, in order to flesh out CFSP acts. The Court does seem to accept a certain subordination of the Community to CFSP, but the CFSP may not encroach on the competences of the Community.[109] This is still broadly the approach of the Court under Article 47 TEU, which explicitly protects the First Pillar against the intergovernmentalism of the Second and Third Pillars, though so far the Court has ruled primarily on questions related to the Third Pillar.[110]

If one looks at the areas where the CFSP is active, it may be noticed that – from a geographical point of view – the West Balkans is an area where the CFSP has been intensively active. A great number of joint actions and common positions of different kinds have been adopted over the years, such as arms embargos and other economic restrictions, visa and travel restrictions for Yugoslavian leaders, specific missions and special representatives, humanitarian help, as well as Union participation in special structures which have been set up in places such as Mostar and

---

105. See R.A. Wessel, *The European Union's Foreign and Security Policy, A Legal Institutional Perspective* (The Hague, 1999), Ch. 4.
106. For ENPI, see *infra* note 306 and Reg. (EC) No 1934/2006 establishing a financing instrument for cooperation with the industrialized countries and other high income countries, O.J. 2007, L 29/16.
107. See also section 3.3.5 *infra*.
108. Reg. (EC) No 1717/2006 establishing an instrument for stability, O.J. 2006, L 327/1.
109. Case C-124/95, *The Queen, ex parte Centro-Com Srl v. HM Treasury and Bank of England*; this case concerned EPC and the EC, but can also be applied to the CFSP; see section 3.3.5 *infra*.
110. See Case C-170/96, *Commission v. Council (transit visas)* and Case C-176/03, *Commission v. Council (criminal sanctions)*. For these and other issues related to the differences and the relationship between the First and Second Pillars: R. Gosalbo Bono, 'Some Reflections on the CFSP Legal Order' (2006) CML Rev., 337–394. Case C-91/05, *Commission v. Council (ECOWAS/ Small Arms and Light Weapons)*, has shed light on the boundary to be drawn between the First and Second Pillars.

Kosovo. The Middle East and support for the peace process in that region is also an important concentration of CFSP measures. But Africa is without doubt head of the list, with a series of acts sparked off by international and civil wars, and the related humanitarian disasters in such areas as the Great Lakes, Angola, Ethiopia-Eritrea, Sierra Leone, Sudan, Nigeria and Libya.

If CFSP activities are viewed from a functional perspective, then one notices – alongside various embargos on arms, whether or not inspired by the UN[111] and other exports, as well as export controls on dual-use goods – a great number of restrictive measures concerning various categories of arms: non-proliferation of nuclear weapons, prohibition on biological and toxin weapons, on blinding laser weapons, and restrictions on landmines and support for mine-clearing activities.[112]

In fact, quite a few of the more operational actions in the Balkans and in Africa referred to above fall in the domain of the European Security and Defence Policy (ESDP) which has really taken off in the last few years. There are presently 11 police and military operations in the field, whereas 8 such missions have come to their end already. Apart from the Political and Security Committee (PSC) that deals with both CFSP and ESDP matters, this side of the Second Pillar is equipped with a Military Committee and the Military Staff of the European Union.[113] It has also been provided with a European Defence Agency in Brussels,[114] a European Union Satellite Centre in Torrejon,[115] and a European Union Institute for Security Studies in Paris.[116]

3   THE COMMON COMMERCIAL POLICY

3.1   THE COMMERCIAL POLICY COMPETENCE OF THE COMMUNITY

3.1.1   The Concept of Commercial Policy

The power to regulate commercial policy relations by unilateral measures concerning imports and exports (autonomous commercial policy) or by agreements with third countries (conventional commercial policy) is expressly included in the EC Treaty in Article 133. The power covers the adoption of autonomous measures

---

111. The common weapons embargo against Sudan, which was not based on a resolution of the Security Council, was also taken on the basis of Art. J.2 (now 12) TEU, O.J. 1994, L 75/1. This Decision reveals that the Member States cling resolutely to the complete exclusion of weapons from the scope of Community law pursuant to Art. 296 EC. The Commission is of the opinion that, if the Council so desires, disparities in the trade in weapons can be eradicated in the same way as obstacles to trade permitted under Art. 30 EC can be overcome by means of harmonization.
112. See the thematic list of CFSP decisions, available (in French) on the website of the Secretariat-General of the Council.
113. Set up by respectively Council Decisions 2001/79/CFSP, O.J. 2001, L 27/4 and 2005/395/CFSP, O.J. 2005, L 132/17.
114. See Joint Action 2004/551/CFSP, O.J. 2004, L 245/17–28 and <www.eda.europa> for information.
115. See Joint Action 2001/555/CFSP, O.J. 2005, L 200/5.
116. See Joint Action 2001/554/CFSP, O.J. 2005, L 200/1.

relating to the common customs tariff under Articles 26 and 27 EC, and the regulation of commercial traffic in agricultural products between the Community and the rest of the world by means, for example, of levies and refunds under common organizations of the market (in accordance with Arts. 34 and 37 EC).

Article 133 EC does not contain a definition of commercial policy but provides a non-exhaustive[117] list of subject matters: changes in tariff rates, the conclusion of tariff and trade agreements, the achievement of uniformity in measures of liberalization, export policy and measures to protect trade such as those to be taken in case of dumping or subsidies. This indicates the core of the common commercial policy, but does not set its boundaries. The Council has advanced the view that only measures whose aim is to influence the volume or flow of trade fall within the scope of commercial policy (a subjective doctrine, looking at the content to identify the objective), whereas the Commission has taken the view that the assessment need only take account of whether a measure is *in fact* an instrument regulating international trade, quite apart from the aim of the measure (an objective or instrumental doctrine).[118] The Court of Justice has not expressly taken a position on this controversy, although elements of both views have been reflected in its case law, and lately the instrumental doctrine seems to be gaining influence.[119] The case law has, though, contributed to further detailing the scope of the field covered by the common commercial policy.

The starting-point is that the concept of commercial policy has 'the same content whether it is applied in the context of the international action of a state or to that of the Community'.[120] There is therefore no reason for interpreting the concept more narrowly in the case of the Community. On the contrary, the proper functioning of the customs union justifies a wide interpretation of *inter alia* Article 133 EC and of the powers thereby conferred on the Community Institutions 'to allow them thoroughly to control external trade by measures taken both

---

117. Cf. Opinion 1/78, *International Agreement on Natural Rubber*.

118. Cf. extensively the exposition of these points of view in Opinion 1/78, *International Agreement on Natural Rubber*. See also Opinion of A.G. Lenz in Case 45/86, *Commission v. Council* (generalized tariff preferences). On this occasion, the Commission in fact presented a more nuanced point of view, where the point of departure was the aim clearly and explicitly to regulate trade with third countries. See also J.H.J. Bourgeois, 'The Common Commercial Policy: Scope and Nature of the Powers', in E.L.M. Völker (ed.), *Protectionism and the European Community* (Deventer, 1983), 4–6.

119. Case C-62/88, *Greece v. Commission*, in which elements of both approaches may be found; Case C-70/94, *Werner v. Germany* and Case C-83/94, *Criminal Proceedings against Peter Leifer, Reinhold Otto Krauskopf and Otto Holzer*, in which the instrumental doctrine seems to be predominant. This controversy is in fact less important now than it used to be, and in retrospect can be seen to have been based on political considerations of the day to some extent. E.g., the TRIPS Agreement could simply have been concluded as a trade agreement on the basis of the Council's teleological approach, i.e., with the aim of promoting trade in goods which contain an important component of intellectual property. The Council, however, clung to the view that this was not a commercial policy competence of the Community; the Court supported that interpretation in Opinion 1/94, *WTO*, this was changed with the new Art. 133 EC, as altered by the Treaty of Nice.

120. Opinion 1/75, *Local Cost Standard*.

independently and by agreement'.[121] Thus the Court concluded that aids for exports to third countries, mentioned in Article 132 EC, and in particular measures concerning export credits necessarily fell within the scope of 'export policy' mentioned in Article 133 EC.[122] The definition of the uniform principles prescribed in Article 133 EC included 'the elimination of national disparities', whether in the field of taxation or of commerce, affecting trade with third countries.[123]

The Court has also held that it is 'not possible to lay down, for Article [133] of the Treaty, an interpretation the effect of which would be to restrict the common commercial policy to the use of instruments intended to have an effect only on the traditional aspects of external trade to the exclusion of more highly developed mechanisms', such as for instance international commodity agreements in the 1970s and, recently, environmental measures. If it were otherwise, observed the Court, the common commercial policy

> would be destined to become nugatory in the course of time. Although it may be thought that at the time when the Treaty was drafted liberalization of trade was the dominant idea, the Treaty nevertheless does not form a barrier to the possibility of the Community's developing a commercial policy aiming at a regulation of the world market for certain products rather than at a mere liberalization of trade.[124]

Development policy and environmental policy are integral aspects of a modern concept of commercial policy. Thus the Court has ruled that the Community system of generalized tariff preferences for developing countries (the Generalized System of Preferences (GSP))[125] and restrictions in trade flows in connection with environmental disasters (e.g., Chernobyl) are part of the common commercial policy, and it is sufficient for these measures to be based on Article 133 EC, without the need to use other provisions of the EC Treaty as joint legal bases.[126] In Opinion 1/78[127] which concerned the Community's competence relating to an international rubber agreement, the Court saw no reason to exclude the agreement from the domain of the common commercial policy because of its possible repercussions on certain sectors of economic policy, such as the supply of certain raw materials to the Union or because the building up of stocks of a product might have a general political importance.[128]

Now that the Treaty also includes provisions on external competence in the area of environmental policy (Arts. 174 et seq. EC), and on development cooperation (Arts. 177 and 179 EC), the choice of correct legal basis is determined by the

---

121. Case 8/73, *Hauptzollamt Bremerhaven v. Massey-Ferguson* (para. 4).
122. Opinion 1/75, *Local Cost Standard.*
123. Joined Cases 37 & 38/73, *Sociaal Fonds voor de Diamantarbeiders v. Indiamex, De Belder et al.* (para. 16).
124. Opinion 1/78, *International Agreement on Natural Rubber* (para. 44).
125. See *infra* text at notes 159–164.
126. Case 45/86, *Commission v. Council* (GTP), and Case C-62/88, *Greece v. Commission.*
127. Opinion 1/78, *International Agreement on Natural Rubber.*
128. Opinion 1/78, *International Agreement on Natural Rubber.*

question which aspect can be said, on objective grounds, to be dominant in a legal act of the Community. Recent case law of the Court reveals that only a careful analysis of the text, context, subject matter and objectives of the agreement can determine the ultimate choice of legal basis. This can lead to divergent results. For instance, the Court ruled that the Cartagena Protocol on Biosafety had to be concluded on the basis of 175 EC,[129] but the so-called Energy-Star Agreement[130] on energy-efficient labelling programmes for office equipment had to be concluded on the basis of Article 133 EC. Recently the Court has rather tended towards a double legal basis, since the cases in which trade and environmental matters are of equal weight and highly intertwined within one and the same agreement seem more prevalent among the newer agreements on the borderline between the two policy areas.[131] There is as yet no new case law on the relation between development cooperation policy and commercial policy since the introduction of Article 177 EC in the Treaty.

The most important controversy in the 1990s concerning the concept of the common commercial policy was about its scope: whether this only covers the external aspects of the customs union, and thus only tariff and non-tariff barriers to trade in goods, or whether it also embraces other aspects of the common market, such as international trade in services and certain external aspects of the right of establishment. The Commission has long taken the view that trade in services comes within the common commercial policy, and also those aspects of the right of establishment and of the free movement of persons which are directly linked to the liberalization of trade in services. The Commission's view was based on the increasing intermingling of trade in services with trade in goods, and also on the increasing importance of international trade in services as such; it built on the Court's evolutionary approach to the concept of the common commercial policy and concluded that international trade in services formed part of the common commercial policy. For a long time, the Council and pretty well all the Member States rejected this view. They remained firmly attached to the narrow view of the concept of the common commercial policy, restricting its scope to trade in goods and some services directly linked thereto.

In Opinion 1/94, *WTO - GATS and TRIPS* the Court sought to give something of a judgment of Solomon on the scope of the Community's commercial policy competence, but in practice the result largely tended towards the approach of the Council and the Member States. The Court recognized that developments in the practice of international trade indicate that trade in services and the trade aspects of intellectual property play an increasingly important role. The common commercial policy must retain an open nature, and evolve together with the practice of international trade. In view of the structure of the EC Treaty, however, the Court was unwilling to draw the full consequences of this approach. It found that the cross-frontier provision of services involving no movement of persons was not unlike trade in goods and, as the latter was unquestionably within the scope of the common

---

129.   Opinion 2/00, *Cartagena Protocol.*
130.   Case C-281/01, *Commission v. Council* (Energy Star).
131.   Case C-94/03, *Commission v. Council* (PICs).

commercial policy, so was the former; but the other forms of provision of services dealt with in the definition of trade in services under Article I(2) General Agreement on Trade in Services (GATS) were, the Court concluded, very closely linked to the free movement of persons, the freedom of undertakings to establish themselves, and the specific EC Treaty provisions on transport. Thus for these modes of providing services and for transport any exclusive Community competence had to be established on the basis of the *ERTA* doctrine or on the basis of the existence of specific clauses in Community legislation relating to the treatment of persons or undertakings from third countries or dealing with negotiations with third countries. The same view was taken in relation to the international aspects of intellectual property rights: here too determination of exclusive external competence depended on the doctrine of implied powers, save in relation to frontier measures against counterfeit goods, which clearly fell under Article 133 EC.[132]

The result of Opinion 1/94 was applied in the conclusion of the WTO agreements; in the years that followed, however, the practice inside that organization hardly reflected the strictures of the Opinion. Its niceties were formally observed, when the occasional legal act had to be adopted, but in the reality of the discussions inside the WTO it was the Commission, representing the Community and/or the collectivity of the Member States, which spoke and negotiated.

The Treaty of Nice confirmed the inclusion of services and intellectual property in the common commercial policy[133] – but, alas, at the price of the uniformity of decision-making, and, in certain circumstances, the exclusive character of commercial policy competence. As long as certain corresponding internal provisions on services and intellectual property have to be adopted by unanimity, commercial policy agreements including such provisions must also be negotiated and concluded on the basis of unanimity, instead of qualified majority.[134] In addition, the new provisions on services and the commercial aspects of intellectual property are said not to affect 'the right of the Member States to maintain and conclude agreements with third countries or international organizations insofar as such agreements comply with Community law and other relevant international agreements.'[135] The Treaty of Lisbon ends any and all quarrels about the scope

---

132. Opinion 1/94, *WTO - GATS and TRIPS.*
133. Art. 133(5), 1st sub-para.
134. Art. 133(5), 2nd and 3rd sub-paras.
135. Art. 133(5), 4th sub-para. It is not fully clear whether this is only an incidental right of the Member States to maintain and perhaps modify national agreements relating to trade in services and commercial aspects of intellectual property, or whether it entitles Member States to co-conclude all agreements in these sectors as mixed agreements. The latter interpretation would seem to go against the clear intention of the first three subparagraphs of Art. 133(5), which establish a system of exclusive Community competence, but with unanimous voting, and against the explicit characterization of mixed agreements in Art. 133(6) as requiring 'the common accord' of Community and Member States. See also Section 3.3.6 *infra.* This and other interpretative issues concerning Art. 133 in its Nice version will be decided in Case C-13/07, *Commission v. Council, Vietnam*, pending.

of the common commercial policy by explicitly including not only trade in services and commercial aspects of intellectual property, but also foreign investment within its scope.

3.1.2   The Exclusivity of Community Competence in the Field of Commercial Policy

The case law demonstrates that in the field of commercial policy the Community has exclusive competence in relation to conventional as well as autonomous measures;[136] indeed, according to the Court's judgment in *Donckerwolcke*, after the end of the transitional period national commercial policy measures are only permissible when specifically authorized by the Community. In Opinion 1/75[137] the Court based this exclusivity on the ground that the common commercial policy was conceived 'in the context of the operation of the Common Market, for the defence of the common interests of the Community, within which the particular interests of the Member States must endeavour to adapt to each other.' 'Quite clearly', continued the Court, 'this conception is incompatible with the freedom to which the Member States could lay claim by invoking a concurrent power, so as to ensure that their own interests were separately satisfied in external relations, at the risk of compromising the effective defence of the common interests of the Community.'

If such a parallel competence were to be accepted, that:

> would amount to recognizing that, in relations with third countries, Member States may adopt positions which differ from those which the Community intends to adopt, and which would thereby distort the institutional framework, call into question the mutual trust within the Community and prevent the latter from fulfilling its task in the defence of the common interest.[138]

That is unless it can be guaranteed that the parallel competences of the Member States are only exercised in accordance with Community law; and this condition has been included in the EC Treaty by the Treaty of Nice, where the last paragraph of Article 133(5) EC permits the Member States to maintain and conclude agreements with third countries or international organizations agreements in the fields of trade in services and the commercial aspects of intellectual property.

In Opinion 1/75, the Court also found that no obstacle to the exclusivity of the Community's common commercial policy competence arises from the fact that the obligations and financial burdens inherent in the execution of conventional autonomous agreements are borne directly by the Member States; such obligations and burdens do not necessarily have to be transferred to the Community Institutions,[139] nor does the implementation of the obligations have to be completely the task of the

---

136. Case 41/76, *Suzanne Criel, née Donckerwolcke and Henri Schou v. Procureur de la République au tribunal de grande instance de Lille and Director General of Customs.*
137. Opinion 1/75, *Local Cost Standard*, part B.2.
138. Opinion 1/75, *Local Cost Standard*, part B.2.
139. Opinion 1/75, *Local Cost Standard*.

Community Institutions.[140] The Community does though have the power to enter into financial obligations charged to the Community budget arising from an instrument of the common commercial policy (even if they are not incidental or subsidiary obligations but are an essential part of the system set up, as, for example, in the case of a buffer stock mechanism which has to be financed as part of the regulatory system of an international commodity agreement).[141]

In fact, Opinion 1/78[142] reveals that in certain circumstances the question whether the financial burdens arising from an agreement fall on the Member States is relevant for the exclusivity or otherwise of the competence.[143] In the case of the financing of buffer stocks in the framework of the international rubber agreement, at issue in Opinion 1/78, the Court held that if the agreement was to be financed from the budgets of the Member States, it was not possible to establish an exclusive competence of the Community to conclude the agreement.[144]

As already indicated above, the new Nice version of Article 133 creates some uncertainty about the continued exclusive character of the common commercial policy in respect of trade in services and commercial aspects of intellectual property.[145] In addition, paragraph 6 of that article states that any trade agreement that would lead to a harmonization of laws and regulations of the Member States in an area for which the Treaty rules out such harmonization is *ultra vires* for the Community.[146] 'In this regard', as the second subparagraph of Article 133(6) puts it, agreements relating to trade in cultural and audiovisual services, educational, social and human health services (all sectors for which the EC Treaty prohibits harmonization) can, in derogation from other provisions of Article 133, only be concluded as mixed agreements. The crucial issue here is the meaning of the words 'in this regard'. Do they refer to the situation described in the preceding subparagraph, namely that an agreement is about to be concluded that envisages a harmonization where that would normally not be allowed? In that case the two

---

140. Opinion 2/91, *ILO Convention.*
141. Opinion 1/78, *International Agreement on Natural Rubber.*
142. Ibid., para. 60.
143. Compare with the findings in Opinion 1/75, *Local Cost Standard,* just discussed.
144. In Opinion 1/94, *WTO,* the Court rejected an abusive use of its Opinion 1/78; given that in the case of the WTO, where there is merely an operating budget of the organization, and no quasi-independent funds or buffer stocks, there is not a sufficient financial interest to justify the conclusion of the agreement jointly by the Member States. This may be the position under Community law, but at the international level, i.e., in the WTO itself, third states preferred a situation where the Member States would continue to pay into the WTO budget rather than the Community. Since contributions are trade-weighted in the WTO, the sum of the individual contributions of the Member States is higher than the contribution of the Community, which would be based on its trade with third States only and not include the trade between Member States. This is an interesting example of a more wide-spread phenomenon, namely that so-called 'international realities' may stand in the way of the normal respect for Community law as interpreted by the Court.
145. See note 133 *supra* and accompanying text.
146. One wonders why such a situation of *ultra vires* could not have been solved through the existing procedure of an Opinion under Art. 300(6) EC.

provisions would be a kind of special procedure replacing Article 300(6). If not, all trade agreements in the sectors mentioned would be mixed, as would be all broader trade agreements containing clauses on these sectors, even without the danger of illicit harmonization being present.[147]

One thing is clear, Article 133, as rewritten at Nice, is not exactly clearly drafted. Viewed from this perspective, it is to be welcomed that the Treaty of Lisbon, taking over the text from the Constitutional Treaty, arrives at a much simpler configuration of powers between the Union and the Member States.

3.1.3   Procedure in the Exercise of the Commercial Policy Competence

Since the new version of Article 300 EC prescribes a general procedure for the exercise of external competence which is largely inspired by the procedure under Article 133 EC, the latter provision refers to the relevant provisions of Article 300 EC as well as containing a special provision on the manner in which commercial negotiations must be opened and conducted. Article 133(3) EC is therefore now virtually identical to Article 300(1) EC.

The importance of the special committee of the Council constituted on the basis of Article 133 EC in the conduct of commercial policy cannot be overestimated. This so-called Article 133 Committee meets monthly at the level of the national Directors General for commercial policy and weekly at the level of their deputies. Further, the Article 133 Committee meets at least weekly in Geneva, the seat of the WTO. It may also meet in various compositions anywhere in the world where the Commission is conducting negotiations on behalf of the Community. The negotiations are opened after the Council has authorized this, acting on the basis of a recommendation from the Commission itself. The Council may also issue directives for the negotiations; it is then the Article 133 Committee which ensures that these are adhered to by the Commission during the negotiations.

In very formal negotiation sessions, the Commission's representatives are accompanied by members of the Article 133 Committee as observers. In certain important informal negotiating situations, the Commission is accompanied by the representative of the Member State currently holding the Presidency of the Council, and thus also of the Article 133 Committee.[148] In all other cases, the Commission negotiates independently, but has to report regularly to the Article 133 Committee. One of the additions made by the Treaty of Nice to Article 133(3) EC explicitly states that 'the Commission shall report regularly to the special committee on the progress of negotiations.' The Article 133 Committee thus functions as a permanent sounding-board for the Commission, not only during negotiations, but also continually, in the conception and execution of the common

---

147. These questions of interpretation are still pending before the Court of Justice in Case C-13/07, *Commission v. Council* (Vietnam).

148. An example of this was the so-called 'Green Room' sessions of the Director-General of the GATT with leaders of delegations during the Uruguay Round.

commercial policy. While the Committee is an advisory committee having no power of decision of its own, it is evident that the Commission will attempt to achieve if not a consensus, at least a qualified majority support for its intended stance, since the latter is after all the majority by which the Council is to approve commercial agreements or adopt autonomous commercial policy measures.

Although, as was noted in section 2.5, above, Article 300(3) EC appears scarcely to accord powers to the European Parliament in the approval of commercial policy agreements, it cannot be excluded that such agreements may establish 'a specific institutional framework' or have 'important budgetary implications for the Community' and thus require the assent of the European Parliament. The Treaty of Lisbon will finally put an end to this situation and require that all trade agreements be approved by the European Parliament.[149]

If both the Community and the Member States are participating in the negotiations (for so-called mixed agreements) then there is a dual leadership of the Community delegation. The mixed delegation includes a representative of the Commission and of the Member State holding the Presidency of the Council, and includes one civil servant from each Member State. This style of delegation – also called the UNCTAD formula – is also used without the participation in the negotiations of separate delegations from each Member State. The Commission tends to be entrusted with the role of common spokesman.

At the close of negotiations, the draft agreement is initialled by the Commission in the name of the Community. Signature by the President of the Council and/or the responsible Commissioner will only occur after conclusion of the agreement has been approved by the Council on the basis of authorization thereto. If, though, the agreement contains a ratification clause then the agreement is signed on behalf of the Community (by the representative of the Commission, authorized by the Council) and then an approval procedure in the Council begins. Approval by the Council is then transmitted either to the other parties to the agreement or deposited with the depositary, in accordance with the provisions of the agreement.

3.2 PRINCIPLES AND DEVELOPMENT OF THE COMMON COMMERCIAL POLICY

3.2.1 The External Framework of the Common Commercial Policy: The WTO

In the arrangements for commercial policy relations by means of autonomous measures, for instance changes in external tariffs or measures concerning imports (autonomous commercial policy), or the conclusion of agreements with third countries (conventional commercial policy), the Community is bound by the applicable international rules. At the time the EEC was created – and this is still the case

---

149. Art. 207(2) TFEU read together with Art. 218(6)(a)(v) TFEU.

today – these rules were laid down in the General Agreement on Tariffs and Trade (GATT).[150]

In *International Fruit Company NV et al. v. Produktschap voor Groenten en Fruit*[151] the Court held that the Community as such was bound by the provisions of the GATT 'in so far as under the EEC Treaty the Community has assumed the powers previously exercised by the Member States in the area covered by the General Agreement'. The Court noted that this fact, resulting from the Community's succession as an international legal person to the rights and obligations of the Member States under the GATT, had been recognized by the other contracting parties to the GATT. This was perfectly correct. The establishment of the Community's Common Customs Tariff occurred largely in tandem with two rounds of tariff negotiations on the basis of the most-favoured-nation principle in the GATT: the Dillon Round (1961–1962) and the Kennedy Round (1964–1967). In these Rounds, the Commission acted as representative of the Community and thus strengthened the confidence of the GATT partners in the Community as such. In this manner the Community also clearly indicated that in the GATT framework it was inspired by the liberal bases of the common commercial policy.[152] In total, as a result of these Rounds, tariff reductions of some 40% were effected in the Common Customs Tariff. Thus in the GATT a situation arose in the 1970s and 1980s, in which the Member States remained contracting parties to the GATT but the Community became in effect also a contracting party which spoke for the Member States in nearly all areas covered by the GATT.[153]

In the framework of the Uruguay Round (1986–1993) the GATT was transformed into the World Trade Organization, which covers pretty well all aspects of international trade. In addition to matters which had been dealt with earlier in the so-called Codes of the Tokyo Round (1973–1979), and which were linked to trade in goods – such as anti-dumping, subsidies, customs valuation and technical barriers to trade[154] – the WTO Agreement also deals with trade in services (GATS) and commercial aspects of intellectual property rights (Trade-Related Intellectual Property Rights (TRIPs)).

As discussed in section 3.1.1. above, the Court of Justice, in its Opinion 1/94, took the view that trade in services and intellectual property rights is not entirely covered by the notion 'commercial policy'. As a result, the WTO Agreement was

---

150. General Agreement on Tariffs and Trade now contained in Annex IA to the WTO Agreement.
151. Joined Cases 21-24/72, *International Fruit Company NV et al. v. Produktschap voor Groenten en Fruit*, cf. paras 10–18. See also Kapteyn's annotation in (1973) SEW, 491.
152. Art. 131 EC.
153. This went so far that, when a Member State expressed an opinion which differed from that of the Community, the chairman of the GATT Council stated that only the representative of the EC could bind the Community to a GATT council decision; see P.J. Kuyper, 'Het GATT en het Volkenrecht', Mededelingen NVIR nr., 107, 26.
154. For the Tokyo Round of trade negotiations, see *The Tokyo Round of Multilateral Trade Negotiations*: Report by the Director-General of GATT, Geneva, GATT 1979 and J.H. Jackson, J.V. Louis and M. Matsushita, *Implementing the Tokyo Round* (Ann Arbor, 1984).

signed and ratified by both the Community and the Member States.[155] The WTO Agreement entered into force on 1 January 1995. The Community is thus a party to the WTO, alongside the Member States.[156]

At the heart of the GATT 1947, and thus also of the WTO Agreement, lie the core standards of the most-favoured nation principle and the national treatment principle. The former obliges the contracting parties to grant the advantages, of whatever kind, which they grant to any other country relating to the import or export of goods, and now also of services, to all other Members of the WTO. Thus, tariff concessions or agreed treatment of providers of services do not merely benefit the contracting party to which they are accorded, but all Members of the WTO. The national treatment principle requires each WTO Member to grant national treatment to its partners in the fields of internal taxation and legislation. In this manner, trade advantages which have been accorded cannot be in fact rendered nugatory through discriminatory national taxation or legislation. Under the national treatment clause in Article XVII GATS, this principle is conditional as far as services are concerned, i.e., national treatment is only accorded to undertakings in those sectors which a country has inscribed in its Schedule of Commitments.[157]

An extremely important exception as far as the Community is concerned is the exception in Article XXIV(4)-(8) GATT and Articles V and Va GATS, relating to the formation of customs unions and free trade areas which satisfy certain conditions. On the occasion of the establishment, and later of the expansions, of the Community, the Member States relied on the provision concerning customs unions as against their GATT partners. Thus they are not obliged to grant the advantages which they accord each other in the Community framework to all their GATT and now WTO partners. The Community itself has also relied on this exception – although it is questionable, now that the Community itself is formally a member of the WTO, whether it still needs to rely on that exception. Community legislation in the internal market field does not necessarily any longer need to be seen as a set of advantages which the Member States confer on each other, but merely as legislation of one member of the WTO.

Nevertheless, the exception for customs unions and free trade areas remains and will in the future remain important for the Community, as it has concluded many such agreements with its neighbouring countries and with developing countries. The EEA Agreement (establishing the EEA) establishes a free trade area in goods and a common market in other sectors of the economy; the agreement with Switzerland concerning trade in goods is a free trade agreement; the agreements concluded with countries of the former Yugoslavia also aim to create a free trade area between the Community and each individual country; only the older agreements with Turkey and Cyprus and the agreement with Malta provided for a customs union with the Community. It is not always clear, though, that these

---

155. Signed in Marrakesh 15 Apr. 1994.
156. See Art. XI:1 of the WTO Agreement.
157. See Art. XVII GATS.

agreements satisfy the requirements of Article XXIV GATT. First, the requirement that 'substantially all the trade' in products originating in the constituent territories must be free is often not met, as trade in agricultural products is to a great degree excluded in connection with the Common Agricultural Policy. Secondly, Article XXIV GATT requires that if the customs union or free trade area which is the aim of the agreement is not formed immediately, a clear plan or schedule must be set out in advance which will achieve this aim. In this respect, too, these agreements do not appear to meet the requirements entirely. Various GATT and WTO working groups have criticized these Community agreements, but so far they have not been clearly condemned. Thus these agreements have long operated in a legally uncertain situation as far as the GATT is concerned, since they could be declared, in part or as a whole, incompatible with GATT or other WTO agreements in so-called panel proceedings at any moment. An example is the customs union with Turkey, which forced that country to impose the same import restrictions on textiles as the EC still maintained under the WTO textiles agreements; these restrictions were wholly condemned by a WTO Panel, and that view was confirmed by a decision of the WTO Appellate Body.[158]

Another important exception to the core principles of the GATT is the Community's GSP. This concept, developed and accepted in the United Nations Conference on Trade and Development (UNCTAD), seeks to abolish tariffs for imports from developing countries, although certain ceilings may apply, in order to raise the export revenue of these countries, to promote their industrialization and to accelerate their economic growth. The GATT authorized such preferences – which are clearly in conflict with the most-favoured-nation principle – originally by means of a so-called 'waiver', that is an exemption from the obligations of the GATT under Article XXV: 5 GATT, and later by adopting a more general exception for differentiated and more favourable treatment of developing countries.[159] These tariff preferences were to be introduced autonomously by all industrialized countries, on a non-reciprocal basis and on the basis of non-discrimination, in relation to finished and semi-finished products from all developing countries. The Community was one of the first developed economies to make use of the possibility to introduce such a GSP, in 1971, even though it had already established association agreements with developing countries in Africa, the Caribbean and the Pacific (the ACP countries), granting them specific preferences, and these countries would not readily wish to see these preferences diminished. Presently, the preferences are granted to more than 140 developing countries, including certain Eastern European countries and countries of the former Soviet Union, as they are so-called economies in transition. Of all these countries, 50 so-called 'least-developed countries' according to the criteria of the UN profit from total freedom of customs duties for 'everything but arms'. This initiative by Commissioner Lamy was first enacted in 2001 and is now an integral part of the latest GSP

---

158. Case concerning Turkey-Textiles, WT/DS 34.
159. The so-called Enabling Clause; see BISD 26S, 203.

Regulation.[160] The Community, like the United States, has always sought to discriminate between different groups of countries profiting from the GSP, but the Community has normally followed the road of positive discrimination. The principle of such positive discrimination has been upheld by a WTO Panel and the Appellate Body in a case brought by India against the GSP regime of the Community that expired in 2004.[161] Next to 'everything but arms' for the least-developed countries, there is now a special incentive arrangement, which provides for additional preferences between the normal regime and the 'everything but arms' treatment for countries that have ratified a number of core human rights and labour conventions, as well as a number of international conventions in the field of environmental protection and good governance (mainly relating to combating illicit drugs and corruption).[162] The special incentive arrangement may be withdrawn when its conditions are no longer fulfilled. Such so-called 'temporary withdrawal' may be applied to other beneficiaries when they commit serious and systematic violations of human rights and core labour rights, export products of prison labour, show serious shortcomings in customs surveillance in respect of illicit drugs and in upholding international anti-money-laundering conventions. Even serious and systematic infringements of regional fisheries agreements of which the Community is a member may lead to such temporary withdrawal.[163] In addition the Commission may also apply a special safeguard procedure when imports of products under the GSP regime cause serious difficulties to Community producers of like products.[164] This new GSP regime of the Community so far has not been subjected to such criticism that a new challenge in the WTO seems likely.

Finally, the new dispute settlement system of the WTO should be mentioned as an important external element influencing the EC's commercial policy. The reports and decisions of the panels and the Appellate Body of the WTO are binding, and can be enforced insofar as the country which has 'won' the case may request an authorization to apply trade sanctions.[165]

It has already been pointed out above that this dispute settlement system leads one to wonder whether the free trade and customs union agreements of the Community are non-discriminatory and in accordance with the exception of Article XXIV GATT. Similarly, the dispute settlement system has contributed to reappraisal of the non-reciprocal character of the preferential system of cooperation

---

160. Reg. (EC) No. 980/2005, O.J. 2005, L 169, 1–43, Art. 12.
161. See Cases WT/DS 242 and 246. While condemning specific aspects of the GSP regime in favour of drugs-producing countries for their discriminatory nature, the Appellate Body accepted that different least-developed countries could be treated differently, if their situations were different. The new Community regime strives to conform to the Appellate Body report. Cf. J. Harrison, 'Incentives for development: The EC's GSP, India's WTO challenge and reform' (2005) CML Rev., 1663 et seq.
162. These conventions are listed in Annexes IIIA and IIIB of Reg. (EC) No. 980/2005.
163. For the full Commission procedure for temporary withdrawal, see Arts. 16–20 of Reg. (EC) No. 980/2005.
164. Art. 21 of Reg. (EC) No. 980/2005.
165. See Arts. 21 and 22 WTO Dispute Settlement Understanding.

with the ACP countries and the countries in the Mediterranean area. In a series of panel proceedings, concerning the EC banana policy and more recently also the sugar policy in favour of certain ACP countries, first the non-reciprocal character of these preferences was characterized as discriminatory vis-à-vis the developing countries that are not part of these systems of cooperation; such discrimination could not be considered permissible under certain GATT provisions. In addition, the specific authorization by the WTO of the retention of the non-reciprocal character of the cooperation with ACP countries turned out eventually to be insufficient. Although undoubtedly there were also political reasons for a re-examination of the non-reciprocal nature of ACP and Mediterranean cooperation, these panel proceedings certainly also had a contributory effect.[166]

3.2.2   The Completion of the Internal Market and the Common Commercial Policy

There is an inseparable link between the internal free movement of goods within the Community and the commercial policy of Member States towards third countries. After all: products from third countries are in free circulation within this market on the same footing as those originating from Member States as soon as the import formalities have been complied with and any customs duties and charges which were due in respect of them have been paid in one Member State.[167] Free movement of these goods as well as of those originating from Member States can be fully maintained only if the import as well as the export regime of Member States is broadly identical not only in the matter of customs tariffs (the Common Customs Tariff), but on other points as well. If there are clear differences, this results in a deflection of trade to the countries whose regime is least restrictive, with all the harmful economic consequences this entails. Since the completion of the internal market within the Community this is no longer acceptable.

How common must the common commercial policy be? This question must be distinguished from that of whether or not the Community has exclusive competence in this field – although in practice and theory such a distinction is not always made. The exclusivity which the Court has conferred on this competence since the end of the transitional period means that the Member States are unable to derive from their national law the competence to take national commercial policy measures. Community exclusivity, however, does not prevent Community law conferring such competence on them,[168] although it has been clear ever since the judgment in *Donckerwolcke*[169] that 'measures of commercial policy of a national

---

166.   WTO litigation may also have a powerful influence on internal policy and legislation of the EC. If important legislation is involved, such as in the Hormones and Biotech Products cases, the adaptation may prove particularly painful and difficult.

167.   Arts. 23 and 24 EC.

168.   Cf. on this P.J.G. Kapteyn, 'The Common Commercial Policy of the European Economic Community: Delimination of the Community's Powers and the European Court of Justice's Opinion of November 11, 1975' (1976) *Texas International Law Journal*, esp. 487–489.

169.   Case 41/76 *Criel, née Donckerwolcke*.

character are only permissible after the end of the transitional period by virtue of specific authorization by the Community.'[170] It can be deduced from this that Article 133 EC excludes the possibility of the Community limiting itself to establishing uniform principles and conferring on the Member States a *general* authorization to apply those principles in their autonomous or conventional commercial policies. The Community must itself adopt measures applying these principles, that is to say must itself take autonomous measures and enter into agreements with third countries and international organizations. Article 133 does not prevent the Community in well-defined cases and subject to well-defined conditions from granting the Member States powers of execution (decentralization) or differentiating these measures from Member State to Member State (differentiation).

Decentralization of the common commercial policy occurs regularly. In particular, all customs aspects of commercial policy are decentralized: the Community does not have its own customs service as such, but uses the customs authorities of the Member States in the implementation of many aspects of its commercial policy.[171] Autonomous commercial policy in particular, considered in the sections below, tends to be executed by the competent authorities of the Member States, which means not just the customs administrations but also the departments responsible for the grant of import and export authorizations (such as the Dutch Centrale Dienst In- en Uitvoer, or in Britain, HM Revenue & Customs). The common provisions that these administrations have to follow ensure that decentralization does not affect the unity of the commercial policy.[172]

Differentiation is a rather more difficult matter, as it means that per Member State a certain flexibility in the common commercial policy is possible. Such differentiation may be the result of remaining aspects of national commercial policies which could not immediately be completely removed on 1 January 1970, or on the day following accession to the Community or the Union, even if this was only because a number of national trade agreements remain in force or

---

170. Ibid., para. 32. However, see Case 174/84, *Bulk Oil (Zug) AG v. Sun International Limited and Sun Oil Trading Company*, where the Court extended the concept 'specific authorization' in a rather dubious way. The Court considered Art. 10 Reg. 2603/69 (establishing common rules for exports), to be such a special authorization, although that provision merely provides that the principle of freedom of export does not, for the time being, apply to certain products, including oil (para. 32). Cf. J.J. Feenstra, annotation in (1987) SEW, 145 et seq., and by E.L.M. Völker, in (1987) CML Rev., 99–109.

171. In comparative constitutional law, this is called executive federalism. It is the form of federalism prevailing in Germany, for instance, in contrast to US federalism, where there is a 'federal layer' in the court system, the police and other agencies, which is specifically charged with enforcing federal law.

172. In practice, that is of course not always the case. For instance, a difference of opinion on the nomenclature of certain computer equipment between the English and Irish customs authorities and the other customs authorities in the EC led to a dispute in the WTO with the USA. The fact that the USA originally started these dispute proceedings against the Member States in question rather than the Community demonstrates that third states have difficulty with the distinction between decentralization and competence in the area of commercial policy, see DS 62, 67 and 68 *EC-Computer Equipment*.

national trade restrictions continue to remain. As has been noted above, a specific authorization from the Community is necessary for such differentiation. Since the completion of the internal market and the conclusion of the Uruguay Round of trade negotiations, there is scarcely any reason to give such a specific authorization for quantitative restrictions per Member State. As far as conventional commercial policy is concerned, there are a small number of decisions addressed to the Member States which permit them to maintain national trade agreements and to conclude national cooperation agreements, provided that these satisfy certain conditions. These are discussed below.

It may thus be seen that in the present situation, after the completion of the internal market, it is not entirely excluded that disparities between the Member States in the field of commercial policy continue to exist. That is the reason why Article 134 (ex 115) EC has still not been removed from the EC Treaty. That provision enables the Commission, if there are such disparities in existence which lead to economic difficulties, to make recommendations 'as to the methods for the requisite cooperation between Member States' or to authorize Member States to take the necessary protective measures. When the Community still had effective internal frontiers, these were usually restrictions on the free transit of goods from third countries placed in free circulation in a Member State. Given that systematic border controls on the movement of goods within the Community have now been abolished, the Commission can do little else than authorize a Member State still to refuse goods having a certain origin when they carry out internal fiscal or other controls.[173] Since the coming into force of the Treaty of Maastricht, this provision has effectively become redundant.

Despite what has been briefly set out above, the Court's case law confirms that the degree of centralization and uniformity of the common commercial policy is completely left to the discretion of the Council. As cited above in section 3.1.2., in Opinion 1/75 *OECD Understanding on a Local Cost Standard for Export Credits*,[174] the Court indicated that the common commercial policy was conceived in Article 133 'in the context of the operation of the Common Market, for the defence of the common interests of the Community within which the particular interests of the Member States must endeavour to adapt to each other.' This means *inter alia* that the promotion of national undertakings on export markets through excessive export credits is not permitted, and that strict uniformity in that field must be maintained. Similarly, the Court has held that the definition of the uniform principles of the common commercial policy involves the elimination of national disparities, whether in the field of taxation or of commerce, affecting trade with third countries.[175] Thus, in trade with third countries the Member States may not impose duties having equivalent effect to tariffs on the basis of their national legislation.[176]

---

173.   Relevant decisions which are only directed to one Member State are usually not published, but these days do contain a prohibition on checks at borders.
174.   Opinion 1/75, *Local Cost Standard*, cf. part B.2.
175.   In Joined Cases 37 & 38/73, *Sociaal Fonds voor de Diamantarbeiders*.
176.   Case C-125/94, *Aprile Srl, in liquidation, v. Amministrazione delle Finanze dello Stato*.

The next step is then that distortions of competition caused by ordinary market participants are also combated in international trade.

If the functioning of the common market is indeed decisive for the common commercial policy, then the question arises once more – both before and, even more forcefully, after the completion of the internal market – of the scope of the latter. After all, a common market, and also an internal market, embrace more than merely a customs union, and if they are decisive for the commercial policy of the Community, then this commercial policy must extend further than only the external aspects of movement of goods, and should embrace the external aspects of all facets of the common market, albeit that the Treaty of Maastricht has introduced specific provisions dealing with the external aspects of capital movements and of monetary policy. As was noted in section 3.1.1 above, the Court was unwilling to go so far in Opinion 1/94 *WTO - GATS and TRIPS*.

The easiest category to visualize has always been the external aspects of the customs union, as the customs union has a naturally uniform external barrier: the Common Customs Tariff. This merely had to be complemented by uniform quantitative barriers and common commercial policy instruments. Most other aspects of the internal market lack such an obvious uniform external barrier. Of these other aspects, the free movement of persons has an obvious external barrier in theory: the external frontier of the Community, where all control of persons should take place according to uniform principles. For a limited number of countries in the Community, this was achieved by the so-called Schengen Convention.[177] The arrangements made under the Schengen Convention – the so-called Schengen 'acquis' – were incorporated into Community and Union law by the Treaty of Amsterdam, and it is clear that in the field of free movement of persons a set of uniform principles and rules for treatment of aliens at the external border of the Schengen area is evolving.[178]

As far as the external aspects of freedom of establishment within the Community is concerned, there has always been the so-called 'gap' in Article 48 EC: each Member State could independently determine which companies were established in accordance with its own law, even if they were subsidiaries of non-Community undertakings. Thus the question whether undertakings linked to third countries may benefit from the freedom of establishment was and indeed still is a question of the national law of the individual Member States.[179] There is

---

177. Schengen Convention, Trb. 1985, nr. 102, and the Implementing Agreement, Trb. 1990, nr. 145.

178. See P.J. Kuijper, 'Some Legal Problems Associated with the Communitarization of Policy on Visas, Asylum and Immigration under the Amsterdam Treaty and Incorporation of the Schengen acquis' (2000) CML Rev., 345–366; id., 'De communautarisering van visa-, asiel-en immigratiepolitiek krachtens het Verdrag van Amsterdam en de incorporatie van het Schengen-acquis' (1999) SEW, 434–442. See *supra* Ch. VIII section 4.2.

179. In the GATS, the Community has tried – *inter alia* by means of the definition of the concept 'legal person from another Member State' – to ensure acceptance of certain criteria from the liberalization programme of 1961, by linking to it the requirement that there must be 'substantive business operations' on the territory of that WTO member; see Art. XXVIII(m) GATS.

virtually no Community law on the right of establishment for nationals of third countries. In relation to international trade in services, where the external barriers are in part based on those in the two last-mentioned areas – establishment of companies and access for personal providers of services – it is even more difficult to draw a clear external border. A first step in this direction was taken with the introduction of reciprocity clauses in the Second Banking Directive and two insurance directives:[180] but these were 'negotiated into non-existence' in the framework of the WTO negotiations on financial services. So far, commercial policy in the services sector has not got any further than these examples of autonomous measures, although a similar reciprocity provision was included in Directive 93/38 on procurement procedures in the field of utilities.[181] Autonomous commercial policy in the field of services and establishment is thus, clearly, still in its infancy, and for that reason the main emphasis in the following discussion is placed on commercial policy measures governing trade in goods.

3.3   COMMERCIAL POLICY ARRANGEMENTS

3.3.1   Autonomous Commercial Policy; Regulation of Imports and Exports

As a result of the completion of the single internal market within the Community on 1 January 1993, and as a result of the negotiations in the Uruguay Round, the Community's import regime has been considerably simplified. The drastic changes in Central and Eastern Europe, as a result of which a great number of countries abandoned the communist planned economy as model, has contributed to a more liberal regime for imports into the Community. In principle, imports into the Community are wholly free from quantitative restrictions. Whereas in the 1980s Community legislation still permitted numerous Member States to restrict the quantity of various imports, the general import regime for industrial products as a whole no longer contains quantitative restrictions.[182] Even for the few countries which still have not introduced a complete market economy, there are hardly any restrictions: only in the case of China was, until recently, the import of certain sensitive products permanently subject to quotas or placed under supervision.[183] This is, of course, bound to change since China has joined the WTO.[184] Similarly, in the textile sector the Community has gone from far-reaching quantitative restrictions to liberalization. In the context of the so-called Multi-Fibre Textile

---

180. Dir. 89/646/EEC, O.J. 1989, L 386; Dir. 90/618/EEC and Dir. 90/619/EEC, O.J. 1990, L 330/44, 50.
181. See Art. 36 of this directive, O.J. 1993, L 199/84. This, too, is primarily a negotiating instrument in the framework of the WTO Agreement on Government Procurement.
182. See Art. 1(2) Reg. 3285/94, O.J. 1994, L 349/53. Cf. Annexe I of Reg. 288/82, O.J. 1982, L 35/1.
183. See Annexes II and III Reg. 519/94, O.J. 1994, L 67/89.
184. See the amendment of Reg. 519/94, proposed by the Commission, including the special safeguard clause for China, COM(2003)24 final.

Arrangement, which was concluded in the framework of the GATT, the Community concluded a large number of bilateral agreements.[185] Pursuant to the WTO Agreement on Textiles and Clothing (ATC), these restrictions were gradually abolished in three stages, so that as of 1 January 2005 the textiles sector was entirely subject to the normal WTO rules – in particular the prohibition on quantitative restrictions contained in Article XI of the GATT. To the extent to which such restrictions were maintained in relation to market economy countries, they were suspended until the goods covered by the Multi-Fibre Arrangement were integrated into the normal GATT system: obviously these quotas were partly symbolic, and were only maintained as a negotiating matter until the date of integration, 1 January 2005.[186] Moreover, only these restrictions not covered by the ATC could still be regarded as being in fact a coordinated system of national protection measures;[187] for the rest, such quantitative restrictions as remain are fixed at Community level, which represents an important step forward.[188]

Long before this uniformization of external policy in relation to quantitative restrictions took place, the Common Customs Tariff was established, much earlier than envisaged in the EEC Treaty, on 1 July 1968. Furthermore, harmonized or common rules have been adopted in the field of customs legislation, and the myriad instruments were codified in the Community Customs Code,[189] in parallel with the completion of the Community's internal market.

The Community's export regime has long been based on the principle that exports to third countries are unrestricted. This was already ensured in 1969, in Regulation 2603/69.[190] The exception, allowing Member States to maintain unilateral export restrictions for a small number of products, including petroleum, lapsed in 1991.[191]

However, the common rules on exports do contain a number of exceptions which are also to be found in Article XX GATT. First, there is the exception on the ground of a 'critical shortage' of certain products in the Community: in such cases

185. See on the Multi-fibre Agreement, N. Blokker, *International Regulation of World Trade in Textiles* (Dordrecht, 1989). For the Community textile agreements, see O.J. 1992, L 410; later amendments in O.J. 1994, L 110.
186. See Reg. 517/94, O.J. 1994, L 67/1.
187. See C.W.A. Timmermans, 'Community Commercial Policy on Textiles: A Legal Imbroglio', in E.L.M. Völker (ed.), *Protectionism and the European Community* (Deventer, 1987), 125–145.
188. For the Community rules for import of certain textile products from third countries, see Reg. 3030/93, frequently amended. A consolidated version may be found on <http://ec.europa.eu/trade/issues/sectoral/industry/textile/legis/index_en.htm>. It is frankly amazing that the legislation on the import of textile products is still based on old regulations dating back to the early 1990s; this seems contrary to the rules on codification and recasting adopted in the 'Better Regulation' programme of the Commission.
189. See *supra* Ch. VIII, section 2.7.
190. O.J. 1969, L 324. As to the export of dual-use goods, see section 3.3.5 *infra*.
191. Reg. 3918/91, O.J. 1991, L 372/31. The Member States retain only the limited possibility to take measures restricting exports in the framework of the 'sharing system' of the International Energy Agency.

quantitative restrictions may be introduced. At the moment no use is made of this provision, which is an exception that has to be invoked at the Community level. There are also exceptions which run parallel not only to Article XX GATT but also to Articles 30 and 297 EC, in that they may be unilaterally invoked by the Member States. The common export regime and also the various common regimes for imports contain a national safeguard measures clause which permits each of the Member States to apply quantitative restrictions or supervisory measures justified on the grounds of public policy, public morality, public security; the health and life of humans, animals and plants; the protection of national treasures possessing artistic, historic or archaeological value; or the protection of industrial and commercial property. Furthermore, Member States may also impose restrictions on imports or exports in connection with special formalities which are introduced, in conformity with the EC Treaty, on the ground of international agreements.[192] This latter category embraces in particular matters such as trade restrictions applying to certain endangered species and hazardous waste.

It is clear that the general regulations on the import and export regimes play only a supplementary role as far as imports and exports of agricultural products are concerned. These are governed in the first instance by the relevant provisions of the rules for the common organization of agricultural markets.[193] The rules for processed agricultural products also establish a special regime for those products. For both types of product this system has been based on a so-called Community preference for products in the common market, the subsidized export of Community surpluses, and specific protective measures against imports from third countries, as long as certain conditions are fulfilled.[194]

In relation to the manner in which the Member States promote exports to third countries relatively little has been done in the way of introducing uniform principles in the sense of Article 133 EC. Pure *export promotion*, in the sense of propaganda for national products is probably still permissible for the Member States.[195] But once propaganda for a Member State's own products develops into the provision of substantive advantages, the realm of distortion of competition between Community undertakings is reached and, in accordance with Article 132 EC, the national aid measures for exports to third countries[196] should be harmonized. In addition, it cannot be excluded that the competitive relationships within the Community are distorted by national aids to exports, and thus Article 87 EC

---

192. See e.g., Art. 24 Reg. 3285/94, O.J. 1994, L 349/53.
193. See Art. 25 Reg. 3285/94, O.J. 1994, L 349/53. As of 1 Jan. 2008, Reg. No. 1234/2007 replaced previous individual common organizations of the market by one horizontal regulation, O.J. 2007, L 299/1; see in particular Part III, Trade with Third Countries.
194. See Ch. XII sections 2.1 and 2.3 *supra.*
195. In fact, in the USA – where the competence in matters of foreign trade belongs to the federation – the states are also empowered to engage in this kind of export promotion activity. States such as Georgia and Michigan etc. even have overseas offices for this.
196. The tying of bilateral (development) aid to purchases in the donor country can come within this, but a Commission initiative to come to an 'unbundling' of help at Community level was not dealt with by the Council, cf. Doc. SEC(91)2273.

may be brought into play.[197] Up to now, there has been pretty well no such harmonization.[198] Myriad proposals from the Commission have been comprehensively buried by the Council. In the closely related field of export credit insurance,[199] credit guarantees and financial credits, a group of officials is entrusted with the coordination of Member States' policies in these matters and an information and consultation procedure is prescribed. The major agreements in this area have been achieved in the framework of the Organization for Economic Cooperation and Development (OECD), and are usually then taken over by the EC. Thus, the Council adopted by a decision on 4 April 1978 on behalf of the Community the OECD consensus called the Arrangement on Guidelines for Officially Supported Export Credits. The adoption of these Guidelines by the Community was on the basis of the Community's exclusive competence recognized by the Court's Opinion 1/75.[200] The OECD regularly updates this arrangement and has expanded it with special annexes on officially supported export credits for ships, for civil aircraft, and for nuclear power plants. The Community never 'concludes' these agreements, but has developed the interesting method of adopting a decision addressed to the Member States making the Guidelines, which formally are not binding, obligatory for them under Community law.[201]

Financial instruments relating to the development of trade with particular countries or territories remain in the hands of the Member States. This can only tally with the Community's exclusive competence in the field of export policy as long as the rules governing the use of such instruments provide for 'a strict uniformity of credit conditions granted to undertakings in the Community whatever their nationality' as required by the Court in Opinion 1/75.[202] After a failed attempt in 1970, which resulted in directives which never entered into force, a first step in this direction has been taken by the adoption of a directive on the harmonization of the most important provisions concerning export credit insurance for transactions with medium and long-term cover.[203]

---

197. Case C-142/87, *Belgium v. Commission*.
198. The most recent legislative special 'discipline' for state aids in shipbuilding was laid down in Council Reg. No 1540/98, establishing new rules on aid to shipbuilding, O.J. 1998, L 202/1. After the expiry of that legislation on 31 Dec. 2003, the matter was regulated by a soft law Commission communication 'Framework on State Aid to Ships', O.J. 2003, C 317/11.
199. These instruments may also come under Arts. 87 and 88 EC (ex 92 and 93), see Case C-63/89, *Les Assurances du Crédit SA and Compagnie Belge d'Assurance Crédit SA v. Council and Commission*.
200. Opinion 1/75, *Local Cost Standard*.
201. The latest such decisions in force are Dec. 2001/76 and 2001/77, O.J. 2001, L 32/1 et seq. and Dec. 2002/634, O.J. 2002, L 206/16 et seq. The Commission has filed a proposal with the Council for the adoption of a new Decision that should make the December 2005 version of the OECD Arrangement binding on the Member States, and which is still pending before the Council, while in the meantime the OECD has already agreed on yet a newer version.
202. See Opinion 1/75, *Local Cost Standard*.
203. Dir. 98/29/EC, O.J. 1998, L 148/22. For the earlier, failed, attempts of 1970, see the previous editions of this book, 785 of the Dutch 5th edition, 1299–1300 of the English 3rd edition.

3.3.2   Autonomous Commercial Policy: Safeguard Measures

The basic Regulation on the common regime for imports[204] provides for the possibility of keeping a weather eye on the import of industrial products – which has been liberalized within the Community framework. First, there are provisions on a Community information and consultation procedure, which forms the first step towards the adoption of surveillance or safeguard measures. In the context of this procedure the Member States may provide information to the Commission and request that such measures be adopted. Such a request is discussed in the Advisory Committee, which consists of representatives of the Member States, and is chaired by a representative of the Commission. If the discussion in the committee gives cause, and if the Commission is of opinion that there is sufficient evidence, a Community investigation procedure may be initiated. The Commission is charged with undertaking this investigation, and is bound to follow the rules laid down in Regulation 3285/94. These rules guarantee a certain transparency of the investigation and permit the Commission to gather information and to undertake verification inspections on the premises of the parties concerned. Interested parties (primarily exporters, importers and producers) may have access to the information collected and can be heard by the Commission. The investigation should be aimed at the importation of the products concerned, particularly looking at the quantities imported (the circumstances under which, and the prices at which goods are imported) and any damage which there may be for Community industry. Within nine months at the most from the opening of the investigation, the Commission has to decide whether Community surveillance measures or safeguard measures should be adopted, or whether the file should be closed without further action. Only in exceptional cases may this deadline be extended, and then by up to two months at the most.[205]

The measures which the Commission may decide to adopt may take one of two forms: Community retrospective surveillance or Community prior surveillance. The latter form of supervisory measures is clearly more restrictive, requiring the presentation of an import document in order to place the goods in free circulation within a Member State, even though the document is to be endorsed free of charge and within five days of request by the importer. In certain cases the Commission may decide to impose regional surveillance measures, which are limited to one or two regions (often Member States) of the Community. The Commission adopts Community and regional surveillance measures according to a special procedure for safeguard measures, laid down in the so-called Comitology decision.[206] This procedure enables a Member State to bring a Commission decision before the Council, which may confirm, amend or revoke the decision, acting by a qualified

---

204. Reg. 3285/94, O.J. 1994, L 349/53.
205. See Title III Reg. 3285/94, ibid. The conditions on which – and the methods whereby – safeguard measures may be taken are based on the provisions of the WTO Agreement on Safeguards, see recitals 3 and 4 of the preamble of the regulation.
206. See Title IV Reg. 3285/94, ibid., esp. Art. 11(2) read with Art. 16(7) and (8) and Art. 6 Decision 1999/468/EC, O.J. 1999, L 184/2, as amended. See Ch. 5 section 4.2 on comitology in general.

majority. If the Council takes no decision within three months of the matter being laid before it, the Commission's decision is deemed to be revoked. Such surveillance measures may only be adopted if the developments on the market for a product originating in a third country cause or threaten to cause serious injury to Community producers of like or directly competing products *and* if the interests of the Community require such action to be taken. This last condition permits the Commission a certain policy discretion.

Safeguard measures may be adopted by the Commission for protection of the interests of the Community if a product is imported into the Community in such increased quantities and/or[207] under such conditions that Community producers of like or directly competing products are serious injured or if such serious injury threatens to occur. Such measures are adopted by the Commission according to the safeguard measures procedure outlined above, and may be of two types:

(i) The period of validity of import documents may be limited after the entry into force of a prior Community surveillance measure.

(ii) The import rules for the product in question may be altered by making its release for free circulation conditional on production of an import authorization, the granting of which is governed by such provisions and subject to such limits as the Commission lays down.

The measures may be of a Community or regional nature. In addition, the Council may, on a proposal from the Commission, decide by a qualified majority to adopt appropriate safeguard measures and measures to allow the exercise of international rights (such as the right of retaliation flowing from certain WTO procedures) or the fulfilment of international obligations of the Community or its Member States, particularly those relating to trade in commodities.[208]

In the regulation on common rules for imports from state trading countries,[209] the conditions for instituting surveillance measures and for the application of safeguard measures are less stringently formulated. This is due to the fact, *inter alia*, that the countries to which that regulation applies are not yet members of the WTO.[210] Community surveillance may be instituted simply whenever the interests

---

207. The text of Art. 16(1) Reg. 3285/94, O.J. 1994, L 349/53, is to a large extent taken from Art. XIX GATT; this makes both conditions mandatory; see also Art. 16(2) of the regulation. Case law of the WTO has in the meantime put renewed emphasis on the unforeseen circumstances in which the increase in imports takes place under Art. XIX GATT, see DS 98 Korea-Dairy. An amendment of the regulation seems necessary.

208. Art. 17 and 23 Reg. 3285/94, O.J. 1994, L 349/53.

209. Council Reg. (EC) No. 519/94 of 7 Mar. 1994 on common rules for imports from certain third countries and repealing Regulations (EEC) Nos. 1765/82, 1766/82 and 3420/83, O.J. 1994, L 67/89.

210. At present Russia and many states of the former Soviet Union are not yet WTO Members, but many of them are not far from becoming so; in that case, a safeguard clause conforming to GATT will also apply for these countries, unless a temporary special safeguard clause is negotiated in their accession protocol to GATT or WTO – as was previously the case for certain East European countries, and now for China. As a consequence there is a special regulation on a transitional product-specific safeguard mechanism for China, Reg. (EC) No. 427/2003, O.J. 2003, L 65/1.

of the Community so require.[211] The Commission may institute such Community or regional surveillance entirely independently, and, if necessary, may strengthen it by restricting the period of validity of import documents or subjecting their endorsement to certain conditions.[212] In the conditions for the adoption of safeguard measures there is a clear choice between importation under such conditions *or* in such increased quantities that the adoption of such measures is justified. The Commission is entitled to make release of the products concerned for free circulation subject to import authorizations, under such conditions and subject to such limits as it may determine, again under the scheme applicable to safeguard measures set out in accordance with the Comitology decision mentioned above. The Council may in such circumstances adopt 'appropriate' measures by qualified majority, on a proposal from the Commission. Regional surveillance or safeguard measures are possible under this regulation as well.[213]

In the framework of the common rules for imports of textile products, in spite of the integration of textile products into the WTO[214] surveillance is pretty well permanent. The Member States have to provide the Commission with monthly reports of the quantities and origin of imports of textiles covered by the regulation, and with annual information about the export of textile products.[215] In this manner the Commission can evaluate at any given moment whether a Community investigation procedure should be initiated; a Member State may also request that this occur. Such a procedure runs in a broadly similar manner to that provided for in the general rules on imports.[216]

In this investigation and in the adoption of any measures which may follow, the Commission is assisted by a committee. The investigation proceedings may be terminated without any measures, or may lead to Community surveillance or safeguard measures. Again, supervision may be prior or retrospective in nature. The safeguard measures consist of the introduction of an authorization system, under which authorizations are granted under the conditions prescribed by the Commission and within the limits it establishes. In certain cases urgent measures or regional safeguards are possible. Again, measures against textile imports from non-market economy countries may be adopted under less stringent conditions than those applicable to imports from market economy countries. The committee procedures used in taking the surveillance or safeguard measures may be of a management nature for the surveillance measures, but usually the special safeguards procedure foreseen in the Comitology decision is used.[217]

As has been noted above, the lion's share of import restrictions of textile products now take the form of Community (as opposed to national) measures;

211. Art. 9 Reg. 519/94, O.J. 1994, L 67/89.
212. Art. 11 Reg. 519/94, ibid.
213. See Arts. 15, 16 and 17 Reg. 519/94, ibid.
214. Again it is mainly Russia and many states of the former USSR which are still outside the WTO.
215. Art. 6 Reg. 517/94, O.J. 1994, L 67/1.
216. Compare Arts. 8–10 Reg. 517/94 with Arts. 5–10 Reg. 3285/94.
217. See *supra* note 206.

the management of these import restrictions is now also regulated at Community level. Thus the Member States inform the Commission of the quantities for which they have received applications for import authorizations; the authorizations are granted centrally by the Commission on a first-come, first-served basis; an advanced data processing system has been set up in the Community for this purpose. The authorizations granted have a limited period of validity, and if they are not used within that period they must be returned to the Member State concerned, which returns them to the pool of available central authorizations. Thus, after the Court on grounds of principle had found against the division of quotas among Member States,[218] even in one of the most sensitive sectors of the economy, for which the Court had originally been prepared to countenance an exception, it has proved possible to introduce a real Community system of quota management.

More generally, the management of quantitative quotas is governed by Regulation 520/94, of 7 March 1994.[219] In addition to the first-come, first-served technique, two other methods of quota management are prescribed in this regulation, the method chosen depending on the circumstances. The method of allocation of quotas according to traditional trading patterns is used for quotas imposed as a result of safeguard measures adopted against imports from other WTO members. Within the GATT, it had become customary that in such cases quotas would be established on the basis of the average trading patterns in the last three representative years, a custom which has been codified in the new WTO Agreement on Safeguards.[220] The final method is division in relation to the quantities requested. This method is primarily applied in cases in which the quota will probably be quickly exhausted. In order to ensure that the quotas are in fact used up as much as possible, Regulation 520/94 permits a combination of methods to be used (limited period of validity of authorizations; return of unused authorizations; and return to the Community pool) so that unused authorizations may be reissued by the Commission.

Despite the increased communitarization of the surveillance and safeguards regimes in the Community, it remains possible to adopt regional measures, that is to say measures limited to one Member State. In some cases this can probably be economically justified,[221] and the Community was able to negotiate this right under the WTO Agreement on Safeguards.[222] Nevertheless, one may wonder whether this right makes sense and whether in practice it will now be very much used, given that it is nowadays so much more difficult to apply Article 134 EC – in

---

218. See Case 51/87, *Commission v. Council.*
219. O.J. 1994, L 66/1.
220. Cf. Arts. 6–11 Reg. 520/94 with Art. 5 of the so-called Agreement on Safeguards of the WTO. In addition, the regulation takes account of individual traditional importers and not just traditional trade flows in general.
221. For instance, the case described in the anti-dumping regulation of a market which is geographically quite separated, because goods cannot be transported over a long distance, Art. 4(1)(ii) Reg. 3283/94, O.J. 1994, L 349/1.
222. See footnote to Art. 2 Agreement on Safeguards.

the present circumstances, where the internal market truly functions as one whole, and the protected product is marketed within the internal market as a whole, such a measure can scarcely be adequate any longer.

It should be noted, finally, that unlike in the case of the commercial policy instruments which are discussed below, there is no provision in the current version of the basic regulations on imports for individuals or Community industry to complain and thus persuade the Commission to initiate proceedings, although they may be heard if they can demonstrate an interest in the matter. This is partly due to the fact that safeguards remain within the realm of 'fair trade' (as opposed to unfair trading practices), and that any complaint can best be left as a matter for a decision of the authorities, taking all elements into account. The anti-dumping and anti-subsidies measures discussed in the next section are designed to combat unfair trading practices, and in such circumstances the initiative in the form of a complaint is best left in the hands of the industry concerned.

3.3.3   Anti-dumping Duties and Countervailing Duties

Dumping and the use of subsidies are regarded as unfair trading practices because a company or a country does not, unlike in the case of safeguards, simply use its comparative advantage to export large quantities of products at low prices, but in fact artificially changes its comparative costs. In the case of subsidization this occurs through state subsidies; in the case of dumping this occurs because a company is prepared to export a product for a long period at a lower price than the sales price applicable on its domestic market, and sometimes even at a lower price than the cost price.[223] It will be evident that this is only possible if the products cannot flow back onto the company's domestic market, and that dumping assumes a certain division of markets, which in international trade is frequently present in the form of tariffs.[224]

In the framework of the so-called 'implementing package' of the Uruguay Round, two new regulations were adopted: an anti-dumping regulation (Regulation 3283/94, later replaced by Regulation 384/96)[225] and a regulation on protection against imports of subsidized goods from third countries (Regulation 3284/94, later replaced by Regulation 2026/97).[226] As is apparent from the preambles of the regulations, they are designed to give effect to the results of the Uruguay Round negotiations in the fields concerned. The obligations flowing from these

---

223. For a certain period of time, sales at prices below the costs of production, or below marginal cost, may be a legitimate market strategy. For this reason, the very basis of anti-dumping law is subject to criticism: see A. Deardorff, 'Economic Perspectives on Antidumping Law', in J.H. Jackson, E.A. Vermulst (eds), *Antidumping Law and Practice, A Comparative Study* (Ann Arbor, 1990), 23–39.
224. Within a common market like the EC, dumping is only possible during a transitional period. Cf. the old Art. 91 EC which was repealed by the Treaty of Amsterdam.
225. O.J. 1994, L 349/1 and O.J. 1996, L 56/1, respectively.
226. O.J. 1994, L 349/22 and O.J. 1997, L 288/1, respectively.

agreements lay down strict requirements with which Community action in both areas must comply.[227]

Under Article 1(1) of Regulation 384/96, anti-dumping duties 'may be applied to any dumped product whose release for free circulation in the Community causes injury'. The concepts of dumping and injury are thus the crucial concepts in the regulation. Under Article 1(2) of Regulation 384/96 a product is considered to have been dumped 'if its export price to the Community is less than a comparable price for the like product, in the ordinary course of trade, as established for the exporting country.' This is the so-called 'normal value' of the product, and is 'based on the prices paid or payable, in the ordinary course of trade, by independent customers in the exporting country', according to Article 2(1). The export price is the 'price actually paid or payable for the product when sold for export from the exporting country to the Community'.[228] The difference between the normal value and the export price is what is called the dumping margin.[229] The anti-dumping duty may not be higher than the dumping margin. In the Community – unlike the United States – the practice has developed of imposing anti-dumping duties that are lower than the dumping margin, but adequate to remove the injury to Community industry.[230] This brings us back to the other crucial concept in the Regulation: injury, which – according to Article 3 of the Regulation – means, material injury to the Community industry, or the threat of such injury, or even the material retardation of the establishment of such an industry. This involves both the volume and price of the dumped imports on the Community market, on the one hand, and the consequent impact on the relevant branch of the Community industry, on the other. In addition to the presence of dumping and injury, it is also required to establish that the imposition of anti-dumping duties is in the Community interest. The most recent version of the Regulation includes, in Article 21, extensive provisions on this score.

Anti-dumping law as set out above might appear fairly simple, but it is in reality extremely complex, as the establishment of the normal value and the export price is usually far from being a straightforward matter, particularly in the case of large multinationals. On their domestic markets they may distribute their products through subsidiaries rather than to independent buyers directly, and on their export markets this also often occurs. In non-market economy countries neither domestic prices nor costs are of much use. In these circumstances recourse is had to a constructed normal value, which is calculated on the basis of production costs plus a reasonable amount for selling, general and administrative costs and for

---

227. Thus Art. 13(10) Reg. 2423/88, the anti-evasion provision, was declared by a GATT panel to be in conflict with Art. III GATT, see EEC Regulation on imports of parts and components, BISD 37S, 132. See J. Willemen, 'De anti-ontduikingsverordening in de relatie EC-Japan' (1993) SEW, 187–214. A new anti-evasion provision is included in Art. 1 Reg. 384/96.
228. Art. 2(8) Reg. 384/96.
229. Art. 2(12) Reg. 384/96. The Commission's practice of calculating the dumping margin without taking account of the so-called positive dumping margin was recently condemned by a WTO panel and the Appellate Body, see WT/DS 141, EC-Bed Linen.
230. Art. 9(4) Reg. 384/96.

profits, or on the basis of export prices to an appropriate third country,[231] or else to a constructed export price calculated on the basis of the price at which the imported products are first resold to an independent buyer.[232] Furthermore, in order to achieve a valid comparison at the same level of trade between the normal value and the export price, adjustments are often necessary on account of discounts and rebates, indirect taxes, transport costs, and differences in physical characteristics of the products concerned between products sold on the domestic market and products sold to the Community market.[233] It will be apparent that in a comparison between two prices, of which frequently one and sometimes both are constructed, and in the calculation of which adjustments are so often necessary, the question may well arise as to just how far there is actually dumping, and how far the result of the investigation is in reality an artifice.

Both the old Agreement on Subsidies and Countervailing Duties concluded as a result of the Tokyo Round, and Regulation 2423/88 failed to include a definition of the concept of a subsidy. This led to considerable friction, particularly in relations between the Community and the United States. The current version of the Agreement on Subsidies and Countervailing Measures, concluded in the framework of the WTO, does however provide for such a definition, and embraces a large number of other improvements. For this reason, it was decided to adopt a separate Community regulation dealing with anti-subsidies measures, permitting countervailing duties to be imposed: Regulation 3284/94, later replaced by Regulation 2026/97, already mentioned above. Thus Articles 2 and 3 of the Regulation largely reflect the definition of a subsidy in the new Agreement, and the conditions under which a subsidy is or is not countervailable. A subsidy is deemed to exist whenever there is 'financial contribution by a government in the country of origin or export',[234] and a benefit is thereby conferred on the subsidized enterprise or body. Subsidies only lead to the imposition of countervailing duties if they are specific, i.e., where access to a subsidy is explicitly limited to certain enterprises and there is no general availability of subsidies according to objective and neutral criteria.[235] Article 3(4) of the Regulation provides that certain types of subsidies, such as those contingent upon export performance or on the use of domestic rather than imported goods, are deemed to be specific. On the other hand, certain specific subsidies are exempt from retaliation in the form of countervailing duties: subsidies for research and technological development up to certain levels, subsidies for regional development subject to stringent conditions, and

---

231.   Art. 2(3) Reg. 384/96. Since such constructed normal value may make it easier to find dumping, countries considered non-market economies strive to be omitted from that list, see e.g., Reg. No. 2117/2005 through which Ukraine was so omitted, O.J. 2005, L 340/17.
232.   Art. 2(9) Reg. 384/96.
233.   Art. 2(10) Reg. 384/96.
234.   This means not just obvious financial benefits, either by means of direct transfers of revenue or non-collection of taxes or levies, but also the provision of goods or services other than general infrastructure, or financial contributions through intermediaries or funding mechanisms; see Reg. 2026/97, Art. 2(1)(a)(i)-(iv).
235.   Art. 3(2) Reg. 2026/97.

certain environmental subsidies. These exceptions have, however, been dropped in the WTO Agreement on Subsidies and Countervailing Measures, because it proved impossible to reach agreement on the extension in time of the relevant clauses. Regulation 2026/97 also contains, in Article 4, detailed criteria as to the calculation of the amount of the countervailable subsidy, derived from the relevant WTO agreement.

The determination of injury, the definition of the concept of the Community industry affected and the procedures leading to the imposition of anti-dumping and countervailing duties are dealt with more or less identically in the two regulations.[236]

In order to establish the existence of material damage, factors will have to be taken into account such as whether there has been a significant increase in the import of dumped or subsidized products, significant price undercutting by these imports as compared with the price of a like product of the Community industry, and the influence of this sort of factor on the development of production, capacity utilization, inventories, sales, market share, productivity, return on investments, and profitability of the relevant branch of Community industry. Of course, a causal link must be demonstrated between the dumping or subsidies and the damage. Damage caused by other factors – such as the amount or prices of imports which are not being dumped or subsidized, or decrease in demand – which either separately or in combination also have negative effects on the industry, may not be attributed to the dumped or subsidized imports.

The term 'Community industry' refers to the Community producers of the like products as a whole, or a number of them whose collective output of the products constitutes a major proportion of the total Community production.

In the procedures potentially leading to the imposition of anti-dumping duties and countervailing duties, the Commission plays a central role – even though at many stages it is obliged to consult an advisory committee, consisting of representatives of each Member State with a representative of the Commission as its chairman.[237] Such consultation only leads to binding legal effects if the Commission proposes to close a proceeding and this proposal is the subject of consultation. If there are objections within the committee from one or more Member States to the proposal to close the proceeding, the Commission must forthwith submit to the Council a proposal that the proceeding be terminated. If within one month the Council, acting by a qualified majority, has not decided otherwise, the proceeding is deemed terminated.[238]

Anti-dumping or anti-subsidy proceedings may be opened *inter alia* on the basis of a complaint by an undertaking or an association of undertakings.[239] In this

---

236. Compare Arts. 3–21 of Reg. 384/96 with Arts. 8–30 of Reg. 2026/97.
237. Art. 15 Reg. 384/96.
238. Art. 9(2) Reg. 384/96.
239. Cf. for the following in particular M.C.E.J. Bronckers, B.H. ter Kuile and J. Steenbergen, 'Ondernemingen en handelspolitieke instrumenten' (1985) SEW, 599–672.

case the so-called sector or representative requirement applies:[240] the natural or legal person or association not having legal personality must be acting on behalf of a Community industry in the sense of the regulation, as set out above.

The complaint must be accompanied by sufficient evidence of the existence of dumping or subsidization and resulting injury. If after consultation it appears that there is sufficient evidence to justify initiating a proceeding, the Commission announces the initiation of proceedings in the *Official Journal*, and advises the exporters and importers which it knows to be concerned as well as representatives of the exporting country and the complaints.[241] The Commission commences the investigation at Community level and may request the Member States to carry out checks and inspections for it. Investigations may also be carried out in third countries, provided that the firms concerned give their consent and the government of the country concerned raises no objection.

Interested parties have the right to provide the Commission with information; to inspect, on written request, information which the Commission has collected, apart from internal documents and confidential information; to be heard (again, on written request); and on request to be given an opportunity to meet the other parties to the proceedings, and – to the extent that they will be concerned thereby – to be informed, at their request, of the most important acts and considerations on the basis of which the imposition of duties is considered. The obligation to respect the confidentiality of certain information[242] may not be interpreted in such a way that the rights which are designed to ensure that interested parties can make their views known are deprived of their substance. Thus the Commission ought to make every effort, as far as is compatible with the obligation not to disclose business secrets, to provide interested parties with information relevant to the defence of their interests.[243]

If the (provisional) investigation reveals the existence of dumping or subsidization, and of damages caused thereby, a provisional anti-dumping or countervailing duty is imposed by the Commission within nine months of the initiation of the proceedings.[244] These provisional measures may be imposed only for a period of six, or exceptionally nine, months. If further investigation confirms the existence of the required conditions, the Commission submits to the Council a proposal for a definitive anti-dumping or countervailing duty. The Council now decides by a negative simple majority.[245] There is however also the further

---

240. For criticism on the requirement of branch or representativeness in relation to the right of appeal and right to damages, see Bronckers et al., op. cit., 641 et seq.
241. Art. 5 Reg. 384/96.
242. Art. 19 Reg. 384/96, see also Art. 287 EC.
243. Case 264/82, *Timex Corporation v. Council and Commission.*
244. Art. 7 Reg. 384/96.
245. Art. 9(4) Reg. 384/96, as amended by Reg. (EC) No. 461/2004, O.J. 2004, L 77/12. This is a remarkable piece of Community law: not only does the procedure go further than the decision-making procedure of its legal basis (Art. 133 EC), as was the case previously, but it also goes further than the positive simple majority rule laid down in the Treaty (Art. 205 EC). This has been defended in the light of Case C-76/01, *Eurocoton*, in which it was decided that a non-

requirement that Community interests make a Community action necessary. In the balancing of interests, besides the interests of the complainant, of consumers and importers and the like, more general considerations of a commercial policy and external relations policy nature may play a part. The decision to impose duties thus clearly has a discretionary character and, more generally, on the basis of these regulations the Commission 'has a very wide discretion to decide, in terms of the interests of the Community, any measures needed to deal with the situation which it has established'.[246]

If it becomes apparent that protective measures are unnecessary or if the firms or governments causing the injury are prepared to enter into 'undertakings' acceptable to the Commission as a result of which the injury is eliminated, the proceedings are terminated.[247] The Commission informs the parties concerned and the termination is announced in appropriate form in the *Official Journal*, together with a summary of the relevant material facts and considerations.

Anti-dumping and countervailing duties are imposed by means of regulations. The case law shows that this does not prevent complainants from bringing an action before the Court.[248] These complainants sometimes allege that Community anti-dumping measures are incompatible with the WTO Anti-dumping Agreement (and previously the GATT Anti-dumping Code). The question then arises whether that Agreement is directly effective; it is a question which has long been the subject of debate, but which has been answered negatively by the Court in relation to all of the WTO Agreement and its annexes, including the Anti-dumping Agreement.[249] In one judgment, however, the Court was willing to examine the anti-dumping regulation in the light of the then GATT Anti-dumping Code, in the context of a plea of illegality under Article 241 EC, in view of the fact that the basic anti-dumping regulation stated explicitly that it was supposed to implement the WTO Anti-dumping Agreement.[250]

Every year, dozens of anti-dumping proceedings are initiated, mainly concerning imports from state trading countries, the United States and Japan and other Asian countries. In many instances definitive or provisional anti-dumping duties are imposed, or undertakings are accepted under which the injurious effects are removed or reduced. The length of a proceeding usually stays well

---

decision by the Council in respect of a proposed anti-dumping measure by the Commission, in view of the limited period of time within which the Council had to decide (15 months) had binding consequences for the complainants in an anti-dumping case and should, therefore, be reviewable in an action for annulment. The negative vote by simple majority had the intention to diminish this risk of non-decision and still respect the letter of Art. 205 EC ('The Council shall act by a majority of its Members').

246. Case 191/82, *EEC Seed Crushers' and Oil Processors' Federation (FEDIOL) v. Commission*, para. 26.
247. Art. 8 Reg. 384/96.
248. See on this, *supra*, Ch. VI, section 2.3.1.2 *in fine*.
249. Case C-149/96, *Portuguese Republic v. Council*.
250. See Case C-69/89, *Nakajima All Precision Co. Ltd v. Council* and Case C-76/00, *Petrotub and Republica v. Council*.

within the 'normal' period of one year from initiation, indicated by the Regulation,[251] with the exception of complex cases. The manner in which the right to start anti-dumping procedures has been exercised by the Community (and by the United States) has however become a matter of increasing controversy.[252] The application of these procedures could sometimes simply find no justification in the WTO Anti-dumping Agreement, as interpreted by the panels and the Appellate Body; both the Community and the United States have had their proverbial knuckles rapped on various occasions, and numerous WTO proceedings on anti-dumping duties and countervailing measures are still pending. Nevertheless, even the WTO Anti-dumping Agreement itself has not been immune from criticism.[253]

3.3.4   The Trade Barriers Regulation[254]

On 20 September 1984, the so-called new commercial policy instrument took effect; ten years later, this was amended and then replaced, in March and December 1994.[255] The immediate cause for the adoption of the regulation was the deterioration in international trade relations in the early 1980s, and in particular the unilateral measures adopted by the United States, on the basis of Section 301 of the Trade Act, against commercial practices which were considered unlawful or damaging to American trade. The new commercial policy instrument was to be the European answer to Section 301, i.e., an instrument with which the closed markets of other states could effectively be forced to open up.[256] This aim seems to have come closer with the amendments made in 1994, as a result of which the Trade Barriers Regulation (TBR) – as it became – was more clearly given the character of

---

251. Art. 11(5) Reg. 384/1996.
252. See for the practice, the annual reports on anti-dumping and anti-subsidy measures, prepared each year since 1984 by the Commission and the overviews by E. Vermulst and F. Graafsma published regularly in EJIL with the title 'Commercial Defence Actions and other International Trade Developments in the European Communities'.
253. See Panel and Appellate Body reports DS 132, Mexico-Corn Syrup, DS 141, EC-Bed Linen, DS 179, US-Stainless Steel (Korea) and DS 184, US-Hot Rolled Steel (Japan) and DS 217 and 234 US Continued Dumping and Subsidy Offset Act. For criticism of the WTO Anti-dumping Agreement, see: G. Horlick, 'How the GATT Became Protectionist' (1993) JWT, 5–17, and P. Waer, E. Vermulst, 'EC Antidumping Law and Practice after the Uruguay Round' (1994) JWT, 5–21.
254. Reg. 3286/94, O.J. 1994, L 349/71. See R. MacLean and B. Volpi, *EU Trade Barrier Regulation, Tackling Unfair Foreign Trade Practices* (Wight, 2000) and G. Zonnekeyn and J.C. Van Eeckhaute, 'De handelsbarrièreverordening en de vernieuwde markttoegangsstrategie van de EC' (1998) SEW, 80–91.
255. Reg. 2641/84 on the strengthening of the common commercial policy with regard in particular to protection against illicit commercial practices, O.J. 1984, L 252/1, amended by Reg. 522/94, O.J. 1994, L 66/10 and later replaced by Reg. 3286/94, O.J. 1994, L 349/71.
256. Although the instrument is indeed used as such, it owes its formulation a great deal to the EC's defensive trade instruments, such as anti-dumping; see on this M.I.B. Arnold, M.C.E.J. Bronckers, 'The EEC New Trade Policy Instruments, Some Comments on its Application' (1988) JWT, 19–51.

an instrument for enforcing the Community's rights according to the rules of international trade law, and in particular those of the WTO Agreement. The TBR is, for the time being, still based on Article 133 EC and thus only covers rights in the field of trade in goods and trade in direct cross-frontier services;[257] since the entry into force of the Treaty of Nice and its extension of the scope of trade policy so as to include trade in services and commercial aspects of intellectual property this is no longer in fact a problem.

The TBR is intended to permit the exercise of the above-mentioned rights of the Community, with two aims in mind a) to remove obstacles to trade that have an effect on the market of the Community, with a view to removing the material injury resulting therefrom; b) removing obstacles to trade that have an effect on the market of a third country, with a view to cancelling the adverse trade effects resulting therefrom.[258] Article 15 of the TBR provides that the regulation does not apply in cases where safeguard measures, anti-dumping duties or countervailing duties may be imposed, and that it is without prejudice to other measures which may be taken pursuant to Article 133 EC.

Obstacles to trade are defined as any trade practice adopted or maintained by a third country in respect of which international trade rules – that is to say the WTO Agreement or bilateral or multilateral treaties of the Community – establish a right of action; a right of action means a right to contest the breach of the rules directly, or a right to seek to eliminate the consequences of the measure.[259] The consequences of such obstacles to trade may be felt directly on the Community market[260] or indirectly through the effects of such measures felt by Community undertakings on the market in third countries.[261] The TBR adds a new dimension to the arsenal of the Community's commercial policy protective measures, which before had only been aimed at avoiding or limiting injury caused by importation into the Community. It enables the Community, *inter alia*, to combat illicit obstacles to Community exports in so far as these are to be imputed to states. The dispute settlement procedures of the appropriate trade agreements, particularly those of the WTO, must be respected.[262]

Proceedings may be initiated in one of three ways: a complaint may be submitted on behalf of a branch of Community industry, or on behalf of individual Community enterprises, or proceedings may be started at the request of a Member State.[263] In the first case, the complaint must concern a breach of the Community's rights under a) above; in the second case, the breach of rights under b). The latter is a change introduced in December 1994: it is reasonable that individual enterprises

---

257. See Opinion 1/94, WTO.
258. Art. 1 Reg. 3286/94. The concept 'adverse trade effects' comes from the WTO Agreement on Subsidies and Countervailing Measures, see Art. 5.
259. The last-mentioned is connected with the so-called 'non-violation' complaints in the framework of the GATT, see Art. XXIII(1) b.
260. Injury, Art. 2(3) Reg. 3286/94.
261. Adverse trade effects, Art. 2(4) Reg. 3286/94.
262. Art. 12(2) Reg. 3286/94.
263. Reg. 3286/94, Arts. 3, 4 and 6 respectively.

should be able to complain about obstacles to Community exports, since usually they are the ones who suffer from such obstacles, without a whole branch of industry or trade being affected. Moreover, in most third countries they are not able to rely on an application to the national courts, because usually the rules of the WTO or other trade agreements are not granted direct effect.[264] Finally, the Member States may ask the Commission to initiate an examination as to the breach of both categories of Community rights.

The Commission conducts the Community examination procedure, assisted by a committee. The latter is purely consultative as regards the initiation of the procedure: if after consultation it appears that an examination procedure is justified as a result of a complaint or referral under one of the three procedures outlined above, the Commission initiates the procedure. In essence the examination follows the same pattern as that for countervailing measures, since – as is the case with subsidies – the TBR concerns practices of third states.[265] Article 10 of the TBR explains in detail what elements must be examined in order to establish injury or adverse trade effects. The examination procedure is terminated or suspended, under Article 11 of the TBR, if the interests of the Community do not require any action to be taken, or if the third country adopts satisfactory measures or if negotiations with that country about a solution seem the most appropriate means. Such a decision is adopted by means of a committee procedure, during which any Member State may refer the Commission's decision to the Council for revision, but if within 30 days the Council is not able to take a decision, by qualified majority, revising the Commission's decision then the latter applies.[266] The same procedure applies to decisions relating to the initiation, conduct or termination of procedures if the Community decides to follow formal international consultation or dispute settlement procedures before resorting to any retaliatory measures.[267] Such retaliatory commercial policy measures, consisting of the suspension or revocation of trade concessions, the raising or introduction of customs duties or levies, or the imposition of quantitative restrictions, may, however, only be adopted under the normal procedure of Article 133 EC.[268]

From the one case in which a decision under the TBR was attacked before the Court of First Instance (CFI) – it concerned a Commission decision terminating a case without further action – one may conclude, on the one hand, that the Commission has a considerable discretion in fashioning its decisions under the TBR Regulation but, on the other hand, that the CFI is willing to go into painstaking

---

264. In Case 70/87, *Fédération de l'industrie de l'huilerie de la CEE (Fediol) v. Commission*, the Court indicated that it will interpret a measure which is based on an instrument that refers to the GATT provisions in the light of those provisions; that does not, though, amount to giving those provisions real direct effect.
265. Art. 8 Reg. 3286/94.
266. Arts. 13(1) and 14 of the TBR. This rule is no longer in accordance with Art. 6 of the new Comitology Decision (Decision 1999/468/EC), which provides that, if the Council cannot reach a decision, the decision of the Commission is deemed to be withdrawn.
267. Art. 13(2) and 14 Reg. 3286/94.
268. Art. 13(3) and 12(2) and (3) Reg. 3286/94.

detail in order to establish that this discretion has been properly used on the basis of all the facts and in respect of all the procedures.[269]

The original new commercial policy instrument of 1984 was not intensively used during its lifetime of about a decade, with some ten disputes being examined. In its new form as TBR, the instrument has been used more regularly. In 12 years (1995–2007) 25 cases were examined. In both forms, the instrument seems to be used mainly for its intended aim, i.e., removing obstacles to trade or unfair commercial practices in third countries. Virtually all the procedures led to an improvement in the situation of Community exporters. The most spectacular cases were undoubtedly those which led to a GATT or WTO panel, with varying success.[270] Some other cases led to a settlement, with positive consequences for the EC.[271]

3.3.5 Community Economic Sanctions

Since the early 1980s, developments have been set in course in the Community which led the Community to adopt, or one should rather say implement, economic sanctions against third countries. This practice was initially based on a combination of a decision taken in the framework of European Political Cooperation and a regulation based on the commercial policy competence of the Community.[272] After gradual codification in the Treaties of Maastricht and Amsterdam, a special Article 301 is now included in the EC Treaty, which expressly provides that where a common position or a joint action adopted under the CFSP provides for an action by the Community to interrupt or to reduce economic relations with one or more third countries, the Council takes the necessary urgent measures; the Council then acts by a qualified majority on a proposal from the Commission. Article 60(1) EC is the corresponding provision for measures in the area of international payments and capital movements. The fact that economic sanctions are initiated by a decision under the CFSP – Article 12 TEU – does not leave Member States the possibility independently to implement sanctions which are different from or more stringent than those of the Community. Once the Community has adopted measures, these

---

269. See Case T-317/02, *Fédération des Industrie Condimentaires de France v. Commission.* A claim for damages from the same trade association was also rejected: Case T-90/03.
270. See GATT Panel US: Section 337 of the Trade Act, BISD 36S, 345 and WTO Panels, DS 136, US-Anti-Dumping Act of 1916 (both won by the EC); DS 160, US-Section 110 of the Copyright Act (mixed result, but broadly favourable to the EC); DS 155, Argentina-Bovine Hides (mixed result), DS 193, Chile-Swordfish (panel proceeding discontinued after reaching agreement with Chile) and DS 332, Brazil-Retreaded Tyres (largely favourable to the EC).
271. See the complaint against the US on the origin of textile products, Decision 97/162/EC, O.J. 1997, L 62/4.
272. This practice started with the unilateral economic sanctions against Argentina in 1982 following the so-called Falklands war (Malvinas war), a case of self-defence using military means by a Member State, accompanied by self-defence using economic means by the Community. For an overview of this practice, with extensive references to the literature, see P.J. Kuyper, 'European Economic Community', in K.M. Meessen (ed.), *The International Law of Export Control* (London), 59–77.

must be respected by the Member States – also as part of the implementation of cooperation under CFSP.[273]

Starting with the sanctions against Iraq, in 1991, the implementation of binding economic sanctions decided by the UN Security Council, was also undertaken by the Community in the manner indicated above. This implementation is often extremely detailed, as the Security Council resolutions are also becoming ever more detailed. The Community then tends to pay less attention than normal to the limits of the common commercial policy as they are usually, at least by the Council, seen to exist.[274] The new Article 301 EC is, however, so broadly formulated – speaking of 'economic relations' and not 'trade relations' – that this issue seems of little importance, the more so because since the entry into force of the Treaty of Nice commercial policy also includes trade in services.

However, Article 301 was considered not sufficiently broad to be able to accommodate so-called 'smart sanctions' of the UN. Such sanctions took precise aim originally at persons in or associated to the government of countries against which the Security Council decided to take economic sanctions under Article 49 of the UN Charter, but later also at persons further removed from the government, or alleged terrorists with no governmental link whatsoever. Article 301 EC, since it spoke about the interruption of economic relations with *one or more third countries*, seemed in this respect more restrictive than Article 49 UN Charter, so that it was considered necessary for the Council to include Article 308 EC as additional legal base when the latter category of individuals was the target. Being directed against individuals or moral persons, as they were, the imposition of sanctions also raised the question whether their imposition was subject to the minimum procedural requirements of Community law. If that were the case, this could lead to considerable tension with the UN and the Security Council in particular, which at its level only reluctantly introduced some improvements in this respect. However, in principle it is possible – and probably even desirable – that the Court would take the view that the protection of minimum procedural rules within the Community is more important than some embarrassment in the relations between the EC and the UN.[275] In the case of smart sanctions adopted by the UN Security Council and implemented through Community law, it is possible to mobilize the action for annulment to this end. In the cases that are of a purely political or military nature, such as arms embargoes directed at individual traders or groups and which have been adopted only under the CFSP provisions of the TEU, the Court has no jurisdiction and no remedy would be available to the individuals concerned. Fortunately the Treaty of Lisbon – disappointing though it may be

---

273. Case 124/95, *Centro-Com* with note by P.J. Kuyper (1998) SEW, 425.
274. Reg. 3541/92, O.J. 1992, L 361/1.
275. See the Opinion of A.G. Maduro of 16 Jan. 2008 on appeal in the most important of the pending sanctions cases, Case T-315/01, *Kadi* (on appeal C-402/05). See on these issues M. Nettesheim, 'UN Sanctions against Individuals: A Challenge to the Architecture of European Union Governance' (2007) CML Rev., 567–600 and M. Bulterman, 'Fundamental Rights and the United Nations Financial Sanction Regime: The Kadi and Yusuf Judgements of the Court of First Instance of the European Communities' (2006) LJIL, 753–772.

that the Court of Justice still has not been given jurisdiction over CFSP matters in general – provides nevertheless a possibility of judicial review of decisions providing for restrictive measures against natural or legal persons taken under the CFSP.[276] Finally, in respect of sanctions measures directed against individuals suspected of being part of a terrorist organization or against these organizations themselves, the problem arose that some of this terrorism was 'home-grown' in Europe. How could Articles 60 and 301 EC, which essentially deal with *international* sanctions, be used as legal basis for such measures?[277]

The implementation of economic sanctions decided by the UN sometimes affects particular categories of persons or enterprises more severely than others. This has raised the question whether the Community is then liable to pay them damages by way of compensation for lawful government acts. The Community legislature could make provision for such damages but has so far not done so. The Court of Justice has declared the usual conditions from its case law on damages for lawful acts applicable to this sort of case.[278] When these principles, however, had to be applied in a specific case, not involving UN sanctions, but WTO authorized countermeasures from the side of the US in the *Hormones case*, the CFI decided that in that situation damages were not justified, since damages resulting from such countermeasures fall within the normal risks operators must accept in international trade. This would seem to apply *a fortiori* to UN economic sanctions.[279]

Finally, there are also categories of economic sanctions which are not reactions to a particular event or circumstance, but are the consequence of longer term security policy considerations. In the new situation without internal frontiers in the Community's internal market, a Member State can no longer itself effectively control the export of certain products which are sensitive from the point of view of security policy, i.e., those products which have both a normal commercial use and a military one. Therefore, rules for dual-use goods and technology – which until fairly recently had been adopted at the level of the Member States, and had as such led to some interesting case law – were organized at Community level, under the same framework.[280] A joint action based on Article 12 TEU (then Art. J.2) drew up a list of sensitive goods, and Regulation 3381/94 based on Article 133 EC (then Art. 113 EC) contained the Community rules for export controls on these goods.[281]

---

276. Art. 275 TFEU.
277. The cases dealing with the last question are the cases dealing with the Dutch so-called 'Hofstad group', Cases T-76/07 & T-362/07, *Hamdi* and Cases T-75/07 & T-363/07, *El Fatmi*, pending; there are also Cases T-37/07 & T-323/07, *Morabit I and II*, pending.
278. Case C 237/98, *Dorsch Consult v. Council and Commission*. The criteria are: damage, causal link with the lawful action, abnormal and special character of the damage.
279. Case T-69/00, *FIAMM et al. v. Council and Commission*, appeal still pending under C-120/06P.
280. The first example was that of the predecessors of chemical weapons, see Reg. 428/89, O.J. 1989, L 50/1. A regulation which was in some ways similar concerning the predecessors of psychotropic substances was, however, simply based on Art. 113 (133) EC: Reg. 3677/90, O.J. 1990, L 357/1, amended by Reg. 900/92, O.J. 1992, L 96/1.
281. Decision 94/942/CFSP and Reg. 381/94, O.J. 1994, L 367/8 and L 367/1. Art. 113 (now 133) EC and not Art. 228A (now 301) EC is the legal basis of the regulation, because the latter article only mentions urgent measures.

After the Court's judgment in *Werner* and *Leifer*,[282] in which it was established that export controls on dual-use goods is a Community competence, and also because the new rules led to a large number of complaints from industry, the Commission presented a proposal in 1998 for a completely communitarized system of export controls for dual-use goods. This proposal was accepted.[283] Recently the Community's dual-use export controls have again been subjected to thorough-going review from the side of the Council (2004 peer review) and the Commission (December 2006 proposal for a new Regulation), but this has not yet led to any result.

3.3.6   Trade and Cooperation Agreements of the Community and the Member States

As mentioned above, after the end of the transitional period competence to conclude trade agreements was put exclusively in the hands of the Community. The Member States are no longer free to conclude such agreements unless they have been specifically authorized to do so by the Community. As a rule, it will not be possible to ensure that such an authorization complies with the requirements which the functioning of the common market imposes on the uniformity of a Community conventional commercial policy. The question remained of what to do about existing trade agreements of the Member States. An investigation made by the Commission in 1969[284] revealed that there were some 128 treaties of friendship, trade and navigation and some 196 trade agreements (in the narrower sense) between Member States and third countries. In addition there were a great many agreements relating to economic, industrial, scientific and technical cooperation, which could also be relevant on certain points for the commercial policy of the Community. For various political and economic reasons, the Member States were not particularly keen to replace these trade agreements by Community agreements all of a sudden, nor to subject their cooperation agreements to examination at Community level. Just before the end of the transitional period, therefore, and after difficult negotiations, Council Decision 69/494 on the progressive standardization of agreements concerning commercial relations was adopted.[285]

This decision provided in Title I for a Community procedure of prior information and consultation with respect to the express or tacit renewal, after the end of the transitional period, of any bilateral agreements in the matter of the trade relations between Member States and third countries. An extension of agreements whose provisions fall under the common commercial policy is permitted only if

---

282. Case C-70/94, *Werner v. Germany* and Case C-83/94, *Criminal Proceedings against Peter Leifer, Reinhold Otto Krauskopf and Otto Holzer.*

283. Reg. 1334/2000, O.J. 2000, L 159/1.

284. SEC(69)1175 Final, 28 Mar. 1969.

285. Council Decision 69/494 of 16 Dec. 1969 on the progressive standardization of agreements concerning commercial relations between Member States and third countries and on the negotiation of Community agreements, O.J. 1969, L 326/39.

the Council has so authorized, and for a period not exceeding one year, unless such agreements contain an EC clause or can be terminated at the end of every year. Authorization can be granted only if the provisions of an agreement do not obstruct the application of the common commercial policy. If they do, the Commission provides the Council with a detailed report, along with appropriate suggestions and, if necessary, recommendations for the Council to grant an authorization to open Community negotiations with the third country concerned.

Most of the other provisions of this decision have become obsolete, but the decision does still have a function: it reminds the Member States that there must be renegotiation at Community level of national trade agreements which could form an obstacle to the common commercial policy. It also reminds the Member States that even though third countries may invoke the first paragraph of Article 307 EC in relation to agreements they have concluded with Member States, the latter are obliged, as a result of the second paragraph of that article, to take all appropriate steps to eliminate any incompatibilities with Community law in such agreements. This is certainly not a superfluous provision: the Commission in more recent years campaigned to remove all the commercial policy provisions from the Member States' agreements with the European Free Trade Association (EFTA) countries – this would have to be done in cooperation with the Member States, of course. The treaties of friendship, commerce and navigation which the United States has concluded on a large scale with Member States have also sometimes turned out to give rise to considerable complications, as they embrace many national treatment clauses which may be incompatible with Community law and with the obligations under the WTO agreement.[286]

It is important to note that the use of classic trade agreements is steadily decreasing. The title of the agreements concluded with the United States, mentioned above, demonstrates that even classic trade agreements often embrace far more than simply trade. Throughout the 1960s and 1970s, parties increasingly began to include, in addition to trade provisions, provisions dealing with industrial cooperation (in agreements with the old Eastern bloc countries) and on technical and development cooperation (in agreements with developing countries): these were then called cooperation agreements. Initially, cooperation agreements were primarily used by the Member States in order to conclude a sort of pseudo-trade agreements with the former Eastern bloc countries and the Arabian oil-producing states, and to circumvent the exclusive competence of the Community in trade policy matters. Now, the stage has been reached where not just the Member States,

---

286. In autumn 1993, the Commission refused to propose the renewed extension of these agreements under Art. 3 of Decision 69/494, as long as the Member States failed to make a declaration that the national treatment clause in the agreements would not be interpreted in such a way as to be an impediment to Community law. This was after an incident whereby Germany withdrew from certain measures concerning public purchasing *vis-à-vis* the US because, allegedly, the US had invoked the provisions of the friendship, commerce and navigation (FCN) treaty. See Decision 93/679/EC, O.J. 1993, L 317/61, and F.M. Abbott, 'Crosscurrents in European Union External Commercial Relations: The Controversy over the Germany-United States Treaty of Friendship' (1994) *ZaöRV*, 756–778.

but the Community itself makes extensive use of cooperation agreements. 'Classic' trade agreements – i.e., agreements which only cover trade in goods – are hardly concluded any more, not even by the Community.

It cannot be denied that to some extent these cooperation agreements have clear commercial policy aspects. Frequently they contain most-favoured-nation-treatment clauses, clauses promoting long-term contracts, the exchange of licences and know-how, compensating transactions for the supply of complete factories, favourable credit terms and so on.[287] The question then arises whether the Member States are still competent to conclude such agreements and to enter into more defined commitments or to take further measures in execution of them.

So far the Council has limited itself to the adoption of Decision 74/393, which lays down that prior notification and, if necessary, consultation is required for the conclusion and implementation of cooperation agreements between Member States and third countries. The consultation has in particular the aim of avoiding interference with the common commercial policy, promoting the coordination of cooperation activities with third countries and investigating the desirability of adopting autonomous commercial policy measures in support of these activities.

It may, with respect, be doubted whether Decision 74/393 is reconcilable with the case law of the Court on the division of competences between the Community and the Member States.[288] The case law justifies a claim by the Community to the exclusive competence to conclude such agreements if, as is the case with most of these agreements, their most important subject matter is of a commercial policy nature in the wide sense in which that term must be used. Community commercial policy is not restricted to the use of traditional commercial policy instruments, such as trade agreements, but should also embrace new instruments which are developed to promote and support external trade. The reasoning of the Court in Case 45/86 *Commission v. Council*[289] appears to apply *mutatis mutandis* in relation to cooperation agreements.

Recognition of exclusive Community competence in this field would have to lead to rules analogous to those in Decision 69/494, on the progressive standardization of policy relating to traditional trade agreements. The willingness on the part of the Member States to adopt such rules has so far been minimal. The Council, until recently, still considered such matters to be partly outside the sphere of operation of Article 133 EC, but it may be wondered whether this viewpoint can be maintained since the entry into force of the broader conception of commercial policy contained in the Treaty of Nice.

---

287.   On these cooperation agreements, see B.R. Bot, 'EEC-CMEA: Is a Meaningful Relationship Possible?' (1976) CML Rev., 335–366, and the authors cited therein. The question of the relationship between the EC and COMECON (CMEA) has now become a historical one, after a short-lived agreement between the two.

288.   See section 2.1.1 and 2.1.2 *supra*. Also: Opinion 1/75, *Local Cost Standard*, Opinion 1/78, *International Agreement on Natural Rubber* and in particular also Case 45/86, *Commission v. Council* (GSP).

289.   Case 45/86, *Commission v. Council* (GSP).

As already briefly mentioned above, the Community has over the years, and following in the footsteps of the Member States, also started to conclude a large number of cooperation agreements. These agreements – like Decision 74/393 itself – are based on Article 133 (ex 113) and 308 (ex 235) EC. They also contain a so-called Canada clause – named after the first cooperation agreement concluded by the Community – which explicitly provides that they do not affect the powers of the Member States to pursue bilateral activities in the field of cooperation with these countries and if necessary to conclude new agreements on such matters.[290] Since the Community's first cooperation agreement, with Canada (1976), the Community has gone on to conclude numerous such agreements, also with groups of states such as the Association of Southeast Asian Nations(ASEAN) countries (1979), with the countries of the Cartagena Agreement (Andean Pact) (1983); with the countries of Central America (1986); and with the Gulf Cooperation Council (1989). In some cases, a second cooperation agreement has even been concluded (e.g., Brazil, 1982 and 1992; India, 1981 and 1994).

In particular cooperation agreements with the major developing countries are these days concluded on the basis of Article 133 EC and Article 181 EC, introduced by the Treaty of Maastricht. That latter provision provides that agreements in the field of development cooperation should be negotiated and concluded on the basis of that article and Article 300 EC. It is also striking that the second paragraph of Article 181 EC expressly states that the Community's competence to conclude such agreements is without prejudice to Member States' competence to negotiate in international bodies and to conclude international agreements. It seems that the Member States, as Community constitutional legislators, have effectively enshrined the Canada clause in the EC Treaty, and thus established at constitutional level the parallel competence in the field of (development) cooperation.[291]

Recently there have been renewed problems between the Commission and the Member States concerning these old trade and cooperation agreements, largely triggered by the fact that the new Member States still had considerable numbers of these agreements on the books. During the accession negotiations, the Commission sought to force the new Member States to do away with these agreements

---

290. This provision can in fact be regarded as superfluous, as Art. 308 EC does not confer exclusive powers in the external field on the Community, but clearly there is felt to be a need to make the situation explicit for the third country concerned.

291. The Member States thus probably also wished to set aside the case law of the ECJ in Opinion 1/78, *International Agreement on Natural Rubber*, which held that development aims could be part of a modern trade policy. On the other hand, Art. 179 EC explicitly states that it applies 'Without prejudice to the other provisions of this Treaty', which includes Art. 133 EC. The judgment in Case C-268/94, *Portuguese Republic v. Council* gives important indications about the scope of Art. 181 EC and permits, among other things, the inclusion of human rights clauses in cooperation agreements with developing countries. It is doubtful, however, whether Art. 181 EC can serve as legal basis for cooperation agreements with developed countries. The Treaty of Nice seems to fill this hiatus by a new Art. 181a EC, which to a large extent corresponds to Art. 181 EC. The Court has expressed itself on the parallel competences in relation to development cooperation in Joined Cases C-181 & 248/91, *Parliament v. Council and Commission*, and Case C-316/91, *Parliament v. Council*.

completely and in some instances even went so far as to help the candidate countries in the necessary negotiations with the third states involved. To some extent, this approach was successful. However, at a certain point both old and new Member States and some important trade partners, such as Japan and the USA, became concerned; they wanted to hold on to those agreements and actually managed to do so. In response, the Commission has refused to propose the renewal of the authorization for existing trade agreements under Decision 69/494, thereby putting their continued validity in jeopardy. It does not require much imagination to make a link between this situation and the Member States' wish to include a clause such as Article 133(5), fourth subparagraph on the right of the Member States to maintain trade agreements with third countries, insofar as such agreements comply with Community law, thus in fact constitutionalizing the exceptional authorization given by Decision 69/494.

4   THE SYSTEM OF COMMUNITY AGREEMENTS

4.1   THE SYSTEM VIEWED GEOGRAPHICALLY: PREPARING FOR ACCESSION

The system of agreements that the Community has concluded over the years is built up in concentric circles. The innermost circle consists of the EEA Agreement. This establishes a free trade area for the movement of goods and a common market in the area of the other freedoms: workers, establishment, and the provision of services. This most far-reaching form of cooperation with the economies of a number of the Community's immediate neighbours, together with a special institutional apparatus, was originally established with countries who were members of the EFTA: Austria, Finland, Iceland, Liechtenstein, Norway and Sweden. Switzerland remained outside, following the negative decision given at a referendum, and – after Austria, Finland and Sweden acceded to the EU – a set of separate agreements were concluded with Switzerland. If one wants to characterize the present remaining Member States of the EEA and Switzerland, one would say that they are countries that do not or no longer want to accede to the European Union.

The second circle of countries is formed by those that are officially recognized as being candidates for accession or of having the calling of becoming a Member. These are the countries of the Western Balkans and Turkey. Accession negotiations have begun with the latter country and Croatia, while those with Macedonia may soon follow. Serbia, including Kosovo, Bosnia/Herzegovina, Montenegro and Albania are still in the waiting room. All these countries may profit from financing under a special financial instrument, the Instrument for Pre-accession Assistance (IPA) and they are subject to the finely balanced accession policy of the European Union.[292] This accession policy is based on a number of criteria which were

---

292.   A good summary is to be found in 'European Union Enlargement: A Historic Opportunity', published by the European Commission.

developed by the European Councils of Copenhagen (1993), Madrid (1995) and Helsinki (1999). According to the Copenhagen criteria, a candidate Member State must first have stable institutions guaranteeing democracy, the rule of law, human rights and respect for minorities; in addition, the country must have a functioning market economy, and the capacity to cope with competition from the common market; finally, the country must be able to undertake the obligations of membership, including adherence to the various political, economic and monetary aims of the European Union. In Madrid, a 'good governance' criterion was added: incorporation of the Community *acquis* is as such not enough; it must be possible for the acquis to be implemented and applied by competent administrative and judicial structures. Last, but not least, in Helsinki, the emphasis was again put on the importance of the political criteria for accession: the candidate countries should share the common values and objectives laid down in the Treaties. The Luxembourg European Council (1997) also made a link between accession and the reform of the Institutions of the Union.

The third circle is formed by the countries of the former Soviet Union (except the Asian ones) and the countries falling under the Mediterranean Policy of the Community. They are the object of the European Neighbourhood Policy (ENP) and have a common financial instrument to serve them: the ENPI. Russia falls outside the ENP and the ENPI, though the PCA concluded with it is a model for similar agreements with the other countries of the former Soviet Union (Ukraine, Belarus, Armenia, Azerbaijan, Georgia and Moldova). These agreements have been concluded on the basis of several articles of the EC Treaty.

So-called development association agreements (based on Art. 310 EC) have been concluded with the Maghreb countries (Algeria, Morocco and Tunisia) and the Mashreq countries (Egypt, Jordan, Syria, Lebanon and the occupied Palestinian territories). These agreements confer free trade concessions, include extensive cooperation provisions in diverse areas and are equipped with decision-making bodies.

Somewhat outside this third circle stand Russia and the countries of the Cotonou Partnership and Association Agreement, the latter being another example of a development association. The PCA with Russia has been on the verge of being comprehensively re-negotiated for quite some time now. There is a connection here with Russia acceding to the WTO. The renewed friction with this country has had the result that both Russia's accession to the WTO and the new PCA have been repeatedly put off. The most well-known example of a development association is the ACP-EC Partnership Agreement of Cotonou; this is a multilateral association agreement with more than 70 countries from Africa, the Caribbean and the Pacific (hence ACP countries).

Finally, the outermost circle of the Community's agreements, geographically, politically and legally, consists of the diverse forms of trade and cooperation agreements with countries of the Americas, the Arabian Peninsula, Asia and the Far East. These agreements are usually based on Articles 133 and 308 EC, and, to the extent they concern development, also on Article 181 EC.

4.2   Agreements Based on Article 310 EC

4.2.1   Article 310 EC

The characteristics of an association agreement under Article 310 EC lie in the reciprocal rights and obligations – albeit that is true of all agreements – and in joint action and special procedures. Given the pluriformity of agreements concluded on the basis of Article 310 EC, it is difficult to point out specific characteristics which these agreements have in common as against other forms of cooperation agreements, and indeed the distinction between association agreements and those other forms has always been a problem for the Community Institutions. On the basis of the practice followed and of the case law, we can make certain statements however: association agreements are concluded with countries with which the Community has or wishes to establish particularly close links. These links may have historic roots, as in the case of the ACP, the Maghreb and the Mashreq countries; they may be geographical or political in nature, as in the case of the EEA countries. Association agreements may involve the whole gamut of Community competence, and thus often embrace broad fields.[293] Nevertheless, they are in practice mostly concluded as mixed agreements; only those with Cyprus and Malta in their time were concluded solely by the Community. Also, as the Court has put it, association agreements presuppose a certain participation in the Community system; certain fundamental rules of Community law, even if sometimes only in the form of free trade, are extended to the association partner. That does not mean, though, that such rules have to be interpreted in the framework of the association in the same manner as in the framework of the Community itself.[294] Finally, association agreements are characterized by their strong institutional structure: they are often equipped with several bodies, including an association council at ministerial level and an association committee at the level of senior civil servants. The association council is often endowed with decision-making powers, and its decisions are binding on the participants in the association. The decisions of the association council form an integral part of Community law, without having to be transposed; they can thus be interpreted by the Court of Justice.[295]

Since the entry into force of the SEA the assent of the European Parliament has been required for the conclusion of association agreements. This requirement is currently to be found in Article 300(3) second subparagraph EC. Article 300(3) third subparagraph provides moreover that the Council and the European Parliament may, in an urgent situation, agree upon a time-limit for the assent to be given. This provision has not yet been relied upon.

---

293.   Case 181/73, *R. & V. Haegeman v. Belgian State* and Case 12/86, *Demirel*.
294.   Case 270/80, *Polydor Ltd and RSO Records Inc. v. Harlequin Records Shops Ltd and Simons Records Ltd*; Case 104/81, *Hauptzollamt Mainz v. Kupferberg*; Case C-207/91, *Eurim-Pharm GmbH v. Bundesgesundheitsamt*.
295.   Case 181/73, *Haegeman* and Case C-192/89, *S.Z. Sevince v. Staatssecretaris van Justitie*.

4.2.2 The EEA Agreement

Initially the Community had simple free trade agreements with its non-communist neighbours in Europe, which were members of the EFTA. The EEA Agreement, however, was designed to create 'a homogeneous EEA',[296] and to this end created an association which provides for the same five freedoms as are found in the EC Treaty, although the free movement of goods remains limited to a free trade area as opposed to a customs union. There is as yet no complete free trade in agricultural products. A system is established whereby undistorted competition and equal compliance with the rules on competition is ensured. There is also provision for close cooperation in fields such as research and technological development, environment, education and social policy.

In order to achieve all this, the EEA Agreement contains a great many provisions which are identical, or virtually so, to the fundamental provisions on the five freedoms in the EC Treaty, as well as to its competition provisions for undertakings and state enterprises, and the provisions on state aids. The EEA partners also take on board almost the whole *acquis communautaire*. For this purpose a number of Protocols and Annexes to the Agreement contain long lists with references to Community secondary legislation in all sorts of areas, which has force in the EEA partner states, sometimes with accompanying notes on the conditions under which this will occur, or with textual adaptations for this purpose.

From the institutional viewpoint, the EEA is extremely well-equipped. There is an EEA Council, consisting of the members of the Council of the European Union, members of the Commission of the European Communities, and one member of the government of each of the EFTA States which are parties to the EEA Agreement. The EEA Council meets twice a year, and is responsible for giving the general political impetus in the implementation of the EEA Agreement and for laying down general guidelines for the Joint Committee. This Joint Committee consists of representatives of the contracting parties, with the Commission representing the Community; it meets in principle at least once a month. Its main task is to keep track of legislative developments within the Community, and continually adapt EEA law to secondary Community law. The relevant Protocols and Annexes to the EEA Agreement are revised accordingly. There is also a Joint Parliamentary Committee, which consists of members of the European Parliament on the one hand and Member of Parliaments (MPs) of the EFTA States which are parties to the EEA on the other.

The EEA Agreement also creates bodies which are competent only in relation to the EFTA States which are parties to the EEA Agreement. Thus the EFTA Surveillance Authority has a role which is somewhat similar to that of the Commission in the Community, namely supervision of the implementation and fulfilment of EEA law by the EFTA States which are parties to the EEA Agreement, and, in particular, supervision of the implementation of competition law. The

---

296. Art. 1(1) EEA, see O.J. 1994, L 1. See also S. Norberg et al., *The European Economic Area, EEA Law, A Commentary of the EEA Agreement* (Stockholm, 1993).

EFTA Court deals with appeals against the surveillance procedure regarding the EFTA States concerned, appeals concerning decisions in the competition field taken by the EFTA Surveillance Authority, and the settlement of disputes between two or more of the EFTA States concerned.

Given that the intention is to maintain a homogeneous interpretation of Community law and EEA law which is identical to it, a special procedure for this purpose has been established. Accordingly, one of the tasks of the Joint Committee is to keep the development of the case law of the Court of Justice and of the EFTA Court under constant review, and to do what may be necessary in order to preserve the homogeneous interpretation of the Agreement.[297] If it is unable to preserve such homogeneous interpretation, the Contracting Parties may, if the dispute concerns provisions of the EEA Agreement which are identical in substance to those of the EC Treaty and secondary legislation adopted thereunder, place the matter before the Court of Justice for a ruling on the interpretation of the relevant rules. If the Contracting Parties are not able to refer the matter to the Court of Justice, a party may take safeguard measures under a special procedure.

This dispute settlement procedure was set up in this form only after the Court of Justice, in proceedings under Article 300(6) EC, had found the dispute settlement procedure originally proposed to be incompatible with the EC Treaty.[298] The initial proposal was to establish an EEA Court, which would draw the majority of its members from the Court of Justice, and which would have had to interpret EEA law in the light of the case law of the Court of Justice as it stood prior to the signature of the EEA Agreement. The Court of Justice found that this was incompatible with the EC Treaty, as in this manner Community law, particularly the provisions on free movement and competition, would be interpreted by a body other than the Court of Justice itself; this was found to be incompatible with Article 220 EC. The fact that judges of the Court of Justice would form the majority of judges of the proposed EEA Court made no difference, because as judges in the EEA Court they would sometimes have to interpret essentially identical provisions in different ways, as the objective of the EEA Agreement is substantially different from the objectives of the EC Treaty. Then, in the Community context, they could not later decide on identical provisions with an open mind and the necessary independence.[299]

Although the practical importance of the EEA Agreement has diminished as a result of accession to the European Union by a large number of the parties (except Liechtenstein, Norway and Iceland), the EEA phase undoubtedly facilitated the accession negotiations (as much work on alignment by the candidate countries had already been undertaken, and the *acquis communautaire* had been already

---

297. In practice, the EFTA Court has so far revealed itself to be very inclined to follow the case law of the Court of Justice, even with respect to such typical Community law matters of doctrine as liability of the Member States for failure to implement directives, see Case E-9/97, *Erla María Sveinbjörnsdóttir v. the Government of Iceland* (EFTA Court).
298. Opinion 1/91, *European Economic Area I.*
299. Opinion 1/91, *European Economic Area I*, see esp. paras 41–53.

accepted); moreover, the EEA remains an interesting model for close integration in a brief pre-accession period.

A special agreement was concluded with Iceland and Norway in the area of asylum and immigration policy – which was brought within the Community system by the Treaty of Amsterdam – as a kind of equivalent of the EEA Agreement.[300]

As mentioned earlier, Switzerland remained outside the EEA, but in the course of 1999, a set of seven agreements were concluded with this country – alongside the old free trade agreement – on free movement of persons, air transport, overland transport (of goods and persons), trade in agricultural products, technical barriers to trade (mutual recognition of conformity to standards), public procurement, research and technological cooperation. Taken together, the substantive content of these agreements does not differ much from the EEA Agreement. The agreements entered into force on 1 June 2002.[301]

4.2.3 The Partnership Agreements with the Eastern European Countries

Very shortly after the first signs of reform appeared in Central and Eastern Europe, the Community concluded trade and cooperation agreements with countries such as Hungary, Poland, Czechoslovakia, Bulgaria and Romania.[302] An autonomous system of economic assistance to promote economic reforms in Poland and Hungary was established in the form of the PHARE programme, which assisted all the Central European countries, including the Baltic States.[303] Once the political reforms took on a permanent character, it was proposed to these countries – and later also the Baltic states – to conclude so-called Europe Agreements.[304] These agreements, of which the Europe Agreement with Poland, concluded in 1993,[305] is a good example, have now served their purpose as instruments preparatory to

---

300. This agreement was concluded on the basis of Art. 6 Schengen Protocol, see Decision 1999/439/EC, O.J. 1999, L 176/5.

301. The seven agreements are published and commented in D. Felder and C. Kaddous, *Accords bilatéraux Suisse – UE (Commentaires)* (Bâle/Bruxelles, 2001). For information on the entry into force and the official publication of the agreements, see O.J. 2002, L 114. S. Breitenmoser, 'Sectoral Agreements between the EC and Switzerland: Contents and Context' (2003) CML Rev., 1137–1186.

302. The first example was the agreement with Hungary (21 Nov. 1988), O.J. 1988, L 327/1. These agreements were still based on the old Arts. 113 and 235 EC. Similar agreements were concluded with the Baltic States in 1992; see O.J. 1992, L 403.

303. See Reg. 3906/89, O.J. 1989, L 375/11, last amended by Reg. 2500/2001, O.J. 2001, L 342/1. The EC in fact also acts in a broader context, the so-called G-24, as coordinator of the aid given by all these 24 states to Central and East Europe.

304. M. Maresceau and E. Montaguti, 'The Relations between the European Union and Central and Eastern Europe: a Legal Appraisal' (1995) CML Rev., 1327–1367; S. Peers, 'An Ever Closer Waiting Room? The Case for Eastern European Accession to the European Economic Area' (1995) CML Rev., 187.

305. See O.J. 1993, L 348/1.

accession. By contrast the remaining agreements with Eastern European countries, Ukraine, Belarus (with which the Partnership Agreement has never been finalized for political reasons), Moldava, and similar agreements with the South Caucasus countries, Armenia, Azerbaijan, and Georgia have as their main aim to link these countries strongly to the European Union in the framework of the ENP and to grant them considerable financial assistance with the help of the corresponding financial instrument,[306] without giving them an immediate perspective of accession.

Taking the PCA with Ukraine[307] as an example, the following picture of these agreements can be sketched. The agreement contains an opening clause that states that democratic principles, respect for human rights and market economy principles underpin the relationship. Breach of these principles can lead to the unilateral suspension or termination of the agreement. The human rights and democratic principles are based on the UN Charter, the Helsinki Final Act and the Charter of Paris for a new Europe.[308] The PCA institutes a political dialogue between the parties. In the field of trade in goods, the PCA anticipates – or in cases where the partner is already a member of that organization, refers to – GATT/WTO principles. The ultimate aim is to establish a free trade area, but that will be decided only at a later stage through discussions in the Association Council; for the moment the agreement restricts itself to a certain liberalization of the mutual economic relations. With respect to services and establishment, the PCA seeks to bring about a certain liberalization, non-discrimination and certain advantages for the employees of service providers and established companies. In respect to intellectual property, much depends on the extent to which the countries concerned have already ratified a certain number of major international conventions on copyright, patents etc.; the objective is to bring them close to the EC standard in this area by adhering to these conventions.

For the rest, the PCAs provide for cooperation in a large number of sectors, from 'hard' industrial cooperation to 'soft' tourism and cultural cooperation. The agreements have a number of institutions, with a Cooperation Council at Ministerial level at the top. These institutions, unlike in association agreements, are not endowed with any decision-making power resulting in decisions binding on the parties. These agreements have been concluded as mixed agreements, with as legal basis a large number of treaty provisions, next to Article 133 EC, reflecting the narrow view of the scope of the common commercial policy prevailing at the end of the 1990s, as well as the unwillingness on the EC side to turn these agreements into associations.[309] That willingness, by contrast, did exist in the case of the new agreements that were concluded in the first years of the twenty-first century with the countries of the Western Balkans, which were given a perspective of accession; they were a new edition of an old phenomenon: the so-called pre-accession association.

---

306.   Reg. No. 1638/2006 establishing a ENPI, O.J. 2006, L 310/1.
307.   See O.J. 1998, L 49/1.
308.   As to the Charter of Paris, see Bull. EC 11–1990, 130–148, point 2.2.1; 30 ILM 190 (1991).
309.   PCAs of a similar type were concluded with the Asian states of the former Soviet Union, which however do not fall under the ENP and its financial instrument.

4.2.4 Association with a View to Accession

It was observed above that the Europe Agreements were a type of pre-accession association; the earliest examples of such associations, however, were with Greece, in 1961 (until Greece acceded to the Communities in 1981) and Turkey, in 1963. The association with Turkey has in many respects a similar structure to that of the Europe Agreements, in the sense that the agreement, albeit in a much simpler manner, limits itself to setting out the objectives in the field of the four freedoms which then have to be achieved through decisions of the Association Council; moreover, it contains similar asymmetrical obligations concerning tariff concessions. The original Agreement with Turkey was however too simple, and a protocol was signed in 1970 which brought a transitional phase into being, designed to lead to a customs union over 20 years. The objectives of the Agreement remained unaltered: a customs union, with free movement of workers, services and capital, as well as freedom of establishment, modelled on the EC Treaty. Because the association was 'frozen' for political reasons for a long time in the 1980s, and because the Association Council could not always muster the necessary decision-making impetus, the establishment of the customs union took rather longer than originally envisaged (twenty-two years). The limited degree of liberalization for Turkish workers lawfully employed in a Member State has also caused such problems,[310] that full free movement of workers does not seem to be a realistic proposition for the foreseeable future.

In the meantime, at the end of the 1980s, Turkey applied to accede.[311] The Commission originally gave its opinion that while accession was in principle possible, it would only be feasible after a number of years.[312] Only at the end of 1995 was the Association Council able to take a decision on the implementation of the final phase of the customs union.[313] The most difficult problem was the necessity of establishing a common commercial policy, which is a *sine qua non* for a customs union. It is astonishing that a country with such increasing economic significance as Turkey should adopt the greatest part of the Community's common commercial policy, without being able to exert much influence on it; only the Joint Committee of the customs union and the Association Council offer limited possibilities for this.[314] In this respect, the Europe Agreements, which did not go beyond the creation of a free trade area, were probably more realistic. In relations with third countries, the customs union with Turkey has already led to considerable

---

310. A number of judgments of the ECJ in which the Decisions of the Association Council concerning the right of access to other employment within the Community were granted direct effect led to an unprecedented strong political reaction from the German authorities. See Case C-192/89, *Sevince*, and Case C-237/91, *Kazim Kus v. Landeshauptstadt Wiesbaden*, and many other such cases; see e.g., D. Martin and E. Guild, *Free Movement of Persons in the European Union*, Ch. 13.
311. Bull. EC 4–1987, points 1.3.1 and 1.3.2.
312. Bull. EC 12/89, 88.
313. Decision No. 1/95 of the Association Council EC-Turkey, O.J. 1995, L 5/1.
314. See Arts. 54–60 of Decision 1/95.

problems: Turkey was obliged to impose restrictions on the import of textile products, following Community policy in this area, which led to a condemnation of Turkey in the WTO dispute settlement procedure.[315]

Nevertheless, these problems did not prevent the Helsinki European Council in 1999 from deciding that Turkey could, in principle, accede. The Council has followed an interesting legal course on this issue, whereby first a Regulation based on Article 308 EC was adopted in February 2001, which laid down that as part of the pre-accession strategy in relation to Turkey, an accession partnership with that country would be realized. That partnership could be adopted by the Council by qualified majority, and would lay down the objectives, principles and priorities and interim objectives for the accession partnership. Although there were certainly negotiations with Turkey in relation to this, the framework for the possible coming accession was laid down in a unilateral legal act of the Council. Many of the same elements found in the Europe Agreements are met within that framework, including the basic principles of democracy, rule of law, human rights and protection of minorities.[316]

The associations with Malta (1970) and Cyprus (1972) were originally associations as substitutes for accession, later supplemented by financial protocols in 1976 and 1973 respectively. Both of these countries later applied to accede and, as was mentioned in Chapter I of this book, acceded in May 2004. In respect of Cyprus, the transformation into a pre-accession association was already started by the adaptation of the association agreement, and the creation of a customs union was proclaimed as the ultimate objective (1986). As a result of political difficulties and changes of government, there was no similar adaptation of the agreement with Malta; that country desired to proceed straight to accession.

As for Cyprus, ultimately it was decided not to make accession dependent on a peaceful, balanced and lasting resolution of the conflict between the two Cypriot communities, as the Commission's opinion on the application originally proposed.[317] Even without such a general resolution of the conflict – and notwithstanding a negative result of a referendum held in the Republic of Cyprus on a deal carefully brokered by the UN in the presence of the old guarantor powers, the UK and Turkey, and the European Commission – the Republic of Cyprus has acceded. Since then the part of the island which is known officially as the areas in which the government of the Republic of Cyprus does not exercise effective control and unofficially as the Turkish Republic of Northern Cyprus, remains *de facto* outside the EU legal system.[318]

---

315. See Panel and Appellate Body reports in Case WT/DS 34 (Turkey-Textiles).
316. See Reg. 390/2001, O.J. 2001, L 58/1 and the Council Decision 2001/235/EC, O.J. 2001, L 85/13–23, based on it.
317. See 27th General Report 1993, paras 642–645, on the accession of Malta and Cyprus.
318. This is provided for in Protocol 10 to the Accession Treaty with Cyprus, O.J. 2003, L 236/955; Reg. No. 866/2004, on the regime on the so-called 'Green Line' dividing the Republic of Cyprus from the North; Reg. No. 389/2006, establishing an instrument of financial support for encouraging the economic development of the Turkish Cypriot Community, O.J. 2006, L 65/5. A Commission proposal for enabling trade between the two parts of the island has never been adopted by the Council, see Doc. COM(2004)466(01).

A new version of the pre-accession association was invented when the Community decided to conclude a series of so-called Stabilization and Association Agreements (SAAs) with the countries of the Western Balkans which were considered candidates for accession in the short run (Croatia and possibly Macedonia) or in the longer run (Serbia, Montenegro, Bosnia and Herzegovina and Albania). These SAAs are clearly more ambitious than the PCAs with Ukraine and others, but fall short of the present state of the Association Agreement with Turkey, which includes the decision establishing the customs union. For the moment, the SAAs do not go further than to aim for a free trade area in full conformity with the relevant articles of the GATT and the GATS in 6 to 10 years time. They are founded on a strongly worded opening article stating that democracy and human rights in line with the Universal Declaration of Human Rights, the Helsinki Final Act and the Paris Charter, as well as the principles of the market economy in line with the Organization for Security and Cooperation in Europe (OSCE) Bonn principles,[319] underlie the association. Another important provision is the one on cooperation with the other countries of the Western Balkans, with which SAAs have been concluded. The high ambitions of the agreements are also expressed in provisions on the movement of workers, establishment and trans-border services. In addition, there are elaborate chapters on approximation of laws and law enforcement, as well as on Justice and Home Affairs. In the SAAs, the Association Councils have the power to take decisions that are binding on both parties.[320] The SAAs are mixed agreements based on Article 310 EC, and like all association agreements are concluded with the assent of Parliament.

4.2.5 Development Association

The classic examples of development association are the successive Yaoundé and Lomé Conventions and the Cotonou Partnership Agreement. After the independence of the French-African states it was felt necessary to continue the association provided for in Article 182 EC in some way or other. This took the form of a combination of a free trade area and the grant of financial and technical assistance, initially contained in the Yaoundé Conventions. After four Lomé Conventions – the last of which was subject to an interim revision in 1995, whereby provisions on human rights were included – the Cotonou Agreement was signed on 2 June 2000, between the Community, its Member States, and more than seventy developing countries in Africa, the Caribbean and the Pacific (the ACP countries). The Agreement was provisionally applied as of 2 August 2000, and entered into force on

---

319. Document of the Bonn Conference on Economic Cooperation in Europe convened in accordance with the relevant provisions of the concluding document of the Vienna Meeting of the Conference on Security and Cooperation in Europe (19 Mar. to 11 Apr. 1990), at <www.osce.org/documents/eea/1990/04/13751_en.pdf>. This document treated the necessary economic reforms in Eastern Europe at the time in relation to the political reforms.
320. Examples are the SAA with FYROM, O.J. 2004, L 84/13, and with Croatia, O.J. 2005, L 26/1.

1 March 2003.[321] The Cotonou Agreement has clearly gained a political dimension as a result of the insertion of a number of articles concerning political dialogue, prevention and resolution of armed conflicts, and peace-building initiatives between the parties – apparently in the hope that this could contribute to the solution of the chaotic situation in a number of – mainly African – countries.

Moreover, the provision included in Lomé IV on respect for human rights, democratic principles and the rule of law has been retained. This has been classified as an 'essential element' of the agreement, so that a breach in this area could be a reason for unilateral suspension of the agreement, or even its termination.[322]

As to free trade, the Agreement is – for the time being at least – non-reciprocal: the Community permits free access to ACP products (except for agricultural products, in respect of which a system of preferential treatment applies), while the ACP countries only grant Community products most-favoured nation treatment. In the future, however, reciprocal freedom of movement must be established in order to meet the GATT requirements for a free trade area. To this end the Community is presently negotiating free trade agreements, called Economic Partnership Agreements (EPAs) with groups of ACP countries. These agreements are supposed not only to reinforce trade links with the European Union, but also among African countries in the same region.[323] The cooperation provisions of the Agreement cover a multitude of areas which are important for development, such as agriculture, fisheries, industrial development, mining, energy, the environment and so on. In the sphere of financial development the European Development Fund has been created in order to support development activities under soft conditions. The amount of this development aid is laid down by contract for five years, and thus grants the ACP countries a degree of the certainty which they need. The special instruments created by the Lomé Conventions, such as a stabilization mechanism for exports of agricultural commodities (STABEX) and a special financing mechanism for countries which are particularly dependent on mining activities (SYSMIN), have been transformed into a more flexible mechanism in order to compensate strong fluctuations in the export income of a country in general.

The implementation of the obligations for access of ACP bananas to the Community market, after the establishment of the Community's internal

---

321. For the text: <ec.europa.eu/development/Geographical/CotonouIntro_en.cfm>. For the conclusion and entry into force, see Council Decision 2003/159/EC, O.J. 2003, L 65/27, read with Art. 93(3) Cotonou. See K. Arts, 'ACP-EU Relations in a New Era: the Cotonou Agreement' (2003) CML Rev., 95–116.

322. See Art. 60 Vienna Convention on the Law of Treaties 1969. Such clauses, whether or not they include the 'essential element' formula, were gradually introduced as of the beginning of the 1990s in various agreements of the EC, first with the Latin American states, and later also with the Baltic and Asian states; see on this, B. Brandtner, A. Rosas, 'Human Rights and the External Relations of the European Community: an Analysis of Doctrine and Practice' (1998) EJIL, 437.

323. There is considerable resistance in many ACP states against these agreements; the progress of the negotiations is very slow.

market,[324] has given rise to major controversy, both within and outside the Community; in the light of the incompatibility of the Lomé Convention and its banana regime with WTO rules – established by a number of WTO panels – it also led to a reform of the Lomé system. The Banana Protocol of the Cotonou Agreement no longer includes the guaranteed sales of specific amounts and concomitant licensing system for imports which was found to be incompatible with WTO law.[325]

The Cotonou Agreement contains a very elaborate system for sanctioning countries that do not conform to the democracy, human rights and rule of law provision which is laid down in Article 96. This provision has been activated for many African countries, when *coups d'état* occurred or civil war broke out.[326]

The most important institutions of the partnership are the Council of Ministers, the Committee of Ambassadors and the Joint Parliamentary Assembly. The members of the Council of the European Union and the members of the Commission on the one hand, and a member of the government of each of the ACP states on the other, comprise the Council of Ministers. The Council of Ministers meets once a year, and acts by agreement between the Community and its Member States on the one hand and the ACP states on the other. The Committee of Ambassadors is composed along the same lines. An internal agreement governs the procedure by which the Community arrives at its position. The Joint Parliamentary Assembly is composed of representatives of the European Parliament on the one hand, and members of parliament (or in their absence other representatives) designated by the ACP states on the other.

A planned revision of the Cotonou Agreement took place in 2005, after 5 years of its intended 20 years of validity. This led to the addition of important political clauses in the agreement, such as those on the cooperation in the realm of antiterrorism, weapons of mass destruction and combating small arms and landmines, as well as an improvement of the mechanism of Article 96 for sanctioning the breach of the fundamental provision of the Convention on democracy and human rights.[327]

---

324. See Reg. 404/93, O.J. 1993, L 47/1, and Case C-280/93 R, *Germany v. Council.*
325. See the series of decisions of WTO Panels and the Appellate Body in the so-called Bananas Case (WT/DS 29); later, under political pressure, a licence system which is contrary to Art. XIII GATT was re-introduced, but this time with the consent of all the parties involved. A WTO waiver was granted for this. In the meantime, this new system is being converted into a tariff only system, but since some limitation of the quantities that can be imported under the lower tariff for ACP countries is desirable, there is a new problem of WTO conformity and new WTO litigation was under way in 2007, when parties asked the Director-General of the WTO, Pascal Lamy, for mediation.
326. See on the application of Art. 96, L. Laakso, T. Kivimäki and M. Seppänen, 'Evaluation of Coordination and Coherence in the Application of Art. 96 of the Cotonou Partnership Agreement', Studies in European Development Cooperation Evaluation No. 6, European Union, 2007. A large number of African states have at one time or another been hit by the application of Art. 96, for instance, Niger, Ivory Coast, Togo, Comores, Chad, Zimbabwe etc.
327. This revision was provisionally applied as from signature by Decision 2/2005 of the ACP-EC Council of Ministers, O.J. 2005, L 287/1, subject to financial reciprocity from the side of the Union in respect of the replenishment of the EDF.

Similar associations, with a clear development character, have existed for a long time with the Maghreb and Mashreq countries. The last 'generation' of these – which were drawn up in the framework of the Mediterranean policy and now function within the ENP – are called Euro-Mediterranean agreements. The agreement with Tunisia may serve as example.[328] First of all, it may be noticed that the agreements contains numerous references to the WTO, the GATT (in particular the provisions on free trade areas) and the GATS; it is clearly the intention of the parties to keep within the framework created by the WTO for regional trade agreements. As far as trade in goods is concerned, a free trade area must come into existence within a period of 12 years – although Tunisia is granted abundant possibilities for temporarily raising customs duties or re-imposing them in favour of 'infant industries' or restructuring with large-scale social consequences. It should also be noted that the free trade in agricultural products is still very limited. In the area of establishment and services, the liberalization is intended to come about through recommendations of the Association Council. In addition, the agreement contains extensive provisions in the area of economic, social and cultural cooperation. These last aspects provide an unobtrusive possibility for provisions on migration and clandestine immigration, but these remain more or less framework provisions. The Community did not manage to include a so-called readmission provision for illegal immigrants; there will have to be negotiations on this issue at a later stage. A special aspect of the agreements with Algeria and Morocco is that they contain specific provisions on migrant workers, in particular non-discrimination provisions concerning social security. The Court has recognized the direct effect of these provisions.[329]

Similar association agreements exist with the Mashrek countries: Egypt Syria, Lebanon, Jordan, as well as with Israel. These agreements have all been re-negotiated between 1997 and 2004 and only the agreement with Syria has not yet been fully finalized due to political considerations.[330] In the framework of the Euro-Mediterranean policy, the Community also concluded a so-called Euro-Mediterranean interim association agreement with the Palestine Liberation Organization (PLO) for the benefit of the Palestinian Authority, at the time Palestinian autonomy began to be realized in 1997. This agreement is not based on the Treaty's association provision (Art. 310), but on Articles 133 and 181 EC (on the commercial policy and international cooperation).[331] A full association agreement was intended to follow at some stage, but after the deterioration of the situation in the Gaza strip and on the West Bank, the Community has not been able

---

328. O.J. 1998, L 97/1.
329. See Case C-18/90, *Office national de l'emploi v. Bahia Kziber* and Case C-58/93, *Zoubir Yousfi v. Belgian State*. Just like Case C-192/89, *Sevince* and Case C-237/91, *Kus*, (see note 310 *supra*) these decisions led to rather negative reactions, this time from the French authorities.
330. The agreement with Jordan is a good example; see O.J. 2002, L 129/1. The agreement with Israel is slightly different, O.J. 2000, L 147/1 and has been complemented with an important agreement on cooperation in science and technology.
331. See O.J. 1997, L 187/1, amended by exchange of letters, O.J. 2005, L 2/6.

to do much more than financially support the Palestinian Authority as best it could, whilst at the same time trying to guarantee that these monies were not diverted from their purpose.

4.3   OTHER COOPERATION AGREEMENTS

4.3.1   Partnership Agreements

The meeting of the European Council on Corfu in June 1994 saw the signature of the PCA with Russia.[332] This agreement was later embedded in the Common Strategy which the European Council adopted in the course of 1999.[333] This is a mixed agreement, which – in the wake of Opinion 1/94 – inevitably came to be based on a whole series of articles (i.e., 44(2), 47(2), 55, 57(2), 71, 80(2), 93, 94, 133 and 308 EC).[334]

    One of its first articles (Art. 2), like that of the PCA with Ukraine discussed earlier, states explicitly that respect for democratic principles and human rights underpins the internal and external policies of the Parties and constitutes an essential element of the partnership and of the agreement. In this context, reference is made to the Helsinki Final Act and the Charter of Paris for a new Europe.[335] The agreement establishes a political dialogue between the partners, and also contains a large number of provisions concerning trade in the broad sense of the word, i.e., trade in goods, in services, establishment, and also provisions concerning payments and capital movements, competition and intellectual property. The fact that Russia, like most of the other CIS states, is not (yet) a member of the WTO, and is still in the middle of the transition to a market economy, plays an important role in this; the content of this part of the agreement is to a large degree determined by these two facts. For example, the most-favoured-nation clause is introduced for trade in goods and for establishment, while at the same time exceptions are possible for special advantages that Russia wishes to grant other CIS countries. Current payments are liberalized, as are capital movements related to direct investments. In addition, the Agreement contains a title on economic cooperation, which provides for cooperation in a diversity of areas. As well as the usual industrial cooperation, other areas for cooperation include transport, science and

---

332. See O.J. 1997, L 327/1
333. See *supra*, section 2.7.
334. This list of ten legal bases was the nicest example of the absurdity of the situation on the external competences of the Community. Now the Treaty of Nice, and the new versions of Art. 133 EC and the new Art. 181a EC for cooperation agreements with developed countries, have entered into force, these two articles will provide sufficient legal basis.
335. Such clauses are not included in the Europe agreements, although similar clauses may be found in the preambles. Membership of the Council of Europe and the European Convention on Human Rights was given as a reason for the lack of such a clause, but that has been overtaken by events insofar as Russia and Ukraine have also acceded to these. As for the 'essential element' formula, see note 322 *supra* and accompanying text.

technology, the nuclear sector, mining and such like. As in the Europe Agreements, drugs and money-laundering are mentioned, and cooperation in the area of prevention of other illegal practices. There is also a title devoted to financial cooperation.

The institutional structure of the agreement resembles that of association agreements, with a Cooperation Council at ministerial level, and a Cooperation Committee at the level of senior civil servants, and a Parliamentary Cooperation Committee. Although the Cooperation Council may make recommendations, it has no power, unlike most association councils, to adopt binding decisions.

By now, similar partnership agreements have been concluded with a number of Asian CIS countries: Kyrgyzstan, Kazakhstan, Turkmenistan and Uzbekistan, and they entered into force on 1 July 1999.[336] There has been a trade and cooperation agreement with Mongolia – which is not a member of the CIS – since 1993.

4.3.2   Diverse Cooperation Agreements

Since the mid-1970s, the Community has hardly signed any further classic trade agreements with non-European States which do not fall under development association; it has only signed cooperation agreements based on Articles 133 and 308 EC. One of the earliest examples was the Cooperation Agreement with Canada (1976), but that has remained an exception in the sense that the Community did not conclude any other general agreements with similar countries such as the United States, Japan, Australia, New Zealand and South Korea, i.e., countries which are not developing countries and with whom trade relations are governed by the GATT. The so-called Transatlantic Declarations were drawn up with the United States and Canada, and a Transatlantic Dialogue is kept going, accompanied by an early warning system for trade conflicts. Comparable declarations have been agreed with Japan, Australia and New Zealand, but these are political documents, which belong more to the CFSP – although they have not been officially included in the CFSP – than Community law.[337]

If this outer circle of the system of agreements of the Community is analysed, it is noticeable first of all that at the end of the 1990s, the Community renewed all its agreements with Latin America.[338] In 1998–1999, the Community established a number of so-called framework agreements with the states parties of three regional economic organizations. The Community renewed its agreements with the countries of the Andean Community (Bolivia, Ecuador, Colombia, Peru and Venezuela) and the countries of the Central America Common Market (Costa Rica,

---

336. For an example of one of these agreements, see O.J. 1999, L 196/1 (Kazakhstan).
337. 24th General Report 1990, para. 693 (US) and para. 712 (Canada); 25th General Report 1991, para. 859 (Japan). Unfortunately, these declarations – which are full of consultation clauses and intentions as to cooperation, and which were stepped up even further in the mid-1990s – have not led in practice to a less confrontational type of trade policy, particularly between the US and the Community. The joint declarations with Australia and New Zealand date from 1997 and 1999 respectively.
338. For the review at the beginning of the 1990s, see the previous edition of this book.

El Salvador, Guatemala, Honduras, Nicaragua and Panama). Thirdly, the Community concluded a new agreement with the Mercosur and its member states Argentina, Brazil, Paraguay and Uruguay. All these agreements follow more or less the same pattern. They are based on Articles 133 and 181 EC, and therefore have a commercial and development character. They start with a provision concerning democratic principles and fundamental human rights as essential elements of the agreement. They contain a clause concerning most-favoured nation treatment, in agreement with GATT (to the extent this is necessary, as not all the Latin American countries involved are parties to the GATT). The agreements also contain very broad provisions on economic, industrial and trade cooperation, and sometimes provisions concerning investments and cooperation in the field of the environment. Obviously, there are also provisions on cooperation with these countries in the field of drugs. The agreements each establish a Joint Committee for the cooperation, in which the Commission represents the Community, but does not have real decision-making powers, unlike in the case of associations.[339] The agreement with Chile is slightly more ambitious, and aims to lead to an association of a political and economic nature between the Community and its Member States on the one hand and Chile on the other. An extremely ambitious agreement was signed with Mexico in 1997 on economic partnership, political coordination and cooperation, but the entry into force ran up against a series of obstacles, which led to the conclusion of an interim agreement in 1998 on trade in goods and services. The main agreement finally entered into force on 1 October 2000.[340] At present the Commission has begun negotiations with Mercosur, the Andean Community and the Central-American Common Market with a view to establishing free trade regimes with these organizations; it thus hopes to contribute to the solidity of these agreements, which are seen as being based on the European model, much in the way as the EU hopes that the EPAs with the ACP countries will contribute to regional integration in Africa, but so far without result.

As far as relations with Asian countries are concerned, the Community has had a cooperation agreement with the five ASEAN countries jointly (Indonesia, Malaysia, the Philippines, Singapore and Thailand) since 1980, which is similar to the agreements with the regional economic organizations in Latin America. After they joined ASEAN, Brunei (1984) and Vietnam (1999) became parties to this cooperation agreement. This does not prevent the Community having a separate cooperation agreement with Vietnam, since 1996. The Community has also completed a revision of the cooperation agreements with the South Asian states: India,[341] Pakistan, Nepal and Sri Lanka. These agreements are now all based on Articles 133 and 181 EC and also contain a clause on democracy and human rights. The Joint Committee of these cooperation agreements does not have decision-making

---

339. The agreement with Mercosur does also have a cooperation council, however, to which the cooperation committee is subordinate, and in which the presidency of the EU Council represents the Community; the cooperation council does not have real decision-making powers either.
340. See O.J. 2000, L 276/45.
341. See Case C-268/94, *Portuguese Republic v. Council*.

power. Trade relations with China are also governed by a cooperation agreement, dating from 1985, but those with Taiwan are regulated on the basis of autonomous measures – even though they are often preceded by unofficial negotiations. In this manner the Community takes account of China's sensitivities, but at the same time it can seek a *modus vivendi* with Taiwan, which is of great importance in all trade. The Community also played a role in enabling 'China-Taipei' to become a Member of the WTO, be it with the status of 'separate customs territory possessing full autonomy in the conduct of its external economic relations'.[342]

Relations between the Community and the countries of the Middle East have not yet been highly developed in contractual terms. A Euro-Arab dialogue has existed since 1976 in the context first of European political cooperation, now of CFSP, with the objective, among other things, of contributing to the Middle Eastern peace process. The old cooperation agreement with North Yemen, dating from 1984, was extended with effect from 1995 to embrace the new Republic of Yemen, resulting from unification of the two Yemens.[343] Finally, in 1989 the Community concluded a cooperation agreement with the states of the Gulf Cooperation Council (Saudi Arabia, Kuwait, Bahrain, Qatar, United Arab Emirates, Oman), which may ultimately lead to the creation of a free trade area.[344] The realization of the objectives of the Agreement faces considerable obstacles, however. Negotiations for an EU-GCC Free Trade Agreement were opened in 1990 and re-launched in 2001 once the Gulf Cooperation Council (GCC) had moved to establish a customs union. These negotiations have yet to be concluded.

Finally, a number of autonomous measures relating to development assistance and humanitarian aid should also be noted in this context. Financial and technical assistance to and economic cooperation with the non-associated developing countries in Asia and Latin America is laid down in a general regulation relating to development cooperation.[345] Here too, strong emphasis is placed on the fact that the Community's development policy is based on democracy and human rights.[346] The Community is also a large-scale provider of food aid, in part on the basis of the World Food Programme and obligations undertaken towards United Nations Relief and Works Agency (UNRWA). The general rules governing such food aid are now included in the general financing instrument for development cooperation. Much of this aid is given in the form of emergency aid. For these purposes the Commission has established the European Commision Humanitarian Aid (ECHO), which is a semi-independent service and is in a position to make money and goods available at short notice to assist in coping with the consequences of disasters.[347]

---

342. Art. XII:1 WTO Agreement.
343. See the exchange of letters in O.J. 1993, C 310/19.
344. O.J. 1989, L 54/1, see esp. Art. 11 of the Agreement.
345. Reg. (EC) 1905/2006 establishing a financing instrument for development cooperation, O.J. 2006, L 387/41.
346. There is even a special financing instrument for democracy and human rights, Reg. (EC) 1889/2006, O.J. 2006, L 386/1.
347. The ECHO is primarily applying Reg. (EC) 1257/96 concerning humanitarian aid, O.J. 1996, L 163/1.

4.4   THE SYSTEM OF AGREEMENTS VIEWED BY SECTOR

This section gives a brief overview of the Community's system of agreements on a sector-by-sector basis; reference is also made from time to time to autonomous external measures in the sectors concerned

As far as *coal and steel* is concerned, it is no longer useful to describe the almost Byzantine complications which resulted from the absence of true external (commercial policy) competences in the ECSC Treaty, since that Treaty ceased to operate in 2002, and thus the relevant products and international trade therein now fall under the normal EC Treaty rules. As for *products falling under the Euratom Treaty*, the situation is still unclear. On the one hand Articles 64–66 Euratom confer far-reaching powers on the Euratom Supply Agency and the Commission in the context of supply contracts or contracts for the supply of ores, source materials and special fissile materials coming from outside the Community, yet on the other hand the Euratom Treaty contains no commercial policy provisions. It is submitted that the better view is that trade in Euratom products falls in principle under the common commercial policy (see Art. 305(2) EC), save as far as supplies of products specified in Article 64 Euratom to the Community from third countries are concerned.[348] In the other areas covered by the Euratom Treaty, such as nuclear safety and nuclear research, the Community has concluded myriad agreements with third countries on the basis of Article 101 Euratom.

In section 3.1.1 above, attention was paid to the question whether *international trade in services and establishment* fell within the concept of the common commercial policy. Sometimes Article 49(2) EC has been seen as a provision which could support an external policy in relation to trade in services, but it is submitted that this provision is too limited in nature to be capable of doing so; it is rather a provision which enables internal rules relating to free movement to be declared also applicable to subjects of third countries who have established themselves in the Community. The admission of persons or undertakings established outside the Community to provision of services within the Community or to the provision of services over the Community's external frontiers cannot be based on this provision. This could instead occur through an *ERTA* approach, as in the case of the agreement with Switzerland on insurance, which was based on Articles 47 and 55 EC.[349] This approach has now been endorsed by the Court in Opinion 1/94. It was already observed in section 3.2.2 above that autonomous policy in this field has so far been limited to reciprocity requirements in banking and insurance directives. According to the Court's Opinion 1/94,[350] such provisions involve the grant of exclusive external competence in the fields which they cover as long as no use has been made of the power in Article 133(5) EC to communitarize this policy. Since the entry into force of the Treaty of Nice, trade in services has been brought

---

348. Opinion 1/94, *WTO*, para. 24, seems to confirm this.
349. O.J. 1991, L 205/1.
350. At para. 95.

within the Community's commercial policy competence and with the Treaty of Lisbon investment and thus establishment will also be part of it.

The application of *free movement of workers* for the benefit of workers from third countries, insofar as it is not limited to what is necessary for the international provision of services, but represents an independent value, has two facets: free movement of such workers within the Community and free movement between the Community and third countries. The former clearly falls under Community competence, as only the Community may extend the preferential treatment granted to nationals of other Member States[351] so as to benefit third country nationals who are already present in the Community. The latter, which embraces the problem of first admission onto the territory of a Member State and thus the Community as a whole, has become potentially a Community competence, following the communitarization of visa and immigration policy brought about by the Treaty of Amsterdam.[352] To the extent that the integration of the Schengen acquis as a result of the relevant Protocol is now realized,[353] the Community has acquired instant secondary law, which may provide a basis for application of the ERTA doctrine. As a result, it may be argued, for example, that the Community has the exclusive competence to conclude treaties on visa policy and the right to remain anywhere in the territory of the Community for three months on the basis of a visa.[354]

The EC Treaty contains fundamental rules on the *movement of capital and of payments with third countries*, and makes it clear that these are separate from the common commercial policy as such. In principle, capital movements and payments to and from third countries are totally liberalized, according to Article 56 EC. Only to the extent that restrictions on capital movements with third countries are directly linked to policy concerning direct investment, provision of services and establishment in relation to third countries, may existing restrictions be maintained or may the Council adopt measures by a qualified majority, on a proposal from the Commission.[355] In this sector, commercial policy on services intersects with external policy on capital movements, and this nexus is quite likely to involve complications.

As far as *international transport policy* is concerned, in Opinion 1/94 the Court expressly stated in clear terms that the whole of transport policy should be based on the *ERTA* doctrine, and thus access to the market for transport services did not fall within the common commercial policy.[356] This situation was not altered by the Treaty of Nice: it is explicitly laid down in the amended version

---

351. See Arts. 16(2) and 19(2) Reg. 1612/68.
352. See Art. 62 EC.
353. See Decisions 1999/435/EC and 1999/436/EC, O.J. 1999, L 176.
354. See the legislation listed at <http://ec.europa.eu/justice_home/doc_centre/freetravel/visa/doc_freetravel_visa_en.htm>.
355. Art. 57 EC. So far the authority given in the second paragraph. of this article has not yet been used, but it seems almost the only authority in the Treaty that could be resorted to in case the actions of foreign 'sovereign' investment and natural resource companies become particularly worrisome.
356. Opinion 1/94, *WTO*, paras 48–52.

of Article133 EC. In fact, it is remarkable that it is only now, more than 30 years after the judgment dealing with the ERTA, that the Community is actually considering acceding to that agreement. In 1992, the Community concluded its first civil air transport agreements, with Norway and Sweden.[357] Since the Court's ruling in the so-called 'Open skies' cases[358] the Community has proceeded to sign or conclude a number of air transport agreements with neighbouring countries and the USA.[359] It is remarkable that in concluding these agreements the Council has finally opted for an integrated Community approach, where formally the mixed character of these agreements may be upheld, but in reality an agreement is concluded as one deal by the Commission. In some cases the power to conclude air transport agreements with smaller third countries is re-delegated to individual Member States subject to scrutiny by the Commission.

As to *competition* policy, many Community agreements, particularly association and free trade agreements with European countries contain provisions, often analogous to Articles 81, 82 and 86 EC, relating to guaranteeing competition in trade between the parties. The procedures laid down in those agreements for this purpose are in fact rarely or never applied; distortions of competition in trade between the contracting parties always involved distortions of competition in trade between Member States as well, so Articles 81 and 82 EC could be applied directly without objection.[360]

There is no doubt that the Community may be a party to agreements of the soft law variety, such as that established in the framework of OECD, concerning notification, information exchange and cooperation in the field of application of the competition laws of the parties involved. As to the question whether the Commission, as the competition authority, could conclude such agreements on its own account, the Court answered this in the negative.[361] In the field of public procurement, Community law has stormed ahead in recent years, not only due to internal pressures but also in response to external pressures. Of the numerous directives which were adopted, a few contained a similar reciprocity provision for the access of tenderers from third countries to those in the banking and insurance directive.[362] Agreements concerning public procurement were originally seen as trade agreements, but their extension in some cases to embrace public procurement of services and to public works contracts caused Article 133 EC alone to be a controversial and ultimately unacceptable (for the Court of Justice) legal basis. One may doubt whether the Court was sufficiently aware of the fact that international agreements on public procurement do not concern the public purchases themselves, but the possibility to take part in the tendering process. Apart from that, the distinction in

---

357. See O.J. 1992, L 200/21 and O.J. 1993, L 212.
358. Case C-471/98, *Commission v. Belgium* etc.
359. Decision on the signature and the provisional application of the agreement with the USA, O.J. 2007, L 134/1.
360. See Joined Cases 89/85 etc., *A. Ahlström Osakeyhtiö and others v. Commission (wood pulp)*.
361. See Case C-327/91, *France v. Commission*.
362. Cf. Art. 36 Dir. 93/38, O.J. 1993, L 199/84.

treatment between public purchases of goods and those of services disappeared with the entry into force of the Treaty of Nice.[363]

External aspects of Community fisheries policy are obviously important: international agreements are an absolute necessity in order to permit the Community's fishing fleet to fish in the exclusive economic zones of third countries. Ever since the judgment in *Kramer et al.*,[364] there is no doubt as to the Community's exclusive competence to deal with fisheries and the conservation of the biological resources of the sea. Accordingly, the Community has concluded numerous bilateral agreements concerning fishing with the Scandinavian, African and South American countries. The main object of these is to ensure access to fishing rights in the exclusive economic zones of the countries in question, in return for granting similar access to the waters of the Community, or in return for payments. The Community is also a party to many agreements concerning fishing or conservation on the High Seas, such as the North Atlantic Fisheries Organization (NAFO).

The Community's international *environmental policy* is characterized by the conclusion of regional or global multilateral environmental agreements, initially on the basis of Article 308 EC, nowadays on the basis of Articles 174(4) or 175 EC. Almost all of these agreements have been concluded in the form of mixed agreements, an approach which is effectively pre-programmed by the text of Article 174(4) EC, particularly its second subparagraph. The subsidiarity principle, which was initially specifically laid down in this provision, disappeared from it when the Treaty of Maastricht made subsidiarity a generally applicable principle for Community action.

As far as international aspects of Community *research and technology policy* are concerned, amendments made by the Treaty of Maastricht continued those introduced by the SEA. The exercise of the power to conclude agreements in this field, contained in Article 170 EC, is directly linked to the execution of the multi-annual framework programmes which, in accordance with Article166 EC, embraces all Community activities in the area of research and technological development. So far, little or no actual use has been made of the competence contained in Article 170 EC. For the rest, there has been a certain variable geometry in the Community's activities in research and technological development: internally, supplementary programmes to the multi-annual framework programmes could only be carried out by the Member States; externally, a flexible cooperation with the European member countries of the OECD was possible in the context of COST (Coopération Scientifique et Technologique) and the EUREKA programme.

The development of the international *energy policy* of the Community is a laborious process. For instance: it has been possible from the start for the Community to accede to the International Energy Agency in Paris, but this was never put into effect. The Community was involved in the drawing up of the European Energy Charter, the initiative for which owed much to the former Dutch Prime

---

363.   Cf. Case C-360/93, *Parliament v. Council*; see annotation by Kuijper in (1997) SEW, 175.
364.   Joined Cases 3, 4 & 6/76, *Kramer*.

Minister, Lubbers. The Community and the Member States signed the non-binding Charter together, and participated in the negotiation of the accompanying European Energy Charter Treaty, which contains rules on trade, investment, technological cooperation and the like concerning energy generation and raw materials for that purpose.[365] It is a mixed agreement, the usefulness of which must be increasingly open to doubt, now that it seems that Russia will never ratify it.

FURTHER READING

EU External relations, General

Bretherton, C., J. Vogler. *The European Union as a Global Actor.* 2nd ed., London: Routledge, 2006.

Cafruny, A., P. Peters. *The Union and the World: The Political Economy of a Common European Foreign Policy.* The Hague: Kluwer, 1998.

Cameron, F. *An Introduction to European Foreign Policy.* London: Routledge, 2007.

Canor, I. *The Limits of Judicial Discretion in the European Court of Justice: Security and Foreign Affairs Issues.* Baden-Baden: Nomos Verlagsgesellschaft, 1998.

Carlsnaes, W., et al. *Contemporary European Foreign Policy.* London: Sage, 2004.

Casarini, N., C. Musu. *European Foreign Policy in an Evolving International System: The Road Towards Convergence.* Basingstoke: Palgrave Macmillan, 2007 (Palgrave studies in European Union Politics).

Chini, M. *European Union Politics.* 2nd ed., Oxford: Oxford University Press, 2007.

Dashwood, A.A., et al. (eds). *The General Law of E.C. External Relations.* London: Sweet and Maxwell, 2000.

Denza, E. *The Intergovernmental Pillars of the European Union.* Oxford: Oxford University Press, 2002.

Dony, M., (réd.), *L'Union européenne et le Monde après.* Brussels: Editions de l'universit de Bruxelles Amsterdam, 1999.

Eeckhout, P. *External Relations of the European Union: Legal and Constitutional Foundations.* Oxford: Oxford University Press, 2004.

Elgström, O., M. Smith (eds.), *The European Union's Roles in International Politics: Concepts and Analysis.* Routledge/ECPR Studies in European Political Science, vol. 45. London: Routledge, 2006.

Griller, S., B. Weidel. *External Economic Relations and Foreign Policy in the European Union.* Wien: Springer, 2002 (Schriftenreihe des Forschungsinstituts für Europafragen der Wirtschaftsuniversität Wien; 20).

Guttman, R.J. *Europe in the New Century: Visions of an Emerging Superpower.* Boulder: Lynne Rienner, 2001.

---

365. 27th General report 1993, para. 293 and O.J. 1994, C 334/1. For the text of the European Energy Charter Treaty, see O.J. 1994, L 380/24; see P. Cameron, 'Het Verdrag inzake het Energiehandvest: een beoordeling na zes jaar' (2001) SEW, 139.

Heliskoski, J. *Mixed Agreements as a Technique for Organizing the International Relations of the European Community and its Member States*. The Hague: Kluwer Law International, 2001 (The Erik Castrén Institute monographs on international law and human rights; 2).

Hill, C., M. Smith. *International Relations and the European Union*. Oxford: Oxford University Press, 2005.

Holdgaard, R. External Relations Law of the European Community: Legal Reasoning and Legal Discourses. Alphen aan den Rijn: Kluwer Law International, 2008 (European Monographs; 57).

Kaddous, C., Le droit des relations extérieures dans la jurisprudence de la Cour de Justice des Communautés européennes, Bâle etc., 1998.

Knodt, M., S.B.M. Princen. *Understanding the European Union's External Relations*. London: Routledge, 2003 (Routledge/ECPR Studies in European Political Science; 29).

Koutrakos, P. *EU International Relations Law*. Oxford: Hart, 2006 (Modern Studies in European Law; 9).

Louis, J.-V., M. Dony, et al., Relations extérieures, 2e éd., Bruxelles: Éd. de l'Université de Bruxelles, 2005 (Commentaire J. Mégret: Le droit de la CE et de l'Union européenne; 12).

Lucarelli, S., I. Manners. *Values and Principles in European Union Foreign Policy*. London: Routledge, 2006 (Routledge Advances in European Politics; 37).

MacGoldrick, D. *International Relations Law of the European Union*. London: Longman, 1997.

Maresceau, M. (ed.). *The European Community's Commercial Policy after 1992: The Legal Dimension*. Dordrecht: Kluwer, 1993.

Maresceau, M. (ed.). *Bilateral Agreements Concluded by the European Community*. Collected Courses of the Hague Academy, Martinus Nijhoff, 2006.

Marsh, S., H. Mackenstein. *The International Relations of the European Union*. Harlow: Pearson Longman, 2005.

Nuttall, S.J. *European Foreign Policy*. Oxford: Oxford University Press, 2000.

O'Keeffe, D., H.G. Schermers (eds). *Mixed Agreements*. Deventer: Kluwer, 1983.

Pitschas, C., Die völkerrechtliche Verantwortlichkeit der Europäischen Gemeinschaft und ihrer Mitgliedstaaten: zugleich ein Beitrag zu den völkerrechtlichen Kompetenzen der Europäischen Gemeinschaft, Berlin, Duncker & Humblot, 2001 (Schriften zum europäischen Recht; Bd. 78).

T.M.C. Asser Instituut, *Externe bevoegdheden van de Europese Unie*, Den Haag, 1994.

Sjursen, H., Special Issue: 'What Kind of Power?: European Foreign Policy in Perspective'. (2006) *Journal of European Public Policy*, 169–327.

Smith, H. European *Union Foreign Policy: What It Is and What it Does*. London: Pluto Press, 2002.

Smith, K.E. *European Union Foreign Policy in a Changing World*. Cambridge: Polity, 2003.

Tonra, B., T. Christiansen. *Rethinking European Union Foreign Policy.* Manchester: Manchester University Press, 2004.
White, B. *Understanding European Foreign Policy.* Basingstoke: Palgrave, 2001.
Wood, D.M., B.A. Yesilada. *The Emerging European Union.* 4th ed. New York: Pearson/Longman, 2007.

External Relations and Internal Market
Dijck, P.V., G. Faber. *The External Economic Dimension of the European Union.* The Hague: Kluwer Law International, 2000 (Legal aspects of international organization 35).
Eeckhout, P. *The European Internal Market and International Trade: A Legal Analysis.* Oxford: Clarendon Press, 1994.
Koutrakos, P. 'The External Dimension of the Internal Market and the Individual'. In *Regulating the Internal Market.* Edited by N.N. Shuibhne. Cheltenham: Edward Elgar, 2006.
Molinier, J., La dimension externe du marché unique européen, Toulouse, Presses de l'Univ. des sciences sociales de Toulouse, 1994.
Völker, E.L.M. *Barriers to External and Internal Community Trade.* Deventer: Kluwer, 1993.

CFSP
Batt, J. *Partners and Neighbours: A CFSP for a Wider Europe.* Paris: Institute for Security Studies European Union, 2003 (Chaillot paper; 64).
Cameron, F. *An Introduction to European Foreign Policy.* London: Routledge, 2007.
Cameron, F. *The Foreign and Security Policy of the European Union: Past, Present and Future.* Sheffield: Sheffield Academic press, 1999 (Contemporary European studies; 7).
Casarini, N., C. Musu. *European Foreign Policy in an Evolving International System: The Road Towards Convergence.* Basingstoke: Palgrave Macmillan, 2007 (Palgrave studies in European Union politics).
Dannreuther, R. *European Union Foreign and Security Policy: Towards a Neighbourhood Strategy.* London: Routledge, 2004.
Dannreuther, R., J. Peterson. *Security Strategy and Transatlantic Relations.* London: Routledge, 2006.
Duke, S. *The Elusive Quest for European Security: From EDC to CFSP.* Basingstoke: Macmillan in association with St. Antony's College Oxford, 2000 (St Antony's series).
Gänzle, S., A.G. Sens. *The Changing Politics of European Security: Europe Alone?* Basingstoke: Palgrave Macmillan, 2007 (Palgrave studies in European Union politics).
Gerteiser, K., Die Sicherheits- und Verteidigungspolitik der Europäischen Union: rechtliche Analyse der gegenwärtigen Struktur und der Optionen zur weiteren Entwicklung, Frankfurt am Main etc.; Peter Lang, 2002 (Europäische Hochschulschriften. Reihe 2, Rechtswissenschaft; Bd. 3430).

Jones, S.G. *The Rise of European Security Cooperation.* Cambridge: Cambridge University Press, 2007.

Keukeleire, S., Het buitenlands beleid van de Europese Unie. Deventer: Kluwer, 1998.

Merlingen, M., R. Ostrauskaite. *The European Security and Defence Policy: An Implementation Perspective.* London: Routledge, 2007 (Routledge advances in European politics).

Münch, L., Die gemeinsame Aktion als Mittel der Gemeinsamen Aussen- und Sicherheitspolitik, Berlin, Duncker & Humblot, 1997 (Schriften zum europäischen Recht; Bd. 45).

Nuttall, S.J. *European Foreign Policy.* Oxford: Oxford University Press, 2000.

Smith, H. *European Union Foreign Policy: What it is and What it Does.* London: Pluto Press, 2002.

Smith, M.E. *Europe's Foreign and Security Policy: The Institutionalization of Cooperation.* Cambridge: Cambridge University Press, 2004.

Soetendorp, R.B. *Foreign Policy in the European Union: Theory, History and Practice.* London: Longman, 1999.

Wessel, R.A. *The European Union's Foreign and Security Policy: A Legal Institutional Perspective.* The Hague: Kluwer Law International, 1999 (Legal aspects of international organization; vol. 33).

Winn, N., C. Lord. *EU Foreign Policy beyond the Nation State: Joint Actions and Institutional Analysis of the Common Foreign and Security Policy.* Basingstoke: Palgrave, 2001.

Common Commercial Policy
a. GATT/WTO

De Búrca, G., J. Scott. *The EU and the WTO: Legal and Constitutional Issues.* Oxford: Hart, 2003.

Dijck, P.v., G. Faber. *The External Economic Dimension of the European Union.* The Hague: Kluwer Law International, 2000 (Legal aspects of international organization 35).

Dillon, S. *International Trade and Economic Law and the European Union.* Oxford: Hart, 2002.

Elsig, M. *The EU's Common Commercial Policy: Institutions, Interests and Ideas.* Aldershot: Ashgate, 2002.

Emch, A., C.E.U. Universidad de San Pablo. *The Biret Cases: What Effects do WTO Dispute Settlement Rulings Have in EU Law?* Instituto de Estudios Europeos de la USP-CEU, 2005 (Documentos de Trabajo / Instituto de Estudios Europeos; 1–2005).

Emiliou, N., D. O'Keeffe. *The European Union and World Trade Law: After the GATT Uruguay Round.* Chichester: John Wiley and Sons, 1996.

Hilf, M., F.G. Jacobs, E.-U. Petersmann (eds). *The European Community and GATT.* Deventer: Kluwer, 1986.

Hofmann, R., G. Tondl. *The European Union and the WTO Doha Round.* Nomos, 2007 (Schriften zur Europäischen Integration und Internationalen Wirtschaftsordnung; Bd. 5).

Hoogmartens, J. *EC Trade Law Following China's Accession to the WTO.* The Hague: Kluwer Law International, 2004 (Global Trade and Finance Series; 6).

Luengo Hernández de Madrid, G.E. *Regulation of Subsidies and State Aids in WTO and EC Law: Conflicts in International Trade Law.* Alphen aan den Rijn: Kluwer Law International, 2007 (European Monographs; 55).

Meunier, S. *Trading Voices: The European Union in International Commercial Negotiations.* Princeton: Princeton University Press, 2007.

Ortino, F. *Basic Legal Instruments for the Liberalisation of Trade: A Comparative Analysis of EC and WTO Law.* Oxford: Hart, 2004 (Studies in international trade law; 1).

Perdikis, N. *The WTO and the Regulation of International Trade: Recent Trade Disputes between the European Union and the United States.* Cheltenham: Elgar, 2005.

Petersmann, E.-U., M.A. Pollack. *Transatlantic Economic Disputes: The EU, the US, and the WTO.* Oxford: Oxford University Press, 2003.

Saunders, C., G.D. Triggs. *Trade and Cooperation with the European Union in the New Millennium.* The Hague: Kluwer Law International, 2002 (Melbourne studies in comparative and international law; vol. 2).

Slotboom, M.M. *A Comparison of WTO and EC Law: Do Different Objects and Purposes Matter for Treaty Interpretation?* London: Cameron May, 2006.

Snyder, F.G. *Regional and Global Regulation of International Trade.* Oxford: Hart, 2002.

Trebilcock, M.J., R. Howse. *The Regulation of International Trade.* 3rd ed. London: Routledge, 2005.

Weiler, J.H.H. *The EU, the WTO and the NAFTA: Towards a Common Law of International Trade?* Oxford: Oxford Univeristy Press, 2000 (The collected courses of the Academy of European Law; 2).

Wiers, J.-J.D. *Trade and Environment in the EC and the WTO: A Legal Analysis.* Groningen: European Law Publishing, 2002.

b. Commercial Policy Instruments

Adamantopoulos, K.A., M.J. Pereyra-Friedrichsen. *EU Anti-subsidy Law & Practice.* 2nd ed. London: Sweet and Maxwell, 2007.

Bael, I.V., J.-F. Bellis. *Anti-dumping and other Trade Protection Laws of the EC.* 4th ed. The Hague: Kluwer Law International, 2004.

Blokker, N.M. *International Regulation of World Trade in Textiles, Lessons for Practice, a Contribution to Theory.* Dordrecht: Kluwer, 1989.

Bronckers, M.C.E.J. *Selective Safeguard Measures in Multilateral Trade Relations.* Kluwer, Deventer, 1985.

Didier, P. *WTO Trade Instruments in EU Law: Commercial Policy Instruments: Dumping, Subsidies, Safeguards, Public Procurement.* London: Cameron May, 1999.

Elsig, M. *The EU's Common Commercial Policy: Institutions, Interests and Ideas.*
     Repr. Aldershot: Ashgate, 2004.
Giannakopoulos, T.K. *A Concise Guide to the EU Anti-dumping, Anti-subsidies
     Procedures.* Alphen aan den Rijn: Kluwer Law International, 2006
     (International competition law series; 23).
Hermann, C.W. 'Common Commercial Policy after Nice: Sisyphus Would Have
     Done a Better Job' (2002) CML Rev. 7–29.
Inama, S., E.A. Vermulst. *Customs and Trade Laws of the European Community.*
     The Hague: Kluwer Law International, 1999 (European business law and
     practice series; 15).
Koutrakos, P. Trade, *Foreign Policy and Defence in EU Constitutional Law: The
     Legal Regulation of Sanctions, Exports of Dual-use Goods and Armaments.*
     Oxford: Hart, 2001.
MacLean, R.M. *EU Trade Barrier Regulation: Tackling Unfair Foreign Trade
     Practices.* 2nd ed. London: Sweet and Maxwell, 2006.
Müller, W., N. Khan and H. A, Neumann. *EC Anti-dumping Law – A Commentary
     on Regulation 384/96.* Chichester: Wiley, 1998.

EU Relations with (Groups of) Countries
Robles, Alfredo C. Jr. *The Political Economy of Interregional Relations*: ASEAN
     and the EU. Aldershot: Ashgate, 2004.
Anderson, P.J., G. Wiessala. *The European Union and Asia: Reflections and Re-
     orientations.* Amsterdam: Rodopi, 2007 (European studies; 25).
Andreosso-O'Callaghan, B., et al. *The Economic Relations between Asia and
     Europe: Organisations, Trade and Investment.* Chandos, 2007 (Chandos
     Asian studies series: contemporary issues and trends).
Antonenko, O., K. Pinnick. *Russia and the European Union: Prospects for a New
     Relationship.* London: Routledge, 2005.
Archer, C. *Norway Outside the European Union: Norway and European Integra-
     tion from 1994 to 2004.* London: Routledge, 2005 (Europe and the nation
     state; 5).
Arikan, H. *Turkey and the EU: An Awkward Candidate for EU Membership?*
     Ashgate, 2006.
Babarinde, O., G. Faber. *The European Union and the Developing Countries: The
     Cotonou Agreement.* Leiden: Martinus Nijhoff Publishers, 2005.
Barysch, K., et al. *Embracing the Dragon: The EU's Partnership with China.*
     London: Centre for European Reform CER, 2005.
Baylis, J., J. Roper. *The United States and Europe: Beyond the Neo-conservative
     Divide?* Routledge, 2006 (Contemporary security studies).
Bersick, S., W.A.L. Stokhof. *Multiregionalism and Multilateralism: Asian-
     European Relations in a Global Context.* Amsterdam: Amsterdam University
     Press, 2006 (ICAS publication series; 1).
Brown, W. *The European Union and Africa: The Restructuring of North-South
     Relations.* London: Tauris, 2002 (Library of international relations; 20).
Burwell, F.G., I.H. Daalder. *The United States and Europe in the Global Arena.*
     Basingstoke: Macmillan Press; New York: St. Martin's Press, 1999.

Calleya, S.C. *Evaluating Euro-Mediterranean Relations.* London, New York: Routledge, 2005 (Routledge advances in European politics; 22).

Church, C.H. *Switzerland and the European Union: A Close, Contradictory and Misunderstood Relationship.* London: Routledge, 2007 (Europe and the nation state; 11).

Coffey, P. *The EC and the United States.* London: Pinter, 1993.

Cosgrove-Sacks, C., C. Santos. *Europe, Diplomacy, and Development: New Issues in EU Relations with Developing Countries.* Basingstoke: Palgrave, 2001.

Cosgrove-Sacks, C., G. Scappucci. *The European Union and Developing Countries: The Challenges of Globalization.* Basingstoke: Macmillan, New York: St. Martin's Press, 1999.

Dent, C.M. *The European Union and East Asia: An Economic Relationship.* London: Routledge, 1999.

Dosenrode-Lynge, S.Z.v., A. Stubkjær. *The European Union and the Middle East.* London: Sheffield Academic Press, 2002 (Contemporary European Studies; 12).

Fabre, T., P. Sant Cassia. *Between Europe and the Mediterranean: The Challenges and the Fears.* Palgrave Macmillan, 2007.

Gebrewold, B. *Africa and Fortress Europe: Threats and Opportunities.* Aldershot: Ashgate, 2007.

Giri, D.K. *European Union and India: A Study in North-South Relations.* New Delhi: Concept Pub. Co., 2001

Grabendorff, W., R. Seidelmann. *Relations between the European Union and Latin America: Biregionalism in a Changing Global System.* Nomos, 2005 (Internationale Politik und Sicherheit/Stiftung Wissenschaft und Politik; 57).

Hillion, C. *The Evolving System of European Union External Relations as Evidenced in the EU Partnerships with Russia and Ukraine.* Leiden: s.n., 2005.

Holland, M. *The European Union and the Third World.* Basingstoke: Palgrave, 2002.

Johnson, D., P. Robinson. *Perspectives on EU-Russia Relations.* London: Routledge, 2004 (Europe and the nation state; 7).

Joseph, J.S. *Turkey and the European Union: Internal Dynamics and External Challenges.* Basingstoke Palgrave Macmillan, 2006.

Kerr, D., L. Fei. *The International Politics of EU-China Relations.* Oxford: Oxford University Press, for the British Academy, 2007 (British Academy occasional papers; 10).

Lister, M. *European Union Development Policy.* 3rd print. Basingstoke: Palgrave, New York: St. Martin's Press, 2001.

Malfliet, K., et al. *The CIS, the EU and Russia: The Challenges of Integration.* Palgrave: Macmillan, 2007 (Studies in Central and Eastern Europe).

Mannin, M. *Pushing Back the Boundaries: The European Union and Central and Eastern Europe.* Manchester: Manchester University Press, 1999.

Maresceau, M., E. Lannon. *The EU's Enlargement and Mediterranean Strategies: A Comparative Analysis.* Basingstoke: Palgrave, 2001.

Mayhew, A. *Recreating Europe: The European Union's Policy Towards Central and Eastern Europe.* 2nd ed. Cambridge: Cambridge University Press, 2008.

Monar, J. *The New Transatlantic Agenda and the Future of EU-US Relations.* London: Kluwer Law International, 1998.

Nello, S.S., K. E. Smith. *The European Union and Central and Eastern Europe: The Implications of Enlargement in Stages.* Aldershot: Ashgate, 1998.

Norberg, S., et al. *The European Economic Area, EEA Law, A Commentary on the EEA Agreement.* Stockholm, 1993.

Preston, P.W., J. Gilson. *The European Union and East Asia: Interregional Linkages in Changing Global System.* Cheltenham: Edward Elgar, 2001.

Prozorov, S. *Understanding Conflict between Russia and the EU: The Limits of Integration.* Basingstoke: Palgrave Macmillan, 2006.

Purcell, S.K., F. Simon. *Europe and Latin America in the World Economy.* Boulder, CO: Lynne Rienner Publishers, 1995.

Rogers, N. *A Practitioner's Guide to the EC-Turkey Association Agreement.* The Hague: Kluwer Law International, 2000.

Seeberg, P. *EU and the Mediterranean: Foreign Policy and Security.* Odense: University Press of Southern Denmark, 2007 (University of Southern Denmark studies in history and social sciences; vol. 342).

Shan, W. *The Legal Framework of EU-China Investment Relations.* Oxford: Hart Publishing, 2005.

Steffenson, R. *Managing EU-US Relations: Actors, Institutions and the New Transatlantic Agenda.* Manchester: Manchester University Press, 2005.

Strange, R., et al. *The European Union and ASEAN: Trade and Investment Issues.* Basingstoke: Macmillan etc., 2000.

Velychenko, S. *Ukraine, the EU and Russia: History, Culture and International Relations.* Palgrave: Macmillan, 2007 (Studies in Central and Eastern Europe).

Wahlers, G., et al. *The United States of America and the European Union.* Washington, DC: Brookings Institution Press, 2007.

Westphal, K. *A Focus on EU-Russian Relations: Towards a Close Partnership on Defined Road Maps.* Frankfurt am Main: Lang, 2005 (Schriften zur internationalen Entwicklungs- und Umweltforschung; 15).

Wouters, J., et al. *The United Nations and the European Union: An Ever Stronger Partnership.* The Hague: T.M.C. Asser Press, 2006.

Youngs, R. *Europe and the Middle East: In the Shadow of September 11.* Boulder, CO: Lynne Rienner Publishers, 2006.

Zippel, W., Die Beziehungen zwischen der EU und den Mercosur-Staaten: Stand und Perspektiven, Baden-Baden, Nomos, 2002 (Schriftenreihe des Arbeitskreises europäische Integration; Bd. 48).

Relations between EU and International Organizations

Frid, R. 'The European Economic Community, A Member of a Specialized Agency of the United Nations'. (1993) *EJIL*, 239–255.

Frid, R. *The Relations between the EC and International Organizations: Legal Theory and Practice.* The Hague: Kluwer Law International, 1995 (Legal aspects of international organization; vol. 24).

Govaere, I., et al. 'In-between Seats: The Participation of the European Union in International Organizations'. (2004) *European Foreign Affairs Review* 155–187.

Hilpold, P., Die EU im GATT/WTO-System: Aspekte einer Beziehung 'sui generis', Frankfurt am Main etc., Lang, 1999 (Europäische Hochschulschriften. Reihe 2; Bd. 2559).

Laatikainen, K.V., K.E. Smith. *The European Union at the United Nations: Intersecting Multilateralisms.* Basingstoke: Palgrave Macmillan, 2006.

Lavranos, N. *Legal Interaction between Decisions of International Organizations and European Law.* Groningen: Europa Law Publishing, 2004.

Michta, A.A. *The Limits of Alliance: The United States, NATO, and the EU in North and Central Europe.* Lanham, MD: Rowman and Littlefield, 2006.

Müller-Graff, P.-C., Die Europäische Gemeinschaft in der Welthandelsorganisation: Globalisierung und Weltmarktrecht als Herausforderung für Europa, Baden-Baden, Nomos, 2000 (Schriftenreihe des Arbeitskreises Europäische Integration; Bd. 47).

Reichard, M. *The EU-NATO Relationship: A Legal and Political Perspective.* Aldershot: Ashgate, 2006.

Wouters, J., et al. The United Nations and the European Union: An Ever Stronger Partnership. The Hague: T.M.C. Asser Press, 2006.

Index